AF342539

ANCIENT HISTORY

WIDENER LIBRARY SHELFLIST, 55

ANCIENT HISTORY

CLASSIFICATION SCHEDULE
CLASSIFIED LISTING BY CALL NUMBER
CHRONOLOGICAL LISTING
AUTHOR AND TITLE LISTING

Published by the Harvard University Library
Cambridge, Massachusetts
Distributed by the Harvard University Press
Cambridge, Massachusetts and London, England
1975

Library of Congress Cataloging in Publication Data

Harvard University.   Library.
   Ancient history.

   (Widener Library shelflist ; 55)
   1. History, Ancient—Bibliography—Catalogs. 2. Harvard University.   Library. I.
Title. II. Series: Harvard University. Library. Widener Library shelflist ; 55.
Z6202.H37   1975   [D57]   016.93   75-21543
ISBN 0-674-03312-4

Preface

As part of its effort to computerize certain of its operations, the Harvard University Library is converting to machine-readable form the shelflist and classification schedules of Widener Library, which houses Harvard's central research collection. After each class or group of related classes is converted, it is published in the *Widener Library Shelflist* series. A list of currently available titles follows this preface.

This volume, the fifty-fifth in the series, lists more than 11,000 titles concerning the history, civilization, government, economic and social conditions, and geography of the Mediterranean region and Western Asia down to the Barbarian invasions in Europe and the Arab conquest in Asia and Africa. Also included are works on Egyptian and Assyro-Babylonian literatures and on the archaeology of Assyria and Babylonia. In general, archaeological works and works on prehistoric times are excluded. More detailed information on the scope and arrangement of this material may be found in the classification schedule section of this book.

This catalogue is arranged in four parts. The classification schedule is the first of these. It serves as an outline of the second part, which presents the entries in shelflist order; that is, in order by call number, as the books are arranged on the shelves. Together these two parts form a classified catalogue and browsing guide to the class. Part three lists the same items (excluding periodicals and other serials) in chronological order by date of publication. In addition to its obvious reference use, this list yields information on the quantity and rate of publication in the field. It can be helpful in determining patterns of collection development and in identifying existing strengths and weaknesses. Access to the collection by author and by title is provided by the alphabetical list which constitutes the fourth part of the catalogue. Computer-generated entries are included for titles of works listed elsewhere by author. (In these added entries the author's name follows the title and is enclosed in parentheses.) This section equips the reader with a subject-oriented subset of the card catalogue — a finding list which offers substantial advantages of conciseness and portability over the catalogue as a whole.

A note of caution is in order. A shelflist has traditionally served as an inventory record of the books in the library and as an indispensable tool for assigning call numbers to books as they are added to the collection. Designed and maintained to fulfill these two functions, the Widener shelflist was never intended to serve the purposes now envisaged for it. The bibliographical standards are not equal to those that prevail in the public card catalogues; shelflist entries are less complete than the public catalogue entries and may contain errors and inconsistencies which have not been eliminated during the conversion process. Cross references and name added entries are not included. Entries for serials rarely reflect changes in title, and serial holding statements give only the year or volume number of the first and last volumes in the library with no indication of gaps. If there is a plus sign after the beginning volume number or date, it can be inferred that the title is being currently received. For a complete record of the holdings of serial titles, the conventional serial records in the Widener Library should be consulted.

The list has other deficiencies. No classification system is perfect, and books are not always classified where the reader would expect to find them. Some books formerly in Widener and subsequently tranferred to the Houghton Library or the New England Deposit Library are still to be found in the list; but others had been dropped from the original shelflist and could not be re-inserted.

Special notations indicate the locations of books which are in the shelflist but not in the Widener building. Books transferred to the Houghton Library (for rare books and special collections) are indicated by the letters *Htn*. Books that have been moved to special storage areas are designated by one of the following notations: *NEDL, X Cg,* or a *V* as the first letter of a call number prefix. These books should be requested, by their current numbers, through the Widener Circulation Desk. The letters *RRC* designate books in the Russian Research Center Library. The letter *A* following a call number in the alphabetical or chronological section indicates that the Library holds more than one copy of the book on this number. The classified list, however, includes all copies.

The shelflists of libraries not having classified catalogues have long been used by librarians and readers as implements for systematically surveying holdings in a particular subject. When perusing a shelflist one sees all the titles that have been classified in a given area, and not merely those which happen to be on the shelves and whose spine lettering is legible. In addition, one can take in at a glance the essential bibliographical description of a book — author, title, place and date of publication. However, the potential bibliographical usefulness of the shelflist has been difficult to exploit because it exists in only one copy, which is generally kept in a relatively inaccessible location. In Widener this problem is intensified because the handwritten sheaf shelflist is peculiarly awkward to read and difficult to interpret. Computer technology has made it possible to enlarge the concept of the shelflist and to expand its usefulness and accessibility while improving the techniques of maintaining it.

This shelflist catalogue will be of greatest utility to those using the libraries at Harvard, but in spite of its limitations, it can serve as a general bibliography of the subject and is therefore being made available to other interested libraries and individuals. The computer-based shelflist files are being maintained on a continuing basis so that updated editions of volumes in the series can be published as the need arises.

CHARLES W. HUSBANDS
Systems Librarian

Shelflist Volumes in Print

Contents

Statistical Summaries of Classes in this Volume

February 1975

Analysis of Shelflist Entries by Language

Entries in the *AH* Class   10,101

English	3,645	Latin	1,604	Yugoslav Languages	5
German	2,600	French	1,520	Czech & Slovak	10
Dutch	58	Italian	675	Bulgarian	10
Swedish	20	Spanish	80	Hungarian	11
Danish	18	Portuguese	13	Turkish	18
Norwegian	4	Rumanian	8	Finnish	1
Icelandic	2	Russian	123	Celtic Languages	1
Greek	71	Ukrainian	1	Uncoded	112
		Polish	13		

Entries in the *Eg* Class   1,034

English	474	French	185	Yugoslav Languages	1
German	259	Italian	32	Hungarian	2
Dutch	8	Spanish	2	Turkish	2
Swedish	4	Russian	22	Uncoded	13
Latin	28	Polish	2		

Entries in the *AHP* Class   75

English	14	Italian	9	Polish	1
German	36	Spanish	2	Hungarian	1
Dutch	2	Portuguese	1	Uncoded	1
French	6	Russian	2		

Entries in the *EgP* Class   32

English	12	Dutch	1	Italian	1
German	7	French	11		

Count of Titles

		Widener	Elsewhere	Total
AH	Monographs	9,207	671	9,878
	Serials	48	0	48
	Pamphlets in Tract Volumes	526	53	579
	Pamphlet Boxes	70	2	72
	Total *AH*	9,851	726	10,577
Eg	Monographs	995	21	1,016
	Serials	5	1	6
	Pamphlets in Tract Volumes	51	0	51
	Pamphlet Boxes	6	0	6
	Total *Eg*	1,057	22	1,079
AHP	Monographs	4	0	4
	Serials	71	0	71
	Total *AHP*	75	0	75
EgP	Monographs	6	0	6
	Serials	26	0	26
	Total *EgP*	32	0	32
Total Titles		11,015	748	11,763

Count of Volumes

		Widener	Elsewhere	Total
AH	Monograph	11,481	1,404	12,885
	Serial	364	0	364
	Tract	88	15	103
	Total *AH*	11,933	1,419	13,352
Eg	Monograph	1,184	27	1,211
	Serial	16	1	17
	Tract	6	0	6
	Total *Eg*	1,206	28	1,234
AHP	Monograph	4	0	4
	Serial	640	0	640
	Total *AHP*	644	0	644
EgP	Monograph	6	0	6
	Serial	177	0	177
	Total *EgP*	183	0	183
Total Volumes		13,966	1,447	15,413

ANCIENT HISTORY

CLASSIFICATION SCHEDULES

NOTE ON THE CLASSIFICATION

The AH class provides for the history of all the countries of the ancient world. It should be noted at once that this refers primarily to the areas surrounding the Mediterranean which were parts of the Graeco-Roman sphere of influence. The class contains works on the history, civilization and social life, government and law, religion, economic conditions, geography and travels and the various races of these countries. The period covered varies with the area - for Asia and Africa, up to the Arab conquest (to ca. 650); for Europe, up to the barbarian invasions (to ca. 500). Works on the prehistoric period and works on archaeology are in the Arc class. The AH class is primarily for monographs; all periodicals, except those of a bibliographical nature, go in the AHP class.

The accompanying Outline shows the overall arrangement of the class, with a general progression from east to west. However, the countries of a continent and the provinces or districts of a country or larger area are arranged alphabetically. Most countries are assigned a series of 50 base numbers, which are arranged according to a common table. The Ancient World in general, Ancient Orient in general, Greece in general, and Rome in general are each assigned a block of 1000 numbers, which allows for a much expanded and more detailed version of the country table. For that, many topics are given a block of 10 numbers, which provides for bibliographies, pamphlet volumes, and a date arrangement of most monographs (Table A).

A few exceptions to what has been written above should be mentioned. The section for Assyria and Babylonia includes works on archaeology and art and on Assyro-Babylonian literature. Works on ancient Egyptian history and literature are in the separate Eg class. Greek and Roman religion are in Class rather than AH.

The typed version of the scheme had numerous elisions and abbreviations, which were a source of confusion. For the present revision, the scheme has been written out in full in order to make it easier for the classifiers. It has not been possible as yet to reclassify all the books which had been wrongly classified.

Bartol Brinkler
Classification Specialist
November 1974

OUTLINE

2-979	Ancient World in general
1002-1979	Ancient Orient in general
2000-2046	Arabia
2050-2096	Armenia
	Asia Minor
2100-2147	General
2150-2999	Special kingdoms, etc.
3000-3195	Assyria and Babylonia
3200-3996	Other western Asia
	Greece and Macedonia
4002-4979	General
5000-6196	Provinces, etc.
	Rome and the Occident
7002-7979	General
8000-8196	North Africa (except Egypt)
8200-9846	Roman Europe

Ancient World in general
[Include also works dealing with ancient
Greece and Rome together. For the
Near East in general, see AH 1002-1979.]

Periodicals. See AHP and AH 2

General bibliographies
2   Periodicals
4-9   Monographs (By date)
15   General pamphlet volumes
24-29   Collected sources, etc. (By date)

Government and administration
30-39   General works (Table A)
              [Include history of political theory]
40-49   Forms of government (Table A)
50-59   Administrative branch (Table A)
60-69   Legislature and legislation (Table A)
70-79   Elections and voting (Table A)
80-89   Provincial government (Table A)
90-99   Municipal government (Table A)
100-109   Public finance (Table A)

           Special topics
114   Classes of citizens
115   Tribes
118   Gentes
120   Secretaries

           Law
130-139   General works (Table A)
                 [See also AH 190-199]
140-149   Public law (Table A)
150-159   Criminal law (Table A)

           Private law
160   General works
161   Family law
162   Inheritance law
163   Marriage law
165-169   Maritime law (By date)
170-179   Agrarian law (Table A)
180-189   Slavery and emancipation (Table A)
190-199   Philosophy of law (Table A)

           Special topics
214   The oath
215   Sacred law
216   Suretyship
217   Public rewards
218   Statutes of limitations
219   Sales
220-229   Legal procedure (Table A)
230-239   Military affairs (Table A)
250-259   Naval affairs (Table A)
260-269   Foreign relations, diplomacy (Table A)
274-279   General history (By date)

           General special
294-299   Miscellany (By date)
                 [Include Festschriften, congresses, etc.]
300-309   Philosophy of history (Table A)
                 [Include historiography]
310-319   Cosmology (Table A)
320-329   Races (Table A)
330-339   Collected biographies (Table A)

           History by periods
400-409   Before 500 B.C. (Table A)
450-459   500 - 1 B.C. (Table A)
500-509   1 A.D. - ca. 500 (Table A)
800-809   Chronology (Table A)

           Civilization, social life
810-819   General works (Table A)
820-829   Private life in general (Table A)
830-839   Athletic games, sports (Table A)

Ancient World in general (cont.)
  Civilization, social life (cont.)

           Special topics
840   The family
841   Writing
842   Books and education
843   Music and dancing
                 [See also Class]
844   Festivals
845   Character and morals
846   Houses, etc.
847   Baths
848   Costume
849   Perfumes
850   Meals
851   Fire and lights
852   Pottery and metalwork
853   Glass
854   Domestic plants and animals
855   Hunting and fishing
856   Guest-friendship
857   Parasites
858   Marriage
859   Condition of women
860   Condition of children
861   Burial
862   Hygiene and medicine
                 [See also Class]
863   Sexual customs, love
864   Games, spectacles
865.1-.499   Vehicles
865.500-.999 Inns
866   Amber
867   Gestures
868   Beverages
869   Names
              Arts and sciences in general. See AH
                 810-819 and Class.
870-879   Religion (Table A)
              [N.B. - See also R and Class]

           Economic conditions
880-889   General works (Table A)
890-899   Agriculture (Table A)
900-909   Commerce and industries (Table A)
910-919   Associations (Table A)
920-929   Weights and measures (Table A)
           Public finance. See AH 100-109
930   Atlases

           Geography and description
931   Bibliographies
932   Pamphlet volumes
933   Collected authors, etc.
934-939   Monographs (By date)

           Travels
950-959   General works (Table A)
960-969   Imaginary travels (Table A)
970-979   Guidebooks (Table A)

Ancient Orient in general
[Include here primarily works on ancient
western Asia, the ancient Near East.]

Periodicals. See AHP and AH 1002

General bibliographies
1002   Periodicals
1004-1009 Monographs (By date)
1015   General pamphlet volumes
1024-1029 Collected sources, etc. (By date)

Government and administration
1030-1039   General works (Table A)
                 [Include history of political theory]
1040-1049 Forms of government (Table A)
1050-1059 Administrative branch (Table A)
1060-1069 Legislature and legislation (Table A)

Ancient Orient in general (cont.)
  Government and administration (cont.)

1070-1079	Elections and voting (Table A)
1080-1089	Provincial government (Table A)
1090-1099	Municipal government (Table A)
1100-1109	Public finance (Table A)

    Special topics

1114	Classes of citizens
1115	Tribes
1118	Gentes

  Law

1130-1139	General works (Table A)
	[See also AH 1190-1199]
1140-1149	Public law (Table A)
1150-1159	Criminal law (Table A)

    Private law

1160	General works
1161	Family law
1162	Inheritance law
1163	Marriage law
1165-1169	Maritime law (By date)
1170-1179	Agrarian law (Table A)
1180-1189	Slavery and emancipation (Table A)
1190-1199	Philosophy of law (Table A)

    Special topics

1214	The oath
1215	Sacred law
1216	Suretyship
1217	Public rewards
1218	Statutes of limitations
1219	Sales
1220-1229	Legal procedure (Table A)
1230-1239	Military affairs (Table A)
1250-1259	Naval affairs (Table A)
1260-1269	Foreign relations, diplomacy (Table A)
1274-1279	General history (By date)

  General special

1294-1299	Miscellany (By date)
	[Include Festschriften, congresses, etc.]
1300-1309	Philosophy of history (Table A)
	[Include historiography]
1310-1319	Cosmology (Table A)
1320-1329	Races (Table A)
	[See also AH 3800-3820]
1330-1339	Collected biographies (Table A)

  History by periods

1400-1409	Before 500 B.C. (Table A)
1450-1459	500 - 1 B.C. (Table A)
1500-1509	1 A.D. - ca. 650 (Table A)
1800-1809	Chronology (Table A)

  Civilization, Social life

1810-1819	General works (Table A)
1820-1829	Private life in general (Table A)
1830-1839	Athletic games, sports (Table A)

    Special topics

1840	The family
1841	Writing
1842	Books and education
1843	Music and dancing
1844	Festivals
1845	Character and morals
1846	Houses, etc.
1847	Baths
1848	Costume
1849	Perfumes
1850	Meals
1851	Fire and lights
1852	Pottery and metalwork
1853	Glass
1854	Domestic plants and animals
1855	Hunting and fishing
1856	Guest-friendship

Ancient Orient in general (cont.)
  Civilization, Social life (cont.)
    Special topics (cont.)

1857	Parasites
1858	Marriage
1859	Condition of women
1860	Condition of children
1861	Burial
1862	Hygiene and medicine
1863	Sexual customs, love
1864	Games, spectacles
1865.1-.499	Vehicles
1865.500-.999	Inns
1866	Amber
1867	Gestures
1868	Beverages
1869	Names
	Arts and sciences in general.
	See AH 1810-1819
1870-1879	Religion (Table A)
	[See also R]

  Economic conditions

1880-1889	General works (Table A)
1890-1899	Agriculture (Table A)
1900-1909	Commerce and industries (Table A)
1910-1919	Associations (Table A)
1920-1929	Weights and measures (Table A)
	Public finance. See AH 1100-1109
1930	Atlases

  Geography and description

1931	Bibliographies
1932	Pamphlet volumes
1933	Collected authors, etc.
1934-1939	Monographs (By date)

  Travels

1950-1959	General works (Table A)
1960-1969	Imaginary travels (Table A)
1970-1979	Guidebooks (Table A)

Countries of ancient Asia

  Arabia
    Periodicals. See AHP

2000	Bibliographies
2001	Pamphlet volumes
2002	Collected source materials
2003	Government and administration
2004	Law
2005	Military affairs
2006	Naval affairs
2007	General history
2008	General special

    History by periods

2009	Before 500 B.C.
2010	500 - 1 B.C.
2011	1 A.D. - ca. 650
2012	Chronology
2013	Civilization
2014	Religion
2015	Economic conditions
2016	Geography
2017	Travels
2018-2020	Special topics (Develop as needed)
2021-2046	Local (A-Z by place)

  Armenia
    Periodicals. See AHP

2050	Bibliographies
2051	Pamphlet volumes
2052	Collected source materials
2053	Government and administration
2054	Law
2055	Military affairs
2056	Naval affairs
2057	General history
2058	General special

Countries of ancient Asia (cont.)
  Armenia (cont.)

	History by periods
2059	Before 500 B.C.
2060	500 - 1 B.C.
2061	1 A.D. - ca. 650
2062	Chronology
2063	Civilization
2064	Religion
2065	Economic conditions
2066	Geography
2067	Travels
2068-2070	Special topics (Develop as needed)
2071-2096	Local (A-Z by place)

  Asia Minor in general

	Periodicals. See AHP
2100	Bibliographies
2101	Pamphlet volumes
2102	Collected source materials
2103	Government and administration
2104	Law
2105	Military affairs
2106	Naval affairs
2107	General history
2108	General special
	History by periods
2109	Before 500 B.C.
2110	500 - 1 B.C.
2111	1 A.D. - ca. 650
2112	Chronology
2113	Civilization
2114	Religion
2115	Economic conditions
2116	Geography
2117	Travels
	Special topics
2120	Ionia (coastal district)
	Cities and towns, etc. See AH 2150-2996
2147	Roman Province of Asia

  Kingdoms of Asia Minor
    Bithynia

	Periodicals. See AHP
2150	Bibliographies
2151	Pamphlet volumes
2152	Collected source materials
2153	Government and administration
2154	Law
2155	Military affairs
2156	Naval affairs
2157	General history
2158	General special
	History by periods
2159	Before 500 B.C.
2160	500 - 1 B.C.
2161	1 A.D. - ca. 650
2162	Chronology
2163	Civilization
2164	Religion
2165	Economic conditions
2166	Geography
2167	Travels
2168-2170	Special topics (Develop as needed)
2171-2196	Local (A-Z by place)

    Cappadocia

	Periodicals. See AHP
2200	Bibliographies
2201	Pamphlet volumes
2202	Collected source materials
2203	Government and administration
2204	Law
2205	Military affairs
2206	Naval affairs
2207	General history
2208	General special

Countries of ancient Asia (cont.)
  Kingdoms of Asia Minor (cont.)
    Cappadocia (cont.)

	History by periods
2209	Before 500 B.C.
2210	500 - 1 B.C.
2211	1 A.D. - ca. 650
2212	Chronology
2213	Civilization
2214	Religion
2215	Economic conditions
2216	Geography
2217	Travels
2218-2220	Special topics (Develop as needed)
2221-2246	Local (A-Z by place)

    Caria

	Periodicals. See AHP
2250	Bibliographies
2251	Pamphlet volumes
2252	Collected source materials
2253	Government and administration
2254	Law
2255	Military affairs
2256	Naval affairs
2257	General history
2258	General special
	History by periods
2259	Before 500 B.C.
2260	500 - 1 B.C.
2261	1 A.D. - ca. 650
2262	Chronology
2263	Civilization
2264	Religion
2265	Economic conditions
2266	Geography
2267	Travels
2268-2270	Special topics (Develop as needed)
2271-2296	Local (A-Z by place)

    Cilicia

	Periodicals. See AHP
2300	Bibliographies
2301	Pamphlet volumes
2302	Collected source materials
2303	Government and administration
2304	Law
2305	Military affairs
2306	Naval affairs
2307	General history
2308	General special
	History by periods
2309	Before 500 B.C.
2310	500 - 1 B.C.
2311	1 A.D. - ca. 650
2312	Chronology
2313	Civilization
2314	Religion
2315	Economic conditions
2316	Geography
2317	Travels
2318-2320	Special topics (Develop as needed)
2321-2346	Local (A-Z by place)

    Galatia

	Periodicals. See AHP
2350	Bibliographies
2351	Pamphlet volumes
2352	Collected source materials
2353	Government and administration
2354	Law
2355	Military affairs
2356	Naval affairs
2357	General history
2358	General special
	History by periods
2359	Before 500 B.C.
2360	500 - 1 B.C.
2361	1 A.D. - ca. 650
2362	Chronology

Countries of ancient Asia (cont.)
  Kingdoms of Asia Minor (cont.)
    Galatia (cont.)

2363	Civilization
2364	Religion
2365	Economic conditions
2366	Geography
2367	Travels
2368-2370	Special topics (Develop as needed)
2371-2396	Local (A-Z by place)
	Ionia. See AH 2120

    Isauria

	Periodicals. See AHP
2400	Bibliographies
2401	Pamphlet volumes
2402	Collected source materials
2403	Government and administration
2404	Law
2405	Military affairs
2406	Naval affairs
2407	General history
2408	General special
	History by periods
2409	Before 500 B.C.
2410	500 - 1 B.C.
2411	1 A.D. - ca. 650
2412	Chronology
2413	Civilization
2414	Religion
2415	Economic conditions
2416	Geography
2417	Travels
2418-2420	Special topics (Develop as needed)
2421-2446	Local (A-Z by place)

    Lycaonia

	Periodicals. See AHP
2450	Bibliographies
2451	Pamphlet volumes
2452	Collected source materials
2453	Government and administration
2454	Law
2455	Military affairs
2456	Naval affairs
2457	General history
2458	General special
	History by periods
2459	Before 500 B.C.
2460	500 - 1 B.C.
2461	1 A.D. - ca. 650
2462	Chronology
2463	Civilization
2464	Religion
2465	Economic conditions
2466	Geography
2467	Travels
2468-2470	Special topics (Develop as needed)
2471-2496	Local (A-Z by place)

    Lycia

	Periodicals. See AHP
2500	Bibliographies
2501	Pamphlet volumes
2502	Collected source materials
2503	Government and administration
2504	Law
2505	Military affairs
2506	Naval affairs
2507	General history
2508	General special
	History by periods
2509	Before 500 B.C.
2510	500 - 1 B.C.
2511	1 A.D. - ca. 650
2512	Chronology
2513	Civilization
2514	Religion
2515	Economic conditions
2516	Geography

Countries of ancient Asia (cont.)
  Kingdoms of Asia Minor (cont.)
    Lycia (cont.)

2517	Travels
2518-2520	Special topics (Develop as needed)
2521-2546	Local (A-Z by place)

    Lydia

	Periodicals. See AHP
2550	Bibliographies
2551	Pamphlet volumes
2552	Collected source materials
2553	Government and administration
2554	Law
2555	Military affairs
2556	Naval affairs
2557	General history
2558	General special
	History by periods
2559	Before 500 B.C.
2560	500 - 1 B.C.
2561	1 A.D. - ca. 650
2562	Chronology
2563	Civilization
2564	Religion
2565	Economic conditions
2566	Geography
2567	Travels
2568-2570	Special topics (Develop as needed)
2571-2596	Local (A-Z by place)

    Mysia

	Periodicals. See AHP
2600	Bibliographies
2601	Pamphlet volumes
2602	Collected source materials
2603	Government and administration
2604	Law
2605	Military affairs
2606	Naval affairs
2607	General history
2608	General special
	History by periods
2609	Before 500 B.C.
2610	500 - 1 B.C.
2611	1 A.D. - ca. 650
2612	Chronology
2613	Civilization
2614	Religion
2615	Economic conditions
2616	Geography
2617	Travels
2618-2620	Special topics (Develop as needed)
2621-2646	Local (A-Z by place)
2648	Osrhoene

    Pamphylia

	Periodicals. See AHP
2650	Bibliographies
2651	Pamphlet volumes
2652	Collected source materials
2653	Government and administration
2654	Law
2655	Military affairs
2656	Naval affairs
2657	General history
2658	General special
	History by periods
2659	Before 500 B.C.
2660	500 - 1 B.C.
2661	1 A.D. - ca. 650
2662	Chronology
2663	Civilization
2664	Religion
2665	Economic conditions
2666	Geography
2667	Travels
2668-2670	Special topics (Develop as needed)
2671-2696	Local (A-Z by place)

Countries of ancient Asia (cont.)
Kingdoms of Asia Minor (cont.)

Paphlogonia
Periodicals. See AHP
2700 Bibliographies
2701 Pamphlet volumes
2702 Collected source materials
2703 Government and administration
2704 Law
2705 Military affairs
2706 Naval affairs
2707 General history
2708 General special
History by periods
2709 Before 500 B.C.
2710 500 - 1 B.C.
2711 1 A.D. - ca. 650
2712 Chronology
2713 Civilization
2714 Religion
2715 Economic conditions
2716 Geography
2717 Travels
2718-2720 Special topics (Develop as needed)
2721-2746 Local (A-Z by place)

Pergamon
Periodicals. See AHP
2750 Bibliographies
2751 Pamphlet volumes
2752 Collected source materials
2753 Government and administration
2754 Law
2755 Military affairs
2756 Naval affairs
2757 General history
2758 General special
History by periods
2759 Before 500 B.C.
2760 500 - 1 B.C.
2761 1 A.D. - ca. 650
2762 Chronology
2763 Civilization
2764 Religion
2765 Economic conditions
2766 Geography
2767 Travels
2768-2770 Special topics (Develop as needed)
2771-2796 Local (A-Z by place)

Phrygia
Periodicals. See AHP
2800 Bibliographies
2801 Pamphlet volumes
2802 Collected source materials
2803 Government and administration
2804 Law
2805 Military affairs
2806 Naval affairs
2807 General history
2808 General special
History by periods
2809 Before 500 B.C.
2810 500 - 1 B.C.
2811 1 A.D. - ca. 650
2812 Chronology
2813 Civilization
2814 Religion
2815 Economic conditions
2816 Geography
2817 Travels
2818-2820 Special topics (Develop as needed)
2821-2846 Local (A-Z by place)

Pisidia
Periodicals. See AHP
2850 Bibliographies
2851 Pamphlet volumes
2852 Collected source materials

Countries of ancient Asia (cont.)
Kingdoms of Asia Minor (cont.)
Pisidia (cont.)
2853 Government and administration
2854 Law
2855 Military affairs
2856 Naval affairs
2857 General history
2858 General special
History by periods
2859 Before 500 B.C.
2860 500 - 1 B.C.
2861 1 A.D. - ca. 650
2862 Chronology
2863 Civilization
2864 Religion
2865 Economic conditions
2866 Geography
2867 Travels
2868-2870 Special topics (Develop as needed)
2871-2896 Local (A-Z by place)

Pontus
Periodicals. See AHP
2900 Bibliographies
2901 Pamphlet volumes
2902 Collected source materials
2903 Government and administration
2904 Law
2905 Military affairs
2906 Naval affairs
2907 General history
2908 General special
History by periods
2909 Before 500 B.C.
2910 500 - 1 B.C.
2911 1 A.D. - ca. 650
2912 Chronology
2913 Civilization
2914 Religion
2915 Economic conditions
2916 Geography
2917 Travels
2918-2920 Special topics (Develop as needed)
2921-2946 Local (A-Z by place)

Troas
Periodicals. See AHP
2950 Bibliographies
2951 Pamphlet volumes
2952 Collected source materials
2953 Government and administration
2954 Law
2955 Military affairs
2956 Naval affairs
2957 General history
2958 General special
History by periods
2959 Before 500 B.C.
2960 500 - 1 B.C.
2961 1 A.D. - ca. 650
2962 Chronology
2963 Civilization
2964 Religion
2965 Economic conditions
2966 Geography
2967 Travels
2968-2970 Special topics (Develop as needed)
2971-2996 Local (A-Z by place)

Assyria and Babylonia
[For the purposes of this scheme, Assyria
and Babylonia are treated together
because at different periods one country
dominated the territory of both countries.
For each period, the general works which deal
with both countries are classed with works on the
dominant country (Babylonia in the first and
third periods, Assyria in the second).
Books on single events not specially provided
for are to be classed with the reigns in which
the events occurred.]

Countries of ancient Asia (cont.)
  Assyria and Babylonia (cont.)

      Periodicals. See AHP
3000   Bibliographies
        [Include also lists of inscriptions.
         See also AH 3170.]
3001   General pamphlet volumes

      Collected sources
3002   General collections
        [Include general compilations of
         inscriptions]
      Special collections (special periods,
        legal, religious, literary, etc.).
        See with the subject in AH 3020,
        3073, 3123-3124, 3154, 3173, etc.

      Assyriology as a discipline
3004   Theory, scope, methods of study
3005.1-.599 History of Assyriology
        [Include the history of the
         decipherment of the inscriptions.]
      Biographies of scholars
3005.600-.699 Collected
3005.700-.999 Individual (299 scheme, A-Z by person)
        [Include a scholar's memoirs and letters]
3006-3009 General histories (By date)
        [Include here general histories dealing
        with Assyria and Babylonia together
        and general histories of Babylonia.
        General histories of Assyria go in AH
        3075.]
3011   Miscellaneous essays
        [Include Festschriften]
3012   General special
        [Include ancient geography and ethnology.
        See also AH 3103-3127, 3143-3195.]

      Assyro-Babylonian archaeology and art
3013   General works (By date, e.g. .960 for 1960)
3014   Architecture
3015   Painting
3016   Sculpture
3017   Other special
        [Include cylinder seals, glyptics, etc.]

      History by periods
      Before 1300 B.C.
        [First period, Babylonian supremacy]
3018   Mythical rulers
        [Include Semiramis, etc. For
        Sardanapalus or Saracus, see AH 3098.]
3020   Sources and documents
        [Include Sumerian and Akkadian texts, etc.]
3021   General histories
        [N.B. - See also AH 3037]
      Sumer and Akkad
        [These two kingdoms formed the southern
        and northern divisions of what later
        became Babylonia.]
      Documents. See AH 3020
3022   General works
        [Include civilization, etc.
        See also AH 3143-3195.]
3023   Early rulers
3024   Sargon I of Akkad, ca. 2637-2582
3025   Later rulers
        [Include Naram-Sin, Gudea, etc.]
      Amorites, ca. 2050-1750
3027   General works
3028   General special
        [See also AH 3143-3195]
3030   Hammurabi, ca. 1955-1913
        [N.B. - His code of laws goes in
        AH 3151.]
3031   Later rulers

Countries of ancient Asia (cont.)
  Assyria and Babylonia (cont.)
    History by periods (cont.)
      Before 1300 B.C. (cont.)
        Kassites, ca. 1750-1200
3032   General works
3033   General special
        [See also AH 3143-3195]
3035   Individual rulers
      Assyria before ca. 1300
3037   General works
3038   Special events, etc.
        [See also AH 3103-3127 and
        3170-3195.]
3041-3066 Local (A-Z by place)
        [Include the city of Babylon,
        Erech, Kish, Lagash, Larsa, Nippur,
        Seleucia, Tello, Umma, Ur, etc. For
        Nineveh, see AH 3073-3098.]
      Special topics for Babylonia. See
        AH 3143-3195
    1300-606 B.C.
      [Second period, Assyrian supremacy]
      Sources and documents
3073   Collected
3074   Individual
3075   General histories
        [N.B. - Include here histories of
        Assyria and Babylonia together during
        this period, histories of Assyria alone
        during this period, and general histories
        of Assyria covering all periods. See also
        AH 3099-3100.]
      Assyria before 1300. See AH 3037-3038
      Special reigns and events
3081   Shalmaneser I, ca. 1320-1290
3082   1290-1140
3084   Tiglath-Pileser I, ca. 1140-1105
3085   1105-889
3086   Tugulti-Ninip II, ca. 889-885
3087   Asshurnazirpal III, ca. 885-860
3088   Shalmaneser III (II), ca. 860-825
3089   Shamshi-Ramman IV, 824-811
3090   811-745
3092   Tiglath-Pileser IV, 745-728
3093   Shalmaneser V, 728-722
3094   Sargon II, 722-705
3095   Sennacherib, 705-681
3096   Esarhaddon, 681-668
        [For the conquest of Egypt, see
        Eg 650-659.]
3097   Asshurbanipal, 668-625
3098   Decline and fall of Nineveh, 625-606
        [Include works on the identity of
        Saracus or Sardanapalus.]
      Babylonia during 1300-606
3099   General works
3100   Special events, etc.
        [See also AH 3143-3195.]
      Local
        Nineveh. See AH 3073-3098
        Others. See AH 3041-3066
      Special topics for Assyria
        [N.B. - Books on these topics dealing
        with Assyria and Babylonia together go
        in AH 3143-3167.]
        Assyriology as a discipline. See
        AH 3004-3005
        Archaeology and art. See AH 3013-3017
3103   Civilization
        [See also AH 3123-3127]
      Government and administration
        [See also AH 3110-3112]
3105   General works
3107   Special topics
3109   Chronology
      Law
3110   General works
        [Include documents]
3112   Special topics

Countries of ancient Asia (cont.)
  Assyria and Babylonia (cont.)
    History by periods (cont.)
      1300-606 B.C. (cont.)
        Special topics for Assyria (cont.)
          Religion. See AH 3154-3160
          Private life
            Documents
3123   Collected
3124   Special
3125   General works
3127   Special topics
          Foreign relations
            With Hittites. See AH 3400-3420
            With Elam. See AH 3650-3670
            With Israel. See AH 3950-3970
            Literature. See AH 3170-3195
      605-538 B.C.
        [Third period, Babylonian supremacy]
3129   Sources and documents
          [See also AH 3150, 3154, 3163, and
          3173-3195.]
3130   General histories
        Special reigns and events
3132   Nebuchadnezzar, 605-562
3133   Amel Marduk, 562-560
3134   560-556
3135   Nabonidus, 556-539
3137   Assyria during 605-538
        Local. See AH 3041-3066
        Special topics. See AH 3103-3127
          and 3143-3195
      538 B.C. - 650 A.D.
        [Fourth period, foreign domination]
3140   Sources and documents
3141   General histories
3142   Special events, etc.
        Local. See AH 3041-3066
        Special topics. See AH 3103-3127 and
          3143-3195

    Special topics for Babylonia
      [N.B. - Include here works on these topics
      relating to Babylonia alone and to Assyria
      and Babylonia together. Works on these topics
      limited to Assyria alone go in AH 3103-3127.]
      Study of Babylonia as a discipline. See
        AH 3004-3005
      Archaeology and art. See AH 3013-3017
3143   Civilization
        [See also AH 3163-3167]
      Government and administration
        [See also AH 3150-3152]
3145   General works
3147   Special topics
3149   Chronology
      Law
3150   General works
        [Include documents]
3151   Code of Hammurabi
        [Include texts and commentaries]
3152   Other special
      Religion and mythology
3154   Documents and sources
        [See also AH 3181 and 3183]
3155   General works
3156   Magic, divination, etc.
        [See also AH 3183-3184]
3158   Ishtar or Astarte
3159   Relations with Jewish religion
3160   Other special
      Private life
3163   Documents
3165   General works
3167   Special topics

    Assyro-Babylonian literature
3170   Bibliographies
3171   Literary history
3173   General anthologies

Countries of ancient Asia (cont.)
  Assyria and Babylonia (cont.)
    Assyro-Babylonian literature (cont.)
      Poetry
        [See also AH 3181-3184]
3175   Anthologies
3176   General history
3177   Gilgamesh epic
3178   Izdubar saga
3179   Other individual poems
      Hymns and psalms
3181   Texts
3182   Commentaries
      Magical incantations
3183   Texts
3184   Commentaries
      Prose literature
3185   Texts
3186   Commentaries
      Laws. See AH 3110, 3150, etc.
      Letters
3187   Texts
3188   Commentaries
      Maxims, Wisdom literature
3189   Texts
3190   Commentaries
      Medicine
3191   Texts
3192   Commentaries
      Astronomy and Astrology
3193   Texts
3194   Commentaries
3195   Other literature

  Bactria
    Periodicals. See AHP
3200   Bibliographies
3201   Pamphlet volumes
3202   Collected source materials
3203   Government and administration
3204   Law
3205   Military affairs
3206   Naval affairs
3207   General history
3208   General special

    History by periods
3209   Before 500 B.C.
3210   500 - 1 B.C.
3211   1 A.D. - ca. 650
3212   Chronology
3213   Civilization
3214   Religion
3215   Economic conditions
3216   Geography
3217   Travels
3218-3220   Special topics (Develop as needed)
3221-3246   Local (A-Z by place)

  Chaldea. See AH 3000-3195
  Colchis
    Periodicals. See AHP
3250   Bibliographies
3251   Pamphlet volumes
3252   Collected source materials
3253   Government and administration
3254   Law
3255   Military affairs
3256   Naval affairs
3257   General history
3258   General special

    History by periods
3259   Before 500 B.C.
3260   500 - 1 B.C.
3261   1 A.D. - ca. 650
3262   Chronology
3263   Civilization
3264   Religion
3265   Economic conditions

	Countries of ancient Asia (cont.)			Countries of ancient Asia (cont.)
	Colchis (cont.)			Hittites (cont.)
3266	Geography		3412	Chronology
3267	Travels		3413	Civilization
3268-3270	Special topics (Develop as needed)		3414	Religion
3271-3296	Local (A-Z by place)		3415	Economic conditions
			3416	Geography
	Cyprus		3417	Travels
	Periodicals. See AHP		3418-3420	Special topics (Develop as needed)
3300	Bibliographies		3421-3446	Local (A-Z by place)
3301	Pamphlet volumes			
3302	Collected source materials			Iberia, Caucasus
3303	Government and administration			Periodicals. See AHP
3304	Law		3450	Bibliographies
3305	Military affairs		3451	Pamphlet volumes
3306	Naval affairs		3452	Collected source materials
3307	General history		3453	Government and administration
3308	General special		3454	Law
			3455	Military affairs
	History by periods		3456	Naval affairs
3309	Before 500 B.C.		3457	General history
3310	500 - 1 B.C.		3458	General special
3311	1 A.D. - ca. 650			
3312	Chronology			History by periods
3313	Civilization		3459	Before 500 B.C.
3314	Religion		3460	500 - 1 B.C.
3315	Economic conditions		3461	1 A.D. - ca. 650
3316	Geography		3462	Chronology
3317	Travels		3463	Civilization
3318-3320	Special topics (Develop as needed)		3464	Religion
3321-3346	Local (A-Z by place)		3465	Economic conditions
			3466	Geography
	Cyrenaica		3467	Travels
	[N.B. - This is in North Africa and		3468-3470	Special topics (Develop as needed)
	properly should be elsewhere; but there		3471-3496	Local (A-Z by place)
	is no room for it in the correct place,			
	so it is left here.]			Iran. See AH 3650-3696
				Iraq. See AH 3000-3195
				Media
	Periodicals. See AHP			Periodicals. See AHP
3350	Bibliographies		3500	Bibliographies
3351	Pamphlet volumes		3501	Pamphlet volumes
3352	Collected source materials		3502	Collected source materials
3353	Government and administration		3503	Government and administration
3354	Law		3504	Law
3355	Military affairs		3505	Military affairs
3356	Naval affairs		3506	Naval affairs
3357	General history		3507	General history
3358	General special		3508	General special
	History by periods			History by periods
3359	Before 500 B.C.		3509	Before 500 B.C.
3360	500 - 1 B.C.		3510	500 - 1 B.C.
3361	1 A.D. - ca. 650		3511	1 A.D. - ca. 650
3362	Chronology		3512	Chronology
3363	Civilization		3513	Civilization
3364	Religion		3514	Religion
3365	Economic conditions		3515	Economic conditions
3366	Geography		3516	Geography
3367	Travels		3517	Travels
3368-3370	Special topics (Develop as needed)		3518-3520	Special topics (Develop as needed)
3371-3396	Local (A-Z by place)		3521-3546	Local (A-Z by place)
	Egypt. See Eg		[3550-3596]	Mesopotamia [Discontinued. See AH 3000-3195]
	Elam. See AH 3850-3896			Palestine. See AH 3950-3996
	Hittites			
	Periodicals. See AHP			Parthia
3400	Bibliographies			Periodicals. See AHP
3401	Pamphlet volumes		3600	Bibliographies
3402	Collected source materials		3601	Pamphlet volumes
3403	Government and administration		3602	Collected source materials
3404	Law		3603	Government and administration
3405	Military affairs		3604	Law
3406	Naval affairs		3605	Military affairs
3407	General history		3606	Naval affairs
3408	General special		3607	General history
			3608	General special
	History by periods			
3409	Before 500 B.C.			
3410	500 - 1 B.C.			
3411	1 A.D. - ca. 650			

Countries of ancient Asia (cont.)
  Parthia (cont.)

    History by periods
3609   Before 500 B.C.
3610   500 - 1 B.C.
3611   1 A.D. - ca. 650
3612   Chronology
3613   Civilization
3614   Religion
3615   Economic conditions
3616   Geography
3617   Travels
3618-3620   Special topics (Develop as needed)
3621-3646   Local (A-Z by place)

  Persia
    Periodicals. See AHP
3650   Bibliographies
3651   Pamphlet volumes
3652   Collected source materials
3653   Government and administration
3654   Law
3655   Military affairs
3656   Naval affairs
3657   General history
3658   General special

    History by periods
3659   Before 500 B.C.
3660   500 - 1 B.C.
3661   1 A.D. - ca. 650
3662   Chronology
3663   Civilization
3664   Religion
3665   Economic conditions
3666   Geography
3667   Travels

    Special topics
3668   Education
3670   Cities in general
3671-3696   Local (A-Z by place)

  Phoenicia
    Periodicals. See AHP
3700   Bibliographies
3701   Pamphlet volumes
3702   Collected source materials
3703   Government and administration
3704   Law
3705   Military affairs
3706   Naval affairs
3707   General history
3708   General special

    History by periods
3709   Before 500 B.C.
3710   500 - 1 B.C.
3711   1 A.D. - ca. 650
3712   Chronology
3713   Civilization
3714   Religion
3715   Economic conditions
3716   Geography
3717   Travels
3718-3720   Special topics (Develop as needed)
3721-3746   Local (A-Z by place)

  Scythia
    [See also Sarmatia in AH 9800-9846]

    Periodicals. See AHP
3750   Bibliographies
3751   Pamphlet volumes
3752   Collected source materials
3753   Government and administration
3754   Law
3755   Military affairs
3756   Naval affairs

Countries of ancient Asia (cont.)
  Scythia (cont.)
3757   General history
3758   General special

    History by periods
3759   Before 500 B.C.
3760   500 - 1 B.C.
3761   1 A.D. - ca. 650
3762   Chronology
3763   Civilization
3764   Religion
3765   Economic conditions
3766   Geography
3767   Travels
3768-3770   Special topics (Develop as needed)
3771-3796   Local (A-Z by place)

  Semites in general
    Periodicals. See AHP
3800   Bibliographies
3801   Pamphlet volumes
3802   Collected source materials
3803   Government and administration
3804   Law
3805   Military affairs
3806   Naval affairs
3807   General history
3808   General special

    History by periods
3809   Before 500 B.C.
3810   500 - 1 B.C.
3811   1 A.D. - ca. 650
3812   Chronology
3813   Civilization
3814   Religion
3815   Economic conditions
3816   Geography
3817   Travels
3818-3820   Special topics (Develop as needed)

  Sumeria. See AH 3000-3195
  Susiana, Elam
    Periodicals. See AHP
3850   Bibliographies
3851   Pamphlet volumes
3852   Collected source materials
3853   Government and administration
3854   Law
3855   Military affairs
3856   Naval affairs
3857   General history
3858   General special

    History by periods
3859   Before 500 B.C.
3860   500 - 1 B.C.
3861   1 A.D. - ca. 650
3862   Chronology
3863   Civilization
3864   Religion
3865   Economic conditions
3866   Geography
3867   Travels
3868-3870   Special topics (Develop as needed)
3871-3896   Local (A-Z by place)

  Syria
    [Include also works covering Syria,
    Palestine, and Phoenicia together.
    See also AH 3700-3746 and 3950-3996.]

    Periodicals. See AHP
3900   Bibliographies
3901   Pamphlet volumes
3902   Collected source materials
3903   Government and administration
3904   Law
3905   Military affairs

Countries of ancient Asia (cont.)
   Syria (cont.)

3906	Naval affairs
3907	General history
3908	General special
	History by periods
3909	Before 500 B.C.
3910	500 - 1 B.C.
3911	1 A.D. - ca. 650
3912	Chronology
3913	Civilization
3914	Religion
3915	Economic conditions
3916	Geography
3917	Travels
3918-3920	Special topics (Develop as needed)
3921-3946	Local (A-Z by place)

   Palestine
      [See also Jud]

	Periodicals. See AHP
3950	Bibliographies
3951	Pamphlet volumes
3952	Collected source materials
3953	Government and administration
3954	Law
3955	Military affairs
3956	Naval affairs
3957	General history
3958	General special
	History by periods
3959	Before 500 B.C.
3960	500 - 1 B.C.
3961	1 A.D. - ca. 650
3962	Chronology
3963	Civilization
3964	Religion
3965	Economic conditions
3966	Geography
3967	Travels
3968-3970	Special topics (Develop as needed)
3971-3996	Local (A-Z by place)

Ancient Greece in general
   [N.B. - Works dealing with ancient Greece
   and Rome together go in AH 2-979.]

	Periodicals. See AHP and AH 4002
	General bibliographies
4002	Periodicals
4004-4009	Monographs (By date)
4015	General pamphlet volumes
[4018]	Miscellany [Discontinued]
4024-4029	Collected sources, etc. (By date)
	Government and administration
4030-4039	General works (Table A)
	[Include history of political theory, general constitutional history.]
4040-4049	Forms of government (Table A)
	[Include democracy, oligarchy, tyrants, etc.]
4050-4059	Administrative branch (Table A)
4060-4069	Legislature and legislation (Table A)
4070-4079	Popular assemblies (Table A)
4080-4089	Provincial government in general (Table A)
4090-4099	Municipal government in general (Table A)
4100-4109	Public finance (Table A)
	Special topics
4112	Amphictyonic League
4114	Classes of citizens
4115	Tribes
4116	Phratries
4117	Demes
4118	Gentes
4119	Satrapies

Ancient Greece in general (cont.)

	Law
4130-4139	General works (Table A)
	[See also AH 4190-4199]
4140-4149	Public law (Table A)
4150-4159	Criminal law (Table A)
	Private law
4160	Bibliographies; Pamphlet volumes
4161	Family law
4162	Inheritance law
4163	Marriage law
4164	Arrha
4165-4169	General works (By date)
4170-4179	Agrarian law (Table A)
4180-4189	Slavery and emancipation (Table A)
4190-4199	Philosophy of law (Table A)
	Special topics
4200	Laws of Lycurgus
4202	Laws of Draco
4204	Laws of Solon
4206	The Areopagus
4208	The Heliaea
4212	Proxenia
4214	The oath
4215	Sacred law
4216	Suretyship
4217	Public rewards
4218	Statutes of limitations
4219	Sales
4220-4229	Legal procedure (Table A)
4230-4239	Military affairs (Table A)
4250-4259	Naval affairs (Table A)
4260-4269	Foreign relations, diplomacy (Table A)
4274-4279	General history (By date)
	General special
4294-4299	Miscellany (By date)
	[Include Festschriften, congresses, etc.]
4300-4309	Philosophy of history (Table A)
	[Include historiography]
4310-4319	Cosmology (Table A)
4320-4329	Races (Table A)
	[See also AH 4410]
4330-4339	Collected biographies (Table A)
	History by periods
	Before 500 B.C.
4400-4409	General works (Table A)
4410	Bronze age, Mycenaean age
4415	Trojan War
4430-4439	7th century (Table A)
4440-4449	6th century (Table A)
	500-146 B.C.
4450-4459	General works (Table A)
	[Include here general works on the period of Athenian supremacy, the Athenian empire, the fifth century in general, etc.]
	Persian Wars, 499-479
4470-4479	General works (Table A)
4481	Battle of Marathon, 490
4482	Battle of Thermopylae, 480
4483	Battle of Salamis, 480
4484	Battle of Plataea, 479
4486	Miltiades
4487	Themistocles
4490-4499	Age of Pericles, 479-431 (Table A)
	[Include biographies of Pericles, works on the Delian League, etc.]
	The Peloponnesian War, 431-404
4510-4519	General works (Table A)
4521	Alcibiades
4522	Mutilation of the Hermae
4523	Sicilian Expedition
4524	The Four Hundred at Athens

Ancient Greece in general (cont.)
  History by periods (cont.)
    500-146 B.C. (cont.)
      Age of Spartan and Theban supremacy, 404-362
        [N.B. - Limit strictly to this period.
        Other works on Sparta and Thebes go in
        AH 5750-5796 and 5390.]
4530-4539   General works (Table A)
        [Include Corinthian War, Battle of
        Leuctra, etc.]
4543   Phocion
      Age of Macedonian supremacy, 359-280
        [N.B. - Limit strictly to this period.
        Other works on Macedonia go in
        AH 6100-6146.]
4545   General works
      Philip II of Macedon, 359-336.
        See AH 6110
4550-4559   Alexander the Great, 336-323 (Table A)
        [Include biographies of Alexander,
        works on his battles and conquests.]
4600-4609   Macedonian Empire after Alexander (Table A)
        [Include primarily works on the immediate
        successors of Alexander to ca. 280.]
      Hellenistic Age, 323-146
4650-4659   General works (Table A)
      323-280. See AH 4600-4609
4700-4709   Achaean and Aetolian Leagues, 280-220
        (Table A)
4710-4719   Macedonian Wars and Roman conquest,
        220-146 (Table A)
4720-4729   146 B.C. - 323 A.D. (Table A)
        [Include here works on the history of
        Greece under Roman rule]

      Since 323. See MG
4800-4809   Chronology (Table A)

    Civilization, social life
4810-4819   General works (Table A)
        [N.B. - Works dealing with a specific
        period, e.g . the Age of Pericles or the
        Hellenistic Age, go preferably with the
        period.]
4820-4829   Private life (Table A)
4830-4839   Athletic games, sports (Table A)
        [Use AH 4833 for Gymnastics]

      Special topics
4840   The family
4841   Writing, scribes
          [See also Arc and Class]
4842   Books and education
4843   Music and dancing
          [See also Class]
4844   Festivals
4845   Character and morals
4846   Houses, etc.
4847   Baths
4848   Costume
4849   Perfumes
4850   Meals
4851   Fire and lights
4852   Pottery and metalwork
4853   Glass
4854   Domestic plants and animals
4855   Hunting and fishing
4856   Guest-friendship
4857   Parasites
4858   Marriage
4859   Condition of women
4860   Condition of children
4861   Burial
4862   Hygiene
          [N.B. - See Class for medicine]
4863   Sexual customs, love
4864   Games, toys
4865.1-.499   Vehicles
4865.500-.999   Inns
4866   Amber

Ancient Greece in general (cont.)
  Civilization, social life (cont.)
    Special topics (cont.)
4867   Gestures
4868   Beverages
4869   Names
        Arts and sciences. See Class

    Religion and mythology. See Class

    Economic conditions
4880-4889   General works (Table A)
4890-4899   Agriculture (Table A)
4900-4909   Commerce and industries (Table A)
4910-4919   Associations (Table A)
4920-4929   Weights and measures (Table A)
      Public finance. See AH 4100-4109

    Geography and description
4930-4939   General works (Table A)
4945-4949   Atlases (By date)

    Travels
4950-4959   General works (Table A)
4960-4969   Imaginary travels (Table A)
4970-4979   Guidebooks (Table A)

Ancient Greek provinces, etc.

  Acarnania
    Periodicals. See AHP
5000   Bibliographies
5001   Pamphlet volumes
5002   Collected source materials
5003   Government and administration
5004   Law
5005   Military affairs
5006   Naval affairs
5007   General history
5008   General special

    History by periods
5009   Before 500 B.C.
5010   500 - 1 B.C.
5011   1 A.D. - ca. 500
5012   Chronology
5013   Civilization
5014   Religion
5015   Economic conditions
5016   Geography
5017   Travels
5018-5020   Special topics (Develop as needed)
5021-5046   Local (A-Z by place)

  Achaia
    Periodicals. See AHP
5050   Bibliographies
5051   Pamphlet volumes
5052   Collected source materials
5053   Government and administration
5054   Law
5055   Military affairs
5056   Naval affairs
5057   General history
5058   General special

    History by periods
5059   Before 500 B.C.
5060   500 - 1 B.C.
5061   1 A.D. - ca. 500
5062   Chronology
5063   Civilization
5064   Religion
5065   Economic conditions
5066   Geography
5067   Travels
5068-5070   Special topics (Develop as needed)
5071-5096   Local (A-Z by place)

Ancient Greek provinces, etc. (cont.)

    Aegean Islands
      [See also AH 4410]

      Periodicals. See AHP
5100   Bibliographies
5101   Pamphlet volumes
5102   Collected source materials
5103   Government and administration
5104   Law
5105   Military affairs
5106   Naval affairs
5107   General history
5108   General special

      History by periods
5109   Before 500 B.C.
5110   500 - 1 B.C.
5111   1 A.D. - ca. 500
5112   Chronology
5113   Civilization
5114   Religion
5115   Economic conditions
5116   Geography
5117   Travels
5118-5120   Special topics (Develop as needed)
5121-5146   Local (A-Z by place)

    Aetolia
      Periodicals. See AHP
5150   Bibliographies
5151   Pamphlet volumes
5152   Collected source materials
5153   Government and administration
5154   Law
5155   Military affairs
5156   Naval affairs
5157   General history
5158   General special

      History by periods
5159   Before 500 B.C.
5160   500 - 1 B.C.
5161   1 A.D. - ca. 500
5162   Chronology
5163   Civilization
5164   Religion
5165   Economic conditions
5166   Geography
5167   Travels
5168-5170   Special topics (Develop as needed)
5171-5196   Local (A-Z by place)

    Arcadia
      Periodicals. See AHP
5200   Bibliographies
5201   Pamphlet volumes
5202   Collected source materials
5203   Government and administration
5204   Law
5205   Military affairs
5206   Naval affairs
5207   General history
5208   General special

      History by periods
5209   Before 500 B.C.
5210   500 - 1 B.C.
5211   1 A.D. - ca. 500
5212   Chronology
5213   Civilization
5214   Religion
5215   Economic conditions
5216   Geography
5217   Travels
5218-5220   Special topics (Develop as needed)
5221-5246   Local (A-Z by place)

Ancient Greek provinces, etc. (cont.)

    Argolis
      Periodicals. See AHP
5250   Bibliographies
5251   Pamphlet volumes
5252   Collected source materials
5253   Government and administration
5254   Law
5255   Military affairs
5256   Naval affairs
5257   General history
5258   General special

      History by periods
5259   Before 500 B.C.
5260   500 - 1 B.C.
5261   1 A.D. - ca. 500
5262   Chronology
5263   Civilization
5264   Religion
5265   Economic conditions
5266   Geography
5267   Travels
5268-5270   Special topics (Develop as needed)
5271-5296   Local (A-Z by place)

    Attica
      [N.B. - The whole set of numbers has been
      used for Athens; the numbers for Local
      are used for particular parts of Athens.
      Note also that many books on Athens,
      especially during its period of supremacy
      in the fifth century B.C., are with
      Greece in general in AH 4000-4979.]

      Periodicals. See AHP
5300   Bibliographies
5301   Pamphlet volumes
5302   Collected source materials
5303   Government and administration
5304   Law
5305   Military affairs
5306   Naval affairs
5307   General history
5308   General special

      History by periods
5309   Before 500 B.C.
5310   500 - 1 B.C.
5311   1 A.D. - ca. 500
5312   Chronology
5313   Civilization
5314   Religion
5315   Economic conditions
5316   Geography
5317   Travels
5318-5320   Special topics (Develop as needed)
5321-5346   Local (A-Z by place)

    Black Sea colonies. See AH 6150-6196
    Boeotia
      Periodicals. See AHP
5350   Bibliographies
5351   Pamphlet volumes
5352   Collected source materials
5353   Government and administration
5354   Law
5355   Military affairs
5356   Naval affairs
5357   General history
5358   General special

      History by periods
5359   Before 500 B.C.
5360   500 - 1 B.C.
5361   1 A.D. - ca. 500
5362   Chronology
5363   Civilization
5364   Religion

Ancient Greek provinces, etc. (cont.)

Boeotia (cont.)

5365	Economic conditions
5366	Geography
5367	Travels
5368-5370	Special topics (Develop as needed)
5371-5396	Local (A-Z by place)

Corinthia

	Periodicals. See AHP
5400	Bibliographies
5401	Pamphlet volumes
5402	Collected source materials
5403	Government and administration
5404	Law
5405	Military affairs
5406	Naval affairs
5407	General history
5408	General special

History by periods

5409	Before 500 B.C.
5410	500 - 1 B.C.
5411	1 A.D. - ca. 500
5412	Chronology
5413	Civilization
5414	Religion
5415	Economic conditions
5416	Geography
5417	Travels
5418-5420	Special topics (Develop as needed)
5421-5446	Local (A-Z by place)

Crete

[See also AH 4410]

	Periodicals. See AHP
5450	Bibliographies
5451	Pamphlet volumes
5452	Collected source materials
5453	Government and administration
5454	Law
5455	Military affairs
5456	Naval affairs
5457	General history
5458	General special

History by periods

5459	Before 500 B.C.
5460	500 - 1 B.C.
5461	1 A.D. - ca. 500
5462	Chronology
5463	Civilization
5464	Religion
5465	Economic conditions
5466	Geography
5467	Travels
5468-5470	Special topics (Develop as needed)
5471-5496	Local (A-Z by place)

Doris

	Periodicals. See AHP
5500	Bibliographies
5501	Pamphlet volumes
5502	Collected source materials
5503	Government and administration
5504	Law
5505	Military affairs
5506	Naval affairs
5507	General history
5508	General special

History by periods

5509	Before 500 B.C.
5510	500 - 1 B.C.
5511	1 A.D. - ca. 500
5512	Chronology
5513	Civilization
5514	Religion
5515	Economic conditions

Ancient Greek provinces, etc. (cont.)

Doris (cont.)

5516	Geography
5517	Travels
5518-5520	Special topics (Develop as needed)
5521-5546	Local (A-Z by place)

Elis

	Periodicals. See AHP
5550	Bibliographies
5551	Pamphlet volumes
5552	Collected source materials
5553	Government and administration
5554	Law
5555	Military affairs
5556	Naval affairs
5557	General history
5558	General special

History by periods

5559	Before 500 B.C.
5560	500 - 1 B.C.
5561	1 A.D. - ca. 500
5562	Chronology
5563	Civilization
5564	Religion
5565	Economic conditions
5566	Geography
5567	Travels
5568-5570	Special topics (Develop as needed)
5571-5596	Local (A-Z by place)

Epirus

	Periodicals. See AHP
5600	Bibliographies
5601	Pamphlet volumes
5602	Collected source materials
5603	Government and administration
5604	Law
5605	Military affairs
5606	Naval affairs
5607	General history
5608	General special

History by periods

5609	Before 500 B.C.
5610	500 - 1 B.C.
5611	1 A.D. - ca. 500
5612	Chronology
5613	Civilization
5614	Religion
5615	Economic conditions
5616	Geography
5617	Travels
5618-5620	Special topics (Develop as needed)
5621-5646	Local (A-Z by place)

Euboea

	Periodicals. See AHP
5650	Bibliographies
5651	Pamphlet volumes
5652	Collected source materials
5653	Government and administration
5654	Law
5655	Military affairs
5656	Naval affairs
5657	General history
5658	General special

History by periods

5659	Before 500 B.C.
5660	500 - 1 B.C.
5661	1 A.D. - ca. 500
5662	Chronology
5663	Civilization
5664	Religion
5665	Economic conditions
5666	Geography
5667	Travels
5668-5670	Special topics (Develop as needed)

	Ancient Greek provinces, etc. (cont.)
	Euboea (cont.)
5671-5696	Local (A-Z by place)
	Ionia district, Asia Minor. See AH 2120
	Ionian Islands
	Periodicals. See AHP
5700	Bibliographies
5701	Pamphlet volumes
5702	Collected source materials
5703	Government and administration
5704	Law
5705	Military affairs
5706	Naval affairs
5707	General history
5708	General special
	History by periods
5709	Before 500 B.C.
5710	500 - 1 B.C.
5711	1 A.D. - ca. 500
5712	Chronology
5713	Civilization
5714	Religion
5715	Economic conditions
5716	Geography
5717	Travels
5718-5720	Special topics (Develop as needed)
5721-5746	Local (A-Z by place)
	Laconia
	[N.B. - The whole set of numbers has been
	used for Sparta. See also AH 4530-4543.]
	Periodicals. See AHP
5750	Bibliographies
5751	Pamphlet volumes
5752	Collected source materials
5753	Government and administration
5754	Law
5755	Military affairs
5756	Naval affairs
5757	General history
5758	General special
	History by periods
5759	Before 500 B.C.
5760	500 - 1 B.C.
5761	1 A.D. - ca. 500
5762	Chronology
5763	Civilization
5764	Religion
5765	Economic conditions
5766	Geography
5767	Travels
5768-5770	Special topics (Develop as needed)
5771-5796	Local (A-Z by place)
	Locris
	Periodicals. See AHP
5800	Bibliographies
5801	Pamphlet volumes
5802	Collected source materials
5803	Government and administration
5804	Law
5805	Military affairs
5806	Naval affairs
5807	General history
5808	General special
	History by periods
5809	Before 500 B.C.
5810	500 - 1 B.C.
5811	1 A.D. - ca. 500
5812	Chronology
5813	Civilization
5814	Religion
5815	Economic conditions
5816	Geography
5817	Travels

	Ancient Greek provinces, etc. (cont.)
	Locris (cont.)
5818-5820	Special topics (Develop as needed)
5821-5846	Local (A-Z by place)
	Macedonia. See AH 6100-6146
	Megaris
	Periodicals. See AHP
5850	Bibliographies
5851	Pamphlet volumes
5852	Collected source materials
5853	Government and administration
5854	Law
5855	Military affairs
5856	Naval affairs
5857	General history
5858	General special
	History by periods
5859	Before 500 B.C.
5860	500 - 1 B.C.
5861	1 A.D. - ca. 500
5862	Chronology
5863	Civilization
5864	Religion
5865	Economic conditions
5866	Geography
5867	Travels
5868-5870	Special topics (Develop as needed)
5871-5896	Local (A-Z by place)
	Messenia
	[See also AH 4410]
	Periodicals. See AHP
5900	Bibliographies
5901	Pamphlet volumes
5902	Collected source materials
5903	Government and administration
5904	Law
5905	Military affairs
5906	Naval affairs
5907	General history
5908	General special
	History by periods
5909	Before 500 B.C.
5910	500 - 1 B.C.
5911	1 A.D. - ca. 500
5912	Chronology
5913	Civilization
5914	Religion
5915	Economic conditions
5916	Geography
5917	Travels
5918-5920	Special topics (Develop as needed)
5921-5946	Local (A-Z by place)
	Northern Shores of the Black Sea.
	See AH 6150-6196
	Peloponnesus in general
	Periodicals. See AHP
5950	Bibliographies
5951	Pamphlet volumes
5952	Collected source materials
5953	Government and administration
5954	Law
5955	Military affairs
5956	Naval affairs
5957	General history
5958	General special
	History by periods
5959	Before 500 B.C.
5960	500 - 1 B.C.
5961	1 A.D. - ca. 500
5962	Chronology
5963	Civilization
5964	Religion
5965	Economic conditions

Ancient Greek provinces, etc. (cont.)
  Peloponnesus in general (cont.)

5966	Geography
5967	Travels
5968-5970	Special topics (Develop as needed)

  Phocis
    Periodicals. See AHP

6000	Bibliographies
6001	Pamphlet volumes
6002	Collected source materials
6003	Government and administration
6004	Law
6005	Military affairs
6006	Naval affairs
6007	General history
6008	General special

    History by periods

6009	Before 500 B.C.
6010	500 - 1 B.C.
6011	1 A.D. - ca. 500
6012	Chronology
6013	Civilization
6014	Religion
6015	Economic conditions
6016	Geography
6017	Travels
6018-6020	Special topics (Develop as needed)
6021-6046	Local (A-Z by place)
6049	Sicyonia

  Thessaly
    Periodicals. See AHP

6050	Bibliographies
6051	Pamphlet volumes
6052	Collected source materials
6053	Government and administration
6054	Law
6055	Military affairs
6056	Naval affairs
6057	General history
6058	General special

    History by periods

6059	Before 500 B.C.
6060	500 - 1 B.C.
6061	1 A.D. - ca. 500
6062	Chronology
6063	Civilization
6064	Religion
6065	Economic conditions
6066	Geography
6067	Travels
6068-6070	Special topics (Develop as needed)
6071-6096	Local (A-Z by place)

  Thrace. See AH 9700-9746
  Macedonia
    [See also AH 4545-4609]

    Periodicals. See AHP

6100	Bibliographies
6101	Pamphlet volumes
6102	Collected source materials
6103	Government and administration
6104	Law
6105	Military affairs
6106	Naval affairs
6107	General history
6108	General special

    History by periods

6109	Before 500 B.C.
6110	500 - 1 B.C.
6111	1 A.D. - ca. 500
6112	Chronology
6113	Civilization
6114	Religion

Ancient Greek provinces, etc. (cont.)
  Macedonia (cont.)

6115	Economic conditions
6116	Geography
6117	Travels
6118-6120	Special topics (Develop as needed)
6121-6146	Local (A-Z by place)

  Northern Shores of the Black Sea
    Periodicals. See AHP

6150	Bibliographies
6151	Pamphlet volumes
6152	Collected source materials
6153	Government and administration
6154	Law
6155	Military affairs
6156	Naval affairs
6157	General history
6158	General special

    History by periods

6159	Before 500 B.C.
6160	500 - 1 B.C.
6161	1 A.D. - ca. 500
6162	Chronology
6163	Civilization
6164	Religion
6165	Economic conditions
6166	Geography
6167	Travels
6168-6170	Special topics (Develop as needed)
6171-6196	Local (A-Z by place)

Ionia district, Asia Minor. See AH 2120
Thrace. See AH 9700-9746
Magna Graecia. See AH 8647, etc.

Ancient Rome in general
    [N.B. - Include here works dealing with the
    ancient Roman Republic or Roman Empire
    as a whole. Works limited to the city of Rome
    go in AH 8650-8696. Works on Italy in
    general go in AH 8600-8617.]

Periodicals. See AHP and AH 7002

	General bibliographies
7002	Periodicals
7004-7009	Monographs (By date)
7015	General pamphlet volumes
7024-7029	Collected sources (By date)

	Government and administration
7030-7039	General works (Table A)
	[Include history of political theory, general constitutional history.]
7040-7049	Forms of government (Table A)
7050-7059	Administrative branch (Table A)
	[Include praefects, consuls, magistrates, tribunes, etc.]
7060-7069	Legislature and legislation (Table A)
	[See also AH 7207]
7070-7079	Popular assemblies (Table A)
7080-7089	Provincial government in general (Table A)
7090-7099	Municipal government in general (Table A)
7100-7109	Public finance (Table A)

	Special topics
7114	Classes of citizens
	[See also AH 7217]
7115	Tribes
7116	Centuries
7118	Gentes

  Law
    [N.B. - Class here only works on the law of
    ancient Rome. Roman law of mediaeval and
    modern Europe goes in Gov.]

7130-7139	General works (Table A)
	[See also AH 7190-7199]

Ancient Rome in general (cont.)
Law (cont.)
7140-7149   Public law (Table A)
7150-7159   Criminal law (Table A)

Private law
7160   Bibliographies; Pamphlet volumes
7161   Family law
7162   Inheritance law
7163   Marriage law
7164-7169   General works (By date)
7170-7179   Agrarian law (Table A)
7180-7189   Slavery and emancipation (Table A)
7190-7199   Philosophy of law (Table A)

Special topics
7200   The Twelve Tables
7201   Early law and jurists
     [Include Gaius, Ulpianus, etc.]
7202   Codex Theodosianus
7203   Justinian's Corpus juris civilis
     [Include also the Institutes and
       Digest.]
7204   Imperial institutes before Justinian
     [Include Caracalla, Marcus
       Aurelius, Vespasiam, etc.]
7205   Theophilus
7206   Other Byzantine laws
     [Include the Ecloga of Leo, the
       Basilica, etc.]
7207   The Senate
7208   The Comitia
7210   Interreges
7212   Leges Annales
7214   The oath
7215   Sacred law
7216   Suretyship
7217   Public rewards; Nobility
7218   Treasure-trove
7219   Sales
7220-7229   Legal procedure (Table A)
7230-7239   Military affairs (Table A)
     [Include military triumphalia, military
       tribunes, etc.]
7250-7259   Naval affairs (Table A)
7260-7269   Foreign relations, diplomacy (Table A)
7274-7279   General history (By date)

General special
7294-7299   Miscellany (By date)
     [Include Festschriften, congresses, etc.]
7300-7309   Philosophy of history (Table A)
     [Include historiography]
7310-7319   Cosmology (Table A)
7320-7329   Races (Table A)
7330-7339   Collected biographies (Table A)

History by periods
7400-7409   Origins and Kings, 753-510 B.C. (Table A)
     [Include Romulus, Tarquinius, etc.]

Republic, 509-27 B.C.
7410-7419   General works (Table A)
7420-7429   509-343 (Table A)
     [Include also works covering the
       period 509-265 as a whole.]
7430-7439   343-265 (Table A)
     [Include Samnite Wars and subjugation of
       Italy, biography of Appius Claudius Caeus.]
7440-7449   264-201 (Table A)
     [Include also works covering the
       period 264-133 as a whole.
       Include 1st and 2nd Punic Wars;
       biography of Marcus Atilius Regulus,
       Hannibal, Scipio Africanus Major]
7450-7459   200-146 (Table A)
     [For the Macedonian Wars and other wars in
       Greece, see AH 4710-4719. Include
       here other wars of the period; biography
       of Scipio Aemilianus, etc.]

Ancient Rome in general (cont.)
History by periods (cont.)
Republic, 509-27 B.C. (cont.)
7460-7469   146-27 (Table A)
     [Include works on the decline of the
       Republic and the establishment of the
       Empire; the Servile Wars, Civil Wars,
       Mithradatic Wars, and other wars
       of the period; biography of the Gracchi,
       Marius and Sulla, Cataline, Lucullus,
       Verres, etc.]
7470-7479   Age of Julius Caesar (Table A)
     [Include Caesar's life and wars; also
       the 1st and 2nd Triumvirates; biography of
       Brutus, Pompey, Marc Antony]

Empire, 27 B.C. - 476 A.D.
7480-7489   General works (Table A)
     [Include also works covering the period
       27 B.C. - 180 A.D. or 27 B.C. -
       284 A.D. as a whole.]
The Caesars, 27 B.C. - 96 A.D.
7490-7499   General works (Table A)
     [Include general works on "the 12
       Caesars"]
7500-7509   Augustus, 27 B.C. - 14 A.D. (Table A)
     [Include also Marcus Agrippa]
7510-7519   Tiberius, 14-37 (Table A)
     [Include also Germanicus
       and Agrippina the elder.]
7520-7529   Caligula, 37-41 (Table A)
7530-7539   Claudius I, 41-54 (Table A)
7540-7549   Nero, 54-68 (Table A)
7550-7559   Galba, Otto, Vitellius, 68-69 (Table A)
7560-7569   Vespasian, 69-79 (Table A)
7570-7579   Titus, 79-81 (Table A)
7580-7589   Domitian, 81-96 (Table A)
The Antonines, 96-180
7590-7599   General works (Table A)
     [Include also works on the 2nd century
       in general]
7600-7609   Nerva, 96-98 (Table A)
7610-7619   Trajan, 98-117 (Table A)
7620-7629   Hadrian, 117-138 (Table A)
7630-7639   Antoninus Pius, 138-161 (Table A)
7640-7649   Marcus Aurelius, 161-180 (Table A)
     [N.B. - For his writings and
       critical works about them, see Ga 73.]
The Decline, 180-476
General works
Gibbon's Decline and Fall
7650   Complete editions in English
7651   Abridgements and Selections
7652   Translations
7653   Criticism
7654   Bibliographies, Pamphlet volumes, etc.
7655-7659   Other general works (By date)
     [N.B. - Class here only works
       on the whole period. For
       particular centuries, see
       AH 7700-7709, 7760-7769,
       and 7790-7799.]
7660-7669   Commodus, 180-192 (Table A)
7670-7679   Pertinax, 192 (Table A)
7680-7689   Didius, Julianus, 193 (Table A)
7690-7699   Septimius Severus, 193-211 (Table A)
7700-7709   Third century in general (Table A)
     [Include also works on individual
       emperors not provided for in
       AH 7710-7749, e.g. Maximinus,
       Gordianus, Gallus, Valerian,
       Gallienus, Claudius II, Probus.]
7710-7719   Caracalla and Macrinus, 211-218 (Table A)
7720-7729   Heliogabalus, 218-222 (Table A)
7730-7739   Severus Alexander, 222-235 (Table A)
     Emperors of 235-284. See AH 7700-7709
       284-476 in general. See AH 7650-7659
7740-7749   Diocletian, 284-305 (Table A)
7750-7759   Constantine I, 306-337 (Table A)
7760-7769   Fourth century in general (Table A)
     [Include also works on individual
       emperors not provided for in
       AH 7770-7789, e.g. the Rival

Ancient Rome in general (cont.)
  History by periods (cont.)
    Empire, 27 B.C. - 476 A.D. (cont.)
      The Decline, 180-476 (cont.)
        Fourth century in general (Table A) (cont.)
          Augusti of 306-324, Constantine II,
          Constans, Valentinian I and II,
          Gratian, Theodosius I.]

7770-7779   Julian, 361-363 (Table A)
7780-7789   Jovian, 363-364 (Table A)
7790-7799   Fifth century in general (Table A)
          [Include also works on individual
          emperors for 395 to 476; also Galla
          Placidia, Attila, etc. See also
          H 440-449; also MG.]

      Since 476. See Ital
7800-7809   Chronology (Table A)

    Civilization, social life
7810-7819   General works (Table A)
        [N.B. - Works dealing with a specific period,
        e.g. the reign of an emperor, go preferably
        with the period.]
7820-7829   Private life (Table A)
7830-7839   Athletic games, sports (Table A)
        [Include also gladiators. Use AH 7833
        for Gymnastics.]

    Special topics
7840   The family
7841   Writing, scribes
        [See also Arc and Class]
7842   Books and education
7843   Music and dancing
        [See also Class]
7844   Festivals, spectacles
        [See also Class for religious festivals]
7845   Character and morals
7846   Houses, etc.
7847   Baths
7848   Costume
7849   Perfumes
7850   Meals
7851   Fire and lights
7852   Pottery and metalwork
7853   Glass
7854   Domestic plants and animals
7855   Hunting and fishing
7856   Guest-friendship
7857   Parasites
7858   Marriage
7859   Condition of women
7860   Condition of children
7861   Burial
7862   Hygiene
        [N.B. - See Class for medicine]
7863   Sexual customs, love
7864   Games, toys
        [See also AH 7844]
7865.1-.499   Vehicles
7865.500-.999   Inns
7866   Amber
7867   Gestures
7868   Beverages
7869   Names
      Arts and sciences. See Class

    Religion. See Class

    Economic conditions
7880-7889   General works (Table A)
7890-7899   Agriculture (Table A)
7900-7909   Commerce and industries (Table A)
7910-7919   Associations (Table A)
7920-7929   Weights and measures (Table A)
      Public finance. See AH 7100-7109

Ancient Rome in general (cont.)

  Geography and description
7930-7939   General works (Table A)
7945-7949   Atlases (By date)

  Travels
7950-7959   General works (Table A)
7960-7969   Imaginary travels (Table A)
7970-7979   Guidebooks (Table A)

Ancient North Africa
  [N.B. - This is the Africa known to the
  Greeks and Romans. For ancient Africa
  as a whole and for ancient central and southern
  Africa, see Afr.]

  General
    Periodicals. See AHP
8000   Bibliographies
8001   Pamphlet volumes
8002   Collected source materials
8003   Government and administration
8004   Law
8005   Military affairs
8006   Naval affairs
8007   General history
8008   General special

    History by periods
8009   Before 500 B.C.
8010   500 - 1 B.C.
8011   1 A.D. - ca. 650
8012   Chronology
8013   Civilization
8014   Religion
8015   Economic conditions
8016   Geography
8017   Travels
8018-8020   Special topics (Develop as needed)

  Hamites in general
    [N.B. - See Afr for works on the Hamitic race
    in post-Roman times]
8047   Bibliographies
8048   General works
8049   Special topics

  Africa Proper (Province); Carthage
    [N.B. - This is approximately the equivalent
    of modern Tunisia. Works on Hannibal and the
    Punic Wars go in AH 7440-7449.]

    Periodicals. See AHP
8050   Bibliographies
8051   Pamphlet volumes
8052   Collected source materials
8053   Government and administration
8054   Law
8055   Military affairs
8056   Naval affairs
8057   General history
8058   General special

    History by periods
8059   Before 500 B.C.
8060   500 - 1 B.C.
8061   1 A.D. - ca. 650
8062   Chronology
8063   Civilization
8064   Religion
8065   Economic conditions
8066   Geography
8067   Travels
8068-8070   Special topics (Develop as needed)
8071-8096   Local (A-Z by place)

  Cyrenaica. See AH 3350-3396
  Egypt. See Eg
  Mauretania
    [N.B. - This is approximately the equivalent
    of modern Morocco.]

	Ancient North Africa (cont.)
	Mauretania (cont.)
	Periodicals. See AHP
8100	Bibliographies
8101	Pamphlet volumes
8102	Collected source materials
8103	Government and administration
8104	Law
8105	Military affairs
8106	Naval affairs
8107	General history
8108	General special
	History by periods
8109	Before 500 B.C.
8110	500 - 1 B.C.
8111	1 A.D. - ca. 650
8112	Chronology
8113	Civilization
8114	Religion
8115	Economic conditions
8116	Geography
8117	Travels
8118-8120	Special topics (Develop as needed)
8121-8146	Local (A-Z by place)
	Numidia
	[N.B. - This is approximately the equivalent of modern Algeria.]
	Periodicals. See AHP
8150	Bibliographies
8151	Pamphlet volumes
8152	Collected source materials
8153	Government and administration
8154	Law
8155	Military affairs
8156	Naval affairs
8157	General history
8158	General special
	History by periods
8159	Before 500 B.C.
8160	500 - 1 B.C.
8161	1 A.D. - ca. 650
8162	Chronology
8163	Civilization
8164	Religion
8165	Economic conditions
8166	Geography
8167	Travels
8168-8170	Special topics (Develop as needed)
8171-8196	Local (A-Z by place)
	Ancient Europe
	General. See AH 7002-7979
	Britain
	[N.B. - Prefer Br for works covering Pre-Roman and Roman times together.]
	Periodicals. See AHP
8200	Bibliographies
8201	Pamphlet volumes
8202	Collected source materials
8203	Government and administration
8204	Law
8205	Military affairs
8206	Naval affairs
8207	General history
8208	General special
	History by periods
8209	Before 500 B.C.
8210	500 - 1 B.C.
8211	1 A.D. - ca. 650
8212	Chronology
8213	Civilization
8214	Religion

	Ancient Europe (cont.)
	Britain (cont.)
8215	Economic conditions
8216	Geography
8217	Travels
8218-8220	Special topics (Develop as needed)
8221-8246	Local (A-Z by place)
	Corsica. See AH 9550-9596
	Dacia. See AH 8300-8346
	Dalmatia. See AH 8574
	Danubian Provinces
	General
	Periodicals. See AHP
8250	Bibliographies
8251	Pamphlet volumes
8252	Collected source materials
8253	Government and administration
8254	Law
8255	Military affairs
8256	Naval affairs
8257	General history
8258	General special
	History by periods
8259	Before 500 B.C.
8260	500 - 1 B.C.
8261	1 A.D. - ca. 500
8262	Chronology
8263	Civilization
8264	Religion
8265	Economic conditions
8266	Geography
8267	Travels
8268-8270	Special topics (Develop as needed)
	Dacia
	Periodicals. See AHP
8300	Bibliographies
8301	Pamphlet volumes
8302	Collected source materials
8303	Government and administration
8304	Law
8305	Military affairs
8306	Naval affairs
8307	General history
8308	General special
	History by periods
8309	Before 500 B.C.
8310	500 - 1 B.C.
8311	1 A.D. - ca.500
8312	Chronology
8313	Civilization
8314	Religion
8315	Economic conditions
8316	Geography
8317	Travels
8318-8320	Special topics (Develop as needed)
8321-8346	Local (A-Z by place)
	Moesia
	Periodicals. See AHP
8350	Bibliographies
8351	Pamphlet volumes
8352	Collected source materials
8353	Government and administration
8354	Law
8355	Military affairs
8356	Naval affairs
8357	General history
8358	General special
	History by periods
8359	Before 500 B.C.
8360	500 - 1 B.C.
8361	1 A.D. - ca. 500
8362	Chronology
8363	Civilization
8364	Religion
8365	Economic conditions
8366	Geography
8367	Travels

Ancient Europe (cont.)
  Danubian Provinces (cont.)
    Moesia (cont.)
8368-8370   Special topics (Develop as needed)
8371-8396   Local (A-Z by place)

    Noricum
      Periodicals. See AHP
8400   Bibliographies
8401   Pamphlet volumes
8402   Collected source materials
8403   Government and administration
8404   Law
8405   Military affairs
8406   Naval affairs
8407   General history
8408   General special
      History by periods
8409   Before 500 B.C.
8410   500 - 1 B.C.
8411   1 A.D. - ca.500
8412   Chronology
8413   Civilization
8414   Religion
8415   Economic conditions
8416   Geography
8417   Travels
8418-8420   Special topics (Develop as needed)
8421-8446   Local (A-Z by place)

    Pannonia
      Periodicals. See AHP
8450   Bibliographies
8451   Pamphlet volumes
8452   Collected source materials
8453   Government and administration
8454   Law
8455   Military affairs
8456   Naval affairs
8457   General history
8458   General special
      History by periods
8459   Before 500 B.C.
8460   500 - 1 B.C.
8461   1 A.D. - ca. 500
8462   Chronology
8463   Civilization
8464   Religion
8465   Economic conditions
8466   Geography
8467   Travels
8468-8470   Special topics (Develop as needed)
8471-8496   Local (A-Z by place)

    Gaul
      [N.B. - Prefer Fr for works covering
      Pre-Roman and Roman times together.
      See also AH 9500-9546 for the Rhenish
      Provinces; also AH 8950-8996 for
      Cisalpine Gaul.]

      Periodicals. See AHP
8500   Bibliographies
8501   Pamphlet volumes
8502   Collected source materials
8503   Government and administration
8504   Law
8505   Military affairs
8506   Naval affairs
8507   General history
8508   General special

      History by periods
8509   Before 500 B.C.
8510   500 - 1 B.C.
8511   1 A.D. - ca. 500
8512   Chronology
8513   Civilization
8514   Religion
8515   Economic conditions

Ancient Europe (cont.)
  Gaul (cont.)
8516   Geography
8517   Travels
8518-8520   Special topics (Develop as needed)
8521-8546   Local (A-Z by place)

    Celts in general
8547   Bibliographies
8548   General works
8549   Religion and mythology; Druidism (By date,
         e.g. .150 for 1950)
      Germany. See AH 9750-9796
      Hispania, Iberian Peninsula. See AH 9650-9696

    Illyricum
      [Include Dalmatia]

      Periodicals. See AHP
8550   Bibliographies
8551   Pamphlet volumes
8552   Collected source materials
8553   Government and administration
8554   Law
8555   Military affairs
8556   Naval affairs
8557   General history
8558   General special

      History by periods
8559   Before 500 B.C.
8560   500 - 1 B.C.
8561   1 A.D. - ca. 500
8562   Chronology
8563   Civilization
8564   Religion
8565   Economic conditions
8566   Geography
8567   Travels
8568-8570   Special topics (Develop as needed)
8571-8596   Local (A-Z by place)

    Italy
      General
        Periodicals. See AHP
8600   Bibliographies
8601   Pamphlet volumes
8602   Collected source materials
8603   Government and administration
8604   Law
8605   Military affairs
8606   Naval affairs
8607   General history
8608   General special
      History by periods
8609   Before 500 B.C.
8610   500 - 1 B.C.
8611   1 A.D. - ca.500
8612   Chronology
8613   Civilization
8614   Religion
8615   Economic conditions
8616   Geography
8617   Travels
8618-8620   Special topics (Develop as needed)
      Cities and towns, etc. See AH 8650-9446

8647   Magna Graecia in general
        [See also AH 8700-8796, 9600-9646, etc.]

      City of Rome
        [N.B. - Include here only works limited
        strictly to Rome as a city. The numbers for
        Local are used for districts and buildings
        of the city.]
        Periodicals. See AHP
8650   Bibliographies
8651   Pamphlet volumes
8652   Collected source materials
8653   Government and administration

	Ancient Europe (cont.)		**Ancient Europe (cont.)**
	Italy (cont.)		Italy (cont.)
	City of Rome (cont.)		Campania (cont.)
8654	Law	8856	Naval affairs
8655	Military affairs	8857	General history
8656	Naval affairs	8858	General special
8657	General history		History by periods
8658	General special	8859	Before 500 B.C.
	History by periods	8860	500 - 1 B.C.
8659	Before 500 B.C.	8861	1 A.D. - ca. 500
8660	500 - 1 B.C.	8862	Chronology
8661	1 A.D. - ca. 500	8863	Civilization
8662	Chronology	8864	Religion
8663	Civilization	8865	Economic conditions
8664	Religion	8866	Geography
8665	Economic conditions	8867	Travels
8666	Geography	8868-8870	Special topics (Develop as needed)
8667	Travels	8871-8896	Local (A-Z by place)
8668-8670	Special topics (Develop as needed)		
8671-8696	Local (A-Z by place)		Etruria
			[Include here works on the ancient Etruscans
	Apulia		and their civlization.]
	[Include Iapigia and Messapia.]		Periodicals. See AHP
	Periodicals. See AHP	8900	Bibliographies
8700	Bibliographies	8901	Pamphlet volumes
8701	Pamphlet volumes	8902	Collected source materials
8702	Collected source materials	8903	Government and administration
8703	Government and administration	8904	Law
8704	Law	8905	Military affairs
8705	Military affairs	8906	Naval affairs
8706	Naval affairs	8907	General history
8707	General history	8908	General special
8708	General special		History by periods
	History by periods	8909	Before 500 B.C.
8709	Before 500 B.C.	8910	500 - 1 B.C.
8710	500 - 1 B.C.	8911	1 A.D. - ca.500
8711	1 A.D. - ca.500	8912	Chronology
8712	Chronology	8913	Civilization
8713	Civilization	8914	Religion
8714	Religion	8915	Economic conditions
8715	Economic conditions	8916	Geography
8716	Geography	8917	Travels
8717	Travels		Special topics
8718-8720	Special topics (Develop as needed)	8918	Medicine
8721-8746	Local (A-Z by place)	8921-8946	Local (A-Z by place)
			[Include works on the Faliscans
	Bruttium		and Volsci.]
	Periodicals. See AHP		
8750	Bibliographies		Gallia Cisalpina
8751	Pamphlet volumes		[Include Lombardy and Piedmont.]
8752	Collected source materials		Periodicals. See AHP
8753	Government and administration	8950	Bibliographies
8754	Law	8951	Pamphlet volumes
8755	Military affairs	8952	Collected source materials
8756	Naval affairs	8953	Government and administration
8757	General history	8954	Law
8758	General special	8955	Military affairs
	History by periods	8956	Naval affairs
8759	Before 500 B.C.	8957	General history
8760	500 - 1 B.C.	8958	General special
8761	1 A.D. - ca. 500		History by periods
8762	Chronology	8959	Before 500 B.C.
8763	Civilization	8960	500 - 1 B.C.
8764	Religion	8961	1 A.D. - ca. 500
8765	Economic conditions	8962	Chronology
8766	Geography	8963	Civilization
8767	Travels	8964	Religion
8768-8770	Special topics (Develop as needed)	8965	Economic conditions
8771-8796	Local (A-Z by place)	8966	Geography
		8967	Travels
[8800-8846]	Calabria [Discontinued. See AH 8750-8796]	8968-8970	Special topics (Develop as needed)
		8971-8996	Local (A-Z by place)
	Campania		
	Periodicals. See AHP		Istria
8850	Bibliographies		Periodicals. See AHP
8851	Pamphlet volumes	9000	Bibliographies
8852	Collected source materials	9001	Pamphlet volumes
8853	Government and administration	9002	Collected source materials
8854	Law	9003	Government and administration
8855	Military affairs	9004	Law

Ancient Europe (cont.)
  Italy (cont.)
    Istria (cont.)

9005	Military affairs
9006	Naval affairs
9007	General history
9008	General special
	History by periods
9009	Before 500 B.C.
9010	500 - 1 B.C.
9011	1 A.D. - ca.500
9012	Chronology
9013	Civilization
9014	Religion
9015	Economic conditions
9016	Geography
9017	Travels
9018-9020	Special topics (Develop as needed)
9021-9046	Local (A-Z by place)

    Latium
      [N.B. - See AH 8650-8696 for the City of
      Rome.]
      Periodicals. See AHP

9050	Bibliographies
9051	Pamphlet volumes
9052	Collected source materials
9053	Government and administration
9054	Law
9055	Military affairs
9056	Naval affairs
9057	General history
9058	General special
	History by periods
9059	Before 500 B.C.
9060	500 - 1 B.C.
9061	1 A.D. - ca. 500
9062	Chronology
9063	Civilization
9064	Religion
9065	Economic conditions
9066	Geography
9067	Travels
9068-9070	Special topics (Develop as needed)
9071-9096	Local (A-Z by place)

    Liguria
      Periodicals. See AHP

9100	Bibliographies
9101	Pamphlet volumes
9102	Collected source materials
9103	Government and administration
9104	Law
9105	Military affairs
9106	Naval affairs
9107	General history
9108	General special
	History by periods
9109	Before 500 B.C.
9110	500 - 1 B.C.
9111	1 A.D. - ca.500
9112	Chronology
9113	Civilization
9114	Religion
9115	Economic conditions
9116	Geography
9117	Travels
9118-9120	Special topics (Develop as needed)
9121-9146	Local (A-Z by place)

    Lucania
      Periodicals. See AHP

9150	Bibliographies
9151	Pamphlet volumes
9152	Collected source materials
9153	Government and administration
9154	Law
9155	Military affairs
9156	Naval affairs
9157	General history

Ancient Europe (cont.)
  Italy (cont.)
    Lucania (cont.)

9158	General special
	History by periods
9159	Before 500 B.C.
9160	500 - 1 B.C.
9161	1 A.D. - ca. 500
9162	Chronology
9163	Civilization
9164	Religion
9165	Economic conditions
9166	Geography
9167	Travels
9168-9170	Special topics (Develop as needed)
9171-9196	Local (A-Z by place)

    Picenum
      [Include the Marches and Emilia.]
      Periodicals. See AHP

9200	Bibliographies
9201	Pamphlet volumes
9202	Collected source materials
9203	Government and administration
9204	Law
9205	Military affairs
9206	Naval affairs
9207	General history
9208	General special
	History by periods
9209	Before 500 B.C.
9210	500 - 1 B.C.
9211	1 A.D. - ca.500
9212	Chronology
9213	Civilization
9214	Religion
9215	Economic conditions
9216	Geography
9217	Travels
9218-9220	Special topics (Develop as needed)
9221-9246	Local (A-Z by place)

    Sabini, Aequi, Paeligni, etc.
      Periodicals. See AHP

9250	Bibliographies
9251	Pamphlet volumes
9252	Collected source materials
9253	Government and administration
9254	Law
9255	Military affairs
9256	Naval affairs
9257	General history
9258	General special
	History by periods
9259	Before 500 B.C.
9260	500 - 1 B.C.
9261	1 A.D. - ca. 500
9262	Chronology
9263	Civilization
9264	Religion
9265	Economic conditions
9266	Geography
9267	Travels
9268-9270	Special topics (Develop as needed)
9271-9296	Local (A-Z by place)

    Samnium
      [Include Abruzzi e Molise.]
      Periodicals. See AHP

9300	Bibliographies
9301	Pamphlet volumes
9302	Collected source materials
9303	Government and administration
9304	Law
9305	Military affairs
9306	Naval affairs
9307	General history
9308	General special

          Ancient Europe (cont.)
            Italy (cont.)
              Samnium (cont.)
                History by periods

9309	Before 500 B.C.
9310	500 - 1 B.C.
9311	1 A.D. - ca.500
9312	Chronology
9313	Civilization
9314	Religion
9315	Economic conditions
9316	Geography
9317	Travels
9318-9320	Special topics (Develop as needed)
9321-9346	Local (A-Z by place)

             Sardinia and Corsica. See AH 9550-9596
             Sicily. See AH 9600-9646
             Umbria
              Periodicals. See AHP

9350	Bibliographies
9351	Pamphlet volumes
9352	Collected source materials
9353	Government and administration
9354	Law
9355	Military affairs
9356	Naval affairs
9357	General history
9358	General special

              History by periods

9359	Before 500 B.C.
9360	500 - 1 B.C.
9361	1 A.D. - ca. 500
9362	Chronology
9363	Civilization
9364	Religion
9365	Economic conditions
9366	Geography
9367	Travels
9368-9370	Special topics (Develop as needed)
9371-9396	Local (A-Z by place)

             Venetia
              Periodicals. See AHP

9400	Bibliographies
9401	Pamphlet volumes
9402	Collected source materials
9403	Government and administration
9404	Law
9405	Military affairs
9406	Naval affairs
9407	General history
9408	General special

              History by periods

9409	Before 500 B.C.
9410	500 - 1 B.C.
9411	1 A.D. - ca.500
9412	Chronology
9413	Civilization
9414	Religion
9415	Economic conditions
9416	Geography
9417	Travels
9418-9420	Special topics (Develop as needed)
9421-9446	Local (A-Z by place)

             Magna Graecia. See AH 8647
             Malta. See AH 9647
             Moesia. See AH 8350-8396
             Noricum. See AH 8400-8446
             Pannonia. See AH 8450-8496

             Rhaetia
              [Include Vindelicia]

              Periodicals. See AHP

9450	Bibliographies
9451	Pamphlet volumes
9452	Collected source materials
9453	Government and administration
9454	Law

          Ancient Europe (cont.)
            Rhaetia (cont.)

9455	Military affairs
9456	Naval affairs
9457	General history
9458	General special

             History by periods

9459	Before 500 B.C.
9460	500 - 1 B.C.
9461	1 A.D. - ca. 500
9462	Chronology
9463	Civilization
9464	Religion
9465	Economic conditions
9466	Geography
9467	Travels
9468-9470	Special topics (Develop as needed)
9471-9496	Local (A-Z by place)

            Rhenish Provinces
             [Include Belgium, etc.]

             Periodicals. See AHP

9500	Bibliographies
9501	Pamphlet volumes
9502	Collected source materials
9503	Government and administration
9504	Law
9505	Military affairs
9506	Naval affairs
9507	General history
9508	General special

             History by periods

9509	Before 500 B.C.
9510	500 - 1 B.C.
9511	1 A.D. - ca. 500
9512	Chronology
9513	Civilization
9514	Religion
9515	Economic conditions
9516	Geography
9517	Travels
9518-9520	Special topics (Develop as needed)
9521-9546	Local (A-Z by place)

            Sardinia and Corsica
             Periodicals. See AHP

9550	Bibliographies
9551	Pamphlet volumes
9552	Collected source materials
9553	Government and administration
9554	Law
9555	Military affairs
9556	Naval affairs
9557	General history
9558	General special

             History by periods

9559	Before 500 B.C.
9560	500 - 1 B.C.
9561	1 A.D. - ca. 500
9562	Chronology
9563	Civilization
9564	Religion
9565	Economic conditions
9566	Geography
9567	Travels
9568-9570	Special topics (Develop as needed)
9571-9596	Local (A-Z by place)

            Sarmatia. See AH 9800-9846
            Sicily
             Periodicals. See AHP

9600	Bibliographies
9601	Pamphlet volumes
9602	Collected source materials
9603	Government and administration
9604	Law

Ancient Europe (cont.)
  Sicily (cont.)
9605	Military affairs
9606	Naval affairs
9607	General history
9608	General special
	History by periods
9609	Before 500 B.C.
9610	500 - 1 B.C.
9611	1 A.D. - ca. 500
9612	Chronology
9613	Civilization
9614	Religion
9615	Economic conditions
9616	Geography
9617	Travels
9618-9620	Special topics (Develop as needed)
9621-9646	Local (A-Z by place)

9647	Malta

Spain
    [N.B. - Prefer Span for works covering
      Pre-Roman and Roman times together.]

	Periodicals. See AHP
9650	Bibliographies
9651	Pamphlet volumes
9652	Collected source materials
9653	Government and administration
9654	Law
9655	Military affairs
9656	Naval affairs
9657	General history
9658	General special
	History by periods
9659	Before 500 B.C.
9660	500 - 1 B.C.
9661	1 A.D. - ca. 500
9662	Chronology
9663	Civilization
9664	Religion
9665	Economic conditions
9666	Geography
9667	Travels
9668-9670	Special topics (Develop as needed)
9671-9696	Local (A-Z by place)

Thrace
	Periodicals. See AHP
9700	Bibliographies
9701	Pamphlet volumes
9702	Collected source materials
9703	Government and administration
9704	Law
9705	Military affairs
9706	Naval affairs
9707	General history
9708	General special
	History by periods
9709	Before 500 B.C.
9710	500 - 1 B.C.
9711	1 A.D. - ca. 500
9712	Chronology
9713	Civilization
9714	Religion
9715	Economic conditions
9716	Geography
9717	Travels
9718-9720	Special topics (Develop as needed)
9721-9746	Local (A-Z by place)

Vindelicia. See AH 9450-9496
Germany
    [N.B. - Prefer Ger for works covering
      Pre-Roman and Roman times together.
      Include in the numbers for Local,
      general works on the Goths and Vandals.]

Ancient Europe (cont.)
  Germany (cont.)
	Periodicals. See AHP
9750	Bibliographies
9751	Pamphlet volumes
9752	Collected source materials
9753	Government and administration
9754	Law
9755	Military affairs
9756	Naval affairs
9757	General history
9758	General special
	History by periods
9759	Before 500 B.C.
9760	500 - 1 B.C.
9761	1 A.D. - ca. 500
9762	Chronology
9763	Civilization
9764	Religion
9765	Economic conditions
9766	Geography
9767	Travels
9768-9770	Special topics (Develop as needed)
9771-9796	Local (A-Z by place)

Sarmatia
    [See also Scythia in AH 3750-3796.]

	Periodicals. See AHP
9800	Bibliographies
9801	Pamphlet volumes
9802	Collected source materials
9803	Government and administration
9804	Law
9805	Military affairs
9806	Naval affairs
9807	General history
9808	General special
	History by periods
9809	Before 500 B.C.
9810	500 - 1 B.C.
9811	1 A.D. - ca. 500
9812	Chronology
9813	Civilization
9814	Religion
9815	Economic conditions
9816	Geography
9817	Travels
9818-9820	Special topics (Develop as needed)
9821-9846	Local (A-Z by place)

Table A

	Periodicals. See AHP
0	Bibliographies
1	Pamphlet volumes
2	Collected authors, sources, etc.
3	Special topic (To be established only rarely]
4-9	Monographs (By date, e.g. 8.75 for 1875, 9.60 for 1960)

NOTE ON THE CLASSIFICATION

The Eg class provides for the history and literature of ancient Egypt. The class contains works on the history, civilization and social life, government and law, religion, economic conditions, geography and travels, and the literature of Egypt up to the time of the Arab conquest in 638. Similar works on Egypt since the Arab conquest are in the Afr class. Works of an archaeological nature are in the Arc class. The Eg class is primarily for monographs; all periodicals, except those of a bibliographical nature or literary anthologies, are in the Eg P class.

The accompanying Outline shows the major divisions of the class. The sections for history are the counterpart of the sections for Greece in general and Rome in general in the AH class; the arrangement and numbering is almost exactly the same, though some details are omitted or modified. The sections for literature are straightforward. Most topics are given a block of 10 numbers, which provides for bibliographies, pamphlet volumes, and a date arrangement of most monographs (Table A).

During the present editing, there have been no major changes or additions. The emphasis has been on making the schedule easier to use by the addition of references and explanatory notes. It has not as yet been possible to reclassify all the books which had been wrongly classified because of ambiguities in the old typed version of the schedule.

Bartol Brinkler
Classification Specialist
November 1974

OUTLINE

	Ancient Egyptian history
2-399	Bibliographies; Sources; Government; Law; General history; etc.
400-799	History by periods
800-959	Chronology; Civilization; Religion; Economic conditions; Geography and travels
971-996	Local history, description, etc.
	Ancient Egyptian literature
1002-1029	General history and anthologies
1030-1199	Special forms, etc.
1300-1309	Unclassified papyri

Ancient Egyptian history
Periodicals. See Eg P and Eg 2

	General bibliographies
2	Periodicals
4-9	Monographs (By date)
	Egyptology as a science. See Arc 550-575
15	General pamphlet volumes
24-29	Collected sources (By date)
	[See also Eg 1024-1029]
30-39	Government and administration (Table A)
	[Include constitutional history, provincial and municipal government in general, public finance, etc.]
130-139	Law (Table A)
	[Include public law, private law, criminal law, slavery, legal procedure, etc.]
230-239	Military affairs (Table A)
250-259	Naval affairs (Table A)
260-269	Foreign relations, diplomacy (Table A)
274-279	General history (By date)
	General special
291	Pamphlet volumes
294-299	Miscellany (By date)
	[Include Festschriften, congresses, etc.]
300-309	Philosophy of history (Table A)
	[Include historiography]
310-319	Cosmology (Table A)
	History by periods
400-409	Predynastic period (Table A)
	[See also Arc]
450-459	Old Kingdom, 1st-10th dynasties, 3200-2160 B.C. (Table A)
	Middle Kingdom, 11th-17th dynasties, 2160-1580 B.C.
500-509	General (Table A)
550-559	Hyksos (Table A)
	New Kingdom, 18th-21st dynasties, 1580-950 B.C.
600	Bibliographies
601	Pamphlet volumes
602	Collected sources, etc.
603	Tell el-Amarna Tablets
604-609	Other works (By date)
	[Include Thotmes III, Amenhetep IV and Nefertete, Tutenkhamun, Rameses II and III, Akhnaton, etc.]
650-659	Later dynastic period, 22d-26th dynasties, 950-525 B.C. (Table A)
690-699	Persian rule, 27th-30th dynasties, 525-332 B.C. (Table A)
700-709	The Ptolemies, 332-30 B.C. (Table A)
	[Include Cleopatra, etc.]
750-759	Roman and Byzantine rule, 30 B.C.-638 A.D. (Table A)
	Since 638 A.D. See Afr
800-809	Chronology (Table A)
	Civilization, social life
810-819	General works (Table A)
820-829	Private life (Table A)
830-839	Burial (Table A)
	Special topics
840	Athletic games, sports
841	Gymnastics
842	Games, toys
843	The family
844	Marriage
845	Condition of women
846	Condition of children
847	Writing, scribes
	[See also Arc and Linguistics class]
848	Books and education
849	Music and dancing
850	Festivals

Ancient Egyptian history (cont.)
    Civilization, social life (cont.)
        Special topics (cont.)

851	Character and morals
852	Houses, etc.
853	Baths
854	Water supplies
855	Hygiene
	[See also Eg 1150-1159]
856	Costume
857	Meals
858	Beverages
859	Fire and lights
860	Pottery
861	Glass
862	Metalwork
863	Domestic plants
864	Domestic animals
865	Hunting and fishing
866	Vehicles
	Sciences. See Eg 1160-1199
[869]	Miscellany [Discontinued]
870-879	Religion and mythology (Table A)
	[Include individual deities. See also
	Eg 1030-1042 and 1060-1069.]
885	Magic (By date, e.g. .960 for 1960)

    Economic conditions

900-909	General works (Table A)
910-919	Agriculture (Table A)
	Commerce and industries. See Eg 900-909
920-929	Weights and measures (Table A)
	Public finance. See Eg 30-39
930-939	Geography and description (Table A)
950-959	Travels (Table A)
971-996	Local history, description, etc. (A-Z
	by place)
	[See also Arc]

Ancient Egyptian literature
    Periodicals. See Eg P and Eg 1024-1029

1002	Bibliographies

    General literary history

1003	Pamphlet volumes
1004-1009	General works (By date)

    General anthologies

1023	Pamphlet volumes
1024-1029	General collections (By date)

    Special forms, etc.
        [For each, include anthologies, editions of
        individual texts, and works about them.]

1030-1039	Book of the Dead (Table A)
1042	Pyramid and Coffin texts (By date, e.g.
	.960 for 1960)

    Poetry

1050-1059	General works (Table A)
1060-1069	Hymns and religious poetry (Table A)
1070-1079	Lyric poetry (Table A)

    Prose literature

1090-1099	General works (Table A)
1100-1109	Romances and tales (Table A)
1120-1129	Maxims (Table A)
1130-1139	Letters (Table A)
1150-1159	Medicine (Table A)

    Sciences

1160-1169	General (Table A)
1170-1179	Astronomy (Table A)
1180-1189	Mathematics (Table A)
1190-1199	Others (Table A)
1300-1309	Unclassified papyri (Table A)

Table A

	Periodicals. See Eg P
0	Bibliographies
1	Pamphlet volumes
2	Collected authors, sources, etc.
3	Special topic (To be established only rarely)
4-9	Monographs (By date, e.g. 8.90 for 1890,
	9.60 for 1960)

NOTE ON THE CLASSIFICATION

The AHP class includes periodicals devoted to ancient history of the world in general or of the Mediterranean area -- primarily the world of ancient Greece and Rome and the countries of the ancient Near East. Periodicals devoted solely to ancient Egypt are in the EgP class. Archaeological periodicals are in the Arc class.

The periodicals are arranged in approximate alphabetical order according to the catalogue entry -- either a distinctive title or the name of a society.

Ancient history periodicals
11-36   Periodicals and society publications (A-Z)

NOTE ON THE CLASSIFICATION

The EgP class contains periodicals devoted to the history and literature of ancient Egypt. Purely archaeological periodicals are in the Arc class. Periodicals devoted to medieval and modern Egypt are in the Afr class.

The periodicals are arranged in approximate alphabetical order according to the catalogue entry -- either a distinctive title or the name of a society.

Egyptology Periodicals
1-150   General periodicals (150 scheme, A-Z)

WIDENER LIBRARY SHELFLIST, 55

ANCIENT HISTORY

CLASSIFIED LISTING BY CALL NUMBER

Classified Listing

AH 4 - 9   Ancient World in general - General bibliographies - Monographs (By date)

AH 7.16A	Fabricius, J.A. Bibliographia antiquaria. Hamburgi, 1716.
AH 7.16B	Fabricius, J.A. Bibliographia antiquaria. Hamburgi, 1716.
AH 7.16.9	Barth, J.M. Mantissa...Fabricii Bibliographiam antiquariam. Ratisbonae, 1751.
AH 8.85	Meyer, P. Premières compilations françaises d'histoire ancienne. Paris, 1885.
AH 8.95	Büdinger, Max. Die Universalhistorie. Wien, 1895.
AH 8.96	Sittl, Karl. Anschauungsmethode...Altertumswissenschaft. Gotha, 1896.
AH 8.98	Tropea, Giacomo. Manuale di fonti letterarie. Messina, 1898.
AH 9.43	Bibliotheca orientalis. Leiden. 1,1943+ 20v.
AH 9.49	Bengtson, Hermann. Einführung in die alte Geschichte. München, 1949.
AH 9.49.2A	Bengtson, Hermann. Einführung in die alte Geschichte. 2. Aufl. München, 1953.
AH 9.49.2B	Bengtson, Hermann. Einführung in die alte Geschichte. 2. Aufl. München, 1953.
AH 9.49.6	Bengtson, Hermann. Introduction to ancient history. Berkeley, 1970.
AH 9.56	Klauser, Theodor. Franz Joseph Dölger. Münster, 1956.
AH 9.59	Petit, Paul. Guide de l'étudiant en histoire ancienne. Paris, 1959.
AH 9.59.2	Petit, Paul. Guide de l'étudiant en histoire ancienne. 2. éd. Paris, 1962.
AH 9.61	Voronkov, A.I. Drevniaia Gretsiia i drevnii Rim. Moskva, 1961.
VAH 9.65	Kočiš, Gejza. Historiografia a bibliografia dejín prvotnopospolnej a otrokárskej spoločnosti. Bratislava, 1965.
AH 9.71	Ancient society: resources for teachers. North Ryde, Australia. 1,1971+

AH 15   Ancient World in general - General pamphlet volumes

AH 15.1	Pamphlet vol. Alte Geschichte. 23 pam.
AH 15.2	Lange, C.C.L. Historia mutationum rei...romanorum. Gottingae, 1846- 12 pam.
AH 15.4	Pamphlet box. Ancient history. Miscellaneous pamphlets. 26 pam.
AH 15.5	Pamphlet box. Ancient history. Miscellaneous pamphlets. 5 pam.
AH 15.6	Pamphlet vol. Miscellany on archaeology. Frankfurt, 1817. 8 pam.
AH 15.8	Pamphlet box. Downey, Glanville 1908- . Miscellaneous pamphlets.
AH 15.10	Pamphlet vol. Ancient history. Miscellaneous pamphlets. 7 pam.

AH 24 - 29   Ancient World in general - Collected sources, etc. (By date)

AH 27.65	Martini, J.C. Thesaurus dissertationum. Norimbergae, 1766. 3v.
AH 28.07	Museum der Alterthums-Wissenschaft. Berlin, 1807. 2v.
AH 28.22	Serapis, oder Abhandlungen betreffend das griechische und römische Alterthum. St. Peterburg, 1822.
AH 28.89	Gutschmid, A. von. Kleine Schriften. Leipzig, 1889. 5v.
AH 28.98	Scala, Rudolf von. Die Staatsverträge des Altertums. Leipzig, 1898.
AH 29.09	Paris. Université. Faculté de Lettres. Mélanges d'histoire ancienne. Photoreproduction. Paris, 1909.
AH 29.14	Kunst und Altertum. Berlin, 1914-25. 6v.
AH 29.23.5A	The Cambridge ancient history. Cambridge, Eng., 1923-1939. 12v.
AH 29.23.5B	The Cambridge ancient history. v.8,10-11. Cambridge, Eng., 1923-1939. 3v.
AH 29.23.7	The Cambridge ancient history. Plates. Cambridge, Eng., 1927-39. 5v.
AH 29.23.10	The Cambridge ancient history. v.3-12. Cambridge, Eng., 1923-1939. 10v.
AH 29.29	Yale University. The legacy of the ancient world. New Haven, 1929.
AH 29.50	Struve, V.V. Geschichte der alten Welt; Christomathie. Berlin, 1954-57. 3v.
AH 29.56	Barker, Ernest. From Alexander to Constantine. Oxford, 1956.
AH 29.62	Akademiia nauk SSSR. Institut narodov Azii. Drevnii mir; sbornik statei. Moskva, 1962.
AH 29.62.5	Bengtson, Hermann. Die Staatsverträge des Altertums. v.2-3. München, 1962. 2v.
AH 29.63	Adademiia nauk SSSR. Otdelenie istoricheskikh nauk. Problemy sotsial'no-ekonomischeskoi istorii drevnego mira. Moskva, 1963.
AH 29.64	Deutsche Historiker-Gesellschaft. Fachgruppe alte Geschichte. Neue Beiträge zur Geschichte der alten Welt. Berlin, 1964-65. 2v.
AH 29.65	Kivilcimli, Hikmet. Tarih, devrim, sosyalizm. Istanbul, 1965.
AH 29.68	Kongress für klassische Philologie, Budapest. Studien zur Geschichte und Philosophie des Altertums. Budapest, 1968.
AH 29.68.5	Nuove questioni de storia antica. Milano, 1968.
AH 29.69	Beiträge zur alten Geschichte und deren Nachleben. Berlin, 1969- 2v.

AH 30 - 39   Ancient World in general - Government and administration - General works (Table A)

AH 32.5	Sociedad Española de Estudios Clásicos. Coloquios sobre teoria política de la antigüedad clásica. Madrid, 1965.
AH 36.08	Zamosci, J. De senatu romano. Argen, 1608.
AH 37.96	Bisset, R. Sketch of democracy. London, 1796.
AH 37.99	Sainte Croix, G.E.J.G. de. Anciens gouvernemens fédératifs. Paris, 1799.
AH 38.20	Hüllmann, K.D. Staatsrecht des Alterthums. Cöln, 1820.
AH 38.29	Reichard, H.G. Erinnerungen aus der Staatskunst. Leipzig, 1829.
AH 38.54.2	Sudre, Alfred. Histoire de la souveraineté. 2. éd. Paris, 1874.
AH 38.64	Fustel de Coulanges, N.D. La cité antique. 3. éd. Paris, 1870.
AH 38.64.2	Fustel de Coulanges, N.D. La cité antique. 4. éd. Paris, 1872.
AH 38.64.4	Fustel de Coulanges, N.D. La cité antique. 10. éd. Paris, 1883.
AH 38.64.5	Fustel de Coulanges, N.D. La cité antique. 16. éd. Paris, 1898.
AH 38.64.6	Fustel de Coulanges, N.D. La cité antique. 18. éd. Paris, 1903.

AH 30 - 39   Ancient World in general - Government and administration - General works (Table A) - cont.

AH 38.64.12	Fustel de Coulanges, N.D. The ancient city. 3. ed. Photoreproduction. Boston, 1877.
AH 38.64.30	Fustel de Coulanges, N.D. La città antica. Firenze, 1924.
AH 39.03	Willoughby, W.W. Political theories of the ancient world. N.Y., 1903.
AH 39.03.2	Boxler, A.A. Précis des institutions publiques...Grèce et Rome. Paris, 1903.
AH 39.10	Arnim, H. Politischen Theorien des Altertums. Wien, 1910.
AH 39.51	Hammond, M. City-state and world state in Greek and Roman political theory until Augustus. Cambridge, Mass., 1951.
AH 39.59	Ehrhardt, Arnold. Politische Metaphysik von Solon bis Augustin. Tübingen, 1959-69. 3v.
AH 39.61	Suerbaum, Werner. Vom Antiken zum frühmittelarlerlichen Staatsbegriff. Münster, 1961.
AH 39.61.2	Suerbaum, Werner. Vom Antiken zum frühmittelalterlichen Staatsbegriff. 2. Aufl. Münster, 1970.
AH 39.64	Anderson, W. Man's quest for political knowledge. Minneapolis, 1964.
AH 39.66	Dvornik, Frantisek. Early Christian and Byzantine political philosophy; origins and background. Washington, 1966. 2v.
AH 39.67	Gaudemon, Jean. Institutions de l'antiquité. Paris, 1967.
AH 39.68	Meyer, Ernst. Einführung in die antike Staatskunde. Darmstadt, 1968.
AH 39.71	Maillet, Jean. Institutions politiques et sociales de l'antiquité. 2. éd. Paris, 1971.
AH 39.71.5	Gaudemet, Jean. Précis des institutions de l'antiquité. Paris, 1971. 2v.
AH 39.73	Rizzo, Silvia. Il lessico filologico degli umanisti. Roma, 1973.

AH 40 - 49   Ancient World in general - Government and administration - Forms of government (Table A)

AH 47.69	Turpin, François H. Histoire du gouvernement des anciennes républiques. Paris, 1769.
AH 48.51	Zell, Karl. Natalia Caroli Friderici. Inaug. Diss. Heidelbergae, 1851.
AH 48.61	Givodan, Léon. Histoire des classes privilégiées. Paris, 1861. 2v.
AH 48.86	Curtius, Ernst. Das Königthum bei dem Alten. Berlin, 1886.
AH 48.93.5	Fowler, W.W. The city-state of the Greeks and Romans. London, 1898.
AH 48.93.7	Fowler, W.W. The city-state of the Greeks and Romans. London, 1921.
AH 48.98	Kaerst, Julius. Studien zur Entwickelung...Monarchie...Altertum. Photoreproduction. München, 1898.
AH 49.26	Hasebroek, Johannus. Der imperialistische Gedanke im Altertum. Stuttgart, 1926.
AH 49.55	Larsen, Jakob A.O. Representative government in Greek and Roman history. Berkeley, 1955.
AH 49.60	Palanque, Jean R. Les imperialismes antiques. Paris, 1960.
AH 49.65	Ritter, Hans-Werner. Diadem und Königsherrschaft. München, 1965.
AH 49.68	Aalders, Gerhard Jean Daniel. Die Theorie der gemischten Verfassung im Altertum. Amsterdam, 1968.

AH 60 - 69   Ancient World in general - Government and administration - Legislature and legislation (Table A)

AH 68.17	Pastoret, C.E.J.P. de. Histoire de la législation. Paris, 1817-37. 11v.
AH 69.09	Radin, Max. Legislation of Greeks and Romans on corporations. N.Y.? 1909.

AH 70 - 79   Ancient World in general - Government and administration - Elections and voting (Table A)

AH 78.87	Borgeaud, C. Plébiscite dans l'antiquité. Genève, 1887.
AH 79.72	Staveley, Eastland Stuart. Greek and Roman voting and elections. London, 1972.

AH 90 - 99   Ancient World in general - Government and administration - Municipal government (Table A)

AH 98.78	Kuhn, Emil. Entstehung der Staedte der Alten. Leipzig, 1878.
AH 98.80	Cognat, René. De municipalibus et provincialibus militis in Imperio Romano. Thesis. Lutetiae Parisiorum, 1880.
AH 99.24	Salvioli, G. La città antica e la sua economia. Napoli, 1924.

AH 100 - 109   Ancient World in general - Government and administration - Public finance (Table A)

AH 109.21	Ciccotti, Ettore. Lineamenti dell'evoluzione tributaria nel mondo antico. Milano, 1921.

AH 115   Ancient World in general - Government and administration - Special topics - Tribes

AH 115.3	Kutorga, M. Essai sur l'organisation de la tribu dans l'antiquité. Paris, 1839.

AH 120   Ancient World in general - Government and administration - Special topics - Secretaries

AH 120.5	Egger, Emile. Observations historiques sur la fonction de secrétaire des princes chez les anciens. Paris, 1858.

AH 130 - 139   Ancient World in general - Law - General works (Table A)

Htn	AH 135.61*	Eustathius Antecessor. De varia...in jure civile observatione. Basileae, 1561.
	AH 136.45	Miscellae defensiones pro Cl. Salmasio. Lugduni Batavorum, 1645.
Htn	AH 137.69*	Pettingal, J. An enquiry into the use and practice of juries. London, 1769.
	AH 138.60A	Béchard, F. Droit municipal dans l'antiquité. Paris, 1860.
NEDL	AH 138.60B	Béchard, F. Droit municipal dans l'antiquité. Paris, 1860.
NEDL	AH 138.61	Maine, Henry S. Ancient law. London, 1861.
	AH 138.61.2	Maine, Henry S. Ancient law. 1. American ed. N.Y., 1864.
	AH 138.61.2.5	Maine, Henry S. Ancient law. 1. American ed. N.Y., 1867.
	AH 138.61.4	Maine, Henry S. Ancient law. 3. American ed. N.Y., 1875.
	AH 138.61.7	Maine, Henry S. Ancient law. London, 1905.
	AH 138.61.9	Maine, Henry S. Ancient law. 10. ed. London, 1906.
	AH 138.61.18	Maine, Henry S. Ancient law. London, 1920.
	AH 138.61.19	Maine, Henry S. Ancient law. London, 1965.

Classified Listing

AH 130 - 139   Ancient World in general - Law - General works (Table A) - cont.

AH 138.62   Mayer, S. Rechte der Israeliten, Athener und Römer. Leipzig, 1862. 2v.

AH 138.70   Hofmann, F. Beiträge zur Geschichte des griechischen und römischen Rechts. Wien, 1870.

AH 138.75A   Maine, Henry S. Lectures on the early history of institutions. N.Y., 1875.

AH 138.75B   Maine, Henry S. Lectures on the early history of institutions. N.Y., 1875.

AH 138.75.2A   Maine, Henry S. Lectures on the early history of institutions. London, 1875.

AH 138.75.2B   Maine, Henry S. Lectures on the early history of institutions. London, 1875.

AH 138.75.3   Maine, Henry S. Lectures on the early history of institutions. N.Y., 1888.

AH 138.75.5   Maine, Henry S. Lectures on the early history of institutions. 3. ed. London, 1880.

AH 138.75.7   Maine, Henry S. Lectures on the early history of institutions. N.Y., 1884.

AH 138.83A   Maine, Henry S. Early law and custom. London, 1883.

AH 138.83B   Maine, Henry S. Early law and custom. London, 1883.

NEDL AH 138.83.3   Maine, Henry S. Dissertations on early law and custom. N.Y., 1883.

NEDL AH 138.83.5   Maine, Henry S. Dissertations on early law and custom. N.Y., 1886.

AH 138.83.8   Maine, Henry S. Études sur l'ancien droit. Paris, 1884.

AH 138.84   Leist, B.W. Graeco-italische Rechtsgeschichte. Jena, 1884.

AH 138.96   Andé, Edouard. La fondation perpetuelle dans l'antiquité. Paris, 1896.

AH 139.00   Rivalta, V. Atticarum et Romanarum legum collatio. Ravennae, 1900.

AH 139.03   Wilutzky, P. Vorgeschichte des Rechts. Breslau, 1903.

AH 139.28   Bill, August. L'évangile et la loi. Thèse. Strasbourg, 1928.

AH 139.34   Ciccotti, Ettore. La formazione della coscienza giuridica e le sue concrete graduali espressioni nel mondo antico. Udine, 1934.

AH 139.56   Monier, Raymond. Histoire des institutions et des faits sociaux des origines à l'aube du Moyen Âge. Paris, 1955.

AH 139.61   Imbert J. Le droit antique et ses prolongements modernes. Paris, 1961.

AH 139.68   Gesellschaft und Recht im griechisch-römischen Altertum. Berlin, 1968- 2v.

AH 140 - 149   Ancient World in general - Law - Public law (Table A)

AH 147.31   Otto, E. De tutela viarum publicarum. Rhenum, 1731.

AH 148.66   Egger, Emile. Traités publics. Paris, 1886.

AH 148.89   Leist, B.W. Alt-arisches jus Gentium. Jena, 1889.

AH 149.11   Phillipson, C. International law and custom. London, 1911. 2v.

AH 150 - 159   Ancient World in general - Law - Criminal law (Table A)

AH 158.69   Thomissen, J.J. Études sur l'histoire du droit criminel. Bruxelles, 1869. 2v.

AH 158.99   Hitzig, H.F. Injuria. München, 1899.

AH 159.05   Mommsen, T. Zum ältesten Strafrecht der Kulturvölker. Leipzig, 1905.

AH 161   Ancient World in general - Law - Private law - Family law

AH 161.5   Hearn, W.E. The Aryan household; an introduction to comparative jurisprudence. London, 1879.

AH 162   Ancient World in general - Law - Private law - Inheritance law

AH 162.3   Schulin, F. Das griechische Testament. Basel, 1882.

AH 162.5   Bruck, E.F. Die Schenkung auf den Todesfall. Breslau, 1909.

AH 162.7   Saumaise, A. Specimen confutationis...sive tractatus. Lugdunum Batavorum, 1648.

AH 163   Ancient World in general - Law - Private law - Marriage law

AH 163.10   Wolff, H.J. Written and unwritten marriages in Hellenistic and postclassical Roman law. Haverford, 1939.

AH 165 - 169   Ancient World in general - Law - Maritime law (By date)

AH 168.56   Goldschmidt, J.G. De nautico foenore. Berolini, 1866.

AH 168.93   Sieveking, H. Seedarlehen. Leipzig, 1893.

AH 169.06   Schlossmann, S. Persona und Prosopon im Recht. Kiliae, 1906.

AH 180 - 189   Ancient World in general - Law - Slavery and emancipation (Table A)

AH 180.5   Vogt, Joseph. Bibliographie zur antiken Sklaverei. Bochum, 1971.

AH 186.56   Pignoria, L. De servis. Patavii, 1656.

AH 186.74   Pignoria, L. De servis. Amstelodami, 1674.

AH 188.40   Venedey, J. Römerthum, Christenthum und Germanenthum. Frankfurt, 1840.

AH 188.88   Maschke, R. Der Freiheitsprozess im klassischen Altertum. Berlin, 1888.

AH 188.96   Keiffer, Jules. L'esclavage à Athènes et à Rome. Luxembourg, 1896.

AH 188.98   Meyer, G. Die Sklaverei im Altertum. Dresden, 1898.

AH 188.99   Ciccotti, Ettore. Il tramonto della schiavitù nel mondo antico. Torino, 1899.

AH 189.03   Jerovšek, Anton. Die antik-heidnische Sklaverei. Marburg, 1903.

AH 189.34   Westermann, W.L. Sklaverei. Stuttgart, 1934.

AH 189.55A   Westermann, W.L. The slave systems of Greek and Roman antiquity. Philadelphia, 1955.

AH 189.55B   Westermann, W.L. The slave systems of Greek and Roman antiquity. Philadelphia, 1955.

AH 189.60   Finley, Moses I. Slavery in classical antiquity. Cambridge, Eng., 1960.

AH 189.71   Meltzer, Milton. Slavery: from the rise of Western civilization to the Renaissance. 1. ed. N.Y., 1971.

AH 190 - 199   Ancient World in general - Law - Philosophy of law (Table A)

AH 198.32   Veder, A. Historia philosophiae juris apud veteres. Lugduni Batavorum, 1832.

AH 199.58   Kuri Breña, Daniel. La filosofía del clericho in la antigüedad cristiana. 2. ed. Mexico, 1958.

AH 214   Ancient World in general - Law - Special topics - The oath

AH 214.5   Schröder, G.A. De praecisis iurandi formis Graecorum. Marienwerder, 1845.

AH 214.7   Curtius, E. Der Zehnte. Berlin, 1885.

AH 230 - 239   Ancient World in general - Military affairs (Table A)

Htn   AH 235.59*   Bartholin, T. De armillis veterum schedion. Amstelodami, 1676. 3 pam.

AH 238.19   Dureau de la Malle, Adolphe. Poliorcéteque des anciens. Paris, 1819.

AH 238.41   Bernd, C.S.T. Die Hauptstücke der Wappenwissenschaft. Bonn, 1841.

AH 238.43   Armandi, C.P. Histoire militaire des éléphants. Paris, 1843.

AH 238.88   Fickelscherer, M. Kriegswesen der Alten. Leipzig, 1888.

AH 238.93   Schneider, R. Legion und Phalanx. Berlin, 1893.

AH 238.95   Liers, Hugo. Kriegswesen der Alten. Breslau, 1895.

AH 239.01   Ciccotti, Ettore. La guerra et la pace. Torino, 1901.

AH 239.10   Daniels, Emil. Das antike Kriegswesen. Leipzig, 1910.

AH 239.10.10   Mastropasqui, O. Assedi e battaglie memorabili dai tempi più remoti al 476. Molfetti, 1910.

AH 239.20   Daniels, Emil. Das antike Kriegswesen. 2. Aufl. Berlin, 1920.

AH 239.27   Wienicke, Arnold. Keltisches Söldnertum in der Mittelmeerwelt bis zur Herrschaft der Römer. Inaug. Diss. Breslau, 1927.

AH 239.37A   Spaulding, O.L. Pen and sword in Greece and Rome. Princeton, 1937.

AH 239.37B   Spaulding, O.L. Pen and sword in Greece and Rome. Princeton, 1937.

AH 239.69   Marsden, Eric W. Greek and Roman artillery; historical development. Oxford, 1969.

AH 239.71   Diesner, Hans-Joachim. Kriege des Altertums. Berlin, 1971.

AH 239.71.5   Marsden, Eric W. Greek and Roman artillery; technical treatises. Oxford, 1971.

AH 239.72   Garlan, Yvon. La guerre dans l'antiquité. Paris, 1972.

AH 250 - 259   Ancient World in general - Naval affairs (Table A)

Htn   AH 255.37*   Baif, Lazare de. De re navali libellus. Lugdunum Batavorum, 1537.

Htn   AH 255.37.5*   Baif, Lazare de. Annotationis in l. ii. Lutetiae, 1549.

Htn   AH 255.40*   Geraldi, L.G. De re nautica libellus. Basiliae, 1540.

Htn   AH 256.33*   Ryves, Thomas. Historia navalis antiqua. Londini, 1633.

Htn   AH 256.40*   Ryves, Thomas. Historia navalis antiqua. Londini, 1640.

Htn   AH 256.85*   Vossius, Isaac. Observationum. Londini, 1685.

Htn   AH 257.68*   Déslandes, A.F.B. Essai sur la marine des anciens. Paris, 1768.

AH 257.77   LeRoy, J.D. La marine des anciens peuples. Paris, 1777.

AH 257.83   LeRoy, J.D. Les navires des anciens. Paris, 1783.

AH 258.55   Goodwin, J.W. De potentiae veterum...maritimae epochis. Gottingae, 1855.

AH 258.86   Jurien de la Graviére, J.P.E. Marine des anciens. Paris, 1886. 2v.

AH 259.24   Shepard, A.M. Sea power in ancient history. Boston, 1924.

AH 259.33   Rose, John Holland. The Mediterranean in the ancient world. Cambridge, Eng., 1933.

AH 259.35   Saint-Denis, E. de. Le vocabulaire des manoeuvres nautiques en Latin. Thèse. Macon, 1935.

AH 259.59   Carson, Lionel. The ancient mariners: seafarers. N.Y., 1959.

AH 259.64   Meirat, Jean. Marines antiques de la Mediterranée. Paris, 1964.

AH 259.68   Rost, Georg Alexander. Von Seewesen und Seehandel in der Antike. Amsterdam, 1968.

AH 274 - 279   Ancient World in general - General history (By date)

Htn   AH 275.39F*   Freculphus. Chronicorum. Cologne, 1539.

Htn   AH 276.14F*   Raleigh, Walter. Historie of the world in five books. London, 1614.

AH 276.14.2F   Raleigh, Walter. Historie of the world in five bookes. London, 1677.

Htn   AH 276.14.3F*   Raleigh, Walter. Historie of the world and Life of the author. London, 1736. 2v.

Htn   AH 276.14.4F*   Raleigh, Walter. The historie of the world. London, 1628.

Htn   AH 276.14.5*   Raleigh, Walter. An abridgment of Raleigh's Historie of the world. London, 1700.

Htn   AH 276.14.7F*   Raleigh, Walter. Historie of the world in five bookes. London, 1634.

AH 276.14.9   Raleigh, Walter. The history of the world. London, 1971.

AH 276.16A   Paiva d'Andrada, Diogo de. Exame d'antiquidades. Lisboa, 1616.

AH 276.16B   Paiva d'Andrada, Diogo de. Exame d'antiquidades. Lisboa, 1616.

NEDL AH 276.28   Pezelio, T. Mellificium historicum. Francofurti, 1628.

Htn   AH 276.46*   Thysius, Antonius. Memorabilia celebriorum veterum rerumpublicarum. Lugduni Batavorum, 1646.

Htn   AH 276.50*   Ussher, James. Annales Veteris Testamenti a prima mundi origine deducti. Londini, 1650-54. 2v.

Htn   AH 276.50.8F*   Ussher, James. Annales Veteris et Novi Testamenti. Genevae, 1722.

Htn   AH 276.58F*   Ussher, James. The annals of the Old and New Testament. London, 1658.

AH 276.61F   Howel, W. An institution of general history. London, 1661.

Htn   AH 276.61.2F*   Howel, W. An institution of general history. London, 1680.

NEDL AH 277.09   Du Pin, L.E. Universal library of historians. London, 1709. 2v.

Htn   AH 277.27.3*   Shuckford, Samuel. The sacred and prophane history of the world connected. London, 1731-37. 3v.

AH 277.27.25   Shuckford, Samuel. The sacred and profane history of the world connected. London, 1858. 2v.

NEDL AH 277.34   Rollin, Charles. Ancient history. London, 1734. 10v.

AH 277.34.2   Rollin, Charles. Histoire ancienne. Paris, 1740. 5v.

AH 277.34.2.3   Rollin, Charles. Histoire ancienne. Amsterdam, 1734-39. 13v.

NEDL AH 277.34.3   Rollin, Charles. Histoire ancienne. Amsterdam, 1759. 3v.

AH 277.34.4   Rollin, Charles. Histoire ancienne. v.4-13. Amsterdam, 1767. 10v.

NEDL AH 277.34.5   Rollin, Charles. Histoire ancienne. v.1-13. Paris, 1758-63. 14v.

NEDL AH 277.34.6   Rollin, Charles. Ancient history. London, 1774. 8v.

NEDL AH 277.34.8   Rollin, Charles. Ancient history. London, 1788. 10v.

AH 277.34.10   Rollin, Charles. Ancient history. Glasgow, 1800. 6v.

NEDL AH 277.34.10.5   Rollin, Charles. Ancient history. 10. ed. London, 1804. 8v.

AH 274 - 279   Ancient World in general - General history (By date) - cont.

NEDL AH 277.34.10.8 Rollin, Charles. Ancient history. Portland, 1805. 8v.
AH 277.34.10.9 Rollin, Charles. Ancient history. v.6. Philadelphia, 1805.
NEDL AH 277.34.11 Rollin, Charles. Ancient history. Boston, 1801. 8v.
AH 277.34.12 Rollin, Charles. Ancient history. Boston, 1807. 8v.
NEDL AH 277.34.13 Rollin, Charles. Ancient history. Boston, 1807. 8v.
NEDL AH 277.34.14 Rollin, Charles. Ancient history. Boston, 1823. 2v.
NEDL AH 277.34.14.3 Rollin, Charles. Ancient history. N.Y., 1828. 2v.
NEDL AH 277.34.14.5 Rollin, Charles. Ancient history. v.2-4,6-8. Philadelphia, 1829. 6v.
NEDL AH 277.34.14.9 Rollin, Charles. Ancient history. N.Y., 1839. 2v.
NEDL AH 277.34.15 Rollin, Charles. Ancient history. N.Y., 1841. 2v.
NEDL AH 277.34.16 Rollin, Charles. Ancient history of the Egyptians. N.Y., 1843-44. 8v.
AH 277.34.17 Rollin, Charles. The ancient history of the Egyptians. Cincinnati, 1850. 2v.
NEDL AH 277.34.19 Rollin, Charles. Ancient history. v.1-4. N.Y., 1857. 2v.
NEDL AH 277.34.21 Rollin, Charles. Ancient history. v.1-4. Cincinnati, 1860. 2v.
AH 277.34.22 Rollin, Charles. The ancient history of the Egyptians. N.Y., 1883. 4v.
AH 277.34.23 Rollin, Charles. The ancient history of the Egyptians. London, 1826. 8v.
NEDL AH 277.34.25 Rollin, Charles. Storia antica. Livorno, 1835. 11v.
NEDL AH 277.34.27 Rollin, Charles. Storia antica e romana. 1. ed. Firenze, 1828-32. 49v.
AH 277.34.30 Rollin, Charles. Ancient history. Atlas. n.p., 1738-40.
AH 277.66.2 Abbt, Thomas. Fragment der aeltesten Begebenheiten des menschlichen Geschlechts. Halle, 1767.
Htn AH 277.88* Newbery, John. A compendious history of the world. London, 1788. 2v.
AH 277.93.3.4 Heeren, Arnold Herman Ludwig. Handbuch der Geschichte der Staaten des Alterthums. 4. Aufl. Göttingen, 1821.
AH 277.93.4 Heeren, Arnold Herman Ludwig. Ideen über Politik, Verbehr und Handel. Göttingen, 1824. 6v.
AH 277.93.10 Heeren, Arnold Herman Ludwig. Historical researches into politics, intercourse and trade. London, 1866. 2v.
AH 277.93.25 Heeren, Arnold Herman Ludwig. Etwas über meine Studien des alten Indiens. Göttingen, 1827.
AH 277.96 Fréret, N. Oeuvres complètes. Paris, 1796. 20v.
Htn AH 278.00* Millot, C.F.X. Elements of ancient history. N.Y., 18- .
NEDL AH 278.10 Heeren, Arnold Herman Ludwig. Handbuch...Geschichte...Staaten. Göttingen, 1810.
AH 278.11 Eichhorn, J.G. Antiqua historia. Lipsiae, 1811. 4v.
NEDL AH 278.11.5 Royou, J.C. Précis de l'histoire ancienne. 2. éd. Paris, 1811. 4v.
AH 278.13 Mayo, R. A view of ancient geography and ancient history. v.1-2. Philadelphia, 1813.
AH 278.15 Schlosser, Friedrich Christoph. Alte Geschichte bis zum Untergang des weströmischen Reiche. Frankfurt am Main, 1815.
AH 278.16 Whepley, S. Lectures on ancient history. N.Y., 1816.
AH 278.17 Heeren, Arnold Herman Ludwig. Handbuch...Geschichte...Staaten. Göttingen, 1817.
AH 278.26 Schlosser, Friedrich Christoph. Geschichte der alten Welt. v.1-3. Frankfurt, 1826. 9v.
NEDL AH 278.26.5 Ertov, I.D. Prodolzhenie v seobshchei istorii drevnikh prosveschennykh narodov. Sankt Peterburg, 1826. 2v.
AH 278.27.12 Poirson, A. Précis de l'histoire ancienne. 12. éd. Paris, 1853. 2v.
AH 278.28 Heeren, Arnold Herman Ludwig. History of the states of antiquity. Northhampton, 1828.
AH 278.28.5 Niebuhr, B.G. Kleine historische und philologische Schriften. Bonn, 1828.
NEDL AH 278.28.9 Outline of general history. v.1-2. London, 1828.
AH 278.35 Pogodin, Mikhail Petrovich. Lektsii po Gerenu o politike. Moskva, 1835.
AH 278.36 Ségur, L.P. Histoire universelle. 5. éd. v.1-10. Atlas. Paris, 1836. 11v.
AH 278.40 Heeren, Arnold Herman Ludwig. A manual of ancient history. 3. ed. Oxford, 1840.
NEDL AH 278.40.5 Heeren, Arnold Herman Ludwig. A manual of ancient history. London, 1847.
NEDL AH 278.41.7 Dielitz, T. Hellas und Rom. 7. Aufl. Berlin, 18- ?
NEDL AH 278.43 True stories from ancient history. N.Y., 1843.
NEDL AH 278.44 Boulet, Jean B.E. Manuel pratique d'histoire ancienne. Paris, 1844.
NEDL AH 278.44.5 Lista y Aragón, A. Elementos de historia antigua. Sevilla, 1844.
AH 278.45 Taylor, W.C. A manual of ancient history. N.Y., 1845.
AH 278.46 Frost, J. Pictorial ancient history of the world. Philadelphia, 1846.
AH 278.47 Goodrich, S.G. Ancient history. Louisville, Ky., 1847.
NEDL AH 278.47.10 Storia antica. Torino, 1847.
AH 278.48 Niebuhr, B.G. Vorträge über alte Geschichte. Berlin, 1847. 2v.
NEDL AH 278.48.5 Vendel-Heyl, L.A. Sumario de la historia de Grecia i de Roma. Santiago, 1848. 2 pam.
AH 278.52 Niebuhr, B.G. Lectures on ancient history. Philadelphia, 1852. 3v.
AH 278.52.3 Niebuhr, B.G. Lectures on ancient history. London, 1852. 3v.
AH 278.52.15 Duncker, M. Geschichte des Alterthums. Berlin, 1863. 4v.
AH 278.52.19 Duncker, M. Geschichte des Alterthums. 4. Aufl. Leipzig, 1874. 9v.
NEDL AH 278.53 Lamé-Fleury, J.R. La storia antica. Venezia, 1853.
NEDL AH 278.54 Boreau, V. Historia antigua. Santiago, 1854.
NEDL AH 278.55 Schmitz, L. A manual of ancient history. Philadelphia, 1855.
NEDL AH 278.56.10 Leva, G. de. Sommario della storia de' popoli antichi. Padova, 1856.
NEDL AH 278.58 Guillemin, J.J. Histoire ancienne. Paris, 1858.
NEDL AH 278.58.4 Flóres, Antonio. Historia universal. Lima, 1858.
NEDL AH 278.58.5 Flóres, Antonio. Curso de historia antigua. 2. ed. Besanyon, 1863.
AH 278.67 Lamé-Fleury, J.R. L'histoire ancienne. Paris, 1867.
AH 278.69A Rawlinson, G. Manual of ancient history. Oxford, 1869.
AH 278.69B Rawlinson, G. Manual of ancient history. Oxford, 1869.
NEDL AH 278.69 Rawlinson, G. Manual of ancient history. Oxford, 1869.
AH 278.69.6 Rawlinson, G. Manual of ancient history. N.Y., 1871.
NEDL AH 278.69.6 Rawlinson, G. Manual of ancient history. N.Y., 1871.
NEDL AH 278.69.9 Lord, J. Ancient states and empire. N.Y., 1869.
NEDL AH 278.69.15 Yonge, Chrlotte M. A book of worthies. London, 1886.
AH 278.70 Lamé-Fleury, J.R. Ancient history. Boston, 1870.
NEDL AH 278.72 Thalheimer, M.E. Ancient history. Cincinnati, 1872.

AH 274 - 279   Ancient World in general - General history (By date) - cont.

NEDL AH 278.72.3 Schieffelin, S.B. Ta themelia tes istorias. Athens, 1872.
NEDL AH 278.72.5 Thalheimer, M.E. A manual of ancient history. Cincinnati, 1872.
NEDL AH 278.74 Smith, Philip. History of the world. N.Y., 1874. 3v.
NEDL AH 278.75 Barton, J.A.G. The ancient world. Edinburgh, 1875.
NEDL AH 278.81.5 Steele, J.D. A brief history of ancient peoples. N.Y., 1881.
NEDL AH 278.82.5 Myers, P.V.N. Outlines of ancient history. N.Y., 1882.
NEDL AH 278.83 Duruy, V. Petite histoire ancienne. Paris, 1883.
AH 278.84 Ranke, L.F. von. Universal history. London, 1884.
AH 278.84.2 Ranke, L.F. von. Universal history. N.Y., 1884.
AH 278.84.3 Meyer, E. Geschichte des Alterthums. Stuttgart, 1884. 5v.
AH 278.84.5 Meyer, E. Geschichte des Alterthums. v.1-5. Stuttgart, 1907-31. 7v.
AH 278.84.7 Meyer, E. Die ältere Chronologie Babyloniens, Assyriens und Ägyptens. Stuttgart, 1925.
AH 278.84.7.2 Meyer, E. Die ältere Chronologie Babyloniens. Stuttgart, 1931.
AH 278.84.10 Meyer, E. Geschichte des Altertums. 5. Aufl. v.1,3,4. Stuttgart, 1925-26. 4v.
NEDL AH 278.84.12 Martinez Silva, Carlos. Compendio de historia antigua. 4. ed. Bogota, 1910.
NEDL AH 278.85 Smith, P. History of the world. N.Y., 1885. 3v.
NEDL AH 278.86 Vuibert, A.J.B. An ancient history. Baltimore, 1886.
NEDL AH 278.90 Allen, W. Ancient history for colleges and high schools. Boston, 1890. 2v.
NEDL AH 278.91 Allen, W. Ancient history for colleges and high schools. Boston, 1891.
NEDL AH 278.92 Eyzaquirre, R. Compendio de historia antigua, griega y romana. Santiago de Chile, 1892.
NEDL AH 278.93 Seignbos, C. Histoire ancienne. Paris, 1903.
NEDL AH 278.93.3 Zeehe, Andreas. Lehrbuch der Geschichte des Alterthums. Laibach, 1893.
NEDL AH 278.93.5 Allen, W. Ancient history for colleges and high schools. pt.2. Boston, 1893.
NEDL AH 278.96 Krüger, C.A. Geschichte der Griechen und Römen. Berlin, 1896.
NEDL AH 278.97 Boughton, W. History of ancient peoples. N.Y., 1896.
NEDL AH 279.02.2 Botsford, G.W. Ancient history for beginners. N.Y., 1902.
NEDL AH 279.02.5 Wolfson, A.M. Essentials in ancient history. N.Y., 1902.
NEDL AH 279.03 Souttar, R. Short history of ancient peoples. London, 1903.
NEDL AH 279.03.2 Souttar, R. Short history of ancient peoples. N.Y., 1904.
NEDL AH 279.03.5 Seignobos, C. Histoire narrative et descriptive de l'antiquité. 8. éd. Paris, 1910.
AH 279.04 Bauer, A. Lehrbuch der Geschichte des Alterthums. Wien, 1904.
AH 279.04.3 Goodspeed, George S. A history of the ancient world. N.Y., 1904.
AH 279.04.5 Myers, Philip Van Ness. The eastern nations and Greece. Boston, 1904.
NEDL AH 279.05 Leadbetter, F. Outlines and studies to accompany Myer's Ancient history. Boston, 1905.
NEDL AH 279.05.5 West, Willis M. The ancient world from the earliest times to 800 A.D. Boston, 1905.
AH 279.06 Myers, Philip Van Ness. A short history of ancient times. Boston, 1906.
NEDL AH 279.06.5 Morey, William Carey. Outlines of ancient history. N.Y., 1906.
NEDL AH 279.08 Snider, D.J. European history, chiefly ancient. St. Louis, 1908.
NEDL AH 279.09 Ulbricht, E. Grundzüge der alten Geschichte. Weissen, 1909. 2v.
AH 279.09.5 Amatucci, A.G. Dalle rive del Nilo ai lidi del "mar nostro". 2. ed. Bari, 1925. 2v.
AH 279.10 Schwahn, W. Geschichte der Griechen und Römer. Berlin, 1910.
AH 279.11 Pöhlmann, R. von. Aus Altertum und Gegenwart. München, 1911.
AH 279.11.15 Botsford, G.W. A history of the ancient world. N.Y., 1925.
AH 279.11.20 Botsford, G.W. A history of the ancient world. N.Y., 1927.
AH 279.12.2 Botsford, G.W. History of the ancient world. N.Y., 1916.
AH 279.12.3 Goodspeed, George S. A history of the ancient world. N.Y., 1912.
AH 279.12.5 Meyer, E. Histoire de l'antiquité. Paris, 1912.
AH 279.12.7 Westermann, William L. The story of ancient nations. N.Y., 1912.
AH 279.13 Cavaignac, E. Histoire de l'antiquité. v.1-3 et index générale. Paris, 1913-20. 5v.
AH 279.13.4 Porzio, G. Una "storia dell'antichità". Milano, 1919.
NEDL AH 279.13.5 Webster, Hutton. Ancient history. N.Y., 1913.
AH 279.13.10 West, Willis M. The ancient world. Boston, 1913.
AH 279.14 Mattingly, H. Outlines of ancient history. Cambridge, Eng., 1914.
AH 279.15 Breasted, James H. A short ancient history. Boston, 1915.
AH 279.16A Breasted, James H. Ancient times, a history of the early world. Boston, 1916.
AH 279.16B Breasted, James H. Ancient times, a history of the early world. Boston, 1916.
AH 279.16C Breasted, James H. Ancient times, a history of the early world. Boston, 1916.
AH 279.16D Breasted, James H. Ancient times, a history of the early world. Boston, 1916.
AH 279.16E Breasted, James H. Ancient times, a history of the early world. Boston, 1916.
AH 279.16.7F Roosevelt, Theodore. Dawn and sunrise of history. N.Y., 1917.
AH 279.16.10 Betten, F.S. The ancient world, from the earliest times to 800 A.D. Boston, 1916.
AH 279.16.15 Breasted, James H. Ancient times. 2. ed. Boston, 1935.
NEDL AH 279.23 Blanchet, D. Histoire de l'Orient et de la Grèce. 7. éd. Paris, 1923.
NEDL AH 279.23.10 Mills, Dorothy. The book of the ancient world for younger readers. N.Y., 1923.
NEDL AH 279.23.15 Mills, Dorothy. The book of the ancient world for younger readers. N.Y., 1926.
AH 279.24 Rostovtsev, Mikhail Ivanovich. Ocherk" istorii drevnego mira. Berlin', 1924.
AH 279.24.5A Rostovtsev, Mikhail Ivanovich. A history of the ancient world. v.2. Oxford, 1927.
AH 279.24.5B Rostovtsev, Mikhail Ivanovich. A history of the ancient world. v.2. Oxford, 1927.
AH 279.24.6 Rostovtsev, Mikhail Ivanovich. A history of the ancient world. Westport, 1971. 2v.

Classified Listing

AH 274 - 279   Ancient World in general - General history (By date) - cont.

AH 279.29 — Laistner, Max L.W. Survey of ancient history to the death of Constantine. Boston, 1929.

AH 279.29.10 — Ebeling, Erich. Geschichte des alten Morgenlandes. Berlin, 1929.

Htn AH 279.30* — Hollins, Elizabeth C.M. History of civilization. Portland, 1930.

AH 279.30.5 — Alfonso I, king of Castile and Leon. General estoria. pt.1-2. Madrid, 1930- 2v.

AH 279.31 — Webster, Hutton. Ancient civilization. Boston, 1931.

AH 279.32 — Sanctis, G. de. Problemi di storia antica. Bari, 1932.

AH 279.33 — Vicini, Antonio. La civiltà antica dal periodo preistorico. Piedimonte d'Alife, 1933.

AH 279.33.5 — Junker, H. Die Völker des Antiken Orients. Freiburg, 1933.

AH 279.35A — Glover, T.R. The ancient world; a beginning. N.Y., 1935.

AH 279.35B — Glover, T.R. The ancient world; a beginning. N.Y., 1935.

AH 279.35C — Glover, T.R. The ancient world; a beginning. N.Y., 1935.

AH 279.35.5 — Glover, T.R. The ancient world. London, 1944.

AH 279.36 — Monteath, K.M. The antiquity of mankind and the modernity of religions. 3. ed. York, 1936.

AH 279.36.5 — Sêcher, J. L'Orient et la Grèce. Paris, 1936.

AH 279.36.10 — Perkins, C. Ancient history. N.Y., 1936.

AH 279.37 — Finkelstein, M.I. A syllabus for ancient history. N.Y., 1937.

AH 279.37.5 — Bevan, E.R. The world of Greece and Rome. London, 1937.

AH 279.39.5 — Taeger, Fritz. Das Altertum. 3. Aufl. v.2. Stuttgart, 1942.

AH 279.39.7 — Taeger, Fritz. Das Altertum. 4. Aufl. Stuttgart, 1950.

AH 279.39.9 — Taeger, Fritz. Das Altertum. 6. Aufl. Stuttgart, 1958. 2v.

AH 279.39.10 — Smith, C.E. A short history of the ancient world. N.Y., 1939.

AH 279.41 — Adademiia nauk SSSR. Institut istorii. Istoriia drevnego mira. Izd. 2. Moskva, 1941.

AH 279.41.5 — Mishuls'a, A.V. Istoriia drevnego mira. Izd. 5. Moskva, 1946.

AH 279.41.10 — Tovar, Antonio. En el primer giro. Madrid, 1941.

AH 279.41.15 — Thiess, Frank. Das Reich der Dämonen. Berlin, 1941.

AH 279.41.15.5 — Thiess, Frank. Das Reich der Dämonen. Wien, 1968.

AH 279.43 — Hjartarson, A. Mannkynssaga. Reykjavik, 1943.

AH 279.43.5 — Altheim, Franz. Die Krise der alten Welt im 3. Jahrhundert n. zw. und ihre Ursachen. v.1,3. Berlin, 1943- 2v.

AH 279.43.10 — Altheim, Franz. Niedergang der alten Welt. Frankfurt am Main, 1952. 2v.

AH 279.45 — Tôrres, Flausino. O mundo mediterrânico do séc. XII a.C. ao séc. III d.C. Lisboa, 1945.

AH 279.46 — Finegan, Jack. Light from the ancient past. Princeton, N.J., 1946.

AH 279.46.2 — Finegan, Jack. Light from the ancient past. 2. ed. Princeton, N.J., 1959.

AH 279.46.4 — Finegan, Jack. Light from the ancient past. Princeton, 1947.

AH 279.46.5 — Burton-Brown, T. Studies in third millennium history. London, 1946.

AH 279.46.10 — Cavaignac, E. Histoire générale de l'antiquité. Paris, 1946.

AH 279.47 — Van Sickle, C.E. A political and cultural history of the ancient world from prehistoric times to the dissolution of the Roman Empire in the West. Boston, 1947-

AH 279.48 — Kornemann, E. Weltgeschichte des Mittelmeer-Raumes von Philipp II. München, 1948-49. 2v.

AH 279.48.5 — Taeger, Fritz. Grundzüge der alten Geschichte. Oberursel, 1948.

AH 279.48.10 — Kocherthaler, E. Das Reich der Antike. Baden-Baden, 1948.

AH 279.48.15 — Kahrstedt, Ulrich. Geschichte der griechiesh-römischen Altertums. München, 1948.

AH 279.49 — Berve, Helmut. Gestaltende Kräfte der Antike. München, 1949.

AH 279.49.2 — Berve, Helmut. Gestaltende Kräfte der Antike. 2. Aufl. München, 1966.

AH 279.50A — Swain, J.W. The ancient world. N.Y., 1950. 2v.

AH 279.50B — Swain, J.W. The ancient world. N.Y., 1950. 2v.

AH 279.51 — Robinson, C.A. Ancient history from prehistoric times to the death of Justinian. N.Y., 1951.

AH 279.52A — Velikovsky, I. Ages in chaos. 1. ed. Garden City, 1952.

AH 279.52B — Velikovsky, I. Ages in chaos. 1. ed. Garden City, 1952.

AH 279.52.5 — Grant, Michael. Ancient history. London, 1952.

AH 279.52.10 — Passerini, Alfredo. Questioni di storia antica. Milano, 1952.

AH 279.54 — Giannelli, G. Le grandi correnti della storia antica. Milano, 1954.

AH 279.55 — Levi, Mario Attilio. La lotta politica nel mondo antico. 1. ed. Milano, 1955.

AH 279.55.5 — Levi, Mario Attilio. Political power in the ancient world. London, 1965.

AH 279.56 — Histoire et historiens dans l'antiquité. Genève, 1956.

AH 279.57 — Schreiber, H. Throne unter Schutt und Sand. Wien, 1957.

AH 279.58 — Cottrell, Leonard. The anvil of civilisation. London, 1958.

AH 279.58.5 — Pareti, Luigi. Studi minori di storia antica. Roma, 1958-69. 4v.

AH 279.58.20 — Chambers, M.H. Greek and Roman history. Washington, 1958.

AH 279.58.25 — Nenci, Giuseppe. Introduzione alle guerre persiane e altri saggi. Pisa, 1958.

AH 279.58.30 — Bignami, Ernesto. Manuale di storia orientale e greca. Milano, 1958.

AH 279.58.35 — Mueller, W.F. Aufstieg und Untergang der Grossreiche des Altertums. 2. Aufl. Stuttgart, 1959.

AH 279.59.5 — Nováková, J. Antika v dokumentech. Praha, 1959-61. 2v.

AH 279.60.5 — Vogt, Joseph. Orbis. Freiburg, 1960.

AH 279.62 — Petit, Paul. Précis d'histoire ancienne. Paris, 1962.

AH 279.63.5 — Schaefer, Hans. Probleme der alten Geschichte. Göttingen, 1963.

AH 279.63.10 — Sverdlovsk, Russia (City). Ural'skii gosudarstvennyi universitet. Antichnaia drevnost' i srednie veka. v.1-2,4-5,7. v.1,5; Photoreproduction. Sverdlovsk, 1963-5v.

AH 279.64 — Haywood, Richard M. Ancient Greece and the Near East. N.Y., 1964.

AH 279.65 — Starr, Chester G. A history of the ancient world. N.Y., 1965.

AH 279.65.5 — Schieder, Oscar. Die alte Welt. Wiesbaden, 1965-69. 2v.

AH 279.65.10 — Preobrazhenskii, Petr F. V mire antichnykh idei i obrazov. Moskva, 1965.

AH 279.66 — Sanctis, Gaetano de. Scritti minori. Roma, 1966- 3v.

AH 274 - 279   Ancient World in general - General history (By date) - cont.

VAH 279.67.5 — Varshavskii, Anatolii S. Goroda raskryvaint tainy. Moskva, 1967.

AH 279.68 — Finley, Moses I. Aspects of antiquity. London, 1968.

AH 279.68.5 — Passman, Franz Anton. Der Durchbruch durch die Völkerwanderung. Bonn, 1968. 2v.

AH 279.69 — Studi di storia antica in memoria di Luca de Regibus. Genova, 1969.

AH 279.71.5 — Lauffer, Siegfried. Kurze Geschichte der antiken Welt. München, 1971.

AH 279.72 — Drevnii Vostok i antichnyi mir. Moskva, 1972.

AH 288.85 — Ranke, L.F. von. Universal history. N.Y., 1885.

AH 294 - 299   Ancient World in general - General special - Miscellany (By date)

Htn AH 295.53* — Postel, G. De originibus, seu De varia...historia. Basiliae, 1553.

Htn AH 295.64* — Porcacchi, T. Il primo volume delle cagioni delle guerre antiche. Vinegia, 1564.

Htn AH 297.02* — Dale, A. van. Dissertationes IX. antiquitatibus. Amstelodami, 1702.

Htn AH 297.24* — Cumberland, R. Origines gentium antiquissimae. Londini, 1724.

AH 297.67 — Bryant, J. Observations and inquiries relating to ancient history. Cambridge, 1767.

AH 298.00 — Bredow, G.G. Untersuchungen...alten Geschichte. pt.1-2. Altona, 1800-02.

AH 298.05 — Fortia d'Urban, A.J. de. Mémoires pour servir à l'histoire ancienne. v.1-10. Paris, 1805-09. 4v.

NEDL AH 298.15 — Heeren, Arnold Herman Ludwig. Ideen über Politik, Verkehr und Handel. v.1-2. Göttingen, 1815. 3v.

AH 298.21 — Volney, C.F. New researches in ancient history. London, 1821. 2v.

AH 298.21.5 — Volney, C.F. Recherches nouvelles sur l'histoire ancienne. Paris, 1814. 3v.

Htn AH 298.22* — Adams, J. Flowers of ancient history. Leesburg, 1822.

AH 298.28 — Herbert, Algernon. Nimrod. London, 1828-30. 4v.

NEDL AH 298.33.3 — Heeren, Arnold Herman Ludwig. Historical researches. Oxford, 1833. 3v.

AH 298.33.5 — Lorentz, R. Gründzüge zu Vorträgen über Geschichte. Leipzig, 1833.

AH 298.34F — Harrison, George. Fragments and scraps of history. London, 1834. 2v.

AH 298.38 — Älteste und alte Zeit. v.1-5. Hanover, 1838. 2v.

AH 298.41 — Gerlach, F.D. Historische Studien. Hamburg, 1841. 2v.

NEDL AH 298.42 — Kollataj, Hugo. Rozbiór krytyczny zazad historyi. Krakow, 1842. 3v.

AH 298.42.2 — Kollataj, Hugo. Rozbiór krytyczny zazad historii. wyd.1. Warszawa, 1972.

AH 298.54 — Lasaulx, Ernest. Studien des classischen Alterthums. Regensburg, 1854.

NEDL AH 298.61 — Stacke, L. Erzählungen aus der alten Geschichte in biographischer Form. 4. Aufl. v.2. Oldenburg, 1861.

NEDL AH 298.65 — Zeller, J. Entretiens sur l'histoire antiquité. Paris, 1865.

AH 298.71 — Mahaffy, J.P. Prolegomena to ancient history. London, 1871.

AH 298.72 — Schmidt, V. Assyriens og Aegyptiens gamle historie. Kjøbenhavn, 1872-77.

AH 298.76 — Cory, I.P. Ancient fragments. London, 1876.

AH 298.82 — Schaefer, Arnold. Abrisz der Quellenkunde der griechischen und römischen Geschichte. Leipzig, 1882.

AH 298.82.4 — Schaefer, Arnold. Abrisz der Quellenkunde der griechischen und römischen Geschichte. v.1, 4. Aufl; v.2, 2. Aufl. Leipzig, 1885-89. 2v.

NEDL AH 298.88 — Wood, C.W. Topics in ancient history. Boston, 1888.

AH 298.88.3 — Schmidt, A. Abhandlungen zur alten Geschichte. Leipzig, 1888.

NEDL AH 298.90 — Sheldon, Mary D. Studies in Greek and Roman history. Boston, 1890.

AH 298.91 — Beloch, J. Studi di storia antica. v.1-7. Roma, 1891. 3v.

AH 298.95 — Wachsmuth, C. Einleitung...der alten Geschichte. Leipzig, 1895.

AH 298.99 — Mücke, C. Vom Euphrat zum Tiber. Leipzig, 1899.

AH 298.99.3 — Zeitschrift für Altegeschichte. Leipzig, 1899.

NEDL AH 299.01 — Strehl, Willy. Grundriss der alten Geschichte. Breslau, 1901. 2v.

AH 299.05 — Winckler, Hugo. Auszug aus der vorderasiatischen Geschichte. Leipzig, 1905.

AH 299.10 — Meyer, E. Kleine Schriften. Halle, 1910.

AH 299.10.2 — Meyer, E. Kleine Schriften. v.1, 2. Aufl. Halle, 1924. 2v.

AH 299.10.3 — Saggi di storia antica e di archeologia. Roma, 1910.

AH 299.12 — Gercke, Alfred. Einleitung in die Altertumswissenschaft. Leipzig, 1912-23. 3v.

AH 299.12.2 — Gercke, Alfred. Einleitung in die Altertumswissenschaft. Leipzig, 1910-12. 3v.

AH 299.12.5 — Gercke, Alfred. Einleitung in die Altertumswissenschaft. 3. Aufl. Leipzig, 1921-27. 3v.

AH 299.13 — Strehl, Willy. Grundriss der alten Geschichte und Quellenkundl. 2. Aufl. Breslau, 1913. 2v.

AH 299.19 — Kornemann, E. Aufsätze und Vorträge. Leipzig, 1919.

AH 299.20 — Preller, Hugo. Das Altertum seine staatliche und geistige Entwicklung und deren Nachwirkungen. Leipzig, 1920.

AH 299.22 — Ure, Percy. The origin of tyranny. Cambridge, 1922.

AH 299.22.2 — Ure, Percy. The origin of tyranny. N.Y., 1962.

AH 299.30 — Chuckerbutty, K. The world on the positive plate. Calcutta, 193-. 5 pam.

AH 299.35 — Ehrenberg, V. Ost und West. Brünn, 1935.

AH 299.38 — Sanford, E.M. The Mediterranean world in ancient times. N.Y., 1938.

AH 299.38.5 — Sanford, E.M. The Mediterranean world in ancient times. N.Y., 1951.

AH 299.39 — Altheim, F. Die Soldatinkaiser. Frankfurt am Main, 1939.

AH 299.39.5 — Teggart, F.J. Rome and China. Berkeley, 1939.

AH 299.45 — Rosenvasser, Abraham. La poesía amatoria en el antiguo egipto. Buenos Aires, 1945.

AH 299.50 — Bertoldi, V. Colonizzazioni nell'antico. Napoli, 1950.

AH 299.62 — Laptev, V.V. Pervobytnoobshchinnyi i rabovladel'cheskii stroi na territorii nashei strany. Leningrad, 1962.

AH 299.64 — Badian, Ernst. Studies in Greek and Roman history. Oxford, 1964.

AH 299.66 — Mélanges d'archéologie d'épigraphie et d'histoire offerts à Jérôme Carcopino. Paris, 1966.

AH 299.67 — Konferentsiia po izucheniiu problem antichnosti, Leningrad, 1964. Antichnoe obshchestvo. Moskva, 1967.

AH 294 - 299   Ancient World in general - General special - Miscellany (By date) - cont.

AH 299.70	Massé, Claude. La colonisation dans l'antiquité. Paris, 1970.
AH 299.71	Studi di storiografia antica. In memoria di Leonardo Ferrero. Torino, 1971.
AH 299.72	Schenk von Stauffenberg, Alexander. Macht und Geist. München, 1972.
AH 299.72.5	De Camp, Lyon S. Great cities of the ancient world. Garden City, N.Y., 1972.
AH 299.72.10A	Hammond, Mason. The city in the ancient world. Cambridge, Mass., 1972.
AH 299.72.10B	Hammond, Mason. The city in the ancient world. Cambridge, Mass., 1972.

AH 300 - 309   Ancient World in general - General special - Philosophy of history (Table A)

	AH 307.59	Montagu, E.W. Reflections on the rise and fall of the ancient republic. London, 1759.
	AH 307.60	Montagu, E.W. Reflections on the rise and fall of the ancient republic. London, 1760.
Htn	AH 307.66*	Voltaire, François Marie Arouet de. The philosophy of history. London, 1766.
Htn	AH 307.69*	Perisonius, J. Animadversiones historicae. Amstelodami, 1685.
	AH 307.87	Bellenden, W. De statu libri tres. 2. ed. Londini, 1787.
	AH 307.87.2	Bellenden, W. De statu libri tres. 2. ed. Londini, 1787.
	AH 307.96.3	Volney, C.F. Les ruines...révolutions des empires. Paris, 1826.
	AH 308.46	Lasaulx, E. von. Über das Studium der griechischen und römischen Alterthümer. München, 1846.
	AH 308.57	Ulm. Gymnasium. Parallelen römischer und griechischen Entwicklungsgeschichte. Ulm, 1857.
	AH 308.64	Negri, C. Memorie storico-politiche. Torino, 1864.
	AH 308.95	Pöhlmann, R. Aus Altertum und Gegenwart. München, 1895.
	AH 308.95.2	Pöhlmann, R. Aus Altertum und Gegenwart. München, 1911.
	AH 308.96	Taylor, H.O. Ancient ideals. N.Y., 1896. 2v.
	AH 308.96.2	Taylor, H.O. Ancient ideals. v.2. N.Y., 1896.
	AH 308.96.5A	Taylor, H.O. Ancient ideals. 2. ed. N.Y., 1921. 2v.
	AH 308.96.5B	Taylor, H.O. Ancient ideals. 2. ed. N.Y., 1921. 2v.
	AH 309.03	Kaerst, J. Antike Idee der Oekumene. Leipzig, 1903.
	AH 309.07	Paterson, W.R. The nemesis of nations. London, 1907.
	AH 309.67	Jones, Tom Bard. Paths to the ancient past: applications of the historical method to ancient history. N.Y., 1967.
	AH 309.67.5	Frolov, Eduard D. Russkaia istoriografiia antichnosti do serediny XIX v. Leningrad, 1967.
	AH 309.70	Slonimskii, Mikhail M. Periodizatsiia drevnei istorii v sovetskoi istoriografii. Voronezh, 1970.

AH 310 - 319   Ancient World in general - General special - Cosmology (Table A)

Htn	AH 316.77F*	Hale, Matthew. Primitive origination of mankind. London, 1677.
	AH 317.93	Delisle de Sales, J.C.I. Historie philosophique du monde primitif. Paris, 1793. 8v.

AH 320 - 329   Ancient World in general - General special - Races (Table A)

AH 328.69	Blyden, E.W. The negro in ancient history. N.Y.? 1869.
AH 328.69.2	Blyden, E.W. The negro in ancient history. Washington, 1869.
AH 328.73	Roget de Belloguet, D.F.L. Ethnogénie gauloise. Paris, 1873. 4v.
AH 328.83	Penka, K. Origines ariacae. Wien, 1883.
AH 328.83.2	Spiegel, F. Arische Periode. Leipzig, 1887.
AH 329.70	Snowden, Frank Martin. Black in antiquity; Ethiopians in the Greco-Roman experience. Cambridge, 1970.

AH 330 - 339   Ancient World in general - General special - Collected biographies (Table A)

Htn	AH 336.02*	Batero, G. Observations upon the lives of Alexander, Caesar, Scipio. London, 1602.
	AH 336.42.5	Heerman, F. Guldene Annotatien. Dordrecht, 1664.
	AH 338.13.2	Beauchamp, A. de. Biographie des jeunes gens. 2. éd. Paris, 1818.
	AH 338.72	Stoll, H.W. Geschichte der Griechen und Römer in Biographien. 2. Aufl. Leipzig, 1872. 2v.
	AH 339.52	Kornemann, E. Grosse Frauen des Altertums. 4. Aufl. Wiesbaden, 1952.
	AH 339.52.5	Toynbee, Arnold Joseph. Twelve men of action in Graeco-Roman history. Freeport, N.Y., 1969.
	AH 339.61	Carcopino, J. Profils de conquérants. Paris, 1961.
	AH 339.63	Sonnet-Altenburg, Helene. Hetären, Mütter, Amazonen. Heidenheim, 1963.

AH 400 - 409   Ancient World in general - History by periods - Before 500 B.C. (Table A)

Htn	AH 405.50*	Nanni, Giovanni. Antichita de beroso sacredote caldeo. Ventiae, 1550.
	AH 407.47	Fourmont, Etienne. Reflexions sur l'origine, histoire. Paris, 1747. 2v.
	AH 407.89	Williams, W. Primitive history. Chichester, 1789.
	AH 408.01	Russell, William. History of ancient Europe. Philadelphia, 1801. 2v.
	AH 408.46	Loebell, J.W. Weltgeschichte. Leipzig, 1846.
	AH 408.46.3	Kenrick, J. Essay on primaeval history. London, 1846.
	AH 408.47.5	Smith, George. The patriarchial age. N.Y., 1851.
	AH 408.55	Duncker, M. Geschichte des Alterthums. Berlin, 1855. 4v.
NEDL	AH 408.58	Menzies, H. Early ancient history. London, 1858.
	AH 408.60	Gerlach, F.D. Sage und Forschung. Basel, 1860.
	AH 408.69	Baldwin, J.D. Pre-historic nations. N.Y., 1869.
	AH 408.77A	Duncker, M. History of antiquity. London, 1877. 6v.
	AH 408.77B	Duncker, M. History of antiquity. London, 1877. 6v.
	AH 408.78.5A	Keary, C.F. The dawn of history. N.Y., 1879?
NEDL	AH 408.78.5B	Keary, C.F. The dawn of history. N.Y., 1879?
NEDL	AH 408.78.7	Keary, C.F. The dawn of history. pt.1-2. N.Y., 1883.
	AH 408.78.8	Keary, C.F. The dawn of history. pt.1. N.Y., 1883.
NEDL	AH 408.78.9	Keary, C.F. The dawn of history. N.Y., 1885.
	AH 408.78.15	Keary, C.F. The dawn of history. N.Y., 1887.
	AH 408.82	Lenormant, F. Beginnings of history. N.Y., 1882.
	AH 408.86	Welzhofer, H. Allgemeine Geschichte des Altertums. v.1-3. Gotha, 1886. 2v.
	AH 408.87	Clodd, E. Childhood of the world. London, 1887.
	AH 408.91	Büchner, L. Das goldene Zeitalter. Berlin, 1891.
	AH 408.92	Laing, S. Human origins. London, 1892.
NEDL	AH 408.99	Ragozin, Z.A. (Mrs.) A history of the world. N.Y., 1899.
NEDL	AH 409.09	Khvostov, M.M. Istoriia drevnago vostoka. Kazan', 1909.
	AH 409.11.5A	Myres, J.L. The dawn of history. N.Y., 1911.

AH 400 - 409   Ancient World in general - History by periods - Before 500 B.C. (Table A) - cont.

	AH 409.11.5B	Myres, J.L. The dawn of history. N.Y., 1911.
	AH 409.20	Van Loon, Hendrik Willem. Ancient man. N.Y., 1920.
	AH 409.22	Van Loon, Hendrik Willem. Ancient man. N.Y., 1922.
	AH 409.25	Weber, Wilhelm. Die Staatenwelt des Mittelmeeres in der Frühzeit des Griechentums. Stuttgart, 1925.
	AH 409.28	Peake, Harold. The steppe and the sown. New Haven, 1928.
	AH 409.43	Wiesner, J. Vor- und Frühzeit der Mittelmeerländer. Berlin, 1943. 2v.

AH 450 - 459   Ancient World in general - History by periods - 500 - 1 B.C. (Table A)

	AH 457.16.5F	Prideaux, H. The Old and New Testament connected in the history of the Jews. 5. ed. London, 1718-19. 2v.
	AH 457.16.10	Prideaux, H. The Old and New Testament connected in the history of the Jews. 10. ed. v.1-2. London, 1729. 4v.
	AH 457.16.15	Prideaux, H. The Old and New Testament connected in the history of the Jews. 13. ed. v.1-2. Glasgow, 1763. 4v.
Htn	AH 457.16.20*	Prideaux, H. The Old and New Testament connected in the history of the Jews. Charlestown, 1815-16. 4v.
	AH 457.49	Prideaux, H. The Old and New Testament connected in the history of the Jews. v.3-4. London, 1749. 2v.
	AH 458.07	Gillies, J. History of the world. London, 1807. 2v.
	AH 458.09	Gillies, J. History of the world. Philadelphia, 1809. 3v.
	AH 459.33	Beloch, Julius. Le monarchie ellenistiche e la repubblica romana. Bari, 1933.
	AH 459.51	Regibus, Luca de. La repubblica romana e gli ultimi re di Macedonia. Genova, 1951.
	AH 459.61	Mourre, Michel. Le monde a la mort de Socrate. Paris, 1961.

AH 500 - 509   Ancient World in general - History by periods - 1 A.D. - ca. 500 (Table A)

AH 507.98	Roesler, C.F. Chronica medii aevi. Tubingae, 1798.

AH 800 - 809   Ancient World in general - Chronology (Table A)

Htn	AH 805.45F*	Funck, J. Chronologia. Norimbergae, 1545.
Htn	AH 805.75*	Lucidus, J. Chronicon seu Emendatio temporum. Venetiis, 1575.
Htn	AH 805.83.2F*	Scaliger, J. De emendatione temporum. Francofurti, 1593.
Htn	AH 805.83.3F*	Scaliger, J. De emendatione temporum. Lugduni Batavorum, 1598.
Htn	AH 805.97*	Pie, Thomas. An houreglasse. London, 1597.
	AH 806.11.5F	Tornielli, A. Annales sacri. Lucae, 1756-57. 4v.
Htn	AH 806.72F*	Marcham, John. Chronicus canon. Londini, 1672.
	AH 807.01	Dodwell, Henry. De veteribus Graecorum Romanorum que cyclis. Oxonii, 1701.
	AH 807.22	Newton, Isaac. Chronology of antient kingdoms. Dublin, 1722.
	AH 807.28A	Hegewisch, D.H. Introduction to historical chronology. Burlington, 1837.
	AH 807.28B	Hegewisch, D.H. Introduction to historical chronology. Burlington, 1837.
Htn	AH 807.28.3*	Newton, Isaac. Chronology of ancient kingdoms. London, 1728.
	AH 807.28.5	Fréret, Nicolas. Défense de la chronologie. Paris, 1758.
	AH 807.52	Jackson, J. Chronological antiquities. London, 1752. 3v.
	AH 807.52.5F	Simson, E. Chronicon historiam catholicam. Amstelodami, 1752.
	AH 807.87	Roncallius, T. Vetustiora Latinorum scriptorum chronica. Patavii, 1787.
	AH 808.25	Ideler, L.C. Handbuch der...Chronologie. Berlin, 1825. 2v.
	AH 808.30	Hales, W. New analysis of chronology and geography. London, 1830. 4v.
	AH 808.31	Ideler, L.C. Lehrbuch der Chronologie. Berlin, 1831.
	AH 808.37	Strauchius, G. Treatise...in chronology. London, 1722.
	AH 808.38	Zumpt, K.G. Annales. Berolini, 1838.
	AH 808.38.3	Zumpt, K.G. Annales. Berolini, 1862.
	AH 808.39	Smith, J.T. Observations on chronological eras. Boston, 1839.
	AH 808.52	Scaliger, J. Olymiadōn anagra. Berolini, 1852.
	AH 808.63	Böckh, A. Sonnenkreise der Alten. Berlin, 1863.
	AH 808.74	Mendelssohn, L. Parallel-Tabellen zur griechischrömischen Chronologie. Leipzig, 1874.
	AH 808.77	Nichol, J. Tables of ancient literature and history. Glasgow, 1877.
	AH 808.79	Cassel, P.S. Phönix und seine Aera. Berlin, 1879.
	AH 808.79.10	Neteler, Bernhard. Zusammenhang der alttestamentlichen Zeitrechnung mit der Profangeschichte. v.1-3. Münster, 1879-86.
	AH 808.87.5	Paganelli, A. Riposta alle osservazione...della civiltà cattolica sulla chronologia rivendicata. Prato, 1889.
	AH 809.10	Elia bar Sinaya. La chronographie. Paris, 1910.
	AH 809.42	Meyer, Frank H. The crux of chronology; an essay to establish the life-time of Jesus Christ and...date of Easter. Boston, 1942.
	AH 809.45	Velikovsky, I. Thesis for the reconstruction of ancient history. N.Y., 1945.
	AH 809.62	Delorme, J. Les grandes dates de l'antiquité. Paris, 1962.
	AH 809.68	Bickerman, Elias Joseph. Chronology of the ancient world. London, 1968.

AH 810 - 819   Ancient World in general - Civilization, social life - General works (Table A)

	AH 812.5	Recherches sur les structures sociales dans l'antiquité classique. Paris, 1970.
	AH 812.10	Archaeological Symposium, American University of Beirut, 1967. The role of the Phoenicians in the interaction of Mediterranean civilizations. Beirut, 1968.
Htn	AH 815.16.3F*	Ricchieri, Lodovico. Digini lectionum antiquarum libri XVI. Basileae, 1517.
Htn	AH 815.16.9F*	Ricchieri, Lodovico. Rhodigini lectionum antiquarum...XXX. Basileae, 1542.
Htn	AH 815.16.11*	Ricchieri, Lodovico. Lectionum antiquarum libri XXX. Ludguni, 1560. 3v.
Htn	AH 815.16.15F*	Ricchieri, Lodovico. Rhodigini lectionum antiquarum. n.p., 1599.
Htn	AH 816.45*	Licetus, F. De anulis antiquis. Utini, 1645.
	AH 816.72F	Ferretti, G.B. Musae lapidariae antiquarum. Veronae, 1672.
Htn	AH 816.76*	Gibson, E. Portus iecius. Oxonii, 1694.
Htn	AH 816.85F*	Spon, J. Miscellanea eruditae antiquitatis. Lugduni, 1685.

Classified Listing

	AH 817.03	Lampe, F.A. De cymbalis veterum. Trajecti, 1703.
	AH 817.37	Rollin, Charles. History of the arts and sciences. London, 1737. 4v.
Htn	AH 817.41*	Athenian letters. London, 1741-43. 4v.
	AH 817.41.5	Athenian letters. London, 1810. 2v.
Htn	AH 817.41.6*	Athenian letters. London, 1798. 2v.
	AH 817.41.7	Athenische Briefe. Leipzig, 1799. 2v.
	AH 817.58	Holberg, Ludwig. Introduction to universal history. London, 1758.
	AH 817.58.3	Goguet, Antoine Y. De l'origine des lois, des arts, et des sciences. Paris, 1758. 3v.
NEDL	AH 817.58.5	Goguet, Antoine Y. De l'origine des lois. 6. éd. Paris, 1820. 3v.
NEDL	AH 817.58.13	Goguet, Antoine Y. Della origine delle leggi, delle arte...antichi popoli. Lucca, 1761. 3v.
NEDL	AH 817.58.17	Goguet, Antoine Y. The origins of laws, arts, and sciences. Edinburgh, 1775. 3v.
NEDL	AH 817.66	Boulanger, N.A. L'antiquité dévoilée par ses usages. Amsterdam, 1766. 3v.
	AH 817.66.5	Boulanger, N.A. L'antiquité dévoilée par ses usages. Amsterdam, 1766.
	AH 817.76	Sabbathier, F. Institutions, manners and customs of ancient nations. London, 1776. 2v.
	AH 817.87	Plessing, F.V.L. Memnonium. Leipzig, 1787. 2v.
NEDL	AH 817.95	Pölitz, K.H.L. Geschichte der Kultur der Menschheit. Leipzig, 1795.
	AH 818.52	Müller, C.O. Ancient art and its remains. London, 1852.
	AH 818.57	Hermann, K.F. Culturgeschichte. Göttingen, 1857.
	AH 818.62	Trottet, J.P. Génie des civilisations. Paris, 1862. 2v.
NEDL	AH 818.62.3	Guhl, Ernst. Leben der Griechen und Römer. Berlin, 1862.
NEDL	AH 818.62.3.5	Guhl, Ernst. Leben der Griechen und Römer. 2. Aufl. Berlin, 1864.
NEDL	AH 818.62.4	Guhl, Ernst. Leben der Griechen und Römer. 3. Aufl. Berlin, 1872.
NEDL	AH 818.62.5	Guhl, Ernst. Leben der Griechen und Römer. Berlin, 1876.
	AH 818.62.6	Guhl, Ernst. Leben der Griechen und Römer. 6. Aufl. Berlin, 1893.
NEDL	AH 818.62.8	Guhl, Ernst. Life of the Greeks and Romans. N.Y., 1876.
	AH 818.62.9	Guhl, Ernst. Life of the Greeks and Romans. London, 188-?
NEDL	AH 818.62.13A	Guhl, Ernst. The life of Greeks and Romans described from antique monuments. N.Y., 1896.
NEDL	AH 818.62.13B	Guhl, Ernst. The life of Greeks and Romans described from antique monuments. N.Y., 1896.
NEDL	AH 818.62.15	Guhl, Ernst. The life of Greeks and Romans described from antique monuments. N.Y., 1902.
	AH 818.67	Dombart, Theodore. Die sieben Weltwunder des Altertums. 2. Aufl. München, 1970.
	AH 818.68	Ozanam, A.F. History of civilization. London, 1868. 2v.
	AH 818.68.5	Ozanam, A.F. La civilisation au cinquième siècle. Paris, 1855. 2v.
	AH 818.69	Mahaffy, J.P. Primitive civilization. London, 1869.
	AH 818.69.3	Göll, Hermann. Kulturbilder. v.1-3. Leipzig, 1869. 2v.
	AH 818.69.4	Göll, Hermann. Kulturbilder. Leipzig, 1880. 2v.
	AH 818.71	Barber, T.C. Aryan civilization. London, 1871.
	AH 818.74	Lenormant, F. Premières civilisations. Paris, 1874. 2v.
	AH 818.74.3	Doublier, L. Geschichte des Altertums. Wien, 1874.
	AH 818.76	Hoyns, G. Die alte Welt. Berlin, 1876.
	AH 818.76.3	Forbiger, A. Hellas und Rom. v.1-2. Leipzig, 1876. 6v.
	AH 818.77	Rawlinson, G. Origins of nations. London, 1877.
	AH 818.77.3	Rawlinson, G. Origin of nations. N.Y., 1881.
	AH 818.77.3.5	Rawlinson, G. Origin of nations. N.Y., 1881.
	AH 818.77.4	Morgan, L.H. Ancient society. N.Y., 1877.
	AH 818.77.5	Morgan, L.H. Ancient society. Chicago, 1877.
	AH 818.77.6	Soury, J. Études historiques sur les religions, les arts, la civilisation. Paris, 1877.
	AH 818.78F	Falke, J. von. Hellas und Rom. Stuttgart, 1878.
	AH 818.78.3FA	Falke, J. von. Greece and Rome. N.Y., 1882.
	AH 818.78.3FB	Falke, J. von. Greece and Rome. N.Y., 1882.
	AH 818.82	Yaggy, Levi M. Museum of antiquity, a description of ancient life. N.Y., 1882.
NEDL	AH 818.82.10	Aguglia, S. Genesi dell'incivilimento. Napoli, 1882.
	AH 818.84.2	Jebb, R.C. Some ancient organs of public opinion. Cambridge, Eng., 1884.
	AH 818.84.5	Rauber, August. Urgeschichte des Menschen. v.1-2. Leipzig, 1884.
	AH 818.86	Spitzer, S. Sitte und Sitten der alten Völker. Budapest, 1886.
NEDL	AH 818.89	Verschoyle, J.S. History of ancient civilization. N.Y., 1889.
	AH 818.90	Reich, Emil. Graeco-Roman institutions. London, 1890.
	AH 818.90.5	Merrians, A.C. Telegraphing among the ancients. Cambridge, 1890.
	AH 818.93	Hittell, J.S. History of mental growth of mankind. N.Y., 1893. 4v.
	AH 818.94	Simcox, E.J. Primitive civilizations. London, 1894. 2v.
	AH 818.97	Holm, A. Kulturgeschichte des...Altertums. Leipzig, 1897.
	AH 818.97.2	Schneidewin, Max. Antike Humanität. Berlin, 1897.
	AH 818.97.5	Schneidewin, Max. Offener Brief au Herrn Professor Theobald Ziegler über "Antike Humanität". Leipzig, 1897.
	AH 819.03	Seignobos, C. Histoire de la civilisation ancienne. Paris, 1903.
	AH 819.03.5	Seignobos, C. Histoire de la civilisation ancienne. 5. éd. Paris, 1910.
	AH 819.05	Hahn, E. Das Alle des wirtschaftlichen Kultur. Heidelberg, 1905.
	AH 819.05.3F	Cybulski, S. Kultur der Griechen und Römer. Leipzig, 1905.
	AH 819.06	Schmidt, M.C.P. Kulturhistorische Beiträge zur Kenntnis des griechischen und römischen Altertums. Leipzig, 1906-12. 2v.
	AH 819.06.2	Schmidt, M.C.P. Kulturhistorische Beiträge zur Kenntnis des griechischen und römischen Altertums. Leipzig, 1914.
NEDL	AH 819.07	Reitzenstein, P. Werden und Wesen der Humanität. Strassburg, 1907.
	AH 819.08	Marett, R.R. Anthropology and the classics. Oxford, 1908.
	AH 819.08.10	Zieliński, Tadeusz. Iz zhizni idei. izd. 2. v.1-2,4, pt.2. Sankt Peterburg, 1908-11. 2v.
	AH 819.08.13	Zieliński, Tadeusz. Iz zhizni idei. izd. 3. Petrograd, 1916.
	AH 819.09	Morgan, J. Premières civilisations. Paris, 1909.

AH 819.12.3	Höhn, G. Die Einteilungsarten der Lebens- und Weltalter bei Griechen und Römer. Würzburg, 1912.
AH 819.13	Baumgarten, F. Die hellistisch-römische Kultur. Leipzig, 1913.
AH 819.15.5	Ashley, R.L. Ancient civilization. N.Y., 1917.
AH 819.16	Wolfson, Arthur M. Ancient civilization. N.Y., 1916.
AH 819.18.2	Birt, Theodor. Aus dem Leben der Antike. 2. Aufl. Leipzig, 1919.
AH 819.19	Petrie, W.M.F. Some sources of human history. London, 1919.
AH 819.19.10	Neuburger, Albert. Die Technik des Altertums. 2. Aufl. Leipzig, 1921.
AH 819.19.15	Neuburger, Albert. The technical arts and sciences of the ancients. London, 1930.
AH 819.19.16	Neuburger, Albert. The technical arts and sciences of the ancients. N.Y., 1969.
AH 819.24	De Burgh, W.G. The legacy of the ancient world. London, 1924.
AH 819.24.3	De Burgh, W.G. The legacy of the ancient world. v.1-2. London, 1953.
AH 819.24.5	Civilizaciones antiguas. Barcelona. 1-3
AH 819.25	Morgan, J. de. La préhistoire orientale. Paris, 1925-27. 3v.
AH 819.25.5	Otto, Walter G.A. Kulturgeschichte des Altertums. München, 1925.
AH 819.27	Mackenzie, D.A. Ancient civilizations from the earliest times to the birth of Christ. London, 1927.
AH 819.27.5	Peake, Harold. Peasants and potters. New Haven, 1927.
AH 819.27.10	Peake, Harold. Priests and kings. New Haven, 1927.
AH 819.28	Dawson, Christopher H. The age of the gods. Boston, 1928.
AH 819.28.5	Dawson, Christopher H. The age of the gods. London, 1933.
AH 819.28.10	Dawson, Christopher H. The age of the gods. 2. ed. N.Y., 1934.
AH 819.29	Waddell, L.A. The makers of civilization in race and history. London, 1929.
AH 819.29.5A	Peake, Harold. The way of the sea. New Haven, 1929.
AH 819.29.5B	Peake, Harold. The way of the sea. New Haven, 1929.
AH 819.30	Smith, G.E. Human history. London, 1930.
AH 819.32	Wright, Frederick A. The romance of life in the ancient world. London, 1932?
AH 819.33	Peake, Harold. Early steps in human progress. London, 1933.
AH 819.33.5	Niemax, Hans. Antike Humanität im Kampfe mit römischen Gesängniseland. Inaug. Diss. Neubrandenburg, 1933.
AH 819.35	Ciccotti, Ettore. La civiltà del mondo antico. Udine, 1935. 2v.
AH 819.35.6	Howard, E. Die Kultur der Antike. 2. Aufl. Zürich, 1948.
AH 819.36	Trever, Albert A. History of ancient civilization. N.Y., 1936-39. 2v.
AH 819.36.5	Hertzler, J.O. The social thought of the ancient civilization. 1. ed. N.Y., 1936.
AH 819.36.10A	Childe, Vere Gordon. Man makes himself. London, 1936.
AH 819.36.10B	Childe, Vere Gordon. Man makes himself. London, 1936.
AH 819.36.11	Childe, Vere Gordon. Man makes himself. London, 1948.
AH 819.36.15	Peake, Harold. The law and the prophets. New Haven, 1936.
AH 819.36.20	Poulsen, Frederik. Fra stille aftener. København, 1936.
AH 819.36.25	Friedell, Egon. Kulturgeschichte des Altertums. Zürich, 1936-
AH 819.36.27	Friedell, Egon. Kulturgeschichte Ägyptens und des alten Orients. 3. Aufl. München, 1951.
AH 819.39	Unger, Eckhard. Welt und Mensch im alten Orient. v.4. Berlin, 1939.
AH 819.40.2	Couch, H.N. Classical civilization. N.Y., 1947.
AH 819.40.4	Couch, H.N. Classical civilization. 2. ed. N.Y., 1950-51. 2v.
AH 819.41A	Turner, R.C. The great cultural traditions. 1. ed. N.Y., 1941. 2v.
AH 819.41B	Turner, R.C. The great cultural traditions. 1. ed. N.Y., 1941. 2v.
AH 819.41.8	Gabriel-Leroux, Jacqueline. Les premières civilisations de la Mediterranée. 6. éd. Paris, 1958.
AH 819.42	Childe, Vere Gordon. What happened in history. Harmondsworth, 1943.
AH 819.42.5	Childe, Vere Gordon. What happened in history. London, 1960.
AH 819.42.6	Childe, Vere Gordon. What happened in history. Harmondsworth, 1948.
AH 819.44	Cavazzana, J.C. Historia de la cultura. Lima, 1944.
AH 819.48	Passerini, A. La civiltà de mondo antico. Milano, 1948.
AH 819.49	Caldwell, W.E. The ancient world. N.Y., 1949.
AH 819.49.5	Taeger, Fritz. Die Kultur der Antike. Köln, 1949.
AH 819.50	Jouguet, Pierre. Les premières civilisations. Paris, 1950.
AH 819.51	National Geographic Magazine. Everyday life in ancient times. Washington, 1951.
AH 819.51.5	Pirenne, J. Civilisations antiques. Paris, 1951.
AH 819.52	Hoare, F.R. Eight decisive books of antiquity. London, 1952.
AH 819.54	Turone, Mario. La prima umanità. Milano, 1954.
AH 819.55	Forbes, Robert James. Studies in ancient technology. Leiden, 1955-64. 9v.
AH 819.55.2	Forbes, Robert James. Studies in ancient technology. 2. ed. v.1,4. Leiden, 1964. 2v.
AH 819.59	Parker, Henry B. Gods and men. 1. ed. N.Y., 1959.
AH 819.59.5	White, Leslie A. The evolution of culture. N.Y., 1959.
AH 819.60	Green, Peter. Essays in antiquity. Cleveland, 1960.
AH 819.60.10A	Guthrie, William K.C. Tradition and personal achievement in classical antiquity. London, 1960.
AH 819.60.10B	Guthrie, William K.C. Tradition and personal achievement in classical antiquity. London, 1960.
AH 819.60.15	Hardy, William. The Greek and Roman world. Cambridge, 1962.
AH 819.61F	Piggott, Stuart. The dawn of civilization. N.Y., 1961.
AH 819.61.4F	Piggott, Stuart. Aux portes de l'histoire. Paris, 1962.
AH 819.61.5	Bibby, Geoffrey. Four thousand years ago. 1. ed. N.Y., 1961.
AH 819.61.10F	Life (Chicago). The epic of man. N.Y., 1961.
AH 819.61.20	Deutsche Historiker-Gesellschaft. Sozialökonomische Verhältnisse in alter Orient. Berlin, 1961.
AH 819.61.25	Lissner, Ivar. Rätselhafte Kulturen. Olten, 1961.
AH 819.62F	Horizon (New York). The Horizon book of lost worlds. N.Y., 1962.
AH 819.62.5	Lissner, Ivar. The silent past. N.Y., 1962.
AH 819.62.10	Gordon, Cyrus. Before the Bible. London, 1962.
AH 819.63F	Bacon, Edward. Vanished civilizations of the ancient world. N.Y., 1963.

Classified Listing

Classified Listing

AH 848 Ancient World in general - Civilization, social life - Special topics - Costume - cont.
AH 848.15 Solerius, A. De pileo. Amstelodami, 1672.
AH 848.17 Paschalius, C. Coronae. Lugduni Batavorum, 1671.

AH 849 Ancient World in general - Civilization, social life - Special topics - Perfumes
AH 849.5 Sigismund, R. Die Aromata. Leipzig, 1884.
AH 849.6 Steuer, R.O. Myrrhe und Stakte. Wien, 1933.

AH 850 Ancient World in general - Civilization, social life - Special topics - Meals
AH 850.3F Stuck, J.G. Antiquitatum convivialium. Lugduni Batavorum, 1695.
AH 850.5 Schuch, C.T. Gemüse und Salate der Alten. Rastatt, 1853.
AH 850.7 Eberl, G. Die Fischkonserven der Alten. Stadtamhof, 1892.
AH 850.9 Bommer, Sigwald. Die Gabe der Demeter. München, 1961.
AH 850.12 Brothwell, Don R. Food in antiquity: a survey of the diet of early peoples. London, 1969.
AH 850.12.5 Brothwell, Don R. Food in antiquity. N.Y., 1969.

AH 854 Ancient World in general - Civilization, social life - Special topics - Domestic plants and animals
AH 854.7 Blatchford, C.H. Butterfly in ancient literature and art. Cambridge, 1889.
AH 854.9A Keller, Otto. Der antike Tierwelt. Leipzig, 1909. 2v.
AH 854.9B Keller, Otto. Die antike Tierwelt. Leipzig, 1909. 2v.
AH 854.9.2 Keller, Otto. Gesamtregister von Eugen Staiger. Leipzig, 1920.
AH 854.11 Keller, Otto. Thiere des...Altertums. Innsbruck, 1887.
AH 854.12 Negelini, J. Das Pferd im arischen Altertum. Königsberg, 1903.
AH 854.13 McDermott, William C. The ape in antiquity. Baltimore, 1938.
AH 854.13.5 McDermott, William C. The ape in antiquity. Thesis. Baltimore, 1938.

AH 855 Ancient World in general - Civilization, social life - Special topics - Hunting and fishing
AH 855.5 Miller, Max. Jagdwesen der alten Griechen und Römer. München, 1883.

AH 856 Ancient World in general - Civilization, social life - Special topics - Guest-friendship
AH 856.5 Tomasini, J.P. De tesseris hospitalitatis. Utini, 1647.

AH 857 Ancient World in general - Civilization, social life - Special topics - Parasites
AH 857.5 Giese, A. De parasiti persona capita selecta. Berolini, 1908.

AH 858 Ancient World in general - Civilization, social life - Special topics - Marriage
AH 858.5 Schmidt, R.O. De hymenaeo et talasio. Kiliae, 1886.

AH 859 Ancient World in general - Civilization, social life - Special topics - Condition of women
AH 859.3 Rainneville, Joseph de. La femme dans l'antiquité et d'après la morale. Paris, 1865.
Htn AH 859.6F* Bachofen, J.J. Das Mutterrecht. Stuttgart, 1861.
AH 859.6.2F Bachofen, J.J. Das Mutterrecht. 2. Aufl. Basel, 1897.
AH 859.7 Kornemann, Ernst. Die Stellung der Frau und der vorgriechischen Mittelmeerkultur. Heidelberg, 1927.
AH 859.8 Leipoldt, J. Die Frau in der antiken Welt und im Urchristentum. Gütersloh, 1962.
AH 859.9 Zinserling, Verena. Die Frau in Hellas und Rom. Stuttgart, 1972.
AH 859.9.1 Zinserling, Verena. Women in Greece and Rome. N.Y., 1973.

AH 860 Ancient World in general - Civilization, social life - Special topics - Condition of children
AH 860.5 Galante, L. Guiochi infantili e giocattoli. Firenze, 1904.
AH 860.7 Hoorn, G. van. De vita atque cultu puerorum monumentis antiquis explanato. Inaug. Diss. Amstelodami, 1909.

AH 861 Ancient World in general - Civilization, social life - Special topics - Burial
Htn AH 861.5* Belon, P. De medicato funere. Parisiis, 1553.
AH 861.7F Feydeau, E. Histoire des usages funèbres. Paris, 1856. 2v.
AH 861.9 Quenstedt, J.A. Septultura veterum. Wittenberge, 1660.
AH 861.10 Fuhrmann, M.D. Begräbniss der Altere. Halle, 1800.
AH 861.13 Vogelives, I.G. De epulis veteruno Christianorum sepulcrabibus. Viternbergae, 1710.
AH 861.14 Haffner, G. De antiquis sepulturae ritibus. Ulmae, 1764.

AH 862 Ancient World in general - Civilization, social life - Special topics - Hygiene and medicine
AH 862.5 Gaupp, W. Sanitätswesen in den Heeren der Alten. Blaubeuren, 1875.
AH 862.6 Grawinkel, Karl J. Zähne und Zahnbehandlung der alten Aegypter, Hebräer, Inder, Babyloner, Assyrer, Griechen und Römer. Berlin, 1906.
AH 862.7 Jones, W.H.S. Malaria. Cambridge, 1907.
AH 862.8 Willson, R.N. Medical men in the time of Christ. Philadelphia, 1910.
AH 862.9 Gordon, B.L. Medicine throughout antiquity. Philadelphia, 1949.
AH 862.10 Crecope, John. Medicine, magic and mythology. London, 1954.
AH 862.11 Esser, Alexander Albert Maria. Das Antlitz der Blindheit in der Antike. Leiden, 1961.
AH 862.12 Hagen, Hansludwig. Die physiologisch und psychologisch Bedeutung der Leber in der Antike. Bonn, 1961.
AH 862.13 Thorwald, Jürgen. Macht und Geheimnis der frühen Arzte. München, 1962.
AH 862.13.5 Thorwald, Jürgen. Science and secrets of early medicine. London, 1962.
AH 862.14 Wells, C. Bones, bodies and disease. London, 1964.
AH 862.16 Hollaender, Eugen. Askulap und Venus. Berlin, 1928.
AH 862.20 Ars medica. Abt. 2: Griechische-lateinische Medizin. Berlin. 1,1968+ 3v.
AH 862.22 Ars medica. Abt. 3: Arabische Medizin. Berlin. 1,1971+ 2v.

AH 863 Ancient World in general - Civilization, social life - Special topics - Sexual customs, love
AH 863.10 Tennodrac, M.J. L'antiquité érotique. Paris, 1952.
AH 863.15 Reynes-Lyons, P. Mitos, ritos y costumbres sexuales en las sociedades antiguas. Buenos Aires, 1964.

AH 864 Ancient World in general - Civilization, social life - Special topics - Games, spectacles
AH 864.1 Becq de Fouquières, L. Les jeux des anciens. Paris, 1869.
AH 864.3 Becq de Fouquières, L. Les jeux des anciens. 2. éd. Paris, 1873.
AH 864.5 Soveri, H.F. De ludorum memoria. Helsingforsiae, 1912.

AH 865.1 - .499 Ancient World in general - Civilization, social life - Special topics - Vehicles
AH 865.5F Ginzrot, J.C. Die Wagen und Fahrwerke. München, 1817.

AH 866 Ancient World in general - Civilization, social life - Special topics - Amber
AH 866.5 Bastelaer, D.A. van. L'ambre taillé ou véritable. Bruxelles, 1876.
AH 866.6 Lohmeyer, K. Ist Preuszen das Bernsteinland der alten Gewesen? Königsberg, 1872.
AH 866.7 Rogge, A. Ist Preussen das Bernsteinland der alten Gewesen? Königsberg, 1880.
AH 866.9 Kuiper, G. Harpocrates. Trajecti, 1687.
AH 866.11 Hasse, J.G. Der aufgefundene Eridanus. Riga, 1796.
AH 866.12 Thilo, M. Isaac. Dissertatio physico-historica de succino borussorum. Lipsiae, 1563.
AH 866.13.1 Waldmann, F. Der Bernstein im Altertum. Walluf bei Weisbaden, 1973.
AH 866.15 Spekke, Arnolds. The ancient amber routes and the geographical discovery of the eastern Baltic. Stockholm, 1957.

AH 867 Ancient World in general - Civilization, social life - Special topics - Gestures
AH 867.5 Sittl, C. Die Gebärden der Griechen und Römer. Leipzig, 1890.
AH 867.10 Jucker, Ines. Der Gestus des Aposkopein. Zürich, 1956.

AH 870 - 879 Ancient World in general - Religion (Table A)
Htn AH 876.77* Howe, John. View of antiquity. London, 1677.
AH 877.75 Meiners, Christoph. Versuch über die Religionsgeschichte der ältesten Völker besonders des Egyptier. Göttingen, 1775.
AH 878.22 Onymus, A.J. Dämonen-Lehre der Alten. Würzburg, 1822.
AH 878.37F Lajard, J.B.F. Recherches sur le culte...de Vénus. Paris, 1837-48. 2v.
AH 878.76A Myriantheus, L. Die Acvins. München, 1876.
AH 878.76B Myriantheus, L. Die Acvins. München, 1876.
AH 878.80 Phillips, H. Worship of the sun. The story told by a coin of Constantine. Philadelphia, 1880.
AH 878.82.3 Rawlinson, G. The religions of the ancient world. N.Y., 1883.
AH 878.84 Rawlinson, G. Religions of the ancient world. N.Y., 1884.
AH 878.85 Rawlinson, G. Religions of the ancient world. N.Y., 1885.
AH 879.09 Schmidt, E. Kultübeitragungen. Giessen, 1909.
AH 879.09.5 Lietzmann, H. Der Weltheiland. Bonn, 1909.
AH 879.14 Kennebicq, Léon. L'idee du juste dans l'orient grec avant Socrate. Bruxelles, 1914.
AH 879.19 Warren, E.P. Alemaeon, Hypermestia, Caeneus. Oxford, 1919.
AH 879.58 Martino, Ernesto de. Morti e pianto rituale nel mondo antico dal lamento pagano al pianto di Maria. Torino, 1958.
AH 879.60 Chakraberty, Chandra. Ancient races and myths. Calcutta, 196-.
AH 879.67 Cilento, Vincenzo. Comprensione della religione antica. Napoli, 1967.
AH 879.69 Brandon, Samuel George Frederick. Religion in ancient history: studies in ideas, men and events. N.Y., 1969.

AH 880 - 889 Ancient World in general - Economic conditions - General works (Table A)
AH 883.2 Altheim, Franz. Entwicklungshilfe im Altertum. Reinbeck, 1962.
AH 888.41 Zumpt, K.G. Über den Stand der Bevölkerung. Berlin, 1841.
AH 888.49 Moreau-Christophe, Louis-Mathurin. Driot à l'oisiveté. Paris, 1849.
AH 888.86 Beloch, J. Bevölkerung der griechisch-römischen Welt. Photoreproduction. Leipzig, 1886.
AH 888.95 Wetzel, M. Bedeutung des klassichen Altertums. Paderborn, 1895.
AH 888.95.3 Meyer, E. Die wirtschaftliche Entwickelung. Jena, 1895.
AH 888.98 Billeter, G. Geschichte des Zinfusses. Leipzig, 1898.
AH 889.05 Guiraud, P. Etudes économiques. Paris, 1905.
AH 889.06 Salvioli, G. Capitalisme dans le monde antique. Paris, 1906.
AH 889.06.5 Neurath, Otto. Zur Anschauung der Antike über Handel, Gewerbe und Landwirtschaft. Jena, 1906.
AH 889.07 Khvostov, M. Istoriia vostochoi torgovli. Kazan', 1907.
AH 889.09 Wolf, H. Geschichte des antike Sozialismus. Gütersloh, 1909.
AH 889.09.5 Neurath, A. Antike Wirtschaftsgeschichte. Leipzig, 1909.
AH 889.19 Appleton, C. Le taux du "fenus unciarum". Paris, 1919.
AH 889.22 Segrè, Angelo. Circolazione monetaria e prezzi nel mondo antico ed in particolare in Egitto. Roma, 1922.
AH 889.23 Cavaignac, E. Population et capital dans le monde mediterranéen antique. Strasbourg, 1923.
AH 889.28 Segrè, Angelo. Metrologia e circolazione monetaria degli antichi. Bologna, 1928.
AH 889.29 Brentano, Lujo. Das Wirtschaftsleben der antiken Welt. Jena, 1929.
AH 889.30 Toutain, J. The economic life of the ancient world. London, 1930.
AH 889.38.2 Heichelheim, Fritz. An ancient economic history from the Palaeolithic age to the migrations of the Germanic, Slavic, and Arabic nations. Leiden, 1958-64. 3v.
AH 889.39A Bullock, C.J. Politics, finance, and consequences. Cambridge, 1939.
AH 889.39B Bullock, C.J. Politics, finance, and consequences. Cambridge, 1939.
AH 889.42 Palumbo, P. Fausto. L'organizzazione del lavoro nel mondo antico. Firenze, 1942.
AH 889.48 Jones, Arnold. Ancient economic history. London, 1948.
AH 889.52 Palumbo, P. Fausto. L'unità economica del mondo antico. Roma, 1952.

AH 880 - 889   Ancient World in general - Economic conditions - General works (Table A) - cont.

AH 889.57   Welskopf, Elisabeth C. Die Produktionsverhältnisse im alten Orient und in der griechisch-römischen Antike. Berlin, 1957.

AH 889.64   Lévy, Jean Philippe. L'économie antique. Paris, 1964.
AH 889.73   Finley, Moses I. The ancient economy. London, 1973.
AH 889.73.1   Finley, Moses I. The ancient economy. Berkeley, 1973.

AH 890 - 899   Ancient World in general - Economic conditions - Agriculture (Table A)

AH 897.30   Goetze, F.L. De pistrinis veterum. Cygneae, 1730.
AH 898.54   Wüstemann, E.F. Unterhaltungen aus der alten Welt. Gotha, 1854.
AH 898.56   Forchhammer, P.W. Landwirthschaftliche Mittheilungen. Kiel, 1856.
AH 898.98   Beaurredon, J. Voyage agricole chez les anciens. Paris, 1898.
AH 899.21   Heitland, William E. Agricola; a study of agriculture and rustic life in the Greco-Roman world. Cambridge, 1921.
AH 899.27F   Acerbo, Giacomo. Studi reassuntivi di agricoltura antica. Roma, 1927.
AH 899.44   Jasny, Naum. The wheats of classical antiquity. Baltimore, 1944.

AH 900 - 909   Ancient World in general - Economic conditions - Commerce and industries (Table A)

AH 907.63   Huet, Pierre D. Histoire du commerce et de la navigation des anciens. Lyon, 1763.
AH 907.63.2   Huet, Pierre D. Histoire du commerce et de la navigation des anciens. 2. éd. Paris, 1716.
AH 908.43   Estrup, H.F.J. De makariske ör og Elisa. Kjøbenhavn, 1843.
AH 908.60   Drumann, W. Die Arbeiter und Communisten. Königsberg, 1860.
AH 908.66   Frohberger, H. De opificum apud veteres Graecas condicione dissertatio. Grimae, 1866.
AH 908.75   Blümner, H. Technologie und Terminologie der Gewerbe. v.1-4. Leipzig, 1875. 3v.
AH 908.75.2   Blümner, H. Technologie und Terminologie der Gewerbe. 2. Aufl. Berlin, 1912.
AH 908.75.3   Guillard, E. Les banquiers athéniens-romains. Paris, 1875.
AH 908.77F   Helbig, W. Il commercio dell'ambra. Roma, 1877.
AH 908.77.3   Sadowski, J.N. Die Handelstrassen der Griechen und Römer. Jena, 1877.
AH 908.79   Cruchon, G. Les banques dans l'antiquité. Paris, 1879.
AH 908.89   Helbig, W. Sopra le relazioni commericali. Roma, 1889.
AH 909.10   Preisigke, F. Girowesen im griechischen Ägypten. Strassburg, 1910.
AH 909.11   Barbagallo, C. Contributo alla storia economica dell'antichità. Roma, 1907.
AH 909.25   Segre, Arturo. Il commercio dei popoli antichi nel bacino del Mediterraneo. Torino, 1925.
AH 909.50   Forbes, R. Metallurgy in antiquity. Leiden, 1950.
AH 909.52F   Wilsdorf, H. Berglente und Hüttenminner im Altertum. Berlin, 1952.
AH 909.58   Moritz, L.A. Grain-mills and flour in classical antiquity. Oxford, 1958.
AH 909.71   Raunig, Walter. Bernstein, Weihrauch, Seide. Wien, 1971.
AH 909.72   Burford, Alison. Craftsmen in Greek and Roman society. London, 1972.

AH 910 - 919   Ancient World in general - Economic conditions - Associations (Table A)

AH 919.09   Sarrazin, Albert. Étude sur les fondations dans l'antiquité en particulier à Rome et à Byzance. Thèse. Paris, 1909.
AH 919.14   Laum, Bernhard. Stiftungen in der griechischen und römischen Antike. Leipzig, 1914. 2v.
AH 919.14.1   Laum, Bernhard. Stiftungen in der griechischen und römischen Antike. v.1-2. Aalen, 1964.
AH 919.14.5   Laum, Bernhard. Uber griechische und römische Stiftungen. Leipzig, 1913.

AH 920 - 929   Ancient World in general - Economic conditions - Weights and measures (Table A)

Htn   AH 925.32*   Senali, R. De liquidorum leguminumque. Parisiis, 1532.
Htn   AH 925.33*   Georgii agricolae medici libri. Parisiis, 1533. 3 pam.
Htn   AH 925.55*   Neander, M. Eynopsis. Basileae, 1555.
AH 926.17   Angelocrator, D. Doctrina de ponderibus. Marpurgi Cattorum, 1617.
Htn   AH 927.08.2*   Eisenschmid, J.C. De ponderibus et mensuris veterum. 2. ed. Argentorati, 1732.
AH 928.13   Ukert, F.A. Entfernungen bei den Alten. Weimar, 1813.
AH 928.21   Wurm, J.F. De ponderum, numerum. Stutgardaie, 1821.
AH 928.36A   Hussey, R. Essay on ancient weights and money. Oxford, 1836.
AH 928.36B   Hussey, R. Essay on ancient weights and money. Oxford, 1836.
AH 928.38   Böckh, August. Metrologische Untersuchungen über Gewichte, Münzfüsse und Masse. Berlin, 1838.
AH 928.59   Müller, H. Uber die heilige Masse des Alterthums. Freiburg, 1859.
AH 928.62   Hultsch, F. Metrologie. Berlin, 1862.
AH 928.62.3   Hultsch, F. Metrologie. Berlin, 1882.
AH 929.23   Viedebandtt, Oskar. Antike Gewichtsnormen und Münzfusse. Berlin, 1923.

AH 930   Ancient World in general - Atlases

AH 930.3F   Jones and Co. Jones' classical atlas. London, 1830.
AH 930.5   Johnston, W. and A.K., publishers. The world; a classical atlas. Edinburgh, 18- .
NEDL   AH 930.7.3   Findlay, Alexander G. A classical atlas, to illustrate ancient geography. London, 1854.
NEDL   AH 930.7.5   Findlay, Alexander G. A classical atlas, to illustrate ancient geography. N.Y., 185-?
NEDL   AH 930.7.6   Findlay, Alexander G. A classical atlas, to illustrate ancient geography. N.Y., 1849.
AH 930.10   Butler, George. The public school's atlas of ancient geography. London, 1889.
AH 930.15   Ginn and Co., publishers. Classical atlas. Boston, 1894.
AH 930.20   Lord, John K. Atlas of the geography and history of the ancient world. Boston, 1902.
AH 930.25   Lelewel, J. Die Entdeckungen der Carthager und Griechen. Berlin, 1821.
AH 930.30   Ramsauer, F. Die antike Vulkankunde. Burghausen, 1906.
AH 930.36   Atlas of ancient and classical geography. London, 1912.

AH 930   Ancient World in general - Atlases - cont.

AH 930.37   Atlas of ancient and classic geography. London, 1952.
AH 930.40F   Heyden, A.A. Atlas van de antieke wereld. Amsterdam, 1958.
AH 930.42   Kampen, Albert van. Die Welt der Antike. 12. Aufl. Gotha, 1958.
AH 930.43   Shepherd, William Robert. Atlas of ancient history. N.Y., 1913.
AH 930.44   Iliff, John G. Maps illustrating ancient history. Topeka, 1915.

AH 934 - 939   Ancient World in general - Geography and description - Monographs (By date)

AH 936.83   Birkerod, J. Timh Timaiov. Altodorfi Noricorum, 1683.
AH 937.68   Anville, Jean B.B. d'. Geographie ancienne abrégée. Paris, 1768. 3v.
AH 937.91   Anville, Jean B.B. d'. Compendium of ancient geography. London, 1791. 2v.
AH 937.91.3   Anville, Jean B.B. d'. Compendium of ancient geography. N.Y., 1814. 2v.
AH 938.16   Ukert, F.A. Geographie der Griechen und Römer. v.1-3. Weimar, 1816-46. 5v.
AH 938.16.5   Schulthess, J. Das Paradies. Zürich, 1816.
AH 938.29   Mannert, K. Geographie. v.1-10. Leipzig, 1799-1829. 14v.
AH 938.29.2   Longe, George. An introduction to the study of Greek and Roman geography. Charlottesville, 1829.
AH 938.31   Butler, Samuel. Geographia classica. Philadelphia, 1831.
AH 938.36   Lelewel, J. Kleinere Schriften. Leipzig, 1836.
AH 938.38   Georgii, L. Alte Geographie. Stuttgart, 1838. 2v.
AH 938.39   Reinganum, H. Geschichte der Erd- und Landerabbildungen. Jena, 1839.
AH 938.47   Curtius, E. Beiträge zur Terminologie...der alten Geographie. Berlin, 1888.
AH 938.49F   Jenks, William. The explanatory Bible atlas and Scripture gazetteer. Boston, 1849.
AH 938.51   Niebuhr, B.G. Vorträge über alte Länder und Volkerkunde. Berlin, 1851.
NEDL   AH 938.53   Niebuhr, B.G. Lectures on ancient ethnography and geography. London, 1853. 2v.
AH 938.54   Niebuhr, B.G. Lectures on ancient ethnography and geography. Boston, 1854. 2v.
NEDL   AH 938.54.2   Smith, William. Dictionary of Greek and Roman geography. London, 1854.
AH 938.54.3   Smith, William. Dictionary of Greek and Roman geography. London, 1854.
NEDL   AH 938.54.4   Smith, William. Dictionary of Greek and Roman geography. London, 1856-57. 2v.
AH 938.54.5   Smith, William. Dictionary of Greek and Roman geography. London, 1870. 2v.
AH 938.54.20   Leake, W.M. On some disputed questions of ancient geography. London, 1857.
AH 938.56   Hughes, William. An atlas of classical geography. Philadelphia, 1856.
NEDL   AH 938.56.3   Hughes, William. An atlas of classical geography. Philadelphia, 1859.
NEDL   AH 938.56.4   Hughes, William. An atlas of classical geography. Philadelphia, 1861.
AH 938.56.5   Hughes, William. An atlas of classical geography. Philadelphia, 1865.
NEDL   AH 938.56.10   Hughes, William. An atlas of classical geography. N.Y., 1867.
NEDL   AH 938.56.12   Hughes, William. An atlas of classical geography. N.Y., 1870.
NEDL   AH 938.56.15   Hughes, William. An atlas of classical geography. N.Y., 1871.
NEDL   AH 938.56.20   Hughes, William. An atlas of classical geography. N.Y., 1856.
AH 938.57   Schmitz, L. Manual of ancient geography. Philadelphia, 1857.
AH 938.60.3   Schmidt, H.I. Course on ancient geography. N.Y., 1860.
AH 938.77A   Tozer, Henry F. Classical geography. N.Y., 1877.
AH 938.77B   Tozer, Henry F. Classical geography. N.Y., 1877.
AH 938.77.5   Tozer, Henry F. Classical geography. N.Y., 1877.
AH 938.79   Bunbury, E.H. A history of ancient geography. London, 1879. 2v.
AH 938.79.10   Bunbury, E.H. A history of ancient geography among the Greeks and Romans. 2. ed. N.Y., 1959. 2v.
AH 938.81   Kiepert, H. Manual of ancient geography. London, 1881.
AH 938.84   Keppel, T. Ansichten der alten Griechen und Römer. Schwienfurt, 1884.
AH 938.87   Schmidt, C.P. Zur Geschichte der geographischen Litteratur bei Griechen und Römer. Breslau, 1887.
AH 938.87.2   Friedrich, R. Begriffsbestimmung des Orbis terarum. Leipzig, 1887.
AH 938.88   Günther, S. Geschichte der antike Naturwissenschaft. Nördlingen, 1888.
AH 938.88.5   Tozer, Henry F. Nociones de geografía antigua. N.Y., 1888.
AH 938.89.5   Hughes, Lugi. Manuali di geografia antica ad uso delle scuole secondarie. v.1-3. Torino, 1889-90.
AH 938.92   Villar, J. Geografia antigua comparada. Santiago, 1892.
AH 938.93   Columba, G.M. Gli studi geografici nel I secolo dell'impero romano. Torino, 1893.
AH 938.97   Tozer, Henry F. History of ancient geography. Cambridge, 1897.
AH 938.97.2   Tozer, Henry F. A history of ancient geography. N.Y., 1964.
AH 938.98   Beiträge zur alten Geschichte und Geographie. Berlin, 1898.
AH 938.99   Heeren, A. De chorographia a Valerio Flacco. Inaug. Diss. Gottingae, 1899.
AH 939.02   Müller, C. Studien zur Geschichte der Erdkunde. Breslau, 1902.
AH 939.02.2   Gautier, E.F. Indici oceani pars. Lutetiia, 1902.
AH 939.02.5   Jobst, D. Scylla und Charybdis, eine geographische Studien. Würzburg, 1902.
AH 939.12   Filek, E. von Wittinghausen. Die geographischen Vorstellungen in Altertum. Wien, 1912.
AH 939.14   Besnier, M. Lexique de géographie ancienne. Paris, 1914.
AH 939.28.5   Browne, Lewis. The graphic Bible, from Genesis to Revelation in animated maps and charts. N.Y., 1941.
AH 939.28.10   Browne, Lewis. The graphic Bible. N.Y., 1942.
AH 939.29   Cary, Max. The ancient explorers. London, 1929.
AH 939.31   Scheliha, Renata von. Die Wassergrenze im Altertum. Breslau, 1931.
AH 939.31.5   Semple, Ellen C. The geography of the Mediterranean region. N.Y., 1937.

AH 934 - 939 Ancient World in general - Geography and description -
Monographs (By date) - cont.

AH 939.49 — Cary, Max. The geographic background of Greek and Roman history. Oxford, 1949.

AH 939.66 — Carpenter, Rhys. Beyond the Pillars of Heracles. N.Y., 1966.

AH 939.68 — Fischer, Rudolf. Das ausseritalische geographische Bild in Vergils Georgica, in den Oden des Horan und in den Elegien des Properz. Zürich, 1968.

AH 950 - 959 Ancient World in general - Travels - General works (Table A)

AH 957.31 — Otto, Everard. De tutela viarum publicarum liber singularis. Rhenum, 1731.

AH 958.72 — Falconer, W. Dissertation on St. Paul's voyage. Photoreproduction. London, 1872.

AH 958.90 — Bencker, Max. Der Anteil der Periegese an den Kuntschrift der Alten. München, 1890.

AH 959.01 — Skeel, C.A.J. Travel in the first century after Christ. Cambridge, 1901.

AH 959.17 — Schoff, Wilfred H. Navigation to the Far East under the Roman Empire. Boston, 1917.

AH 959.20 — Mooney, William West. Travel among the ancient Romans. Boston, 1920.

AH 959.61 — Seel, Otto. Antike Entdeckerfahrten. Zürich, 1961.

AH 960 - 969 Ancient World in general - Travels - Imaginary travels
(Table A)

NEDL AH 968.55 — Wheeler, J. Life and travels of Herodotus. London, 1855. 2v.

AH 968.55.5 — Wheeler, J. Life and travels of Herodotus. N.Y., 1856. 2v.

AH 969.55 — Sestios, Maarkos. Journal. Paris, 1955.

AH 1004 - 1009 Ancient Orient in general - General bibliographies -
Monographs (By date)

AH 1009.66 — Mayrhofer, Manfred. Die Indo-Arier im alten Vorderasien. Mit einer analytischen Bibliographie. Wiesbaden, 1966.

AH 1015 Ancient Orient in general - General pamphlet volumes

AH 1015.01 — Pamphlet box. Ancient history. Orient. Tracts.

AH 1024 - 1029 Ancient Orient in general - Collected sources, etc. (By
date)

AH 1028.32.3 — Cory, I.P. Ancient fragments. London, 1832.

AH 1028.35A — The Phenix. N.Y., 1835.

AH 1028.35B — The Phenix. N.Y., 1835.

AH 1029.50F — Pritchard, James B. Ancient Near Eastern texts relating to the Old Testament. Princeton, 1950.

AH 1029.50.2 — Pritchard, James B. Ancient Near Eastern texts relating to the Old Testament. 2. ed. Princeton, 1955.

AH 1029.58 — Pritchard, James B. The ancient Near East; an anthology of texts and pictures. Princeton, 1958.

AH 1029.69 — Pritchard, James B. The ancient Near East; supplementary texts and pictures. Princeton, 1969.

AH 1040 - 1049 Ancient Orient in general - Government and administration -
Forms of government (Table A)

AH 1049.48A — Gadd, Cyril John. Ideas of divine rule in the ancient East. London, 1948.

AH 1049.48B — Gadd, Cyril John. Ideas of divine rule in the ancient East. London, 1948.

AH 1130 - 1139 Ancient Orient in general - Law - General works (Table A)

AH 1130.36.5 — Studia et documenta ad iura orientia antiqui pertinentia. Leiden. 1-9 7v.

AH 1180 - 1189 Ancient Orient in general - Law - Slavery and emancipation
(Table A)

AH 1189.36 — Lauterbach, W. Der Arbeiter in Recht und Rechtspraxis des Alten Testaments und des alten Orients. Inaug. Diss. Heidelberg, 1936.

AH 1189.49A — Mendelsohn, I. Slavery in the ancient Near East. N.Y., 1949.

AH 1189.49B — Mendelsohn, I. Slavery in the ancient Near East. N.Y., 1949.

AH 1230 - 1239 Ancient Orient in general - Military affairs (Table A)

AH 1233.65 — Amadasi, Maria Giulia. L'iconografia del carro da guerra in Siria e Palestina. Roma, 1965.

AH 1239.63 — Yadin, Y. The art of warfare in Biblical lands. N.Y., 1963. 2v.

AH 1274 - 1279 Ancient Orient in general - General history (By date)

AH 1278.62 — Rawlinson, G. Five great monarchies of the ancient Eastern World. London, 1862-1867. 4v.

NEDL AH 1278.62.2A — Rawlinson, G. Five great monarchies of the ancient Eastern World. 2. ed. London, 1871. 3v.

AH 1278.62.2B — Rawlinson, G. Five great monarchies of the ancient Eastern World. 2. ed. London, 1871. 3v.

AH 1278.62.4 — Rawlinson, G. Five great monarchies of the ancient Eastern World. N.Y., 1880. 3v.

AH 1278.62.6 — Rawlinson, G. Five great monarchies of the ancient Eastern World. N.Y., 190-? 3v.

NEDL AH 1278.62.6 — Rawlinson, G. Five great monarchies of the ancient Eastern World. N.Y., 1881. 3v.

AH 1278.68.7 — Lenormant, F. Histoire ancienne de l'Orient. Paris, 1881-86. 6v.

AH 1278.71.3 — Smith, Philip. Ancient history of the East. N.Y., 1871.

AH 1278.71.4 — Smith, Philip. Smaller history of the East. N.Y., 1872.

AH 1278.71.7 — Smith, Philip. The student's ancient history. The ancient history of the East. N.Y., 1894.

AH 1278.76 — Maspero, Gaston. Histoire ancienne des peuples de l'Orient. Paris, 1876.

AH 1278.76.4 — Maspero, Gaston. Histoire ancienne des peuples de l'Orient. Paris, 1886.

AH 1278.76.7 — Maspero, Gaston. Historie ancienne des peuples de l'Orient. 7e éd. Paris, 1905.

NEDL AH 1278.76.8 — Maspero, Gaston. Histoire ancienne des peuples de l'Orient. 3. éd. Paris, 1878.

AH 1278.76.15 — Maspero, Gaston. Struggle of the nations, Egypt, Syria and Assyria. N.Y., 1897.

NEDL AH 1278.78 — Van Den Berg, E. Petite histoire ancienne des peuples de l'Orient. Paris, 1878.

AH 1278.78.2 — Van Den Berg, E. Petite histoire ancienne des peuples de l'Orient. 2. éd. Paris, 1881.

AH 1278.83 — Fontane, M. Histoire universelle les Asiatiques. Paris, 1883.

AH 1278.89A — Sayce, A.H. Ancient empires of the East. London, 1884.

AH 1274 - 1279 Ancient Orient in general - General history (By date) - cont.

AH 1278.89B — Sayce, A.H. Ancient empires of the East. London, 1884.

NEDL AH 1278.89.5 — Sayce, A.H. Ancient empires of the East. N.Y., 1904.

NEDL AH 1278.89.7 — Sayce, A.H. Ancient empires of the East. N.Y., 1907.

AH 1278.95 — Maspero, Gaston. Histoire ancienne des peuples de l'Orient. Paris, 1895. 3v.

AH 1278.99 — Krall, J. Grundriss der altorientalischen Geschichte. Wien, 1899.

AH 1279.00 — Maspero, Gaston. The passing of the empires, 850 B.C.-330 B.C. London, 1900.

AH 1279.06 — Sayce, A.H. Ancient empires of the East. Philadelphia, 1906.

AH 1279.07 — King, Leonard. History of Egypt, Chaldea, Syria, Babylonia and Assyria in the light of recent discovery. London, 1907.

AH 1279.19 — Hanslik, E. Einleitung und Geschichte des alten Orients. Gotha, 1919.

AH 1279.31 — Stewart-Vargas, Guillermo. Historia del Oriente antiguo y Medo Persa. Montevideo, 1931.

AH 1279.36 — Capart, Jean. Histoire de l'Orient ancien. Paris, 1936.

AH 1279.37 — Snegirev, I.L. Drevnii Vostok; atlas. Leningrad, 1937.

AH 1279.38 — Les peuples de l'Orient méditerranéen. Paris, 1938. 2v.

AH 1279.39 — Ebeling, Erich. Geschichte des Orients vom Tode Alexanders des Grossen bis zum Einbruch des Islams. Berlin, 1939.

AH 1279.41 — Struve, Vasilii V. Istoriia drevnego Vostoka. Leningrad, 1941.

AH 1279.50 — Cornelius, F. Geschichte des alten Orients. Stuttgart, 1950.

AH 1279.53 — Altheim, Franz. Alexander und Asien. Tübingen, 1953.

AH 1279.53.5 — Gordon, Cyrus H. Introduction to Old Testament times. Ventnor, N.J., 1953.

AH 1279.57.3 — Cerfaux, Lucien. L'antiquité: le Proche-Orient. 3. éd. Tournai, 1960.

AH 1279.62 — Gray, John. Archaeology and the Old Testament world. London, 1962.

AH 1279.63 — Tovar, Antonio. Historia del antiguo oriente. Barcelona, 1963.

AH 1279.69 — Garelli, Paul. Le Proche-Orient asiatique. Paris, 1969.

AH 1279.69.5 — Nützel, Werner. Von der Sintflut bis Byzanz. Darmstadt, 1969.

AH 1279.70 — Altheim, Franz. Geschichte Mittelasiens im Altertum. Berlin, 1970.

AH 1279.70.5 — Arnaud, Daniel. Le Proche-Orient ancien, de l'invention de l'écriture à l'hellénisation. Paris, 1970.

AH 1279.71 — Hallo, William W. The ancient Near East. N.Y., 1971.

AH 1279.72 — Die altorientalischen Reiche. Frankfurt, 1972-73. 3v.

AH 1294 - 1299 Ancient Orient in general - General special - Miscellany
(By date)

AH 1298.24 — Drummond, W. Origines. London, 1824. 4v.

AH 1298.61 — Quatremère, Etienne M. Mélanges d'histoire et de philologie orientale. Paris, 1861.

AH 1298.86 — Wright, William B. Ancient cities from dawn to the daylight. Boston, 1886.

AH 1298.89 — Winckler, H. Untersuchungen zur altorientalischen Geschichte. Leipzig, 1889.

AH 1298.93 — Winckler, H. Altorientalische Forschungen. v.1-2,3,4,5,6. Leipzig, 1893. 5v.

AH 1298.93.2 — Winckler, H. Altorientalische Forschungen. Zweite Reihe. Leipzig, 1898. 3v.

AH 1298.93.3 — Winckler, H. Altorientalische Forschungen. Dritte Reihe. Leipzig, 1902. 3v.

AH 1298.93.7 — Winckler, H. Altorientalische Forschungen. Leipzig, 1897-1901. 2v.

AH 1298.94 — Niebuhr, Carl. Studien und Bemerkungen zur Geschichte des alten Orients. Leipzig, 1894.

AH 1298.95 — Vinogradov, Aleksy. Drevne patriarhalnyja. St. Petersburg, 1895.

AH 1299.05 — Winckler, H. Ex Oriente Lux. Leipzig. 1-6,1905-1931 4v.

AH 1299.63 — Akademiia nauk SSSR. Institut Archeologii. Antichnyi gorod. Moskva, 1963.

AH 1299.67 — Speiser, Ephraim A. Oriental and Biblical studies. Philadelphia, 1967.

AH 1299.68 — Struve, Vasilii V. Etudy po istorii Severnogo Prichernomor'ia, Kavkazo i Srednei Azii. Leningrad, 1968.

AH 1299.71 — Hommages à Andre Dupont-Sommer. Paris, 1971.

AH 1300 - 1309 Ancient Orient in general - General special - Philosophy of
history (Table A)

AH 1309.58 — Avdièv, Vsevolod I. Sovietskaia nauka s drevnene Vostoke za 40 let. Moskva, 1958.

AH 1309.58.3 — Avdièv, Vsevolod I. L'étude de l'ancien Orient en U.R.S.S. 1917-1957. Moscou, 1958.

AH 1309.61 — Postovskaia, N.M. Izuchenie drevnei istorii Blizhnego Vostoka. Moskva, 1961.

AH 1320 - 1329 Ancient Orient in general - General special - Races (Table
A)

AH 1329.64 — Imparati, Fiorella. I Hurriti. Firenze, 1964.

AH 1329.65 — Phillips, Eustace Dockray. The royal hordes. London, 1965.

AH 1400 - 1409 Ancient Orient in general - History by periods - Before 500
B.C. (Table A)

VAH 1402.5 — Zabłocka, Julia. Wybór źródet do historii starozytnego wschodu do poł. Wyd. 2. Poznań, 1966.

AH 1407.50 — Scharff, A. Ägypten und Vorderasien im Altertum. München, 1950.

AH 1408.56 — Krüger, J. Geschichte der Assyrier und Iranier. Frankfurt, 1856.

NEDL AH 1408.68 — Lenormant, F. Manuel d'histoire ancienne de l'Orient. Paris, 1868. 2v.

AH 1408.68.5 — Lenormant, F. Manual of the ancient history of the East. Philadelphia, 1869.

AH 1408.69 — Lenormant, F. Manual of the ancient history of the East. 3. ed. Paris, 1869. 3v.

AH 1408.69.3 — Lenormant, F. Manual of the ancient history of the East. London, 1869.

AH 1408.80 — Lenormant, F. Les origines de l'histoire. v.1; v.2, pt.1-2. Paris, 1880. 3v.

AH 1408.88 — Duruy, J.V. Histoire ancienne des peuples de l'Orient. Paris, 1888.

AH 1408.95 — Hommel, Fritz. Geschichte des alten Morgenlandes. Stuttgart, 1895.

AH 1408.95.2 — Hommel, Fritz. Geschichte des alten Morgenlandes. 2. Aufl. Leipzig, 1898.

Classified Listing

AH 1400 - 1409   Ancient Orient in general - History by periods - Before 500 B.C. (Table A) - cont.

AH 1409.06   Olmstead, Albert T. Western Asia in the days of Sargon of Assyria. Thesis. Lancaster, Pa., 1908.

AH 1409.06.1   Olmstead, Albert T. Western Asia in the days of Sargon of Assyria, 722-705 B.C. N.Y., 1908.

AH 1409.13   Hall, Harry R. The ancient history of the Near East from the earliest times to the Battle of Salamis. London, 1913.

AH 1409.13.1   Hall, Harry R. The ancient history of the Near East from the earliest times to the Battle of Salamis. N.Y., 1913.

AH 1409.13.5   Hall, Harry R. The ancient history of the Near East from the earliest times to the Battle of Salamis. 5. ed. London, 1920.

AH 1409.14   Hogarth, D.G. The ancient East. London, 1914.

AH 1409.14.2   Hogarth, D.G. The ancient East. 2. ed. London, 1950.

AH 1409.20   Grant, Elihu. The Orient in Bible times. Philadelphia, 1920.

AH 1409.27   Turaev, V.A. Russkaia nauka odrevnem Vostoke do 1917 g. Leningrad, 1927.

AH 1409.27.5   Bilabel, Friedrich. Geschichte Vorderasiens und Ägyptens vom 16. Jahrhundert vor Christ bis auf die Neuzeit. Heidelberg, 1927.

AH 1409.35   Turaev, V.A. Istoriia drevnago Vostoka. Leningrad, 1935. 2v.

AH 1409.36   Götze, Albrecht. Hethiter, Churriter und Assyrer. Oslo, 1936.

AH 1409.63.10   Liverani, M. Introduzione alla storia dell'Asia anteriore antica. Roma, 1963.

AH 1409.65   Schwantes, Siegfried J. A short history of the ancient Near East. Grand Rapids, 1965.

AH 1450 - 1459   Ancient Orient in general - History by periods - 500 - 1 B.C. (Table A)

AH 1457.5   Klaproth, J. Tableau historique de l'Asie. Paris, 1826.

AH 1457.5F   Klaproth, J. Tableau historique de l'Asie. Atlas. Paris, 1826.

AH 1459.47   Altheim, Franz. Weltgeschichte Asiens ein griechischen Zeitalter. Halle, 1947-48. 2v.

AH 1800 - 1809   Ancient Orient in general - Chronology (Table A)

AH 1801.1   Pamphlet box. The Orient. Chronology.

AH 1806.83   Seldeni Joannis DeArmo civili et calendario. Lugdunum Batavorum, 1683.

AH 1807.38   Vignolles, A. Chronologie de l'histoire sainte. Berlin, 1738. 2v.

AH 1808.30   Yeates, T. Remarks of Bible chronology. London, 1830.

AH 1808.82   Floigl, Victor. Geschichte des semitischen Altertums in Tabellen. Leipzig, 1882.

AH 1808.96   Krug, Carl. Die Chronologie der Geschichte Israels, Aegyptens. Leipzig, 1896.

AH 1810 - 1819   Ancient Orient in general - Civilization, Social life - General works (Table A)

AH 1812.5   Symposium on Urbanization and Cultural Development in the Ancient Near East, University of Chicago, 1958. City invincible. Chicago, 1960.

AH 1818.72   Twesten, C. Religiösen, politischen und socialen Ideen. v.1-2. Berlin, 1872.

AH 1818.82   Geiger, W. Ostiranische Kultur im Altertum. Erlangen, 1882.

AH 1818.82.5   Geiger, W. Civilization of the eastern Iranians. London, 1885.

AH 1819.23A   Baikie, James. The life of the ancient East. N.Y., 1923.

AH 1819.23B   Baikie, James. The life of the ancient East. N.Y., 1923.

AH 1819.26   Daunt, Hew D. The centre of ancient civilization. London, 1926.

AH 1819.28.5   Childe, Vere G. The most ancient East. London, 1929.

AH 1819.34A   Childe, Vere G. New light on the most ancient East. London, 1934.

AH 1819.34B   Childe, Vere G. New light on the most ancient East. London, 1934.

AH 1819.34.5   Childe, Vere G. New light on the most ancient East. 4. ed. London, 1952.

AH 1819.34.10   Childe, Vere G. New light on the most ancient East. N.Y., 1934.

AH 1819.36   Ungnad, Arthur. Subartu; Beiträge zur Kulturgeschichte und Völkerkunde Vorderasiens. Berlin, 1936.

AH 1819.45.4   Contenau, Georges. Les civilisations anciennes du Proche-Orient. 5. éd. Paris, 1963.

AH 1819.51   Frankfort, Henri. The birth of civilization in the Near East. Bloomington, 1951.

AH 1819.51.1   Frankfort, Henri. The birth of civilization in the Near East. London, 1951.

AH 1819.51.2   Frankfort, Henri. The birth of civilization in the Near East. Bloomington, 1954.

AH 1819.52   Braidwood, Robert J. The Near East and the foundations for civilization. Eugene, 1952.

AH 1819.54   Pritchard, James B. The ancient Near East in pictures. Princeton, N.J., 1954.

AH 1819.56   Moscati, Sabatino. Il profilo dell'Oriente mediterraneo. Torino, 1956.

AH 1819.56.3   Moscati, Sabatino. The face of the ancient Orient. Chicago, 1960.

AH 1819.61A   Muller, H.J. Freedom in the ancient world. 1. ed. N.Y., 1961.

AH 1819.61B   Muller, H.J. Freedom in the ancient world. 1. ed. N.Y., 1961.

AH 1819.61.5   Schmökel, Hartmut. Kulturgeschichte des alten Orient. Stuttgart, 1961.

AH 1819.70.1   Peters, Francis E. The harvest of Hellenism. N.Y., 1971.

AH 1819.71   Beitraege zur sozialen Struktur des alten Vorderasien. Berlin, 1971.

AH 1819.72   Oberhuber, Karl. Die Kultur des alten Orients. Frankfurt, 1974.

AH 1819.73   Hawkes, Jacquetta Hopkins. The first great civilizations. 1. ed. N.Y., 1973.

AH 1842   Ancient Orient in general - Civilization, Social life - Special topics - Books and education

AH 1842.5   Kuehnert, F. Allgemeinbildung und Fachbildung in der Antike. Berlin, 1961.

AH 1866   Ancient Orient in general - Civilization, Social life - Special topics - Amber

AH 1866.5   Oppert, J. L'ambre jaune chez les Assyriens. Paris, 1880.

AH 1870 - 1879   Ancient Orient in general - Religion (Table A)

AH 1872.22   Munter, Friederich. Sendschreiben an Friedrich Creuzer, über einige sardische Idole. Kopenhagen, 1822.

AH 1878.89   Ablaing van Giessenburg, R.C. Évolution des idées religieuses dans la Mésopotamie et dans l'Egypte. Amsterdam, 1889.

AH 1879.30   Semper, Max. Rassen und Religionen im alten Vorderasien. Heidelberg, 1930.

AH 1879.58   James, E.O. Myth and ritual in the ancient Near East. London, 1958.

AH 1879.63   Hooke, S.H. Middle Eastern mythology. Harmondsworth, 1963.

AH 1879.65   Vanal, Antoine. L'iconographie du dieu de l'orage. Paris, 1965.

AH 1900 - 1909   Ancient Orient in general - Economic conditions - Commerce and industries (Table A)

AH 1909.24   Köster, A. Schiffahrt und Handelsverkehr des östlichen Mittelmeeres. Leipzig, 1924.

AH 1920 - 1929   Ancient Orient in general - Economic conditions - Weights and measures (Table A)

AH 1928.75   Skinner, J.R. Key to the Hebrew-Egyptian mystery in the source of measures. Cincinnati, 1875.

AH 1934 - 1939   Ancient Orient in general - Geography and description - Monographs (By date)

AH 1939.30   Berthelot, A. L'Asie ancienne, centrale et sud-orientale d'après Ptolémée. Paris, 1930.

AH 1950 - 1959   Ancient Orient in general - Travels - General works (Table A)

AH 1958.38   Ainsworth, W. Researches in Assyria...Euphrates expedition. London, 1838.

AH 2003   Countries of ancient Asia - Arabia - Government and administration

AH 2003.5   Ryckmans, Jacques. L'institution monarchique en Arabie méridionale avant l'Islam. Louvain, 1951.

AH 2007   Countries of ancient Asia - Arabia - General history

AH 2007.2   Rohden, P. De Palaestina e Arabia. Berolini, 1885.

AH 2007.3   Glaser, E. Skizze der Geschichte und Geographie Arabiens. Berlin, 1890.

AH 2007.4   Price, David. Essay towards the history of Arabia. London, 1824.

AH 2007.5   Pocock, E. Historia imperii vetustissimi. v.1-2. Harderovici Gebrorum, 1786.

AH 2007.6   Altheim, Franz. Die Araber in der alten Welt. v.2-5, pt.1-2. Berlin, 1964. 5v.

AH 2007.7   Çagatay, Neş'et. Islâmdan önce Arap tarihi. Ankara, 1957.

AH 2007.7.2   Çagatay, Neş'et. Islâmdan önce Arap tarihi. 2. ed. Ankara, 1963.

AH 2008   Countries of ancient Asia - Arabia - General special

AH 2008.5   Fresnel, F. Lettres sur l'histoire des Arabes. Paris, 1836.

AH 2008.7   Margoliouth, D.S. The relations between Arabs and Israelites prior to the rise of Islam. London, 1924.

AH 2008.9   Kammerer, Albert. Pétra et la Nabatène. Plates, maps and atlas. Paris, 1929-30. 2v.

AH 2008.12   Glueck, Nelson. Deities and dolphins; the story of the Nabataeans. N.Y., 1965.

AH 2008.14   Montgomery, James Alan. Arabia and the Bible. N.Y., 1969.

AH 2009   Countries of ancient Asia - Arabia - History by periods - Before 500 B.C.

AH 2009.5   Abu Ubaid al-Bakri. Die Wohnsetze und Wanderungen der arabischen Stämme. Göttingen, 1869.

AH 2009.6   Kremer, A. von. Über die südarabische Sage. Leipzig, 1866.

AH 2009.6.5   Kremer, A. von. Über die südarabische Sage. Leipzig, 1866.

AH 2011   Countries of ancient Asia - Arabia - History by periods - 1 A.D. - ca. 650

AH 2011.5   Lammens, H. Le berceau de l'Islam. Romae, 1914.

AH 2011.5.5   Lammens, H. L'Arabie occidentale avant l'hégire. Beyrouth, 1928.

AH 2011.6   Reiske, J.J. Primae lineae historiae regnorum arabicorum. Gottingae, 1847.

AH 2011.8   Jochum, Johannes. Geschichte de Familie El-'Abbâs bin 'Abd El-Muttalib. Inaug. Diss. Berlin, 1933.

AH 2011.9   Bräunlich, Erich. Bistäm ibn Qais. Leipzig, 1923.

AH 2011.10   Jamme, Albert. La dynastie de Sarahbi il Yakuf et la documentation épigraphique sud-arabe. Istanbul, 1961.

AH 2012   Countries of ancient Asia - Arabia - Chronology

AH 2012.2   Ryckmans, Jacques. La chronologie des rois de Saba et dü-Raydän. Istanbul, 1964.

AH 2012.4   Lundin, Avraam G. Gosudarstvo mukarribov Saba'. Moskva, 1971.

AH 2013   Countries of ancient Asia - Arabia - Civilization

AH 2013.5   Wilken, G.A. Het matriarchaat bij de Oude Arabieren. Amsterdam, 1884.

AH 2013.5.7   Wilken, G.A. Das Matriarchat...bei den Alten Arabern. Leipzig, 1884.

AH 2013.7   Farès, Edouard. L'honneur chez les Arabes avant l'Islam. Thèse. Paris, 1932.

AH 2013.7.5   Farès, Edouard. L'honneur chez les Arabes avant l'Islam. Paris, 1932.

AH 2013.7.8   Guidi, Ignazio. L'Arabie antéislamique. Paris, 1921.

AH 2013.10   Proksch, Otto. Über die Blutrache bei den vorislamischen Arabern und Mohammeds Stellung zu Christ. Leipzig, 1899.

AH 2014   Countries of ancient Asia - Arabia - Religion

AH 2014.5   Blochet, E. Le culte d'Aphrodite-Anahita. Chalon-sur-Saône, 1902.

AH 2014.6   Hommel, Fritz. Der Gestirndienst der alten Araber. München, 1901.

AH 2014.7.2   Wellhausen, Julius. Reste arabischen Heidentums. Berlin, 1897.

AH 2014.7.5   Wellhausen, Julius. Reste arabischen Heidentums. Berlin, 1927.

AH 2014   Countries of ancient Asia - Arabia - Religion - cont.
    AH 2014.8   Ryckmans, G. Les religiones arabes préislamiques. 2. éd. Louvain, 1951.

AH 2016   Countries of ancient Asia - Arabia - Geography
    AH 2016.5   Forster, Charles. The historical geography of Arabia. London, 1844. 2v.

AH 2017   Countries of ancient Asia - Arabia - Travels
    AH 2017.5   Beke, Charles. The late Dr. Charles Beke's discoveries of Sinai in Arabia. London, 1878.

AH 2057   Countries of ancient Asia - Armenia - General history
    AH 2057.5   Burney, Charles Allen. The peoples of the hills: ancient Ararat and Caucasus. London, 1971.

AH 2058   Countries of ancient Asia - Armenia - General special
Htn   AH 2058.5*   Görres, J. Die Japhetiden. München, 1844.

AH 2060   Countries of ancient Asia - Armenia - History by periods - 500 - 1 B.C.
    AH 2060.5   Armen, H.K. Tigranes the Great. Detroit, 1940.
    AH 2060.10   Manandian, I. Tigran Vtoroi i Rim. Erevan, 1943.

AH 2061   Countries of ancient Asia - Armenia - History by periods - 1 A.D. - ca. 650
    AH 2061.3   Elisaeus. History of Varton and of the Battle of the Armenians. London, 1830.
    AH 2061.3.5   Yeghisheh, Elisha Vardapet. The epic of St. Vardan the brave. N.Y., 1951.

AH 2102   Countries of ancient Asia - Asia Minor in general - Collected source materials
    AH 2102.10A   Calder, W.M. Anatolian studies presented to William H. Buckler. Manchester, 1939.
    AH 2102.10B   Calder, W.M. Anatolian studies presented to William H. Buckler. Photoreproduction. Manchester, 1939.

AH 2103   Countries of ancient Asia - Asia Minor in general - Government and administration
    AH 2103.2   Paris, P. Feminae res republicas. Paris, 1891.

AH 2104   Countries of ancient Asia - Asia Minor in general - Law
    AH 2104.5   Eyuboğlu, Ismet Zeki. Tanri yaratan toprak; Anadolu. Istanbul, 1973.

AH 2107   Countries of ancient Asia - Asia Minor in general - General history
    AH 2107.5   Cramer, J.A. Geographical and historical description of Asia Minor. Oxford, 1832. 2v.
    AH 2107.7   Le Bas, P. Asie Mineure. Paris, 1878.
    AH 2107.9A   Bittel, Kurt. Grundzüge der Vor- und Frühgeschichte Kleinasiens. 2. Aufl. Tübingen, 1950.
    AH 2107.9B   Bittel, Kurt. Grundzüge der Vor- und Frühgeschichte Kleinasiens. 2. Aufl. Tübingen, 1950.
    AH 2107.10   Metzger, Henri. Anatolia II. London, 1969.

AH 2108   Countries of ancient Asia - Asia Minor in general - General special
    AH 2108.5   Vaux, W.S.W. Great cities and islands of Asia Minor. London, 1877.
    AH 2108.7   Meyer, Ernst. Die Grenzen der hellenistischen Staaten in Kleinasien. Zürich, 1925.
    AH 2108.8   Stark, Freya. Rome on the Euphrates. London, 1966.
    AH 2108.10   Grantovskii, E.A. Ranniaia istoriia iranskikh plemen Perednei Azii. Moskva, 1970.
    AH 2108.15   Cozzoli, Umberto. I Cimmeri. Roma, 1968.

AH 2109   Countries of ancient Asia - Asia Minor in general - History by periods - Before 500 B.C.
    AH 2109.5   Karolides, Paul. Die sogenannten Assyro-Chaldäer und Hittiten. Athens, 1898.
    AH 2109.7F   Forschungen. 1,1926
    AH 2109.9   Götze, Albrecht. Kleinasien zur Hethiterzeit. Heidelberg, 1924.
    AH 2109.10   Lloyd, Seton Howard. Early highland peoples of Anatolia. London, 1967.
    AH 2109.15   Balikçisi, Halikarnas. Anadolu'nun sesi. Istanbul, 1971.

AH 2110   Countries of ancient Asia - Asia Minor in general - History by periods - 500 - 1 B.C.
    AH 2110.5   Judeich, W. Kleinasiastische Studien. Marburg, 1892.
    AH 2110.7   Cousin, J. Kyros le jeune en Asie mineure. Nancy, 1904.
    AH 2110.10   Pagi. Histoire de Cyrus le jeune. Paris, 1736.
    AH 2110.15   Kinal, Füruzan. Eski Anadolu tarihi. Ankara, 1962.

AH 2111   Countries of ancient Asia - Asia Minor in general - History by periods - 1 A.D. - ca. 650
    AH 2111.5   Levick, Barbara Mary. Roman colonies in Southern Asia Minor. Oxford, 1967.

AH 2113   Countries of ancient Asia - Asia Minor in general - Civilization
    AH 2113.2   Klengel, Evelyn. Die Hethiter. Geschichte und Umwelt. Wien, 1970.

AH 2114   Countries of ancient Asia - Asia Minor in general - Religion
    AH 2114.2   Steinleitner, Franz Seraph. Die Beicht im Zusammenhange mit der sakralen Rechtspflege in der Antike. Inaug. Diss. München, 1913.

AH 2117   Countries of ancient Asia - Asia Minor in general - Travels
    AH 2117.5F   Paton, David. Egyptian records of travel in Western Asia. v.1-3. Princeton, 1915-18. 4v.

AH 2120   Countries of ancient Asia - Asia Minor in general - Special topics - Ionia (coastal district)
    AH 2120.3   Stark, Freya. Ionia; a quest. 1. ed. London, 1954.
    AH 2120.5   Cassola, Filippo. La Ionia nel mondo miceneo. Napoli, 1957.
    AH 2120.7F   Roebuck, Carl A. Ionian trade and colonization. N.Y., 1959.

AH 2147   Countries of ancient Asia - Asia Minor in general - Roman Province of Asia
    AH 2147.2   Bergmann, R. Asiae Romanorum provinciae civitatibus liberis. Brandenburg, 1855.
    AH 2147.2.5   Bergmann, R. Asiae Romanorum provinciae civitatibus liberis. Berolini, n.d.
    AH 2147.3   Merckens, G. De Asia Provincia. Vratislaviae, 1860.
    AH 2147.4   Foucart, P. Formation de province romaine d'Asie. Paris, 1903.

AH 2147   Countries of ancient Asia - Asia Minor in general - Roman Province of Asia - cont.
    AH 2147.5   Chapot, V. Province romaine proconsulaire d'Asie. Paris, 1904.
    AH 2147.6   Monceaux, P. Communi asiae provinciae. Paris, 1885.
    AH 2147.7   Ramsay, W.M. The social basis of Roman power in Asia Minor. Aberdeen, 1941.
    AH 2147.8   Magie, D. Roman rule in Asia Minor. Princeton, 1950. 2v.
    AH 2147.9   Golubtsova, E.S. Ocherki sotsial'no-politicheskoi istorii Maloi Asii v I-III vv. Moskva, 1962.
    AH 2147.10   Zabłocka, Julia. Podstawy gospodarcze anatolijskiej arystokraeji w świetle inskrypcji fundacyjnych okresu wczesnegocesarstwa. Wyd. 1. Poznań, 1968.
    AH 2147.12   Lanza, Michele. Roma e l'eredita di Alessandro. Milano, 1971.

AH 2157   Countries of ancient Asia - Kingdoms of Asia Minor - Bithynia - General history
    AH 2157.2   Schoemann, A.G.O. Bithynia et Ponto. Gottingae, 1855.

AH 2158   Countries of ancient Asia - Kingdoms of Asia Minor - Bithynia - General special
    AH 2158.2   Faber, A. Quaestionum propontiacarum. Herford, 1858.
    AH 2158.5   Lauria, Guiseppe A. La Bitinia - la Lidia. Napoli, 1874.

AH 2171 - 2196   Countries of ancient Asia - Kingdoms of Asia Minor - Bithynia - Local (A-Z by place)
    AH 2173.5   Göttingen. Universitat. Index Scholarum...Academia Georgia Augusta. Gottingae, 1879.

AH 2207   Countries of ancient Asia - Kingdoms of Asia Minor - Cappadocia - General history
    AH 2207.5   Karolidos, G.K. Kappadokias. Könstantinople, 1874.

AH 2209   Countries of ancient Asia - Kingdoms of Asia Minor - Cappadocia - History by periods - Before 500 B.C.
    AH 2209.2   Gorelli, P. Les assyriens en Cappadoce. Paris, 1963.
    AH 2209.4   Orlin, Louis Lawrence. Assyrian colonies in Cappadocia. The Hague, 1970.

AH 2211   Countries of ancient Asia - Kingdoms of Asia Minor - Cappadocia - History by periods - 1 A.D. - ca. 650
    AH 2211.5   Gwatkin, William E. Cappadocia as a Roman procuratorial province. Diss. Princeton, 1930.

AH 2221 - 2246   Countries of ancient Asia - Kingdoms of Asia Minor - Cappadocia - Local (A-Z by place)
    AH 2231.5   Balkan, Kemal. Letter of King Anum-Hirbi of Mama to King Warshama of Kanish. Ankara, 1957.
    AH 2231.5.5   Balkan, Kemal. Kanis Karumunun kronoloji problemleri Hakkinda Musahedeler. Ankara, 1955.

AH 2257   Countries of ancient Asia - Kingdoms of Asia Minor - Caria - General history
    AH 2257.5   Robert, L. La Carie. v.2. Paris, 1954.

AH 2264   Countries of ancient Asia - Kingdoms of Asia Minor - Caria - Religion
    AH 2264.5   Laumonier, A. Les cultes indigènes en Carie. Paris, 1958.

AH 2271 - 2296   Countries of ancient Asia - Kingdoms of Asia Minor - Caria - Local (A-Z by place)
    AH 2271.5   Vagts, Rudolph. Aphrodisias in Karien. Diss. Borna, 1920.

AH 2302   Countries of ancient Asia - Kingdoms of Asia Minor - Cilicia - Collected source materials
    AH 2302.2   Hartung, Caspar. De proconsulatu Ciceronis Ciliciensi. Wirceburgi, 1868. 3 pam.

AH 2321 - 2346   Countries of ancient Asia - Kingdoms of Asia Minor - Cilicia - Local (A-Z by place)
    AH 2321.2   Kinal, F. Géographie et l'histoire des pays d'Arzava. Ankara, 1953.

AH 2353   Countries of ancient Asia - Kingdoms of Asia Minor - Galatia - Government and administration
    AH 2353.2   Zwintscher, A. De Galatarum tetarchis. Lipsiae, 1892.

AH 2357   Countries of ancient Asia - Kingdoms of Asia Minor - Galatia - General history
    AH 2357.4   Gelder, H. van. Galatarum res in Graecia et Asia gestae. Inaug. Diss. Amstelaedami, 1888.
    AH 2357.5   Staehelin, Felix. Geschichte der kleinasiatischen Galater. Basel, 1897.
    AH 2357.7   Chevalier, L. Die Gallier in Kleinasien. Prag, 1883.
    AH 2357.9   Robiou, F. Histoire des Gaulois d'Orient. Paris, 1866.
    AH 2357.11.3   Staehelin, Felix. Geschichte der kleinasiatischen Galater. 2. Aufl. Osnabrück, 1973.
    AH 2357.13   Perrot, G. De Galatia provincia romana. Lutetiae, 1867.
    AH 2357.15   Wernsdoff, G. Republica Galatarum. Norimbergae, 1743.
    AH 2357.16   Schmidt, G.A. De fontibus. Berolini, 1834.

AH 2358   Countries of ancient Asia - Kingdoms of Asia Minor - Galatia - General special
    AH 2358.5   Haerne, D. de. Les Belges en Asie-Mineure. Louvain, n.d.

AH 2503   Countries of ancient Asia - Kingdoms of Asia Minor - Lycia - Government and administration
    AH 2503.5   Fougères, G. De Lyciorum communi. Lutetiae, 1898.

AH 2507   Countries of ancient Asia - Kingdoms of Asia Minor - Lycia - General history
    AH 2507.5   Bachofen, J.J. Das lykische Volk. Freiburg, 1862.
    AH 2507.5.5   Bachofen, J.J. Das lykische Volk. Leipzig, 1924.
    AH 2507.7   Treuber, O. Geschichte der Lykier. Stuttgart, 1887.
    AH 2507.10   Stark, Freya. The Lycian shore. N.Y., 1956.
    AH 2507.15   Akşit, Oktay. Likya tarihi. Istanbul, 1967.

AH 2557   Countries of ancient Asia - Kingdoms of Asia Minor - Lydia - General history
    AH 2557.5   Schubert, R.J.W. Könige von Lydien. Breslau, 1884.
    AH 2557.7   Hogarth, D.G. Ionia and the East. Oxford, 1909.

AH 2558   Countries of ancient Asia - Kingdoms of Asia Minor - Lydia - General special
AH 2558.5   Alexander, L. The kings of Lydia. Oberlin, 1914.

AH 2571 - 2596   Countries of ancient Asia - Kingdoms of Asia Minor - Lydia - Local (A-Z by place)
AH 2573.5   Pertz, C.A. Colophoniaca. Gottingae, 1848.
AH 2575.5   Guhl, Ernestus. Ephesiaca. Berolini, 1843.
AH 2575.7   Gaebler, H. Erythrä. Berlin, 1892.
AH 2575.9   Menadier, J. Qua condicione Ephesii. Berolini, 1880.
AH 2583.5F   Kern, Otto. Magnesia am Maiandros. Berlin, 1894.
AH 2583.7   Haussoulier, B. L'histoire de Milet. Photoreproduction. Paris, 1902.
AH 2583.8   Dunham, A.G. History of Miletus down to the anabasis of Alexander. Thesis. London, 1915.
AH 2583.9   Mezger, Fridericus. Inscriptio milesiaca de pace cum magnetibus facta. Inaug. Diss. Monaci, 1913.
AH 2583.10   Kobylina, Mariia M. Milet. Moskva, 1965.
AH 2589.5   Lane, G.M. Smyrnaeorum res gestae et antiquitates. Gottingae, 1851.
AH 2589.7   Mylonas, C.D. De Smyrnaeorum rebus gestis. Inaug. Diss. Gottingae, 1866.
AH 2589.9   Cadaux, Cecil J. Ancient Smyrna. Oxford, 1938.
AH 2589.10   Pedley, John. Sardis in the age of Croesus. 1. ed. Norman, 1968.

AH 2621 - 2646   Countries of ancient Asia - Kingdoms of Asia Minor - Mysia - Local (A-Z by place)
AH 2623.5   Marquarat, J. Cyzicus und sein Gebiet. Berlin, 1836.
AH 2623.7   Hasluck, Fredrick William. Cyzicus. Cambridge, 1910.

AH 2648   Countries of ancient Asia - Kingdoms of Asia Minor - Osrhoene
AH 2648.5   Bayer, G.S. Historia osrhoëna et edessena ex numis illustrata. Petropoli, 1734.

AH 2757   Countries of ancient Asia - Kingdoms of Asia Minor - Pergamon - General history
AH 2757.5   Thraemer, E. Pergamos. Leipzig, 1888.
AH 2757.7   Pedroli, D.U. Il regno di Pergamo. Torino, 1896.
AH 2757.9   Brinkgreve, I.G. De regno Pergameno deque eius dynastis. Rhenum, 1893.
AH 2757.15   Cardinali, Guiseppe. Il regno di Pergamo. Roma, 1968.

AH 2760   Countries of ancient Asia - Kingdoms of Asia Minor - Pergamon - History by periods - 500 - 1 B.C.
AH 2760.5   Meischke, Kurt. Symbolae ad Eumenis II. Pergamenorum regis historiam. Inaug. Diss. Lipsiae, 1892.
AH 2760.5.5   Meischke, Kurt. Zur Geschichte des Königs Eumenes II von Pergamon. Pirna, 1905.

AH 2763   Countries of ancient Asia - Kingdoms of Asia Minor - Pergamon - Civilization
AH 2763.5   Reifferscheid, August. Pergamon und seine Kunstschätze. Breslau, 1881-82.

AH 2764   Countries of ancient Asia - Kingdoms of Asia Minor - Pergamon - Religion
AH 2764.5   Ohlemutz, Erwin. Die Kulte und Heiligtumer der Gotter in Pergamon. 2. Aufl. Darmstadt, 1968.

AH 2807   Countries of ancient Asia - Kingdoms of Asia Minor - Phrygia - General history
AH 2807.5   Lauria, G.A. La Frigia. Naples, 1874.
AH 2807.7   Ramsay, W.M. Early historical relations between Phrygia and Cappadocia. n.p., n.d.

AH 2808   Countries of ancient Asia - Kingdoms of Asia Minor - Phrygia - General special
AH 2808.5A   Ramsay, W.M. Cities and bishoprics of Phrygia. Oxford, 1895. 2v.
AH 2808.5B   Ramsay, W.M. Cities and bishoprics of Phrygia. Oxford, 1895. 2v.
AH 2808.5C   Ramsay, W.M. Cities and bishoprics of Phrygia. Oxford, 1895.

AH 2816   Countries of ancient Asia - Kingdoms of Asia Minor - Phrygia - Geography
AH 2816.5   Anderson, J.G.C. A summer in Phrygia. n.p., 1897.

AH 2907   Countries of ancient Asia - Kingdoms of Asia Minor - Pontus - General history
AH 2907.2   Meyer, E. Geschichte des Königreichs Pontos. Leipzig, 1879.
AH 2907.4   Gologlu, Mahmut. Anadolunun milli devleti Pontos. Istanbul, 1973.

AH 2910   Countries of ancient Asia - Kingdoms of Asia Minor - Pontus - History by periods - 500 - 1 B.C.
AH 2910.2   Duggan, Alfred Leo. He died old. London, 1958.

AH 2921 - 2946   Countries of ancient Asia - Kingdoms of Asia Minor - Pontus - Local (A-Z by place)
AH 2928.5   Steinmann, W. Das Gebiet von Heraklea Pontica. Rostock, 1869.

AH 2951   Countries of ancient Asia - Kingdoms of Asia Minor - Troas - Pamphlet volumes
AH 2951.1   Pamphlet box. Ancient history. Troas.

AH 2957   Countries of ancient Asia - Kingdoms of Asia Minor - Troas - General history
AH 2957.3   Chandler, R. History of Illium or Troy. London, 1802.
AH 2957.5A   Benjamin, S. Troy. N.Y., 1880.
AH 2957.5B   Benjamin, S. Troy. N.Y., 1880.
AH 2957.5.3   Benjamin, S. Troy. N.Y., 1893.
AH 2957.5.5   Benjamin, S. Troy. N.Y., 1895.
AH 2957.7   Meyer, E. Geschichte von Troas. Leipzig, 1877.
AH 2957.9   Lauth, F.J. Troja's Epoche. München, 1877.
AH 2957.11   Haubold, P. De rebus Iliensium. Lipsiae, 1888.
AH 2957.13   Macurdy, Grace H. Troy and Paeonia. N.Y., 1925.

AH 2958   Countries of ancient Asia - Kingdoms of Asia Minor - Troas - General special
AH 2958.5   Maclaren, Charles. The plain of Troy described. Edinburgh, 1863.
AH 2958.6   Levillain, Jean. Etude sur la localisation d'Ilion d'apres l'Iliade d'Homere. Istanbul, 1962.

AH 2959   Countries of ancient Asia - Kingdoms of Asia Minor - Troas - History by periods - Before 500 B.C.
AH 2959.5   Weigel, Hildegard. Der trojanische Krieg. Darmstadt, 1970.

AH 2963   Countries of ancient Asia - Kingdoms of Asia Minor - Troas - Civilization
AH 2963.5   Gomperz, T. Zur Entzifferung der Schliemann sehen Inschriften. Wien, 1874.

AH 2966   Countries of ancient Asia - Kingdoms of Asia Minor - Troas - Geography
AH 2966.2   Degen, H. De Troianis Scaenicis. Lipsiae, 1900.

AH 3000   Countries of ancient Asia - Assyria and Babylonia - Bibliographies
AH 3000.3   British Museum. Catalog of cuneiform tablets in the Kouyunjik collection. London, 1889-99. 5v.
AH 3000.3.2   British Museum. Catalog of cuneiform tablets in the Kouyunjik collection. Supplement. London, 1914.
AH 3000.3.3   British Museum. Catalog of cuneiform tablets in the Kouyunjik collection. 2d supplement. London, 1968.
AH 3000.3.5   British Museum. Department of Western Asiatic Antiquities. A bibliography of the cuneiform tablets of the Kuyunjik collection. London, 1964.
AH 3000.4   Ménant, J. Rapport...sur les inscriptions assyriens. v.1-2. Paris, 1862.
AH 3000.5   Morgan, J.P. Cuneiform inscriptions : Chaldean, Babylonian. N.Y., 1908.
AH 3000.6   Bibliographie analytique de l'assyriologie et de l'archéologie du Proche-Orient. Leyde. 1,1954+
AH 3000.10   Weidner, Ernst. Die Assyriologie, 1914-1922. Leipzig, 1922-23.

AH 3001   Countries of ancient Asia - Assyria and Babylonia - General pamphlet volumes
AH 3001.1   Pamphlet vol. Babylonia and Assyria. 3 pam.
AH 3001.2   Pamphlet vol. Babylonia and Assyria. 12 pam.
AH 3001.3   Pamphlet vol. Babylonia and Assyria. 13 pam.
AH 3001.4   Hincks, E. On the polyphony of the Assyric-Babylonian cuneiform writing. Dublin, 1863. 10 pam.
AH 3001.5   Bruston, Charles. Le dechiffrement des inscriptions cuneiform. Paris, 1873. 13 pam.
AH 3001.6   Pamphlet vol. Assyriology. 13 pam.
AH 3001.7   Pamphlet vol. Assyriology. 12 pam.
AH 3001.8   Pamphlet box. Babylonia and Assyria.

AH 3002   Countries of ancient Asia - Assyria and Babylonia - Collected sources - General collections
AH 3002.2.1   Haupt, Paul. Akkadische und sumerische Keilschrifttexte. Leipzig, 1881-82.
AH 3002.2.2   Bezold, Carl. Die Achämenideninschriften. Leipzig, 1882.
AH 3002.2.3   Haupt, Paul. Das babylonische Nimrodepos. Leipzig, 1884-91.
AH 3002.2.4   Strassmaier, J.N. Alphabetisches Verzeichniss. Leipzig, 1886.
AH 3002.2.5A   Sargon, king of Assyria. Keilschrifttexte: Sargon's Königs von Assyrien. Leipzig, 1883.
AH 3002.2.5B   Sargon, king of Assyria. Keilschrifttexte: Sargon's Königs von Assyrien. Leipzig, 1883.
AH 3002.2.5C   Sargon, king of Assyria. Keilschrifttexte: Sargon's Königs von Assyrien. Leipzig, 1883.
AH 3002.2.6   Zimmern, Heinrich. Babylonische Busspsalmen. Leipzig, 1885.
AH 3002.2.7   Delitzsch, Friedrich. Assyrisches Wörterbuch. Leipzig, 1887-
AH 3002.2.8   Lehmann-Haupt, C.F. Šeamaššumukîn, König von Babylonien. Leipzig, 1892.
AH 3002.2.9   Weissbach, F.H. Die Achämenideninschriften zweiter Art. Leipzig, 1890.
AH 3002.2.10   Weissbach, F.H. Die altpersischen Keilinschriften. Leipzig, 1908.
AH 3002.2.11   Meissner, Bruno. Beiträge zum altbabylonischen Privatrecht. Leipzig, 1893.
AH 3002.2.12   Zimmern, Heinrich. Beiträge zur Kenntnis der babylonischen Religion. Leipzig, 1901.
AH 3002.2.13   Craig, James A. Assyrian and Babylonian religious texts. Leipzig, 1895-97.
AH 3002.2.14   Craig, James A. Astrological-astronomical texts. Leipzig, 1899.
AH 3002.2.15   Price, Ira M. The great cylinder inscriptions A and B of Gudea. Pt.1-2. Leipzig, 1899-1927. 2v.
AH 3002.2.16   Delitzsch, Friedrich. Assyrische Lesestücke, mit grammatische Tabellen. 4. Aufl. Leipzig, 1900.
AH 3002.2.16.2   Delitzsch, Friedrich. Assyrische Lesestücke. 5. Aufl. Leipzig, 1912.
AH 3002.2.17   Johns, Claude H. An Assyrian doomsday book. Leipzig, 1901.
AH 3002.2.18   Küchler, Friedrich. Beiträge zur Kenntnis der assyrisch-babylonischen Medizin. Leipzig, 1904.
AH 3002.2.19   Prince, John D. Materials for a Sumerian lexicon. Leipzig, 1905-08.
AH 3002.2.20   Meissner, Bruno. Seltene assyrische Ideogramme. Leipzig, 1906.
AH 3002.2.21   Huber, Engelbert. Die Personennamen in der Keilschrifturkunden. Leipzig, 1907.
AH 3002.2.22   Dennefeld, L. Babylonisch-assyrische Geburts-Omina. Leipzig, 1914.
AH 3002.2.23F   Weidner, Ernst F. Handbuch der babylonischen Astronomus. Leipzig, 1915.
AH 3002.2.25   Nies, James B. Ur dynasty tablets. Leipzig, 1920.
AH 3002.2.100F   Assyriologische Bibliothek. Leipzig.
AH 3002.3   Delattre, A. Les inscriptions historiques de Nineve. Paris, 1879.
AH 3002.4   New York Metropolitan Museum of Art. Cuneiform texts in the Metropolitan Museum. N.Y., 1903.
AH 3002.4.5   Moldenke, A.B. Babylonian contract tablets in the Metropolitan Museum of Art. N.Y., 1893.
AH 3002.5A   Records of the past. London, 1873. 12v.
AH 3002.5B   Records of the past. v.11-12. London, 1873. 2v.
AH 3002.5.2   Records of the past. London, 1873.
AH 3002.5.5A   Records of the past. London, 1889. 6v.
AH 3002.5.5B   Records of the past. London, 1889. 6v.
AH 3002.6FA   Winckler, H. Sammlung von Keilschrifttexten. Leipzig, 1893. 2v.
AH 3002.6FB   Winckler, H. Sammlung von Keilschrifttexten. Leipzig, 1893.
AH 3002.6.5   Winckler, H. Keilinschriftliches Textbuch zum Alten Testament. Leipzig, 1892.

Classified Listing

AH 3002   Countries of ancient Asia - Assyria and Babylonia - Collected sources - General collections - cont.

AH 3002.7F — Morgan, J.P. Babylonian records in the library of J.P. Morgan. N.Y., 1912. 4v.

AH 3002.7.5 — Clay, A.T. Hebrew deluge story in cuneiform...Morgan Library. New Haven, 1922.

AH 3002.8 — University of Pennsylvania. Publications of the Babylonian section...Museum. Philadelphia. 1-16,1911-1930 20v.

AH 3002.12 — University of Pennsylvania. Babylonian Expedition. The Babylonian expedition. Series A: Cuneiform texts. Philadelphia. 1-29,1893-1913 10v.

AH 3002.12F — University of Pennsylvania. Babylonian Expedition. The Babylonian expedition. Series A: Cuneiform texts. Philadelphia. 30-31,1913-1914 2v.

AH 3002.15 — University of Pennsylvania. Babylonian Expedition. Babylonian expedition. Series D: Researches and treatises. Philadelphia. 1-4,1904-1907 3v.

AH 3002.18 — Hilprecht, H.V. The so-called Peters-Hilprecht controversy. Pt.1-2. Philadelphia, 1908.

AH 3002.25F — British Museum. Department of Egyptian and Assyrian Antiquities. Cuneiform texts from Babylonian tablets. London. 1,1896+ 35v.

AH 3002.25.5F — British Museum. Department of Egyptian and Assyrian Antiquities. Cuneiform texts from Babylonian tablets. London. 13,1901+ 25v.

AH 3002.25.6F — British Museum. Department of Egyptian and Assyrian Antiquities. Cuneiform texts from Babylonian tablets. Index to registration numbers of texts, pt.1-25. n.p., n.d.

AH 3002.26F — British Museum. Department of Egytpian and Assyrian Antiquities. Hittite texts in the cuneiform character. London, 1920.

AH 3002.26.5F — British Museum. Department of Egyptian and Assyrian Antiquities. Cuneiform texts from Cappadocian tablets. London. 1-4,1921-1927 3v.

AH 3002.26.10 — British Museum. Department of Egyptian and Assyrian Antiquities. Chronicles of Chaldaean kings. London, 1956.

AH 3002.27 — Schrader, E. Sammlung von assyrischen und babylonsichen Texten. Berlin. 1-6,1889-1915 6v.

AH 3002.27.5 — Keilinschriftliche Bibliothek. Berlin. 2-5,1890-1896 4v.

AH 3002.28 — Rogers, R.W. Cuneiform parallels to the Old Testament. N.Y., 1912.

AH 3002.29 — Lenormant, F. Choix de textes cunéiformes. Paris, 1873-75.

AH 3002.30F — Rawlinson, H.C. Cuneiform inscriptions of Western Asia. v.1-5. London, 1861-64. 3v.

AH 3002.30.2F — Rawlinson, H.C. Cuneiform inscriptions of Western Asia. v.4. London, 1891.

AH 3002.32F — Yale Oriental series. Babylonian texts. New Haven. 1-10,1915-1947 10v.

AH 3002.33 — Yale Oriental series. Researches. New Haven. 2-24,1916-1949 20v.

AH 3002.34F — Nies, James B. Babylonian inscriptions. v.1-2, 4-9. New Haven, 1918-42. 8v.

AH 3002.35F — Paris. Musée National du Louvre. Département des Antiquités Orientales et de la Céramique Antique. Textes cunéiformes. v.3, photoreproduction. Paris. 1-30 28v.

AH 3002.37 — Chiera, Edward. Selected temple accounts from Tellohyokha and Drehem. Philadelphia, 1921.

AH 3002.38F — Goucher College cuneiform inscriptions. New Haven. 1-2,1923-1933 2v.

AH 3002.40 — Grant, Elihu. Cuneiform documents in Smith Library. Haverford, 1918.

AH 3002.50 — Luckenbill, D.D. Ancient records of Assyria and Babylonia. Chicago, 1926. 2v.

AH 3002.55F — Oxford University. Ashmolean Museum. Oxford editions of cuneiform inscriptions. London. 1-8 5v.

AH 3002.60F — Amherst of Hackney, W.A.T.A. The Amherst tablets. London, 1908.

AH 3002.65F — Lewy, Julius. Studien zu den altassyrischen Texten aus Kappadokien. Berlin, 1922.

AH 3002.65.5 — Stephens, Ferris J. Studies of the cuneiform tablets from Cappadocia. n.p., 1925.

AH 3002.70 — American Schools of Oriental Research. Publications - Texts. Paris. 1-6,1927-1939 6v.

AH 3002.75F — Joint Expedition of the British Museum and the Museum of the University of Pennyslvania to Mesopotamia. Ur excavations. Texts and plates. v.1-4; 6, pt.1-2; 8. Philadelphia, 1920-35. 10v.

AH 3002.80 — Smith, Sidney. Babylonian historical texts relating to the capture and downfall of Babylon. London, 1924.

AH 3002.81 — Waterman, L. Royal correspondence of the Assyrian empire. Ann Arbor, 1930-36. 4v.

AH 3002.82F — Keilschrifturkunden aus Boghazköi. Berlin. 1-37 14v.

AH 3002.83 — Belck, Waldemar. Die Kelischin-Stele und ihre chaldisch-assyrischen Keilinschriften. Freienwald, 1904.

AH 3002.84 — Dhorme, Paul. Choix de textes religieux assyro-babylonies. Paris, 1907.

AH 3002.86F — Lehmann-Haupt, C.F. Corpus inscriptionum Chaldicarum. Berlin, 1928-35.

AH 3002.87 — Brussels. Musées Royaux du Cinquantenaire. Recueil des inscriptions de l'Asie des Musées Royaux du Cinquantenaire à Bruxelles. Bruxelles, 1925.

AH 3002.88F — Gelb, I.J. Inscriptions from Alishar and vicinity. Chicago, 1935.

AH 3002.89F — Luckenbill, Daniel D. Inscriptions from Adab. Chicago, 1930.

AH 3002.92 — Jacobsen, T. Cuneiform texts in the National Museum. Copenhagen, 1939.

AH 3002.94 — British Museum. Department of Egyptian and Assyrian Antiquities. Annals of the kings of Assyria. London, 1902-

AH 3002.96 — Peiser, F. Urkunden aus der Zeit der dritten babylonischen Dynastie. Berlin, 1905.

AH 3002.98 — Fossey, C. Syllabaire cunéiforme. Paris, 1901.

AH 3002.100 — Manchester cuneiform studies. Manchester. 1-3,1951-1953 2v.

AH 3002.102 — Archives royales de Mari. v.1-9, 11-13, 15. Paris, 1950-9v.

AH 3002.105 — Keilschriftliche Miscellanea. Roma, 1933.

AH 3002.110 — Aberhuber, Karl. Innsbrucher Keilschrifttexte. Innsbruck, 1956.

AH 3002.115F — Genouillac, Henri de. Tablettes de Dréhem. Paris, 1911.

AH 3002.120F — Berlin. Staatliche Museen. Vorderasiatische Schriftdenckmaler der Museen. Leipzig. 1-16, 1907-1917 16v.

AH 3002   Countries of ancient Asia - Assyria and Babylonia - Collected sources - General collections - cont.

AH 3002.125F — Deimel, Anton. Tabulae signorum cuneiformium in usum scholae. Romae, 1910.

AH 3002.135A — Nederkands Institut voor het Nabije Oosten, Leyden. Studia ad tabulas cuneiformas collectas ab De Liagre Böhl pertinentia. v.1, pt.1-2; 3. Leiden, 1952- 3v.

AH 3002.135B — Nederkands Institut voor het Nabije Oosten, Leyden. Studia ad tabulas cuneiformas collectas ab De Liagre Böhl pertinentia. v.1, pt.1-2; 3. Leiden, 1952- 3v.

AH 3002.136F — Böhl, Franz M.T. Tabulae cuneiformae a F.M.T. de Liagre Böhl. v.1; 2, pt.1; 3-4. Leiden, 1957. 4v.

AH 3002.140 — Altbabylonische Briefe in Umschrift und Übersetzung. Leiden. 1,1964+ 4v.

AH 3002.144 — Borger, Riekele. Handbuch der Keilschriftliteratur. Berlin, 1967-

AH 3002.150 — Baghdad. Iraq Museum. Texts in the Iraq Museum. Baghdad, 1964- 7v.

AH 3002.152 — Pettinato, Giovanni. Texte zur Verwaltung der Landwirtschaft in der Ur-III Zeit. Habilitationsschrift. Roma, 1969.

AH 3002.154 — Sollberger, Edmond. Inscriptions royales sumériennes et akkadiennes. Paris, 1971.

AH 3002.154.5 — The claremont Ras Shamra tablets. Roma, 1971.

AH 3002.155 — Rashid, Fawzi. Archiv des Nûrsămăs und andere Darlehensurkunden aus der altbabylonischen Zeit. Inaug. Diss. Heidelberg, 1965.

AH 3002.158 — Cuneiform texts from Nimrud. London. 1,1972+

AH 3004   Countries of ancient Asia - Assyria and Babylonia - Assyriology as a discipline - Theory, scope, methods of study

AH 3004.3 — Brandis, J. Über den historischen Gewinn...assyrischen Inschriften. Berlin, 1856.

AH 3004.4 — Winckler, H. Ein Beitrag zur Geschichte des Assyriologie im Deutschland. Leipzig, 1894.

AH 3004.5 — Pinches, Theodore G. The Babylonian chronicle. London, 1887.

AH 3004.7 — Brown, F. Assyriology - its use and abuse in Old Testament study. N.Y., 1885.

AH 3005.1 - .599   Countries of ancient Asia - Assyria and Babylonia - Assyriology as a discipline - History of Assyriology

AH 3005.3.01 — Pamphlet box. Assyriological scholars.

AH 3005.5 — Booth, A.J. Discovery...of trilingual cuneiform inscriptions. London, 1902.

AH 3005.6 — Fossey, Charles. Manuel d'Assyriologie. v.1-2. Paris, 1904-26. 3v.

AH 3005.7 — Gutschmid, A. Neue Beiträge zur Geschichte des alten Orients; die Assyriologie in Deutschland. Leipzig, 1876.

AH 3005.8 — Budge, E.A.T.N. The rise and progress of Assyriology. London, 1925.

AH 3005.9F — Hommel, Fritz. Beiträge zur morgenländischen Altentum. München, 1920.

AH 3005.10 — Ebeling, Erich. Keallexikon der Assyriologie. Berlin, 1928-38. 4v.

AH 3005.11 — Lloyd, Seton. Foundations in the dust. London, 1947.

AH 3005.13 — Scheil, Vincent. Au service de Clio. Chalon-sur-Saone, 1937.

AH 3005.14 — Wiseman, D.J. The expansion of Assyrian studies. London, 1962.

AH 3005.15 — Garelli, Paul. L'assyriologie. Paris, 1964.

AH 3005.16 — Saggs, Henry William. Assyriology and the study of the Old Testament. Cardiff, 1969.

AH 3005.700 - .999   Countries of ancient Asia - Assyria and Babylonia - Assyriology as a discipline - Biographies of scholars - Individual (299 scheme, A-Z by person)

AH 3005.828 — Hincks, Edward. Edward Hincks; a selection from his correspondence. London, 1933.

AH 3005.830 — Matouš, Lubor. Bedřich Hrozný; the life and work of a Czech Oriental scholar. Prague, 1949.

AH 3005.830.5 — Hrozný, Bedřich. Stručný přehled mých vědeckých objevů. Praha, 1848.

AH 3005.855 — Layard, Austen Henry. Sir A. Henry Layard; autobiography and letters. London, 1903. 2v.

AH 3005.855.5 — Waterfield, Gordon. Layard of Nineveh. London, 1963.

AH 3005.913 — Pillet, Maurice. Un pionnier de l'assyriologie: Victor Place. Paris, 1962.

AH 3006 - 3009   Countries of ancient Asia - Assyria and Babylonia - General histories (By date)

AH 3007.11A — Perizonius, J. Origines Babylonicae et Aegypticae. Lugdunum Batavorum, 1711. 2v.

AH 3007.11B — Perizonius, J. Origines Babylonicae et Aegypticae. Lugdunum Batavorum, 1711. 2v.

AH 3008.54 — Gumpach, J. von. Abriss der babylonisch-assyrischen Geschichte. Mannheim, 1854.

AH 3008.57 — Niebuhr, M.K.N. Geschichte Assur's und Babel's seit Phiel. Berlin, 1857.

AH 3008.65 — Oppert, J. Histoire des empires de Chaldée et d'Assyrie. Versailles, 1865.

AH 3008.67 — Oppert, J. Babylone et les Babyloniens. Paris, 1867.

AH 3008.68 — Wattenbach, W. Ninive und Babylon. Heidelberg, 1868.

AH 3008.71 — Robion, F.M.L.J. L'histoire de la Chaldée et de l'Assyrie. n.p., 1871.

AH 3008.75.5 — Menant, J. Babylone et la Chaldée. Paris, 1875.

AH 3008.77 — Smith, George. The history of Babylonia. London, 1877.

AH 3008.80 — Hommel, F. Abriss der babylonisch-assyrischen und israelitischen Geschichte. Leipzig, 1880.

AH 3008.82 — Mürdter, F. Kurzgefasste Geschichte Babyloniens und Assyriens. Stuttgart, 1882.

AH 3008.82.5 — Mürdter, F. Geschichte Babyloniens und Assyriens. 2. Aufl. Stuttgart, 1891.

AH 3008.82.7 — Kausen, F. Assyrien und Babylonien. 2. Aufl. Freiburg, 1885.

AH 3008.84 — Budge, E.A.W. Babylonian life and history. London, 1884. 2v.

AH 3008.84.5 — Budge, E.A.W. Babylonian life and history. 2. ed. London, 1925.

NEDL AH 3008.85 — Brunengo, G. L'impero di Babilonia e di Ninive. v.1-2. Prato, 1885.

AH 3008.86A — Tiele, C.P. Babylonisch-assyrische Geschicte. Gotha, 1886. 2v.

AH 3008.86B — Tiele, C.P. Babylonisch-assyrische Geschichte. v.1-2. Gotha, 1886.

AH 3008.86.5 — Boscawen, William. From under the dust of ages. London, 1886.

Classified Listing

AH 3006 - 3009   Countries of ancient Asia - Assyria and Babylonia - General
histories (By date) - cont.

AH 3008.92 — Winckler, H. Geschichte Babyloniens und Assyriens. Leipzig, 1892.

AH 3008.92.7A — Winckler, H. The history of Babylonia and Assyria. N.Y., 1907.

AH 3008.92.7B — Winckler, H. The history of Babylonia and Assyria. N.Y., 1907.

AH 3009.00 — Rogers, R.W. A history of Babylonia and Assyria. N.Y., 1900. 2v.

AH 3009.02 — Goodspeed, G.S. A history of the Babylonians and Assyrians. N.Y., 1902.

AH 3009.03 — Bezold, C. Ninive und Babylon. Bielefeld, 1903.

AH 3009.06 — Goodspeed, G.S. A history of the Babylonians and Assyrians. 2. ed. N.Y., 1906.

AH 3009.07 — Starck, C. von. Babylonien und Assyrien. Marburg, 1907.

AH 3009.10 — King, L.W. History of Babylon from foundation...to Persian conquest. N.Y., 1915.

AH 3009.13 — Johns, C.H.W. Ancient Babylonia. Cambridge, Eng., 1913.

AH 3009.15 — Rogers. R.W. A history of Babylonia and Assyria. 6. ed. N.Y., 1915. 2v.

AH 3009.26 — Meissner, Bruno. Könige Babyloniens und Assyriens. Leipzig, 1926.

AH 3009.33 — Boulton, W.H. Babylonia. London, 1933.

AH 3009.55 — Schmökel, H. Ur, Assur und Babylon. Stuttgart, 1953.

AH 3009.57 — Champdor, Albert. Babylone. Paris, 1957.

AH 3009.58 — Rutten, M. Babylone. Paris, 1958.

AH 3009.60F — Beek, Martinus A. Atlas van het Tweestromland. Amsterdam, 1960.

AH 3009.60.1F — Beek, Martinus A. Atlas of Mesopotamia; a survey of the history and civilization of Mesopotamia from the Stone Age to the fall of Babylon. London, 1962.

AH 3009.60.3F — Beek, Martinus A. Bildatlas der assyrisch-bablonischen Kultur. Gütersloh, 1961.

AH 3009.64 — Roux, Georges. Ancient Iraq. London, 1964.

AH 3009.71 — Beliavskii, Vatalii A. Vavilon legendarnyi i Vavilon istoricheskii. Moskva, 1971.

AH 3009.72 — Wellard, James Howard. By the waters of Babylon. London, 1972.

AH 3011   Countries of ancient Asia - Assyria and Babylonia - Miscellaneous essays

AH 3011.3 — Fenzi, F. Ricerche per lo Studio dell'antichità Assira. Roma, 1872.

AH 3011.4 — Hilprecht, H.V. Assyriaca eine Nachlese...Assyriologie. Berlin, 1894.

AH 3011.5F — Grotefend, G.F. Erläuterung der Keilinschriften babylonischer Backsteine. Hannover, 1852.

AH 3011.5.5F — Grotefend, G.F. Erläuterung einer Inschrift des letzten assyrisch-babylonischen Königs aus Nimrud. Hannover, 1853.

AH 3011.6 — Witzel, M. Keilinschriftliche Studien. Leipzig. 1-7,1918-1930// 7v.

AH 3011.8 — Dhorme, E.P. Recueil Edouard Dhorme. Paris, 1951.

AH 3011.15 — Böhl, F.M.T. Opera minora. Groningen, 1953.

AH 3011.16 — McCullough, W.S. The seed of wisdom. Toronto, 1964.

AH 3011.17 — Leningrad. Universitet. Kafedra stran Drevnego Vostoka. Assiriologiia i egiptologiia. Leningrad, 1964.

AH 3011.18 — Chicago. University. Studies presented to A. Leo Oppenheim, June 7, 1964. Chicago, 1964.

AH 3011.20 — Heidelberger Studien zum Alten Orient. Adam Falkenstein zum (60 Geburtstag) 17 September 1966. Wiesbaden, 1967.

AH 3011.21 — Lišan Mithurti. Festschrift Wolfram Freiherr von Soden. Kevelaer, 1969.

AH 3011.22 — Jacobsen, Thorkild. Toward the image of Tammuz, and other essays on Mesopotamian history and culture. Cambridge, 1970.

AH 3011.24 — Beitraege zu Geschichte, Kultur und Religion des alten Orients; in Memoriam Eckhard Unger. 1. Aufl. Baden-Baden, 1971.

AH 3012   Countries of ancient Asia - Assyria and Babylonia - General special

AH 3012.3 — Rawlinson, H.C. Commentary on cuneiform inscriptions. London, 1850.

AH 3012.4 — Berliner, A. Beiträge zur Geographie und Ethnographie Babyloniens. Berlin, 1884.

AH 3012.5 — Tofteen, O.A. Researches in Assyrian and Babylonian geography. Chicago, 1908.

AH 3012.6 — Schrader, E. Keilinschriften und Geschichtsforschung. Giessen, 1878.

AH 3012.7 — Sayce, A.H. The archaeology of cuneiform inscriptions. London, 1907.

AH 3012.9A — Speiser, Ephraim A. Mesopotamian origins. Philadelphia, 1930.

AH 3012.9B — Speiser, Ephraim A. Mesopotamian origins. Philadelphia, 1930.

AH 3012.9.1 — Speiser, Ephraim A. Mesopotamian origins. Philadelphia, 1930. Ann Arbor, 1973.

AH 3012.10 — Zimmermann, Carl. Babylon. Basel, 1859.

AH 3012.11 — Jung, H.W.M. Demonische ziekten in Babylon en Bijbel. Leiden, 1959.

AH 3012.13 — Sulayman, Tawfiq. Die Entstehung und Entwicklung der Götterwaffen im alten Mesopotamien und ihre Bedeutung. Berlin, 1964.

AH 3012.17 — Laessøe, J. People of ancient Assyria. London, 1963.

AH 3012.19 — O'Callaghan, Roger T. Aram Naharaim. Roma, 1948.

AH 3012.20 — Larsen, Morgens. Old Assyrian caravan procedures. Istanbul, 1967.

AH 3012.21 — Rupper, Jean R. Les nomades en Mésopotamia au temps des rois de Mari. Paris, 1957.

AH 3012.22 — Labłocha, Yulia. Stosunki agrarne w paristure Sargonidów. Wyd. 1. Poznan, 1971.

AH 3013   Countries of ancient Asia - Assyria and Babylonia - Assyro-Babylonian
archaeology and art - General works (By date, e.g. .960 for 1960)

AH 3013.1 — Pamphlet box. Babylonia and Assyria. General archaeology.

AH 3013.4F — Heuzey, Leon A. Les origines orientales de l'art. Pt.1-4. Paris, 1891-1915.

AH 3013.5 — Cavaniol, C.H. Les monuments en Chaldée, en Assyrie. Paris, 1870.

AH 3013.6.2 — Kaulen, Franz. Assyrien und Babylonien. 2. Aufl. Freiburg, 1882.

AH 3013.6.4A — Kaulen, Franz. Assyrien und Babylonien. 4. Aufl. Freiburg, 1891.

AH 3013.6.4B — Kaulen, Franz. Assyrien und Babylonien. 4. Aufl. Freiburg, 1891.

AH 3013.6.5 — Kaulen, Franz. Assyrien und Babylonien. 5. Aufl. Freiburg, 1899.

AH 3013.7 — Rassam, H. Asshur and the land of Nimrod. N.Y., 1897.

AH 3013   Countries of ancient Asia - Assyria and Babylonia - Assyro-Babylonian
archaeology and art - General works (By date, e.g. .960 for 1960) - cont.

AH 3013.8 — Gaugengigl, I. Erklärung der König Ludwig's Inschriften in der Münchner Glyptothek. München, 1870.

AH 3013.9 — British Museum. Assyrian antiquities - guide to Koujunjik Gallery. London, 1883.

AH 3013.9.5A — British Museum. Guide to the Babylonian and Assyrian antiquities. London, 1900.

AH 3013.9.5B — British Museum. Guide to the Babylonian and Assyrian antiquities. London, 1900.

AH 3013.9.6 — British Museum. Guide to the Babylonian and Assyrian antiquities. 2. ed. London, 1908.

AH 3013.10A — Hilprecht, H.V. Explorations in Bible lands. Philadelphia, 1903.

AH 3013.10B — Hilprecht, H.V. Explorations in Bible lands. Philadelphia, 1903.

AH 3013.10.7 — Hilprecht, H.V. Die Ausgrabungen in Assyrien und Babylonien. Leipzig, 1904.

AH 3013.11F — Oppert, J. Expédition scientifique en Mésopotamie. v.1-2; plates. Paris, 1863. 3v.

AH 3013.12 — Delitzsch, F. Ex Oriente lux! Leipzig, 1898.

AH 3013.12.15 — Delitzsch, F. Im Lande des einstigen Paradieses. Stuttgart, 1903.

AH 3013.13.5 — Paris. Musée Nationale du Louvre. Catalogue des antiquités chaldéennes. Paris, 1902.

AH 3013.14 — Weissenborn, H.J.C. Ninive und sein Gebiet. Erfurt, 1851.

AH 3013.15 — Landseer, J. Sabaean researches. London, 1823.

AH 3013.17A — Handcock, P.S.P. Mesopotamian archaeology. N.Y., 1912.

AH 3013.17B — Handcock, P.S.P. Mesopotamian archaeology. N.Y., 1912.

AH 3013.17C — Handcock, P.S.P. Mesopotamian archaeology. N.Y., 1912.

AH 3013.17D — Handcock, P.S.P. Mesopotamian archaeology. N.Y., 1912.

AH 3013.17E — Handcock, P.S.P. Mesopotamian archaeology. N.Y., 1912.

AH 3013.18 — Circourt, A. de. Decouvertes dans les ruines de Ninive et de Babylone. Paris, 1854.

AH 3013.19 — Kiepert, J.S.H. Begleitworte zur Karte de Ruinenfelder von Babylon. Berlin, 1883.

AH 3013.20.3 — Rich, C.J. Memoir on the ruins of Babylon. 3. ed. v.1-2. London, 1818.

AH 3013.20.7 — Rich, C.J. Narrative of a journey to the site of Babylon. London, 1839.

AH 3013.22 — Streber, F. Über die Mauern von Babylon. München, 1849.

AH 3013.23 — Smith, A. Ruins of Nineveh. n.p., 1845?

AH 3013.23.15 — Smith, G. Assyrian discoveries. N.Y., 1875.

AH 3013.24 — Eichhoff, F.G. Etudes sur Ninive et Persepolis. Lyon, 1852.

AH 3013.25 — Hoefer, J.C.F. Premier memoire sur les ruines de Ninive. Paris, 1850.

AH 3013.26 — Buckingham, J.S. The buried city of the East-Nineveh. London, 1851?

AH 3013.27.4 — Vaux, W.S.W. Nineveh and Persepolis. 4. ed. London, 1855.

AH 3013.28 — Fergusson, J. The palaces of Nineveh and Persepolis restored. London, 1851.

AH 3013.29F — Ledrain, E. Les antiquités chaldéennes du Louvre. Paris, 1882.

AH 3013.30 — Lehmann-Haupt, C.F. Materialen zur Kultur...der Chalder...Ausgrabungen. Berlin, 1901.

AH 3013.31 — Chicago, Illinois. University. Oriental Exploration Fund. Expedition of Oriental Exploration Fund (Babylonian section). Reports 1-4, 6. Chicago? 1904.

AH 3013.31.7 — Pamphlet box. Chicago, Illinois. University. Oriental Exploration Fund.

AH 3013.32 — Bonomi, J. Nineveh and its palaces. London, 1852.

AH 3013.32.3 — Bonomi, J. Nineveh and its palaces. 3. ed. London, 1875.

AH 3013.33A — Layard, A.H. Nineveh and its remains. N.Y., 1849. 2v.

AH 3013.33B — Layard, A.H. Nineveh and its remains. N.Y., 1849. 2v.

AH 3013.33.2 — Layard, A.H. Nineveh and its remains. 2. ed. London, 1849. 2v.

AH 3013.33.3 — Layard, A.H. Nineveh and its remains. N.Y., 1852.

AH 3013.33.4 — Layard, A.H. Nineveh and its remains. v.1-2. N.Y., 1853.

NEDL AH 3013.33.5 — Layard, A.H. Nineveh and its remains. 6. ed. London, 1854. 2v.

AH 3013.33.6A — Layard, A.H. Discoveries among the ruins of Nineveh and Babylon. N.Y., 1853.

AH 3013.33.6B — Layard, A.H. Discoveries among the ruins of Nineveh and Babylon. N.Y., 1853.

AH 3013.33.6C — Layard, A.H. Discoveries among the ruins of Nineveh and Babylon. N.Y., 1853.

AH 3013.33.7A — Layard, A.H. Discoveries among the ruins of Nineveh and Babylon. N.Y., 1853.

AH 3013.33.7B — Layard, A.H. Discoveries among the ruins of Nineveh and Babylon. N.Y., 1853.

AH 3013.33.8 — Layard, A.H. Discoveries among the ruins of Nineveh and Babylon. N.Y., 1853.

AH 3013.33.9 — Layard, A.H. Discoveries among the ruins of Nineveh and Babylon. 2. ed. N.Y., 1856.

AH 3013.33.10 — Layard, A.H. Nineveh and Babylon; a narrative of a second expedition to Assyria...1849, 1850 and 1851. London, 1867.

AH 3013.33.15PF — Layard, A.H. The monuments of Nineveh. London, 1849.

AH 3013.33.17PF — Layard, A.H. The monuments of Nineveh. 2d series. London, 1853.

AH 3013.33.24 — Layard, A.H. A popular account of discoveries at Nineveh. London, 1851.

AH 3013.33.25 — Layard, A.H. Popular account of discoveries at Nineveh. N.Y., 1852.

AH 3013.33.27 — Layard, A.H. A popular account of discoveries at Nineveh. N.Y., 1855.

AH 3013.35PF — Botta, P.E. Monument de Ninive. Text and plates. Paris, 1849-50. 5v.

AH 3013.35.5 — Botta, P.E. Lettres de...sur ses decouvertes a Khorsabad. Paris, 1845.

AH 3013.36PF — Place, V. Ninive et l'Assyrie. Paris, 1867. 3v.

AH 3013.37 — Peters, J.P. Nippur or explorations...on the Euphrates. N.Y., 1898. 2v.

AH 3013.38 — Oppert, J. Grundgüge des Assyrischen Kunst. Basel, 1872.

AH 3013.39PF — Pennsylvania. University. Babylonian Expeditions. Excavations at Nippur. Pt.1-2. Philadelphia, 1905.

AH 3013.40 — Rassam, H. Babylonian cities. London, 1884?

AH 3013.41 — Smith, George. Assyrian discoveries. London, 1875.

AH 3013.42F — Clercq, Louis de. Collection De Clercq. v.3-6, 7, pt.1-2. Paris, 1905-11. 6v.

AH 3013.42PF — Clercq, Louis de. Collection De Clercq. Paris, 1885-1908. 2v.

AH 3013.42.2F — Clercq, Louis de. Collection De Clercq. Paris, 1912.

AH 3013.43 — Gregory, John M. An account of the sepulchres of the antients. London, 1712.

Classified Listing

AH 3013   Countries of ancient Asia - Assyria and Babylonia - Assyro-Babylonian archaeology and art - General works (By date, e.g. .960 for 1960) - cont.

AH 3013.45PF   Sarzec, E. de. Decouvertes en Chaldée. Facsimile. Paris, 1884-93.

AH 3013.801   Hager, Joseph. A dissertation of the newly discovered Babylonian inscriptions. London, 1801.

AH 3013.855   Pillet, M. L'expedition scientifique et artistique de Mésopotamie et de Médie. Paris, 1922.

AH 3013.888   Menant, J. Les fausses antiquités de l'Assyrie et de la Chaldée. Paris, 1888.

AH 3013.907   Delitzsch, F. Mehr Licht; die bedeutsamsten Ergebnisse der babylonisch-assyrischen Grabungen für Geschichte, Kultur und Religion. Leipzig, 1907.

AH 3013.909   Assyriologische und archaeologische Studien Hermann V. Hilprecht. Leipzig, 1909.

AH 3013.912   Boissier, Alfred. Notice sur quelques monuments assyriens a l'Université de Zurich. Genève, 1912.

AH 3013.913F   Bell, Gertrude. Churches and monasteries of the Tûr 'Abdîn and neighbouring districts. Heidelberg, 1913.

AH 3013.914   Koldewey, Robert. The excavations at Babylon. London, 1914.

AH 3013.923   Lane, William H. Babylonian problems. N.Y., 1923.

AH 3013.924   Langdon, S.H. Excavations at Kish. v.1, 3, 4. Paris, 1924-34. 3v.

AH 3013.925   Koldewey, Robert. Das wieder erstehende Babylon. Leipzig, 1925.

AH 3013.925.3   Koldewey, Robert. Das wieder erstehende Babylon. 3. Aufl. Leipzig, 1914.

AH 3013.927F   Hall, Harry R. Ur excavations. v.1-10. Oxford, 1927-39. 9v.

AH 3013.928   Harvard University. Fogg Art Museum. Kirkuk excavations conducted by the Fogg Museum of Art. Preliminary report. n.p., 1928.

AH 3013.928.5.2   Harcourt-Smith, S. Babylonian art. N.Y., 1928.

AH 3013.929   Woolley, Charles L. The excavations at Ur and the Hebrew records. London, 1929.

AH 3013.929.5A   Thompson, R.C. A century of exploration at Nineveh. London, 1929.

AH 3013.929.5B   Thompson, R.C. A century of exploration at Nineveh. London, 1929.

AH 3013.929.10   Gadd, Cyril J. History and monuments of Ur. London, 1929.

AH 3013.930   Iraq. Ministry of Education. Report on excavations in Iraq during the season. Baghdad. 1928-1929

AH 3013.930.5   Woolley, Charles L. Ur of the Chaldees. Washington, 1930.

AH 3013.930.10   Woolley, Charles L. Ur of the Chaldees. N.Y., 1930.

AH 3013.931   Waterman, Leroy. Preliminary report upon excavations at Tel Umar, Iraq. Ann Arbor, 1931-33. 2v.

AH 3013.931.5   Oppenheim, Max. Der Tell Halaf. Leipzig, 1931.

AH 3013.931.10F   Tompson, Reginald C. The prisms of Esarhaddon and Ashurbanipal found at Nineveh. London, 1931.

AH 3013.935F   Jacobsen, T. Sennacherib's aqueduct at Jerwan. Chicago, 1935.

AH 3013.935.5F   Zervos, C. L'art de la Mésopotamie de la fin du quatrième millénaire au XVe siècle avant notre ère. Paris, 1935.

AH 3013.936   Lloyd, Seton. Mesopotamia. London, 1936.

AH 3013.937F   Starr, R.F.S. Nuzi; report on the excavations at Yorgan Tepa near Kirkuk, Iraq, conducted by Harvard University. Cambridge, 1937-39. 2v.

AH 3013.937.5   Cross, Dorothy. Movable property in the Nuzi documents. Diss. Philadelphia, 1937.

AH 3013.937.10   Iraq. Department of Antiquities. Guide thru the ruins of Babylon and Borsippa. Baghdad, 1937.

AH 3013.938   Unger, E. Altindogermanisches Kulturgut in Nordmesopotamien. Leipzig, 1938.

AH 3013.938.5   Busink, T.A. De Toren van Babel. Batavia, 1938.

AH 3013.940   Christian, V. Altertumskunde des Zweistromlandes von der Vorzeit bis zum Ende der Achamenidenherrschaft. v.1; pt.2. Leipzig, 1940.

AH 3013.942   Perkins, Ann L. The comparative stratigraphy of prehistoric Mesopotamia. Chicago, 1942.

AH 3013.942F   Delougaz, Pinhas. Pre-Sargonia temples in the Diyala region. Chicago, 1942.

AH 3013.942.12   Lloyd, Seton. Ruined cities of Iraq. 3. ed. London, 1945.

AH 3013.943F   Oppenheim, Max. Tell Halaf. Berlin, 1943. 4v.

AH 3013.943.5   Iraq. Department of Antiquities. Babylon. Baghdad, 1943.

AH 3013.944   Baqir, Taha. Excavations at 'Aqar Quf, 1942-1943, 1943-1944. 1st and 2nd interim report. London, 1944-45.

AH 3013.949F   Perkins, Ann L. The comparative archaeology of early Mesopotamia. Chicago, 1949.

AH 3013.949.5   Castellino, Giorgio. Corso di lezioni di assiriologia. Roma, 1949.

AH 3013.949.10   Parrot, André. Ziggurats et Tour de Babel. Paris, 1949.

AH 3013.950PF   Eliot, H.W. Excavations in Mesopotamia and Western Iran. Cambridge, 1950.

AH 3013.955   Woolley, Charles L. Excavations at Ur. London, 1955.

AH 3013.956   Pallis, Svend Aage. The antiquity of Iraq. Copenhagen, 1956.

AH 3013.958F   Chicago. University. Oriental Institute. Soundings at Tell Fakhariyah. Chicago, 1958.

AH 3013.958.10   Flittner, N.D. Kul'tura i iskusstvo Dvurech'ia. Leningrad, 1958.

AH 3013.959   Moortgat, Anton. Archäologische Forschungen der Max Freiherr von Oppenheim - Stiftung in nördlichen Mesopotamien 1956. Köln, 1959.

AH 3013.960.5   Parrot, André. Sumer. London, 1960.

AH 3013.965.5   Margueron, Jean Claude. Mesopotamia. London, 1965.

AH 3013.966   Nissen, Hans Jörg. Zur Datierung des Königsfreidhofes von Ur besonderer Berücksichtigung der Stratigraphie der Privatgräber. Bonn, 1966.

AH 3013.971   Moortgat, Anton. Einführung in die vorderasiatische Archäologie. Darmstadt, 1971.

AH 3014   Countries of ancient Asia - Assyria and Babylonia - Assyro-Babylonian archaeology and art - Architecture

AH 3014.3   Meissner, B. Noch einmal das Bît-Hillâne und assyrische Säule. Leipzig, 1893.

AH 3014.5   Bell, Edward. Early architecture in western Asia: Chaldaean, Hittite, Assyrian, Persian. London, 1924.

AH 3014.7F   Andrae, Walter. Das Gotteshaus und die Urformen des Bauens im alten Orient. Berlin, 1930.

AH 3014.15F   Martiny, G. Die Kulturichtung in Mesopotamien. Diss. Berlin, 1932.

AH 3014.16   Delougaz, Pinhas. Plano-convex bricks and the methods of their employment. Chicago, 1933.

AH 3014.17F   Heinrich, Ernst. Schilf und Lehm. Diss. Berlin, 1934.

AH 3014.19   Woolley, Charles L. The development of Sumerian art. N.Y., 1935.

AH 3014   Countries of ancient Asia - Assyria and Babylonia - Assyro-Babylonian archaeology and art - Architecture - cont.

AH 3014.21F   Delougaz, Pinhas. The temple oval at Khafâjah. Chicago, 1940.

AH 3014.23F   Frankfort, Henri. The Gimilsin temple and the palace of the rulers at Tell Asmar. Chicago, 1940.

AH 3014.25   Layard, A.H. The Nineveh court in the crystal palace. London, 1854.

AH 3014.30   Busink, T.A. Die Babylonische Tempeltoren. Leiden, 1949.

AH 3016   Countries of ancient Asia - Assyria and Babylonia - Assyro-Babylonian archaeology and art - Sculpture

AH 3016.5   Descemet, C. Bas-reliefs assyriens. Rome, 1883.

X Cg   AH 3016.7   Meissner, Bruno. Grundzüge der babylonisch-assyrischen Plastik. Leipzig, 1915.

AH 3016.7.5F   Meissner, Bruno. Die babylonischen Kleinplastiken. Leipzig, 1934.

AH 3016.9F   British Museum. Department of Egyptian and Assyrian Antiquities. Assyrian sculptures in British Museum. London, 1914.

AH 3016.13F   Gadd, C.J. The stones of Assyria. London, 1936.

AH 3016.15F   Van Buren, Elizabeth D. Foundation figurines and offerings. Berlin, 1931.

AH 3016.25   Van Buren, Elizabeth D. The flowing vase and the god with streams. Berlin, 1933.

AH 3016.30   Frankfort, Henri. Sculpture of the third millennium B.C. from Tell Asmar and Khafâjah. Chicago, 1939.

AH 3016.35F   Frankfort, Henri. More sculpture from the Diyala region. Chicago, 1943.

AH 3016.40   Loseva, I.M. Iskusstvo drevnei Mesopotamii; ocherki. Moskva, 1946.

AH 3016.45   Contenau, Georges. Monuments mésopotamiens. Paris, 1934.

AH 3016.48   Schnitzler, Ludwig. Frühe Plastik im Zweistromland. 1. Aufl. Stuttgart, 1959.

AH 3016.50F   Hall, Harry R. Babylonian and Assyrian sculpture in the British Museum. Paris, 1928.

AH 3016.52   Barnett, Richard. Assyrian palace reliefs and their influence on the sculptures of Babylonia and Persia. London, 1960.

AH 3016.55   Moortgat, Anton. Tammuz. Berlin, 1949.

AH 3016.58   Potratz, J.A.H. Die menschliche Rundskulptur in der sumero-akkadischen Kunst. Istanbul, 1960.

AH 3017   Countries of ancient Asia - Assyria and Babylonia - Assyro-Babylonian archaeology and art - Other special

Htn   AH 3017.4F*   Morgan, John P. Cylinders and oriental seals in library. N.Y., 1909.

AH 3017.5F   Heuzey, L. La stèle des vautours. Paris, 1884.

AH 3017.6F   Fischer, H. Über Babylonische "Talismane". Stuttgart, 1881.

AH 3017.7   Menant, J. Recherches sur la glyphique orientale. Pt.1-2. Paris, 1883. 2v.

AH 3017.7.5   Menant, J. Notice sur quelques empreintes de cylindres. Paris, 1879.

AH 3017.7.9   Menant, J. Empreintes de cylindres assyro-chaldéens. Paris, 1880.

AH 3017.7.11F   Menant, J. Catalogue des cylindres orientaux du cabinet royal des medailles de la Haye. La Haye, 1878.

AH 3017.7.12   Menant, J. Les cylindres orientaux. Paris, 1879.

AH 3017.7.15   Menant, J. Notice sur quelques cylindres orientaux. Paris, 1878.

AH 3017.7.18   Menant, J. Observations sur trois cylindres orientaux. Paris, 1880.

AH 3017.8.1   Frankfort, Henri. Cylinder seals. Furnborough, 1965.

AH 3017.9   Cullimore, A. Oriental cylinders. London, 1842.

AH 3017.10   Le Brun-Dalbanne. De l'intérêt de pierres gravées. Besançon, 1872.

AH 3017.11   Heidenreich, R. Beiträge zur Geschichte der vorderasiatischen Steinschneidekunst. Inaug. Diss. Heidelberg, 1925.

AH 3017.15.1   Steinmetzer, Franz Xaver. Die babylonischen Kudurru (Grenzsteine) als Urkundenform. Paderborn, 1968.

AH 3017.19   Brussels. Musée des Arts Décoratifs et Industriels. Catalogue des intailles et empreintes orientales des Musées royaux du cinquantenaire. Bruxelles, 1917.

AH 3017.25   Waddell, L.A. The Indo-Sumerian seals deciphered. London, 1925.

AH 3017.27   Gadd, Cyril J. Seals of ancient Indian style found at Ur. London, 1933.

AH 3017.30F   Andrae, W. Farbige Keramik aus Assur und ihre Vorstafen in altassyrischen Wandmalereien. Berlin, 1923.

AH 3017.35   Rome (City). Pontificio Instituto Biblico. The cylinder seals of the Pontifical Institute. Roma, 1940.

AH 3017.40   Pierpont Morgan Library, New York. Mesopotamian art in cylinder seals of the Pierpont Morgan Library. N.Y., 1947.

AH 3017.45   Borowski, E. Cylindres et cachets orientaux conservés dans la collection suisses. Ascona, 1947.

AH 3017.49   Gudea, patesi of Lagash. Die Inschriften Gudeas von Lagaš. Roma, 1966.

AH 3017.50   Falkenstein, Adams. Grammatik der Sprache Gudeas von Lagaš. Roma, 1949-50. 2v.

AH 3017.55   Van Buren, Elizabeth D. The fauna of ancient Mesopotamia as represented in art. Roma, 1939.

AH 3017.60   Hague. Kabinet van Munten. Catalogue sommaire des cylindres orientaux au Cabinet. La Haye, 1952.

AH 3017.65   Limet, Henri. Le travail du métal au pays de Sumer au temps de la III dynastie d'Ur. Paris, 1960.

AH 3017.70F   Ravn, Otto E. A catalogue of oriental cylinder seals and seal impressions in the Danish National Museum. København, 1960.

AH 3017.75F   Amiet, Pierre. La glyphique mesopotamienne archaïque. Paris, 1961.

AH 3017.80   Hilzheimer, Max. Animal remains from Tell Asmar. Chicago, 1941.

AH 3017.85   Moortgat, Anton. Vorderasiatische Rollsiegel; ein Beitrag zur Geschichte der Steinschneidekunst. 2. Aufl. Berlin, 1966.

AH 3018   Countries of ancient Asia - Assyria and Babylonia - History by periods - Before 1300 B.C. - Mythical rulers

AH 3018.3F   Lenormant, F. La legende de Sémiramis - mythologie comparative. Bruxelles, 1873.

AH 3018.5   Lehmann-Haupt, C.F. Die historische Semiramis und ihre Zeit. Tübingen, 1910.

Classified Listing

AH 3020 Countries of ancient Asia - Assyria and Babylonia - History by periods - Before 1300 B.C. - Sources and documents

AH 3020.01   Pamphlet box. Babylonia and Assyria. Period of 1st Babylonian supremacy.

AH 3020.3   Legrain, L. Le temps des rois d'Ur. Text and plates. Paris, 1912. 2v.

AH 3020.4   Thureau-Dangin, F. Die sumerische und akkadischen Königsinschriften. Leipzig, 1907.

AH 3020.5   Haupt, Paul. Die sumerischen Familiengesetze. Leipzig, 1879.

AH 3020.6   Margolis, E. Sumerian temple documents. N.Y., 1915.

AH 3020.7F   John Rylands Library. Manchester. Sumerian tablets from Umma. Manchester, 1915.

AH 3020.7.10   John Rylands Library. Manchester. Catalogue of Sumerian tablets in the John Rylands Library. Manchester, 1932.

AH 3020.8   Ungnad, A. Babylonische Briefe aus der Zeit der Hammurapidynastie. Leipzig, 1914.

AH 3020.9PF   Heuzey, Léon A. Restitution matérielle de la stèle des vautours. Paris, 1909.

AH 3020.10FA   Harvard University. Semitic Museum. Sumerian tablets in the Harvard Semitic Museum. Pt.1-2. Cambridge, Mass., 1912. 2v.

AH 3020.10FB   Harvard University. Semitic Museum. Sumerian tablets in the Harvard Semitic Museum. Cambridge, Mass., 1912.

AH 3020.11   Jean, Charles Francois. Sumer et Akkad. Paris, 1923.

AH 3020.13A   Chiera, Edward. Excavations at Nuzi. v.2-8. Cambridge, 1932-62. 7v.

AH 3020.13B   Chiera, Edward. Excavations at Nuzi. v.8. Cambridge, 1962.

AH 3020.13.7   Pfeiffer, R.H. Nuzi and the Hurrians. Washington, 1936.

AH 3020.13.9A   Pfeiffer, R.H. One hundred new selected Nuzi texts. n.p., 1936.

AH 3020.13.9B   Pfeiffer, R.H. One hundred new selected Nuzi texts. n.p., 1936.

AH 3020.14   Lutz, H.F. Sumerian temple records of the late Ur dynasty. Berkeley, 1928.

AH 3020.15F   Chiera, Edward. Sumerian lexical texts from the temple school of Nippur. Chicago, 1929.

AH 3020.16F   Chiera, Edward. Sumerian epics and myths. Chicago, 1934.

AH 3020.17F   Chiera, Edward. Sumerian texts of varied contents. Chicago, 1934.

AH 3020.18F   Allotte de la Fuÿe, Francois N. Documents présargoniques. Paris, 1908-20. 5v.

AH 3020.19F   Pohl, A. Vorsargonische und sargonische Wirtschaftstexte. Leipzig, 1935.

AH 3020.20   Steele, Francis Rue. Nuzi real estate transactions. Thesis. Philadelphia, 1943.

AH 3020.22.1   King, Leonard W. Chronicles concerning early Babylonian kings. v.1-2. London, 1972.

AH 3020.23   Jestin, Raymond. Textes économiques sumériens de la 11e dynastie d'Ur. Paris, 1935.

AH 3020.25F   Sollberger, E. Corpus des inscriptions royales présargoniques de Lagas. Genève, 1956.

AH 3020.28   Istanbul. Asari atika Müzeleri. Nouvelles tablettes sumeriennes. Paris, 1957.

AH 3020.30   Jones, Tom B. Sumerian economic texts from the third Ur dynasty. Minneapolis, 1961.

AH 3020.40   Çiğ, Muazzez. Yeni Sumer çağina ait Nippur hukukî ve idarî belgeleri. Ankara, 1965.

AH 3020.40.5   Çiğ, Muazzez. Eski Babill zamanina ait Nippur menşeli iki okul kitabi. Ankara, 1959.

AH 3020.45   Iankovskaia, N.B. Klinopisnye teksty iz Koul'-Tepe v sobraniiakh SSSR. Moskva, 1968.

AH 3020.50   Rosengarten, Yvonne. Répertoire commenté des signes présargoniques sumériens de Lagaš. Paris, 1967.

AH 3020.55   Virolleaud, Charles. Tablettes économiques de Lagash (époque de la IIIe dynastie d'Ur). Paris, 1968.

AH 3020.55.5   Bauer, Josef. Altsumerische Wirtschaftstexte aus Lagasch. Rome, 1972.

AH 3020.70   Sauren, Herbert. Wirtschaftsurkunden aus der Zeit der III. Dynastie von Ur im Besitz des Musée d'Art et d'Histoire in Genf. Napoli, 1969.

AH 3020.75   Çiğ, Muazzez. Istanbul arkeoloji müzelerinde bulunan Sumer edebi tablet parçalari. Ankara, 1969.

AH 3020.76   Sumerian and Akkadian cuneiform texts in the collection of the World Heritage Museum of the University of Illinois. Urbana, 1972. 2v.

AH 3021 Countries of ancient Asia - Assyria and Babylonia - History by periods - Before 1300 B.C. - General histories

AH 3021.2A   Ragozin, Zénaide A. The story of the nations: story of Chaldea. N.Y., 1886.

AH 3021.2B   Ragozin, Zénaide A. The story of the nations: story of Chaldea. N.Y., 1886.

AH 3021.2.5   Ragozin, Zénaide A. The story of Chaldea. 2. ed. N.Y., 1890.

AH 3021.2.10   Ragozin, Zénaide A. The story of Chaldea from the earliest times to the rise of Assyria. 2. ed. N.Y., 1896.

AH 3021.3   Radar, H. Early Babylonian history. N.Y., 1899.

AH 3021.3.3   Radar, H. Early Babylonian history. N.Y., 1900.

AH 3021.4   Boscawen, W. St. C. The first of empires. London, 1903.

AH 3021.21   Edzard, Dietz O. Die "zweite Zwischenzeit" Babyloniens. Wiesbaden, 1957.

AH 3022 Countries of ancient Asia - Assyria and Babylonia - History by periods - Before 1300 B.C. - Sumer and Akkad - General works

AH 3022.5   King, Leonard W. A history of Sumer and Akkad. N.Y., 1910?

AH 3022.7   Gadd, C.J. The early dynasties of Sumer and Akkad. London, 1921.

AH 3022.9A   Woolley, Charles L. The Sumerians. Oxford, 1928.

AH 3022.9B   Woolley, Charles L. The Sumerians. Oxford, 1928.

AH 3022.11   Pallis, Svend Aage. Chronology of the Shuk-ad culture. Kobenhavn, 1941.

AH 3022.15   Aldrey Pereira, M.L. Pensamiento idiomatico šumero-akkadico. Series 1. v.1, pt.1-2. Madrid, 1953. 2v.

AH 3022.17   Kramer, S.N. From the tablets of Sumer. Indian Hills, 1956.

AH 3022.17.5   Kramer, S.N. Dve elegii na tablichke muzeia im A.S. Pushkina. Moskva, 1960.

AH 3022.17.10   Kramer, S.N. The Sumerians: their history. Chicago, 1963.

AH 3022.20   D'iakonov, I.M. Obshchestvennyi i gosudarstvennyi stroi drevnego Dvurech'ia. Moskva, 1959.

AH 3022.24   Resina, Guiseppe. Sumer e Akkad; la vita economica. Catania, 1958.

AH 3022.25   Rosengarten, Yvonne. Le concept sumérien de consommation. Paris, 1960.

AH 3022 Countries of ancient Asia - Assyria and Babylonia - History by periods - Before 1300 B.C. - Sumer and Akkad - General works - cont.

AH 3022.26   Rosengarten, Yvonne. Le regime des offrandes dans la société sumerienne d'après les textes présargoniques de Lagas. Paris, 1960.

AH 3022.27   Ankara. Universite. Sümeroloji arastirmalari, 1940-1941. Istanbul, 1941.

AH 3022.28   Cottrell, Leonard. The land of Shinar. London, 1965.

AH 3022.29   Schmökel, Hartmut. Das Land Sumer. 2. Aufl. Stuttgart, 1956.

AH 3022.30   Mallowan, Max Edgar. Early Mesopotamia and Iran. N.Y., 1965.

AH 3022.38   Pettinato, Giovanni. Untersuchungen zur neusumarischen Landwirtschaft. Napoli, 1967.

AH 3024 Countries of ancient Asia - Assyria and Babylonia - History by periods - Before 1300 B.C. - Sumer and Akkad - Sargon I of Akkad, ca. 2637-2582

AH 3024.5   Weidner, Ernst F. Der Zug Sargons von Akkad nach Kleinasien. Leipzig, 1922.

AH 3027 Countries of ancient Asia - Assyria and Babylonia - History by periods - Before 1300 B.C. - Amorites, ca. 2050-1750 - General works

AH 3027.5F   Bauer, Theo. Die Oskanaanäer. Leipzig, 1926.

AH 3027.10   Buccellati, Biorgio. The Amorites of the Ur III period. Naples, 1966.

AH 3027.11   Haldar, Alfred Ossian. Who were the Amorites? Leiden, 1971.

AH 3028 Countries of ancient Asia - Assyria and Babylonia - History by periods - Before 1300 B.C. - Amorites, ca. 2050-1750 - General special

AH 3028.5   Clay, A.T. The antiquity of Amorite civilization. New Haven, 1924.

AH 3030 Countries of ancient Asia - Assyria and Babylonia - History by periods - Before 1300 B.C. - Amorites, ca. 2050-1750 - Hammurabi, ca. 1955-1913

AH 3030.3   King, L.W. Letters and inscriptions of Hammourabi. London, 1898-1900. 3v.

AH 3030.4   Menant, J. Inscriptions de Hammourabi. Paris, 1863.

AH 3030.4.5F   Menant, J. Une novelle inscription de Hammourabi. Paris, 1880.

AH 3030.5   Schnöbel, Hartmut. Hammurabi von Babylon. München, 1958.

AH 3037 Countries of ancient Asia - Assyria and Babylonia - History by periods - Before 1300 B.C. - Assyria before ca. 1300 - General works

AH 3037.5   Smith, S.M.A. Early history of Assyria to 1000 B.C. London, 1928.

AH 3038 Countries of ancient Asia - Assyria and Babylonia - History by periods - Before 1300 B.C. - Assyria before ca. 1300 - Special events, etc.

AH 3038.5   Jawal, Abd al-Jalil. The advent of the era of townships in northern Mesopotamia. Leiden, 1965.

AH 3041 - 3066 Countries of ancient Asia - Assyria and Babylonia - History by periods - Before 1300 B.C. - Local (A-Z by place)

AH 3041.2   Mueller, Manfred. Die Erlässe und Instruktionen aus dem Lande Arrapha, ein Beitrag zur Rechtsgeschichte des Alten Vorderen Orients. Inaug. Diss. Leipzig? 1968?

AH 3042.3   Baermstark, A. Babylon zur Stadtgeschichte. Stuttgart, 1896.

AH 3042.3.5   McGee, D.G. De topographia urbis Babylonis. Lipsiae, 1895.

AH 3042.3.10   Unger, Eckhard. Babylon. Berlin, 1931.

AH 3042.3.12   Unger, Eckhard. Babylon. 2e Aufl. Berlin, 1970.

AH 3044.2F   Adams, Robert McCormick. Land behind Bagyhdad. Chicago, 1965.

AH 3044.3   Delougaz, Pinhas. Private houses and graves in the Digala region. Chicago, 1967.

AH 3045.5F   Jordan, J. Dritter vorläufiger Bericht über die von der Notgemeinschaft die deutschen Wissenschaft in Uruk unternommenen Ausgrabungen. Berlin, 1932.

AH 3045.5.5F   Deutsches Archäologisches Institut. Vorläufiger Bericht über die von dem Deutschen Archäologischen Institut und der Deutschen Orient-Gesellschaft aus Mitteln der Deutschen Forschungsgemeinschaft unternommenen Ausgrabungen in Uruk-Warka. Berlin. 12,1953+ 9v.

AH 3045.10   Bohtz, C. Helmut. In den Ruinen von Warka. Leipzig, 1941.

AH 3045.15   Keiser, Helen. Die Stadt der Grossen Götin 4000 Jahre Uruk. Olten, 1967.

AH 3045.20   Adams, Robert McCormick. The Uruk countryside. Chicago, 1972.

AH 3045.100.5   Eshnunna. Laws, statutes, etc. The laws of Eshnunna. Jerusalem, 1969.

AH 3045.150   Segal, Judah B. Edessa and Harran. London, 1963.

AH 3046.5F   Heinrich, Ernst. Fara; Ergebnisse der Ausgrabungen der Deutschen Orient-Gesellschaft in Fara. Berlin, 1931.

AH 3051.5F   Genouillac, H. de. Premières recherches archéologiques à Kich. Paris, 1924.

AH 3052.3F   Allotte, C. Les sceaux de Longalanda. Paris, 1907.

AH 3052.5A   Price, I.M. Some literary remains of Rim-Sin...king of Larsa. Chicago, 1904.

AH 3052.5B   Price, I.M. Some literary remains of Rim-Sin...king of Larsa. Chicago, 1904.

AH 3052.5.5   Walters, Stanley D. Water for Larsa; an old Babylonian archive dealing with irrigation. New Haven, 1970.

AH 3052.6   Grégoire, J.P. La province méridionale de l'état de Lagash. Luxembourg, 1962.

AH 3052.6.5   Struve, Vasilii V. Gosudarstvo Lagash. Moskva, 1961.

AH 3052.9F   Toscanne, P. Les cylindres de Gudéa. Paris, 1901.

AH 3053.5   Iahdun-Lim, king of Mari. L'inscription de fondation de Iahdun-Lim, roi de Mari. Paris, 1955.

AH 3053.10   Reinaud, Joseph T. Mémoire sur le commencement et la fin de la Mésène et de la Kharacène. Paris, 1861.

AH 3054.5   McCown, Donald E. Nippur; excavations at the site of the Joint Expedition to Nippur of the University Museum of Philadelphia and the Oriental Institute of the University of Chicago. Chicago, 1967-

AH 3054.10   Dietrich, Manfried. Nuzi-Bibliographie. Kevelaer, 1972.

AH 3054.10.5   Eichler, Barry L. Indenture at Nuzi. New Haven, 1973.

AH 3059.5   Billerbeck, A. Das Sandschak Suliemania. Leipzig, 1898.

AH 3059.7   Fabian, E.A. De Seleucia Babylonia. Lipsiae, 1869.

AH 3059.7.5   McDowell, R.H. Stamped and inscribed objects from Seleucia. Ann Arbor, 1935.

AH 3059.7.10   Van Ingen, W. Figurines from Seleucia on the Tigris. Ann Arbor, 1939.

AH 3060.3   Heuzey, L. Un nouveau roi de Tello. Paris, 1884.

AH 3060.3.5   Heuzey, L. Un palais Chaldéen. Paris, 1888.

AH 3060.3.9   Heuzey, L. Une villa royal Chaldéenne. Paris, 1900.

X Cg   AH 3060.3.13F   Cros, Gaston. Nouvelle fouilles de Tello. Paris, 1910-14.

Classified Listing

AH 3041 - 3066   Countries of ancient Asia - Assyria and Babylonia - History by periods - Before 1300 B.C. - Local (A-Z by place) - cont.

AH 3060.3.15F Barton, George A. Haverford Library collection of cuneiform tablets. New Haven, 1918. 3v.

AH 3060.3.20 Parrot, André. Tello. Paris, 1948.

AH 3061.1 Contenau, Georges. Contribution à l'histoire économique d'Umma. Paris, 1915.

AH 3061.2 Contenau, Georges. Umma sous la dynastie d'Ur. Paris, 1916.

AH 3061.5 Sauren, Herbert. Topographie der Provinz Umma nach den Urkunden der Zeit der III. Dynastie von Ur. Bamberg, 1966.

AH 3073   Countries of ancient Asia - Assyria and Babylonia - History by periods - 1300-606 B.C. - Sources and documents - Collected

AH 3073.3A Kellner, M. The Assyrian monuments illustrating sermons of Isaiah. Boston, 1900.

AH 3073.3B Kellner, M. The Assyrian monuments illustrating sermons of Isaiah. Boston, 1900.

AH 3073.3.5 Kellner, M. The prophecies of Isaiah. Cambridge, 1895.

AH 3073.4 Smith, S.A. Miscellaneous Assyrian texts on the British Museum. Leipzig, 1887.

AH 3073.5 Menant, J. Annales des rois d'Assyrie. Paris, 1874.

AH 3073.7 Klauber, Ernst. Politisch-religiöse Texte aus der Sargonidenzeit. Leipzig, 1913.

AH 3074   Countries of ancient Asia - Assyria and Babylonia - History by periods - 1300-606 B.C. - Sources and documents - Individual

AH 3074.5F British Museum. Photograph of Assyrian tablet. London, n.d.

AH 3075   Countries of ancient Asia - Assyria and Babylonia - History by periods - 1300-606 B.C. - General histories

AH 3075.2 Cooper, William R. The resurrection of Assyria. London, 1875.

AH 3075.3 Smith, George. Ancient history...Assyria. London, 1875.

AH 3075.3.2 Smith, George. Assyria from the earliest time to the fall of Nineveh. London, 1875.

AH 3075.3.3 Smith, George. Ancient history...Asyria. N.Y., 1876.

NEDL AH 3075.4 Massaroli, G. Phiel e Tuklatpalasar II. Roma, 1882.

AH 3075.5 Strauss, Otto. Ninive und das Wort Gottes. Berlin, 1855.

AH 3075.6 Sayce, A.H. Assyria, its princes, priests and people. London, 1885.

AH 3075.7 Robertson, H.S. Voices of the past from Assyria and Babylonia. London, 1900.

AH 3075.8 Bible. Prophets. The prophecies relating to Nineveh and the Assyrians. London, 1857.

AH 3075.9 Breiteneicher, M. Ninive und Nahum. München, 1861.

AH 3075.10 Ragozin, Z.A. The story of the nations: story of Assyria. N.Y., 1887.

AH 3075.11 Naster, Paul. L'Asie Mineure et l'Assyrie aux VIIIe et VIIe siècles avant Jésus Christ. Louvain, 1938.

AH 3075.12 Maspero, Gaston. Histoire ancienne, Égypte, Assyrie; lectures historiques. Paris, 1890.

AH 3075.13 Olmstead, Albert T. History of Assyria. N.Y., 1923.

AH 3075.14 Brinkman, J.A. A political history of post-Kassite Babylonia, 1158-722 B.C. Roma, 1968.

AH 3084   Countries of ancient Asia - Assyria and Babylonia - History by periods - 1300-606 B.C. - Special reigns and events - Tiglath-Pileser I, ca. 1140-1105

AH 3084.3A Lotz, W. Die Inschriften Tiglathpileser's. Leipzig, 1880.

AH 3084.3B Lotz, W. Die Inschriften Tiglathpileser's. Leipzig, 1880.

AH 3086   Countries of ancient Asia - Assyria and Babylonia - History by periods - 1300-606 B.C. - Special reigns and events - Tugulti-Ninip II, ca. 889-885

AH 3086.5 Annales de Tukulti Ninip II. Paris, 1909.

AH 3087   Countries of ancient Asia - Assyria and Babylonia - History by periods - 1300-606 B.C. - Special reigns and events - Asshurnazirpal III, ca. 885-860

AH 3087.3 Le Gag, Y. Les inscriptions d'Assur Nasir Aplu III. Paris, 1907.

AH 3088   Countries of ancient Asia - Assyria and Babylonia - History by periods - 1300-606 B.C. - Special reigns and events - Shalmaneser III (II), ca. 860-825

AH 3088.3 Rasmussen, N. Salmanasser den II's Indskrifter. Kjøbenhavn, 1897.

AH 3088.4PF Birch, S. Bronze ornaments of the Gates of Balawat. London, 1880.

AH 3088.5F King, L.W. Bronze reliefs from the Gates of Shalmaneser. London, 1915.

AH 3088.10 Shalmaneser II, king of Assyria. Les inscriptions de Salmanasar II, roi d'Assyrie, 860-824. Paris, 1890.

AH 3089   Countries of ancient Asia - Assyria and Babylonia - History by periods - 1300-606 B.C. - Special reigns and events - Shamshi-Ramman IV, 824-811

AH 3089.3 Schell, P. Inscription Assyrienne...de Sämší-Ramman IV. Paris, 1889.

AH 3092   Countries of ancient Asia - Assyria and Babylonia - History by periods - 1300-606 B.C. - Special reigns and events - Tiglath-Pileser IV, 745-728

AH 3092.2 Rost, P. Die Keilschrifttexte Tiglat-Pilesers III. Leipzig, 1893. 2v.

AH 3092.3 Schrader, E. Zur Kritik der Inschriften Tiglath-Pilesers II des Asarhaddon. Berlin, 1880.

AH 3094   Countries of ancient Asia - Assyria and Babylonia - History by periods - 1300-606 B.C. - Special reigns and events - Sargon II, 722-705

AH 3094.3F Lyon, D.G. Die Cylinder-Inschrift Sargons II. Leipzig, 1882.

AH 3094.4F Oppert, J. Les fastes de Sargon roi d'Assyrie. Paris, 1863. 2 pam.

AH 3094.4.2F Oppert, J. Les fastes de Sargon roi d'Assyrie. Paris, 1863.

AH 3094.5F Menant, J. Inscriptions...du palais de Khorsabad. Paris, 1865.

NEDL AH 3094.6F Winckler, Hugo. Die Keilschrifttexte Sargons. Leipzig, 1889.

AH 3094.6.5 Sargon, king of Assyria. De inscriptione Sargonis. Berolini, 1886.

AH 3095   Countries of ancient Asia - Assyria and Babylonia - History by periods - 1300-606 B.C. - Special reigns and events - Sennacherib, 705-681

AH 3095.3 Meissner, B. Die Bauinschriften Sanheribs. Leipzig, 1893.

AH 3095.4 Hoerning, K.J.R. Das sechsseitige Prisma des Sanherib. Leipzig, 1878.

AH 3095.5 Pognon, H. L'inscription de Bavian. Paris, 1879.

AH 3095.6 Smith, George. History of Sennacherib. London, 1878.

AH 3095.7F Sennacherib, king of Assyria. The annals of Sennacherib. Chicago, 1924.

AH 3095.8 Sennacherib, king of Assyria. The first campaign of Sennacherib. London, 1921.

AH 3095.10 Dietrich, Manfried. Die Aramäer Südbabyloniens in der Sargonidenzeit, 700-648. Kevelaer, 1970.

AH 3096   Countries of ancient Asia - Assyria and Babylonia - History by periods - 1300-606 B.C. - Special reigns and events - Esarhaddon, 681-668

AH 3096.3 Scheil, V. Le prisme d'Assaraddon...681-668. Paris, 1914.

AH 3096.4 Budge, E.A. The history of Esarhaddon...681-668. London, 1880.

AH 3096.5 Schmidtke, Friedrich. Asarhaddons Statthalterschaft in Babylonien und seine Thronbesteigung in Assyrien. Inaug. Diss. Leiden, 1916.

AH 3096.6 Hirschberg, Hans. Studien zur Geschichte Esarhaddons König von Assyrien (681-669). Inaug. Diss. Ohlau, 1932.

AH 3096.7 Esarhaddon, king of Assyria. Cylinder A of the Esarhaddon inscriptions. New Haven, 1888.

AH 3096.8 Esarhaddon, king of Assyria. The Vassal-treaties of Esarhaddon. London, 1958.

AH 3096.10 Parpola, Simo. Letters from Assyrian scholars to the Kings Esarhaddon and Assurbanipal. Neukirchen-Vluyn, 1970.

AH 3097   Countries of ancient Asia - Assyria and Babylonia - History by periods - 1300-606 B.C. - Special reigns and events - Asshurbanipal, 668-625

AH 3097.3 Lau, R.J. The annals of Ashurbanapal. Leiden, 1903.

AH 3097.4 Smith, George. History of Assurbanipal. Leiden, 1871.

AH 3097.5 Streck, Maximilian. Assurbanipal und die letzen assyrischen Könige. Leipzig, 1916. 3v.

AH 3097.6 Ashurbanapal, king of Assyria. Editions E, B and K of the annals of Ashurbanipal. Diss. Chicago, 1933.

AH 3097.7 Ashurbanapal, king of Assyria. Le prisme du Louvre AO 19.939. Paris, 1957.

AH 3098   Countries of ancient Asia - Assyria and Babylonia - History by periods - 1300-606 B.C. - Special reigns and events - Decline and fall of Nineveh, 625-606

AH 3098.3 Koopmans, W.C. Disputatio historico-critica de Sardanapalo. Amsterdam, 1819.

AH 3100   Countries of ancient Asia - Assyria and Babylonia - History by periods - 1300-606 B.C. - Babylonia during 1300-606 - Special events, etc.

AH 3100.5 al-Ahmad, Sami S. Southern Mesopotamia in the time of Ashurbanipal. The Hague, 1968.

AH 3103   Countries of ancient Asia - Assyria and Babylonia - History by periods - 1300-606 B.C. - Special topics for Assyria - Civilization

NEDL AH 3103.3 Gosse, P.H. Assyria: her manners, customs. London, 1852.

AH 3103.4 Maspero, G. Life in ancient Egypt and Assyria. N.Y., 1899.

AH 3103.6 Harkness, M.E. Assyrian life and history. London, 1883.

AH 3105   Countries of ancient Asia - Assyria and Babylonia - History by periods - 1300-606 B.C. - Special topics for Assyria - Government and administration - General works

AH 3105.5A Pfeiffer, R.H. State letters of Assyria. New Haven, 1935.

AH 3105.5B Pfeiffer, R.H. State letters of Assyria. New Haven, 1935.

AH 3107   Countries of ancient Asia - Assyria and Babylonia - History by periods - 1300-606 B.C. - Special topics for Assyria - Government and administration - Special topics

AH 3107.01 Pamphlet box. Babylonia and Assyria.

AH 3107.3 Oberziner, L.A. Divisione politica e militare dell'antica Assiria. Trento, 1884.

AH 3107.5 Godbey, A.H. Notes on some officials of the Sargonid period. Chicago, 1906.

AH 3107.7 Forrer, Emil. Die Provinzeiteilung des assyrischen Reiches. Leipzig, 1920.

AH 3109   Countries of ancient Asia - Assyria and Babylonia - History by periods - 1300-606 B.C. - Special topics for Assyria - Chronology

AH 3109.3 Brandis, J. Rerum Assyriarum tempora emendata. Bonn, 1853.

AH 3109.4F Haerdtl, E. Astronomische Beiträge zur assyrischen Chronologie. Wien, 1884.

AH 3109.5 Bosanquet, J.W. The fall of Nineveh and the reign of Sennacherib chronologically considered. London, 1853.

AH 3109.6 Smith, George. Assyrian Eponym Canon. London, 1875.

AH 3110   Countries of ancient Asia - Assyria and Babylonia - History by periods - 1300-606 B.C. - Special topics for Assyria - Law - General works

AH 3110.5 San Nicoló, Mariano. Beiträge zur Rechtsgeschichte im Brereiche der keilschriftlichen Rechtsquellen. Cambridge, 1931.

AH 3123   Countries of ancient Asia - Assyria and Babylonia - History by periods - 1300-606 B.C. - Special topics for Assyria - Private life - Documents - Collected

AH 3123.6 Virolleaud, C. Comptabilité Chaldienne. Poitiers, 1903.

AH 3123.8 Meek, Theophile J. Old Babylonian business and legal documents. Thesis. Chicago, 1917.

AH 3125   Countries of ancient Asia - Assyria and Babylonia - History by periods - 1300-606 B.C. - Special topics for Assyria - Private life - General works

AH 3125.3 Glimpses of Nineveh. N.Y., 1857.

AH 3127   Countries of ancient Asia - Assyria and Babylonia - History by periods - 1300-606 B.C. - Special topics for Assyria - Private life - Special topics

AH 3127.5 Oppert, J. L'Etalon des mesures Assyriennes. Paris, 1875.

AH 3129   Countries of ancient Asia - Assyria and Babylonia - History by periods - 605-538 B.C. - Sources and documents

AH 3129.3 Langdon, S. Building inscriptions of the Neo-Babylonian Empire: Nabopolassar and Nebuchadnezzar. Paris, 1905.

AH 3129.3.5 Langdon, S. Die neubabylonischen Königsinschriften. Leipzig, 1912.

AH 3129.7 Moore, Ellen W. Neo-Babylonian business and administrative documents. Ann Arbor, 1935.

Classified Listing

AH 3129   Countries of ancient Asia - Assyria and Babylonia - History by periods - 605-538 B.C. - Sources and documents - cont.
AH 3129.7.5A   Moore, Ellen W. Neo-Babylonian documents in the University of Michigan collection. Ann Arbor, 1939.
AH 3129.7.5B   Moore, Ellen W. Neo-Babylonian documents in the University of Michigan collection. Ann Arbor, 1939.
AH 3129.8   Berger, Paul. Die neubabylonischen Königsinschriften. Kevelaer, 1973-

AH 3132   Countries of ancient Asia - Assyria and Babylonia - History by periods - 605-538 B.C. - Special reigns and events - Nebuchadnezzar, 605-562
AH 3132.3   O'Connor, J.F.X. Cuneiform text...cylinder of Nebuchadnezzar. n.p., 1885.
AH 3132.4F   Hasse, G.R. Dissertatio de prima Nebucednezaris adversus Hierosolyma expeditione. Bonn, 1856.
AH 3132.5   Hilprecht, H.V. Freibrief Nebukadnezars I. Leipzig, 1883.
AH 3132.6   Buchwald, R. Nebuchodnosor II von Babylon. n.p., 1898.
AH 3132.7   Grotefend, G.F. Erläuterung zweier Ausschreiben des Königes Nebukadnezar. Göttingen, 1853.
AH 3132.8   Bernstein, G. König Nebucadnezar von Babel in der judischen Tradition. Berlin, 1907.

AH 3133   Countries of ancient Asia - Assyria and Babylonia - History by periods - 605-538 B.C. - Special reigns and events - Amel Marduk, 562-560
AH 3133.1   Sack, Ronald Herbert. Amel-Marduk, 562-560 B.C. Kevelaer, 1972.

AH 3135   Countries of ancient Asia - Assyria and Babylonia - History by periods - 605-538 B.C. - Special reigns and events - Nabonidus, 556-539
AH 3135.3   Nabonidus king of Babylonia. Leiden, 1905.

AH 3140   Countries of ancient Asia - Assyria and Babylonia - History by periods - 538 B.C. - 650 A.D. - Sources and documents
AH 3140.3   Demuth, L. Fünfzig babylonische Rechts- und Verwaltungsurkunden. Leipzig, 1896.
AH 3140.4   Lincke, A.A. Assyrien und Ninive...Mittelmeervölker. Berlin, 1894.

AH 3142   Countries of ancient Asia - Assyria and Babylonia - History by periods - 538 B.C. - 650 A.D. - Special events, etc.
AH 3142.3   Rothstein, G. Die Dynastie der Lahmiden in al-Hira. Halle, 1898.
AH 3142.3.3   Rothstein, G. Die Dynastie der Lahmiden in al-Hira. Berlin, 1899.
AH 3142.4   Lamy, T.J. Concilium Seleuciae et Ctesiphonti Habitum. Levanii, 1868.
AH 3142.17   Cardascia, Guillaume. Les archives des Murašû, une famille d'hommes d'affaires babyloniens à l'époque perse (455-403 avant J.C.). Paris, 1951.
AH 3142.20   Weisberg, David B. Guild structure and political allegiance in early Achaemenid Mesopotamia. New Haven, 1967.

AH 3143   Countries of ancient Asia - Assyria and Babylonia - Special topics for Babylonia - Civilization
AH 3143.3   Dubor, Georges de. Assyrie et Chaldée. Montauban, 1878.
AH 3143.4   Menant, J. Ninive et Babylone. Paris, 1888.
AH 3143.5   Winckler, H. Die babylonische Geisteskultur. Leipzig, 1907.
AH 3143.6   Köberle, J. Beziehungen zwischen Israel und Babylonien. Wismar, 1908.
AH 3143.7   Sayce, A.H. Babylonians and Assyrians. N.Y., 1899.
AH 3143.8   Jastrow, Morris. The civilization of Babylonia and Assyria. Philadelphia, 1915.
AH 3143.8.2   Jastrow, Morris. The civilization of Babylonia and Assyria. Philadephia, 1915.
AH 3143.9   Contenau, Georges. La civilisation assyro-babylonienne. Paris, 1922.
AH 3143.9.5   Contenau, Georges. La civilisation d'Assur et de Babylone. Paris, 1937.
AH 3143.10   Meissner, Bruno. Babylonien und Assyrien. Heidelberg, 1920. 2v.
AH 3143.11   Delitzsch, Friedrich. Handel und Wandel in Altbabylonien. Stuttgart, 1910.
AH 3143.12   Jeremias, Alfred. Handbuch der altorientalischen Geisteskultur. Leipzig, 1913.
AH 3143.12.5A   Jeremias, Alfred. Handbuch der altorientalischen Geisteskultur. 2e Aufl. Berlin, 1929.
AH 3143.12.5B   Jeremias, Alfred. Handbuch der altorientalischen Geisteskultur. 2e Aufl. Berlin, 1929.
AH 3143.13   Chiera, Edward. They wrote on clay. Chicago, 1938.
AH 3143.14   Beek, Martinus A. Aan Babylons stromen. Amsterdam, 1955.
AH 3143.15   Saggs, H.W. The greatness that was Babylon. N.Y., 1962.
AH 3143.16   Appenheim, Adolf L. Ancient Mesopotamia. Chicago, 1964.
AH 3143.17   Nikol'skii, Nikolai M. Kultura drevnei Vavilonii. Minsk, 1959.
AH 3143.18.1   Delaporte, Louis. Mesopotamia; the Babylonian and Assyrian civilization. N.Y., 1970.
AH 3143.19   Sayce, Archibald H. A primer of Assyriology. London, 1894.
AH 3143.19.1   Sayce, Archibald H. A primer of Assyriology. N.Y., 1894.
AH 3143.20   Landersdorfer, Simon. Die Kultur der Babylonier und Assyrier. Kempten, 1913.
AH 3143.21   Schneider, Hermann. Kultur und Denken der Babylonier und Juden. Leipzig, 1910.
AH 3143.22   Fischer, Hugo. Die Geburt der Hochkultur in Ägypten und Mesopotamien. Stuttgart, 1960.
AH 3143.23.3   Klima, Josef. Gesellschaft und Kultur des alten Mesopotamien. Prag, 1964.
AH 3143.25   Klengel, Evelyn. Reise in das alte Babylon. 1. Aufl. Leipzig, 1970.

AH 3145   Countries of ancient Asia - Assyria and Babylonia - Special topics for Babylonia - Government and administration - General works
AH 3145.5   Soden, W.F. von. Herrscher im alten Orient. Berlin, 1954.

AH 3147   Countries of ancient Asia - Assyria and Babylonia - Special topics for Babylonia - Government and administration - Special topics
AH 3147.3   Lindl, Ernest. Das Priester- und Beamtentum der altbabylonischen Kontrakte. Paderborn, 1913.
AH 3147.5   Labat, René. Le caractère religieux de la royauté assyrobabylonienne. Thèse. Paris, 1939.

AH 3149   Countries of ancient Asia - Assyria and Babylonia - Special topics for Babylonia - Chronology
AH 3149.05   Pamphlet box. Babylonia-Chronology. Miscellaneous pamphlets.
AH 3149.3   Oppert, J. Chronologie des Assyriens et des Babyloniens. Paris, n.d.
AH 3149.4   Deimels, A. Veteris testamenti chronologia. Roma, 1912.
AH 3149.5   Gumpach, J. Die Zeitrechnung der Babylonier und Assyrier. Heidelberg, 1852.
AH 3149.6   Toffteen, O.A. Ancient chronology. Chicago, 1907.
AH 3149.7   Sidersky, David. Etude sur la chronologie Assyro-Babylonienne. Paris, 1916.
AH 3149.8F   Langdon, Stephen. The Venus tablets of Ammizaduga. London, 1928.
AH 3149.9   Smith, S. Alalakh and chronology. London, 1940.
AH 3149.10   Mercer, Samuel A. Lumero-Babylonian year-formulae. London, 1946.
AH 3149.11   Deimel, Anton. Die altbabylonische Königsliste und ihre Bedeutung für die Chronologie. Rom, 1935.
AH 3149.12   Schneider, N. Die Zeitbestimmungen der Wirtschaftsurkunden von Ur. III. Rom, 1936.
AH 3149.13   Schmidtke, Friedrich. Der Aufbau der babylonischen Chronologie. Münster, 1952.
AH 3149.14   Parker, Richard A. Babylonian chronology 626 B.C.-A.D. 45. Chicago, 1946.
AH 3149.14.5   Parker, Richard A. Babylonian chronology 626 B.C.-A.D. 75. Providence, 1956.

AH 3150   Countries of ancient Asia - Assyria and Babylonia - Special topics for Babylonia - Law - General works
AH 3150.01   Pamphlet box. Assyro-Babylonian law. Miscellaneous pamphlets.
AH 3150.3   Oppert, J. Documents juridiques de l'Assyrie et de la Chaldée. Paris, 1877.
AH 3150.4   Peiser, F.E. Jurisprudentiae Babylonicae quae supersunt. Cöthen, 1890.
AH 3150.5   Kohler, J. Aus dem babylonischen Rechtsleben. Leipzig, 1890.
AH 3150.7A   Stevenson, J.H. Assyrian and Babylonian contracts. N.Y., 1902.
AH 3150.7B   Stevenson, J.H. Assyrian and Babylonian contracts. N.Y., 1902.
AH 3150.8   Johns, C.H.W. Babylonian and Assyrian laws, contracts and letters. N.Y., 1904.
AH 3150.9   Schorr, M. Urkunden des altbabylonischen Zivil- und Prozessrechts. Leipzig, 1913.
AH 3150.11F   Walther, Arnold. Zum altbabylonischen Gerichtswesen. Inaug. Diss. Leipzig, 1915.
AH 3150.12F   Augapfel, J. BabylonischeRechtsurkunden aus der Regierungszeit Artaxerxes I und Darius II. Wien, 1917.
AH 3150.13   Pohl, Alfred. Neubabylonische Achtsurkunden aus den Berliner Staatlichen Museum. v.1-2. Roma, 1933-34.
AH 3150.14   Haase, Richard. Einführung in das Studium keilschriftlicher Rechtsquellen. Wiesbaden, 1965.

AH 3151   Countries of ancient Asia - Assyria and Babylonia - Special topics for Babylonia - Law - Code of Hammurabi
AH 3151.1.3F   Hammurabi, king of Babylonia. Codex Hammurabi. Romae, 1953.
AH 3151.2.3F   Hammurabi, king of Babylonia. Codex Hammurabi. Romae, 1950.
AH 3151.2.5   Hammurabi, king of Babylonia. The Babylonian laws. Oxford, 1960. 2v.
AH 3151.2.10   Hammurabi, king of Babylonia. The Hammurabi code and the Sinaitic legislation. Port Washington, 1971.
AH 3151.3   Stooss, Carl. Das babylonische Strafrecht Hammurabis. Bern, 1903.
AH 3151.4   Hammurabi, king of Babylonia. The oldest code of laws in the world. Edinburgh, 1903.
AH 3151.4.5   Hammurabi, king of Babylonia. The oldest code of laws in the world. Edinburgh, 1903.
AH 3151.5   Lyon, D.G. Structure of the Hammurabi code. New Haven, 1904.
AH 3151.6   Hammurabi, king of Babylonia. Die Gesetze Hammurabis in Urnschrift. Leipzig, 1904.
AH 3151.7   Hammurabi, king of Babylonia. Hammurabis Gesetz. v.1-6. Leipzig, 1904-23. 4v.
AH 3151.8   Müller, D.H. Die Gesetze Hammurabis. Wien, 1903.
X Cg   AH 3151.9.2   Hammurabi, king of Babylonia. The code of Hammurabi...about 2250 B.C. 2. ed. Chicago, 1904.
AH 3151.10   Colgecen, M.C. Le code d'Hammourabi. Fribourg, 1949.
AH 3151.11   Hammurabi, king of Babylonia. La loi de Hammourabi. Paris, 1904.
AH 3151.12   Gordon, Cyrus. Hammurabi's code. N.Y., 1957.
AH 3151.14   Hammurabi, king of Babylonia. The code of Hammurabi. Chicago, 1904.

AH 3152   Countries of ancient Asia - Assyria and Babylonia - Special topics for Babylonia - Law - Other special
AH 3152.3   Nesbit, William M. Sumerian records from Drehem. N.Y., 1914.
AH 3152.5   Grant, Elihu. Babylonian business documents of the classical period. Philadelphia, 1919.
AH 3152.7   Praag, A. Droit matrimonial assyro-Babylonien. Amsterdam, 1945.

AH 3154   Countries of ancient Asia - Assyria and Babylonia - Special topics for Babylonia - Religion and mythology - Documents and sources
AH 3154.01   Pamphlet box. Babylonian religion.
AH 3154.2   Halevy, J. Documents religieux. Paris, 1882.
AH 3154.3   Pognon, H. Les inscriptions babyloniennes du Wade Brissa. Paris, 1887.
AH 3154.4   Arnold, William R. Ancient Babylonian temple records. N.Y., 1896.
AH 3154.5   Martin, F. Textes religieux assyriens et babyloniens. Paris, 1900.
AH 3154.7   Lau, Robert J. Old Babylonian temple records. N.Y., 1906.
AH 3154.7.5   Thompson, Reginald Campbell. The reports of the magicians and astrologers of Nineveh and Babylon in the British Museum. Ann Arbor, 1974.
AH 3154.8   Luckenbill, D.D. Study of temple documents from Cassite period. Chicago, 1907.
AH 3154.11   Tallqvist, K.L. Die assyrische Beschwörungsserie Maqlû. Leipzig, 1895.
NEDL AH 3154.12F   Knudtzon, J.A. Assyrische Gebete an den Sonnengott. Leipzig, 1893. 2v.
AH 3154.13   Deimel, Anton. Pantheon Babylonicum. Nomina deorum. Romae, 1914.

AH 3154   Countries of ancient Asia - Assyria and Babylonia - Special topics for Babylonia - Religion and mythology - Documents and sources - cont.

AH 3154.14   Nikel, Johannes. Ein neuer Ninkarrak. Paderborn, 1918.
AH 3154.15   Thureau-Dangin, F. Rituels accadiens. Paris, 1921.
AH 3154.16F   Boissier, A. Documents assyriens relatifs aux Présages. Paris, 1894-96.
AH 3154.17   Kunstmann, W.G. Die babylonische Gebetsbeschwörung. Inaug. Diss. Gräfenhainichen, 1930.
AH 3154.25   Maynard, John A. Studies in religious texts from Assur. Thesis. Chicago, 1917.
AH 3154.27   Ebeling, Erich. Tod und Leben nach den Vorstellungen der Babylonier. Berlin, 1931.
AH 3154.30   Labat, René. Hémérologies et ménologies d'Assur. Thèse. Paris, 1939.
AH 3154.30.5   Labat, René. Hémérologies et ménologies d'Assur. Paris, 1939.
AH 3154.35   Witzel, M. Texte zum Studium sumerischer Tempel und Kulturzentren. Roma, 1932.
AH 3154.40   Laessoee, Joergen. Studies on the Assyrian ritual and series lûtrimki. København, 1955.

AH 3155   Countries of ancient Asia - Assyria and Babylonia - Special topics for Babylonia - Religion and mythology - General works

AH 3155.1   Bollenrücher, J. Gebete und Hymnen an Nergal. Leipzig, n.d. 6 pam.
AH 3155.3   Münter, D.F. Religion der Babylonier. Kopenhagen, 1827.
AH 3155.4   Jensen, P. Die Kosmologie der Babylonier. Strassburg, 1890.
AH 3155.4.5   Zimmern, Heinrich. The Babylonian and the Hebrew genesis. London, 1901.
AH 3155.5   Sayce, A.H. Lecture on...religion of...Babylonians. London, 1887.
AH 3155.5.2   Sayce, A.H. Lectures on the origin and growth of religion as illustrated by the religion of the ancient Babylonians. 2d ed. London, 1888.
AH 3155.5.5   Sayce, A.H. Lectures on...growth of religion...ancient Babylonians. 5. ed. London, 1898.
AH 3155.6   Jastrow, Morris. Die Religion Babyloniens und Assyriens. Giessen, 1905-12. 3v.
AH 3155.6.2FA   Jastrow, Morris. Bildermappe...zur Religion Babyloniens und Assyriens. Giessen, 1912.
AH 3155.6.2FB   Jastrow, Morris. Bildermappe...zur Religion Babyloniens und Assyriens. Giessen, 1912.
AH 3155.6.3   Jastrow, Morris. The religion of Babylonia and Assyria. v.1-2. Boston, 1898.
AH 3155.6.5A   Jastrow, Morris. Aspects of religious belief and practice in Babylonia and Assyria. N.Y., 1911.
AH 3155.6.5B   Jastrow, Morris. Aspects of religious belief and practice in Babylonia and Assyria. N.Y., 1911.
AH 3155.7   Pinches, T.G. The religion of Babylonia and Assyria. London, 1906.
AH 3155.8   King, L.W. Babylonian religion and mythology. London, 1903.
AH 3155.9   Paffrath, T. Zur Götterlehre in den altbabylonischen Königsinschriften. Paderborn, 1913.
AH 3155.11   Tiele, C.P. Die Assyriologie...verleichende Religionsgeschichte. Leipzig, 1878.
AH 3155.11.5   Tiele, C.P. De vrucht der assyriologie. Amsterdam, 1877.
AH 3155.12   Spence, Lewis. Myths and legends of Babylonia and Assyria. London, 1916.
AH 3155.12.5A   Spence, Lewis. Myths and legends of Babylonia and Assyria. N.Y., 1916.
AH 3155.12.5B   Spence, Lewis. Myths and legends of Babylonia and Assyria. N.Y., 1916.
AH 3155.13   Mercer, Samuel A. Religious and moral ideas in Babylonia and Assyria. Milwaukee, 1919.
AH 3155.14   Radau, Hugo. Bel, the Christ of ancient times. Chicago, 1908.
AH 3155.15   Brooks, Beatrice A. A contribution to the study of moral practices of certain social groups in ancient Mesopotamia. Diss. Leipzig, 1921.
AH 3155.16   Briem, Efraim. Babyloniska myter och sagor med kulturhistorisk inledning. Stockholm, 1927.
AH 3155.17   Tooke, W. The loves of Othniel and Achsah. London, 1769. 2v.
AH 3155.18   Dhorme, E. Les religions de Babylonie et d'Assyrie. 2. ed. Paris, 1949.
AH 3155.19   Rogers, R.W. The religion of Babylonia and Assyria. N.Y., 1908.
AH 3155.20   Contenau, G. Le déluge babylonier. Paris, 1952.
AH 3155.21   Hoake, S.H. Babylonian and Assyrian religion. London, 1953.
AH 3155.23   Battero, Jean. La religion babylonienne. 1. ed. Paris, 1952.
AH 3155.28   Kramer, Samuel N. Sumerian mythology. Philadelphia, 1944.
AH 3155.29   Castellino, Giorgio R. Mitologia sumerico-accadica. Torino, 1967.
AH 3155.30   Spycket, Agnès. Les statues de culte dans les textes mésopotamiens, des origines à la 1er dynastie de Babylone. Paris, 1968.
AH 3155.31   Piesl, Helga. Vom Präanthropomorphismus zum Anthropomorphismus. Innsbruck, 1969.
AH 3155.32   Rosengarten, Yvonne. Trois aspects de la pensée religieuse sumérienne. Paris, 1971.

AH 3156   Countries of ancient Asia - Assyria and Babylonia - Special topics for Babylonia - Religion and mythology - Magic, divination, etc.

AH 3156.5   Lenormant, F. La magie chez les Chaldéens. Paris, 1874.
AH 3156.5.5   Lenormant, F. Chaldean magic. London, 1877.
AH 3156.5.9   Lenormant, F. La divination et la science des présages. Paris, 1875.
AH 3156.6   King, Leonard W. Babylonian magic and sorcery. London, 1896.
AH 3156.6.5   King, Leonard W. Babylonian magic and sorcery. Lieden, 1952.
AH 3156.7   Laurent, A. La magie et la divination chez les chaldéo-assyriens. Paris, 1894.
AH 3156.8   Bassi, D. Mitologia babilonese-assira. Milano, 1899.
AH 3156.9   Jastrow, M. Babylonian-Assyrian birth omens. Giessen, 1914.
AH 3156.10   Fossey, C. La magie assyrienne. Paris, 1902.
AH 3156.11   Stübe, R. Judisch-Babylonische Zaubertexte. Halle, 1895.
AH 3156.13   Kraus, F.R. Die physiognomischen Omina der Babylonier. Inaug. Diss. Gräfenhainichen, 1935.
AH 3156.14   Boissier, A. Mantique babylonienne et mantique hittite. Paris, 1935.
AH 3156.15   Labat, René. Commentaires assyro-babyloniens sur les présages. Bordeux, 1933.

AH 3156   Countries of ancient Asia - Assyria and Babylonia - Special topics for Babylonia - Religion and mythology - Magic, divination, etc. - cont.

AH 3156.16   Rencontre Assyriologique Internationale, 14th, Strasbourg 1965. La divination en Mésopotamie ancienne et dans les régions voisines. Paris, 1966.
AH 3156.18   Pettinato, Giovanni. Die Ölwahrsagung bei den Babyloniern. Roma, 1966. 2v.

AH 3158   Countries of ancient Asia - Assyria and Babylonia - Special topics for Babylonia - Religion and mythology - Ishtar or Astarte

AH 3158.7   Contenau, G. La déesse nue babylonienne. Paris, 1914.

AH 3159   Countries of ancient Asia - Assyria and Babylonia - Special topics for Babylonia - Religion and mythology - Relations with Jewish religion

AH 3159.5.3   Delitzsch, F. Babel und Bibel. Leipzig, 1902.
AH 3159.5.5   Delitzsch, F. Babel and Bible. N.Y., 1903.
AH 3159.5.6   Delitzsch, F. Babel and Bible. Chicago, 1903.
AH 3159.5.8   Delitzsch, F. Babel und Bibel. Leipzig, 1905.
AH 3159.5.10   Babel und Bibel. n.p., 1903. 2 pam.
AH 3159.5.12   Jeremias, A. In Kämpfe um Babel und Bibel. 3. Aufl. Leipzig, 1903.
AH 3159.5.15   Tänzer, Aaron. Judentum und Entwicklungslehre. Berlin, 1903.
AH 3159.5.20   Schreiber, Emilio. Bibbia e babele. Trieste, 1904.
AH 3159.6.3   Smith, George. The Chaldean account of genesis. 3. ed. London, 1876.
AH 3159.6.3.5   Smith, George. The Chaldean account of genesis. N.Y., 1876.
AH 3159.6.9   Smith, George. George Smith's Chaldaische Genesis. Leipzig, 1876.
AH 3159.7   Loisy, Alfred. Les mythes babyloniens. Paris, 1901.
AH 3159.8   Scholz, A. Die Keilschrift-Urkunden und die Genesis. Würzburg, 1877.
AH 3159.10.3   Jeremias, A. Die Panbabylonisten der alte Orient. Leipzig, 1907.
AH 3159.10.5   Winckler, H. Die jüngsten Kämpfer wider den Panbabylonismus. Leipzig, 1907.
AH 3159.11   Schrader, E. Die Keilinschriften und das Alte Testament. Giessen, 1872.
AH 3159.11.2A   Schrader, E. Die Keilinschriften und das Alte Testament. 2e Aufl. Giessen, 1883.
AH 3159.11.2B   Schrader, E. Die Keilinschriften und das Alte Testament. 2e Aufl. Giessen, 1883.
AH 3159.11.5   Schrader, E. The cuneiform inscriptions and the Old Testament. London, 1885-88. 2v.
AH 3159.12   Bonnet, E. Les découvertes assyriennes et le livre de la genèse. Montauban, 1884.
AH 3159.14   Pinches, T.G. The Old Testament in the light of the historical records. London, 1902.
AH 3159.15   Price, I.M. The monuments and the Old Testament. 2. ed. Chicago, 1900.
AH 3159.15.5   Price, I.M. The monuments and the Old Testament. Chicago, 1899.
AH 3159.16   Ball, C.J. Light from the East, or Witness of the monuments. London, 1899.
AH 3159.17   Lyon, D.G. Assyriology and the Old Testament. Boston, 1887.
AH 3159.18   Mac Whorter, Alexander. The Edenic period of man. N.Y., 1880.
AH 3159.19   Barton, G.A. Archaeology and the Bible. Philadelphia, 1916.
AH 3159.19.10   Barton, G.A. Archaelogy and the Bible. Philadelphia, 1925.
AH 3159.21   Willcocks, W. From the Garden of Eden to the crossing of the Jordan. 1st ed. Cairo, 1918.
AH 3159.22   Rawlinson, George. Historical illustrations of the Old Testament. London, 18- .
AH 3159.23F   Bedford, A. The scripture chronology demonstrated by astronomical calculations. London, 1730.
AH 3159.24F   Laborde, L. de. Commentaire geographique sur l'exode et les nombres. Paris, 1841.
AH 3159.25   Sayce, A.H. Fresh light from the ancient monuments. 2d ed. London, 1884.
AH 3159.26   Kinns, Samuel. Graven in the rock. London, 1895.
AH 3159.28   Stamm, J.J. Das Leiden des Unschuldigen in Babylon und Israel. Zürich, 1946.
AH 3159.34   Blome, Friedrich. Die Opfermaterie in Babylonien und Israel. Thesis. Romae, 1934.
AH 3159.36   Gressmann, Hugo. Altorientalische Texte zum Alten Testament. Berlin, 1965.

AH 3160   Countries of ancient Asia - Assyria and Babylonia - Special topics for Babylonia - Religion and mythology - Other special

AH 3160.5   Boissier, A. Note sur un monument babylonien. Genève, 1899.
AH 3160.6   Chevolson, D.A. Über Tammuz und die Menschenverehrung. St. Petersburg, 1860.
AH 3160.6.5   Lenormant, F. Sur le nom de...Tammouz. Paris, 1873.
AH 3160.7   Zimmern, H. Vater, Sohn und Fursprecher. Leipzig, 1896.
AH 3160.8   Oppert, J. L'inmortalité de l'âme chez les chaldéens. Paris, 1875.
AH 3160.8.5   Delitzsch, F. Das Land ohne Heimkehr. Stuttgart, 1911.
AH 3160.11   Kugler, F.X. Im Bannkreis Babels. Münster, 1910.
AH 3160.12   Combe, E. Histoire du culte de Sin. Paris, 1908.
AH 3160.13   Walz, C. Turibuli Assyrii descriptio. Tubingae, 1856.
AH 3160.14   Selms, A. van. De babylonische termini voor zonde. Proefschrift. Wageningen, 1933.
AH 3160.16   Van Buren, Elizabeth. Symbols of the gods in Mesopotamian art. Roma, 1945.
AH 3160.18   Witzel, M. Tammuz-Liturgien und Verwandtes. Roma, 1935.
AH 3160.19   Schneider, Nikolaus. Die Götternamen von Ur III. Roma, 1939.
AH 3160.20   Frankena, R. Takultu. Leiden, 1954.
AH 3160.21   García de la Fuente, Oligario. Los dioses y el pecado en Babilonia. El Escorial, 1961.
AH 3160.22   Sjoeberg, Ake. Der mondgott nanna-suen in der sumerischen uberliefeung Uppsala. Uppsala, 1960.
AH 3160.23   Reder, Dimitrii G. Mity i legendy drevnego Dvurech'ia. Moskva, 1965.
AH 3160.24   Driel, G. van. The cult of Aššur. Assen, 1969.
AH 3160.25   Kramer, Samuel N. The sacred marriage rite. Bloomington, 1969.
AH 3160.26F   Paulus, Witold. Marduk, Urtyp Christi? Romae, 1928.
AH 3160.28   Weiher, Egbert von. Der babylonische Gott Nergal. Kevelaer, 1971.
AH 3160.29   Roberts, Jimmy J.M. The earliest Semitic pantheon. Baltimore, 1972.

AH 3163   Countries of ancient Asia - Assyria and Babylonia - Special topics for Babylonia - Private life - Documents
AH 3163.5   Hinke, W.J. Selected Babylonian Kudurrie inscriptions. Leiden, 1911.
AH 3163.6   Pinches, T.G. The Babylonian tables of the Berens collection. London, 1915.
AH 3163.7   Oppert, Jules. Les inscriptions commerciales en caractères cuneiformes. Paris, 1866.
AH 3163.8   Peisir, Felix E. Keilschriftliche Actenstücke aus babylonischen Städten. Berlin, 1889.

AH 3165   Countries of ancient Asia - Assyria and Babylonia - Special topics for Babylonia - Private life - General works
AH 3165.5   Sayce, A.H. Social life among the Assyrians and Babylonians. London, 1893.
AH 3165.10   Contenau, G. La vie quotidienne à Babylone et en Assyrie. 16. éd. Paris, 1950.
AH 3165.10.5   Contenau, G. Everyday life in Babylon and Assyria. N.Y., 1954.
AH 3165.10.6   Contenau, G. Everyday life. London, 1954.
AH 3165.15   Saggs, Henry William Frederick. Everyday life in Babylonia and Assyria. London, 1967.

AH 3167   Countries of ancient Asia - Assyria and Babylonia - Special topics for Babylonia - Private life - Special topics
AH 3167.5F   Lepsius, K.R. Die babylonisch-assyrischen Längenmasse. Berlin, 1877.
AH 3167.7   Weitemeyer, M. Some aspects of the hiring of workers in the Sippar region at the time of Hammorati. Copenhagen, 1962.
AH 3167.10   Seibert, Ilse. Hirt, Herde, Konig; zur Hirausbildung des Königtums in Mesopotamien. Berlin, 1969.
AH 3167.11   Dandamaev, Mukhammed A. Rabstvo v Vavilonii VII-IV vv. do n.e. (661-331 gg). Moskva, 1974.

AH 3170   Countries of ancient Asia - Assyria and Babylonia - Assyro-Babylonian literature - Bibliographies
AH 3170.5   Orlin, Louis L. Ancient Near Eastern literature; a bibliography of one thousand items on the cuneiform literatures of the ancient world. Ann Arbor, 1969.

AH 3171   Countries of ancient Asia - Assyria and Babylonia - Assyro-Babylonian literature - Literary history
AH 3171.5   Sayce, A.H. Babylonian literature. London, 1879.
AH 3171.5.5   Sayce, A.H. Babylonian literature. London, 1877.
AH 3171.6   Bezold, E. Kurzgefasster Uberblick...Babylonisch-Assyrische Literatur. Leipzig, 1886.
AH 3171.7A   Menant, J. La bibliothèque du palais de Ninive. Paris, 1880.
AH 3171.7B   Menant, J. La bibliothèque du palais de Ninive. Paris, 1880.
AH 3171.9   Dhorme, E. La littérature babylonienne et assyrienne. Thèse. Paris, 1937.
AH 3171.10   Rinaldi, Giovanni. Storia delle letterature dell'antica mesopotamia. Milano, 1957.
AH 3171.11   Fiore, Silvestro. Voices from the clay. 1st ed. Norman, 1965.
AH 3171.12   Güterbock, Hans G. Die historische Tradition und ihre literarische Gestaltung bei Babyloniern und Hethitern bis 1200. Inaug. Diss. Glückstadt, 1934.

AH 3173   Countries of ancient Asia - Assyria and Babylonia - Assyro-Babylonian literature - General anthologies
AH 3173.5A   Assyrian and Babylonian literature. N.Y., 1901.
AH 3173.5B   Assyrian and Babylonian literature. N.Y., 1901.
AH 3173.6A   Assyrian and Babylonian literature. N.Y., 1904.
AH 3173.6B   Assyrian and Babylonian literature. N.Y., 1904.
AH 3173.7   Jean, C.F. La littérature des Babyloniens et des Assyriens. Paris, 1924.
AH 3173.10   Eveling, Erich. Literarische Keilschrifttexte aus Assur. Berlin, 1953.
AH 3173.12   Bezold, Carl. Babylonisch-assyrische Texte: Die Schöpfungeslegende. Bonn, 1904.
AH 3173.15   Mendelsohn, I. Religions of the ancient Near East. N.Y., 1955.

AH 3175   Countries of ancient Asia - Assyria and Babylonia - Assyro-Babylonian literature - Poetry - Anthologies
AH 3175.5   Witzel, Maurus. Auswohl sumerischer Dichtungen. Roma, 1938.
AH 3175.10   Poemetti mitologici babilonesi e assiri. Firenze, 1954.
AH 3175.20A   Sanders, Nancy K. Poems of heaven and hell from ancient Mesopotamia. Harmondsworth, 1971.
AH 3175.20B   Sanders, Nancy K. Poems of heaven and hell from ancient Mesopotamia. Harmondsworth, 1971.

AH 3176   Countries of ancient Asia - Assyria and Babylonia - Assyro-Babylonian literature - Poetry - General history
AH 3176.2   Krecher, Joachim. Sumerische Kultlyrik. Wiesbaden, 1966.

AH 3177   Countries of ancient Asia - Assyria and Babylonia - Assyro-Babylonian literature - Poetry - Gilgamesh epic
AH 3177.3F   Smith, George. Chaldaean account of the deluge. London, 1872.
AH 3177.4   Rencontre assyriologique, 7, Paris, 1958. Gilgames et sa légende. Paris, 1960.
AH 3177.5   Gilgamesh. Le poème Chaldéen du deluge. Paris, 1885.
AH 3177.7   Kellner, M.L. The deluge in the Izdubar epic. N.Y., 1888.
AH 3177.8   Ishtar and Izdubar; the epic of Babylon. London, 1884.
AH 3177.9   Peserico, Luigi. Indagini sul poema di Gilgames. Vicenza, 1919.
X Cg   AH 3177.10F   Gilgamesh. The epic of Gilgamesh. Oxford, 1930.
AH 3177.11   Ungnod, Arthur. Gilgamesch - Epos und Odysee. Breslau, 1923.
AH 3177.12   Gilgamesh. Gilgamesch. Leipzig, 1916.
AH 3177.13   Heidel, Alexander. The Gilgamesh epic and Old Testament parallels. Chicago, 1946.
AH 3177.13.5   Heidel, Alexander. The Gilgamesh epic and Old Testament parallels. 2d ed. Chicago, 1949.
AH 3177.14   Gilgamesh. Epos o Gil'gameshe. Moskva, 1961.
AH 3177.14.5   Gilgamesh. Das Gilgamesh Epos. Stuttgart, 1966.
AH 3177.15   Mason, Herbert. Gilgamesh: a verse narrative. Boston, 1971.
AH 3177.16   Gilgamesh. The epic of Gilgamesh. Harmondsworth, 1960.

AH 3178   Countries of ancient Asia - Assyria and Babylonia - Assyro-Babylonian literature - Poetry - Izdubar saga
AH 3178.5   Schrader, E. Die Höllenfahrt der Istar. Giessen, 1874.
AH 3178.6   Jeremias, A. Izdubar-Nimrod...Heldensage. Leipzig, 1891.

AH 3179   Countries of ancient Asia - Assyria and Babylonia - Assyro-Babylonian literature - Poetry - Other individual poems
AH 3179.5   Jastrow, M. A fragment of Babylonian "Dibbarra" epic. Philadelphia, 1891.
AH 3179.7   Langdon, S. The Babylonian epic of creation restored from the recently recovered tablets of Assur. Oxford, 1923.
AH 3179.7.10   King, Leonard W. Seven tablets of creation. London, 1902.
AH 3179.7.17   Heidel, Alexander. The Babylonian Genesis. 2d ed. Chicago, 1965.
AH 3179.10   Enuma elish. Le poème babylonien de la création. Paris, 1935.
AH 3179.10.2   Enuma elish. Enuma eliš. Oxford, 1966.
AH 3179.10.8   Furlani, Giuseppe. Mite babilonesi e assiri. Firenze, 1958.
AH 3179.10.15   Deimel, Anton. Enuma eliš und Hexaëmeron. Rom, 1934.
AH 3179.12   Jordan, F. In den Lagen des Tammuz. München, 1950.
AH 3179.13   Hallo, William W. The exaltation of Inanna. New Haven, 1968.
AH 3179.14   Wilcke, Claus. Dan Lugalbandaepos. Wiesbaden, 1969.
AH 3179.16   Kramer, Samuel Noah. Enmerkar and the Lord of Aratta. Ann Arbor, 1973.
AH 3179.18   Ferrara, A.J. Nanna-Suen's journey to Nippur. Rome, 1973.

AH 3181   Countries of ancient Asia - Assyria and Babylonia - Assyro-Babylonian literature - Hymns and psalms - Texts
AH 3181.5   Vanderburgh, F.A. Sumerian hymns. Thesis. N.Y., 1908.
AH 3181.5.2   Vanderburgh, F.A. Sumerian hymns. N.Y., 1908.
AH 3181.6   Messerschmidt, L. Tabula Babylonica V.A. Th 246 Musei Berolinensis. Kirchain, 1896.
AH 3181.7   Banks, E.J. Sumerisch Babylonische Hymnen. Leipzig, 1897.
AH 3181.9   Schollmeyer, A. Sumerisch-babylonische Hymnen und Gebete an Samas. Paderborn, 1912.
AH 3181.10   Langdon, S. Sumerian and Babylonian psalms. Paris, 1909.
NEDL AH 3181.10.5F   Langdon, S. Babylonian liturgies. Paris, 1913.
AH 3181.11.1   Stummer, Friedrich. Sumerisch-akkadische Parallelen zum Aufbau alttestamentlicher Psalmen. Diss. Paderborn, 1968.
AH 3181.12   Edelkoort, A.H. Het zondebesef in de Babylonische boetepsalmen. Utrecht, 1918.
AH 3181.13   Falkenstein, Adam. Sumerische und akkadische Hymnen und Gebete. Zurich, 1953.
AH 3181.14   Castellino, Giorgio R. Two Šulgi hymns [and] Be. Roma, 1972.
AH 3181.15   Römer, Willem H.P. Sumerische Königshymnen, der Isin-Zeit. Leiden, 1965.

AH 3182   Countries of ancient Asia - Assyria and Babylonia - Assyro-Babylonian literature - Hymns and psalms - Commentaries
AH 3182.5   Widengren, Georg. The Accadian and Hebrew Psalms of lamentation as religious documents. Inaug. Diss. Uppsala, 1936.

AH 3183   Countries of ancient Asia - Assyria and Babylonia - Assyro-Babylonian literature - Magical incantations - Texts
AH 3183.5   Thompson, Reginald C. The devils and evil spirits of Babylonia. London, 1903- 2v.
AH 3183.10   Meier, G. Die assyrische Beschwörungssammlung Maglû. Inaug. Diss. Horn, 1937.
AH 3183.15   Die Labartu-Texte. Strassburg, 1902.

AH 3187   Countries of ancient Asia - Assyria and Babylonia - Assyro-Babylonian literature - Letters - Texts
AH 3187.5A   Harper, R.F. Assyrian and Babylonian letters. London, 1892- 14v.
AH 3187.5B   Harper, R.F. Assyrian and Babylonian letters. v.2-8. London, 1892- 7v.
AH 3187.6   Berry, George R. The letters of the Room 2 collection in the British Museum. Chicago, 1896.
AH 3187.7   Johnston, C. Epistolary literature of Assyrians and Babylonians. Baltimore, 1898.
AH 3187.8   Landersdorfer, S. Altbabylonische Privatbriefe. Paderborn, 1908.
AH 3187.9   Martin, F. Lettres néo-babyloniennes. Paris, 1909.
AH 3187.10F   Tallquist, K.L. Babylonische Schenkungsbriefe. Helsingfors, 1891.
AH 3187.12   Thompson, Reginald C. Late Babylonian letters. London, 1906.
AH 3187.13   Waschow, H. Babylonische Briefe aus der Kassitenzeit. Inaug. Diss. Berlin, 1936.
AH 3187.14   McKnight, Robert J.G. Selected letters from Sargonid period. Chicago, 1909.
AH 3187.15   al-Zibari, Akram. Altbabylonische Briefe des Iraq-Museums. Köln, 1964.
AH 3187.16   Römer, Willem H.P. Frauenbriefe über Religion, Politik und Privatleben in Mari. Kevelaer, 1971.
AH 3187.17   Oppenheim, Adolf L. Letters from Mesopotamia. Chicago, 1967.

AH 3188   Countries of ancient Asia - Assyria and Babylonia - Assyro-Babylonian literature - Letters - Commentaries
AH 3188.5   Schawe, Joseph. Untersuchung der Elambriefe aus dem Archiv Assurbanîpals. Inaug. Diss. Berlin, 1927.

AH 3189   Countries of ancient Asia - Assyria and Babylonia - Assyro-Babylonian literature - Maxims, Wisdom literature - Texts
AH 3189.3A   Gordon, Edmund I. Sumerian proverbs. Philadelphia, 1959.
AH 3189.3B   Gordon, Edmund I. Sumerian proverbs. Philadelphia, 1959.
AH 3189.5   Lambert, Wilfred G. Babylonian wisdom literature. Oxford, 1960.

AH 3190   Countries of ancient Asia - Assyria and Babylonia - Assyro-Babylonian literature - Maxims, Wisdom literature - Commentaries
AH 3190.5   Dijk, Johannes J.A. van. La sagesse suméro-accadienne. Proefschrift. Leiden, 1953.
AH 3190.5.1   Dijk, Johannes J.A. van. La sagesse suméro-accadienne. Leiden, 1953.

AH 3191   Countries of ancient Asia - Assyria and Babylonia - Assyro-Babylonian literature - Medicine - Texts
AH 3191.01   Pamphlet box. Babylonia and Assyria. Medicine.
AH 3191.7F   British Museum. Department of Egyptian and Assyrian Antiquities. Assyrian medical texts. London, 1923.
AH 3191.9F   Labat, René. Traite akkadien de diagnostics et pronostics mestiaux. Paris, 1951. 2v.

Classified Listing

AH 3191   Countries of ancient Asia - Assyria and Babylonia - Assyro-Babylonian literature - Medicine - Texts - cont.
AH 3191.10F   Koecher, F. Die babylonisch-assyrische Medizin in Texten. Berlin, 1963- 4v.

AH 3192   Countries of ancient Asia - Assyria and Babylonia - Assyro-Babylonian literature - Medicine - Commentaries
AH 3192.5   Oefele, F.F. Keilschriftmedicin. Breslan, 1902.

AH 3193   Countries of ancient Asia - Assyria and Babylonia - Assyro-Babylonian literature - Astronomy and Astrology - Texts
AH 3193.6F   Virolleaud, C. L'astrologie chaldéenne. v.1-14. Paris, 1908. 3v.
AH 3193.7   Pinches, T.G. Late Babylonian astronomical and related texts. Providence, 1955.
AH 3193.8   Labat, René. Un calendrier babylonien des travaux des signes et des mois. Paris, 1965.

AH 3194   Countries of ancient Asia - Assyria and Babylonia - Assyro-Babylonian literature - Astronomy and Astrology - Commentaries
AH 3194.1   Weir, John D. The Venus tablets of Ammizaduga. Istanbul, 1972.

AH 3195   Countries of ancient Asia - Assyria and Babylonia - Assyro-Babylonian literature - Other literature
AH 3195.3   Renan, Ernest. An essay on the age and antiquity of the book of Nabathaean agriculture. London, 1862.
AH 3195.7   Ebeling, Erich. Die babylonische Fabel. Leipzig, 1927.
AH 3195.10F   Era. Das Erra-Epos. Würzburg, 1956.
AH 3195.10.2   Era. Das Erra-Epos. Rom, 1970.
AH 3195.10.3   Era. L'epopea di Erra. Roma, 1969.
AH 3195.12   Kramer, Samuel Noah. Schooldays. Philadelphia, 1950?
AH 3195.14   Hunger, Hermann. Babylonische und assyrische Kolophone. Neukirchen, 1968.

AH 3207   Countries of ancient Asia - Bactria - General history
AH 3207.5   Rawlinson, H.G. Bactria. The history of a forgotten empire. London, 1912.
AH 3207.6   Masson, Vadim M. Strana tysiachi gorodov. Moskva, 1966.

AH 3210   Countries of ancient Asia - Bactria - History by periods - 500 - 1 B.C.
AH 3210.5   Narain, A.K. The Indo-Greeks. Oxford, 1957.
AH 3210.5.2   Narain, A.K. The Indo-Greeks. Oxford, 1962.

AH 3250   Countries of ancient Asia - Colchis - Bibliographies
AH 3250.5   Margwelaschwili, T. von. Colchis, Iberien und Albanien um die Wende des 1. Jahrhunderts vor Christ. Inaug. Diss. Halle, 1914.

AH 3302   Countries of ancient Asia - Cyprus - Collected source materials
AH 3302.1   Chatzeioannou, Kyriakos. He archaia Kypros eis tas Hellenikas pegas. Leukosia, 1971.

AH 3307   Countries of ancient Asia - Cyprus - General history
AH 3307.5   Engel, W.H. Kypros. Berlin, 1841. 2v.
AH 3307.7   Lauria, G.A. Cipro. Napoli, 1879.

AH 3308   Countries of ancient Asia - Cyprus - General special
AH 3308.5   Davidson, J.T. Cyprus: its place in Bible history. London, 1878.

AH 3309   Countries of ancient Asia - Cyprus - History by periods - Before 500 B.C.
AH 3309.5   Lichtenberg, R.F. Beiträge zur...Geschichte von Kypros. Berlin, 1906.

AH 3310   Countries of ancient Asia - Cyprus - History by periods - 500 - 1 B.C.
AH 3310.5   Spyridakis, K. Euagaros I van Salamis. Stuttgart, 1935.
AH 3310.5.5   Spyridakis, K. Kyprioi basileis tou 4 aiv. P. Ch. Leukosia, 1963.

AH 3313   Countries of ancient Asia - Cyprus - Civilization
AH 3313.2   Bisi, Anna Maria. Kuopiaká; contributi allo studio della componente cipriota della civiltá punica. Roma, 1966.

AH 3354   Countries of ancient Asia - Cyrenaica - Law
AH 3354.5   Luzzatto, G.I. La "Lex Cathartica" di Cirene. Milano, 1936.

AH 3357   Countries of ancient Asia - Cyrenaica - General history
AH 3357.5   Thrige, Johann P. Historia Cyrenes. Hauniae, 1819.
AH 3357.7   Thrige, Johann P. Res Cyrenensium. Hauniae, 1828.
AH 3357.7.5   Thrige, Johann P. Res Cyrenensium. Verbania, 1940.
AH 3357.8   Thrige, Johann P. Storia di Cirene. Verbania, 1948.
AH 3357.9   Gottschick, A.F. Geschichte der Gründung...des Hellenischen Staates. Leipzig, 1858.

AH 3358   Countries of ancient Asia - Cyrenaica - General special
AH 3358.5F   Bates, O. The Eastern Libyans; essay. London, 1914.
AH 3358.9   Fantoli, A. La Libia negli scritti degli antiche. Roma, 1933.

AH 3359   Countries of ancient Asia - Cyrenaica - History by periods - Before 500 B.C.
AH 3359.5   Malten, L. Cyrenarum origines. n.p., 1904.
AH 3359.10   Chamoux, J. Cyrène sour la monarchie des Battiades. Paris, 1952.

AH 3361   Countries of ancient Asia - Cyrenaica - History by periods - 1 A.D. - ca. 650
AH 3361.5   Rossberg, W. Quaestiones de rebus Cyrenarum. Frankenbergae, 1876.

AH 3366   Countries of ancient Asia - Cyrenaica - Geography
AH 3366.5   Bertrand, Louis. Vers Cyrène, terre d'Apollon. Paris, 1935.

AH 3400   Countries of ancient Asia - Hittites - Bibliographies
AH 3400.5   Contenau, G. Eléments de bibliograhie Hittite. Thèse. Paris, 1922.
AH 3400.5.5   Contenau, G. Eléments de bibliographie Hittite. Paris, 1922.
AH 3400.10   Schwartz, Benjamin. The Hittites; a list of references in the New York Public Library. N.Y., 1939.
AH 3400.15F   Gelb, Ignace J. Hittite hieroglyphic monuments. Chicago, 1939.

AH 3401   Countries of ancient Asia - Hittites - Pamphlet volumes
AH 3401.2   Pamphlet box. Hittites.

AH 3404   Countries of ancient Asia - Hittites - Law
AH 3404.5   Hittites. Laws, statutes, etc. The Hittite laws. London, 1951.
AH 3404.6   Hittites. Laws, statutes, etc. Der Telipinu-Erlass. Diss. München? 1970?

AH 3407   Countries of ancient Asia - Hittites - General history
AH 3407.3   Hethitica. Paris. 1,1922
AH 3407.5   Wright, W. Empire of Hittites. London, 1884.
AH 3407.5.3   Wright, W. Empire of Hittites. 2d ed. London, 1886.
AH 3407.6   Sayce, A.H. The Hittites. London, 1888.
AH 3407.6.5   Sayce, A.H. The Hittites. 2d ed. London, 1892.
AH 3407.7   Campbell, J. Hittites. London, 1891. 2v.
AH 3407.9   Lantsheere, L. De la race...langue des Hittites. Bruxelles, 1891.
AH 3407.10   Walser, G. Neuere Hethiterforschung. Wiesbaden, 1964.
AH 3407.11   Conder, C.R. Hittites and their language. N.Y., 1898.
AH 3407.13   Fossey, C. Quid de Hethaeis. Versailles, 1902.
AH 3407.17   Cowley, Arthur E. The Hittites. London, 1920.
AH 3407.20   Cavaignac, E. Les Hittites. Paris, 1950.
AH 3407.22   Cavaignac, Eugène. Le problème hittite. Paris, 1936.
AH 3407.25   Revue hittite et asianique. Paris. 1,1930+ 10v.
AH 3407.30   Gurney, O.R. The Hittites. London, 1952.
AH 3407.33   Marek, Kurt W. Enge Schlucht und schwarzer Berg. Hamburg, 1955.
AH 3407.33.5   Marek, Kurt W. Enge Schlucht und schwarzer Berg. Reinbek, 1966.
AH 3407.34   Menabde, Eduard A. Khettskoe obshchestvo. Tbilisi, 1965.
AH 3407.35   Zamarovsky, Voitech. Tainy khettov. Moskva, 1968.
AH 3407.36   Dovgialo, Gennadii I. K istorii vozniknoveniia gosudarstva. Minsk, 1968.

AH 3408   Countries of ancient Asia - Hittites - General special
AH 3408.5   Jensen, P. Hittiter und Armenier. Strassburg, 1898.
AH 3408.7   Leonard, W. Hittiter und Amazonen. Leipzig, 1911.
AH 3408.9   Cara, Cesare A. de. Gli Hethei-Palasgi. Roma, 1894. 3v.
AH 3408.13   Hogarth, D.G. Kings of the Hittites. London, 1926.
AH 3408.17   Matter, E.P. Die Bedeutung der Hethiter für das Alti Testament. Diss. Bottrop, 1933.
AH 3408.19   Giorgadze, Grigorii G. Ocherki po sotsial'no-ekonomicheskoi istorii Khettskogo gosudarstva. Tbilisi, 1973.

AH 3409   Countries of ancient Asia - Hittites - History by periods - Before 500 B.C.
AH 3409.5   Cavaignac, Eugène. Subbiluliuma et son temps. Paris, 1932.

AH 3413   Countries of ancient Asia - Hittites - Civilization
AH 3413.5   Pottier, E. L'art hittite. Paris, 1926.
AH 3413.9   Weber, Otto. Die Kunst der Hethiter. Berlin, 1922.
AH 3413.12   Contenau, Georges. La civilisation des Hitties et des Mitanniens. Paris, 1934.
AH 3413.12.5   Contenau, Georges. La civilisation des Hittites. Paris, 1948.
AH 3413.15   Riemschneider, M. Die Welt der Hethiter. Stuttgart, 1954.

AH 3414   Countries of ancient Asia - Hittites - Religion
AH 3414.5   Furlani, G. La religione degli Hittite. Bologna, 1936.
AH 3414.10   Gueterbock, H.G. Kumarki. Zürich, 1946.
AH 3414.10.5   Gueterbock, H.G. The song of Ullikummi. New Haven, 1952.
AH 3414.15   Bossert, Helmuth. Janus und der Mann mit derer Adler; oder Greifenmaske. Istanbul, 1959.
AH 3414.20   Haas, Volkert. Der Kult von Nerik. Rom, 1970.

AH 3421 - 3446   Countries of ancient Asia - Hittites - Local (A-Z by place)
AH 3423.1F   British Museum. Carchemish: report on excavations at Djerabis. London, 1914. 3v.

AH 3507   Countries of ancient Asia - Media - General history
AH 3507.5   Delattre, A. L'empire des Mèdes. Bruxelles, 1883.
AH 3507.7   Ragozin, Z.A. Story of Media, Babylon and Persia. N.Y., 1888.
AH 3507.7.5   Ragozin, Z.A. Media, Babylon, and Persia. N.Y., 1900.
AH 3507.7.7   Ragozin, Z.A. Media, Babylon, and Persia. N.Y., 1903.
AH 3507.10   Diakonov, I. Istoriia Midii. Moskva, 1956.
AH 3507.15   Aliev, Igrar. Istoriia Midii. Baku, 1960.

AH 3550 - 3596   Countries of ancient Asia - Mesopotamia [Discontinued]
AH 3565.10   Akademiia nauk SSSR. Institut narodov Azii. Ancient Mesopotamia: socio-economic history. Moscow, 1969.

AH 3607   Countries of ancient Asia - Parthia - General history
AH 3607.5   Vaillant, J.F. Regum Parthorum historia. Parisiis, 1725. 2v.
AH 3607.7   Vaillant, J.F. Regum Parthorum historia. Parisiis, 1728.
AH 3607.9A   Rawlinson, G. Sixth great oriental monarchy. London, 1873.
AH 3607.9B   Rawlinson, G. Sixth great oriental monarchy. London, 1873.
AH 3607.9.5   Rawlinson, G. Sixth great oriental monarchy. N.Y., 190-?
AH 3607.11A   Rawlinson, G. Story of Parthia. N.Y., 1893.
AH 3607.11B   Rawlinson, G. Story of Parthia. N.Y., 1893.
AH 3607.12   Rawlinson, G. Parthia. N.Y., 1903.
AH 3607.13   Debevoise, Neilson Carel. Parthian problems. An abstract of a thesis. n.p., 1931.
AH 3607.13.7   Debevoise, Neilson Carel. A political history of Parthia. Chicago, 1938.
AH 3607.15   Colledge, Malcom A.R. The Parthians. London, 1967.

AH 3608   Countries of ancient Asia - Parthia - General special
AH 3608.5   Bokshchanin, A.G. Parfiia i Rim. Moskva, 1960. 2v.

AH 3609   Countries of ancient Asia - Parthia - History by periods - Before 500 B.C.
AH 3609.5   Lozinski, B.P. The original homeland of the Parthians. 's Gravenhage, 1959.

AH 3613   Countries of ancient Asia - Parthia - Civilization
AH 3613.5   Koshelenko, Gennadii A. Kul'tura Parfii. Moskva, 1966.

Classified Listing

AH 3651 Countries of ancient Asia - Persia - Pamphlet volumes
AH 3651.2 Pamphlet box. Ancient Persia.

AH 3653 Countries of ancient Asia - Persia - Government and administration
AH 3653.5 Buchholz, A. Quaestiones de Persarum satrapis satrapiiseque. Lipsiae, 1894.
AH 3653.7 Ehtécham, Mortéza. L'Iran sous les Achéménides. Fribourg, 1946.

AH 3654 Countries of ancient Asia - Persia - Law
AH 3654.5 Roth, R. De More Pensarum aquam. Jenae, 1670.
AH 3654.10 Nasr, Taghi. Essai sur l'histoire du droit persan des l'origine a l'invasion arabe. Paris, 1933.

AH 3657 Countries of ancient Asia - Persia - General history
AH 3657.3 Ohsson. Tableau historique de l'Orient. Paris, 1804. 2v.
AH 3657.5 Spiegel, F. Éran. Berlin, 1863.
AH 3657.7 Gobineau, J.A. Histoire des Perses. Paris, 1869. 2v.
AH 3657.9 Spiegel, F. Franische Alterthumskunde. Leipzig, 1871. 3v.
AH 3657.11 Vaux, William Sandys Wright. Persia. London, 1875.
AH 3657.11.5 Vaux, William Sandys Wright. Persia. London, 1893.
AH 3657.12 Rawlinson, G. Seventh great oriental monarchy. London, 1876.
NEDL AH 3657.13 Rawlinson, G. Seventh great oriental monarchy. N.Y., 1882. 2v.
AH 3657.13.5 Rawlinson, G. Seventh great oriental monarchy. v.1-2. N.Y., 190-?
AH 3657.15 Benjamin, S.G.W. Story of Persia. N.Y., 1887.
AH 3657.17.1 Gutschmid, Alfred von. Geschichte Irans. Graz, 1973.
AH 3657.18 Brisson, B. De regio Persarum. Argentoratum, 1710.
Htn AH 3657.18.5* Brisson, B. De regio Persarum. Heidelberg, 1595.
AH 3657.20 Prášek, J.V. Geschichte der Meder und Perser. Gotha, 1906. 2v.
AH 3657.25 Ahl, Augustus W. Outline of Persian history. N.Y., 1922.
AH 3657.29 Rogers, Robert W. A history of ancient Persia. N.Y., 1929.
AH 3657.31A Olmstead, A.T.E. History of the Persian empire. Chicago, 1948.
AH 3657.31B Olmstead, A.T.E. History of the Persian empire. Chicago, 1948.
AH 3657.35 Huart, Clément. La Perse antique et la civilisation iranienne. Paris, 1925.
AH 3657.38 Frye, R.N. The heritage of Persia. London, 1962.
AH 3657.39 Mirkhoud. History of the early kings of Persia. London, 1832.
AH 3657.40A Foye, R.N. The heritage of Persia. Cleveland, 1963.
AH 3657.40B Foye, R.N. The heritage of Persia. Cleveland, 1963.
AH 3657.42 Verbruggen, Hendrick. Zoeklicht op Oud-Perzie. Hasselt, 1964.
AH 3657.44 Herzfeld, Ernst Emil. The Persian empire. Wiesbaden, 1968.
AH 3657.46 Collins, Robert J. The Medes and Persians, conquerors and diplomats. N.Y., 1972.

AH 3658 Countries of ancient Asia - Persia - General special
AH 3658.5 Nöldeke, T. Aufsätze zur Persischen Geschichte. Leipzig, 1887.
AH 3658.6 Menaut, J. Les achemenides et les inscriptions de la Perse. Paris, 1872.
AH 3658.7 Krumbholz, Paul. De discriptione regni achaemenidarum. Eisnach, 1891.
AH 3658.8 Krumbholz, Paul. De Asiae Minoras satrapis Persicis. Inaug. Diss. Lipsiae, 1883.

AH 3659 Countries of ancient Asia - Persia - History by periods - Before 500 B.C.
AH 3659.3 Büdinger. Die neuentdckten Inscription über Cyrus. Wien, 1881.
AH 3659.5 Prášek, J.V. Forschungen zur Geschichte des Alterthums. Leipzig, 1897. 3v.
AH 3659.7 Evers, E. Das Emporkommen der persischen Macht. Berlin, 1884.
AH 3659.8 Silvestre de Sacy, A.I. Memoires sur diverses antiquités de la Perse. Paris, 1793.
AH 3659.9 Hoffmenn-Kutschke, A. Die Wahrheit über Kyros, Darius und Zarathuschatra. Berlin, 1910.
AH 3659.10 Lindl, Ernest. Enstehung und Blüte...des altorientalischen Kulturwelt: Cyrus. München, 1903.
AH 3659.12 Champdor, A. Cyrus. Paris, 1952.
AH 3659.14 Lamb, Harold. Cyrus the Great. 1st ed. Garden City, N.Y., 1960.
AH 3659.15 Abbott, Jacob. History of Cyrus the Great. N.Y., 1850.
AH 3659.15.2 Abbott, Jacob. History of Cyrus the Great. N.Y., 1852.
AH 3659.15.6 Abbott, Jacob. History of Cyrus the Great. N.Y., 1877.
AH 3659.20 Abbott, Jacob. History of Darius the Great. N.Y., 1850.
AH 3659.20.3 Abbott, Jacob. History of Darius the Great. N.Y., 1854.
AH 3659.20.6 Abbott, Jacob. History of Darius the Great. N.Y., 1871.
AH 3659.21 Walser, Gerold. Audienz beim persischen Grosskönig. Zürich, 1965.

AH 3660 Countries of ancient Asia - Persia - History by periods - 500 - 1 B.C.
AH 3660.3 Abbott, Jacob. History of Xerxes the Great. N.Y., 1850.
AH 3660.3.2 Abbott, Jacob. History of Xerxes the Great. N.Y., 1852.
AH 3660.3.5 Abbott, Jacob. History of Xerxes the Great. N.Y., 1872.
AH 3660.5 Poncritius, M. Studien über die Schlacht bei Kunaxa. Berlin, 1906.
AH 3660.10 Schneiderwirth, J.H. Die persische Politik gegen die Griechen seit dem Ende der Perserkriege. Heiligenstadt, 1863.
AH 3660.15 Dandamaev, M.A. Iran pri perviykh akhemenidakh. Moskva, 1963.
AH 3660.20 Walser, Gerold. Beiträge zur Achämenidengeschichte. Wiesbaden, 1972.

AH 3661 Countries of ancient Asia - Persia - History by periods - 1 A.D. - ca. 650
AH 3661.5 Christensen, A. L'empire des Sassanides. København, 1907.
AH 3661.6.1 Tabari, Muhammed Ibn. Geschichte der Perser und Araber. Leyden, 1973.
AH 3661.10 Altheim, Franz. Ein asiatischer Staat. Wiesbaden, 1954.
AH 3661.10.5 Altheim, Franz. Utopie und Wirtschaft. Frankfurt, 1957.
AH 3661.14 Lukonin, Vladimir G. Kul'tura sasanidskogo Irana. Moskva, 1969.
AH 3661.15 Lukonin, Vladimir G. Iran v epokhu pervykh Sasanidov. Leningrad, 1961.

AH 3661 Countries of ancient Asia - Persia - History by periods - 1 A.D. - ca. 650 - cont.
AH 3661.15.5 Gagé, Jean. La montée des Sassanides et l'heure de Palmyre. Paris, 1964.
AH 3661.20 Gumilev, L.N. Podvig Bakhrama Chubiny. Leningrad, 1962.

AH 3663 Countries of ancient Asia - Persia - Civilization
AH 3663.5 Modi, J.J. Wine among the ancient Persians. Bombay, 1888.
AH 3663.7 Dhalla, M.N. Loroastrian civilization. N.Y., 1922.
AH 3663.9 Pithawalla, M. The light of ancient Persia. Adyar, 1923.
AH 3663.11 Osten, H.H. von der. Die Welt der Perser. Stuttgart, 1956.
AH 3663.12 Gobineau, Arthur. The world of the Persians. London, 1971.
AH 3663.14 Katrak, Jamshed C. Marriage in ancient Iran. Bombay, 1965.

AH 3664 Countries of ancient Asia - Persia - Religion
AH 3664.5 Rosny, L. L'origine du langage. Paris, 1869. 2 pam.
AH 3664.8 Korn, Friedrich. Mythen der alten Perser. Leipzig, 1835.
Htn AH 3664.10* Meiners, Christoph. Commentatio de...religionis Persarum. n.p., n.d.
AH 3664.11 Reitzenstein, R. Das iranische Erlösungsmysterium. Bonn, 1921.
AH 3664.12 Duchesne-Guillemin, J. La religion de l'Iran ancien. Paris, 1962.
AH 3664.13 Güntert, Hermann. Der arische Weltkönig und Heiland. Halle, 1923.
AH 3664.14 Widengren, George. Iranische Geisteswelt von der Anfängen bis zum Islam. Baden-Baden, 1961.
AH 3664.15 Clemen, Carolus. Fontes historiae religionum Persicae. Bonnae, 1920.
AH 3664.16 Widengren, G. Hochgottglaube im alten Iran. Uppsala, 1938.
AH 3664.17.1 Wesendonk, Otto Günther von. Urmensch und Seele in der iranischen Überlieferung. Osnabrück, 1971.

AH 3667 Countries of ancient Asia - Persia - Travels
AH 3667.7 Buckingham, J.S. Travels in Assyria, Media and Persia. London, 1829.

AH 3668 Countries of ancient Asia - Persia - Special topics - Education
AH 3668.5 Modi, J.J. Education among the ancient Iranians. Bombay, 1905.

AH 3670 Countries of ancient Asia - Persia - Special topics - Cities in general
AH 3670.5 Pigulevskaia, N.V. Goroda Irana v rannem srednevekove. Moskva, 1956.
AH 3670.5.5 Pigulevskaia, N.V. Les villes de l'état iranien. Paris, 1963.

AH 3707 Countries of ancient Asia - Phoenicia - General history
AH 3707.5 Cumberland, R. Sanchoniatho's Phoenician history. London, 1720.
AH 3707.7 Movers, F.K. Die Phönizier. v.1-2, pt.1-3. Bonn, 1841. 4v.
AH 3707.9 Kenrick, J. Phoenicia. London, 1855.
AH 3707.11A Rawlinson, G. Story of Phoenicia. N.Y., 1889.
AH 3707.11B Rawlinson, G. Story of Phoenicia. N.Y., 1889.
AH 3707.11.2 Rawlinson, G. Story of Phoenicia. N.Y., 1896.
AH 3707.11.3A Rawlinson, G. History of Phoenicia. London, 1889.
AH 3707.11.3B Rawlinson, G. History of Phoenicia. London, 1889.
AH 3707.12 L'espansione fenicia nel Mediterraneo. Roma, 1971.
AH 3707.15 Berger, P. Phénicie. Paris, 1881.
AH 3707.17 Pereira de Lima, J.M. Phenicios a carthaginezes. Lisboa, 1904.
AH 3707.19F Autran, C. Phéniciens. Paris, 1920.
AH 3707.21 Landau, W. Die Phönizier. Leipzig, 1901.
AH 3707.22 Moscati, Sabatino. The world of the Phoenicians. London, 1968.
AH 3707.25 Weill, R. La Phenicie et l'Asie occidentale. Paris, 1939.
AH 3707.25.5 Weill, R. Phoenicia and western Asia to the Macedonian conquest. London, 1940.
AH 3707.26 Baramki, D.C. Phoenicia and the Phoenicians. Beirut, 1961.
AH 3707.28 Harden, Donald B. The Phoenicians. London, 1962.
AH 3707.28.1 Harden, Donald B. The Phoenicians. Harmondsworth, 1971.
AH 3707.29 Shifman, Il'ia. Finikliskie morekhody. Moskva, 1965.

AH 3708 Countries of ancient Asia - Phoenicia - General special
AH 3708.5 Nibbi, Alessandra. The Tyrrhenians. Cowley, 1969.

AH 3713 Countries of ancient Asia - Phoenicia - Civilization
AH 3713.5 Barges, J.J.L. Colonies phéniciennes. Paris, 1878.
AH 3713.10 Contenau, G. La civilisation phénicienne. Paris, 1926.
AH 3713.15 Wilkins, A.S. Phoenicia and Israel. London, 1871.

AH 3714 Countries of ancient Asia - Phoenicia - Religion
AH 3714.5 Landersdorfer, S. Der baal tetramorphos und die Kerube des Ezechiel. Paderborn, 1918.

AH 3715 Countries of ancient Asia - Phoenicia - Economic conditions
AH 3715.5 Schmülling, T. Der phönizische Handel in den griechischen Gewässern. Münster, 1884-85.

AH 3716 Countries of ancient Asia - Phoenicia - Geography
AH 3716.5 Bochart, S. Geographia sacra. Francofurti, 1681.

AH 3721 - 3746 Countries of ancient Asia - Phoenicia - Local (A-Z by place)
AH 3739.5 Eiselen, F.C. Sidon. N.Y., 1907.
AH 3739.5.2 Eiselen, F.C. Sidon. N.Y., 1907.
AH 3739.10 Jidejian, Nina. Sidon through the ages. Beirut, 1971.
AH 3740.5 Ryhinerus, E. De Tyro. Basilae, 1715.
AH 3740.6 Tyre; its rise, glory, and desolation. Philadelphia, 1852.
AH 3740.6.3 Tyre; its rise, glory, and desolation. Nashville, 1856.
AH 3740.7 Jeremias, F. Tyrus. Leipzig, 1891.
AH 3740.8 Fleming, Wallace B. The history of Tyre. N.Y., 1915.
AH 3740.9 Jidejian, Nina. Tyre through the ages. Beirut, 1969.
AH 3740.10 Tarbox, Increase N. Tyre and Alexandria. Boston, 1865.

AH 3757 Countries of ancient Asia - Scythia - General history
AH 3757.5 Pinkerton, J. Seythians or Goths. London, 1787.
AH 3757.7 Bergmann, F.G. Les Serythes. Halle, 1858.
AH 3757.9 Fressl, J. Skythen-Saken. München, 1886.
AH 3757.10 Potratz, Johannes A.H. Die Skythen in Südrussland. Basel, 1963.
AH 3757.11 Földvary, A. Les ancêtres d'Attila. Paris, 1875.

Classified Listing

AH 3757 Countries of ancient Asia - Scythia - General history - cont.
AH 3757.12 Remennikov, A.M. Bor'ba plenen severnogo prichernomor'ia s rimon v III veke n.e. Moskva, 1954.
AH 3757.13 Latyshev, B. Scythica et Cancasica. Petrograd. 1-2,1890-1906
AH 3757.14 Gibellino Krasceninnicowa, Maria. Gli sciti. Roma, 1942.
AH 3757.15 Rice, Tamara. The Scythians. London, 1957.
AH 3757.20 Shikov, A.F. Shifskoe vosstanie na Bospore. Voronezh, 1960.
AH 3757.22 Elderkin, George. Migration in the Mycenaean Age. n.p., 1963.
AH 3757.24 Junge, Julius. Saka-Studien: der Ferne Nordasten im Weltbild der Antike. Aalen, 1962.

AH 3759 Countries of ancient Asia - Scythia - History by periods - Before 500 B.C.
AH 3759.5 Walch, G.B. De cyri expeditione in Massagetas. Goettingae, 1767.
AH 3759.6 Bonnell, Ernst. Beiträge zur Alterthumskunde Russlands. St. Petersburg, 1882.

AH 3801 Countries of ancient Asia - Semites in general - Pamphlet volumes
AH 3801.2 Pamphlet box. Semites.

AH 3803 Countries of ancient Asia - Semites in general - Government and administration
AH 3803.5 Cohen, Kadmi. Introduction à l'histoire des institutions sociales et politiques chez les Semites. Paris, 1922.

AH 3804 Countries of ancient Asia - Semites in general - Law
AH 3804.5 Schaeffer, Henry. The social legislation of the primitive Semites. N.Y., 1971.

AH 3807 Countries of ancient Asia - Semites in general - General history
AH 3807.5 Vibert, C.T. La race sémitique. Paris, 1883.
AH 3807.6 Hommel, Fritz. Die semitischen Völker und Sprachen. Leipzig, 1883.
AH 3807.10 Moscati, Sabatino. Storia e civiltà dei Semiti. Bari, 1949.
AH 3807.15 Moscati, Sabatino. Ancient Semitic civilizations. 1st American ed. N.Y., 1957.
AH 3807.15.2 Moscati, Sabatino. Ancient Semitic civilizations. London, 1957.
AH 3807.20 Moscati, Sabatino. The Semites in ancient history. Cardiff, 1959.

AH 3808 Countries of ancient Asia - Semites in general - General special
AH 3808.3 Halévy, J. Melanges de critique et d'histoire. Paris, 1883.

AH 3809 Countries of ancient Asia - Semites in general - History by periods - Before 500 B.C.
AH 3809.5 Rougemont, F. L'age du bronze ou Semites en occident. Paris, 1866.

AH 3813 Countries of ancient Asia - Semites in general - Civilization
AH 3813.5 Röntsch, J. Indogermann und Semitenthum. Leipzig, 1872.
AH 3813.7 Morgenstern, Julian. Rites of birth, marriage, death, and kindred occasions among the Semites. Cincinnati, 1966.
AH 3813.8 Moscati, Sabatino. Le antiche civiltà semitiche. Bari, 1958.
AH 3813.10 Dussel, Enrique D. El humanismo semita. Buenos Aires, 1969.

AH 3863 Countries of ancient Asia - Susiana, Elam - Civilization
AH 3863.5 Cruveilhier, P. Les principaux résultats des nouvelles fouilles de Suse. Paris, 1921.

AH 3867 Countries of ancient Asia - Susiana, Elam - Travels
AH 3867.5F Dieulafoy, J.A. A Suse journal des fouilles, 1884-86. Paris, 1888.

AH 3871 - 3896 Countries of ancient Asia - Susiana, Elam - Local (A-Z by place)
AH 3889.5 Billerbeck, A. Susa. Leipzig, 1893.

AH 3902 Countries of ancient Asia - Syria - Collected source materials
AH 3902.3 Gordon, Cyrus H. Ugarit and Minoan Crete; the bearing of their texts on the origins of Western culture. N.Y., 1966.
AH 3902.5 Brown, John Pairman. The Lebanon and Phoenicia; ancient texts illustrating their physical geography and native industries. Beirut, 1969.

AH 3907 Countries of ancient Asia - Syria - General history
AH 3907.3F Terzidi Lavria, B. Siria sacra. Roma, 1695.

AH 3908 Countries of ancient Asia - Syria - General special
AH 3908.5 Schiffer, Sina. Die Aramäer. Leipzig, 1911.
AH 3908.5.5 Dupont-Sommer, Andre. Les Araméens. Paris, 1949.
AH 3908.5.10 Unger, Merrill F. Israel and the Aramaeans of Damascus. London, 1957.

AH 3909 Countries of ancient Asia - Syria - History by periods - Before 500 B.C.
AH 3909.4 Cormack, George. Egypt in Asia; a plain account of pre-biblical Syria and Palestine. London, 1908.
AH 3909.5 Petrie, W.M.F. Syria and Egypt from the Tell el Amarna letters. London, 1908.
AH 3909.6 Schmidt, V. Indledning til Syriens historie i oldtiden. Kjobenhavn, 1872.
AH 3909.7A Paton, L.B. The early history of Syria and Palestine. N.Y., 1901.
AH 3909.7B Paton, L.B. The early history of Syria and Palestine. N.Y., 1901.
AH 3909.8 Maisler, Benjamin. Untersuchungen zur alten Geschichte und Ethnographie Syriens und Palästinas. Giessen, 1930.
AH 3909.9 Michelini, T.F. La Siria nell'eta di Mari. Roma, 1960.
AH 3909.10 Buccellati, Giorgio. Cities and nations of ancient Syria. Roma, 1967.

AH 3910 Countries of ancient Asia - Syria - History by periods - 500 - 1 B.C.
Htn AH 3910.3* Foy-Vaillant. Seleucidarum imperium. Luteciae Parisiorum, 1681.
AH 3910.4F Noris, F.H. Annus et epochae Syromacedonum. Florence, 1689.
AH 3910.5F Foy-Vaillant. Seleucidarum imperium. Hagae, 1732.
AH 3910.6 Kuhn, Adolf. Beiträge zur Geschichte der Seleukiden. Altkirch, 1891.

AH 3910 Countries of ancient Asia - Syria - History by periods - 500 - 1 B.C. - cont.
AH 3910.7 Bevan, E.R. The house of Seleucus. London, 1902. 2v.
AH 3910.8 Bouché-Leclercq, A. Histoire des Seleucides. Paris, 1913-14. 2v.
AH 3910.9 Majo, U. Antioco IV Epifane re di Siria. Sassari, 1907.
AH 3910.9.5 Mørkholm, Otto. Antiochus IV of Syria. Thesis. København, 1966.
AH 3910.10 Kolbe, Walther. Beiträge sur syrischen und jüdischen Geschichte. Stuttgart, 1926.
AH 3910.11 Rostovtsev, M.I. O blizhnem Vostoke. Parizh, 1931.
AH 3910.12 Farn, W.W. Selencid-Parthian studies. London, 1930.
AH 3910.13 Heyden, E.A. Res ab Antiocho III Magno. Monasterii, 1877.
AH 3910.14 Kümpel, Eduard. Die Quellen zur Geschichte des Krieges der Römer gegen Antiochus III. Hamburg, 1893.
AH 3910.15 Tetzlaff, N.J. De Antiochi III. Magni Syriae. Monasterii, 1874.
AH 3910.16 Schmitt, H.H. Untersuchungen zur Geschichte Antiochos des Grossen. Wiesbaden, 1964.
AH 3910.25 Krüger, F. Orient und Hellas in den Denkmälern und Inschriften des Königs Antiochos I. von Kommagene. Greifswald, 1937.
AH 3910.26 Aymard, André. Les grandes monarchies hellenistiques en Asie. Paris, 1965.
AH 3910.27 Fisher, Thomas. Untersuchungen zum Partherkrieg. Diss. Tübingen, 1970.

AH 3911 Countries of ancient Asia - Syria - History by periods - 1 A.D. - ca. 650
AH 3911.5 Bormann, E. De Syriae provinciae romanae partibus capita Nonnulla. Berolini, n.d.
AH 3911.6 Bouchier, E.S. Syria as Roman province. Oxford, 1916.
AH 3911.7 Dobias, J. Dějiny Rimské provincie Syrske. Praha, 1924.
AH 3911.8 Harper, George M. Village administration in the Roman province of Syria. Diss. Princeton, 1928.
AH 3911.9A Downey, G. A study of the Comites orientis and the Consulares Syriae. Diss. Princeton, 1939.
AH 3911.9B Downey, G. A study of the Comites orientis and the Consulares Syriae. Diss. Princeton, 1939.
AH 3911.10 Sournia, Jean Charles. L'Orient des premiers chrétiens. Paris, 1966.

AH 3913 Countries of ancient Asia - Syria - Civilization
AH 3913.5 Selms, A. van. Marriage and family life in Ugaritic literature. London, 1954.

AH 3914 Countries of ancient Asia - Syria - Religion
Htn AH 3914.2* Selden, John. De dis Syris syntagmata II. London, 1617.
AH 3914.3 Selden, John. De dis Syris. Lugdunum Batavorum, 1629.
AH 3914.3.3 Selden, John. De dis Syris. 3. ed. Lipsiae, 1662.
AH 3914.3.6 Selden, John. De dis Syris. Lipsiae, 1672.
AH 3914.3.8 Selden, John. De dis Syris. Amsterdam, 1680.
AH 3914.5 Korn, F. Die Götter Syriens. Stuttgart, 1842.
AH 3914.6 Dussaud, R. Notes de mythologie syrienne. Paris, 1903.
AH 3914.7 Obermann, Julian. Ugaritic mythology. New Haven, 1948.
AH 3914.7.5 Xella, Paolo. Il mito di Shre Slm. Saggio sulla mitologia ugaritica. Roma, 1973.

AH 3915 Countries of ancient Asia - Syria - Economic conditions
AH 3915.5 Dürst, J.U. Die Rinder von Babylonien, Assyrien. Berlin, 1899.

AH 3916 Countries of ancient Asia - Syria - Geography
AH 3916.5 Honigmann, Ernst. Historische Topographie von Nordsyrien im Altertum. Leipzig, 1923.

AH 3917 Countries of ancient Asia - Syria - Travels
AH 3917.5 Maundrell, H. Journey from Allepo to Jerusalem. Oxford, 1740.

AH 3921 - 3946 Countries of ancient Asia - Syria - Local (A-Z by place)
AH 3921.5F Hug, A. Antiochia und der Aufstand des Jahres 387 nach Christus. Winterthur, 1863.
AH 3921.6 Harnack, A. De Zeit des Ignatius. Leipzig, 1878.
AH 3921.7 Haddad, G. Aspects of social life in Antioch in the Hellenistic Roman period. Thesis. Chicago, 1949.
AH 3921.8 Downey, Glanville. A history of Antioch in Syria. Princeton, 1961.
AH 3921.8.5 Downey, Glanville. Ancient Antioch. Princeton, 1963.
AH 3921.9 Downey, Glanville. Antioch in the age of Thedosius the Great. Norman, 1962.
AH 3921.9.5 Kurbatov, G.L. Rannevizantiiskii gorod. Leningrad, 1962.
AH 3921.10F Petet, Paul. Libanius et la vie municipale à Antioche au IV. siècle après J.-C. Paris, 1955.
AH 3921.11 Ceran, Waldemar. Rzemieslnicy i kupcy w Antiochii i ich ranga spoleczna (II polowa IV wieku). Wrocław, 1969.
AH 3921.12 Liebsschuetz, John Hugo Wolfgang Gideon. Antiochi city and imperial administration in the later Roman Empire. Oxford, 1972.
AH 3925.5F Texier, C.F.M. Édesse et ses monuments. Paris, 1859.
AH 3928.45 Goossens, Godefroy. Hiérapolis de Syrie. Louvain, 1943.
AH 3933.2 Sasson, Jack Murad. The military establishments at Mari. Rome, 1969.
AH 3936.2 Double, L. Césars de Palmyre. Paris, 1877.
AH 3936.5 Wright, W. Palmyra and Zenobia. N.Y., 1895.
AH 3936.7 Müller, F. Studien über Zenobia und Palmyra. Kirchain, 1902.
AH 3936.9 Février, J.G. Essai sur l'histoire politique et economique de Palmyre. Paris, 1931.
AH 3936.9.5 Février, J.G. Essai sur l'histoire politique et economique de Palmyre. Thèse. Paris, 1931.
AH 3936.9.7 Février, J.G. La religion des Palmyrénies. Thèse. Paris, 1931.
AH 3936.10 Starcky, J. Palmyre. Paris, 1952.
AH 3941.5 Liverari, Mario. Storia di Ugarit nell'età degli archivi politici. Roma, 1962.

AH 3951 Countries of ancient Asia - Palestine - Pamphlet volumes
AH 3951.1 Pamphlet box. Palestine.
AH 3951.2 Pamphlet box. Palestine.

AH 3953 Countries of ancient Asia - Palestine - Government and administration
Htn AH 3953.9* Sigonio, Carlo. De republica hebralarum libri VII. Francofurti, 1585.

Classified Listing

AH 3954   Countries of ancient Asia - Palestine - Law
AH 3954.11   Zucrow, S. Women, slaves and the ignorant in rabbinic literature. Boston, 1932.

AH 3955   Countries of ancient Asia - Palestine - Military affairs
AH 3955.5A   Abrahams, Israel. Campaigns in Palestine from Alexander the Great. London, 1927.
AH 3955.5B   Abrahams, Israel. Campaigns in Palestine from Alexander the Great. London, 1927.

AH 3957   Countries of ancient Asia - Palestine - General history
Htn   AH 3957.20*   Tappan, David. Lectures on Jewish antiquities. Cambridge, 1807.
AH 3957.23   Rappoport, A.S. History of Palestine. N.Y., 1931.
AH 3957.24   Schofield, J.N. The historical background of the Bible. London, 1938.
AH 3957.24.3   Schofield, J.N. The historical background of the Bible. London, 1946.
AH 3957.25   Causse, A. Du groupe ethnique à la communaté religieuse. Paris, 1937.
AH 3957.30   Ragaz, L. Die Bibel. Zürich, 1947-50. 7v.
AH 3957.35   Rolla, Armando. L'ambiente biblico. Brescia, 1959.
VAH 3957.38   Beöthy, Leó. Júda, Izrael és Aram. Budapest, 1874.

AH 3958   Countries of ancient Asia - Palestine - General special
Htn   AH 3958.2.5F*   Fuller, T. A Pisgah-sight of Palestine. London, 1662.
AH 3958.5F   Hitzig, F. Zur ältesten Völker und Mythengeschichte - Urgeschichte...der Philistäer. Leipzig, 1845.
AH 3958.5.5   Stark, Karl B. Gaza und die philistäische Küste. Jena, 1852.
Htn   AH 3958.8.20*   Caussin, N. The unfortunate politique [or the life of Herod]. Oxford, 1638.
AH 3958.10   Meyer, E. Die Israeliten und ihre Nachbarstämme. Halle, 1906.
AH 3958.12A   Kraeling, E.G.H. Aram and Israel. N.Y., 1918.
AH 3958.12B   Kraeling, E.G.H. Aram and Israel. N.Y., 1918.
AH 3958.20   Nordisk Teologkonferanse, Utstein Kloster, 1971. Israel, kirken og verden. Oslo, 1972.
AH 3958.23   Bergman, A. The Israelite tribe of Half-Manasseh. Diss. Jerusalem, 1936.

AH 3959   Countries of ancient Asia - Palestine - History by periods - Before 500 B.C.
AH 3959.4   Gray, J. The Canaanites. London, 1964.
AH 3959.5   Weiss, H. Index lectionum in lyceo regio hosiano Brunsbergensi. Brunsbergae, 1880.
AH 3959.22   Volkov, I.M. Arameiskie dokumenty Iudeiskoi Kolonii. Moskva, 1915.
AH 3959.23A   Robinson, T.H. Palestine in general history. Oxford, 1929.
AH 3959.23B   Robinson, T.H. Palestine in general history. Oxford, 1929.
AH 3959.31   Michaelis, J.D. Commentationes societati regiae scientiarum Goettingensi per armas 1758-62. Bremae, 1763.
AH 3959.31.5   Michaelis, J.D. Commentationes societati regiae scientiarum Goettingensi per armas 1758-62. Bremae, 1769.
AH 3959.35   Moscati, Sabatino. I predecessori d'Israele. Roma, 1956.
AH 3959.36   Kenyon, Kathleen Mary. Amorites and Canaanites. London, 1966.

AH 3960   Countries of ancient Asia - Palestine - History by periods - 500 - 1 B.C.
AH 3960.5   Fassinus, V. De Alexandro Magno ingresso Hierosolyma. Florentiae, 1780.
AH 3960.7   Hölscher, G. Palästina in der persischen und hellenistischen Zeit. Berlin, 1903.
AH 3960.8.5   Mathews, S. A history of New Testament times in Palestine, 175 B.C.-70 A.D. N.Y., 1914.
AH 3960.16   Motzo, B. Saggi di storia e letteratura guideo-ellenistica. Firenze, 1925.
AH 3960.22   Apotowitzer, V. Parteipolitik der Hasmonäerzeit im rabbinischen und pseudoepigraphischen Schriftlum. Wien, 1927.
AH 3960.23   Abel, F.M. Histoire de la Palestine. Paris, 1952. 2v.
AH 3960.24   Busch, Fritz-Otto. The fine Herods. London, 1958.

AH 3961   Countries of ancient Asia - Palestine - History by periods - 1 A.D. - ca. 650
AH 3961.3   Couret, A. La Palestine sur les empereurs grecs, 326-636. Grenoble, 1869.
AH 3961.4   Derenbourg, M.J. Quelques notes sur la guerre de Bar Kôzèbâ. Paris, 1878.
AH 3961.5   Feuerlein, J.J. Dissertatio...de Christian orum migratione in Oppidum Pellam. Jenae, 1694.

AH 3962   Countries of ancient Asia - Palestine - Chronology
Htn   AH 3962.16*   Vossius, G.J. Chronologiae sacrae isagoge. Hagae-Comitum, 1659. 2 pam.
AH 3962.22   Panin, I.N. Bible chronology. pt.1-3. Lowestoft, 19- ?

AH 3963   Countries of ancient Asia - Palestine - Civilization
AH 3963.7   Frohnmeyer. Bilder Atlas zur Bibelkunde. Stuttgart, 1905.
AH 3963.12   Macalister, R.A.S. A history of civilization in Palestine. Cambridge, Eng., 1912.
AH 3963.12.5   Macalister, R.A.S. A history of civilization in Palestine. Cambridge, Eng., 1921.
AH 3963.19   Geikie, J.C. The Holy Land and the Bible. N.Y., 1888. 2v.
AH 3963.24   North, Martin. Aufsätze zur biblischen Landes- und Altertumskunde. Neukirchen, 1971.
AH 3963.30   Jirku, Anton. Die Welt der Bibel. Stuttgart, 1957.
AH 3963.30.1   Jirku, Anton. The world of the Bible. London, 1967.
AH 3963.76   Sayce, A.H. The races of the Old Testament. London, 1891.
AH 3963.77   Daniel-Rops, H. Daily life in the time of Jesus. N.Y., 1962.
AH 3963.80.2   Szeke'hyi, Lajos. A bibliaí régiségtudomany kézikönyve. 2. kiadas. v.1-2. Budapest, 1896.
AH 3963.140   Studi sull'Oriente e la Bibbia. Genova, 1967.
AH 3963.150F   Scaccho, F. Thesaurus antiquitas sacro-prophanarum. Hagae-Comitum, 1725.
AH 3963.150.5F   Scaccho, F. Sacrorum elaeochrismatwn myrothecia tria. Amstelaedami, 1701.
AH 3963.162   Stockholm. Statens Historiska Museum. Från bibelns land. 2. uppl. Stockholm, 1955.
AH 3963.165   Lattes, Aldo. La civiltà ebraica e le origini del cristianesimo, ad uso delle scuole medie. Firenze, 1924.

AH 3963   Countries of ancient Asia - Palestine - Civilization - cont.
AH 3963.175   Küchenmeister, F. Die Totenbestattungen der Bibel. Stuttgart, 1893.

AH 3964   Countries of ancient Asia - Palestine - Religion
AH 3964.01   Pamphlet box. Religions of ancient Palestine.
AH 3964.5   Blaw, L. Das altjüdische Zauberwesen. Strassburg, 1898.
AH 3964.11   Schulze, B. Coniecturae historiae criticae sadducaeorum inter indaeos sectae novam lucem accendentes. Halae, 1779.
AH 3964.12   Popper, Julius. Der Ursprung des Monotheismus. Berlin, 1879.
AH 3964.14   Dibelius, Martin. Die Lade Jahnes. Inaug. Diss. Göttingen, 1906.
AH 3964.15   Langen, Joseph. Das Judentherm in Palästina zur Zeit Christi. Freiburg im Breisgau, 1866.
AH 3964.16   Weber, F. System des Altsynagogalen palästinischen Theologie aus Targum. Leipzig, 1880.
AH 3964.16.5   Weber, F. Jüdische Theologie auf Grund des Talmud. Leipzig, 1897.
AH 3964.17   Edersheim, A. The temple; its ministry and services as they were at the time of Jesus Christ. 2. ed. London, 1874.
AH 3964.17.10F   Kitto, John. The tabernacle and its furniture. London, 1849.
AH 3964.17.15F   Eversull, H.K. The temples in Jerusalem. Cincinnati, Ohio, 1946.
AH 3964.18   Graham, William C. Culture and conscience. Chicago, 1936.
AH 3964.19   Dhorme, E. L'evolution religieuse d'Israël. Thèse. Bruxelles, 1937.
AH 3964.20   Albright, William F. Archaeology and the religion of Israel. Baltimore, 1942.
AH 3964.25   Thomas, Joseph. Le mouvement baptiste en Palestine et Syrie. Gembloux, 1935.
AH 3964.30.5   Jirku, Anton. Der Mythus der Kanaanäer. Bonn, 1966.
AH 3964.32   Paoli, P.A. Della religione de Gentili per riguardo ad alcuni animali e specialmente a topi. Napoli, 1771.
AH 3964.34   Rodén, Nils. Bibliska städer. Stockholm, 1932.
AH 3964.36   Thompson, Henry O. Mekal, the God of Beth-Shan. Leiden, 1970.

AH 3965   Countries of ancient Asia - Palestine - Economic conditions
AH 3965.5   Lauré, M.J. The property concepts of the early Hebrews. Iowa City, 1915.
Htn   AH 3965.6*   Cumberland, R. An essay towards the recovery of the Jewish measures and weights. London, 1686.
AH 3965.6.9   Moors, B.P. Le système des poids, mesures et monnaies des israélites d'apres la Bible. Paris, 1904.
AH 3965.7   Ejges, Simcha. Das Geld im Talmud. Diss. Wilna, 1930.
AH 3965.9   Verinder, Frederick. My neighbor's landmark. Cincinnati, 1917.
AH 3965.13   Sulzberger, M. The status of labor in ancient Israel. Philadelphia, 1923.
AH 3965.15   Peppercorne, J.W. Testimonies to the fertility of ancient Palestine. London, 1838.
AH 3965.16   Ginzberg, Eli. Studies in the economics of the Bible. Philadelphia, 1932.
AH 3965.18   Ben-David, Arye. Jerusalem und Tyros. Basel, 1969.

AH 3966   Countries of ancient Asia - Palestine - Geography
AH 3966.2F   Bible atlas and gazetteer. N.Y., 1862.
AH 3966.3   Coleman, L. An historical text book and atlas of Biblical geography. Philadelphia, 1868.
AH 3966.4F   Clark, Samuel. The Bible atlas of maps and plans to illustrate geography and topography of O.T. and N.T. and Apocrypha. London, 1868.
AH 3966.5.3   Smith, George A. The historical geography of the Holy Land. 3. ed. N.Y., 1895.
AH 3966.5.5   Smith, George A. The historical geography of the Holy Land. 3d ed. London, 1897.
AH 3966.5.6   Smith, George A. The historical geography of the Holy Land. 4. ed. N.Y., 1897.
AH 3966.5.7   Smith, George A. The historical geography of the Holy Land. 7. ed. N.Y., 1900.
AH 3966.5.26   Smith, George A. The historical geography of the Holy Land. 26. ed. N.Y., 1937?
AH 3966.6.2   Lagarde, Pauli. Onomastica sacra. Gottingae, 1887.
AH 3966.7   Armstrong, G. Names and places in the Old and New Testament. London, 1888.
Htn   AH 3966.8*   Carpenter, L. An introduction to the geography of the New Testament. Cambridge, 1811.
AH 3966.8.5   Carpenter, L. An introduction to the geography of the New Testament. 6. ed. London, 1830.
Htn   AH 3966.9*   Parish, Elijah. Sacred geography: or, A gazetteer of the Bible. Boston, 1813.
AH 3966.10   Baikie, James. Lands and peoples of the Bible. London, 1914.
AH 3966.14   Gans, J. Kěnään nach der Stammeintheilung. Paderborn, 1843.
AH 3966.15   Headley, J.T. The sacred mountains. N.Y., 1847.
AH 3966.16.3   Headley, J.T. The sacred plains. Buffalo, 1856.
AH 3966.17   Quistorpius, J. Nebo, undi tota perlustratur Terra Sancta. Rostochi, 1663.
AH 3966.18   Herrmann, A. Die Erdkarte der Urbibel. Braunschweig, 1931.
AH 3966.19   Saulcy, F. de. Dictionnaire topographique. Paris, 1877.
AH 3966.20   Gosse, Philip H. Sacred streams; or, The ancient and modern history of the rivers of the Bible. N.Y., 1852.
Htn   AH 3966.21*   The Holy Land and Egypt. Vernon, N.Y., 1927.
AH 3966.22   Ben-Har, Bezalel. The concealed map of the land of Israel. Jerusalem, 1964?
AH 3966.23   Saarisalo, Aapeli. Boundary between Issachar and Naphtali. Helsinki, 1927.
AH 3966.24F   Jenks, William. The explanatory Bible atlas and scripture gazetteer. Boston, 1847.
AH 3966.25   Wells, Edward. An historical geography of the Old Testament. London, 1711-12. 3v.
AH 3966.26   Hackett, H.B. Illustrations of scripture. Boston, 1855.
AH 3966.27   Rawlinson, George. Biblical topography. London, 1887.
AH 3966.28F   Wright, G.E. The Westminster historical atlas to the Bible. Philadelphia, 1945.
AH 3966.28.2F   Wright, G.E. The Westminster historical atlas to the Bible. Philadelphia, 1956.
AH 3966.29   Halbwachs, M. La topographie légendaire des Évangiles en Terre Sainte. Paris, 1941.
AH 3966.30F   Simons, Jan. The geographical and topographical texts of the Old Testament. Leiden, 1959.
AH 3966.31   Kopp, Clemens. The holy places of the Gospels. N.Y., 1963.

AH 3966   Countries of ancient Asia - Palestine - Geography - cont.
AH 3966.32	Pidal Rios, Carlos. Los paises legendarios de la Biblia. Buenos Aires, 1962.
AH 3966.33	North, Martin. The Old Testament world. Philadelphia, 1966.
AH 3966.35	Aharoni, Jochanan. The Macmillan Bible atlas. N.Y., 1968.
AH 3966.38	Rowley, Harold Henry. Dictionary of Bible place names. London, 1970.
AH 3966.40	Kok, Johannes. Det hellige land og dets Mabolande i fortid og mutid. Kjøbenhavn, 1878.

AH 3968 - 3970   Countries of ancient Asia - Palestine - Special topics (Develop as needed)
AH 3968.1	Macalister, Robert Alexander Stewart. The Philistines. London, 1914.

AH 3971 - 3996   Countries of ancient Asia - Palestine - Local (A-Z by place)
	AH 3977.3	Merrill, S. Galilee in the time of Christ. 2. ed. London, 1886.
	AH 3977.5	Linder, Sven. Sauls Gibea. Uppsala, 1922.
Htn	AH 3980.2*	Aldrichem, C. von. A briefe description of Hierusalem and of the suburbs thereof. London, 1595.
	AH 3980.3	Fergusson, J. Essay on ancient topography of Jerusalem. London, 1847.
	AH 3980.5	Warburton, William. Julian. London, 1750.
	AH 3980.5.1	Warburton, William. Julian, or Discourse...earthquake...temple at Jerusalem. London, 1750.
	AH 3980.5.2	Warburton, William. Julian, or Discourse...earthquake...temple at Jerusalem. London, 1751.
	AH 3980.7	Manual to accompany the pictorial view of ancient Jerusalem and its vicinity. n.p., n.d.
	AH 3980.8	Meigs, Charles D. Lecture on Jerusalem at the commencement of the Christian era. Philadelphia, 1841. 2 pam.
	AH 3980.9	Derby, H.W. Selous' two grand pictures of Jerusalem. N.Y., 1872.
	AH 3980.12	Howe, Fisher. The true site of Calvary. N.Y., 1871.
	AH 3980.12.3	Howe, Fisher. The true site of Calvary. N.Y., 1889.
	AH 3980.12.5	Wilson, C.W. Golgotha and the holy sepulchre. London, 1906.
	AH 3980.12.10	Scholz, J.M.A. Commentatio de Golgothae et sanctissimi D.N.J.C. sepulcri situ. Bonnae, 1825.
	AH 3980.15	Holford, George Peter. The destruction of Jerusalem. 10. American ed. Boston, 1817.
	AH 3980.17	Kirmis, F. Die Lage der alten Davidsstadt und die Mauern des Alten Jerusalem. Breslau, 1919.
	AH 3980.50	Parent, A. Siege de Jotapata. Paris, 1866.
	AH 3981.3	Trumbull, H.C. Kadesh-Barnea - its importance. N.Y., 1884.
	AH 3983.5	Zwl, A.D. van. The Moabites. Leiden, 1960.
	AH 3999.59	Guignebert, Charles. The Jewish world in the time of Jesus. 7th American ed. N.Y., 1959.

AH 4004 - 4009   Ancient Greece in general - General bibliographies - Monographs (By date)
AH 4006.51	Vossius, G.J. De historicis Graecis. Lugdunum Batavorum, 1651.
AH 4008.99	Bauer, A. Forsuchungen zur griechischen Geschichten. München, 1899.
AH 4009.20	Tilden, F.W. Greek life; bibliography and review questions. Bloomington, 1920.
AH 4009.27	Cary, Max. The documentary sources of Greek history. Oxford, 1927.
AH 4009.36	Zmigryder-Konopka, Z. Bibliografia historii starozytnej. pt.1-3. Lwow, 1936-38.
AH 4009.52	Manni, Eugenio. Introduzione allo studio della staria greca e romana. Palermo, 1952.
AH 4009.52.2	Manni, Eugenio. Introduzione allo studio della storia greca e romana. 2. ed. Palermo, 1959.

AH 4015   Ancient Greece in general - General pamphlet volumes
AH 4015.2	Pamphlet vol. Ancient Greece. 21 pam.
AH 4015.3	Pamphlet vol. Greek history. Göttingen. 12 pam.
AH 4015.3.5	Pamphlet vol. Greek history. Göttingen, 1850. 7 pam.
AH 4015.10	Pamphlet vol. Grecian history. 3 pam.
AH 4015.12	Pamphlet box. Ancient history. Greece.
AH 4015.13	Pamphlet box. Ancient history. Greece. Miscellaneous quarto pamphlets.

AH 4018   Ancient Greece in general - Miscellany [Discontinued]
AH 4018.1	Pamphlet vol. Greek antiquities. 6 pam.
AH 4018.2	Pamphlet vol. Greek antiquities. 5 pam.
AH 4018.3	Pamphlet vol. Antiquities of the Greeks. 5 pam.
AH 4022.3	Ancient society and institutions: studies presented to Victor Ehrenberg on his 75th birthday. Oxford, 1966.

AH 4024 - 4029   Ancient Greece in general - Collected sources, etc. (By date)
AH 4027.32F	Gronovio, J. Thesaurus Graecarum antiquitatum. Venetiis, 1732. 12v.
AH 4028.97	Toepffer, J. Griechischen Altertumswissenschaft. Berlin, 1897.
VAH 4029.60	Borzsák, István. Görög történeti chrestomathia. Budapest, 1960.
AH 4029.71	Lewis, Naphtali. The fifth century B.C. Toronto, 1971.

AH 4030 - 4039   Ancient Greece in general - Government and administration - General works (Table A)
	AH 4031.01	Pamphlet box. Ancient history. Greek government.
	AH 4031.5	Saal, N. De demorum atticae per tribus distributione. Coloniae-Agrippinensim, 1860. 3 pam.
Htn	AH 4036.32*	Emmus, Vbbonis. Graecorum republicae. Lugdunum Batavorum, 1632.
Htn	AH 4036.44*	Emmus, Vbbonis. Republica Graecorum. Luden, 1644. 2v.
	AH 4038.21	Kortüm, Friedrich. Zur Geschichte hellenischen Staatsverfassungen hauptsächlich Während des peloponnesischen Krieges. Heidelberg, 1821.
	AH 4038.22	Tittmann, F.W. Staatsverfassungen. Leipzig, 1822.
	AH 4038.36	Hermann, C.F. Manuel of political antiquities. Oxford, 1836.
	AH 4038.54	Schömann, G.F. Verfassungsgeschichte Athen's. Leipzig, 1854.
	AH 4038.54.3	Schömann, G.F. Athenian constitutional history. Oxford, 1878.

AH 4030 - 4039   Ancient Greece in general - Government and administration - General works (Table A) - cont.
	AH 4038.54.7	Filon, A. Histoire de la démocratie athénienne. Paris, 1854.
	AH 4038.63A	Freeman, E.A. History of federal government. London, 1863.
	AH 4038.63B	Freeman, E.A. History of federal government. London, 1863.
	AH 4038.63.2	Freeman, E.A. History of federal government. 2. ed. London, 1893.
	AH 4038.63.9	Vischer, W. Ueber C.A. Freeman's History of federal governemnt. n.p., 1864.
	AH 4038.72.2	Henkel, H. Studien zur Geschichte...vom Staat. Leipzig, 1872.
	AH 4038.76F	Pamphlet vol. Greek political antiquities. 23 pam.
	AH 4038.78	Pamphlet box. Political antiquities. 5 pam.
	AH 4038.81	Gilbert, G. Griechischen Staatsalterthümer. Leipzig, 1881. 2v.
	AH 4038.81.3	Gilbert, G. Constitutional antiquities. London, 1895.
	AH 4038.81.4	Gilbert, G. Constitutional antiquities. London, 1895.
	AH 4038.81.5	Gilbert, G. Handbuch der griechischen Staatsalterthümer. Leipzig, 1893.
	AH 4038.84	Schvarcz, J. Die Demokratie. v.1-2. Leipzig, 1884. 3v.
	AH 4038.86	Koenig, C. Ta teah et oi en telei. Diss. Jenae, 1886.
	AH 4038.91	Hammond, B.E. Greek constitutions. Cambridge, 1891.
NEDL	AH 4038.91.3	Headlam-Morley, J.W. Election by lot at Athens. Cambridge, 1891.
	AH 4038.91.5	Headlam-Morley, J.W. Election by lot at Athens. 2. ed. Cambridge, 1933.
	AH 4038.93	Kopp, W. Griechische Staatsaltertümer. Berlin, 1893.
	AH 4038.93.3	Raeder, A. Athens politiske udvikling. Christiania, 1893.
	AH 4038.93.7	Botsford, G.W. Development of the Athenian constitution. Boston, 1893.
	AH 4038.95	Hammond, B.E. Political institutions of ancient Greeks. London, 1895.
	AH 4038.96	Greenidge, A.H.J. Greek constitutional history. London, 1896.
	AH 4038.96.10	Greenidge, A.H.J. A handbook of Greek constitutional history. London, 1920.
	AH 4038.97	Herzog, E. Verwaltung...des attischen Staats. Tübingen, 1897.
	AH 4039.07	Francotte, H. La polis grecque. Paderborn, 1907.
	AH 4039.09	Croiset, A. Les démocraties antiques. Paris, 1909.
	AH 4039.13A	Ferguson, W.S. Greek imperialism. Boston, 1913.
	AH 4039.13B	Ferguson, W.S. Greek imperialism. Boston, 1913.
	AH 4039.13C	Ferguson, W.S. Greek imperialism. Boston, 1913.
	AH 4039.13D	Ferguson, W.S. Greek imperialism. Boston, 1913.
	AH 4039.13.3	Ferguson, W.S. Greek imperialism. London, 1913.
	AH 4039.14	Ledl, Arthur. Studien zur älteren athenischen Verfassungsgeschichte. Heidelberg, 1914.
	AH 4039.15	Swoboda, H. Die griechischen Bünde und der moderne Bundesstaat. Prag, 1915.
	AH 4039.22	Menzel, Adolf. Kallikles. Wien, 1922.
	AH 4039.22.5	Strohm, Gustav. Demos und Monarch. Stuttgart, 1922.
	AH 4039.23	Pohlenz, Max. Staatsgedanke und Staatslehre der Griechen. Leipzig, 1923.
	AH 4039.27	Myres, John L. The political ideas of the Greeks. N.Y., 1927.
	AH 4039.27.5	Glover, T.R. Democracy in the ancient world. Cambridge, 1927.
	AH 4039.30	Loenen, Dirk. Vrijheid en gelijkheid in Athene. Amsterdam, 1930.
	AH 4039.32	Schaefer, Hans. Staatsform und Politik. Leipzig, 1932.
	AH 4039.35	Beccari, A. La fondazione delle dottrine politiche in Grecia. Napoli, 1935.
	AH 4039.35.5	Carcopino, J. L'ostracisme athénien. Paris, 1935.
	AH 4039.39	Romero, J.L. El estado y las facciones en la antiquedad. Buenos Aires, 1938.
	AH 4039.40A	Jones, A.H.M. The Greek city from Alexander to Justinian. Oxford, 1940.
	AH 4039.40B	Jones, A.H.M. The Greek city from Alexander to Justinian. Oxford, 1940.
	AH 4039.40.5	Krauss, B. Staat und Mensch in Hellas. 2. Aufl. Berlin, 1949.
	AH 4039.41	The Greek political experience. Princeton, 1941.
	AH 4039.43	Balogh, Elemér. Political refugees in ancient Greece from the period of the tyrants to Alexander the Great. Johannesburg, 1943.
	AH 4039.49	Ryffel, Heinrich. Metabolē politeiōn. Bern, 1949.
	AH 4039.51	Sinclair, Thomas Alan. A history of Greek political thought. London, 1951.
	AH 4039.51.2	Sinclair, Thomas Alan. A history of Greek political thought. 2. ed. Cleveland, 1968.
	AH 4039.51.5	Reesor, M.E. The political theory of the old and middle Stoa. N.Y., 1951.
	AH 4039.51.10	Sartori, F. La crisi del 411 a.C. nell'Anthenaeon politeia di Aristotele. Padova, 1951.
	AH 4039.52	Hignett, C. A history of the Athenian constitution to the end of the fifth century B.C. Oxford, 1952.
	AH 4039.52.5	Hignett, C. A history of the Athenian constitution to the end of the fifth century B.C. Oxford, 1958.
	AH 4039.53	Fuks, Alexander. The ancestral constitution. London, 1953.
	AH 4039.54	Ténékidès, G. La notion juridique d'independance et la tradition hellenique. Athenes, 1954.
	AH 4039.57	Havelock, E.A. The liberal temper in Greek politics. London, 1957.
	AH 4039.57.5	Ehrenberg, Victor. Der Staat der Griechen. Leipzig, 1957- 2v.
	AH 4039.58	Jones, Arnold H.M. Athenian democracy. N.Y., 1958.
	AH 4039.58.5	Pavar, Massiniliaro. La grecità politica da Jucidide ad Aristotele. Roma, 1958.
	AH 4039.59	Tarkiainen, Tuttu. Demokratia. Helsinki, 1959.
	AH 4039.60	Ehrenberg, Victor. The Greek state. Oxford, 1960.
	AH 4039.60.2	Ehrenberg, Victor. The Greek state. 2. ed. London, 1969.
	AH 4039.60.5	Oliver, James H. Demokratia, the gods and the free world. Baltimore, 1960.
	AH 4039.60.10A	Barker, E. Greek political theory. London, 1960.
	AH 4039.60.10B	Barker, E. Greek political theory. London, 1960.
	AH 4039.60.11	Barker, E. Greek political theory. 5. ed. London, 1960.
	AH 4039.64A	Strauss, L. The city and man. Chicago, 1964.
	AH 4039.64B	Strauss, L. The city and man. Chicago, 1964.
	AH 4039.64C	Strauss, L. The city and man. Chicago, 1964.
	AH 4039.65	Kagan, Donald. The great dialogue; history of Greek political thought from Homer to Polybius. N.Y., 1965.
	AH 4039.65.5	Ryder, Timothy Thomas Bennett. Koine Eirene. London, 1965.

AH 4030 - 4039   Ancient Greece in general - Government and administration - General works (Table A) - cont.

AH 4039.66	Berger, Anatolii K. Politicheskaia mysl' drevnegrecheskoi demokratii. Moskva, 1966.
AH 4039.67	Larsen, Jakob Aall Ottesen. Greek federal states. Oxford, 1968.
VAH 4039.68	Turasiewicz, Romuald. Gycie politzczne w Atenach V i IV w. przed n.e. w ocenie krytzcznej wspólczesnych autorow atenskich. 1. wyd. Wrocław, 1968.
AH 4039.69	Gschnitzer, Fritz. Zur griechischen Staatskunde. Darmstadt, 1969.
AH 4039.69.5	Weber-Schäfer, Peter. Das politische Denken der Griechen. München, 1969.
AH 4039.69.10	Ceechin, Sergio A. Patrios politeia. Torino, 1969.
AH 4039.70	Ghinatti, Franco. I gruppi politici ateniesi fino alle guerre persiane. Roma, 1970.
AH 4039.70.5	Damsgaard-Madsen, Aksel. Det athenske demokrati. København, 1970.
AH 4039.71	Finley, Moses. The ancestral constitution. London, 1971.
AH 4039.72	Akarca, Aşkidil. Yunan arkeolojisinin ana çirgileri. Ankara, 1972.

AH 4040 - 4049   Ancient Greece in general - Government and administration - Forms of government (Table A)

AH 4043.5	Berve, Helmut. Die Tyrannis bei den Griechen. München, 1967. 2v.
AH 4043.5.5	Andrews, Anthony. The Greek tyrants. London, 1956.
AH 4043.5.10	Plass, Hermann. Die Tyrannis in ihren beiden Perioden. Bremen, 1852. 2v.
AH 4043.5.12	Plass, Hermann. Die Tyrannis in ihren beiden Perioden. v.1-2. 2. Ausg. Leipzig, 1859.
AH 4043.5.15	Mossé, Claude. La tyrannie dans la Grèce antique. Paris, 1969.
AH 4043.5.20	Frolov, Eduard D. Grecheskie tirany IV v. do n.e. Leningrad, 1972.
AH 4047.94	Drummond, W. Review of government of Sparta and Athens. London, 1794.
AH 4048.53	Jurrjens, D.H. Democratiae apud Athenienses. Rhenum, 1853.
AH 4048.60	Reynald, M.H. Recherches sur ce qui manquait a la liberté...grecque. Paris, 1860.
AH 4048.86	Jevons, F.B. Development of Athenian democracy. London, 1886.
AH 4048.96A	Whibley, L. Greek oligarchies. N.Y., 1896.
AH 4048.96B	Whibley, L. Greek oligarchies. N.Y., 1896.
AH 4049.04	Léotard, M.E. La démocratie. Lyon, 1904.
AH 4049.09	Buzeskul, V. Istoria afinskoi demokratia. Sankt Peterburg, 1909.
AH 4049.33	Bonner, R.J. Aspects of Athenian democracy. Berkeley, 1933.
AH 4049.37	Friedel, H. Untersuchungen zum Tyrannenmord in Gesetzgebung und Volksmeinung der Griechen. Inaug. Diss. Würzburg, 1937.
AH 4049.38	English, B.R. The problem of freedom in Greece from Homer to Pindar. Toronto, 1938.
AH 4049.42A	Agard, W.R. What democracy meant to the Greeks. Chapel Hill, 1942.
AH 4049.42B	Agard, W.R. What democracy meant to the Greeks. Chapel Hill, 1942.
AH 4049.43	Levitt, Bella. Supreme political power in Greek literature of the fourth century B.C. Thesis. Philadelphia, 1943.
AH 4049.45	Isaac, Jules. Les oligarques. Paris, 1945.
AH 4049.45.5	Isaac, Jules. Les oligarques. Paris, 1946.
AH 4049.57	Taeger, Fritz. Charisma. Stuttgart, 1951-60. 2v.
AH 4049.69	Ostwald, Martin. Namos and the beginnings of the Athenian democracy. Oxford, 1969.
AH 4049.71	Giovannini, Adalberto. Untersuchungen über die Natur und die Anfange der bundesstaatlichen Sympolitie in Griechenland. Göttingen, 1971.
AH 4049.72	Díaz Tejera, Alberto. Encrucijada de lo político y lo humano, un momento histórico de Grecia. Sevilla, 1972.

AH 4050 - 4059   Ancient Greece in general - Government and administration - Administrative branch (Table A)

AH 4056.22	Meursius, J. Archontes athenienses. Lugdunum Batavorum, 1622.
AH 4058.65	Kubicki, C. De magistratu decem strategorum. Berolini, 1865.
AH 4058.78	Hille, C.A. De scribis atheniensium publicis. v.1-2. Lipsiae, 1878.
AH 4058.80	Starker, J. De nomophylacibus atheniensium. Nissae, 1880.
AH 4058.93	Lecoutere, C. L'archontat athénien. Louvain, 1893.

AH 4060 - 4069   Ancient Greece in general - Government and administration - Legislature and legislation (Table A)

AH 4068.34	Osenburgen, C. Senatu atheniensium. Hagae Comitum, 1834.
AH 4068.80	Heydemann, Victor. De senatu atheniensium quaestiones epigraphicae selectae. Argentorati, 1880.

AH 4070 - 4079   Ancient Greece in general - Government and administration - Popular assemblies (Table A)

AH 4078.19	Schömann, G.F. De comitiis atheniensium. Gryphiswaldiae, 1819.
AH 4078.19.3	Schömann, G.F. Assemblies of the Athenians. Cambridge, 1838.
AH 4078.36	Schömann, G.F. De ecclesiis lacedaemoniorum. Gryphiswaldiae, 1836.
AH 4078.90	Swoboda, H. Griechischen Volksbeschlüsse. Leipzig, 1890.
AH 4079.27	Laqueur, Richard. Epigraphische Untersuchungen zu den griechischen Volksbeschlüssen. Leipzig, 1927.

AH 4090 - 4099   Ancient Greece in general - Government and administration - Municipal government in general (Table A)

AH 4098.80	Mueller, O. De demis atticis. Nordhusae, 1880.
AH 4098.85	Feldmann, W. Analecta epigraphica...synoecismorum. Argentorati, 1885.
AH 4098.98	Gertz, M.C. Statog statsforfatninger. Kjøbenhavn, 1898.

AH 4100 - 4109   Ancient Greece in general - Government and administration - Public finance (Table A)

AH 4103.2	Buchanan, James. Theorika. N.Y., 1962.
AH 4103.3	Thomsen, Rudi. Eisphora; a study of direct taxation in ancient Athens. København, 1964.
AH 4108.17	Böckh, August. Staatshaushaltung der Athener. Berlin, 1817. 2v.
AH 4108.17.2	Böckh, August. Staatshaushaltung der Athener. 2. Aufl. Berlin, 1851. 3v.

AH 4100 - 4109   Ancient Greece in general - Government and administration - Public finance (Table A) - cont.

AH 4108.17.3	Böckh, August. Public economy of Athens. 2. ed. London, 1842.
AH 4108.17.4	Böckh, August. Public economy of Athenians. Boston, 1857.
AH 4108.17.5	Böckh, August. Die Staatshaushaltung der Athener. 3. Aufl. Berlin, 1967. 2v.
AH 4108.17.7F	Böckh, August. Sieben Tafeln zum 11 Bande Staatshaushaltung. Berlin, 1851.
AH 4108.18	Hüllmann, K.D. Ursprünge der Besteurung. Cöln, 1818.
AH 4108.73	Schoell, R. Quaestiones fiscales iuris attici. Berolini, 1873.
AH 4108.76	Pflug, C. Einführung des Soldes. Waldenburg, 1876.
AH 4108.79	Christ, Johann. De publicis populi atheniensis rationibus saeculo A. Ch. quinto et quarto. Gryphiswaldiae, 1879.
AH 4108.80	Thumser, V. De livium atheniensium. Vindobonae, 1880.
AH 4108.85	Goodwin, W.W. Value of Attic talent in modern money. v.1-2. n.p., 1885.
NEDL AH 4108.86	Böckh, August. Staatshaushaltung der Athener. 3. Aufl. Berlin, 1886. 2v.
AH 4108.90	Lehner, H. Athenischen Schatzverzeichnisse. Strassburg, 1890.
AH 4108.90.5	Panske, Petrus Paulus. De magistratibus atticis qui saeculo A. Chr. n. quarto pecunias publicas curabant. pt.1. Inaug. Diss. Lipsiae, 1890.
AH 4109.04	Dahms, R. De atheniensium sociorum tributi quaestiones septem. Berolini, 1904.
AH 4109.09	Francotte, H. Les finances des cités grecques. Liège, 1909.
AH 4109.18	Andreadès, Andreas M. Istoría tēs 'Ellēnikēs. Athens, 1918.
AH 4109.18.2	Andreadès, Andreas M. Istoría tēs Hellēnikēs. Athēnai, 1928-30. 2v.
AH 4109.18.5	Andreadès, Andreas M. Geschichte der griechischen Staatswirtschaft. Hildesheim, 1965.
AH 4109.26	Meritt, B.D. Studies in the Athenian tribute lists. Diss. Princeton, N.J., 1926.
AH 4109.32	Meritt, B.D. Athenian financial documents of the 5th century. Ann Arbor, 1932.
AH 4109.32.5	Ferguson, William S. Athenian war finance. Boston, 1932.
AH 4109.51	Finley, M.I. Studies in land and credit in ancient Athens. New Brunswick, N.J., 1951.

AH 4112   Ancient Greece in general - Government and administration - Special topics - Amphictyonic League

AH 4112.5	Tittman, F.W. Bund der Amphiktyonen. Berlin, 1812.
AH 4112.7	Göttingen. De amphictionia delphica. Gottingae, 1873.
AH 4112.9	Gürgel, H. Die...Amphiktyonie. München, 1877.
AH 4112.11	Walek, T. Die delphische Amphiktyonie in der Zeit den aitolischen Herrschaft. Berlin, 1912.
AH 4112.13	Flacelière, R. Les Aitoliens a Delphes. Thèse. Paris, 1937.
AH 4112.14	Zulhofer, Gerhard. Sparta, Delphoi und die Amphiktyonen im 5. Jahrhundert. Erlangen? 1959?

AH 4114   Ancient Greece in general - Government and administration - Special topics - Classes of citizens

AH 4114.5	Dirichlet, G.J. De equititus atticis. Regimonti, 1882.
AH 4114.7	Schömann, G.F. Recognitio quaestionis de Spartanis Homoeis. Gryphiswaldiae, 1855.
AH 4114.9	Buermann, H. De titulis atticis. Lipsiae, 1879.
AH 4114.11	Toepffer, J. Attische Genealogie. Berlin, 1889.
AH 4114.13	Seebohm, H.E. On the structure of the Greek Tribal Society. London, 1895.
AH 4114.16	Hermann, G.F. Natalem zum quagesimum nonum. Marburgi, 1835.
AH 4114.17	Billheimer, A. Naturalization in Athenian law and practice. Diss. Gettysburg, 1922.
AH 4114.18	Gerhardt, Paul. Die attische Metoikie im vierten Jahrhundert. Inaug. Diss. Königsberg, 1933.
AH 4114.19A	Haarhoff, T.J. The stranger at the gate. London, 1938.
AH 4114.19B	Haarhoff, T.J. The stranger at the gate. London, 1938.
AH 4114.19.5	Haarhoff, T.J. The stranger at the gate. Oxford, 1948.
AH 4114.20	Loenen, Dirk. Eugeneia; adel en adeldom binnen de atheense demokratie. Amsterdam, 1965.

AH 4115   Ancient Greece in general - Government and administration - Special topics - Tribes

AH 4115.2	Pritchett, William Kendrick. The five Attic tribes after Kleisthenes. Thesis. Photoreproduction. Baltimore, 1942.

AH 4116   Ancient Greece in general - Government and administration - Special topics - Phratries

AH 4116.5	Sauppe, H. De phratriis atticis. Gottingae, 1886.
AH 4116.7	Schaefer, C. Die attischen Phratrien. Naumburg, 1888.

AH 4117   Ancient Greece in general - Government and administration - Special topics - Demes

AH 4117.5	Meursius, J. Populis atticae. Lugdunum Batavorum, 1616.
AH 4117.6	Edwards, J.B. Demesman in Attic life. Thesis. Menasha, 1916.
AH 4117.7	Kastromenos, P. Die Demen von Attika. Diss. Leipzig, 1886.
AH 4117.8	Hanriot, Charles. Recherches sur la topographie des dèmes de l'Attique. Napoléon-Vendée, 1853.

AH 4118   Ancient Greece in general - Government and administration - Special topics - Gentes

AH 4118.5	Platner, E. De gentibus atticis. Marburgi, 1811.
AH 4118.7	Meier, M.H.E. De gentilitate attica. Halis, 1835.
AH 4118.9	Meier, M.H.E. De gentilitate attica. Halis, 1835.
AH 4118.11	Petersen, J.C.G. De historia gentium atticarum. Slesvici, 1880.

AH 4119   Ancient Greece in general - Government and administration - Special topics - Satrapies

AH 4119.5	Julien, Paul. Zur Verwaltung der Satrapien unter Alexander dem Grossen. Leipzig, 1914.

AH 4130 - 4139   Ancient Greece in general - Law - General works (Table A)

AH 4130.5	Calhoun, George M. A working bibliography of Greek law. Cambridge, 1927.
AH 4131.01	Pamphlet box. Ancient history. Greece. 4 pam.
AH 4132.5	Graezistische Abhandlungn. Weimar. 1,1965+ 2v.
Htn AH 4135.43*	Postel, G.F. Libro di magistrati de gli Atheniesi. Venetia, 1543.
Htn AH 4136.35F*	Petitus, S. Leges Atticae. Paris, 1635.
NEDL AH 4136.35.2F	Petitus, S. Leges Atticae. Lugdunum Batavorum, 1742.

Classified Listing

AH 4130 - 4139		**Ancient Greece in general - Law - General works (Table A) - cont.**
AH 4136.35.4F	Jurisprudentia Romana et Attica. Lugdunum Batavorum, 1741.
AH 4136.84	Meurs, Johannes van. Theseus. n.p., 1684. 3 pam.
AH 4136.85	Meurs, Johannes van. Themis Attica. Rhenum, 1685. 4 pam.
AH 4136.85.5	Meurs, Johannes van. Ioannis Meursii Themis Attica, sive De legibus Atticii libri II. Rhenum, 1685.
AH 4138.22	Heffter, A.W. Athenäische Gerichtsverfassung. Cöln, 1822.
AH 4138.29A	Hermann, C.F. De jure et Auctoritate Magistratum. Heidelbergae, 1829.
AH 4138.29B	Hermann, C.F. De jure et Auctoritate Magistratum. Heidelbergae, 1829.
AH 4138.41	Halbertsma, P. De Magistratum Probatione. Daventriae, 1841.
AH 4138.68	Télfy, I. Corpus juris Attici. Lipsiae, 1868.
AH 4138.86	Pamphlet vol. Legal institutions. 4 pam.
AH 4138.94	Gantzer, P. Verfassungs- und Gesetzevision in Athen. Halle, 1894.
AH 4138.95	Dareste, R. Recueil des inscriptions juridiques grecques. Paris, 1895.
AH 4138.95.2	Dareste, R. Recueil des inscriptions juridiques grecques. Paris, 1898. 2v.
AH 4139.05	Lipsius, Justus Hermann. Attische Recht. Leipzig, 1905. 4v.
AH 4139.05.1	Lipsius, Justus Hermann. Das attische Recht und Rechtsverfahren. v.1-3. Hildesheim, 1966.
AH 4139.06	Hitzig, Hermann F. Die Bedeutung des altgriechischen Rechtes für die vergleichende Rechtswissenschaft. Stuttgart, 1906.
AH 4139.08	Leisi, Ernst. Zeuge im attischen Recht. Frauenfeld, 1908.
AH 4139.17	Haussoullier, B. Traité entre Delphes et Pellana. Paris, 1917.
AH 4139.30	Paoli, Ugo Enrico. Studi di diritto attico. Firenze, 1930.
AH 4139.46	Périphanakis, C. La théorie grecque du droit et le classicisme actuel. Athènes, 1946.
AH 4139.49	Frisch, Hortvig. Might and right in antiquity. København, 1949.
AH 4139.56	Jones, J.W. The law and legal theory of the Greeks. Oxford, 1956.
AH 4139.68	Harrison, A.R.W. The law of Athens. Oxford, 1968. 2v.
AH 4139.71	Ramilly, Jacqueline de. La loi dans la pensée grecque des origines à Aristote. Paris, 1971.

AH 4140 - 4149		**Ancient Greece in general - Law - Public law (Table A)**
AH 4147.45	Bougainville. Droits des metropolis sur colonies. Paris, 1745.
AH 4147.85	Biagi Cremonensi. De Decretis Atheniensium. Romae, 1785.
AH 4148.38	Schoemann, G.F. Iuris publici Graecorum. Gryphiswaldiae, 1838.
AH 4148.69	Perrot, G. Droit public d'Athènes. Paris, 1869.
AH 4148.70	Philippi, A. Attischen Bürgerrechtes. Berlin, 1870.
AH 4148.77	Fränkel, M. Attischen Geschworenengerichte. Berlin, 1877.
AH 4148.78	Hartel, W. Attisches Staatsrecht. Wien, 1878.
AH 4148.78.3	Fränkel, A. Condicione, jure...sociorum atheniensium. Rostochii, 1878.
AH 4148.80	Lenz, Emil. Synedrien der Bundesgenossen. Elbing, 1880.
AH 4148.81	Stahl, J.M. De sociorum Atheniensum judiciis. Monasterii Guestfalorum, 1881.
AH 4148.81.3	Szántó, Emil. Untersuchungen über die attische Bürgerrecht. Wien, 1881.
AH 4148.85	Poland, F. De legationibus Graecorum publicis. Lipsiae, 1885.
AH 4148.88	Sonne, E. De arbitris externis. Gottingae, 1888.
AH 4148.92	Szántó, Emil. Griechische Bürgerrecht. Freiburg, 1892.
AH 4148.94	Berard, V. Liberas Graecorum civitates. Lutetiae, 1894.
AH 4148.98	Lögdberg, L.E. Animadversiones de Aetione. Upsaliae, 1898.
AH 4148.99	Arvanitopullo, A. Questioni di diritto Attico. Roma, 1899.
AH 4149.05	Rost, M. De vocibus quibusdam publici iuris Attici. Inaug. Diss. München, 1905.
AH 4149.07	Hitzig, H.F. Altgriechische Staatsverträge. Zürich, 1907.
AH 4149.10	Francotte, H. Mélanges droit public grec. Liège, 1910.
AH 4149.13	Tod, Marcus N. International arbitration amongst the Greeks. Oxford, 1913.
AH 4149.22	Kahrstedt, U. Griechisches Staatsrecht. Göttingen, 1922.
AH 4149.32	Stratēegas autokratōr. Inaug. Diss. Engelsdorf, 1932. 4v.

AH 4150 - 4159		**Ancient Greece in general - Law - Criminal law (Table A)**
AH 4158.19	Meier, M.H.E. Historiae juris Attici. Berolini, 1819.
AH 4158.35	Lelyveld, P. De Infama jure Attico. Amsterdam, 1835.
AH 4158.75	Thonissen, J.J. Le droit pénal. Bruxelles, 1875.
AH 4158.83	Herrlich, S. Verbrechen gegen das Leben. Berlin, 1883.
AH 4158.86	Passow, W. De crimine Bouleuseôs. Leipzig, 1886.
AH 4158.88	Barth, B. De Graecorum Asylis. Argentorati, 1888.
AH 4158.92	Thalheim, T. Griechischen Rechtsaltertümern. v.1-2. Schneidemühl, 1892.
AH 4159.09	Bruck, E.F. Zur Geschichte der Verfügungen von Todeswegen. Breslau, 1909.
AH 4159.23	Keramopoullos, A.D. Ho apotympanismos. Athēnai, 1923.
AH 4159.27A	Calhoun, G.M. The growth of criminal law in ancient Greece. Berkeley, Calif., 1927.
AH 4159.27B	Calhoun, G.M. The growth of criminal law in ancient Greece. Berkeley, Calif., 1927.
AH 4159.33	Schlesinger, E. Die griechische Asylie. Diss. Giessen, 1933.
AH 4159.46	Freeman, Kathleen. The murder of Herodes and other trials from the Athenian law courts. London, 1946.
AH 4159.63	MacDowell, D. Athenian homicide law in the age of the orators. Manchester, 1963.

AH 4161		**Ancient Greece in general - Law - Private law - Family law**
AH 4161.5	Glotz, Gustave. Solidarité de la famille. Paris, 1904.
AH 4161.7	Timmermann, R. De nothorum Athenis condicione. Mederici, 1886.
AH 4161.9	Es Vanden, A.H.G.P. De iure familiarum. Lugdunum Batavorum, 1864.
AH 4161.11	Hruza, Ernst. Familienrechts. Erlangen, 1892. 2v.
AH 4161.13	Savage, C.A. The Athenian family. Baltimore, 1907.

AH 4162		**Ancient Greece in general - Law - Private law - Inheritance law**
AH 4162.5	Bunsen, C.C. De iure hereditario Atheniensium. Gottingae, 1813.

AH 4162		**Ancient Greece in general - Law - Private law - Inheritance law - cont.**
AH 4162.9	Steigertahl, G.H.C.L. De vi et usu Parachatabolès in causis Atheniensium hereditariis commentatio. Cellis, 1832.
AH 4162.11	Boor, Carl de. Attische Intestat Erbrecht. Hamburg, 1838.
AH 4162.13	Grasshof, W. Doctrin am iuris Attici de hereditatibus. Berolini, 1877.
AH 4162.15	Caillemer, E. Droit de succession légitime. v.1-2. Paris, 1879.
AH 4162.17	Hafter, Eugen. Die Erbtochter. Leipzig, 1887.
AH 4162.19	Ledl, Arthur. Studien zum attischen Epiklerenrechte. Graz, 1907.
AH 4162.25	Schneider, E. De jure hereditario Atheniensium. Monachii, 1851.

AH 4164		**Ancient Greece in general - Law - Private law - Arrha**
AH 4164.5	Caloziron, Georges. Die Arrha im Vermögensrecht. Leipzig, 1911.
AH 4164.7	Bergold, Friedrich. Geschichte und Wesen des Arrabons und der Arrha im griechischen und römischen Recht. Gernsback, 1923.

AH 4165 - 4169		**Ancient Greece in general - Law - Private law - General works (By date)**
AH 4168.62	Bétant, C. An fuerint apud Graecos indices certi. Berolini, 1862.
AH 4168.67	Dareste, R. Du pret a la grosse. Paris, 1867.
AH 4168.95	Hitzig, H.F. Griechische Pfandrecht. München, 1895.
AH 4168.95.5	Wilbrandt, M. De rerum privatarum ante solonis tempus. Rostochii, 1895.
AH 4168.97.2	Beauchet, Ludovic. Histoire du droit privé de la République Athenienne. Amsterdam, 1969.
AH 4169.12	Raape, L. Der Verfall des griechischen Pfandes. Halle, 1912.
AH 4169.14	Meurs, Johann van. Rechtsgedingen over Bepaalde Goederen. Amsterdam, 1914.
AH 4169.62	Mannzmann, Anneliese. Griechische Stiftungsurkunden. Münster, 1962.

AH 4170 - 4179		**Ancient Greece in general - Law - Agrarian law (Table A)**
AH 4178.34	Hermann, C.F. Causis turbatae apud Lacedaemonios agrorum aequalitatis. Marburgi, 1834.
AH 4179.70	Behrend, Diederich. Attische Pachturkunden. München, 1970.

AH 4180 - 4189		**Ancient Greece in general - Law - Slavery and emancipation (Table A)**
AH 4188.67	Foucart, P. L'affranchissement des esclaves. Paris, 1867.
AH 4188.75	Schück, J. Sklaverei bei den Griechen. Breslau, 1875.
AH 4188.96	Foucart, G. De libertorum conditione apud Athenienses. Lutetiae, 1896.
AH 4188.98	Waszynski, S. De servis Atheniensium publicis. v.1-2. Berolini, 1898.
AH 4189.04	Francke, I. De manumissionibus Delphicis. Monasterii Guestfalorum, 1904.
AH 4189.08	Calderini, A. Condizione dei liberti in Grecia. Milano, 1908.
AH 4189.23	Sargent, R.L. The size of the slave population at Athens during the 5th and 4th century B.C. Thesis. Urbana? 1923?
AH 4189.23.5	Sargent, R.L. The size of the slave population at Athens. Urbana, 1924.
AH 4189.28	Jacob, Oscar. Les esclaves publics à Athènes. Liége, 1928.
AH 4189.37	Valmin, N.S. Arbete och slaveri i antiken. Stockholm, 1937.
AH 4189.59	Lotze, D. Metaxy eleutherōn kai doulōn. Berlin, 1959.
AH 4189.63	Turasiewicz, R. De servis testibus in Atheniensium. Wrocław, 1963.
AH 4189.63.5	Lentsman, Iakov A. Rabstvo v mikenskoi i gomerovskoi Gretsii. Moskva, 1963.
AH 4189.68	Rabstvo na periferii antichnogo mira. Leningrad, 1968.
AH 4189.69	Blavatskaia, Tat'iana v. Rabstvo v ellinisticheskikh gosudarstvakh v III-I vv do n.e. Moskva, 1969.
AH 4189.69.5	Rädle, Herbert. Untersuchungen zum griechischen Freilassungswesen. Inaug. Diss. München, 1969.

AH 4190 - 4199		**Ancient Greece in general - Law - Philosophy of law (Table A)**
AH 4199.50	Wolf, E. Griechisches Rechtsdenken. v.1-4. Frankfurt am Main, 1950-52. 5v.

AH 4200		**Ancient Greece in general - Law - Special topics - Laws of Lycurgus**
AH 4200.5	Kopstadt, A. Constitutionis Lycurgae. Gryphiae, 1849.
AH 4200.7	Stein, H.K. Kritik der Überlieferung über...Lykurg. Glatz, 1882.
AH 4200.9	Bazin, H. De Lycurgo. Paris, 1895.
AH 4200.11	Busson, A. Lykurgos. Innsbruck, 1887.
AH 4200.13	Attinger, G. Essai sur Lycurgue. Neuchatel, 1892.
AH 4200.15	Tsopanakis, A. La Rhètre de Lycurgue. Tyrtée, 1954.

AH 4202		**Ancient Greece in general - Law - Special topics - Laws of Draco**
AH 4202.7	Fritzsche, F.V. De sortitione judicum. Lipsiae, 1835.
AH 4202.9	Hüllmann, K.D. Griechische Denkwürdigkeiten. Bonn, 1840.
AH 4202.11	Hofmann, I. Studien zur drakontischen Verfassung. Straubing, 1899.
AH 4202.15	Stroud, Ronald S. Drakon's law on homicide. Berkeley, 1968.

AH 4204		**Ancient Greece in general - Law - Special topics - Laws of Solon**
AH 4204.5	Prantl, C. De Solonis legibus. Monachii, 1841.
AH 4204.7	Schelling, H. De Solonis legibus. Berolini, 1842.
AH 4204.9	Dramburg. Verfassungskämpfe Athens. Dramburg, 1870.
AH 4204.11	Anfossi, P.C. Legislazioni di Solone e Servio Tullo. Torino, 1899.
AH 4204.12	Schreiner, Iosephus: de corpore iuris Atheniensium. Bonn, 1913.
AH 4204.15	Dondorff, H. Aphorismen zur Beurtheilung der solonischen Verfassung. Berlin, 1880.
AH 4204.17	Makrygiannè, E.S. Meletè peri tès politeias tou Solonos. Ermoupolei, Syrou, 1888.
AH 4204.20	Jonas, J. De Solone Atheniensi. Dissertatio historica. Monasterii Guestfalorum, 1884.

AH 4206   Ancient Greece in general - Law - Special topics - The Areopagus
AH 4206.5   Forchhammer, P.W. De Areopago. Kiliae, 1828.
AH 4206.7   Philippi, A. Areopagu...Epheten. Berlin, 1874.
AH 4206.8   Gleue, H. De homicidarum in Areopago Atheniensi judicio.
   Gottingae, 1894.
AH 4206.9   Terwen, J.J. De Areopago Atheniensium. Ultraiecti, 1894.

AH 4208   Ancient Greece in general - Law - Special topics - The Heliaea
AH 4208.3   Vömel, Johann T. Examina solemnia gymnasii Francofurtani.
   Disseritur de Heliaea. Francofurti, 1822.
AH 4208.5   Westermann, A. De iuris iurandi iudicium Atheniensium
   formula. Lipsiae, 1858.

AH 4212   Ancient Greece in general - Law - Special topics - Proxenia
AH 4212.5   Schubert, J.G. De proxenia Attica. Lipsiae, 1881.
AH 4212.6   Monceaux, P. Les proxénies grecques. Paris, 1885.
AH 4212.7   D'André, J. La proxénie. Toulouse, 1911.

AH 4214   Ancient Greece in general - Law - Special topics - The oath
AH 4214.5   Martin, Albert. Foedera publica. Lutetiae
   Parisiorum, 1886.
AH 4214.7   Ziebarth, E. De iureiurando in iure Graeco.
   Gottingae, 1892.
AH 4214.9   Ott, Ludwig. Kenntnis der griechischen Eid.
   Leipzig, 1896.
AH 4214.11   Hirzel, R. Der Eid. Leipzig, 1902.
AH 4214.17   Hofmann, G. De iurandi apud Athenienses formulis.
   Darmatadii, 1886.
AH 4214.19   Prott, J. de. Fasti Graecorum sacri. Lipsiae, 1893.

AH 4215   Ancient Greece in general - Law - Special topics - Sacred law
AH 4215.5   Ploeg, G.L.J. De veterum Graecorum. Groningae, n.d.
   3 pam.
AH 4215.7   Latte, Kurt. Heiliges Recht. Tübingen, 1920.
AH 4215.9   Oliver, James H. The Athenian expounders of sacred and
   ancestral law. Baltimore, 1950.

AH 4216   Ancient Greece in general - Law - Special topics - Suretyship
AH 4216.5   Beasley, T.W. Le cautionnement. Paris, 1902.
AH 4216.7   Partsch, Josef. Griechisches Bürgschaftsrecht.
   Leipzig, 1909.
AH 4216.10   Bastid, Paul. L'hypothèque grecque et sa signification
   historique. Thèse. Tours, 1917.

AH 4217   Ancient Greece in general - Law - Special topics - Public rewards
AH 4217.5   Hagemann, G. De Graecorum pryteneis capita Tria.
   Vrateslaviae, 1881.
AH 4217.7   Westermann, A. De publicis Atheniensium honoribus ae
   Praemais commutaico. Lipsiae, 1830.
AH 4217.9   Schmitthenner, W. De coronarum apud Athenienses honoribus.
   Berolini, 1891.
AH 4217.10   Şenel, Alaeddin. Eshi yunondo eşitlitove eşitsrilik.
   Ankara, 1970.

AH 4218   Ancient Greece in general - Law - Special topics - Statutes of limitations
AH 4218.5   Charles, John F. Statutes of limitations at Athens. Diss.
   Chicago, 1938.

AH 4219   Ancient Greece in general - Law - Special topics - Sales
AH 4219.5   Pringsheim, F. The Greek law of sale. Weimar, 1950.

AH 4220 - 4229   Ancient Greece in general - Law - Legal procedure (Table A)
AH 4228.12   Hudtwalcker, M.H. Privat-Schiedsrichter-Diäteten.
   Jena, 1812.
AH 4228.20   Otto, C.E. De Atheniensium actionibus forensibus.
   Lipsiae, 1820.
AH 4228.24   Platner, E. Process und Klagen. Darmstaat, 1824. 2v.
AH 4228.24.3   Meier, M.H.E. Attische Process. Halle, 1824.
AH 4228.24.5   Meier, M.H.E. Attische Process. Berlin, 1883. 2v.
AH 4228.46   Meier, M.H.E. Privatschiedsrichter. Halle, 1846.
AH 4228.52   Otto, C.E. De Atheniensium actionibus forensibus publicis.
   Dorpati, 1852.
AH 4228.72   Bohm, H. De Eisaggeliais. Inaug. Diss. Halae, 1874.
AH 4228.77   Höffler, R.J.A. De nomothesia Attica. Kiliae, 1877.
AH 4228.83   Sauppe, Herman. Atheniensium...suffragia.
   Gottingae, 1883.
AH 4228.86   Heikel, I.A. Boyleusis in Mordprocessen.
   Helsingfors, 1886.
AH 4228.93   Pischinger, A. De arbitris Atheniensium publicis.
   München, 1893.
AH 4228.94   Teusch, T. De sortitione indicum apud Atheniensis.
   Gottingae, 1894.
AH 4229.05   Bonner, Robert Johnson. Evidence in Athenian courts.
   Chicago, 1905.
AH 4229.08   Weber, Hans. Attisches Prozessrecht. Paderborn, 1908.
AH 4229.08.2   Weber, Hans. Die Rezeption des attischen Prozessrechts.
   Paderborn, 1908.
AH 4229.21   Schultheiss, Otto. Das attische Volksgericht. Bern, 1921.
AH 4229.24   Smith, Gertrude. The administration of justice from Hesiod
   to Solon. Diss. Chicago, 1924.
AH 4229.27.1   Bonner, Robert Johnson. Lawyers and litigants in ancient
   Athens. N.Y., 1969.
AH 4229.30   Bonner, Robert Johnson. The administration of justice from
   Homer to Aristotle. Chicago, 1930-38. 2v.
AH 4229.30.10   Derenne, Eudore. Les procès d'impiété. Liége, 1930.
AH 4229.33   Paoli, U.E. Studi sul processo attico. Padova, 1933.
AH 4229.36   Harrell, Hansen C. Public arbitration in Athenian Law.
   Chicago, 1936.
AH 4229.36.3   Harrell, Hansen C. Public arbitration in Athenian Law.
   Columbia, 1936.
AH 4229.36.5   Cronin, James F. The Athenian juror and his oath. Diss.
   Chicago, 1936.
AH 4229.41   Ralph, J.D. Ephesus in Athenian litigation. Thesis.
   Chicago, 1941.

AH 4230 - 4239   Ancient Greece in general - Military affairs (Table A)
AH 4231.1   Pamphlet box. Military affairs. German Dissertations.
AH 4237.60   Guischardt, Karl. Mémoires militaires sur les
   Grecs...Romains. Lyon, 1760.
AH 4238.37   Kreenen, J.J. Cohortis Sacrae apud Thebanos Histobiam.
   Arnhemiae, 1837.
Htn   AH 4238.51*   Herbert, Henry W. The captains of the Old World.
   N.Y., 1851.
AH 4238.52   Rüstow, W. Geschichte des griechischen Kriegswesens.
   Aarau, 1852.
AH 4238.52.5   Herbert, Henry W. The captains of the Old World.
   N.Y., 1852.

AH 4230 - 4239   Ancient Greece in general - Military affairs (Table A) - cont.
AH 4238.57   Dansin, H. De mercenariis militibus apud antiquas Graeciae
   civitates...Thesim proponebat. Argentorati, 1857.
AH 4238.69   Chevalier, L. Entstehung...der griechischen Söldnerheere
   und ihre Teilnahme. Prag, 1869.
AH 4238.69.2   Bohstedt, E. Uber das Söldnerwesen. Rendsburg, 1873.
AH 4238.72   Stettin, Prussia. Festungen und Festungskrieg der
   Griechen. Stettin, 1872.
AH 4238.77   Lorenz, A. Sölderei bei den Griechen. Eichstätt, 1876-77.
AH 4238.77.5   Le civilización griega y la ciencia militar entre los
   griegos. Barcelona, 1877.
AH 4238.81   Kopp, W. Griechische Kriegsaltertümer. Berlin, 1881.
AH 4238.82   Müller, K.K. Griechisches Fragment über Kriegswesen.
   Würzburg, 1882.
AH 4238.86   Myska, G.L. De antiquiorum historicorum Graecorum
   vocabulis. Inaug. Diss. Regimonti, 1886.
AH 4238.88   Gülde, O. Die Kriegsverfassung der ersten attischen
   Bundes. Neukaldensleben, 1888.
AH 4238.93   Ringnalda, H.F.T. De exercitu Laeedaemoniorum.
   Leovardiae, 1893.
AH 4239.00.5   Church, A.J. Helmet and spear. N.Y., 1914.
AH 4239.03   Roloff, G. Probleme aus der griechischen Kriegsgeschichte.
   Berlin, 1903.
AH 4239.03.2   Kromayer, J. Antike Schlachtfelder. v.1-4.
   Berlin, 1903-31. 5v.
AH 4239.08   Müller, B. Beiträge zur Geschichte...Söldnerwesens.
   Frankfurt am Main, 1908.
AH 4239.30   Tarn, William W. Hellenistic military and naval
   developments. Cambridge, Eng., 1930.
AH 4239.33   Parke, H. William. Greek mercenary soldiers.
   Oxford, 1933.
AH 4239.35   Griffith, G.T. The mercenaries of the Hellenistic world.
   Cambridge, Eng., 1935.
AH 4239.53   Sarikakēs, Theodōros Christou. The hoplite general in
   Athens. Athens, 1953.
AH 4239.57   Adcock, F.E. The Greek and Macedonian art of war.
   Berkeley, 1957.
AH 4239.61   Brelich, A. Guerra. Bonn, 1961.
AH 4239.65   Pritchett, William Kendrick. Studies in ancient Greek
   topography. Berkeley, 1965- 2v.
AH 4239.68   Problèmes de la guerre en Grèce ancienne, sous la direction
   de Jean-Pierre Vernant. Paris, 1968.
AH 4239.68.5   Ducrey, Pierre. Le traitement des prisonniers de guerre
   dans la Grèce antique des origines à la conquête romaine.
   Paris, 1968.
AH 4239.69.5   Best, Jan. Thracian Peltasts and their influence on Greek
   warfare. Proefschrift. Groningen, 1969.
AH 4239.70   Anderson, John Kinloch. Military theory and practice in
   the age of Xenophon. Berkeley, 1970.
AH 4239.71.5   Pritchett, William Kendrick. Ancient Greek military
   practice. Berkeley, 1971-

AH 4250 - 4259   Ancient Greece in general - Naval affairs (Table A)
AH 4258.40   Böckh, August. Urkunden. Berlin, 1840.
AH 4258.40.2F   Böckh, August. Tafeln zu Urkunden. Berlin, 1840.
AH 4258.55   Goodwin, G.W. De potentiae...maritimae Epochis.
   Gottingae, 1855.
AH 4258.82   Müller, K.K. Griechischen Schrift über Seekrieg.
   Würzburg, 1882.
AH 4258.99   Kolbe, G. De Atheniensium re navali quaestiones.
   Tubingae, 1899.
AH 4259.05   Taru, William W. The Greek warship I-II. n.p., 1905.
   3 pam.
AH 4259.15   Tenne, A. Kriegsschiffe zu den zeiten der alten Griechen.
   Oldenburg, 1915.
AH 4259.19   Custance, Reginald Neville. War at sea. Edinburgh, 1919.
AH 4259.31   Schmidt, Kurt. Die Namen der attischen Kriegsschiffe.
   Inaug. Diss. Engelsdorf, 1931.
AH 4259.37   Döpel, G. Die attische Flotte im peloponnesischen Kriege.
   Inaug. Diss. Borna, 1937.
AH 4259.47   Hyde, Walter W. Ancient Greek mariners. N.Y., 1947.
AH 4259.50   Alexandiēs, K.A. He Thalassia dynamis eis ten historia tēs
   archaias Hellados. Athēnai, 1950.
AH 4259.57   Labarbe, Jules. La loi navale de Themistocle.
   Paris, 1957.
AH 4259.60   Potamianos, Phōkiōn. The sea as a factor of the Greek
   life. Athens? 1960?
AH 4259.65   Amit, M. Athens and the sea. Bruxelles, 1965.
AH 4259.68   Morrison, John Sinclair. Greek oared ships, 900-322 B.C.
   Cambridge, Eng., 1968.

AH 4260 - 4269   Ancient Greece in general - Foreign relations, diplomacy (Table A)
AH 4269.73   Mosley, Derek J. Envoys and diplomacy in ancient Greece.
   Wiesbaden, 1973.

AH 4274 - 4279   Ancient Greece in general - General history (By date)
Htn   AH 4277.51*   Stanyan, T. Grecian history. London, 1751. 2v.
AH 4277.68   Robertson, W. History of ancient Greece. Edinburgh, 1768.
Htn   AH 4277.74*   Goldsmith, Oliver. The Grecian history from the earliest
   state to the death of Alexander the Great. London, 1774.
   2v.
AH 4277.84   Denina, C. Istoria...della Graecia. Venezia, 1784.
   4v.
AH 4277.86F   Gillies, J. History of ancient Greece. London, 1786.
   2v.
AH 4277.86.3   Gillies, J. History of ancient Greece. Dublin, 1786.
   3v.
NEDL   AH 4277.86.4   Gillies, J. History of ancient Greece. Basil, 1790.
   5v.
NEDL   AH 4277.86.5   Gillies, J. History of ancient Greece. 4. ed.
   London, 1801. 4v.
AH 4277.86.7   Gillies, J. History of ancient Greece. 1. American ed.
   N.Y., 1814. 4v.
NEDL   AH 4277.86.10   Gillies, J. History of ancient Greece. 6. ed. v.1-8.
   London, 1820. 4v.
AH 4277.86.12   Gillies, J. History of ancient Greece. 2. American ed.
   Philadelphia, 1822. 4v.
AH 4277.95   Mitford, W. History of Greece. London, 1795. 10v.
AH 4277.95.3   Mitford, W. History of Greece. London, 1814. 8v.
NEDL   AH 4277.95.4   Mitford, W. History of Greece. v.9-10, 3. ed.
   London, 1821-22. 10v.
AH 4277.95.5   Mitford, W. History of Greece. Boston, 1823. 8v.
NEDL   AH 4277.95.5.5   Mitford, W. History of Greece. Boston, 1823. 8v.
NEDL   AH 4277.95.6   Mitford, W. The history of Greece from the earliest period
   to the death of Agesilaus. London, 1835. 8v.
AH 4277.95.7   Mitford, W. History of Greece with final additions and
   corrections. London, 1838. 8v.

AH 4274 - 4279   Ancient Greece in general - General history (By date) - cont.

AH 4278.00 — Goldsmith, Oliver. Grecian history. London, 1800. 2v.
NEDL AH 4278.00.2 — Goldsmith, Oliver. Grecian history. v.1-2. Philadelphia, 1805.
NEDL AH 4278.00.3 — Goldsmith, Oliver. Grecian history. v.1-2. Philadelphia, 1808.
NEDL AH 4278.00.5 — Goldsmith, Oliver. Grecian history from earliest state. v.1-2. Hallowell, 1818.
NEDL AH 4278.00.7 — Goldsmith, Oliver. History of Greece. London, 1821. 2v.
NEDL AH 4278.00.8 — Goldsmith, Oliver. Grecian history from earliest state to the death of Alexander. Hartford, 1824.
AH 4278.00.9 — Goldsmith, Oliver. The history of Greece from the earliest state to the death of Alexander the Great. London, 1825.
AH 4278.00.10 — Goldsmith, Oliver. History of Greece. 11. ed. London, 1825.
AH 4278.00.11 — Goldsmith, Oliver. Pinnock's improved edition of Goldsmith's History of Greece. Philadelphia, 1846.
AH 4278.00.15 — Goldsmith, Oliver. Pinnock's improved edition of Goldsmith's History of Greece. Philadelphia, 1854.
AH 4278.02 — Mavor, W. History of Greece. London, 1802. 2v.
AH 4278.07 — Epitome historia tēs Hellados. En Benetia, 1807. 2v.
AH 4278.19 — Morell, T. Studies in history...Greece. Philadelphia, 1819.
AH 4278.24 — Heeren, A.H.L. Reflections on politics of ancient Greece. Boston, 1824.
NEDL AH 4278.24.2 — Heeren, A.H.L. Sketch of political history of ancient Greece. Oxford, 1829.
AH 4278.24.4 — Heeren, A.H.L. Ancient Greece. 2. ed. Boston, 1842.
AH 4278.24.5 — Heeren, A.H.L. Ancient Greece. London, 1847.
AH 4278.25 — Pinnock, W. Catechism of history of Greece. London, 1822.
AH 4278.29 — Malkin, F. History of Greece from earliest times. London, 1829.
NEDL AH 4278.29.7 — Lamé Fleury, J.R. L'histoire grecque, racontée aux enfants. 4e éd. Paris, 1837.
AH 4278.29.13 — Lamé Fleury, J.R. L'histoire grecque, racontée aux enfants. Paris, 1873.
AH 4278.31 — Plass, H.G. Geschichte des alten Griech. Leipzig, 1831. 3v.
NEDL AH 4278.35 — Thirlwall, C. Cabinet of history. London, 1835. 8v.
AH 4278.35.3 — Thirlwall, C. History of Greece. London, 1845. 8v.
AH 4278.35.3.5 — Thirlwall, C. History of Greece. N.Y., 1845. 2v.
NEDL AH 4278.35.4 — Thirlwall, C. Greece. London, 1844. 2v.
NEDL AH 4278.35.5 — Thirlwall, C. Histoire de la Grèce ancienne. Paris, 1847.
AH 4278.39 — Keightley, T. History of Greece. Boston, 1839.
AH 4278.46 — Grote, George. History of Greece. London, 1846. 12v.
AH 4278.46.3 — Grote, George. History of Greece. 2. ed. London, 1849. 12v.
NEDL AH 4278.46.5 — Grote, George. History of Greece. 2. ed. London, 1849. 12v.
NEDL AH 4278.46.7 — Grote, George. History of Greece. Boston, 1851.
NEDL AH 4278.46.11 — Grote, George. History of Greece. v.2-12. N.Y., 1859. 11v.
AH 4278.46.15 — Grote, George. History of Greece. N.Y., 1852-71. 12v.
AH 4278.46.16 — Grote, George. A history of Greece. London, 1862. 8v.
AH 4278.46.17 — Grote, George. Histoire de la Grece. v.1-19. Paris, 1864. 9v.
NEDL AH 4278.46.19 — Grote, George. History of Greece. N.Y., 1867. 12v.
NEDL AH 4278.46.21 — Grote, George. History of Greece. London, 1869. 12v.
AH 4278.46.23A — Grote, George. History of Greece. London, 1869. 12v.
NEDL AH 4278.46.23B — Grote, George. History of Greece. v.1-7,12. London, 1869. 8v.
NEDL AH 4278.46.27 — Grote, George. History of Greece. 4. ed. London, 1872. 10v.
NEDL AH 4278.46.29 — Grote, George. History of Greece. v.1-6,8-10. London, 1872. 9v.
NEDL AH 4278.46.34 — Grote, George. Greece. N.Y., 1899-1901. 2v.
AH 4278.46.36 — Grote, George. History of Greece. London, 1906. 12v.
AH 4278.46.37 — Grote, George. History of Greece. London, 1906. 3v.
AH 4278.46.75 — Grote, George. A history of Greece from the time of Solon to 403 B.C. London, 1907.
AH 4278.50 — Keightley, T. Historia tēs Archaias Hellados. En Athēnais, 1850.
AH 4278.53 — Durdent, René Jean. Beautés de l'histoire grecque. 7. éd. Paris, 1853.
AH 4278.55 — Boreau, V. Historia griega. Santiago, 1855.
NEDL AH 4278.56 — History of ancient Greece. London, 1856.
AH 4278.56.4 — Duruy, V. Histoire grecque. 5. éd. Paris, 1866.
NEDL AH 4278.56.5 — Duruy, V. Histoire grecque. 4. éd. Paris, 1864.
NEDL AH 4278.56.6 — Duruy, V. Histoire grecque. 6. éd. Paris, 1867.
AH 4278.56.7 — Duruy, V. Histoire de la Grèce ancienne. Paris, 1888.
AH 4278.56.9 — Duruy, V. Histoire grecque. Paris, 1856.
AH 4278.56.13 — Duruy, V. Histoire grecque. Paris, 1889.
NEDL AH 4278.56.15 — Duruy, V. Historia de los Griegos. Barcelona, 1890. 2v.
AH 4278.56.25 — Duruy, V. Histoire grecque. 32. éd. Paris, 1901.
AH 4278.56.35F — Duruy, V. History of Greece. v.1-4. Boston, 1890. 8v.
AH 4278.57 — Mone, F. Kritische Bemerkung von Ernest Curtius. Berlin, 1858.
AH 4278.57.5 — Curtius, Ernest. Griechische Geschichte. Berlin, 1857. 3v.
NEDL AH 4278.57.6 — Curtius, Ernest. Griechische Geschichte. Berlin, 1878. 3v.
AH 4278.57.7A — Curtius, Ernest. Griechische Geschichte. 6. Aufl. Berlin, 1887. 3v.
AH 4278.57.7B — Curtius, Ernest. Griechische Geschichte. 6. Aufl. Berlin, 1887. 3v.
AH 4278.57.12 — Curtius, Ernest. History of Greece. London, 1868. 5v.
NEDL AH 4278.57.13 — Curtius, Ernest. History of Greece. N.Y., 1871. 5v.
NEDL AH 4278.57.13.5 — Curtius, Ernest. History of Greece. N.Y., 1868?-1873? 5v.
NEDL AH 4278.57.14A — Curtius, Ernest. History of Greece. N.Y., 1876. 5v.
NEDL AH 4278.57.14B — Curtius, Ernest. History of Greece. N.Y., 1876. 5v.
NEDL AH 4278.57.16 — Curtius, Ernest. History of Greece. N.Y., 1883. 5v.
NEDL AH 4278.57.17A — Curtius, Ernest. History of Greece. N.Y., 1886. 5v.
NEDL AH 4278.57.17B — Curtius, Ernest. History of Greece. N.Y., 1886. 5v.
NEDL AH 4278.57.17.5 — Curtius, Ernest. History of Greece. N.Y., 1892. 5v.
NEDL AH 4278.57.18 — Curtius, Ernest. History of Greece. N.Y., 1897. 5v.
NEDL AH 4278.57.19 — Smith, William. A history of Greece. Boston, 1855.
NEDL AH 4278.57.19.5A — Smith, William. A history of Greece. Boston, 1855.
NEDL AH 4278.57.19.5B — Smith, William. A history of Greece. Boston, 1855.
AH 4278.57.20 — Smith, William. History of Greece. Boston, 1857.
NEDL AH 4278.57.21 — Smith, William. History of Greece. Boston, 1857.
NEDL AH 4278.57.22 — Smith, William. History of Greece. Boston, 1860.

AH 4274 - 4279   Ancient Greece in general - General history (By date) - cont.

NEDL AH 4278.57.23 — Smith, William. History of Greece. N.Y., 1860.
NEDL AH 4278.57.23.10 — Smith, William. History of Greece. N.Y., 1861.
NEDL AH 4278.57.23.15 — Smith, William. History of Greece. N.Y., 1863.
NEDL AH 4278.57.24.7 — Smith, William. History of Greece. N.Y., 1885.
NEDL AH 4278.57.24.9 — Smith, William. History of Greece. N.Y., 1886.
NEDL AH 4278.57.25 — Smith, William. History of Greece. London, 1900.
NEDL AH 4278.57.28 — Smith, William. Smaller history of Greece. N.Y., 1860.
NEDL AH 4278.57.32 — Smith, William. Smaller history of Greece. N.Y., 1886.
NEDL AH 4278.68.2 — Stoll, H.W. Geschichte der Griechen bis zur Unterwerfung unter Rom. 2. Aufl. Hannover, 1871. 2v.
AH 4278.74.5 — Cox, George W. History of Greece. London, 1878. 2v.
AH 4278.76 — Cox, George W. General history of Greece. N.Y., 1876.
NEDL AH 4278.76.4 — Pennell, R.F. Ancient Greece. Boston, 1876.
AH 4278.76.5 — Pennell, R.F. Ancient Greece. Boston, 1886.
AH 4278.76.10 — Pennell, R.F. Ancient Greece from the earliest times down to 146 B.C. Boston, 1895.
AH 4278.77 — Cox, George W. History of Greece. London, 1874. 2v.
AH 4278.78 — Fyffe, C.A. History of Greece. N.Y., 1878.
NEDL AH 4278.78.4 — Fyffe, C.A. History of Greece. N.Y., 1883.
NEDL AH 4278.78.5 — Fyffe, C.A. History of Greece. N.Y., 1875.
NEDL AH 4278.78.7 — Fyffe, C.A. History of Greece. N.Y., 1890.
NEDL AH 4278.78.8 — Fyffe, C.A. History of Greece. N.Y., 1885.
NEDL AH 4278.78.10 — Fyffe, C.A. Nociones de Historia de Grecia. N.Y., 1880.
AH 4278.79 — Hertzberg, G.F. Geschichte von Hellas und Rom. Berlin, 1879. 2v.
AH 4278.80 — Combers, L. La Grèce. Paris, 1880.
AH 4278.80.5 — Van den Berg. Petite histoire des Grecs. Paris, 1880.
AH 4278.81 — Timayenis, T.T. History of Greece. N.Y., 1881. 2v.
NEDL AH 4278.81.2 — Timayenis, T.T. History of Greece. N.Y., 1883. 2v.
NEDL AH 4278.81.3 — Timayenis, T.T. History of Greece. N.Y., 1884. 2v.
NEDL AH 4278.81.4 — Timayenis, T.T. History of Greece. N.Y., 1882-83. 2v.
AH 4278.83 — Duncker, M.W. History of Greece. London, 1883. 2v.
AH 4278.83.5 — Willson, M. Mosaics of Grecian history. N.Y., 1883.
AH 4278.85 — Busolt, G. Griechische Geschichte. Gotha, 1885-97. 3v.
AH 4278.85.3 — Busolt, G. Griechische Geschichte. v.1-3. Gotha, 1893-1904. 4v.
AH 4278.85.5 — Harrison, J.A. The story of Greece. N.Y., 1885.
AH 4278.85.7 — Harrison, J.A. The story of Greece. N.Y., 1887.
AH 4278.86 — Ménard, L. Histoire des Grecs. Paris, 1886. 2v.
AH 4278.86.5 — Holm, Adolf. Griechische Geschichte. Berlin, 1886. 4v.
AH 4278.86.7A — Holm, Adolf. History of Greece. London, 1894. 4v.
NEDL AH 4278.86.7B — Holm, Adolf. History of Greece. London, 1894. 4v.
NEDL AH 4278.86.8 — Holm, Adolf. History of Greece. London, 1896-99. 4v.
NEDL AH 4278.86.9 — Holm, Adolf. The history of Greece. London, 1906. 4v.
NEDL AH 4278.86.10 — Holm, Adolf. The history of Greece. London, 1899-1902. 4v.
AH 4278.87 — Jäger, O.E.F. Geschichte der Griechen. Gütersloh, 1887.
NEDL AH 4278.87.5A — Duruy, J.V. Histoire des Grecs. Paris, 1887. 3v.
NEDL AH 4278.87.5B — Duruy, J.V. Histoire des Grecs. Paris, 1887. 3v.
AH 4278.87.7 — Rose, D. A popular history of Greece. London, 1887.
AH 4278.88 — Abbott, Evelyn. History of Greece. v.2, photoreproduction. London, 1888-1900. 3v.
NEDL AH 4278.90.5 — Oman, C.W.C. History of Greece. Rivingtons, 1890.
AH 4278.90.6 — Oman, C.W.C. History of Greece. 2. ed. London, 1891.
AH 4278.90.6.3 — Oman, C.W.C. History of Greece. 3. ed. London, 1892.
AH 4278.90.6.4 — Oman, C.W.C. History of Greece. 4. ed. London, 1893.
AH 4278.90.7.5 — Oman, C.W.C. History of Greece. 7. ed. N.Y., 1901.
AH 4278.90.9 — Oman, C.W.C. Greece. v.2. Philadelphia, 1906.
AH 4278.91.5 — Roth, K.L. Griechische Geschichte. München, 1891.
AH 4278.92 — Joy, James R. Grecian history. N.Y., 1892.
AH 4278.93A — Beloch, J. Grecian history. v.1-3. Strassburg, 1893- 4v.
AH 4278.93B — Beloch, J. Grecian history. Strassburg, 1893- 2v.
AH 4278.93.2 — Beloch, J. Grecian history. v.1-4. Strassburg, 1912-27. 8v.
AH 4278.96 — Swoboda, H. Griechische Geschichte. Leipzig, 1896.
AH 4278.96.7 — Brelet, H. Historiae Graecae. Paris, 1896.
AH 4278.98 — Myers, P. Van Ness. A history of Greece for colleges and high schools. Boston, 1898.
AH 4278.98.10 — Coleridge, E.P. Res graecae. London, 1898.
AH 4278.99A — Botsford, George W. History of Greece. N.Y., 1899.
AH 4278.99B — Botsford, George W. History of Greece. N.Y., 1899.
AH 4278.99.3 — Botsford, George W. A history of Greece for high schools and academies. N.Y., 1900.
AH 4278.99.5 — Botsford, George W. A history of the Orient and Greece. N.Y., 1911.
AH 4279.00.4A — Bury, John Bagnell. History of Greece. London, 1902. 2v.
AH 4279.00.4B — Bury, John Bagnell. History of Greece. London, 1902. 2v.
AH 4279.00.30 — Bury, John Bagnell. A history of Greece to the death of Alexander the Great. 3. ed. London, 1951.
AH 4279.00.31 — Bury, John Bagnell. A history of Greece to the death of Alexander the Great. 3. ed. London, 1972.
AH 4279.06 — Shuckburgh, E.S. Greece. N.Y., 1906.
AH 4279.06.5 — Shuckburgh, E.S. Greece from the coming of the Hellenes to A.D. 14. 1. ed. London, 1922.
AH 4279.09.5 — Pöhlmann, R. von. Grundriss der griechischen Geschichte nebst Quellenkunde. 4. Aufl. München, 1909.
X Cg AH 4279.12 — Soteriades, G. Historia tēs Archaiotētos. Athēnai, 1912.
AH 4279.14 — Jardé, A. Grèce antique et la vie grecque. Paris, 1914.
AH 4279.14.5 — Thallon, Ida C. Readings in Greek history. Boston, 1914.
AH 4279.15A — Botsford, George W. Hellenic civilization. N.Y., 1915.
AH 4279.15B — Botsford, George W. Hellenic civilization. N.Y., 1915.
AH 4279.20 — Ciccotti, Ettore. Griechische Geschichte. Gotha, 1920.
AH 4279.21 — James, Henry R. Our Hellenic heritage. London, 1921-30. 2v.
AH 4279.21.2 — James, Henry R. Our Hellenic heritage. v.1-2. N.Y., 1927.
AH 4279.21.5 — Walker, E.M. Greek history. Oxford, 1921.
AH 4279.22A — Botsford, George W. Hellenic history. N.Y., 1922.
AH 4279.22B — Botsford, George W. Hellenic history. N.Y., 1922.
AH 4279.22C — Botsford, George W. Hellenic history. N.Y., 1922.
AH 4279.22.2A — Botsford, George W. Hellenic history. N.Y., 1926.
AH 4279.22.2B — Botsford, George W. Hellenic history. N.Y., 1926.
AH 4279.22.3 — Botsford, George W. Hellenic history. N.Y., 1930.
AH 4279.22.4 — Botsford, George W. Hellenic history. N.Y., 1928.
AH 4279.22.5 — Botsford, George W. Hellenic history. N.Y., 1939.
AH 4279.22.8 — Botsford, George W. Hellenic history. 3. ed. N.Y., 1948.
AH 4279.22.9 — Botsford, George W. Hellenic history. 4. ed. N.Y., 1956.
AH 4279.22.9.5 — Botsford, George W. Botsford and Robinson's Hellenic history. 5. ed. N.Y., 1969.
AH 4279.22.10 — Ciccotti, Ettore. Storia greca. Firenze, 1922.

Classified Listing

AH 4274 - 4279   Ancient Greece in general - General history (By date) - cont.

AH 4279.24	Wilcken, U. Griechische Geschichte im Rahmen der Altertumsgeschichte. München, 1924.
AH 4279.24.5	Wilcken, U. Griechische Geschichte im Rahmen der Altertumsgeschichte. 7. Aufl. München, 1951.
AH 4279.25	Grundy, G.B. A history of the Greek and Roman world. N.Y., 1925.
AH 4279.26	Grundy, G.B. A history of the Greek and Roman world. London, 1926.
AH 4279.26.5	Hatzfeld, Jean. Histoire de la Grèce ancienne. Paris, 1926.
AH 4279.26.5.3	Hatzfeld, Jean. Histoire de la Grèce ancienne. Paris, 1950.
AH 4279.26.5.4	Hatzfeld, Jean. Histoire de la Grèce ancienne. 3. éd. Paris, 1962.
AH 4279.26.9	Hamilton, M.A. (Mrs.). Greece. Oxford, 1926.
AH 4279.28.5	Puech, Aimé. Ce qu'il faut connaître de la Grèce antique. Paris, 1928.
AH 4279.29.4.5	Robinson, Cyril E. A history of Greece. 9. ed. London, 1957.
AH 4279.29.5	Ferrabino, Aldo. La dissoluzione della libertà nella Grecia antica. Padova, 1929.
AH 4279.29.10	Warg, Hans. Griechische Geschichte. Leipzig, 1929.
AH 4279.29.15	Hallynck, P. L'Orient et la Grèce. Paris, 1929.
AH 4279.31	Berve, Helmut. Griechische Geschichte. Freiburg, 1931-33. 2v.
AH 4279.31.2	Berve, Helmut. Griechische Geschichte. 2. Aufl. Freiburg, 1951- 2v.
AH 4279.32	Petrie, Alexander. An introduction to Greek history. London, 1932.
AH 4279.32.5	Laistner, M.L.W. Greek history. Boston, 1932.
AH 4279.34A	Lavell, C.F. A biography of the Greek people. Boston, 1934.
AH 4279.34B	Lavell, C.F. A biography of the Greek people. Boston, 1934.
AH 4279.36	Robinson, D.M. A short history of Greece. N.Y., 1936.
AH 4279.38.7	Secco Ellauri, Oscar. Historia de los griegos. Montevideo, 1945.
AH 4279.40A	Prentice, William K. The ancient Greeks. London, 1940.
AH 4279.40B	Prentice, William K. The ancient Greeks. London, 1940.
AH 4279.42	Sanctis, G. de. Storia dei greci dalle origini alla fine del secolo V. 3. ed. Firenze, 1942. 2v.
AH 4279.46	Robinson, Cyril E. Zíto Hellas. London, 1946.
AH 4279.46.2	Robinson, Cyril E. Hellas. N.Y., 1948.
AH 4279.46.5	Ehrenberg, V. Aspects of the ancient world. N.Y., 1946.
AH 4279.46.10	Laache, Rolv. Om hellener og barbarer og om Athens herlighet. Oslo, 1946.
AH 4279.47	Bruwaene, M. Le miracle grec. Bruxelles, 1947.
AH 4279.51	Kitto, H.D.F. The Greeks. Harmondsworth, 1951.
AH 4279.53	Accame, Silvio. Problemi di storia greca. Rome, 1953.
AH 4279.53.5	Loenen, Dirk. Stasis. Amsterdam, 1953.
AH 4279.54	Giannelli, Giulio. Trattato di storia greca. 3. ed. Roma, 1954.
AH 4279.58.5	Wade-Gery, H.T. Essays in Greek history. Oxford, 1958.
AH 4279.58.10	Woodhouse, W.J. The tutorial history of Greece. 3. ed. London, 1958.
AH 4279.58.15	Grant, Michael. Greeks. Edinburgh, 1958.
AH 4279.58.20	Zielinski, Tadeusz. Grecja niepodległa. 1. wyd. Warszawa, 1958.
AH 4279.59	Hammond, Nicholas Geoffrey Lemprière. A history of Greece. Oxford, 1959.
AH 4279.59.5	Hammond, Nicholas Geoffrey Lemprière. A history of Greece to 322 B.C. 2. ed. Oxford, 1967.
AH 4279.60	Smith, Morton. The ancient Greeks. Ithaca, N.Y., 1960.
AH 4279.60.5	Crossland, R.A. New background to the study of ancient Greece. Sheffield, 1960.
AH 4279.60.10	Schachermeyr, Fritz. Griechische Geschichte. Stuttgart, 1960.
AH 4279.60.12	Schachermeyr, Fritz. Griechische Geschichte. 2. Aufl. Stuttgart, 1969.
AH 4279.61A	Barr, Stringfellow. The will of Zeus. Philadelphia, 1961.
AH 4279.62	De Silincourt, A. The world of Herodotus. London, 1962.
AH 4279.62.3	De Silincourt, A. The world of Herodotus. 1. ed. Boston, 1963.
AH 4279.63	Badi, Amiz Mehdi. Les Grecs et les barbares. v.1-3. Lausanne, 1963-66. 2v.
AH 4279.66	Blavatskaia, Tat'iana V. Akheiskaia Gretsiia vo vtorom tysiacheletii do nie. Moskva, 1966.
AH 4279.67	Pugliese Carratelli, Giovanni. Storia greca. Milano, 1967.
AH 4279.67.5	Levi, Mario Attilio. Quattro studi spartani e altri scritti di storia greca. Milano, 1967.
AH 4279.68	Senel, Alâeddin. Eski Yunanda siyasal düşünüş. Ankara, 1968.
AH 4279.68.5	Burn, Andrew Robert. The warring states of Greece from their rise to the Roman conquest. London, 1968.
AH 4279.69	Bengtson, Hermann. Griechische Geschichte. 2. Aufl. München, 1969.
AH 4279.73	Green, Peter. A concise history of Ancient Greece to the close of the classical era. London, 1973.
AH 4279.73.5	Chambers, Mortimer Hardin. Ancient Greece. Washington, 1973.

AH 4294 - 4299   Ancient Greece in general - General special - Miscellany (By date)

AH 4296.26	Emmius, U. Vetus Graecia. Lugdunum Batavorum, 1626.
AH 4298.08	Hegewisch, D.H. Colonien der Griechen. Altona, 1808.
AH 4298.11	Hegewisch, D.H. Griechischen Colonien. Altona, 1811.
AH 4298.21F	Bertocchi, F. Raccolta di 100 soggetti li piú remarche. Roma, 1821.
AH 4298.26.5	Heeren, Arnold H.L. The historical works of Arnold H.L. Heeren. London, 1846?-50? 6v.
AH 4298.40	Wordsworth, C. Greece; pictorial, descriptive, and historical. London, 1840.
NEDL AH 4298.40.2	Wordsworth, C. Greece; pictorial, descriptive, and historical. 2. ed. London, 1844.
AH 4298.44	Weissenborn, J.C. Hellen. Jena, 1844.
AH 4298.44.5	Müller, K.O. Geschichten hellenische Stämme und Städte-Karten. Breslau, 1844. 4v.
AH 4298.52	Jacobs, Friedrich. Hellas; Vorträge über Heimath, Geschichte, Literatur und Kunst der Hellenen. Berlin, 1852.
AH 4298.52.2	Jacobs, Friedrich. Hellas; Geographie, Geschichte und Literatur Griechenlands. Stuttgart, 1897.
AH 4298.52.5	Jacobs, Friedrich. Hellas; or, The home, history, literature, and art of the Greeks. London, 1855.
AH 4298.53	Wordsworth, C. Greece; pictorial, descriptive, and historical. London, 1853.

AH 4294 - 4299   Ancient Greece in general - General special - Miscellany (By date) - cont.

AH 4298.53.2	Wordsworth, C. Greece; pictorial, descriptive, and historical. London, 1859.
NEDL AH 4298.53.3	Wordsworth, C. Greece; pictorial, descriptive and historical. 5. ed. London, 1868.
AH 4298.53.5	Turner, D.W. Heads of an analogy of the history of Greece. 2. ed. London, 1860.
AH 4298.56	Reynald, H. Libertati apud veteres Graeciae populos quid defuerit. Parisiis, 1856.
AH 4298.58	Paparrēgópanlos, K. Istorikai pragmateiai. v.1-6. Athēnai, 1858.
AH 4298.62	Bässler, F. Hellenischer Heldensaal. 2. Aufl. Berlin, 1862.
AH 4298.76	Loeschcke, G. De titulis aliquot Atticis. Bonnae, 1876.
AH 4298.83	Steele, J.D. Brief history of Greece. N.Y., 1883.
AH 4298.83.2	Steele, J.D. Brief history of Greece. N.Y., 1883.
AH 4298.83.10	Erdmann, M. Zur Kunde der hellenistischen Städtegründungen. Strassburg, 1883.
AH 4298.84	Lamprog, S. Meletēllata. Athēnai, 1884.
AH 4298.84.5	Thiriou, M. De civitatibus quae a Graecis in Chersoneso taurica conditae fuerunt. Thesim. Nancy, 1884.
AH 4298.87	Duncker, Max. Abhandlungen aus der griechische Geschichte. Leipzig, 1887.
AH 4298.88	Paganelēs. Athēnaikai nyktes. Athēnai, 1888.
AH 4298.90	Lévi, Sylvain. Quid de Graecis veterum indorum. Paris, 1890.
AH 4298.92A	Mahaffy, J.P. Problems in Greek history. Photoreproduction. London, 1892.
AH 4298.92B	Mahaffy, J.P. Problems in Greek history. Photoreproduction. London, 1892.
AH 4298.92.5	Hertzberg, G.F. Altgriechische Kolonisation. Gütersloh, 1892.
AH 4298.92.7	Meyer, E. Forschungen zur alten Geschichte. Halle, 1892. 2v.
AH 4298.92.11	Gardner, P. New chapters in Greek history. London, 1892.
AH 4298.93	Wiedemann, A. Beziehungen zwischen Aegypten und Griechenland. Leipzig, 1883.
AH 4298.95	Butzer, H. Quellenbuch. Dresden, 1895.
AH 4299.00.4	Swoboda, H. Greek history. London, 1920.
AH 4299.07	Huber, Peter. Griechische Geschichte bis 449. München, 1907.
AH 4299.10	Myres, John L. Greek lands and the Greek people. Oxford, 1910.
AH 4299.10.3	Syllogos pros. Eikones ek tēs archaias. Athēnai, n.d.
AH 4299.11	Billeter, G. Die Anschauungen von Wesen des Griechentums. Leipzig, 1911.
X Cg AH 4299.13	Haverfield, F. Ancient town-planning. Oxford, 1913.
AH 4299.14	Tillyard, E. The Athenian empire and the great illusion. Cambridge, 1914.
AH 4299.21.4	Birt, T. Von Homer bis Sokrates. 4. Aufl. Leipzig, 1929.
AH 4299.23	Halliday, William R. The growth of the city state. Liverpool, 1923.
AH 4299.29	Ferrarino, Aldo. La dissoluzione della libertà nella Grecia antica. Padova, 1929.
AH 4299.30	Myres, John L. Who were the Greeks? Berkeley, Calif., 1930.
AH 4299.34	Cohen, R. La grèce et l'hellénisation du monde antique. Paris, 1934.
AH 4299.34.5	Cohen, R. La grèce et l'hellénisation du monde antique. 3. éd. Paris, 1948.
AH 4299.36	Bullock, Charles J. The new deal in ancient Greece. Cambridge, 1936.
AH 4299.37A	Gomme, Arnold W. Essays in Greek history and literature. Oxford, 1937.
AH 4299.37B	Gomme, Arnold W. Essays in Greek history and literature. Oxford, 1937.
AH 4299.45	Hatzfeld, Jean. La Grèce et son héritage. Paris, 1945.
AH 4299.47	Wason, Margaret O. Class struggles in ancient Greece. London, 1947.
AH 4299.47.5	Mazzarino, S. Fra Ceriente e Occidente; ricerche di storia greca arcaica. Firenze, 1947.
AH 4299.50	Freeman, K. Greek city-states. London, 1950.
AH 4299.50.5	Freeman, K. Greek city-states. 1. ed. N.Y., 1950.
AH 4299.53	Myres, John L. Geographical history in Greek lands. Oxford, 1953.
AH 4299.53.5	Murray, Gilbert. Hellenism and the modern world. London, 1953.
AH 4299.53.7	Murray, Gilbert. Hellenism and the modern world. Boston, 1954.
AH 4299.56	Martin, Roland. L'urbanisme dans la Grèce antique. Paris, 1956.
AH 4299.58.5	Seltman, Charles T. Riot in Ephesus; writings on the heritage of Greece. London, 1958.
AH 4299.60	Berard, Jean. L'expansion et la colonisation. Paris, 1960.
AH 4299.61	Grècs et barbares. Genève, 1961.
AH 4299.62	Woodhead, Arthur Geoffrey. The Greeks in the West. London, 1962.
AH 4299.62.5	Gomme, Arnold W. More essays in Greek history and literature. Oxford, 1962.
AH 4299.62.10	Moretti, Luigi. Ricerche sulle leghe greche: peloponnesiaca-beotica-licia. Roma, 1962.
AH 4299.64	Bauer, Walter. Lorbeer für Hallas. Stuttgart, 1964.
AH 4299.64.5	Graham, Alexander John. Colony and mother city in ancient Greece. N.Y., 1964.
AH 4299.69	Gorbunova, Vseniia S. Drevnie greki na ostrove Berezan'. Leningrad, 1969.
AH 4299.71	Baaccesi, Lorenzo. Grecità adriatica. Bologna, 1971.
AH 4299.71.5	Estudios sobre el mundo helenístico. Swilla, 1971.
AH 4299.73	Amit, M. Great and small poleis. Bruxelles, 1973.

AH 4300 - 4309   Ancient Greece in general - General special - Philosophy of history (Table A)

AH 4303.6	Touloumakos, Johannes. Zum Geschichtsbewusstsein der Griechen in der Zeit der römischen Herrschaft. Bonn, 1971.
AH 4307.49	Mably, G.B. Observations sur les Grecs. Genève, 1749.
AH 4307.87	Pauw, C. Recherches philosophiques sur les Grecs. Berlin, 1787. 2v.
AH 4307.87.5	Pauw, C. Philosophical dissertations on the Greeks. London, 1793. 2v.
AH 4308.15	Drumann, K.U. Ideen zur Geschichte des Verfalls. Berlin, 1815.
AH 4308.65	Oncken, W. Athen und Hellas. Leipzig, 1865.
AH 4308.69	Curtius, Ernst. Festrede. Berlin, 1869.
AH 4309.00	Bouché-Leclercq, A. Leçons d'histoire grecque. Paris, 1900.

AH 4300 - 4309   Ancient Greece in general - General special - Philosophy of history (Table A) - cont.

AH 4309.00.2	Bouché-Leclercq, A. Leçons d'histoire grecque. 2. éd. Paris, 1913.
AH 4309.02	Pöhlmann, R. Griechische Geschichte. München, 1902.
AH 4309.21	Toynbee, A.J. The tragedy of Greece. Oxford, 1921.
AH 4309.54A	Gomme, Arnold W. The attitude to poetry and history. Berkeley, 1954.
AH 4309.54B	Gomme, Arnold W. The attitude to poetry and history. Berkeley, 1954.
AH 4309.54.5	Arias, Paolo E. Storiografia e fonti della storia greca. Bologna, 1954.
AH 4309.62	Châtelet, François. La naissance de l'histoire. Paris, 1962.
AH 4309.65	Fabricius, Johannes. Oldtidens idéhistorie. København, 1965.
AH 4309.67	Fritz, Kurt von. Die griechische Geschichtsschreibung. Text and notes. Berlin, 1967- 2v.

AH 4310 - 4319   Ancient Greece in general - General special - Cosmology (Table A)

AH 4318.51.1	Pococke, Edward. India in Greece. Delhi, 1972.

AH 4320 - 4329   Ancient Greece in general - General special - Races (Table A)

AH 4323.5	Nixon, Ivor G. The rise of the Dorians. N.Y., 1968.
AH 4328.30	Müller, K.O. History and antiquities of Dorie Race. Oxford, 1830. 2v.
AH 4328.30.2	Müller, K.O. History and antiquities of Dorie Race. 2. ed. London, 1839. 2v.
AH 4328.37	Uebelen, G. Jonische Stamms. Stuttgart, 1837.
AH 4328.48	Ow, J. Die Abstammung der Griechen und die Errthüme und Tausch. München, 1848.
AH 4328.49	Mueller, E.H.O. De populi Atheniensis tribuum origine. Marburgi, 1849.
AH 4328.55	Curtius, Ernst. Die Ionier. Berlin, 1855.
AH 4328.56	Schoemann, G.F. Animadversiones de Ionibus. Gryphisivaldiae, 1856.
AH 4328.61	Nitzsch, Otto. Jonischen Städteleben. Greifswald, 1861.
AH 4328.84	Bruck, Sylvius. De Pelasgis. Vratislaviae, 1884.
AH 4328.91F	Schwartz, E. Quaestiones Ionicas. Adleranis, 1891.
AH 4329.06	Peroutka, E. Pelasgove'. Praze, 1906.
AH 4329.20	Bilabel, Friedrich. Die ionische Kolonisation. Leipzig, 1920.
AH 4329.26	Jardé, Auguste. The formation of the Greek people. N.Y., 1926.
AH 4329.27	Mucke, J.R. Die Urbevölkerung Griechenlands und ihre allmähliche Entwickelung zu Volksstämen. Leipzig, 1927-29.
AH 4329.29	Günther, H.F.K. Rassengeschichte des hellenischen und des römischen Volkes. München, 1929.
AH 4329.37	Diller, A. Race mixture among the Greeks before Alexander. Urbana, 1937.
AH 4329.56	Will, Edouard. Doriens et Ioniens. Strasbourg, 1956.
AH 4329.56.5	Will, Edouard. Doriens et Ioniens. Paris, 1956.
AH 4329.66	Huxley, George. The early Ionians. N.Y., 1966.
AH 4329.71	Bourgeois, Alain. La Grèce antique devant la négritude. Paris, 1971.

AH 4330 - 4339   Ancient Greece in general - General special - Collected biographies (Table A)

AH 4333.5	Broadbent, Molly. Studies in Greek genealogy. Leiden, 1968.
AH 4338.49	Bässler, Ferdinand. Hellenischer Heldensaal. v.2. Berlin, 1851.
AH 4338.85A	Cox, George W. Lives of Greek statesmen. N.Y., 1885. 2v.
AH 4338.85B	Cox, George W. Lives of Greek statesmen. N.Y., 1885. 2v.
AH 4339.13	Poralla, Paul. Prosopographie der Lakedaimonier bis auf die Zeit Alexanders des Grossen. Inaug. Diss. Breslau, 1913.
AH 4339.18	Hopkinson, L.W. Greek leaders. Boston, 1918.
AH 4339.23	Pohlenz, M. Gestalten aus Hellas. München, 1950.
AH 4339.71	Kanellopoulos, Panagiötes. Five men - five centuries; essays on Solon. London, 1971.
AH 4339.71.5	Davies, John K. Athenian propertied families, 600-300 B.C. Oxford, 1971.
AH 4339.72	Bicknell, P.J. Studies in Athenian politics and genealogy. Wiesbaden, 1972.

AH 4400 - 4409   Ancient Greece in general - History by periods - Before 500 B.C. - General works (Table A)

AH 4403.54	Oliva, Pavel. Raná řecká tyrannis. Praha, 1954.
AH 4407.87	Rabaut, J.P. L'histoire primitive de la Grèce. Paris, 1787.
AH 4408.09.5	Clavier, M. Histoire des premiers temps de la Grèce. 2. éd. Paris, 1822. 3v.
AH 4408.14	Hüllmann, K.D. Anfänge der griechischen Geschichte. Königsberg, 1814.
AH 4408.25	Eissner, C.G. Die alten Pelasger und ihre Mysterien. Leipzig, 1825.
AH 4408.27	Petit-Radel, C.F. Examen analytique...de l'histoire...de la Grèce. Paris? 1827.
AH 4408.56	Behr, Par M. L'histoire des temps heroïques. Paris, 1856.
AH 4408.60	Volkmuth, P. Pelasger als Semiten. Schaffhausen, 1860.
AH 4408.75	Pyne, J. Pre-historic Greece. N.Y., 1875.
AH 4408.89F	Corcia, N. Frammento della storia graecia. Napoli, 1889.
AH 4408.90	Hesselmeyer, E. Die Pelasgerfrage und ihre Lösbarkeit. Tübingen, 1890.
AH 4408.91	Beloch, J. Storia greca. Roma, 1891.
AH 4408.91.5	Allcroft, A.H. Early Grecian history. London, 1891.
AH 4408.91.7	Prigge, E. De thesei rebus gestis quaestionum. Marpurgi, 1891.
AH 4408.92	Müller, H.D. Historisch-mythologischen Untersuchungen. Göttingen, 1892.
AH 4409.01A	Ridgeway, W. Early age of Greece. Cambridge, 1901-31. 2v.
AH 4409.01B	Ridgeway, W. Early age of Greece. Cambridge, 1901.
AH 4409.06	Wilamowitz-Moellendorff, Ulrich von. Uber die ionische Wanderung. n.p., 1906.
AH 4409.09	Fimmen, D. Zeit und Dauer der kretisch-mykenischen Kultur. Leipzig, 1909.
AH 4409.11	Penka, K. Die vorhellenische Bevölkerung Griechenlands. Hildburg, 1911.
AH 4409.15	Snyder, William L. The military annals of Greece from the earliest times to the beginning of the Pelopormesian War. Boston, 1915. 2v.
AH 4409.20	Forsdyke, E.J. Greece before Homer. London, 1956.

AH 4400 - 4409   Ancient Greece in general - History by periods - Before 500 B.C. - General works (Table A) - cont.

AH 4409.65	Accame, Silvio. Ricerche di storia greca. Napoli, 1965?
AH 4409.66	Forest, William George Grieve. The emergence of Greek democracy, 800-400 B.C. N.Y., 1966.
AH 4409.70	Finley, Moses I. Early Greece; the bronze and archaic ages. London, 1970.
AH 4409.72	Desborough, Vincent Robin d'Arba. The Greek dark ages. London, 1972.

AH 4410   Ancient Greece in general - History by periods - Before 500 B.C. - Bronze age, Mycenaean age

AH 4410.1	Moon, Brenda Elizabeth. Mycenaean civilization, publications...1935-1960, a bibliography. v.1-2. London, 1957-61.
AH 4410.5	Schachermeyr, Fritz. Die ältesten kulturen Griechenlands. Stuttgart, 1955.
AH 4410.10.5	Matz, Friedrich. Le monde egéen. Paris, 1956.
AH 4410.10.15	Matz, Friedrich. Kreta, Mykene, Troja. 5. Aufl. Stuttgart, 1962.
AH 4410.15	Severyns, Albert. Grece et Proche Orient avant Homère. Bruxelles, 1960.
AH 4410.20.5	Huxley, George Leonard. Achaeans and Hittites. Belfast, 1965.
AH 4410.25	Starr, Chester. The origins of Greek civilization, 1100-650 B.C. N.Y., 1961.
AH 4410.30	Cottrell, L. Realms of gold; a journey in search of the Mycenaeans. 1. ed. Greenwich, 1963.
AH 4410.31	Taylour, William. The Mycenaeans. London, 1964.
AH 4410.31.5	Webster, Thomas Bertram Lonsdale. From Mycenae to Homer. N.Y., 1964.
AH 4410.31.7	Webster, Thomas Bertram Lonsdale. From Mycenae to Homer. 2. ed. London, 1964.
AH 4410.32	Vermeule, Emily. Greece in the bronze age. Chicago, 1964.
AH 4410.32.1	Vermeule, Emily. Greece in the bronze age. Chicago, 1966.
AH 4410.33	Astour, Michael C. Hellenosemitica. Leiden, 1965.
AH 4410.34	Luce, John Victor. The end of Atlantis: a new light on an old legend. London, 1969.
AH 4410.35	McDonald, William Andrew. Progress into the past: the rediscovery of Mycenaean civilization. N.Y., 1967.
AH 4410.36	Wundsam, Klaus. Die politische und soziale Struktur in den mykenischen Residenzen nach den Linear B. Texten. Wien, 1968.
AH 4410.37	Harrel-Courtès, Henry. Les fils de Minos. Paris, 1967.
AH 4410.38	Renfrew, Colin. The emergence of civilisation: the Cyclades and the Aegean in the third millennium B.C. London, 1972.
AH 4410.40.3	Emmrich, Kurt. An den Küsten des Lichts. 3. Aufl. München, 1961.
AH 4410.41	Zafiropulo, Jean. Mead and wine. N.Y., 1966.
AH 4410.42	Kerschensteiner, Jula. Die mykenische Welt in ihren schriftlichen Zeugnissen. 1. Aufl. München, 1970.

AH 4415   Ancient Greece in general - History by periods - Before 500 B.C. - Trojan War

AH 4415.5	Uschold, Johannes N. Geschichte des trojanischen Krieges. Stuttgart, 1836.
AH 4415.7.5	Witt, Karl. The Trojan War. London, 1884.
AH 4415.7.9	Witt, Karl. The Trojan War. 5. ed. London, 1896.

AH 4430 - 4439   Ancient Greece in general - History by periods - Before 500 B.C. - 7th century (Table A)

AH 4438.92A	Wright, J.H. Date of Cylon...early Athenian history. Boston, 1892.
AH 4438.92B	Wright, J.H. Date of Cylon...early Athenian history. Boston, 1892.
AH 4439.52	Lindemann, H. Generale machen Politik. 1. Aufl. Bonn, 1952.
AH 4439.60.1	Burn, Andrew Robert. The lyric age of Greece. London, 1967.

AH 4440 - 4449   Ancient Greece in general - History by periods - Before 500 B.C. - 6th century (Table A)

AH 4441.3	Pamphlet box. Ancient history. Greece. Sixth century.
AH 4448.40	Dietrich, A. De Clisthene. Halis Saxonum, 1840.
AH 4448.75	Grunder, C. Bellum Salaminium. Ienae, 1875.
AH 4448.86	Toepffer, J. Quaestiones pisistrateae. Dorpati, 1886.
AH 4449.03	Oddo, Antonino. Pisistrato. Palermo, 1903.
AH 4449.04	Hauser, F. Harmodios und Aristogeiton. Rom, 1904.
AH 4449.25	Ehrenberg, Victor. Neugründer des Staates. München, 1925.
AH 4449.29	Cornelius, Friedrich. Die Tyrannis in Athen. München, 1929.
AH 4449.36	Nilsson, M.P. The age of the early Greek tyrants. Belfast, 1936.
AH 4449.68	Ehrenberg, Victor. From Solon to Socrates. London, 1968.
AH 4449.68.2	Ehrenberg, Victor. From Solon to Socrates. 2. ed. London, 1973.

AH 4450 - 4459   Ancient Greece in general - History by periods - 500-146 B.C. - General works (Table A)

AH 4458.5	Cloché, Paul. Étude chronologique sur la troisième guerre sacrée. Thèse. Paris, 1915.
AH 4458.76.5	Cox, George W. The Athenian empire. N.Y., 1876.
AH 4458.76.6	Cox, George W. The Athenian empire. London, 1876.
AH 4458.76.7	Cox, George W. The Athenian empire. 5. ed. London, 1887.
AH 4458.76.9	Cox, George W. Athenian empire. 6. ed. London, 1888.
AH 4458.76.10	Cox, George W. Athenian empire. N.Y., 1889.
AH 4458.76.15	Cox, George W. Athenian empire. N.Y., 1895.
AH 4458.98	Allcroft, Arthur H. The making of Athens; a history of Greece, 495-431 B.C. Photoreproduction. London, 1898.
AH 4459.06.5	Croiset, Maurice. Aristophanes and the political parties at Athens. London, 1909.
AH 4459.17	Glover, Terrot R. From Pericles to Philip. London, 1917.
AH 4459.17.5	Glover, Terrot R. From Pericles to Philip. N.Y., 1917.
AH 4459.21	Holleaux, M. Rome, la Grèce et les monarchies hellénistiques. Thèse. Paris, 1921.
AH 4459.27	Ferrabino, A. L'impero atheniese. Torino, 1927.
AH 4459.36	Laistner, M.L.W. A history of the Greek world from 479 to 323 B.C. London, 1936.
AH 4459.36.2	Laistner, M.L.W. A history of the Greek world from 479 to 323 B.C. 2. ed. London, 1947.
AH 4459.36.3	Laistner, M.L.W. A history of the Greek world. 3. ed. London, 1957.
AH 4459.46	Dorjohn, A.P. Political forgiveness in old Athens. Evanston, 1946.
AH 4459.58	Cloché, Paul. Le monde grec aux temps classiques. Paris, 1958.

AH 4450 - 4459   Ancient Greece in general - History by periods - 500-146 B.C. - General works (Table A) - cont.

AH 4459.59	Berve, Helmuf. Griechische Geschichte. Freiburg, 1959. 2v.
AH 4459.60	Hackl, Ursula. Die oligarchische Bewegung in Athen am Ausgang des 5. Jahrhunderts. München, 1960.
AH 4459.63	Kanellopoulos, Panagiōtēs. Apo ton Marathōna sten Pydna ki'ōs ten katastrophe tēs Korivthou 490-146 p.ch. Athēnai, 1963. 3v.
AH 4459.64	Frolov, Eduard Davidovich. Sotsial'no-politicheskaia bor'ba v Afinakh v kontse V veka do n.e. Leningrad, 1964.
AH 4459.66	Fliess, Peter J. Thueydides and the politics of bipolarity. Baton Rouge, 1966.

AH 4470 - 4479   Ancient Greece in general - History by periods - 500-146 B.C. - Persian Wars, 499-479 - General works (Table A)

AH 4473.5	Witkowski, S. De pace quae dicitur cimonica. Leopoli, 1900.
AH 4478.60	Kutorga, M.S. Parti persan dans la Grèce ancienne. Paris, 1860.
AH 4478.61	Cox, George W. Great Persian War. London, 1861.
AH 4478.71	Berg, C.A. Aristides. Göttingen, 1871.
AH 4478.76A	Cox, George W. Greeks and Persians. 5. ed. London, 1886.
AH 4478.76B	Cox, George W. Greeks and Persians. 5. ed. London, 1886.
AH 4478.76.2	Cox, George W. Greeks and Persians. N.Y., 1876.
AH 4478.76.3	Cox, George W. Greeks and Persians. London, 1876.
AH 4478.76.5	Cox, George W. Greeks and Persians. N.Y., 1892.
AH 4478.76.15	Wecklein, N. Ueber die Tradition der Perserkriege. München, 1876.
AH 4478.87	Delbrück, H. Die Perserkriege. Berlin, 1887.
AH 4479.00	Agricola, Ernest. De Aristidis censu. Berolini, 1900.
AH 4479.01.1	Grundy, George Beardoe. The great Persian War and its preliminaries. N.Y., 1969.
AH 4479.02	Reuther, H. Pausanias, Sohn des Kleombrotos. Bonn, 1902.
AH 4479.13	Obst, E. Der Feldzug des Xerxes. Kapitel V. Leipzig, 1913.
AH 4479.23	Nolte, Ferdinand. Die historisch-politischen Voraussetzungen des Konigsfriedens von 386 v. Chr. Bamberg, 1923.
AH 4479.24	Giannelli, Giulio. La spedizione di serse da terme a Salamina. Milano, 1924.
AH 4479.34	Lombardo, G. Cimone. Roma, 1934.
AH 4479.62	Burn, Andrew. Persia and the Greeks. London, 1962.
AH 4479.63	Hignett, Charles. Xerxes' invasion of Greece. Oxford, 1963.

AH 4481   Ancient Greece in general - History by periods - 500-146 B.C. - Persian Wars, 499-479 - Battle of Marathon, 490

AH 4481.5	Noethe, H. De Pugnia Marathonia. Susati, 1881.
AH 4481.7	Duncker, M. Die Schlacht von Marathon. München, 1881.
AH 4481.9	Boucher, Arthur. La bataille de la Marne de l'antiquité; Marathon d'aprés Hérodote. Nancy, 1920.
AH 4481.11	Sotiriadis, G. L'expédition de Marathon. Salonique, 1934.
AH 4481.13	Mackenzie, C. Marathon and Salamis. Photoreproduction. London, 1934.

AH 4482   Ancient Greece in general - History by periods - 500-146 B.C. - Persian Wars, 499-479 - Battle of Thermopylae, 480

AH 4482.2	Daskalakēs, A.B. Problèmes historiques autour de la bataille des Thermopyles. Paris, 1962.

AH 4483   Ancient Greece in general - History by periods - 500-146 B.C. - Persian Wars, 499-479 - Battle of Salamis, 480

AH 4483.1	Pamphlet box. Ancient history. Greece. Salamis.
AH 4483.7	Raase, Hans. Beitrag zur Darstellung der Schacht bei Salamis. Rostock, 1904.
AH 4483.9	Rediades, P.D. Hē en Salamini Naumachia. Athens, 1911.
AH 4483.12	Rados, C.N. La bataille de Salamine. Thèse. Paris, 1915.
AH 4483.14	Baelen, Jean. L'an 480, Salamine. Paris, 1961.
AH 4483.15	Papadopoulos, Nikos M. Hē naumachia tēs Salaminos. Athēnai, 1961.
AH 4483.16	Green, Peter. The year of Salamis, 480-479 B.C. London, 1970.
AH 4483.16.5	Green, Peter. Xerxes at Salamis. N.Y., 1970.

AH 4484   Ancient Greece in general - History by periods - 500-146 B.C. - Persian Wars, 499-479 - Battle of Plataea, 479

AH 4484.5	Frick, Otto. Plataeische Weihgeschenk. Leipzig, 1859.
AH 4484.7	Grundy, G.B. Topography of Battle of Plataea. London, 1894.
AH 4484.9	Rudolph, F. Schlacht von Platää. Dresden, 1895.
AH 4484.11	Olsen, W. Schlacht bei Plataeae. Greifswald, 1903.
AH 4484.13	Wright, H.B. Campaign of Plataea. New Haven, 1904.
AH 4484.15	Winter, L. Platää. Berlin, 1909.
AH 4484.15.2	Winter, L. Die Schacht von Platää. Berlin, 1909.
AH 4484.16	Siewert, Peter. Der Eid von Plataiai. München, 1972.

AH 4486   Ancient Greece in general - History by periods - 500-146 B.C. - Persian Wars, 499-479 - Miltiades

AH 4486.5	Kinzl, Kourad. Miltiades-Forschungen. Wien, 1968.

AH 4487   Ancient Greece in general - History by periods - 500-146 B.C. - Persian Wars, 499-479 - Themistocles

AH 4487.5	Nieberding, K. De Themiestocle quaestio duplex. Gleiwitz, 1864.
AH 4487.7	Wolff, E. De vita Themiestoclis Atheniensis. Monasteii, 1871.
AH 4487.9	Bauer, Adolf. Themistokles. Merseburg, 1881.
AH 4487.11	Nordin, R. Studien in der Themistoklesfrage. Upsala, 1893.
AH 4487.13	Frank, T. Themistokles. Mannheim, 1898.
AH 4487.15	Braccesi, Lorenzo. Il problema del decreto di Temistocle. Bologna, 1968.

AH 4490 - 4499   Ancient Greece in general - History by periods - 500-146 B.C. - Age of Pericles, 479-431 (Table A)

AH 4491.5	Probandt, K. Beiträge zur Geschichte der Pentekontaetie. Halle, 1908. 3 pam.
AH 4498.21	Boeckh, A. De Pericle, artium et letterarum slatore. Berolini, 1821.
AH 4498.60	Gause, A. Societatis Atheniensis historia. Berolini, 1860.
AH 4498.62	Bissing, F. Athen und die Politik seiner Staatsmeiner. Heidelberg, 1862.
AH 4498.62.2	Capefigue, M. Aspasie et le siècle de Périclès. Paris, 1862.
AH 4498.65	Schaefer, A. Rerum post Bellum Persicum. Lipsiae, 1865.

AH 4490 - 4499   Ancient Greece in general - History by periods - 500-146 B.C. - Age of Pericles, 479-431 (Table A) - cont.

AH 4498.70F	Köhler, U. Geschichte des delisch-attischen Bundes. Berlin, 1870.
AH 4498.72	Becq de Fouquières. Aspasie de Milet. Paris, 1872.
AH 4498.73	Filleul, E. Siècle der Périclès. Paris, 1873. 2v.
AH 4498.75	Lloyd, W.W. Age of Pericles. London, 1875. 2v.
AH 4498.77	Schmidt, A. Perikleische Zeitalter. Jena, 1877. 2v.
AH 4498.83	Larocque, J. La Grèce. Paris, 1883.
AH 4498.84	Pflugk-Harttung, J. Perikles als Feldherr. Stuttgart, 1884.
AH 4498.87	Fischer, P. De Atheniensium sociis. Bonnae, 1887.
AH 4498.87.3	Frey, Karl. Leben des Perikles. Bern, 1887.
AH 4498.89	Nöthe, Heinrich. Delische Bund. Magdeburg, 1889.
AH 4498.89.5	Nedwed, E. Perikles. Iglau, 1889.
AH 4498.90	Mosler, I. Chronologie der Pentekontaëtie. Berlin, 1890.
AH 4498.90.5	Nöthe, Heinrich. Bundesrat, Bundessteuer und Kriegsdienst der delischen Bündner. Magdeburg, 1890.
AH 4498.91	Abbott, E. Pericles and golden age of Athens. N.Y., 1891.
AH 4498.93	Grant, A.J. Greece in age of Pericles. London, 1893.
AH 4498.94	Östlye, P. Zahl der Bürger von Athen. Kristiania, 1894.
AH 4498.97	Hill, G. Sources for Greek history. Oxford, 1897.
AH 4498.97.5	Hill, G. Sources for Greek history between the Persian and Pelopormesian wars. Oxford, 1951.
AH 4499.02	Keil, Bruno. Anonymus Argentinensis. Strassburg, 1902.
AH 4499.19	Schulte-Vaërting, H. Die Friedenspolitik des Perikles. München, 1919.
AH 4499.32	Taeger, Fritz. Ein Beitrag zur Geschichte der Pentekontaetie. Stuttgart, 1932.
AH 4499.34	Stier, Hans E. Eine Grosstat der attischen Geschichte, die sog. Schlacht bei Oinoë. Stuttgart, 1934.
AH 4499.36	Willrich, Hugo. Perikles. Göttingen, 1936.
AH 4499.37	Mackenzie, Compton. Pericles. London, 1937.
AH 4499.40	Delcourt, Marie. Périclès. Paris, 1940.
AH 4499.41	Jouguet, Pierre. L'Athènes de Périclès et les destinées de la Grèce. Le Caire, 1941.
AH 4499.44	Sanctis, G. de. Pericle. Milano, 1944.
AH 4499.48	Burn, A.R. Pericles and Athens. London, 1948.
AH 4499.54	Homo, León. Périclès. Paris, 1954.
AH 4499.59	Dienelt, Karl. Die Friedenspolitik des Perikles. Wien, 1959.
AH 4499.65	Athènes au temps de Périclès. Paris, 1965.
AH 4499.68	Accame, Silvio. Ricerche intorno alla Pentecontaetia. Napoli, 1968.
AH 4499.69	Schachermeyr, Fritz. Perikles. Stuttgart, 1969.
AH 4499.71	Bowra, Cecil Maurice. Periclean Athens. N.Y., 1971.
AH 4499.71.5	Schachermeyr, Fritz. Geistesgeschichte der Perikleischen Zeit. Stuttgart, 1971.
AH 4499.72A	Meiggs, Russell. The Athenian empire. Oxford, 1972.
AH 4499.72B	Meiggs, Russell. The Athenian empire. Oxford, 1972.

AH 4510 - 4519   Ancient Greece in general - History by periods - 500-146 B.C. - The Peloponnesian War, 431-404 - General works (Table A)

AH 4511.5	Schimmelpfeng, G. De Brasidae Spartani. Marburgi Cattorum, 1857. 4 pam.
AH 4511.6	Pamphlet box. Peloponnesian War.
AH 4518.55	Herbst, L.F. Die Schlacht bei den Arginusen. Hamburg, 1855.
AH 4518.58	Metropulos, C. Schacht bei Mantinea. Göttingen, 1858.
AH 4518.70	Haussding, F. De Demosthenes Atheniensium. Halae, 1870.
AH 4518.77	Gilbert, G. Beiträge zur Innerngeschichte Athens. Leipzig, 1877.
AH 4518.86	Belser. Altischen Strategen in Vfahrk. v.1-2. Ellivangen, 1886.
AH 4518.89	Whibley, L. Political parties in Athens. 2. ed. Cambridge, 1889.
AH 4518.94	Müller, Emil. Sokrates in der Volksversammlung. Zittau, 1894.
AH 4518.94.3	Boerner, A. De rebus a Graecis. Gottingae, 1894.
AH 4518.95	Allcroft, A.H. Peloponnesian War. London, 1895.
AH 4519.10	Kahrstedt, U. Forschungen zur Geschichte des ausgehenden fünften und des vierten Jahrhunderts. Berlin, 1910.
AH 4519.13	Pokorny, Erich. Studien zur griechischen Geschichte im sechsten und fünften Jahrzehnt des vierten Jahrhunderts vor Christ. Inaug Diss. Greifswald, 1913.
AH 4519.19	Murray, Gilbert. Aristophanes and the war party. Photoreproduction. London, 1919.
AH 4519.19.2	Murray, Gilbert. Our great war and the war of the ancient Greeks. N.Y., 1920.
AH 4519.22	Laskarus, K.A. Phōs eis tò Thoukydídeiou erhebos. Athēnai, 1922.
AH 4519.27	Henderson, B.W. The great war between Athens and Sparta. London, 1927.
AH 4519.33	Brauer, H. Die Kriegschuldfrage in der geschichtlichen Uberlieferung des peloponnesischen Krieges. Inaug. Diss. Emsdetten, 1933.
AH 4519.33.5	Woodhouse, William J. King Agis of Sparta and his campaign in Arkadia in 418 B.C. Oxford, 1933.
AH 4519.69	Kagan, Doanld. The outbreak of the Peloponnesian War. Ithaca, 1969.
AH 4519.72	De Ste. Croix, Geoffrey Ernest Maurice. The origins of the Peloponnesian War. London, 1972.
AH 4519.72.1	De Ste. Croix, Geoffrey Ernest Maurice. The origins of the Peloponnesian War. Ithaca, 1972.

AH 4521   Ancient Greece in general - History by periods - 500-146 B.C. - The Peloponnesian War, 431-404 - Alcibiades

	AH 4521.5	Bischer, W. Alkibiades und Lysandros. Basel, 1845.
	AH 4521.7	Hertzberg, G.F. Alkibiades als Staatsmann und Feldhen. Halle, 1853.
	AH 4521.9	Houssaye, H. Histoire d'Alcibiade. Paris, 1874. 2v.
	AH 4521.11	Fokke, A. Rettungen des Alkibiades. Emden, 1883.
	AH 4521.13	Oberziner, G. Alcibiade. Genova, 1891.
	AH 4521.15	Taeger, Fritz. Alkibiades. Stuttgart, 1925.
	AH 4521.15.5	Taeger, Fritz. Alkibiades. München, 1943.
Htn	AH 4521.16*	Malvezzi, V. Considerations upon the lives of Alcibiades and Coriolanus. London, 1650.
	AH 4521.17	Herbst, L.F. Die Rückkehr des Alcibiades. Hamburg, 1843.
	AH 4521.18	Hatzfeld, Jean. Alcibiade, étude sur l'histoire d'Athènes à la fin du Ve siècle. Paris, 1940.
	AH 4521.18.2	Hatzfeld, Jean. Alcibiade. 2. éd. Paris, 1951.
	AH 4521.19	Benson, E.F. The life of Alcibiades. N.Y., 1929.
	AH 4521.20	Bloedow, Edmund F. Alcibiades reexamined. Wiesbaden, 1973.

AH 4522   Ancient Greece in general - History by periods - 500-146 B.C. - The Peloponnesian War, 431-404 - Mutilation of the Hermae

AH 4522.5   Hartman, I.I. Hermocipidarum mysterior. Lugdunum Batavorum, 1880.

AH 4522.7   Weil, Henri. Hermocopides. Paris, 1891.

AH 4523   Ancient Greece in general - History by periods - 500-146 B.C. - The Peloponnesian War, 431-404 - Sicilian Expedition

AH 4523.5   Rottsahl, C. Expedition der Athener nach Sicilien. Langensalza, 1878.

AH 4523.7   Church, A.J. Nicias and Sicilian expedition. London, 1899.

AH 4523.9   Schübeler, P. De Syracusarum oppugnatione quaestiones criticae. Geestemüde, 1910.

AH 4523.10   Odermann, E. Der Festungskrieg vor Syrakus in den Jahren 414-413 v.C. Inaug. Diss. Leipzig, 1927.

AH 4523.12   Green, Peter. Armada from Athens. 1st ed. Garden City, N.Y., 1970.

AH 4524   Ancient Greece in general - History by periods - 500-146 B.C. - The Peloponnesian War, 431-404 - The Four Hundred at Athens

AH 4524.5   Scheibe, J.F. Oligarchische Umwälzung. Leipzig, 1841.

AH 4524.7   Wattenbach, G. Quadringentorum Athenis factione. Berolini, 1842.

NEDL AH 4524.9   Micheli, Horace. Révolution oligarchique des quatre-cents. Genève, 1893.

AH 4524.11   Sadl, A. Die oligarchische Revolution vom Jahre 411. Pola, 1910.

AH 4530   -   4539   Ancient Greece in general - History by periods - 500-146 B.C. - Age of Spartan and Theban supremacy, 404-362 - General works (Table A)

AH 4531.1   Pamphlet box. Spartan and Theban supremacies.

AH 4538.40   Sievers, G.R. Geschichte Griechenlandes. Kiel, 1840.

AH 4538.42   Schröder, H. Abbildungen des Demosthenes. Braunschweig, 1842.

AH 4538.45   Rehdantz, C. Iphicratis Chabriae Timothei. Berolini, 1845.

AH 4538.54   Lachmann, J.H. Geschichte Griechenlands. v.1-2. Leipzig, 1854.

AH 4538.70   Pomtow, L. Leben des Epaminondas. Berlin, 1870.

AH 4538.81   Brückler, C.A. De chronologia Belli...Corinthiaci. Halis Saxonum, 1881.

AH 4538.81.3   Luebbert, G.A. De amnestia. Kiliae, 1881.

AH 4538.84   Sankey, C. Spartan and Theban supremacies. 3. ed. London, 1884.

AH 4538.84.2   Sankey, C. Spartan and Theban supremacies. N.Y., 1886.

AH 4538.84.5   Sankey, C. Spartan and Theban supremacies. N.Y., 1894.

AH 4538.85   Blass, F.W. Die sozialen Zustände Athens. Kiel, 1885.

AH 4538.95   Allcroft, A.H. Sparta and Thebes. London, 1895.

AH 4538.95.3   Weise, Richard. Athenische Bundesgenossenkrieg. Berlin, 1895.

AH 4538.97   Reichenbächer, W. Geschichte der athenischen...Politik. Halle, 1897.

AH 4539.03   Motzki, A. Eubulos von Probalinthos. Königsberg, 1903.

AH 4539.05   Marshall, F.H. Second Athenian Confederacy. Cambridge, 1905.

AH 4539.07   Grillnberger, P.O. Griechische Studien. Wilhering, 1906.

AH 4539.08   Radüge, E. Zur Zeitbestimmung des euböischen...Krieges. Giessen, 1908.

AH 4539.09   Hengweld, A. De conone Atheniensi. Traiecti ad Rhenum, 1909.

AH 4539.10   Rügg, A. Thermaenes. Basel, 1910.

AH 4539.36.2   Glotz, Gustave. La Grèce au IVe siècle; la lutte pour l'hégémonie, 404-336. Paris, 1941.

AH 4539.51   Accame, Silvio. Ricerche intorno alla guerra corinzia. Napoli, 1951.

AH 4539.55   Barbieri, Guido. Conone. Roma, 1955.

AH 4539.59   Farina, Antonio. Il processo di Frine. Napoli, 1959.

AH 4539.62   Mossé, C. La fin de la démocratie athénienne. Paris, 1962.

AH 4539.67   Fol, Aleksandur. Epaminoud. Sofiia, 1967.

AH 4539.70   Beister, Hartmut. Untersuchungen zu der Zeit der thebanischen Hegemonie. Inaug. Diss. Bonn, 1970.

AH 4543   Ancient Greece in general - History by periods - 500-146 B.C. - Age of Spartan and Theban supremacy, 404-362 - Phocion

AH 4543.5   Morell, L.J. Vita Phocionis. Lugdunum Batavorum, 1869.

AH 4543.7   Klotz, W.O.R. Quellen zur Geschichte Phokions. Zittau, 1877.

AH 4543.9   Bernays, J. Phokion. Berlin, 1881.

AH 4543.10   Candidus, Isaums. Vie de Phocion. Paris, 1948.

AH 4545   Ancient Greece in general - History by periods - 500-146 B.C. - Age of Macedonian supremacy, 359-280 - General works

AH 4545.5   Aymard, André. Le monde grec aux temps de Philippe II de Macédoine et d'Alexandre le Grand (359-323 avant J.-C.). Paris, 1964.

AH 4550   -   4559   Ancient Greece in general - History by periods - 500-146 B.C. - Age of Macedonian supremacy, 359-280 - Alexander the Great, 336-323 (Table A)

AH 4550.2   Burich, Nancy J. Alexander the Great: a bibliography. 1st ed. Kent, Ohio, 1970.

AH 4551.1   Pamphlet box. Alexander the Great.

AH 4551.5   Crämer, H. Beiträge zur Geschichte Alexanders der Grossen. Marburg, 1893. 3 pam.

AH 4558.04   Sainte-Croix, Guillaume Emmanuel Joseph de. Examen critique. Paris, 1804.

AH 4558.04.2   Sainte-Croix, Guillaume Emmanuel Joseph de. Examen critique. 2. éd. Paris, 1810.

AH 4558.22   Gobdelas, D. Histoire d'Alexandre le Grand. Varsovie, 1822.

NEDL AH 4558.29   Williams, John. Alexander the Great, life and actions. London, 1829.

AH 4558.29.3   Williams, John. Alexander the Great, life and actions. 2. ed. London, 1829.

NEDL AH 4558.29.4   Williams, John. Alexander the Great, life and actions. N.Y., 1830.

NEDL AH 4558.29.5   Williams, John. Alexander the Great, life and actions. N.Y., 1832.

AH 4558.29.6   Williams, John. Life and actions of Alexander the Great. N.Y., 1836.

AH 4558.29.50   Williams, John. The life and actions of Alexander the Great. N.Y., 1900.

AH 4558.33   Droysen, J.G. Alexanders des Grossen. Hamburg, 1833.

AH 4558.33.6   Droysen, J.G. Geschichte Alexanders des Grossen. Berlin, 1917.

AH 4550   -   4559   Ancient Greece in general - History by periods - 500-146 B.C. - Age of Macedonian supremacy, 359-280 - Alexander the Great, 336-323 (Table A) - cont.

AH 4558.48   Geier, S.R. Erziehung und Unterricht Alexanders des Grossen. Halle, 1848.

AH 4558.48.5   Abbott, J. History of Alexander the Great. N.Y., 1848.

AH 4558.58   Alexandrou. Istoria. Venetia, 1858.

AH 4558.61   Jäger. Bemerkungen zur Geschichte Alexanders des Grossen. Wetzlar, 1861.

AH 4558.75   Hertzberg, F.F. Asiatischen Feldzüge Alexanders des Grossen. Halle, 1875. 2v.

AH 4558.75.3   Zolling, T. Alexanders des Grossen Feldzug in centralischen Asien. Leipzig, 1875.

AH 4558.83   Jurien, J.P.E. Les campagnes d'Alexandre; drame macédonien. Paris, 1883. 5v.

AH 4558.83.2   Jurien, J.P.E. Le drame macédonien. 2. éd. Paris, 1891.

AH 4558.85   Droysen, H. Alexanders des Grossen Heerwesen. Freiburg, 1885.

AH 4558.86F   Schuffert. Alexanders des Grossen indischer Feldzug. Colberg, 1886.

AH 4558.87A   Mahaffy, J.P. Alexander's empire. London, 1887.

AH 4558.87B   Mahaffy, J.P. Alexander's empire. London, 1887.

AH 4558.87.3   Mahaffy, J.P. Story of Alexander's empire. N.Y., 1887.

AH 4558.91   Adler, Maximilian. De Alexandri Magni epistularum commercio. Inaug. Diss. Lipsiae, 1891.

AH 4558.93   Schwarz, F. Alexanders des Grossen Feldzüge in Turkestan. München, 1893.

AH 4558.93.2   Schwarz, F. Alexanders des Grossen Feldzüge in Turkestan. 2. Aufl. Stuttgart, 1906.

AH 4558.93.3   M'Crindle, J.W. Invasion of India by Alexander the Great. Westminster, 1893.

AH 4558.93.5A   M'Crindle, J.W. Invasion of India by Alexander the Great. Westminster, 1896.

AH 4558.93.5B   M'Crindle, J.W. Invasion of India by Alexander the Great. Westminster, 1896.

AH 4558.94   Allcroft, A.H. Decline of Hellas. London, 1894.

AH 4558.97   Yorck, M.G. Feldzüge Alexanders des Grossen. Berlin, 1897.

AH 4558.97.3   Hogarth, D.G. Philip and Alexander of Macedon. N.Y., 1897.

AH 4558.98   Emerson, A. Portraiture of Alexander the Great. Baltimore, 1886.

AH 4558.98.3   Wulff, Oskar. Alexander mit der Lanze. Berlin, 1898.

AH 4558.99   Koepp, F. Alexander der Grosse. Bielefeld, 1899.

AH 4558.99.5   Wheeler, B.I. Alexander the Great. n.p., n.d.

AH 4559.00A   Wheeler, B.I. Alexander the Great. N.Y., 1900.

AH 4559.00B   Wheeler, B.I. Alexander the Great. N.Y., 1900.

AH 4559.00.2   Wheeler, B.I. Alexander the Great. London, 1925.

AH 4559.02   Hackmann, F. Schlacht bei Gaugamela. Halle, 1902.

X Cg   AH 4559.02.3F   Ujfalvy, C. d'. Type physique d'Alexandre le Grand. Paris, 1902.

AH 4559.03   Anspach, A.E. De Alexandri Magni expeditionis Indiea. Lipsiae, 1903.

AH 4559.03.3   Waldhauer, O. Porträts Alexanders des Grossen. München, 1903.

AH 4559.03.7   Schreiber, T. Studien über das Bildniss Alexanders des Grossen. Leipzig, 1903.

AH 4559.04   Janke, A. Alexanders des Grossen. Berlin, 1904.

AH 4559.04.5   Keller, Erich. Alexander der Grosse. Berlin, 1904.

AH 4559.05   Müller, K.F. Leichenwagen Alexanders des Grossen. Leipzig, 1905.

AH 4559.05.3   Bernoulli, J.J. Darstellungen Alexanders des Grossen. München, 1905.

AH 4559.05.7   Gruhn, Albert. Das Schlachtfeld von Issus. Jena, 1905.

AH 4559.07   Hoffmann, W. Literarische Porträt Alexanders des Grossen. Leipzig, 1907.

AH 4559.07.2   Hoffmann, W. Literarische Porträt Alexanders des Grossen. Quelle, 1907.

AH 4559.08   Dittberner, W. Issos. Ein Beiträge zur Geschichte Alexanders des Grossen. Berlin, 1908.

AH 4559.09   Weber, F. Alexander der Grosse im Urteil der Griechen und Römer. Borna, 1909.

AH 4559.09.3   Eicke, L. Veterum philosophorum qualia fuerint de Alexandero Magno iudicia. Rostochii, 1909.

AH 4559.13   Kirkman, M.M. History of Alexander the Great. Chicago, 1913.

AH 4559.16   Otto, Walter. Alexander der Grosse. Marburg, 1916.

AH 4559.24   Birt, Theodor. Alexander der Grosse und das Weltgriechentum bis zum erscheinen Jesu. Leipzig, 1924.

AH 4559.24.5   Endres, Heinrich. Geographischer Horizont und Politik bei Alexander der Grossen in den Jahren 330/323. Würzburg, 1924.

AH 4559.25   Radet, Georges. Notes critiques sur l'histoire d'Alexandre. Bordeaux, 1925-27.

AH 4559.26   Berve, H. Das Alexanderreich auf prosopographischer Grundlage. v.1-2. München, 1926.

AH 4559.28A   Bercovici, Konrad. Alexander; a romantic biography. N.Y., 1928.

AH 4559.28B   Bercovici, Konrad. Alexander; a romantic biography. N.Y., 1928.

AH 4559.28.3   Bercovici, Konrad. La vie de Alexandre le Grand. 3. éd. Paris, 1931.

AH 4559.28.5   Petković, Živko D. Aleksandr Veliki. Beograd, 1928.

AH 4559.29   Stein, Mark Aurel. Alexander's campaign on the Indian north-west frontier. London, 1929.

AH 4559.29.5   Robson, Edgar. Alexander the Great. London, 1929.

AH 4559.31   Wilcken, Ulrich. Alexander der Grosse. Leipzig, 1931.

AH 4559.31.5   Wilcken, Ulrich. Alexander the Great. London, 1932.

AH 4559.31.10A   Radet, Georges. Alexandre le Grand. 5. éd. Paris, 1931.

AH 4559.31.10B   Radet, Georges. Alexandre le Grand. 5. éd. Paris, 1931.

AH 4559.31.12   Radet, Georges. Alexandre le Grand. 5. éd. Paris, 1950.

AH 4559.32A   Robinson, Charles A. The Ephemerides of Alexander's expedition. Providence, 1932.

AH 4559.32B   Robinson, Charles A. The Ephemerides of Alexander's expedition. Providence, 1932.

AH 4559.32.5   Risi, Arnaldo de. Alessandro Magno, 356-331. Roma, 1932.

AH 4559.33   Tarn, W.W. Alexander the Great and the unity of mankind. London, 1933.

AH 4559.33.7   Weigall, A.E.P.B. Alexander the Great. N.Y., 1933.

AH 4559.33.8   Weigall, A.E.P.B. Alexander the Great. Garden City, 1933.

AH 4559.33.9   Weigall, A.E.P.B. Alexandre le Grand. Paris, 1934.

AH 4559.33.10   Andreotti, R. Il problema politico di Alessandro Magno. Torino, 1933.

AH 4559.34   Wright, Frederick A. Alexander the Great. London, 1934.

AH 4559.34.5   Strasburger, H. Ptolemaios und Alexander. Leipzig, 1934.

AH 4559.36   Tritsch, Walther. Olympias, die Mutter Alexanders des Grossen; das Schicksal eines Weltreiches. Frankfurt, 1936.

**AH 4550 - 4559 Ancient Greece in general - History by periods - 500-146
B.C. - Age of Macedonian supremacy, 359-280 - Alexander the Great,
336-323 (Table A) - cont.**

AH 4559.37 Bungard, R. L'expedition d'Alexandre et la conquête de l'Asie. Paris, 1937.

AH 4559.38 Ehrenberg, Victor. Alexander and the Greeks. Oxford, 1938.

AH 4559.38.5 Ivánka, E. Die aristotelische Politik und die Städtegründungen Alexanders des Grossen. Budapest, 1938.

AH 4559.38.10 Glotz, Gustone. Alexandre et l'hellenisation du monde antique. 2. éd. Paris, 1945.

AH 4559.39A Berzunza, J. A tentative classification of books. n.p., 1939.

AH 4559.39B Berzunza, J. A tentative classification of books. n.p., 1939.

AH 4559.40 Cummings, L.V. Alexander the Great. Boston, 1940.

AH 4559.40.5 Gregor, Joseph. Alexander der Grosse. München, 1940.

AH 4559.41 Brelaer, B. Alexanders Bund mit Paros. Leipzig, 1941.

AH 4559.42 Grabowsky, Adolf. Dialoge um Alexander. Zurich, 1942.

AH 4559.46 Lamb, Harold. Alexander of Macedon, the journey to world's end. 1st ed. Garden City, N.Y., 1946.

AH 4559.47A Robinson, C.A. Alexander the Great. 1st ed. N.Y., 1947.

AH 4559.47B Robinson, C.A. Alexander the Great. 1st ed. N.Y., 1947.

AH 4559.47.5 Burn, A.R. Alexander the Great and the Hellenistic Empire. London, 1947.

AH 4559.48 Tarn, William W. Alexander the Great. Cambridge, 1948. 2v.

AH 4559.49 Instensky, H.U. Alexander der Grosse am Hellespont. Godesberg, 1949.

AH 4559.49.5 Schachermeyer, F. Alexander der Grosse. Graz, 1949.

AH 4559.51 Gitti, Alberto. Alessandro Magno all'oasi di Siwah. Bari, 1951.

AH 4559.51.5 Homo, Léon Pol. Alexandre le Grand. Paris, 1951.

AH 4559.53 Robinson, C.A. The history of Alexander the Great. v.2. Providence, 1953.

AH 4559.53.5 Cloché, Paul. Alexandre le Grand et les essais de fusion entre l'occident gréco-macédonien. Neuchatel, 1953.

AH 4559.55 Savill, A.F. Alexander the Great and his time. Rockliff, 1955.

AH 4559.56 Pfister, F. Alexander der Grosse in den Offenbarungen der Griechen. Berlin, 1956.

AH 4559.58 Fuller, J.F. The generalship of Alexander the Great. London, 1958.

AH 4559.58.5 Hempl, Franz. Alexander der Grosse. Göttingen, 1958.

AH 4559.60 Altheim, F. Zarathustra und Alexander. Frankfurt, 1960.

AH 4559.60.5 Pearson, Lionel. The lost histoire of Alexander the Great. N.Y., 1960-

AH 4559.60.10 Pagliaro, Antonino. Alessandro Magno. Torino, 1960.

AH 4559.61 Gleixner, H.J. Das Alexanderbild der Byzantiner. München, 1961.

AH 4559.62 Alexandre le Grand. Paris, 1962.

AH 4559.63 Daskalakēs, Apostolos Basileiou. O Mégas Aléxandros kaí o Hellēniphios. Athēnai, 1963.

AH 4559.63.5 Dzięciot, Witold. Aleksander Wielki Macedoński. Londyn, 1963.

AH 4559.64 Marsden, E.W. The campaign of Gaugamela. Liverpool, 1964.

AH 4559.64.5 Bieber, Margarete. Alexander the Great in Greek and Roman art. Chicago, 1964.

AH 4559.65 Bamm, Peter. Alexander; oder Die Vewandlung der Welt. Zürich, 1966.

AH 4559.66 Griffith, Guy Thompson. Alexander the Great: the main problems. Cambridge, 1966.

AH 4559.66.5 Daskalakēs, Apostolos Basileiou. Alexander the Great and Hellenism. Thessalonikē, 1966.

AH 4559.67 Michel, Dorothea. Alexander als Vorbild für Pompeius. Brussel, 1967.

AH 4559.68 Milns, R.D. Alexander the Great. London, 1968.

AH 4559.68.10 Emmrich, Kurt. Alexander the Great: power as destiny. London, 1968.

AH 4559.68.15 Emmrich, Kurt. Alexander der Grosse. Zürich, 1968.

AH 4559.70 Green, Peter. Alexander the Great. London, 1970.

AH 4559.70.1 Green, Peter. Alexander of Macedon, 356-323 B.C. Harmondsworth, 1974.

AH 4559.70.5 Welles, Charles Bradford. Alexander and the Hellenistic world. Toronto, 1970.

AH 4559.71 Kraft, Konrad. Der rationale Alexander. Kallmünz, 1971.

AH 4559.71.5 Zalokōstas, Chrēstos Petrou. Megas Alexandros. Athēnai, 1971?

AH 4559.72 Seibert, Jakob. Alexander der Grosse. Darmstadt, 1972.

AH 4559.73 Fox, Robin Lane. Alexander the Great. London, 1973.

**AH 4600 - 4609 Ancient Greece in general - History by periods - 500-146
B.C. - Age of Macedonian supremacy, 359-280 - Macedonian Empire after
Alexander (Table A)**

AH 4608.61 Nicolas, B. De ingenio et fortuna Graecarum apud Thraces coloniarum. Thesim proponebat. Lutetiae Parisiorum, 1861.

AH 4608.84 Spangenberg, E. De Atheniensium publicis institutis aetate Macedonum commutatis. Diss. inaug. Halis Saxonum, 1884.

AH 4609.00 Hünerwadel, W. Geschichte des Königs Lysimachos. Zürich, 1900.

AH 4609.03 Breccia, Evaristo. Il diritto dinastico nelle monarchie dei successori d'Alexxandro Magno. Roma, 1903.

AH 4609.06 Rutgers, A. De Eumene Cardiano. Amsterdam, 1906.

AH 4609.07 Vezin, A. Eumenes von Kardia. Münster, 1907.

AH 4609.13 Tarn, W.W. Antigonos Gonatas. Oxford, 1913.

AH 4609.14 Schubert, R. Die Quellen zur Geschichte der Diadochenzeit. Leipzig, 1914.

AH 4609.26.5 Jouguet, P. Macedonian imperialism and the Hellenization of the East. London, 1928.

AH 4609.26.10 Jouguet, P. L'impérialism macédonien. Paris, 1961.

AH 4609.29 Kincaid, Charles A. Successors of Alexander. London, 1930.

AH 4609.30 Fellmann, W. Antigonos Gonatas, König der Makedonen. Inaug. Diss. Würzburg, 1930.

AH 4609.34 Edson, C.F. The Antigonids, Heracles, and Beroea. n.p., 1934.

AH 4609.40 Walbank, F.W. Philip V of Macedon. Cambridge, Eng., 1940.

AH 4609.51 Manni, E. Demetrio Paliorcete. Roma, 1951.

AH 4609.59 Cloché, Paul. La dislocation d'un empire. Paris, 1959.

AH 4609.59.5 Gyiokos, P.K. Philippos ho He. Thessalonikē, 1959.

AH 4609.65 Aymard, André. Le royaume de Macédoine de la mort d'Alexandre à sa disparition, 323-168 avant J.-C. Paris, 1965.

AH 4609.67 Seibert, Jakob. Historische Beiträge zu den dynastischen Verbindungen in hellenistischer Zeit. Wiesbaden, 1967.

AH 4609.68 Wehrli, Claude. Antigone et Démétrios. Genéve, 1968.

AH 4609.73 Müller, Olaf. Antigonos Monophthalmos und "Das Jahr der Könige". Bonn, 1973.

**AH 4650 - 4659 Ancient Greece in general - History by periods - 500-146
B.C. - Hellenistic Age, 323-146 - General works (Table A)**

AH 4658.36 Droysen, J.G. Geschichte des Hellenismus. Hamburg, 1836. 2v.

AH 4658.36.2 Droysen, J.G. Geschichte des Hellenismus. v.1-6. 2. Aufl. Gotha, 1877-78. 4v.

AH 4658.36.5 Droysen, J.G. Histoire de l'hellénisme. Paris, 1883. 3v.

AH 4659.00 Niese, B. Welt des Hellenismus. Marburg, 1900.

AH 4659.01 Kaerst, Julius. Geschichte des hellenistischen Zeitalters. Leipzig, 1901. 2v.

AH 4659.01.2 Kaerst, Julius. Geschichte des Hellenismus. 2. Aufl. Leipzig, 1917-26. 2v.

AH 4659.05 Mahaffy, J.P. Progress of Hellenism in Alexander's empire. Chicago, 1905.

AH 4659.06 Mahaffy, J.P. Silver age of the Greek world. Chicago, 1906.

AH 4659.06.5 Mahaffy, J.P. The silver age of the Greek world. Chicago, 1911.

AH 4659.23 The Hellenistic age. Cambridge, Eng., 1923.

AH 4659.24 Cohen, D. Universalisme en particularisme in den aarwang van het hellenistisch tijdperk. Groningen, 1924.

AH 4659.25 Laqueur, R. Hellenismus. Giessen, 1925.

AH 4659.27 Tarn, William W. Hellenistic civilization. London, 1927.

AH 4659.27.3 Tarn, William W. Hellenistic civilization. 2. ed. London, 1930.

AH 4659.27.10 Tarn, William W. Hellenistic civilization. London, 1947.

AH 4659.27.15 Tarn, William W. Hellenistic civilization. 3. ed. London, 1952.

AH 4659.28 Oliveira Martins, J.P. O hellenismo e a civilisação christan. 4. ed. Lisboa, 1928.

AH 4659.29.10 Corradi, G. Studi ellenistíci. Torino, 1929.

AH 4659.32A Macurdy, G.H. Hellenistic queens. Baltimore, 1932.

AH 4659.32B Macurdy, G.H. Hellenistic queens. Baltimore, 1932.

AH 4659.32.10A Cary, Max. A history of the Greek world from 325-146 B.C. London, 1932.

AH 4659.32.10B Cary, Max. A history of the Greek world from 325-146 B.C. London, 1932.

AH 4659.32.15 Cary, Max. A history of the Greek world from 323-146 B.C. 2. ed. London, 1951.

AH 4659.32.20 Cary, Max. A history of the Greek world from 323-146 B.C. N.Y., 1939.

AH 4659.38.5 Tarn, William W. The Greeks in Bactria and India. 2. ed. Cambridge, Eng., 1951.

AH 4659.41A Rostovtsev, Mikhail Ivanovich. The social and economic history of the Hellenistic world. Oxford, Eng., 1941. 3v.

AH 4659.41B Rostovtsev, Mikhail Ivanovich. The social and economic history of the Hellenistic world. v.1,3. Oxford, Eng., 1941. 2v.

AH 4659.41.2 Rostovtsev, Mikhail Ivanovich. The social and economic history of the Hellenistic world. Oxford, 1967. 3v.

AH 4659.41.5 Rostovtsev, Mikhail Ivanovich. Gesellschafts- und Wirtschaftsgeschichte der hellenistischen Welt. Darmstadt, 1955-56. 3v.

AH 4659.50 Ranovich, A.B. Der Hellenismus und seine geschichtliche Ralle. Berlin, 1958.

AH 4659.59 Toynbee, A.J. Hellenism. London, 1959.

AH 4659.59.2 Toynbee, A.J. Hellenism. N.Y., 1959.

AH 4659.59.5 Hadas, Moses. Hellenistic culture. N.Y., 1959.

AH 4659.61 Eddy, S.K. The king is dead. Lincoln, 1961.

AH 4659.61.5 Welles, Charles B. The Hellenistic world. Photoreproduction. New Haven, 1961.

AH 4659.62 Petit, Paul. La civilisation hellénistique. Paris, 1962.

AH 4659.67 Schneider, Carl. Kulturgeschichte des Hellenismus. München, 1967- 2v.

AH 4659.72 Heinen, Heinz. Untersuchungen zur hellenistischen Geschichte des 3. Jahrhunderts. Wiesbaden, 1972.

**AH 4700 - 4709 Ancient Greece in general - History by periods - 500-146
B.C. - Hellenistic Age, 323-146 - Achaean and Aetolian Leagues, 280-220
(Table A)**

AH 4708.33 Schorn, W. Geschichte Griechenlands. Bonn, 1833.

AH 4708.44 Paparrēgopoulos, Konstantinos. To telegtaion etos tēs ellēnikēs eleutherias. Athēnai, 1844.

AH 4708.77 Klatt, Max. Forschungen zur Geschichte des achäischen Bundes. Berlin, 1877.

AH 4708.81 Weinert, A. Die achäische Bundesverstallung. Demmin, 1881.

AH 4708.83 Klatt, Max. Chronologische Beiträge zur Geschichte des achäischen Bundes. Berlin, 1883.

AH 4708.85 Baier, B. Studien zur achaeischen Bundes-Verfassung. Inaug. Diss. Würzburg, 1885.

AH 4708.94 Sanctis, G. Questioni politiche e reforme sociali. v.1-2. Roma, 1894.

AH 4708.96 Gillischewski, H. De Aetolorum praetorubus. Berolini, 1896.

AH 4709.14 Niccolini, G. La confederazione Achea. Paris, 1914.

AH 4709.21 Ferrabino, A. Il problema dell'unita nazionale nella Grecia antica I. Firenze, 1921.

AH 4709.33 Walbank, Frank William. Aratos of Sicyon. Thirwall prize essay 1933. Cambridge, Eng., 1933.

AH 4709.38 Aymard, A. Les assemblées de la confédération achaienne. Bordeaux, 1938.

AH 4709.38.2 Aymard, A. Les assemblées de la confédération achaienne. Thèse. Bordeaux, 1938.

AH 4709.38.5 Aymard, A. Les premiers rapports de Rome et de la confédération achaienne. 198-189 avant J.C. Thèse. Bordeaux, 1938.

**AH 4710 - 4719 Ancient Greece in general - History by periods - 500-146
B.C. - Hellenistic Age, 323-146 - Macedonian Wars and Roman conquest,
220-146 (Table A)**

AH 4719.03 Mundt, Johannes. Nabis, König von Sparta. Köln, 1903. 2v.

AH 4719.09 Nicolaus, M. Zwei Beiträge zur Geschichte König Philipps V. von Makedonien. Berlin, 1909.

AH 4719.14 Theiler, Wilhelm. Die politische Lage in den beiden makedonischen Kriegen (200-197 v.C. und 171-168 v.C.). Diss. Halle, 1914.

AH 4719.40.2 Petzold, Karl E. Die Eröffnung des zweiten römisch-makedonischen Krieges. 2. Aufl. Darmstadt, 1968.

AH 4719.54 Oost, S.I. Roman policy in Epirus and Acarmania in the age of the Roman conquest of Greece. Dallas, 1954.

AH 4719.69 Errington, Robert. Philopormen. Oxford, Eng., 1969.

AH 4719.69.6 Deininger, Jürgen. Der politische Widerstand gegen Rom in Griechenland. Habilitationsschrift. Berlin, 1971.

AH 4720 - 4729   Ancient Greece in general - History by periods - 146 B.C. - 323 A.D. (Table A)

AH 4721.5 — Pamphlet box. Greece. B.C. 146-A.D. 476.
AH 4727.99 — Romans in Greece. Boston, 1799.
AH 4728.29 — Ahrens, F.H.L. Athenarum statu politico. Gottingae, 1829.
AH 4728.52 — Hermann, C.F. Conditione Graeciae post captam Corinthun. Gottingae, 1852.
AH 4728.66 — Hertzberg, G.F. Geschichte Griechenlands. Halle, 1866. 3v.
AH 4728.66.5 — Hertzberg, G.F. Histoire de la Grèce. Paris, 1887. 2v.
AH 4728.75 — Petit de Julleville, L. Histoire de la Grèce. Paris, 1875.
AH 4728.75.2 — Petit de Julleville, L. Histoire de la Grèce sou la domination romaine. 2. éd. Paris, 1879.
AH 4728.78 — Chevalier, L. Einfälle der Gallier in Griechen. Prag, 1878.
AH 4728.80 — Petit de Julleville, L. Histoire grecque. Paris, 1880.
AH 4728.90 — Mahaffy, J.P. Greek world under Roman sway. London, 1890.
AH 4729.05 — Barbagallo, C. La fine della Grecia antica. Bari, 1905.
AH 4729.05.5 — Barbaballo, C. Le declin d'une civilisation, ou La fin de la Grèce antique. Paris, 1927.
AH 4729.46 — Accame, Silvio. Il domino romano in Grecia dalla guerra acaica ad Augusto. Roma, 1946.
AH 4729.59 — Kordatos, G.K. Istoría tōn Ellēnistikōn chronōn. Athēnai, 1959.

AH 4800 - 4809   Ancient Greece in general - Chronology (Table A)

Htn   AH 4805.36* — Gaze Thessalo. Liber de Mensibus Atticis. Basileae, 1536.
AH 4807.32F — Maittaire, M. Marmorum. London, 1732.
Htn   AH 4807.41* — Squire, Samuel. Two essays, a defense of ancient Greek chronologies. Cambridge, 1741.
AH 4807.44 — Corsine, E. Fastiattici in quibus Archantum. Florentiae, 1744. 4v.
AH 4807.88 — Robertson, Joseph. Parian chronicle. London, 1788.
AH 4808.21 — Dalzel, A. Substance of lecture on ancient Greece. Edinburgh, 1821.
AH 4808.34 — Clinton, H.F. Fasti Hellenici. Oxford, 1834. 3v.
AH 4808.34.3 — Clinton, H.F. Fasti Hellenici. Lipsiae, 1830.
AH 4808.35 — Peter, C.L. Zeittafeln der griechischen Geschichte. v.1-2. Halle, 1835.
AH 4808.35.3 — Peter, C.L. Zeittafeln der griechischen Geschichte. 3. Aufl. v.1-2. Halle, 1866.
AH 4808.35.4 — Peter, C.L. Zeittafeln der griechischen Geschichte. 4. Aufl. Halle, 1873.
AH 4808.35.6 — Peter, C.L. Zeittafeln der griechischen Geschichte. 6. Aufl. Halle, 1886.
AH 4808.44 — Hermann, K.F. Griechische Monatskunde. Göttingen, 1844.
AH 4808.45 — Bergk, T. Beiträge zur griechischen Monatskunde. Giefsen, 1845.
AH 4808.51 — Clinton, H.F. Epitome...civil and literary chronicle of Greece. Oxford, 1851.
AH 4808.57 — Brandis, J. De temporum graecorum antiquissimorum rationibus. Bonnae, 1857.
AH 4808.61 — Faselius, A. Attische Kalender. Weimar, 1861.
AH 4808.70 — Dumont, A. Essai sur la chronologie des archontes athéniens. Paris, 1870.
AH 4808.74 — Dumont, A. Fastes éponymiques d'Athènes. Paris, 1874.
AH 4808.79 — Reusch, A. De Dilbus Contionum Ordmarium. Argentorali, 1879.
AH 4808.82A — Peter, C.L. Chronological tables of Greek history. Cambridge, 1882.
AH 4808.82B — Peter, C.L. Chronological tables of Greek history. Cambridge, 1882.
AH 4808.83 — Mommsen, A. Chronologie. Leipzig, 1883.
AH 4808.84 — Parian Chronicle. Chronicon Parium. Tubingae, 1884.
AH 4808.85 — Kubicki, K. Das Schaltjahr in der grossen Rechnungs-Urkunde. v.1-2. Ratibor, 1885.
AH 4808.88 — Schmidt, A. Handbuch der griechischen Chronologie. Jena, 1888.
AH 4808.92 — Israel-Holtzwart, Karl. Das System der attischen Zeitrechnung auf neuer Grundlage. Frankfurt, 1892.
AH 4808.92.5 — Gnaedinger, G. De Graecorum Magistratibus Eponymis. Argentorali, 1892.
AH 4808.98 — Solari, Arcturus. Fasti Ephororum spartanorum. Pisis, 1898.
AH 4808.99 — Svoronos, J.M. Der athenische Volkskalender. Athens, 1899.
AH 4809.03 — Roscher, W.H. Die enneadischen und hebdomadischen Fristen und Wochen der ältesten Griechen. Leipzig, 1903.
AH 4809.06 — Ferguson, W.S. The priests of Asklepios; a new method of dating Athenian archons. Berkeley, 1906.
AH 4809.22 — Boethius, Axel. Der argivische Kalender. Uppsala, 1922.
AH 4809.31F — Dinsmoor, William B. The archons of Athens in the Hellenistic age. Cambridge, 1931.
AH 4809.32A — Ferguson, W.S. Athenian tribal cycles in the Hellenistic age. Cambridge, 1932.
AH 4809.32B — Ferguson, W.S. Athenian tribal cycles in the Hellenistic age. Cambridge, 1932.
AH 4809.39F — Dinsmoor, William B. The Athenian archon list in the light of recent discoveries. N.Y., 1939.
AH 4809.39.2 — Dinsmoor, William B. The Athenian archon list in the light of recent discoveries. Westport, 1974.
AH 4809.43 — Prakken, D.W. Studies in Greek genealogical chronology. Lancaster, Pa., 1943.
AH 4809.47 — Pritchett, W.K. The calendars of Athens. Cambridge, Mass., 1947.
AH 4809.51 — Winniczuh, L. Kalendarz starozy tnych Greków i Rzymian. Warszawa, 1951.
AH 4809.61 — Meritt, Benjamin Dean. The Athenian year. Berkeley, Calif., 1961.
AH 4809.70 — Miller, Molly. The Sicilian colony dates. Albany, 1970.
AH 4809.71 — Miller, Molly. The Thalassocracies; studies in chronography. Albany, 1971.

AH 4810 - 4819   Ancient Greece in general - Civilization, social life - General works (Table A)

AH 4810.5 — Wheeler, B.I. Life of the ancient Greeks. Ithaca, 1890.
AH 4811.2 — Pamphlet box. Greek civilization.
Htn   AH 4815.57* — Sardi, Alessandro. De moribus et ritibus gentium. Venetiis, 1557.
Htn   AH 4815.99* — Sardi, Alessandro. De moribus et ritibus gentium. Ambergae, 1599.
AH 4817.06 — Potter, J. Antiquities of Greece. 2. ed. London, 1706. 2v.
NEDL   AH 4817.06.2 — Potter, J. Antiquities of Greece. 4th ed. London, 1722.
AH 4817.06.4 — Potter, J. Antiquities of Greece. 5th ed. London, 1728. 2v.

AH 4810 - 4819   Ancient Greece in general - Civilization, social life - General works (Table A) - cont.

AH 4817.06.5 — Potter, J. Antiquities of Greece. 6th ed. London, 1740. 2v.
NEDL   AH 4817.06.5 — Potter, J. Antiquities of Greece. 6th ed. London, 1740. 2v.
AH 4817.06.6 — Potter, J. Antiquities of Greece. 8th ed. London, 1764. 2v.
AH 4817.06.8 — Potter, J. Antiquities of Greece. 9th ed. London, 1775. 2v.
AH 4817.06.10 — Potter, J. Antiquities of Greece. London, 1795. 2v.
AH 4817.06.12 — Potter, J. Antiquities of Greece. Edinburgh, 1804. 2v.
NEDL   AH 4817.06.14 — Potter, J. Antiquities of Greece. Edinburgh, 1808.
AH 4817.06.15 — Potter, J. Archaeologia Graeca. Edinburgh, 1813. 2v.
NEDL   AH 4817.06.16 — Potter, J. Archaeologia Graeca. Edinburgh, 1832. 2v.
NEDL   AH 4817.06.17 — Potter, J. Archaeologia Graeca. v.2. Edinburgh, 1818.
AH 4817.06.18 — Potter, J. Archaeologia Graeca. 3. ed. London, 1837.
AH 4817.34 — Bruyn, C. Compendium Antiquitatum Graecum. Francofurti, 1734.
AH 4817.69 — Jackson, R. Literatura Graeca. London, 1769.
AH 4817.72 — Bos, L. Antiquities of Greece. London, 1772.
AH 4817.91 — Nitsch, P.F.A. Kurzer Entwurf der griechische Alterthümer. Altenburg, 1791.
AH 4817.91.4 — Nitsch, P.F.A. Beschriebung...der Griechen. Erfurt, 1806. 4v.
AH 4818.01 — Harwood, T. Grecian antiquities. London, 1801.
AH 4818.05 — Leuliette, J.J. Essai sur...supériorité des Grecs. Paris, 1805.
AH 4818.07.2 — Robinson, J. Antiquities of Greece. London, 1807.
AH 4818.22 — Irving, C. Catechism of Grecian antiquities. N.Y., 1822.
AH 4818.23 — Wessenberg, I.H. Volksleben zu Athen. Zürich, 1823.
AH 4818.26 — Wachsmuth, W. Hellenische Alterthumskunde. Halle, 1826. 4v.
AH 4818.26.3 — Wachsmuth, W. Hellenische Alterthumskunde. Halle, 1846. 2v.
AH 4818.26.6 — Wachsmuth, W. Historical antiquities of Greeks. Oxford, 1837. 2v.
AH 4818.26.7 — Petersen, F.C. De statu culturae. Havniae, 1826.
AH 4818.27 — Cleveland, C.D. Epitome of Grecian antiquities. Boston, 1827.
AH 4818.27.4 — Cleveland, C.D. Compendium of Grecian antiquities. 2. ed. Boston, 1831.
AH 4818.27.6 — Clevland, C.D. Compendium of Grecian antiquities. 2. ed. Boston, 1836.
AH 4818.30 — Geijer, Erik Gustof. Mores heroicae aetatis apud veteres Graecas et Scandinavas comjsaroti. Upsaliae, 1830.
AH 4818.35 — Pouqueville, F.C.H.L. Grèce. Paris, 1835.
AH 4818.35.5 — Pouqueville, F.C.H.L. Grèce. Paris, 1843.
NEDL   AH 4818.35.9 — Pouqueville, F.C.H.L. La Grecia. Venezia, 1836.
AH 4818.36 — Hase, H. Public and private life of ancient Greeks. London, 1836.
NEDL   AH 4818.41 — Hermann, K.F. Lehrbuch der griechischen Antiquitäten. 3. Aufl. Heidelberg, 1841. 2v.
AH 4818.41.3 — Hermann, K.F. Lehrbuch der griechischen Antiquitäten. 4. Aufl. Heidelberg, 1855. 3v.
NEDL   AH 4818.41.5 — Hermann, K.F. Lehrbuch der griechischen Antiquitäten. 5. Aufl. Heidelberg, 1875. 3v.
NEDL   AH 4818.41.6 — Hermann, K.F. Lehrbuch der griechischen Antiquitäten. v.1,3. Heidelberg, 1875. 2v.
AH 4818.41.9A — Hermann, K.F. Lehrbuch der griechischen Antiquitäten. v.1-4. 6. Aufl. Freiburg, 1889. 7v.
AH 4818.41.9B — Hermann, K.F. Lehrbuch der griechischen Antiquitäten. v.1, pt.3. 6. Aufl. Freiburg, 1889.
AH 4818.41.10 — Hermann, K.F. Lehrbuch der griechischen Antiquitäten. 4. Aufl. Freiburg, 1895.
AH 4818.43F — Panofka, Theodor. Bilder Antiken Lebens. Berlin, 1843.
AH 4818.43.5 — Schönwalder. Darstellung des Religiösen...Bildungszustandes. Brieg, 1843.
AH 4818.44F — Panofka, Theodor. Griechinnnen und Griechen. Berlin, 1844.
AH 4818.44.3 — Panofka, Theodor. Manners and customs of Greeks. London, 1849.
AH 4818.51 — Schoemann, G.F. Griechische Alterthümer. Berlin, 1855. 2v.
NEDL   AH 4818.51.3A — Schoemann, G.F. Griechische Alterthümer. 2. Aufl. Berlin, 1861.
AH 4818.51.3B — Schoemann, G.F. Griechische Alterthümer. 2. Aufl. Berlin, 1861-63. 2v.
AH 4818.51.5 — Schoemann, G.F. Griechische Alterthümer. 3. Aufl. Berlin, 1871. 2v.
AH 4818.51.8 — Schoemann, G.F. Griechische Alterthümer. 4. Aufl. Berlin, 1897. 2v.
AH 4818.51.10 — Schoemann, G.F. Antiquities of Greece. Oxford, 1879.
AH 4818.54 — Schwalbe, K.F.H. Handbuch der Griechischen Antiquitäten. Magdeburg, 1854.
AH 4818.55 — Rousopoulos, A.S. Ellēnikēs archaiologias. Patrais, 1855.
AH 4818.67A — Felton, C.C. Greece, ancient and modern. Boston, 1867. 2v.
NEDL   AH 4818.67B — Felton, C.C. Greece, ancient and modern. Boston, 1867.
NEDL   AH 4818.67.10 — Felton, C.C. Greece, ancient and modern. v.1-2. Boston, 1896.
AH 4818.70 — Stoll, H.W. Bilder aus dem altgriechischen Leben. Leipzig, 1870.
AH 4818.73 — Wägner, W. Hellas. v.1-2. Leipzig, 1873.
NEDL   AH 4818.73.2 — Esvanden, A.H.G.P. Grieksche antiquiteiten. Groningen, 1873.
AH 4818.75 — Rousopoulos, A.S. Manual of Greek archaeology. Athens, 1875?
AH 4818.76 — Döring, E. Hellas. Frankfurt, 1876.
NEDL   AH 4818.76.2.5 — Mahaffy, J.P. Old Greek life. N.Y., 1876.
NEDL   AH 4818.76.2.9 — Mahaffy, J.P. Old Greek life. N.Y., 1885.
NEDL   AH 4818.76.3 — Mahaffy, J.P. Old Greek life. N.Y., 1888.
NEDL   AH 4818.76.4 — Mahaffy, J.P. Old Greek life. N.Y., 18- .
NEDL   AH 4818.76.5 — Mahaffy, J.P. Antiguedades clasicas I. Antiguedades griegas. N.Y., 1889.
AH 4818.79 — Houssaye, H. Athènes, Rome, Paris. Paris, 1879.
AH 4818.80 — Mather, R.H. Abstract of lectures upon Greek life. n.p., 188-.
AH 4818.83 — Kuhnert, E. De cura statuarum. Berolini, 1883.
AH 4818.83.5 — Kuhnert, E. De cura statuarum apud Graecos. Berolini, 1883.
AH 4818.87.2 — Gache, F. Petit manuel d'archéologie grecque. Paris, 1887.
AH 4818.87.3A — Blümner, H. Leben und Sitten der Griechen. Leipzig, 1887. 3v.
AH 4818.87.3B — Blümner, H. Leben und Sitten der Griechen. Leipzig, 1887.
AH 4818.87.5 — Blümner, H. Home life of ancient Greeks. London, 1893.
AH 4818.87.7A — Blümner, H. Home life of ancient Greeks. London, 1895.

Classified Listing

AH 4810 - 4819   Ancient Greece in general - Civilization, social life - General works (Table A) - cont.

AH 4818.87.7B — Blümner, H. Home life of ancient Greeks. London, 1895.
AH 4818.87.10A — Mahaffy, J.P. Greek life and thought. London, 1887.
AH 4818.87.10B — Mahaffy, J.P. Greek life and thought. London, 1887.
AH 4818.87.11A — Mahaffy, J.P. Greek life and thought. 2nd ed. London, 1896.
AH 4818.87.11B — Mahaffy, J.P. Greek life and thought. 2nd ed. London, 1896.
AH 4818.87.11C — Mahaffy, J.P. Greek life and thought. 2nd ed. London, 1896.
AH 4818.87.11D — Mahaffy, J.P. Greek life and thought. 2nd ed. London, 1896.
AH 4818.89 — Robiou, F. Les institutions de la Grèce antique. Paris, 1889.
AH 4818.92 — Busolt, G. Griechischen Staats- und Rechtsaltertümer. München, 1892.
AH 4818.94 — Guiraud, P. Lectures historiques. Paris, 1894.
AH 4818.94.3 — Kleemann, M. Ein Tag in alten Athen. Gütersloh, 1894.
AH 4818.95.5 — Gardner, P. A manual of Greek antiquities. Books 1-5. N.Y., 1895.
AH 4818.96A — Mahaffy, J.P. Survey of Greek civilization. N.Y., 1896.
AH 4818.96B — Mahaffy, J.P. Survey of Greek civilization. N.Y., 1896.
AH 4818.96.5A — Mahaffy, J.P. Survey of Greek civilization. N.Y., 1899.
AH 4818.96.5B — Mahaffy, J.P. Survey of Greek civilization. N.Y., 1899.
AH 4818.96.15 — Dickinson, G.L. The Greek view of life. 5th ed. N.Y., 1906.
AH 4818.97 — Maisch, R. Griechische Altertumskunde. Leipzig, 1897.
AH 4818.98 — Dickinson, G.L. Greek view of life. 2nd ed. London, 1898.
AH 4818.98.3 — Burckhardt, J. Griechische Kulturgeschichte. 3. Aufl. Berlin, 1898. 4v.
AH 4818.98.5A — Burckhardt, J. Griechische Kulturgeschichte. Stuttgart, 1930-31. 4v.
AH 4818.98.5B — Burckhardt, J. Griechische Kulturgeschichte. Stuttgart, 1930. 2v.
AH 4818.98.5.15 — Burckhardt, J. Kulturgeschichte Griechenlands. Berlin, 1934.
AH 4818.98.10 — Burckhardt, J. Griechische Kulturgeschichte. Stuttgart, 1952. 3v.
AH 4818.98.20 — Burckhardt, J. History of Greek culture. N.Y., 1963.
AH 4818.98.25 — Schmid, Wilhelm. Über den kulturgeschichtlichen Zusammenhang. Leipzig, 1898.
AH 4819.00 — Lefèvre, A. Grèce antique. Paris, 1900.
AH 4819.02A — Gulick, C.B. Life of ancient Greeks. N.Y., 1902.
AH 4819.02B — Gulick, C.B. Life of ancient Greeks. N.Y., 1902.
AH 4819.02C — Gulick, C.B. Life of ancient Greeks. N.Y., 1902.
AH 4819.02.2 — Wagner, J. Realien aus Griechischesk Alterthums. 4. Aufl. Brünn, 1902.
AH 4819.02.3A — Gulick, Charles B. Life of the ancient Greeks. N.Y., 1902.
AH 4819.02.3B — Gulick, Charles B. Life of the ancient Greeks. N.Y., 1902.
AH 4819.02.3C — Gulick, Charles B. Life of the ancient Greeks. N.Y., 1902.
AH 4819.02.5 — Gulick, C.B. Life of the ancient Greeks. N.Y., 1905.
AH 4819.05 — Baumgarten, F. Hellenische Kultur. Leipzig, 1905.
AH 4819.05.2 — Baumgarten, F. Hellenische Kultur. Leipzig, 1908.
AH 4819.05.3 — Whibley, Leonard. Companion to Greek studies. Cambridge, 1905.
AH 4819.05.3.5 — Whibley, Leonard. Companion to Greek studies. 2nd ed. Cambridge, 1906.
AH 4819.05.3.6 — Whibley, Leonard. Companion to Greek studies. Cambridge, 1916.
AH 4819.05.5 — Baumgarten, F. Die hellenische Kultur. 3. Aufl. Leipzig, 1913.
AH 4819.05.8 — Dickinson, G.L. The Greek view of life. 3d ed. N.Y., 1905.
AH 4819.05.12 — Dickinson, G.L. The Greek view of life. N.Y., 1916.
AH 4819.05.17 — Dickinson, G.L. The Greek view of life. 7th ed. Garden City, N.Y., 1925.
AH 4819.05.20 — Dickinson, G.L. The Greek view of life. 7th ed. Garden City, N.Y., 1927.
AH 4819.05.30 — Dickinson, G.L. The Greek view of life. 22d ed. London, 1949.
AH 4819.05.31 — Dickinson, G.L. The Greek view of life. 23d ed. London, 1957.
AH 4819.06 — Glotz, G. Études...sur l'antiquité grecque. Paris, 1906.
AH 4819.06.3A — Tucker, T.G. Life in ancient Athens. N.Y., 1906.
AH 4819.06.3B — Tucker, T.G. Life in ancient Athens. N.Y., 1906.
AH 4819.06.7 — Tucker, T.G. Life in ancient Athens. Handbooks of archaeology and antiquities. Chautauqua, 1917.
AH 4819.07 — Wendland, P. Hellenistisch-Römische Kultur. Tübingen, 1907.
AH 4819.07.2A — Wendland, P. Hellenistisch-römische Kultur. Tübingen, 1912.
AH 4819.07.2B — Wendland, P. Hellenistisch-römische Kultur. Tübingen, 1912.
AH 4819.08 — Amatucci, A.G. Hellás. v.1-2. Bari, 1908.
AH 4819.08.2 — Inama, V. Amtichita greche. Milano, 1908.
AH 4819.09 — Mahaffy, J.P. What have the Greeks done for modern civilization? N.Y., 1909.
AH 4819.09.3 — Dickinson, G.L. The Greek view of life. 6th ed. N.Y., 1909.
AH 4819.10 — Monceaux, Paul. La Grèce avant Alexandre. Paris, 1892.
AH 4819.11.2.5A — Zimmern, A.E. The Greek commonwealth. 4th ed. Oxford, 1924.
AH 4819.11.2.5B — Zimmern, A.E. The Greek commonwealth. 4th ed. Oxford, 1924.
AH 4819.11.2.10A — Zimmern, A.E. The Greek commonwealth. 5th ed. Oxford, 1931.
AH 4819.11.2.10B — Zimmern, A.E. The Greek commonwealth. 5th ed. Oxford, 1931.
AH 4819.11.3A — Stobart, J.C. The glory that was Greece. London, 1911.
AH 4819.11.3B — Stobart, J.C. The glory that was Greece. London, 1911.
AH 4819.11.4 — Stobart, J.C. The glory that was Greece. London, 1921.
AH 4819.11.5 — Stobart, J.C. The glory that was Greece. N.Y., 1935.
AH 4819.12 — Prato, E. Vita e civilta digh Elleni. Livorno, 1912.
AH 4819.13A — Cotterill, H.B. Ancient Greece. London, 1913.
AH 4819.13B — Cotterill, H.B. Ancient Greece. London, 1913.
AH 4819.13.5 — Bianchi, Enrico. La Grecia nella letteratura, nella religione. Milano, 1913-14.
AH 4819.13.10 — Beaunier, André. La Grèce et nous. Paris, 1913.
AH 4819.14 — Stephens, Kate. The Greek spirit. N.Y., 1914.
AH 4819.14.5 — Lamer, Hans. Griechische Kultur im Bilde. Leipzig, 1914.
AH 4819.14.8 — L'hellénisation du monde antique. Paris, 1914.
AH 4819.14.10 — Davis, William S. A day in old Athens. 1. ed. Boston, 1914.

AH 4810 - 4819   Ancient Greece in general - Civilization, social life - General works (Table A) - cont.

AH 4819.17 — Burns, Cecil D. Greek ideals; study of social life. London, 1917.
AH 4819.17.8 — Gernet, Louis. Recherches sur le développement de la pensée juridique...en Grèce. Thèse. Paris, 1917.
AH 4819.21 — Thomson, J.A.K. Greeks and Barbarians. London, 1921.
AH 4819.21.5A — Ure, Percy N. The Greek renaissance. London, 1921.
AH 4819.21.5B — Ure, Percy N. The Greek renaissance. London, 1921.
AH 4819.22 — Croiset, M. La civilisation hellénique. Paris, 1922. 2v.
AH 4819.22.5 — Casson, S. Ancient Greece. London, 1922.
AH 4819.22.6 — Casson, S. Ancient Greece. Oxford, 1939.
AH 4819.22.7 — Poland, Franz. Die antike Kultur. Leipzig, 1922.
AH 4819.22.9 — Poland, Franz. The culture of ancient Greece and Rome. London, 1926.
AH 4819.22.10A — Poland, Franz. The culture of ancient Greece and Rome. Boston, 1926.
AH 4819.22.10B — Poland, Franz. The culture of ancient Greece and Rome. Boston, 1926.
AH 4819.23A — Greene, William Chase. The achievement of Greece. Cambridge, 1923.
AH 4819.23B — Greene, William Chase. The achievement of Greece. Cambridge, 1923.
AH 4819.23.2 — Greene, William Chase. The achievement of Greece. Cambridge, 1924.
AH 4819.23.5 — Greene, William Chase. The achievement of Greece; a chapter in human experience. N.Y., 1967.
AH 4819.24 — Lönborg, Sven. Dike und Eros. München, 1924.
AH 4819.24.5 — Lönborg, Sven. Dike och Eros. v.1-2,3. Uppsala, 1932-37. 2v.
AH 4819.25A — Hutton, Maurice. The Greek point of view. London, 1925.
AH 4819.25B — Hutton, Maurice. The Greek point of view. London, 1925.
AH 4819.25.5 — Rose, H.J. Primitive culture in Greece. London, 1925.
AH 4819.25.10 — Peyronnet, Raymond. Méditerranée au temps de l'Iliade; civilisation hellène. Paris, 1924.
AH 4819.25.15 — Croiset, Maurice. Hellenic civilization. N.Y., 1925.
AH 4819.27A — Gulick, Charles B. Modern traits in old Greek life. N.Y., 1927.
AH 4819.27B — Gulick, Charles B. Modern traits in old Greek life. N.Y., 1927.
AH 4819.27.5A — Ramsay, W.M. Asianic elements in Greek civilization. London, 1927.
AH 4819.27.5B — Ramsay, W.M. Asianic elements in Greek civilization. London, 1927.
AH 4819.27.7 — Ramsay, W.M. Asianic elements in Greek civilization. New Haven, 1928.
AH 4819.27.8A — Weigall, A. Personalities of antiquity. Garden City, N.Y., 1928.
AH 4819.27.8B — Weigall, A. Personalities of antiquity. Garden City, N.Y., 1928.
AH 4819.27.10 — Zane, J.M. The grandeur that was Rome. Chicago, 1927.
AH 4819.28A — Zimmern, A.E. Solon and Croesus, and other Greek essays. London, 1928.
AH 4819.28B — Zimmern, A.E. Solon and Croesus, and other Greek essays. London, 1928.
AH 4819.28.5 — Birt, Theodor. Das Kulturleben der Griechen und Römer in ihrer Entwicklung. Leipzig, 1928.
AH 4819.29 — Earp, F.R. The way of the Greeks. London, 1929.
AH 4819.29.5 — Lur'e, Sol. Iak. Istoriia antichnoi obshchestvennoi mysli. Moskva, 1929.
AH 4819.30 — Moscow. Gosudarstvennyi Muzei Iziashchnykh Iskusstv. Drevniaia gretsiia. Moskva, 1930.
AH 4819.31 — La vie publique et privée des anciens Grecs. Paris. 5-8 2v.
AH 4819.31.5 — Brodeur, A.G. The pageant of civilization. Garden City, 1934?
AH 4819.31.6 — Brodeur, A.G. The pageant of civilization. N.Y., 1931.
AH 4819.32 — Glover, Terrot R. Greek byways. Cambridge, Eng., 1932.
AH 4819.32.5A — Glover, Terrot R. Greek byways. N.Y., 1932.
AH 4819.32.5B — Glover, Terrot R. Greek byways. N.Y., 1932.
AH 4819.32.5C — Glover, Terrot R. Greek byways. N.Y., 1932.
AH 4819.32.7 — Rostovtsev, M.I. Out of the past of Greece and Rome. New Haven, 1934.
AH 4819.32.15 — Croiset, Maurice. La civilisation de la Grèce antique. Paris, 1932.
AH 4819.32.20 — Dickinson, G.L. The contribution of ancient Greece to modern life. London, 1932.
AH 4819.33 — Drerup, Engelbert. Kulturprobleme des klassischen Griechentums. Paderborn, 1933-34. 2v.
AH 4819.33.5 — Robinson, C.E. Everyday life in ancient Greece. Oxford, 1934.
AH 4819.33.10 — Bethe, E. Tausend Jahre altgriechischen Lebens. München, 1933.
AH 4819.33.15 — Quennell, M.C. Everday things in classical Greece. N.Y., 1933.
AH 4819.33.16 — Quennell, M.C. Everday things in ancient Greece. 2. ed. London, 1954.
AH 4819.36 — Vlachos, N.P. Hellas and Hellenism. Boston, 1936.
AH 4819.36.5 — Burn, Andrew Robert. The world of Hesiod. London, 1936.
AH 4819.36.6 — Burn, Andrew Robert. The world of Hesiod. 2. ed. N.Y., 1966.
AH 4819.39 — Boas, G. The Greek tradition. Baltimore, 1939.
AH 4819.39.5 — Durant, Will. The life of Greece. N.Y., 1939.
AH 4819.41.5 — Mewaldt, J. Hellenische Weltanschauung. Wien, 1941.
AH 4819.42A — Glover, Terrot R. The challenge of the Greek. Cambridge, Eng., 1942.
AH 4819.42B — Glover, Terrot R. The challenge of the Greek. Cambridge, Eng., 1942.
AH 4819.42.5 — Hommages à la Grèce. Lausanne, 1942.
AH 4819.42.10 — Grønbech, Vilhelm. Hellas; kultur og religion. v.1-5. København, 1942-45. 3v.
AH 4819.42.15 — Grønbech, Vilhelm. Hellas. Hamburg, 1965.
AH 4819.43 — Mondolfo, Rodolfo. El genio helénico y las caracteres de sus creaciones espirituales. Tucuman, 1943.
AH 4819.43.5 — Kranz, Walther. Die Kultur der Griechen. Leipzig, 1943.
AH 4819.46 — Marinatos, S.W. Greece and Greek civilization as results of economic expansion. Athens, 1946.
AH 4819.46.5 — Baynes, Norman H. The Hellenistic civilization and East Rome. London, 1946.
AH 4819.47.5 — Paoli, Ugo E. Uomini e cose del mondo antico. Firenze, 1947.
AH 4819.47.6 — Paoli, Ugo E. Cane del popolo. 2. ed. Firenze, 1958.
AH 4819.47.10 — Pohlenz, Max. Der hellenische Mensch. Göttingen, 1947?
AH 4819.47.15 — Farrington, B. Head and hand in ancient Greece. London, 1947.
AH 4819.48 — Rhodokanakês, K.P. Athens and the Greek miracle. London, 1948.

AH 4819.48.3	Rhodakanakēs, K.P. Athens and the Greek miracle. 1. American ed. Boston, 1951.
AH 4819.48.5	Permanence de la Grèce. Paris, 1948.
AH 4819.49A	Thomson, G.D. Studies in ancient Greek society. London, 1949. 2v.
AH 4819.49B	Thomson, G.D. Studies in ancient Greek society. London, 1949.
AH 4819.49.2	Thomson, G.D. Studies in ancient Greek society. London, 1954. 2v.
AH 4819.49.5	Friedell, Egon. Kulturgeschichte Griechenlands. München, 1949.
AH 4819.49.10	Solle, Miloš. Počátky helénské civilozace. Praha, 1949.
AH 4819.50A	Miami, Florida. University. Lectures of evaluations of the enduring qualities of Greek civilization. Miami, Fla., 1950.
AH 4819.50B	Miami, Florida. University. Lectures of evaluations of the enduring qualities of Greek civilization. Miami, Fla., 1950.
AH 4819.50.10	Wifsbrand, Albert. Den grekiska kulturhistoriens faser. Stockholm, 1950.
AH 4819.51	Dodds, Eric Robertson. The Greeks and the irrational. Berkeley, Calif., 1951.
AH 4819.51.2	Dodds, Eric Robertson. The Greeks and the irrational. 1st ed. Boston, 1957. 2v.
AH 4819.51.3	Dodds, Eric Robertson. The Greeks and the irrational. Berkeley, 1959.
AH 4819.52	Freeman, K. God, man and state. London, 1952.
AH 4819.52.5	Huxley, Michael. The root of Europe. London, 1952.
AH 4819.52.10	Diano, Carlo. Forma ed evento. 1. ed. Veneia, 1952.
AH 4819.52.12	Diano, Carlo. Forma ed evento. 2. ed. Venezia, 1960.
AH 4819.52.15	Deichgräber, Karl. Der listensinnede Trug des Gottes. Göttingen, 1952.
AH 4819.52.20	Kranz, W. Griechentum. Baden-Baden, 1952.
AH 4819.53	Hiebel, F. Die Botschaft von Hellas. Bern, 1953.
AH 4819.54	Finley, Moses I. The world of Odysseus. N.Y., 1954.
AH 4819.54.1	Finley, Moses I. The world of Odysseus. Harmondsworth, 1972.
AH 4819.54.2	Finley, Moses I. The world of Odysseus. Harmondsworth, 1962.
AH 4819.54.5	Bonnard, André. Civilization grecque. Lausanne, 1954. 3v.
AH 4819.54.6	Bonnard, André. Greek civilization from the Iliad to the Parthenon. London, 1957. 3v.
AH 4819.54.7	Bonnard, André. Civilization grecque. v.2-3. Paris, 1963. 2v.
AH 4819.54.10	Mireaux, Émile. La vie quotidienne du temps d'Homère. Paris, 1954.
AH 4819.54.12	Mireaux, Émile. Daily life in the time of Homer. London, 1959.
AH 4819.55	Pohlenz, Max. Griechische Freiheit. Heidelberg, 1955.
AH 4819.55.5	Fernandez-Galiano, M. El concepto del hombre en la antigua Grecia. Madrid, 1955.
AH 4819.57	Hamilton, Edith. The echo of Greece. 1st ed. N.Y., 1957.
AH 4819.57.5	Agard, W.R. The Greek mind. Princeton, N.J., 1957.
AH 4819.57.10	Bowra, Cecil Maurice. The Greek experience. London, 1957.
AH 4819.57.12	Bowra, Cecil Maurie. The Greek experience. 1st ed. Cleveland, 1958.
AH 4819.57.15	Kerényi, Karoly. Griechische Miniaturen. Zürich, 1957.
AH 4819.57.20	Lambrechts, Pierre. Wat Hellas en Rome ons gaven. 2. Druk. Antwerpen, 1957.
AH 4819.58	Stokes, Adrian Durham. Greek culture and the ego. London, 1958.
AH 4819.59	Messinesi, X.L. Meet the ancient Greeks. Caldwell, 1959.
AH 4819.59.5	Webster, Thomas. Greek art and literature, 700-530 B.C. Dunedin, 1959.
AH 4819.59.10	Flacelière, Robert. La vie quotidienne en Grèce au siècle de Périclès. Paris, 1959.
AH 4819.59.15	Zschietzschmann, Willy. Hellas und Rom. Zürich, 1959.
AH 4819.60	Doedeus, T.P. Ontmoeting met het oude Hellas. Amsterdam, 1960.
AH 4819.60.5	Aigrisse, Gilbert. Psychanalyse de la Grèce antique. Paris, 1960.
AH 4819.60.10	Godel, Roger. Une Grèce secrete. Paris, 1960.
AH 4819.60.15	Polska Akademia nauk Oddział w Krakowie. Grecja współczesna i starozytna. Kraków, 1960.
AH 4819.60.20	Sprey, Karel. De weg van Hellas. Den Haag, 1960.
AH 4819.60.26	Payne, Robert. The splendor of Greece. London, 1961.
AH 4819.60.30	Payne, Robert. The splendor of Greece. 1st ed. N.Y., 1960.
AH 4819.61.5	Conley, P.M. America's debt to Greece. Charleston, 1961.
AH 4819.61.10	Problemas del mundo helenistico. Madrid, 1961.
AH 4819.62	Riesterer, Peter P. Griechisches Erbe. Zürich, 1962.
AH 4819.62.5	Nolthenius, Hélène. In het voorportaal van de Akropolis. Den Haag, 1962.
AH 4819.62.10	Samivel. The glory of Greece. N.Y., 1962.
AH 4819.62.15	Harder, Richard. Eigenart der Griechen. Freiburg, 1962.
AH 4819.62.20	Boer, Willem den. Eros en Amor. Den Haag, 1962.
AH 4819.62.25	Vernant, J.P. Les origines de la pensée grecque. Paris, 1962.
AH 4819.63	Finley, Moses I. The ancient Greeks. N.Y., 1963.
AH 4819.63.5	Lloyd-Jones, H. The Greeks. 1. ed. Cleveland, 1963.
AH 4819.63.10F	Zadoks, A.N. Ontieke cultuur in beeld. 7. Druk. Bussum, 1963.
AH 4819.63.15	Chamoux, François. La civilisation grecque. Paris, 1963.
AH 4819.63.16	Chamoux, François. The civilization of Greece. London, 1965.
AH 4819.63.25	Peremans, Willy. Hellas en de Westeuropese cultuur. Kasterlee, 1963.
AH 4819.64	Payne, R. Ancient Greece. 1st ed. N.Y., 1964.
AH 4819.64.5	Ehrenberg, V. Society and civilization in Greece and Rome. Cambridge, 1964.
AH 4819.64.10	Groningen, Bernhard Abraham van. Bedwongen hartstocht. Leiden, 1964.
AH 4819.64.15	Lévêque, Pierre. The Greek adventure. Cleveland, 1968.
AH 4819.65	Hale, William Harlan. The Horizon book of ancient Greece. N.Y., 1965.
AH 4819.65.5	Pereira, Maria Helena Rocha. Estudos de história da cultura clássica. Lisboa, 1965.
AH 4819.65.10	Gouldner, Alvin Ward. Enter Plato. N.Y., 1965.
AH 4819.65.15	Bowra, Cecil Maurice. Classical Greece. N.Y., 1965.
AH 4819.66	Flacelière, Robert. Daily life in Greece at the time of Pericles. N.Y., 1966.
AH 4819.66.5	Pohlenz, Max. Freedom in Greek life and thought. Dordrecht, 1966.
AH 4819.66.10	Carpenter, Rhys. Discontinuity in Greek civilization. Cambridge, Eng., 1966.

AH 4819.66.15	Browning, Robert. Greece - ancient and medieval: an inaugural lecture delivered at Birkbeck College, 15th June, 1966. London, 1966.
AH 4819.66.21F	The world of classical Athens. London, 1970.
AH 4819.67	Hooper, Finley Allison. Greek realities; life and thought in ancient Greece. N.Y., 1967.
AH 4819.67.5	European Cultural Foundation. L'héritage vivant de l'antiquité grecque. La Haye, 1967.
AH 4819.67.10	La civilisation grecque de l'antiquité à nos jours. Bruxelles, 1967. 2v.
AH 4819.67.15	Andrewes, Anthony. The Greeks. N.Y., 1967.
AH 4819.67.20	Moebius, Hans. Studia varia. Auftsätze zur Kunst und Kultur der Antike mit Nachträgen. Wiesbaden, 1967.
AH 4819.67.25	Archaeologia Homerica. Die Denkmäler und das frühgriechischen Epos. Göttingen, 1967- 5v.
AH 4819.68	Lindsay, Jack. The ancient world; manners and morals. London, 1968.
AH 4819.68.5	Gernet, Louis. Anthropologie de la Grèce antique. Paris, 1968.
AH 4819.68.12	Scheliha, Renata von. Freiheit und Freundschaft in Hellas. 2. Aufl. Amsterdam, 1968.
AH 4819.69	Mackendrick, Paul Lachlan. The Athenian aristocracy, 399 to 31 B.C. Cambridge, 1969.
AH 4819.69.15	Krause, Wilhelm. Die Griechen von Mykene bis Byzanz. Wien, 1969.
AH 4819.69.20	Toynbee, Arnold Joseph. Some problems of Greek history. London, 1969.
AH 4819.70	Crow, John Armstrong. Greece: the magic spring. 1st ed. N.Y., 1970.
AH 4819.71	Starr, Chester G. The ancient Greeks. N.Y., 1971.
AH 4819.72	Warner, Rex. Men of Athens: the story of fifth century Athens. London, 1972.
AH 4819.72.5	Miller, Helen (Hill). Greece through the ages. N.Y., 1972.
AH 4819.72.10	Van Duyn, Janet H. (Dunning). The Greeks: their legacy. N.Y., 1972.
AH 4819.72.15	Hurmuziadis, Jorge. La cultura de Grecia: antigua, bizantia, moderna. Buenos Aires, 1972.
AH 4819.73	Ferguson, John. The heritage of Hellenism. 1st American ed. N.Y., 1973.

AH 4827.96	Barthelemy, J.J. Carite et Polydore. Lausanne, 1796.
AH 4828.01	Chaussard, J.B. Fetes et courtisanes. Paris, 1801. 4v.
AH 4828.01.4	Chaussard, J.B. Fetes et courtisanes. 4. éd. Paris, 1821. 4v.
AH 4828.40	Becker, W.A. Charikles. Leipzig, 1840.
AH 4828.40.2	Becker, W.A. Charikles. 2. Aufl. Leipzig, 1854. 3v.
AH 4828.40.3	Becker, W.A. Charikles. Berlin, 1877-78. 3v.
AH 4828.40.5	Becker, W.A. Charicles. London, 1845.
AH 4828.40.7	Becker, W.A. Charicles. London, 1854.
AH 4828.40.8A	Becker, W.A. Charicles. London, 1854.
NEDL AH 4828.40.8B	Becker, W.A. Charicles. London, 1854.
AH 4828.40.11A	Becker, W.A. Charicles. 3. ed. London, 1866.
AH 4828.40.11B	Becker, W.A. Charicles. 3. ed. London, 1866.
NEDL AH 4828.40.12	Becker, W.A. Charicles. 4. ed. London, 1874.
AH 4828.40.14	Becker, W.A. Charicles. 6. ed. London, 1882.
AH 4828.40.20	Becker, W.A. Charicles. London, 1899.
AH 4828.42	St. John, J.A. History of manners and customs of ancient Greece. London, 1842. 3v.
AH 4828.42.3	St. John, J.A. Hellenes. History of manners and customs of ancient Greece. London, 1844. 3 pam.
AH 4828.73	Benizelos, T.B. Peri tou idōtikou Biou. Athēnai, 1873.
AH 4828.74A	Mahaffy, J.P. Social life in Greece. London, 1874.
AH 4828.74B	Mahaffy, J.P. Social life in Greece. London, 1874.
AH 4828.74C	Mahaffy, J.P. Social life in Greece. London, 1874.
AH 4828.74.2A	Mahaffy, J.P. Social life in Greece. 2. ed. London, 1875.
AH 4828.74.2B	Mahaffy, J.P. Social life in Greece. 2. ed. London, 1875.
AH 4828.74.4	Mahaffy, J.P. Social life in Greece from Homer to Menander. 5. ed. London, 1883.
AH 4828.74.5	Mahaffy, J.P. Social life in Greece. London, 1898.
AH 4828.74.8	Mahaffy, J.P. Social life in Greece from Homer to Menander. London, 1902.
AH 4828.74.12	Mahaffy, J.P. Social life in Greece from Homer to Menander. London, 1925.
AH 4828.75	Boudodēnou, Charalampous. Dokimion. Odēssō, 1875. 2v.
AH 4828.85	Timayenis, T.T. Greece in times of Homer. N.Y., 1885.
AH 4828.93.5	Gilbert, Gustav. Egcheiridion Archaiologias toù demosiou biou. Tom A', Teux.1-3. Athēnai, 1897-99.
AH 4828.94	Pernice, E. Griechische Gewichte. Berlin, 1894.
AH 4829.16.5	Robinson, C.E. The days of Alkibiades. 3. ed. London, 1925.
AH 4829.23	Van Rook, La Rue. Greek life and thought. N.Y., 1923.
AH 4829.25A	Wright, F.A. Greek social life. London, 1925.
AH 4829.25B	Wright, F.A. Greek social life. London, 1925.
Htn AH 4829.26F*A	Licht, Hans. Sittengeschichte Griechenlands. Dresden, 1926-28. 3v.
AH 4829.26FB	Licht, Hans. Sittengeschichte Griechenlands. Dresden, 1926-28. 3v.
AH 4829.31A	Picard, Charles. La vie privée dans la Grèce classique. Paris, 1931.
AH 4829.31B	Picard, Charles. La vie privée dans la Grèce classique. Paris, 1931.
AH 4829.33	Demopoulos, P.N. Ho dnmodios...tōn hargaiōy Hellenōn. Athēnai, 1933.
X Cg AH 4829.34	Licht, Hans. Sexual life in ancient Greece. N.Y., 1934.
AH 4829.60	Flacelière, Robert. L'amour en Grèce. Paris, 1960.

AH 4831.1	Pamphlet box. Athletic games. 3 pam.
AH 4833.5	Loebker, G. Gymnastik der Hellenen. Münster, 1835.
AH 4833.7	Brugsma, A.L. Gymasiorum apud Graecos descriptionem. Groningae, 1855.
AH 4833.9	Petersen, C. Gymnasium der Griechen. Hamburg, 1858.
AH 4833.10	Basiades, C.H. De veterum Graecorum gymnastice. Berolini, 1858.
AH 4833.11	Seitz, F. Leibesübungen der alten Griechen. Ansbach, 1872.
AH 4833.13	Bintz, J. Gymnastik der Hellenen. Gütersloh, 1878.
AH 4833.15	Jaeger, O.H. Die Gymnastik der Hellenen. Stuttgart, 1881.
AH 4833.17	Schneider, K. Griechischen Gymnasien und Palästren. Diss. Solothurn, 1909.

Classified Listing

AH 4830 - 4839   Ancient Greece in general - Civilization, social life -
Athletic games, sports (Table A) - cont.

AH 4833.19   Rabath, Joseph. Artis gymnicae quae fuerit origo.
Gleiwitz, 1851.
AH 4833.22   Zschietzschmann, W. Weltkampf- und Übungsstätten in
Griechenland. Schomdorf, 1961. 2v.
AH 4837.56   Paciavdi, M. De athletarum. Romae, 1756. 4 pam.
AH 4838.38   Krause, J.H. Olympia. Wien, 1838.
AH 4838.39   Hermanno, G. De hippodromo olympiaco. Lipsiae, 1839.
AH 4838.41   Krause, J.H. Pythien, Nemeen und Isthmien. Leipzig, 1841.
AH 4838.41.3   Krause, J.H. Institute, Sitten und Bräuche des alten
Hellas. v.1-2. Leipzig, 1841. 3v.
AH 4838.41.5   Dissenio, L. De ordine certaminum. Gottingae, 1841.
AH 4838.48   Wieseler, F. Satyrspiel. Göttingen, 1848.
AH 4838.67   Pinder, E. Fünfkampf der Hellenen. Berlin, 1867.
AH 4838.76   Lehndorff, G.G. Hippodromos. Berlin, 1876.
AH 4838.80   Karikoulas. Peri chrēseōs toū stephanou. Erlangen, 1880.
AH 4838.81   Knapp, P. Traditionen über Stiftung der olympischen
Spiele. Tübingen, 1881.
AH 4838.86   Marquardt, H. Zum Pentathlon der Hellenen. Güstrow, 1886.
AH 4838.88   Mie, F. Quaestiones Agonisticae. Rostochii, 1888.
AH 4838.89.5   Fedde, F. Über den Fünfkampf der Hellenen. Leipzig, 1889.
AH 4838.90   Pollack, E. Hippodromica. Diss. Lipsiae, 1890.
AH 4838.90.5   Pollack, E. Hippodromica. Lipsiae, 1891.
AH 4838.91   Förster, H. Sieger in den olympischen Spielen.
Zwickau, 1891.
AH 4838.92   Henrich, K.E. Pentathlon der Griechen. Würzburg, 1892.
AH 4838.93   Sartori, K. Studien...der griechischen Privataltertümer.
München, 1893.
AH 4838.96F   Lambros and Polites. Olympic games. Athens, 1896.
AH 4838.96.5   Pamphlet box. Olympian Games at Athens, 1896.
AH 4838.98   Plummer, E.M. Athletics and games of ancient Greece.
Cambridge, Mass., 1898.
AH 4839.05   Gaspar, C. Olympia. Paris, 1905.
AH 4839.05.3   Seliger, M. Interesse Hellenen am Sport. Tilsit, 1905.
AH 4839.06F   Grützner. Fünfkampf der Griechen. v.1-2. Leipzig, 1906.
AH 4839.10   Gardiner, Edward Norman. Greek athletic sport.
London, 1910.
AH 4839.10.1   Gardiner, Edward Norman. Greek athletic sports and
festivals. London, 1973.
AH 4839.18   Klee, Theophil. Zur Geschichte der gymnischen Agone an
griechischen Festen. Leipzig, 1918.
AH 4839.25   New York Metropolitan Museum of Art. Greek athletics.
N.Y., 1925.
AH 4839.25.5   Wright, Frederick A. Greek athletics. London, 1925.
AH 4839.27   Robinson, Rachel Louisa. Sources for the history of Greek
athletics. Cincinnati, 1955.
AH 4839.33   Forbes, C.A. Neoi. Middletown, Conn., 1933.
AH 4839.34   Knab, Rudolf. Die Periodoniken. Diss. Boltrop, 1934.
AH 4839.35   Ridington, William R. The Minoan-Mycenaean background of
Greek athletics. Diss. Philadelphia, 1935.
AH 4839.35.5   Curtius, E. Olympia. Berlin, 1935.
AH 4839.61   Anderson, John K. Ancient Greek horsemanship.
Berkeley, 1961.
AH 4839.61.5   Popplow, Ulrich. Leibesübungen und Leibeserziehung in der
griechischen Antike. 3. Aufl. Stuttgart, 1961.
AH 4839.62   Drees, Ludwig. Der Ursprung der olympischen Spiele.
Stuttgart, 1962.
AH 4839.64   Harris, Harold Arthur. Greek athletes and athletics.
London, 1964.
AH 4839.64.5   Spaak, Bob. Goden in het stadion. Amsterdam, 1964.
AH 4839.65   Schöbel, Heinz. Olympia und seine Spiele. Berlin, 1965.
AH 4839.65.5   Rudolph, Werner. Olympischer Kampfsport in der Antike.
Berlin, 1965.
AH 4839.71   Bengston, Hermann. Die olympischen Spiele in der Antike.
Zürich, 1972.

AH 4840   Ancient Greece in general - Civilization, social life - Special topics -
The family

AH 4840.5   Szymanski, M. De natura familiae Graecae. Berolini, 1840.
AH 4840.8   Lacey, Walter K. The family in classical Greece.
London, 1968.
AH 4840.10A   Slater, Philip Elliot. The glory of Hera. Boston, 1968.
AH 4840.10B   Slater, Philip Elliot. The glory of Hera. Boston, 1968.
AH 4840.15   Eichhoff, Karl. Ueber die Blutrache bei den Griechen.
Duisburg, 1873.
AH 4840.15.5   Treston, Hubert J. Poine; a study in ancient Greek
blood-vengeance. London, 1923.

AH 4841   Ancient Greece in general - Civilization, social life - Special topics -
Writing, scribes

AH 4841.5   Kornitzer, A. De scribis publicis Atheniensium.
Wien, 1883.
AH 4841.6   Brillant, M. Les secretaires atheniens. Paris, 1911.

AH 4842   Ancient Greece in general - Civilization, social life - Special topics -
Books and education

AH 4842.01   Pamphlet box. Greece. Education.
AH 4842.5   Girard, P. L'éducation athénienne. Paris, 1889.
AH 4842.6   Girard, P. L'éducation athénienne. 2. éd. Paris, 1891.
AH 4842.7   Bach, A. De institutione...scholastica. Bonnae, 1841.
AH 4842.9   Dittenberger, W. De Ephebis Atticis. Gottingae, 1863.
AH 4842.11   Leiber, T. von. Professoren, Studenten und Studentleben.
Bern, 1867.
AH 4842.13   Petit de Julleville. L'ecole d'Athènes. Paris, 1868.
AH 4842.15   Wilkins, A.S. National education in Greece. London, 1873.
AH 4842.17   Dumont, A. Essai sur l'Ephébie Attique. Paris, 1876.
2v.
AH 4842.19   Schmitz, W. Schriftsteller und Buchshändler.
Heidelberg, 1876.
X Cg AH 4842.21   Capes, W.W. University life in Athens. N.Y., 1877.
AH 4842.23   Martin, A. Doctrines pédagogiques. Paris, 1881.
AH 4842.25   Paley, F.A. Bibliographia Graeca. Lugdunum
Batavorum, 1881.
AH 4842.26   Mahaffy, J.P. Old Greek education. N.Y., 188-.
AH 4842.27A   Mahaffy, J.P. Old Greek education. N.Y., 1882.
AH 4842.27B   Mahaffy, J.P. Old Greek education. N.Y., 1882.
AH 4842.29   Mahaffy, J.P. Old Greek education. N.Y., 1905.
AH 4842.31   Hochheimers, C.F.A. System der griechische Pädagogik.
v.1-2. Göttingen, 1788.
AH 4842.33   Haebeilin, C. Beiträge zur Kenntniss des Bibliographies
und Buchwesens. Leipzig, 1890.
AH 4842.35   Davidson, T. Education of the Greek people. N.Y., 1894.
AH 4842.35.5   Davidson, T. Education of the Greek people. N.Y., 1903.
AH 4842.37   Aus dem pädagogischen Universität-Seminar zu Jena.
Langenzala, 1904.
AH 4842.39   Freeman, Kenneth John. Schools of Hellas. London, 1907.
AH 4842.39.1   Freeman, Kenneth John. Schools of Hellas. London, 1908.

AH 4842   Ancient Greece in general - Civilization, social life - Special topics -
Books and education - cont.

AH 4842.39.1.2   Freeman, Kenneth John. Schools of Hellas. 2. ed.
London, 1912.
AH 4842.39.2   Freeman, Kenneth John. Schools of Hellas. 3. ed.
London, 1922.
AH 4842.39.5   Freeman, Kenneth John. Schools of Hellas. N.Y., 1969.
AH 4842.41   Grousset, P. L'ecole d'Athens. Paris, 1908.
AH 4842.43A   Walden, J.W.H. University of ancient Greece. N.Y., 1909.
AH 4842.43B   Walden, J.W.H. University of ancient Greece. N.Y., 1909.
AH 4842.43.2   Walden, J.W.H. University of ancient Greece. N.Y., 1912.
AH 4842.45   Ziebarth, E. Aus dem griechischen Schulwesen.
Leipzig, 1909.
AH 4842.45.2   Ziebarth, E. Aus dem griechischen Schulwesen. 2. Aufl.
Leipzig, 1914.
AH 4842.47   Sakellaropoulou, S.K. Peri tes Latinikes glōssēs kai
philologias. Athēnai, 1878.
AH 4842.50   Möller. De eruditione Graecorum. v.1-2. Weimar, 1863.
AH 4842.52   Stallbaum, G. De veterum Graecorum institutione.
Lipsiae, 1858.
AH 4842.54A   Drever, J. Greek education, its practice and principles.
Cambridge, 1912.
AH 4842.54B   Drever, J. Greek education, its practice and principles.
Cambridge, 1912.
AH 4842.56   Lane, F.H. Elementary Greek education. Syracuse,
N.Y., 1895.
AH 4842.58   Terzaghi, N. L'educazione in Grecia. Milano, 1910.
AH 4842.60   Bernot, Alice. Recherches sur l'Éphébie attique.
Paris, 1920.
AH 4842.63   Hudson-Williams, T. An education bill from ancient Greece.
Cambridge, 1917.
AH 4842.65   Weinstock, Heinrich. Antike Bildungsideale. Berlin, 1925.
AH 4842.67   Reinmuth, O.W. The foreigners in the Albanian Ephebia.
Lincoln, Neb., 1929.
AH 4842.69   Bendel, Paulus. Qua ratione Graeci liberos docuerint.
Monasterii Guestfalorum, 1911.
AH 4842.71   Dobson, J.F. Ancient education and its meaning to us.
N.Y., 1932.
AH 4842.72   Jaeger, Werner Wilhelm. Paideia: die Formung des
griechischen Menschen. Berlin, 1936.
AH 4842.72.3A   Jaeger, Werner Wilhelm. Paideia. 2. Aufl. Berlin, 1936-
3v.
AH 4842.72.3B   Jaeger, Werner Wilhelm. Paideia. 2. Aufl. Berlin, 1936-
3v.
AH 4842.72.3C   Jaeger, Werner Wilhelm. Paideia. 2. Aufl. Berlin, 1936-
2v.
X Cg AH 4842.72.10A   Jaeger, Werner Wilhelm. Paideia: the ideals of Greek
culture. N.Y., 1939.
AH 4842.72.10A   Jaeger, Werner Wilhelm. Paideia: the ideals of Greek
culture. v.2-3. N.Y., 1939-43. 2v.
AH 4842.72.10B   Jaeger, Werner Wilhelm. Paideia: the ideals of Greek
culture. v.2-3. N.Y., 1939-1943. 2v.
AH 4842.72.10C   Jaeger, Werner Wilhelm. Paideia: the ideals of Greek
culture. v.3. N.Y., 1943.
AH 4842.72.15A   Jaeger, Werner Wilhelm. Paideia: the ideals of Greek
culture. 2. ed. N.Y., 1945.
AH 4842.72.15B   Jaeger, Werner Wilhelm. Paideia: the ideals of Greek
culture. 2. ed. N.Y., 1945.
AH 4842.72.15C   Jaeger, Werner Wilhelm. Paideia: the ideals of Greek
culture. 2. ed. N.Y., 1945.
AH 4842.72.20   Jaeger, Werner Wilhelm. Paideia; the ideals of Greek
culture. 2. English ed. Oxford, 1965.
AH 4842.73   Jaeger, Werner Wilhelm. Early Christianity and Greek
Paideia. Cambridge, 1961.
AH 4842.73.15   Jaeger, Werner Wilhelm. Das frühe Christentum und die
griechische Beldung. Berlin, 1963.
AH 4842.75A   Moore, E.C. The story of instruction. N.Y., 1936.
AH 4842.75B   Moore, E.C. The story of instruction. N.Y., 1936.
AH 4842.77   Jeanmaire, H. Couroi et courètes. Thèse. Lille, 1939.
AH 4842.80   Seel, Otto. Die plotonische Akademie. Stuttgart, 1953.
AH 4842.85   Nilsson, M.P. Die hellenistische Schule. München, 1955.
AH 4842.85.5   Nilsson, M.P. Den grekiska skolan. Stockholm, 1954.
AH 4842.87.1   Forbes, Clarence Allen. Greek physical education.
N.Y., 1971.
AH 4842.88   Greco, Felice. La pedagogia presso i Greci.
Bologna, 1959.
AH 4842.89   Pélékidis, Chrysis. Histoire de l'Éphébie attique.
Paris, 1962.
AH 4842.90   Pélékidis, Chrysis. Histoire de l'Éphébie attique.
Paris, 1962.
AH 4842.91   Beck, F.A.G. Greek education. London, 1964.
AH 4842.92   Sant'Anna Dionisio, J.A. Pedagogia culminante dos gregos.
Porto, 1962.
AH 4842.93   Exarchopoulos, Nikolaos. Das athenische und das
spartanische Erziehungssystem, im 5. und 6. Jahrhundert vor
Christ. Langensalza, 1909.
AH 4842.95   Pfeiffer, Rudolf. History of classical scholarship from
the beggining to the end of the Hellenistic age.
Oxford, 1968.
AH 4842.98   Lynch, John Patrick. Aristotle's school. Berkeley, 1972.

AH 4843   Ancient Greece in general - Civilization, social life - Special topics -
Music and dancing

AH 4843.2   Emmanuel, M. Saltationis disciplina. Paris, 1895.
AH 4843.3   Emmanuel, M. L'orchestique grecque. Paris, 1895.
AH 4843.4   Weitzmann, C.F. Geschichte der griechischen Musik.
Berlin, 1855.
AH 4843.5   Emmanuel, M. Danse grecque. Paris, 1896.
AH 4843.5.8A   Emmanuel, M. The antique Greek dance. N.Y., 1916.
AH 4843.5.8B   Emmanuel, M. The antique Greek dance. N.Y., 1916.
AH 4843.5.10   Emmanuel, M. The antique Greek dance. London, 1927.
AH 4843.6F   Krüger, E. De musicis Graecorum organis. Gottingae, 1830.
AH 4843.7   Karl von Jan. Griechische Saiteninstrumente.
Leipzig, 1882.
AH 4843.8   Dionysius, A. Hymnen. Berlin, 1840.
AH 4843.9   Hymne à Apollon. Paris, 1894.
AH 4843.10F   Hymnus an Apollo. Leipzig, 1896.
AH 4843.11   Poirée, E. Nouvelle interprétation rythmique.
Solesmes, 1901.
AH 4843.12   Latte, K. De saltationibus Graecorum. Giessen, 1913.
AH 4843.15   Waldenburg. Gymnasium. Geschichte der Aulodik bie den
Griechen. Waldenburg, 1879.
AH 4843.16   Bojesen, E.F. De Tonis S. Harmoniis Graecorum commentario.
Kjobenhavn, 1843.
AH 4843.18   Schnabel, H. Kordap. München, 1910.
AH 4843.19   Wright, F.A. The arts in Greece. London, 1923.
AH 4843.20F   Weege, Fritz. Der Tanz in der Antike. Halle, 1926.
AH 4843.21   Séchan, Louis. La danse greque antique. Paris, 1930.

Classified Listing

**AH 4843   Ancient Greece in general - Civilization, social life - Special topics -
Music and dancing - cont.**

AH 4843.22	Moens, P.W. De twee delphische hymnen. Purmerend, 1930.
AH 4843.23	Fortlage, Karl. Das musikalische System der Griechen in seiner Urgestalt. Leipzig, 1847.
AH 4843.24	Lawler, Lillian B. The dance in ancient Greece. London, 1964.
AH 4843.26	Webster, Thomas Bertram Lonsdale. The Greek chorus. London, 1970.

**AH 4844   Ancient Greece in general - Civilization, social life - Special topics -
Festivals**

AH 4844.2	Hirt, A.L. Die Hierodulen. Berlin, 1818.
AH 4844.3	Panofka, T. Die griechischen Trinkhörner. Berlin, 1851.
AH 4844.4	Ringwood, I.C. Agonistic features of local Greek festivals chiefly from inscriptional evidence. Poughkeepsie, N.Y., 1927.
AH 4844.6	Robert, Louis. Les gladiateurs dans l'Orient grec. Paris, 1940.
AH 4844.8	Vandoni, Mariangela. Feste pubbliche e private nei documenti greci. Milano, 1964.

**AH 4845   Ancient Greece in general - Civilization, social life - Special topics -
Character and morals**

AH 4845.5F	Eichstädt, H.C. Humanitate Graecorum. Ienae, 1825.
AH 4845.7	Zander, A.G.B. Luxu Atheniensium. Gryphiae, 1828.
AH 4845.9	Schömann, G.F. Sittlich-religiöse Verhalten. Greifswald, 1848.
AH 4845.11	Debay, A. Nuits corinthiennes. Paris, 1877.
AH 4845.13	Foerster, P. Physiognomik der Griechen. Kiel, 1884.
AH 4845.15	Ribbeck, O.J.K. Agroikos. Leipzig, 1885.
AH 4845.17F	Curtius, E. Conservative Zug. Berlin, 1890.
AH 4845.19	Wolff, E. Philanthropie bei den Griechen. Berlin, 1902.
AH 4845.21	Muller, E. Einleitung zu einer Darstellung der nationalen Ethik. n.p., n.d.
AH 4845.23	Delepierre, O.J. Dissertation sur les idées morales des grecs. Rouen, 1879.
AH 4845.26	Walcot, Peter. Greek peasants, ancient and modern: a camparison of social and moral values. Manchester, Eng., 1970.
AH 4845.28	Goebel, Maximilianus. Ethnica, pars prima: De Graecorum civitatum proprietatibus proverbio notatis. Vratislaviae, 1915.

**AH 4846   Ancient Greece in general - Civilization, social life - Special topics -
Houses, etc.**

AH 4846.5	Allatius, L. De templis Graecorum. Colonia Agrippina, 1645.
AH 4846.7	Winckler, A. Wohnhäuser der Hellenen. Berlin, 1868.
AH 4846.8	Rider, B.C. Greek house, its history and development from Neolithic period to Hellenistic. Thesis. Cambridge, 1916.
AH 4846.9	Wycherley, Richard Ernest. How the Greeks built cities. 2. ed. London, 1967.
AH 4846.10	Boersma, Johannes Sipko. Athenian building policy from 561-560 to 405-404 B.C. Groningen, 1970.

**AH 4847   Ancient Greece in general - Civilization, social life - Special topics -
Baths**

AH 4847.5	Mauri, A. I cittadini lavoratori. Milano, 1895.
AH 4847.7	Esveld, C. De Balneis Lavationibusque Graecorum. Amersfortiae, 1908.
AH 4847.15	Ginouvès, René. Balaesytike. Paris, 1962.

**AH 4848   Ancient Greece in general - Civilization, social life - Special topics -
Costume**

AH 4848.1	Pamphlet box. Costume special.
AH 4848.4	Baxter, Thomas. An illustration of the Egyptian, Grecian and Roman costume. London, 1810.
AH 4848.5	Klein, G. Der Kranz bei den alten Griechen. Günzburg, 1912.
AH 4848.5.5	Müller, V.K. Der Polos, die griechische Gotterkrone. Inaug. Diss. Berlin, 1915.
AH 4848.6	Köchling, J. De coronarum apud antiquos. Giessen, 1914.
AH 4848.7	Braungarten, F. Untersuchung und der Tracht die Athener am Grundlage. n.p., 1876.
AH 4848.8	Walch, C.F. Antiquitates pallii philosophici verterum Christianorum. Ienae, 1746.
AH 4848.9	Evans, M.M. Chapters on Greek dress. London, 1893.
AH 4848.10	Smith, J.M. Ancient Greek female costume. London, 1882.
AH 4848.10.3	Smith, J.M. Ancient Greek female costume. 2. ed. London, 1883.
AH 4848.11	Boelhau, I. Quaestionum de re vestiaria graecorum specimen. Diss. Wimariae, 1884.
AH 4848.12	Sambon, A. La toilette des femmes grecques. Paris, 1904.
AH 4848.13	Abrahams, E.B. Greek dress. London, 1908.
AH 4848.13.5	Johnson, Marie. Ancient Greek. Chicago, 1964.
AH 4848.14F	Bieber, Margarete. Griechische Kleidung. Berlin, 1928.
AH 4848.14.5F	Bieber, Margarete. Entwicklungsgeschichte der griechischen Tracht. Berlin, 1934.

**AH 4850   Ancient Greece in general - Civilization, social life - Special topics -
Meals**

AH 4850.5	Hollaender, A. Anaglyphis Sepulcraliebus Graecis. Berolini, 1865.
AH 4850.7	Bielschowsky, A. De Spartanorum syssitiis. Vratislaviae, 1869.
AH 4850.9	Pervanoglu, P. Familienmahl. Leipzig, 1872.
AH 4850.11	Maltou. Tōn Symposion. Athēnai, 1880.
AH 4850.13	Rankin, E.M. Role of Mageiroi in life of ancient Greece. Chicago, 1907.
AH 4850.14	Fendius, M. Oratio de Appellationibus panum. Vitebergae, 1549.
AH 4850.15	Vickery, Kenton F. Food in early Greece. Urbana, 1936.

**AH 4852   Ancient Greece in general - Civilization, social life - Special topics -
Pottery and metalwork**

AH 4852.5	Huddilston, J.H. Lessons from Greek pottery. N.Y., 1902.
AH 4852.9	Hansen, I.H. De Metallis Atticis. Hamburgi, 1885.

**AH 4854   Ancient Greece in general - Civilization, social life - Special topics -
Domestic plants and animals**

AH 4854.5	Hömschemeyer, Orloys. Die Pferdezucht im klassischen Altertum. Diss. Giessen, 1929.
AH 4854.7	Brendel, Otto. Die Schafzucht im alten Griechenland. Diss. Würzburg, 1934.
AH 4854.9	Vickery, Kenton F. Food in early Greece. Thesis. Urbana? 1936.

**AH 4855   Ancient Greece in general - Civilization, social life - Special topics -
Hunting and fishing**

AH 4855.5	Manns, O. Jagd bei den Griechen. Cassel, 1888. 3 pam.
AH 4855.7	Schneider, K. Fischer in der antiken Literatur. Aachen, 1892.
AH 4855.9	Johannes, R. De studio Venandi apud Graecos et Romanos. Gottingae, 1907.
AH 4855.11	Butler, Alfred J. Sport in classic times. London, 1930.
AH 4855.13	Höppener, Frank. Halieutica. Proefschrift. Amsterdam, 1931.
AH 4855.15	Hull, Denison B. Hounds and hunting in ancient Greece. Chicago, 1964.

**AH 4857   Ancient Greece in general - Civilization, social life - Special topics -
Parasites**

AH 4857.5	Knorr, A. De parasitis Graecorum. Colbergae, 1873.
AH 4857.7	Knorr, A. Parisiten bei den Griechen. Belgard, 1875.
AH 4857.9	Ribbeck, O. Kolax. Leipzig, 1883.

**AH 4858   Ancient Greece in general - Civilization, social life - Special topics -
Marriage**

AH 4858.7	Georgopoulos. Otamos tōn ellēnōn. Tripolei, 1880.
AH 4858.9	Buddenhagen, F. Peri gamou. pt.1. Turici, 1919.
AH 4858.11	Mulder, J.J.B. Quaestiones nonnullae ad Atheniensium matrimonia vetamque conjugalem pertinentes. Inaug. Diss. Traiecti ad Rhenum, 1920?
AH 4858.13	Geurts, Nico. Het huwelijk bij de Griekse en Romeinse moralisten. Proefschrift. Amsterdam, 1928.
AH 4858.14	Lasaulx, E. von. Zur Geschichte und Philosophie der Ehe bei den Griechen. München, 1852.
AH 4858.15	Klinz, A. Hieros gamos. Diss. Halis Saxonum, 1933.
AH 4858.17	Vatin, Claude. Recherches sur le mariage et la condition de la femme mariée à l'epoque hellénistique. Thèse. Paris, 1970.
AH 4858.17.1	Vatin, Claude. Recherches sur le mariage et la condition de la femme mariée à l'epoque hellénistique. Paris, 1970.

**AH 4859   Ancient Greece in general - Civilization, social life - Special topics -
Condition of women**

	AH 4859.5	Lenz, C.G. Weiber in heroischen Zeitalter. Hannover, 1790.
	AH 4859.7	Fickler, C.B.A. Griechischen Frauen. Heidelberg, 1848.
	AH 4859.9	Mähly, J.A. Frauen des griechischen Alterthums. Basel, 1853.
X Cg	AH 4859.11	Bader, C. Femme grecque. Paris, 1872. 2v.
	AH 4859.13	Bruns, Ivo. Frauenemancipation in Athen. Kiliae, 1900.
	AH 4859.15	Navarre, O. Mulieres Athenienses. Tolosae, 1900.
	AH 4859.17F	Notor, G. La femme. Paris, 1901.
	AH 4859.19	Matthias, T. Stellung der griechischen Frau. Zittau, 1893.
	AH 4859.21	Balabanoff, A. Untersuchungen zur Geschäftsfähigkeit. Borna, 1905.
	AH 4859.22	Herfst, Pieter. La travail de la femme dans la Grèce ancienne. Proefschrift. Utrecht, 1922.
	AH 4859.23	Braunstein, O. Die politische Wirksamkeit der griechischen Frau. Leipzig, 1911.
	AH 4859.25	Vries, M. de. Pallake proef. Amsterdam, 1927.

**AH 4860   Ancient Greece in general - Civilization, social life - Special topics -
Condition of children**

AH 4860.5	Surecicki, H. Pflege der Kinder bei den Griechen. Breslau, 1877.
AH 4860.7	Bryant, A.A. Boyhood and youth in days of Aristophanes. n.p., 1907.
AH 4860.8	Bryant, A.A. Boyhood and youth in days of Aristophanes. n.p., 1907.
AH 4860.9	Mary Rosaria, sister. The nurse in Greek life. Diss. Boston, 1917.
AH 4860.10	Bork, Arnold. Der junge Grieche. Zürich, 1959.
AH 4860.10.5	Bork, Arnold. Der junge Grieche. Zürich, 1961.

**AH 4861   Ancient Greece in general - Civilization, social life - Special topics -
Burial**

AH 4861.5	Nathusius, C.H.A. More Humandi and Cencremandi Mortuos. Halis Saxonum, 1864?
AH 4861.6	Graves, F.R. The burial customs of the ancient Greeks. Thesis. Brooklyn, 1891.
AH 4861.7	Kriesche, W. Darstellung der griechische Grabsitte. Braunau, 1878.
AH 4861.8	Nicolai, J. Johannis Nicolai Tractatus de Graecorum luctu. Thielae, 1697.
AH 4861.9	Kurtz, Donna Carol. Greek burial customs. London, 1971.

**AH 4862   Ancient Greece in general - Civilization, social life - Special topics -
Hygiene**

AH 4862.5	Hueppe, F. Rassen und Sozialhygiene. Wiesbaden, 1897.
AH 4862.7	Roper, Allen George. Ancient eugenics. Oxford, 1913.

**AH 4863   Ancient Greece in general - Civilization, social life - Special topics -
Sexual customs, love**

AH 4863.7	Kittredge, G.L. Armpitting among the Greeks. Baltimore, 1885.
AH 4863.9	Meier, M.H.E. Histoire de l'amour grec. Paris, 1930.
AH 4863.11	Vèze, Raoul. Le baiser en Grèce. Paris, 1906.
AH 4863.13.5	Flacelière, Robert. Love in ancient Greece. N.Y., 1962.

**AH 4864   Ancient Greece in general - Civilization, social life - Special topics -
Games, toys**

	AH 4864.7	Boehm, C. De cottabo. Bonnae, 1893.
Htn	AH 4864.9*	Christie, J. Inquiry into ancient Greek game. London, 1801.

**AH 4865.1 - .499   Ancient Greece in general - Civilization, social
life - Special topics - Vehicles**

AH 4865.5	Pownall, Thomas. Dissertations on the ancient chariot. London, 1771.

**AH 4880 - 4889   Ancient Greece in general - Economic conditions - General
works (Table A)**

AH 4881.1	Pamphlet box. Economics. Greece.
AH 4881.5	Amzalak, Moses B. Historia das doutrinas económicas da antiga Grécia. n.p., n.d. 3 pam.
AH 4882.5	Austin, Michel. Économies et sociétés en Grèce ancienne. Paris, 1972.
AH 4888.56	Roscher, Wilhelm. De dogtrinae oeconomico-politicae apud Graecos primordiis. Diss. Lipsiae, 1856.
AH 4888.65	Glaser, J.C. Wirtschafts-Verhältnisse. Berlin, 1865.

AH 4880 - 4889 Ancient Greece in general - Economic conditions - General works (Table A) - cont.

AH 4888.69	Büchsenschütz, B. Besitz und Erwerb. Halle, 1869.
AH 4888.93	Guiraud, P. Propriété foncière. Paris, 1893.
AH 4888.95	Platon, G. Socialisme en Grèce. Paris, 1895.
AH 4889.00	Guiraud, P. Main d'oeuvre industrielle. Paris, 1900.
AH 4889.01	Pestalozza, U. Vita economica Ateniese. Milano, 1901.
AH 4889.03	Huch, G. Die Organisation der offentlichen Arbeit. Schlesien, 1903.
AH 4889.18.25A	Andreades, Andreas Michaël. History of Greek public finance. Cambridge, 1933.
AH 4889.18.25B	Andreades, Andreas Michaël. History of Greek public finance. Cambridge, 1933.
AH 4889.20	Glotz, G. Le travail dans la Grèce ancienne. Paris, 1920.
AH 4889.23	Bolkestein, H. Het economisch leven in Griekenlands bloeitijd. Haarlem, 1923.
AH 4889.23.3	Bolkestein, H. Economic life in Greece's golden age. Leiden, 1958.
AH 4889.26	Calhoun, G.M. The business life of ancient Athens. Chicago, 1926.
AH 4889.31	Hasebroeck, J. Griechische Wirtschafts- und Gesellschaftsgeschichte bis zur Perserzeit. Tübingen, 1931.
AH 4889.34	Korver, J. De terminologie van het crediet-wezen in het Grieksch. Amsterdam, 1934.
AH 4889.35	Brake, J. Wirtschaften und Charakter in der antiken Bildung. Frankfurt, 1935.
AH 4889.37	Endenburg, P.J. Koinoonia. Amsterdam, 1937.
AH 4889.40	Michell, Humfrey. The economics of ancient Greece. Cambridge, 1940.
AH 4889.40.2	Michell, Humfrey. The economics of ancient Greece. 2. ed. Cambridge, 1957.
AH 4889.64	French, A. The growth of the Athenian economy. London, 1964.
AH 4889.68	Bogaert, Raymond. Banques et banquiers dans les cités grecques. Leyde, 1968.

AH 4890 - 4899 Ancient Greece in general - Economic conditions - Agriculture (Table A)

AH 4892.1	Problèmes de la terre en Grèce ancienne. Paris, 1973.
AH 4899.25	Jardé, A. Les céréales dans l'antiquité grecque. Thèse. Paris, 1925.

AH 4900 - 4909 Ancient Greece in general - Economic conditions - Commerce and industries (Table A)

AH 4908.27	Baumstark, A. Curatoribus emporii et nautodicis. Friburgi, 1827.
AH 4908.39	Hüllmann, K.D. Handelsgeschichte. Bonn, 1839.
AH 4908.59	Kutorga, M. Trapézites. Paris, 1859.
AH 4908.67	Jahn, Otto. Darstellungen des Handwerks. Leipzig, 1868.
AH 4908.86	Häderli, R. Astynomen und Agoranomen. Leipzig, 1886.
AH 4909.00	Francotte, Henri. L'industrie dans la Grèce ancienne. Bruxelles, 1900-01. 2v.
AH 4909.07	Riezler, Kurt. Finanzen und Monopole in Griechenland. Berlin, 1907.
AH 4909.26A	Calhoun, G.M. The ancient Greeks and the evolution of standards in business. Boston, 1926.
AH 4909.26B	Calhoun, G.M. The ancient Greeks and the evolution of standards in business. Boston, 1926.
AH 4909.26.5	Knorringa, H. Emporos. Amsterdam, 1926.
AH 4909.27	Brashinskii, I.P. Afiny i Severnoe Prichernomor'e v VI-II vv. do n.e. Moskva, 1963.
AH 4909.28	Hasebroek, J. Staat und Handel im alten Griechenland. Tübingen, 1928.
AH 4909.28.5	Hasebroek, J. Trade and politics in ancient Greece. London, 1933.
AH 4909.29	Ziebarth, Erich. Beiträge zur Geschichte des Seeraubs und Seehandels im alten Griechenland. Hamburg, 1929.
AH 4909.34	Ziebarth, Erich. Der griechische Kaufmann im Altertum. München, 1934.
AH 4909.57	Canarache, V. Importul amforelor stampilate la Istria. Bucureşti, 1957.

AH 4910 - 4919 Ancient Greece in general - Economic conditions - Associations (Table A)

AH 4919.05	Oehler, J. Griechischen Vereinwesen. Wien, 1905.

AH 4920 - 4929 Ancient Greece in general - Economic conditions - Weights and measures (Table A)

AH 4929.01	Lehmann, C.F. Gewichte aus Thera. Berlin, 1901.

AH 4930 - 4939 Ancient Greece in general - Geography and description - General works (Table A)

Htn	AH 4935.45F*	Gerbelius, N. Descriptio Graeciae. Basiliae, 1545.
	AH 4937.90F	Gossellin, M. Geographie des Grècs analysée. Paris, 1790.
	AH 4938.25	Kruse, F.C.H. Hellas. Leipzig, 1825. 3v.
	AH 4938.25.3	Cramer, J.A. Ancient Greece. Oxford, 1828. 3v.
	AH 4938.34	Harrison, G. Lectures on geography of ancient Greece. Charlottesville, 1834.
	AH 4938.41	Hoffmann, S. Griechenland. Leipzig, 1841. 2v.
	AH 4938.42	Bobrik, H. Griechenland. Leipzig, 1842.
	AH 4938.43	Fiedler, F. Geographie und Geschichte von Altgriechenland. Leipzig, 1843.
	AH 4938.53	Hanriot, Charles. Geographia Graecorum antiquissima Napoleonopoli qualis ab Homero...Thesim proponebat. Pictavorum, 1853.
	AH 4938.62	Bursian, Konrad. Geographie von Griechenland. v.1-2. Leipzig, 1862. 3v.
	AH 4938.62.5	Bursian, Konrad. Geographie von Griechenland. Leipzig, 1862-72. 2v.
	AH 4938.73	Tozer, H.F. Lecture on geography of Greece. London, 1873.
	AH 4938.82	Curtius, E. Die Griechen in der Diaspora. v.1-2. Berlin, 1882.
	AH 4938.87	Berger, H. Geschichte der...Erdkunde der Griechen. Leipzig, 1903.
	AH 4938.87.2	Berger, H. Geschichte der...Erdkunde der Griechen. Leipzig, 1887.
	AH 4938.89	Lolling, H.G. Geographie und Geschichte des griechisches Altertums. Athen? 1889.
	AH 4938.92	Urban, K. Geographischen Forschungen und Märchen. Gütersloh, 1892.
	AH 4939.13	Oberhummer, E. Hellas abs Wiege der wissenschaftliche Geographie. Wien, 1913.
	AH 4939.52A	Diller, A. The tradition of the minor Greek geographers. Lancaster, Pa., 1952.
	AH 4939.52B	Diller, A. The tradition of the minor Greek geographers. Lancaster, Pa., 1952.

AH 4930 - 4939 Ancient Greece in general - Geography and description - General works (Table A) - cont.

AH 4939.56	Kirsten, Ernst. Die griechische Polis als historisch-geographisches Problem des Mittelmeerraumes. Bonn, 1956.
AH 4939.57	Briand de Crèvecaeur, Emmanuél. Havets pionerer. København, 1957.

AH 4945 - 4949 Ancient Greece in general - Geography and description - Atlases (By date)

AH 4948.83	Bouché-Leclercq, Auguste. Atlas pour servir à l'histoire grecque de E. Curtius. Paris, 1883.
AH 4949.11	Blümner, Hugo. Karte von Griechenland zur Zeit des Pausanias. Bern, 1911.

AH 4950 - 4959 Ancient Greece in general - Travels - General works (Table A)

AH 4957.77	Chandler, R. Reisen in Griechenland. Leipzig, 1777.
AH 4958.22	Muller, C. Voyage en Grèce et dans les Iles Ioniennes. Paris, 1822.
AH 4958.35	Leake, W.M. Travels in northern Greece. London, 1835. 4v.
AH 4958.43	Stephani, L. Reise durch...nördlichen Griechenlandes. Leipzig, 1843.
AH 4958.65	Welcker, F.G. Tagebuch einer griechische Reise. Berlin, 1865.
AH 4959.00A	Frazer, James G. Pausanias and other Greek sketches. London, 1900.
AH 4959.00B	Frazer, James G. Pausanias and other Greek sketches. London, 1900.
AH 4959.00.2	Frazer, James G. Studies in Greek scenery, legend and history, selected from his commentary on Pausanias. London, 1919.
AH 4959.00.7	Frazer, James G. Sur les traces de Pausanias a travers la Grèce ancienne. Paris, 1923.
AH 4959.08A	Gardner, W.A. In Greece with the classics. Boston, 1908.
AH 4959.08B	Gardner, W.A. In Greece with the classics. Boston, 1908.
AH 4959.09A	Allinson, Francis Greenleaf. Greek lands and letters. Boston, 1909.
AH 4959.09B	Allinson, Francis Greenleaf. Greek lands and letters. Boston, 1909.
AH 4959.09.5	Allinson, Francis Greenleaf. Greek lands and letters. Boston, 1912.
AH 4959.09.10	Allinson, Francis Greenleaf. Greek lands and letters. 3. ed. Boston, 1931.
AH 4959.30	Frazer, James G. Graecia antiqua. London, 1930.

AH 4960 - 4969 Ancient Greece in general - Travels - Imaginary travels (Table A)

Htn	AH 4967.88*	Barthélemy, J.J. Voyage de jeune Anacharsis. Paris, 1788. 5v.
	AH 4967.88.2	Barthélemy, J.J. Voyage de jeune Anacharsis. 3. éd. Paris, 1790. 7v.
NEDL	AH 4967.88.3F	Barthélemy, J.J. Voyage de jeune Anacharsis. 4. éd. Paris, 1799. 7v.
NEDL	AH 4967.88.4	Barthélemy, J.J. Voyage de jeune Anacharsis. Paris, 1788.
NEDL	AH 4967.88.5F	Barthélemy, J.J. Recueil de cartes géographiques. Paris, 1799.
	AH 4967.88.5.10	Barbié du Bocage, J.D. Recueil de cartes géographiques. Paris, 1807.
	AH 4967.88.6	Barbié du Bocage, J.D. Voyage du jeune Anacharsis en Grèce. Londres, 1796. 3v.
	AH 4967.88.6.5	Barbié du Bocage, J.D. Voyage du jeune Anacharsis en Grèce. Londres, 1798.
	AH 4967.88.7	Barbié du Bocage, J.D. Voyage du jeune Anacharsis et recueil de cartes. 3. éd. Paris, 1790. 8v.
	AH 4967.88.8	Barbié du Bocage, J.D. Oeuvres diverses. Paris, 1798. 4v.
	AH 4967.88.9	Barbié du Bocage, J.D. Oeuvres de Barthélemy. v.1-4, Atlas. Paris, 1821. 5v.
	AH 4967.88.10	Barbié du Bocage, J.D. Voyage du jeune Anacharsis en Grèce. 3. éd. Londres, 1806.
	AH 4967.88.11	Barthélemy, J.J. Voyage du jeune Anacharsis. Paris, 1822. 7v.
	AH 4967.88.13	Barthélemy, J.J. Voyage du jeune Anacharsis. v.1-7, Atlas. Paris, 1825. 8v.
NEDL	AH 4967.88.14	Barthélemy, J.J. Voyage du jeune Anacharsis en Grèce. Paris, 1830. 7v.
NEDL	AH 4967.88.15	Barthélemy, J.J. Voyage du jeune Anacharsis en Grèce. Aux Deux-Ponts, 1791. 9v.
	AH 4967.88.17	Barthélemy, J.J. Viaggio d'Anacarsi. v.1, 3-12. Venezia, 1791. 11v.
	AH 4967.88.19A	Barthélemy, J.J. Travels of Anacharsis the younger. Philadelphia, 1804. 4v.
	AH 4967.88.19B	Barthélemy, J.J. Travels of Anacharsis the younger. Philadelphia, 1804. 4v.
	AH 4967.88.23	Barthélemy, J.J. Travels of Anacharsis the younger. 4. ed. London, 1806. 8v.
	AH 4967.88.24	Barthélemy, J.J. Travels of Anacharsis the younger. 6. ed. London, 1825. 6v.
	AH 4967.88.25	Barthélemy, J.J. Travels of Anacharsis the younger. Baltimore, 1829.
	AH 4967.88.35	Barthélemy, J.J. Nouvel abrégé du Voyage du jeune Anacharsis en Grèce. v.2. Paris, 18- ?
	AH 4967.88.40	Barthélemy, J.J. Periëgesis toü Néou Anacharsidos eis Ten Hellada. v.1-7, Atlas. En Bienne, 1819. 3v.
	AH 4967.88.150	Barbié du Bocage, J.D. Maps, plans, views and coins, illustrative of the travels of Anacharsis the younger in Greece. 2. ed. London, 1793.

AH 4970 - 4979 Ancient Greece in general - Travels - Guidebooks (Table A)

AH 4978.41	Aldenhoven, F. Itineraire descriptif. Athènes, 1841.
AH 4978.90	Haussoullier, Bernard. Grèce. Collection des guides - Joanne. Paris, 1890. 2v.
AH 4978.90.2	Haussoullier, Bernard. Grèce. Collection des guides - Joanne. Paris, 1896. 2v.

AH 5007 Ancient Greek provinces, etc. - Acarnania - General history

AH 5007.5	Oberhummer, E. Akarnanien. München, 1887.

AH 5057 Ancient Greek provinces, etc. - Achaia - General history

	AH 5057.2	Gothofreedus, J. History of united provinces of Achaia. London, 1673.
Htn	AH 5057.5*	Schoockius, M. Respublicae Achaeorum. Trajani ad Rhenum, 1664.

Classified Listing

AH 5101   Ancient Greek provinces, etc. - Aegean Islands - Pamphlet volumes
 AH 5101.1   Pamphlet box. Aegean Islands. Greece.

AH 5107   Ancient Greek provinces, etc. - Aegean Islands - General history
 AH 5107.5   Waltz, Pierre. Le monde égéen avant les Grècs. Paris, 1934.
 AH 5107.9F   Instituto Storico-Archeologico di Rodi. Memorie. Rodi. 1,1933

AH 5113   Ancient Greek provinces, etc. - Aegean Islands - Civilization
 AH 5113.4   Lunn, H.S. Aegean civilizations. London, 1925.
 AH 5113.5A   Lunn, H.S. Aegean civilizations. 2. ed. London, 1927.
 AH 5113.5B   Lunn, H.S. Aegean civilizations. 2. ed. London, 1927.
 AH 5113.15A   Glotz, Gustave. The Aegean civilization. N.Y., 1925.
 AH 5113.15B   Glotz, Gustave. The Aegean civilization. N.Y., 1925.

AH 5121 - 5146   Ancient Greek provinces, etc. - Aegean Islands - Local (A-Z by place)
 AH 5121.5   Mueller, C. Aegineticorum. Berolini, 1817.
 AH 5123.5   Susini, Giancarlo. Nuove scoperte sulla storia di Coo. Bologna, 1957.
 AH 5124.5   Daenius, A. Specimen litterarum de Insula delo. Lugdunum Batavorum, 1851. 2 pam.
 AH 5124.6.5   Roussel, Pierre. Délos. Paris, 1925.
 AH 5124.7   Laidlaw, W.A. A history of Delos. Oxford, 1933.
 AH 5132.5   Plehn, S.L. Lesbiacorum liber. Berolini, 1826.
 AH 5132.7   Cichorius, Conrad. Rom und Mytilene. Leipzig, 1888.
 AH 5134.5   Dugit, E. De Insula Naxo. Lutetiae Parisiorum, 1867.
 AH 5134.7   Stumpf, Phil. De Nesistarum republica commentatio. Monachii, 1881.
 AH 5136.5   Oikonomos, S.A. He Nēsos Peparēthos. Ienae, 1883.
 AH 5138.5   Schryver, P.A. Loi Rhodia de Jactu. Bruxelles, 1844.
 AH 5138.7   Schneiderwirth, J.H. Geschichte der Insel Rhodus. Heiligenstadt, 1868.
 AH 5138.9   Torr, Cecil. Rhodes in ancient times. Photoreproduction. Cambridge, 1885.
 AH 5138.11   Schumacher, C. Republica Rhodiorum commentatio. Heidelbergae, 1886.
 AH 5138.13   Gelder, H. Geschichte der alten Rhodier. Haag, 1900.
 AH 5138.14   Fraser, P.M. The Rhodian Peraen and island. London, 1954.
 AH 5138.15   Nomos Rodiōn, Nautikos. Rhodian law. Oxford, 1909.
 AH 5138.17F   Clara Rhodes. 1-9,1928-1938 10v.
 AH 5139.5   Curtius, C. Urkunden zur Geschichte von Samos. Wesel, 1873.
 AH 5139.7   Curtius, C. Inschriften zur Geschichte von Samos. Lübeck, 1877.
 AH 5139.7.5   Curtius, C. Inschriften und Studien zur Geschichte von Samos. Lübeck, 1877.
 AH 5140.5   Hiller, F. Archaische Kultur der Insel Thera. Berlin, 1897.
 AH 5140.7   Jacobs, Emil. Thasiaca. Berolini, 1893.
 AH 5140.7.1   Jacobs, Emil. Thasiaca. Inaug. Diss. Berolini, 1893.
 AH 5140.9   Moschatos, A. De Insula Teno Eiusque historia. Gottingae, 1855.

AH 5157   Ancient Greek provinces, etc. - Aetolia - General history
 AH 5157.5   Hohmann, W. Aitolien und die Aitoler bis zum lamischen Kriege. Halle, 1908.
 AH 5157.10   Brandstäter, F.A. Die Geschichten des aetolischen Landes. Berlin, 1844.
 AH 5157.15   Benecke, H.H. Die Seepolitik der Aitoler. Inaug. Diss. Hamburg, 1934.
 AH 5157.20   Stergiopoulos, K.D. He archaia aitōlia. En Athēnais, 1939.

AH 5207   Ancient Greek provinces, etc. - Arcadia - General history
 AH 5207.5   Schwab, C.T. Arkadien. Stuttgart, 1852.
 AH 5207.10   Callmer, C. Studien zur Geschichte Arkadiens. Lund, 1943.

AH 5210   Ancient Greek provinces, etc. - Arcadia - History by periods - 500 - 1 B.C.
 AH 5210.5   Dušanić, Slobodan. Arkadski savez IV veka. Beograd, 1970.

AH 5221 - 5246   Ancient Greek provinces, etc. - Arcadia - Local (A-Z by place)
 AH 5233.5   Herthum, P. De megalopolitarum rebus gestis. Lipsiae, 1893.

AH 5253   Ancient Greek provinces, etc. - Argolis - Government and administration
 AH 5253.5   Zwolski, Edward. Ustrój państwowy w starożytnym Argos. Lublin, 1967.

AH 5257   Ancient Greek provinces, etc. - Argolis - General history
 AH 5257.1   Tomlinson, Richard Allan. Argos and the Argolid. Ithaca, N.Y., 1972.

AH 5271 - 5296   Ancient Greek provinces, etc. - Argolis - Local (A-Z by place)
 AH 5271.5   Schneiderwirth, J.H. Polische Geschichte des dorischen Argos. v.1-2. Heiligenstadt, 1865.
 AH 5271.7   Kophiniōtēs, I.K. Historia tou Argous. Athēnai, 1892.
 AH 5271.10   Woerrle, Michael. Untersuchungen zur Verfassungsgeschichte von Argos im 5. Jahrhundert vor Christus. Diss. Erlangen? 196-.

AH 5301   Ancient Greek provinces, etc. - Attica - Pamphlet volumes
 AH 5301.1   Pamphlet box. Attica. Greece.
 AH 5301.7   Arnim, I. Hans. Ad scholas ad civitatis Atticae historiam symbole. Rostock, 1895. 3 pam.

AH 5303   Ancient Greek provinces, etc. - Attica - Government and administration
 Htn   AH 5303.5*   Postel, G. Republica seu magistratibus. Lugdunum Batavorum, 1635.
 Htn   AH 5303.5.3*   Postel, G. Republica seu magistratibus Atheniensium. Lugdunum Batavorum, 1645.
 AH 5303.6   Rhodes, P.J. The Athenian boule. Oxford, 1972.
 AH 5303.7   Büttner, H. Polische Hetärieen in Athen. Leipzig, 1840.
 AH 5303.8   De Laix, Roger. Probouleusis at Athens. Berkeley, 1973.
 AH 5303.9   Canet, V. Institutions d'Athènes. Lille, 1888. 2v.
 AH 5303.10   Warncke, F. Die demokratische Staatsidee in der Verfassung von Athens. Bonn, 1951.
 AH 5303.11   Méautis, G. L'aristocratie athénienne. Paris, 1927.
 AH 5303.12   Andria, N. La démocratie athénienne. Thèse. Paris, 1935.
 AH 5303.13   Ferguson, William S. The treasurers of Athena. Cambridge, Mass., 1932.
 AH 5303.14   Cloché, Paul. La démocratie athénienne. Paris, 1951.
 AH 5303.15   Ferguson, William S. The Athenian secretaries. Photoreproduction. N.Y., 1898.

AH 5303   Ancient Greek provinces, etc. - Attica - Government and administration - cont.
 AH 5303.16   Jones, Arnold H.M. Athenian democracy. Oxford, 1957.
 AH 5303.20   Loenen, Dirk. De Atheense democratie. Amsterdam, 1946.
 AH 5303.25   Sartori, Franco. Le eterie nella vita politica ateniese del VI e V secolo A.C. Roma, 1957.
 AH 5303.30   Connor, Walter Robert. The new politicians of fifth-century Athens. Princeton, 1971.
 AH 5303.32   Pecorella Longo, Chiara. Eterie e gruppi politici nell'Atene del IV sec. A.C. Firenze, 1971.

AH 5304   Ancient Greek provinces, etc. - Attica - Law
 AH 5304.2   Cohen, Edward E. Ancient Athenian maritime courts. Princeton, 1973.

AH 5305   Ancient Greek provinces, etc. - Attica - Military affairs
 AH 5305.5   Fornara, Charles W. The Athenian board of generals from 501 to 404. Wiesbaden, 1971.

AH 5306   Ancient Greek provinces, etc. - Attica - Naval affairs
 AH 5306.5   Curtius, E. De portubus Athenarum. Halis, 1842.
 AH 5306.7F   Marstand, Vilhelm. Arsenalet i Piraeus og oldtidens byggereqler. København, 1922.

AH 5307   Ancient Greek provinces, etc. - Attica - General history
 AH 5307.5   Fanelli, F. Athene Attica. Venezia, 1707.
 AH 5307.7   Young, W. History of Athens. London, 1786.
 AH 5307.7.3   Young, W. History of Athens. 3. ed. London, 1804.
 AH 5307.9   Bulwer, E. Athens. Its rise and fall. London, 18- . 2v.
 AH 5307.11   Creuzeri, F. Oratio de civitate Athenarum. Francofurti, 1826.
 AH 5307.13   Bulwer, E. Athens. Its rise and fall. Paris, 1837.
 AH 5307.14.2   Bulwer, E. Athens. Its rise and fall. N.Y., 1837. 2v.
 AH 5307.14.6   Bulwer, E. Athens. Its rise and fall. v.1-2. Leipzig, 1843.
 AH 5307.15   Müller, K.O. De munimentis Athenarum. Gottingae, 1836.
 AH 5307.17   Müller, K.O. Attica and Athens. London, 1842.
 AH 5307.19   Hoeck, A. De rebus ab Atheniensibus in Thracia et in Ponto. Kiliae, 1876.
 AH 5307.21   Hertzberg, G.F. Athen. Halle, 1885.
 AH 5307.22   Curtius, Ernst. Die Stadtgeschichte von Athen. Berlin, 1891.
 AH 5307.23   Butler, Howard C. Story of Athens. London, 1902.
 AH 5307.23.5   Butler, Howard C. Story of Athens. N.Y., 1902.
 AH 5307.25   Felton, C.C. Athens. n.p., 18- .
 AH 5307.27   Jardé, A. Athènes ancienne. Paris, 1930.
 AH 5307.29   Guy, Noël. Athènes. Illustrations en couleurs de Marilac. Paris, 1935.
 AH 5307.30   Cohen, R. Athènes, une démocratie. Paris, 1936.
 AH 5307.34   Sealey, Raphael. Essays in Greek politics. N.Y., 1967.

AH 5308   Ancient Greek provinces, etc. - Attica - General special
 AH 5308.5   Droysen, H. Athen und der Westen. Berlin, 1882.
 AH 5308.6   Lofberg, John O. Sycophancy in Athens. Thesis. Chicago, 1917.
 AH 5308.7   Stauffer, A. Zwölf Gestalten der Glanzzeit Athens. München, 1896.
 AH 5308.8   Schroeder, Otto. De laudibus Athenarum a poetis. Gottingae, 1914.
 AH 5308.9   Calhoun, G.M. Athenian clubs in politics and litigation. Austin, 1913.
 AH 5308.9.2   Calhoun, G.M. Athenian clubs in politics and litigation. Austin, 1913.
 AH 5308.10   Eliot, C.W.J. Coastal demes of Attika. Toronto, 1962.
 AH 5308.11   Powers, H.H. The hill of Athena. N.Y., 1924.
 AH 5308.12   Hoffmeister, E.E.W. Kritische Untersuchung der Charakterentwicklung der Athener. Hamburg, 1932.

AH 5309   Ancient Greek provinces, etc. - Attica - History by periods - Before 500 B.C.
 AH 5309.5   Büchenschütz, A.B. Könige von Athen. Berlin, 1855.
 AH 5309.6   Zel'in, K.K. Bor'ba politicheskikh gruppirovok v Attike. Moskva, 1964.
 AH 5309.7   Schjøtt, P.O. Athen for Solon. Kristiania, 1880.
 AH 5309.9   Kausel, T. Thesei Synoecismo. Dillenburg, 1882.
 AH 5309.11   Sanctis, G. Atthis. Roma, 1898.
 AH 5309.11.2   Sanctis, G. Atthis. 2. ed. Torino, 1912.
 AH 5309.12   Cataudella, Michele R. Atene fra il VII e il VI secolo. Catania, 1966.

AH 5310   Ancient Greek provinces, etc. - Attica - History by periods - 500 - 1 B.C.
 AH 5310.3.2   Accame, Silvio. L'imperialismo ateniese all'inizio del secolo IV A.C. e la crisi della Polis. 2. ed. Napoli, 1966.
 AH 5310.5A   Ferguson, William S. Hellenistic Athens. London, 1911.
 AH 5310.5B   Ferguson, William S. Hellenistic Athens. London, 1911.
 AH 5310.6   Cloché, Paul. Le restauration democratique à Athènes en 403 avant J.C. Paris, 1915.
 AH 5310.7   Gilbert, Gustav. Beiträge zur innern Geschichte Athens. Leipzig, 1877.
 AH 5310.11   Sundwall, J. Epigraphische Beiträge zur sozial-politischen Geschichte Athens im Zeitalter des Demosthenes. Leipzig, 1906.
 AH 5310.15   Cloché, Paul. La politique étrangère d'Athènes de 404 à 338 avant Jesus Christ. Paris, 1934.

AH 5311   Ancient Greek provinces, etc. - Attica - History by periods - 1 A.D. - ca. 500
 AH 5311.5   Neubauer, F. Atheniensium Reipublicae quaenam romanorum temporibus fuerit condicio. Halis Saxonum, 1882.
 AH 5311.7   Graindor, Paul. Athènes sous Hadrieu. Le Caire, 1934.

AH 5312   Ancient Greek provinces, etc. - Attica - Chronology
 AH 5312.5F   Pritchett, William K. The chronology of Hellenistic Athens. Cambridge, Mass., 1940.

AH 5313   Ancient Greek provinces, etc. - Attica - Civilization
 AH 5313.10   Robinson, Charles. Athens in the age of Pericles. 1st ed. Norman, 1959.
 AH 5313.12   Massachusetts Institute of Technology. Department of English and History. Athens in the fifth century B.C. Cambridge, Mass., 1950.
 AH 5313.15   Halsberghe, Gaston. Zoeklicht op het oude Athene. Hasselt, 1960.
 AH 5313.20   Webster, Thomas Bertham Lonsdale. Everyday life in classical Athens. London, 1969.

AH 5315   Ancient Greek provinces, etc. - Attica - Economic conditions
AH 5315.5   Gomme, A.W. Population of Athens in the fifth and fourth
                 centuries B.C. Oxford, 1933.
AH 5315.7   Hansen, J.H. Über die Bevölkerungsdichtigkeit Attika's und
                 ihre politische Bedeutung im Altertum. Hamburg, 1885?
AH 5315.20   Woodhouse, William J. Solon the liberator; a study of the
                 Agrarian problem in Attika in the seventh century.
                 London, 1938.
AH 5315.25   Calhoun, G.M. Ancient Athenian mining. Cambridge,
                 Mass., 1931.
AH 5315.30   Lugones, Leopoldo. Las industrias de Atenas. Buenos
                 Aires, 1919.
AH 5315.35   Day, John. An economic history of Athens under Roman
                 domination. N.Y., 1942.
AH 5315.40A   Marsh, T.B. Modern problems in the ancient world.
                 Austin, 1943.
AH 5315.40B   Marsh, T.B. Modern problems in the ancient world.
                 Austin, 1943.
AH 5315.40C   Marsh, T.B. Modern problems in the ancient world.
                 Austin, 1943.

AH 5316   Ancient Greek provinces, etc. - Attica - Geography
AH 5316.5   Holmberg, Erik J. Aten och Delfi. Lund, 1953.

**AH 5321 - 5346   Ancient Greek provinces, etc. - Attica - Local (A-Z by
place)**
AH 5333.5   Curtius, Carl. Metroon in Athen. Berlin, 1868.
AH 5335.5   Dunbach, F. Cropo et Amphiarae Sacro. Parisiis, 1890.
AH 5336.6   Curtius, Ernst. Attische Studien; Pnyx und Stadtmauer.
                 Göttingen, 1862.
AH 5336.7   Hagemann, G. De Prytaneo. Vratislaviae, 1880.
AH 5343.2   Frickenhaus, A. Athens Mauern. Bonn, 1905.

AH 5357   Ancient Greek provinces, etc. - Boeotia - General history
AH 5357.5A   Roberts, W.R. Ancient Bocotians. Cambridge, 1895.
AH 5357.5B   Roberts, W.R. Ancient Bocotians. Cambridge, 1895.
AH 5357.10   Guillon, P. La Béotie antique. Paris, 1948.

**AH 5360   Ancient Greek provinces, etc. - Boeotia - History by periods - 500 - 1
B.C.**
AH 5360.5   Braake, G.J. Theilnahme der Böoter. Rostock, 1874.

AH 5363   Ancient Greek provinces, etc. - Boeotia - Civilization
AH 5363.5   Newmann, G. De nominibus boeotorum propriis.
                 Regimonti, 1908.

**AH 5371 - 5396   Ancient Greek provinces, etc. - Boeotia - Local (A-Z by
place)**
AH 5372.5   Aubert, L.M.B. Et graesk Senatsconsult om Thisbaeerne.
                 n.p., 1875.
AH 5386.5   Stanhope, J.S. Battle of Plataea. v.1-2. London, 1835.
AH 5386.7   Fritzsche, G. Geschichte Platääs. Bautzen, 1898.
AH 5390.5   Müller, M. Geschichte Thebens. Leipzig, 1879.
AH 5390.7   Fabricius, E. Theben. Freiburg, 1890.
AH 5390.9   Funk, Emil. De Thebanorum. Berlin, 1890.
AH 5390.11   Werenka, D. Kritische Bemerkungen. Czernowitz, 1907.
AH 5390.13   Schäfer, Alexander. Die Berichte Xenophons, Plutarchs und
                 Diodors über die Besetzung und Befreiung. Inaug. Diss.
                 München, 1930.
AH 5390.15   Prickard, A.O. The return of the Theban exiles, 379-378
                 B.C. Oxford, 1926.
AH 5390.17   Cloché, Paul. Thèbes de Béotie. Namur, 1952?
AH 5390.19   Reimer, P.J. Zeven tegen Thebe. Gouda, 1953.
AH 5390.20   Roesch, Paul. Thespies et la confédération béotienne.
                 Paris, 1965.
VAH 5390.21   Krawczuk, Aleksander. Siedurin pneciw Tebom. 1. wyd.
                 Warszawa, 1968.

**AH 5403   Ancient Greek provinces, etc. - Corinthia - Government and
administration**
AH 5403.5   Porzio, Guido. La più antica aristocrazia Corintiaca.
                 Milano, 1919.

AH 5407   Ancient Greek provinces, etc. - Corinthia - General history
AH 5407.5   Wilisch, E. Beiträge zur...Geschichte des...Korinth.
                 Zittau, 1887.

**AH 5409   Ancient Greek provinces, etc. - Corinthia - History by periods - Before
500 B.C.**
AH 5409.5   Schubring, J.J. Cypsello Corinthiorum tyranno.
                 Gottingae, 1862.
AH 5409.6   Porzio, Guido. I Cipselidi. Bologna, 1912.
AH 5409.6.15   Porzio, Guido. Corinto. Padova, 1907.
AH 5409.7   Well, Edouard. Korinthiaka. Paris, 1955.
AH 5409.8   Phouriötës, Angelos. Korinthos. Athēnai, 1972.

**AH 5410   Ancient Greek provinces, etc. - Corinthia - History by periods - 500 - 1
B.C.**
AH 5410.5   Wilisch, E. Geschichte Korinths. Zittau, 1896.

AH 5415   Ancient Greek provinces, etc. - Corinthia - Economic conditions
AH 5415.5   Barth, H. Corinthiorum. Berolini, 1844.

**AH 5421 - 5446   Ancient Greek provinces, etc. - Corinthia - Local (A-Z by
place)**
AH 5436.2   Alexander, J.A. Potidaea. Athens, 1963.

AH 5453   Ancient Greek provinces, etc. - Crete - Government and administration
AH 5453.5   Muttelsee, M. Zur Verfassungsgeschichte Kretas im
                 Zeitalter des Hellenismus. Glückstadt, 1925.
AH 5453.7A   Mijnsbrugge, M. van der. The Cretan koinon. N.Y., 1931.
AH 5453.7B   Mijnsbrugge, M. van der. The Cretan koinon. N.Y., 1931.

AH 5457   Ancient Greek provinces, etc. - Crete - General history
AH 5457.5   Meursius, J. Creta, Cyprus, Rhodus. Amstelodami, 1675.
AH 5457.7   Koeck, K. Kreta. Göttingen, 1823. 3v.

AH 5458   Ancient Greek provinces, etc. - Crete - General special
AH 5458.5   Willetts, Ronald Frederick. Ancient Crete. London, 1965.

**AH 5459   Ancient Greek provinces, etc. - Crete - History by periods - Before 500
B.C.**
AH 5459.5   Huxley, George Leonard. Crete and the Lumians.
                 Oxford, 1961.

**AH 5460   Ancient Greek provinces, etc. - Crete - History by periods - 500 - 1
B.C.**
AH 5460.5   Effenterre, H. van. La Crète et le monde grec.
                 Paris, 1948.
AH 5460.10   Mikrogiannakes, E.I. Hē Krētē kara toys Ellēnistikoys
                 chronoys. Thesis. Athēnai, 1967.

AH 5463   Ancient Greek provinces, etc. - Crete - Civilization
AH 5463.5   Hogarth, D.G. The twilight of history. London, 1926.
AH 5463.10   Willetts, Ronald Frederick. Aristocratic society in
                 ancient Crete. London, 1955.
AH 5463.10.5   Willetts, Ronald Frederick. Everyday life in ancient
                 Crete. London, 1969.
AH 5463.15   Glotz, Gustave. La civilisation égéenne. Paris, 1952.
AH 5463.20   Branigan, Keith. The foundations of palatial Crete: a
                 survey of Crete in the early Bronze Age. London, 1970.
AH 5463.25   Hood, Sinclair. The Minoans. N.Y., 1971.
AH 5463.30   Huxley, George Leonard. Minoans in Greek sources.
                 Belfast, 1968.
AH 5463.35   Cottrell, Leonard. The mystery of Minoan civilization.
                 N.Y., 1971.
AH 5463.36   Mellersh, Harold E.L. The destruction of Knossos: the rise
                 and fall of Minoan Crete. London, 1970.

**AH 5471 - 5496   Ancient Greek provinces, etc. - Crete - Local (A-Z by
place)**
AH 5479.2   Spyridakēs, Stylianos Basileiou. Ptolemaic Itanos and
                 Hellenistic Crete. Berkeley, 1970.

AH 5553   Ancient Greek provinces, etc. - Elis - Government and administration
AH 5553.7   Curtius, Ernst. Der Synoikismos von Elis. Berlin, 1895.

AH 5557   Ancient Greek provinces, etc. - Elis - General history
AH 5557.5   Schiller, L. Elis, Arkadien, Achaja. Erlangen, 1855.

AH 5603   Ancient Greek provinces, etc. - Epirus - Government and administration
AH 5603.5   Cross, Geoffrey N. Epirus; a study in Greek constitutional
                 development. Cambridge, 1932.

AH 5607   Ancient Greek provinces, etc. - Epirus - General history
AH 5607.5   Schmidt, H. Epeirotika...Geschichte des alten Epeiros.
                 Marburg, 1894.
AH 5607.7   Klotzsch, C. Epirotische Geschichte. Boston, 1911.
AH 5607.8   Hammond, Nicholas Geoffrey Lempriere. Epirus: the
                 geography, the ancient remains, the history. Oxford, 1967.

AH 5608   Ancient Greek provinces, etc. - Epirus - General special
AH 5608.2   Lepore, Ettore. Recherche sull'antico-epiro.
                 Napoli, 1962.

**AH 5610   Ancient Greek provinces, etc. - Epirus - History by periods - 500 - 1
B.C.**
AH 5610.5   Schubert, R. Geschichte der Pyrrhus. Königsberg, 1894.
AH 5610.6.2   Garouphalias, Petros Euagelov. Pyrros, ho Basilias tēs
                 Epeirov. 2. ed. Athēnai, 1972.
AH 5610.7   Abbott, Jacob. History of Pyrrhus. N.Y., 1871.
AH 5610.7.5   Abbott, Jacob. History of Pyrrhus. N.Y., 1854.
AH 5610.9   Hamburger, Oswald. Untersuchungen über den pynhischen
                 Krieg. Inaug. Diss. Würzburg, 1927.
AH 5610.12   Hassell, Ulrich von. Pyrrhus. München, 1947.
AH 5610.14   Bartsos, Iōannēs A. Ho Pyrros en Italia, skopoi kai drasis
                 autou. Diss. Athēnai, 1967.
AH 5610.15   Léveque, P. Pyrrhos. Paris, 1957.
AH 5610.20   Franke, Peter R. Alt-Epirus und des Königtum der Molosser.
                 Kallmünz, 1954.
AH 5610.21   Sandberger, Frank. Prosopographie zur Geschichte des
                 Pyrrhos. Diss. Stuttgart, 1970.

AH 5616   Ancient Greek provinces, etc. - Epirus - Geography
AH 5616.5   Treidler, Hans. Epirus im Altertum; Studien zur
                 historischen Topographie. Inaug. Diss. Leipzig, 1917.

AH 5657   Ancient Greek provinces, etc. - Euboea - General history
AH 5657.4   Geyer, F. Topographie...der Insel Euboia. Kirchain, 1902.
AH 5657.5   Geyer, F. Topographie...der Insel Euboia. Berlin, 1903.

AH 5658   Ancient Greek provinces, etc. - Euboea - General special
AH 5658.5   Bursian, C. Quaestionum Euboicarum. Lipsiae, 1856.

AH 5666   Ancient Greek provinces, etc. - Euboea - Geography
AH 5666.5   Baumeister, A. Topographische Skizze der Insel Euboia.
                 Lübeck, 1864.

**AH 5671 - 5696   Ancient Greek provinces, etc. - Euboea - Local (A-Z by
place)**
AH 5673.5   Bakhuizen, Simon Cornelis. Chalcidian studies.
                 Proefschrift. v.2. Groningen, 1970-
AH 5673.10   Zahrnt, Michael. Olynth und die Chalkidier.
                 München, 1971.

AH 5708   Ancient Greek provinces, etc. - Ionian Islands - General special
AH 5708.5   Sakellariou, M.B. La migration grecque en Ionie.
                 Athènes, 1958.
AH 5708.7   Cook, John. The Greeks in Ionia and the East.
                 London, 1962.

**AH 5721 - 5746   Ancient Greek provinces, etc. - Ionian Islands - Local (A-Z
by place)**
AH 5723.5   Giurini, A.M. Primordia Corcyrae. Lycij, 1725.
Htn AH 5723.7* Giurini, A.M. Primordia Corcyrae. Brixiae, 1738.
AH 5723.15   Biedermann, Georg. Die Insel Kephallenia im Altertum.
                 Inaug. Diss. München, 1887.

AH 5751   Ancient Greek provinces, etc. - Laconia - Pamphlet volumes
AH 5751.1   Pamphlet box. Laconia.

AH 5753   Ancient Greek provinces, etc. - Laconia - Government and administration
AH 5753.5   Dum, Georg. Spartanischen Ephorats. Innsbruck, 1878.
AH 5753.7   Kuchtner, K. Spartanischen Ephorats. München, 1897.
AH 5753.9   Frick, C. Ephoris Spartanis. Gottingae, 1872.
AH 5753.15   Gachon, Paul. De ephoris Spartanis. Diss.
                 Monspelii, 1888.

Classified Listing

AH 5754   Ancient Greek provinces, etc. - Laconia - Law
AH 5754.5   Hermann, C.F. Antiquitatum Laconicarum. Marburgi, 1841.
AH 5754.7   Trieber, C. Forschungen zur spartanischen Verfassungsgeschichte. Berlin, 1871.
AH 5754.9   Fustel de Coulanges. Propriété a Sparte. Paris, 1880.
AH 5754.11   Lachmann, K.H. Spartnisches Staatsverfassung. Breslau, 1836.
AH 5754.13   Solari, Arturo. Ricerche spartane. Livorno, 1907.

AH 5757   Ancient Greek provinces, etc. - Laconia - General history
AH 5757.5   Manso, J.K.F. Sparta. v.1-3. Leipzig, 1800. 5v.
AH 5757.7   Krag, Niels. De republica Lacedaemoniorum. Lugdunum Batavorum, 1670.
AH 5757.9   Busolt, G. Lakedaimonier. Leipzig, 1878.
AH 5757.10   Tigerstedt, Eugène Napoleon. The legend of Sparta in classical antiquity. Stockholm, 1965.
AH 5757.11   Ollier, F. Le mirage spartiate. Thèse. Paris, 1933.
AH 5757.11.5 Ollier, F. Le mirage spartiate. Paris, 1943.
AH 5757.13   Däubler, T. Sparta; ein Versuch. Leipzig, 1923.
AH 5757.15   Berve, H. Sparta. Leipzig, 1937.
AH 5757.17   Lüdemann, Hans. Sparta, Lebensordnung und Schicksal. Leipzig, 1939.
AH 5757.19   Cavaignac, E. Sparte. 25. éd. Paris, 1948.
AH 5757.20   Forrest, William George Grieve. A history of Sparta, 950-192 B.C. N.Y., 1969.
AH 5757.21   Chrimes, K.M.T. Ancient Sparta. Manchester, 1949.
AH 5757.25   Boer, W. den. Laconian studies. Amsterdam, 1954.
AH 5757.26   Jones, Arnold Hugh Martin. Sparta. Cambridge, 1967.

AH 5758   Ancient Greek provinces, etc. - Laconia - General special
AH 5758.5   Jannet, C. Institutions sociales. Paris, 1880.
AH 5758.10   Rawson, Elizabeth. The Spartan tradition in European thought. Oxford, 1969.
AH 5758.16   Oliva, Pavel. Sparta and her social problems. Prague, 1971.
AH 5758.16.1 Oliva, Pavel. Sparta and her social problems. Amsterdam, 1971.

AH 5759   Ancient Greek provinces, etc. - Laconia - History by periods - Before 500 B.C.
AH 5759.5   Gilbert, G. Altspartanishen Geschichte. Göttingen, 1872.
AH 5759.7   Pareti, Luigi. Storia di Sparta arcaica. Firenze, 1917.
AH 5759.9   Doukas, P.C. He Sparte dia mesou tōn aiōnon. Nea Yorkē, 1922.
AH 5759.12A   Huxley, G.L. Early Sparta. Cambridge, 1962.
AH 5759.12B   Huxley, G.L. Early Sparta. Cambridge, 1962.
AH 5759.13   Kiele, F. Lakonien und Sparta. München, 1963.

AH 5760   Ancient Greek provinces, etc. - Laconia - History by periods - 500 - 1 B.C.
AH 5760.5   Nordin, R. Äussere Politik Spartas. Upsala, 1895.
AH 5760.7   Löwy, A. Sparta. Rostock, 1873.
AH 5760.8   Senfftleben, Franz. Sparta und sein Bund von 479 bis 445 vor Christ. Jena, 1872.
AH 5760.9   Kaegi, Adolph. Kritische Geschichte des spartanischen Staates von 500-431 vor Christ. Leipzig, 1873.
AH 5760.11   Hertzberg, G.F. Königs Agesilaos II von Sparta. Halle, 1856.
AH 5760.13   Buttmann, A. Agesilaus. Halle, 1872.
AH 5760.15   Petit-Dutaillis, C. Laecedaemoniorum Reipublicae. Lutetiae Parisiorum, 1894.

AH 5762   Ancient Greek provinces, etc. - Laconia - Chronology
AH 5762.5   Dum, Georg. Spartanischen Königslisten. Innsbruck, 1878.

AH 5763   Ancient Greek provinces, etc. - Laconia - Civilization
AH 5763.3   Willing, Karl. Die Geist Spartas. 1. Aufl. Berlin, 1935.
AH 5763.5A   Michell, Humfrey. Sparta. Cambridge, Eng., 1952.
AH 5763.5B   Michell, Humfrey. Sparta. Cambridge, Eng., 1952.
AH 5763.6   Michell, Humfrey. Sparta. Cambridge, Eng., 1964.
AH 5763.8   Janni, Pietro. La cultura di Sparta arcaica. Roma, 1965. 2v.
AH 5763.10   Stibbe, C.M. Sparta. Geschiedenis en cultuur der Spartanen van praehistorie tot Perzische oorlogen. Bussum, 1969.

AH 5765   Ancient Greek provinces, etc. - Laconia - Economic conditions
AH 5765.5   Andreadès, A.M. He demosia oikonomia tōn Spartiatōn. Athēnai, n.d.

AH 5766   Ancient Greek provinces, etc. - Laconia - Geography
AH 5766.5   Heidemann, L. Die territoriale Entwicklung. Berlin, 1904.

AH 5807   Ancient Greek provinces, etc. - Locris - General history
AH 5807.5   Bauer, Edmund. Untersuchungen zur Geographie...der norwestlichen Land. Inaug. Diss. Halle, 1907.
AH 5807.7   Roltsch, Otto. Die Westlokrer. Inaug. Diss. Weida, 1914.

AH 5853   Ancient Greek provinces, etc. - Megaris - Government and administration
AH 5853.5   Ullrich, F.W. Megarische Psephisma. Hamburg, 1838.
AH 5853.7   Cauer, F. Parteien und Politiker. Stuttgart, 1890.

AH 5857   Ancient Greek provinces, etc. - Megaris - General history
AH 5857.5   Reinganum, H. Alte Megaris. Berlin, 1825.
AH 5857.7   Vogt, G. Rebus Megarensium. Marburgi, 1857.
AH 5857.9   Thamm, M. Republica ac Magistratibus Megarensium. Halis Saxonum, 1885.
AH 5857.11   Highbarger, E.L. The history and civilization of ancient Megara. Baltimore, 1927.
AH 5857.11.5 Highbarger, E.L. Chapters in the history and civilization of ancient Megara. Baltimore, 1927.
AH 5857.12   Hanell, Krister. Megarische Studien. Lund, 1934.

AH 5858   Ancient Greek provinces, etc. - Megaris - General special
AH 5858.5   Levègue, J. A. De oppidis et portibus Megaridis ac Boeotiae. Thesim proponebat. Parisiis, 1875.

AH 5905   Ancient Greek provinces, etc. - Messenia - Military affairs
AH 5905.5   Dundaczek, Raimund. Beiträge zur Geschichte der...messenischen Kriege. Czernowitz, 1882.

AH 5909   Ancient Greek provinces, etc. - Messenia - History by periods - Before 500 B.C.
AH 5909.59   Kiechle, Franz. Messenische Studien. Kallmünz, 1959.

AH 5910   Ancient Greek provinces, etc. - Messenia - History by periods - 500 - 1 B.C.
AH 5910.5   Seeliger, K. Messenien und der achäische Bund. Zittau, 1897.
AH 5910.10   Roebuck, Carl A. A history of Messenia from 369 to 146 B.C. Thesis. Chicago, 1941.

AH 5916   Ancient Greek provinces, etc. - Messenia - Geography
AH 5916.5   Valmin, M.N. Études topographiques sur la Messénie ancienne. Lund, 1930.

AH 5957   Ancient Greek provinces, etc. - Peloponnesus in general - General history
AH 5957.5   Curtius, Ernst. Peloponnesos. Gotha, 1851. 2v.
AH 5957.7   Beulé, E. Études sur Péloponésé. Paris, 1855.
NEDL AH 5957.9   Clark, W.G. Peloponnesus. London, 1858.

AH 5958   Ancient Greek provinces, etc. - Peloponnesus in general - General special
AH 5958.5   Vitalis, Gerhard. Die Entwicklung der Sage von der Rückkehr der Herakliden. Griefswald, 1930.
Htn   AH 5958.10*   Pasiaudi, P.M. Monumenta Peloponnesia. Romae, 1761. 2v.

AH 5967   Ancient Greek provinces, etc. - Peloponnesus in general - Travels
AH 5967.5A   Leake, W.M. Travels in the Morea. London, 1830. 3v.
AH 5967.5B   Leake, W.M. Travels in the Morea. London, 1830. 3v.
AH 5967.7   Leake, W.M. Peloponnesiaca. London, 1846.

AH 6007   Ancient Greek provinces, etc. - Phocis - General history
AH 6007.5   Kazarow, G. Foederis Phocensium institutis. Lipsiae, 1899.
AH 6007.10   Schober, Friedrick. Phokis. Inaug. Diss. Crossen, 1924.

AH 6009   Ancient Greek provinces, etc. - Phocis - History by periods - Before 500 B.C.
AH 6009.5   Flathe, Theodor. Der phokische Krieg. Plauen, 1854.

AH 6021 - 6046   Ancient Greek provinces, etc. - Phocis - Local (A-Z by place)
AH 6024.5   Curtius, Ernst. Anecdota Delphica. Berolini, 1843.
AH 6024.7   Bourguet, Emile. De rebus Delphicis imperatoriae aetatis capita duo. Diss. Montepessulano, 1905.
AH 6024.9   Hiller von Gaertringen, F. Geschichte von Delphi. Stuttgart, 1899.
AH 6024.11   Daux, Georges. Delphes au IIe et au Ier siècle depuis l'abaissement de l'Etolie jusqu'à la paix romaine 191-31 avant J.C. Thèse. Paris, 1936.
AH 6024.15   Hoyle, Peter. Delphi. London, 1967.

AH 6049   Ancient Greek provinces, etc. - Sicyonia
AH 6049.5   Skalet, Charles H. Chapters in history of ancient Sicyon. Baltimore, 1928.
AH 6049.5.5   Skalet, Charles H. Ancient Sicyon, with a prosopographia Sicyonia. Baltimore, 1928.

AH 6053   Ancient Greek provinces, etc. - Thessaly - Government and administration
AH 6053.5   Kroog, G. Foederis Thessalorum praetoribus. Halis Saxonum, 1908.

AH 6057   Ancient Greek provinces, etc. - Thessaly - General history
AH 6057.5   Kriegk, G.L. Thessalische Ebene. Frankfurt am Main, 1858.
AH 6057.7F   Costanzi, V. Saggio di storia tessalica. Pisa, 1906.
AH 6057.9   Kent, R.G. History of Thessaly. Lancaster, Pa., 1904.
AH 6057.11   Kip, G. Thessalische Studien. Halle, 1910.
AH 6057.13   Stählin, F. Das hellenische Thessalien. Stuttgart, 1924.
AH 6057.15   Solari, Arturo. La lega tessalica. Pisa, 1912.
AH 6057.17   Sordi, Marta. La lega tessala fino ad Afessundro-Magno. Roma, 1958.

AH 6060   Ancient Greek provinces, etc. - Thessaly - History by periods - 500 - 1 B.C.
AH 6060.5   Westlake, Henry Dickinson. Thessaly in the fourth century B.C. London, 1935.
AH 6060.5.2   Westlake, Henry Dickinson. Thessaly in the fourth century B.C. Groningen, 1969.

AH 6071 - 6096   Ancient Greek provinces, etc. - Thessaly - Local (A-Z by place)
AH 6082.5   Axenidès, T.D. He pelasgis Larissa kai he archaia Thessalia. Athēnai, 1947.
AH 6086.5   Stählin, Friedrich. Pagasai und Demetrios. Berlin, 1934.

AH 6103   Ancient Greek provinces, etc. - Macedonia - Government and administration
AH 6103.5   Hampl, Franz. Der König der Makedonien. Inaug. Diss. Weida, 1934.
AH 6103.7   Zancan, P. Il monarcato ellenistico nei suoi elementi federativi. Padova, 1934.

AH 6104   Ancient Greek provinces, etc. - Macedonia - Law
AH 6104.5   Engelhardt, Hans. Das senatus consultum Macedonianum. Inaug. Diss. Bamberg, 1930.

AH 6107   Ancient Greek provinces, etc. - Macedonia - General history
AH 6107.5   Abel, O. Makedonien. Leipzig, 1847.
AH 6107.6   Daskalakès, Apostolos Basileiou. Ho Hellenismos tēs archaias Makedonias. Athēnai, 1960.
AH 6107.6.2   Daskalakès, Apostolos Basileiou. The Hellenism of the ancient Macedonians. Thessalonikē, 1965.
AH 6107.7   Flathe, L. Geschichte Macedoniens. Leipzig, 1832. 2v.
AH 6107.8   Curteis, A.M. Rise of the Macedonian empire. London, 1877.
AH 6107.9   Curteis, A.M. Rise of the Macedonian empire. N.Y., 1880.
AH 6107.10   Cloché, Paul. Histoire de la Macédoine. Paris, 1960.
AH 6107.11   Curteis, A.M. Rise of the Macedonian empire. 4. ed. London, 1886.
AH 6107.11.5 Curteis, A.M. Rise of the Macedonian empire. N.Y., 1896.
AH 6107.12   Kanatsoulès, Dèmètrios. He Makedonia mechri tou thanatou tou Archelaou. Thessalonikē, 1964.
AH 6107.13   Niese, B. Geschichte der griechischen und makedonischen Staaten. Gotha, 1893. 3v.
AH 6107.14   Hammond, Nicholas Geoffrey Lempriere. A history of Macedonia. Oxofrd, 1972-
AH 6107.15   Kalléris, J.N. Les anciens Macédoniens. Athènes, 1954-
AH 6107.20   Kanatsoulès, Dèmètrios. He dytikē Makedonia kata tous archaious chronous. Thessalonikē, 1958.

Classified Listing

AH 6107   Ancient Greek provinces, etc. - Macedonia - General history - cont.
AH 6107.21   Kanatsoulēs, Dēmētrios. Historia tēs Makedonias. Thessalonikē, 1964.
AH 6107.25   International Symposium, 1st, Salonika, 1968. Ancient Macedonia. Thessaloniki, 1970.
AH 6107.55   Paribeni, Roberto. La Macedonia sino ad Alessandro Magno. Milano, 1947.
AH 6107.60   Shofman, A.S. Istoriia antichnoi Makedonii. Kazan', 1960- 2v.

AH 6108   Ancient Greek provinces, etc. - Macedonia - General special
AH 6108.7   Radet, Georges. De coloniis a Macedonibus in Asiam cis Taurum deductis. Thesim. Parisiis, 1892.
AH 6108.9   Barzoni, V. I Romani nella Grecia. 11. ed. Londra, 1799.

AH 6110   Ancient Greek provinces, etc. - Macedonia - History by periods - 500 - 1 B.C.
AH 6110.5F   Leland, T. History of life and reign of Philip. 2. ed. London, 1761. 2v.
AH 6110.7F   Leland, T. History of life and reign of Philip. London, 1758.
AH 6110.8   Leland, T. History of life and reign of Philip. 2. ed. London, 1775. 2v.
AH 6110.9   Brückner, K.A.F. König Philipp. Göttingen, 1837.
AH 6110.10   Wüst, F.R. Philipp II. München, 1938.
AH 6110.11   Gerlach, F.D. Perseus König von Makedonien. Basel, 1857.
AH 6110.12   Heiland, Paul. Untersuchungen zur Geschichte des Königs Perseus von Makedonien. Diss. Jena, 1913.
AH 6110.13   Walek, T.B. Dzieje upadku monarchji macedonskiej. Krakow, 1924.
AH 6110.14   Elson, Charles F. Perseus and Demetrius. n.p., 1935.
AH 6110.15   Schubert, R. Untersuchungen über die Quellen zur Geschichte Philipps II von Macedonien. Konigsberg, 1904.
AH 6110.17   Bettingen, W. König Antigonos Doson von Makedonien. Inaug. Diss. Weida, 1912.
AH 6110.19   Momigliano, A. Filippo il Macedone. Firenze, 1934.
AH 6110.20   Rane, H.O. Untersuchungen zur Geschichte des koituthischen Bundes. Inaug. Diss. Marburg, 1937.
AH 6110.21   Cloché, Paul. Un fondateur d'empire. Saint Etienne, 1955.
AH 6110.22   Katsarov, G.I. Tsar Filipp II Makedonski. Sofiia, 1922.
AH 6110.24   Naltsas, Christophoros A. Philippos deuteros ho Makedōn. Thessalonikē, 1970.
AH 6110.26   Perlman, Samuel. Philip and Athens. Cambridge, 1973.

AH 6113   Ancient Greek provinces, etc. - Macedonia - Civilization
AH 6113.5   Casson, Stanley. Macedenia, Thrace and Illyria. Oxford, 1926.
AH 6113.8   Keramopoullos, A.D. Arigia of the Macedonians. Detroit, 1946.

AH 6116   Ancient Greek provinces, etc. - Macedonia - Geography
AH 6116.5   Desdevises-du-dezert. Géographie ancienne de la Macedoine. Paris, 1863.
AH 6116.7   Döll, M. Studien zur Geographie des alten Makedoniens. Stadtamhof, 1891.

AH 6121 - 6146   Ancient Greek provinces, etc. - Macedonia - Local (A-Z by place)
AH 6136.5   Katsarov, G.I. Peoniia. Sofiia, 1921.
AH 6136.10   Collart, Paul. Philippes, ville de Macédoine. Atlas. Paris, 1937. 2v.
AH 6140.2   Tafel, F. Thessalonica. Berolini, 1839.
AH 6140.6   Fafralé, O. Thessalonique des origines au XIVe siècle. Paris, 1919.

AH 6150   Ancient Greek provinces, etc. - Northern Shores of the Black Sea - Bibliographies
AH 6150.5   Belin de Ballu, Eugène. L'histoire des colonies grecques du littoral nord de la Mer Noire; bibliographie...1940 à 1957. Paris, 1960.
AH 6150.5.2   Belin de Ballu, Eugène. L'histoire des colonies grecques du littoral nord de la Mer Noire; bibliographie...1940 à 1962. Leiden, 1965.

AH 6157   Ancient Greek provinces, etc. - Northern Shores of the Black Sea - General history
AH 6157.5   Neumann, K. Hellenen in Skythenlande. Berlin, 1855.
AH 6157.7   Ortmann, K. De regno bosperano Spartocedarum. Halis Saxonum, 1894.
AH 6157.9   Klym, P. Die milesischen Kolonien im Skythenlande his zum III. nachchristliche Jahrhundert. Czernowitz, 1914.
AH 6157.10   Izvestiia vizantiiskikh pisatelei o Severnom Prichernomor'e. Moskva, 1934.

AH 6158   Ancient Greek provinces, etc. - Northern Shores of the Black Sea - General special
AH 6158.5   Ritter, C. Vorhalle europäischer Völkerges. Berlin, 1820.

AH 6168 - 6170   Ancient Greek provinces, etc. - Northern Shores of the Black Sea - Special topics (Develop as needed)
AH 6168.5   Komitee zur Förderung der Klassischen Studien. Griechesche Städte und einheimische Völker des Schwarzmengebietes. Berlin, 1961.

AH 7002   Ancient Rome in general - General bibliographies - Periodicals
AH 7002.5   Bulletin analytique d'histoire romaine. Strasbourg. 1,1962+ 4v.

AH 7004 - 7009   Ancient Rome in general - General bibliographies - Monographs (By date)
AH 7007.40   Beaufort, L. Dissertation upon uncertainty. London, 1740.
AH 7008.38   Le Clerc, J.V. Des journaux chez les romaines. Paris, 1838.
AH 7008.40   Lieberkuehn, Wilhelm. Inest commentatio de diurnis. Vimariae, 1840.
AH 7008.55   Hulleman, I.G. Disputatio critica de Annalibus. n.p., 1855.
AH 7008.57   Renssen, J.G. Disputatio de diurnis aliisque. Groningen, 1857.
AH 7008.57.5   Heinze, H. De spuriis actorum diurnorum. Gryphiae, 1860.
AH 7008.58   Hübner, E.W. De senatus populiue romani actis. Lipsiae, 1858.
AH 7008.61   Peter, K. Mommsen. Studien zur römische Geschichte. Naumburg, 1861.
AH 7008.73   Nitzsch, K.W. Die römische Annalistik. Berlin, 1873.
AH 7008.79   Bonghi, R. Bibliografia storica di Roma attica. Roma, 1879.
AH 7008.79.3   Bonghi, R. Monografia della citta di Roma. Roma, 1881.

AH 7004 - 7009   Ancient Rome in general - General bibliographies - Monographs (By date) - cont.
AH 7008.84   Cauer, F. De fabulis graecis ad romam. Berolini, 1884.
AH 7008.90   Volkmar, A. De annalibus romanis quaestiones. Marburgi, 1890.
AH 7009.02   Platner, S.B. Credibility of early Roman history. n.p., 1902.
AH 7009.03   Schwartz, E. Ad praemiorum...publicam renuntiationem. Gottingae, 1903.
AH 7009.04   Munro, D.C. Source book of Roman history. Boston, 1904.
AH 7009.05   Gamurrin, G.F. Bibliografia dell'Italia antica. Arezzo, 1905.
AH 7009.05.5   Gamurrin, G.F. Bibliografia dell'Italia antica. pt.1. Roma, 1933.
AH 7009.07   Loesche, J. Die Abfassung des Faits des Romains. Halle, 1907.
AH 7009.09   Soltau, W. Anfänge der roemischen Geschichtsschreibung. Leipzig, 1909.
AH 7009.09.3   Hayes, C.H. Introduction to the sources relating to the Germanic invasions. N.Y., 1909.
AH 7009.09.5A   Hayes, C.H. Introduction to the sources relating to the Germanic invasions. N.Y., 1909.
AH 7009.09.5B   Hayes, C.H. Introduction to the sources relating to the Germanic invasions. N.Y., 1909.
AH 7009.11   Parducci, P. La genesi degli annales Maximi. Pisa, 1911.
AH 7009.47   Ceccarelli, G. Saggio di bibliografia romana. Roma. 2-12,1946-1957// 5v.
AH 7009.53   Arias, P.E. Bibliografia e fonti. Bologna, 1953?
AH 7009.57   French Bibliographic Digest. History III. Roman history. N.Y., 1957.

AH 7015   Ancient Rome in general - General pamphlet volumes
AH 7015.1   Pamphlet vol. Ancient and mediaeval Rome. 16 pam.
AH 7015.3   Pamphlet vol. Rome republic and empire. 3 pam.
AH 7015.4   Pamphlet vol. Aspects of Roman history. 14 pam.
AH 7015.5   Pamphlet vol. Rome past and present. 17 pam.
AH 7015.6   Pamphlet vol. Roman history. 14 pam.
Htn   AH 7015.7*   Pamphlet vol. Rome. 11 pam.
AH 7015.8   Pamphlet vol. Rome. 16 pam.
AH 7015.9   Pamphlet box. Roman history. 7 pam.
AH 7015.10   Pamphlet vol. Roman history. 10 pam.
AH 7015.11F   Götz, Georg. C. Maecenas. Rede...zur Feier der akademischen Preisvertheilung. Jena, 1902. 3 pam.
AH 7015.13F   Pamphlet box. Roman antiquities.
AH 7015.15F   Pamphlet box. In antiquitatis romanas.
AH 7015.18   Pamphlet vol. Rome ancient and modern. 3 pam.
AH 7015.20   Pamphlet vol. Scramuzza, V.M. Roman studies. 14 pam.

AH 7024 - 7029   Ancient Rome in general - Collected sources (By date)
AH 7026.94F   Graevio, J.G. Thesaurus antiquitatum rom. Lugdunum Batavorum, 1694. 12v.
AH 7027.16F   Sallengre, Albert Hendrik de. Novus thesaurus antiquitatum. Hagae, 1716-19. 3v.
AH 7029.04   Sanders, Henry. Roman historical sources. N.Y., 1904.
AH 7029.08   Giorni, C. Epitome rerum romanarum. Firenze, 1908.
AH 7029.10   Sanders, Henry. Roman history and mythology. N.Y., 1910.
AH 7029.69   Charles-Picard, Gilbert. Textes et documents relatifs à la vie économique et sociale dans l'empire romain. Paris, 1969.
AH 7029.69.5   Sherk, Robert K. Roman documents from the Greek East; senatus consulta and epistolae to the age of Augustus. Baltimore, 1969.

AH 7030 - 7039   Ancient Rome in general - Government and administration - General works (Table A)
AH 7031.01   Pamphlet box. Roman history. Government.
AH 7031.7F   Frandsen, P.S. Über die Politik des Marcus Agrippa. Altona, 1833. 5 pam.
Htn   AH 7035.29*   Fiocco, A.D. L. Fenestellae, de magistratibus, sacerdotisq. Lutetiae, 1529.
Htn   AH 7035.38*   Fiocco, A.D. L. Fenestellae, de magistratibus, sacerdotisq. Basileae, 1538.
Htn   AH 7035.38.3*   Fiocco, A.D. L. Fenestellae, de magistratibus, sacerdotisq. Basileae, n.d.
Htn   AH 7035.38.6*   Fiocco, A.D. L. Fenestellae, de magistratibus, sacerdotisq. Venetiis, n.d.
Htn   AH 7035.42*   Fiocco, A.D. L. Fenestellae, de magistrattibus, sacerdotisq. Parisiis, 1542. 4 pam.
Htn   AH 7035.49*   Fiocco, A.D. L. Fenestellae, de magistratibus, sacerdotisq. Lutetiae, 1549.
AH 7035.85   Manuzio, Paolo. Antiquitatum romanorum. Romae, 1585.
Htn   AH 7035.88*   Panvino, O. Civitas romana. Parisiis, 1588.
AH 7035.99   Paruta, P. Discorsi politici. Bologna, 1943.
Htn   AH 7036.29*   Schrijver, Pieter. Republica romana. Lugdunum Batavorum, 1629.
AH 7037.03   Spanhem, Ezekiel. Orbis romanus. London, 1703.
AH 7037.34.30   Montesquieu, Charles L. Consideratione on the causes of the greatness of the Romans. N.Y., 1965.
Htn   AH 7037.63*   Duni, E. Origini del cittadino di Roma. Roma, 1763. 2v.
AH 7037.67   Beaufort, L. La republique romaine. Paris, 1767. 6v.
AH 7037.76   Kearney, M. Lectures concerning history read during the year 1775 in Trinity College, Dublin. London, 1776.
AH 7038.24   Rovers, J.A.C. De censaum apud romanos auctoritate. Trajecti ad Rhenum, 1824.
AH 7038.32   Hüllmann, Karl. Römische Grundverfassung. Bonn, 1832.
AH 7038.32.2   Hüllmann, Karl. Römische Grundverfassung. Bonn, 1832.
AH 7038.33   Schultz, C.L. Grundlegung-Staatswissenschaft. Köln, 1833.
AH 7038.38   Huschke, G. Die Verfassung des Servius Tullius. Heidelberg, 1838.
AH 7038.39   Rubino, J. Untersuchungen und römische Verfassung. Cassel, 1839.
AH 7038.40   Göttling, K. Geschichte der römischen Staatsverfassung. Halle, 1840.
AH 7038.41   Römer, H.G. De consulum Romanorum auctoritate. Trajecti ad Rhenum, 1841.
AH 7038.41.2   Peter, C.L. Die Epochen der Verfassungsgeschichte. Leipzig, 1841.
AH 7038.42   Gerlach, F.D. Die römische Censur. Basel, 1842.
AH 7038.42.2   Terpstra, D. Quaestiones literariae. Rotterdami, 1842.
AH 7038.42.3   Bröcker, L.O. Vorarbeiten zur römische Geschichte. Tübingen, 1842.
AH 7038.46   Raumer, F. Die römische Staatsverfassung. Berlin, 1846.
AH 7038.47   Ihne, W. Forschungen - römischen Vergassungsgeschichte. Frankfurt, 1847.
AH 7038.49   Kuhn, E. Verfassung des römischen Reichs. Leipzig, 1849.
AH 7038.49.2   Nägele, M. Studien über Staatsleben. Schaffhausen, 1849.

AH 7030 - 7039   Ancient Rome in general - Government and administration -
General works (Table A) - cont.

	AH 7038.58	Bröcker, L. Altrömische Verfassungsgeschichte. Hamburg, 1858.
	AH 7038.71	Gerlach, F. Verfassungsgeschichte. Basel, 1871.
	AH 7038.77	Dupond, A. De la constitution. Paris, 1877.
	AH 7038.77.5	Naudet, Joseph. De l'etat des personnes et des peuples sous les empereurs romains. Paris, 1877.
	AH 7038.81	Madvig, J.N. Die Verfassung und Verwaltung. Leipzig, 1881. 2v.
	AH 7038.81.4	Madvig, J.N. L'etat romain. v.1-5. Paris, 1882. 4v.
	AH 7038.82	Bernhöft, F. Staat und Recht. Stuttgart, 1882.
	AH 7038.82.2	Mispoulet, J.B. Les institutions politiques. Paris, 1882. 2v.
X Cg	AH 7038.84	Herzog, Ernst. Geschichte und System der römischen Staatsverfassung. Leipzig, 1884. 3v.
	AH 7038.86	Bouché-Leclercq, A. Manuel des institutions romaines. Paris, 1886.
	AH 7038.86.3	Tighe, A. Development of Roman constitution. N.Y., 1889.
	AH 7038.86.5	Tighe, A. The development of the Roman constitution. N.Y., 1886.
	AH 7038.86.9	Tighe, A. The development of the Roman constitution. N.Y., 1886.
	AH 7038.87	Misporelet, J.B. Études d'institutions romaines. Paris, 1887.
	AH 7038.95	Zoeller, Max. Römische Staats und Rechtsaltertümer. Breslau, 1895.
	AH 7038.96	Decley, Ferdinand. Histoire de la centralisation dans l'empire romain. Thèse. Caen, 1896.
	AH 7038.99	Lengle, Joseph. Untersuchungen über die sulianische Verfassung. Freiburg, 1899.
	AH 7038.99.2	Taylor, Thomas M. Constitutional and political history of Rome. London, 1899.
	AH 7038.99.3	Taylor, Thomas M. A constitutional and political history of Rome. London, 1911.
	AH 7039.01	Abbott, Frank F. History and description of Roman political institutions. Boston, 1901.
	AH 7039.01.2	Abbott, Frank F. History and description of Roman political institutions. Boston, 1901.
	AH 7039.01.5	Greenidge, Abel Hendy Jones. Roman public life. London, 1922.
	AH 7039.02	Granrud, John E. Roman constitutional history, 753-44 B.C. Boston, 1902.
	AH 7039.05	Chudzinski, A. Staatseinrichtungen...Kaiserreichs. Gutersloh, 1905.
	AH 7039.10	Bury, J.B. Constitution of the later Roman empire. Cambridge, 1910.
	AH 7039.10.2A	Bussell, F.W. Roman empire. London, 1910. 2v.
	AH 7039.11	Fabricius, Ernest. Über die Entwicklung der römischen Verfassung im republikanischer Zeit. Freiburg, 1911.
	AH 7039.12	Leuze, O. Zur Geschichte der römischen Censur. Halle, 1912.
	AH 7039.23A	Abbott, Frank F. Roman politics. Boston, 1923.
	AH 7039.23B	Abbott, Frank F. Roman politics. Boston, 1923.
	AH 7039.24	Gelzer, Matthias. Gemeindestaat und Reichsstaat in der römischen Geschichte. Frankfurt, 1924.
	AH 7039.25	Heinze, Richard. Von den Ursachen der grösse Roms. Leipzig, 1925.
	AH 7039.28	Levi, Mario A. La costituzione romana dai gracchi a Giulio Cesare. Firenze, 1928.
	AH 7039.29	Homs, Léon. Roman political institutions from city to state. London, 1929.
	AH 7039.45	Lombardi, Gabrio. Lo sviluppo costituzionale di Roma dalle origini alla fine della repubblica. Roma, 1945.
	AH 7039.48	Meyer, Ernst. Römischer Staat und Staatsgedanke. Zurich, 1948.
	AH 7039.50	Wirszubski, C. Libertas as a political idea. Cambridge, 1950.
	AH 7039.53	Béranger, J. Recherches sur l'aspect ideologique su principat. Basel, 1953.
	AH 7039.53.5	Tibiletti, G. Principe e magistrati repubblicani. Roma, 1953.
	AH 7039.57	Wirszubski, C. Libertas. Bari, 1957.
	AH 7039.58	Martino, Francesco de. Storia della costituzione romana. v.1-6. Napoli, 1958-72. 7v.
	AH 7039.59	Adcock, Frank. Roman political ideas and practice. Ann Arbor, 1959.
	AH 7039.60	Jones, A.H.M. Studies in Roman government and law. Oxford, 1960.
	AH 7039.62	Timpe, D. Untersuchungen zur Kontinuität. Wiesbaden, 1962.
	AH 7039.63	Rouvier, J. Du pouvoir dans la république romaine. Paris, 1963.
	AH 7039.66	Klein, Richard. Das Staatsdenken der Römer. Darmstadt, 1966.
	AH 7039.66.5	Meier, Christian. Res publica amissa. Eine Studie zu Verfassung und Geschichte der späten römischen Republik. Wiesbaden, 1966.
	AH 7039.67	Earl, Donald Charles. The moral and political tradition of Rome. London, 1967.
	AH 7039.69	Michel, Alain. La philosophie politique à Rome d'Auguste à Marc Aurèle. Paris, 1969.
	AH 7039.71	Krarup, Per. Romersk politik i oldtiden. København, 1971.

AH 7040 - 7049   Ancient Rome in general - Government and administration -
Forms of government (Table A)

	AH 7048.75	Paillard, A. Histoire de le transmission du pouvoir impérial. Paris, 1875.
	AH 7049.27	Münzner, Friedrich. Die Entstehung des römischen Principats; ein Beispiel des Wandels von Staatsformen. Münster, 1927.
	AH 7049.33.2	Hammond, Mason. The Augustan Principate in theory and practice during the Julio-Claudian period. N.Y., 1968.

AH 7050 - 7059   Ancient Rome in general - Government and administration -
Administrative branch (Table A)

	AH 7051.1	Pamphlet box. Roman history. Government. Administration.
Htn	AH 7055.10*	Fiocco, A.D. L. Fenestellae, de Romanorum magistratibus. n.p., n.d.
Htn	AH 7055.10.2*	Fiocco, A.D. L. Fenestellae, de Romanorum magistratibus. Lugduni, 1551.
Htn	AH 7055.10.3*	Fiocco, A.D. L. Fenestellae, de Romanrum magistratibus. Basileae, 1581.
Htn	AH 7055.10.4*	Fiocco, A.D. L. Fenestellae, de Romanorum magistratibus. n.p., n.d.
Htn	AH 7055.93F*	Notitia utraque dignitatum. Venetiis, 1593.
	AH 7055.93.3	Böcking, Edvardus. Notitia dignitatum. Bonnae, 1839-53. 3v.

AH 7050 - 7059   Ancient Rome in general - Government and administration -
Administrative branch (Table A) - cont.

	AH 7055.93.5	Böcking, D. Eduard. Über die Notitia Dignitatum. Bonn, 1834.
	AH 7055.93.6	Omont, H. Le plus ancien manuscrit de la Notitia dignitatum. Paris, 1891.
	AH 7055.93.6.5	Seeck, Otto. Quaestiones de Notitia dignitatum. Berolini, 1872.
	AH 7055.93.7	Notitia dignitatum. Berolini, 1876.
	AH 7055.93.8	Notitia dignitatum, or Register. Philadelphia, 1899.
	AH 7055.93.9	Goutière, Jacques. De officiis domus Augustae. Parisiis, 1628.
	AH 7055.93.10	Notitia dignitatum imperii Romani. Parisiis, 1651.
	AH 7058.14F	Thorlacius, B. De irenarchis. Aavniae, 1814.
	AH 7058.17	Naudet, Joseph. Des changemens...de l'empire romain. Paris, 1817. 2v.
	AH 7058.18	Harencarspel, R.S. van. De propria reipublicae romanae. Trajecti ad Rhenum, 1818.
	AH 7058.28	Schubert, F.G. De romanorum aedilibus. Regimontii, 1828.
	AH 7058.28.2	Hofmann, F. De aedilibus romanorum. Berolini, 1842.
	AH 7058.28.3	Seidel, Joseph. Fasti aedilicii. Inaug. Diss. Breslau, 1908.
	AH 7058.29	Magistratum et sacerdotiorum. Vratislaviae, 1829.
	AH 7058.29.2	Incerti auctoris magistratuum. Diss. Vratislaviae, 1829.
	AH 7058.29.3	Schaefer, A. Zur Geschichte des römischen Consulates. Leipzig, 1876.
	AH 7058.39	Breuk, H.R. de. Dissertatio historica...de quaestione. Lugduni-Batavorum, 1839.
	AH 7058.39.2	Brambach, G. De consulatus romani mutata. Bonnae, 1864.
	AH 7058.46	Mommsen, T. De apparitoribus magistratum romanorum. Romae, 1846.
	AH 7058.53	Linker, G. Über die Wahl...Praefectus urbis feriarum. Wien? 1853.
	AH 7058.63	Degli uficiali e degli ufidii di Roma. Padova, 1863.
	AH 7058.72	Belot, Émile. De tribunis plebis. n.p., n.d.
	AH 7058.72.5	Stobbe, H.F. Zum Capitel von den Consules Suffecti unter den Kaisern. n.p., n.d.
	AH 7058.77	Hirschfeld, O. Untersuchungen...römischen Verwaltungsgeschichte. Berlin, 1877.
	AH 7058.78	Hudemann, E.E. Geschichte des Römischen Postwesens. Berlin, 1878.
	AH 7058.78.5	Faure, F. Essai historique sur le préteur romain. Paris, 1878.
	AH 7058.83	Zippel, Gustav. Die Losung der konsularischen Prokonsuln in der früheren Kaizerzeit. Königsberg, 1883.
	AH 7058.86	Liebenam, W. Die Laufbahn der Procuratoren. Jena, 1886.
	AH 7058.86.2	Liebenam, W. Beiträge zur Verwaltungsgeschichte. Jena, 1886.
	AH 7058.87	Wehrmann, P. Programm des Konig-Wilhelms-Gymnasiums. Stettin, 1887.
	AH 7058.87.3	Niccolini, I. Tasti tribunorum plebis. Pisis, 1898.
	AH 7058.87.5	Stella Maranca, F. Il tribunato della Plebe. Lanciano, 1901.
	AH 7058.88	Liebenam, W. Forschungen zur Verwaltungsgeschichte. Leipzig, 1888.
	AH 7058.91	Stückelberg, E.A. Der Constantinische Patriciat. Basel, 1891.
	AH 7058.94	Mentz, M. De magistratuum romanorum. Ienae, 1894.
	AH 7059.03F	Cantarelli, L. La diocesi italiana. Roma, 1901.
	AH 7059.05	Hirschfeld, O. Die kaiserlichen Verwaltungsbeamten. Berlin, 1905.
	AH 7059.05.2	Cosenza, M.E. Official positions after the time of Constantine. Lancaster, 1905.
	AH 7059.09	Sobeck, T. Die Quästoren der Römischen Republik. Trebnitz, 1909.
	AH 7059.10	Mattingly, H. The imperial civil service of Rome. Cambridge, 1910.
	AH 7059.18	Holleaux, M. Stratëgos Ypatos. Thèse. Paris, 1918.
	AH 7059.19	Boak, A.E.R. The master of the offices in the later Roman and Byzantine empires. N.Y., 1919.
	AH 7059.20	McFayden, Donald. The history of the title imperator under the Roman empire. Thesis. Chicago, 1920.
	AH 7059.24A	Boak, A.E.R. Two studies in later Roman and Byzantine administration. N.Y., 1924.
	AH 7059.24B	Boak, A.E.R. Two studies in later Roman and Byzantine administration. N.Y., 1924.
	AH 7059.24.5	Dunlap, J.E. The office of the grand chamberlain in the later Roman and Byzantine empires. London, 1924.
	AH 7059.33	Palanque, Jean-Rémy. Essai sur la préfecture du prétoire du Bas-Empire. Thèse. Paris, 1933.
	AH 7059.34	Kruse, Helmut. Studien zur offiziellen Geltung des Kaiserbildes im römischen Reiche. Paderborn, 1934.
	AH 7059.37	Schmähling, E. Untersuchungen zur Sittenaufsicht der Censoren. Inaug. Diss. Würzburg, 1937.
	AH 7059.37.5	Lotti Faravelli, A. Origine della censura romana. Como, 1937.
	AH 7059.55	Crook, J.A. Consilium principis. Cambridge, Eng., 1955.
	AH 7059.63	Parsi, Blanche. Désignation et investiture de l'empéreur romain, Ier et IIe siècles après J.C. Paris, 1963.
	AH 7059.66	Combès, Robert. Imperator; recherches sur l'emploi et la signification du titre d'imperator dans la Rome republicaine. Thèse. Paris, 1966.
	AH 7059.68	Pieri, Georges. L'histoire du cens jusqu'à la fin de la République romaine. Paris, 1968.
	AH 7059.69	Kneissl, Peter. Die Siegestitulatur der römischen Kaiser. Göttingen, 1969.
	AH 7059.70	Jahn, Joachim. Intenegnum und Wahldiktatur. Kallmünz, 1970.

AH 7060 - 7069   Ancient Rome in general - Government and administration -
Legislature and legislation (Table A)

	AH 7068.99	Mispoulet, J.B. La vie parlementaire a Rome. Paris, 1899.

AH 7070 - 7079   Ancient Rome in general - Government and administration -
Popular assemblies (Table A)

	AH 7078.15	Schulze, C.F. Von den Volksdersammlungen. Gotha, 1815.
	AH 7078.48	Casar aux elections. Paris, 1848.
	AH 7078.75	Berns, Carolus. De cometorum tributorum. Wetzlariae, 1875.
	AH 7078.76	Labatut, E. La corruption électorale. Paris, 1876.
	AH 7078.79	Gentile, I. Le elezioni e il Broglio. Milan, 1879.
	AH 7078.80	Soltau, W. Über Entstehung und Zusammensetzung der altrömischen Volksversamlungen. Berlin, 1880.
	AH 7079.09	Botsford, G.W. The Roman assemblies. N.Y., 1909.
	AH 7079.11	Chaigne, G. Sous la robe blanche. Paris, 1911.
	AH 7079.66	Linderski, Jerzy. Rzymskie zgromadzenie wyborcze od Sulli do Cezara. Wrocław, 1966.

**AH 7070 - 7079   Ancient Rome in general - Government and administration -
Popular assemblies (Table A) - cont.**

AH 7079.66.5 — Taylor, Lily Ross. Roman voting assemblies from the Hannibalic war to the dictatorship of Caesar. Ann Arbor, 1966.

AH 7079.67 — Frei-Stolba, Regula. Untersuchungen zur den Wahlen in der römischen Kaiserzeit. Zürich, 1967.

**AH 7080 - 7089   Ancient Rome in general - Government and administration -
Provincial government in general (Table A)**

AH 7081.1 — Pamphlet box. Roman government.

AH 7085.98F — Lazius, W. Reipublicae Romanae in exteris provinciis. v.1-3. Francofurti, 1598.

AH 7088.29 — Hopfensack, J.C.W.A. Staatsrecht der Unterthonen der Römer. Düsseldorf, 1829.

AH 7088.43 — Fontein, P. Disputatio...de provinciis romanorum. Rhenum, 1843.

AH 7088.46 — Poinsignon, A.M. Essai sur le nombre et l'origine des provinces romaines. Paris, 1846.

AH 7088.62 — Grant, A. How the ancient Roman governed their provinces. Bombay, 1862.

AH 7088.72 — Waddington, W.H. Fastes des provinces asiatiques de l'empire romain. pt.1. Paris, 1872.

AH 7088.77 — Person, E. Essai...des provinces romaines. Paris, 1877.

AH 7088.79A — Arnold, W.T. Roman system of provincial administration. London, 1879.

AH 7088.79B — Arnold, W.T. Roman system of provincial administration. London, 1879.

AH 7088.79C — Arnold, W.T. Roman system of provincial administration. London, 1879.

AH 7088.79D — Arnold, W.T. Roman system of provincial administration. London, 1879.

AH 7088.79.5 — Arnold, W.T. Roman system of provincial administration. Oxford, 1906.

AH 7088.79.9 — Arnold, W.T. Roman system of provincial administration. 3rd ed. Oxford, 1914.

AH 7088.80 — Marx, Edgarel. Essai sur les pouvoirs du gouverneur. Paris, 1880.

AH 7088.81A — Jung, Julius. Die romanischen Landschaften. Innsbruck, 1881.

AH 7088.81B — Jung, Julius. Die romanischen Lanschaften. Innsbruck, 1881.

AH 7088.85 — Wilcken, U. Observationes ad historiam Aegypti. Berolinii, 1885.

AH 7088.85.5 — Bourgeois, Émile. Quomodo provinciarum Romanarum. Paris, 1885.

AH 7088.87 — Guiraud, Paul. Les assemblées provinciales. Paris, 1887.

AH 7088.98 — Halgan, C. Essai sur l'administration des provinces sénatoriales. Paris, 1898.

AH 7089.09 — Regnault, Henri. Une province procuratorienne. Paris, 1909.

AH 7089.12 — Letz, Emil. Die Provinzialverwaltung Caesars. Strassburg, 1912.

AH 7089.26 — Mierow, Herbert E. The roman provincial governor as he appears in the Digest and Code of Justinian. Colorado Springs, 1926.

AH 7089.33 — Bon, Alessio de. La colonizzazione romana dal Brenta al Piave. Bassagno del Grappe, 1933.

AH 7089.39A — Stevenson, G.H. Roman provincial administration. Oxford, 1939.

AH 7089.39B — Stevenson, G.H. Roman provincial administration. Oxford, 1939.

AH 7089.50 — Jashemski, W.M. The origins and history of the pro-consular. Chicago, 1950.

**AH 7090 - 7099   Ancient Rome in general - Government and administration -
Municipal government in general (Table A)**

AH 7091.1 — Pamphlet box. Roman history. Government. Municipal.

AH 7097.66 — Corsinii, Eduardi. De praefectis urbis. Pisis, 1766.

AH 7098.32 — Madvig, J.N. De coloniarum populi Romani iure et condicione quaestionis historicae pars prior. Hauniae, 1832. 2 pam.

AH 7098.36 — Schmidt. Über römische Colonien. pt.1-2. Potsdam, 1836.

AH 7098.44 — Jordans, G.H.H. De publicis urbium Romae et Constantinapolis. Bonnae, 1844.

AH 7098.47 — Potsdam. Gymnasiums. Zuder öffentlichen Prüsung der Zöglinge. Potsdam, 1847.

AH 7098.47.5 — Reinii, W. Dissertatio de Romanorum Municipiis. Eisenach, 1847.

AH 7098.50 — Zumptii, A.W. Commentationum epigraphicarum. Berolini, 1850.

AH 7098.60 — Voigt, Moritz. Drei epigraphische Constitutionen. Leipzig, 1860.

AH 7098.60.5 — Henzen, Wilhelm. Intorno alcuni magistrati municipali de romani. n.p., 1860? 2 pam.

AH 7098.64 — Kuhn, Emil. Die stadtische...Verfassung. Leipzig, 1864.

AH 7098.66 — Zoeller, M. De civitate sine suffragio et municipio Romanorum. Heidelbergae, 1866.

AH 7098.75 — Houdoy, R.J.A. De la condition et...chez les romains. Paris, 1875.

AH 7098.75.4 — Houdoy, R.J.A. Le droit municipal. Paris, 1876.

AH 7098.82 — Mantey, Otto. De gradu et statu quaestorum im municipiis colonisque. Diss. Inaug. Halis Saxonum, 1882.

AH 7098.83 — Bloch, G. De decretis functorum magistratum ornamentis. Lutetiae Parisiorum, 1883.

AH 7098.92 — Schulten, Adolf. De conventibus civium romanorum. Berolini, 1892.

AH 7098.92.1 — Schulten, Adolf. De conventibus civium romanorum. Diss. Lipsiae, 1892.

AH 7098.92.2 — Henze, Walter. De civitatibus liberis. Berolini, 1892.

AH 7098.94 — Cyprès, Imbert. Droit romain de la curie. Paris, 1894.

AH 7098.96 — Ruggiero, E. de. Le colonie dei romani. Spoleto, 1896.

AH 7098.96.2 — Vigneaux, P.E. Essai sur l'histoire de la Praefectura Urbis. Paris, 1896.

AH 7098.96.3 — Boutet, Paul. De la police et de la voirie. Paris, 1896.

AH 7098.98 — Kornemann, Ernst. Zur Stadtentstehung. Giessen, 1898.

AH 7099.00 — Tanfani, L. Ricerche storiche-epigrafiche. Taranto, 1900.

AH 7099.00.2 — Leogrande, P. I cognomi delle colonie romane militari. Trani, 1900.

AH 7099.00.4 — Liebenam, W. Stadtverwaltung in römischen Kaiserreiche. Leipzig, 1900.

X Cg   AH 7099.13 — Reid, J.S. The municipalities of the Roman empire. Cambridge, 1913.

AH 7099.26 — Reynolds, P.K.B. The vigiles of imperial Rome. London, 1926.

AH 7099.26.5 — Abbott, Frank F. Municipal administration in the Roman empire. Princeton, 1926.

**AH 7090 - 7099   Ancient Rome in general - Government and administration -
Municipal government in general (Table A) - cont.**

AH 7099.28 — Heitland, William E. Last wards on the Roman municipalities. Cambridge, Eng., 1928.

AH 7099.30 — Heitland, Willian E. Repetita. Cambridge, Eng., 1930.

AH 7099.35 — Rudolph, Hans. Stadt und Staat im römischen Italien. Leipzig, 1935.

AH 7099.39 — Sherwin-White, A.N. The Roman citizenship. Oxford, 1939.

AH 7099.43 — Sanchez-Albornoz y Menduiña, C. Ruina y extención del municipio. Buenos Aires, 1943.

AH 7099.56 — Vitucci, Giovanni. Ricerche sulla praefectura urbi in età imperiale. Roma, 1956.

AH 7099.63 — Ganghoffer, Roland. L'evolution des institutions municipales en Occident et en Orient au Bas-Empire. Thèse. Paris, 1963.

AH 7099.65 — Colin, Jean. Les villes libres de l'Orient gréco-romain et l'envoi au supplice par acclamations populaires. Bruxelles, 1965.

AH 7099.66 — Laffi, Umberto. Adtributio e contributio. 1a ed. Pisa, 1966.

AH 7099.67 — Storoni Mazzolani, Lidia. L'idea di città nel mondo romano. Milano, 1967.

AH 7099.67.1 — Storoni Mazzolani, Lidia. The idea of the city in Roman thought. London, 1970.

AH 7099.72 — Grelle, Francesco. L'autonomia cittadina fra Traiano e Adriano. Napoli, 1972.

**AH 7100 - 7109   Ancient Rome in general - Government and administration -
Public finance (Table A)**

AH 7101.1 — Pamphlet box. Roman government and finance.

Htn   AH 7105.22* — Budé, G. Libri V de asse et partibus eius. Venice, 1522.

Htn   AH 7105.22.3* — Budé, G. Libri V de asse et partibus eius. Venetiis, 1522.

Htn   AH 7105.22.5* — Budé, G. Extrait ou abregé du Livre de assé de feu mons. Lyon, 1554.

Htn   AH 7106.12* — Bonlenger, J.C. De tributis ac vetigalis populi Romani liber. Tolosae, 1612.

AH 7107.34 — Burmani, Petro. Vectigalia Popule Romani. Leidae, 1734.

AH 7107.34.2 — Zornii, Petri. Historia fisci judaici. Altonaviae, 1734.

AH 7107.40 — Traité des finances et de la fausse monnoie des romains. Paris, 1740.

AH 7107.66 — Dissertation historique et critique touchant l'état de l'immunité ecclésiastique sous les empereurs romains. Soissions, 1766.

AH 7108.03 — Bosse, R.H.B. Grundzüge des Finanzwesens. Braunschweig, 1803.

AH 7108.04 — Hegewisch, D.H. Historische Versuch. Altona, 1804.

AH 7108.43 — Coppi, A. Discorso sopra alcune tasse...degli antichi romani. Roman, 1843.

AH 7108.47 — Huschke, P.E. Über den Census und die Steuerverfassung. Berlin, 1847.

AH 7108.72 — Bouchard, L. Étude sur l'adminstration des finances. Paris, 1872.

AH 7108.75 — Naquet, Henri. Des impots indirects. Paris, 1875.

AH 7108.79 — Hahn, G. De censorum locationibus. Lipsiae, 1879.

AH 7108.80 — Cagnat, René. Le portorium...chez les Romains. Paris, 1880.

AH 7108.82 — Cagnat, René. Étude historique sur les impots. Paris, 1882.

AH 7108.86 — Humbert, G. Essai sur les finances. Paris, 1886. 2v.

AH 7108.87 — Mendes, José Amando. Droit romain des douanes chez les Romains. v.1-2. Libourne, 1887.

AH 7108.88 — Marsault, A. Droit romain des magistrats monétaires. Paris, 1888.

AH 7108.88.5 — Thibault, Fabien. Les douanes chez les romains. Paris, 1888.

AH 7108.90 — Bachofen, J.J. Die Grundlagen...Reichs. n.p., n.d.

AH 7108.94 — Moulin, C.D. Droit romain. Des impots indirectes. Poitiers, 1894.

AH 7109.00 — Leo, Fritz. Die Capitatio Plebeia. Berlin, 1900.

AH 7109.00.2 — Thibault, F. Les impots directs. Paris, 1900.

AH 7109.15 — Böttcher, Kurt. Die Einnahmen der römischen Republic im letzten Jahrhundert ihres Bestehens. Weida, 1915.

AH 7109.16 — Piganiol, André. L'impot de capitation sons le Bas-Empire romain. Chambéry, 1916.

AH 7109.43 — Clerici, Luigi. Economici e finanza dei romani. Bologna, 1943-

AH 7109.45 — Déléage, A. La capitation du Bas-Empire. Macon, 1945.

**AH 7114   Ancient Rome in general - Government and administration - Special
topics - Classes of citizens**

AH 7114.2 — Heuermann, O.L. Programm...Gymnasii Arnoldini. Münster, 1856.

AH 7114.3 — Voigt, Moritz. Über die Clientel und Libertinität. Leipzig, 1878.

AH 7114.4 — Pellegrino, D. Andeutungen...der römischen Patricier. Leipzig, 1842.

AH 7114.5 — Raumer, R. De. De servii tullii censu. Erlangae, 1840.

AH 7114.6 — Burchardi, G.C. Bemerkungen über den Census. Kiel, 1824.

AH 7114.7 — Swingar, G.H.D. Commentatio de Patronatus. Groningae, 1823.

AH 7114.8 — Marquardt, I. Historiae equitum romanorum. Berolini, 1840.

AH 7114.8.2 — Marquardt, I. Historiea equitum romanorum. Berolini, 1840.

AH 7114.9 — Schuermans, Henri. Histoire de la lutte entre les patriciens. Bruxelles, 1845.

AH 7114.10 — Hennebert, A. Histoire de la lutte entre les patriciens. Gand, 1845.

AH 7114.11 — Niemeyer, K. De equitibus romanis. Gryphiae, 1851.

AH 7114.12 — Gomont, H. Les chevaliers romains. Paris, 1854.

AH 7114.13 — Gerathewohl, Bernhard. Die Reiter und die Rittercenturien. München, 1886.

AH 7114.14 — Oberziner, G. Origine della Plebe Romana. Leipzig, 1901.

AH 7114.15 — Vinder, Julius. Die Plebs. Leipzig, 1909.

AH 7114.16 — Belot, E.J. Histoire des chevaliers romains. Paris, 1866.

AH 7114.17 — Francke, G.K. De tribuum, curiarum atque. Slesvici, 1824.

AH 7114.18 — Strafser, G. Versuch über die römische Plebejer. Elberfeld, 1832.

AH 7114.19 — Kappes, K. Erläuterungen...zur römischen Ritter. Freiburg, 1835.

AH 7114.20 — Pardon, L. De aerariis. Berolini, 1853.

AH 7114.21 — Lefèvre, Eugene. Du role des tribuns de la plebe. Paris, 1910.

AH 7114.22 — Hesselmeyer, Ellis. Vermischte Beiträge zur Geschichte des Reiteradels bei Römern und Deutschen. Tübingen, 1911.

AH 7114.23 — Oberziner, G. Patrizisto e plebe. Milano, 1912.

Classified Listing

AH 7114   Ancient Rome in general - Government and administration - Special topics - Classes of citizens - cont.

AH 7114.24   Menser, C.F. Dissertatio de annua equitum romanorum. Lipsiae, 1734.

AH 7114.25   Park, Marion E. The plebs in Cicero's day. Diss. Cambridge, 1918.

AH 7114.26   Münzer, F. Römische Adelsparteien und Adelsfamilien. Stuttgart, 1920.

AH 7114.27   Genz, Hermann. Das patrische Rom. Berlin, 1878.

AH 7114.28   Moinier, Gilbert. Les pérégrins déditices dans les premiers siècles de la Republique et sous le Haut-Empire. Thèse. Paris, 1930.

AH 7114.29   Niccolini, G. Il tribunato della plebe. Milano, 1932.

AH 7114.30   Niccolini, G. I fasti dei tribuni della plebe. Milano, 1934.

AH 7114.31   Muhlert, Fridericus. De equitibus Romanis. Diss. Hildesiae, 1831.

AH 7114.32   Zumpt, Karl G. Über die römischen Ritter und den Ritterstand in Rom. v.1-2. Berlin, 1841.

AH 7114.34.5   Hill, Herbert. The Roman middle class in the Republican period. Ann Arbor, 1967.

AH 7114.35   Badian, E. Foreign clientelae, 264-70 B.C. Oxford, 1958.

AH 7114.35.1   Badian, E. Foreign clientelae, 264-70 B.C. Oxford, 1972.

AH 7114.36   Sardi, Marta. I rapporti romano-ceriti e l'origine della civitas sino suffragio. Roma, 1960.

AH 7114.37   Pflaum, Hans Georg. Essai sur les procurateurs equestres sous le Haut-Empire romain. Paris, 1950.

AH 7114.38   Gagé, Jean. Les classes sociales dans l'empire romain. Paris, 1964.

AH 7114.40   Yavetz, Z. Plebs and princeps. London, 1969.

AH 7114.42   Pistor, Hans Henning. Prinzeps und Patriziat in den Zeit von Augustus bis Commodus. Thesis. Freiburg, 1965?

AH 7114.44.2   Bleicken, Jochen. Das Volkstribunat der klassischen Republik. 2e Aufl. München, 1968.

AH 7114.46   Brunt, Peter Astbury. Social conflicts in the Roman Republic. London, 1971.

AH 7114.48   Alföldi, Andras. Der Vater des Vaterlandes im römischen Denken. Darmstadt, 1971.

AH 7115   Ancient Rome in general - Government and administration - Special topics - Tribes

AH 7115.2   Mommsen, T. Die römischen Tribus. Altona, 1844.

AH 7115.3   Grotefend, C.L. Imperium Romanum. Hannover, 1863.

AH 7115.4   Kubitschek, W. Imperium Romanum tributim discriptum. Pragae, 1889.

AH 7116   Ancient Rome in general - Government and administration - Special topics - Centuries

AH 7116.2   Plüss, H.T. Die Entwicklung. Leipzig, 1870.

AH 7116.3   Troll, M.J. De non metata classium centuriarum. Asciburgi, 1830.

AH 7116.4   Breda, O. Die Centurienverfassung des Servius Tullius. Bromberg, 1848. 2 pam.

AH 7116.5   Schmidt, F. De mutatis centuriis servianis. Gissae, 1890.

AH 7116.6   Rosenberg, A. Untersuchungen zur römischen Zenturienverfassung. Berlin, 1911.

AH 7118   Ancient Rome in general - Government and administration - Special topics - Gentes

AH 7118.2   Ruggiero, E. de. La gens in Roma. Napoli, 1872.

AH 7118.3   Giraud, Charles. Dissertation sur la gentilité romaine. n.p., n.d.

AH 7118.4   Rieu, G.N. du. Dissertatio...de gente fabia. Lugduni-Batavorum, 1856.

AH 7118.5   Lohse, G. Die Häupter des patrizischen Claudiergeschlechts. Chemnitz, 1891.

AH 7118.6   Luebberti, E. Dissertatio de gentis claudiae. Kiliae, 1878.

AH 7118.8   Heiter, C. De patriciis gentibres. Berolini, 1909.

AH 7118.9   Münzer, F. De gente valeria. Oppoliae, 1891.

AH 7118.10   Wende, Martin. De Caeciliis metellis commentationis pars I. Inaug. Diss. Bonnae, 1875.

AH 7130   -   7139   Ancient Rome in general - Law - General works (Table A)

AH 7130.2   Caes, Lucien. Collectio bibliographica operum ad ius romanum pertienetium. v.1-20. Bruxelles, 1949- 13v.

AH 7131.1   Pamphlet box. Roman history. Law.

AH 7131.7   Soldan, A. De reipublicae romanae legatis. Marburg, 1854. 6 pam.

AH 7132.10   Sympotica Franz Wieacker sexagenario Sasbachwaldeni a suis libata. Göttingen, 1970.

Htn   AH 7135.48*   Budé, G. Forensia. Lutetiae, 1548. 2 pam.

AH 7135.59.7F   Brisson, B. De verborum quae ad jus pertinent significatione. Lipsiae, 1721.

AH 7135.59.10F   Brisson, B. B. Brissonii...De verborum quae ad ivs civile pertinent significatione. Halae Magdeburgicae, 1743.

AH 7135.59.20F   Wunderlich, I. Additamentorum ad Barnabae Brissonii. Hamburgi, 1778.

Htn   AH 7135.68*   Sigonio, C. De antiquo iure provinciarum. Venetiis, 1568.

Htn   AH 7135.69*   Manuzio, P. Antiquitatem romanarum. Venetiis, 1569.

Htn   AH 7135.73*   Sigonio, C. De antiquo iure civium romanorum. Paris, 1573.

AH 7135.74F   Sigonio, C. De antiquo iure populi romani. Bononiae, 1574.

Htn   AH 7136.60*   Zouche, R. Juris civilis. Oxoniae, 1660.

AH 7137.09   Bynkershoek, C. von. Opuscula varii argumenti. Lugdunum Batavorum, 1719.

AH 7137.10   Bynkershoek, C. von. Observationum juris romani. Lugdunum Batavorum, 1710. 2v.

AH 7137.11   Duker, K.A. Opuscula varia de Latimitate. Lugdunum Batavorum, 1711.

Htn   AH 7137.11.2*   Duker, K.A. Opuscula varia de Latinate. 2. ed. n.p., 1761.

AH 7137.15   Sigonio, C. De antiquo iure populi romani. Lipsiae, 1715. 2v.

AH 7137.18.5   Ferriere, M.C.J. The history of the Roman or civil law. London, 1724.

AH 7137.21.2F   Brisson, B. Formulis et solennibul populi romani verbis. Halae, 1731.

AH 7137.22.2F   Domat, Jean. The civil law in its natural order together with the publick law. London, 1737. 2v.

AH 7137.22.5F   Domat, Jean. Les loix civiles. Paris, 1756.

AH 7137.22.15   Domat, Jean. The civil law in its natural order together with the publick law. 2. ed. Boston, 1850. 2v.

AH 7137.32   Taylor, J. Summary of the Roman law. London, 1772.

AH 7137.35F   Domat, Jean. Les loix civiles dans leur ordre naturel. v.1-2. Paris, 1735.

AH 7130   -   7139   Ancient Rome in general - Law - General works (Table A) - cont.

AH 7137.41   Heineccius, J.G. Antiquitatum Romanarum iurisprudentiam. Argentorati, 1741.

AH 7137.41.5   Heineccius, J.G. Antiquitatum Romanarum jurisprudentiam. Leovardiae, 1777.

AH 7137.41.15   Bello, Andrés. Institciones de derecho romano. Santiago, 1843.

Htn   AH 7137.49F*   Brisson, B. Opera minora. Lugdunum, 1749.

Htn   AH 7137.55*   Taylor, J. Elements of the civil law. Cambridge, 1755.

AH 7137.55.3   Taylor, J. Elements of the civil law. 3. ed. London, 1769.

AH 7137.55.5   Taylor, J. Elements of the civil law. 3. ed. London, 1786.

AH 7137.57   Selchow, J.H.C. Elementa antiquitatum iuris Romani publici et privati. Gottingae, 1757.

AH 7138.03.9   Thibaut, F.J. System des Pandekten-Rechts. Jena, 1846. 2v.

AH 7138.06   Godefroy, J. Manuale juris. Parisiis, 1806.

AH 7138.09   Hauboldi, C.G. Institutiones iuris Romani. Lipsiae, 1809.

AH 7138.20   Dirksen, H.E. Civilistische Abhandlungen. Berlin, 1820. 2v.

AH 7138.22   Doneau, H. Commentarii de iure civili. Norimberg, 1822. 16v.

AH 7138.23   Dirksen, H.E. Auslegung...des römischen Rechts Versuch zu Kritik. Leipzig, 1823.

AH 7138.24   Pernice, L. Geschichte...römischen Rechts. Halle, 1824.

AH 7138.25   Hugo, G. Histoire du droit romain. Paris, 1825. 2v.

AH 7138.27   Gans, E. System des römischen Civilrechts. Berlin, 1827.

AH 7138.29   Gaius. Institutiones iuris Romani. Berolini, 1829.

AH 7138.30   Huschke, E. Studien des römischen Rechts. Breslau, 1830.

AH 7138.30.5   Bloudeau, M. Chrestomathie ou choix de textes. Paris, 1830.

AH 7138.32   Hugo, G. Lehrbuch der Geschichte des römischen Rechts. Berlin, 1832.

AH 7138.32.3   Schweppe, A. Römische Rechtsgeschichte. Göttingen, 1832.

AH 7138.36   Halifax, S. An analysis of the civil law. Cambridge, 1836.

AH 7138.37F   Dirksen, H.E. Manuale iuris civilis Romani. Berolini, 1837.

AH 7138.38   Zumpt, C.G. Über Ursprung, Form und Bedeutung. Berlin, 1838.

AH 7138.40.3   Zachariä, K.E. Geschichte des griechisch-römischen Rechts. Berlin, 1892.

AH 7138.41   Heineccius, J.G. Antiquitatum Romanarum. Francofurti, 1841.

AH 7138.41.5   Burchardi, G.C. Lehrbuch des römischen Rechts. v.1-2, pt.1-3. Stuttgart, 1841. 3v.

AH 7138.41.10   Thibaut, A.F.J. Juristischer Nachlass. Berlin, 1841-42. 2v.

AH 7138.45   Walter, F. Geschichte des römischen Rechts. 2e Aufl. Bonn, 1845.

AH 7138.45.3   Puchta, G.F. Cursus der Institutionen. Leipzig, 1845. 2v.

AH 7138.45.8   Puchta, G.F. Cursus der Institutionen. 6. Aufl. Leipzig, 1865. 3v.

AH 7138.45.9   Puchta, G.F. Cursus der Institutionen. Leipzig, 1871. 3v.

AH 7138.45.10   Puchta, G.F. Cursus der Institutionen. Leipzig, 1875.

AH 7138.45.15   Boujean, L.B. Traité des actions, ou Exposition historique de l'organization judiciaire. Paris, 1845. 2v.

AH 7138.47   Pfund, T.G. Rechts Alterthümer. Weimar, 1847.

AH 7138.47.5   Lange, C.F.W. Examinations über die römischen Rechtsgeschichte. Halle, 1847.

AH 7138.48.5   Secco, A.L. de S.H. Manual histórico de directo romano. Coimbra, 1848.

AH 7138.49   Colquhoun, P. Summary of Roman civil law. London, 1849. 4v.

AH 7138.49.5   Deurer, E.F.F.W. Grundriss für Äussere Geschichte und Institutionen. Heidelberg, 1849.

AH 7138.49.9   Warnkoenig, Leopold A. Historia externa del derecho romano para el uso de los estudiantes de jurisprudencia. Habana, 1849.

AH 7138.50   Heineccius, J.G. Elementos de derecho romano. 3. ed. Paris, 1850.

AH 7138.51   Puchta, G.F. Kleine civilistische Schriften. Leipzig, 1851.

AH 7138.53   Scheurl, C.G.A. Beiträge zur...römischen Rechts. Erlangen, 1853. 2v.

AH 7138.54   Fresquet, R. Traité élémentaire de droit romain. Paris, 1854.

AH 7138.54.3   Cushing, L.S. Introduction to study of Roman law. Boston, 1854.

AH 7138.54.16   Humphreys, E.R. Manual of civil law for...schools. 2. ed. London, 1856.

AH 7138.55   Troplong, R.T. De l'influence du christianisme. Paris, 1855.

AH 7138.55.5   Asher, G.M. Disquisitionum de fontibus juris romani historicarum. Heidelbergae, 1855.

AH 7138.56   Esmach, K. Römischen Rechtsgeschichte. Göttingen, 1856.

AH 7138.56.3   Machelard, E. Textes de droit roman. v.1-2. Paris, 1856.

AH 7138.56.15   Matthiae, C. Controversen Lexikon des römischen Civilrechts. Leipzig, 1856. 3v.

AH 7138.57   Rudorff, A.F. Römischen Rechtsgeschichte. Leipzig, 1857.

AH 7138.59   Leapingwell, George. Manual of Roman civil law. Cambridge, 1859.

AH 7138.60   Walter, F. Geschichte der römische Rechte. Bonn, 1860. 2v.

AH 7138.64   Barinetti, P. Dritto romano. Milano, 1864.

AH 7138.64.6   Namur, P. Cours d'institutes. v.1-2. Bruxelles, 1873.

AH 7138.64.10   Beckhaus, F.W.K. Repetitorium der ausseren römischen Rechtsgeschichte. Berlin, 1873.

AH 7138.66   Demangeat, C. Cours élémentaire de droit romain. 2. ed. Paris, 1866. 2v.

AH 7138.67   Brocher, H. Del'enseignment du droit romain. Lausanne, 1867. 7 pam.

AH 7138.67.5   Tompkins, F. The institutes of Roman law. London, 1867.

AH 7138.68   Arnold W. Cultur und Recht der Römer. Berlin, 1868.

AH 7138.68.3   Troplong, R.T. Influence du christianisme. Paris, 1868.

AH 7138.70   Mackenzie, L. Studies in Roman law. 3. ed. Edinburgh, 1870.

AH 7138.70.3   Maynz, C. Cours de droit romain. Bruxelles, 1870. 3v.

AH 7138.70.5   Krüger, P. Römischen Rechts, kritische Versuche. Berlin, 1870.

AH 7138.71   Rivier, A. Introduction historique au droit romain. Bruxelles, 1871.

NEDL   AH 7138.71.3   Accarias, C. Précis de droit romain. v.1-2. Paris, 1871. 3v.

AH 7130 - 7139 Ancient Rome in general - Law - General works (Table A) - cont.

AH 7138.71.5   Wetter, P. Cours élémentaire de droit romain. Gand, 1871. 2v.

AH 7138.71.6   Wetter, P. Cours élémentaire de droit romain. Gand, 1875. 2v.

AH 7138.71.7   Danz, H.A.A. Lehrbuch der Geschichte des römischen Rechts. v.1-2. Leipzig, 1871.

AH 7138.71.9   Dirksen, H.E. Hinterlassene Schriften. v.1-2. Leipzig, 1871.

AH 7138.71.11   Bryer, J. The academical study of the civil law. London, 1871.

AH 7138.72   Clark, E.C. Early Roman law. London, 1872.

NEDL AH 7138.72.2   Rivier, A. Introduction historique droit romain. Paris, 1872.

AH 7138.72.3   Puntschart, V. Civilrechts der Römer. Erlangen, 1872.

AH 7138.72.5   Accarias, C. Précis de droit romain. Paris, 1872.

AH 7138.73   Goudsmit, J.E. Pandects; treatise on Roman law. London, 1873.

AH 7138.73.3   Hadley, James. Introduction to Roman law. N.Y., 1873.

AH 7138.73.3.5   Hadley, James. Introduction to Roman law, in twelve academical lectures. N.Y., 1893.

AH 7138.73.4   Hadley, James. Introduction to Roman law. New Haven, 1931.

AH 7138.73.5   Giraud, C. Novum enchiridion juris Romani. Paris, 1873.

AH 7138.73.10   Arndts, L. Gesammelte civilistische Schriften. Stuttgart, 1873. 3v.

AH 7138.74   Pellat, C.A. Manuale juris synopticum. Paris, 1874.

AH 7138.74.3   Molitor, J.P. Obligations en droit romain. Paris, 1874. 3v.

AH 7138.75   Harris, S.F. Elements of Roman law. London, 1875.

AH 7138.76   Demangeat, C. Cours élémentaire de droit romain. 3. éd. Paris, 1876. 2v.

AH 7138.76.3   Vignali, G. Del corpo del diritto romano. Napoli, 1876.

AH 7138.76.5   Massol, H. La règle catonienne. Toulouse, 1876. 2 pam.

AH 7138.76.7   Hunter, W.A. Roman law. London, 1876.

AH 7138.76.8   Hunter, W.A. Roman law. London, 1876.

AH 7138.76.9   Ortolan, J.L.E. Institutes of Justinian including history...of Roman law. Toulouse, 1876.

AH 7138.76.10   Ortolan, J.L.E. Institutes of Justinian including history...of Roman law. Analysis. London, 1876.

AH 7138.76.11   Cubain, R. Lois civiles de Rome. Angers, 1876.

AH 7138.76.13   Bruns, C.G. Unterschriften in römischen Rechts-Urkunden. Berlin, 1876.

AH 7138.76.15   Marynz, K.G. Cours de droit romain. 4. éd. Bruxelles, 1876. 3v.

AH 7138.76.20F   Bonjean, G. Tavleaux synoptiques de droit romain. Paris, 1876.

AH 7138.78   Pailhé, E.D. Cours élémentaire de droit romain. Paris, 1878.

AH 7138.78.5   Raisini, G. Programma di diritto romano. Bologna, 1878.

AH 7138.78.10   Padelletti, G. Storia del diritto romano. Firenze, 1878.

AH 7138.78.11   Padelletti, G. Lehrbuch der römischen Rechtsgeschichte. Berlin, 1879.

AH 7138.79   Heumann, H.G. Quellen des römischen Rechts. Jena, 1879.

AH 7138.79.3   Kuntze, J.E. Cursus des römischen Rechts. Leipzig, 1879.

AH 7138.79.7F   Hirschfeld, O. Zur Geschichte des lateinischen Rechts. Wien, 1879. 2 pam.

AH 7138.80   Esmarch, K. Römische Rechtsgeschichte. Kassel, 1880.

AH 7138.80.3   Kuntze, J.E. Excurse über römischen Recht. 2. Aufl. Leipzig, 1880.

AH 7138.80.4   Gneist, R. Institutionum et regularum iuris Romani syntagma. Lipsiae, 1880.

AH 7138.80.5A   Hunter, W.A. Introduction to Roman law. London, 1880.

AH 7138.80.5B   Hunter, W.A. Introduction to Roman law. London, 1880.

AH 7138.81   Marezoll. Lehrbuch der Institutionen. Brussel, 1881.

AH 7138.81.3   Rivier, A. Introduction historique au droit romain. Bruxelles, 1881.

AH 7138.81.8   Merkel, J. Abhandlungen aus dem Gebiete des römischen Rechts. v.1-3. Halle, 1888. 2v.

AH 7138.82   Ruben de Couder, M.J. Droit romain. Paris, 1882.

AH 7138.83   Mackeldey, F. Handbook of Roman law. v.1-2. Philadelphia, 1883.

AH 7138.83.3   Amos, S. History and principles of the civil law of Rome. London, 1883.

AH 7138.83.5.3   Sohm, R. Institutionen des römischen Rechts. 3e Aufl. Leipzig, 1888.

AH 7138.84   Baron, J. Geschichte des römischen Rechts. Berlin, 1884.

AH 7138.84.3   Appleton, C. Cours de droit romain. Paris, 1884.

AH 7138.84.5   Sohm, R. Institutionen des römischen Rechts. Leipzig, 1884.

AH 7138.84.15   Hölder, E. Zwei Abhandlungen aus dem römischen Rechte. Freiburg, 1884.

AH 7138.84.20   Wlassak, M. Kritische Studien zur Theorie des Rechtsquellen. Graz, 1884.

AH 7138.85   Scrutton, T.E. Influence of Roman law on the law of England. Cambridge, 1885.

AH 7138.85.3   Karlowa, O. Römische Rechtsgeschichte. Leipzig, 1885. 2v.

AH 7138.86   Harmann, O.E. Ordo judiciorum. Göttingen, 1886.

AH 7138.87.7   Poiret, J. L'eloquence judiciaire. Paris, 1887.

AH 7138.88   Garsonnet, E. Textes de droit romain. Paris, 1888.

AH 7138.88.3   Jörs, Paul. Römische Rechtswissenschaft. Berlin, 1888.

AH 7138.88.5   Krüger, Paul. Geschichte der Quellen...römischen Rechts. Leipzig, 1888.

AH 7138.89   Schulin, F. Lehrbuch des römischen Rechts. Stuttgart, 1889.

AH 7138.89.3   Bulletino dell'Istituto di diritto romano. Roma. 1,1889+ 41v.

AH 7138.89.10   Girard, P.F. Textes de droit romain. Paris, 1895.

AH 7138.89.15   Mispoulet, J.B. Manuel des textes de droit romain. Paris, 1889.

AH 7138.90   Flach, J. Études critiques sur histoire du droit romain. Paris, 1890.

AH 7138.90.5   Tardif, A. Histoire des sources du droit français. Paris, 1890.

AH 7138.91   Cuq, E. Institutions juridiques. Paris, 1891. 2v.

AH 7138.91.2   Cuq, E. Institutions juridiques. Paris, 1904. 2v.

AH 7138.91.3   Mitteis, L. Reichsrecht und Volksrecht. Leipzig, 1891.

AH 7138.91.15   Bry, Georges. Principes de droit romain. 6. éd. v.1-2. Paris, 1927-30.

AH 7138.92   Voigt, M. Römische Rechtsgeschichte. Leipzig, 1892. 3v.

AH 7138.92.5   Sohm, R. Institutes of Roman law. Oxford, 1892.

AH 7138.93   Chamier, D. Manual of Roman law. London, 1893.

AH 7138.93.5F   Voigt, M. Über die Leges Iuliae iudiciorum privatorum et publicorum. Leipzig, 1893.

AH 7130 - 7139 Ancient Rome in general - Law - General works (Table A) - cont.

AH 7138.95   Landucci, L. Storia del diritto romano. 2. ed. Verona, 1898. 2v.

AH 7138.95.3   Girard, P.F. Manuel élémentaire de droit romain. 3. éd. Paris, 1906.

AH 7138.95.4   Girard, P.F. Manuel élémentaire de droit romain. 4. éd. Paris, 1906.

AH 7138.95.5   Girard, P.F. Textes de droit romain. 3. éd. Paris, 1903.

AH 7138.95.6   Girard, P.F. Manuel élémentaire de droit romain. 5e éd. Paris, 1911.

AH 7138.95.10   Girard, P.F. Manuel élémentaire de droit romain. 8e éd. Paris, 1929.

AH 7138.96   Eisele, F. Beiträge zur römischen Rechtsgeschichte. Freiburg, 1896.

AH 7138.96.5F   Alibrandi, I. Opere giuridiche e storiche. Roma, 1896.

AH 7138.97   Hunter, W.A. Roman law. 3. ed. London, 1897.

AH 7138.99   Czyhlarz, Karl. Lehrbuch der Institutionen des römischen Rechtes. 4. Aufl. Leipzig, 1899.

AH 7138.99.2   Czyhlarz, Karl. Lehrbuch der Institutionen des römischen Rechtes. 7-8. Aufl. Wien, 1905.

AH 7138.99.3   Czyhlarz, Karl. Lehrbuch der Institutionen des römischen Rechtes. 19. Aufl. Wien, 1933.

AH 7138.99.5   Gilson, J. L'étude du droit romain comparé aux autres droits de l'antiquité. Paris, 1899.

AH 7139.01.3   Costa, E. Storia del diritto romano. Bologna, 1901. 2v.

AH 7139.01.5   May, Gaston. Éléments de droit romain. 7e éd. Paris, 1901.

AH 7139.01.6   May, Gaston. Éléments de droit romain. Paris, 1907.

AH 7139.01.8   Theophanopoulos, D. Susthema pomaikou dikaiou. Athens, 1900. 3 pam.

AH 7139.02   Brassloff, S. Kenntniss des Volksrechtes. Weimar, 1902.

AH 7139.02.5   Zoll, F. Historya Prawodawstwa Rzymskiego. Kraków, 1902. 2v.

AH 7139.03   Kipp, T. Geschichte...des römischen Rechts. Leipzig, 1903.

AH 7139.03.3   Walton, F.P. Historical introduction to Roman law. Edinburgh, 1903.

AH 7139.03.4   Walton, F.P. Historical introduction to Roman law. 2. ed. Edinburgh, 1912.

AH 7139.03.5   Conrat, M. Breviarium Alaricianum. Leipzig, 1903.

AH 7139.03.10   Vocabularium jurisprudentiae Romanae. v.1-4. Berolini, 1903-39. 2v.

AH 7139.04   Knappe, O. Grundriss der römischen Rechtsgeschichte. Berlin, 1904.

AH 7139.04.5   Hirschfeld, B. Die Gesta municipalia. Marburg, 1904.

AH 7139.05   Robinson, J.J. Selections from the public and private law of the Romans. N.Y., 1905.

AH 7139.05.3   Wenger, L. Römische und antike Rechtsgeschichte. Graz, 1905.

AH 7139.05.5   Robinson, J.J. Selections from the public and private law of the Romans. N.Y., 1905.

AH 7139.05.10   Triebs, Franz. Studien zur Lex Dei. Freiburg, 1905. 2v.

AH 7139.06   Girard, P.F. Short history of Roman law. Oxford, 1906.

AH 7139.06.3   Bernard, F. First year of Roman law. Oxford, 1906.

AH 7139.07   Mélanges Gerardin. Paris, 1907.

AH 7139.09   Velsen, F. von. Beiträge zur...edictum Pratoris urbani. Leipzig, 1909.

AH 7139.10   Kuhlenbeck, L. Die Entwicklungsgeschichte des römischen Rechts. München, 1910. 2v.

NEDL AH 7139.11   Hardy, E.G. Six Roman laws. Oxford, 1911.

AH 7139.12   Girard, P.F. Mélanges. Paris, 1912. 2v.

AH 7139.12.3   Girard, P.F. Mélanges du droit romain. Paris, 1912-23. 2v.

AH 7139.12.5   Revillont, E. Les origines égyptiennes. Paris, 1912.

AH 7139.12.7   Hardy, E.G. Roman laws and charters. Oxford, 1912.

AH 7139.12.9   Girard, P.F. Études d'histoire juridique. Paris, 1913. 2v.

AH 7139.17.2   Cuq, Edouard. Manuel des institutions juridiques des Romains. Paris, 1928.

AH 7139.23   Francisci, P. de. Il diritto romano. Roma, 1923.

AH 7139.25   Kübler, Bernhard. Geschichte des römischen Rechts; ein Lehrbuch. Leipzig, 1925.

AH 7139.26   Siber, Heinrich. Römisches Recht in Grundzügen für die Vorlesung. Berlin, 1925-28. 2v.

AH 7139.26.5   Mélanges de droit romain dédiés à Georges Cornil. Gand, 1926. 2v.

AH 7139.26.10   Declareuil, J. Rome, the law giver. N.Y., 1926.

AH 7139.27   Radin, Max. Handbook of Roman law. St. Paul, 1927.

AH 7139.28   Rodriguez, José S. Elementos de derecho romano. Caracas, 1928. 2v.

AH 7139.32.2   Jolowicz, Herbert Felix. Historical introduction to the study of Roman law. 2. ed. Cambridge, Eng., 1952.

AH 7139.32.3   Jolowicz, Herbert Felix. Historical introduction to the study of Roman law. 2. ed. Cambridge, Eng., 1965.

AH 7139.32.5   Kreller, Hans. Das Probelm der Juristenrechts in der römischen Rechtsgeschichte. Tübingen, 1932.

AH 7139.34   Mackintosh, J. Some aspects of Roman law. Patna, 1934.

AH 7139.34.5   Fürst, Fritz. Die Bedeutung der Auctoritas im privaten und öffentlichen Leben der römischen Republik. Inaug. Diss. Marburg, 1934.

AH 7139.34.15   Schulz, Fritz. Principles of Roman law. Oxford, 1936.

AH 7139.34.20   Schulz, Fritz. Prinzipien des römischen Rechts. München, 1934.

AH 7139.45   Arangio Ruiz, V. Parerga. Napoli, 1945.

AH 7139.46   Schulz, Fritz. History of Roman legal science. Oxford, 1946

AH 7139.46.2   Schulz, Fritz. Geschichte der römischen Rechtswissenschaft. Weimar, 1961.

AH 7139.51   Schulz, Fritz. Classical Roman law. Oxford, 1951.

AH 7139.51.5   Wolff, Hans J. Roman law. Oklahoma, 1951.

AH 7139.53F   Schulz, F. Die Quellen des römischen Rechts. Wien, 1953.

AH 7139.53.10F   Berger, Adolf. Encyclopedia dictionary of Roman law. Philadelphia, 1953.

AH 7139.54   Bruck, E.F. Über römisches Recht im Rahmen der Kulturgeschichte. Berlin, 1954.

AH 7139.56   Riccobono, Salvatore. Profilo storico del diritto romano. Palermo, 1956.

AH 7139.58   Scherillo, Gaetano. Manuele di storia del dirito romano. Milano, 1958.

AH 7139.61F   Rome (Ancient). Laws, statutes, etc. Ancient Roman statutes. Austin, 1961.

AH 7139.62A   Nicholas, B. An introduction to Roman law. Oxford, 1962.

AH 7139.62B   Nicholas, B. An introduction to Roman law. Oxford, 1962.

AH 7139.63   Levy, Ernst. Gesammelte Schriften. Köln, 1963. 2v.

AH 7139.67   Crook, John A. Law and life of Rome. Ithaca, 1967.

Classified Listing

AH 7130 - 7139   Ancient Rome in general - Law - General works (Table A) - cont.
AH 7139.67.5   Puglisi Cosentino, Alfio. Influenza del primo cristianesimo sul diritto romano dell'epoca classica. Palermo, 1967?
AH 7139.68.5   Brink, Herman van den. Ex iure quiritium. Deventer, 1968.
AH 7139.71   Soellner, Alfred. Römische Rechtsgeschichte. 1e Aufl. Freiburg, 1971.

AH 7140 - 7149   Ancient Rome in general - Law - Public law (Table A)
AH 7147.19   Harlessen, A. Jure colonario. Jenae, 1719.
AH 7148.29   Eisendecher, W. Über die Entstehung...des Burgerrechts. Hamburg, 1829.
AH 7148.33   Vaugerow, C.A. Latini Juniani. Marburg, 1833.
AH 7148.34   Weiske, C.A. Considérations historique...sur les ambassades. Zwickau, 1834.
AH 7148.36   Roulez, J. Observations sur divers points de l'histoire de la constitution. Bruxelles, 1836.
AH 7148.38   Giraud, C. Droit de propriété. Aix, 1838.
AH 7148.40   Römer, J.W. Defensaibus plebis seu civitatium. Trajecti ad Rhenum, 1840.
AH 7148.43   Thermann. De iure praetorio. Lipsiae, 1843. 2 pam.
AH 7148.43.5   Mommsen, Theodor. Ad legem de scribis et viatoribus et de anectoritate commentationes. Kiliae, 1843.
AH 7148.45   Beaujon, J.H. Specimen juridicum inaugurale, de variis modis, quibus...jus civitatis Romanae...potuerit. Lugdunum-Batavorum, 1845.
AH 7148.56   Voigt, M. Jus naturale. Leipzig, 1856. 4v.
AH 7148.56.3   Voigt, M. Jus naturale. v.3-4. Leipzig, 1871.
AH 7148.59   Quinion, L. Du municipe romain. Paris, 1859.
AH 7148.60   Rudorff, A. De maiore ac minori latio. Berolini, 1860.
AH 7148.62   Serrigny, D. Droit public et administratif. Paris, 1862. 2v.
AH 7148.70.2   Willems, P. Le droit public romain. 2e éd. Louvain, 1872.
AH 7148.70.3   Willems, P. Le droit public romain. 3e éd. Louvain, 1874.
AH 7148.70.4   Willems, P. Le droit public romain. 4e éd. Louvain, 1880.
AH 7148.70.5   Willems, P. Le droit public romain. 5e éd. Louvain, 1883.
AH 7148.70.6   Willems, P. Le droit public romain. 6e éd. Louvain, 1888.
AH 7148.70.7   Willems, P. Le droit public romain. 7e éd. Louvain, 1910.
AH 7148.71   Clason, D.O. Kristische Erörterungen über den römischen Staat. Rostock, 1871.
AH 7148.75   Ruggier de Ettore. Diritto publico romano. Firenze, 1875.
AH 7148.75.2   Eigenbrodt, A. De magistratuum Romanorum. Lipsiae, 1875.
AH 7148.76   Bohn, Oscar. Qua condicione iuris reges. Berolini, 1877.
AH 7148.78   Grévy, L. Des municipes. Versailles, 1878.
AH 7148.79   Hoffmann, E. Patricische und plebeische Curien. Wien, 1879.
AH 7148.80.2   Lindet, T. De l'aquisition et de la perte. Paris, 1880.
AH 7148.80.4   Pollack, Erich. Der Majestätsgedanke. Leipzig, 1908.
AH 7148.80.5   Dürr, F. Die Majestätsprocesse unter dem Kaiser. Heilbronn, 1880.
AH 7148.81   Heyrovský, Leopold. Über die rechtliche Grundlage der Leges contractus. Leipzig, 1881.
AH 7148.83   Weiss, André. Le droit fétial et les fétiaux. Paris, 1883.
AH 7148.83.2   Thurm, A.A. De Romanorum legatis. Lipsiae, 1883.
AH 7148.83.3   Létourville, G. de. Étude sur le droit de cité à Rome. Paris, 1883.
AH 7148.83.4   Houwing, J.F. De Romanorum legibus. Lugdunum Batavorum, 1883.
AH 7148.84   Roques, Charles. Droit romain des juridictions. Paris, 1884.
AH 7148.85   Michel, N.H. Du droit de cité romaine. Paris, 1885.
AH 7148.85.2   Pinvert, L. Droit romain du droit de cité. Paris, 1885.
AH 7148.86   Dorsch, E. De civitatis Romanae apud Graecos. Vratislaviae, 1886.
AH 7148.87   Hartmann, L.M. De exilio apud Romanos. Berolini, 1887.
AH 7148.87.5   Bachofen. Das römische Pfandrecht. Baseel, 1887.
AH 7148.87.7   Taddei, A. Roma e isuoi municipi. Firenze, 1887.
AH 7148.88   Kromayer, J. Die rechtliche Begründung. Marburg, 1888.
AH 7148.89   Appleton, C. Histoire de la propriété prétorien. Paris, 1889. 2v.
AH 7148.91   Kappeyne van de Coppello, Johann. Drei Abhandlungen zum römischen Staats- und Privatrecht. Berlin, 1891.
AH 7148.91.5   Kornemann, E. De civibus Romanes in provinciis. Berolini, 1891.
AH 7148.93   Roy, C. Les fétiaux du peuple romain. Poitiers, 1893.
AH 7148.93.5   Ruggiero, E. de. L'arbitrato pubblico. Roma, 1893.
AH 7148.94   Politis, N.E. Les triumvirs capitaux. Paris, 1894.
AH 7148.95   Ferrenbach, V. Die Amici Populi Romani. Strassburg, 1895.
AH 7149.01   Kuhn, F.J. Betrachtungen über Majestäten. München, 1901.
AH 7149.06   Costa, Emilio. Storia del diritto romano. Firenze, 1906.
AH 7149.07   Mommsen, Theodor. Abriss des römischen Staatsrechts. Leipzig, 1907.
AH 7149.11   Boissière, G. L'accusation publique...chez les Romains. Niort, 1911.
AH 7149.12   Rotondi, G. Leges publicae populi Romani. Photoreproduction. Hildesheim, 1962.
AH 7149.14   Leifer, Franz. Die Einheit des Gewaltgedankens im römischen Staatsrecht. München, 1914.
AH 7149.15   Pais, E. Ricerche sulla storia e sul diritto pubblico di Roma. Roma, 1915. 4v.
AH 7149.16   Krug, Erich. Die Senatsboten der römischen Republik. Inaug. Diss. Breslau, 1916.
AH 7149.35   Goodfellow, C.E. Roman citizenship. Thesis. Lancaster, 1935.
AH 7149.36   De Robertis, F.M. La espropriazione per pubblica utilità nel diritto romano. Bari, 1936.
AH 7149.68   Magdelain, André. Recherches sur l'imperium. 1e éd. Paris, 1968.
AH 7149.72   Bleicken, Jochen. Staatliche Ordnung und Freiheit in der römischen Republik. Kallmünz, 1972.

AH 7150 - 7159   Ancient Rome in general - Law - Criminal law (Table A)
AH 7158.15.2   Hasse, J.C. Die Eulpa des römischen Rechts. Bonn, 1838.
AH 7158.25   Fragmenta Klenze. Legis serviliae. Berolini, 1825.
AH 7158.36   Invernizi, P. De publicis et criminalibus iudiciis Romanorum. Lipsiae, 1846.
AH 7158.38   Burckhardt, Adolf. Die Kriminalgerichtsbarkeit. Basel, 1838.
AH 7158.41   Osenbüggen, E. Das altrömisches Paricidium. Kiel, 1841.
AH 7158.42   Geib, G. Römische Criminalprocesses. Leipzig, 1842.
AH 7158.44   Rein, W. Criminalrecht der Römer. Leipzig, 1844.
AH 7158.45   Laboulaye, E. Lois criminelles des Romains. Paris, 1845.
AH 7158.45.15   Zumpt, Karl G. Commentationis de legibus judiciisque repetundarum. Berolini, 1845. 2 pam.
AH 7158.58   Eisenlohr, C. Die Provocatio ad Populum. Schwerin, 1858.
AH 7158.65   Zumpt, A.W. Criminalrecht der römischen Republik. v.1-2. Berlin, 1865. 4v.

AH 7150 - 7159   Ancient Rome in general - Law - Criminal law (Table A) - cont.
AH 7158.71   Zumpt, A.W. Criminalprocess der römischen Republik. Leipzig, 1871.
AH 7158.74   Huschke, E. Die Multa und das Sacramentum. Leipzig, 1874.
AH 7158.75   Hohl, A. Kriminalgerichtswesen der römischen Republik. Burghausen, 1875.
AH 7158.83   Montagnon, E. Essai sur la nature des condamnations civiles. Lyon, 1883.
AH 7158.85   Zedler, K.A.G.I. De memoriae damnatione quae dicitur. Darmstaadiae, 1885.
AH 7158.87   Brunnenmeister, E. Das Tödtungsverbrechen im alten Rechts. Leipzig, 1887.
AH 7158.88   Weihmayr, W. Über Lex Plantia de VI und Lex Lutatia. Augsburg, 1888.
AH 7158.89   Bruyant, E. Juridictions criminelles à Rome. Paris, 1889.
AH 7158.93   Justinianus I. De Furtis. Cantabrigiae, 1893.
AH 7158.94   Greenidge, A.H.J. Infamia. Oxford, 1894.
AH 7158.95   Hallensleben, P.W. Das Vitium Furti und seine Purgatio. Aachen, 1895.
AH 7158.99   Mommsen, Theodor. Römisches Strafrecht. Leipzig, 1899.
AH 7159.06   Binsbergen, J. De legibus ablatae Pecuniae. Trajecti ad Rhenum, 1906.
AH 7159.09   Hitzig, H.F. Die Herkunft des Schwurgerichts. Zürich, 1909.
AH 7159.12A   Strachan-Davidson, J.L. Problems of the Roman criminal law. Oxford, 1912. 2v.
AH 7159.12B   Strachan-Davidson, J.L. Problems of the Roman criminal law. Oxford, 1912. 2v.
AH 7159.15   Huvelin, Paul. Études sur le fortum dans le très ancien droit romain. Lyon, 1915.
AH 7159.26   Schisas, P.M. Offences against the state in Roman law. London, 1926.
AH 7159.34   Mellor, A. Les conceptions du crime politique sous la République romaine. Thèse. Paris, 1934.
AH 7159.35   Rogers, R.S. Crimial trials and criminal legislation under Tiberius. Middletown, Conn., 1935.
AH 7159.35.5   Coster, C.H. The indicium quinquevirale. Cambridge, 1935.
AH 7159.36   Vittinghoff, F. Der Staatsfeind in der römischen Kaiserzeit. Inaug. Diss. Speyer, 1936.
AH 7159.37   Brasiello, U. La repressione penale in diritto romano. Napoli, 1937.
AH 7159.40   Robinson, L. Freedom of speech in the Roman republic. Thesis. Baltimore, 1940.
AH 7159.61   Crifò, Giuliano. Richerche sull'"exilium" nel periodo repubblicano. Milano, 1961.
AH 7159.67   Lebigne, Arlette. Quelques aspects de la responsabilité pénale en droit romain classique. Paris, 1967.
AH 7159.67.5   Bauman, Richard A. The crimen maiestatis in the Roman Republic and Augustan Principate. Johannesburg, 1967.
AH 7159.68   Gruen, Erich Stephen. Roman politics and criminal courts, 149-78 B.C. Cambridge, 1968.
AH 7159.69   Eder, Walter. Das vorsullanische Repetundenverfahren. Inaug. Diss. München, 1969.
AH 7159.69.5   Bauman, Richard. The duumviri in the Roman criminal law. Wiesbaden, 1969.
AH 7159.72   Jones, Arnold Hugh Martin. The criminal curts of the Roman Republic and Principate. Oxford, 1972.

AH 7160   Ancient Rome in general - Law - Private law - Bibliographies; Pamphlet volumes
AH 7160.01   Pamphlet box. Private Roman law.

AH 7161   Ancient Rome in general - Law - Private law - Family law
AH 7161.2   Meyer, Paul. Der römische Konkubinat. Leipzig, 1895.
AH 7161.3   Rossbach, A. Untersuchungen über die römische Ehe. Stuttgart, 1853.
AH 7161.4   Rivier, Alphonse. Précis du droit de famille romain. Paris, 1891.
AH 7161.5   Maanen, J.M. van. De muliere in manu in tutela secundum Gaji Veronensis institutionum principis. Lugdunum Batavorum, 1823.
AH 7161.7   Hase, E.F. De manu iuris romani antiquioris commentatis. Halis, 1847.
AH 7161.9   La Fort, Charles. Essai historique sur la tutelle en droit romain. Genève, 1850.
AH 7161.11   Thön, Karl. Die römische Familie. Kronstadt, 1857.
AH 7161.12   Rossbach, August. Römische Hochzeits- und Ehedenkmäler. Leipzig, 1871.
AH 7161.13   Schupfer, F. La famiglia secondo il diritto romano. Padova, 1876.
AH 7161.14   Fitting, H. Das castrense peculium. Halle, 1871.
AH 7161.15   Maranges, J.M. Estudios jurídicos. Madrid, 1878.
AH 7161.17   Leist, B.W. Zur Geschichte der römischen Societas. Jena, 1881.
AH 7161.19   Jhering, R. Entwicklungsgeschichte des römischen Rechts. Leipzig, 1894.
AH 7161.20   Heiberg, C.F. De familiari patriciorum. Slesvici, 1829.
AH 7161.21   Laënnec, R. Droit des patresfamilias. Saint-Amand, 1899.
AH 7161.23   Stockar, H. Entzug der väterlichen Gewalt. Zürich, 1903.
AH 7161.27   Schmidt, K.A. Das Hauskind in Mancipio. Leipzig, 1879.
AH 7161.29   Westrup, Carl W. Introduction to early Roman law; the patriarchal joint family. London, 1934-55. 5v.
AH 7161.32   Kuleczka, Gerard. Prawo rzymskie epoki pryncypatu wobec dizeci pozamalzeńskich. Wrocław, 1969.

AH 7162   Ancient Rome in general - Law - Private law - Inheritance law
AH 7162.5   Rosshirt, K.F. Erbrecht. Landshut, 1831.
AH 7162.7   Syntrophius, T.F. Instrumentum donationis ineditum. Vratislaviae, 1838.
AH 7162.9   Bachofen, J.J. Lex voconia. Basel, 1843.
AH 7162.11   Vering, F.H. Römische Erbrecht. Heidelberg, 1861.
AH 7162.13   Flach, J. Bonorum possessio. Paris, 1870.
AH 7162.15   Kahn, F. Römischen Frauen-Erbrechts. Leipzig, 1884.
AH 7162.17   Franke, W. Commentar über den Paudie de Heeredetatis Petitione. Göttingen, 1864.
AH 7162.21   Rivier, A. Traité élémentarie des successions. Bruxelles, 1878.
AH 7162.22   Dropsie, M.A. Roman law of testaments. Philadelphia, 1892.
AH 7162.24   Jarriand, E. Histoire de la novelle 118. Paris, 1889.
AH 7162.27   Machalard, E. Dissertation sur l'accroissement. Paris, 1858.
AH 7162.29   Wetter, P.A.H. Droit d'accroissement. Bruxelles, 1866.
AH 7162.31   Deutsch, H. Die Vorläufer der heutigen Testamentsvollstrecker. Berlin, 1899.
AH 7162.32   Wöll, W. Über die regula Catoiana. Strassburg, 1894.
AH 7162.33   Rivier, A. De descrimine quod inter regulam Cotonianem. Berolini, n.d.

AH 7162   Ancient Rome in general - Law - Private law - Inheritance law - cont.

AH 7162.34   Coli, Ugo. Lo suiluppo delle varie forme di legato nel diritto romano. Parigi, 1920.

AH 7162.35   Segrè, Angelo. Richerche di diritto ereditario romano. Roma, 1930.

AH 7162.36   Huber, Paul. Die Ausdehnung der Normen der Senatus Consultum Juventianum auf die private Heredetatis petitio klassischen Rechts. Inaug. Diss. Erlangen, 1933.

AH 7162.37   Longo, G. L'hereditatis pelitio. Padova, 1933.

AH 7162.38   Simonius, Pascal. Die Donatio Mortis Causa im klassischen römischen Recht. Basel, 1958.

Htn   AH 7162.39*   Provera, Giuseppe. La Vindicatio caducorum; contributo allo studio del processo fiscale romano. Torino, 1964.

AH 7162.40   Wistrand, Erik Karl Hilding. Aru och testamenten i romarnas sociala liu. Göteborg, 1966.

AH 7162.42   Meinhart, Marianne. Die Senatusconsulta Tertullianum und Orfitianum in ihre Bedeutung für das klassische römische Erbrecht. Habilitationsschrift. Graz, 1967.

AH 7162.44   Watson, Alan. The law of succession in the later Roman Republic. Oxford, 1971.

AH 7163   Ancient Rome in general - Law - Private law - Marriage law

AH 7163.5   Perizonius, J. Dissertationes. Lugdunum Batavorum, 1710.

AH 7163.7   Wächter-Spittler, K. Ehescheidungen. Stuttgart, 1822.

AH 7163.9   Hasse, J.C. Güterrecht der Ehegatten. Berlin, 1824.

AH 7163.11   Grupen, C.U. De uxore romana. Hannoverae, 1727.

AH 7163.13   Eggers, F.W.T. Alt-römischen Ehe mit Manus. Altona, 1833.

AH 7163.15   Gerlach, F. De romanorum conubio. Halis, 1851.

AH 7163.17   Hölder, E. Römische Ehe. Zürich, 1874.

AH 7163.18   Karlowa, O. Die Formen der römischen Ehe. Bonn, 1868.

AH 7163.19   Morael, G.L.M. Du divorce. Paris, 1888.

AH 7163.20   Beverland, H. De stolatae virginitatis. Lugdunum Batavorum, 1680.

Htn   AH 7163.20.5*   Beverland, H. De stolatae virginitatis. Lugdunum Batavorum, 1680.

AH 7163.21   Jörs, Paul. Ehe Gesetze des Augustus. Marburg, 1894.

AH 7163.23   Dervilers, P. Des peines de l'adultère. Paris, 1893.

AH 7163.25   Sontag, C.R. De sponsalibus apud Romanos. Halae, 1860.

AH 7163.27.2 Pellat, C.A. Textes sur la dot. 2e éd. Paris, 1853.

AH 7163.28   Kirchmaier, G.C. Papia Poppoea lex, e ruderibus exposita. Wittenbeergae, 1694.

AH 7163.29   Corbett, Percy E. The Roman law of marriage. Oxford, 1930.

AH 7163.30   Spagnolo, C.A. Richerche sulle diverse maniere di contrarre matrimonio. Roma, 1807.

AH 7163.32   Soraci, Rosario. Ricerche sui Conubia tra romani e germani nei secoli IV-VI. Catania, 1968.

AH 7164   -   7169   Ancient Rome in general - Law - Private law - General works
(By date)

AH 7167.42   Taylor, John. Commentarius ad Leges decemvirdem. Cantabrigiae, 1742.

AH 7168.11   Löhr, E. Constitutionen der römischen Kaiser. v.1-2. Wetzlar, 1811.

AH 7168.15.2 Bucher, K. Das Recht der Forderungen. 2e Aufl. Leipzig, 1830.

AH 7168.17.3 Mühlenbruch, C.F. Die Lehre von der Cession. 3e Aufl. Stuttgart, 1836.

AH 7168.26   Zimmern, S.W. Geschichte der römischen Privatrechts. v.1,3. Heidelberg, 1826. 2v.

AH 7168.26.5 Zimmern, M. Traité des actions, ou Théorie de la procédure privée. Paris, 1843.

AH 7168.34   Schilling, F.A. Lehrbuch für Institutionen und Geschichte. Leipzig, 1834. 3v.

AH 7168.36   Rein, W. Römisches Privatrecht. Leipzig, 1836.

AH 7168.37.2 Pellat, C.A. Exposé...du droit romain sur la propriété. Paris, 1853.

AH 7168.37.7 Fabricius, C.F. Historische Forschungen im Gebiete des römischen Privat-Rechts. Berlin, 1837.

AH 7168.40   Marezoll, T. Droit privé des Romains. Paris, 1840.

AH 7168.41   Wening Ingenheim, J.N. von. Lehre vom Schadensersatze nach römischen Rechte. Heidelberg, 1841.

AH 7168.41.6 Sell, K. Römische Lehre der dinglichen Rechte. Bonn, 1852.

AH 7168.43   Christiansen, J. Institutionen des römischen Rechts. Altona, 1843.

AH 7168.46   Huschke, P.E. Ueber das Recht des Nexum. Leipzig, 1846.

AH 7168.50   Dernburg, H. Emtio Bonorum. Heidelberg, 1850.

AH 7168.52   Marezoll, T. Du droit privé. 2. éd. Paris, 1852.

AH 7168.52.5 Grotefend, G.A.A. De exceptione Disionis. Gottingae, 1852.

AH 7168.53   Delbrück, E.L.B. Uebernahme fremder Schulden. Berlin, 1853.

AH 7168.58   Rein, W. Privatrecht...der Römer. Leipzig, 1858.

AH 7168.58.5 Demangeat, C. Des obligations solidaires. Paris, 1858.

AH 7168.58.10 Massol, M. De l'obligation naturelle. Paris, 1858.

AH 7168.59   Mommsen, Theodor. Erörterungen aus dem Obligationenrecht. v.1-2. Braunschweig, 1859.

AH 7168.61   Staedtler, H. De la restitution. Bruxelles, 1861.

AH 7168.61.5 Schwanert, H.A. Die Naturalobligationen der römischen Recht. Göttingen, 1861.

AH 7168.61.10 Machelard, E. Des obligations naturelles. Paris, 1861.

AH 7168.62   Böcking, E. Römischen Privatrecht. Bonn, 1862.

AH 7168.63   Phillimore, J.G. Private law among Romans. London, 1863.

AH 7168.64   Sulpius, B. von. Novation und Delegation. Berlin, 1864.

AH 7168.65   Vernet, R. Textes choisis sur la Théorie des obligations. Paris, 1865.

AH 7168.66   Accarias, C. Théorie des contrats innommis. Paris, 1866.

AH 7168.66.5 Salkowski, C. Zur Lehre von der Novation. Leipzig, 1866.

AH 7168.67   Jhering, R. Schuldmoment im römischen Privatrecht. Giessen, 1867.

AH 7168.68   Schupfer da Chioggia, F. Il diritto delle obbligazioni. Padova, 1868.

AH 7168.70   Schwanert, H.A. Compensation nach römischen Recht. Rostock, 1870.

AH 7168.70.5 Glasson, E. Étude sur les donations. Paris, 1870.

AH 7168.70.10 Ubbelohde, A. Zur Geschichte der...Realcontracte auf Rückgabe. Marburg, 1870.

AH 7168.71   Bekker, E.I. Die Aktionen der römischen Privatrechts. Berlin, 1871.

AH 7168.72   Bechmann, A. Das Ius Postliminii und die Lex Cornelia. Erlangen, 1872.

AH 7168.74   Rambaud de Larocque, Marcel. Étude sur la société de crédit foncier de France. Paris, 1874.

AH 7168.76   Jourdan, A. L'Hypothèque. Paris, 1876.

AH 7168.76.5 Eisele, F.H. Compensation nach römischen und gemeinem Recht. Berlin, 1876.

AH 7164   -   7169   Ancient Rome in general - Law - Private law - General works
(By date) - cont.

AH 7168.77   Zródlowski, F. Römischen Privatrecht. Prag, 1877. 2v.

AH 7168.77.3 Merkel, J. Konkurs der Abtionen. Halle, 1877.

AH 7168.78   Scialoja, V. Il precarium nel diritto romano. Roma, 1878.

AH 7168.78.5 Artur, E. De la cause en droit romain et en droit français. Paris, 1878.

AH 7168.79   Koeppen, K.F.A. Institutionen und Geschichte. Strassburg, 1879.

AH 7168.79.5 Leist, B.W. Das römische Patronatrecht. Erlangen, 1879. 2v.

AH 7168.79.7 Flach, J. La table de bronze d'Aljustrel. Paris, 1879.

AH 7168.79.10 Gide, P. Etude sur la novation. Paris, 1879.

AH 7168.79.15 Brissaud, J.B. La notion de cause...obligations conventionnelles en droit romain et...français. Thèse. Bordeaux, 1879.

AH 7168.80   Hoelder, E. Die Entwickelungsformen des römischen Privatrechtes. Erlangen, 1880.

AH 7168.80.5 Dürr, Julius. Die Majestätsprocesse unter dem Kaiser Tiberius. Heilbronn, 1880.

AH 7168.81   Cabonat, J. De la Successio in locum creditorum. Paris, 1881.

AH 7168.82   Trinbal, J. Le la cause dans les contrats et les obligations. Toulouse, 1882.

AH 7168.83   Salkowski, C. Lehrbuch der Institutionen. 4. Aufl. Leipzig, 1883.

AH 7168.83.2 Salkowski, C. Institutionen. 8. Aufl. Leipzig, 1902.

AH 7168.83.7 Dernburg, H. Entwicklung und Begriff des juristischen Besitzes des römischen Rechts. Halle, 1883.

AH 7168.85   Waaser, M. Die Colonia Partiaria des römischen Rechts. Berlin, 1885.

AH 7168.86   Salkowski, C. Roman private law. London, 1886.

AH 7168.86.3 Grueber, E. Roman law of damage to property. Oxford, 1886.

AH 7168.86.5 Muirhead, J. Historical introduction to the private law of Rome. Edinburgh, 1886.

AH 7168.86.6 Muirhead, J. Historical introduction to the private law of Rome. 2. ed. London, 1899.

AH 7168.86.10 Esmein, A. Mélanges de l'histoire du droit et de critique. Paris, 1886.

AH 7168.86.15 Appleton, C. Essai de restitution de l'Edit publicien. Paris, 1886.

AH 7168.88   Matthiass, B. Entwicklung des römischen Schiedgerichts. Rostock, 1888.

AH 7168.89   Burckhardt, Karl. Zur Geschichte der Socatio Conductio. Basel, 1889.

AH 7168.92   Audibert, A. L'histoire du droit romain. Paris, 1892.

AH 7168.92.3 Appleton, C. Fou et prodigue en droit romain. Paris, 1893.

AH 7168.92.7 Appleton, J. Droit romain; essai sur le fondement de la protection possessoire. Paris, 1892.

AH 7168.92.10 Merkel, R. Der römisch-rechtliche Begriff. Strassburg, 1892.

AH 7168.94   Björling, C.G.E. Penning deposition enligt justiniansk Rätt. Lund, 1894.

AH 7168.94.5 Cantacuzène, M.G. Droit romain de l'impot sur l'importation et l'exportation des marchandises à Rome sous la république et sous l'empire. Paris, 1894.

AH 7168.95   Buckler, W.H. Contract in Roman law. London, 1895.

AH 7168.95.3 Appleton, C. Compensation en droit romain. Paris, 1895.

AH 7168.95.10 Henry, René. Étude sur la compensation en droit romain. Paris, 1895.

AH 7168.96   Fleischmann, M. Pignus in causa judicati captum. Breslau, 1896.

AH 7168.97   Wünsch, P. Zur Lehre vom Beneficium Competentiae. Diss. Leipzig, 1897.

AH 7168.98   Duquesne, J. Possession et de la détention en droit romain. Paris, 1898.

AH 7169.02   Roby, H.J. Roman private law. Cambridge, 1902. 2v.

AH 7169.04   Schlossmann, S. Altrömische Schuldrecht und Schuldverfahren. Leipzig, 1904.

AH 7169.04.3 Stintzing, W. Mancipatio. Leipzig, 1904.

AH 7169.05   Cornil, G. Possession dans le droit romain. Paris, 1905.

AH 7169.05.2 Appleton, C. Les lois romains sur le cautionnement. Weimar, 1905.

AH 7169.06   Leage, Richard William. Roman private law. London, 1906.

AH 7169.06.3 Leage, Richard William. Leage's Roman private law. London, 1961.

AH 7169.06.5 Clark, E.C. History of Roman private law. pt.1-2. Cambridge, 1906-19. 4v.

AH 7169.08   Mitteis, L. Römisches Privatrecht. Leipzig, 1908.

AH 7169.09   Partsch, J. De l'édit sur l'alienatio judicii mutandi causa facta. Genève, 1909.

AH 7169.10   Fehr, M. Beiträge zur römischen Pfandrecht. Upsala, 1910.

AH 7169.21.2 Buckland, W.W. A text-book of Roman law from Augustus to Justinian. 2. ed. Cambridge, Eng., 1932.

AH 7169.28   Del Chiaro, E. Le contrat de société en droit privé romain sous la République. Paris, 1928.

AH 7169.30   Hollfelder, H. Die Confusio im römischen Recht. Inaug. Diss. Kallmünz, 1930.

AH 7169.30.5 Poggi, Agostino. Il contratto di società in diritto romano classico. Torino, 1930-34. 2v.

AH 7169.32   Meyer-Collings, J.J. Dereletio. Inaug. Diss. Kallmünz, 1932.

AH 7169.33   Romano, S. Studi sulla derelizione nel diritto romano. Padova, 1933.

AH 7169.33.5 Bussmann, M. L'obligation de délivrance du vendeur. Thèse. Lausanne, 1933.

AH 7169.33.10 Cavin, P.E. L'extinction de l'usufruit "rei mutatione". Thèse. Lausanne, 1933.

AH 7169.34   Longo, G. Diritto romano. Catania, 1934.

AH 7169.35   Jörs, Paul. Römisches Privatrecht. 2. Aufl. Berlin, 1935.

AH 7169.37   Beretta, M. L'esecuzione contro il debitore nel diritto romano ed il nexum. Udine, 1937.

AH 7169.45   Hornby, J.A. Questions and answers on Roman law. London, 1945.

AH 7169.51A   Levy, Ernst. West Roman vulgar law. Phildelphia, 1951.

AH 7169.51B   Levy, Ernst. West Roman vulgar law. Phildelphia, 1951.

AH 7169.55   Betti, Emilio. La struttura dell'obbligazione romana e il problema della sua genesi. Milano, 1955.

AH 7169.59   Endemann, W. Der Begriff der Delegation im klassischen, römischen Recht. Marburg, 1959.

AH 7169.61   Volterra, Edoardo. Istituzioni di diritto privato romano. Roma, 1961.

AH 7169.64   Hausmaninger, H. Die bona fides des Ersitzungsbesitzers im klassischen römischen Recht. Wien, 1964.

AH 7164 - 7169   **Ancient Rome in general - Law - Private law - General works**
(By date) - cont.

AH 7169.65	Watson, Alan. The law of obligations in the later Roman Republic. Oxford, 1965.
AH 7169.67	Watson, Alan. The law of persons in the later Roman Republic. Oxford, 1967.
AH 7169.68	Watson, Alan. The law of property in the later Roman Republic. Oxford, 1968.
AH 7169.71	Watson, Alan. Roman private law around 200 B.C. Edinburgh, 1971.

AH 7170 - 7179   **Ancient Rome in general - Law - Agrarian law (Table A)**

AH 7178.39	Rudorff, A.A.F. Ackergesetz der S. Thorius. Berlin, 1839.
AH 7178.41	Zeiss, Gustavo. Commentatio de Lege Thoria Agraria. Vimariae, 1841.
AH 7178.42	Engelbregt, C.A. Legibus Agrariis. Lugduni Batavorum, 1842.
AH 7178.46	Macé, A.P.L. Lois agraires. Paris, 1846.
AH 7178.56	Revillout, Charles. Etude sur l'histoire du Colonat. Paris, 1856.
AH 7178.56.3	Heisterbergk, B. Die Entstehung des Colonats. Leipzig, 1876.
AH 7178.56.5	Bolkestein, H. De Colonatu Romano ejusque origine. Amstelodami, 1906.
AH 7178.62	Hildebrand, B. De antiquiisimae agri Romani. Jenae, 1862.
AH 7178.70	Jürgens. Ueber der Ursprung und die Werwendung. Blankeburg, 1870.
AH 7178.78	Buhl, Heinrich. Die agrarische Frage. Heidelberg, 1878.
AH 7178.82	Baillierie, P. Du domaine public del'état. Paris, 1882.
AH 7178.82.3	Pelham, Henry. Imperial domains and the Colonate. London, 1890.
AH 7178.82.4	His, Rudolph. Die Domänen der römischen Kaiserzeit. Leipzig, 1896.
AH 7178.82.5	Beaudouin, E. Les grands domains dans l'Empire Romain. Paris, 1899.
AH 7178.82.7	Matthiass, B. Die römische Grundsteuer. Erlangen, 1882.
AH 7178.83	Freund, F. Die gesetzlichen Beschränkungen. Berlin, 1883.
AH 7178.87	Legnazzi, E.N. Del catasto romano. Verona, 1887.
AH 7178.91A	Stephenson, A. Public lands and agrarian laws. Baltimore, 1891.
AH 7178.91B	Stephenson, A. Public lands and agrarian laws. Baltimore, 1891.
AH 7178.91.6	Weber, Max. Die römische Agrargeschichte in ihrer Bedeutung für das Staats- und Privatrecht. Amsterdam, 1966.
AH 7178.94	Beaudouin, E. La limitation des fonds de terre. Paris, 1894.
AH 7178.96	Schulten, A. Die römischen Grundherrschaften. Weimar, 1896.
AH 7178.98	Ossig, A. Römisches Wasserecht. Leipzig, 1898.
AH 7178.98.2	Dreyfus, Robert. Essae sur les lois agraires. Paris, 1898.
AH 7178.99	Salvioli, G. Sulla distribuzione della proprietà fondiaria in Italia al tempo dell'impero romano. Modena, 1899.
AH 7179.00	Neumann, K.J. Die Grundherrschaft der Römischen Republik. Strassburg, 1900.
AH 7179.01	Angelis Mangano, E. Sulle forme primitive. Catania, 1901.
AH 7179.06	Fleischmann, Wilhelm. Altgermanische...Agrarverhältnisse. Leipzig, 1906.
AH 7179.06.5	Maschke, R. Zur Theorie und Geschichte der römischen Agrargesetze. Tübingen, 1906.
AH 7179.08	Quillfeldt, W. Altrömisches Landwirtschaftsrecht. Inaug. Diss. Heidelberg? 1908?
AH 7179.12	Cardinali, G. Studi graccani. Roma, 1912.
AH 7179.13	Guenoun, L. La cessio bonorum. Paris, 1913.
AH 7179.14	Pfeifer, Gerhard. Agrargeschichtlicher Beitrag. Inaug. Diss. Altenburg, 1914.
AH 7179.20	Pachtere, F.G. La table hypothécaire de Valeia. Paris, 1920.
AH 7179.27	Kaïla, E. L'unité foncière en droit romain. Paris, 1927.
AH 7179.27.5	Brissaud, J. Le régime de la terre dans la société étatiste du Bas-Empire. Thèse. Paris, 1927.
AH 7179.35	Zancan, L. Ager publicus. Padova, 1935.

AH 7180 - 7189   **Ancient Rome in general - Law - Slavery and emancipation**
(Table A)

AH 7188.26	Böcking, E. De mancipii causis. Berolini, 1826.
AH 7188.33.2	Blair, William. An inquiry into the state of slavery amongst the Romans. Detroit, 1969?
AH 7188.38	Hoffmann, E. Lehre von den Servituten. v.1-2. Darmstadt, 1838.
AH 7188.38.5	Schüller, C.L. Necessitudine cum moralitum civili. Rhenum, 1838.
AH 7188.40	Bierregaard, L. De libertinorum hominum conditione. Hauniae, 1840.
AH 7188.41	Böger, G. De manciporum commercio apud Romanos. Berolini, 1841.
AH 7188.44	Gessner, Aemilius. De servis Romanorum publicis. Berolini, 1844.
AH 7188.56	Elvers, R. Römische Servitutenlehre. Marburg, 1856.
AH 7188.61	Bechmann, C.G.A. Personalservitut des Usus. Nürnberg, 1861.
AH 7188.66	Adams. Über die Sklaverie und Sklavenentlassung bei den Römern. Tübingen, 1866.
AH 7188.68	Schmidt, A. Pflichttheilsrecht. Heidelberg, 1868.
AH 7188.68.3	Machelard, E. Distinctions admises. Paris, 1868.
AH 7188.77	Ferrero, E. Dei libertini dissertazione. Torino, 1877.
AH 7188.78	Duchauffour, A. De la condition des esclaves. Paris, 1878.
AH 7188.87	Krüger, H. Geschichte des capitis deminutio. Breslau, 1887.
AH 7188.87.2	Lemonnier, H. Étude historique sur la condition des esclaves. Paris, 1887.
AH 7188.89	Lehmann, Eduard. De publica romanorum servitute quaestiones. Diss inaug. Lipsiae, 1889.
AH 7188.90	Vollmann, Franz. Uber das Verhaltnis der späteren Stoa zur Sklaverei im römischen Reiche. Stadtamhof, 1890.
AH 7188.91	Salkowski, C. Lehre vom Sklavenerwerb. Leipzig, 1891.
AH 7188.92.1	Schneider, Albert. Zur Geschichte der Sclaverei im alten Rom. Frankfurt, 1970.
AH 7188.97	Halkin, Léon. Les esclaves publics chez les Romains. Bruxelles, 1897.
AH 7189.02	Juglar, L. Zuomodo per servos...negotiarentur Romani. Paris, 1902.
AH 7189.06	Crumley, J.J. On the social standing of freedmen. Baltimore, 1906.
AH 7189.08	Buckland, William Warwick. The Roman law of slavery. Cambridge, Eng., 1908.

AH 7180 - 7189   **Ancient Rome in general - Law - Slavery and emancipation**
(Table A) - cont.

AH 7189.08.1	Buckland, William Warwick. The Roman law of slavery. Cambridge, Eng., 1970.
AH 7189.25.2	Duff, Arnold Mackay. Freedmen in the early Roman Empire. Oxford, 1928.
AH 7189.25.5	Duff, Arnold Mackay. Freedmen in the early Roman Empire. Cambridge, 1958.
AH 7189.28	Barrow, R.H. Slavery in the Roman Empire. London, 1928.
AH 7189.29	Basanoff, V. Partus ancillae. Paris, 1929.
AH 7189.56	Kotsevalov, A.S. Antichnoe rabstvo i revoliutsii rabov v sovetskoi istoricheskoi literature. Miunkhen, 1956.
AH 7189.57.5	Shtaerman, Elena. Krizis rabovladel'cheskogo stroia v zapadn'ikh provinschchiiakh rimskoi imperii. Moskva, 1957.
AH 7189.59	Aleksishvili, M.M. Iz glubiny vekov. Tbilisi, 1959.
AH 7189.64	El'nitskii, L.A. Voznknovenie i razvitie rabstva v Rime v XIII - III v do n.e. Moskva, 1964.
AH 7189.64.5	Shtaerman, Elena. Rastzvet rabovladel'cheskikh otnoshenii v Rimskoi respublike. Moskva, 1964.
AH 7189.65	Wolf, Manfred. Untersuchungen zur Stellung der kaiserlichen Freigelassenen und Sklaven in Italien und der Westprovinzen. Munster? 1965.
AH 7189.66	Capozza, Maria. Movimenti servili nel mondo romano in età repubblicana. Roma, 1966.
AH 7189.66.5	Wachtel, Klaus. Freigelassene und Sklaven in der staatlichen Finanzverwaltung der römischen Kaeserzeit von Augustus bis Diokletian. Berlin, 1966.
AH 7189.67	Chantraine, Heinrich. Freigelassene und Sklaven im Dienst der römischen Kaiser. Wiesbaden, 1967.
AH 7189.69	Treggiari, Susan. Roman freedmen during the late republic. Oxford, 1969.
AH 7189.69.5	Kiechle, Franz. Sklavenarbeit und technischen Fortschritt im Römischen Reich. Wiesbaden, 1969.
AH 7189.69.10	Zel'in, Konstantin K. Formy zavisimosti v Vostochnom Sredi zemnomor'e ellinistisheskogo perioda. Moskva, 1969.
AH 7189.71	Shtaerman, Elena. Rabovladel'cheskie otnosheniia v romner Rimskoi imperii (Italiia). Moskva, 1971.
AH 7189.71.5	Bellen, Heinz. Studien zur Sklavenflucht im römischen Kaiserreich. Wiesbaden, 1971.
AH 7189.72	Weaver, Paul Richard Carey. Family Caesaris; a social study of the Emperor's freedom and slaves. Cambridge, Eng., 1972.

AH 7190 - 7199   **Ancient Rome in general - Law - Philosophy of law (Table A)**

AH 7198.38	Christiansen, J. Wissenschaft des römischen Rechtsgeschichte. Altona, 1838.
AH 7198.66	Bufnoir, C. Théorie de la condition...en droit romain. Paris, 1866.
AH 7198.66.3	Ihering, R. Geist des römischen Rechts. v.1-3. Leipzig, 1866. 4v.
AH 7198.66.8	Ihering, R. Geist des römischen Rechts. Leipzig, 1891. 3v.
AH 7198.77.2A	Ihering, R. L'esprit du droit romain. Paris, 1877. 4v.
AH 7198.77.2B	Ihering, R. L'esprit du droit romain. Paris, 1877. 4v.
AH 7198.77.3	Ihering, R. L'esprit du droit romain. v.1-2. Paris, 1880-82.
AH 7198.97	Affolter, F.X. Römischen Institutionen-System. Berlin, 1897.
AH 7199.47	Magdelain, A. Auctoritas principis. Paris, 1947.
AH 7199.60	Honig, Richard. Humanitas und Rhetorik in spät römischen Kaisergesetzen; Studien zur Gesinnungsgrundlage des Dominats. Göttingen, 1960.
AH 7199.66	Thomas, Joseph A.C. Form and substance in Roman law. London, 1966.

AH 7200   **Ancient Rome in general - Law - Special topics - The Twelve Tables**

AH 7200.5	Wolff, Emil. Rättshistoriska studier till den tolf taflanaslag. Göteborg, 1883.
AH 7200.7	Dirksen, H.E. Zwölf-Tafel-Fragmente. Leipzig, 1824.
AH 7200.9	Kokkinos, E. Lege XII Tabularum. Heidelbergae, 1836.
AH 7200.11	Valeriani, J. Leggi delle dodici tavole. Firenze, 1839.
AH 7200.12	Duodecim Tabulae. Legis Duodecim Tabularum. Lipsiae, 1866.
AH 7200.13	Voigt, M. Die XII Tafeln. Leipzig, 1883. 2v.
AH 7200.15	Lambert, E. L'origine des XII tables. Paris, 1902.
AH 7200.16	Boesch, F. De XII Tabularum Lege a Graecio Petita. Gottingae, 1893.
AH 7200.17	Nikol'skii, B.V. Sistema i teket "XII tablin". Sankt Peterbug, 1897.
AH 7200.18	Täubler, Eugen. Untersuchungen zur Geschichte des Decemvirats und der zwölft Afdu. Berlin, 1921.
AH 7200.19.2	Leges XII Tabularum. Das Zwölftafelgesetz. 2. Aufl. München, 1953.
AH 7200.19.4	Leges XII Tabularum. Das Zwölftafelgesetz. 4. Aufl. München, 1971.

AH 7201   **Ancient Rome in general - Law - Special topics - Early law and jurists**

	AH 7201.1.5	Studia Gaiana. Leiden. 1,1948+ 4v.
Htn	AH 7201.3*	Gaius. Gai Codex Rescripticus...numero XV. Lipsiae, 1909.
	AH 7201.4.2	Schulting, A. Jurisprudentia vetus Ante-Justinianea. Lipsiae, 1737.
	AH 7201.4.35	Ulpianus. Fragmenta. Notas adjecit Joannes Canregieter. Trajecti ad Rhenum, 1768.
	AH 7201.4.50	Beck, I.L.G. De Fabio Mela Iuris Consulto. Lipsiae, 1806.
	AH 7201.5	Ulpiani, D. Fragmenta. v.1-2. Berolini, 1811.
	AH 7201.6	Hugo, G. Jus civile antejustinianeum. Berolini, 1815. 2v.
	AH 7201.7	Gans, E. Scholien zum Gajus. Berlin, 1821.
	AH 7201.9	Schrader, E. Wasgewimit die römische Rechtsgeschichte. Heidelberg, 1823.
	AH 7201.11	Bluhme, A.F. Gaius Institutionum. Berolini, 1824.
	AH 7201.11.5	Honoré, Antony. Gaius. Oxford, 1962.
	AH 7201.13	Gaius. Institutionum...sive de actionibus. Berolini, 1827.
	AH 7201.15	Gaius. Institutionum. Paris, 1827.
	AH 7201.17	Vaticana fragmenta. Borussorum, 1828.
	AH 7201.18	Fragmenta vaticana. Locorum exiure Romano anteiustiniano ab incerto scriptore coll. fragmenta quae dicuntur vaticana. Bonnae, 1833.
	AH 7201.19	Haubold, C.G. Antiquitatis Romanae monumenta legalia. Berolini, 1830.
	AH 7201.19.6	Kriegel, C.J. Antiqua versio latina. Lipsiae, 1830.
	AH 7201.21	Paulus, Julius. Receptarum sententiarum. Bonnae, 1833.
NEDL	AH 7201.21	Paulus, Julius. Receptarum sententiarum. Bonnae, 1833.
	AH 7201.21.5	Levy, Ernst. Pauli sententiae. Ithaca, 1945.

AH 7201   Ancient Rome in general - Law - Special topics - Early law and jurists - cont.

AH 7201.21.10   Kaser, Max. Die Interpretatio zu den Paulussentenzen. Köln, 1956.

AH 7201.22   Unger, F.W. De duorum praecipuorum iurisprudentiae. Inaug. Diss. Hannoverae, 1834.

AH 7201.23   Ulpiani, D. Fragmenta. Bonnae, 1836.

AH 7201.23.4   Ulpiani, D. Fragmenta. Leipsiae, 1855.

AH 7201.24   Gaius. 1839. Laboulaye. Flores juris antejustianei. Paris, 1839.

AH 7201.25F   Corpus Iuris Romani. Anteiustiniani. Bonnae, 1841.

AH 7201.27   Gaius. Institutionum commentarius quattuor. Bonnae, 1841.

AH 7201.27.5   Gaius. Institutionum commentarius quattuor Goeschen. 3. ed. Berolini, 1842.

AH 7201.29   Pomponius. De origine iuris. Gissae, 1848.

AH 7201.31   Gaius. Institutionum commentarii quattuor. Lipsiae, 1855.

AH 7201.31.2   Gaius. Beiträge zur Kritik und zum Veret. Leipzig, 1855.

AH 7201.32   Demelius, G. Legum quae ad ius civile. Vimariae, 1857.

AH 7201.33   Fragmenta vaticana Iuris anteiustiniani. Berolini, 1860.

AH 7201.33.10   Gaius. Institutionum juris civilis commentarii quattuor. Lipsiae, 1861.

AH 7201.33.15   Gaius. Institutionum iuris civilis commentarii quattuor. 5th ed. Lipsiae, 1886.

AH 7201.34   Domenget, M.L. Institutes de Gaius. Paris, 1866.

AH 7201.35   Gaius. Institutiones. Lipsiae, 1866.

AH 7201.37   Gaius. Institutiones. Lipsiae, 1866.

AH 7201.39   Huschke, P.E. Indices. Lipsiae, 1868.

AH 7201.40   Huschke, P.E. Iurisprudentiae anteiustinianae. Lipsiae, 1867.

AH 7201.40.2   Huschke, P.E. Iurisprudentiae anteiustinianae. Lipsiae, 1867.

AH 7201.40.4   Huschke, P.E. Iurisprudentiae anteiustinianae. Lipsiae, 1879.

AH 7201.40.6   Huschke, P.E. Iurisprudentiae anteiustinianae. v.1-2. Lipsiae, 1908-27. 3v.

AH 7201.41   Dernburg, H. Institutionenen des Cajus. Halle, 1869.

AH 7201.43   Gaius. Commentaries. Cambridge, 1870.

AH 7201.45   Gaius. Elements of Roman law. Oxford, 1871.

AH 7201.47.2   Bruns, C.G. Fontes Juris Romani Antiqui. 2. ed. Tubingae, 1871.

AH 7201.47.3   Bruns, C.G. Fontes Juris Romani Antiqui. 3. ed. Tubingae, 1876.

AH 7201.47.4   Bruns, C.G. Fontes Juris Romani Antiqui. 4. ed. Friburg, 1879.

AH 7201.47.5   Bruns, C.G. Fontes Juris Romani Antiqui. 5. ed. Friburg, 1871.

AH 7201.47.6   Bruns, C.G. Fontes Juris Romani Antiqui. 6. ed. Friburg, 1893.

AH 7201.47.7   Bruns, C.G. Fontes Juris Romani Antiqui. 7. ed. Tubingae, 1909.

AH 7201.47.12   Bruns, C.G. Fontes Juris Romani Antiqui. Index. Tubingae, 1912.

AH 7201.47.12F   Bruns, C.G. Fontes Juris Romani Antiqui. v.2. Plates. Tubingae, 1912.

AH 7201.48   Pernice, A. Marcus Antistius Labeo. v.2. Halle, 1873. 3v.

AH 7201.49   Gaius. Commentaries. Cambridge, 1874.

AH 7201.50   Gaius. Institutionum. Lipsiae, 1874.

AH 7201.51A   Gaius. Elements of Roman law. 2. ed. Oxford, 1875.

AH 7201.51B   Gaius. Elements of Roman law. 2. ed. Oxford, 1875.

AH 7201.53   Polenaar, B.J. Gai institutiones iuris civilis Rom. Lugduni Batavorum, 1876.

AH 7201.54   Julianus. Fragments of the perpetual edict. Cambridge, Eng., 1877.

AH 7201.55   Gaius. Institutiones. Berolini, 1877.

AH 7201.55.7   Gaius. 1923. Krueger and Studemund. Institutiones ad codicus veronensis apographum studemundianum novis curis auctum. Berolini, 1923.

AH 7201.57A   Ulpianus. Fragmenta minora. Berolini, 1878.

AH 7201.57B   Ulpianus. Fragmenta minora. Berolini, 1878.

AH 7201.63A   Gaius. Institutes of and rules of Ulpian. Edinburgh, 1880.

AH 7201.63B   Gaius. Institutes of and rules of Ulpian. Edinburgh, 1880.

AH 7201.64   Schilling, F.A. Dissertatio critica de Ulpiani fragmentis. Vratislaviae, 1824. 3 pam.

AH 7201.65   Glasson, E. Étude sur Gaius. Paris, 1885.

AH 7201.67   Buhl, H. Salvius Julianus. Heidelberg, 1886.

AH 7201.69   Mommsen, T. Fragmenta Vaticana III. Berolini, 1890.

AH 7201.71   Gaius. Institutiones I. Berolini, 1884.

AH 7201.73   Gaius. Elements of Roman law. Oxford, 1890.

AH 7201.74   Cantarelli, L. Il frammento Berlinese "De Dediticus". Roma, 1894.

AH 7201.75   Bremer, F.P. Iurisprudentiae Antehadrianae. v.1-2, pt.1-2. Lipsiae, 1896. 3v.

AH 7201.77   Kipp, T. Quellenkunde des römischen Rechts. Leipzig, 1896.

AH 7201.79   Gaius. Institutiones. 4th ed. Berolini, 1899. 7v.

AH 7201.81.5   Gaius. Institutiones. 4th ed. London, 1925.

AH 7201.83   Gaius. Institutiones. 5th ed. Berolini, 1905.

AH 7201.85   Sabinus, M. Fragmente in Ulpians Sabinus Commentar. Halle, 1906.

AH 7201.87   Gaius. Institutionum commentarius quattuor. 2. ed. Lipsiae, 1908.

AH 7201.88   Gaius. Institutionum commentarius primus. Jena, 1911.

AH 7201.89   Gaius. Institutionum commentarii quattuor. Lipsiae, 1928.

AH 7201.90   Haeckermann, G.A.A.G. De legislatione decemoirali. Gryphiae, 1843.

AH 7201.92   Heimbach, C. Aelii Galli icti de verborum. Lipsiae, 1823.

AH 7201.94   Mantellini, G. Papiniano. 2. ed. Roma, 1885.

AH 7201.95   Beaudouin, E. Le majus et le minus latium. Paris, 1879.

AH 7201.95.50   Balog, E. Über das alter der Ediktskommentare des Gaius. Hannover, 1914.

AH 7201.96   Kooiman, C.L. Fragmenta juris quiritum 1913. Amstelodami, 1914.

AH 7201.97   Gaius. 1912. Krueger and Studemund. Gai institutiones. 6. ed. Berolini, 1912.

AH 7201.98   Gaius. 1937. Bizoukides. Opera. v.1-3, pt.1-2. Thessalonicae, 1937-39. 5v.

AH 7201.98.5   Bisoukides, P.K. O gaïos kai aieisēgeseis autou. Thessalonikē, 1937.

AH 7201.99   Gaius. 1937. Bizoukides. Les nouveaux fragments des institutes de Gaius. Paris, 1933.

AH 7201.100   Gaius. 1937. Bizoukides. Gai institutiones. Lipsiae, 1939.

AH 7201.106   Gaius. 1946. Zuleta. The institutes of Gaius. pt.1-2. Oxford, 1946-53. 2v.

AH 7201.108   Gaius. 1950. Reinach. Institutes. Paris, 1950.

AH 7201   Ancient Rome in general - Law - Special topics - Early law and jurists - cont.

AH 7201.109   Bretone, Mario. Linee dell'Enchiridion di Pomponio. Bari, 1965.

AH 7201.110   Capito, G.A. Fragmenta. Wratislaviae, 1960.

AH 7201.111   Wołodkiewicz, Witold. Obligationes ex variis causarum figuris. Warszawa, 1968.

AH 7201.113   Ortiz Márquez, Julio. Comentarios a las Instituciones de Gayo. 1. ed. Bogota, 1968.

AH 7201.115   Lex Rubria. Studien zur der Lex Rubria. Utrecht? 1971?

AH 7202   Ancient Rome in general - Law - Special topics - Codex Theodosianus

AH 7202.5F   Codex Theodosianus. Codex. Lugduni Batavorum, 1665. 6v.

AH 7202.7F   Codex Theodusianus. Codex. Lipsiae, 1743. 6v.

AH 7202.9   Codex Theodosianus. Theodosianus Codex genuina fragmenta. Bonnae, 1825.

AH 7202.11   Codex Theodosianus. Codicis Theodosiani libri v priores. Lipsiae, 1825.

AH 7202.13   Codex Theodosianus. Antiqua summaria Codicis Theodosiani. Lipsiae, 1834.

AH 7202.15   Codex Theodosianus. Gregorianus Hermogenianus. Bonn, 1842.

AH 7202.15.2   Codex Theodosianus. Gregorianus Hermogenianus. Bonn, 1844.

AH 7202.16   Maasen, F. Ein Commentar des Florus von Lyon zu einigen der sogenannten Sermondschen Constitutionen. Wien, 1879.

AH 7202.17   Codex Theodosianus. Theodosiani. Berolini, 1905. 2v.

AH 7202.18   Codex Theodosianus. Theodosiani libri XVI. Berolini, 1905.

AH 7202.20   Rome. Laws, statutes, etc. Theodosius II. Codex Theodosianus. Facsimile 1-2. Berolini, 1923-26.

AH 7202.25F   Gradenwitz, Otto. Heidelberger Index zum Theodosianus. Berlin, 1925.

AH 7202.30F   Codex Theodosianus. The Theodosian code and novels and the Sermondian constitutions. Princeton, N.J., 1952.

AH 7202.35   Capito, Caius Ateius. C. Atei Capitonis fragmenta. Wratislaviae, 1960.

AH 7202.36   Seyfarth, W. Soziale Fragen der spätrömischen Kaiserzeit im Spiegel des Theodosianus. Berlin, 1963.

AH 7203   Ancient Rome in general - Law - Special topics - Justinian's Corpus juris civilis

AH 7203.01   Pamphlet box. Corpus juris civilis.

Htn   AH 7203.2*   Institutionis imperiales Justiniani. Venetiis, 1483.

Htn   AH 7203.4PF*   Corpus juris civilis. Digesta. Digestorum seu Pandectarum codex Florentinus. v.1-2. Roma, 1902-10. 10v.

Htn   AH 7203.4.6*   Corpus juris civilis. Digesta. Digestum vetus. Colophon, 1513.

Htn   AH 7203.4.7*   Corpus juris civilis. Justiniani Leges de re rustica. Lobanii, 1542.

Htn   AH 7203.4.7.5*   Baudoin, François. Breves commentarii, in praecipuas Justiniani imp. Novellas. Ludguni, 1548.

AH 7203.4.8F   Corpus juris civilis. Leges Justiniani. Parisiis, 1559. 5v.

Htn   AH 7203.4.9*   Corpus juris civilis. Institutiones. Institutionum D. Justiniani. Parisiis, 1560.

Htn   AH 7203.5*   Corpus juris civilis. Codex. Codicis Justiniani. Ludguni, 1571.

AH 7203.6F   Baudoin, François. Institutiones. Ingolstadt, 1573.

AH 7203.6.5F   Corpus juris civilis. Juris civilis septimus tomus. Venetiis, 1610. 2v.

AH 7203.6.9   Corpus juris civilis. Corpus juris civilis in iiii partes distinctum. Genevae, 1619.

Htn   AH 7203.7*   Corvini, A. Digesta per aphoumos. Amstelodami, 1642.

AH 7203.7.5   Corvini, A. Digesta per aphoumos. Amstelodami, 1664.

AH 7203.7.10   Corvini, A. Elementa juris civilis. Amstelodami, 1664.

AH 7203.7.15   Corvini, A. Euchiridium seu institutiones imperiales. Amstelodami, 1644.

AH 7203.8.10   Vinnii, A. In quatuor libros institutionum. Lugdunum Batavorum, 1709.

AH 7203.9   Perez, A. Institutiones imperiales erotematibus. Amstelodami, 1657.

AH 7203.9.2   Perez, A. Institutiones imperiales erotematibus. Amstelodami, 1662.

Htn   AH 7203.10F*   Zoesius. Commentarius ad digestorum. Bruxelles, 1717.

AH 7203.11   Perez, A. Codicis justiniani imperiales. Amstelodami, 1761.

Htn   AH 7203.11.3*   Perez, A. Codicis justiniani imperiales. Amstelodami, 1671. 2v.

AH 7203.12   Corpus juris civilis. Corpus juris civilis in iv partes distinctum. Lugduni, 1652. 2v.

AH 7203.13F   Favre, A. Rationalias in pandectas. Lugduni, 1559. 4v.

AH 7203.14   Corpus juris civilis. Institutiones. Imp. Justiniani Institutionum sive Elementorum. Tremoniae, 1663.

AH 7203.15A   Corpus juris civilis. Corpus juris civilis. Amstelaedami, 1663-64. 2v.

AH 7203.15B   Corpus juris civilis. Corpus juris civilis. Amstelaedami, 1663-64. 2v.

AH 7203.19   Corpus juris civilis. Corpus juris civilis. Amstelodami, 1700. 2v.

AH 7203.19.5   Corpus juris civilis. Institutiones. Elementa juris secundum ordinem Institutionum Justiniani. Lugduni Batavorum, 1700.

AH 7203.20   Triglandius, T. Paedia juris sive Examen Institutiones. Oxoniae, 1710.

AH 7203.21   Corpus juris civilis. Institutiones. Der teutsche Justinianus...Der Grund-lehren dess römischen Rechts. Augspurg, 1718. 2v.

AH 7203.22   Perezl, A. Juris civilis Antecessoris. Vesaliae, 1670.

AH 7203.23   Brenkmann, H. Historia Pandectarum. Trajecta ad Rhenum, 1722.

AH 7203.24   Corpus juris civilis. Digesta. Jacobi Labitti index legum omnium. Francoforti, 1724. 2v.

AH 7203.25   Corpus juris civilis. Jurisprudentia restituta, sive Index chronologicus in totum juris Justinianaei corpus. Amstelaedami, 1727.

AH 7203.26   Eden, R. Jurisprudentia Philologica. Oxonii, 1744.

AH 7203.27   Eck, Cornelius van. Principia juris civilis. Trajecta ad Rhenum, 1756. 2v.

Htn   AH 7203.29F*   Corpus juris civilis. Corpus juris civilis. Amstelodami, 1663. 2v.

AH 7203.31   Corpus juris civilis. Institutiones. D. Justiniani Institutionum libri quatuor. London, 1761.

AH 7203.32.5   Heineccius, J.G. Elementa juris civilis. 5. ed. Trajecti ad Rhenum, 1772.

AH 7203.33F   Corpus juris civilis. Corpus juris civilis Romani. Coloniae Munatianae, 1781.

AH 7206   Ancient Rome in general - Law - Special topics - Other Byzantine laws - cont.
Htn   AH 7206.21F*   Rome. Laws, statutes, etc. Basil I. Lx librorum Basilikōn.
                Basileae, 1575.
        AH 7206.23   Tipucitus. M. Kritoy Patzē Tipoy Keitos. Romae, 1914-29.
                5v.
        AH 7206.27F   Heimbach, G.E. Anekdota. v.1-2. Lipsiae, 1838.
Htn   AH 7206.31*   Monvéron, Charles de. Observationes et emendationes in
                synopsim Basilicum. Paris, 1607.
        AH 7206.33   Pringsheim, Fritz. Zum Plan einer neuen Ausgabe der
                Basiliken. Berlin, 1956.
        AH 7206.34   Byzantine Empire. Laws, statutes, etc. Ekloga.
                Moskva, 1965.
        AH 7206.35   Law of Justinian. Loi de judgement. Bucarest, 1971.

AH 7207   Ancient Rome in general - Law - Special topics - The Senate
        AH 7207.01   Pamphlet box. Rome. Senate.
        AH 7207.1   Oko, Jan. De senatoribus Pedariis. Livowie, 1911.
Htn   AH 7207.2*   Mannuccius, P. Antiquitatum Romanarum...Liber de Senatu.
                Venetiis, 1581.
        AH 7207.5   Middleton, Conyers. A treatise on the Roman senate.
                London, 1747.
        AH 7207.7   Chapman, Thomas. An essay on the Roman senate.
                Cambridge, 1750.
        AH 7207.15   Ihne, W. Uber die Patres Conscripti. n.p., n.d.
        AH 7207.17   Hofmann, Friedrich. Der römische Senat. Berlin, 1847.
        AH 7207.19   Dumeril, Adfred E.S. De senatu romano sub imperatoribus
                Augusto Tiberioque. Duaci, 1859.
        AH 7207.20A   Diaz, José F. Historia del Senado romano.
                Barcelona, 1867.
        AH 7207.20B   Diaz, José F. Historia del Senado romano.
                Barcelona, 1867.
        AH 7207.21   Pantaleoni, Diomede. Dell'auctoritas patrum.
                Bologna, 1882.
        AH 7207.23.1   Williams, Pierre. Le sénat de la République romaine.
                Aalen, 1968. 2v.
        AH 7207.25   Abele, Theodor Anton. Der Senat unter Augustus.
                Paderborn, 1907.
        AH 7207.27   Fischer, Frideric. Senatus Romanus, qui fuerit Augusti
                temporibus. Diss. inaug. Berolini, 1908.
        AH 7207.29   Lullius, Georgius. De senatorum Romanorum patria.
                Romae, 1918.
        AH 7207.31   Lange, Ludwig. De plebiscitis ovinio et atinio disputatio.
                Lipsiae, 1879.
        AH 7207.33   Lambrechts, P. La composition du sénat romain de
                l'accession au trône d'Hadrien à la mort de Commode,
                117-192. Antwerpen, 1936.
        AH 7207.35   Cobban, J.M. Senate and provinces, 78-49 B.C. Cambridge,
                Eng., 1935.
        AH 7207.38   Piaget, Robert. Le sénatus-consulte neronien. Thèse.
                Lausanne, 1936.
        AH 7207.40   Barbieri, Guido. L'albo senatorio da Settimino Severo a
                Carino. Roma, 1952.
        AH 7207.42   Bergener, Alfred. Die führende Senatorenschicht im frühen
                Prinzipat. Bonn, 1965.
        AH 7207.46.1   Stein, Paul. Die Senatssitzungen der ciceronischen Zeit
                68-43. Photoreproduction. Münster, 1930.
        AH 7207.48   Eck, Werner. Senatoren von Vespasian bis Hadrian. Diss.
                München, 1970.
        AH 7207.50   Ungern-Sternberg von Pürkel, Jürgen. Untersuchungen zum
                spatrepublikanischen Notstandsrecht. Diss. München, 1970.
        AH 7207.52   Wiseman, Timothy Peter. New men in the Roman senate 139
                B.C. - A.D. 14. London, 1971.
        AH 7207.53   Arnheim, M.T.W. The senatorial aristocracy in the later
                Roman empire. Oxford, 1972.

AH 7208   Ancient Rome in general - Law - Special topics - The Comitia
        AH 7208.2   Zumpt, Karl G. Uber Abstimmung des römischen Volks.
                Berlin, 1837.
        AH 7208.3   Hallays, André. Les comices à Rome. Paris, 1890.
        AH 7208.4   Marlot, Emile. Les comices électoraux. Paris, 1884.
        AH 7208.6   Palmer, Robert E.A. The King and the comitium; a study of
                Rome's oldest public documents. Wiesbaden, 1969.
        AH 7208.8A   Palmer, Robert E.A. The archaic community of the Romans.
                Cambridge, 1970.
        AH 7208.8B   Palmer, Robert E.A. The archaic community of the Romans.
                Cambridge, 1970.

AH 7210   Ancient Rome in general - Law - Special topics - Interreges
        AH 7210.2   Bamberger, F. De Interregibus Romanis. Brunsvigae, 1844.

AH 7212   Ancient Rome in general - Law - Special topics - Leges Annales
        AH 7212.2   Nipperdey, Karl. Die Leges Annales. Leipzig, 1865.
        AH 7212.5*   Astin, A.E. The Lex Annalis before Sulla.
                Brussells, 1958.

AH 7214   Ancient Rome in general - Law - Special topics - The oath
        AH 7214.2   Mercklin, D. Die Cooptation der Römer. Mitau, 1848.
        AH 7214.3   Maschke, R. De magistratuum Romanorum iure.
                Berolini, 1884.
        AH 7214.5   Peter, R. Quaestionum pontificatium specimen.
                Argentorati, 1886. 2 pam.
        AH 7214.7   Grosser, G. De spectione et nuntiatione.
                Vratislaviae, 1851.
        AH 7214.9   Demelius, G. Schiedseid und Beweiseid. Leipzig, 1887.
        AH 7214.10   Ioachmiovici, V.E. Juspirandum...du droit romain.
                Paris, 1912.
        AH 7214.12   Herrmann, Peter. Der römische Kaisereid.
                Habilitationsschrift. Göttingen, 1968.

AH 7215   Ancient Rome in general - Law - Special topics - Sacred law
        AH 7215.5   Schwede, C. De pontificum collegii pontifisque Maximi in
                re publica potestate. Diss. inaug. Lipsiae, 1875.
        AH 7215.6   Danz, H.A.A. Der sacrale Schutz im römischen
                Rechtsverkehr. Jena, 1857.
        AH 7215.7   Lefèvre, R. Ses sacre privata en droit romain. Thèse.
                Paris, 1923.

AH 7217   Ancient Rome in general - Law - Special topics - Public rewards;
    Nobility
        AH 7217.5   Gaupp, E.T. De professoribus et medicis eorumgue.
                Vratislaviae, 1827.
        AH 7217.11   Bonolis, G. I titoli di nobiltà. Firenze, 1905.
        AH 7217.13   Naudet, Joseph. De la noblesse et des récompenses.
                Paris, 1863.
        AH 7217.13.5   Naudet, Joseph. De la noblesse chez les Romains.
                Paris, 1868.
        AH 7217.15   Gelzer, Matthias. Die Nobilität der römischen Republik.
                Leipzig, 1912.

AH 7217   Ancient Rome in general - Law - Special topics - Public rewards;
    Nobility - cont.
        AH 7217.15.5   Gelzer, Matthias. The Roman nobility. Oxford, 1969.
        AH 7217.16   Heil, Wilhelm. Der konstantinische Patriziat. Diss.
                Basel, 1966.
        AH 7217.18   Nuyens, Michel. Le statut obligatoire des décurions dans
                le droit constantinien. Louvain, 1964.

AH 7218   Ancient Rome in general - Law - Special topics - Treasure-trove
        AH 7218.5   Hill, George. Treasure-trove; the law and practice of
                antiquity. London, 1934.

AH 7219   Ancient Rome in general - Law - Special topics - Sales
        AH 7219.5   Daube, David. Studies in the Roman law of sale.
                Oxford, 1959.

AH 7220 - 7229   Ancient Rome in general - Law - Legal procedure (Table A)
        AH 7228.25.3   Heffter, A.W. System des römischen und deutschen
                Civil-Processrechts. 2. Aufl. Bonn, 1843.
        AH 7228.27   Keller, F.L. Litis Contestation und Ultheil.
                Zürich, 1827.
        AH 7228.35   Schneider, K.A. De centumviralis judicii apud romani
                origine. Rostochii, 1835.
        AH 7228.36   Wasserschleben, W.H. Historia quaestionum pertormenta.
                Berolini, 1836.
        AH 7228.41   Walter, F. Histoire de la procédure civile. Paris, 1841.
        AH 7228.42   Escher, J.H.A. De testium ratione. Turici, 1842.
        AH 7228.45   Wetzell, G.W. Der römische Vindicationsprocess.
                Leipzig, 1845.
        AH 7228.50   Erxleben, A. Condictiones sine causa. pt.1-2.
                Leipzig, 1850.
        AH 7228.52.3   Keller, Friedrich. Der römische Civilprocess und die
                Actionen. 3. Aufl. Leipzig, 1863.
        AH 7228.52.4   Keller, Friedrich. Der römische Civilprocess und die
                Actionen. 4. Aufl. Leipzig, 1871.
        AH 7228.52.5   Keller, Friedrich. Der römische Civilprocess und die
                Actionen. Leipzig, 1876.
        AH 7228.52.9   Keller, Firedrich. Der römische Civilprocess und die
                Actionen. Leipzig, 1883.
        AH 7228.53   Schmidt, K.A. Interdiktenverfahren der Römer.
                Leipzig, 1853.
        AH 7228.56   Windscheid, B. Die Actio des römischen Civilrechts.
                Düsseldorf, 1856.
        AH 7228.57   Windscheid, B. Die Actio. Düsseldorf, 1857.
        AH 7228.58   Daniel, C.G.F. Legisactionen und Formularprozess.
                Schwerin, 1858.
        AH 7228.58.2   Grellet Dumageau, J.B.M. Le barreau romain. Paris, 1858.
        AH 7228.59   Hartmann, O.E. Ordo judiciorum. Göttingen, 1859.
        AH 7228.61   Degenkolb, H. Die Lex Hieronica. Berlin, 1861.
        AH 7228.62   Voigt, M. Ueber die condictiones ob causam.
                Leipzig, 1862.
        AH 7228.64   Machelard, E. Théorie général interdits en droit romain.
                Paris, 1864.
        AH 7228.64.5   Bethmann-Hollweg, M.A. von. Der Civilprozess des gemeinen
                Rechts. Bonn, 1864. 6v.
        AH 7228.70   Keller, F.L. von. De procédure civile et des actions.
                Paris, 1870.
        AH 7228.70.5   Latreille, J. Histoire des institutions judiciaires.
                Paris, 1870.
        AH 7228.71.5   Eisele, F. Materielle Grundlage der Exceptio.
                Berlin, 1871.
        AH 7228.72   Karlowa, O. Der römische Civilprozess. Berlin, 1872.
        AH 7228.75   Eisele, F. Zur Geschichte der processualen Behandlung der
                Exceptionen. Berlin, 1875.
        AH 7228.76   Lohse, S.C. De quaestionum perpetuarum origine.
                Plaviae, 1876.
        AH 7228.79   Wlassak, M. Zur Geschichte der Negotiorum Gestio.
                Jena, 1879.
        AH 7228.81.5   Baron, J. Abhandlungen aus dem römischen Civilprozess.
                Berlin, 1881. 3v.
        AH 7228.81.9   Tardif, E.J. Etude sur la Litis Contestatio en droit
                romain. Paris, 1881.
        AH 7228.82   Wlassak, M. Edict und Klageform. Jena, 1882.
        AH 7228.86   Poiret, J. De Centumvoris et Causio Centumviralibus.
                Parisiis, 1886.
        AH 7228.88   Pfersche, E. Interdicte des römischen Civilprocesses.
                Graz, 1888.
        AH 7228.88.5   Wlassak, M. Römische Processgesetze. Leipzig, 1888.
        AH 7228.89   Bechmann, A. Studie...Legis actio sacramenti in rem.
                München, 1889.
        AH 7228.93   Hitzig, H.F. Die Assessoren der römischen Magistrate.
                München, 1893.
        AH 7228.93.5   Koschembahr-Lyskowski, J. Die Theorie der Exceptionen.
                Berlin, 1893.
        AH 7228.96   Jobbé-Duval, E. La procédure civil. Paris, 1896.
        AH 7228.98   Marzo, D.S. Procedura criminale romana. Palermo, 1898.
        AH 7228.98.5   Louvet, F. Juridictions criminelles à Rome. Paris, 1898.
        AH 7228.99   Erman, Karl. Conceptio formularum, actio in factum und
                ipso iure-Consumption. Weimar, 1899.
        AH 7229.01   Girard, P.F. Histoire de l'organization judiciaire.
                Paris, 1901.
        AH 7229.04   Schott, R. Römischen Zivilprozess. München, 1904.
        AH 7229.05   Partsch, J. Schriftformel im römischen Provinzialprozesse.
                Breslau, 1905.
        AH 7229.05.3   Koschaker, P. Translatio iudicii. Graz, 1905.
        AH 7229.05.5   Schlossmann, S. Litis Contestatio. Leipzig, 1905.
        AH 7229.27   Johnson, H.D. The Roman tribunal. Baltimore, 1927.
        AH 7229.66   Kelly, John Maurice. Roman litigation. Oxford, 1966.
        AH 7229.70   Behrends, Okko. Die römische Geschworenenverfassung. Diss.
                Göttingen, 1970.
        AH 7229.70.5   Garnsey, Peter. Social status and legal privilege in the
                Roman Empire. Oxford, 1970.

AH 7230 - 7239   Ancient Rome in general - Military affairs (Table A)
        AH 7231.01   Pamphlet box. Roman history. Military affairs.
        AH 7231.9   Kuthe, A. Römische Kriegsaltertümer. Wismar, 1884.
                4 pam.
Htn   AH 7235.59*   Du Choul, G. Discorso...sopra la castrametatione.
                n.p., 1559. 2 pam.
Htn   AH 7235.59.3*   Du Choul, G. Discorso...sopra la castrametatione.
                n.p., 1579.
Htn   AH 7235.59.5*   Du Choul, G. Discorso...sopra la castrametatione.
                Vinegia, 1582. 5 pam.
Htn   AH 7235.96*   Lipsius, J. De militia Romana. Antverpiae, 1596.
Htn   AH 7235.97*   Valtrimus, J.A. De re militari veterum Romanorum.
                n.p., 1597.
Htn   AH 7236.57*   Saumaise, C. de. De re militari Romanorum.
                Lugdunum, 1657.

Classified Listing

AH 7230 - 7239 Ancient Rome in general - Military affairs (Table A) - cont.

AH 7236.86 Du Choul, G. Veterum Romanorum religio. Amstelodami, 1686.

Htn AH 7237.34* Ainsworth, R. De Clypeo Camilli. London, 1734.

AH 7237.64.5 Stierneman. Principes de l'art de la guerre. Strasbourg, 1765.

AH 7238.30 Wiener, P.E.A. De legione Romanorum vicesima secunda. Darmstadii, 1830.

AH 7238.35 Cardinali, Clemente. Diplomi imperiali di privilegj accordatiai militari. Velletri, 1835.

AH 7238.39 Klenze, C.A.C. Philologische Abhandlungen. Berlin, 1839.

AH 7238.50 Rabus, J.M. Ad solemia anniversaria gymnasii. n.p., 1850.

AH 7238.50.2 Stolze, F. Triumph and ovation. Rostock, 1874.

AH 7238.50.3 Pamphlet box. Roman triumph. 2 pam.

AH 7238.51 Simpson, J.Y. Was the Roman army provided with any medical officers? Edinburgh, 1851.

AH 7238.54 Herbert, H.W. The captains of the Roman republic. N.Y., 1854.

AH 7238.55 Pamphlet box. Tribuni militares. 2 pam.

AH 7238.60 Rein, A. De phaleris et de argenteis e arum exemplaribus haud praculcalone et Asaburgio. Romae, 1860.

AH 7238.63 Lamarre, Claude. De la milice romaine depuis la fondation de Rome jusqu'à Constantin. Thèse. Paris, 1863.

AH 7238.64 Eichhorst, Otto. De Cohortibus urbanis imperatorum Romanorum. Danzig, 1864.

AH 7238.64.5 Steinike, Heinrich. De equitatu romano. Diss. Halis Saxonum, 1864.

AH 7238.64.10 Masquelez, Alfred Émile A.E. Étude sur la castramétation des romains. Paris, 1864.

AH 7238.66 Briau, René. Du service de santé militaire chez les romains. Paris, 1866.

AH 7238.67F Robert, Charles. Les légions du Rhin et les inscriptions des carrières. Paris, 1867.

AH 7238.68 Hirschfeld, Otto. Das Aerarium Militare und die Verwaltung der Heeresgelder in der römischen Kaiserzeit. Leipzig, 1868.

AH 7238.70 Naudet, Joseph. Études d'histoire romaine. Paris, 1870.

AH 7238.72 Geppert, P. De tribunis miletum. Berolini, 1872.

AH 7238.74 Genz, Hermann. Die servianische Centurien-Verfassung. Sorau, 1874. 2 pam.

AH 7238.77 Stille, Wilhelm. Historia legionum auxiliorumqui ende ab excessu divi Augusti usque ad Vespasiani tempora. Kiliae, 1877.

AH 7238.81 Pfitzner, W. Geschichte der römischen Kaiserlegionen. Leipzig, 1881.

AH 7238.81.2 Schambach, O. Gymnasium zu Mühlhausen - Jahres-Bericht. Mühlhausen, 1881.

AH 7238.82 Lindenschmit, Ludwig. Tracht und Bewaffnung. Braunschweig, 1882.

AH 7238.82.5 Fiegel, M. Historia legionis III. Augustae. Inaug. Diss. Berolini, 1882.

AH 7238.83 Fontaine, L. L'armée romaine. Paris, 1883.

AH 7238.83.2 Schambach, O. Sechsundsiebenzigste Nachricht. Altenburg, 1883.

AH 7238.83.5 Jullian, C. De protectoribus et domesticis Augustorum. Thesis. Paris, 1883.

AH 7238.84 Kraner, F. L'armée romaine au temps de César. Paris, 1884.

AH 7238.85 Ritterling, E.H.E. De legione Romanorum X Genima. Lipsiae, 1855.

AH 7238.87 Schultze, E. De legione Romanorum XIII Genima. Kiliae, 1887.

AH 7238.88.1 Judson, Harry P. Caesar's army; a study of the military art of the Romans in the last days of the Republic. N.Y., 1961.

AH 7238.89 Stürenburg, H. Zu den Schlachtfeldern am trasionenischen See. Leipzig, 1889.

AH 7238.92 Beniamin, C. De iustmiani imperatoris aetale. Berolini, 1892.

AH 7238.93 Vaders, Joseph. Einundvierzigster Jahresbericht...Realgymnasium. Münster, 1893.

AH 7238.94 Fröhlich, F. Feldheeren des Altertums. v. 1-2, 3-5. Zürich, 1894. 4v.

AH 7238.94.2 Bray, Joseph. Essai sur le droit penal militaire. Paris, 1894.

AH 7238.95 Luterbacher, F. Die römischen Legionen und Kriegsschiffe. Burgdorf, 1895.

AH 7238.95.5 Gündel, Friedrich. De legione II adiutrice. Inaug. Diss. Lipsiae, 1895.

AH 7239.00 Baehr, W. De centurionibus legionariis. Berolini, 1900.

AH 7239.03 Weichert, A. Die Legio XXII Primigenia. Ein Beitrag. Trier, 1903.

AH 7239.03.2 Beuchel, F. De legione Romanorum i Italica. Lipsiae, 1903.

AH 7239.03.3 Renel, Charles. Cultes militaires de Rome. Les enseignes. Lyon, 1903.

AH 7239.03.4 Helbig, W. Sur l'aes pararium. Paris, 1903. 2 pam.

AH 7239.04 Koeser, E. De captivis Romanorum. Gissae, 1904.

AH 7239.05 Steiner, Paul. De Dona Militaria. Bonn, 1905.

AH 7239.06 Bang, Martin. Die Germanen im römischen Dienst. Berlin, 1906.

AH 7239.06.5 Smith, F. Römische Heeresverfassung und Timokratie. Berlin, 1906.

AH 7239.06.7 Bang, Martin. Die Germanen im römischen Dienst. Berlin, 1906.

AH 7239.07 Tschauschmer, Carl. Legionare Kriegsvexillationen. Breslau, 1907.

AH 7239.07.5 Weerd, Hubert van de. Étude historique sur trois legions romaines du Bas-Danube. Louvain, 1907.

AH 7239.08 Steinwender, T. Ursprung und Heerwirkung. Danzig, 1908.

AH 7239.08.5 De Rebus Bellicis. Anonymi de rebus bellicis liber. Berlin, 1908.

AH 7239.08.7 Domaszewski, Alfred von. Die Anlage der Limeskastelle. Heidelberg, 1908.

AH 7239.08.9 Wolks, Josef. Beiträge zur Geschichte der Legio XI Claudia. Breslau, 1908.

AH 7239.12 Stolle, F. Das Lager und Heer der Römer. Strassburg, 1912.

AH 7239.13 Steinwender, T. Die römische Taktik zur Zeit der Manipularstellung. Danzig, 1913.

AH 7239.13.5 Wegeleben, Theodor. Die Rangordnung der römischen Centurionen. Berlin, 1913.

AH 7239.14 Cheesman, G.L. The auxilia of the Roman imperial army. Oxford, 1914.

AH 7239.14.4 Fischer, W. Das römische Lager insbesondere nach Livius. Leipzig, 1914.

AH 7239.20 Pais, Ettore. Fasti triumphales populi Romani. v.1-2. Roma, 1920.

AH 7230 - 7239 Ancient Rome in general - Military affairs (Table A) - cont.

AH 7239.20.5 Grosse, Robert. Römische Militärgeschichte. Berlin, 1920.

AH 7239.20.7 Sulser, Jakob. Disciplina, Beiträge zur inneren Geschichte des römischen Heeres von Augustus bis Vespasian. Inaug. Diss. Dachau, 1920.

AH 7239.23 McCartney, E.S. Warfare by land and sea. Boston, 1923.

AH 7239.26 Couissin, Paul. Les armes romaines. Paris, 1926.

AH 7239.26.5 Couissin, Paul. Les armes romaines. Thèse. Paris, 1926.

AH 7239.26.9 Vliet, Jacobus van. De praetoria atque amicorum cohortibus. Diss. Traiecti ad Rhenum, 1926.

AH 7239.28 Parker, Henry M.D. The Roman legions. Oxford, 1928.

AH 7239.30 Horn, Heinrich. Foederati. Inaug. Diss. Frankfurt, 1930.

AH 7239.36 Lorenz, H. Untersuchung zum Prätorium. Inaug. Diss. Halle, 1936.

AH 7239.38 Durry, Marcel. Les cohortes pretoriennes. Thèse. Paris, 1938.

AH 7239.38.5 Westington, M.M. Atrocities in Roman warfare to 133 B.C. Diss. Chicago, 1938.

AH 7239.39 Passerini, A. Le coorti pretorie. Roma, 1939.

AH 7239.40 Adcock, F.E. The Roman art of war under the republic. Cambridge, 1940.

AH 7239.52A De Rebus Billicis. A Roman reformer and inventor. Oxford, 1952.

AH 7239.52B De Rebus Billicis. A Roman reformer and inventor. Oxford, 1952.

AH 7239.52.5 Barini, C. Triumphalia. Torino, 1952.

AH 7239.53 Focni, G. Il reclatamento delle legioni da Augusto a Diocleziano. 1. ed. Milano, 1953.

AH 7239.56 Morin y Peña, Manuel. Instituciones militares romanas. Madrid, 1956.

AH 7239.56.5 Webster, Graham. The Roman army. Chester, 1956.

AH 7239.58 Smith, Richard. Service in the past - Marian Roman Army. Manchester, 1958.

AH 7239.59 Hackl, Othmar. Die sogenannte servianische Heeresreform. München, 1959.

AH 7239.61 Várady, Lazló. Késórómai hadügyek es társadalmi alapjaik. Budapest, 1961.

AH 7239.63A MacMullen, R. Soldier and civilian in the later Roman Empire. Cambridge, 1963.

AH 7239.63B MacMullen, R. Soldier and civilian in the later Roman Empire. Cambridge, 1963.

AH 7239.65 Mellersh, Harold Edward Leslie. The Roman soldier. N.Y., 1965.

AH 7239.65.5 Waas, Manfred. Germanen im römischen Dienst im 4. Jahrhundert nach Christus. Bonn, 1965.

AH 7239.65.10 Speidel, Michael. Die equites singulares Augusti. Bonn, 1965.

AH 7239.66 Crescenti, Giovanni. Obiettori di coscienza e martiri militari nei primi cinque secoli del cristianesimo. Polermo, 1966.

AH 7239.67 Harmand, Jacques. L'armée et le soldat à Rome de 107 à 50 avant notre ere. Paris, 1967.

AH 7239.68 Brand, Clarence E. Roman military law. Austin, 1968.

AH 7239.69 Webster, Graham. The Roman Imperial Army of the first and second centuries, A.D. London, 1969.

AH 7239.69.5 Watson, G.R. The Roman soldier. London, 1969.

AH 7239.69.10 Problèmes de la guerre à Rome. Paris, 1969.

AH 7239.71 Fink, Robert O. Roman military records on Papyrus. Cleveland, 1971.

AH 7239.71.5F Claustra Alpium Iuliarum. Ljubljana, 1971.

AH 7239.72 Barker, Phil. The armies and enemies of imperial Rome. Goring by Sea, 1972.

AH 7250 - 7259 Ancient Rome in general - Naval affairs (Table A)

AH 7251.01 Pamphlet box. Roman Naval affairs.

AH 7258.78F Ferrero, E. L'ordinamento delle armate romane. Torino, 1878.

AH 7258.78.2F Ferrero, E. Iscrizioni e ricerche nuove. Torino, 1884.

AH 7258.85 Jurien de la Gravière. Marine des Ptolémées et...Romains. Paris, 1885. 2v.

AH 7258.87 La Berge, Camille de. Étude sur l'organisation des flottes romaines. Vienne, 1887.

AH 7258.96 Chapot, Victor. La flotte de misène. Paris, 1896.

AH 7259.13 Vescovini, Adolfo. Le flotte romane in Africa. Roma, 1913.

AH 7259.15 Clark, F.W. The influence of sea power on...Roman republic. Menasha, 1915.

AH 7259.41.5 Starr, Chester G. The Roman imperial navy. 2. ed. N.Y., 1960.

AH 7259.46 Thiel, J.H. Studies on the history of Roman sea-power in Republican times. Amsterdam, 1946.

AH 7259.54 Thiel, J.H. A history of Roman sea-power before the second Pernic War. Amsterdam, 1954.

AH 7259.56 Wallinga, Herman Tammo. The boarding-bridge of the Romans. Groningen, 1956.

AH 7260 - 7269 Ancient Rome in general - Foreign relations, diplomacy (Table A)

AH 7269.33 Winkler, Heinz. Rom und Aegypten im 2. Jahrhundert v. Chr. Engelsdorf, 1933.

AH 7269.57 Kampe, Otto. Die römische Republik und ihre Auseinandersetzung mit den Grossmächten des Mittelmeerraumes bis 168. Stuttgart, 1957.

AH 7269.65.1 Dahlheim, Werner. Struktur und Entwicklung des römischen Volkerrechte im dritten und zweiten Jahrhundert v. Chr. München, 1968.

AH 7269.67 Lemosse, Maxime. Le regime des relations internationales dans le Haut-Empire romain. Paris, 1967.

AH 7272.2 Aufstieg und Niedergang der römischen Welt. Berlin, 1972-6v.

AH 7274 - 7279 Ancient Rome in general - General history (By date)

Htn AH 7276.25* Alciati, Andrea. Rerum patriae libri IIII. Mediolani, 1625.

Htn AH 7276.34F* Bellendenus, G. Supplicum libellorum August regis. Paris, 1634.

AH 7276.64 Alveri, Gasparo. Roma in ogni stato. Roma, 1664. 2v.

AH 7277.13 Echard, L. Roman history. London, 1713. 5v.

AH 7277.25 Catrou, François. Histoire romaine. Paris, 1725. 17v.

AH 7277.25.3 Catrou, François. Histoire romaine. v.18-21. Paris, 1734. 4v.

AH 7277.25.5F Catrou, François. Roman history. London, 1728. 6v.

AH 7277.27 A new essay on the Roman history. London, 1727.

AH 7277.38.2 Hooke, N. The Roman history. London, 1745-64. 3v.

AH 7277.38.3 Hooke, N. The Roman history. London, 1757. 4v.

AH 7277.38.9 Hooke, N. The Roman history. London, 18- . 3v.

AH 7277.42 Algemeene histori. Ultrecht, 1744.

Classified Listing

		Ancient Rome in general - General history (By date) - cont.
AH 7274 - 7279		**Ancient Rome in general - General history (By date) - cont.**
	AH 7277.52	Rollin, Charles. Histoire romaine. Paris, 1752. 8v.
NEDL	AH 7277.52.1	Rollin, Charles. Histoire romaine. Paris, 1758-68. 16v.
	AH 7277.52.2	Rollin, Charles. Histoire romaine. Paris, 1803-05. 16v.
	AH 7277.52.3	Rollin, Charles. Roman history. 2. ed. London, 1754. 16v.
	AH 7277.53	Holberg, Ludvig. Conjectures sur les causes de la grandeur des Romains. Leipzig, 1752.
	AH 7277.60	Macquer, P. Chronological abridgement of Roman history. London, 1760.
Htn	AH 7277.69*	Goldsmith, O. The Roman history, from the foundation of the city of Rome to the destruction of the western empire. London, 1769. 2v.
	AH 7277.70	Goldsmith, O. Roman history. London, 1770. 2v.
	AH 7277.70.3	Goldsmith, O. Roman history. London, 1786. 2v.
	AH 7277.70.5	Goldsmith, O. Roman history. London, 1805. 2v.
NEDL	AH 7277.70.7	Goldsmith, O. Roman history. London, 1821. 2v.
NEDL	AH 7277.70.9	Goldsmith, O. Roman history. Dublin, 1781.
NEDL	AH 7277.70.21	Goldsmith, O. Roman history. 35. American ed. Philadelphia, 1853.
NEDL	AH 7277.70.25	Goldsmith, O. Rōmaïkēs istorias. Athēnai, 1852.
	AH 7277.92	Adams, J. History of Rome. Dublin, 1792. 2v.
	AH 7277.95	Abrégé de l'histoire romaine. Londres, 1795.
	AH 7277.95.3	Abrégé de l'histoire romaine. 1. American ed. Baltimore, 1812.
	AH 7278.10F	Mirys, S.D. Histoire de la république romaine. Paris, 1810.
Htn	AH 7278.11*	Niebuhr, B.G. Römische Geschichte. Berlin, 1811. 2v.
Htn	AH 7278.11.3*	Schlegel, August W. Recension von Niebuhr's Römische Geschichte. n.p., 1816.
	AH 7278.11.5	Niebuhr, B.G. Römische Geschichte. 2. Aufl. Berlin, 1827.
NEDL	AH 7278.11.7	Niebuhr, B.G. Römische Geschichte. 3. Aufl. Berlin, 1828. 3v.
	AH 7278.11.9	Niebuhr, B.G. Vorträge über römische Geschichte. Berlin, 1846. 3v.
	AH 7278.11.11	Niebuhr, B.G. Römische Geschichte. Berlin, 1873. 3v.
	AH 7278.11.13	Niebuhr, B.G. History of Rome. Cambridge, 1828. 3v.
	AH 7278.11.15	Niebuhr, B.G. History of Rome. Philadelphia, 1835. 2v.
	AH 7278.11.16	Niebuhr, B.G. History of Rome. Philadelphia, 1844. 2v.
	AH 7278.11.18A	Niebuhr, B.G. History of Rome. London, 1851. 3v.
	AH 7278.11.18B	Niebuhr, B.G. History of Rome. v.3. London, 1851.
	AH 7278.11.21	Niebuhr, B.G. History of Rome. London, 1844. 2v.
	AH 7278.11.23	Niebuhr, B.G. Römische Geschichte. Jena, 1844. 2v.
	AH 7278.11.24	Niebuhr, B.G. Lectures on the History of Rome. London, 1848.
	AH 7278.11.25	Niebuhr, B.G. Lectures on the History of Rome. 2. ed. London, 1849. 3v.
	AH 7278.11.26	Niebuhr, B.G. Lectures of Roman history. London, 1850. 3v.
	AH 7278.11.27	Niebuhr, B.G. Lectures on the History of Rome. 3. ed. London, 1852. 3v.
	AH 7278.11.29	Niebuhr, B.G. Lectures on the History of Rome. 4. ed. London, 1873?
	AH 7278.18	Bankes, H. History of Rome. London, 1818. 2v.
	AH 7278.18.5F	Rogers, Eliza. History of the Roman Empire. Atlas. London, 1818.
VAH	7278.20	Stories from Roman history, by a lady. Boston, 182-?
	AH 7278.24	Irving, C. Catechism of Roman history. 2. American ed. N.Y., 1824.
	AH 7278.28	Cobbett, W. Elements of Roman history. London, 1828.
	AH 7278.28.2	Cobbett, W. Abridged history of emperors. London, 1829.
	AH 7278.30	History of Rome. v.1-5. London, 1830-
	AH 7278.32.5	Lamé Fleury, J.R. L'histoire romaine racontée aux enfants. Paris, 1869-70. 2v.
	AH 7278.33	Michelet, J. Histoire romaine. 2. ed. Paris, 1833. 2v.
	AH 7278.33.3	Michelet, J. Histoire romaine. 3. ed. Paris, 1843. 2v.
	AH 7278.33.5	Michelet, J. History of the Roman Republic. London, 1847.
	AH 7278.33.6	Michelet, J. History of the Roman Republic. N.Y., 1847.
	AH 7278.33.15	Michelet, J. History of the Roman Republic. N.Y., 1859.
	AH 7278.37	Bell, R. History of Rome. Philadelphia, 1837.
NEDL	AH 7278.37.3	Lardner, D. Cabinet cyclopedia. London, 1833. 2v.
	AH 7278.39	Hetherington, W.M. History of Rome. Edinburgh, 1839.
	AH 7278.39.5	Keightley, T. History of Rome. Boston, 1839.
	AH 7278.39.7	Fiedler, F.A.M. Geschichte des römischen Staates. Leipzig, 1839.
	AH 7278.39.9	Fiedler, F.A.M. Geschichte der Römer. 2. Aufl. Leipzig, 1854.
	AH 7278.40	Arnold, T. History of Rome. London, 1840. 3v.
	AH 7278.40.3A	Arnold, T. History of Rome. v.1-3. N.Y., 1846. 2v.
	AH 7278.40.3B	Arnold, T. History of Rome. v.1-3. N.Y., 1846. 2v.
	AH 7278.40.7	Arnold, T. History of Rome. N.Y., 1857.
	AH 7278.43	Kortüm, F. Römische Geschichte. Heidelberg, 1843.
	AH 7278.44	Roth, C.L. Römische Geschichte. v.1-4. Nürnberg, 1844. 3v.
	AH 7278.45	Society for Promoting Christian Knowledge, London. The Roman Empire. London, 1845.
	AH 7278.46	Arnold, T. History of the Roman Commonwealth. N.Y., 1846.
	AH 7278.46.5	Arnold, T. History of the later Roman Commonwealth. London, 1857. 2v.
	AH 7278.46.10	Laurian, A.T. Coup d'oeil sur l'histoire des roumains. Bucuresti, 1846.
	AH 7278.47	Schmitz, L. History of Rome. N.Y., 1847.
	AH 7278.47.2	Schmitz, L. A history of Rome from the earliest times to the death of Commodus, A.D. 192. Andover, 1847.
	AH 7278.51	Segur. Histoire romaine. Paris, 1851. 2v.
	AH 7278.53.3	Peter, C. Geschichte Roms. Halle, 1853. 2v.
	AH 7278.53.5	Peter, C. Geschichte Roms. v.1-2; v.3, pt.1-2. 2. Aufl. Halle, 1865. 4v.
	AH 7278.53.7	Peter, C. Geschichte Roms. 3. Aufl. Halle, 1870. 3v.
	AH 7278.53.9	Peter, C. Geschichte Roms. 4. Aufl. Halle, 1881. 3v.
	AH 7278.53.10	Schwegler, A. Römische Geschichte. Tübingen, 1853. 4v.
	AH 7278.53.11	Schwegler, A. Römische Geschichte. 2. Aufl. Tubingen, 1867-1872. 3v.
Htn	AH 7278.54*	Mommsen, T. Römische Geschichte. v.1-3, 5. Leipzig, 1954. 4v.
	AH 7278.54.3	Mommsen, T. Römische Geschichte. 2. Aufl. Berlin, 1856. 3v.
	AH 7278.54.4	Mommsen, T. Römische Geschichte. 4. Aufl. Berlin, 1865. 4v.
	AH 7278.54.5	Mommsen, T. Inhalts-Verzeichniss. Römische Geschichte. n.p., n.d.
	AH 7278.54.6	Mommsen, T. Römische Geschichte. 3. Aufl. Berlin, 1861. 3v.
	AH 7278.54.7	Mommsen, T. Römische Geschichte. 5. Aufl. v.1, pt.1-2; v.2-3. Berlin, 1868. 4v.
NEDL	AH 7278.54.9	Mommsen, T. Römische Geschichte. 6. Aufl. Berlin, 1874. 3v.
	AH 7278.54.9.5	Mommsen, T. Römische Geschichte. v.1-3, 7. Aufl. v.5, 3. Aufl. Berlin, 1881-86. 4v.
	AH 7278.54.10	Mommsen, T. Römische Geschichte. v.5. Berlin, 1885.
	AH 7278.54.10.15	Mommsen, T. Römische Geschichte. v.1-3, 5. Berlin, 1933. 4v.
	AH 7278.54.11.2	Mommsen, T. History of Rome. 2. ed. v.1-3; v.4, pt.1-2. London, 1864-67. 5v.
	AH 7278.54.12	Mommsen, T. History of Rome. London, 1868. 4v.
	AH 7278.54.13	Mommsen, T. Index to History of Rome. London, 1870.
NEDL	AH 7278.54.15	Mommsen, T. History of Rome. N.Y., 1869-70. 4v.
	AH 7278.54.16	Mommsen, T. History of Rome. N.Y., 1868. 4v.
	AH 7278.54.16.5	Mommsen, T. History of Rome. N.Y., 1871. 4v.
NEDL	AH 7278.54.17	Mommsen, T. History of Rome. N.Y., 1873. 2v.
	AH 7278.54.18	Mommsen, T. History of Rome. N.Y., 1885. 4v.
NEDL	AH 7278.54.18.9	Mommsen, T. History of Rome. Provinces of the Roman Empire from Caesar to Diocletian. N.Y., 1887. 2v.
	AH 7278.54.18.15	Mommsen, T. History of Rome. N.Y., 1894. 4v.
	AH 7278.54.19	Mommsen, T. History of Rome. N.Y., 1895. 5v.
	AH 7278.54.21	Mommsen, T. History of Rome. N.Y., 1900. 5v.
	AH 7278.54.23	Mommsen, T. Rome. v.3. Philadelphia, 1906.
	AH 7278.54.24	Mommsen, T. The history of Rome. N.Y., 1908. 5v.
	AH 7278.54.27	Mommsen, T. The history of Rome. London, 1920.
	AH 7278.54.28	Mommsen, T. The history of Rome. N.Y., 1958.
	AH 7278.54.28.10	Mommsen, T. The history of Rome. London, 1908-12. 5v.
	AH 7278.54.29	Mommsen, T. Histoire romaine. v.1-8. Paris, 1863. 4v.
	AH 7278.54.30	Mommsen, T. Histoire romaine. v.1-2, 3-4, 5-6, 7. Paris, 1882. 4v.
	AH 7278.54.30.5A	Mommsen, T. Das Weltreich der Caesaren. Wien, 1933.
	AH 7278.54.30.5B	Mommsen, T. Das Weltreich der Caesaren. Wien, 1933.
	AH 7278.54.30.10	Mommsen, T. Römische Geschichte. Wien, 1932.
	AH 7278.54.30.12	Mommsen, T. Römische Geschichte. Wien, 1934.
	AH 7278.54.30.15	Mommsen, T. Römische Geschichte. Wien, 1954.
	AH 7278.54.31	Mommsen, T. Historia de Roma. Madrid, 1877.
	AH 7278.54.32	Mommsen, T. Storia romana. Torino, 1857-63. 3v.
	AH 7278.54.32.5	Mommsen, T. Storia di Roma antica. Torino, 1943. 3v.
	AH 7278.54.33	Peter, Carl. Studien zur römische Geschichte. 2. Aufl. Halle, 1863.
	AH 7278.54.35	Nöldeke, T. Mommsen's Darstellung der römische Herrschaft. Leipzig, 1885.
	AH 7278.54.37	Pais, Ettore. Ottantaduesimo anniversario di Theodor Mommsen. Messina, 1899.
	AH 7278.54.39	Zangmeister, K. Theodor Mommsen als Schriftsteller. Berlin, 1905.
	AH 7278.54.41	Hirschfeld, O. Gedächtnisrede auf Theodor Mommsen. Berlin, 1904.
	AH 7278.54.46	Straeuli, Hans Heinrich. Theodor Mommsen's Römische Geschichte. Zuerich, 1948.
	AH 7278.55	Liddell, H.G. History of Rome. London, 1855. 2v.
NEDL	AH 7278.55.2A	Liddell, H.G. History of Rome. N.Y., 1857.
	AH 7278.55.2B	Liddell, H.G. History of Rome. N.Y., 1857.
NEDL	AH 7278.55.2.5	Liddell, H.G. History of Rome. N.Y., 1864.
NEDL	AH 7278.55.9A	Liddell, H.G. History of Rome. N.Y., 1879.
NEDL	AH 7278.55.9B	Liddell, H.G. History of Rome. N.Y., 1879.
	AH 7278.61	Turner, D.W. Roman history. 3. ed. London, 1861.
	AH 7278.62	Ampère, J.J. Histoire romaine. Paris, 1862. 4v.
	AH 7278.62.3	Ampère, J.J. L'histoire romaine à Rome. 3. éd. Paris, 1866-72. 4v.
	AH 7278.67	Duruy, V. Histoire romaine. Paris, 1867.
NEDL	AH 7278.67.3	Duruy, V. Histoire universelle. Paris, 1876.
	AH 7278.67.17	Duruy, V. Histoire romaine. Paris, 1889.
	AH 7278.67.27	Duruy, V. Histoire romaine. Paris, 1899.
	AH 7278.68	Ihne, W. Römische Geschichte. v.1-6, 7-8. Leipzig, 1868. 7v.
	AH 7278.68.3A	Ihne, W. History of Rome. London, 1871. 5v.
	AH 7278.68.3B	Ihne, W. History of Rome. London, 1871. 5v.
NEDL	AH 7278.68.3C	Ihne, W. History of Rome. v.2, 5. London, 1871. 2v.
	AH 7278.68.7	Ihne, W. Römische Geschichte. 2. Aufl. v.1-2. Leipzig, 1893.
Htn	AH 7278.69.2*	Stoll, H.W. Geschichte der Römer bis zum Untergange der Republik. 2. Aufl. Hannover, 1871. 2v.
	AH 7278.70	Duruy, V. Histoire des romains. Paris, 1870. 7v.
	AH 7278.70.3	Duruy, V. Histoire des romains. Paris, 1881-90. 7v.
NEDL	AH 7278.70.5	Duruy, V. History of Rome. v.1-6, pt.1-2. London, 1884- 12v.
	AH 7278.70.9	Duruy, V. History of Rome. Boston, 1883. 16v.
	AH 7278.70.15F	Duruy, V. History of Rome. v.1-8, pt.1-2. Boston, 1884-87. 16v.
	AH 7278.72	Thalheimer, Mary Elsie. Manual of ancient history. Pt.3. Cincinnati, 1872.
	AH 7278.74	Smith, William. Smaller history of Rome. N.Y., 1874.
NEDL	AH 7278.74.8	Smith, William. A smaller history of Rome. N.Y., 1881.
	AH 7278.75	Merivale, C. General history of Rome. N.Y., 1875.
	AH 7278.76	Pennell, R.F. Rome. Boston, 1876.
	AH 7278.76.1	Pennell, R.F. Rome. Boston, 1886.
	AH 7278.76.2	Pennell, R.F. Ancient Rome. Boston, 1890.
	AH 7278.76.10	Talbot, E. Histoire romaine. Paris, 1876.
	AH 7278.79	Leighton, R.F. History of Rome. N.Y., 1879.
NEDL	AH 7278.79.4	Leighton, R.F. History of Rome. N.Y., 1880.
	AH 7278.79.12	Leighton, R.F. A history of Rome. N.Y., 1901.
	AH 7278.80F	Formby, Henry. Ancient Rome and its connection with the Christian religion. London, 1880.
	AH 7278.81	Pantaleoni, D. Storia...di Roma. Torino, 1881.
	AH 7278.83	Duruy, V. Petite histoire grecque. Paris, 1883.
	AH 7278.84	Matheson, P.E. Skeleton outline of Roman history. London, 1884.
	AH 7278.84.10	Matheson, P.E. Skeleton outline of Roman history down A.D. 180. London, 1922.
	AH 7278.85	Creighton, M. History of Rome. N.Y., 1885.
	AH 7278.85.2	Creighton, M. History of Rome. N.Y., 1888.
NEDL	AH 7278.85.2.5	Creighton, M. History of Rome. London, 1888.
	AH 7278.85.3A	Creighton, M. History of Rome. N.Y., 1875.
	AH 7278.85.3B	Creighton, M. History of Rome. N.Y., 1875.
	AH 7278.85.3.4	Creighton, M. History of Rome. N.Y., 1877.
	AH 7278.85.3.5	Creighton, M. History of Rome. N.Y., 1879.

Classified Listing

AH 7294 - 7299   Ancient Rome in general - General special - Miscellany (By date)

Htn   AH 7295.72*   Serdonati, Francesco. De' fatti d'arme de' Romani. Venetia, 1572.

Htn   AH 7295.89F*   Glandorp. Onomasticon historicae Romanae. Francofurti, 1859.

AH 7297.20   Vertot, R.A. History of revolutions of the Roman Republic. London, 1720. 2v.

AH 7297.20.2   Vertot, R.A. History of revolutions of the Roman Republic. London, 1721.

AH 7297.20.5   Vertot, R.A. Histoire des révolutions. Paris, 1796. 4v.

AH 7297.20.6   Vertot, R.A. Histoire des révolutions. 6e éd. Paris, 1767. 3v.

AH 7297.20.6.5   Vertot, R.A. Histoire des révolutions. 8e éd. Paris, 1786. 2v.

AH 7297.20.7   Vertot, R.A. Histoire des révolutions. Paris, 1833. 4v.

NEDL   AH 7297.20.15   Vertot, R.A. Historia de las revoluciones. Paris, 1825.

AH 7297.47   Zell, Carolus. Elogiorum Romae reliquae. Stuttgartie, 1847.

AH 7297.71   Perizonius, I. Animadversiones historicae. Altenburgi, 1771.

AH 7297.97   Wilcocks, J. Roman conversations. London, 1797. 2v.

AH 7298.21   Bertocchi, Fulvia. Racollta...istoria romana. Roma, 1821.

Htn   AH 7298.52*   À Beckett, G.A. The comic history of Rome. London, 1852?

AH 7298.55   Lewis, George C. An inquiry...early Roman history. London, 1855. 2v.

AH 7298.55.3   Lewis, George C. Untersuchungen...altrömischen Geschichte. Hannover, 1863.

AH 7298.63   Labberton, R.H. Historical questions. Philadelphia, 1863.

AH 7298.64   Kingsley, Charles. The Roman and the Teuton. Cambridge, 1864.

NEDL   AH 7298.64.1   Kingsley, Charles. The Roman and the Teuton. London, 1879.

NEDL   AH 7298.64.2   Kingsley, Charles. The Roman and the Teuton. London, 1890.

AH 7298.64.3   Kingsley, Charles. The Roman and the Teuton. London, 1881.

AH 7298.64.5   Kingsley, Charles. The Roman and the Teuton. London, 1889.

AH 7298.65   Wolterstonff, A. Bilder aus dem römischen Alterthum. Halberstadt, 1865.

AH 7298.71A   À Beckett, G.A. Comic history of Rome. London, n.d.

AH 7298.71B   À Beckett, G.A. Comic history of Rome. London, n.d.

AH 7298.76   Büttner-Wobst, Theodor. De legationibus reipublicae liberae temporibus Romam missis. Diss. Lipsiae, 1876.

AH 7298.81.1   Budinszky, Alexander. Die Ausbreitung der lateinischen Sprache über Italien und die Provinzen des römischen Reiches. Berlin, Wiesbaden, 1973.

AH 7298.82   Kuntze, J.E. Prolegomena zur Geschichte Roms. Leipzig, 1882.

AH 7298.86.2   Mommsen, Theodor. The provinces of the Roman empire, from Caesar to Diocletian. N.Y., 1899. 2v.

AH 7298.86.3   Mommsen, Theodor. The provinces of the Roman empire from Caesar to Diocletian. London, 1909. 2v.

AH 7298.86.5   Mommsen, Theodor. The provinces of the Roman Empire; the European provinces. Chicago, 1968.

AH 7298.90   Hübner, Emil. Römische Herrschaft in Westeuropa. Berlin, 1890.

AH 7298.99F   Gubernatis, A. de. Roma e l'Oriente. Roma, 1899.

AH 7299.01   Barbagallo, C. Le relazioni politiche di Roma con l'egitto. Roma, 1901.

AH 7299.04   Garofalo, F.P. Studi storici. Noto, 1904.

AH 7299.05   Mommsen, Theodor. Gesammelte Schriften. Berlin, 1905. 8v.

AH 7299.05.2   Assmann, J. Dissertatio Historica. Langensalzae, 1905.

AH 7299.05.4   Mommsen, Theodor. Reden und Aufsätze. Berlin, 1905.

AH 7299.05.5   Mommsen, Theodor. Reden und Aufsätze. 2. Aufl. Berlin, 1905.

AH 7299.05.7   Mommsen, Theodor. Reden und Aufsätze. Berlin, 1912.

AH 7299.06   Hardy, E.G. Studies in Roman history. London, 1906.

AH 7299.06.2   Hardy, E.G. Studies in Roman history. London, 1909.

AH 7299.11   Pflüger, P. Die soziale Frage im alten Rom. Zürich, 1911.

AH 7299.16   Piganiol, André. Essai sur les origines de Rome. Thèse. Paris, 1916.

AH 7299.22   Cichorius, C. Römische Studien, historisches, epigraphisches, literargeschichtliches. Leipzig, 1922.

AH 7299.23   Jerome, Thomas S. Aspects of the study of Roman history. N.Y., 1923.

AH 7299.26   Barbagallo, C. Il problema delle origini di Roma. Milano, 1926.

AH 7299.33.5   Heuss, Alfred. Amicitia. Inaug. Diss. Gräfenhainichen, 1933.

AH 7299.33.10   Regano, A. Origine e creazione del fascio. Napoli, 1933.

AH 7299.36.2   Levi, Mario A. La pooitica imperiale di Roma. 2. ed. Torino, 1936.

AH 7299.37.5   Jones, Arnold H.M. The cities of the eastern Roman provinces. Oxford, 1937.

AH 7299.37.6   Jones, Arnold H.M. The cities of the eastern Roman provinces. 2. ed. Oxford, 1971.

AH 7299.38   Fucho, Harold. Der geistige Widerstand gegen Rom. Berlin, 1938.

AH 7299.39   Haskell, Henry J. The new deal in old Rome; how government in the ancient world tried to deal with modern problems. N.Y., 1939.

AH 7299.40   Curotto, Ernest. Antichità classica. Torino, 1940.

NEDL   AH 7299.41   Calestoni, V. Origini della razza italiana. Milano, 1941.

NEDL   AH 7299.42   Canavesi, Manlio. La politica estera di Roma antica. Milano, 1942. 2v.

NEDL   AH 7299.44A   Gelzer, Matthias. Vom romanischen Staat. Leipzig, 1944. 2v.

NEDL   AH 7299.44B   Gelzer, Matthias. Vom romanischen Staat. Leipzig, 1944. 2v.

AH 7299.49.2   Barrow, R.H. The Romans. Harmondsworth, 1958.

AH 7299.49.3   Barrow, R.H. The Romans. Chicago, 1964.

AH 7299.55   International Congress of Roman Frontier Studies, 2d, Carnuntum, 1955. Carnuntina; Ergebnisse der Forschung über die Grenzprovinzen des Römischen Reiches. Graz, 1956.

AH 7299.57   Alföldi, Andras. Die trojanischen Urahnen der Römer. Basel, 1957.

AH 7299.57.5   Harmond, Louis. Le patronat sur les collectivités publiques des origines au Bas-Empire. Paris, 1957.

AH 7299.57.6   Harmond, Louis. Le patronat sur les collectivités publiques des origines au Bas-Empire. Paris, 1957.

AH 7299.62   Gelzer, Matthias. Kleine Schriften. Wiesbaden, 1962-64. 3v.

AH 7294 - 7299   Ancient Rome in general - General special - Miscellany (By date) - cont.

AH 7299.64   Ziegber, K.H. Die Beziehungen zwischen Rom und dem Partherreich. Wiesbaden, 1964.

AH 7299.65   Deininger, Jürgen. Die Provinziallandtage der römischen Kaiserzeit von Augustus bis zum Ende des dritten Jahrhunderts nach Christ. München, 1965.

AH 7299.66   MacMullen, Ramsay. Enemies of the Roman order. Cambridge, 1966.

AH 7299.68   Benzinger, Josef. Invectiva in Romam. Lübeck, 1968.

AH 7299.69   Salmon, Edward T. Roman colonization under the Republic. London, 1969.

AH 7299.71   Korpanty, Jósef. Rozwòj politycznej roli jednostki w republice rsymskiej i jego olkicije w literaturze. Wyd. 1. Wrocław, 1970.

AH 7299.71.5   Maiak, I.L. Vzaimsotnosheniia Rima i italiitsev v III-II vv. do n.e. (do grakhanskogo dvisheniia). Moskva, 1971.

AH 7299.71.10   Thompson, David. The idea of Rome; from antiquity to the Renaissance. Albuquerque, 1971.

AH 7299.72   Storoni Mazzalani. L'impero sena fine. Milano, 1972.

AH 7299.72.5   Aufstieg und Niedergang der römischen Welt. v.1-2. Berlin, 1972- 6v.

AH 7299.73   Piganiol, André. Scripta varia. Bruxelles, 1973. 3v.

AH 7300 - 7309   Ancient Rome in general - General special - Philosophy of history (Table A)

Htn   AH 7307.34*   Montesquieu, Charles de. Considérations sur les causes de la grandeur des Romains. 2. éd. Amsterdam, 1734.

Htn   AH 7307.34.3*   Montesquieu, Charles de. Considérations sur les causes de la grandeur des Romains. 2. éd. Amsterdam, 1935.

AH 7307.34.5   Montesquieu, Charles de. Considérations sur les causes de la grandeur des Romains. Amsterdam, 1759.

AH 7307.34.7   Montesquieu, Charles de. Considérations sur les causes de la grandeur des Romains. Amsterdam, 1761.

AH 7307.34.9   Montesquieu, Charles de. De la grandeur des Romains. Paris, 1870.

AH 7307.34.11   Montesquieu, Charles de. Considérations sur les causes de la grandeur des Romains. Paris, 1876.

AH 7307.34.12   Montesquieu, Charles de. Considérations sur les causes de la grandeur des Romains. Paris, 1876.

AH 7307.34.12.5   Montesquieu, Charles de. De la grandeur des Romains. Paris, 1879.

AH 7307.34.13   Montesquieu, Charles de. Considérations sur les causes de la grandeur des Romains. Paris, 1887.

AH 7307.34.14   Montesquieu, Charles de. Considérations sur les causes de la grandeur des Romains. Paris, 1894.

AH 7307.34.15   Montesquieu, Charles de. Considérations sur les causes de la grandeur des Romains. Paris, 1896.

AH 7307.34.17   Montesquieu, Charles de. Reflections on the causes of the rise and fall of the Romans. London, 1752.

AH 7307.34.18   Montesquieu, Charles de. Considérations sur les causes de la grandeur des Romains, et de leur décadence. Paris, 1771.

AH 7307.34.19   Montesquieu, Charles de. Considerations on the causes of the grandeur of the Romans. N.Y., 1882.

AH 7307.34.30   Montesquieu, Charles de. Considérations sur les causes de la grandeur des Romains. Paris, 1945.

AH 7307.34.31   Montesquieu, Charles de. Betrachtungen über die Ursachen von Grösse und Niedergang der Römer. Bremen, 1962.

AH 7307.51   Mably, G.B. Observations on the Romans. London, 1751.

AH 7308.49   Eliot, Samuel. Liberty of Rome. N.Y., 1849. 2v.

AH 7308.49.2   Eliot, Samuel. History of the liberty of the ancient Romans. Boston, 1853.

AH 7308.61   Lasaulx, E. von. Zur Philosophie der römischen Geschichte. München, 1861.

AH 7308.65   Thierry, M. Amédée. Tableau de l'Empire Romain. Paris, 1865.

NEDL   AH 7308.76A   Thierry, A.S.D. Tableau de l'Empire Romain. Paris, 1876.

NEDL   AH 7308.76B   Thierry, A.S.D. Tableau de l'Empire Romain. Paris, 1876.

AH 7308.76.2   Thierry, A.S.D. Tableau de l'Empire Romair. Paris, 1862.

AH 7308.76.3A   Thierry, A.S.D. Tableau de l'Empire Romain. 6e éd. Paris, 1872.

NEDL   AH 7308.76.3B   Thierry, A.S.D. Tableau de l'Empire Romain. 6e éd. Paris, 1872.

AH 7308.82   Graf, A. Roma. Torino, 1882. 2v.

AH 7309.04   Ferrero, G. Grandeur et décadence de Rome. Paris, 1904. 6v.

NEDL   AH 7309.04.1   Ferrero, G. Grandeur et décadence de Rome. Paris, 1907. 5v.

AH 7309.04.2   Ferrero, G. Grandezza e decadenza di Roma. Milano, 1907. 5v.

AH 7309.04.3A   Ferrero, G. Greatness and decline of Rome. v.1-3,5. N.Y., 1907-09. 4v.

NEDL   AH 7309.04.3B   Ferrero, G. Greatness and decline of Rome. v.1-2,5. N.Y., 1907-09. 3v.

AH 7309.04.4   Ferrero, G. Greatness and decline of Rome. N.Y., 1909-10. 5v.

NEDL   AH 7309.04.6   Ferrero, G. Greatness and decline of Rome. N.Y., 1908. 4v.

AH 7309.04.7   Ferrero, G. Greatness and decline of Rome. London, 1909. 5v.

AH 7309.04.8A   Ferrero, G. Greatness and decline of Rome. N.Y., 1909. 5v.

AH 7309.04.8B   Ferrero, G. Greatness and decline of Rome. N.Y., 1909. 5v.

AH 7309.04.10   Ferrero, G. Grösse und Niedergang Roms. Stuttgart, 1908-09. 5v.

AH 7309.09   Ferrero, G. Characters and events of Roman history. N.Y., 1909.

AH 7309.09.5   Ferrero, G. Characters and events of Roman history. N.Y., 1922.

AH 7309.14   Ferrero, G. Ancient Rome and modern America. N.Y., 1914.

AH 7309.21A   Ferrero, G. The ruin of the ancient civilization and the triumph of Christianity. N.Y., 1921.

AH 7309.21B   Ferrero, G. The ruin of the ancient civilization and the triumph of Christianity. N.Y., 1921.

AH 7309.21.3   Ferrero, G. La ruine de la civilisation antique. Paris, 1921.

AH 7309.21.5   Heinze, Richard. Von den Ursachen der Grösse Roms. Leipzig, 1921.

AH 7309.22   Heitland, William E. The Roman fate; an essay. Cambridge, 1922.

AH 7309.25   Sorel, Georges. La ruine du monde antique. 2e éd. Paris, 1925.

AH 7309.25.5   Heitland, W.E. Iterum, or A further discussion of the Roman fate. Cambridge, 1925.

AH 7309.38   Heinze, Richard. Vom Geist des Römertums. Leipzig, 1938.

Classified Listing

AH 7300 - 7309   Ancient Rome in general - General special - Philosophy of history (Table A) - cont.

AH 7309.38.3   Heinze, Richard. Vom Geist des Römertums. 3. Aufl. Darmstadt, 1960.

AH 7309.38.5   Momigliano, Arnaldo. La formazione della moderna storiografia sull'impiro romano. Torino, 1938.

AH 7309.54   Mazzarino, Santo. Storia romana e storiografia moderna. Napoli, 1954.

AH 7309.61   Espadas Burgos, Manuel. La periodización de la historiagrafia romana. Madrid, 1961.

AH 7309.66   Schoenlein, Peter Wilhelm. Sittliches Bewusstsein als Handlungsmotiv bei römischen Historiken. Erlangen, 1966.

AH 7320 - 7329   Ancient Rome in general - General special - Races (Table A)

AH 7328.78   Cuno, J.G. Vorgeschichte Roms. Leipzig, 1878. 2v.

AH 7328.82   Hudson, E.H. A history of the Jews in Rome. London, 1882.

AH 7328.84   Hudson, E.H. History of the Jews in Rome. London, 1884.

AH 7329.12   Juster, Jean. Les droits politiques des juifs dans L'empire romain. Paris, 1912.

AH 7329.14   Juster, Jean. Les juifs dans l'empire romain. Paris, 1914. 2v.

AH 7329.27   La Piana, George. Foreign groups in Rome during the first centuries of the empire. Cambridge, 1927.

AH 7329.60   Leon, Harry J. The Jews of ancient Rome. 1. ed. Philadelphia, 1960.

AH 7329.67   Sherwin-White, Adrian N. Racial prejudice in imperial Rome. Cambridge, 1967.

AH 7330 - 7339   Ancient Rome in general - General special - Collected biographies (Table A)

AH 7338.14   Berwick, Edward. Lives of Caius A. Pollio. London, 1814.

AH 7338.18   Rogers, Eliza. History of the Roman Empire. London, 1818. 5v.

AH 7338.97   Klebs, E. Prosopographia Imperii Romani. Berolini, 1897-98. 3v.

AH 7338.97.5   Groag, E. Prosopographia Imperii Romani. 2. ed. v.1-4, pt.1-3. Berolini, 1933-52. 4v.

AH 7339.13   Birt, Theodor. Römische Charakterköpfe. Leipzig, 1913.

AH 7339.13.3   Birt, Theodor. Römische Charakterköpfe. 3. Aufl. Leipzig, 1918.

AH 7339.13.4   Birt, Theodor. Zur Kulturgeschichte Roms. 4. Aufl. Leipzig, 1919.

AH 7339.13.7   Birt, Theodor. Römische Charakterköpfe. Leipzig, 1927.

AH 7339.19.2   Birt, Theodor. Charakterbilder Spätroms. 2. Aufl. Leipzig, 1920.

AH 7339.19.3   Birt, Theodor. Charakterbilder Spätroms. 3. Aufl. Leipzig, 1923.

AH 7339.22   Hamilton, M.A. Ancient Rome. Oxford, 1922.

AH 7339.35A   Showerman, G. Monuments and men of ancient Rome. N.Y., 1935.

AH 7339.35B   Showerman, G. Monuments and men of ancient Rome. N.Y., 1935.

AH 7339.51   Broughton, Thomas R.S. The magistrates of the Roman Republic. N.Y., 1951-52. 2v.

AH 7339.51.1   Broughton, Thomas R.S. The magistrates of the Roman Republic. Supplement. N.Y., 1960.

AH 7339.56   Lissner, Ivar. Die Casaren. Olten, 1956.

AH 7339.56.2   Lissner, Ivar. The Caesars: might and madness. N.Y., 1958.

AH 7339.71   Jones, Arnold Hugh Martin. The prosopography of the later Roman Empire. Cambridge, Eng., 1971-

AH 7339.72   Saklatvala, Beram. The Caesars: the Roman Empire and its rulers. Newton Abbott, 1972.

AH 7400 - 7409   Ancient Rome in general - History by periods - Origins and Kings, 753-510 B.C. (Table A)

Htn   AH 7406.32*   Malvezzi, V. Il Tarquinio superbo. Bologna, 1632.

Htn   AH 7406.36*   Malvezzi, V. Princeps, eiusque arcana. n.p., n.d. 2 pam.

Htn   AH 7406.37*   Malvezzi, V. Romulus and Tarquin. London, 1637.

Htn   AH 7406.38*   Malvezzi, V. Romulus and Tarquin. London, 1638.

Htn   AH 7406.47*   Malvezzi, V. Il Romulo. Geneva, 1647. 5 pam.

Htn   AH 7406.48*   Malvezzi, V. Romulus and Tarquin. 3. ed. London, 1648.

AH 7408.21   Pöhlmann, Robert. Die Anfange Roms. Erlangen, 1887.

AH 7408.21.5   Micali, G. L'Italia avanti il Domino dei Romani. 2. ed. v.1-2, 3-4. Firenze, 1821. 2v.

AH 7408.21.6F   Micali, G. Antichi monumenti per servire all'opera intitolata l'Italia. Firenze, 1821.

AH 7408.28   Blum, K.L. Einleitung im Rom's alte Geschichte. Berlin, 1828.

AH 7408.39   Orioli, F. Dei sette re di Roma e del cominciamento del Consolato. Fiesole, 1839.

AH 7408.47   Schoemann, G.F. De tullo hostilio. Gryphiswaldiae, 1847.

AH 7408.51   Gerlach, F.D. Von den Quellen der ältesten römischen Geschichte. Basel, 1853.

AH 7408.52   Newman, F.W. Regal Rome. London, 1852.

AH 7408.52.5   Abbott, Jacob. History of Romulus. N.Y., 1852.

AH 7408.53   Gerlach, F.D. Quellen der altesten römischen Geschichte. Basel, 1853.

AH 7408.58   Linker, G. Die älteste Sagengeschichte Roms. Wien, 1858.

AH 7408.68A   Dyer, Thomas H. History of the kings of Rome. London, 1868.

NEDL   AH 7408.68B   Dyer, Thomas H. History of the kings of Rome. London, 1868.

NEDL   AH 7408.68.3   Dyer, Thomas H. History of the kings of Rome. Philadelphia, 1868.

AH 7408.68.5   Rawlinson, George. Recent histories of early Rome. London, 1868.

AH 7408.71   Modestow, B. Der Gebrauch der Schrift unter den römischen Königen. Berlin, 1871.

AH 7408.72   Laing, C.H.B. Seven kings of the seven hills. Philadelphia, 1872.

AH 7408.77   Abbott, Jacob. History of Romulus. N.Y., 1877.

NEDL   AH 7408.77.2   Abbott, Jacob. History of Romulus. N.Y., 1852.

NEDL   AH 7408.77.25   Ihne, W. Early Rome. 2. ed. London, 1877.

NEDL   AH 7408.78   Ihne, W. Early Rome. N.Y., 1878.

NEDL   AH 7408.78.2   Ihne, W. Early Rome. London, 1876.

NEDL   AH 7408.78.3   Ihne, W. Early Rome. 4th ed. London, 1886.

NEDL   AH 7408.78.5   Ihne, W. Early Rome. N.Y., 1892.

AH 7408.78.7   Ihne, W. Early Rome. N.Y., 1896.

AH 7408.78.11   Ihne, W. Early Rome. London, 1913.

AH 7408.81   Lange, C.C.L. Das römische Königthum. Leipzig, 1881.

AH 7408.84   Bonghi, R. Storia di Roma. v.3. Milano, 1896.

AH 7408.87   Jordan, Henri. Die Könige im alten Italien. Berlin, 1887.

AH 7408.97   Potter, G.S. The founders of Rome. Buffalo, 1897.

AH 7409.12   Kornemann, E. Der Priester Codex in der Regia. Tübingen, 1912.

AH 7400 - 7409   Ancient Rome in general - History by periods - Origins and Kings, 753-510 B.C. (Table A) - cont.

AH 7409.14   Lloyd, Thomas. The making of the Roman people. London, 1914.

AH 7409.38   Colonna di Cesaro, G.A. Il mistero delle origini di Roma. Milano, 1938.

AH 7409.49   Cardinali, Giuseppe. Le origini di Roma. Roma, 1949.

AH 7409.51   Bömer, Franz. Rom und Troia. Baden Baden, 1951.

AH 7409.57   Accame, Silvio. Le origini di Roma. Napoli, 1957.

AH 7409.58   Bloch, Raymond. Les origins de Rome. 3. ed. Paris, 1958.

AH 7409.58.5   Bloch, Raymond. The origins of Rome. London, 1960.

AH 7409.59   Accame, Silvio. I re di Roma nella leggenda e nella storia. Napoli, 1959.

AH 7409.59.5   Francisci, Pietro. Primordia civitates. Romae, 1959.

AH 7409.60   Franzero, A.M. The life and times of Tarquin the Etruscan. London, 1960.

AH 7409.62   Erasmus, Hendrik. The origins of Rome. Assen, 1962.

AH 7409.65A   Alföldi, Andras. Early Rome and the Latins. Ann Arbor, 1965.

AH 7409.65B   Alföldi, Andras. Early Rome and the Latins. Ann Arbor, 1965.

AH 7409.67   Poucet, Jacques. Recherches sur la légende sabine des origines de Rome. Louvain, 1967.

AH 7409.70   Lukan, Karl. Romulus, oder Auf den Spuren der Gründer Roms. Wien, 1970.

AH 7409.70.5   Peruzzi, Emilio. Origini di Roma. Firenze, 1970- 2v.

AH 7410 - 7419   Ancient Rome in general - History by periods - Republic, 509-27 B.C. - General works (Table A)

AH 7411.01   Pamphlet box. Roman republic.

Htn   AH 7416.01*   Fulbeck, William. An historical collection of the continuall factions...of the Romans and Italians...before Augustus Caesar. London, 1601.

AH 7417.83   Ferguson, A. History of...Roman republic. London, 1783. 3v.

AH 7417.83.3   Ferguson, A. A history of...Roman republic. Dublin, 1783. 3v.

NEDL   AH 7417.83.5A   Ferguson, A. A history of...Roman republic. 1. American ed. Philadelphia, 1805. 3v.

NEDL   AH 7417.83.5B   Ferguson, A. A history of...Roman republic. 1. American ed. Philadelphia, 1805. 3v.

NEDL   AH 7417.83.9   Ferguson, A. History of...Roman republic. Philadelphia, 1811. 3v.

AH 7417.83.11   Ferguson, A. History of...Roman republic. London, 1825.

NEDL   AH 7417.83.13   Ferguson, A. History of...Roman republic. Philadelphia, 1830.

NEDL   AH 7417.83.14   Ferguson, A. History of the progress and termination of the Roman republic. N.Y., 1836.

NEDL   AH 7417.83.15   Ferguson, A. A history of the progress and termination of the Roman republic. N.Y., 1841.

NEDL   AH 7417.83.17   Ferguson, A. History of the progress and termination of the Roman republic. N.Y., 1852.

AH 7418.14   Ferrer, V.P. Historia de los dictadores de la republica romana. Cartagena de Indias, 1814.

AH 7418.60   Moule, H. The Roman republic. London, 1860.

AH 7418.68   Scholtze, A. Die Beziehungen zwischen Rom und Hellas. Leipzig, 1868.

AH 7418.77   Hinstin, G. Les romains à Athènes avant l'empire. Paris, 1877.

AH 7418.84   Nitzsch, K.W. Geschichte der römischen Republik. Leipzig, 1884.

AH 7418.85.3   Oliveira Martins, J.P. Historia da republica romana. 3. ed. v.1-2. Lisboa, 1919.

AH 7418.89   Mommsen, T. The history of the Roman republic. N.Y., 1889.

AH 7418.98.2   Woodhouse, Mason A. History of Rome, 390-202 B.C. London, 1911.

AH 7418.99   Tegge, August. Die Staatsgewalten der römischen Republik. Bunzlau, 1899.

AH 7419.08   Sands, P.C. Client princes of the Roman empire. Cambridge, 1908.

AH 7419.09   Heitland, W.E. Roman republic. Cambridge, 1909. 3v.

AH 7419.09.2   Heitland, W.E. Roman republic. Cambridge, 1923. 3v.

AH 7419.11   Vargas Vila, J.M. La república romana. Paris, 1911.

AH 7419.13   Lewis, J.H. The two great republics - Rome and the United States. Chicago, 1913.

AH 7419.13.5   Bloch, Gustave. La république romaine. Paris, 1913.

AH 7419.13.10   Gröseling, Johannes. Rom und Eturien von der Eroberung Vejis bis zur Mitte des 3. Jahrhunderts vor Christus. Borna, 1913.

AH 7419.14   Havell, Herbert L. Republican Rome. N.Y., 1914.

AH 7419.14.2A   Havell, Herbert L. Republican Rome. London, 1914.

AH 7419.14.2B   Havell, Herbert L. Republican Rome. London, 1914.

AH 7419.18   Pais, Ettore. Dalle guerre puniche a Cesare Augusto. v.1-2. Roma, 1918.

AH 7419.23   Holmes, T. Rice E. The Roman republic and the founder of the empire. Oxford, 1923. 3v.

AH 7419.26   Beloch, Julius. Römische Geschichte. Berlin, 1926.

AH 7419.27.5   Piganiol, André. La conquête romaine. 5. éd. Paris, 1967.

AH 7419.32   Robinson, Cyril E. A history of the Roman republic. N.Y., 1932.

AH 7419.37   Giannelli, Giulio. La repubblica romana. Milano, 1937.

AH 7419.40   Pais, Ettore. Des origines à l'achievement de la conquête. Paris, 1940.

AH 7419.44   Becerra Oliva, Guillermo. La republica romana. Cordoba, 1944.

AH 7419.48   Cowell, Frank R. Cicero and the Roman republic. London, 1948.

AH 7419.48.5   Cowell, Frank R. Cicero and the Roman republic. N.Y., 1948.

AH 7419.51   Calderini, A. L'espansione romana in occidente durante la repubblica. Milano, 1951.

AH 7419.55   Clerici, André. La république romaine. 1. éd. Paris, 1955.

AH 7419.62   Cassola, F. I gruppi politici romani nel III secolo A.C. Triesti, 1962.

AH 7419.63   Pieri, Piero. Genesi e sviluppi dell'imperialismo. Torino, 1963.

AH 7419.63.5   Werner, Robert. Der Beginn der römischen Republik. München, 1963.

AH 7419.64   Halsberghe, Gaston H. Zoeklicht op het oude Rome. Hasselt, 1964.

AH 7419.65   Boren, Henry Charles. The Roman republic. Princeton, 1965.

AH 7419.66   McDonald, Alex. Republican Rome. London, 1966.

AH 7419.67   Les origines de la république romaine. Vandoeuvres, 1967.

AH 7419.67.5   Ooteghem, Jules van. Les Crecilii Metelli de la république. Namur, 1967?

AH 7410 - 7419   Ancient Rome in general - History by periods - Republic,
509-27 B.C. - General works (Table A) - cont.

AH 7419.68   Lintott, Andrew W. Violence in republican Rome.
Oxford, 1968.

AH 7419.72   Combès, Robert. La république à Rome, 509-29 avant
Jésus-Christ. Paris, 1972.

AH 7419.72.5   Nechai, Fedor M. Obrazovanie rimskogo gosudarstva.
Minsk, 1972.

AH 7419.72.10   Gruen, Erich Stephen. The Roman republic.
Washington, 1972.

AH 7420 - 7429   Ancient Rome in general - History by periods - Republic,
509-27 B.C. - 509-343 (Table A)

AH 7428.19   Wachsmuth, W. Ältere Geschichte des römischen Staates.
Halle, 1819.

AH 7428.91   Burger, Combertus P. Sechzig Jahre aus der älteren
Geschichte Roms. Amsterdam, 1891.

AH 7428.94   Burger, Combertus P. Neue Forschungen zur älteren
Geschichte Roms. Amsterdam, 1894. 2v.

AH 7430 - 7439   Ancient Rome in general - History by periods - Republic,
509-27 B.C. - 343-265 (Table A)

AH 7438.42   Saal, N. De appio Claudio Caeco commentatio historica.
Köln, 1842.

AH 7438.63   Siebert, W. Ueber Appius Claudius Caecus. Kassel, 1863.
AH 7438.72   Gerlach, F.D. Griechischer Einfluss in Rom. Basel, 1872.
AH 7438.84   Burger, Combertus P. De bello cum Samnitibus secundo.
Harlemi, 1884.

AH 7438.90   Sieke, Carl. Appius Claudius Caesar Censor.
Marburg, 1890.

AH 7438.93   Binneboessel, P. Untersuchungen über...Geschichte.
Halle, 1893.

AH 7438.98   Burger, Combertus P. Der Kampf zwischen Rom und Samnium.
Amsterdam, 1898.

AH 7438.98.5   Pirro, A. La seconda guerra samnitica. Salerno, 1898.
AH 7439.26   Spaeth, John W. A study of the causes of Rome's wars from
343 to 265 B.C. Diss. Princeton, 1926.

AH 7440 - 7449   Ancient Rome in general - History by periods - Republic,
509-27 B.C. - 264-201 (Table A)

Htn   AH 7445.02*   Acciajuoli, D. Hannibalis atque Scipionis...ducum historie
eleganti dulcique stilo coscriptac. Swollensi, 1502.

Htn   AH 7445.44*   Cope, Anthony. The historie of two the moste noble
capitaines. Londini, 1544.

Htn   AH 7445.48*   Cope, Anthony. Historie of two the moste noble
capitaines...Anniball...Scipio. Londini, 1548.

AH 7446.17   Scipio, L.C. Vetustissima inscriptio. Romae, 1617.
AH 7447.94   Whitaker, J. Course of Hannibal over the Alps.
London, 1794. 2v.

AH 7448.12F   Vaudoncourt, F. Guillaume. Histoire des campagnes
d'Annibal. Milan, 1812. 3v.

AH 7448.18   DeLuc, J.A. Histoire du passage des Alpes par Annibal.
Genève, 1818.

Htn   AH 7448.18.2*   Long, H.L. March of Hannibal from Rome. London, 1831.
4 pam.

AH 7448.18.3   Ellis, Robert. Treatise on Hannibal's Passage.
Cambridge, 1853.

AH 7448.18.4   Rauchenstein, F. Nochmals Hannibals Alpenübergang.
Aarau, 1864.

AH 7448.18.5   Law, William J. The Alps of Hannibal. London, 1866.
2v.

AH 7448.18.6   Ellis, Robert. An inquiry into the ancient routes between
Italy and Gaul. Cambridge, Eng., 1867.

AH 7448.18.7   Linke, Otto. Die Controverse über Hannibals Alpenübergang.
Breslau, 1873.

AH 7448.18.8   Perrin, J.B. Marche d'Annibal. Paris, 1887.
AH 7448.18.9   Fuchs, J. Hannibals Alpenübergang. Wien, 1897.
AH 7448.18.10   Osiander, W. Der Hannibalweg. Berlin, 1901.
AH 7448.18.11A   Azan, Paul. Annibal dans les Alpes. Oran, 1902.
AH 7448.18.11B   Azan, Paul. Annibal dans les Alpes. Oran, 1902.
AH 7448.18.12   Montanari, T. Punto per Punto. Mantova, 1903.
AH 7448.18.13   Colin, J. Annibal en Gaule. Paris, 1904.
AH 7448.18.14   Hesselmeyer, E. Hannibals Alpenübergang. Tübingen, 1906.
AH 7448.18.15   Wilkinson, S. Hannibal's march through the Alps.
Oxford, 1911.

AH 7448.20   Wickham, Henry L. A dissertation on the passage of
Hannibal over the Alps. Oxford, 1820.

AH 7448.24   Giani, G.B. Battaglia del Ticino tra Annibale e Scipione.
Appendice. Milano, 1824-26.

AH 7448.26   Larauza, J.L. Histoire critique du passage des Alpes par
Annibal. Paris, 1826.

AH 7448.32   Beaujour, F. De l'expédition d'Annibal en Italie.
Paris, 1832.

AH 7448.41   Vincke, Ludwig. Der zweite punische Krieg und der
Kriegsplan der Carthager. Berlin, 1841.

AH 7448.48   Wijmre, J.A. Quaestiones criticae de belli punici.
Groningae, 1848.

AH 7448.49   Abbott, Jacob. History of Hannibal the Carthaginian.
N.Y., 1849.

AH 7448.64   Voigt, G. De primis Hannibalici belli annis quaestiones.
Berlin, 1864.

AH 7448.67   Müller, H. Die Schlacht an der Trebia. Berlin, 1867.
AH 7448.67.3   Pohle, R. De Pugna ad Trebiam Flumen. Inaug. Diss. Halis
Saxonum, 1872.

AH 7448.68   Alames, H. Hannibal sive disputatio. Dublin, 1868.
AH 7448.69   Jäger, Oskar. Die punischen Kriege. Halle, 1869.
AH 7448.70   Hennebert, E. Histoire d'Annibal. Paris, 1870. 3v.
AH 7448.70F   Hennebert, E. Histoire d'Annibal. Atlas. Paris, 1870.
AH 7448.70.5   Nissen, Heinrich. Commentatio de pace anno 201 a. Chr.
Carthaginiensibus data. Marburgi, 1870.

AH 7448.72   Vollmer, A. Quaeritur unde belli punici secundi.
Gottingae, 1872.

AH 7448.72.5   Gilles, I. Annibal et Publins Cornelius Scipion.
Paris, 1872.

AH 7448.72.10   Buchholz. Die Quellen des Appian und Dio Cassius für die
Geschichte des zweiten punischen Krieges. Pyritz, 1872.

AH 7448.73   Neuling, I. De belli punici primi scriptorum.
Gottingae, 1873.

AH 7448.73.10   Scott, Austin. Macedonien und Rom während des
Hannibalischen Krieges. Berlin, 1873.

AH 7448.74   Hesselbarth, H. De Pugna Cannensi. Gottingae, 1874.
AH 7448.74.2   Breyton, A. La bataille de Cannes. Paris, 1884.
AH 7448.74.3   Wilms, A. Die Schlacht bei Cannae. Hamburg, 1895.
AH 7448.74.4   Fried, F. Uber die Schlacht bei Cannä. Leipzig, 1898.
AH 7448.74.5   Schwab, Otto. Das Schlachtfeld von Cannä. München, 1898.
AH 7448.74.6   Schutz, Karl. Die Schlacht bei Cannä.
Donaueschingen, 1899.

AH 7448.75   Keller, Ludwig. Der zweite punische Krieg. Marburg, 1875.

AH 7440 - 7449   Ancient Rome in general - History by periods - Republic,
509-27 B.C. - 264-201 (Table A) - cont.

AH 7448.75.5   Schemann, Ludwig. De legionum per alterum bellum punicum
historium quae investigari posse videntur. Bonnae, 1875.

AH 7448.76   Gilbert, Otto. Rom und Karthago in ihren gegenseitigen
Veziehungen 513-536 von Christus. (241-218 von Christus).
Leipzig, 1876.

AH 7448.77   Person, Emile. De P. Cornelio Scipione Aemiliano Africano
et Numantino. Thesim. Sancti-Clodoaldi, 1877.

AH 7448.78   Sieglin, W. Die Chronologie der Belagerung von Sagunt.
Leipzig, 1878.

AH 7448.78.3   Buzello, J. De oppugnatione sagunti quaestiones
chronologicae. Inaug. Diss. Regimonti, 1886.

AH 7448.80   Zielinski, T. Letzten Jahre des zweiten punischen Krieges.
Leipzig, 1880.

AH 7448.81   Smith, R.B. Rome and Carthage. N.Y., 1880.
NEDL   AH 7448.81.2A   Smith, R.B. Rome and Carthage. 5. ed. London, 1887.
NEDL   AH 7448.81.2B   Smith, R.B. Rome and Carthage. 5. ed. London, 1887.
AH 7448.81.5   Smith, R.B. Rome and Carthage. N.Y., 1896.
AH 7448.83   Frantz, Johann. Die Kriege der Scipionen in Spanien.
München, 1883.

AH 7448.83.10   Neumann, Karl. Das Zeitalter der punischen Kriege.
Breslau, 1883.

AH 7448.83.15   Stuerenburg, Heinrich. Der Romanorum cladibus Trasumenna
et Cannensi. Leipzig, 1883.

AH 7448.84   Fröhlich, F. Die Bedeutung des zweiten punischen Krieges.
Leipzig, 1884.

AH 7448.85   Meltzer, Otto. De belli Punici secundi primordiis
adversariorum capita quattuor. Dresden, 1885.

AH 7448.86   Arnold, Thomas. The second Punic War. London, 1886.
AH 7448.88   Koehn, M. De Pugna ad Zamam Commissa. Halis
Saxonum, 1888.

AH 7448.91A   Dodge, T.A. Hannibal - history of the art of war.
Boston, 1891.

AH 7448.91B   Dodge, T.A. Hannibal - history of the art of war.
Boston, 1891.

AH 7448.91C   Dodge, T.A. Hannibal - history of the art of war.
Boston, 1891. 2v.

AH 7448.91.10F   Bossi, Gaetano. La guerra d'Annibale in Italia da Canne al
Metauro. Roma, 1891.

AH 7448.92   Boguth, Walter. M. Valerius Laevinus (Ein Beitrag).
Krems, 1892.

AH 7448.92.2   Jumpertz, M. Der römisch-karthagische Krieg.
Berlin, 1892.

AH 7448.94   Fuchs, Josef. Der zweite punische Krieg.
Wienerneustadt, 1894.

AH 7448.94.2   Masom, W.J. The struggle for Empire. London, 1894.
AH 7448.97A   Morris, William C. Hannibal; soldier, statesman.
N.Y., 1897.

AH 7448.97B   Morris, William C. Hannibal; soldier, statesman.
N.Y., 1897.

AH 7448.98.5   Garmendia, J.I. Estudios históricos y militares sobre las
compañas de Anibal. Buenos Aires, 1898.

AH 7448.98.10   Fried, Friedrich. Über Die schlacht bei Cannä. Inaug.
Diss. Leipzig, 1898.

AH 7448.99   How, W.W. Hannibal and the Great War. London, 1899.
AH 7448.99.5   Gaez, H. Nachmals des Schlachtfeld von Cannä.
Frankfurt, 1899.

AH 7449.01   Montanari, T. Annibale. Rovigo, 1900-01.
AH 7449.05   Schermann, Max. Der erste punische Krieg.
Stuttgart, 1905.

AH 7449.05.2   Lehmann, K. Die Angriffe der drei Bardiken.
Leipzig, 1905.

AH 7449.05.3   Lauterbach, A. Untersuchungen...Unterwerfung von
Oberitalien. Breslau, 1905.

AH 7449.07   Mordtmann, A.D. Historische Bilder vom Bosporus.
Konstantinopel, 1907.

AH 7449.08   Meyer, P. Der Ausbruch des ersten punischen Krieges.
Berlin, 1908.

AH 7449.12   Kromayer, I. Roms Kampf um die Welthenschaft.
Leipzig, 1912.

AH 7449.14   Freshfield, D.w. Hannibal once more. London, 1914.
AH 7449.14.5   Brewitz, Walther. Scipio Africanus maior in Spanien.
Inaug. Diss. Tübingen, 1914.

AH 7449.14.7   Sann, Georg. Untersuchungen zu Scipios Feldzug in Afrika.
Inaug. Diss. Berlin, 1914.

AH 7449.17   Huvelin, Paul. Une guerre d'usure. Paris, 1917.
AH 7449.21   Täubler, Eugen. Die Vorgeschichte des zweiten punischen
Krieges. Berlin, 1921.

AH 7449.22   Egelhauf, G. Hannibal. Stuttgart, 1922.
AH 7449.25   Torr, Cecil. Hannibal crosses the Alps 2. ed.
Cambridge, 1925.

AH 7449.25.5   Bonus, A.R. Where Hannibal passed. London, 1925.
AH 7449.26   Liddell Hart, B.H. A greater than Napoleon, Scipio
Africanus. Edinburgh, 1926.

AH 7449.26.3   Liddell Hart, B.H. A greater than Napoleon, Scipio
Africanus. Boston, 1927.

AH 7449.26.5   Liddell Hart, B.H. A greater than Napoleon, Scipio
Africanus. Boston, 1928.

AH 7449.27   Pais, Ettore. Storia de Roma durante le guerre puniche. 2.
ed. Torino, 1935. 2v.

AH 7449.29   Groag, Edmund. Hannibal als Politiker. Wien, 1929.
AH 7449.29.5   Scharf, Alfred. Der Ausgang des tarentinischen Krieges als
Wendepunkt. Inaug. Diss. Bremen, 1929.

AH 7449.29.10   Branchini, A. Studio critico-polemico su la precisazione
storica della battaglia del Metauro. Fano, 1929.

AH 7449.29.12   Branchini, A. La battaglia del Metauro. Pesaro, 1934.
AH 7449.29.15   Baker, George Philip. Hannibal. N.Y., 1929.
AH 7449.30   Scullard, Howard Hayes. Scipio Africanus in the second
Punic War. Cambridge, Eng., 1930.

AH 7449.31   Guarnieri, L. Roma e Cartagine sul mare. Roma, 1931.
AH 7449.33   Cappis, F. Zum Alpenübergang Hannibals. Aarau, 1933.
AH 7449.35   Nap, J.M. Die römische Republik um das Jahr 225 vor
Christus. Leiden, 1935.

AH 7449.40   Ciaceri, Emanuele. Scipione Africano e l'idea imperiale di
Roma. Napoli, 1940.

AH 7449.41   Grazioli, Francesco. Scipione l'Africano. Torino, 1941.
AH 7449.42   Bonarelli, G. La battaglia del Metauro. Ancona, 1942.
AH 7449.45   Blaettler, Pirmin. Studien zur Regulusgeschichte.
Sarnen, 1945.

AH 7449.47   Zeller, Eberhard. Hannibal. Uberlingen, 1948.
AH 7449.48   Valori, F. Scipione l'Africano. Torino, 1948.
AH 7449.51   Gómez, N.P. Guerras de Anibal preparatorias del sitio de
Saguntum. Valencia, 1951.

AH 7449.53   Grimal, P. Le siècle des Scipions. Paris, 1953.
AH 7449.55   De Beer, Gavin Rylands. Alps and elephants. 1. American
ed. N.Y., 1956.

AH 7449.55.5   De Beer, Gavin Rylands. Hannibal's march. London, 1967.

AH 7440 - 7449   Ancient Rome in general - History by periods - Republic, 509-27 B.C. - 264-201 (Table A) - cont.

	AH 7449.59	Veitskivs'kyi, I.I. Zovnishnia polityka krain Zakhidnogo Ceredzemnomor'ia v 264-219 rr. do n.e. L'viv, 1959.
	AH 7449.59.5F	Ludovico, D. La battaglia di Canne. Roma, 1959.
	AH 7449.61	Cottrell, Leonard. Hannibal, enemy of Rome. 1. American ed. N.Y., 1961.
	AH 7449.63	Lippold, A. Consules. Bonn, 1963.
	AH 7449.69	De Beer, Gavin Rylands. Hannibal; the struggle for power in the Mediterranean. London, 1969.
	AH 7449.70	Scullard, Howard Hayes. Scipio Africanus: soldier and politician. Ithaca, 1970.
	AH 7449.70.5	Goerlitz, Walter. Hannibal; eine politische Biographie. Stuttgart, 1970.
	AH 7449.70.10	Mix, Erving R. Marcus Atilius Regulus; exemplum historicum. The Hague, 1970.
	AH 7449.71	Proctor, Dennis. Hannibal's march in history. Oxford, 1971.
	AH 7449.71.5	Dorey, Thomas Alan. Rome against Carthage. London, 1971.
	AH 7449.71.10	Errington, Robert Malcolm. The dawn of empire; Rome's rise to world power. London, 1971.

AH 7450 - 7459   Ancient Rome in general - History by periods - Republic, 509-27 B.C. - 200-146 (Table A)

	AH 7458.36	Heerwagen, H.G. De P. et L. Scipionum accusation de quaestio. Baruthi, 1836.
	AH 7458.73	Mendelssohn, L. De senati consulti Romanorum. Lipsiae, 1873.
	AH 7458.79	Genzken, H. De rebus a P. et Cn. Corneliis Scipionibus in Hispania gestis. Diss. inaug. Fribergae, 1879.
NEDL	AH 7458.92	Allcroft, A.H. Rome under the Oligarchs. London, 1892.
	AH 7458.96	Pascal, Carlo. Studi romani. Torino, 1896.
	AH 7458.98	Lincke, E. Martin. P. Cornelius Scipio Amilianus. Dresden, 1898.
	AH 7459.18	Leffingwell, G.W. Social...life in Rome in the time of Plautus. N.Y., 1918.
	AH 7459.33	Haywood, R.M. Studies on Scipio Africanus. Diss. Baltimore, 1933.
	AH 7459.33.5	Haywood, R.M. Studies on Scipio Africanus. Baltimore, 1933.
	AH 7459.51	Scullard, Howard Hayes. Roman politics, 220-150 B.C. Oxford, 1951.
	AH 7459.51.2	Scullard, Howard Hayes. Roman politics, 220-150 B.C. 2. ed. Oxford, 1973.
	AH 7459.56	Utchenko, S.L. Der weltanschaulich politische Kampf in Rom. Berlin, 1956.
	AH 7459.66	Armstrong, Donald Budd. The reluctant warriors. N.Y., 1966.
	AH 7459.67	Astin, A.E. Scipio Aemilianus. Oxford, 1967.
	AH 7459.68	Schlag, Ursula. Regnum in senatu; das Wirken römischen Staatsmänner von 200 bis 191 vor Christus. Stuttgart, 1968.

AH 7460 - 7469   Ancient Rome in general - History by periods - Republic, 509-27 B.C. - 146-27 (Table A)

	AH 7461.5	Rothke, G. De Romanorum Bellis Servilibus. Berlin, 1904. 6 pam.
	AH 7462.5.2	Greenidge, Abel H.J. Sources for Roman history, 133-70 B.C. 2. ed. Oxford, 1960.
	AH 7462.10.2	Hawthorn, John R. Roman politics, 80-44 B.C.; a selection of Latin passages. London, 1965.
	AH 7467.21	Britannicus. Conspirators. London, 1721.
	AH 7467.21.2	Gordon, T. The conspirators. 2. ed. London, 1721.
	AH 7467.21.2.2	Gordon, T. The conspirators. 2. ed. London, 1721.
	AH 7468.01	Hegewisch, D.H. Geschichte der gracchischen Unruhen. Hamburg, 1801.
	AH 7468.10	Luzac, L.C. Specimen...Q. Hortensio Oratore, Ciceronis. Lugduni Batavorum, 1810.
	AH 7468.25	Reiff, H.C. Geschichte der römischen Burgerkreige. Berlin, 1825.
	AH 7468.29	Emperius, A.C.W. De temporum Belli Mithridatici. Gottingae, 1829.
X Cg	AH 7468.29.3	Reinach, T. Mithradates Eupator. Paris, 1890.
	AH 7468.29.5	Reinach, T. Mithradates Eupator. Leipzig, 1895.
	AH 7468.29.7	Bernhardt, H. Chronologie der mithridatischen Kriege. Marburg, 1896.
	AH 7468.34	Lau, Thaddeus. Lucius Cornelius Sulla. Hamburg, 1855.
	AH 7468.34.2	Gerlach, F.D. Marius and Sulla. Basel, 1856.
	AH 7468.34.4	Drumann, W. Geschichte Roms. Koenigsberg, 1834. 6v.
	AH 7468.34.5	Drumann, W. Geschichte Roms. v.1-6. Berlin, 1899. 5v.
	AH 7468.34.6	Zacharia, K.S. Lucius Cornelius Sulla. Heidelberg, 1834.
	AH 7468.34.7	Zacharia, K.S. Lucius Cornelius Sulla. Mannheim, 1850.
	AH 7468.36	Ahrens, E.A.J. Die drei Volkstribunen Tib. Gracchus, M. Drusus und P. Sulpicius. Leipzig, 1836.
	AH 7468.44	Plutarch. Civil wars of Rome. London, 1844. 3v.
	AH 7468.44.2	Mérimée, P. Etudes sur l'histoire romaine. Paris, 1844. 2v.
	AH 7468.44.3	Mérimée, P. Etudes sur l'histoire romaine. Paris, 1853.
	AH 7468.45	Kiene, Adolf. Der römische Bundesgenossenkrieg. Leipzig, 1845.
	AH 7468.47	Nitzsch, K.W. Die Gracchen und ihre...Vorgänger. Berlin, 1847.
	AH 7468.54	Lau, Thaddeus. Die Gracchen und ihre Zeit. Hamburg, 1854.
	AH 7468.54.25	Hagen, E. Untersuchungen über römische Geschichte. Königsberg, 1854.
	AH 7468.64	Long, George. Decline of the Roman Republic. v.3, photoreproduction. London, 1864. 5v.
NEDL	AH 7468.64	Long, George. Decline of the Roman Republic. London, 1684. 5v.
	AH 7468.69	Backmund, J. Catilina und die Parteikämpfe in Rom im Jahre 63 vor Christus. Würzburg, 1869.
	AH 7468.70	Merivale, Charles. Fall of the Roman Republic. London, 1870.
	AH 7468.70.5	Gilles, I. Campagne de Marius dans la Gaule. Paris, 1870.
	AH 7468.71	Gilles, I. Marius et Jules César. Marseille, 1871.
	AH 7468.74	Gilles, I. La legende des Saintes Maries. Paris, 1874.
	AH 7468.74.5	Schmidt, Robert. Kritik der Quellen...gracchischen Unruhen. Berlin, 1874.
	AH 7468.74.7	Simon, H.O. Vita Q. Lutatii Q.F. Catuli. Berlin, 1874.
	AH 7468.76	Hugues, G.D. Une province romaine sous la Republique. Paris, 1876.
	AH 7468.76.2	Dubois-Guchan, E.P. Rome et Cicéron. Paris, 1880.
	AH 7468.77	Beesly, A.H. The Gracchi, Marius and Sulla. London, 1877.
NEDL	AH 7468.77.3	Beesly, A.H. The Gracchi, Marius and Sulla. London, 1887.
NEDL	AH 7468.77.4	Beesly, A.H. The Gracchi, Marius and Sulla. N.Y., 1891.
NEDL	AH 7468.77.4.5A	Beesly, A.H. The Gracchi, Marius and Sulla. N.Y., 1892.
	AH 7468.77.4.5B	Beesly, A.H. The Gracchi, Marius and Sulla. N.Y., 1892.

AH 7460 - 7469   Ancient Rome in general - History by periods - Republic, 509-27 B.C. - 146-27 (Table A) - cont.

	AH 7468.77.5	Beesly, A.H. The Gracchi, Marius and Sulla. N.Y., 1895.
	AH 7468.78	Beesly, E.S. Catiline, Clodius and Tiberius. London, 1878.
	AH 7468.79	Byvanck, W.G.C. Studia in Ti. Gracchi historiam. Lugdunum Batavorum, 1879.
	AH 7468.79.5	Bürcklein, A. Quellen und Chronologie der römisch-parthischen Feldzüge in den Jahren 713-718. Inaug. Diss. Berlin, 1879.
	AH 7468.81	Neumann, Carl. Geschichte Roms. Breslau, 1881.
	AH 7468.82	Fritzsche, Hermann. Die sulianische Gesetzgebung. Essen, 1882.
	AH 7468.83	Stern, Ernst von. Catilina und die Parterkämpfe. Dorpat, 1883.
	AH 7468.84	Bardey, Ernst. Das sechste Consulat des Marius. Brandenburg, 1884.
	AH 7468.85	Ritter, Georg. Untersuchungen zu dem allobrogischen Krieg. Hof, 1885.
	AH 7468.87	Strehl, Willy. M. Livius Drusus. Marburg, 1887.
	AH 7468.88A	Lacour-Gayet, G. De P. Clodis Pulchris tribuno plebis. Thèse. Lutetiae Parisiorum, 1888.
	AH 7468.88B	Lacour-Gayet, G. De P. Clodis Pulchris tribuno plebis. Thèse. Lutetiae Parisiorum, 1888.
	AH 7468.92	Klimke, Karl. Beiträge zur Geschichte der Gracchen. Sagen, 1892.
	AH 7468.93	Willrich, H. De conjurationis Catilinariae fontibus. Gottingae, 1893.
NEDL	AH 7468.95	Masom, W.F. Decline of the oligarchy: History of Rome. London, 1895.
	AH 7468.96	Lewandowski, M. La question sociale à Rome. Paris, 1896.
	AH 7468.96.5	Linden, E. De bello civili Sullano. Friburgi Brisigavorum, 1896.
	AH 7468.98	Tarantino, Mario. Questioni cronologiche. Catania, 1898.
	AH 7468.98.5	Tarantino, Mario. La congiura catilinaria. Catania, 1898.
	AH 7468.99	Regling, Kurt L. De belli Parthici Crassiani fontibus. Berolini, 1899.
	AH 7469.00	Hubel, Karl. Die Beiffragmente der Cornelia. Erlangen, 1900.
	AH 7469.00.3	Kappler, Carl. Uber die unter dem Namen der Cornelia überlieferten Brieffragmente. Weiden, 1905.
	AH 7469.01	Deknatel, Christian. De vita M. Lucinis Crassi. Lugduni-Batavorum, 1901.
	AH 7469.02	Oman, Charles. Seven Roman statesmen of the later Republic. London, 1902.
	AH 7469.02.2	Oman, Charles. Seven Roman statesmen of the later Republic. N.Y., 1902.
	AH 7469.02.3	Oman, Charles. Seven Roman statesmen of the later Republic. N.Y., 191-?
	AH 7469.02.3.5	Oman, Charles. Seven Roman statesmen of the later Republic. London, 1927.
	AH 7469.02.4	Oman, Charles. Seven Roman statesmen of the later Republic. London, 1929.
	AH 7469.02.5	Neunheuser, J. Aemilius Lepidus. Essen, 1902.
	AH 7469.02.6	Oman, Charles. Seven Roman statesmen of the later Republic: the Gracchi, Sulla, Crassus, Cato, Pompey and Caesar. Freeport, 1971.
	AH 7469.03	Greenidge, A.H.J. Sources for Roman history, B.C. 133-70. Oxford, 1903.
	AH 7469.05	Boissier, Gaston. La conjuration de Catilina. Paris, 1905.
	AH 7469.05.2	Boissier, Gaston. La conjuration de Catilina. 2. éd. Paris, 1908.
	AH 7469.06	Mühll, F.V. De L. Appuleio Saturnino Tribuno Plebis. Basileae, 1906.
	AH 7469.06.5	Clerc, Michel. La bataille d'Aix. Paris, 1906.
	AH 7469.08	Prodinger, Karl. Das Tribunat des C. Gracchus. Gottschee, 1908.
	AH 7469.09	Gatti, Giuseppe. Lamina di bronzo con iscrizione...guerra dei socii italici. Roma, 1909.
	AH 7469.09.5	Paladino, G. La guerra dei gladiatori (73-71 a.C.). Napoli, 1909.
	AH 7469.13.5	Bloch, G. La République romaine. Paris, 1919.
	AH 7469.14	Fraccaro, P. Studi sull'età dei Gracchi. Città di Castello, 1914.
	AH 7469.15A	Howard, A.A. Latin selections illustrating public life in the Roman Commonwealth in the time of Cicero. Boston, 1915.
	AH 7469.15B	Howard, A.A. Latin selections illustrating public life in the Roman Commonwealth in the time of Cicero. Boston, 1915.
	AH 7469.15.5	Lanzani, C. Mario e Silla. Catania, 1915.
	AH 7469.17	Cowles, F.H. Gaius Verres. Thesis. Ithaca, 1917.
	AH 7469.19	Koehler, M.A. Catilina in classic tradition. Thesis. N.Y., 1919.
	AH 7469.19.5	Jolliffe, Richard. Phases of corruption in Roman administration. Menasha, 1919.
	AH 7469.19.7	Hartwig, Wilhelm. Spartakus und der Glatiatorenkrieg 73-71 vor Christus. Leipzig, 1919.
	AH 7469.19.9	Thomas, S.P. Den antikke tradition om Graecherne. Kristiania, 1919.
	AH 7469.21	Constans, L.A. Un correspondant de Cicérone. Thèse. Paris, 1921.
	AH 7469.22	Marsh, F.B. The founding of the Roman empire. Austin, 1922.
	AH 7469.22.2A	Marsh, F.B. The founding of the Roman empire. 2. ed. London, 1927.
	AH 7469.22.2B	Marsh, F.B. The founding of the Roman empire. 2. ed. London, 1927.
	AH 7469.23	Bennett, Harold. Cinna and his times. Menasha, 1923.
	AH 7469.23.5	Dobiás, J. Synoský prokonsulát M. Calpurnia Bibula. Praha, 1923.
	AH 7469.24	Hardy, E.G. The Catilinarian conspiracy in its context. Oxford, 1924.
	AH 7469.25	Pareti, Luigi. La congiura di Catilina alle soglie dell'impero. Catania, 1934.
	AH 7469.26	Groener, Franz. Der Fremdenverkehr in Rom zur Zeit Ciceros. Inaug. Diss. Bonn, 1926.
	AH 7469.27	Baker, George P. Sulla the fortunate, the great dictator. London, 1927.
	AH 7469.28	Holmes, T.R.E. The architect of the Roman Empire. Oxford, 1928-31. 2v.
	AH 7469.28.5	Taeger, Fritz. Untersuchungen zur römischen Geschichte und Quellenkunde. Stuttgart, 1928.
	AH 7469.28.10	Binder, Max. Studien zur Geschichte des zweiten Bürgerkriegs. Inaug. Diss. Uberlingen am Bodensee, 1928.
	AH 7469.28.15	Carcopino, Jérôme. Autour des Gracques, études critiques. Paris, 1928.

AH 7460 - 7469   Ancient Rome in general - History by periods - Republic, 509-27 B.C. - 146-27 (Table A) - cont.

AH 7469.29   Balbo, Emilio. Catilina nel giudizio della critica demagogica. Roma, 1929.

AH 7469.29.5   Block, Gustave. La République romaine de 133 avant J.C. à la mort de César. Pt.1. Paris, 1929.

AH 7469.29.10   Bloch, Gustave. La République romaine de 133 avant J.C. à la mort de César. v.1-2. 2.-3. ed. Paris, 1940-43.

AH 7469.31   Carcopino, Jérôme. Sylla; ou, La monarchie manquée. Paris, 1931.

AH 7469.31.4   Weigall, Arthur E.P.B. The life and times of Marc Antony. N.Y., 1931.

AH 7469.31.5   Weigall, Arthur E.P.B. The life and times of Marc Antony. Garden City, 1931.

AH 7469.31.10   Graindor, P. La guerre d'Alexandrie. Le Caire, 1931.

AH 7469.31.11   Pamphlet vol. Université Égyptienne. Recueil de travaux par la faculté des lettres. 2 pam.

AH 7469.33   Brun-Laloire, Louis. La vie tragique des Gracques. Paris, 1933.

AH 7469.34   Pavano Amato, Giovanni. La rivolta di Catalina. Messina, 1934.

AH 7469.34.5   Mainzer, Ferdinand. Der Kampf um Caesars Erbe. Leipzig, 1936.

AH 7469.34.5.3   Mainzer, Ferdinand. Caesar's mantle. N.Y., 1936.

AH 7469.35   Marsh, Frank B. A history of the Roman world from 146 to 30 B.C. London, 1935.

AH 7469.35.1   Marsh, Frank B. A history of the Roman world from 146 to 30 B.C. N.Y., 1939.

AH 7469.35.2   Marsh, Frank B. A history of the Roman world from 146 to 30 B.C. 2. ed. London, 1953.

AH 7469.35.3   Marsh, Frank B. A history of the Roman world from 146 to 30 B.C. 3. ed. London, 1963.

AH 7469.36   Lanzani, C. Lucio Cornelio Silla, dittatore. Milano, 1936.

AH 7469.37   Lindsay, Jack. Marc Antony; his world and his contemporaries. N.Y., 1937.

AH 7469.38.6   Vogt, Joseph. Cicero und Sallust über die Catilinarische Verschwurung. Darmstadt, 1973.

AH 7469.39   Syme, Ronald. The Roman revolution. Oxford, 1939.

AH 7469.39.3   Syme, Ronald. The Roman revolution. Oxford, 1956.

AH 7469.39.10   Sheldon, E.L. Publius Cornelius Dolabella. N.Y., 1939.

AH 7469.39.15   Manni, Eugenio. Lucio Sergio Catilina. Firenze, 1939.

AH 7469.39.20   Villoresi, Mario. Lucullo. Firenze, 1939.

AH 7469.40   Andreotti, Roberto. Cajo Mario. Gubbio, 1940.

AH 7469.41   Passerini, Alfredo. Caio Mario. Roma, 1941.

AH 7469.47   Rimscha, Hans von. Die Gracchen. München, 1947.

AH 7469.52   Brion, M. La révolte des gladiateurs. Paris, 1952.

AH 7469.54.5   Mainzer, Ferdinand. Clodia. Braunschweig, 1954.

AH 7469.54.10   Garzetti, Albino. Verso il principato. Milano, 1954.

AH 7469.55   Smith, R.E. The failure of the Roman Republic. Cambridge, Eng., 1955.

AH 7469.56   Valgiglio, E. Silla e la crisi repubblicana. 1. ed. Firenze, 1956.

AH 7469.58   Volkmann, Hans. Sullas Marsch auf Rom. München, 1958.

AH 7469.59   Ooteghem, Jules van. Lucius Licinius Lucullus. Namur, 1959.

AH 7469.59.5   Chantraine, Heinrich. Untersuchungen zur römischen Geschichte am Ende des 2. Jahrhunderts vor Christus. Kallmünz, 1959.

AH 7469.60   Krawczuk, A. Kolonizacja sullańska. Wrocław, 1960.

AH 7469.60.5   Linderski, Jerzy. Państwo a kolegia. Kraków, 1961.

AH 7469.60.10   Weil, Bruno. Clodia. Zürich, 1960.

AH 7469.61   Ooteghem, Jules van. Lucius Marcius Phillipus et sa famille. Namur, 1961.

AH 7469.63   Hawthorn, J.R. The Republican empire. London, 1963.

AH 7469.63.5   Earl, D.C. Tiberius Gracchus; a study in politics. Bruxelles, 1963.

AH 7469.64   Ooteghem, Jules van. Caius Marius. Namur, 1964.

AH 7469.65   Utchenko, S. Krizis; padenie Rimskoi respubliki. Moskva, 1965.

AH 7469.66   Hutchinson, Lester. The conspiracy of Catiline. London, 1966.

AH 7469.66.5   Adcock, Frank Ezra. Marcus Crassus, millionaire. Cambridge, 1966.

AH 7469.67   Nicolet, Claude. Les gracques ou Crise agraire et révolution à Rome. Paris, 1967.

AH 7469.68   Kaplan, Arthur. Catiline; the man and his role in the Roman revolution. N.Y., 1968.

AH 7469.68.5   Perowne, Stewart. Death of the Roman republic. 1. ed. Garden City, 1968.

AH 7469.68.12   Badian, Ernst. Roman imperialism in the late republic. 2. ed. Oxford, 1968.

AH 7469.69   Holliday, Vivian L. Pompey in Cicero's correspondence and Lucan's civil war. Thesis. The Hague, 1969.

AH 7469.69.5   Boren, Henry Charles. The Gracchi. N.Y., 1969.

AH 7469.69.10   Roedl, Bernd. Das Senatus Consultum Ultimun und der Tod der Gracchen. Thesis. Bonn, 1969.

AH 7469.70   Badian, Ernst. Lucius Sulla. Sydney, 1970.

AH 7469.71   Christiansen, Erik. Den romerske republiks sidste hundrede år. København, 1971.

AH 7469.71.5   Fonti su Caio Mario. Milano, 1971.

AH 7469.71.10   Odahl, Charles Matson. The Catilinarian conspiracy. New Haven, 1971.

AH 7470 - 7479   Ancient Rome in general - History by periods - Republic, 509-27 B.C. - Age of Julius Caesar (Table A)

AH 7476.32.5   Guarino, Alessandro. L'apologia di Cesare. Roma, 1929.

AH 7477.24   The life and actions of Caius Julius Caesar. London, 1724.

Htn   AH 7477.38*   Hill, Aaron. An enquiry into the merit of assassination...character of Caesar. London, 1738.

AH 7477.74   Guischard, Charles. Memoires...plusieurs points d'antiquités militaires. Paris, 1774. 4v.

AH 7478.26   Knowles, J.S. Character of Julius Caesar. Boston, 1826.

AH 7478.27   Petrarca, F. Historia Iulii Caesaris. Lipsiae, 1827.

AH 7478.36   Napoléon III, emperor of the French. Précis des guerres de César. Paris, 1836.

AH 7478.36.3   Napoléon III, emperor of the French. Précis des guerres de César. Bruxelles, 1836.

AH 7478.41   Berlin. Friedrichs Werderschen Gymnasiums. Programm...De C. Iulii Caesaris Coloniis. Berlin, 1841.

AH 7478.49   Abbott, Jacob. History of Julius Caesar. N.Y., 1849.

AH 7478.49.9   Abbott, Jacob. History of Julius Caesar. N.Y., 1877.

AH 7478.54A   Mommsen, T. History of Rome. London, 1886. 2v.

AH 7478.54B   Mommsen, T. History of Rome. London, 1886. 2v.

AH 7478.54.2   Mommsen, T. History of Rome. N.Y., 1899. 2v.

AH 7478.57   Mommsen, T. Die Rechtsfrage zwischen Caesar und dem Senat. Breslau, 1857.

AH 7478.60   Liddell, H.G. Life of Julius Caesar. N.Y., 1860.

AH 7470 - 7479   Ancient Rome in general - History by periods - Republic, 509-27 B.C. - Age of Julius Caesar (Table A) - cont.

AH 7478.61   Göler, F.A. Bürgerkrieg zwischen Cäsar und Pompejus. Heidelberg, 1861.

AH 7478.61.2   Oliver y Hurtado, J. y D. Munda Pompeiana. Madrid, 1861.

AH 7478.62   De Damas, Nicolas. La mort de César. Paris, 1862.

AH 7478.63   Dressel, E. Über die politische Rolle des Gnaeus Pompejus Magnus. Coburg, 1863.

AH 7478.63.8   Gastineau, Benjamin. Les femmes de Jules César. 2. éd. Paris, 1865.

AH 7478.65   Napoléon III, emperor of the French. Histoire de Jules César. N.Y., 1865. 2v.

AH 7478.65.2   Napoléon III, emperor of the French. Histoire de Jules César. Paris, 1865-66. 2v.

AH 7478.65.2F   Napoléon III, emperor of the French. Histoire de Jules César. Atlas. Paris, 1865-66.

AH 7478.65.2.5F   Napoléon III, emperor of the French. Histoire de Jules César. Atlas. v.1-2. Paris, 1865-66.

AH 7478.65.3F   Napoléon III, emperor of the French. Histoire de Jules César. Paris, 1865-66. 2v.

AH 7478.65.4   Napoléon III, emperor of the French. History of Julius Caesar. London, 1865. 2v.

AH 7478.65.5F   Napoléon III, emperor of the French. History of Julius Caesar. Atlas. London, n.d.

AH 7478.65.6   Napoléon III, emperor of the French. Geschichte Julius Cäsars. Wien, 1865. 2v.

AH 7478.65.7A   Napoléon III, emperor of the French. History of Julius Caesar. N.Y., 1865-66. 2v.

AH 7478.65.7B   Napoléon III, emperor of the French. History of Julius Caesar. N.Y., 1865.

AH 7478.65.50   Fallue, Léon. Études archéologiques sur l'histoire de Jules César par l'empereur Napoleon III. Paris, 1867.

AH 7478.66   Rose, M. Renaud. Le theatre de la dernière guerre des bellovaques contre Jules César. Beauvais, 1866.

AH 7478.69   Delorme, S. César et ses contemporains. Paris, 1869.

AH 7478.70.3   Ramée, D. César. Paris, 1870.

NEDL   AH 7478.77.2   Merivale, Charles. Roman triumvirates. London, 1876.

AH 7478.77.3A   Merivale, Charles. Roman triumvirates. 5. ed. London, 1887.

AH 7478.77.3B   Merivale, Charles. Roman triumvirates. 5. ed. London, 1887.

NEDL   AH 7478.77.5   Merivale, Charles. Roman triumvirates. N.Y., 1889.

NEDL   AH 7478.77.6   Merivale, Charles. Roman triumvirates. N.Y., 1893.

AH 7478.77.7   Merivale, Charles. Roman triumvirates. N.Y., 1895.

AH 7478.78   Guiraud, Paul. Le différend entre César et le sénat (59-49 avant J.C.). Thèse. Paris, 1878.

AH 7478.79A   Froude, J.A. Caesar; a sketch. N.Y., 1879.

AH 7478.79B   Froude, J.A. Caesar; a sketch. N.Y., 1879.

NEDL   AH 7478.79.1A   Froude, J.A. Caesar; a sketch. London, 1879.

AH 7478.79.1B   Froude, J.A. Caesar; a sketch. London, 1879.

AH 7478.79.2A   Froude, J.A. Caesar; a sketch. London, 1880.

AH 7478.79.2B   Froude, J.A. Caesar; a sketch. London, 1880.

NEDL   AH 7478.79.3   Froude, J.A. Caesar; a sketch. N.Y., 1881.

AH 7478.79.4   Wesemann, H. Caesarfabeln des Mittelalters. Löwenberg, 1879.

AH 7478.80   Göler, F.A. Caesars gallischer Krieg. v.1-2. Freiburg, 1880.

AH 7478.81   Froude, J.A. Caesar; a sketch. N.Y., 1881.

NEDL   AH 7478.81.7A   Froude, J.A. Caesar; a sketch. N.Y., 189-?

AH 7478.81.7B   Froude, J.A. Caesar; a sketch. N.Y., 189-?

AH 7478.81.9   Froude, J.A. Caesar; a sketch. London, 1893.

AH 7478.81.10   Froude, J.A. Julius Caesar. N.Y., 1900.

AH 7478.81.15   Garrido, Luiz. L'histoire romaine au septième siècle, 622-677. Lisbonne, 1881.

AH 7478.81.20   Liddell, H.G. Life of Julius Caesar. Biographical series. Boston, 1881.

AH 7478.82   Plathner, J. Zur Quellenkritik der...Bürgerkrieges. Bernburg, 1882.

AH 7478.83   Wendelmuth, Richard. T. Labienus. Inaug. Diss. Marburg, 1883.

AH 7478.83.5   Schelle, Emil. De M. Antonii triumveri quae supersunt epistalis. Pt.1. Frankenberg, 1883.

AH 7478.86   Heuzey, L.A. Les operations militaires de Jules César. Paris, 1886.

AH 7478.86.2   Schneider, R. Ilerda. Beitrag zur römische Kriegsgeschichte. Berlin, 1886.

AH 7478.86.5   Jullien, Emile. De L. Cornelio Balbo majore. Thesim. Lutetiae Parisiorum, 1886.

AH 7478.87   Stoffel. Histoire de Jules César. Atlas. Paris, 1887. 3v.

AH 7478.87.5   Stocchi, Giuseppe. Due studî di storia romana. Firenze, 1887.

AH 7478.89   Salvatierra. Lo mundo de los romanos. Ronda, 1889.

NEDL   AH 7478.92.2   Dodge, T.A. Caesar. A History of the art of war. Boston, 1892.

AH 7478.93   Allcroft, A.H. Making of the monarchy. London, 1893.

AH 7478.95   Ciccotti, E. Donne e politica. Milano, 1895.

AH 7478.98   Wiegandt, L. Studien zur staatsrechtlichen Stellung. Dresden, 1898.

AH 7478.99   Holmes, T.R.E. Caesar's conquest of Gaul. London, 1899.

AH 7478.99.5   Holmes, T.R.E. Caesar's conquest of Gaul. 2. ed. Oxford, 1911.

AH 7479.00   Moineville, L. Deux campagnes de César. Paris, 1900.

AH 7479.03   Scott, F.J. Portraitures of Julius Caesar. London, 1903.

AH 7479.04   Fowler, W.W. Julius Caesar and the foundation of the Roman imperial system. N.Y., 1904.

AH 7479.04.5   Fowler, W.W. Julius Caesar and the foundation of the Roman imperial system. N.Y., 1891.

AH 7479.07   Bondurant, B.C. Decimus Junius Brutus Albinus. Chicago, 1907.

AH 7479.07.5   Volquardsen, C. Rom im Übergange von der Republik. Kiel, 1907.

AH 7479.10   Hardinge, Hilary. Julius Caesar. London, 191-.

AH 7479.10.5   Gans, Maximilian E. Studien zu Schlacht bei Pharsalus. Lundenberg, 1910.

AH 7479.14   Müller, Ernst. Cäsaren-Porträts. v.1-2, 3. Bonn, 1914-27. 2v.

AH 7479.18.2   Meyer, Eduard. Caesars Monarchie und das Principat des Pompejus. 2. Aufl. Stuttgart, 1919.

AH 7479.18.3   Meyer, Eduard. Caesars Monarchie und das Principat des Pompejus. 3. Aufl. Stuttgart, 1963.

AH 7479.20   Veith, Georg. Der Feldrug von Dyrrhachium. Wien, 1920.

AH 7479.21   Gelzer, Matthias. Cäsar, der Politiker und Staatsmann. Stuttgart, 1921.

AH 7479.21.7   Gelzer, Matthias. Cäsar, der Politiker und Staatsmann. 4. Aufl. München, 1942.

AH 7479.21.9   Gelzer, Matthias. Cäsar, der Politiker und Staatsmann. 6. Aufl. Wiesbaden, 1960.

AH 7470 - 7479   Ancient Rome in general - History by periods - Republic, 509-27 B.C. - Age of Julius Caesar (Table A) - cont.

AH 7479.21.12	Gelzer, Matthias. Caesar, politician and statesman. Cambridge, 1968.
AH 7479.24	Hardy, E.G. Some problems in Roman history. Oxford, 1924.
AH 7479.24.5	Gundolf, F. Caesar. Berlin, 1924.
AH 7479.24.7	Gundolf, F. Caesar; Geschichte seines Ruhms. 2. Aufl. Berlin, 1925.
AH 7479.24.10	Gundolf, F. The mantle of Caesar. London, 1929.
AH 7479.27	Thaddeus, V. Julius Caesar. N.Y., 1927.
AH 7479.30	Silvagni, V. Giulio Cesare. Torino, 1930.
AH 7479.30.10	Afzelius, Adam. Pompeius og hans modstandere. København, 1930.
AH 7479.31.5	Duncan, Renée. The love life of Julius Caesar. N.Y., 1931.
AH 7479.32	Bailly, Auguste. Jules César. Paris, 1932.
AH 7479.32.5	Sonnet, Paul. Gaius Trebatius Testa. Diss. Jena, 1932.
AH 7479.33F	Pasquini, Luigi. Rimini e Giulio Cesare. Rimini, 1933.
AH 7479.34	Vassalli, Pietro. Lucio Munazio Planco, generale di Giulio Cesare, console 42 a. C. Cassino, 1934.
AH 7479.34.5	Larrouy, Maurice. Antoine et Cléopatre; La bataille d'Actium. Paris, 1934.
AH 7479.36	Foschini, Antonino. Cesare. Milano, 1936.
AH 7479.38	Viviani, Alberto. Caio Guilio Cesare. Firenze, 1938.
AH 7479.38.6	Strasburger, Hermann. Caesars Eintritt in die Geschichte. Darmstadt, 1966.
AH 7479.38.10	Walter, Gérard, Brutus et la fin de la république. Paris, 1938.
AH 7479.39	Klass, J. Cicero und Caesar. Berlin, 1939.
AH 7479.39.5	Radin, Max. Marcus Brutus. N.Y., 1939.
AH 7479.45	Ferrabino, Aldo. Cesare. Torino, 1945.
AH 7479.45.5	Vollenweider, H. Caesars Entwicklung bis zum Consulat im Urteil seiner Zeitgenossen. Zürich, 1945.
AH 7479.45.10	Delogu, Giuseppe. Bruto. Lugano, 1945.
AH 7479.45.18	Breuil, Roger. Brutus. 7. éd. Paris, 1945.
AH 7479.49.2	Gelzer, Matthias. Pompeius. 2. Aufl. München, 1959.
AH 7479.49.5	Taylor, Lily Ross. Party politics in the age of Caesar. Berkeley, 1949.
AH 7479.52	Walter, G. Caesar. N.Y., 1952.
AH 7479.54	Ooteghem, Jules van. Pompée le grand, bâtisseur d'empire. Namur, 1954.
AH 7479.55A	Duggan, A.L. Julius Caesar. 1. ed. N.Y., 1955.
AH 7479.55B	Duggan, A.L. Julius Caesar. 1. ed. N.Y., 1955.
AH 7479.55.5	Portalupi, Felicita. Bruto e i neo-atticisti. Torino, 1955.
AH 7479.56	Radio Italiana. Cesare nel brimillenario della morte. Torino, 1956.
AH 7479.57	Schmittlein, Raymond. La première campagne de César contre les Germaines. Paris, 1957.
AH 7479.58	Opermann, Hans. Caesar. Göttingen, 1958.
AH 7479.59	Madaule, Jacques. César. Paris, 1959.
AH 7479.59.5	Rossi, Ruggero F. Marco Antonio nella lotta politica della tarda republica romana. Trieste, 1959.
AH 7479.60	Thevenot, Emile. Les éduens n'ont pas trahi. Bruxelles, 1960.
AH 7479.61	Madaule, Jacques. Jules César. Paris, 1961.
AH 7479.62	Bocheński, J. Boski Juliusz. Wyd. 2. Warszawa, 1962.
AH 7479.63	Dickinson, J. Death of a republic. N.Y., 1963.
AH 7479.65	Carcopino, Jérôme. Jules César. Paris, 1965.
AH 7479.67	Balsdon, John Percy Vyvian. Julius Caesar; a political biography. 1. American ed. N.Y., 1967.
AH 7479.68	Gesche, Helga. Die Vergottung Caesars. Kallmünz, 1968.
AH 7479.69	Grant, Michael. Julius Caesar. London, 1969.
AH 7479.69.5	Holliday, Vivian L. Pompey in Cicero's correspondence and Lucan's civil war. The Hague, 1969.
AH 7479.70	Szidat, Joachim. Caesars diplomatische Tätigkeit im gallischen Krieg. Wiesbaden, 1970.
AH 7479.70.5	Carter, John M. The battle of Actium. London, 1970.
AH 7479.71	Sabben-Clare, James. Caesar and Roman politics 60-50 B.C. London, 1971.

AH 7480 - 7489   Ancient Rome in general - History by periods - Empire, 27 B.C. - 476 A.D. - General works (Table A)

	AH 7480.2	Sanna, G. Bibliografia generale dell'età romana imperiale. Firenze, 1938.
	AH 7481.01	Pamphlet box. Roman empire.
Htn	AH 7485.61F*	Mexia, Pedro. Historia imperial y Cesarea. Anvers, 1561.
Htn	AH 7485.61.10F*	Cuspinianus, J. De Caesaribus. Basileae, 1561?
Htn	AH 7486.36*	Brathuaite, R. The lives of all the Roman emperors. London, 1636.
	AH 7486.57F	Tristan, Jean. Commentaires historiques contenans l'histoire générale des empereurs, impératrices, Caesars, et tyrans de l'Empire Romain. Paris, 1657.
X Cg	AH 7486.85F	Angeloni, F. L'historia augusta. Roma, 1685.
	AH 7487.00	Lenain, L.S. Histoire des empereurs. Paris, 1700. 6v.
	AH 7487.07F	Lotich, J.P. Historicae Augusta imperatorum Rom. Amstelodami, 1707.
	AH 7487.20	Lemain de Tillemont. Histoire des empereurs. Paris, 1720-38. 6v.
	AH 7487.29	Comazzi, G.B. The morals of princes. London, 1729.
	AH 7487.32.2F	Lemain de Tillemont. Histoire des empereurs. v.1-6. Bruxelles, 1732. 3v.
	AH 7487.50	Crevier, J.B.L. Histoire des empereurs romains. Paris, 1750. 6v.
	AH 7487.50.3	Crevier, J.B.L. History of Roman emperors. London, 1755. 10v.
NEDL	AH 7487.50.10	Crevier, J.B.L. Histoire des empereurs romains. Paris, 1753-66. 12v.
	AH 7488.25	Elton, C.A. History of Roman emperors...to...last Constantine. London, 1825.
	AH 7488.28	Die Römischen Kaiser. v.1-4. Leipzig, 1828-29.
	AH 7488.41	Hoeck, K.F.C. Römische Geschichte. Braunschweig, 1841.
NEDL	AH 7488.41.3	Hoeck, K.F.C. Römische Geschichte. Braunschweig, 1841.
	AH 7488.41.5	Keightley, Thomas. History of the Roman empire, from the accession of Augustus to the end of the empire of the West. Boston, 1841.
	AH 7488.42	Garzetti, G.B. Römische Geschichte von den Unruhen. Landshut, 1842.
	AH 7488.43	Garzetti, G.B. Della condizione di Roma, d'Italia. Capologo, 1843. 5v.
	AH 7488.50	Lynam, R. The history of the Roman emperors, from Augustus to the death of Marcus Antoninus. London, 1850. 2v.
	AH 7488.52A	Merivale, Charles. History of the Romans. 2. ed. London, 1852. 7v.
NEDL	AH 7488.52B	Merivale, Charles. History of the Romans. 2. ed. London, 1852. 7v.

AH 7480 - 7489   Ancient Rome in general - History by periods - Empire, 27 B.C. - 476 A.D. - General works (Table A) - cont.

NEDL	AH 7488.52C	Merivale, Charles. History of the Romans. 2. ed. London, 1852. 7v.
NEDL	AH 7488.52.2	Merivale, Charles. History of the Romans. London, 1850. 4v.
NEDL	AH 7488.52.5	Merivale, Charles. History of the Romans. 4. London ed. N.Y., 1863. 7v.
NEDL	AH 7488.52.7	Merivale, Charles. History of Romans under the Empire. London, 1865-68. 8v.
	AH 7488.52.9	Merivale, Charles. History of the Romans under the Empire. 4. London ed. N.Y., 1866. 7v.
	AH 7488.52.9.3	Merivale, Charles. History of the Romans under the Empire. 4. London ed. N.Y., 1866. 7v.
NEDL	AH 7488.52.10	Merivale, Charles. History of the Romans under the Empire. N.Y., 1872-74. 7v.
	AH 7488.52.10.2	Merivale, Charles. History of the Romans under the Empire. London, 1872-74. 8v.
	AH 7488.55	Lamé Fleury, J.R. La storia romana. Milano, 1855.
	AH 7488.63	Reinaud, J.T. Relations politiques...de la empire romain. Paris, 1863.
	AH 7488.63.3	Zeller, J.S. Les empereurs romains. 2. ed. Paris, 1863.
	AH 7488.63.4	Zeller, J.S. Les empereurs romains. 3. ed. Paris, 1869.
	AH 7488.67	Ampère, J.J. L'empire romain à Rome. Paris, 1867. 2v.
	AH 7488.68	Büdinger, M. Untersuchungen zur Römischen Kaesergeschichte. Leipzig, 1868. 3v.
	AH 7488.70	Sievers, G.R. Studien zur Geschichte der Römischen Kaiserreiches. Berlin, 1870.
NEDL	AH 7488.75.3A	Curteis, A.M. History of Roman Empire. Philadelphia, 1875.
NEDL	AH 7488.75.3B	Curteis, A.M. History of Roman Empire. Philadelphia, 1875.
	AH 7488.80	Hertzberg, G.F. Geschichte des Römischen Kaiserreiches. Berlin, 1880.
	AH 7488.83	Schiller, K.H.F.H. Geschichte der Römischen Kaiserzeit. Gotha, 1883. 2v.
	AH 7488.83.2	Schiller, K.H.F.H. Geschichte der Römischen Kaiserzeit. v.1,pt.1-2. Gotha, 1883. 2v.
	AH 7488.83.5	Proudhon, P.J. Césarisme et Christianisme. Paris, 1883. 2v.
Htn	AH 7488.92*	Saltus, E. Imperial purple. Chicago, 1892.
	AH 7488.93	Bury, J.B. History of the Roman Empire. N.Y., 1893.
	AH 7488.93.2	Bury, J.B. History of the Roman Empire. N.Y., 1893.
	AH 7488.97	Peter, H. Die geschichtliche Literatur...Kaiserzeit. Leipzig, 1897.
	AH 7488.97.2	Vienna. Heraldischen Gesellschaft "Adler". Jahrbuch. Wien, 1897.
	AH 7488.97.5	Stueckelberg, Ernst Alfred. Die Thronfolge von Augustus bis Constantin. Wien, 1897.
	AH 7489.06	Arnold, W.T. Studies of Roman imperialism. Manchester, 1906.
	AH 7489.08.5	Jones, H.S. Roman Empire B.C. 29-A.D. 476. N.Y., 192-?
	AH 7489.09	Domaszewski, A. von. Geschichte der Römischen Kaiser. Leipzig, 1909. 2v.
	AH 7489.09.2	Domaszewski, A. von. Geschichte der Römischen Kaiser. 2. Aufl. Leipzig, 1914. 2v.
	AH 7489.09.10	Davis, W.S. Outline history of the Roman Empire. N.Y., 1909.
	AH 7489.10	McCabe, Joseph. The empresses of Rome. N.Y., 1911.
NEDL	AH 7489.11A	McCabe, Joseph. The empresses of Rome. London, 1911.
NEDL	AH 7489.11B	McCabe, Joseph. The empresses of Rome. London, 1911.
	AH 7489.11C	McCabe, Joseph. The empresses of Rome. London, 1911.
	AH 7489.13	Hahn, L. Das Kaisertum. Leipzig, 1913.
	AH 7489.13.3	Täubler, E. Imperium Romanum. Leipzig, 1913.
	AH 7489.14	Frank, Tenny. Roman imperialism. N.Y., 1914.
	AH 7489.16	Schulz, Otto T. Das Wesen des Römischen Kaisertums. Paderborn, 1916.
	AH 7489.21	Nilsson, Martin. Den romerska kejsartiden. Stockholm, 1921.
	AH 7489.22	Bloch, G. L'empire romain; évolution et decadence. Paris, 1922.
	AH 7489.22.5	Guenther, Adolf. Beiträge zur Geschichte der Kriege zwischen Römern und Parthern. Photoreproduction. Berlin, 1922.
	AH 7489.23	Vipper, R.Iu. Ocherki istorii rimskoi imperii. Berlin, 1923.
	AH 7489.24	Dessau, Hermann. Geschichte der römischen Kaiserzeit. v.1-2. Berlin, 1924-30. 3v.
	AH 7489.25	Homo, Léon P. L'empire romain. Paris, 1925.
	AH 7489.26	Nilsson, Martin. Imperial Rome. London, 1926.
	AH 7489.27	Chapot, Victor. Le monde romain. Paris, 1927.
	AH 7489.27.5	Chapot, Victor. The Roman world. N.Y., 1928.
	AH 7489.29.4	Albertini, Eugène. L'empire romain. 4. éd. Paris, 1970.
	AH 7489.30	Stevenson, G.H. The Roman Empire. London, 1930.
	AH 7489.30.5	Laqueur, Richard. Probleme der Spätantike. Stuttgart, 1930.
	AH 7489.30.9	Wagenvoort, H. Pax Augusta. Groningen, 1930.
	AH 7489.31	Kornemann, E. Doppelprinzipat und Reichsteilung im Imperium Romanum. Leipzig, 1931.
	AH 7489.31.5	Wells, Joseph. A short history of the Roman Empire to the death of Marcus Aurelius. N.Y., 1931.
	AH 7489.33.5	Brassloff, Stephen. Staat und Gesellschaft in der Römischen Kaiserzeit. Wien, 1933.
	AH 7489.33.10	Homo, Léon P. Le haut-empire. Paris, 1941.
	AH 7489.34	Carcopino, J. Points de vue sur l'impérialisme romain. Paris, 1934.
	AH 7489.35	Parker, Henry M.D. A history of the Roman world from A.D. 138 to 337. London, 1935.
	AH 7489.35.2	Parker, Henry M.D. A history of the Roman world from A.D. 138 to 337. 2. ed. London, 1958.
	AH 7489.35.3	Parker, Henry M.D. A history of the Roman world from A.D. 138 to 337. N.Y., 1939.
	AH 7489.36	Charlesworth, M.P. Five men. Cambridge, Mass., 1936.
	AH 7489.37A	Macurdy, G.H. Vassal-queens and some contemporary women in Roman Empire. Baltimore, 1937.
	AH 7489.37B	Macurdy, G.H. Vassal-queens and some contemporary women in Roman Empire. Baltimore, 1937.
	AH 7489.37.5	Charlesworth, M.P. The virtues of a Roman emperor. London, 1937.
	AH 7489.38	Pariheni, R. L'Italia imperiale da Ottaviano a Teodosio. Milano, 1938.
	AH 7489.39	Strank, J.A. Vom Herrscherideal in der Spätantike. Stuttgart, 1939.
	AH 7489.40	Solari, Arturo. L'impero romano. Genova, 1940.
	AH 7489.41	Birt, Theodor. Das römische Weltreich. Berlin, 1941.
	AH 7489.44	Salmon, E.T. A history of the Roman world from 30 B.C. to A.D. 138. N.Y., 1944.

AH 7480 - 7489 Ancient Rome in general - History by periods - Empire, 27
B.C. - 476 A.D. - General works (Table A) - cont.

AH 7489.44.1.5 Salmon, E.T. A history of the Roman world. 3. ed.
London, 1957.

AH 7489.44.5 Columba, G.M. L'impero romano. 3. ed. pt.1. Milano, 1944.

AH 7489.46.1 Walbank, Frank William. The decline of the Roman Empire in
the West. N.Y., 1953.

AH 7489.48 Schenk von Stauffenberg, A. Das Imperium und die
Völkerwanderung. München, 1948.

AH 7489.50 Toynbee, Arnold J. The cold war in the Roman Empire.
Claremont, Calif., 1950.

AH 7489.51A Charlesworth, M.P. The Roman Empire. London, 1951.
AH 7489.51B Charlesworth, M.P. The Roman Empire. London, 1951.
AH 7489.51.5 Hartke, W. Römische Kinderkaiser. Berlin, 1951.
AH 7489.53.2 Walbank, Frank William. The awful revolution: the decline
of the Roman Empire in the West. Liverpool, 1969.

AH 7489.59 Scullard, Howard Hayes. From the Gracchi to Nero.
London, 1959.

AH 7489.59.2 Scullard, Howard Hayes. From the Gracchi to Nero. 2. ed.
N.Y., 1963.

AH 7489.59.3 Scullard, Howard Hayes. From the Gracchi to Nero. 3. ed.
London, 1970.

AH 7489.60 Harmand, Louis. L'occident romain. Paris, 1960.
AH 7489.63 Behn, Friedrich. Romertum und Völkerwanderung.
Zürich, 1963.

AH 7489.64 Burdeau, François. Aspects de l'empire romain.
Paris, 1964.

AH 7489.65 Picard, Gilbert Charles. Augustus and Nero. N.Y., 1966.
AH 7489.66.1 Millar, Fergus. The Roman Empire and its neighbours.
London, 1967.

AH 7489.67.5 Petit, Paul. La paix romaine. Paris, 1967.
AH 7489.68 Grant, Michael. The climax of Rome. 1. American ed.
Boston, 1968.

AH 7489.69 Utchenko, Sergei L. Drevnii Rim. Moskva, 1969.
AH 7489.69.5 Demaugeot, Emilienne. La formation de l'Europe et les
invasions barbares. Paris, 1969.

AH 7489.69.10 Koch, Wilhelm. Caesaren, Herren am Limes.
Stuttgart, 1969.

AH 7489.70 Montherlant, Henry de. Le treizieme César. Paris, 1970.
AH 7489.74 Garzetti, Albino. From Tiberius to the Antoninos.
London, 1974.

AH 7490 - 7499 Ancient Rome in general - History by periods - Empire, 27
B.C. - 476 A.D. - The Caesars, 27 B.C. - 96 A.D. - General works (Table
A)

AH 7492.5 McCrum, M. Select documents of the principates.
Cambridge, Eng., 1961.

Htn AH 7495.26* Hüttich, J. Romische Keyser abcontra Vegt.
Strassburg, 1526.

Htn AH 7495.34* Hüttich, J. Imperatorum et Caesarum vitae.
Argentorati, 1534.

Htn AH 7495.57* Guevara, A. A chronicle, conteyning the lives of tenne
emperours of Rome. London, 1577.

Htn AH 7495.98* Lipsus, Justus. Admiranda. v.1-2. Antwerpen, 1598.
AH 7497.21 Serviez, J.R. de. Les femmes des douze Cesars.
Amsterdam, 1721.

AH 7497.21.4 Serviez, J.R. de. Les femmes des douze Cesars. 4. éd.
Amsterdam, 1722-24. 3v.

AH 7497.21.6 Serviez, J.R. de. Roman empresses, or History of lives.
Dublin, 1752. 3v.

Htn AH 7497.21.7* Serviez, J.R. de. Roman empresses, or History of lives.
London, 1752. 3v.

AH 7497.21.25 Serviez, J.R. de. The Roman empresses. London, 1899.
2v.

Htn AH 7497.84* Hancarville, Pierre François Hugues. Monumens du culte
secret des dames romaines. Nancy, 1784.

Htn AH 7497.84.5* Hancarville, Pierre François Hugues. Monumens du culte
secret des dames romaines. Rome, 1790.

Htn AH 7497.85* Hancarville, Pierre François Hugues. Monumens de la vie
privée des douze Césars. pt.1-2. Rome, 1785. 2v.

Htn AH 7497.85.5* Hancarville, Pierre François Hugues. Monumens de la vie
privée des douze Césars. Rome, 1786.

AH 7498.00F Die Römischen Kaiser. Leipzig, 18- .
AH 7498.26 Chateaubriand, François August René. Discours servant
d'introduction à l'histoire de France. Paris, 1826.

AH 7498.46 Cesare, G. di. Lettere romane dall'anno 818 della 830.
Prato, 1846.

AH 7498.52 Arnold, Thomas. Pictorial history of Rome. London, 1852.
AH 7498.53 Duruy, V. Etat du monde romain. Paris, 1853.
AH 7498.59 Champagny, F.J.M.T. Les Césars. Paris, 1859.
AH 7498.59.4 Champagny, F.J.M.T. Les Césars. 4. éd. v.1-4.
Paris, 1867. 2v.

AH 7498.61 Dubois Guchan, E.P. Tacite et son siècle. Paris, 1861.
2v.

AH 7498.65 Stahr, Adolf. Römische Kaiserfrauen. Berlin, 1865.
AH 7498.66 Peter, Carl Eduard. De fontibus historiae imperatorem
Flaviorum. Diss. Halis, 1866.

AH 7498.69.2 Beule, Ernest. Le sang de Germanicus. 2. éd. Paris, 1869.
AH 7498.75 Wiedemeister, F. Der Cäsarenwahnsinn. Hannover, 1875.
AH 7498.75.5 Boissier, Gaston. L'opposition sous les Césars.
Paris, 1875.

AH 7498.76 Capes, William W. Roman history, early empire.
London, 1876.

AH 7498.77 Capes, William W. Roman history, early empire. 2. ed.
London, 1877.

AH 7498.85A Boissier, Gaston. L'opposition sous les Césars.
Paris, 1885.

AH 7498.85B Boissier, Gaston. L'opposition sous les Césars. 3. éd.
Paris, 1892.

AH 7498.87 Capes, William W. Roman history: the early empire.
London, 1887.

AH 7498.87.4 Capes, William W. Roman history: the early empire.
N.Y., 1892.

AH 7498.87.5 Capes, William W. Roman history: the early empire.
N.Y., 1895.

AH 7498.92 Baring-Gould, Sabine. The tragedy of the Caesars.
London, 1892. 2v.

NEDL AH 7498.92.3 Baring-Gould, Sabine. The tragedy of the Caesars.
N.Y., 1892. 2v.

AH 7498.92.6 Baring-Gould, Sabine. The tragedy of the Caesars.
N.Y., 1907.

AH 7498.93 Allcroft, A.H. Early principate: history of Rome 31
B.C.-96 A.D. London, 1892.

AH 7498.93.5 Beaujeu, Maurice. Psychologie des premiers Césars.
Lyon, 1893.

AH 7499.02A Van Santvoord, S. The house of Caesar. Troy, 1902.
AH 7499.02B Van Santvoord, S. The house of Caesar. Troy, 1902.

AH 7490 - 7499 Ancient Rome in general - History by periods - Empire, 27
B.C. - 476 A.D. - The Caesars, 27 B.C. - 96 A.D. - General works (Table
A) - cont.

AH 7499.04 Greenidge, A.H.J. History of Rome during later republic.
London, 1904.

AH 7499.09 Schmaus, J. Charakterbilder römischer Kaiser.
Bamberg, 1909.

AH 7499.09.5 Silvagni, K. L'impero e le donne dei Cesari. 2. ed.
Torino, 1909.

AH 7499.11A Ferrero, G. The women of the Caesars. N.Y., 1911.
NEDL AH 7499.11B Ferrero, G. The women of the Caesars. N.Y., 1911.
AH 7499.11C Ferrero, G. The women of the Caesars. N.Y., 1911.
AH 7499.12 Ferrero, G. Die Frauen der Caesaren. Stuttgart, 1912.
AH 7499.13 Bardt, C. Römische Charakterpöpfe in Briefen.
Leipzig, 1913.

AH 7499.38 Pietrangeli, Carlo. La famiglia di Augusto. Roma, 1938.
AH 7499.46 Bourne, Frank C. The public works of the Julio-Claudians
and Flavians. Thesis. Princeton, 1946.

AH 7499.58 Carcopino, Jerôme. Passion et politique chez les Césars.
Paris, 1958.

AH 7499.58.5 Esser, A.A.M. Cäsar und die julisch-claudischen Kaiser im
biologisc-härztichen Blickfeld. Leiden, 1958.

AH 7499.64 Grenzheuser, Bruno. Kaiser und Senat in der Zeit von Nero
bis Nerva. Münster? 1964.

AH 7499.65 Africa, Thomas W. Rome of the Caesars. N.Y., 1965.
AH 7499.69 Meise, Erkhard. Untersuchungen zur Geschichte der
julisch-claudischen Dynastie. München, 1969.

AH 7500 - 7509 Ancient Rome in general - History by periods - Empire, 27
B.C. - 476 A.D. - The Caesars, 27 B.C. - 96 A.D. - Augustus, 27 B.C. -
14 A.D. (Table A)

AH 7501.2 Pamphlet box. Augustus.
AH 7502.5.4 Ehrenberg, Victor. Documents illustrating the reigns of
Augustus and Tiberius. 2. ed. Oxofrd, 1967.

AH 7506.45 Lentulus, Cyriaeus. Augustus. Amsteledami, 1645.
AH 7507.41 Rose, Christianne. Dissertationem sollemnem de Augusto.
Halae Magdeburgecae, 1741.

Htn AH 7507.53* Blackwell, Thomas. Memoirs of the courts of Augustus.
Edinburgh, 1753. 3v.

AH 7508.39 Meigs, C.D. The Augustan age. Philadelphia, 1841.
AH 7508.44 Egger, A.E. Examen critique des historiens anciens.
Paris, 1844.

AH 7508.61 Anton, A.F.M. De sideribus Augusti nataliciis quae
coniiciendo videantur. Halle, 1861.

AH 7508.66 Wutzdorff, R. Wiegestaltete sich der Caesarismus.
Langensalza, 1866.

AH 7508.67.6 Beulé, C. Ernest. Auguste, sa famille et ses amis. 6. éd.
Paris, 1895.

AH 7508.68 Beulé, C. Ernest. Auguste, sa famille et ses amis.
Paris, 1868.

AH 7508.76 Doetsch, P. Leben und Treiben am Hofe des Kaisers
Augustus, nach Tacitus. Malmedy, 1876.

AH 7508.76.7 Blaze de Bury, H. Les femmes...au temps d'Auguste. 2. éd.
Paris, 1876.

AH 7508.87 Hagen, M. von. Quaestiones criticae de belle mutinensi.
Marburgi Cattorum, 1887.

AH 7508.91 Gardthausen, V. Augustus und seine Zeit. Leipzig, 1891.
2v.

AH 7508.92 Jullien, Emile. Le fondateur de Lyon. Paris, 1892.
AH 7509.00 Gabrici, E. Il secondo viaggio di Augusto in Oriente.
Napoli, 1900.

NEDL AH 7509.00.7F Oberziner, G. Le guerre di Augusto contro i populi alpini.
Roma, 1900.

AH 7509.02 Seeck, Otto. Kaiser Augustus. Bielefeld, 1902.
AH 7509.02.8 Firth, John B. Augustus Caesar and the organization of the
empire of Rome. Freeport, 1972.

AH 7509.03 Firth, John B. Augustus Caesar. N.Y., 1903.
AH 7509.03.2 Firth, John B. Augustus Caesar. London, 1925.
AH 7509.03.3 Meyer, Eduard. Kaiser Augustus. Heidelberg, 1903.
AH 7509.03.5A Shuckburgh, E.S. Augustus...(B.C. 63-A.D. 14).
London, 1903.

AH 7509.03.5B Shuckburgh, E.S. Augustus...(B.C. 63-A.D. 14).
London, 1903.

AH 7509.11 Willrich, H. Livia. Leipzig, 1911.
AH 7509.11.5 Poupé, E. Le lieu de la rencontre de Lépide et d'Antoine.
Droguignan, 1911.

AH 7509.21 Kornemann, Ernst. Mausoleum und Tatenbericht des Augustus.
Leipzig, 1921.

AH 7509.22.3 Hadley, H.S. Rome and the world today. 3. ed. N.Y., 1934.
AH 7509.23 Nicolaus Damascenus. Nicolaus of Damascus' life of
Augustus. Northampton, 1923.

AH 7509.23.5 Nicolaus Damascenus. Nicolaus of Damascus' life of
Augustus. Menasha, 1923.

AH 7509.29 Levi, Mario A. Augusto. Roma, 1929.
AH 7509.30 Heinze, Richard. Die augusteische Kultur. Leipzig, 1930.
AH 7509.30.2 Heinze, Richard. Die augusteische Kultur. 2. Aufl.
Leipzig, 1933.

AH 7509.30.5 Hadas, Moses. Sextus Pompey. N.Y., 1930.
AH 7509.31 Brendel, Otto. Ikonographie des Kaisers Augustus. Inaug.
Diss. Nürnberg, 1931.

AH 7509.33 Daniel, Rudolf. Mareus Vipsanius Agrippa. Inaug. Diss.
Breslau, 1933.

AH 7509.33.5 Reinhold, M. Marcus Agrippa. Geneva, 1933.
AH 7509.33.7 Shipley, F.W. Agrippa's building activities in Rome. St.
Louis, 1933.

AH 7509.33.9 Levi, Mario A. Attaviano capoparti. Firenze, 1933.
2v.

AH 7509.34 Vaubel, T. Untersuchungen zu Augustus' Politik und
Staatsauffassung nach den autobiographischen Schriften.
Inaug. Diss. Düsseldorf, 1934.

AH 7509.34.5 Schur, Werner. Augustus. Lübeck, 1934.
AH 7509.34.10 Berve, H. Kaiser Augustus. Leipzig, 1934.
AH 7509.34.20 Stella, A. Druso. Gleno, 1934.
AH 7509.35 Homo, L. Auguste. Paris, 1935.
AH 7509.36 Weber, W. Princeps; Studien zur Geschichte des Augustus.
Stuttgart, 1936.

AH 7509.37A Wright, F.A. Marcus Agrippa, organizer of victory.
N.Y., 1937.

AH 7509.37B Wright, F.A. Marcus Agrippa, organizer of victory.
N.Y., 1937.

AH 7509.37.5A Buchan, J. Augustus. Boston, 1937.
AH 7509.37.5B Buchan, J. Augustus. Boston, 1937.
AH 7509.37.7 Buchan, J. Augustus. London, 1937.
AH 7509.37.10 Baker, G.P. Augustus; the golden age of Rome. N.Y., 1937.
AH 7509.37.15 Allen, B.M. Augustus Caesar. London, 1937.
AH 7509.37.20 Kornemann, E. Gli studi germanici sulla figura e l'opera
di Augusto e sulla fondazione dell'Impero romano.
Spoleto, 1937.

AH 7500   -   7509   Ancient Rome in general - History by periods - Empire, 27
B.C. - 476 A.D. - The Caesars, 27 B.C. - 96 A.D. - Augustus, 27 B.C. -
14 A.D. (Table A) - cont.

AH 7509.37.25	Bergman, J. Augustus. Stockholm, 1937.
AH 7509.37.30	Rehrmann, F.A. Kaiser Augustus. Hildesheim, 1937.
AH 7509.38.5	Hönn, Karl. Augustus. 2. Aufl. Wien, 1938.
AH 7509.38.7	Hönn, Karl. Augustus und seine Zeit. 3. Aufl. Wien, 1943.
AH 7509.38.8	Hönn, Karl. Augustus und seine Zeit. 4. Aufl. Wien, 1953.
AH 7509.38.10	Accademia dei Lincei, Rome. Augustus. Roma, 1938.
AH 7509.38.12	Trapani, Sicily. Augusto. Palermo, 1938.
AH 7509.38.15	Poplawskii, M. Oktawian August. Lublin, 1938.
AH 7509.39	Piccarolo, A. Augusto e seu século. São Paulo, 1939.
AH 7509.39.5	Augusto. Padova, 1939.
AH 7509.44	Laet, S.J. de. Aspects de la vie sociale et économique sous Auguste et Tibère. Bruxelles, 1944.
AH 7509.45	Benuzzi, Valerio. La tragedia familiare di Augusto. Milano, 1945.
AH 7509.51	Levi, Mario A. Il tempo di Augusto. Firenze, 1951.
AH 7509.52	Wagenvoot, Hendrik. Augustus. Amsterdam, 1952.
AH 7509.53	Treves, Piero. Il mito di Alessandro e la Roma d'Augusto. Milano, 1953.
AH 7509.55	Grimal, Pierre. Le siècle d'Auguste. 1. éd. Paris, 1955.
AH 7509.56	Mashkin, N.A. Il principato di Augusto. Roma, 1956. 2v.
AH 7509.56.5	Christ, Karl. Drusus und Germanicus. Paderborn, 1956.
AH 7509.59	Vittinghoff, Friedrich. Kaiser Augustus. Göttingen, 1959.
AH 7509.60	Sattler, Peter. Augustus und der Senat. Göttingen, 1960.
AH 7509.62	Rowell, H.T. Rome in the Augustan Age. Norman, 1962.
AH 7509.62.5	Picard, G.C. Auguste et Néron. Paris, 1962.
AH 7509.63	Brancati, Antonio. Augusto e la guerra di Spagna. Urbino, 1963.
AH 7509.65.1	Bowersock, Glen Warren. Augustus and the Greek world. Oxofrd, 1966.
AH 7509.68.5	Earl, Donald Charles. The age of Augustus. N.Y., 1968.
AH 7509.69	Schmitthenner, Walter. Augustus. Darmstadt, 1969.
AH 7509.69.5	Fadinger, Volker. Quellenuntersuchungen zur Geschichte des 2. Triumvirats. Inaug. Diss. München, 1969.
AH 7509.70.5	Jones, Arnold Hugh Martin. Augustus. London, 1970.

AH 7510   -   7519   Ancient Rome in general - History by periods - Empire, 27
B.C. - 476 A.D. - The Caesars, 27 B.C. - 96 A.D. - Tiberius, 14-37
(Table A)

	AH 7516.18.4	Matthieu, P. Aelius Sejanus. Histoire romaine. 4. éd. Rouen, 1626.
	AH 7516.18.6	Matthieu, P. Aelius Sejanus. Histoire romaine. Rouen, 1628.
	AH 7516.18.10	Matthieu, P. Aelius Seianus. Rouen, 1642.
Htn	AH 7516.28*	Matthieu, P. The powerfull favorite...Aelius Seianus. Paris, 1628.
Htn	AH 7516.28.2*	Matthieu, P. Unhappy prosperity express'd in History of Aelius Sejanus. 2. ed. London, 1639.
Htn	AH 7516.34*	Manzini, G.B. Political observations upon the fall of Seianus. London, 1634.
	AH 7518.04	Hamilton, E. Memoirs of the life of Agrippina. Bath, 1804. 3v.
	AH 7518.63	Stahr, Adolf. Tiberius. Berlin, 1863.
	AH 7518.63.3	Stahr, Adolf. Tiberius. 2. Aufl. Berlin, 1873.
	AH 7518.68	Beulé, C.E. Tibère et l'héritage d'Auguste. Paris, 1868.
	AH 7518.68.3	Beulé, C.E. Tibère et l'héritage d'Auguste. 2. éd. Paris, 1868.
	AH 7518.68.4	Beulé, C.E. Tibère et l'héritage d'Auguste. 4. éd. Paris, 1883.
	AH 7518.70	Freytag, L. Tiberius und Tacitus. Berlin, 1870.
	AH 7518.74	Thamm, M. De Fontibus ad Tiberii historiam pertinentibus. Halis Saxonum, 1874.
	AH 7518.80	Stahr, Adolf. Agrippina, die Mutter Neros. 2. Aufl. Berlin, 1880.
	AH 7518.82	Weisse, J. P. Populaere forelaesninger over Tiberius og Nero. Kristiania, 1882.
	AH 7518.90	Ferber, Curtius. Utrum metuerit Tiberius Germanicum necne quaeritur. Inaug. Diss. Hamburgi, 1890.
	AH 7518.92	Ihne, Wilhelm. Zur Ehrenrettung des Kaisers Tiberius. Strassburg, 1892.
	AH 7518.93	Schott, W. Kriminaljustiz und des Kaisers Tiberius. Erlangen, 1893.
	AH 7518.96	Willenbucher, H. Tiberius und die Verschwörung des Sejan. Gütersloh, 1896.
	AH 7519.01	Viertel, A. Tiberius und Germanicus. Göttingen, 1901.
	AH 7519.01.5	Lévy, L. Quo modo Tiberius Claudius Nero. Paris, 1901.
	AH 7519.02	Tarver, J.C. Tiberius the tyrant. N.Y., 1902.
	AH 7519.03.2	Bergmans, Jan. Die Quellen der Vita Tiberii. Bockhandel, 1903.
	AH 7519.12	Schwab, J. Leben und Charakter des Tiberius Claudius Nero nach Velleius. Tetschen, 1912.
	AH 7519.29	Baker, G.P. Tiberius Caesar. N.Y., 1929.
	AH 7519.31	Marsh, Frank Burr. The reign of Tiberius. London, 1931.
	AH 7519.34	Ciaceri, E. Tiberio, successore di Augusto. Milano, 1934.
	AH 7519.34.5	Ciaceri, E. Tiberio, successore di Augusto. 2. ed. Roma, 1944.
	AH 7519.42	Smith, Charles E. Tiberius and the Roman Empire. Baton Rouge, 1942.
	AH 7519.43	Rogers, R.S. Studies in the reign of Tiberius. Baltimore, 1943.
	AH 7519.47	Franzero, Charles M. The memoirs of Pontius Pilate. London, 1947.
	AH 7519.52	Marañón, G. Tiberius. München, 1952.
	AH 7519.52.3	Marañón, G. Tiberius. London, 1956.
	AH 7519.56	Pezzella, Federico. L'imperatore Tiberio. Santa Maria, 1956.
	AH 7519.59	Gollub, Wilhelm. Tiberius. München, 1959.
	AH 7519.60	Kornemann, Ernst. Tiberius. Stuttgart, 1960.
	AH 7519.68	Meissner, Erhard. Sejan, Tiberius und die Nachfolge im Punzipat. Erlangen, 1968.
	AH 7519.72	Seager, Robin. Tiberius. London, 1972.

AH 7520   -   7529   Ancient Rome in general - History by periods - Empire, 27
B.C. - 476 A.D. - The Caesars, 27 B.C. - 96 A.D. - Caligula, 37-41
(Table A)

NEDL	AH 7528.94	Quidde, L. Caligula. Leipzig, 1894.
	AH 7529.06	Venturini, L. Caligola. Milano, 1906.
	AH 7529.09	Linnert, U. Beiträge zur Geschichte Caligulas. Nürnberg, 1909.
	AH 7529.30.5	Sachs, Hanns. Bubi Caligula. 2. Aufl. Wien, 1932.
	AH 7529.30.15	Sachs, Hanns. Caligula. London, 1931.
	AH 7529.34	Balsdom, John Percy Vyvian D. The Emperor Gaius Caligula. Oxford, 1934.
	AH 7529.34.6	Balsdom, John Percy Vyvian D. The Emperor Gaius Caligula. Oxford, 1964.

AH 7530   -   7539   Ancient Rome in general - History by periods - Empire, 27
B.C. - 476 A.D. - The Caesars, 27 B.C. - 96 A.D. - Claudius I, 41-54
(Table A)

AH 7532.2	Smallwood, Edith Mary. Documents illustrating the principates of Gaius Claudius and Nero. Cambridge, 1967.
AH 7538.58	Lehmann, H. Claudius und Nero und ihre Zeit. Gotha, 1858.
AH 7538.58.2	Lehmann, H. Claudius und seine Zeit. Leipzig, 1877.
AH 7538.76	Double, L. L'empereur Claude. Paris, 1876.
AH 7538.85	Ziegler, A. Die Regierung des Kaisers Claudius I. Wien, 1885.
AH 7539.11	Vivell, Karl. Chronoligisch-kritische Untersuchungen zur Geschichte des Kaisers Claudius. Diss. Freiburg, 1911.
AH 7539.24	Ruth, Thomas De C. The problem of Claudius. Diss. Baltimore, 1924.
AH 7539.27	Zielinski, T. L'empereur Claude et l'idée de la domination mondiale des Juifs. Bruxelles, 1927.
AH 7539.29	Stroux, J. Eine Gerichtsreform des Kaisers Claudius. München, 1929.
AH 7539.32	Momigliano, A. L'opera dell'imperatore Claudio. Firenze, 1932.
AH 7539.32.5	Momigliano, A. Claudius, the emperor. Oxford, 1934.
AH 7539.38	Stuart, Meriwether. Portraiture of Claudius. Thesis. N.Y., 1938.
AH 7539.39	Charlesworth, M.P. Documents illustrating the reigns of Cladius and Nero. Cambridge, Eng., 1939.
AH 7539.40A	Scramuzza, V.M. The emperor Claudius. Cambridge, 1940.
AH 7539.40B	Scramuzza, V.M. The emperor Claudius. Cambridge, 1940.
AH 7539.52	Gordon, A.E. Quintus Veranius. Berkeley, 1952.

AH 7540   -   7549   Ancient Rome in general - History by periods - Empire, 27
B.C. - 476 A.D. - The Caesars, 27 B.C. - 96 A.D. - Nero, 54-68 (Table A)

Htn	AH 7546.27*	Bolton, Edmund. Nero Caesar. London, 1627.
	AH 7548.39	Reinhold, K.W. Die Römische Kaisergeschichte. Pasewalf, 1839.
	AH 7548.53	Abbott, Jacob. History of Nero. N.Y., 1853.
	AH 7548.72	Raabe, A.H. Geschichte und Bild von Nero. Utrecht, 1872.
	AH 7548.72.5	Abbott, Jacob. History of Nero. N.Y., 1872.
	AH 7548.72.7	Schiller, H. Geschichte des Römischen Kaiserreichs. Berlin, 1872.
	AH 7548.96	Nordmeyer, G. Der Tod Neros in der Legende. Mors, 1896.
	AH 7549.00	Sabatini, F. Pascal. L'incendio di Roma. Roma, 1901. 5 pam.
	AH 7549.00.2	Pascal, Carlo. L'incendio di Roma e i primi christiani. Milano, 1900.
	AH 7549.00.3	Pascal, Carlo. L'incendie de Rome et premiers chrétiens. Paris, 1902.
	AH 7549.02	Cavazzi, C.G. Sull'incendio di Roma. Roma, 1902.
	AH 7549.02.5	Difesa dei primi cristiani e martiri. Roma, 1902.
	AH 7549.04	Allard, Paul. Les chrétiens ont-ils incendie Rome sous Néron. Paris, 1904.
	AH 7549.05F	Profumo, A. Le fonti ed i tempi d'incendio. Roma, 1905.
	AH 7549.07	Klette, E.T. Die Christenkatastrophe unter Nero. Tübingen, 1907.
	AH 7549.15	Barbagallo, C. La catastrofe di Nerone. Catania, 1915.
	AH 7549.16	Caiti, G. Una nuova ipotesi sulle origini dell'incendio Nerone ano. Roma, 1916.
	AH 7549.20	Jahn, John Nicholas H. A critical study of the history of the Emperor Nero. Thesis. N.Y.? 1920.
	AH 7549.23	Pascal, Carlo. Nerone. Milano, 1923.
	AH 7549.30	Schumann, Gerhard. Hellenistische und griechische Elemente in der Regierung Neros. Inaug. Diss. Leipzig, 1930.
	AH 7549.30.5	Weigall, Arthur E.P.B. Nero, emperor of Rome. London, 1930.
	AH 7549.30.10	Weigall, Arthur E.P.B. Nero. N.Y., 1930.
	AH 7549.30.11	Weigall, Arthur E.P.B. Nero, the singing emperor of Rome. N.Y., 1930.
	AH 7549.35	Hermant, Abel. Poppée, l'amante de l'Antéchrist. Paris, 1935.
	AH 7549.45	Cananesi, M. Nerone. Milano, 1945.
	AH 7549.48	Heinz, Kurt. Das Bild Kaiser Neros bei Seneca. Inaug. Diss. Biel, 1948.
	AH 7549.49	Levi, Mario A. Nerone e i suoi tempi. Milano, 1949.
	AH 7549.54	Franzero, Charles M. The life and times of Nero. London, 1954.
	AH 7549.55	Walter, Gérard. Néron. Paris, 1955.
	AH 7549.55.2	Walter, Gérard. Nero. London, 1957.
	AH 7549.60	Beaujeu, J. L'incendie de Rome. Bruxelles, 1960.
	AH 7549.62	Pichon, Jean Charles. Néron et le mystère des origines chrétiennes. Paris, 1971.
	AH 7549.64	Bishop, John H. Nero; the man and the legend. London, 1964.
	AH 7549.64.2	Bishop, John H. Nero, the man and the legend. N.Y., 1965.
	AH 7549.69	Warmington, Brian Herbert. Nero: reality and legend. London, 1969.
	AH 7549.70	Grant, Michael. Nero. London, 1970.
	AH 7549.72	Cizek, Eugen. L'époque de Néron et ses controverses idéologiques. Leiden, 1972.

AH 7550   -   7559   Ancient Rome in general - History by periods - Empire, 27
B.C. - 476 A.D. - The Caesars, 27 B.C. - 96 A.D. - Galba, Otto,
Vitellius, 68-69 (Table A)

AH 7558.58	Champagny, F.J.M.T.N. Rome et la Judée au temps de la chute de Néron. Paris, 1858.
AH 7558.80	Beckurts, F. Zur Quellenkritik des Tacitus, Sueton. Braunschweig, 1880.
AH 7558.80.7	Krauss, L. De Vitarum Imperatoris Othonis. Zweibrücken, 1880.
AH 7559.08	Henderson, B.W. Civil war and rebellion in Roman Empire. London, 1908.
AH 7559.39	Zancan, P. La crisi del principato nell'anno. Padova, 1939.
AH 7559.47	Manfri, Guglielmo. La crisi politica dell'anno 68-69 d. C. Bologna, 1947.
AH 7559.63	Hallermann, Burkhard. Untersuchungen zu den Truppenbewegungen in den Jahren 68/69 nach Christ. Inaug. Diss. Würzburg, 1963.

AH 7560   -   7569   Ancient Rome in general - History by periods - Empire, 27
B.C. - 476 A.D. - The Caesars, 27 B.C. - 96 A.D. - Vespasian, 69-79
(Table A)

AH 7567.85	Cramero, A.W.D. Vespasianus sive de vita et legislatione. Ienae, 1785.
AH 7569.11	Menrad, K. Gestaltung des römischen Staats...Flairer Vespasian. München, 1911.
AH 7569.41	Bersanetti, G.M. Vespasiano. Roma, 1941.
AH 7569.49	Homo, Léon P. Vespasien. Paris, 1949.

AH 7560 - 7569   Ancient Rome in general - History by periods - Empire, 27 B.C. - 476 A.D. - The Caesars, 27 B.C. - 96 A.D. - Vespasian, 69-79 (Table A) - cont.

AH 7569.65   Vanella, Giovanni. L'Adventus di Vespasiano nei suoi aspetti mistico-religiosi e giundico-costituzionali. Napoli, 1965.

AH 7570 - 7579   Ancient Rome in general - History by periods - Empire, 27 B.C. - 476 A.D. - The Caesars, 27 B.C. - 96 A.D. - Titus, 79-81 (Table A)

AH 7571.01   Pamphlet box. Roman history. The Caesars. Titus.

AH 7578.67   Renier, Léon. Mémoire sur les officiers qui assistèrent au conseil de guerre. Paris, 1867.

AH 7578.83   Hoffman, O.A. De Imperatoris Titi temporibus. Marpeogi, 1883.

AH 7579.00   Mayor, G. Kaiser Titus. Eger, 1900.

AH 7579.05   Wolff-Beckh, B. Kaiser Titus und der jüdische Krieg. Berlin, 1905.

AH 7579.55   Fortina, M. L'imperatore Tito. Torino, 1955.

AH 7580 - 7589   Ancient Rome in general - History by periods - Empire, 27 B.C. - 476 A.D. - The Caesars, 27 B.C. - 96 A.D. - Domitian, 81-96 (Table A)

AH 7581.01   Pamphlet box. Roman history. The Caesars. Domitian.

AH 7588.57   Imhof, Albert T. Flavius Domitianus. Halle, 1857.

AH 7588.75   Krauss, J.E. Zur Charakteristik des Kaisers Domitianus. Amberg, 1875.

AH 7589.02   Vieze, H. Domitians Chattenkrieg. Berlin, 1902.

AH 7589.45   Arias, P. Domiziano. Catania, 1945.

AH 7590 - 7599   Ancient Rome in general - History by periods - Empire, 27 B.C. - 476 A.D. - The Antonines, 96-180 - General works (Table A)

AH 7592.2   Smallwood, Edith Mary. Documents illustrating the principates of Nerva Trajan and Hadrian. Cambridge, Eng., 1966.

AH 7598.00   Hegewisch, D.H. Über die Menscheit...Epoche in der römischen Geschichte. Hamburg, 1800.

AH 7598.00.3   Hegewisch, D.H. Essai sur l'epoque de l'histoire romaine. Paris, 1834.

AH 7598.66   Champagny, F.J.M.T. Les Antonins. Paris, 1866. 3v.

NEDL AH 7598.76   Capes, William W. The Roman Empire of the second century. London, 1876.

NEDL AH 7598.76.9   Capes, William W. The Roman Empire of the second century. N.Y., 1887.

AH 7598.76.12   Capes, William W. The Roman Empire of the second century. N.Y., 1891.

AH 7598.76.15   Capes, William W. The Roman Empire of the second century. N.Y., 1895.

AH 7599.03   Henderson, B.W. Life and principate of Emperor Nero. London, 1903.

AH 7599.27   Henderson, B.W. Five Roman emperors. Cambridge, Eng., 1927.

AH 7599.37   Weber, William. Rom; Herrschertum und Reich in zweiten Jahrhundert. Stuttgart, 1937.

AH 7599.47   Homo, Léon P. Le siècle d'or de l'empire romain. 3. éd. Paris, 1947.

AH 7599.47.2   Homo, Léon P. Le siècle d'or de l'empire romain. Paris, 1969.

AH 7599.65   Les empéreurs romains d'Espagne. Paris, 1965.

AH 7600 - 7609   Ancient Rome in general - History by periods - Empire, 27 B.C. - 476 A.D. - The Antonines, 96-180 - Nerva, 96-98 (Table A)

AH 7607.48   Lampe, H. Dissertatio juridica prior de Marco Coccejo Nerva Roman. Bremae, 1748? 2 pam.

AH 7609.50   Garzetti, A. Nerva. Roma, 1950.

AH 7610 - 7619   Ancient Rome in general - History by periods - Empire, 27 B.C. - 476 A.D. - The Antonines, 96-180 - Trajan, 98-117 (Table A)

AH 7617.93   Mannert, K. Res Traiani imperatoris ad Danubium gestae. Norimbergae, 1793.

NEDL AH 7618.37   Francke, J.F. Zur Geschichte Trajans. Gustrow, 1837.

AH 7618.37.3   Francke, J.F. Zur Geschichte Trajans. 2. Aufl. Quedlinburg, 1840.

AH 7618.77   La Berge, C. de. Essai sur le regne de Trajan. Paris, 1877.

AH 7618.86   Pellisson, M. Rome sous Trajan. Paris, 1886.

AH 7618.95   Cantarelli, Luigi. Le fonti per la storia dell'imperatore Traiano. Roma, 1895.

AH 7619.26   Paribeni, R. Optimus princeps. Messina, 1926-27.

AH 7619.37   Gross, W.H. Studien zu den Bildnissen Trajans. Inaug. Diss. Würzburg? 1937.

AH 7619.40   Carrea d'Oliveira, E. Roma imperiale ai tempi di Traiano. Milano, 1940.

AH 7619.48   Lepper, F.A. Trajan's Paethian war. London, 1948.

AH 7620 - 7629   Ancient Rome in general - History by periods - Empire, 27 B.C. - 476 A.D. - The Antonines, 96-180 - Hadrian, 117-138 (Table A)

AH 7626.92   Dadwell, Henry. Praelectiones academicae in schola historices camdeniana. Oxonii, 1692.

AH 7628.51   Gregorovius, F.A. Geschichte des römischen Kaisers Hadrian. Königsberg, 1851.

AH 7628.57   Caillet, Jules. De ratione in imperio Romano ordinando ab Hadriano imperatore adhibita. Diss. Parisiis, 1857.

AH 7628.69   Lucas, Charles. L'empereur-architecte Adrien. Paris, 1869.

AH 7628.83   Schurz, Wilhelm. De mutationibus in imperio romano ordinando ab imperatore Hadriano factis. pt.1. Bonnae, 1883.

AH 7628.84.3   Gregorovius, F.A. Der Kaiser Hadrian. 2. Aufl. Stuttgart, 1884.

AH 7628.92   Hitzig, H.F. Stellung Kaiser Hadrians. Zürich, 1892.

AH 7628.97   Schurz, Wilhelm. Die Militärreorganisation Hadrians. Leipzig, 1897.

AH 7628.98   Gregorovius, F.A. The Emperor Hadrian. London, 1898.

AH 7628.99   Schulz, O.T. Leben des Kaisers Hadrian. Leipzig, 1904.

AH 7629.04   Mecklin, J.M. Hadrians Rescript an Minicius Fundanus. Leipzig, 1899.

AH 7629.05   Kornemann, E. Kaiser Hadrian. Leipzig, 1905.

AH 7629.07   Weber, W. Untersuchungen zur Geschichte...Hadrianus. Leipzig, 1907.

AH 7629.07.5   Kornemann, E. Anax mainôs â Hadrhinôs. Leipzig, 1907.

AH 7629.07.7   Weber, W. Die Adoption Kaiser Hadrians. Leipzig, 1907.

AH 7629.17   Lacey, R.H. The equestrian officials of Trajan and Hadrian. Thesis. Princeton, 1917.

AH 7629.20   Gray, William D. A study...life of Hadrian prior...accession. Northampton, 1919?

AH 7620 - 7629   Ancient Rome in general - History by periods - Empire, 27 B.C. - 476 A.D. - The Antonines, 96-180 - Hadrian, 117-138 (Table A) - cont.

AH 7629.23   Henderson, B.W. The life and principate of the Emperor Hadrian. London, 1923.

AH 7629.29   Perret, Louis. La titulature impériale d'Hadrien. Paris, 1929.

AH 7629.46   Corradi, Guiseppe. Adriano. Roma, 1946.

AH 7629.50   Orgeval, B. L'empereur Hadrien. Paris, 1950.

AH 7629.60   Perowne, Stewart. Hadrian. London, 1960.

AH 7630 - 7639   Ancient Rome in general - History by periods - Empire, 27 B.C. - 476 A.D. - The Antonines, 96-180 - Antoninus Pius, 138-161 (Table A)

AH 7636.67   Keuchenius, R. Antoninus Pius. Amstelaedami, 1667.

AH 7638.95   Bryant, E.E. Reign of Antoninus Pius. Cambridge, 1895.

AH 7639.10   Leszynsky, R. Die Lösung des Antoninusrätsels. Berlin, 1910.

AH 7639.33   Hüttl, Willy. Antoninus Pius. Prag, 1933-36.

AH 7639.46   Regibus, Luca de. Antonino Pio. Rome, 1946.

AH 7640 - 7649   Ancient Rome in general - History by periods - Empire, 27 B.C. - 476 A.D. - The Antonines, 96-180 - Marcus Aurelius, 161-180 (Table A)

AH 7648.08   Thomas, A.L. Eulogium on Marcus Aurelius. N.Y., 1808.

Htn   AH 7648.08.5*   Thomas, A.L. Eulogium on Marcus Aurelius. N.Y., 1808.

AH 7648.60   Des Vergers, M.J.A. Essai sur Marc Aurèle. Paris, 1860.

AH 7648.68   Bodek, Arnold. Marcus Aurelius Antoninus als Zeitgenosse und Freund des Rabbi Jehuda ha-Nasi. Leipzig, 1868.

AH 7648.90   Dimmock, Thomas. Marcus Aurelius; an address...1890. St. Louis, 1890.

AH 7648.97   Dartique-Peyroux, J. Marc Aurèle dans ses rapports avec le christianisme. Paris, 1897.

AH 7649.14   Eberlein, Hellmut. Kaiser Mark Aurel und die Christen. Inaug. Diss. Breslau, 1914.

AH 7649.23   Schwendemann, J. Der historische Wert der Vita Marci bei Scriptores Historiae Augustae. Photoreproduction. Heidelberg, 1923.

AH 7649.35   Hayward, F.H. Marcus Aurelius, a saviour of men. London, 1935.

AH 7649.51   Farquharson, A.S.L. Marcus Aurelius. Oxford, 1951.

AH 7649.53   Carrata Thomes, Franco. Il regno di Marco Aurelio. Torino, 1953.

AH 7649.54   Goerlitz, W. Marc Aurel, Kaiser und Philosoph. Stuttgart, 1954.

AH 7649.62   Proyart, Pierre de. Marc Aurèle. Paris, 1962.

AH 7649.66   Birley, Anthony Richard. Marcus Aurelius. London, 1966.

AH 7649.68   Schrempf, Claus. Weisheit und Weltherrschaft. München, 1968.

AH 7650   Ancient Rome in general - History by periods - Empire, 27 B.C. - 476 A.D. - The Decline, 180-476 - General works - Gibbon's Decline and Fall - Complete editions in English

AH 7650.3F   Gibbon, Edward. History of decline and fall of the Roman Empire. v.1, 2. ed. London, 1776-78. 6v.

NEDL AH 7650.7   Gibbon, Edward. History of decline and fall of the Roman Empire. London, 1782. 3v.

NEDL AH 7650.8   Gibbon, Edward. History of the decline and fall of the Roman Empire. London, 1783. 6v.

NEDL AH 7650.13   Gibbon, Edward. The history of the decline and fall of the Roman Empire. London, 1802. 12v.

AH 7650.17   Gibbon, Edward. History of decline and fall of Roman Empire. Philadelphia, 1804. 8v.

NEDL AH 7650.17   Gibbon, Edward. History of decline and fall of Roman Empire. Philadelphia, 1804. 8v.

NEDL AH 7650.24   Gibbon, Edward. History of decline and fall of Roman Empire. London, 1820. 12v.

NEDL AH 7650.24.5   Gibbon, Edward. History of decline and fall of Roman Empire. London, 1820. 12v.

NEDL AH 7650.25   Gibbon, Edward. History of decline and fall of Roman Empire. London, 1821. 2v.

NEDL AH 7650.26   Gibbon, Edward. History of decline and fall of Roman Empire. London, 1821. 12v.

NEDL AH 7650.27   Gibbon, Edward. History of decline and fall of Roman Empire. London, 1825. 8v.

NEDL AH 7650.29   Gibbon, Edward. History of the decline and fall of the Roman Empire. London, 1826-28. 4v.

NEDL AH 7650.31   Gibbon, Edward. The history of the decline and fall of the Roman Empire. London, 1827. 11v.

AH 7650.32A   Gibbon, Edward. History of decline and fall of Roman Empire. Oxford, 1827. 8v.

AH 7650.32B   Gibbon, Edward. History of decline and fall of Roman Empire. Oxford, 1827. 8v.

NEDL AH 7650.33   Gibbon, Edward. History of decline and fall of Roman Empire. 6. American ed. Philadelphia, 1830. 4v.

AH 7650.34   Gibbon, Edward. History of decline and fall of Roman Empire. v.2-8. London, 1862. 7v.

NEDL AH 7650.36   Gibbon, Edward. History of decline and fall of Roman Empire. Paris, 1840. 8v.

NEDL AH 7650.37   Gibbon, Edward. History of decline and fall of Roman Empire. Paris, 1840. 8v.

NEDL AH 7650.38   Gibbon, Edward. History of decline and fall of Roman Empire. v.3-8. Paris, 1840. 3v.

NEDL AH 7650.38.5   Gibbon, Edward. History of decline and fall of Roman Empire. Cincinnati, 1840.

NEDL AH 7650.39   Gibbon, Edward. History of decline and fall of Roman Empire. N.Y., 1841-43. 4v.

NEDL AH 7650.40   Gibbon, Edward. History of decline and fall of Roman Empire. N.Y., 1843-44. 4v.

NEDL AH 7650.40.5   Gibbon, Edward. History of the decline and fall of the Roman Empire. N.Y., 1845-46. 4v.

AH 7650.41   Gibbon, Edward. History of decline and fall of the Roman Empire. Chicago, 1845. 5v.

NEDL AH 7650.41.5   Gibbon, Edward. History of decline and fall of the Roman Empire. Philadelphia, 1845. 5v.

NEDL AH 7650.43   Gibbon, Edward. History of the decline and fall of the Roman Empire. v.3. N.Y., 1847.

NEDL AH 7650.46   Gibbon, Edward. History of decline and fall of Roman Empire. Boston, 1850.

NEDL AH 7650.49   Gibbon, Edward. History of decline and fall of Roman Empire. Boston, 1851. 6v.

NEDL AH 7650.53   Gibbon, Edward. History of decline and fall of Roman Empire. London, 1853. 7v.

NEDL AH 7650.54   Gibbon, E. History of decline and fall of Roman Empire. Boston, 1854. 8v.

NEDL AH 7650.60   Gibbon, Edward. History of decline and fall of Roman Empire. London, 1872. 3v.

NEDL AH 7650.65   Gibbon, Edward. History of decline and fall of Roman Empire. London, 1872. 3v.

AH 7650   Ancient Rome in general - History by periods - Empire, 27 B.C. - 476
A.D. - The Decline, 180-476 - General works - Gibbon's Decline and
Fall - Complete editions in English - cont.

NEDL	AH 7650.67	Gibbon, Edward. History of decline and fall of Roman Empire. N.Y., 1880. 6v.
	AH 7650.70	Gibbon, Edward. The history of the decline and fall of the Roman Empire. London, 1887. 8v.
	AH 7650.72	Gibbon, Edward. The history of the decline and fall of the Roman Empire. London, 1898-1901. 7v.
NEDL	AH 7650.75	Gibbon, Edward. History of decline and fall of Roman Empire. N.Y., 1902. 5v.
	AH 7650.80.5A	Gibbon, Edward. History of decline and fall of Roman Empire. v.2. London, 1910.
	AH 7650.80.5B	Gibbon, Edward. History of decline and fall of Roman Empire. v.2. London, 1910.
	AH 7650.85	Gibbon, Edward. History of decline and fall of Roman Empire. N.Y., 1914. 7v.
	AH 7650.88A	Gibbon, Edward. The decline and fall of the Roman Empire. N.Y., 1932. 2v.
	AH 7650.88B	Gibbon, Edward. The decline and fall of the Roman Empire. N.Y., 1932. 2v.
	AH 7650.90	Gibbon, Edward. The decline and fall of the Roman Empire. London, 1929-36. 6v.

AH 7651   Ancient Rome in general - History by periods - Empire, 27 B.C. - 476
A.D. - The Decline, 180-476 - General works - Gibbon's Decline and
Fall - Abridgements and Selections

NEDL	AH 7651.2	Gibbon, Edward. Abridgement of Gibbon's History of Roman Empire. London, 1790. 2v.
NEDL	AH 7651.5	Gibbon, Edward. Abridgement of Gibbon's History of Roman Empire. 2. ed. London, 1807. 2v.
NEDL	AH 7651.10A	Gibbon, Edward. Student's Gibbon. N.Y., 1857.
NEDL	AH 7651.10B	Gibbon, Edward. Student's Gibbon. N.Y., 1857.
NEDL	AH 7651.10.5	Gibbon, Edward. The history of the decline and fall of the Roman Empire. N.Y., 1860.
NEDL	AH 7651.11	Gibbon, Edward. History of the decline and fall of the Roman Empire. N.Y., 1862.
NEDL	AH 7651.12	Gibbon, Edward. Student's Gibbon. History of Roman Empire. N.Y., 1859.
NEDL	AH 7651.12.5	Gibbon, Edward. Student's Gibbon. History of Roman Empire. N.Y., 1867.
NEDL	AH 7651.13	Gibbon, Edward. Student's Gibbon. History of Roman Empire. N.Y., 1868.
NEDL	AH 7651.15	Gibbon, Edward. Student's Gibbon. History of Roman Empire. London, 1868.
	AH 7651.19	Gibbon, Edward. The history of the decline and fall of the Roman Empire. v.2. London, 1899.
	AH 7651.22	Gibbon, Edward. Selections from the decline and fall of the Roman Empire. London, 1947.
	AH 7651.25	Gibbon, Edward. Decline and fall of the Roman Empire. London, 1953.
	AH 7651.25.1	Gibbon, Edward. The decline and fall of the Roman Empire. 1. American ed. N.Y., 1960.
	AH 7651.25.2	Gibbon, Edward. The decline and fall of the Roman Empire. N.Y., 1963.
	AH 7651.26	Gibbon, Edward. The history of the decline and fall of the Roman Empire. 2. ed. v.2-7. London, 1926-29. 6v.
	AH 7651.28	Gibbon, Edward. The decline and fall of the Roman Empire. London, 1960.

AH 7652   Ancient Rome in general - History by periods - Empire, 27 B.C. - 476
A.D. - The Decline, 180-476 - General works - Gibbon's Decline and
Fall - Translations

NEDL	AH 7652.8	Gibbon, Edward. Histoire de la décadence et de la chute de l'Empire Romain. Paris, 1812. 13v.
NEDL	AH 7652.10	Gibbon, Edward. Histoire de la décadence et de la chute de l'Empire Romain. Paris, 1839. 2v.
NEDL	AH 7652.16	Gibbon, Edward. Geschichte...des Römischen Rechts. Frankfurt, 1800. 13v.

AH 7653   Ancient Rome in general - History by periods - Empire, 27 B.C. - 476
A.D. - The Decline, 180-476 - General works - Gibbon's Decline and
Fall - Criticism

	AH 7653.8	Davis, H.E. Reply to Gibbon's vindication. London, 1779.
Htn	AH 7653.10*	Chelsum, J. Remarks on 2 last chapters of Gibbon's History of Roman Empire. London, 1776.
	AH 7653.15	Evans, J. Attempt to account for infidelity of Edward Gibbon. London, n.d.
	AH 7653.16	Milner, Joseph. Gibbon's account of Christianity. York, 1781.
	AH 7653.17	White, Lynn Townsend. The transformation of the Roman world; Gibbon's problem after two centuries. Berkeley, 1966.
	AH 7653.18	Whitaker, J. Gibbon's History of decline and fall of Roman Empire. London, 1791.
	AH 7653.20	Collins, William M. The student's companion to Gibbon. Melbourne, 1957.
	AH 7653.35	Ringeling, Hans G. Pragmatismus in Edward Gibbons Geschichte vom Verfall und Untergang des romischen Reiches. Inaug. Diss. Schönberg, 1915.
	AH 7653.38	Jordan, David. Gibbon and his Roman Empire. Urbana, 1971.
	AH 7653.40	Lyon, Bryce Dale. The origins of the Middle Ages; Pirenne's challenge to Gibbon. 1. ed. N.Y., 1972.

AH 7655 - 7659   Ancient Rome in general - History by periods - Empire, 27
B.C. - 476 A.D. - The Decline, 180-476 - General works - Other general
works (By date)

Htn	AH 7655.15*	Leto, G.P. Romanae historiae compendium. Argentorati, 1515.
Htn	AH 7655.44*	Biondo, F. Historie da la declinatione. Venetia, 1544. 2v.
Htn	AH 7655.93F*	Sigonio, Carlo. Caroli Sigonii historiarum de occidentali imperio libri XX. Francofurti, 1591-93. 2 pam.
	AH 7658.35	Simonde de Simondi, J.C.L. History of the fall of the Roman Empire. Philadelphia, 1835.
	AH 7658.36	Simonde de Simondi, J.C.L. Histoire de la chute de l'Empire romain. Bruxelles, 1836.
	AH 7658.59	Wietersheim, E. von. Geschichte der Völkerwanderung. Leipzig, 1859. 4v.
	AH 7658.61	Sheppard, J.G. The fall of Rome. London, 1861.
	AH 7658.61.5	Sheppard, J.G. The fall of Rome. London, 1892.
	AH 7658.95	Seeck, Otto. Geschichte des Untergangs der antiken Welt. v.1-6. Appendix. Berlin, 1895. 8v.
	AH 7658.95.5	Seeck, Otto. Geschichte des Untergangs der antiken Welt. v.1-6. Appendix 1-6. Stuttgart, 1920-23. 12v.
	AH 7659.03	Hartmann, L.M. Untergang der antiken Welt. Wien, 1903.
	AH 7659.03.2	Hartmann, L.M. Untergang der antiken Welt. Wien, 1910.

AH 7655 - 7659   Ancient Rome in general - History by periods - Empire, 27
B.C. - 476 A.D. - The Decline, 180-476 - General works - Other general
works (By date) - cont.

	AH 7659.03.5	Schulz, Otto. Beiträge zur Kritik unserer litterarischen Überlieferung fur die Zeit von Commodus' Sturze bis auf den Tod des M. Aurelius Antonius. Leipzig, 1903.
	AH 7659.13	Pais, E. Storia critica di Roma durante i primi cinque secoli. v.1-4. Roma, 1913- 5v.
	AH 7659.16	Woodward, E.L. Christianity and nationalism in...Roman Empire. Photoreproduction. London, 1916.
	AH 7659.19F	Seeck, Otto. Regesten der Kaiser und Päpste für die Jahre 311 bis 476 nach Christ. Stuttgart, 1919.
	AH 7659.27	White, Edward L. Why Rome fell. N.Y., 1927.
	AH 7659.28	Stein, Ernst. Geschichte der spätrömischen Reiches I. Wien, 1928.
	AH 7659.28.5	Stein, Ernst. Histoire du Bas-Empire. v.1-2. Paris, 1949. 3v.
	AH 7659.30	Rehm, Walther. Der Untergang Roms im abendländischen Denken. Leipzig, 1930.
	AH 7659.31.5	Lot, Ferdinand. La fin du monde antique et le début du moyen âge. Paris, 1951.
	AH 7659.31.10	Lot, Ferdinand. The end of the ancient world and the beginnings of the Middle Ages. N.Y., 1961.
	AH 7659.36A	Arragon, R.F. The transition from the ancient to the medieval world. N.Y., 1936.
	AH 7659.36B	Arragon, R.F. The transition from the ancient to the medieval world. N.Y., 1936.
	AH 7659.39	Werner, H. Der Untergang Roms. Stuttgart, 1939.
	AH 7659.39.5	Solari, A. Il rinnovamento dell'impero romano. Milano, 1938-
	AH 7659.47	Kaphahn, Fritz. Zwischen Antike und Mittelalter. München, 1947.
	AH 7659.47.5	Kaphahn, Fritz. Zwischen Antike und Mittelalter. München, 1944.
	AH 7659.51	Demougeot, E. De l'unité à la division de l'Empire romain. Paris, 1951.
	AH 7659.55	Katz, Solomon. The decline of Rome and the rise of mediaeval Europe. Ithaca, N.Y., 1955.
	AH 7659.58	Haywood, R.M. The myth of Rome's fall. N.Y., 1958.
	AH 7659.62	Centro Italiano di Studi Sull'alto Medioevo. Il passaggio dall'antichita al Medioevo in occidente. Spoleto, 1962.
	AH 7659.62.5	Perowne, Stewart. Caesars and saints. 1. ed. N.Y., 1963.
	AH 7659.62.10	Kagan, Donald. Decline and fall of the Roman Empire. Boston, 1962.
	AH 7659.63	Chambers, M.H. The fall of Rome. N.Y., 1963.
	AH 7659.64	Rémondon, Roger. La crise de l'Empire romain. Paris, 1964.
	AH 7659.64.2	Rémondon, Roger. La crise de l'Empire romain de Marc Aurèle à Anastase. 2. éd. Paris, 1970.
	AH 7659.67.5	Grant, Michael. The climax of Rome. Saskatoon, 1967.
	AH 7659.68	Coster, Charles Henry. Late Roman studies. Cambridge, 1968.
	AH 7659.69	Downey, Glanville. The late Roman Empire. N.Y., 1969.
	AH 7659.70	Christ, Karl. Der Untergang des Romischen Reiches. Darmstadt, 1970.

AH 7660 - 7669   Ancient Rome in general - History by periods - Empire, 27
B.C. - 476 A.D. - The Decline, 180-476 - Commodus, 180-192 (Table A)

	AH 7668.76	Ceuleneer, A. de. Marcia la favorite de Commode. Paris, 1876.

AH 7670 - 7679   Ancient Rome in general - History by periods - Empire, 27
B.C. - 476 A.D. - The Decline, 180-476 - Pertinax, 192 (Table A)

	AH 7678.83	Hundertmark, J. De imperatore Pertinace; dissertatio historica. Monasterii Guestfalorum, 1883.

AH 7690 - 7699   Ancient Rome in general - History by periods - Empire, 27
B.C. - 476 A.D. - The Decline, 180-476 - Septimius Severus, 193-211
(Table A)

	AH 7693.1	Balty, Janine. Essai d'iconographie de l'empereur Clodius Albinus. Bruxelles, 1966.
	AH 7693.5	Severus, Lucius Septimius. Apokrimata; decisions of Septimius Severus on legal matters. N.Y., 1954.
	AH 7698.80	Ceuleneer, A. de. Essai sur la vie et le regne de Septime Sévère. Bruxelles, 1880.
	AH 7698.84	Fuchs, C. Geschichte des Kaisers L. Septimius Severus. Wien, 1884.
	AH 7698.88	Wirth, A. Quaestiones severianae. Lipsiae, 1888.
	AH 7699.18A	Platnauer, Maurice. Life and reign of the Emperor Lucius Septimius Severus. London, 1918.
	AH 7699.18B	Platnauer, Maurice. Life and reign of the Emperor Lucius Septimius Severus. London, 1918.
	AH 7699.18.2	Platnauer, Maurice. The life and reign of the Emperor Lucius Septimius Severus. Westport, 1970.
	AH 7699.21	Haselroeck, J. Untersuchungen zur Geschichte des Kaisers Septimius Severus. Heidelberg, 1921.
	AH 7699.45	Murphy, G.J. The reign of the Emperor L. Septimius Severus. Philadelphia, 1945.
	AH 7699.71	Birley, Anthony Richard. Septimus Severus: the African emperor. London, 1971.

AH 7700 - 7709   Ancient Rome in general - History by periods - Empire, 27
B.C. - 476 A.D. - The Decline, 180-476 - Third century in general (Table
A)

	AH 7700.5	Walser, Gerold. Die Krise des römischen Reiches; Bericht über die Forschungen zur Geschichte des 3. Jahrhunderts. Berlin, 1962.
	AH 7707.66	Montégut, J.F. Essai historique sur la famille de l'Empereur Valérien. n.p., 1766. 2 pam.
	AH 7708.49	Ware, William. Aurelian. v.2. N.Y., 1849.
	AH 7708.52	Hoyns, Georg. Geschichte der s.g. driessig Inrannen. Göttingen, 1852.
	AH 7708.67	Bernhardt, T. Geschichte Roms von Valerian. Berlin, 1867.
	AH 7708.70.3	Champagny, F.J.M.T. Les Césars du troisieme siècle. Paris, 1878. 3v.
	AH 7708.74	Feugère, A.C. A.C. Cilnius Maecenas G. Octaviano Augusto ad adipiscendum gerendumque principatum quantum profuerit. Thesis. Paris, 1874.
	AH 7708.91	Meyer, Paul. De Maecenatis oratione a Dione ficta. Inaug. Diss. Berolini, 1891.
	AH 7709.03	Homo, Léon P. De Claudio Gothico, Romanorum. Lutetiae Parisiorum, 1903.
	AH 7709.05.1	Forquet de Dorne, Charles B. Les Césars africains et syriens et l'anarchie militaire. [Ristampa anastatica]. Roma, 1970.
	AH 7709.09	Dannhäuser, Erich. Geschichte des Kaisers Probus (276-282). Jena, 1909.

AH 7700 - 7709   Ancient Rome in general - History by periods - Empire, 27 B.C. - 476 A.D. - The Decline, 180-476 - Third century in general (Table A) - cont.

AH 7709.11	Lehmann, Karl Friedrich Wilhelm. Kaiser Gordian III. Berlin, 1911.
AH 7709.11.3	Lehmann, Karl Friedrich Wilhelm. Kaiser Gordian III. Berlin, 1911.
AH 7709.11.5	Crees, J.H.E. The reign of the Emperor Probus. London, 1911.
AH 7709.19	Schulz, Otto T. Vom Prinzipat zum Dominat. Das Wesen des römischen Kaisertums. Paderborn, 1919.
AH 7709.36	Regibus, L. Problemi d'impero nella storia romana del terzo secolo. Torino, 1936.
AH 7709.39	Regibus, L. La monarchia militare di Gallieno. Recco, 1939.
AH 7709.42A	Howe, L.L. The pretorian prefect from Commodus to Diocletian (A.D. 180-305). Chicago, 1942.
AH 7709.42B	Howe, L.L. The pretorian prefect from Commodus to Diocletian (A.D. 180-305). Thesis. Chicago, 1942.
AH 7709.45	Passerini, Alfredo. I Severi da Caracalla ad Alessandro Severo. Roma, 1945.
AH 7709.49	Manni, Eugenio. L'impero di Gallieno. Roma, 1949.
AH 7709.51	Pollione, T. Le vite di Valeriano e di Gallieno. Palermo, 1951.
AH 7709.52.5	Vitucci, G. L'imperatore Probo. Roma, 1952.
AH 7709.57	Bebelon, Jean. Impératrices syriennes. Paris, 1957.
AH 7709.61	Sotgiu, Giovanna. Studi sull'epigrafia di Aureliano. Palmero, 1961.
AH 7709.64	Jones, A.H.M. The later Roman Empire. v.1-3, Atlas. Oxford, 1964. 3v.
AH 7709.64.5	Bellezza, Angela. Massimino il Trace. Genova, 1964.
AH 7709.67	Alföldi, András. Studien zur Geschichte der Weltkrise des 3. Jahrhunderts nach Christus. Darmstadt, 1967-
AH 7709.67.5	Brauer, George C. The young emperors, Rome, A.D. 193-244. N.Y., 1967.
AH 7709.68	Merten, Elke W. Zwei Herrscherfeste in der Historia Augusta. Thesis. Bonn, 1968.
AH 7709.70	Mazza, Mario. Lotte sociali e restaurazione autoritaria nel 3. secolo d. C. Catania, 1970.

AH 7710 - 7719   Ancient Rome in general - History by periods - Empire, 27 B.C. - 476 A.D. - The Decline, 180-476 - Caracalla and Macrinus, 211-218 (Table A)

AH 7718.90	Schneider, C. Beiträge zur Geschichte Caracallas. Marburg, 1890.
AH 7719.09	Schulz, O.T. Der römische Kaiser Caracalla. Leipzig, 1909.

AH 7720 - 7729   Ancient Rome in general - History by periods - Empire, 27 B.C. - 476 A.D. - The Decline, 180-476 - Heliogabalus, 218-222 (Table A)

AH 7727.11	Valsecchi, V. De M. Aurelii Antonine Elaggbali tribunitici potestate V. Florentiae, 1711.
AH 7728.02	Chaussard, P.J.B. Héliogabale, ou Esquisse morale. Paris, 1802.
AH 7729.03	Duviquet, Georges. Héliogabale. Paris, 1903.
AH 7729.11	Hönn, K. Quellenuntersuchungen zu den Viten des Heliogabalus. Leipzig, 1911.
AH 7729.11.3	Hay, J.S. The amazing emperor Heliogabalus. London, 1911.
AH 7729.34A	Artaud, Antonin. Héliogabale. Paris, 1934.
AH 7729.34B	Artaud, Antonin. Héliogabale. Photoreproduction. Paris, 1934.
AH 7729.57	Villeneuve, Roland. Héliogabale. Paris, 1957.
AH 7729.69	Optendrenk, Theo. Die Religionspolitik des Kaisers Elagabal im Spiegel der Historia Augusta. Bonn, 1969.

AH 7730 - 7739   Ancient Rome in general - History by periods - Empire, 27 B.C. - 476 A.D. - The Decline, 180-476 - Severus Alexander, 222-235 (Table A)

AH 7738.34	Grepps, J.G.H. Dissertation sur les laraires de l'empereur Sévère Alexandre. Belley, 1834.
AH 7738.73	Muche, Eugenius. Forschungen über den römischen Kaiser M.A. Severus Alexander. Schweidnitz, 1873.
AH 7738.76	Porrath, Otto. Der Kaiser Alexander Severus. Halle, 1876.
AH 7739.07A	Hopkins, R.V.N. Life of Alexander Severus. Cambridge, 1907.
AH 7739.07B	Hopkins, R.V.N. Life of Alexander Severus. Cambridge, 1907.
AH 7739.08	Thiele, W. De Severo Alexandro Imperatore. Berolini, 1908.
AH 7739.09	Thiele, W. De Severo Alexandro Imperatore. Berolini, 1909.
AH 7739.11	Boer, H.G.W. De Julia Mamaea Severi A. Matre. Rhenum, 1911.
AH 7739.12	Stein, Arthur. Die kaiserlichen Verwaltungsbeamten unter Severus Alexander, 222-235. Prag, 1912.
AH 7739.25	Jardé, Auguste. Etudes critiques sur la vie et le règne de Sévère Alexandre. Thèse. Paris, 1925.
AH 7739.25.5	Jardé, Auguste. Etudes critiques sur la vie et le règne de Sévère Alexandre. Paris, 1925.

AH 7740 - 7749   Ancient Rome in general - History by periods - Empire, 27 B.C. - 476 A.D. - The Decline, 180-476 - Diocletian, 284-305 (Table A)

AH 7748.61	Mommsen, Theodor. Uber die Zeitfolge der Verordnungen Diocletians. Berlin, 1861.
AH 7748.69	Preuss, Theodor. Kaiser Diocletan. Leipzig, 1869.
AH 7749.18	Bulić, F. Car Dijoklecijan. Zagreb, 1918.
AH 7749.20	Costa, Giovanni. Diocleziano. Roma, 1920.
AH 7749.23	Bjarnason, T.H. Diocletianus keisari. Reykjavík, 1923.
AH 7749.26	Stade, Kurt. Der Politiker Diokletian und die letzte grosse Christenverfolgung. Wiesbaden, 1926.
AH 7749.58	Gigli, Guido. L'impero romano dall'abdicazione di Diocleziano alla morte di Costantino (305-337). Roma, 1958.

AH 7750 - 7759   Ancient Rome in general - History by periods - Empire, 27 B.C. - 476 A.D. - The Decline, 180-476 - Constantine I, 306-337 (Table A)

	AH 7751.01	Pamphlet box. Roman history. The Decline.
	AH 7752.5	Internationaler Konstantinorden. Schriftenreihe. Zürich. 1,1959+
	AH 7757.27	Balduini, F. Constantinus Magnus. Lipsiae, 1727.
	AH 7758.17	Mauso, J.C.F. Leben Constantins des Grossen. Breslau, 1817.
	AH 7758.53	Burckhardt, Jacob. Die Zeit Konstantins des Grossen. Leipzig, 1853.
Htn	AH 7758.53.2*	Burckhardt, Jacob. Die Zeit Konstantins des Grossen. Basel, 1853.

AH 7750 - 7759   Ancient Rome in general - History by periods - Empire, 27 B.C. - 476 A.D. - The Decline, 180-476 - Constantine I, 306-337 (Table A) - cont.

AH 7758.61	Aube, B. De Constantino imperatore, pontifice max. Lutetiae, 1861.
AH 7758.80	Burckhardt, Jacob. Die Zeit Constantins des Grossen. Leipzig, 1880.
AH 7758.98	Burckhardt, Jacob. Die Zeit Constantins des Grossen. Leipzig, 1898.
AH 7759.05	Firth, J.B. Constantine the Great. N.Y., 1905.
AH 7759.08	Jenks, J. Heidentum und Christianismus des Kaisers Konstantin des Grossen. Sereth, 1907.
AH 7759.11	Couzard, R. Sainte Hélène d'après l'histoire et la tradition. Paris, 1911.
AH 7759.12	Centonze, L. L'imperatore Costantino e la chiesa cattolica. Bari, 1912.
AH 7759.24	Burckhardt, Jacob. DieZeit Konstantins des Grossen. 4e Aufl. Leipzig, 1924.
AH 7759.24.3	Burckhardt, Jacob. Die Zeit Konstantins des Grossen. Stuttgart, 1929.
AH 7759.27	Burch, Vacher. Myth and Constantine the Great. London, 1927.
AH 7759.28	Salvatorelli, Luigi. Costantino il Grande. Roma, 1928.
AH 7759.30	Baker, G.P. Constantine the Great and the Christian revolution. N.Y., 1930.
AH 7759.30.5	Baynes, N.H. Constantine the Great and the Christian Church. London, 1930.
AH 7759.31	Koch, J.A. Studien ouer den tijd von Constantijn den Grooten. Dordrecht, 1931.
AH 7759.32	Piganiol, A. L'empereur Constantin. Paris, 1932.
AH 7759.40.5	Hönn, Karl. Konstantin der Grosse. Leipzig, 1945.
AH 7759.42A	Holsapple, L.B. Constantine the Great. N.Y., 1942.
AH 7759.42B	Holsapple, L.B. Constantine the Great. N.Y., 1942.
AH 7759.48	Alfoldi, Andras. The conversion of Constantine and pagan Rome. Oxford, 1948.
AH 7759.49	Burckhardt, Jacob. The age of Constantine the Great. N.Y., 1949.
AH 7759.49.5	Vogt, J. Constantin der Grosse. München, 1949.
AH 7759.49.6	Vogt, J. Constantin der Grosse und sein Jahrhundert. 2. Aufl. München, 1960.
AH 7759.50	Burckhardt, Jacob. Die Zeit Constantins des Grossen. Bern, 1950.
AH 7759.53	Franchi de' Cavalieri, P. Constantiniana. Roma, 1953.
AH 7759.55	Instinsky, H.U. Beschafsstuhl und Kaiserthron. 1. Aufl. München, 1955.
AH 7759.57	Voelkl, Ludwig. Der Kaiser Konstantin. München, 1957.
AH 7759.58	Doerries, Hermann. Konstantin der Grosse. Stuttgart, 1958.
AH 7759.60	Doerries, Hermann. Constantine and religious liberty. New Haven, 1960.
AH 7759.62	Calderone, S. Costantino e il cattolicesimo. Firenze, 1962.
AH 7759.64	Fera, Giovanni. Constantino e il cristianesimo. Milano, 1964.
AH 7759.69	MacMullen, Ramsay. Constantine. N.Y., 1969.
AH 7759.69.5	Kyriazēs, Kōstas D. Kōnstantinos ho Megas. Athēnai, 1969.
AH 7759.71	Smith, John Holland. Constantine the Great. London, 1971.

AH 7760 - 7769   Ancient Rome in general - History by periods - Empire, 27 B.C. - 476 A.D. - The Decline, 180-476 - Fourth century in general (Table A)

AH 7762.5	Abinnaeus, Flavius. The Abinnaeus archive; papers of a Roman officer in the reign of Constantius II. Oxford, 1962.
AH 7766.81	Fléchier, E. Histoire de Theodose le Grand. Paris, 1681.
AH 7768.65	Richter, H. Das weströmische Reich. Berlin, 1865.
AH 7768.73	Léotard, E. Essae sur la condition des barbares. Paris, 1873.
AH 7768.78	Güldenpenning, A. Der Kaiser Theodosius der Grosse. Halle, 1878.
AH 7768.85	Löffler, Eduard. Der Comes Theodosius. Inaug. Diss. Halle, 1885.
AH 7768.89	Gimazane, Joannes. De secundo sallustio promoto. Diss. Tolosae, 1889.
AH 7769.03	Runkel, F. Schlacht bei Adrianapel. Rostock, 1903.
AH 7769.13	Cherniavskii, N.F. Imperator Feodosii Velikii i ego tsaratvovanie v tserkovno istoricheskom otnoshenii. Sergiev Posad, 1913.
AH 7769.15	Olivetti, Alberto. Sulle stragi di Costantinopoli succedute alla morte di Costantino il Grande. n.p., n.d.
AH 7769.15.5	Olivetti, Alberto. Osservazioni storiche cronologiche sulla guerra di Costanzo II contro i Persiani. Torino, 1915.
AH 7769.27	Heering, Walter. Kaiser Valentinian I (364-375). Inaug. Diss. Magdeburg, 1927.
AH 7769.33	Solari, A. La crisi dell'impero romano. Milano, 1933-37. 5v.
AH 7769.47.2	Piganiol, André. L'empire chrétien (325-395). 2. éd. Paris, 1972.
AH 7769.52	Alföldi, Andras. A conflict of ideas in the late Roman Empire. Oxford, 1952.
AH 7769.53	Fortina, M. L'imperatore Graziano. Torino, 1953.
AH 7769.59	Gigli, Guido. La dinastia die secondi Flavii: Costantino II, Costante, Costanzo II, 337-361. Roma, 1959.
AH 7769.61	Kohns, Hans Peter. Versorgungskrisen und Hungerrevolten im spätantiken Rom. Bonn, 1961.
AH 7769.64	Paven, Massimiliano. La politica gotica di Teodosio nella publiastica del suo tempo. Roma, 1964.
AH 7769.65	Stroheker, Karl Friedrich. Germanentum und Spätantike. Zürich, 1965.
AH 7769.67	Perowne, Stewart. The end of the Roman world. N.Y., 1967.
AH 7769.67.5	Paschoud, François. Roma aeterna. Rome, 1967.
AH 7769.68	Lippold, Adolf. Theodosius der Grosse und seine Zeit. Stuttgart, 1968.
AH 7769.69	Castritius, Helmut. Studien zu Maximinus Daia. Diss. Kallmünz, 1969.
AH 7769.69.5	Stallknecht, Bernt. Untersuchungen zur römischen Aussenpolitik in der Spätantike (306-395). Bonn, 1969.
AH 7769.72	Krawczuk, Aleksander. Ród konstantgna. Wyd. 1. Warszawa, 1972. 2v.

AH 7770 - 7779   Ancient Rome in general - History by periods - Empire, 27 B.C. - 476 A.D. - The Decline, 180-476 - Julian, 361-363 (Table A)

	AH 7776.81	Freher, Marquard. Sapphirus Constantii imp. Aug. exposita anno 1602. Heidelbergae, 1681.
Htn	AH 7776.83.5*	Hickes, George. Jovian. 2. ed. London, 1683.
Htn	AH 7776.89*	Johnson, Samuel. Julian's arts to undermine and extirpate Christianity. London, 1689.

Classified Listing

AH 7770 - 7779   Ancient Rome in general - History by periods - Empire, 27 B.C. - 476 A.D. - The Decline, 180-476 - Julian, 361-363 (Table A) - cont.

AH 7777.46	La Bleterie. Vie de l'Empereur Julien. Paris, 1746.
AH 7778.12.5	Neander, A. The Emperor Julian and his generation. N.Y., 1850.
AH 7778.77	Naville, Henri Adrien. Julien l'apostat. Paris, 1877.
AH 7778.79	Rendall, Gerald Henry. Emperor Julian, paganism and Christianity. Cambridge, 1879.
AH 7778.92	Reinhardt, G. Der Perserkreig des Kaisers Julian. Dessau, 1892.
AH 7778.97	Scholl, Karl. Ein Kaiser im Kampf mit seiner Zeit. 2. Aufl. Bamberg, 1897?
AH 7779.01.3	Negri, G. L'imperatore Giuliano L'Apostata. Milano, 1902.
AH 7779.01.4	Negri, G. Julian the Apostate. 2. ed. N.Y., 1905. 2v.
AH 7779.07	Nostitz-Rieneck, R.G. Vom Tode des Kaisers Julian. Feldkirch, 1907.
AH 7779.12	Barbagallo, C. Giuliano l'Apostata. Genova, 1912.
AH 7779.14	Geffcken, J. Kaiser Julianus. Leipzig, 1914.
AH 7779.19	Martin, Edward J. The emperor Julian. London, 1919.
AH 7779.30	Bidez, Joseph. La vie de l'empereur Julien. Paris, 1930.
AH 7779.30.5	Bidez, Joseph. Kaiser Julian. Hamburg, 1956.
NEDL AH 7779.30.10	Bidez, Joseph. Julian der Abtrünnige. 5. Aufl. München, 1946?
AH 7779.33	Weis, B.K. Das Restitutions-Edict Kaiser Julians. Inaug. Diss. Bruchsal, 1933.
AH 7779.34	Farney, R. La religion de l'empereur Julien et le mysticisme du temps. Paris, 1934.
AH 7779.36	Andreotti, R. Il regno dell'imperatore Giuliano. Bologna, 1936.
AH 7779.37	Ridley, F.A. Julian the Apostate and the rise of Christianity. London, 1937.
AH 7779.40	Nicolaas, T.W.J. Praetextatus. Proefschrift. Nijmegen, 1940.
AH 7779.49	Gigli, Guido. L'artodossia. Roma, 1949.
AH 7779.56	Ricciotti, Giuseppe. L'imperatore Giuliano l'Apostata secondo i documenti. Milano, 1956.
AH 7779.56.4	Riciotti, Giuseppe. Julian the Apostate. Milwaukee, 1960.
AH 7779.71	Manacorda, Mario Alighiero. La paideia di Achille. Roma, 1971.

AH 7780 - 7789   Ancient Rome in general - History by periods - Empire, 27 B.C. - 476 A.D. - The Decline, 180-476 - Jovian, 363-364 (Table A)

AH 7787.50	La Bleterie. Histoire de l'Empereur Jovien. Amsterdam, 1750.

AH 7790 - 7799   Ancient Rome in general - History by periods - Empire, 27 B.C. - 476 A.D. - The Decline, 180-476 - Fifth century in general (Table A)

AH 7797.50	Bel, C.A. De avitis Hungarorum sedibus. n.p., n.d.
AH 7798.41	Gaupp, E.T. De occupatione et divisione. Vratislaviae, 1841.
AH 7798.48	Pavirani, D.P. Memorie istoriche della vita e governo. Ravenna, 1848.
AH 7798.56	Thierry, A.S.D. Histoire d'Attila. Paris, 1856. 2v.
AH 7798.56.6	Thierry, A.S.D. Histoire d'Attila et de ses successeurs. 6. éd. Paris, 1884. 2v.
AH 7798.60	Thierry, A.S.D. Récits de l'histoire romaine. Paris, 1860.
AH 7798.60.3	Thierry, A.S.D. Récits de l'histoire romaine. 2. éd. Paris, 1862.
AH 7798.60.7	Thierry, A.S.D. Récits de l'histoire romaine. 5. éd. Paris, 1876.
AH 7798.65	Thierry, A.S.D. Nouveaux récits de l'histoire romaine. Paris, 1865.
AH 7798.68	Aretin, J.C.F. Diplomatische Abhandlung. Prag, 1868.
AH 7798.78	Foss, Rudolph. Attila in der Geschichte und Sage. Düsseldorf, 1878.
AH 7798.78.5	Foss, Rudolph. Attila in der Geschichte und Sage. Gütersloh, 1910?
AH 7798.80	Thierry, A.S.D. Alaric; l'agonie de l'empire. 2. éd. Paris, 1880.
AH 7798.82	Jornandes. De origine actibusque Getarum. Freiburg, 1882.
AH 7798.84	Keller, Rudolf. Stilicho. Berlin, 1884.
AH 7798.85	Birt, Theodor. De moribus christianis quantum Stilichonis. Marburg, 1885.
AH 7798.89	Hodgkin, T. Dynasty of Theodosius. Oxford, 1889.
AH 7798.97	Schild, W. Galla Placidia. Halle, 1897.
AH 7799.00	Hossner, K. Die letzten Kaiser des römischen Abendlandes. Bielitz, 1900.
AH 7799.04A	Freeman, E.A. Western Europe in the fifth century. London, 1904.
AH 7799.04B	Freeman, E.A. Western Europe in the fifth century. London, 1904.
AH 7799.05	Bugiani, Carlo. Storia di Ezio generale dell'Impero Sotto Valentiniano III. Firenze, 1905.
AH 7799.06	Bierbach, Karl. Die letzten Jahre Attilas. Berlin, 1906.
AH 7799.08	Nagl, M.A. Galla Placidia. Paderborn, 1908.
AH 7799.09	Bugiani, Carlo. L'Imperatore Avito. Pistoia, 1909.
AH 7799.15	Sundwall, J. Weströmische Studien. Berlin, 1915.
AH 7799.15.5	Hutton, Edward. Attila and the Huns. N.Y., 1915.
AH 7799.16	Solari, Arturo. Gli unni e Attila. Pisa, 1916.
AH 7799.28	Brion, Marcel. La vie d'Attila. 2. éd. Paris, 1928.
AH 7799.30	Brion, Marcel. La vie d'Alaric. 7. éd. Paris, 1930.
AH 7799.40	Németh, Gyula. Attila és hunjai. Budapest, 1940.
AH 7799.40.5	Németh, Gyula. Attila és Hunlari. Istanbul, 1962.
AH 7799.48	Thompson, E.A. A history of Attila and the Huns. Oxford, 1948.
AH 7799.51	Homeyer, H. Attila der Hunnenkönig von seinen Zeitgenossen dargestellt. Berlin, 1951.
AH 7799.51.5	Altheim, F. Attila und die Hunne. Baden-Baden, 1951.
AH 7799.51.10	Mazzarino, S. Aspetti sociali del quarto secolo. Roma, 1951.
AH 7799.53	Dévignes, G. Ici, le monde changea de maitre. Paris, 1953.
AH 7799.55	Boak, A.E.R. Manpower shortage and the fall of the Roman Empire in the West. Ann Arbor, 1955.
AH 7799.61	Sirago, V.A. Galla Placidia e la trasformazione politica dell'Occidente. Louvain, 1961.
AH 7799.67	Wes, Marinus Antony. Das Ende des Kaisertums im Westen des Römischen Reichs. 's-Gravenhage, 1967.
AH 7799.68	Oost, Stewart Irvin. Galla Placidia Augusta. Chicago, 1968.
AH 7799.68.5	Kaegi, Walter Emil. Byzantium and the decline of Rome. Princeton, 1968.
AH 7799.71	Lafferty, Raphael A. The fall of Rome. Garden City, N.Y., 1971.

AH 7790 - 7799   Ancient Rome in general - History by periods - Empire, 27 B.C. - 476 A.D. - The Decline, 180-476 - Fifth century in general (Table A) - cont.

AH 7799.71.5	Luponiac, Pierre de. La disparition de l'Empire romain en Occident. Paris, 1971.

AH 7800 - 7809   Ancient Rome in general - Chronology (Table A)

Htn	AH 7805.57.2F*	Panvinio, Onofrio. Fasti et triumphi. Venetiis, 1557.
Htn	AH 7805.99F*	Piglius, S.V. Annales magistratuum. Antverpiae, 1599.
	AH 7805.99.2F	Piglius, S.V. Annales romanorum qui commentarii vicem supplent in omnes veteres historiae romanae scriptores. Antverpiae, 1599-1615. 3v.
	AH 7806.35	Nagel, J.A.M. Fastorum Romanorum formula post consulatum. Altorfii, 1635.
Htn	AH 7807.61PF*	Piranesii, I.B. Lapides capitolini sive fasti. Romae, 1761.
	AH 7807.98	Calendriers de Rome ancienne et moderne. Paris. 1798
	AH 7808.01	Sigonio, Carlo. Mutinensis fasti consulares ac triumphi acti. Oxonii, 1801.
	AH 7808.15	Golbrig, Karl Friedrich. Über Jahrform und Jahrrechnung bei den Römern. Salzwedel, 1815.
	AH 7808.18	Borghesi, Bartolomeo. Nuovi frammenti dei fasti consolari capitolini. Milano, 1818.
	AH 7808.18.3	Borghesi, Bartolomeo. Nuovi frammenti dei fasti consolari capitolini. Milano, 1820.
	AH 7808.20F	Fea, Carlo. Frammenti di fasti consolari e trionfali ultimamente scaperti nel faro romano e altrove. Roma, 1820.
	AH 7808.33	Fasti consulares capitolini. Altonae, 1833.
	AH 7808.35.5	Peter, Carl. Zeittafeln der römischen Geschichte. Halle, 1864.
	AH 7808.35.6	Peter, Carl. Zeittafeln der römischen Geschichte. 5. Aufl. Halle, 1875.
	AH 7808.35.7	Peter, Carl. Zeittafeln der römischen Geschichte. Halle, 1882.
	AH 7808.40	Fischer, Ernst. Griechische und römische Zeittafeln. Altona, 1840-46. 2v.
	AH 7808.41	Peter, C.L. Zeittafeln der römischen Geschichte. 6. Aufl. Halle, 1882.
	AH 7808.45	Clinton, Henry Fynes. Fasti Romani, the civil and literary chronology of Rome and Constantinople. v.2. Oxford, 1845.
	AH 7808.53	Scheiffele, A. Jahrbücher der römischen Geschichte. Nördlingen, 1853.
	AH 7808.53.5	Clinton, Henry Fynes. An epitome of the civil and literary chronology of Rome and Constantinople. Oxford, 1853.
	AH 7808.57	Simon, Heinrich O. Fastorum Romanorum Specimen. Berlin, 1857.
	AH 7808.58.3	Mommsen, Theodor. Römische Chronologie bis auf Caesar. 2. Aufl. Berlin, 1859.
	AH 7808.60	Hartmann, O.E. Zum römischen Kalender. Eine Entgegnung auf Th. Mommsen's Angriffe. Göttingen, 1860.
	AH 7808.61	Hermann, F.C. Der römische Schalttag seit Julius Caesar. Berlin, 1861.
	AH 7808.69	Helfferich, A. Der altroemische Kalender. Frankfurt, 1869.
	AH 7808.69.5	Huschke, G.P.E. Das alte römische Jahr und seine Tage. Breslau, 1869.
	AH 7808.72	Boor, C. de. Fasti censorii. Berolini, 1873.
	AH 7808.75	Wehrmann, Petrus. Fasti Praetorii ab A.V. DLXXXVIII ad A.V. DCCX. Berolini, 1875.
	AH 7808.75.2	Hölzl, M. Fasti Praetorii ad A.V. DLXXXVII ad A.V. DCCX. Lipsiae, 1876.
	AH 7808.75.3	Levison, Hans. Fasti Praetorii inde ab Octaviani imperii singularis intro usque ad Hadriani Exitum. Vratislaviae, 1892.
	AH 7808.76	Hofmann, A. Drei synchronistische Daten des römischen Kalenders vor der julianischen Reform. Triest, 1876.
	AH 7808.80	Hex, Rudolph. Die älteste Monatseintheilung der Römer. Jena, 1883.
	AH 7808.81	Klein, Joseph. Fasti Consularis inde a Caesaris nece usque ad imperium Diocletiani. Lipsiae, 1881.
	AH 7808.82	Hartmann, O.E. Der römische Kalender. Leipzig, 1882.
	AH 7808.83	Matzat, H. Römische Chronologie. Berlin, 1883. 2v.
	AH 7808.85	Holzapfel, L. Römische Chronologie. Leipzig, 1885.
	AH 7808.86	Soltau, Wilhelm. Prolegomena zu einer römische Chronologie. Berlin, 1886.
	AH 7808.87	Thouret, Georg. Die Chronologie von 218/217 v. Chr. Berlin, 1887.
	AH 7808.88	Soltau, Wilhelm. Die römischen Amstjahre auf ihren natürlichen Zeitwerth reducirt. Freiburg, 1888.
	AH 7808.88.5	Werner, C. De feriis Latinis. Coloniae, 1888.
	AH 7808.89	Matzat, Heinrich. Römische Zeitrechnung für die Jahre 219 bis 1 v. Chr. Berlin, 1880.
	AH 7808.89.15	Soltau, Wilhelm. Römische Chronologie. Freiburg, 1889.
	AH 7808.90	Kaestner, O. De aeris quae ab imperio Caesaris. Lipsiae, 1890.
	AH 7808.91	Goyau, G. Chronologie de l'Empire romain. Paris, 1891.
	AH 7808.91.3F	Wissowa, Georgius. De feriis anni Romanorum vetustissimi observationes selectae. Marburgi, 1891.
	AH 7808.93	Groebe, P. De legibus et senatus consultis anno 710. Lipsiae, 1893.
	AH 7808.99.3	Rolando, A. Chronologia storica Roma. Torino, 1899.
	AH 7809.02	Pais, Ettore. Saggio di illustrazione del calendario romano. Napoli, 1902.
	AH 7809.05	Schön, Georg. Die Differenzen zwischen der kapitolinischen Magistrats- und Triumphliste. Wien, 1905.
	AH 7809.08	Bülz, Martin. Dem Jahresberichte geht eine wissenschaftliche Abhandlung des Oberlehrers. Zittau, 1908.
	AH 7809.08.5	Varese, P. Cronologia romana. Roma, 1908.
	AH 7809.09	Leuzl, Oscar. Die römische Jahrzählung. Tübingen, 1909.
	AH 7809.09.5	Fasti Consulares. Fasti consulares imperii romani von 30 v. Chr. bis 565 n. Chr. Bonn, 1909.
	AH 7809.10	Casta, G. L'originale dei Fasti Consolari. Roma, 1910.
	AH 7809.10.5	Caosta, G. I Fasti Consolari Romani. Milano, 1910.
	AH 7809.10.7	Heiligenstaedt, F. Fasti aedilicii inde a Caesaris nece usque ad imperium A. Severi. Halis Saxonum, 1910.
	AH 7809.36	Geiger, Karl. Der römische Kalender und seine Verbesserung durch Julius Caesar. München, 1936.
	AH 7809.44	Odom, R.L. Sunday in Roman paganism, a history of the planetary week and its "day of the sun". Washington, D.C., 1944.
	AH 7809.52	Degrassi, A. I fasti consolari dell'Impero Romano. Roma, 1952.
	AH 7809.54	Degrassi, A. Fasti capitolini. 1. ed. Torino, 1954.
	AH 7809.67	Michels, Agnes Kirsopp. The calendar of the Roman republic. Princeton, 1967.

**AH 7810 - 7819   Ancient Rome in general - Civilization, social life -
General works (Table A)**

	AH 7811.2	Pamphlet box. Roman history. Civilization.
Htn	AH 7815.21*	Laeti, Pomponii. Opera varia - quorum catalogum. Moguntiae, 1521.
Htn	AH 7815.31F*	Biondo, Flavio. De Roma triumphante libri deceon. Basileae, 1531.
	AH 7816.20	Rossfeld, J. Anitiqvitatvm Romanarvm liber pumus, de vrbeetpopulo. Coloniae, 1620.
	AH 7816.20.5	Rossfeld, J. Anitiqvitatvm Romanarvm liber pumus, de vrbeetpopulo. Coloniae, 1669.
Htn	AH 7816.28*	Godwyn, Thomas. Romanae historiae anthologia. Oxford, 1628. 2 pam.
Htn	AH 7816.28.5*	Godwyn, Thomas. Romanae historiae anthologia. 15th ed. London, 1689.
Htn	AH 7816.77*	Bell, T. Roma restituta. London, 1677.
	AH 7816.88.3	Cantel, P.J. De Romana Republica sive de re militari et Civili Romanorum ad explicandos scriptores antiquos. Ultrajecti, 1691.
	AH 7816.96.3	Kennett, Basil. Romae antiquae notitia. 3. ed. Oxford, 1704.
NEDL	AH 7816.96.6	Kennett, Basil. Romae antiquae notitia. 6th ed. London, 1717.
NEDL	AH 7816.96.11	Kennett, Basil. Romae antiquae notitia. 11th ed. London, 1746.
NEDL	AH 7816.96.13	Kennett, Basil. Romae antiquae notitia. 13th ed. London, 1763.
	AH 7816.96.14	Kennett, Basil. Romae antiquae notitia. 14th ed. London, 1769.
	AH 7816.96.16	Kennett, Basil. Romae antiquae notitia. 1st American ed. Philadelphia, 1822.
	AH 7816.96.17	Kennett, Basil. Romae antiquae notitia. 2nd American ed. Baltimore, 18- .
	AH 7817.12.3	Nieupoort, W.H. Rituum qui olim apud Romanos. 3rd ed. Rhenum, 1723.
	AH 7817.12.6	Nieupoort, W.H. Rituum qui olim apud Romanos obtinuerunt. 13. ed. Venetiis, 1748.
NEDL	AH 7817.12.9	Nieupoort, W.H. Rituum qui olim apud Romanos obtinuerunt. 9. ed. Berolini, 1751.
	AH 7817.12.13	Nieupoort, W.H. Rituum qui olim apud Romanos obtinuerunt. Berolini, 1767.
Htn	AH 7817.13F*	Pitisco, Samuel. Lexicon antiquitatum Romanarum. Leovardiae, 1713. 2v.
	AH 7817.13.5F	Pitisco, Samuel. Lexicon antiquitatum Romanarum. Venetiis, 1719. 3v.
	AH 7817.23	Oudaans, J. Roomsche mogentheid. Leiden, 1723.
	AH 7817.26	Baxteri, W. Reliquiae Baxterianae. London, 1726.
Htn	AH 7817.32*	Vaslet, L. Introduzzione alla scienza d'antichita. Venezia, 1732.
	AH 7817.32.5	Vaslet, L. Introduzzione alla scienza d'antichita. Venezia, 1828.
	AH 7817.42	Chladenii, E.M. De gentilitate vetervm Romanorum liber singvlaris. Lipsiae, 1742.
	AH 7817.42.10	Cellarii, Christophori. Christophori Cellarii Breviarium antiquitatum romanarum, accurante. Augustae Taurinorum, 1742.
	AH 7817.43.3	Rossfeld, J. Antiquitatum Romanarum corpus. Amstelodami, 1743.
	AH 7817.46	Gruneri, J.F. Introductio in antiquitates romanas. Ienae, 1746.
	AH 7817.91	Meiners, C. Geschichte des Verfalls der Sitten. Wien, 1791.
	AH 7817.91.5	Moritz, K.P. Anthoysa, oder Roms Alterthümer. Berlin, 1791. 2v.
NEDL	AH 7817.91.5	Moritz, K.P. Anthoysa, oder Roms Alterthümer. Berlin, 1791.
	AH 7817.92.2	Adam, Alexander. Roman antiquities. 2nd ed. Edinburgh, 1792.
	AH 7817.92.5	Adam, Alexander. Roman antiquities. 1st American ed. Philadelphia, 1807.
	AH 7817.92.6	Adam, Alexander. Roman antiquities. 2nd American ed. N.Y., 1814.
	AH 7817.92.7	Adam, Alexander. Roman antiquities. N.Y., 1826.
NEDL	AH 7817.92.9	Adam, Alexander. Roman antiquities. N.Y., 1830.
	AH 7817.92.10	Adam, Alexander. Roman antiquities. 6th ed. Glasgow, 1835.
NEDL	AH 7817.92.11	Adam, Alexander. Roman antiquities. N.Y., 1837.
	AH 7817.92.12	Adam, Alexander. Roman antiquities. 7th ed. N.Y., 1836.
	AH 7817.92.13	Adam, Alexander. Handbuch der römischen Alterthümer. Erlangen, 1805-06. 2v.
	AH 7817.92.18	Nitsch, P.F. Beschreibung...Zustandes der Römer. Wien, 1792. 4v.
	AH 7817.92.20	Nitsch, P.F. Beschreibung...Zustandes der Römer. Erfurt, 1807- 2v.
	AH 7818.20.3	Fuss, J.D. Antiquitates Romanae compendio. Leodii, 1836.
	AH 7818.20.6	Fuss, J.D. Roman antiquities. Oxford, 1840.
	AH 7818.24	Creuzers, G.F. Abriss der römischen Antiquitäten. Leipzig, 1824.
	AH 7818.24.3	Creuzers, G.F. Abriss der römischen Antiquitäten. 2. Aufl. Leipzig, 1829.
	AH 7818.28.3	Lanktree, J. Synopsis of Roman antiquities. London, 1857.
	AH 7818.31	Irving, C. Catechism of Roman antiquities. 4th American ed. N.Y., 1831.
	AH 7818.32.3	Dillaway, C.K. Roman antiquities and ancient mythology. 2nd ed. Boston, 1833.
	AH 7818.40.3	Ozaneaux, J.G. Les Romains...République romaine. 2. éd. Paris, 1845.
	AH 7818.41	Ruperte, F.F.F. Handbuch der römischen Alterthümer. Hannover, 1841. 3v.
	AH 7818.43	Mommsen, T. De Collegiis et Sodaliciis Romanorum. Kiliae, 1843. 3 pam.
	AH 7818.43.5	Becker, W.A. Handbuch der römischen Alterthümer. v.1-9. Leipzig, 1843. 5v.
	AH 7818.46	Wannowski, A. Antiquitates Romanas. London, 1846.
	AH 7818.46.3	Dezobry, Charles. Rome au siècle d'Auguste. Paris, 1846. 4v.
	AH 7818.46.5	Dezobry, Charles. Rome au siècle d'Auguste. Göttingen, 1850.
	AH 7818.46.7	Dezobry, Charles. Rome au siècle d'Auguste. Paris, 1870. 4v.
	AH 7818.48.10	Ramsay, William. Manual of Roman antiquities. 10th ed. London, 1876.
	AH 7818.48.15	Ramsay, William. Manual of Roman antiquities. 15th ed. N.Y., 1895.
NEDL	AH 7818.48.17A	Ramsay, William. Manual of Roman antiquities. 17th ed. London, 1901.
NEDL	AH 7818.48.17B	Ramsay, William. Manual of Roman antiquities. 17th ed. London, 1901.

**AH 7810 - 7819   Ancient Rome in general - Civilization, social life -
General works (Table A) - cont.**

	AH 7818.53	Schmidt, C. Essai historique sur la société civile. Strasbourg, 1853.
	AH 7818.54	Tounsend, F. Letters from Rome. N.Y., 1854.
	AH 7818.56	Lange, C.C.L. Römische Alterthümer. Berlin, 1856-71. 3v.
	AH 7818.56.3	Lange, C.C.L. Römische Alterthümer. v.1-2, 2. Aufl; v.3, 1. Aufl. Berlin, 1863-71. 3v.
	AH 7818.56.5	Lange, C.C.L. Römische Alterthüsmer. v.1-2, 3. Aufl; v.3, 2. Aufl. Berlin, 1871-79. 3v.
	AH 7818.58	Niebuhr, B.G. Vorträge über römische Alterthümer. Berlin, 1858.
	AH 7818.58.5	Castelar y Ripoll, E. La civilizacion en los cinco primeros siglos del cristianismo. 2. ed. Madrid, 1865. 4v.
	AH 7818.59	Ramsay, William. Elementary manual of Roman antiquities. London, 1859.
	AH 7818.59.3	Ramsay, William. Elementary manual of Roman antiquities. 3. ed. London, 1863.
	AH 7818.63	Mommsen, T. Römische Forschungen. Berlin, 1864-79. 2v.
	AH 7818.63.3	Mommsen, T. Römische Forschungen. v.1, 2. Aufl.; v.2, 1. Aufl. Berlin, 1864. 2v.
	AH 7818.64.4	Marquardt, Joachim. Handbuch der römischen Alterthümer. v.1-7. Leipzig, 1871-1888. 9v.
	AH 7818.64.7	Marquardt, Joachim. Handbuch der römischen Alterthümer. 2. Aufl. Leipzig, 1876- 2v.
	AH 7818.64.9	Marquardt, Joachim. Handbuch der römischen Alterthümer. 2. Aufl. v.1-7. Leipzig, 1876. 10v.
	AH 7818.64.11	Marquardt, Joachim. Handbuch der römischen Alterthümer. 3. Aufl. Leipzig, 1887. 3v.
NEDL	AH 7818.64.13	Marquardt, Joachim. Manual des antiquités romaines. v.1-19. Paris, 1887-1907. 20v.
	AH 7818.64.15	Marquardt, Joachim. Römische Privatalterthümer. Leipzig, 1864-67.
	AH 7818.64.18	Marquardt, Joachim. Handbuch der römischen Alterthümer. 3. Aufl. v.1-3. Graz, 1952-53. 5v.
	AH 7818.65	Friedlaender, Ludwig. Darstellungen aus der Sittengeschichte Roms. v.2-3. Leipzig, 1864-1871. 2v.
	AH 7818.65.2	Friedlaender, Ludwig. Darstellungen aus der Sittengeschichte Roms. 2. Aufl. Leipzig, 1865-1867. 2v.
	AH 7818.65.3	Friedlaender, Ludwig. Darstellungen aus der Sittengeschichte Roms. 3. Aufl. Leipzig, 1869.
	AH 7818.65.6	Friedlaender, Ludwig. Darstellungen aus der Sittengeschichte Roms. v.1, 4. Aufl; v.2, 3. Aufl. Leipzig, 1873-1874. 2v.
	AH 7818.65.9	Friedlaender, Ludwig. Darstellungen aus der Sittengeschichte Roms. 6. Aufl. Leipzig, 1888. 3v.
	AH 7818.65.11	Friedlaender, Ludwig. Darstellungen aus der Sittengeschichte Roms. 7. Aufl. Leipzig, 1901. 2v.
	AH 7818.65.13	Friedlaender, Ludwig. Darstellungen aus der Sittengeschichte Roms. 8. Aufl. Leipzig, 1910. 4v.
	AH 7818.65.15	Friedlaender, Ludwig. Darstellungen aus der Sittengeschichte Roms. 9.-10. Aufl. Leipzig, 1919. 4v.
	AH 7818.65.16	Friedlaender, Ludwig. Darstellungen aus der Sittengeschichte Roms. 10. Aufl. Aalen, 1964. 4v.
	AH 7818.65.17	Friedlaender, Ludwig. Roman life and manners. London, 190-. 4v.
	AH 7818.65.18	Friedlaender, Ludwig. Roman life and manners under the early empire. N.Y., 1968. 4v.
NEDL	AH 7818.65.19A	Friedlaender, Ludwig. Moeurs romaines du règne d'Auguste. Paris, 1865. 4v.
NEDL	AH 7818.65.19B	Friedlaender, Ludwig. Moeurs romaines du règne d'Auguste. Paris, 1865. 4v.
	AH 7818.65.23	Friedlaender, Ludwig. Vida íntima de los Romanos. Primera version española. Barcelona, 1876.
	AH 7818.65.27	Friedlaender, Ludwig. Town life in ancient Italy. Boston, 1902.
	AH 7818.66	Bojesen, E.F.C. Handbuch der römischen Antiquitaten. Wien, 1866.
	AH 7818.67	Lord, John. The old Roman world. N.Y., 1867.
	AH 7818.71	Stoll, H.W. Bilder aus dem altrömischen Leben. Leipzig, 1877.
NEDL	AH 7818.77.8	Wilkins, Augustus S. Antigüedades clásicas II. Antigüedades Romanas. N.Y., 1883.
NEDL	AH 7818.77.15	Wilkins, Augustus S. Antigüedades clásicas II. Antigüedades Romanas. N.Y., 1903.
	AH 7818.79	Bender, H. Rom und römisches Leben im Alterthumen. Tübingen, 1879.
	AH 7818.79.3	Bender, H. Rom und römisches Leben im Alterthumen. 2. Aufl. Tübingen, 1893.
	AH 7818.79.5	Rydberg, V. Roman days. N.Y., 1879.
	AH 7818.80	Dupuy, Antoine. De Graecis Romanorum amicis aut praeceptoribus a secundo punico bello ad Augustum. Thesim. Parisiis, 1880.
NEDL	AH 7818.83	Jung, I. Leben und Sitten der Römer. Prag, 1883. 2v.
	AH 7818.83.15	Wilkins, A.S. Classical antiquities. N.Y., 1883.
NEDL	AH 7818.84	Wilkins, A.S. Roman antiquities. N.Y., 1884.
NEDL	AH 7818.84.2A	Wilkins, A.S. Roman Antiquities. N.Y., 1892?
NEDL	AH 7818.84.2B	Wilkins, A.S. Roman antiquities. N.Y., 1892?
	AH 7818.84.3	Robiow, F.M.C.J. Les institutions de l'ancienne Rome. Paris, 1884. 3v.
NEDL	AH 7818.84.5	Church, Alfred J. Roman life in the days of Cicero. London, 1884.
	AH 7818.84.6	Church, Alfred J. Roman life in the days of Cicero. N.Y., 1883.
	AH 7818.84.10	Saalfeld, G.A.E.A. Haus und Hof in Rom im Spiegel griechischen Kultur. Paderborn, 1884.
	AH 7818.85	Shumway, E.S. A day in ancient Rome. N.Y., 1885.
	AH 7818.88A	Inge, W.R. Society in Rome under the Caesars. N.Y., 1888.
	AH 7818.88B	Inge, W.R. Society in Rome under the Caesars. N.Y., 1888.
	AH 7818.91	Lovatelli, E.C. (Contessa). Miscellanea archeologica. Roma, 1891.
	AH 7818.91.2	Lovatelli, E.C. (Contessa). Nuova miscellanea archeologica. Roma, 1894.
	AH 7818.91.3	Lovatelli, E.C. (Contessa). Römische Essays. Leipzig, 1891.
	AH 7818.95	Bloch, Leo. Römische Altertumskunde. Stuttgart, 1895.
	AH 7818.95.5	Bloch, Leo. Römische Altertumskunde. 2. Aufl. Leipzig, 1898.
	AH 7818.97	Thomas, Émile. Rome et l'empire. Paris, 1897.
	AH 7818.97.5	Thomas, Émile. Roman life under the Caesars. N.Y., 1899.
	AH 7818.98	Dill, Samuel. Roman society in the last century of the Western Empire. London, 1898.

Classified Listing

AH 7820 - 7829   Ancient Rome in general - Civilization, social life - Private life (Table A) - cont.

	AH 7828.38.9A	Becker, W.A. Gallus or Roman scenes. London, 1849.
	AH 7828.38.9B	Becker, W.A. Gallus or Roman scenes. London, 1849.
NEDL	AH 7828.38.13A	Becker, W.A. Gallus, or Roman scenes. 4th ed. London, 1873.
	AH 7828.38.13B	Becker, W.A. Gallus, or Roman scenes. 4th ed. London, 1873.
NEDL	AH 7828.38.15	Becker, W.A. Gallus or Roman scenes. 5th ed. London, 1876.
NEDL	AH 7828.38.18	Becker, W.A. Gallus or Roman scenes. 10th ed. London, 1891.
	AH 7828.38.20	Becker, W.A. Gallus or Roman scenes. London, 1903.
	AH 7828.38.25	Becker, W.A. Gallus or Roman scenes. London, 1915.
	AH 7828.42	Schuch, C.T. Privatalterthümer. Karlsruhe, 1842.
	AH 7828.59	Friedlaender, L. Dissertatio de appellatione doninis. Regimonti Borussorum, 1859.
	AH 7828.75	Koppoy, G. Pegitou idiōtikoy bioytōn rōmaiōn. Athēnai, 1875.
	AH 7828.79	Marquardt, J. Das Privatleben der Römer. Leipzig, 1879.
	AH 7828.82	Pellisson, M. Les Romains au temps de Pline. Paris, 1882.
	AH 7828.82.3A	Pellisson, M. Roman life in Pliny's time. Meadville, Pa., 1897.
	AH 7828.82.3B	Pellisson, M. Roman life in Pliny's time. Meadville, Pa., 1897.
	AH 7828.85	Giachi, V. Amori e costumi latini. Citta di Castello, 1885.
	AH 7828.90F	Brunet, P. Mémoires d'un romain vie. Tours, 1890.
	AH 7828.93	Preston, H.W. Private life of the Romans. Boston, 1893.
	AH 7829.03A	Johnston, Harold W. Private life of the Romans. Chicago, 1903.
	AH 7829.03B	Johnston, Harold W. Private life of the Romans. Chicago, 1903.
	AH 7829.03.2	Johnston, Harold W. Private life of the Romans. Chicago, 1903.
	AH 7829.03.7	Johnston, Harold W. The private life of the Romans. Chicago, 1907.
	AH 7829.03.9	Johnston, Harold W. The private life of the Romans. N.Y., 1973.
	AH 7829.08.3	Fowler, W.W. Social life at Rome in the age of Cicero. N.Y., 1909.
	AH 7829.08.4	Fowler, W.W. Social life at Rome in the age of Cicero. N.Y., 1922.
	AH 7829.08.5	Fowler, W.W. Social life at Rome in the age of Cicero. N.Y., 1933.
	AH 7829.08.6	Preibisch, J. De sermonis cotidiani formulis. Halis Saxonum, 1908.
	AH 7829.10	Kuehn, G. De opificum romanorum condicione privata quaestiones. Diss. inaug. Halis, 1910.
NEDL	AH 7829.13A	Allinson, A.C.E. Roads from Rome. N.Y., 1913.
	AH 7829.13B	Allinson, A.C.E. Roads from Rome. N.Y., 1913.
NEDL	AH 7829.13C	Allinson, A.C.E. Roads from Rome. N.Y., 1913.
	AH 7829.24	McDaniel, W.B. Roman private life and its survivals. Boston, 1924.
	AH 7829.24.5	McDaniel, W.B. Roman private life and its survivals. N.Y., 1929.
	AH 7829.24.6	McDaniel, W.B. Roman private life and its survivals. N.Y., 1963.
	AH 7829.53	Grimal, Pierre. La vie à Rome dans l'antiquité. 2. éd. Paris, 1957.
	AH 7829.53.3	Grimal, Pierre. La vie à Rome dans l'antiquité. 3. éd. Paris, 1960.

AH 7830 - 7839   Ancient Rome in general - Civilization, social life - Athletic games, sports (Table A)

	AH 7833.5	Huber, Karl. Theorie des gymnischen Erziehung bei den Römern. Langensalza, 1934.
Htn	AH 7835.98*	Boulenger, J.C. De Circo Romano Ludisque. Lutetiae Parisiorum, 1598.
Htn	AH 7836.00F*	Panvinio, O. De Ludis Circensibus. Venetia, 1600.
	AH 7836.81F	Onuphrii Panvinii Veronensis. Patanii, 1681.
	AH 7838.25F	Eichstadius, H.C.A. De Votis X, XX, et XXX Imperatoum Romanorum. Ienae, 1825.
	AH 7838.37	Ademollo, A. Gli spettacoli dell'antica Roma. pt.1-6. Firenze, 1837.
	AH 7838.64	Ritschl, F. Die Tessarae Gladiatoriae. München, 1864.
	AH 7838.66	Planck, M. Über den Ursprung der römischen Gladiatorenspiele. Ulm, 1866.
	AH 7838.68	Hübner, Émile. Revue archéologique - nouvelles tessères. Paris, 1868.
	AH 7838.69	Goguel, Edward. Les gladiateurs romains. Paris, 1869.
	AH 7838.72	Friedlaender, L. De certamine cercensi diversio appellato. Regimonti, 1872.
	AH 7838.81	Meier, P.J. De gladiatura romana. Bonnae, 1881.
	AH 7838.82	Rasch, Franz. De ludo Troiae. v.1-2. Jena, 1882.
	AH 7839.23	Piganiol, A. Recherches sur les jeux romains. Strasbourg, 1923.
	AH 7839.38	Wegner, Ernst. Das Ballspiel der Römer. Würzburg, 1938.
	AH 7839.61	Balil, Albert. La ley gladiatoria de Italica. Madrid, 1961.
	AH 7839.67.2	Grant, Michael. Gladiators. Harmondsworth, Eng., 1971.

AH 7840   Ancient Rome in general - Civilization, social life - Special topics - The family

	AH 7840.2	Lacombe, P. La famille dans la société romaine. Paris, 1889.
	AH 7840.5.4	Paribeni, Roberto. Le famiglia romana. 4. ed. Bologna, 1948.

AH 7842   Ancient Rome in general - Civilization, social life - Special topics - Books and education

	AH 7842.01	Pamphlet box. Roman history. Civilization. Books and education.
	AH 7842.2	Clarke, George. The education of children at Rome. N.Y., 1896.
	AH 7842.3	Jullien, E. Professeurs de littérature dans l'ane Rome. Paris, 1885.
NEDL	AH 7842.4	Gerini, G.B. Le dottrine pedagogiche. Torino, 1894.
	AH 7842.5.2	Haenny, L. Schriftsteller und Buchhändler. 2. Aufl. Leipzig, 1885.
	AH 7842.6	Bremer, F.P. Die Rechtslehrer und Rechtsschulen. Berlin, 1868.
	AH 7842.7	Egger, Emile. Étude sur l'éducation. Paris, 1833.
	AH 7842.8	Lazic, G.S. Pogled na shkolu i polozhaj. Karlovuima, 1895.
	AH 7842.10A	Wilkins, A.S. Roman education. Cambridge, 1905.
	AH 7842.10B	Wilkins, A.S. Roman education. Cambridge, 1905.
	AH 7842.10.5	Wilkins, A.S. Roman education. Cambridge, 1914.

AH 7842   Ancient Rome in general - Civilization, social life - Special topics - Books and education - cont.

	AH 7842.12	Barbagallo, C. Lo stato e l'istruzione pubblica. Catania, 1911.
	AH 7842.14	Cole, P.R. Later Roman education in Ausonius, Capella. N.Y., 1909.
	AH 7842.16	Boyd, C.E. Public libraries and literary culture in ancient Rome. Chicago, 1915.
	AH 7842.16.5	Boyd, C.E. Public libraries and literary culture in ancient Rome. Thesis. Chicago, 1916.
	AH 7842.19	Gwynn, Aubrey. Roman education from Cicero to Quintilian. Oxford, 1926.
	AH 7842.19.5	Gwynn, Aubrey. Roman education from Cicero to Quintilian. N.Y., 1966.
	AH 7842.20	Pavan, M. La crisi della scuola nel IV secolo d.C. Bari, 1952.
	AH 7842.22	Hulsebos, G.A. Disputatio antiquabis de educatione et institutione apud Romanos. n.p., 1867.
	AH 7842.24	Norman, Albert Francis. Teachers and administrators. Hall, 1969.

AH 7844   Ancient Rome in general - Civilization, social life - Special topics - Festivals, spectacles

	AH 7844.2	Schulze, E. Die Schauspiele zur Unterhaltung. Gütersloh, 1895.
	AH 7844.3	Wissowa, G. Die Saecularfeier des Augustus. Marburg, 1894.
	AH 7844.4	Vollbrecht, W. Das Sakularfest des Augustus. Gütersloh, 1900.
	AH 7844.5F	Mommsen, T. Commentarium ludorum. Milano, 1891.
	AH 7844.5.5F	Mommsen, T. I commentarii dei ludi secolari. Roma, 1891.
	AH 7844.6	Amante, B. Il natale di Roma. Roma, 1879.
	AH 7844.6.15	Vaccari, A. Il natale de Roma nelle leggende e nella storia. Verona, 1934.
	AH 7844.7	Brissonius, B. Commentarius de spectaculis. Lugdini Batavorum, 1742.
	AH 7844.8	Gagé, J. Recherches sur les jeux séculaires. Paris, 1934.
	AH 7844.9.2	Pighi, Giovanni B. De ludis saecularibus populi Romani quiritium. Amstelodami, 1965.
	AH 7844.10	Piccoluga, Giulia. Elementi speltocolori nei rihuoli festivi Romani. Roma, 1965.
	AH 7844.11	Meslin, Michel. La fete des kalendes de janvier dans l'Empire romain. Bruxelles, 1970.
	AH 7844.12	Bollinger, Traugott. Theatralis licentia. Die Publikumsdemonstrationen an den öffentlichen Spielen im Rom der früheren Kaiserzeit und ihrer Bedeutung im politischen Leben. Winterthur, 1969.
	AH 7844.13	Auguet, Roland. Cruanté et civilisation: les jeux romains. Paris, 1970.

AH 7845   Ancient Rome in general - Civilization, social life - Special topics - Character and morals

	AH 7845.5	Rome galante, ou Histoire...de J. Cesar. Paris, 1696.
	AH 7845.9	Brouwer, P.C. De Romanorum indole e litteris cognascenda. n.p., 1911.
	AH 7845.15	Rech, H. Mos maiorum; Wesen und Wirkung der Tradition in Rom. Inaug. Diss. Marburg, 1936.
	AH 7845.20	André, Jean Marie. L'otium dans la vie morale et intellectuelle romaine. Paris, 1966.

AH 7846   Ancient Rome in general - Civilization, social life - Special topics - Houses, etc.

	AH 7846.4	Lanz-Liebenfels. Wie heizten die Römer ihre Wohnraume. Umschau, 1902.
	AH 7846.5	Becker, Philipp. Der römische Villenbesitz in Italien zur Keiserzeit. Inaug. Diss. Bonn, 1925.
	AH 7846.6	Peignot, Gabriel. Recherches sur le luxe des Romains dans leur ameublement. Dijon, 1837.

AH 7847   Ancient Rome in general - Civilization, social life - Special topics - Baths

	AH 7847.2	Morgan, M.H. Remarks on water supply of ancient Rome. Boston, 1902.

AH 7848   Ancient Rome in general - Civilization, social life - Special topics - Costume

	AH 7848.2	Figrelills, E. De statius illustrium Romanorum. v.1-2. Holmiae, 1656.
	AH 7848.3	Fisch, R. Die Walker oder Leben und Treiben. Berlin, 1891.
	AH 7848.5	Nötling, E. Studie über altrömische Thur. Mannheim, 1870.
	AH 7848.7	Helbig, W. Toga und Trabea. v.1-2. Berlin, 1904.
	AH 7848.8	Hula, Eduard. Die Toga der späteren Kaiserzeit. Brünn, 1895.
	AH 7848.9	Wilson, L.M. The Roman toga. Baltimore, 1924.
	AH 7848.9.5	Wilson, L.M. A study of the Roman toga. Diss. Baltimore, 1924.
	AH 7848.9.10	Wilson, L.M. The clothing of the ancient Romans. Baltimore, 1938.

AH 7850   Ancient Rome in general - Civilization, social life - Special topics - Meals

	AH 7850.2A	Chacon, P. De Triclinio rive de modo convivandi. Amsterdam, 1664.
	AH 7850.2B	Chacon, P. De Triclinio rive de modo convivandi. Amsterdam, 1664.
	AH 7850.3	Harcum, C.G. Roman cooks. Diss. Baltimore, 1914.
	AH 7850.4	Lacombe, Paul. Fragments d'une histoire des moeurs. Cahors, 1880.
	AH 7850.5	Peignot, Gabriel. Des coinestebles et des vins de la Grèce et de l'Italie, en usage chez les Romains. Dijon, 1822.
	AH 7850.6	Deouna, Waldemar. Croyances et superstitions de table dans la Rome antique. Bruxelles, 1961.
	AH 7850.7	André, Jacques. L'alimentation et la cuisine à Rome. Paris, 1961.

AH 7851   Ancient Rome in general - Civilization, social life - Special topics - Fire and lights

	AH 7851.2	Krell, Otto. Altrömische Heizungen. München, 1901.

AH 7852   Ancient Rome in general - Civilization, social life - Special topics - Pottery and metalwork

	AH 7852.5	Namur, A. De lacrymatoriis sive de lagenulis. Luciliburgi, 1855.
Htn	AH 7852.8*	Baïf, L. De vasculis libellus. Paris, 1535.

Classified Listing

AH 7854   Ancient Rome in general - Civilization, social life - Special topics - Domestic plants and animals

AH 7854.1   Toynbee, Jocelyn Mary Catherine. Animals in Roman life and art. London, 1973.

AH 7854.2   Jennison, George. Animals for show and pleasure in ancient Rome. Manchester, 1937.

AH 7855   Ancient Rome in general - Civilization, social life - Special topics - Hunting and fishing

AH 7855.2   Aymard, Jacques. Essai sur les chasses romaines, des origines à la fin du siècle des Antonins (Cynegetica). Thèse. Paris, 1957.

AH 7859   Ancient Rome in general - Civilization, social life - Special topics - Condition of women

AH 7859.1   Pamphlet box. Roman history, civilization, condition of women.

AH 7859.2   Ludovici, C.G. De ritu osculis explorandi...mulierum. Lipsie, 1733.

AH 7859.3   Pitacco, G. De mulierum romanorum cultu. Görz, 1907.

AH 7859.4.2   Bader, Clarisse. La femme romaine. 2. éd. Paris, 1877.

AH 7859.5   Paternò-Paterno, S. La donna nella storia del diritto romano. Roma, 1932.

AH 7859.6   Hoffsten, R.B. Roman women of rank of the early empire in public life as portrayed by Dio. Diss. Philadelphia, 1939.

AH 7859.7   Balsdon, John Percy V.D. Roman women. London, 1962.

AH 7859.8   Herrmann, Claudine. Le role judiciaire et politique des femmes sous la République romaine. Bruxelles, 1964.

AH 7859.9   Sandels, Friedrich. Die Stellung der kaiserlichen Frauen aus dem julisch-claudischen Wause. Darmstadt, 1912.

AH 7861   Ancient Rome in general - Civilization, social life - Special topics - Burial

Htn   AH 7861.3*   Kirchmann, J. De funeribus Romanorum. Hamburg, 1605.

Htn   AH 7861.4*   Kirchmann, J. De funeribus Romanorum cum appendice. Lugduni Batavorum, 1672.

Htn   AH 7861.6*   Rigalt, N. Funus Parasiticum. Lutetiae, 1601. 4 pam.

AH 7861.8   Schiess, T. Die römischen Collegia Funeraticia. München, 1888.

AH 7861.10   Santoro, B. La Nenia Latina. Acireale, 1902.

AH 7861.12   Nock, A.D. Cremation and burial in the Roman Empire. Cambridge, 1932.

AH 7861.13   Gautière, J. De jure manium. Lipsiae, 1671.

AH 7861.14   Toynbee, Jocelyn Mary Catherine. Death and burial in the Roman world. London, 1971.

AH 7863   Ancient Rome in general - Civilization, social life - Special topics - Sexual customs, love

AH 7863.6   Grinial, P. L'amour à Rome. Paris, 1963.

AH 7863.7   Pike, Edgar R. Love in ancient Rome. London, 1965.

AH 7865.500 - .999   Ancient Rome in general - Civilization, social life - Special topics - Inns

AH 7865.502   Kleberg, Tounes. Hôtels, restaurants et cabarets dans l'antiquité romaine. Uppsala, 1957.

AH 7867   Ancient Rome in general - Civilization, social life - Special topics - Gestures

AH 7867.5   Struve, B.G. Antiquitatum Romanorum syntagma. Jenae, 1701.

AH 7868   Ancient Rome in general - Civilization, social life - Special topics - Beverages

AH 7868.2   Curtel, G. La vigne et le vin chez les Romains. Paris, 1903.

AH 7869   Ancient Rome in general - Civilization, social life - Special topics - Names

AH 7869.2   Ellendt, F. Cognomine et agnomine Romano. Regimontii Borussorum, 1853.

AH 7869.5   Hübner, Emil. Quaestiones onomatologicae Latinae. Bonnae, 1854.

AH 7869.7   Hübner, Emil. Quaestiones onomatologicae Latinae. Berolini, 1874. 2 pam.

AH 7880 - 7889   Ancient Rome in general - Economic conditions - General works (Table A)

AH 7881.2   Pamphlet box. Roman History. Economics.

AH 7881.5   Pamphlet vol. Amzalak, Moses B. Historia das doutrines económicas da antiga Roma. 4 pam.

AH 7888.40   Dureau, A.J. Économie politique des Romains. Paris, 1840. 2v.

AH 7888.84   Bücher, Karl. Die Aüfstande der unfreien Arbeiter. Frankfurt, 1874.

AH 7888.85   Belot, E. De la révolution économique et monétaire. Paris, 1885.

AH 7888.86   Büchsenschütz, A.B. Bemerkungen über die römische Volkswirtschaft. Berlin, 1886.

AH 7888.91   Oertmann, P. Die Volkswirtschaftslehre. Berlin, 1891.

AH 7888.92.2   Deloume, Antonin. Les manieurs d'argent à Rome. 2. éd. Rome, 1970.

AH 7888.95   Vanlaer, M. La fin d'un peuple. Paris, 1895. 2v.

AH 7888.97   Pfaff, Ivo. Über den rechtlichen Schutz. Weimar, 1897.

AH 7888.98   Levison, W. Die Buerkundung des Civilstandes. Bonn, 1898.

AH 7888.99   Hoffmeister, K. Die wirtschaftliche Entwicklung Roms. Wien, 1899.

AH 7888.99.3   Thomas, Paul. Essai sur...théories économiques. Paris, 1899.

AH 7889.00   Bloch, Leo. Die ständlichen und sozialen Kämpfe. Leipzig, 1900.

AH 7889.00.2   Bloch, Leo. Soziale Kämpfe im alten Rom. 2. Aufl. Leipzig, 1908.

AH 7889.02   Esser, J.J. De Pauperum cura apud Romanos. Campis, 1902.

AH 7889.04   Beigel, R. Rechnungswesen und Buchführung. Karlsruhe, 1904.

AH 7889.07   Oliver, E.H. Roman economic conditions. Toronto, 1907.

AH 7889.10   Davis, William S. Influence of wealth in imperial Rome. N.Y., 1910.

AH 7889.10.5   Davis, William S. Influence of wealth in imperial Rome. N.Y., 1933.

AH 7889.15A   MacFarlane, Charles W. Some observations on the economic interpretation of early Roman history. Philadelphia, 1915.

AH 7889.15B   MacFarlane, Charles W. Some observations on the economic interpretation of early Roman history. Philadelphia, 1915.

AH 7889.16A   Simklovich, V.G. Rome's fall reconsidered. N.Y., 1916.

AH 7889.16B   Simklovich, V.G. Rome's fall reconsidered. N.Y., 1916.

AH 7889.19   Herzog, R. Aus der Geschichte des Bankwesens im Altertum. Giessen, 1919.

AH 7880 - 7889   Ancient Rome in general - Economic conditions - General works (Table A) - cont.

AH 7889.20A   Frank, Tenney. An economic history of Rome. Baltimore, 1920.

AH 7889.20B   Frank, Tenney. An economic history of Rome. Baltimore, 1920.

AH 7889.20.2   Frank, Tenney. An economic history of Rome. 2. ed. Baltimore, 1927.

AH 7889.22   Homs, Léon. Problèmes sociaux de jadis et d'à présent. Paris, 1922.

AH 7889.26A   Rostovtsev, M.I. The social and economic history of the Roman Empire. Oxford, 1926.

AH 7889.26B   Rostovtsev, M.I. The social and economic history of the Roman Empire. Oxford, 1926.

AH 7889.26.10   Rostovtsev, M.I. Gesellschaft und Wirtschaft im Römischen Reich. Leipzig, 1929. 2v.

AH 7889.26.15   Rostovtsev, M.I. Storia economica e sociale dell'Impero romano. Firenze, 1946.

AH 7889.31   Cassimatis, Grégoire. Les intérêts dans la législation de Justinien et dans le droit byzantin. Paris, 1931.

AH 7889.33A   Frank, Tenney. An economic survey of ancient Rome. Baltimore, 1933-40. 3v.

AH 7889.33B   Frank, Tenney. An economic survey of ancient Rome. Baltimore, 1933-40. 3v.

AH 7889.33.2   Frank, Tenney. An economic survey of ancient Rome. General index. Baltimore, 1940.

AH 7889.33.5   Frank, Tenney. An economic survey of ancient Rome. Paterson, N.J., 1959.

AH 7889.33.10   Jonkers, Engbert. Economische en sociale toestanden in het Romeinsche rijk. Proefschrift. Wageningen, 1933.

AH 7889.36   Bernard, Antoine. La rémunération des professions liberales en droit romain classique. Paris, 1936.

AH 7889.64   Halsberghe, Gaston H. Het republikeinse Rome; de grondslagen van het antieke wirtschaftswunder (509-31 v. Chr.). Hasselt, 1964.

AH 7889.72   Badian, Ernst. Publicans and sinners; private enterprise in the service of the Roman Republic. Ithaca, N.Y., 1972.

AH 7889.73.1   Kolendo, Jerzy. Le traité d'agronomie des Saserna. Wroclaw, 1973.

AH 7889.74   Duncan-Jones, Richard. The economy of the Roman Empire: quantitative studies. Cambridge, Eng., 1924.

AH 7890 - 7899   Ancient Rome in general - Economic conditions - Agriculture (Table A)

AH 7890.2   White, Kenneth Douglas. A bibliography of Roman agriculture. Reading, 1970.

AH 7897.88   Dickson, Adam. Husbandry of the ancients. Edinburgh, 1788.

AH 7897.88.15   Dickson, Adam. De l'agriculture des anciens. Paris, 1802. 2v.

AH 7898.57   Daubeny, Charles. Lectures on Roman husbandry. Oxford, 1857.

AH 7898.58   Magerstedt, A.F. Bilder aus der römischen Landwirtschaft. Sondershausen, 1858. 6v.

AH 7898.59   Michon, L.A.J. Des céréales en Italie sous les Romains. Paris, 1859.

AH 7898.66   Beheim-Schwarzbach, H. Beitrag zur Kenntnitz des Ackerbaues der Römer. Cassel, 1866.

AH 7898.98   Wurm, A. De villa rustica. Kempten, 1898.

AH 7899.10   Pamphlet box. Roman History. Economics. Agriculture.

AH 7899.12   Schwarze, K. Beiträge zur Geschichte altrömische Agrarprobleme. Halle, 1912.

AH 7899.21.5   Hanger, A. Zur römischen Landwirtschaft und Haustierzucht. Hanover, 1921.

AH 7899.39   Ghigi, A. Poultry farming as described by the writers of ancient Rome. Milano, 1939.

AH 7899.42   Papàsogli, G. L'agricoltura degli etruschi e dei Romani. Roma, 1942.

AH 7899.51   García-Badell, Gabriel. La agricultura en la Roma. Madrid, 1951.

AH 7899.67   White, K.D. Agricultural implements of the Roman world. Cambridge, 1967.

AH 7899.68   Kolendo, Jerzy. Postep techniczky a problem rify robocrej w roluicture starozytnej Helii. Wroctaw, 1968.

AH 7899.69   Brockmeyer, Norbert. Arbeitsorganisation und ökonomisches Denken in der Gutswirtschaft des römischen Reiches. Inaug. Diss. Bachum? 1969?

AH 7899.70   White, Kenneth Douglas. Roman farming. London, 1970.

AH 7899.71   Martin, René. Recherches sur les agronomes latins et leurs conceptions économiques et sociàles. Paris, 1971.

AH 7900 - 7909   Ancient Rome in general - Economic conditions - Commerce and industries (Table A)

AH 7903.5.2   Diocletianus. Edictum Diocletiani de pretiis rerum venalium. Berolini, 1893.

AH 7903.5.5F   Diocletianus. Édit de Dioclétien, établissant le maximum dans l'Empire romain. Paris, 1864.

AH 7903.5.10   Diocletianus. Diokletians Preisedikt. Berlin, 1971.

AH 7903.6   Giacchero, Marta. Note sull'Editto-calmiere di Diocleziano. Genova, 1962.

AH 7908.51   Mommsen, Theodor. Das Edict Diocletians de Pretiis Rerum Venalium. Leipzig, 1851.

AH 7908.65   Zacharia von Lingenthal, K.E. Eine Verordnung Justinian's über den Seidenhandel. v.1-2. St. Petersburg, 1865. 2 pam.

AH 7908.74   Krakauer, G. Das Verpflegungswesen der Stadt Rom. Berlin, 1874.

AH 7908.74.3   Pigeonneau, H. De convectione urbanae annonae. Sancti-Clodoaldi, 1876.

AH 7908.74.5   Gebhardt, E. Studien über das Verpflegungswesen. Dorpat, 1881.

AH 7908.74.7   Babled, H. De la cura annonae. Paris, 1892.

AH 7908.74.9   Friedlaender, L. Dissertatio de mercatura Romanorum. Regimonti Prussorum, 1874.

AH 7908.80   Herbermann, Charles G. Business life in ancient Rome. N.Y., 1880.

AH 7909.01F   Forcella, V. Le industrie e il commercio. Milano, 1901.

AH 7909.02   Juglar, L. Quamodo per servos libertosque negotiarentur Romani imperii temporibus. Paris, 1902.

AH 7909.05   Solbisky. Voraus geht eine Abhandlung. Weimar, 1905.

AH 7909.09   Parvan, Vasile. Die Nationalität der Kaufleute. Breslau, 1909.

AH 7909.17.1   Brewster, Ethel Hampson. Roman craftsmen and tradesmen of the early empire. N.Y., 1972.

AH 7909.19   Hatzfeld, Jean. Les trafiquants italiens dans l'Orient hellénique. Photoreproduction. Paris, 1919.

AH 7909.24A   Charlesworth, M.P. Trade-routes and commerce of the Roman Empire. Cambridge, 1924.

Classified Listing

AH 7900 - 7909 Ancient Rome in general - Economic conditions - Commerce and industries (Table A) - cont.

AH 7909.24B   Charlesworth, M.P. Trade-routes and commerce of the Roman Empire. Cambridge, 1924.

AH 7909.24.5   Charlesworth, M.P. Trade-routes and commerce of the Roman Empire. Hildesheim, 1961.

AH 7909.28   Warmington, E.H. The commerce between the Roman Empire and India. Cambridge, 1928.

AH 7909.32   Perali, P. Le origini artigiane industriali e mercantili di Roma. Roma, 1932.

AH 7909.32.5   Perali, P. Vestigia dell'antico artigianato nelle regioni dell 'Egeo e dell'Italia. Roma, 1934.

AH 7909.33   Holmberg, E.J. Zur Geschichte des Cursus publicus. Uppsala, 1933.

AH 7909.38   Loane, Helen J. Industry and commerce in the city of Rome, 50 B.C.-200 A.D. Baltimore, 1938.

AH 7909.38.2   Loane, Helen J. Industry and commerce in the city of Rome, 50 B.C.-200 A.D. Baltimore, 1938.

AH 7909.58   Calabi Limentani, Ida. Studi sulla società romana; il lavoro artistico. Milano, 1958.

AH 7909.66   Rougé, Jean. Recherches sur l'organisation du commerce maritime en Méditerranée sous l'Empire romain. Thèse. Paris, 1966.

AH 7909.70   Wild, J.P. Textile manufacture in the northern Roman provinces. Cambridge, Eng., 1970.

AH 7910 - 7919 Ancient Rome in general - Economic conditions - Associations (Table A)

AH 7918.41   Rabanis, J.F. Recherches sur les dendrophores et sur les corporations romaines en général. Bordeaux, 1841.

AH 7918.43   Mommsen, Theodor. De Collegiis et sodalicis Romanorum. Kiliae, 1843.

AH 7918.66   Friedlaender, L. De pretiis frumentis apud Romanos. Regimonti, 1866.

AH 7918.87   Maué, H.C. Der Praefectus Fabrum. Halle, 1887.

AH 7918.90   Liebenam, W. Zur Geschichte...des römischen Vereinswesens. Leipzig, 1890.

AH 7918.93   Liebenam, W. Aus dem Vereinswesen im römischen Reiche. Berlin, 1893.

AH 7918.93.3   Labat, P. Etude sur les Collèges d'artisans. Toulouse, 1893.

AH 7918.95   Waltzing, J.P. Etude...sur les corporations professionnelles. Louvain, 1895. 4v.

AH 7918.95.3   Waltzing, J.P. Les corporations romaines. Louvain, 1895.

AH 7918.95.5   Waltzing, J.P. Étude historique sur les corporations professionnelles chez les Romains depuis les origines jusqu'à la chute de l'Empire d'Occident. Bologne, 1968.

AH 7918.97   Floss, Antonius. De collegiis iuvenum quaestiones. Bonnae, 1897.

AH 7918.97.3   Demoulin, H. Les Collegia Juvenum. Louvain, 1897.

AH 7918.99   Levasseur, E. L'organisation des métiers. Paris, 1899.

AH 7919.02   Rossi, G.B. de. La villa di silio italico ed il collegio. n.p., 1902.

AH 7920 - 7929 Ancient Rome in general - Economic conditions - Weights and measures (Table A)

AH 7926.47   Greaves, John. Pyramidographia. London, 1646. 2 pam.

AH 7930 - 7939 Ancient Rome in general - Geography and description - General works (Table A)

AH 7939.01   Bessem, E. De terminis et terminationibus. Groningae, 1901.

AH 7950 - 7959 Ancient Rome in general - Travels - General works (Table A)

AH 7956.00   Itinerarium Antonini Augusti. Coloniae Agrippinae, 1600.

AH 7957.35   Wesseling, P. Vetera Romanorum itineraria. Amstelodami, 1735.

AH 7958.64   Bernard, E. Les voyages de Saint Jérome. Paris, 1864.

AH 7959.72   O'Sullivan, Firmin. The Egnation Way. Newton Abbot, 1972.

AH 7970 - 7979 Ancient Rome in general - Travels - Guidebooks (Table A)

AH 7979.16F   Miller, Konrad. Itineraria romana. Stuttgart, 1916.

AH 7979.29   Itineraria romana. Lipsiae, 1929. 2v.

AH 8003 Ancient North Africa - General - Government and administration

AH 8003.1   Gascou, Jacques. La politique municipale de l'empire romain en Afrique proconsulaire de Trajan à Septime-Sévère. Rome, 1972.

AH 8005 Ancient North Africa - General - Military affairs

AH 8005.2   Cagnat, René. L'armée romaine d'Afrique. Paris, 1892.

AH 8005.2.2   Cagnat, René. L'armée romaine d'Afrique. 2. éd. Paris, 1912. 2v.

AH 8005.2.7   Cagnat, René. La frontière militaire de la Tripolitaine à l'époque romaine. Paris, 1912.

AH 8007 Ancient North Africa - General - General history

AH 8007.01   Pamphlet box. Roman Africa.

NEDL AH 8007.2   Graham, A. Roman Africa...Roman occupation of Africa. London, 1902.

AH 8007.3   Vivien de Saint-Martin, L. Le Nord de l'Afrique. Paris, 1863.

AH 8007.5   Heeren, A.H.L. Historical researches...politics. Oxford, 1852. 2v.

AH 8007.5.2   Heeren, A.H.L. Historical researches...politics. 2. ed. Oxford, 1838. 2v.

AH 8007.7   Boissier, Gaston. L'Afrique romaine. Paris, 1895.

AH 8007.7.4   Boissier, Gaston. L'Afrique romaine. 5. éd. Paris, 1912.

AH 8007.7.5   Boissier, Gaston. Roman Africa. N.Y., 1899.

AH 8007.11   Baale, C.H. De provinciis Africanis. Groningae, 1896.

AH 8007.12   Gsell, Stéphane. Histoire ancienne de l'Afrique du nord. Paris, 1913-28. 8v.

AH 8007.12.5   Gsell, Stéphane. Histoire ancienne de l'Afrique du nord. Paris, 1920. 4v.

AH 8007.12.6   Gsell, Stéphane. Histoire ancienne de l'Afrique du nord. Osnabrück, 1972. 8v.

AH 8007.15   Broughton, T.R.S. The romanization of Africa Proconsularis. Baltimore, 1929.

AH 8007.15.5   Broughton, T.R.S. The romanization of Africa Proconsularis. Diss. Baltimore, 1929.

AH 8007.17   Africa romana. Milano, 1935.

AH 8007.18   Albertini, Eugène. L'Afrique romaine. Alger, 1937.

AH 8007.18.5   Albertini, Eugène. L'Afrique romaine. Alger? 1950.

AH 8007.18.7   Albertini, Eugène. L'Afrique romaine. Alger, 1955.

AH 8007.18.10   Albertini, Eugène. L'Afrique romaine. Alger, 1955.

AH 8007.19   Kruglikova, I.T. Dakiia v epokhu rinskoi okkupatsii. Moskva, 1955.

AH 8007 Ancient North Africa - General - General history - cont.

AH 8007.21   Romanelli, P. Storia delle province romane dell'Africa. Roma, 1959.

AH 8007.23   Brisson, Jean Paul. Autonomisme et christianisme dans l'Afrique romaine de Septime Sévère à l'invasion vandale. Paris, 1958.

AH 8007.25   Ayache, Albert. Histoire ancienne de l'Afrique du nord. Paris, 1964.

AH 8008 Ancient North Africa - General - General special

AH 8008.7   Berlioux, E.F. Les atlantes. Histoire de l'Atlantis. Paris, 1883.

AH 8008.9   Leglay, Marcel. Les gaulois en Afrique. Bruxelles, 1962.

AH 8008.10   Desanges, J. Catalogue des tribus africaines de l'antiquité classique à l'ouest du Nil. Dakar, 1962.

AH 8008.11   Teutsch, Leo. Das Stadtewesen in Nordafrika. Berlin, 1962.

AH 8008.12   Overbeck, Hechtild. Untersuchungen zum afrikanischen Senatsadel in der Spätantike. Kallmünz, 1973.

AH 8011 Ancient North Africa - General - History by periods - 1 A.D. - ca. 650

AH 8011.2   Martroye, F. Genséric la conquête vandale. Paris, 1707.

AH 8011.3   Papencordt, F. Geschichte der vandalischen Herrschaft. Berlin, 1837.

AH 8011.4   Schmidt, L. Geschichte der Wandalen. Leipzig, 1901.

AH 8011.5   Marcus, Ludwig. Histoire des wandales. Paris, 1836.

AH 8011.6   Warmington, B.H. The North African province from Diocletian to the Vandal conquest. Cambridge, Eng., 1954.

AH 8011.7   Courtois, C. Les Vandales et l'Afrique. Paris, 1955.

AH 8011.8   Diligenskii, G.G. Severnaia Afrika v IV-V vekakh. Moskva, 1961.

AH 8011.9   Diesner, Hans J. Der Untergang der römischen Herrschaft in Nordafrika. Weimar, 1964.

AH 8011.9.5   Diesner, Hans J. Des Vandalenreich, Aufstieg und Untergang. Stuttgart, 1966.

AH 8011.10   Rachet, Marguerite. Rome et les berbères. Bruxelles, 1970.

AH 8012 Ancient North Africa - General - Chronology

AH 8012.2   Pallu de Lessert, A.C. Fastes des provinces africaines. Paris, 1896-1901. 2v.

AH 8012.5   Pallu de Lessert, A.C. Vicaires et comtes d'Afrique. Constantine, 1892.

AH 8013 Ancient North Africa - General - Civilization

AH 8013.2   Barthel, W. Zur Geschichte der römischen Städte in Africa. Griefswald, 1904.

AH 8013.3   Bouchier, E.S. Life and letters in Roman Africa. Oxford, 1913.

AH 8013.4   Charles-Picard, Gilbert. La civilisation de l'Afrique romaine. Paris, 1959.

AH 8013.6   Raven, Susan. Rome in Africa. London, 1969.

AH 8014 Ancient North Africa - General - Religion

AH 8014.5   Charles-Picard, Gilbert. Les religions de l'Afrique antique. Paris, 1954.

AH 8015 Ancient North Africa - General - Economic conditions

AH 8015.5   Camps-Fabrer, Henriette. L'olivier et l'huile dans l'Afrique romaine. Alger, 1953.

AH 8016 Ancient North Africa - General - Geography

AH 8016.2   Detlefsen, D. Die Geographie Afrikas. Berlin, 1908.

AH 8016.3   Rabusson, A. De la geographie du nord de l'Afrique. Paris, 1856.

AH 8016.5F   Nau de Champlouis, A.V. Notice sur la carte de l'Afrique. Paris, 1854.

AH 8016.7   Knötel, A. Der Niger der alten und andere wichtige Fragen der alten Geographie Afrika's. Glogau, 1866.

AH 8016.9   Berthelot, André. L'Afrique saharienne et sondanaise. Paris, 1927.

AH 8016.10   Gsell, Stéphane. Le climat de l'Afrique du nord dans l'antiquité. Alger, 1911.

AH 8017 Ancient North Africa - General - Travels

AH 8017.5   Fischer, C.T. De Hannonis Carthagoniensis. Lipsiae, 1893.

AH 8048 Ancient North Africa - Hamites in general - General works

AH 8048.2   Honea, K.K. A contribution to the history of Hamitic peoples. Horn, 1958.

AH 8048.3   Vibert, Théodore. La race chamitique. Paris, 1916.

AH 8048.5   Adametz, Leopold. Herkunft und Wanderungen der Hamiten erschlossen aus ihren Haustierrassen. Wien, 1920.

AH 8057 Ancient North Africa - Africa Proper (Province); Carthage - General history

AH 8057.3   Flatters, P. L'Afrique septentrionale ancienne. Alger, 1879.

AH 8057.5   Charles-Picard, Gilbert. Le monde de Carthage. Paris, 1956.

AH 8057.5.6   Charles-Picard, Gilbert. Carthage. N.Y., 1965.

AH 8058 Ancient North Africa - Africa Proper (Province); Carthage - General special

AH 8058.5   Mesnage, R.J. Romanisation de l'Afrique, Tunisie. Paris, 1913.

AH 8060 Ancient North Africa - Africa Proper (Province); Carthage - History by periods - 500 - 1 B.C.

AH 8060.5   Vega, Luis A. de. Amilcar Barca. Madrid, 1960.

AH 8063 Ancient North Africa - Africa Proper (Province); Carthage - Civilization

AH 8063.5   Mahjouhi, Ammar. Les cités romaines de Tunisie. Tunis, 1969?

AH 8064 Ancient North Africa - Africa Proper (Province); Carthage - Religion

AH 8064.1   Münter, F. Religion der Karthager. Kopenhagen, 1816.

AH 8064.1.5   Münter, F. Religion der Karthager. Kopenhagen, 1821.

AH 8066 Ancient North Africa - Africa Proper (Province); Carthage - Geography

AH 8066.3   Tissot, Charles. Exploration scientifique de la Tunisie. Atlas. Paris, 1884-88. 2v.

Classified Listing

AH 8071 - 8096   Ancient North Africa - Africa Proper (Province); Carthage - Local (A-Z by place)

AH 8073.2   Botticher, J.F.W. Geschichte der Carthager. Berlin, 1827.

AH 8073.3   Meltzer, Otto. Geschichte der Karthager. Berlin, 1879.
3v.

AH 8073.4   Smith, R.B. Carthage and the Carthaginians. 2. ed.
London, 1879.

AH 8073.5   Littré, M.P.E. Comment...les sémites entrèrent.
Leipzig, 1879.

AH 8073.6   Friedrich, T. Biographie des Barkiden Mago. Wien, 1880.

AH 8073.7   Church, A.J. Story of Carthage. Photoreproduction.
N.Y., 1886.

AH 8073.7.5   Church, A.J. Carthage, or The empire of Africa.
Photoreproduction. London, 1887.

AH 8073.8   Seibel, V. Der Söldner-Krieg der Karthager.
Dilingen, 1848.

AH 8073.9   Drapeyron, L. La condition de Carthage. Paris, 1882.

AH 8073.11   Hannon, G. Antigüedad maritima de...Cartago.
Madrid, 1756.

AH 8073.13   Hendreich, C. Carthage, sive Carthaginensium respublica.
Francofurti ad Oderam, 1664.

AH 8073.14   Lüdemann, Hans. Untersuchungen zur Verfassungsgeschichte
Karthagos bis auf Aristoteles. Inaug. Diss. Bottrop, 1933.

AH 8073.15   Hurd, H.P. The topography of Punic Carthage.
Williamsport, 1934.

AH 8073.16   Schmidt, W. L'empire carthaginois. Paris, 1940.

AH 8073.17   Hubac, Pierre. Carthage. Paris, 1946.

AH 8073.18   Vogt, Josef. Rom und Karthago. Leipzig, 1943.

AH 8073.19   Walter, Gerard. La destruction de Carthage. 264-146.
Paris, 1947.

AH 8073.20   Picard, Colette. Carthage. Paris, 1951.

AH 8073.21   Hours-Miedan, Madeleine. Carthage. 1. éd. Paris, 1949.

AH 8073.22   Charles-Picard, Gilbert. La vie quotidienne à Carthage en
temps d'Hannibal. Paris, 1958.

AH 8073.22.5 Charles-Picard, Gilbert. La Carthage de Saint Augustin.
Paris, 1965.

AH 8073.22.9 Charles-Picard, Gilbert. Vie et mort de Carthage.
Paris, 1970.

AH 8073.22.10 Charles-Picard, Gilbert. The life and death of Carthage.
London, 1968.

AH 8073.22.15 Charles-Picard, Gilbert. Daily life in Carthage at the
time of Hannibal. London, 1961.

AH 8073.23   Warmington, Brian Herbert. Carthage. London, 1960.

AH 8073.23.2 Warmington, Brian Herbert. Carthage. 2. ed. London, 1969.

AH 8073.24   Shifman, I.S. Vozniknovenie Karfagenskoi derzhavy.
Leningrad, 1963.

AH 8073.25   Barreca, Ferruccio. La civiltà di Cartagine.
Cagliari, 1964.

AH 8073.28   Fantar, Mhamed. Carthage, la prestigieuse cité d'Elissa.
Tunis, 1970.

AH 8107   Ancient North Africa - Mauretania - General history

AH 8107.5   Poulle, M.A. A travers la Mauritanie sétifienne.
Constantine, 1863.

AH 8107.10   Carcopino, J. Le Maroc antique. 8. éd. Paris, 1948.

AH 8116   Ancient North Africa - Mauretania - Geography

AH 8116.5   Roget, Raymond. Le Maroc chez les auteurs anciens.
Paris, 1924.

AH 8157   Ancient North Africa - Numidia - General history

AH 8157.2   Boissière, G. Esquisse d'une histoire dans la nord de
l'Afrique. Paris, 1878.

AH 8157.3   Boissière, G. L'Algérie romaine. Paris, 1883.
2v.

AH 8157.4   Gsell, Stéphane. L'Algérie dans l'antique. Alger, 1903.

AH 8157.5F   France. Ministère de la guerre. Précis analytique de
l'histoire ancienne de l'Afrique septent. Paris, 1842.

AH 8157.7   Dureau de la Malle, A. L'Algérie. Paris, 1852.

AH 8157.9   Kaddache, Mahfoud. L'Algérie dans l'antiquité.
Alger, 1972.

AH 8161   Ancient North Africa - Numidia - History by periods - 1 A.D. - ca. 650

AH 8161.2   Kolbe, H.G. Die Statthalter Numidiens von Gallien bis
Konstantin, 268-320. München, 1962.

AH 8162   Ancient North Africa - Numidia - Chronology

AH 8162.5   Pallu de Lessert, A.C. Les fastes de la Numidie sous la
domination romaine. Constantine, 1888.

AH 8171 - 8196   Ancient North Africa - Numidia - Local (A-Z by place)

AH 8182.5   Cagnat, René. Les deux camps de la légion IIIe Auguste à
Lambèse. Paris, 1908.

AH 8200   Ancient Europe - Britain - Bibliographies

AH 8200.2   Bonsen, Wilfrid. A Romano-British bibliography.
Oxford, 1964. 2v.

AH 8202   Ancient Europe - Britain - Collected source materials

AH 8202.5   Moore, Ralph W. The Romans in Britain; a selection of
Latin texts. London, 1938.

AH 8202.8   Mann, John C. The northern frontier in Britain from
Hadrian to Honorius; literary and epigraphic sources.
Newcastle-upon-Tyne, 1969.

AH 8205   Ancient Europe - Britain - Military affairs

AH 8205.2   Airy, George B. Essays on the invasion of Britain by
Julius Caesar; the invasion of Britain by Plautius, and by
Claudius Caesar; the early military policy of the Romans in
Britain; the battle of Hastings. London, 1865.

AH 8205.3   Le Roux, L. L'armée romaine de Bretagne. Paris, 1911.

AH 8205.4   Birley, Eric. Roman Britain and the Roman army.
Kendal, 1953.

AH 8205.5   Divine, Arthur D. The north-west frontier of Rome: a
military study of Hadrian's Wall. London, 1969.

AH 8207   Ancient Europe - Britain - General history

Htn   AH 8207.5*   Langhorne, D. Elenchus antiquitatum albionensium.
Londini, 1675.

AH 8207.8   Sagot, François. La Bretagne romaine. Paris, 1911.

AH 8207.10.2 Windle, Bertram C.A. The Romans in Britain. 2. ed.
London, 1923.

AH 8207.12   Collingwood, Robin G. Roman Britain. London, 1923.

AH 8207.15   Haverfield, F.J. The Roman occupation of Britain.
Oxford, 1924.

AH 8207.21   Winbolt, Samuel E. Britain under the Romans.
Harmondsworth, 1945.

AH 8207   Ancient Europe - Britain - General history - cont.

AH 8207.25   Charlesworth, M.P. The lost province. Cardiff,
Wales, 1949.

AH 8207.27   Lindsay, Jack. The Romans were here. London, 1956.

AH 8207.30   Welch, G.P. Britannia, the Roman conquest. 1. ed.
Middletown, 1963.

AH 8207.34   Priestley, Harold E. Britain under the Romans.
London, 1967.

AH 8207.35   Frere, Sheppard. Britannia; a history of Roman Britain.
Cambridge, 1967.

AH 8207.36   Rowland, Thomas Henry. The Romans in North Britain.
Newcastle upon Tyne, 1970.

AH 8208   Ancient Europe - Britain - General special

AH 8208.10   Young, Douglas. Romanisation in Scotland. Tayport, 1955?

AH 8208.15   Jarrett, Michael G. Britain and Rome; essays presented to
Eric Birley on his sixteenth birthday. Kendal, 1966.

AH 8208.20   Salway, Peter. The frontier people of Roman Britain.
Cambridge, Eng., 1965.

AH 8210   Ancient Europe - Britain - History by periods - 500 - 1 B.C.

AH 8210.2   Guest, Edwin. The invasion of Britain by Julius Caesar.
London, 1864.

AH 8210.4   Caesar's campaigns in Britain. London, 1881.

AH 8210.5   Vine, Francis T. Caesar in Kent, the landing of Julius
Caesar and his battles with the ancient Britons.
Edinburgh, 1886.

AH 8210.5.2   Vine, Francis T. Caesar in Kent, an account of the landing
of Julius Caesar and his battles with the ancient Britons.
2. ed. London, 1887.

AH 8210.7   Tamblyn, William F. The establishment of Roman power in
Britain. Hamilton, Ont., 1899.

AH 8211   Ancient Europe - Britain - History by periods - 1 A.D. - ca. 650

AH 8211.2   Guest, Edwin. The campaign of Aulus Plautius in Britain,
A.D. 43. London, 1866.

AH 8211.5   Burn, A.R. Agricola and Roman Britain. London, 1953.

AH 8211.7   Cottrell, Leonard. The great invasion. London, 1958.

AH 8211.9   Dudley, Donald R. The Roman conquest of Britain, A.D.
43-57. London, 1965.

AH 8211.10A   Foord, Edward A. The last age of Roman Britain.
London, 1925.

AH 8211.10B   Foord, Edward A. The last age of Roman Britain.
London, 1925.

AH 8213   Ancient Europe - Britain - Civilization

AH 8213.2   Haverfield, Francis J. The romanization of Roman Britain.
London, 1906.

AH 8213.2.2   Haverfield, Francis J. The romanization of Roman Britain.
2. ed. Oxford, 1912.

AH 8213.2.4   Haverfield, Francis J. The romanization of Roman Britain.
4. ed. Oxford, 1923.

AH 8213.4   Birley, Anthony R. Life in Roman Britain. London, 1964.

AH 8213.10   Liversidge, Joan. Britain in the Roman empire.
London, 1968.

AH 8217   Ancient Europe - Britain - Travels

Htn   AH 8217.5*   Burton, William. Commentary on Antoninus...itinerary.
London, 1658.

AH 8221 - 8246   Ancient Europe - Britain - Local (A-Z by place)

AH 8222.10   Howard, Peter. Birdoswald Fort on Hadrian's Wall.
Huddersfield, 1969.

AH 8228.2   Davies, Hunter. A walk along the wall. London, 1974.

AH 8229.5   Fletcher, Elsie. The story of Ilkley in Roman times.
Skipton, 1966.

AH 8232.5   Merrifield, Ralph. Roman London. N.Y., 1969.

AH 8233.5   Sharpe, Montagu. Middlesex in British, Roman and Saxon
times. London, 1919.

AH 8257   Ancient Europe - Danubian Provinces - General - General history

AH 8257.3   Fuhrmann, M. Allgemeine Kirchen- und...Oesterreich.
Wien, 1769.

AH 8257.4   Dischendorffer, F. Kritische
Staatsgeschichte...Oesterreich. pt.1-2. Wien, 1783.

AH 8257.5   Gross-Hoffinger, A. Urgeschichte der österreichischen
Länder. Meissen, 1846.

AH 8257.7   Nischer, Ernst. Die Römer im Gebiete des ehenmaligen
Österreich-Ungarn. Wien, 1923.

AH 8258   Ancient Europe - Danubian Provinces - General - General special

AH 8258.1   Syme, Ronald. Danubian papers. Bucharest, 1971.

AH 8305   Ancient Europe - Danubian Provinces - Dacia - Military affairs

AH 8305.5   Christescu, V. Istoria militară a Daciei romane.
Bucureşti, 1937.

AH 8305.7   Rossi, Lino. Trajan's column and the Dacian wars.
London, 1971.

AH 8307   Ancient Europe - Danubian Provinces - Dacia - General history

AH 8307.2   Vaschide, V. Histoire de la conquête...de la Dacie.
Paris, 1903.

AH 8307.3   Daicoviciu, Hadrian. Dacii. Bucureşti, 1965.

AH 8307.4   Maior, Petru. Istoria pentru începutul românillor in
Dacia. Bucureşti, 1971. 2v.

AH 8307.5   Király, Pál. Dacia provincia Augusti.
Nagy-Becskerek, 1893-94. 2v.

AH 8307.6   Király, Pál. Ulpia Trajana Augusta colonia Dacica.
Budapest, 1891.

AH 8307.10   Macrea, Mihail. Viata in Dacia romana. Bucureşti, 1969.

AH 8308   Ancient Europe - Danubian Provinces - Dacia - General special

AH 8308.5   Daicoviciu, Constantin. Le Transylvanie dans l'antiquité.
Bucarest, 1938.

AH 8308.5.1   Daicoviciu, Constantin. Siebenbürgen im Altertum.
Bukarest, 1943.

AH 8308.10   Tudor, D. Istoria sclavajului in Dacia romana.
Bucureşti, 1957.

AH 8311   Ancient Europe - Danubian Provinces - Dacia - History by periods - 1 A.D. - ca.500

AH 8311.2   Alfoldi, András. A gót mozgalom és Dácia feladása.
Budapest, 1930?

Classified Listing

AH 8548 **Ancient Europe - Celts in general - General works - cont.**

AH 8548.20   Lemière, P.L. Étude sur les Celtes et les Gaulois. St. Brieuc, 187-?

AH 8548.22   Maclear, George F. The Celts. London, 1878.

AH 8548.25   Valroger, L. de. Les Celtes, la Gaule celtique. Paris, 1879.

AH 8548.30   Becker, K. von. Versuch einer Lösung der Celtenfrage. Karlsruhe, 1883.

AH 8548.35   Lizeray, Henri. Fondation du pan-celtisme. Paris, 1884. 2 pam.

AH 8548.38   Scott, A. The Celts and Druids and their story from the earliest times. North Shields, 1894.

AH 8548.40   Dias Pinheiro, Alfredo. Os celtas e povos com êles relacionados. Guimarães, 1928.

AH 8548.48   Adam, Maurice. La tradition celtique et ses adversaires. Paris, 1901.

AH 8548.50   Roessler, C. Les influences celtiques. Paris, 1902.

AH 8548.52   Sculfort de Beaurepas, Serge. La panceltisme universel et pacifique contre le pangermanisme envahisseur et l'imperialisme anglais. Paris, 1903. 2v.

AH 8548.55   Arbois de Jubainville, Henry d'. Les Celtes. Paris, 1904.

AH 8548.55.1   Arbois de Jubainville, Henry d'. Les Celtes depuis le temps les plus anciens. Osnabrück, 1968.

AH 8548.57   Dottin, Georges. Manuel pour servir à l'étude de la antiquité celtique. Paris, 1906.

AH 8548.57.2   Dottin, Georges. Manuel pour servir à l'étude de l'antiquité celtique. 2. éd. Paris, 1915.

AH 8548.65   Dinan, W. Monumenta historica celtica. London, 1911.

AH 8548.75   Leslie, S. Celt and the world. N.Y., 1917.

AH 8548.80   Rott, Joseph. Ueber die Nationalität der Kelten. Passau, 1866?

AH 8548.90   Paniagua, A. de. Les Celtes bretons et les Phocéens dans le sud ouest de la Gaule. Paris, 1926.

AH 8548.95   Chotzen, T.M. Primitieve Keltistiek in de Nederlanden. 's-Gravenhage, 1931.

AH 8548.100   O'Rahilly, T.F. The Guidels and their predecessors. London, 1936.

AH 8548.105   Elston, C.S. The earliest relations between Celts and Germans. London, 1934.

AH 8548.110   Navarro, J.M. de. A survey of research on an early phase of Celtic culture. London, 1936.

AH 8548.115   Mone, F.J. Celtische Forschungen zur Geschichte Mitteleuropas. Freiburg, 1857.

AH 8548.120   Dillon, Myles. The archaism of Irish tradition. London, 1947.

AH 8548.120.5   Dillon, Myles. The Celtic realms. London, 1967.

AH 8548.125   Gaulle, C. de. Les Celtes au XIX. siècle. Paris, 1903.

AH 8548.130   Rivoallan, A. Présence des Celtes. Paris, 1957.

AH 8548.135   Moreau, Jacques. Die Welt der Kelten. Stuttgart, 1958.

AH 8548.140   Powell, Terence G.E. The Celts. London, 1958.

AH 8548.141   Filip, Jan. Celtic civilization and its heritage. Prague, 1960.

AH 8548.141.5   Filip, Jan. Keltská civilisace a její dědictví. Praha, 1959.

AH 8548.142   Raftery, Joseph. The Celts. Cork, 1964.

AH 8548.145   Cailleux, Théophile. Origine celtique de la civilisation de tous les peuples: théorie nouvelle. Paris, 1878.

AH 8548.147   Markale, Jean. Les Celtes et la civilisation celtique; mythe et histoire. Paris, 1969.

AH 8548.149   Ross, Anne. Everyday life of the pagan Celts. London, 1970.

AH 8548.150   Lengyel, Lancelot. Le secret des Celtes. 1. éd. Le Jas du Revest-Saint-Martin, 1969.

AH 8548.152   Chadwick, Nora (Kershaw). The Celts. Harmondsworth, Eng., 1970.

AH 8548.154   Harmond, Jacques. Les Celtes au second âge du fer. Paris, 1970.

AH 8548.155   Hubert, Henri. The greatness and decline of the Celts. New York, 1972.

AH 8549 **Ancient Europe - Celts in general - Religion and mythology; Druidism (By date, e.g. .150 for 1950)**

AH 8549.2   Eyring, Elias M. Veterum instituta druidum. Lipsiae, 1698.

AH 8549.3   La Saussaye, L. de. Dissertation sur le lieu de l'assemblée des druides. n.p., n.d.

AH 8549.5   Frick, J.G. De druidis occidentalium popularum philosophis. Ulmae, 1731.

AH 8549.10   Frick, J.G. Commentatio de Druidis. Ulmae, 1744.

AH 8549.12   Martin, Jacques. La religion des Gaulois, tirée des plus pures sources de l'antiquité. Amsterdam, 1750. 2v.

AH 8549.15   Pelloutier, S. Die Religion der Celten. Frankfurt am Mayn, 1784.

AH 8549.17   Travels of a British druid. London, 1811. 2v.

AH 8549.17.50   Toland, John. A critical history of the Celtic religion. London, 174-?

AH 8549.18   Toland, John. A critical history of the Celtic religion. Edinburgh, 1815.

AH 8549.20   Barth, C.K. Ueber die Druiden der Kelten. Erlangen, 1826.

AH 8549.25   Bowles, W.L. A dissertation on the Celtic deity Teutates. London, 1828.

AH 8549.36   James, D. The patriarchal religion of Britain; or A complete manual of ancient British Druidism. London, 1836.

AH 8549.42   Williams, J. An essay on the question "Whether the British Druids offered human sacrifices". Bala, 1842.

AH 8549.42.5   Roberts, J. Druidical remains and antiquities of the ancient Britons. Swansea, 1842.

AH 8549.45   Smith, John. Histoire des druides et...Calédonie. Arbois, 1845.

AH 8549.45.5   David de St. Georges, J.J.A. Histoire des druides et...Calédonie. Arbois, 1845.

AH 8549.50   Herrig, L. De Druidibus, eine Abhandlung. Berlin, 1853.

AH 8549.65   Panchaud, Edouard. Le druidisme; ou Religion des anciens gaulois. Lausanne, 1865.

AH 8549.69   Leflocq, J. Etudes de mythologie celtique. Orléans, 1869.

AH 8549.71   Smiddy, Richard. An essay on the Druids. Dublin, 1871.

Htn   AH 8549.76*   Vallentin, F. Essai sur les divinités indigètes du Vocontium. Grenoble, 1877.

AH 8549.77   Ferk, F. Über Druidismus in Noricum. Graz, 1877.

AH 8549.79   Fustel de Coulanges, N.D. Comment le druidisme a disparu. Paris, 1879.

AH 8549.79.5   Arbois de Jubainville, Henry d'. Le dieu de la mort et les origines mythologiques. Paris, 1879.

AH 8549.80   Gaidoz, Henri. La religion gauloise et de Gui de Chêne. Paris, 1880.

AH 8549.80.5   Howard, John E. The Druids and their religion. London, 1880?

AH 8549 **Ancient Europe - Celts in general - Religion and mythology; Druidism (By date, e.g. .150 for 1950) - cont.**

AH 8549.81   Cerquand, J.F. Taranis Lithobole; étude de mythologie celtique. Avignon, 1881.

AH 8549.85   Macbain, A. Celtic mythology and religion. Photoreproduction. Inverness, 1885.

AH 8549.85.5   Macbain, A. Celtic mythology and religion. Stirling, 1917.

AH 8549.86   Pufendorf, E. A dissertation upon the Druids. Edinburgh, 1886.

AH 8549.86.1A   Pufendorf, E. A dissertation upon the Druids. Edinburgh, 1886.

AH 8549.86.1B   Pufendorf, E. A dissertation upon the Druids. Edinburgh, 1886.

AH 8549.87   Morgan, O. The light of Britannia. Cardiff, 1894.

AH 8549.94   Bonwick, James. Irish Druids and old Irish religions. London, 1894.

Htn   AH 8549.102*   Gaidoz, Henri. Le grand dieu gaulois...Allobroges. n.p., 1902.

AH 8549.103   Robinson, F.N. Human sacrifice among the Irish Celts. Boston, 1913.

AH 8549.104   Callegari, G.V. Il druidismo nell'antica Gallia. Padova, 1904.

AH 8549.104.5   Dottin, Georges. La religion des Celtes. 2. éd. Paris, 1904.

AH 8549.106   Arbois de Jubainville, Henry d'. Les druides et les dieux celtiques. Paris, 1906.

AH 8549.106.5   Arnoyl, E. Celtic religion in pre-Christian times. London, 1906.

AH 8549.110   Bosc, Ernest. Belisama, ou L'occultisme cetique. Paris, 1910.

AH 8549.111   Pokorny, J. The origin of druidism. Washington, 1911.

AH 8549.111.5   MacCulloch, John A. The religion of the ancient Celts. Edinburgh, 1911.

AH 8549.122   Memminger, A. Das Erbe der Druiden. 7. Aufl. Würzburg, 1922.

AH 8549.124   Wright, D. Druidism; the ancient faith of Britain. London, 1924.

AH 8549.125.5   Hubert, Henri. Divinités gauloises. Epona, 1925.

AH 8549.127   Kendrick, T.D. The Druids. London, 1927.

AH 8549.127.5   Kendrick, T.D. The Druids. N.Y., 1927.

AH 8549.127.10   Daniel, J. The philosophy of ancient Britain. London, 1927.

AH 8549.128   Spence, Lewis. The mysteries of Britain. London, 1928.

AH 8549.135   Hamel, Anton G. van. Aspects of Celtic mythology. London, 1935.

AH 8549.135.5   MacNiell, Evin. Celtic and Teutonic religions. London, 1935.

AH 8549.142   Lambrechts, P. Contributions à l'étude des divinités celtiques. Brügge, 1942.

AH 8549.145   Spence, Lewis. The magic arts in Celtic Britain. London, 1945.

AH 8549.148   MacCulloch, John A. The Celtic and Scandinavian religions. London, 1948.

AH 8549.149   Spence, Lewis. The history and origins of druidism. N.Y., 1949.

AH 8549.149.5   Spence, Lewis. The history and origins of druidism. N.Y., 1949.

AH 8549.157   Duval, Paul Marie. Les dieux de la Gaule. 1. éd. Paris, 1957.

AH 8549.161   Le Roux, F. Les druides. Paris, 1961.

AH 8549.163.1   Vries, Jan de. La religion des Celtes. Paris, 1963.

AH 8549.166   Chadwick, Nora (Kershaw). The Druids. Cardiff, 1966.

AH 8549.167   Genty, Patrice. Etudes sur le celtisme. Paris, 1967.

AH 8549.168   Piggott, Stuart. The Druids. N.Y., 1968.

AH 8549.168.5   Thévenot, Emile. Divinités et sanctuaires de la Gaule. Paris, 1968.

AH 8549.168.10   Serbanesco, Demeter Gérard Roger. Les Celtes et les druides. Paris, 1968.

AH 8549.170.5   Benoît, Fernand. Le symbolisme dans les sanctuaires de la Gaule. Bruxelles, 1970.

AH 8549.171   Coarer-Kalondan, Edmond. Le druidisme, ou La lumière del l'Occident. Paris, 1971.

AH 8549.173.1   Lochner-Huettenbach, Fritz. Keltische Grottheit auf norischem Inschriftstein. Photoreproduction. Graz, 1973.

AH 8549.174   Gilbert, Max. "Les roches aux fées" dans l'ancienne Gaule. Fécamp, 1971.

AH 8557 **Ancient Europe - Illyricum - General history**

AH 8557.2   Zippel, B. Römische Herrschaft in Illyrien. Leipzig, 1877.

AH 8557.4   Schütt, C. Untersuchungen zur Geschichte der alten Illyrien. Inaug. Diss. Breslau, 1910.

AH 8557.5   Hohenhausen, S.J. Illyrien. Essegg, 1777.

AH 8557.7   Poinsignon, A.M. Quid praicipue apud Romanos adusque Diocletiani tempora Illyricum fuerit breviter disseritur. Parisiis, 1896.

AH 8557.10   Rogošić, Roko. Veliki Illirik (284-395) i njegova konačna dioba (396-437). Zagreb, 1962.

AH 8566 **Ancient Europe - Illyricum - Geography**

AH 8566.5   Almerigotti, Francesco. Della estensione dell'antico Ilirico. pt.1-2. Venezia, 17- .

AH 8571 - 8596 **Ancient Europe - Illyricum - Local (A-Z by place)**

AH 8574.2   Cons, Henri. La province romaine de Dalmatie. Paris, 1881.

AH 8574.4   Alföldy, Géza. Bevölkerung und Gesellschaft der römischen Provinz Dalmatien. Budapest, 1965.

AH 8574.5   Wilkes, J.J. Dalmatia. Cambridge, 1969.

AH 8603 **Ancient Europe - Italy - General - Government and administration**

AH 8603.2   Rosenberg, A. Der Staat der alten Italiker. Berlin, 1913.

AH 8607 **Ancient Europe - Italy - General - General history**

AH 8607.2   Pais, Ettore. Ancient Italy. Chicago, 1908.

AH 8607.2.5   Pais, Ettore. Storia dell'Italia antica. Roma, 1925. 2v.

AH 8607.2.7   Pais, Ettore. Storia dell'Italia antica e della Sicilia per l'età anteriore al dominio romano. 2. ed. Torino, 1933. 2v.

AH 8607.2.10F   Pais, Ettore. Gli elementi ilaliati sannitici e campani nella più antica civiltà romana. Napoli, 1900.

AH 8607.5   Vannucci, A. Storia d'Italia. Firenze, 1851. 4v.

AH 8607.5.5   Vannucci, A. Storia dell'Italia antica. 3. ed. Milano, 1873-76. 4v.

AH 8607.7   Puglisi-Marino, S. Sul nome Italia. Catania, 1901.

Classified Listing

AH 8607   Ancient Europe - Italy - General - General history - cont.
AH 8607.8   Micali, G. L'Italia avanti il dominio dei romani. 3. ed. Milano, 1826. 3v.
AH 8607.9   Panciera, D. Lezioni di storia patria. Grosseto, 1867.
AH 8607.10   Ducati, P. L'Italia antica dalle prime civiltà alla morte di Cesare, 44 a.C. Milano, 1936.
AH 8607.11   Ferrabino, Aldo. L'Italia romana. Milano, 1934.
AH 8607.12   Sesti, Luigi. Storia d'Italia dalle origini alla conquista romana. Milano, 1960.

AH 8608   Ancient Europe - Italy - General - General special
AH 8608.2   Fligier, C. Zur praehistorischen Ethnologie Italiens. Wien, 1877.
AH 8608.3   Lamarre, C. Étude sur peuples anciens de l'Italie. Paris, 1899.
AH 8608.4   Grotefend, G.F. Zur Geographie und Geschichte von Alt-Italien. v.1-3. Hannover, 1840-42.
AH 8608.5   Guarnacci, Mario. Origini italiche. Roma, 1785-87. 3v.
AH 8608.5.5   Guarnacci, Mario. Delle origini italiche. Venezia, 1773.
AH 8608.6   Mazzoldi, Angelo. Delle origini italiche. Livorno, 1849. 2v.
AH 8608.6.5   Bianchi Giovini, A. Sulle Origini italiche di Angelo Mazzoldi; osservazioni. Milano, 1841.
AH 8608.6.10   Mazzoldi, Angelo. Riposta alle osservazioni di Bianchi-Giovini sulle Origini. Milano, 1841.
AH 8608.7F   Bardetti, S. De primi abitatori dell'Italia; opera postuma. pt.1-2. Modena, 1769.
AH 8608.8F   Italy. Ministero della marina. Monografia storica dei porti dell'antichità nell'Italia insulare. Roma, 1906.
AH 8608.8.10   Stella, Luigia A. Italia antica sul mare. Milano, 1930.
AH 8608.9   Misiano, D.B. I popoli preistorici dell'Italia. Bova Marina, 1930.
AH 8608.10   Devoto, Giacomo. Gli antichi italici. Firenze, 1931.
AH 8608.10.2   Devoto, Giacomo. Gli antichi italici. 2. ed. Firenze, 1951.
AH 8608.11   Miscosi, G. Origini italiche; testimonianze storiche sull'esistenza di Roma e Genova prerumulee. Genova, 1934.
AH 8608.12   Arias, Paolo E. La civiltà gallica in Italia. L'impero di Severo Alessandro. Bologna, 1953.

AH 8609   Ancient Europe - Italy - General - History by periods - Before 500 B.C.
AH 8609.2   Rubino, J. Beiträge zur Vorgeschichte Italiens. Leipzig, 1868.
AH 8609.3   Mommsen, Theodor. Earliest inhabitants of Italy. London, 1858.
AH 8609.4   Modestov, V.I. Vvednie v rimskuiu. Sankt Peterburg, 1902-04. 2v.
AH 8609.5   Modestov, V.I. Introduction à l'histoire romaine. Paris, 1907.

AH 8610   Ancient Europe - Italy - General - History by periods - 500 - 1 B.C.
AH 8610.2   Beloch, J. Der italische Bund...Roms Hegemonie. Leipzig, 1880.

AH 8611   Ancient Europe - Italy - General - History by periods - 1 A.D. - ca.500
AH 8611.5   Thomsen, Rudi. The Italic regions. København, 1947.

AH 8613   Ancient Europe - Italy - General - Civilization
AH 8613.5   Gerlach, F.D. Zaleukos, Charondas, Pythagoras. Basel, 1858.

AH 8615   Ancient Europe - Italy - General - Economic conditions
AH 8615.5   Sirago, Vito A. L'Italia agraria sotto Traiano. Louvain, 1958.
AH 8615.7   Ruggini, Lallia. Economia e società nell'Italia annonaria. Milano, 1961.
AH 8615.10   Wilson, A.J.N. Emigration from Italy in the republican age of Rome. Manchester, Eng., 1966.
AH 8615.15   Brunt, Peter A. Italian manpower, 225 B.C.-A.D. 14. Oxford, 1971.

AH 8616   Ancient Europe - Italy - General - Geography
AH 8616.2F   Cluneri, P. Italiae antiquae. Lugduni Batavorum, 1624.
AH 8616.4   Nissen, H. Italische Landeskunde. v.1-2. Berlin, 1883. 3v.
AH 8616.6   Cramer, J.A. Geographical...description of ancient Italy. Oxford, 1826. 2v.
AH 8616.9A   Sabin, Frances E. Classical associations of places in Italy. Madison, Wis., 1921.
AH 8616.9B   Sabin, Frances E. Classical associations of places in Italy. Madison, Wis., 1921.
AH 8616.10   Wikén, Erik. Die Kunde der Hellenen von dem Lande und den Völkern der Apenninenhalbinsel bis 300 v. Chr. Lund, 1937.

AH 8617   Ancient Europe - Italy - General - Travels
AH 8617.5   Cuoco, Vincenzo. Platone in Italia. Bari, 1916-24. 2v.
AH 8617.5.2   Cuoco, Vincenzo. Platone in Italia. 2. ed. Parma, 1820.
AH 8617.5.5   Cuoco, Vincenzo. Voyage de Platon en Italie. Paris, 1807. 3v.
AH 8617.7   Tulelli, E. Il filadelfos de Giovanni Gemelli. Napoli, 1882.

AH 8647   Ancient Europe - Italy - Magna Graecia in general
AH 8647.5   Lenormant, F. Grand-Grèce paysages. Paris, 1881. 3v.
AH 8647.5.3   Lenormant, F. Grande-Grèce paysages. 2. éd. Paris, 1881. 2v.
AH 8647.5.15   Lenormant, F. La Magna Grecia, paesaggio e storia. Crotone, 1931-33. 3v.
AH 8647.9   Byvanck, A.W. De Magnae Graeciae historia antiquissima. Hagae, 1912.
AH 8647.10.5   Ciaceri, E. Storia della Magna Grecia. Milano, 1927-32. 3v.
AH 8647.11   Società Magna Grecia. Campagne della Società Magna Grecia, 1926 e 1927. Roma, 1928.
AH 8647.12   Randall-MacIver, D. Greek cities in Italy and Sicily. Oxford, 1931.
AH 8647.13F   Larizza, Pietro. La Magna Grecia. Roma, 1929.
AH 8647.14   Olivieri, A. Civiltà greca nell'Italia meridionale. Napoli, 1931.
AH 8647.15   Marincola Pistoja, D. Di Cautonia, repubblica della Magna Grecia. Catanzaro, 1866. 2 pam.
AH 8647.16   Schereschewsky, J. Die politischen Beziehungen der unter italischen Griechenstädte. Inaug. Diss. Leipzig, 1934.
AH 8647.17A   Dunabin, T.J. The western Greeks. Oxford, 1948.
AH 8647.17B   Dunabin, T.J. The western Greeks. Oxford, 1948. 2v.

AH 8647   Ancient Europe - Italy - Magna Graecia in general - cont.
AH 8647.20   Sartori, F. Problemi di storia costituzionale italiata. Roma, 1953.
AH 8647.21   Kahrstedt, Ulrich. Die wirtschaftliche Lage. Grossgriechenlands in der Kaiserzeit. Wiesbaden, 1960.
AH 8647.22   Bérard, Jean. La colonisation grecque de l'Italie meridionale et de la Sicile dans l'antiquité. Paris, 1957.
AH 8647.22.5   Bérard, Jean. Bibliographie topographique des principales cités grecque de l'Italie. Paris, 1941.
AH 8647.25   Convegno di Studi sulla Magna Grecia. Atti. Napoli. 1,1961+ 9v.
AH 8647.26   Maiuri, Amedeo. Passeggiate in Magna Grecia. Napoli, 1963.

AH 8653   Ancient Europe - Italy - City of Rome - Government and administration
AH 8653.5   Chastagnol, André. La préfecture urbaine à Rome sous le Bas-Empire. 1. éd. Paris, 1960.

AH 8657   Ancient Europe - Italy - City of Rome - General history
AH 8657.3   Gilbert, Otto. Geschichte...der Stadt Rom im Altertum. Leipzig, 1883. 3v.
AH 8657.5   Dyer, Thomas H. History of the city of Rome. London, 1865.
AH 8657.5.3   Dyer, Thomas H. The city of Rome. 2. ed. London, 1883.

AH 8658   Ancient Europe - Italy - City of Rome - General special
AH 8658.2   Elliot, F.D.G. Pictures of old Rome. Leipzig, 1882.
AH 8658.5   Historical pictures of pagan and Christian Rome. Rome, 1855.

AH 8662   Ancient Europe - Italy - City of Rome - Chronology
AH 8662.5   Chastagnol, André. Les fastes de la préfecture de Rome au Bas-Empire. Paris, 1962.

AH 8663   Ancient Europe - Italy - City of Rome - Civilization
AH 8663.2   Shumway, E.S. A day in ancient Rome. Boston, 1897.

AH 8666   Ancient Europe - Italy - City of Rome - Geography
AH 8666.3   Victor, Pubblius (pseud.). De regionibus urbis Romae. 1. ed. Romae? 1500.
AH 8666.5   Castagnoli, Ferdinando. Topografia e urbanistica di Roma antica. Bologna, 1969.

AH 8667   Ancient Europe - Italy - City of Rome - Travels
AH 8667.2   Jones, H.S. Classical Rome. N.Y., 1910.
AH 8667.3   Theis, A. di. Viaggio di Policleto a Roma. Milano, 1824. 4v.
AH 8667.4   Stuart-Jones, H. Classical Rome. London, 1910.

AH 8671 - 8696   Ancient Europe - Italy - City of Rome - Local (A-Z by place)
AH 8673.3   Elter, A. Cremera und Porta Carmentalis. Bonn, 1910.
AH 8676.2   Schulze, E. Römische Forum als Mittelpunkt. Gütersloh, 1893.
Htn   AH 8676.3*   Lauro, G. Antiquae urbis splendor. Romae, 1610.
AH 8679.2   Werner, P. De incendiis urbis Romae. Lipsiae, 1906.
AH 8683.2   Becker, G.A. De Romae veteris muris...portis. Lipsiae, 1842.
AH 8689.5F   Colini, Antonio. Stadium Domitiani. Roma, 1943.

AH 8708   Ancient Europe - Italy - Apulia - General special
AH 8708.5   Maggiulli, Pasquale. Sull'origine dei Messapi. Lecce, 1934.

AH 8716   Ancient Europe - Italy - Apulia - Geography
AH 8716.5   Lucarelli, Antonio. Saggio sulla geografia storica dell Japigia. Trani, 1903.

AH 8721 - 8746   Ancient Europe - Italy - Apulia - Local (A-Z by place)
AH 8740.2   Lorentz, Rudolf. De civitate veterum Tarentinorum. Lipsiae, 1833.
AH 8740.2.5   Lorentz, Rudolf. De rebus sacris et artibus veterum Tarentinorum. Elberfeldiae, 1836.
AH 8740.3   Doehle. Geschichte Tarents bis auf seine Unterwerfung unter Rom. Strassburg, 1877.

AH 8771 - 8796   Ancient Europe - Italy - Bruttium - Local (A-Z by place)
AH 8788.2   Axt, Otto. Zur Topographie von Rhegion und Messana. Grimma, 1887.
AH 8789.5   Callaway, Joseph S. Sybaris. Baltimore, 1950.
AH 8789.7   Tabouis, Geneviève R. Sybaris, les grecs en Italie. Paris, 1958.

AH 8857   Ancient Europe - Italy - Campania - General history
AH 8857.2   Beloch, Julius. Campanien. Geschichte und Topographie des antiken Neapel und seiner Umgebung. Berlin, 1879.
AH 8857.2F   Beloch, Julius. Campanien. Geschichte und Topographie des antiken Neapel und seiner Umgebung. Atlas. Berlin, 1879.
AH 8857.3   Beloch, Julius. Campanien. Geschichte und Topogrpahie des antiken Neapel und seiner Umgebung. Breslau, 1890.
AH 8857.4   Pellegrini, C. Apparato alle antichità di Capua o vero discorsi della campania. Napoli, 1651.
AH 8857.4.5   Pellegrini, C. Apparato alle antichità di Capua o vero discorsi della campania. Napoli, 1771. 2v.
AH 8857.5   Jerome, Thomas S. Roman memories in the landscape seen from Capri. Detroit, 1914.

AH 8858   Ancient Europe - Italy - Campania - General special
AH 8858.7   Fricke, Karl. Die Hellenen in Campanien. Hildesheim, 1873.

AH 8863   Ancient Europe - Italy - Campania - Civilization
Htn   AH 8863.5*   Mazochi, P.S. In mutilum Campani amphitheatri. Neapoli, 1727.
AH 8863.10   D'Arms, John Houghton. Romans and the Bay of Naples; a social and cultural study of the villas and their owners from 150 B.C. to A.D. 400. Cambridge, 1970.

AH 8864   Ancient Europe - Italy - Campania - Religion
AH 8864.16   Peterson, Roy M. The cults of Campania. Rome, 1919.

AH 8871 - 8896   Ancient Europe - Italy - Campania - Local (A-Z by place)
AH 8873.2   Zoeller, Max. Das Senatusconsultum über Capua. Mulhausen, 1875.
AH 8873.5   Weyer, G.A. Die staatsrechtlichen Beziehungen Kapuas zu Rom. Inaug. Diss. Bonn, 1913.
AH 8873.10   Stein, J.J. De Capuae gentisque Campanorum. Diss. Vratislaviae, 1838.

AH 8871 - 8896   Ancient Europe - Italy - Campania - Local (A-Z by place) - cont.
AH 8879.5   Monti, Pietro. Ischia preistorica, greca, romana, paleocristiana. Napoli, 1968.
AH 8886.5   Willems, Pierre. Les élections municipales à Pompéi. Paris, 1887.

AH 8900   Ancient Europe - Italy - Etruria - Bibliographies
AH 8900.5   Lopes Pegna, M. Saggio di bibliografia etrusca. Firenze, 1953.

AH 8902   Ancient Europe - Italy - Etruria - Collected source materials
AH 8902.5   Convegno di studi etruschi. Atti. Firenze. 1-2

AH 8903   Ancient Europe - Italy - Etruria - Government and administration
AH 8903.5   Pfiffig, Ambros Josef. Die Ausbreitung des römischen Städtewesens in Etrurien und die Frage der Unterwerfung der Etrusker. Firenze, 1966.
AH 8903.6   Liou, Bernard. Praetores Etruriae XV populorum (étude d'épigraphie). Bruxelles, 1969.

AH 8904   Ancient Europe - Italy - Etruria - Law
AH 8904.5   Lambrechts, R. Essai sur les magistratures des républiques étrusques. Bruxelles, 1959.

AH 8907   Ancient Europe - Italy - Etruria - General history
AH 8907.2   Spadoni, O.L. The Etruscans. Rome, 1887.
AH 8907.3   Conestabile, G. Degli etruschi dell'agricoltura. Perugia, 1859.
AH 8907.4   Des Vergers, M.J.A.N. L'Étrurie et les Étrusques. Paris, 1862-64. 2v.
AH 8907.4PF   Des Vergers, M.J.A.N. L'Étrurie et les Étrusques. v.3. Atlas. Paris, 1862-64.
Htn   AH 8907.5F*   Ethruscarum antiquitatum fragmenta. Francofurti, 1637.
AH 8907.5.5   Inghirami, C. Discorso...sopra l'opposizioni. Firenze, 1645.
AH 8907.6   Gray, E.C.H. History of Etruria. London, 1843. 3v.
Htn   AH 8907.7*   Postell, G. De Etruriae regionis. Florentiae, 1551.
AH 8907.8   Müller, Karl O. Die Etrusker. v.1-2. Breslau, 1828.
AH 8907.8.5   Müller, Karl O. Die Etrusker. Stuttgart, 1877. 2v.
AH 8907.8.10   Müller, Karl O. Die Etrusker. Graz, 1965. 2v.
AH 8907.9   Casati, Charles. Les Étrusques, leur langue...civilisation. Paris, 1914.
AH 8907.11.5   Pallottino, Massimo. The Etruscans. 3d Italian ed. Harmondsworth, 1955.
AH 8907.11.10   Pallottino, Massimo. Etruscologia. 6. ed. Milano, 1968.
AH 8907.12   Peserico, Luigi. Ricerche di storia etrusca. Vicenza, 1919.
AH 8907.13   Fell, R.A.L. Etruria and Rome. Cambridge, Eng., 1924.
AH 8907.14   Pareti, Luigi. Le origine etrusche. Firenze, 1926.
AH 8907.15   Ducati, Pericule. Etruria antica. Torino, 1925.
AH 8907.16   Buonamici, G. L'Etruria e gli Etruschi. Firenze, 1926.
AH 8907.17   Cooley, Julia. The forgotten Etruscans. N.Y., 1927.
AH 8907.18   Schachermeyer, F. Etruskische Frühgeschichte. Berlin, 1929.
AH 8907.19   Johnstone, M.A. Etruria past and present. London, 1930.
AH 8907.20   Nogara, Bartolemeo. Gli Etruschi e la loro civiltà. Milano, 1933.
AH 8907.21F   Solari, Arturo. Vita pubblica e privata degli Etruschi. Firenze, 1931.
AH 8907.22   Bulanda, E. Etrurja i Etruskowie. Lwów, 1934.
AH 8907.23   Ducati, Pericule. Le problème étrusque. Paris, 1938.
AH 8907.25   Bloch, Raymond. Les Étrusques. Paris, 1954.
AH 8907.26   Cles-Reden, S. Les Étrusques. Paris, 1955.
AH 8907.26.5   Cles-Reden, S. The buried people. N.Y., 1955.
AH 8907.27   Pfister, Kurt. Die Etrusker. München, 1940.
AH 8907.30   Hus, Alain. Les Étrusques. Paris, 1957.
AH 8907.30.5   Hus, Alain. The Etruscans. N.Y., 1961.
AH 8907.35   Zalesskii, Nikolai N. Etruski v severnoi Italii. Leningrad, 1959.
AH 8907.40   Istituto lombardo di scienze e lettere. Tyrrhenica. Milano, 1957.
AH 8907.41   Vaughan, A.C. Those mysterious Etruscans. 1. ed. Garden City, N.Y., 1964.
AH 8907.42   Études étrusco-italiques. Louvain, 1963.
AH 8907.44   Signorelli, Mario. Storia degli Etruschi. Roma, 1969.
AH 8907.46   Keller, Werner. Denn die Entzündeten das Licht. München, 1970.
AH 8907.48   Nemirovskii, Aleksandr I. Etruski. Voronezh, 1969.
AH 8907.50   Burian, Ján. Zagadochnye etruski. Moskva, 1970.

AH 8908   Ancient Europe - Italy - Etruria - General special
AH 8908.01   Pamphlet box. Roman history. Etruria.
AH 8908.3   Brunet y Bellet, J. Els gregs, els etruscos. Barcelona, 1895.
AH 8908.5   Rühle, J.J.O.A. Zur Geschichte der Pelasger und Etrusker. Berlin, 1831.
AH 8908.7   Lepsius, K.R. Ueber die tyrrhenischen Pelasger. Leipzig, 1842.
AH 8908.9   Körte, G. Etrusker. Stuttgart, 1877.
AH 8908.11   Herbig, G. Zum heutigen Stand der etruskischen Frage. München, 1907.
AH 8908.12   Cserèp, J. De Pelasgis Etruscisqui. Budapestini, 1912.
AH 8908.13   Betham, William. Etruria. Celtica Etruscan literature and antiquities. Dublin, 1842. 2v.
AH 8908.14   Haury, Jacob. Neues über die Herkunft der Etrusker und über Homer. Kaiserslautern, 1926.
AH 8908.14.5   Haùry, Jacob. Über die Herkunft der Etrusker. Kaiserslautern, 1922.
AH 8908.15   Mühlestein, H. Über die Herkunft der Etrusker. Berlin, 1929.
AH 8908.16   Pallottino, Massimo. L'origine degli Etruschi. Roma, 1947.
AH 8908.17   Altheim, F. Der Ursprung der Etrusker. Baden, 1950.

AH 8909   Ancient Europe - Italy - Etruria - History by periods - Before 500 B.C.
AH 8909.2   Gardthausen, V. Mastarna öder Servius Tullius. Leipzig, 1882.
AH 8909.5   Ciba Foundation. Ciba Foundation on medical biology and Etruscan origins. London, 1959.

AH 8910   Ancient Europe - Italy - Etruria - History by periods - 500 - 1 B.C.
AH 8910.5   Zalesskii, Nikolai N. K istorii etrusskoi kolonizatsii Italii v VII-IV vv. Leningrad, 1965.
AH 8910.8   Harris, William Vernon. Rome in Etruria and Umbria. Oxford, 1971.

AH 8913   Ancient Europe - Italy - Etruria - Civilization
AH 8913.5   Bloch, Raymond. L'art et la civilisation étrusques. Paris, 1955.
AH 8913.5.5   Bloch, Raymond. Le mystère étrusque. Paris, 1956.
AH 8913.5.6   Bloch, Raymond. The Etruscans. London, 1958.
AH 8913.5.7   Bloch, Raymond. The Etruscans. London, 1969.
AH 8913.5.8   Bloch, Raymond. The ancient civilization of the Etruscans. N.Y., 1969.
AH 8913.10   Vacano, Otto Wilhelm von. Die Etrusker. Stuttgart, 1955.
AH 8913.10.5   Vacano, Otto Wilhelm von. Die Etrusker in der Welt der Antike. Hamburg, 1957.
AH 8913.10.10   Vacano, Otto Wilhelm von. The Etruscans in the ancient world. N.Y., 1960.
AH 8913.12   Pallottino, Massimo. La civilisation étrusque. Paris, 1949.
AH 8913.15   Heurgon, Jacques. La vie quotidienne chez les Étrusques. Paris, 1961.
AH 8913.20F   Svenska Institutet i Rom. Etruscan culture, land and people. N.Y., 1963.
AH 8913.25   Richardson, Emeline H. The Etruscans; their art and civilization. Chicago, 1964.
AH 8913.28   Scullard, Howard. The Etruscan cities and Rome. Ithaca, 1967.
AH 8913.28.5   Convegno di studi sulla città etrusca e italica preromana. Studi sulla città antica. Bologna, 1970.
AH 8913.30   Strong, Donald Emrys. The early Etruscans. London, 1968.
AH 8913.32   Gaudio, Attilio. Les Étrusques. Une civilisation retrouvée. Verviers, 1969.
AH 8913.34   Mayani, Zecharia. La fin du mystère étrusque; les origines, la langue et la vie des Étrusques. Paris, 1970.

AH 8914   Ancient Europe - Italy - Etruria - Religion
AH 8914.5   Rossi, S. Il tipo e l'ufficio del charun etrusco. Messina, 1900.
AH 8914.10   Clemen, Carl. Die Religion der Etrusker. Bonn, 1936.
AH 8914.16   Taylor, Lily R. Local cults in Etruria. Rome, 1923.
AH 8914.20   Herbig, G. Religion und Kultur der Etrusker. Breslau, 1922.

AH 8915   Ancient Europe - Italy - Etruria - Economic conditions
AH 8915.2   Genthe, H.F. Ueber den etruskischen Tauschhandel. Heibronn, 1874.

AH 8917   Ancient Europe - Italy - Etruria - Travels
AH 8917.5   Harrel-Courtès, Henry. L'Italie des Étrusques. Paris, 1960.

AH 8918   Ancient Europe - Italy - Etruria - Special topics - Medicine
AH 8918.1   Tabanelli, Mario. La medicina nel mondo degli Etruschi. Firenze, 1963.

AH 8921 - 8946   Ancient Europe - Italy - Etruria - Local (A-Z by place)
NEDL AH 8922.2   Grenier, A. Bologne, Villanovienne et Étrusque. Thèse. Paris, 1912.
AH 8926.2   Deecke, W. Die Falisker, eine geschichtlich-sprachliche Untersuchung. Strassburg, 1888.
Htn   AH 8936.2F*   Noris, Enrico. Cenotaphia Piasana Caii et Lucii Caesarum. Venetiis, 1681.
AH 8940.2   Carchidio, F. Memorie storichi dell'...Telamone. Firenze, 1824.
AH 8942.2   Riccobaldi del Bana, G.M. Dissertazione istorico-etrusca...della città di Volterra. Firenze, 1758.
AH 8942.5   Hubaux, Jean. Rome et Véies. Paris, 1958.
AH 8942.7   Rossi Danielli, Luigi. Gli Etruschi del Viterbese. Viterbo, 1959. 2v.
AH 8942.9   Ricchi, Antonio. La reggia de' Volsci. Bologna, 1967.

AH 8954   Ancient Europe - Italy - Gallia Cisalpina - Law
AH 8954.5F   Ritschl, F. Legis rubriae pars superstes. Bonae, 1851.
AH 8954.10F   Lama, Pietro de. Tavola legislativa della Gallia Cisalpina. Parma, 1820.

AH 8955   Ancient Europe - Italy - Gallia Cisalpina - Military affairs
AH 8955.2   Lackner, G. De incursionibus a Gallis in Italiani factis. Regimonti, 1887.

AH 8957   Ancient Europe - Italy - Gallia Cisalpina - General history
AH 8957.5   Rovelli, G. Das cisalpinische Gallien. Leipzig, 1791.
Htn   AH 8957.10*   Castiglione, B. Gallorum Insubrum antiquae sedes. Mediolani, 1541.

AH 8963   Ancient Europe - Italy - Gallia Cisalpina - Civilization
AH 8963.5   Mansuelli, Guido Achille. I Cisalpini. Firenze, 1962.

AH 8964   Ancient Europe - Italy - Gallia Cisalpina - Religion
AH 8964.3   Bladé, J.F. Mémoire sur l'histoire religieuse. Bordeaux, 1885.

AH 8965   Ancient Europe - Italy - Gallia Cisalpina - Economic conditions
AH 8965.5   Chilver, G.E.F. Cisalpine Gaul. Oxford, 1941.

AH 8971 - 8996   Ancient Europe - Italy - Gallia Cisalpina - Local (A-Z by place)
AH 8971.5   De-Vit, Vincenzo. La provincia romana dell'Ossola, ossia Delle Alpi Atrezziane. Firenze, 1892.
AH 8972.5   Maluasia, C.C. Marmora felsinea...Bononiae senatu. Bononiae, 1690.
AH 8972.7   Rota, G. Dell'origine e della storia antica di Bergamo. Bergamo, 1804.
AH 8986.5   Salomonius, J. Agri Patavini inscriptiones sacrae et prophanae. Patavius, 1696.
AH 8986.10   Storia romana 1962-63. Epigrafia latina; il Piemonte preromano e romano. Milano, 1962.
AH 8990.5   Promis, Carlo. Storia dell'antica Torino, Julia Augusta Taurinorum. Torino, 1869.

AH 9057   Ancient Europe - Italy - Latium - General history
AH 9057.2   Zoeller, Max. Latium und Rom. Leipzig, 1878.
AH 9057.5   Corradini, Pietro M. Petri Marcellini Corradini. Romae, 1748. 2v.

AH 9065   Ancient Europe - Italy - Latium - Economic conditions
AH 9065.5   Adams, Louise E.W. A study of commerce in Latium from the early iron age through the sixth century B.C. Thesis. Northampton, Mass., 1921.

AH 9066   Ancient Europe - Italy - Latium - Geography
  AH 9066.2   Bormann, A.K.E. Altlatinische Chorographie. Halle, 1852.
  AH 9066.5   Desjardins, Ernest. Essai sur la topographie du Latium.
                             Thèse. Paris, 1854.

AH 9071 - 9096   Ancient Europe - Italy - Latium - Local (A-Z by place)
  AH 9071.2   Schmidt, Otto Eduard. Arpinum, eine
                             topographischhistorische Skizze. Meissen, 1900.
  AH 9071.2.5   Schmidt, Otto Eduard. Arpinum. Arpino, 1907.
  AH 9085.5   Meiggs, Russell. Roman Ostia. Oxford, 1960.
  AH 9086.5   La Blanchère, R. Un chapitre d'histoire pontine.
                             Paris, 1889.
  AH 9089.5   Serafini, P. Intorno a Sulmona del Lazio distrutta da
                             Lucio Silla. 2. ed. Sulmona, 1901.
  AH 9090.2   Bourne, Ella. Study of Tibur. Diss. Menasha, 1916.
  AH 9090.3   Le Gall, Joël. Le Tibre, fleuve de Rome, dans l'antiquité.
                             Thèse. Paris, 1952.

AH 9108   Ancient Europe - Italy - Liguria - General special
  AH 9108.2   Lamboglia, Nino. Liguria romana; studi storico
                             topografici. Roma, 1939-

AH 9109   Ancient Europe - Italy - Liguria - History by periods - Before 500 B.C.
  AH 9109.5   Tromp, S.P.C. De Romanorum piaculis. Lugduni
                             Batavorum, 1921.

AH 9113   Ancient Europe - Italy - Liguria - Civilization
  AH 9113.5   Sereni, Emilio. Comunità rurali nell'Italia antica.
                             Roma, 1955.

AH 9121 - 9146   Ancient Europe - Italy - Liguria - Local (A-Z by place)
  AH 9121.2   Lamboglia, Nino. Topografia storica dell'Ingaunia
                             nell'antichità. Albenga, 1933.

AH 9157   Ancient Europe - Italy - Lucania - General history
  AH 9157.5   Tropea, G. Storia dei lucani. Messina, 1894.

AH 9171 - 9196   Ancient Europe - Italy - Lucania - Local (A-Z by place)
  AH 9186.5   Grazia, Paolo di. La città di Pandosia. Napoli, 1918.
  AH 9192.5   Jacobone, Nunzio. Venusia, storia e topografia.
                             Trani, 1909.

AH 9221 - 9246   Ancient Europe - Italy - Picenum - Local (A-Z by place)
  AH 9221.5   Maretti, N. Ancona. Roma, 1945.
  AH 9221.5.5   Natalucci, Mario. Ancona antica. Città di Castello, 1960.
  AH 9225.5   Rome. Istituto di studi romani. Sezione emiliana. Italia
                             romana: Emilia romana. Firenze, 1941.

AH 9271 - 9296   Ancient Europe - Italy - Sabini, Aequi, Paeligni, etc. -
Local (A-Z by place)
  AH 9273.5   Passeri, T. La colonia Carseolana. Roma, 1883.
  AH 9283.5   Fernique, Emmanuel. De regione Marsorum. Thesis. Lutetiae
                             Parisiorum, 1880.
  AH 9286.2   Besnier, M. De regione Paelignorum. Lutetiae
                             Parisiorum, 1902.

AH 9307   Ancient Europe - Italy - Samnium - General history
  AH 9307.5   Ring, B.J.J.M. de. Histoire des peuples opiques.
                             Paris, 1859.
  AH 9307.10   Salmon, Edward Togo. Samnium and the Samnites.
                             Cambridge, 1967.

AH 9308   Ancient Europe - Italy - Samnium - General special
  AH 9308.5   Del Rosso, G. Storia politica civile...di Trentani.
                             Campobasso, 1887.

AH 9313   Ancient Europe - Italy - Samnium - Civilization
  AH 9313.5   Bertolé Viale, Giovanni. La civiltà latina in Abruzzo.
                             Pescara, 1956.

AH 9371 - 9396   Ancient Europe - Italy - Umbria - Local (A-Z by place)
  AH 9379.5   Rosenzweig, I. Ritual and cults of pre-Roman Iguvium.
                             London, 1937.
  AH 9379.10   Cagiano de Azenado, M. Interamna Lirenas vel Sucasina.
                             Roma, 1947.
  AH 9385.1   Borziani, G. Dell'antica città di Ostra. Cefalu, 1911.
  AH 9389.5.4F   Naudé, Gabriel. Exercitatio. Lugduni Batavorum, 1722.

AH 9421 - 9446   Ancient Europe - Italy - Venetia - Local (A-Z by place)
  AH 9421.5   De-Vit, Vincenzo. Adria e le sue antiche epigrafi. v.1-2.
                             Firenze, 1888.
  AH 9421.10   Panciera, Silvio. Vita economica de Aquileia in età
                             romana. Venezia, 1957.
  AH 9421.10.5   Herfurth, Karl. De Aquileiae commercio. Inaug. Diss.
                             Halis Saxonum, 1889.
  AH 9423.5   Stucchi, S. Forum Iulii (Cividale del Friuli).
                             Roma, 1951.
  AH 9426.5F   Fistulario, P. Della geografia antica del Friuli dalle
                             età più rimote sino ai tempi di Costantino il grande.
                             Udine, 1775.
  AH 9440.5   Scrinari, V. Tergeste. Roma, 1951.
  AH 9446.5   Moro, Placida Maria. Iulium Carnicum (Zuglio).
                             Roma, 1956.

AH 9458   Ancient Europe - Rhaetia - General special
  AH 9458.5   Whatmough, J. "Tusca origo Raetis". n.p., 1937.

AH 9471 - 9496   Ancient Europe - Rhaetia - Local (A-Z by place)
  AH 9471.3   Buckhardt-Biedermann, T. Die Kolonie Augusta Raurica.
                             Basel, 1910.
  AH 9475.2   Schreiner, W. Blick in die Geschichte...Eining's von
                             Trajan bis Diocletian. v.1-2. Landshut, 1896.

AH 9505   Ancient Europe - Rhenish Provinces - Military affairs
  AH 9505.2   Ring, B.J.J.M. de. Mémoire sur les établissements romains.
                             Paris, 1852. 2v.

AH 9508   Ancient Europe - Rhenish Provinces - General special
  AH 9508.5   Riese, A. Forschungen zur Geschichte der Rheinlande in der
                             Römerzeit. Frankfurt am Main, 1889.
  AH 9508.6   Schell, Günther. Die römische Besiedlung von Rheingau und
                             Welterau. Mainz, 1962.

AH 9551   Ancient Europe - Sardinia and Corsica - Pamphlet volumes
  AH 9551.1   Pamphlet box. Sardinia and Corsica.

AH 9557   Ancient Europe - Sardinia and Corsica - General history
  AH 9557.1   Bouchier, E.S. Sardinia in ancient times. Oxford, 1917.
  AH 9557.5   Bellieni, C. La Sardegna e i sardi nella civiltà del mondo
                             antico. Cagliari, 1928-31. 2v.

AH 9558   Ancient Europe - Sardinia and Corsica - General special
  AH 9558.2   Pais, Ettore. La Sardegna prima del dominio romano.
                             Roma, 1881.
  AH 9558.3   Pais, Ettore. Storia della Sardegna e della Corsica
                             durante il dominio romano. Roma, 1923. 2v.

AH 9560   Ancient Europe - Sardinia and Corsica - History by periods - 500 - 1
B.C.
  AH 9560.2   Eliaeson, Ake. Beiträge zur Geschichte Sardiniens.
                             Uppsala, 1906.

AH 9563   Ancient Europe - Sardinia and Corsica - Civilization
  AH 9563.5   Zervos, C. La civilisation de la Sardaigne. Paris, 1954.
  AH 9563.6   Lilliu, G. La civiltà dei Sardi dal neolitico all'età dei
                             nuraghi. Torino, 1963.
  AH 9563.7F   Serra, Marcello. Il popolo dei nuraghi. Cagliari, 1965.

AH 9603   Ancient Europe - Sicily - Government and administration
  AH 9603.2   Dareste de la Chavanne, R. De forma et conditione Siciliae
                             provinciae Romanae. Thesis. Lutetiae, 1850.
  AH 9603.3   Klein, Josef. Die Verwaltungsbeamten der
                             Provinzen...Sicilien und Sardinien. Bonn, 1878.

AH 9604   Ancient Europe - Sicily - Law
  AH 9604.5   Scicilano-Villanueva, L. Sul diritto greco-romano
                             (privato) in Sicilia. Palermo, 1902.

AH 9607   Ancient Europe - Sicily - General history
Htn AH 9607.5F*   Goltzius, H. Sicilia et Magna Graecia. Brugis, 1576.
Htn AH 9607.6F*   Goltzius, H. Sicilia historia posterior. Brugis
                             Flandrorum, 1576.
  AH 9607.7   Brunet de Presle, W. Recherches sur les établissements des
                             grecs. Paris, 1845.
  AH 9607.9   Holm, A. Geschichte Siciliens in Alterthum.
                             Leipzig, 1870. 3v.
  AH 9607.9.25   Revelli, P. La storia della Sicilia nell'antichità.
                             Pinerolo, 1902.
NEDL AH 9607.11   Lloyd, W.W. History of Sicily to the Athenian war.
                             London, 1872.
  AH 9607.13A   Freeman, E.A. History of Sicily from earliest times.
                             Oxford, 1891. 4v.
  AH 9607.13B   Freeman, E.A. History of Sicily from earliest times.
                             Oxford, 1891. 4v.
  AH 9607.13C   Freeman, E.A. History of Sicily from earliest times.
                             Oxford, 1891. 4v.
  AH 9607.15A   Freeman, E.A. Story of Sicily, Phoenician, Greek and
                             Roman. N.Y., 1892.
  AH 9607.15B   Freeman, E.A. Story of Sicily, Phoenician, Greek and
                             Roman. N.Y., 1892.
  AH 9607.17   Pais, Ettore. Storia della Sicilia. Torino, 1894.
  AH 9607.19   Perry, W.C. Sicily in fable, history, art and song.
                             London, 1908.
  AH 9607.21   Jenison, E.S. The history of the province of Sicily.
                             Boston, 1919.
  AH 9607.23   Borzi, Salvatore. Sicilia Schiava; panoramica azione
                             critico-storica. Paternò, 1962.
  AH 9607.24   Schenk von Stauffenberg, Alexander. Trinakria.
                             München, 1963.

AH 9608   Ancient Europe - Sicily - General special
  AH 9608.5   Pareti, Luigi. Studi siciliani ed italioti.
                             Firenze, 1920.
  AH 9608.5.5F   Pareti, Luigi. Sicilia antica. Palermo, 1959.
  AH 9608.7   Soraci, Rosario. I proconsoli di Sicilia da Augusto a
                           Traiano. Catania, 1958?

AH 9609   Ancient Europe - Sicily - History by periods - Before 500 B.C.
  AH 9609.3   Compernolle, René van. Etude de chronologie et
                             d'historiographie siciliotes...concernant la fondation des
                             colonies siciliotes. Bruxelles, 1960.
  AH 9609.4   Sjoeqvist, Erik. Sicily and the Greeks. Ann Arbor, 1973.
  AH 9609.5   Puglisi Marino, S. Siculi e greci nella Sicilia orientale.
                             Catania, 1909.
  AH 9609.5.5   Brea, L.B. Sicily before the Greeks. N.Y., 1957.
  AH 9609.5.7   Brea, L.B. Sicily before the Greeks. London, 1957.

AH 9610   Ancient Europe - Sicily - History by periods - 500 - 1 B.C.
Htn AH 9610.3*   Perrinchief, Richard. The Sicilian tyrant. London, 1676.
  AH 9610.5   Lau, T. Leben der Surakusaners Dion. Prag, 1860.
  AH 9610.7   Beloch, Julius. L'imperio siciliano di Dionisio.
                             Roma, 1881.
  AH 9610.9   Bass, Josef. Dionysios I. von Syrakus. Wien, 1881.
  AH 9610.11   Schubert, R.J.W. Geschichte des Agathokles.
                           Breslau, 1887.
  AH 9610.13   Allcroft, A.H. History of Sicily 491-289 B.C.
                           London, 1890.
  AH 9610.15   Krug, Otto. Quellenuntersuchung zur Geschichte des
                           jüngeren Dionys. Kattowitz, 1891.
  AH 9610.17   Clasen, C. Timoleon, eine historische Untersuchung.
                           Glückstadt, 1896.
  AH 9610.18   Westlake, H.D. Timoleon and his relations with tyrants.
                           Manchester, Eng., 1952.
  AH 9610.19   Loncao, E. La Sicilia romana. Palermo, 1905.
  AH 9610.21   Tillyard, H.J.W. Agathocles. Cambridge, 1908.
  AH 9610.22   Stroheker, Karl. Dionysios I. Wiesbaden, 1958.
  AH 9610.22.5   Meier-Welcker, Hans. Dionysios I., Tyrann von Syrakus.
                           Göttingen, 1971.
  AH 9610.23   Felice-Guiffrida, G. de. Le guerre servili in Sicilia.
                           Catania, 1911.
  AH 9610.24   Märker, Martin. Die Kämpfe der Karthager auf Sizilien in
                           den Jahren 409-405 v. Chr. Inaug. Diss. Weida, 1930.
  AH 9610.25   Völkerling, A. De rebus Siculis ab Atheniensium
                           expeditione usque ad prioris belli Punice finem gestia.
                           Inaug. Diss. Vratislaviae, 1868.
  AH 9610.26   Bayet, Jean. La Sicile greque. Paris, 1930.
  AH 9610.27   Schenk von Stauffenberg, Alexander. König Hieron der
                           Zweite von Syrakus. Stuttgart, 1933.
  AH 9610.28   Ciaceri, Emanuele. Esame critico della storia...guerre
                           servili. Catania, 1907.

Classified Listing

AH 9610   Ancient Europe - Sicily - History by periods - 500 - 1 B.C. - cont.
AH 9610.28.5   Ciaceri, Emanuele. Intorno alle più antiche relazioni fra
    la Sicilia e la Persia. Pisa, 1912.
AH 9610.29   Wentker, Hermann. Sizilien und Athen. Heidelberg, 1956.

AH 9613   Ancient Europe - Sicily - Civilization
AH 9613.5   Pace, Biagio. Arte e civiltà della Sicilia antica.
    Milano, 1935-49. 4v.
AH 9613.5.5   Pace, Biagio. Arte e civiltà della Sicilia antica. 2. ed.
    Milano, 1958.
AH 9613.10   Hardouin di Belmonte, F. Trinacria olimpica.
    Palermo, 1951.

AH 9614   Ancient Europe - Sicily - Religion
AH 9614.5   Tropea, G. Carta teotopiche della Sicilia antica.
    Padova, 1902.

AH 9615   Ancient Europe - Sicily - Economic conditions
AH 9615.5   Rauber, H. Die agrarischen Verhaltnisse Siziliens in
    Altertume besonders zur Zeit Ciceros. Bayreuth, 1919.

AH 9616   Ancient Europe - Sicily - Geography
AH 9616.5   Holm, A. Beiträge zur Berichtung der Karte des alten
    Siciliens. Lübeck, 1866.

AH 9621 - 9646   Ancient Europe - Sicily - Local (A-Z by place)
AH 9621.5   Bindseil, R. Geschichte der Stadt Akragas.
    Neustettin, 1882.
AH 9621.7   Hagt, W. van de. De urbe Agrigentinorum.
    Roterodami, 1903.
AH 9621.9   Torremuzza, G.L.C. Dissertazione sopra una statua di
    Marmo. Palermo, 1749.
AH 9621.12   Waele, J.A. de. Acragas Graeca. 's-Gravenhage, 1971-
AH 9627.2   Navarra, Giuseppe. Città sicane, sicule e greche nella
    zona di Gela. Palermo, 1964.
AH 9632.5   Libertini, Guido. Le isole Eolie nell'antichità greca e
    romana. Firenze, 1921.
AH 9633.5F   Reina, Placido. Delle notizie istoriche della città della
    Messina. Messina, 1739.
AH 9633.6   Vallet, Georges. Rhégion et Zancle. Paris, 1958.
AH 9633.7   Giacomazzi, Rosaria. Considerazione sopra la storia dei
    Mamerlini. Messina, 1935.
AH 9634.5   Rizzo, P. Naxos siceliota. Catania, 1894.
AH 9639.5   Reinganum, H. Selinus und sein Gebiet. Leipzig, 1827.
AH 9639.6   Arendt, A. Syrakus im zweiten peinischen Kriege.
    Königsberg, 1899.
AH 9639.6.5   Muess, H. De Syracusanorum statu. Inaug. Diss.
    Ienae, 1867.
AH 9639.8   Salinas, A. Solunto ricordi storici. Palermo, 1884.
AH 9639.9.5   Giuliano, Luigi. Storia di Siracusa antica. 2. ed.
    Milano, 1928.
AH 9639.12   Mansuelli, Guido Achille. La politica estera di Siracusa.
    Bologna, 1958.
AH 9639.14   Droegemueller, Hans-Peter. Syrakus; zur Topographie und
    Geschichte einer griechischer Stadt. Heidelberg, 1969.
AH 9639.15   Fiori, Alberto. Siracusa greca. Roma, 1971.
AH 9640.2   Parisi, G. Tyndaris. Messina, 1950.
AH 9646.5   Lazonder, A. Zande-Messana. Rhenum, 1903.
AH 9646.10   Ryolo di Maria, Domenico. L'espansione di Zande sulla
    costa settentrionale della Sicilia dalla metà dell'VIII
    secolo a.C. agli albori del V secolo a.C. Messina, 1968.

AH 9647   Ancient Europe - Malta
AH 9647.5   Bres, Onorato. Malta antica illustrata cò monumenti, e
    coll'istoria. Roma, 1816.

AH 9653   Ancient Europe - Spain - Government and administration
AH 9653.2   Braun, F. Provinzialeinteilung Spaniens in römischer Zeit.
    Berlin, 1908.
AH 9653.5F   Galsterer, Hartmut. Untersuchungen zum römischen
    Städtewesen auf der iberieschen Halbinsel. Berlin, 1971.

AH 9654   Ancient Europe - Spain - Law
AH 9654.5   Mommsen, T. Die Stadtrechte der latinischen Gemeinden
    Salkensa und Malaca. Leipzig, 1855.

AH 9657   Ancient Europe - Spain - General history
AH 9657.5   Bouchier, E.S. Spain under the Roman empire.
    Oxford, 1914.

AH 9658   Ancient Europe - Spain - General special
AH 9658.2   Othmer, W. Die Wölkerstämme von Hispania. Berlin, 1904.
AH 9658.5   García y Bellido, Antonio. Las colonias romanas de
    Hispania. Madrid, 1959.

AH 9660   Ancient Europe - Spain - History by periods - 500 - 1 B.C.
AH 9660.2   Gotzfried, K. Annalen der römischen Provinzen...Spanien.
    Erlangen, 1907.
AH 9660.5   Schulten, Adolf. Los Cantabras y Astures y su guerra con
    Roma. Madrid, 1943.
AH 9660.7   Barco, Alejandro del. Las colonias gemelas reintegradas en
    la mitad de sua respectivas publaciones. Madrid, 1788.

AH 9661   Ancient Europe - Spain - History by periods - 1 A.D. - ca. 500
AH 9661.2   García y Bellido, Antonio. Las España del siglo primero de
    nustra era. Madrid, 1947.

AH 9662   Ancient Europe - Spain - Chronology
AH 9662.5   Wilsdorf, D. Tasti Hispaniarum provinciarum. Inaug. Diss.
    Lipsiae, 1878.

AH 9664   Ancient Europe - Spain - Religion
AH 9664.5   Gonzalez Echegaray, Joaquin. Origenes del cristianismo en
    Cantabria. Santander, 1969.

AH 9665   Ancient Europe - Spain - Economic conditions
AH 9665.5   West, Louis C. Imperial Roman Spain; the objects of trade.
    Oxford, 1929.

AH 9666   Ancient Europe - Spain - Geography
AH 9666.2   Braun, F. Die Entwicklung der spanischen
    Provinzialgrenzen. Berlin, 1909.
AH 9666.4   Alemany y Bolufer, J. La geografía de la peninsula
    ibérica. Madrid, 1912.
AH 9666.5   Cortés y López, Miguel. Diccionario...de la Espana
    antigua. Madrid, 1835-36. 3v.
AH 9666.7   Albertini, E. Les divisions administratives de l'Espagne
    romaine. Thèse. Paris, 1923.

AH 9666   Ancient Europe - Spain - Geography - cont.
AH 9666.9   Haebler, Albin. Die Nord- und Westküste Hispaniens; ein
    Beitrag zur Geschichte der antiken Geographie.
    Leipzig, 1886.
AH 9666.10   Saa, Mário. As grandes vias da Lusitania.
    Lisboa, 1956-60. 5v.

AH 9668 - 9670   Ancient Europe - Spain - Special topics (Develop as needed)
AH 9668.2   Morales Belda, Francisco. La marina vándala.
    Barcelona, 1969.

AH 9671 - 9696   Ancient Europe - Spain - Local (A-Z by place)
AH 9675.2   Botet y Siso, J. Noticia histórica y arqueológica de la
    antigua ciudad de Emporion. Madrid, 1879.
AH 9677.2   Barros Sivélo, Ramón. Antigüedades de Galicia.
    Coruña, 1875.
AH 9682.2   Ursin, Nils R. De Lusitania provincia Romana.
    Helsingiae, 1884.
AH 9682.4   Vázquez Seijas, M. Lugo bajo el imperio romano.
    Lugo, 1939.
AH 9684.5F   Schulten, Adolf. Numantia...1905-1912. v.1-4 and atlas.
    München, 1914-31. 7v.
AH 9684.5.2F   Hofmann, H. Panorama von Numantia. München, 1922.
AH 9684.7   Mélida, José R. Excursión a Numancia pasando por Soria.
    Madrid, 1922.
AH 9684.9   Schulten, Adolf. Geschichte von Numantia. München, 1933.
AH 9684.10   Gómez Santa Cruz, S. El solar numantino. Madrid, 1914.
Htn   AH 9692.2*   Blade, J.F. Géographie historique de la Vasconie
    espagnole. Auch, 1891.

AH 9701   Ancient Europe - Thrace - Pamphlet volumes
AH 9701.5   Kalopothakes, D. De Thracia provincia Romana.
    Lipsiae, 1893. 2 pam.

AH 9705   Ancient Europe - Thrace - Military affairs
AH 9705.1   Fol, Aleksandur. Trakiisko voenno izkustvo. Sofiia, 1969.

AH 9707   Ancient Europe - Thrace - General history
AH 9707.5   Gatterer, J.C. Abhandlung von Thracien. Göttingen, 1800.
AH 9707.7   Kalopothakes, D. De Thracia provincia Romana.
    Lipsiae, 1893.
AH 9707.7.5   Kalopothakes, D. De Thracia provincia Romana.
    Berlin, 1893.
AH 9707.7.10   Kalopothakes, D. O chörismos. Athēnai, 1894.
AH 9707.8   Randa, A. Der Balkan. 1. Aufl. Graz, 1949.
AH 9707.9   Wieser, J. Die Thraker. Stuttgart, 1963.
AH 9707.10   Fol, Aleksandur. Demografska i sotsialna struktura na
    drevna Trakiia. Sofiia, 1970.
AH 9707.11   Zlatkovskaia, Tat'iana D. Vozniknovenie gosudarstva u
    trakiitsev. VII-V vv do n.e. Moskva, 1971.
AH 9707.12   Danov, Khristo M. Drevna Trakiia. Sofiia, 1968.
AH 9707.13   Fol, Aleksandur. Policheska istoriia na Trakite.
    Sofiia, 1972.
AH 9707.14   Mikhailov, Georgei I. Trakite. Sofiia, 1972.

AH 9708   Ancient Europe - Thrace - General special
AH 9708.5   Velkov, Velizar I. Robstvoto v Trakiia i Miziia prez
    antichnostta. Sofiia, 1967.

AH 9710   Ancient Europe - Thrace - History by periods - 500 - 1 B.C.
AH 9710.5   Solari, A. Sui dinasti degli Odrisi (V-IV secolo a.C.).
    Pisa, 1912.

AH 9713   Ancient Europe - Thrace - Civilization
AH 9713.5   Kazaroev, G.I. Beiträge zur Kulturgeschichte der Thraker.
    Sarajevo, 1916.
AH 9713.6   Fol, Aleksandur. Pesenta za Sitalk. Sofiia, 1968.

AH 9714   Ancient Europe - Thrace - Religion
AH 9714.5   Balaschev, Georgi D. Staro-trakiiski svetilishta i
    bozhestva v Mezek, Glava, Panega, Madara, Tsarichina i
    drugade i tekhnsto znachenie. Sofiia, 1932.

AH 9721 - 9746   Ancient Europe - Thrace - Local (A-Z by place)
AH 9722.5   Falk, F.W.A. De origine Byzantie dissertatio.
    Vratislaviae, 1829.
AH 9722.6   Schultze, V. Altchristliche Städte und Landschaften.
    Leipzig, 1913-22. 3v.
AH 9722.7   Merle, Heinrich. Die Geschichte der Städte Byzantion und
    Kalchedon. Inaug. Diss. Kiel, 1916.
AH 9722.8   Nevskaia, V.P. Byzanz in der klassichen und
    hellenistischen Epoche. Leipzig, 1955.
AH 9722.9A   Nevskaia, V.P. Bizantii v klassicheskuiu i
    ellinisticheskuiu epokhi. Moskva, 1953.
AH 9722.9B   Nevskaia, V.P. Bizantii v klassicheskuiu i
    ellinisticheskuiu epokhi. Moskva, 1953.
AH 9727.15   Rousopoulos, A.S. Peri Zamolxidos. Inaug. Diss.
    Gottingae, 1852.

AH 9754   Ancient Europe - Germany - Law
AH 9754.3   Davoud-Oghlou, G.A. Histoire de la legislation des anciens
    germains. Berlin, 1845. 2v.

AH 9757   Ancient Europe - Germany - General history
AH 9757.5   Dragendorff, H. Westdeutschland zur Römerzeit.
    Leipzig, 1912.
AH 9757.5.5   Dragendorff, H. Westdeutschland zur Römerzeit. 2. Aufl.
    Leipzig, 1919.
AH 9757.6   Cramer, F. Römisch-germanische Studien. Breslau, 1914.
AH 9757.7   Eidam, Heinrich. Deutschlands Besetzung durch die Römer.
    Dinkelsbühl, 1928.
AH 9757.8   Martin, Charles. Les deux Germanies cis-rhénanes. Étude
    d'histoire et de géographie anciennes. Paris, 1863.

AH 9758   Ancient Europe - Germany - General special
AH 9758.3   Wersebe, August von. Ueber die Völker und Völkerbundnisse
    des alten Teutschlands. Hannover, 1826.
AH 9758.5   Riese, A. Idealiserung der Naturvölker des Nordens.
    Frankfurt, 1875.
AH 9758.6   Horkel, J. Die Geschichtschreiber der deutschen Vorzeit.
    Berlin, 1847.
AH 9758.7   Capelle, Wilhelm. Das alte Germanien. Jena, 1929.
AH 9758.8   Gutenbrunner, S. Germanische Frühzeit in den Berichten der
    Antike. Halle, 1939.

Classified Listing

AH 9760   Ancient Europe - Germany - History by periods - 500 - 1 B.C.
AH 9760.1   Wells, Colin Michael. The German policy of Augustus: an examination of the archaeological evidence. Oxford, 1972.

AH 9765   Ancient Europe - Germany - Economic conditions
AH 9765.5   Wollheim, Günther. Germania oeconomica; das Bild der germanischen Wirtschaft bei Caesar und Tacitus. Freiburg, 1958.

AH 9771   -   9796   Ancient Europe - Germany - Local (A-Z by place)
AH 9773.5   Pedersen, N. Cimbrorum et Gothorum origines. Lipsiae, 1695.
AH 9773.13   La Baume, Peter. Colonia Agrippinensis. 3. Aufl. Köln, 1964.
AH 9773.13.5   Signon, Helmut. Die Römer in Köln. Frankfurt, 1971.
AH 9777.5   Gothicarum et Langobardicarum. Lugduni Batavorum, 1618.
AH 9777.6   Jordanes. De getarum sive Gothorum. Lugduni Batavorum, 1732.
AH 9777.7   Aschbach, J. Geschichte der Westgothen. Frankfurt, 1827.
AH 9777.8   Freudensprung, S. Commentatio Jornande sive Jordane libellorum natalibus. Monaci, 1837.
AH 9777.9   Jordanes. De la succession des royaumes...les Goths. Paris, 1842.
AH 9777.11   Glöden, I. von. Das römische Recht im östgothischen Reiche. Jena, 1843.
AH 9777.13   Bessell, G. De rebus geticis. Gottingae, 1854.
AH 9777.14   Leake, Jane. The Geats of Beowulf. Madison, 1967.
AH 9777.15   Simonis, Carl. Versuch einer Geschichte des Alarich. Göttingen, 1858.
AH 9777.17   Köpke, R. Die Anfänge des Königthums bei den Gothen. Berlin, 1859.
AH 9777.18   Jordanes. Diversarum...historiae antiquae scriptores tres. Hamburgi, 1611.
AH 9777.19   Jordanes. Getarum sive Gothorum. Stuttgart, 1861.
AH 9777.19.2   Jordanes. Getarum sive Gothorum. 2. ed. Stuttgart, 1866.
AH 9777.19.3   Jordanes. Getarum sive Gothorum. 3. ed. Reutlingen, 1888.
AH 9777.19.5   Jordanes. O proiskhozhdenii i deianiiakh getov. Moskva, 1960.
AH 9777.19.10   Svensson, Jacob Vilhelm. De sydsvenska folknammen hos Jordanes. Karlstad, 1914.
AH 9777.20   Roesler, E. Die Geten und ihre Nachbarn. Wien, 1864.
AH 9777.21   Eicken, H. von. Der Kampf der Westgothen und Römer. Leipzig, 1876.
AH 9777.23A   Bradley, Henry. Story of the Goths. N.Y., 1888.
AH 9777.23B   Bradley, Henry. Story of the Goths. N.Y., 1888.
AH 9777.24   Bradley, Henry. The Goths from the earliest times to the end of the Gothic dominion. N.Y., 1899.
AH 9777.29A   Jordanes. Origins and deeds of the Goths. Princeton, 1908.
AH 9777.29B   Jordanes. Origins and deeds of the Goths. Princeton, 1908.
AH 9777.29.5A   Jordanes. The Gothic history of Jordanes. Princeton, 1915.
AH 9777.29.5B   Jordanes. The Gothic history of Jordanes. Princeton, 1915.
AH 9777.29.6   Jordanes. The Gothic history of Jordanes. N.Y., 1960.
AH 9777.31A   Rappaport, B. De Gotorum usque ad decium imperatorem. Berlin, 1899.
AH 9777.31B   Rappaport, B. De Gotorum usque ad decium imperatorem. Berlin, 1899.
AH 9777.33   Rappaport, B. Die Einfälle der Goten in die römische Reich. Leipzig, 1899.
AH 9777.35   Braun, F.A. Toty i ikh' sosedidov. Sankt Peterburg, 1899.
AH 9777.36   Ropaligero, D. I Goti illustrati o vero Istoria de Goti antichi. Verona, 1679.
AH 9777.37   Paulinus a Sancto Bartholomaeo. Jornandes vindiciae de Var Hunnorum. Romae, 1800.
AH 9777.38   Eicke, Hermann. Heerführer und Könige. Leipzig, 193-?
AH 9777.40   Rackus, A.M. Guthones (the Goths), kinsmen of the Lithuanian people. Chicago, 1929.
AH 9777.41   Cazzaniga, I. Dispense relative alla lettura del testo di Iordanes Historia getarum. Milano, 1963.
AH 9777.42   Thompson, Edward Arthur. The Visigoths in the time of Ulfila. Oxford, 1966.
AH 9790.5   Muchau, H. Das 4000 Jährige alter des Volkes der Hermunduringer (Thüringer). Jena, 1910.
AH 9790.5.10   Schneeberger, H. Die Brunnenschlacht. Bad Kissingen, 1931.
AH 9792.5   Schulze, H. De testamento Genserici (Vandali). Jenae, 1859.
AH 9792.6A   Bigelow, Poultney. Genseric, king of the Vandals. N.Y., 1918.
AH 9792.6B   Bigelow, Poultney. Genseric, king of the Vandals. N.Y., 1918.
AH 9792.7   Gautier, E.F. Genséric, roi des Vandals. Paris, 1932.
AH 9792.7.5   Gautier, E.F. Geiserich, König der Wandalen. Frankfurt am Main, 1934.
AH 9792.8   Gitti, Alberto. Ricerche sui rapporti tra i vandali e l'impero romano. Bari, 1953.

AH 9807   Ancient Europe - Sarmatia - General history
AH 9807.5   Harmatta, Janos. Studies on the history of Sarmatians. Budapest, 1950.
AH 9807.6   Gyárfás, István Tihamér. A jasz-kunok története. v.1-2,4. Kecskemét, 1870-85. 3v.

Eg 4   -   9   Ancient Egyptian history - General bibliographies - Monographs (By date)
Eg 8.50   Seyffarth, G. Altertumskunde. n.p., 1850?
X Cg   Eg 8.61   Palmer, W. Egyptian chronicles. London, 1861. 2v.
Eg 8.80   Trübner and Co. Catalogue of...books on Egypt and Egyptology. London, 1880.
Eg 8.93   Boston, Mass. Public Library. List of works on Egypt. Boston, 1893.
Eg 9.10   Farina, G. Bollettino. Roma, 1910.
Eg 9.24   Cook, William B. Catalogue of the Egyptological library and other books from the collection of the late Charles E. Wilbour. Brooklyn, 1924.
Eg 9.25A   New York. Public Library. Ancient Egypt. N.Y., 1925.
Eg 9.25B   New York. Public Library. Ancient Egypt. N.Y., 1925.
Eg 9.25.5A   New York. Public Library. Ancient Egypt, 1925-1941. Supplement. N.Y., 1942.
Eg 9.25.5B   New York. Public Library. Ancient Egypt, 1925-1941. Supplement. N.Y., 1942.
Eg 9.60   Proosdij, Boricus Antonius van. Als een goet instrument. Leiden, 1960.
Eg 9.70   Cairo. Musée des Antiquités Égyptiennes. Catalogue de la Bibliothek...1927-1958. Le Caire, 1970.

Eg 15   Ancient Egyptian history - General pamphlet volumes
Eg 15.1   Pamphlet vol. Egypt. 24 pam.
Eg 15.2F   Pamphlet box. Egypt.
Eg 15.3   Pamphlet box. Egypt.
Eg 15.5   Pamphlet vol. Egypt, ancient and modern. 2 pam.

Eg 24   -   29   Ancient Egyptian history - Collected sources (By date)
Eg 27.82   Stroth, F.A. Aegyptiaca sev veterum scriptorum. Gothae, 1782.
Eg 28.97   Bondi, J.H. Aegyptiaca. Leipzig, 1897.
Eg 29.06.1   Breasted, James Henry. Ancient records of Egypt. N.Y., 1962. 5v.
Eg 29.11   Pick, Robert F. Egyptological tracts. N.Y., 1911.

Eg 30   -   39   Ancient Egyptian history - Government and administration (Table A)
Eg 39.03   Preisigke, Friedrich. Städtisches Beamtenwesen im römischen Agypten. Halle, 1903.
Eg 39.09   Engers, M. De Aegyptiarum...administratione. Groningae, 1909.
Eg 39.11   Martin, V. Les Épistratèges. Genève, 1911.
Eg 39.12   Cohen, D. De magistratibus Aegyptiis externas Lagidarum regni provincias administrantibus. 's Gravenhage, n.d.
Eg 39.16   Modica, Marco. Contribute papirologici. Roma, 1916.
Eg 39.23   Rouillard, G. L'administration civile de l'Égypte Byzantine. Thèse. Paris, 1923.
Eg 39.25   Collomp, Paul. Recherches sur la chancellerie et la diplomatique des Lagides. Thèse. Strasbourg, 1925.
Eg 39.26   Collomp, Paul. Recherches sur la chancellerie et la diplomatique des Lagides. Paris, 1926.
Eg 39.29   Gabra, Sami. Les conseils de fonctionnaires dans l'Égypte pharaonique. Le Caire, 1929.
Eg 39.32   Pirenne, Jacques. Histoire des institutions et du droit privé de l'ancienne Egypte. v.1-3. Bruxelles, 1932-35. 4v.
Eg 39.41   Dubois-Richard, Paul. Essai sur les gouvernements de l'Egypte. Le Caire, 1941.
Eg 39.54F   Helck, W. Untersuchungen zu den Beamtentiteln des ägyptischen alten Reichs. Glückstadt, 1954.
Eg 39.70   Vandoni, Mariangela. Gli epistrategi nell'Egitto greco-romano. Milano, 1970?

Eg 130   -   139   Ancient Egyptian history - Law (Table A)
Eg 132.53   Malinine, Michel. Choix de textes juridiques en hiératique et en démotique. pt.1. Paris, 1953-
Eg 133.70   Drath, Juergen. Untersuchungen zum Wohnungseigentum auf Grund der gräko-ägyptischen Papyri. Diss. Marburg, 1970?
Eg 137.06   Nicolai, J. Tractatus de Synedrio Aegyptiorum. Lugdunum Batavorum, 1706.
Eg 138.68   Devéria, T. Le papyrus judiciaire de Turin. Paris, 1868.
Eg 138.81   Krall, J. Demotische und Assyrische Contracte. Wien, 1881.
Eg 138.82   Revillout, Eugène. Le procès d'Hermias d'après les documents démotiques et grecs. pt.1-2. Paris, 1882.
Eg 138.84   Revillout, Eugène. Cours de droit égyptien. Paris, 1884.
Eg 138.86   Revillout, Eugène. Les obligations en droit égyptien. Paris, 1886.
Eg 138.92F   Spiegelberg, Wilhelm. Studien und Materialien zum Rechtswesen des Pharaohenreiches. Hannover, 1892.
Eg 138.98   Griffith, F.L. Wills in ancient Egypt. London, 1898.
Eg 138.99   Uah. Oldest known will. Philadelphia, 19- .
Eg 139.02   Revillout, Eugène. Les rapports historiques et legaux des Quirites et des Egyptiens. Paris, 1902.
Eg 139.06   Arangio-Ruiz, V. Successione testamentaria. Napoli, 1906.
Eg 139.12   Frese, Benedict. Ocherki greko-egipetskago prava. Iaroslavl', 1912.
Eg 139.14   Dagallier, Jean. Les institutions judiciaires de l'Egypte ancienne. Thèse. Paris, 1914.
Eg 139.24   Segrè, Angelo. Note sul documento nel diritto greco-egizio. Roma, 1924.
Eg 139.29.5   Seidl, Erwin. Der Eid im ptolemäischen Recht. München, 1929.
Eg 139.44   Taubenschlag, R. The law of Greco-Roman Egypt in the light of the papyri 332 B.C.-640 A.D. v.2: supplement. N.Y., 1944. 2v.
Eg 139.44.2   Taubenschlag, R. The law of Greco-Roman Egypt in the light of the papyri. 2. ed. Warszawa, 1955.
Eg 139.51F   Seidl, Erwin. Einführung in die ägyptische Rechtsgeschichte. 2. Aufl. Glückstadt, 1951.
Eg 139.60   Lur'e, I.M. Ocherki drevneegipetskogo prava. Leningrad, 1960.
Eg 139.62F   Seidl, F. Ptolemäische Rechtgeschichte. 2. Aufl. Glückstadt, 1962.
Eg 139.63   Kaplony-Heckel, U. Die demotischen Tempeleide. Wiesbaden, 1963. 2v.
Eg 139.70   Menu, Bernadette. Le regime juridique des terres et du personnel attaché à la terre dans le Papyrus Wilbour. Lille, 1970.

Eg 230   -   239   Ancient Egyptian history - Military affairs (Table A)
Eg 232.5   Daris, Sergio. Documenti per la storia dell'esercito romano in Egitto. Milano, 1964.
Eg 239.12   Maspero, J. Organisation militaire de l'Egypte Byzantine. Paris, 1912.
Eg 239.68   Cottrell, Leonard. The warrior pharaohs. London, 1968.

Eg 260   -   269   Ancient Egyptian history - Foreign relations, diplomacy (Table A)
Eg 269.22   Lazzaridès, C.A. De l'évolution des relations internationales de l'Egypte pharaonique. Thèse. Paris, 1922.
Eg 269.54   Vercoutter, Jean. Essai sur les relations entre Egyptiens et Préhellènes. Paris, 1954.
Eg 269.62   Helck, Hans Wolfgang. Die Beziehungen Ägyptens zu Vorderasien im 3. und 2. Jahrtausend vor Christ. Wiesbaden, 1962.
Eg 269.71   Ward, William A. Egypt and the east Mediterranean world, 2200-1900 B.C.; studies in Egyptian foreign relations during the first intermediate period. Beirut, 1971.

Eg 274   -   279   Ancient Egyptian history - General history (By date)
Eg 276.66.10   Murtada ibn al-Kafif. L'Egypte de Murtadi. Facsimile. Paris, 1953.
Htn   Eg 276.66.15*   Murtada ibn al-Kafif. The Egyptian history. London, 1672.
Eg 278.14   Champollion, J.J. L'Égypte. Paris, 1814. 2v.
Eg 278.14.3   Champollion, J.J. Egypte ancienne. Paris, 1839.
Eg 278.35   Yeates, T. Ancient Egypt. London, 1835.
Eg 278.36   Sharpe, S. Early history of Egypt. London, 1836.

Eg 294 - 299   Ancient Egyptian history - General special - Miscellany (By date) - cont.

Eg 299.22.5   Schubart, W. Ägypten von Alexander dem Grossen bis auf Mohammed. Berlin, 1922.

Eg 299.22.10   Recueil d'études égyptologiques dédiées à la mémoire de Jean-François Champollion. Paris, 1922.

Eg 299.26   Kings and queens of ancient Egypt. London, 1926.

Eg 299.29   Great ones of ancient Egypt. London, 1929.

Eg 299.37   Kutter, Carl. Alt Egypten spricht. Basel, 1937.

Eg 299.37.10   Brodrick, M. Egypt, papers and lectures. London, 1937.

Eg 299.39   Brundage, B.C. Notes on some blocks from the excavation of Medinet Habu. Diss. Chicago, 1939.

Eg 299.41   Savë-Soderbergh, T. Agypten und Nubien. Lund, 1941.

Eg 299.42   Steindorff, G. When Egypt ruled the East. Chicago, 1942.

Eg 299.42.5   Steindorff, G. When Egypt ruled the East. Chicago, 1957.

Eg 299.57   Drioton, Etienne. Pages d'égyptologie. Le Caire, 1957.

Eg 299.60   Akademiia nauk SSSR. Institut Narodov Azii. Drevnii Egypet; sbornik statei. Moskva, 1960.

Eg 299.66   Stuchevskii, Iosif A. Zavisimoe naselenie drevnego Egipta. Moskva, 1966.

Eg 299.67   Akademiia nauk SSSR. Institut Narodov Azii. Drevnii Egipet i drevniaia Afrika. Moskva, 1967.

Eg 299.68   Festschrift für Siegfried Schott zu seinem 70. Geburtstag am 20. August 1967. Wiesbaden, 1968.

Eg 299.69   Studies in honor of John A. Wilson, September 12, 1969. Chicago, 1969.

Eg 300 - 309   Ancient Egyptian history - General special - Philosophy of history (Table A)

X Cg Eg 308.68   Dall, C. (Mrs.). Egypt's place in history. Boston, 1868.

Eg 309.63   Donadoni, Sergio. Le fonti indirette della storia egiziana. Roma, 1963.

Eg 310 - 319   Ancient Egyptian history - General special - Cosmology (Table A)

Eg 318.81.5   Massey, G. Preface to, with extracts from, A book of the beginnings. London, 1881.

NEDL Eg 318.83   Massey, G. The natural genesis. London, 1883. 2v.

Eg 400 - 409   Ancient Egyptian history - History by periods - Predynastic period (Table A)

Eg 409.08   Reinach, A.J. L'Égypte préhistorique. Paris, 1908.

Eg 409.55   Baumgärtel, E. The cultures of prehistoric Egypt. London, 1955.

Eg 409.65   Weissen-Szumlanska, Marcelle. Origines atlantiques des anciens Égyptiens. Paris, 1965.

Eg 450 - 459   Ancient Egyptian history - History by periods - Old Kingdom, 1st-10th dynasties, 3200-2160 B.C. (Table A)

Eg 452.5   Fischer, Henry G. Inscriptions from the Coptite Nome dynasties VI-XI. Rome, 1964.

Eg 452.6   Schenkel, Wolfgang. Memphis, Herakleopolis, Theben; die epigraphischen Zeugnisse der 7.-11. Dynastie Agyptens. Wiesbaden, 1965.

Eg 458.61   Knötel, August. Cheops der Pyramidenerbauer und seine Nachfolger. Leipzig, 1861.

Eg 458.74   Dümichen, J. Die erste bis...aufgefundene...Angabe über die Regierungszeit...Königs...alten Reich. Leipzig, 1874.

Eg 459.49F   Studia aegyptiaca. v.1-2. Roma, 1938-49.

Eg 459.55   Julien, Max. Le tombeau du Pharaon, en l'an 2800 av. J.-C. Paris, 1955.

Eg 459.58   Muck, O.H. Cheops und die grosse Pyramide. Olten, 1958.

Eg 459.60   Baer, Klaus. Rank and title in the Old Kingdom. Chicago, 1960.

Eg 459.60.5   Grediche, Hans. Die Stellung des Königs im alten Reich. Weisbaden, 1960.

Eg 459.61   Gardiner, Alan. Egypt of the pharaohs. Oxford, 1961.

Eg 459.62   Stuchevskii, Iosef A. Khramovaia forma tsarskogo khoz. drevnego Egypta. Moskva, 1962.

Eg 459.65.5   Aldred, Cyril. Egypt to the end of the Old Kingdom. London, 1965.

Eg 500 - 509   Ancient Egyptian history - History by periods - Middle Kingdom, 11th-17th dynasties, 2160-1580 B.C. - General (Table A)

Eg 502.5   Brunner, Hellmut. Die Texte aus den Gräbern der Herakleopolitenzeit von Suit. Glückstadt, 1937.

Eg 502.12PF   Papyrus Reisner II. Papyrus Reisner II; accounts of the dockyard workshop at This in the reign of Sesostris I. Boston, 1965.

Eg 509.18   Weill, Raymond. La fin du moyen empire égyptien. v.1-2. Paris, 1918.

Eg 509.42F   Stock, Hanns. Studien zur Geschichte und Archäologie. Glückstadt, 1942.

Eg 509.47A   Winlock, H.E. The rise and fall of the middle kingdom in Thebes. N.Y., 1947.

Eg 509.47B   Winlock, H.E. The rise and fall of the middle kingdom in Thebes. N.Y., 1947.

Eg 509.62   Omlin, J. Amenemhet I. und Sesostris I. Heidelberg, 1962.

Eg 509.63   Margulies, H. Der Pharao Josefs. Herrenalb, 1963.

Eg 509.64   Beckerath, Jürgen von. Untersuchungen zur politischen Geschichte der Zweiten Zwischenzeit in Ägypten. Glückstadt, 1964.

Eg 550 - 559   Ancient Egyptian history - History by periods - Middle Kingdom, 11th-17th dynasties, 2160-1580 B.C. - Hyksos (Table A)

Eg 558.56   Uhlemann, M. Israeliten und Hyksos in Aegypten. Leipzig, 1856.

Eg 558.68   Chabas, F. Les pasteurs en Egypte. Amsterdam, 1868. 2 pam.

Eg 558.75   Brugsch-Bey, H. L'éxode et les monuments égyptiens. Leipzig, 1875.

Eg 559.39   Engberg, R.M. The Hyksos reconsidered. Diss. Chicago, 1939.

Eg 559.41   Montet, Pierre. Le drame d'Avaris; essai sur la pénétration des Sémites en Égypte. Paris, 1941.

Eg 559.66   Seters, John van. The Hyksos. New Haven, 1966.

Eg 602   Ancient Egyptian history - History by periods - New Kingdom, 18th-21st dynasties, 1580-950 B.C. - Collected sources, etc.

Eg 602.5   Sethe, Kurt. Urkunden des 18. Dynastie. (Heft 1-22). Leipzig, 1906- 6v.

Eg 602.5.2   Sethe, Kurt. Urkunden der 18. Dynastie. Übersetzung zu den Heften 17-22...von Wolfgang Helck. Berlin, 1961.

Eg 602.10   Edgerton, William F. Historical records of Ramses III. Chicago, 1936.

Eg 602.14   Gardiner, Alan H. Ramesside administrative documents. London, 1940.

Eg 602   Ancient Egyptian history - History by periods - New Kingdom, 18th-21st dynasties, 1580-950 B.C. - Collected sources, etc. - cont.

Eg 602.15   Gardiner, Alan H. The Kadesh inscriptions of Ramesses II. Oxford, 1960.

Eg 603   Ancient Egyptian history - History by periods - New Kingdom, 18th-21st dynasties, 1580-950 B.C. - Tell el-Amarna Tablets

Eg 603.5A   British Museum. Tell el-Amarna tablets. London, 1892.

Eg 603.5B   British Museum. Tell el-Amarna tablets. London, 1892.

Eg 603.6   Halevy, J. Correspondance d'Amenophis III. Paris, 1899.

Eg 603.7   Bezold, C. Oriental diplomacy. London, 1893.

Eg 603.8   Knudtzon, J.A. Die el Amarna-Tafeln. Leipzig, 1907-08. 2v.

Eg 603.9   Klostermann, A. Diplomatischer Briefwechsel aus dem zweiten Jahrhundert vor Christo. Kiel, 1898.

Eg 603.10   Pendlebury, J.D.S. Tell el-Amarna. Photoreproduction. London, 1935.

Eg 603.10.5   Mercer, S.A.B. The Tell el-Amarna tablets. Toronto, 1939. 2v.

Eg 603.11   Tell el-Amarna Tablets. El Amarna tablets, 359-379. Neukirchen-Vluyn, 1970.

Eg 603.15   Tut'ankhomien's tomb series. Oxford. 1,1963+ 9v.

Eg 603.17   Campbell, E.F. The chronology of the Amarna letters. Baltimore, 1964.

Eg 603.19   Kühne, Cord. Die Chronologie der internationalen Korrespondenz von El-Amarna. Kevelaer, 1973.

Eg 604 - 609   Ancient Egyptian history - History by periods - New Kingdom, 18th-21st dynasties, 1580-950 B.C. - Other works (By date)

Eg 607.04   Historia Pharaonis. Helmstadt? 1704.

Eg 608.53F   Birch, S. Thothmes III. London, 1853.

Eg 608.58   Rougé, E. de. Etude sur une stèle égyptienne. Paris, 1858.

Eg 608.70   Tugnot de Lanoye, Ferdinand. Rameses the Great. N.Y., 1870.

Eg 608.86   King, James. Cleopatra's needle. London, 1886.

Eg 608.86.10F   Maspero, G. Mummy of Rameses II. Boston, 1886.

Eg 609.08F   Weil, A. Veziere Aegyptens. Strassburg, 1908.

Eg 609.11.5   Weigall, Arthur E.P.B. The life and times of Akhnaton, pharaoh of Egypt. Edinburgh, 1911.

Eg 609.13   Nelson, Harold H. The battle of Megiddo. Diss. Chicago, 1921.

Eg 609.22F   Siemens, Clara. Koenig Echnaton in el-Amarna. Leipzig, 1922.

Eg 609.23   Budge, Ernest Alfred Wallis. Tutankhamen, Amenism, Atenism and Egyptian monotheism. London, 1923.

Eg 609.23.5   Smith, G.E. Tutankhamen and the discovery of his tomb. London, 1923.

Eg 609.23.6   Capart, Jean. The tomb of Tutankhamen. London, 1923.

Eg 609.23.6.5   Capart, Jean. Tout-Ankh-Amon. 2. éd. Bruxelles, 1950.

Eg 609.23.7   Carter, Howard. The tomb of Tut-Ankh-Amen. London, 1923-33. 3v.

Eg 609.23.8A   Carter, Howard. The tomb of Tut-Ankh-Amen. N.Y., 1923.

Eg 609.23.8B   Carter, Howard. The tomb of Tut-Ankh-Amen. N.Y., 1923.

Eg 609.23.9   Weigall, Arthur E.P.B. The life and times of Akhnaton, pharaoh of Egypt. London, 1923.

Eg 609.23.10A   Weigall, Arthur E.P.B. The life and times of Akhnaton. N.Y., 1923.

Eg 609.23.10B   Weigall, Arthur E.P.B. The life and times of Akhnaton. N.Y., 1923.

Eg 609.23.11   Mercer, S.A.B. Tutankhamen and Egyptology. Milwaukee, 1923.

Eg 609.23.15   Nahas, Bishara. The life and times of Tut-Ankh-Amen. N.Y., 1923.

Eg 609.26F   Mr. Howard Carter's triumph: the superb coffins of Tutankhamen. London, 1926.

Eg 609.26.5   Baikie, J. The Amarna age. N.Y., 1926.

Eg 609.30   Parain, Charles. La vie de Ramsès II. 5. éd. Paris, 1930.

Eg 609.33A   Edgerton, William F. The Thutmosid succession. Chicago, 1933.

Eg 609.33B   Edgerton, William F. The Thutmosid succession. Chicago, 1933.

Eg 609.40F   Hermann, Alfred. Die Stelen der thebanischen Felsgräber. Glückstadt, 1940.

Eg 609.40.5   Seele, Keith C. The coregency of Ramses II with Seti I and the date of the great hypostyle hall at Karnak. Chicago, 1940.

Eg 609.48   Janssen, J.M.A. Ramses III. Leiden, 1948.

Eg 609.51   Lange, Kurt. König Echnaton und die Amarnazeit. München, 1951.

Eg 609.55F   The shrines of Tut-Ankh-Amen. N.Y., 1955.

Eg 609.59   Bertram, J. Echnaton der Grosse im Schauen. Hamburg, 1959.

Eg 609.59.5   Montet, Pierre. L'Égypte et la Bible. Neuchâtel, 1959.

Eg 609.61   Vergote, J. Toutankhamon dans les archives hittites. Istanbul, 1961.

Eg 609.61.5   Bratton, Fred. The first heretic...Ikhnaton the king. Boston, 1961.

Eg 609.64   Hornung, E. Untersuchungen zur Chronologie und Geschichte des Neuen Reiches. Wiesbaden, 1964.

Eg 609.64.5   Wells, Evelyn. Nefertiti. Garden City, N.Y., 1964.

Eg 609.65   Hawkes, Jacquetta Hopkins. Pharaohs of Egypt. 1. ed. N.Y., 1965.

Eg 609.67   Perepelkin, Iurii I. Perevorot Amen-Khotpa IV. Moskva, 1967.

Eg 609.67.5   Redford, Donald B. History and chronology of the eighteenth dynasty of Egypt. Toronto, 1967.

Eg 609.67.10   Bille-De-Mot, Eléonore. The age of Akhenaten. London, 1967.

Eg 609.68   Aldred, Cyrill. Akhenaten, pharaoh of Egypt: a new study. London, 1968.

Eg 609.68.5   Perepelkin, Iurii I. Taina zolotogo groba. Moskva, 1968.

Eg 609.70   Giles, Frederick John. Ikhnaton: legend and history. London, 1970.

Eg 609.71   Vandersleyen, Claude. Les guerres d'Amoses. Bruxelles, 1971.

Eg 609.72   Wynne, Barry. Behind the mask of Tutankhamen. London, 1972.

Eg 609.72.5   Carter, Michael. The golden monarch; Tutankhamun. Christchurch, 1972.

Eg 650 - 659   Ancient Egyptian history - History by periods - Later dynastic period, 22d-26th dynasties, 950-525 B.C. (Table A)

Eg 658.65   Ebers, Georg. Disquisitiones de dynastia vicesima sexta regum Aegyptiarum. Berolini, 1865.

Eg 658.98   Marucchi, Orazio. La biografia di un personaggio politico dell'antico Egitto scritta sopra la sua statua. Roma, 1898.

Classified Listing

Eg 650 - 659 Ancient Egyptian history - History by periods - Later dynastic period, 22d-26th dynasties, 950-525 B.C. (Table A) - cont.

Eg 659.03	Moret, A. De Bocchori Rege. Paris, 1903.
Eg 659.44F	Zeisel, Helene von. Athiopen und Assyrer in Ägypten. Glüchstadt, 1944.
Eg 659.51	Elgood, P.G. Later dynasties of Egypt. Oxford, 1951.
Eg 659.73	Kitchen, Kenneth Anderson. The third intermediate perio⌐ in Egypt. (1100-650 B.C.). Warminster, 1973.

Eg 690 - 699 Ancient Egyptian history - History by periods - Persian rule, 27th-30th dynasties, 525-332 B.C. (Table A)

Eg 691.2	Pamphlet box. Egyptian history. Persian supremacy.

Eg 700 - 709 Ancient Egyptian history - History by periods - The Ptolemies, 332-30 B.C. (Table A)

Eg 702.10	Hutmacher, Rudolf. Das Ehrendekret für den Strategen Kallimachos. Meisenheim am Glan, 1965.
Eg 707.01	Vaillant, J. Historia Ptolemaeorum. Amstelodami, 1701.
Eg 708.19	Champollion, J.J. Annales des Lagides. Paris, 1819. 2v.
Eg 708.23	Drumann, Wilhelm. Historisch-antiquarische Untersuchungen über Aegypten, oder Die Inschrift von Rosette. Königsberg, 1823.
Eg 708.38	Sharpe, S. Egypt under the Ptolemies. London, 1838.
Eg 708.51	Abbott, Jacob. History of Cleopatra, queen of Egypt. N.Y., 1851.
Eg 708.51.2	Abbott, Jacob. History of Cleopatra, queen of Egypt. N.Y., 1860.
Eg 708.51.5	Abbott, Jacob. History of Cleopatra, queen of Egypt. N.Y., 1874.
Eg 708.52	Robiou, Felix. Aegypti regimen quo anno susceperunt et qua ratione tractaverint Ptolemai. Rhedonis, 1852.
Htn Eg 708.58*	Pennsylvania. University. Philomathean Society. Report of the committee...to translate...the Rosetta Stone. Philadelphia, 1858.
Htn Eg 708.58.5*	Pennsylvania. University. Philomathean Society. Report of the committee. Manuscript. n.p., n.d.
Eg 708.64	Stahr, Adolf. Cleopatra. Berlin, 1864.
Eg 708.64.2	Stahr, Adolf. Cleopatra. 2. Aufl. Berlin, 1879.
Eg 708.68	Lumbroso, Giacomo. Seconda lettera al Gaspare Garresio intorno ad alcuni punti della storia dei Tolemei. Torino, 1868.
Eg 708.70	Lumbroso, Giacomo. Recherches sur l'économie politique de l'Egypte sous les Lagides. Turin, 1870.
Eg 708.90.5	Houssaye, Henry. Cleopatra. N.Y., 1890.
Htn Eg 708.90.7*	Houssaye, Henry. Cleopatra. N.Y., 1890.
Eg 708.93	Bandelin, Erich. De rebus inter Aegyptios et Romanos...usque ad bellum Alexandrinum a Caesare gestum. Inaug. Diss. Halis Saxonum, 1893.
Eg 708.95A	Mahaffy, J.P. The empire of the Ptolemies. London, 1895.
Eg 708.95B	Mahaffy, J.P. The empire of the Ptolemies. London, 1895.
Eg 708.97	Strack, M.L. Die Dynastie der Ptolemäer. Berlin, 1897.
Eg 709.00	Schubart, W. Quaestiones de rebus militaribus...in regno Lagidarum. Trebnitz, 1900.
Eg 709.00.5	Meyer, Paul M. Das Heerwesen der Ptolemäer und Römer in Ägypten. Leipzig, 1900.
Eg 709.03	Bouché-Leclercq, A. Histoire des Lagides. v.4, photoreproduction. Paris, 1903. 4v.
Eg 709.03.5	De Bernáth, D. Cléopâtre; sa vie, son règne. Paris, 1903.
Eg 709.04	Budge, Ernest Alfred Wallis. The decrees of Memphis and Canopus. London, 1904. 3v.
Eg 709.05	Maspéro, Henri. Les finances de l'Égypte sous les Lagides. Paris, 1905.
Eg 709.06	Wolf, Josef. Aus Inschriften und Papyren der Ptolemaierzeit. Feldkirch, 1906.
Eg 709.09	Otto, P.W. Die wirtschaftliche Lage und die Bildnis der Priester im hellenischen Agypten. Leipzig, 1907.
Eg 709.09.15	Sergeant, P.W. Cleopatra of Egypt. N.Y., 1909.
Eg 709.10F	Plaumann, Gerhard. Ptolemais in Oberägypten. Leipzig, 1910.
Eg 709.11	Lesquier, Jean. Les institutions militaires de l'Égypte sous les Lagides. Paris, 1911.
Eg 709.12	Gradenwitz, O. Griechische und demotische Papyri. Strassburg, 1912.
Eg 709.12.3	Oertel, Friedrich. Die Liturgie; Studien zur ptolemäischen...Verwaltung Agyptens. Leipzig, 1912.
Eg 709.12.5	Oertel, Friedrich. Die Liturgie. Leipzig, 1917.
Eg 709.13	Biedermann, Erhard. Studien zur ägyptischen Verwaltungsgeschichte in ptolemäisch-römischen Zeit. Berlin, 1913.
Eg 709.13.3	Steiner, A. Der Fiskus der Ptolemaeer. v.1-3. Leipzig, 1913.
Eg 709.13.5	Semeka, G. Ptolemäisches Prozessrecht. München, 1913.
Eg 709.14	Weigall, Arthur E.P.B. The life and times of Cleopatra, queen of Egypt. N.Y., 1914.
Eg 709.14.5A	Weigall, Arthur E.P.B. The life and times of Cleopatra. N.Y., 1924.
Eg 709.14.5B	Weigall, Arthur E.P.B. The life and times of Cleopatra. N.Y., 1924.
Eg 709.14.7	Weigall, Arthur E.P.B. The life and times of Cleopatra. London, 1926.
Eg 709.23	Koch, Walter. Ein Ptolemaeerkrieg. Stuttgart, 1923.
Eg 709.26	Harry, Myriam (pseud.). La vie amoureuse de Cléopâtre. Paris, 1926.
Eg 709.30	Wertheimer, O.V. Kleopatra. Zürich, 1930.
Eg 709.37.3	Ludwig, E. Cleopatra, Geschichte einer Königin. Amsterdam, 1937.
Eg 709.37.5A	Ludwig, E. Cleopatra, the story of a queen. N.Y., 1937.
Eg 709.37.5B	Ludwig, E. Cleopatra, the story of a queen. N.Y., 1937.
Eg 709.37.10	Peremans, W. Vreemdelingen en Egyptenaren. Louvain, 1937.
Eg 709.38	Elgood, P.G. The Ptolemies of Egypt. Bristol, 1938.
Eg 709.38.5F	Otto, Walter. Zur Geschichte des Niedergangs des Ptolemäerreiches. München, 1938.
Eg 709.44	Jouguet, P. Trois études sur l'hellénisme. Le Caire, 1944.
Eg 709.53	Volkmann, Hans. Kleopatra. München, 1953.
Eg 709.53.2	Volkmann, Hans. Kleopatra. N.Y., 1958.
Eg 709.60	Daix, Pierre. Cléopatre. Paris, 1960.
Eg 709.60.5	Zel'in, Konstantin K. Issledovaniia po istorii zemel'nykh otnoshenii v ellinisticheskom Egipte, II-I vv. do n.e. Moskva, 1960.
Eg 709.63	Bloedow, Edmund. Beiträge zur Geschichte der Ptolemaios XII. Würzburg, 1963.
Eg 709.66	Thissen, Heinz Josef. Studien zum Raphiadekret. Meisenheim am Glan, 1966.
Eg 709.66.5	Heinen, Heinz. Rom und Ägypten vom 51 bis 47 vor Christ; Untersuchungen zur Regierungszeit der 7. Kleopatra und des 13. Ptolemäers. Tübingen, 1966.

Eg 700 - 709 Ancient Egyptian history - History by periods - The Ptolemies, 332-30 B.C. (Table A) - cont.

Eg 709.68	Longega, Gabriella. Arsinoe II. Roma, 1968.
Eg 709.71	Lindsay, Jack. Cleopatra. London, 1971.
Eg 709.71.5	Desmond, Alice Curtis. Cleopatra's children. N.Y., 1971.
Eg 709.71.10	Bradford, Ernle Dusgate Selby. Cleopatra. London, 1971.
Eg 709.72	Grant, Michael. Cleopatra. London, 1972.

Eg 750 - 759 Ancient Egyptian history - History by periods - Roman and Byzantine rule, 30 B.C.-638 A.D. (Table A)

Eg 752.5	Acta Alexandrinorum. The acts of the pagan martyrs. Oxford, 1954.
Eg 752.5.2	Acta Alexandrinorum. Acta Alexandrinorum de mortibus Alexandriae nobilium; fragmenta papyracea Graeca. Lipsiae, 1961.
Eg 752.10	Skeat, T.C. Papyri from Panopolis in the Chester Beatty Library. Dublin, 1964.
Eg 752.15	L'Archivio di Kronion. Milano, 1971.
Eg 758.42	Sharpe, S. Egypt under the Romans. London, 1842.
Eg 758.79	Peabody, F.G. Christianity in Egypt. n.p., n.d.
Eg 758.82	Lumbroso, Giacomo. L'Egitto al tempo dei Greci e dei Romani. Roma, 1882.
Eg 758.83	Merriam, A.C. The Obelisk-Crab. N.Y., 1883.
Eg 758.92	Simaika, A. Province Romaine d'Egypte. Paris, 1892.
Eg 759.06	Boulard, L. Les instructions écrites du Magistrat au juge-commissaire dans l'Egypte Romaine. Paris, 1906.
Eg 759.09	Studien zur byzantinischen Verwaltung Ägyptens. Leipzig, 1909.
Eg 759.15	Stein, Arthur. Untersuchungen zur Geschichte und Verwaltung Ägyptens unter roemischer Herrschaft. Stuttgart, 1915.
Eg 759.22	Piotrowicz, L. Stanowisko nomarchów w administracji Egiptu. Poznan, 1922.
Eg 759.22.5	Wenger, L. Volk und Staat in Ägypten am Ausgang der Römerherrschaft. München, 1922.
Eg 759.24.5	Segrè, Angelo. Il mutuo e il tasso d'interesse nell'Egitto greco-romano. Firenze, 1924.
Eg 759.31	Hardy, E.R. The large estates of Byzantine Egypt. N.Y., 1931.
Eg 759.37.3	Breccia, Evaristo. Egitto greco e romano. 3. ed. Pisa, 1957.
Eg 759.38	Wallace, S.L. Taxation in Egypt from Augustus to Diocletian. Princton, 1938.
Eg 759.47	Jouguet, P. La domination romaine en Égypte aux deux premiers siècles. Alexandrie, 1947.
Eg 759.51	Johnson, A.C. Egypt and the Roman Empire. Ann Arbor, 1951.
Eg 759.55	Burr, Viktor. Tiberius Iulius Alexander. Bonn, 1955.
Eg 759.64	Chalon, Gérard. L'édit de Tiberius Julius Alexander; étude historique et exégétique. Olten, 1964.

Eg 800 - 809 Ancient Egyptian history - Chronology (Table A)

Eg 807.37	Averani, N. De mensibus Aegyptiorum. Florentiae, 1737.
Eg 807.65	Schmidt, F.S. de. Opuscula Aegyptiacae. Caroleruhae, 1765.
Eg 808.45	Böskh, A. Manetho und die Hundssternperiode. Berlin, 1845.
Eg 808.49F	Lepsius, K.R. Die Chronologie der Ägypter. Berlin, 1849.
Eg 808.49.5F	Lepsius, K.R. Königsbuch der alten Ägypter. Berlin, 1858.
Eg 808.57	Knötel, A. System der ägyptischen Chronologie. Leipzig, 1857.
Eg 808.63	Lieblein, J. Agyptische Chronologie. Christiania, 1863.
Eg 808.65	Henne, A. Manethós...Geschichte und Chronologie. Gotha, 1865.
Eg 808.67	Unger, G.F. Chronologie des Manetho. Berlin, 1867.
Eg 808.73	Lieblein, J. Chronologie égyptienne. Christiania, 1873.
Eg 808.77	Lauth, F.J. Agyptische Chronologie. Strassburg, 1877.
Eg 808.78	Pessl, H. von. Das chronologisches System Manetho's. Leipzig, 1878.
Eg 808.96	Torr, C. Memphis and Mycenae. Cambridge, Eng., 1896.
Eg 809.00	Schmidt, Orlando P. A self-verifying chronological history of ancient Egypt. Cincinnati, 1900.
Eg 809.08	Budge, Ernest Alfred Wallis. The book of the kings of Egypt. London, 1908. 2v.
Eg 809.17F	Quellen und Forschungen zur Zeitbestimmung der ägyptischen Geschichte. Berlin. 1-2,1917-1935 2v.
Eg 809.26	Weill, R. Bases, méthodes, et résultats de la chronologie égyptienne. pt.1-2. Paris, 1926-28.
Eg 809.28	Nicklin, T. Studies in Egyptian chronology. v.1-2. Blackburn, 1928-29.
Eg 809.32	Macnaughton, D. A scheme of Egyptian chronology. London, 1932.
Eg 809.62	Vanderslayen, Claude. Chronologie des préfets d'Égypte de 284 à 395. Bruxelles, 1962.

Eg 810 - 819 Ancient Egyptian history - Civilization, social life - General works (Table A)

Eg 817.67	Terrasson, J. Sethos. Paris, 1767. 2v.
Eg 818.37	Wilkinson, J.G. Manners and customs of the ancient Egyptians. London, 1837. 3v.
Eg 818.37.2	Wilkinson, J.G. Manners and customs of the ancient Egyptians. 2. series. London, 1841. 3v.
Eg 818.37.3	Wilkinson, J.G. Manners and customs of the ancient Egyptians. 3. ed. London, 1847. 5v.
Eg 818.37.6A	Wilkinson, J.G. Manners and customs of the ancient Egyptians. London, 1878. 3v.
Eg 818.37.6B	Wilkinson, J.G. Manners and customs of the ancient Egyptians. London, 1878. 3v.
Eg 818.37.10	Wilkinson, J.G. The manners and customs of the ancient Egyptians. Boston, 1883. 3v.
Eg 818.37.12	Wilkinson, J.G. A popular account of the ancient Egyptians. London, 1854. 2v.
Eg 818.37.13	Wilkinson, J.G. A popular account of the ancient Egyptians. N.Y., 1854. 2v.
Eg 818.37.15	Wilkinson, J.G. A popular account of the ancient Egyptians. London, 1871. 2v.
Eg 818.37.17	Wilkinson, J.G. A popular account of the ancient Egyptians. London, 1874. 2v.
Eg 818.37.25	Wilkinson, J.G. A popular account of the ancient Egyptians. London, 1878. 2v.
Eg 818.44	Haskins, Roswell W. The arts, sciences, and civilization, anterior to Greece and Rome. Buffalo, 1844.
Eg 818.57	Wilkinson, J.G. The Egyptians in the time of the pharaohs. London, 1857.
Eg 818.91	Brugsch, H. Die Ägyptologie. Leipzig, 1891.
Eg 818.92.2	Maspéro, Gaston. Life in ancient Egypt and Assyria. N.Y., 1895.

Classified Listing

Eg 810 - 819   Ancient Egyptian history - Civilization, social life -
General works (Table A) - cont.

Eg 818.92.3	Hommel, F. Der babylonische Ursprung der ägyptischen Kultur. München, 1895.
Eg 818.94A	Maspéro, Gaston. The dawn of civilization. N.Y., 1894.
Eg 818.94B	Maspéro, Gaston. The dawn of civilization. N.Y., 1894.
Eg 818.94.4	Maspéro, Gaston. The dawn of civilization. N.Y., 1897.
Eg 818.94.6	Maspéro, Gaston. The dawn of civilization. 2. ed. London, 1896.
Eg 819.07	Schneider, H. Kultur und Denken der alten Ägypter. Leipzig, 1907.
Eg 819.09	Rustafjaell, R. de. The light of Egypt. London, 1909.
Eg 819.10	Lieblein, J. Recherches sur l'histoire et la civilisation de l'ancien Égypte. Leipzig, 1910. 3v.
Eg 819.11	Smith, G.E. Ancient Egyptians. London, 1911.
Eg 819.11.3	Poertner, D.B. Die agyptischen Totenstelen. Paderborn, 1911.
Eg 819.12	Baillet, J. Introduction à l'étude des idées morales dans l'Égypte antique. Thèse. Blois, 1912.
Eg 819.12.3	Röder, G. Aus dem Leben vornehmer Ägypter. Leipzig, n.d.
Eg 819.13	Baillet, J. Le régime pharaonique...avec l'evolution de la morale en Egypte. Thèse. Blois, 1913.
Eg 819.13.5	Bissing, F.W. von. Die Kultur des alten Ägyptens. 2. Aufl. Leipzig, 1919.
Eg 819.16	Gosse, A.B. The civilization of the ancient Egyptians. N.Y., 1916.
Eg 819.16.5	Rozanov, V.V. Iz vostochykh motivov. pt.1-3. Petrograd, 1916-17.
Eg 819.20	Wiedemann, A. Das alte Ägypten. Heidelberg, 1920.
Eg 819.23A	Petrie, William M.F. Social life in ancient Egypt. Boston, 1923.
Eg 819.23B	Petrie, William M.F. Social life in ancient Egypt. Boston, 1923.
Eg 819.23.2	Petrie, William M.F. Social life in ancient Egypt. London, 1932.
Eg 819.23.5	Blackman, A.M. Luxor and its temples. N.Y., 1923.
Eg 819.24	Wilson, R.F. The living pageant of the Nile. Indianapolis, 1924.
Eg 819.25	Jequier, Gustave. Histoire de la civilisation égyptienne des origines à la conquête d'Alexandre. Paris, 1925.
Eg 819.26.5	Moret, Alexandre. The Nile and Egyptian civilization. N.Y., 1927.
Eg 819.30	Waddell, L.A. Egyptian civilization. London, 1930.
Eg 819.33	Rydh, H. Hur man levde i Faraos land. Stockholm, 1933.
Eg 819.36	Erman, Adolf. Die Welt am Nil. Leipzig, 1936.
Eg 819.37	Cumont, Franz. L'Égypt des astrologues. Bruxelles, 1937.
Eg 819.39	Petrie, William M.F. The making of Egypt. London, 1939.
Eg 819.40	Akademiia nauk SSSR. Ocherki po istorii tekhniki drevnei Egipta. Moskva, 1940.
Eg 819.42A	Glanville, S.R.K. The legacy of Egypt. Oxford, 1942.
Eg 819.42B	Glanville, S.R.K. The legacy of Egypt. Oxford, 1942.
Eg 819.44	Scott, N.E. The home life of the ancient Egyptians. N.Y., 1944.
Eg 819.49	Murray, Margaret Alice. The splendour that was Egypt. London, 1949.
Eg 819.49.2	Murray, Margaret Alice. The splendour that was Egypt. 2. ed. London, 1964.
Eg 819.51	Wilson, J. The burden of Egypt. Chicago, 1951.
Eg 819.51.5	Davis, Simon. Race-relations in ancient Egypt. London, 1951.
Eg 819.54.4	Neubert, Otto. Tutankhamun and the Valley of the Kings. London, 1972.
Eg 819.55	Wolf, Walther. Die Welt der Ägypter. Stuttgart, 1955.
Eg 819.55.5	Kees, Hermann. Das alte Ägypten. Berlin, 1955.
Eg 819.55.10	Cottrell, L. Life under the pharaohs. London, 1955.
Eg 819.59	Garnot, Jean Sainte F. Aspects de l'Égypte antique. Cairo, 1959.
Eg 819.59.5	Posener, Georges. Dictionnaire de la civilisation égyptienne. Paris, 1959.
Eg 819.61	Pirenne, Jacques. Histoire de la civilisation de l'Égypte. Neuchâtel, 1961. 3v.
Eg 819.62.5	Wolf, Walther. Kulturgeschichte des alten Ägypten. Stuttgart, 1962.
Eg 819.63	Nolli, G. Civiltà dell'antico Egitto. Tolino, 1963.
Eg 819.64	Sämih, Wali al Din. Daily life in ancient Egypt. N.Y., 1964.
Eg 819.64.5	Montet, Pierre. Eternal Egypt. N.Y., 1969.
Eg 819.65	Ward, William A. The spirit of ancient Egypt. Beirut, 1965.
Eg 819.65.5	Daumas, François. La civilisation de l'Égypte pharaonique. Paris, 1965.
Eg 819.67	Säve-Söderbergh, Torgny. Faraoner och människor. Stockholm, 1967.
Eg 819.67.7	Makram, Rizg. Kulturgeist und Kulturleib. 2. Aufl. Tübingen, 1970.
Eg 819.67.10	Hofmann, Inge. Die Kulturen des Niltals von Aswan bis Sennar. Hamburg, 1967.
Eg 819.69	Otto, Eberhard. Wesen und Wandel der ägyptischen Kultur. Berlin, 1969.
Eg 819.70.1F	Barocas, Claudio. Egypt. N.Y., 1972.
Eg 819.71	Savel'eva, Tat'iana N. Kak zhili egiptiane vo vremena stroitel'stva piramid. Moskva, 1971.
Eg 819.71.7	Harris, James Renel. The legacy of Egypt. 2. ed. Oxford, 1971.
Eg 819.72	Aldred, Cyril. Tatankhamun's Egypt. London, 1972.
Eg 819.73	Obenga, Théophile. L'Afrique dans l'antiquité: Egypte pharaonique. Paris, 1973.

Eg 820 - 829   Ancient Egyptian history - Civilization, social life -
Private life (Table A)

Eg 829.25	Montet, Pierre. Les scènes de la vie privée dans les tombeaux égyptiens de l'ancien empire. Londres, 1925.
Eg 829.25.5	Montet, Pierre. Les scènes de la vie privée dans les tombeaux égyptiens de l'ancien empire. Thèse. Strasbourg, 1925.
Eg 829.32	Shorter, Alan W. Everyday life in ancient Egypt. London, 1932.
Eg 829.46	Montet, Pierre. La vie quotidienne en Égypt au temps des Ramsès (XIII-XII siècles avant J.C.). Paris, 1946.
Eg 829.46.5	Montet, Pierre. Everyday life in Egypt in the days of Ramesses the Great. N.Y., 1958.
Eg 829.55	Winlock, H.E. Models of daily life in ancient Egypt. Cambridge, Mass., 1955.
Eg 829.60	Grapow, Herman. Wie die alten Ägypter sich anredeten. Berlin, 1960.
Eg 829.65	Lindsay, Jack. Leisure and pleasure in Roman Egypt. London, 1965.

Eg 830 - 839   Ancient Egyptian history - Civilization, social life -
Burial (Table A)

Eg 839.13	Sottas, H. La préservation de la propriété funéraire. Paris, 1913.
Eg 839.24	Smith, G.E. Egyptian mummies. London, 1924.
Eg 839.56	Smith, J.L. Tombs, temples and ancient art. 1. ed. Norman, 1956.

Eg 841   Ancient Egyptian history - Civilization, social life - Special topics -
Gymnastics

Eg 841.5	Schmidt, Karl F.W. Das griechische Gymnasium in Ägypten. Halle, 1926?
Eg 841.10	Sijpesteijn, Pieter Johannes. Liste des gymnasiarques des métropoles de l'Égypte romaine. Amsterdam, 1967.

Eg 844   Ancient Egyptian history - Civilization, social life - Special topics -
Marriage

Eg 844.5	Edgerton, W.F. Notes on Egyptian marriage chiefly in the Plotemaic period. Chicago, 1931.
Eg 844.71	Lüddeckens, E. Agyptische Eheverträge. Wiesbaden, 1960.

Eg 845   Ancient Egyptian history - Civilization, social life - Special topics -
Condition of women

Eg 845.5A	Buttles, Janet R. The queens of Egypt. N.Y., 1908.
Eg 845.5B	Buttles, Janet R. The queens of Egypt. N.Y., 1908.
Eg 845.7	Paturet, G. La condition juridique. Paris, 1886.
Eg 845.10	Bingmann, Lea. Die Frau in ptolemäisch-kaiserlicher Agypter. Bonn, 1939.

Eg 847   Ancient Egyptian history - Civilization, social life - Special topics -
Writing, scribes

Eg 847.1	Schmidt, Karl F.W. Die Kunst Hieroglyphen zu Lesen. Breslau, 1828.
Eg 847.2	Schwartze, Moritz Gotthilf. Das alte Agypten...altägyptischen Original-Schriften und den Mittheilungen der nichtägyptischen alten Schriftsteller bearbeitet. Leipzig, 1843. 2v.
Eg 847.3	Rougé, Emman. Essai sur une stèle junéraire. Berlin, 1849.
Eg 847.4F	Möller, G. Hieratische Paläographie. Leipzig, 1909-12. 3v.
Eg 847.4.5F	Möller, G. Hieratische Paläographie. Ergänzungsheft zu Bd. 1-2. Leipzig, 1936.
Eg 847.4.10	Möller, G. Hieratische Lesestücke für den akademischen Gebrauch. v.1-3. Berlin, 1961.
Eg 847.5	Essai sur le symbolisme antique. Paris, 1847.
Eg 847.6	Candar, Aaoni Ali. Eti hiyeroglifi üzerinde tetkikler 534 idéogramme. Ankara, 1933.
Eg 847.7	Reisner, M. Inscribed monuments from Gebel Barkal. Leipzig, 1934.
Eg 847.8	Waangstedt, Stev von. Ausgewählte demotische Ostraka. Inaug. Diss. Uppsala, 1954.
Eg 847.9	Davies, N.M. Picture writing in ancient Egypt. London, 1958.
Eg 847.10	Iversen, Erik. The myth of Egypt and its hieroglyphs in European tradition. Copenhagen, 1961.
Eg 847.11F	Gardiner, Alan Henderson. Catalogue des caractères d'impression hiéroglyphiques égyptiens. Bruxelles, 1928.
Eg 847.12	Waangstedt, Stev von. Die demotischen Ostraka der Universität zu Zürich. Uppsala, 1965.

Eg 848   Ancient Egyptian history - Civilization, social life - Special topics -
Books and education

Eg 848.2	Uhlemann, M. Thoth oder die Wissenschaft der alten Agypter. Göttingen, 1855.
Eg 848.3	Majer-Leonhard, E. Agrammatoi in Aegypto qui litteras sciverint qui nesciverint ex papyris graecis quantum fieri potest exploratur. Francofurti, 1913.
Eg 848.3.2	Majer-Leonhard, E. Agrammatoi. Marpurgi Chattorum, 1913.
Eg 848.4	Moreux, T. La science mystérieuse des pharaons. Paris, 1923.
Eg 848.4.5	Moreux, T. La science mystérieuse des pharaons. Paris, 1926.
Eg 848.4.10	Moreux, T. La science mystérieuse des pharaons. Paris, 1938.
Eg 848.5	Brunner, Hellmut. Altägyptische Erziehung. Wiesbaden, 1957.
Eg 848.6	Milne, J.G. Relics of Graeco-Egyptian schools. n.p., 1908.
Eg 848.7	Galé, José Miguel. Las escuelas del antiguo Egipto a través de los papiros griegos. Madrid, 1961.

Eg 849   Ancient Egyptian history - Civilization, social life - Special topics -
Music and dancing

Eg 849.5F	Brunner-Traut, E. Der Tanz im alten Ägypten nach bildlichen und inschriftlichen Zeugnissen. N.Y., 1938.
Eg 849.10	Lexová, Irena. Ancient Egyptian dances. Praha, 1935.

Eg 850   Ancient Egyptian history - Civilization, social life - Special topics -
Festivals

Eg 850.1	Brygseh, H. Drei Fest-Kalender. Leipzig, 1877.
Eg 850.5	Bleeker, Claas J. Egyptian festivals. Leiden, 1967.
Eg 850.8F	Cairo. Musée des antiquités égyptiennes. M'n.(Papyrus 86637). The Cairo calendar, no. 86637. Cairo, 1966.

Eg 851   Ancient Egyptian history - Civilization, social life - Special topics -
Character and morals

Eg 851.5	Rosenvasser, A. Las ideas morales en el antiquo Egipto. Santa Fé, 1938.

Eg 855   Ancient Egyptian history - Civilization, social life - Special topics -
Hygiene

Eg 855.1	Caton, R. Ancient Egyptian medicine. London, 1904.
Eg 855.2	Dauson, Warren R. Magician and leech. London, 1929.
Eg 855.3	Garry, Thomas G. Egypt. London, 1931.

Eg 856   Ancient Egyptian history - Civilization, social life - Special topics -
Costume

Eg 856.2	Bonnet, Hans. Die altägyptische Schurztracht. Leipzig, 1916.
Eg 856.3	Abubakr, Abdel Monem Jooussef. Untersuchungen über die ägyptischen Kronen. Inaug. Diss. Glückstadt, 1937.
Eg 856.4F	Keimer, Ludwig. Remarques sur le tatouage dans l'Égypte ancienne. Caire, 1948.

Classified Listing

Eg 860   Ancient Egyptian history - Civilization, social life - Special topics -
Pottery
    Eg 860.5F — Raphael, M. Prehistoric pottery and civilization in Egypt. N.Y., 1947.

Eg 862   Ancient Egyptian history - Civilization, social life - Special topics -
Metalwork
    Eg 862.1 — Lepsius, C.R. Les métaux dans les inscriptions égyptiennes. Paris, 1877.
    Eg 862.5 — Garland, H. Ancient Egyptian metallurgy. London, 1927.

Eg 863   Ancient Egyptian history - Civilization, social life - Special topics -
Domestic plants
    Eg 863.5 — Laurent-Täckholm, Vini. Faraos blomster. Stockholm, 1951.
    Eg 863.7 — Ismail, Ismail Moustafa. Die Gärten der alten Agypter und die Entwicklung der Bewässerung bis zum Hochdamm bei Assuan. München? 1960?

Eg 866   Ancient Egyptian history - Civilization, social life - Special topics -
Vehicles
    Eg 866.2 — Gamer-Wallert, Ingrid. Fische und Fischkulte im alten Agypten. Wiesbaden, 1970.

Eg 869   Ancient Egyptian history - Civilization, social life - Special topics -
Miscellany [Discontinued]
    VEg 869.09 — Giesswein, Sándor. Egiptom és a biblia. Budapest, 1909.

Eg 870 - 879   Ancient Egyptian history - Religion and mythology (Table A)
    Eg 870.1 — Garnot, J. St. F. Religions égyptiennes antiques; bibliographie analytique. Paris, 1952.
    Eg 871.1 — Pamphlet box. Egyptian religion.
    Eg 872.5 — Hopfner, Theodor. Fontes historiae religionis aegypticae. Bonnae, 1922-25. 5v.
    Eg 872.10 — Schott, Siegfried. Urkunden mythologischen Inhalts. Heft 1-2. Leipzig, 1929-39.
Htn   Eg 876.08* — Pignorio, L. Characteres Aegyptii hoc est sacrorum. Francofurti, 1608.
Htn   Eg 876.69* — Pignorio, L. Mensa isiaca qua sacrorum. Amstelodami, 1669.
Htn   Eg 876.76F* — Kircher, A. Sphinx mystagoga. Amstelodami, 1676.
    Eg 877.17 — Witsi, H. Aegyptiaca et dekaphylon de...sacrorum. Herbornae Nassaviorum, 1717.
    Eg 877.19 — Basheysen, H. Natales XI Deo consecrat disputatione paradox de Isicle. pt.1-2. Servestae, 1719.
    Eg 877.50 — Iablonski, P.E. Pantheon Aegyptiorum. Francofurti, 1750.
    Eg 877.73 — Schumacher, J.H. De cultu animalium. Brunsvigiis, 1773.
    Eg 878.18 — Babor, Johann. Über die philosophische Historiographie der neuesten Zeit. Olmütz, 1818.
    Eg 878.19 — Prichard, J.C. An analysis of Egyptian mythology. London, 1819.
    Eg 878.19.5 — Prichard, J.C. An analysis of Egyptian mythology. London, 1838.
    Eg 878.46 — Henry, D.M.J. L'Égypte pharaonique. Paris, 1846. 2v.
    Eg 878.46.5 — Schwenck, K. Die Mythologie der Aegypter für gebildete und die studirende Jugend. Frankfurt am Main, 1846. 5v.
    Eg 878.55 — Seyffarth, G. Theologische Schriften der alten Aegypter. Gotha, 1855.
    Eg 878.58 — Heavlin, R.A. (Mrs.). The mysteries of Isis. N.Y., 1858.
    Eg 878.63 — Sharpe, Samuel. Egyptian mythology. London, 1863.
    Eg 878.75 — Meyer, E. Set-Typhon. Leipzig, 1875.
    Eg 878.75.5 — Ancessi, Victor. L'Egypte et Moïse. Paris, 1875.
    Eg 878.77.5 — Ancessi, Victor. Job et l'Égypte, le redempteur et la vie future. Paris, 1877.
    Eg 878.77.10 — Schiaparelli, Ernesto. Del sentimento religioso degli antichi Egiziani secondo i monumenti. Torino, 1877.
    Eg 878.80 — Renouf, P. le P. Lectures on the origin and growth of religion...of ancient Egypt. London, 1880.
    Eg 878.81 — Lauzone, R.N. Dizionario di mitologia egizia. v.1-5. Torino, 1881. 3v.
    Eg 878.82 — Tiele, C.R. History of the Egyptian religion. London, 1882.
    Eg 878.82.4 — Lemm, O. von. Studien zum Ritualbuche des Ammondienstes. Leipzig, 1882.
    Eg 878.85 — Brugsch, H. Religion und Mythologie der alten Ägypter. Leipzig, 1885. 2v.
    Eg 878.85.3 — Brugsch, H. Religion und Mythologie der alten Ägypter. Leipzig, 1891.
    Eg 878.89 — Strauss, V. von. Der altägyptische Götterglaube. Heidelberg, 1889. 2v.
    Eg 878.90 — Lefébure, E. Rites égyptiens. Paris, 1890.
    Eg 878.90.5 — Drexler, W. Der Cultus der Aegyptischen Gottheiten. Leipzig, 1890.
    Eg 878.94 — Jequier, G. Le livre de ce qu'il y a dans l'hadès. Paris, 1894.
    Eg 878.95 — Wiedemann, A. The ancient Egyptian doctrine of the immortality of the soul. N.Y., 1895.
    Eg 878.95.15 — Wiedemann, A. The ancient Egyptian doctrine of the immortality of the soul. 1895.
    Eg 878.97A — Wiedemann, A. Religion of the ancient Egyptians. Photoreproduction. N.Y., 1897.
    VEg 878.97B — Wiedemann, A. Religion of the ancient Egyptians. Photoreproduction. N.Y., 1897.
    Eg 878.98 — Petrie, William M.F. Religion and conscience in ancient Egypt. London, 1898.
    Eg 878.98.5 — St. Clair, G. Creation records discovered in Egypt. London, 1898.
    Eg 879.00 — Budge, Ernest Alfred Wallis. Egyptian ideas of the future life. 2. ed. London, 1900.
    Eg 879.00.5 — Blackden, M.W. Ritual of the mystery of the judgment of the soul. London, 19- .
    Eg 879.02.5 — Sayce, Archibald H. The religions of ancient Egypt and Babylonia. Edinburgh, 1903.
    Eg 879.03 — Palanque, C. Le Nil...son rôle et son culte en Égypt. Paris, 1903.
    Eg 879.04 — Budge, Ernest Alfred Wallis. The gods of the Egyptians. Chicago, 1904.
X Cg   Eg 879.04 — Budge, Ernest Alfred Wallis. The gods of the Egyptians. v.2. Chicago, 1904.
    Eg 879.04.2 — Budge, Ernest Alfred Wallis. The gods of the Egyptians. London, 1904. 2v.
    Eg 879.04.2.2 — Budge, Ernest Alfred Wallis. The gods of the Egyptians. N.Y., 1969. 2v.
    Eg 879.04.5 — Wreszinski, W. Die Hohenpriester des Amon. Berlin, 1904.
    Eg 879.05 — Otto, Walter. Priester und Tempel im Hellenistischen Agypten. Leipzig, 1905. 2v.
    Eg 879.05.5 — Steindorff, Georg. The religion of the ancient Egyptians. N.Y., 1905.

Eg 870 - 879   Ancient Egyptian history - Religion and mythology (Table A) - cont.
    Eg 879.05.10 — Capart, Jean. Bulletin critique des religions de l'Égypte. v.1-5. Leiden, 1905-39.
    Eg 879.06 — Budge, Ernest Alfred Wallis. The Egyptian heaven and hell. London, 1906. 3v.
    Eg 879.06.5 — Petrie, William M.F. The religion of ancient Egypt. London, 1906.
    Eg 879.07 — Erman, A. Handbook of Egyptian religion. London, 1907.
    Eg 879.07.5 — Massey, Gerald. Ancient Egypt, the light of the world. London, 1907. 2v.
    Eg 879.07.10 — Pamphlet vol. Massey, Gerald. Lectures. 6 pam.
    Eg 879.08 — Amélineau, Emile. Prolegomènes a l'étude de la religion egyptienne. pt.2. Paris, 1916.
    Eg 879.09 — Budge, Ernest Alfred Wallis. The book of the opening of the mouth. London, 1909. 2v.
    Eg 879.09.5 — Budge, Ernest Alfred Wallis. The liturgy of funerary offerings. London, 1909.
    Eg 879.10 — Virey, P. La religion de l'ancienne Égypte. Paris, 1910.
    Eg 879.11 — Budge, Ernest Alfred Wallis. Osiris and the Egyptian resurrection. London, 1911. 2v.
    Eg 879.12 — Breasted, James Henry. Development of religion and thought in ancient Egypt. N.Y., 1912.
    Eg 879.12.2 — Breasted, James Henry. Development of religion and thought in ancient Egypt. N.Y., 1912.
    Eg 879.12.3 — Zimmermann, F. Die ägyptische Religion. Paderborn, 1912.
    Eg 879.12.5 — Kees, Hermann. Der Opfertanz des ägyptischen Königs. München, 1912.
    Eg 879.14 — Amélineau, Emile. L'enfer egyptien et l'enfer virgilien. Paris, 1914.
    Eg 879.14.5F — Hopfner, Theodor. Der Tierkult der alten Ägypter. Wien, 1913.
    Eg 879.15A — Spence, Lewis. Myths and legends of ancient Egypt. N.Y., 1915.
    Eg 879.15B — Spence, Lewis. Myths and legends of ancient Egypt. N.Y., 1915.
    Eg 879.15.4 — Knight, A.E. Amentet; account of gods, amulets of ancient Egyptians. London, 1915.
    Eg 879.16 — Allen, T.G. Horus in the pyramid texts. Diss. Chicago, 1916.
    Eg 879.17F — Junker, H. Die Onurislegende. Wien, 1917.
    Eg 879.17.5 — Frank-Kamenetskii, I.G. Pamiatniki egipetskoi religii v fivanskii period. Moskva, 1917- 2v.
    Eg 879.24 — Amenopë. The teaching of Amen-em-Apt. London, 1924.
    Eg 879.26 — Weynants-Ronday, M. (Mrs.). Les statues vivantes. Bruxelles, 1926.
    Eg 879.26.5 — Kees, Hermann. Totenglauben und Jenseitsvorstellungen der alten Ägypter. Leipzig, 1926.
    Eg 879.26.7 — Kees, Hermann. Totenglauben und Jenseitsvorstellungen der alten Ägypter. 2. Aufl. Berlin, 1956.
    Eg 879.29.5 — Lefebure, G. Inscriptions concernant les grands prêtres d'Amon. Thèse. v.1-2. Paris, 1929.
    Eg 879.30A — Spence, Lewis. The mysteries of Egypt. Philadelphia, 1930.
    Eg 879.30B — Spence, Lewis. The mysteries of Egypt. Philadelphia, 1930.
    Eg 879.30.5 — Cazemier, L.J. Oud-Egyptiese voorstellingen aangaande de ziel. Proefschrift. Wageningen, 1930.
    Eg 879.31 — Kevin, Robert O. Wisdom of Amen-em-Apt and its possible dependence upon Hebrew book of proverbs. Thesis. Philadelphia, 1931.
    Eg 879.31.5 — Gauthier, Henri. Les fêtes du dieu Min. Thèse. Le Caire, 1931. 2 pam.
    Eg 879.31.10 — Cooke, Harold P. Osiris. London, 1931.
    Eg 879.33A — Breasted, James Henry. The dawn of conscience. N.Y., 1933.
    Eg 879.33B — Breasted, James Henry. The dawn of conscience. N.Y., 1933.
    Eg 879.33.5A — Breasted, James Henry. The dawn of conscience. N.Y., 1934.
    Eg 879.33.5B — Breasted, James Henry. The dawn of conscience. N.Y., 1934.
    Eg 879.33.5C — Breasted, James Henry. The dawn of conscience. N.Y., 1934.
    Eg 879.33.6 — Breasted, James Henry. The dawn of conscience. N.Y., 1935.
    Eg 879.34 — Budge, Ernest Alfred Wallis. From fetish to God in ancient Egypt. London, 1934.
    Eg 879.35 — Gardiner, Alan H. The attitude of the ancient Egyptians to death and the dead. Cambridge, Eng., 1935.
    Eg 879.36 — Weill, R. Le champ des roseaux et le champ des offrandes dans la religion funéraire. Paris, 1936.
    Eg 879.36.5 — Schaedel, Herbert D. Die Listen des grossen Papyrus Harris. Glückstadt, 1936.
    Eg 879.37 — Badawi, Ahmod M. Der Gott Chnum. Inaug. Diss. Glückstadt, 1937.
    Eg 879.37.5 — Shorter, A.W. The Egyptian gods. London, 1937.
    Eg 879.38 — Visser, Cornelia E. Götter und Kulte im ptolemäischen Alexandrien. Thesis. Amsterdam, 1938.
    Eg 879.38.5 — Visser, Cornelia E. Götter und Kulte im ptolemäischen Alexandrien. Amsterdam, 1938.
    Eg 879.38.10 — Wainwright, G.A. The sky-religion in Egypt. Cambridge, Eng., 1938.
    Eg 879.39 — McGlinchey, J.M. The teaching of Amen-em-Apt. Washington, 1939.
    Eg 879.39.5 — Jacobsohn, Helmuth. Die dogmatische Stellung des Königs. Glückstadt, 1939.
    Eg 879.42 — Mercer, S.A.B. Horus, royal god of Egypt. Grafton, 1942.
    Eg 879.42.10 — Grdseloff, Bernhard. Les débuts du culte de Rechef en Égypte. Le Caire, 1942.
    Eg 879.44 — Vondier, Jacques. La religion égyptienne. Paris, 1944.
    Eg 879.46 — Jéquier, Gustave. Considérations sur les religions égyptiennes. Neuchâtel, 1946.
    Eg 879.48 — Garnot, J.S.F. La vie religieuse dans l'ancienne Égypte. 1. éd. Paris, 1948.
    Eg 879.48.5 — Frankfort, Henri. Ancient Egyptian religion. N.Y., 1961.
    Eg 879.49 — Junker, H. Pyramidenzeit. Einsiedeln, 1949.
    Eg 879.52 — Bonnet, H. Reallexikon der ägyptischen Religionsgeschichte. Berlin, 1952.
    Eg 879.52.5 — Roeder, G. Volksglaube in Pharaonenreich. Stuttgart, 1952.
    Eg 879.52.10 — Cerný, J. Ancient Egyptian religion. London, 1952.
    Eg 879.52.15F — Greven, L. Der Ka in Theologie und Königs Kult. Glückstadt, 1952.
    Eg 879.53.2 — Bell, H.I. Cults and creeds in Graeco-Roman Egypt. N.Y., 1953.
    Eg 879.53.5 — Spiegel, J. Das Werden der Altägyptischen Hochkultur. Heidelberg, 1953.
    Eg 879.54A — Morenz, S. Der Gatt auf der Blume. Ascona, 1954.

Classified Listing

Eg 870 - 879   Ancient Egyptian history - Religion and mythology (Table A) - cont.

Eg 879.54B	Morenz, S. Der Gatt auf der Blume. Ascona, 1954.
Eg 879.54.5	Bertram, Johannes. Die Urweisheit der alten Ägypter. Hamburg, 1954.
Eg 879.54.10	Sainte Fare Garnot, Jean. L'hommage aux dieux sous l'ancien empire egyptien. 1. éd. Paris, 1954.
Eg 879.55	Donadoni, S. Le religione dell'Egitto antico. Milano, 1955.
Eg 879.55.5	Cramer, Maria. Das altägyptische Lebenszeichen. 3. Aufl. Wiesbaden, 1955.
Eg 879.56	Kees, Hermann. Der Götterglaube im alten Ägypten. 2. Aufl. Berlin, 1956.
Eg 879.56.5	Bleeker, C.J. Die Geburt eines Gottes. Leiden, 1956.
Eg 879.56.10	Bonwick, James. Egyptian belief and modern thought. Indian Hills, 1956.
Eg 879.57	Mayassis, S. Mystéres et initiations de l'Egypte ancienne. Athènes, 1957.
Eg 879.57.5	Sauneron, Serge. Les prêtres de l'ancienne Égypte. Paris, 1957.
Eg 879.57.7	Sauneron, Serge. The priests of ancient Egypt. N.Y., 1960.
Eg 879.57.10	Uxkull, Woldemar. Die Einweihung im alten Ägypten. Büdingen-Gettenbach, 1957.
Eg 879.57.15	Bernard, J.L. L'Égypte et la genèse du surhomme. Paris, 1957.
Eg 879.58	Daumas, François. Les mammisis des temples égyptiens. Paris, 1958.
Eg 879.58.2F	Daumas, François. Les mammisis de Dendara. Le Caire, 1959.
Eg 879.59A	Clark, R.T. Myth and symbol in ancient Egypt. v.4. London, 1959.
Eg 879.59B	Clark, R.T. Myth and symbol in ancient Egypt. v.4. London, 1959.
Eg 879.59.5	Roeder, Günther. Die ägyptische Religion in Texten und Bildern. v.1-3. Zürich, 1959-
Eg 879.59.10	Gollob, Hedwig. Die Götter am Nil. Wien, 1959.
Eg 879.59.15	Andrzejewski, Tadeusz. Le papyrus mythologique de Te-hem-en-Mout. Warszawa, 1959.
Eg 879.60	Zandee, Jan. Death as an enemy. Leiden, 1960.
Eg 879.60.5	Doresse, Jean. Des hieroglyphes à la croix. Istanbul, 1960.
Eg 879.60.10	Griffiths, J.G. The conflict of Horus and Seth. Liverpool, 1960.
Eg 879.60.15	Posener, Georges. De la divinité du pharaon. Paris, 1960.
Eg 879.60.20	Lanozkowski, Guenter. Altägyptischer Prophetismus. Wiesbaden, 1960.
Eg 879.61	Rachewiltz, Boris de. I miti e i luoghi dell'antico Egitto. Milano, 1961.
Eg 879.62F	Brooklyn Institute of Arts and Sciences. Museum. Mss. (Papyrus 47.218.3). A Saite oracle papyrus from Thebes. Providence, R.I., 1962.
Eg 879.63F	Book of That Which is in the Nether World. Das Amduat. v.1-3. Wiesbaden, 1963. 2v.
Eg 879.63.5	Énel (pseud.). Les origines de la Genèse et l'enseignement des temples de l'ancienne Égypte. Paris, 1963.
Eg 879.63.10	Merkelbach, Reinhold. Isisfeste in griechisch-römischer Zeit; Daten und Riten. Meisenheim am Glan, 1963.
Eg 879.64	Bonneau, D. La crue du Nil. Paris, 1964.
Eg 879.64.5	Brunner, Hellmut. Die Geburt des Gottkonigs. Wiesbaden, 1964.
Eg 879.65	Pirenne, Jacques. La religion et la morale dans l'Égypte antique. Neuchâtel, 1965.
Eg 879.65.5	Daumas, François. Les dieux de l'Égypte. Paris, 1965.
Eg 879.65.10F	Chassinat, Emile G. Le temple de Dendara. v.6. Le Caire, 1965-
Eg 879.65.15	Altenmueller, Hartwig. Die Atropaia und die Götter Mittelägypten. v.1-2. München, 1965.
Eg 879.66F	Chassinat, Emile G. Le mystère d'Osiris au mois de Khoiak. Le Caire, 1966-68. 2v.
Eg 879.68	Lindsay, Jack. Men and gods on the Roman Nile. London, 1968.
Eg 879.68.5	Žabkar, Louis V. A study of the Ba concept in ancient Egyptian texts. Chicago, 1968.
Eg 879.68.10	Barta, Winfried. Aufbau und Bedeutung der altägyptischen Opferformel. Glückstadt, 1968.
Eg 879.69	Reymond, Eve A.E. The mythical origin of the Egyptian temple. N,Y., 1969.
Eg 879.69.5	Religions en Égypte hellenistique et romaine, colloque de Strasbourg, 16-18 mai 1967. Paris, 1969.
Eg 879.70.5	Guilmot, Max. Le message spirituel de l'Égypte ancienne. Paris, 1970.
Eg 879.70.10	Horstmann, Erwin. Beiträge zur Bewusstseinsgeschichte des alten Ägypten. Stuttgart, 1970.
Eg 879.70.15	George, Beate. Zu den altägyptischen Vorstellungen vom Schatten als Seele. Bonn, 1970.
Eg 879.71	Witt, Reginald Eldred. Isis in the Graeco-Roman world. Ithaca, N.Y., 1971.
Eg 879.71.5	Olsson, Albert. I faraos land-på faraos tid. Solna, 1971.
Eg 879.71.10	Thausing, Gertrud. Sein und Werden. Wien, 1971.
Eg 879.72	Derchain, Philippe. Hathor Quadrifons. Istanbul, 1972.
Eg 879.73	Hornung, Erik. Der Eine und die Vielen. Darmstadt, 1973.
Eg 879.73.5	Bleeker, Chaes. Hathor and Thoth. Leiden, 1973.

Eg 885   Ancient Egyptian history - Magic (By date, e.g. .960 for 1960)

Eg 885.899.2	Budge, Ernest Alfred Wallis. Egyptian magic. London, 1901.
Eg 885.899.4	Budge, Ernest Alfred Wallis. Egyptian magic. Evanston, 1958.
Eg 885.899.6	Budge, Ernest Alfred Wallis. Egyptian magic. N.Y., 1971.
Eg 885.925	Lexa, Frantisek. La magie dans l'Egypte antique. v.1-2, Atlas. Paris, 1925. 3v.
Eg 885.925.5	Obbink, H.W. De magische beteekenis van den naam inzonderheid in het oude Egypte. Amsterdam, 1925.
Eg 885.933A	Bell, H.I. Magical texts from a bilingual papyrus in the British museum. London, 1933.
Eg 885.933B	Bell, H.I. Magical texts from a bilingual papyrus in the British museum. London, 1933.
Eg 885.959	Piantanida, Danato. La chiave perduta. Milano, 1959.
Eg 885.967	Feucht-Putz, Erika. Die königlichen Pektorale; Motive, Sinngehalt und Zweck. Inaug. Diss. Bamberg, 1967.
VEg 885.969	Kákosy, László. Varázslás az ókori Egyiptomban. Budapest, 1969.
Eg 885.971F	Feucht-Putz, Erika. Pektorale nichtköniglicher Personen. Wiesbaden, 1971.

Eg 900 - 909   Ancient Egyptian history - Economic conditions - General works (Table A)

Eg 907.66	Armeilhon, H.P. Histoire du commerce et de la navigation des Égyptiens. Paris, 1766.
Eg 909.03	Hultsch, F. Die ptolemäischen Münz und Rechnungswerte. Leipzig, 1903.
Eg 909.10	Fitzler, Kurt. Steinbrüche und Bergwerke im ptolemäischen und römischen Agypten. Thesis. Leipzig, 1910.
Eg 909.10.1	Fitzler, Kurt. Steinbrüche und Bergwerke im ptolemäischen und römischen Agypten. Leipzig, 1910.
Eg 909.13.5	Reil, Theodor. Beiträge zur Kenntnis des Gewerbes im hellenistischen Agypten. Borna, 1913.
Eg 909.31	Kortenbeutel, H. Der ägyptische Süd und Osthandel in der Politik der Ptolemäer und römischen Kaiser. Inaug. Diss. Charlottenburg, 1931.
Eg 909.33	Dairanes, Serge. L'Égypte economique sous la XVIIIe dynastie pharaonique. Thèse. Paris, 1933.
Eg 909.35	Lewis, Naphtali. L'industrie du papyrus dans l'Égypte gréco-romaine. Thèse. Paris, 1934.
Eg 909.36.5	Dykmans, G.L. Histoire économique et social de l'ancienne Égypte. Paris, 1936-37. 3v.
Eg 909.38	Wallace, S. Le Roy. Census and poll-tax in Ptolemaic and Roman Egypt. Princeton, 1938.
Eg 909.39	Preaux, C. L'économie royale des Lagides. Bruxelles, 1939.
Eg 909.49	Johnson, A.C. Byzantine Egypt: economic studies. Princeton, 1949.
Eg 909.64	Braunert, Horst. Die Binnenwanderung. Bonn, 1964.
Eg 909.65	Wipszycka, Ewa. L'industrie textile dans l'Egypte romaine. Wrocław, 1965.
Eg 909.65.5	Fikhman, Itskhok. Egipet na rubezhe dvukh epokh. Moskva, 1965.

Eg 910 - 919   Ancient Egyptian history - Economic conditions - Agriculture (Table A)

Eg 919.22	Westermann, W.L. The "dryland" in Ptolemaic and Roman Egypt. n.p., 1922.
Eg 919.23	Hartmann, Fernande. L'agriculture dans l'ancienne Égypte. Thèse. Paris, 1923.
Eg 919.52	Hughes, George. Saite demotic land leases. Chicago, 1952.
Eg 919.60	Smiderkówna, Anna. La propriété foncière privée dans l'Égypte de Vespasien et technique agricole d'après. Wroclaw, 1960.
Eg 919.62	Savel'eva, T.N. Agrarnyi stroi Egipta. Moskva, 1962.
Eg 919.72	Pikus, Nikolai N. Tsanskie zemledel'tsy (nepossedstvennye proisvoditeli) i nemeslenniki v Egipte III v. do n.e. Moskva, 1972.
Eg 919.72.5	Berlev, Oleg D. Trudovoe naselenie Egipta v epokhn srednego tsarstva. Moskva, 1972.

Eg 920 - 929   Ancient Egyptian history - Economic conditions - Weights and measures (Table A)

Eg 928.59	Taylor, J. The great pyramid. London, 1859.
Eg 928.95	Revillout, Eugène. Mélanges sur la métrologie, l'économie politique et l'histoire de l'ancienne Égypte. Paris, 1895.

Eg 930 - 939   Ancient Egyptian history - Geography and description (Table A)

Eg 931.1	Pamphlet box. Egyptian geography.
Eg 938.57	Brugsch, H. Geographische Inschriften. v.1-3. Leipzig, 1857. 2v.
Eg 938.65	Rougé, J. de. Textes géographiques du temple d'Edfou. Paris, 1865.
Eg 938.85	Dawson, J.W. Egypt and Syria. London, 1885.
Eg 938.91	Rougé, J. de. Géographie ancienne de la Basse-Égypte. Paris, 1891.
Eg 938.93	Amélineau, Emile. La géographie de l'Égypte. Paris, 1893.
Eg 938.94.1	Dümichen, Johannes. Zur Geographie des alten Agypten. Wiesbaden, 1973.
Eg 939.42	Ball, J. Egypt in the classical geographers. Cairo, 1942.
Eg 939.57	Montet, Pierre. Géographie de l'Egypte ancienne. pt.1-2. Paris, 1957. 2v.
Eg 939.61	Kees, Hermann. Ancient Egypt. Chicago, 1961.

Eg 950 - 959   Ancient Egyptian history - Travels (Table A)

Eg 958.47	Wilkinson, G. Hand-book for travellers in Egypt. London, 1847.
Eg 958.66F	Chabas, F. Voyage d'un égyptien. Paris, 1866.
Eg 958.72	Ebers, G. Durch Gosen zum Sinai. Leipzig, 1872.
Eg 958.79	Bartlett, S.C. From Egypt to Palestine. N.Y., 1879.
Eg 959.60	Unamun. Puteshestvie Un-Amuna v Bibl; egipetskii ieraticheskii papirus no.120. Moskva, 1960.

Eg 971 - 996   Ancient Egyptian history - Local history, description, etc. (A-Z by place)

Eg 971.2F	Winlock, H.E. The temper of Ramesses I at Abydos. N.Y., 1937.
Eg 971.5	Kübler, B. Antinoupolis, aus dem alten Städteleben. Leipzig, 1914.
Eg 971.7	Lübbert, E. Alexandre unter Ptolemaeus, Philadelphus und Energetes. Kiel, 1880.
Eg 971.7.5	Leider, Erich. Der Handel von Alexandreia. Hamburg, 1933.
Eg 971.7.6	Leider, Erich. Der Handel von Alexandreia. Diss. Hamburg, 1934.
Eg 971.7.10	Davis, H.T. Alexandria, the golden city. Evanston, 1957. 2v.
Eg 971.7.15	Marlowe, John. The golden age of Alexandria: from its foundation by Alexander the Great in 1331 B.C. to its capture by the Arabs in 642 A.D. London, 1971.
Eg 971.7.20	Heuer, Kenneth. City of the stargazers. N.Y., 1972.
Eg 971.7.25	Fraser, Peter Marshall. Ptolemaic Alexandria. Oxford, 1972. 3v.
Eg 971.9	Gayet, A.J. Fantomes d'Antinoe. Paris, 1904.
Eg 971.9.5	Gayet, A.J. Antinoï et les sepultures de Thaïs et Serapion. Paris, 1902.
Eg 971.11F	Monneret de Villard, Ugo. La Necrapoli musulmana di Aswán. Le Caire, 1930.
Eg 971.15	Monneret de Villard, Ugo. Aksum. Roma, 1938.
Eg 971.15PF	United Arab Republic. Centre of Documentation and Studies on Ancient Egypt. Le petit temple d'Abou Simbel. Le Caire, 1968. 2v.
Eg 972.5	Knudtzon, E.J. Bakchiastexte und andere Papyri. Lund, 1946.
Eg 974.5	Fakhry, A. The bent pyramid of Dahshûr. Le Caire, 1954.
Eg 974.5.5F	Fakhry, A. The monuments of Sneferu at Dahshur. Cairo, 1959-61. 2v.

Classified Listing

Eg 971 - 996   Ancient Egyptian history - Local history, description, etc.
(A-Z by place) - cont.

Eg 974.6	Fischer, Henry George. Dendera in the third millennium B.C., down to the Theban domination of Upper Egypt. Locust Valley, N.Y., 1968.
Eg 978.5	Méautis, G. Hermoupolis-la-Grande. Lausanne, 1918.
Eg 981.2	Geremek, Hanna. Karanis; communsuté rurale. Wrocław, 1969.
Eg 981.5	Crawford, Dorothy. Kerkeosiris. Cambridge, Eng., 1971.
Eg 981.10	Siegler, Karl Georg. Kalabsha; Architektur und Baugeschichte des Tempels. Berlin, 1970.
Eg 983.5	Shinnie, Peter L. Meroe; a civilization of the Sudan. London, 1967.
Eg 983.10PF	Berlin. Universität. Institut für Ägyptologie. Musawwart es sufra. Humboldt-Universität zu Berlin. v.1, pt.2. Berlin, 1971.
Eg 983.15	Hofmann, Inge. Studien zum meroitischen Königtum. Bruxelles, 1971.
Eg 984.2	Farag, Nagib. The discovery of Neferuptah. Cairo, 1971.
Eg 985.5	MacLennan, Hugh. Oxyrhynchos. Diss. Princeton, 1935.
Eg 986.5A	Plaumann, G. Ptolemais in Oberägypten. Leipzig, 1910.
Eg 986.5B	Plaumann, G. Ptolemais in Oberägypten. Leipzig, 1910.
Eg 989.5	Mallet, D. Le culte de Neit à Saïs. Paris, 1888.
Eg 989.10F	Breccia, E. With King Fuad to the oasis of Ammon [Siwa]. Milano, 1929.
Eg 990.5F	Robichon, C. Le temple du scribe royal Amenhotep. pt.1. Le Caire, 1936.
Eg 990.7	Riefstahl, E. Thebes in the time of Amunhotep III. 1. ed. Norman, 1964.
Eg 990.10F	Beckerath, J. von. Tanis und Theben. Glückstadt, 1951.
Eg 990.16	Bataille, André. Les memnonia. Le Caire, 1952.
Eg 990.20PF	Seele, Keith. The tomb of Tjanefer at Thebes. Chicago, 1959.
Eg 990.21	Helck, Hans Wolfgang. Die Ritualdarstellungen des Ramesseums. [Thebes]. Wiesbaden, 1972-

Eg 1004 - 1009   Ancient Egyptian literature - General literary history -
General works (By date)

Eg 1008.83	Rouge, Jacques de. Littérature de l'ancienne Égypte. Paris, 1883.
Eg 1009.31A	Peet, Thomas Eric. Comparative study of the literature of Egypt, Palestine and Mesopotamia. London, 1931.
Eg 1009.31B	Peet, Thomas Eric. Comparative study of the literature of Egypt, Palestine and Mesopotamia. London, 1931.
Eg 1009.42	Drioton, Etienne. Le théâtre egyptien. Le Caire, 1942.
Eg 1009.48	Walle, Baudouin van de. La transmission des textes littéraires égyptiens. Bruxelles, 1948.
Eg 1009.56	Posener, Georges. Littérature et politique dans l'Égypte de la XII dynastie. Paris, 1956.
Eg 1009.62	Korostovtsev, M.A. Pistsy Drevnego Egipta. Moskva, 1962.
Eg 1009.66	Brunner, Hellmut. Grundzüge einer Geschichte der altägyptischen Literatur. Darmstadt, 1966.
Eg 1009.68	Donadoni, Sergio. La letteratura egizia. Firenze, 1968.
Eg 1009.69	Walle, Baudouin van de. L'humour dans la littérature et dans l'art de l'ancienne Égypte. Leiden, 1969.

Eg 1024 - 1029   Ancient Egyptian literature - General anthologies - General
collections (By date)

Eg 1028.97	Griffith, Francis L. Egyptian literature. N.Y., 1897.
Eg 1029.01F	Spiegelberg, W. Demotische Studien. Hefte 1-8 and plates 5-6. Leipzig, 1901- 10v.
Eg 1029.01.5FA	Berlin. Koniglichen Museen. Hieratische Papyrus. Leipzig, 1901- 5v.
Eg 1029.01.5FB	Berlin. Koniglichen Museen. Hieratische Papyrus. Leipzig, 1901- 5v.
Eg 1029.01.15	Egyptian literature. London, 1901.
Eg 1029.06PF	Dedekind, A. Photographische Reproduktionen der Inschriften. Wien, 1906.
Eg 1029.14	Budge, Ernest Alfred Wallis. The literature of the ancient Egyptians. London, 1914.
Eg 1029.21	Spiegelberg, W. Agyptische und andere Graffiti. Heidelberg, 1921.
Eg 1029.23A	Erman, Adolf. Die Literatur der Ägypter. Leipzig, 1923.
Eg 1029.23B	Erman, Adolf. Die Literatur der Ägypter. Leipzig, 1923.
Eg 1029.23.5	Erman, Adolf. The literature of the ancient Egyptians. London, 1927.
Eg 1029.25	Gaskell, G.A. Egyptian scriptures interpreted through the language of symbolism. London, 1925.
Eg 1029.32	Biblioteca aegyptiaca. Leiden. 6-8,1936-1938 2v.
X Cg Eg 1029.32	Biblioteca aegyptiaca. Leiden. 1-5,1932-1933
Eg 1029.38	Mayer, Josephine. Never to die; the Egyptians in their own words. N.Y., 1938.
Eg 1029.50F	Erichsen, W. Auswahl frühdemotischer Texte. Kopenhagen, 1950.
Eg 1029.57PF	Černý, Jaroslav. Hieratic ostraca. Oxford, 1957.
Eg 1029.58	Andrzejewski, Tad. Opowiadaniia egipskie. Warszawa, 1958.
Eg 1029.61	Riesterer, Peter P. Kostbarkeiten aus Agypten. Zürich, 1961.
Eg 1029.63	Kaplony, Peter. Die Inschriften der ägyptischen Frühzeit. Wiesbaden, 1963. 3v.
Eg 1029.63.1	Kaplony, Peter. Die Inschriften der ägyptischen Frühzeit. Supplement. Wiesbaden, 1964.
Eg 1029.63.5	Kaplony, Peter. Kleine Beiträge zu der Inschriften der ägyptischen Frühzeit. Wiesbaden, 1966.
Eg 1029.68	Kaster, Joseph. Wings of the falcon; Life and thought of ancient Egypt. N.Y., 1968.
Eg 1029.68.1	Kaster, Joseph. The literature and mythology of ancient Egypt. London, 1970.
Eg 1029.72	Simpson, William Kelly. The literature of ancient Egypt; an anthology of stories, instructions, and poetry. New Haven, 1972.
Eg 1029.73	Lichtheim, Miriam. Ancient Egyptian literature; a book of readings. Berkeley, 1973-

Eg 1030 - 1039   Ancient Egyptian literature - Special forms, etc. - Book of
the Dead (Table A)

Eg 1038.42	Book of the Dead. Das Todtenbuch der Ägypter. Leipzig, 1842.
Eg 1038.77F	Book of the Dead. Le papyrus funéraire de Soutimès. Paris, 1877.
Eg 1038.86	Book of the Dead. Das ägyptische Todtenbuch. Berlin, 1886. 3v.
Eg 1038.88F	Marucchi, Orazio. Il grande papiro egizio della Biblioteca Vaticana. Roma, 1888.
Eg 1038.95F	Book of the Dead. The book of the dead. London, 1895.
NEDL Eg 1038.98	Book of the Dead. The book of the dead. London, 1898. 3v.
Eg 1038.98.9	Adams, W.M. The book of the master. London, 1898.

Eg 1030 - 1039   Ancient Egyptian literature - Special forms, etc. - Book of
the Dead (Table A) - cont.

Eg 1038.99	Book of the Dead. The book of the dead. London, 1899.
Eg 1038.99.2	Book of the Dead. The book of the dead. 2. ed. London, 1969.
Eg 1039.04	Book of the Dead. The Egyptian book of the dead. London, 1904.
Eg 1039.07.2	Book of the Dead. Le livre des morts des anciens Égyptiens. 2. éd. Paris, 1907.
Eg 1039.10	Book of the Dead. Theban recension of the book of the dead. London, 1910. 3v.
Eg 1039.10.5	Budge, Ernest Alfred Wallis. A hieroglyphic vocabulary to the Theban recension of the book of the dead. London, 1911.
Eg 1039.13	Book of the Dead. The papyrus of Ani. London, 1913. 2v.
Eg 1039.13.2	Book of the Dead. The papyrus of Ani. N.Y., 1913. 3v.
Eg 1039.13.4	Book of the Dead. The book of the dead. New Hyde Park, N.Y., 1960.
Eg 1039.15F	Grapow, Hermann. Religiöse Urkunden. Heft 1-3. Leipzig, 1915.
Eg 1039.20	British Museum. Department of Egyptian and Assyrian Antiquities. The book of the dead. London, 1920.
Eg 1039.23A	Book of the Dead. The coming forth by day. Boston, 1923.
Eg 1039.23B	Book of the Dead. The coming forth by day. Boston, 1923.
Eg 1039.33	Adams, W.M. The book of the master of the hidden places. London, 1933.
Eg 1039.54	Book of the Dead. Livre des morts des anciens Égyptiens. Paris, 1954.
Eg 1039.54.5	Book of the Dead. Ägyptisches Totenbuch. München, 1955.
Eg 1039.55	Mayassis, S. Le livre des morts de l'Égypte ancienne est un livre d'initiation. Athènes, 1955.
Eg 1039.60F	Book of the Dead. The Egyptian book of the dead. Chicago, 1960.
Eg 1039.63	Champdor, Albert. Le livre des morts. Paris, 1963.

Eg 1042   Ancient Egyptian literature - Special forms, etc. - Pyramid and Coffin
texts (By date, e.g. .960 for 1960)

Eg 1042.908	Pyramid Texts. Die altägyptischen Pyramidentexte. v.1-4. Leipzig, 1908-22. 3v.
Eg 1042.923F	Pyramid Texts. Les textes des pyramides egyptiennes. v.1-2. Bruxelles, 1923-24.
Eg 1042.926F	Schott, Siegfried. Untersuchungen zur Schriftgeschichte der Pyramidentexte. Inaug. Diss. Heidelberg, 1926.
Eg 1042.935F	Pyramid Texts. Ubersetzung und Kommentar zu den altägyptischen Pyramidentexten. Glückstadt, 1935-1962. 6v.
Eg 1042.935.10F	Buck, Adriaan de. The Egyptian coffin texts. Chicago, 1935. 7v.
Eg 1042.935.20	Gundlach, Rolf. Lexikalisch-grammatische Liste zu Spruch 335a der altägyptischen Sargtexte LL/CT. Darmstadt, 1970. 2v.
Eg 1042.944	Goyon, G. Les inscriptions et graffiti des voyageurs sur la grande pyramide. Le Caire, 1944.
Eg 1042.946A	Coffin Texts (Egyptian). Textes des cercueils du Moyen Empire égyptien. Bruxelles, 1946.
Eg 1042.946B	Coffin Texts (Egyptian). Textes des cercueils du Moyen Empire égyptien. Bruxelles, 1946.
Eg 1042.950	Allen, Thomas G. Occurrences of pyramid texts. Chicago, 1950.
Eg 1042.952	Pyramid Texts. The pyramid texts in translation and commentary. 1. ed. N.Y., 1952. 4v.
Eg 1042.957PF	Davies, Norman de Garis. A corpus of inscribed Egyptian funerary cones. pt.1. Oxford, 1957.
Eg 1042.968F	Pyramid texts: the pyramid of Unas. Princeton, 1968.
Eg 1042.968.5	Helck, Hans Wolfgang. Die Ritualszenen auf der Umfassungsmauer Ramses' II. Wiesbaden, 1968.
Eg 1042.969	Pyramid Texts. The ancient Egyptian pyramid texts. Oxford, 1969.
Eg 1042.969.2	Pyramid Texts. The ancient Egyptian pyramid texts. Supplement of hieroglyphic texts. Oxford, 1969.
Eg 1042.970	Kuentz, Charles. La face sud du massif est du pylône de Ramse's II à Louxor. Le Caire, 1970.
Eg 1042.970.5	Grieshammer, Reinhard. Das Jenseitsgericht in der Sargtexten. Wiesbaden, 1970.
Eg 1042.970.10	Gundlach, Rolf. Lexikalisch-grammatische Liste zu Spruch 335a der altägyptischen Sargtexte LL/CT 335a. Darmstadt, 1970. 2v.
Eg 1042.971	Spiegel, Joachim. Das Auferstehungsritual der Unas-Pyramide. Wiesbaden, 1971.
Eg 1042.972	Altenmüller, Hartwig. Die Texte zum Begrabensritual in den Pyramiden des alten Reiches. Wiesbaden, 1972.
Eg 1042.972.5	Book of Two Ways. The ancient Egyptian book of two ways. Berkeley, 1972.
Eg 1042.973	Munro, Peter. Die spätägyptischen Totenstelen. v.1-2. Glückstadt, 1973.

Eg 1050 - 1059   Ancient Egyptian literature - Special forms, etc. -
Poetry - General works (Table A)

Eg 1058.77	Shaï-en-Sinsin. Le livre des respirations. Paris, 1877.
Eg 1058.85	Revillout, E. Un poeme satyrique. Paris, 1885.
F 1059.04	Vogelsang, F. Die Klagen des Bauern. Berlin, 1904.
Eg 1059.25	Sharpley, C.E. Anthology of ancient Egyptian poems. London, 1925.
Eg 1059.29	Hassan, S. Le poème dit de Pentaour et le rapport officiel. Le Caire, 1929.
Eg 1059.55	Aafjes, B. De blinde harpenaar. Amsterdam, 1955.
Eg 1059.59.5	Flora, Francesco. La poesia dell'Egitto e della Mesopotamia. Milano, 1959.

Eg 1060 - 1069   Ancient Egyptian literature - Special forms, etc. -
Poetry - Hymns and religious poetry (Table A)

Eg 1068.74	Hymne à Ammon-Ra. Paris, 1874.
Eg 1069.10	Dennis, J.T. The burden of Isis. London, 1910.
Eg 1069.30	Hassan, Sélim. Hymnes religieux du moyen empire. La Caire, 1928.
Eg 1069.39	Seele, K.C. The tomb of Čanefer at Thebes (no.158). Chicago, 1939.
Eg 1069.48F	Zandee, J. De hymnen aan Amon van papyrus Leiden I 350. Leiden, 1948.
Eg 1069.49	Murray, Margaret A. Egyptian religious poetry. London, 1949.
Eg 1069.58	British Museum. Department of Manuscripts. Mss. (Papyrus 10569). An ancient Egyptian book of hours. Oxford, 1958.
Eg 1069.64F	The litany of Re. N.Y., 1964.

Classified Listing

Eg 1070 - 1079   Ancient Egyptian literature - Special forms, etc. -
Poetry - Lyric poetry (Table A)

Eg 1078.99F	Müller, W.M. Die Liebespoisie der alten Ägypter. Leipzig, 1899.
Eg 1079.50	Schott, Siegfried. Altägyptische Liebeslieder. Zürich, 1950.
Eg 1079.55	Schott, Siegfried. Liebeslieder der Pharaonenzeit. Zürich, 1959.
Eg 1079.59	Hermann, Alfred. Altägyptische Liebesdichtung. Wiesbaden, 1959.
Eg 1079.62	Pound, Ezra. Love poems of ancient Egypt. Norfolk, Conn., 1962.
Eg 1079.72.1	McCoy, Raymond Aloysius. The golden goddess. Menomonie, 1972.

Eg 1090 - 1099   Ancient Egyptian literature - Special forms, etc. - Prose
literature - General works (Table A)

Eg 1098.81	Brugsch, H.K. Die neue Weltordnung nach Vernichtung. Berlin, 1881.
Eg 1099.44F	Brunner, Hellmut. Die Lehre des Cheti. Glückstadt, 1944.
Eg 1099.46	Janssen, Jozef. De traditionelle egyptische autobiografie. v.2. Leiden, 1946.
Eg 1099.46F	Janssen, Jozef. De traditionelle egyptische autobiografie. Leiden, 1946.
Eg 1099.53	Suys, Émile. Étude sur le Conte du Fellah Plaideur. Roma, 1933.
Eg 1099.58	Caminos, R.A. The chronicle of Prince Osorkon. Roma, 1958.
Eg 1099.61	Korostovtsev, M.A. Ieraticheskii papirus 127 iz sobraniia GMII im A.S. Pushkina. Moskva, 1961.

Eg 1100 - 1109   Ancient Egyptian literature - Special forms, etc. - Prose
literature - Romances and tales (Table A)

	Eg 1108.90	Papyrus d'Orbiney. The tale of the two brothers. [Egyptian fairy-tale]. n.p., 189-?
Htn	Eg 1108.98*	Papyrus d'Orbiney. The tale of the two brothers. Watchung, N.J., 1898.
	Eg 1109.00	Griffith, F.L. Stories of the high priests of Memphis. [Sethon-Khamuas]. v.1, Atlas. Oxford, 1900. 2v.
	Eg 1109.00.5	Papyrus d'Orbiney. Papyrus d'Orbiney. The hieroglyphic transcription. Watchung, N.J., 1900.
	Eg 1109.15	Turaev, B.A. Razskaz Egiptiianina Sinukheta. Moskva, 1915.
	Eg 1109.31	Budge, Ernest Alfred Wallis. Egyptian tales and romances, pagan, Christian and Muslim. London, 1931.
	Eg 1109.52PF	Sanehet. The Ashmolean ostracon of Sinuhe. London, 1952.
	Eg 1109.56F	Caminos, R.A. Literary fragments in the hieratic script. Oxford, 1956.
	Eg 1109.59.2	Brunner-Traut, Emma. Altägyptische Tiergeschichte und Fabel. 2. Aufl. Darmstadt, 1968.

Eg 1120 - 1129   Ancient Egyptian literature - Special forms, etc. - Prose
literature - Maxims (Table A)

Eg 1128.76F	Ani. L'égyptologie - maximes du scribe Ani. Paris, 1876.
Eg 1128.76.5	Ani. La sagesse d'Ani. Roma, 1935.
Eg 1128.87	Virey, P. Études sur le papyrus Prisse. Paris, 1887.
Eg 1128.87.8	"The oldest book in the world"...Papyrus Prisse. n.p., 1888.
Eg 1128.87.15PF	Papyrus Prisse. Le papyrus Prisse et ses variantes. Paris, 1911.
Eg 1129.55	Bissing, Friedrich W. von. Altägyptische Lebensweisheit. Zürich, 1955.
Eg 1129.56F	Ptah-Hetep. Les maximes de Ptahhotep. Prague, 1956.

Eg 1130 - 1139   Ancient Egyptian literature - Special forms, etc. - Prose
literature - Letters (Table A)

Eg 1139.67	Wente, Edward F. Late Ramesside letters. Chicago, 1967.

Eg 1150 - 1159   Ancient Egyptian literature - Special forms, etc. -
Medicine (Table A)

	Eg 1158.63	Brugsch, H. Notice raisonnée d'un traité médical datant du XIVme siècle. Leipzig, 1863.
Htn	Eg 1158.75F*	Ebers, G.M. Papyros Ebers...Arzeneimittel der alten Agypter. Leipzig, 1875. 2v.
	Eg 1158.78	Dutrieux, P.J. Egyptian ophthalmia. Cairo, 1878.
	Eg 1158.90.1	Papyrus Ebers. Papyros Ebers; das älteste Buch über Heilkunde. Berlin 1890. Berlin, 1973.
	Eg 1159.15	Weindler, Fritz. Geburts- und Wochenbettsdarstellungen auf altägyptischen Tempelreliefs. München, 1915.
	Eg 1159.28	Hurry, Jamieson Boyd. Imhotep. 2. ed. Oxford, 1928.
	Eg 1159.31F	Breasted, James Henry. The Edwin Smith surgical papyrus. Chicago, 1931. 2v.
	Eg 1159.37	Papyrus Ebers. The Papyrus Ebers. Copenhagen, 1957.
	Eg 1159.52	Leake, C.D. The old Egyptian medical papyri. Lawrence, 1952.
	Eg 1159.52.5F	Klasens, Adolf. A magical statue base. Leiden, 1952.
	Eg 1159.54	Grapow, H. Grundriss der Medizin der alten Ägypter. v.1-9. Berlin, 1954- 10v.
	Eg 1159.55	Riad, Naguib. La médecine au temps des pharaons. Paris, 1955.
	Eg 1159.56	Bitschai, J. A history of urology in Egypt. Cambridge, 1956.
	Eg 1159.58	Jonckheere, Frans. Les médecins de l'Égypte pharaonique. Bruxelles, 1958.
	Eg 1159.59	Steuer, Robert. Ancient Egyptian and Cnidian medicine. Berkeley, 1959.
	Eg 1159.66	Edwin Smith Surgical Papyrus. Ein medizinisches Lehrbuch aus dem alten Agypten! Wund- und Unfallchirurgie. Bern, 1966.

Eg 1170 - 1179   Ancient Egyptian literature - Special forms, etc. -
Sciences - Astronomy (Table A)

Eg 1179.30	Pogo, A. Astronomical ceiling decoration in the tomb of Senmut. Bruges, 1930.
Eg 1179.31	Pogo, A. Zum Problem der Identifikation der nördlichen Sternbilder der alter Ägypter. Bruges, 1931.
Eg 1179.32	Pogo, A. Calendars on coffin lids from Asyut. Bruges, 1932.
Eg 1179.34	Antoniadi, E.M. L'astronomie égyptienne. Paris, 1934.
Eg 1179.60F	Neugebauer, Otto. Egyptian astronomical texts. v.2-3, pt.1-2. Providence, 1960- 3v.

Eg 1180 - 1189   Ancient Egyptian literature - Special forms, etc. -
Sciences - Mathematics (Table A)

Eg 1180.5	Archibald, Raymond C. Bibliography of Egyptian mathematics. Supplement. Oberlin, 1927.
Eg 1188.77	Eisenlohr, August. Ein mathematisches Handbuch der alten Ägypter. Leipzig, 1877. 2v.
Eg 1188.96F	Spiegelberg, Wilhelm. Rechnungen aus der Zeit Setis I. v.1, Atlas. Strassburg, 1896. 2v.
Eg 1189.20F	Scharff, A. Ein Rechnungsbuch des königlichen Hofes aus der 13 Dynastie. Berlin, 192-.
Eg 1189.23F	Papyrus Rhind. The Rhind mathematical papyrus. London, 1923.
Eg 1189.23.5FA	Papyrus Rhind. The Rhind mathematical papyrus. British Museum, 10057 and 10058. Oberlin, 1927-29. 2v.
Eg 1189.23.5FB	Papyrus Rhind. The Rhind mathematical papyrus. British Museum, 10057 and 10058. Oberlin, 1927-29. 2v.
Eg 1189.27	Gillain, O. La science égyptienne; L'arithmetique au Moyen Empire. Bruxelles, 1927.
Eg 1189.29	Vogel, Kurt. Die Grundlagen der ägyptischen Arithmetik. Inaug. Diss. München, 1929.
Eg 1189.30	Vogel, Kurt. Die Algebra der Agypter des mittleren Reiches. Roma, 1930.
Eg 1189.72F	Parker, Richard Anthony. Demotic mathematical papyri. Providence, R.I., 1972.
Eg 1189.72.5	Gillings, Richard J. Mathematics in the time of the pharaohs. Cambridge, 1972.

Eg 1300 - 1309   Ancient Egyptian literature - Unclassified papyri (Table A)

	Eg 1300.5	Champollion-Figeae, Jacques J. Catalogo de' papiri egiziani della Biblioteca Vaticana e notizia piu estesa di uno d'essi. Roma, 1825.
	Eg 1300.10	British Museum. Department of Egyptian and Assyrian Antiquities. Catalogue of Egyptian religious papyri in the British Museum. London, 1938.
	Eg 1300.11F	British Museum. Department of Egyptian and Assyrian Antiquities. Catalogue of demotic papyri in the British Museum. v.1-2. London, 1939-
	Eg 1307.85F	Mingarelli, Giovanni L. Aegyptiorum codicum reliquae. Bononiae, 1785.
	Eg 1307.85.2F	Mingarelli, Giovanni L. Aegyptiorum codicum reliquae. Bononiae, 1785.
	Eg 1308.85F	Revillout, Eugène. Corpus papyrorum Egyptii. v.1-3. Parisiis, 1885-1902.
	Eg 1308.91	Marucchi, Orazio. Monumenta papyracea. Romae, 1891.
	Eg 1308.98	Griffith, F.L. Hieratic papyri. London, 1898. 2v.
	Eg 1308.99	Newberry, R.E. The Amherst papyri. London, 1899.
	Eg 1308.99.5	Erman, Adolf. Aus den Papyrus der Königlichen Museen. Berlin, 1899.
	Eg 1309.07	Spiegelberg, W. Der Papyrus Libbey. Strassburg, 1907.
	Eg 1309.07.5	Staerk, Willy. Die jüische-arameischen Papyri von Assuan. Bonn, 1907.
	Eg 1309.09	Spiegelberg, W. Die demotischen Papyrus. Bruxelles, 1909.
	Eg 1309.09.5F	Admonitions of an Egyptian Sage. The admonitions of an Egyptian sage. Leipzig, 1909.
	Eg 1309.11	Gardiner, A.H. Egyptian hieratic texts. Leipzig, 1911-
	Eg 1309.20PF	Peet, T. Eric. The Mayer papyri A and B. London, 1920.
	Eg 1309.21F	Sottas, Henri. Papyrus démotiques de Lille. Paris, 1921.
	Eg 1309.25	Baikie, James. Egyptian papyri and papyrus-hunting. N.Y., 1925?
	Eg 1309.26F	Papyrus Insinger. Papyrus Insinger. v.1-2. Paris, 1926.
	Eg 1309.27F	Turaev, B.A. Papyrus Prachov. Leningrad, 1927.
	Eg 1309.28F	Botti, Giuseppe. Il giornale della necropoli di Tebe. Torino, 1928.
	Eg 1309.31PFA	Gardiner, A.H. The library of A. Chester Beatty. London, 1931.
	Eg 1309.31PFB	Gardiner, A.H. The library of A. Chester Beatty. London, 1931.
	Eg 1309.31.5F	Otto, Walter. Papyri der Universität München. München. 1,1931
	Eg 1309.32	Gardiner, A.H. The Astarte papyrus. London, 1932.
	Eg 1309.34F	Thompson, H. A family archive from Siut from papyri in the British Museum. Oxford, 1934. 2v.
	Eg 1309.38.5	Nims, C.F. Notes on University of Michigan demotic papyri from Rhila. Chicago, 1938.
Htn	Eg 1309.39PF*	Papyrus Leopold II. Le papyrus Leopold II. N.Y., 1939.
	Eg 1309.40F	Analecta aegyptiaca, consilio Instituti Aegyptologici Hafnaensis edita. Kopenhagen. 1-6 2v.
	Eg 1309.41F	Botti, Giuseppe. Testi demotici. Firenze, 1941.
	Eg 1309.41.5F	The Wilbour papyrus. v.2-4. London, 1941-52. 3v.
	Eg 1309.41.5PF	The Wilbour papyrus. London, 1941.
	Eg 1309.54	Caminos, R.A. Late-Egyptian miscellanies. London, 1954.
	Eg 1309.55F	Gardiner, A.H. The Ramesseum papyri. Oxford, 1955.
	Eg 1309.56F	Barns, J.W. Five Ramesseum papyri. Oxford, 1956.
	Eg 1309.59PF	Book of the kings of Egypt. Oxford, 1959.
	Eg 1309.59.5F	Vienna. National-Bibliothek. Papyrussammlung. A Vienna demotic papyrus on eclipse- and lunar-omina. Providence, 1959.
	Eg 1309.60F	Otto, Eberhard. Das ägyptische Mundöffnungsritual. Wiesbaden, 1960. 2v.
	Eg 1309.62F	Vandier, Jacques. Le papyrus Jumilhac. Paris, 1962.
	Eg 1309.63PF	Papyrus Reimer I. Papyrus Reimer I. Boston, 1963.
	Eg 1309.64.5F	Kaplony-Heckel, Ursula. Die demotischen Gebelen-Urkunden der Heidelberger Papyrus-Sammlung. Heidelberg, 1964.

AHP 11 - 36   Ancient history periodicals and society publications (A-Z)

AHP 11.5F	Archiv für Keilschriftforschung. Berlin. 1,1923+ 13v.
AHP 11.5.10	Archiv für Keilschriftforschung. Beiband. Berlin. 1,1933+ 10v.
AHP 11.6	Antike und Christentum. Münster. 1-7,1929-1942
AHP 11.6.10	Antike und Christentum. Ergänzungsband. Münster. 1,1939
AHP 11.7	Antique review. Bengal. 1-3,1931-1933
AHP 11.8	Chicago. University. Oriental Institute. Assyriological studies. Chicago. 1-11,1935-1939 5v.
AHP 11.9	Anales de historia antigua y medieval. Buenos Aires. 1948+ 5v.
AHP 11.10	Antike Welt; Zeitschrift für Archäologie und Urgeschichte. Zürich. 1,1970+
AHP 11.11	Ancient society. Louvain. 1,1970+
AHP 11.13	Ancient society: resources for teachers. North Ryde, Australia. 1,1971+
AHP 12.3	Babyloniaca. Paris. 1-17,1906-1937 10v.
AHP 12.5	Beiträge zur Assyriologie. Leipzig. 1-10,1889-1927 11v.
AHP 12.10	Beiträge zur Altertumskunde. Berlin.
AHP 12.12	Britannica. London. 1,1970+ 3v.
AHP 13.1	Catania. Universita. Instituto di Storia del Diritto Romano. Annuario. Catania. 13-14,1914-1915

Classified Listing

AHP 11 - 36   Ancient history periodicals and society publications (A-Z) - cont.

AHP 13.5	Columbia University. Ancient Near Eastern Society. Journal. N.Y. 1,1969+ 3v.
AHP 13.7	Chiron. München. 1,1971+ 4v.
AHP 13.8	Cahiers des études anciennes. Montréal. 1,1972+
AHP 14.5F	Deutsche Forschungsgemeinschaft. Ausgraben der deutschen Froschungsgemeinschaft in Uruk-Warka. Leipzig. 1,1936+ 6v.
AHP 14.6F	Documenta et Monumenta orientis antiqui. Leiden. 3,1948+ 11v.
AHP 14.7	Deutsche Beiträge zur Altertumswissenschaft. Baden-Baden. 1,1951+ 5v.
AHP 14.8	Dacoromania. Freiburg. 1,1973+
AHP 15.9F	Atlas der Urgeschichte. Hamburg. 1,1951+
AHP 15.9.2F	Atlas der Urgeschichte. Beiheft. Hamburg. 1,1953+ 7v.
AHP 17.1	Gymnasial-Bibliothek. Gütersloh. 1-58,1892-1920 4v.
AHP 18.3	Historia. Zeitschrift für alte Geschichte. Baden-Baden. 1,1950+ 25v.
AHP 18.5	Hermeneus, Maandblad voor de antieke cultuur. Zwolle. 1,1928+ 29v.
AHP 19.1	Iraq. London. 1,1934+ 16v.
AHP 19.1.2	Iraq. Index, v.1-30. London, 1970.
AHP 20.1	Janus. Wien. 1-2,1920-1921
AHP 20.2	Journal of cuneiform studies. New Haven. 1,1947+ 10v.
AHP 20.4	Jahrbuch für Antike und Christentum. Münster. 1,1958+ 13v.
AHP 20.5	Jahrbuch für Antike und Christentum. Ergänzungsband. Münster. 1,1964+ 2v.
AHP 21.1	Klio, beiträge zur alten Geschichte. Leipzig. 1,1902+ 42v.
AHP 21.2	Klio, beiträge zur alten Geschichte. Beihefte. Leipzig. 1-49,1903-1944 20v.
AHP 21.5	Kokalos, studi publicati dall Istituto di Storia Antica dell Universita di Palermo. Palermo. 3,1957+ 10v.
AHP 21.7	Kokalos. Supplement I. Palermo. 2v.
AHP 22.3	Lebendiges Altertum. Berlin. 1,1963+ 3v.
AHP 23.4	Magyar keleti Társaság Kiadvanyai. Budapest. 5,1945+
AHP 23.10	Meander, Miestiecnik posw. kulturze świata starózyta. Warszawa. 3,1948+ 25v.
AHP 23.12	Milan. Universita Cattolica del Sacro Cuore. Istituto di Filologia Classica. Sezione di Storia Antica. Contributi. Milano. 1,1963+
AHP 23.14	Myers memorial lecture. Oxford. 2v.
AHP 24.15	Neue deutsche Forschungen. Abteilungen alte Geschichte. Berlin. 1-7,1935-1939 8v.
AHP 24.16	Nortsiia. Voronezh. 1,1971+
AHP 25.3	Oriens antiquus. Roma. 1,1962+ 10v.
AHP 25.4	Oriens antiquus. Collectio. Roma. 1,1962+ 9v.
AHP 26.5	Pontos, revue internationale des études pontiques. Athenes.
AHP 27.5	Quaderni dell'impero; La scienza e la tecnica di tempi di Roma imperiale. Roma. 10-20 2v.
AHP 28.2	Revue d'assyriologie. Paris. 1,1884+ 31v.
AHP 28.3	Rivista di storia antica e scienze affini. Messina. 1-13 13v.
AHP 28.4	Rivista storica dell'antichità. Bologna. 1,1971+
AHP 28.5	Revue des études semitiques et babyloniaca. Paris. 1934-1945 3v.
AHP 28.6	Religion und Kultur der alten Arier. Frankfurt a.M. 1,1935 2v.
AHP 28.8	Roma, guida allo studio della civilta romana. Roma.
AHP 28.11	Romanitas. Rio de Janeiro. 1-5 5v.
AHP 29.5	Schriften zur Geschichte und Kultur der Antike. Berlin. 1,1970+ 3v.
AHP 29.10	Sources and monographs. Monographs in history: ancient Near East. Los Angeles. 1,1974+
AHP 29.51	McDermott, William C. Readings in the history of the Ancient World. N.Y., 1951.
AHP 30.5	Talanta; proceedings of the Dutch Archaeological and Historical Society. Groningen. 1,1969+
AHP 30.6	Teiresias. Montreal. 1,1971+
AHP 30.7	Teiresias. Supplement. Montreal. 1,1972+
AHP 30.8	Thracia. Serdicae. 1,1972+
AHP 31.3	Ugarit-Forschungen. Neukirchen. 1,1969+ 5v.
AHP 31.4	Untersuchungen zur römischen Geschichte. Frankfurt a.M. 1,1961+ 4v.
AHP 31.5	Untersuchungen zur Assyriologie und vorderasiatischen Archäologie. Berlin. 1,1960+ 5v.
AHP 31.6	Übersetzungen ausländischer Arbeiten zur antiken Sklaverei. Wiesbaden. 1,1966+ 4v.
AHP 32.1	Vestinik drevnei istorii. Moskva. 1,1937+ 51v.
AHP 34.1	Dissertationes bernenses. Historian orbis antiqui. Ser.1. Bern. 1950-1959 9v.
AHP 34.2	Dissertationes Bernenses. Historian orbis antiqui. Ser.2. Bern. 1952
AHP 36.1	Zeitschrift für Keilschriftforschung. Leipzig. 1-2,1884-1885
AHP 36.2	Zeitschrift für Assyriologie. Leipzig. 1886+ 31v.
AHP 36.3	Zeitschrift für die alttestamentliche Wissenschaft. Giessen. 1881+ 58v.
AHP 36.3.3	Zeitschrift für die alttestamentliche Wissenschaft. Register, Bd. 1-25. Giessen, 1910.
AHP 36.3.4	Zeitschrift für die alttestamentliche Wissenschaft. Register, 26-50 (1906-1932). Berlin, 1970.
AHP 36.3.5	Zeitschrift für die alttestamentliche Wissenschaft. Beihefte. Giessen. 1,1896+ 75v.

EgP 1 - 150   Egyptology periodicals - General periodicals (150 scheme, A-Z)

EgP 3.10	Aegyptus, rivista italiana di egittologia e di papirologia. Milano. 1,1921+ 23v.
EgP 6.5	American Research Center in Egypt. Journal. Boston. 1,1962+ 2v.
EgP 7.5	Ancient Egypt. London. 1914-1935 6v.
EgP 9.5	Annuaire de l'égyptologie. Le Caire. 1971+
EgP 22.3PF	British Museum. Department of Egyptian Antiquities. Hieratic papyri in the British Museum. London. 1,1935+ 7v.
EgP 27.2	Chronique d'Egypte. Bruxelles. 4-11,1928-1936 4v.
EgP 39.41	Dubois-Richard, P. Essai sur les gouvernements de l'Egypte. Le Caire, 1941.
EgP 40.5	Egyptian Society of Historical Studies, Gezireh, Cairo. Proceedings. Cairo.
EgP 41.5	Egyptian religion. N.Y., 1-4,1933-1936 3v.
EgP 43.9	Enchoria. Wiesbaden. 1,1971+
EgP 60.5	Göttinger Orientforschungen. Reihe IV: Ägypten. Wiesbaden. 1,1973+

EgP 1 - 150   Egyptology periodicals - General periodicals (150 scheme, A-Z) - cont.

EgP 66.5	International Association of Egyptologists. Annual Egyptological bibliography. Leiden. 1947+ 13v.
EgP 66.6A	International Association of Egyptologists. Annual Egyptological bibliography. Indexes, 1947-56. Leiden, 1960.
EgP 66.6B	International Association of Egyptologists. Annual Egyptological bibliography. Indexes, 1947-56. Leiden, 1960.
EgP 79.2	Kemi, revue de philologie et d'archeologie. Paris. 1,1928+ 5v.
EgP 83.25	Leipziger ägyptologische Studien. Glueckstadt. 1-8,1935-1937
EgP 87.6	Manchester Egyptian and Oriental Society. Journal. Manchester. 1912-1938 4v.
EgP 89.5F	Mizraim. N.Y. 1-3,1933-1936
EgP 93.5	Münchner ägyptologische Studien. Berlin. 1+ 13v.
EgP 111.5	Probleme der Aegyptologie. Leiden. 1,1953+ 5v.
EgP 117.3	Recueil de travaux...egyptiennes. Paris. 1-40 25v.
EgP 117.3.5	Recueil de travaux...egyptiennes. Index, v. XVII-XXXII. Paris, 1911.
EgP 120.1	Revue egyptologique. Paris. 1-9,1880-1924 5v.
EgP 120.3	Revue de l'Egypte ancienne. Paris. 1-3,1927-1931 3v.
EgP 120.4	Revue d'Egyptologie. Paris. 1,1933+ 8v.
EgP 133.15F	Société fouadier de papyrologie. Publications. Textes et documents. Caire. 1-6,1931-1945 3v.
EgP 133.15	Société fouadier de papyrologie. Publications. Textes et documents. Caire. 7-9,1947-1949
EgP 137.50	Syro-Egyptian Society of London. Original papers read before. London, 1845.
EgP 142.2	Tübinger ägyptologische Beiträge. Bonn. 1,1973+
EgP 143.2	Université de Lille III. Institut de papyrologie et d'égyptologie. Cahier de recherches. Lille. 1,1973+ 2v.
EgP 149.5	Zeitschrift für ägyptische Altertumskunde. Leipzig. 1,1863+ 43v.
EgP 149.5.2	Zeitschrift für ägyptische Altertumskunde. Index, 1863-1943. Ösnabrück, 1970.

ANCIENT HISTORY

CHRONOLOGICAL LISTING

No date

	AH 7298.71A	À Beckett, G.A. Comic history of Rome. London, n.d.
	AH 4881.5	Amzalak, Moses B. Historia das doutrinas económicas da antiga Grécia. n.p., n.d. 3 pam.
	AH 5765.5	Andreadès, A.M. He demosia oikonomia tōn Spartiatōn. Athēnai, n.d.
	AH 7108.90	Bachofen, J.J. Die Grundlagen...Reichs. n.p., n.d.
	AH 7797.50	Bel, C.A. De avitis Hungarorum sedibus. n.p., n.d.
	AH 7058.72	Belot, Émile. De tribunis plebis. n.p., n.d.
	AH 2147.2.5	Bergmann, R. Asiae Romanorum provinciae civitatibus liberis. Berolini, n.d.
	AH 3155.1	Bollenrücher, J. Gebete und Hymnen an Nergal. Leipzig, n.d. 6 pam.
	AH 3911.5	Bormann, E. De Syriae provinciae romanae partibus capita Nonnulla. Berolini, n.d.
	AH 3074.5F	British Museum. Photograph of Assyrian tablet. London, n.d.
	AH 3002.25.6F	British Museum. Department of Egyptian and Assyrian Antiquities. Cuneiform texts from Babylonian tablets. Index to registration numbers of texts, pt.1-25. n.p., n.d.
	Eg 39.12	Cohen, D. De magistratibus Aegyptiis externas Lagidarum regni provincias administrantibus. 's Gravenhage, n.d.
	AH 7653.15	Evans, J. Attempt to account for infidelity of Edward Gibbon. London, n.d.
Htn	AH 7035.38.3*	Fiocco, A.D. L. Fenestellae, de magistratibus, sacerdotisq. Basileae, n.d.
Htn	AH 7035.38.6*	Fiocco, A.D. L. Fenestellae, de magistratibus, sacerdotisq. Venetiis, n.d.
Htn	AH 7055.10*	Fiocco, A.D. L. Fenestellae, de Romanorum magistratibus. n.p., n.d.
Htn	AH 7055.10.4*	Fiocco, A.D. L. Fenestellae, de Romanorum magistratibus. n.p., n.d.
	AH 7118.3	Giraud, Charles. Dissertation sur la gentilité romaine. n.p., n.d.
	AH 2358.5	Haerne, D. de. Les Belges en Asie-Mineure. Louvain, n.d.
	AH 7207.15	Ihne, W. Über die Patres Conscripti. n.p., n.d.
	AH 8549.3	La Saussaye, L. de. Dissertation sur le lieu de l'assemblée des druides. n.p., n.d.
Htn	AH 7406.36*	Malvezzi, V. Princeps, eiusque arcana. n.p., n.d. 2 pam.
	AH 3980.7	Manual to accompany the pictorial view of ancient Jerusalem and its vicinity. n.p., n.d.
Htn	AH 3664.10*	Meiners, Christoph. Commentatio de...religionis Persarum. n.p., n.d.
	AH 7278.54.5	Mommsen, T. Inhalts-Verzeichniss. Römische Geschichte. n.p., n.d.
	AH 4845.21	Muller, E. Einleitung zu einer Darstellung der nationalen Ethik. n.p., n.d.
	AH 7478.65.5F	Napoléon III, emperor of the French. History of Julius Caesar. Atlas. London, n.d.
	AH 7769.15	Olivetti, Alberto. Sulle stragi di Costantinopoli succedute alla morte di Costantino il Grande. n.p., n.d.
	AH 3149.3	Oppert, J. Chronologie des Assyriens et des Babyloniens. Paris, n.d.
	Eg 758.79	Peabody, F.G. Christianity in Egypt. n.p., n.d.
Htn	Eg 708.58.5*	Pennsylvania. University. Philomathean Society. Report of the committee. Manuscript. n.p., n.d.
	AH 4215.5	Ploeg, G.L.J. De veterum Graecorum. Groningae, n.d. 3 pam.
	AH 2807.7	Ramsay, W.M. Early historical relations between Phrygia and Cappadocia. n.p., n.d.
	AH 7162.33	Rivier, A. De descrimine quod inter regulam Cotonianem. Berolini, n.d.
	Eg 819.12.3	Röder, G. Aus dem Leben vornehmer Ägypter. Leipzig, n.d.
NEDL	AH 7278.85.4	Steele, J.D. Brief history of Rome. N.Y., n.d.
	AH 7058.72.5	Stobbe, H.F. Zum Capitel von den Consules Suffecti unter den Kaisern. n.p., n.d.
	AH 4299.10.3	Syllogos pros. Eikones ek tēs archaias. Athēnai, n.d.
	AH 4558.99.5	Wheeler, B.I. Alexander the Great. n.p., n.d.

1480-1489

Htn	AH 7203.2*	Institutionis imperiales Justiniani. Venetiis, 1483.

1500-1509

	AH 8666.3	Victor, Pubblius (pseud.). De regionibus urbis Romae. 1. ed. Romae? 1500.
Htn	AH 7445.02*	Acciajuoli, D. Hannibalis atque Scipionis...ducum historie eleganti dulcique stilo coscriptac. Swollensi, 1502.
Htn	AH 846.4*	Grapaldi, F.M. De partibus Aedium dictionari. Argentinae, 1508.

1510-1519

Htn	AH 7203.4.6*	Corpus juris civilis. Digesta. Digestum vetus. Colophon, 1513.
Htn	AH 7655.15*	Leto, G.P. Romanae historiae compendium. Argentorati, 1515.
Htn	AH 846.5*	Grapaldi, F.M. De partibus Aedium. Venetiis, 1517.
Htn	AH 815.16.3F*	Ricchieri, Lodovico. Digini lectionum antiquarum libri XVI. Basileae, 1517.

1520-1529

Htn	AH 7815.21*	Laeti, Pomponii. Opera varia - quorum catalogum. Moguntiae, 1521.
Htn	AH 7105.22.3*	Budé, G. Libri V de asse et partibus eius. Venetiis, 1522.
Htn	AH 7105.22*	Budé, G. Libri V de asse et partibus eius. Venice, 1522.
Htn	AH 7495.26*	Hüttich, J. Romische Keyser abcontra Vegt. Strassburg, 1526.
Htn	AH 7035.29*	Fiocco, A.D. L. Fenestellae, de magistratibus, sacerdotisq. Lutetiae, 1529.

1530-1539

Htn	AH 7815.31F*	Biondo, Flavio. De Roma triumphante libri deceon. Basileae, 1531.
Htn	AH 925.32*	Senali, R. De liquidorum leguminumque. Parisiis, 1532.
Htn	AH 925.33*	Georgii agricolae medici libri. Parisiis, 1533. 3 pam.
Htn	AH 846.6*	Grapaldi, F.M. De partibus Aedium lexicon. Basil, 1533.
Htn	AH 7203.125*	Budé, G. Annotationes in quatuor et viginti Pandectarum libros. Pt.1. Basiliae, 1534.
Htn	AH 7495.34*	Hüttich, J. Imperatorum et Caesarum vitae. Argentorati, 1534.

1530-1539 - cont.

Htn	AH 7205.5*	Theophilus Antecessor. Institutiones iuris civilis. Paris, 1534.
Htn	AH 7852.8*	Baïf, L. De vasculis libellus. Paris, 1535.
Htn	AH 4805.36*	Gaze Thessalo. Liber de Mensibus Atticis. Basileae, 1536.
Htn	AH 255.37*	Baif, Lazare de. De re navali libellus. Lugdunum Batavorum, 1537.
Htn	AH 7035.38*	Fiocco, A.D. L. Fenestellae, de magistratibus, sacerdotisq. Basileae, 1538.
Htn	AH 275.39F*	Freculphus. Chronicorum. Cologne, 1539.

1540-1549

Htn	AH 255.40*	Geraldi, L.G. De re nautica libellus. Basiliae, 1540.
Htn	AH 8957.10*	Castiglione, B. Gallorum Insubrum antiquae sedes. Mediolani, 1541.
Htn	AH 7203.4.7*	Corpus juris civilis. Justiniani Leges de re rustica. Lobanii, 1542.
Htn	AH 7035.42*	Fiocco, A.D. L. Fenestellae, de magistrattibus, sacerdotisq. Parisiis, 1542. 4 pam.
Htn	AH 815.16.9F*	Ricchieri, Lodovico. Rhodigini lectionum antiquarum...XXX. Basileae, 1542.
Htn	AH 4135.43*	Postel, G.F. Libro de magistrati de gli Atheniesi. Venetia, 1543.
Htn	AH 7655.44*	Biondo, F. Historie da la declinatione. Venetia, 1544. 2v.
Htn	AH 7445.44*	Cope, Anthony. The historie of two the moste noble capitaines. Londini, 1544.
Htn	AH 805.45F*	Funck, J. Chronologia. Norimbergae, 1545.
Htn	AH 4935.45F*	Gerbelius, N. Descriptio Graeciae. Basiliae, 1545.
Htn	AH 7203.4.7.5*	Baudoin, François. Breves commentarii, in praecipuas Justiniani imp. Novellas. Ludguni, 1548.
Htn	AH 7135.48*	Budé, G. Forensia. Lutetiae, 1548. 2 pam.
Htn	AH 7445.48*	Cope, Anthony. Historie of two the moste noble capitaines...Anniball...Scipio. Londini, 1548.
Htn	AH 255.37.5*	Baif, Lazare de. Annotationis in l. ii. Lutetiae, 1549.
	AH 4850.14	Fendius, M. Oratio de Appellationibus panum. Vitebergae, 1549.
Htn	AH 7035.49*	Fiocco, A.D. L. Fenestellae, de magistratibus, sacerdotisq. Lutetiae, 1549.

1550-1559

Htn	AH 405.50*	Nanni, Giovanni. Antichita de beroso sacredote caldeo. Ventiae, 1550.
Htn	AH 7055.10.2*	Fiocco, A.D. L. Fenestellae, de Romanorum magistratibus. Lugduni, 1551.
Htn	AH 8907.7*	Postell, G. De Etruriae regionis. Florentiae, 1551.
Htn	AH 848.13*	Baif, L. de. De revestaria. Lutetiae, 1553.
Htn	AH 861.5*	Belon, P. De medicato funere. Parisiis, 1553.
Htn	AH 295.53*	Postel, G. De originibus, seu De varia...historia. Basiliae, 1553.
Htn	AH 7105.22.5*	Budé, G. Extrait ou abregé du Livre de assé de feu mons. Lyon, 1554.
Htn	AH 925.55*	Neander, M. Eynopsis. Basileae, 1555.
Htn	AH 8548.1.100*	Picard, Jean. De prisca Celtopaedia. Parisiis, 1556.
Htn	AH 7805.57.2F*	Panvinio, Onafrio. Fasti et triumphi. Venetiis, 1557.
Htn	AH 4815.57*	Sardi, Alessandro. De moribus et ritibus gentium. Venetiis, 1557.
	AH 7203.4.8F	Corpus juris civilis. Leges Justiniani. Parisiis, 1559. 5v.
Htn	AH 7235.59*	Du Choul, G. Discorso...sopra la castrametatione. n.p., 1559. 2 pam.
	AH 7203.13F	Favre, A. Rationalias in pandectas. Lugduni, 1559. 4v.

1560-1569

Htn	AH 7203.4.9*	Corpus juris civilis. Institutiones. Institutionum D. Justiniani. Parisiis, 1560.
Htn	AH 815.16.11*	Ricchieri, Lodovico. Lectionum antiquarum libri XXX. Ludguni, 1560. 3v.
Htn	AH 7485.61.10F*	Cuspinianus, J. De Caesaribus. Basileae, 1561?
Htn	AH 135.61*	Eustathius Antecessor. De varia...in jure civile observatione. Basileae, 1561.
Htn	AH 7485.61F*	Mexia, Pedro. Historia imperial y Cesarea. Anvers, 1561.
Htn	AH 8513.11*	La Ramée, P. de. Liber de moribus veterum Gallorum. Parisiis, 1562.
	AH 866.12	Thilo, M. Isaac. Dissertatio physico-historica de succino borussorum. Lipsiae, 1563.
Htn	AH 295.64*	Porcacchi, T. Il primo volume delle cagioni delle guerre antiche. Vinegia, 1564.
Htn	AH 7135.68*	Sigonio, C. De antiquo iure provinciarum. Venetiis, 1568.
Htn	AH 7135.69*	Manuzio, P. Antiquitatem romanarum. Venetiis, 1569.
Htn	AH 833.1*	Mercuriale, G. Artis gymnasticae. Venetijs, 1569.

1570-1579

Htn	AH 7203.5*	Corpus juris civilis. Codex. Codicis Justiniani. Lugduni, 1571.
Htn	AH 7295.72*	Serdonati, Francesco. De' fatti d'arme de' Romani. Venetia, 1572.
	AH 7203.6F	Baudoin, François. Institutiones. Ingolstadt, 1573.
Htn	AH 7206.1*	Bonefidius, E. Tog A'natoli. Geneva, 1573.
Htn	AH 833.4*	Mercuriale, G. Hieronymi...de arte gymnastica. 2. ed. Venetiis, 1573.
	AH 7203.128	Pinelus, Arius. Ad constitutiones codicis de bonis maternis doctissimus. Venetiis, 1573.
Htn	AH 7135.73*	Sigonio, C. De antiquo iure civium romanorum. Paris, 1573.
	AH 7135.74F	Sigonio, C. De antiquo iure populi romani. Bononiae, 1574.
Htn	AH 805.75*	Lucidus, J. Chronicon seu Emendatio temporum. Venetiis, 1575.
Htn	AH 7206.21F*	Rome. Laws, statutes, etc. Basil I. Lx librorum Basilikōn. Basileae, 1575.
Htn	AH 9607.5F*	Goltzius, H. Sicilia et Magna Graecia. Brugis, 1576.
Htn	AH 9607.6F*	Goltzius, H. Sicilia historia posterior. Brugis Flandrorum, 1576.
Htn	AH 7495.57*	Guevara, A. A chronicle, conteyning the lives of tenne emperours of Rome. London, 1577.
Htn	AH 7235.59.3*	Du Choul, G. Discorso...sopra la castrametatione. n.p., 1579.

Chronological Listing

1580-1589

Htn AH 7055.10.3* Fiocco, A.D. L. Fenestellae, de Romanarum magistratibus. Basileae, 1581.

Htn AH 7207.2* Mannuccius, P. Antiquitatum Romanarum...Liber de Senatu. Venetiis, 1581.

Htn AH 7235.59.5* Du Choul, G. Discorso...sopra la castrametatione. Vinegia, 1582. 5 pam.

AH 7035.85 Manuzio, Paolo. Antiquitatum romanorum. Romae, 1585.

Htn AH 3953.9* Sigonio, Carlo. De republica hebralarum libri VII. Francofurti, 1585.

Htn AH 833.6* Mercuriale, G. De arte gymnastica. Venetiis, 1587.

Htn AH 7035.88* Panvino, O. Civitas romana. Parisiis, 1588.

1590-1599

Htn AH 7655.93F* Sigonio, Carlo. Caroli Sigonii historiarum de occidentali imperio libri XX. Francofurti, 1591-93. 2 pam.

Htn AH 844.8F* Hospinian, Rudolph. De origine, progressu, ceremoniis. Tiguri, 1592.

Htn AH 844.8.3F* Hospinian, Rudolph. De origine, progressu, ceremoniis. Tiguri, 1593.

Htn AH 7055.93F* Notitia utraque dignitatum. Venetiis, 1593.

Htn AH 805.83.2F* Scaliger, J. De emendatione temporum. Francofurti, 1593.

Htn AH 3980.2* Aldrichem, C. von. A briefe description of Hierusalem and of the suburbs thereof. London, 1595.

Htn AH 3657.18.5* Brisson, B. De regio Persarum. Heidelberg, 1595.

Htn AH 7235.96* Lipsius, J. De militia Romana. Antverpiae, 1596.

Htn AH 7206.19F* Loewenklau, J. Juris Graeco-Romani tam Canonici quam Civilis. Francofurti, 1596.

Htn AH 805.97* Pie, Thomas. An houreglasse. London, 1597.

Htn AH 7235.97* Valtrimus, J.A. De re militari veterum Romanorum. n.p., 1597.

Htn AH 7835.98* Boulenger, J.C. De Circo Romano Ludisque. Lutetiae Parisiorum, 1598.

AH 7085.98F Lazius, W. Reipublicae Romanae in exteris provinciis. v.1-3. Francofurti, 1598.

Htn AH 7495.98* Lipsus, Justus. Admiranda. v.1-2. Antwerpen, 1598.

Htn AH 805.83.3F* Scaliger, J. De emendatione temporum. Lugduni Batavorum, 1598.

Htn AH 7805.99F* Piglius, S.V. Annales magistratuum. Antverpiae, 1599.

AH 7805.99.2F Piglius, S.V. Annales romanorum qui commentarii vicem supplent in omnes veteres historiae romanae scriptores. Antverpiae, 1599-1615. 3v.

Htn AH 815.16.15F* Ricchieri, Lodovico. Rhodigini lectionum antiquarum. n.p., 1599.

Htn AH 4815.99* Sardi, Alessandro. De moribus et ritibus gentium. Ambergae, 1599.

1600-1609

AH 7956.00 Itinerarium Antonini Augusti. Coloniae Agrippinae, 1600.

Htn AH 7836.00F* Panvinio, O. De Ludis Circensibus. Venetia, 1600.

Htn AH 7416.01* Fulbeck, William. An historical collection of the continuall factions...of the Romans and Italians...before Augustus Caesar. London, 1601.

Htn AH 833.2* Mercuriale, G. Hieronymi...de arte gymnastica. Venetijs, 1601.

Htn AH 7861.6* Rigalt, N. Funus Parasiticum. Lutetiae, 1601. 4 pam.

Htn AH 336.02* Batero, G. Observations upon the lives of Alexander, Caesar, Scipio. London, 1602.

Htn AH 7861.3* Kirchmann, J. De funeribus Romanorum. Hamburg, 1605.

Htn AH 7206.31* Monvéron, Charles de. Observationes et emendationes in synopsim Basilicum. Paris, 1607.

Htn Eg 876.08* Pignorio, L. Characteres Aegyptii hoc est sacrorum. Francofurti, 1608.

AH 36.08 Zamosci, J. De senatu romano. Argen, 1608.

1610-1619

AH 7203.6.5F Corpus juris civilis. Juris civilis septimus tomus. Venetiis, 1610. 2v.

Htn AH 8676.3* Lauro, G. Antiquae urbis splendor. Romae, 1610.

AH 9777.18 Jordanes. Diversarum...historiae antiquae scriptores tres. Hamburgi, 1611.

Htn AH 7106.12* Bonlenger, J.C. De tributis ac vetigalis populi Romani liber. Tolosae, 1612.

Htn AH 276.14F* Raleigh, Walter. Historie of the world in five bookes. London, 1614.

AH 4117.5 Meursius, J. Populis atticae. Lugdunum Batavorum, 1616.

AH 276.16A Paiva d'Andrada, Diogo de. Exame d'antiquidades. Lisboa, 1616.

AH 926.17 Angelocrator, D. Doctrina de ponderibus. Marpurgi Cattorum, 1617.

AH 7446.17 Scipio, L.C. Vetustissima inscriptio. Romae, 1617.

Htn AH 3914.2* Selden, John. De dis Syris syntagmata II. London, 1617.

AH 9777.5 Gothicarum et Langobardicarum. Lugduni Batavorum, 1618.

AH 7203.6.9 Corpus juris civilis. Corpus juris civilis in iiii partes distinctum. Genevae, 1619.

1620-1629

AH 7816.20 Rossfeld, J. Anitiqvitatvm Romanarvm liber pumus, de vrbeetpopulo. Coloniae, 1620.

AH 4056.22 Meursius, J. Archontes athenienses. Lugdunum Batavorum, 1622.

AH 8616.2F Cluneri, P. Italiae antiquae. Lugduni Batavorum, 1624.

Htn AH 7276.25* Alciati, Andrea. Rerum patriae libri IIII. Mediolani, 1625.

AH 4296.26 Emmius, U. Vetus Graecia. Lugdunum Batavorum, 1626.

AH 7516.18.4 Matthieu, P. Aelius Sejanus. Histoire romaine. 4. éd. Rouen, 1626.

Htn AH 7546.27* Bolton, Edmund. Nero Caesar. London, 1627.

Htn AH 7816.28* Godwyn, Thomas. Romanae historiae anthologia. Oxford, 1628. 2 pam.

AH 7055.93.9 Goutière, Jacques. De officiis domus Augustae. Parisiis, 1628.

AH 7516.18.6 Matthieu, P. Aelius Sejanus. Histoire romaine. Rouen, 1628.

Htn AH 7516.28* Matthieu, P. The powerfull favorite...Aelius Seianus. Paris, 1628.

NEDL AH 276.28 Pezelio, T. Mellificium historicum. Francofurti, 1628.

Htn AH 276.14.4F* Raleigh, Walter. The historie of the world. London, 1628.

Htn AH 7036.29* Schrijver, Pieter. Republica romana. Lugdunum Batavorum, 1629.

AH 3914.3 Selden, John. De dis Syris. Lugdunum Batavorum, 1629.

1630-1639

Htn AH 4036.32* Emmus, Vbbonis. Graecorum republicae. Lugdunum Batavorum, 1632.

Htn AH 7406.32* Malvezzi, V. Il Tarquinio superbo. Bologna, 1632.

Htn AH 256.33* Ryves, Thomas. Historia navalis antiqua. Londini, 1633.

Htn AH 7276.34F* Bellendenus, G. Supplicum libellorum August regis. Paris, 1634.

Htn AH 7516.34* Manzini, G.B. Political observations upon the fall of Seianus. London, 1634.

Htn AH 276.14.7F* Raleigh, Walter. Historie of the world in five bookes. London, 1634.

AH 7806.35 Nagel, J.A.M. Fastorum Romanorum formula post consulatum. Altorfii, 1635.

Htn AH 4136.35F* Petitus, S. Leges Atticae. Paris, 1635.

Htn AH 5303.5* Postel, G. Republica seu magistratibus. Lugdunum Batavorum, 1635.

Htn AH 7486.36* Brathuaite, R. The lives of all the Roman emperors. London, 1636.

Htn AH 8907.5F* Ethruscarum antiquitatum fragmenta. Francofurti, 1637.

Htn AH 7406.37* Malvezzi, V. Romulus and Tarquin. London, 1637.

Htn AH 3958.8.20* Caussin, N. The unfortunate politique [or the life of Herod]. Oxford, 1638.

Htn AH 7406.38* Malvezzi, V. Romulus and Tarquin. London, 1638.

Htn AH 7516.28.2* Matthieu, P. Unhappy prosperity express'd in History of Aelius Sejanus. 2. ed. London, 1639.

1640-1649

Htn AH 256.40* Ryves, Thomas. Historia navalis antiqua. Londini, 1640.

Htn AH 7203.7* Corvini, A. Digesta per aphoumos. Amstelodami, 1642.

AH 7516.18.10 Matthieu, P. Aelius Seianus. Rouen, 1642.

AH 7203.7.15 Corvini, A. Euchiridium seu institutiones imperiales. Amstelodami, 1644.

Htn AH 4036.44* Emmus, Vbbonis. Republica Graecorum. Luden, 1644. 2v.

AH 8516.11 Labbe, Philippe. Pharus Galliae antiquae. Molinis, 1644.

AH 4846.5 Allatius, L. De templis Graecorum. Colonia Agrippina, 1645.

AH 8907.5.5 Inghirami, C. Discorso...sopra l'opposizioni. Firenze, 1645.

AH 7506.45 Lentulus, Cyriaeus. Augustus. Amstelodami, 1645.

Htn AH 816.45* Licetus, F. De anulis antiquis. Utini, 1645.

AH 136.45 Miscellae defensiones pro Cl. Salmasio. Lugduni Batavorum, 1645.

Htn AH 5303.5.3* Postel, G. Republica seu magistratibus Atheniensium. Lugdunum Batavorum, 1645.

AH 7926.47 Greaves, John. Pyramidographia. London, 1646. 2 pam.

Htn AH 276.46* Thysius, Antonius. Memorabilia celebriorum veterum rerumpublicarum. Lugduni Batavorum, 1646.

Htn AH 7406.47* Malvezzi, V. Il Romulo. Geneva, 1647. 5 pam.

AH 856.5 Tomasini, J.P. De tesseris hospitalitatis. Utini, 1647.

Htn AH 7406.48* Malvezzi, V. Romulus and Tarquin. 3. ed. London, 1648.

AH 162.7 Saumaise, A. Specimen confutationis...sive tractatus. Lugdunum Batavorum, 1648.

1650-1659

Htn AH 4521.16* Malvezzi, V. Considerations upon the lives of Alcibiades and Coriolanus. London, 1650.

Htn AH 276.50* Ussher, James. Annales Veteris Testamenti a prima mundi origine deducti. Londini, 1650-54. 2v.

AH 7055.93.10 Notitia dignitatum imperii Romani. Parisiis, 1651.

AH 8857.4 Pellegrini, C. Apparato alle antichità di Capua o vero discorsi della campania. Napoli, 1651.

AH 4006.51 Vossius, G.J. De historicis Graecis. Lugdunum Batavorum, 1651.

AH 7203.12 Corpus juris civilis. Corpus juris civilis in iv partes distinctum. Lugduni, 1652. 2v.

AH 7848.2 Figrelills, E. De statius illustrium Romanorum. v.1-2. Holmiae, 1656.

AH 186.56 Pignoria, L. De servis. Patavii, 1656.

AH 836.57 Lydii, J. Agonistica sacra. Roterdami, 1657.

AH 7203.9 Perez, A. Institutiones imperiales erotematibus. Amstelodami, 1657.

Htn AH 7236.57* Saumaise, C. de. De re militari Romanorum. Lugdunum, 1657.

AH 7486.57F Tristan, Jean. Commentaires historiques contenans l'histoire générale des empereurs, impératrices, Caesars, et tyrans de l'Empire Romain. Paris, 1657.

Htn AH 8217.5* Burton, William. Commentary on Antoninus...itinerary. London, 1658.

Htn AH 276.58F* Ussher, James. The annals of the Old and New Testament. London, 1658.

Htn AH 3962.16* Vossius, G.J. Chronologiae sacrae isagoge. Hagae-Comitum, 1659. 2 pam.

1660-1669

AH 861.9 Quenstedt, J.A. Septultura veterum. Wittenberge, 1660.

Htn AH 7136.60* Zouche, R. Juris civilis. Oxoniae, 1660.

AH 276.61F Howel, W. An institution of general history. London, 1661.

Htn AH 3958.2.5F* Fuller, T. A Pisgah-sight of Palestine. London, 1662.

AH 7203.9.2 Perez, A. Institutiones imperiales erotematibus. Amstelodami, 1662.

AH 3914.3.3 Selden, John. De dis Syris. 3. ed. Lipsiae, 1662.

AH 7203.15A Corpus juris civilis. Corpus juris civilis. Amstelaedami, 1663-64. 2v.

Htn AH 7203.29F* Corpus juris civilis. Corpus juris civilis. Amstelodami, 1663. 2v.

AH 7203.14 Corpus juris civilis. Institutiones. Imp. Justiniani Institutionum sive Elementorum. Tremoniae, 1663.

AH 3966.17 Quistorpius, J. Nebo, undi tota perlustratur Terra Sancta. Rostochi, 1663.

AH 7276.64 Alveri, Gasparo. Roma in ogni stato. Roma, 1664. 2v.

AH 7850.2A Chacon, P. De Triclinio rive de modo convivandi. Amsterdam, 1664.

AH 7203.7.5 Corvini, A. Digesta per aphoumos. Amstelodami, 1664.

AH 7203.7.10 Corvini, A. Elementa juris civilis. Amstelodami, 1664.

AH 336.42.5 Heerman, F. Guldene Annotatien. Dordrecht, 1664.

AH 8073.13 Hendreich, C. Carthago, sive Carthaginensium respublica. Francofurti ad Oderam, 1664.

Htn AH 5057.5* Schoockius, M. Respublicae Achaeorum. Trajani ad Rhenum, 1664.

AH 7202.5F Codex Theodosianus. Codex. Lugduni Batavorum, 1665. 6v.

AH 7636.67 Keuchenius, R. Antoninus Pius. Amstelaedami, 1667.

Chronological Listing

1660-1669 - cont.

Htn Eg 876.69* — Pignorio, L. Mensa isiaca qua sacrorum. Amstelodami, 1669.

AH 7816.20.5 — Rossfeld, J. Anitiqvitatvm Romanarvm liber pumus, de vrbeetpopulo. Coloniae, 1669.

1670-1679

AH 5757.7 — Krag, Niels. De republica Lacedaemoniorum. Lugdunum Batavorum, 1670.

AH 7203.22 — Perezl, A. Juris civilis Antecessoris. Vesaliae, 1670.

AH 3654.5 — Roth, R. De More Pensarum aquam. Jenae, 1670.

AH 7861.13 — Gautière, J. De jure manium. Lipsiae, 1671.

AH 848.17 — Paschalius, C. Coronae. Lugduni Batavorum, 1671.

Htn AH 7203.11.3* — Perez, A. Codicis justiniani imperiales. Amstelodami, 1671. 2v.

AH 7203.127 — Bronchorst, E. In tit. digestorum de...regulis juris antiqui. Parisiis, 1672.

AH 816.72F — Ferretti, G.B. Musae lapidariae antiquarum. Veronae, 1672.

Htn AH 7861.4* — Kirchmann, J. De funeribus Romanorum cum appendice. Lugduni Batavorum, 1672.

Htn AH 806.72F* — Marcham, John. Chronicus canon. Londini, 1672.

Htn AH 833.3* — Mercuriale, G. Arte gymnastica. Amstelodami, 1672.

Htn Eg 276.66.15* — Murtada ibn al-Kafif. The Egyptian history. London, 1672.

AH 3914.3.6 — Selden, John. De dis Syris. Lipsiae, 1672.

AH 848.15 — Solerius, A. De pileo. Amstelodami, 1672.

AH 5057.2 — Gothofreedus, J. History of united provinces of Achaia. London, 1673.

AH 186.74 — Pignoria, L. De servis. Amstelodami, 1674.

Htn AH 8207.5* — Langhorne, D. Elenchus antiquitatum albionensium. Londini, 1675.

AH 5457.5 — Meursius, J. Creta, Cyprus, Rhodus. Amstelodami, 1675.

Htn AH 235.59* — Bartholin, T. De armillis veterum schedion. Amstelodami, 1676. 3 pam.

Htn Eg 876.76F* — Kircher, A. Sphinx mystagoga. Amstelodami, 1676.

Htn AH 9610.3* — Perrinchief, Richard. The Sicilian tyrant. London, 1676.

Htn AH 7816.77* — Bell, T. Roma restituta. London, 1677.

Htn AH 316.77F* — Hale, Matthew. Primitive origination of mankind. London, 1677.

Htn AH 876.77* — Howe, John. View of antiquity. London, 1677.

AH 276.14.2F — Raleigh, Walter. Historie of the world in five bookes. London, 1677.

AH 9777.36 — Ropaligero, D. I Goti illustrati o vero Istoria de Goti antichi. Verona, 1679.

1680-1689

Htn AH 7163.20.5* — Beverland, H. De stolatae virginitatis. Lugdunum Batavorum, 1680.

AH 7163.20 — Beverland, H. De stolatae virginitatis. Lugdunum Batavorum, 1680.

Htn AH 276.61.2F* — Howel, W. An institution of general history. London, 1680.

AH 3914.3.8 — Selden, John. De dis Syris. Amsterdam, 1680.

AH 3716.5 — Bochart, S. Geographia sacra. Francofurti, 1681.

AH 7203.145 — Corpus juris civilis. Institutiones. Theophili antecessoris Institutionum libri quatuor. Parisiis, 1681.

AH 7766.81 — Fléchier, E. Histoire de Theodose le Grand. Paris, 1681.

Htn AH 3910.3* — Foy-Vaillant. Seleucidarum imperium. Luteciae Parisiorum, 1681.

AH 7776.81 — Freher, Marquard. Sapphirus Constantii imp. Aug. exposita anno 1602. Heidelbergae, 1681.

Htn AH 8936.2F* — Noris, Enrico. Cenotaphia Piasana Caii et Lucii Caesarum. Venetiis, 1681.

AH 7836.81F — Onuphrii Panvinii Veronensis. Patanii, 1681.

AH 936.83 — Birkerod, J. Timh Timaiov. Altodorfi Noricorum, 1683.

Htn AH 7776.83.5* — Hickes, George. Jovian. 2. ed. London, 1683.

AH 1806.83 — Seldeni Joannis DeArmo civili et calendario. Lugdunum Batavorum, 1683.

NEDL AH 7468.64 — Long, George. Decline of the Roman Republic. London, 1684. 5v.

AH 4136.84 — Meurs, Johannes van. Theseus. n.p., 1684. 3 pam.

X Cg AH 7486.85F — Angeloni, F. L'historia Augusta. Roma, 1685.

AH 4136.85.5 — Meurs, Johannes van. Ioannis Meursii Themis Attica, sive De legibus Atticii libri II. Rhenum, 1685.

AH 4136.85 — Meurs, Johannes van. Themis Attica. Rhenum, 1685. 4 pam.

Htn AH 307.69* — Perisonius, J. Animadversiones historicae. Amstelodami, 1685.

Htn AH 816.85F* — Spon, J. Miscellanea eruditae antiquitatis. Lugduni, 1685.

Htn AH 256.85* — Vossius, Isaac. Observationum. Londini, 1685.

Htn AH 3965.6* — Cumberland, R. An essay towards the recovery of the Jewish measures and weights. London, 1685.

AH 7236.86 — Du Choul, G. Veterum Romanorum religio. Amstelodami, 1686.

AH 866.9 — Kuiper, G. Harpocrates. Trajecti, 1687.

Htn AH 7816.28.5* — Godwyn, Thomas. Romanae historiae anthologia. 15th ed. London, 1689.

Htn AH 7776.89* — Johnson, Samuel. Julian's arts to undermine and extirpate Christianity. London, 1689.

AH 3910.4F — Noris, F.H. Annus et epochae Syromacedonum. Florence, 1689.

1690-1699

AH 8972.5 — Maluasia, C.C. Marmora felsinea...Bononiae senatu. Bononiae, 1690.

AH 7816.88.3 — Cantel, P.J. De Romana Republica sive de re militari et Civili Romanorum ad explicandos scriptores antiquos. Ultrajecti, 1691.

AH 7626.92 — Dadwell, Henry. Praelectiones academicae in schola historices camdeniana. Oxonii, 1692.

AH 3961.5 — Feuerlein, J.J. Dissertatio...de Christian orum migratione in Oppidum Pellam. Jenae, 1694.

Htn AH 816.76* — Gibson, E. Portus iecius. Oxonii, 1694.

AH 7026.94F — Graevio, J.G. Thesaurus antiquitatum rom. Lugdunum Batavorum, 1694. 12v.

AH 7163.28 — Kirchmaier, G.C. Papia Poppoea lex, e ruderibus exposita. Wittenbeergae, 1694.

AH 9773.5 — Pedersen, N. Cimbrorum et Gothorum origines. Lipsiae, 1695.

Htn AH 850.3F — Stuck, J.G. Antiquitatum convivialium. Lugduni Batavorum, 1695.

AH 3907.3F — Terzidi Lavria, B. Siria sacra. Roma, 1695.

AH 7845.5 — Rome galante, ou Histoire...de J. Cesar. Paris, 1696.

1690-1699 - cont.

AH 8986.5 — Salomonius, J. Agri Patavini inscriptiones sacrae et prophanae. Patavius, 1696.

AH 4861.8 — Nicolai, J. Johannis Nicolai Tractatus de Graecorum luctu. Thielae, 1697.

AH 8549.2 — Eyring, Elias M. Veterum instituta druidum. Lipsiae, 1698.

17-

AH 8566.5 — Almerigotti, Francesco. Della estensione dell'antico Ilirico. pt.1-2. Venezia, 17- .

1700-1709

AH 7203.19 — Corpus juris civilis. Corpus juris civilis. Amstelodami, 1700. 2v.

AH 7203.19.5 — Corpus juris civilis. Institutiones. Elementa juris secundum ordinem Institutionum Justiniani. Lugduni Batavorum, 1700.

AH 7487.00 — Lenain, L.S. Histoire des empereurs. Paris, 1700. 6v.

Htn AH 276.14.5* — Raleigh, Walter. An abridgment of Raleigh's Historie of the world. London, 1700.

AH 7203.140.5F — Brunnermann, J. Commentoris in Pandectas. Wittenburgae, 1701.

AH 807.01 — Dodwell, Henry. De veteribus Graecorum Romanorum que cyclis. Oxonii, 1701.

AH 3963.150.5F — Scaccho, F. Sacrorum elaeochrismatwn myrothecia tria. Amstelaedami, 1701.

AH 7867.5 — Struve, B.G. Antiquitatum Romanorum syntagma. Jenae, 1701.

Eg 707.01 — Vaillant, J. Historia Ptolemaeorum. Amstelodami, 1701.

Htn AH 297.02* — Dale, A. van. Dissertationes IX. antiquitatibus. Amstelodami, 1702.

AH 817.03 — Lampe, F.A. De cymbalis veterum. Trajecti, 1703.

AH 7037.03 — Spanhem, Ezekiel. Orbis romanus. London, 1703.

Eg 607.04 — Historia Pharaonis. Helmstadt? 1704.

AH 7816.96.3 — Kennett, Basil. Romae antiquae notitia. 3. ed. Oxford, 1704.

Htn AH 8514.5* — Boze, C.G. de. Explications...sacrifices...les anciens. Paris, 1705.

Eg 137.06 — Nicolai, J. Tractatus de Synedrio Aegyptiorum. Lugdunum Batavorum, 1706.

AH 8548.2 — Pezron, P. Antiquité de la nation et de la langue des Celtes. Paris, 1706.

AH 8548.2.5 — Pezron, P. Antiquities of nations. London, 1706.

AH 4817.06 — Potter, J. Antiquities of Greece. 2. ed. London, 1706. 2v.

AH 5307.5 — Fanelli, F. Athene Attica. Venezia, 1707.

AH 7487.07F — Lotich, J.P. Historicae Augusta imperatorum Rom. Amstelodami, 1707.

AH 8011.2 — Martroye, F. Genséric la conquête vandale. Paris, 1707.

NEDL AH 277.09 — Du Pin, L.E. Universal library of historians. London, 1709. 2v.

AH 7203.8.10 — Vinnii, A. In quatuor libros institutionum. Lugdunum Batavorum, 1709.

1710-1719

AH 3657.18 — Brisson, B. De regio Persarum. Argentoratum, 1710.

AH 7137.10 — Bynkershoek, C. von. Observationum juris romani. Lugdunum Batavorum, 1710. 2v.

AH 7163.5 — Perizonius, J. Dissertationes. Lugdunum Batavorum, 1710.

AH 7203.20 — Triglandius, T. Paedia juris sive Examen Institutiones. Oxoniae, 1710.

AH 861.13 — Vogelives, I.G. De epulis veteruno Christianorum sepulcrabibus. Viternbergae, 1710.

AH 7137.11 — Duker, K.A. Opuscula varia de Latimitate. Lugdunum Batavorum, 1711.

AH 3007.11A — Perizonius, J. Origines Babylonicae et Aegyptiacae. Lugdunum Batavorum, 1711. 2v.

AH 7727.11 — Valsecchi, V. De M. Aurelii Antonine Elaggbali tribunitici potestate V. Florentiae, 1711.

AH 3966.25 — Wells, Edward. An historical geography of the Old Testament. London, 1711-12. 3v.

AH 3013.43 — Gregory, John M. An account of the sepulchres of the antients. London, 1712.

AH 7277.13 — Echard, L. Roman history. London, 1713. 5v.

Htn AH 7817.13F* — Pitisco, Samuel. Lexicon antiquitatum Romanarum. Leovardiae, 1713. 2v.

AH 3740.5 — Ryhinerus, E. De Tyro. Basilae, 1715.

AH 7137.15 — Sigonio, C. De antiquo iure populi romani. Lipsiae, 1715. 2v.

AH 7.16A — Fabricius, J.A. Bibliographia antiquaria. Hamburgi, 1716.

AH 907.63.2 — Huet, Pierre D. Histoire du commerce et de la navigation des anciens. 2. éd. Paris, 1716.

AH 7027.16F — Sallengre, Albert Hendrik de. Novus thesaurus antiquitatum. Hagae, 1716-19. 3v.

NEDL AH 7816.96.6 — Kennett, Basil. Romae antiquae notitia. 6th ed. London, 1717.

AH 8315.2 — Köleséri, Sámuel. Auraria Romano-Dacica. Cibinii, 1717.

Eg 877.17 — Witsi, H. Aegyptiaca et dekaphylon de...sacrorum. Herbornae Nassaviorum, 1717.

Htn AH 7203.10F* — Zoesius. Commentarius ad digestorum. Bruxelles, 1717.

AH 7203.21 — Corpus juris civilis. Institutiones. Der teutsche Justinianus...Der Grund-lehren dess römischen Rechts. Augspurg, 1718. 2v.

AH 457.16.5F — Prideaux, H. The Old and New Testament connected in the history of the Jews. 5. ed. London, 1718-19. 2v.

AH 7203.143.2 — Struve, G.A. Syntagmatis juris civilis. 2. ed. Francofurti, 1718.

Eg 877.19 — Basheysen, H. Natales XI Deo consecrat disputatione paradox de Isicle. pt.1-2. Servestae, 1719.

AH 7137.09 — Bynkershoek, C. von. Opuscula varii argumenti. Lugdunum Batavorum, 1719.

AH 7147.19 — Harlessen, A. Jure colonario. Jenae, 1719.

AH 7817.13.5F — Pitisco, Samuel. Lexicon antiquitatum Romanarum. Venetiis, 1719. 3v.

1720-1729

AH 3707.5 — Cumberland, R. Sanchoniatho's Phoenician history. London, 1720.

AH 7487.20 — Lemain de Tillemont. Histoire des empereurs. Paris, 1720-38. 6v.

Chronological Listing

1720-1729 - cont.

AH 7297.20 — Vertot, R.A. History of revolutions of the Roman Republic. London, 1720. 2v.

AH 7135.59.7F — Brisson, B. De verhorum quae ad jus pertinent significatione. Lipsiae, 1721.

AH 7467.21 — Britannicus. Conspirators. London, 1721.

AH 7467.21.2 — Gordon, T. The conspirators. 2. ed. London, 1721.

AH 7467.21.2.2 — Gordon, T. The conspirators. 2. ed. London, 1721.

AH 7497.21 — Serviez, J.R. de. Les femmes des douze Cesars. Amsterdam, 1721.

AH 7297.20.2 — Vertot, R.A. History of revolutions of the Roman Republic. London, 1721.

AH 7203.23 — Brenkmann, H. Historia Pandectarum. Trajecta ad Rhenum, 1722.

AH 9389.5.4F — Naudé, Gabriel. Exercitatio. Lugduni Batavorum, 1722.

AH 807.22 — Newton, Isaac. Chronology of antient kingdoms. Dublin, 1722.

NEDL AH 4817.06.2 — Potter, J. Antiquities of Greece. 4th ed. London, 1722.

AH 7497.21.4 — Serviez, J.R. de. Les femmes des douze Cesars. 4. éd. Amsterdam, 1722-24. 3v.

AH 808.37 — Strauchius, G. Treatise...in chronology. London, 1722.

Htn AH 276.50.8F* — Ussher, James. Annales Veteris et Novi Testamenti. Genevae, 1722.

AH 7817.12.3 — Nieupoort, W.H. Rituum qui olim apud Romanos. 3rd ed. Rhenum, 1723.

AH 7817.23 — Oudaans, J. Roomsche mogentheid. Leiden, 1723.

AH 7203.24 — Corpus juris civilis. Digesta. Jacobi Labitti index legum omnium. Francoforti, 1724. 2v.

Htn AH 297.24* — Cumberland, R. Origines gentium antiquissimae. Londini, 1724.

AH 7137.18.5 — Ferriere, M.C.J. The history of the Roman or civil law. London, 1724.

AH 7477.24 — The life and actions of Caius Julius Caesar. London, 1724.

AH 7277.25 — Catrou, François. Histoire romaine. Paris, 1725. 17v.

AH 5723.5 — Giurini, A.M. Primordia Corcyrae. Lycij, 1725.

AH 3963.150F — Scaccio, F. Thesaurus antiquitas sacro-prophanarum. Hagae-Comitum, 1725.

AH 3607.5 — Vaillant, J.F. Regum Parthorum historia. Parisiis, 1725. 2v.

AH 7817.26 — Baxteri, W. Reliquiae Baxterianae. London, 1726.

AH 7757.27 — Balduini, F. Constantinus Magnus. Lipsiae, 1727.

AH 7203.25 — Corpus juris civilis. Jurisprudentia restituta, sive Index chronologicus in totum juris Justinianaei corpus. Amstelaedami, 1727.

AH 7163.11 — Grupen, C.U. De uxore romana. Hannoverae, 1727.

Htn AH 8863.5* — Mazochi, P.S. In mutilum Campani amphitheatri. Neapoli, 1727.

AH 7277.27 — A new essay on the Roman history. London, 1727.

AH 7277.25.5F — Catrou, François. Roman history. London, 1728. 6v.

Htn AH 807.28.3* — Newton, Isaac. Chronology of ancient kingdoms. London, 1728.

AH 4817.06.4 — Potter, J. Antiquities of Greece. 5th ed. London, 1728. 2v.

AH 3607.7 — Vaillant, J.F. Regum Parthorum historia. Parisiis, 1728.

AH 7487.29 — Comazzi, G.B. The morals of princes. London, 1729.

AH 457.16.10 — Prideaux, H. The Old and New Testament connected in the history of the Jews. 10. ed. v.1-2. London, 1729. 4v.

1730-1739

AH 3159.23F — Bedford, A. The scripture chronology demonstrated by astronomical calculations. London, 1730.

AH 897.30 — Goetze, F.L. De pistrinis veterum. Cygneae, 1730.

AH 7137.21.2F — Brisson, B. Formulis et solennibul populi romani verbis. Halae, 1731.

AH 8549.5 — Frick, J.G. De druidis occidentalium popularum philosophis. Ulmae, 1731.

AH 147.31 — Otto, E. De tutela viarum publicarum. Rhenum, 1731.

AH 957.31 — Otto, Everard. De tutela viarum publicarum liber singularis. Rhenum, 1731.

Htn AH 277.27.3* — Shuckford, Samuel. The sacred and prophane history of the world connected. London, 1731-37. 3v.

Htn AH 7203.138.6F* — Voet, J. Commentarius ad Pandectas. Hagae, 1731. 2v.

Htn AH 927.08.2* — Eisenschmid, J.C. De ponderibus et mensuris veterum. 2. ed. Argentorati, 1732.

AH 3910.5F — Foy-Vaillant. Seleucidarum imperium. Hagae, 1732.

AH 4027.32F — Gronovio, J. Thesaurus Graecarum antiquitatum. Venetiis, 1732. 12v.

AH 9777.6 — Jordanes. De getarum sive Gothorum. Lugduni Batavorum, 1732.

AH 7487.32.2F — Lemain de Tillemont. Histoire des empereurs. v.1-6. Bruxelles, 1732. 3v.

AH 4807.32F — Maittaire, M. Marmorum. London, 1732.

Htn AH 7817.32* — Vaslet, L. Introduzzione alla scienza d'antichita. Venezia, 1732.

AH 7859.2 — Ludovici, C.G. De ritu osculis explorandi...mulierum. Lipsie, 1733.

Htn AH 7237.34* — Ainsworth, R. De Clypeo Camilli. London, 1734.

AH 2648.5 — Bayer, G.S. Historia osrhoëna et edessena ex numis illustrata. Petropoli, 1734.

AH 4817.34 — Bruyn, C. Compendium Antiquitatum Graecum. Francofurti, 1734.

AH 7107.34 — Burmani, Petro. Vectigalia Popule Romani. Leidae, 1734.

AH 7277.25.3 — Catrou, François. Histoire romaine. v.18-21. Paris, 1734. 4v.

AH 7114.24 — Menser, C.F. Dissertatio de annua equitum romanorum. Lipsiae, 1734.

Htn AH 7307.34* — Montesquieu, Charles de. Considérations sur les causes de la grandeur des Romains. 2. éd. Amsterdam, 1734.

Eg 297.34 — Révérend, Dominique. Letters to Monsieur H*** [Hénrich] concerning the most ancient gods...Egypt. London, 1734.

NEDL AH 277.34 — Rollin, Charles. Ancient history. London, 1734. 10v.

AH 277.34.2.3 — Rollin, Charles. Histoire ancienne. Amsterdam, 1734-39. 13v.

AH 7107.34.2 — Zornii, Petri. Historia fisci judaici. Altonaviae, 1734.

AH 7137.35F — Domat, Jean. Les loix civiles dans leur ordre naturel. v.1-2. Paris, 1735.

AH 7957.35 — Wesseling, P. Vetera Romanorum itineraria. Amstelodami, 1735.

AH 2110.10 — Pagi. Histoire de Cyrus le jeune. Paris, 1736.

Htn AH 276.14.3F* — Raleigh, Walter. Historie of the world and Life of the author. London, 1736. 2v.

Eg 807.37 — Averani, N. De antiquis Aegyptiorum. Florentiae, 1737.

AH 7137.22.2F — Domat, Jean. The civil law in its natural order together with the publick law. London, 1737. 2v.

1730-1739 - cont.

AH 817.37 — Rollin, Charles. History of the arts and sciences. London, 1737. 4v.

AH 7201.4.2 — Schulting, A. Jurisprudentia vetus Ante-Justinianea. Lipsiae, 1737.

Htn AH 5723.7* — Giurini, A.M. Primordia Corcyrae. Brixiae, 1738.

Htn AH 7477.38* — Hill, Aaron. An enquiry into the merit of assassination...character of Caesar. London, 1738.

AH 277.34.30 — Rollin, Charles. Ancient history. Atlas. n.p., 1738-40.

AH 1807.38 — Vignolles, A. Chronologie de l'histoire sainte. Berlin, 1738. 2v.

AH 9633.5F — Reina, Placido. Delle notizie istoriche della città della Messina. Messina, 1739.

1740-1749

AH 8549.17.50 — Toland, John. A critical history of the Celtic religion. London, 174-?

AH 7007.40 — Beaufort, L. Dissertation upon uncertainty. London, 1740.

AH 3917.5 — Maundrell, H. Journey from Allepo to Jerusalem. Oxford, 1740.

AH 4817.06.5 — Potter, J. Antiquities of Greece. 6th ed. London, 1740. 2v.

NEDL AH 4817.06.5 — Potter, J. Antiquities of Greece. 6th ed. London, 1740.

AH 277.34.2 — Rollin, Charles. Histoire ancienne. Paris, 1740. 5v.

AH 7107.40 — Traité des finances et de la fausse monnoie des romains. Paris, 1740.

AH 8516.9 — Anville, J.B.B. Éclaircissemens géographiques sur l'ancienne Gaule. Paris, 1741.

Htn AH 817.41* — Athenian letters. London, 1741-43. 4v.

AH 7137.41 — Heineccius, J.G. Antiquitatum Romanarum iurisprudentiam. Argentorati, 1741.

AH 4136.35.4F — Jurisprudentia Romana et Attica. Lugdunum Batavorum, 1741.

AH 7507.41 — Rose, Christianne. Dissertationem sollemnem de Augusto. Halae Magdeburgecae, 1741.

Htn AH 4807.41* — Squire, Samuel. Two essays, a defense of ancient Greek chronologies. Cambridge, 1741.

AH 7844.7 — Brissonius, B. Commentarius de spectaculis. Lugdini Batavorum, 1742.

AH 7817.42.10 — Cellarii, Christophori. Christophori Cellarii Breviarium antiquitatum romanarum, accurante. Augustae Taurinorum, 1742.

AH 7817.42 — Chladenii, E.M. De gentilitate vetervm Romanorum liber singvlaris. Lipsiae, 1742.

NEDL AH 4136.35.2F — Petitus, S. Leges Atticae. Lugdunum Batavorum, 1742.

AH 7167.42 — Taylor, John. Commentarius ad Leges decemvirdem. Cantabrigiae, 1742.

AH 7135.59.10F — Brisson, B. B. Brissonii...De verhorum quae ad ivs civile pertinent significatione. Halae Magdeburgicae, 1743.

AH 7202.7F — Codex Theodusianus. Codex. Lipsiae, 1743. 6v.

AH 7817.43.3 — Rossfeld, J. Antiquitatum Romanarum corpus. Amstelodami, 1743.

AH 2357.15 — Wernsdoff, G. Republica Galatarum. Norimbergae, 1743.

AH 7277.42 — Algemeene histori. Ultrecht, 1744.

AH 4807.44 — Corsine, E. Fastiattici in quibus Archantum. Florentiae, 1744. 4v.

AH 7203.26 — Eden, R. Jurisprudentia Philologica. Oxonii, 1744.

AH 8549.10 — Frick, J.G. Commentatio de Druidis. Ulmae, 1744.

AH 4147.45 — Bougainville. Droits des metropolis sur colonies. Paris, 1745.

AH 7277.38.2 — Hooke, N. The Roman history. London, 1745-64. 3v.

AH 7817.46 — Gruneri, J.F. Introductio in antiquitates romanas. Ienae, 1746.

NEDL AH 7816.96.11 — Kennett, Basil. Romae antiquae notitia. 11th ed. London, 1746.

AH 7777.46 — La Bleterie. Vie de l'Empereur Julien. Paris, 1746.

AH 4848.8 — Walch, C.F. Antiquitates pallii philosophici verterum Christianorum. Ienae, 1746.

AH 407.47 — Fourmont, Étienne. Reflexions sur l'origine, histoire. Paris, 1747. 2v.

AH 7207.5 — Middleton, Conyers. A treatise on the Roman senate. London, 1747.

AH 9057.5 — Corradini, Pietro M. Petri Marcellini Corradini. Romae, 1748. 2v.

AH 7607.48 — Lampe, H. Dissertatio juridica prior de Marco Coccejo Nerva Roman. Bremae, 1748? 2 pam.

AH 7817.12.6 — Nieupoort, W.H. Rituum qui olim apud Romanos obtinuerunt. 13. ed. Venetiis, 1748.

Htn AH 7137.49F* — Brisson, B. Opera minora. Lugdunum, 1749.

AH 4307.49 — Mably, G.B. Observations sur les Grecs. Genève, 1749.

AH 457.49 — Prideaux, H. The Old and New Testament connected in the history of the Jews. v.3-4. London, 1749. 2v.

AH 9621.9 — Torremuzza, G.L.C. Dissertazione sopra una statua di Marmo. Palermo, 1749.

1750-1759

AH 7207.7 — Chapman, Thomas. An essay on the Roman senate. Cambridge, 1750.

AH 7487.50 — Crevier, J.B.L. Histoire des empereurs romains. Paris, 1750. 6v.

Eg 877.50 — Iablonski, P.E. Pantheon Aegyptiorum. Francofurti, 1750.

AH 7787.50 — La Bleterie. Histoire de l'Empereur Jovien. Amsterdam, 1750.

AH 8549.12 — Martin, Jacques. La religion des Gaulois, tirée des plus pures sources de l'antiquité. Amsterdam, 1750. 2v.

AH 3980.5.1 — Warburton, William. Julian, or Discourse...earthquake...temple at Jerusalem. London, 1750.

AH 3980.5 — Warburton, William. Julian. London, 1750.

AH 7.16.9 — Barth, J.M. Mantissa...Fabricii Bibliographiam antiquariam. Ratisbonae, 1751.

AH 7307.51 — Mably, G.B. Observations on the Romans. London, 1751.

NEDL AH 7817.12.9 — Nieupoort, W.H. Rituum qui olim apud Romanos obtinuerunt. 9. ed. Berolini, 1751.

Htn AH 4277.51* — Stanyan, T. Grecian history. London, 1751. 2v.

AH 7205.7 — Theophilus Antecessor. Paraphrasis Graeca Institutionum Caesarearum. Hagae, 1751.

AH 3980.5.2 — Warburton, William. Julian, or Discourse...earthquake...temple at Jerusalem. London, 1751.

AH 7277.53 — Holberg, Ludvig. Conjectures sur les causes de la grandeur des Romains. Leipzig, 1752.

AH 807.52 — Jackson, J. Chronological antiquities. London, 1752. 3v.

AH 7307.34.17 — Montesquieu, Charles de. Reflections on the causes of the rise and fall of the Romans. London, 1752.

Chronological Listing

1750-1759 - cont.

AH 7277.52 — Rollin, Charles. Histoire romaine. Paris, 1752. 8v.

AH 7497.21.6 — Serviez, J.R. de. Roman empresses, or History of lives. Dublin, 1752. 3v.

Htn AH 7497.21.7* — Serviez, J.R. de. Roman empresses, or History of lives. London, 1752. 3v.

AH 807.52.5F — Simson, E. Chronicon historiam catholicam. Amstelodami, 1752.

Htn AH 7507.53* — Blackwell, Thomas. Memoirs of the courts of Augustus. Edinburgh, 1753. 3v.

NEDL AH 7487.50.10 — Crevier, J.B.L. Histoire des empereurs romains. Paris, 1753-66. 12v.

AH 7277.52.3 — Rollin, Charles. Roman history. 2. ed. London, 1754. 16v.

AH 8548.6 — Schoepflin, J.D. Vindiciae Celticae. Argentorati, 1754.

AH 7487.50.3 — Crevier, J.B.L. History of Roman emperors. London, 1755. 10v.

Htn AH 7137.55* — Taylor, J. Elements of the civil law. Cambridge, 1755.

AH 7137.22.5F — Domat, Jean. Les loix civiles. Paris, 1756.

AH 7203.27 — Eck, Cornelius van. Principia juris civilis. Trajecta ad Rhenum, 1756. 2v.

AH 8073.11 — Hannon, G. Antigüedad maritima de...Cartago. Madrid, 1756.

AH 4837.56 — Paciavdi, M. De athletarum. Romae, 1756. 4 pam.

AH 806.11.5F — Tornielli, A. Annales sacri. Lucae, 1756-57. 4v.

AH 7277.38.3 — Hooke, N. The Roman history. London, 1757. 4v.

AH 7137.57 — Selchow, J.H.C. Elementa antiquitatum iuris Romani publici et privati. Gottingae, 1757.

AH 807.28.5 — Fréret, Nicolas. Défense de la chronologie. Paris, 1758.

AH 817.58.3 — Goguet, Antoine Y. De l'origine des lois, des arts, et des sciences. Paris, 1758. 3v.

AH 817.58 — Holberg, Ludwig. Introduction to universal history. London, 1758.

Htn AH 7206.2* — Hooke, N. Observations on the answer. London, 1758.

AH 6110.7F — Leland, T. History of life and reign of Philip. London, 1758.

AH 8942.2 — Riccobaldi del Bana, G.M. Dissertazione istorico-etrusca...della città di Volterra. Firenze, 1758.

NEDL AH 277.34.5 — Rollin, Charles. Histoire ancienne. v.1-13. Paris, 1758-63. 14v.

NEDL AH 7277.52.1 — Rollin, Charles. Histoire romaine. Paris, 1758-68. 16v.

AH 307.59 — Montagu, E.W. Reflections on the rise and fall of the ancient republic. London, 1759.

AH 7307.34.5 — Montesquieu, Charles de. Considérations sur les causes de la grandeur des Romains. Amsterdam, 1759.

NEDL AH 277.34.3 — Rollin, Charles. Histoire ancienne. Amsterdam, 1759. 3v.

1760-1769

AH 4237.60 — Guischardt, Karl. Mémoires militaires sur les Grecs...Romains. Lyon, 1760.

AH 7277.60 — Macquer, P. Chronological abridgement of Roman history. London, 1760.

AH 307.60 — Montagu, E.W. Reflections on the rise and fall of the ancient republic. London, 1760.

AH 7203.31 — Corpus juris civilis. Institutiones. D. Justiniani Institutionum libri quatuor. London, 1761.

Htn AH 7137.11.2* — Duker, K.A. Opuscula varia de Latinate. 2. ed. n.p., 1761.

NEDL AH 817.58.13 — Goguet, Antoine Y. Della origine delle leggi, delle arte...antichi popoli. Lucca, 1761. 3v.

AH 6110.5F — Leland, T. History of life and reign of Philip. 2. ed. London, 1761. 2v.

AH 7307.34.7 — Montesquieu, Charles de. Considérations sur les causes de la grandeur des Romains. Amsterdam, 1761.

Htn AH 5958.10* — Pasiaudi, P.M. Monumenta Peloponnesia. Romae, 1761. 2v.

AH 7203.11 — Perez, A. Codicis justiniani imperiales. Amstelodami, 1761.

Htn AH 7807.61PF* — Piranesii, I.B. Lapides capitolini sive fasti. Romae, 1761.

Htn AH 7037.63* — Duni, E. Origini del cittadino di Roma. Roma, 1763. 2v.

AH 907.63 — Huet, Pierre D. Histoire du commerce et de la navigation des anciens. Lyon, 1763.

NEDL AH 7816.96.13 — Kennett, Basil. Romae antiquae notitia. 13th ed. London, 1763.

AH 3959.31 — Michaelis, J.D. Commentationes societati regiae scientiarum Goettingensi per armas 1758-62. Bremae, 1763.

AH 457.16.15 — Prideaux, H. The Old and New Testament connected in the history of the Jews. 13. ed. v.1-2. Glasgow, 1763. 4v.

AH 7827.59.3 — D'Arnay, J.R. Private life of the Romans. 2. ed. London, 1764.

AH 861.14 — Haffner, G. De antiquis sepulturae ritibus. Ulmae, 1764.

AH 4817.06.6 — Potter, J. Antiquities of Greece. 8th ed. London, 1764. 2v.

Eg 807.65 — Schmidt, F.S. de. Opuscula Aegyptiacae. Caroleruhae, 1765.

AH 7237.64.5 — Stierneman. Principes de l'art de la guerre. Strasbourg, 1765.

Eg 907.66 — Armeilhon, H.P. Histoire du commerce et de la navigation des Égyptiens. Paris, 1766.

AH 817.66.5 — Boulanger, N.A. L'antiquité dévoilée par ses usages. Amsterdam, 1766.

NEDL AH 817.66 — Boulanger, N.A. L'antiquité dévoilée par ses usages. Amsterdam, 1766. 3v.

AH 7097.66 — Corsinii, Eduardi. De praefectis urbis. Pisis, 1766.

AH 7107.66 — Dissertation historique et critique touchant l'état de l'immunité ecclésiastique sous les empereurs romains. Soissions, 1766.

AH 27.65 — Martini, J.C. Thesaurus dissertationum. Norimbergae, 1766. 3v.

AH 7707.66 — Montégut, J.F. Essai historique sur la famille de l'Empereur Valérien. n.p., 1766. 2 pam.

Htn AH 307.66* — Voltaire, François Marie Arouet de. The philosophy of history. London, 1766.

AH 277.66.2 — Abbt, Thomas. Fragment der aeltesten Begebenheiten des menschlichen Geschlechts. Halle, 1767.

AH 7037.67 — Beaufort, L. La republique romaine. Paris, 1767. 6v.

AH 297.67 — Bryant, J. Observations and inquiries relating to ancient history. Cambridge, 1767.

AH 7817.12.13 — Nieupoort, W.H. Rituum qui olim apud Romanos obtinuerunt. Berolini, 1767.

AH 277.34.4 — Rollin, Charles. Histoire ancienne. v.4-13. Amsterdam, 1767. 10v.

1760-1769 - cont.

Eg 817.67 — Terrasson, J. Sethos. Paris, 1767. 2v.

AH 7297.20.6 — Vertot, R.A. Histoire des révolutions. 6e éd. Paris, 1767. 3v.

AH 3759.5 — Walch, G.B. De cyri expeditione in Massagetas. Goettingae, 1767.

AH 937.68 — Anville, Jean B.B. d'. Geographie ancienne abrégée. Paris, 1768. 3v.

Htn AH 257.68* — Déslandes, A.F.B. Essai sur la marine des anciens. Paris, 1768.

AH 4277.68 — Robertson, W. History of ancient Greece. Edinburgh, 1768.

AH 7201.4.35 — Ulpianus. Fragmenta. Notas adjecit Joannes Canregieter. Trajecti ad Rhenum, 1768.

AH 8608.7F — Bardetti, S. De primi abitatori dell'Italia; opera postuma. pt.1-2. Modena, 1769.

AH 8257.3 — Fuhrmann, M. Allgemeine Kirchen- und...Oesterreich. Wien, 1769.

Htn AH 7277.69* — Goldsmith, O. The Roman history, from the foundation of the city of Rome to the destruction of the western empire. London, 1769. 2v.

AH 4817.69 — Jackson, R. Literatura Graeca. London, 1769.

AH 7816.96.14 — Kennett, Basil. Romae antiquae notitia. 14th ed. London, 1769.

AH 3959.31.5 — Michaelis, J.D. Commentationes societati regiae scientiarum Goettingensi per armas 1758-62. Bremae, 1769.

Htn AH 137.69* — Pettingal, J. An enquiry into the use and practice of juries. London, 1769.

AH 7137.55.3 — Taylor, J. Elements of the civil law. 3. ed. London, 1769.

AH 3155.17 — Tooke, W. The loves of Othniel and Achsah. London, 1769. 2v.

AH 47.69 — Turpin, François H. Histoire du gouvernement des anciennes républiques. Paris, 1769.

1770-1779

AH 7277.70 — Goldsmith, O. Roman history. London, 1770. 2v.

AH 8548.3 — Pelloutier, S. Histoire des Celtes. Paris, 1770-71. 8v.

AH 7307.34.18 — Montesquieu, Charles de. Considérations sur les causes de la grandeur des Romains, et de leur décadence. Paris, 1771.

AH 3964.32 — Paoli, P.A. Della religione de Gentili per riguardo ad alcuni animali e specialmente a topi. Napoli, 1771.

AH 8857.4.5 — Pellegrini, C. Apparato alle antichità di Capua o vero discorsi della campania. Napoli, 1771. 2v.

AH 8548.3.2 — Pelloutier, S. Histoire des Celtes. Paris, 1771. 2v.

AH 7297.71 — Perizonius, I. Animadversiones historicae. Altenburgi, 1771.

AH 4865.5 — Pownall, Thomas. Dissertations on the ancient chariot. London, 1771.

AH 4817.72 — Bos, L. Antiquities of Greece. London, 1772.

AH 7203.32.5 — Heineccius, J.G. Elementa juris civilis. 5. ed. Trajecti ad Rhenum, 1772.

AH 7204.19 — Malmeri, J.P. De Marco Aurelio Centonio. Halae, 1772. 2v.

AH 7137.32 — Taylor, J. Summary of the Roman law. London, 1772.

AH 8608.5.5 — Guarnacci, Mario. Delle origini italiche. Venezia, 1773.

Eg 877.73 — Schumacher, J.H. De cultu animalium. Brunsvigiis, 1773.

Htn AH 4277.74* — Goldsmith, Oliver. The Grecian history from the earliest state to the death of Alexander the Great. London, 1774. 2v.

AH 7477.74 — Guischard, Charles. Memoires...plusieurs points d'antiquités militaires. Paris, 1774. 4v.

AH 8548.7 — Robin, Claude C. Le Mont-Glonne; ou Recherches historiques sur l'origine des Celtes. Paris, 1774. 2v.

NEDL AH 277.34.6 — Rollin, Charles. Ancient history. London, 1774. 8v.

AH 9426.5F — Fistulario, P. Della geografia antica del Friuli dalle età più rimote sino ai tempi di Costantino il grande. Udine, 1775.

NEDL AH 817.58.17 — Goguet, Antoine Y. The origins of laws, arts, and sciences. Edinburgh, 1775. 3v.

AH 6110.8 — Leland, T. History of life and reign of Philip. 2. ed. London, 1775. 2v.

AH 877.75 — Meiners, Christoph. Versuch über die Religionsgeschichte der ältesten Völker besonders des Egyptier. Göttingen, 1775.

AH 4817.06.8 — Potter, J. Antiquities of Greece. 9th ed. London, 1775. 2v.

Htn AH 7653.10* — Chelsum, J. Remarks on 2 last chapters of Gibbon's History of Roman Empire. London, 1776.

AH 7650.3F — Gibbon, Edward. History of decline and fall of the Roman Empire. v.1, 2. ed. London, 1776-78. 6v.

AH 7037.76 — Kearney, M. Lectures concerning history read during the year 1775 in Trinity College, Dublin. London, 1776.

AH 817.76 — Sabbathier, F. Institutions, manners and customs of ancient nations. London, 1776. 2v.

AH 4957.77 — Chandler, R. Reisen in Griechenland. Leipzig, 1777.

AH 7137.41.5 — Heineccius, J.G. Antiquitatum Romanarum jurisprudentiam. Leovardiae, 1777.

AH 8557.5 — Hohenhausen, S.J. Illyrien. Essegg, 1777.

AH 257.77 — LeRoy, J.D. La marine des anciens peuples. Paris, 1777.

AH 7135.59.20F — Wunderlich, I. Additamentorum ad Barnabae Brissonii. Hamburgi, 1778.

AH 7653.8 — Davis, H.E. Reply to Gibbon's vindication. London, 1779.

AH 3964.11 — Schulze, B. Coniecturae historiae criticae sadducaeorum inter indaeos sectae novam lucem accendentes. Halae, 1779.

1780-1789

AH 3960.5 — Fassinus, V. De Alexandro Magno ingresso Hierosolyma. Florentiae, 1780.

AH 8315.2.5 — Köleséri, Sámuel. Auraria Romano-Dacica. Posonii, 1780.

AH 7203.33F — Corpus juris civilis. Corpus juris civilis Romani. Coloniae Munatianae, 1781.

NEDL AH 7277.70.9 — Goldsmith, O. Roman history. Dublin, 1781.

AH 8407.1 — Klein, Magnus. Notitia Austriae antiquae et mediae. Tegernsee, 1781. 2v.

AH 7653.16 — Milner, Joseph. Gibbon's account of Christianity. York, 1781.

NEDL AH 7650.7 — Gibbon, Edward. History of decline and fall of the Roman Empire. London, 1782. 3v.

Eg 27.82 — Stroth, F.A. Aegyptiaca sev veterum scriptorum. Gothae, 1782.

AH 8257.4 — Dischendorffer, F. Kritische Staatsgeschichte...Oesterreich. pt.1-2. Wien, 1783.

Chronological Listing

1780-1789 - cont.

AH 7417.83.3 — Ferguson, A. A history of...Roman republic. Dublin, 1783. 3v.

AH 7417.83 — Ferguson, A. History of...Roman republic. London, 1783. 3v.

NEDL AH 7650.8 — Gibbon, Edward. History of the decline and fall of the Roman Empire. London, 1783. 6v.

AH 257.83 — LeRoy, J.D. Les navires des anciens. Paris, 1783.

AH 4277.84 — Denina, C. Istoria...della Graecia. Venezia, 1784. 4v.

Htn AH 7497.84* — Hancarville, Pierre François Hugues. Monumens du culte secret des dames romaines. Nancy, 1784.

AH 8549.15 — Pelloutier, S. Die Religion der Celten. Frankfurt am Mayn, 1784.

AH 4147.85 — Biagi Cremonensi. De Decretis Atheniensium. Romae, 1785.

AH 7567.85 — Cramero, A.W.D. Vespasianus sive de vita et legislatione. Ienae, 1785.

AH 8608.5 — Guarnacci, Mario. Origini italiche. Roma, 1785-87. 3v.

Htn AH 7497.85* — Hancarville, Pierre François Hugues. Monumens de la vie privée des douze Césars. pt.1-2. Rome, 1785. 2v.

Eg 1307.85.2F — Mingarelli, Giovanni L. Aegyptiorum codicum reliquae. Bononiae, 1785.

Eg 1307.85F — Mingarelli, Giovanni L. Aegyptiorum codicum reliquae. Bononiae, 1785.

AH 4277.86.3 — Gillies, J. History of ancient Greece. Dublin, 1786. 3v.

AH 4277.86F — Gillies, J. History of ancient Greece. London, 1786. 2v.

AH 7277.70.3 — Goldsmith, O. Roman history. London, 1786. 2v.

Htn AH 7497.85.5* — Hancarville, Pierre François Hugues. Monumens de la vie privée des douze Césars. Rome, 1786.

AH 2007.5 — Pocock, E. Historia imperii vetustissimi. v.1-2. Harderovici Gebrorum, 1786.

AH 7137.55.5 — Taylor, J. Elements of the civil law. 3. ed. London, 1786.

AH 7297.20.6.5 — Vertot, R.A. Histoire des révolutions. 8e éd. Paris, 1786. 2v.

AH 5307.7 — Young, W. History of Athens. London, 1786.

AH 307.87.2 — Bellenden, W. De statu libri tres. 2. ed. Londini, 1787.

AH 307.87 — Bellenden, W. De statu libri tres. 2. ed. Londini, 1787.

AH 4307.87 — Pauw, C. Recherches philosophiques sur les Grecs. Berlin, 1787. 2v.

AH 3757.5 — Pinkerton, J. Scythians or Goths. London, 1787.

AH 817.87 — Plessing, F.V.L. Memnonium. Leipzig, 1787. 2v.

AH 4407.87 — Rabaut, J.P. L'histoire primitive de la Grèce. Paris, 1787.

AH 807.87 — Roncallius, T. Vetustiora Latinorum scriptorum chronica. Patavii, 1787.

AH 9660.7 — Barco, Alejandro del. Las colonias gemelas reintegradas en la mitad de sua respectivas publaciones. Madrid, 1788.

NEDL AH 4967.88.4 — Barthélemy, J.J. Voyage de jeune Anacharsis. Paris, 1788.

Htn AH 4967.88* — Barthélemy, J.J. Voyage de jeune Anacharsis. Paris, 1788. 5v.

AH 7897.88 — Dickson, Adam. Husbandry of the ancients. Edinburgh, 1788.

AH 4842.31 — Hochheimers, C.F.A. System der griechische Pädagogik. v.1-2. Göttingen, 1788.

Htn AH 277.88* — Newbery, John. A compendious history of the world. London, 1788. 2v.

AH 4807.88 — Robertson, Joseph. Parian chronicle. London, 1788.

NEDL AH 277.34.8 — Rollin, Charles. Ancient history. London, 1788. 10v.

AH 407.89 — Williams, W. Primitive history. Chichester, 1789.

1790

AH 4967.88.7 — Barbié du Bocage, J.D. Voyage du jeune Anacharsis et recueil de cartes. 3. éd. Paris, 1790. 8v.

AH 4967.88.2 — Barthélemy, J.J. Voyage de jeune Anacharsis. 3. éd. Paris, 1790. 7v.

NEDL AH 7651.2 — Gibbon, Edward. Abridgement of Gibbon's History of Roman Empire. London, 1790. 2v.

NEDL AH 4277.86.4 — Gillies, J. History of ancient Greece. Basil, 1790. 5v.

AH 4937.90F — Gossellin, M. Geographie des Grècs analysée. Paris, 1790.

Htn AH 7497.84.5* — Hancarville, Pierre François Hugues. Monumens du culte secret des dames romaines. Rome, 1790.

AH 4859.5 — Lenz, C.G. Weiber in heroischen Zeitalter. Hannover, 1790.

1791

AH 937.91 — Anville, Jean B.B. d'. Compendium of ancient geography. London, 1791. 2v.

AH 4967.88.17 — Barthélemy, J.J. Viaggio d'Anacarsi. v.1, 3-12. Venezia, 1791. 11v.

NEDL AH 4967.88.15 — Barthélemy, J.J. Voyage du jeune Anacharsis en Grèce. Aux Deux-Ponts, 1791. 9v.

AH 7817.91 — Meiners, C. Geschichte des Verfalls der Sitten. Wien, 1791.

AH 7817.91.5 — Moritz, K.P. Anthoysa, oder Roms Alterthümer. Berlin, 1791. 2v.

NEDL AH 7817.91.5 — Moritz, K.P. Anthoysa, oder Roms Alterthümer. Berlin, 1791.

AH 4817.91 — Nitsch, P.F.A. Kurzer Entwurf der griechische Alterthümer. Altenburg, 1791.

AH 8957.5 — Rovelli, G. Das cisalpinische Gallien. Leipzig, 1791.

AH 7653.18 — Whitaker, J. Gibbon's History of decline and fall of Roman Empire. London, 1791.

1792

AH 7817.92.2 — Adam, Alexander. Roman antiquities. 2nd ed. Edinburgh, 1792.

AH 7277.92 — Adams, J. History of Rome. Dublin, 1792. 2v.

AH 7817.92.18 — Nitsch, P.F. Beschreibung...Zustandes der Römer. Wien, 1792. 4v.

1793

AH 4967.88.150 — Barbié du Bocage, J.D. Maps, plans, views and coins, illustrative of the travels of Anacharsis the younger in Greece. 2. ed. London, 1793.

AH 317.93 — Delisle de Sales, J.C.I. Historie philosophique du monde primitif. Paris, 1793. 8v.

AH 7617.93 — Mannert, K. Res Traiani imperatoris ad Danubium gestae. Norimbergae, 1793.

1793 - cont.

AH 4307.87.5 — Pauw, C. Philosophical dissertations on the Greeks. London, 1793. 2v.

AH 3659.8 — Silvestre de Sacy, A.I. Memoires sur diverses antiquités de la Perse. Paris, 1793.

1794

AH 4047.94 — Drummond, W. Review of government of Sparta and Athens. London, 1794.

AH 7447.94 — Whitaker, J. Course of Hannibal over the Alps. London, 1794. 2v.

1795

AH 7277.95 — Abrégé de l'histoire romaine. Londres, 1795.

AH 7827.95 — D'Arnay, J.R. Habitudes et moeurs privées. Paris, 1795.

AH 4277.95 — Mitford, W. History of Greece. London, 1795. 10v.

NEDL AH 817.95 — Pölitz, K.H.L. Geschichte der Kultur der Menschheit. Leipzig, 1795.

AH 4817.06.10 — Potter, J. Antiquities of Greece. London, 1795. 2v.

1796

AH 4967.88.6 — Barbié du Bocage, J.D. Voyage du jeune Anacharsis en Grèce. Londres, 1796. 3v.

AH 4827.96 — Barthelemy, J.J. Carite et Polydore. Lausanne, 1796.

AH 37.96 — Bisset, R. Sketch of democracy. London, 1796.

AH 277.96 — Fréret, N. Oeuvres complètes. Paris, 1796. 20v.

AH 866.11 — Hasse, J.G. Der aufgefundene Eridanus. Riga, 1796.

AH 7297.20.5 — Vertot, R.A. Histoire des révolutions. Paris, 1796. 4v.

1797

AH 7203.141 — Glück, D.C.F. Ausführliche Erläuterung der Pandecten. Erlangen, 1797-1868. 46v.

AH 7297.97 — Wilcocks, J. Roman conversations. London, 1797. 2v.

1798

Htn AH 817.41.6* — Athenian letters. London, 1798. 2v.

AH 4967.88.8 — Barbié du Bocage, J.D. Oeuvres diverses. Paris, 1798. 4v.

AH 4967.88.6.5 — Barbié du Bocage, J.D. Voyage du jeune Anacharsis en Grèce. Londres, 1798.

AH 507.98 — Roesler, C.F. Chronica medii aevi. Tubingae, 1798.

1799

AH 817.41.7 — Athenische Briefe. Leipzig, 1799. 2v.

NEDL AH 4967.88.5F — Barthélemy, J.J. Recueil de cartes géographiques. Paris, 1799.

NEDL AH 4967.88.3F — Barthélemy, J.J. Voyage de jeune Anacharsis. 4. éd. Paris, 1799. 7v.

AH 6108.9 — Barzoni, V. I Romani nella Grecia. 11. ed. Londra, 1799.

AH 938.29 — Mannert, K. Geographie. v.1-10. Leipzig, 1799-1829. 14v.

AH 4727.99 — Romans in Greece. Boston, 1799.

AH 37.99 — Sainte Croix, G.E.J.G. de. Anciens gouvernemens fédératifs. Paris, 1799.

18-

AH 4967.88.35 — Barthélemy, J.J. Nouvel abrégé du Voyage du jeune Anacharsis en Grèce. v.2. Paris, 18- ?

AH 5307.9 — Bulwer, E. Athens. Its rise and fall. London, 18- . 2v.

NEDL AH 278.41.7 — Dielitz, T. Hellas und Rom. 7. Aufl. Berlin, 18- ?

AH 5307.25 — Felton, C.C. Athens. n.p., 18- .

AH 7277.38.9 — Hooke, N. The Roman history. London, 18- . 3v.

AH 930.5 — Johnston, W. and A.K., publishers. The world; a classical atlas. Edinburgh, 18- .

AH 7816.96.17 — Kennett, Basil. Romae antiquae notitia. 2nd American ed. Baltimore, 18- .

NEDL AH 4818.76.4 — Mahaffy, J.P. Old Greek life. N.Y., 18- .

Htn AH 278.00* — Millot, C.F.X. Elements of ancient history. N.Y., 18- .

AH 3159.22 — Rawlinson, George. Historical illustrations of the Old Testament. London, 18- .

AH 7498.00F — Die Römischen Kaiser. Leipzig, 18- .

1800

AH 298.00 — Bredow, G.G. Untersuchungen...alten Geschichte. pt.1-2. Altona, 1800-02.

AH 861.10 — Fuhrmann, M.D. Begräbniss der Altere. Halle, 1800.

AH 9707.5 — Gatterer, J.C. Abhandlung von Thracien. Göttingen, 1800.

NEDL AH 7652.16 — Gibbon, Edward. Geschichte...des Römischen Rechts. Frankfurt, 1800. 13v.

AH 4278.00 — Goldsmith, Oliver. Grecian history. London, 1800. 2v.

AH 7598.00 — Hegewisch, D.H. Über die Menscheit...Epoche in der römischen Geschichte. Hamburg, 1800.

AH 5757.5 — Manso, J.K.F. Sparta. v.1-3. Leipzig, 1800. 5v.

AH 9777.37 — Paulinus a Sancto Bartholomaeo. Jornandes vindiciae de Var Hunnorum. Romae, 1800.

AH 277.34.10 — Rollin, Charles. Ancient history. Glasgow, 1800. 6v.

1801

AH 4828.01 — Chaussard, J.B. Fetes et courtisanes. Paris, 1801. 4v.

Htn AH 4864.9* — Christie, J. Inquiry into ancient Greek game. London, 1801.

NEDL AH 4277.86.5 — Gillies, J. History of ancient Greece. 4. ed. London, 1801. 4v.

AH 3013.801 — Hager, Joseph. A dissertation of the newly discovered Babylonian inscriptions. London, 1801.

AH 4818.01 — Harwood, T. Grecian antiquities. London, 1801.

AH 7468.01 — Hegewisch, D.H. Geschichte der gracchischen Unruhen. Hamburg, 1801.

NEDL AH 277.34.11 — Rollin, Charles. Ancient history. Boston, 1801. 8v.

AH 408.01 — Russell, William. History of ancient Europe. Philadelphia, 1801. 2v.

AH 7808.01 — Sigonio, Carlo. Mutinensis fasti consulares ac triumphi acti. Oxonii, 1801.

Chronological Listing

1802

AH 2957.3 — Chandler, R. History of Illium or Troy. London, 1802.

AH 7728.02 — Chaussard, P.J.B. Héliogabale, ou Esquisse morale. Paris, 1802.

AH 7897.88.15 — Dickson, Adam. De l'agriculture des anciens. Paris, 1802. 2v.

NEDL AH 7650.13 — Gibbon, Edward. The history of the decline and fall of the Roman Empire. London, 1802. 12v.

AH 4278.02 — Mavor, W. History of Greece. London, 1802. 2v.

AH 7827.76.2 — Meierotto, J.H.L. Ueber Sitten und Lebensart der Römer. Berlin, 1802.

1803

AH 7828.03 — Böttiger, C.A. Sabina, oder Morgenscenen. Leipzig, 1803.

AH 7108.03 — Bosse, R.H.B. Grundzüge des Finanzwesens. Braunschweig, 1803.

AH 7277.52.2 — Rollin, Charles. Histoire romaine. Paris, 1803-05. 16v.

1804

AH 4967.88.19A — Barthélemy, J.J. Travels of Anacharsis the younger. Philadelphia, 1804. 4v.

Htn AH 8548.4* — Davies, E. Celtic researches on the origin, traditions and languages. London, 1804.

AH 8548.4 — Davies, E. Celtic researches on the origin, traditions and languages. London, 1804.

NEDL AH 7650.17 — Gibbon, Edward. History of decline and fall of Roman Empire. Philadelphia, 1804. 8v.

AH 7650.17 — Gibbon, Edward. History of decline and fall of Roman Empire. Philadelphia, 1804. 8v.

AH 7518.04 — Hamilton, E. Memoirs of the life of Agrippina. Bath, 1804. 3v.

AH 7108.04 — Hegewisch, D.H. Historische Versuch. Altona, 1804.

AH 3657.3 — Ohsson. Tableau historique de l'Orient. Paris, 1804. 2v.

AH 4817.06.12 — Potter, J. Antiquities of Greece. Edinburgh, 1804. 2v.

NEDL AH 277.34.10.5 — Rollin, Charles. Ancient history. 10. ed. London, 1804. 8v.

AH 8972.7 — Rota, G. Dell'origine e della storia antica di Bergamo. Bergamo, 1804.

AH 4558.04 — Sainte-Croix, Guillaume Emmanuel Joseph de. Examen critique. Paris, 1804.

AH 7203.35 — Schultingii, A. Notae ad...pandectas. v.1-7, pt.1-2. Lugdunum Batavorum, 1804. 8v.

AH 5307.7.3 — Young, W. History of Athens. 3. ed. London, 1804.

1805

AH 7817.92.13 — Adam, Alexander. Handbuch der römischen Alterthümer. Erlangen, 1805-06. 2v.

AH 7203.36 — Corpus juris civilis. Institutiones. Justiniani Institutiones. Parisiis, 1805.

NEDL AH 7417.83.5A — Ferguson, A. A history of...Roman republic. 1. American ed. Philadelphia, 1805. 3v.

AH 298.05 — Fortia d'Urban, A.J. de. Mémoires pour servir à l'histoire ancienne. v.1-10. Paris, 1805-09. 4v.

AH 7277.70.5 — Goldsmith, O. Roman history. London, 1805. 2v.

NEDL AH 4278.00.2 — Goldsmith, Oliver. Grecian history. v.1-2. Philadelphia, 1805.

AH 4818.05 — Leuliette, J.J. Essai sur...supériorité des Grecs. Paris, 1805.

NEDL AH 277.34.10.8 — Rollin, Charles. Ancient history. Portland, 1805. 8v.

AH 277.34.10.9 — Rollin, Charles. Ancient history. v.6. Philadelphia, 1805.

1806

AH 4967.88.10 — Barbié du Bocage, J.D. Voyage du jeune Anacharsis en Grèce. 3. éd. Londres, 1806.

AH 4967.88.23 — Barthélemy, J.J. Travels of Anacharsis the younger. 4. ed. London, 1806. 8v.

AH 7201.4.50 — Beck, I.L.G. De Fabio Mela Iuris Consulto. Lipsiae, 1806.

AH 7828.03.4 — Böttiger, C.A. Sabina, oder Morgenscenen. Leipzig, 1806.

Eg 291.5 — Champollion, J.J. A collection of 15 tracts. Grenoble, 1806. 15 pam.

AH 7138.06 — Godefroy, J. Manuale juris. Parisiis, 1806.

AH 4817.91.4 — Nitsch, P.F.A. Beschriebung...der Griechen. Erfurt, 1806. 4v.

1807

AH 7817.92.5 — Adam, Alexander. Roman antiquities. 1st American ed. Philadelphia, 1807.

AH 4967.88.5.10 — Barbié du Bocage, J.D. Recueil de cartes géographiques. Paris, 1807.

AH 8617.5.5 — Cuoco, Vincenzo. Voyage de Platon en Italie. Paris, 1807. 3v.

AH 4278.07 — Epitome historia tès Hellados. En Benetia, 1807. 2v.

NEDL AH 7651.5 — Gibbon, Edward. Abridgement of Gibbon's History of Roman Empire. 2. ed. London, 1807. 2v.

AH 458.07 — Gillies, J. History of the world. London, 1807. 2v.

AH 28.07 — Museum der Alterthums-Wissenschaft. Berlin, 1807. 2v.

AH 7817.92.20 — Nitsch, P.F. Beschreibung...Zustandes der Römer. Erfurt, 1807- 2v.

AH 4818.07.2 — Robinson, J. Antiquities of Greece. London, 1807.

AH 277.34.12 — Rollin, Charles. Ancient history. Boston, 1807. 8v.

NEDL AH 277.34.13 — Rollin, Charles. Ancient history. Boston, 1807. 8v.

AH 7163.30 — Spagnolo, C.A. Richerche sulle diverse maniere di contrarre matrimonio. Roma, 1807.

Htn AH 3957.20* — Tappan, David. Lectures on Jewish antiquities. Cambridge, 1807.

AH 841.3 — Weber, C.F. Versuch einer Geschichte der Schreibkunst. Göttingen, 1807.

1808

AH 842.5 — Goess, G.F.D. Erziehungswissenschaft. Ansbach, 1808.

NEDL AH 4278.00.3 — Goldsmith, Oliver. Grecian history. v.1-2. Philadelphia, 1808.

AH 4298.08 — Hegewisch, D.H. Colonien der Griechen. Altona, 1808.

NEDL AH 4817.06.14 — Potter, J. Antiquities of Greece. Edinburgh, 1808.

Htn AH 7648.08.5* — Thomas, A.L. Eulogium on Marcus Aurelius. N.Y., 1808.

AH 7648.08 — Thomas, A.L. Eulogium on Marcus Aurelius. N.Y., 1808.

1809

AH 458.09 — Gillies, J. History of the world. Philadelphia, 1809. 3v.

AH 7138.09 — Hauboldi, C.G. Institutiones iuris Romani. Lipsiae, 1809.

1810

AH 817.41.5 — Athenian letters. London, 1810. 2v.

AH 4848.4 — Baxter, Thomas. An illustration of the Egyptian, Grecian and Roman costume. London, 1810.

NEDL AH 278.10 — Heeren, Arnold Herman Ludwig. Handbuch...Geschichte...Staaten. Göttingen, 1810.

AH 7468.10 — Luzac, L.C. Specimen...Q. Hortensio Oratore, Ciceronis. Lugduni Batavorum, 1810.

AH 7278.10F — Mirys, S.D. Histoire de la république romaine. Paris, 1810.

AH 4558.04.2 — Sainte-Croix, Guillaume Emmanuel Joseph de. Examen critique. 2. éd. Paris, 1810.

1811

Htn AH 3966.8* — Carpenter, L. An introduction to the geography of the New Testament. Cambridge, 1811.

AH 7203.37 — Cramer, A.W. Verborum significatione. Kiliae, 1811.

AH 278.11 — Eichhorn, J.G. Antiqua historia. Lipsiae, 1811. 4v.

NEDL AH 7417.83.9 — Ferguson, A. History of...Roman republic. Philadelphia, 1811. 3v.

AH 4298.11 — Hegewisch, D.H. Griechischen Colonien. Altona, 1811.

AH 7168.11 — Löhr, E. Constitutionen der römischen Kaiser. v.1-2. Wetzlar, 1811.

Htn AH 7278.11* — Niebuhr, B.G. Römische Geschichte. Berlin, 1811. 2v.

AH 4118.5 — Platner, E. De gentibus atticis. Marburgi, 1811.

NEDL AH 278.11.5 — Royou, J.C. Précis de l'histoire ancienne. 2. éd. Paris, 1811. 4v.

AH 8549.17 — Travels of a British druid. London, 1811. 2v.

AH 7201.5 — Ulpiani, D. Fragmenta. v.1-2. Berolini, 1811.

1812

AH 7277.95.3 — Abrégé de l'histoire romaine. 1. American ed. Baltimore, 1812.

AH 7203.39 — Corpus juris civilis. Institutiones. Justiniani Institutionum libri IV. Berolini, 1812.

NEDL AH 7652.8 — Gibbon, Edward. Histoire de la décadence et de la chute de l'Empire Romain. Paris, 1812. 13v.

AH 4228.12 — Hudtwalcker, M.H. Privat-Schiedsrichter-Diäteten. Jena, 1812.

AH 4112.5 — Tittman, F.W. Bund der Amphiktyonen. Berlin, 1812.

AH 7448.12F — Vaudoncourt, F. Guillaume. Histoire des campagnes d'Annibal. Milan, 1812. 3v.

1813

AH 7828.03.6 — Böttiger, C.A. Sabine, ou Matinée d'une dame romaine. Paris, 1813.

AH 4162.5 — Bunsen, C.C. De iure hereditario Atheniensium. Gottingae, 1813.

AH 278.13 — Mayo, R. A view of ancient geography and ancient history. v.1-2. Philadelphia, 1813.

AH 842.7 — Niemeyer, A.H. Originalstellen...über Theorie der Erziehung. Halle, 1813.

Htn AH 3966.9* — Parish, Elijah. Sacred geography: or, A gazetteer of the Bible. Boston, 1813.

AH 4817.06.15 — Potter, J. Archaeologia Graeca. Edinburgh, 1813. 2v.

AH 928.13 — Ukert, F.A. Entfernungen bei den Alten. Weimar, 1813.

1814

AH 7817.92.6 — Adam, Alexander. Roman antiquities. 2nd American ed. N.Y., 1814.

AH 937.91.3 — Anville, Jean B.B. d'. Compendium of ancient geography. N.Y., 1814. 2v.

AH 7338.14 — Berwick, Edward. Liyes of Caius A. Pollio. London, 1814.

Eg 278.14 — Champollion, J.J. L'Égypte. Paris, 1814. 2v.

AH 7418.14 — Ferrer, V.P. Historia de los dictadores de la republica romana. Cartagena de Indias, 1814.

AH 4277.86.7 — Gillies, J. History of ancient Greece. 1. American ed. N.Y., 1814. 4v.

AH 4408.14 — Hüllmann, K.D. Anfänge der griechische Geschichte. Königsberg, 1814.

AH 7827.76.3 — Meierotto, J.H.L. Ueber Sitten und Lebensart der Römer. Berlin, 1814.

AH 4277.95.3 — Mitford, W. History of Greece. London, 1814. 8v.

AH 7058.14F — Thorlacius, B. De irenarchis. Aavniae, 1814.

AH 298.21.5 — Volney, C.F. Recherches nouvelles sur l'histoire ancienne. Paris, 1814. 3v.

1815

AH 4308.15 — Drumann, K.U. Ideen zur Geschichte des Verfalls. Berlin, 1815.

AH 7808.15 — Golbrig, Karl Friedrich. Über Jahrform und Jahrrechnung bei den Römern. Salzwedel, 1815.

NEDL AH 298.15 — Heeren, Arnold Herman Ludwig. Ideen über Politik, Verkehr und Handel. v.1-2. Göttingen, 1815. 3v.

AH 7201.6 — Hugo, G. Jus civile antejustinianeum. Berolini, 1815. 2v.

Htn AH 457.16.20* — Prideaux, H. The Old and New Testament connected in the history of the Jews. Charlestown, 1815-16. 4v.

AH 278.15 — Schlosser, Friedrich Christoph. Alte Geschichte bis zum Untergang des weströmischen Reiche. Frankfurt am Main, 1815.

AH 7078.15 — Schulze, C.F. Von den Volksdersammlungen. Gotha, 1815.

AH 8549.18 — Toland, John. A critical history of the Celtic religion. Edinburgh, 1815.

1816

AH 9647.5 — Bres, Onorato. Malta antica illustrata cò monumenti, e coll'istoria. Roma, 1816.

AH 8064.1 — Münter, F. Religion der Karthager. Kopenhagen, 1816.

Htn AH 7278.11.3* — Schlegel, August W. Recension von Niebuhr's Römische Geschichte. n.p., 1816.

AH 938.16.5 — Schulthess, J. Das Paradies. Zürich, 1816.

AH 938.16 — Ukert, F.A. Geographie der Griechen und Römer. v.1-3. Weimar, 1816-46. 5v.

Chronological Listing

1816 - cont.

AH 278.16   Whepley, S. Lectures on ancient history. N.Y., 1816.

1817

AH 4108.17   Böckh, August. Staatshaushaltung der Athener. Berlin, 1817. 2v.

AH 7203.39.6   Corpus juris civilis. Institutiones. Einleitung in das römisch-justinianische Sbuch Recht. Hannover, 1817.

AH 865.5F   Ginzrot, J.C. Die Wagen und Fahrwerke. München, 1817.

AH 278.17   Heeren, Arnold Herman Ludwig. Handbuch...Geschichte...Staaten. Göttingen, 1817.

AH 3980.15   Holford, George Peter. The destruction of Jerusalem. 10. American ed. Boston, 1817.

AH 7758.17   Mauso, J.C.F. Leben Constantins des Grossen. Breslau, 1817.

AH 5121.5   Mueller, C. Aegineticorum. Berolini, 1817.

AH 7058.17   Naudet, Joseph. Des changemens...de l'empire romain. Paris, 1817. 2v.

AH 68.17   Pastoret, C.E.J.P. de. Histoire de la législation. Paris, 1817-37. 11v.

1818

Eg 878.18   Babor, Johann. Über die philosophische Historiographie der neuesten Zeit. Olmütz, 1818.

AH 7278.18   Bankes, H. History of Rome. London, 1818. 2v.

AH 338.13.2   Beauchamp, A. de. Biographie des jeunes gens. 2. éd. Paris, 1818.

AH 7808.18   Borghesi, Bartolomeo. Nuovi frammenti dei fasti consolari capitolini. Milano, 1818.

AH 7203.40F   Corpus juris civilis. Digesta. Pandectae Justinianae. Parisiis, 1818. 3v.

AH 7203.40.9   Corpus juris civilis. Digesta. Pandectae Justinianae. Parisiis, 1818-20. 5v.

AH 7448.18   DeLuc, J.A. Histoire du passage des Alpes par Annibal. Genève, 1818.

NEDL AH 4278.00.5   Goldsmith, Oliver. Grecian history from earliest state. v.1-2. Hallowell, 1818.

AH 7058.18   Harencarspel, R.S. van. De propria reipublicae romanae. Trajecti ad Rhenum, 1818.

AH 4844.2   Hirt, A.L. Die Hierodulen. Berlin, 1818.

AH 4108.18   Hüllmann, K.D. Ursprünge der Besteurung. Cöln, 1818.

NEDL AH 4817.06.17   Potter, J. Archaeologia Graeca. v.2. Edinburgh, 1818.

AH 3013.20.3   Rich, C.J. Memoir on the ruins of Babylon. 3. ed. v.1-2. London, 1818.

AH 7338.18   Rogers, Eliza. History of the Roman Empire. London, 1818. 5v.

AH 7278.18.5F   Rogers, Eliza. History of the Roman Empire. Atlas. London, 1818.

1819

AH 4967.88.40   Barthélemy, J.J. Periëgesis toū Néou Anacharsidos eis Ten Hellada. v.1-7, Atlas. En Bienne, 1819. 3v.

Eg 708.19   Champollion, J.J. Annales des Lagides. Paris, 1819. 2v.

AH 238.19   Dureau de la Malle, Adolphe. Poliorcéteque des anciens. Paris, 1819.

AH 7206.13   Haubold, G.G. Manuale Basilicorum. Lipsiae, 1819.

AH 3098.3   Koopmans, W.C. Disputatio historico-critica de Sardanapalo. Amsterdam, 1819.

AH 4158.19   Meier, M.H.E. Historiae juris Attici. Berolini, 1819.

AH 4278.19   Morell, T. Studies in history...Greece. Philadelphia, 1819.

Eg 878.19   Prichard, J.C. An analysis of Egyptian mythology. London, 1819.

AH 4078.19   Schömann, G.F. De comitiis atheniensium. Gryphiswaldiae, 1819.

AH 3357.5   Thrige, Johann P. Historia Cyrenes. Hauniae, 1819.

AH 7428.19   Wachsmuth, W. Ältere Geschichte des römischen Staates. Halle, 1819.

182-

VAH 7278.20   Stories from Roman history, by a lady. Boston, 182-?

1820

AH 7808.18.3   Borghesi, Bartolomeo. Nuovi frammenti dei fasti consolari capitolini. Milano, 1820.

AH 8617.5.2   Cuoco, Vincenzo. Platone in Italia. 2. ed. Parma, 1820.

AH 7138.20   Dirksen, H.E. Civilistische Abhandlungen. Berlin, 1820. 2v.

AH 7808.20F   Fea, Carlo. Frammenti di fasti consolari e trionfali ultimamente scaperti nel faro romano e altrove. Roma, 1820.

NEDL AH 7650.24.5   Gibbon, Edward. History of decline and fall of Roman Empire. London, 1820. 12v.

NEDL AH 7650.24   Gibbon, Edward. History of decline and fall of Roman Empire. London, 1820. 12v.

NEDL AH 4277.86.10   Gillies, J. History of ancient Greece. 6. ed. v.1-8. London, 1820. 4v.

NEDL AH 817.58.5   Goguet, Antoine Y. De l'origine des lois. 6. éd. Paris, 1820. 3v.

AH 38.20   Hüllmann, K.D. Staatsrecht des Alterthums. Cöln, 1820.

AH 8954.10F   Lama, Pietro de. Tavola legislativa della Gallia Cisalpina. Parma, 1820.

AH 4228.20   Otto, C.E. De Atheniensium actionibus forensibus. Lipsiae, 1820.

AH 6158.5   Ritter, C. Vorhalle europäischer Völkerges. Berlin, 1820.

AH 848.5   Stieglitz, C.L. Archäologische Unterhaltungen. Leipzig, 1820.

AH 7448.20   Wickham, Henry L. A dissertation on the passage of Hannibal over the Alps. Oxford, 1820.

1821

AH 4967.88.9   Barbié du Bocage, J.D. Oeuvres de Barthélemy. v.1-4, Atlas. Paris, 1821. 5v.

AH 4298.21F   Bertocchi, F. Raccolta di 100 soggetti li piú remarche. Roma, 1821.

AH 7298.21   Bertocchi, Fulvia. Racollta...istoria romana. Roma, 1821.

AH 4498.21   Boeckh, A. De Pericle, artium et letterarum slatore. Berolini, 1821.

AH 4828.01.4   Chaussard, J.B. Fetes et courtisanes. 4. éd. Paris, 1821. 4v.

1821 - cont.

AH 4808.21   Dalzel, A. Substance of lecture on ancient Greece. Edinburgh, 1821.

AH 7201.7   Gans, E. Scholien zum Gajus. Berlin, 1821.

NEDL AH 7650.26   Gibbon, Edward. History of decline and fall of Roman Empire. London, 1821. 12v.

NEDL AH 7650.25   Gibbon, Edward. History of decline and fall of Roman Empire. London, 1821. 2v.

NEDL AH 7277.70.7   Goldsmith, O. Roman history. London, 1821. 2v.

NEDL AH 4278.00.7   Goldsmith, Oliver. History of Greece. London, 1821. 2v.

AH 277.93.3.4   Heeren, Arnold Herman Ludwig. Handbuch der Geschichte der Staaten des Alterthums. 4. Aufl. Göttingen, 1821.

AH 4038.21   Kortüm, Friedrich. Zur Geschichte hellenischen Staatsverfassungen hauptsächlich Während des peloponnesischen Krieges. Heidelberg, 1821.

AH 930.25   Lelewel, J. Die Entdeckungen der Carthager und Griechen. Berlin, 1821.

AH 7408.21.6F   Micali, G. Antichi monumenti per servire all'opera intitolata l'Italia. Firenze, 1821.

AH 7408.21.5   Micali, G. L'Italia avanti il Domino dei Romani. 2. ed. v.1-2, 3-4. Firenze, 1821. 2v.

NEDL AH 4277.95.4   Mitford, W. History of Greece. v.9-10, 3. ed. London, 1821-22. 10v.

AH 8064.1.5   Münter, F. Religion der Karthager. Kopenhagen, 1821.

AH 298.21   Volney, C.F. New researches in ancient history. London, 1821. 2v.

AH 928.21   Wurm, J.F. De ponderum, numerum. Stutgardaie, 1821.

1822

Htn AH 298.22*   Adams, J. Flowers of ancient history. Leesburg, 1822.

AH 4967.88.11   Barthélemy, J.J. Voyage du jeune Anacharsis. Paris, 1822. 7v.

AH 4408.09.5   Clavier, M. Histoire des premiers temps de la Grèce. 2. éd. Paris, 1822. 3v.

AH 7203.40.15   Corpus juris civilis. Juris civilis ecloga. Parisiis, 1822.

AH 7138.22   Doneau, H. Commentarii de iure civili. Norimberg, 1822. 16v.

AH 4277.86.12   Gillies, J. History of ancient Greece. 2. American ed. Philadelphia, 1822. 4v.

AH 4558.22   Gobdelas, D. Histoire d'Alexandre le Grand. Varsovie, 1822.

AH 4138.22   Heffter, A.W. Athenäische Gerichtsverfassung. Cöln, 1822.

AH 4818.22   Irving, C. Catechism of Grecian antiquities. N.Y., 1822.

AH 7816.96.16   Kennett, Basil. Romae antiquae notitia. 1st American ed. Philadelphia, 1822.

AH 4958.22   Muller, C. Voyage en Grèce et dans les Iles Ioniennes. Paris, 1822.

AH 1872.22   Munter, Friederich. Sendschreiben an Friedrich Creuzer, über einige sardische Idole. Kopenhagen, 1822.

AH 878.22   Onymus, A.J. Dämonen-Lehre der Alten. Würzburg, 1822.

AH 7850.5   Peignot, Gabriel. Des coinestebles et des vins de la Grèce et de l'Italie, en usage chez les Romains. Dijon, 1822.

AH 4278.25   Pinnock, W. Catechism of history of Greece. London, 1822.

AH 28.22   Serapis, oder Abhandlungen betreffend das griechische und römische Alterthum. St. Peterburg, 1822.

AH 7828.22   Sketches of domestic manners. Philadelphia, 1822.

AH 4038.22   Tittmann, F.W. Staatsverfassungen. Leipzig, 1822.

AH 4208.3   Vömel, Johann T. Examina solemnia gymnasii Francofurtani. Disseritur de Heliaea. Francofurti, 1822.

AH 7163.7   Wächter-Spittler, K. Ehescheidungen. Stuttgart, 1822.

1823

AH 7138.23   Dirksen, H.E. Auslegung...des römischen Rechts Versuch zu Kritik. Leipzig, 1823.

Eg 708.23   Drumann, Wilhelm. Historisch-antiquarische Untersuchungen über Aegypten, oder Die Inschrift von Rosette. Königsberg, 1823.

AH 7201.92   Heimbach, C. Aelii Galli icti de verborum. Lipsiae, 1823.

AH 5457.7   Koeck, K. Kreta. Göttingen, 1823. 3v.

AH 3013.15   Landseer, J. Sabaean researches. London, 1823.

AH 7161.5   Maanen, J.M. van. De muliere in manu in tutela secundum Gaji Veronensis institutionum principis. Lugdunum Batavorum, 1823.

NEDL AH 4277.95.5.5   Mitford, W. History of Greece. Boston, 1823. 8v.

AH 4277.95.5   Mitford, W. History of Greece. Boston, 1823. 8v.

NEDL AH 277.34.14   Rollin, Charles. Ancient history. Boston, 1823. 2v.

AH 7201.9   Schrader, E. Wasgewimit die römische Rechtsgeschichte. Heidelberg, 1823.

AH 7828.22.3A   Sketches of domestic manners. 2. American ed. Philadelphia, 1823.

AH 7114.7   Swingar, G.H.D. Commentatio de Patronatus. Groningae, 1823.

AH 4818.23   Wessenberg, I.H. Volksleben zu Athen. Zürich, 1823.

1824

AH 7203.41   Biener, F.A. Geschichte der novellen Justinian's. Berlin, 1824.

AH 7201.11   Bluhme, A.F. Gaius Institutionum. Berolini, 1824.

AH 7114.6   Burchardi, G.C. Bemerkungen über den Census. Kiel, 1824.

AH 8940.2   Carchidio, F. Memorie storichi dell'...Telamone. Firenze, 1824.

AH 7818.24   Creuzers, G.F. Abriss der römischen Antiquitäten. Leipzig, 1824.

AH 7200.7   Dirksen, H.E. Zwölf-Tafel-Fragmente. Leipzig, 1824.

AH 1298.24   Drummond, W. Origines. London, 1824. 4v.

AH 7114.17   Francke, G.K. De tribuum, curiarum atque. Slesvici, 1824.

AH 7448.24   Giani, G.B. Battaglia del Ticino tra Annibale e Scipione. Appendice. Milano, 1824-26.

NEDL AH 4278.00.8   Goldsmith, Oliver. Grecian history from earliest state to the death of Alexander. Hartford, 1824.

AH 7163.9   Hasse, J.C. Güterrecht der Ehegatten. Berlin, 1824.

AH 4278.24   Heeren, A.H.L. Reflections on politics of ancient Greece. Boston, 1824.

AH 277.93.4   Heeren, Arnold Herman Ludwig. Ideen über Politik, Verkehr und Handel. Göttingen, 1824. 6v.

AH 7278.24   Irving, C. Catechism of Roman history. 2. American ed. N.Y., 1824.

AH 4228.24.3   Meier, M.H.E. Attische Process. Halle, 1824.

AH 7138.24   Pernice, L. Geschichte...römischen Rechts. Halle, 1824.

AH 4228.24   Platner, E. Process und Klagen. Darmstaat, 1824. 2v.

AH 2007.4   Price, David. Essay towards the history of Arabia. London, 1824.

1824 - cont.

AH 7038.24 Rovers, J.A.C. De censaum apud romanos auctoritate.
Trajecti ad Rhenum, 1824.

AH 7201.64 Schilling, F.A. Dissertatio critica de Ulpiani fragmentis.
Vratislaviae, 1824. 3 pam.

AH 8667.3 Theis, A. di. Viaggio di Policleto a Roma. Milano, 1824.
4v.

1825

AH 4967.88.24 Barthélemy, J.J. Travels of Anacharsis the younger. 6. ed.
London, 1825. 6v.

AH 4967.88.13 Barthélemy, J.J. Voyage du jeune Anacharsis. v.1-7, Atlas.
Paris, 1825. 8v.

Eg 1300.5 Champollion-Figeae, Jacques J. Catalogo de' papiri
egiziani della Biblioteca Vaticana e notizia piu estesa di
uno d'essi. Roma, 1825.

AH 7202.11 Codex Theodosianus. Codicis Theodosiani libri v priores.
Lipsiae, 1825.

AH 7202.9 Codex Theodosianus. Theodosianus Codex genuina fragmenta.
Bonnae, 1825.

AH 7838.25F Eichstadius, H.C.A. De Votis X, XX, et XXX Imperatoum
Romanorum. Ienae, 1825.

AH 4845.5F Eichstädt, H.C. Humanitate Graecorum. Ienae, 1825.

AH 4408.25 Eissner, C.G. Die alten Pelasger und ihre Mysterien.
Leipzig, 1825.

AH 7488.25 Elton, C.A. History of Roman emperors...to...last
Constantine. London, 1825.

AH 7417.83.11 Ferguson, A. History of...Roman republic. London, 1825.

AH 7158.25 Fragmenta Klenze. Legis serviliae. Berolini, 1825.

NEDL AH 7650.27 Gibbon, Edward. History of decline and fall of Roman
Empire. London, 1825. 8v.

AH 4278.00.10 Goldsmith, Oliver. History of Greece. 11. ed.
London, 1825.

AH 4278.00.9 Goldsmith, Oliver. The history of Greece from the earliest
state to the death of Alexander the Great. London, 1825.

AH 7138.25 Hugo, G. Histoire du droit romain. Paris, 1825. 2v.

AH 808.25 Ideler, L.C. Handbuch der...Chronologie. Berlin, 1825.
2v.

AH 4938.25 Kruse, F.C.H. Hellas. Leipzig, 1825. 3v.

AH 8407.2 Muchar, A.A. Das römische Norikum. Gratz, 1825.
2v.

AH 7468.25 Reiff, H.C. Geschichte der römischen Burgerkreige.
Berlin, 1825.

AH 5857.5 Reinganum, H. Alte Megaris. Berlin, 1825.

AH 3980.12.10 Scholz, J.M.A. Commentatio de Golgothae et sanctissimi
D.N.J.C. sepulcri situ. Bonnae, 1825.

NEDL AH 7297.20.15 Vertot, R.A. Historia de las revoluciones. Paris, 1825.

1826

AH 7817.92.7 Adam, Alexander. Roman antiquities. N.Y., 1826.

AH 8549.20 Barth, C.K. Ueber die Druiden der Kelten. Erlangen, 1826.

AH 7188.26 Böcking, E. De mancipii causis. Berolini, 1826.

AH 7498.26 Chateaubriand, François August René. Discours servant
d'introduction à l'histoire de France. Paris, 1826.

AH 8616.6 Cramer, J.A. Geographical...description of ancient Italy.
Oxford, 1826. 2v.

AH 5307.11 Creuzer, F. Oratio de civitate Athenarum.
Francofurti, 1826.

NEDL AH 278.26.5 Ertov, I.D. Prodolzhenie v seobshchei istorii drevnikh
prosveschennykh narodov. Sankt Peterburg, 1826. 2v.

NEDL AH 7650.29 Gibbon, Edward. History of the decline and fall of the
Roman Empire. London, 1826-28. 4v.

AH 1457.5 Klaproth, J. Tableau historique de l'Asie. Paris, 1826.

AH 1457.5F Klaproth, J. Tableau historique de l'Asie. Atlas.
Paris, 1826.

AH 7478.26 Knowles, J.S. Character of Julius Caesar. Boston, 1826.

AH 7448.26 Larauza, J.L. Histoire critique du passage des Alpes par
Annibal. Paris, 1826.

AH 8607.8 Micali, G. L'Italia avanti il dominio dei romani. 3. ed.
Milano, 1826. 3v.

AH 4818.26.7 Petersen, F.C. De statu culturae. Havniae, 1826.

AH 5132.5 Plehn, S.L. Lesbiacorum liber. Berolini, 1826.

AH 277.34.23 Rollin, Charles. The ancient history of the Egyptians.
London, 1826. 8v.

AH 278.26 Schlosser, Friedrich Christoph. Geschichte der alten Welt.
v.1-3. Frankfurt, 1826. 9v.

AH 307.96.3 Volney, C.F. Les ruines...révolutions des empires.
Paris, 1826.

AH 4818.26 Wachsmuth, W. Hellenische Alterthumskunde. Halle, 1826.
4v.

AH 9758.3 Wersebe, August von. Ueber die Völker und Völkerbundnisse
des alten Teutschlands. Hannover, 1826.

AH 7168.26 Zimmern, S.W. Geschichte der römischen Privatrechts.
v.1,3. Heidelberg, 1826. 2v.

1827

AH 9777.7 Aschbach, J. Geschichte der Westgothen. Frankfurt, 1827.

AH 4908.27 Baumstark, A. Curatoribus emporii et nautodicis.
Friburgi, 1827.

AH 8073.2 Botticher, J.F.W. Geschichte der Carthager. Berlin, 1827.

AH 4818.27 Cleveland, C.D. Epitome of Grecian antiquities.
Boston, 1827.

AH 7201.13 Gaius. Institutionum...sive de actionibus.
Berolini, 1827.

AH 7201.15 Gaius. Institutionum. Paris, 1827.

AH 7138.27 Gans, E. System des römischen Civilrechts. Berlin, 1827.

AH 7217.5 Gaupp, E.T. De professoribus et medicis eorumgue.
Vratislaviae, 1827.

AH 7650.32A Gibbon, Edward. History of decline and fall of Roman
Empire. Oxford, 1827. 8v.

NEDL AH 7650.31 Gibbon, Edward. The history of the decline and fall of the
Roman Empire. London, 1827. 11v.

AH 277.93.25 Heeren, Arnold Herman Ludwig. Etwas über meine Studien des
alten Indiens. Göttingen, 1827.

AH 7228.27 Keller, F.L. Litis Contestation und Ultheil.
Zürich, 1827.

AH 3155.3 Münter, D.F. Religion der Babylonier. Kopenhagen, 1827.

AH 7278.11.5 Niebuhr, B.G. Römische Geschichte. 2. Aufl. Berlin, 1827.

AH 4408.27 Petit-Radel, C.F. Examen analytique...de l'histoire...de
la Grèce. Paris? 1827.

AH 7478.27 Petrarca, F. Historia Iulii Caesaris. Lipsiae, 1827.

AH 9639.5 Reinganum, H. Selinus und sein Gebiet. Leipzig, 1827.

AH 8548.5 Ritson, J. Memoirs of the Celts or Gauls. London, 1827.

1828

AH 7408.28 Blum, K.L. Einleitung im Rom's alte Geschichte.
Berlin, 1828.

AH 8549.25 Bowles, W.L. A dissertation on the Celtic deity Teutates.
London, 1828.

AH 7278.28 Cobbett, W. Elements of Roman history. London, 1828.

AH 4938.25.3 Cramer, J.A. Ancient Greece. Oxford, 1828. 3v.

AH 4206.5 Forchhammer, P.W. De Areopago. Kiliae, 1828.

AH 278.28 Heeren, Arnold Herman Ludwig. History of the states of
antiquity. Northhampton, 1828.

Eg 298.28 Henry, Dominique Marie Joseph. Lettre à M. Champollion le
jeune...avant l'invasion de Cambyse. Paris, 1828.

AH 298.28 Herbert, Algernon. Nimrod. London, 1828-30. 4v.

AH 8907.8 Müller, Karl O. Die Etrusker. v.1-2. Breslau, 1828.

AH 7278.11.13 Niebuhr, B.G. History of Rome. Cambridge, 1828. 3v.

AH 278.28.5 Niebuhr, B.G. Kleine historische und philologische
Schriften. Bonn, 1828.

NEDL AH 7278.11.7 Niebuhr, B.G. Römische Geschichte. 3. Aufl. Berlin, 1828.
3v.

AH 278.28.9 Outline of general history. v.1-2. London, 1828.

AH 7488.28 Die Römischen Kaiser. v.1-4. Leipzig, 1828-29.

NEDL AH 277.34.14.3 Rollin, Charles. Ancient history. N.Y., 1828. 2v.

NEDL AH 277.34.27 Rollin, Charles. Storia antica e romana. 1. ed.
Firenze, 1828-32. 49v.

Eg 847.1 Schmidt, Karl F.W. Die Kunst Hieroglyphen zu Lesen.
Breslau, 1828.

AH 7058.28 Schubert, F.G. De romanorum aedilibus. Regimontii, 1828.

AH 3357.7 Thrige, Johann P. Res Cyrenensium. Hauniae, 1828.

AH 7817.32.5 Vaslet, L. Introduzzione alla scienza d'antichita.
Venezia, 1828.

AH 7201.17 Vaticana fragmenta. Borussorum, 1828.

AH 4845.7 Zander, A.G.B. Luxu Atheniensium. Gryphiae, 1828.

1829

AH 4728.29 Ahrens, F.H.L. Athenarum statu politico. Gottingae, 1829.

AH 4967.88.25 Barthélemy, J.J. Travels of Anacharsis the younger.
Baltimore, 1829.

AH 3667.7 Buckingham, J.S. Travels in Assyria, Media and Persia.
London, 1829.

AH 7278.28.2 Cobbett, W. Abridged history of emperors. London, 1829.

AH 7203.43 Corpus juris civilis. Institutiones. Corpus juris civilis.
Lipsiae, 1829-37. 2v.

AH 7818.24.3 Creuzers, G.F. Abriss der römischen Antiquitäten. 2. Aufl.
Leipzig, 1829.

AH 7148.29 Eisendecher, W. Über die Entstehung...des Burgerrechts.
Hamburg, 1829.

AH 7468.29 Emperius, A.C.W. De temporum Belli Mithridatici.
Gottingae, 1829.

AH 9722.5 Falk, F.W.A. De origine Byzantie dissertatio.
Vratislaviae, 1829.

AH 7138.29 Gaius. Institutiones iuris Romani. Berolini, 1829.

NEDL AH 4278.24.2 Heeren, A.H.L. Sketch of political history of ancient
Greece. Oxford, 1829.

AH 7161.20 Heiberg, C.F. De familiari patriciorum. Slesvici, 1829.

AH 4138.29A Hermann, C.F. De jure et Auctoritate Magistratum.
Heidelbergae, 1829.

AH 7088.29 Hopfensack, J.C.W.A. Staatsrecht der Unterthonen der
Römer. Düsseldorf, 1829.

AH 7058.29.2 Incerti auctoris magistratuum. Diss. Vratislaviae, 1829.

AH 938.29.2 Longe, George. An introduction to the study of Greek and
Roman geography. Charlottesville, 1829.

AH 7058.29 Magistratum et sacerdotiorum. Vratislaviae, 1829.

AH 4278.29 Malkin, F. History of Greece from earliest times.
London, 1829.

AH 38.29 Reichard, H.G. Erinnerungen aus der Staatskunst.
Leipzig, 1829.

NEDL AH 277.34.14.5 Rollin, Charles. Ancient history. v.2-4,6-8.
Philadelphia, 1829. 6v.

NEDL AH 4558.29 Williams, John. Alexander the Great, life and actions.
London, 1829.

AH 4558.29.3 Williams, John. Alexander the Great, life and actions. 2.
ed. London, 1829.

1830

Adam, Alexander. Roman antiquities. N.Y., 1830.

NEDL AH 7817.92.9 Adam, Alexander. Roman antiquities. N.Y., 1830.

NEDL AH 4967.88.14 Barthélemy, J.J. Voyage du jeune Anacharsis en Grèce.
Paris, 1830. 7v.

AH 7138.30.5 Bloudeau, M. Chrestomathie ou choix de textes.
Paris, 1830.

AH 7168.15.2 Bucher, K. Das Recht der Forderungen. 2e Aufl.
Leipzig, 1830.

AH 3966.8.5 Carpenter, L. An introduction to the geography of the New
Testament. 6. ed. London, 1830.

AH 4808.34.3 Clinton, H.F. Fasti Hellenici. Lipsiae, 1830.

AH 2061.3 Elisaeus. History of Varton and of the Battle of the
Armenians. London, 1830.

NEDL AH 7417.83.13 Ferguson, A. History of...Roman republic.
Philadelphia, 1830.

AH 4818.30 Geijer, Erik Gustof. Mores heroicae aetatis apud veteres
Graecas et Scandinavas comjsaroti. Upsaliae, 1830.

NEDL AH 7650.33 Gibbon, Edward. History of decline and fall of Roman
Empire. 6. American ed. Philadelphia, 1830. 4v.

AH 808.30 Hales, W. New analysis of chronology and geography.
London, 1830. 4v.

AH 7201.19 Haubold, C.G. Antiquitatis Romanae monumenta legalia.
Berolini, 1830.

AH 7278.30 History of Rome. v.1-5. London, 1830-

AH 7138.30 Huschke, E. Studien des römischen Rechts. Breslau, 1830.

AH 930.3F Jones and Co. Jones' classical atlas. London, 1830.

AH 7201.19.6 Kriegel, C.J. Antiqua versio latina. Lipsiae, 1830.

AH 4843.6F Krüger, S. De musicis Graecorum organis. Gottingae, 1830.

AH 5967.5A Leake, W.M. Travels in the Morea. London, 1830. 3v.

AH 4328.30 Müller, K.O. History and antiquities of Dorie Race.
Oxford, 1830. 2v.

AH 7116.3 Troll, M.J. De non metata classium centuriarum.
Asciburgi, 1830.

AH 4217.7 Westermann, A. De publicis Atheniensium honoribus ae
Praemais commutaico. Lipsiae, 1830.

AH 7238.30 Wiener, P.E.A. De legione Romanorum vicesima secunda.
Darmstadii, 1830.

NEDL AH 4558.29.4 Williams, John. Alexander the Great, life and actions.
N.Y., 1830.

AH 1808.30 Yeates, T. Remarks of Bible chronology. London, 1830.

Chronological Listing

1831

	AH 938.31	Butler, Samuel. Geographia classica. Philadelphia, 1831.
	AH 4818.27.4	Cleveland, C.D. Compendium of Grecian antiquities. 2. ed. Boston, 1831.
	AH 7203.44	Corpus juris civilis. Das Corpus Juris Civilis. Leipzig, 1831-39. 7v.
	AH 808.31	Ideler, L.C. Lehrbuch der Chronologie. Berlin, 1831.
	AH 7818.31	Irving, C. Catechism of Roman antiquities. 4th American ed. N.Y., 1831.
Htn	AH 7448.18.2*	Long, H.L. March of Hannibal from Rome. London, 1831. 4 pam.
	AH 7114.31	Muhlert, Fridericus. De equitibus Romanis. Diss. Hildesiae, 1831.
	AH 4278.31	Plass, H.G. Geschichte des alten Griech. Leipzig, 1831. 3v.
	AH 7162.5	Rosshirt, K.F. Erbrecht. Landshut, 1831.
	AH 8908.5	Rühle, J.J.O.A. Zur Geschichte der Pelasger und Etrusker. Berlin, 1831.

1832

AH 7448.32	Beaujour, F. De l'expédition d'Annibal en Italie. Paris, 1832.
AH 7203.43.6	Corpus juris civilis. Institutiones. Justiniani Institutionum libri IV. Berolini, 1832.
AH 1028.32.3	Cory, I.P. Ancient fragments. London, 1832.
AH 842.34	Cramer, Friedrich. Geschichte der Erziehung und des Unterrichts im Alterthume. Elberfeld, 1832-38. 2v.
AH 2107.5	Cramer, J.A. Geographical and historical description of Asia Minor. Oxford, 1832. 2v.
AH 6107.7	Flathe, L. Geschichte Macedoniens. Leipzig, 1832. 2v.
AH 7038.32.2	Hüllmann, Karl. Römische Grundverfassung. Bonn, 1832.
AH 7038.32	Hüllmann, Karl. Römische Grundverfassung. Bonn, 1832.
AH 7138.32	Hugo, G. Lehrbuch der Geschichte des römischen Rechts. Berlin, 1832.
AH 7098.32	Madvig, J.N. De coloniarum populi Romani iure et condicione quaestionis historicae pars prior. Hauniae, 1832. 2 pam.
AH 3657.39	Mirkhoud. History of the early kings of Persia. London, 1832.

NEDL	AH 4817.06.16	Potter, J. Archaeologia Graeca. Edinburgh, 1832. 2v.
	AH 7138.32.3	Schweppe, A. Römische Rechtsgeschichte. Göttingen, 1832.
	AH 4162.9	Steigertahl, G.H.C.L. De vi et usu Parachatabolès in causis Atheniensium hereditariis commentatio. Cellis, 1832.
	AH 7114.18	Strafser, G. Versuch über die römische Plebejer. Elberfeld, 1832.
	AH 198.32	Veder, A. Historia philosophiae juris apud veteres. Lugduni Batavorum, 1832.
NEDL	AH 4558.29.5	Williams, John. Alexander the Great, life and actions. N.Y., 1832.

1833

	AH 7206.9F	Basilicorum libri LX. Lipsiae, 1833-1850. 5v.
	AH 7818.32.3	Dillaway, C.K. Roman antiquities and ancient mythology. 2nd ed. Boston, 1833.
	AH 4558.33	Droysen, J.G. Alexanders des Grossen. Hamburg, 1833.
	AH 7842.7	Egger, Emile. Étude sur l'éducation. Paris, 1833.
	AH 7163.13	Eggers, F.W.T. Alt-römischen Ehe mit Manus. Altona, 1833.
	AH 7808.33	Fasti consulares capitolini. Altonae, 1833.
	AH 7201.18	Fragmenta vaticana. Locorum exiure Romano anteiustiniano ab incerto scriptore coll. fragmenta quae dicuntur vaticana. Bonnae, 1833.
	AH 7031.7F	Frandsen, P.S. Über die Politik des Marcus Agrippa. Altona, 1833. 5 pam.
NEDL	AH 298.33.3	Heeren, Arnold Herman Ludwig. Historical researches. Oxford, 1833. 3v.
NEDL	AH 7278.37.3	Lardner, D. Cabinet cyclopedia. London, 1833. 2v.
	AH 298.33.5	Lorentz, R. Gründzüge zu Vorträgen über Geschichte. Leipzig, 1833.
	AH 8740.2	Lorentz, Rudolf. De civitate veterum Tarentinorum. Lipsiae, 1833.
	AH 7278.33	Michelet, J. Histoire romaine. 2. ed. Paris, 1833. 2v.
	AH 7201.21	Paulus, Julius. Receptarum sententiarum. Bonnae, 1833.
NEDL	AH 7201.21	Paulus, Julius. Receptarum sententiarum. Bonnae, 1833.
	AH 4708.33	Schorn, W. Geschichte Griechenlands. Bonn, 1833.
	AH 7038.33	Schultz, C.L. Grundlegung-Staatswissenschaft. Köln, 1833.
	AH 7148.33	Vaugerow, C.A. Latini Juniani. Marburg, 1833.
	AH 7297.20.7	Vertot, R.A. Histoire des révolutions. Paris, 1833. 4v.

1834

AH 7055.93.5	Böcking, D. Eduard. Über die Notitia Dignitatum. Bonn, 1834.
AH 4808.34	Clinton, H.F. Fasti Hellenici. Oxford, 1834. 3v.
AH 7202.13	Codex Theodosianus. Antiqua summaria Codicis Theodosiani. Lipsiae, 1834.
AH 7468.34.4	Drumann, W. Geschichte Roms. Koenigsberg, 1834. 6v.
AH 7738.34	Grepps, J.G.H. Dissertation sur les laraires de l'empereur Sévère Alexandre. Belley, 1834.
AH 4938.34	Harrison, G. Lectures on geography of ancient Greece. Charlottesville, 1834.
AH 298.34F	Harrison, George. Fragments and scraps of history. London, 1834. 2v.
AH 7598.00.3	Hegewisch, D.H. Essai sur l'epoque de l'histoire romaine. Paris, 1834.
AH 4178.34	Hermann, C.F. Causis turbatae apud Lacedaemonios agrorum aequalitatis. Marburgi, 1834.
AH 4118.7	Meier, M.H.E. De gentilitate attica. Halis, 1834.
AH 4068.34	Osenburgen, C. Senatu atheniensium. Hagae Comitum, 1834.
AH 842.4.2	Peignot, E.G. Reliure des livres. Dijon, 1834.
AH 842.4	Peignot, E.G. Reliure des livres. Dijon, 1834.
AH 7168.34	Schilling, F.A. Lehrbuch für Institutionen und Geschichte. Leipzig, 1834. 3v.
AH 2357.16	Schmidt, G.A. De fontibus. Berolini, 1834.
AH 7201.22	Unger, F.W. De duorum praecipuorum iurisprudentiae. Inaug. Diss. Hannoverae, 1834.
AH 7148.34	Weiske, C.A. Considérations historique...sur les ambassades. Zwickau, 1834.
AH 7468.34.6	Zacharia, K.S. Lucius Cornelius Sulla. Heidelberg, 1834.

1835

	AH 7817.92.10	Adam, Alexander. Roman antiquities. 6th ed. Glasgow, 1835.
	AH 7238.35	Cardinali, Clemente. Diplomi imperiali di privilegj accordatiai militari. Velletri, 1835.
	AH 9666.5	Cortés y López, Miguel. Diccionario...de la Espana antigua. Madrid, 1835-36. 3v.
	AH 4202.7	Fritzsche, F.V. De sortitione judicum. Lipsiae, 1835.
	AH 4114.16	Hermann, G.F. Natalem zum quagesimum nonum. Marburgi, 1835.
	AH 3664.8	Korn, Friedrich. Mythen der alten Perser. Leipzig, 1835.
	AH 4958.35	Leake, W.M. Travels in northern Greece. London, 1835. 4v.
	AH 4158.35	Lelyveld, P. De Infama jure Attico. Amsterdam, 1835.
	AH 4833.5	Loebker, G. Gymnastik der Hellenen. Münster, 1835.
	AH 4118.9	Meier, M.H.E. De gentilitate attica. Halis, 1835.
NEDL	AH 4277.95.6	Mitford, W. The history of Greece from the earliest period to the death of Agesilaus. London, 1835. 8v.
	AH 7278.11.15	Niebuhr, B.G. History of Rome. Philadelphia, 1835. 2v.
	AH 4808.35	Peter, C.L. Zeittafeln der griechischen Geschichte. v.1-2. Halle, 1835.
	AH 1028.35A	The Phenix. N.Y., 1835.
	AH 278.35	Pogodin, Mikhail Petrovich. Lektsii po Gerenu o politike. Moskva, 1835.
	AH 4818.35	Pouqueville, F.C.H.L. Grèce. Paris, 1835.
NEDL	AH 277.34.25	Rollin, Charles. Storia antica. Livorno, 1835. 11v.
	AH 7228.35	Schneider, K.A. De centumviralis judicii apud romani origine. Rostochii, 1835.
	AH 7658.35	Simonde de Simondi, J.C.L. History of the fall of the Roman Empire. Philadelphia, 1835.
	AH 5386.5	Stanhope, J.S. Battle of Plataea. v.1-2. London, 1835.
	AH 8508.7.2	Thierry, A.S.D. Histoire des Gaulois. 2. éd. Paris, 1835. 3v.
NEDL	AH 4278.35	Thirlwall, C. Cabinet of history. London, 1835. 8v.
Eg	278.35	Yeates, T. Ancient Egypt. London, 1835.

1836

	AH 7817.92.12	Adam, Alexander. Roman antiquities. 7th ed. N.Y., 1836.
	AH 7468.36	Ahrens, E.A.J. Die drei Volkstribunen Tib. Gracchus, M. Drusus und P. Sulpicius. Leipzig, 1836.
	AH 4818.27.6	Clevland, C.D. Compendium of Grecian antiquities. 2. ed. Boston, 1836.
	AH 4658.36	Droysen, J.G. Geschichte des Hellenismus. Hamburg, 1836. 2v.
NEDL	AH 7417.83.14	Ferguson, A. History of the progress and termination of the Roman republic. N.Y., 1836.
	AH 2008.5	Fresnel, F. Lettres sur l'histoire des Arabes. Paris, 1836.
	AH 7818.20.3	Fuss, J.D. Antiquitates Romanae compendio. Leodii, 1836.
	AH 7138.36	Halifax, S. An analysis of the civil law. Cambridge, 1836.
	AH 4818.36	Hase, H. Public and private life of ancient Greeks. London, 1836.
	AH 7458.36	Heerwagen, H.G. De P. et L. Scipionum accusation de quaestio. Baruthi, 1836.
	AH 4038.36	Hermann, C.F. Manuel of political antiquities. Oxford, 1836.
	AH 928.36A	Hussey, R. Essay on ancient weights and money. Oxford, 1836.
	AH 8549.36	James, D. The patriarchal religion of Britain; or A complete manual of ancient British Druidism. London, 1836.
	AH 7200.9	Kokkinos, E. Lege XII Tabularum. Heidelbergae, 1836.
	AH 5754.11	Lachmann, K.H. Spartnisches Staatsverfassung. Breslau, 1836.
	AH 938.36	Lelewel, J. Kleinere Schriften. Leipzig, 1836.
	AH 8740.2.5	Lorentz, Rudolf. De rebus sacris et artibus veterum Tarentinorum. Elberfeldiae, 1836.
	AH 8011.5	Marcus, Ludwig. Histoire des wandales. Paris, 1836.
	AH 2623.5	Marquarat, J. Cyzicus und sein Gebiet. Berlin, 1836.
	AH 7168.17.3	Mühlenbruch, C.F. Die Lehre von der Cession. 3e Aufl. Stuttgart, 1836.
	AH 5307.15	Müller, K.O. De munimentis Athenarum. Gottingae, 1836.
	AH 7478.36.3	Napoléon III, emperor of the French. Précis des guerres de César. Bruxelles, 1836.
	AH 7478.36	Napoléon III, emperor of the French. Précis des guerres de César. Paris, 1836.
NEDL	AH 4818.35.9	Pouqueville, F.C.H.L. La Grecia. Venezia, 1836.
	AH 7168.36	Rein, W. Römisches Privatrecht. Leipzig, 1836.
	AH 7148.36	Roulez, J. Observations sur divers points de l'histoire de la constitution. Bruxelles, 1836.
	AH 7098.36	Schmidt. Über römische Colonien. pt.1-2. Potsdam, 1836.
	AH 4078.36	Schömann, G.F. De ecclesiis lacedaemoniorum. Gryphiswaldiae, 1836.
	AH 278.36	Ségur, L.P. Histoire universelle. 5. éd. v.1-10. Atlas. Paris, 1836. 11v.
Eg	278.36	Sharpe, S. Early history of Egypt. London, 1836.
	AH 7658.36	Simonde de Simondi, J.C.L. Histoire de la chute de l'Empire romain. Bruxelles, 1836.
	AH 7201.23	Ulpiani, D. Fragmenta. Bonnae, 1836.
	AH 4415.5	Uschold, Johannes N. Geschichte des trojanischen Krieges. Stuttgart, 1836.
	AH 7228.36	Wasserschleben, W.H. Historia quaestionum pertormenta. Berolini, 1836.
	AH 4558.29.6	Williams, John. Life and actions of Alexander the Great. N.Y., 1836.

1837

NEDL	AH 7817.92.11	Adam, Alexander. Roman antiquities. N.Y., 1837.
	AH 7838.37	Ademollo, A. Gli spettacoli dell'antica Roma. pt.1-6. Firenze, 1837.
	AH 7278.37	Bell, R. History of Rome. Philadelphia, 1837.
	AH 6110.9	Brückner, K.A.F. König Philipp. Göttingen, 1837.
	AH 5307.14.2	Bulwer, E. Athens. Its rise and fall. N.Y., 1837. 2v.
	AH 5307.13	Bulwer, E. Athens. Its rise and fall. Paris, 1837.
	AH 7138.37F	Dirksen, H.E. Manuale iuris civilis Romani. Berolini, 1837.
	AH 7168.37.7	Fabricius, C.F. Historische Forschungen im Gebiete des römischen Privat-Rechts. Berlin, 1837.
NEDL	AH 7618.37	Francke, J.F. Zur Geschichte Trajans. Gustrow, 1837.
	AH 9777.8	Freudensprung, S. Commentatio Jornande sive Jordane libellorum natalibus. Monaci, 1837.
	AH 807.28A	Hegewisch, D.H. Introduction to historical chronology. Burlington, 1837.

1837 - cont.

AH 7206.15	Hertzog, Emil. Pragmateia. Monachō, 1837.
AH 4238.37	Kreenen, J.J. Cohortis Sacrae apud Thebanos Histobiam. Arnhemiae, 1837.
AH 878.37F	Lajard, J.B.F. Recherches sur le culte...de Vénus. Paris, 1837-48. 2v.
NEDL AH 4278.29.7	Lamé Fleury, J.R. L'histoire grecque, racontée aux enfants. 4e éd. Paris, 1837.
AH 8011.3	Papencordt, F. Geschichte der vandalischen Herrschaft. Berlin, 1837.
AH 7846.6	Peignot, Gabriel. Recherches sur le luxe des Romains dans leur ameublement. Dijon, 1837.
AH 4817.06.18	Potter, J. Archaeologia Graeca. 3. ed. London, 1837.
AH 4328.37	Uebelen, G. Jonische Stamms. Stuttgart, 1837.
AH 4818.26.6	Wachsmuth, W. Historical antiquities of Greeks. Oxford, 1837. 2v.
Eg 818.37	Wilkinson, J.G. Manners and customs of the ancient Egyptians. London, 1837. 3v.
AH 7208.2	Zumpt, Karl G. Über Abstimmung des römischen Volks. Berlin, 1837.

1838

AH 298.38	Älteste und alte Zeit. v.1-5. Hanover, 1838. 2v.
AH 1958.38	Ainsworth, W. Researches in Assyria...Euphrates expedition. London, 1838.
AH 7828.38	Becker, W.A. Gallus, oder Römische Scenen. Leipzig, 1838. 2v.
AH 928.38	Böckh, August. Metrologische Untersuchungen über Gewichte, Münzfüsse und Masse. Berlin, 1838.
AH 4162.11	Boor, Carl de. Attische Intestat Erbrecht. Hamburg, 1838.
AH 7158.38	Burckhardt, Adolf. Die Kriminalgerichtsbarkeit. Basel, 1838.
AH 7198.38	Christiansen, J. Wissenschaft des römischen Rechtsgeschichte. Altona, 1838.
AH 938.38	Georgii, L. Alte Geographie. Stuttgart, 1838. 2v.
AH 7148.38	Giraud, C. Droit de propriété. Aix, 1838.
AH 7158.15.2	Hasse, J.C. Die Eulpa des römischen Rechts. Bonn, 1838.
AH 8007.5.2	Heeren, A.H.L. Historical researches...politics. 2. ed. Oxford, 1838. 3v.
AH 7206.27F	Heimbach, G.E. Anekdota. v.1-2. Lipsiae, 1838.
AH 7188.38	Hoffmann, E. Lehre von den Servituten. v.1-2. Darmstadt, 1838.
AH 7038.38	Huschke, G. Die Verfassung der Servius Tullius. Heidelberg, 1838.
AH 4838.38	Krause, J.H. Olympia. Wien, 1838.
AH 7008.38	Le Clerc, J.V. Des journaux chez les romaines. Paris, 1838.
AH 4277.95.7	Mitford, W. History of Greece with final additions and corrections. London, 1838. 8v.
AH 7203.42	Mühlenbruch, C.F. Doctriia Pandectarum. Bruxelles, 1838.
AH 3965.15	Peppercorne, J.W. Testimonies to the fertility of ancient Palestine. London, 1838.
Eg 878.19.5	Prichard, J.C. An analysis of Egyptian mythology. London, 1838.
AH 4078.19.3	Schömann, G.F. Assemblies of the Athenians. Cambridge, 1838.
AH 4148.38	Schoemann, G.F. Iuris publici Graecorum. Gryphiswaldiae, 1838.
AH 7188.38.5	Schüller, C.L. Necessitudine cum moralitum civili. Rhenum, 1838.
Eg 708.38	Sharpe, S. Egypt under the Ptolemies. London, 1838.
AH 8873.10	Stein, J.J. De Capuae gentisque Campanorum. Diss. Vratislaviae, 1838.
AH 7162.7	Syntrophius, T.F. Instrumentum donationis ineditum. Vratislaviae, 1838.
AH 5853.5	Ullrich, F.W. Megarische Psephisma. Hamburg, 1838.
AH 7138.38	Zumpt, C.G. Über Ursprung, Form und Bedeutung. Berlin, 1838.
AH 808.38	Zumpt, K.G. Annales. Berolini, 1838.

1839

AH 7055.93.3	Böcking, Edvardus. Notitia dignitatum. Bonnae, 1839-53. 3v.
AH 7058.39	Breuk, H.R. de. Dissertatio historica...de quaestione. Lugduni-Batavorum, 1839.
Eg 278.14.3	Champollion, J.J. Égypte ancienne. Paris, 1839.
AH 7278.39.7	Fiedler, F.A.M. Geschichte des römischen Staates. Leipzig, 1839.
AH 7201.24	Gaius. 1839. Laboulaye. Flores juris antejustianei. Paris, 1839.
NEDL AH 7652.10	Gibbon, Edward. Histoire de la décadence et de la chute de l'Empire Romain. Paris, 1839. 2v.
AH 4838.39	Hermanno, G. De hippodromo olympiaco. Lipsiae, 1839.
AH 7278.39	Hetherington, W.M. History of Rome. Edinburgh, 1839.
AH 4908.39	Hüllmann, K.D. Handelsgeschichte. Bonn, 1839.
AH 4278.39	Keightley, T. History of Greece. Boston, 1839.
AH 7278.39.5	Keightley, T. History of Rome. Boston, 1839.
AH 7238.39	Klenze, C.A.C. Philologische Abhandlungen. Berlin, 1839.
AH 115.3	Kutorga, M. Essai sur l'organisation de la tribu dans l'antiquité. Paris, 1839.
AH 4328.30.2	Müller, K.O. History and antiquities of Dorie Race. 2. ed. London, 1839. 2v.
AH 7408.39	Orioli, F. Dei sette re di Roma e del cominciamento del Consolato. Fiesole, 1839.
AH 938.39	Reinganum, H. Geschichte der Erd- und Landerabbildungen. Jena, 1839.
AH 7548.39	Reinhold, K.W. Die Römische Kaisergeschichte. Pasewalf, 1839.
AH 3013.20.7	Rich, C.J. Narrative of a journey to the site of Babylon. London, 1839.
NEDL AH 277.34.14.9	Rollin, Charles. Ancient history. N.Y., 1839. 2v.
AH 845.5	Rosenbaum, J. Die Lustseuche im Alterthume. Halle, 1839.
AH 7038.39	Rubino, J. Untersuchungen und römische Verfassung. Cassel, 1839.
AH 7178.39	Rudorff, A.A.F. Ackergesetz der S. Thorius. Berlin, 1839.
AH 808.39	Smith, J.T. Observations on chronological eras. Boston, 1839.
AH 6140.2	Tafel, F. Thessalonica. Berolini, 1839.
AH 7200.11	Valeriani, L. Leggi delle dodici tavole. Firenze, 1839.

1840

AH 7278.40	Arnold, T. History of Rome. London, 1840. 3v.
AH 4828.40	Becker, W.A. Charikles. Leipzig, 1840.

1840 - cont.

AH 7188.40	Bierregaard, L. De libertinorum hominum conditione. Hauniae, 1840.
AH 4258.40.2F	Böckh, August. Tafeln zu Urkunden. Berlin, 1840.
AH 4258.40	Böckh, August. Urkunden. Berlin, 1840.
AH 5303.7	Büttner, H. Polische Hetärieen in Athen. Leipzig, 1840.
AH 4448.40	Dietrich, A. De Clisthene. Halis Saxonum, 1840.
AH 4843.8	Dionysius, A. Hymnen. Berlin, 1840.
AH 7888.40	Dureau, A.J. Économie politique des Romains. Paris, 1840. 2v.
AH 7808.40	Fischer, Ernst. Griechische und römische Zeittafeln. Altona, 1840-46. 2v.
AH 7618.37.3	Francke, J.F. Zur Geschichte Trajans. 2. Aufl. Quedlinburg, 1840.
AH 7818.20.6	Fuss, J.D. Roman antiquities. Oxford, 1840.
NEDL AH 7650.38.5	Gibbon, Edward. History of decline and fall of Roman Empire. Cincinnati, 1840.
NEDL AH 7650.37	Gibbon, Edward. History of decline and fall of Roman Empire. Paris, 1840. 8v.
NEDL AH 7650.36	Gibbon, Edward. History of decline and fall of Roman Empire. Paris, 1840. 8v.
NEDL AH 7650.38	Gibbon, Edward. History of decline and fall of Roman Empire. v.3-8. Paris, 1840. 3v.
AH 7038.40	Göttling, K. Geschichte der römischen Staatsverfassung. Halle, 1840.
AH 8608.4	Grotefend, G.F. Zur Geographie und Geschichte von Alt-Italien. v.1-3. Hannover, 1840-42.
AH 278.40	Heeren, Arnold Herman Ludwig. A manual of ancient history. 3. ed. Oxford, 1840.
AH 4202.9	Hüllmann, K.D. Griechische Denkwürdigkeiten. Bonn, 1840.
AH 7008.40	Lieberkuehn, Wilhelm. Inest commentatio de diurnis. Vimariae, 1840.
AH 7168.40	Marezoll, T. Droit privé des Romains. Paris, 1840.
AH 7114.8	Marquardt, I. Historiae equitum romanorum. Berolini, 1840.
AH 7114.8.2	Marquardt, I. Historiea equitum romanorum. Berolini, 1840.
AH 7114.5	Raumer, R. De. De servii tullii censu. Erlangae, 1840.
AH 7148.40	Römer, J.W. Defensaibus plebis seu civitatium. Trajecti ad Rhenum, 1840.
AH 4538.40	Sievers, G.R. Geschichte Griechenlandes. Kiel, 1840.
AH 4840.5	Szymanski, M. De natura familiae Graecae. Berolini, 1840.
AH 188.40	Venedey, J. Römerthum, Christenthum und Germanenthum. Frankfurt, 1840.
AH 7206.17	Walter, F. Geschichte des römischen Rechts. Bonn, 1840.
AH 4298.40	Wordsworth, C. Greece; pictorial, descriptive, and historical. London, 1840.

1841

AH 4978.41	Aldenhoven, F. Itineraire descriptif. Athènes, 1841.
AH 4842.7	Bach, A. De institutione...scholastica. Bonnae, 1841.
AH 7478.41	Berlin. Friedrichs Werderschen Gymnasiums. Programm...De C. Iulii Caesaris Coloniis. Berlin, 1841.
AH 238.41	Bernd, C.S.T. Die Hauptstücke der Wappenwissenschaft. Bonn, 1841.
AH 8608.6.5	Bianchi Giovini, A. Sulle Origini italiche di Angelo Mazzoldi; osservazioni. Milano, 1841.
AH 7188.41	Böger, G. De manciporum commercio apud Romanos. Berolini, 1841.
AH 7138.41.5	Burchardi, G.C. Lehrbuch des römischen Rechts. v.1-2, pt.1-3. Stuttgart, 1841. 3v.
AH 7201.25F	Corpus Iuris Romani. Anteiustiniani. Bonnae, 1841.
AH 4838.41.5	Dissenio, L. De ordine certaminum. Gottingae, 1841.
AH 3307.5	Engel, W.H. Kypros. Berlin, 1841. 2v.
NEDL AH 7417.83.15	Ferguson, A. A history of the progress and termination of the Roman republic. N.Y., 1841.
AH 7201.27	Gaius. Institutionum commentarius quattuor. Bonnae, 1841.
AH 7798.41	Gaupp, E.T. De occupatione et divisione. Vratislaviae, 1841.
AH 298.41	Gerlach, F.D. Historische Studien. Hamburg, 1841. 2v.
NEDL AH 7650.39	Gibbon, Edward. History of decline and fall of Roman Empire. N.Y., 1841-43. 4v.
AH 4138.41	Halbertsma, P. De Magistratum Probatione. Daventriae, 1841.
AH 7138.41	Heineccius, J.G. Antiquitatum Romanarum. Francofurti, 1841.
AH 5754.5	Hermann, C.F. Antiquitatum Laconicarum. Marburgi, 1841.
NEDL AH 4818.41	Hermann, K.F. Lehrbuch der griechischen Antiquitäten. 3. Aufl. Heidelberg, 1841. 2v.
AH 7488.41	Hoeck, K.F.C. Römische Geschichte. Braunschweig, 1841.
NEDL AH 7488.41.3	Hoeck, K.F.C. Römische Geschichte. Braunschweig, 1841.
AH 4938.41	Hoffmann, S. Griechenland. Leipzig, 1841. 2v.
AH 7488.41.5	Keightley, Thomas. History of the Roman empire, from the accession of Augustus to the end of the empire of the West. Boston, 1841.
AH 4838.41.3	Krause, J.H. Institute, Sitten und Bräuche des alten Hellas. v.1-2. Leipzig, 1841. 3v.
AH 4838.41	Krause, J.H. Pythien, Nemeen und Isthmien. Leipzig, 1841.
AH 3159.24F	Laborde, L. de. Commentaire geographique sur l'exode et les nombres. Paris, 1841.
AH 8608.6.10	Mazzoldi, Angelo. Riposta alle osservazioni di Bianchi-Giovini sulle Origini. Milano, 1841.
AH 7508.39	Meigs, C.D. The Augustan age. Philadelphia, 1841.
AH 3980.8	Meigs, Charles D. Lecture on Jerusalem at the commencement of the Christian era. Philadelphia, 1841. 2 pam.
AH 3707.7	Movers, F.K. Die Phönizier. v.1-2, pt.1-3. Bonn, 1841. 4v.
AH 7158.41	Osenbüggen, E. Das altrömisches Paricidium. Kiel, 1841.
AH 7038.41.2	Peter, C.L. Die Epochen der Verfassungsgeschichte. Leipzig, 1841.
AH 4204.5	Prantl, C. De Solonis legibus. Monachii, 1841.
AH 7918.41	Rabanis, J.F. Recherches sur les dendrophores et sur les corporations romaines en général. Bordeaux, 1841.
AH 7038.41	Römer, H.G. De consulum Romanorum auctoritate. Trajecti ad Rhenum, 1841.
NEDL AH 277.34.15	Rollin, Charles. Ancient history. N.Y., 1841. 2v.
AH 7818.41	Ruperte, F.F.F. Handbuch der römischen Alterthümer. Hannover, 1841. 3v.
AH 4524.5	Scheibe, J.F. Oligarchische Umwälzung. Leipzig, 1841.
AH 7138.41.10	Thibaut, A.F.J. Juristischer Nachlass. Berlin, 1841-42. 2v.
AH 7448.41	Vincke, Ludwig. Der zweite punische Krieg und der Kriegsplan der Carthager. Berlin, 1841.
AH 7203.138.25F	Voet, J. Table des Commentaires. Bruxelles, 1841.
AH 7228.41	Walter, F. Histoire de la procédure civile. Paris, 1841.

1841 - cont.

AH 7168.41 — Wening Ingenheim, J.N. von. Lehre vom Schadensersatze nach römischen Rechte. Heidelberg, 1841.

Eg 818.37.2 — Wilkinson, J.G. Manners and customs of the ancient Egyptians. 2. series. London, 1841. 3v.

AH 7178.41 — Zeiss, Gustavo. Commentatio de Lege Thoria Agraria. Vimariae, 1841.

AH 888.41 — Zumpt, K.G. Über den Stand der Bevölkerung. Berlin, 1841.

AH 7114.32 — Zumpt, Karl G. Über die römischen Ritter und den Ritterstand in Rom. v.1-2. Berlin, 1841.

1842

AH 8683.2 — Becker, G.A. De Romae veteris muris...portis. Lipsiae, 1842.

AH 8908.13 — Betham, William. Etruria. Celtica Etruscan literature and antiquities. Dublin, 1842. 2v.

AH 4938.42 — Bobrik, H. Griechenland. Leipzig, 1842.

AH 4108.17.3 — Böckh, August. Public economy of Athens. 2. ed. London, 1842.

Eg 1038.42 — Book of the Dead. Das Todtenbuch der Ägypter. Leipzig, 1842.

AH 7038.42.3 — Bröcker, L.O. Vorarbeiten zur römische Geschichte. Tübingen, 1842.

AH 7202.15 — Codex Theodosianus. Gregorianus Hermogenianus. Bonn, 1842.

AH 3017.9 — Cullimore, A. Oriental cylinders. London, 1842.

AH 5306.5 — Curtius, E. De portubus Athenarum. Halis, 1842.

AH 7178.42 — Engelbregt, C.A. Legibus Agrariis. Lugduni Batavorum, 1842.

AH 7228.42 — Escher, J.H.A. De testium ratione. Turici, 1842.

AH 8157.5F — France. Ministère de la guerre. Précis analytique de l'histoire ancienne de l'Afrique septent. Paris, 1842.

AH 7201.27.5 — Gaius. Institutionum commentarius quattuor Goeschen. 3. ed. Berolini, 1842.

AH 7488.42 — Garzetti, G.B. Römische Geschichte von den Unruhen. Landshut, 1842.

AH 7158.42 — Geib, G. Römische Criminalprocesses. Leipzig, 1842.

AH 7038.42 — Gerlach, F.D. Die römische Censur. Basel, 1842.

AH 4278.24.4 — Heeren, A.H.L. Ancient Greece. 2. ed. Boston, 1842.

AH 7058.28.2 — Hofmann, F. De aedilibus romanorum. Berolini, 1842.

AH 9777.9 — Jordanes. De la succession des royaumes...les Goths. Paris, 1842.

NEDL AH 298.42 — Kołłątaj, Hugo. Rozbiór krytyczny zazad historyi. Krakow, 1842. 3v.

AH 3914.5 — Korn, F. Die Götter Syriens. Stuttgart, 1842.

AH 8908.7 — Lepsius, K.R. Ueber die tyrrhenischen Pelasger. Leipzig, 1842.

AH 5307.17 — Müller, K.O. Attica and Athens. London, 1842.

AH 7114.4 — Pellegrino, D. Andeutungen...der römischen Patricier. Leipzig, 1842.

AH 8549.42.5 — Roberts, J. Druidical remains and antiquities of the ancient Britons. Swansea, 1842.

AH 7438.42 — Saal, N. De appio Claudio Caeco commentatio historica. Köln, 1842.

AH 4828.42 — St. John, J.A. History of manners and customs of ancient Greece. London, 1842. 3v.

AH 4204.7 — Schelling, H. De Solonis legibus. Berolini, 1842.

AH 4538.42 — Schröder, H. Abbildungen des Demosthenes. Braunschweig, 1842.

AH 7828.42 — Schuch, C.T. Privatalterthümer. Karlsruhe, 1842.

Eg 758.42 — Sharpe, S. Egypt under the Romans. London, 1842.

AH 7038.42.2 — Terpstra, D. Quaestiones literariae. Rotterdami, 1842.

AH 4524.7 — Wattenbach, G. Quadringentorum Athenis factione. Berolini, 1842.

AH 8549.42 — Williams, J. An essay on the question "Whether the British Druids offered human sacrifices". Bala, 1842.

AH 8532.7 — Wilthemius, A. Luciliburgensia sive Luxemburgum Romanum...nunc primum in lucem editum. Luxemburgi, 1842.

1843

AH 238.43 — Armandi, C.P. Histoire militaire des éléphants. Paris, 1843.

AH 7162.9 — Bachofen, J.J. Lex voconia. Basel, 1843.

AH 7818.43.5 — Becker, W.A. Handbuch der römischen Alterthümer. v.1-9. Leipzig, 1843. 5v.

AH 7137.41.15 — Bello, Andrés. Institutciones de derecho romano. Santiago, 1843.

AH 4843.16 — Bojesen, E.F. De Tonis S. Harmoniis Graecorum commentario. Kjobenhavn, 1843.

AH 5307.14.6 — Bulwer, E. Athens. Its rise and fall. v.1-2. Leipzig, 1843.

AH 7168.43 — Christiansen, J. Institutionen des römischen Rechts. Altona, 1843.

AH 7108.43 — Coppi, A. Discorso sopra alcune tasse...degli antichi romani. Roman, 1843.

AH 6024.5 — Curtius, Ernst. Anecdota Delphica. Berolini, 1843.

AH 908.43 — Estrup, H.F.J. De makariske ör og Elisa. Kjøbenhavn, 1843.

AH 4938.43 — Fiedler, F. Geographie und Geschichte von Altgriechenland. Leipzig, 1843.

AH 7088.43 — Fontein, P. Disputatio...de provinciis romanorum. Rhenum, 1843.

AH 3966.14 — Gans, J. Kěnään nach der Stammeintheilung. Paderborn, 1843.

AH 7488.43 — Garzetti, G.B. Della condizione di Roma, d'Italia. Capologo, 1843. 5v.

NEDL AH 7650.40 — Gibbon, Edward. History of decline and fall of Roman Empire. N.Y., 1843-44. 4v.

Eg 278.43.3 — Gliddon, G.R. Ancient Egypt. N.Y., 1843.

Eg 278.43A — Gliddon, G.R. Ancient Egypt. N.Y., 1843.

AH 9777.11 — Glöden, I. von. Das römische Recht im östgothischen Reiche. Jena, 1843.

AH 8907.6 — Gray, E.C.H. History of Etruria. London, 1843. 3v.

AH 2575.5 — Guhl, Ernestus. Ephesiaca. Berolini, 1843.

AH 7201.90 — Haeckermann, G.A.A.G. De legislatione decemoirali. Gryphiae, 1843.

AH 7228.25.3 — Heffter, A.W. System des römischen und deutschen Civil-Processrechts. 2. Aufl. Bonn, 1843.

AH 4521.17 — Herbst, L.F. Die Rückkehr des Alcibiades. Hamburg, 1843.

AH 7278.43 — Kortüm, F. Römische Geschichte. Heidelberg, 1843.

AH 7278.33.3 — Michelet, J. Histoire romaine. 3. ed. Paris, 1843. 2v.

AH 7818.43 — Mommsen, T. De Collegiis et Sodaliciis Romanorum. Kiliae, 1843. 3 pam.

1843 - cont.

AH 7148.43.5 — Mommsen, Theodor. Ad legem de scribis et viatoribus et de anectoritate commentationes. Kiliae, 1843.

AH 7918.43 — Mommsen, Theodor. De Collegiis et sodalicis Romanorum. Kiliae, 1843.

AH 4818.43F — Panofka, Theodor. Bilder Antiken Lebens. Berlin, 1843.

AH 4818.35.5 — Pouqueville, F.C.H.L. Grèce. Paris, 1843.

NEDL AH 277.34.16 — Rollin, Charles. Ancient history of the Egyptians. N.Y., 1843-44. 8v.

AH 4818.43.5 — Schönwalder. Darstellung des Religiösen...Bildungszustandes. Brieg, 1843.

Eg 847.2 — Schwartze, Moritz Gotthilf. Das alte Agypten...altägyptischen Original-Schriften und den Mittheilungen der nichtägyptischen alten Schriftsteller bearbeitet. Leipzig, 1843. 2v.

AH 4958.43 — Stephani, L. Reise durch...nördlichen Griechenlandes. Leipzig, 1843.

AH 7148.43 — Thermann. De iure praetorio. Lipsiae, 1843. 2 pam.

NEDL AH 278.43 — True stories from ancient history. N.Y., 1843.

AH 8508.6 — Vincent, F.V. Recherches sur l'origine des Boies. Paris, 1843.

AH 7168.26.5 — Zimmern, M. Traité des actions, ou Théorie de la procédure privée. Paris, 1843.

1844

Eg 278.44 — Ancient history. Egypt. N.Y., 1844.

AH 7210.2 — Bamberger, F. De Interregibus Romanis. Brunsvigae, 1844.

AH 5415.5 — Barth, H. Corinthiorum. Berolini, 1844.

AH 7828.38.7 — Becker, W.A. Gallus or Roman scenes. London, 1844.

NEDL AH 278.44 — Boulet, Jean B.E. Manuel pratique d'histoire ancienne. Paris, 1844.

AH 5157.10 — Brandstäter, F.A. Die Geschichten des aetolischen Landes. Berlin, 1844.

AH 7202.15.2 — Codex Theodosianus. Gregorianus Hermogenianus. Bonn, 1844.

AH 7203.42.10 — Corpus juris civilis. Lehrbuch des Pandecten-Rechts. 4. Aufl. Halle, 1844. 3v.

AH 7203.43.9 — Corpus juris civilis. Institutiones. Imperatoris Justiniani Institutionum libri IV. Berolini, 1844.

AH 7508.44 — Egger, A.E. Examen critique des historiens anciens. Paris, 1844.

AH 2016.5 — Forster, Charles. The historical geography of Arabia. London, 1844. 2v.

AH 7188.44 — Gessner, Aemilius. De servis Romanorum publicis. Berolini, 1844.

Eg 278.43.2 — Gliddon, G.R. Ancient Egypt. N.Y., 1844.

Htn AH 2058.5* — Görres, J. Die Japhetiden. München, 1844.

AH 847.5 — Guenther, O. De balneis veterum. Berolini, 1844.

Eg 818.44 — Haskins, Roswell W. The arts, sciences, and civilization, anterior to Greece and Rome. Buffalo, 1844.

AH 4808.44 — Hermann, K.F. Griechische Monatskunde. Göttingen, 1844.

AH 7098.44 — Jordans, G.H.H. De publicis urbium Romae et Constantinapolis. Bonnae, 1844.

NEDL AH 278.44.5 — Lista y Aragón, A. Elementos de historia antigua. Sevilla, 1844.

AH 7468.44.2 — Mérimée, P. Etudes sur l'histoire romaine. Paris, 1844. 2v.

AH 7115.2 — Mommsen, T. Die römischen Tribus. Altona, 1844.

AH 4298.44.5 — Müller, K.O. Geschichten hellenische Stämme und Städte-Karten. Breslau, 1844. 4v.

AH 7278.11.21 — Niebuhr, B.G. History of Rome. London, 1844. 2v.

AH 7278.11.16 — Niebuhr, B.G. History of Rome. Philadelphia, 1844. 2v.

AH 7278.11.23 — Niebuhr, B.G. Römische Geschichte. Jena, 1844. 2v.

AH 4818.44F — Panofka, Theodor. Griechinnnnen und Griechen. Berlin, 1844.

AH 4708.44 — Paparrēgopoulos, Konstantinos. To telegtaion etos tēs ellēnikēs eleutherias. Athēnai, 1844.

AH 7468.44 — Plutarch. Civil wars of Rome. London, 1844. 3v.

AH 7158.44 — Rein, W. Criminalrecht der Römer. Leipzig, 1844.

AH 7278.44 — Roth, C.L. Römische Geschichte. v.1-4. Nürnberg, 1844. 3v.

AH 4828.42.3 — St. John, J.A. Hellenes. History of manners and customs of ancient Greece. London, 1844. 3 pam.

AH 5138.5 — Schryver, P.A. Loi Rhodia de Jactu. Bruxelles, 1844.

NEDL AH 4278.35.4 — Thirlwall, C. Greece. London, 1844. 2v.

AH 4298.44 — Weissenborn, J.C. Hellen. Jena, 1844.

NEDL AH 4298.40.2 — Wordsworth, C. Greece; pictorial, descriptive, and historical. 2. ed. London, 1844.

1845

AH 7148.45 — Beaujon, J.H. Specimen juridicum inaugurale, de variis modis, quibus...jus civitatis Romanae...potuerit. Lugdunum-Batavorum, 1845.

AH 4828.40.5 — Becker, W.A. Charicles. London, 1845.

AH 4808.45 — Bergk, T. Beiträge zur griechischen Monatskunde. Giefsen, 1845.

AH 4521.5 — Bischer, W. Alkibiades und Lysandros. Basel, 1845.

Eg 808.45 — Böskh, A. Manetho und die Hundssternperiode. Berlin, 1845.

AH 3013.35.5 — Botta, P.E. Lettres de...sur ses decouvertes a Khorsabad. Paris, 1845.

AH 7138.45.15 — Boujean, L.B. Traité des actions, ou Exposition historique de l'organization judiciaire. Paris, 1845. 2v.

AH 9607.7 — Brunet de Presle, W. Recherches sur les établissements des grecs. Paris, 1845.

Eg 278.45 — Bunsen, C.C.J. Aegyptens Stelle. v.1-5. Hamburg, 1845. 3v.

AH 7808.45 — Clinton, Henry Fynes. Fasti Romani, the civil and literary chronology of Rome and Constantinople. v.2. Oxford, 1845.

AH 8549.45.5 — David de St. Georges, J.J.A. Histoire des druides et...Calédonie. Arbois, 1845.

AH 9754.3 — Davoud-Oghlou, G.A. Histoire de la legislation des anciens germains. Berlin, 1845. 2v.

AH 7650.41 — Gibbon, Edward. History of decline and fall of the Roman Empire. Chicago, 1845. 5v.

NEDL AH 7650.41.5 — Gibbon, Edward. History of decline and fall of the Roman Empire. Philadelphia, 1845. 5v.

NEDL AH 7650.40.5 — Gibbon, Edward. History of the decline and fall of the Roman Empire. N.Y., 1845-46. 4v.

AH 7114.10 — Hennebert, A. Histoire de la lutte entre les patriciens. Gand, 1845.

AH 3958.5F — Hitzig, F. Zur ältesten Völker und Mythengeschichte - Urgeschichte...der Philistäer. Leipzig, 1845.

1845 - cont.

AH 7468.45 — Kiene, Adolf. Der römische Bundesgenossenkrieg. Leipzig, 1845.

AH 7158.45 — Laboulaye, E. Lois criminelles des Romains. Paris, 1845.

AH 7818.40.3 — Ozaneaux, J.G. Les Romains...République romaine. 2. éd. Paris, 1845.

AH 7138.45.3 — Puchta, G.F. Cursus der Institutionen. Leipzig, 1845. 2v.

AH 4538.45 — Rehdantz, C. Iphicratis Chabriae Timothei. Berolini, 1845.

AH 214.5 — Schröder, G.A. De praecisis iurandi formis Graecorum. Marienwerder, 1845.

AH 7114.9 — Schuermans, Henri. Histoire de la lutte entre les patriciens. Bruxelles, 1845.

AH 3013.23 — Smith, A. Ruins of Nineveh. n.p., 1845?

AH 8549.45 — Smith, John. Histoire des druides et...Calédonie. Arbois, 1845.

AH 7278.45 — Society for Promoting Christian Knowledge, London. The Roman Empire. London, 1845.

EgP 137.50 — Syro-Egyptian Society of London. Original papers read before. London, 1845.

AH 278.45 — Taylor, W.C. A manual of ancient history. N.Y., 1845.

AH 4278.35.3 — Thirlwall, C. History of Greece. London, 1845. 8v.

AH 4278.35.3.5 — Thirlwall, C. History of Greece. N.Y., 1845. 2v.

AH 7138.45 — Walter, F. Geschichte des römischen Rechts. 2e Aufl. Bonn, 1845.

AH 7228.45 — Wetzell, G.W. Der römische Vindicationsprocess. Leipzig, 1845.

AH 7158.45.15 — Zumpt, Karl G. Commentationis de legibus judiciisque repetundarum. Berolini, 1845. 2 pam.

1846

AH 7278.40.3A — Arnold, T. History of Rome. v.1-3. N.Y., 1846. 2v.

AH 7278.46 — Arnold, T. History of the Roman Commonwealth. N.Y., 1846.

AH 7498.46 — Cesare, G. di. Lettere romane dall'anno 818 della 830. Prato, 1846.

AH 7818.46.3 — Dezobry, Charles. Rome au siècle d'Auguste. Paris, 1846. 4v.

AH 278.46 — Frost, J. Pictorial ancient history of the world. Philadelphia, 1846.

AH 4278.00.11 — Goldsmith, Oliver. Pinnock's improved edition of Goldsmith's History of Greece. Philadelphia, 1846.

AH 8257.5 — Gross-Hoffinger, A. Urgeschichte der österreichischen Länder. Meissen, 1846.

AH 4278.46 — Grote, George. History of Greece. London, 1846. 12v.

AH 4298.26.5 — Heeren, Arnold H.L. The historical works of Arnold H.L. Heeren. London, 1846?-50? 6v.

Eg 878.46 — Henry, D.M.J. L'Egypte pharaonique. Paris, 1846. 2v.

AH 7168.46 — Huschke, P.E. Ueber das Recht des Nexum. Leipzig, 1846.

AH 7158.36 — Invernizi, P. De publicis et criminalibus iudiciis Romanorum. Lipsiae, 1846.

AH 408.46.3 — Kenrick, J. Essay on primaeval history. London, 1846.

AH 15.2 — Lange, C.C.L. Historia mutationum rei...romanorum. Gottingae, 1846- 12 pam.

AH 308.46 — Lasaulx, E. von. Uber das Studium der griechischen und römischen Alterthümer. München, 1846.

AH 7278.46.10 — Laurian, A.T. Coup d'oeil sur l'histoire des roumains. Bucuresti, 1846.

AH 5967.7 — Leake, W.M. Peloponnesiaca. London, 1846.

AH 408.46 — Loebell, J.W. Weltgeschichte. Leipzig, 1846.

AH 7178.46 — Macé, A.P.L. Lois agraires. Paris, 1846.

AH 4228.46 — Meier, M.H.E. Privatschiedsrichter. Halle, 1846.

AH 7058.46 — Mommsen, T. De apparitoribus magistratum romanorum. Romae, 1846.

AH 7278.11.9 — Niebuhr, B.G. Vorträge über römische Geschichte. Berlin, 1846. 3v.

AH 7088.46 — Poinsignon, A.M. Essai sur le nombre et l'origine des provinces romaines. Paris, 1846.

AH 7038.46 — Raumer, F. Die römische Staatsverfassung. Berlin, 1846.

Eg 878.46.5 — Schwenck, K. Die Mythologie der Aegypter für gebildete und die studirende Jugend. Frankfurt am Main, 1846. 5v.

Eg 278.36.3 — Sharpe, S. History of Egypt. London, 1846.

AH 7138.03.9 — Thibaut, F.J. System des Pandekten-Rechts. Jena, 1846. 2v.

AH 4818.26.3 — Wachsmuth, W. Hellenische Alterthumskunde. Halle, 1846. 2v.

AH 7818.46 — Wannowski, A. Antiquitates Romanas. London, 1846.

1847

AH 6107.5 — Abel, O. Makedonien. Leipzig, 1847.

AH 7203.44.5 — Corpus juris civilis. Institutes. Paris, 1847.

Eg 847.5 — Essai sur le symbolisme antique. Paris, 1847.

AH 3980.3 — Fergusson, J. Essay on ancient topography of Jerusalem. London, 1847.

AH 4843.23 — Fortlage, Karl. Das musikalische System der Griechen in seiner Urgestalt. Leipzig, 1847.

NEDL AH 7650.43 — Gibbon, Edward. History of the decline and fall of the Roman Empire. v.3. N.Y., 1847.

Eg 278.43.8 — Gliddon, G.R. Ancient Egypt. N.Y., 1847.

AH 278.47 — Goodrich, S.G. Ancient history. Louisville, Ky., 1847.

AH 7161.7 — Hase, E.F. De manu iuris romani antiquioris commentatis. Halis, 1847.

AH 3966.15 — Headley, J.T. The sacred mountains. N.Y., 1847.

AH 4278.24.5 — Heeren, A.H.L. Ancient Greece. London, 1847.

NEDL AH 278.40.5 — Heeren, Arnold Herman Ludwig. A manual of ancient history. London, 1847.

AH 7207.17 — Hofmann, Friedrich. Der römische Senat. Berlin, 1847.

AH 9758.6 — Horkel, J. Die Geschichtschreiber der deutschen Vorzeit. Berlin, 1847.

AH 7108.47 — Huschke, P.E. Über den Census und die Steuerverfassung. Berlin, 1847.

AH 7038.47 — Ihne, W. Forschungen - römischen Vergassungsgeschichte. Frankfurt, 1847.

AH 3966.24F — Jenks, William. The explanatory Bible atlas and scripture gazetteer. Boston, 1847.

AH 7138.47.5 — Lange, C.F.W. Examinations über die römischen Rechtsgeschichte. Halle, 1847.

AH 7278.33.5 — Michelet, J. History of the Roman Republic. London, 1847.

AH 7278.33.6 — Michelet, J. History of the Roman Republic. N.Y., 1847.

AH 278.48 — Niebuhr, B.G. Vorträge über alte Geschichte. Berlin, 1847. 2v.

AH 7468.47 — Nitzsch, K.W. Die Gracchen und ihre...Vorgänger. Berlini, 1847.

AH 7138.47 — Pfund, T.G. Rechts Alterthümer. Weimar, 1847.

1847 - cont.

AH 7098.47 — Potsdam. Gymnasiums. Zuder öffentlichen Prüsung der Zöglinge. Potsdam, 1847.

AH 7098.47.5 — Reinii, W. Dissertatio de Romanorum Municipiis. Eisenach, 1847.

AH 2011.6 — Reiske, J.J. Primae lineae historiae regnorum arabicorum. Gottingae, 1847.

AH 7278.47 — Schmitz, L. History of Rome. N.Y., 1847.

AH 7278.47.2 — Schmitz, L. A history of Rome from the earliest times to the death of Commodus, A.D. 192. Andover, 1847.

AH 7408.47 — Schoemann, G.F. De tullo hostilio. Gryphiswaldiae, 1847.

NEDL AH 278.47.10 — Storia antica. Torino, 1847.

AH 7205.9 — Theophilus Antecessor. Paraphrase grecque des Institutes de Justinien. Paris, 1847.

NEDL AH 4278.35.5 — Thirlwall, C. Histoire de la Grèce ancienne. Paris, 1847.

Eg 958.47 — Wilkinson, G. Hand-book for travellers in Egypt. London, 1847.

Eg 818.37.3 — Wilkinson, J.G. Manners and customs of the ancient Egyptians. 3. ed. London, 1847. 5v.

AH 7297.47 — Zell, Carolus. Elogiorum Romae reliquae. Stuttgartie, 1847.

1848

AH 4558.48.5 — Abbott, J. History of Alexander the Great. N.Y., 1848.

AH 7116.4 — Breda, O. Die Centurienverfassung des Servius Tullius. Bromberg, 1848. 2 pam.

Eg 278.48 — Bunsen, C.C.J. Egypt's place in universal history. London, 1848. 5v.

AH 7078.48 — Casar aux elections. Paris, 1848.

AH 7203.44.6 — Corpus juris civilis. Corpus juris civilis. Lipsiae, 1848-49. 3v.

AH 4859.7 — Fickler, C.B.A. Griechischen Frauen. Heidelberg, 1848.

AH 4558.48 — Geier, S.R. Erziehung und Unterricht Alexanders des Grossen. Halle, 1848.

AH 3005.830.5 — Hrozný, Bedřich. Stručný přehled mých vědeckých objevu. Praha, 1848.

AH 8514.12 — Martin, L.A. Histoire morale de la Gaule. Paris, 1848.

AH 7214.2 — Mercklin, D. Die Cooptation der Römer. Mitau, 1848.

AH 7278.11.24 — Niebuhr, B.G. Lectures on the History of Rome. London, 1848.

AH 4328.48 — Ow, J. Die Abstammung der Griechen und die Errthüme und Tausch. München, 1848.

AH 7798.48 — Pavirani, D.P. Memorie istoriche della vita e governo. Ravenna, 1848.

AH 2573.5 — Pertz, C.A. Colophoniaca. Gottingae, 1848.

AH 7201.29 — Pomponius. De origine iuris. Gissae, 1848.

AH 4845.9 — Schömann, G.F. Sittlich-religiöse Verhalten. Greifswald, 1848.

AH 7138.48.5 — Secco, A.L. de S.H. Manual histórico de directo romano. Coimbra, 1848.

AH 8073.8 — Seibel, V. Der Söldner-Krieg der Karthager. Dilingen, 1848.

NEDL AH 278.48.5 — Vendel-Heyl, L.A. Sumario de la historia de Grecia i de Roma. Santiago, 1848. 2 pam.

AH 4838.48 — Wieseler, F. Satyrspiel. Göttingen, 1848.

AH 7448.48 — Wijmre, J.A. Quaestiones criticae de belli punici. Groningae, 1848.

1849

AH 7448.49 — Abbott, Jacob. History of Hannibal the Carthaginian. N.Y., 1849.

AH 7478.49 — Abbott, Jacob. History of Julius Caesar. N.Y., 1849.

AH 7828.38.3 — Becker, W.A. Gallus, oder Römische Scenen. 2. Aufl. Leipzig, 1849. 3v.

AH 7828.38.9A — Becker, W.A. Gallus or Roman scenes. London, 1849.

AH 3013.35PF — Botta, P.E. Monument de Ninive. Text and plates. Paris, 1849-50. 5v.

AH 7138.49 — Colquhoun, P. Summary of Roman civil law. London, 1849. 4v.

AH 7138.49.5 — Deurer, E.F.F.W. Grundriss für Äussere Geschichte und Institutionen. Heidelberg, 1849.

AH 7308.49 — Eliot, Samuel. Liberty of Rome. N.Y., 1849. 2v.

NEDL AH 930.7.6 — Findlay, Alexander G. A classical atlas, to illustrate ancient geography. N.Y., 1849.

NEDL AH 4278.46.5 — Grote, George. History of Greece. 2. ed. London, 1849. 12v.

AH 4278.46.3 — Grote, George. History of Greece. 2. ed. London, 1849. 12v.

AH 938.49F — Jenks, William. The explanatory Bible atlas and Scripture gazetteer. Boston, 1849.

AH 3964.17.10F — Kitto, John. The tabernacle and its furniture. London, 1849.

AH 4200.5 — Kopstadt, A. Constitutionis Lycurgae. Gryphiae, 1849.

AH 7038.49 — Kuhn, E. Verfassung des römischen Reichs. Leipzig, 1849.

AH 3013.33.15PF — Layard, A.H. The monuments of Nineveh. London, 1849.

AH 3013.33A — Layard, A.H. Nineveh and its remains. N.Y., 1849. 2v.

AH 3013.33.2 — Layard, A.H. Nineveh and its remains. 2. ed. London, 1849. 2v.

Eg 808.49F — Lepsius, K.R. Die Chronologie der Ägypter. Berlin, 1849.

AH 8608.6 — Mazzoldi, Angelo. Delle origini italiche. Livorno, 1849. 2v.

AH 888.49 — Moreau-Christophe, Louis-Mathurin. Driot à l'oisiveté. Paris, 1849.

AH 4328.49 — Mueller, E.H.O. De populi Atheniensis tribuum origine. Marburgi, 1849.

AH 7038.49.2 — Nägele, M. Studien über Staatsleben. Schaffhausen, 1849.

AH 7278.11.25 — Niebuhr, B.G. Lectures on the History of Rome. 2. ed. London, 1849. 3v.

AH 4818.44.3 — Panofka, Theodor. Manners and customs of Greeks. London, 1849.

Eg 847.3 — Rougé, Emman. Essai sur une stèle junéraire. Berlin, 1849.

AH 3013.22 — Streber, F. Über die Mauern von Babylon. München, 1849.

AH 7708.49 — Ware, William. Aurelian. v.2. N.Y., 1849.

AH 7138.49.9 — Warnkoenig, Leopold A. Historia externa del derecho romano para el uso de los estudiantes de jurisprudencia. Habana, 1849.

185-

NEDL AH 930.7.5 — Findlay, Alexander G. A classical atlas, to illustrate ancient geography. N.Y., 185-?

1850

AH 3659.15 — Abbott, Jacob. History of Cyrus the Great. N.Y., 1850.
AH 3659.20 — Abbott, Jacob. History of Darius the Great. N.Y., 1850.
AH 3660.3 — Abbott, Jacob. History of Xerxes the Great. N.Y., 1850.
AH 9603.2 — Dareste de la Chavanne, R. De forma et conditione Siciliae provinciae Romanae. Thesis. Lutetiae, 1850.
AH 7168.50 — Dernburg, H. Emtio Bonorum. Heidelberg, 1850.
AH 7818.46.5 — Dezobry, Charles. Rome au siècle d'Auguste. Göttingen, 1850.
AH 7137.22.15 — Domat, Jean. The civil law in its natural order together with the publick law. 2. ed. Boston, 1850. 2v.
AH 7228.50 — Erxleben, A. Condictiones sine causa. pt.1-2. Leipzig, 1850.
NEDL AH 7650.46 — Gibbon, Edward. History of decline and fall of Roman Empire. Boston, 1850.
AH 7138.50 — Heineccius, J.G. Elementos de derecho romano. 3. ed. Paris, 1850.
AH 3013.25 — Hoefer, J.C.F. Premier memoire sur les ruines de Ninive. Paris, 1850.
AH 4278.50 — Keightley, T. Historia tēs Archaias Hellados. En Athēnais, 1850.
AH 7161.9 — La Fort, Charles. Essai historique sur la tutelle en droit romain. Genève, 1850.
AH 7488.50 — Lynam, R. The history of the Roman emperors, from Augustus to the death of Marcus Antoninus. London, 1850. 2v.
NEDL AH 7488.52.2 — Merivale, Charles. History of the Romans. London, 1850. 4v.
AH 7778.12.5 — Neander, A. The Emperor Julian and his generation. N.Y., 1850.
AH 7278.11.26 — Niebuhr, B.G. Lectures of Roman history. London, 1850. 3v.
AH 7238.50 — Rabus, J.M. Ad solemia anniversaria gymnasii. n.p., 1850.
AH 3012.3 — Rawlinson, H.C. Commentary on cuneiform inscriptions. London, 1850.
AH 277.34.17 — Rollin, Charles. The ancient history of the Egyptians. Cincinnati, 1850. 2v.
AH 7203.44.15 — Scheurl, C.G. von. Lehrbuch der Institutionen. Erlangen, 1850.
Eg 8.50 — Seyffarth, G. Altertumskunde. n.p., 1850?
AH 7468.34.7 — Zacharia, K.S. Lucius Cornelius Sulla. Mannheim, 1850.
AH 7098.50 — Zumptii, A.W. Commentationum epigraphicarum. Berolini, 1850.

1851

Eg 708.51 — Abbott, Jacob. History of Cleopatra, queen of Egypt. N.Y., 1851.
AH 4338.49 — Bässler, Ferdinand. Hellenischer Heldensaal. v.2. Berlin, 1851.
AH 4108.17.7F — Böckh, August. Sieben Tafeln zum 11 Bande Staatshaushaltung. Berlin, 1851.
AH 4108.17.2 — Böckh, August. Staatshaushaltung der Athener. 2. Aufl. Berlin, 1851. 3v.
AH 3013.26 — Buckingham, J.S. The buried city of the East-Nineveh. London, 1851?
AH 4808.51 — Clinton, H.F. Epitome...civil and literary chronicle of Greece. Oxford, 1851.
AH 7203.45 — Corpus juris civilis. Institutiones. Institutes de Justinien. Paris, 1851. 2v.
AH 5957.5 — Curtius, Ernst. Peloponnesos. Gotha, 1851. 2v.
AH 5124.5 — Daenius, A. Specimen litterarum de Insula delo. Lugdunum Batavorum, 1851. 2 pam.
AH 3013.28 — Fergusson, J. The palaces of Nineveh and Persepolis restored. London, 1851.
AH 7163.15 — Gerlach, F. De romanorum conubio. Halis, 1851.
NEDL AH 7650.49 — Gibbon, Edward. History of decline and fall of Roman Empire. Boston, 1851. 6v.
AH 7628.51 — Gregorovius, F.A. Geschichte des römischen Kaisers Hadrian. Königsberg, 1851.
AH 7214.7 — Grosser, G. De spectione et nuntiatione. Vratislaviae, 1851.
NEDL AH 4278.46.7 — Grote, George. History of Greece. Boston, 1851.
Htn AH 4238.51* — Herbert, Henry W. The captains of the Old World. N.Y., 1851.
AH 842.9 — Krause, J.H. Geschichte der Erziehung. Halle, 1851.
AH 2589.5 — Lane, G.M. Smyrnaeorum res gestae et antiquitates. Gottingae, 1851.
AH 3013.33.24 — Layard, A.H. A popular account of discoveries at Nineveh. London, 1851.
AH 7908.51 — Mommsen, Theodor. Das Edict Diocletians de Pretiis Rerum Venalium. Leipzig, 1851.
AH 7278.11.18A — Niebuhr, B.G. History of Rome. London, 1851. 3v.
AH 938.51 — Niebuhr, B.G. Vorträge über alte Länder und Volkerkunde. Berlin, 1851.
AH 7114.11 — Niemeyer, K. De equitibus romanis. Gryphiae, 1851.
AH 4844.3 — Panofka, T. Die griechischen Trinkhörner. Berlin, 1851.
AH 7138.51 — Puchta, G.F. Kleine civilistische Schriften. Leipzig, 1851.
AH 4833.19 — Rabath, Joseph. Artis gymnicae quae fuerit origo. Gleiwitz, 1851.
AH 8954.5F — Ritschl, F. Legis rubriae pars superstes. Bonae, 1851.
AH 4162.25 — Schneider, E. De jure hereditario Atheniensium. Monachii, 1851.
AH 7278.51 — Segur. Histoire romaine. Paris, 1851. 2v.
AH 7238.51 — Simpson, J.Y. Was the Roman army provided with any medical officers? Edinburgh, 1851.
AH 408.47.5 — Smith, George. The patriarchial age. N.Y., 1851.
AH 8607.5 — Vannucci, A. Storia d'Italia. Firenze, 1851. 4v.
AH 3013.14 — Weissenborn, H.J.C. Ninive und sein Gebiet. Erfurt, 1851.
AH 48.51 — Zell, Karl. Natalia Caroli Friderici. Inaug. Diss. Heidelbergae, 1851.

1852

Htn AH 7298.52* — À Beckett, G.A. The comic history of Rome. London, 1852?
AH 3659.15.2 — Abbott, Jacob. History of Cyrus the Great. N.Y., 1852.
NEDL AH 7408.77.2 — Abbott, Jacob. History of Romulus. N.Y., 1852.
AH 7408.52.5 — Abbott, Jacob. History of Romulus. N.Y., 1852.
AH 3660.3.2 — Abbott, Jacob. History of Xerxes the Great. N.Y., 1852.
AH 7498.52 — Arnold, Thomas. Pictorial history of Rome. London, 1852.
AH 3013.32 — Bonomi, J. Nineveh and its palaces. London, 1852.
AH 9066.2 — Bormann, A.K.E. Altlatinische Chorographie. Halle, 1852.

1852 - cont.

AH 8157.7 — Dureau de la Malle, A. L'Algérie. Paris, 1852.
AH 3013.24 — Eichhoff, F.G. Etudes sur Ninive et Persepolis. Lyon, 1852.
NEDL AH 7417.83.17 — Ferguson, A. History of the progress and termination of the Roman republic. N.Y., 1852.
AH 848.9 — Fuchs, W.H. De ratione quam veteres artifices. Gottingae, 1852.
NEDL AH 7277.70.25 — Goldsmith, O. Rōmaïkēs istorias. Athēnai, 1852.
NEDL AH 3103.3 — Gosse, P.H. Assyria: her manners, customs. London, 1852.
AH 3966.20 — Gosse, Philip H. Sacred streams; or, The ancient and modern history of the rivers of the Bible. N.Y., 1852.
AH 4278.46.15 — Grote, George. History of Greece. N.Y., 1852-71. 12v.
AH 7168.52.5 — Grotefend, G.A.A. De exceptione Disionis. Gottingae, 1852.
AH 3011.5F — Grotefend, G.F. Erläuterung der Keilinschriften babylonischer Backsteine. Hannover, 1852.
AH 3149.5 — Gumpach, J. Die Zeitrechnung der Babylonier und Assyrier. Heidelberg, 1852.
AH 8007.5 — Heeren, A.H.L. Historical researches...politics. Oxford, 1852. 2v.
AH 4238.52.5 — Herbert, Henry W. The captains of the Old World. N.Y., 1852.
AH 4728.52 — Hermann, C.F. Conditione Graeciae post captam Corinthun. Gottingae, 1852.
AH 7708.52 — Hoyns, Georg. Geschichte der s.g. driessig Inrannen. Göttingen, 1852.
AH 4298.52 — Jacobs, Friedrich. Hellas; Vorträge über Heimath, Geschichte, Literatur und Kunst der Hellenen. Berlin, 1852.
Eg 278.52 — Kenrick, J. Ancient Egypt. N.Y., 1852. 2v.
AH 4858.14 — Lasaulx, E. von. Zur Geschichte und Philosophie der Ehe bei den Griechen. München, 1852.
AH 3013.33.3 — Layard, A.H. Nineveh and its remains. N.Y., 1852.
AH 3013.33.25 — Layard, A.H. Popular account of discoveries at Nineveh. N.Y., 1852.
AH 7168.52 — Marezoll, T. Du droit privé. 2. éd. Paris, 1852.
AH 7488.52A — Merivale, Charles. History of the Romans. 2. ed. London, 1852. 7v.
AH 818.52 — Müller, C.O. Ancient art and its remains. London, 1852.
AH 7408.52 — Newman, F.W. Regal Rome. London, 1852.
AH 278.52.3 — Niebuhr, B.G. Lectures on ancient history. London, 1852. 3v.
AH 278.52 — Niebuhr, B.G. Lectures on ancient history. Philadelphia, 1852. 3v.
AH 7278.11.27 — Niebuhr, B.G. Lectures on the History of Rome. 3. ed. London, 1852. 3v.
AH 4228.52 — Otto, C.E. De Atheniensium actionibus forensibus publicis. Dorpati, 1852.
AH 4043.5.10 — Plass, Hermann. Die Tyrannis in ihren beiden Perioden. Bremen, 1852. 2v.
AH 9505.2 — Ring, B.J.J.M. de. Mémoire sur les établissements romains. Paris, 1852. 2v.
Eg 708.52 — Robiou, Felix. Aegypti regimen quo anno susceperunt et qua ratione tractaverint Ptolemai. Rhedonis, 1852.
AH 9727.15 — Rousopoulos, A.S. Peri Zamolxidos. Inaug. Diss. Gottingae, 1852.
AH 4238.52 — Rüstow, W. Geschichte des griechischen Kriegswesens. Aarau, 1852.
AH 808.52 — Scaliger, J. Olymiadōn anagra. Berolini, 1852.
AH 5207.5 — Schwab, C.T. Arkadien. Stuttgart, 1852.
AH 7168.41.6 — Sell, K. Römische Lehre der dinglichen Rechte. Bonn, 1852.
AH 3958.5.5 — Stark, Karl B. Gaza und die philistäische Küste. Jena, 1852.
AH 3740.6 — Tyre; its rise, glory, and desolation. Philadelphia, 1852.
AH 7206.7 — Zacharia, K.E. Collectio librorum juris Graeco-Romanum. Lipsiae, 1852.

1853

AH 7548.53 — Abbott, Jacob. History of Nero. N.Y., 1853.
Eg 608.53F — Birch, S. Thothmes III. London, 1853.
AH 3109.5 — Bosanquet, J.W. The fall of Nineveh and the reign of Sennacherib chronologically considered. London, 1853.
AH 3109.3 — Brandis, J. Rerum Assyriarum tempora emendata. Bonn, 1853.
Htn AH 7758.53.2* — Burckhardt, Jacob. Die Zeit Constantins des Grossen. Basel, 1853.
AH 7758.53 — Burckhardt, Jacob. Die Zeit Constantins des Grossen. Leipzig, 1853.
AH 7808.53.5 — Clinton, Henry Fynes. An epitome of the civil and literary chronology of Rome and Constantinople. Oxford, 1853.
AH 7203.46 — Corpus juris civilis. Institutiones. Institutes of Justinian. London, 1853.
AH 7168.53 — Delbrück, E.L.B. Uebernahme fremder Schulden. Berlin, 1853.
AH 4278.53 — Durdent, René Jean. Beautés de l'histoire grecque. 7. éd. Paris, 1853.
AH 7498.53 — Duruy, V. Etat du monde romain. Paris, 1853.
AH 7308.49.2 — Eliot, Samuel. History of the liberty of the ancient Romans. Boston, 1853.
AH 7869.2 — Ellendt, F. Cognomine et agnomine Romano. Regimontii Borussorum, 1853.
AH 7448.18.3 — Ellis, Robert. Treatise on Hannibal's Passage. Cambridge, 1853.
AH 7408.53 — Gerlach, F.D. Quellen der altesten römischen Geschichte. Basel, 1853.
AH 7408.51 — Gerlach, F.D. Von den Quellen der ältesten römischen Geschichte. Basel, 1853.
NEDL AH 7650.53 — Gibbon, Edward. History of decline and fall of Roman Empire. London, 1853. 7v.
NEDL AH 7277.70.21 — Goldsmith, O. Roman history. 35. American ed. Philadelphia, 1853.
AH 3011.5.5F — Grotefend, G.F. Erläuterung einer Inschrift des letzten assyrisch-babylonischen Königs aus Nimrud. Hannover, 1853.
AH 3132.7 — Grotefend, G.F. Erläuterung zweier Ausschreiben des Königes Nebukadnezar. Göttingen, 1853.
AH 4938.53 — Hanriot, Charles. Geographia Graecorum antiquissima Napoleonopoli qualis ab Homero...Thesim proponebat. Pictavorum, 1853.
AH 4117.8 — Hanriot, Charles. Recherches sur la topographie des dèmes de l'Attique. Napoléon-Vendée, 1853.
AH 8549.50 — Herrig, L. De Druidibus, eine Abhandlung. Berlin, 1853.
AH 4521.7 — Hertzberg, G.F. Alkibiades als Staatsmann und Feldhen. Halle, 1853.

Chronological Listing

1853 - cont.

AH 4048.53 Jurrjens, D.H. Democratiae apud Athenienses. Rhenum, 1853.

NEDL AH 278.53 Lamé-Fleury, J.R. La storia antica. Venezia, 1853.

AH 3013.33.7A Layard, A.H. Discoveries among the ruins of Nineveh and Babylon. N.Y., 1853.

AH 3013.33.6A Layard, A.H. Discoveries among the ruins of Nineveh and Babylon. N.Y., 1853.

AH 3013.33.8 Layard, A.H. Discoveries among the ruins of Nineveh and Babylon. N.Y., 1853.

AH 3013.33.17PF Layard, A.H. The monuments of Nineveh. 2d series. London, 1853.

AH 3013.33.4 Layard, A.H. Nineveh and its remains. v.1-2. N.Y., 1853.

AH 7058.53 Linker, G. Über die Wahl...Praefectus urbis feriarum. Wien? 1853.

AH 828.53 Lionnet, A. Palaion, die alte Welt. Berlin, 1853.

AH 4859.9 Mähly, J.A. Frauen des griechischen Alterthums. Basel, 1853.

AH 7468.44.3 Mérimée, P. Etudes sur l'histoire romaine. Paris, 1853.

NEDL AH 938.53 Niebuhr, B.G. Lectures on ancient ethnography and geography. London, 1853. 2v.

AH 7114.20 Pardon, L. De aerariis. Berolini, 1853.

AH 7168.37.2 Pellat, C.A. Exposé...du droit romain sur la propriété. Paris, 1853.

AH 7163.27.2 Pellat, C.A. Textes sur la dot. 2e éd. Paris, 1853.

AH 7278.53.3 Peter, C. Geschichte Roms. Halle, 1853. 2v.

AH 278.27.12 Poirson, A. Précis de l'histoire ancienne. 12. éd. Paris, 1853. 2v.

AH 7161.3 Rossbach, A. Untersuchungen über die römische Ehe. Stuttgart, 1853.

AH 7808.53 Scheiffele, A. Jahrbücher der römischen Geschichte. Nördlingen, 1853.

AH 7138.53 Scheurl, C.G.A. Beiträge zur...römischen Rechts. Erlangen, 1853. 2v.

AH 7818.53 Schmidt, C. Essai historique sur la société civile. Strasbourg, 1853.

AH 7228.53 Schmidt, K.A. Interdiktenverfahren der Römer. Leipzig, 1853.

AH 850.5 Schuch, C.T. Gemüse und Salate der Alten. Rastatt, 1853.

AH 7278.53.10 Schwegler, A. Römische Geschichte. Tübingen, 1853. 4v.

AH 4298.53 Wordsworth, C. Greece; pictorial, descriptive, and historical. London, 1853.

1854

AH 3659.20.3 Abbott, Jacob. History of Darius the Great. N.Y., 1854.

AH 5610.7.5 Abbott, Jacob. History of Pyrrhus. N.Y., 1854.

AH 4828.40.8A Becker, W.A. Charicles. London, 1854.

AH 4828.40.7 Becker, W.A. Charicles. London, 1854.

AH 4828.40.2 Becker, W.A. Charikles. 2. Aufl. Leipzig, 1854. 3v.

AH 9777.13 Bessell, G. De rebus geticis. Gottingae, 1854.

NEDL AH 278.54 Boreau, V. Historia antigua. Santiago, 1854.

AH 3013.18 Circourt, A. de. Decouvertes dans les ruines de Ninive et de Babylone. Paris, 1854.

AH 7138.54.3 Cushing, L.S. Introduction to study of Roman law. Boston, 1854.

AH 9066.5 Desjardins, Ernest. Essai sur la topographie du Latium. Thèse. Paris, 1854.

AH 7278.39.9 Fiedler, F.A.M. Geschichte der Römer. 2. Aufl. Leipzig, 1854.

AH 4038.54.7 Filon, A. Histoire de la démocratie athénienne. Paris, 1854.

NEDL AH 930.7.3 Findlay, Alexander G. A classical atlas, to illustrate ancient geography. London, 1854.

AH 6009.5 Flathe, Theodor. Der phokische Krieg. Plauen, 1854.

AH 7138.54 Fresquet, R. Traité élémentaire de droit romain. Paris, 1854. 2v.

NEDL AH 7650.54 Gibbon, E. History of decline and fall of Roman Empire. Boston, 1854. 8v.

AH 4278.00.15 Goldsmith, Oliver. Pinnock's improved edition of Goldsmith's History of Greece. Philadelphia, 1854.

AH 7114.12 Gomont, H. Les chevaliers romains. Paris, 1854.

AH 3008.54 Gumpach, J. von. Abriss der babylonisch-assyrischen Geschichte. Mannheim, 1854.

AH 7468.54.25 Hagen, E. Untersuchungen über römische Geschichte. Königsberg, 1854.

AH 7238.54 Herbert, H.W. The captains of the Roman republic. N.Y., 1854.

AH 7869.5 Hübner, Emil. Quaestiones onomatologicae Latinae. Bonnae, 1854.

AH 4538.54 Lachmann, J.H. Geschichte Griechenlands. v.1-2. Leipzig, 1854.

AH 298.54 Lasaulx, Ernest. Studien des classischen Alterthums. Regensburg, 1854.

AH 7468.54 Lau, Thaddeus. Die Gracchen und ihre Zeit. Hamburg, 1854.

NEDL AH 3013.33.5 Layard, A.H. Nineveh and its remains. 6. ed. London, 1854. 2v.

AH 3014.25 Layard, A.H. The Nineveh court in the crystal palace. London, 1854.

AH 938.54 Niebuhr, B.G. Lectures on ancient ethnography and geography. Boston, 1854. 2v.

Eg 278.54 Osburn, W. The monumental history of Egypt. London, 1854. 2v.

AH 4038.54 Schömann, G.F. Verfassungsgeschichte Athen's. Leipzig, 1854.

AH 4818.54 Schwalbe, K.F.H. Handbuch der Griechischen Antiquitäten. Magdeburg, 1854.

NEDL AH 938.54.2 Smith, William. Dictionary of Greek and Roman geography. London, 1854.

AH 938.54.3 Smith, William. Dictionary of Greek and Roman geography. London, 1854.

AH 7131.7 Soldan, A. De reipublicae romanae legatis. Marburg, 1854. 6 pam.

AH 7818.54 Tounsend, F. Letters from Rome. N.Y., 1854.

Eg 818.37.12 Wilkinson, J.G. A popular account of the ancient Egyptians. London, 1854. 2v.

Eg 818.37.13 Wilkinson, J.G. A popular account of the ancient Egyptians. N.Y., 1854. 2v.

AH 898.54 Wüstemann, E.F. Unterhaltungen aus der alten Welt. Gotha, 1854.

1855

AH 7138.55.5 Asher, G.M. Disquisitionum de fontibus juris romani historicarum. Heidelbergae, 1855.

AH 2147.2 Bergmann, R. Asiae Romanorum provinciae civitatibus liberis. Brandenburg, 1855.

AH 5957.7 Beulé, E. Etudes sur Péloponésé. Paris, 1855.

AH 4278.55 Boreau, V. Historia griega. Santiago, 1855.

AH 4833.7 Brugsma, A.L. Gymasiorum apud Graecos descriptionem. Groningae, 1855.

AH 5309.5 Büchenschütz, A.B. Könige von Athen. Berlin, 1855.

AH 4328.55 Curtius, Ernst. Die Ionier. Berlin, 1855.

AH 408.55 Duncker, M. Geschichte des Alterthums. Berlin, 1855. 4v.

AH 7201.31.2 Gaius. Beiträge zur Kritik und zum Veret. Leipzig, 1855.

AH 7201.31 Gaius. Institutionum commentarii quattuor. Lipsiae, 1855.

AH 7203.46.10 Goldschmidt, L. Untersuchungen. Heidelberg, 1855.

AH 4258.55 Goodwin, G.W. De potentiac...maritimae Epochis. Gottingae, 1855.

AH 258.55 Goodwin, J.W. De potentiae veterum...maritimae epochis. Gottingae, 1855.

AH 3966.26 Hackett, H.B. Illustrations of scripture. Boston, 1855.

AH 4518.55 Herbst, L.F. Die Schlacht bei den Arginusen. Hamburg, 1855.

AH 4818.41.3 Hermann, K.F. Lehrbuch der griechischen Antiquitäten. 4. Aufl. Heidelberg, 1855. 3v.

AH 8658.5 Historical pictures of pagan and Christian Rome. Rome, 1855.

AH 8507.5 Holtzmann, A. Kelten und Germanen. Stuttgart, 1855.

AH 7008.55 Hulleman, I.G. Disputatio critica de Annalibus. n.p., 1855.

AH 4298.52.5 Jacobs, Friedrich. Helias; or, The home, history, literature, and art of the Greeks. London, 1855.

AH 7114.19 Kappes, K. Erläuterungen...zur römischen Ritter. Freiburg, 1855.

AH 3707.9 Kenrick, J. Phoenicia. London, 1855.

AH 7488.55 Lamé Fleury, J.R. La storia romana. Milano, 1855.

AH 7468.34 Lau, Thaddeus. Lucius Cornelius Sulla. Hamburg, 1855.

AH 3013.33.27 Layard, A.H. A popular account of discoveries at Nineveh. N.Y., 1855.

AH 7298.55 Lewis, George C. An inquiry...early Roman history. London, 1855. 2v.

AH 7278.55 Liddell, H.G. History of Rome. London, 1855. 2v.

AH 9654.5 Mommsen, T. Die Stadtrechte der latinischen Gemeinden Salkensa und Malaca. Leipzig, 1855.

AH 5140.9 Moschatos, A. De Insula Teno Eiusque historia. Gottingae, 1855.

AH 7852.5 Namur, A. De lacrymatoriis sive de lagenulis. Luciliburgi, 1855.

AH 6157.5 Neumann, K. Hellenen in Skythenlande. Berlin, 1855.

AH 818.68.5 Ozanam, A.F. La civilisation au cinquième siècle. Paris, 1855. 2v.

AH 7238.85 Ritterling, E.H.E. De legione Romanorum X Genima. Lipsiae, 1855.

AH 4818.55 Rousopoulos, A.S. Ellenikès archaiologias. Patrais, 1855.

AH 5557.5 Schiller, L. Elis, Arkadien, Achaja. Erlangen, 1855.

NEDL AH 278.55 Schmitz, L. A manual of ancient history. Philadelphia, 1855.

AH 2157.2 Schoemann, A.G.O. Bithynia et Ponto. Gottingae, 1855.

AH 4818.51 Schoemann, G.F. Griechische Alterthümer. Berlin, 1855. 2v.

AH 4114.7 Schömann, G.F. Recognitio quaestionis de Spartanis Homoeis. Gryphiswaldiae, 1855.

Eg 878.55 Seyffarth, G. Theologische Schriften der alten Aegypter. Gotha, 1855.

NEDL AH 4278.57.19.5A Smith, William. A history of Greece. Boston, 1855.

NEDL AH 4278.57.19 Smith, William. A history of Greece. Boston, 1855.

AH 3075.5 Strauss, Otto. Ninive und das Wort Gottes. Berlin, 1855.

AH 7138.55 Troplong, R.T. De l'influence du christianisme. Paris, 1855.

Eg 848.2 Uhlemann, M. Thoth oder die Wissenschaft der alten Ägypter. Göttingen, 1855.

AH 7201.23.4 Ulpiani, D. Fragmenta. Leipsiae, 1855.

AH 3013.27.4 Vaux, W.S.W. Nineveh and Persepolis. 4. ed. London, 1855.

AH 4843.4 Weitzmann, C.F. Geschichte der griechischen Musik. Berlin, 1855.

NEDL AH 968.55 Wheeler, J. Life and travels of Herodotus. London, 1855. 2v.

1856

AH 4408.56 Behr, Par M. L'histoire des temps heroïques. Paris, 1856.

AH 3004.3 Brandis, J. Über den historischen Gewinn...assyrischen Inschriften. Berlin, 1856.

AH 8525.2 Bulliot, J.G. Essai sur le système défensif...pays Éduen. Paris, 1856.

AH 5658.5 Bursian, C. Quaestionum Euboicarum. Lipsiae, 1856.

AH 4278.56.9 Duruy, V. Histoire grecque. Paris, 1856.

AH 7188.56 Elvers, R. Römischen Servitutenlehre. Marburg, 1856.

AH 7138.56 Esmach, K. Römischen Rechtsgeschichte. Göttingen, 1856.

AH 861.7F Feydeau, E. Histoire des usages funèbres. Paris, 1856. 2v.

AH 898.56 Forchhammer, P.W. Landwirthschaftliche Mittheilungen. Kiel, 1856.

AH 7468.34.2 Gerlach, F.D. Marius and Sulla. Basel, 1856.

AH 3132.4F Hasse, G.R. Dissertatio de prima Nebucednezaris adversus Hierosolyma expeditione. Bonn, 1856.

AH 3966.16.3 Headley, J.T. The sacred plains. Buffalo, 1856.

AH 5760.11 Hertzberg, G.F. Königs Agesilaos II von Sparta. Halle, 1856.

AH 7114.2 Heuermann, O.L. Programm...Gymnasii Arnoldini. Münster, 1856.

NEDL AH 4278.56 History of ancient Greece. London, 1856.

NEDL AH 938.56.20 Hughes, William. An atlas of classical geography. N.Y., 1856.

AH 938.56 Hughes, William. An atlas of classical geography. Philadelphia, 1856.

AH 7138.54.16 Humphreys, E.R. Manual of civil law for...schools. 2. ed. London, 1856.

Eg 298.90 Ibn Abd al Hakam, Abd al Rahman. Libellus de Historia Aegypti antiqua. Gottingae, 1856.

AH 1408.56 Krüger, J. Geschichte der Assyrier und Iranier. Frankfurt, 1856.

AH 7818.56 Lange, C.C.L. Römische Alterthümer. Berlin, 1856-71. 3v.

AH 3013.33.9 Layard, A.H. Discoveries among the ruins of Nineveh and Babylon. 2. ed. N.Y., 1856.

Chronological Listing

1856 - cont.

NEDL AH 278.56.10   Leva, G. de. Sommario della storia de' popoli antichi. Padova, 1856.

AH 7138.56.3   Machelard, E. Textes de droit romain. v.1-2. Paris, 1856.

AH 7138.56.15   Matthiae, C. Controversen Lexikon des römischen Civilrechts. Leipzig, 1856. 3v.

AH 7278.54.3   Mommsen, T. Römische Geschichte. 2. Aufl. Berlin, 1856. 3v.

AH 8016.3   Rabusson, A. De la geographie du nord de l'Afrique. Paris, 1856.

AH 7178.56   Revillout, Charles. Étude sur l'histoire du Colonat. Paris, 1856.

AH 4298.56   Reynald, H. Libertati apud veteres Graeciae populos quid defuerit. Parisiis, 1856.

AH 7118.4   Rieu, G.N. du. Dissertatio...de gente fabia. Lugduni-Batavorum, 1856.

AH 4888.56   Roscher, Wilhelm. De dogtrinae oeconomico-politicae apud Graecos primordiis. Diss. Lipsiae, 1856.

AH 4328.56   Schoemann, G.F. Animadversiones de Ionibus. Gryphisvaldiae, 1856.

NEDL AH 938.54.4   Smith, William. Dictionary of Greek and Roman geography. London, 1856-57. 2v.

AH 7798.56   Thierry, A.S.D. Histoire d'Attila. Paris, 1856. 2v.

AH 3740.6.3   Tyre; its rise, glory, and desolation. Nashville, 1856.

Eg 558.56   Uhlemann, M. Israeliten und Hyksos in Aegypten. Leipzig, 1856.

AH 7148.56   Voigt, M. Jus naturale. Leipzig, 1856. 4v.

AH 3160.13   Walz, C. Turibuli Assyrii descriptio. Tubingae, 1856.

AH 968.55.5   Wheeler, J. Life and travels of Herodotus. N.Y., 1856. 2v.

AH 7228.56   Windscheid, B. Die Actio des römischen Civilrechts. Düsseldorf, 1856.

AH 7206.6   Zacharia, K.E. Innere Geschichte des griechisch römische Rechts. Leipzig, 1856.

AH 7206.5   Zacharia, K.E. Jus Graeco-Romanum. v.1-3. Lipsiae, 1856. 2v.

1857

AH 7278.40.7   Arnold, T. History of Rome. N.Y., 1857.

AH 7278.46.5   Arnold, T. History of the later Roman Commonwealth. London, 1857. 2v.

AH 3075.8   Bible. Prophets. The prophecies relating to Nineveh and the Assyrians. London, 1857.

AH 4108.17.4   Böckh, August. Public economy of Athenians. Boston, 1857.

AH 4808.57   Brandis, J. De temporum graecorum antiquissimorum rationibus. Bonnae, 1857.

AH 8548.10   Braudes, C. Das ethnographische Verhältniss der Kelten und Germanen. Leipzig, 1857.

Eg 938.57   Brugsch, H. Geographische Inschriften. v.1-3. Leipzig, 1857. 2v.

AH 7628.57   Caillet, Jules. De ratione in imperio Romano ordinando ab Hadriano imperatore adhibita. Diss. Parisiis, 1857.

AH 4278.57.5   Curtius, Ernest. Griechische Geschichte. Berlin, 1857. 3v.

AH 4238.57   Dansin, H. De mercenariis militibus apud antiquas Graeciae civitates...Thesim proponebat. Argentorati, 1857.

AH 7215.6   Danz, H.A.A. Der sacrale Schutz im römischen Rechtsverkehr. Jena, 1857.

AH 7898.57   Daubeny, Charles. Lectures on Roman husbandry. Oxford, 1857.

AH 7201.32   Demelius, G. Legum quae ad ius civile. Vimariae, 1857.

AH 6110.11   Gerlach, F.D. Perseus König von Makedonien. Basel, 1857.

NEDL AH 7651.10A   Gibbon, Edward. Student's Gibbon. N.Y., 1857.

AH 3125.3   Glimpses of Nineveh. N.Y., 1857.

AH 7204.5F   Haenel, G.F. Corpus legem. Lipsiae, 1857.

AH 818.57   Hermann, K.F. Culturgeschichte. Göttingen, 1857.

AH 7588.57   Imhof, Albert T. Flavius Domitianus. Halle, 1857.

Eg 808.57   Knötel, A. System der ägyptischen Chronologie. Leipzig, 1857.

AH 7818.28.3   Lanktree, J. Synopsis of Roman antiquities. London, 1857.

AH 938.54.20   Leake, W.M. On some disputed questions of ancient geography. London, 1857.

NEDL AH 7278.55.2A   Liddell, H.G. History of Rome. N.Y., 1857.

AH 7478.57   Mommsen, T. Die Rechtsfrage zwischen Caesar und dem Senat. Breslau, 1857.

AH 7278.54.32   Mommsen, T. Storia romana. Torino, 1857-63. 3v.

AH 8548.115   Mone, F.J. Celtische Forschungen zur Geschichte Mitteleuropas. Freiburg, 1857.

AH 3008.57   Niebuhr, M.K.N. Geschichte Assur's und Babel's seit Phiel. Berlin, 1857.

AH 7008.57   Renssen, J.G. Disputatio de diurnis aliisque. Groningen, 1857.

NEDL AH 277.34.19   Rollin, Charles. Ancient history. v.1-4. N.Y., 1857. 2v.

AH 7138.57   Rudorff, A.F. Römischen Rechtsgeschichte. Leipzig, 1857.

AH 4511.5   Schimmelpfeng, G. De Brasidae Spartani. Marburgi Cattorum, 1857. 4 pam.

AH 938.57   Schmitz, L. Manual of ancient geography. Philadelphia, 1857.

AH 7808.57   Simon, Heinrich O. Fastorum Romanorum Specimen. Berlin, 1857.

NEDL AH 4278.57.21   Smith, William. History of Greece. Boston, 1857.

AH 4278.57.20   Smith, William. History of Greece. Boston, 1857.

AH 7161.11   Thön, Karl. Die römische Familie. Kronstadt, 1857.

AH 308.57   Ulm. Gymnasium. Parallelen römischer und griechischen Entwicklungsgeschichte. Ulm, 1857.

AH 5857.7   Vogt, G. Rebus Megarensium. Marburgi, 1857.

Eg 818.57   Wilkinson, J.G. The Egyptians in the time of the pharaohs. London, 1857.

AH 7228.57   Windscheid, B. Die Actio. Düsseldorf, 1857.

1858

AH 4558.58   Alexandrou. Istoria. Venetia, 1858.

AH 4833.10   Basiades, C.H. De veterum Graecorum gymnastice. Berolini, 1858.

AH 3757.7   Bergmann, F.G. Les Serythes. Halle, 1858.

AH 7038.58   Bröcker, L. Altrömische Verfassungsgeschichte. Hamburg, 1858.

AH 7558.58   Champagny, F.J.M.T.N. Rome et la Judée au temps de la chute de Néron. Paris, 1858.

NEDL AH 5957.9   Clark, W.G. Peloponnesus. London, 1858.

AH 7228.58   Daniel, C.G.F. Legisactionen und Formularprozess. Schwerin, 1858.

AH 7168.58.5   Demangeat, C. Des obligations solidaires. Paris, 1858.

1858 - cont.

AH 120.5   Egger, Emile. Observations historiques sur la fonction de secrétaire des princes chez les anciens. Paris, 1858.

AH 7158.58   Eisenlohr, C. Die Provocatio ad Populum. Schwerin, 1858.

AH 2158.2   Faber, A. Quaestionum propontiacarum. Herford, 1858.

NEDL AH 278.58.4   Flóres, Antonio. Historia universal. Lima, 1858.

AH 8613.5   Gerlach, F.D. Zaleukos, Charondas, Pythagoras. Basel, 1858.

AH 3357.9   Gottschick, A.F. Geschichte der Gründung...des Hellenischen Staates. Leipzig, 1858.

AH 7228.58.2   Grellet Dumageau, J.B.M. Le barreau romain. Paris, 1858.

NEDL AH 278.58   Guillemin, J.J. Histoire ancienne. Paris, 1858.

Eg 878.58   Heavlin, R.A. (Mrs.). The mysteries of Isis. N.Y., 1858.

AH 7008.58   Hübner, E.W. De senatus populique romani actis. Lipsiae, 1858.

AH 6057.5   Kriegk, G.L. Thessalische Ebene. Frankfurt am Main, 1858.

AH 7538.58   Lehmann, H. Claudius und Nero und ihre Zeit. Gotha, 1858.

Eg 808.49.5F   Lepsius, K.R. Königsbuch der alten Ägypter. Berlin, 1858.

AH 7408.58   Linker, G. Die älteste Sagengeschichte Roms. Wien, 1858.

AH 7162.27   Machalard, E. Dissertation sur l'accroissement. Paris, 1858.

AH 7898.58   Magerstedt, A.F. Bilder aus der römischen Landwirtschaft. Sondershausen, 1858. 6v.

AH 7168.58.10   Massol, M. De l'obligation naturelle. Paris, 1858.

NEDL AH 408.58   Menzies, H. Early ancient history. London, 1858.

AH 4518.58   Metropulos, C. Schacht bei Mantinea. Göttingen, 1858.

AH 8609.3   Mommsen, Theodor. Earliest inhabitants of Italy. London, 1858.

AH 4278.57   Mone, F. Kritische Bemerkung von Ernest Curtius. Berlin, 1858.

AH 7818.58   Niebuhr, B.G. Vorträge über römische Alterthümer. Berlin, 1858.

AH 4298.58   Paparrēgópanlos, K. Istorikai pragmateiai. v.1-6. Athēnai, 1858.

Htn Eg 708.58*   Pennsylvania. University. Philomathean Society. Report of the committee...to translate...the Rosetta Stone. Philadelphia, 1858.

AH 4833.9   Petersen, C. Gymnasium der Griechen. Hamburg, 1858.

AH 7168.58   Rein, W. Privatrecht...der Römer. Leipzig, 1858.

Eg 608.58   Rougé, E. de. Etude sur une stèle égyptienne. Paris, 1858.

AH 7203.123   Schemmelpfeng, T. Hommel Redivivus. Cassel, 1858. 3v.

AH 277.27.25   Shuckford, Samuel. The sacred and profane history of the world connected. London, 1858. 2v.

AH 9777.15   Simonis, Carl. Versuch einer Geschichte des Alarich. Göttingen, 1858.

AH 4842.52   Stallbaum, G. De veterum Graecorum institutione. Lipsiae, 1858.

AH 4208.5   Westermann, A. De iuris iurandi iudicium Atheniensium formula. Lipsiae, 1858.

1859

AH 8514.10   Barry, A.E. Monographie du dieu Leherenn d'Ardiége. Paris, 1859.

Eg 278.59   Brugsch, H. Histoire d'Égypte. Leipzig, 1859.

AH 7498.59   Champagny, F.J.M.T. Les Césars. Paris, 1859.

AH 8907.3   Conestabile, G. Degli etruschi dell'agricoltura. Perugia, 1859.

AH 7203.47   Corpus juris civilis. Institutiones. Institutes of Justinian. 2. ed. London, 1859.

AH 7207.19   Dumeril, Adfred E.S. De senatu romano sub imperatoribus Augusto Tiberiano. Duaci, 1859.

AH 4484.5   Frick, Otto. Plataeische Weihgeschenk. Leipzig, 1859.

AH 7828.59   Friedlaender, L. Dissertatio de appellatione doninis. Regimonti Borussorum, 1859.

NEDL AH 7651.12   Gibbon, Edward. Student's Gibbon. History of Roman Empire. N.Y., 1859.

Htn AH 7295.89F*   Glandorp. Onomasticon historicae Romanae. Francofurti, 1859.

NEDL AH 4278.46.11   Grote, George. History of Greece. v.2-12. N.Y., 1859. 11v.

AH 7228.59   Hartmann, O.E. Ordo judiciorum. Göttingen, 1859.

NEDL AH 938.56.3   Hughes, William. An atlas of classical geography. Philadelphia, 1859.

AH 9777.17   Köpke, R. Die Anfänge des Königthums bei den Gothen. Berlin, 1859.

AH 4908.59   Kutorga, M. Trapézites. Paris, 1859.

AH 7138.59   Leapingwell, George. Manual of Roman civil law. Cambridge, 1859.

AH 7278.33.15   Michelet, J. History of the Roman Republic. N.Y., 1859.

AH 7898.59   Michon, L.A.J. Des céréales en Italie sous les Romains. Paris, 1859.

AH 7168.59   Mommsen, Theodor. Erörterungen aus dem Obligationenrecht. v.1-2. Braunschweig, 1859.

AH 7808.58.3   Mommsen, Theodor. Römische Chronologie bis auf Caesar. 2. Aufl. Berlin, 1859.

AH 928.59   Müller, H. Über die heilige Masse des Alterthums. Freiburg, 1859.

AH 4043.5.12   Plass, Hermann. Die Tyrannis in ihren beiden Perioden. v.1-2. 2. Ausg. Leipzig, 1859.

AH 7148.59   Quinion, L. Du municipe romain. Paris, 1859.

AH 7818.59   Ramsay, William. Elementary manual of Roman antiquities. London, 1859.

AH 9307.5   Ring, B.J.J.M. de. Histoire des peuples opiques. Paris, 1859.

AH 9792.5   Schulze, H. De testamento Genserici (Vandali). Jenae, 1859.

Eg 278.59.12   Seyffarth, G. Summary of recent discoveries in biblical chronology. 2. ed. N.Y., 1859.

Eg 278.36.4A   Sharpe, S. History of Egypt. London, 1859. 2v.

Eg 928.59   Taylor, J. The great pyramid. London, 1859.

AH 3925.5F   Texier, C.F.M. Edesse et ses monuments. Paris, 1859.

AH 7658.59   Wietersheim, E. von. Geschichte der Völkerwanderung. Leipzig, 1859. 4v.

AH 4298.53.2   Wordsworth, C. Greece; pictorial, descriptive, and historical.

AH 3012.10   Zimmermann, Carl. Babylon. Basel, 1859.

AH 8507.3   Zumpt, A.W. Studi Romana. Berolini, 1859.

1860

Eg 708.51.2   Abbott, Jacob. History of Cleopatra, queen of Egypt. N.Y., 1860.

AH 138.60A   Béchard, F. Droit municipal dans l'antiquité. Paris, 1860.

Chronological Listing

1860 - cont.

AH 3160.6 — Chevolson, D.A. Über Tammuz und die Menschenverehrung. St. Petersburg, 1860.

AH 7648.60 — Des Vergers, M.J.A. Essai sur Marc Aurèle. Paris, 1860.

AH 908.60 — Drumann, W. Die Arbeiter und Communisten. Königsberg, 1860.

AH 7201.33 — Fragmenta vaticana Iuris anteiustiniani. Berolini, 1860.

AH 4498.60 — Gause, A. Societatis Atheniensis historia. Berolini, 1860.

AH 408.60 — Gerlach, F.D. Sage und Forschung. Basel, 1860.

NEDL AH 7651.10.5 — Gibbon, Edward. The history of the decline and fall of the Roman Empire. N.Y., 1860.

AH 7808.60 — Hartmann, O.E. Zum römischen Kalender. Eine Entgegnung auf Th. Mommsen's Angriffe. Göttingen, 1860.

AH 7008.57.5 — Heinze, H. De spuriis actorum diurnorum. Gryphiae, 1860.

AH 7098.60.5 — Henzen, Wilhelm. Intorno alcuni magistrati municipali de romani. n.p., 1860? 2 pam.

AH 4478.60 — Kutorga, M.S. Parti persan dans la Grèce ancienne. Paris, 1860.

AH 9610.5 — Lau, T. Leben der Surakusaners Dion. Prag, 1860.

AH 7478.60 — Liddell, H.G. Life of Julius Caesar. N.Y., 1860.

AH 2147.3 — Merckens, G. De Asia Provincia. Vratislaviae, 1860.

AH 7418.60 — Moule, H. The Roman republic. London, 1860.

AH 7238.60 — Rein, A. De phaleris et de argenteis e arum exemplaribus haud praculcalone et Asaburgio. Romae, 1860.

AH 4048.60 — Reynald, M.H. Recherches sur ce qui manquait a la liberté...grecque. Paris, 1860.

NEDL AH 277.34.21 — Rollin, Charles. Ancient history. v.1-4. Cincinnati, 1860. 2v.

AH 7148.60 — Rudorff, A. De maiore ac minori latio. Berolini, 1860.

AH 4031.5 — Saal, N. De demorum atticae per tribus distributione. Coloniae-Agrippinensim, 1860. 3 pam.

AH 938.60.3 — Schmidt, H.I. Course on ancient geography. N.Y., 1860.

NEDL AH 4278.57.22 — Smith, William. History of Greece. Boston, 1860.

NEDL AH 4278.57.23 — Smith, William. History of Greece. N.Y., 1860.

NEDL AH 4278.57.28 — Smith, William. Smaller history of Greece. N.Y., 1860.

AH 7163.25 — Sontag, C.R. De sponsalibus apud Romanos. Halae, 1860.

AH 7798.60 — Thierry, A.S.D. Récits de l'histoire romaine. Paris, 1860.

AH 4298.53.5 — Turner, D.W. Heads of an analogy of the history of Greece. 2. ed. London, 1860.

AH 7098.60 — Voigt, Moritz. Drei epigraphische Constitutionen. Leipzig, 1860.

AH 4408.60 — Volkmuth, P. Pelasger als Semiten. Schaffhausen, 1860.

AH 7138.60 — Walter, F. Geschichte der römische Rechte. Bonn, 1860. 2v.

1861

AH 7508.61 — Anton, A.F.M. De sideribus Augusti nataliciis quae coniiciendo videantur. Halle, 1861.

AH 7758.61 — Aube, B. De Constantino imperatore, pontifice max. Lutetiae, 1861.

Htn AH 859.6F* — Bachofen, J.J. Das Mutterrecht. Stuttgart, 1861.

AH 7188.61 — Bechmann, C.G.A. Personalservitut des Usus. Nürnberg, 1861.

AH 3075.9 — Breiteneicher, M. Ninive und Nahum. München, 1861.

AH 8548.15 — Coutzen, L. Die Wanderungen der Kelten. Leipzig, 1861.

AH 4478.61 — Cox, George W. Great Persian War. London, 1861.

AH 7228.61 — Degenkolb, H. Die Lex Hieronica. Leipzig, 1861.

AH 7498.61 — Dubois Guchan, E.P. Tacite et son siècle. Paris, 1861. 2v.

AH 4808.61 — Faselius, A. Attische Kalender. Weimar, 1861.

AH 7201.33.10 — Gaius. Institutionum juris civilis commentarii quattuor. Lipsiae, 1861.

AH 48.61 — Givodan, Léon. Histoire des classes privilégiées. Paris, 1861. 2v.

AH 7478.61 — Göler, F.A. Bürgerkrieg zwischen Cäsar und Pompejus. Heidelberg, 1861.

AH 7808.61 — Hermann, F.C. Der römische Schalttag seit Julius Caesar. Berlin, 1861.

NEDL AH 938.56.4 — Hughes, William. An atlas of classical geography. Philadelphia, 1861.

AH 4558.61 — Jäger. Bemerkungen zur Geschichte Alexanders des Grossen. Wetzlar, 1861.

AH 9777.19 — Jordanes. Getarum sive Gothorum. Stuttgart, 1861.

Eg 458.61 — Knötel, August. Cheops der Pyramidenbauer und seine Nachfolger. Leipzig, 1861.

AH 7308.61 — Lasaulx, E. von. Zur Philosophie der römischen Geschichte. München, 1861.

AH 7168.61.10 — Machelard, E. Des obligations naturelles. Paris, 1861.

NEDL AH 138.61 — Maine, Henry S. Ancient law. London, 1861.

AH 7278.54.6 — Mommsen, T. Römische Geschichte. 3. Aufl. Berlin, 1861. 3v.

AH 7748.61 — Mommsen, Theodor. Über die Zeitfolge der Verordnungen Diocletians. Berlin, 1861.

AH 4608.61 — Nicolas, B. De ingenio et fortuna Graecarum apud Thraces coloniarum. Thesim proponebat. Lutetiae Parisiorum, 1861.

AH 4328.61 — Nitzsch, Otto. Jonischen Städteleben. Greifswald, 1861.

AH 7478.61.2 — Oliver y Hurtado, J. y D. Munda Pompeiana. Madrid, 1861.

X Cg Eg 8.61 — Palmer, W. Egyptian chronicles. London, 1861. 2v.

AH 7008.61 — Peter, K. Mommsen. Studien zur römischen Geschichte. Naumburg, 1861.

AH 1298.61 — Quatremère, Etienne M. Mélanges d'histoire et de philologie orientale. Paris, 1861.

AH 3002.30F — Rawlinson, H.C. Cuneiform inscriptions of Western Asia. v.1-5. London, 1861-64. 3v.

AH 3053.10 — Reinaud, Joseph T. Mémoire sur le commencement et la fin de la Mésène et de la Kharacène. Paris, 1861.

NEDL AH 4818.51.3A — Schoemann, G.F. Griechische Alterthümer. 2. Aufl. Berlin, 1861.

AH 7168.61.5 — Schwanert, H.A. Die Naturalobligationen der römischen Recht. Göttingen, 1861.

AH 7658.61 — Sheppard, J.G. The fall of Rome. London, 1861.

NEDL AH 4278.57.23.10 — Smith, William. History of Greece. N.Y., 1861.

NEDL AH 298.61 — Stacke, L. Erzählungen aus der alten Geschichte in biographischer Form. 4. Aufl. v.2. Oldenburg, 1861.

AH 7168.61 — Staedtler, H. De la restitution. Bruxelles, 1861.

AH 7278.61 — Turner, D.W. Roman history. 3. ed. London, 1861.

AH 7162.11 — Vering, F.H. Römische Erbrecht. Heidelberg, 1861.

1862

AH 7278.62 — Ampère, J.J. Histoire romaine. Paris, 1862. 4v.

AH 2507.5 — Bachofen, J.J. Das lykische Volk. Freiburg, 1862.

AH 4298.62 — Bässler, F. Hellenischer Heldensaal. 2. Aufl. Berlin, 1862.

1862 - cont.

AH 4168.62 — Bétant, C. An fuerint apud Graecos indices certi. Berolini, 1862.

AH 3966.2F — Bible atlas and gazetteer. N.Y., 1862.

AH 4498.62 — Bissing, F. Athen und die Politik seiner Staatsmeiner. Heidelberg, 1862.

AH 7168.62 — Böcking, E. Römischen Privatrecht. Bonn, 1862.

AH 4938.62.5 — Bursian, Konrad. Geographie von Griechenland. Leipzig, 1862-72. 2v.

AH 4938.62 — Bursian, Konrad. Geographie von Griechenland. v.1-2. Leipzig, 1862. 3v.

AH 4498.62.2 — Capefigue, M. Aspasie et le siècle de Périclès. Paris, 1862.

AH 5336.6 — Curtius, Ernst. Attische Studien; Pnyx und Stadtmauer. Göttingen, 1862.

AH 7478.62 — De Damas, Nicolas. La mort de César. Paris, 1862.

AH 8907.4 — Des Vergers, M.J.A.N. L'Étrurie et les Étrusques. Paris, 1862-64. 2v.

AH 8907.4PF — Des Vergers, M.J.A.N. L'Étrurie et les Étrusques. v.3. Atlas. Paris, 1862-64.

AH 7650.34 — Gibbon, Edward. History of decline and fall of Roman Empire. v.2-8. London, 1862. 7v.

NEDL AH 7651.11 — Gibbon, Edward. History of the decline and fall of the Roman Empire. N.Y., 1862.

AH 7088.62 — Grant, A. How the ancient Roman governed their provinces. Bombay, 1862.

AH 4278.46.16 — Grote, George. A history of Greece. London, 1862. 8v.

NEDL AH 818.62.3 — Guhl, Ernst. Leben der Griechen und Römer. Berlin, 1862.

AH 7178.62 — Hildebrand, B. De antiquiisimae agri Romani. Jenae, 1862.

AH 928.62 — Hultsch, F. Metrologie. Berlin, 1862.

AH 138.62 — Mayer, S. Rechte der Israeliten, Athener und Römer. Leipzig, 1862. 2v.

AH 3000.4 — Ménant, J. Rapport...sur les inscriptions assyriens. v.1-2. Paris, 1862.

AH 1278.62 — Rawlinson, G. Five great monarchies of the ancient Eastern World. London, 1862-1867. 4v.

AH 3195.3 — Renan, Ernest. An essay on the age and antiquity of the book of Nabathaean agriculture. London, 1862.

AH 5409.5 — Schubring, J.J. Cypsello Corinthiorum tyranno. Gottingae, 1862.

AH 7148.62 — Serrigny, D. Droit public et administratif. Paris, 1862. 2v.

AH 7798.60.3 — Thierry, A.S.D. Récits de l'histoire romaine. 2. éd. Paris, 1862.

AH 7308.76.2 — Thierry, A.S.D. Tableau de l'Empire Romain. Paris, 1862.

AH 818.62 — Trottet, J.P. Génie des civilisations. Paris, 1862. 2v.

AH 7228.62 — Voigt, M. Ueber die condictiones ob causam. Leipzig, 1862.

AH 808.38.3 — Zumpt, K.G. Annales. Berolini, 1862.

1863

AH 808.63 — Böckh, A. Sonnenkreise der Alten. Berlin, 1863.

Eg 1158.63 — Brugsch, H. Notice raisonnée d'un traité médical datant du XIVme siècle. Leipzig, 1863.

AH 7058.63 — Degli uficiali e degli uficii di Roma. Padova, 1863.

AH 6116.5 — Desdevises-du-dezert. Géographie ancienne de la Macedoine. Paris, 1863.

AH 4842.9 — Dittenberger, W. De Ephebis Atticis. Gottingae, 1863.

AH 7478.63 — Dressel, E. Über die politische Rolle des Gnaeus Pompejus Magnus. Coburg, 1863.

AH 278.52.15 — Duncker, M. Geschichte des Alterthums. Berlin, 1863. 4v.

Eg 298.63 — Early Egyptian history, for the young. London, 1863.

NEDL AH 278.58.5 — Flóres, Antonio. Curso de historia antigua. 2. ed. Besanyon, 1863.

AH 4038.63A — Freeman, E.A. History of federal government. London, 1863.

AH 7115.3 — Grotefend, C.L. Imperium Romanum. Hannover, 1863.

AH 3001.4 — Hincks, E. On the polyphony of the Assyric-Babylonian cuneiform writing. Dublin, 1863. 10 pam.

AH 3921.5F — Hug, A. Antiochia und der Aufstand des Jahres 387 nach Christus. Winterthur, 1863.

AH 7228.52.3 — Keller, Friedrich. Der römische Civilprocess und die Actionen. 3. Aufl. Leipzig, 1863.

AH 7298.63 — Labberton, R.H. Historical questions. Philadelphia, 1863.

AH 7238.63 — Lamarre, Claude. De la milice romaine depuis la fondation de Rome jusqu'à Constantin. Thèse. Paris, 1863.

AH 7818.56.3 — Lange, C.C.L. Römische Alterthümer. v.1-2, 2. Aufl; v.3, 1. Aufl. Berlin, 1863-71. 3v.

AH 7298.55.3 — Lewis, George C. Untersuchungen...altrömischen Geschichte. Hannover, 1863.

Eg 808.63 — Lieblein, J. Ägyptische Chronologie. Christiania, 1863.

AH 2958.5 — Maclaren, Charles. The plain of Troy described. Edinburgh, 1863.

AH 9757.8 — Martin, Charles. Les deux Germanies cis-rhénanes. Étude d'histoire et de géographie anciennes. Paris, 1863.

AH 3030.4 — Menant, J. Inscriptions de Hammourabi. Paris, 1863.

NEDL AH 7488.52.5 — Merivale, Charles. History of the Romans. 4. London ed. N.Y., 1863. 7v.

AH 4842.50 — Möller. De eruditione Graecorum. v.1-2. Weimar, 1863.

AH 7278.54.29 — Mommsen, T. Histoire romaine. v.1-8. Paris, 1863. 4v.

AH 7217.13 — Naudet, Joseph. De la noblesse et des récompenses. Paris, 1863.

AH 3013.11F — Oppert, J. Expédition scientifique en Mésopotamie. v.1-2; plates. Paris, 1863. 3v.

AH 3094.4F — Oppert, J. Les fastes de Sargon roi d'Assyrie. Paris, 1863. 2 pam.

AH 3094.4.2F — Oppert, J. Les fastes de Sargon roi d'Assyrie. Paris, 1863.

AH 7278.54.33 — Peter, Carl. Studien zur römische Geschichte. 2. Aufl. Halle, 1863.

AH 7168.63 — Phillimore, J.G. Private law among Romans. London, 1863.

AH 8107.5 — Poulle, M.A. À travers la Mauritaine sétifienne. Constantine, 1863.

AH 7818.59.3 — Ramsay, William. Elementary manual of Roman antiquities. 3. ed. London, 1863.

AH 7488.63 — Reinaud, J.T. Relations politiques...de la empire romain. Paris, 1863.

AH 3660.10 — Schneiderwirth, J.H. Die persische Politik gegen die Griechen seit dem Ende der Perserkriege. Heiligenstadt, 1863.

Eg 878.63 — Sharpe, Samuel. Egyptian mythology. London, 1863.

AH 7438.63 — Siebert, W. Ueber Appius Claudius Caecus. Kassel, 1863.

NEDL AH 4278.57.23.15 — Smith, William. History of Greece. N.Y., 1863.

Chronological Listing

1863 - cont.

AH 3657.5 — Spiegel, F. Éran. Berlin, 1863.
AH 7518.63 — Stahr, Adolf. Tiberius. Berlin, 1863.
AH 8007.3 — Vivien de Saint-Martin, L. Le Nord de l'Afrique. Paris, 1863.
AH 7488.63.3 — Zeller, J.S. Les empereurs romains. 2. ed. Paris, 1863.

1864

AH 7138.64 — Barinetti, P. Dritto romano. Milano, 1864.
AH 5666.5 — Baumeister, A. Topographische Skizze der Insel Euboia. Lübeck, 1864.
AH 7958.64 — Bernard, E. Les voyages de Saint Jérome. Paris, 1864.
AH 7228.64.5 — Bethmann-Hollweg, M.A. von. Der Civilprozess des gemeinen Rechts. Bonn, 1864. 6v.
AH 7058.39.2 — Brambach, G. De consulatus romani mutata. Bonnae, 1864.
AH 8516.5 — Creuly, Casimir. Carte de la Gaule sous le proconsulat de César. Paris, 1864.
AH 7903.5.5F — Diocletianus. Édit de Dioclétien, établissant le maximum dans l'Empire romain. Paris, 1864.
NEDL AH 4278.56.5 — Duruy, V. Histoire grecque. 4. éd. Paris, 1864.
AH 7238.64 — Eichhorst, Otto. De Cohortibus urbanis imperatorum Romanorum. Danzig, 1864.
AH 4161.9 — Es Vanden, A.H.G.P. De iure familiarum. Lugdunum Batavorum, 1864.
AH 8507.13 — Fallue, Léon. Annales de la Gaule avant et pendant la domination romaine. Paris, 1864.
AH 7162.17 — Franke, W. Commentar über den Paudie de Heeredetatis Petitione. Göttingen, 1864.
AH 7818.65 — Friedlaender, Ludwig. Darstellungen aus der Sittengeschichte Roms. v.2-3. Leipzig, 1864-1871. 2v.
AH 842.11 — Grasberger, L. Erziehung und Unterricht. Würzburg, 1864. 3v.
AH 4278.46.17 — Grote, George. Histoire de la Grece. v.1-19. Paris, 1864. 9v.
AH 8210.2 — Guest, Edwin. The invasion of Britain by Julius Caesar. London, 1864.
NEDL AH 818.62.3.5 — Guhl, Ernst. Leben der Griechen und Römer. 2. Aufl. Berlin, 1864.
AH 7298.64 — Kingsley, Charles. The Roman and the Teuton. Cambridge, 1864.
AH 7098.64 — Kuhn, Emil. Die stadtische...Verfassung. Leipzig, 1864.
NEDL AH 7278.55.2.5 — Liddell, H.G. History of Rome. N.Y., 1864.
AH 7468.64 — Long, George. Decline of the Roman Republic. v.3, photoreproduction. London, 1864. 5v.
AH 7228.64 — Machelard, E. Théorie général interdits en droit romain. Paris, 1864.
AH 138.61.2 — Maine, Henry S. Ancient law. 1. American ed. N.Y., 1864.
AH 7818.64.15 — Marquardt, Joachim. Römische Privatalterthümer. Leipzig, 1864-67.
AH 7238.64.10 — Masquelez, Alfred Émile A.E. Étude sur la castramétation des romains. Paris, 1864.
AH 7278.54.11.2 — Mommsen, T. History of Rome. 2. ed. v.1-3; v.4, pt.1-2. London, 1864-67. 5v.
AH 7818.63 — Mommsen, T. Römische Forschungen. Berlin, 1864-79. 2v.
AH 7818.63.3 — Mommsen, T. Römische Forschungen. v.1, 2. Aufl.; v.2, 1. Aufl. Berlin, 1864. 2v.
AH 4861.5 — Nathusius, C.H.A. More Humandi and Cencremandi Mortuos. Halis Saxonum, 1864?
AH 8016.5F — Nau de Champlouis, A.V. Notice sur la carte de l'Afrique. Paris, 1864.
AH 308.64 — Negri, C. Memorie storico-politiche. Torino, 1864.
AH 4487.5 — Nieberding, K. De Themiestocle quaestio duplex. Gleiwitz, 1864.
AH 7808.35.5 — Peter, Carl. Zeittafeln der römischen Geschichte. Halle, 1864.
AH 7448.18.4 — Rauchenstein, F. Nochmals Hannibals Alpenübergang. Aarau, 1864.
AH 7838.64 — Ritschl, F. Die Tessarae Gladiatoriae. München, 1864.
AH 9777.20 — Roesler, E. Die Geten und ihre Nachbarn. Wien, 1864.
Eg 708.64 — Stahr, Adolf. Cleopatra. Berlin, 1864.
AH 7238.64.5 — Steinike, Heinrich. De equitatu romano. Diss. Halis Saxonum, 1864.
AH 7168.64 — Sulpius, B. von. Novation und Delegation. Berlin, 1864.
AH 4038.63.9 — Vischer, W. Ueber C.A. Freeman's History of federal governemnt. n.p., 1864.
AH 7448.64 — Voigt, G. De primis Hannibalici belli annis quaestiones. Berlin, 1864.

1865

AH 8205.2 — Airy, George B. Essays on the invasion of Britain by Julius Caesar; the invasion of Britain by Plautius, and by Claudius Caesar; the early military policy of the Romans in Britain; the battle of Hastings. London, 1865.
AH 7818.58.5 — Castelar y Ripoll, E. La civilizacion en los cinco primeros siglos del cristianismo. 2. ed. Madrid, 1865. 4v.
AH 8657.5 — Dyer, Thomas H. History of the city of Rome. London, 1865.
Eg 658.65 — Ebers, Georg. Disquisitiones de dynastia vicesima sexta regum Aegyptiarum. Berolini, 1865.
AH 7818.65.2 — Friedlaender, Ludwig. Darstellungen aus der Sittengeschichte Roms. 2. Aufl. Leipzig, 1865-1867. 2v.
NEDL AH 7818.65.19A — Friedlaender, Ludwig. Moeurs romaines du règne d'Auguste. Paris, 1865. 4v.
AH 7478.63.8 — Gastineau, Benjamin. Les femmes de Jules César. 2. éd. Paris, 1865.
AH 4888.65 — Glaser, J.C. Wirtschafts-Verhältnisse. Berlin, 1865.
Eg 808.65 — Henne, A. Manethós...Geschichte und Chronologie. Gotha, 1865.
AH 4850.5 — Hollaender, A. Anaglyphis Sepulcraliebus Graecis. Berolini, 1865.
AH 938.56.5 — Hughes, William. An atlas of classical geography. Philadelphia, 1865.
AH 4058.65 — Kubicki, C. De magistratu decem strategorum. Berolini, 1865.
AH 3094.5F — Menant, J. Inscriptions...du palais de Khorsabad. Paris, 1865.
NEDL AH 7488.52.7 — Merivale, Charles. History of Romans under the Empire. London, 1865-68. 8v.
AH 7278.54.4 — Mommsen, T. Römische Geschichte. 4. Aufl. Berlin, 1865. 4v.
AH 7478.65.6 — Napoléon III, emperor of the French. Geschichte Julius Cäsars. Wien, 1865. 2v.

1865 - cont.

AH 7478.65 — Napoléon III, emperor of the French. Histoire de Jules César. N.Y., 1865. 2v.
AH 7478.65.3F — Napoléon III, emperor of the French. Histoire de Jules César. Paris, 1865-66. 2v.
AH 7478.65.2 — Napoléon III, emperor of the French. Histoire de Jules César. Paris, 1865-66. 2v.
AH 7478.65.2F — Napoléon III, emperor of the French. Histoire de Jules César. Atlas. Paris, 1865-66.
AH 7478.65.2.5F — Napoléon III, emperor of the French. Histoire de Jules César. Atlas. v.1-2. Paris, 1865-66.
AH 7478.65.4 — Napoléon III, emperor of the French. History of Julius Caesar. London, 1865. 2v.
AH 7478.65.7A — Napoléon III, emperor of the French. History of Julius Caesar. N.Y., 1865. 2v.
AH 7212.2 — Nipperdey, Karl. Die Leges Annales. Leipzig, 1865.
AH 4308.65 — Oncken, W. Athen und Hellas. Leipzig, 1865.
AH 3008.65 — Oppert, J. Histoire des empires de Chaldée et d'Assyrie. Versailles, 1865.
AH 8549.65 — Panchaud, Édouard. Le druidisme; ou Religion des anciens gaulois. Lausanne, 1865.
AH 7278.53.5 — Peter, C. Geschichte Roms. v.1-2; v.3, pt.1-2. 2. Aufl. Halle, 1865. 4v.
AH 7138.45.8 — Puchta, G.F. Cursus der Institutionen. 6. Aufl. Leipzig, 1865. 3v.
AH 859.3 — Rainneville, Joseph de. La femme dans l'antiquité et d'après la morale. Paris, 1865.
AH 7768.65 — Richter, H. Das weströmische Reich. Berlin, 1865.
Eg 938.65 — Rougé, J. de. Textes géographiques du temple d'Edfou. Paris, 1865.
AH 4498.65 — Schaefer, A. Rerum post Bellum Persicum. Lipsiae, 1865.
AH 5271.5 — Schneiderwirth, J.H. Polische Geschichte des dorischen Argos. v.1-2. Heiligenstadt, 1865.
AH 7498.65 — Stahr, Adolf. Römische Kaiserfrauen. Berlin, 1865.
AH 3740.10 — Tarbox, Increase N. Tyre and Alexandria. Boston, 1865.
AH 7798.65 — Thierry, A.S.D. Nouveaux récits de l'histoire romaine. Paris, 1865.
AH 7308.65 — Thierry, M. Amédée. Tableau de l'Empire Romain. Paris, 1865.
AH 7168.65 — Vernet, R. Textes choisis sur la Théorie des obligations. Paris, 1865.
AH 4958.65 — Welcker, F.G. Tagebuch einer griechische Reise. Berlin, 1865.
AH 7298.65 — Wolterstonff, A. Bilder aus dem römischen Alterthum. Halberstadt, 1865.
AH 7908.65 — Zacharia von Lingenthal, K.E. Eine Verordnung Justinian's über den Seidenhandel. v.1-2. St. Petersburg, 1865. 2 pam.
NEDL AH 298.65 — Zeller, J. Entretiens sur l'histoire antiquité. Paris, 1865.
AH 7158.65 — Zumpt, A.W. Criminalrecht der römischen Republik. v.1-2. Berlin, 1865. 4v.

1866

AH 7168.66 — Accarias, C. Théorie des contrats innommis. Paris, 1866.
AH 7188.66 — Adams. Über die Sklaverie und Sklavenentlassung bei den Römern. Tübingen, 1866.
AH 7278.62.3 — Ampère, J.J. L'histoire romaine à Rome. 3. éd. Paris, 1866-72. 4v.
AH 4828.40.11A — Becker, W.A. Charicles. 3. ed. London, 1866.
AH 7898.66 — Beheim-Schwarzbach, H. Beitrag zur Kenntnitz des Ackerbaues der Römer. Cassel, 1866.
AH 7114.16 — Belot, E.J. Histoire des chevaliers romains. Paris, 1866.
AH 7818.66 — Bojesen, E.F.C. Handbuch der römischen Antiquitaten. Wien, 1866.
AH 7238.66 — Briau, René. Du service de santé militaire chez les romains. Paris, 1866.
AH 7198.66 — Bufnoir, C. Théorie de la condition...en droit romain. Paris, 1866.
Eg 958.66F — Chabas, F. Voyage d'un égyptien. Paris, 1866.
AH 7598.66 — Champagny, F.J.M.T. Les Antonins. Paris, 1866. 3v.
AH 7203.50 — Corpus juris civilis. Institutiones. Corpus juris civilis. Lipsiae, 1866. 3v.
AH 7138.66 — Demangeat, C. Cours élémentaire de droit romain. 2. ed. Paris, 1866. 2v.
AH 7201.34 — Domenget, M.L. Institutes de Gaius. Paris, 1866.
AH 7200.12 — Duodecim Tabulae. Legis Duodecim Tabularum. Lipsiae, 1866.
AH 4278.56.4 — Duruy, V. Histoire grecque. 5. éd. Paris, 1866.
AH 7918.66 — Friedlaender, L. De pretiis frumentis apud Romanos. Regimonti, 1866.
AH 908.66 — Frohberger, H. De opificum apud veteres Graecas condicione dissertatio. Grimae, 1866.
AH 7201.37 — Gaius. Institutiones. Lipsiae, 1866.
AH 7201.35 — Gaius. Institutiones. Lipsiae, 1866.
AH 168.56 — Goldschmidt, J.G. De nautico foenore. Berolini, 1866.
AH 8211.2 — Guest, Edwin. The campaign of Aulus Plautius in Britain, A.D. 43. London, 1866.
AH 277.93.10 — Heeren, Arnold Herman Ludwig. Historical researches into politics, intercourse and trade. London, 1866. 2v.
AH 4728.66 — Hertzberg, G.F. Geschichte Griechenlands. Halle, 1866. 3v.
AH 9616.5 — Holm, A. Beiträge zur Berichtung der Karte des alten Siciliens. Lübeck, 1866.
AH 7198.66.3 — Ihering, R. Geist des römischen Rechts. v.1-3. Leipzig, 1866. 4v.
AH 9777.19.2 — Jordanes. Getarum sive Gothorum. 2. ed. Stuttgart, 1866.
AH 8016.7 — Knötel, A. Der Niger der alten und andere wichtige Fragen der alten Geographie Afrika's. Glogau, 1866.
AH 2009.6 — Kremer, A. von. Über die südarabische Sage. Leipzig, 1866.
AH 2009.6.5 — Kremer, A. von. Über die südarabische Sage. Leipzig, 1866.
AH 3964.15 — Langen, Joseph. Das Judentherm in Palästina zur Zeit Christi. Freiburg im Breisgau, 1866.
AH 7448.18.5 — Law, William J. The Alps of Hannibal. London, 1866. 2v.
AH 8647.15 — Marincola Pistoja, D. Di Cautonia, republica della Magna Grecia. Catanzaro, 1866. 2 pam.
AH 7488.52.9.3 — Merivale, Charles. History of the Romans under the Empire. 4. London ed. N.Y., 1866. 7v.
AH 7488.52.9 — Merivale, Charles. History of the Romans under the Empire. 4. London ed. N.Y., 1866. 7v.
AH 2589.7 — Mylonas, C.D. De Smyrnaeorum rebus gestis. Inaug. Diss. Gottingae, 1866.

Chronological Listing

1866 - cont.

AH 3163.7 — Oppert, Jules. Les inscriptions commerciales en caractères cuneiformes. Paris, 1866.

AH 3980.50 — Parent, A. Siege de Jotapata. Paris, 1866.

AH 7203.52 — Pellat, C.A. Textes choisis des pandectes. 2. ed. Paris, 1866.

AH 4808.35.3 — Peter, C.L. Zeittafeln der griechischen Geschichte. 3. Aufl. v.1-2. Halle, 1866.

AH 7498.66 — Peter, Carl Eduard. De fontibus historiae imperatorem Flaviorum. Diss. Halis, 1866.

AH 7838.66 — Planck, M. Über den Ursprung der römischen Gladiatorenspiele. Ulm, 1866.

AH 2357.9 — Robiou, F. Histoire des Gaulois d'Orient. Paris, 1866.

AH 842.33 — Rordam, H.F. Skolens og opdragelsens historie. Kjobenhavn, 1866.

AH 7478.66 — Rose, M. Renaud. Le theatre de la dernière guerre des bellovaques contre Jules César. Beauvais, 1866.

AH 8548.80 — Rott, Joseph. Ueber die Nationalität der Kelten. Passau, 1866?

AH 3809.5 — Rougemont, F. L'age du bronze ou Semites en occident. Paris, 1866.

AH 7168.66.5 — Salkowski, C. Zur Lehre von der Novation. Leipzig, 1866.

AH 7162.29 — Wetter, P.A.H. Droit d'accroissement. Bruxelles, 1866.

AH 7508.66 — Wutzdorff, R. Wiegestaltete sich der Caesarismus. Langensalza, 1866.

AH 7098.66 — Zoeller, M. De civitate sine suffragio et municipio Romanorum. Heidelbergae, 1866.

1867

AH 7488.67 — Ampère, J.J. L'empire romain à Rome. Paris, 1867. 2v.

AH 7708.67 — Bernhardt, T. Geschichte Roms von Valerian. Berlin, 1867.

AH 7138.67 — Brocher, H. Del'enseignment du droit romain. Lausanne, 1867. 7 pam.

Eg 278.48.5 — Bunsen, C.C.J. Egypt's place in universal history. v.1,5. London, 1867. 2v.

AH 7498.59.4 — Champagny, F.J.M.T. Les Césars. 4. éd. v.1-4. Paris, 1867. 2v.

AH 4168.67 — Dareste, R. Du pret a la grosse. Paris, 1867.

AH 7207.20A — Diaz, José F. Historia del Senado romano. Barcelona, 1867.

AH 5134.5 — Dugit, E. De Insula Naxo. Lutetiae Parisiorum, 1867.

NEDL AH 4278.56.6 — Duruy, V. Histoire grecque. 6. éd. Paris, 1867.

AH 7278.67 — Duruy, V. Histoire romaine. Paris, 1867.

AH 7448.18.6 — Ellis, Robert. An inquiry into the ancient routes between Italy and Gaul. Cambridge, Eng., 1867.

AH 7478.65.50 — Fallue, Léon. Etudes archéologiques sur l'histoire de Jules César par l'empereur Napoleon III. Paris, 1867.

AH 4818.67A — Felton, C.C. Greece, ancient and modern. Boston, 1867. 2v.

AH 4188.67 — Foucart, P. L'affranchissement des esclaves. Paris, 1867.

NEDL AH 7651.12.5 — Gibbon, Edward. Student's Gibbon. History of Roman Empire. N.Y., 1867.

NEDL AH 4278.46.19 — Grote, George. History of Greece. N.Y., 1867. 12v.

Eg 298.67 — Guigniaut, J.D. Progrès des etudes relatives à l'Égypte et à l'Orient. Paris, 1867.

NEDL AH 938.56.10 — Hughes, William. An atlas of classical geography. N.Y., 1867.

AH 7842.22 — Hulsebos, G.A. Disputatio antiquabis de educatione et institutione apud Romanos. n.p., 1867.

AH 7201.40 — Huschke, P.E. Iurisprudentiae anteiustinianae. Lipsiae, 1867.

AH 7201.40.2 — Huschke, P.E. Iurisprudentiae anteiustinianae. Lipsiae, 1867.

AH 7168.67 — Jhering, R. Schuldmoment im römischen Privatrecht. Giessen, 1867.

AH 278.67 — Lamé-Fleury, J.R. L'histoire ancienne. Paris, 1867.

AH 3013.33.10 — Layard, A.H. Nineveh and Babylon; a narrative of a second expedition to Assyria...1849, 1850 and 1851. London, 1867.

AH 4842.11 — Leiber, T. von. Professoren, Studenten und Studentleben. Bern, 1867.

AH 7818.67 — Lord, John. The old Roman world. N.Y., 1867.

AH 138.61.2.5 — Maine, Henry S. Ancient law. 1. American ed. N.Y., 1867.

Eg 278.67 — Mariette, A. Égypte. Paris, 1867.

AH 7448.67 — Müller, H. Die Schlacht an der Trebia. Berlin, 1867.

AH 9639.6.5 — Muess, H. De Syracusanorum statu. Inaug. Diss. Ienae, 1867.

AH 3008.67 — Oppert, J. Babylone et les Babyloniens. Paris, 1867.

AH 8607.9 — Panciera, D. Lezioni di storia patria. Grosseto, 1867.

AH 2357.13 — Perrot, G. De Galatia provincia romana. Lutetiae, 1867.

AH 4838.67 — Pinder, E. Fünfkampf der Hellenen. Berlin, 1867.

AH 3013.36PF — Place, V. Ninive et l'Assyrie. Paris, 1867. 3v.

Eg 278.67.20 — Regaldi, G. L'oriente antico. Torino, 1867.

AH 7578.67 — Renier, Léon. Mémoire sur les officiers qui assistèrent au conseil de guerre. Paris, 1867.

AH 7238.67F — Robert, Charles. Les légions du Rhin et les inscriptions des carrières. Paris, 1867.

AH 7278.53.11 — Schwegler, A. Römische Geschichte. 2. Aufl. Tubingen, 1867-1872. 3v.

AH 7138.67.5 — Tompkins, F. The institutes of the Roman law. London, 1867.

Eg 808.67 — Unger, G.F. Chronologie des Manetho. Berlin, 1867.

1868

AH 7448.68 — Alames, H. Hannibal sive disputatio. Dublin, 1868.

AH 7798.68 — Aretin, J.C.F. Diplomatische Abhandlung. Prag, 1868.

AH 7138.68 — Arnold W. Cultur und Recht der Römer. Berlin, 1868.

AH 7508.68 — Beulé, C. Ernest. Auguste, sa famille et ses amis. Paris, 1868.

AH 7518.68 — Beulé, C.E. Tibère et l'héritage d'Auguste. Paris, 1868.

AH 7518.68.3 — Beulé, C.E. Tibère et l'héritage d'Auguste. 2. éd. Paris, 1868.

AH 7648.68 — Bodek, Arnold. Marcus Aurelius Antoninus als Zeitgenosse und Freund des Rabbi Jehuda ha-Nasi. Leipzig, 1868.

AH 7842.6 — Bremer, F.P. Die Rechtslehrer und Rechtsschulen. Berlin, 1868.

AH 7488.68 — Büdinger, M. Untersuchungen zur Römischen Kaesergeschichte. Leipzig, 1868. 3v.

Eg 558.68 — Chabas, F. Les pasteurs en Egypte. Amsterdam, 1868. 2 pam.

AH 3966.4F — Clark, Samuel. The Bible atlas of maps and plans to illustrate geography and topography of O.T. and N.T. and Apocrypha. London, 1868.

AH 3966.3 — Coleman, L. An historical text book and atlas of Biblical geography. Philadelphia, 1868.

1868 - cont.

AH 7203.51 — Corpus juris civilis. Institutiones. Imp. Iustiniani Institutionum libri quattuor. Lipsiae, 1868.

AH 5333.5 — Curtius, Carl. Metroon in Athen. Berlin, 1868.

AH 4278.57.12 — Curtius, Ernest. History of Greece. London, 1868. 5v.

NEDL AH 4278.57.13.5 — Curtius, Ernest. History of Greece. N.Y., 1868?-1873? 5v.

X Cg Eg 308.68 — Dall, C. (Mrs.). Egypt's place in history. Boston, 1868.

Eg 138.68 — Devéria, T. Le papyrus judiciaire de Turin. Paris, 1868.

AH 7408.68A — Dyer, Thomas H. History of the kings of Rome. London, 1868.

NEDL AH 7408.68.3 — Dyer, Thomas H. History of the kings of Rome. Philadelphia, 1868.

Eg 298.68 — Ebers, G. Aegypten und die Bücher Mose's. Leipzig, 1868.

NEDL AH 7651.15 — Gibbon, Edward. Student's Gibbon. History of Roman Empire. London, 1868.

NEDL AH 7651.13 — Gibbon, Edward. Student's Gibbon. History of Roman Empire. N.Y., 1868.

AH 2302.2 — Hartung, Caspar. De proconsulatu Ciceronis Ciliciensi. Wirceburgi, 1868. 3 pam.

AH 7238.68 — Hirschfeld, Otto. Das Aerarium Militare und die Verwaltung der Heeresgelder in der römischen Kaiserzeit. Leipzig, 1868.

AH 7838.68 — Hübner, Emile. Revue archéologique - nouvelles tessères. Paris, 1868.

AH 7201.39 — Huschke, P.E. Indices. Lipsiae, 1868.

AH 7278.68 — Ihne, W. Römische Geschichte. v.1-6, 7-8. Leipzig, 1868. 7v.

AH 4908.67 — Jahn, Otto. Darstellungen des Handwerks. Leipzig, 1868.

AH 7163.18 — Karlowa, O. Die Formen der römischen Ehe. Bonn, 1868.

AH 3142.4 — Lamy, T.J. Concilium Seleuciae et Ctesiphonti Habitum. Levanii, 1868.

NEDL AH 1408.68 — Lenormant, F. Manuel d'histoire ancienne de l'Orient. Paris, 1868. 2v.

Eg 708.68 — Lumbroso, Giacomo. Seconda lettera al Gaspare Garresio intorno ad alcuni punti della storia dei Tolemei. Torino, 1868.

AH 7188.68.3 — Machelard, E. Distinctions admises. Paris, 1868.

AH 7278.54.12 — Mommsen, T. History of Rome. London, 1868. 4v.

AH 7278.54.16 — Mommsen, T. History of Rome. N.Y., 1868. 4v.

AH 7278.54.7 — Mommsen, T. Römische Geschichte. 5. Aufl. v.1, pt.1-2; v.2-3. Berlin, 1868. 4v.

AH 7217.13.5 — Naudet, Joseph. De la noblesse chez les Romains. Paris, 1868.

Eg 298.68.5 — Oppel, K. Wunderland der Pyramiden. Leipzig, 1868.

AH 818.68 — Ozanam, A.F. History of civilization. London, 1868. 2v.

AH 4842.13 — Petit de Julleville. L'ecole d'Athènes. Paris, 1868.

AH 7408.68.5 — Rawlinson, George. Recent histories of early Rome. London, 1868.

AH 8609.2 — Rubino, J. Beiträge zur Vorgeschichte Italiens. Leipzig, 1868.

AH 7188.68 — Schmidt, A. Pflichttheilsrecht. Heidelberg, 1868.

AH 5138.7 — Schneiderwirth, J.H. Geschichte der Insel Rhodus. Heiligenstadt, 1868.

AH 7418.68 — Scholtze, A. Die Beziehungen zwischen Rom und Hellas. Leipzig, 1868.

AH 7168.68 — Schupfer da Chioggia, F. Il diritto delle obbligazioni. Padova, 1868.

AH 4138.68 — Télfy, I. Corpus juris Attici. Lipsiae, 1868.

AH 7138.68.3 — Troplong, R.T. Influence du christianisme. Paris, 1868.

AH 9610.25 — Völkerling, A. De rebus Siculis ab Atheniensium expeditione usque ad prioris belli Punice finem gestia. Inaug. Diss. Vratislaviae, 1868.

AH 3008.68 — Wattenbach, W. Ninive und Babylon. Heidelberg, 1868.

AH 4846.7 — Winckler, A. Wohnhäuser der Hellenen. Berlin, 1868.

NEDL AH 4298.53.3 — Wordsworth, C. Greece; pictorial, descriptive and historical. 5. ed. London, 1868.

1869

AH 2009.5 — Abu Ubaid al-Bakri. Die Wohnsetze und Wanderungen der arabischen Stämme. Göttingen, 1869.

AH 7468.69 — Backmund, J. Catilina und die Parteikämpfe in Rom im Jahre 63 vor Christus. Würzburg, 1869.

AH 408.69 — Baldwin, J.D. Pre-historic nations. N.Y., 1869.

AH 864.1 — Becq de Fouquières, L. Les jeux des anciens. Paris, 1869.

AH 7498.69.2 — Beule, Ernest. Le sang de Germanicus. 2. éd. Paris, 1869.

AH 4850.7 — Bielschowsky, A. De Spartanorum syssitiis. Vratislaviae, 1869.

AH 328.69 — Blyden, E.W. The negro in ancient history. N.Y.? 1869.

AH 328.69.2 — Blyden, E.W. The negro in ancient history. Washington, 1869.

AH 4888.69 — Büchsenschütz, B. Besitz und Erwerb. Halle, 1869.

AH 4238.69 — Chevalier, L. Entstehung...der griechischen Söldnerheere und ihre Teilnahme. Prag, 1869.

AH 3961.3 — Couret, A. La Palestine sur les empereurs grecs, 326-636. Grenoble, 1869.

AH 4308.69 — Curtius, Ernst. Festrede. Berlin, 1869.

AH 7478.69 — Delorme, S. César et ses contemporains. Paris, 1869.

AH 7201.41 — Dernburg, H. Institutionenen des Cajus. Halle, 1869.

AH 8516.3 — Desjardins, E. Géographie de la Gaule d'après la Table de Peutinger. Paris, 1869.

AH 3059.7 — Fabian, E.A. De Seleucia Babylonia. Lipsiae, 1869.

AH 7818.65.3 — Friedlaender, Ludwig. Darstellungen aus der Sittengeschichte Roms. 3. Aufl. Leipzig, 1869.

AH 3657.7 — Gobineau, J.A. Histoire des Perses. Paris, 1869. 2v.

AH 818.69.3 — Göll, Hermann. Kulturbilder. v.1-3. Leipzig, 1869. 2v.

AH 7838.69 — Goguel, Edward. Les gladiateurs romains. Paris, 1869.

NEDL AH 4278.46.21 — Grote, George. History of Greece. London, 1869. 12v.

AH 4278.46.23A — Grote, George. History of Greece. London, 1869. 12v.

AH 7808.69 — Helfferich, A. Der altroemische Kalender. Frankfurt, 1869.

AH 7808.69.5 — Huschke, G.P.E. Das alte römische Jahr und seine Tage. Breslau, 1869.

AH 7448.69 — Jäger, Oskar. Die punischen Kriege. Halle, 1869.

AH 7204.7 — Julianus, S. Edicti perpetui. Lipsiae, 1869.

AH 7278.32.5 — Lamé Fleury, J.R. L'histoire romaine racontée aux enfants. Paris, 1869-70. 2v.

AH 8549.69 — Leflocq, J. Études de mythologie celtique. Orléans, 1869.

AH 1408.69.3 — Lenormant, F. Manual of the ancient history of the East. London, 1869.

AH 1408.68.5 — Lenormant, F. Manual of the ancient history of the East. Philadelphia, 1869.

Chronological Listing

1869 - cont.

AH 1408.69 — Lenormant, F. Manual of the ancient history of the East. 3. ed. Paris, 1869. 3v.
NEDL AH 278.69.9 — Lord, J. Ancient states and empire. N.Y., 1869.
AH 7628.69 — Lucas, Charles. L'empereur-architecte Adrien. Paris, 1869.
AH 818.69 — Mahaffy, J.P. Primitive civilization. London, 1869.
NEDL AH 7278.54.15 — Mommsen, T. History of Rome. N.Y., 1869-70. 4v.
AH 4543.5 — Morell, L.J. Vita Phocionis. Lugdunum Batavorum, 1869.
AH 4148.69 — Perrot, G. Droit public d'Athènes. Paris, 1869.
AH 7748.69 — Preuss, Theodor. Kaiser Diocletan. Leipzig, 1869.
AH 8990.5 — Promis, Carlo. Storia dell'antica Torino, Julia Augusta Taurinorum. Torino, 1869.
AH 278.69A — Rawlinson, G. Manual of ancient history. Oxford, 1869.
NEDL AH 278.69 — Rawlinson, G. Manual of ancient history. Oxford, 1869.
AH 3664.5 — Rosny, L. L'origine du langage. Paris, 1869. 2 pam.
AH 2928.5 — Steinmann, W. Das Gebiet von Heraklea Pontica. Rostock, 1869,
AH 158.69 — Thomissen, J.J. Études sur l'histoire du droit criminel. Bruxelles, 1869. 2v.
AH 7488.63.4 — Zeller, J.S. Les empereurs romains. 3. ed. Paris, 1869.

187-

AH 8548.20 — Lemière, P.L. Étude sur les Celtes et les Gaulois. St. Brieuc, 187-?

1870

AH 3013.5 — Cavaniol, C.H. Les monuments en Chaldée, en Assyrie. Paris, 1870.
AH 7203.57 — Corpus juris civilis. Digesta. Digesta Iustiniani Augusti. Berolini, 1870. 2v.
AH 7818.46.7 — Dezobry, Charles. Rome au siècle d'Auguste. Paris, 1870. 4v.
AH 4204.9 — Dramburg. Verfassungskämpfe Athens. Dramburg, 1870.
AH 4808.70 — Dumont, A. Essai sur la chronologie des archontes athéniens. Paris, 1870.
AH 7278.70 — Duruy, V. Histoire des romains. Paris, 1870. 7v.
AH 7162.13 — Flach, J. Bonorum possessio. Paris, 1870.
AH 7518.70 — Freytag, L. Tiberius und Tacitus. Berlin, 1870.
AH 38.64 — Fustel de Coulanges, N.D. La cité antique. 3. éd. Paris, 1870.
AH 7201.43 — Gaius. Commentaries. Cambridge, 1870.
AH 3013.8 — Gaugengigl, I. Erklärung der König Ludwig's Inschriften in der Münchner Glyptothek. München, 1870.
AH 7468.70.5 — Gilles, I. Campagne de Marius dans la Gaule. Paris, 1870.
AH 7168.70.5 — Glasson, E. Etude sur les donations. Paris, 1870.
AH 9807.6 — Gyárfás, István Tihamér. A jasz-kunok története. v.1-2,4. Kecskemét, 1870-85. 3v.
AH 843.2F — Hasenderer, R. Grundzüge der...Harmoniks...des Altertums. Cologne, 1870.
AH 4518.70 — Haussding, F. De Demosthenes Atheniensium. Halae, 1870.
AH 7448.70 — Hennebert, E. Histoire d'Annibal. Paris, 1870. 3v.
AH 7448.70F — Hennebert, E. Histoire d'Annibal. Atlas. Paris, 1870.
AH 138.70 — Hofmann, F. Beiträge zur Geschichte des griechischen und römischen Rechts. Wien, 1870.
AH 9607.9 — Holm, A. Geschichte Siciliens in Alterthum. Leipzig, 1870. 3v.
NEDL AH 938.56.12 — Hughes, William. An atlas of classical geography. N.Y., 1870.
AH 7178.70 — Jürgens. Ueber der Ursprung und die Werwendung. Blankeburg, 1870.
AH 7228.70 — Keller, F.L. von. De procédure civile et des actions. Paris, 1870.
AH 4498.70F — Köhler, U. Geschichte des delisch-attischen Bundes. Berlin, 1870.
AH 7138.70.5 — Krüger, P. Römischen Rechts, kritische Versuche. Berlin, 1870.
AH 278.70 — Lamé-Fleury, J.R. Ancient history. Boston, 1870.
AH 7228.70.5 — Latreille, J. Histoire des institutions judiciaires. Paris, 1870.
Eg 708.70 — Lumbroso, Giacomo. Recherches sur l'économie politique de l'Égypte sous les Lagides. Turin, 1870.
AH 7138.70 — Mackenzie, L. Studies in Roman law. 3. ed. Edinburgh, 1870.
Eg 278.67.3 — Mariette, A. Aperçu de l'histoire d'Égypte. 2. éd. Paris, 1870.
AH 7138.70.3 — Maynz, C. Cours de droit romain. Bruxelles, 1870. 3v.
AH 7468.70 — Merivale, Charles. Fall of the Roman Republic. London, 1870.
AH 7278.54.13 — Mommsen, T. Index to History of Rome. London, 1870.
AH 7307.34.9 — Montesquieu, Charles de. De la grandeur des Romains. Paris, 1870.
AH 7238.70 — Naudet, Joseph. Études d'histoire romaine. Paris, 1870.
AH 7448.70.5 — Nissen, Heinrich. Commentatio de pace anno 201 a. Chr. Carthaginiensibus data. Marburgi, 1870.
AH 7848.5 — Nötling, E. Studie über altrömische Thur. Mannheim, 1870.
AH 7203.53 — Ortolan, J.L.E. Explication..des Instituts. 8. ed. Paris, 1870. 3v.
AH 7203.55 — Ortolan, J.L.E. Explication..des Instituts. 8. ed. Paris, 1870. 3v.
AH 7278.53.7 — Peter, C. Geschichte Roms. 3. Aufl. Halle, 1870. 3v.
AH 4148.70 — Philippi, A. Attischen Bürgerrechtes. Berlin, 1870.
AH 7116.2 — Plüss, H.T. Die Entwicklung. Leipzig, 1870.
AH 4538.70 — Pomtow, L. Leben des Epaminondas. Berlin, 1870.
AH 7478.70.3 — Ramée, D. César. Paris, 1870.
AH 7168.70 — Schwanert, H.A. Compensation nach römischen Recht. Rostock, 1870.
Eg 278.36.6 — Sharpe, S. History of Egypt. London, 1870. 2v.
AH 7488.70 — Sievers, G.R. Studien zur Geschichte der Römischen Kaiserreiches. Berlin, 1870.
AH 938.54.5 — Smith, William. Dictionary of Greek and Roman geography. London, 1870. 2v.
AH 4818.70 — Stoll, H.W. Bilder aus dem altgriechischen Leben. Leipzig, 1870.
Eg 608.70 — Tugnot de Lanoye, Ferdinand. Rameses the Great. N.Y., 1870.
AH 7168.70.10 — Ubbelohde, A. Zur Geschichte der...Realcontracte auf Rückgabe. Marburg, 1870.
AH 842.13 — Ussing, J.L. Darstellung des Erziehungs- und Unterrichtwesens. Altona, 1870.

1871

AH 3659.20.6 — Abbott, Jacob. History of Darius the Great. N.Y., 1871.
AH 5610.7 — Abbott, Jacob. History of Pyrrhus. N.Y., 1871.
NEDL AH 7138.71.3 — Accarias, C. Précis de droit romain. v.1-2. Paris, 1871. 3v.
AH 818.71 — Barber, T.C. Aryan civilization. London, 1871.
AH 7168.71 — Bekker, E.I. Die Aktionen der römischen Privatrechts. Berlin, 1871.
AH 4478.71 — Berg, C.A. Aristides. Göttingen, 1871.
AH 7201.47.2 — Bruns, C.G. Fontes Juris Romani Antiqui. 2. ed. Tubingae, 1871.
AH 7201.47.5 — Bruns, C.G. Fontes Juris Romani Antiqui. 5. ed. Friburg, 1871.
AH 7138.71.11 — Bryer, J. The academical study of the civil law. London, 1871.
AH 7148.71 — Clason, D.O. Kristische Erörterungen über den römischen Staat. Rostock, 1871.
NEDL AH 4278.57.13 — Curtius, Ernest. History of Greece. N.Y., 1871. 5v.
AH 7138.71.7 — Danz, H.A.A. Lehrbuch der Geschichte des römischen Rechts. v.1-2. Leipzig, 1871.
AH 7138.71.9 — Dirksen, H.E. Hinterlassene Schriften. v.1-2. Leipzig, 1871.
AH 7228.71.5 — Eisele, F. Materielle Grundlage der Exceptio. Berlin, 1871.
AH 7161.14 — Fitting, H. Das castrense peculium. Halle, 1871.
AH 7201.45 — Gaius. Elements of Roman law. Oxford, 1871.
AH 7038.71 — Gerlach, F. Verfassungsgeschichte. Basel, 1871.
AH 7468.71 — Gilles, I. Marius et Jules César. Marseille, 1871.
AH 7203.141.2 — Glück, D.C.F. Ausführliche Erläuterung der Pandecten und Hellfeld ein Commentar. Erlangen, 1871-87. 6v.
AH 3980.12 — Howe, Fisher. The true site of Calvary. N.Y., 1871.
NEDL AH 938.56.15 — Hughes, William. An atlas of classical geography. N.Y., 1871.
AH 7278.68.3A — Ihne, W. History of Rome. London, 1871. 5v.
AH 7228.52.4 — Keller, Friedrich. Der römische Civilprocess und die Actionen. 4. Aufl. Leipzig, 1871.
AH 7818.56.5 — Lange, C.C.L. Römische Alterthümer. v.1-2, 3. Aufl; v.3, 2. Aufl. Berlin, 1871-79. 3v.
AH 298.71 — Mahaffy, J.P. Prolegomena to ancient history. London, 1871.
AH 7818.64.4 — Marquardt, Joachim. Handbuch der römischen Alterthümer. v.1-7. Leipzig, 1871-1888. 9v.
AH 7408.71 — Modestow, B. Der Gebrauch der Schrift unter den römischen Königen. Berlin, 1871.
AH 7278.54.16.5 — Mommsen, T. History of Rome. N.Y., 1871. 4v.
AH 7138.45.9 — Puchta, G.F. Cursus der Institutionen. Leipzig, 1871. 3v.
NEDL AH 1278.62.2A — Rawlinson, G. Five great monarchies of the ancient Eastern World. 2. ed. London, 1871. 3v.
NEDL AH 278.69.6 — Rawlinson, G. Manual of ancient history. N.Y., 1871.
AH 278.69.6 — Rawlinson, G. Manual of ancient history. N.Y., 1871.
AH 7138.71 — Rivier, A. Introduction historique au droit romain. Bruxelles, 1871.
AH 3008.71 — Robion, F.M.L.J. L'histoire de la Chaldée et de l'Assyrie. n.p., 1871.
AH 7161.12 — Rossbach, August. Römische Hochzeits- und Ehedenkmäler. Leipzig, 1871.
AH 4818.51.5 — Schoemann, G.F. Griechische Alterthümer. 3. Aufl. Berlin, 1871. 2v.
AH 8549.71 — Smiddy, Richard. An essay on the Druids. Dublin, 1871.
AH 3097.4 — Smith, George. History of Assurbanipal. Leiden, 1871.
AH 1278.71.3 — Smith, Philip. Ancient history of the East. N.Y., 1871.
AH 3657.9 — Spiegel, F. Franische Alterthumskunde. Leipzig, 1871. 3v.
NEDL AH 4278.68.2 — Stoll, H.W. Geschichte der Griechen bis zur Unterwerfung unter Rom. 2. Aufl. Hannover, 1871. 2v.
Htn AH 7278.69.2* — Stoll, H.W. Geschichte der Römer bis zum Untergange der Republik. 2. Aufl. Hannover, 1871. 2v.
AH 5754.7 — Trieber, C. Forschungen zur spartanischen Verfassungsgeschichte. Berlin, 1871.
AH 7148.56.3 — Voigt, M. Jus naturale. v.3-4. Leipzig, 1871.
AH 7138.71.5 — Wetter, P. Cours élémentaire de droit romain. Gand, 1871. 2v.
AH 3713.15 — Wilkins, A.S. Phoenicia and Israel. London, 1871.
Eg 818.37.15 — Wilkinson, J.G. A popular account of the ancient Egyptians. London, 1871. 2v.
AH 4487.7 — Wolff, E. De vita Themiestoclis Atheniensis. Monasteii, 1871.
AH 7158.71 — Zumpt, A.W. Criminalprocess der römischen Republik. Leipzig, 1871.

1872

AH 7548.72.5 — Abbott, Jacob. History of Nero. N.Y., 1872.
AH 3660.3.5 — Abbott, Jacob. History of Xerxes the Great. N.Y., 1872.
AH 7138.72.5 — Accarias, C. Précis de droit romain. Paris, 1872.
X Cg AH 4859.11 — Bader, C. Femme grecque. Paris, 1872.
AH 7168.72 — Bechmann, A. Das Ius Postliminii und die Lex Cornelia. Erlangen, 1872.
AH 4498.72 — Becq de Fouquières. Aspasie de Milet. Paris, 1872.
AH 7108.72 — Bouchard, L. Etude sur l'adminstration des finances. Paris, 1872.
AH 7448.72.10 — Buchholz. Die Quellen des Appian und Dio Cassius für die Geschichte des zweiten punischen Krieges. Pyritz, 1872.
AH 5760.13 — Buttmann, A. Agesilaus. Halle, 1872.
AH 7138.72 — Clark, E.C. Early Roman law. London, 1872.
AH 3980.9 — Derby, H.W. Selous' two grand pictures of Jerusalem. N.Y., 1872.
Eg 958.72 — Ebers, G. Durch Gosen zum Sinai. Leipzig, 1872.
AH 958.72 — Falconer, W. Dissertation on St. Paul's voyage. Photoreproduction. London, 1872.
AH 3011.3 — Fenzi, F. Ricerche per lo Studio dell'antichità Assira. Roma, 1872.
AH 5753.9 — Frick, C. Ephoris Spartanis. Gottingae, 1872.
AH 7838.72 — Friedlaender, G. De certamine cercensi diversio appellato. Regimonti, 1872.
AH 38.64.2 — Fustel de Coulanges, N.D. La cité antique. 4. éd. Paris, 1872.
AH 7238.72 — Geppert, P. De tribunis miletum. Berolini, 1872.
AH 7438.72 — Gerlach, F.D. Griechischer Einfluss in Rom. Basel, 1872.
NEDL AH 7650.65 — Gibbon, Edward. History of decline and fall of Roman Empire. London, 1872. 3v.
NEDL AH 7650.60 — Gibbon, Edward. History of decline and fall of Roman Empire. London, 1872. 3v.
AH 5759.5 — Gilbert, G. Altspartanishen Geschichte. Göttingen, 1872.
AH 7448.72.5 — Gilles, I. Annibal et Publins Cornelius Scipion. Paris, 1872.

Chronological Listing

1872 - cont.

NEDL AH 4278.46.29   Grote, George. History of Greece. v.1-6,8-10. London, 1872. 9v.

NEDL AH 4278.46.27   Grote, George. History of Greece. 4. ed. London, 1872. 10v.

NEDL AH 818.62.4   Guhl, Ernst. Leben der Griechen und Römer. 3. Aufl. Berlin, 1872.

AH 4038.72.2   Henkel, H. Studien zur Geschichte...vom Staat. Leipzig, 1872.

AH 7228.72   Karlowa, O. Der römische Civilprozess. Berlin, 1872.

AH 7408.72   Laing, C.H.B. Seven kings of the seven hills. Philadelphia, 1872.

AH 3017.10   Le Brun-Dalbanne. De l'intérêt de pierres gravées. Besançon, 1872.

NEDL AH 9607.11   Lloyd, W.W. History of Sicily to the Athenian war. London, 1872.

AH 866.6   Lohmeyer, K. Ist Preuszen das Bernsteinland der alten Gewesen? Königsberg, 1872.

Eg 278.67.5   Mariette, A. Aperçu de l'histoire d'Égypte. 3. éd. Alexandrie, 1872.

AH 3658.6   Menaut, J. Les achemenides et les inscriptions de la Perse. Paris, 1872.

AH 7488.52.10.2   Merivale, Charles. History of the Romans under the Empire. London, 1872-74. 8v.

NEDL AH 7488.52.10   Merivale, Charles. History of the Romans under the Empire. N.Y., 1872-74. 7v.

AH 3013.38   Oppert, J. Grundgüge des Assyrischen Kunst. Basel, 1872.

AH 4850.9   Pervanoglu, P. Familienmahl. Leipzig, 1872.

AH 7448.67.3   Pohle, R. De Pugna ad Trebiam Flumen. Inaug. Diss. Halis Saxonum, 1872.

AH 7138.72.3   Puntschart, V. Civilrechts der Römer. Erlangen, 1872.

AH 7548.72   Raabe, A.H. Geschichte und Bild von Nero. Utrecht, 1872.

NEDL AH 7138.72.2   Rivier, A. Introduction historique droit romain. Paris, 1872.

AH 3813.5   Röntsch, J. Indogermann und Semitenthum. Leipzig, 1872.

AH 7118.2   Ruggiero, E. de. La gens in Roma. Napoli, 1872.

NEDL AH 278.72.3   Schieffelin, S.B. Ta themelia tes istorias. Athens, 1872.

AH 7548.72.7   Schiller, H. Geschichte des Römischen Kaisereichs. Berlin, 1872.

AH 298.72   Schmidt, V. Assyriens og Aegyptiens gamle historie. Kjøbenhavn, 1872-7?.

AH 3909.6   Schmidt, V. Indledning til Syriens historie i oldtiden. Kjobenhavn, 1872.

AH 3159.11   Schrader, E. Die Keilinschriften und das Alte Testament. Giessen, 1872.

AH 7055.93.6.5   Seeck, Otto. Quaestiones de Notitia dignitatum. Berolini, 1872.

AH 4833.11   Seitz, F. Leibesübungen der alten Griechen. Ansbach, 1872.

AH 5760.8   Senfftleben, Franz. Sparta und sein Bund von 479 bis 445 vor Christ. Jena, 1872.

AH 3177.3F   Smith, George. Chaldaean account of the deluge. London, 1872.

AH 1278.71.4   Smith, Philip. Smaller history of the East. N.Y., 1872.

AH 4238.72   Stettin, Prussia. Festungen und Festungskrieg der Griechen. Stettin, 1872.

AH 338.72   Stoll, H.W. Geschichte der Griechen und Römer in Biographien. 2. Aufl. Leipzig, 1872. 2v.

NEDL AH 278.72   Thalheimer, M.E. Ancient history. Cincinnati, 1872.

NEDL AH 278.72.5   Thalheimer, M.E. A manual of ancient history. Cincinnati, 1872.

AH 7278.72   Thalheimer, Mary Elsie. Manual of ancient history. Pt.3. Cincinnati, 1872.

AH 7308.76.3A   Thierry, A.S.D. Tableau de l'Empire Romain. 6e éd. Paris, 1872.

AH 1818.72   Twesten, C. Religiösen, politischen und socialen Ideen. v.1-2. Berlin, 1872.

AH 7448.72   Vollmer, A. Quaeritur unde belli punici secundi. Gottingae, 1872.

AH 7088.72   Waddington, W.H. Fastes des provinces asiatiques de l'empire romain. pt.1. Paris, 1872.

AH 7148.70.2   Willems, P. Le droit public romain. 2e éd. Louvain, 1872.

1873

AH 7138.73.10   Arndts, L. Gesammelte civilistische Schriften. Stuttgart, 1873. 3v.

NEDL AH 7828.38.13A   Becker, W.A. Gallus, or Roman scenes. 4th ed. London, 1873.

AH 7138.64.10   Beckhaus, F.W.K. Repetitorium der ausseren römischen Rechtsgeschichte. Berlin, 1873.

AH 864.3   Becq de Fouquières, L. Les jeux des anciens. 2. éd. Paris, 1873.

AH 4828.73   Benizelos, T.B. Peri tou idôtikou Biou. Athēnai, 1873.

AH 4238.69.2   Bohstedt, E. Uber das Söldnerwesen. Rendsburg, 1873.

AH 7808.72   Boor, C. de. Fasti censorii. Berolini, 1873.

AH 3001.5   Bruston, Charles. Le dechiffrement des inscriptions cuneiform. Paris, 1873. 13 pam.

AH 7203.61A   Corpus juris civilis. Institutiones. Institutes of Justinian. Oxford, 1873.

AH 7203.60F   Corpus juris civilis. Novellae Constitutiones. Iuliani epilome latina Novellarum Iustiniani. Lipsiae, 1873.

AH 5139.5   Curtius, C. Urkunden zur Geschichte von Samos. Wesel, 1873.

AH 4840.15   Eichhoff, Karl. Ueber die Blutrache bei den Griechen. Duisburg, 1873.

NEDL AH 4818.73.2   Esvanden, A.H.G.P. Grieksche antiquiteiten. Groningen, 1873.

AH 4498.73   Filleul, E. Siècle de Périclès. Paris, 1873. 2v.

AH 8858.7   Fricke, Karl. Die Hellenen in Campanien. Hildesheim, 1873.

AH 7818.65.6   Friedlaender, Ludwig. Darstellungen aus der Sittengeschichte Roms. v.1, 4. Aufl; v.2, 3. Aufl. Leipzig, 1873-1874. 2v.

AH 7138.73.5   Giraud, C. Novum enchiridion juris Romani. Paris, 1873.

AH 4112.7   Göttingen. De amphictionia delphica. Gottingae, 1873.

AH 7138.73   Goudsmit, J.E. Pandects; treatise on Roman law. London, 1873.

AH 7138.73.3   Hadley, James. Introduction to Roman law. N.Y., 1873.

AH 5760.9   Kaegi, Adolph. Kritische Geschichte des spartanischen Staates von 500-431 vor Christ. Leipzig, 1873.

AH 4857.5   Knorr, A. De parasitis Graecorum. Colbergae, 1873.

AH 4278.29.13   Lamé Fleury, J.R. L'histoire grecque, racontée aux enfants. Paris, 1873.

AH 3002.29   Lenormant, F. Choix de textes cunéiformes. Paris, 1873-75.

1873 - cont.

AH 3018.3F   Lenormant, F. La legende de Sémiramis - mythologie comparative. Bruxelles, 1873.

AH 3160.6.5   Lenormant, F. Sur le nom de...Tammouz. Paris, 1873.

AH 7768.73   Léotard, E. Essae sur la condition des barbares. Paris, 1873.

Eg 808.73   Lieblein, J. Chronologie égyptienne. Christiania, 1873.

AH 7448.18.7   Linke, Otto. Die Controverse über Hannibals Alpenübergang. Breslau, 1873.

AH 5760.7   Löwy, A. Sparta. Rostock, 1873.

AH 7458.73   Mendelssohn, L. De senati consulti Romanorum. Lipsiae, 1873.

NEDL AH 7278.54.17   Mommsen, T. History of Rome. N.Y., 1873. 2v.

AH 7738.73   Muche, Eugenius. Forschungen über den römischen Kaiser M.A. Severus Alexander. Schweidnitz, 1873.

AH 7138.64.6   Namur, P. Cours d'institutes. Bruxelles, 1873.

AH 7448.73   Neuling, I. De belli punici primi scriptorum. Gottingae, 1873.

AH 7278.11.29   Niebuhr, B.G. Lectures on the History of Rome. 4. ed. London, 1873?

AH 7278.11.11   Niebuhr, B.G. Römische Geschichte. Berlin, 1873. 3v.

AH 7008.73   Nitzsch, K.W. Die römische Annalistik. Berlin, 1873.

AH 7201.48   Pernice, A. Marcus Antistius Labeo. v.2. Halle, 1873. 3v.

AH 4808.35.4   Peter, C.L. Zeittafeln der griechischen Geschichte. 4. Aufl. Halle, 1873.

AH 3607.9A   Rawlinson, G. Sixth great oriental monarchy. London, 1873.

AH 3002.5A   Records of the past. London, 1873. 12v.

AH 3002.5.2   Records of the past. London, 1873.

AH 328.73   Roget de Belloguet, D.F.L. Ethnogénie gauloise. Paris, 1873. 4v.

AH 4108.73   Schoell, R. Quaestiones fiscales iuris attici. Berolini, 1873.

AH 7448.73.10   Scott, Austin. Macedonien und Rom während des Hannibalischen Krieges. Berlin, 1873.

AH 7518.63.3   Stahr, Adolf. Tiberius. 2. Aufl. Berlin, 1873.

AH 7203.59   Thézard, L. Droit romain. 2. ed. Paris, 1873.

AH 4938.73   Tozer, H.F. Lecture on geography of Greece. London, 1873.

AH 8607.5.5   Vannucci, A. Storia dell'Italia antica. 3. ed. Milano, 1873-76. 4v.

AH 4818.73   Wägner, W. Hellas. v.1-2. Leipzig, 1873.

AH 4842.15   Wilkins, A.S. National education in Greece. London, 1873.

1874

Eg 708.51.5   Abbott, Jacob. History of Cleopatra, queen of Egypt. N.Y., 1874.

NEDL AH 4828.40.12   Becker, W.A. Charicles. 4. ed. London, 1874.

VAH 3957.38   Beöthy, Leó. Júda, Izrael és Aram. Budapest, 1874.

AH 4228.72   Bohm, H. De Eisaggeliais. Inaug. Diss. Halae, 1874.

AH 5360.5   Braake, G.J. Theilnahme der Böoter. Rostock, 1874.

AH 7888.84   Bücher, Karl. Die Aüfstande der unfreien Arbeiter. Frankfurt, 1874.

AH 4278.77   Cox, George W. History of Greece. London, 1874. 2v.

AH 818.74.3   Doublier, L. Geschichte des Altertums. Wien, 1874.

Eg 458.74   Dümichen, J. Die erste bis...aufgefundene...Angabe über die Regierungszeit...Königs...alten Reich. Leipzig, 1874.

AH 4808.74   Dumont, A. Fastes éponymiques d'Athènes. Paris, 1874.

AH 278.52.19   Duncker, M. Geschichte des Alterthums. 4. Aufl. Leipzig, 1874. 9v.

AH 3964.17   Edersheim, A. The temple; its ministry and services as they were at the time of Jesus Christ. 2. ed. London, 1874.

AH 7708.74   Feugère, A.C. C. Cilnius Maecenas G. Octaviano Augusto ad adipiscendum gerendumque principatum quantum profuerit. Thesis. Paris, 1874.

AH 7908.74.9   Friedlaender, L. Dissertatio de mercatura Romanorum. Regimonti Prussorum, 1874.

AH 7201.49   Gaius. Commentaries. Cambridge, 1874.

AH 7201.50   Gaius. Institutionum. Lipsiae, 1874.

AH 8915.2   Genthe, H.F. Ueber den etruskischen Tauschhandel. Heibronn, 1874.

AH 7238.74   Genz, Hermann. Die servianische Centurien-Verfassung. Sorau, 1874. 2 pam.

AH 7468.74   Gilles, I. La legende des Saintes Maries. Paris, 1874.

AH 2963.5   Gomperz, T. Zur Entzifferung der Schliemann sehen Inschriften. Wien, 1874.

AH 7448.74   Hesselbarth, H. De Pugna Cannensi. Gottingae, 1874.

AH 7163.17   Hölder, E. Römische Ehe. Zürich, 1874.

AH 4521.9   Houssaye, H. Histoire d'Alcibiade. Paris, 1874. 2v.

AH 7869.7   Hübner, Emil. Quaestiones onomatologicae Latinae. Berolini, 1874. 2 pam.

AH 7158.74   Huschke, E. Die Multa und das Sacramentum. Leipzig, 1874.

Eg 1068.74   Hymme is Ammon-Ra. Paris, 1874.

AH 2207.5   Karolidos, G.K. Kappadokias. Könstantinople, 1874.

AH 7908.74   Krakauer, G. Das Verpflegungswesen der Stadt Rom. Berlin, 1874.

AH 2807.5   Lauria, G.A. La Frigia. Naples, 1874.

AH 2158.5   Lauria, Guiseppe A. La Bitinia - la Lidia. Napoli, 1874.

AH 3156.5   Lenormant, F. La magie chez les Chaldéens. Paris, 1874.

AH 818.74   Lenormant, F. Premières civilisations. Paris, 1874. 2v.

AH 4828.74A   Mahaffy, J.P. Social life in Greece. London, 1874.

AH 3073.5   Menant, J. Annales des rois d'Assyrie. Paris, 1874.

AH 808.74   Mendelssohn, L. Parallel-Tabellen zur griechischrömischen Chronologie. Leipzig, 1874.

AH 7138.74.3   Molitor, J.P. Obligations en droit romain. Paris, 1874. 3v.

NEDL AH 7278.54.9   Mommsen, T. Römische Geschichte. 6. Aufl. Berlin, 1874. 3v.

AH 7138.74   Pellat, C.A. Manuale juris synopticum. Paris, 1874.

AH 4206.7   Philippi, A. Areopagu...Epheten. Berlin, 1874.

AH 7168.74   Rambaud de Larocque, Marcel. Étude sur la société de crédit foncier de France. Paris, 1874.

AH 3178.5   Schmidt, Robert. Kritik der Quellen...gracchischen Unruhen. Berlin, 1874.

AH 7468.74.7   Schrader, E. Die Höllenfahrt der Istar. Giessen, 1874.

AH 38.54.2   Simon, H.O. Vita Q. Lutatii Q.F. Catuli. Berlin, 1874.

NEDL AH 278.74   Smith, Philip. History of the world. N.Y., 1874. 3v.

AH 7278.74   Smith, William. Smaller history of Rome. N.Y., 1874.

AH 7238.50.2   Stolze, F. Triumph and ovation. Rostock, 1874.

AH 38.54.2   Sudre, Alfred. Histoire de la souveraineté. 2. éd. Paris, 1874.

AH 3910.15   Tetzlaff, N.J. De Antiochi III. Magni Syriae. Monasterii, 1874.

Chronological Listing

1874 - cont.

AH 7518.74   Thamm, M. De Fontibus ad Tiberii historiam pertinentibus. Halis Saxonum, 1874.

Eg 818.37.17   Wilkinson, J.G. A popular account of the ancient Egyptians. London, 1874. 2v.

AH 7148.70.3   Willems, P. Le droit public romain. 3e éd. Louvain, 1874.

1875

Eg 878.75.5   Ancessi, Victor. L'Égypte et Moïse. Paris, 1875.

AH 5372.5   Aubert, L.M.B. Et graesk Senatsconsult om Thisbaeerne. n.p., 1875.

AH 9677.2   Barros Sivélo, Ramón. Antigüedades de Galicia. Coruña, 1875.

NEDL AH 278.75   Barton, J.A.G. The ancient world. Edinburgh, 1875.

AH 7078.75   Berns, Carolus. De cometorum tributorum. Wetzlariae, 1875.

Eg 278.75   Birch, S. Egypt. N.Y., 1875.

AH 908.75   Blümner, H. Technologie und Terminologie der Gewerbe. v.1-4. Leipzig, 1875. 3v.

AH 7498.75.5   Boissier, Gaston. L'opposition sous les Césars. Paris, 1875.

AH 3013.32.3   Bonomi, J. Nineveh and its palaces. 3. ed. London, 1875.

AH 4828.75   Boudodénou, Charalampous. Dokimion. Odéssó, 1875. 2v.

Eg 558.75   Brugsch-Bey, H. L'éxode et les monuments égyptiens. Leipzig, 1875.

AH 8505.5   Castagne, E. Mémoire sur les ouvrages de fortification des appidum gaulois. Tours, 1875.

AH 3075.2   Cooper, William R. The resurrection of Assyria. London, 1875.

AH 7203.62   Corpus juris civilis. Institutiones. Corpus juris civilis. pt.1-3. Lipsiae, 1875. 2v.

AH 7278.85.3A   Creighton, M. History of Rome. N.Y., 1875.

NEDL AH 7488.75.3A   Curteis, A.M. History of Roman Empire. Philadelphia, 1875.

Htn   Eg 1158.75F*   Ebers, G.M. Papyros Ebers...Arzeneimittel der alten Ägypter. Leipzig, 1875. 2v.

AH 7148.75.2   Eigenbrodt, A. De magistratuum Romanorum. Lipsiae, 1875.

AH 7228.75   Eisele, F. Zur Geschichte der processualen Behandlung der Exceptionen. Berlin, 1875.

AH 7203.62.5   Esmarch, K. Pandekten-Exegeticum. Prag, 1875.

AH 3757.11   Földvary, A. Les ancêtres d'Attila. Paris, 1875.

NEDL AH 4278.78.5   Fyffe, C.A. History of Greece. N.Y., 1875.

AH 7201.51A   Gaius. Elements of Roman law. 2. ed. Oxford, 1875.

AH 862.5   Gaupp, W. Sanitätswesen in den Heeren der Alten. Blaubeuren, 1875.

AH 843.3   Gevaert, F.A. La musique de l'antiquité. Gand, 1875. 2v.

AH 4448.75   Grunder, C. Bellum Salaminium. Ienae, 1875.

AH 908.75.3   Guillard, E. Les banquiers athéniens-romains. Paris, 1875.

AH 7138.75   Harris, S.F. Elements of Roman law. London, 1875.

NEDL AH 4818.41.6   Hermann, K.F. Lehrbuch der griechischen Antiquitäten. v.1,3. Heidelberg, 1875. 2v.

NEDL AH 4818.41.5   Hermann, K.F. Lehrbuch der griechischen Antiquitäten. 5. Aufl. Heidelberg, 1875. 3v.

AH 4558.75   Hertzberg, F.F. Asiatischen Feldzüge Alexanders des Grossen. Halle, 1875. 2v.

AH 7158.75   Hohl, A. Kriminalgerichtswesen der römischen Republik. Burghausen, 1875.

AH 7098.75   Houdoy, R.J.A. De la condition et...chez les romains. Paris, 1875.

AH 7448.75   Keller, Ludwig. Der zweite punische Krieg. Marburg, 1875.

AH 4857.7   Knorr, A. Parisiten bei den Griechen. Belgard, 1875.

AH 7828.75   Koppoy, G. Pegitou idiótikoy bioytón rómaión. Athénai, 1875.

AH 7588.75   Krauss, J.E. Zur Charakteristik des Kaisers Domitianus. Amberg, 1875.

AH 3156.5.9   Lenormant, F. La divination et la science des présages. Paris, 1875.

AH 5858.5   Levègue, J. A. De oppidis et portibus Megaridis ac Boeotiae. Thesim proponebat. Parisiis, 1875.

AH 4498.75   Lloyd, W.W. Age of Pericles. London, 1875. 2v.

AH 4828.74.2A   Mahaffy, J.P. Social life in Greece. 2. ed. London, 1875.

AH 138.61.4   Maine, Henry S. Ancient law. 3. American ed. N.Y., 1875.

AH 138.75.2A   Maine, Henry S. Lectures on the early history of institutions. London, 1875.

AH 138.75A   Maine, Henry S. Lectures on the early history of institutions. N.Y., 1875.

AH 3008.75.5   Menant, J. Babylone et la Chaldée. Paris, 1875.

AH 7278.75   Merivale, C. General history of Rome. N.Y., 1875.

Eg 878.75   Meyer, E. Set-Typhon. Leipzig, 1875.

AH 7108.75   Naquet, Henri. Des impots indirects. Paris, 1875.

AH 3127.5   Oppert, J. L'Etalon des mesures Assyriennes. Paris, 1875.

AH 3160.8   Oppert, J. L'inmortalité de l'âme chez les chaldéens. Paris, 1875.

AH 7048.75   Paillard, A. Histoire de le transmission du pouvoir impérial. Paris, 1875.

AH 7808.35.6   Peter, Carl. Zeittafeln der römischen Geschichte. 5. Aufl. Halle, 1875.

AH 4728.75   Petit de Julleville, L. Histoire de la Grèce. Paris, 1875.

AH 7138.45.10   Puchta, G.F. Cursus der Institutionen. Leipzig, 1875.

AH 4408.75   Pyne, J. Pre-historic Greece. N.Y., 1875.

AH 9758.5   Riese, A. Idealiserung der Naturvölker des Nordens. Frankfurt, 1875.

AH 4818.75   Rousopoulos, A.S. Manual of Greek archaeology. Athens, 1875?

AH 7148.75   Ruggier de Ettore. Diritto publico romano. Firenze, 1875.

AH 7448.75.5   Schemann, Ludwig. De legionum per alterum bellum punicum historium quae investigari posse videntur. Bonnae, 1875.

AH 4188.75   Schück, J. Sklaverei bei den Griechen. Breslau, 1875.

AH 7215.5   Schwede, C. De pontificum collegii pontifisque Maximi in re publica potestate. Diss. inaug. Lipsiae, 1875.

AH 1928.75   Skinner, J.R. Key to the Hebrew-Egyptian mystery in the source of measures. Cincinnati, 1875.

AH 3013.23.15   Smith, G. Assyrian discoveries. N.Y., 1875.

AH 3075.3   Smith, George. Ancient history...Assyria. London, 1875.

AH 3075.3.2   Smith, George. Assyria from the earliest time to the fall of Nineveh. London, 1875.

AH 3013.41   Smith, George. Assyrian discoveries. London, 1875.

AH 3109.6   Smith, George. Assyrian Eponym Canon. London, 1875.

AH 4158.75   Thonissen, J.J. Le droit pénal. Bruxelles, 1875.

AH 3657.11   Vaux, William Sandys Wright. Persia. London, 1875.

AH 7808.75   Wehrmann, Petrus. Fasti Praetorii ab A.V. DLXXXVIII ad A.V. DCCX. Berolini, 1875.

1875 - cont.

AH 7118.10   Wende, Martin. De Caeciliis metellis commentationis pars I. Inaug. Diss. Bonnae, 1875.

AH 7138.71.6   Wetter, P. Cours élémentaire de droit romain. Gand, 1875. 2v.

AH 7498.75   Wiedemeister, F. Der Cäsarenwahnsinn. Hannover, 1875.

AH 8873.2   Zoeller, Max. Das Senatusconsultum über Capua. Mulhausen, 1875.

AH 4558.75.3   Zolling, T. Alexanders des Grossen Feldzug in centralischen Asien. Leipzig, 1875.

1876

Eg 1128.76F   Ani. L'égyptologie - maximes du scribe Ani. Paris, 1876.

AH 866.5   Bastelaer, D.A. van. L'ambre taillé ou véritable. Bruxelles, 1876.

NEDL AH 7828.38.15   Becker, W.A. Gallus or Roman scenes. 5th ed. London, 1876.

Eg 278.76   Birch, S. Monumental history of Egypt. London, 1876.

AH 7508.76.7   Blaze de Bury, H. Les femmes...au temps d'Auguste. 2. éd. Paris, 1876.

AH 7138.76.20F   Bonjean, G. Tavleaux synoptiques de droit romain. Paris, 1876.

AH 4848.7   Braungarten, F. Untersuchung und der Tracht die Athener am Grundlage. n.p., 1876.

AH 7201.47.3   Bruns, C.G. Fontes Juris Romani Antiqui. 3. ed. Tubingae, 1876.

AH 7138.76.13   Bruns, C.G. Unterschriften in römischen Rechts-Urkunden. Berlin, 1876.

AH 848.11   Buchholtz, F. De aulaeorum velorum que usu. Gottingae, 1876.

AH 7298.76   Büttner-Wobst, Theodor. De legationibus reipublicae liberae temporibus Romam missis. Diss. Lipsiae, 1876.

NEDL AH 7598.76   Capes, William W. The Roman Empire of the second century. London, 1876.

AH 7498.76   Capes, William W. Roman history, early empire. London, 1876.

AH 8536.9   Carré, G. Le régime municipal à Périgueux. Périgueux, 1876.

AH 7668.76   Ceuleneer, A. de. Marcia la favorite de Commode. Paris, 1876.

AH 7203.63   Corpus juris civilis. Institutiones. Institutes of Justinian. Cambridge, Eng., 1876.

AH 7203.46.5   Corpus juris civilis. Institutiones. Institutes of Justinian. 5. London ed. Chicago, 1876.

AH 298.76   Cory, I.P. Ancient fragments. London, 1876.

AH 4458.76.6   Cox, George W. The Athenian empire. London, 1876.

AH 4458.76.5   Cox, George W. The Athenian empire. N.Y., 1876.

AH 4278.76   Cox, George W. General history of Greece. N.Y., 1876.

AH 4478.76.3   Cox, George W. Greeks and Persians. London, 1876.

AH 4478.76.2   Cox, George W. Greeks and Persians. N.Y., 1876.

AH 7138.76.11   Cubain, R. Lois civiles de Rome. Angers, 1876.

NEDL AH 4278.57.14A   Curtius, Ernest. History of Greece. N.Y., 1876. 5v.

AH 7138.76   Demangeat, C. Cours élémentaire de droit romain. 3. éd. Paris, 1876. 2v.

AH 4818.76   Döring, E. Hellas. Frankfurt, 1876.

AH 7508.76   Doetsch, P. Leben und Treiben am Hofe des Kaisers Augustus, nach Tacitus. Malmedy, 1876.

AH 7538.76   Double, L. L'empereur Claude. Paris, 1876.

AH 4842.17   Dumont, A. Essai sur l'Ephébie Attique. Paris, 1876. 2v.

NEDL AH 7278.67.3   Duruy, V. Histoire universelle. Paris, 1876.

AH 9777.21   Eicken, H. von. Der Kampf der Westgothen und Römer. Leipzig, 1876.

AH 7168.76.5   Eisele, F.H. Compensation nach römischen und gemeinem Recht. Berlin, 1876.

AH 818.76.3   Forbiger, A. Hellas und Rom. v.1-2. Leipzig, 1876. 6v.

AH 7818.65.23   Friedlaender, Ludwig. Vida íntima de los Romanos. Primera version española. Barcelona, 1876.

AH 7448.76   Gilbert, Otto. Rom und Karthago in ihren gegenseitigen Veziehungen 513-536 von Christus. (241-218 von Christus). Leipzig, 1876.

NEDL AH 818.62.5   Guhl, Ernst. Leben der Griechen und Römer. Berlin, 1876.

NEDL AH 818.62.8   Guhl, Ernst. Life of the Greeks and Romans. N.Y., 1876.

AH 3005.7   Gutschmid, A. Neue Beiträge zur Geschichte des alten Orients; die Assyriologie in Deutschland. Leipzig, 1876.

AH 7178.56.3   Heisterbergk, B. Die Entstehung des Colonats. Leipzig, 1876.

AH 5307.19   Hoeck, A. De rebus ab Atheniensibus in Thracia et in Ponto. Kiliae, 1876.

AH 7808.75.2   Hölzl, M. Fasti Praetorii ad A.V. DLXXXVII ad A.V. DCCX. Lipsiae, 1876.

AH 7808.76   Hofmann, A. Drei synchronistische Daten des römischen Kalenders vor der julianischen Reform. Triest, 1876.

AH 7098.75.4   Houdoy, R.J.A. Le droit municipal. Paris, 1876.

AH 818.76   Hoyns, G. Die alte Welt. Berlin, 1876.

AH 7468.76   Hugues, G.D. Une province romaine sous la Republique. Paris, 1876.

AH 7138.76.8   Hunter, W.A. Roman law. London, 1876.

AH 7138.76.7   Hunter, W.A. Roman law. London, 1876.

NEDL AH 4278.78.2   Ihne, W. Early Rome. London, 1876.

AH 7168.76   Jourdan, A. L'Hypothèque. Paris, 1876.

AH 7228.52.5   Keller, Friedrich. Der römische Civilprocess und die Actionen. Leipzig, 1876.

AH 7078.76   Labatut, E. La corruption électorale. Paris, 1876.

AH 4838.76   Lehndorff, G.G. Hippodromos. Berlin, 1876.

AH 4298.76   Loeschcke, G. De titulis aliquot Atticis. Bonnae, 1876.

AH 7228.76   Lohse, S.C. De quaestionum perpetuarum origine. Plaviae, 1876.

AH 4238.77   Lorenz, A. Sölderei bei den Griechen. Eichstätt, 1876-77.

NEDL AH 4818.76.2.5   Mahaffy, J.P. Old Greek life. N.Y., 1876.

AH 7818.64.7   Marquardt, Joachim. Handbuch der römischen Alterthümer. 2. Aufl. Leipzig, 1876- 2v.

AH 7818.64.9   Marquardt, Joachim. Handbuch der römischen Alterthümer. 2. Aufl. v.1-7. Leipzig, 1876. 10v.

AH 7138.76.15   Marynz, K.G. Cours de droit romain. 4. éd. Bruxelles, 1876. 3v.

AH 1278.76   Maspero, Gaston. Histoire ancienne des peuples de l'Orient. Paris, 1876.

AH 7138.76.5   Massol, H. La règle catonienne. Toulouse, 1876. 2 pam.

NEDL AH 7478.77.2   Merivale, Charles. Roman triumvirates. London, 1876.

AH 7307.34.12   Montesquieu, Charles. Considérations sur les causes de la grandeur des Romains. Paris, 1876.

AH 7307.34.11   Montesquieu, Charles de. Considérations sur les causes de la grandeur des Romains. Paris, 1876.

Chronological Listing

1876 - cont.

AH 878.76A   Myriantheus, L. Die Acvins. München, 1876.
AH 7055.93.7   Notitia dignitatum. Berolini, 1876.
AH 7138.76.9   Ortolan, J.L.E. Institutes of Justinian including history...of Roman law. Toulouse, 1876.
AH 7138.76.10   Ortolan, J.L.E. Institutes of Justinian including history...of Roman law. Analysis. London, 1876.
NEDL AH 4278.76.4   Pennell, R.F. Ancient Greece. Boston, 1876.
AH 7278.76   Pennell, R.F. Rome. Boston, 1876.
AH 4108.76   Pflug, C. Einführung des Soldes. Waldenburg, 1876.
AH 7908.74.3   Pigeonneau, H. De convectione urbanae annonae. Sancti-Clodoaldi, 1876.
AH 7201.53   Polenaar, B.J. Gai institutiones iuris civilis Rom. Lugduni Batavorum, 1876.
AH 7738.76   Porrath, Otto. Der Kaiser Alexander Severus. Halle, 1876.
AH 7818.48.10   Ramsay, William. Manual of Roman antiquities. 10th ed. London, 1876.
AH 3657.12   Rawlinson, G. Seventh great oriental monarchy. London, 1876.
AH 3361.5   Rossberg, W. Quaestiones de rebus Cyrenarum. Frankenbergae, 1876.
AH 7058.29.3   Schaefer, A. Zur Geschichte des römischen Consulates. Leipzig, 1876.
AH 4842.19   Schmitz, W. Schriftsteller und Buchshändler. Heidelberg, 1876.
AH 7161.13   Schupfer, F. La famiglia secondo il diritto romano. Padova, 1876.
AH 3075.3.3   Smith, George. Ancient history...Asyria. N.Y., 1876.
AH 3159.6.3.5   Smith, George. The Chaldean account of genesis. N.Y., 1876.
AH 3159.6.3   Smith, George. The Chaldean account of genesis. 3. ed. London, 1876.
AH 3159.6.9   Smith, George. George Smith's Chaldaische Genesis. Leipzig, 1876.
AH 7278.76.10   Talbot, E. Histoire romaine. Paris, 1876.
AH 7798.60.7   Thierry, A.S.D. Récits de l'histoire romaine. 5. éd. Paris, 1876.
NEDL AH 7308.76A   Thierry, A.S.D. Tableau de l'Empire Romain. Paris, 1876.
AH 846.7   Ussing, J.L. Graekernes og Romernes huse. Kjøbenhavn, 1876.
AH 7203.143.5   Vangerow, K.A. von. Lehrbuch der Pandekten. 7. Aufl. Marburg, 1876. 3v.
AH 7138.76.3   Vignali, G. Del corpo del diritto romano. Napoli, 1876.
AH 4478.76.15   Wecklein, N. Ueber die Tradition der Perserkriege. München, 1876.

1877

AH 3659.15.6   Abbott, Jacob. History of Cyrus the Great. N.Y., 1877.
AH 7478.49.9   Abbott, Jacob. History of Julius Caesar. N.Y., 1877.
AH 7408.77   Abbott, Jacob. History of Romulus. N.Y., 1877.
Eg 878.77.5   Ancessi, Victor. Job et l'Égypte, le redempteur et la vie future. Paris, 1877.
AH 7859.4.2   Bader, Clarisse. La femme romaine. 2. éd. Paris, 1877.
AH 4828.40.3   Becker, W.A. Charikles. Berlin, 1877-78. 3v.
AH 7468.77   Beesly, A.H. The Gracchi, Marius and Sulla. London, 1877.
AH 7148.76   Bohn, Oscar. Qua condicione iuris reges. Berolini, 1877.
Eg 1038.77F   Book of the Dead. Le papyrus funéraire de Soutimès. Paris, 1877.
Eg 278.59.4   Brugsch, H. Geschichte Aegypten's. Leipzig, 1877.
Eg 850.1   Brygseh, H. Drei Fest-Kalender. Leipzig, 1877.
X Cg   AH 4842.21   Capes, W.W. University life in Athens. N.Y., 1877.
AH 7498.77   Capes, William W. Roman history, early empire. 2. ed. London, 1877.
AH 7203.67   Corpus juris civilis. Codex. Codex Iustinianus. Berolini, 1877.
AH 7203.65.3   Corpus juris civilis. Digesta. Das zwanzigste Buch der Pandekten. Bonn, 1877.
AH 7278.85.3.4   Creighton, M. History of Rome. N.Y., 1877.
AH 6107.8   Curteis, A.M. Rise of the Macedonian empire. London, 1877.
AH 5139.7.5   Curtius, C. Inschriften und Studien zur Geschichte von Samos. Lübeck, 1877.
AH 5139.7   Curtius, C. Inschriften zur Geschichte von Samos. Lübeck, 1877.
AH 4845.11   Debay, A. Nuits corinthiennes. Paris, 1877.
AH 8740.3   Doehle. Geschichte Tarents bis auf seine Unterwerfung unter Rom. Strassburg, 1877.
AH 3936.2   Double, L. Césars de Palmyre. Paris, 1877.
AH 4658.36.2   Droysen, J.G. Geschichte des Hellenismus. v.1-6. 2. Aufl. Gotha, 1877-78. 4v.
AH 408.77A   Duncker, M. History of antiquity. London, 1877. 6v.
AH 7038.77   Dupond, A. De la constitution. Paris, 1877.
Eg 1188.77   Eisenlohr, August. Ein mathematisches Handbuch der alten Agypter. Leipzig, 1877. 2v.
AH 8549.77   Ferk, F. Über Driudismus in Noricum. Graz, 1877.
AH 7188.77   Ferrero, E. Dei libertini dissertazione. Torino, 1877.
AH 8608.2   Fligier, C. Zur praehistorischen Ethnologie Italiens. Wien, 1877.
AH 4148.77   Fränkel, M. Attischen Geschworenengerichte. Berlin, 1877.
AH 38.64.12   Fustel de Coulanges, N.D. The ancient city. 3. ed. Photoreproduction. Boston, 1877.
AH 7201.55   Gaius. Institutiones. Berolini, 1877.
AH 4518.77   Gilbert, G. Beiträge zur Innerngeschichte Athens. Leipzig, 1877.
AH 5310.7   Gilbert, Gustav. Beiträge zur innern Geschichte Athens. Leipzig, 1877.
AH 4162.13   Grasshof, W. Doctrin am iuris Attici de hereditatibus. Berolini, 1877.
AH 4112.9   Gürgel, H. Die...Amphiktyonie. München, 1877.
AH 908.77F   Helbig, W. Il commercio dell'ambra. Roma, 1877.
AH 3910.13   Heyden, E.A. Res ab Antiocho III Magno. Monasterii, 1877.
AH 7418.77   Hinstin, G. Les romains à Athènes avant l'empire. Paris, 1877.
AH 7058.77   Hirschfeld, O. Untersuchungen...römischen Verwaltungsgeschichte. Berlin, 1877.
AH 4228.77   Höffler, R.J.A. De nomothesia Attica. Kiliae, 1877.
AH 7198.77.2A   Ihering, R. L'esprit du droit romain. Paris, 1877. 4v.
NEDL AH 7408.77.25   Ihne, W. Early Rome. 2. ed. London, 1877.
AH 7201.54   Julianus. Fragments of the perpetual edict. Cambridge, Eng., 1877.
AH 4708.77   Klatt, Max. Forschungen zur Geschichte des achäischen Bundes. Berlin, 1877.
AH 4543.7   Klotz, W.O.R. Quellen zur Geschichte Phokions. Zittau, 1877.
AH 8908.9   Körte, G. Etrusker. Stuttgart, 1877.

1877 - cont.

AH 7618.77   La Berge, C. de. Essai sur le regne de Trajan. Paris, 1877.
Eg 808.77   Lauth, F.J. Ägyptische Chronologie. Strassburg, 1877.
AH 2957.9   Lauth, F.J. Troja's Epoche. München, 1877.
AH 4238.77.5   Le civilización griega y la ciencia militar entre los griegos. Barcelona, 1877.
AH 7538.58.2   Lehmann, H. Claudius und seine Zeit. Leipzig, 1877.
AH 3156.5.5   Lenormant, F. Chaldean magic. London, 1877.
Eg 862.1   Lepsius, C.R. Les métaux dans les inscriptions égyptiennes. Paris, 1877.
AH 3167.5F   Lepsius, K.R. Die babylonisch-assyrischen Längenmasse. Berlin, 1877.
AH 7168.77.3   Merkel, J. Konkurs der Abtionen. Halle, 1877.
AH 2957.7   Meyer, E. Geschichte von Troas. Leipzig, 1877.
AH 7278.54.31   Mommsen, T. Historia de Roma. Madrid, 1877.
AH 818.77.5   Morgan, L.H. Ancient society. Chicago, 1877.
AH 818.77.4   Morgan, L.H. Ancient society. N.Y., 1877.
AH 8907.8.5   Müller, Karl O. Die Etrusker. Stuttgart, 1877. 2v.
AH 7038.77.5   Naudet, Joseph. De l'etat des personnes et des peuples sous les empereurs romains. Paris, 1877.
AH 7778.77   Naville, Henri Adrien. Julien l'apostat. Paris, 1877.
AH 808.77   Nichol, J. Tables of ancient literature and history. Glasgow, 1877.
AH 3150.3   Oppert, J. Documents juridiques de l'Assyrie et de la Chaldée. Paris, 1877.
AH 7088.77   Person, E. Essai...des provinces romaines. Paris, 1877.
AH 7448.77   Person, Emile. De P. Cornelio Scipione Aemiliano Africano et Numantino. Thesim. Sancti-Clodoaldi, 1877.
AH 818.77   Rawlinson, G. Origins of nations. London, 1877.
AH 908.77.3   Sadowski, J.N. Die Handelsstrassen der Griechen und Römer. Jena, 1877.
AH 3966.19   Saulcy, F. de. Dictionnaire topographique. Paris, 1877.
AH 3171.5.5   Sayce, A.H. Babylonian literature. London, 1877.
Eg 878.77.10   Schiaparelli, Ernesto. Del sentimento religioso degli antichi Egiziani secondo i monumenti. Torino, 1877.
AH 4498.77   Schmidt, A. Perikleische Zeitalter. Jena, 1877. 2v.
AH 3159.8   Scholz, A. Die Keilschrift-Urkunden und die Genesis. Würzburg, 1877.
Eg 1058.77   Shaï-en-Sinsin. Le livre des respirations. Paris, 1877.
AH 308.77   Smith, George. The history of Babylonia. London, 1877.
AH 818.77.6   Soury, J. Etudes historiques sur les religions, les arts, la civilisation. Paris, 1877.
AH 7238.77   Stille, Wilhelm. Historia legionum auxiliorumqui ende ab excecssu divi Augusti usque ad Vespasiani tempora. Kiliae, 1877.
AH 7818.71   Stoll, H.W. Bilder aus dem altrömischen Leben. Leipzig, 1877.
AH 4860.5   Sureciciki, H. Pflege der Kinder bei den Griechen. Breslau, 1877.
AH 3155.11.5   Tiele, C.P. De vrucht der assyriologie. Amsterdam, 1877.
AH 938.77A   Tozer, Henry F. Classical geography. N.Y., 1877.
AH 938.77.5   Tozer, Henry F. Classical geography. N.Y., 1877.
Htn   AH 8549.76*   Vallentin, F. Essai sur les divinités indigètes du Vocontium. Grenoble, 1877.
AH 2108.5   Vaux, W.S.W. Great cities and islands of Asia Minor. London, 1877.
AH 8557.2   Zippel, B. Römische Herrschaft in Illyrien. Leipzig, 1877.
AH 7168.77   Zródłowski, F. Römischen Privatrecht. Prag, 1877. 2v.

1878

AH 7168.78.5   Artur, E. De la cause en droit romain et en droit français. Paris, 1878.
AH 3713.5   Barges, J.J.L. Colonies phéniciennes. Paris, 1878.
AH 7468.78   Beesly, E.S. Catiline, Clodius and Tiberius. London, 1878.
AH 2017.5   Beke, Charles. The late Dr. Charles Beke's discoveries of Sinai in Arabia. London, 1878.
AH 4833.13   Bintz, J. Gymnastik der Hellenen. Gütersloh, 1878.
AH 8157.2   Boissière, G. Esquisse d'une histoire dans la nord de l'Afrique. Paris, 1878.
AH 7203.68   Bonjean, G. Institutes de Justien. Paris, 1878. 2v.
AH 7178.78   Buhl, Heinrich. Die agrarische Frage. Heidelberg, 1878.
AH 5757.9   Busolt, G. Lakedaimonier. Leipzig, 1878.
AH 8548.145   Cailleux, Théophile. Origine celtique de la civilisation de tous les peuples: théorie nouvelle. Paris, 1878.
AH 7708.70.3   Champagny, F.J.M.T. Les Césars du troisieme siècle. Paris, 1878. 3v.
AH 4728.78   Chevalier, L. Einfälle der Gallier in Griechen. Prag, 1878.
AH 4278.74.5   Cox, George W. History of Greece. London, 1878. 2v.
AH 7328.78   Cuno, J.G. Vorgeschichte Roms. Leipzig, 1878. 2v.
NEDL AH 4278.57.6   Curtius, Ernest. Griechische Geschichte. Berlin, 1878. 3v.
AH 3308.5   Davidson, J.T. Cyprus: its place in Bible history. London, 1878.
AH 3961.4   Derenbourg, M.J. Quelques notes sur la guerre de Bar Kôzêbâ. Paris, 1878.
AH 3143.3   Dubor, Georges de. Assyrie et Chaldée. Montauban, 1878.
AH 7188.78   Duchauffour, A. De la condition des esclaves. Paris, 1878.
AH 5753.5   Dum, Georg. Spartanischen Ephorats. Innsbruck, 1878.
AH 5762.5   Dum, Georg. Spartanischen Königslisten. Innsbruck, 1878.
Eg 1158.78   Dutrieux, P.J. Egyptian ophthalmia. Cairo, 1878.
AH 818.78F   Falke, J. von. Hellas und Rom. Stuttgart, 1878.
AH 7058.78.5   Faure, F. Essai historique sur le préteur romain. Paris, 1878.
AH 7258.78F   Ferrero, E. L'ordinamento delle armate romane. Torino, 1878.
AH 7798.78   Foss, Rudolph. Attila in der Geschichte und Sage. Düsseldorf, 1878.
AH 4148.78.3   Fränkel, A. Condicione, jure...sociorum atheniensium. Rostochii, 1878.
AH 4278.78   Fyffe, C.A. History of Greece. N.Y., 1878.
AH 7114.27   Genz, Hermann. Das patrische Rom. Berlin, 1878.
AH 8321.5   Gooss, Carl. Die römische Lagerstadt Apulum in Dacien. Schassburg, 1878.
AH 7148.78   Grévy, L. Des municipes. Versailles, 1878.
AH 7768.78   Güldenpenning, A. Der Kaiser Theodosius der Grosse. Halle, 1878.
AH 7478.78   Guiraud, Paul. Le différend entre César et le sénat (59-49 avant J.C.). Thèse. Paris, 1878.
AH 3921.6   Harnack, A. De Zeit des Ignatius. Leipzig, 1878.

Chronological Listing

1878 - cont.

AH 4148.78 — Hartel, W. Attisches Staatsrecht. Wien, 1878.
AH 4058.78 — Hille, C.A. De scribis atheniensium publicis. v.1-2. Lipsiae, 1878.
AH 3095.4 — Hoerning, K.J.R. Das sechsseitige Prisma des Sanherib. Leipzig, 1878.
AH 7058.78 — Hudemann, E.E. Geschichte des Römischen Postwesens. Berlin, 1878.
NEDL AH 7408.78 — Ihne, W. Early Rome. N.Y., 1878.
AH 9603.3 — Klein, Josef. Die Verwaltungsbeamten der Provinzen...Sicilien und Sardinien. Bonn, 1878.
AH 3966.40 — Kok, Johannes. Det hellige land og dets Mabolande i fortid og mutid. Kjøbenhavn, 1878.
AH 4861.7 — Kriesche, W. Darstellung der griechische Grabsitte. Braunau, 1878.
AH 98.78 — Kuhn, Emil. Entstehung der Staedte der Alten. Leipzig, 1878.
AH 846.9 — Lange, W. Antike...Wohnhaus. Leipzig, 1878.
AH 2107.7 — Le Bas, P. Asie Mineure. Paris, 1878.
AH 7118.6 — Luebberti, E. Dissertatio de gentis claudiae. Kiliae, 1878.
AH 8548.22 — Maclear, George F. The Celts. London, 1878.
AH 7161.15 — Maranges, J.M. Estudios jurídicos. Madrid, 1878.
NEDL AH 1278.76.8 — Maspero, Gaston. Histoire ancienne des peuples de l'Orient. 3. éd. Paris, 1878.
AH 3017.7.11F — Menant, J. Catalogue des cylindres orientaux du cabinet royal des medailles de la Haye. La Haye, 1878.
AH 3017.7.15 — Menant, J. Notice sur quelques cylindres orientaux. Paris, 1878.
AH 7138.78.10 — Padelletti, G. Storia del diritto romano. Firenze, 1878.
AH 7138.78 — Pailhé, E.D. Cours élémentaire de droit romain. Paris, 1878.
Eg 808.78 — Pessl, H. von. Das chronologisches System Manetho's. Leipzig, 1878.
AH 7138.78.5 — Raisini, G. Programma di diritto romano. Bologna, 1878.
AH 7162.21 — Rivier, A. Traité élémentarie des successions. Bruxelles, 1878.
AH 4523.5 — Rottsahl, C. Expedition der Athener nach Sicilien. Langensalza, 1878.
AH 7203.69 — Ruben der Couder. Droit romain. Paris, 1878.
AH 4842.47 — Sakellaropoulou, S.K. Peri tes Latinikes glossès kai philologias. Athènai, 1878.
AH 4038.54.3 — Schömann, G.F. Athenian constitutional history. Oxford, 1878.
AH 3012.6 — Schrader, E. Keilinschriften und Geschichtsforschung. Giessen, 1878.
AH 7168.78 — Scialoja, V. Il precarium nel diritto romano. Roma, 1878.
AH 7448.78 — Sieglin, W. Die Chronologie der Belagerung von Sagunt. Leipzig, 1878.
AH 3095.6 — Smith, George. History of Sennacherib. London, 1878.
AH 7203.71 — Thézard, L. Droit romain. 3. éd. Paris, 1878.
AH 3155.11 — Tiele, C.P. Die Assyriologie...verleichende Religionsgeschichte. Leipzig, 1878.
AH 7201.57A — Ulpianus. Fragmenta minora. Berolini, 1878.
NEDL AH 1278.78 — Van Den Berg, E. Petite histoire ancienne des peuples de l'Orient. Paris, 1878.
AH 7114.3 — Voigt, Moritz. Uber die Clientel und Libertinität. Leipzig, 1878.
Eg 818.37.6A — Wilkinson, J.G. Manners and customs of the ancient Egyptians. London, 1878. 3v.
Eg 818.37.25 — Wilkinson, J.G. A popular account of the ancient Egyptians. London, 1878. 2v.
AH 9662.5 — Wilsdorf, D. Tasti Hispaniarum provinciarum. Inaug. Diss. Lipsiae, 1878.
AH 9057.2 — Zoeller, Max. Latium und Rom. Leipzig, 1878.

1879

AH 7844.6 — Amante, B. Il natale di Roma. Roma, 1879.
AH 8549.79.5 — Arbois de Jubainville, Henry d'. Le dieu de la mort et les origines mythologiques. Paris, 1879.
AH 7088.79A — Arnold, W.T. Roman system of provincial administration. London, 1879.
Eg 958.79 — Bartlett, S.C. From Egypt to Palestine. N.Y., 1879.
AH 7201.95 — Beaudouin, E. Le majus et le minus latium. Paris, 1879.
AH 8857.2 — Beloch, Julius. Campanien. Geschichte und Topographie des antiken Neapel und seiner Umgebung. Berlin, 1879.
AH 8857.2F — Beloch, Julius. Campanien. Geschichte und Topographie des antiken Neapel und seiner Umgebung. Atlas. Berlin, 1879.
AH 7818.79 — Bender, H. Rom und römisches Leben im Alterthumen. Tübingen, 1879.
AH 7008.79 — Bonghi, R. Bibliografia storica di Roma attica. Roma, 1879.
AH 9675.2 — Botet y Siso, J. Noticia histórica y arqueológica de la antigua ciudad de Emporion. Madrid, 1879.
AH 7168.79.15 — Brissaud, J.B. La notion de cause...obligations conventionnelles en droit romain et...français. Thèse. Bordeaux, 1879.
Eg 278.59.6 — Brugsch, H. A history of Egypt. London, 1879. 2v.
AH 7201.47.4 — Bruns, C.G. Fontes Juris Romani Antiqui. 4. ed. Friburg, 1879.
AH 7468.79.5 — Bürcklein, A. Quellen und Chronologie der römisch-parthischen Feldzüge in den Jahren 713-718. Inaug. Diss. Berlin, 1879.
AH 4114.9 — Buermann, H. De titulis atticis. Lipsiae, 1879.
AH 938.79 — Bunbury, E.H. A history of ancient geography. London, 1879. 2v.
AH 7468.79 — Byvanck, W.G.C. Studia in Ti. Gracchi historiam. Lugdunum Batavorum, 1879.
AH 4162.15 — Caillemer, E. Droit de succession légitime. v.1-2. Paris, 1879.
AH 808.79 — Cassel, P.S. Phönix und seine Aera. Berlin, 1879.
AH 4108.79 — Christ, Johann. De publicis populi atheniensis rationibus saeculo A. Ch. quinto et quarto. Gryphiswaldiae, 1879.
AH 7203.100 — Corpus juris civilis. Digesta. Selected titles from the Digest...XVII. Cambridge, Eng., 1879.
AH 7278.85.3.5 — Creighton, M. History of Rome. N.Y., 1879.
AH 908.79 — Cruchon, G. Les banques dans l'antiquité. Paris, 1879.
AH 3002.3 — Delattre, A. Les inscriptions historiques de Nineve. Paris, 1879.
AH 4845.23 — Delepierre, O.J. Dissertation sur les idées morales des grecs. Rouen, 1879.
AH 7168.79.7 — Flach, J. La table de bronze d'Aljustrel. Paris, 1879.
AH 8057.3 — Flatters, P. L'Afrique septentrionale ancienne. Alger, 1879.
NEDL AH 7478.79.1A — Froude, J.A. Caesar; a sketch. London, 1879.
AH 7478.79A — Froude, J.A. Caesar; a sketch. N.Y., 1879.

1879 - cont.

AH 8549.79 — Fustel de Coulanges, N.D. Comment le druidisme a disparu. Paris, 1879.
AH 7078.79 — Gentile, I. Le elezioni et il Broglio. Milan, 1879.
AH 7458.79 — Genzken, H. De rebus a P. et Cn. Corneliis Scipionibus in Hispania gestis. Diss. inaug. Fribergae, 1879.
AH 7168.79.10 — Gide, P. Etude sur la novation. Paris, 1879.
AH 2173.5 — Göttingen. Universitat. Index Scholarum...Academia Georgia Augusta. Gottingae, 1879.
AH 7108.79 — Hahn, G. De censorum locationibus. Lipsiae, 1879.
AH 3020.5 — Haupt, Paul. Die sumerischen Familiengesetze. Leipzig, 1879.
AH 161.5 — Hearn, W.E. The Aryan household; an introduction to comparative jurisprudence. London, 1879.
AH 4278.79 — Hertzberg, G.F. Geschichte von Hellas und Rom. Berlin, 1879. 2v.
AH 7138.79 — Heumann, H.G. Quellen des römischen Rechts. Jena, 1879.
AH 7138.79.7F — Hirschfeld, O. Zur Geschichte des lateinischen Rechts. Wien, 1879. 2 pam.
AH 7148.79 — Hoffmann, E. Patricische und plebeische Curien. Wien, 1879.
AH 4818.79 — Houssaye, H. Athènes, Rome, Paris. Paris, 1879.
AH 7201.40.4 — Huschke, P.E. Iurisprudentiae anteiustinianae. Lipsiae, 1879.
AH 408.78.5A — Keary, C.F. The dawn of history. N.Y., 1879?
NEDL AH 7298.64.1 — Kingsley, Charles. The Roman and the Teuton. London, 1879.
AH 7168.79 — Koeppen, K.F.A. Institutionen und Geschichte. Strassburg, 1879.
AH 7138.79.3 — Kuntze, J.E. Cursus des römischen Rechts. Leipzig, 1879.
AH 7207.31 — Lange, Ludwig. De plebiscitis ovinio et atinio disputatio. Lipsiae, 1879.
AH 3307.7 — Lauria, G.A. Cipro. Napoli, 1879.
AH 7278.79 — Leighton, R.F. History of Rome. N.Y., 1879.
AH 7168.79.5 — Leist, B.W. Das römische Patronatrecht. Erlangen, 1879. 2v.
NEDL AH 7278.55.9A — Liddell, H.G. History of Rome. N.Y., 1879.
AH 8073.5 — Littré, M.P.E. Comment...les sémites entrèrent. Leipzig, 1879.
AH 7202.16 — Maasen, F. Ein Commentar des Florus von Lyon zu einigen der sogenannten Sermondschen Constitutionen. Wien, 1879.
AH 7828.79 — Marquardt, J. Das Privatleben der Römer. Leipzig, 1879.
Eg 298.79 — Maspero, G. Études égyptiennes. Paris, 1879-86. 2v.
AH 8073.3 — Meltzer, Otto. Geschichte der Karthager. Berlin, 1879. 3v.
AH 3017.7.12 — Menant, J. Les cylindres orientaux. Paris, 1879.
AH 3017.7.5 — Menant, J. Notice sur quelques empreintes de cylindres. Paris, 1879.
AH 2907.2 — Meyer, E. Geschichte des Königreichs Pontos. Leipzig, 1879.
AH 7307.34.12.5 — Montesquieu, Charles de. De la grandeur des Romains. Paris, 1879.
AH 5390.5 — Müller, M. Geschichte Thebens. Leipzig, 1879.
AH 808.79.10 — Neteler, Bernhard. Zusammenhang der alttestamentlichen Zeitrechnung mit der Profangeschichte. v.1-3. Münster, 1879-86.
AH 7138.78.11 — Padelletti, G. Lehrbuch der römischen Rechtsgeschichte. Berlin, 1879.
AH 4728.75.2 — Petit de Julleville, L. Histoire de la Grèce sou la domination romaine. 2. éd. Paris, 1879.
AH 3095.5 — Pognon, H. L'inscription de Bavian. Paris, 1879.
AH 3964.12 — Popper, Julius. Der Ursprung des Monotheismus. Berlin, 1879.
AH 7778.79 — Rendall, Gerald Henry. Emperor Julian, paganism and Christianity. Cambridge, 1879.
AH 4808.79 — Reusch, A. De Dilbus Contionum Ordmarium. Argentorali, 1879.
AH 7818.79.5 — Rydberg, V. Roman days. N.Y., 1879.
AH 3171.5 — Sayce, A.H. Babylonian literature. London, 1879.
AH 7161.27 — Schmidt, K.A. Das Hauskind in Mancipio. Leipzig, 1879.
AH 4818.51.10 — Schoemann, G.F. Antiquities of Greece. Oxford, 1879.
AH 8073.4 — Smith, R.B. Carthage and the Carthaginians. 2. ed. London, 1879.
Eg 708.64.2 — Stahr, Adolf. Cleopatra. 2. Aufl. Berlin, 1879.
AH 8548.25 — Valroger, L. de. Les Celtes, la Gaule celtique. Paris, 1879.
AH 4843.15 — Waldenburg. Gymnasium. Geschichte der Aulodik bie den Griechen. Waldenburg, 1879.
AH 7478.79.4 — Wesemann, H. Caesarfabeln des Mittelalters. Löwenberg, 1879.
AH 7228.79 — Wlassak, M. Zur Geschichte der Negotiorum Gestio. Jena, 1879.

188-

AH 818.62.9 — Guhl, Ernst. Life of the Greeks and Romans. London, 188-?
AH 4842.26 — Mahaffy, J.P. Old Greek education. N.Y., 188-.
AH 4818.80 — Mather, R.H. Abstract of lectures upon Greek life. n.p., 188-.
Eg 278.81.5 — Rawlinson, George. History of ancient Egypt. N.Y., 188-? 2v.

1880

AH 7828.38.5 — Becker, W.A. Gallus, oder Römische Scenen. v.1-3. Berlin, 1880. 2v.
AH 7558.80 — Beckurts, F. Zur Quellenkritik des Tacitus, Sueton. Braunschweig, 1880.
AH 8610.2 — Beloch, J. Der italische Bund...Roms Hegemonie. Leipzig, 1880.
AH 2957.5A — Benjamin, S. Troy. N.Y., 1880.
AH 3088.4PF — Birch, S. Bronze ornaments of the Gates of Balawat. London, 1880.
NEDL Eg 278.59.10 — Brugsch, H. The true story of the exodus of Israel. Boston, 1880.
AH 3096.4 — Budge, E.A. The history of Esarhaddon...681-668. London, 1880.
AH 7758.80 — Burckhardt, Jacob. Die Zeit Constantins des Grossen. Leipzig, 1880.
AH 7108.80 — Cagnat, René. Le portorium...chez les Romains. Paris, 1880.
AH 7698.80 — Ceuleneer, A. de. Essai sur la vie et le regne de Septime Sévère. Bruxelles, 1880.
AH 98.80 — Cognat, René. De municipalibus et provincialibus militus in Imperio Romano. Thesis. Lutetiae Parisiorum, 1880.
AH 4278.80 — Combers, L. La Grèce. Paris, 1880.

Chronological Listing

Chronological Listing

1881 - cont.

AH 2763.5 — Reifferscheid, August. Pergamon und seine Kunstschätze. Breslau, 1881-82.

AH 7138.81.3 — Rivier, A. Introduction historique au droit romain. Bruxelles, 1881.

AH 7238.81.2 — Schambach, O. Gymnasium zu Mühlhausen - Jahres-Bericht. Mühlhausen, 1881.

AH 4212.5 — Schubert, J.G. De proxenia Attica. Lipsiae, 1881.

NEDL AH 7278.74.8 — Smith, William. A smaller history of Rome. N.Y., 1881.

AH 4148.81 — Stahl, J.M. De sociorum Atheniensum judiciis. Monasterii Guestfalorum, 1881.

NEDL AH 278.81.5 — Steele, J.D. A brief history of ancient peoples. N.Y., 1881.

AH 5134.7 — Stumpf, Phil. De Nesistarum republica commentatio. Monachii, 1881.

AH 4148.81.3 — Szántó, Emil. Untersuchungen über die attische Bürgerrecht. Wien, 1881.

AH 7228.81.9 — Tardif, E.J. Etude sur la Litis Contestatio en droit romain. Paris, 1881.

AH 4278.81 — Timayenis, T.T. History of Greece. N.Y., 1881. 2v.

AH 1278.78.2 — Van Den Berg, E. Petite histoire ancienne des peuples de l'Orient. 2. éd. Paris, 1881.

AH 4708.81 — Weinert, A. Die achäische Bundesverstallung. Demmin, 1881.

Eg 278.81.50 — Wilson, E. The Egypt of the past. London, 1881.

1882

NEDL AH 818.82.10 — Aguglia, S. Genesi dell'incivilimento. Napoli, 1882.

AH 7178.82 — Baillierie, P. Du domaine public del'état. Paris, 1882.

AH 4828.40.14 — Becker, W.A. Charicles. 6. ed. London, 1882.

AH 7038.82 — Bernhöft, F. Staat und Recht. Stuttgart, 1882.

AH 3002.2.2 — Bezold, Carl. Die Achämenideninschriften. Leipzig, 1882.

AH 9621.5 — Bindseil, R. Geschichte der Stadt Akragas. Neustettin, 1882.

AH 3759.6 — Bonnell, Ernst. Beiträge zur Alterthumskunde Russlands. St. Petersburg, 1882.

AH 7108.82 — Cagnat, René. Etude historique sur les impots. Paris, 1882.

AH 842.15 — Cassan, K. Pädagogik der Alten. Leipzig, 1882.

AH 4938.82 — Curtius, E. Die Griechen in der Diaspora. v.1-2. Berlin, 1882.

AH 4114.5 — Dirichlet, G.J. De equititus atticis. Regimonti, 1882.

AH 8073.9 — Drapeyron, L. La condition de Carthage. Paris, 1882.

AH 5308.5 — Droysen, H. Athen und der Westen. Berlin, 1882.

AH 5905.5 — Dundaczek, Raimund. Beiträge zur Geschichte der...messenischen Kriege. Czernowitz, 1882.

AH 8658.2 — Elliot, F.D.G. Pictures of old Rome. Leipzig, 1882.

AH 818.78.3FA — Falke, J. von. Greece and Rome. N.Y., 1882.

AH 7238.82.5 — Fiegel, M. Historia legionis III. Augustae. Inaug. Diss. Berolini, 1882.

AH 1808.82 — Floigl, Victor. Geschichte des semitischen Altertums in Tabellen. Leipzig, 1882.

AH 7468.82 — Fritzsche, Hermann. Die sulianische Gesetzgebung. Essen, 1882.

AH 8909.2 — Gardthausen, V. Mastarna öder Servius Tullius. Leipzig, 1882.

AH 1818.82 — Geiger, W. Ostiranische Kultur im Altertum. Erlangen, 1882.

AH 7308.82 — Graf, A. Roma. Torino, 1882. 2v.

AH 3154.2 — Halevy, J. Documents religieux. Paris, 1882.

AH 7808.82 — Hartmann, O.E. Der römische Kalender. Leipzig, 1882.

AH 7328.82 — Hudson, E.H. A history of the Jews in Rome. London, 1882.

AH 928.62.3 — Hultsch, F. Metrologie. Berlin, 1882.

AH 7798.82 — Jornandes. De origine actibusque Getarum. Freiburg, 1882.

AH 4843.7 — Karl von Jan. Griechische Saiteninstrumente. Leipzig, 1882.

AH 3013.6.2 — Kaulen, Franz. Assyrien und Babylonien. 2. Aufl. Freiburg, 1882.

AH 5309.9 — Kausel, T. Thesej Synoecismo. Dillenburg, 1882.

AH 8516.7 — Kerviler, René. Etudes critiques sur l'ancienne géographie armoricaine. Saint-Brieuc, 1882.

AH 7298.82 — Kuntze, J.E. Prolegomena zur Geschichte Roms. Leipzig, 1882.

AH 3013.29F — Ledrain, E. Les antiquités chaldéennes du Louvre. Paris, 1882.

Eg 878.82.4 — Lemm, O. von. Studien zum Ritualbuche des Ammondienstes. Leipzig, 1882.

AH 408.82 — Lenormant, F. Beginnings of history. N.Y., 1882.

AH 7238.82 — Lindenschmit, Ludwig. Tracht und Bewaffnung. Braunschweig, 1882.

Eg 758.82 — Lumbroso, Giacomo. L'Egitto al tempo dei Greci e dei Romani. Roma, 1882.

AH 3094.3F — Lyon, D.G. Die Cylinder-Inschrift Sargons II. Leipzig, 1882.

AH 7038.81.4 — Madvig, J.N. L'etat romain. v.1-5. Paris, 1882. 4v.

AH 4842.27A — Mahaffy, J.P. Old Greek education. N.Y., 1882.

AH 7098.82 — Mantey, Otto. De gradu et statu quaestorum im municipiis colonisque. Diss. Inaug. Halis Saxonum, 1882.

NEDL AH 3075.4 — Massaroli, G. Phiel e Tuklatpalasar II. Roma, 1882.

AH 7178.82.7 — Matthiass, B. Die römische Grundsteuer. Erlangen, 1882.

AH 7038.82.2 — Mispoulet, J.B. Les institutions politiques. Paris, 1882. 2v.

AH 7278.54.30 — Mommsen, T. Histoire romaine. v.1-2, 3-4, 5-6, 7. Paris, 1882. 4v.

AH 7307.34.19 — Montesquieu, Charles de. Considerations on the causes of the grandeur of the Romans. N.Y., 1882.

AH 4258.82 — Müller, K.K. Griechischen Schrift über Seekrieg. Würzburg, 1882.

AH 4238.82 — Müller, K.K. Griechisches Fragment über Kriegswesen. Würzburg, 1882.

AH 3008.82 — Mürdter, F. Kurzgefasste Geschichte Babyloniens und Assyriens. Stuttgart, 1882.

NEDL AH 278.82.5 — Myers, P.V.N. Outlines of ancient history. N.Y., 1882.

AH 5311.5 — Neubauer, F. Atheniensium Reipublicae quaenam romanorum temporibus fuerit condicio. Halis Saxonum, 1882.

AH 7207.21 — Pantaleoni, Diomede. Dell'auctoritas patrum. Bologna, 1882.

AH 7828.82 — Pellisson, M. Les Romains au temps de Pline. Paris, 1882.

AH 4808.82A — Peter, C.L. Chronological tables of Greek history. Cambridge, 1882.

AH 7808.41 — Peter, C.L. Zeittafeln der römischen Geschichte. 6. Aufl. Halle, 1882.

AH 7808.35.7 — Peter, Carl. Zeittafeln der römischen Geschichte. Halle, 1882.

AH 7478.82 — Plathner, J. Zur Quellenkritik der...Bürgerkrieges. Bernburg, 1882.

1882 - cont.

AH 7838.82 — Rasch, Franz. De ludo Troiae. v.1-2. Jena, 1882.

NEDL AH 3657.13 — Rawlinson, G. Seventh great oriental monarchy. N.Y., 1882. 2v.

Eg 278.81.3 — Rawlinson, George. History of ancient Egypt. Boston, 1882. 2v.

Eg 138.82 — Revillout, Eugène. Le procès d'Hermias d'après les documents démotiques et grecs. pt.1-2. Paris, 1882.

AH 845.5.3 — Rosenbaum, J. Geschichte der Lustseuche im Alterthume. 3. Aufl. Halle, 1882.

AH 7138.82 — Ruben de Couder, M.J. Droit romain. Paris, 1882.

AH 298.82 — Schaefer, Arnold. Abrisz der Quellenkunde der griechischen und römischen Geschichte. Leipzig, 1882.

AH 162.3 — Schulin, F. Das griechische Testament. Basel, 1882.

AH 4848.10 — Smith, J.M. Ancient Greek female costume. London, 1882.

AH 4200.7 — Stein, H.K. Kritik der Überlieferung über...Lykurg. Glatz, 1882.

Eg 878.82 — Tiele, C.R. History of the Egyptian religion. London, 1882.

NEDL AH 4278.81.4 — Timayenis, T.T. History of Greece. N.Y., 1882-83. 2v.

AH 7168.82 — Trinbal, J. Le la cause dans les contrats et les obligations. Toulouse, 1882.

AH 8617.7 — Tulelli, E. Il filadelfos de Giovanni Gemelli. Napoli, 1882.

AH 7203.76 — Violet, W. Juristen-Bibliothek. Leipzig, 1882.

AH 7518.82 — Weisse, J. P. Populaere forelaesninger over Tiberius og Nero. Kristiania, 1882.

AH 7228.82 — Wlassak, M. Edict und Klageform. Jena, 1882.

AH 818.82 — Yaggy, Levi M. Museum of antiquity, a description of ancient life. N.Y., 1882.

1883

AH 7138.83.3 — Amos, S. History and principles of the civil law of Rome. London, 1883.

AH 8548.30 — Becker, K. von. Versuch einer Lösung der Celtenfrage. Karlsruhe, 1883.

Eg 278.83 — Berkley, E. The pharaohs and their people. N.Y., 1883.

AH 8008.7 — Berlioux, E.F. Les atlantes. Histoire de l'Atlantis. Paris, 1883.

AH 7518.68.4 — Beulé, C.E. Tibère et l'héritage d'Auguste. 4. éd. Paris, 1883.

Eg 278.75.9 — Birch, S. Egypt. London, 1883.

AH 7098.83 — Bloch, G. De decretis functorum magistratum ornamentis. Lutetiae Parisiorum, 1883.

AH 8157.3 — Boissière, G. L'Algérie romaine. Paris, 1883. 2v.

AH 4948.83 — Bouché-Leclercq, Auguste. Atlas pour servir à l'histoire grecque de E. Curtius. Paris, 1883.

AH 3013.9 — British Museum. Assyrian antiquities - guide to Koujunjik Gallery. London, 1883.

AH 2357.7 — Chevalier, L. Die Gallier in Kleinasien. Prag, 1883.

AH 7818.84.6 — Church, Alfred J. Roman life in the days of Cicero. N.Y., 1883.

AH 7203.90 — Corpus juris civilis. Institutiones. Justinian: Institutionum libri quattuor. Oxford, 1883. 2v.

AH 7278.85.3.6 — Creighton, M. History of Rome. N.Y., 1883.

NEDL AH 4278.57.16 — Curtius, Ernest. History of Greece. N.Y., 1883. 5v.

AH 3507.5 — Delattre, A. L'empire des Mèdes. Bruxelles, 1883.

AH 7168.83.7 — Dernburg, H. Entwicklung und Begriff des juristischen Besitzes des römischen Rechts. Halle, 1883.

AH 3016.5 — Descemet, C. Bas-reliefs assyriens. Rome, 1883.

AH 4658.36.5 — Droysen, J.G. Histoire de l'hellénisme. Paris, 1883. 3v.

AH 4278.83 — Duncker, M.W. History of Greece. London, 1883. 2v.

AH 7278.70.9 — Duruy, V. History of Rome. Boston, 1883. 16v.

NEDL AH 278.83 — Duruy, V. Petite histoire ancienne. Paris, 1883.

AH 7278.83 — Duruy, V. Petite histoire grecque. Paris, 1883.

AH 8657.5.3 — Dyer, Thomas H. The city of Rome. 2. ed. London, 1883.

AH 4298.83.10 — Erdmann, M. Zur Kunde der hellenistischen Städtegründungen. Strassburg, 1883.

AH 4521.11 — Fokke, A. Rettungen des Alkibiades. Emden, 1883.

AH 7238.83 — Fontaine, L. L'armée romaine. Paris, 1883.

AH 1278.83 — Fontane, M. Histoire universelle les Asiatiques. Paris, 1883.

AH 7448.83 — Frantz, Johann. Die Kriege der Scipionen in Spanien. München, 1883.

AH 7178.83 — Freund, F. Die gesetzlichen Beschränkungen. Berlin, 1883.

AH 38.64.4 — Fustel de Coulanges, N.D. La cité antique. 10. éd. Paris, 1883.

NEDL AH 4278.78.4 — Fyffe, C.A. History of Greece. N.Y., 1883.

AH 8657.3 — Gilbert, Otto. Geschichte...der Stadt Rom im Altertum. Leipzig, 1883. 3v.

AH 3808.3 — Halévy, J. Melanges de critique et d'histoire. Paris, 1883.

AH 3103.6 — Harkness, M.E. Assyrian life and history. London, 1883.

AH 4158.83 — Herrlich, S. Verbrechen gegen das Leben. Berlin, 1883.

AH 7808.80 — Hex, Rudolph. Die älteste Monatseintheilung der Römer. Jena, 1883.

AH 3132.5 — Hilprecht, H.V. Freibrief Nebukadnezars I. Leipzig, 1883.

AH 7578.83 — Hoffman, O.A. De Imperatoris Titi temporibus. Marpeogi, 1883.

AH 3807.6 — Hommel, Fritz. Die semitischen Völker und Sprachen. Leipzig, 1883.

AH 7148.83.4 — Houwing, J.F. De Romanorum legibus. Lugdunum Batavorum, 1883.

AH 7678.83 — Hundertmark, J. De imperatore Pertinace; dissertatio historica. Monasterii Guestfalorum, 1883.

AH 7238.83.5 — Jullian, C. De protectoribus et domesticis Augustorum. Thesis. Paris, 1883.

NEDL AH 7818.83 — Jung, I. Leben und Sitten der Römer. Prag, 1883. 2v.

AH 4558.83 — Jurien, J.P.E. Les campagnes d'Alexandre; drame macédonien. Paris, 1883. 5v.

AH 408.78.8 — Keary, C.F. The dawn of history. pt.1. N.Y., 1883.

NEDL AH 408.78.7 — Keary, C.F. The dawn of history. pt.1-2. N.Y., 1883.

AH 7228.52.9 — Keller, Friedrich. Der römische Civilprocess und die Actionen. Leipzig, 1883.

AH 3013.19 — Kiepert, J.S.H. Begleitworte zur Karte de Ruinenfelder von Babylon. Berlin, 1883.

AH 4708.83 — Klatt, Max. Chronologische Beiträge zur Geschichte des achäischen Bundes. Berlin, 1883.

AH 4841.5 — Kornitzer, A. De scribis publicis Atheniensium. Wien, 1883.

AH 3658.8 — Krumbholz, Paul. De Asiae Minoras satrapis Persicis. Inaug. Diss. Lipsiae, 1883.

1883 - cont.

AH 4818.83 — Kuhnert, E. De cura statuarum. Berolini, 1883.
AH 4818.83.5 — Kuhnert, E. De cura statuarum apud Graecos. Berolini, 1883.
AH 4498.83 — Larocque, J. La Grèce. Paris, 1883.
AH 7204.9 — Lenel, Otto. Edictum perpetuum. Leipzig, 1883.
AH 7148.83.3 — Létourville, G. de. Étude sur le droit de cité à Rome. Paris, 1883.
AH 7138.83 — Mackeldey, F. Handbook of Roman law. v.1-2. Philadelphia, 1883.
AH 4828.74.4 — Mahaffy, J.P. Social life in Greece from Homer to Menander. 5. ed. London, 1883.
NEDL AH 138.83.3 — Maine, Henry S. Dissertations on early law and custom. N.Y., 1883.
AH 138.83A — Maine, Henry S. Early law and custom. London, 1883.
NEDL Eg 318.83 — Massey, G. The natural genesis. London, 1883. 2v.
AH 7808.83 — Matzat, H. Römische Chronologie. Berlin, 1883. 2v.
AH 4228.24.5 — Meier, M.H.E. Attische Process. Berlin, 1883. 2v.
AH 3017.7 — Menant, J. Recherches sur la glyphique orientale. Pt.1-2. Paris, 1883. 2v.
Eg 758.83 — Merriam, A.C. The Obelisk-Crab. N.Y., 1883.
AH 855.5 — Miller, Max. Jagdwesen der alten Griechen und Römer. München, 1883.
AH 4808.83 — Mommsen, A. Chronologie. Leipzig, 1883.
AH 7158.83 — Montagnon, E. Essai sur la nature des condamnations civiles. Lyon, 1883.
AH 7448.83.10 — Neumann, Karl. Das Zeitalter der punischen Kriege. Breslau, 1883.
AH 8616.4 — Nissen, H. Italische Landeskunde. v.1-2. Berlin, 1883. 3v.
AH 5136.5 — Oikonomos, S.A. He Nēsos Peparēthos. Ienae, 1883.
Eg 298.83 — Osborn, H.S. Ancient Egypt. Cincinnati, 1883.
AH 9273.5 — Passeri, T. La colonia Carseolana. Roma, 1883.
AH 328.83 — Penka, K. Origines ariacae. Wien, 1883.
AH 7488.83.5 — Proudhon, P.J. Césarisme et Christianisme. Paris, 1883. 2v.
AH 878.82.3 — Rawlinson, G. The religions of the ancient world. N.Y., 1883.
AH 4857.9 — Ribbeck, O. Kolax. Leipzig, 1883.
AH 277.34.22 — Rollin, Charles. The ancient history of the Egyptians. N.Y., 1883. 4v.
Eg 1008.83 — Rouge, Jacques de. Littérature de l'ancienne Égypte. Paris, 1883.
AH 7168.83 — Salkowski, C. Lehrbuch der Institutionen. 4. Aufl. Leipzig, 1883.
AH 3002.2.5A — Sargon, king of Assyria. Keilschrifttexte: Sargon's Königs von Assyrien. Leipzig, 1883.
AH 4228.83 — Sauppe, Herman. Atheniensium...suffragia. Gottingae, 1883.
AH 7238.83.2 — Schambach, O. Sechsundsiebenzigste Nachricht. Altenburg, 1883.
AH 7478.83.5 — Schelle, Emil. De M. Antonii triumveri quae supersunt epistalis. Pt.1. Frankenberg, 1883.
AH 7488.83 — Schiller, K.H.F.H. Geschichte der Römischen Kaiserzeit. Gotha, 1883. 2v.
AH 7488.83.2 — Schiller, K.H.F.H. Geschichte der Römischen Kaiserzeit. v.1,pt.1-2. Gotha, 1883. 2v.
AH 3159.11.2A — Schrader, E. Die Keilinschriften und das Alte Testament. 2e Aufl. Giessen, 1883.
AH 7628.83 — Schurz, Wilhelm. De mutationibus in imperio romano ordinando ab imperatore Hadriano factis. pt.1. Bonnae, 1883.
AH 4848.10.3 — Smith, J.M. Ancient Greek female costume. 2. ed. London, 1883.
AH 4298.83 — Steele, J.D. Brief history of Greece. N.Y., 1883.
AH 4298.83.2 — Steele, J.D. Brief history of Greece. N.Y., 1883.
AH 7468.83 — Stern, Ernst von. Catilina und die Parterkämpfe. Dorpat, 1883.
AH 7448.83.15 — Stuerenburg, Heinrich. Der Romanorum cladibus Trasumenna et Cannensi. Leipzig, 1883.
AH 7148.83.2 — Thurm, A.A. De Romanorum legatis. Lipsiae, 1883.
NEDL AH 4278.81.2 — Timayenis, T.T. History of Greece. N.Y., 1883. 2v.
AH 8516.12 — Vallentin, Florian. Les Alpes cottiennes et graies; géographie gallo-romaine. Paris, 1883.
AH 3807.5 — Vibert, C.T. La race sémitique. Paris, 1883.
AH 7200.13 — Voigt, M. Die XII Tafeln. Leipzig, 1883. 2v.
AH 7148.83 — Weiss, André. Le droit fétial et les fétiaux. Paris, 1883.
AH 7478.83 — Wendelmuth, Richard. T. Labienus. Inaug. Diss. Marburg, 1883.
AH 4298.93 — Wiedemann, A. Beziehungen zwischen Aegypten und Griechenland. Leipzig, 1883.
AH 7818.83.15 — Wilkins, A.S. Classical antiquities. N.Y., 1883.
NEDL AH 7818.77.8 — Wilkins, Augustus S. Antigüedades clásicas II. Antigüedades Romanas. N.Y., 1883.
Eg 818.37.10 — Wilkinson, J.G. The manners and customs of the ancient Egyptians. Boston, 1883. 3v.
AH 7148.70.5 — Willems, P. Le droit public romain. 5e éd. Louvain, 1883.
AH 7203.77 — Williams, J. Institutes of Justinian. London, 1883.
AH 4278.83.5 — Willson, M. Mosaics of Grecian history. N.Y., 1883.
AH 7200.5 — Wolff, Emil. Rättshistoriska studier till den tolf taflanaslag. Göteborg, 1883.
AH 7058.83 — Zippel, Gustav. Die Losung der konsularischen Prokonsuln in der früheren Kaizerzeit. Königsberg, 1883.

1884

AH 7138.84.3 — Appleton, C. Cours de droit romain. Paris, 1884.
AH 7468.84 — Bardey, Ernst. Das sechste Consulat des Marius. Brandenburg, 1884.
AH 7138.84 — Baron, J. Geschichte des römischen Rechts. Berlin, 1884.
AH 3012.4 — Berliner, A. Beiträge zur Geographie und Ethnographie Babyloniens. Berlin, 1884.
AH 4848.11 — Boelhau, I. Quaestionum de re vestiaria graecorum specimen. Diss. Wimariae, 1884.
AH 3159.12 — Bonnet, E. Les découvertes assyriennes et le livre de la genèse. Montauban, 1884.
AH 7448.74.2 — Breyton, A. La bataille de Cannes. Paris, 1884.
AH 4328.84 — Bruck, Sylvius. De Pelasgis. Vratíclaviae, 1884.
AH 3008.84 — Budge, E.A.W. Babylonian life and history. London, 1884. 2v.
AH 7438.84 — Burger, Combertus P. De bello cum Samnitibus secundo. Harlemi, 1884.
AH 7008.84 — Cauer, F. De fabulis graecis ad romam. Berolini, 1884.
NEDL AH 7818.84.5 — Church, Alfred J. Roman life in the days of Cicero. London, 1884.

1884 - cont.

AH 7203.95 — Corpus juris civilis. Novellae constitutiones. Appendix ad editionem novellarum Iustiniani. Lipsiae, 1884.
NEDL AH 7278.70.5 — Duruy, V. History of Rome. v.1-6, pt.1-2. London, 1884-12v.
AH 7278.70.15F — Duruy, V. History of Rome. v.1-8, pt.1-2. Boston, 1884-87. 16v.
AH 3659.7 — Evers, E. Das Emporkommen der persischen Macht. Berlin, 1884.
AH 7258.78.2F — Ferrero, E. Iscrizioni e ricerche nuove. Torino, 1884.
AH 4845.13 — Foerster, P. Physiognomik der Griechen. Kiel, 1884.
AH 7448.84 — Fröhlich, F. Die Bedeutung des zweiten punischen Krieges. Leipzig, 1884.
AH 7698.84 — Fuchs, C. Geschichte des Kaisers L. Septimius Severus. Wien, 1884.
AH 7201.71 — Gaius. Institutiones I. Berolini, 1884.
AH 7628.84.3 — Gregorovius, F.A. Der Kaiser Hadrian. 2. Aufl. Stuttgart, 1884.
AH 3109.4F — Haerdtl, E. Astronomische Beiträge zur assyrischen Chronologie. Wien, 1884.
AH 3002.2.3 — Haupt, Paul. Das babylonische Nimrodepos. Leipzig, 1884-91.
X Cg AH 7038.84 — Herzog, Ernst. Geschichte und System der römischen Staatverfassung. Leipzig, 1884. 3v.
AH 3060.3 — Heuzey, L. Un nouveau roi de Tello. Paris, 1884.
AH 3017.5F — Heuzey, L. La stèle des vautours. Paris, 1884.
AH 7138.84.15 — Hölder, E. Zwei Abhandlungen aus dem römischen Rechte. Freiburg, 1884.
AH 7328.84 — Hudson, E.H. History of the Jews in Rome. London, 1884.
AH 3177.8 — Ishtar and Izdubar; the epic of Babylon. London, 1884.
AH 818.84.2 — Jebb, R.C. Some ancient organs of public opinion. Cambridge, Eng., 1884.
AH 4204.20 — Jonas, J. De Solone Atheniensi. Dissertatio historica. Monasterii Guestfalorum, 1884.
AH 7162.15 — Kahn, F. Römischen Frauen-Erbrechts. Leipzig, 1884.
AH 7798.84 — Keller, Rudolf. Stilicho. Berlin, 1884.
AH 938.84 — Keppel, T. Ansichten der alten Griechen und Römer. Schwienfurt, 1884.
AH 7238.84 — Kraner, F. L'armée romaine au temps de César. Paris, 1884.
AH 7231.9 — Kuthe, A. Römische Kriegsaltertümer. Wismar, 1884. 4 pam.
AH 4298.84 — Lamprog, S. Meletēllata. Athēnai, 1884.
AH 138.84 — Leist, B.W. Graeco-italische Rechtsgeschichte. Jena, 1884.
AH 8548.35 — Lizeray, Henri. Fondation du pan-celtisme. Paris, 1884. 2 pam.
AH 138.83.8 — Maine, Henry S. Études sur l'ancien droit. Paris, 1884.
AH 138.75.7 — Maine, Henry S. Lectures on the early history of institutions. N.Y., 1884.
AH 7208.4 — Marlot, Emile. Les comices électoraux. Paris, 1884.
AH 7214.3 — Maschke, R. De magistratuum Romanorum iure. Berolini, 1884.
AH 7278.84 — Matheson, P.E. Skeleton outline of Roman history. London, 1884.
AH 278.84.3 — Meyer, E. Geschichte des Alterthums. Stuttgart, 1884. 5v.
AH 7418.84 — Nitzsch, K.W. Geschichte der römischen Republik. Leipzig, 1884.
AH 3107.3 — Oberziner, L.A. Divisione politica e militare dell'antica Assiria. Trento, 1884.
AH 4808.84 — Parian Chronicle. Chronicon Parium. Tubingae, 1884.
AH 4498.84 — Pflugk-Harttung, J. Perikles als Feldherr. Stuttgart, 1884.
AH 278.84 — Ranke, L.F. von. Universal history. London, 1884.
AH 278.84.2 — Ranke, L.F. von. Universal history. N.Y., 1884.
AH 3013.40 — Rassam, H. Babylonian cities. London, 1884?
AH 818.84.5 — Rauber, August. Urgeschichte des Menschen. v.1-2. Leipzig, 1884.
AH 878.84 — Rawlinson, G. Religions of the ancient world. N.Y., 1884.
Eg 138.84 — Revillout, Eugène. Cours de droit égyptien. Paris, 1884.
AH 7818.84.3 — Robiow, F.M.C.J. Les institutions de l'ancienne Rome. Paris, 1884. 3v.
AH 7203.79 — Roby, H.J. Introduction to study of Justinian's Digest. Cambridge, 1884.
AH 7148.84 — Roques, Charles. Droit romain des juridictions. Paris, 1884.
AH 7818.84.10 — Saalfeld, G.A.E.A. Haus und Hof in Rom im Spiegel griechischen Kultur. Paderborn, 1884.
AH 9639.8 — Salinas, A. Solunto ricordi storici. Palermo, 1884.
AH 4538.84 — Sankey, C. Spartan and Theban supremacies. 3. ed. London, 1884.
AH 3013.45PF — Sarzec, E. de. Decouvertes en Chaldée. Facsimile. Paris, 1884-93.
AH 1278.89A — Sayce, A.H. Ancient empires of the East. London, 1884.
AH 3159.25 — Sayce, A.H. Fresh light from the ancient monuments. 2d ed. London, 1884.
AH 3715.5 — Schmülling, T. Der phönizische Handel in den griechischen Gewässern. Münster, 1884-85.
AH 2557.5 — Schubert, R.J.W. Könige von Lydien. Breslau, 1884.
AH 4038.84 — Schvarcz, J. Die Demokratie. v.1-2. Leipzig, 1884. 3v.
AH 849.5 — Sigismund, R. Die Aromata. Leipzig, 1884.
AH 7138.84.5 — Sohm, R. Institutionen des römischen Rechts. Leipzig, 1884.
AH 4608.84 — Spangenberg, E. De Atheniensium publicis institutis aetate Macedonum commutatis. Diss. inaug. Halis Saxonum, 1884.
AH 7205.11 — Theophilus Antecessor. Institutionum Graeca paraphrasis. Berolini, 1884.
AH 7798.56.6 — Thierry, A.S.D. Histoire d'Attila et de ses successeurs. 6. éd. Paris, 1884. 2v.
AH 4298.84.5 — Thiriou, M. De civitatibus quae a Graecis in Chersoneso taurica conditae fuerunt. Thesim. Nancy, 1884.
NEDL AH 4278.81.3 — Timayenis, T.T. History of Greece. N.Y., 1884. 2v.
AH 8066.3 — Tissot, Charles. Exploration scientifique de la Tunisie. Atlas. Paris, 1884-88. 2v.
AH 3981.3 — Trumbull, H.C. Kadesh-Barnea - its importance. N.Y., 1884.
AH 9682.2 — Ursin, Nils R. De Lusitania provincia Romana. Helsingiae, 1884.
Eg 278.84 — Wiedemann, A. Ägyptische Geschichte. Gotha, 1884. 2v.
AH 2013.5 — Wilken, G.A. Het matriarchaat bij de Oude Arabieren. Amsterdam, 1884.
AH 2013.5.7 — Wilken, G.A. Das Matriarchat...bei den Alten Arabern. Leipzig, 1884.
NEDL AH 7818.84 — Wilkins, A.S. Roman antiquities. N.Y., 1884.

Chronological Listing

1884 - cont.

AH 4415.7.5 — Witt, Karl. The Trojan War. London, 1884.
AH 7138.84.20 — Wlassak, M. Kritische Studien zur Theorie des Rechtsquellen. Graz, 1884.
AH 3407.5 — Wright, W. Empire of Hittites. London, 1884.

1885

AH 4708.85 — Baier, B. Studien zur achaeischen Bundes-Verfassung. Inaug. Diss. Würzburg, 1885.
AH 7888.85 — Belot, E. De la révolution économique et monétaire. Paris, 1885.
AH 7798.85 — Birt, Theodor. De moribus christianis quantum Stilichonis. Marburg, 1885.
AH 8964.3 — Bladé, J.F. Mémoire sur l'histoire religieuse. Bordeaux, 1885.
AH 4538.85 — Blass, F.W. Die sozialen Zustände Athens. Kiel, 1885.
AH 7498.85A — Boissier, Gaston. L'opposition sous les Césars. Paris, 1885.
AH 7088.85.5 — Bourgeois, Émile. Quomodo provinciarum Romanarum. Paris, 1885.
AH 3004.7 — Brown, F. Assyriology - its use and abuse in Old Testament study. N.Y., 1885.
Eg 878.85 — Brugsch, H. Religion und Mythologie der alten Ägypter. Leipzig, 1885. 2v.
NEDL AH 3008.85 — Brunengo, G. L'impero di Babilonia e di Ninive. v.1-2. Prato, 1885.
X Cg Eg 278.85.3 — Budge, Ernest Alfred Wallis. The dwellers on the Nile. London, 1885.
AH 4278.85 — Busolt, G. Griechische Geschichte. Gotha, 1885-97. 3v.
AH 3013.42PF — Clercq, Louis de. Collection De Clercq. Paris, 1885-1908. 2v.
AH 4338.85A — Cox, George W. Lives of Greek statesmen. N.Y., 1885. 2v.
AH 7278.85 — Creighton, M. History of Rome. N.Y., 1885.
AH 214.7 — Curtius, E. Der Zehnte. Berlin, 1885.
Eg 938.85 — Dawson, J.W. Egypt and Syria. London, 1885.
AH 4558.85 — Droysen, H. Alexanders des Grossen Heerwesen. Freiburg, 1885.
Eg 278.85 — Erman, A. Ägypten. Tübingen, 1885.
Eg 278.85.1 — Erman, A. Ägypten. Tübingen, 1885-87. 2v.
AH 4098.85 — Feldmann, W. Analecta epigraphica...synoecismorum. Argentorati, 1885.
NEDL AH 4278.78.8 — Fyffe, C.A. History of Greece. N.Y., 1885.
AH 1818.82.5 — Geiger, W. Civilization of the eastern Iranians. London, 1885.
AH 7828.85 — Giachi, V. Amori e costumi latini. Citta di Castello, 1885.
AH 3177.5 — Gilgamesh. Le poème Chaldéen du deluge. Paris, 1885.
AH 7278.85.21 — Gilman, A. Story of Rome. N.Y., 1885.
AH 7201.65 — Glasson, E. Étude sur Gaius. Paris, 1885.
AH 4108.85 — Goodwin, W.W. Value of Attic talent in modern money. v.1-2. n.p., 1885.
AH 7278.85.23 — Guiraud, Paul. Histoire romaine. Paris, 1885.
AH 7842.5.2 — Haenny, L. Schriftsteller und Buchhändler. 2. Aufl. Leipzig, 1885.
AH 4852.9 — Hansen, I.H. De Metallis Atticis. Hamburgi, 1885.
AH 5315.7 — Hansen, J.H. Über die Bevölkerungsdichtigkeit Attika's und ihre politische Bedeutung im Altertum. Hamburg, 1885?
AH 4278.85.5 — Harrison, J.A. The story of Greece. N.Y., 1885.
AH 5307.21 — Hertzberg, G.F. Athen. Halle, 1885.
AH 7808.85 — Holzapfel, L. Römische Chronologie. Leipzig, 1885.
AH 7842.3 — Jullien, E. Professeurs de littérature dans l'ane Rome. Paris, 1885.
AH 7258.85 — Jurien de la Gravière. Marine des Ptolémées et...Romains. Paris, 1885. 2v.
AH 7138.85.3 — Karlowa, O. Römische Rechtsgeschichte. Leipzig, 1885. 2v.
AH 3008.82.7 — Kausen, F. Assyrien und Babylonien. 2. Aufl. Freiburg, 1885.
NEDL AH 408.78.9 — Keary, C.F. The dawn of history. N.Y., 1885.
AH 4863.7 — Kittredge, G.L. Armpitting among the Greeks. Baltimore, 1885.
AH 4808.85 — Kubicki, K. Das Schaltjahr in der grossen Rechnungs-Urkunde. v.1-2. Ratibor, 1885.
AH 7278.85.6 — Lange, Ludwig. Histoire intérieure de Rome. Paris, 1885. 2v.
AH 7768.85 — Löffler, Eduard. Der Comes Theodosius. Inaug. Diss. Halle, 1885.
AH 8549.85 — Macbain, A. Celtic mythology and religion. Photoreproduction. Inverness, 1885.
NEDL AH 4818.76.2.9 — Mahaffy, J.P. Old Greek life. N.Y., 1885.
AH 7201.94 — Mantellini, G. Papiniano. 2. ed. Roma, 1885.
AH 7448.85 — Meltzer, Otto. De belli Punici secundi primordiis adversariorum capita quattuor. Dresden, 1885.
AH 8.85 — Meyer, P. Premières compilations françaises d'histoire ancienne. Paris, 1885.
AH 7148.85 — Michel, N.H. Du droit de cité romaine. Paris, 1885.
AH 7278.54.18 — Mommsen, T. History of Rome. N.Y., 1885. 4v.
AH 7278.54.10 — Mommsen, T. Römische Geschichte. v.5. Berlin, 1885.
AH 2147.6 — Monceaux, P. Communi asiae provinciae. Paris, 1885.
AH 4212.6 — Monceaux, P. Les proxénies grecques. Paris, 1885.
AH 7278.54.35 — Nöldeke, T. Mommsen's Darstellung der römischen Herrschaft. Leipzig, 1885.
AH 3132.3 — O'Connor, J.F.X. Cuneiform text...cylinder of Nebuchadnezzar. n.p., 1885.
AH 7148.85.2 — Pinvert, L. Droit romain du droit de cité. Paris, 1885.
AH 4148.85 — Poland, F. De legationibus Graecorum publicis. Lipsiae, 1885.
AH 288.85 — Ranke, L.F. von. Universal history. N.Y., 1885.
AH 878.85 — Rawlinson, G. Religions of the ancient world. N.Y., 1885.
Eg 298.85.5 — Rawlinson, George. Egypt and Babylon. N.Y., 1885.
Eg 1058.85 — Revillout, E. Un poeme satyrique. Paris, 1885.
Eg 1308.85F — Revillout, Eugène. Corpus papyrorum Egyptii. v.1-3. Parisiis, 1885-1902.
AH 4845.15 — Ribbeck, O.J.K. Agroikos. Leipzig, 1885.
AH 7468.85 — Ritter, Georg. Untersuchungen zu dem allobrogischen Krieg. Hof, 1885.
AH 2007.2 — Rohden, P. De Palaestina e Arabia. Berolini, 1885.
AH 3075.6 — Sayce, A.H. Assyria, its princes, priests and people. London, 1885.
AH 298.82.4 — Schaefer, Arnold. Abrisz der Quellenkunde der griechischen und römischen Geschichte. v.1, 4. Aufl; v.2, 2. Aufl. Leipzig, 1885-89. 2v.
AH 3159.11.5 — Schrader, E. The cuneiform inscriptions and the Old Testament. London, 1885-88. 2v.

1885 - cont.

AH 7138.85 — Scrutton, T.E. Influence of Roman law on the law of England. Cambridge, 1885.
Eg 278.36.10 — Sharpe, S. History of Egypt. 6. ed. London, 1885. 2v.
AH 7818.85 — Shumway, E.S. A day in ancient Rome. N.Y., 1885.
NEDL AH 278.85 — Smith, P. History of the world. N.Y., 1885. 3v.
NEDL AH 4278.57.24.7 — Smith, William. History of Greece. N.Y., 1885.
AH 5857.9 — Thamm, M. Republica ac Magistratibus Megarensium. Halis Saxonum, 1885.
AH 4828.85 — Timayenis, T.T. Greece in times of Homer. N.Y., 1885.
Eg 298.85 — Tomkins, H.G. Egyptological research. London, 1885?
AH 5138.9 — Torr, Cecil. Rhodes in ancient times. Photoreproduction. Cambridge, 1885.
AH 842.14 — Ussing, J.L. Erziehung und Jugendunterricht. Berlin, 1885.
AH 7168.85 — Waaser, M. Die Colonia Partiaria des römischen Rechts. Berlin, 1885.
AH 7088.85 — Wilcken, U. Observationes ad historiam Aegypti. Berolinii, 1885.
AH 7158.85 — Zedler, K.A.G.I. De memoriae damnatione quae dicitur. Darmstaadiae, 1885.
AH 7538.85 — Ziegler, A. Die Regierung des Kaisers Claudius I. Wien, 1885.
AH 3002.2.6 — Zimmern, Heinrich. Babylonische Busspsalmen. Leipzig, 1885.

1886

AH 7168.86.15 — Appleton, C. Essai de restitution de l'Edit publicien. Paris, 1886.
AH 7448.86 — Arnold, Thomas. The second Punic War. London, 1886.
AH 888.86 — Beloch, J. Bevölkerung der griechisch-römischen Welt. Photoreproduction. Leipzig, 1886.
AH 4518.86 — Belser. Altischen Strategen in Vfahrk. v.1-2. Ellivangen, 1886.
AH 3171.6 — Bezold, E. Kurzgefasster Uberblick...Babylonisch-Assyrische Literatur. Leipzig, 1886.
NEDL AH 4108.86 — Böckh, August. Staatshaushaltung der Athener. 3. Aufl. Berlin, 1886. 2v.
Eg 1038.86 — Book of the Dead. Das ägyptische Todtenbuch. Berlin, 1886. 3v.
AH 3008.86.5 — Boscawen, William. From under the dust of ages. London, 1886.
AH 7038.86 — Bouché-Leclercq, A. Manuel des institutions romaines. Paris, 1886.
AH 7205.13 — Brokate, Henricus. De Theophilinae quae fertur Iustiniani Institutionum Graecae paraphraseos compositione. Argentorati, 1886.
AH 7888.86 — Büchsenschütz, A.B. Bemerkungen über die römische Volkswirtschaft. Berlin, 1886.
AH 7201.67 — Buhl, H. Salvius Julianus. Heidelberg, 1886.
AH 7448.78.3 — Buzello, J. De oppugnatione sagunti quaestiones chronologicae. Inaug. Diss. Regimonti, 1886.
AH 8073.7 — Church, A.J. Story of Carthage. Photoreproduction. N.Y., 1886.
AH 4478.76A — Cox, George W. Greeks and Persians. 5. ed. London, 1886.
AH 7278.85.3.8 — Creighton, M. History of Rome. N.Y., 1886.
AH 6107.11 — Curteis, A.M. Rise of the Macedonian empire. 4. ed. London, 1886.
NEDL AH 4278.57.17A — Curtius, Ernest. History of Greece. N.Y., 1886. 5v.
AH 48.86 — Curtius, Ernst. Das Königthum bei den Alten. Berlin, 1886.
AH 7148.86 — Dorsch, E. De civitatis Romanae apud Graecos. Vratislaviae, 1886.
AH 148.66 — Egger, Emile. Traités publics. Paris, 1886.
AH 4558.98 — Emerson, A. Portraiture of Alexander the Great. Baltimore, 1886.
AH 7168.86.10 — Esmein, A. Mélanges de l'histoire du droit et de critique. Paris, 1886.
AH 3757.9 — Fressl, J. Skythen-Saken. München, 1886.
AH 8514.7 — Gaidoz, H. Etudes de mythologie gauloise. Paris, 1886.
AH 7201.33.15 — Gaius. Institutionum iuris civilis commentarii quattuor. 5th ed. Lipsiae, 1886.
AH 7114.13 — Gerathewohl, Bernhard. Die Reiter und die Rittercenturien. München, 1886.
AH 7168.86.3 — Grueber, E. Roman law of damage to property. Oxford, 1886.
AH 9666.9 — Haebler, Albin. Die Nord- und Westküste Hispaniens; ein Beitrag zur Geschichte der antiken Geographie. Leipzig, 1886.
AH 4908.86 — Häderli, R. Astynomen und Agoranomen. Leipzig, 1886.
AH 7138.86 — Harmann, O.E. Ordo judiciorum. Göttingen, 1886.
AH 4228.86 — Heikel, I.A. Boyleusis in Mordprocessen. Helsingfors, 1886.
AH 7478.86 — Heuzey, L.A. Les operations militaires de Jules César. Paris, 1886.
AH 4214.17 — Hofmann, G. De iurandi apud Athenienses formulis. Darmatadii, 1886.
AH 4278.86.5 — Holm, Adolf. Griechische Geschichte. Berlin, 1886. 4v.
AH 7108.86 — Humbert, G. Essai sur les finances. Paris, 1886. 2v.
NEDL AH 7408.78.3 — Ihne, W. Early Rome. 4th ed. London, 1886.
AH 4048.86 — Jevons, F.B. Development of Athenian democracy. London, 1886.
AH 7478.86.5 — Jullien, Émile. De L. Cornelio Balbo majore. Thesim. Lutetiae Parisiorum, 1886.
AH 258.86 — Jurien de la Graviére, J.P.E. Marine des anciens. Paris, 1886. 2v.
AH 4117.7 — Kastromenos, P. Die Demen von Attika. Diss. Leipzig, 1886.
Eg 608.86 — King, James. Cleopatra's needle. London, 1886.
AH 4038.86 — Koenig, C. Ta teah et oi en telei. Diss. Jenae, 1886.
AH 7058.86.2 — Liebenam, W. Beiträge zur Verwaltungsgeschichte. Jena, 1886.
AH 7058.86 — Liebenam, W. Die Laufbahn der Procuratoren. Jena, 1886.
NEDL AH 138.83.5 — Maine, Henry S. Dissertations on early law and custom. N.Y., 1886.
AH 4838.86 — Marquardt, H. Zum Pentathlon der Hellenen. Güstrow, 1886.
AH 4214.5 — Martin, Albert. Foedera publica. Lutetiae Parisiorum, 1886.
Eg 608.86.10F — Maspero, G. Mummy of Rameses II. Boston, 1886.
AH 1278.76.4 — Maspero, Gaston. Histoire ancienne des peuples de l'Orient. Paris, 1886.
AH 4278.86 — Ménard, L. Histoire des Grecs. Paris, 1886. 2v.
AH 8514.9 — Mérimée, E. De antiquis aquarum religionibus. Parisiis, 1886.

Chronological Listing

1886 - cont.

AH 3977.3 — Merrill, S. Galilee in the time of Christ. 2. ed. London, 1886.

AH 7478.54A — Mommsen, T. History of Rome. London, 1886. 2v.

AH 7168.86.5 — Muirhead, J. Historical introduction to the private law of Rome. Edinburgh, 1886.

AH 4238.86 — Myska, G.L. De antiquiorum historicorum Graecorum vocabulis. Inaug. Diss. Regimonti, 1886.

AH 4158.86 — Passow, W. De crimine Bouleuseōs. Leipzig, 1886.

Eg 845.7 — Paturet, G. La condition juridique. Paris, 1886.

AH 7618.86 — Pellisson, M. Rome sous Trajan. Paris, 1886.

AH 4278.76.5 — Pennell, R.F. Ancient Greece. Boston, 1886.

AH 7278.76.1 — Pennell, R.F. Rome. Boston, 1886.

AH 4808.35.6 — Peter, C.L. Zeittafeln der griechischen Geschichte. 6. Aufl. Halle, 1886.

AH 7214.5 — Peter, R. Quaestionum pontificatium specimen. Argentorati, 1886. 2 pam.

AH 7228.86 — Poiret, J. De Centumvoris et Causio Centumviralibus. Parisiis, 1886.

AH 8549.86.1A — Pufendorf, E. A dissertation upon the Druids. Edinburgh, 1886.

AH 8549.86 — Pufendorf, E. A dissertation upon the Druids. Edinburgh, 1886.

AH 3021.2A — Ragozin, Zénaide A. The story of the nations: story of Chaldea. N.Y., 1886.

Eg 278.81.6 — Rawlinson, George. History of ancient Egypt. N.Y., 1886. 2v.

Eg 138.86 — Revillout, Eugène. Les obligations en droit égyptien. Paris, 1886.

AH 7168.86 — Salkowski, C. Roman private law. London, 1886.

AH 4538.84.2 — Sankey, C. Spartan and Theban supremacies. N.Y., 1886.

AH 3094.6.5 — Sargon, king of Assyria. De inscriptione Sargonis. Berolini, 1886.

AH 4116.5 — Sauppe, H. De phratriis atticis. Gottingae, 1886.

AH 858.5 — Schmidt, R.O. De hymenaeo et talasio. Kiliae, 1886.

AH 7478.86.2 — Schneider, R. Ilerda. Beitrag zur römische Kriegsgeschichte. Berlin, 1886.

AH 4558.86F — Schuffert. Alexanders des Grossen indischer Feldzug. Colberg, 1886.

AH 5138.11 — Schumacher, C. Republica Rhodiorum commentatio. Heidelbergae, 1886.

NEDL AH 4278.57.24.9 — Smith, William. History of Greece. N.Y., 1886.

NEDL AH 4278.57.32 — Smith, William. Smaller history of Greece. N.Y., 1886.

AH 7808.86 — Soltau, Wilhelm. Prolegomena zu einer römische Chronologie. Berlin, 1886.

AH 818.86 — Spitzer, S. Sitte und Sitten der alten Völker. Budapest, 1886.

AH 3002.2.4 — Strassmaier, J.N. Alphabetisches Verzeichniss. Leipzig, 1886.

AH 3008.86A — Tiele, C.P. Babylonisch-assyrische Geschicte. Gotha, 1886. 2v.

AH 7038.86.5 — Tighe, A. The development of the Roman constitution. N.Y., 1886.

AH 7038.86.9 — Tighe, A. The development of the Roman constitution. N.Y., 1886.

AH 4161.7 — Timmermann, R. De nothorum Athenis condicione. Mederici, 1886.

AH 4448.86 — Toepffer, J. Quaestiones pisistrateae. Dorpati, 1886.

AH 8210.5 — Vine, Francis T. Caesar in Kent, the landing of Julius Caesar and his battles with the ancient Britons. Edinburgh, 1886.

NEDL AH 278.86 — Vuibert, A.J.B. An ancient history. Baltimore, 1886.

AH 408.86 — Welzhofer, H. Allgemeine Geschichte des Altertums. v.1-3. Gotha, 1886. 2v.

AH 3407.5.3 — Wright, W. Empire of Hittites. 2d ed. London, 1886.

AH 1298.86 — Wright, William B. Ancient cities from dawn to the daylight. Boston, 1886.

NEDL AH 278.69.15 — Yonge, Chrlotte M. A book of worthies. London, 1886.

1887

AH 8788.2 — Axt, Otto. Zur Topographie von Rhegion und Messana. Grimma, 1887.

AH 7148.87.5 — Bachofen, Das römische Pfandrecht. Baseel, 1887.

NEDL AH 7468.77.3 — Beesly, A.H. The Gracchi, Marius and Sulla. London, 1887.

AH 3657.15 — Benjamin, S.G.W. Story of Persia. N.Y., 1887.

AH 4938.87.2 — Berger, H. Geschichte der...Erdkunde der Griechen. Leipzig, 1887.

AH 5723.15 — Biedermann, Georg. Die Insel Kephallenia im Altertum. Inaug. Diss. München, 1887.

AH 4818.87.3A — Blümner, H. Leben und Sitten der Griechen. Leipzig, 1887. 3v.

AH 78.87 — Borgeaud, C. Plébiscite dans l'antiquité. Genève, 1887.

AH 7158.87 — Brunnenmeister, E.` Das Tödtungsverbrechen im alten Rechts. Leipzig, 1887.

AH 4200.11 — Busson, A. Lykurgos. Innsbruck, 1887.

NEDL AH 7598.76.9 — Capes, William W. The Roman Empire of the second century. N.Y., 1887.

AH 7498.87 — Capes, William W. Roman history: the early empire. London, 1887.

AH 8073.7.5 — Church, A.J. Carthage, or The empire of Africa. Photoreproduction. London, 1887.

AH 408.87 — Clodd, E. Childhood of the world. London, 1887.

AH 4458.76.7 — Cox, George W. The Athenian empire. 5. ed. London, 1887.

AH 4278.57.7A — Curtius, Ernest. Griechische Geschichte. 6. Aufl. Berlin, 1887. 3v.

AH 4478.87 — Delbrück, H. Die Perserkriege. Berlin, 1887.

AH 3002.2.7 — Delitzsch, Friedrich. Assyrisches Wörterbuch. Leipzig, 1887-

AH 9308.5 — Del Rosso, G. Storia politica civile...di Trentani. Campobasso, 1887.

AH 7214.9 — Demelius, G. Schiedseid und Beweiseid. Leipzig, 1887.

AH 4298.87 — Duncker, Max. Abhandlungen aus der griechische Geschichte. Leipzig, 1887.

NEDL AH 4278.87.5A — Duruy, J.V. Histoire des Grecs. Paris, 1887. 3v.

AH 4498.87 — Fischer, P. De Atheniensium sociis. Bonnae, 1887.

AH 4498.87.3 — Frey, Karl. Leben des Perikles. Bern, 1887.

AH 938.87.2 — Friedrich, R. Begriffsbestimmung des Orbis terearum. Leipzig, 1887.

AH 4818.87.2 — Gache, F. Petit manuel d'archéologie grecque. Paris, 1887.

AH 7650.70 — Gibbon, Edward. The history of the decline and fall of the Roman Empire. London, 1887. 8v.

AH 7203.83 — Gradenwitz, O. Interpolationen in den Pandekten. Berlin, 1887.

AH 7088.87 — Guiraud, Paul. Les assemblées provinciales. Paris, 1887.

AH 4162.17 — Hafter, Eugen. Die Erbtochter. Leipzig, 1887.

1887 - cont.

AH 7508.87 — Hagen, M. von. Quaestiones criticae de belle mutinensi. Marburgi Cattorum, 1887.

AH 4278.85.7 — Harrison, J.A. The story of Greece. N.Y., 1887.

AH 7148.87 — Hartmann, L.M. De exilio apud Romanos. Berolini, 1887.

AH 4728.66.5 — Hertzberg, G.F. Histoire de la Grèce. Paris, 1887. 2v.

AH 4278.87 — Jäger, O.E.F. Geschichte der Griechen. Gütersloh, 1887.

AH 7408.87 — Jordan, Henri. Die Könige im alten Italien. Berlin, 1887.

AH 408.78.15 — Keary, C.F. The dawn of history. N.Y., 1887.

AH 854.11 — Keller, Otto. Thiere des...Altertums. Innsbruck, 1887.

AH 7188.87 — Krüger, H. Geschichte des capitis deminutio. Breslau, 1887.

AH 7258.87 — La Berge, Camille de. Étude sur l'organisation des flottes romaines. Vienne, 1887.

AH 8955.2 — Lackner, G. De incursionibus a Gallis in Italiani factis. Regimonti, 1887.

AH 3966.6.2 — Lagarde, Pauli. Onomastica sacra. Gottingae, 1887.

AH 7178.87 — Legnazzi, E.N. Del catasto romano. Verona, 1887.

AH 7188.87.2 — Lemonnier, H. Étude historique sur la condition des esclaves. Paris, 1887.

AH 3159.17 — Lyon, D.G. Assyriology and the Old Testament. Boston, 1887.

AH 4558.87A — Mahaffy, J.P. Alexander's empire. London, 1887.

AH 4818.87.10A — Mahaffy, J.P. Greek life and thought. London, 1887.

AH 4558.87.3 — Mahaffy, J.P. Story of Alexander's empire. N.Y., 1887.

AH 7818.64.11 — Marquardt, Joachim. Handbuch der römischen Alterthümer. 3. Aufl. Leipzig, 1887. 3v.

NEDL AH 7818.64.13 — Marquardt, Joachim. Manual des antiquités romaines. v.1-19. Paris, 1887-1907. 20v.

AH 7918.87 — Maué, H.C. Der Praefectus Fabrum. Halle, 1887.

AH 7203.81 — Meinhold, K. Animadversiones in Justiniani Institutiones. Diedenhofen, 1887.

AH 7108.87 — Mendes, José Amando. Droit romain des douanes chez les Romains. v.1-2. Libourne, 1887.

AH 7478.77.3A — Merivale, Charles. Roman triumvirates. 5. ed. London, 1887.

AH 7038.87 — Misporelet, J.B. Études d'institutions romaines. Paris, 1887.

NEDL AH 7278.54.18.9 — Mommsen, T. History of Rome. Provinces of the Roman Empire from Caesar to Diocletian. N.Y., 1887. 2v.

AH 7307.34.13 — Montesquieu, Charles de. Considérations sur les causes de la grandeur des Romains. Paris, 1887.

AH 3658.5 — Nöldeke, T. Aufsätze zur Persischen Geschichte. Leipzig, 1887.

AH 5007.5 — Oberhummer, E. Akarnanien. München, 1887.

AH 7448.18.8 — Perrin, J.B. Marche d'Annibal. Paris, 1887.

AH 3004.5 — Pinches, Theodore G. The Babylonian chronicle. London, 1887.

AH 7408.21 — Pöhlmann, Robert. Die Anfange Roms. Erlangen, 1887.

AH 3154.3 — Pognon, H. Les inscriptions babyloniennes du Wade Brissa. Paris, 1887.

AH 7138.87.7 — Poiret, J. L'eloquence judiciaire. Paris, 1887.

AH 3075.10 — Ragozin, Z.A. The story of the nations: story of Assyria. N.Y., 1887.

AH 3966.27 — Rawlinson, George. Biblical topography. London, 1887.

Eg 278.87 — Rawlinson, George. The story of ancient Egypt. N.Y., 1887.

AH 838.87.3 — Richter, W. Die Spiele der Griechen und Römer. Leipzig, 1887.

Eg 278.87.5 — Robinson, Charles S. The pharaohs of the bondage and the Exodus. N.Y., 1887.

AH 7203.79.10 — Roby, H.J. Introduzione allo studio del Digesto giustinianeo. Firenze, 1887.

AH 4278.87.7 — Rose, D. A popular history of Greece. London, 1887.

AH 3155.5 — Sayce, A.H. Lecture on...religion of...Babylonians. London, 1887.

AH 938.87 — Schmidt, C.P. Zur Geschichte der geographischen Litteratur bei Griechen und Römer. Breslau, 1887.

AH 9610.11 — Schubert, R.J.W. Geschichte des Agathokles. Breslau, 1887.

AH 7238.87 — Schultze, E. De legione Romanorum XIII Genima. Kiliae, 1887.

NEDL AH 7448.81.2A — Smith, R.B. Rome and Carthage. 5. ed. London, 1887.

AH 3073.4 — Smith, S.A. Miscellaneous Assyrian texts on the British Museum. Leipzig, 1887.

AH 8907.2 — Spadoni, O.L. The Etruscans. Rome, 1887.

AH 328.83.2 — Spiegel, F. Arische Periode. Leipzig, 1887.

AH 7478.87.5 — Stocchi, Giuseppe. Due studî di storia romana. Firenze, 1887.

AH 7478.87 — Stoffel. Histoire de Jules César. Atlas. Paris, 1887. 3v.

AH 7468.87 — Strehl, Willy. M. Livius Drusus. Marburg, 1887.

AH 7148.87.7 — Taddei, A. Roma e isuoi municipi. Firenze, 1887.

AH 7808.87 — Thouret, Georg. Die Chronologie von 218/217 v. Chr. Berlin, 1887.

AH 2507.7 — Treuber, O. Geschichte der Lykier. Stuttgart, 1887.

Eg 1128.87 — Viery, P. Études sur le papyrus Prisse. Paris, 1887.

AH 8210.5.2 — Vine, Francis T. Caesar in Kent, an account of the landing of Julius Caesar and his battles with the ancient Britons. 2. ed. London, 1887.

AH 7058.87 — Wehrmann, P. Programm des Konig-Wilhelms-Gymnasiums. Stettin, 1887.

AH 5407.5 — Wilisch, E. Beiträge zur...Geschichte des...Korinth. Zittau, 1887.

AH 8886.5 — Willems, Pierre. Les élections municipales à Pompéi. Paris, 1887.

AH 828.87 — Zoeller, Max. Privataltertümer. Breslau, 1887.

1888

AH 4278.88 — Abbott, Evelyn. History of Greece. v.2, photoreproduction. London, 1888-1900. 3v.

AH 3966.7 — Armstrong, G. Names and places in the Old and New Testament. London, 1888.

AH 838.87 — Augé de Lassus, Lucien. Spectacles antiques. Paris, 1888.

AH 4158.88 — Barth, B. De Graecorum Asylis. Argentorati, 1888.

AH 8513.8 — Bonnemère, L. Les jeux et le théâtre chez les Gaulois en Provence. Paris, 1888.

AH 9777.23A — Bradley, Henry. Story of the Goths. N.Y., 1888.

AH 5303.9 — Canet, V. Institutions d'Athènes. Lille, 1888. 2v.

AH 5132.7 — Cichorius, Conrad. Rom und Mytilene. Leipzig, 1888.

AH 7203.85 — Corpus juris civilis. Institutiones. Institutes of Justinian. 8th ed. London, 1888.

AH 4458.76.9 — Cox, George W. Athenian empire. 6. ed. London, 1888.

NEDL AH 7278.85.2.5 — Creighton, M. History of Rome. London, 1888.

AH 7278.85.2 — Creighton, M. History of Rome. N.Y., 1888.

Chronological Listing

1888 - cont.

AH 938.47 — Curtius, E. Beiträge zur Terminologie...der alten Geographie. Berlin, 1888.

AH 9421.5 — De-Vit, Vincenzo. Adria e le sue antiche epigrafi. v.1-2. Firenze, 1888.

AH 8926.2 — Deecke, W. Die Falisker, eine geschichtlich-sprachliche Untersuchung. Strassburg, 1888.

AH 3867.5F — Dieulafoy, J.A. A Suse journal des fouilles, 1884-86. Paris, 1888.

AH 1408.88 — Duruy, J.V. Histoire ancienne des peuples de l'Orient. Paris, 1888.

AH 4278.56.7 — Duruy, V. Histoire de la Grèce ancienne. Paris, 1888.

AH 3096.7 — Esarhaddon, king of Assyria. Cylinder A of the Esarhaddon inscriptions. New Haven, 1888.

AH 238.88 — Fickelscherer, M. Kriegswesen der Alten. Leipzig, 1888.

AH 7818.65.9 — Friedlaender, Ludwig. Darstellungen aus der Sittengeschichte Roms. 6. Aufl. Leipzig, 1888. 3v.

AH 5753.15 — Gachon, Paul. De ephoris Spartanis. Diss. Monspelii, 1888.

AH 7138.88 — Garsonnet, E. Textes de droit romain. Paris, 1888.

AH 3963.19 — Geikie, J.C. The Holy Land and the Bible. N.Y., 1888. 2v.

AH 2357.4 — Gelder, H. van. Galatarum res in Graecia et Asia gestae. Inaug. Diss. Amstelaedami, 1888.

NEDL AH 7278.88 — Gilman, A. The story of Rome. N.Y., 1888.

AH 4238.88 — Gülde, O. Die Kriegsverfassung der ersten attischen Bundes. Neukaldensleben, 1888.

AH 938.88 — Günther, S. Geschichte der antike Naturwissenschaft. Nördlingen, 1888.

AH 2957.11 — Haubold, P. De rebus Iliensium. Lipsiae, 1888.

AH 3060.3.5 — Heuzey, L. Un palais Chaldéen. Paris, 1888.

AH 7818.88A — Inge, W.R. Society in Rome under the Caesars. N.Y., 1888.

AH 7138.88.3 — Jörs, Paul. Römische Rechtswissenschaft. Berlin, 1888.

AH 9777.19.3 — Jordanes. Getarum sive Gothorum. 3. ed. Reutlingen, 1888.

AH 3177.7 — Kellner, M.L. The deluge in the Izdubar epic. N.Y., 1888.

AH 7448.88 — Koehn, M. De Pugna ad Zamam Commissa. Halis Saxonum, 1888.

AH 7148.88 — Kromayer, J. Die rechtliche Begründung. Marburg, 1888.

AH 7138.88.5 — Krüger, Paul. Geschichte der Quellen...römischen Rechts. Leipzig, 1888.

AH 7468.88A — Lacour-Gayet, G. De P. Clodis Pulchris tribuno plebis. Thèse. Lutetiae Parisiorum, 1888.

AH 7058.88 — Liebenam, W. Forschungen zur Verwaltungsgeschichte. Leipzig, 1888.

NEDL AH 4818.76.3 — Mahaffy, J.P. Old Greek life. N.Y., 1888.

AH 138.75.3 — Maine, Henry S. Lectures on the early history of institutions. N.Y., 1888.

AH 4204.17 — Makrygiannė, E.S. Meletė peri tēs politeias tou Solonos. Ermoupolei, Syrou, 1888.

Eg 989.5 — Mallet, D. Le culte de Neit à Saïs. Paris, 1888.

AH 4855.5 — Manns, O. Jagd bei den Griechen. Cassel, 1888. 3 pam.

AH 7108.88 — Marsault, A. Droit romain des magistrats monétaires. Paris, 1888.

Eg 1038.88F — Marucchi, Orazio. Il grande papiro egizio della Biblioteca Vaticana. Roma, 1888.

AH 188.88 — Maschke, R. Der Freiheitsprozess im klassischen Altertum. Berlin, 1888.

AH 7168.88 — Matthiass, B. Entwicklung des römischen Schiedgerichts. Rostock, 1888.

AH 3013.888 — Menant, J. Les fausses antiquités de l'Assyrie et de la Chaldée. Paris, 1888.

AH 3143.4 — Menant, J. Ninive et Babylone. Paris, 1888.

AH 7138.81.8 — Merkel, J. Abhandlungen aus dem Gebiete des römischen Rechts. v.1-3. Halle, 1888. 2v.

AH 4838.88 — Mie, F. Quaestiones Agonisticae. Rostochii, 1888.

AH 3663.5 — Modi, J.J. Wine among the ancient Persians. Bombay, 1888.

AH 7163.19 — Morael, G.L.M. Du divorce. Paris, 1888.

AH 8542.2 — Morel, Charles. Genève et la colonie de Vienne. Genève, 1888.

Eg 1128.87.8 — "The oldest book in the world"...Papyrus Prisse. n.p., 1888.

AH 4298.88 — Paganelès. Athēnaikai nyktes. Athēnai, 1888.

AH 8162.5 — Pallu de Lessert, A.C. Les fastes de la Numidie sous la domination romaine. Constantine, 1888.

AH 7228.88 — Pfersche, E. Interdicte des römischen Civilprocesses. Graz, 1888.

AH 3507.7 — Ragozin, Z.A. Story of Media, Babylon and Persia. N.Y., 1888.

AH 3407.6 — Sayce, A.H. The Hittites. London, 1888.

AH 3155.5.2 — Sayce, A.H. Lectures on the origin and growth of religion as illustrated by the religion of the ancient Babylonians. 2d ed. London, 1888.

AH 4116.7 — Schaefer, D. Die attischen Phratrien. Naumburg, 1888.

AH 7861.8 — Schiess, T. Die römischen Collegia Funeraticia. München, 1888.

AH 298.88.3 — Schmidt, A. Abhandlungen zur alten Geschichte. Leipzig, 1888.

AH 4808.88 — Schmidt, A. Handbuch der griechischen Chronologie. Jena, 1888.

AH 7138.83.5.3 — Sohm, R. Institutionen des römischen Rechts. 3e Aufl. Leipzig, 1888.

AH 7808.88 — Soltau, Wilhelm. Die römischen Amstjahre auf ihren natürlichen Zeitwerth reducirt. Freiburg, 1888.

AH 4148.88 — Sonne, E. De arbitris externis. Gottingae, 1888.

AH 7108.88.5 — Thibault, Fabien. Les douanes chez les romains. Paris, 1888.

AH 2757.5 — Thraemer, E. Pergamos. Leipzig, 1888.

AH 938.88.5 — Tozer, Henry F. Nociones de geografía antigua. N.Y., 1888.

AH 7158.88 — Weihmayr, W. Über Lex Plantia de VI und Lex Lutatia. Augsburg, 1888.

AH 7808.88.5 — Werner, C. De feriis Latinis. Coloniae, 1888.

Eg 278.84.2 — Wiedemann, A. Ägyptische Geschichte. Supplement. Gotha, 1888.

AH 7148.70.6 — Willems, P. Le droit public romain. 6e éd. Louvain, 1888.

AH 7698.88 — Wirth, A. Quaestiones severianae. Lipsiae, 1888.

AH 7228.88.5 — Wlassak, M. Römische Processgesetze. Leipzig, 1888.

NEDL AH 298.88 — Wood, C.W. Topics in ancient history. Boston, 1888.

1889

AH 1878.89 — Ablaing van Giessenburg, R.C. Évolution des idées religieuses dans la Mésopotamie et dans l'Égypte. Amsterdam, 1889.

AH 7148.89 — Appleton, C. Histoire de la propriété prétorien. Paris, 1889. 2v.

1889 - cont.

AH 7228.89 — Bechmann, A. Studie...Legis actio sacramenti in rem. München, 1889.

AH 854.7 — Blatchford, C.H. Butterfly in ancient literature and art. Cambridge, 1889.

AH 3000.3 — British Museum. Catalog of cuneiform tablets in the Kouyunjik collection. London, 1889-99. 5v.

AH 7158.89 — Bruyant, E. Juridictions criminelles à Rome. Paris, 1889.

AH 7168.89 — Burckhardt, Karl. Zur Geschichte der Socatio Conductio. Basel, 1889.

AH 930.10 — Butler, George. The public school's atlas of ancient geography. London, 1889.

AH 4408.89F — Corcia, N. Frammento della storia graecia. Napoli, 1889.

AH 7203.78 — Corpus juris civilis. Institutiones. The institutes of Justinian. 2. ed. Oxford, 1889.

AH 7203.87 — Corpus juris civilis. Institutiones. Institutes of Moyle. 2. ed. Oxford, 1889.

AH 4458.76.10 — Cox, George W. Athenian empire. N.Y., 1889.

AH 4278.56.13 — Duruy, V. Histoire grecque. Paris, 1889.

AH 7278.67.17 — Duruy, V. Histoire romaine. Paris, 1889.

AH 4838.89.5 — Fedde, F. Über den Fünfkampf der Hellenen. Leipzig, 1889.

AH 7768.89 — Gimazane, Joannes. De secundo sallustio promoto. Diss. Tolosae, 1889.

AH 4842.5 — Girard, P. L'éducation athénienne. Paris, 1889.

AH 28.89 — Gutschmid, A. von. Kleine Schriften. Leipzig, 1889. 5v.

AH 908.89 — Helbig, W. Sopra le relazioni commericali. Roma, 1889.

AH 9421.10.5 — Herfurth, Karl. De Aquileiae commercio. Inaug. Diss. Halis Saxonum, 1889.

AH 4818.41.9A — Hermann, K.F. Lehrbuch der griechischen Antiquitäten. v.1-4. 6. Aufl. Freiburg, 1889. 7v.

AH 7798.89 — Hodgkin, T. Dynasty of Theodosius. Oxford, 1889.

AH 3980.12.3 — Howe, Fisher. The true site of Calvary. N.Y., 1889.

AH 938.89.5 — Hughes, Lugi. Manuali di geografia antica ad uso delle scuole secondarie. v.1-3. Torino, 1889-90.

AH 7162.24 — Jarriand, E. Histoire de la novelle 118. Paris, 1889.

AH 7298.64.5 — Kingsley, Charles. The Roman and the Teuton. London, 1889.

AH 7115.4 — Kubitschek, W. Imperium Romanum tributim discriptum. Pragae, 1889.

AH 9086.5 — La Blanchère, R. Un chapitre d'histoire pontine. Paris, 1889.

AH 7840.2 — Lacombe, P. La famille dans la société romaine. Paris, 1889.

AH 7188.89 — Lehmann, Eduard. De publica romanorum servitute quaestiones. Diss inaug. Lipsiae, 1889.

AH 148.89 — Leist, B.W. Alt-arisches jus Gentium. Jena, 1889.

AH 7206.11 — Leonis. Ecloga. Athenis, 1889.

AH 4938.89 — Lolling, H.G. Geographie und Geschichte des griechisches Altertums. Athen? 1889.

NEDL AH 4818.76.5 — Mahaffy, J.P. Antiguedades clasicas I. Antiguedades griegas. N.Y., 1889.

NEDL AH 7478.77.5 — Merivale, Charles. Roman triumvirates. N.Y., 1889.

AH 7138.89.15 — Mispoulet, J.B. Manuel des textes de droit romain. Paris, 1889.

AH 7418.89 — Mommsen, T. The history of the Roman republic. N.Y., 1889.

AH 4498.89.5 — Nedwed, E. Perikles. Iglau, 1889.

AH 4498.89 — Nöthe, Heinrich. Delische Bund. Magdeburg, 1889.

AH 808.87.5 — Paganelli, A. Riposta alla osservazione...della civiltà cattolica sulla chronologia rivendicata. Prato, 1889.

AH 3163.8 — Peisir, Felix E. Keilschriftliche Actenstücke aus babylonischen Städten. Berlin, 1889.

AH 3707.11.3A — Rawlinson, G. History of Phoenicia. London, 1889.

AH 3707.11A — Rawlinson, G. Story of Phoenicia. N.Y., 1889.

Eg 278.87.3 — Rawlinson, George. The story of ancient Egypt. N.Y., 1889.

AH 3002.5.5A — Records of the past. London, 1889. 6v.

AH 9508.5 — Riese, A. Forschungen zur Geschichte der Rheinlande in der Römerzeit. Frankfurt am Main, 1889.

AH 4818.89 — Robiou, F. Les institutions de la Grèce antique. Paris, 1889.

AH 7478.89 — Salvatierra. Lo mundo de los romanos. Ronda, 1889.

AH 3089.3 — Schell, P. Inscription Assyrienne...de Sămšî-Ramman IV. Paris, 1889.

AH 7138.89 — Schulin, F. Lehrbuch des römischen Rechts. Stuttgart, 1889.

AH 7808.89.15 — Soltau, Wilhelm. Römische Chronologie. Freiburg, 1889.

Eg 878.89 — Strauss, V. von. Der altägyptische Götterglaube. Heidelberg, 1889. 2v.

AH 7238.89 — Stürenburg, H. Zu den Schlachtfeldern am trasionenischen See. Leipzig, 1889.

AH 7038.86.3 — Tighe, A. Development of Roman constitution. N.Y., 1889.

AH 4114.11 — Toepffer, J. Attische Genealogie. Berlin, 1889.

NEDL AH 818.89 — Verschoyle, J.S. History of ancient civilization. N.Y., 1889.

AH 4518.89 — Whibley, L. Political parties in Athens. 2. ed. Cambridge, 1889.

AH 1298.89 — Winckler, H. Untersuchungen zur altorientalischen Geschichte. Leipzig, 1889.

NEDL AH 3094.6F — Winckler, Hugo. Die Keilschrifttexte Sargons. Leipzig, 1889.

189-

AH 7278.85.3.7A — Creighton, M. History of Rome. N.Y., 189-?

NEDL AH 7478.81.7A — Froude, J.A. Caesar; a sketch. N.Y., 189-?

Eg 1108.90 — Papyrus d'Orbiney. The tale of the two brothers. [Egyptian fairy-tale]. n.p., 189-?

1890

AH 9610.13 — Allcroft, A.H. History of Sicily 491-289 B.C. London, 1890.

NEDL AH 278.90 — Allen, W. Ancient history for colleges and high schools. Boston, 1890. 2v.

NEDL AH 7278.90.2 — Allen, W.T. Ancient history for colleges and high schools. Boston, 1890-91. 2v.

AH 8857.3 — Beloch, Julius. Campanien. Geschichte und Topogrpahie des antiken Neapel und seiner Umgebung. Breslau, 1890.

AH 958.90 — Bencker, Max. Der Anteil der Periegese an den Kuntschrift der Alten. München, 1890.

AH 7828.90F — Brunet, P. Mémoires d'un romain vie. Tours, 1890.

AH 5853.7 — Cauer, F. Parteien und Politiker. Stuttgart, 1890.

AH 7203.91 — Corpus juris civilis. Institutiones. Justiniani Institutionum libri quattuor. 2. ed. Oxford, 1890.

AH 7278.85.3.10 — Creighton, M. History of Rome. N.Y., 1890.

Chronological Listing

1890 - cont.

AH 4845.17F — Curtius, E. Conservative Zug. Berlin, 1890.

AH 7648.90 — Dimmock, Thomas. Marcus Aurelius; an address...1890. St. Louis, 1890.

Eg 878.90.5 — Drexler, W. Der Cultus der Aegyptischen Gottheiten. Leipzig, 1890.

AH 5335.5 — Dunbach, F. Cropo et Amphiarae Sacro. Parisiis, 1890.

NEDL AH 4278.56.15 — Duruy, V. Historia de los Griegos. Barcelona, 1890. 2v.

AH 4278.56.35F — Duruy, V. History of Greece. v.1-4. Boston, 1890. 8v.

AH 5390.7 — Fabricius, E. Theben. Freiburg, 1890.

AH 7518.90 — Ferber, Curtius. Utrum metuerit Tiberius Germanicum necne quaeritur. Inaug. Diss. Hamburgi, 1890.

AH 7138.90 — Flach, J. Études critiques sur histoire du droit romain. Paris, 1890.

AH 5390.9 — Funk, Emil. De Thebanorum. Berlin, 1890.

NEDL AH 4278.78.7 — Fyffe, C.A. History of Greece. N.Y., 1890.

AH 7201.73 — Gaius. Elements of Roman law. Oxford, 1890.

AH 2007.3 — Glaser, E. Skizze der Geschichte und Geographie Arabiens. Berlin, 1890.

AH 4842.33 — Haebeilin, C. Beiträge zur Kenntniss des Bibliographies und Buchwesens. Leipzig, 1890.

AH 7208.3 — Hallays, André. Les comices à Rome. Paris, 1890.

AH 4978.90 — Haussoullier, Bernard. Grèce. Collection des guides - Joanne. Paris, 1890. 2v.

AH 4408.90 — Hesselmeyer, E. Die Pelasgerfrage und ihre Lösbarkeit. Tübingen, 1890.

Eg 708.90.5 — Houssaye, Henry. Cleopatra. N.Y., 1890.

Htn Eg 708.90.7* — Houssaye, Henry. Cleopatra. N.Y., 1890.

AH 7298.90 — Hübner, Emil. Römische Herrschaft in Westeuropa. Berlin, 1890.

AH 3155.4 — Jensen, P. Die Kosmologie der Babylonier. Strassburg, 1890.

AH 7808.90 — Kaestner, O. De aeris quae ab imperio Caesaris. Lipsiae, 1890.

NEDL AH 7298.64.2 — Kingsley, Charles. The Roman and the Teuton. London, 1890.

AH 3150.5 — Kohler, J. Aus dem babylonischen Rechtsleben. Leipzig, 1890.

Eg 878.90 — Lefébure, E. Rites égyptiens. Paris, 1890.

AH 4108.90 — Lehner, H. Athenischen Schatzverzeichnisse. Strassburg, 1890.

AH 4298.90 — Lévi, Sylvain. Quid de Graecis veterum indorum. Paris, 1890.

AH 7918.90 — Liebenam, W. Zur Geschichte...des römischen Vereinswesens. Leipzig, 1890.

AH 4728.90 — Mahaffy, J.P. Greek world under Roman sway. London, 1890.

AH 3075.12 — Maspero, Gaston. Histoire ancienne, Égypte, Assyrie; lectures historiques. Paris, 1890.

AH 818.90.5 — Merrians, A.C. Telegraphing among the ancients. Cambridge, 1890.

AH 7201.69 — Mommsen, T. Fragmenta Vaticana III. Berolini, 1890.

AH 4498.90 — Mosler, I. Chronologie der Pentekontaëtie. Berlin, 1890.

AH 4498.90.5 — Nöthe, Heinrich. Bundesrat, Bundessteuer und Kriegsdienst der delischen Bündner. Magdeburg, 1890.

NEDL AH 4278.90.5 — Oman, C.W.C. History of Greece. Rivingtons, 1890.

AH 4108.90.5 — Panske, Petrus Paulus. De magistratibus atticis qui saeculo A. Chr. n. quarto pecunias publicas curabant. pt.1. Inaug. Diss. Lipsiae, 1890.

AH 3150.4 — Peiser, F.E. Jurisprudentiae Babylonicae quae supersunt. Cöthen, 1890.

AH 7178.82.3 — Pelham, Henry. Imperial domains and the Colonate. London, 1890.

AH 7278.76.2 — Pennell, R.F. Ancient Rome. Boston, 1890.

AH 4838.90 — Pollack, E. Hippodromica. Diss. Lipsiae, 1890.

AH 3021.2.5 — Ragozin, Zénaide A. The story of Chaldea. 2. ed. N.Y., 1890.

AH 818.90 — Reich, Emil. Graeco-Roman institutions. London, 1890.

X Cg AH 7468.29.3 — Reinach, T. Mithradates Eupator. Paris, 1890.

AH 7116.5 — Schmidt, F. De mutatis centuriis servianis. Gissae, 1890.

AH 7718.90 — Schneider, C. Beiträge zur Geschichte Caracallas. Marburg, 1890.

AH 3088.10 — Shalmaneser II, king of Assyria. Les inscriptions de Salmanasar II, roi d'Assyrie, 860-824. Paris, 1890.

NEDL AH 298.90 — Sheldon, Mary D. Studies in Greek and Roman history. Boston, 1890.

AH 7438.90 — Sieke, Carl. Appius Claudius Caesar Censor. Marburg, 1890.

AH 867.5 — Sittl, C. Die Gebärden der Griechen und Römer. Leipzig, 1890.

AH 4078.90 — Swoboda, H. Griechischen Volksbeschlüsse. Leipzig, 1890.

AH 7138.90.5 — Tardif, A. Histoire des sources du droit français. Paris, 1890.

AH 7008.90 — Volkmar, A. De annalibus romanis quaestiones. Marburgi, 1890.

AH 7188.90 — Vollmann, Franz. Über das Verhaltnis der späteren Stoa zur Sklaverei im römischen Reiche. Stadtamhof, 1890.

AH 3002.2.9 — Weissbach, F.H. Die Achämenideninschriften zweiter Art. Leipzig, 1890.

Eg 278.90A — Wendel, F.C.H. History of Egypt. N.Y., 1890.

AH 4810.5 — Wheeler, B.I. Life of the ancient Greeks. Ithaca, 1890.

1891

AH 4498.91 — Abbott, E. Pericles and golden age of Athens. N.Y., 1891.

AH 4558.91 — Adler, Maximilian. De Alexandri Magni epistularum commercio. Inaug. Diss. Lipsiae, 1891.

AH 4408.91.5 — Allcroft, A.H. Early Grecian history. London, 1891.

NEDL AH 278.91 — Allen, W. Ancient history for colleges and high schools. Boston, 1891.

AH 7204.2 — Appleton, Charles. Les sources des Institutes de Justinien. Paris, 1891.

NEDL AH 7828.38.18 — Becker, W.A. Gallus or Roman scenes. 10th ed. London, 1891.

NEDL AH 7468.77.4 — Beesly, A.H. The Gracchi, Marius and Sulla. N.Y., 1891.

AH 4408.91 — Beloch, J. Storia greca. Roma, 1891.

AH 298.91 — Beloch, J. Studi di storia antica. v.1-7. Roma, 1891. 3v.

Htn AH 9692.2* — Blade, J.F. Géographie historique de la Vasconie espagnole. Auch, 1891.

AH 7448.91.10F — Bossi, Gaetano. La guerra d'Annibale in Italia da Canne al Metauro. Roma, 1891.

Eg 818.91 — Brugsch, H. Die Ägyptologie. Leipzig, 1891.

Eg 278.59.9 — Brugsch, H. Egypt under the pharaohs. London, 1891.

Eg 878.85.3 — Brugsch, H. Religion und Mythologie der alten Agypter. Leipzig, 1891.

1891 - cont.

AH 408.91 — Büchner, L. Das goldene Zeitalter. Berlin, 1891.

AH 7428.91 — Burger, Combertus P. Sechzig Jahre aus der älteren Geschichte Roms. Amsterdam, 1891.

AH 3407.7 — Campbell, J. Hittites. London, 1891. 2v.

AH 7598.76.12 — Capes, William W. The Roman Empire of the second century. N.Y., 1891.

AH 7138.91 — Cuq, E. Institutions juridiques. Paris, 1891. 2v.

AH 5307.22 — Curtius, Ernst. Die Stadtgeschichte von Athen. Berlin, 1891.

AH 7448.91A — Dodge, T.A. Hannibal - history of the art of war. Boston, 1891.

AH 6116.7 — Döll, M. Studien zur Geographie des alten Makedoniens. Stadtamhof, 1891.

AH 7848.3 — Fisch, R. Die Walker oder Leben und Treiben. Berlin, 1891.

AH 4838.91 — Förster, H. Sieger in den olympischen Spielen. Zwickau, 1891.

AH 7479.04.5 — Fowler, W.W. Julius Caesar and the foundation of the Roman imperial system. N.Y., 1891.

AH 9607.13A — Freeman, E.A. History of Sicily from earliest times. Oxford, 1891. 4v.

AH 8533.5 — Fröhner, W. Scolies latines relatives à l'histoire...de Marseille. Paris, 1891.

AH 7508.91 — Gardthausen, V. Augustus und seine Zeit. Leipzig, 1891. 2v.

AH 4842.6 — Girard, P. L'éducation athénienne. 2. éd. Paris, 1891.

AH 7808.91 — Goyau, G. Chronologie de l'Empire romain. Paris, 1891.

AH 4861.6 — Graves, F.R. The burial customs of the ancient Greeks. Thesis. Brooklyn, 1891.

AH 4038.91 — Hammond, B.E. Greek constitutions. Cambridge, 1891.

NEDL AH 4038.91.3 — Headlam-Morley, J.W. Election by lot at Athens. Cambridge, 1891.

AH 3013.4F — Heuzey, Leon A. Les origines orientales de l'art. Pt.1-4. Paris, 1891-1915.

AH 7198.66.8 — Ihering, R. Geist des römischen Rechts. Leipzig, 1891. 3v.

AH 3179.5 — Jastrow, M. A fragment of Babylonian "Dibbarra" epic. Philadelphia, 1891.

AH 3178.6 — Jeremias, A. Izdubar-Nimrod...Heldensage. Leipzig, 1891.

AH 3740.7 — Jeremias, F. Tyrus. Leipzig, 1891.

AH 4558.83.2 — Jurien, J.P.E. Le drame macédonien. 2. éd. Paris, 1891.

AH 7148.91 — Kappeyne van de Coppello, Johann. Drei Abhandlungen zum römischen Staats- und Privatrecht. Berlin, 1891.

AH 3013.6.4A — Kaulen, Franz. Assyrien und Babylonien. 4. Aufl. Freiburg, 1891.

AH 8307.6 — Király, Pál. Ulpia Trajana Augusta colonia Dacica. Budapest, 1891.

AH 7148.91.5 — Kornemann, E. De civibus Romanes in provinciis. Berolini, 1891.

AH 9610.15 — Krug, Otto. Quellenuntersuchung zur Geschichte des jüngeren Dionys. Kattowitz, 1891.

AH 3658.7 — Krumbholz, Paul. De discriptione regni achaemenidarum. Eisnach, 1891.

AH 3910.6 — Kuhn, Adolf. Beiträge zur Geschichte der Seleukiden. Altkirch, 1891.

AH 3407.9 — Lantsheere, L. De la race...langue des Hittites. Bruxelles, 1891.

AH 7118.5 — Lohse, G. Die Häupter des patrizischen Claudiergeschlechts. Chemnitz, 1891.

AH 7818.91 — Lovatelli, E.C. (Contessa). Miscellanea archeologica. Roma, 1891.

AH 7818.91.3 — Lovatelli, E.C. (Contessa). Römische Essays. Leipzig, 1891.

Eg 1308.91 — Marucchi, Orazio. Monumenta papyracea. Romae, 1891.

AH 7708.91 — Meyer, Paul. De Maecenatis oratione a Dione ficta. Inaug. Diss. Berolini, 1891.

AH 7138.91.3 — Mitteis, L. Reichsrecht und Volksrecht. Leipzig, 1891.

AH 7844.5.5F — Mommsen, T. I commentarii dei ludi secolari. Roma, 1891.

AH 7844.5F — Mommsen, T. Commentarium ludorum. Milano, 1891.

AH 7118.9 — Münzer, F. De gente valeria. Oppoliae, 1891.

AH 3008.82.5 — Mürdter, F. Geschichte Babyloniens und Assyriens. 2. Aufl. Stuttgart, 1891.

AH 4521.13 — Oberziner, G. Alcibiade. Genova, 1891.

AH 7888.91 — Oertmann, P. Die Volkswirtschaftslehre. Berlin, 1891.

AH 4278.90.6 — Oman, C.W.C. History of Greece. 2. ed. London, 1891.

AH 7055.93.6 — Omont, H. Le plus ancien manuscrit de la Notitia dignitatum. Paris, 1891.

AH 2103.2 — Paris, P. Feminae res republicas. Paris, 1891.

AH 4838.90.5 — Pollack, E. Hippodromica. Lipsiae, 1891.

AH 4408.91.7 — Prigge, E. De thesei rebus gestis quaestionum. Marpurgi, 1891.

Eg 278.91 — Rawlinson, George. Ancient Egypt. N.Y., 1891.

AH 3002.30.2F — Rawlinson, H.C. Cuneiform inscriptions of Western Asia. v.4. London, 1891.

AH 7161.4 — Rivier, Alphonse. Précis du droit de famille romain. Paris, 1891.

AH 4278.91.5 — Roth, K.L. Griechische Geschichte. München, 1891.

Eg 938.91 — Rougé, J. de. Géographie ancienne de la Basse-Egypte. Paris, 1891.

AH 7188.91 — Salkowski, C. Lehre vom Sklavenerwerb. Leipzig, 1891.

AH 3963.76 — Sayce, A.H. The races of the Old Testament. London, 1891.

AH 4217.9 — Schmitthenner, W. De coronarum apud Athenienses honoribus. Berolini, 1891.

AH 4328.91F — Schwartz, E. Quaestiones Ionicas. Adleranis, 1891.

AH 7178.91A — Stephenson, A. Public lands and agrarian laws. Baltimore, 1891.

AH 7058.91 — Stückelberg, E.A. Der Constantinische Patriciat. Basel, 1891.

AH 3187.10F — Tallquist, K.L. Babylonische Schenkungsbriefe. Helsingfors, 1891.

AH 4522.7 — Weil, Henri. Hermocopides. Paris, 1891.

AH 7808.91.3F — Wissowa, Georgius. De feriis anni Romanorum vetustissimi observationes selectae. Marburgi, 1891.

1892

AH 7498.93 — Allcroft, A.H. Early principate: history of Rome 31 B.C.-96 A.D. London, 1892.

NEDL AH 7458.92 — Allcroft, A.H. Rome under the Oligarchs. London, 1892.

AH 7168.92.7 — Appleton, J. Droit romain; essai sur le fondement de la protection possessoire. Paris, 1892.

AH 4200.13 — Attinger, G. Essai sur Lycurgue. Neuchatel, 1892.

AH 7168.92 — Audibert, A. L'histoire du droit romain. Paris, 1892.

AH 7908.74.7 — Babled, H. De la cura annonae. Paris, 1892.

AH 7498.92 — Baring-Gould, Sabine. The tragedy of the Caesars. London, 1892. 2v.

Chronological Listing

1892 - cont.

NEDL AH 7498.92.3 — Baring-Gould, Sabine. The tragedy of the Caesars. N.Y., 1892. 2v.

NEDL AH 7468.77.4.5A — Beesly, A.H. The Gracchi, Marius and Sulla. N.Y., 1892.

AH 7238.92 — Beniamin, C. De iustmiani imperatoris aetale. Berolini, 1892.

AH 7448.92 — Boguth, Walter. M. Valerius Laevinus (Ein Beitrag). Krems, 1892.

Eg 603.5A — British Museum. Tell el-Amarna tablets. London, 1892.

AH 4818.92 — Busolt, G. Griechischen Staats- und Rechtsaltertümer. München, 1892.

AH 8005.2 — Cagnat, René. L'armée romaine d'Afrique. Paris, 1892.

AH 7498.87.4 — Capes, William W. Roman history: the early empire. N.Y., 1892.

AH 7203.93 — Corpus juris civilis. Digesta. Roman law of sale with modern illustrations. Digest XVIII.1 and XIX.1 translated. Edinburgh, 1892.

AH 4478.76.5 — Cox, George W. Greeks and Persians. N.Y., 1892.

NEDL AH 4278.57.17.5 — Curtius, Ernest. History of Greece. N.Y., 1892. 5v.

AH 8971.5 — De-Vit, Vincenzo. La provincia romana dell'Ossola, ossia Delle Alpi Atrezziane. Firenze, 1892.

NEDL AH 7478.92.2 — Dodge, T.A. Caesar. A History of the art of war. Boston, 1892.

AH 7162.22 — Dropsie, M.A. Roman law of testaments. Philadelphia, 1892.

AH 850.7 — Eberl, G. Die Fischkonserven der Alten. Stadtamhof, 1892.

NEDL AH 278.92 — Eyzaquirre, R. Compendio de historia antigua, griega y romana. Santiago de Chile, 1892.

AH 9607.15A — Freeman, E.A. Story of Sicily, Phoenician, Greek and Roman. N.Y., 1892.

AH 2575.7 — Gaebler, H. Erythrä. Berlin, 1892.

AH 4298.92.11 — Gardner, P. New chapters in Greek history. London, 1892.

AH 4808.92.5 — Gnaedinger, G. De Graecorum Magistratibus Eponymis. Argentorali, 1892.

AH 3187.5A — Harper, R.F. Assyrian and Babylonian letters. London, 1892- 14v.

AH 4838.92 — Henrich, K.E. Pentathlon der Griechen. Würzburg, 1892.

AH 7098.92.2 — Henze, Walter. De civitatibus liberis. Berolini, 1892.

AH 4298.92.5 — Hertzberg, G.F. Altgriechische Kolonisation. Gütersloh, 1892.

AH 7628.92 — Hitzig, H.F. Stellung Kaiser Hadrians. Zürich, 1892.

AH 4161.11 — Hruza, Ernst. Familienrechts. Erlangen, 1892. 2v.

NEDL AH 7408.78.5 — Ihne, W. Early Rome. N.Y., 1892.

AH 7518.92 — Ihne, Wilhelm. Zur Ehrenrettung des Kaisers Tiberius. Strassburg, 1892.

AH 4808.92 — Israel-Holtzwart, Karl. Das System der attischen Zeitrechnung auf neuer Grundlage. Frankfurt, 1892.

AH 4278.92 — Joy, James R. Grecian history. N.Y., 1892.

AH 2110.5 — Judeich, W. Kleinasiastische Studien. Marburg, 1892.

AH 7508.92 — Jullien, Emile. Le fondateur de Lyon. Paris, 1892.

AH 7448.92.2 — Jumpertz, M. Der römisch-karthagische Krieg. Berlin, 1892.

AH 7468.92 — Klimke, Karl. Beiträge zur Geschichte der Gracchen. Sagen, 1892.

AH 5271.7 — Kophiniôtēs, I.K. Historia tou Argous. Athēnai, 1892.

AH 408.92 — Laing, S. Human origins. London, 1892.

AH 3002.2.8 — Lehmann-Haupt, C.F. Seamaššumukîn, König von Babylonien. Leipzig, 1892.

AH 7808.75.3 — Levison, Hans. Fasti Praetorii inde ab Octaviani imperii singularis intro usque ad Hadriani Exitum. Vratislaviae, 1892.

AH 4298.92A — Mahaffy, J.P. Problems in Greek history. Photoreproduction. London, 1892.

Eg 278.67.10A — Mariette, A. Outline of ancient Egyptian history. N.Y., 1892.

AH 2760.5 — Meischke, Kurt. Symbolae ad Eumenis II. Pergamenorum regis historiam. Inaug. Diss. Lipsiae, 1892.

AH 7168.92.10 — Merkel, R. Der römisch-rechtliche Begriff. Strassburg, 1892.

AH 4298.92.7 — Meyer, E. Forschungen zur alten Geschichte. Halle, 1892. 2v.

AH 4819.10 — Monceaux, Paul. La Grèce avant Alexandre. Paris, 1892.

AH 4408.92 — Müller, H.D. Historisch-mythologischen Untersuchungen. Göttingen, 1892.

AH 4278.90.6.3 — Oman, C.W.C. History of Greece. 3. ed. London, 1892.

AH 8012.5 — Pallu de Lessert, A.C. Vicaires et comtes d'Afrique. Constantine, 1892.

AH 6108.7 — Radet, Georges. De coloniis a Macedonibus in Asiam cis Taurum deductis. Thesim. Parisiis, 1892.

AH 7778.92 — Reinhardt, G. Der Perserkrieg des Kaisers Julian. Dessau, 1892.

Htn AH 7488.92* — Saltus, E. Imperial purple. Chicago, 1892.

AH 3407.6.5 — Sayce, A.H. The Hittites. 2d ed. London, 1892.

AH 4855.7 — Schneider, K. Fischer in der antiken Literatur. Aachen, 1892.

AH 7098.92 — Schulten, Adolf. De conventibus civium romanorum. Berolini, 1892.

AH 7098.92.1 — Schulten, Adolf. De conventibus civium romanorum. Diss. Lipsiae, 1892.

AH 7658.61.5 — Sheppard, J.G. The fall of Rome. London, 1892.

Eg 758.92 — Simaika, A. Province Romaine d'Égypte. Paris, 1892.

AH 7138.92.5 — Sohm, R. Institutes of Roman law. Oxford, 1892.

Eg 138.92F — Spiegelberg, Wilhelm. Studien und Materialien zum Rechtswesen des Pharaohenreiches. Hannover, 1892.

AH 4148.92 — Szántó, Emil. Griechische Bürgerrecht. Freiburg, 1892.

AH 4158.92 — Thalheim, T. Griechischen Rechtsaltertümern. v.1-2. Schneidemühl, 1892.

AH 4938.92 — Urban, K. Geographischen Forschungen und Märchen. Gütersloh, 1892.

AH 938.92 — Villar, J. Geografia antigua comparada. Santiago, 1892.

AH 7138.92 — Voigt, M. Römische Rechtsgeschichte. Leipzig, 1892. 3v.

NEDL AH 7818.84.2A — Wilkins, A.S. Roman Antiquities. N.Y., 1892?

AH 3008.92 — Winckler, H. Geschichte Babyloniens und Assyriens. Leipzig, 1892.

AH 3002.6.5 — Winckler, H. Keilinschriftliches Textbuch zum Alten Testament. Leipzig, 1892.

AH 4438.92A — Wright, H.M. Date of Cylon...early Athenian history. Boston, 1892.

AH 7138.40.3 — Zachariä, K.E. Geschichte des griechisch-römischen Rechts. Berlin, 1892.

AH 4214.7 — Ziebarth, E. De iureiurando in iure Graeco. Gottingae, 1892.

AH 2353.2 — Zwintscher, A. De Galatarum tetarchis. Lipsiae, 1892.

1893

AH 7478.93 — Allcroft, A.H. Making of the monarchy. London, 1893.

NEDL AH 278.93.5 — Allen, W. Ancient history for colleges and high schools. pt.2. Boston, 1893.

Eg 938.93 — Amélineau, Emile. La géographie de l'Égypte. Paris, 1893.

AH 7168.92.3 — Appleton, C. Fou et prodigue en droit romain. Paris, 1893.

Eg 708.93 — Bandelin, Erich. De rebus inter Aegyptios et Romanos...usque ad bellum Alexandrinum a Caesare gestum. Inaug. Diss. Halis Saxonum, 1893.

AH 7498.93.5 — Beaujeu, Maurice. Psychologie des premiers Césars. Lyon, 1893.

AH 4278.93A — Beloch, J. Grecian history. v.1-3. Strassburg, 1893-4v.

AH 7818.79.3 — Bender, H. Rom und römisches Leben im Alterthumen. 2. Aufl. Tübingen, 1893.

AH 2957.5.3 — Benjamin, S. Troy. N.Y., 1893.

Eg 603.7 — Bezold, C. Oriental diplomacy. London, 1893.

AH 3889.5 — Billerbeck, A. Susa. Leipzig, 1893.

AH 7438.93 — Binneboessel, P. Untersuchungen über...Geschichte. Halle, 1893.

AH 4818.87.5 — Blümner, H. Home life of ancient Greeks. London, 1893.

AH 4864.7 — Boehm, C. De cottabo. Bonnae, 1893.

AH 7200.16 — Boesch, F. De XII Tabularum Lege a Graecio Petita. Gottingae, 1893.

Eg 8.93 — Boston, Mass. Public Library. List of works on Egypt. Boston, 1893.

AH 4038.93.7 — Botsford, G.W. Development of the Athenian constitution. Boston, 1893.

AH 2757.9 — Brinkgreve, I.G. De regno Pergameno deque eius dynastis. Rhenum, 1893.

AH 7201.47.6 — Bruns, C.G. Fontes Juris Romani Antiqui. 6. ed. Friburg, 1893.

AH 7488.93.2 — Bury, J.B. History of the Roman Empire. N.Y., 1893.

AH 7488.93 — Bury, J.B. History of the Roman Empire. N.Y., 1893.

AH 4278.85.3 — Busolt, G. Griechische Geschichte. v.1-3. Gotha, 1893-1904. 4v.

AH 8503.2 — Carette, E. Les assemblées provinciales de la Gaule romaine. Paris, 1893.

AH 7138.93 — Chamier, D. Manual of Roman law. London, 1893.

AH 938.93 — Columba, G.M. Gli studi geografici nel I secolo dell'impero romano. Torino, 1893.

AH 4551.5 — Crämer, H. Beiträge zur Geschichte Alexanders der Grossen. Marburg, 1893. 3 pam.

AH 7163.23 — Dervilers, P. Des peines de l'adultère. Paris, 1893.

AH 7903.5.2 — Diocletianus. Edictum Diocletiani de pretiis rerum venalium. Berolini, 1893.

AH 4848.9 — Evans, M.M. Chapters on Greek dress. London, 1893.

AH 8017.5 — Fischer, C.T. De Hannonis Carthagoniensis. Lipsiae, 1893.

AH 4038.63.2 — Freeman, E.A. History of federal government. 2. ed. London, 1893.

AH 7478.81.9 — Froude, J.A. Caesar; a sketch. London, 1893.

AH 4038.81.5 — Gilbert, G. Handbuch der griechischen Staatsalterthümer. Leipzig, 1893.

AH 4498.93 — Grant, A.J. Greece in age of Pericles. London, 1893.

AH 7808.93 — Groebe, P. De legibus et senatus consultis anno 710. Lipsiae, 1893.

AH 818.62.6 — Guhl, Ernst. Leben der Griechen und Römer. 6. Aufl. Berlin, 1893.

AH 4888.93 — Guiraud, P. Propriété foncière. Paris, 1893.

AH 7138.73.3.5 — Hadley, James. Introduction to Roman law, in twelve academical lectures. N.Y., 1893.

AH 5233.5 — Herthum, P. De megalopolitarum rebus gestis. Lipsiae, 1893.

AH 818.93 — Hittell, J.S. History of mental growth of mankind. N.Y., 1893. 4v.

AH 7228.93 — Hitzig, H.F. Die Assessoren der römischen Magistrate. München, 1893.

AH 7278.68.7 — Ihne, W. Römische Geschichte. 2. Aufl. v.1-2. Leipzig, 1893.

AH 5140.7 — Jacobs, Emil. Thasiaca. Berolini, 1893.

AH 5140.7.1 — Jacobs, Emil. Thasiaca. Inaug. Diss. Berolini, 1893.

AH 7158.93 — Justinianus I. De Furtis. Cantabrigiae, 1893.

AH 9707.7.5 — Kalopothakes, D. De Thracia provincia Romana. Berlin, 1893.

AH 9701.5 — Kalopothakes, D. De Thracia provincia Romana. Lipsiae, 1893. 2 pam.

AH 9707.7 — Kalopothakes, D. De Thracia provincia Romana. Lipsiae, 1893.

AH 8307.5 — Király, Pál. Dacia provincia Augusti. Nagy-Becskerek, 1893-94. 2v.

NEDL AH 3154.12F — Knudtzon, J.A. Assyrische Gebete an den Sonnengott. Leipzig, 1893. 2v.

AH 4038.93 — Kopp, W. Griechische Staatsaltertümer. Berlin, 1893.

AH 7228.93.5 — Koschembahr-Lyskowski, J. Die Theorie der Exceptionen. Berlin, 1893.

AH 3963.175 — Küchenmeister, F. Die Totenbestattungen der Bibel. Stuttgart, 1893.

AH 3910.14 — Kümpel, Eduard. Die Quellen zur Geschichte des Krieges der Römer gegen Antiochus III. Hamburg, 1893.

AH 7918.93.3 — Labat, P. Etude sur les Collèges d'artisans. Toulouse, 1893.

AH 4058.93 — Lecoutere, C. L'archontat athénien. Louvain, 1893.

AH 7918.93 — Liebenam, W. Aus dem Vereinswesen im römischen Reiche. Berlin, 1893.

AH 4558.93.3 — M'Crindle, J.W. Invasion of India by Alexander the Great. Westminster, 1893.

AH 4859.19 — Matthias, T. Stellung der griechischen Frau. Zittau, 1893.

AH 3095.3 — Meissner, B. Die Bauinschriften Sanheribs. Leipzig, 1893.

AH 3014.3 — Meissner, B. Noch einmal das Bît-Hillâne und assyrische Säule. Leipzig, 1893.

AH 3002.2.11 — Meissner, Bruno. Beiträge zum altbabylonischen Privatrecht. Leipzig, 1893.

NEDL AH 7478.77.6 — Merivale, Charles. Roman triumvirates. N.Y., 1893.

NEDL AH 4524.9 — Micheli, Horace. Révolution oligarchique des quatre-cents. Genève, 1893.

AH 3002.4.5 — Moldenke, A.B. Babylonian contract tablets in the Metropolitan Museum of Art. N.Y., 1893.

Eg 298.93 — Müller, W.M. Asien und Europa nach altägyptischen Denkmälern. Leipzig, 1893.

AH 3002.4 — New York Metropolitan Museum of Art. Cuneiform texts in the Metropolitan Museum. N.Y., 1893.

AH 6107.13 — Niese, B. Geschichte der griechischen und makedonischen Staaten. Gotha, 1893. 3v.

AH 4487.11 — Nordin, R. Studien in der Themistoklesfrage. Upsala, 1893.

Chronological Listing

1893 - cont.

	AH 4278.90.6.4	Oman, C.W.C. History of Greece. 4. ed. London, 1893.
	AH 7278.85.7A	Pelham, H.F. Outlines of Roman history. N.Y., 1893.
	AH 7278.85.7.5	Pelham, H.F. Outlines of Roman history. N.Y., 1893.
	AH 4228.93	Pischinger, A. De arbitris Atheniensium publicis. München, 1893.
	AH 7828.93	Preston, H.W. Private life of the Romans. Boston, 1893.
	AH 4214.19	Prott, J. de. Fasti Graecorum sacri. Lipsiae, 1893.
	AH 4038.93.3	Raeder, A. Athens politiske udvikling. Christiania, 1893.
	AH 3607.11A	Rawlinson, G. Story of Parthia. N.Y., 1893.
	Eg 278.93	Rawlinson, George. The story of ancient Egypt. N.Y., 1893.
	AH 4238.93	Ringnalda, H.F.T. De exercitu Laeedaemoniorum. Leovardiae, 1893.
	AH 3092.2	Rost, P. Die Keilschrifttexte Tiglat-Pilesers III. Leipzig, 1893. 2v.
	AH 7148.93	Roy, C. Les fétiaux du peuple romain. Poitiers, 1893.
	AH 7148.93.5	Ruggiero, E. de. L'arbitrato pubblico. Roma, 1893.
	AH 4838.93	Sartori, K. Studien...der griechischen Privataltertümer. München, 1893.
	AH 3165.5	Sayce, A.H. Social life among the Assyrians and Babylonians. London, 1893.
	AH 238.93	Schneider, R. Legion und Phalanx. Berlin, 1893.
	AH 7518.93	Schott, W. Kriminaljustiz und des Kaisers Tiberius. Erlangen, 1893.
	AH 8676.2	Schulze, E. Römische Forum als Mittelpunkt. Gütersloh, 1893.
	AH 4558.93	Schwarz, F. Alexanders des Grossen Feldzüge in Turkestan. München, 1893.
	AH 168.93	Sieveking, H. Seedarlehen. Leipzig, 1893.
	AH 7238.93	Vaders, Joseph. Einundvierzigster Jahresbericht...Realgymnasium. Münster, 1893.
	AH 3657.11.5	Vaux, William Sandys Wright. Persia. London, 1893.
	AH 7138.93.5F	Voigt, M. Uber die Leges Iuliae iudiciorum privatorum et publicorum. Leipzig, 1893.
	AH 7468.93	Willrich, H. De conjurationis Catilinariae fontibus. Gottingae, 1893.
	AH 1298.93	Winckler, H. Altorientalische Forschungen. v.1-2,3,4,5,6. Leipzig, 1893. 5v.
	AH 3002.6FA	Winckler, H. Sammlung von Keilschrifttexten. Leipzig, 1893. 2v.
NEDL	AH 278.93.3	Zeehe, Andreas. Lehrbuch der Geschichte des Alterthums. Laibach, 1893.

1894

	AH 4558.94	Allcroft, A.H. Decline of Hellas. London, 1894.
	AH 7178.94	Beaudouin, E. La limitation des fonds de terre. Paris, 1894.
	AH 4148.94	Berard, V. Liberas Graecorum civitates. Lutetiae, 1894.
	AH 7168.94	Björling, C.G.E. Penning deposition enligt justiniansk Rätt. Lund, 1894.
	AH 4518.94.3	Boerner, A. De rebus a Graecis. Gottingae, 1894.
	AH 3154.16F	Boissier, A. Documents assyriens relatifs aux Présages. Paris, 1894-96.
	AH 8549.94	Bonwick, James. Irish Druids and old Irish religions. London, 1894.
	AH 7238.94.2	Bray, Joseph. Essai sur le droit penal militaire. Paris, 1894.
	AH 3653.5	Buchholz, A. Quaestiones de Persarum satrapis satrapiiiseque. Lipsiae, 1894.
	AH 7428.94	Burger, Combertus P. Neue Forschungen zur älteren Geschichte Roms. Amsterdam, 1894. 2v.
	AH 7168.94.5	Cantacuzène, M.G. Droit romain de l'impot sur l'importation et l'exportation des marchandises à Rome sous la république et sous l'empire. Paris, 1894.
	AH 7201.74	Cantarelli, L. Il frammento Berlinese "De Dediticus". Roma, 1894.
	AH 3408.9	Cara, Cesare A. de. Gli Hethei-Palasgi. Roma, 1894. 3v.
	AH 7098.94	Cyprès, Imbert. Droit romain de la curie. Paris, 1894.
	AH 4842.35	Davidson, T. Education of the Greek people. N.Y., 1894.
	Eg 278.85.4A	Erman, A. Life in ancient Egypt. London, 1894.
	AH 7238.94	Fröhlich, F. Feldheeren des Altertums. v. 1-2, 3-5. Zürich, 1894. 4v.
	AH 7448.94	Fuchs, Josef. Der zweite punische Krieg. Wienerneustadt, 1894.
	AH 4138.94	Gantzer, P. Verfassungs- und Gesetzevision in Athen. Halle, 1894.
NEDL	AH 7842.4	Gerini, G.B. Le dottrine pedagogiche. Torino, 1894.
	AH 930.15	Ginn and Co., publishers. Classical atlas. Boston, 1894.
	AH 4206.8	Gleue, H. De homicidarum in Areopago Atheniensi judicio. Gottingae, 1894.
	AH 7158.94	Greenidge, A.H.J. Infamia. Oxford, 1894.
	AH 4484.7	Grundy, G.B. Topography of Battle of Plataea. London, 1894.
	AH 4818.94	Guiraud, P. Lectures historiques. Paris, 1894.
	AH 3011.4	Hilprecht, H.V. Assyriaca eine Nachlese...Assyriologie. Berlin, 1894.
	AH 4278.86.7A	Holm, Adolf. History of Greece. London, 1894. 4v.
	AH 4843.9	Hymne à Apollon. Paris, 1894.
	Eg 878.94	Jequier, G. Le livre de ce qu'il y a dans l'hadès. Paris, 1894.
	AH 7161.19	Jhering, R. Entwicklungsgeschichte des römischen Rechts. Leipzig, 1894.
	AH 7163.21	Jörs, Paul. Ehe Gesetze des Augustus. Marburg, 1894.
	AH 8312.2	Jung, Julius. Fasten der Provinz Dacien. Innsbruck, 1894.
	AH 9707.7.10	Kalopothakes, D. O chörismos. Athénai, 1894.
	AH 2583.5F	Kern, Otto. Magnesia am Maiandros. Berlin, 1894.
	AH 4818.94.3	Kleemann, M. Ein Tag in alten Athen. Gütersloh, 1894.
	AH 3156.7	Laurent, A. La magie et la divination chez les chaldéo-assyriens. Paris, 1894.
	AH 3140.4	Lincke, A.A. Assyrien und Ninive...Mittelmeervölker. Berlin, 1894.
	AH 7818.91.2	Lovatelli, E.C. (Contessa). Nuova miscellanea archeologica. Roma, 1894.
	AH 842.16	Marr, F. Chauvinismus und Schulreform im Altertum. Breslau, 1894.
	AH 7448.94.2	Masom, W.J. The struggle for Empire. London, 1894.
	Eg 818.94A	Maspéro, Gaston. The dawn of civilization. N.Y., 1894.
	AH 7058.94	Mentz, M. De magistratuum romanorum. Ienae, 1894.
	AH 7278.54.18.15	Mommsen, T. History of Rome. N.Y., 1894. 4v.
	AH 7307.34.14	Montesquieu, Charles de. Considérations sur les causes de la grandeur des Romains. Paris, 1894.
	AH 8549.87	Morgan, O. The light of Britannia. Cardiff, 1894.
	AH 7108.94	Moulin, C.D. Droit romain. Des impots indirectes. Poitiers, 1894.

1894 - cont.

	AH 4518.94	Müller, Emil. Sokrates in der Volksversammlung. Zittau, 1894.
	AH 1298.94	Niebuhr, Carl. Studien und Bemerkungen zur Geschichte des alten Orients. Leipzig, 1894.
	AH 4498.94	Östlye, P. Zahl der Bürger von Athen. Kristiania, 1894.
	AH 840.5	Opitz, R. Häusliche Leben. Leipzig, 1894.
	AH 6157.7	Ortmann, K. De regno bosperano Spartocedarum. Halis Saxonum, 1894.
	AH 9607.17	Pais, Ettore. Storia della Sicilia. Torino, 1894.
	AH 4828.94	Pernice, E. Griechische Gewichte. Berlin, 1894.
	AH 5760.15	Petit-Dutaillis, C. Laecedaemoniorum Reipublicae. Lutetiae Parisiorum, 1894.
	Eg 278.94	Petrie, William M.F. A history of Egypt from earliest times to the XVIth dynasty. v.1. London, 1894.
	AH 7148.94	Politis, N.E. Les triumvirs capitaux. Paris, 1894.
NEDL	AH 7528.94	Quidde, L. Caligula. Leipzig, 1894.
	AH 9634.5	Rizzo, P. Naxos siceliota. Catania, 1894.
	AH 4708.94	Sanctis, G. Questioni politiche e reforme sociali. v.1-2. Roma, 1894.
	AH 4538.84.5	Sankey, C. Spartan and Theban supremacies. N.Y., 1894.
	AH 3143.19	Sayce, Archibald H. A primer of Assyriology. London, 1894.
	AH 3143.19.1	Sayce, Archibald H. A primer of Assyriology. N.Y., 1894.
	AH 5607.5	Schmidt, H. Epeirotika...Geschichte des alten Epeiros. Marburg, 1894.
	AH 5610.5	Schubert, R. Geschichte der Pyrrhus. Königsberg, 1894.
	AH 8548.38	Scott, A. The Celts and Druids and their story from the earliest times. North Shields, 1894.
NEDL	AH 7278.94A	Shuckburgh, E.S. History of Rome. N.Y., 1894.
	AH 818.94	Simcox, E.J. Primitive civilizations. London, 1894. 2v.
	AH 1278.71.7	Smith, Philip. The student's ancient history. The ancient history of the East. N.Y., 1894.
	AH 4206.9	Terwen, J.J. De Areopago Atheniensium. Ultraiecti, 1894.
	AH 4228.94	Teusch, T. De sortitione indicum apud Atheniensis. Gottingae, 1894.
	AH 9157.5	Tropea, G. Storia dei lucani. Messina, 1894.
	AH 3004.4	Winckler, H. Ein Beitrag zur Geschichte des Assyriologie im Deutschland. Leipzig, 1894.
	AH 7844.3	Wissowa, G. Die Saecularfeier des Augustus. Marburg, 1894.
	AH 7162.32	Wöll, W. Uber die regula Catoiana. Strassburg, 1894.

1895

	AH 4518.95	Allcroft, A.H. Peloponnesian War. London, 1895.
	AH 4538.95	Allcroft, A.H. Sparta and Thebes. London, 1895.
NEDL	AH 7278.90.5	Allen, W.T. A short history of the Roman people. Boston, 1895.
	AH 7168.95.3	Appleton, C. Compensation en droit romain. Paris, 1895.
	AH 5301.7	Arnim, I. Hans. Ad scholas ad civitatis Atticae historiam symbole. Rostock, 1895. 3 pam.
	AH 4200.9	Bazin, H. De Lycurgo. Paris, 1895.
	AH 7468.77.5	Beesly, A.H. The Gracchi, Marius and Sulla. N.Y., 1895.
	AH 2957.5.5	Benjamin, S. Troy. N.Y., 1895.
	AH 7508.67.6	Beulé, C. Ernest. Auguste, sa famille et ses amis. 6. éd. Paris, 1895.
	AH 7818.95	Bloch, Leo. Römische Altertumskunde. Stuttgart, 1895.
	AH 4818.87.7A	Blümner, H. Home life of ancient Greeks. London, 1895.
	AH 842.17	Bohatta, H. Erziehung und Unterricht bei den Griechen und Römern. Gütersloh, 1895.
	AH 8007.7	Boissier, Gaston. L'Afrique romaine. Paris, 1895.
	Eg 1038.95F	Book of the Dead. The book of the dead. London, 1895.
	AH 8908.3	Brunet y Bellet, J. Els gregs, els etruscos. Barcelona, 1895.
	AH 7638.95	Bryant, E.E. Reign of Antoninus Pius. Cambridge, 1895.
	AH 7168.95	Buckler, W.H. Contract in Roman law. London, 1895.
	AH 8.95	Büdinger, Max. Die Universalhistorie. Wien, 1895.
	AH 4298.95	Butzer, H. Quellenbuch. Dresden, 1895.
	AH 7618.95	Cantarelli, Luigi. Le fonti per la storia dell'imperatore Traiano. Roma, 1895.
	AH 7598.76.15	Capes, William W. The Roman Empire of the second century. N.Y., 1895.
	AH 7498.87.5	Capes, William W. Roman history: the early empire. N.Y., 1895.
	AH 7478.95	Ciccotti, E. Donne e politica. Milano, 1895.
	AH 4458.76.15	Cox, George W. Athenian empire. N.Y., 1895.
	AH 3002.2.13	Craig, James A. Assyrian and Babylonian religious texts. Leipzig, 1895-97.
	AH 5553.7	Curtius, Ernst. Der Synoikismos von Elis. Berlin, 1895.
	AH 4138.95	Dareste, R. Recueil des inscriptions juridiques grecques. Paris, 1895.
	AH 4843.3	Emmanuel, M. L'orchestique grecque. Paris, 1895.
	AH 4843.2	Emmanuel, M. Saltationis disciplina. Paris, 1895.
	AH 7148.95	Ferrenbach, V. Die Amici Populi Romani. Strassburg, 1895.
	AH 4818.95.5	Gardner, P. A manual of Greek antiquities. Books 1-5. N.Y., 1895.
	AH 843.4	Gevaert, F.A. Mélopée antique. Gand, 1895.
	AH 4038.81.3	Gilbert, G. Constitutional antiquities. London, 1895.
	AH 4038.81.4	Gilbert, G. Constitutional antiquities. London, 1895.
	AH 7138.89.10	Girard, P.F. Textes de droit romain. Paris, 1895.
	AH 7238.95.5	Gündel, Friedrich. De legione II adiutrice. Inaug. Diss. Lipsiae, 1895.
	AH 7158.95	Hallensleben, P.W. Das Vitium Furti und seine Purgatio. Aachen, 1895.
	AH 4038.95	Hammond, B.E. Political institutions of ancient Greeks. London, 1895.
	AH 7168.95.10	Henry, René. Étude sur la compensation en droit romain. Paris, 1895.
	AH 4818.41.10	Hermann, K.F. Lehrbuch der griechischen Antiquitäten. 4. Aufl. Freiburg, 1895.
	AH 4168.95	Hitzig, H.F. Griechische Pfandrecht. München, 1895.
	Eg 818.92.3	Hommel, F. Der babylonische Ursprung der ägyptischen Kultur. München, 1895.
	AH 1408.95	Hommel, Fritz. Geschichte des alten Morgenlandes. Stuttgart, 1895.
	AH 7848.8	Hula, Eduard. Die Toga der späteren Kaiserzeit. Brünn, 1895.
	AH 3073.3.5	Kellner, M. The prophecies of Isaiah. Cambridge, 1895.
	AH 3159.26	Kinns, Samuel. Graven in the rock. London, 1895.
	AH 4842.56	Lane, F.H. Elementary Greek education. Syracuse, N.Y., 1895.
	AH 842.32	Laurie, S.S. Historical survey of pre-Christian education. London, 1895.
	AH 7842.8	Lazic, G.S. Pogled na shkolu i polozhaj. Karlovuima, 1895.

Chronological Listing

1895 - cont.

AH 238.95	Liers, Hugo. Kriegswesen der Alten. Breslau, 1895.
AH 7238.95	Luterbacher, F. Die römischen Legionen und Kriegsschiffe. Burgdorf, 1895.
AH 3042.3.5	McGee, D.G. De topographia urbis Babylonis. Lipsiae, 1895.
Eg 708.95A	Mahaffy, J.P. The empire of the Ptolemies. London, 1895.
NEDL AH 7468.95	Masom, W.F. Decline of the oligarchy: History of Rome. London, 1895.
AH 1278.95	Maspero, Gaston. Histoire ancienne des peuples de l'Orient. Paris, 1895.
Eg 818.92.2	Maspéro, Gaston. Life in ancient Egypt and Assyria. N.Y., 1895.
AH 4847.5	Mauri, A. I cittadini lavoratori. Milano, 1895.
AH 7478.77.7	Merivale, Charles. Roman triumvirates. N.Y., 1895.
AH 888.95.3	Meyer, E. Die wirtschaftliche Entwickelung. Jena, 1895.
AH 7161.2	Meyer, Paul. Der römische Konkubinat. Leipzig, 1895.
AH 7204.15	Michaelis, H. Kritische Nürdigung der Kriese. Köln, 1895.
AH 7278.54.19	Mommsen, T. History of Rome. N.Y., 1895. 5v.
AH 5760.5	Nordin, R. Aussere Politik Spartas. Upsala, 1895.
AH 4278.76.10	Pennell, R.F. Ancient Greece from the earliest times down to 146 B.C. Boston, 1895.
Eg 278.94.9	Petrie, William M.F. A history of Egypt from the earliest times to the XVIth dynasty. 2. ed. London, 1895.
AH 4888.95	Platon, G. Socialisme en Grèce. Paris, 1895.
AH 308.95	Pöhlmann, R. Aus Altertum und Gegenwart. München, 1895.
AH 2808.5A	Ramsay, W.M. Cities and bishoprics of Phrygia. Oxford, 1895. 2v.
AH 7818.48.15	Ramsay, William. Manual of Roman antiquities. 15th ed. N.Y., 1895.
AH 7468.29.5	Reinach, T. Mithradates Eupator. Leipzig, 1895.
Eg 928.95	Revillout, Eugène. Mélanges sur la métrologie, l'économie politique et l'histoire de l'ancienne Égypte. Paris, 1895.
AH 5357.5A	Roberts, W.R. Ancient Bocotians. Cambridge, 1895.
AH 4484.9	Rudolph, F. Schlacht von Platää. Dresden, 1895.
Eg 298.95	Sayce, A.H. The Egypt of the Hebrews and Herodotos. N.Y., 1895.
AH 7844.2	Schulze, E. Die Schauspiele zur Unterhaltung. Gütersloh, 1895.
AH 4114.13	Seebohm, H.E. On the structure of the Greek Tribal Society. London, 1895.
AH 7658.95	Seeck, Otto. Geschichte des Untergangs der antiken Welt. v.1-6. Appendix. Berlin, 1895. 8v.
AH 3966.5.3	Smith, George A. The historical geography of the Holy Land. 3. ed. N.Y., 1895.
AH 3156.11	Stübe, R. Judisch-Babylonische Zaubertexte. Halle, 1895.
AH 3154.11	Tallqvist, K.L. Die assyrische Beschwörungsserie Maqlû. Leipzig, 1895.
AH 7278.95	Trask, C.W. Reference handbook of Roman history. Boston, 1895.
AH 7888.95	Vanlaer, M. La fin d'un peuple. Paris, 1895. 2v.
AH 1298.95	Vinogradov, Aleksy. Drevne patriarhalnyja. St. Petersburg, 1895.
AH 298.95	Wachsmuth, C. Einleitung...der alten Geschichte. Leipzig, 1895.
AH 7918.95.3	Waltzing, J.P. Les corporations romaines. Louvain, 1895.
AH 7918.95	Waltzing, J.P. Etude...sur les corporations professionnelles. Louvain, 1895. 4v.
AH 4538.95.3	Weise, Richard. Athenische Bundesgenossenkrieg. Berlin, 1895.
AH 888.95	Wetzel, M. Bedeutung des klassichen Altertums. Paderborn, 1895.
Eg 878.95.15	Wiedemann, A. The ancient Egyptian doctrine of the immortality of the soul. London, 1895.
Eg 878.95	Wiedemann, A. The ancient Egyptian doctrine of the immortality of the soul. N.Y., 1895.
AH 4168.95.5	Wilbrandt, M. De rerum privatarum ante solonis tempus. Rostochii, 1895.
AH 7448.74.3	Wilms, A. Die Schlacht bei Cannae. Hamburg, 1895.
AH 3936.5	Wright, W. Palmyra and Zenobia. N.Y., 1895.
AH 7038.95	Zoeller, Max. Römische Staats und Rechtsaltertümer. Breslau, 1895.

1896

AH 7138.96.5F	Alibrandi, I. Opere giuridiche e storiche. Roma, 1896.
AH 138.96	Andé, Edouard. La fondation perpetuelle dans l'antiquité. Paris, 1896.
AH 3154.4	Arnold, William R. Ancient Babylonian temple records. N.Y., 1896.
AH 8007.11	Baale, C.H. De provinciis Africanis. Groningae, 1896.
AH 3042.3	Baermstark, A. Babylon zur Stadtgeschichte. Stuttgart, 1896.
AH 7468.29.7	Bernhardt, H. Chronologie der mithridatischen Kriege. Marburg, 1896.
AH 3187.6	Berry, George R. The letters of the Room 2 collection in the British Museum. Chicago, 1896.
AH 7408.84	Bonghi, R. Storia di Roma. v.3. Milano, 1896.
NEDL AH 278.97	Boughton, W. History of ancient peoples. N.Y., 1896.
AH 7098.96.3	Boutet, Paul. De la police et de la voirie. Paris, 1896.
AH 4278.96.7	Brelet, H. Historiae Graecae. Paris, 1896.
AH 7201.75	Bremer, F.P. Iurisprudentiae Antehadrianae. v.1-2, pt.1-2. Lipsiae, 1896. 3v.
AH 7258.96	Chapot, Victor. La flotte de misène. Paris, 1896.
AH 7842.2	Clarke, George. The education of children at Rome. N.Y., 1896.
AH 9610.17	Clasen, C. Timoleon, eine historische Untersuchung. Glückstadt, 1896.
AH 7278.96.10	Coleridge, E.P. Res Romanae. London, 1896.
AH 6107.11.5	Curteis, A.M. Rise of the Macedonian empire. N.Y., 1896.
AH 7038.96	Decly, Ferdinand. Histoire de la centralisation dans l'empire romain. Thèse. Caen, 1896.
AH 3140.3	Demuth, L. Fünfzig babylonische Rechts- und Verwaltungsurkunden. Leipzig, 1896.
AH 7138.96	Eisele, F. Beiträge zur römischen Rechtsgeschichte. Freiburg, 1896.
AH 4843.5	Emmanuel, M. Danse grecque. Paris, 1896.
AH 842.19	Fegerl, J. Die physikalischen Kenntnisse der Alten. Mähr, 1896.
NEDL AH 4818.67.10	Felton, C.C. Greece, ancient and modern. v.1-2. Boston, 1896.
AH 7168.96	Fleischmann, M. Pignus in causa judicati captum. Breslau, 1896.
AH 4188.96	Foucart, G. De libertorum conditione apud Athenienses. Lutetiae, 1896.
AH 4708.96	Gillischewski, H. De Aetolorum praetorubus. Berolini, 1896.

1896 - cont.

AH 4038.96	Greenidge, A.H.J. Greek constitutional history. London, 1896.
NEDL AH 7278.96	Guerber, H.A. Story of Romans. N.Y., 1896.
NEDL AH 818.62.13A	Guhl, Ernst. The life of Greeks and Romans described from antique monuments. N.Y., 1896.
AH 4978.90.2	Haussoullier, Bernard. Grèce. Collection des guides - Joanne. Paris, 1896. 2v.
AH 7178.82.4	His, Rudolph. Die Domänen der römischen Kaiserzeit. Leipzig, 1896.
NEDL AH 4278.86.8	Holm, Adolf. History of Greece. London, 1896-99. 4v.
AH 4843.10F	Hymnus an Apollo. Leipzig, 1896.
AH 7408.78.7	Ihne, W. Early Rome. N.Y., 1896.
AH 7228.96	Jobbé-Duval, E. La procédure civil. Paris, 1896.
AH 188.96	Keiffer, Jules. L'esclavage à Athènes et à Rome. Luxembourg, 1896.
AH 3156.6	King, Leonard W. Babylonian magic and sorcery. London, 1896.
AH 7201.77	Kipp, T. Quellenkunde des römischen Rechts. Leipzig, 1896.
NEDL AH 278.96	Krüger, C.A. Geschichte der Griechen und Römen. Berlin, 1896.
AH 1808.96	Krug, Carl. Die Chronologie der Geschichte Israels, Aegyptens. Leipzig, 1896.
AH 4838.96F	Lambros and Polites. Olympic games. Athens, 1896.
AH 7468.96	Lewandowski, M. La question sociale à Rome. Paris, 1896.
AH 7468.96.5	Linden, E. De bello civili Sullano. Friburgi Brisigavorum, 1896.
AH 4558.93.5A	M'Crindle, J.W. Invasion of India by Alexander the Great. Westminster, 1896.
AH 4818.87.11A	Mahaffy, J.P. Greek life and thought. 2nd ed. London, 1896.
AH 4818.96A	Mahaffy, J.P. Survey of Greek civilization. N.Y., 1896.
Eg 818.94.6	Maspéro, Gaston. The dawn of civilization. 2. ed. London, 1896.
AH 3181.6	Messerschmidt, L. Tabula Babylonica V.A. Th 246 Musei Berolinensis. Kirchain, 1896.
AH 7307.34.15	Montesquieu, Charles de. Considérations sur les causes de la grandeur des Romains. Paris, 1896.
AH 7548.96	Nordmeyer, G. Der Tod Neros in der Legende. Mors, 1896.
AH 4214.9	Ott, Ludwig. Kenntnis der griechischen Eid. Leipzig, 1896.
AH 8012.2	Pallu de Lessert, A.C. Fastes des provinces africaines. Paris, 1896-1901. 2v.
AH 7458.96	Pascal, Carlo. Studi romani. Torino, 1896.
AH 2757.7	Pedroli, D.U. Il regno di Pergamo. Torino, 1896.
AH 8557.7	Poinsignon, A.M. Quid praicipue apud Romanos adusque Diocletiani tempora Illyricum fuerit breviter disseritur. Parisiis, 1896.
AH 3021.2.10	Ragozin, Zénaide A. The story of Chaldea from the earliest times to the rise of Assyria. 2. ed. N.Y., 1896.
AH 3707.11.2	Rawlinson, G. Story of Phoenicia. N.Y., 1896.
AH 7098.96	Ruggiero, E. de. Le colonie dei romani. Spoleto, 1896.
Eg 298.95.4	Sayce, A.H. The Egypt of the Hebrews and Herodotos. London, 1896.
AH 9475.2	Schreiner, W. Blick in die Geschichte...Eining's von Trajan bis Diocletian. v.1-2. Landshut, 1896.
AH 7178.96	Schulten, A. Die römischen Grundherrschaften. Weimar, 1896.
AH 8.96	Sittl, Karl. Anschauungsmethode...Altertumswissenschaft. Gotha, 1896.
AH 7448.81.5	Smith, R.B. Rome and Carthage. N.Y., 1896.
Eg 1188.96F	Spiegelberg, Wilhelm. Rechnungen aus der Zeit Setis I. v.1, Atlas. Strassburg, 1896. 2v.
AH 5308.7	Stauffer, A. Zwölf Gestalten der Glanzzeit Athens. München, 1896.
AH 4278.96	Swoboda, H. Griechische Geschichte. Leipzig, 1896.
AH 3963.80.2	Szeke'hyi, Lajos. A bibliaí régiségtudomany kézikönyve. 2. kiadas. v.1-2. Budapest, 1896.
AH 308.96	Taylor, H.O. Ancient ideals. N.Y., 1896. 2v.
AH 308.96.2	Taylor, H.O. Ancient ideals. v.2. N.Y., 1896.
Eg 808.96	Torr, C. Memphis and Mycenae. Cambridge, Eng., 1896.
Eg 278.96F	Untersuchungen zur Geschichte...Aegyptens. v.1-10. Leipzig, 1896-1928. 5v.
AH 7098.96.2	Vigneaux, P.E. Essai sur l'histoire de la Praefectura Urbis. Paris, 1896.
AH 7278.96.5	Wells, J. History of Rome. London, 1896.
AH 4048.96A	Whibley, L. Greek oligarchies. N.Y., 1896.
AH 5410.5	Wilisch, E. Geschichte Korinths. Zittau, 1896.
AH 7518.96	Willenbucher, H. Tiberius und die Verschwörung des Sejan. Gütersloh, 1896.
AH 4415.7.9	Witt, Karl. The Trojan War. 5. ed. London, 1896.
AH 3160.7	Zimmern, H. Vater, Sohn und Fursprecher. Leipzig, 1896.

1897

AH 7198.97	Affolter, F.X. Römischen Institutionen-System. Berlin, 1897.
AH 2816.5	Anderson, J.G.C. A summer in Phrygia. n.p., 1897.
AH 859.6.2F	Bachofen, J.J. Das Mutterrecht. 2. Aufl. Basel, 1897.
AH 3181.7	Banks, E.J. Sumerisch Babylonische Hymnen. Leipzig, 1897.
Eg 28.97	Bondi, J.H. Aegyptiaca. Leipzig, 1897.
NEDL AH 4278.57.18	Curtius, Ernest. History of Greece. N.Y., 1897. 5v.
AH 7648.97	Dartique-Peyroux, J. Marc Aurèle dans ses rapports avec le christianisme. Paris, 1897.
AH 7918.97.3	Demoulin, H. Les Collegia Juvenum. Louvain, 1897.
AH 7918.97	Floss, Antonius. De collegiis iuvenum quaestiones. Bonnae, 1897.
AH 7448.18.9	Fuchs, J. Hannibals Alpenübergang. Wien, 1897.
AH 4828.93.5	Gilbert, Gustav. Egcheiridion Archaiologias toū demosiou biou. Tom A', Teux.1-3. Athēnai, 1897-99.
Eg 1028.97	Griffith, Francis L. Egyptian literature. N.Y., 1897.
AH 7188.97	Halkin, Léon. Les esclaves publics chez les Romains. Bruxelles, 1897.
AH 4038.97	Herzog, E. Verwaltung...des attischen Staats. Tübingen, 1897.
AH 4498.97	Hill, G. Sources for Greek history. Oxford, 1897.
AH 5140.5	Hiller, F. Archaische Kultur der Insel Thera. Berlin, 1897.
AH 4558.97.3	Hogarth, D.G. Philip and Alexander of Macedon. N.Y., 1897.
AH 818.97	Holm, A. Kulturgeschichte des...Altertums. Leipzig, 1897.
AH 4862.5	Hueppe, F. Rassen und Sozialhygiene. Wiesbaden, 1897.
AH 7138.97	Hunter, W.A. Roman law. 3. ed. London, 1897.
AH 4298.52.2	Jacobs, Friedrich. Hellas; Geographie, Geschichte und Literatur Griechenlands. Stuttgart, 1897.

1897 - cont.

AH 7338.97	Klebs, E. Prosopographia Imperii Romani. Berolini, 1897-98. 3v.
AH 5753.7	Kuchtner, K. Spartanischen Ephorats. München, 1897.
AH 4818.97	Maisch, R. Griechische Altertumskunde. Leipzig, 1897.
Eg 818.94.4	Maspéro, Gaston. The dawn of civilization. N.Y., 1897.
AH 1278.76.15	Maspero, Gaston. Struggle of the nations, Egypt, Syria and Assyria. N.Y., 1897.
AH 7448.97A	Morris, William C. Hannibal; soldier, statesman. N.Y., 1897.
AH 7200.17	Nikol'skii, B.V. Sistema i teket "XII tablin". Sankt Peterburg, 1897.
AH 7828.82.3A	Pellisson, M. Roman life in Pliny's time. Meadville, Pa., 1897.
AH 7488.97	Peter, H. Die geschichtliche Literatur...Kaiserzeit. Leipzig, 1897.
AH 7888.97	Pfaff, Ivo. Über den rechtlichen Schutz. Weimar, 1897.
AH 7408.97	Potter, G.S. The founders of Rome. Buffalo, 1897.
AH 3659.5	Prášek, J.V. Forschungen zur Geschichte des Alterthums. Leipzig, 1897. 3v.
AH 3088.3	Rasmussen, N. Salmanasser den II's Indskrifter. Kjøbenhavn, 1897.
AH 3013.7	Rassam, H. Asshur and the land of Nimrod. N.Y., 1897.
AH 4538.97	Reichenbächer, W. Geschichte der athenischen...Politik. Halle, 1897.
AH 842.21	Saffroy, (Mlle.). Écrivans, pédagogues de l'antiquité. Paris, 1897.
AH 7798.97	Schild, W. Galla Placidia. Halle, 1897.
AH 818.97.2	Schneidewin, Max. Antike Humanität. Berlin, 1897.
AH 818.97.5	Schneidewin, Max. Offener Brief au Herrn Professor Theobald Ziegler über "Antike Humanität". Leipzig, 1897.
AH 4818.51.8	Schoemann, G.F. Griechische Alterthümer. 4. Aufl. Berlin, 1897. 2v.
AH 7778.97	Scholl, Karl. Ein Kaiser im Kampf mit seiner Zeit. 2. Aufl. Bamberg, 1897?
AH 7628.97	Schurz, Wilhelm. Die Militärreorganisation Hadrians. Leipzig, 1897.
AH 5910.5	Seeliger, K. Messenien und der achäische Bund. Zittau, 1897.
AH 8663.2	Shumway, E.S. A day in ancient Rome. Boston, 1897.
AH 3966.5.5	Smith, George A. The historical geography of the Holy Land. 3d ed. London, 1897.
AH 3966.5.6	Smith, George A. The historical geography of the Holy Land. 4. ed. N.Y., 1897.
AH 2357.5	Staehelin, Felix. Geschichte der kleinasiatischen Galater. Basel, 1897.
Eg 708.97	Strack, M.L. Die Dynastie der Ptolemäer. Berlin, 1897.
AH 7488.97.5	Stueckelberg, Ernst Alfred. Die Thronfolge von Augustus bis Constantin. Wien, 1897.
AH 7818.97	Thomas, Émile. Rome et l'empire. Paris, 1897.
AH 4028.97	Toepffer, J. Griechischen Altertumswissenschaft. Berlin, 1897.
AH 938.97	Tozer, Henry F. History of ancient geography. Cambridge, 1897.
AH 7488.97.2	Vienna. Heraldischen Gesellschaft "Adler". Jahrbuch. Wien, 1897.
AH 3964.16.5	Weber, F. Jüdische Theologie auf Grund des Talmud. Leipzig, 1897.
AH 2014.7.2	Wellhausen, Julius. Reste arabischen Heidentums. Berlin, 1897.
Eg 878.97A	Wiedemann, A. Religion of the ancient Egyptians. Photoreproduction. N.Y., 1897.
AH 1298.93.7	Winckler, H. Altorientalische Forschungen. Leipzig, 1897-1901. 2v.
AH 7168.97	Wünsch, P. Zur Lehre vom Beneficium Competentiae. Diss. Leipzig, 1897.
AH 4558.97	Yorck, M.G. Feldzüge Alexanders des Grossen. Berlin, 1897.

1898

Eg 1038.98.9	Adams, W.M. The book of the master. London, 1898.
AH 4458.98	Allcroft, Arthur H. The making of Athens; a history of Greece, 495-431 B.C. Photoreproduction. London, 1898.
AH 898.98	Beaurredon, J. Voyage agricole chez les anciens. Paris, 1898.
AH 938.98	Beiträge zur alten Geschichte und Geographie. Berlin, 1898.
AH 3059.5	Billerbeck, A. Das Sandschak Suliemania. Leipzig, 1898.
AH 888.98	Billeter, G. Geschichte des Zinfusses. Leipzig, 1898.
AH 3964.5	Blaw, L. Das altjüdische Zauberwesen. Strassburg, 1898.
AH 7818.95.5	Bloch, Leo. Römische Altertumskunde. 2. Aufl. Leipzig, 1898.
NEDL Eg 1038.98	Book of the Dead. The book of the dead. London, 1898. 3v.
AH 3132.6	Buchwald, R. Nebuchodnosor II von Babylon. n.p., 1898.
AH 4818.98.3	Burckhardt, J. Griechische Kulturgeschichte. 3. Aufl. Berlin, 1898. 4v.
AH 7758.98	Burckhardt, Jacob. Die Zeit Constantins des Grossen. Leipzig, 1898.
AH 7438.98	Burger, Combertus P. Der Kampf zwischen Rom und Samnium. Amsterdam, 1898.
AH 4278.98.10	Coleridge, E.P. Res graecae. London, 1898.
AH 3407.11	Conder, C.R. Hittites and their language. N.Y., 1898.
AH 4138.95.2	Dareste, R. Recueil des inscriptions juridiques grecques. Paris, 1898. 2v.
AH 3013.12	Delitzsch, F. Ex Oriente lux! Leipzig, 1898.
AH 4818.98	Dickinson, G.L. Greek view of life. 2nd ed. London, 1898.
AH 7818.98	Dill, Samuel. Roman society in the last century of the Western Empire. London, 1898.
AH 7178.98.2	Dreyfus, Robert. Essae sur les lois agraires. Paris, 1898.
AH 7168.98	Duquesne, J. Possession et de la détention en droit romain. Paris, 1898.
AH 5303.15	Ferguson, William S. The Athenian secretaries. Photoreproduction. N.Y., 1898.
AH 2503.5	Fougères, G. De Lyciorum communi. Lutetiae, 1898.
AH 48.93.5	Fowler, W.W. The city-state of the Greeks and Romans. London, 1898.
AH 4487.13	Frank, T. Themistokles. Mannheim, 1898.
AH 7448.74.4	Fried, F. Uber die Schlacht bei Cannä. Leipzig, 1898.
AH 7448.98.10	Fried, Friedrich. Über Die schlacht bei Cannä. Inaug. Diss. Leipzig, 1898.
AH 5386.7	Fritzsche, G. Geschichte Platääs. Bautzen, 1898.
AH 38.64.5	Fustel de Coulanges, N.D. La cité antique. 16. éd. Paris, 1898.

1898 - cont.

AH 7448.98.5	Garmendia, J.I. Estudios históricos y militares sobre las compañas de Anibal. Buenos Aires, 1898.
AH 4098.98	Gertz, M.C. Statog statsforfatninger. Kjøbenhavn, 1898.
AH 7650.72	Gibbon, Edward. The history of the decline and fall of the Roman Empire. London, 1898-1901. 7v.
AH 7628.98	Gregorovius, F.A. The Emperor Hadrian. London, 1898.
Eg 1308.98	Griffith, F.L. Hieratic papyri. London, 1898. 2v.
Eg 138.98	Griffith, F.L. Wills in ancient Egypt. London, 1898.
AH 7088.98	Halgan, C. Essai sur l'administration des provinces sénatoriales. Paris, 1898.
AH 8538.2	Hall, William H. Romans on the Riviera and the Rhone. London, 1898.
AH 1408.95.2	Hommel, Fritz. Geschichte des alten Morgenlandes. 2. Aufl. Leipzig, 1898.
AH 7278.96.7	How, W.W. History of Rome. London, 1898.
AH 3155.6.3	Jastrow, Morris. The religion of Babylonia and Assyria. v.1-2. Boston, 1898.
AH 3408.5	Jensen, P. Hittiter und Armenier. Strassburg, 1898.
AH 3187.7	Johnston, C. Epistolary literature of Assyrians and Babylonians. Baltimore, 1898.
AH 48.98	Kaerst, Julius. Studien zur Entwickelung...Monarchie...Altertum. Photoreproduction. München, 1898.
AH 2109.5	Karolides, Paul. Die sogenannten Assyro-Chaldäer und Hittiten. Athens, 1898.
AH 3030.3	King, L.W. Letters and inscriptions of Hammourabi. London, 1898-1900. 3v.
Eg 603.9	Klostermann, A. Diplomatischer Briefwechsel aus dem zweiten Jahrhundert vor Christo. Kiel, 1898.
AH 7098.98	Kornemann, Ernst. Zur Stadtentstehung. Giessen, 1898.
AH 7138.95	Landucci, L. Storia del diritto romano. 2. ed. Verona, 1898. 2v.
AH 7888.98	Levison, W. Die Buerkundung des Civilstandes. Bonn, 1898.
AH 7458.98	Lincke, E. Martin. P. Cornelius Scipio Amilianus. Dresden, 1898.
AH 4148.98	Lögdberg, L.E. Animadversiones de Aetione. Upsaliae, 1898.
AH 7228.98.5	Louvet, F. Juridictions criminelles à Rome. Paris, 1898.
AH 4828.74.5	Mahaffy, J.P. Social life in Greece. London, 1898.
Eg 658.98	Marucchi, Orazio. La biografia d'un personaggio politico dell'antico Egitto scritta sopra la sua statua. Roma, 1898.
AH 7228.98	Marzo, D.S. Procedura criminale romana. Palermo, 1898.
AH 188.98	Meyer, G. Die Sklaverei im Altertum. Dresden, 1898.
AH 4278.98	Myers, P. Van Ness. A history of Greece for colleges and high schools. Boston, 1898.
AH 7058.87.3	Niccolini, I. Tasti tribunorum plebis. Pisis, 1898.
AH 7178.98	Ossig, A. Römisches Wasserecht. Leipzig, 1898.
AH 7278.98	Pais, Ettore. Storia di Roma. v.1, pt.1-2. Torino, 1898. 2v.
Htn Eg 1108.98*	Papyrus d'Orbiney. The tale of the two brothers. Watchung, N.J., 1898.
AH 3013.37	Peters, J.P. Nippur or explorations...on the Euphrates. N.Y., 1898. 2v.
Eg 878.98	Petrie, William M.F. Religion and conscience in ancient Egypt. London, 1898.
AH 7438.98.5	Pirro, A. La seconda guerra samnitica. Salerno, 1898.
AH 4838.98	Plummer, E.M. Athletics and games of ancient Greece. Cambridge, Mass., 1898.
AH 3142.3	Rothstein, G. Die Dynastie der Lahmiden in al-Hira. Halle, 1898.
Eg 878.98.5	St. Clair, G. Creation records discovered in Egypt. London, 1898.
AH 5309.11	Sanctis, G. Atthis. Roma, 1898.
AH 3155.5.5	Sayce, A.H. Lectures on...growth of religion...ancient Babylonians. 5. ed. London, 1898.
AH 28.98	Scala, Rudolf von. Die Staatsverträge des Altertums. Leipzig, 1898.
AH 4818.98.25	Schmid, Wilhelm. Über den kulturgeschichtlichen Zusammenhang. Leipzig, 1898.
AH 7448.74.5	Schwab, Otto. Das Schlachtfeld von Cannä. München, 1898.
AH 4808.98	Solari, Arcturus. Fasti Ephororum spartanorum. Pisis, 1898.
AH 7468.98.5	Tarantino, Mario. La congiura catilinaria. Catania, 1898.
AH 7468.98	Tarantino, Mario. Questioni cronologiche. Catania, 1898.
AH 8.98	Tropea, Giacomo. Manuale di fonti letterarie. Messina, 1898.
AH 4188.98	Waszynski, S. De servis Atheniensium publicis. v.1-2. Berolini, 1898.
AH 7478.98	Wiegandt, L. Studien zur staatsrechtlichen Stellung. Dresden, 1898.
AH 1298.93.2	Winckler, H. Altorientalische Forschungen. Zweite Reihe. Leipzig, 1898. 3v.
AH 4558.98.3	Wulff, Oskar. Alexander mit der Lanze. Berlin, 1898.
AH 7898.98	Wurm, A. De villa rustica. Kempten, 1898.

1899

AH 4204.11	Anfossi, P.C. Legislazioni di Solone e Servio Tullo. Torino, 1899.
AH 9639.6	Arendt, A. Syrakus im zweiten peinischen Kriege. Königsberg, 1899.
AH 4148.99	Arvanitopullo, A. Questioni di diritto Attico. Roma, 1899.
AH 3159.16	Ball, C.J. Light from the East, or Witness of the monuments. London, 1899.
AH 3156.8	Bassi, D. Mitologia babilonese-assira. Milano, 1899.
AH 4008.99	Bauer, A. Forsuchungen zur griechischen Geschichten. München, 1899.
AH 7178.82.5	Beaudouin, E. Les grands domains dans l'Empire Romain. Paris, 1899.
AH 4828.40.20	Becker, W.A. Charicles. London, 1899.
AH 3160.5	Boissier, A. Note sur un monument babylonien. Genève, 1899.
AH 8007.7.5	Boissier, Gaston. Roman Africa. N.Y., 1899.
Eg 1038.99	Book of the Dead. The book of the dead. London, 1899.
AH 4278.99A	Botsford, George W. History of Greece. N.Y., 1899.
AH 9777.24	Bradley, Henry. The Goths from the earliest times to the end of the Gothic dominion. N.Y., 1899.
AH 9777.35	Braun, F.A. Toty i ikh' sosedidov. Sankt Peterburg, 1899.
AH 4523.7	Church, A.J. Nicias and Sicilian expedition. London, 1899.
AH 188.99	Ciccotti, Ettore. Il tramonto della schiavitù nel mondo antico. Torino, 1899.
AH 3002.2.14	Craig, James A. Astrological-astronomical texts. Leipzig, 1899.

1899 - cont.

AH 7138.99 — Czyhlarz, Karl. Lehrbuch der Institutionen des römischen Rechtes. 4. Aufl. Leipzig, 1899.

AH 7162.31 — Deutsch, H. Die Vorläufer der heutigen Testamentsvollstrecker. Berlin, 1899.

AH 7468.34.5 — Drumann, W. Geschichte Roms. v.1-6. Berlin, 1899. 5v.

AH 3915.5 — Dürst, J.U. Die Rinder von Babylonien, Assyrien. Berlin, 1899.

AH 7278.67.27 — Duruy, V. Histoire romaine. Paris, 1899.

Eg 1308.99.5 — Erman, Adolf. Aus den Papyrus der Königlichen Museen. Berlin, 1899.

AH 7228.99 — Erman, Karl. Conceptio formularum, actio in factum und ipso iure-Consumption. Weimar, 1899.

AH 7448.99.5 — Gaez, H. Nachmals des Schlachtfeld von Cannä. Frankfurt, 1899.

AH 7201.79 — Gaius. Institutiones. 4th ed. Berolini, 1899. 7v.

AH 7651.19 — Gibbon, Edward. The history of the decline and fall of the Roman Empire. v.2. London, 1899.

AH 7138.99.5 — Gilson, J. L'étude du droit romain comparé aux autres droits de l'antiquité. Paris, 1899.

NEDL AH 4278.46.34 — Grote, George. Greece. N.Y., 1899-1901. 2v.

AH 7298.99F — Gubernatis, A. de. Roma e l'Oriente. Roma, 1899.

Eg 603.6 — Halevy, J. Correspondance d'Amenophis III. Paris, 1899.

AH 938.99 — Heeren, A. De chorographia a Valerio Flacco. Inaug. Diss. Gottingae, 1899.

AH 6024.9 — Hiller von Gaertringen, F. Geschichte von Delphi. Stuttgart, 1899.

AH 158.99 — Hitzig, H.F. Injuria. München, 1899.

AH 7888.99 — Hoffmeister, K. Die wirtschaftliche Entwicklung Roms. Wien, 1899.

AH 4202.11 — Hofmann, I. Studien zur drakontischen Verfassung. Straubing, 1899.

NEDL AH 4278.86.10 — Holm, Adolf. The history of Greece. London, 1899-1902. 4v.

AH 7478.99 — Holmes, T.R.E. Caesar's conquest of Gaul. London, 1899.

AH 7448.99 — How, W.W. Hannibal and the Great War. London, 1899.

AH 3013.6.5 — Kaulen, Franz. Assyrien und Babylonien. 5. Aufl. Freiburg, 1899.

AH 6007.5 — Kazarow, G. Foederis Phocensium institutis. Lipsiae, 1899.

AH 4558.99 — Koepp, F. Alexander der Grosse. Bielefeld, 1899.

AH 4258.99 — Kolbe, G. De Atheniensium re navali quaestiones. Tubingae, 1899.

AH 1278.99 — Krall, J. Grundriss der altorientalischen Geschichte. Wien, 1899.

AH 7161.21 — Laënnec, R. Droit des patresfamilias. Saint-Amand, 1899.

AH 8608.3 — Lamarre, C. Étude sur peuples anciens de l'Italie. Paris, 1899.

AH 7038.99 — Lengle, Joseph. Untersuchungen über die sulianische Verfassung. Freiburg, 1899.

AH 7918.99 — Levasseur, E. L'organisation des métiers. Paris, 1899.

Eg 278.94.4 — Mahaffy, J.P. A history of Egypt under the Ptolemaic dynasty. v.4. London, 1899.

AH 4818.96.5A — Mahaffy, J.P. Survey of Greek civilization. N.Y., 1899.

Eg 278.99 — Marucchi, Orazio. Lo scarabeo onorario di una regina d'Egitto nel Museo egizio vaticano. Roma, 1899.

AH 3103.4 — Maspero, G. Life in ancient Egypt and Assyria. N.Y., 1899.

AH 7629.04 — Mecklin, J.M. Hadrians Rescript an Minicius Fundanus. Leipzig, 1899.

AH 7068.99 — Mispoulet, J.B. La vie parlementaire a Rome. Paris, 1899.

AH 7478.54.2 — Mommsen, T. History of Rome. N.Y., 1899. 2v.

AH 7298.86.2 — Mommsen, Theodor. The provinces of the Roman empire, from Caesar to Diocletian. N.Y., 1899. 2v.

AH 7158.99 — Mommsen, Theodor. Römisches Strafrecht. Leipzig, 1899.

AH 298.99 — Mücke, C. Vom Euphrat zum Tiber. Leipzig, 1899.

Eg 1078.99F — Müller, W.M. Die Liebespoisie der alten Ägypter. Leipzig, 1899.

AH 7168.86.6 — Muirhead, J. Historical introduction to the private law of Rome. 2. ed. London, 1899.

Eg 1308.99 — Newberry, R.E. The Amherst papyri. London, 1899.

AH 7055.93.8 — Notitia dignitatum, or Register. Philadelphia, 1899.

AH 7278.54.37 — Pais, Ettore. Ottantaduesimo anniversario di Theodor Mommsen. Messina, 1899.

AH 3159.15.5 — Price, I.M. The monuments and the Old Testament. Chicago, 1899.

AH 3002.2.15 — Price, Ira M. The great cylinder inscriptions A and B of Gudea. Pt.1-2. Leipzig, 1899-1927. 2v.

AH 2013.10 — Proksch, Otto. Über die Blutrache bei den vorislamischen Arabern und Mohammeds Stellung zu Christ. Leipzig, 1899.

AH 3021.3 — Radar, H. Early Babylonian history. N.Y., 1899.

NEDL AH 408.99 — Ragozin, Z.A. (Mrs.). A history of the world. N.Y., 1899.

AH 9777.31A — Rappaport, B. De Gotorum usque ad decium imperatorem. Berlin, 1899.

AH 9777.33 — Rappaport, B. Die Einfälle der Goten in der römische Reich. Leipzig, 1899.

AH 7468.99 — Regling, Kurt L. De belli Parthici Crassiani fontibus. Berolini, 1899.

AH 7808.99.3 — Rolando, A. Chronologia storica Roma. Torino, 1899.

AH 3142.3.3 — Rothstein, G. Die Dynastie der Lahmiden in al-Hira. Berlin, 1899.

AH 7178.99 — Salvioli, G. Sulla distribuzione della proprietà fondiaria in Italia al tempo dell'impero romano. Modena, 1899.

AH 3143.7 — Sayce, A.H. Babylonians and Assyrians. N.Y., 1899.

AH 7448.74.6 — Schutz, Karl. Die Schlacht bei Cannä. Donaueschingen, 1899.

AH 7497.21.25 — Serviez, J.R. de. The Roman empresses. London, 1899. 2v.

AH 4808.99 — Svoronos, J.M. Der athenische Volkskalender. Athens, 1899.

AH 8210.7 — Tamblyn, William F. The establishment of Roman power in Britain. Hamilton, Ont., 1899.

AH 7038.99.2 — Taylor, Thomas M. Constitutional and political history of Rome. London, 1899.

AH 7418.99 — Tegge, August. Die Staatsgewalten der römischen Republik. Bunzlau, 1899.

AH 7818.97.5 — Thomas, Emile. Roman life under the Caesars. N.Y., 1899.

AH 7888.99.3 — Thomas, Paul. Essai sur...théories économiques. Paris, 1899.

AH 7818.99 — Thomas, Paul. Moeurs romaines. Bruxelles, 1899.

AH 298.99.3 — Zeitschrift für Altegeschichte. Leipzig, 1899.

19-

Eg 879.00.5 — Blackden, M.W. Ritual of the mystery of the judgment of the soul. London, 19- .

AH 3962.22 — Panin, I.N. Bible chronology. pt.1-3. Lowestoft, 19- ?

Eg 138.99 — Uah. Oldest known will. Philadelphia, 19- .

190-

AH 7818.65.17 — Friedlaender, Ludwig. Roman life and manners. London, 190-. 4v.

AH 1278.62.6 — Rawlinson, G. Five great monarchies of the ancient Eastern World. N.Y., 190-? 3v.

AH 3657.13.5 — Rawlinson, G. Seventh great oriental monarchy. v.1-2. N.Y., 190-?

AH 3607.9.5 — Rawlinson, G. Sixth great oriental monarchy. N.Y., 190-?

1900

AH 4479.00 — Agricola, Ernest. De Aristidis censu. Berolini, 1900.

AH 7239.00 — Baehr, W. De centurionibus legionariis. Berolini, 1900.

AH 7889.00 — Bloch, Leo. Die ständlichen und sozialen Kämpfe. Leipzig, 1900.

AH 4278.99.3 — Botsford, George W. A history of Greece for high schools and academies. N.Y., 1900.

AH 4309.00 — Bouché-Leclercq, A. Leçons d'histoire grecque. Paris, 1900.

AH 3013.9.5A — British Museum. Guide to the Babylonian and Assyrian antiquities. London, 1900.

AH 4859.13 — Bruns, Ivo. Frauenemancipation in Athen. Kiliae, 1900.

Eg 879.00 — Budge, Ernest Alfred Wallis. Egyptian ideas of the future life. 2. ed. London, 1900.

AH 7203.97 — Corpus juris civilis. Digesta. Digest XLI. Cambridge, Eng., 1900.

AH 2966.2 — Degen, H. De Troianis Scaenicis. Lipsiae, 1900.

AH 3002.2.16 — Delitzsch, Friedrich. Assyrische Lesestücke, mit grammatische Tabellen. 4. Aufl. Leipzig, 1900.

AH 4909.00 — Francotte, Henri. L'industrie dans la Grèce ancienne. Bruxelles, 1900-01. 2v.

AH 4959.00A — Frazer, James G. Pausanias and other Greek sketches. London, 1900.

AH 7478.81.10 — Froude, J.A. Julius Caesar. N.Y., 1900.

AH 7509.00 — Gabrici, E. Il secondo viaggio di Augusto in Oriente. Napoli, 1900.

AH 5138.13 — Gelder, H. Geschichte der alten Rhodier. Haag, 1900.

Eg 1109.00 — Griffith, F.L. Stories of the high priests of Memphis. [Sethon-Khamuas]. v.1, Atlas. Oxford, 1900. 2v.

AH 4889.00 — Guiraud, P. Main d'oeuvre industrielle. Paris, 1900.

AH 3060.3.9 — Heuzey, L. Une villa royal Chaldéenne. Paris, 1900.

AH 7203.99 — Hofmann, F. Digesten Justinians. Wien, 1900.

AH 7799.00 — Hossner, K. Die letzten Kaiser des römischen Abendlandes. Bielitz, 1900.

AH 7469.00 — Hubel, Karl. Die Beiffragmente der Cornelia. Erlangen, 1900.

AH 4609.00 — Hünerwadel, W. Geschichte des Königs Lysimachos. Zürich, 1900.

AH 3073.3A — Kellner, M. The Assyrian monuments illustrating sermons of Isaiah. Boston, 1900.

AH 842.32.2 — Laurie, S.S. Historical survey of pre-Christian education. 2. ed. N.Y., 1900.

AH 4819.00 — Lefèvre, A. Grèce antique. Paris, 1900.

AH 7109.00 — Leo, Fritz. Die Capitatio Plebeia. Berlin, 1900.

AH 7099.00.2 — Leogrande, P. I cognomi delle colonie romane militari. Trani, 1900.

AH 7099.00.4 — Liebenam, W. Stadtsverwaltung in römischen Kaiserreiche. Leipzig, 1900.

AH 3154.5 — Martin, F. Textes religieux assyriens et babyloniens. Paris, 1900.

AH 1279.00 — Maspero, Gaston. The passing of the empires, 850 B.C.-330 B.C. London, 1900.

AH 7579.00 — Mayor, G. Kaiser Titus. Eger, 1900.

Eg 709.00.5 — Meyer, Paul M. Das Heerwesen der Ptolemäer und Römer in Ägypten. Leipzig, 1900.

AH 7479.00 — Moineville, L. Deux campagnes de César. Paris, 1900.

AH 7278.54.21 — Mommsen, T. History of Rome. N.Y., 1900. 5v.

AH 7449.01 — Montanari, T. Annibale. Rovigo, 1900-01.

AH 7279.00 — Myers, P.V.N. Rome; its rise and fall. Boston, 1900.

AH 4859.15 — Navarre, O. Mulieres Athenienses. Tolosae, 1900.

AH 7179.00 — Neumann, K.J. Die Grundherrschaft der Römischen Republik. Strassburg, 1900.

AH 4659.00 — Niese, B. Welt des Hellenismus. Marburg, 1900.

NEDL AH 7509.00.7F — Oberziner, G. Le guerre di Augusto contro i populi alpini. Roma, 1900.

AH 8607.2.10F — Pais, Ettore. Gli elementi ilaliati sanniciti e campani nella più antica civiltà romana. Napoli, 1900.

Eg 1109.00.5 — Papyrus d'Orbiney. Papyrus d'Orbiney. The hieroglyphic transcription. Watchung, N.J., 1900.

AH 7549.00.2 — Pascal, Carlo. L'incendio di Roma e i primi christiani. Milano, 1900.

AH 3159.15 — Price, I.M. The monuments and the Old Testament. 2. ed. Chicago, 1900.

AH 3021.3.3 — Radar, H. Early Babylonian history. N.Y., 1900.

AH 3507.7.5 — Ragozin, Z.A. Media, Babylon, and Persia. N.Y., 1900.

AH 842.23 — Rauschen, G. Griechisch-römische Schulwesen. Bonn, 1900.

AH 139.00 — Rivalta, V. Atticarum et Romanarum legum collatio. Ravennae, 1900.

AH 3075.7 — Robertson, H.S. Voices of the past from Assyria and Babylonia. London, 1900.

AH 3009.00 — Rogers, R.W. A history of Babylonia and Assyria. N.Y., 1900. 2v.

AH 8914.5 — Rossi, S. Il tipo e l'ufficio del charun etrusco. Messina, 1900.

Eg 809.00 — Schmidt, Orlando P. A self-verifying chronological history of ancient Egypt. Cincinnati, 1900.

AH 9071.2 — Schmidt, Otto Eduard. Arpinum, eine topographischhistorische Skizze. Meissen, 1900.

Eg 709.00 — Schubart, W. Quaestiones de rebus militaribus...in regno Lagidarum. Trebnitz, 1900.

AH 3966.5.7 — Smith, George A. The historical geography of the Holy Land. 7. ed. N.Y., 1900.

NEDL AH 4278.57.25 — Smith, William. History of Greece. London, 1900.

Eg 279.00 — Steindorff, G. Die Blütezeit des Pharaohenreichs. Bielefeld, 1900.

AH 7203.98 — Suchier, H. Die Handschriften der castilianischen Übersetzung des Codi. Halis, 1900.

AH 7099.00 — Tanfani, L. Ricerche storiche-epigrafiche. Taranto, 1900.

AH 7139.01.8 — Theophanopoulos, D. Susthema pomaikou dikaiou. Athens, 1900. 3 pam.

Chronological Listing

1900 - cont.

AH 7109.00.2 — Thibault, F. Les impots directs. Paris, 1900.
AH 7844.4 — Vollbrecht, W. Das Sakularfest des Augustus. Gütersloh, 1900.
AH 4559.00A — Wheeler, B.I. Alexander the Great. N.Y., 1900.
AH 4558.29.50 — Williams, John. The life and actions of Alexander the Great. N.Y., 1900.
AH 4473.5 — Witkowski, S. De pace quae dicitur cimonica. Leopoli, 1900.

1901

AH 7039.01.2 — Abbott, Frank F. History and description of Roman political institutions. Boston, 1901.
AH 7039.01 — Abbott, Frank F. History and description of Roman political institutions. Boston, 1901.
AH 8548.48 — Adam, Maurice. La tradition celtique et ses adversaires. Paris, 1901.
AH 7179.01 — Angelis Mangano, E. Sulle forme primitive. Catania, 1901.
AH 3173.5A — Assyrian and Babylonian literature. N.Y., 1901.
AH 7299.01 — Barbagallo, C. Le relazioni politiche di Roma con l'egitto. Roma, 1901.
Eg 1029.01.5FA — Berlin. Koniglichen Museen. Hieratische Papyrus. Leipzig, 1901- 5v.
AH 7939.01 — Bessem, E. De terminis et terminationibus. Groningae, 1901.
NEDL AH 7279.01 — Botsford, G.W. History of Rome. N.Y., 1901.
Eg 885.899.2 — Budge, Ernest Alfred Wallis. Egyptian magic. London, 1901.
AH 7059.03F — Cantarelli, L. La diocesi italiana. Roma, 1901.
AH 239.01 — Ciccotti, Ettore. La guerra et la pace. Torino, 1901.
AH 7139.01.3 — Costa, E. Storia del diritto romano. Bologna, 1901. 2v.
AH 7469.01 — Deknatel, Christian. De vita M. Lucinis Crassi. Lugduni-Batavorum, 1901.
AH 4278.56.25 — Duruy, V. Histoire grecque. 32. éd. Paris, 1901.
Eg 1029.01.15 — Egyptian literature. London, 1901.
AH 7909.01F — Forcella, V. Le industrie e il commercio. Milano, 1901.
AH 3002.98 — Fossey, C. Syllabaire cunéiforme. Paris, 1901.
AH 7818.65.11 — Friedlaender, Ludwig. Darstellungen aus der Sittengeschichte Roms. 7. Aufl. Leipzig, 1901. 2v.
AH 7229.01 — Girard, P.F. Histoire de l'organization judiciaire. Paris, 1901.
AH 2014.6 — Hommel, Fritz. Der Gestirndienst der alten Araber. München, 1901.
AH 3002.2.17 — Johns, Claude H. An Assyrian doomsday book. Leipzig, 1901.
AH 4659.01 — Kaerst, Julius. Geschichte des hellenistischen Zeitalters. Leipzig, 1901. 2v.
AH 7851.2 — Krell, Otto. Altrömische Heizungen. München, 1901.
AH 7149.01 — Kuhn, F.J. Betrachtungen über Majestäten. München, 1901.
AH 3707.21 — Landau, W. Die Phönizier. Leipzig, 1901.
Eg 278.94.21 — Lane-Poole, Stanley. A history of Egypt in the Middle Ages. N.Y., 1901.
Eg 278.94.6A — Lane-Poole, Stanley. A history of Egypt in the Middle Ages. v.6. London, 1901.
AH 4929.01 — Lehmann, C.F. Gewichte aus Thera. Berlin, 1901.
AH 3013.30 — Lehmann-Haupt, C.F. Materialen zur Kultur...der Chalder...Ausgrabungen. Berlin, 1901.
AH 7278.79.12 — Leighton, R.F. A history of Rome. N.Y., 1901.
AH 7204.11 — Lenel, Otto. L'édit perpétuel. Paris, 1901. 2v.
AH 7519.01.5 — Lévy, L. Quo modo Tiberius Claudius Nero. Paris, 1901.
AH 3159.7 — Loisy, Alfred. Les mythes babyloniens. Paris, 1901.
AH 7139.01.5 — May, Gaston. Éléments de droit romain. 7e éd. Paris, 1901.
AH 842.25 — Monroe, Paul. Source book of the history of education. N.Y., 1901.
AH 7279.00.5 — Myers, P.V.N. Rome; its rise and fall. 2. ed. Boston, 1901.
AH 4859.17F — Notor, G. La femme. Paris, 1901.
AH 7114.14 — Oberziner, G. Origine della Plebe Romana. Leipzig, 1901.
AH 4278.90.7.5 — Oman, C.W.C. History of Greece. 7. ed. N.Y., 1901.
AH 7448.18.10 — Osiander, W. Der Hannibalweg. Berlin, 1901.
AH 3909.7A — Paton, L.B. The early history of Syria and Palestine. N.Y., 1901.
AH 4889.01 — Pestalozza, U. Vita economica Ateniese. Milano, 1901.
AH 4843.11 — Poirée, E. Nouvelle interprétation rythmique. Solesmes, 1901.
AH 8607.7 — Puglisi-Marino, S. Sul nome Italia. Catania, 1901.
NEDL AH 7818.48.17A — Ramsay, William. Manual of Roman antiquities. 17th ed. London, 1901.
AH 842.23.5 — Rauschen, G. Das griechisch-römische Schulwesen zur zeit des ausgehenden Heidentums. Bonn, 1901.
AH 4409.01A — Ridgeway, W. Early age of Greece. Cambridge, 1901-31. 2v.
AH 7549.00 — Sabatini, F. Pascal. L'incendio di Roma. Roma, 1901. 5 pam.
AH 840.7 — Samter, Ernst. Familienfeste. Berlin, 1901.
AH 8011.4 — Schmidt, L. Geschichte der Wandalen. Leipzig, 1901.
AH 9089.5 — Serafini, P. Intorno a Sulmona del Lazio distrutta da Lucio Silla. 2. ed. Sulmona, 1901.
AH 959.01 — Skeel, C.A.J. Travel in the first century after Christ. Cambridge, 1901.
Eg 1029.01F — Spiegelberg, W. Demotische Studien. Hefte 1-8 and plates 5-6. Leipzig, 1901- 10v.
AH 7058.87.5 — Stella Maranca, F. Il tribunato della Plebe. Lanciano, 1901.
NEDL AH 299.01 — Strehl, Willy. Grundriss der alten Geschichte. Breslau, 1901. 2v.
AH 3052.9F — Toscanne, P. Les cylindres de Gudéa. Paris, 1901.
AH 7519.01 — Viertel, A. Tiberius und Germanicus. Göttingen, 1901.
AH 3155.4.5 — Zimmern, Heinrich. The Babylonian and the Hebrew genesis. London, 1901.
AH 3002.2.12 — Zimmern, Heinrich. Beiträge zur Kenntnis der babylonischen Religion. Leipzig, 1901.

1902

AH 7448.18.11A — Azan, Paul. Annibal dans les Alpes. Oran, 1902.
AH 4216.5 — Beasley, T.W. Le cautionnement. Paris, 1902.
AH 9286.2 — Besnier, M. De regione Paelignorum. Lutetiae Parisiorum, 1902.
AH 3910.7 — Bevan, E.R. The house of Seleucus. London, 1902. 2v.
AH 2014.5 — Blochet, E. Le culte d'Aphrodite-Anahita. Chalon-sur-Saône, 1902.

1902 - cont.

AH 3005.5 — Booth, A.J. Discovery...of trilingual cuneiform inscriptions. London, 1902.
NEDL AH 279.02.2 — Botsford, G.W. Ancient history for beginners. N.Y., 1902.
AH 7139.02 — Brassloff, S. Kenntniss des Volksrechtes. Weimar, 1902.
AH 3002.94 — British Museum. Department of Egyptian and Assyrian Antiquities. Annals of the kings of Assyria. London, 1902-
Eg 279.02 — Budge, Ernest Alfred Wallis. A history of Egypt. London, 1902. 8v.
AH 4279.00.4A — Bury, John Bagnell. History of Greece. London, 1902. 2v.
AH 5307.23 — Butler, Howard C. Story of Athens. London, 1902.
AH 5307.23.5 — Butler, Howard C. Story of Athens. N.Y., 1902.
AH 7549.02 — Cavazzi, C.G. Sull'incendio di Roma. Roma, 1902.
AH 7203.101 — Corpus juris civilis. Digesta. Digest XVII. Cambridge, Eng., 1902.
Htn AH 7203.4PF* — Corpus juris civilis. Digesta. Digestorum seu Pandectarum codex Florentinus. v.1-2. Roma, 1902-10. 10v.
AH 3159.5.3 — Delitzsch, F. Babel und Bibel. Leipzig, 1902.
AH 7549.02.5 — Difesa dei primi cristiani e martiri. Roma, 1902.
AH 7889.02 — Esser, J.J. De Pauperum cura apud Romanos. Campis, 1902.
AH 3156.10 — Fossey, C. La magie assyrienne. Paris, 1902.
AH 3407.13 — Fossey, C. Quid de Hethaeis. Versailles, 1902.
AH 7818.65.27 — Friedlaender, Ludwig. Town life in ancient Italy. Boston, 1902.
Htn AH 8549.102* — Gaidoz, Henri. Le grand dieu gaulois...Allobroges. n.p., 1902.
AH 939.02.2 — Gautier, E.F. Indici oceani pars. Lutetiia, 1902.
Eg 971.9.5 — Gayet, A.J. Antinoï et les sepultures de Thaïs et Serapion. Paris, 1902.
AH 5657.4 — Geyer, F. Topographie...der Insel Euboia. Kirchain, 1902.
NEDL AH 7650.75 — Gibbon, Edward. History of decline and fall of Roman Empire. N.Y., 1902. 5v.
AH 7015.11F — Götz, Georg. C. Maecenas. Rede...zur Feier der akademischen Preisvertheilung. Jena, 1902. 3 pam.
AH 3009.02 — Goodspeed, G.S. A history of the Babylonians and Assyrians. N.Y., 1902.
NEDL AH 8007.2 — Graham, A. Roman Africa...Roman occupation of Africa. London, 1902.
AH 7039.02 — Granrud, John E. Roman constitutional history, 753-44 B.C. Boston, 1902.
NEDL AH 818.62.15 — Guhl, Ernst. The life of Greeks and Romans described from antique monuments. N.Y., 1902.
AH 4819.02A — Gulick, C.B. Life of ancient Greeks. N.Y., 1902.
AH 4819.02.3A — Gulick, Charles B. Life of the ancient Greeks. N.Y., 1902.
AH 4559.02 — Hackmann, F. Schlacht bei Gaugamela. Halle, 1902.
AH 2583.7 — Haussoulier, B. L'histoire de Milet. Photoreproduction. Paris, 1902.
AH 7204.21 — Hellems, F.B.R. Lex de Imperio Vespasiani. Chicago, 1902.
AH 4214.11 — Hirzel, R. Der Eid. Leipzig, 1902.
AH 4852.5 — Huddilston, J.H. Lessons from Greek pottery. N.Y., 1902.
AH 939.02.5 — Jobst, D. Scylla und Charybdis, eine geographische Studien. Würzburg, 1902.
AH 7909.02 — Juglar, L. Quamodo per servos libertosque negotiarentur Romani imperii temporibus. Paris, 1902.
AH 7189.02 — Juglar, L. Zuomodo per servos...negotiarentur Romani. Paris, 1902.
AH 4499.02 — Keil, Bruno. Anonymus Argentinensis. Strassburg, 1902.
AH 3179.7.10 — King, Leonard W. Seven tablets of creation. London, 1902.
AH 3183.15 — Die Labartu-Texte. Strassburg, 1902.
AH 7200.15 — Lambert, E. L'origine des XII tables. Paris, 1902.
AH 7846.4 — Lanz-Liebenfels. Wie heizten die Römer ihre Wohnraume. Umschau, 1902.
AH 930.20 — Lord, John K. Atlas of the geography and history of the ancient world. Boston, 1902.
AH 4828.74.8 — Mahaffy, J.P. Social life in Greece from Homer to Menander. London, 1902.
AH 8609.4 — Modestov, V.I. Vvednie v rimskuiu. Sankt Peterburg, 1902-04. 2v.
AH 7847.2 — Morgan, M.H. Remarks on water supply of ancient Rome. Boston, 1902.
AH 939.02 — Müller, C. Studien zur Geschichte der Erdkunde. Breslau, 1902.
AH 3936.7 — Müller, F. Studien über Zenobia und Palmyra. Kirchain, 1902.
AH 7779.01.3 — Negri, G. L'imperatore Giuliano L'Apostata. Milano, 1902.
AH 7469.02.5 — Neunheuser, J. Aemilius Lepidus. Essen, 1902.
AH 3192.5 — Oefele, F.F. Keilschriftmedicin. Breslan, 1902.
AH 7469.02 — Oman, Charles. Seven Roman statesmen of the later Republic. London, 1902.
AH 7469.02.2 — Oman, Charles. Seven Roman statesmen of the later Republic. N.Y., 1902.
AH 7809.02 — Pais, Ettore. Saggio di illustrazione del calendario romano. Napoli, 1902.
AH 3013.13.5 — Paris. Musée Nationale du Louvre. Catalogue des antiquités chaldéennes. Paris, 1902.
AH 7549.00.3 — Pascal, Carlo. L'incendie de Rome et premiers chrétiens. Paris, 1902.
AH 3159.14 — Pinches, T.G. The Old Testament in the light of the historical records. London, 1902.
AH 7009.02 — Platner, S.B. Credibility of early Roman history. n.p., 1902.
AH 4309.02 — Pöhlmann, R. Griechische Geschichte. München, 1902.
AH 4479.02 — Reuther, H. Pausanias, Sohn des Kleombrotos. Bonn, 1902.
AH 9607.9.25 — Revelli, P. La storia della Sicilia nell'antichità. Pinerolo, 1902.
Eg 139.02 — Revillout, Eugène. Les rapports historiques et legaux des Quirites et des Egyptiens. Paris, 1902.
AH 7169.02 — Roby, H.J. Roman private law. Cambridge, 1902. 2v.
AH 8548.50 — Roessler, C. Les influences celtiques. Paris, 1902.
AH 7919.02 — Rossi, G.B. de. La villa di silio italico ed il collegio. n.p., 1902.
AH 7168.83.2 — Salkowski, C. Institutionen. 8. Aufl. Leipzig, 1902.
AH 7861.10 — Santoro, B. La Nenia Latina. Acireale, 1902.
AH 9604.5 — Scicilano-Villanueva, L. Sul diritto greco-romano (privato) in Sicilia. Palermo, 1902.
AH 7509.02 — Seeck, Otto. Kaiser Augustus. Bielefeld, 1902.
AH 3150.7A — Stevenson, J.H. Assyrian and Babylonian contracts. N.Y., 1902.
AH 7519.02 — Tarver, J.C. Tiberius the tyrant. N.Y., 1902.
AH 9614.5 — Tropea, G. Carta teotopiche della Sicilia antica. Padova, 1902.
X Cg AH 4559.02.3F — Ujfalvy, C. d'. Type physique d'Alexandre le Grand. Paris, 1902.
AH 7499.02A — Van Santvoord, S. The house of Caesar. Troy, 1902.

Chronological Listing

1902 - cont.

AH 7589.02 — Vieze, H. Domitians Chattenkrieg. Berlin, 1902.
AH 4819.02.2 — Wagner, J. Realien aus Griechischesk Alterthums. 4. Aufl. Brünn, 1902.
AH 1298.93.3 — Winckler, H. Altorientalische Forschungen. Dritte Reihe. Leipzig, 1902. 3v.
AH 4845.19 — Wolff, E. Philanthropie bei den Griechen. Berlin, 1902.
NEDL AH 279.02.5 — Wolfson, A.M. Essentials in ancient history. N.Y., 1902.
AH 7139.02.5 — Zoll, F. Historya Prawodawstwa Rzymskiego. Kraków, 1902. 2v.

1903

AH 4559.03 — Anspach, A.E. De Alexandri Magni expeditionis Indiea. Lipsiae, 1903.
AH 3159.5.10 — Babel und Bibel. n.p., 1903. 2 pam.
AH 7828.38.20 — Becker, W.A. Gallus or Roman scenes. London, 1903.
AH 4938.87 — Berger, H. Geschichte der...Erdkunde der Griechen. Leipzig, 1903.
AH 7519.03.2 — Bergmans, Jan. Die Quellen der Vita Tiberii. Bockhandel, 1903.
AH 7239.03.2 — Beuchel, F. De legione Romanorum i Italica. Lipsiae, 1903.
AH 3009.03 — Bezold, C. Ninive und Babylon. Bielefeld, 1903.
AH 3021.4 — Boscawen, W. St. C. The first of empires. London, 1903.
AH 7279.01.3 — Botsford, G.W. Story of Rome. N.Y., 1903.
Eg 709.03 — Bouché-Leclercq, A. Histoire des Lagides. v.4, photoreproduction. Paris, 1903. 4v.
AH 39.03.2 — Boxler, A.A. Précis des institutions publiques...Grèce et Rome. Paris, 1903.
AH 4609.03 — Breccia, Evaristo. Il diritto dinastico nelle monarchie dei successori d'Alexxandro Magno. Roma, 1903.
AH 7139.03.5 — Conrat, M. Breviarium Alaricianum. Leipzig, 1903.
AH 7203.91.5 — Corpus juris civilis. Institutiones. Imperatoris Justiniani Institutionum libri quattuor. 4th ed. Oxford, 1903.
NEDL AH 7278.85.3.15 — Creighton, M. Nociones de historia de Roma. N.Y., 1903.
AH 7868.2 — Curtel, G. La vigne et le vin chez les Romains. Paris, 1903.
AH 4842.35.5 — Davidson, T. Education of the Greek people. N.Y., 1903.
Eg 709.03.5.6 — De Bernáth, D. Cléopâtre; sa vie, son règne. Paris, 1903.
AH 3159.5.6 — Delitzsch, F. Babel and Bible. Chicago, 1903.
AH 3159.5.5 — Delitzsch, F. Babel and Bible. N.Y., 1903.
AH 3013.12.15 — Delitzsch, F. Im Lande des einstigen Paradieses. Stuttgart, 1903.
AH 3914.6 — Dussaud, R. Notes de mythologie syrienne. Paris, 1903.
AH 7729.03 — Duviquet, Georges. Héliogabale. Paris, 1903.
AH 7509.03 — Firth, John B. Augustus Caesar. N.Y., 1903.
AH 2147.4 — Foucart, P. Formation de province romaine d'Asie. Paris, 1903.
AH 38.64.6 — Fustel de Coulanges, N.D. La cité antique. 18. éd. Paris, 1903.
AH 8548.125 — Gaulle, C. de. Les Celtes au XIX. siècle. Paris, 1903.
AH 5657.5 — Geyer, F. Topographie...der Insel Euboia. Berlin, 1903.
AH 7138.95.5 — Girard, P.F. Textes de droit romain. 3. éd. Paris, 1903.
AH 7469.03 — Greenidge, A.H.J. Sources for Roman history, B.C. 133-70. Oxford, 1903.
AH 7819.03.3 — Grupp, G. Kulturgeschichte...Kaiserzeit. München, 1903. 2v.
AH 8157.4 — Gsell, Stéphane. L'Algérie dans l'antique. Alger, 1903.
AH 9621.7 — Hagt, W. van de. De urbe Agrigentinorum. Roterodami, 1903.
AH 3151.4 — Hammurabi, king of Babylonia. The oldest code of laws in the world. Edinburgh, 1903.
AH 3151.4.5 — Hammurabi, king of Babylonia. The oldest code of laws in the world. Edinburgh, 1903.
AH 7659.03 — Hartmann, L.M. Untergang der antiken Welt. Wien, 1903.
AH 7239.03.4 — Helbig, W. Sur l'aes pararium. Paris, 1903. 2 pam.
AH 7599.03 — Henderson, B.W. Life and principate of Emperor Nero. London, 1903.
AH 3013.10A — Hilprecht, H.V. Explorations in Bible lands. Philadelphia, 1903.
AH 3960.7 — Hölscher, G. Palästina in der persischen und hellenistischen Zeit. Berlin, 1903.
AH 7709.03 — Homo, Léon P. De Claudio Gothico, Romanorum. Lutetiae Parisiorum, 1903.
AH 4889.03 — Huch, G. Die Organisation der offentlichen Arbeit. Schlesien, 1903.
Eg 909.03 — Hultsch, F. Die ptolemäischen Münz und Rechnungswerte. Leipzig, 1903.
AH 3159.5.12 — Jeremias, A. In Kämpfe um Babel und Bibel. 3. Aufl. Leipzig, 1903.
AH 189.03 — Jerovšek, Anton. Die antik-heidnische Sklaverei. Marburg, 1903.
AH 7829.03.2 — Johnston, Harold W. Private life of the Romans. Chicago, 1903.
AH 7829.03A — Johnston, Harold W. Private life of the Romans. Chicago, 1903.
AH 8514.8 — Jullian, C. Recherches sur la religion gauloise. Bordeaux, 1903.
AH 309.03 — Kaerst, J. Antike Idee der Oekumene. Leipzig, 1903.
AH 3155.8 — King, L.W. Babylonian religion and mythology. London, 1903.
AH 7139.03 — Kipp, T. Geschichte...des römischen Rechts. Leipzig, 1903.
AH 4239.03.2 — Kromayer, J. Antike Schlachtfelder. v.1-4. Berlin, 1903-31. 5v.
AH 3097.3 — Lau, R.J. The annals of Ashurbanapal. Leiden, 1903.
AH 3005.855 — Layard, Austen Henry. Sir A. Henry Layard; autobiography and letters. London, 1903. 2v.
AH 9646.5 — Lazonder, A. Zande-Messana. Rhenum, 1903.
AH 3659.10 — Lindl, Ernest. Enstehung und Blüte...des altorientalischen Kulturwelt: Cyrus. München, 1903.
AH 8716.5 — Lucarelli, Antonio. Saggio sulla geografia storica dell Japigia. Trani, 1903.
AH 7509.03.3 — Meyer, Eduard. Kaiser Augustus. Heidelberg, 1903.
AH 7448.18.12 — Montanari, T. Punto per Punto. Mantova, 1903.
Eg 659.03 — Moret, A. De Bocchori Rege. Paris, 1903.
AH 4539.03 — Motzki, A. Eubulos von Probalinthos. Königsberg, 1903.
AH 3151.8 — Müller, D.H. Die Gesetze Hammurabis. Wien, 1903.
AH 4719.03 — Mundt, Johannes. Nabis, König von Sparta. Köln, 1903. 2v.
AH 854.12 — Negelini, J. Das Pferd im arischen Altertum. Königsberg, 1903.
AH 4449.03 — Oddo, Antonino. Pisistrato. Palermo, 1903.
AH 4484.11 — Olsen, W. Schlacht bei Plataeae. Greifswald, 1903.

1903 - cont.

Eg 879.03 — Palanque, C. Le Nil...son rôle et son culte en Égypt. Paris, 1903.
Eg 39.03 — Preisigke, Friedrich. Städtisches Beamtenwesen im römischen Ägypten. Halle, 1903.
AH 3507.7.7 — Ragozin, Z.A. Media, Babylon, and Persia. N.Y., 1903.
AH 3607.12 — Rawlinson, G. Parthia. N.Y., 1903.
AH 7239.03.3 — Renel, Charles. Cultes militaires de Rome. Les enseignes. Lyon, 1903.
AH 4239.03 — Roloff, G. Probleme aus der griechischen Kriegsgeschichte. Berlin, 1903.
AH 4809.03 — Roscher, W.H. Die enneadischen und hebdomadischen Fristen und Wochen der ältesten Griechen. Leipzig, 1903.
AH 7769.03 — Runkel, F. Schlacht bei Adrianapel. Rostock, 1903.
AH 7819.03 — Rydberg, V. Kulturhistoriska förekäsningar. Stockholm, 1903. 6v.
Eg 879.02.5 — Sayce, Archibald H. The religions of ancient Egypt and Babylonia. Edinburgh, 1903.
AH 4559.03.7 — Schreiber, T. Studien über das Bildniss Alexanders des Grossen. Leipzig, 1903.
AH 7659.03.5 — Schulz, Otto. Beiträge zur Kritik unserer litterarischen Überlieferung fur die Zeit von Commodus' Sturze bis auf den Tod des M. Aurelius Antonius. Leipzig, 1903.
AH 7009.03 — Schwartz, E. Ad praemiorum...publicam renuntiationem. Gottingae, 1903.
AH 7479.03 — Scott, F.J. Portraitures of Julius Caesar. London, 1903.
AH 8548.52 — Sculfort de Beaurepas, Serge. La panceltisme universel et pacifique contre le pangermanisme envahisseur et l'imperialisme anglais. Paris, 1903. 2v.
NEDL AH 278.93 — Seignbos, C. Histoire ancienne. Paris, 1903.
AH 7279.03 — Seignobos, C. Antiquité romaine. Paris, 1903.
AH 819.03 — Seignobos, C. Histoire de la civilisation ancienne. Paris, 1903.
AH 7509.03.5A — Shuckburgh, E.S. Augustus...(B.C. 63-A.D. 14). London, 1903.
NEDL AH 279.03 — Souttar, R. Short history of ancient peoples. London, 1903.
AH 7161.23 — Stockar, H. Entzug der väterlichen Gewalt. Zürich, 1903.
AH 3151.3 — Stooss, Carl. Das babylonische Strafrecht Hammurabis. Bern, 1903.
AH 3159.5.15 — Tänzer, Aaron. Judentum und Entwicklungslehre. Berlin, 1903.
AH 3183.5 — Thompson, Reginald C. The devils and evil spirits of Babylonia. London, 1903- 2v.
AH 8307.2 — Vaschide, V. Histoire de la conquête...de la Dacie. Paris, 1903.
AH 3123.6 — Virolleaud, C. Comptabilité Chaldienne. Poitiers, 1903.
AH 7139.03.10 — Vocabularium jurisprudentiae Romanae. v.1-4. Berolini, 1903-39. 2v.
AH 4559.03.3 — Waldhauer, O. Porträts Alexanders des Grossen. München, 1903.
AH 7139.03.3 — Walton, F.P. Historical introduction to Roman law. Edinburgh, 1903.
AH 7239.03 — Weichert, A. Die Legio XXII Primigenia. Ein Beitrag. Trier, 1903.
NEDL AH 7818.77.15 — Wilkins, Augustus S. Antigüedades clásicas II. Antigüedades Romanas. N.Y., 1903.
AH 39.03 — Willoughby, W.W. Political theories of the ancient world. N.Y., 1903.
AH 139.03 — Wilutzky, P. Vorgeschichte des Rechts. Breslau, 1903.

1904

AH 7549.04 — Allard, Paul. Les chrétiens ont-ils incendie Rome sous Néron. Paris, 1904.
AH 8548.55 — Arbois de Jubainville, Henry d'. Les Celtes. Paris, 1904.
AH 3173.6A — Assyrian and Babylonian literature. N.Y., 1904.
AH 4842.37 — Aus den pädagogischen Universität-Seminar zu Jena. Langenzala, 1904.
AH 8013.2 — Barthel, W. Zur Geschichte der römischen Städte in Africa. Griefswald, 1904.
AH 279.04 — Bauer, A. Lehrbuch der Geschichte des Alterthums. Wien, 1904.
AH 7889.04 — Beigel, R. Rechnungswesen und Buchführung. Karlsruhe, 1904.
AH 3002.83 — Belck, Waldemar. Die Kelischin-Stele und ihre chaldisch-assyrischen Keilinschriften. Freienwald, 1904.
AH 3173.12 — Bezold, Carl. Babylonisch-assyrische Texte: Die Schöpfungeslegende. Bonn, 1904.
Eg 279.04 — Bissing, F.W. von. Geschichte Ägyptens. Berlin, 1904.
Eg 1039.04 — Book of the Dead. The Egyptian book of the dead. London, 1904.
Eg 709.04 — Budge, Ernest Alfred Wallis. The decrees of Memphis and Canopus. London, 1904. 3v.
Eg 879.04 — Budge, Ernest Alfred Wallis. The gods of the Egyptians. Chicago, 1904.
Eg 879.04.2 — Budge, Ernest Alfred Wallis. The gods of the Egyptians. London, 1904. 2v.
X Cg Eg 879.04 — Budge, Ernest Alfred Wallis. The gods of the Egyptians. v.2. Chicago, 1904.
AH 8549.104 — Callegari, G.V. Il druidismo nell'antica Gallia. Padova, 1904.
Eg 855.1 — Caton, R. Ancient Egyptian medicine. London, 1904.
AH 2147.5 — Chapot, V. Province romaine proconsulaire d'Asie. Paris, 1904.
AH 3013.31 — Chicago, Illinois. University. Oriental Exploration Fund. Expedition of Oriental Exploration Fund (Babylonian section). Reports 1-4, 6. Chicago? 1904.
AH 7448.18.13 — Colin, J. Annibal en Gaule. Paris, 1904.
AH 7203.107 — Corpus juris civilis. Digesta. Digest of Justinian. Cambridge, Eng., 1904-09. 2v.
AH 2110.7 — Cousin, J. Kyros le jeune en Asie mineure. Nancy, 1904.
AH 7138.91.2 — Cuq, E. Institutions juridiques. Paris, 1904. 2v.
AH 4109.04 — Dahms, R. De atheniensium sociorum tributis quaestiones septem. Berolini, 1904.
AH 7819.04A — Dill, Samuel. Roman society from Nero to Marcus Aurelius. London, 1904.
AH 8549.104.5 — Dottin, Georges. La religion des Celtes. 2. éd. Paris, 1904.
AH 7309.04 — Ferrero, G. Grandeur et décadence de Rome. Paris, 1904. 6v.
AH 3005.6 — Fossey, Charles. Manuel d'Assyriologie. v.1-2. Paris, 1904-26. 3v.
AH 7479.04 — Fowler, W.W. Julius Caesar and the foundation of the Roman imperial system. N.Y., 1904.
AH 4189.04 — Francke, I. De manumissionibus Delphicis. Monasterii Guestfalorum, 1904.

1904 - cont.

AH 7799.04A   Freeman, E.A. Western Europe in the fifth century. London, 1904.

AH 860.5   Galante, L. Guiochi infantili e giocattoli. Firenze, 1904.

AH 7299.04   Garofalo, F.P. Studi storici. Noto, 1904.

Eg 971.9   Gayet, A.J. Fantomes d'Antinoe. Paris, 1904.

AH 4161.5   Glotz, Gustave. Solidarité de la famille. Paris, 1904.

AH 279.04.3   Goodspeed, George S. A history of the ancient world. N.Y., 1904.

AH 7499.04   Greenidge, A.H.J. History of Rome during later republic. London, 1904.

X Cg   AH 3151.9.2   Hammurabi, king of Babylonia. The code of Hammurabi...about 2250 B.C. 2. ed. Chicago, 1904.

AH 3151.14   Hammurabi, king of Babylonia. The code of Hammurabi. Chicago, 1904.

AH 3151.6   Hammurabi, king of Babylonia. Die Gesetze Hammurabis in Urnschrift. Leipzig, 1904.

AH 3151.7   Hammurabi, king of Babylonia. Hammurabis Gesetz. v.1-6. Leipzig, 1904-23. 4v.

AH 3151.11   Hammurabi, king of Babylonia. La loi de Hammourabi. Paris, 1904.

AH 4449.04   Hauser, F. Harmodios und Aristogeiton. Rom, 1904.

AH 5766.5   Heidemann, L. Die territoriale Entwicklung. Berlin, 1904.

AH 7848.7   Helbig, W. Toga und Trabea. v.1-2. Berlin, 1904.

AH 3013.10.7   Hilprecht, H.V. Die Ausgrabungen in Assyrien und Babylonien. Leipzig, 1904.

AH 7139.04.5   Hirschfeld, B. Die Gesta municipalia. Marburg, 1904.

AH 7278.54.41   Hirschfeld, O. Gedächtnisrede auf Theodor Mommsen. Berlin, 1904.

AH 4559.04   Janke, A. Alexanders des Grossen. Berlin, 1904.

AH 3150.8   Johns, C.H.W. Babylonian and Assyrian laws, contracts and letters. N.Y., 1904.

AH 4559.04.5   Keller, Erich. Alexander der Grosse. Berlin, 1904.

AH 6057.9   Kent, R.G. History of Thessaly. Lancaster, Pa., 1904.

AH 7139.04   Knappe, O. Grundriss der römischen Rechtsgeschichte. Berlin, 1904.

AH 7239.04   Koeser, E. De captivis Romanorum. Gissae, 1904.

AH 3002.2.18   Küchler, Friedrich. Beiträge zur Kenntnis der assyrisch-babylonischen Medizin. Leipzig, 1904.

AH 842.32.3   Laurie, S.S. Historical survey of pre-Christian education. N.Y., 1904.

AH 4049.04   Léotard, M.E. La démocratie. Lyon, 1904.

AH 3151.5   Lyon, D.G. Structure of the Hammurabi code. New Haven, 1904.

AH 3359.5   Malten, L. Cyrenarum origines. n.p., 1904.

AH 3965.6.9   Moors, B.P. Le système des poids, mesures et monnaies des israélites d'apres la Bible. Paris, 1904.

AH 7009.04   Munro, D.C. Source book of Roman history. Boston, 1904.

AH 7279.04.2   Myers, P.V.N. Ancient history. Boston, 1904.

AH 279.04.5   Myers, Philip Van Ness. The eastern nations and Greece. Boston, 1904.

AH 9658.2   Othmer, W. Die Wölkerstämme von Hispania. Berlin, 1904.

AH 3707.17   Pereira de Lima, J.M. Phenicios a carthaginezes. Lisboa, 1904.

AH 3052.5A   Price, I.M. Some literary remains of Rim-Sin...king of Larsa. Chicago, 1904.

AH 4483.7   Raase, Hans. Beitrag zur Darstellung der Schacht bei Salamis. Rostock, 1904.

AH 845.5.7   Rosenbaum, J. Geschichte der Lustseuche im Altertume. Berlin, 1904.

AH 7461.5   Rothke, G. De Romanorum Bellis Servilibus. Berlin, 1904. 6 pam.

AH 4848.12   Sambon, A. La toilette des femmes grecques. Paris, 1904.

AH 7029.04   Sanders, Henry. Roman historical sources. N.Y., 1904.

NEDL   AH 1278.89.5   Sayce, A.H. Ancient empires of the East. N.Y., 1904.

AH 7169.04   Schlossmann, S. Altrömische Schuldrecht und Schuldverfahren. Leipzig, 1904.

AH 7229.04   Schott, R. Römischen Zivilprozess. München, 1904.

AH 3159.5.20   Schreiber, Emilio. Bibbia e babele. Trieste, 1904.

AH 6110.15   Schubert, R. Untersuchungen über die Quellen zur Geschichte Philipps II von Macedonien. Konigsberg, 1904.

AH 7628.99   Schulz, O.T. Leben des Kaisers Hadrian. Leipzig, 1904.

NEDL   AH 7299.03.2   Souttar, R. Short history of ancient peoples. N.Y., 1904.

AH 7169.04.3   Stintzing, W. Mancipatio. Leipzig, 1904.

Eg 1059.04   Vogelsang, F. Die Klagen des Bauern. Berlin, 1904.

Eg 879.04.5   Wreszinski, W. Die Hohenpriester des Amon. Berlin, 1904.

AH 4484.13   Wright, H.B. Campaign of Plataea. New Haven, 1904.

1905

AH 7169.05.2   Appleton, C. Les lois romains sur le cautionnement. Weimar, 1905.

AH 7299.05.2   Assmann, J. Dissertatio Historica. Langensalzae, 1905.

AH 4859.21   Balabanoff, A. Untersuchungen zur Geschäftsfähigkeit. Borna, 1905.

AH 4729.05   Barbagallo, C. La fine della Grecia antica. Bari, 1905.

AH 4819.05   Baumgarten, F. Hellenische Kultur. Leipzig, 1905.

AH 4559.05.3   Bernoulli, J.J. Darstellungen Alexanders des Grossen. München, 1905.

AH 7469.05   Boissier, Gaston. La conjuration de Catilina. Paris, 1905.

AH 4229.05   Bonner, Robert Johnson. Evidence in Athenian courts. Chicago, 1905.

AH 7217.11   Bonolis, G. I titoli di nobiltà. Firenze, 1905.

AH 6024.7   Bourguet, Émile. De rebus Delphicis imperatoriae aetatis capita duo. Diss. Montepessulano, 1905.

Eg 279.05A   Breasted, James Henry. A history of Egypt. N.Y., 1905.

AH 7799.05   Bugiani, Carlo. Storia di Ezio generale dell'Impero Sotto Valentiniano III. Firenze, 1905.

AH 8513.9   Camau, E. Moeurs et institutions romaines. Paris, 1905.

Eg 879.05.10   Capart, Jean. Bulletin critique des religions de l'Égypte. v.1-5. Leiden, 1905-39.

AH 7039.05   Chudzinski, A. Staatseinrichtungen...Kaiserreichs. Gutersloh, 1905.

AH 3013.42F   Clercq, Louis de. Collection De Clercq. v.3-6, 7, pt.1-2. Paris, 1905-11. 6v.

AH 7202.17   Codex Theodosianus. Theodosiani. Berolini, 1905. 2v.

AH 7202.18   Codex Theodosianus. Theodosiani libri XVI. Berolini, 1905.

AH 7169.05   Cornil, G. Possession dans le droit romain. Paris, 1905.

AH 7059.05.2   Cosenza, M.E. Official positions after the time of Constantine. Lancaster, 1905.

AH 819.05.3F   Cybulski, S. Kultur der Griechen und Römer. Leipzig, 1905.

AH 7138.99.2   Czyhlarz, Karl. Lehrbuch der Institutionen des römischen Rechtes. 7-8. Aufl. Wien, 1905.

1905 - cont.

AH 3159.5.8   Delitzsch, F. Babel und Bible. Leipzig, 1905.

AH 4819.05.8   Dickinson, G.L. The Greek view of life. 3d ed. N.Y., 1905.

AH 7819.04.2   Dill, Samuel. Roman society from Nero to Marcus Aurelius. 2. ed. London, 1905.

AH 7818.98.3A   Dill, Samuel. Roman society in the last century of the Western Empire. 2. ed. London, 1905.

AH 7759.05   Firth, J.B. Constantine the Great. N.Y., 1905.

AH 5343.2   Frickenhaus, A. Athens Mauern. Bonn, 1905.

AH 3963.7   Frohnmeyer. Bilder Atlas zur Bibelkunde. Stuttgart, 1905.

AH 7201.83   Gaius. Institutiones. 5th ed. Berolini, 1905.

AH 7009.05   Gamurrin, G.F. Bibliografia dell'Italia antica. Arezzo, 1905.

AH 4839.05   Gaspar, C. Olympia. Paris, 1905.

AH 4559.05.7   Gruhn, Albert. Das Schlachtfeld von Issus. Jena, 1905.

AH 889.05   Guiraud, P. Études économiques. Paris, 1905.

AH 4819.02.5   Gulick, C.B. Life of the ancient Greeks. N.Y., 1905.

AH 819.05   Hahn, E. Das Alle des wirtschaftlichen Kultur. Heidelberg, 1905.

AH 7059.05   Hirschfeld, O. Die kaiserlichen Verwaltungsbeamten. Berlin, 1905.

AH 3155.6   Jastrow, Morris. Die Religion Babyloniens und Assyriens. Giessen, 1905-12. 3v.

AH 7469.00.3   Kappler, Carl. Über die unter dem Namen der Cornelia überlieferten Brieffragmente. Weiden, 1905.

AH 7629.05   Kornemann, E. Kaiser Hadrian. Leipzig, 1905.

AH 7229.05.3   Koschaker, P. Translatio iudicii. Graz, 1905.

AH 3129.3   Langdon, S. Building inscriptions of the Neo-Babylonian Empire: Nabopolassar and Nebuchadnezzar. Paris, 1905.

AH 7449.05.3   Lauterbach, A. Untersuchungen...Unterwerfung von Oberitalien. Breslau, 1905.

NEDL   AH 279.05   Leadbetter, F. Outlines and studies to accompany Myer's Ancient history. Boston, 1905.

AH 7449.05.2   Lehmann, K. Die Angriffe der drei Bardiken. Leipzig, 1905.

AH 4139.05   Lipsius, Justus Hermann. Attische Recht. Leipzig, 1905. 4v.

AH 9610.19   Loncao, E. La Sicilia romana. Palermo, 1905.

AH 4842.29   Mahaffy, J.P. Old Greek education. N.Y., 1905.

AH 4659.05   Mahaffy, J.P. Progress of Hellenism in Alexander's empire. Chicago, 1905.

AH 138.61.7   Maine, Henry S. Ancient law. London, 1905.

AH 4539.05   Marshall, F.H. Second Athenian Confederacy. Cambridge, 1905.

AH 1278.76.7   Maspero, Gaston. Historie ancienne des peuples de l'Orient. 7e éd. Paris, 1905.

Eg 709.05   Maspéro, Henri. Les finances de l'Égypte sous les Lagides. Paris, 1905.

AH 2760.5.5   Meischke, Kurt. Zur Geschichte des Königs Eumenes II von Pergamon. Pirna, 1905.

AH 3668.5   Modi, J.J. Education among the ancient Iranians. Bombay, 1905.

AH 159.05   Mommsen, T. Zum altesten Strafrecht der Kulturvölker. Leipzig, 1905.

AH 7299.05   Mommsen, Theodor. Gesammelte Schriften. Berlin, 1905. 8v.

AH 7299.05.4   Mommsen, Theodor. Reden und Aufsätze. Berlin, 1905.

AH 7299.05.5   Mommsen, Theodor. Reden und Aufsätze. 2. Aufl. Berlin, 1905.

AH 4559.05   Müller, K.F. Leichenwagen Alexanders des Grossen. Leipzig, 1905.

AH 3135.3   Nabonidus king of Babylonia. Leiden, 1905.

AH 7779.01.4   Negri, G. Julian the Apostate. 2. ed. N.Y., 1905. 2v.

AH 4919.05   Oehler, J. Griechischen Vereinwesen. Wien, 1905.

Eg 879.05   Otto, Walter. Priester und Tempel im Hellenistischen Agypten. Leipzig, 1905. 2v.

AH 7278.98.3   Pais, Ettore. Ancient legends of Roman history. N.Y., 1905.

AH 7229.05   Partsch, J. Schriftformel im römischen Provinzialprozesse. Breslau, 1905.

AH 3002.96   Peiser, F. Urkunden aus der Zeit der dritten babylonischen Dynastie. Berlin, 1905.

NEDL   AH 7278.85.13   Pelham, H.F. Outlines of Roman history. 4. ed. London, 1905.

AH 7278.85.15   Pelham, H.F. Outlines of Roman history. 4. ed. N.Y., 1905.

AH 3013.39PF   Pennsylvania. University. Babylonian Expeditions. Excavations at Nippur. Pt.1-2. Philadelphia, 1905.

AH 3002.2.19   Prince, John D. Materials for a Sumerian lexicon. Leipzig, 1905-08.

AH 7549.05F   Profumo, A. Le fonti ed i tempi d'incendio. Roma, 1905.

AH 7139.05   Robinson, J.J. Selections from the public and private law of the Romans. N.Y., 1905.

AH 7139.05.5   Robinson, J.J. Selections from the public and private law of the Romans. N.Y., 1905.

AH 4149.05   Rost, M. De vocibus quibusdam publici iuris Attici. Inaug. Diss. München, 1905.

AH 7449.05   Schermann, Max. Der erste punische Krieg. Stuttgart, 1905.

AH 7229.05.5   Schlossmann, S. Litis Contestatio. Leipzig, 1905.

AH 844.5   Schmidt, G. De die natali apud veteres. Hannoverae, 1905.

AH 7809.05   Schön, Georg. Die Differenzen zwischen der kapitolinischen Magistrats- und Triumphliste. Wien, 1905.

AH 4839.05.3   Seliger, M. Interesse Hellenen am Sport. Tilsit, 1905.

AH 7909.05   Solbisky. Voraus geht eine Abhandlung. Weimar, 1905.

Eg 879.05.5   Steindorff, Georg. The religion of the ancient Egyptians. N.Y., 1905.

AH 7239.05   Steiner, Paul. Die Dona Militaria. Bonn, 1905.

AH 4259.05   Taru, William W. The Greek warship I-II. n.p., 1905. 3 pam.

AH 7139.05.10   Triebs, Franz. Studien zur Lex Dei. Freiburg, 1905. 2v.

AH 7139.05.3   Wenger, L. Römische und antike Rechtsgeschichte. Graz, 1905.

NEDL   AH 279.05.5   West, Willis M. The ancient world from the earliest times to 800 A.D. Boston, 1905.

AH 4819.05.3   Whibley, Leonard. Companion to Greek studies. Cambridge, 1905.

AH 7842.10A   Wilkins, A.S. Roman education. Cambridge, 1905.

AH 299.05   Winckler, Hugo. Auszug aus der vorderasiatischen Geschichte. Leipzig, 1905.

AH 7579.05   Wolff-Beckh, B. Kaiser Titus und der jüdische Krieg. Berlin, 1905.

AH 7278.54.39   Zangmeister, K. Theodor Mommsen als Schriftsteller. Berlin, 1905.

Chronological Listing

1906

AH 842.27	Adam, L. Die Unsicherheit literarischen Eigentums. Düsseldorf, 1906.
Eg 139.06	Arangio-Ruiz, V. Successione testamentaria. Napoli, 1906.
AH 8549.106	Arbois de Jubainville, Henry d'. Les druides et les dieux celtiques. Paris, 1906.
AH 7088.79.5	Arnold, W.T. Roman system of provincial administration. Oxford, 1906.
AH 7489.06	Arnold, W.T. Studies of Roman imperialism. Manchester, 1906.
AH 8549.106.5	Arnoyl, E. Celtic religion in pre-Christian times. London, 1906.
AH 7239.06	Bang, Martin. Die Germanen im römischen Dienst. Berlin, 1906.
AH 7239.06.7	Bang, Martin. Die Germanen im römischen Dienst. Berlin, 1906.
AH 7139.06.3	Bernard, F. First year of Roman law. Oxford, 1906.
AH 7799.06	Bierbach, Karl. Die letzten Jahre Attilas. Berlin, 1906.
AH 7159.06	Binsbergen, J. De legibus ablatae Pecuniae. Trajecti ad Rhenum, 1906.
AH 7178.56.5	Bolkestein, H. De Colonatu Romano ejusque origine. Amstelodami, 1906.
Eg 759.06	Boulard, L. Les instructions écrites du Magistrat au juge-commissaire dans l'Egypte Romaine. Paris, 1906.
Eg 279.05.10	Breasted, James Henry. Ancient records of Egypt. Chicago, 1906-07. 2v.
Eg 879.06	Budge, Ernest Alfred Wallis. The Egyptian heaven and hell. London, 1906. 3v.
AH 7169.06.5	Clark, E.C. History of Roman private law. pt.1-2. Cambridge, 1906-19. 4v.
AH 7469.06.5	Clerc, Michel. La bataille d'Aix. Paris, 1906.
AH 7149.06	Costa, Emilio. Storia del diritto romano. Firenze, 1906.
AH 6057.7F	Costanzi, V. Saggio di storia tessalica. Pisa, 1906.
AH 7189.06	Crumley, J.J. On the social standing of freedmen. Baltimore, 1906.
Eg 1029.06PF	Dedekind, A. Photographische Reproduktionen der Inschriften. Wien, 1906.
AH 3964.14	Dibelius, Martin. Die Lade Jahnes. Inaug. Diss. Göttingen, 1906.
AH 4818.96.15	Dickinson, G.L. The Greek view of life. 5th ed. N.Y., 1906.
AH 7818.98.5A	Dill, Samuel. Roman society in the last century of the Western Empire. London, 1906.
AH 8548.57	Dottin, Georges. Manuel pour servir à l'étude de la antiquité celtique. Paris, 1906.
AH 9560.2	Eliaeson, Ake. Beiträge zur Geschichte Sardiniens. Uppsala, 1906.
AH 4809.06	Ferguson, W.S. The priests of Asklepios; a new method of dating Athenian archons. Berkeley, 1906.
AH 8355.2	Filow, B. Die Legionen der Provinz Moesia. Leipzig, 1906.
AH 7179.06	Fleischmann, Wilhelm. Altergermanische...Agrarverhältnisse. Leipzig, 1906.
AH 7138.95.3	Girard, P.F. Manuel élémentaire de droit romain. 3. éd. Paris, 1906.
AH 7138.95.4	Girard, P.F. Manuel élémentaire de droit romain. 4. éd. Paris, 1906.
AH 7139.06	Girard, P.F. Short history of Roman law. Oxford, 1906.
AH 4819.06	Glotz, G. Études...sur l'antiquité grecque. Paris, 1906.
AH 3107.5	Godbey, A.H. Notes on some officials of the Sargonid period. Chicago, 1906.
AH 3009.06	Goodspeed, G.S. A history of the Babylonians and Assyrians. 2. ed. N.Y., 1906.
AH 862.6	Grawinkel, Karl J. Zähne und Zahnbehandlung der alten Aegypter, Hebräer, Inder, Babyloner, Assyrer, Griechen und Römer. Berlin, 1906.
AH 4539.07	Grillnberger, P.O. Griechische Studien. Wilhering, 1906.
AH 4278.46.36	Grote, George. History of Greece. London, 1906. 12v.
AH 4278.46.37	Grote, George. History of Greece. London, 1906. 3v.
AH 4839.06F	Grützner. Fünfkampf der Griechen. v.1-2. Leipzig, 1906.
AH 7299.06	Hardy, E.G. Studies in Roman history. London, 1906.
AH 8213.2	Haverfield, Francis J. The romanization of Roman Britain. London, 1906.
AH 7448.18.14	Hesselmeyer, E. Hannibals Alpenübergang. Tübingen, 1906.
AH 4139.06	Hitzig, Hermann F. Die Bedeutung des altgriechischen Rechtes für die vergleichende Rechtswissenschaft. Stuttgart, 1906.
NEDL AH 4278.86.9	Holm, Adolf. The history of Greece. London, 1906. 4v.
AH 8608.8F	Italy. Ministero della marina. Monografia storica dei porti dell'antichità nell'Italia insulare. Roma, 1906.
AH 3154.7	Lau, Robert J. Old Babylonian temple records. N.Y., 1906.
AH 7169.06	Leage, Richard William. Roman private law. London, 1906.
AH 3309.5	Lichtenberg, R.F. Beiträge zur...Geschichte von Kypros. Berlin, 1906.
AH 4659.06	Mahaffy, J.P. Silver age of the Greek world. Chicago, 1906.
AH 138.61.9	Maine, Henry S. Ancient law. 10. ed. London, 1906.
AH 7179.06.5	Maschke, R. Zur Theorie und Geschichte der römischen Agrargesetze. Tübingen, 1906.
AH 3002.2.20	Meissner, Bruno. Seltene assyrische Ideogramme. Leipzig, 1906.
AH 3958.10	Meyer, E. Die Israeliten und ihre Nachbarstämme. Halle, 1906.
AH 7278.54.23	Mommsen, T. Rome. v.3. Philadelphia, 1906.
AH 842.25.5	Monroe, Paul. Source book of the history of education for the Greek and Roman period. N.Y., 1906.
NEDL AH 279.06.5	Morey, William Carey. Outlines of ancient history. N.Y., 1906.
AH 7469.06	Mühll, F.V. De L. Appuleio Saturnino Tribuno Plebis. Basileae, 1906.
AH 279.06	Myers, Philip Van Ness. A short history of ancient times. Boston, 1906.
AH 889.06.5	Neurath, Otto. Zur Anschauung der Antike über Handel, Gewerbe und Landwirtschaft. Jena, 1906.
AH 4278.90.9	Oman, C.W.C. Greece. v.2. Philadelphia, 1906.
AH 7278.98.5	Pais, Ettore. Ancient legends of Roman history. London, 1906.
AH 4329.06	Peroutka, E. Pelasgove'. Praze, 1906.
Eg 879.06.5	Petrie, William M.F. The religion of ancient Egypt. London, 1906.
AH 3155.7	Pinches, T.G. The religion of Babylonia and Assyria. London, 1906.
AH 3660.5	Poncritus, M. Studien über die Schlacht bei Kunaxa. Berlin, 1906.
AH 3657.20	Prášek, J.V. Geschichte der Meder und Perser. Gotha, 1906. 2v.
AH 930.30	Ramsauer, F. Die antike Vulkankunde. Burghausen, 1906.

1906 - cont.

AH 4609.06	Rutgers, A. De Eumene Cardiano. Amsterdam, 1906.
AH 7201.85	Sabinus, M. Fragmente in Ulpians Sabinus Commentar. Halle, 1906.
AH 889.06	Salvioli, G. Capitalisme dans le monde antique. Paris, 1906.
AH 1279.06	Sayce, A.H. Ancient empires of the East. Philadelphia, 1906.
AH 169.06	Schlossmann, S. Persona und Prosópon im Recht. Kiliae, 1906.
AH 819.06	Schmidt, M.C.P. Kulturhistorische Beiträge zur Kenntnis des griechischen und römischen Altertums. Leipzig, 1906-12. 2v.
AH 4558.93.2	Schwarz, F. Alexanders des Grossen Feldzüge in Turkestan. 2. Aufl. Stuttgart, 1906.
Eg 602.5	Sethe, Kurt. Urkunden des 18. Dynastie. (Heft 1-22). Leipzig, 1906- 6v.
AH 4279.06	Shuckburgh, E.S. Greece. N.Y., 1906.
AH 7239.06.5	Smith, F. Römische Heeresverfassung und Timokratie. Berlin, 1906.
AH 5310.11	Sundwall, J. Epigraphische Beiträge zur sozial-politischen Geschichte Athens im Zeitalter des Demosthenes. Leipzig, 1906.
AH 3187.12	Thompson, Reginald C. Late Babylonian letters. London, 1906.
AH 4819.06.3A	Tucker, T.G. Life in ancient Athens. N.Y., 1906.
AH 7529.06	Venturini, L. Caligola. Milano, 1906.
AH 4863.11	Vèze, Raoul. Le baiser en Grèce. Paris, 1906.
AH 8679.2	Werner, P. De incendiis urbis Romae. Lipsiae, 1906.
AH 4819.05.3.5	Whibley, Leonard. Companion to Greek studies. 2nd ed. Cambridge, 1906.
AH 4409.06	Wilamowitz-Moellendorff, Ulrich von. Über die ionische Wanderung. n.p., 1906.
AH 3980.12.5	Wilson, C.W. Golgotha and the holy sepulchre. London, 1906.
Eg 709.06	Wolf, Josef. Aus Inschriften und Papyren der Ptolemaierzeit. Feldkirch, 1906.

1907

AH 7207.25	Abele, Theodor Anton. Der Senat unter Augustus. Paderborn, 1907.
AH 3052.3F	Allotte, C. Les sceaux de Longalanda. Paris, 1907.
AH 909.11	Barbagallo, C. Contributo alla storia economica dell'antichità. Roma, 1907.
AH 7498.92.6	Baring-Gould, Sabine. The tragedy of the Caesars. N.Y., 1907.
AH 5807.5	Bauer, Edmund. Untersuchungen zur Geographie...der norwestlichen Land. Inaug. Diss. Halle, 1907.
AH 3132.8	Bernstein, G. König Nebucadnezar von Babel in der judischen Tradition. Berlin, 1907.
AH 7479.07	Bondurant, B.C. Decimus Junius Brutus Albinus. Chicago, 1907.
Eg 1039.07.2	Book of the Dead. Le livre des morts des anciens Égyptiens. 2. éd. Paris, 1907.
AH 4860.8	Bryant, A.A. Boyhood and youth in days of Aristophanes. n.p., 1907.
AH 4860.7	Bryant, A.A. Boyhood and youth in days of Aristophanes. n.p., 1907.
AH 3661.5	Christensen, A. L'empire des Sassanides. København, 1907.
AH 9610.28	Ciaceri, Emanuele. Esame critico della storia...guerre servili. Catania, 1907.
AH 3013.907	Delitzsch, F. Mehr Licht; die bedeutsamsten Ergebnisse der babylonisch-assyrischen Grabungen für Geschichte, Kultur und Religion. Leipzig, 1907.
AH 3002.84	Dhorme, Paul. Choix de textes religieux assyro-babylonies. Paris, 1907.
AH 3739.5.2	Eiselen, F.C. Sidon. N.Y., 1907.
AH 3739.5	Eiselen, F.C. Sidon. N.Y., 1907.
Eg 879.07	Erman, A. Handbook of Egyptian religion. London, 1907.
NEDL AH 7309.04.1	Ferrero, G. Grandeur et décadence de Rome. Paris, 1907. 5v.
AH 7309.04.2	Ferrero, G. Grandezza e decadenza di Roma. Milano, 1907. 5v.
AH 7309.04.3A	Ferrero, G. Greatness and decline of Rome. v.1-3,5. N.Y., 1907-09. 4v.
AH 4039.07	Francotte, H. La polis grecque. Paderborn, 1907.
AH 4842.39	Freeman, Kenneth John. Schools of Hellas. London, 1907.
AH 9660.2	Gotzfried, K. Annalen der römischen Provinzen...Spanien. Erlangen, 1907.
AH 4278.46.75	Grote, George. A history of Greece from the time of Solon to 403 B.C. London, 1907.
AH 8908.11	Herbig, G. Zum heutigen Stand der etruskischen Frage. München, 1907.
AH 4149.07	Hitzig, H.F. Altgriechische Staatsverträge. Zürich, 1907.
AH 4559.07	Hoffmann, W. Literarische Porträt Alexanders des Grossen. Leipzig, 1907.
AH 4559.07.2	Hoffmann, W. Literarische Porträt Alexanders des Grossen. Quelle, 1907.
AH 7739.07A	Hopkins, R.V.N. Life of Alexander Severus. Cambridge, 1907.
Eg 299.07	Horrack, Philippe Jacques de. Oeuvres diverses. Paris, 1907.
NEDL AH 7278.96.8	How, W.W. A history of Rome to the death of Caesar. N.Y., 1907.
AH 3002.2.21	Huber, Engelbert. Die Personennamen in der Keilschrifturkunden. Leipzig, 1907.
AH 4299.07	Huber, Peter. Griechische Geschichte bis 449. München, 1907.
AH 7759.08	Jenks, J. Heidentum und Christianismus des Kaisers Konstantin des Grossen. Sereth, 1907.
AH 3159.10.3	Jeremias, A. Die Panbabylonisten die alte Orient. Leipzig, 1907.
AH 4855.9	Johannes, R. De studio Venandi apud Graecos et Romanos. Gottingae, 1907.
AH 7829.03.7	Johnston, Harold W. The private life of the Romans. Chicago, 1907.
AH 862.7	Jones, W.H.S. Malaria. Cambridge, 1907.
AH 889.07	Khvostov, M. Istoriia vostochoi torgovli. Kazan', 1907.
AH 1279.07	King, Leonard. History of Egypt, Chaldea, Syria, Babylonia and Assyria in the light of recent discovery. London, 1907.
AH 7549.07	Klette, E.T. Die Christenkatastrophe unter Nero. Tübingen, 1907.
Eg 603.8	Knudtzon, J.A. Die el Amarna-Tafeln. Leipzig, 1907-08. 2v.
AH 7629.07.5	Kornemann, E. Anax mainós â Hadrhinós. Leipzig, 1907.

Chronological Listing

1907 - cont.

AH 4162.19 — Ledl, Arthur. Studien zum attischen Epiklerenrechte. Graz, 1907.

AH 7204.4 — Lefranc, André. L'édit d'Antonin Caracalla. Bordeaux, 1907.

AH 3087.3 — Le Gag, Y. Les inscriptions d'Assur Nasir Aplu III. Paris, 1907.

AH 7204.13 — Lenel, Otto. Edictum perpetuum. 2. Aufl. Leipzig, 1907.

AH 7009.07 — Loesche, J. Die Abfassung des Faits des Romains. Halle, 1907.

AH 3154.8 — Luckenbill, D.D. Study of temple documents from Cassite period. Chicago, 1907.

AH 3910.9 — Majo, U. Antioco IV Epifane re di Siria. Sassari, 1907.

Eg 879.07.5 — Massey, Gerald. Ancient Egypt, the light of the world. London, 1907. 2v.

AH 7139.01.6 — May, Gaston. Eléments de droit romain. Paris, 1907.

AH 7139.07 — Mélanges Gerardin. Paris, 1907.

AH 278.84.5 — Meyer, E. Geschichte des Alterthums. v.1-5. Stuttgart, 1907-31. 7v.

AH 8609.5 — Modestov, V.I. Introduction à l'histoire romaine. Paris, 1907.

AH 7149.07 — Mommsen, Theodor. Abriss des römischen Staatsrechts. Leipzig, 1907.

AH 7449.07 — Mordtmann, A.D. Historische Bilder vom Bosporus. Konstantinopel, 1907.

Eg 279.07 — Newberry, P.E. Ancient Egypt. London, 1907.

AH 7779.07 — Nostitz-Rieneck, R.G. Vom Tode des Kaisers Julian. Feldkirch, 1907.

AH 7889.07 — Oliver, E.H. Roman economic conditions. Toronto, 1907.

Eg 709.09 — Otto, P.W. Die wirtschaftliche Lage und die Bildnis der Priester im hellenischen Ägypten. Leipzig, 1907.

AH 309.07 — Paterson, W.R. The nemesis of nations. London, 1907.

AH 8403.2 — Peaks, M.B. General, civil and military administration. Chicago, 1907.

AH 7859.3 — Pitacco, G. De mulierum romanorum cultu. Görz, 1907.

AH 5409.6.15 — Porzio, Guido. Corinto. Padova, 1907.

AH 4850.13 — Rankin, E.M. Role of Mageiroi in life of ancient Greece. Chicago, 1907.

NEDL AH 819.07 — Reitzenstein, P. Werden und Wesen der Humanität. Strassburg, 1907.

AH 4909.07 — Riezler, Kurt. Finanzen und Monopole in Griechenland. Berlin, 1907.

AH 7279.07 — Sanctis, G. de. Storia dei Romani. v.1-4, pt.1-3. Torino, 1907. 8v.

AH 4161.13 — Savage, C.A. The Athenian family. Baltimore, 1907.

NEDL AH 1278.89.7 — Sayce, A.H. Ancient empires of the East. N.Y., 1907.

AH 3012.7 — Sayce, A.H. The archaeology of cuneiform inscriptions. London, 1907.

AH 9071.2.5 — Schmidt, Otto Eduard. Arpinum. Arpino, 1907.

Eg 819.07 — Schneider, H. Kultur und Denken der alten Ägypter. Leipzig, 1907.

AH 842.46.5 — Schubart, Wilhelm. Das Buch bei den Griechen und Römern. Berlin, 1907.

AH 5754.13 — Solari, Arturo. Ricerche spartane. Livorno, 1907.

Eg 1309.07 — Spiegelberg, W. Der Papyrus Libbey. Strassburg, 1907.

Eg 1309.07.5 — Staerk, Willy. Die jüische-arameischen Papyri von Assuan. Bonn, 1907.

AH 3009.07 — Starck, C. von. Babylonien und Assyrien. Marburg, 1907.

AH 7203.105 — Taschenwörterbuch. Corpus juris civilis. Berlin, 1907.

AH 3020.4 — Thureau-Dangin, F. Die sumerische und akkadischen Königsinschriften. Leipzig, 1907.

AH 3149.6 — Toffteen, O.A. Ancient chronology. Chicago, 1907.

AH 7239.07 — Tschauschmer, Carl. Legionare Kriegsvexillationen. Breslau, 1907.

AH 4609.07 — Vezin, A. Eumenes von Kardia. Münster, 1907.

AH 7479.07.5 — Volquardsen, C. Rom im Übergange von der Republik. Kiel, 1907.

AH 7629.07.7 — Weber, W. Die Adoption Kaiser Hadrians. Leipzig, 1907.

AH 7629.07 — Weber, W. Untersuchungen zur Geschichte...Hadrianus. Leipzig, 1907.

AH 7239.07.5 — Weerd, Hubert van de. Étude historique sur trois legions romaines du Bas-Danube. Louvain, 1907.

AH 4819.07 — Wendland, P. Hellenistisch-Römische Kultur. Tübingen, 1907.

AH 5390.11 — Werenka, D. Kritische Bemerkungen. Czernowitz, 1907.

AH 3143.5 — Winckler, H. Die babylonische Geisteskultur. Leipzig, 1907.

AH 3008.92.7A — Winckler, H. The history of Babylonia and Assyria. N.Y., 1907.

AH 3159.10.5 — Winckler, H. Die jüngsten Kämpfer wider den Panbabylonismus. Leipzig, 1907.

1908

AH 4848.13 — Abrahams, E.B. Greek dress. London, 1908.

AH 3020.18F — Allotte de la Fuÿe, Francois N. Documents présargoniques. Paris, 1908-20. 5v.

AH 4819.08 — Amatucci, A.G. Hellás. v.1-2. Bari, 1908.

AH 3002.60F — Amherst of Hackney, W.A.T.A. The Amherst tablets. London, 1908.

Eg 279.08.5 — Baikie, James. The story of the pharaohs. London, 1908.

AH 4819.05.2 — Baumgarten, F. Hellenische Kultur. Leipzig, 1908.

AH 7889.00.2 — Bloch, Leo. Soziale Kämpfe im alten Rom. 2. Aufl. Leipzig, 1908.

AH 7469.05.2 — Boissier, Gaston. La conjuration de Catilina. 2. éd. Paris, 1908.

AH 9653.2 — Braun, F. Provinzialeinteilung Spaniens in römischer Zeit. Berlin, 1908.

Eg 279.08.2 — Breasted, James Henry. A history of the ancient Egyptians. London, 1908.

Eg 279.08A — Breasted, James Henry. A history of the ancient Egyptians. N.Y., 1908.

AH 3013.9.6 — British Museum. Guide to the Babylonian and Assyrian antiquities. 2. ed. London, 1908.

AH 7189.08 — Buckland, William Warwick. The Roman law of slavery. Cambridge, Eng., 1908.

Eg 809.08 — Budge, Ernest Alfred Wallis. The book of the kings of Egypt. London, 1908. 2v.

AH 7809.08 — Bülz, Martin. Dem Jahresberichte geht eine wissenschaftliche Abhandlung des Oberlehrers. Zittau, 1908.

Eg 845.5A — Buttles, Janet R. The queens of Egypt. N.Y., 1908.

AH 8182.5 — Cagnat, René. Les deux camps de la légion IIIe Auguste à Lambèse. Paris, 1908.

AH 4189.08 — Calderini, A. Condizione dei liberti in Grecia. Milano, 1908.

AH 3160.12 — Combe, E. Histoire du culte de Sin. Paris, 1908.

1908 - cont.

AH 3909.4 — Cormack, George. Egypt in Asia; a plain account of pre-biblical Syria and Palestine. London, 1908.

AH 7239.08.5 — De Rebus Bellicis. Anonymi de rebus bellicis liber. Berlin, 1908.

AH 8016.2 — Detlefsen, D. Die Geographie Afrikas. Berlin, 1908.

AH 4559.08 — Dittberner, W. Issos. Ein Beiträge zur Geschichte Alexanders des Grossen. Berlin, 1908.

AH 7239.08.7 — Domaszewski, Alfred von. Die Anlage der Limeskastelle. Heidelberg, 1908.

AH 4847.7 — Esveld, C. De Balneis Lavationibusque Graecorum. Amersfortiae, 1908.

NEDL AH 7309.04.6 — Ferrero, G. Greatness and decline of Rome. N.Y., 1908. 4v.

AH 7309.04.10 — Ferrero, G. Grösse und Niedergang Roms. Stuttgart, 1908-09. 5v.

AH 7207.27 — Fischer, Frideric. Senatus Romanus, qui fuerit Augusti temporibus. Diss. inaug. Berolini, 1908.

AH 4842.39.1 — Freeman, Kenneth John. Schools of Hellas. London, 1908.

AH 7201.87 — Gaius. Institutionum commentarius quattuor. 2. ed. Lipsiae, 1908.

AH 4959.08A — Gardner, W.A. In Greece with the classics. Boston, 1908.

AH 857.5 — Giese, A. De parasiti persona capita selecta. Berolini, 1908.

AH 7029.08 — Giorni, C. Epitome rerum romanarum. Firenze, 1908.

AH 4842.41 — Grousset, P. L'ecole d'Athens. Paris, 1908.

AH 7559.08 — Henderson, B.W. Civil war and rebellion in Roman Empire. London, 1908.

AH 3002.18 — Hilprecht, H.V. The so-called Peters-Hilprecht controversy. Pt.1-2. Philadelphia, 1908.

AH 5157.5 — Hohmann, W. Aitolien und die Aitoler bis zum lamischen Kriege. Halle, 1908.

AH 7201.40.6 — Huschke, P.E. Iurisprudentiae anteiustinianae. v.1-2. Lipsiae, 1908-27. 3v.

AH 4819.08.2 — Inama, V. Amtichita greche. Milano, 1908.

AH 9777.29A — Jordanes. Origins and deeds of the Goths. Princeton, 1908.

AH 3143.6 — Köberle, J. Beziehungen zwischen Israel und Babylonien. Wismar, 1908.

AH 6053.5 — Kroog, G. Foederis Thessalorum praetoribus. Halis Saxonum, 1908.

AH 3187.8 — Landersdorfer, S. Altbabylonische Privatbriefe. Paderborn, 1908.

AH 842.29 — Langie, A. Bibliothèques publiques. Fribourg, 1908.

AH 4139.08 — Leisi, Ernst. Zeuge im attischen Recht. Frauenfeld, 1908.

AH 819.08 — Marett, R.R. Anthropology and the classics. Oxford, 1908.

AH 7819.08 — Meissner, A. Altrömisches Kulturleben. Leipzig, 1908.

AH 7449.08 — Meyer, P. Der Ausbruch des ersten punischen Krieges. Berlin, 1908.

Eg 848.6 — Milne, J.G. Relics of Graeco-Egyptian schools. n.p., 1908.

AH 7169.08 — Mitteis, L. Römisches Privatrecht. Leipzig, 1908.

AH 7278.54.28.10 — Mommsen, T. The history of Rome. London, 1908-12. 5v.

AH 7278.54.24 — Mommsen, T. The history of Rome. N.Y., 1908. 5v.

AH 3000.5 — Morgan, J.P. Cuneiform inscriptions : Chaldean, Babylonian. N.Y., 1908.

AH 4239.08 — Müller, B. Beiträge zur Geschichte...Söldnerwesens. Frankfurt am Main, 1908.

AH 7799.08 — Nagl, M.A. Galla Placidia. Paderborn, 1908.

AH 5363.5 — Newmann, G. De nominibus boeotorum propriis. Regimonti, 1908.

AH 1409.06.1 — Olmstead, Albert T. Western Asia in the days of Sargon of Assyria, 722-705 B.C. N.Y., 1908.

AH 1409.06 — Olmstead, Albert T. Western Asia in the days of Sargon of Assyria. Thesis. Lancaster, Pa., 1908.

AH 8607.2 — Pais, Ettore. Ancient Italy. Chicago, 1908.

AH 9607.19 — Perry, W.C. Sicily in fable, history, art and song. London, 1908.

AH 3909.5 — Petrie, W.M.F. Syria and Egypt from the Tell el Amarna letters. London, 1908.

AH 7148.80.4 — Pollack, Erich. Der Majestätsgedanke. Leipzig, 1908.

AH 7829.08.6 — Preibisch, J. De sermonis cotidiani formulis. Halis Saxonum, 1908.

AH 4491.5 — Probandt, K. Beiträge zur Geschichte der Pentekontaetie. Halle, 1908. 3 pam.

AH 7469.08 — Prodinger, Karl. Das Tribunat des C. Gracchus. Gottschee, 1908.

Eg 1042.908 — Pyramid Texts. Die altägyptischen Pyramidentexte. v.1-4. Leipzig, 1908-22. 3v.

AH 7179.08 — Quillfeldt, W. Altrömisches Landwirtschaftsrecht. Inaug. Diss. Heidelberg? 1908?

AH 3155.14 — Radau, Hugo. Bel, the Christ of ancient times. Chicago, 1908.

AH 4539.08 — Radüge, E. Zur Zeitbestimmung des euböischen...Krieges. Giessen, 1908.

Eg 409.08 — Reinach, A.J. L'Égypte préhistorique. Paris, 1908.

AH 8514.11 — Rodet, P. Culte des sources thermales. Paris, 1908.

AH 3155.19 — Rogers, R.W. The religion of Babylonia and Assyria. N.Y., 1908.

AH 7419.08 — Sands, P.C. Client princes of the Roman empire. Cambridge, 1908.

AH 844.7 — Schmidt, W. Geburtstag im Altertum. Giessen, 1908.

AH 7058.28.3 — Seidel, Joseph. Fasti aedilicii. Inaug. Diss. Breslau, 1908.

NEDL AH 279.08 — Snider, D.J. European history, chiefly ancient. St. Louis, 1908.

AH 7239.08 — Steinwender, T. Ursprung und Entwickelung. Danzig, 1908.

AH 7739.08 — Thiele, W. De Severo Alexandro Imperatore. Berolini, 1908.

AH 9610.21 — Tillyard, H.J.W. Agathocles. Cambridge, 1908.

AH 3012.5 — Tofteen, O.A. Researches in Assyrian and Babylonian geography. Chicago, 1908.

AH 3181.5.2 — Vanderburgh, F.A. Sumerian hymns. N.Y., 1908.

AH 3181.5 — Vanderburgh, F.A. Sumerian hymns. Thesis. N.Y., 1908.

AH 7809.08.5 — Varese, P. Cronologia romana. Roma, 1908.

AH 3193.6F — Virolleaud, C. L'astrologie chaldéenne. v.1-14. Paris, 1908. 3v.

AH 4229.08 — Weber, Hans. Attisches Prozessrecht. Paderborn, 1908.

AH 4229.08.2 — Weber, Hans. Die Rezeption des attischen Prozessrechts. Paderborn, 1908.

Eg 609.08F — Weil, A. Veziere Aegyptens. Strassburg, 1908.

AH 3002.2.10 — Weissbach, F.H. Die altpersischen Keilinschriften. Leipzig, 1908.

AH 7239.08.9 — Wolks, Josef. Beiträge zur Geschichte der Legio XI Claudia. Breslau, 1908.

Chronological Listing

1908 - cont.

AH 819.08.10 — Zieliński, Tadeusz. Iz zhizni idei. izd. 2. v.1-2,4, pt.2. Sankt Peterburg, 1908-11. 2v.

1909

Eg 1309.09.5F — Admonitions of an Egyptian Sage. The admonitions of an Egyptian sage. Leipzig, 1909.

AH 4959.09A — Allinson, Francis Greenleaf. Greek lands and letters. Boston, 1909.

AH 3086.5 — Annales de Tukulti Ninip II. Paris, 1909.

AH 3013.909 — Assyriologische und archaeologische Studien Hermann V. Hilprecht. Leipzig, 1909.

Eg 299.09 — Bevan, J.O. Egypt and the Egyptians. London, 1909.

AH 7079.09 — Botsford, G.W. The Roman assemblies. N.Y., 1909.

AH 7279.09 — Bouché-Leclerq, A. Leçons d'histoire romaine. Paris, 1909.

AH 9666.2 — Braun, F. Die Entwicklung der spanischen Provinzialgrenzen. Berlin, 1909.

Eg 279.05.5 — Breasted, James Henry. A history of Egypt. N.Y., 1909.

AH 162.5 — Bruck, E.F. Die Schenkung auf den Todesfall. Breslau, 1909.

AH 4159.09 — Bruck, E.F. Zur Geschichte der Verfügungen von Todeswegen. Breslau, 1909.

AH 7201.47.7 — Bruns, C.G. Fontes Juris Romani Antiqui. 7. ed. Tubingae, 1909.

Eg 879.09 — Budge, Ernest Alfred Wallis. The book of the opening of the mouth. London, 1909. 2v.

Eg 879.09.5 — Budge, Ernest Alfred Wallis. The liturgy of funerary offerings. London, 1909.

AH 7799.09 — Bugiani, Carlo. L'Imperatore Avito. Pistoia, 1909.

AH 4049.09 — Buzeskul, V. Istoria afinskoi demokratia. Sankt Peterburg, 1909.

AH 7842.14 — Cole, P.R. Later Roman education in Ausonius, Capella. N.Y., 1909.

AH 4039.09 — Croiset, A. Les démocraties antiques. Paris, 1909.

AH 4459.06.5 — Croiset, Maurice. Aristophanes and the political parties at Athens. London, 1909.

AH 7709.09 — Dannhäuser, Erich. Geschichte des Kaisers Probus (276-282). Jena, 1909.

AH 7489.09.10 — Davis, W.S. Outline history of the Roman Empire. N.Y., 1909.

AH 4819.09.3 — Dickinson, G.L. The Greek view of life. 6th ed. N.Y., 1909.

AH 7489.09 — Domaszewski, A. von. Geschichte der Römischen Kaiser. Leipzig, 1909. 2v.

AH 4559.09.3 — Eicke, L. Veterum philosophorum qualia fuerint de Alexandero Magno iudicia. Rostochii, 1909.

Eg 39.09 — Engers, M. De Aegyptiarum...administratione. Groningae, 1909.

AH 4842.93 — Exarchopoulos, Nikolaos. Das athenische und das spartanische Erziehungssystem, im 5. und 6. Jahrhundert vor Christ. Langensalza, 1909.

AH 7809.09.5 — Fasti Consulares. Fasti consulares imperii romani von 30 v. Chr. bis 565 n. Chr. Bonn, 1909.

AH 7309.09 — Ferrero, G. Characters and events of Roman history. N.Y., 1909.

AH 7309.04.7 — Ferrero, G. Greatness and decline of Rome. London, 1909. 5v.

AH 7309.04.8A — Ferrero, G. Greatness and decline of Rome. N.Y., 1909. 5v.

AH 7309.04.4 — Ferrero, G. Greatness and decline of Rome. N.Y., 1909-10. 5v.

AH 4409.09 — Fimmen, D. Zeit und Dauer der kretisch-mykenischen Kultur. Leipzig, 1909.

AH 7829.08.3 — Fowler, W.W. Social life at Rome in the age of Cicero. N.Y., 1909.

AH 4109.09 — Francotte, H. Les finances des cités grecques. Liège, 1909.

Htn AH 7201.3* — Gaius. Gai Codex Rescripticus...numero XV. Lipsiae, 1909.

AH 7469.09 — Gatti, Giuseppe. Lamina di bronzo con iscrizione...guerra dei socii italici. Roma, 1909.

VEg 869.09 — Giesswein, Sándor. Egiptom és a biblia. Budapest, 1909.

AH 7299.06.2 — Hardy, E.G. Studies in Roman history. London, 1909.

AH 7009.09.5A — Hayes, C.H. Introduction to the sources relating to the Germanic invasions. N.Y., 1909.

AH 7009.09.3 — Hayes, C.H. Introduction to the sources relating to the Germanic invasions. N.Y., 1909.

AH 7118.8 — Heiter, C. De patriciis gentibres. Berolini, 1909.

AH 7419.09 — Heitland, W.E. Roman republic. Cambridge, 1909. 3v.

AH 4539.09 — Hengweld, A. De conone Atheniensi. Traiecti ad Rhenum, 1909.

AH 3020.9PF — Heuzey, Léon A. Restitution matérielle de la stèle des vautours. Paris, 1909.

AH 7159.09 — Hitzig, H.F. Die Herkunft des Schwurgerichts. Zürich, 1909.

AH 2557.7 — Hogarth, D.G. Ionia and the East. Oxford, 1909.

AH 860.7 — Hoorn, G. van. De vita atque cultu puerorum monumentis antiquis explanato. Inaug. Diss. Amstelodami, 1909.

AH 9192.5 — Jacobone, Nunzio. Venusia, storia e topografia. Trani, 1909.

AH 854.9A — Keller, Otto. Der antike Tierwelt. Leipzig, 1909. 2v.

NEDL AH 409.09 — Khvostov, M.M. Istoriia drevnago vostoka. Kazan', 1909.

AH 3181.10 — Langdon, S. Sumerian and Babylonian psalms. Paris, 1909.

AH 840.9 — Léotard, E. La famille. Lyon, 1909.

AH 7809.09 — Leuzl, Oscar. Die römische Jahrzählung. Tübingen, 1909.

AH 846.10 — Lichtenberg, F. Haus, Dorf, Stadt. Leipzig, 1909.

AH 879.09.5 — Lietzmann, H. Der Weltheiland. Bonn, 1909.

AH 7529.09 — Linnert, U. Beiträge zur Geschichte Caligulas. Nürnberg, 1909.

AH 3187.14 — McKnight, Robert J.G. Selected letters from Sargonid period. Chicago, 1909.

AH 4819.09 — Mahaffy, J.P. What have the Greeks done for modern civilization? N.Y., 1909.

AH 3187.9 — Martin, F. Lettres néo-babyloniennes. Paris, 1909.

Eg 847.4F — Möller, G. Hieratische Paläographie. Leipzig, 1909-12. 3v.

AH 7298.86.3 — Mommsen, Theodor. The provinces of the Roman empire from Caesar to Diocletian. London, 1909. 2v.

AH 819.09 — Morgan, J. Premières civilisations. Paris, 1909.

Htn AH 3017.4F* — Morgan, John P. Cylinders and oriental seals in library. N.Y., 1909.

AH 889.09.5 — Neurath, A. Antike Wirtschaftsgeschichte. Leipzig, 1909.

AH 4719.09 — Nicolaus, M. Zwei Beiträge zur Geschichte König Philipps V. von Makedonien. Berlin, 1909.

AH 5138.15 — Nomos Rodion, Nautikos. Rhodian law. Oxford, 1909.

1909 - cont.

AH 7469.09.5 — Paladino, G. La guerra dei gladiatori (73-71 a.C.). Napoli, 1909.

AH 29.09 — Paris. Université. Faculté de Lettres. Mélanges d'histoire ancienne. Photoreproduction. Paris, 1909.

AH 7169.09 — Partsch, J. De l'édit sur l'alienatio judicii mutandi causa facta. Genève, 1909.

AH 4216.7 — Partsch, Josef. Griechisches Bürgschaftsrecht. Leipzig, 1909.

AH 7909.09 — Parvan, Vasile. Die Nationalität der Kaufleute. Breslau, 1909.

AH 4279.09.5 — Pöhlmann, R. von. Grundriss der griechischen Geschichte nebst Quellenkunde. 4. Aufl. München, 1909.

AH 9609.5 — Puglisi Marino, S. Siculi e greci nella Sicilia orientale. Catania, 1909.

AH 69.09 — Radin, Max. Legislation of Greeks and Romans on corporations. N.Y.? 1909.

AH 7089.09 — Regnault, Henri. Une province procuratorienne. Paris, 1909.

AH 7819.09.5 — Rockwell, J.C. Private Baustiftungen. Jena, 1909.

Eg 819.09 — Rustafjaell, R. de. The light of Egypt. London, 1909.

AH 919.09 — Sarrazin, Albert. Étude sur les fondations dans l'antiquité en particulier à Rome et à Byzance. Thèse. Paris, 1909.

AH 7499.09 — Schmaus, J. Charakterbilder römischer Kaiser. Bamberg, 1909.

AH 879.09 — Schmidt, E. Kultübeitragungen. Giessen, 1909.

AH 4833.17 — Schneider, K. Griechischen Gymnasien und Palästren. Diss. Solothurn, 1909.

AH 7719.09 — Schulz, O.T. Der römische Kaiser Caracalla. Leipzig, 1909.

Eg 709.09.15 — Sergeant, P.W. Cleopatra of Egypt. N.Y., 1909.

AH 7499.09.5 — Silvagni, K. L'impero e le donne dei Cesari. 2. ed. Torino, 1909.

AH 7059.09 — Sobeck, T. Die Quästoren der Römischen Republik. Trebnitz, 1909.

AH 7009.09 — Soltau, W. Anfänge der roemischen Geschichtsschreibung. Leipzig, 1909.

Eg 1309.09 — Spiegelberg, W. Die demotischen Papyrus. Bruxelles, 1909.

Eg 759.09 — Studien zur byzantinischen Verwaltung Ägyptens. Leipzig, 1909.

AH 7739.09 — Thiele, W. De Severo Alexandro Imperatore. Berolini, 1909.

NEDL AH 279.09 — Ulbricht, E. Grundzüge der alten Geschichte. Weissen, 1909. 2v.

AH 7139.09 — Velsen, F. von. Beiträge zur...edictum Pratoris urbani. Leipzig, 1909.

AH 7114.15 — Vinder, Julius. Die Plebs. Leipzig, 1909.

AH 4842.43A — Walden, J.W.H. University of ancient Greece. N.Y., 1909.

AH 4559.09 — Weber, F. Alexander der Grosse im Urteil der Griechen und Römer. Borna, 1909.

AH 4484.15 — Winter, L. Platää. Berlin, 1909.

AH 4484.15.2 — Winter, L. Die Schacht von Platää. Berlin, 1909.

AH 889.09 — Wolf, H. Geschichte des antike Sozialismus. Gütersloh, 1909.

AH 4842.45 — Ziebarth, E. Aus dem griechischen Schulwesen. Leipzig, 1909.

191-

AH 7479.10 — Hardinge, Hilary. Julius Caesar. London, 191-.

AH 7469.02.3 — Oman, Charles. Seven Roman statesmen of the later Republic. N.Y., 191-?

1910

AH 7819.09.10 — Abbott, F.F. Society and politics in ancient Rome. N.Y., 1910.

AH 39.10 — Arnim, H. Politischen Theorien des Altertums. Wien, 1910.

Eg 1039.10 — Book of the Dead. Theban recension of the book of the dead. London, 1910. 3v.

AH 8549.110 — Bosc, Ernest. Belisama, ou L'occultisme cetique. Paris, 1910.

AH 7279.01.10 — Botsford, G.W. A history of Rome for high schools. N.Y., 1910.

AH 9471.3 — Buckhardt-Biedermann, T. Die Kolonie Augusta Raurica. Basel, 1910.

AH 7039.10 — Bury, J.B. Constitution of the later Roman empire. Cambridge, 1910.

AH 7039.10.2A — Bussell, F.W. Roman empire. London, 1910. 2v.

AH 7809.10.5 — Caosta, G. I Fasti Consolari Romani. Milano, 1910.

AH 7809.10 — Casta, G. L'originale dei Fasti Consolari. Roma, 1910.

X Cg AH 3060.3.13F — Cros, Gaston. Nouvelle fouilles de Tello. Paris, 1910-14.

AH 239.10 — Daniels, Emil. Das antike Kriegswesen. Leipzig, 1910.

AH 7889.10 — Davis, William S. Influence of wealth in imperial Rome. N.Y., 1910.

AH 3002.125F — Deimel, Anton. Tabulae signorum cuneiformium in usum scholae. Romae, 1910.

AH 3143.11 — Delitzsch, Friedrich. Handel und Wandel in Altbabylonien. Stuttgart, 1910.

Eg 1069.10 — Dennis, J.T. The burden of Isis. London, 1910.

AH 809.10 — Elia bar Sinaya. La chronographie. Paris, 1910.

AH 8673.3 — Elter, A. Cremera und Porta Carmentalis. Bonn, 1910.

Eg 9.10 — Farina, G. Bollettino. Roma, 1910.

AH 7169.10 — Fehr, M. Beiträge zur römischen Pfandrecht. Upsala, 1910.

Eg 909.10 — Fitzler, Kurt. Steinbrüche und Bergwerke im ptolemäischen und römischen Ägypten. Thesis. Leipzig, 1910.

Eg 909.10.1 — Fitzler, Kurt. Steinbrüche und Bergwerke im ptolemäischen und römischen Ägypten. Leipzig, 1910.

AH 7798.78.5 — Foss, Rudolph. Attila in der Geschichte und Sage. Gütersloh, 1910?

AH 4149.10 — Francotte, H. Mélanges droit public grec. Liège, 1910.

AH 7818.65.13 — Friedlaender, Ludwig. Darstellungen aus der Sittengeschichte Roms. 8. Aufl. Leipzig, 1910. 4v.

AH 7479.10.5 — Gans, Maximilian E. Studien zu Schlacht bei Pharsalus. Lundenberg, 1910.

AH 4839.10 — Gardiner, Edward Norman. Greek athletic sport. London, 1910.

AH 299.12.2 — Gercke, Alfred. Einleitung in die Altertumswissenschaft. Leipzig, 1910-12. 3v.

AH 7650.80.5A — Gibbon, Edward. History of decline and fall of Roman Empire. v.2. London, 1910.

AH 7279.10 — Hamilton, M.A. A junior history of Rome. Oxford, 1910.

AH 7659.03.2 — Hartmann, L.M. Untergang der antiken Welt. Wien, 1910.

AH 2623.7 — Hasluck, Fredrick William. Cyzicus. Cambridge, 1910.

AH 7809.10.7 — Heiligenstaedt, F. Fasti aedilicii inde a Caesaris nece usque ad imperium A. Severi. Halis Saxonum, 1910.

Chronological Listing

1910 - cont.

AH 842.31 — Hobhouse, W. Theory and practise of ancient education. N.Y., 1910.

AH 3659.9 — Hoffmenn-Kutschke, A. Die Wahrheit über Kyros, Darius und Zarathuschatra. Berlin, 1910.

AH 8667.2 — Jones, H.S. Classical Rome. N.Y., 1910.

AH 4519.10 — Kahrstedt, U. Forschungen zur Geschichte des ausgehenden fünften und des vierten Jahrhunderts. Berlin, 1910.

AH 3022.5 — King, Leonard W. A history of Sumer and Akkad. N.Y., 1910?

AH 6057.11 — Kip, G. Thessalische Studien. Halle, 1910.

AH 7829.10 — Kuehn, G. De opificum romanorum condicione privata quaestiones. Diss. inaug. Halis, 1910.

AH 3160.11 — Kugler, F.X. Im Bannkreis Babels. Münster, 1910.

AH 7139.10 — Kuhlenbeck, L. Die Entwicklungsgeschichte des römischen Rechts. München, 1910. 2v.

AH 7114.21 — Lefèvre, Eugene. Du role des tribuns de la plebe. Paris, 1910.

AH 3018.5 — Lehmann-Haupt, C.F. Die historische Semiramis und ihre Zeit. Tübingen, 1910.

AH 7639.10 — Leszynsky, R. Die Lösung des Antoninusträtsels. Berlin, 1910.

Eg 819.10 — Lieblein, J. Recherches sur l'histoire et la civilisation de l'ancien Égypte. Leipzig, 1910. 3v.

NEDL AH 278.84.12 — Martinez Silva, Carlos. Compendio de historia antigua. 4. ed. Bogota, 1910.

AH 239.10.10 — Mastropasqui, O. Assedi e battaglie memorabili dai tempi più remoti al 476. Molfetti, 1910.

AH 7059.10 — Mattingly, H. The imperial civil service of Rome. Cambridge, 1910.

AH 299.10 — Meyer, E. Kleine Schriften. Halle, 1910.

AH 9790.5 — Muchau, H. Das 4000 Jährige alter des Volkes der Hermunduringer (Thüringer). Jena, 1910.

AH 4299.10 — Myres, John L. Greek lands and the Greek people. Oxford, 1910.

Eg 986.5A — Plaumann, G. Ptolemais in Oberägypten. Leipzig, 1910.

Eg 709.10 — Plaumann, Gerhard. Ptolemais in Oberägypten. Leipzig, 1910.

AH 909.10 — Preisigke, F. Girowesen im griechischen Ägypten. Strassburg, 1910.

AH 4539.10 — Rügg, A. Thermaenes. Basel, 1910.

AH 4524.11 — Sadl, A. Die oligarchische Revolution vom Jahre 411. Pola, 1910.

AH 299.10.3 — Saggi di storia antica e di archeologia. Roma, 1910.

AH 7029.10 — Sanders, Henry. Roman history and mythology. N.Y., 1910.

AH 7819.10 — Sandys, J.E. Companion to Latin studies. Cambridge, 1910.

AH 4843.18 — Schnabel, H. Kordap. München, 1910.

AH 3143.21 — Schneider, Hermann. Kultur und Denken der Babylonier und Juden. Leipzig, 1910.

AH 4523.9 — Schübeler, P. De Syracusarum oppugnatione quaestiones criticae. Geestemüde, 1910.

AH 8557.4 — Schütt, C. Untersuchungen zur Geschichte der alten Illyrien. Inaug. Diss. Breslau, 1910.

AH 279.10 — Schwahn, W. Geschichte der Griechen und Römer. Berlin, 1910.

AH 819.03.5 — Seignobos, C. Histoire de la civilisation ancienne. 5. éd. Paris, 1910.

NEDL AH 279.03.5 — Seignobos, C. Histoire narrative et descriptive de l'antiquité. 8. éd. Paris, 1910.

AH 8667.4 — Stuart-Jones, H. Classical Rome. London, 1910.

AH 4842.58 — Terzaghi, N. L'educazione in Grecia. Milano, 1910.

AH 7819.10.2 — Tucker, T.G. Life in the Roman world of Nero and St. Paul. London, 1910.

Eg 879.10 — Virey, P. La religion de l'ancienne Égypte. Paris, 1910.

AH 7148.70.7 — Willems, P. Le droit public romain. 7e éd. Louvain, 1910.

AH 862.8 — Willson, R.N. Medical men in the time of Christ. Philadelphia, 1910.

AHP 36.3.3 — Zeitschrift für die alttestamentliche Wissenschaft. Register, Bd. 1-25. Giessen, 1910.

1911

AH 7819.11 — Abbott, F.F. The common people of ancient Rome. N.Y., 1911.

AH 7842.12 — Barbagallo, C. Lo stato e l'istruzione pubblica. Catania, 1911.

AH 4842.69 — Bendel, Paulus. Qua ratione Graeci liberos docuerint. Monasterii Guestfalorum, 1911.

AH 4299.11 — Billeter, G. Die Anschauungen von Wesen des Griechentums. Leipzig, 1911.

AH 4949.11 — Blümner, Hugo. Karte von Griechenland zur Zeit des Pausanias. Bern, 1911.

AH 7739.11 — Boer, H.G.W. De Julia Mamaea Severi A. Matre. Rhenum, 1911.

AH 7149.11 — Boissière, G. L'accusation publique...chez les Romains. Niort, 1911.

AH 9385.1 — Borziani, G. Dell'antica città di Ostra. Cefalu, 1911.

AH 4278.99.5 — Botsford, George W. A history of the Orient and Greece. N.Y., 1911.

AH 4859.23 — Braunstein, O. Die politische Wirksamkeit der griechischen Frau. Leipzig, 1911.

AH 4841.6 — Brillant, M. Les secretaires atheniens. Paris, 1911.

AH 7845.9 — Brouwer, P.C. De Romanorum indole e litteris cognascenda. n.p., 1911.

Eg 1039.10.5 — Budge, Ernest Alfred Wallis. A hieroglyphic vocabulary to the Theban recension of the book of the dead. London, 1911.

Eg 879.11 — Budge, Ernest Alfred Wallis. Osiris and the Egyptian resurrection. London, 1911. 2v.

AH 4164.5 — Caloziron, Georges. Die Arrha im Vermögensrecht. Leipzig, 1911.

AH 7079.11 — Chaigne, G. Sous la robe blanche. Paris, 1911.

AH 7759.11 — Couzard, R. Sainte Hélène d'après l'histoire et la tradition. Paris, 1911.

AH 7709.11.5 — Crees, J.H.E. The reign of the Emperor Probus. London, 1911.

AH 4212.7 — D'André, J. La proxénie. Toulouse, 1911.

AH 3160.8.5 — Delitzsch, F. Das Land ohne Heimkehr. Stuttgart, 1911.

AH 7819.04.3 — Dill, Samuel. Roman society from Nero to Marcus Aurelius. 2. ed. London, 1911.

AH 8548.65 — Dinan, W. Monumenta historica celtica. London, 1911.

AH 7039.11 — Fabricius, Ernest. Über die Entwicklung der römischen Verfassung im republikanischer Zeit. Freiburg, 1911.

AH 9610.23 — Felice-Guiffrida, G. de. Le guerre servili in Sicilia. Catania, 1911.

AH 5310.5A — Ferguson, William S. Hellenistic Athens. London, 1911.

AH 7499.11A — Ferrero, G. The women of the Caesars. N.Y., 1911.

1911 - cont.

AH 7201.88 — Gaius. Institutionum commentarius primus. Jena, 1911.

Eg 1309.11 — Gardiner, A.H. Egyptian hieratic texts. Leipzig, 1911-

AH 3002.115F — Genouillac, Henri de. Tablettes de Dréhem. Paris, 1911.

AH 7138.95.6 — Girard, P.F. Manuel élémentaire de droit romain. 5e éd. Paris, 1911.

AH 8016.10 — Gsell, Stéphane. Le climat de l'Afrique du nord dans l'antiquité. Alger, 1911.

NEDL AH 7139.11 — Hardy, E.G. Six Roman laws. Oxford, 1911.

AH 7729.11.3 — Hay, J.S. The amazing emperor Heliogabalus. London, 1911.

AH 7114.22 — Hesselmeyer, Ellis. Vermischte Beiträge zur Geschichte des Reiteradels bei Römern und Deutschen. Tübingen, 1911.

AH 3163.5 — Hinke, W.J. Selected Babylonian Kudurrie inscriptions. Leiden, 1911.

AH 7729.11 — Hönn, K. Quellenuntersuchungen zu den Viten des Heliogabalus. Leipzig, 1911.

AH 7478.99.5 — Holmes, T.R.E. Caesar's conquest of Gaul. 2. ed. Oxford, 1911.

AH 3155.6.5A — Jastrow, Morris. Aspects of religious belief and practice in Babylonia and Assyria. N.Y., 1911.

AH 5607.7 — Klotzsch, C. Epirotische Geschichte. Boston, 1911.

AH 7709.11 — Lehmann, Karl Friedrich Wilhelm. Kaiser Gordian III. Berlin, 1911.

AH 7709.11.3 — Lehmann, Karl Friedrich Wilhelm. Kaiser Gordian III. Berlin, 1911.

AH 3408.7 — Leonard, W. Hittiter und Amazonen. Leipzig, 1911.

AH 8205.3 — Le Roux, L. L'armée romaine de Bretagne. Paris, 1911.

Eg 709.11 — Lesquier, Jean. Les institutions militaires de l'Egypte sous les Lagides. Paris, 1911.

NEDL AH 7489.11A — McCabe, Joseph. The empresses of Rome. London, 1911.

AH 7489.10 — McCabe, Joseph. The empresses of Rome. N.Y., 1911.

AH 8549.111.5 — MacCullock, John A. The religion of the ancient Celts. Edinburgh, 1911.

AH 4659.06.5 — Mahaffy, J.P. The silver age of the Greek world. Chicago, 1911.

Eg 39.11 — Martin, V. Les Épistratèges. Genève, 1911.

AH 7569.11 — Menrad, K. Gestaltung des römischen Staats...Flairer Vespasian. München, 1911.

AH 409.11.5A — Myres, J.L. The dawn of history. N.Y., 1911.

AH 7207.1 — Oko, Jan. De senatoribus Pedariis. Livowie, 1911.

Eg 1128.87.15PF — Papyrus Prisse. Le papyrus Prisse et ses variantes. Paris, 1911.

AH 7009.11 — Parducci, P. La genesi degli annales Maximi. Pisa, 1911.

AH 7278.85.19 — Pelham, H.F. Essays. Oxford, 1911.

AH 4409.11 — Penka, K. Die vorhellenische Bevölkerung Griechenlands. Hildburg, 1911.

Eg 299.11 — Petrie, William M.F. Egypt and Israel. London, 1911.

AH 7299.11 — Pflüger, P. Die soziale Frage im alten Rom. Zürich, 1911.

AH 149.11 — Phillipson, C. International law and custom. London, 1911. 2v.

Eg 29.11 — Pick, Robert F. Egyptological tracts. N.Y., 1911.

AH 308.95.2 — Pöhlmann, R. Aus Altertum und Gegenwart. München, 1911.

AH 279.11 — Pöhlmann, R. von. Aus Altertum und Gegenwart. München, 1911.

Eg 819.11.3 — Poertner, D.B. Die agyptischen Totenstelen. Paderborn, 1911.

AH 8549.111 — Pokorny, J. The origin of druidism. Washington, 1911.

AH 7509.11.5 — Poupé, E. Le lieu de la rencontre de Lépide et d'Antoine. Droguignan, 1911.

EgP 117.3.5 — Recueil de travaux...egyptiennes. Index, v. XVII-XXXII. Paris, 1911.

AH 4483.9 — Rediades, P.D. Hē en Salamini Naumachia. Athens, 1911.

AH 7116.6 — Rosenberg, A. Untersuchungen zur römischen Zenturienverfassung. Berlin, 1911.

AH 8207.8 — Sagot, François. La Bretagne romaine. Paris, 1911.

AH 3908.5 — Schiffer, Sina. Die Aramäer. Leipzig, 1911.

Eg 819.11 — Smith, G.E. Ancient Egyptians. London, 1911.

AH 4819.11.3A — Stobart, J.C. The glory that was Greece. London, 1911.

AH 8353.2 — Stout, S.E. Governors of Moesia. Princeton, 1911.

AH 7038.99.3 — Taylor, Thomas M. A constitutional and political history of Rome. London, 1911.

AH 7819.11.3 — Thiersch, H. An den Rändern des römischen Reichs. München, 1911.

AH 7419.11 — Vargas Vila, J.M. La república romana. Paris, 1911.

AH 7539.11 — Vivell, Karl. Chronoligisch-kritische Untersuchungen zur Geschichte des Kaisers Claudius. Diss. Freiburg, 1911.

Eg 609.11.5 — Weigall, Arthur E.P.B. The life and times of Akhnaton, pharaoh of Egypt. Edinburgh, 1911.

AH 7448.18.15 — Wilkinson, S. Hannibal's march through the Alps. Oxford, 1911.

AH 7509.11 — Willrich, H. Livia. Leipzig, 1911.

AH 7418.98.2 — Woodhouse, Mason A. History of Rome, 390-202 B.C. London, 1911.

1912

AH 7819.09.3 — Abbott, F.F. Society and politics in ancient Rome. London, 1912.

AH 9666.4 — Alemany y Bolufer, J. La geografía de la peninsula ibérica. Madrid, 1912.

AH 4959.09.5 — Allinson, Francis Greenleaf. Greek lands and letters. Boston, 1912.

AH 930.36 — Atlas of ancient and classical geography. London, 1912.

Eg 819.12 — Baillet, J. Introduction à l'étude des idées morales dans l'Egypte antique. Thèse. Blois, 1912.

AH 7779.12 — Barbagallo, C. Giuliano l'Apostata. Genova, 1912.

AH 4278.93.2 — Beloch, J. Grecian history. v.1-4. Strassburg, 1912-27. 8v.

AH 6110.17 — Bettingen, W. König Antigonos Doson von Makedonien. Inaug. Diss. Weida, 1912.

AH 908.75.2 — Blümner, H. Technologie und Terminologie der Gewerbe. 2. Aufl. Berlin, 1912.

AH 3013.912 — Boissier, Alfred. Notice sur quelques monuments assyriens a l'Université de Zurich. Genève, 1912.

AH 8007.7.4 — Boissier, Gaston. L'Afrique romaine. 5. éd. Paris, 1912.

Eg 879.12.2 — Breasted, James Henry. Development of religion and thought in ancient Egypt. N.Y., 1912.

Eg 879.12 — Breasted, James Henry. Development of religion and thought in ancient Egypt. N.Y., 1912.

Eg 279.05.9 — Breasted, James Henry. A history of Egypt. 2. ed. N.Y., 1912.

AH 7201.47.12 — Bruns, C.G. Fontes Juris Romani Antiqui. Index. Tubingae, 1912.

AH 7201.47.12F — Bruns, C.G. Fontes Juris Romani Antiqui. v.2. Plates. Tubingae, 1912.

AH 8647.9 — Byvanck, A.W. De Magnae Graeciae historia antiquissima. Hagae, 1912.

Chronological Listing

1912 - cont.

AH 8005.2.2   Cagnat, René. L'armée romaine d'Afrique. 2. éd. Paris, 1912. 2v.

AH 8005.2.7   Cagnat, René. La frontière militaire de la Tripolitaine à l'époque romaine. Paris, 1912.

AH 7179.12   Cardinali, G. Studi graccani. Roma, 1912.

AH 7759.12   Centonze, L. L'imperatore Costantino e la chiesa cattolica. Bari, 1912.

AH 9610.28.5   Ciaceri, Emanuele. Intorno alle più antiche relazioni fra la Sicilia e la Persia. Pisa, 1912.

AH 3013.42.2F   Clercq, Louis de. Collection De Clercq. Paris, 1912.

AH 8908.12   Cserèp, J. De Pelasgis Etruscisqui. Budapestini, 1912.

AH 3149.4   Deimels, A. Veteris testamenti chronologia. Roma, 1912.

AH 3002.2.16.2   Delitzsch, Friedrich. Assyrische Lesestücke. 5. Aufl. Leipzig, 1912.

AH 9757.5   Dragendorff, H. Westdeutschland zur Römerzeit. Leipzig, 1912.

AH 4842.54A   Drever, J. Greek education, its practice and principles. Cambridge, 1912.

AH 7499.12   Ferrero, G. Die Frauen der Caesaren. Stuttgart, 1912.

AH 939.12   Filek, E. von Wittinghausen. Die geographischen Vorstellungen in Altertum. Wien, 1912.

AH 7279.11.15A   Fowler, W.W. Rome. N.Y., 1912.

AH 4842.39.1.2   Freeman, Kenneth John. Schools of Hellas. 2. ed. London, 1912.

Eg 139.12   Frese, Benedict. Ocherki greko-egipetskago prava. Iaroslavl', 1912.

AH 7201.97   Gaius. 1912. Krueger and Studemund. Gai institutiones. 6. ed. Berolini, 1912.

AH 7217.15   Gelzer, Matthias. Die Nobilität der römischen Republik. Leipzig, 1912.

AH 299.12   Gercke, Alfred. Einleitung in die Altertumswissenschaft. Leipzig, 1912-23. 3v.

AH 7139.12   Girard, P.F. Mélanges. Paris, 1912. 2v.

AH 7139.12.3   Girard, P.F. Mélanges du droit romain. Paris, 1912-23. 2v.

AH 279.12.3   Goodspeed, George S. A history of the ancient world. N.Y., 1912.

Eg 709.12   Gradenwitz, O. Griechische und demotische Papyri. Strassburg, 1912.

NEDL AH 8922.2   Grenier, A. Bologne, Villanovienne et Étrusque. Thèse. Paris, 1912.

AH 3013.17A   Handcock, P.S.P. Mesopotamian archaeology. N.Y., 1912.

AH 7139.12.7   Hardy, E.G. Roman laws and charters. Oxford, 1912.

AH 3020.10FA   Harvard University. Semitic Museum. Sumerian tablets in the Harvard Semitic Museum. Pt.1-2. Cambridge, Mass., 1912. 2v.

AH 8213.2.2   Haverfield, Francis J. The romanization of Roman Britain. 2. ed. Oxford, 1912.

AH 819.12.3   Höhn, G. Die Einteilungsarten der Lebens- und Weltalter bei Griechen und Römer. Würzburg, 1912.

AH 7214.10   Ioachmiovici, V.E. Juspirandum...du droit romain. Paris, 1912.

AH 3155.6.2FA   Jastrow, Morris. Bildermappe...zur Religion Babyloniens und Assyriens. Giessen, 1912.

AH 7279.12A   Jones, H.S. Companion to Roman history. Oxford, 1912.

AH 7329.12   Juster, Jean. Les droits politiques des juifs dans L'empire romain. Paris, 1912.

Eg 879.12.5   Kees, Hermann. Der Opfertanz des ägyptischen Königs. München, 1912.

AH 4848.5   Klein, G. Der Kranz bei den alten Griechen. Günzburg, 1912.

AH 7409.12   Kornemann, E. Der Priester Codex in der Regia. Tübingen, 1912.

AH 7449.12   Kromayer, I. Roms Kampf um die Welthenschaft. Leipzig, 1912.

AH 3129.3.5   Langdon, S. Die neubabylonischen Königsinschriften. Leipzig, 1912.

AH 3020.3   Legrain, L. Le temps des rois d'Ur. Text and plates. Paris, 1912. 2v.

AH 7089.12   Letz, Emil. Die Provinzialverwaltung Caesars. Strassburg, 1912.

AH 7039.12   Leuze, O. Zur Geschichte der römischen Censur. Halle, 1912.

AH 7819.12   Louis, Paul. Travail dans le monde romaine. Paris, 1912.

AH 3963.12   Macalister, R.A.S. A history of civilization in Palestine. Cambridge, Eng., 1912.

Eg 239.12   Maspero, J. Organisation militaire de l'Egypte Byzantine. Paris, 1912.

AH 279.12.5   Meyer, E. Histoire de l'antiquité. Paris, 1912.

AH 7299.05.7   Mommsen, Theodor. Reden und Aufsätze. Berlin, 1912.

Eg 299.12   Moret, Alexandre. Kings and gods of Egypt. N.Y., 1912.

AH 3002.7F   Morgan, J.P. Babylonian records in the library of J.P. Morgan. N.Y., 1912. 4v.

AH 7114.23   Oberziner, G. Patrizisto e plebe. Milano, 1912.

Eg 709.12.3   Oertel, Friedrich. Die Liturgie; Studien zur ptolemäischen...Verwaltung Agyptens. Leipzig, 1912.

AH 5409.6   Porzio, Guido. I Cipselidi. Bologna, 1912.

AH 4819.12   Prato, E. Vita e civilta degli Elleni. Livorno, 1912.

AH 4169.12   Raape, L. Der Verfall des griechischen Pfandes. Halle, 1912.

AH 3207.5   Rawlinson, H.G. Bactria. The history of a forgotten empire. London, 1912.

AH 7139.12.5   Revillont, E. Les origines égyptiennes. Paris, 1912.

AH 3002.28   Rogers, R.W. Cuneiform parallels to the Old Testament. N.Y., 1912.

AH 5309.11.2   Sanctis, G. Atthis. 2. ed. Torino, 1912.

AH 7859.9   Sandels, Friedrich. Die Stellung der kaiserlichen Frauen aus dem julisch-claudischen Wause. Darmstadt, 1912.

AH 3181.9   Schollmeyer, A. Sumerisch-babylonische Hymnen und Gebete an Samas. Paderborn, 1912.

AH 7519.12   Schwab, J. Leben und Charakter des Tiberius Claudius Nero nach Velleius. Tetschen, 1912.

AH 7899.12   Schwarze, K. Beiträge zur Geschichte altrömische Agrarprobleme. Halle, 1912.

AH 9710.5   Solari, A. Sui dinasti degli Odrisi (V-IV secolo a.C.). Pisa, 1912.

AH 6057.15   Solari, Arturo. La lega tessalica. Pisa, 1912.

X Cg AH 4279.12   Soteriades, G. Historia tès Archaiotétos. Athènai, 1912.

AH 864.5   Soveri, H.F. De ludorum nomina. Helsingforsiae, 1912.

AH 7739.12   Stein, Arthur. Die kaiserlichen Verwaltungsbeamten unter Severus Alexander, 222-235. Prag, 1912.

AH 7819.11.5A   Stobart, J.C. The grandeur that was Rome; a survey of Roman culture. London, 1912.

AH 7239.12   Stolle, F. Das Lager und Heer der Römer. Strassburg, 1912.

1912 - cont.

AH 7159.12A   Strachan-Davidson, J.L. Problems of the Roman criminal law. Oxford, 1912. 2v.

AH 4842.43.2   Walden, J.W.H. University of ancient Greece. N.Y., 1912.

AH 4112.11   Walek, T. Die delphische Amphiktyonie in der Zeit den aitolischen Herrschaft. Berlin, 1912.

AH 7139.03.4   Walton, F.P. Historical introduction to Roman law. 2. ed. Edinburgh, 1912.

AH 4819.07.2A   Wendland, P. Hellenistisch-römische Kultur. Tübingen, 1912.

AH 279.12.7   Westermann, William L. The story of ancient nations. N.Y., 1912.

Eg 879.12.3   Zimmermann, F. Die ägyptische Religion. Paderborn, 1912.

1913

NEDL AH 7829.13A   Allinson, A.C.E. Roads from Rome. N.Y., 1913.

Eg 819.13   Baillet, J. Le régime pharaonique...avec l'evolution de la morale en Egypte. Thèse. Blois, 1913.

AH 7499.13   Bardt, C. Römische Charakterpöfe in Briefen. Leipzig, 1913.

AH 4819.05.5   Baumgarten, F. Die hellenische Kultur. 3. Aufl. Leipzig, 1913.

AH 819.13   Baumgarten, F. Die hellistisch-römische Kultur. Leipzig, 1913.

AH 4819.13.10   Beaunier, André. La Grèce et nous. Paris, 1913.

AH 3013.913F   Bell, Gertrude. Churches and monasteries of the Tûr 'Abdîn and neighbouring districts. Heidelberg, 1913.

AH 4819.13.5   Bianchi, Enrico. La Grecia nella letteratura, nella religione. Milano, 1913-14.

Eg 709.13   Biedermann, Erhard. Studien zur ägyptischen Verwaltungsgeschichte in ptolemäisch-römischen Zeit. Berlin, 1913.

AH 7339.13   Birt, Theodor. Römische Charakterköpfe. Leipzig, 1913.

AH 7419.13.5   Bloch, Gustave. La république romaine. Paris, 1913.

Eg 1039.13   Book of the Dead. The papyrus of Ani. London, 1913. 2v.

Eg 1039.13.2   Book of the Dead. The papyrus of Ani. N.Y., 1913. 3v.

AH 3910.8   Bouché-Leclercq, A. Histoire des Seleucides. Paris, 1913-14. 2v.

AH 4309.00.2   Bouché-Leclercq, A. Leçons d'histoire grecque. 2. éd. Paris, 1913.

AH 8013.3   Bouchier, E.S. Life and letters in Roman Africa. Oxford, 1913.

AH 5308.9.2   Calhoun, G.M. Athenian clubs in politics and litigation. Austin, 1913.

AH 5308.9   Calhoun, G.M. Athenian clubs in politics and litigation. Austin, 1913.

AH 279.13   Cavaignac, E. Histoire de l'antiquité. v.1-3 et index générale. Paris, 1913-20. 5v.

AH 7769.13   Cherniavskii, N.F. Imperator Feodosii Velikii i ego tsaratvovanie v tserkovno istoricheskom otnoshenii. Sergiev Posad, 1913.

AH 4819.13A   Cotterill, H.B. Ancient Greece. London, 1913.

AH 7279.13   Davis, W.S. Readings in ancient history. v.2. Boston, 1913.

AH 4039.13A   Ferguson, W.S. Greek imperialism. Boston, 1913.

AH 4039.13.3   Ferguson, W.S. Greek imperialism. London, 1913.

AH 7139.12.9   Girard, P.F. Études d'histoire juridique. Paris, 1913. 2v.

AH 7419.13.10   Gröseling, Johannes. Rom und Eturien von der Eroberung Vejis bis zur Mitte des 3. Jahrhunderts vor Christus. Borna, 1913.

AH 8007.12   Gsell, Stéphane. Histoire ancienne de l'Afrique du nord. Paris, 1913-28. 8v.

AH 7179.13   Guenoun, L. La cessio bonorum. Paris, 1913.

AH 7489.13   Hahn, L. Das Kaisertum. Leipzig, 1913.

AH 1409.13.1   Hall, Harry R. The ancient history of the Near East from the earliest times to the Battle of Salamis. N.Y., 1913.

AH 1409.13   Hall, Harry R. The ancient history of the Near East from the earliest times to the Battle of Salamis. London, 1913.

X Cg AH 4299.13   Haverfield, F. Ancient town-planning. Oxford, 1913.

AH 6110.12   Heiland, Paul. Untersuchungen zur Geschichte des Königs Perseus von Makedonien. Diss. Jena, 1913.

Eg 879.14.5F   Hopfner, Theodor. Der Tierkult der alten Ägypter. Wien, 1913.

AH 7408.78.11   Ihne, W. Early Rome. London, 1913.

AH 3143.12   Jeremias, Alfred. Handbuch der altorientalischen Geisteskultur. Leipzig, 1913.

AH 3009.13   Johns, C.H.W. Ancient Babylonia. Cambridge, Eng., 1913.

AH 4559.13   Kirkman, M.M. History of Alexander the Great. Chicago, 1913.

AH 3073.7   Klauber, Ernst. Politisch-religiöse Texte aus der Sargonidenzeit. Leipzig, 1913.

AH 3143.20   Landersdorfer, Simon. Die Kultur der Babylonier und Assyrier. Kempten, 1913.

NEDL AH 3181.10.5F   Langdon, S. Babylonian liturgies. Paris, 1913.

AH 4843.12   Latte, K. De saltationibus Graecorum. Giessen, 1913.

AH 919.14.5   Laum, Bernhard. Uber griechische und römische Stiftungen. Leipzig, 1913.

AH 7419.13   Lewis, J.H. The two great republics - Rome and the United States. Chicago, 1913.

AH 3147.3   Lindl, Ernest. Das Priester- und Beamtentum der altbabylonischen Kontrakte. Paderborn, 1913.

Eg 848.3.2   Majer-Leonhard, E. Agrammatoi. Marpurgi Chattorum, 1913.

Eg 848.3   Majer-Leonhard, E. Agrammatoi in Aegypto qui litteras sciverint qui nesciverint ex papyris graecis quantum fieri potest exploratur. Francofurti, 1913.

AH 829.13   Ménard, René J. La Grèce et l'Italie. Paris, 1913.

AH 828.80.4   Ménard, René J. Le travail dans l'antiquité. Paris, 1913? 2v.

AH 8058.5   Mesnage, R.J. Romanisation de l'Afrique, Tunisie. Paris, 1913.

AH 2583.9   Mezger, Fridericus. Inscriptio milesiaca de pace cum magnetibus facta. Inaug. Diss. Monaci, 1913.

AH 4939.13   Oberhummer, E. Hellas abs Wiege der wissenschaftliche Geographie. Wien, 1913.

AH 4479.13   Obst, E. Der Feldzug des Xerxes. Kapitel V. Leipzig, 1913.

AH 3155.9   Paffrath, T. Zur Götterlehre in den altbabylonischen Königsinschriften. Paderborn, 1913.

AH 7659.13   Pais, E. Storia critica di Roma durante i primi cinque secoli. v.1-4. Roma, 1913- 5v.

AH 4519.13   Pokorny, Erich. Studien zur griechischen Geschichte im sechsten und fünften Jahrzehnt des vierten Jahrhunderts vor Christ. Inaug Diss. Greifswald, 1913.

Chronological Listing

1913 - cont.

AH 4339.13 — Poralla, Paul. Prosopographie der Lakedaimonier bis auf die Zeit Alexanders des Grossen. Inaug. Diss. Breslau, 1913.

X Cg AH 7099.13 — Reid, J.S. The municipalities of the Roman empire. Cambridge, 1913.

Eg 909.13.5 — Reil, Theodor. Beiträge zur Kenntnis des Gewerbes im hellenistischen Agypten. Borna, 1913.

AH 8549.103 — Robinson, F.N. Human sacrifice among the Irish Celts. Boston, 1913.

AH 4862.7 — Roper, Allen George. Ancient eugenics. Oxford, 1913.

AH 8603.2 — Rosenberg, A. Der Staat der alten Italiker. Berlin, 1913.

AH 7819.13 — Sandys, J.E. A companion to Latin studies. 2. ed. Cambridge, 1913.

AH 3150.9 — Schorr, M. Urkunden des altbabylonischen Zivil- und Prozessrechts. Leipzig, 1913.

AH 4204.12 — Schreiner, Iosephus: de corpore iuris Atheniensium. Bonn, 1913.

AH 9722.6 — Schultze, V. Altchristliche Städte und Landschaften. Leipzig, 1913-22. 3v.

Eg 709.13.5 — Semeka, G. Ptolemäisches Prozessrecht. München, 1913.

AH 930.43 — Shepherd, William Robert. Atlas of ancient history. N.Y., 1913.

Eg 839.13 — Sottas, H. La préservation de la propriété funéraire. Paris, 1913.

Eg 709.13.3 — Steiner, A. Der Fiskus der Ptolemaeer. v.1-3. Leipzig, 1913.

AH 2114.2 — Steinleitner, Franz Seraph. Die Beicht im Zusammenhange mit der sakralen Rechtspflege in der Antike. Inaug. Diss. München, 1913.

AH 7239.13 — Steinwender, T. Die römische Taktik zur Zeit der Manipularstellung. Danzig, 1913.

AH 299.13 — Strehl, Willy. Grundriss der alten Geschichte und Quellenkundl. 2. Aufl. Breslau, 1913. 2v.

AH 7489.13.3 — Täubler, E. Imperium Romanum. Leipzig, 1913.

AH 4609.13 — Tarn, W.W. Antigonos Gonatas. Oxford, 1913.

AH 4149.13 — Tod, Marcus N. International arbitration amongst the Greeks. Oxford, 1913.

AH 7259.13 — Vescovini, Adolfo. Le flotte romane in Africa. Roma, 1913.

NEDL AH 279.13.5 — Webster, Hutton. Ancient history. N.Y., 1913.

AH 7239.13.5 — Wegeleben, Theodor. Die Rangordnung der römischen Centurionen. Berlin, 1913.

AH 279.13.10 — West, Willis M. The ancient world. Boston, 1913.

AH 8873.5 — Weyer, G.A. Die staatsrechtlichen Beziehungen Kapuas zu Rom. Inaug. Diss. Bonn, 1913.

1914

AH 2558.5 — Alexander, L. The kings of Lydia. Oberlin, 1914.

Eg 879.14 — Amélineau, Emile. L'enfer egyptien et l'enfer virgilien. Paris, 1914.

AH 7088.79.9 — Arnold, W.T. Roman system of provincial administration. 3rd ed. Oxford, 1914.

AH 3966.10 — Baikie, James. Lands and peoples of the Bible. London, 1914.

AH 7201.95.50 — Balog, E. Uber das alter der Ediktskommentare des Gaius. Hannover, 1914.

AH 3358.5F — Bates, O. The Eastern Libyans; essay. London, 1914.

AH 939.14 — Besnier, M. Lexique de géographie ancienne. Paris, 1914.

AH 7279.14.3 — Botsford, G.W. A history of Rome for high schools and academies. N.Y., 1914.

AH 9657.5 — Bouchier, E.S. Spain under the Roman empire. Oxford, 1914.

AH 7449.14.5 — Brewitz, Walther. Scipio Africanus maior in Spanien. Inaug. Diss. Tübingen, 1914.

AH 3423.1F — British Museum. Carchemish: report on excavations at Djerabis. London, 1914. 3v.

AH 3000.3.2 — British Museum. Catalog of cuneiform tablets in the Kouyunjik collection. Supplement. London, 1914.

AH 3016.9F — British Museum. Department of Egyptian and Assyrian Antiquities. Assyrian sculptures in British Museum. London, 1914.

Eg 1029.14 — Budge, Ernest Alfred Wallis. The literature of the ancient Egyptians. London, 1914.

Eg 279.14 — Budge, Ernest Alfred Wallis. A short history of the Egyptian people. London, 1914.

AH 8907.9 — Casati, Charles. Les Etrusques, leur langue...civilisation. Paris, 1914.

AH 7239.14 — Cheesman, G.L. The auxilia of the Roman imperial army. Oxford, 1914.

AH 4239.00.5 — Church, A.J. Helmet and spear. N.Y., 1914.

AH 3158.7 — Contenau, G. La déesse nue babylonienne. Paris, 1914.

AH 9757.6 — Cramer, F. Römisch-germanische Studien. Breslau, 1914.

AH 8522.5 — Cumont, Franz. Comment la Belgique fut romanisée. Paris, 1914.

Eg 139.14 — Dagallier, Jean. Les institutions judiciaires de l'Egypte ancienne. Thèse. Paris, 1914.

AH 4819.14.10 — Davis, William S. A day in old Athens. 1. ed. Boston, 1914.

AH 3154.13 — Deimel, Anton. Pantheon Babylonicum. Nomina deorum. Romae, 1914.

AH 3002.2.22 — Dennefeld, L. Babylonisch-assyrische Geburts-Omina. Leipzig, 1914.

AH 7489.09.2 — Domaszewski, A. von. Geschichte der Römischen Kaiser. 2. Aufl. Leipzig, 1914. 2v.

AH 7649.14 — Eberlein, Hellmut. Kaiser Mark Aurel und die Christen. Inaug. Diss. Breslau, 1914.

AH 7309.14 — Ferrero, G. Ancient Rome and modern America. N.Y., 1914.

AH 7239.14.4 — Fischer, W. Das römische Lager insbesondere nach Livius. Leipzig, 1914.

AH 7469.14 — Fraccaro, P. Studi sull'età dei Gracchi. Città di Castello, 1914.

AH 7489.14 — Frank, Tenny. Roman imperialism. N.Y., 1914.

AH 7449.14 — Freshfield, D.w. Hannibal once more. London, 1914.

AH 8536.5 — Ganter, F.L. Cäsars fahrt nach Britannien. Düsseldorf, 1914.

AH 7779.14 — Geffcken, J. Kaiser Julianus. Leipzig, 1914.

AH 7650.85 — Gibbon, Edward. History of decline and fall of Roman Empire. N.Y., 1914. 7v.

AH 7279.14 — Giles, A.F. A history of Rome. London, 1914.

AH 9684.10 — Gómez Santa Cruz, S. El solar numantino. Madrid, 1914.

AH 7850.3 — Harcum, C.G. Roman cooks. Diss. Baltimore, 1914.

AH 7419.14.2A — Havell, Herbert L. Republican Rome. London, 1914.

AH 7419.14 — Havell, Herbert L. Republican Rome. N.Y., 1914.

AH 4819.14.8 — L'hellénisation du monde antique. Paris, 1914.

AH 1409.14 — Hogarth, D.G. The ancient East. London, 1914.

1914 - cont.

AH 4279.14 — Jardé, A. Grèce antique et la vie grecque. Paris, 1914.

AH 3156.9 — Jastrow, M. Babylonian-Assyrian birth omens. Giessen, 1914.

AH 8857.5 — Jerome, Thomas S. Roman memories in the landscape seen from Capri. Detroit, 1914.

AH 4119.5 — Julien, Paul. Zur Verwaltung der Satrapien unter Alexander dem Grossen. Leipzig, 1914.

AH 7329.14 — Juster, Jean. Les juifs dans l'empire romain. Paris, 1914. 2v.

AH 879.14 — Kennebicq, Léon. L'idee du juste dans l'orient grec avant Socrate. Bruxelles, 1914.

AH 6157.9 — Klym, P. Die milesischen Kolonien im Skythenlande his zum III. nachchristliche Jahrhundert. Czernowitz, 1914.

AH 4848.6 — Köchling, J. De coronarum apud antiquos. Giessen, 1914.

AH 3013.914 — Koldewey, Robert. The excavations at Babylon. London, 1914.

AH 3013.925.3 — Koldewey, Robert. Das wieder erstehende Babylon. 3. Aufl. Leipzig, 1914.

AH 7201.96 — Kooiman, C.L. Fragmenta juris quiritum 1913. Amstelodami, 1914.

Eg 971.5 — Kübler, B. Antinoupolis, aus dem alten Städteleben. Leipzig, 1914.

AH 29.14 — Kunst und Altertum. Berlin, 1914-25. 6v.

AH 4819.14.5 — Lamer, Hans. Griechische Kultur im Bilde. Leipzig, 1914.

AH 2011.5 — Lammens, H. Le berceau de l'Islam. Romae, 1914.

AH 919.14 — Laum, Bernhard. Stiftungen in der griechischen und römischen Antike. Leipzig, 1914. 2v.

AH 4039.14 — Ledl, Arthur. Studien zur älteren athenischen Verfassungsgeschichte. Heidelberg, 1914.

AH 7149.14 — Leifer, Franz. Die Einheit des Gewaltgedankens im römischen Staatsrecht. München, 1914.

AH 7409.14 — Lloyd, Thomas. The making of the Roman people. London, 1914.

AH 3968.1 — Macalister, Robert Alexander Stewart. The Philistines. London, 1914.

AH 3250.5 — Margwelaschwili, T. von. Colchis, Iberien und Albanien um die Wende des 1. Jahrhunderts vor Christ. Inaug. Diss. Halle, 1914.

AH 3960.8.5 — Mathews, S. A history of New Testament times in Palestine, 175 B.C.-70 A.D. N.Y., 1914.

AH 279.14 — Mattingly, H. Outlines of ancient history. Cambridge, Eng., 1914.

AH 4169.14 — Meurs, Johann van. Rechtsgedingen over Bepaalde Goederen. Amsterdam, 1914.

AH 7479.14 — Müller, Ernst. Cäsaren-Porträts. v.1-2, 3. Bonn, 1914-27. 2v.

AH 3152.3 — Nesbit, William M. Sumerian records from Drehem. N.Y., 1914.

AH 4709.14 — Niccolini, G. La confederazione Achea. Paris, 1914.

AH 7179.14 — Pfeifer, Gerhard. Agrargeschichtlicher Beitrag. Inaug. Diss. Altenburg, 1914.

AH 5807.7 — Roltsch, Otto. Die Westlokrer. Inaug. Diss. Weida, 1914.

AH 7449.14.7 — Sann, Georg. Untersuchungen zu Scipios Feldzug in Afrika. Inaug. Diss. Berlin, 1914.

AH 3096.3 — Scheil, V. Le prisme d'Assaraddon...681-668. Paris, 1914.

AH 819.06.2 — Schmidt, M.C.P. Kulturhistorische Beiträge zur Kenntnis des griechischen und römischen Altertums. Leipzig, 1914.

AH 5308.8 — Schroeder, Otto. De laudibus Athenarum a poetis. Gottingae, 1914.

AH 4609.14 — Schubert, R. Die Quellen zur Geschichte der Diadochenzeit. Leipzig, 1914.

AH 9684.5F — Schulten, Adolf. Numantia...1905-1912. v.1-4 and atlas. München, 1914-31. 7v.

AH 4819.14 — Stephens, Kate. The Greek spirit. N.Y., 1914.

AH 9777.19.10 — Svensson, Jacob Vilhelm. De sydsvenska folknammen hos Jordanes. Karlstad, 1914.

AH 4279.14.5 — Thallon, Ida C. Readings in Greek history. Boston, 1914.

AH 4719.14 — Theiler, Wilhelm. Die politiche Lage in den beiden makedonischen Kriegen (200-197 v.C. und 171-168 v.C.). Diss. Halle, 1914.

AH 4299.14 — Tillyard, E. The Athenian empire and the great illusion. Cambridge, 1914.

AH 7206.23 — Tipucitus. M. Kritoy Patzē Tipoy Keitos. Romae, 1914-29. 5v.

AH 3020.8 — Ungnad, A. Babylonische Briefe aus der Zeit der Hammurapidynastie. Leipzig, 1914.

Eg 709.14 — Weigall, Arthur E.P.B. The life and times of Cleopatra, queen of Egypt. N.Y., 1914.

AH 7842.10.5 — Wilkins, A.S. Roman education. Cambridge, 1914.

AH 4842.45.2 — Ziebarth, E. Aus dem griechischen Schulwesen. 2. Aufl. Leipzig, 1914.

1915

AH 7549.15 — Barbagallo, C. La catastrofe di Nerone. Catania, 1915.

AH 7828.38.25 — Becker, W.A. Gallus or Roman scenes. London, 1915.

AH 7109.15 — Böttcher, Kurt. Die Einnahmen der römischen Republic im letzten Jahrhundert ihres Bestehens. Weida, 1915.

AH 4279.15A — Botsford, George W. Hellenic civilization. N.Y., 1915.

AH 7842.16 — Boyd, C.E. Public libraries and literary culture in ancient Rome. Chicago, 1915.

AH 279.15 — Breasted, James H. A short ancient history. Boston, 1915.

AH 7259.15 — Clark, F.W. The influence of sea power on...Roman republic. Menasha, 1915.

AH 4458.5 — Cloché, Paul. Etude chronologique sur la troisième guerre sacrée. Thèse. Paris, 1915.

AH 5310.6 — Cloché, Paul. Le restauration democratique à Athènes en 403 avant J.C. Paris, 1915.

AH 3061.1 — Contenau, Georges. Contribution à l'histoire économique d'Umma. Paris, 1915.

AH 8548.57.2 — Dottin, Georges. Manuel pour servir à l'étude de l'antiquité celtique. 2. éd. Paris, 1915.

AH 2583.8 — Dunham, A.G. History of Miletus down to the anabasis of Alexander. Thesis. London, 1915.

AH 3740.8 — Fleming, Wallace B. The history of Tyre. N.Y., 1915.

AH 4845.28 — Goebel, Maximilianus. Ethnica, pars prima: De Graecorum civitatum proprietatibus proverbio notatis. Vratislaviae, 1915.

Eg 1039.15F — Grapow, Hermann. Religiöse Urkunden. Heft 1-3. Leipzig, 1915.

AH 7469.15A — Howard, A.A. Latin selections illustrating public life in the Roman Commonwealth in the time of Cicero. Boston, 1915.

AH 7799.15.5 — Hutton, Edward. Attila and the Huns. N.Y., 1915.

AH 7159.15 — Huvelin, Paul. Etudes sur le fortum dans le très ancien droit romain. Lyon, 1915.

Chronological Listing

1915 - cont.

AH 930.44 — Iliff, John G. Maps illustrating ancient history. Topeka, 1915.

AH 3143.8 — Jastrow, Morris. The civilization of Babylonia and Assyria. Philadelphia, 1915.

AH 3143.8.2 — Jastrow, Morris. The civilization of Babylonia and Assyria. Philadephia, 1915.

AH 3020.7F — John Rylands Library. Manchester. Sumerian tablets from Umma. Manchester, 1915.

AH 9777.29.5A — Jordanes. The Gothic history of Jordanes. Princeton, 1915.

AH 3088.5F — King, L.W. Bronze reliefs from the Gates of Shalmaneser. London, 1915.

AH 3009.10 — King, L.W. History of Babylon from foundation...to Persian conquest. N.Y., 1915.

Eg 879.15.4 — Knight, A.E. Amentet; account of gods, amulets of ancient Egyptians. London, 1915.

AH 7819.15 — Lamer, Hans. Römische Kultur im Bilde. Leipzig, 1915.

AH 7469.15.5 — Lanzani, C. Mario e Silla. Catania, 1915.

AH 3965.5 — Lauré, M.J. The property concepts of the early Hebrews. Iowa City, 1915.

AH 7889.15A — MacFarlane, Charles W. Some observations on the economic interpretation of early Roman history. Philadelphia, 1915.

AH 3020.6 — Margolis, E. Sumerian temple documents. N.Y., 1915.

X Cg AH 3016.7 — Meissner, Bruno. Grundzüge der babylonisch-assyrischen Plastik. Leipzig, 1915.

AH 4848.5.5 — Müller, V.K. Der Polos, die griechische Gotterkrone. Inaug. Diss. Berlin, 1915.

AH 7769.15.5 — Olivetti, Alberto. Osservazioni storiche cronologiche sulla guerra di Costanzo II contro i Persiani. Torino, 1915.

AH 7149.15 — Pais, E. Ricerche sulla storia e sul diritto pubblico di Roma. Roma, 1915. 4v.

AH 2117.5F — Paton, David. Egyptian records of travel in Western Asia. v.1-3. Princeton, 1915-18. 4v.

AH 3163.6 — Pinches, T.G. The Babylonian tables of the Berens collection. London, 1915.

AH 4483.12 — Rados, C.N. La bataille de Salamine. Thèse. Paris, 1915.

AH 7653.35 — Ringeling, Hans G. Pragmatismus in Edward Gibbons Geschichte vom Verfall und Untergang des romischen Reiches. Inaug. Diss. Schönberg, 1915.

AH 3009.15 — Rogers, R.W. A history of Babylonia and Assyria. 6. ed. N.Y., 1915. 2v.

AH 4409.15 — Snyder, William L. The military annals of Greece from the earliest times to the beginning of the Peloporrnesian War. Boston, 1915. 2v.

Eg 879.15A — Spence, Lewis. Myths and legends of ancient Egypt. N.Y., 1915.

Eg 759.15 — Stein, Arthur. Untersuchungen zur Geschichte und Verwaltung Ägyptens unter roemischer Herrschaft. Stuttgart, 1915.

AH 7799.15 — Sundwall, J. Weströmische Studien. Berlin, 1915.

AH 4039.15 — Swoboda, H. Die griechischen Bünde und der moderne Bundesstaat. Prag, 1915.

AH 4259.15 — Tenne, A. Kriegsschiffe zu den zeiten der alten Griechen. Oldenburg, 1915.

Eg 1109.15 — Turaev, B.A. Razskaz Egiptiianina Sinukheta. Moskva, 1915.

AH 3959.22 — Volkov, I.M. Arameiskie dokumenty Iudeiskoi Kolonii. Moskva, 1915.

AH 3150.11F — Walther, Arnold. Zum altbabylonischen Gerichtswesen. Inaug. Diss. Leipzig, 1915.

AH 3002.2.23F — Weidner, Ernst F. Handbuch der babylonischen Astronomus. Leipzig, 1915.

Eg 1159.15 — Weindler, Fritz. Geburts- und Wochenbettsdarstellungen auf altägyptischen Tempelreliefs. München, 1915.

1916

Eg 879.16 — Allen, T.G. Horus in the pyramid texts. Diss. Chicago, 1916.

Eg 879.08 — Amélineau, Emile. Prolegomènes a l'étude de la religion egyptienne. pt.2. Paris, 1916.

AH 3159.19 — Barton, G.A. Archaeology and the Bible. Philadelphia, 1916.

AH 279.16.10 — Betten, F.S. The ancient world, from the earliest times to 800 A.D. Boston, 1916.

Eg 856.2 — Bonnet, Hans. Die altägyptische Schurztracht. Leipzig, 1916.

AH 279.12.2 — Botsford, G.W. History of the ancient world. N.Y., 1916.

AH 3911.6 — Bouchier, E.S. Syria as Roman province. Oxford, 1916.

AH 9090.2 — Bourne, Ella. Study of Tibur. Diss. Menasha, 1916.

AH 7842.16.5 — Boyd, C.E. Public libraries and literary culture in ancient Rome. Thesis. Chicago, 1916.

AH 279.16A — Breasted, James H. Ancient times, a history of the early world. Boston, 1916.

NEDL AH 7819.16 — Cagnat, René. Manual d'archeologie romaine. Paris, 1916-20. 2v.

AH 7549.16 — Caiti, G. Una nuova ipotesi sulle origini dell'incendio Nerone ano. Roma, 1916.

AH 3061.2 — Contenau, Georges. Umma sous la dynastie d'Ur. Paris, 1916.

AH 8617.5 — Cuoco, Vincenzo. Platone in Italia. Bari, 1916-24. 2v.

AH 4819.05.12 — Dickinson, G.L. The Greek view of life. N.Y., 1916.

AH 4117.6 — Edwards, J.B. Demesman in Attic life. Thesis. Menasha, 1916.

AH 4843.5.8A — Emmanuel, M. The antique Greek dance. N.Y., 1916.

AH 3177.12 — Gilgamesh. Gilgamesch. Leipzig, 1916.

Eg 819.16 — Gosse, A.B. The civilization of the ancient Egyptians. N.Y., 1916.

AH 9713.5 — Kazaroev, G.I. Beiträge zur Kulturgeschichte der Thraker. Sarajevo, 1916.

AH 7149.16 — Krug, Erich. Die Senatsboten der römischen Republik. Inaug. Diss. Breslau, 1916.

AH 9722.7 — Merle, Heinrich. Die Geschichte der Städte Byzantion und Kalchedon. Inaug. Diss. Kiel, 1916.

AH 7979.16F — Miller, Konrad. Itineraria romana. Stuttgart, 1916.

Eg 39.16 — Modica, Marco. Contribute papirologici. Roma, 1916.

AH 7279.04.5 — Myers, P.V.N. Ancient history. 2. ed. Boston, 1916.

AH 4559.16 — Otto, Walter. Alexander der Grosse. Marburg, 1916.

AH 7299.16 — Piganiol, André. Essai sur les origines de Rome. Thèse. Paris, 1916.

AH 7109.16 — Piganiol, André. L'impot de capitation sons le Bas-Empire romain. Chambéry, 1916.

AH 4846.8 — Rider, B.C. Greek house, its history and development from Neolithic period to Hellenistic. Thesis. Cambridge, 1916.

1916 - cont.

Eg 819.16.5 — Rozanov, V.V. Iz vostochykh motivov. pt.1-3. Petrograd, 1916-17.

AH 3096.5 — Schmidtke, Friedrich. Asarhaddons Statthalterschaft in Babylonien und seine Thronbesteigung in Assyrien. Inaug. Diss. Leiden, 1916.

AH 7489.16 — Schulz, Otto T. Das Wesen des Römischen Kaisertums. Paderborn, 1916.

AH 3149.7 — Sidersky, David. Étude sur la chronologie Assyro-Babylonienne. Paris, 1916.

AH 7889.16A — Simklovich, V.G. Rome's fall reconsidered. N.Y., 1916.

AH 7799.16 — Solari, Arturo. Gli unni e Attila. Pisa, 1916.

AH 3155.12 — Spence, Lewis. Myths and legends of Babylonia and Assyria. London, 1916.

AH 3155.12.5A — Spence, Lewis. Myths and legends of Babylonia and Assyria. N.Y., 1916.

AH 3097.5 — Streck, Maximilian. Assurbanipal und die letzen assyrischen Könige. Leipzig, 1916. 3v.

AH 8048.3 — Vibert, Théodore. La race chamitique. Paris, 1916.

AH 4819.05.3.6 — Whibley, Leonard. Companion to Greek studies. Cambridge, 1916.

AH 819.16 — Wolfson, Arthur M. Ancient civilization. N.Y., 1916.

AH 7659.16 — Woodward, E.L. Christianity and nationalism in...Roman Empire. Photoreproduction. London, 1916.

AH 819.08.13 — Zieliński, Tadeusz. Iz zhizni idei. izd. 3. Petrograd, 1916.

1917

AH 819.15.5 — Ashley, R.L. Ancient civilization. N.Y., 1917.

AH 3150.12F — Augapfel, J. BabylonischeRechtsurkunden aus der Regierungszeit Artaxerxes I und Darius II. Wien, 1917.

Eg 279.17 — Baikie, James. The story of the pharaohs. 2. ed. London, 1917.

AH 4216.10 — Bastid, Paul. L'hypothèque grecque et sa signification historique. Thèse. Tours, 1917.

AH 9557.1 — Bouchier, E.S. Sardinia in ancient times. Oxford, 1917.

AH 3017.19 — Brussels. Musée des Arts Décoratifs et Industriels. Catalogue des intailles et empreintes orientales des Musées royaux du cinquantenaire. Bruxelles, 1917.

AH 4819.17 — Burns, Cecil D. Greek ideals; study of social life. London, 1917.

AH 7469.17 — Cowles, F.H. Gaius Verres. Thesis. Ithaca, 1917.

AH 4558.33.6 — Droysen, J.G. Geschichte Alexanders des Grossen. Berlin, 1917.

Eg 879.17.5 — Frank-Kamenetskii, I.G. Pamiatniki egipetskoi religii v fivanskii period. Moskva, 1917- 2v.

AH 4819.17.8 — Gernet, Louis. Recherches sur le développement de la pensée juridique...en Grèce. Thèse. Paris, 1917.

AH 4459.17 — Glover, Terrot R. From Pericles to Philip. London, 1917.

AH 4459.17.5 — Glover, Terrot R. From Pericles to Philip. N.Y., 1917.

AH 4139.17 — Haussoullier, B. Traité entre Delphes et Pellana. Paris, 1917.

AH 4842.63 — Hudson-Williams, T. An education bill from ancient Greece. Cambridge, 1917.

AH 7449.17 — Huvelin, Paul. Une guerre d'usure. Paris, 1917.

Eg 879.17F — Junker, H. Die Onurislegende. Wien, 1917.

AH 4659.01.2 — Kaerst, Julius. Geschichte des Hellenismus. 2. Aufl. Leipzig, 1917-26. 2v.

AH 7629.17 — Lacey, R.H. The equestrian officials of Trajan and Hadrian. Thesis. Princeton, 1917.

AH 8548.75 — Leslie, S. Celt and the world. N.Y., 1917.

AH 5308.6 — Lofberg, John O. Sycophancy in Athens. Thesis. Chicago, 1917.

AH 8549.85.5 — Macbain, A. Celtic mythology and religion. Stirling, 1917.

AH 4860.9 — Mary Rosaria, sister. The nurse in Greek life. Diss. Boston, 1917.

AH 3154.25 — Maynard, John A. Studies in religious texts from Assur. Thesis. Chicago, 1917.

AH 3123.8 — Meek, Theophile J. Old Babylonian business and legal documents. Thesis. Chicago, 1917.

Eg 709.12.5 — Oertel, Friedrich. Die Liturgie. Leipzig, 1917.

AH 5759.7 — Pareti, Luigi. Storia di Sparta arcaica. Firenze, 1917.

AH 279.16.7F — Roosevelt, Theodore. Dawn and sunrise of history. N.Y., 1917.

AH 959.17 — Schoff, Wilfred H. Navigation to the Far East under the Roman Empire. Boston, 1917.

AH 7278.94.2 — Shuckburgh, E.S. A history of Rome to the battle of Actium. N.Y., 1917.

AH 5616.5 — Treidler, Hans. Epirus im Altertum; Studien zur historischen Topographie. Inaug. Diss. Leipzig, 1917.

AH 4819.06.7 — Tucker, T.G. Life in ancient Athens. Handbooks of archaeology and antiquities. Chautauqua, 1917.

AH 7819.10.4A — Tucker, T.G. Life in the Roman world of Nero and St. Paul. N.Y., 1917.

AH 3965.9 — Verinder, Frederick. My neighbor's landmark. Cincinnati, 1917.

1918

NEDL AH 7819.09.2 — Abbott, F.F. Society and politics in ancient Rome. N.Y., 1918.

AH 4109.18 — Andreadès, Andreas M. Istoría tēs 'Ellēnikēs. Athens, 1918.

AH 3060.3.15F — Barton, George A. Haverford Library collection of cuneiform tablets. New Haven, 1918. 3v.

AH 9792.6A — Bigelow, Poultney. Genseric, king of the Vandals. N.Y., 1918.

AH 7339.13.3 — Birt, Theodor. Römische Charakterköpfe. 3. Aufl. Leipzig, 1918.

AH 7749.18 — Bulić, F. Car Dijoklecijan. Zagreb, 1918.

AH 3181.12 — Edelkoort, A.H. Het zondebesef in de Babylonische boetepsalmen. Utrecht, 1918.

AH 8532.5 — Fabia, Philippe. La garnison romaine de Lyon. Lyon, 1918.

AH 7279.18 — Ferrero, Guglielmo. Short history of Rome. N.Y., 1918-19. 2v.

AH 7819.18 — Gilis, Alexander A. The Roman civilization. Edinburgh, 1918.

AH 3002.40 — Grant, Elihu. Cuneiform documents in Smith Library. Haverford, 1918.

AH 9186.5 — Grazia, Paolo di. La città di Pandosia. Napoli, 1918.

AH 7059.18 — Holleaux, M. Strátegos Ypatos. Thèse. Paris, 1918.

AH 4339.18 — Hopkinson, L.W. Greek leaders. Boston, 1918.

AH 4839.18 — Klee, Theophil. Zur Geschichte der gymnischen Agone an griechischen Festen. Leipzig, 1918.

AH 3958.12A — Kraeling, E.G.H. Aram and Israel. N.Y., 1918.

1918 - cont.

AH 3714.5 — Landersdorfer, S. Der baal tetramorphos und die Kerube des Ezechiel. Paderborn, 1918.

AH 7459.18 — Leffingwell, G.W. Social...life in Rome in the time of Plautus. N.Y., 1918.

AH 7207.29 — Lullius, Georgius. De senatorum Romanorum patria. Romae, 1918.

Eg 978.5 — Méautis, G. Hermoupolis-la-Grande. Lausanne, 1918.

AH 3002.34F — Nies, James B. Babylonian inscriptions. v.1-2, 4-9. New Haven, 1918-42. 8v.

AH 3154.14 — Nikel, Johannes. Ein neuer Ninkarrak. Paderborn, 1918.

AH 7419.18 — Pais, Ettore. Dalle guerre puniche a Cesare Augusto. v.1-2. Roma, 1918.

AH 7114.25 — Park, Marion E. The plebs in Cicero's day. Diss. Cambridge, 1918.

AH 7699.18A — Platnauer, Maurice. Life and reign of the Emperor Lucius Septimius Severus. London, 1918.

Eg 509.18 — Weill, Raymond. La fin du moyen empire égyptien. v.1-2. Paris, 1918.

AH 3159.21 — Willcocks, W. From the Garden of Eden to the crossing of the Jordan. 1st ed. Cairo, 1918.

1919

AH 889.19 — Appleton, C. Le taux du "fenus unciarum". Paris, 1919.

AH 819.18.2 — Birt, Theodor. Aus dem Leben der Antike. 2. Aufl. Leipzig, 1919.

AH 7339.13.4 — Birt, Theodor. Zur Kulturgeschichte Roms. 4. Aufl. Leipzig, 1919.

Eg 819.13.5 — Bissing, F.W. von. Die Kultur des alten Ägyptens. 2. Aufl. Leipzig, 1919.

AH 7469.13.5 — Bloch, G. La République romaine. Paris, 1919.

AH 7059.19 — Boak, A.E.R. The master of the offices in the later Roman and Byzantine empires. N.Y., 1919.

AH 4858.9 — Buddenhagen, F. Peri gamou. pt.1. Turici, 1919.

AH 4259.19 — Custance, Reginald Neville. War at sea. Edinburgh, 1919.

AH 7818.98.10 — Dill, Samuel. Roman society in the last century of the Western Empire. 2. ed. London, 1919.

AH 9757.5.5 — Dragendorff, H. Westdeutschland zur Römerzeit. 2. Aufl. Leipzig, 1919.

AH 6140.6 — Fafralé, O. Thessalonique des origines au XIVe siècle. Paris, 1919.

AH 4959.00.2 — Frazer, James G. Studies in Greek scenery, legend and history, selected from his commentary on Pausanias. London, 1919.

AH 7818.65.15 — Friedlaender, Ludwig. Darstellungen aus der Sittengeschichte Roms. 9.-10. Aufl. Leipzig, 1919. 4v.

AH 3152.5 — Grant, Elihu. Babylonian business documents of the classical period. Philadelphia, 1919.

AH 7629.20 — Gray, William D. A study...life of Hadrian prior...accession. Northampton, 1919?

AH 1279.19 — Hanslik, E. Einleitung und Geschichte des alten Orients. Gotha, 1919.

AH 7279.19 — Hartmann, Ludo. Römische Geschichte. Gotha, 1919.

AH 7469.19.7 — Hartwig, Wilhelm. Spartakus und der Glatiatorenkrieg 73-71 vor Christus. Leipzig, 1919.

AH 7909.19 — Hatzfeld, Jean. Les trafiquants italiens dans l'Orient hellénique. Photoreproduction. Paris, 1919.

AH 7889.19 — Herzog, R. Aus der Geschichte des Bankwesens im Altertum. Giessen, 1919.

AH 9607.21 — Jenison, E.S. The history of the province of Sicily. Boston, 1919.

AH 7469.19.5 — Jolliffe, Richard. Phases of corruption in Roman administration. Menasha, 1919.

AH 3980.17 — Kirmis, F. Die Lage der alten Davidsstadt und die Mauern des Alten Jerusalem. Breslau, 1919.

AH 7469.19 — Koehler, M.A. Catilina in classic tradition. Thesis. N.Y., 1919.

AH 299.19 — Kornemann, E. Aufsätze und Vorträge. Leipzig, 1919.

AH 5315.30 — Lugones, Leopoldo. Las industrias de Atenas. Buenos Aires, 1919.

AH 7779.19 — Martin, Edward J. The emperor Julian. London, 1919.

AH 3155.13 — Mercer, Samuel A. Religious and moral ideas in Babylonia and Assyria. Milwaukee, 1919.

AH 7479.18.2 — Meyer, Eduard. Caesars Monarchie und das Principat des Pompejus. 2. Aufl. Stuttgart, 1919.

AH 4519.19 — Murray, Gilbert. Aristophanes and the war party. Photoreproduction. London, 1919.

AH 7418.85.3 — Oliveira Martins, J.P. Historia da republica romana. 3. ed. v.1-2. Lisboa, 1919.

AH 3177.9 — Peserico, Luigi. Indagini sul poema di Gilgames. Vicenza, 1919.

AH 8907.12 — Peserico, Luigi. Ricerche di storia etrusca. Vicenza, 1919.

AH 8864.16 — Peterson, Roy M. The cults of Campania. Rome, 1919.

AH 819.19 — Petrie, W.M.F. Some sources of human history. London, 1919.

AH 279.13.4 — Porzio, G. Una "storia dell'antichità". Milano, 1919.

AH 5403.5 — Porzio, Guido. La più antica aristocrazia Corintiaca. Milano, 1919.

AH 9615.5 — Rauber, H. Die agrarischen Verhaltnisse Siziliens in Altertume besonders zur Zeit Ciceros. Bayreuth, 1919.

AH 4499.19 — Schulte-Vaërting, H. Die Friedenspolitik des Perikles. München, 1919.

AH 7709.19 — Schulz, Otto T. Vom Prinzipat zum Dominat. Das Wesen des römischen Kaisertums. Paderborn, 1919.

AH 7659.19F — Seeck, Otto. Regesten der Kaiser und Päpste für die Jahre 311 bis 476 nach Christ. Stuttgart, 1919.

AH 8233.5 — Sharpe, Montagu. Middlesex in British, Roman and Saxon times. London, 1919.

AH 7469.19.9 — Thomas, S.P. Den antikke tradition om Graecherne. Kristiania, 1919.

AH 879.19 — Warren, E.P. Alemaeon, Hypermestia, Caeneus. Oxford, 1919.

192-

AH 7279.20.5 — Cardona, Chiara. Roma antica attraverso la sua storia e i suoi monumenti. 2. ed. Roma, 192-.

AH 7489.08.5 — Jones, H.S. Roman Empire B.C. 29-A.D. 476. N.Y., 192-?

Eg 1189.20F — Scharff, A. Ein Rechnungsbuch des königlichen Hofes aus der 13 Dynastie. Berlin, 192-.

1920

AH 8048.5 — Adametz, Leopold. Herkunft und Wanderungen der Hamiten erschlossen aus ihren Haustierrassen. Wien, 1920.

AH 3707.19F — Autran, C. Phéniciens. Paris, 1920.

AH 4842.60 — Bernot, Alice. Recherches sur l'Éphébie attique. Paris, 1920.

AH 4329.20 — Bilabel, Friedrich. Die ionische Kolonisation. Leipzig, 1920.

AH 7339.19.2 — Birt, Theodor. Charakterbilder Spätroms. 2. Aufl. Leipzig, 1920.

AH 4481.9 — Boucher, Arthur. La bataille de la Marne de l'antiquité; Marathon d'aprés Hérodote. Nancy, 1920.

Eg 1039.20 — British Museum. Department of Egyptian and Assyrian Antiquities. The book of the dead. London, 1920.

AH 3002.26F — British Museum. Department of Egytpian and Assyrian Antiquities. Hittite texts in the cuneiform character. London, 1920.

AH 4279.20 — Ciccotti, Ettore. Griechische Geschichte. Gotha, 1920.

AH 3664.15 — Clemen, Carolus. Fontes historiae religionum Persicae. Bonnae, 1920.

AH 7162.34 — Coli, Ugo. Lo suiluppo delle varie forme di legato nel diritto romano. Parigi, 1920.

AH 7749.20 — Costa, Giovanni. Diocleziano. Roma, 1920.

AH 3407.17 — Cowley, Arthur E. The Hittites. London, 1920.

AH 239.20 — Daniels, Emil. Das antike Kriegswesen. 2. Aufl. Berlin, 1920.

AH 7819.04.5 — Dill, Samuel. Roman society from Nero to Marcus Aurelius. London, 1920.

AH 3107.7 — Forrer, Emil. Die Provinzeiteilung des assyrischen Reiches. Leipzig, 1920.

AH 7889.20A — Frank, Tenney. An economic history of Rome. Baltimore, 1920.

AH 4889.20 — Glotz, G. Le travail dans la Grèce ancienne. Paris, 1920.

AH 1409.20 — Grant, Elihu. The Orient in Bible times. Philadelphia, 1920.

AH 4038.96.10 — Greenidge, A.H.J. A handbook of Greek constitutional history. London, 1920.

AH 7239.20.5 — Grosse, Robert. Römische Militärgeschichte. Berlin, 1920.

AH 8007.12.5 — Gsell, Stéphane. Histoire ancienne de l'Afrique du nord. Paris, 1920. 4v.

AH 1409.13.5 — Hall, Harry R. The ancient history of the Near East from the earliest times to the Battle of Salamis. 5. ed. London, 1920.

AH 3005.9F — Hommel, Fritz. Beiträge zur morgenländischen Altentum. München, 1920.

AH 7549.20 — Jahn, John Nicholas H. A critical study of the history of the Emperor Nero. Thesis. N.Y.? 1920.

AH 3002.75F — Joint Expedition of the British Museum and the Museum of the University of Pennyslvania to Mesopotamia. Ur excavations. Texts and plates. v.1-4; 6, pt.1-2; 8. Philadelphia, 1920-35. 10v.

AH 854.9.2 — Keller, Otto. Gesamtregister von Eugen Staiger. Leipzig, 1920.

AH 4215.7 — Latte, Kurt. Heiliges Recht. Tübingen, 1920.

AH 7059.20 — McFayden, Donald. The history of the title imperator under the Roman empire. Thesis. Chicago, 1920.

AH 138.61.18 — Maine, Henry S. Ancient law. London, 1920.

AH 3143.10 — Meissner, Bruno. Babylonien und Assyrien. Heidelberg, 1920. 2v.

AH 7278.54.27 — Mommsen, T. The history of Rome. London, 1920.

AH 7279.20.7 — Monaci, Ernesto. Storie de Troja et de Roma altrimenti dette Liber ystoriarum Romanorum. Roma, 1920.

AH 959.20 — Mooney, William West. Travel among the ancient Romans. Boston, 1920.

AH 7114.26 — Münzer, F. Römische Adelsparteien und Adelsfamilien. Stuttgart, 1920.

AH 4858.11 — Mulder, J.J.B. Quaestiones nonnullae ad Atheniensium matrimonia vetamque conjugalem pertinentes. Inaug. Diss. Traiecti ad Rhenum, 1920?

AH 4519.19.2 — Murray, Gilbert. Our great war and the war of the ancient Greeks. N.Y., 1920.

AH 3002.2.25 — Nies, James B. Ur dynasty tablets. Leipzig, 1920.

AH 7179.20 — Pachtere, F.G. La table hypothécaire de Valeia. Paris, 1920.

AH 7239.20 — Pais, Ettore. Fasti triumphales populi Romani. v.1-2. Roma, 1920.

AH 9608.5 — Pareti, Luigi. Studi siciliani ed italioti. Firenze, 1920.

Eg 1309.20PF — Peet, T. Eric. The Mayer papyri A and B. London, 1920.

AH 299.20 — Preller, Hugo. Das Altertum seine staatliche und geistige Entwicklung und deren Nachwirkungen. Leipzig, 1920.

AH 7658.95.5 — Seeck, Otto. Geschichte des Untergangs der antiken Welt. v.1-6. Appendix 1-6. Stuttgart, 1920-23. 12v.

AH 7239.20.7 — Sulser, Jakob. Disciplina, Beiträge zur inneren Geschichte des römischen Heeres von Augustus bis Vespasian. Inaug. Diss. Dachau, 1920.

AH 4299.00.4 — Swoboda, H. Greek history. London, 1920.

AH 4009.20 — Tilden, F.W. Greek life; bibliography and review questions. Bloomington, 1920.

AH 2271.5 — Vagts, Rudolph. Aphrodisias in Karien. Diss. Borna, 1920.

AH 409.20 — Van Loon, Hendrik Willem. Ancient man. N.Y., 1920.

AH 7479.20 — Veith, Georg. Der Feldrug von Dyrrhachium. Wien, 1920.

Eg 819.20 — Wiedemann, A. Das alte Agypten. Heidelberg, 1920.

1921

AH 9065.5 — Adams, Louise E.W. A study of commerce in Latium from the early iron age through the sixth century B.C. Thesis. Northampton, Mass., 1921.

AH 7279.21 — Boak, Arthur E.R. A history of Rome to 565 A.D. N.Y., 1921.

AH 7819.21 — Bornecque, H. Rome et les romains (littérature, histoire, antiquités publiques et privées). Paris, 1921.

AH 3155.15 — Brooks, Beatrice A. A contribution to the study of moral practices of certain social groups in ancient Mesopotamia. Diss. Leipzig, 1921.

AH 3002.37 — Chiera, Edward. Selected temple accounts from Tellohyokha and Drehem. Philadelphia, 1921.

AH 109.21 — Ciccotti, Ettore. Lineamenti dell'evoluzione tributaria nel mondo antico. Milano, 1921.

AH 7469.21 — Constans, L.A. Un correspondant de Cicérone. Thèse. Paris, 1921.

AH 3863.5 — Cruveilhier, P. Les principaux résultats des nouvelles fouilles de Suse. Paris, 1921.

AH 4709.21 — Ferrabino, A. Il problema dell'unita nazionale nella Grecia antica I. Firenze, 1921.

Chronological Listing

1921 - cont.

AH 7309.21A   Ferrero, G. The ruin of the ancient civilization and the triumph of Christianity. N.Y., 1921.

AH 7309.21.3   Ferrero, G. La ruine de la civilisation antique. Paris, 1921.

AH 7279.21.5   Ferrero, Guglielmo. Roma antica. Firenze, 1921-22. 3v.

AH 48.93.7   Fowler, W.W. The city-state of the Greeks and Romans. London, 1921.

AH 3022.7   Gadd, C.J. The early dynasties of Sumer and Akkad. London, 1921.

AH 7479.21   Gelzer, Matthias. Cäsar, der Politiker und Staatsmann. Stuttgart, 1921.

AH 299.12.5   Gercke, Alfred. Einleitung in die Altertumswissenschaft. 3. Aufl. Leipzig, 1921-27. 3v.

AH 2013.7.8   Guidi, Ignazio. L'Arabie antéislamique. Paris, 1921.

AH 7899.21.5   Hanger, A. Zur römischen Landwirtschaft und Haustierzucht. Hanover, 1921.

AH 7699.21   Haselroeck, J. Untersuchungen zur Geschichte des Kaisers Septimius Severus. Heidelberg, 1921.

AH 7309.21.5   Heinze, Richard. Von den Ursachen der Grösse Roms. Leipzig, 1921.

AH 899.21   Heitland, William E. Agricola; a study of agriculture and rustic life in the Greco-Roman world. Cambridge, 1921.

AH 7279.20.2A   Henderson, Bernard W. The study of Roman history. London, 1921.

AH 4459.21   Holleaux, M. Rome, la Grèce et les monarchies hellénistiques. Thèse. Paris, 1921.

AH 4279.21   James, Henry R. Our Hellenic heritage. London, 1921-30. 2v.

AH 6136.5   Katsarov, G.I. Peoniia. Sofiia, 1921.

Eg 299.21   Knight, G.A. Frank. Nile and Jordan. London, 1921.

AH 7509.21   Kornemann, Ernst. Mausoleum und Tatenbericht des Augustus. Leipzig, 1921.

AH 9632.5   Libertini, Guido. Le isole Eolie nell'antichità greca e romana. Firenze, 1921.

AH 3963.12.5   Macalister, R.A.S. A history of civilization in Palestine. Cambridge, Eng., 1921.

Eg 609.13   Nelson, Harold H. The battle of Megiddo. Diss. Chicago, 1921.

AH 819.19.10   Neuburger, Albert. Die Technik des Altertums. 2. Aufl. Leipzig, 1921.

AH 7489.21   Nilsson, Martin. Den romerska kejsartiden. Stockholm, 1921.

AH 3664.11   Reitzenstein, R. Das iranische Erlösungsmysterium. Bonn, 1921.

AH 7279.21.7   Rosenberg, Arthur. Einleitung und Quellenkunde zur römischen Geschichte. Berlin, 1921.

AH 8616.9A   Sabin, Frances E. Classical associations of places in Italy. Madison, Wis., 1921.

AH 7819.13.3   Sandys, J.E. A companion to Latin studies. 3. ed. Cambridge, 1921.

AH 4229.21   Schulthess, Otto. Das attische Volksgericht. Bern, 1921.

AH 3095.8   Sennacherib, king of Assyria. The first campaign of Sennacherib. 1921.

Eg 1309.21F   Sottas, Henri. Papyrus démotiques de Lille. Paris, 1921.

Eg 1029.21   Spiegelberg, W. Ägyptische und andere Graffiti. Heidelberg, 1921.

AH 4819.11.4   Stobart, J.C. The glory that was Greece. London, 1921.

AH 7200.18   Täubler, Eugen. Untersuchungen zur Geschichte des Decemvirats und der zwölft Afdu. Berlin, 1921.

AH 7449.21   Täubler, Eugen. Die Vorgeschichte des zweiten punischen Krieges. Berlin, 1921.

AH 308.96.5A   Taylor, H.O. Ancient ideals. 2. ed. N.Y., 1921. 2v.

AH 4819.21   Thomson, J.A.K. Greeks and Barbarians. London, 1921.

AH 3154.15   Thureau-Dangin, F. Rituels accadiens. Paris, 1921.

AH 4309.21   Toynbee, A.J. The tragedy of Greece. Oxford, 1921.

AH 9109.5   Tromp, S.P.C. De Romanorum piaculis. Lugduni Batavorum, 1921.

AH 4819.21.5A   Ure, Percy N. The Greek renaissance. London, 1921.

AH 4279.21.5   Walker, E.M. Greek history. Oxford, 1921.

1922

AH 3657.25   Ahl, Augustus W. Outline of Persian history. N.Y., 1922.

AH 4114.17   Billheimer, A. Naturalization in Athenian law and practice. Diss. Gettysburg, 1922.

AH 7489.22   Bloch, G. L'empire romain; évolution et decadence. Paris, 1922.

AH 4809.22   Boethius, Axel. Der argivische Kalender. Uppsala, 1922.

AH 4279.22A   Botsford, George W. Hellenic history. N.Y., 1922.

AH 4819.22.5   Casson, S. Ancient Greece. London, 1922.

AH 4279.22.10   Ciccotti, Ettore. Storia greca. Firenze, 1922.

AH 7299.22   Cichorius, C. Römische Studien, historisches, epigraphisches, literargeschichtliches. Leipzig, 1922.

AH 3002.7.5   Clay, A.T. Hebrew deluge story in cuneiform...Morgan Library. New Haven, 1922.

AH 3803.5   Cohen, Kadmi. Introduction à l'histoire des institutions sociales et politiques chez les Semites. Paris, 1922.

AH 3400.5   Contenau, G. Eléments de bibliograhie Hittite. Thèse. Paris, 1922.

AH 3400.5.5   Contenau, G. Eléments de bibliographie Hittite. Paris, 1922.

AH 3143.9   Contenau, Georges. La civilisation assyro-babylonienne. Paris, 1922.

AH 4819.22   Croiset, M. La civilisation hellénique. Paris, 1922. 2v.

AH 3663.7   Dhalla, M.N. Loroastrian civilization. N.Y., 1922.

AH 5759.9   Doukas, P.C. He Sparte dia mesou tòn aiònon. Nea Yorkè, 1922.

AH 7449.22   Egelhauf, G. Hannibal. Stuttgart, 1922.

AH 7309.09.5   Ferrero, G. Characters and events of Roman history. N.Y., 1922.

VAH 842.50.2   Finácsy, Ernö. Az ókori newelés törteneti. 2. kiad. Budapest, 1922.

AH 7829.08.4   Fowler, W.W. Social life at Rome in the age of Cicero. N.Y., 1922.

AH 4842.39.2   Freeman, Kenneth John. Schools of Hellas. 3. ed. London, 1922.

AH 7039.01.5   Greenidge, Abel Hendy Jones. Roman public life. London, 1922.

AH 7489.22.5   Guenther, Adolf. Beiträge zur Geschichte der Kriege zwischen Römern und Parthern. Photoreproduction. Berlin, 1922.

AH 7339.22   Hamilton, M.A. Ancient Rome. Oxford, 1922.

AH 8908.14.5   Haury, Jacob. Über die Herkunft der Etrusker. Kaiserslautern, 1922.

1922 - cont.

AH 7309.22   Heitland, William E. The Roman fate; an essay. Cambridge, 1922.

AH 8914.20   Herbig, G. Religion und Kultur der Etrusker. Breslau, 1922.

AH 4859.22   Herfst, Pieter. La travail de la femme dans la Grèce ancienne. Proefschrift. Utrecht, 1922.

AH 9684.5.2F   Hofmann, H. Panorama von Numantia. München, 1922.

AH 7889.22   Homs, Léon. Problèmes sociaux de jadis et d'à présent. Paris, 1922.

Eg 872.5   Hopfner, Theodor. Fontes historiae religionis aegypticae. Bonnae, 1922-25. 5v.

AH 4149.22   Kahrstedt, U. Griechisches Staatsrecht. Göttingen, 1922.

AH 6110.22   Katsarov, G.I. Tsar Filipp II Makedonski. Sofiia, 1922.

AH 7203.130   Krüger, Hugo. Die Herstellung der Digesten Justinians und der Gang der Exzerption. Münster, 1922.

AH 4519.22   Laskarus, K.A. Phòs eis tò Thoukydídeiou erhebos. Athènai, 1922.

Eg 269.22   Lazzaridès, C.A. De l'évolution des relations internationales de l'Égypte pharaonique. Thèse. Paris, 1922.

AH 3002.65F   Lewy, Julius. Studien zu den altassyrischen Texten aus Kappadokien. Berlin, 1922.

AH 3977.5   Linder, Sven. Sauls Gibea. Uppsala, 1922.

AH 7469.22   Marsh, F.B. The founding of the Roman empire. Austin, 1922.

AH 5306.7F   Marstand, Vilhelm. Arsenalet i Piraeus og oldtidens byggereqler. København, 1922.

AH 7279.22A   Matheson, P.E. The growth of Rome. London, 1922.

AH 7278.84.10   Matheson, P.E. Skeleton outline of Roman history down A.D. 180. London, 1922.

AH 9684.7   Mélida, José R. Excursión a Numancia pasando por Soria. Madrid, 1922.

AH 8549.122   Memminger, A. Das Erbe der Druiden. 7. Aufl. Würzburg, 1922.

AH 4039.22   Menzel, Adolf. Kallikles. Wien, 1922.

AH 7279.22.10   Pais, Ettore. Italia antica. Bologna, 1922. 2v.

AH 3013.855   Pillet, M. L'expedition scientifique et artistique de Mésopotamie et de Médie. Paris, 1922.

Eg 759.22   Piotrowicz, L. Stanowisko nomarchów w administracji Egiptu. Poznan, 1922.

AH 4819.22.7   Poland, Franz. Die antike Kultur. Leipzig, 1922.

Eg 299.22.10   Recueil d'études égyptologiques dédiées à la mémoire de Jean-François Champollion. Paris, 1922.

Eg 299.22.5   Schubart, W. Ägypten von Alexander dem Grossen bis auf Mohammed. Berlin, 1922.

AH 889.22   Segrè, Angelo. Circolazione monetaria e prezzi nel mondo antico ed in particolare in Egitto. Roma, 1922.

AH 4279.06.5   Shuckburgh, E.S. Greece from the coming of the Hellenes to A.D. 14. 1. ed. London, 1922.

Eg 609.22F   Siemens, Clara. Koenig Echnaton in el-Amarna. Leipzig, 1922.

AH 4039.22.5   Strohm, Gustav. Demos und Monarch. Stuttgart, 1922.

AH 299.22   Ure, Percy. The origin of tyranny. Cambridge, 1922.

AH 409.22   Van Loon, Hendrik Willem. Ancient man. N.Y., 1922.

AH 3413.9   Weber, Otto. Die Kunst der Hethiter. Berlin, 1922.

AH 3000.10   Weidner, Ernst. Die Assyriologie, 1914-1922. Leipzig, 1922-23.

AH 3024.5   Weidner, Ernst F. Der Zug Sargons von Akkad nach Kleinasien. Leipzig, 1922.

Eg 759.22.5   Wenger, L. Volk und Staat in Ägypten am Ausgang der Römerherrschaft. München, 1922.

Eg 919.22   Westermann, W.L. The "dryland" in Ptolemaic and Roman Egypt. n.p., 1922.

1923

AH 7039.23A   Abbott, Frank F. Roman politics. Boston, 1923.

AH 9666.7   Albertini, E. Les divisions administratives de l'Espagne romaine. Thèse. Paris, 1923.

AH 3017.30F   Andrae, W. Farbige Keramik aus Assur und ihre Vorstafen in altassyrischen Wandmalereien. Berlin, 1923.

AH 1819.23A   Baikie, James. The life of the ancient East. N.Y., 1923.

AH 7819.23A   Bailey, Cyril. The legacy of Rome. Oxford, 1923.

AH 7469.23   Bennett, Harold. Cinna and his times. Menasha, 1923.

AH 4164.7   Bergold, Friedrich. Geschichte und Wesen des Arrabons und der Arrha im griechischen und römischen Recht. Gernsback, 1923.

AH 7339.19.3   Birt, Theodor. Charakterbilder Spätroms. 3. Aufl. Leipzig, 1923.

AH 7749.23   Bjarnason, T.H. Diocletianus keisari. Reykjavík, 1923.

Eg 819.23.5   Blackman, A.M. Luxor and its temples. N.Y., 1923.

NEDL AH 279.23   Blanchet, D. Histoire de l'Orient et de la Grèce. 7. éd. Paris, 1923.

AH 4889.23   Bolkestein, H. Het economisch leven in Griekenlands bloeitijd. Haarlem, 1923.

Eg 1039.23A   Book of the Dead. The coming forth by day. Boston, 1923.

AH 2011.9   Bräunlich, Erich. Bistäm ibn Qais. Leipzig, 1923.

AH 3191.7F   British Museum. Department of Egyptian and Assyrian Antiquities. Assyrian medical texts. London, 1923.

Eg 609.23   Budge, Ernest Alfred Wallis. Tutankhamen, Amenism, Atenism and Egyptian monotheism. London, 1923.

AH 29.23.5A   The Cambridge ancient history. Cambridge, Eng., 1923-1939. 12v.

AH 29.23.10   The Cambridge ancient history. v.3-12. Cambridge, Eng., 1923-1939. 10v.

Eg 609.23.6   Capart, Jean. The tomb of Tutankhamen. London, 1923.

Eg 609.23.7   Carter, Howard. The tomb of Tut-Ankh-Amen. London, 1923-33. 3v.

Eg 609.23.8A   Carter, Howard. The tomb of Tut-Ankh-Amen. N.Y., 1923.

AH 889.23   Cavaignac, E. Population et capital dans le monde mediterranéen antique. Strasbourg, 1923.

AH 8207.12   Collingwood, Robin G. Roman Britain. London, 1923.

AH 5757.13   Däubler, T. Sparta; ein Versuch. Leipzig, 1923.

AH 7469.23.5   Dobiás, J. Synoský prokonsulát M. Calpurnia Bibula. Praha, 1923.

Eg 278.85.2A   Erman, A. Agypten und ägyptisches Leben im Altertum. Tübingen, 1923.

Eg 1029.23A   Erman, Adolf. Die Literatur der Ägypter. Leipzig, 1923.

AH 7139.23   Francisci, P. de. Il diritto romano. Roma, 1923.

AH 7279.23.1   Frank, Tenney. A history of Rome. London, 1923.

AH 7279.23A   Frank, Tenney. A history of Rome. N.Y., 1923.

AH 4959.00.7   Frazer, James G. Sur les traces de Pausanias a travers la Grèce ancienne. Paris, 1923.

AH 7201.55.7   Gaius. 1923. Krueger and Studemund. Institutiones ad codicis veronensis apographum studemundianum novis curis auctum. Berolini, 1923.

Chronological Listing

1923 - cont.

AH 4819.23A	Greene, William Chase. The achievement of Greece. Cambridge, 1923.
AH 3664.13	Güntert, Hermann. Der arische Weltkönig und Heiland. Halle, 1923.
AH 4299.23	Halliday, William R. The growth of the city state. Liverpool, 1923.
Eg 919.23	Hartmann, Fernande. L'agriculture dans l'ancienne Égypte. Thèse. Paris, 1923.
AH 8213.2.4	Haverfield, Francis J. The romanization of Roman Britain. 4. ed. Oxford, 1923.
AH 7419.09.2	Heitland, W.E. Roman republic. Cambridge, 1923. 3v.
AH 4659.23	The Hellenistic age. Cambridge, Eng., 1923.
AH 7629.23	Henderson, B.W. The life and principate of the Emperor Hadrian. London, 1923.
AH 7419.23	Holmes, T. Rice E. The Roman republic and the founder of the empire. Oxford, 1923. 3v.
AH 3916.5	Honigmann, Ernst. Historische Topographie von Nordsyrien im Altertum. Leipzig, 1923.
AH 3020.11	Jean, Charles Francois. Sumer et Akkad. Paris, 1923.
AH 7299.23	Jerome, Thomas S. Aspects of the study of Roman history. N.Y., 1923.
AH 4159.23	Keramopoullos, A.D. Ho apotympanismos. Athēnai, 1923.
Eg 709.23	Koch, Walter. Ein Ptolemaeerkrieg. Stuttgart, 1923.
AH 3013.923	Lane, William H. Babylonian problems. N.Y., 1923.
AH 3179.7	Langdon, S. The Babylonian epic of creation restored from the recently recovered tablets of Assur. Oxford, 1923.
AH 7215.7	Lefèvre, R. Ses sacre privata en droit romain. Thèse. Paris, 1923.
AH 7239.23	McCartney, E.S. Warfare by land and sea. Boston, 1923.
AH 7203.129	Mayr, Robert. Vocabularium codicis Iustiniani. Pragae, 1923-25. 2v.
Eg 609.23.11	Mercer, S.A.B. Tutankhamen and Egyptology. Milwaukee, 1923.
NEDL AH 279.23.10	Mills, Dorothy. The book of the ancient world for younger readers. N.Y., 1923.
Eg 848.4	Moreux, T. La science mystérieuse des pharaons. Paris, 1923.
Eg 609.23.15	Nahas, Bishara. The life and times of Tut-Ankh-Amen. N.Y., 1923.
AH 7509.23.5	Nicolaus Damascenus. Nicolaus of Damascus' life of Augustus. Menasha, 1923.
AH 7509.23	Nicolaus Damascenus. Nicolaus of Damascus' life of Augustus. Northampton, 1923.
AH 8257.7	Nischer, Ernst. Die Römer im Gebiete des ehenmaligen Österreich-Ungarn. Wien, 1923.
AH 4479.23	Nolte, Ferdinand. Die historisch-politischen Voraussetzungen des Konigsfriedens von 386 v. Chr. Bamberg, 1923.
AH 3075.13	Olmstead, Albert T. History of Assyria. N.Y., 1923.
AH 9558.3	Pais, Ettore. Storia della Sardegna e della Corsica durante il dominio romano. Roma, 1923. 2v.
Eg 1189.23F	Papyrus Rhind. The Rhind mathematical papyrus. London, 1923.
AH 7549.23	Pascal, Carlo. Nerone. Milano, 1923.
Eg 278.94.10	Petrie, William M.F. A history of Egypt from the earliest kings to the XVIth dynasty. 10. ed. London, 1923.
Eg 819.23A	Petrie, William M.F. Social life in ancient Egypt. Boston, 1923.
AH 7839.23	Piganiol, A. Recherches sur les jeux romains. Strasbourg, 1923.
AH 3663.9	Pithawalla, M. The light of ancient Persia. Adyar, 1923.
AH 4039.23	Pohlenz, Max. Staatsgedanke und Staatslehre der Griechen. Leipzig, 1923.
Eg 1042.923F	Pyramid Texts. Les textes des pyramides egyptiennes. v.1-2. Bruxelles, 1923-24.
AH 7202.20	Rome. Laws, statutes, etc. Theodosius II. Codex Theodosianus. Facsimile 1-2. Berolini, 1923-26.
Eg 39.23	Rouillard, G. L'administration civile de l'Égypte Byzantine. Thèse. Paris, 1923.
AH 4189.23	Sargent, R.L. The size of the slave population at Athens during the 5th and 4th century B.C. Thesis. Urbana? 1923?
Eg 299.12.15	Schubart, W. Ein Jahrtausend am Nil. 2. Aufl. Berlin, 1923.
AH 7649.23	Schwendemann, J. Der historische Wert der Vita Marci bei Scriptores Historiae Augustae. Photoreproduction. Heidelberg, 1923.
Eg 609.23.5	Smith, G.E. Tutankhamen and the discovery of his tomb. London, 1923.
AH 3965.13	Sulzberger, M. The status of labor in ancient Israel. Philadelphia, 1923.
AH 8914.16	Taylor, Lily R. Local cults in Etruria. Rome, 1923.
AH 4840.15.5	Treston, Hubert J. Poine; a study in ancient Greek blood-vengeance. London, 1923.
AH 3177.11	Ungnod, Arthur. Gilgamesch - Epos und Odysee. Breslau, 1923.
AH 4829.23	Van Rook, La Rue. Greek life and thought. N.Y., 1923.
AH 929.23	Viedebandtt, Oskar. Antike Gewichtsnormen und Münzfusse. Berlin, 1923.
AH 7489.23	Vipper, R.Iu. Ocherki istorii rimskoi imperii. Berlin, 1923.
Eg 609.23.9	Weigall, Arthur E.P.B. The life and times of Akhnaton, pharaoh of Egypt. London, 1923.
Eg 609.23.10A	Weigall, Arthur E.P.B. The life and times of Akhnaton. N.Y., 1923.
AH 8207.10.2	Windle, Bertram C.A. The Romans in Britain. 2. ed. London, 1923.
AH 4843.19	Wright, F.A. The arts in Greece. London, 1923.

1924

Eg 879.24	Amenopë. The teaching of Amen-em-Apt. London, 1924.
AH 2507.5.5	Bachofen, J.J. Das lykische Volk. Leipzig, 1924.
AH 3014.5	Bell, Edward. Early architecture in western Asia: Chaldaean, Hittite, Assyrian, Persian. London, 1924.
AH 4559.24	Birt, Theodor. Alexander der Grosse und das Weltgriechentum bis zum erscheinen Jesu. Leipzig, 1924.
AH 7059.24A	Boak, A.E.R. Two studies in later Roman and Byzantine administration. N.Y., 1924.
AH 7759.24	Burckhardt, Jacob. DieZeit Konstantins des Grossen. 4e Aufl. Leipzig, 1924.
AH 7909.24A	Charlesworth, M.P. Trade-routes and commerce of the Roman Empire. Cambridge, 1924.
AH 3028.5	Clay, A.T. The antiquity of Amorite civilization. New Haven, 1924.
AH 4659.24	Cohen, D. Universalisme en particularisme in den aarwang van het hellenistisch tijdperk. Groningen, 1924.

1924 - cont.

Eg 9.24	Cook, William B. Catalogue of the Egyptological library and other books from the collection of the late Charles E. Wilbour. Brooklyn, 1924.
AH 819.24	De Burgh, W.G. The legacy of the ancient world. London, 1924.
AH 7489.24	Dessau, Hermann. Geschichte der römischen Kaiserzeit. v.1-2. Berlin, 1924-30. 3v.
AH 3911.7	Dobias, J. Dějiny Řimské provincie Syrske. Praha, 1924.
AH 7889.74	Duncan-Jones, Richard. The economy of the Roman Empire: quantitative studies. Cambridge, Eng., 1924.
AH 7059.24.5	Dunlap, J.E. The office of the grand chamberlain in the later Roman and Byzantine empires. London, 1924.
AH 4559.24.5	Endres, Heinrich. Geographischer Horizont und Politik bei Alexander der Grossen in den Jahren 330/323. Würzburg, 1924.
AH 8907.13	Fell, R.A.L. Etruria and Rome. Cambridge, Eng., 1924.
AH 38.64.30	Fustel de Coulanges, N.D. La città antica. Firenze, 1924.
AH 7039.24	Gelzer, Matthias. Gemeindestaat und Reichsstaat in der römischen Geschichte. Frankfurt, 1924.
AH 3051.5F	Genouillac, H. de. Premières recherches archéologiques à Kich. Paris, 1924.
AH 4479.24	Giannelli, Giulio. La spedizione di serse da terme a Salamina. Milano, 1924.
AH 2109.9	Götze, Albrecht. Kleinasien zur Hethiterzeit. Heidelberg, 1924.
AH 4819.23.2	Greene, William Chase. The achievement of Greece. Cambridge, 1924.
AH 7479.24.5	Gundolf, F. Caesar. Berlin, 1924.
AH 7469.24	Hardy, E.G. The Catilinarian conspiracy in its context. Oxford, 1924.
AH 7479.24	Hardy, E.G. Some problems in Roman history. Oxford, 1924.
AH 8207.15	Haverfield, F.J. The Roman occupation of Britain. Oxford, 1924.
AH 3173.7	Jean, C.F. La littérature des Babyloniens et des Assyriens. Paris, 1924.
Eg 279.24	Klippel, Ernst. Das alte Ägypten. Berlin, 1924.
AH 1909.24	Köster, A. Schiffahrt und Handelsverkehr des östlichen Mittelmeeres. Leipzig, 1924.
AH 3013.924	Langdon, S.H. Excavations at Kish. v.1, 3, 4. Paris, 1924-34. 3v.
AH 3963.165	Lattes, Aldo. La civiltà ebraica e le origini del cristianesimo, ad uso delle scuole medie. Firenze, 1924.
AH 4819.24	Lönborg, Sven. Dike und Eros. München, 1924.
AH 7829.24	McDaniel, W.B. Roman private life and its survivals. Boston, 1924.
AH 2008.7	Margoliouth, D.S. The relations between Arabs and Israelites prior to the rise of Islam. London, 1924.
AH 299.10.2	Meyer, E. Kleine Schriften. v.1, 2. Aufl. Halle, 1924. 2v.
Eg 278.94.19	Milne, Joseph G. A history of Egypt under Roman rule. 3. ed. London, 1924.
Eg 278.94.16	Petrie, William M.F. A history of Egypt during the XVIIth and XVIIIth dynasties. 7. ed. London, 1924.
AH 4819.25.10	Peyronnet, Raymond. Méditerranée au temps de l'Iliade; civilisation hellène. Paris, 1924.
AH 5308.11	Powers, H.H. The hill of Athena. N.Y., 1924.
AH 8116.5	Roget, Raymond. Le Maroc chez les auteurs anciens. Paris, 1924.
AH 279.24	Rostovtsev, Mikhail Ivanovich. Ocherk" istorii drevnego mira. Berlin', 1924.
AH 7539.24	Ruth, Thomas De C. The problem of Claudius. Diss. Baltimore, 1924.
AH 99.24	Salvioli, G. La città antica e la sua economia. Napoli, 1924.
AH 4189.23.5	Sargent, R.L. The size of the slave population at Athens. Urbana, 1924.
AH 6007.10	Schober, Friedrick. Phokis. Inaug. Diss. Crossen, 1924.
Eg 759.24.5	Segrè, Angelo. Il mutuo e il tasso d'interesse nell'Egitto greco-romano. Firenze, 1924.
Eg 139.24	Segrè, Angelo. Note sul documento nel diritto greco-egizio. Roma, 1924.
AH 3095.7F	Sennacherib, king of Assyria. The annals of Sennacherib. Chicago, 1924.
AH 259.24	Shepard, A.M. Sea power in ancient history. Boston, 1924.
Eg 839.24	Smith, G.E. Egyptian mummies. London, 1924.
AH 4229.24	Smith, Gertrude. The administration of justice from Hesiod to Solon. Diss. Chicago, 1924.
AH 3002.80	Smith, Sidney. Babylonian historical texts relating to the capture and downfall of Babylon. London, 1924.
AH 6057.13	Stählin, F. Das hellenische Thessalien. Stuttgart, 1924.
AH 6110.13	Walek, T.B. Dzieje upadku monarchji macedonskiej. Krakow, 1924.
Eg 709.14.5A	Weigall, Arthur E.P.B. The life and times of Cleopatra. N.Y., 1924.
AH 4279.24	Wilcken, U. Griechische Geschichte im Rahmen der Altertumsgeschichte. München, 1924.
AH 7848.9	Wilson, L.M. The Roman toga. Baltimore, 1924.
AH 7848.9.5	Wilson, L.M. A study of the Roman toga. Diss. Baltimore, 1924.
Eg 819.24	Wilson, R.F. The living pageant of the Nile. Indianapolis, 1924.
AH 8549.124	Wright, D. Druidism; the ancient faith of Britain. London, 1924.
AH 4819.11.2.5A	Zimmern, A.E. The Greek commonwealth. 4th ed. Oxford, 1924.

1925

AH 279.09.5	Amatucci, A.G. Dalle rive del Nilo ai lidi del "mar nostro". 2. ed. Bari, 1925. 2v.
Eg 1309.25	Baikie, James. Egyptian papyri and papyrus-hunting. N.Y., 1925?
AH 3159.19.10	Barton, G.A. Archaelogy and the Bible. Philadelphia, 1925.
AH 7846.5	Becker, Philipp. Der römische Villenbesitz in Italien zur Keiserzeit. Inaug. Diss. Bonn, 1925.
AH 7449.25.5	Bonus, A.R. Where Hannibal passed. London, 1925.
AH 279.11.15	Botsford, G.W. A history of the ancient world. N.Y., 1925.
AH 3002.87	Brussels. Musées Royaux du Cinquantenaire. Recueil des inscriptions de l'Asie des Musées Royaux du Cinquantenaire à Bruxelles. Bruxelles, 1925.
AH 3005.8	Budge, E.A.T.N. The rise and progress of Assyriology. London, 1925.
AH 3008.84.5	Budge, E.A.W. Babylonian life and history. 2. ed. London, 1925.

Chronological Listing

1925 - cont.

Eg 279.25 — Budge, Ernest Alfred Wallis. Egypt. London, 1925.
AH 7279.25 — Cauer, Friedrich. Römische Geschichte. München, 1925.
Eg 39.25 — Collomp, Paul. Recherches sur la chancellerie et la diplomatique des Lagides. Thèse. Strasbourg, 1925.
AH 4819.25.15 — Croiset, Maurice. Hellenic civilization. N.Y., 1925.
AH 7819.25.5A — Davis, William S. A day in old Rome. Boston, 1925.
AH 4819.05.17 — Dickinson, G.L. The Greek view of life. 7th ed. Garden City, N.Y., 1925.
AH 7819.04.7A — Dill, Samuel. Roman society from Nero to Marcus Aurelius. London, 1925.
AH 8907.15 — Ducati, Pericule. Etruria antica. Torino, 1925.
AH 4449.25 — Ehrenberg, Victor. Neugründer des Staates. München, 1925.
AH 7509.03.2 — Firth, John B. Augustus Caesar. London, 1925.
AH 8211.10A — Foord, Edward A. The last age of Roman Britain. London, 1925.
AH 7201.81.5 — Gaius. Institutiones. 4th ed. London, 1925.
Eg 1029.25 — Gaskell, G.A. Egyptian scriptures interpreted through the language of symbolism. London, 1925.
AH 5113.15A — Glotz, Gustave. The Aegean civilization. N.Y., 1925.
AH 7202.25F — Gradenwitz, Otto. Heidelberger Index zum Theodosianus. Berlin, 1925.
AH 4279.25 — Grundy, G.B. A history of the Greek and Roman world. N.Y., 1925.
AH 7479.24.7 — Gundolf, F. Caesar; Geschichte seines Ruhms. 2. Aufl. Berlin, 1925.
AH 3017.11 — Heidenreich, R. Beiträge zur Geschichte der vorderasiatischen Steinschneidekunst. Inaug. Diss. Heidelberg, 1925.
AH 7039.25 — Heinze, Richard. Von den Ursachen der grösse Roms. Leipzig, 1925.
AH 7309.25.5 — Heitland, W.E. Iterum, or A further discussion of the Roman fate. Cambridge, 1925.
AH 7489.25 — Homo, Léon P. L'empire romain. Paris, 1925.
AH 3657.35 — Huart, Clément. La Perse antique et la civilisation iranienne. Paris, 1925.
AH 8549.125.5 — Hubert, Henri. Divinités gauloises. Epona, 1925.
AH 4819.25A — Hutton, Maurice. The Greek point of view. London, 1925.
AH 4899.25 — Jardé, A. Les céreales dans l'antiquité grecque. Thèse. Paris, 1925.
AH 7739.25.5 — Jardé, Auguste. Études critiques sur la vie et le règne de Sévère Alexandre. Paris, 1925.
AH 7739.25 — Jardé, Auguste. Études critiques sur la vie et le règne de Sévère Alexandre. Thèse. Paris, 1925.
Eg 819.25 — Jequier, Gustave. Histoire de la civilisation égyptienne des origines à la conquête d'Alexandre. Paris, 1925.
AH 3013.925 — Koldewey, Robert. Das wieder erstehende Babylon. Leipzig, 1925.
AH 7139.25 — Kübler, Bernhard. Geschichte des römischen Rechts; ein Lehrbuch. Leipzig, 1925.
AH 7819.25 — Lanciani, R. Ancient and modern Rome. Boston, 1925.
AH 7819.25.3 — Lanciani, R. Ancient and modern Rome. London, 1925.
Eg 278.94.20 — Lane-Poole, Stanley. A history of Egypt in the Middle Ages. 4. ed. London, 1925.
AH 4659.25 — Laqueur, R. Hellenismus. Giessen, 1925.
Eg 885.925 — Lexa, Frantisek. La magie dans l'Egypte antique. v.1-2, Atlas. Paris, 1925. 3v.
AH 5113.4 — Lunn, H.S. Aegean civilizations. London, 1925.
AH 2957.13 — Macurdy, Grace H. Troy and Paeonia. N.Y., 1925.
AH 4828.74.12 — Mahaffy, J.P. Social life in Greece from Homer to Menander. London, 1925.
AH 7279.22.5A — Matheson, P.E. The growth of Rome. London, 1925.
AH 278.84.7 — Meyer, E. Die ältere Chronologie Babyloniens, Assyriens und Agyptens. Stuttgart, 1925.
AH 278.84.10 — Meyer, E. Geschichte des Altertums. 5. Aufl. v.1,3,4. Stuttgart, 1925-26. 4v.
AH 2108.7 — Meyer, Ernst. Die Grenzen der hellenistischen Staaten in Kleinasien. Zürich, 1925.
Eg 829.25 — Montet, Pierre. Les scènes de la vie privée dans les tombeaux égyptiens de l'ancien empire. Londres, 1925.
Eg 829.25.5 — Montet, Pierre. Les scènes de la vie privée dans les tombeaux égyptiens de l'ancien empire. Thèse. Strasbourg, 1925.
Eg 299.11.10 — Moret, Alexandre. Au temps des pharaons. 5. éd. Paris, 1925.
Eg 299.12.3 — Moret, Alexandre. Rais et dieux d'Égypte. 5. éd. Paris, 1925.
AH 819.25 — Morgan, J. de. La préhistoire orientale. Paris, 1925-27. 3v.
AH 3960.16 — Motzo, B. Saggi di storia e letteratura guideo-ellenistica. Firenze, 1925.
AH 5453.5 — Muttelsee, M. Zur Verfassungsgeschichte Kretas im Zeitalter des Hellenismus. Glückstadt, 1925.
Eg 9.25A — New York. Public Library. Ancient Egypt. N.Y., 1925.
AH 4839.25 — New York Metropolitan Museum of Art. Greek athletics. N.Y., 1925.
Eg 885.925.5 — Obbink, H.W. De magische beteekenis van den naam inzonderheid in het oude Egypte. Amsterdam, 1925.
AH 819.25.5 — Otto, Walter G.A. Kulturgeschichte des Altertums. München, 1925.
AH 8607.2.5 — Pais, Ettore. Storia dell'Italia antica. Roma, 1925. 2v.
Eg 278.94.17 — Petrie, William M.F. A history of Egypt from the XIXth to the XXXth dynasties. 3. ed. London, 1925.
AH 4559.25 — Radet, Georges. Notes critiques sur l'histoire d'Alexandre. Bordeaux, 1925-27.
AH 4829.16.5 — Robinson, C.E. The days of Alkibiades. 3. ed. London, 1925.
AH 4819.25.5 — Rose, H.J. Primitive culture in Greece. London, 1925.
AH 5124.6.5 — Roussel, Pierre. Délos. Paris, 1925.
AH 909.25 — Segre, Arturo. Il commercio dei popoli antichi nel bacino del Mediterraneo. Torino, 1925.
Eg 1059.25 — Sharpley, C.E. Anthology of ancient Egyptian poems. London, 1925.
AH 7139.26 — Siber, Heinrich. Römisches Recht in Grundzügen für die Vorlesung. Berlin, 1925-28. 2v.
AH 7309.25 — Sorel, Georges. La ruine du monde antique. 2e éd. Paris, 1925.
AH 3002.65.5 — Stephens, Ferris J. Studies of the cuneiform tablets from Cappadocia. n.p., 1925.
AH 4521.15 — Taeger, Fritz. Alkibiades. Stuttgart, 1925.
AH 7449.25 — Torr, Cecil. Hannibal crosses the Alps 2. ed. Cambridge, 1925.
AH 3017.25 — Waddell, L.A. The Indo-Sumerian seals deciphered. London, 1925.
AH 409.25 — Weber, Wilhelm. Die Staatenwelt des Mittelmeeres in der Frühzeit des Griechentums. Stuttgart, 1925.

1925 - cont.

Eg 279.25.5 — Weigall, A.E.P.B. A history of the pharaohs. London, 1925-27? 2v.
AH 4842.65 — Weinstock, Heinrich. Antike Bildungsideale. Berlin, 1925.
AH 4559.00.2 — Wheeler, B.I. Alexander the Great. London, 1925.
AH 4829.25A — Wright, F.A. Greek social life. London, 1925.
AH 4839.25.5 — Wright, Frederick A. Greek athletics. London, 1925.
AH 7203.131 — Zitelmann, E. Digestenexegese; 20 Fälle aus dem Römischen Recht. Berlin, 1925.

1926

AH 7099.26.5 — Abbott, Frank F. Municipal administration in the Roman empire. Princeton, 1926.
Eg 609.26.5 — Baikie, J. The Amarna age. N.Y., 1926.
AH 7299.26 — Barbagallo, C. Il problema delle origini di Roma. Milano, 1926.
AH 3027.5F — Bauer, Theo. Die Oskanaanäer. Leipzig, 1926.
AH 7419.26 — Beloch, Julius. Römische Geschichte. Berlin, 1926.
AH 4559.26 — Berve, H. Das Alexanderreich auf prosopographischer Grundlage. v.1-2. München, 1926.
AH 4279.22.2A — Botsford, George W. Hellenic history. N.Y., 1926.
Eg 278.85.3.5 — Budge, Ernest Alfred Wallis. The dwellers on the Nile. London, 1926.
AH 8907.16 — Buonamici, G. L'Etruria e gli Etruschi. Firenze, 1926.
AH 4909.26A — Calhoun, G.M. The ancient Greeks and the evolution of standards in business. Boston, 1926.
AH 4889.26 — Calhoun, G.M. The business life of ancient Athens. Chicago, 1926.
AH 6113.5 — Casson, Stanley. Macedenia, Thrace and Illyria. Oxford, 1926.
Eg 39.26 — Collomp, Paul. Recherches sur la chancellerie et la diplomatique des Lagides. Paris, 1926.
AH 3713.10 — Contenau, G. La civilisation phénicienne. Paris, 1926.
AH 7239.26 — Couissin, Paul. Les armes romaines. Paris, 1926.
AH 7239.26.5 — Couissin, Paul. Les armes romaines. Thèse. Paris, 1926.
AH 1819.26 — Daunt, Hew D. The centre of ancient civilization. London, 1926.
AH 7139.26.10 — Declareuil, J. Rome, the law giver. N.Y., 1926.
AH 7651.26 — Gibbon, Edward. The history of the decline and fall of the Roman Empire. 2. ed. v.2-7. London, 1926-29. 6v.
AH 7469.26 — Groener, Franz. Der Fremdenverkehr in Rom zur Zeit Ciceros. Inaug. Diss. Bonn, 1926.
AH 4279.26 — Grundy, G.B. A history of the Greek and Roman world. London, 1926.
AH 7842.19 — Gwynn, Aubrey. Roman education from Cicero to Quintilian. Oxford, 1926.
AH 4279.26.9 — Hamilton, M.A. (Mrs.). Greece. Oxford, 1926.
Eg 709.26 — Harry, Myriam (pseud.). La vie amoureuse de Cléopâtre. Paris, 1926.
AH 49.26 — Hasebroek, Johannus. Der imperialistische Gedanke im Altertum. Stuttgart, 1926.
AH 4279.26.5 — Hatzfeld, Jean. Histoire de la Grèce ancienne. Paris, 1926.
AH 8908.14 — Haury, Jacob. Neues über die Herkunft der Etrusker und über Homer. Kaiserslautern, 1926.
AH 3408.13 — Hogarth, D.G. Kings of the Hittites. London, 1926.
AH 5463.5 — Hogarth, D.G. The twilight of history. London, 1926.
AH 4329.26 — Jardé, Auguste. The formation of the Greek people. N.Y., 1926.
Eg 879.26.5 — Kees, Hermann. Totenglauben und Jenseitsvorstellungen der alten Ägypter. Leipzig, 1926.
Eg 299.26 — Kings and queens of ancient Egypt. London, 1926.
AH 4909.26.5 — Knorringa, H. Emporos. Amsterdam, 1926.
AH 3910.10 — Kolbe, Walther. Beiträge sur syrischen und jüdischen Geschichte. Stuttgart, 1926.
Htn AH 4829.26F*A — Licht, Hans. Sittengeschichte Griechenlands. Dresden, 1926-28. 3v.
AH 7449.26 — Liddell Hart, B.H. A greater than Napoleon, Scipio Africanus. Edinburgh, 1926.
AH 3002.50 — Luckenbill, D.D. Ancient records of Assyria and Babylonia. Chicago, 1926. 2v.
AH 3009.26 — Meissner, Bruno. Könige Babyloniens und Assyriens. Leipzig, 1926.
AH 7139.26.5 — Mélanges de droit romain dédiés à Georges Cornil. Gand, 1926. 2v.
AH 4109.26 — Meritt, B.D. Studies in the Athenian tribute lists. Diss. Princeton, N.J., 1926.
AH 7089.26 — Mierow, Herbert E. The roman provincial governor as he appears in the Digest and Code of Justinian. Colorado Springs, 1926.
NEDL AH 279.23.15 — Mills, Dorothy. The book of the ancient world for younger readers. N.Y., 1926.
Eg 848.4.5 — Moreux, T. La science mystérieuse des pharaons. Paris, 1926.
Eg 609.26F — Mr. Howard Carter's triumph: the superb coffins of Tutankhamen. London, 1926.
AH 7489.26 — Nilsson, Martin. Imperial Rome. London, 1926.
AH 8548.90 — Paniagua, A. de. Les Celtes bretons et les Phocéens dans le sud ouest de la Gaule. Paris, 1926.
Eg 1309.26F — Papyrus Insinger. Papyrus Insinger. v.1-2. Paris, 1926.
AH 8907.14 — Pareti, Luigi. Le origine etrusche. Firenze, 1926.
AH 7619.26 — Paribeni, R. Optimus princeps. Messina, 1926-27.
AH 4819.22.10A — Poland, Franz. The culture of ancient Greece and Rome. Boston, 1926.
AH 4819.22.9 — Poland, Franz. The culture of ancient Greece and Rome. London, 1926.
AH 3413.5 — Pottier, E. L'art hittite. Paris, 1926.
AH 5390.15 — Prickard, A.O. The return of the Theban exiles, 379-378 B.C. Oxford, 1926.
AH 7099.26 — Reynolds, P.K.B. The vigiles of imperial Rome. London, 1926.
AH 846.25FA — Richter, G.M.A. Ancient furniture; a history of Greek. Oxford, 1926.
AH 7819.26 — Rose, Herbert J. Primitive culture in Italy. London, 1926.
AH 7889.26A — Rostovtsev, M.I. The social and economic history of the Roman Empire. Oxford, 1926.
AH 7159.26 — Schisas, P.M. Offences against the state in Roman law. London, 1926.
Eg 841.5 — Schmidt, Karl F.W. Das griechische Gymnasium in Ägypten. Halle, 1926?
Eg 1042.926F — Schott, Siegfried. Untersuchungen zur Schriftgeschichte der Pyramidentexte. Inaug. Diss. Heidelberg, 1926.
Eg 279.26 — Schubart, F. Von der Flügelsonne zum Halbmond. Leipzig, 1926.

1926 - cont.

AH 7439.26 — Spaeth, John W. A study of the causes of Rome's wars from 343 to 265 B.C. Diss. Princeton, 1926.

AH 7749.26 — Stade, Kurt. Der Politiker Diokletian und die letzte grosse Christenverfolgung. Wiesbaden, 1926.

AH 7239.26.9 — Vliet, Jacobus van. De praetoria atque amicorum cohortibus. Diss. Traiecti ad Rhenum, 1926.

AH 4843.20F — Weege, Fritz. Der Tanz in der Antike. Halle, 1926.

Eg 709.14.7 — Weigall, Arthur E.P.B. The life and times of Cleopatra. London, 1926.

Eg 809.26 — Weill, R. Bases, méthodes, et résultats de la chronologie égyptienne. pt.1-2. Paris, 1926-28.

Eg 879.26 — Weynants-Ronday, M. (Mrs.). Les statues vivantes. Bruxelles, 1926.

1927

AH 3955.5A — Abrahams, Israel. Campaigns in Palestine from Alexander the Great. London, 1927.

AH 899.27F — Acerbo, Giacomo. Studi reassuntivi di agricoltura antica. Roma, 1927.

AH 3960.22 — Apotowitzer, V. Parteipolitik der Hasmonäerzeit im rabbinischen und pseudoepigraphischen Schriftlum. Wien, 1927.

Eg 1180.5 — Archibald, Raymond C. Bibliography of Egyptian mathematics. Supplement. Oberlin, 1927.

AH 7469.27 — Baker, George P. Sulla the fortunate, the great dictator. London, 1927.

AH 4729.05.5 — Barbaballo, C. Le declin d'une civilisation, ou La fin de la Grèce antique. Paris, 1927.

AH 8016.9 — Berthelot, André. L'Afrique saharienne et sondanaise. Paris, 1927.

Eg 278.94.25 — Bevan, E.R. A history of Egypt under the Ptolemaic dynasty. v.4. London, 1927.

AH 1409.27.5 — Bilabel, Friedrich. Geschichte Vorderasiens und Ägyptens vom 16. Jahrhundert vor Christ bis auf die Neuzeit. Heidelberg, 1927.

AH 7339.13.7 — Birt, Theodor. Römische Charakterköpfe. Leipzig, 1927.

AH 279.11.20 — Botsford, G.W. A history of the ancient world. N.Y., 1927.

AH 3155.16 — Briem, Efraim. Babyloniska myter och sagor med kulturhistorisk inledning. Stockholm, 1927.

AH 7179.27.5 — Brissaud, J. Le régime de la terre dans la société étatiste du Bas-Empire. Thèse. Paris, 1927.

AH 7138.91.15 — Bry, Georges. Principes de droit romain. 6. éd. v.1-2. Paris, 1927-30.

AH 7759.27 — Burch, Vacher. Myth and Constantine the Great. London, 1927.

AH 4159.27A — Calhoun, G.M. The growth of criminal law in ancient Greece. Berkeley, Calif., 1927.

AH 4130.5 — Calhoun, George M. A working bibliography of Greek law. Cambridge, 1927.

AH 29.23.7 — The Cambridge ancient history. Plates. Cambridge, Eng., 1927-39. 5v.

AH 4009.27 — Cary, Max. The documentary sources of Greek history. Oxford, 1927.

AH 7489.27 — Chapot, Victor. Le monde romain. Paris, 1927.

AH 8647.10.5 — Ciaceri, E. Storia della Magna Grecia. Milano, 1927-32. 3v.

AH 8907.17 — Cooley, Julia. The forgotten Etruscans. N.Y., 1927.

AH 8549.127.10 — Daniel, J. The philosophy of ancient Britain. London, 1927.

AH 4819.05.20 — Dickinson, G.L. The Greek view of life. 7th ed. Garden City, N.Y., 1927.

AH 3195.7 — Ebeling, Erich. Die babylonische Fabel. Leipzig, 1927.

AH 4843.5.10 — Emmanuel, M. The antique Greek dance. London, 1927.

Eg 1029.23.5 — Erman, Adolf. The literature of the ancient Egyptians. London, 1927.

AH 4459.27 — Ferrabino, A. L'impero ateniese. Torino, 1927.

AH 7889.20.2 — Frank, Tenney. An economic history of Rome. 2. ed. Baltimore, 1927.

Eg 862.5 — Garland, H. Ancient Egyptian metallurgy. London, 1927.

Eg 1189.27 — Gillain, O. La science égyptienne; L'arithmetique au Moyen Empire. Bruxelles, 1927.

AH 4039.27.5 — Glover, T.R. Democracy in the ancient world. Cambridge, 1927.

AH 4819.27A — Gulick, Charles B. Modern traits in old Greek life. N.Y., 1927.

AH 8504.5 — Hajje, Antoine. Histoire de la justice seigneuriale en France; les origines romaines. Paris, 1927.

AH 3013.927F — Hall, Harry R. Ur excavations. v.1-10. Oxford, 1927-39. 9v.

AH 5610.9 — Hamburger, Oswald. Untersuchungen über den pynhischen Krieg. Inaug. Diss. Würzburg, 1927.

AH 7769.27 — Heering, Walter. Kaiser Valentinian I (364-375). Inaug. Diss. Magdeburg, 1927.

AH 7599.27 — Henderson, B.W. Five Roman emperors. Cambridge, Eng., 1927.

AH 4519.27 — Henderson, B.W. The great war between Athens and Sparta. London, 1927.

AH 5857.11.5 — Highbarger, E.L. Chapters in the history and civilization of ancient Megara. Baltimore, 1927.

AH 5857.11 — Highbarger, E.L. The history and civilization of ancient Megara. Baltimore, 1927.

Htn — AH 3966.21* — The Holy Land and Egypt. Vernon, N.Y., 1927.

AH 4279.21.2 — James, Henry R. Our Hellenic heritage. v.1-2. N.Y., 1927.

AH 7229.27 — Johnson, H.D. The Roman tribunal. Baltimore, 1927.

AH 7179.27 — Kaïla, E. L'unité foncière en droit romain. Paris, 1927.

AH 8549.1201 — Kendrick, T.D. The Druids. London, 1927.

AH 8549.127.5 — Kendrick, T.D. The Druids. N.Y., 1927.

AH 859.7 — Kornemann, Ernst. Die Stellung der Frau und der vorgriechischen Mittelmeerkultur. Heidelberg, 1927.

AH 7329.27 — La Piana, George. Foreign groups in Rome during the first centuries of the empire. Cambridge, 1927.

AH 4079.27 — Laqueur, Richard. Epigraphische Untersuchungen zu den griechischen Volksbeschlüssen. Leipzig, 1927.

AH 7449.26.3 — Liddell Hart, B.H. A greater than Napoleon, Scipio Africanus. Boston, 1927.

AH 7819.27 — Louis, Paul. Ancient Rome at work. N.Y., 1927.

AH 5113.5A — Lunn, H.S. Aegean civilizations. 2. ed. London, 1927.

AH 819.27 — Mackenzie, D.A. Ancient civilizations from the earliest times to the birth of Christ. London, 1927.

AH 7469.22.2A — Marsh, F.B. The founding of the Roman empire. 2. ed. London, 1927.

AH 5303.11 — Méautis, G. L'aristocratie athénienne. Paris, 1927.

Eg 279.13.5 — Moret, A. Mystères égyptiens. Paris, 1927.

1927 - cont.

Eg 819.26.5 — Moret, Alexandre. The Nile and Egyptian civilization. N.Y., 1927.

Eg 279.27 — Much, Hans. Das ewige Ägypten. Dresden, 1927.

AH 4329.27 — Mucke, J.R. Die Urbevölkerung Griechenlands und ihre allmähliche Entwickelung zu Volksstämen. Leipzig, 1927-29.

AH 7049.27 — Münzer, Friedrich. Die Entstehung des römischen Principats; ein Beispiel des Wandels von Staatsformen. Münster, 1927.

AH 4039.27 — Myres, John L. The political ideas of the Greeks. N.Y., 1927.

AH 4523.10 — Odermann, E. Der Festungskrieg vor Syrakus in den Jahren 414-413 v.C. Inaug. Diss. Leipzig, 1927.

AH 7469.02.3.5 — Oman, Charles. Seven Roman statesmen of the later Republic. London, 1927.

Eg 1189.23.5FA — Papyrus Rhind. The Rhind mathematical papyrus. British Museum, 10057 and 10058. Oberlin, 1927-29. 2v.

AH 819.27.5 — Peake, Harold. Peasants and potters. New Haven, 1927.

AH 819.27.10 — Peake, Harold. Priests and kings. New Haven, 1927.

AH 7139.27 — Radin, Max. Handbook of Roman law. St. Paul, 1927.

AH 4819.27.5A — Ramsay, W.M. Asianic elements in Greek civilization. London, 1927.

AH 4844.4 — Ringwood, I.C. Agonistic features of local Greek festivals chiefly from inscriptional evidence. Poughkeepsie, N.Y., 1927.

AH 279.24.5A — Rostovtsev, Mikhail Ivanovich. A history of the ancient world. v.2. Oxford, 1927.

AH 3966.23 — Saarisalo, Aapeli. Boundary between Issachar and Naphtali. Helsinki, 1927.

AH 3188.5 — Schawe, Joseph. Untersuchung der Elambriefe aus dem Archiv Assurbanîpals. Inaug. Diss. Berlin, 1927.

AH 839.27 — Schröder, B. Der Sport im Altertum. 1. Aufl. Berlin, 1927.

AH 4659.27 — Tarn, William W. Hellenistic civilization. London, 1927.

AH 7479.27 — Thaddeus, V. Julius Caesar. N.Y., 1927.

Eg 1309.27F — Turaev, B.A. Papyrus Prachov. Leningrad, 1927.

AH 1409.27 — Turaev, V.A. Russkaia nauka odrevnem Vostoke do 1917 g. Leningrad, 1927.

AH 4859.25 — Vries, M. de. Pallake proef. Amsterdam, 1927.

Eg 279.25.7A — Weigall, A.E.P.B. A history of the pharaohs. N.Y., 1927. 2v.

AH 2014.7.5 — Wellhausen, Julius. Reste arabischen Heidentums. Berlin, 1927.

AH 7659.27 — White, Edward L. Why Rome fell. N.Y., 1927.

AH 239.27 — Wienicke, Arnold. Keltisches Söldnertum in der Mittelmeerwelt bis zur Herrschaft der Römer. Inaug. Diss. Breslau, 1927.

AH 4819.27.10 — Zane, J.M. The grandeur that was Rome. Chicago, 1927.

AH 7539.27 — Zielinski, T. L'empereur Claude et l'idée de la domination mondiale des Juifs. Bruxelles, 1927.

1928

AH 4109.18.2 — Andreadēs, Andreas M. Istoría tēs Hellēnikēs. Athēnai, 1928-30. 2v.

AH 7819.23.3 — Bailey, Cyril. The legacy of Rome. Oxford, 1928.

AH 7189.28 — Barrow, R.H. Slavery in the Roman Empire. London, 1928.

AH 9557.5 — Bellieni, C. La Sardegna e i sardi nella civiltà del mondo antico. Cagliari, 1928-31. 2v.

AH 4559.28A — Bercovici, Konrad. Alexander; a romantic biography. N.Y., 1928.

AH 4848.14F — Bieber, Margarete. Griechische Kleidung. Berlin, 1928.

AH 139.28 — Bill, August. L'évangile et la loi. Thèse. Strasbourg, 1928.

AH 7469.28.10 — Binder, Max. Studien zur Geschichte des zweiten Bürgerkriegs. Inaug. Diss. Überlingen am Bodensee, 1928.

AH 4819.28.5 — Birt, Theodor. Das Kulturleben der Griechen und Römer in ihrer Entwicklung. Leipzig, 1928.

AH 4279.22.4 — Botsford, George W. Hellenic history. N.Y., 1928.

Eg 1309.28F — Botti, Giuseppe. Il giornale della necropoli di Tebe. Torino, 1928.

AH 7799.28 — Brion, Marcel. La vie d'Attila. 2. éd. Paris, 1928.

AH 7469.28.15 — Carcopino, Jérôme. Autour des Gracques, études critiques. Paris, 1928.

AH 7489.27.5 — Chapot, Victor. The Roman world. N.Y., 1928.

AH 7139.17.2 — Cuq, Edouard. Manuel des institutions juridiques des Romains. Paris, 1928.

AH 819.28 — Dawson, Christopher H. The age of the gods. Boston, 1928.

AH 7169.28 — Del Chiaro, E. Le contrat de société en droit privé romain sous la République. Paris, 1928.

AH 8548.40 — Dias Pinheiro, Alfredo. Os celtas e povos com êles relacionados. Guimarães, 1928.

AH 7189.25.2 — Duff, Arnold Mackay. Freedmen in the early Roman Empire. Oxford, 1928.

AH 3005.10 — Ebeling, Erich. Keallexikon der Assyriologie. Berlin, 1928-38. 4v.

AH 9757.7 — Eidam, Heinrich. Deutschlands Besetzung durch die Römer. Dinkelsbühl, 1928.

AH 7279.23.10 — Frank, Tenney. A history of Rome. N.Y., 1928.

AH 7201.89 — Gaius. Institutionum commentarii quattuor. Lipsiae, 1928.

Eg 847.11F — Gardiner, Alan Henderson. Catalogue des caractères d'impression hiéroglyphiques égyptiens. Bruxelles, 1928.

AH 4858.13 — Geurts, Nico. Het huwelijk bij de Griekse en Romeinse moralisten. Proefschrift. Amsterdam, 1928.

AH 9639.9.5 — Giuliano, Luigi. Storia di Siracusa antica. 2. ed. Milano, 1928.

AH 3016.50F — Hall, Harry R. Babylonian and Assyrian sculpture in the British Museum. Paris, 1928.

AH 3013.928.5.2 — Harcourt-Smith, S. Babylonian art. N.Y., 1928.

AH 3911.8 — Harper, George M. Village administration in the Roman province of Syria. Diss. Princeton, 1928.

AH 3013.928 — Harvard University. Fogg Art Museum. Kirkuk excavations conducted by the Fogg Museum of Art. Preliminary report. n.p., 1928.

AH 4909.28 — Hasebroek, J. Staat und Handel im alten Griechenland. Tübingen, 1928.

Eg 1069.30 — Hassan, Sélim. Hymnes religieux du moyen empire. La Caire, 1928.

AH 7099.28 — Heitland, William E. Last wards on the Roman municipalities. Cambridge, Eng., 1928.

AH 862.16 — Hollaender, Eugen. Askulap und Venus. Berlin, 1928.

AH 7469.28 — Holmes, T.R.E. The architect of the Roman Empire. Oxford, 1928-31. 2v.

Eg 1159.28 — Hurry, Jamieson Boyd. Imhotep. 2. ed. Oxford, 1928.

AH 4189.28 — Jacob, Oscar. Les esclaves publics à Athènes. Liége, 1928.

Chronological Listing

1928 - cont.

AH 4609.26.5   Jouguet, P. Macedonian imperialism and the Hellenization of the East. London, 1928.

AH 2011.5.5   Lammens, H. L'Arabie occidentale avant l'hégire. Beyrouth, 1928.

AH 3149.8F   Langdon, Stephen. The Venus tablets of Ammizaduga. London, 1928.

AH 3002.86F   Lehmann-Haupt, C.F. Corpus inscriptionum Chaldicarum. Berlin, 1928-35.

AH 7039.28   Levi, Mario A. La costituzione romana dai gracchi a Giulio Cesare. Firenze, 1928.

AH 7449.26.5   Liddell Hart, B.H. A greater than Napoleon, Scipio Africanus. Boston, 1928.

AH 3020.14   Lutz, H.F. Sumerian temple records of the late Ur dynasty. Berkeley, 1928.

Eg 809.28   Nicklin, T. Studies in Egyptian chronology. v.1-2. Blackburn, 1928-29.

AH 4659.28   Oliveira Martins, J.P. O hellenismo e a civilisação christan. 4. ed. Lisboa, 1928.

AH 7239.28   Parker, Henry M.D. The Roman legions. Oxford, 1928.

AH 3160.26F   Paulus, Witold. Marduk, Urtyp Christi? Romae, 1928.

AH 409.28   Peake, Harold. The steppe and the sown. New Haven, 1928.

AH 7278.85.25   Pelham, H.F. Outlines of Roman history. 5. ed. London, 1928.

AH 4559.28.5   Petković, Živko D. Aleksandr Veliki. Beograd, 1928.

AH 4279.28.5   Puech, Aimé. Ce qu'il faut connaître de la Grèce antique. Paris, 1928.

AH 4819.27.7   Ramsay, W.M. Asianic elements in Greek civilization. New Haven, 1928.

AH 7139.28   Rodriguez, José S. Elementos de derecho romano. Caracas, 1928. 2v.

AH 7759.28   Salvatorelli, Luigi. Costantino il Grande. Roma, 1928.

AH 889.28   Segrè, Angelo. Metrologia e circolazione monetaria degli antichi. Bologna, 1928.

AH 6049.5.5   Skalet, Charles H. Ancient Sicyon, with a prosopographia Sicyonia. Baltimore, 1928.

AH 6049.5   Skalet, Charles H. Chapters in history of ancient Sicyon. Baltimore, 1928.

AH 3037.5   Smith, S.M.A. Early history of Assyria to 1000 B.C. London, 1928.

AH 8647.11   Società Magna Grecia. Campagne della Società Magna Grecia, 1926 e 1927. Roma, 1928.

AH 8549.128   Spence, Lewis. The mysteries of Britain. London, 1928.

AH 7659.28   Stein, Ernst. Geschichte der spätrömischen Reiches I. Wien, 1928.

AH 7469.28.5   Taeger, Fritz. Untersuchungen zur römischen Geschichte und Quellenkunde. Stuttgart, 1928.

AH 7909.28   Warmington, E.H. The commerce between the Roman Empire and India. Cambridge, 1928.

AH 4819.27.8A   Weigall, A. Personalities of antiquity. Garden City, N.Y., 1928.

AH 3022.9A   Woolley, Charles L. The Sumerians. Oxford, 1928.

AH 4819.28A   Zimmern, A.E. Solon and Croesus, and other Greek essays. London, 1928.

1929

AH 7279.29   Ambrosi, A. Histoire romaine. Paris, 1929.

Eg 279.29   Baikie, James. A history of Egypt from the earliest times to the end of the 18th dynasty. N.Y., 1929. 2v.

AH 7519.29   Baker, G.P. Tiberius Caesar. N.Y., 1929.

AH 7449.29.15   Baker, George Philip. Hannibal. N.Y., 1929.

AH 7469.29   Balbo, Emilio. Catilina nel giudizio della critica demagogica. Roma, 1929.

AH 7189.29   Basanoff, V. Partus ancillae. Paris, 1929.

AH 4521.19   Benson, E.F. The life of Alcibiades. N.Y., 1929.

AH 4299.21.4   Birt, T. Von Homer bis Sokrates. 4. Aufl. Leipzig, 1929.

AH 7469.29.5   Block, Gustave. La République romaine de 133 avant J.C. à la mort de César. Pt.1. Paris, 1929.

AH 7279.21.3   Boak, Arthur E.R. A history of Rome to 565 A.D. N.Y., 1929.

AH 7449.29.10   Branchini, A. Studio critico-polemico su la precisazione storica della battaglia del Metauro. Fano, 1929.

Eg 989.10F   Breccia, E. With King Fuad to the oasis of Ammon [Siwa]. Milano, 1929.

AH 889.29   Brentano, Lujo. Das Wirtschaftsleben der antiken Welt. Jena, 1929.

AH 8007.15   Broughton, T.R.S. The romanization of Africa Proconsularis. Baltimore, 1929.

AH 8007.15.5   Broughton, T.R.S. The romanization of Africa Proconsularis. Diss. Baltimore, 1929.

AH 7759.24.3   Burckhardt, Jacob. Die Zeit Constantins des Grossen. Stuttgart, 1929.

AH 9758.7   Capelle, Wilhelm. Das alte Germanien. Jena, 1929.

AH 939.29   Cary, Max. The ancient explorers. London, 1929.

AH 3020.15F   Chiera, Edward. Sumerian lexical texts from the temple school of Nippur. Chicago, 1929.

AH 1819.28.5   Childe, Vere G. The most ancient East. London, 1929.

AH 4449.29   Cornelius, Friedrich. Die Tyrannis in Athen. München, 1929.

AH 7203.134   Corpus juris civilis. Digesta. Index interpolationum. Supplement. Weimar, 1929.

AH 7203.133   Corpus juris civilis. Digesta. Index interpolationum quae in Iustiniani Digestis inesse dicuntur. Weimar, 1929-35. 3v.

AH 7203.132   Corpus juris civilis. Digesta. Lex aquilia. Cambridge, 1929.

AH 4659.29.10   Corradi, G. Studi ellenistíci. Torino, 1929.

Eg 855.2   Dauson, Warren R. Magician and leech. London, 1929.

AH 4819.29   Earp, F.R. The way of the Greeks. London, 1929.

AH 279.29.10   Ebeling, Erich. Geschichte des alten Morgenlandes. Berlin, 1929.

AH 4279.29.5   Ferrabino, Aldo. La dissoluzione della libertà nella Grecia antica. Padova, 1929.

AH 4299.29   Ferrarino, Aldo. La dissoluzione della libertà nella Grecia antica. Padova, 1929.

Eg 39.29   Gabra, Sami. Les conseils de fonctionnaires dans l'Égypte pharaonique. Le Caire, 1929.

AH 3013.929.10   Gadd, Cyril J. History and monuments of Ur. London, 1929.

AH 7650.90   Gibbon, Edward. The decline and fall of the Roman Empire. London, 1929-36. 6v.

AH 7138.95.10   Girard, P.F. Manuel élémentaire de droit romain. 8e éd. Paris, 1929.

Eg 299.29   Great ones of ancient Egypt. London, 1929.

AH 7449.29   Groag, Edmund. Hannibal als Politiker. Wien, 1929.

AH 7476.32.5   Guarino, Alessandro. L'apologia di Cesare. Roma, 1929.

1929 - cont.

AH 4329.29   Günther, H.F.K. Rassengeschichte des hellenischen und des römischen Volkes. München, 1929.

AH 7479.24.10   Gundolf, F. The mantle of Caesar. London, 1929.

AH 4279.29.15   Hallynck, P. L'Orient et la Grèce. Paris, 1929.

Eg 1059.29   Hassan, S. Le poème dit de Pentaour et le rapport officiel. Le Caire, 1929.

AH 4854.5   Hömschemeyer, Orloys. Die Pferdezucht im klassischen Altertum. Diss. Giessen, 1929.

AH 7039.29   Homs, Léon. Roman political institutions from city to state. London, 1929.

AH 7979.29   Itineraria romana. Lipsiae, 1929. 2v.

AH 3143.12.5A   Jeremias, Alfred. Handbuch der altorientalischen Geisteskultur. 2e Aufl. Berlin, 1929.

AH 2008.9   Kammerer, Albert. Pétra et la Nabatène. Plates, maps and atlas. Paris, 1929-30. 2v.

AH 279.29   Laistner, Max L.W. Survey of ancient history to the death of Constantine. Boston, 1929.

AH 8647.13F   Larizza, Pietro. La Magna Grecia. Roma, 1929.

Eg 879.29.5   Lefebure, G. Inscriptions concernant les grands prêtres d'Amon. Thèse. v.1-2. Paris, 1929.

AH 7509.29   Levi, Mario A. Augusto. Roma, 1929.

AH 4819.29.5   Lur'e, Sol. Iak. Istoriia antichnoi obshchestvennoi mysli. Moskva, 1929.

AH 7829.24.5   McDaniel, W.B. Roman private life and its survivals. N.Y., 1929.

AH 7819.29   MacKail, J.W. The lesson of imperial Rome. London, 1929.

AH 8908.15   Mühlestein, H. Über die Herkunft der Etrusker. Berlin, 1929.

AH 7469.02.4   Oman, Charles. Seven Roman statesmen of the later Republic. London, 1929.

AH 819.29.5A   Peake, Harold. The way of the sea. New Haven, 1929.

AH 7629.29   Perret, Louis. La titulature impériale d'Hadrien. Paris, 1929.

AH 9777.40   Rackus, A.M. Guthones (the Goths), kinsmen of the Lithuanian people. Chicago, 1929.

AH 4842.67   Reinmuth, O.W. The foreigners in the Albanian Ephebia. Lincoln, Neb., 1929.

AH 3959.23A   Robinson, T.H. Palestine in general history. Oxford, 1929.

AH 4559.29.5   Robson, Edgar. Alexander the Great. London, 1929.

AH 3657.29   Rogers, Robert W. A history of ancient Persia. N.Y., 1929.

AH 7889.26.10   Rostovtsev, M.I. Gesellschaft und Wirtschaft im Römischen Reich. Leipzig, 1929. 2v.

AH 8907.18   Schachermeyer, F. Etruskische Frühgeschichte. Berlin, 1929.

AH 7449.29.5   Scharf, Alfred. Der Ausgang des tarentinischen Krieges als Wendepunkt. Inaug. Diss. Bremen, 1929.

Eg 872.10   Schott, Siegfried. Urkunden mythologischen Inhalts. Heft 1-2. Leipzig, 1929-39.

Eg 139.29.5   Seidl, Erwin. Der Eid im ptolemäischen Recht. München, 1929.

AH 4559.29   Stein, Mark Aurel. Alexander's campaign on the Indian north-west frontier. London, 1929.

AH 7539.29   Stroux, J. Eine Gerichtsreform des Kaisers Claudius. München, 1929.

AH 3013.929.5A   Thompson, R.C. A century of exploration at Nineveh. London, 1929.

AH 7819.10.5   Tucker, T.G. Life in the Roman world of Nero and St. Paul. N.Y., 1929.

Eg 1189.29   Vogel, Kurt. Die Grundlagen der ägyptischen Arithmetik. Inaug. Diss. München, 1929.

AH 819.29   Waddell, L.A. The makers of civilization in race and history. London, 1929.

AH 4279.29.10   Warg, Hans. Griechische Geschichte. Leipzig, 1929.

AH 9665.5   West, Louis C. Imperial Roman Spain; the objects of trade. Oxford, 1929.

AH 3013.929   Woolley, Charles L. The excavations at Ur and the Hebrew records. London, 1929.

AH 29.29   Yale University. The legacy of the ancient world. New Haven, 1929.

AH 4909.29   Ziebarth, Erich. Beiträge zur Geschichte des Seeraubs und Seehandels im alten Griechenland. Hamburg, 1929.

193-

AH 299.30   Chuckerbutty, K. The world on the positive plate. Calcutta, 193-. 5 pam.

AH 9777.38   Eicke, Hermann. Heerführer und Könige. Leipzig, 193-?

1930

AH 7479.30.10   Afzelius, Adam. Pompeius og hans modstandere. København, 1930.

AH 8311.2   Alfoldi, András. A gót mozgalom és Dácia feladása. Budapest, 1930?

AH 279.30.5   Alfonso I, king of Castile and Leon. General estoria. pt.1-2. Madrid, 1930- 2v.

AH 3014.7F   Andrae, Walter. Das Gotteshaus und die Urformen des Bauens im alten Orient. Berlin, 1930.

AH 7759.30   Baker, G.P. Constantine the Great and the Christian revolution. N.Y., 1930.

AH 9610.26   Bayet, Jean. La Sicile greque. Paris, 1930.

AH 7759.30.5   Baynes, N.H. Constantine the Great and the Christian Church. London, 1930.

AH 1939.30   Berthelot, A. L'Asie ancienne, centrale et sud-orientale d'après Ptolémée. Paris, 1930.

AH 7779.30   Bidez, Joseph. La vie de l'empereur Julien. Paris, 1930.

AH 4229.30   Bonner, Robert Johnson. The administration of justice from Homer to Aristotle. Chicago, 1930-38. 2v.

AH 4279.22.3   Botsford, George W. Hellenic history. N.Y., 1930.

AH 7799.30   Brion, Marcel. La vie d'Alaric. 7. éd. Paris, 1930.

AH 4818.98.5A   Burckhardt, J. Griechische Kulturgeschichte. Stuttgart, 1930-31. 4v.

AH 4855.11   Butler, Alfred J. Sport in classic times. London, 1930.

Eg 879.30.5   Cazemier, L.J. Oud-Egyptiese voorstellingen aangaande de ziel. Proefschrift. Wageningen, 1930.

AH 7163.29   Corbett, Percy E. The Roman law of marriage. Oxford, 1930.

AH 4229.30.10   Derenne, Eudore. Les procès d'impiété. Liége, 1930.

AH 3965.7   Ejges, Simcha. Das Geld im Talmud. Diss. Wilna, 1930.

AH 6104.5   Engelhardt, Hans. Das senatus consultum Macedonianum. Inaug. Diss. Bamberg, 1930.

AH 3910.12   Farn, W.W. Selencid-Parthian studies. London, 1930.

AH 4609.30   Fellmann, W. Antigonos Gonatas, König der Makedonen. Inaug. Diss. Würzburg, 1930.

Chronological Listing

1930 - cont.

AH 4959.30 — Frazer, James G. Graecia antiqua. London, 1930.

AH 839.30 — Gardiner, Edward Norman. Athletics of the ancient world. Oxford, 1930.

X Cg AH 3177.10F — Gilgamesh. The epic of Gilgamesh. Oxford, 1930.

AH 2211.5 — Gwatkin, William E. Cappadocia as a Roman procuratorial province. Diss. Princeton, 1930.

AH 7509.30.5 — Hadas, Moses. Sextus Pompey. N.Y., 1930.

AH 7509.30 — Heinze, Richard. Die augusteische Kultur. Leipzig, 1930.

AH 7099.30 — Heitland, Willian E. Repetita. Cambridge, Eng., 1930.

AH 7169.30 — Hollfelder, H. Die Confusio im römischen Recht. Inaug. Diss. Kallmünz, 1930.

Htn AH 279.30* — Hollins, Elizabeth C.M. History of civilization. Portland, 1930.

AH 7819.30.10 — Homs, Léon. La civilisation romaine. Paris, 1930.

AH 7239.30 — Horn, Heinrich. Foederati. Inaug. Diss. Frankfurt, 1930.

AH 5307.27 — Jardé, A. Athènes ancienne. Paris, 1930.

AH 8907.19 — Johnstone, M.A. Etruria past and present. London, 1930.

AH 4609.29 — Kincaid, Charles A. Successors of Alexander. London, 1930.

AH 3154.17 — Kunstmann, W.G. Die babylonische Gebetsbeschwörung. Inaug. Diss. Gräfenhainichen, 1930.

AH 7489.30.5 — Laqueur, Richard. Probleme der Spätantike. Stuttgart, 1930.

AH 4039.30 — Loenen, Dirk. Vrijheid en gelijkheid in Athene. Amsterdam, 1930.

AH 3002.89F — Luckenbill, Daniel D. Inscriptions from Adab. Chicago, 1930.

AH 9610.24 — Märker, Martin. Die Kämpfe der Karthager auf Sizilien in den Jahren 409-405 v. Chr. Inaug. Diss. Weida, 1930.

AH 3909.8 — Maisler, Benjamin. Untersuchungen zur alten Geschichte und Ethnographie Syriens und Palästinas. Giessen, 1930.

AH 4863.9 — Meier, M.H.E. Histoire de l'amour grec. Paris, 1930.

AH 8608.9 — Misiano, D.B. I popoli preistorici dell'Italia. Bova Marina, 1930.

AH 4843.22 — Moens, P.W. De twee delphische hymnen. Purmerend, 1930.

AH 7114.28 — Moinier, Gilbert. Les pérégrins déditices dans les premiers siècles de la Republique et sous le Haut-Empire. Thèse. Paris, 1930.

Eg 971.11F — Monneret de Villard, Ugo. La Necropoli musulmana di Aswán. Le Caire, 1930.

AH 4819.30 — Moscow. Gosudarstvennyi Muzei Iziashchnykh Iskusstv. Drevniaia gretsiia. Moskva, 1930.

AH 4299.30 — Myres, John L. Who were the Greeks? Berkeley, Calif., 1930.

AH 819.19.15 — Neuburger, Albert. The technical arts and sciences of the ancients. London, 1930.

AH 4139.30 — Paoli, Ugo Enrico. Studi di diritto attico. Firenze, 1930.

Eg 609.30 — Parain, Charles. La vie de Ramsès II. 5. éd. Paris, 1930.

AH 7169.30.5 — Poggi, Agostino. Il contratto di società in diritto romano classico. Torino, 1930-34. 2v.

Eg 1179.30 — Pogo, A. Astronomical ceiling decoration in the tomb of Senmut. Bruges, 1930.

AH 7819.30.15 — Preston, H.W. The private life of the Romans. Chicago, 1930.

AH 7659.30 — Rehm, Walther. Der Untergang Roms im abendländischen Denken. Leipzig, 1930.

AH 5390.13 — Schäfer, Alexander. Die Berichte Xenophons, Plutarchs und Diodors über die Besetzung und Befreiung. Inaug. Diss. München, 1930.

AH 7549.30 — Schumann, Gerhard. Hellenistische und griechische Elemente in der Regierung Neros. Inaug. Diss. Leipzig, 1930.

AH 7449.30 — Scullard, Howard Hayes. Scipio Africanus in the second Punic War. Cambridge, Eng., 1930.

AH 4843.21 — Séchan, Louis. La danse greque antique. Paris, 1930.

AH 7162.35 — Segrè, Angelo. Richerche di diritto ereditario romano. Roma, 1930.

AH 1879.30 — Semper, Max. Rassen und Religionen im alten Vorderasien. Heidelberg, 1930.

AH 7479.30 — Silvagni, V. Giulio Cesare. Torino, 1930.

AH 819.30 — Smith, G.E. Human history. London, 1930.

AH 3012.9A — Speiser, Ephraim A. Mesopotamian origins. Philadelphia, 1930.

Eg 879.30A — Spence, Lewis. The mysteries of Egypt. Philadelphia, 1930.

AH 7207.46.1 — Stein, Paul. Die Senatssitzungen der ciceronischen Zeit 68-43. Photoreproduction. Münster, 1930.

AH 8608.8.10 — Stella, Luigia A. Italia antica sul mare. Milano, 1930.

AH 7489.30 — Stevenson, G.H. The Roman Empire. London, 1930.

AH 4659.27.3 — Tarn, William W. Hellenistic civilization. 2. ed. London, 1930.

AH 4239.30 — Tarn, William W. Hellenistic military and naval developments. Cambridge, Eng., 1930.

AH 7279.30.10 — Terrail, Gabriel. Histoire romaine. Paris, 1930.

AH 889.30 — Toutain, J. The economic life of the ancient world. London, 1930.

AH 7819.30A — Treble, H.A. Everyday life in Rome in the time of Caesar and Cicero. Oxford, 1930.

AH 5916.5 — Valmin, M.N. Études topographiques sur la Messénie ancienne. Lund, 1930.

AH 5958.5 — Vitalis, Gerhard. Die Entwicklung der Sage von der Rückkehr der Herakliden. Griefswald, 1930.

Eg 1189.30 — Vogel, Kurt. Die Algebra der Ägypter des mittleren Reiches. Roma, 1930.

Eg 819.30 — Waddell, L.A. Egyptian civilization. London, 1930.

AH 7489.30.9 — Wagenvoort, H. Pax Augusta. Groningen, 1930.

AH 3002.81 — Waterman, L. Royal correspondence of the Assyrian empire. Ann Arbor, 1930-36. 4v.

AH 7549.30.5 — Weigall, Arthur E.P.B. Nero, emperor of Rome. London, 1930.

AH 7549.30.11 — Weigall, Arthur E.P.B. Nero, the singing emperor of Rome. N.Y., 1930.

AH 7549.30.10 — Weigall, Arthur E.P.B. Nero. N.Y., 1930.

Eg 709.30 — Wertheimer, O.V. Kleopatra. Zürich, 1930.

AH 3013.930.10 — Woolley, Charles L. Ur of the Chaldees. N.Y., 1930.

AH 3013.930.5 — Woolley, Charles L. Ur of the Chaldees. Washington, 1930.

1931

AH 4959.09.10 — Allinson, Francis Greenleaf. Greek lands and letters. 3. ed. Boston, 1931.

AH 4559.28.3 — Bercovici, Konrad. La vie de Alexandre le Grand. 3. éd. Paris, 1931.

AH 4279.31 — Berve, Helmut. Griechische Geschichte. Freiburg, 1931-33. 2v.

1931 - cont.

Eg 1159.31F — Breasted, James Henry. The Edwin Smith surgical papyrus. Chicago, 1931. 2v.

AH 7509.31 — Brendel, Otto. Ikonographie des Kaisers Augustus. Inaug. Diss. Nürnberg, 1931.

AH 4819.31.6 — Brodeur, A.G. The pageant of civilization. N.Y., 1931.

Eg 1109.31 — Budge, Ernest Alfred Wallis. Egyptian tales and romances, pagan, Christian and Muslim. London, 1931.

AH 5315.25 — Calhoun, G.M. Ancient Athenian mining. Cambridge, Mass., 1931.

AH 7469.31 — Carcopino, Jérôme. Sylla; ou, La monarchie manquée. Paris, 1931.

AH 7889.31 — Cassimatis, Grégoire. Les intérêts dans la législation de Justinien et dans le droit byzantin. Paris, 1931.

AH 8548.95 — Chotzen, T.M. Primitieve Keltistiek in de Nederlanden. 's-Gravenhage, 1931.

Eg 879.31.10 — Cooke, Harold P. Osiris. London, 1931.

AH 7203.135 — Corpus juris civilis. Digesta. Digesta Justiniani Augusti. Mediolani, 1931.

AH 3607.13 — Debevoise, Neilson Carel. Parthian problems. An abstract of a thesis. n.p., 1931.

AH 8608.10 — Devoto, Giacomo. Gli antichi italici. Firenze, 1931.

AH 4809.31F — Dinsmoor, William B. The archons of Athens in the Hellenistic age. Cambridge, 1931.

AH 7479.31.5 — Duncan, Renée. The love life of Julius Caesar. N.Y., 1931.

AH 3154.27 — Ebeling, Erich. Tod und Leben nach den Vorstellungen der Babylonier. Berlin, 1931.

Eg 844.5 — Edgerton, W.F. Notes on Egyptian marriage chiefly in the Plotemaic period. Chicago, 1931.

AH 3936.9 — Février, J.G. Essai sur l'histoire politique et economique de Palmyre. Paris, 1931.

AH 3936.9.5 — Février, J.G. Essai sur l'histoire politique et economique de Palmyre. Thèse. Paris, 1931.

AH 3936.9.7 — Février, J.G. La religion des Palmyrénies. Thèse. Paris, 1931.

AH 7279.23.4 — Frank, Tenney. A history of Rome. N.Y., 1931.

Eg 1309.31PFA — Gardiner, A.H. The library of A. Chester Beatty. London, 1931.

Eg 855.3 — Garry, Thomas G. Egypt. London, 1931.

Eg 879.31.5 — Gauthier, Henri. Les fêtes du dieu Min. Thèse. Le Caire, 1931. 2 pam.

AH 7469.31.10 — Graindor, P. La guerre d'Alexandrie. Le Caire, 1931.

AH 7449.31 — Guarnieri, L. Roma e Cartagine sul mare. Roma, 1931.

AH 7138.73.4 — Hadley, James. Introduction to Roman law. New Haven, 1931.

Eg 759.31 — Hardy, E.R. The large estates of Byzantine Egypt. N.Y., 1931.

AH 4889.31 — Hasebroeck, J. Griechische Wirtschafts- und Gesellschaftsgeschichte bis zur Perserzeit. Tübingen, 1931.

AH 3046.5F — Heinrich, Ernst. Fara; Ergebnisse der Ausgrabungen der Deutschen Orient-Gesellschaft in Fara. Berlin, 1931.

AH 3966.18 — Herrmann, A. Die Erdkarte der Urbibel. Braunschweig, 1931.

AH 4855.13 — Höppener, Frank. Halieutica. Proefschrift. Amsterdam, 1931.

Eg 879.31 — Kevin, Robert O. Wisdom of Amen-em-Apt and its possible dependence upon Hebrew book of proverbs. Thesis. Philadelphia, 1931.

AH 7759.31 — Koch, J.A. Studien ouer den tijd von Constantijn den Grooten. Dordrecht, 1931.

AH 7489.31 — Kornemann, E. Doppelprinzipat und Reichsteilung im Imperium Romanum. Leipzig, 1931.

Eg 909.31 — Kortenbeutel, H. Der ägyptische Süd und Osthandel in der Politik der Ptolemäer und römischen Kaiser. Inaug. Diss. Charlottenburg, 1931.

AH 8647.5.15 — Lenormant, F. La Magna Grecia, paesaggio e storia. Crotone, 1931-33. 3v.

AH 7819.31.5 — Marchi, Attilio de. I romani nelle istituzioni e nel costume. Milano, 1931.

AH 7519.31 — Marsh, Frank Burr. The reign of Tiberius. London, 1931.

AH 278.84.7.2 — Meyer, E. Die ältere Chronologie Babyloniens. Stuttgart, 1931.

AH 5453.7A — Mijnsbrugge, M. van der. The Cretan koinon. N.Y., 1931.

AH 8647.14 — Olivieri, A. Civiltà greca nell'Italia meridionale. Napoli, 1931.

AH 3013.931.5 — Oppenheim, Max. Der Tell Halaf. Leipzig, 1931.

Eg 1009.31A — Peet, Thomas Eric. Comparative study of the literature of Egypt, Palestine and Mesopotamia. London, 1931.

AH 4829.31A — Picard, Charles. La vie privée dans la Grèce classique. Paris, 1931.

Eg 1179.31 — Pogo, A. Zum Problem der Identifikation der nördlichen Sternbilder der alter Ägypter. Bruges, 1931.

AH 4559.31.10A — Radet, Georges. Alexandre le Grand. 5. éd. Paris, 1931.

AH 8647.12 — Randall-MacIver, D. Greek cities in Italy and Sicily. Oxford, 1931.

AH 3957.23 — Rappoport, A.S. History of Palestine. N.Y., 1931.

AH 3910.11 — Rostovtsev, M.I. O blizhnem Vostoke. Parizh, 1931.

AH 7529.30.15 — Sachs, Hanns. Caligula. London, 1931.

AH 3110.5 — San Nicoló, Mariano. Beiträge zur Rechtsgeschichte im Brereiche der keilschriftlichen Rechtsquellen. Cambridge, 1931.

AH 939.31 — Scheliha, Renata von. Die Wassergrenze im Altertum. Breslau, 1931.

AH 4259.31 — Schmidt, Kurt. Die Namen der attischen Kriegsschiffe. Inaug. Diss. Engelsdorf, 1931.

AH 9790.5.10 — Schneeberger, H. Die Brunnenschlacht. Bad Kissingen, 1931.

AH 7819.31.2 — Showerman, Grant. Rome and the Romans. N.Y., 1931.

AH 8907.21F — Solari, Arturo. Vita pubblica e privata degli Etruschi. Firenze, 1931.

AH 1279.31 — Stewart-Vargas, Guillermo. Historia del Oriente antiguo y Medo Persa. Montevideo, 1931.

AH 3013.931.10F — Tompson, Reginald C. The prisms of Esarhaddon and Ashurbanipal found at Nineveh. London, 1931.

AH 3042.3.10 — Unger, Eckhard. Babylon. Berlin, 1931.

AH 3016.15F — Van Buren, Elizabeth D. Foundation figurines and offerings. Berlin, 1931.

AH 3013.931 — Waterman, Leroy. Preliminary report upon excavations at Tel Umar, Iraq. Ann Arbor, 1931-33. 2v.

AH 279.31 — Webster, Hutton. Ancient civilization. Boston, 1931.

AH 7469.31.5 — Weigall, Arthur E.P.B. The life and times of Marc Antony. Garden City, 1931.

AH 7469.31.4 — Weigall, Arthur E.P.B. The life and times of Marc Antony. N.Y., 1931.

Chronological Listing

1931 - cont.

AH 7489.31.5 — Wells, Joseph. A short history of the Roman Empire to the death of Marcus Aurelius. N.Y., 1931.
AH 4559.31 — Wilcken, Ulrich. Alexander der Grosse. Leipzig, 1931.
AH 4819.11.2.10A — Zimmern, A.E. The Greek commonwealth. 5th ed. Oxford, 1931.

1932

AH 7479.32 — Bailly, Auguste. Jules César. Paris, 1932.
AH 9714.5 — Balaschev, Georgi D. Staro-trakiiski svetilishta i bozhestva v Mezek, Glava, Panega, Madara, Tsarichina i drugade i tekhnsto znachenie. Sofiia, 1932.
AH 7203.136 — Boháček, Miroslav. Un esempio dell'insegnamento di Berito ai compilatori. Palermo, 1932.
AH 7169.21.2 — Buckland, W.W. A text-book of Roman law from Augustus to Justinian. 2. ed. Cambridge, Eng., 1932.
AH 7819.32 — Carcopino, Jérôme. Ce que Rome et l'empire romain doivent à la Gaule. Oxford, 1932.
AH 4659.32.10A — Cary, Max. A history of the Greek world from 325-146 B.C. London, 1932.
AH 3409.5 — Cavaignac, Eugène. Subbiluliuma et son temps. Paris, 1932.
AH 3020.13A — Chiera, Edward. Excavations at Nuzi. v.2-8. Cambridge, 1932-62. 7v.
AH 4819.32.15 — Croiset, Maurice. La civilisation de la Grèce antique. Paris, 1932.
AH 5603.5 — Cross, Geoffrey N. Epirus; a study in Greek constitutional development. Cambridge, 1932.
AH 4819.32.20 — Dickinson, G.L. The contribution of ancient Greece to modern life. London, 1932.
AH 4842.71 — Dobson, J.F. Ancient education and its meaning to us. N.Y., 1932.
AH 2013.7.5 — Farès, Edouard. L'honneur chez les Arabes avant l'Islam. Paris, 1932.
AH 2013.7 — Farès, Edouard. L'honneur chez les Arabes avant l'Islam. Thèse. Paris, 1932.
AH 4809.32A — Ferguson, W.S. Athenian tribal cycles in the Hellenistic age. Cambridge, 1932.
AH 4109.32.5 — Ferguson, William S. Athenian war finance. Boston, 1932.
AH 5303.13 — Ferguson, William S. The treasurers of Athena. Cambridge, Mass., 1932.
AH 7819.32.5 — Frank, Tenney. Aspects of social behavior in ancient Rome. Cambridge, Mass., 1932.
Eg 1309.32 — Gardiner, A.H. The Astarte papyrus. London, 1932.
AH 9792.7 — Gautier, E.F. Genséric, roi des Vandales. Paris, 1932.
AH 7650.88A — Gibbon, Edward. The decline and fall of the Roman Empire. N.Y., 1932. 2v.
AH 3965.16 — Ginzberg, Eli. Studies in the economics of the Bible. Philadelphia, 1932.
AH 4819.32 — Glover, Terrot R. Greek byways. Cambridge, Eng., 1932.
AH 4819.32.5A — Glover, Terrot R. Greek byways. N.Y., 1932.
AH 3096.6 — Hirschberg, Hans. Studien zur Geschichte Esarhaddons König von Assyrien (681-669). Inaug. Diss. Ohlau, 1932.
AH 5308.12 — Hoffmeister, E.E.W. Kritische Untersuchung der Charakterentwicklung der Athener. Hamburg, 1932.
AH 3020.7.10 — John Rylands Library. Manchester. Catalogue of Sumerian tablets in the John Rylands Library. Manchester, 1932.
AH 3045.5F — Jordan, J. Dritter vorläufiger Bericht über die von der Notgemeinschaft die deutschen Wissenschaft in Uruk unternommenen Ausgrabungen. Berlin, 1932.
AH 7278.98.15 — Koch, Julius. Römische Geschichte. Berlin, 1932. 2v.
AH 7139.32.5 — Kreller, Hans. Das Probelm der Juristenrechts in der römischen Rechtsgeschichte. Tübingen, 1932.
AH 4279.32.5 — Laistner, M.L.W. Greek history. Boston, 1932.
AH 4819.24.5 — Lönborg, Sven. Dike och Eros. v.1-2,3. Uppsala, 1932-37. 2v.
Eg 809.32 — Macnaughton, D. A scheme of Egyptian chronology. London, 1932.
AH 4659.32A — Macurdy, G.H. Hellenistic queens. Baltimore, 1932.
AH 3014.15F — Martiny, G. Die Kulturichtung in Mesopotamien. Diss. Berlin, 1932.
AH 4109.32 — Meritt, B.D. Athenian financial documents of the 5th century. Ann Arbor, 1932.
AH 7169.32 — Meyer-Collings, J.J. Deretictio. Inaug. Diss. Kallmünz, 1932.
AH 7539.32 — Momigliano, A. L'opera dell'imperatore Claudio. Firenze, 1932.
AH 7278.54.30.10 — Mommsen, T. Römische Geschichte. Wien, 1932.
AH 7114.29 — Niccolini, G. Il tribunato della plebe. Milano, 1932.
AH 7861.12 — Nock, A.D. Cremation and burial in the Roman Empire. Cambridge, 1932.
AH 7859.5 — Paternò-Paterno, S. La donna nella storia del diritto romano. Roma, 1932.
AH 7909.32 — Perali, P. Le origini artigiane industriali e mercantili di Roma. Roma, 1932.
AH 4279.32 — Petrie, Alexander. An introduction to Greek history. London, 1932.
Eg 819.23.2 — Petrie, William M.F. Social life in ancient Egypt. London, 1932.
AH 7759.32 — Piganiol, A. L'empereur Constantin. Paris, 1932.
Eg 39.32 — Pirenne, Jacques. Histoire des institutions et du droit privé de l'ancienne Égypte. v.1-3. Bruxelles, 1932-35. 4v.
Eg 1179.32 — Pogo, A. Calendars on coffin lids from Asyut. Bruges, 1932.
AH 4559.32.5 — Risi, Arnaldo de. Alessandro Magno, 356-331. Roma, 1932.
AH 4559.32A — Robinson, Charles A. The Ephemerides of Alexander's expedition. Providence, 1932.
AH 7419.32 — Robinson, Cyril E. A history of the Roman republic. N.Y., 1932.
AH 3964.34 — Rodén, Nils. Bibliska städer. Stockholm, 1932.
AH 7279.32 — Römische Geschichte. Freiburg, 1932. 2v.
AH 7529.30.5 — Sachs, Hanns. Bubi Caligula. 2. Aufl. Wien, 1932.
AH 279.32 — Sanctis, G. de. Problemi di storia antica. Bari, 1932.
AH 4039.32 — Schaefer, Hans. Staatsform und Politik. Leipzig, 1932.
Eg 829.32 — Shorter, Alan W. Everyday life in ancient Egypt. London, 1932.
AH 7479.32.5 — Sonnet, Paul. Gaius Trebatius Testa. Diss. Jena, 1932.
AH 4149.32 — Stratéegas autokratòr. Inaug. Diss. Engelsdorf, 1932. 4v.
AH 4499.32 — Taeger, Fritz. Ein Beitrag zur Geschichte der Pentekontaetie. Stuttgart, 1932.
AH 8514.13 — Vaillat, Claudius. Le culte des sources dans la Gaule antique. Paris, 1932.
AH 4559.31.5 — Wilcken, Ulrich. Alexander the Great. London, 1932.

1932 - cont.

AH 3154.35 — Witzel, M. Texte zum Studium sumerischer Tempel und Kulturzentren. Roma, 1932.
AH 819.32 — Wright, Frederick A. The romance of life in the ancient world. London, 1932?
AH 3954.11 — Zucrow, S. Women, slaves and the ignorant in rabbinic literature. Boston, 1932.

1933

Eg 1039.33 — Adams, W.M. The book of the master of the hidden places. London, 1933.
AH 4889.18.25A — Andreades, Andreas Michaël. History of Greek public finance. Cambridge, 1933.
AH 4559.33.10 — Andreotti, R. Il problema politico di Alessandro Magno. Torino, 1933.
AH 3097.6 — Ashurbanapal, king of Assyria. Editions E, B and K of the annals of Ashurbanipal. Diss. Chicago, 1933.
Eg 885.933A — Bell, H.I. Magical texts from a bilingual papyrus in the British museum. London, 1933.
AH 459.33 — Beloch, Julius. Le monarchie ellenistiche e la repubblica romana. Bari, 1933.
AH 4819.33.10 — Bethe, E. Tausend Jahre altgriechischen Lebens. München, 1933.
AH 7089.33 — Bon, Alessio de. La colonizzazione romana dal Brenta al Piave. Bassagno del Grappe, 1933.
AH 4049.33 — Bonner, R.J. Aspects of Athenian democracy. Berkeley, 1933.
AH 3009.33 — Boulton, W.H. Babylonia. London, 1933.
AH 7489.33.5 — Brassloff, Stephen. Staat und Gesellschaft in der Römischen Kaiserzeit. Wien, 1933.
AH 4519.33 — Brauer, H. Die Kriegschuldfrage in der geschichtlichen Überlieferung des peloponnesischen Krieges. Inaug. Diss. Emsdetten, 1933.
Eg 879.33A — Breasted, James Henry. The dawn of conscience. N.Y., 1933.
AH 7469.33 — Brun-Laloire, Louis. La vie tragique des Gracques. Paris, 1933.
AH 7169.33.5 — Bussmann, M. L'obligation de délivrance du vendeur. Thèse. Lausanne, 1933.
Eg 847.6 — Candar, Aaoni Ali. Eti hiyeroglifi üzerinde tetkikler 534 idéogramme. Ankara, 1933.
AH 7449.33 — Cappis, F. Zum Alpenübergang Hannibals. Aarau, 1933.
AH 7279.25.5 — Cauer, Friedrich. Römische Geschichte. 2. Aufl. München, 1933.
AH 7169.33.10 — Cavin, P.E. L'extinction de l'usufruit "rei mutatione". Thèse. Lausanne, 1933.
AH 7203.137 — Chiazzese, L. Confronti testuali contributo alla dottrina delle interpolazioni giustinianee. Cortona, 1933.
AH 7138.99.3 — Czyhlarz, Karl. Lehrbuch der Institutionen des römischen Rechtes. 19. Aufl, Wien, 1933.
Eg 909.33 — Dairanes, Serge. L'Égypte economique sous la XVIIIe dynastie pharaonique. Thèse. Paris, 1933.
AH 7509.33 — Daniel, Rudolf. Mareus Vipsanius Agrippa. Inaug. Diss. Breslau, 1933.
AH 7889.10.5 — Davis, William S. Influence of wealth in imperial Rome. N.Y., 1933.
AH 819.28.5 — Dawson, Christopher H. The age of the gods. London, 1933.
AH 3014.16 — Delougaz, Pinhas. Plano-convex bricks and the methods of their employment. Chicago, 1933.
AH 4829.33 — Demopoulos, P.N. Ho dnmodios...tòn hargaiòy Hellenòn. Athènai, 1933.
AH 4819.33 — Drerup, Engelbert. Kulturprobleme des klassischen Griechentums. Paderborn, 1933-34. 2v.
Eg 609.33A — Edgerton, William F. The Thutmosid succession. Chicago, 1933.
AH 3358.9 — Fantoli, A. La Libia negli scritti degli antiche. Roma, 1933.
AH 7279.21.6 — Ferrero, Guglielmo. Roma antica. 2. ed. Firenze, 1933. 3v.
AH 4839.33 — Forbes, C.A. Neoi. Middletown, Conn., 1933.
AH 7829.08.5 — Fowler, W.W. Social life at Rome in the age of Cicero. N.Y., 1933.
AH 7889.33A — Frank, Tenney. An economic survey of ancient Rome. Baltimore, 1933-40. 3v.
AH 7279.23.5 — Frank, Tenney. A history of Rome. N.Y., 1933.
AH 3017.27 — Gadd, Cyril J. Seals of ancient Indian style found at Ur. London, 1933.
AH 7201.99 — Gaius. 1937. Bizoukides. Les nouveaux fragments des institutes de Gaius. Paris, 1933.
AH 7009.05.5 — Gamurrin, G.F. Bibliografia dell'Italia antica. pt.1. Roma, 1933.
AH 4114.18 — Gerhardt, Paul. Die attische Metoikie im vierten Jahrhundert. Inaug. Diss. Berlin, 1933.
AH 5315.5 — Gomme, A.W. Population of Athens in the fifth and fourth centuries B.C. Oxford, 1933.
AH 7819.33A — Greene, William C. Achievement of Rome. Cambridge, 1933.
AH 7338.97.5 — Groag, E. Prosopographia Imperii Romani. 2. ed. v.1-4, pt.1-3. Berolini, 1933-52. 4v.
AH 4909.28.5 — Hasebroek, J. Trade and politics in ancient Greece. London, 1933.
AH 7459.33.5 — Haywood, R.M. Studies on Scipio Africanus. Baltimore, 1933.
AH 7459.33 — Haywood, R.M. Studies on Scipio Africanus. Diss. Baltimore, 1933.
AH 4038.91.5 — Headlam-Morley, J.W. Election by lot at Athens. 2. ed. Cambridge, 1933.
AH 7509.30.2 — Heinze, Richard. Die augusteische Kultur. 2. Aufl. Leipzig, 1933.
AH 7299.33.5 — Heuss, Alfred. Amicitia. Inaug. Diss. Gräfenhainichen, 1933.
AH 3005.828 — Hincks, Edward. Edward Hincks; a selection from his correspondence. London, 1933.
AH 7909.33 — Holmberg, E.J. Zur Geschichte des Cursus publicus. Uppsala, 1933.
AH 7162.36 — Huber, Paul. Die Ausdehnung der Normen der Senatus Consultum Juventianum auf die private Heredetatis petitio klassischen Rechts. Inaug. Diss. Erlangen, 1933.
AH 7639.33 — Hüttl, Willy. Antoninus Pius. Prag, 1933-36.
AH 2011.8 — Jochum, Johannes. Geschichte de Familie El-'Abbâs bin 'Abd El-Muttalib. Inaug. Diss. Berlin, 1933.
AH 7889.33.10 — Jonkers, Engbert. Economische en sociale toestanden in het Romeinsche rijk. Proefschrift. Wageningen, 1933.
AH 279.33.5 — Junker, H. Die Völker des Antiken Orients. Freiburg, 1933.
AH 3002.105 — Keilschriftliche Miscellanea. Roma, 1933.

Chronological Listing

1933 - cont.

AH 7819.33.5 — Kiefer, Otto. Kulturgeschichte Roms, unter besonderer Berücksichtigung der römischen Sitten. Berlin, 1933.

AH 4858.15 — Klinz, A. Hieros gamos. Diss. Halis Saxonum, 1933.

AH 3156.15 — Labat, René. Commentaires assyro-babyloniens sur les présages. Bordeux, 1933.

AH 5124.7 — Laidlaw, W.A. A history of Delos. Oxford, 1933.

AH 9121.2 — Lamboglia, Nino. Topografia storica dell'Ingaunia nell'antichità. Albenga, 1933.

Eg 971.7.5 — Leider, Erich. Der Handel von Alexandreia. Hamburg, 1933.

AH 7509.33.9 — Levi, Mario A. Attaviano capoparti. Firenze, 1933. 2v.

AH 7162.37 — Longo, G. L'hereditatis pelitio. Padova, 1933.

AH 8073.14 — Lüdemann, Hans. Untersuchungen zur Verfassungsgeschichte Karthagos bis auf Aristoteles. Inaug. Diss. Bottrop, 1933.

AH 3408.17 — Matter, E.P. Die Bedeutung der Hethiter für das Alti Testament. Diss. Bottrop, 1933.

AH 7278.54.10.15 — Mommsen, T. Römische Geschichte. v.1-3, 5. Berlin, 1933. 4v.

AH 7278.54.30.5A — Mommsen, T. Das Weltreich der Caesaren. Wien, 1933.

AH 3654.10 — Nasr, Taghi. Essai sur l'histoire du droit persan des l'origine a l'invasion arabe. Paris, 1933.

AH 819.33.5 — Niemax, Hans. Antike Humanität im Kampfe mit römischen Gesängniseland. Inaug. Diss. Neubrandenburg, 1933.

AH 8907.20 — Nogara, Bartolemeo. Gli Etruschi e la loro civiltà. Milano, 1933.

AH 5757.11 — Ollier, F. Le mirage spartiate. Thèse. Paris, 1933.

AH 8607.2.7 — Pais, Ettore. Storia dell'Italia antica e della Sicilia per l'età anteriore al dominio romano. 2. ed. Torino, 1933. 2v.

AH 7059.33 — Palanque, Jean-Rémy. Essai sur la préfecture du prétoire du Bas-Empire. Thèse. Paris, 1933.

AH 4229.33 — Paoli, U.E. Studi sul processo attico. Padova, 1933.

AH 4239.33 — Parke, H. William. Greek mercenary soldiers. Oxford, 1933.

AH 7479.33F — Pasquini, Luigi. Rimini e Giulio Cesare. Rimini, 1933.

AH 819.33 — Peake, Harold. Early steps in human progress. London, 1933.

AH 3150.13 — Pohl, Alfred. Neubabylonische Achturkunden aus den Berliner Staatlichen Museum. v.1-2. Roma, 1933-34.

AH 4819.33.15 — Quennell, M.C. Everday things in classical Greece. N.Y., 1933.

AH 7299.33.10 — Regano, A. Origine e creazione del fascio. Napoli, 1933.

AH 7509.33.5 — Reinhold, M. Marcus Agrippa. Geneva, 1933.

AH 7169.33 — Romano, S. Studi sulla derelizione nel diritto romano. Padova, 1933.

AH 259.33 — Rose, John Holland. The Mediterranean in the ancient world. Cambridge, Eng., 1933.

Eg 819.33 — Rydh, H. Hur man levde i Faraos land. Stockholm, 1933.

AH 9610.27 — Schenk von Stauffenberg, Alexander. König Hieron der Zweite von Syrakus. Stuttgart, 1933.

AH 4159.33 — Schlesinger, E. Die griechische Asylie. Diss. Giessen, 1933.

AH 9684.9 — Schulten, Adolf. Geschichte von Numantia. München, 1933.

AH 3160.14 — Selms, A. van. De babylonische termini voor zonde. Proefschrift. Wageningen, 1933.

AH 7509.33.7 — Shipley, F.W. Agrippa's building activities in Rome. St. Louis, 1933.

AH 7769.33 — Solari, A. La crisi dell'impero romano. Milano, 1933-37. 5v.

AH 849.6 — Steuer, R.O. Myrrhe und Stakte. Wien, 1933.

Eg 1099.53 — Suys, Émile. Etude sur le Conte du Fellah Plaideur. Roma, 1933.

AH 4559.33 — Tarn, W.W. Alexander the Great and the unity of mankind. London, 1933.

AH 3016.25 — Van Buren, Elizabeth D. The flowing vase and the god with streams. Berlin, 1933.

AH 279.33 — Vicini, Antonio. La civiltà antica dal periodo preistorico. Piedimonte d'Alife, 1933.

AH 4709.33 — Walbank, Frank William. Aratos of Sicyon. Thirwall prize essay 1933. Cambridge, Eng., 1933.

AH 4559.33.8 — Weigall, A.E.P.B. Alexander the Great. Garden City, 1933.

AH 4559.33.7 — Weigall, A.E.P.B. Alexander the Great. London, 1933.

AH 7779.33 — Weis, B.K. Das Restitutions-Edict Kaiser Julians. Inaug. Diss. Bruchsal, 1933.

AH 7269.33 — Winkler, Heinz. Rom und Aegypten im 2. Jahrhundert v. Chr. Engelsdorf, 1933.

AH 4519.33.5 — Woodhouse, William J. King Agis of Sparta and his campaign in Arkadia in 418 B.C. Oxford, 1933.

1934

Eg 1179.34 — Antoniadi, E.M. L'astronomie égyptienne. Paris, 1934.

AH 7729.34A — Artaud, Antonin. Héliogabale. Paris, 1934.

AH 7279.34 — Baker, G.P. Twelve centuries of Rome. N.Y., 1934.

AH 7529.34 — Balsdom, John Percy Vyvian D. The Emperor Gaius Caligula. Oxford, 1934.

AH 5157.15 — Benecke, H.H. Die Seepolitik der Aitoler. Inaug. Diss. Hamburg, 1934.

AH 7279.34.15F — Bertolini, F. Storia di Roma. Milano, 1934.

AH 7509.34.10 — Berve, H. Kaiser Augustus. Leipzig, 1934.

AH 4848.14.5F — Bieber, Margarete. Entwicklungsgeschichte der griechischen Tracht. Berlin, 1934.

AH 3159.34 — Blome, Friedrich. Die Opfermaterie in Babylonien und Israel. Thesis. Romae, 1934.

AH 7449.29.12 — Branchini, A. La battaglia del Metauro. Pesaro, 1934.

Eg 879.33.5A — Breasted, James Henry. The dawn of conscience. N.Y., 1934.

AH 4854.7 — Brendel, Otto. Die Schafzucht im alten Griechenland. Diss. Würzburg, 1934.

AH 4819.31.5 — Brodeur, A.G. The pageant of civilization. Garden City, 1934?

Eg 879.34 — Budge, Ernest Alfred Wallis. From fetish to God in ancient Egypt. London, 1934.

AH 8907.22 — Bulanda, E. Etrurja i Etruskowie. Lwów, 1934.

AH 4818.98.5.15 — Burckhardt, J. Kulturgeschichte Griechenlands. Berlin, 1934.

AH 7489.34 — Carcopino, J. Points de vue sur l'impérialisme romain. Paris, 1934.

AH 3020.16F — Chiera, Edward. Sumerian epics and myths. Chicago, 1934.

AH 3020.17F — Chiera, Edward. Sumerian texts of varied content. Chicago, 1934.

AH 1819.34A — Childe, Vere G. New light on the most ancient East. London, 1934.

AH 1819.34.10 — Childe, Vere G. New light on the most ancient East. N.Y., 1934.

AH 7519.34 — Ciaceri, E. Tiberio, successore di Augusto. Milano, 1934.

1934 - cont.

AH 139.34 — Ciccotti, Ettore. La formazione della coscienza giuridica e le sue concrete graduali espressioni nel mondo antico. Udine, 1934.

AH 5310.15 — Cloché, Paul. La politique étrangère d'Athènes de 404 à 338 avant Jesus Christ. Paris, 1934.

AH 4299.34 — Cohen, R. La grèce et l'hellénisation du monde antique. Paris, 1934.

AH 3413.12 — Contenau, Georges. La civilisation des Hitties et des Mitanniens. Paris, 1934.

AH 3016.45 — Contenau, Georges. Monuments mésopotamiens. Paris, 1934.

AH 819.28.10 — Dawson, Christopher H. The age of the gods. 2. ed. N.Y., 1934.

AH 3179.10.15 — Deimel, Anton. Enuma eliš und Hexaëmeron. Rom, 1934.

AH 8514.14 — Drioux, Georges. Cultes indigènes des Lingons. Paris, 1934.

AH 8514.14.5 — Drioux, Georges. Cultes indigénes des Lingons. Thèse. Paris, 1934.

AH 4609.34 — Edson, C.F. The Antigonids, Heracles, and Beroea. n.p., 1934.

AH 8548.105 — Elston, C.S. The earliest relations between Celts and Germans. London, 1934.

AH 7779.34 — Farney, R. La religion de l'empereur Julien et le mysticisme du temps. Paris, 1934.

AH 8607.11 — Ferrabino, Aldo. L'Italia romana. Milano, 1934.

AH 7139.34.5 — Fürst, Fritz. Die Bedeutung der Auctoritas im privaten und öffentlichen Leben der römischen Republik. Inaug. Diss. Marburg, 1934.

AH 7844.8 — Gagé, J. Recherches sur les jeux séculaires. Paris, 1934.

AH 9792.7.5 — Gautier, E.F. Geiserich, König der Wandalen. Frankfurt am Main, 1934.

AH 5311.7 — Graindor, Paul. Athènes sous Hadrieu. Le Caire, 1934.

AH 3171.12 — Güterbock, Hans G. Die historische Tradition und ihre literarische Gestaltung bei Babyloniern und Hethitern bis 1200. Inaug. Diss. Glückstadt, 1934.

AH 7509.22.3 — Hadley, H.S. Rome and the world today. 3. ed. N.Y., 1934.

AH 6103.5 — Hampl, Franz. Der König der Makedonien. Inaug. Diss. Weida, 1934.

AH 5857.12 — Hanell, Krister. Megarische Studien. Lund, 1934.

AH 3014.17F — Heinrich, Ernst. Schilf und Lehm. Diss. Berlin, 1934.

AH 7218.5 — Hill, George. Treasure-trove; the law and practice of antiquity. London, 1934.

AH 7833.5 — Huber, Karl. Theorie des gymnischen Erziehung bei den Römern. Langensalza, 1934.

AH 8073.15 — Hurd, H.P. The topography of Punic Carthage. Williamsport, 1934.

AH 6157.10 — Izvestiia vizantiiskikh pisatelei o Severnom Prichernomor'e. Moskva, 1934.

AH 4842.72 — Jaeger, Werner Wilhelm. Paideia: die Formung des griechischen Menschen. Berlin, 1934.

AH 7819.33.5.3 — Kiefer, Otto. Sexual life in ancient Rome. London, 1934.

AH 4839.34 — Knab, Rudolf. Die Periodoniken. Diss. Boltrop, 1934.

AH 4889.34 — Korver, J. De terminologie van het crediet-wezen in het Grieksch. Amsterdam, 1934.

AH 7059.34 — Kruse, Helmut. Studien zur offiziellen Geltung des Kaiserbildes im römischen Reiche. Paderborn, 1934.

AH 7479.34.5 — Larrouy, Maurice. Antoine et Cléopatre; La bataille d'Actium. Paris, 1934.

AH 4279.34A — Lavell, C.F. A biography of the Greek people. Boston, 1934.

Eg 971.7.6 — Leider, Erich. Der Handel von Alexandreia. Diss. Hamburg, 1934.

Eg 909.35 — Lewis, Naphtali. L'industrie du papyrus dans l'Égypte gréco-romaine. Thèse. Paris, 1934.

X Cg AH 4829.34 — Licht, Hans. Sexual life in ancient Greece. N.Y., 1934.

AH 4479.34 — Lombardo, G. Cimone. Roma, 1934.

AH 7169.34 — Longo, G. Diritto romano. Catania, 1934.

AH 4481.13 — Mackenzie, C. Marathon and Salamis. Photoreproduction. London, 1934.

AH 7139.34 — Mackintosh, J. Some aspects of Roman law. Patna, 1934.

AH 8708.5 — Maggiulli, Pasquale. Sull'origine dei Messapi. Lecce, 1934.

Htn AH 8511.5* — Manley, Inza J. Effects of the Germanic invasions on Gaul. Berkeley, 1934.

AH 8511.5.2 — Manley, Inza J. Effects of the Germanic invasions on Gaul. Berkeley, 1934.

AH 3016.7.5F — Meissner, Bruno. Die babylonischen Kleinplastiken. Leipzig, 1934.

AH 7159.34 — Mellor, A. Les conceptions du crime politique sous la République romaine. Thèse. Paris, 1934.

AH 8608.11 — Miscosi, G. Origini italiche; testimonianze storiche sull'esistenza di Roma e Genova prerumulee. Genova, 1934.

AH 7539.32.5 — Momigliano, A. Claudius, the emperor. Oxford, 1934.

AH 6110.19 — Momigliano, A. Filippo il Macedone. Firenze, 1934.

AH 7278.54.30.12 — Mommsen, T. Römische Geschichte. Wien, 1934.

AH 7114.30 — Niccolini, G. I fasti dei tribuni della plebe. Milano, 1934.

AH 7469.25 — Pareti, Luigi. La congiura di Catilina alle soglie dell'impero. Catania, 1934.

AH 7469.34 — Pavano Amato, Giovanni. La rivolta di Catalina. Messina, 1934.

AH 7909.32.5 — Perali, P. Vestigia dell'antico artigianato nelle regioni dell 'Egeo e dell'Italia. Roma, 1934.

Eg 847.7 — Reisner, M. Inscribed monuments from Gebel Barkal. Leipzig, 1934.

AH 4819.33.5 — Robinson, C.E. Everyday life in ancient Greece. Oxford, 1934.

AH 4819.32.7 — Rostovtsev, M.I. Out of the past of Greece and Rome. New Haven, 1934.

AH 8647.16 — Scherechewsky, J. Die politischen Beziehungen der unter italischen Griechenstädte. Inaug. Diss. Leipzig, 1934.

AH 7139.34.20 — Schulz, Fritz. Prinzipien des römischen Rechts. München, 1934.

AH 7509.34.5 — Schur, Werner. Augustus. Lübeck, 1934.

AH 7203.142 — Simonius, A. Was bedeuten für uns die Pandekten? Basel, 1934.

AH 4481.11 — Sotiriadis, G. L'expédition de Marathon. Salonique, 1934.

AH 6086.5 — Stählin, Friedrich. Pagasai und Demetrios. Berlin, 1934.

AH 7509.34.20 — Stella, L.A. Druso. Gleno, 1934.

AH 4499.34 — Stier, Hans E. Eine Grosstat der attischen Geschichte, die sog. Schlacht bei Oinoë. Stuttgart, 1934.

AH 4559.34.5 — Strasburger, H. Ptolemaios und Alexander. Leipzig, 1934.

Eg 1309.34F — Thompson, H. A family archive from Siut from papyri in the British Museum. Oxford, 1934. 2v.

AH 7844.6.15 — Vaccari, A. Il natale de Roma nelle leggende e nella storia. Verona, 1934.

Chronological Listing

1934 - cont.

AH 7479.34 — Vassalli, Pietro. Lucio Munazio Planco, generale di Giulio Cesare, console 42 a. C. Cassino, 1934.

AH 7509.34 — Vaubel, T. Untersuchungen zu Augustus' Politik und Staatsauffassung nach den autobiographischen Schriften. Inaug. Diss. Düsseldorf, 1934.

AH 5107.5 — Waltz, Pierre. Le monde égéen avant les Grècs. Paris, 1934.

AH 4559.33.9 — Weigall, A.E.P.B. Alexandre le Grand. Paris, 1934.

Eg 279.34 — Weigall, A.E.P.B. A short history of ancient Egypt. London, 1934.

AH 189.34 — Westermann, W.L. Sklaverei. Stuttgart, 1934.

AH 7161.29 — Westrup, Carl W. Introduction to early Roman law; the patriarchal joint family. London, 1934-55. 5v.

AH 4559.34 — Wright, Frederick A. Alexander the Great. London, 1934.

AH 6103.7 — Zancan, P. Il monarcato ellenistico nei suoi elementi federativi. Padova, 1934.

AH 4909.34 — Ziebarth, Erich. Der griechische Kaufmann im Altertum. München, 1934.

1935

AH 8007.17 — Africa romana. Milano, 1935.

AH 5303.12 — Andria, N. La démocratie athénienne. Thèse. Paris, 1935.

Eg 1128.76.5 — Ani. La sagesse d'Ani. Roma, 1935.

AH 4039.35 — Beccari, A. La fondazione delle dottrine politiche in Grecia. Napoli, 1935.

AH 3366.5 — Bertrand, Louis. Vers Cyrène, terre d'Apollon. Paris, 1935.

AH 7279.21.4 — Boak, Arthur E.R. A history of Rome to 565 A.D. N.Y., 1935.

AH 3156.14 — Boissier, A. Mantique babylonienne et mantique hittite. Paris, 1935.

AH 4889.35 — Brake, J. Wirtschaften und Charakter in der antiken Bildung. Frankfurt, 1935.

AH 279.16.15 — Breasted, James H. Ancient times. 2. ed. Boston, 1935.

Eg 879.33.6 — Breasted, James Henry. The dawn of conscience. N.Y., 1935.

Eg 1042.935.10F — Buck, Adriaan de. The Egyptian coffin texts. Chicago, 1935. 7v.

AH 4039.35.5 — Carcopino, J. L'ostracisme athénien. Paris, 1935.

AH 819.35 — Ciccotti, Ettore. La civiltà del mondo antico. Udine, 1935. 2v.

AH 7207.35 — Cobban, J.M. Senate and provinces, 78-49 B.C. Cambridge, Eng., 1935.

AH 7203.109 — Corpus juris civilis. Institutiones. Les Institutes de Justinien. Paris, 1935.

AH 7159.35.5 — Coster, C.H. The indicium quinquevirale. Cambridge, 1935.

AH 4839.35.5 — Curtius, E. Olympia. Berlin, 1935.

AH 3149.11 — Deimel, Anton. Die altbabylonische Königsliste und ihre Bedeutung für die Chronologie. Rom, 1935.

AH 299.35 — Ehrenberg, V. Ost und West. Brünn, 1935.

AH 6110.14 — Elson, Charles F. Perseus and Demetrius. n.p., 1935.

AH 3179.10 — Enuma elish. Le poème babylonien de la création. Paris, 1935.

AH 7819.35 — Fraenkel, Eduard. Rome and Greek culture. Oxford, 1935.

Eg 879.35 — Gardiner, Alan H. The attitude of the ancient Egyptians to death and the dead. Cambridge, Eng., 1935.

AH 3002.88F — Gelb, I.J. Inscriptions from Alishar and vicinity. Chicago, 1935.

AH 9633.7 — Giacomazzi, Rosaria. Considerazione sopra la storia dei Mamerlini. Messina, 1935.

AH 279.35A — Glover, T.R. The ancient world; a beginning. N.Y., 1935.

AH 7149.35 — Goodfellow, C.E. Roman citizenship. Thesis. Lancaster, 1935.

AH 4239.35 — Griffith, G.T. The mercenaries of the Hellenistic world. Cambridge, Eng., 1935.

AH 5307.29 — Guy, Noël. Athènes. Illustrations en couleurs de Marilac. Paris, 1935.

AH 8549.135 — Hamel, Anton G. van. Aspects of Celtic mythology. London, 1935.

AH 7649.35 — Hayward, F.H. Marcus Aurelius, a saviour of men. London, 1935.

AH 7549.35 — Hermant, Abel. Poppée, l'amante de l'Antéchrist. Paris, 1935.

AH 7509.35 — Homo, L. Auguste. Paris, 1935.

AH 3013.935F — Jacobsen, T. Sennacherib's aqueduct at Jerwan. Chicago, 1935.

AH 3020.23 — Jestin, Raymond. Textes économiques sumériens de la 11e dynastie d'Ur. Paris, 1935.

AH 7169.35 — Jörs, Paul. Römisches Privatrecht. 2. Aufl. Berlin, 1935.

AH 7819.33.5.2 — Kiefer, Otto. Sexual life in ancient Rome. N.Y., 1935.

AH 3156.13 — Kraus, F.R. Die physiognomischen Omina der Babylonier. Inaug. Diss. Gräfenhainichen, 1935.

Eg 849.10 — Lexová, Irena. Ancient Egyptian dances. Praha, 1935.

AH 3059.7.5 — McDowell, R.H. Stamped and inscribed objects from Seleucia. Ann Arbor, 1935.

Eg 985.5 — MacLennan, Hugh. Oxyrhynchos. Diss. Princeton, 1935.

AH 8549.135.5 — MacNiell, Evin. Celtic and Teutonic religions. London, 1935.

AH 7469.35 — Marsh, Frank B. A history of the Roman world from 146 to 30 B.C. London, 1935.

Htn   AH 7307.34.3* — Montesquieu, Charles de. Considérations sur les causes de la grandeur des Romains. 2. éd. Amsterdam, 1935.

AH 3129.7 — Moore, Ellen W. Neo-Babylonian business and administrative documents. Ann Arbor, 1935.

AH 7449.35 — Nap, J.M. Die römische Republik um das Jahr 225 vor Christus. Leiden, 1935.

AH 9613.5 — Pace, Biagio. Arte e civiltà della Sicilia antica. Milano, 1935-49. 4v.

AH 7449.27 — Pais, Ettore. Storia de Roma durante le guerre puniche. 2. ed. Torino, 1935. 2v.

AH 7489.35 — Parker, Henry M.D. A history of the Roman world from A.D. 138 to 337. London, 1935.

Eg 603.10 — Pendleburg, J.D.S. Tell el-Amarna. Photoreproduction. London, 1935.

AH 3105.5A — Pfeiffer, R.H. State letters of Assyria. New Haven, 1935.

AH 3020.19F — Pohl, A. Vorsargonische und sargonische Wirtschaftstexte. Leipzig, 1935.

Eg 1042.935F — Pyramid Texts. Übersetzung und Kommentar zu den altägyptischen Pyramidentexten. Glückstadt, 1935-1962. 6v.

AH 4839.35 — Ridington, William R. The Minoan-Mycenaean background of Greek athletics. Diss. Philadelphia, 1935.

AH 7279.35 — Robinson, C.E. A history of Rome. N.y., 1935.

AH 7159.35 — Rogers, R.S. Crimial trials and criminal legislation under Tiberius. Middletown, Conn., 1935.

1935 - cont.

AH 7099.35 — Rudolph, Hans. Stadt und Staat im römischen Italien. Leipzig, 1935.

AH 259.35 — Saint-Denis, E. de. Le vocabulaire des manoeuvres nautiques en Latin. Thèse. Macon, 1935.

AH 7279.35.10A — Scullard, H.H. A history of the Roman world from 753 to 146 B.C. London, 1935.

AH 7339.35A — Showerman, G. Monuments and men of ancient Rome. N.Y., 1935.

AH 3310.5 — Spyridakis, K. Euagaros I van Salamis. Stuttgart, 1935.

AH 4819.11.5 — Stobart, J.C. The glory that was Greece. N.Y., 1935.

AH 7819.11.9A — Stobart, J.C. The grandeur that was Rome; a survey of Roman culture. N.Y., 1935.

AH 3964.25 — Thomas, Joseph. Le mouvement baptiste en Palestine et Syrie. Gembloux, 1935.

AH 1409.35 — Turaev, V.A. Istoriia drevnago Vostoka. Leningrad, 1935. 2v.

AH 8515.5 — West, L.C. Roman Gaul; the objects of trade. Oxford, 1935.

AH 6060.5 — Westlake, Henry Dickinson. Thessaly in the fourth century B.C. London, 1935.

AH 5763.3 — Willing, Karl. Die Geist Spartas. 1. Aufl. Berlin, 1935.

AH 3160.18 — Witzel, M. Tammuz-Liturgien und Verwandtes. Roma, 1935.

AH 3014.19 — Woolley, Charles L. The development of Sumerian art. N.Y., 1935.

AH 7179.35 — Zancan, L. Ager publicus. Padova, 1935.

AH 3013.935.5F — Zervos, C. L'art de la Mésopotamie de la fin du quatrième millénaire au XVe siècle avant notre ère. Paris, 1935.

1936

AH 8313.5 — Alfoldi, András. Magyarország hépei es a Római biródolom. Budapest, 1936.

AH 7779.36 — Andreotti, R. Il regno dell'imperatore Giuliano. Bologna, 1936.

AH 7659.36A — Arragon, R.F. The transition from the ancient to the medieval world. N.Y., 1936.

AH 3958.23 — Bergman, A. The Israelite tribe of Half-Manasseh. Diss. Jerusalem, 1936.

AH 7889.36 — Bernard, Antoine. La rémunération des professions liberales en droit romain classique. Paris, 1936.

Eg 279.05.15 — Breasted, James Henry. Geschichte Ägyptens. Zürich, 1936.

AH 4299.36 — Bullock, Charles J. The new deal in ancient Greece. Cambridge, 1936.

AH 4819.36.5 — Burn, Andrew Robert. The world of Hesiod. London, 1936.

AH 1279.36 — Capart, Jean. Histoire de l'Orient ancien. Paris, 1936.

AH 3407.22 — Cavaignac, Eugène. Le problème hittite. Paris, 1936.

AH 7489.36 — Charlesworth, M.P. Five men. Cambridge, Mass., 1936.

AH 819.36.10A — Childe, Vere Gordon. Man makes himself. London, 1936.

AH 8914.10 — Clemen, Carl. Die Religion der Etrusker. Bonn, 1936.

AH 5307.30 — Cohen, R. Athènes, une démocratie. Paris, 1936.

AH 4229.36.5 — Cronin, James F. The Athenian juror and his oath. Diss. Chicago, 1936.

AH 6024.11 — Daux, Georges. Delphes au IIe et au Ier siècle depuis l'abaissement de l'Etolie jusqu'à la paix romaine 191-31 avant J.C. Thèse. Paris, 1936.

AH 7149.36 — De Robertis, F.M. La espropriazione per pubblica utilità nel diritto romano. Bari, 1936.

AH 8607.10 — Ducati, P. L'Italia antica dalle prime civiltà alla morte di Cesare, 44 a.C. Milano, 1936.

Eg 909.36.5 — Dykmans, G.L. Histoire économique et social de l'ancienne Égypte. Paris, 1936-37. 3v.

Eg 602.10 — Edgerton, William F. Historical records of Ramses III. Chicago, 1936.

Eg 819.36 — Erman, Adolf. Die Welt am Nil. Leipzig, 1936.

AH 7479.36 — Foschini, Antonino. Cesare. Milano, 1936.

AH 819.36.25 — Friedell, Egon. Kulturgeschichte des Altertums. Zürich, 1936-

AH 3414.5 — Furlani, G. La religione degli Hittite. Bologna, 1936.

AH 3016.13F — Gadd, C.J. The stones of Assyria. London, 1936.

AH 7809.36 — Geiger, Karl. Der römische Kalender und seine Verbesserung durch Julius Caesar. München, 1936.

AH 1409.36 — Götze, Albrecht. Hethiter, Churriter und Assyrer. Oslo, 1936.

AH 3964.18 — Graham, William C. Culture and conscience. Chicago, 1936.

AH 4229.36 — Harrell, Hansen C. Public arbitration in Athenian Law. Chicago, 1936.

AH 4229.36.3 — Harrell, Hansen C. Public arbitration in Athenian Law. Columbia, 1936.

AH 819.36.5 — Hertzler, J.O. The social thought of the ancient civilization. 1. ed. N.Y., 1936.

AH 4842.72.3A — Jaeger, Werner Wilhelm. Paideia. 2. Aufl. Berlin, 1936- 3v.

AH 4459.36 — Laistner, M.L.W. A history of the Greek world from 479 to 323 B.C. London, 1936.

AH 7207.33 — Lambrechts, P. La composition du sénat romain de l'accession au trône d'Hadrien à la mort de Commode, 117-192. Antwerpen, 1936.

AH 7469.36 — Lanzani, C. Lucio Cornelio Silla, dittatore. Milano, 1936.

AH 1189.36 — Lauterbach, W. Der Arbeiter in Recht und Rechtspraxis des Alten Testaments und des alten Orients. Inaug. Diss. Heidelberg, 1936.

AH 7299.36.2 — Levi, Mario A. La pooitica imperiale di Roma. 2. ed. Torino, 1936.

AH 3013.936 — Lloyd, Seton. Mesopotamia. London, 1936.

AH 7239.36 — Lorenz, H. Untersuchung zum Prätorium. Inaug. Diss. Halle, 1936.

AH 3354.5 — Luzzatto, G.I. La "Lex Cathartica" di Cirene. Milano, 1936.

AH 7469.34.5.3 — Mainzer, Ferdinand. Caesar's mantle. N.Y., 1936.

AH 7469.34.5 — Mainzer, Ferdinand. Der Kampf um Caesars Erbe. Leipzig, 1936.

Eg 847.4.5F — Möller, G. Hieratische Paläographie. Ergänzungsheft zu Bd. 1-2. Leipzig, 1936.

AH 279.36 — Monteath, K.M. The antiquity of mankind and the modernity of religions. 3. ed. York, 1936.

AH 4842.75A — Moore, E.C. The story of instruction. N.Y., 1936.

AH 7819.36A — Moore, F.G. The Roman's world. N.Y., 1936.

AH 8548.110 — Navarro, J.M. de. A survey of research on an early phase of Celtic culture. London, 1936.

AH 4449.36 — Nilsson, M.P. The age of the early Greek tyrants. Belfast, 1936.

AH 8548.100 — O'Rahilly, T.F. The Guidels and their predecessors. London, 1936.

AH 819.36.15 — Peake, Harold. The law and the prophets. New Haven, 1936.

AH 279.36.10 — Perkins, C. Ancient history. N.Y., 1936.

Chronological Listing

1936 - cont.

AH 3020.13.7 — Pfeiffer, R.H. Nuzi and the Hurrians. Washington, 1936.

AH 3020.13.9A — Pfeiffer, R.H. One hundred new selected Nuzi texts. n.p., 1936.

AH 7207.38 — Piaget, Robert. Le sénatus-consulte neronien. Thèse. Lausanne, 1936.

AH 819.36.20 — Poulsen, Frederik. Fra stille aftener. København, 1936.

AH 7845.15 — Rech, H. Mos maiorum; Wesen und Wirkung der Tradition in Rom. Inaug. Diss. Marburg, 1936.

AH 7709.36 — Regibus, L. Problemi d'impero nella storia romana del terzo secolo. Torino, 1936.

Eg 990.5F — Robichon, C. Le temple du scribe royal Amenhotep. pt.1. Le Caire, 1936.

AH 4279.36 — Robinson, D.M. A short history of Greece. N.Y., 1936.

Eg 879.36.5 — Schaedel, Herbert D. Die Listen des grossen Papyrus Harris. Glückstadt, 1936.

AH 3149.12 — Schneider, N. Die Zeitbestimmungen der Wirtschaftsurkunden von Ur. III. Rom, 1936.

AH 7139.34.15 — Schulz, Fritz. Principles of Roman law. Oxford, 1936.

AH 279.36.5 — Sêcher, J. L'Orient et la Grèce. Paris, 1936.

AH 819.36 — Trever, Albert A. History of ancient civilization. N.Y., 1936-39. 2v.

AH 4559.36 — Tritsch, Walther. Olympias, die Mutter Alexanders des Grossen; das Schicksal eines Weltreiches. Frankfurt, 1936.

AH 1819.36 — Ungnad, Arthur. Subartu; Beiträge zur Kulturgeschichte und Völkerkunde Vorderasiens. Berlin, 1936.

AH 4850.15 — Vickery, Kenton F. Food in early Greece. Urbana, 1936.

AH 4854.9 — Vickery, Kenton F. Food in early Greece. Thesis. Urbana? 1936.

AH 7159.36 — Vittinghoff, F. Der Staatsfeind in der römischen Kaiserzeit. Inaug. Diss. Speyer, 1936.

AH 4819.36 — Vlachos, N.P. Hellas and Hellenism. Boston, 1936.

AH 3187.13 — Waschow, H. Babylonische Briefe aus der Kassitenzeit. Inaug. Diss. Berlin, 1936.

AH 7509.36 — Weber, W. Princeps; Studien zur Geschichte des Augustus. Stuttgart, 1936.

Eg 879.36 — Weill, R. Le champ des roseaux et le champ des offrandes dans la religion funéraire. Paris, 1936.

AH 3182.5 — Widengren, Georg. The Accadian and Hebrew Psalms of lamentation as religious documents. Inaug. Diss. Uppsala, 1936.

AH 4499.36 — Willrich, Hugo. Perikles. Göttingen, 1936.

AH 4009.36 — Zmigryder-Konopka, Z. Bibliografia historii starozytnej. pt.1-3. Lwow, 1936-38.

1937

Eg 856.3 — Abubakr, Abdel Monem Jooussef. Untersuchungen über die ägyptischen Kronen. Inaug. Diss. Glückstadt, 1937.

AH 8007.18 — Albertini, Eugène. L'Afrique romaine. Alger, 1937.

AH 7509.37.15 — Allen, B.M. Augustus Caesar. London, 1937.

Eg 879.37 — Badawi, Ahmod M. Der Gott Chnum. Inaug. Diss. Glückstadt, 1937.

AH 7509.37.10 — Baker, G.P. Augustus; the golden age of Rome. N.Y., 1937.

AH 7169.37 — Beretta, A. L'esecuzione contro il debitore nel diritto romano ed il nexum. Udine, 1937.

AH 7509.37.25 — Bergman, J. Augustus. Stockholm, 1937.

AH 5757.15 — Berve, H. Sparta. Leipzig, 1937.

AH 279.37.5 — Bevan, E.R. The world of Greece and Rome. London, 1937.

AH 7201.98.5 — Bisoukides, P.K. O gaïos kai aieisêgeseis autou. Thessalonikê, 1937.

AH 7159.37 — Brasiello, U. La repressione penale in diritto romano. Napoli, 1937.

Eg 299.37.10 — Brodrick, M. Egypt, papers and lectures. London, 1937.

Eg 502.5 — Brunner, Hellmut. Die Texte aus den Gräbern der Herakleopolitenzeit von Suit. Glückstadt, 1937.

AH 7509.37.5A — Buchan, J. Augustus. Boston, 1937.

AH 7509.37.7 — Buchan, J. Augustus. London, 1937.

AH 4559.37 — Bungard, R. L'expedition d'Alexandre et la conquête de l'Asie. Paris, 1937.

AH 3957.25 — Causse, A. Du groupe ethnique à la communaté religieuse. Paris, 1937.

AH 7489.37.5 — Charlesworth, M.P. The virtues of a Roman emperor. London, 1937.

AH 8305.5 — Christescu, V. Istoria militară a Daciei romane. Bucureşti, 1937.

AH 7279.37 — Ciaceri, Emanuele. Le origini di Roma. Milano, 1937.

AH 6136.10 — Collart, Paul. Philippes, ville de Macédoine. Atlas. Paris, 1937. 2v.

AH 3143.9.5 — Contenau, Georges. La civilisation d'Assur et de Babylone. Paris, 1937.

AH 7203.144 — Corpus juris civilis. Digesta. Digest XII...XIII...De condictionibus. Cambridge, Eng., 1937.

AH 3013.937.5 — Cross, Dorothy. Movable property in the Nuzi documents. Diss. Philadelphja, 1937.

Eg 819.37 — Cumont, Franz. L'Egypt des astroloques. Bruxelles, 1937.

AH 3964.19 — Dhorme, E. L'evolution religieuse d'Israël. Thèse. Bruxelles, 1937.

AH 3171.9 — Dhorme, E. La littérature babylonienne et assyrienne. Thèse. Paris, 1937.

AH 4329.37 — Diller, A. Race mixture among the Greeks before Alexander. Urbana, 1937.

AH 4259.37 — Döpel, G. Die attische Flotte im peloponnesischen Kriege. Inaug. Diss. Borna, 1937.

AH 4889.37 — Endenburg, P.J. Koinoonia. Amsterdam, 1937.

AH 279.37 — Finkelstein, M.I. A syllabus for ancient history. N.Y., 1937.

AH 4112.13 — Flacelière, R. Les Aitoliens a Delphes. Thèse. Paris, 1937.

AH 4049.37 — Friedel, H. Untersuchungen zum Tyrannenmord in Gesetzgebung und Volksmeinung der Griechen. Inaug. Diss. Würzburg, 1937.

AH 7201.98 — Gaius. 1937. Bizoukides. Opera. v.1-3, pt.1-2. Thessalonicae, 1937-39. 5v.

AH 7419.37 — Giannelli, Giulio. La repubblica romana. Milano, 1937.

AH 4299.37A — Gomme, Arnold W. Essays in Greek history and literature. Oxford, 1937.

AH 7619.37 — Gross, W.H. Studien zu den Bildnissen Traians. Inaug. Diss. Würzburg? 1937.

AH 3013.937.10 — Iraq. Department of Antiquities. Guide thru the ruins of Babylon and Borsippa. Baghdad, 1937.

AH 7854.2 — Jennison, George. Animals for show and pleasure in ancient Rome. Manchester, 1937.

AH 7299.37.5 — Jones, Arnold H.M. The cities of the eastern Roman provinces. Oxford, 1937.

1937 - cont.

AH 7509.37.20 — Kornemann, E. Gli studi germanici sulla figura e l'opera di Augusto e sulla fondazione dell'Impero romano. Spoleto, 1937.

AH 3910.25 — Krüger, F. Orient und Hellas in den Denkmälern und Inschriften des Königs Antiochos I. von Kommagene. Greifswald, 1937.

Eg 299.37 — Kutter, Carl. Alt Egypten spricht. Basel, 1937.

AH 7469.37 — Lindsay, Jack. Marc Antony; his world and his contemporaries. N.Y., 1937.

AH 7059.37.5 — Lotti Faravelli, A. Origine della censura romana. Como, 1937.

Eg 709.37.3 — Ludwig, E. Cleopatra, Geschichte einer Königin. Amsterdam, 1937.

Eg 709.37.5A — Ludwig, E. Cleopatra, the story of a queen. N.Y., 1937.

AH 4499.37 — Mackenzie, Compton. Pericles. London, 1937.

AH 7489.37A — Macurdy, G.H. Vassal-queens and some contemporary women in Roman Empire. Baltimore, 1937.

AH 3183.10 — Meier, G. Die assyrische Beschwörungssammlung Maglû. Inaug. Diss. Horn, 1937.

Eg 709.37.10 — Peremans, W. Vreemdelingen en Egyptenaren. Louvain, 1937.

AH 6110.20 — Rane, H.O. Untersuchungen zur Geschichte des koituthischen Bundes. Inaug. Diss. Marburg, 1937.

AH 7509.37.30 — Rehrmann, F.A. Kaiser Augustus. Hildesheim, 1937.

AH 7779.37 — Ridley, F.A. Julian the Apostate and the rise of Christianity. London, 1937.

AH 9379.5 — Rosenzweig, I. Ritual and cults of pre-Roman Iguvium. London, 1937.

AH 3005.13 — Scheil, Vincent. Au service de Clio. Chalon-sur-Saone, 1937.

AH 7059.37 — Schmähling, E. Untersuchungen zur Sittenaufsicht der Censoren. Inaug. Diss. Würzburg, 1937.

AH 7279.37.5 — Sécher, J. Rome. Paris, 1937.

AH 939.31.5 — Semple, Ellen C. The geography of the Mediterranean region. N.Y., 1937.

Eg 879.37.5 — Shorter, A.W. The Egyptian gods. London, 1937.

AH 3966.5.26 — Smith, George A. The historical geography of the Holy Land. 26. ed. N.Y., 1937?

AH 1279.37 — Snegirev, I.L. Drevnii Vostok; atlas. Leningrad, 1937.

AH 239.37A — Spaulding, O.L. Pen and sword in Greece and Rome. Princeton, 1937.

AH 3013.937F — Starr, R.F.S. Nuzi; report on the excavations at Yorgan Tepa near Kirkuk, Iraq, conducted by Harvard University. Cambridge, 1937-39. 2v.

AH 4189.37 — Valmin, N.S. Arbete och slaveri i antiken. Stockholm, 1937.

AH 7599.37 — Weber, William. Rom; Herrschertum und Reich in zweiten Jahrhundert. Stuttgart, 1937.

AH 9458.5 — Whatmough, J. "Tusca origo Raetis". n.p., 1937.

AH 8616.10 — Wikén, Erik. Die Kunde der Hellenen von dem Lande und den Völkern der Apenninenhalbinsel bis 300 v. Chr. Lund, 1937.

Eg 971.2F — Winlock, H.E. The temper of Ramesses I at Abydos. N.Y., 1937.

AH 7509.37A — Wright, F.A. Marcus Agrippa, organizer of victory. N.Y., 1937.

1938

AH 7509.38.10 — Accademia dei Lincei, Rome. Augustus. Roma, 1938.

AH 4709.38 — Aymard, A. Les assemblées de la confédération achaienne. Bordeaux, 1938.

AH 4709.38.2 — Aymard, A. Les assemblées de la confédération achaienne. Thèse. Bordeaux, 1938.

AH 4709.38.5 — Aymard, A. Les premiers rapports de Rome et de la confédération achaienne, 198-189 avant J.C. Thèse. Bordeaux, 1938.

Eg 1300.10 — British Museum. Department of Egyptian and Assyrian Antiquities. Catalogue of Egyptian religious papyri in the British Museum. London, 1938.

Eg 849.5F — Brunner-Traut, E. Der Tanz im alten Ägypten nach bildlichen und inschriftlichen Zeugnissen. N.Y., 1938.

AH 3013.938.5 — Busink, T.A. De Toren van Babel. Batavia, 1938.

AH 2589.9 — Cadaux, Cecil J. Ancient Smyrna. Oxford, 1938.

AH 7279.35.8 — Cary, Max. A history of Rome down to the reign of Constantine. London, 1938.

AH 4218.5 — Charles, John F. Statutes of limitations at Athens. Diss. Chicago, 1938.

AH 3143.13 — Chiera, Edward. They wrote on clay. Chicago, 1938.

AH 7409.38 — Colonna di Cesaro, G.A. Il mistero delle origini di Roma. Milano, 1938.

AH 8308.5 — Daicoviciu, Constantin. Le Transylvanie dans l'antiquité. Bucarest, 1938.

AH 3607.13.7 — Debevoise, Neilson Carel. A political history of Parthia. Chicago, 1938.

AH 8907.23 — Ducati, Pericule. Le problème étrusque. Paris, 1938.

AH 7239.38 — Durry, Marcel. Les cohortes pretoriennes. Thèse. Paris, 1938.

AH 4559.38 — Ehrenberg, Victor. Alexander and the Greeks. Oxford, 1938.

Eg 709.38 — Elgood, P.G. The Ptolemies of Egypt. Bristol, 1938.

AH 4049.38 — English, B.R. The problem of freedom in Greece from Homer to Pindar. Toronto, 1938.

AH 7299.38 — Fucho, Harold. Der geistige Widerstand gegen Rom. Berlin, 1938.

AH 4114.19A — Haarhoff, T.J. The stranger at the gate. London, 1938.

AH 7309.38 — Heinze, Richard. Vom Geist des Römertums. Leipzig, 1938.

AH 7509.38.5 — Hönn, Karl. Augustus. 2. Aufl. Wien, 1938.

AH 4559.38.5 — Ivánka, E. Die aristotelische Politik und die Städtegründungen Alexanders des Grossen. Budapest, 1938.

AH 7909.38.2 — Loane, Helen J. Industry and commerce in the city of Rome, 50 B.C.-200 A.D. Baltimore, 1938.

AH 7909.38 — Loane, Helen J. Industry and commerce in the city of Rome, 50 B.C.-200 A.D. Baltimore, 1938.

AH 854.13 — McDermott, William C. The ape in antiquity. Baltimore, 1938.

AH 854.13.5 — McDermott, William C. The ape in antiquity. Thesis. Baltimore, 1938.

Eg 1029.38 — Mayer, Josephine. Never to die; the Egyptians in their own words. N.Y., 1938.

AH 7309.38.5 — Momigliano, Arnaldo. La formazione della moderna storiografia sull'impiro romano. Torino, 1938.

Eg 971.15 — Monneret de Villard, Ugo. Aksum. Roma, 1938.

AH 8202.5 — Moore, Ralph W. The Romans in Britain; a selection of Latin texts. London, 1938.

Eg 848.4.10 — Moreux, T. La science mystérieuse des pharaons. Paris, 1938.

Chronological Listing

1938 - cont.

Eg 299.12.5F   Müller, Hugo. Die formale Entwicklung der Titulatur der ägyptischen Könige. Inaug. Diss. Glückstadt, 1938.

AH 3075.11   Naster, Paul. L'Asie Mineure et l'Assyrie aux VIIIe et VIIe siècles avant Jésus Christ. Louvain, 1938.

Eg 1309.38.5   Nims, C.F. Notes on University of Michigan demotic papyri from Rhila. Chicago, 1938.

Eg 709.38.5F   Otto, Walter. Zur Geschichte des Niedergangs des Ptolemäerreiches. München, 1938.

AH 7489.38   Pariheni, R. L'Italia imperiale da Ottaviano a Teodosio. Milano, 1938.

AH 1279.38   Les peuples de l'Orient méditerranéen. Paris, 1938. 2v.

AH 7499.38   Pietrangeli, Carlo. La famiglia di Augusto. Roma, 1938.

AH 7509.38.15   Popławskii, M. Oktawian August. Lublin, 1938.

AH 7279.38   Rome. Instituto di Studi Romani. Storia di Roma. Bologna, 1938.

AH 7279.38.5   Rome. Instituto di Studi Romani. Storia di Roma. v.1-. Bologna, 1938- 23v.

AH 4039.39   Romero, J.L. El estado y las facciones en la antiquedad. Buenos Aires, 1938.

Eg 851.5   Rosenvasser, A. Las ideas morales en el antiquo Egipto. Santa Fé, 1938.

AH 299.38   Sanford, E.M. The Mediterranean world in ancient times. N.Y., 1938.

AH 7480.2   Sanna, G. Bibliografia generale dell'età romana imperiale. Firenze, 1938.

AH 3957.24   Schofield, J.N. The historical background of the Bible. London, 1938.

AH 7659.39.5   Solari, A. Il rinnovamento dell'impero romano. Milano, 1938-

AH 7539.38   Stuart, Meriwether. Portraiture of Claudius. Thesis. N.Y., 1938.

Eg 459.49F   Studia aegyptiaca. v.1-2. Roma, 1938-49.

AH 7509.38.12   Trapani, Sicily. Augusto. Palermo, 1938.

AH 3013.938   Unger, E. Altindogermanisches Kulturgut in Nordmesopotamien. Leipzig, 1938.

Eg 879.38.5   Visser, Cornelia E. Götter und Kulte im ptolemäischen Alexandrien. Amsterdam, 1938.

Eg 879.38   Visser, Cornelia E. Götter und Kulte im ptolemäischen Alexandrien. Thesis. Amsterdam, 1938.

AH 7479.38   Viviani, Alberto. Caio Guilio Cesare. Firenze, 1938.

Eg 879.38.10   Wainwright, G.A. The sky-religion in Egypt. Cambridge, Eng., 1938.

Eg 909.38   Wallace, S. Le Roy. Census and poll-tax in Ptolemaic and Roman Egypt. Princeton, 1938.

Eg 759.38   Wallace, S.L. Taxation in Egypt from Augustus to Diocletian. Princton, 1938.

AH 7479.38.10   Walter, Gérard, Brutus et la fin de la république. Paris, 1938.

AH 7839.38   Wegner, Ernst. Das Ballspiel der Römer. Würzburg, 1938.

AH 7239.38.5   Westington, M.M. Atrocities in Roman warfare to 133 B.C. Diss. Chicago, 1938.

AH 3664.16   Widengren, G. Hochgottglaube im alten Iran. Uppsala, 1938.

AH 7848.9.10   Wilson, L.M. The clothing of the ancient Romans. Baltimore, 1938.

AH 3175.5   Witzel, Maurus. Auswohl sumerischer Dichtungen. Roma, 1938.

AH 5315.20   Woodhouse, William J. Solon the liberator; a study of the Agrarian problem in Attika in the seventh century. London, 1938.

AH 6110.10   Wüst, F.R. Philipp II. München, 1938.

1939

AH 299.39   Altheim, F. Die Soldatinkaiser. Frankfurt am Main, 1939.

AH 7509.39.5   Augusto. Padova, 1939.

AH 4559.39A   Berzunza, J. A tentative classification of books. n.p., 1939.

Eg 845.10   Bingmann, Lea. Die Frau in ptolemäisch-kaiserlicher Agypter. Bonn, 1939.

AH 4819.39   Boas, G. The Greek tradition. Baltimore, 1939.

AH 4279.22.5   Botsford, George W. Hellenic history. N.Y., 1939.

Eg 1300.11F   British Museum. Department of Egyptian and Assyrian Antiquities. Catalogue of demotic papyri in the British Museum. v.1-2. London, 1939-

Eg 299.39   Brundage, B.C. Notes on some blocks from the excavation of Medinet Habu. Diss. Chicago, 1939.

AH 889.39A   Bullock, C.J. Politics, finance, and consequences. Cambridge, 1939.

AH 2102.10A   Calder, W.M. Anatolian studies presented to William H. Buckler. Manchester, 1939.

AH 7819.39   Carcopino, J. La vie quotidienne à Rome à l'apogée de l'empire. Paris, 1939.

AH 4659.32.20   Cary, Max. A history of the Greek world from 323-146 B.C. N.Y., 1939.

AH 4819.22.6   Casson, S. Ancient Greece. Oxford, 1939.

AH 7539.39   Charlesworth, M.P. Documents illustrating the reigns of Cladius and Nero. Cambridge, Eng., 1939.

AH 4809.39F   Dinsmoor, William B. The Athenian archon list in the light of recent discoveries. N.Y., 1939.

AH 3911.9A   Downey, G. A study of the Comites orientis and the Consulares Syriae. Diss. Princeton, 1939.

AH 4819.39.5   Durant, Will. The life of Greece. N.Y., 1939.

AH 1279.39   Ebeling, Erich. Geschichte des Orients vom Tode Alexanders des Grossen bis zum Einbruch des Islams. Berlin, 1939.

Eg 559.39   Engberg, R.M. The Hyksos reconsidered. Diss. Chicago, 1939.

AH 3016.30   Frankfort, Henri. Sculpture of the third millennium B.C. from Tell Asmar and Khafajah. Chicago, 1939.

AH 7201.100   Gaius. 1937. Bizoukides. Gai institutiones. Lipsiae, 1939.

AH 3400.15F   Gelb, Ignace J. Hittite hieroglyphic monuments. Chicago, 1939.

AH 7899.39   Ghigi, A. Poultry farming as described by the writers of ancient Rome. Milano, 1939.

AH 9758.8   Gutenbrunner, S. Germanische Frühzeit in den Berichten der Antike. Halle, 1939.

AH 7299.39   Haskell, Henry J. The new deal in old Rome; how government in the ancient world tried to deal with modern problems. N.Y., 1939.

AH 7859.6   Hoffsten, R.B. Roman women of rank of the early empire in public life as portrayed by Dio. Diss. Philadelphia, 1939.

AH 3002.92   Jacobsen, T. Cuneiform texts in the National Museum. Copenhagen, 1939.

1939 - cont.

Eg 879.39.5   Jacobsohn, Helmuth. Die dogmatische Stellung des Königs. Glückstadt, 1939.

X Cg   AH 4842.72.10A   Jaeger, Werner Wilhelm. Paideia: the ideals of Greek culture. N.Y., 1939.

AH 4842.72.10A   Jaeger, Werner Wilhelm. Paideia: the ideals of Greek culture. v.2-3. N.Y., 1939-43. 2v.

AH 4842.77   Jeanmaire, H. Couroi et courètes. Thèse. Lille, 1939.

AH 7479.39   Klass, J. Cicero und Caesar. Berlin, 1939.

AH 8458.5   Kovrig, Ilona. Pannonia. Budapest, 1939.

AH 3147.5   Labat, René. Le caractère religieux de la royauté assyrobabylonienne. Thèse. Paris, 1939.

AH 3154.30   Labat, René. Hémérologies et ménologies d'Assur. Thèse. Paris, 1939.

AH 3154.30.5   Labat, René. Hémérologies et ménologies d'Assur. Paris, 1939.

AH 9108.2   Lamboglia, Nino. Liguria romana; studi storico topografici. Roma, 1939-

AH 5757.17   Lüdemann, Hans. Sparta, Lebensordnung und Schicksal. Leipzig, 1939.

Eg 879.39   McGlinchey, J.M. The teaching of Amen-em-Apt. Washington, 1939.

AH 7469.39.15   Manni, Eugenio. Lucio Sergio Catilina. Firenze, 1939.

AH 7469.35.1   Marsh, Frank B. A history of the Roman world from 146 to 30 B.C. N.Y., 1939.

Eg 603.10.5   Mercer, S.A.B. The Tell el-Amarna tablets. Toronto, 1939. 2v.

AH 3129.7.5A   Moore, Ellen W. Neo-Babylonian documents in the University of Michigan collection. Ann Arbor, 1939.

Htn   Eg 1309.39PF*   Papyrus Leopold II. Le papyrus Leopold II. N.Y., 1939.

AH 7489.35.3   Parker, Henry M.D. A history of the Roman world from A.D. 138 to 337. N.Y., 1939.

AH 7239.39   Passerini, A. Le coorti pretorie. Roma, 1939.

Eg 819.39   Petrie, William M.F. The making of Egypt. London, 1939.

AH 7509.39   Piccarolo, A. Augusto e seu século. São Paulo, 1939.

AH 7279.39   Piganiol, André. Histoire de Rome. Paris, 1939.

Eg 909.39   Preaux, C. L'économie royale des Lagides. Bruxelles, 1939.

AH 7479.39.5   Radin, Max. Marcus Brutus. N.Y., 1939.

AH 7709.39   Regibus, L. La monarchia militare di Gallieno. Recco, 1939.

AH 3160.19   Schneider, Nikolaus. Die Götternamen von Ur III. Roma, 1939.

AH 3400.10   Schwartz, Benjamin. The Hittites; a list of references in the New York Public Library. N.Y., 1939.

AH 7279.35.10.6   Scullard, H.H. A history of the Roman world from 753 to 146 B.C. N.Y., 1939.

Eg 1069.39   Seele, K.C. The tomb of Čanefer at Thebes (no.158). Chicago, 1939.

AH 7469.39.10   Sheldon, E.L. Publius Cornelius Dolabella. N.Y., 1939.

AH 7099.39   Sherwin-White, A.N. The Roman citizenship. Oxford, 1939.

AH 279.39.10   Smith, C.E. A short history of the ancient world. N.Y., 1939.

AH 5157.20   Stergiopoulos, K.D. He archaia aitōlia. En Athēnais, 1939.

AH 7089.39A   Stevenson, G.H. Roman provincial administration. Oxford, 1939.

AH 7489.39   Strank, J.A. Vom Herrscherideal in der Spätantike. Stuttgart, 1939.

AH 7469.39   Syme, Ronald. The Roman revolution. Oxford, 1939.

AH 299.39.5   Teggart, F.J. Rome and China. Berkeley, 1939.

AH 819.39   Unger, Eckhard. Welt und Mensch im alten Orient. v.4. Berlin, 1939.

AH 3017.55   Van Buren, Elizabeth D. The fauna of ancient Mesopotamia as represented in art. Roma, 1939.

AH 3059.7.10   Van Ingen, W. Figurines from Seleucia on the Tigris. Ann Arbor, 1939.

AH 9682.4   Vázquez Seijas, M. Lugo bajo el imperio romano. Lugo, 1939.

AH 7469.39.20   Villoresi, Mario. Lucullo. Firenze, 1939.

AH 3707.25   Weill, R. La Phenicie et l'Asie occidentale. Paris, 1939.

AH 7659.39   Werner, H. Der Untergang Roms. Stuttgart, 1939.

AH 163.10   Wolff, H.J. Written and unwritten marriages in Hellenistic and postclassical Roman law. Haverford, 1939.

AH 7559.39   Zancan, P. La crisi del principato nell'anno. Padova, 1939.

1940

AH 7239.40   Adcock, F.E. The Roman art of war under the republic. Cambridge, 1940.

Eg 819.40   Akademiia nauk SSSR. Ocherki po istorii tekhniki drevnei Egipta. Moskva, 1940.

AH 7469.40   Andreotti, Roberto. Cajo Mario. Gubbio, 1940.

AH 2060.5   Armen, H.K. Tigranes the Great. Detroit, 1940.

AH 7469.29.10   Bloch, Gustave. La République romaine de 133 avant J.C. à la mort de César. v.1-2. 2.-3. ed. Paris, 1940-43.

AH 7819.41.2   Carcopino, J. Daily life in ancient Rome. New Haven, 1940.

AH 7619.40   Carrea d'Oliveira, E. Roma imperiale ai tempi di Traiano. Milano, 1940.

AH 3013.940   Christian, V. Altertumskunde des Zweistromlandes von der Vorzeit bis zum Ende der Achamenidenherrschaft. v.1; pt.2. Leipzig, 1940.

AH 7449.40   Ciaceri, Emanuele. Scipione Africano e l'idea imperiale di Roma. Napoli, 1940.

AH 4559.40   Cummings, L.V. Alexander the Great. Boston, 1940.

AH 7299.40   Curotto, Ernest. Antichità classica. Torino, 1940.

AH 4499.40   Delcourt, Marie. Périclès. Paris, 1940.

AH 3014.21F   Delougaz, Pinhas. The temple oval at Khafājah. Chicago, 1940.

AH 8513.12   DeWitt, N.J. Urbanization and the franchise in Roman Gaul. Lancaster, Pa., 1940.

AH 7889.33.2   Frank, Tenney. An economic survey of ancient Rome. General index. Baltimore, 1940.

AH 3014.23F   Frankfort, Henri. The Gimilsin temple and the palace of the rulers at Tell Asmar. Chicago, 1940.

Eg 602.14   Gardiner, Alan H. Ramesside administrative documents. London, 1940.

AH 4559.40.5   Gregor, Joseph. Alexander der Grosse. München, 1940.

AH 4521.18   Hatzfeld, Jean. Alcibiade, étude sur l'histoire d'Athènes à la fin du Ve siècle. Paris, 1940.

Eg 609.40F   Hermann, Alfred. Die Stelen der thebanischen Felsgräber. Glüchstadt, 1940.

AH 4039.40A   Jones, A.H.M. The Greek city from Alexander to Justinian. Oxford, 1940.

Chronological Listing

1940 - cont.

AH 4889.40 — Michell, Humfrey. The economics of ancient Greece. Cambridge, 1940.

AH 7799.40 — Németh, Gyula. Attila és hunjai. Budapest, 1940.

AH 7779.40 — Nicolaas, T.W.J. Praetextatus. Proefschrift. Nijmegen, 1940.

AH 7419.40 — Pais, Ettore. Des origines à l'achievement de la conquête. Paris, 1940.

AH 8907.27 — Pfister, Kurt. Die Etrusker. München, 1940.

AH 4279.40A — Prentice, William K. The ancient Greeks. London, 1940.

AH 5312.5F — Pritchett, William K. The chronology of Hellenistic Athens. Cambridge, Mass., 1940.

AH 4844.6 — Robert, Louis. Les gladiateurs dans l'Orient grec. Paris, 1940.

AH 7159.40 — Robinson, L. Freedom of speech in the Roman republic. Thesis. Baltimore, 1940.

AH 3017.35 — Rome (City). Pontificio Instituto Biblico. The cylinder seals of the Pontifical Institute. Roma, 1940.

AH 8073.16 — Schmidt, W. L'empire carthaginois. Paris, 1940.

AH 7539.40A — Scramuzza, V.M. The emperor Claudius. Cambridge, 1940.

Eg 609.40.5 — Seele, Keith C. The coregency of Ramses II with Seti I and the date of the great hypostyle hall at Karnak. Chicago, 1940.

AH 3149.9 — Smith, S. Alalakh and chronology. London, 1940.

AH 7489.40 — Solari, Arturo. L'impero romano. Genova, 1940.

AH 3357.7.5 — Thrige, Johann P. Res Cyrenensium. Verbania, 1940.

AH 4609.40 — Walbank, F.W. Philip V of Macedon. Cambridge, Eng., 1940.

AH 3707.25.5 — Weill, R. Phoenicia and western Asia to the Macedonian conquest. London, 1940.

1941

AH 279.41 — Adademiia nauk SSSR. Institut istorii. Istoriia drevnego mira. Izd. 2. Moskva, 1941.

AH 7279.41 — Altheim, Franz. Italien und Rom. Leipzig, 1941-44. 2v.

AH 3022.27 — Ankara. Universite. Sümeroloji arastirmalari, 1940-1941. Istanbul, 1941.

AH 8534.5 — Benedict, Coleman H. A history of Narbo. Thesis. Princeton, 1941.

AH 8647.22.5 — Bérard, Jean. Bibliographie topographique des principales cités grecque de l'Italie. Paris, 1941.

AH 7569.41 — Bersanetti, G.M. Vespasiano. Roma, 1941.

AH 7489.41 — Birt, Theodor. Das römische Weltreich. Berlin, 1941.

AH 3045.10 — Bohtz, C. Helmut. In den Ruinen von Warka. Leipzig, 1941.

Eg 1309.41F — Botti, Giuseppe. Testi demotici. Firenze, 1941.

AH 4559.41 — Brelaer, B. Alexanders Bund mit Paros. Leipzig, 1941.

AH 939.28.5 — Browne, Lewis. The graphic Bible, from Genesis to Revelation in animated maps and charts. N.Y., 1941.

NEDL AH 7299.41 — Calestoni, V. Origini della razza italiana. Milano, 1941.

AH 7819.41 — Carcopino, J. Daily life in ancient Rome. New Haven, 1941.

AH 8965.5 — Chilver, G.E.F. Cisalpine Gaul. Oxford, 1941.

EgP 39.41 — Dubois-Richard, P. Essai sur les gouvernements de l'Egypte. Le Caire, 1941.

Eg 39.41 — Dubois-Richard, Paul. Essai sur les gouvernements de l'Egypte. Le Caire, 1941.

AH 4539.36.2 — Glotz, Gustave. La Grèce au IVe siècle; la lutte pour l'hégémonie, 404-336. Paris, 1941.

AH 7449.41 — Grazioli, Francesco. Scipione l'Africano. Torino, 1941.

AH 4039.41 — The Greek political experience. Princeton, 1941.

AH 3966.29 — Halbwachs, M. La topographie légendaire des Evangiles en Terre Sainte. Paris, 1941.

AH 3017.80 — Hilzheimer, Max. Animal remains from Tell Asmar. Chicago, 1941.

AH 7489.33.10 — Homo, Léon P. Le haut-empire. Paris, 1941.

AH 4499.41 — Jouguet, Pierre. L'Athènes de Périclès et les destinées de la Grèce. Le Caire, 1941.

AH 7819.41.5 — Klingner, Friedrich. Vom Geistes Leben im Rom des ausgehenden Alterthums. Halle an der Saale, 1941.

AH 7279.42 — Kornemann, Ernst. Römische Geschichte. Stuttgart, 1941-42. 2v.

AH 4819.41.5 — Mewaldt, J. Hellenische Weltanschauung. Wien, 1941.

Eg 559.41 — Montet, Pierre. Le drame d'Avaris; essai sur la pénétration des Sémites en Égypte. Paris, 1941.

AH 3022.11 — Pallis, Svend Aage. Chronology of the Shuk-ad culture. Kobenhavn, 1941.

AH 7469.41 — Passerini, Alfredo. Caio Mario. Roma, 1941.

AH 4229.41 — Ralph, J.D. Ephesus in Athenian litigation. Thesis. Chicago, 1941.

AH 2147.7 — Ramsay, W.M. The social basis of Roman power in Asia Minor. Aberdeen, 1941.

AH 5910.10 — Roebuck, Carl A. A history of Messenia from 369 to 146 B.C. Thesis. Chicago, 1941.

AH 9225.5 — Rome. Istituto di studi romani. Sezione emiliana. Italia romana: Emilia romana. Firenze, 1941.

AH 4659.41A — Rostovtsev, Mikhail Ivanovich. The social and economic history of the Hellenistic world. Oxford, Eng., 1941. 3v.

Eg 299.41 — Savë-Soderbergh, T. Ägypten und Nubien. Lund, 1941.

AH 1279.41 — Struve, Vasilii V. Istoriia drevnego Vostoka. Leningrad, 1941.

AH 279.41.15 — Thiess, Frank. Das Reich der Dämonen. Berlin, 1941.

AH 279.41.10 — Tovar, Antonio. En el primer giro. Madrid, 1941.

AH 819.41A — Turner, R.C. The great cultural traditions. 1. ed. N.Y., 1941. 2v.

Eg 1309.41.5PF — The Wilbour papyrus. London, 1941.

Eg 1309.41.5F — The Wilbour papyrus. v.2-4. London, 1941-52. 3v.

1942

AH 4049.42A — Agard, W.R. What democracy meant to the Greeks. Chapel Hill, 1942.

AH 3964.20 — Albright, William F. Archaeology and the religion of Israel. Baltimore, 1942.

AH 7819.42.10 — Atheim, F. Rom und der Hellenismus. Amsterdam, 1942.

Eg 939.42 — Ball, J. Egypt in the classical geographers. Cairo, 1942.

AH 7449.42 — Bonarelli, G. La battaglia del Metauro. Ancona, 1942.

AH 939.28.10 — Browne, Lewis. The graphic Bible. N.Y., 1942.

NEDL AH 7299.42 — Canavesi, Manlio. La politica estera di Roma antica. Milano, 1942. 2v.

AH 7819.41.3 — Carcopino, J. La vida catidiana en Roma en el apogeo del imperio. Buenos Aires, 1942.

AH 5315.35 — Day, John. An economic history of Athens under Roman domination. N.Y., 1942.

AH 3013.942F — Delougaz, Pinhas. Pre-Sargonia temples in the Diyala region. Chicago, 1942.

1942 - cont.

Eg 1009.42 — Drioton, Etienne. Le théâtre egyptien. Le Caire, 1942.

AH 7279.42.10 — Ferrabino, Aldo. Nuova storia di Roma. Roma, 1942- 2v.

AH 7479.21.7 — Gelzer, Matthias. Cäsar, der Politiker und Staatsmann. 4. Aufl. München, 1942.

AH 3757.14 — Gibellino Krasceninnicowa, Maria. Gli sciti. Roma, 1942.

Eg 819.42A — Glanville, S.R.K. The legacy of Egypt. Oxford, 1942.

AH 4819.42A — Glover, Terrot R. The challenge of the Greek. Cambridge, Eng., 1942.

AH 4559.42 — Grabowsky, Adolf. Dialoge um Alexander. Zurich, 1942.

Eg 879.42.10 — Grdseloff, Bernhard. Les débuts du culte de Rechef en Égypte. Le Caire, 1942.

AH 4819.42.10 — Grønbech, Vilhelm. Hellas; kultur og religion. v.1-5. København, 1942-45. 3v.

AH 7759.42A — Holsapple, L.B. Constantine the Great. N.Y., 1942.

AH 4819.42.5 — Hommages à la Grèce. Lausanne, 1942.

AH 7709.42A — Howe, L.L. The pretorian prefect from Commodus to Diocletian (A.D. 180-305). Chicago, 1942.

AH 8549.142 — Lambrechts, P. Contributions à l'étude des divinités celtiques. Brügge, 1942.

Eg 879.42 — Mercer, S.A.B. Horus, royal god of Egypt. Grafton, 1942.

AH 809.42 — Meyer, Frank H. The crux of chronology; an essay to establish the life-time of Jesus Christ and...date of Easter. Boston, 1942.

AH 7819.42.5 — Moore, R.W. The Roman commonwealth. London, 1942.

Eg 9.25.5A — New York. Public Library. Ancient Egypt, 1925-1941. Supplement. N.Y., 1942.

AH 889.42 — Palumbo, P. Fausto. L'organizzazione del lavoro nel mondo antico. Firenze, 1942.

AH 7899.42 — Papàsogli, G. L'agricoltura degli etruschi e dei Romani. Roma, 1942.

AH 3013.942 — Perkins, Ann L. The comparative stratigraphy of prehistoric Mesopotamia. Chicago, 1942.

AH 4115.2 — Pritchett, William Kendrick. The five Attic tribes after Kleisthenes. Thesis. Photoreproduction. Baltimore, 1942.

AH 4279.42 — Sanctis, G. de. Storia dei greci dalle origini alla fine del secolo V. 3. ed. Firenze, 1942. 2v.

AH 7519.42 — Smith, Charles E. Tiberius and the Roman Empire. Baton Rouge, 1942.

Eg 299.42 — Steindorff, G. When Egypt ruled the East. Chicago, 1942.

Eg 509.42F — Stock, Hanns. Studien zur Geschichte und Archäologie. Glüchstadt, 1942.

AH 279.39.5 — Taeger, Fritz. Das Altertum. 3. Aufl. v.2. Stuttgart, 1942.

AH 7819.42 — White, George W. Roman history, life and literature. London, 1942.

1943

AH 279.43.5 — Altheim, Franz. Die Krise der alten Welt im 3. Jahrhundert n. zw. und ihre Ursachen. v.1,3. Berlin, 1943- 2v.

AH 4039.43 — Balogh, Elemér. Political refugees in ancient Greece from the period of the tyrants to Alexander the Great. Johannesburg, 1943.

AH 7279.21.4.5A — Boak, Arthur E.R. A history of Rome to 565 A.D. 3. ed. N.Y., 1943.

AH 5207.10 — Callmer, C. Studien zur Geschichte Arkadiens. Lund, 1943.

AH 819.42 — Childe, Vere Gordon. What happened in history. Harmondsworth, 1943.

AH 7109.43 — Clerici, Luigi. Economici e finanza dei romani. Bologna, 1943-

AH 8689.5F — Colini, Antonio. Stadium Domitiani. Roma, 1943.

AH 8308.5.1 — Daicoviciu, Constantin. Siebenbürgen im Altertum. Bukarest, 1943.

AH 3016.35F — Frankfort, Henri. More sculpture from the Diyala region. Chicago, 1943.

AH 3928.45 — Goossens, Godefroy. Hiérapolis de Syrie. Louvain, 1943.

AH 279.43 — Hjartarson, A. Mannkynssaga. Reykjavik, 1943.

AH 7509.38.7 — Hönn, Karl. Augustus und seine Zeit. 3. Aufl. Wien, 1943.

AH 3013.943.5 — Iraq. Department of Antiquities. Babylon. Baghdad, 1943.

AH 4819.43.5 — Kranz, Walther. Die Kultur der Griechen. Leipzig, 1943.

AH 4049.43 — Levitt, Bella. Supreme political power in Greek literature of the fourth century B.C. Thesis. Philadelphia, 1943.

AH 2060.10 — Manandian, I. Tigran Vtoroi i Rim. Erevan, 1943.

AH 5315.40A — Marsh, T.B. Modern problems in the ancient world. Austin, 1943.

AH 7278.54.32.5 — Mommsen, T. Storia di Roma antica. Torino, 1943. 3v.

AH 4819.43 — Mondolfo, Rodolfo. Il genio helénico y las caracteres de sus creaciones espirituales. Tucuman, 1943.

AH 5757.11.5 — Ollier, F. Le mirage spartiate. Paris, 1943.

AH 3013.943F — Oppenheim, Max. Tell Halaf. Berlin, 1943. 4v.

AH 7035.99 — Paruta, P. Discorsi politici. Bologna, 1943.

AH 4809.43 — Prakken, D.W. Studies in Greek genealogical chronology. Lancaster, Pa., 1943.

AH 7519.43 — Rogers, R.S. Studies in the reign of Tiberius. Baltimore, 1943.

AH 7099.43 — Sanchez-Albornoz y Menduiña, C. Ruina y extención del municipio. Buenos Aires, 1943.

AH 9660.5 — Schulten, Adolf. Los Cantabras y Astures y su guerra con Roma. Madrid, 1943.

AH 3020.20 — Steele, Francis Rue. Nuzi real estate transactions. Thesis. Philadelphia, 1943.

Eg 279.43F — Steindorff, G. Egypt. N.Y., 1943.

AH 4521.15.5 — Taeger, Fritz. Alkibiades. München, 1943.

AH 8073.18 — Vogt, Josef. Rom und Karthago. Leipzig, 1943.

AH 409.43 — Wiesner, J. Vor- und Frühzeit der Mittelmeerländer. Berlin, 1943. 2v.

1944

AH 3013.944 — Baqir, Taha. Excavations at 'Aqar Quf, 1942-1943, 1943-1944. 1st and 2nd interim report. London, 1944-45.

AH 7419.44 — Becerra Oliva, Guillermo. La republica romana. Cordoba, 1944.

Eg 1099.44F — Brunner, Hellmut. Die Lehre des Cheti. Glückstadt, 1944.

AH 819.44 — Cavazzana, J.C. Historia de la cultura. Lima, 1944.

AH 7519.34.5 — Ciaceri, E. Tiberio, successore di Augusto. 2. ed. Roma, 1944.

AH 7489.44.5 — Columba, G.M. L'impero romano. 3. ed. pt.1. Milano, 1944.

AH 7499.44A — Durant, W. Caesar and Christ. N.Y., 1944.

NEDL AH 7299.44A — Gelzer, Matthias. Vom romanischen Staat. Leipzig, 1944. 2v.

AH 279.35.5 — Glover, T.R. The ancient world. London, 1944.

Eg 1042.944 — Goyon, G. Les inscriptions et graffiti des voyageurs sur la grande pyramide. Le Caire, 1944.

Chronological Listing

1944 - cont.

AH 7819.44 — Grose-Hodge, Hamfrey. Roman panorama. Cambridge, Eng., 1944.

AH 899.44 — Jasny, Naum. The wheats of classical antiquity. Baltimore, 1944.

Eg 709.44 — Jouguet, P. Trois études sur l'hellénisme. Le Caire, 1944.

AH 7819.44.5 — Kahrstedt, Ulrich. Kulturgeschichte der römischen Kaiserzeit. München, 1944.

AH 7659.47.5 — Kaphahn, Fritz. Zwischen Antike und Mittelalter. München, 1944.

AH 3155.28 — Kramer, Samuel N. Sumerian mythology. Philadelphia, 1944.

AH 7509.44 — Laet, S.J. de. Aspects de la vie sociale et économique sous Auguste et Tibère. Bruxelles, 1944.

AH 7809.44 — Odom, R.L. Sunday in Roman paganism, a history of the planetary week and its "day of the sun". Washington, D.C., 1944.

AH 7489.44 — Salmon, E.T. A history of the Roman world from 30 B.C. to A.D. 138. N.Y., 1944.

AH 4499.44 — Sanctis, G. de. Pericle. Milano, 1944.

Eg 819.44 — Scott, N.E. The home life of the ancient Egyptians. N.Y., 1944.

Eg 139.44 — Taubenschlag, R. The law of Greco-Roman Egypt in the light of the papyri 332 B.C.-640 A.D. v.2: supplement. N.Y., 1944. 2v.

Eg 879.44 — Vondier, Jacques. La religion égyptienne. Paris, 1944.

Eg 659.44F — Zeisel, Helene von. Äthiopen und Assyrer in Agypten. Glückstadt, 1944.

1945

AH 7139.45 — Arangio Ruiz, V. Parerga. Napoli, 1945.

AH 7589.45 — Arias, P. Domiziano. Catania, 1945.

AH 7509.45 — Benuzzi, Valerio. La tragedia familiare di Augusto. Milano, 1945.

AH 7449.45 — Blaettler, Pirmin. Studien zur Regulusgeschichte. Sarnen, 1945.

AH 7479.45.18 — Breuil, Roger. Brutus. 7. éd. Paris, 1945.

AH 7549.45 — Cananesi, M. Nerone. Milano, 1945.

AH 7819.41.10 — Carcopino, J. Daily life in ancient Rome. New Haven, 1945.

AH 7109.45 — Déléage, A. La capitation du Bas-Empire. Macon, 1945.

AH 7479.45.10 — Delogu, Giuseppe. Bruto. Lugano, 1945.

AH 7479.45 — Ferrabino, Aldo. Cesare. Torino, 1945.

AH 4559.38.10 — Glotz, Gustone. Alexandre et l'hellenisation du monde antique. 2. éd. Paris, 1945.

AH 4299.45 — Hatzfeld, Jean. La Grèce et son héritage. Paris, 1945.

AH 7759.40.5 — Hönn, Karl. Konstantin der Grosse. Leipzig, 1945.

AH 7169.45 — Hornby, J.A. Questions and answers on Roman law. London, 1945.

AH 4049.45 — Isaac, Jules. Les oligarques. Paris, 1945.

AH 4842.72.15A — Jaeger, Werner Wilhelm. Paideia: the ideals of Greek culture. 2. ed. N.Y., 1945.

AH 7201.21.5 — Levy, Ernst. Pauli sententiae. Ithaca, 1945.

AH 3013.942.12 — Lloyd, Seton. Ruined cities of Iraq. 3. ed. London, 1945.

AH 7039.45 — Lombardi, Gabrio. Lo sviluppo costituzionale di Roma dalle origini alla fine della repubblica. Roma, 1945.

AH 9221.5 — Maretti, N. Ancona. Roma, 1945.

AH 7307.34.30 — Montesquieu, Charles de. Considérations sur les causes de la grandeur des Romains. Paris, 1945.

AH 7699.45 — Murphy, G.J. The reign of the Emperor L. Septimius Severus. Philadelphia, 1945.

AH 7279.40.5 — Paoli, U.E. Vita romana. 4. ed. Firenze, 1945.

AH 7709.45 — Passerini, Alfredo. I Severi da Caracalla ad Alessandro Severo. Roma, 1945.

AH 3152.7 — Praag, A. Droit matrimonial assyro-Babylonien. Amsterdam, 1945.

AH 299.45 — Rosenvasser, Abraham. La poesía amatoria en el antiguo egipto. Buenos Aires, 1945.

AH 4279.38.7 — Secco Ellauri, Oscar. Historia de los griegos. Montevideo, 1945.

AH 8549.145 — Spence, Lewis. The magic arts in Celtic Britain. London, 1945.

AH 279.45 — Tôrres, Flausino. O mundo mediterrânico do séc. XII a.C. ao séc. III d.C. Lisboa, 1945.

AH 3160.16 — Van Buren, Elizabeth. Symbols of the gods in Mesopotamian art. Roma, 1945.

AH 809.45 — Velikovsky, I. Thesis for the reconstruction of ancient history. N.Y., 1945.

AH 7479.45.5 — Vollenweider, H. Caesars Entwicklung bis zum Consulat im Urteil seiner Zeitgenossen. Zürich, 1945.

AH 8207.21 — Winbolt, Samuel E. Britain under the Romans. Harmondsworth, 1945.

AH 3966.28F — Wright, G.E. The Westminster historical atlas to the Bible. Philadelphia, 1945.

1946

AH 4729.46 — Accame, Silvio. Il domino romano in Grecia dalla guerra acaica ad Augusto. Roma, 1946.

AH 4819.46.5 — Baynes, Norman H. The Hellenistic civilization and East Rome. London, 1946.

NEDL AH 7779.30.10 — Bidez, Joseph. Julian der Abtrünnige. 5. Aufl. München, 1946?

AH 7499.46 — Bourne, Frank C. The public works of the Julio-Claudians and Flavians. Thesis. Princeton, 1946.

AH 279.46.5 — Burton-Brown, T. Studies in third millennium history. London, 1946.

AH 279.46.10 — Cavaignac, E. Histoire générale de l'antiquité. Paris, 1946.

Eg 1042.946A — Coffin Texts (Egyptian). Textes des cercueils du Moyen Empire égyptien. Bruxelles, 1946.

AH 7203.43.10 — Corpus juris civilis. Institutiones. Imperatoris Justiniani Institutionum libri IV. 5th ed. Oxford, 1946.

AH 7629.46 — Corradi, Guiseppe. Adriano. Roma, 1946.

AH 4459.46 — Dorjohn, A.P. Political forgiveness in old Athens. Evanston, 1946.

AH 4279.46.5 — Ehrenberg, V. Aspects of the ancient world. N.Y., 1946.

AH 3653.7 — Ehtécham, Mortéza. L'Iran sous les Achéménides. Fribourg, 1946.

AH 3964.17.15F — Eversull, H.K. The temples in Jerusalem. Cincinnati, Ohio, 1946.

AH 279.46 — Finegan, Jack. Light from the ancient past. Princeton, N.J., 1946.

AH 4159.46 — Freeman, Kathleen. The murder of Herodes and other trials from the Athenian law courts. London, 1946.

1946 - cont.

AH 7201.106 — Gaius. 1946. Zuleta. The institutes of Gaius. pt.1-2. Oxford, 1946-53. 2v.

AH 3414.10 — Gueterbock, H.G. Kumarki. Zürich, 1946.

AH 3177.13 — Heidel, Alexander. The Gilgamesh epic and Old Testament parallels. Chicago, 1946.

AH 8073.17 — Hubac, Pierre. Carthage. Paris, 1946.

AH 4049.45.5 — Isaac, Jules. Les oligarques. Paris, 1946.

Eg 1099.46F — Janssen, Jozef. De traditionelle egyptische autobiografie. Leiden, 1946.

Eg 1099.46 — Janssen, Jozef. De traditionelle egyptische autobiografie. v.2. Leiden, 1946.

Eg 879.46 — Jéquier, Gustave. Considérations sur les religions égyptiennes. Neuchâtel, 1946.

AH 6113.8 — Keramopoullos, A.D. Arigia of the Macedonians. Detroit, 1946.

Eg 972.5 — Knudtzon, E.J. Bakchiastexte und andere Papyri. Lund, 1946.

AH 4279.46.10 — Laache, Rolv. Om hellener og barbarer og om Athens herlighet. Oslo, 1946.

AH 4559.46 — Lamb, Harold. Alexander of Macedon, the journey to world's end. 1st ed. Garden City, N.Y., 1946.

AH 5303.20 — Loenen, Dirk. De Atheense democratie. Amsterdam, 1946.

AH 3016.40 — Loseva, I.M. Iskusstvo drevnei Mesopotamii; ocherki. Moskva, 1946.

AH 4819.46 — Marinatos, S.W. Greece and Greek civilization as results of economic expansion. Athens, 1946.

AH 3149.10 — Mercer, Samuel A. Lumero-Babylonian year-formulae. London, 1946.

AH 279.41.5 — Mishuls'a, A.V. Istoriia drevnego mira. Izd. 5. Moskva, 1946.

Eg 829.46 — Montet, Pierre. La vie quotidienne en Égypt au temps des Ramsès (XIII-XII siècles avant J.C.). Paris, 1946.

AH 3149.14 — Parker, Richard A. Babylonian chronology 626 B.C.-A.D. 45. Chicago, 1946.

AH 4139.46 — Périphanakis, C. La théorie grecque du droit et le classicisme actuel. Athènes, 1946.

AH 7639.46 — Regibus, Luca de. Antonino Pio. Rome, 1946.

AH 4279.46 — Robinson, Cyril E. Zito Hellas. London, 1946.

AH 7889.26.15 — Rostovtsev, M.I. Storia economica e sociale dell'Impero romano. Firenze, 1946.

AH 3957.24.3 — Schofield, J.N. The historical background of the Bible. London, 1946.

AH 7139.46 — Schulz, Fritz. History of Roman legal science. Oxford, 1946.

AH 3159.28 — Stamm, J.J. Das Leiden des Unschuldigen in Babylon und Israel. Zürich, 1946.

AH 7259.46 — Thiel, J.H. Studies on the history of Roman sea-power in Republican times. Amsterdam, 1946.

1947

AH 1459.47 — Altheim, Franz. Weltgeschichte Asiens ein griechischen Zeitalter. Halle, 1947-48. 2v.

AH 6082.5 — Axenidès, T.D. He pelasgis Larissa kai he archaia Thessalia. Athénai, 1947.

AH 7279.21.4.6 — Boak, Arthur E.R. A history of Rome to 565 A.D. 3. ed. N.Y., 1947.

AH 3017.45 — Borowski, E. Cylindres et cachets orientaux conservés dans la collection suisses. Ascona, 1947.

AH 4279.47 — Bruwaene, M. Le miracle grec. Bruxelles, 1947.

AH 4559.47.5 — Burn, A.R. Alexander the Great and the Hellenistic Empire. London, 1947.

AH 9379.10 — Cagiano de Azenado, M. Interamna Lirenas vel Sucasina. Roma, 1947.

AH 7819.38.5 — Carcopino, J. La vita quotidiana a Roma. 2. ed. Bari, 1947.

AH 819.40.2 — Couch, H.N. Classical civilization. N.Y., 1947.

AH 8548.120 — Dillon, Myles. The archaism of Irish tradition. London, 1947.

AH 4819.47.15 — Farrington, B. Head and hand in ancient Greece. London, 1947.

AH 279.46.4 — Finegan, Jack. Light from the ancient past. Princeton, 1947.

AH 7519.47 — Franzero, Charles M. The memoirs of Pontius Pilate. London, 1947.

AH 9661.2 — García y Bellido, Antonio. Las España del siglo primero de nustra era. Madrid, 1947.

AH 7651.22 — Gibbon, Edward. Selections from the decline and fall of the Roman Empire. London, 1947.

AH 7819.47.5 — Gonella, Guido. Pace romana e pace cartaginese. Roma, 1947.

AH 5610.12 — Hassell, Ulrich von. Pyrrhus. München, 1947.

AH 7599.47 — Homo, Léon P. Le siècle d'or de l'empire romain. 3. éd. Paris, 1947.

AH 4259.47 — Hyde, Walter W. Ancient Greek mariners. N.Y., 1947.

Eg 759.47 — Jouguet, P. La domination romaine en Égypte aux deux premiers siècles. Alexandrie, 1947.

AH 7659.47 — Kaphahn, Fritz. Zwischen Antike und Mittelalter. München, 1947.

AH 4459.36.2 — Laistner, M.L.W. A history of the Greek world from 479 to 323 B.C. 2. ed. London, 1947.

AH 3005.11 — Lloyd, Seton. Foundations in the dust. London, 1947.

AH 7199.47 — Magdelain, A. Auctoritas principis. Paris, 1947.

AH 7559.47 — Manfri, Guglielmo. La crisi politica dell'anno 68-69 d. C. Bologna, 1947.

AH 7819.47A — Mattingly, Harold. The man in the Roman street. N.Y., 1947.

AH 4299.47.5 — Mazzarino, S. Fra Ceriente e Occidente; ricerche di storia greca arcaica. Firenze, 1947.

AH 8908.16 — Pallottino, Massimo. L'origine degli Etruschi. Roma, 1947.

AH 4819.47.5 — Paoli, Ugo E. Uomini e cose del mondo antico. Firenze, 1947.

AH 6107.55 — Paribeni, Roberto. La Macedonia sino ad Alessandro Magno. Milano, 1947.

AH 3017.40 — Pierpont Morgan Library, New York. Mesopotamian art in cylinder seals of the Pierpont Morgan Library. N.Y., 1947.

AH 4819.47.10 — Pohlenz, Max. Der hellenische Mensch. Göttingen, 1947?

AH 4809.47 — Pritchett, W.K. The calendars of Athens. Cambridge, Mass., 1947.

AH 3957.30 — Ragaz, L. Die Bibel. Zürich, 1947-50. 7v.

Eg 860.5F — Raphael, M. Prehistoric pottery and civilization in Egypt. N.Y., 1947.

AH 7469.47 — Rimscha, Hans von. Die Gracchen. München, 1947.

AH 4559.47A — Robinson, C.A. Alexander the Great. 1st ed. N.Y., 1947.

AH 4659.27.10 — Tarn, William W. Hellenistic civilization. London, 1947.

Chronological Listing

1947 - cont.

AH 8611.5 — Thomsen, Rudi. The Italic regions. København, 1947.

AH 279.47 — Van Sickle, C.E. A political and cultural history of the ancient world from prehistoric times to the dissolution of the Roman Empire in the West. Boston, 1947-

AH 8073.19 — Walter, Gerard. La destruction de Carthage. 264-146. Paris, 1947.

AH 4299.47 — Wason, Margaret O. Class struggles in ancient Greece. London, 1947.

Eg 509.47A — Winlock, H.E. The rise and fall of the middle kingdom in Thebes. N.Y., 1947.

1948

AH 7759.48 — Alfoldi, Andras. The conversion of Constantine and pagan Rome. Oxford, 1948.

AH 7279.48.10 — Altheim, Franz. Römische Geschichte. Berlin, 1948. 2v.

Eg 279.48A — Bell, Harold. Egypt from Alexander the Great to the Arab conquest. Oxford, 1948.

AH 4279.22.8 — Botsford, George W. Hellenic history. 3. ed. N.Y., 1948.

AH 4499.48 — Burn, A.R. Pericles and Athens. London, 1948.

AH 4543.10 — Candidus, Isaums. Vie de Phocion. Paris, 1948.

AH 8107.10 — Carcopino, J. Le Maroc antique. 8. éd. Paris, 1948.

AH 5757.19 — Cavaignac, E. Sparte. 25. éd. Paris, 1948.

AH 819.36.11 — Childe, Vere Gordon. Man makes himself. London, 1948.

AH 819.42.6 — Childe, Vere Gordon. What happened in history. Harmondsworth, 1948.

AH 4299.34.5 — Cohen, R. La grèce et l'hellénisation du monde antique. 3. éd. Paris, 1948.

AH 3413.12.5 — Contenau, Georges. La civilisation des Hittites. Paris, 1948.

AH 7419.48 — Cowell, Frank R. Cicero and the Roman republic. London, 1948.

AH 7419.48.5 — Cowell, Frank R. Cicero and the Roman republic. N.Y., 1948.

AH 8647.17A — Dunabin, T.J. The western Greeks. Oxford, 1948.

AH 5460.5 — Effenterre, H. van. La Crète et le monde grec. Paris, 1948.

AH 1049.48A — Gadd, Cyril John. Ideas of divine rule in the ancient East. London, 1948.

Eg 879.48 — Garnot, J.S.F. La vie religieuse dans l'ancienne Égypte. 1. éd. Paris, 1948.

AH 5357.10 — Guillon, P. La Béotie antique. Paris, 1948.

AH 4114.19.5 — Haarhoff, T.J. The stranger at the gate. Oxford, 1948.

AH 7549.48 — Heinz, Kurt. Das Bild Kaiser Neros bei Seneca. Inaug. Diss. Biel, 1948.

AH 819.35.6 — Howard, E. Die Kultur der Antike. 2. Aufl. Zürich, 1948.

Eg 609.48 — Janssen, J.M.A. Ramses III. Leiden, 1948.

AH 889.48 — Jones, Arnold. Ancient economic history. London, 1948.

AH 279.48.15 — Kahrstedt, Ulrich. Geschichte der griechiesh-römischen Altertums. München, 1948.

Eg 856.4F — Keimer, Ludwig. Remarques sur le tatouage dans l'Égypte ancienne. Caire, 1948.

AH 279.48.10 — Kochethaler, E. Das Reich der Antike. Baden-Baden, 1948.

AH 279.48 — Kornemann, E. Weltgeschichte des Mittelmeer-Raumes von Philipp II. München, 1948-49. 2v.

AH 7619.48 — Lepper, F.A. Trajan's Paethian war. London, 1948.

AH 8549.148 — MacCulloch, John A. The Celtic and Scandinavian religions. London, 1948.

AH 842.35 — Marrow, Henri Irenée. Histoire de l'éducation dans l'antiquité. Paris, 1948.

AH 7039.48 — Meyer, Ernst. Römischer Staat und Staatsgedanke. Zurich, 1948.

AH 3914.7 — Obermann, Julian. Ugaritic mythology. New Haven, 1948.

AH 3012.19 — O'Callaghan, Roger T. Aram Naharaim. Roma, 1948.

AH 3657.31A — Olmstead, A.T.E. History of the Persian empire. Chicago, 1948.

AH 7840.5.4 — Paribeni, Roberto. Le famiglia romana. 4. ed. Bologna, 1948.

AH 3060.3.20 — Parrot, André. Tello. Paris, 1948.

AH 819.48 — Passerini, A. La civiltà de mondo antico. Milano, 1948.

AH 4819.48.5 — Permanence de la Grèce. Paris, 1948.

AH 4819.48 — Rhodokanakès, K.P. Athens and the Greek miracle. London, 1948.

AH 4279.46.2 — Robinson, Cyril E. Hellas. N.Y., 1948.

AH 7489.48 — Schenk von Stauffenberg, A. Das Imperium und die Völkerwanderung. München, 1948.

AH 7279.48 — Stauffer, Ethelbert. Christus und die Caesaren. 2. Aufl. Hamburg, 1948.

AH 7278.54.46 — Straeuli, Hans Heinrich. Theodor Mommsen's Römische Geschichte. Zuerich, 1948.

AH 8503.4 — Stroheker, Karl Friedrich. Der senatorische Adel in spätaniken Gallien. Tübingen, 1948.

AH 279.48.5 — Taeger, Fritz. Grundzüge der alten Geschichte. Oberursel, 1948.

AH 4559.48 — Tarn, William W. Alexander the Great. Cambridge, 1948. 2v.

AH 7799.48 — Thompson, E.A. A history of Attila and the Huns. Oxford, 1948.

AH 3357.8 — Thrige, Johann P. Storia di Cirene. Verbania, 1948.

AH 7449.48 — Valori, F. Scipione l'Africano. Torino, 1948.

AH 7819.48 — Vangenechten, K. Het antieke Rome. Antwerpen, 1948.

Eg 1009.48 — Walle, Baudouin van de. La transmission des textes littéraires égyptiens. Bruxelles, 1948.

Eg 1069.48F — Zandee, J. De hymnen aan Amon van papyrus Leiden I 350. Leiden, 1948.

AH 7449.47 — Zeller, Eberhard. Hannibal. Uberlingen, 1948.

1949

AH 9.49 — Bengtson, Hermann. Einführung in die alte Geschichte. München, 1949.

AH 279.49 — Berve, Helmut. Gestaltende Kräfte der Antike. München, 1949.

AH 7759.49 — Burckhardt, Jacob. The age of Constantine the Great. N.Y., 1949.

AH 3014.30 — Busink, T.A. Die Babylonische Tempeltoren. Leiden, 1949.

AH 7130.2 — Caes, Lucien. Collectio bibliograf.ica operum ad ius romanum pertienetium. v.1-20. Bruxelles, 1949- 13v.

AH 819.49 — Caldwell, W.E. The ancient world. N.Y., 1949.

AH 7409.49 — Cardinali, Giuseppe. Le origini di Roma. Roma, 1949.

AH 939.49 — Cary, Max. The geographic background of Greek and Roman history. Oxford, 1949.

AH 3013.949.5 — Castellino, Giorgio. Corso di lezioni di assiriologia. Roma, 1949.

1949 - cont.

AH 8207.25 — Charlesworth, M.P. The lost province. Cardiff, Wales, 1949.

AH 5757.21 — Chrimes, K.M.T. Ancient Sparta. Manchester, 1949.

AH 3151.10 — Colgecen, M.C. Le code d'Hammourabi. Fribourg, 1949.

AH 3155.18 — Dhorme, E. Les religions de Babylonie et d'Assyrie. 2. ed. Paris, 1949.

AH 4819.05.30 — Dickinson, G.L. The Greek view of life. 22d ed. London, 1949.

AH 3908.5.5 — Dupont-Sommer, Andre. Les Araméens. Paris, 1949.

AH 3017.50 — Falkenstein, Adams. Grammatik der Sprache Gudeas von Lagaš. Roma, 1949-50. 2v.

AH 7279.11.12 — Fowler, W.W. Rome. 2. ed. London, 1949.

AH 4819.49.5 — Friedell, Egon. Kulturgeschichte Griechenlands. München, 1949.

AH 4139.49 — Frisch, Hortvig. Might and right in antiquity. København, 1949.

AH 7779.49 — Gigli, Guido. L'artodossia. Roma, 1949.

AH 862.9 — Gordon, B.L. Medicine throughout antiquity. Philadelphia, 1949.

AH 3921.7 — Haddad, G. Aspects of social life in Antioch in the Hellenistic Roman period. Thesis. Chicago, 1949.

AH 3177.13.5 — Heidel, Alexander. The Gilgamesh epic and Old Testament parallels. 2d ed. Chicago, 1949.

AH 7279.49 — Homo, Léon. Nouvelle histoire romaine. 48. éd. Paris, 1949.

AH 7569.49 — Homo, Léon P. Vespasien. Paris, 1949.

AH 8073.21 — Hours-Miedan, Madeleine. Carthage. 1. éd. Paris, 1949.

AH 4559.49 — Instensky, H.U. Alexander der Grosse am Hellespont. Godesberg, 1949.

Eg 279.48.7 — Iskander, Z. Brief history of ancient Egypt. 2. ed. Cairo, 1949.

Eg 909.49 — Johnson, A.C. Byzantine Egypt: economic studies. Princeton, 1949.

Eg 879.49 — Junker, H. Pyramidenzeit. Einsiedeln, 1949.

AH 4039.40.5 — Krauss, B. Staat und Mensch in Hellas. 2. Aufl. Berlin, 1949.

AH 8510.5 — Lélu, Georges. Vercingétorix et la résistance gauloise. Clamecy, 1949.

AH 7549.49 — Levi, Mario A. Nerone e i suoi tempi. Milano, 1949.

AH 7709.49 — Manni, Eugenio. L'impero di Gallieno. Roma, 1949.

AH 3005.830 — Matouš, Lubor. Bedřich Hrozný; the life and work of a Czech Oriental scholar. Prague, 1949.

AH 1189.49A — Mendelsohn, I. Slavery in the ancient Near East. N.Y., 1949.

AH 3016.55 — Moortgat, Anton. Tammuz. Berlin, 1949.

AH 3807.10 — Moscati, Sabatino. Storia e civiltà dei Semiti. Bari, 1949.

Eg 1069.49 — Murray, Margaret A. Egyptian religious poetry. London, 1949.

Eg 819.49 — Murray, Margaret Alice. The splendour that was Egypt. London, 1949.

AH 8913.12 — Pallottino, Massimo. La civilisation étrusque. Paris, 1949.

AH 3013.949.10 — Parrot, André. Ziggurats et Tour de Babel. Paris, 1949.

AH 3013.949F — Perkins, Ann L. The comparative archaeology of early Mesopotamia. Chicago, 1949.

AH 7279.39.8 — Piganiol, André. Histoire de Rome. 3. éd. Paris, 1949.

AH 7819.49 — Poulsen, F. Römische Kulterbilder. Kobenhagen, 1949.

AH 9707.8 — Randa, A. Der Balkan. 1. Aufl. Graz, 1949.

AH 4039.49 — Ryffel, Heinrich. Metabolē politeiōn. Bern, 1949.

AH 4559.49.5 — Schachermeyer, F. Alexander der Grosse. Graz, 1949.

AH 4819.49.10 — Solle, Miloš. Počátky helénské civilozace. Praha, 1949.

AH 8549.149 — Spence, Lewis. The history and origins of druidism. N.Y., 1949.

AH 8549.149.5 — Spence, Lewis. The history and origins of druidism. N.Y., 1949.

AH 7659.28.5 — Stein, Ernst. Histoire du Bas-Empire. v.1-2. Paris, 1949. 3v.

AH 819.49.5 — Taeger, Fritz. Die Kultur der Antike. Köln, 1949.

AH 7479.49.5 — Taylor, Lily Ross. Party politics in the age of Caesar. Berkeley, 1949.

AH 4819.49A — Thomson, G.D. Studies in ancient Greek society. London, 1949. 2v.

Eg 279.49 — Vercoutter, Jean. L'Egypte ancienne. Paris, 1949.

AH 7759.49.5 — Vogt, J. Constantin der Grosse. München, 1949.

1950

AH 8007.18.5 — Albertini, Eugène. L'Afrique romaine. Alger? 1950.

AH 4259.50 — Alexandiēs, K.A. He Thalassia dynamis eis ten historia tès archaias Hellados. Athēnai, 1950.

Eg 1042.950 — Allen, Thomas G. Occurrences of pyramid texts. Chicago, 1950.

AH 8908.17 — Altheim, F. Der Ursprung der Etrusker. Baden, 1950.

AH 3002.102 — Archives royales de Mari. v.1-9, 11-13, 15. Paris, 1950-9v.

AH 299.50 — Bertoldi, V. Colonizzazioni nell'antico. Napoli, 1950.

AH 2107.9A — Bittel, Kurt. Grundzüge der Vor- und Frühgeschichte Kleinasiens. 2. Aufl. Tübingen, 1950.

Eg 279.05.8 — Breasted, James Henry. A history of Egypt from the earliest times to the Persian conquest. 2. ed. London, 1950.

AH 7759.50 — Burckhardt, Jacob. Die Zeit Constantins des Grossen. Bern, 1950.

AH 8789.5 — Callaway, Joseph S. Sybaris. Baltimore, 1950.

Eg 609.23.6.5 — Capart, Jean. Tout-Ankh-Amon. 2. éd. Bruxelles, 1950.

AH 3407.20 — Cavaignac, E. Les Hittites. Paris, 1950.

AH 3165.10 — Contenau, G. La vie quotidienne à Babylone et en Assyrie. 16. éd. Paris, 1950.

AH 1279.50 — Cornelius, F. Geschichte des alten Orients. Stuttgart, 1950.

AH 819.40.4 — Couch, H.N. Classical civilization. 2. ed. N.Y., 1950-51. 2v.

AH 3013.950PF — Eliot, H.W. Excavations in Mesopotamia and Western Iran. Cambridge, 1950.

Eg 1029.50F — Erichsen, W. Auswahl frühdemotischer Texte. Kopenhagen, 1950.

AH 909.50 — Forbes, R. Metallurgy in antiquity. Leiden, 1950.

AH 4299.50 — Freeman, K. Greek city-states. London, 1950.

AH 4299.50.5 — Freeman, K. Greek city-states. 1. ed. N.Y., 1950.

AH 7201.108 — Gaius. 1950. Reinach. Institutes. Paris, 1950.

AH 7609.50 — Garzetti, A. Nerva. Roma, 1950.

AH 3151.2.3F — Hammurabi, king of Babylonia. Codex Hammurabi. Romae, 1950.

AH 9807.5 — Harmatta, Janos. Studies on the history of Sarmatians. Budapest, 1950.

1950 - cont.

AH 4279.26.5.3	Hatzfeld, Jean. Histoire de la Grèce ancienne. Paris, 1950.
AH 1409.14.2	Hogarth, D.G. The ancient East. 2. ed. London, 1950.
AH 7089.50	Jashemski, W.M. The origins and history of the pro-consular. Chicago, 1950.
AH 3179.12	Jordan, F. In den Lagen des Tammuz. München, 1950.
AH 819.50	Jouguet, Pierre. Les premières civilisations. Paris, 1950.
AH 3195.12	Kramer, Samuel Noah. Schooldays. Philadelphia, 1950?
AH 2147.8	Magie, D. Roman rule in Asia Minor. Princeton, 1950. 2v.
AH 842.35.2	Marrow, Henri Irenée. Histoire de l'éducation dans l'antiquité. 2. éd. Paris, 1950.
AH 5313.12	Massachusetts Institute of Technology. Department of English and History. Athens in the fifth century B.C. Cambridge, Mass., 1950.
AH 4819.50A	Miami, Florida. University. Lectures of evaluations of the enduring qualities of Greek civilization. Miami, Fla., 1950.
AH 4215.9	Oliver, James H. The Athenian expounders of sacred and ancestral law. Baltimore, 1950.
AH 7629.50	Orgeval, B. L'empereur Hadrien. Paris, 1950.
AH 9640.2	Parisi, G. Tyndaris. Messina, 1950.
AH 7114.37	Pflaum, Hans Georg. Essai sur les procurateurs equestres sous le Haut-Empire romain. Paris, 1950.
AH 4339.23	Pohlenz, M. Gestalten aus Hellas. München, 1950.
AH 7819.49.5	Poulsen, F. Glimpses of Roman culture. Leiden, 1950.
AH 4219.5	Pringsheim, F. The Greek law of sale. Weimar, 1950.
AH 1029.50F	Pritchard, James B. Ancient Near Eastern texts relating to the Old Testament. Princeton, 1950.
AH 4559.31.12	Radet, Georges. Alexandre le Grand. 7. éd. Paris, 1950.
AH 1407.50	Scharff, A. Ägypten und Vorderasien im Altertum. München, 1950.
Eg 1079.50	Schott, Siegfried. Altägyptische Liebeslieder. Zürich, 1950.
AH 7279.50	Starr, Chester G. The emergence of Rome as ruler of the Western world. Ithaca, 1950.
AH 279.50A	Swain, J.W. The ancient world. N.Y., 1950. 2v.
AH 279.39.7	Taeger, Fritz. Das Altertum. 4. Aufl. Stuttgart, 1950.
AH 7489.50	Toynbee, Arnold J. The cold war in the Roman Empire. Claremont, Calif., 1950.
AH 7279.50.5	Waddy, Lawrence. Pax Romana and world peace. N.Y., 1950?
AH 4819.50.10	Wifsbrand, Albert. Den grekiska kulturhistoriens faser. Stockholm, 1950.
AH 7039.50	Wirszubski, C. Libertas as a political idea. Cambridge, 1950.
AH 4199.50	Wolf, E. Griechisches Rechtsdenken. v.1-4. Frankfurt am Main, 1950-52. 5v.

1951

AH 4539.51	Accame, Silvio. Ricerche intorno alla guerra corinzia. Napoli, 1951.
AH 7799.51.5	Altheim, F. Attila und die Hunne. Baden-Baden, 1951.
AH 7279.51	Altheim, Franz. Römische Geschichte. Frankfurt, 1951-53. 2v.
Eg 990.10F	Beckerath, J. von. Tanis und Theben. Glückstadt, 1951.
AH 4279.31.2	Berve, Helmut. Griechische Geschichte. 2. Aufl. Freiburg, 1951- 2v.
AH 7409.51	Bömer, Franz. Rom und Troia. Baden Baden, 1951.
AH 7339.51	Broughton, Thomas R.S. The magistrates of the Roman Republic. N.Y., 1951-52. 2v.
AH 4279.00.30	Bury, John Bagnell. A history of Greece to the death of Alexander the Great. 3. ed. London, 1951.
AH 7419.51	Calderini, A. L'espansione romana in occidente durante la repubblica. Milano, 1951.
AH 3142.17	Cardascia, Guillaume. Les archives des Murašû, une famille d'hommes d'affaires babyloniens à l'époque perse (455-403 avant J.C.). Paris, 1951.
AH 4659.32.15	Cary, Max. A history of the Greek world from 323-146 B.C. 2. ed. London, 1951.
AH 7489.51A	Charlesworth, M.P. The Roman Empire. London, 1951.
AH 5303.14	Cloché, Paul. La démocratie athénienne. Paris, 1951.
Eg 819.51.5	Davis, Simon. Race-relations in ancient Egypt. London, 1951.
AH 7659.51	Demougeot, E. De l'unité à la division de l'Empire romain. Paris, 1951.
AH 8608.10.2	Devoto, Giacomo. Gli antichi italici. 2. ed. Firenze, 1951.
AH 3011.8	Dhorme, E.P. Recueil Edouard Dhorme. Paris, 1951.
AH 4819.51	Dodds, Eric Robertson. The Greeks and the irrational. Berkeley, Calif., 1951.
Eg 659.51	Elgood, P.G. Later dynasties of Egypt. Oxford, 1951.
AH 7649.51	Farquharson, A.S.L. Marcus Aurelius. Oxford, 1951.
AH 4109.51	Finley, M.I. Studies in land and credit in ancient Athens. New Brunswick, N.J., 1951.
AH 1819.51	Frankfort, Henri. The birth of civilization in the Near East. Bloomington, 1951.
AH 1819.51.1	Frankfort, Henri. The birth of civilization in the Near East. London, 1951.
AH 819.36.27	Friedell, Egon. Kulturgeschichte Ägyptens und des alten Orients. 3. Aufl. München, 1951.
AH 7899.51	García-Badell, Gabriel. La agricultura en la Roma. Madrid, 1951.
AH 4559.51	Gitti, Alberto. Alessandro Magno all'oasi di Siwah. Bari, 1951.
AH 7449.51	Gómez, N.P. Guerras de Anibal preparatorias del sitio de Saguntum. Valencia, 1951.
AH 39.51	Hammond, M. City-state and world state in Greek and Roman political theory until Augustus. Cambridge, Mass., 1951.
AH 9613.10	Hardouin di Belmonte, F. Trinacria olimpica. Palermo, 1951.
AH 7489.51.5	Hartke, W. Römische Kinderkaiser. Berlin, 1951.
AH 4521.18.2	Hatzfeld, Jean. Alcibiade. 2. éd. Paris, 1951.
AH 4498.97.5	Hill, G. Sources for Greek history between the Persian and Pelopormesian wars. Oxford, 1951.
AH 3404.5	Hittites. Laws, statutes, etc. The Hittite laws. London, 1951.
AH 7799.51	Homeyer, H. Attila der Hunnenkönig von seinen Zeitgenossen dargestellt. Berlin, 1951.
AH 4559.51.5	Homo, Léon Pol. Alexandre le Grand. Paris, 1951.
Eg 759.51	Johnson, A.C. Egypt and the Roman Empire. Ann Arbor, 1951.
AH 4279.51	Kitto, H.D.F. The Greeks. Harmondsworth, 1951.
AH 3191.9F	Labat, René. Traite akkadien de diagnostics et pronostics mestiaux. Paris, 1951. 2v.

1951 - cont.

Eg 609.51	Lange, Kurt. König Echnaton und die Amarnazeit. München, 1951.
Eg 863.5	Laurent-Täckholm, Vini. Faraos blomster. Stockholm, 1951.
AH 7509.51	Levi, Mario A. Il tempo di Augusto. Firenze, 1951.
AH 7169.51A	Levy, Ernst. West Roman vulgar law. Phildelphia, 1951.
AH 7659.31.5	Lot, Ferdinand. La fin du monde antique et le début du moyen âge. Paris, 1951.
AHP 29.51	McDermott, William C. Readings in the history of the Ancient World. N.Y., 1951.
AH 4609.51	Manni, E. Demetrio Paliorcete. Roma, 1951.
AH 7799.51.10	Mazzarino, S. Aspetti sociali del quarto secolo. Roma, 1951.
AH 819.51	National Geographic Magazine. Everyday life in ancient times. Washington, 1951.
AH 7279.40.7	Paoli, U.E. Vita romana. 6. ed. Firenze, 1951.
AH 8073.20	Picard, Colette. Carthage. Paris, 1951.
AH 819.51.5	Pirenne, J. Civilisations antiques. Paris, 1951.
AH 7709.51	Pollione, T. Le vite di Valeriano e di Gallieno. Palermo, 1951.
AH 4039.51.5	Reesor, M.E. The political theory of the old and middle Stoa. N.Y., 1951.
AH 459.51	Regibus, Luca de. La repubblica romana e gli ultimi re di Macedonia. Genova, 1951.
AH 4819.48.3	Rhodakanakès, K.P. Athens and the Greek miracle. 1. American ed. Boston, 1951.
AH 279.51	Robinson, C.A. Ancient history from prehistoric times to the death of Justinian. N.Y., 1951.
AH 2014.8	Ryckmans, G. Les religiones arabes préislamiques. 2. éd. Louvain, 1951.
AH 2003.5	Ryckmans, Jacques. L'institution monarchique en Arabie méridionale avant l'Islam. Louvain, 1951.
AH 299.38.5	Sanford, E.M. The Mediterranean world in ancient times. N.Y., 1951.
AH 4039.51.10	Sartori, F. La crisi del 411 a.C. nell'Anthenaeon politeia di Aristotele. Padova, 1951.
AH 7139.51	Schulz, Fritz. Classical Roman law. Oxford, 1951.
AH 9440.5	Scrinari, V. Tergeste. Roma, 1951.
AH 7279.35.10.5	Scullard, H.H. A history of the Roman world from 753 to 146 B.C. 2. ed. London, 1951.
AH 7459.51	Scullard, Howard Hayes. Roman politics, 220-150 B.C. Oxford, 1951.
Eg 139.51F	Seidl, Erwin. Einführung in die ägyptische Rechtsgeschichte. 2. Aufl. Glückstadt, 1951.
AH 4039.51	Sinclair, Thomas Alan. A history of Greek political thought. London, 1951.
AH 9423.5	Stucchi, S. Forum Iulii (Cividale del Friuli). Roma, 1951.
AH 4049.57	Taeger, Fritz. Charisma. Stuttgart, 1951-60. 2v.
AH 4659.38.5	Tarn, William W. The Greeks in Bactria and India. 2. ed. Cambridge, Eng., 1951.
AH 5303.10	Warncke, F. Die demokratische Staatsidee in der Verfassung von Athens. Bonn, 1951.
AH 4279.24.5	Wilcken, U. Griechische Geschichte im Rahmen der Altertumsgeschichte. 7. Aufl. München, 1951.
Eg 819.51	Wilson, J. The burden of Egypt. Chicago, 1951.
AH 4809.51	Winniczuh, L. Kalendarz starozy tnych Greków i Rzymian. Warszawa, 1951.
AH 7139.51.5	Wolff, Hans J. Roman law. Oklahoma, 1951.
AH 2061.3.5	Yeghisheh, Elisha Vardapet. The epic of St. Vardan the brave. N.Y., 1951.

1952

AH 3960.23	Abel, F.M. Histoire de la Palestine. Paris, 1952. 2v.
AH 7769.52	Alföldi, Andras. A conflict of ideas in the late Roman Empire. Oxford, 1952.
AH 279.43.10	Altheim, Franz. Niedergang der alten Welt. Frankfurt am Main, 1952. 2v.
AH 930.37	Atlas of ancient and classic geography. London, 1952.
AH 7207.40	Barbieri, Guido. L'albo senatorio da Settimino Severo a Carino. Roma, 1952.
AH 7239.52.5	Barini, C. Triumphalia. Torino, 1952.
Eg 990.16	Bataille, André. Les memnonia. Le Caire, 1952.
AH 3155.23	Battero, Jean. La religion babylonienne. 1. ed. Paris, 1952.
Eg 879.52	Bonnet, H. Reallexikon der ägyptischen Religionsgeschichte. Berlin, 1952.
AH 1819.52	Braidwood, Robert J. The Near East and the foundations for civilization. Eugene, 1952.
AH 7469.52	Brion, M. La révolte des gladiateurs. Paris, 1952.
AH 4818.98.10	Burckhardt, J. Griechische Kulturgeschichte. Stuttgart, 1952. 3v.
Eg 879.52.10	Cerný, J. Ancient Egyptian religion. London, 1952.
AH 3359.10	Chamoux, J. Cyrène sour la monarchie des Battiades. Paris, 1952.
AH 3659.12	Champdor, A. Cyrus. Paris, 1952.
AH 1819.34.5	Childe, Vere G. New light on the most ancient East. 4. ed. London, 1952.
AH 5390.17	Cloché, Paul. Thèbes de Béotie. Namur, 1952?
AH 7202.30F	Codex Theodosianus. The Theodosian code and novels and the Sermondian constitutions. Princeton, N.J., 1952.
AH 3155.20	Contenau, G. Le déluge babylonier. Paris, 1952.
AH 7809.52	Degrassi, A. I fasti consolari dell'Impero Romano. Roma, 1952.
AH 4819.52.15	Deichgräber, Karl. Der listensinnede Trug des Gottes. Göttingen, 1952.
AH 7239.52A	De Rebus Billicis. A Roman reformer and inventor. Oxford, 1952.
AH 4819.52.10	Diano, Carlo. Forma ed evento. 1. ed. Veneia, 1952.
AH 4939.52A	Diller, A. The tradition of the minor Greek geographers. Lancaster, Pa., 1952.
AH 4819.52	Freeman, K. God, man and state. London, 1952.
Eg 870.1	Garnot, J. St. F. Religions égyptiennes antiques; bibliographie analytique. Paris, 1952.
AH 5463.15	Glotz, Gustave. La civilisation égéenne. Paris, 1952.
AH 7539.52	Gordon, A.E. Quintus Veranius. Berkeley, 1952.
AH 279.52.5	Grant, Michael. Ancient history. London, 1952.
Eg 879.52.15F	Greven, L. Der Ka in Theologie und Königs Kult. Glückstadt, 1952.
AH 3414.10.5	Gueterbock, H.G. The song of Ullikummi. New Haven, 1952.
AH 3407.30	Gurney, O.R. The Hittites. London, 1952.
AH 3017.60	Hague. Kabinet van Munten. Catalogue sommaire des cylindres orientaux au Cabinet. La Haye, 1952.
AH 4039.52	Hignett, C. A history of the Athenian constitution to the end of the fifth century B.C. Oxford, 1952.

Chronological Listing

1952 - cont.

AH 819.52 — Hoare, F.R. Eight decisive books of antiquity. London, 1952.

AH 7279.52.5 — Hocquard, G. Guide romain antique. Paris 1952.

AH 7819.52.10 — Homo, Léon. Scenes de la vie romaine sous la République. Paris, 1952.

Eg 919.52 — Hughes, George. Saite demotic land leases. Chicago, 1952.

AH 4819.52.5 — Huxley, Michael. The root of Europe. London, 1952.

AH 7139.32.2 — Jolowicz, Herbert Felix. Historical introduction to the study of Roman law. 2. ed. Cambridge, Eng., 1952.

AH 3156.6.5 — King, Leonard W. Babylonian magic and sorcery. Lieden, 1952.

Eg 1159.52.5F — Klasens, Adolf. A magical statue base. Leiden, 1952.

AH 339.52 — Kornemann, E. Grosse Frauen des Altertums. 4. Aufl. Wiesbaden, 1952.

AH 4819.52.20 — Kranz, W. Griechentum. Baden-Baden, 1952.

Eg 1159.52 — Leake, C.D. The old Egyptian medical papyri. Lawrence, 1952.

AH 9090.3 — Le Gall, Joël. Le Tibre, fleuve de Rome, dans l'antiquité. Thèse. Paris, 1952.

AH 4439.52 — Lindemann, H. Generale machen Politik. 1. Aufl. Bonn, 1952.

AH 4009.52 — Manni, Eugenio. Introduzione allo studio della staria greca e romana. Palermo, 1952.

AH 7519.52 — Marañón, G. Tiberius. München, 1952.

AH 7818.64.18 — Marquardt, Joachim. Handbuch der römischen Alterthümer. 3. Aufl. v.1-3. Graz, 1952-53. 5v.

AH 5763.5A — Michell, Humfrey. Sparta. Cambridge, Eng., 1952.

AH 3002.135A — Nederlands Institut voor het Nabije Oosten, Leyden. Studia ad tabulas cuneiformas collectas ab De Liagre Böhl pertinentia. v.1, pt.1-2; 3. Leiden, 1952- 3v.

AH 889.52 — Palumbo, P. Fausto. L'unità economica del mondo antico. Roma, 1952.

AH 7279.52 — Pareti, L. Storia di Roma e del mondo romana. Torino, 1952- 6v.

AH 279.52.10 — Passerini, Alfredo. Questioni di storia antica. Milano, 1952.

AH 7842.20 — Pavan, M. La crisi della scuola nel IV secolo d.C. Bari, 1952.

Eg 1042.952 — Pyramid Texts. The pyramid texts in translation and commentary. 1. ed. N.Y., 1952. 4v.

Eg 879.52.5 — Roeder, G. Volksglaube in Pharaonenreich. Stuttgart, 1952.

Eg 1109.52PF — Sanehet. The Ashmolean ostracon of Sinuhe. London, 1952.

AH 3149.13 — Schmidtke, Friedrich. Der Aufbau der babylonischen Chronologie. Münster, 1952.

AH 3936.10 — Starcky, J. Palmyre. Paris, 1952.

AH 4659.27.15 — Tarn, William W. Hellenistic civilization. 3. ed. London, 1952.

AH 863.10 — Tennodrac, M.J. L'antiquité érotique. Paris, 1952.

AH 7819.52 — Ussani, Vincenzo. Guida allo studio della civiltà romana antica. Napoli, 1952-54. 2v.

AH 279.52A — Velikovsky, I. Ages in chaos. 1. ed. Garden City, 1952.

AH 7709.52.5 — Vitucci, G. L'imperatore Probo. Roma, 1952.

AH 7509.52 — Wagenvoot, Hendrik. Augustus. Amsterdam, 1952.

AH 7479.52 — Walter, G. Caesar. N.Y., 1952.

AH 9610.18 — Westlake, H.D. Timoleon and his relations with tyrants. Manchester, Eng., 1952.

Eg 279.52A — White, Jon M. Ancient Egypt. London, 1952.

AH 909.52F — Wilsdorf, H. Berglente und Hüttenminner im Altertum. Berlin, 1952.

1953

AH 4279.53 — Accame, Silvio. Problemi di storia greca. Rome, 1953.

AH 3022.15 — Aldrey Pereira, M.L. Pensamiento idiomatico šumero-akkadico. Series 1. v.1, pt.1-2. Madrid, 1953. 2v.

AH 1279.53 — Altheim, Franz. Alexander und Asien. Tübingen, 1953.

AH 7009.53 — Arias, P.E. Bibliografia e fonti. Bologna, 1953?

AH 8608.12 — Arias, Paolo E. La civiltà gallica in Italia. L'impero di Severo Alessandro. Bologna, 1953.

Eg 879.53.2 — Bell, H.I. Cults and creeds in Graeco-Roman Egypt. N.Y., 1953.

AH 9.49.2A — Bengtson, Hermann. Einführung in die alte Geschichte. 2. Aufl. München, 1953.

AH 7039.53 — Béranger, J. Recherches sur l'aspect ideologique su principat. Basel, 1953.

AH 7139.53.10F — Berger, Adolf. Encyclopedia dictionary of Roman law. Philadelphia, 1953.

AH 8205.4 — Birley, Eric. Roman Britain and the Roman army. Kendal, 1953.

AH 3011.15 — Böhl, F.M.T. Opera minora. Groningen, 1953.

AH 8507.10.2A — Brogan, O. Roman Gaul. Cambridge, Mass., 1953.

AH 8507.10 — Brogan, O. Roman Gaul. London, 1953.

AH 8211.5 — Burn, A.R. Agricola and Roman Britain. London, 1953.

AH 7206.10 — Byzantine Empire. Laws, statutes, etc. Basilicorum libri LX. Groningen, 1953- 13v.

AH 8015.5 — Camps-Fabrer, Henriette. L'olivier et l'huile dans l'Afrique romaine. Alger, 1953.

AH 7649.53 — Carrata Thomes, Franco. Il regno di Marco Aurelio. Torino, 1953.

AH 4559.53.5 — Cloché, Paul. Alexandre le Grand et les essais de fusion entre l'occident gréco-macédonien. Neuchatel, 1953.

AH 819.24.3 — De Burgh, W.G. The legacy of the ancient work. v.1-2. London, 1953.

AH 833.7 — Deonna, W. Le symbolisme de l'acrobatie antique. Berchem, 1953.

AH 7799.53 — Dévignes, G. Ici, le monde changea de maitre. Paris, 1953.

AH 3190.5.1 — Dijk, Johannes J.A. van. La sagesse suméro-accadienne. Leiden, 1953.

AH 3190.5 — Dijk, Johannes J.A. van. La sagesse suméro-accadienne. Proefschrift. Leiden, 1953.

AH 8513.13 — Duval, Paul Marie. La vie quotidienne en Gaule pendant la paix romaine. Paris, 1953.

AH 3173.10 — Eveling, Erich. Literarische Keilschrifttexte aus Assur. Berlin, 1953.

AH 3181.13 — Falkenstein, Adam. Sumerische und akkadische Hymnen und Gebete. Zurich, 1953.

AH 7239.53 — Focni, G. Il reclatamento delle legioni da Augusto a Diocleziano. 1. ed. Milano, 1953.

AH 7769.53 — Fortina, M. L'imperatore Graziano. Torino, 1953.

AH 7759.53 — Franchi de' Cavalieri, P. Constantiniana. Roma, 1953.

AH 4039.53 — Fuks, Alexander. The ancestral constitution. London, 1953.

1953 - cont.

AH 7651.25 — Gibbon, Edward. Decline and fall of the Roman Empire. London, 1953.

AH 9792.8 — Gitti, Alberto. Ricerche sui rapporti tra i vandali e l'impero romano. Bari, 1953.

AH 1279.53.5 — Gordon, Cyrus H. Introduction to Old Testament times. Ventnor, N.J., 1953.

AH 7449.53 — Grimal, P. Le siècle des Scipions. Paris, 1953.

AH 8511.10 — Grossi, Georges. Deux siècles décisifs! Vaison-la-Romaine, 1953.

AH 3151.1.3F — Hammurabi, king of Babylonia. Codex Hammurabi. Romae, 1953.

AH 4819.53 — Hiebel, F. Die Botschaft von Hellas. Bern, 1953.

AH 3155.21 — Hoake, S.H. Babylonian and Assyrian religion. London, 1953.

AH 7509.38.8 — Hönn, Karl. Augustus und seine Zeit. 4. Aufl. Wien, 1953.

AH 5316.5 — Holmberg, Erik J. Aten och Delfi. Lund, 1953.

AH 7279.25.11 — Homo, Léon. L'Italie primitive et les débuts de l'impérialisme romain. Paris, 1953.

Eg 279.53 — Kienitz, F.K. Die politische Geschichte Ägyptens. Berlin, 1953.

AH 2321.2 — Kinal, F. Géographie et l'histoire des pays d'Arzava. Ankara, 1953.

AH 7200.19.2 — Leges XII Tabularum. Das Zwölftafelgesetz. 2. Aufl. München, 1953.

AH 4279.53.5 — Loenen, Dirk. Stasis. Amsterdam, 1953.

AH 8900.5 — Lopes Pegna, M. Saggio di bibliografia etrusca. Firenze, 1953.

Eg 132.53 — Malinine, Michel. Choix de textes juridiques en hiératique et en démotique. pt.1. Paris, 1953-

AH 7469.35.2 — Marsh, Frank B. A history of the Roman world from 146 to 30 B.C. 2. ed. London, 1953.

AH 7279.53.5 — Mashkin, Nikolai A. Römische Geschichte. Berlin, 1953.

AH 4299.53.5 — Murray, Gilbert. Hellenism and the modern world. London, 1953.

Eg 276.66.10 — Murtadi ibn al-Kafif. L'Égypte de Murtadi. Facsimile. Paris, 1953.

AH 4299.53 — Myres, John L. Geographical history in Greek lands. Oxford, 1953.

AH 9722.9A — Nevskaia, V.P. Bizantii v klassicheskuiu i ellinisticheskuiu epokhi. Moskva, 1953.

Eg 279.53.5 — Otto, Eberhard. Agypten. Stuttgart, 1953.

AH 7203.146 — Palazzini Fivetti, Luigi. Storia della ricerca delle interpolazioninel Corpus iuris Giustinianeo. Milano, 1953.

AH 5390.19 — Reimer, P.J. Zeven tegen Thebe. Gouda, 1953.

AH 4559.53 — Robinson, C.A. The history of Alexander the Great. v.2. Providence, 1953.

AH 4239.53 — Sarikakës, Theodoros Christou. The hoplite general in Athens. Athens, 1953.

AH 8647.20 — Sartori, F. Problemi di storia costituzionale italiata. Roma, 1953.

AH 3009.55 — Schmökel, H. Ur, Assur und Babylon. Stuttgart, 1953.

AH 4842.80 — Seel, Otto. Die plotonische Akademie. Stuttgart, 1953.

Eg 879.53.5 — Spiegel, J. Das Werden der Altägyptischen Hochkultur. Heidelberg, 1953.

AH 7279.50.3 — Starr, Chester G. The emergence of Rome as ruler of the Western world. 2. ed. Ithaca, 1953.

AH 7039.53.5 — Tibiletti, G. Principe e magistrati repubblicani. Roma, 1953.

AH 7509.53 — Treves, Piero. Il mito di Alessandro e la Roma d'Augusto. Milano, 1953.

Eg 709.53 — Volkmann, Hans. Kleopatra. München, 1953.

AH 7489.46.1 — Walbank, Frank William. The decline of the Roman Empire in the West. N.Y., 1953.

AH 7139.53F — Wenger, L. Die Quellen des römischen Rechts. Wien, 1953.

AH 8532.5.5 — Wuilleumier, P. Lyon. Paris, 1953.

1954

Eg 752.5 — Acta Alexandrinorum. The acts of the pagan martyrs. Oxford, 1954.

AH 3661.10 — Altheim, Franz. Ein asiatischer Staat. Wiesbaden, 1954.

AH 4309.54.5 — Arias, Paolo E. Storiografia e fonti della storia greca. Bologna, 1954.

Eg 879.54.5 — Bertram, Johannes. Die Urweisheit der alten Ägypter. Hamburg, 1954.

AH 8907.25 — Bloch, Raymond. Les Étrusques. Paris, 1954.

AH 5757.25 — Boer, W. den. Laconian studies. Amsterdam, 1954.

AH 4819.54.5 — Bonnard, André. Civilization grecque. Lausanne, 1954. 3v.

Eg 1039.54 — Book of the Dead. Livre des morts des anciens Égyptiens. Paris, 1954.

Eg 279.54 — Brion, M. Histoire de l'Egypte. Paris, 1954.

AH 7139.54 — Bruck, E.F. Uber römisches Recht im Rahmen der Kulturgeschichte. Berlin, 1954.

Eg 1309.54 — Caminos, R.A. Late-Egyptian miscellanies. London, 1954.

AH 8014.5 — Charles-Picard, Gilbert. Les religions de l'Afrique antique. Paris, 1954.

AH 3165.10.6 — Contenau, G. Everyday life. London, 1954.

AH 3165.10.5 — Contenau, G. Everyday life in Babylon and Assyria. N.Y., 1954.

AH 862.10 — Crecope, John. Medicine, magic and mythology. London, 1954.

AH 7809.54 — Degrassi, A. Fasti capitolini. 1. ed. Torino, 1954.

Eg 974.5 — Fakhry, A. The bent pyramid of Dahshûr. Le Caire, 1954.

AH 4819.54 — Finley, Moses I. The world of Odysseus. N.Y., 1954.

AH 5610.20 — Franke, Peter R. Alt-Epirus und des Königtum der Molosser. Kallmünz, 1954.

AH 3160.20 — Frankena, R. Takultu. Leiden, 1954.

AH 1819.51.2 — Frankfort, Henri. The birth of civilization in the Near East. Bloomington, 1954.

AH 7549.54 — Franzero, Charles M. The life and times of Nero. London, 1954.

AH 5138.14 — Fraser, P.M. The Rhodian Peraen and island. London, 1954.

AH 7469.54.10 — Garzetti, Albino. Verso il principato. Milano, 1954.

AH 279.54 — Giannelli, G. Le grandi correnti della storia antica. Milano, 1954.

AH 4279.54 — Giannelli, Giulio. Trattato di storia greca. 3. ed. Roma, 1954.

AH 7649.54 — Goerlitz, W. Marc Aurel, Kaiser und Philosoph. Stuttgart, 1954.

AH 4309.54A — Gomme, Arnold W. The attitude to poetry and history. Berkeley, 1954.

Eg 1159.54 — Grapow, H. Grundriss der Medizin der alten Ägypter. v.1-9. Berlin, 1954- 10v.

Eg 39.54F — Helck, W. Untersuchungen zu den Beamtentiteln des ägyptischen alten Reichs. Glückstadt, 1954.

Chronological Listing

1954 - cont.

AH 4499.54	Homo, León. Périclès. Paris, 1954.
AH 6107.15	Kalléris, J.N. Les anciens Macédoniens. Athènes, 1954-
AH 7279.54.5	Levi, Mario Attilio. Lineamenti di storia romana. 2. ed. Milano, 1954.
AH 7469.54.5	Mainzer, Ferdinand. Clodia. Braunschweig, 1954.
AH 7309.54	Mazzarino, Santo. Storia romana e storiografia moderna. Napoli, 1954.
AH 4819.54.10	Mireaux, Émile. La vie quotidienne du temps d'Homère. Paris, 1954.
AH 7278.54.30.15	Mommsen, T. Römische Geschichte. Wien, 1954.
Htn AH 7278.54*	Mommsen, T. Römische Geschichte. v.1-3, 5. Leipzig, 1954. 4v.
Eg 879.54A	Morenz, S. Der Gatt auf der Blume. Ascona, 1954.
AH 4299.53.7	Murray, Gilbert. Hellenism and the modern world. Boston, 1954.
AH 4842.85.5	Nilsson, M.P. Den grekiska skolan. Stockholm, 1954.
AH 4403.54	Oliva, Pavel. Raná řecká tyrannis. Praha, 1954.
AH 4719.54	Oost, S.I. Roman policy in Epirus and Acarmania in the age of the Roman conquest of Greece. Dallas, 1954.
AH 7479.54	Ooteghem, Jules van. Pompée le grand, bâtisseur d'empire. Namur, 1954.
AH 7279.39.9	Piganiol, André. Histoire de Rome. 4. éd. Paris, 1954.
AH 3175.10	Poemetti mitologici babilonesi e assiri. Firenze, 1954.
AH 1819.54	Pritchard, James B. The ancient Near East in pictures. Princeton, N.J., 1954.
AH 4819.33.16	Quennell, M.C. Everday things in ancient Greece. 2. ed. London, 1954.
AH 3757.12	Remennikov, A.M. Bor'ba plenen severnogo prichernomor'ia s rimon v III veke n.e. Moskva, 1954.
AH 3413.15	Riemschneider, M. Die Welt der Hethiter. Stuttgart, 1954.
AH 2257.5	Robert, L. La Carie. v.2. Paris, 1954.
Eg 879.54.10	Sainte Fare Garnot, Jean. L'hommage aux dieux sous l'ancien empire egyptien. 1. éd. Paris, 1954.
AH 3913.5	Selms, A. van. Marriage and family life in Ugaritic literature. London, 1954.
AH 7693.5	Severus, Lucius Septimius. Apokrimata; decisions of Septimius Severus on legal matters. N.Y., 1954.
AH 3145.5	Soden, W.F. von. Herrscher im alten Orient. Berlin, 1954.
AH 2120.3	Stark, Freya. Ionia; a quest. 1. ed. London, 1954.
AH 7819.54	Starr, C.G. Civilization and the Caesars. Ithaca, 1954.
AH 29.50	Struve, V.V. Geschichte der alten Welt; Christomathie. Berlin, 1954-57. 3v.
AH 4039.54	Ténékidès, G. La notion juridique d'independance et la tradition hellenique. Athenes, 1954.
AH 7259.54	Thiel, J.H. A history of Roman sea-power before the second Pernic War. Amsterdam, 1954.
AH 4819.49.2	Thomson, G.D. Studies in ancient Greek society. London, 1954. 2v.
AH 4200.15	Tsopanakis, A. La Rhètre de Lycurgue. Tyrtée, 1954.
AH 819.54	Turone, Mario. La prima umanità. Milano, 1954.
Eg 269.54	Vercoutter, Jean. Essai sur les relations entre Egyptiens et Préhellènes. Paris, 1954.
Eg 847.8	Waangstedt, Stev von. Ausgewählte demotische Ostraka. Inaug. Diss. Uppsala, 1954.
AH 8011.6	Warmington, B.H. The North African province from Diocletian to the Vandal conquest. Cambridge, Eng., 1954.
AH 9563.5	Zervos, C. La civilisation de la Sardaigne. Paris, 1954.

1955

Eg 1059.55	Aafjes, B. De blinde harpenaar. Amsterdam, 1955.
AH 8007.18.7	Albertini, Eugène. L'Afrique romaine. Alger, 1955.
AH 8007.18.10	Albertini, Eugène. L'Afrique romaine. Alger, 1955.
AH 2231.5.5	Balkan, Kemal. Kanis Karumunun kronoloji problemleri Hakkinda Musahedeler. Ankara, 1955.
AH 4539.55	Barbieri, Guido. Conone. Roma, 1955.
Eg 409.55	Baumgärtel, E. The cultures of prehistoric Egypt. London, 1955.
AH 3143.14	Beek, Martinus A. Aan Babylons stromen. Amsterdam, 1955.
AH 7169.55	Betti, Emilio. La struttura dell'obbligazione romana e il problema della sua genesi. Milano, 1955.
Eg 1129.55	Bissing, Friedrich W. von. Altägyptische Lebensweisheit. Zürich, 1955.
AH 8913.5	Bloch, Raymond. L'art et la civilisation étrusques. Paris, 1955.
AH 7799.55	Boak, A.E.R. Manpower shortage and the fall of the Roman Empire in the West. Ann Arbor, 1955.
Eg 1039.54.5	Book of the Dead. Ägyptisches Totenbuch. München, 1955.
AH 7819.55	Bruwaene, M. van den. La société romaine. Bruxelles, 1955.
Eg 759.55	Burr, Viktor. Tiberius Iulius Alexander. Bonn, 1955.
AH 7419.55	Clerici, André. La république romaine. 1. éd. Paris, 1955.
AH 8907.26.5	Cles-Reden, S. The buried people. N.Y., 1955.
AH 8907.26	Cles-Reden, S. Les Etrusques. Paris, 1955.
AH 6110.21	Cloché, Paul. Un fondateur d'empire. Saint Etienne, 1955.
Eg 819.55.10	Cottrell, L. Life under the pharaohs. London, 1955.
AH 8011.7	Courtois, C. Les Vandales et l'Afrique. Paris, 1955.
Eg 879.55.5	Cramer, Maria. Das altägyptische Lebenszeichen. 3. Aufl. Wiesbaden, 1955.
AH 7059.55	Crook, J.A. Consilium principis. Cambridge, Eng., 1955.
Eg 879.55	Donadoni, S. Le religione dell'Egitto antico. Milano, 1955.
AH 7479.55A	Duggan, A.L. Julius Caesar. 1. ed. N.Y., 1955.
AH 4819.55.5	Fernandez-Galiano, M. El concepto del hombre en la antigua Grecia. Madrid, 1955.
AH 819.55	Forbes, Robert James. Studies in ancient technology. Leiden, 1955-64. 9v.
AH 7579.55	Fortina, M. L'imperatore Tito. Torino, 1955.
Eg 1309.55F	Gardiner, A.H. The Ramesseum papyri. Oxford, 1955.
AH 7509.55	Grimal, Pierre. Le siècle d'Auguste. 1. éd. Paris, 1955.
AH 3053.5	Iahdun-Lim, king of Mari. L'inscription de fondation de Iahdun-Lim, roi de Mari. Paris, 1955.
AH 7759.55	Instinsky, H.U. Beschafsstuhl und Kaiserthron. 1. Aufl. München, 1955.
Eg 459.55	Julien, Max. Le tombeau du Pharaon, en l'an 2800 av. J.-C. Paris, 1955.
AH 7659.55	Katz, Solomon. The decline of Rome and the rise of mediaeval Europe. Ithaca, N.Y., 1955.
Eg 819.55.5	Kees, Hermann. Das alte Ägypten. Berlin, 1955.
AH 8007.19	Kruglikova, I.T. Dakiia v epokhu rinskoi okkupatsii. Moskva, 1955.
AH 3154.40	Laessoee, Joergen. Studies on the Assyrian ritual and series lûtrimki. København, 1955.
AH 49.55	Larsen, Jakob A.O. Representative government in Greek and Roman history. Berkeley, 1955.

1955 - cont.

AH 279.55	Levi, Mario Attilio. La lotta politica nel mondo antico. 1. ed. Milano, 1955.
AH 7819.51	Lewis, N. Roman civilization. N.Y., 1955-67. 2v.
AH 3407.33	Marek, Kurt W. Enge Schlucht und schwarzer Berg. Hamburg, 1955.
Eg 1039.55	Mayassis, S. Le livre des morts de l'Égypte ancienne est un livre d'initiation. Athènes, 1955.
AH 3173.15	Mendelsohn, I. Religions of the ancient Near East. N.Y., 1955.
AH 139.56	Monier, Raymond. Histoire des institutions et des faits sociaux des origines à l'aube du Moyen Âge. Paris, 1955.
AH 9722.8	Nevskaia, V.P. Byzanz in der klassischen und hellenistischen Epoche. Leipzig, 1955.
AH 4842.85	Nilsson, M.P. Die hellenistische Schule. München, 1955.
AH 8907.11.5	Pallottino, Massimo. The Etruscans. 3d Italian ed. Harmondsworth, 1955.
AH 3921.10F	Petet, Paul. Libanius et la vie municipale à Antioche au IV. siècle après J.-C. Paris, 1955.
AH 3193.7	Pinches, T.G. Late Babylonian astronomical and related texts. Providence, 1955.
AH 4819.55	Pohlenz, Max. Griechische Freiheit. Heidelberg, 1955.
AH 7479.55.5	Portalupi, Felicita. Bruto e i neo-atticisti. Torino, 1955.
AH 1029.50.2	Pritchard, James B. Ancient Near Eastern texts relating to the Old Testament. 2. ed. Princeton, 1955.
Eg 1159.55	Riad, Naguib. La médecine au temps des pharaons. Paris, 1955.
AH 7819.55.5	Robertis, Francesco Maria de. Il fenomeno associativo nel mondo romano. Napoli, 1955.
AH 4839.27	Robinson, Rachel Louisa. Sources for the history of Greek athletics. Cincinnati, 1955.
AH 4659.41.5	Rostovtsev, Mikhail Ivanovich. Gesellschafts- und Wirtschaftsgeschichte der hellenistischen Welt. Darmstadt, 1955-56. 3v.
AH 4559.55	Savill, A.F. Alexander the Great and his time. Rockliff, 1955.
AH 4410.5	Schachermeyr, Fritz. Die ältesten kulturen Griechenlands. Stuttgart, 1955.
AH 8411.5	Schober, Arnold. Die Römerzeit in Österreich und in den augreuzenden Gebieten von Slowenien. 2. Aufl. Wien, 1955.
AH 9113.5	Sereni, Emilio. Communità rurali nell'Italia antica. Roma, 1955.
AH 969.55	Sestios, Maarkos. Journal. Paris, 1955.
Eg 609.55F	The shrines of Tut-Ankh-Amen. N.Y., 1955.
AH 7469.55	Smith, R.E. The failure of the Roman Republic. Cambridge, Eng., 1955.
AH 3963.162	Stockholm. Statens Historiska Museum. Från bibelns land. 2. uppl. Stockholm, 1955.
Eg 139.44.2	Taubenschlag, R. The law of Greco-Roman Egypt in the light of the papyri. 2. ed. Warszawa, 1955.
AH 8913.10	Vacano, Otto Wilhelm von. Die Etrusker. Stuttgart, 1955.
AH 7279.32.5	Vogt, Joseph. Römische Geschichte. 3. Aufl. Freiburg, 1955.
AH 7549.55	Walter, Gérard. Néron. Paris, 1955.
AH 5409.7	Well, Edouard. Korinthiaka. Paris, 1955.
AH 189.55A	Westermann, W.L. The slave systems of Greek and Roman antiquity. Philadelphia, 1955.
AH 5463.10	Willetts, Ronald Frederick. Aristocratic society in ancient Crete. London, 1955.
Eg 829.55	Winlock, H.E. Models of daily life in ancient Egypt. Cambridge, Mass., 1955.
Eg 819.55	Wolf, Walther. Die Welt der Ägypter. Stuttgart, 1955.
AH 3013.955	Woolley, Charles L. Excavations at Ur. London, 1955.
AH 8208.10	Young, Douglas. Romanisation in Scotland. Tayport, 1955?

1956

AH 3002.110	Aberhuber, Karl. Innsbrucher Keilschrifttexte. Innsbruck, 1956.
AH 846.30	Ambrosio, Raffaele d'. Alle origini della città. Napoli, 1956.
AH 4043.5.5	Andrews, Anthony. The Greek tyrants. London, 1956.
AH 29.56	Barker, Ernest. From Alexander to Constantine. Oxford, 1956.
Eg 1309.56F	Barns, J.W. Five Ramesseum papyri. Oxford, 1956.
AH 9313.5	Bertolé Viale, Giovanni. La civiltà latina in Abruzzo. Pescara, 1956.
AH 7779.30.5	Bidez, Joseph. Kaiser Julian. Hamburg, 1956.
Eg 1159.56	Bitschai, J. A history of urology in Egypt. Cambridge, 1956.
Eg 879.56.5	Bleeker, C.J. Die Geburt eines Gottes. Leiden, 1956.
AH 8913.5.5	Bloch, Raymond. Le mystère étrusque. Paris, 1956.
Eg 879.56.10	Bonwick, James. Egyptian belief and modern thought. Indian Hills, 1956.
AH 4279.22.9	Botsford, George W. Hellenic history. 4. ed. N.Y., 1956.
AH 3002.26.10	British Museum. Department of Egyptian and Assyrian Antiquities. Chronicles of Chaldaean kings. London, 1956.
Eg 1109.56F	Caminos, R.A. Literary fragments in the hieratic script. Oxford, 1956.
AH 8057.5	Charles-Picard, Gilbert. Le monde de Carthage. Paris, 1956.
AH 7509.56.5	Christ, Karl. Drusus und Germanicus. Paderborn, 1956.
AH 7449.55	De Beer, Gavin Rylands. Alps and elephants. 1. American ed. N.Y., 1956.
AH 3507.10	Diakonov, I. Istoriia Midii. Moskva, 1956.
AH 7819.56	Dill, Samuel. Roman society. N.Y., 1956.
AH 3195.10F	Era. Das Era-Epos. Würzburg, 1956.
AH 4409.20	Forsdyke, E.J. Greece before Homer. London, 1956.
AH 7279.56	Giannelli, Giulio. Trattato di storia romana. Roma, 1956- 2v.
AH 7279.56.5	Hadas, Moses. A history of Rome. 1. ed. Garden City, 1956.
AH 279.56	Histoire et historiens dans l'antiquité. Genève, 1956.
AH 7299.55	International Congress of Roman Frontier Studies, 2d, Carnuntum, 1955. Carnuntina; Ergebnisse der Forschung über die Grenzprovinzen des Römischen Reiches. Graz, 1956.
AH 4139.56	Jones, J.W. The law and legal theory of the Greeks. Oxford, 1956.
AH 867.10	Jucker, Ines. Der Gestus des Aposkopein. Zürich, 1956.
AH 7201.21.10	Kaser, Max. Die Interpretatio zu den Paulussentenzen. Köln, 1956.
Eg 879.56	Kees, Hermann. Der Götterglaube im alten Ägypten. 2. Aufl. Berlin, 1956.
Eg 879.26.7	Kees, Hermann. Totenglauben und Jenseitsvorstellungen der alten Ägypter. 2. Aufl. Berlin, 1956.

Chronological Listing

1956 - cont.

AH 4939.56 Kirsten, Ernst. Die griechische Polis als historisch-geographisches Problem des Mittelmeerraumes. Bonn, 1956.

AH 9.56 Klauser, Theodor. Franz Joseph Dölger. Münster, 1956.

AH 7189.56 Kotsevalov, A.S. Antichnoe rabstvo i revoliutsii rabov v sovetskoi istoricheskoi literature. Miunkhen, 1956.

AH 3022.17 Kramer, S.N. From the tablets of Sumer. Indian Hills, 1956.

AH 8207.27 Lindsay, Jack. The Romans were here. London, 1956.

AH 7339.56 Lissner, Ivar. Die Casaren. Olten, 1956.

AH 7519.52.3 Marañón, G. Tiberius. London, 1956.

AH 842.35.4 Marrow, Henri Irenée. A history of education in antiquity. London, 1956.

AH 4299.56 Martin, Roland. L'urbanisme dans la Grèce antique. Paris, 1956.

AH 7509.56 Mashkin, N.A. Il principato di Augusto. Roma, 1956. 2v.

AH 4410.10.5 Matz, Friedrich. Le monde egéen. Paris, 1956.

AH 7239.56 Morin y Peña, Manuel. Instituciones militares romanas. Madrid, 1956.

AH 9446.5 Moro, Placida Maria. Iulium Carnicum (Zuglio). Roma, 1956.

AH 3959.35 Moscati, Sabatino. I predecessori d'Israele. Roma, 1956.

AH 1819.56 Moscati, Sabatino. Il profilo dell'Oriente mediterraneo. Torino, 1956.

AH 3663.11 Osten, H.H. von der. Die Welt der Perser. Stuttgart, 1956.

AH 3013.956 Pallis, Svend Aage. The antiquity of Iraq. Copenhagen, 1956.

AH 3149.14.5 Parker, Richard A. Babylonian chronology 626 B.C.-A.D. 75. Providence, 1956.

AH 7519.56 Pezzella, Federico. L'imperatore Tiberio. Santa Maria, 1956.

AH 4559.56 Pfister, F. Alexander der Grosse in den Offenbarungen der Griechen. Berlin, 1956.

AH 3670.5 Pigulevskaia, N.V. Goroda Irana v rannem srednevekove. Moskva, 1956.

Eg 1009.56 Posener, Georges. Littérature et politique dans l'Égypte de la XII dynastie. Paris, 1956.

AH 7206.33 Pringsheim, Fritz. Zum Plan einer neuen Ausgabe der Basiliken. Berlin, 1956.

Eg 1129.56F Ptah-Hetep. Les maximes de Ptahhotep. Prague, 1956.

AH 7479.56 Radio Italiana. Cesare nel brimillenario della morte. Torino, 1956.

AH 8453.5 Reidinger, Walter. Die Statthalter der ungeteilten Pannonien und Oberpannoniens von Augustus bis Diokletian. Bonn, 1956.

AH 7779.56 Ricciotti, Giuseppe. L'imperatore Giuliano l'Apostata secondo i documenti. Milano, 1956.

AH 7139.56 Riccobono, Salvatore. Profilo storico del diritto romano. Palermo, 1956.

AH 9666.10 Saa, Mário. As grandes vias da Lusitania. Lisboa, 1956-60. 5v.

AH 3022.29 Schmökel, Hartmut. Das Land Sumer. 2. Aufl. Stuttgart, 1956.

Eg 839.56 Smith, J.L. Tombs, temples and ancient art. 1. ed. Norman, 1956.

AH 3020.25F Sollberger, E. Corpus des inscriptions royales présargoniques de Lagas. Genève, 1956.

AH 2507.10 Stark, Freya. The Lycian shore. N.Y., 1956.

AH 7469.39.3 Syme, Ronald. The Roman revolution. Oxford, 1956.

AH 7459.56 Utchenko, S.L. Der weltanschaulich politische Kampf in Rom. Berlin, 1956.

AH 7469.56 Valgiglio, E. Silla e la crisi repubblicana. 1. ed. Firenze, 1956.

AH 7099.56 Vitucci, Giovanni. Ricerche sulla praefectura urbi in età imperiale. Roma, 1956.

AH 7259.56 Wallinga, Herman Tammo. The boarding-bridge of the Romans. Groningen, 1956.

AH 7239.56.5 Webster, Graham. The Roman army. Chester, 1956.

AH 9610.29 Wentker, Hermann. Sizilien und Athen. Heidelberg, 1956.

AH 4329.56.5 Will, Edouard. Doriens et Ioniens. Paris, 1956.

AH 4329.56 Will, Edouard. Doriens et Ioniens. Strasbourg, 1956.

AH 3966.28.2F Wright, G.E. The Westminster historical atlas to the Bible. Philadelphia, 1956.

1957

AH 7409.57 Accame, Silvio. Le origini di Roma. Napoli, 1957.

AH 4239.57 Adcock, F.E. The Greek and Macedonian art of war. Berkeley, 1957.

AH 4819.57.5 Agard, W.R. The Greek mind. Princeton, N.J., 1957.

AH 7299.57 Alföldi, Andras. Die trojanischen Urahnen der Römer. Basel, 1957.

AH 3661.10.5 Altheim, Franz. Utopie und Wirtschaft. Frankfurt, 1957.

AH 3097.7 Ashurbanapal, king of Assyria. Le prisme du Louvre AO 19.939. Paris, 1957.

AH 7855.2 Aymard, Jacques. Essai sur les chasses romaines, des origines à la fin du siècle des Antonins (Cynegetica). Thèse. Paris, 1957.

AH 2231.5 Balkan, Kemal. Letter of King Anum-Hirbi of Mama to King Warshama of Kanish. Ankara, 1957.

AH 7709.57 Bebelon, Jean. Impératrices syriennes. Paris, 1957.

AH 8647.22 Bérard, Jean. La colonisation grecque de l'Italie méridionale et de la Sicile dans l'antiquité. Paris, 1957.

Eg 879.57.15 Bernard, J.L. L'Égypte et la genèse du surhomme. Paris, 1957.

AH 3002.136F Böhl, Franz M.T. Tabulae cuneiformae a F.M.T. de Liagre Böhl. v.1; 2, pt.1; 3-4. Leiden, 1957. 4v.

AH 4819.54.6 Bonnard, André. Greek civilization from the Iliad to the Parthenon. London, 1957. 3v.

AH 4819.57.10 Bowra, Cecil Maurice. The Greek experience. London, 1957.

AH 9609.5.7 Brea, L.B. Sicily before the Greeks. London, 1957.

AH 9609.5.5 Brea, L.B. Sicily before the Greeks. N.Y., 1957.

Eg 759.37.3 Breccia, Evaristo. Egitto greco e romano. 3. ed. Pisa, 1957.

AH 4939.57 Briand de Crèvecaeur, Emmanuél. Havets pionerer. København, 1957.

Eg 848.5 Brunner, Hellmut. Altägyptische Erziehung. Wiesbaden, 1957.

AH 2007.7 Çagatay, Neş'et. Islâmdan önce Arap tarihi. Ankara, 1957.

AH 4909.57 Canarache, V. Importul amforelor stampilate la Istria. Bucureşti, 1957.

AH 2120.5 Cassola, Filippo. La Ionia nel mondo miceneo. Napoli, 1957.

Eg 1029.57PF Červý, Jaroslav. Hieratic ostraca. Oxford, 1957.

1957 - cont.

AH 8532.5.10 Chagny, André. Au cours de l'automne de 43 avant notre ere Lucius Munatius Plancus. Lyon, 1957.

AH 3009.57 Champdor, Albert. Babylone. Paris, 1957.

AH 7653.20 Collins, William M. The student's companion to Gibbon. Melbourne, 1957.

Eg 1042.957PF Davies, Norman de Garis. A corpus of inscribed Egyptian funerary cones. pt.1. Oxford, 1957.

Eg 971.7.10 Davis, H.T. Alexandria, the golden city. Evanston, 1957. 2v.

AH 4819.05.31 Dickinson, G.L. The Greek view of life. 23d ed. London, 1957.

AH 4819.51.2 Dodds, Eric Robertson. The Greeks and the irrational. 1st ed. Boston, 1957. 2v.

Eg 299.57 Drioton, Etienne. Pages d'égyptologie. Le Caire, 1957.

AH 8549.157 Duval, Paul Marie. Les dieux de la Gaule. 1. éd. Paris, 1957.

AH 3021.21 Edzard, Dietz O. Die "zweite Zwischenzeit" Babyloniens. Wiesbaden, 1957.

AH 4039.57.5 Ehrenberg, Victor. Der Staat der Griechen. Leipzig, 1957- 2v.

AH 7279.57 Ferrabino, Aldo. L'essenza del romanesimo. Roma, 1957.

AH 7009.57 French Bibliographic Digest. History III. Roman history. N.Y., 1957.

AH 3151.12 Gordon, Cyrus. Hammurabi's code. N.Y., 1957.

AH 7829.53 Grimal, Pierre. La vie à Rome dans l'antiquité. 2. éd. Paris, 1957.

AH 4819.57 Hamilton, Edith. The echo of Greece. 1st ed. N.Y., 1957.

AH 7299.57.5 Harmond, Louis. Le patronat sur les collectivités publiques des origines au Bas-Empire. Paris, 1957.

AH 7299.57.6 Harmond, Louis. Le patronat sur les collectivités publiques des origines au Bas-Empire. Paris, 1957.

AH 4039.57 Havelock, E.A. The liberal temper in Greek politics. London, 1957.

AH 8907.30 Hus, Alain. Les Étrusques. Paris, 1957.

AH 3020.28 Istanbul. Asari atika Müzeleri. Nouvelles tablettes sumeriennes. Paris, 1957.

AH 8907.40 Istituto lombardo di scienze e lettere. Tyrrhenica. Milano, 1957.

AH 3963.30 Jirku, Anton. Die Welt der Bibel. Stuttgart, 1957.

AH 5303.16 Jones, Arnold H.M. Athenian democracy. Oxford, 1957.

AH 7269.57 Kampe, Otto. Die römische Republik und ihre Auseinandersetzung mit den Grossmächten des Mittelmeerraumes bis 168. Stuttgart, 1957.

AH 4819.57.15 Kerényi, Karoly. Griechische Miniaturen. Zürich, 1957.

AH 7865.502 Kleberg, Tounes. Hôtels, restaurants et cabarets dans l'antiquité romaine. Uppsala, 1957.

AH 4259.57 Labarbe, Jules. La loi navale de Themistocle. Paris, 1957.

AH 4459.36.3 Laistner, M.L.W. A history of the Greek world. 3. ed. London, 1957.

AH 4819.57.20 Lambrechts, Pierre. Wat Hellas in Rome ons gaven. 2. Druk. Antwerpen, 1957.

AH 5610.15 Léveque, P. Pyrrhos. Paris, 1957.

AH 7819.57 Mattingly, Harold. Roman imperial civilization. London, 1957.

Eg 879.57 Mayassis, S. Mystéres et initiations de l'Egypte ancienne. Athènes, 1957.

AH 4889.40.2 Michell, Humfrey. The economics of ancient Greece. 2. ed. Cambridge, 1957.

Eg 939.57 Montet, Pierre. Géographie de l'Égypte ancienne. pt.1-2. Paris, 1957. 2v.

AH 4410.1 Moon, Brenda Elizabeth. Mycenaean civilization, publications...1935-1960, a bibliography. v.1-2. London, 1957-61.

AH 3807.15.2 Moscati, Sabatino. Ancient Semitic civilizations. London, 1957.

AH 3807.15 Moscati, Sabatino. Ancient Semitic civilizations. 1st American ed. N.Y., 1957.

AH 3210.5 Narain, A.K. The Indo-Greeks. Oxford, 1957.

AH 9421.10 Panciera, Silvio. Vita economica de Aquileia in età romana. Venezia, 1957.

Eg 1159.37 Papyrus Ebers. The Papyrus Ebers. Copenhagen, 1957.

AH 3757.15 Rice, Tamara. The Scythians. London, 1957.

AH 3171.10 Rinaldi, Giovani. Storia delle letterature dell'antica mesopotamia. Milano, 1957.

AH 8548.130 Rivoallan, A. Présence des Celtes. Paris, 1957.

AH 4279.29.4.5 Robinson, Cyril E. A history of Greece. 9. ed. London, 1957.

AH 3012.21 Rupper, Jean R. Les nomades en Mésopotamia au temps des rois de Mari. Paris, 1957.

AH 7489.44.1.5 Salmon, E.T. A history of the Roman world. 3. ed. London, 1957.

AH 5303.25 Sartori, Franco. Le eterie nella vita politica ateniese del VI e V secolo A.C. Roma, 1957.

Eg 879.57.5 Sauneron, Serge. Les prêtres de l'ancienne Égypte. Paris, 1957.

AH 7479.57 Schmittlein, Raymond. La première campagne de César contre les Germaines. Paris, 1957.

AH 279.57 Schreiber, H. Throne unter Schutt und Sand. Wien, 1957.

AH 7189.57.5 Shtaerman, Elena. Krizis rabovladel'cheskogo stroia v zapadn'ikh provinschchiiakh rimskoi imperii. Moskva, 1957.

AH 866.15 Spekke, Arnolds. The ancient amber routes and the geographical discovery of the eastern Baltic. Stockholm, 1957.

Eg 299.42.5 Steindorff, G. When Egypt ruled the East. Chicago, 1957.

AH 5123.5 Susini, Giancarlo. Nuove scoperte sulla storia di Coo. Bologna, 1957.

AH 8308.10 Tudor, D. Istoria sclavajului in Dacia romana. Bucureşti, 1957.

AH 3908.5.10 Unger, Merrill F. Israel and the Aramaeans of Damascus. London, 1957.

Eg 879.57.10 Uxkull, Woldemar. Die Einweihung im alten Ägypten. Büdingen-Gettenbach, 1957.

AH 8913.10.5 Vacano, Otto Wilhelm von. Die Etrusker in der Welt der Antike. Hamburg, 1957.

AH 7729.57 Villeneuve, Roland. Héliogabale. Paris, 1957.

AH 7759.57 Voelkl, Ludwig. Der Kaiser Konstantin. München, 1957.

AH 7549.55.2 Walter, Gérard. Nero. London, 1957.

AH 889.57 Welskopf, Elisabeth C. Die Produktionsverhältnisse im alten Orient und in der griechisch-römischen Antike. Berlin, 1957.

AH 7039.57 Wirszubski, C. Libertas. Bari, 1957.

Chronological Listing

1958

Eg 1029.58   Andrzejewski, Tad. Opowiadaniia egipskie. Warszawa, 1958.

AH 7212.5   Astin, A.E. The Lex Annalis before Sulla. Brussells, 1958.

AH 1309.58.3   Avdièv, Vsevolod I. L'étude de l'ancien Orient en U.R.S.S. 1917-1957. Moscou, 1958.

AH 1309.58   Avdièv, Vsevolod I. Sovietskaia nauka s drevnene Vostoke za 40 let. Moskva, 1958.

AH 7114.35   Badian, E. Foreign clientelae, 264-70 B.C. Oxford, 1958.

AH 7299.49.2   Barrow, R.H. The Romans. Harmondsworth, 1958.

AH 279.58.30   Bignami, Ernesto. Manuale di storia orientale e greca. Milano, 1958.

AH 7279.58   Bignami, Ernesto. Manuale di storia romana. Milano, 1958.

AH 8913.5.6   Bloch, Raymond. The Etruscans. London, 1958.

AH 7409.58   Bloch, Raymond. Les origins de Rome. 3. ed. Paris, 1958.

AH 4889.23.3   Bolkestein, H. Economic life in Greece's golden age. Leiden, 1958.

AH 4819.57.12   Bowra, Cecil Maurie. The Greek experience. 1st ed. Cleveland, 1958.

AH 8007.23   Brisson, Jean Paul. Autonomisme et christianisme dans l'Afrique romaine de Septime Sévère à l'invasion vandale. Paris, 1958.

Eg 1069.58   British Museum. Department of Manuscripts. Mss. (Papyrus 10569). An ancient Egyptian book of hours. Oxford, 1958.

Eg 885.899.4   Budge, Ernest Alfred Wallis. Egyptian magic. Evanston, 1958.

AH 3960.24   Busch, Fritz-Otto. The fine Herods. London, 1958.

AH 7909.58   Calabi Limentani, Ida. Studi sulla società romana; il lavoro artistico. Milano, 1958.

Eg 1099.58   Caminos, R.A. The chronicle of Prince Osorkon. Roma, 1958.

AH 7499.58   Carcopino, Jerôme. Passion et politique chez les Césars. Paris, 1958.

AH 279.58.20   Chambers, M.H. Greek and Roman history. Washington, 1958.

AH 8073.22   Charles-Picard, Gilbert. La vie quotidienne à Carthage en temps d'Hannibal. Paris, 1958.

AH 3013.958F   Chicago. University. Oriental Institute. Soundings at Tell Fakhariyah. Chicago, 1958.

AH 4459.58   Cloché, Paul. Le monde grec aux temps classiques. Paris, 1958.

AH 279.58   Cottrell, Leonard. The anvil of civilisation. London, 1958.

AH 8211.7   Cottrell, Leonard. The great invasion. London, 1958.

Eg 879.58   Daumas, François. Les mammisis des temples égyptiens. Paris, 1958.

Eg 847.9   Davies, N.M. Picture writing in ancient Egypt. London, 1958.

AH 7759.58   Doerries, Hermann. Konstantin der Grosse. Stuttgart, 1958.

AH 7189.25.5   Duff, Arnold Mackay. Freedmen in the early Roman Empire. Cambridge, 1958.

AH 2910.2   Duggan, Alfred Leo. He died old. London, 1958.

AH 3096.8   Esarhaddon, king of Assyria. The Vassal-treaties of Esarhaddon. London, 1958.

AH 7499.58.5   Esser, A.A.M. Cäsar und die julisch-claudischen Kaiser im biologisc-härztichen Blickfeld. Leiden, 1958.

AH 845.10   Ferguson, John. Moral values in the ancient world. London, 1958.

AH 3013.958.10   Flittner, N.D. Kul'tura i iskusstvo Dvurech'ia. Leningrad, 1958.

AH 4559.58   Fuller, J.F. The generalship of Alexander the Great. London, 1958.

AH 3179.10.8   Furlani, Giuseppe. Mite babilonesi e assiri. Firenze, 1958.

AH 819.41.8   Gabriel-Leroux, Jacqueline. Les premières civilisations de la Mediterranée. 6. éd. Paris, 1958.

AH 7749.58   Gigli, Guido. L'impero romano dall'abdicazione di Diocleziano alla morte di Costantino (305-337). Roma, 1958.

AH 4279.58.15   Grant, Michael. Greeks. Edinburgh, 1958.

AH 7659.58   Haywood, R.M. The myth of Rome's fall. N.Y., 1958.

AH 889.38.2   Heichelheim, Fritz. An ancient economic history from the Palaeolithic age to the migrations of the Germanic, Slavic, and Arabic nations. Leiden, 1958-64. 3v.

AH 4559.58.5   Hempl, Franz. Alexander der Grosse. Göttingen, 1958.

AH 930.40F   Heyden, A.A. Atlas van de antieke wereld. Amsterdam, 1958.

AH 4039.52.5   Hignett, C. A history of the Athenian constitution to the end of the fifth century B.C. Oxford, 1958.

AH 8048.2   Honea, K.K. A contribution to the history of Hamitic peoples. Horn, 1958.

AH 8942.5   Hubaux, Jean. Rome et Véies. Paris, 1958.

AH 1879.58   James, E.O. Myth and ritual in the ancient Near East. London, 1958.

Eg 1159.58   Jonckheere, Frans. Les médecins de l'Égypte pharaonique. Bruxelles, 1958.

AH 4039.58   Jones, Arnold H.M. Athenian democracy. N.Y., 1958.

AH 7819.44.6   Kahrstedt, Ulrich. Kulturgeschichte der römischen Kaiserzeit. 2. Aufl. Bern, 1958.

AH 930.42   Kampen, Albert van. Die Welt der Antike. 12. Aufl. Gotha, 1958.

AH 6107.20   Kanatsoulēs, Dēmētrios. He dytikē Makedonia kata tous archaious chronous. Thessalonikē, 1958.

AH 199.58   Kuri Breña, Daniel. La filosofia del clericho in la antigüedad cristiana. 2. ed. Mexico, 1958.

AH 2264.5   Laumonier, A. Les cultes indigènes en Carie. Paris, 1958.

AH 7339.56.2   Lissner, Ivar. The Caesars: might and madness. N.Y., 1958.

AH 7819.58   McKendrick, Paul Lachlan. The Roman mind at work. Princeton, N.J., 1958.

AH 9639.12   Mansuelli, Guido Achille. La politica estera di Siracusa. Bologna, 1958.

AH 842.35.6   Marrow, Henri Irenée. Histoire de l'éducation dans l'antiquité. 4. éd. Paris, 1958.

AH 879.58   Martino, Ernesto de. Morti e pianto rituale nel mondo antico dal lamento pagano al pianto di Maria. Torino, 1958.

AH 7039.58   Martino, Francesco de. Storia della costituzione romana. v.1-6. Napoli, 1958-72. 7v.

AH 7278.54.28   Mommsen, T. The history of Rome. N.Y., 1958.

Eg 829.46.5   Montet, Pierre. Everyday life in Egypt in the days of Ramesses the Great. N.Y., 1958.

AH 8548.135   Moreau, Jacques. Die Welt der Kelten. Stuttgart, 1958.

AH 909.58   Moritz, L.A. Grain-mills and flour in classical antiquity. Oxford, 1958.

AH 3813.8   Moscati, Sabatino. Le antiche civiltà semitiche. Bari, 1958.

1958 - cont.

Eg 459.58   Muck, O.H. Cheops und die grosse Pyramide. Olten, 1958.

AH 279.58.25   Nenci, Giuseppe. Introduzione alle guerre persiane e altri saggi. Pisa, 1958.

AH 7479.58   Opermann, Hans. Caesar. Göttingen, 1958.

AH 9613.5.5   Pace, Biagio. Arte e civiltà della Sicilia antica. 2. ed. Milano, 1958.

AH 4819.47.6   Paoli, Ugo E. Cane del popolo. 2. ed. Firenze, 1958.

VAH 7819.58.5   Paoli, Ugo Enrico. Ciceronis Jilius. Firenze, 1958.

AH 279.58.5   Pareti, Luigi. Studi minori di storia antica. Roma, 1958-69. 4v.

AH 7489.35.2   Parker, Henry M.D. A history of the Roman world from A.D. 138 to 337. 2. ed. London, 1958.

AH 4039.58.5   Pavar, Massiniliaro. La grecità politica da Jucidide ad Aristotele. Roma, 1958.

AH 8548.140   Powell, Terence G.E. The Celts. London, 1958.

AH 1029.58   Pritchard, James B. The ancient Near East; an anthology of texts and pictures. Princeton, 1958.

AH 4659.50   Ranovich, A.B. Der Hellenismus und seine geschichtliche Ralle. Berlin, 1958.

AH 3022.24   Resina, Guiseppe. Sumer e Akkad; la vita economica. Catania, 1958.

AH 3009.58   Rutten, M. Babylone. Paris, 1958.

AH 5708.5   Sakellariou, M.B. La migration grecque en Ionie. Athènes, 1958.

AH 7204.4.5   Sasse, Christoph. De Constitutio Antoniniana. Wiesbaden, 1958.

AH 7139.58   Scherillo, Gaetano. Manuele di storia del dirito romano. Milano, 1958.

AH 3030.5   Schnöbel, Hartmut. Hammurabi von Babylon. München, 1958.

AH 4299.58.5   Seltman, Charles T. Riot in Ephesus; writings on the heritage of Greece. London, 1958.

AH 7162.38   Simonius, Pascal. Die Donatio Mortis Causa im klassischen römischen Recht. Basel, 1958.

AH 8615.5   Sirago, Vito A. L'Italia agraria sotto Traiano. Louvain, 1958.

AH 7239.58   Smith, Richard. Service in the past - Marian Roman Army. Manchester, 1958.

AH 9608.7   Soraci, Rosario. I proconsoli di Sicilia da Augusto a Traiano. Catania, 1958?

AH 6057.17   Sordi, Marta. La lega tessala fino ad Afessundro-Magno. Roma, 1958.

AH 4819.58   Stokes, Adrian Durham. Greek culture and the ego. London, 1958.

AH 9610.22   Stroheker, Karl. Dionysios I. Wiesbaden, 1958.

AH 8789.7   Tabouis, Geneviève R. Sybaris, les grecs en Italie. Paris, 1958.

AH 279.39.9   Taeger, Fritz. Das Altertum. 6. Aufl. Stuttgart, 1958. 2v.

AH 9633.6   Vallet, Georges. Rhégion et Zancle. Paris, 1958.

Eg 709.53.2   Volkmann, Hans. Kleopatra. N.Y., 1958.

AH 7469.58   Volkmann, Hans. Sullas Marsch auf Rom. München, 1958.

AH 4279.58.5   Wade-Gery, H.T. Essays in Greek history. Oxford, 1958.

AH 9765.5   Wollheim, Günther. Germania oeconomica; das Bild der germanischen Wirtschaft bei Caesar und Tacitus. Freiburg, 1958.

AH 4279.58.10   Woodhouse, W.J. The tutorial history of Greece. 3. ed. London, 1958.

AH 4279.58.20   Zielinski, Tadeusz. Grecja niepodlegɪa. 1. wyd. Warszawa, 1958.

1959

AH 7409.59   Accame, Silvio. I re di Roma nella leggenda e nella storia. Napoli, 1959.

AH 7039.59   Adcock, Frank. Roman political ideas and practice. Ann Arbor, 1959.

AH 7189.59   Aleksishvili, M.M. Iz glubiny vekov. Tbilisi, 1959.

Eg 879.59.15   Andrzejewski, Tadeusz. Le papyrus mythologique de Te-hem-en-Mout. Warszawa, 1959.

AH 842.45   Barclay, William. Educational ideals in the ancient world. London, 1959.

Eg 609.59   Bertram, J. Echnaton der Grosse im Schauen. Hamburg, 1959.

AH 4459.59   Berve, Helmuf. Griechische Geschichte. Freiburg, 1959. 2v.

Eg 1309.59PF   Book of the kings of Egypt. Oxford, 1959.

AH 4860.10   Bork, Arnold. Der junge Grieche. Zürich, 1959.

AH 3414.15   Bossert, Helmuth. Janus und der Mann mit derer Adler; oder Greifenmaske. Istanbul, 1959.

AH 938.79.10   Bunbury, E.H. A history of ancient geography among the Greeks and Romans. 2. ed. N.Y., 1959. 2v.

AH 259.59   Carson, Lionel. The ancient mariners: seafarers. N.Y., 1959.

AH 7469.59.5   Chantraine, Heinrich. Untersuchungen zur römischen Geschichte am Ende des 2. Jahrhunderts vor Christus. Kallmünz, 1959.

AH 8013.4   Charles-Picard, Gilbert. La civilisation de l'Afrique romaine. Paris, 1959.

AH 8909.5   Ciba Foundation. Ciba Foundation on medical biology and Etruscan origins. London, 1959.

AH 3020.40.5   Çiğ, Muazzez. Eski Babill zamanina ait Nippur menşeli iki okul kitabi. Ankara, 1959.

Eg 879.59A   Clark, R.T. Myth and symbol in ancient Egypt. v.4. London, 1959.

AH 4609.59   Cloché, Paul. La dislocation d'un empire. Paris, 1959.

AH 7219.5   Daube, David. Studies in the Roman law of sale. Oxford, 1959.

Eg 879.58.2F   Daumas, François. Les mammisis de Dendara. Le Caire, 1959.

AH 3022.20   D'iakonov, I.M. Obshchestvennyi i gosudarstvennyi stroi drevnego Dvurech'ia. Moskva, 1959.

AH 4499.59   Dienelt, Karl. Die Friedenspolitik des Perikles. Wien, 1959.

AH 4819.51.3   Dodds, Eric Robertson. The Greeks and the irrational. Berkeley, 1959.

Eg 279.59   Drioton, Etienne. L'Egypte pharaonique. Paris, 1959.

AH 39.59   Ehrhardt, Arnold. Politische Metaphysik von Solon bis Augustin. Tübingen, 1959-69. 3v.

AH 7169.59   Endemann, W. Der Begriff der Delegation im klassischen römischen Recht. Marburg, 1959.

Eg 974.5.5F   Fakhry, A. The monuments of Sneferu at Dahshur. Cairo, 1959-61. 2v.

AH 4539.59   Farina, Antonio. Il processo di Frine. Napoli, 1959.

AH 8548.141.5   Filip, Jan. Keltská civilisace a její dědictví. Praha, 1959.

Chronological Listing

1959 - cont.

AH 279.46.2   Finegan, Jack. Light from the ancient past. 2. ed. Princeton, N.J., 1959.

AH 4819.59.10   Flacelière, Robert. La vie quotidienne en Grèce au siècle de Périclès. Paris, 1959.

Eg 1059.59.5   Flora, Francesco. La poesia dell'Egitto e della Mesopotamia. Milano, 1959.

AH 7409.59.5   Francisci, Pietro. Primordia civitates. Romae, 1959.

AH 7889.33.5   Frank, Tenney. An economic survey of ancient Rome. Paterson, N.J., 1959.

AH 9658.5   García y Bellido, Antonio. Las colonias romanas de Hispania. Madrid, 1959.

Eg 819.59   Garnot, Jean Sainte F. Aspects de l'Égypte antique. Cairo, 1959.

AH 7479.49.2   Gelzer, Matthias. Pompeius. 2. Aufl. München, 1959.

AH 7769.59   Gigli, Guido. La dinastia die secondi Flavii: Costantino II, Costante, Costanzo II, 337-361. Roma, 1959.

Eg 879.59.10   Gollob, Hedwig. Die Götter am Nil. Wien, 1959.

AH 7519.59   Gollub, Wilhelm. Tiberius. München, 1959.

AH 3189.3A   Gordon, Edmund I. Sumerian proverbs. Philadelphia, 1959.

AH 4842.88   Greco, Felice. La pedagogia presso i Greci. Bologna, 1959.

AH 3999.59   Guignebert, Charles. The Jewish world in the time of Jesus. 7th American ed. N.Y., 1959.

AH 4609.59.5   Gyiokos, P.K. Philippos ho He. Thessalonikē, 1959.

AH 7239.59   Hackl, Othmar. Die sogenannte servianische Heeresreform. München, 1959.

AH 4659.59.5   Hadas, Moses. Hellenistic culture. N.Y., 1959.

AH 4279.59   Hammond, Nicholas Geoffrey Lemprière. A history of Greece. Oxford, 1959.

AH 8507.12   Hatt, Jean Jacques. Histoire de la Gaule romaine, 120 avant J.C. Paris, 1959.

Eg 1079.59   Hermann, Alfred. Altägyptische Liebesdichtung. Wiesbaden, 1959.

AH 3012.11   Jung, H.W.M. Demonische ziekten in Babylon en Bijbel. Leiden, 1959.

AH 5909.59   Kiechle, Franz. Messenische Studien. Kallmünz, 1959.

AH 4729.59   Kordatos, G.K. Istoría tōn Ellēnistikōn chronōn. Athēnai, 1959.

AH 8904.5   Lambrechts, R. Essai sur les magistratures des républiques étrusques. Bruxelles, 1959.

AH 4189.59   Lotze, D. Metaxy eleutherōn kai doulōn. Berlin, 1959.

AH 3609.5   Lozinski, B.P. The original homeland of the Parthians. 's Gravenhage, 1959.

AH 7449.59.5F   Ludovico, D. La battaglia di Canne. Roma, 1959.

AH 7479.59   Madaule, Jacques. César. Paris, 1959.

AH 4009.52.2   Manni, Eugenio. Introduzione allo studio della storia greca e romana. 2. ed. Palermo, 1959.

AH 4819.59   Messinesi, X.L. Meet the ancient Greeks. Caldwell, 1959.

AH 4819.54.12   Mireaux, Émile. Daily life in the time of Homer. London, 1959.

AH 8458.6   Mócsy, András. Die Bevolkerung von Pannonien bis zu den Markommenkriegen. Budapest, 1959.

Eg 609.59.5   Montet, Pierre. L'Égypte et la Bible. Neuchâtel, 1959.

AH 3013.959   Moortgat, Anton. Archäologische Forschungen der Max Freiherr von Oppenheim - Stiftung in nördlichen Mesopotamien 1956. Köln, 1959.

AH 3807.20   Moscati, Sabatino. The Semites in ancient history. Cardiff, 1959.

AH 279.58.35   Mueller, W.F. Aufstieg und Untergang der Grossreiche des Altertums. 2. Aufl. Stuttgart, 1959.

AH 3143.17   Nikol'skii, Nikolai M. Kultura drevnei Vavilonii. Minsk, 1959.

AH 279.59.5   Nováková, J. Antika v dokumentech. Praha, 1959-61. 2v.

AH 8457.5   Oliva, Pavel. Pannonie a počátky krize Řemskeho imperia. Praha, 1959.

AH 7469.59   Ooteghem, Jules van. Lucius Licinius Lucullus. Namur, 1959.

AH 9608.5.5F   Pareti, Luigi. Sicilia antica. Palermo, 1959.

AH 819.59   Parker, Henry B. Gods and men. 1. ed. N.Y., 1959.

AH 9.59   Petit, Paul. Guide de l'étudiant en histoire ancienne. Paris, 1959.

Eg 885.959   Piantanida, Danato. La chiave perduta. Milano, 1959.

Eg 819.59.5   Posener, Georges. Dictionnaire de la civilisation égyptienne. Paris, 1959.

AH 8515.10   Renard, Marcel. Technique et agriculture en pays trévire et rémois. Bruxelles, 1959.

AH 5313.10   Robinson, Charles. Athens in the age of Pericles. 1st ed. Norman, 1959.

AH 2120.7F   Roebuck, Carl A. Ionian trade and colonization. N.Y., 1959.

Eg 879.59.5   Roeder, Günther. Die ägyptische Religion in Texten und Bildern. v.1-3. Zürich, 1959-

AH 3957.35   Rolla, Armando. L'ambiente biblico. Brescia, 1959.

AH 8007.21   Romanelli, P. Storia delle province romane dell'Africa. Roma, 1959.

AH 7479.59.5   Rossi, Ruggero F. Marco Antonio nella lotta politica della tarda republica romana. Trieste, 1959.

AH 8942.7   Rossi Danielli, Luigi. Gli Etruschi del Viterbese. Viterbo, 1959. 2v.

AH 3016.48   Schnitzler, Ludwig. Frühe Plastik im Zweistromland. 1. Aufl. Stuttgart, 1959.

Eg 1079.55   Schott, Siegfried. Liebeslieder der Pharaonenzeit. Zürich, 1959.

AH 7489.59   Scullard, Howard Hayes. From the Gracchi to Nero. London, 1959.

Eg 990.20PF   Seele, Keith. The tomb of Tjanefer at Thebes. Chicago, 1959.

AH 3966.30F   Simons, Jan. The geographical and topographical texts of the Old Testament. Leiden, 1959.

Eg 1159.59   Steuer, Robert. Ancient Egyptian and Cnidian medicine. Berkeley, 1959.

AH 4039.59   Tarkiainen, Tuttu. Demokratia. Helsinki, 1959.

AH 4659.59   Toynbee, A.J. Hellenism. London, 1959.

AH 4659.59.2   Toynbee, A.J. Hellenism. N.Y., 1959.

AH 7449.59   Veitskivs'kyi, I.I. Zovnishnia polityka krain Zakhidnogo Ceredzemnomor'ia v 264-219 rr. do n.e. L'viv, 1959.

Eg 1309.59.5F   Vienna. National-Bibliothek. Papyrussammlung. A Vienna demotic papyrus on eclipse- and lunar-omina. Providence, 1959.

AH 7509.59   Vittinghoff, Friedrich. Kaiser Augustus. Göttingen, 1959.

AH 4819.59.5   Webster, Thomas. Greek art and literature, 700-530 B.C. Dunedin, 1959.

AH 819.59.5   White, Leslie A. The evolution of culture. N.Y., 1959.

AH 8907.35   Zalesskii, Nikolai N. Etruski v severnoi Italii. Leningrad, 1959.

1959 - cont.

AH 4819.59.15   Zschietzschmann, Willy. Hellas und Rom. Zürich, 1959.

AH 4112.14   Zulhofer, Gerhard. Sparta, Delphoi und die Amphiktyonen im 5. Jahrhundert. Erlangen? 1959?

196-

AH 879.60   Chakraberty, Chandra. Ancient races and myths. Calcutta, 196-.

AH 5271.10   Woerrle, Michael. Untersuchungen zur Verfassungsgeschichte von Argos im 5. Jahrhundert vor Christus. Diss. Erlangen? 196-.

1960

AH 4819.60.5   Aigrisse, Gilbert. Psychanalyse de la Grèce antique. Paris, 1960.

Eg 299.60   Akademiia nauk SSSR. Institut Narodov Azii. Drevnii Egypet; sbornik statei. Moskva, 1960.

AH 3507.15   Aliev, Igrar. Istoriia Midii. Baku, 1960.

AH 4559.60   Altheim, F. Zarathustra und Alexander. Frankfurt, 1960.

Eg 459.60   Baer, Klaus. Rank and title in the Old Kingdom. Chicago, 1960.

AH 4039.60.10A   Barker, E. Greek political theory. London, 1960.

AH 4039.60.11   Barker, E. Greek political theory. 5. ed. London, 1960.

AH 3016.52   Barnett, Richard. Assyrian palace reliefs and their influence on the sculptures of Babylonia and Persia. London, 1960.

AH 7549.60   Beaujeu, J. L'incendie de Rome. Bruxelles, 1960.

AH 3009.60F   Beek, Martinus A. Atlas van het Tweestromland. Amsterdam, 1960.

AH 6150.5   Belin de Ballu, Eugène. L'histoire des colonies grecques du littoral nord de la Mer Noire; bibliographie...1940 à 1957. Paris, 1960.

AH 4299.60   Berard, Jean. L'expansion et la colonisation. Paris, 1960.

AH 7409.58.5   Bloch, Raymond. The origins of Rome. London, 1960.

AH 7279.60.20   Bloch, Raymond. Rome et son destin. Paris, 1960.

AH 3608.5   Bokshchanin, A.G. Parfiia i Rim. Moskva, 1960. 2v.

Eg 1039.13.4   Book of the Dead. The book of the dead. New Hyde Park, N.Y., 1960.

Eg 1039.60F   Book of the Dead. The Egyptian book of the dead. Chicago, 1960.

VAH 4029.60   Borzsák, István. Görög történeti chrestomathia. Budapest, 1960.

AH 7339.51.1   Broughton, Thomas R.S. The magistrates of the Roman Republic. Supplement. N.Y., 1960.

AH 7202.35   Capito, Caius Ateius. C. Atei Capitonis fragmenta. Wratislaviae, 1960.

AH 7201.110   Capito, G.A. Fragmenta. Wratislaviae, 1960.

AH 1279.57.3   Cerfaux, Lucien. L'antiquité: le Proche-Orient. 3. éd. Tournai, 1960.

AH 8653.5   Chastagnol, André. La préfecture urbaine à Rome sous le Bas-Empire. 1. éd. Paris, 1960.

AH 819.42.5   Childe, Vere Gordon. What happened in history. London, 1960.

AH 6107.10   Cloché, Paul. Histoire de la Macédoine. Paris, 1960.

AH 9609.3   Compernolle, René van. Étude de chronologie et d'historiographie siciliotes...concernant la fondation des colonies siciliotes. Bruxelles, 1960.

AH 4279.60.5   Crossland, R.A. New background to the study of ancient Greece. Sheffield, 1960.

Eg 709.60   Daix, Pierre. Cléopatre. Paris, 1960.

AH 6107.6   Daskalakēs, Apostolos Basileiou. Ho Hellenismos tēs archaias Makedonias. Athēnai, 1960.

AH 4819.52.12   Diano, Carlo. Forma ed evento. 2. ed. Venezia, 1960.

AH 4819.60   Doedeus, T.P. Ontmoeting met het oude Hellas. Amsterdam, 1960.

AH 7759.60   Doerries, Hermann. Constantine and religious liberty. New Haven, 1960.

Eg 879.60.5   Doresse, Jean. Des hieroglyphes à la croix. Istanbul, 1960.

AH 7819.60.5   Dudley, Donald R. The civilization of Rome. N.Y., 1960.

AH 4039.60   Ehrenberg, Victor. The Greek state. Oxford, 1960.

AH 8548.141   Filip, Jan. Celtic civilization and its heritage. Prague, 1960.

AH 189.60   Finley, Moses I. Slavery in classical antiquity. Cambridge, Eng., 1960.

AH 3143.22   Fischer, Hugo. Die Geburt der Hochkultur in Ägypten und Mesopotamien. Stuttgart, 1960.

AH 4829.60   Flacelière, Robert. L'amour en Grèce. Paris, 1960.

AH 7409.60   Franzero, A.M. The life and times of Tarquin the Etruscan. London, 1960.

Eg 602.15   Gardiner, Alan H. The Kadesh inscriptions of Ramesses II. Oxford, 1960.

AH 7479.21.9   Gelzer, Matthias. Cäsar, der Politiker und Staatsmann. 6. Aufl. Wiesbaden, 1960.

AH 7651.28   Gibbon, Edward. The decline and fall of the Roman Empire. London, 1960.

AH 7651.25.1   Gibbon, Edward. The decline and fall of the Roman Empire. 1. American ed. N.Y., 1960.

AH 3177.16   Gilgamesh. The epic of Gilgamesh. Harmondsworth, 1960.

AH 4819.60.10   Godel, Roger. Une Grèce secrete. Paris, 1960.

Eg 829.60   Grapow, Herman. Wie die alten Ägypter sich anredeten. Berlin, 1960.

Eg 459.60.5   Grediche, Hans. Die Stellung des Königs im alten Reich. Weisbaden, 1960.

AH 819.60   Green, Peter. Essays in antiquity. Cleveland, 1960.

AH 7462.5.2   Greenidge, Abel H.J. Sources for Roman history, 133-70 B.C. 2. ed. Oxford, 1960.

Eg 879.60.10   Griffiths, J.G. The conflict of Horus and Seth. Liverpool, 1960.

AH 7819.60.10   Grimal, Pierre. La civilisation romaine. Paris, 1960.

AH 7829.53.3   Grimal, Pierre. La vie à Rome dans l'antiquité. 3. éd. Paris, 1960.

AH 819.60.10A   Guthrie, William K.C. Tradition and personal achievement in classical antiquity. London, 1960.

AH 4459.60   Hackl, Ursula. Die oligarchische Bewegung in Athen am Ausgang des 5. Jahrhunderts. München, 1960.

AH 5313.15   Halsberghe, Gaston. Zoeklicht op het oude Athene. Hasselt, 1960.

AH 3151.2.5   Hammurabi, king of Babylonia. The Babylonian laws. Oxford, 1960. 2v.

AH 7489.60   Harmand, Louis. L'occident romain. Paris, 1960.

AH 8917.5   Harrel-Courtès, Henry. L'Italie des Étrusques. Paris, 1960.

Chronological Listing

1960 - cont.

AH 7309.38.3 — Heinze, Richard. Vom Geist des Römertums. 3. Aufl. Darmstadt, 1960.

AH 7279.60.5 — Heuss, Alfred. Römische Geschichte. Braunschweig, 1960.

AH 7199.60 — Honig, Richard. Humanitas und Rhetorik in spät römischen Kaisergesetzen; Studien zur Gesinnungsgrundlage des Dominats. Göttingen, 1960.

EgP 66.6A — International Association of Egyptologists. Annual Egyptological bibliography. Indexes, 1947-56. Leiden, 1960.

Eg 863.7 — Ismail, Ismail Moustafa. Die Gärten der alten Ägypter und die Entwicklung der Bewässerung bis zum Hochdamm bei Assuan. München? 1960?

AH 7279.60.10F — Johannes Victoriensis. Cronica romanorum. Klagenfurt, 1960.

AH 7039.60 — Jones, A.H.M. Studies in Roman government and law. Oxford, 1960.

AH 9777.29.6 — Jordanes. The Gothic history of Jordanes. N.Y., 1960.

AH 9777.19.5 — Jordanes. O proiskhozhdenii i deianiiakh getov. Moskva, 1960.

AH 8647.21 — Kahrstedt, Ulrich. Die wirtschaftliche Lage. Grossgriechenlands in der Kaiserzeit. Wiesbaden, 1960.

AH 7279.42.4 — Kornemann, Ernst. Römische Geschichte. 4. Aufl. Stuttgart, 1960. 2v.

AH 7519.60 — Kornemann, Ernst. Tiberius. Stuttgart, 1960.

AH 3022.17.5 — Kramer, S.N. Dve elegii na tablichke muzeia im A.S. Pushkina. Moskva, 1960.

AH 7469.60 — Krawczuk, A. Kolonizacja sullańska. Wrocław, 1960.

AH 3659.14 — Lamb, Harold. Cyrus the Great. 1st ed. Garden City, N.Y., 1960.

AH 3189.5 — Lambert, Wilfred G. Babylonian wisdom literature. Oxford, 1960.

Eg 879.60.20 — Lanozkowski, Guenter. Altägyptischer Prophetismus. Wiesbaden, 1960.

AH 7329.60 — Leon, Harry J. The Jews of ancient Rome. 1. ed. Philadelphia, 1960.

AH 7279.60 — Levi, Mario Attilio. Storia romana dagli etruschi a Tedosio. Milano, 1960.

AH 3017.65 — Limet, Henri. Le travail du métal au pays de Sumer au temps de la III dynastie d'Ur. Paris, 1960.

Eg 844.71 — Lüddeckens, E. Ägyptische Eheverträge. Wiesbaden, 1960.

Eg 139.60 — Lur'e, I.M. Ocherki drevneegipetskogo prava. Leningrad, 1960.

AH 9085.5 — Meiggs, Russell. Roman Ostia. Oxford, 1960.

AH 3909.9 — Michelini, T.F. La Siria nell'eta di Mari. Roma, 1960.

AH 1819.56.3 — Moscati, Sabatino. The face of the ancient Orient. Chicago, 1960.

AH 9221.5.5 — Natalucci, Mario. Ancona antica. Città di Castello, 1960.

Eg 1179.60F — Neugebauer, Otto. Egyptian astronomical texts. v.2-3, pt.1-2. Providence, 1960- 3v.

AH 4039.60.5 — Oliver, James H. Demokratia, the gods and the free world. Baltimore, 1960.

Eg 1309.60F — Otto, Eberhard. Das ägyptische Mundöffnungsritual. Wiesbaden, 1960. 2v.

AH 4559.60.10 — Pagliaro, Antonino. Alessandro Magno. Torino, 1960.

AH 49.60 — Palanque, Jean R. Les imperialismes antiques. Paris, 1960.

AH 7279.40.2 — Paoli, U.E. Vita romana. 2. ed. Paris, 1960.

AH 3013.960.5 — Parrot, André. Sumer. London, 1960.

AH 4819.60.30 — Payne, Robert. The splendor of Greece. 1st ed. N.Y., 1960.

AH 4559.60.5 — Pearson, Lionel. The lost histoire of Alexander the Great. N.Y., 1960-

AH 7629.60 — Perowne, Stewart. Hadrian. London, 1960.

AH 4819.60.15 — Polska Akademia nauk Oddział w Krakowie. Grecja współczesna i starozytna. Kraków, 1960.

Eg 879.60.15 — Posener, Georges. De la divinité du pharaon. Paris, 1960.

AH 4259.60 — Potamianos, Phōkiōn. The sea as a factor of the Greek life. Athens? 1960?

AH 3016.58 — Potratz, J.A.H. Die menschliche Rundskulptur in der sumero-akkadischen Kunst. Istanbul, 1960.

Eg 9.60 — Proosdij, Boricus Antonius van. Als een goet instrument. Leiden, 1960.

AH 3017.70F — Ravn, Otto E. A catalogue of oriental cylinder seals and seal impressions in the Danish National Museum. København, 1960.

AH 3177.4 — Rencontre assyriologique, 7, Paris, 1958. Gilgames et sa légende. Paris, 1960.

AH 7779.56.4 — Riciotti, Giuseppe. Julian the Apostate. Milwaukee, 1960.

AH 3022.25 — Rosengarten, Yvonne. Le concept sumérien de consommation. Paris, 1960.

AH 3022.26 — Rosengarten, Yvonne. Le regime des offrandes dans la société sumerienne d'après les textes présargoniques de Lagas. Paris, 1960.

AH 7114.36 — Sardi, Marta. I rapporti romano-ceriti e l'origine della civitas sino suffragio. Roma, 1960.

AH 7509.60 — Sattler, Peter. Augustus und der Senat. Göttingen, 1960.

Eg 879.57.7 — Sauneron, Serge. The priests of ancient Egypt. N.Y., 1960.

AH 4279.60.10 — Schachermeyr, Fritz. Griechische Geschichte. Stuttgart, 1960.

AH 842.46 — Schubart, Wilhelm. Das Buch bei den Griechen. 3. Aufl. Heidelberg, 1960.

AH 8607.12 — Sesti, Luigi. Storia d'Italia dalle origini alla conquista romana. Milano, 1960.

AH 4410.15 — Severyns, Albert. Grece et Proche Orient avant Homère. Bruxelles, 1960.

AH 3757.20 — Shikov, A.F. Shifskoe vosstanie na Bospore. Voronezh, 1960.

AH 6107.60 — Shofman, A.S. Istoriia antichnoi Makedonii. Kazan', 1960- 2v.

AH 3160.22 — Sjoeberg, Ake. Der mondgott nanna-suen in der sumerischen uberliefeung Uppsala. Uppsala, 1960.

Eg 919.60 — Smiderkówna, Anna. La propriété foncière privée dans l'Égypte de Vespasien et technique agricole d'après. Wroclaw, 1960.

AH 4279.60 — Smith, Morton. The ancient Greeks. Ithaca, N.Y., 1960.

AH 7203.149 — Soubie, André. Recherches sur les origines des rubriques du Digeste. Tarbes, 1960.

AH 4819.60.20 — Sprey, Karel. De weg van Hellas. Den Haag, 1960.

AH 7259.41.5 — Starr, Chester G. The Roman imperial navy. 2. ed. N.Y., 1960.

AH 1812.5 — Symposium on Urbanization and Cultural Development in the Ancient Near East, University of Chicago, 1958. City invincible. Chicago, 1960.

AH 7479.60 — Thevenot, Emile. Les éduens n'ont pas trahi. Bruxelles, 1960.

1960 - cont.

Eg 959.60 — Unamun. Puteshestvie Un-Amuna v Bibl; egipetskii ieraticheskii papirus no.120. Moskva, 1960.

AH 8913.10.10 — Vacano, Otto Wilhelm von. The Etruscans in the ancient world. N.Y., 1960.

AH 8060.5 — Vega, Luis A. de. Amilcar Barca. Madrid, 1960.

AH 7759.49.6 — Vogt, J. Constantin der Grosse und sein Jahrhundert. 2. Aufl. München, 1960.

AH 279.60.5 — Vogt, Joseph. Orbis. Freiburg, 1960.

AH 8073.23 — Warmington, Brian Herbert. Carthage. London, 1960.

AH 7469.60.10 — Weil, Bruno. Clodia. Zürich, 1960.

Eg 879.60 — Zandee, Jan. Death as an enemy. Leiden, 1960.

Eg 709.60.5 — Zel'in, Konstantin K. Issledovaniia po istorii zemel'nykh otnoshenii v ellinisticheskom Egipte, II-I vv. do n.e. Moskva, 1960.

AH 3983.5 — Zwl, A.D. van. The Moabites. Leiden, 1960.

1961

Eg 752.5.2 — Acta Alexandrinorum. Acta Alexandrinorum de mortibus Alexandriae nobilium; fragmenta papyracea Graeca. Lipsiae, 1961.

AH 7819.61 — Adcock, Frank Ezra. The character of the Romans in their history and their literature. Sydney, 1961.

Eg 279.61 — Aldred, Cyril. The Egyptians. London, 1961.

AH 7279.52.12 — Allcroft, Arthur. Tutorial history of Rome (to A.D. 69). 6. ed. London, 1961.

AH 3017.75F — Amiet, Pierre. La glyphique mesopotamienne archaïque. Paris, 1961.

AH 4839.61 — Anderson, John K. Ancient Greek horsemanship. Berkeley, 1961.

AH 7850.7 — André, Jacques. L'alimentation et la cuisine à Rome. Paris, 1961.

AH 4483.14 — Baelen, Jean. L'an 480, Salamine. Paris, 1961.

AH 7839.61 — Balil, Albert. La ley gladiatoria de Italica. Madrid, 1961.

AH 3707.26 — Baramki, D.C. Phoenicia and the Phoenicians. Beirut, 1961.

AH 4279.61A — Barr, Stringfellow. The will of Zeus. Philadelphia, 1961.

AH 3009.60.3F — Beek, Martinus A. Bildatlas der assyrisch-bablonischen Kultur. Gütersloh, 1961.

AH 819.61.5 — Bibby, Geoffrey. Four thousand years ago. 1. ed. N.Y., 1961.

AH 850.9 — Bommer, Sigwald. Die Gabe der Demeter. München, 1961.

AH 4860.10.5 — Bork, Arnold. Der junge Grieche. Zürich, 1961.

Eg 609.61.5 — Bratton, Fred. The first heretic...Ikhnaton the king. Boston, 1961.

AH 4239.61 — Brelich, A. Guerra. Bonn, 1961.

AH 339.61 — Carcopino, J. Profils de conquérants. Paris, 1961.

AH 7279.61 — Carcopino, Jérôme. Les étapes de l'impérialisme romaine. Paris, 1961.

AH 8073.22.15 — Charles-Picard, Gilbert. Daily life in Carthage at the time of Hannibal. London, 1961.

AH 7909.24.5 — Charlesworth, M.P. Trade-routes and commerce of the Roman Empire. Hildesheim, 1961.

AH 4819.61.5 — Conley, P.M. America's debt to Greece. Charleston, 1961.

AH 7449.61 — Cottrell, Leonard. Hannibal, enemy of Rome. 1. American ed. N.Y., 1961.

AH 7159.61 — Crifò, Giuliano. Richerche sull'"exilium" nel periodo repubblicano. Milano, 1961.

AH 7850.6 — Deouna, Waldemar. Croyances et superstitions de table dans la Rome antique. Bruxelles, 1961.

AH 819.61.20 — Deutsche Historiker-Gesellschaft. Sozialökonomische Verhältnisse in alter Orient. Berlin, 1961.

AH 8011.8 — Diligenskii, G.G. Severnaia Afrika v IV-V vekakh. Moskva, 1961.

AH 3921.8 — Downey, Glanville. A history of Antioch in Syria. Princeton, 1961.

AH 4659.61 — Eddy, S.K. The king is dead. Lincoln, 1961.

AH 4410.40.3 — Emmrich, Kurt. An den Küsten des Lichts. 3. Aufl. München, 1961.

AH 7309.61 — Espadas Burgos, Manuel. La periodización de la historiografía romana. Madrid, 1961.

AH 862.11 — Esser, Alexander Albert Maria. Das Antlitz der Blindheit in der Antike. Leiden, 1961.

Eg 879.48.5 — Frankfort, Henri. Ancient Egyptian religion. N.Y., 1961.

Eg 848.7 — Galé, José Miguel. Las escuelas del antiguo Egipto a través de los papiros griegos. Madrid, 1961.

AH 3160.21 — García de la Fuente, Oligario. Los dioses y el pecado en Babilonia. El Escorial, 1961.

Eg 459.61 — Gardiner, Alan. Egypt of the pharaohs. Oxford, 1961.

AH 842.40 — Gil, Luis. Censura en el mundo antiguo. Madrid, 1961.

AH 3177.14 — Gilgamesh. Epos o Gil'gameshe. Moskva, 1961.

AH 4559.61 — Gleixner, H.J. Das Alexanderbild der Byzantiner. München, 1961.

AH 4299.61 — Grècs et barbares. Genève, 1961.

AH 862.12 — Hagen, Hansludwig. Die physiologisch und psychologisch Bedeutung der Leber in der Antike. Paris, 1961.

AH 8913.15 — Heurgon, Jacques. La vie quotidienne chez les Etrusques. Paris, 1961.

AH 8907.30.5 — Hus, Alain. The Etruscans. N.Y., 1961.

AH 5459.5 — Huxley, George Leonard. Crete and the Lumians. Oxford, 1961.

AH 139.61 — Imbert J. Le droit antique et ses prolongements modernes. Paris, 1961.

Eg 847.10 — Iversen, Erik. The myth of Egypt and its hieroglyphs in European tradition. Copenhagen, 1961.

AH 4842.73 — Jaeger, Werner Wilhelm. Early Christianity and Greek Paideia. Cambridge, 1961.

AH 2011.10 — Jamme, Albert. La dynastie de Sarahbi il Yakuf et la documentation épigraphique sud-arabe. Istanbul, 1961.

AH 3020.30 — Jones, Tom B. Sumerian economic texts from the third Ur dynasty. Minneapolis, 1961.

AH 4609.26.10 — Jouguet, P. L'impérialism macédonien. Paris, 1961.

AH 7238.88.1 — Judson, Harry P. Caesar's army; a study of the military art of the Romans in the last days of the Republic. N.Y., 1961.

Eg 939.61 — Kees, Hermann. Ancient Egypt. Chicago, 1961.

AH 7769.61 — Kohns, Hans Peter. Versorgungskrisen und Hungerrevolten im spätantiken Rom. Bonn, 1961.

AH 6168.5 — Komitee zur Förderung der Klassischen Studien. Griechesche Städte und einheimische Völker des Schwarzmengebietes. Berlin, 1961.

Eg 1099.61 — Korostovtsev, M.A. Ieraticheskii papirus 127 iz sobraniia GMII im A.S. Pushkina. Moskva, 1961.

AH 1842.5 — Kuehnert, F. Allgemeinbildung und Fachbildung in der Antike. Berlin, 1961.

Chronological Listing

1961 - cont.

AH 7169.06.3 — Leage, Richard William. Leage's Roman private law. London, 1961.

AH 8549.161 — Le Roux, F. Les druides. Paris, 1961.

AH 819.61.10F — Life (Chicago). The epic of man. N.Y., 1961.

AH 7469.60.5 — Linderski, Jerzy. Państwo a kolegia. Kraków, 1961.

AH 819.61.25 — Lissner, Ivar. Rätselhafte Kulturen. Olten, 1961.

AH 7659.31.10 — Lot, Ferdinand. The end of the ancient world and the beginnings of the Middle Ages. N.Y., 1961.

AH 3661.15 — Lukonin, Vladimir G. Iran v epokhu pervykh Sasanidov. Leningrad, 1961.

AH 7492.5 — McCrum, M. Select documents of the principates. Cambridge, Eng., 1961.

AH 7479.61 — Madaule, Jacques. Jules César. Paris, 1961.

AH 4809.61 — Meritt, Benjamin Dean. The Athenian year. Berkeley, Calif., 1961.

Eg 847.4.10 — Möller, G. Hieratische Lesestücke für den akademischen Gebrauch. v.1-3. Berlin, 1961.

AH 459.61 — Mourre, Michel. Le monde a la mort de Socrate. Paris, 1961.

AH 1819.61A — Muller, H.J. Freedom in the ancient world. 1. ed. N.Y., 1961.

AH 7469.61 — Ooteghem, Jules van. Lucius Marcius Phillipus et sa famille. Namur, 1961.

AH 4483.15 — Papadopoulos, Nikos M. Hē naumachia tēs Salaminos. Athēnai, 1961.

AH 4819.60.26 — Payne, Robert. The splendor of Greece. London, 1961.

VAH 7823.2 — Peoli, Ugo Enrico. Ciceronis Jilius. 5. ed. Florentiae, 1961.

AH 819.61F — Piggott, Stuart. The dawn of civilization. N.Y.,]1961.

Eg 819.61 — Pirenne, Jacques. Histoire de la civilisation de l'Égypte. Neuchâtel, 1961. 3v.

AH 4839.61.5 — Popplow, Ulrich. Leibesübungen und Leibeserziehung in der griechischen Antike. 3. Aufl. Stuttgart, 1961.

AH 1309.61 — Postovskaia, N.M. Izuchenie drevnei istorii Blizhnego Vostoka. Moskva, 1961.

AH 4819.61.10 — Problemas del mundo helenistico. Madrid, 1961.

Eg 879.61 — Rachewiltz, Boris de. I miti e i luoghi dell'antico Egitto. Milano, 1961.

Eg 1029.61 — Riesterer, Peter P. Kostbarkeiten aus Ägypten. Zürich, 1961.

AH 7139.61F — Rome (Ancient). Laws, statutes, etc. Ancient Roman statutes. Austin, 1961.

AH 8615.7 — Ruggini, Lallia. Economia e società nell'Italia annonaria. Milano, 1961.

AH 1819.61.5 — Schmökel, Hartmut. Kulturgeschichte des alten Orient. Stuttgart, 1961.

AH 7139.46.2 — Schulz, Fritz. Geschichte der römischen Rechtswissenschaft. Weimar, 1961.

AH 7279.35.10.3 — Scullard, H.H. A history of the Roman world from 753 to 146 B.C. 3. ed. London, 1961.

AH 959.61 — Seel, Otto. Antike Entdeckerfahrten. Zürich, 1961.

Eg 602.5.2 — Sethe, Kurt. Urkunden der 18. Dynastie. Übersetzung zu den Heften 17-22...von Wolfgang Helck. Berlin, 1961.

AH 7799.61 — Sirago, V.A. Galla Placidia e la trasformazione politica dell'Occidente. Louvain, 1961.

AH 7709.61 — Sotgiu, Giovanna. Studi sull'epigrafia di Aureliano. Palmero, 1961.

AH 4410.25 — Starr, Chester. The origins of Greek civilization, 1100-650 B.C. N.Y., 1961.

AH 7819.11.12 — Stobart, J.C. The grandeur that was Rome. 4. ed. London, 1961.

AH 3052.6.5 — Struve, Vasilii V. Gosudarstvo Lagash. Moskva, 1961.

AH 39.61 — Suerbaum, Werner. Vom Antiken zum frühmittelatlerlichen Staatsbegriff. Münster, 1961.

AH 7819.52.5 — Ussani, Vincenzo. Guida allo studio della civiltà romana antica. 2. ed. Torino, 1961-64. 2v.

AH 7239.61 — Várady, Lazló. Késórómai hadügyek es társadalmi alapjaik. Budapest, 1961.

Eg 609.61 — Vergote, J. Toutankhamon dans les archives hittites. Istanbul, 1961.

AH 7169.61 — Volterra, Edoardo. Istituzioni di diritto privato romano. Roma, 1961.

AH 9.61 — Voronkov, A.I. Drevniaia Gretsiia i drevnii Rim. Moskva, 1961.

AH 4659.61.5 — Welles, Charles B. The Hellenistic world. Photoreproduction. New Haven, 1961.

AH 3664.14 — Widengren, George. Iranische Geisteswelt von der Anfängen bis zum Islam. Baden-Baden, 1961.

AH 4833.22 — Zschietzschmann, W. Weltkampf- und Übungsstätten in Griechenland. Schomdorf, 1961. 2v.

1962

AH 7762.5 — Abinnaeus, Flavius. The Abinnaeus archive; papers of a Roman officer in the reign of Constantius II. Oxford, 1962.

AH 29.62 — Akademiia nauk SSSR. Institut narodov Azii. Drevnii mir; sbornik statei. Moskva, 1962.

AH 4559.62 — Alexandre le Grand. Paris, 1962.

AH 883.2 — Altheim, Franz. Entwicklungshilfe im Altertum. Reinbeck, 1962.

AH 7859.7 — Balsdon, John Percy V.D. Roman women. London, 1962.

AH 3009.60.1F — Beek, Martinus A. Atlas of Mesopotamia; a survey of the history and civilization of Mesopotamia from the Stone Age to the fall of Babylon. London, 1962.

AH 29.62.5 — Bengtson, Hermann. Die Staatsverträge des Altertums. v.2-3. München, 1962. 2v.

AH 7479.62 — Bocheński, J. Boski Juliusz. Wyd. 2. Warszawa, 1962.

AH 4819.62.20 — Boer, Willem den. Eros en Amor. Den Haag, 1962.

AH 9607.23 — Borzi, Salvatore. Sicilia Schiava; panoramica azione critico-storica. Paternò, 1962.

Eg 29.06.1 — Breasted, James Henry. Ancient records of Egypt. N.Y., 1962. 5v.

Eg 879.62F — Brooklyn Institute of Arts and Sciences. Museum. Mss. (Papyrus 47.218.3). A Saite oracle papyrus from Thebes. Providence, R.I., 1962.

AH 4103.2 — Buchanan, James. Theorika. N.Y., 1962.

AH 4479.62 — Burn, Andrew. Persia and the Greeks. London, 1962.

AH 7759.62 — Calderone, S. Costantino e il cattolicesimo. Firenze, 1962.

AH 7419.62 — Cassola, F. I gruppi politici romani nel III secolo A.C. Triesti, 1962.

AH 7659.62 — Centro Italiano di Studi Sull'alto Medioevo. Il passaggio dall'antichita al Medioevo in occidente. Spoleto, 1962.

AH 8662.5 — Chastagnol, André. Les fastes de la préfecture de Rome au Bas-Empire. Paris, 1962.

1962 - cont.

AH 4309.62 — Châtelet, François. La naissance de l'histoire. Paris, 1962.

AH 5708.7 — Cook, John. The Greeks in Ionia and the East. London, 1962.

AH 3963.77 — Daniel-Rops, H. Daily life in the time of Jesus. N.Y., 1962.

AH 4482.2 — Daskalakès, A.B. Problèmes historiques autour de la bataille des Thermopyles. Paris, 1962.

AH 809.62 — Delorme, J. Les grandes dates de l'antiquité. Paris, 1962.

AH 8008.10 — Desanges, J. Catalogue des tribus africaines de l'antiquité classique à l'ouest du Nil. Dakar, 1962.

AH 4279.62 — De Silincourt, A. The world of Herodotus. London, 1962.

AH 3921.9 — Downey, Glanville. Antioch in the age of Thedosius the Great. Norman, 1962.

AH 4839.62 — Drees, Ludwig. Der Ursprung der olympischen Spiele. Stuttgart, 1962.

AH 3664.12 — Duchesne-Guillemin, J. La religion de l'Iran ancien. Paris, 1962.

AH 7819.60.6 — Dudley, Donald R. The civilization of Rome. N.Y., 1962.

AH 5308.10 — Eliot, C.W.J. Coastal demes of Attika. Toronto, 1962.

AH 7409.62 — Erasmus, Hendrik. The origins of Rome. Assen, 1962.

AH 8513.14 — Eydaux, Henri. La France antique. Paris, 1962.

AH 4819.54.2 — Finley, Moses I. The world of Odysseus. Harmondsworth, 1962.

AH 4863.13.5 — Flacelière, Robert. Love in ancient Greece. N.Y., 1962.

AH 3657.38 — Frye, R.N. The heritage of Persia. London, 1962.

AH 7299.62 — Gelzer, Matthias. Kleine Schriften. Wiesbaden, 1962-64. 3v.

AH 7903.6 — Giacchero, Marta. Note sull'Editto-calmiere di Diocleziano. Genova, 1962.

AH 4847.15 — Ginouvès, Renè. Balaestyike. Paris, 1962.

AH 2147.9 — Golubtsova, E.S. Ocherki sotsial'no-politicheskoi istorii Maloi Asii v I-III vv. Moskva, 1962.

AH 4299.62.5 — Gomme, Arnold W. More essays in Greek history and literature. Oxford, 1962.

AH 819.62.10 — Gordon, Cyrus. Before the Bible. London, 1962.

AH 1279.62 — Gray, John. Archaeology and the Old Testament world. London, 1962.

AH 3052.6 — Grégoire, J.P. La province méridionale de l'état de Lagash. Luxembourg, 1962.

AH 3661.20 — Gumilev, L.N. Podvig Bakhrama Chubiny. Leningrad, 1962.

AH 3707.28 — Harden, Donald B. The Phoenicians. London, 1962.

AH 4819.62.15 — Harder, Richard. Eigenart der Griechen. Freiburg, 1962.

AH 819.60.15 — Hardy, William. The Greek and Roman world. Cambridge, 1962.

AH 4279.26.5.4 — Hatzfeld, Jean. Histoire de la Grèce ancienne. 3. éd. Paris, 1962.

AH 7279.62 — Heichelheim, F. A history of the Roman people. Englewood Cliffs, 1962.

Eg 269.62 — Helck, Hans Wolfgang. Die Beziehungen Ägyptens zu Vorderasien im 3. und 2. Jahrtausend vor Christ. Wiesbaden, 1962.

AH 7201.11.5 — Honoré, Antony. Gaius. Oxford, 1962.

AH 819.62F — Horizon (New York). The Horizon book of lost worlds. N.Y., 1962.

AH 5759.12A — Huxley, G.L. Early Sparta. Cambridge, 1962.

AH 7819.62.5 — Jones, Tom Bard. The silver-plated age. Sandoval, 1962.

AH 3757.24 — Junge, Julius. Saka-Studien: der Ferne Nordasten im Weltbild der Antike. Aalen, 1962.

AH 7659.62.10 — Kagan, Donald. Decline and fall of the Roman Empire. Boston, 1962.

AH 2110.15 — Kinal, Füruzan. Eski Anadolu tarihi. Ankara, 1962.

AH 842.47 — Kleberg, Tönnes. Bokhandel och bokforlag i antiken. Stockholm, 1962.

AH 7819.62 — Knoche, Ulrich. Vom Selbstverständnis der Römer. Heidelberg, 1962.

AH 8161.2 — Kolbe, H.G. Die Statthalter Numidiens von Gallien bis Konstantin, 268-320. München, 1962.

Eg 1009.62 — Korostovtsev, M.A. Pistsy Drevnego Egipta. Moskva, 1962.

AH 3921.9.5 — Kurbatov, G.L. Rannevizantiiskii gorod. Leningrad, 1962.

AH 299.62 — Laptev, V.V. Pervobytnoobshchinnyi i rabovladel'cheskii stroi na territorii nashei strany. Leningrad, 1962.

AH 8008.9 — Leglay, Marcel. Les gaulois en Afrique. Bruxelles, 1962.

AH 859.8 — Leipoldt, J. Die Frau in der antiken Welt und im Urchristentum. Gütersloh, 1962.

AH 5608.2 — Lepore, Ettore. Recherche sull'antico-epiro. Napoli, 1962.

AH 2958.6 — Levillain, Jean. Étude sur la localisation d'Ilion d'apres l'Iliade d'Homere. Istanbul, 1962.

AH 819.62.5 — Lissner, Ivar. The silent past. N.Y., 1962.

AH 3941.5 — Liverari, Mario. Storia di Ugarit nell'età degli archivi politici. Roma, 1962.

AH 4169.62 — Mannzmann, Anneliese. Griechische Stiftungsurkunden. Münster, 1962.

AH 8963.5 — Mansuelli, Guido Achille. I Cisalpini. Firenze, 1962.

AH 4410.10.15 — Matz, Friedrich. Kreta, Mykene, Troja. 5. Aufl. Stuttgart, 1962.

AH 7307.34.31 — Montesquieu, Charles de. Betrachtungen über die Ursachen von Grösse und Niedergang der Römer. Bremen, 1962.

AH 4299.62.10 — Moretti, Luigi. Ricerche sulle leghe greche: peloponnesiaca-beotica-licia. Roma, 1962.

AH 4539.62 — Mossé, C. La fin de la démocratie athénienne. Paris, 1962.

AH 3210.5.2 — Narain, A.K. The Indo-Greeks. Oxford, 1962.

AH 7799.40.5 — Németh, Gyula. Attila ve Hunlari. Istanbul, 1962.

AH 7139.62A — Nicholas, B. An introduction to Roman law. Oxford, 1962.

AH 4819.62.5 — Noltenius, Hélène. In het voorportaal van de Akropolis. Den Haag, 1962.

AH 8457.6 — Oliva, Pavel. Pannonia and the onset of crisis in the Roman empire. Praha, 1962.

Eg 509.62 — Omlin, J. Amenemhet I. und Sesostris I. Heidelberg, 1962.

AH 4842.89 — Pélékidis, Chrysis. Histoire de l'Ephébie attique. Paris, 1962.

AH 4842.90 — Pélékidis, Chrysis. Histoire de l'Éphébie attique. Paris, 1962.

AH 4659.62 — Petit, Paul. La civilisation hellénistique. Paris, 1962.

AH 9.59.2 — Petit, Paul. Guide de l'étudiant en histoire ancienne. 2. éd. Paris, 1962.

AH 279.62 — Petit, Paul. Précis d'histoire ancienne. Paris, 1962.

AH 7509.62.5 — Picard, G.C. Auguste et Néron. Paris, 1962.

AH 3966.32 — Pidal Rios, Carlos. Los paises legendarios de la Biblia. Buenos Aires, 1962.

AH 7279.39.10 — Piganiol, André. Histoire de Rome. 5. éd. Paris, 1962.

AH 819.61.4F — Piggott, Stuart. Aux portes de l'histoire. Paris, 1962.

Chronological Listing

1962 - cont.

AH 3005.913   Pillet, Maurice. Un pionnier de l'assyriologie: Victor Place. Paris, 1962.

AH 8379.2   Pippidi, D.M. Epigraphische Beiträge zur Geschichte Histrias in hellenistischer und römanischer Zeit. Berlin, 1962.

Eg 1079.62   Pound, Ezra. Love poems of ancient Egypt. Norfolk, Conn., 1962.

AH 7649.62   Proyart, Pierre de. Marc Aurèle. Paris, 1962.

AH 4819.62   Riesterer, Peter P. Griechisches Erbe. Zürich, 1962.

AH 8557.10   Rogošić, Roko. Veliki Illirik (284-395) i njegova konačna dioba (396-437). Zagreb, 1962.

AH 7149.12   Rotondi, G. Leges publicae populi Romani. Photoreproduction. Hildesheim, 1962.

AH 7509.62   Rowell, H.T. Rome in the Augustan Age. Norman, 1962.

AH 3143.15   Saggs, H.W. The greatness that was Babylon. N.Y., 1962.

AH 4819.62.10   Samivel. The glory of Greece. N.Y., 1962.

AH 4842.92   Sant'Anna Dionisio, J.A. Pedagogia culminante dos gregos. Porto, 1962.

Eg 919.62   Savel'eva, T.N. Agrarnyi stroi Egipta. Moskva, 1962.

AH 9508.6   Schell, Günther. Die römische Besiedlung von Rheingau und Welterau. Mainz, 1962.

Eg 139.62F   Seidl, F. Ptolemäische Rechtgeschichte. 2. Aufl. Glückstadt, 1962.

AH 8986.10   Storia romana 1962-63. Epigrafia latina; il Piemonte preromano e romano. Milano, 1962.

Eg 459.62   Stuchevskii, Iosef A. Khramovaia forma tsarskogo khoz. drevnego Egypta. Moskva, 1962.

AH 8008.11   Teutsch, Leo. Das Stadtewesen in Nordafrika. Berlin, 1962.

AH 862.13   Thorwald, Jürgen. Macht und Geheimnis der frühen Arzte. München, 1962.

AH 862.13.5   Thorwald, Jürgen. Science and secrets of early medicine. London, 1962.

AH 7039.62   Timpe, D. Untersuchungen zur Kontinuität. Wiesbaden, 1962.

AH 299.22.2   Ure, Percy. The origin of tyranny. N.Y., 1962.

Eg 809.62   Vanderslayen, Claude. Chronologie des préfets d'Égypte de 284 à 395. Bruxelles, 1962.

Eg 1309.62F   Vandier, Jacques. Le papyrus Jumilhac. Paris, 1962.

AH 4819.62.25   Vernant, J.P. Les origines de la pensée grecque. Paris, 1962.

AH 7700.5   Walser, Gerold. Die Krise des römischen Reiches; Bericht über die Forschungen zur Geschichte des 3. Jahrhunderts. Berlin, 1962.

AH 3167.7   Weitemeyer, M. Some aspects of the hiring of workers in the Sippar region at the time of Hammorati. Copenhagen, 1962.

AH 3005.14   Wiseman, D.J. The expansion of Assyrian studies. London, 1962.

Eg 819.62.5   Wolf, Walther. Kulturgeschichte des alten Ägypten. Stuttgart, 1962.

AH 4299.62   Woodhead, Arthur Geoffrey. The Greeks in the West. London, 1962.

1963

AH 29.63   Adademiia nauk SSSR. Otdelenie istoricheskikh nauk. Problemy sotsial'no-ekonomischeskoi istorii drevnego mira. Moskva, 1963.

AH 1299.63   Akademiia nauk SSSR. Institut Archeologii. Antichnyï gorod. Moskva, 1963.

AH 5436.2   Alexander, J.A. Potidaea. Athens, 1963.

AH 819.63F   Bacon, Edward. Vanished civilizations of the ancient world. N.Y., 1963.

AH 4279.63   Badi, Amiz Mehdi. Les Grecs et les barbares. v.1-3. Lausanne, 1963-66. 2v.

AH 7819.63   Bardon, H. Le génie latin. Bruxelles, 1963.

AH 7489.63   Behn, Friedrich. Romertum und Völkerwanderung. Zürich, 1963.

Eg 709.63   Bloedow, Edmund. Beiträge zur Geschichte der Ptolemaios XII. Würzburg, 1963.

AH 4819.54.7   Bonnard, André. Civilization grecque. v.2-3. Paris, 1963. 2v.

Eg 879.63F   Book of That Which is in the Nether World. Das Amduat. v.1-3. Wiesbaden, 1963. 2v.

AH 7509.63   Brancati, Antonio. Augusto e la querra di Spagna. Urbino, 1963.

AH 4909.27   Brashinskii, I.P. Afiny i Severnoe Prichernomor'e v VI-II vv. do n.e. Moskva, 1963.

AH 4818.98.20   Burckhardt, J. History of Greek culture. N.Y., 1963.

AH 2007.7.2   Çagatay, Neş'et. Islâmdan önce Arap tarihi. 2. ed. Ankara, 1963.

AH 9777.41   Cazzaniga, I. Dispense relative alla lettura del testo di Iordanes Historia getarum. Milano, 1963.

AH 7659.63   Chambers, M.H. The fall of Rome. N.Y., 1963.

AH 4819.63.15   Chamoux, François. La civilisation grecque. Paris, 1963.

Eg 1039.63   Champdor, Albert. Le livre des morts. Paris, 1963.

AH 1819.45.4   Contenau, Georges. Les civilisations anciennes du Proche-Orient. 5. éd. Paris, 1963.

AH 4410.30   Cottrell, L. Realms of gold; a journey in search of the Mycenaeans. 1. ed. Greenwich, 1963.

AH 3660.15   Dandamaev, M.A. Iran pri perviykh akhemenidakh. Moskva, 1963.

AH 4559.63   Daskalakēs, Apostolos Basileiou. O Mégas Alexandros kaí o Hellēniphios. Athēnai, 1963.

AH 4279.62.3   De Silincourt, A. The world of Herodotus. 1. ed. Boston, 1963.

AH 7479.63   Dickinson, J. Death of a republic. N.Y., 1963.

Eg 309.63   Donadoni, Sergio. Le fonti indirette della storia egiziana. Roma, 1963.

AH 3921.8.5   Downey, Glanville. Ancient Antioch. Princeton, 1963.

AH 4559.63.5   Dzięciot, Witold. Aleksander Wielki Macedoński. Londyn, 1963.

AH 7469.63.5   Earl, D.C. Tiberius Gracchus; a study in politics. Bruxelles, 1963.

AH 3757.22   Elderkin, George. Migration in the Mycenaean Age. n.p., 1963.

Eg 879.63.5   Énel (pseud.). Les origines de la Genèse et l'enseignement des temples de l'ancienne Egypte. Paris, 1963.

AH 8907.42   Études étrusco-italiques. Louvain, 1963.

AH 4819.63   Finley, Moses I. The ancient Greeks. N.Y., 1963.

AH 3657.40A   Foye, R.N. The heritage of Persia. Cleveland, 1963.

AH 7099.63   Ganghoffer, Roland. L'evolution des institutions municipales en Occident et en Orient au Bas-Empire. Thèse. Paris, 1963.

1963 - cont.

AH 7651.25.2   Gibbon, Edward. The decline and fall of the Roman Empire. N.Y., 1963.

AH 2209.2   Gorelli, P. Les assyriens en Cappadoce. Paris, 1963.

AH 7819.60.11   Grimal, Pierre. The civilization of Rome. N.Y., 1963.

AH 7863.6   Grinial, P. L'amour à Rome. Paris, 1963.

AH 7559.63   Hallermann, Burkhard. Untersuchungen zu den Truppenbewegungen in den Jahren 68/69 nach Christ. Inaug. Diss. Würzburg, 1963.

AH 7469.63   Hawthorn, J.R. The Republican empire. London, 1963.

AH 7819.63.5   Helm, Ruddle. Römisches Alltagsleben im 1. und 2. Jahrhundert nach Christ nach martial und juvenal. Zürich, 1963.

AH 4479.63   Hignett, Charles. Xerxes' invasion of Greece. Oxford, 1963.

AH 1879.63   Hooke, S.H. Middle Eastern mythology. Harmondsworth, 1963.

AH 4842.73.15   Jaeger, Werner Wilhelm. Das frühe Christentum und die griechische Beldung. Berlin, 1963.

AH 819.63.5   Jones, Tom Bard. Ancient civilization. Chicago, 1963.

AH 4459.63   Kanellopoulos, Panagiōtēs. Apo ton Marathōna sten Pydna ki'ōs ten katastrophe tēs Korivthou 490-146 p.ch. Athēnai, 1963. 3v.

Eg 1029.63   Kaplony, Peter. Die Inschriften der ägyptischen Frühzeit. Wiesbaden, 1963. 3v.

Eg 139.63   Kaplony-Heckel, U. Die demotischen Tempeleide. Wiesbaden, 1963. 2v.

AH 5759.13   Kiele, F. Lakonien und Sparta. München, 1963.

AH 3191.10F   Koecher, F. Die babylonisch-assyrische Medizin in Texten. Berlin, 1963- 4v.

AH 3966.31   Kopp, Clemens. The holy places of the Gospels. N.Y., 1963.

AH 3022.17.10   Kramer, S.N. The Sumerians: their history. Chicago, 1963.

AH 3012.17   Laessøe, J. People of ancient Assyria. London, 1963.

AH 4189.63.5   Lentsman, Iakov A. Rabstvo v mikenskoi i gomerovskoi Gretsii. Moskva, 1963.

AH 7139.63   Levy, Ernst. Gesammelte Schriften. Köln, 1963. 2v.

AH 9563.6   Lilliu, G. La civiltà dei Sardi dal neolitico all'età dei nuraghi. Torino, 1963.

AH 7449.63   Lippold, A. Consules. Bonn, 1963.

AH 1409.63.10   Liverani, M. Introduzione alla storia dell'Asia anteriore antica. Roma, 1963.

AH 4819.63.5   Lloyd-Jones, H. The Greeks. 1. ed. Cleveland, 1963.

AH 7829.24.6   McDaniel, W.B. Roman private life and its survivals. N.Y., 1963.

AH 4159.63   MacDowell, D. Athenian homicide law in the age of the orators. Manchester, 1963.

AH 7239.63A   MacMullen, R. Soldier and civilian in the later Roman Empire. Cambridge, 1963.

AH 8647.26   Maiuri, Amedeo. Passeggiate in Magna Grecia. Napoli, 1963.

Eg 509.63   Margulies, H. Der Pharao Josefs. Herrenalb, 1963.

AH 7469.35.3   Marsh, Frank B. A history of the Roman world from 146 to 30 B.C. 3. ed. London, 1963.

Eg 879.63.10   Merkelbach, Reinhold. Isisfeste in griechisch-römischer Zeit; Daten und Riten. Meisenheim am Glan, 1963.

AH 7479.18.3   Meyer, Eduard. Caesars Monarchie und das Principat des Pompejus. 3. Aufl. Stuttgart, 1963.

Eg 819.63   Nolli, G. Civiltà dell'antico Egitto. Tolino, 1963.

Eg 1309.63PF   Papyrus Reimer I. Papyrus Reimer I. Boston, 1963.

AH 7059.63   Parsi, Blanche. Désignation et investiture de l'empéreur romain, Ier et IIe siècles après J.C. Paris, 1963.

AH 4819.63.25   Peremans, Willy. Hellas en de Westeuropese cultuur. Kasterlee, 1963.

AH 7659.62.5   Perowne, Stewart. Caesars and saints. 1. ed. N.Y., 1963.

AH 7279.63   Pialouse, B. De Romulus à Romulus. Paris, 1963.

AH 7419.63   Pieri, Piero. Genesi e sviluppi dell'imperialismo. Torino, 1963.

AH 3670.5.5   Pigulevskaia, N.V. Les villes de l'état iranien. Paris, 1963.

AH 3757.10   Potratz, Johannes A.H. Die Skythen in Südrussland. Basel, 1963.

AH 7819.63.10   Robertis, Francesco Maria de. Lavore e lavoratori nel mondo romano. Bari, 1963.

AH 7039.63   Rouvier, J. Du pouvoir dans la république romaine. Paris, 1963.

AH 279.63.5   Schaefer, Hans. Probleme der alten Geschichte. Göttingen, 1963.

AH 9607.24   Schenk von Stauffenberg, Alexander. Trinakria. München, 1963.

AH 7489.59.2   Scullard, Howard Hayes. From the Gracchi to Nero. 2. ed. N.Y., 1963.

AH 3045.150   Segal, Judah B. Edessa and Harran. London, 1963.

AH 7202.36   Seyfarth, W. Soziale Fragen der spätrömischen Kaiserzeit im Spiegel des Theodosianus. Berlin, 1963.

AH 8073.24   Shifman, I.S. Vozniknovenie Karfagenskoi derzhavy. Leningrad, 1963.

AH 339.63   Sonnet-Altenburg, Helene. Hetären, Mütter, Amazonen. Heidenheim, 1963.

AH 3310.5.5   Spyridakis, K. Kyprioi basileis tou 4 aiv. P. Ch. Leukōsia, 1963.

AH 8913.20F   Svenska Institutet i Rom. Etruscan culture, land and people. N.Y., 1963.

AH 279.63.10   Sverdlovsk, Russia (City). Ural'skii gosudarstvennyi universitet. Antichnaia drevnost' i srednie veka. v.1-2,4-5,7. v.1,5; Photoreproduction. Sverdlovsk, 1963- 5v.

AH 8918.1   Tabanelli, Mario. La medicina nel mondo degli Etruschi. Firenze, 1963.

AH 1279.63   Tovar, Antonio. Historia del antiguo oriente. Barcelona, 1963.

AH 4189.63   Turasiewicz, R. De servis testibus in Atheniensium. Wrocław, 1963.

AH 8549.163.1   Vries, Jan de. La religion des Celtes. Paris, 1963.

AH 3005.855.5   Waterfield, Gordon. Layard of Nineveh. London, 1963.

AH 8207.30   Welch, G.P. Britannia, the Roman conquest. 1. ed. Middletown, 1963.

AH 7419.63.5   Werner, Robert. Der Beginn der römischen Republik. München, 1963.

AH 9707.9   Wieser, J. Die Thraker. Stuttgart, 1963.

AH 1239.63   Yadin, Y. The art of warfare in Biblical lands. N.Y., 1963. 2v.

AH 4819.63.10F   Zadoks, A.N. Ontieke cultuur in beeld. 7. Druk. Bussum, 1963.

Chronological Listing

1964

AH 2007.6	Altheim, Franz. Die Araber in der alten Welt. v.2-5, pt.1-2. Berlin, 1964. 5v.
AH 39.64	Anderson, W. Man's quest for political knowledge. Minneapolis, 1964.
AH 3143.16	Appenheim, Adolf L. Ancient Mesopotamia. Chicago, 1964.
AH 8007.25	Ayache, Albert. Histoire ancienne de l'Afrique du nord. Paris, 1964.
AH 4545.5	Aymard, André. Le monde grec aux temps de Philippe II de Macédoine et d'Alexandre le Grand (359-323 avant J.-C.). Paris, 1964.
AH 299.64	Badian, Ernst. Studies in Greek and Roman history. Oxford, 1964.
AH 3002.150	Baghdad. Iraq Museum. Texts in the Iraq Museum. Baghdad, 1964- 7v.
AH 7529.34.6	Balsdom, John Percy Vyvian D. The Emperor Gaius Caligula. Oxford, 1964.
AH 8073.25	Barreca, Ferruccio. La civiltà di Cartagine. Cagliari, 1964.
AH 7299.49.3	Barrow, R.H. The Romans. Chicago, 1964.
AH 4299.64	Bauer, Walter. Lorbeer für Hallas. Stuttgart, 1964.
AH 4842.91	Beck, F.A.G. Greek education. London, 1964.
Eg 509.64	Beckerath, Jürgen von. Untersuchungen zur politischen Geschichte der Zweiten Zwischenzeit in Ägypten. Glückstadt, 1964.
AH 7709.64.5	Bellezza, Angela. Massimino il Trace. Genova, 1964.
AH 3966.22	Ben-Har, Bezalel. The concealed map of the land of Israel. Jerusalem, 1964?
AH 4559.64.5	Bieber, Margarete. Alexander the Great in Greek and Roman art. Chicago, 1964.
AH 8213.4	Birley, Anthony R. Life in Roman Britain. London, 1964.
AH 7549.64	Bishop, John H. Nero; the man and the legend. London, 1964.
AH 7279.64.10	Bonde, Cecil von. The splendour that was Rome. Capetown, 1964.
Eg 879.64	Bonneau, D. La crue du Nil. Paris, 1964.
AH 8200.2	Bonsen, Wilfrid. A Romano-British bibliography. Oxford, 1964. 2v.
Eg 909.64	Braunert, Horst. Die Binnenwanderung. Bonn, 1964.
AH 3000.3.5	British Museum. Department of Western Asiatic Antiquities. A bibliography of the cuneiform tablets of the Kuyunjik collection. London, 1964.
Eg 879.64.5	Brunner, Hellmut. Die Geburt des Gottkonigs. Wiesbaden, 1964.
AH 7489.64	Burdeau, François. Aspects de l'empire romain. Paris, 1964.
Eg 603.17	Campbell, E.F. The chronology of the Amarna letters. Baltimore, 1964.
AH 819.64.10	Capovilla, G. Praehomerica et praeitalica. Roma, 1964.
Eg 759.64	Chalon, Gérard. L'édit de Tiberius Julius Alexander; étude historique et exégétique. Olten, 1964.
AH 3011.18	Chicago. University. Studies presented to A. Leo Oppenheim, June 7, 1964. Chicago, 1964.
AH 7203.147F	Cino da Pistoia. Cyni Pistoriensis in codicem et aliquot titulos primi pandectorum tomi. Torino, 1964. 2v.
AH 8514.15	Colin, J. L'empire des Antonins et les martyrs gaulois de 177. Bonn, 1964.
Eg 232.5	Daris, Sergio. Documenti per la storia dell'esercito romano in Egitto. Milano, 1964.
AH 29.64	Deutsche Historiker-Gesellschaft. Fachgruppe alte Geschichte. Neue Beiträge zur Geschichte der alten Welt. Berlin, 1964-65. 2v.
AH 8011.9	Diesner, Hans J. Der Untergang der römischen Herrschaft in Nordafrika. Weimar, 1964.
AH 819.64.20	Eastwood, Charles Cyril. Life and thought in the ancient world. London, 1964.
AH 4819.64.5	Ehrenberg, V. Society and civilization in Greece and Rome. Cambridge, 1964.
AH 7189.64	El'nitskii, L.A. Voznknovenie i razvitie rabstva v Rime v XIII - III v do n.e. Moskva, 1964.
AH 7759.64	Fera, Giovanni. Constantino e il cristianesimo. Milano, 1964.
Eg 452.5	Fischer, Henry G. Inscriptions from the Coptite Nome dynasties VI-XI. Rome, 1964.
AH 819.55.2	Forbes, Robert James. Studies in ancient technology. 2. ed. v.1,4. Leiden, 1964. 2v.
AH 4889.64	French, A. The growth of the Athenian economy. London, 1964.
AH 7818.65.16	Friedlaender, Ludwig. Darstellungen aus der Sittengeschichte Roms. 10. Aufl. Aalen, 1964. 4v.
AH 4459.64	Frolov, Eduard Davidovich. Sotsial'no-politicheskaia bor'ba v Afinakh v kontse V veka do n.e. Leningrad, 1964.
AH 7114.38	Gagé, Jean. Les classes sociales dans l'empire romain. Paris, 1964.
AH 3661.15.5	Gagé, Jean. La montée des Sassanides et l'heure de Palmyre. Paris, 1964.
AH 3005.15	Garelli, Paul. L'assyriologie. Paris, 1964.
AH 4299.64.5	Graham, Alexander John. Colony and mother city in ancient Greece. N.Y., 1964.
AH 819.64.5F	Grant, M. The birth of Western civilization. London, 1964.
AH 3959.4	Gray, J. The Canaanites. London, 1964.
AH 7499.64	Grenzheuser, Bruno. Kaiser und Senat in der Zeit von Nero bis Nerva. Münster? 1964.
AH 4819.64.10	Groningen, Bernhard Abraham van. Bedwongen hartstocht. Leiden, 1964.
AH 7889.64	Halsberghe, Gaston H. Het republikeinse Rome; de grondslagen van het antieke wirtschaftswunder (509-31 v. Chr.). Hasselt, 1964.
AH 7419.64	Halsberghe, Gaston H. Zoeklicht op het oude Rome. Hasselt, 1964.
AH 4839.64	Harris, Harold Arthur. Greek athletes and athletics. London, 1964.
AH 7169.64	Hausmaninger, H. Die bona fides des Ersitzungsbeseitzers im klassischen römischen Recht. Wien, 1964.
AH 279.64	Haywood, Richard M. Ancient Greece and the Near East. N.Y., 1964.
AH 7859.8	Herrmann, Claudine. Le role judiciaire et politique des femmes sous la République romaine. Bruxelles, 1964.
AH 7279.60.5.2	Heuss, Alfred. Römische Geschichte. 2. Aufl. Braunschweig, 1964.
Eg 609.64	Hornung, E. Untersuchungen zur Chronologie und Geschichte des Neuen Reiches. Wiesbaden, 1964.
AH 4855.15	Hull, Denison B. Hounds and hunting in ancient Greece. Chicago, 1964.
AH 1329.64	Imparati, Fiorella. I Hurriti. Firenze, 1964.
AH 4848.13.5	Johnson, Marie. Ancient Greek. Chicago, 1964.

1964 - cont.

AH 7709.64	Jones, A.H.M. The later Roman Empire. v.1-3, Atlas. Oxford, 1964. 3v.
AH 6107.21	Kanatsoulès, Dēmètrios. Historia tēs Makedonias. Thessalonikē, 1964.
AH 6107.12	Kanatsoulès, Dēmètrios. He Makedonia mechri tou thanatou tou Archelaou. Thessalonikē, 1964.
Eg 1029.63.1	Kaplony, Peter. Die Inschriften der ägyptischen Frühzeit. Supplement. Wiesbaden, 1964.
Eg 1309.64.5F	Kaplony-Heckel, Ursula. Die demotischen Gebelen-Urkunden der Heidelberger Papyrus-Sammlung. Heidelberg, 1964.
AH 3143.23.3	Klima, Josef. Gesellschaft und Kultur des alten Mesopotamien. Prag, 1964.
AH 819.64.16	Kumaniecki, Kazimierz F. Historia kultury strożytnej Grecji i Rzymu. wyd. 2. Warszawa, 1964.
AH 9773.13	La Baume, Peter. Colonia Agrippinensis. 3. Aufl. Köln, 1964.
AH 919.14.1	Laum, Bernhard. Stiftungen in der griechischen und römischen Antike. v.1-2. Aalen, 1964.
AH 4843.24	Lawler, Lillian B. The dance in ancient Greece. London, 1964.
AH 3011.17	Leningrad. Universitet. Kafedra stran Drevnego Vostoka. Assiriologiia i egiptologiia. Leningrad, 1964.
AH 889.64	Lévy, Jean Philippe. L'économie antique. Paris, 1964.
Eg 1069.64F	The litany of Re. N.Y., 1964.
AH 3011.16	McCullough, W.S. The seed of wisdom. Toronto, 1964.
AH 7819.64.10	MacQueron, Jean. Le travail des hommes libres dans l'antiquite romaine. Aix-en-Provence, 1964.
AH 4559.64	Marsden, E.W. The campaign of Gaugamela. Liverpool, 1964.
AH 259.64	Meirat, Jean. Marines antiques de la Mediterranée. Paris, 1964.
Eg 279.64	Mertz, Barbara. Temples, tombs, and hieroglyphs. N.Y., 1964.
AH 5763.6	Michell, Humfrey. Sparta. Cambridge, Eng., 1964.
Eg 819.49.2	Murray, Margaret Alice. The splendour that was Egypt. 2. ed. London, 1964.
AH 9627.2	Navarra, Giuseppe. Città sicane, sicule e greche nella zona di Gela. Palermo, 1964.
AH 7819.64.5	Nemirovskii, Aleksandr. Ideologiia i kul'tura rannego Rima. Voronezh, 1964.
AH 7217.18	Nuyens, Michel. Le statut obligatoire des décurions dans le droit constantinien. Louvain, 1964.
AH 7469.64	Ooteghem, Jules van. Caius Marius. Namur, 1964.
AH 7769.64	Paven, Massimiliano. La politica gotica di Teodosio nella publiastica del suo tempo. Roma, 1964.
AH 4819.64	Payne, R. Ancient Greece. 1st ed. N.Y., 1964.
Htn AH 7162.39*	Provera, Giuseppe. La Vindicatio caducorum; contributo allo studio del processo fiscale romano. Torino, 1964.
AH 8548.142	Raftery, Joseph. The Celts. Cork, 1964.
AH 7659.64	Rémondon, Roger. La crise de l'Empire romain. Paris, 1964.
AH 863.15	Reynes-Lyons, P. Mitos, ritos y costumbres sexuales en las sociedades antiguas. Buenos Aires, 1964.
AH 8913.25	Richardson, Emeline H. The Etruscans; their art and civilization. Chicago, 1964.
Eg 990.7	Riefstahl, E. Thebes in the time of Amunhotep III. 1. ed. Norman, 1964.
AH 819.64	Riemschneider, M. Von Olympia bis Ninive im Zeitalter Homeis. Heidelberg, 1964.
AH 3009.64	Roux, Georges. Ancient Iraq. London, 1964.
AH 2012.2	Ryckmans, Jacques. La chronologie des rois de Saba et dū-Raydān. Istanbul, 1964.
Eg 819.64	Sāmih, Wali al Din. Daily life in ancient Egypt. N.Y., 1964.
AH 7819.64	Schefold, K. Römische Kunst als religioses Phänomen. Reinbek, 1964.
AH 3910.16	Schmitt, H.H. Untersuchungen zur Geschichte Antiochos des Grossen. Wiesbaden, 1964.
AH 7279.64.6	Sergeenko, Mariia E. Prostye liudi drevnei Italii. Leningrad, 1964.
AH 7279.64.5	Sergeenko, Mariia E. Zhizn' drevnego Rima. Leningrad, 1964.
AH 7189.64.5	Shtaerman, Elena. Rastzvet rabovladel'cheskikh otnoshenii v Rimskoi respublike. Moskva, 1964.
Eg 752.10	Skeat, T.C. Papyri from Panopolis in the Chester Beatty Library. Dublin, 1964.
AH 4839.64.5	Spaak, Bob. Goden in het stadion. Amsterdam, 1964.
AH 4039.64A	Strauss, L. The city and man. Chicago, 1964.
AH 3012.13	Sulayman, Tawfiq. Die Entstehung und Entwicklung der Götterwaffen im alten Mesopotamien und ihre Bedeutung. Berlin, 1964.
AH 4410.31	Taylour, William. The Mycenaeans. London, 1964.
AH 4103.3	Thomsen, Rudi. Eisphora; a study of direct taxation in ancient Athens. København, 1964.
AH 938.97.2	Tozer, Henry F. A history of ancient geography. N.Y., 1964.
AH 4844.8	Vandoni, Mariangela. Feste pubbliche e private nei documenti greci. Milano, 1964.
AH 8907.41	Vaughan, A.C. Those mysterious Etruscans. 1. ed. Garden City, N.Y., 1964.
AH 3657.42	Verbruggen, Hendrick. Zoeklicht op Oud-Perzie. Hasselt, 1964.
AH 4410.32	Vermeule, Emily. Greece in the bronze age. Chicago, 1964.
AH 3407.10	Walser, G. Neuere Hethiterforschung. Wiesbaden, 1964.
AH 4410.31.5	Webster, Thomas Bertram Lonsdale. From Mycenae to Homer. N.Y., 1964.
AH 4410.31.7	Webster, Thomas Bertram Lonsdale. From Mycenae to Homer. 2. ed. London, 1964.
AH 862.14	Wells, C. Bones, bodies and disease. London, 1964.
Eg 609.64.5	Wells, Evelyn. Nefertiti. Garden City, N.Y., 1964.
AH 5309.6	Zel'in, K.K. Bor'ba politicheskikh gruppirovok v Attike. Moskva, 1964.
AH 3187.15	al-Zibari, Akram. Altbabylonische Briefe des Iraq-Museums. Köln, 1964.
AH 7299.64	Ziegber, K.H. Die Beziehungen zwischen Rom und dem Partherreich. Wiesbaden, 1964.

1965

AH 4409.65	Accame, Silvio. Ricerche di storia greca. Napoli, 1965?
AH 3044.2F	Adams, Robert McCormick. Land behind Bagyhdad. Chicago, 1965.
AH 7499.65	Africa, Thomas W. Rome of the Caesars. N.Y., 1965.
Eg 459.65.5	Aldred, Cyril. Egypt to the end of the Old Kingdom. London, 1965.
AH 8574.4	Alföldy, Géza. Bevölkerung und Gesellschaft der römischen Provinz Dalmatien. Budapest, 1965.

Chronological Listing

1965 - cont.

AH 7409.65A — Alföldi, Andras. Early Rome and the Latins. Ann Arbor, 1965.

Eg 879.65.15 — Altenmueller, Hartwig. Die Atropaia und die Götter Mittelägypten. v.1-2. München, 1965.

AH 1233.65 — Amadasi, Maria Giulia. L'iconografia del carro da guerra in Siria e Palestina. Roma, 1965.

AH 4259.65 — Amit, M. Athens and the sea. Bruxelles, 1965.

AH 4109.18.5 — Andreadès, Andreas M. Geschichte der griechischen Staatswirtschaft. Hildesheim, 1965.

AH 4410.33 — Astour, Michael C. Hellenosemitica. Leiden, 1965.

AH 4499.65 — Athènes au temps de Périclès. Paris, 1965.

AH 3910.26 — Aymard, André. Les grandes monarchies hellenistiques en Asie. Paris, 1965.

AH 4609.65 — Aymard, André. Le royaume de Macédoine de la mort d'Alexandre à sa disparition, 323-168 avant J.-C. Paris, 1965.

AH 6150.5.2 — Belin de Ballu, Eugène. L'histoire des colonies grecques du littoral nord de la Mer Noire; bibliographie...1940 à 1962. Leiden, 1965.

AH 7207.42 — Bergener, Alfred. Die führende Senatorenschicht im frühen Prinzipat. Bonn, 1965.

AH 7549.64.2 — Bishop, John H. Nero, the man and the legend. N.Y., 1965.

AH 7279.21.4.9 — Boak, Arthur E.R. A history of Rome to 565 A.D. 5. ed. N.Y., 1965.

AH 7419.65 — Boren, Henry Charles. The Roman republic. Princeton, 1965.

AH 4819.65.15 — Bowra, Cecil Maurice. Classical Greece. N.Y., 1965.

AH 7201.109 — Bretone, Mario. Linee dell'Enchiridion di Pomponio. Bari, 1965.

AH 7206.34 — Byzantine Empire. Laws, statutes, etc. Ekloga. Moskva, 1965.

AH 7479.65 — Carcopino, Jérôme. Jules César. Paris, 1965.

AH 4819.63.16 — Chamoux, François. The civilization of Greece. London, 1965.

AH 8057.5.6 — Charles-Picard, Gilbert. Carthage. N.Y., 1965.

AH 8073.22.5 — Charles-Picard, Gilbert. La Carthage de Saint Augustin. Paris, 1965.

Eg 879.65.10F — Chassinat, Emile G. Le temple de Dendara. v.6. Le Caire, 1965-

AH 3020.40 — Çiğ, Muazzez. Yeni Sumer çağina ait Nippur hukukî ve idarî belgeleri. Ankara, 1965.

AH 7099.65 — Colin, Jean. Les villes libres de l'Orient gréco-romain et l'envoi au supplice par acclamations populaires. Bruxelles, 1965.

AH 3022.28 — Cottrell, Leonard. The land of Shinar. London, 1965.

AH 8307.3 — Daicoviciu, Hadrian. Dacii. Bucureşti, 1965.

AH 6107.6.2 — Daskalakès, Apostolos Basileiou. The Hellenism of the ancient Macedonians. Thessalonike, 1965.

Eg 819.65.5 — Daumas, François. La civilisation de l'Égypte pharaonique. Paris, 1965.

Eg 879.65.5 — Daumas, François. Les dieux de l'Égypte. Paris, 1965.

AH 7299.65 — Deininger, Jürgen. Die Provinziallandtage der römischen Kaiserzeit von Augustus bis zum Ende des dritten Jahrhunderts nach Christ. München, 1965.

AH 8211.9 — Dudley, Donald R. The Roman conquest of Britain, A.D. 43-57. London, 1965.

AH 819.65 — Ehrenberg, Victor. Polis und Imperium. Zürich, 1965.

AH 7599.65 — Les empéreurs romains d'Espagne. Paris, 1965.

AH 8416.5 — Ertl, Franz. Topographia Norici. Kremsmünster, 1965-69. 2v.

AH 4309.65 — Fabricius, Johannes. Oldtidens idéhistorie. København, 1965.

Eg 909.65.5 — Fikhman, Itskhok. Egipet na rubezhe dvukh epokh. Moskva, 1965.

AH 3171.11 — Fiore, Silvestro. Voices from the clay. 1st ed. Norman, 1965.

AH 3017.8.1 — Frankfort, Henri. Cylinder seals. Furnborough, 1965.

AH 2008.12 — Glueck, Nelson. Deities and dolphins; the story of the Nabataeans. N.Y., 1965.

AH 4819.65.10 — Gouldner, Alvin Ward. Enter Plato. N.Y., 1965.

AH 3159.36 — Gressmann, Hugo. Altorientalische Texte zum Alten Testament. Berlin, 1965.

AH 4819.42.15 — Grønbech, Vilhelm. Hellas. Hamburg, 1965.

AH 3150.14 — Haase, Richard. Einführung in das Studium keilschriftlicher Rechtsquellen. Wiesbaden, 1965.

AH 4819.65 — Hale, William Harlan. The Horizon book of ancient Greece. N.Y., 1965.

Eg 609.65 — Hawkes, Jacquetta Hopkins. Pharaohs of Egypt. 1. ed. N.Y., 1965.

AH 7462.10.2 — Hawthorn, John R. Roman politics, 80-44 B.C.; a selection of Latin passages. London, 1965.

AH 3179.7.17 — Heidel, Alexander. The Babylonian Genesis. 2d ed. Chicago, 1965.

Eg 702.10 — Hutmacher, Rudolf. Das Ehrendekret für den Strategen Kallimachos. Meisenheim am Glan, 1965.

AH 4410.20.5 — Huxley, George Leonard. Achaeans and Hittites. Belfast, 1965.

AH 4842.72.20 — Jaeger, Werner Wilhelm. Paideia; the ideals of Greek culture. 2. English ed. Oxford, 1965.

AH 5763.8 — Janni, Pietro. La cultura di Sparta arcaica. Roma, 1965. 2v.

AH 3038.5 — Jawal, Abd al-Jalil. The advent of the era of townships in northern Mesopotamia. Leiden, 1965.

AH 7139.32.3 — Jolowicz, Herbert Felix. Historical introduction to the study of Roman law. 2. ed. Cambridge, Eng., 1965.

AH 4039.65 — Kagan, Donald. The great dialogue; history of Greek political thought from Homer to Polybius. N.Y., 1965.

AH 3663.14 — Katrak, Jamshed C. Marriage in ancient Iran. Bombay, 1965.

AH 29.65 — Kivilcimli, Hikmet. Tarih, devrim, sosyalizm. Istanbul, 1965.

AH 2583.10 — Kobylina, Mariia M. Milet. Moskva, 1965.

VAH 9.65 — Kočiš, Gejza. Historiografia a bibliografia dejín prvotnopospolnej a otrokárskej spoločnosti. Bratislava, 1965.

AH 3193.8 — Labat, René. Un calendrier babylonien des travaux des signes et des mois. Paris, 1965.

AH 279.55.5 — Levi, Mario Attilio. Political power in the ancient world. London, 1965.

Eg 829.65 — Lindsay, Jack. Leisure and pleasure in Roman Egypt. London, 1965.

AH 4114.20 — Loenen, Dirk. Eugeneia; adel en adeldom binnen de atheense demokratie. Amsterdam, 1965.

AH 138.61.19 — Maine, Henry S. Ancient law. London, 1965.

AH 3022.30 — Mallowan, Max Edgar. Early Mesopotamia and Iran. N.Y., 1965.

1965 - cont.

AH 3013.965.5 — Margueron, Jean Claude. Mesopotamia. London, 1965.

AH 7239.65 — Mellersh, Harold Edward Leslie. The Roman soldier. N.Y., 1965.

AH 3407.34 — Menabde, Eduard A. Khettskoe obshchestvo. Tbilisi, 1965.

AH 7037.34.30 — Montesquieu, Charles L. Consideratione on the causes of the greatness of the Romans. N.Y., 1965.

AH 8907.8.10 — Müller, Karl O. Die Etrusker. Graz, 1965. 2v.

Eg 502.12PF — Papyrus Reisner II. Papyrus Reisner II; accounts of the dockyard workshop at This in the reign of Sesostris I. Boston, 1965.

AH 4819.65.5 — Pereira, Maria Helena Rocha. Estudos de história da cultura clássica. Lisboa, 1965.

AH 1329.65 — Phillips, Eustace Dockray. The royal hordes. London, 1965.

AH 7844.10 — Piccoluga, Giulia. Elementi speltocolori nei rihuoli festivi Romani. Roma, 1965.

AH 7844.9.2 — Pighi, Giovanni B. De ludis saecularibus populi Romani quiritium. Amstelodami, 1965.

AH 7863.7 — Pike, Edgar R. Love in ancient Rome. London, 1965.

Eg 879.65 — Pirenne, Jacques. La religion et la morale dans l'Égypte antique. Neuchâtel, 1965.

AH 7114.42 — Pistor, Hans Henning. Prinzeps und Patriziat in den Zeit von Augustus bis Commodus. Thesis. Freiburg, 1965?

AH 279.65.10 — Preobrazhenskii, Petr F. V mire antichnykh idei i obrazov. Moskva, 1965.

AH 4239.65 — Pritchett, William Kendrick. Studies in ancient Greek topography. Berkeley, 1965- 2v.

AH 3002.155 — Rashid, Fawzi. Archiv des Nūrsāmās und andere Darlehensurkunden aus der altbabylonischen Zeit. Inaug. Diss. Heidelberg, 1965.

AH 3160.23 — Reder, Dimitrii G. Mity i legendy drevnego Dvurech'ia. Moskva, 1965.

AH 49.65 — Ritter, Hans-Werner. Diadem und Königsherrschaft. München, 1965.

AH 3181.15 — Römer, Willem H.P. Sumerische Königshymnen, der Isin-Zeit. Leiden, 1965.

AH 5390.20 — Roesch, Paul. Thespies et la confédération béotienne. Paris, 1965.

AH 4839.65.5 — Rudolph, Werner. Olympischer Kampfsport in der Antike. Berlin, 1965.

AH 4039.65.5 — Ryder, Timothy Thomas Bennett. Koine Eirene. London, 1965.

AH 8208.20 — Salway, Peter. The frontier people of Roman Britain. Cambridge, Eng., 1965.

Eg 452.6 — Schenkel, Wolfgang. Memphis, Herakleopolis, Theben; die epigraphischen Zeugnisse der 7.-11. Dynastie Ägyptens. Wiesbaden, 1965.

AH 279.65.5 — Schieder, Oscar. Die alte Welt. Wiesbaden, 1965-69. 2v.

AH 4839.65 — Schöbel, Heinz. Olympia und seine Spiele. Berlin, 1965.

AH 1409.65 — Schwantes, Siegfried J. A short history of the ancient Near East. Grand Rapids, 1965.

AH 9563.7F — Serra, Marcello. Il popolo dei nuraghi. Cagliari, 1965.

AH 3707.29 — Shifman, Il'ia. Finikliskie morekhody. Moskva, 1965.

AH 32.5 — Sociedad Española de Estudios Clásicos. Coloquios sobre teoria política de la antigüedad clásica. Madrid, 1965.

AH 7239.65.10 — Speidel, Michael. Die equites singulares Augusti. Bonn, 1965.

AH 279.65 — Starr, Chester G. A history of the ancient world. N.Y., 1965.

AH 7769.65 — Stroheker, Karl Friedrich. Germanentum und Spätantike. Zürich, 1965.

AH 7819.65.5 — Suzdal'skii, Jurii P. Na semi kholmakh. 2. izd. Moskva, 1965.

AH 5757.10 — Tigerstedt, Eugène Napoleon. The legend of Sparta in classical antiquity. Stockholm, 1965.

AH 7819.65 — Toynbee, Arnold Joseph. Hannibal's legacy. London, 1965. 2v.

AH 7469.65 — Utchenko, S. Krizis; padenie Rimskoi respubliki. Moskva, 1965.

AH 1879.65 — Vanal, Antoine. L'iconographie du dieu de l'orage. Paris, 1965.

AH 7569.65 — Vanella, Giovanni. L'Adventus di Vespasiano nei suoi aspetti mistico-religiosi e giundico-costituzionali. Napoli, 1965.

AH 7819.65.10 — Vogt, Joseph. Der Niedergang Roms; Metamorphose der antiken Kultur. Zürich, 1965.

AH 7279.65.4 — Volkmann, Hans. Grundzuge der römischen Geschichte. 4. Aufl. Darmstadt, 1965.

Eg 847.12 — Waangstedt, Stev von. Die demotischen Ostraka der Universität zu Zürich. Uppsala, 1965.

AH 7239.65.5 — Waas, Manfred. Germanen im römischen Dienst im 4. Jahrhundert nach Christus. Bonn, 1965.

AH 3659.21 — Walser, Gerold. Audienz beim persischen Grosskönig. Zürich, 1965.

Eg 819.65 — Ward, William A. The spirit of ancient Egypt. Beirut, 1965.

AH 7169.65 — Watson, Alan. The law of obligations in the later Roman Republic. Oxford, 1965.

Eg 409.65 — Weissen-Szumlanska, Marcelle. Origines atlantiques des anciens Égyptiens. Paris, 1965.

AH 5458.5 — Willetts, Ronald Frederick. Ancient Crete. London, 1965.

Eg 909.65 — Wipszycka, Ewa. L'industrie textile dans l'Égypte romaine. Wrocław, 1965.

AH 7189.65 — Wolf, Manfred. Untersuchungen zur Stellung der kaiserlichen Freigelassenen und Sklaven in Italien und der Westprovinzen. Munster? 1965.

AH 8910.5 — Zalesskii, Nikolai N. K istorii etrusskoi kolonizatsii Italii v VII-IV vv. Leningrad, 1965.

1966

AH 5310.3.2 — Accame, Silvio. L'imperialismo ateniese all'inizio del secolo IV A.C. e la crisi della Polis. 2. ed. Napoli, 1966.

AH 7469.66.5 — Adcock, Frank Ezra. Marcus Crassus, millionaire. Cambridge, 1966.

AH 819.66.5 — Akademiia nauk SSSR. Institut arkheologii. Kul'tura antichnogo mira. Moskva, 1966.

AH 4022.3 — Ancient society and institutions: studies presented to Victor Ehrenberg on his 75th birthday. Oxford, 1966.

AH 7845.20 — André, Jean Marie. L'otium dans la vie morale et intellectuelle romaine. Paris, 1966.

AH 7459.66 — Armstrong, Donald Budd. The reluctant warriors. N.Y., 1966.

Chronological Listing

1966 - cont.

AH 7693.1 — Balty, Janine. Essai d'iconographie de l'empereur Clodius Albinus. Bruxelles, 1966.

AH 4559.65 — Bamm, Peter. Alexander; oder Die Vewandlung der Welt. Zürich, 1966.

AH 4039.66 — Berger, Anatolii K. Politicheskaia mysl' drevnegrecheskoi demokratii. Moskva, 1966.

AH 279.49.2 — Berve, Helmut. Gestaltende Kräfte der Antike. 2. Aufl. München, 1966.

AH 7649.66 — Birley, Anthony Richard. Marcus Aurelius. London, 1966.

AH 3313.2 — Bisi, Anna Maria. Kuopiaká; contributi allo studio della componente cipriota della civiltá punica. Roma, 1966.

AH 4279.66 — Blavatskaia, Tat'iana V. Akheiskaia Gretsiia vo vtorom tysiacheletii do nie. Moskva, 1966.

AH 7279.66 — Bourne, Frank C. A history of the Romans. Boston, 1966.

AH 7509.65.1 — Bowersock, Glen Warren. Augustus and the Greek world. Oxofrd, 1966.

AH 819.66.10 — Brodskii, Boris I. Romanticheskie veduty. Moskva, 1966.

AH 4819.66.15 — Browning, Robert. Greece - ancient and medieval: an inaugural lecture delivered at Birkbeck College, 15th June, 1966. London, 1966.

Eg 1009.66 — Brunner, Hellmut. Grundzüge einer Geschichte der altägyptischen Literatur. Darmstadt, 1966.

AH 3027.10 — Buccellati, Biorgio. The Amorites of the Ur III period. Naples, 1966.

AH 4819.36.6 — Burn, Andrew Robert. The world of Hesiod. 2. ed. N.Y., 1966.

Eg 850.8F — Cairo. Musée des antiquités égyptiennes. M'n.(Papyrus 86637). The Cairo calendar, no. 86637. Cairo, 1966.

AH 7189.66 — Capozza, Maria. Movimenti servili nel mondo romano in età repubblicana. Roma, 1966.

AH 939.66 — Carpenter, Rhys. Beyond the Pillars of Heracles. N.Y., 1966.

AH 4819.66.10 — Carpenter, Rhys. Discontinuity in Greek civilization. Cambridge, Eng., 1966.

AH 5309.12 — Cataudella, Michele R. Atene fra il VII e il VI secolo. Catania, 1966.

AH 8549.166 — Chadwick, Nora (Kershaw). The Druids. Cardiff, 1966.

Eg 879.66F — Chassinat, Emile G. Le mystère d'Osiris au mois de Khoiak. Le Caire, 1966-68. 2v.

AH 7059.66 — Combès, Robert. Imperator; recherches sur l'emploi et la signification du titre d'imperator dans la Rome republicaine. Thèse. Paris, 1966.

AH 7239.66 — Crescenti, Giovanni. Obiettori di coscienza e martiri militari nei primi cinque secoli del cristianesimo. Polermo, 1966.

AH 4559.66.5 — Daskalakès, Apostolos Basileiou. Alexander the Great and Hellenism. Thessaloníkē, 1966.

AH 8011.9.5 — Diesner, Hans J. Des Vandalenreich, Aufstieg und Untergang. Stuttgart, 1966.

AH 39.66 — Dvornik, Frantisek. Early Christian and Byzantine political philosophy; origins and background. Washington, 1966. 2v.

Eg 1159.66 — Edwin Smith Surgical Papyrus. Ein medizinisches Lehrbuch aus dem alten Agypten! Wund- und Unfallchirurgie. Bern, 1966.

AH 3179.10.2 — Enuma elish. Enuma eliš. Oxford, 1966.

AH 8461.5 — Fitz, Jenö. Ingenuus et Régalien. Bruxelles, 1966.

AH 8353.4 — Fitz, Jenö. Die Laufbahn der Statthalter in der römischen Provinz Moesia Inferior. Weimar, 1966.

AH 4819.66 — Flacelière, Robert. Daily life in Greece at the time of Pericles. N.Y., 1966.

AH 8229.5 — Fletcher, Elsie. The story of Ilkley in Roman times. Skipton, 1966.

AH 4459.66 — Fliess, Peter J. Thueydides and the politics of bipolarity. Baton Rouge, 1966.

AH 4409.66 — Forest, William George Grieve. The emergence of Greek democracy, 800-400 B.C. N.Y., 1966.

AH 3177.14.5 — Gilgamesh. Das Gilgamesh Epos. Stuttgart, 1966.

AH 3902.3 — Gordon, Cyrus H. Ugarit and Minoan Crete; the bearing of their texts on the origins of Western culture. N.Y., 1966.

AH 4559.66 — Griffith, Guy Thompson. Alexander the Great: the main problems. Cambridge, 1966.

AH 3017.49 — Gudea, patesi of Lagash. Die Inschriften Gudeas von Lagaš. Roma, 1966.

AH 7842.19.5 — Gwynn, Aubrey. Roman education from Cicero to Quintilian. N.Y., 1966.

AH 7217.16 — Heil, Wilhelm. Der konstantinische Patriziat. Diss. Basel, 1966.

Eg 709.66.5 — Heinen, Heinz. Rom und Ägypten vom 51 bis 47 vor Christ; Untersuchungen zur Regierungszeit der 7. Kleopatra und des 13. Ptolemäers. Tübingen, 1966.

AH 7469.66 — Hutchinson, Lester. The conspiracy of Catiline. London, 1966.

AH 4329.66 — Huxley, George. The early Ionians. N.Y., 1966.

AH 8208.15 — Jarrett, Michael G. Britain and Rome; essays presented to Eric Birley on his sixteenth birthday. Kendal, 1966.

AH 3964.30.5 — Jirku, Anton. Der Mythus der Kanaanäer. Bonn, 1966.

Eg 1029.63.5 — Kaplony, Peter. Kleine Beiträge zu der Inschriften der ägyptischen Frühzeit. Wiesbaden, 1966.

AH 7229.66 — Kelly, John Maurice. Roman litigation. Oxford, 1966.

AH 3959.36 — Kenyon, Kathleen Mary. Amorites and Canaanites. London, 1966.

AH 842.47.10 — Kleberg, Tönnes. Romerska antikvariat. Stockholm, 1966.

AH 7039.66 — Klein, Richard. Das Staatsdenken der Römer. Darmstadt, 1966.

AH 3613.5 — Koshelenko, Gennadii A. Kul'tura Parfii. Moskva, 1966.

AH 3176.2 — Krecher, Joachim. Sumerische Kultlyrik. Wiesbaden, 1966.

AH 7099.66 — Laffi, Umberto. Adtributio e contributio. 1a ed. Pisa, 1966.

AH 819.66.20 — Levi, Mario Attilio. La società nel mondo classico. Torino, 1966.

AH 7079.66 — Linderski, Jerzy. Rzymskie zgromadzenie wyborcze od Sulli do Cezara. Wrocław, 1966.

AH 4139.05.1 — Lipsius, Justus Hermann. Das attische Recht und Rechtsverfahren. v.1-3. Hildesheim, 1966.

AH 7419.66 — McDonald, Alex. Republican Rome. London, 1966.

AH 7299.66 — MacMullen, Ramsay. Enemies of the Roman order. Cambridge, 1966.

AH 3407.33.5 — Marek, Kurt W. Enge Schlucht und schwarzer Berg. Reinbek, 1966.

AH 3207.6 — Masson, Vadim M. Strana tysiachi gorodov. Moskva, 1966.

AH 1009.66 — Mayrhofer, Manfred. Die Indo-Arier im alten Vorderasien. Mit einer analytischen Bibliographie. Wiesbaden, 1966.

AH 7039.66.5 — Meier, Christian. Res publica amissa. Eine Studie zu Verfassung und Geschichte der späten römischen Republik. Wiesbaden, 1966.

1966 - cont.

AH 299.66 — Mélanges d'archéologie d'épigraphie et d'histoire offerts à Jérôme Carcopîno. Paris, 1966.

AH 3910.9.5 — Mørkholm, Otto. Antiochus IV of Syria. Thesis. København, 1966.

AH 3017.85 — Moortgat, Anton. Vorderasiatische Rollsiegel; ein Beitrag zur Geschichte der Steinschneidekunst. 2. Aufl. Berlin, 1966.

AH 3813.7 — Morgenstern, Julian. Rites of birth, marriage, death, and kindred occasions among the Semites. Cincinnati, 1966.

AH 846.31 — Neikhardt, Aleksandra A. Sem' chudes drevnego mira. Leningrad, 1966.

AH 3013.966 — Nissen, Hans Jörg. Zur Datierung des Königsfreidhofes von Ur besonderer Berücksichtigung der Stratigraphie der Privatgräber. Bonn, 1966.

AH 3966.33 — North, Martin. The Old Testament world. Philadelphia, 1966.

AH 3156.18 — Pettinato, Giovanni. Die Ölwahrsagung bei den Babyloniern. Roma, 1966. 2v.

AH 8903.5 — Pfiffig, Ambros Josef. Die Ausbreitung des römischen Städtewesens in Etrurien und die Frage der Unterwerfung der Etrusker. Firenze, 1966.

AH 7489.65 — Picard, Gilbert Charles. Augustus and Nero. N.Y., 1966.

AH 4819.66.5 — Pohlenz, Max. Freedom in Greek life and thought. Dordrecht, 1966.

AH 3156.16 — Rencontre Assyriologique Internationale, 14th, Strasbourg 1965. La divination en Mésopotamie ancienne et dans les régions voisines. Paris, 1966.

AH 7909.66 — Rougé, Jean. Recherches sur l'organisation du commerce maritime en Méditerranée sous l'Empire romain. Thèse. Paris, 1966.

AH 279.66 — Sanctis, Gaetano de. Scritti minori. Roma, 1966- 3v.

AH 3061.5 — Sauren, Herbert. Topographie der Provinz Umma nach den Urkunden der Zeit der III. Dynastie von Ur. Bamberg, 1966.

AH 7309.66 — Schoenlein, Peter Wilhelm. Sittliches Bewusstsein als Handlungsmotiv bei römischen Historiken. Erlangen, 1966.

Eg 559.66 — Seters, John van. The Hyksos. New Haven, 1966.

AH 7592.2 — Smallwood, Edith Mary. Documents illustrating the principates of Nerva Trajan and Hadrian. Cambridge, Eng., 1966.

AH 3911.10 — Sournia, Jean Charles. L'Orient des premiers chrétiens. Paris, 1966.

AH 819.66.15 — Spengler, Oswald. Frühzeit der Weltgeschichte. Faksimile. München, 1966.

AH 2108.8 — Stark, Freya. Rome on the Euphrates. London, 1966.

AH 819.66 — Stewart, Z. The ancient world. Englewood Cliffs, 1966.

AH 7479.38.6 — Strasburger, Hermann. Caesars Eintritt in die Geschichte. Darmstadt, 1966.

Eg 299.66 — Stuchevskii, Iosif A. Zavisimoe naselenie drevnego Egipta. Moskva, 1966.

AH 7079.66.5 — Taylor, Lily Ross. Roman voting assemblies from the Hannibalic war to the dictatorship of Caesar. Ann Arbor, 1966.

Eg 709.66 — Thissen, Heinz Josef. Studien zum Raphiadekret. Meisenheim am Glan, 1966.

AH 7199.66 — Thomas, Joseph A.C. Form and substance in Roman law. London, 1966.

AH 9777.42 — Thompson, Edward Arthur. The Visigoths in the time of Ulfila. Oxford, 1966.

AH 4410.32.1 — Vermeule, Emily. Greece in the bronze age. Chicago, 1966.

AH 7189.66.5 — Wachtel, Klaus. Freigelassene und Sklaven in der staatlichen Finanzverwaltung der römischen Kaeserzeit von Augustus bis Diokletian. Berlin, 1966.

AH 7178.91.6 — Weber, Max. Die römische Agrargeschichte in ihrer Bedeutung für das Staats- und Privatrecht. Amsterdam, 1966.

AH 7653.17 — White, Lynn Townsend. The transformation of the Roman world; Gibbon's problem after two centuries. Berkeley, 1966.

AH 8615.10 — Wilson, A.J.N. Emigration from Italy in the republican age of Rome. Manchester, Eng., 1966.

AH 7162.40 — Wistrand, Erik Karl Hilding. Aru och testamenten i romarnas sociala liu. Göteborg, 1966.

VAH 1402.5 — Zabłocka, Julia. Wybór źfodet do historii starozytnego wschodu do pol. Wyd. 2. Poznań, 1966.

AH 4410.41 — Zafiropulo, Jean. Mead and wine. N.Y., 1966.

1967

Eg 299.67 — Akademiia nauk SSSR. Institut Narodov Azii. Drevnii Egipet i drevniaia Afrika. Moskva, 1967.

AH 2507.15 — Akşit, Oktay. Likya tarihi. Istanbul, 1967.

AH 7709.67 — Alföldi, András. Studien zur Geschichte der Weltkrise des 3. Jahrhunderts nach Christus. Darmstadt, 1967-

AH 4819.67.15 — Andrewes, Anthony. The Greeks. N.Y., 1967.

AH 4819.67.25 — Archaeologia Homerica. Die Denkmäler und das frühgriechischen Epos. Göttingen, 1967- 5v.

AH 7459.67 — Astin, A.E. Scipio Aemilianus. Oxford, 1967.

AH 7479.67 — Balsdon, John Percy Vyvian. Julius Caesar; a political biography. 1. American ed. N.Y., 1967.

AH 5610.14 — Bartsos, Iōannes A. Ho Pyrros en Italia, skopoi kai drasis autou. Diss. Athēnai, 1967.

AH 7159.67.5 — Bauman, Richard A. The crimen maiestatis in the Roman Republic and Augustan Principate. Johannesburg, 1967.

AH 4043.5 — Berve, Helmut. Die Tyrannis bei den Griechen. München, 1967. 2v.

Eg 609.67.10 — Bille-de-Mot, Eléonore. The age of Akhenaten. London, 1967.

Eg 850.5 — Bleeker, Claas J. Egyptian festivals. Leiden, 1967.

AH 4108.17.5 — Böckh, August. Die Staatshaushaltung der Athener. 3. Aufl. Berlin, 1967. 2v.

AH 3002.144 — Borger, Riekele. Handbuch der Keilschriftliteratur. Berlin, 1967-

AH 7709.67.5 — Brauer, George C. The young emperors, Rome, A.D. 193-244. N.Y., 1967.

AH 3909.10 — Buccellati, Giorgio. Cities and nations of ancient Syria. Roma, 1967.

AH 4439.60.1 — Burn, Andrew Robert. The lyric age of Greece. London, 1967.

AH 3155.29 — Castellino, Giorgio R. Mitologia sumerico-accadica. Torino, 1967.

AH 7189.67 — Chantraine, Heinrich. Freigelassene und Sklaven im Dienst der römischen Kaiser. Wiesbaden, 1967.

AH 879.67 — Cilento, Vincenzo. Comprensione della religione antica. Napoli, 1967.

AH 4819.67.10 — La civilisation grecque de l'antiquité à nos jours. Bruxelles, 1967. 2v.

Chronological Listing

1967 - cont.

AH 3607.15 — Colledge, Malcom A.R. The Parthians. London, 1967.
AH 7139.67 — Crook, John A. Law and life of Rome. Ithaca, 1967.
AH 7449.55.5 — De Beer, Gavin Rylands. Hannibal's march. London, 1967.
AH 3044.3 — Delougaz, Pinhas. Private houses and graves in the Digala region. Chicago, 1967.
AH 8548.120.5 — Dillon, Myles. The Celtic realms. London, 1967.
AH 7039.67 — Earl, Donald Charles. The moral and political tradition of Rome. London, 1967.
AH 7502.5.4 — Ehrenberg, Victor. Documents illustrating the reigns of Augustas and Tiberius. 2. ed. Oxofrd, 1967.
AH 4819.67.5 — European Cultural Foundation. L'héritage vivant de l'antiquité grecque. La Haye, 1967.
Eg 885.967 — Feucht-Putz, Erika. Die königlichen Pektorale; Motive, Sinngehalt und Zweck. Inaug. Diss. Bamberg, 1967.
AH 4539.67 — Fol, Aleksandur. Epaminoud. Sofiia, 1967.
AH 7079.67 — Frei-Stolba, Regula. Untersuchungen zur den Wahlen in der römischen Kaiserzeit. Zürich, 1967.
AH 8207.35 — Frere, Sheppard. Britannia; a history of Roman Britain. Cambridge, 1967.
AH 4309.67 — Fritz, Kurt von. Die griechische Geschichtsschreibung. Text and notes. Berlin, 1967- 2v.
AH 309.67.5 — Frolov, Eduard D. Russkaia istoriografiia antichnosti do serediny XIX v. Leningrad, 1967.
AH 39.67 — Gaudement, Jean. Institutions de l'antiquité. Paris, 1967.
AH 8549.167 — Genty, Patrice. Études sur le celtisme. Paris, 1967.
AH 7659.67.5 — Grant, Michael. The climax of Rome. Saskatoon, 1967.
AH 4819.23.5 — Greene, William Chase. The achievement of Greece; a chapter in human experience. N.Y., 1967.
AH 5607.8 — Hammond, Nicholas Geoffrey Lempriere. Epirus: the geography, the ancient remains, the history. Oxford, 1967.
AH 4279.59.5 — Hammond, Nicholas Geoffrey Lemprière. A history of Greece to 322 B.C. 2. ed. Oxford, 1967.
AH 7239.67 — Harmand, Jacques. L'armée et le soldat à Rome de 107 à 50 avant notre ere. Paris, 1967.
AH 4410.37 — Harrel-Courtès, Henry. Les fils de Minos. Paris, 1967.
AH 3011.20 — Heidelberger Studien zum Alten Orient. Adam Falkenstein zum (60 Geburtstag) 17 September 1966. Wiesbaden, 1967.
AH 7114.34.5 — Hill, Herbert. The Roman middle class in the Republican period. Ann Arbor, 1967.
AH 7279.67.10 — Hoffter, Heinz. Römische Politik und römische Politiker. Heidelberg, 1967.
Eg 819.67.10 — Hofmann, Inge. Die Kulturen des Niltals von Aswan bis Sennar. Hamburg, 1967.
AH 819.67.5 — Hood, Sinclair. The home of heroes: the Aegean before the Greeks. London, 1967.
AH 4819.67 — Hooper, Finley Allison. Greek realities; life and thought in ancient Greece. N.Y., 1967.
AH 6024.15 — Hoyle, Peter. Delphi. London, 1967.
AH 3963.30.1 — Jirku, Anton. The world of the Bible. London, 1967.
AH 5757.26 — Jones, Arnold Hugh Martin. Sparta. Cambridge, 1967.
AH 309.67 — Jones, Tom Bard. Paths to the ancient past: applications of the historical method to ancient history. N.Y., 1967.
AH 3045.15 — Keiser, Helen. Die Stadt der Grossen Götin 4000 Jahre Uruk. Olten, 1967.
AH 7279.67.5 — Kiechle, Franz. Römische Geschichte. Stuttgart, 1967.
AH 842.47.5 — Kleberg, Tönnes. Buchhandel und Verlagswesen in der Antike. Darmstadt, 1967.
AH 299.67 — Konferentsiia po izucheniiu problem antichnosti, Leningrad, 1964. Antichnoe obshchestvo. Moskva, 1967.
AH 3012.20 — Larsen, Morgens. Old Assyrian caravan procedures. Istanbul, 1967.
AH 9777.14 — Leake, Jane. The Geats of Beowulf. Madison, 1967.
AH 7159.67 — Lebigne, Arlette. Quelques aspects de la responsabilité pénale en droit romain classique. Paris, 1967.
AH 7269.67 — Lemosse, Maxime. Le regime des relations internationales dans le Haut-Empire romain. Paris, 1967.
AH 4279.67.5 — Levi, Mario Attilio. Quattro studi spartani e altri scritti di storia greca. Milano, 1967.
AH 2111.5 — Levick, Barbara Mary. Roman colonies in Southern Asia Minor. Oxford, 1967.
AH 2109.10 — Lloyd,,Seton Howard. Early highland peoples of Anatolia. London, 1967.
AH 3054.5 — McCown, Donald E. Nippur; excavations of the Joint Expedition to Nippur of the University Museum of Philadelphia and the Oriental Institute of the University of Chicago. Chicago, 1967-
AH 4410.35 — McDonald, William Andrew. Progress into the past: the rediscovery of Mycenaean civilization. N.Y., 1967.
AH 819.67 — Mansuelli, Guido Achille. Les civilisations de l'Europe ancienne. Paris, 1967.
AH 7162.42 — Meinhart, Marianne. Die Senatusconsulta Tertullianum und Orfitianum in ihre Bedeutung für das klassische römische Erbrecht. Habilitationsschrift. Graz, 1967.
AH 4559.67 — Michel, Dorothea. Alexander als Vorbild für Pompeius. Brussel, 1967.
AH 7809.67 — Michels, Agnes Kirsopp. The calendar of the Roman republic. Princeton, 1967.
AH 5460.10 — Mikrogiannakes, E.I. Hē Krētē kara toys Ellēnistikoys chronoys. Thesis. Athēnai, 1967.
AH 7489.66.1 — Millar, Fergus. The Roman Empire and its neighbours. London, 1967.
AH 4819.67.20 — Moebius, Hans. Studia varia. Auftsätze zur Kunst und Kultur der Antike mit Nachträgen. Wiesbaden, 1967.
AH 7469.67 — Nicolet, Claude. Les gracques ou Crise agraire et révolution à Rome. Paris, 1967.
VEg 279.67 — Novak, Grga. Egipat. Zagreb, 1967.
AH 7419.67.5 — Ooteghem, Jules van. Les Crecilii Metelli de la république. Namur, 1967?
AH 3187.17 — Oppenheim, Adolf L. Letters from Mesopotamia. Chicago, 1967.
AH 7419.67 — Les origines de la république romaine. Vandoeuvres, 1967.
AH 7769.67.5 — Paschoud, François. Roma aeterna. Rome, 1967.
Eg 609.67 — Perepelkin, Iurii I. Perevorot Amen-Khotpa IV. Moskva, 1967.
AH 7769.67 — Perowne, Stewart. The end of the Roman world. N.Y., 1967.
AH 7489.67.5 — Petit, Paul. La paix romaine. Paris, 1967.
AH 3022.38 — Pettinato, Giovanni. Untersuchungen zur neusumarischen Landwirtschaft. Napoli, 1967.
AH 7419.27.5 — Piganiol, André. La conquête romaine. 5. éd. Paris, 1967.
AH 7409.67 — Poucet, Jacques. Recherches sur la légende sabine des origines de Rome. Louvain, 1967.
AH 8207.34 — Priestley, Harold E. Britain under the Romans. London, 1967.
AH 4279.67 — Pugliese Carratelli, Giovanni. Storia greca. Milano, 1967.

1967 - cont.

AH 7139.67.5 — Puglisi Cosentino, Alfio. Influenza del primo cristianesino sul diritto romano dell'epoca classica. Palermo, 1967?
Eg 609.67.5 — Redford, Donald B. History and chronology of the eighteenth dynasty of Egypt. Toronto, 1967.
AH 8942.9 — Ricchi, Antonio. La reggia de' Volsci. Bologna, 1967.
AH 3020.50 — Rosengarten, Yvonne. Répertoire commenté des signes présargoniques sumériens de Lagaš. Paris, 1967.
AH 4659.41.2 — Rostovtsev, Mikhail Ivanovich. The social and economic history of the Hellenistic world. Oxford, 1967. 3v.
Eg 819.67 — Säve-Söderbergh, Torgny. Faraoner och människor. Stockholm, 1967.
AH 3165.15 — Saggs, Henry William Frederick. Everyday life in Babylonia and Assyria. London, 1967.
AH 9307.10 — Salmon, Edward Togo. Samnium and the Samnites. Cambridge, 1967.
AH 4659.67 — Schneider, Carl. Kulturgeschichte des Hellenismus. München, 1967- 2v.
AH 8913.28 — Scullard, Howard. The Etruscan cities and Rome. Ithaca, 1967.
AH 5307.34 — Sealey, Raphael. Essays in Greek politics. N.Y., 1967.
AH 4609.67 — Seibert, Jakob. Historische Beiträge zu den dynastischen Verbindungen in hellenistischer Zeit. Wiesbaden, 1967.
AH 7329.67 — Sherwin-White, Adrian N. Racial prejudice in imperial Rome. Cambridge, 1967.
Eg 983.5 — Shinnie, Peter L. Meroe; a civilization of the Sudan. London, 1967.
Eg 841.10 — Sijpesteijn, Pieter Johannes. Liste des gymnasiarques des métropoles de l'Egypte romaine. Amsterdam, 1967.
AH 7532.2 — Smallwood, Edith Mary. Documents illustrating the principates of Gaius Claudius and Nero. Cambridge, 1967.
AH 1299.67 — Speiser, Ephraim A. Oriental and Biblical studies. Philadelphia, 1967.
AH 7099.67 — Storoni Mazzolani, Lidia. L'idea di città nel mondo romano. Milano, 1967.
AH 3963.140 — Studi sull'Oriente e la Bibbia. Genova, 1967.
VAH 279.67.5 — Varshavskii, Anatolii S. Goroda raskryvaint tainy. Moskva, 1967.
AH 9708.5 — Velkov, Velizar I. Robstvoto v Trakiia i Miziia prez antichnostta. Sofiia, 1967.
AH 7169.67 — Watson, Alan. The law of persons in the later Roman Republic. Oxford, 1967.
AH 3142.20 — Weisberg, David B. Guild structure and political allegiance in early Achaemenid Mesopotamia. New Haven, 1967.
Eg 1139.67 — Wente, Edward F. Late Ramesside letters. Chicago, 1967.
AH 7799.67 — Wes, Marinus Antony. Das Ende des Kaisertums im Westen des Römischen Reichs. 's-Gravenhage, 1967.
AH 7899.67 — White, K.D. Agricultural implements of the Roman world. Cambridge, 1967.
AH 4846.9 — Wycherley, Richard Ernest. How the Greeks built cities. 2. ed. London, 1967.
AH 5253.5 — Zwolski, Edward. Ustrój państwowy w starożytnym Argos. Lublin, 1967.

1968

AH 49.68 — Aalders, Gerhard Jean Daniel. Die Theorie der gemischten Verfassung im Altertum. Amsterdam, 1968.
AH 4499.68 — Accame, Silvio. Ricerche intorno alla Pentecontaetia. Napoli, 1968.
AH 3966.35 — Aharoni, Jochanan. The Macmillan Bible atlas. N.Y., 1968.
AH 3100.5 — al-Ahmad, Sami S. Southern Mesopotamia in the time of Ashurbanipal. The Hague, 1968.
Eg 609.68 — Aldred, Cyrill. Akhenaten, pharaoh of Egypt: a new study. London, 1968.
AH 8548.55.1 — Arbois de Jubainville, Henry d'. Les Celtes depuis le temps les plus anciens. Osnabrück, 1968.
AH 812.10 — Archaeological Symposium, American University of Beirut, 1967. The role of the Phoenicians in the interaction of Mediterranean civilizations. Beirut, 1968.
AH 7469.68.12 — Badian, Ernst. Roman imperialism in the late republic. 2. ed. Oxford, 1968.
Eg 879.68.10 — Barta, Winfried. Aufbau und Bedeutung der altägyptischen Opferformel. Glückstadt, 1968.
AH 7299.68 — Benzinger, Josef. Invectiva in Romam. Lübeck, 1968.
AH 809.68 — Bickerman, Elias Joseph. Chronology of the ancient world. London, 1968.
AH 7114.44.2 — Bleicken, Jochen. Das Volkstribunat der klassischen Republik. 2e Aufl. München, 1968.
AH 4889.68 — Bogaert, Raymond. Banques et banquiers dans les cités grecques. Leyde, 1968.
AH 4487.15 — Braccesi, Lorenzo. Il problema del decreto di Temistocle. Bologna, 1968.
AH 7239.68 — Brand, Clarence E. Roman military law. Austin, 1968.
AH 7139.68.5 — Brink, Herman van den. Ex iure quiritium. Deventer, 1968.
AH 3075.14 — Brinkman, J.A. A political history of post-Kassite Babylonia, 1158-722 B.C. Roma, 1968.
AH 3000.3.3 — British Museum. Catalog of cuneiform tablets in the Kouyunjik collection. 2d supplement. London, 1968.
AH 4333.5 — Broadbent, Molly. Studies in Greek genealogy. Leiden, 1968.
Eg 1109.59.2 — Brunner-Traut, Emma. Altägyptische Tiergeschichte und Fabel. 2. Aufl. Darmstadt, 1968.
AH 4279.68.5 — Burn, Andrew Robert. The warring states of Greece from their rise to the Roman conquest. London, 1968.
AH 2757.15 — Cardinali, Guiseppe. Il regno di Pergamo. Roma, 1968.
AH 8073.22.10 — Charles-Picard, Gilbert. The life and death of Carthage. London, 1968.
AH 7659.68 — Coster, Charles Henry. Late Roman studies. Cambridge, 1968.
Eg 239.68 — Cottrell, Leonard. The warrior pharaohs. London, 1968.
AH 2108.15 — Cozzoli, Umberto. I Cimmeri. Roma, 1968.
AH 7269.65.1 — Dahlheim, Werner. Struktur und Entwicklung des römischen Volkerrechte im dritten und zweiten Jahrhundert v. Chr. München, 1968.
AH 9707.12 — Danov, Khristo M. Drevna Trakiia. Sofiia, 1968.
AH 8453.10 — Dobó, Árpád. Der Verwaltung der römischen Provinz Pannonien von Augustus bis Diocletianus. Amsterdam, 1968.
Eg 1009.68 — Donadoni, Sergio. La letteratura egizia. Firenze, 1968.
AH 3407.36 — Dovgialo, Gennadii I. K istorii vozniknoveniia gosudarstva. Minsk, 1968.
AH 4239.68.5 — Ducrey, Pierre. Le traitement des prisonniers de guerre dans la Grèce antique des origines à la conquête romaine. Paris, 1968.
AH 7509.68.5 — Earl, Donald Charles. The age of Augustus. N.Y., 1968.

Chronological Listing

1968 - cont.

AH 4449.68 — Ehrenberg, Victor. From Solon to Socrates. London, 1968.

AH 4559.68.15 — Emmrich, Kurt. Alexander der Grosse. Zürich, 1968.

AH 4559.68.10 — Emmrich, Kurt. Alexander the Great: power as destiny. London, 1968.

Eg 299.68 — Festschrift für Siegfried Schott zu seinem 70. Geburtstag am 20. August 1967. Wiesbaden, 1968.

AH 279.68 — Finley, Moses I. Aspects of antiquity. London, 1968.

Eg 974.6 — Fischer, Henry George. Dendera in the third millennium B.C., down to the Theban domination of Upper Egypt. Locust Valley, N.Y., 1968.

AH 939.68 — Fischer, Rudolf. Das ausseritalische geographische Bild in Vergils Georgica, in den Oden des Horan und in den Elegien des Properz. Zürich, 1968.

AH 9713.6 — Fol, Aleksandur. Pesenta za Sitalk. Sofiia, 1968.

AH 7818.65.18 — Friedlaender, Ludwig. Roman life and manners under the early empire. N.Y., 1968. 4v.

AH 7479.21.12 — Gelzer, Matthias. Caesar, politician and statesman. Cambridge, 1968.

AH 4819.68.5 — Gernet, Louis. Anthropologie de la Grèce antique. Paris, 1968.

AH 7479.68 — Gesche, Helga. Die Vergottung Caesars. Kallmünz, 1968.

AH 139.68 — Gesellschaft und Recht im griechisch-römischen Altertum. Berlin, 1968- 2v.

AH 7489.68 — Grant, Michael. The climax of Rome. 1. American ed. Boston, 1968.

AH 7159.68 — Gruen, Erich Stephen. Roman politics and criminal courts, 149-78 B.C. Cambridge, 1968.

AH 3179.13 — Hallo, William W. The exaltation of Inanna. New Haven, 1968.

AH 7049.33.2 — Hammond, Mason. The Augustan Principate in theory and practice during the Julio-Claudian period. N.Y., 1968.

AH 4139.68 — Harrison, A.R.W. The law of Athens. Oxford, 1968. 2v.

Eg 1042.968.5 — Helck, Hans Wolfgang. Die Ritualszenen auf der Umfassungsmauer Ramses' II. Wiesbaden, 1968.

AH 7214.12 — Herrmann, Peter. Der römische Kaisereid. Habilitationsschrift. Göttingen, 1968.

AH 3657.44 — Herzfeld, Ernst Emil. The Persian empire. Wiesbaden, 1968.

AH 3195.14 — Hunger, Hermann. Babylonische und assyrische Kolophone. Neukirchen, 1968.

AH 5463.30 — Huxley, George Leonard. Minoans in Greek sources. Belfast, 1968.

AH 3020.45 — Iankovskaia, N.B. Klinopisnye teksty iz Koul'-Tepe v sobraniiakh SSSR. Moskva, 1968.

AH 7799.68.5 — Kaegi, Walter Emil. Byzantium and the decline of Rome. Princeton, 1968.

AH 7469.68 — Kaplan, Arthur. Catiline; the man and his role in the Roman revolution. N.Y., 1968.

Eg 1029.68 — Kaster, Joseph. Wings of the falcon; Life and thought of ancient Egypt. N.Y., 1968.

AH 4486.5 — Kinzl, Kourad. Miltiades-Forschungen. Wien, 1968.

AH 7899.68 — Kolendo, Jerzy. Postep techniczky a problem rify robocrej w roluicture starozytnej Helii. Wroctaw, 1968.

AH 819.68 — Kondratov, Aleksandr M. Pogibskie tsivilizatsii. Moskva, 1968.

AH 29.68 — Kongress für klassische Philologie, Budapest. Studien zur Geschichte und Philosophie des Altertums. Budapest, 1968.

VAH 5390.21 — Krawczuk, Aleksander. Siedurin pneciw Tebom. 1. wyd. Warszawa, 1968.

AH 4840.8 — Lacey, Walter K. The family in classical Greece. London, 1968.

Eg 278.94.22 — Lane-Poole, Stanley. A history of Egypt in the Middle Ages. 4. ed. London, 1968.

AH 4039.67 — Larsen, Jakob Aall Ottesen. Greek federal states. Oxford, 1968.

AH 4819.64.15 — Lévêque, Pierre. The Greek adventure. Cleveland, 1968.

AH 4819.68 — Lindsay, Jack. The ancient world; manners and morals. London, 1968.

Eg 879.68 — Lindsay, Jack. Men and gods on the Roman Nile. London, 1968.

AH 7419.68 — Lintott, Andrew W. Violence in republican Rome. Oxford, 1968.

AH 7769.68 — Lippold, Adolf. Theodosius der Grosse und seine Zeit. Stuttgart, 1968.

AH 8213.10 — Liversidge, Joan. Britain in the Roman empire. London, 1968.

Eg 709.68 — Longega, Gabriella. Arsinoe II. Roma, 1968.

AH 7149.68 — Magdelain, André. Recherches sur l'imperium. 1e éd. Paris, 1968.

AH 7519.68 — Meissner, Erhard. Sejan, Tiberius und die Nachfolge im Punzipat. Erlangen, 1968.

AH 7709.68 — Merten, Elke W. Zwei Herrscherfeste in der Historia Augusta. Thesis. Bonn, 1968.

AH 39.68 — Meyer, Ernst. Einführung in die antike Staatskunde. Darmstadt, 1968.

AH 4559.68 — Milns, R.D. Alexander the Great. London, 1968.

AH 8358.5 — Mirkovič, Miroslava. Rimski gradovi no Dunavu u Gornjoi Meziji. Thesis. Beograd, 1968.

AH 7298.86.5 — Mommsen, Theodor. The provinces of the Roman Empire; the European provinces. Chicago, 1968.

AH 8879.5 — Monti, Pietro. Ischia preistorica, greca, romana, paleocristiana. Napoli, 1968.

AH 4259.68 — Morrison, John Sinclair. Greek oared ships, 900-322 B.C. Cambridge, Eng., 1968.

AH 3707.22 — Moscati, Sabatino. The world of the Phoenicians. London, 1968.

AH 3041.2 — Mueller, Manfred. Die Erlässe und Instruktionen aus dem Lande Arrapha, ein Beitrag zur Rechtsgeschichte des Alten Vorderen Orients. Inaug. Diss. Leipzig? 1968?

AH 4323.5 — Nixon, Ivor G. The rise of the Dorians. N.Y., 1968.

AH 29.68.5 — Nuove questioni de storia antica. Milano, 1968.

AH 2764.5 — Ohlemutz, Erwin. Die Kulte und Heiligtumer der Gotter in Pergamon. 2. Aufl. Darmstadt, 1968.

AH 7799.68 — Oost, Stewart Irvin. Galla Placidia Augusta. Chicago, 1968.

AH 7201.113 — Ortiz Márquez, Julio. Comentarios a las Instituciones de Gayo. 1. ed. Bogota, 1968.

AH 8907.11.10 — Pallottino, Massimo. Etruscologia. 6. ed. Milano, 1968.

AH 279.68.5 — Passman, Franz Anton. Der Durchbruch durch die Völkerwanderung. Bonn, 1968. 2v.

AH 2589.10 — Pedley, John. Sardis in the age of Croesus. 1. ed. Norman, 1968.

Eg 609.68.5 — Perepelkin, Iurii I. Taina zolotogo groba. Moskva, 1968.

AH 7469.68.5 — Perowne, Stewart. Death of the Roman republic. 1. ed. Garden City, 1968.

1968 - cont.

AH 4719.40.2 — Petzold, Karl E. Die Eröffnung des zweiten römisch-makedonischen Krieges. 2. Aufl. Darmstadt, 1968.

AH 4842.95 — Pfeiffer, Rudolf. History of classical scholarship from the beggining to the end of the Hellenistic age. Oxford, 1968.

AH 7059.68 — Pieri, Georges. L'histoire du cens jusqu'à la fin de la République romaine. Paris, 1968.

AH 8549.168 — Piggott, Stuart. The Druids. N.Y., 1968.

AH 4239.68 — Problèmes de la guerre en Grèce ancienne, sous la direction de Jean-Pierre Vernant. Paris, 1968.

Eg 1042.968F — Pyramid texts: the pyramid of Unas. Princeton, 1968.

AH 4189.68 — Rabstvo na periferii antichnogo mira. Leningrad, 1968.

AH 259.68 — Rost, Georg Alexander. Von Seewesen und Seehandel in der Antike. Amsterdam, 1968.

AH 9646.10 — Ryolo di Maria, Domenico. L'espansione di Zande sulla costa settentrionale della Sicilia dalla metà dell'VIII secolo a.C. agli albori del V secolo a.C. Messina, 1968.

AH 4819.68.12 — Scheliha, Renata von. Freiheit und Freundschaft in Hellas. 2. Aufl. Amsterdam, 1968.

AH 7459.68 — Schlag, Ursula. Regnum in senatu; das Wirken römischen Staatsmänner von 200 bis 191 vor Christus. Stuttgart, 1968.

AH 7649.68 — Schrempf, Claus. Weisheit und Weltherrschaft. München, 1968.

AH 4279.68 — Senel, Alâeddin. Eski Yunanda siyasal düşünüş. Ankara, 1968.

AH 819.68.15 — Senel, Alâeddin. Uygarlik çizgisi. Ankara, 1968.

AH 8549.168.10 — Šerbanesco, Demeter Gérard Roger. Les Celtes et les druides. Paris, 1968.

AH 7279.68 — Sergeenko, Mariia E. Remeslenniki drevnego Rima. Leningrad, 1968.

AH 4039.51.2 — Sinclair, Thomas Alan. A history of Greek political thought. 2. ed. Cleveland, 1968.

AH 4840.10A — Slater, Philip Elliot. The glory of Hera. Boston, 1968.

AH 7163.32 — Soraci, Rosario. Ricerche sui Conubia tra romani e germani nei secoli IV-VI. Catania, 1968.

AH 3155.30 — Spycket, Agnès. Les statues de culte dans les textes mésopotamiens, des origines à la 1er dynastie de Babylone. Paris, 1968.

AH 3017.15.1 — Steinmetzer, Franz Xaver. Die babylonische Kudurru (Grenzsteine) als Urkundenform. Paderborn, 1968.

AH 8913.30 — Strong, Donald Emrys. The early Etruscans. London, 1968.

AH 4202.15 — Stroud, Ronald S. Drakon's law on homicide. Berkeley, 1968.

AH 1299.68 — Struve, Vasilii V. Etudy po istorii Severnogo Prichernomor'ia, Kavkazo i Srednei Azii. Leningrad, 1968.

AH 3181.11.1 — Stummer, Friedrich. Sumerisch-akkadische Parallelen zum Aufbau ajttestamentlicher Psalmen. Diss. Paderborn, 1968.

AH 8549.168.5 — Thévenot, Emile. Divinités et sanctuaires de la Gaule. Paris, 1968.

AH 279.41.15.5 — Thiess, Frank. Das Reich der Dämonen. Wien, 1968.

VAH 4039.68 — Turasiewicz, Romuald. Gycie politzczne w Atenach V i IV w. przed n.e. w ocenie krytzcznej wspólczesnych autorow atenskich. 1. wyd. Wrocław, 1968.

Eg 971.15PF — United Arab Republic. Centre of Documentation and Studies on Ancient Egypt. Le petit temple d'Abou Simbel. Le Caire, 1968. 2v.

AH 3020.55 — Virolleaud, Charles. Tablettes économiques de Lagash (époque de la IIIe dynastie d'Ur). Paris, 1968.

AH 819.68.5 — Vlahos, Olivia. The battle-ax people. N.Y., 1968.

AH 7918.95.5 — Waltzing, J.P. Étude historique sur les corporations professionnelles chez les Romains depuis les origines jusqu'à la chute de l'Empire d'Occident. Bologne, 1968.

AH 7169.68 — Watson, Alan. The law of property in the later Roman Republic. Oxford, 1968.

AH 4609.68 — Wehrli, Claude. Antigone et Démétrios. Genéve, 1968.

AH 7207.23.1 — Williams, Pierre. Le sénat de la République romaine. Aalen, 1968. 2v.

AH 7201.111 — Wolodkiewicz, Witold. Obligationes ex variis causarum figuris. Warszawa, 1968.

AH 4410.36 — Wundsam, Klaus. Die politische und soziale Struktur in den mykenischen Residenzen nach den Linear B. Texten. Wien, 1968.

Eg 879.68.5 — Žabkar, Louis V. A study of the Ba concept in ancient Egyptian texts. Chicago, 1968.

AH 2147.10 — Zabłocka, Julia. Podstawy gospodarcze anatolijskiej arystokraeji w świetle inskrypcji fundacyjnych okresu wczesnegocesarstwa. Wyd. 1. Poznań, 1968.

AH 3407.35 — Zamarovsky, Voitech. Tainy khettov. Moskva, 1968.

1969

AH 3565.10 — Akademiia nauk SSSR. Institut narodov Azii. Ancient Mesopotamia: socio-economic history. Moscow, 1969.

AH 7819.69 — Balsdon, John Percy Vyvian Dacre. Life and leisure in ancient Rome. 1st ed. N.Y., 1969.

AH 8508.12 — Barruol, Guy. Les peuples préromains du Sud-Est de la Gaule. Paris, 1969.

AH 7159.69.5 — Bauman, Richard. The duumviri in the Roman criminal law. Wiesbaden, 1969.

AH 4168.97.2 — Beauchet, Ludovic. Histoire du droit privé de la République Athenienne. Amsterdam, 1969.

AH 29.69 — Beiträge zur alten Geschichte und deren Nachleben. Berlin, 1969- 2v.

AH 3965.18 — Ben-David, Arye. Jerusalem und Tyros. Basel, 1969.

AH 4279.69 — Bengtson, Hermann. Griechische Geschichte. 2. Aufl. München, 1969.

AH 4239.69.5 — Best, Jan. Thracian Peltasts and their influence on Greek warfare. Proefschrift. Groningen, 1969.

AH 7188.33.2 — Blair, William. An inquiry into the state of slavery amongst the Romans. Detroit, 1969?

AH 4189.69 — Blavatskaia, Tat'iana v. Rabstvo v ellinisticheskikh gosudarstvakh v III-I vv do n.e. Moskva, 1969.

AH 8913.5.8 — Bloch, Raymond. The ancient civilization of the Etruscans. N.Y., 1969.

AH 8913.5.7 — Bloch, Raymond. The Etruscans. London, 1969.

AH 7844.12 — Bollinger, Traugott. Theatralis licentia. Die Publikumsdemonstrationen an den öffentlichen Spielen im Rom der früheren Kaiserzeit und ihrer Bedeutung im politischen Leben. Winterthur, 1969.

AH 4229.27.1 — Bonner, Robert Johnson. Lawyers and litigants in ancient Athens. N.Y., 1969.

Eg 1038.99.2 — Book of the Dead. The book of the dead. 2. ed. London, 1969.

AH 7279.69 — Bordet, Marcel. Précis d'histoire romaine. Paris, 1969.

AH 7469.69.5 — Boren, Henry Charles. The Gracchi. N.Y., 1969.

Chronological Listing

1969 - cont.

AH 4279.22.9.5 — Botsford, George W. Botsford and Robinson's Hellenic history. 5. ed. N.Y., 1969.

AH 879.69 — Brandon, Samuel George Frederick. Religion in ancient history: studies in ideas, men and events. N.Y., 1969.

AH 7899.69 — Brockmeyer, Norbert. Arbeitsorganisation und ökonomisches Denken in der Gutswirtschaft des römischen Reiches. Inaug. Diss. Bachum? 1969?

AH 850.12.5 — Brothwell, Don R. Food in antiquity. N.Y., 1969.

AH 850.12 — Brothwell, Don R. Food in antiquity: a survey of the diet of early peoples. London, 1969.

AH 3902.5 — Brown, John Pairman. The Lebanon and Phoenicia; ancient texts illustrating their physical geography and native industries. Beirut, 1969.

Eg 879.04.2.2 — Budge, Ernest Alfred Wallis. The gods of the Egyptians. N.Y., 1969. 2v.

AH 8666.5 — Castagnoli, Ferdinando. Topografia e urbanistica di Roma antica. Bologna, 1969.

AH 7769.69 — Castritius, Helmut. Studien zu Maximinus Daia. Diss. Kallmünz, 1969.

AH 4039.69.10 — Ceechin, Sergio A. Patrios politeia. Torino, 1969.

AH 3921.11 — Ceran, Waldemar. Rzemieslnicy i kupcy w Antiochii i ich ranga społeczna (II połowa IV wieku). Wrocław, 1969.

AH 7819.69.11 — Charles-Picard, Gilbert. The ancient civilization of Rome. N.Y., 1969.

AH 7029.69 — Charles-Picard, Gilbert. Textes et documents relatifs à la vie économique et sociale dans l'empire romain. Paris, 1969.

AH 3020.75 — Çiğ, Muazzez. Istanbul arkeoloji müzelerinde bulunan Sumer edebi tablet parçalari. Ankara, 1969.

AH 7449.69 — De Beer, Gavin Rylands. Hannibal; the struggle for power in the Mediterranean. London, 1969.

AH 7489.69.5 — Demaugeot, Emilienne. La formation de l'Europe et les invasions barbares. Paris, 1969.

AH 8205.5 — Divine, Arthur D. The north-west frontier of Rome: a military study of Hadrian's Wall. London, 1969.

AH 7659.69 — Downey, Glanville. The late Roman Empire. N.Y., 1969.

AH 3160.24 — Driel, G. van. The cult of Aššur. Assen, 1969.

AH 9639.14 — Droegemueller, Hans-Peter. Syrakus; zur Topographie und Geschichte einer griechischer Stadt. Heidelberg, 1969.

AH 7819.69.5 — Dumézil, Georges. Idées romaines. Paris, 1969.

AH 3813.10 — Dussel, Enrique D. El humanismo semita. Buenos Aires, 1969.

AH 7159.69 — Eder, Walter. Das vorsullanische Repetundenverfahren. Inaug. Diss. München, 1969.

AH 4039.60.2 — Ehrenberg, Victor. The Greek state. 2. ed. London, 1969.

AH 3195.10.3 — Era. L'epopea di Erra. Roma, 1969.

AH 4719.69 — Errington, Robert. Philopormen. Oxford, Eng., 1969.

AH 3045.100.5 — Eshnunna. Laws, statutes, etc. The laws of Eshnunna. Jerusalem, 1969.

AH 7509.69.5 — Fadinger, Volker. Quellenuntersuchungen zur Geschichte des 2. Triumvirats. Inaug. Diss. München, 1969.

AH 9705.1 — Fol, Aleksandur. Trakiisko voenno izkustvo. Sofiia, 1969.

AH 5757.20 — Forrest, William George Grieve. A history of Sparta, 950-192 B.C. N.Y., 1969.

AH 4842.39.5 — Freeman, Kenneth John. Schools of Hellas. N.Y., 1969.

AH 1279.69 — Garelli, Paul. Le Proche-Orient asiatique. Paris, 1969.

AH 8913.32 — Gaudio, Attilio. Les Etrusques. Une civilisation retrouvée. Verviers, 1969.

AH 7217.15.5 — Gelzer, Matthias. The Roman nobility. Oxford, 1969.

Eg 981.2 — Geremek, Hanna. Karanis; communsuté rurale. Wrocław, 1969.

AH 9664.5 — Gonzalez Echegaray, Joaquin. Origenes del cristianismo en Cantabria. Santiander, 1969.

AH 4299.69 — Gorbunova, Vseniia S. Drevnie greki na ostrove Berezan'. Leningrad, 1969.

AH 819.69.15 — Grant, Michael. The ancient Mediterranean. London, 1969.

AH 7479.69 — Grant, Michael. Julius Caesar. London, 1969.

AH 4479.01.1 — Grundy, George Beardoe. The great Persian War and its preliminaries. N.Y., 1969.

AH 4039.69 — Gschnitzer, Fritz. Zur griechischen Staatskunde. Darmstadt, 1969.

AH 7279.69.5 — Heurgon, Jacques. Rome et la Méditerranée occidentale jusqu'aux guerres puniques. 1. éd. Paris, 1969.

AH 7479.69.5 — Holliday, Vivian L. Pompey in Cicero's correspondence and Lucan's civil war. The Hague, 1969.

AH 7469.69 — Holliday, Vivian L. Pompey in Cicero's correspondence and Lucan's civil war. Thesis. The Hague, 1969.

AH 7599.47.2 — Homo, Léon P. Le siècle d'or de l'empire romain. Paris, 1969.

AH 8222.10 — Howard, Peter. Birdoswald Fort on Hadrian's Wall. Huddersfield, 1969.

AH 3740.9 — Jidejian, Nina. Tyre through the ages. Beirut, 1969.

AH 4519.69 — Kagan, Doanld. The outbreak of the Peloponnesian War. Ithaca, 1969.

VEg 885.969 — Kákosy, László. Varázslás az ókori Egyiptomban. Budapest, 1969.

AH 7189.69.5 — Kiechle, Franz. Sklavenarbeit und technischen Fortschritt im römischen Reich. Wiesbaden, 1969.

AH 7059.69 — Kneissl, Peter. Die Siegestitulatur der römischen Kaiser. Göttingen, 1969.

AH 7489.69.10 — Koch, Wilhelm. Caesaren, Herren am Limes. Stuttgart, 1969.

AH 3160.25 — Kramer, Samuel N. The sacred marriage rite. Bloomington, 1969.

AH 4819.69.15 — Krause, Wilhelm. Die Griechen von Mykene bis Byzanz. Wien, 1969.

AH 7161.32 — Kuleczka, Gerard. Prawo rzymskie epoki pryncypatu wobec dizeci pozamałżeńskich. Wrocław, 1969.

AH 819.69 — Die Kultur des klassischen Altertums. Frankfurt am Main, 1969.

AH 7759.69.5 — Kyriazes, Kostas D. Konstantinos ho Megas. Athēnai, 1969.

AH 8548.150 — Lengyel, Lancelot. Le secret des Celtes. 1. éd. Le Jas du Revest-Saint-Martin, 1969.

AH 8903.6 — Liou, Bernard. Praetores Etruriae XV populorum (étude d'épigraphie). Bruxelles, 1969.

AH 3011.21 — Lišan Mithurti. Festschrift Wolfram Freiherr von Soden. Kevelaer, 1969.

AH 819.69.10 — Lonis, Raoul. Des origines au vie siècle après J.C. Paris, 1969.

AH 4410.34 — Luce, John Victor. The end of Atlantis: a new light on an old legend. London, 1969.

AH 839.69 — Lukas, Gerhard. Die Körperkultur in frühen Epochen der Menschheitsentwicklung. 1. Aufl. Berlin, 1969.

AH 3661.14 — Lukonin, Vladimir G. Kul'tura sasanidskogo Irana. Moskva, 1969.

AH 4819.69 — Mackendrick, Paul Lachlan. The Athenian aristocracy, 399 to 31 B.C. Cambridge, 1969.

AH 7759.69 — MacMullen, Ramsay. Constantine. N.Y., 1969.

AH 8307.10 — Macrea, Mihail. Viata in Dacia romana. Bucureşti, 1969.

AH 8063.5 — Mahjouhi, Ammar. Les cités romaines de Tunisie. Tunis, 1969?

AH 8202.8 — Mann, John C. The northern frontier in Britain from Hadrian to Honorius; literary and epigraphic sources. Newcastle-upon-Tyne, 1969.

AH 8548.147 — Markale, Jean. Les Celtes et la civilisation celtique; mythe et histoire. Paris, 1969.

AH 239.69 — Marsden, Eric W. Greek and Roman artillery; historical development. Oxford, 1969.

AH 7499.69 — Meise, Erkhard. Untersuchungen zur Geschichte der julisch-claudischen Dynastie. München, 1969.

AH 8232.5 — Merrifield, Ralph. Roman London. N.Y., 1969.

AH 2107.10 — Metzger, Henri. Anatolia II. London, 1969.

AH 7039.69 — Michel, Alain. La philosophie politique à Rome d'Auguste à Marc Aurèle. Paris, 1969.

Eg 819.64.5 — Montet, Pierre. Eternal Egypt. N.Y., 1969.

AH 2008.14 — Montgomery, James Alan. Arabia and the Bible. N.Y., 1969.

AH 9668.2 — Morales Belda, Francisco. La marina vándala. Barcelona, 1969.

AH 4043.5.15 — Mossé, Claude. La tyrannie dans la Grèce antique. Paris, 1969.

AH 8907.48 — Nemirovskii, Aleksandr I. Etruski. Voronezh, 1969.

AH 819.19.16 — Neuburger, Albert. The technical arts and sciences of the ancients. N.Y., 1969.

AH 3708.5 — Nibbi, Alessandra. The Tyrrhenians. Cowley, 1969.

AH 7842.24 — Norman, Albert Francis. Teachers and administrators. Hall, 1969.

AH 1279.69.5 — Nützel, Werner. Von der Sintflut bis Byzanz. Darmstadt, 1969.

AH 7729.69 — Optendrenk, Theo. Die Religionspolitik des Kaisers Elagabal im Spiegel der Historia Augusta. Bonn, 1969.

AH 3170.5 — Orlin, Louis L. Ancient Near Eastern literature; a bibliography of one thousand items on the cuneiform literatures of the ancient world. Ann Arbor, 1969.

AH 4049.69 — Ostwald, Martin. Namos and the beginnings of the Athenian democracy. Oxford, 1969.

Eg 819.69 — Otto, Eberhard. Wesen und Wandel der ägyptischen Kultur. Berlin, 1969.

AH 7208.6 — Palmer, Robert E.A. The King and the comitium; a study of Rome's oldest public documents. Wiesbaden, 1969.

AH 3002.152 — Pettinato, Giovanni. Texte zur Verwaltung der Landwirtschaft in der Ur-III Zeit. Habilitationsschrift. Roma, 1969.

AH 3155.31 — Piesl, Helga. Vom Präanthropomorphismus zum Anthropomorphismus. Innsbruck, 1969.

AH 1029.69 — Pritchard, James B. The ancient Near East; supplementary texts and pictures. Princeton, 1969.

AH 7239.69.10 — Problèmes de la guerre à Rome. Paris, 1969.

Eg 1042.969 — Pyramid Texts. The ancient Egyptian pyramid texts. Oxford, 1969.

Eg 1042.969.2 — Pyramid Texts. The ancient Egyptian pyramid texts. Supplement of hieroglyphic texts. Oxford, 1969.

AH 4189.69.5 — Rädle, Herbert. Untersuchungen zum griechischen Freilassungswesen. Inaug. Diss. München, 1969.

AH 8013.6 — Raven, Susan. Rome in Africa. London, 1969.

AH 5758.10 — Rawson, Elizabeth. The Spartan tradition in European thought. Oxford, 1969.

Eg 879.69.5 — Religions en Egypte hellenistique et romaine, colloque de Strasbourg, 16-18 mai 1967. Paris, 1969.

Eg 879.69 — Reymond, Eve A.E. The mythical origin of the Egyptian temple. N.Y., 1969.

AH 819.69.5 — Riley, Carroll L. The origins of civilization. Carbondale, 1969.

AH 7469.69.10 — Roedl, Bernd. Das Senatus Consultum Ultimun und der Tod der Gracchen. Thesis. Bonn, 1969.

AH 3005.16 — Saggs, Henry William. Assyriology and the study of the Old Testament. Cardiff, 1969.

AH 7299.69 — Salmon, Edward T. Roman colonization under the Republic. London, 1969.

AH 3933.2 — Sasson, Jack Murad. The military establishments at Mari. Rome, 1969.

AH 3020.70 — Sauren, Herbert. Wirtschaftsurkunden aus der Zeit der III. Dynastie von Ur im Besitz des Musée d'Art et d'Histoire in Genf. Napoli, 1969.

AH 4279.60.12 — Schachermeyr, Fritz. Griechische Geschichte. 2. Aufl. Stuttgart, 1969.

AH 4499.69 — Schachermeyr, Fritz. Perikles. Stuttgart, 1969.

AH 7509.69 — Schmitthenner, Walter. Augustus. Darmstadt, 1969.

AH 7819.69.15 — Schottlaender, Rudolf. Römisches Gesellschaftsdenken. Weimar, 1969.

AH 3167.10 — Seibert, Ilse. Hirt, Herde, Konig; zur Hirausbildung des Königtums in Mesopotamien. Berlin, 1969.

AH 7029.69.5 — Sherk, Robert K. Roman documents from the Greek East; senatus consulta and epistolae to the age of Augustus. Baltimore, 1969.

AH 8907.44 — Signorelli, Mario. Storia degli Etruschi. Roma, 1969.

AH 7769.69.5 — Stallknecht, Bernt. Untersuchungen zur römischen Aussenpolitik in der Spätantike (306-395). Bonn, 1969.

AH 5763.10 — Stibbe, C.M. Sparta. Geschiedenis en cultuur der Spartanen van praehistorie tot Perzische oorlogen. Bussum, 1969.

AH 279.69 — Studi di storia antica in memoria di Luca de Regibus. Genova, 1969.

Eg 299.69 — Studies in honor of John A. Wilson, September 12, 1969. Chicago, 1969.

AH 4819.69.20 — Toynbee, Arnold Joseph. Some problems of Greek history. London, 1969.

AH 339.52.5 — Toynbee, Arnold Joseph. Twelve men of action in Graeco-Roman history. Freeport, N.Y., 1969.

AH 7189.69 — Treggiari, Susan. Roman freedmen during the late republic. Oxford, 1969.

AH 7489.69 — Utchenko, Sergei L. Drevnii Rim. Moskva, 1969.

AH 8461.10 — Várady, Lászlo. Das letzte Jahrhundert Pannoniens, 376-476. Budapest, 1969.

AH 7819.65.11 — Vogt, Joseph. The decline of Rome. The metamorphosis of ancient civilization. N.Y., 1969.

AH 7489.53.2 — Walbank, Frank William. The awful revolution: the decline of the Roman Empire in the West. Liverpool, 1969.

Eg 1009.69 — Walle, Baudouin van de. L'humour dans la littérature et dans l'art de l'ancienne Égypte. Leiden, 1969.

AH 8073.23.2 — Warmington, Brian Herbert. Carthage. 2. ed. London, 1969.

AH 7549.69 — Warmington, Brian Herbert. Nero: reality and legend. London, 1969.

Chronological Listing

1969 - cont.

AH 7239.69.5 Watson, G.R. The Roman soldier. London, 1969.

AH 4039.69.5 Weber-Schäfer, Peter. Das politische Denken der Griechen. München, 1969.

AH 7239.69 Webster, Graham. The Roman Imperial Army of the first and second centuries, A.D. London, 1969.

AH 5313.20 Webster, Thomas Bertham Lonsdale. Everyday life in classical Athens. London, 1969.

AH 6060.5.2 Westlake, Henry Dickinson. Thessaly in the fourth century B.C. Groningen, 1969.

AH 3179.14 Wilcke, Claus. Dan Lugalbandaepos. Wiesbaden, 1969.

AH 8574.5 Wilkes, J.J. Dalmatia. Cambridge, 1969.

AH 5463.10.5 Willetts, Ronald Frederick. Everyday life in ancient Crete. London, 1969.

AH 7114.40 Yavetz, Z. Plebs and princeps. London, 1969.

AH 7189.69.10 Zel'in, Konstantin K. Formy zavisimosti v Vostochnom Sredi zemnomor'e ellinisticheskogo perioda. Moskva, 1969.

1970

AH 7489.29.4 Albertini, Eugène. L'empire romain. 4. éd. Paris, 1970.

AH 1279.70 Altheim, Franz. Geschichte Mittelasiens im Altertum. Berlin, 1970.

AH 4239.70 Anderson, John Kinloch. Military theory and practice in the age of Xenophon. Berkeley, 1970.

AH 1279.70.5 Arnaud, Daniel. Le Proche-Orient ancien, de l'invention de l'écriture à l'hellénisation. Paris, 1970.

AH 7844.13 Auguet, Roland. Cruauté et civilisation: les jeux romains. Paris, 1970.

AH 7469.70 Badian, Ernst. Lucius Sulla. Sydney, 1970.

AH 5673.5 Bakhuizen, Simon Cornelis. Chalcidian studies. Proefschrift. v.2. Groningen, 1970-

AH 4179.70 Behrend, Diederich. Attische Pachturkunden. München, 1970.

AH 7229.70 Behrends, Okko. Die römische Geschworenenverfassung. Diss. Göttingen, 1970.

AH 4539.70 Beister, Hartmut. Untersuchungen zu der Zeit der thebanischen Hegemonie. Inaug. Diss. Bonn, 1970.

AH 9.49.6 Bengtson, Hermann. Introduction to ancient history. Berkeley, 1970.

AH 8549.170.5 Benoît, Fernand. Le symbolisme dans les sanctuaires de la Gaule. Bruxelles, 1970.

AH 4846.10 Boersma, Johannes Sipko. Athenian building policy from 561-560 to 405-404 B.C. Groningen, 1970.

AH 5463.20 Branigan, Keith. The foundations of palatial Crete: a survey of Crete in the early Bronze Age. London, 1970.

AH 7189.08.1 Buckland, William Warwick. The Roman law of slavery. Cambridge, Eng., 1970.

AH 8907.50 Burian, Ján. Zagadochnye etruski. Moskva, 1970.

AH 4550.2 Burich, Nancy J. Alexander the Great: a bibliography. 1st ed. Kent, Ohio, 1970.

AH 819.70.15 Burton-Brown, Theodore. Diffusion of ideas. Wootton, 1970-

Eg 9.70 Cairo. Musée des Antiquités Égyptiennes. Catalogue de la Bibliothek...1927-1958. Le Caire, 1970.

AH 7479.70.5 Carter, John M. The battle of Actium. London, 1970.

AH 8548.152 Chadwick, Nora (Kershaw). The Celts. Harmondsworth, Eng., 1970.

AH 8073.22.9 Charles-Picard, Gilbert. Vie et mort de Carthage. Paris, 1970.

AH 7659.70 Christ, Karl. Der Untergang des Romischen Reiches. Darmstadt, 1970.

AH 8913.28.5 Convegno di studi sulla città etrusca e italica preromana. Studi sulla città antica. Bologna, 1970.

AH 7203.75.5 Corpus juris civilis. Corpus juris civilis. 10.-22. ed. Dublin, 1970-73. 3v.

AH 4819.70 Crow, John Armstrong. Greece: the magic spring. 1st ed. N.Y., 1970.

AH 4039.70.5 Damsgaard-Madsen, Aksel. Det athenske demokrati. København, 1970.

AH 8863.10 D'Arms, John Houghton. Romans and the Bay of Naples; a social and cultural study of the villas and their owners from 150 B.C. to A.D. 400. Cambridge, 1970.

AH 3143.18.1 Delaporte, Louis. Mesopotamia; the Babylonian and Assyrian civilization. N.Y., 1970.

AH 7888.92.2 Deloume, Antonin. Les manieurs d'argent à Rome. 2. éd. Rome, 1970.

AH 3095.10 Dietrich, Manfried. Die Aramäer Südbabyloniens in der Sargonidenzeit, 700-648. Kevelaer, 1970.

AH 818.67 Dombart, Theodore. Die sieben Weltwunder des Altertums. 2. Aufl. München, 1970.

Eg 133.70 Drath, Juergen. Untersuchungen zum Wohnungseigentum auf Grund der gräko-ägyptischen Papyri. Diss. Marburg, 1970?

AH 7279.70 Dudley, Donald Reynolds. The Romans. London, 1970.

AH 5210.5 Dušanić, Slobodan. Arkadski savez IV veka. Beograd, 1970.

AH 7207.48 Eck, Werner. Senatoren von Vespasian bis Hadrian. Diss. München, 1970.

AH 8314.2 Eliade, Mircea. De Zalmoxis à Gengis-Khan. Paris, 1970.

AH 3195.10.2 Era. Das Erra-Epos. Rom, 1970.

AH 8073.28 Fantar, Mhamed. Carthage, la prestigieuse cité d'Elissa. Tunis, 1970.

AH 4409.70 Finley, Moses I. Early Greece; the bronze and archaic ages. London, 1970.

AH 3910.27 Fisher, Thomas. Untersuchungen zum Partherkrieg. Diss. Tübingen, 1970.

AH 9707.10 Fol, Aleksandur. Demografska i sotsialna struktura na drevna Trakiia. Sofiia, 1970.

AH 7709.05.1 Forquet de Dorne, Charles B. Les Césars africains et syriens et l'anarchie militaire. [Ristampa anastatica]. Roma, 1970.

AH 7819.70.5 Gallini, Clara. Protesta e integrazione nella Roma antica. Bari, 1970.

Eg 866.2 Gamer-Wallert, Ingrid. Fische und Fischkulte im alten Ägypten. Wiesbaden, 1970.

AH 7229.70.5 Garnsey, Peter. Social status and legal privilege in the Roman Empire. Oxford, 1970.

Eg 879.70.15 George, Beate. Zu den altägyptischen Vorstellungen vom Schatten als Seele. Bonn, 1970.

AH 4039.70 Ghinatti, Franco. I gruppi politici ateniesi fino alle guerre persiane. Roma, 1970.

Eg 609.70 Giles, Frederick John. Ikhnaton: legend and history. London, 1970.

AH 7449.70.5 Goerlitz, Walter. Hannibal; eine politische Biographie. Stuttgart, 1970.

AH 7549.70 Grant, Michael. Nero. London, 1970.

AH 2108.10 Grantovskii, E.A. Ranniaia istoriia iranskikh plemen Perednei Azii. Moskva, 1970.

1970 - cont.

AH 4559.70 Green, Peter. Alexander the Great. London, 1970.

AH 4523.12 Green, Peter. Armada from Athens. 1st ed. Garden City, N.Y., 1970.

AH 4483.16.5 Green, Peter. Xerxes at Salamis. N.Y., 1970.

AH 4483.16 Green, Peter. The year of Salamis, 480-479 B.C. London, 1970.

Eg 1042.970.5 Grieshammer, Reinhard. Das Jenseitsgericht in der Sargtexten. Wiesbaden, 1970.

Eg 879.70.5 Guilmot, Max. Le message spirituel de l'Égypte ancienne. Paris, 1970.

Eg 1042.970.10 Gundlach, Rolf. Lexikalisch-grammatische Liste zu Spruch 335a der altägyptischen Sargtexte LL/CT 335a. Darmstadt, 1970. 2v.

Eg 1042.935.20 Gundlach, Rolf. Lexikalisch-grammatische Liste zu Spruch 335a der altägyptischen Sargtexte LL/CT. Darmstadt, 1970. 2v.

AH 3414.20 Haas, Volkert. Der Kult von Nerik. Rom, 1970.

AH 8548.154 Harmond, Jacques. Les Celtes au second âge du fer. Paris, 1970.

AH 8513.16.1 Hatt, Jean Jacques. Celts and Gallo-Romans. London, 1970.

AH 3404.6 Hittites. Laws, statutes, etc. Der Telipinu-Erlass. Diss. München? 1970?

AH 819.70 Hodges, Henry W.M. Technology in the ancient world. London, 1970.

Eg 879.70.10 Horstmann, Erwin. Beiträge zur Bewusstseinsgeschichte des alten Ägypten. Stuttgart, 1970.

AH 6107.25 International Symposium, 1st, Salonika, 1968. Ancient Macedonia. Thessaloniki, 1970.

AHP 19.1.2 Iraq. Index, v.1-30. London, 1970.

AH 3011.22 Jacobsen, Thorkild. Toward the image of Tammuz, and other essays on Mesopotamian history and culture. Cambridge, 1970.

AH 7059.70 Jahn, Joachim. Intenegnum und Wahldiktatur. Kallmünz, 1970.

AH 7509.70.5 Jones, Arnold Hugh Martin. Augustus. London, 1970.

Eg 1029.68.1 Kaster, Joseph. The literature and mythology of ancient Egypt. London, 1970.

AH 8907.46 Keller, Werner. Denn die Entzündeten das Licht. München, 1970.

AH 4410.42 Kerschensteiner, Jula. Die mykenische Welt in ihren schriftlichen Zeugnissen. 1. Aufl. München, 1970.

AH 2113.2 Klengel, Evelyn. Die Hethiter. Geschichte und Umwelt. Wien, 1970.

AH 3143.25 Klengel, Evelyn. Reise in das alte Babylon. 1. Aufl. Leipzig, 1970.

AH 7299.71 Korpanty, Józef. Rozwòj politycznej roli jednostki w republice rsymskiej i jego olkicije w literaturze. Wyd. 1. Wrocław, 1970.

Eg 1042.970 Kuentz, Charles. La face sud du massif est du pylône de Ramse's II à Louxor. Le Caire, 1970.

AH 7409.70 Lukan, Karl. Romulus, oder Auf den Spuren der Gründer Roms. Wien, 1970.

Eg 819.67.7 Makram, Rizg. Kulturgeist und Kulturleib. 2. Aufl. Tübingen, 1970.

AH 299.70 Massé, Claude. La colonisation dans l'antiquité. Paris, 1970.

AH 8913.34 Mayani, Zecharia. La fin du mystère étrusque; les origines, la langue et la vie des Etrusques. Paris, 1970.

AH 7709.70 Mazza, Mario. Lotte sociali e restaurazione autoritaria nel 3. secolo d. C. Catania, 1970.

AH 5463.36 Mellersh, Harold E.L. The destruction of Knossos: the rise and fall of Minoan Crete. London, 1970.

Eg 139.70 Menu, Bernadette. Le regime juridique des terres et du personnel attaché à la terre dans le Papyrus Wilbour. Lille, 1970.

AH 7844.11 Meslin, Michel. La fete des kalendes de janvier dans l'Empire romain. Bruxelles, 1970.

AH 7819.70 Michaux, Maurice. L'antiquité, Rome et les debuts du Moyen Âge. 6. éd. Paris, 1970.

AH 4809.70 Miller, Molly. The Sicilian colony dates. Albany, 1970.

AH 7449.70.10 Mix, Erving R. Marcus Atilius Regulus; exemplum historicum. The Hague, 1970.

AH 8357.2 Mócsy, András. Gesellschaft und Romanisation in der römischen Provinz Moesia Superior. Amsterdam, 1970.

AH 7489.70 Montherlant, Henry de. Le treizieme César. Paris, 1970.

AH 6110.24 Naltsas, Christophoros A. Philippos deuteros ho Makedòn. Thessolonikè, 1970.

AH 2209.4 Orlin, Louis Lawrence. Assyrian colonies in Cappadocia. The Hague, 1970.

AH 7208.8A Palmer, Robert E.A. The archaic community of the Romans. Cambridge, 1970.

AH 3096.10 Parpola, Simo. Letters from Assyrian scholars to the Kings Esarhaddon and Assurbanipal. Neukirchen-Vluyn, 1970.

AH 7409.70.5 Peruzzi, Emilio. Origini di Roma. Firenze, 1970- 2v.

AH 7699.18.2 Platnauer, Maurice. The life and reign of the Emperor Lucius Septimius Severus. Westport, 1970.

AH 8011.10 Rachet, Marguerite. Rome et les berbères. Bruxelles, 1970.

AH 812.5 Recherches sur les structures sociales dans l'antiquité classique. Paris, 1970.

AH 7659.64.2 Rémondon, Roger. La crise de l'Empire romain de Marc Aurèle à Anastase. 2. éd. Paris, 1970.

AH 8548.149 Ross, Anne. Everyday life of the pagan Celts. London, 1970.

AH 8207.36 Rowland, Thomas Henry. The Romans in North Britain. Newcastle upon Tyne, 1970.

AH 3966.38 Rowley, Harold Henry. Dictionary of Bible place names. London, 1970.

AH 5610.21 Sandberger, Frank. Prosopographie zur Geschichte des Pyrrhos. Diss. Stuttgart, 1970.

AH 7188.92.1 Schneider, Albert. Zur Geschichte der Sclaverei im alten Rom. Frankfurt, 1970.

AH 7489.59.3 Scullard, Howard Hayes. From the Gracchi to Nero. 3. ed. London, 1970.

AH 7449.70 Scullard, Howard Hayes. Scipio Africanus: soldier and politician. Ithaca, 1970.

AH 4217.10 Şenel, Alaeddin. Eshi yunondo eşitlitove eşitsrilik. Ankara, 1970.

Eg 981.10 Siegler, Karl Georg. Kalabsha; Architektur und Baugeschichte des Tempels. Berlin, 1970.

AH 309.70 Slonimskii, Mikhail M. Periodizatsiia drevnei istorii v sovetskoi istoriografii. Voronezh, 1970.

AH 329.70 Snowden, Frank Martin. Black in antiquity; Ethiopians in the Greco-Roman experience. Cambridge, 1970.

AH 5479.2 Spyridakès, Stylianos Basileiou. Ptolemaic Itanos and Hellenistic Crete. Berkeley, 1970.

1970 - cont.

AH 7099.67.1 — Storoni Mazzolani, Lidia. The idea of the city in Roman thought. London, 1970.

AH 39.61.2 — Suerbaum, Werner. Vom Antiken zum frühmittelalterlichen Staatsbegriff. 2. Aufl. Münster, 1970.

AH 7132.10 — Sympotica Franz Wieacker sexagenario Sasbachwaldeni a suis libata. Göttingen, 1970.

AH 7479.70 — Szidat, Joachim. Caesars diplomatische Tätigkeit im gallischen Krieg. Wiesbaden, 1970.

Eg 603.11 — Tell el-Amarna Tablets. El Amarna tablets, 359-379. Neukirchen-Vluyn, 1970.

AH 3964.36 — Thompson, Henry O. Mekal, the God of Beth-Shan. Leiden, 1970.

AH 3042.3.12 — Unger, Eckhard. Babylon. 2e Aufl. Berlin, 1970.

AH 7207.50 — Ungern-Sternberg von Pürkel, Jürgen. Untersuchungen zum spätrepublikanischen Notstandsrecht. Diss. München, 1970.

Eg 39.70 — Vandoni, Mariangela. Gli epistrategi nell'Egitto greco-romano. Milano, 1970?

AH 4858.17 — Vatin, Claude. Recherches sur le mariage et la condition de la femme mariée à l'époque hellénistique. Thèse. Paris, 1970.

AH 4858.17.1 — Vatin, Claude. Recherches sur le mariage et la condition de la femme mariée à l'époque hellénistique. Paris, 1970.

AH 4845.26 — Walcot, Peter. Greek peasants, ancient and modern: a comparison of social and moral values. Manchester, Eng., 1970.

AH 3052.5.5 — Walters, Stanley D. Water for Larsa; an old Babylonian archive dealing with irrigation. New Haven, 1970.

AH 4843.26 — Webster, Thomas Bertram Lonsdale. The Greek chorus. London, 1970.

AH 2959.5 — Weigel, Hildegard. Der trojanische Krieg. Darmstadt, 1970.

AH 4559.70.5 — Welles, Charles Bradford. Alexander and the Hellenistic world. Toronto, 1970.

AH 7890.2 — White, Kenneth Douglas. A bibliography of Roman agriculture. Reading, 1970.

AH 7899.70 — White, Kenneth Douglas. Roman farming. London, 1970.

AH 7909.70 — Wild, J.P. Textile manufacture in the northern Roman provinces. Cambridge, Eng., 1970.

AH 4819.66.21F — The world of classical Athens. London, 1970.

EgP 149.5.2 — Zeitschrift für ägyptische Altertumskunde. Index, 1863-1943. Osnabrück, 1970.

AHP 36.3.4 — Zeitschrift für die alttestamentliche Wissenschaft. Register, 26-50 (1906-1932). Berlin, 1970.

AH 819.70.5 — Zieliński, Tadeusz. Po co Homer? wyd. 1. Kraków, 1970.

1971

AH 7114.48 — Alföldi, Andras. Der Vater des Vaterlandes im römischen Denken. Darmstadt, 1971.

Eg 752.15 — L'Archivio di Kronion. Milano, 1971.

AH 4299.71 — Baaccesi, Lorenzo. Grecità adriatica. Bologna, 1971.

AH 2109.15 — Balikçisi, Halikarnas. Anadolu'nun sesi. Istanbul, 1971.

AH 3011.24 — Beitraege zu Geschichte, Kultur und Religion des alten Orients; in Memoriam Eckhard Unger. 1. Aufl. Baden-Baden, 1971.

AH 1819.71 — Beitraege zur sozialen Struktur des alten Vorderasien. Berlin, 1971.

AH 3009.71 — Beliavskii, Vatalii A. Vavilon legendarnyi i Vavilon istoricheskii. Moskva, 1971.

AH 7189.71.5 — Bellen, Heinz. Studien zur Sklavenflucht im römischen Kaiserreich. Wiesbaden, 1971.

Eg 983.10PF — Berlin. Universität. Institut für Ägyptologie. Musawwart es sufra. Humboldt-Universität zu Berlin. v.1, pt.2. Berlin, 1971.

AH 7699.71 — Birley, Anthony Richard. Septimus Severus: the African emperor. London, 1971.

AH 8511.18 — Bordet, Marcel. La Gaule romaine. Paris, 1971.

AH 4329.71 — Bourgeois, Alain. La Grèce antique devant la négritude. Paris, 1971.

AH 4499.71 — Bowra, Cecil Maurice. Periclean Athens. N.Y., 1971.

Eg 709.71.10 — Bradford, Ernle Dusgate Selby. Cleopatra. London, 1971.

AH 8615.15 — Brunt, Peter A. Italian manpower, 225 B.C.-A.D. 14. Oxford, 1971.

AH 7114.46 — Brunt, Peter Astbury. Social conflicts in the Roman Republic. London, 1971.

Eg 885.899.6 — Budge, Ernest Alfred Wallis. Egyptian magic. N.Y., 1971.

AH 2057.5 — Burney, Charles Allen. The peoples of the hills: ancient Ararat and Caucasus. London, 1971.

AH 846.36 — Castagnoli, Ferdinando. Orthogonal town planning in antiquity. Cambridge, 1971.

AH 3302.1 — Chatzeioannou, Kyriakos. He archaia Kypros eis tas Hellenikas pegas. Leukosia, 1971.

AH 7469.71 — Christiansen, Erik. Den romerske republiks sidste hundrede år. København, 1971.

AH 3002.154.5 — The claremont Ras Shamra tablets. Roma, 1971.

AH 842.52 — Clarke, Martin Lowther. Higher education in the ancient world. London, 1971.

AH 7239.71.5F — Claustra Alpium Iuliarum. Ljubljana, 1971.

AH 8549.171 — Coarer-Kalondan, Edmond. Le druidisme, ou La lumière del l'Occident. Paris, 1971.

AH 5303.30 — Connor, Walter Robert. The new politicians of fifth-century Athens. Princeton, 1971.

AH 5463.35 — Cottrell, Leonard. The mystery of Minoan civilization. N.Y., 1971.

Eg 981.5 — Crawford, Dorothy. Kerkeosiris. Cambridge, Eng., 1971.

AH 4339.71.5 — Davies, John K. Athenian propertied families, 600-300 B.C. Oxford, 1971.

AH 4719.69.6 — Deininger, Jürgen. Der politische Widerstand gegen Rom in Griechenland. Habilitationsschrift. Berlin, 1971.

Eg 709.71.5 — Desmond, Alice Curtis. Cleopatra's children. N.Y., 1971.

AH 239.71 — Diesner, Hans-Joachim. Kriege des Altertums. Berlin, 1971.

AH 7903.5.10 — Diocletianus. Diokletians Preisedikt. Berlin, 1971.

AH 7449.71.5 — Dorey, Thomas Alan. Rome against Carthage. London, 1971.

AH 7449.71.10 — Errington, Robert Malcolm. The dawn of empire; Rome's rise to world power. London, 1971.

AH 3707.12 — L'espansione fenicia nel Mediterraneo. Roma, 1971.

AH 4299.71.5 — Estudios sobre el mundo helenístico. Swilla, 1971.

Eg 984.2 — Farag, Nagib. The discovery of Neferuptah. Cairo, 1971.

AH 7279.71.5 — Fernau, Joachim. Cäsar lässt Grüssen. München, 1971.

Eg 885.971F — Feucht-Putz, Erika. Pektorale nichtköniglicher Personen. Wiesbaden, 1971.

AH 7239.71 — Fink, Robert O. Roman military records on Papyrus. Cleveland, 1971.

AH 4039.71 — Finley, Moses. The ancestral constitution. London, 1971.

AH 9639.15 — Fiori, Alberto. Siracusa greca. Roma, 1971.

1971 - cont.

AH 7469.71.5 — Fonti su Caio Mario. Milano, 1971.

AH 4842.87.1 — Forbes, Clarence Allen. Greek physical education. N.Y., 1971.

AH 5305.5 — Fornara, Charles W. The Athenian board of generals from 501 to 404. Wiesbaden, 1971.

AH 9653.5F — Galsterer, Hartmut. Untersuchungen zum römischen Städtewesen auf der iberieschen Halbinsel. Berlin, 1971.

AH 839.30.1 — Gardiner, Edward Norman. Athletics of the ancient world. Oxford, 1971.

AH 39.71.5 — Gaudemet, Jean. Précis des institutions de l'antiquité. Paris, 1971. 2v.

AH 8549.174 — Gilbert, Max. "Les roches aux fées" dans l'ancienne Gaule. Fécamp, 1971.

AH 4049.71 — Giovannini, Adalberto. Untersuchungen über die Natur und die Anfange der bundesstaatlichen Sympolitie in Griechenland. Göttingen, 1971.

AH 3663.12 — Gobineau, Arthur. The world of the Persians. London, 1971.

AH 7839.67.2 — Grant, Michael. Gladiators. Harmondsworth, Eng., 1971.

AH 819.71.5 — Grimal, Pierre. La civilisation hellénistique et la montée de Rome. Paris, 1971.

AH 3027.11 — Haldar, Alfred Ossian. Who were the Amorites? Leiden, 1971.

AH 1279.71 — Hallo, William W. The ancient Near East. N.Y., 1971.

AH 3151.2.10 — Hammurabi, king of Babylonia. The Hammurabi code and the Sinaitic legislation. Port Washington, 1971.

AH 3707.28.1 — Harden, Donald B. The Phoenicians. Harmondsworth, 1971.

Eg 819.71.7 — Harris, James Renel. The legacy of Egypt. 2. ed. Oxford, 1971.

AH 8910.8 — Harris, William Vernon. Rome in Etruria and Umbria. Oxford, 1971.

Eg 983.15 — Hofmann, Inge. Studien zum meroitischen Königtum. Bruxelles, 1971.

AH 1299.71 — Hommages à Andre Dupont-Sommer. Paris, 1971.

AH 7203.148 — Honoré, Antony Maurice. Justinian's Digest. Oxford, 1971.

AH 5463.25 — Hood, Sinclair. The Minoans. N.Y., 1971.

AH 3739.10 — Jidejian, Nina. Sidon through the ages. Beirut, 1971.

AH 7299.37.6 — Jones, Arnold H.M. The cities of the eastern Roman provinces. 2. ed. Oxford, 1971.

AH 7339.71 — Jones, Arnold Hugh Martin. The prosopography of the later Roman Empire. Cambridge, Eng., 1971-

AH 7653.38 — Jordan, David. Gibbon and his Roman Empire. Urbana, 1971.

AH 4339.71 — Kanellopoulos, Panagiötës. Five men - five centuries; essays on Solon. London, 1971.

AH 4559.71 — Kraft, Konrad. Der rationale Alexander. Kallmünz, 1971.

AH 7039.71 — Krarup, Per. Romersk politik i oldtiden. København, 1971.

AH 4861.9 — Kurtz, Donna Carol. Greek burial customs. London, 1971.

AH 3012.22 — Labłocha, Yulia. Stosunki agrarne w paristure Sargonidów. Wyd. 1. Poznan, 1971.

AH 7799.71 — Lafferty, Raphael A. The fall of Rome. Garden City, N.Y., 1971.

AH 2147.12 — Lanza, Michele. Roma e l'eredita di Alessandro. Milano, 1971.

AH 279.71.5 — Lauffer, Siegfried. Kurze Geschichte der antiken Welt. München, 1971.

AH 7206.35 — Law of Justinian. Loi de judgement. Bucarest, 1971.

AH 7200.19.4 — Leges XII Tabularum. Das Zwölftafelgesetz. 4. Aufl. München, 1971.

AH 4029.71 — Lewis, Naphtali. The fifth century B.C. Toronto, 1971.

AH 7201.115 — Lex Rubria. Studien zur der Lex Rubria. Utrecht? 1971?

Eg 709.71 — Lindsay, Jack. Cleopatra. London, 1971.

AH 2012.4 — Lundin, Avraam G. Gosudarstvo mukarribov Saba'. Moskva, 1971.

AH 7799.71.5 — Luponiac, Pierre de. La disparition de l'Empire romain en Occident. Paris, 1971.

AH 7299.71.5 — Maiak, I.L. Vzaimsotnosheniia Rima i italiitsev v III-II vv. do n.e. (do grakhanskogo dvisheniia). Moskva, 1971.

AH 39.71 — Maillet, Jean. Institutions politiques et sociales de l'antiquité. 2. éd. Paris, 1971.

AH 8307.4 — Maior, Petru. Istoria pentru începutul românillor in Dacia. Bucureşti, 1971. 2v.

AH 7779.71 — Manacorda, Mario Alighiero. La paideia di Achille. Roma, 1971.

Eg 971.7.15 — Marlowe, John. The golden age of Alexandria: from its foundation by Alexander the Great in 1331 B.C. to its capture by the Arabs in 642 A.D. London, 1971.

AH 239.71.5 — Marsden, Eric W. Greek and Roman artillery; technical treatises. Oxford, 1971.

AH 7899.71 — Martin, René. Recherches sur les agronomes latins et leurs conceptions économiques et sociales. Paris, 1971.

AH 3177.15 — Mason, Herbert. Gilgamesh: a verse narrative. Boston, 1971.

AH 9610.22.5 — Meier-Welcker, Hans. Dionysios I, Tyrann von Syrakus. Göttingen, 1971.

AH 189.71 — Meltzer, Milton. Slavery: from the rise of Western civilization to the Renaissance. 2. ed. N.Y., 1971.

AH 4809.71 — Miller, Molly. The Thalassocracies; studies in chronology. Albany, 1971.

AH 3013.971 — Moortgat, Anton. Einführung in die vorderasiatische Archäologie. Darmstadt, 1971.

AH 819.71.10 — Moscati, Sabatino. Civiltà sul Mediterraneo. Novara, 1971.

AH 3963.24 — North, Martin. Aufsätze zur biblischen Landes- und Altertumskunde. Neukirchen, 1971.

AH 7469.71.10 — Odahl, Charles Matson. The Catilinarian conspiracy. New Haven, 1971.

AH 5758.16.1 — Oliva, Pavel. Sparta and her social problems. Amsterdam, 1971.

AH 5758.16 — Oliva, Pavel. Sparta and her social problems. Prague, 1971.

Eg 879.71.5 — Olsson, Albert. I faraos land-på faraos tid. Solna, 1971.

AH 7469.02.6 — Oman, Charles. Seven Roman statesmen of the later Republic: the Gracchi, Sulla, Crassus, Cato, Pompey and Caesar. Freeport, 1971.

AH 819.71.2 — Parandowski, Yan. Z antycznego świata. wyd. 2. Warszawa, 1971.

AH 5303.32 — Pecorella Longo, Chlara. Eterie e gruppi politici nell'Atene del IV sec. A.C. Firenze, 1971.

AH 1819.70.1 — Peters, Francis E. The harvest of Hellenism. N.Y., 1971.

AH 7549.62 — Pichon, Jean Charles. Néron et le mystère des origines chrétiennes. Paris, 1971.

AH 4239.71.5 — Pritchett, William Kendrick. Ancient Greek military practice. Berkeley, 1971-

AH 7449.71 — Proctor, Dennis. Hannibal's march in history. Oxford, 1971.

AH 276.14.9 — Raleigh, Walter. The history of the world. London, 1971.

Chronological Listing

1971 - cont.

AH 4139.71 — Ramilly, Jacqueline de. La loi dans la pensée grecque des origines à Aristote. Paris, 1971.

AH 909.71 — Raunig, Walter. Bernstein, Weihrauch, Seide. Wien, 1971.

AH 3187.16 — Römer, Willem H.P. Frauenbriefe über Religion, Politik und Privatleben in Mari. Kevelaer, 1971.

AH 3155.32 — Rosengarten, Yvonne. Trois aspects de la pensée religieuse sumérienne. Paris, 1971.

AH 8305.7 — Rossi, Lino. Trajan's column and the Dacian wars. London, 1971.

AH 279.24.6 — Rostovtsev, Mikhail Ivanovich. A history of the ancient world. Westport, 1971. 2v.

AH 7479.71 — Sabben-Clare, James. Caesar and Roman politics 60-50 B.C. London, 1971.

AH 3175.20A — Sanders, Nancy K. Poems of heaven and hell from ancient Mesopotamia. Harmondsworth, 1971.

Eg 819.71 — Savel'eva, Tat'iana N. Kak zhili egiptiane vo vremena stroitel'stva piramid. Moskva, 1971.

AH 4499.71.5 — Schachermeyr, Fritz. Geistesgeschichte der Perikleischen Zeit. Stuttgart, 1971.

AH 3804.5 — Schaeffer, Henry. The social legislation of the primitive Semites. N.Y., 1971.

AH 7189.71 — Shtaerman, Elena. Rabovladel'cheskie otnosheniia v romner Rimskoi imperii (Italiia). Moskva, 1971.

AH 9773.13.5 — Signon, Helmut. Die Römer in Köln. Frankfurt, 1971.

AH 7759.71 — Smith, John Holland. Constantine the Great. London, 1971.

AH 7139.71 — Soellner, Alfred. Römische Rechtsgeschichte. 1e Aufl. Freiburg, 1971.

AH 3002.154 — Sollberger, Edmond. Inscriptions royales sumériennes et akkadiennes. Paris, 1971.

Eg 1042.971 — Spiegel, Joachim. Das Auferstehungsritual der Unas-Pyramide. Wiesbaden, 1971.

AH 4819.71 — Starr, Chester G. The ancient Greeks. N.Y., 1971.

AH 7279.71 — Starr, Chester G. The ancient Romans. N.Y., 1971.

AH 299.71 — Studi di storiografia antica. In memoria di Leonardo Ferrero. Torino, 1971.

AH 8258.1 — Syme, Ronald. Danubian papers. Bucharest, 1971.

Eg 879.71.10 — Thausing, Gertrud. Sein und Werden. Wien, 1971.

AH 7299.71.10 — Thompson, David. The idea of Rome; from antiquity to the Renaissance. Albuquerque, 1971.

AH 4303.6 — Touloumakos, Johannes. Zum Geschichtsbewusstsein der Griechen in der Zeit der römischen Herrschaft. Bonn, 1971.

AH 7861.14 — Toynbee, Jocelyn Mary Catherine. Death and burial in the Roman world. London, 1971.

Eg 609.71 — Vandersleyen, Claude. Les guerres d'Amoses. Bruxelles, 1971.

AH 180.5 — Vogt, Joseph. Bibliographie zur antiken Sklaverei. Bochum, 1971.

AH 9621.12 — Waele, J.A. de. Acragas Graeca. 's-Gravenhage, 1971-

Eg 269.71 — Ward, William A. Egypt and the east Mediterranean world, 2200-1900 B.C.; studies in Egyptian foreign relations during the first intermediate period. Beirut, 1971.

AH 7162.44 — Watson, Alan. The law of succession in the later Roman Republic. Oxford, 1971.

AH 7169.71 — Watson, Alan. Roman private law around 200 B.C. Edinburgh, 1971.

AH 3160.28 — Weiher, Egbert von. Der babylonische Gott Nergal. Kevelaer, 1971.

AH 3664.17.1 — Wesendonk, Otto Günther von. Urmensch und Seele in der iranischen Überlieferung. Osnabrück, 1971.

AH 7207.52 — Wiseman, Timothy Peter. New men in the Roman senate 139 B.C. - A.D. 14. London, 1971.

Eg 879.71 — Witt, Reginald Eldred. Isis in the Graeco-Roman world. Ithaca, N.Y., 1971.

Eg 279.71 — Wolf, Walther. Das alte Ägypten. München, 1971.

AH 5673.10 — Zahrnt, Michael. Olynth und die Chalkidier. München, 1971.

AH 4559.71.5 — Zalokòstas, Chrēstos Petrou. Megas Alexandros. Athēnai, 1971?

AH 819.70.10 — Zieliński, Tadeusz. Szkice antyezne. wyd. 1. Kraków, 1971.

AH 9707.11 — Zlatkovskaia, Tat'iana D. Vozniknovenie gosudarstva u trakiitsev. VII-V vv do n.e. Moskva, 1971.

1972

AH 3045.20 — Adams, Robert McCormick. The Uruk countryside. Chicago, 1972.

AH 4039.72 — Akarca, Aşkidil. Yunan arkeolojisinin ana çirgileri. Ankara, 1972.

Eg 819.72 — Aldred, Cyril. Tatankhamun's Egypt. London, 1972.

Eg 1042.972 — Altenmüller, Hartwig. Die Texte zum Begrabensritual in den Pyramiden des alten Reiches. Wiesbaden, 1972.

AH 1279.72 — Die altorientalischen Reiche. Frankfurt, 1972-73. 3v.

AH 7207.53 — Arnheim, M.T.W. The senatorial aristocracy in the later Roman empire. Oxford, 1972.

AH 7272.2 — Aufstieg und Niedergang der römischen Welt. Berlin, 1972- 6v.

AH 7299.72.5 — Aufstieg und Niedergang der römischen Welt. v.1-2. Berlin, 1972- 6v.

AH 4882.5 — Austin, Michel. Economies et sociétés en Grèce ancienne. Paris, 1972.

AH 7114.35.1 — Badian, E. Foreign clientelae, 264-70 B.C. Oxford, 1972.

AH 7889.72 — Badian, Ernst. Publicans and sinners; private enterprise in the service of the Roman Republic. Ithaca, N.Y., 1972.

AH 7239.72 — Barker, Phil. The armies and enemies of imperial Rome. Goring by Sea, 1972.

Eg 819.70.1F — Barocas, Claudio. Egypt. N.Y., 1972.

AH 3020.55.5 — Bauer, Josef. Altsumerische Wirtschaftstexte aus Lagasch. Rome, 1972.

AH 4839.71 — Bengston, Hermann. Die olympischen Spiele in der Antike. Zürich, 1972.

Eg 919.72.5 — Berlev, Oleg D. Trudovoe naselenie Egipta v epokhn srednego tsarstva. Moskva, 1972.

AH 4339.72 — Bicknell, P.J. Studies in Athenian politics and genealogy. Wiesbaden, 1972.

AH 7149.72 — Bleicken, Jochen. Staatliche Ordnung und Freiheit in der römischen Republik. Kallmünz, 1972.

Eg 1042.972.5 — Book of Two Ways. The ancient Egyptian book of two ways. Berkeley, 1972.

AH 7909.17.1 — Brewster, Ethel Hampson. Roman craftsmen and tradesmen of the early empire. N.Y., 1972.

AH 909.72 — Burford, Alison. Craftsmen in Greek and Roman society. London, 1972.

AH 4279.00.31 — Bury, John Bagnell. A history of Greece to the death of Alexander the Great. 3. ed. London, 1972.

1972 - cont.

Eg 609.72.5 — Carter, Michael. The golden monarch; Tutankhamun. Christchurch, 1972.

AH 3181.14 — Castellino, Giorgio R. Two Šulgi hymns [and] Be. Roma, 1972.

AH 7549.72 — Cizek, Eugen. L'époque de Néron et ses controverses idéologiques. Leiden, 1972.

AH 3657.46 — Collins, Robert J. The Medes and Persians, conquerors and diplomats. N.Y., 1972.

AH 7419.72 — Combès, Robert. La république à Rome, 509-29 avant Jésus-Christ. Paris, 1972.

AH 299.72.5 — De Camp, Lyon S. Great cities of the ancient world. Garden City, N.Y., 1972.

Eg 879.72 — Derchain, Philippe. Hathor Quadrifons. Istanbul, 1972.

AH 4409.72 — Desborough, Vincent Robin d'Arba. The Greek dark ages. London, 1972.

AH 4519.72.1 — De Ste. Croix, Geoffrey Ernest Maurice. The origins of the Peloponnesian War. Ithaca, 1972.

AH 4519.72 — De Ste. Croix, Geoffrey Ernest Maurice. The origins of the Peloponnesian War. London, 1972.

AH 4049.72 — Díaz Tejera, Alberto. Encrucijada de lo político y lo humano, un momento histórico de Grecia. Sevilla, 1972.

AH 3054.10 — Dietrich, Manfried. Nuzi-Bibliographie. Kevelaer, 1972.

AH 279.72 — Drevnii Vostok i antichnyi mir. Moskva, 1972.

AH 8314.2.1 — Eliade, Mircea. Zalmoxis, the vanishing god. Chicago, 1972.

AH 4819.54.1 — Finley, Moses I. The world of Odysseus. Harmondsworth, 1972.

AH 7509.02.8 — Firth, John B. Augustus Caesar and the organization of the empire of Rome. Freeport, 1972.

AH 9707.13 — Fol, Aleksandur. Policheska istoriia na Trakite. Sofiia, 1972.

Eg 971.7.25 — Fraser, Peter Marshall. Ptolemaic Alexandria. Oxford, 1972. 3v.

AH 4043.5.20 — Frolov, Eduard D. Grecheskie tirany IV v. do n.e. Leningrad, 1972.

AH 239.72 — Garlan, Yvon. La guerre dans l'antiquité. Paris, 1972.

AH 5610.6.2 — Garouphalias, Petros Euagelov. Pyrros, ho Basilias tēs Epeirov. 2. ed. Athēnai, 1972.

AH 8003.1 — Gascou, Jacques. La politique municipale de l'empire romain en Afrique proconsulaire de Trajan à Septime-Sévère. Rome, 1972.

Eg 1189.72.5 — Gillings, Richard J. Mathematics in the time of the pharaohs. Cambridge, 1972.

Eg 709.72 — Grant, Michael. Cleopatra. London, 1972.

AH 819.72.10 — Green, Peter. The shadow of the Parthenon; studies in ancient history and literature. London, 1972.

AH 7099.72 — Grelle, Francesco. L'autonomia cittadina fra Traiano e Adriano. Napoli, 1972.

AH 7419.72.10 — Gruen, Erich Stephen. The Roman republic. Washington, 1972.

AH 8007.12.6 — Gsell, Stéphane. Histoire ancienne de l'Afrique du nord. Osnabrück, 1972. 8v.

AH 299.72.10A — Hammond, Mason. The city in the ancient world. Cambridge, Mass., 1972.

AH 6107.14 — Hammond, Nicholas Geoffrey Lempriere. A history of Macedonia. Oxfrd, 1972-

AH 839.72 — Harris, Harold A. Sport in Greece and Rome. Ithaca, 1972.

AH 4659.72 — Heinen, Heinz. Untersuchungen zur hellenistischen Geschichte des 3. Jahrhunderts. Wiesbaden, 1972.

Eg 990.21 — Helck, Hans Wolfgang. Die Ritualdarstellungen des Ramesseums. [Thebes]. Wiesbaden, 1972-

Eg 279.72 — Helek, Hans Wolfgang. Lexikon der Agyptologie. v.1, pt.1-6. Wiesbaden, 1972-

Eg 971.7.20 — Heuer, Kenneth. City of the stargazers. N.Y., 1972.

AH 8548.155 — Hubert, Henri. The greatness and decline of the Celts. New York, 1972.

AH 4819.72.15 — Hurmuziadis, Jorge. La cultura de Grecia: antigua, bizantia, moderna. Buenos Aires, 1972.

AH 7159.72 — Jones, Arnold Hugh Martin. The criminal curts of the Roman Republic and Principate. Oxford, 1972.

AH 8157.9 — Kaddache, Mahfoud. L'Algérie dans l'antiquité. Alger, 1972.

AH 3020.22.1 — King, Leonard W. Chronicles concerning early Babylonian kings. v.1-2. London, 1972.

AH 298.42.2 — Kollataj, Hugo. Rozbiór krytyczny zazad historii. wyd.1. Warszawa, 1972.

AH 7769.72 — Krawczuk, Aleksander. Ród konstantgna. Wyd. 1. Warszawa, 1972. 2v.

AH 3921.12 — Liebsschuetz, John Hugo Wolfgang Gideon. Antiochi city and imperial administration in the later Roman Empire. Oxford, 1972.

AH 4842.98 — Lynch, John Patrick. Aristotle's school. Berkeley, 1972.

AH 7653.40 — Lyon, Bryce Dale. The origins of the Middle Ages; Pirenne's challenge to Gibbon. 1. ed. N.Y., 1972.

Eg 1079.72.1 — McCoy, Raymond Aloysius. The golden goddess. Menomonie, 1972.

AH 4499.72A — Meiggs, Russell. The Athenian empire. Oxford, 1972.

AH 9707.14 — Mikhailov, Georgei I. Trakite. Sofiia, 1972.

AH 4819.72.5 — Miller, Helen (Hill). Greece through the ages. N.Y., 1972.

AH 7419.72.5 — Nechai, Fedor M. Obrazovanie rimskogo gosudarstva. Minsk, 1972.

Eg 819.54.4 — Neubert, Otto. Tutankhamun and the Valley of the Kings. London, 1972.

AH 3958.20 — Nordisk Teologkonferanse, Utstein Kloster, 1971. Israel, kirken og verden. Oslo, 1972.

AH 1819.72 — Oberhuber, Karl. Die Kultur des alten Orients. Frankfurt, 1972.

AH 7959.72 — O'Sullivan, Firmin. The Egnation Way. Newton Abbot, 1972.

Eg 1189.72F — Parker, Richard Anthony. Demotic mathematical papyri. Providence, R.I., 1972.

AH 5409.8 — Phouriōtēs, Angelos. Korinthos. Athēnai, 1972.

AH 7769.47.2 — Piganiol, André. L'empire chrétien (325-395). 2. éd. Paris, 1972.

Eg 919.72 — Pikus, Nikolai N. Tsanskie zemledel'tsy (nepossedstvennye proisvoditeli) i nemeslenniki v Egipte III v. do n.e. Moskva, 1972.

AH 4318.51.1 — Pococke, Edward. India in Greece. Delhi, 1972.

AH 4410.38 — Renfrew, Colin. The emergence of civilisation: the Cyclades and the Aegean in the third millennium B.C. London, 1972.

AH 5303.6 — Rhodes, P.J. The Athenian boule. Oxford, 1972.

AH 3160.29 — Roberts, Jimmy J.M. The earliest Semitic pantheon. Baltimore, 1972.

AH 3133.1 — Sack, Ronald Herbert. Amel-Marduk, 562-560 B.C. Kevelaer, 1972.

Chronological Listing

1972 - cont.

AH 7339.72 — Saklatvala, Beram. The Caesars: the Roman Empire and its rulers. Newton Abbott, 1972.

AH 299.72 — Schenk von Stauffenberg, Alexander. Macht und Geist. München, 1972.

AH 7519.72 — Seager, Robin. Tiberius. London, 1972.

AH 4559.72 — Seibert, Jakob. Alexander der Grosse. Darmstadt, 1972.

AH 4484.16 — Siewert, Peter. Der Eid von Plataiai. München, 1972.

Eg 1029.72 — Simpson, William Kelly. The literature of ancient Egypt; an anthology of stories, instructions, and poetry. New Haven, 1972.

AH 819.72.5 — Sotsial'no-ekonomicheskie problemy istorii drevnego mira i srednikh vekov. Moskva, 1972.

AH 79.72 — Staveley, Eastland Stuart. Greek and Roman voting and elections. London, 1972.

AH 7299.72 — Storoni Mazzalani. L'impero sena fine. Milano, 1972.

AH 3020.76 — Sumerian and Akkadian cuneiform texts in the collection of the World Heritage Museum of the University of Illinois. Urbana, 1972. 2v.

AH 5257.1 — Tomlinson, Richard Allan. Argos and the Argolid. Ithaca, N.Y., 1972.

AH 819.72 — Valeurs antiques et temps modernes. Classical values and the modern world. Ottawa, 1972.

AH 4819.72.10 — Van Duyn, Janet H. (Dunning). The Greeks: their legacy. N.Y., 1972.

AH 3660.20 — Walser, Gerold. Beiträge zur Achämenidengeschichte. Wiesbaden, 1972.

AH 4819.72 — Warner, Rex. Men of Athens: the story of fifth century Athens. London, 1972.

AH 7189.72 — Weaver, Paul Richard Carey. Family Caesaris; a social study of the Emperor's freedom and slaves. Cambridge, Eng., 1972.

AH 3194.1 — Weir, John D. The Venus tablets of Ammizaduga. Istanbul, 1972.

AH 3009.72 — Wellard, James Howard. By the waters of Babylon. London, 1972.

AH 9760.1 — Wells, Colin Michael. The German policy of Augustus: an examination of the archaeological evidence. Oxford, 1972.

Eg 609.72 — Wynne, Barry. Behind the mask of Tutankhamen. London, 1972.

AH 859.9 — Zinserling, Verena. Die Frau in Hellas und Rom. Stuttgart, 1972.

1973

AH 4299.73 — Amit, M. Great and small poleis. Bruxeiles, 1973.

AH 819.73 — Antichnaia tsivilizatsiia. Moskva, 1973.

AH 3129.8 — Berger, Paul. Die neubabylonischen Königsinschriften. Kevelaer, 1973-

Eg 879.73.5 — Bleeker, Chaes. Hathor and Thoth. Leiden, 1973.

AH 4521.20 — Bloedow, Edmund F. Alcibiades reexamined. Wiesbaden, 1973.

AH 7298.81.1 — Budinszky, Alexander. Die Ausbreitung der lateinischen Sprache über Italien und die Provinzen des römischen Reiches. Berlin. Wiesbaden, 1973.

AH 4279.73.5 — Chambers, Mortimer Hardin. Ancient Greece. Washington, 1973.

AH 5304.2 — Cohen, Edward E. Ancient Athenian maritime courts. Princeton, 1973.

AH 5303.8 — De Laix, Roger. Probouleusis at Athens. Berkeley, 1973.

Eg 938.94.1 — Dümichen, Johannes. Zur Geographie des alten Ägypten. Wiesbaden, 1973.

AH 4449.68.2 — Ehrenberg, Victor. From Solon to Socrates. 2. ed. London, 1973.

AH 3054.10.5 — Eichler, Barry L. Indenture at Nuzi. New Haven, 1973.

AH 2104.5 — Eyuboğlu, Ismet Zeki. Tanri yaratan toprak; Anadolu. Istanbul, 1973.

AH 4819.73 — Ferguson, John. The heritage of Hellenism. 1st American ed. N.Y., 1973.

AH 3179.18 — Ferrara, A.J. Nanna-Suen's journey to Nippur. Rome, 1973.

AH 889.73.1 — Finley, Moses I. The ancient economy. Berkeley, 1973.

AH 889.73 — Finley, Moses I. The ancient economy. London, 1973.

AH 4559.73 — Fox, Robin Lane. Alexander the Great. London, 1973.

AH 4839.10.1 — Gardiner, Edward Norman. Greek athletic sports and festivals. London, 1973.

AH 3408.19 — Giorgadze, Grigorii G. Ocherki po sotsial'no-ekonomicheskoi istorii Khettskogo gosudarstva. Tbilisi, 1973.

AH 2907.4 — Gologlu, Mahmut. Anadolunun milli devleti Pontos. Istanbul, 1973.

AH 4279.73 — Green, Peter. A concise history of Ancient Greece to the close of the classical era. London, 1973.

AH 3657.17.1 — Gutschmid, Alfred von. Geschichte Irans. Graz, 1973.

AH 1819.73 — Hawkes, Jacquetta Hopkins. The first great civilizations. 1. ed. N.Y., 1973.

Eg 879.73 — Hornung, Erik. Der Eine und die Vielen. Darmstadt, 1973.

AH 7829.03.9 — Johnston, Harold W. The private life of the Romans. N.Y., 1973.

Eg 659.73 — Kitchen, Kenneth Anderson. The third intermediate period in Egypt. (1100-650 B.C.). Warminster, 1973.

AH 7889.73.1 — Kolendo, Jerzy. Le traité d'agronomie des Saserna. Wroclaw, 1973.

AH 3179.16 — Kramer, Samuel Noah. Enmerkar and the Lord of Aratta. Ann Arbor, 1973.

Eg 603.19 — Kühne, Cord. Die Chronologie der internationalen Korrespondenz von El-Amarna. Kevelaer, 1973.

Eg 1029.73 — Lichtheim, Miriam. Ancient Egyptian literature; a book of readings. Berkeley, 1973-

AH 8549.173.1 — Lochner-Huettenbach, Fritz. Keltische Grottheit auf norischem Inschriftstein. Photoreproduction. Graz, 1973.

AH 7279.73 — Martin, Jean Pierre. La Rome ancienne. 1. éd. Paris, 1973.

AH 7819.72 — Menen, Aubrey. Cities in the sand. N.Y., 1973.

AH 4269.73 — Mosley, Derek J. Envoys and diplomacy in ancient Greece. Wiesbaden, 1973.

AH 4609.73 — Müller, Olaf. Antigonos Monophthalmos und "Das Jahr der Könige". Bonn, 1973.

Eg 1042.973 — Munro, Peter. Die spätägyptischen Totenstelen. v.1-2. Glückstadt, 1973.

Eg 819.73 — Obenga, Théophile. L'Afrique dans l'antiquité: Egypte pharaonique. Paris, 1973.

AH 8008.12 — Overbeck, Hechtild. Untersuchungen zum afrikanischen Senatsadel in der Spätantike. Kallmünz, 1973.

Eg 1158.90.1 — Papyrus Ebers. Papyros Ebers; das älteste Buch über Heilkunde. Berlin 1890. Berlin, 1973.

AH 6110.26 — Perlman, Samuel. Philip and Athens. Cambridge, 1973.

1973 - cont.

AH 7299.73 — Piganiol, André. Scripta varia. Bruxelles, 1973. 3v.

AH 4892.1 — Problèmes de la terre en Grèce ancienne. Paris, 1973.

AH 39.73 — Rizzo, Silvia. Il lessico filologico degli umanisti. Roma, 1973.

AH 7459.51.2 — Scullard, Howard Hayes. Roman politics, 220-150 B.C. 2. ed. Oxford, 1973.

AH 9609.4 — Sjoeqvist, Erik. Sicily and the Greeks. Ann Arbor, 1973.

AH 3012.9.1 — Speiser, Ephraim A. Mesopotamian origins. Philadelphia, 1930. Ann Arbor, 1973.

AH 2357.11.3 — Staehelin, Felix. Geschichte der kleinasiatischen Galater. 2. Aufl. Osnabrück, 1973.

AH 3661.6.1 — Tabari, Muhammed Ibn. Geschichte der Perser und Araber. Leyden, 1973.

AH 7854.1 — Toynbee, Jocelyn Mary Catherine. Animals in Roman life and art. London, 1973.

AH 7469.38.6 — Vogt, Joseph. Cicero und Sallust über die Catilinarische Verschworung. Darmstadt, 1973.

AH 866.13.1 — Waldmann, F. Der Bernstein im Altertum. Walluf bei Weisbaden, 1973.

AH 819.73.5 — White, Hayden V. The Greco-Roman tradition. N.Y., 1973.

AH 3914.7.5 — Xella, Paolo. Il mito di Shre Šlm. Saggio sulla mitologia ugaritica. Roma, 1973.

AH 859.9.1 — Zinserling, Verena. Women in Greece and Rome. N.Y., 1973.

1974

AH 3167.11 — Dandamaev, Mukhammed A. Rabstvo v Vavilonii VII-IV vv. do n.e. (661-331 gg). Moskva, 1974.

AH 8228.2 — Davies, Hunter. A walk along the wall. London, 1974.

AH 4809.39.2 — Dinsmoor, William B. The Athenian archon list in the light of recent discoveries. Westport, 1974.

AH 7489.74 — Garzetti, Albino. From Tiberius to the Antoninos. London, 1974.

AH 4559.70.1 — Green, Peter. Alexander of Macedon, 356-323 B.C. Harmondsworth, 1974.

AH 7823.3 — Liefeld, Walter Lewis. The wandering preacher as a social figure in the Roman Empire. Ann Arbor, 1974.

AH 7819.74 — MacMullen, Ramsay. Roman social relations, 50 B.C. to A.D. 284. New Haven, 1974.

AH 7279.73.10 — Masson, Georgina. Ancient Rome, from Romulus to Augustus. N.Y., 1974.

AH 3154.7.5 — Thompson, Reginald Campbell. The reports of the magicians and astrologers of Nineveh and Babylon in the British Museum. Ann Arbor, 1974.

WIDENER LIBRARY SHELFLIST, 55

ANCIENT HISTORY

AUTHOR AND TITLE LISTING

Author and Title Listing

AH 7298.71A | À Beckett, G.A. Comic history of Rome. London, n.d.
Htn AH 7298.52* | À Beckett, G.A. The comic history of Rome. London, 1852?
AH 8107.5 | À travers la Mauritanie sétifienne. (Poulle, M.A.) Constantine, 1863.
Eg 1059.55 | Aafjes, B. De blinde harpenaar. Amsterdam, 1955.
AH 49.68 | Aalders, Gerhard Jean Daniel. Die Theorie der gemischten Verfassung im Altertum. Amsterdam, 1968.
AH 3143.14 | Aan Babylons stromen. (Beek, Martinus A.) Amsterdam, 1955.
AH 4538.42 | Abbildungen des Demosthenes. (Schröder, H.) Braunschweig, 1842.
AH 4498.91 | Abbott, E. Pericles and golden age of Athens. N.Y., 1891.
AH 4278.88 | Abbott, Evelyn. History of Greece. v.2, photoreproduction. London, 1888-1900. 3v.
AH 7819.11 | Abbott, F.F. The common people of ancient Rome. N.Y., 1911.
AH 7819.09.3 | Abbott, F.F. Society and politics in ancient Rome. London, 1912.
AH 7819.09.10 | Abbott, F.F. Society and politics in ancient Rome. N.Y., 1910.
NEDL AH 7819.09.2 | Abbott, F.F. Society and politics in ancient Rome. N.Y., 1918.
AH 7039.01 | Abbott, Frank F. History and description of Roman political institutions. Boston, 1901.
AH 7039.01.2 | Abbott, Frank F. History and description of Roman political institutions. Boston, 1901.
AH 7099.26.5 | Abbott, Frank F. Municipal administration in the Roman empire. Princeton, 1926.
AH 7039.23A | Abbott, Frank F. Roman politics. Boston, 1923.
AH 4558.48.5 | Abbott, J. History of Alexander the Great. N.Y., 1848.
Eg 708.51 | Abbott, Jacob. History of Cleopatra, queen of Egypt. N.Y., 1851.
Eg 708.51.2 | Abbott, Jacob. History of Cleopatra, queen of Egypt. N.Y., 1860.
Eg 708.51.5 | Abbott, Jacob. History of Cleopatra, queen of Egypt. N.Y., 1874.
AH 3659.15 | Abbott, Jacob. History of Cyrus the Great. N.Y., 1850.
AH 3659.15.2 | Abbott, Jacob. History of Cyrus the Great. N.Y., 1852.
AH 3659.15.6 | Abbott, Jacob. History of Cyrus the Great. N.Y., 1877.
AH 3659.20 | Abbott, Jacob. History of Darius the Great. N.Y., 1850.
AH 3659.20.3 | Abbott, Jacob. History of Darius the Great. N.Y., 1854.
AH 3659.20.6 | Abbott, Jacob. History of Darius the Great. N.Y., 1871.
AH 7448.49 | Abbott, Jacob. History of Hannibal the Carthaginian. N.Y., 1849.
AH 7478.49 | Abbott, Jacob. History of Julius Caesar. N.Y., 1849.
AH 7478.49.9 | Abbott, Jacob. History of Julius Caesar. N.Y., 1877.
AH 7548.53 | Abbott, Jacob. History of Nero. N.Y., 1853.
AH 7548.72.5 | Abbott, Jacob. History of Nero. N.Y., 1872.
AH 5610.7.5 | Abbott, Jacob. History of Pyrrhus. N.Y., 1854.
AH 5610.7 | Abbott, Jacob. History of Pyrrhus. N.Y., 1871.
NEDL AH 7408.77.2 | Abbott, Jacob. History of Romulus. N.Y., 1852.
AH 7408.52.5 | Abbott, Jacob. History of Romulus. N.Y., 1852.
AH 7408.77 | Abbott, Jacob. History of Romulus. N.Y., 1877.
AH 3660.3 | Abbott, Jacob. History of Xerxes the Great. N.Y., 1850.
AH 3660.3.2 | Abbott, Jacob. History of Xerxes the Great. N.Y., 1852.
AH 3660.3.5 | Abbott, Jacob. History of Xerxes the Great. N.Y., 1872.
AH 277.66.2 | Abbt, Thomas. Fragment der aeltesten Begebenheiten des menschlichen Geschlechts. Halle, 1767.
AH 3960.23 | Abel, F.M. Histoire de la Palestine. Paris, 1952. 2v.
AH 6107.5 | Abel, O. Makedonien. Leipzig, 1847.
AH 7207.25 | Abele, Theodor Anton. Der Senat unter Augustus. Paderborn, 1907.
AH 3002.110 | Aberhuber, Karl. Innsbrucher Keilschrifttexte. Innsbruck, 1956.
AH 7009.07 | Die Abfassung des Faits des Romains. (Loesche, J.) Halle, 1907.
AH 9707.5 | Abhandlung von Thracien. (Gatterer, J.C.) Göttingen, 1800.
AH 7138.81.8 | Abhandlungen aus dem Gebiete des römischen Rechts. v.1-3. (Merkel, J.) Halle, 1888. 2v.
AH 7228.81.5 | Abhandlungen aus dem römischen Civilprozess. (Baron, J.) Berlin, 1881. 3v.
AH 4298.87 | Abhandlungen aus der griechische Geschichte. (Duncker, Max.) Leipzig, 1887.
AH 298.88.3 | Abhandlungen zur alten Geschichte. (Schmidt, A.) Leipzig, 1888.
AH 7762.5 | Abinnaeus, Flavius. The Abinnaeus archive; papers of a Roman officer in the reign of Constantius II. Oxford, 1962.
AH 7762.5 | The Abinnaeus archive; papers of a Roman officer in the reign of Constantius II. (Abinnaeus, Flavius.) Oxford, 1962.
AH 1878.89 | Ablaing van Giessenburg, R.C. Évolution des idées religieuses dans la Mésopotamie et dans l'Égypte. Amsterdam, 1889.
AH 4848.13 | Abrahams, E.B. Greek dress. London, 1908.
AH 3955.5A | Abrahams, Israel. Campaigns in Palestine from Alexander the Great. London, 1927.
AH 7277.95 | Abrégé de l'histoire romaine. Londres, 1795.
AH 7277.95.3 | Abrégé de l'histoire romaine. 1. American ed. Baltimore, 1812.
AH 7278.28.2 | Abridged history of emperors. (Cobbett, W.) London, 1829.
NEDL AH 7651.2 | Abridgment of Gibbon's History of Roman Empire. (Gibbon, Edward.) London, 1790. 2v.
NEDL AH 7651.5 | Abridgment of Gibbon's History of Roman Empire. 2. ed. (Gibbon, Edward.) London, 1807. 2v.
Htn AH 276.14.5* | An abridgment of Raleigh's Historie of the world. (Raleigh, Walter.) London, 1700.
AH 3008.54 | Abriss der babylonisch-assyrischen Geschichte. (Gumpach, J. von.) Mannheim, 1854.
AH 3008.80 | Abriss der babylonisch-assyrischen und israelitischen Geschichte. (Hommel, F.) Leipzig, 1880.
AH 7818.24 | Abriss der römischen Antiquitäten. (Creuzers, G.F.) Leipzig, 1824.
AH 7818.24.3 | Abriss der römischen Antiquitäten. 2. Aufl. (Creuzers, G.F.) Leipzig, 1829.
AH 7149.07 | Abriss des römischen Staatsrechts. (Mommsen, Theodor.) Leipzig, 1907.
AH 298.82 | Abrisz der Quellenkunde der griechischen und römischen Geschichte. (Schaefer, Arnold.) Leipzig, 1882.
AH 298.82.4 | Abrisz der Quellenkunde der griechischen und römischen Geschichte. v.1, 4. Aufl; v.2, 2. Aufl. (Schaefer, Arnold.) Leipzig, 1885-89. 2v.
AH 4328.48 | Die Abstammung der Griechen und die Errthüme und Tausch. (Ow, J.) München, 1848.
AH 4818.80 | Abstract of lectures upon Greek life. (Mather, R.H.) n.p., 188-.

AH 2009.5 | Abu Ubaid al-Bakri. Die Wohnsetze und Wanderungen der arabischen Stämme. Göttingen, 1869.
Eg 856.3 | Abubakr, Abdel Monem Jooussef. Untersuchungen über die ägyptischen Kronen. Inaug. Diss. Glückstadt, 1937.
AH 7138.71.11 | The academical study of the civil law. (Bryer, J.) London, 1871.
AH 7509.38.10 | Accademia dei Lincei, Rome. Augustus. Roma, 1938.
AH 3182.5 | The Accadian and Hebrew Psalms of lamentation as religious documents. Inaug. Diss. (Widengren, Georg.) Uppsala, 1936.
AH 4729.46 | Accame, Silvio. Il domino romano in Grecia dalla guerra acaica ad Augusto. Roma, 1946.
AH 5310.3.2 | Accame, Silvio. L'imperialismo ateniese all'inizio del secolo IV A.C. e la crisi della Polis. 2. ed. Napoli, 1966.
AH 7409.57 | Accame, Silvio. Le origini di Roma. Napoli, 1957.
AH 4279.53 | Accame, Silvio. Problemi di storia greca. Rome, 1953.
AH 7409.59 | Accame, Silvio. I re di Roma nella leggenda e nella storia. Napoli, 1959.
AH 4409.65 | Accame, Silvio. Ricerche di storia greca. Napoli, 1965?
AH 4539.51 | Accame, Silvio. Ricerche intorno alla guerra corinzia. Napoli, 1951.
AH 4499.68 | Accame, Silvio. Ricerche intorno alla Pentecontaetia. Napoli, 1968.
AH 7138.72.5 | Accarias, C. Précis de droit romain. Paris, 1872.
NEDL AH 7138.71.3 | Accarias, C. Précis de droit romain. v.1-2. Paris, 1871. 3v.
AH 7168.66 | Accarias, C. Théorie des contrats innommis. Paris, 1866.
Htn AH 7445.02* | Acciajuoli, D. Hannibalis atque Scipionis...ducum historie eleganti dulcique stilo coscriptac. Swollensi, 1502.
AH 3013.43 | An account of the sepulchres of the antients. (Gregory, John M.) London, 1712.
AH 7149.11 | L'accusation publique...chez les Romains. (Boissière, G.) Niort, 1911.
AH 899.27F | Acerbo, Giacomo. Studi reassuntivi di agricoltura antica. Roma, 1927.
AH 4410.20.5 | Achaeans and Hittites. (Huxley, George Leonard.) Belfast, 1965.
AH 4708.81 | Die achäische Bundesverstallung. (Weinert, A.) Demmin, 1881.
AH 3002.2.2 | Die Achämenideninschriften. (Bezold, Carl.) Leipzig, 1882.
AH 3002.2.9 | Die Achämenideninschriften zweiter Art. (Weissbach, F.H.) Leipzig, 1890.
AH 3658.6 | Les achemenides et les inscriptions de la Perse. (Menaut, J.) Paris, 1872.
AH 4819.23.5 | The achievement of Greece; a chapter in human experience. (Greene, William Chase.) N.Y., 1967.
AH 4819.23A | The achievement of Greece. (Greene, William Chase.) Cambridge, 1923.
AH 4819.23.2 | The achievement of Greece. (Greene, William Chase.) Cambridge, 1924.
AH 7819.33A | Achievement of Rome. (Greene, William C.) Cambridge, 1933.
AH 7178.39 | Ackergesetz der S. Thorius. (Rudorff, A.A.F.) Berlin, 1839.
AH 9621.12 | Acragas Graeca. (Waele, J.A. de.) 's-Gravenhage, 1971-
Eg 752.5.2 | Acta Alexandrinorum. Acta Alexandrinorum de mortibus Alexandriae nobilium; fragmenta papyracea Graeca. Lipsiae, 1961.
Eg 752.5 | Acta Alexandrinorum. The acts of the pagan martyrs. Oxford, 1954.
Eg 752.5.2 | Acta Alexandrinorum de mortibus Alexandriae nobilium; fragmenta papyracea Graeca. (Acta Alexandrinorum.) Lipsiae, 1961.
AH 7228.57 | Die Actio. (Windscheid, B.) Düsseldorf, 1857.
AH 7228.56 | Die Actio des römischen Civilrechts. (Windscheid, B.) Düsseldorf, 1856.
Eg 752.5 | The acts of the pagan martyrs. (Acta Alexandrinorum.) Oxford, 1954.
AH 878.76A | Die Acvins. (Myriantheus, L.) München, 1876.
AH 7203.128 | Ad constitutiones codicis de bonis maternis doctissimus. (Pinelus, Arius.) Venetiis, 1573.
AH 7148.43.5 | Ad legem de scribis et viatoribus et de anectoritate commentations. (Mommsen, Theodor.) Kiliae, 1843.
AH 7009.03 | Ad praemiorum...publicam renuntiationem. (Schwartz, E.) Gottingae, 1903.
AH 5301.7 | Ad scholas ad civitatis Atticae historiam symbole. (Arnim, I. Hans.) Rostock, 1895. 3 pam.
AH 7238.50 | Ad solemia anniversaria gymnasii. (Rabus, J.M.) n.p., 1850.
AH 279.41 | Adademiia nauk SSSR. Institut istorii. Istoriia drevnego mira. Izd. 2. Moskva, 1941.
AH 29.63 | Adademiia nauk SSSR. Otdelenie istoricheskikh nauk. Problemy sotsial'no-ekonomicheskoi istorii drevnego mira. Moskva, 1963.
AH 7817.92.13 | Adam, Alexander. Handbuch der römischen Alterthümer. Erlangen, 1805-06. 2v.
AH 7817.92.7 | Adam, Alexander. Roman antiquities. N.Y., 1826.
NEDL AH 7817.92.9 | Adam, Alexander. Roman antiquities. N.Y., 1830.
NEDL AH 7817.92.11 | Adam, Alexander. Roman antiquities. N.Y., 1837.
AH 7817.92.5 | Adam, Alexander. Roman antiquities. 1st American ed. Philadelphia, 1807.
AH 7817.92.6 | Adam, Alexander. Roman antiquities. 2nd American ed. N.Y., 1814.
AH 7817.92.2 | Adam, Alexander. Roman antiquities. 2nd ed. Edinburgh, 1792.
AH 7817.92.10 | Adam, Alexander. Roman antiquities. 6th ed. Glasgow, 1835.
AH 7817.92.12 | Adam, Alexander. Roman antiquities. 7th ed. N.Y., 1836.
AH 842.27 | Adam, L. Die Unsicherheit literarischen Eigentums. Düsseldorf, 1906.
AH 8548.48 | Adam, Maurice. La tradition celtique et ses adversaires. Paris, 1901.
AH 8048.5 | Adametz, Leopold. Herkunft und Wanderungen der Hamiten erschlossen aus ihren Haustierrassen. Wien, 1920.
Htn AH 298.22* | Adams, J. Flowers of ancient history. Leesburg, 1822.
AH 7277.92 | Adams, J. History of Rome. Dublin, 1792. 2v.
AH 9065.5 | Adams, Louise E.W. A study of commerce in Latium from the early iron age through the sixth century B.C. Thesis. Northampton, Mass., 1921.
AH 3044.2F | Adams, Robert McCormick. Land behind Bagyhdad. Chicago, 1965.
AH 3045.20 | Adams, Robert McCormick. The Uruk countryside. Chicago, 1972.
Eg 1038.98.9 | Adams, W.M. The book of the master. London, 1898.
Eg 1039.33 | Adams, W.M. The book of the master of the hidden places. London, 1933.

Author and Title Listing

Author and Title Listing

Eg 299.60 — Akademiia nauk SSSR. Institut Narodov Azii. Drevnii Egypet; sbornik statei. Moskva, 1960.

AH 29.62 — Akademiia nauk SSSR. Institut narodov Azii. Drevnii mir; sbornik statei. Moskva, 1962.

AH 4039.72 — Akarca, Aşkidil. Yunan arkeolojisinin ana çirgileri. Ankara, 1972.

AH 5007.5 — Akarnanien. (Oberhummer, E.) München, 1887.

AH 4279.66 — Akheiskaia Gretsiia vo vtorom tysiacheletii do nie. (Blavatskaia, Tat'iana V.) Moskva, 1966.

Eg 609.68 — Akhenaten, pharaoh of Egypt: a new study. (Aldred, Cyrill.) London, 1968.

AH 3002.2.1 — Akkadische und sumerische Keilschrifttexte. (Haupt, Paul.) Leipzig, 1881-82.

AH 2507.15 — Akşit, Oktay. Likya tarihi. Istanbul, 1967.

Eg 971.15 — Aksum. (Monneret de Villard, Ugo.) Roma, 1938.

AH 7168.71 — Die Aktionen der römischen Privatrechts. (Bekker, E.I.) Berlin, 1871.

AH 3149.9 — Alalakh and chronology. (Smith, S.) London, 1940.

AH 7448.68 — Alames, H. Hannibal sive disputatio. Dublin, 1868.

AH 7798.80 — Alaric; l'agonie de l'empire. 2. éd. (Thierry, A.S.D.) Paris, 1880.

AH 9666.7 — Albertini, E. Les divisions administratives de l'Espagne romaine. Thèse. Paris, 1923.

AH 8007.18 — Albertini, Eugène. L'Afrique romaine. Alger, 1937.

AH 8007.18.7 — Albertini, Eugène. L'Afrique romaine. Alger, 1955.

AH 8007.18.10 — Albertini, Eugène. L'Afrique romaine. Alger, 1955.

AH 8007.18.5 — Albertini, Eugène. L'Afrique romaine. Alger? 1950.

AH 7489.29.4 — Albertini, Eugène. L'empire romain. 4. éd. Paris, 1970.

AH 3964.20 — Albright, William F. Archaeology and the religion of Israel. Baltimore, 1942.

Htn AH 7276.25* — Alciati, Andrea. Rerum patriae libri IIII. Mediolani, 1625.

AH 4521.18 — Alcibiade, étude sur l'histoire d'Athènes à la fin du Ve siècle. (Hatzfeld, Jean.) Paris, 1940.

AH 4521.13 — Alcibiade. (Oberziner, G.) Genova, 1891.

AH 4521.18.2 — Alcibiade. 2. éd. (Hatzfeld, Jean.) Paris, 1951.

AH 4521.20 — Alcibiades reexamined. (Bloedow, Edmund F.) Wiesbaden, 1973.

AH 4978.41 — Aldenhoven, F. Itineraire descriptif. Athènes, 1841.

Eg 459.65.5 — Aldred, Cyril. Egypt to the end of the Old Kingdom. London, 1965.

Eg 279.61 — Aldred, Cyril. The Egyptians. London, 1961.

Eg 819.72 — Aldred, Cyril. Tatankhamun's Egypt. London, 1972.

Eg 609.68 — Aldred, Cyrill. Akhenaten, pharaoh of Egypt: a new study. London, 1968.

AH 3022.15 — Aldrey Pereira, M.L. Pensamiento idiomatico šumero-akkadico. Series 1. v.1, pt.1-2. Madrid, 1953. 2v.

Htn AH 3980.2* — Aldrichem, C. von. A briefe description of Hierusalem and of the suburbs thereof. London, 1595.

AH 4559.63.5 — Aleksander Wielki Macedoński. (Dzięciot, Witold.) Londyn, 1963.

AH 4559.28.5 — Aleksandr Veliki. (Petković, Živko D.) Beograd, 1928.

AH 7189.59 — Aleksishvili, M.M. Iz glubiny vekov. Tbilisi, 1959.

AH 879.19 — Alemaeon, Hypermestia, Caeneus. (Warren, E.P.) Oxford, 1919.

AH 9666.4 — Alemany y Bolufer, J. La geografía de la peninsula ibérica. Madrid, 1912.

AH 4559.32.5 — Alessandro Magno, 356-331. (Risi, Arnaldo de.) Roma, 1932.

AH 4559.60.10 — Alessandro Magno. (Pagliaro, Antonino.) Torino, 1960.

AH 4559.51 — Alessandro Magno all'oasi di Siwah. (Gitti, Alberto.) Bari, 1951.

AH 4559.28A — Alexander; a romantic biography. (Bercovici, Konrad.) N.Y., 1928.

AH 5436.2 — Alexander, J.A. Potidaea. Athens, 1963.

AH 2558.5 — Alexander, L. The kings of Lydia. Oberlin, 1914.

AH 4559.65 — Alexander; oder Die Vewandlung der Welt. (Bamm, Peter.) Zürich, 1966.

AH 4559.67 — Alexander als Vorbild für Pompeius. (Michel, Dorothea.) Brussel, 1967.

AH 4559.38 — Alexander and the Greeks. (Ehrenberg, Victor.) Oxford, 1938.

AH 4559.70.5 — Alexander and the Hellenistic world. (Welles, Charles Bradford.) Toronto, 1970.

AH 4559.68.15 — Alexander der Grosse. (Emmrich, Kurt.) Zürich, 1968.

AH 4559.40.5 — Alexander der Grosse. (Gregor, Joseph.) München, 1940.

AH 4559.58.5 — Alexander der Grosse. (Hempl, Franz.) Göttingen, 1958.

AH 4559.04.5 — Alexander der Grosse. (Keller, Erich.) Berlin, 1904.

AH 4558.99 — Alexander der Grosse. (Koepp, F.) Bielefeld, 1899.

AH 4559.16 — Alexander der Grosse. (Otto, Walter.) Marburg, 1916.

AH 4559.49.5 — Alexander der Grosse. (Schachermeyer, F.) Graz, 1949.

AH 4559.72 — Alexander der Grosse. (Seibert, Jakob.) Darmstadt, 1972.

AH 4559.31 — Alexander der Grosse. (Wilcken, Ulrich.) Leipzig, 1931.

AH 4559.49 — Alexander der Grosse am Hellespont. (Instensky, H.U.) Godesberg, 1949.

AH 4559.09 — Alexander der Grosse im Urteil der Griechen und Römer. (Weber, F.) Borna, 1909.

AH 4559.56 — Alexander der Grosse in den Offenbarungen der Griechen. (Pfister, F.) Berlin, 1956.

AH 4559.24 — Alexander der Grosse und das Weltgriechentum bis zum erscheinen Jesu. (Birt, Theodor.) Leipzig, 1924.

AH 4558.98.3 — Alexander mit der Lanze. (Wulff, Oskar.) Berlin, 1898.

AH 4559.46 — Alexander of Macedon, the journey to world's end. 1st ed. (Lamb, Harold.) Garden City, N.Y., 1946.

AH 4559.70.1 — Alexander of Macedon, 356-323 B.C. (Green, Peter.) Harmondsworth, 1974.

NEDL AH 4558.29 — Alexander the Great, life and actions. (Williams, John.) London, 1829.

NEDL AH 4558.29.4 — Alexander the Great, life and actions. (Williams, John.) N.Y., 1830.

NEDL AH 4558.29.5 — Alexander the Great, life and actions. (Williams, John.) N.Y., 1832.

AH 4558.29.3 — Alexander the Great, life and actions. 2. ed. (Williams, John.) London, 1829.

AH 4551.1 — Pamphlet box. Alexander the Great.

AH 4559.40 — Alexander the Great. (Cummings, L.V.) Boston, 1940.

AH 4559.73 — Alexander the Great. (Fox, Robin Lane.) London, 1973.

AH 4559.70 — Alexander the Great. (Green, Peter.) London, 1970.

AH 4559.68 — Alexander the Great. (Milns, R.D.) London, 1968.

AH 4559.29.5 — Alexander the Great. (Robson, Edgar.) London, 1929.

AH 4559.48 — Alexander the Great. (Tarn, William W.) Cambridge, 1948. 2v.

AH 4559.33.8 — Alexander the Great. (Weigall, A.E.P.B.) Garden City, 1933.

AH 4559.33.7 — Alexander the Great. (Weigall, A.E.P.B.) London, 1933.

AH 4559.00.2 — Alexander the Great. (Wheeler, B.I.) London, 1925.

AH 4558.99.5 — Alexander the Great. (Wheeler, B.I.) n.p., n.d.

AH 4559.00A — Alexander the Great. (Wheeler, B.I.) N.Y., 1900.

AH 4559.31.5 — Alexander the Great. (Wilcken, Ulrich.) London, 1932.

AH 4559.34 — Alexander the Great. (Wright, Frederick A.) London, 1934.

AH 4550.2 — Alexander the Great: a bibliography. 1st ed. (Burich, Nancy J.) Kent, Ohio, 1970.

AH 4559.68.10 — Alexander the Great: power as destiny. (Emmrich, Kurt.) London, 1968.

AH 4559.66 — Alexander the Great: the main problems. (Griffith, Guy Thompson.) Cambridge, 1966.

AH 4559.47A — Alexander the Great. 1st ed. (Robinson, C.A.) N.Y., 1947.

AH 4559.66.5 — Alexander the Great and Hellenism. (Daskalakès, Apostolos Basileiou.) Thessaloníkè, 1966.

AH 4559.55 — Alexander the Great and his time. (Savill, A.F.) Rockliff, 1955.

AH 4559.47.5 — Alexander the Great and the Hellenistic Empire. (Burn, A.R.) London, 1947.

AH 4559.33 — Alexander the Great and the unity of mankind. (Tarn, W.W.) London, 1933.

AH 4559.64.5 — Alexander the Great in Greek and Roman art. (Bieber, Margarete.) Chicago, 1964.

AH 1279.53 — Alexander und Asien. (Altheim, Franz.) Tübingen, 1953.

AH 4559.61 — Das Alexanderbild der Byzantiner. (Gleixner, H.J.) München, 1961.

AH 4559.26 — Das Alexanderreich auf prosopographischer Grundlage. v.1-2. (Berve, H.) München, 1926.

AH 4559.41 — Alexanders Bund mit Paros. (Brelaer, B.) Leipzig, 1941.

AH 4559.29 — Alexander's campaign on the Indian north-west frontier. (Stein, Mark Aurel.) London, 1929.

AH 4558.33 — Alexanders des Grossen. (Droysen, J.G.) Hamburg, 1833.

AH 4559.04 — Alexanders des Grossen. (Janke, A.) Berlin, 1904.

AH 4558.93 — Alexanders des Grossen Feldzüge in Turkestan. (Schwarz, F.) München, 1893.

AH 4558.93.2 — Alexanders des Grossen Feldzüge in Turkestan. 2. Aufl. (Schwarz, F.) Stuttgart, 1906.

AH 4558.75.3 — Alexanders des Grossen Feldzug in centralischen Asien. (Zolling, T.) Leipzig, 1875.

AH 4558.85 — Alexanders des Grossen Heerwesen. (Droysen, H.) Freiburg, 1885.

AH 4558.86F — Alexanders des Grossen indischer Feldzug. (Schuffert.) Colberg, 1886.

AH 4558.87A — Alexander's empire. (Mahaffy, J.P.) London, 1887.

AH 4259.50 — Alexandiès, K.A. He Thalassia dynamis eis ten historia tès archaias Hellados. Athènai, 1950.

AH 4559.38.10 — Alexandre et l'hellenisation du monde antique. 2. éd. (Glotz, Gustone.) Paris, 1945.

AH 4559.51.5 — Alexandre le Grand. (Homo, Léon Pol.) Paris, 1951.

AH 4559.33.9 — Alexandre le Grand. (Weigall, A.E.P.B.) Paris, 1934.

AH 4559.62 — Alexandre le Grand. Paris, 1962.

AH 4559.31.10A — Alexandre le Grand. 5. éd. (Radet, Georges.) Paris, 1931.

AH 4559.31.12 — Alexandre le Grand. 7. éd. (Radet, Georges.) Paris, 1950.

AH 4559.53.5 — Alexandre le Grand et les essais de fusion entre l'occident gréco-macédonien. (Cloché, Paul.) Neuchatel, 1953.

Eg 971.7 — Alexandre unter Ptolemaeus, Philadelphus und Energetes. (Lübbert, E.) Kiel, 1880.

Eg 971.7.10 — Alexandria, the golden city. (Davis, H.T.) Evanston, 1957. 2v.

AH 4558.58 — Alexandrou. Istoria. Venetia, 1858.

AH 7709.67 — Alföldi, András. Studien zur Geschichte der Weltkrise des 3. Jahrhunderts nach Christus. Darmstadt, 1967-

AH 7114.48 — Alföldi, Andras. Der Vater des Vaterlandes im römischen Denken. Darmstadt, 1971.

AH 8574.4 — Alföldy, Géza. Bevölkerung und Gesellschaft der römischen Provinz Dalmatien. Budapest, 1965.

AH 7769.52 — Alföldi, Andras. A conflict of ideas in the late Roman Empire. Oxford, 1952.

AH 7759.48 — Alföldi, Andras. The conversion of Constantine and pagan Rome. Oxford, 1948.

AH 7409.65A — Alföldi, András. Early Rome and the Latins. Ann Arbor, 1965.

AH 8311.2 — Alföldi, András. A gót mozgalom és Dácia feladása. Budapest, 1930?

AH 8313.5 — Alföldi, András. Magyarország hépei es a Római biródolom. Budapest, 1936.

AH 7299.57 — Alföldi, Andras. Die trojanischen Urahnen der Römer. Basel, 1957.

AH 279.30.5 — Alfonso I, king of Castile and Leon. General estoria. pt.1-2. Madrid, 1930- 2v.

Eg 1189.30 — Die Algebra der Ägypter des mittleren Reiches. (Vogel, Kurt.) Roma, 1930.

AH 7277.42 — Algemeene histori. Ultrecht, 1744.

AH 8157.7 — L'Algérie. (Dureau de la Malle, A.) Paris, 1852.

AH 8157.4 — L'Algérie dans l'antique. (Gsell, Stéphane.) Alger, 1903.

AH 8157.9 — L'Algérie dans l'antiquité. (Kaddache, Mahfoud.) Alger, 1972.

AH 8157.3 — L'Algérie romaine. (Boissière, G.) Paris, 1883. 2v.

AH 7138.96.5F — Alibrandi, I. Opere giuridiche e storiche. Roma, 1896.

AH 3507.15 — Aliev, Igrar. Istoriia Midii. Baku, 1960.

AH 7850.7 — L'alimentation et la cuisine à Rome. (André, Jacques.) Paris, 1961.

AH 4521.15.5 — Alkibiades. (Taeger, Fritz.) München, 1943.

AH 4521.15 — Alkibiades. (Taeger, Fritz.) Stuttgart, 1925.

AH 4521.7 — Alkibiades als Staatsmann und Feldhen. (Hertzberg, G.F.) Halle, 1853.

AH 4521.5 — Alkibiades und Lysandros. (Bischer, W.) Basel, 1845.

AH 7549.04 — Allard, Paul. Les chrétiens ont-ils incendie Rome sous Néron. Paris, 1904.

AH 4846.5 — Allatius, L. De templis Graecorum. Colonia Agrippina, 1645.

AH 4558.94 — Allcroft, A.H. Decline of Hellas. London, 1894.

AH 4408.91.5 — Allcroft, A.H. Early Grecian history. London, 1891.

AH 7498.93 — Allcroft, A.H. Early principate: history of Rome 31 B.C.-96 A.D. London, 1892.

AH 9610.13 — Allcroft, A.H. History of Sicily 491-289 B.C. London, 1890.

AH 7478.93 — Allcroft, A.H. Making of the monarchy. London, 1893.

AH 4518.95 — Allcroft, A.H. Peloponnesian War. London, 1895.

NEDL AH 7458.92 — Allcroft, A.H. Rome under the Oligarchs. London, 1892.

AH 4538.95 — Allcroft, A.H. Sparta and Thebes. London, 1895.

AH 7279.52.12 — Allcroft, Arthur. Tutorial history of Rome (to A.D. 69). 6. ed. London, 1961.

AH 4458.98 — Allcroft, Arthur H. The making of Athens; a history of Greece, 495-431 B.C. Photoreproduction. London, 1898.

AH 819.05 — Das Alle des wirtschaftlichen Kultur. (Hahn, E.) Heidelberg, 1905.

AH 846.30 — Alle origini della città. (Ambrosio, Raffaele d'.) Napoli, 1956.

AH 7509.37.15 — Allen, B.M. Augustus Caesar. London, 1937.

Author and Title Listing

Eg 879.16 — Allen, T.G. Horus in the pyramid texts. Diss. Chicago, 1916.

Eg 1042.950 — Allen, Thomas G. Occurrences of pyramid texts. Chicago, 1950.

NEDL AH 278.90 — Allen, W. Ancient history for colleges and high schools. Boston, 1890. 2v.

NEDL AH 278.91 — Allen, W. Ancient history for colleges and high schools. Boston, 1891.

NEDL AH 278.93.5 — Allen, W. Ancient history for colleges and high schools. pt.2. Boston, 1893.

NEDL AH 7278.90.2 — Allen, W.T. Ancient history for colleges and high schools. Boston, 1890-91. 2v.

NEDL AH 7278.90.5 — Allen, W.T. A short history of the Roman people. Boston, 1895.

AH 1842.5 — Allgemeinbildung und Fachbildung in der Antike. (Kuehnert, F.) Berlin, 1961.

AH 408.86 — Allgemeine Geschichte des Altertums. v.1-3. (Welzhofer, H.) Gotha, 1886. 2v.

AH 8257.3 — Allgemeine Kirchen- und...Oesterreich. (Fuhrmann, M.) Wien, 1769.

NEDL AH 7829.13A — Allinson, A.C.E. Roads from Rome. N.Y., 1913.

AH 4959.09A — Allinson, Francis Greenleaf. Greek lands and letters. Boston, 1909.

AH 4959.09.5 — Allinson, Francis Greenleaf. Greek lands and letters. Boston, 1912.

AH 4959.09.10 — Allinson, Francis Greenleaf. Greek lands and letters. 3. ed. Boston, 1931.

AH 3052.3F — Allotte, C. Les sceaux de Longalanda. Paris, 1907.

AH 3020.18F — Allotte de la Fuÿe, Francois N. Documents présargoniques. Paris, 1908-20. 5v.

AH 8566.5 — Almerigotti, Francesco. Della estensione dell'antico Ilirico. pt.1-2. Venezia, 17- .

AH 8516.12 — Les Alpes cottiennes et graies; géographie gallo-romaine. (Vallentin, Florian.) Paris, 1883.

AH 3002.2.4 — Alphabetisches Verzeichniss. (Strassmaier, J.N.) Leipzig, 1886.

AH 7449.55 — Alps and elephants. 1. American ed. (De Beer, Gavin Rylands.) N.Y., 1956.

AH 7448.18.5 — The Alps of Hannibal. (Law, William J.) London, 1866. 2v.

Eg 9.60 — Als een goet instrument. (Proosdij, Boricus Antonius van.) Leiden, 1960.

AH 148.89 — Alt-arisches jus Gentium. (Leist, B.W.) Jena, 1889.

Eg 299.37 — Alt Egypten spricht. (Kutter, Carl.) Basel, 1937.

AH 5610.20 — Alt-Epirus und des Königtum der Molosser. (Franke, Peter R.) Kallmünz, 1954.

AH 7163.13 — Alt-römischen Ehe mit Manus. (Eggers, F.W.T.) Altona, 1833.

Eg 848.5 — Altägyptische Erziehung. (Brunner, Hellmut.) Wiesbaden, 1957.

Eg 878.89 — Der altägyptische Götterglaube. (Strauss, V. von.) Heidelberg, 1889.

Eg 1129.55 — Altägyptische Lebensweisheit. (Bissing, Friedrich W. von.) Zürich, 1955.

Eg 879.55.5 — Das altägyptische Lebenszeichen. 3. Aufl. (Cramer, Maria.) Wiesbaden, 1955.

Eg 1079.59 — Altägyptische Liebesdichtung. (Hermann, Alfred.) Wiesbaden, 1959.

Eg 1079.50 — Altägyptische Liebeslieder. (Schott, Siegfried.) Zürich, 1950.

Eg 856.2 — Die altägyptische Schurztracht. (Bonnet, Hans.) Leipzig, 1916.

Eg 1109.59.2 — Altägyptische Tiergeschichte und Fabel. 2. Aufl. (Brunner-Traut, Emma.) Darmstadt, 1968.

Eg 1042.908 — Die altägyptischen Pyramidentexte. v.1-4. (Pyramid Texts.) Leipzig, 1908-22. 3v.

Eg 879.60.20 — Altägyptischer Prophetismus. (Lanozkowski, Guenter.) Wiesbaden, 1960.

AH 3187.15 — Altbabylonische Briefe des Iraq-Museums. (al-Zibari, Akram.) Köln, 1964.

AH 3002.140 — Altbabylonische Briefe in Umschrift und Übersetzung. Leiden. 1,1964+ 4v.

AH 3149.11 — Die altbabylonische Königsliste und ihre Bedeutung für die Chronologie. (Deimel, Anton.) Rom, 1935.

AH 3187.8 — Altbabylonische Privatbriefe. (Landersdorfer, S.) Paderborn, 1908.

AH 9722.6 — Altchristliche Städte und Landschaften. (Schultze, V.) Leipzig, 1913-22. 3v.

Eg 847.2 — Das alte Agypten...altägyptischen Original-Schriften und den Mittheilungen der nichtägyptischen alten Schriftsteller bearbeitet. (Schwartze, Moritz Gotthilf.) Leipzig, 1843. 2v.

Eg 819.55.5 — Das alte Ägypten. (Kees, Hermann.) Berlin, 1955.

Eg 279.24 — Das alte Ägypten. (Klippel, Ernst.) Berlin, 1924.

Eg 819.20 — Das alte Ägypten. (Wiedemann, A.) Heidelberg, 1920.

Eg 279.71 — Das alte Ägypten. (Wolf, Walther.) München, 1971.

AH 938.38 — Alte Geographie. (Georgii, L.) Stuttgart, 1838. 2v.

AH 9758.7 — Das alte Germanien. (Capelle, Wilhelm.) Jena, 1929.

AH 15.1 — Pamphlet vol. Alte Geschichte. 23 pam.

AH 278.15 — Alte Geschichte bis zum Untergang des weströmischen Reiche. (Schlosser, Friedrich Christoph.) Frankfurt am Main, 1815.

AH 5857.5 — Alte Megaris. (Reinganum, H.) Berlin, 1825.

AH 7808.69.5 — Das alte römische Jahr und seine Tage. (Huschke, G.P.E.) Breslau, 1869.

AH 818.76 — Die alte Welt. (Hoyns, G.) Berlin, 1876.

AH 279.65.5 — Die alte Welt. (Schieder, Oscar.) Wiesbaden, 1965-69. 2v.

AH 4408.25 — Die alten Pelasger und ihre Mysterien. (Eissner, C.G.) Leipzig, 1825.

Eg 879.65.15 — Altenmueller, Hartwig. Die Atropaia und die Götter Mittelägypten. v.1-2. München, 1965.

Eg 1042.972 — Altenmüller, Hartwig. Die Texte zum Begrabensritual in den Pyramiden des alten Reiches. Wiesbaden, 1972.

AH 7179.06 — Altgermanische...Agrarverhältnisse. (Fleischmann, Wilhelm.) Leipzig, 1906.

AH 279.39.5 — Das Altertum. 3. Aufl. v.2. (Taeger, Fritz.) Stuttgart, 1942.

AH 279.39.7 — Das Altertum. 4. Aufl. (Taeger, Fritz.) Stuttgart, 1950.

AH 279.39.9 — Das Altertum. 6. Aufl. (Taeger, Fritz.) Stuttgart, 1958. 2v.

AH 299.20 — Das Altertum seine staatliche und geistige Entwicklung und deren Nachwirkungen. (Preller, Hugo.) Leipzig, 1920.

Eg 8.50 — Altertumskunde. (Seyffarth, G.) n.p., 1850?

AH 3013.940 — Altertumskunde des Zweistromlandes von der Vorzeit bis zum Ende der Achamenidenherrschaft. v.1; pt.2. (Christian, V.) Leipzig, 1940.

AH 4298.92.5 — Altgriechische Kolonisation. (Hertzberg, G.F.) Gütersloh, 1892.

AH 4149.07 — Altgriechische Staatsverträge. (Hitzig, H.F.) Zürich, 1907.

AH 7799.51.5 — Altheim, F. Attila und die Hunne. Baden-Baden, 1951.

AH 299.39 — Altheim, F. Die Soldatinkaiser. Frankfurt am Main, 1939.

AH 8908.17 — Altheim, F. Der Ursprung der Etrusker. Baden, 1950.

AH 4559.60 — Altheim, F. Zarathustra und Alexander. Frankfurt, 1960.

AH 1279.53 — Altheim, Franz. Alexander und Asien. Tübingen, 1953.

AH 2007.6 — Altheim, Franz. Die Araber in der alten Welt. v.2-5, pt.1-2. Berlin, 1964. 5v.

AH 3661.10 — Altheim, Franz. Ein asiatischer Staat. Wiesbaden, 1954.

AH 883.2 — Altheim, Franz. Entwicklungshilfe im Altertum. Reinbeck, 1962.

AH 1279.70 — Altheim, Franz. Geschichte Mittelasiens im Altertum. Berlin, 1970.

AH 7279.41 — Altheim, Franz. Italien und Rom. Leipzig, 1941-44. 2v.

AH 279.43.5 — Altheim, Franz. Die Krise der alten Welt im 3. Jahrhundert n. zw. und ihre Ursachen. v.1,3. Berlin, 1943- 2v.

AH 279.43.10 — Altheim, Franz. Niedergang der alten Welt. Frankfurt am Main, 1952. 2v.

AH 7279.48.10 — Altheim, Franz. Römische Geschichte. Berlin, 1948. 2v.

AH 7279.51 — Altheim, Franz. Römische Geschichte. Frankfurt, 1951-53. 2v.

AH 3661.10.5 — Altheim, Franz. Utopie und Wirtschaft. Frankfurt, 1957.

AH 1459.47 — Altheim, Franz. Weltgeschichte Asiens ein griechischen Zeitalter. Halle, 1947-48. 2v.

AH 3013.938 — Altindogermanisches Kulturgut in Nordmesopotamien. (Unger, E.) Leipzig, 1938.

AH 4518.86 — Altischen Strategen in Vfahrk. v.1-2. (Belser.) Ellivangen, 1886.

AH 3964.5 — Das altjüdische Zauberwesen. (Blaw, L.) Strassburg, 1898.

AH 9066.2 — Altlatinische Chorographie. (Bormann, A.K.E.) Halle, 1852.

AH 1298.93.7 — Altorientalische Forschungen. (Winckler, H.) Leipzig, 1897-1901. 2v.

AH 1298.93.3 — Altorientalische Forschungen. Dritte Reihe. (Winckler, H.) Leipzig, 1902. 3v.

AH 1298.93 — Altorientalische Forschungen. v.1-2,3,4,5,6. (Winckler, H.) Leipzig, 1893. 5v.

AH 1298.93.2 — Altorientalische Forschungen. Zweite Reihe. (Winckler, H.) Leipzig, 1898. 3v.

AH 3159.36 — Altorientalische Texte zum Alten Testament. (Gressmann, Hugo.) Berlin, 1965.

AH 1279.72 — Die altorientalischen Reiche. Frankfurt, 1972-73. 3v.

AH 3002.2.10 — Die altpersischen Keilinschriften. (Weissbach, F.H.) Leipzig, 1908.

AH 7851.2 — Altrömische Heizungen. (Krell, Otto.) München, 1901.

AH 7808.69 — Der altroemische Kalender. (Helfferich, A.) Frankfurt, 1869.

AH 7169.04 — Altrömische Schuldrecht und Schuldverfahren. (Schlossmann, S.) Leipzig, 1904.

AH 7038.58 — Altrömische Verfassungsgeschichte. (Bröcker, L.) Hamburg, 1858.

AH 7819.08 — Altrömisches Kulturleben. (Meissner, A.) Leipzig, 1908.

AH 7179.08 — Altrömisches Landwirtschaftsrecht. Inaug. Diss. (Quillfeldt, W.) Heidelberg? 1908?

AH 7158.41 — Das altrömische Paricidium. (Osenbüggen, E.) Kiel, 1841.

AH 5759.5 — Altspartanishen Geschichte. (Gilbert, G.) Göttingen, 1872.

AH 3020.55.5 — Altsumerische Wirtschaftstexte aus Lagasch. (Bauer, Josef.) Rome, 1972.

AH 7276.64 — Alveri, Gasparo. Roma in ogni stato. Roma, 1664. 2v.

AH 1233.65 — Amadasi, Maria Giulia. L'iconografia del carro da guerra in Siria e Palestina. Roma, 1965.

AH 7844.6 — Amante, B. Il natale di Roma. Roma, 1879.

Eg 609.26.5 — The Amarna age. (Baikie, J.) N.Y., 1926.

AH 279.09.5 — Amatucci, A.G. Dalle rive del Nilo ai lidi del "mar nostro". 2. ed. Bari, 1925. 2v.

AH 4819.08 — Amatucci, A.G. Hellás. v.1-2. Bari, 1908.

AH 7729.11.3 — The amazing emperor Heliogabalus. (Hay, J.S.) London, 1911.

AH 3957.35 — L'ambiente biblico. (Rolla, Armando.) Brescia, 1959.

AH 1866.5 — L'ambre jaune chez les Assyriens. (Oppert, J.) Paris, 1880.

AH 866.5 — L'ambre taillé ou véritable. (Bastelaer, D.A. van.) Bruxelles, 1876.

AH 7279.29 — Ambrosi, A. Histoire romaine. Paris, 1929.

AH 846.30 — Ambrosio, Raffaele d'. Alle origini della città. Napoli, 1956.

Eg 879.63F — Das Amduat. v.1-3. (Book of That Which is in the Nether World.) Wiesbaden, 1963. 2v.

AH 3133.1 — Amel-Marduk, 562-560 B.C. (Sack, Ronald Herbert.) Kevelaer, 1972.

Eg 879.14 — Amélineau, Emile. L'enfer egyptien et l'enfer virgilien. Paris, 1914.

Eg 938.93 — Amélineau, Emile. La géographie de l'Égypte. Paris, 1893.

Eg 879.08 — Amélineau, Emile. Prolegomènes a l'étude de la religion egyptienne. pt.2. Paris, 1916.

Eg 509.62 — Amenemhet I. und Sesostris I. (Omlin, J.) Heidelberg, 1962.

Eg 879.24 — Amenopë. The teaching of Amen-em-Apt. London, 1924.

Eg 879.15.4 — Amentet; account of gods, amulets of ancient Egyptians. (Knight, A.E.) London, 1915.

EgP 6.5 — American Research Center in Egypt. Journal. Boston. 1,1962+ 2v.

AH 3002.70 — American Schools of Oriental Research. Publications - Texts. Paris. 1-6,1927-1939 6v.

AH 4819.61.5 — America's debt to Greece. (Conley, P.M.) Charleston, 1961.

AH 3002.60F — Amherst of Hackney, W.A.T.A. The Amherst tablets. London, 1908.

Eg 1308.99 — The Amherst papyri. (Newberry, R.E.) London, 1899.

AH 3002.60F — The Amherst tablets. (Amherst of Hackney, W.A.T.A.) London, 1908.

AH 7148.95 — Die Amici Populi Romani. (Ferrenbach, V.) Strassburg, 1895.

AH 7299.33.5 — Amicitia. Inaug. Diss. (Heuss, Alfred.) Gräfenhainichen, 1933.

AH 3017.75F — Amiet, Pierre. La glyphique mesopotamienne archaïque. Paris, 1961.

AH 8060.5 — Amilcar Barca. (Vega, Luis A. de.) Madrid, 1960.

AH 4259.65 — Amit, M. Athens and the sea. Bruxelles, 1965.

AH 4299.73 — Amit, M. Great and small poleis. Bruxelles, 1973.

AH 7828.85 — Amori e costumi latini. (Giachi, V.) Citta di Castello, 1885.

AH 3959.36 — Amorites and Canaanites. (Kenyon, Kathleen Mary.) London, 1966.

AH 3027.10	The Amorites of the Ur III period. (Buccellati, Biorgio.) Naples, 1966.
AH 7138.83.3	Amos, S. History and principles of the civil law of Rome. London, 1883.
AH 7863.6	L'amour à Rome. (Grinial, P.) Paris, 1963.
AH 4829.60	L'amour en Grèce. (Flacelière, Robert.) Paris, 1960.
AH 7488.67	Ampère, J.J. L'empire romain à Rome. Paris, 1867. 2v.
AH 7278.62	Ampère, J.J. Histoire romaine. Paris, 1862. 4v.
AH 7278.62.3	Ampère, J.J. L'histoire romaine à Rome. 3. éd. Paris, 1866-72. 4v.
AH 4819.08.2	Amtichita greche. (Inama, V.) Milano, 1908.
AH 4881.5	Amzalak, Moses B. Historia das doutrinas económicas da antiga Grécia. n.p., n.d. 3 pam.
AH 7881.5	Pamphlet vol. Amzalak, Moses B. Historia das doutrines económicas da antiga Roma. 4 pam.
AH 4410.40.3	An den Küsten des Lichts. 3. Aufl. (Emmrich, Kurt.) München, 1961.
AH 7819.11.3	An den Rändern des römischen Reichs. (Thiersch, H.) München, 1911.
AH 4168.62	An fuerint apud Graecos indices certi. (Bétant, C.) Berolini, 1862.
AH 4483.14	L'an 480, Salamine. (Baelen, Jean.) Paris, 1961.
AH 2907.4	Anadolunun milli devleti Pontos. (Gologlu, Mahmut.) Istanbul, 1973.
AH 2109.15	Anadolu'nun sesi. (Balikçisi, Halikarnas.) Istanbul, 1971.
AH 4850.5	Anaglyphis Sepulcraliebus Graecis. (Hollaender, A.) Berolini, 1865.
Eg 1309.40F	Analecta aegyptiaca, consilio Instituti Aegyptologici Hafnaensis edita. Kopenhagen. 1-6 2v.
AH 4098.85	Analecta epigraphica...synoecismorum. (Feldmann, W.) Argentorati, 1885.
AHP 11.9	Anales de historia antigua y medieval. Buenos Aires. 1948+ 5v.
Eg 878.19	An analysis of Egyptian mythology. (Prichard, J.C.) London, 1819.
Eg 878.19.5	An analysis of Egyptian mythology. (Prichard, J.C.) London, 1838.
AH 7138.36	An analysis of the civil law. (Halifax, S.) Cambridge, 1836.
AH 2107.10	Anatolia II. (Metzger, Henri.) London, 1969.
AH 2102.10A	Anatolian studies presented to William H. Buckler. (Calder, W.M.) Manchester, 1939.
AH 7629.07.5	Anax mainòs â Hadrhinòs. (Kornemann, E.) Leipzig, 1907.
Eg 878.75.5	Ancessi, Victor. L'Égypte et Moïse. Paris, 1875.
Eg 878.77.5	Ancessi, Victor. Job et l'Égypte, le redempteur et la vie future. Paris, 1877.
AH 4039.71	The ancestral constitution. (Finley, Moses.) London, 1971.
AH 4039.53	The ancestral constitution. (Fuks, Alexander.) London, 1953.
AH 3757.11	Les ancêtres d'Attila. (Földvary, A.) Paris, 1875.
AH 37.99	Anciens gouvernemens fédératifs. (Sainte Croix, G.E.J.G. de.) Paris, 1799.
AH 6107.15	Les anciens Macédoniens. (Kalléris, J.N.) Athènes, 1954-
AH 866.15	The ancient amber routes and the geographical discovery of the eastern Baltic. (Spekke, Arnolds.) Stockholm, 1957.
AH 7015.1	Pamphlet vol. Ancient and mediaeval Rome. 16 pam.
AH 7819.25	Ancient and modern Rome. (Lanciani, R.) Boston, 1925.
AH 7819.25.3	Ancient and modern Rome. (Lanciani, R.) London, 1925.
AH 3921.8.5	Ancient Antioch. (Downey, Glanville.) Princeton, 1963.
AH 818.52	Ancient art and its remains. (Müller, C.O.) London, 1852.
AH 5304.2	Ancient Athenian maritime courts. (Cohen, Edward E.) Princeton, 1973.
AH 5315.25	Ancient Athenian mining. (Calhoun, G.M.) Cambridge, Mass., 1931.
AH 3009.13	Ancient Babylonia. (Johns, C.H.W.) Cambridge, Eng., 1913.
AH 3154.4	Ancient Babylonian temple records. (Arnold, William R.) N.Y., 1896.
AH 5357.5A	Ancient Bocotians. (Roberts, W.R.) Cambridge, 1895.
AH 3149.6	Ancient chronology. (Toffteen, O.A.) Chicago, 1907.
AH 1298.86	Ancient cities from dawn to the daylight. (Wright, William B.) Boston, 1886.
AH 38.64.12	The ancient city. 3. ed. Photoreproduction. (Fustel de Coulanges, N.D.) Boston, 1877.
AH 819.15.5	Ancient civilization. (Ashley, R.L.) N.Y., 1917.
AH 819.63.5	Ancient civilization. (Jones, Tom Bard.) Chicago, 1963.
AH 279.31	Ancient civilization. (Webster, Hutton.) Boston, 1931.
AH 819.16	Ancient civilization. (Wolfson, Arthur M.) N.Y., 1916.
AH 7819.69.11	The ancient civilization of Rome. (Charles-Picard, Gilbert.) N.Y., 1969.
AH 8913.5.8	The ancient civilization of the Etruscans. (Bloch, Raymond.) N.Y., 1969.
AH 819.27	Ancient civilizations from the earliest times to the birth of Christ. (Mackenzie, D.A.) London, 1927.
AH 5458.5	Ancient Crete. (Willetts, Ronald Frederick.) London, 1965.
AH 1409.14	The ancient East. (Hogarth, D.G.) London, 1914.
AH 1409.14.2	The ancient East. 2. ed. (Hogarth, D.G.) London, 1950.
AH 889.48	Ancient economic history. (Jones, Arnold.) London, 1948.
AH 889.38.2	An ancient economic history from the Palaeolithic age to the migrations of the Germanic, Slavic, and Arabic nations. (Heichelheim, Fritz.) Leiden, 1958-64. 3v.
AH 889.73.1	The ancient economy. (Finley, Moses I.) Berkeley, 1973.
AH 889.73	The ancient economy. (Finley, Moses I.) London, 1973.
AH 4842.71	Ancient education and its meaning to us. (Dobson, J.F.) N.Y., 1932.
Eg 879.07.5	Ancient Egypt, the light of the world. (Massey, Gerald.) London, 1907. 2v.
Eg 9.25.5A	Ancient Egypt, 1925-1941. Supplement. (New York. Public Library.) N.Y., 1942.
Eg 278.43A	Ancient Egypt. (Gliddon, G.R.) N.Y., 1843.
Eg 278.43.3	Ancient Egypt. (Gliddon, G.R.) N.Y., 1843.
Eg 278.43.2	Ancient Egypt. (Gliddon, G.R.) N.Y., 1844.
Eg 278.43.8	Ancient Egypt. (Gliddon, G.R.) N.Y., 1847.
Eg 939.61	Ancient Egypt. (Kees, Hermann.) Chicago, 1961.
Eg 278.52	Ancient Egypt. (Kenrick, J.) N.Y., 1852. 2v.
Eg 9.25A	Ancient Egypt. (New York. Public Library.) N.Y., 1925.
Eg 279.07	Ancient Egypt. (Newberry, P.E.) London, 1907.
Eg 298.83	Ancient Egypt. (Osborn, H.S.) Cincinnati, 1883.
Eg 278.91	Ancient Egypt. (Rawlinson, George.) N.Y., 1891.
Eg 279.52A	Ancient Egypt. (White, Jon M.) London, 1952.
Eg 278.35	Ancient Egypt. (Yeates, T.) London, 1835.
EgP 7.5	Ancient Egypt. London. 1914-1935 6v.
Eg 1159.59	Ancient Egyptian and Cnidian medicine. (Steuer, Robert.) Berkeley, 1959.
Eg 1069.58	An ancient Egyptian book of hours. (British Museum. Department of Manuscripts. Mss. (Papyrus 10569).) Oxford, 1958.
Eg 1042.972.5	The ancient Egyptian book of two ways. (Book of Two Ways.) Berkeley, 1972.
Eg 849.10	Ancient Egyptian dances. (Lexová, Irena.) Praha, 1935.
Eg 878.95.15	The ancient Egyptian doctrine of the immortality of the soul. (Wiedemann, A.) London, 1895.
Eg 878.95	The ancient Egyptian doctrine of the immortality of the soul. (Wiedemann, A.) N.Y., 1895.
Eg 1029.73	Ancient Egyptian literature; a book of readings. (Lichtheim, Miriam.) Berkeley, 1973-
Eg 855.1	Ancient Egyptian medicine. (Caton, R.) London, 1904.
Eg 862.5	Ancient Egyptian metallurgy. (Garland, H.) London, 1927.
Eg 1042.969	The ancient Egyptian pyramid texts. (Pyramid Texts.) Oxford, 1969.
Eg 1042.969.2	The ancient Egyptian pyramid texts. Supplement of hieroglyphic texts. (Pyramid Texts.) Oxford, 1969.
Eg 879.52.10	Ancient Egyptian religion. (Cerný, J.) London, 1952.
Eg 879.48.5	Ancient Egyptian religion. (Frankfort, Henri.) N.Y., 1961.
Eg 819.11	Ancient Egyptians. (Smith, G.E.) London, 1911.
AH 1278.89A	Ancient empires of the East. (Sayce, A.H.) London, 1884.
NEDL AH 1278.89.5	Ancient empires of the East. (Sayce, A.H.) N.Y., 1904.
NEDL AH 1278.89.7	Ancient empires of the East. (Sayce, A.H.) N.Y., 1907.
AH 1279.06	Ancient empires of the East. (Sayce, A.H.) Philadelphia, 1906.
AH 4862.7	Ancient eugenics. (Roper, Allen George.) Oxford, 1913.
AH 939.29	The ancient explorers. (Cary, Max.) London, 1929.
AH 1028.32.3	Ancient fragments. (Cory, I.P.) London, 1832.
AH 298.76	Ancient fragments. (Cory, I.P.) London, 1876.
AH 846.25FA	Ancient furniture; a history of Greek. (Richter, G.M.A.) Oxford, 1926.
AH 4015.2	Pamphlet vol. Ancient Greece. 21 pam.
AH 4819.22.5	Ancient Greece. (Casson, S.) London, 1922.
AH 4819.22.6	Ancient Greece. (Casson, S.) Oxford, 1939.
AH 4279.73.5	Ancient Greece. (Chambers, Mortimer Hardin.) Washington, 1973.
AH 4819.13A	Ancient Greece. (Cotterill, H.B.) London, 1913.
AH 4938.25.3	Ancient Greece. (Cramer, J.A.) Oxford, 1828. 3v.
AH 4278.24.5	Ancient Greece. (Heeren, A.H.L.) London, 1847.
NEDL AH 4278.76.4	Ancient Greece. (Pennell, R.F.) Boston, 1876.
AH 4278.76.5	Ancient Greece. (Pennell, R.F.) Boston, 1886.
AH 4819.64	Ancient Greece. 1st ed. (Payne, R.) N.Y., 1964.
AH 4278.24.4	Ancient Greece. 2. ed. (Heeren, A.H.L.) Boston, 1842.
AH 279.64	Ancient Greece and the Near East. (Haywood, Richard M.) N.Y., 1964.
AH 4278.76.10	Ancient Greece from the earliest times down to 146 B.C. (Pennell, R.F.) Boston, 1895.
AH 4848.13.5	Ancient Greek. (Johnson, Marie.) Chicago, 1964.
AH 4848.10	Ancient Greek female costume. (Smith, J.M.) London, 1882.
AH 4848.10.3	Ancient Greek female costume. 2. ed. (Smith, J.M.) London, 1883.
AH 4839.61	Ancient Greek horsemanship. (Anderson, John K.) Berkeley, 1961.
AH 4259.47	Ancient Greek mariners. (Hyde, Walter W.) N.Y., 1947.
AH 4239.71.5	Ancient Greek military practice. (Pritchett, William Kendrick.) Berkeley, 1971-
AH 4819.63	The ancient Greeks. (Finley, Moses I.) N.Y., 1963.
AH 4279.40A	The ancient Greeks. (Prentice, William K.) London, 1940.
AH 4279.60	The ancient Greeks. (Smith, Morton.) Ithaca, N.Y., 1960.
AH 4819.71	The ancient Greeks. (Starr, Chester G.) N.Y., 1971.
AH 4909.26A	The ancient Greeks and the evolution of standards in business. (Calhoun, G.M.) Boston, 1926.
AH 3075.3	Ancient history...Assyria. (Smith, George.) London, 1875.
AH 3075.3.3	Ancient history...Asyria. (Smith, George.) N.Y., 1876.
AH 278.47	Ancient history. (Goodrich, S.G.) Louisville, Ky., 1847.
AH 279.52.5	Ancient history. (Grant, Michael.) London, 1952.
AH 278.70	Ancient history. (Lamé-Fleury, J.R.) Boston, 1870.
AH 7279.04.2	Ancient history. (Myers, P.V.N.) Boston, 1904.
AH 279.36.10	Ancient history. (Perkins, C.) N.Y., 1936.
NEDL AH 277.34.11	Ancient history. (Rollin, Charles.) Boston, 1801. 8v.
NEDL AH 277.34.13	Ancient history. (Rollin, Charles.) Boston, 1807. 8v.
AH 277.34.12	Ancient history. (Rollin, Charles.) Boston, 1807. 8v.
NEDL AH 277.34.14	Ancient history. (Rollin, Charles.) Boston, 1823. 2v.
AH 277.34.10	Ancient history. (Rollin, Charles.) Glasgow, 1800. 6v.
NEDL AH 277.34	Ancient history. (Rollin, Charles.) London, 1734. 10v.
NEDL AH 277.34.6	Ancient history. (Rollin, Charles.) London, 1774. 8v.
NEDL AH 277.34.8	Ancient history. (Rollin, Charles.) London, 1788. 10v.
NEDL AH 277.34.14.3	Ancient history. (Rollin, Charles.) N.Y., 1828. 2v.
NEDL AH 277.34.14.9	Ancient history. (Rollin, Charles.) N.Y., 1839. 2v.
NEDL AH 277.34.15	Ancient history. (Rollin, Charles.) N.Y., 1841. 2v.
NEDL AH 277.34.10.8	Ancient history. (Rollin, Charles.) Portland, 1805. 8v.
AH 278.72	Ancient history. (Thalheimer, M.E.) Cincinnati, 1872.
AH 278.86	An ancient history. (Vuibert, A.J.B.) Baltimore, 1886.
AH 279.13.5	Ancient history. (Webster, Hutton.) N.Y., 1913.
AH 277.34.30	Ancient history. Atlas. (Rollin, Charles.) n.p., 1738-40.
AH 8548.01	Pamphlet box. Ancient history. Celts.
Eg 278.44	Ancient history. Egypt. N.Y., 1844.
AH 4015.12	Pamphlet box. Ancient history. Greece.
AH 4131.01	Pamphlet box. Ancient history. Greece. 4 pam.
AH 4015.13	Pamphlet box. Ancient history. Greece. Miscellaneous quarto pamphlets.
AH 4483.1	Pamphlet box. Ancient history. Greece. Salamis.
AH 4441.3	Pamphlet box. Ancient history. Greece. Sixth century.
AH 4031.01	Pamphlet box. Ancient history. Greek government.
AH 15.5	Pamphlet box. Ancient history. Miscellaneous pamphlets. 5 pam.
AH 15.4	Pamphlet box. Ancient history. Miscellaneous pamphlets. 26 pam.
AH 15.10	Pamphlet vol. Ancient history. Miscellaneous pamphlets. 7 pam.
AH 1015.01	Pamphlet box. Ancient history. Orient. Tracts.
AH 2951.1	Pamphlet box. Ancient history. Troas.
NEDL AH 277.34.21	Ancient history. v.1-4. (Rollin, Charles.) Cincinnati, 1860. 2v.
NEDL AH 277.34.19	Ancient history. v.1-4. (Rollin, Charles.) N.Y., 1857. 2v.
NEDL AH 277.34.14.5	Ancient history. v.2-4,6-8. (Rollin, Charles.) Philadelphia, 1829. 6v.
AH 277.34.10.9	Ancient history. v.6. (Rollin, Charles.) Philadelphia, 1805.
AH 7279.04.5	Ancient history. 2. ed. (Myers, P.V.N.) Boston, 1916.

Author and Title Listing

	Call No.	Entry
	AH 806.11.5F	Annales sacri. (Tornielli, A.) Lucae, 1756-57. 4v.
Htn	AH 276.50.8F*	Annales Veteris et Novi Testamenti. (Ussher, James.) Genevae, 1722.
Htn	AH 276.50*	Annales Veteris Testamenti a prima mundi origine deducti. (Ussher, James.) Londini, 1650-54. 2v.
	AH 3097.3	The annals of Ashurbanapal. (Lau, R.J.) Leiden, 1903.
	AH 3095.7F	The annals of Sennacherib. (Sennacherib, king of Assyria.) Chicago, 1924.
	AH 3002.94	Annals of the kings of Assyria. (British Museum. Department of Egyptian and Assyrian Antiquities.) London, 1902-
Htn	AH 276.58F*	The annals of the Old and New Testament. (Ussher, James.) London, 1658.
	AH 7448.18.11A	Annibal dans les Alpes. (Azan, Paul.) Oran, 1902.
	AH 7448.18.13	Annibal en Gaule. (Colin, J.) Paris, 1904.
	AH 7448.72.5	Annibal et Publins Cornelius Scipion. (Gilles, I.) Paris, 1872.
	AH 7449.01	Annibale. (Montanari, T.) Rovigo, 1900-01.
Htn	AH 7203.125*	Annotationes in quatuor et viginti Pandectarum libros. Pt.1. (Budé, G.) Basiliae, 1534.
Htn	AH 255.37.5*	Annotationis in l. ii. (Baif, Lazare de.) Lutetiae, 1549.
	EgP 9.5	Annuaire de l'égyptologie. Le Caire. 1971+
	EgP 66.5	Annual Egyptological bibliography. (International Association of Egyptologists.) Leiden. 1947+ 13v.
	EgP 66.6A	Annual Egyptological bibliography. Indexes, 1947-56. (International Association of Egyptologists.) Leiden, 1960.
	AHP 13.1	Annuario. (Catania. Universita. Instituto di Storia del Diritto Romano.) Catania. 13-14,1914-1915
	AH 3910.4F	Annus et epochae Syromacedonum. (Noris, F.H.) Florence, 1689.
	AH 7239.08.5	Anonymi de rebus bellicis liber. (De Rebus Bellicis.) Berlin, 1908.
	AH 4499.02	Anonymus Argentinensis. (Keil, Bruno.) Strassburg, 1902.
	AH 4299.11	Die Anschauungen von Wesen des Griechentums. (Billeter, G.) Leipzig, 1911.
	AH 8.96	Anschauungsmethode...Altertumswissenschaft. (Sittl, Karl.) Gotha, 1896.
	AH 938.84	Ansichten der alten Griechen und Römer. (Keppel, T.) Schwienfurt, 1884.
	AH 4559.03	Anspach, A.E. De Alexandri Magni expeditionis Indiea. Lipsiae, 1903.
	AH 958.90	Der Anteil der Periegese an den Kuntschrift der Alten. (Bencker, Max.) München, 1890.
	AH 7201.25F	Anteiustiniani. (Corpus Iuris Romani.) Bonnae, 1841.
	Eg 1059.25	Anthology of ancient Egyptian poems. (Sharpley, C.E.) London, 1925.
NEDL	AH 7817.91.5	Anthoysa, oder Roms Alterthümer. (Moritz, K.P.) Berlin, 1791.
	AH 7817.91.5	Anthoysa, oder Roms Alterthümer. (Moritz, K.P.) Berlin, 1791. 2v.
	AH 4819.68.5	Anthropologie de la Grèce antique. (Gernet, Louis.) Paris, 1968.
	AH 819.08	Anthropology and the classics. (Marett, R.R.) Oxford, 1908.
	AH 3813.8	Le antiche civiltà semitiche. (Moscati, Sabatino.) Bari, 1958.
	AH 8608.10	Gli antichi italici. (Devoto, Giacomo.) Firenze, 1931.
	AH 8608.10.2	Gli antichi italici. 2. ed. (Devoto, Giacomo.) Firenze, 1951.
	AH 7408.21.6F	Antichi monumenti per servire all'opera intitolata l'Italia. (Micali, G.) Firenze, 1821.
	AH 7299.40	Antichità classica. (Curotto, Ernest.) Torino, 1940.
Htn	AH 405.50*	Antichita de beroso sacredote caldeo. (Nanni, Giovanni.) Ventiae, 1550.
	AH 279.63.10	Antichnaia drevnost' i srednie veka. v.1-2,4-5,7. v.1,5; Photoreproduction. (Sverdlovsk, Russia (City). Ural'skii gosudarstvennyi universitet.) Sverdlovsk, 1963- 5v.
	AH 819.73	Antichnaia tsivilizatsiia. Moskva, 1973.
	AH 299.67	Antichnoe obshchestvo. (Konferentsiia po izucheniiu problem antichnosti, Leningrad, 1964.) Moskva, 1967.
	AH 7189.56	Antichnoe rabstvo i revoliutsii rabov v sovetskoi istoricheskoi literature. (Kotsevalov, A.S.) Miunkhen, 1956.
	AH 1299.63	Antichnyi gorod. (Akademiia nauk SSSR. Institut Archeologii.) Moskva, 1963.
	AH 7819.48	Het antieke Rome. (Vangenechten, K.) Antwerpen, 1948.
	AH 4609.68	Antigone et Démétrios. (Wehrli, Claude.) Genéve, 1968.
	AH 4609.34	The Antigonids, Heracles, and Beroea. (Edson, C.F.) n.p., 1934.
	AH 4609.30	Antigonos Gonatas, König der Makedonen. Inaug. Diss. (Fellmann, W.) Würzburg, 1930.
	AH 4609.13	Antigonos Gonatas. (Tarn, W.W.) Oxford, 1913.
	AH 4609.73	Antigonos Monophthalmos und "Das Jahr der Könige". (Müller, Olaf.) Bonn, 1973.
	AH 8073.11	Antigüedad maritima de...Cartago. (Hannon, G.) Madrid, 1756.
NEDL	AH 4818.76.5	Antiguedades clasicas I. Antiguedades griegas. (Mahaffy, J.P.) N.Y., 1889.
NEDL	AH 7818.77.8	Antigüedades clásicas II. Antigüedades Romanas. (Wilkins, Augustus S.) N.Y., 1883.
NEDL	AH 7818.77.15	Antigüedades clásicas II. Antigüedades Romanas. (Wilkins, Augustus S.) N.Y., 1903.
	AH 9677.2	Antigüedades de Galicia. (Barros Sivélo, Ramón.) Coruña, 1875.
	AH 7201.19	Antiguitatis Romanae monumenta legalia. (Haubold, C.G.) Berolini, 1830.
	AH 189.03	Die antik-heidnische Sklaverei. (Jerovšek, Anton.) Marburg, 1903.
	AH 279.59.5	Antika v dokumentech. (Nováková, J.) Praha, 1959-61. 2v.
	AH 846.9	Antike...Wohnhaus. (Lange, W.) Leipzig, 1878.
	AH 4842.65	Antike Bildungsideale. (Weinstock, Heinrich.) Berlin, 1925.
	AH 959.61	Antike Entdeckerfahrten. (Seel, Otto.) Zürich, 1961.
	AH 929.23	Antike Gewichtsnormen und Münzfusse. (Viedebandtt, Oskar.) Berlin, 1923.
	AH 818.97.2	Antike Humanität. (Schneidewin, Max.) Berlin, 1897.
	AH 819.33.5	Antike Humanität im Kampfe mit römischen Gesängniseland. Inaug. Diss. (Niemax, Hans.) Neubrandenburg, 1933.
	AH 309.03	Antike Idee der Oekumene. (Kaerst, J.) Leipzig, 1903.
	AH 239.10	Das antike Kriegswesen. (Daniels, Emil.) Leipzig, 1910.
	AH 239.20	Das antike Kriegswesen. 2. Aufl. (Daniels, Emil.) Berlin, 1920.
	AH 4819.22.7	Die antike Kultur. (Poland, Franz.) Leipzig, 1922.
	AH 4239.03.2	Antike Schlachtfelder. v.1-4. (Kromayer, J.) Berlin, 1903-31. 5v.
	AH 854.9A	Der antike Tierwelt. (Keller, Otto.) Leipzig, 1909. 2v.
	AHP 11.6	Antike und Christentum. Münster. 1-7,1929-1942
	AHP 11.6.10	Antike und Christentum. Ergänzungsband. Münster. 1,1939
	AH 930.30	Die antike Vulkankunde. (Ramsauer, F.) Burghausen, 1906.
	AHP 11.10	Antike Welt; Zeitschrift für Archäologie und Urgeschichte. Zürich. 1,1970+
	AH 889.09.5	Antike Wirtschaftsgeschichte. (Neurath, A.) Leipzig, 1909.
	AH 7469.19.9	Den antikke tradition om Graecherne. (Thomas, S.P.) Kristiania, 1919.
	Eg 971.9.5	Antinoï et les sepultures de Thaïs et Serapion. (Gayet, A.J.) Paris, 1902.
	Eg 971.5	Antinoupolis, aus dem alten Städteleben. (Kübler, B.) Leipzig, 1914.
	AH 3921.9	Antioch in the age of Thedosius the Great. (Downey, Glanville.) Norman, 1962.
	AH 3921.12	Antiochi city and imperial administration in the later Roman Empire. (Liebsschuetz, John Hugo Wolfgang Gideon.) Oxford, 1972.
	AH 3921.5F	Antiochia und der Aufstand des Jahres 387 nach Christus. (Hug, A.) Winterthur, 1863.
	AH 3910.9.5	Antiochus IV of Syria. Thesis. (Mørkholm, Otto.) København, 1966.
	AH 3910.9	Antioco IV Epifane re di Siria. (Majo, U.) Sassari, 1907.
	AH 278.11	Antiqua historia. (Eichhorn, J.G.) Lipsiae, 1811. 4v.
	AH 7202.13	Antiqua summaria Codicis Theodosiani. (Codex Theodosianus.) Lipsiae, 1834.
Htn	AH 7201.19.6 AH 8676.3*	Antiqua versio latina. (Kriegel, C.J.) Lipsiae, 1830. Antiquae urbis splendor. (Lauro, G.) Romae, 1610.
	AH 4843.5.10	The antique Greek dance. (Emmanuel, M.) London, 1927.
	AH 4843.5.8A	The antique Greek dance. (Emmanuel, M.) N.Y., 1916.
	AHP 11.7	Antique review. Bengal. 1-3,1931-1933
Htn	AH 7135.69*	Antiquitatem romanarum. (Manuzio, P.) Venetiis, 1569.
	AH 4848.8	Antiquitates pallii philosophici verterum Christianorum. (Walch, C.F.) Ienae, 1746.
	AH 7818.20.3	Antiquitates Romanae compendio. (Fuss, J.D.) Leodii, 1836.
	AH 7818.46	Antiquitates Romanas. (Wannowski, A.) London, 1846.
	AH 850.3F	Antiquitatum convivialium. (Stuck, J.G.) Lugduni Batavorum, 1695.
	AH 5754.5	Antiquitatum Laconicarum. (Hermann, C.F.) Marburgi, 1841.
Htn	AH 7207.2*	Antiquitatum Romanarum...Liber de Senatu. (Mannuccius, P.) Venetiis, 1581.
	AH 7138.41	Antiquitatum Romanarum. (Heineccius, J.G.) Francofurti, 1841.
	AH 7817.43.3	Antiquitatum Romanarum corpus. (Rossfeld, J.) Amstelodami, 1743.
	AH 7137.41	Antiquitatum Romanarum iurisprudentiam. (Heineccius, J.G.) Argentorati, 1741.
	AH 7137.41.5	Antiquitatum Romanarum jurisprudentiam. (Heineccius, J.G.) Leovardiae, 1777.
	AH 7035.85	Antiquitatum romanorum. (Manuzio, Paolo.) Romae, 1585.
	AH 7867.5	Antiquitatum Romanorum syntagma. (Struve, B.G.) Jenae, 1701.
	AH 7819.70	L'antiquité, Rome et les debuts du Moyen Âge. 6. éd. (Michaux, Maurice.) Paris, 1970.
	AH 1279.57.3	L'antiquité: le Proche-Orient. 3. éd. (Cerfaux, Lucien.) Tournai, 1960.
	AH 8548.2	Antiquité de la nation et de la langue des Celtes. (Pezron, P.) Paris, 1706.
NEDL	AH 817.66	L'antiquité dévoilée par ses usages. (Boulanger, N.A.) Amsterdam, 1766. 3v.
	AH 817.66.5	L'antiquité dévoilée par ses usages. (Boulanger, N.A.) Amsterdam, 1766.
	AH 863.10	L'antiquité érotique. (Tennodrac, M.J.) Paris, 1952.
	AH 7279.03	Antiquité romaine. (Seignobos, C.) Paris, 1903.
	AH 3013.29F	Les antiquités chaldéennes du Louvre. (Ledrain, E.) Paris, 1882.
	AH 4817.72	Antiquities of Greece. (Bos, L.) London, 1772.
	AH 4817.06.12	Antiquities of Greece. (Potter, J.) Edinburgh, 1804. 2v.
NEDL	AH 4817.06.14	Antiquities of Greece. (Potter, J.) Edinburgh, 1808.
	AH 4817.06.10	Antiquities of Greece. (Potter, J.) London, 1795. 2v.
	AH 4818.07.2	Antiquities of Greece. (Robinson, J.) London, 1807.
	AH 4818.51.10	Antiquities of Greece. (Schoemann, G.F.) Oxford, 1879.
	AH 4817.06	Antiquities of Greece. 2. ed. (Potter, J.) London, 1706. 2v.
NEDL	AH 4817.06.2	Antiquities of Greece. 4th ed. (Potter, J.) London, 1722.
	AH 4817.06.4	Antiquities of Greece. 5th ed. (Potter, J.) London, 1728. 2v.
	AH 4817.06.5	Antiquities of Greece. 6th ed. (Potter, J.) London, 1740. 2v.
NEDL	AH 4817.06.5	Antiquities of Greece. 6th ed. (Potter, J.) London, 1740.
	AH 4817.06.6	Antiquities of Greece. 8th ed. (Potter, J.) London, 1764. 2v.
	AH 4817.06.8	Antiquities of Greece. 9th ed. (Potter, J.) London, 1775. 2v.
	AH 8548.2.5	Antiquities of nations. (Pezron, P.) London, 1706.
	AH 4018.3	Pamphlet vol. Antiquities of the Greeks. 5 pam.
	AH 3028.5	The antiquity of Amorite civilization. (Clay, A.T.) New Haven, 1924.
	AH 3013.956	The antiquity of Iraq. (Pallis, Svend Aage.) Copenhagen, 1956.
	AH 279.36	The antiquity of mankind and the modernity of religions. 3. ed. (Monteath, K.M.) York, 1936.
	AH 862.11	Das Antlitz der Blindheit in der Antike. (Esser, Alexander Albert Maria.) Leiden, 1961.
	AH 7479.34.5	Antoine et Cléopatre; La bataille d'Actium. (Larrouy, Maurice.) Paris, 1934.
	AH 7508.61	Anton, A.F.M. De sideribus Augusti nataliciis quae coniiciendo videantur. Halle, 1861.
	Eg 1179.34	Antoniadi, E.M. L'astronomie égyptienne. Paris, 1934.
	AH 7639.46	Antonino Pio. (Regibus, Luca de.) Rome, 1946.
	AH 7598.66	Les Antonins. (Champagny, F.J.M.T.) Paris, 1866. 3v.
	AH 7639.33	Antoninus Pius. (Hüttl, Willy.) Prag, 1933-36.
	AH 7636.67	Antoninus Pius. (Keuchenius, R.) Amstelaedami, 1667.
	AH 279.58	The anvil of civilisation. (Cottrell, Leonard.) London, 1958.
	AH 8516.9	Anville, J.B.B. Eclaircissemens géographiques sur l'ancienne Gaule. Paris, 1741.
	AH 937.91	Anville, Jean B.B. d'. Compendium of ancient geography. London, 1791. 2v.
	AH 937.91.3	Anville, Jean B.B. d'. Compendium of ancient geography. N.Y., 1814. 2v.

AH 937.68	Anville, Jean B.B. d'. Geographie ancienne abrégée. Paris, 1768. 3v.
AH 854.13	The ape in antiquity. (McDermott, William C.) Baltimore, 1938.
AH 854.13.5	The ape in antiquity. Thesis. (McDermott, William C.) Baltimore, 1938.
Eg 278.67.3	Aperçu de l'histoire d'Égypte. 2. éd. (Mariette, A.) Paris, 1870.
Eg 278.67.5	Aperçu de l'histoire d'Égypte. 3. éd. (Mariette, A.) Alexandrie, 1872.
AH 4204.15	Aphorismen zur Beurtheilung der solonischen Verfassung. (Dondorff, H.) Berlin, 1880.
AH 2271.5	Aphrodisias in Karien. Diss. (Vagts, Rudolph.) Borna, 1920.
AH 4459.63	Apo ton Marathōna sten Pydna ki'ōs ten katastrophe tēs Korivthou 490-146 p.ch. (Kanellopoulos, Panagiōtēs.) Athēnai, 1963. 3v.
AH 7693.5	Apokrimata; decisions of Septimius Severus on legal matters. (Severus, Lucius Septimius.) N.Y., 1954.
AH 7476.32.5	L'apologia di Cesare. (Guarino, Alessandro.) Roma, 1929.
AH 3960.22	Apotowitzer, V. Parteipolitik der Hasmonäerzeit im rabbinischen und pseudoepigraphischen Schriftlum. Wien, 1927.
AH 4159.23	Ho apotympanismos. (Keramopoullos, A.D.) Athēnai, 1923.
AH 8857.4	Apparato alle antichità di Capua o vero discorsi della campania. (Pellegrini, C.) Napoli, 1651.
AH 8857.4.5	Apparato alle antichità di Capua o vero discorsi della campania. (Pellegrini, C.) Napoli, 1771. 2v.
AH 7203.95	Appendix ad editionem novellarum Iustiniani. (Corpus juris civilis. Novellae constitutiones.) Lipsiae, 1884.
AH 3143.16	Appenheim, Adolf L. Ancient Mesopotamia. Chicago, 1964.
AH 7438.90	Appius Claudius Caesar Censor. (Sieke, Carl.) Marburg, 1890.
AH 889.19	Appleton, C. Le taux du "fenus unciarum". Paris, 1919.
AH 7168.95.3	Appleton, C. Compensation en droit romain. Paris, 1895.
AH 7138.84.3	Appleton, C. Cours de droit romain. Paris, 1884.
AH 7168.86.15	Appleton, C. Essai de restitution de l'Edit publicien. Paris, 1886.
AH 7168.92.3	Appleton, C. Fou et prodigue en droit romain. Paris, 1893.
AH 7148.89	Appleton, C. Histoire de la propriété prétorien. Paris, 1889. 2v.
AH 7169.05.2	Appleton, C. Les lois romains sur le cautionnement. Weimar, 1905.
AH 7204.2	Appleton, Charles. Les sources des Institutes de Justinien. Paris, 1891.
AH 7168.92.7	Appleton, J. Droit romain; essai sur le fondement de la protection possessoire. Paris, 1892.
AH 2007.6	Die Araber in der alten Welt. v.2-5, pt.1-2. (Altheim, Franz.) Berlin, 1964. 5v.
AH 2008.14	Arabia and the Bible. (Montgomery, James Alan.) N.Y., 1969.
AH 2013.7.8	L'Arabie antéislamique. (Guidi, Ignazio.) Paris, 1921.
AH 2011.5.5	L'Arabie occidentale avant l'hégire. (Lammens, H.) Beyrouth, 1928.
AH 3958.12A	Aram and Israel. (Kraeling, E.G.H.) N.Y., 1918.
AH 3012.19	Aram Naharaim. (O'Callaghan, Roger T.) Roma, 1948.
AH 3908.5	Die Aramäer. (Schiffer, Sina.) Leipzig, 1911.
AH 3095.10	Die Aramäer Südbabyloniens in der Sargonidenzeit, 700-648. (Dietrich, Manfred.) Kevelaer, 1970.
AH 3908.5.5	Les Araméens. (Dupont-Sommer, Andre.) Paris, 1949.
AH 3959.22	Arameiskie dokumenty Iudeiskoi Kolonii. (Volkov, I.M.) Moskva, 1915.
AH 7139.45	Arangio Ruiz, V. Parerga. Napoli, 1945.
Eg 139.06	Arangio-Ruiz, V. Successione testamentaria. Napoli, 1906.
AH 4709.33	Aratos of Sicyon. Thirwall prize essay 1933. (Walbank, Frank William.) Cambridge, Eng., 1933.
AH 1189.36	Der Arbeiter in Recht und Rechtspraxis des Alten Testaments und des alten Orients. Inaug. Diss. (Lauterbach, W.) Heidelberg, 1936.
AH 908.60	Die Arbeiter und Communisten. (Drumann, W.) Königsberg, 1860.
AH 7899.69	Arbeitsorganisation und ökonomisches Denken in der Gutswirtschaft des römischen Reiches. Inaug. Diss. (Brockmeyer, Norbert.) Bachum? 1969?
AH 4189.37	Arbete och slaveri i antiken. (Valmin, N.S.) Stockholm, 1937.
AH 7148.93.5	L'arbitrato pubblico. (Ruggiero, E. de.) Roma, 1893.
AH 8548.55	Arbois de Jubainville, Henry d'. Les Celtes. Paris, 1904.
AH 8548.55.1	Arbois de Jubainville, Henry d'. Les Celtes depuis le temps les plus anciens. Osnabrück, 1968.
AH 8549.79.5	Arbois de Jubainville, Henry d'. Le dieu de la mort et les origines mythologiques. Paris, 1879.
AH 8549.106	Arbois de Jubainville, Henry d'. Les druides et les dieux celtiques. Paris, 1906.
AH 3159.19.10	Archaelogy and the Bible. (Barton, G.A.) Philadelphia, 1925.
AH 4817.06.15	Archaeologia Graeca. (Potter, J.) Edinburgh, 1813. 2v.
NEDL AH 4817.06.16	Archaeologia Graeca. (Potter, J.) Edinburgh, 1832. 2v.
NEDL AH 4817.06.17	Archaeologia Graeca. v.2. (Potter, J.) Edinburgh, 1818.
AH 4817.06.18	Archaeologia Graeca. 3. ed. (Potter, J.) London, 1837.
AH 4819.67.25	Archaeologia Homerica. Die Denkmäler und das frühgriechischen Epos. Göttingen, 1967- 5v.
AH 812.10	Archaeological Symposium, American University of Beirut, 1967. The role of the Phoenicians in the interaction of Mediterranean civilizations. Beirut, 1968.
AH 3013.959	Archäologische Forschungen der Max Freiherr von Oppenheim - Stiftung in nördlichen Mesopotamien 1956. (Moortgat, Anton.) Köln, 1959.
AH 848.5	Archäologische Unterhaltungen. (Stieglitz, C.L.) Leipzig, 1820.
AH 3159.19	Archaeology and the Bible. (Barton, G.A.) Philadelphia, 1916.
AH 1279.62	Archaeology and the Old Testament world. (Gray, John.) London, 1962.
AH 3964.20	Archaeology and the religion of Israel. (Albright, William F.) Baltimore, 1942.
AH 3012.7	The archaeology of cuneiform inscriptions. (Sayce, A.H.) London, 1907.
AH 5157.20	He archaia aitōlia. (Stergiopoulos, K.D.) En Athēnais, 1939.
AH 3302.1	He archaia Kypros eis tas Hellenikas pegas. (Chatzeioannou, Kyriakos.) Leukosia, 1971.
AH 7208.8A	The archaic community of the Romans. (Palmer, Robert E.A.) Cambridge, 1970.
AH 5140.5	Archaische Kultur der Insel Thera. (Hiller, F.) Berlin, 1897.
AH 8548.120	The archaism of Irish tradition. (Dillon, Myles.) London, 1947.
Eg 1180.5	Archibald, Raymond C. Bibliography of Egyptian mathematics. Supplement. Oberlin, 1927.
AH 7469.28	The architect of the Roman Empire. (Holmes, T.R.E.) Oxford, 1928-31. 2v.
AH 3002.155	Archiv des Nūrsămăs und andere Darlehensurkunden aus der altbabylonischen Zeit. Inaug. Diss. (Rashid, Fawzi.) Heidelberg, 1965.
AHP 11.5F	Archiv für Keilschriftforschung. Berlin. 1,1923+ 13v.
AHP 11.5.10	Archiv für Keilschriftforschung. Beiband. Berlin. 1,1933+ 10v.
AH 3142.17	Les archives des Murašû, une famille d'hommes d'affaires babyloniens à l'époque perse (455-403 avant J.C.). (Cardascia, Guillaume.) Paris, 1951.
AH 3002.102	Archives royales de Mari. v.1-9, 11-13, 15. Paris, 1950- 9v.
Eg 752.15	L'Archivio di Kronion. Milano, 1971.
AH 4809.31F	The archons of Athens in the Hellenistic age. (Dinsmoor, William B.) Cambridge, 1931.
AH 4058.93	L'archontat athénien. (Lecoutere, C.) Louvain, 1893.
AH 4056.22	Archontes athenienses. (Meursius, J.) Lugdunum Batavorum, 1622.
AH 9639.6	Arendt, A. Syrakus im zweiten peinischen Kriege. Königsberg, 1899.
AH 4206.7	Areopagu...Epheten. (Philippi, A.) Berlin, 1874.
AH 7798.68	Aretin, J.C.F. Diplomatische Abhandlung. Prag, 1868.
AH 4809.22	Der argivische Kalender. (Boethius, Axel.) Uppsala, 1922.
AH 5257.1	Argos and the Argolid. (Tomlinson, Richard Allan.) Ithaca, N.Y., 1972.
AH 7589.45	Arias, P. Domiziano. Catania, 1945.
AH 7009.53	Arias, P.E. Bibliografia e fonti. Bologna, 1953?
AH 8608.12	Arias, Paolo E. La civiltà gallica in Italia. L'impero di Severo Alessandro. Bologna, 1953.
AH 4309.54.5	Arias, Paolo E. Storiografia e fonti della storia greca. Bologna, 1954.
AH 6113.8	Arigia of the Macedonians. (Keramopoullos, A.D.) Detroit, 1946.
AH 328.83.2	Arische Periode. (Spiegel, F.) Leipzig, 1887.
AH 3664.13	Der arische Weltkönig und Heiland. (Güntert, Hermann.) Halle, 1923.
AH 4478.71	Aristides. (Berg, C.A.) Göttingen, 1871.
AH 5463.10	Aristocratic society in ancient Crete. (Willetts, Ronald Frederick.) London, 1955.
AH 5303.11	L'aristocratie athénienne. (Méautis, G.) Paris, 1927.
AH 4459.06.5	Aristophanes and the political parties at Athens. (Croiset, Maurice.) London, 1909.
AH 4519.19	Aristophanes and the war party. Photoreproduction. (Murray, Gilbert.) London, 1919.
AH 4559.38.5	Die aristotelische Politik und die Städtegründungen Alexanders des Grossen. (Ivánka, E.) Budapest, 1938.
AH 4842.98	Aristotle's school. (Lynch, John Patrick.) Berkeley, 1972.
AH 5207.5	Arkadien. (Schwab, C.T.) Stuttgart, 1852.
AH 5210.5	Arkadski savez IV veka. (Dušanić, Slobodan.) Beograd, 1970.
AH 4523.12	Armada from Athens. 1st ed. (Green, Peter.) Garden City, N.Y., 1970.
AH 238.43	Armandi, C.P. Histoire militaire des éléphants. Paris, 1843.
AH 7239.67	L'armée et le soldat à Rome de 107 à 50 avant notre ere. (Harmand, Jacques.) Paris, 1967.
AH 7238.83	L'armée romaine. (Fontaine, L.) Paris, 1883.
AH 7238.84	L'armée romaine au temps de César. (Kraner, F.) Paris, 1884.
AH 8005.2	L'armée romaine d'Afrique. (Cagnat, René.) Paris, 1892.
AH 8005.2.2	L'armée romaine d'Afrique. 2. éd. (Cagnat, René.) Paris, 1912. 2v.
AH 8205.3	L'armée romaine de Bretagne. (Le Roux, L.) Paris, 1911.
Eg 907.66	Armeilhon, H.P. Histoire du commerce et de la navigation des Égyptiens. Paris, 1766.
AH 2060.5	Armen, H.K. Tigranes the Great. Detroit, 1940.
AH 7239.26	Les armes romaines. (Couissin, Paul.) Paris, 1926.
AH 7239.26.5	Les armes romaines. Thèse. (Couissin, Paul.) Paris, 1926.
AH 7239.72	The armies and enemies of imperial Rome. (Barker, Phil.) Goring by Sea, 1972.
AH 4863.7	Armpitting among the Greeks. (Kittredge, G.L.) Baltimore, 1885.
AH 7459.66	Armstrong, Donald Budd. The reluctant warriors. N.Y., 1966.
AH 3966.7	Armstrong, G. Names and places in the Old and New Testament. London, 1888.
AH 1279.70.5	Arnaud, Daniel. Le Proche-Orient ancien, de l'invention de l'écriture à l'hellénisation. Paris, 1970.
AH 7138.73.10	Arndts, L. Gesammelte civilistische Schriften. Stuttgart, 1873. 3v.
AH 7207.53	Arnheim, M.T.W. The senatorial aristocracy in the later Roman empire. Oxford, 1972.
AH 39.10	Arnim, H. Politischen Theorien des Altertums. Wien, 1910.
AH 5301.7	Arnim, I. Hans. Ad scholas ad civitatis Atticae historiam symbole. Rostock, 1895. 3 pam.
AH 7278.40	Arnold, T. History of Rome. London, 1840. 3v.
AH 7278.40.7	Arnold, T. History of Rome. N.Y., 1857.
AH 7278.40.3A	Arnold, T. History of Rome. v.1-3. N.Y., 1846. 2v.
AH 7278.46.5	Arnold, T. History of the later Roman Commonwealth. London, 1857. 2v.
AH 7278.46	Arnold, T. History of the Roman Commonwealth. N.Y., 1846.
AH 7498.52	Arnold, Thomas. Pictorial history of Rome. London, 1852.
AH 7448.86	Arnold, Thomas. The second Punic War. London, 1886.
AH 7088.79A	Arnold, W.T. Roman system of provincial administration. London, 1879.
AH 7088.79.5	Arnold, W.T. Roman system of provincial administration. Oxford, 1906.
AH 7088.79.9	Arnold, W.T. Roman system of provincial administration. 3rd ed. Oxford, 1914.
AH 7489.06	Arnold, W.T. Studies of Roman imperialism. Manchester, 1906.
AH 3154.4	Arnold, William R. Ancient Babylonian temple records. N.Y., 1896.
AH 7138.68	Arnold W. Cultur und Recht der Römer. Berlin, 1868.
AH 8549.106.5	Arnoyl, E. Celtic religion in pre-Christian times. London, 1906.
AH 849.5	Die Aromata. (Sigismund, R.) Leipzig, 1884.
AH 9071.2	Arpinum, eine topographischhistorische Skizze. (Schmidt, Otto Eduard.) Meissen, 1900.

Author and Title Listing

AH 5307.30   Athènes, une démocratie. (Cohen, R.) Paris, 1936.
AH 5307.29   Athènes. Illustrations en couleurs de Marilac. (Guy, Noël.) Paris, 1935.
AH 5307.27   Athènes ancienne. (Jardé, A.) Paris, 1930.
AH 4499.65   Athènes au temps de Périclès. Paris, 1965.
AH 4499.41   L'Athènes de Périclès et les destinées de la Grèce. (Jouguet, Pierre.) Le Caire, 1941.
AH 5311.7   Athènes sous Hadrieu. (Graindor, Paul.) Le Caire, 1934.
AH 4809.39F   The Athenian archon list in the light of recent discoveries. (Dinsmoor, William B.) N.Y., 1939.
AH 4809.39.2   The Athenian archon list in the light of recent discoveries. (Dinsmoor, William B.) Westport, 1974.
AH 4819.69   The Athenian aristocracy, 399 to 31 B.C. (Mackendrick, Paul Lachlan.) Cambridge, 1969.
AH 5305.5   The Athenian board of generals from 501 to 404. (Fornara, Charles W.) Wiesbaden, 1971.
AH 5303.6   The Athenian boule. (Rhodes, P.J.) Oxford, 1972.
AH 4846.10   Athenian building policy from 561-560 to 405-404 B.C. (Boersma, Johannes Sipko.) Groningen, 1970.
AH 5308.9.2   Athenian clubs in politics and litigation. (Calhoun, G.M.) Austin, 1913.
AH 5308.9   Athenian clubs in politics and litigation. (Calhoun, G.M.) Austin, 1913.
AH 4038.54.3   Athenian constitutional history. (Schömann, G.F.) Oxford, 1878.
AH 4039.58   Athenian democracy. (Jones, Arnold H.M.) N.Y., 1958.
AH 5303.16   Athenian democracy. (Jones, Arnold H.M.) Oxford, 1957.
AH 4458.76.6   The Athenian empire. (Cox, George W.) London, 1876.
AH 4458.76.5   The Athenian empire. (Cox, George W.) N.Y., 1876.
AH 4458.76.10   Athenian empire. (Cox, George W.) N.Y., 1889.
AH 4458.76.15   Athenian empire. (Cox, George W.) N.Y., 1895.
AH 4499.72A   The Athenian empire. (Meiggs, Russell.) Oxford, 1972.
AH 4458.76.7   The Athenian empire. 5. ed. (Cox, George W.) London, 1887.
AH 4458.76.9   Athenian empire. 6. ed. (Cox, George W.) London, 1888.
AH 4299.14   The Athenian empire and the great illusion. (Tillyard, E.) Cambridge, 1914.
AH 4215.9   The Athenian expounders of sacred and ancestral law. (Oliver, James H.) Baltimore, 1950.
AH 4161.13   The Athenian family. (Savage, C.A.) Baltimore, 1907.
AH 4109.32   Athenian financial documents of the 5th century. (Meritt, B.D.) Ann Arbor, 1932.
AH 4159.63   Athenian homicide law in the age of the orators. (MacDowell, D.) Manchester, 1963.
AH 4229.36.5   The Athenian juror and his oath. Diss. (Cronin, James F.) Chicago, 1936.
Htn   AH 817.41*   Athenian letters. London, 1741-43. 4v.
Htn   AH 817.41.6*   Athenian letters. London, 1798. 2v.
AH 817.41.5   Athenian letters. London, 1810. 2v.
AH 4339.71.5   Athenian propertied families, 600-300 B.C. (Davies, John K.) Oxford, 1971.
AH 5303.15   The Athenian secretaries. Photoreproduction. (Ferguson, William S.) N.Y., 1898.
AH 4809.32A   Athenian tribal cycles in the Hellenistic age. (Ferguson, W.S.) Cambridge, 1932.
AH 4109.32.5   Athenian war finance. (Ferguson, William S.) Boston, 1932.
AH 4809.61   The Athenian year. (Meritt, Benjamin Dean.) Berkeley, Calif., 1961.
AH 4228.83   Atheniensium...suffragia. (Sauppe, Herman.) Gottingae, 1883.
AH 5311.5   Atheniensium Reipublicae quaenam romanorum temporibus fuerit condicio. (Neubauer, F.) Halis Saxonum, 1882.
AH 817.41.7   Athenische Briefe. Leipzig, 1799. 2v.
AH 4538.95.3   Athenische Bundesgenossenkrieg. (Weise, Richard.) Berlin, 1895.
AH 4842.93   Das athenische und das spartanische Erziehungssystem, im 5. und 6. Jahrhundert vor Christ. (Exarchopoulos, Nikolaos.) Langensalza, 1909.
AH 4808.99   Der athenische Volkskalender. (Svoronos, J.M.) Athens, 1899.
AH 4108.90   Athenischen Schatzverzeichnisse. (Lehner, H.) Strassburg, 1890.
AH 5307.25   Athens. (Felton, C.C.) n.p., 18- .
AH 5307.9   Athens. Its rise and fall. (Bulwer, E.) London, 18- . 2v.
AH 5307.14.2   Athens. Its rise and fall. (Bulwer, E.) N.Y., 1837. 2v.
AH 5307.13   Athens. Its rise and fall. (Bulwer, E.) Paris, 1837.
AH 5307.14.6   Athens. Its rise and fall. v.1-2. (Bulwer, E.) Leipzig, 1843.
AH 4819.48   Athens and the Greek miracle. (Rhodokanakès, K.P.) London, 1948.
AH 4819.48.3   Athens and the Greek miracle. 1. American ed. (Rhodakanakès, K.P.) Boston, 1951.
AH 4259.65   Athens and the sea. (Amit, M.) Bruxelles, 1965.
AH 5313.10   Athens in the age of Pericles. 1st ed. (Robinson, Charles.) Norman, 1959.
AH 5313.12   Athens in the fifth century B.C. (Massachusetts Institute of Technology. Department of English and History.) Cambridge, Mass., 1950.
AH 5343.2   Athens Mauern. (Frickenhaus, A.) Bonn, 1905.
AH 4038.93.3   Athens politiske udvikling. (Raeder, A.) Christiania, 1893.
AH 4039.70.5   Det athenske demokrati. (Damsgaard-Madsen, Aksel.) København, 1970.
AH 4831.1   Pamphlet box. Athletic games. 3 pam.
AH 4838.98   Athletics and games of ancient Greece. (Plummer, E.M.) Cambridge, Mass., 1898.
AH 839.30   Athletics of the ancient world. (Gardiner, Edward Norman.) Oxford, 1930.
AH 839.30.1   Athletics of the ancient world. (Gardiner, Edward Norman.) Oxford, 1971.
AH 8008.7   Les atlantes. Histoire de l'Atlantis. (Berlioux, E.F.) Paris, 1883.
AHP 15.9F   Atlas der Urgeschichte. Hamburg. 1,1951+
AHP 15.9.2F   Atlas der Urgeschichte. Beiheft. Hamburg. 1,1953+ 7v.
AH 930.37   Atlas of ancient and classic geography. London, 1952.
AH 930.36   Atlas of ancient and classical geography. London, 1912.
AH 930.43   Atlas of ancient history. (Shepherd, William Robert.) N.Y., 1913.
NEDL   AH 938.56.20   An atlas of classical geography. (Hughes, William.) N.Y., 1856.
NEDL   AH 938.56.10   An atlas of classical geography. (Hughes, William.) N.Y., 1867.
NEDL   AH 938.56.12   An atlas of classical geography. (Hughes, William.) N.Y., 1870.
NEDL   AH 938.56.15   An atlas of classical geography. (Hughes, William.) N.Y., 1871.
AH 938.56   An atlas of classical geography. (Hughes, William.) Philadelphia, 1856.
NEDL   AH 938.56.3   An atlas of classical geography. (Hughes, William.) Philadelphia, 1859.
NEDL   AH 938.56.4   An atlas of classical geography. (Hughes, William.) Philadelphia, 1861.
AH 938.56.5   An atlas of classical geography. (Hughes, William.) Philadelphia, 1865.
AH 3009.60.1F   Atlas of Mesopotamia; a survey of the history and civilization of Mesopotamia from the Stone Age to the fall of Babylon. (Beek, Martinus A.) London, 1962.
AH 930.20   Atlas of the geography and history of the ancient world. (Lord, John K.) Boston, 1902.
AH 4948.83   Atlas pour servir à l'histoire grecque de E. Curtius. (Bouché-Leclercq, Auguste.) Paris, 1883.
AH 930.40F   Atlas van de antieke wereld. (Heyden, A.A.) Amsterdam, 1958.
AH 3009.60F   Atlas van het Tweestromland. (Beek, Martinus A.) Amsterdam, 1960.
AH 7239.38.5   Atrocities in Roman warfare to 133 B.C. Diss. (Westington, M.M.) Chicago, 1938.
Eg 879.65.15   Die Atropaia und die Götter Mittelägypten. v.1-2. (Altenmueller, Hartwig.) München, 1965.
AH 7509.33.9   Attaviano capoparti. (Levi, Mario A.) Firenze, 1933. 2v.
AH 7653.15   Attempt to account for infidelity of Edward Gibbon. (Evans, J.) London, n.d.
AH 5309.11   Atthis. (Sanctis, G.) Roma, 1898.
AH 5309.11.2   Atthis. 2. ed. (Sanctis, G.) Torino, 1912.
AH 8902.5   Atti. (Convegno di studi etruschi.) Firenze. 1-2
AH 8647.25   Atti. (Convegno di Studi sulla Magna Grecia.) Napoli. 1,1961+ 9v.
AH 5301.1   Pamphlet box. Attica. Greece.
AH 5307.17   Attica and Athens. (Müller, K.O.) London, 1842.
AH 139.00   Atticarum et Romanarum legum collatio. (Rivalta, V.) Ravennae, 1900.
AH 7799.15.5   Attila and the Huns. (Hutton, Edward.) N.Y., 1915.
AH 7799.51   Attila und der Hunnenkönig von seinen Zeitgenossen dargestellt. (Homeyer, H.) Berlin, 1951.
AH 7799.40   Attila és hunjai. (Németh, Gyula.) Budapest, 1940.
AH 7798.78   Attila in der Geschichte und Sage. (Foss, Rudolph.) Düsseldorf, 1878.
AH 7798.78.5   Attila in der Geschichte und Sage. (Foss, Rudolph.) Gütersloh, 1910?
AH 7799.51.5   Attila und die Hunne. (Altheim, F.) Baden-Baden, 1951.
AH 7799.40.5   Attila ve Hunlari. (Németh, Gyula.) Istanbul, 1962.
AH 4200.13   Attinger, G. Essai sur Lycurgue. Neuchatel, 1892.
AH 4259.37   Die attische Flotte im peloponnesischen Kriege. Inaug. Diss. (Döpel, G.) Borna, 1937.
AH 4114.11   Attische Genealogie. (Toepffer, J.) Berlin, 1889.
AH 4162.11   Attische Intestat Erbrecht. (Boor, Carl de.) Hamburg, 1838.
AH 4808.61   Attische Kalender. (Faselius, A.) Weimar, 1861.
AH 4114.18   Die attische Metoikie im vierten Jahrhundert. Inaug. Diss. (Gerhardt, Paul.) Königsberg, 1933.
AH 4179.70   Attische Pachturkunden. (Behrend, Diederich.) München, 1970.
AH 4228.24.5   Attische Process. (Meier, M.H.E.) Berlin, 1883. 2v.
AH 4228.24.3   Attische Process. (Meier, M.H.E.) Halle, 1824.
AH 4139.05   Attische Recht. (Lipsius, Justus Hermann.) Leipzig, 1905. 4v.
AH 4139.05.1   Das attische Recht und Rechtsverfahren. v.1-3. (Lipsius, Justus Hermann.) Hildesheim, 1966.
AH 5336.6   Attische Studien; Pnyx und Stadtmauer. (Curtius, Ernst.) Göttingen, 1862.
AH 4229.21   Das attische Volksgericht. (Schulthess, Otto.) Bern, 1921.
AH 4148.70   Attischen Bürgerrechtes. (Philippi, A.) Berlin, 1870.
AH 4148.77   Attischen Geschworenengerichte. (Fränkel, M.) Berlin, 1877.
AH 4116.7   Die attischen Phratrien. (Schaefer, C.) Naumburg, 1888.
AH 4229.08   Attisches Prozessrecht. (Weber, Hans.) Paderborn, 1908.
AH 4148.78   Attisches Staatsrecht. (Hartel, W.) Wien, 1878.
Eg 879.35   The attitude of the ancient Egyptians to death and the dead. (Gardiner, Alan H.) Cambridge, Eng., 1935.
AH 4309.54A   The attitude to poetry and history. (Gomme, Arnold W.) Berkeley, 1954.
AH 8532.5.10   Au cours de l'automne de 43 avant notre ere Lucius Munatius Plancus. (Chagny, André.) Lyon, 1957.
AH 3005.13   Au service de Clio. (Scheil, Vincent.) Chalon-sur-Saone, 1937.
Eg 299.11.10   Au temps des pharaons. 5. éd. (Moret, Alexandre.) Paris, 1925.
AH 7758.61   Aube, B. De Constantino imperatore, pontifice max. Lutetiae, 1861.
AH 5372.5   Aubert, L.M.B. Et graesk Senatsconsult om Thisbaeerne. n.p., 1875.
AH 7199.47   Auctoritas principis. (Magdelain, A.) Paris, 1947.
AH 7168.92   Audibert, A. L'histoire du droit romain. Paris, 1892.
AH 3659.21   Audienz beim persischen Grosskönig. (Walser, Gerold.) Zürich, 1965.
AH 7888.84   Die Aüfstande der unfreien Arbeiter. (Bücher, Karl.) Frankfurt, 1874.
AH 3149.13   Der Aufbau der babylonischen Chronologie. (Schmidtke, Friedrich.) Münster, 1952.
Eg 879.68.10   Aufbau und Bedeutung der altägyptischen Opferformel. (Barta, Winfried.) Glückstadt, 1968.
Eg 1042.971   Das Auferstehungsritual der Unas-Pyramide. (Spiegel, Joachim.) Wiesbaden, 1971.
AH 866.11   Der aufgefundene Eridanus. (Hasse, J.G.) Riga, 1796.
AH 299.19   Aufsätze und Vorträge. (Kornemann, E.) Leipzig, 1919.
AH 3963.24   Aufsätze zur biblischen Landes- und Altertumskunde. (North, Martin.) Neukirchen, 1971.
AH 3658.5   Aufsätze zur Persischen Geschichte. (Nöldeke, T.) Leipzig, 1887.
AH 7272.2   Aufstieg und Niedergang der römischen Welt. Berlin, 1972-6v.
AH 7299.72.5   Aufstieg und Niedergang der römischen Welt. v.1-2. Berlin, 1972- 6v.
AH 279.58.35   Aufstieg und Untergang der Grossreiche des Altertums. 2. Aufl. (Mueller, W.F.) Stuttgart, 1959.
AH 3150.12F   Augapfel, J. Babylonische Rechtsurkunden aus der Regierungszeit Artaxerxes I und Darius II. Wien, 1917.
AH 838.87   Augé de Lassus, Lucien. Spectacles antiques. Paris, 1888.

Author and Title Listing

AH 3151.2.5 — The Babylonian laws. (Hammurabi, king of Babylonia.) Oxford, 1960. 2v.

AH 3008.84 — Babylonian life and history. (Budge, E.A.W.) London, 1884. 2v.

AH 3008.84.5 — Babylonian life and history. 2. ed. (Budge, E.A.W.) London, 1925.

AH 3171.5.5 — Babylonian literature. (Sayce, A.H.) London, 1877.

AH 3171.5 — Babylonian literature. (Sayce, A.H.) London, 1879.

NEDL AH 3181.10.5F — Babylonian liturgies. (Langdon, S.) Paris, 1913.

AH 3156.6.5 — Babylonian magic and sorcery. (King, Leonard W.) Lieden, 1952.

AH 3156.6 — Babylonian magic and sorcery. (King, Leonard W.) London, 1896.

AH 3013.923 — Babylonian problems. (Lane, William H.) N.Y., 1923.

AH 3002.7F — Babylonian records in the library of J.P. Morgan. (Morgan, J.P.) N.Y., 1912. 4v.

AH 3154.01 — Pamphlet box. Babylonian religion.

AH 3155.8 — Babylonian religion and mythology. (King, L.W.) London, 1903.

AH 3163.6 — The Babylonian tables of the Berens collection. (Pinches, T.G.) London, 1915.

AH 3189.5 — Babylonian wisdom literature. (Lambert, Wilfred G.) Oxford, 1960.

AH 3143.7 — Babylonians and Assyrians. (Sayce, A.H.) N.Y., 1899.

AH 3143.10 — Babylonien und Assyrien. (Meissner, Bruno.) Heidelberg, 1920. 2v.

AH 3009.07 — Babylonien und Assyrien. (Starck, C. von.) Marburg, 1907.

AH 3002.2.22 — Babylonisch-assyrische Geburts-Omina. (Dennefeld, L.) Leipzig, 1914.

AH 3008.86A — Babylonisch-assyrische Geschicte. (Tiele, C.P.) Gotha, 1886. 2v.

AH 3191.10F — Die babylonisch-assyrische Medizin in Texten. (Koecher, F.) Berlin, 1963- 4v.

AH 3173.12 — Babylonisch-assyrische Texte: Die Schöpfungeslegende. (Bezold, Carl.) Bonn, 1904.

AH 3167.5F — Die babylonisch-assyrischen Längenmasse. (Lepsius, K.R.) Berlin, 1877.

AH 3187.13 — Babylonische Briefe aus der Kassitenzeit. Inaug. Diss. (Waschow, H.) Berlin, 1936.

AH 3020.8 — Babylonische Briefe aus der Zeit der Hammurapidynastie. (Ungnad, A.) Leipzig, 1914.

AH 3002.2.6 — Babylonische Busspsalmen. (Zimmern, Heinrich.) Leipzig, 1885.

AH 3195.7 — Die babylonische Fabel. (Ebeling, Erich.) Leipzig, 1927.

AH 3154.17 — Die babylonische Gebetsbeschwörung. Inaug. Diss. (Kunstmann, W.G.) Gräfenhainichen, 1930.

AH 3143.5 — Die babylonische Geisteskultur. (Winckler, H.) Leipzig, 1907.

AH 3160.28 — Der babylonische Gott Nergal. (Weiher, Egbert von.) Kevelaer, 1971.

AH 3002.2.3 — Das babylonische Nimrodepos. (Haupt, Paul.) Leipzig, 1884-91.

AH 3150.12F — BabylonischeRechtsurkunden aus der Regierungszeit Artaxerxes I und Darius II. (Augapfel, J.) Wien, 1917.

AH 3187.10F — Babylonische Schenkungsbriefe. (Tallquist, K.L.) Helsingfors, 1891.

AH 3151.3 — Das babylonische Strafrecht Hammurabis. (Stooss, Carl.) Bern, 1903.

AH 3014.30 — Die Babylonische Tempeltoren. (Busink, T.A.) Leiden, 1949.

AH 3160.14 — De babylonische termini voor zonde. Proefschrift. (Selms, A. van.) Wageningen, 1933.

AH 3195.14 — Babylonische und assyrische Kolophone. (Hunger, Hermann.) Neukirchen, 1968.

Eg 818.92.3 — Der babylonische Ursprung der ägyptischen Kultur. (Hommel, F.) München, 1895.

AH 3016.7.5F — Die babylonischen Kleinplastiken. (Meissner, Bruno.) Leipzig, 1934.

AH 3017.15.1 — Die babylonischen Kudurru (Grenzsteine) als Urkundenform. (Steinmetzer, Franz Xaver.) Paderborn, 1968.

AH 3155.16 — Babyloniska myter och sagor med kulturhistorisk inledning. (Briem, Efraim.) Stockholm, 1927.

AH 4842.7 — Bach, A. De institutione...scholastica. Bonnae, 1841.

AH 7108.90 — Bachofen, J.J. Die Grundlagen...Reichs. n.p., n.d.

AH 7162.9 — Bachofen, J.J. Lex voconia. Basel, 1843.

AH 2507.5 — Bachofen, J.J. Das lykische Volk. Freiburg, 1862.

AH 2507.5.5 — Bachofen, J.J. Das lykische Volk. Leipzig, 1924.

Htn AH 859.6F* — Bachofen, J.J. Das Mutterrecht. Stuttgart, 1861.

AH 859.6.2F — Bachofen, J.J. Das Mutterrecht. 2. Aufl. Basel, 1897.

AH 7148.87.5 — Bachofen. Das römische Pfandrecht. Basel, 1887.

AH 7468.69 — Backmund, J. Catilina und die Parteikämpfe in Rom im Jahre 63 vor Christus. Würzburg, 1869.

AH 819.63F — Bacon, Edward. Vanished civilizations of the ancient world. N.Y., 1963.

AH 3207.5 — Bactria. The history of a forgotten empire. (Rawlinson, H.G.) London, 1912.

Eg 879.37 — Badawi, Ahmod M. Der Gott Chnum. Inaug. Diss. Glückstadt, 1937.

X Cg AH 4859.11 — Bader, C. Femme grecque. Paris, 1872. 2v.

AH 7859.4.2 — Bader, Clarisse. La femme romaine. 2. éd. Paris, 1877.

AH 4279.63 — Badi, Amiz Mehdi. Les Grecs et les barbares. v.1-3. Lausanne, 1963-66. 2v.

AH 7114.35 — Badian, E. Foreign clientelae, 264-70 B.C. Oxford, 1958.

AH 7114.35.1 — Badian, E. Foreign clientelae, 264-70 B.C. Oxford, 1972.

AH 7469.70 — Badian, Ernst. Lucius Sulla. Sydney, 1970.

AH 7889.72 — Badian, Ernst. Publicans and sinners; private enterprise in the service of the Roman Republic. Ithaca, N.Y., 1972.

AH 7469.68.12 — Badian, Ernst. Roman imperialism in the late republic. 2. ed. Oxford, 1968.

AH 299.64 — Badian, Ernst. Studies in Greek and Roman history. Oxford, 1964.

AH 7239.00 — Baehr, W. De centurionibus legionariis. Berolini, 1900.

AH 4483.14 — Baelen, Jean. L'an 480, Salamine. Paris, 1961.

Eg 459.60 — Baer, Klaus. Rank and title in the Old Kingdom. Chicago, 1960.

AH 3042.3 — Baermstark, A. Babylon zur Stadtgeschichte. Stuttgart, 1896.

AH 4298.62 — Bässler, F. Hellenischer Heldensaal. 2. Aufl. Berlin, 1862.

AH 4338.49 — Bässler, Ferdinand. Hellenischer Heldensaal. v.2. Berlin, 1851.

AH 3002.150 — Baghdad. Iraq Museum. Texts in the Iraq Museum. Baghdad, 1964- 7v.

AH 4708.85 — Baier, B. Studien zur achaeischen Bundes-Verfassung. Inaug. Diss. Würzburg, 1885.

Htn AH 7852.8* — Baïf, L. De vasculis libellus. Paris, 1535.

Htn AH 848.13* — Baif, L. de. De revestaria. Lutetiae, 1553.

Htn AH 255.37.5* — Baif, Lazare de. Annotationis in l. ii. Lutetiae, 1549.

Htn AH 255.37* — Baif, Lazare de. De re navali libellus. Lugdunum Batavorum, 1537.

Eg 609.26.5 — Baikie, J. The Amarna age. N.Y., 1926.

Eg 1309.25 — Baikie, James. Egyptian papyri and papyrus-hunting. N.Y., 1925?

Eg 279.29 — Baikie, James. A history of Egypt from the earliest times to the end of the 18th dynasty. N.Y., 1929. 2v.

AH 3966.10 — Baikie, James. Lands and peoples of the Bible. London, 1914.

AH 1819.23A — Baikie, James. The life of the ancient East. N.Y., 1923.

Eg 279.08.5 — Baikie, James. The story of the pharaohs. London, 1908.

Eg 279.17 — Baikie, James. The story of the pharaohs. 2. ed. London, 1917.

AH 7819.23A — Bailey, Cyril. The legacy of Rome. Oxford, 1923.

AH 7819.23.3 — Bailey, Cyril. The legacy of Rome. Oxford, 1928.

Eg 819.12 — Baillet, J. Introduction à l'étude des idées morales dans l'Egypte antique. Thèse. Blois, 1912.

Eg 819.13 — Baillet, J. Le régime pharaonique...avec l'evolution de la morale en Egypte. Thèse. Blois, 1913.

AH 7178.82 — Baillierie, P. Du domaine public del'état. Paris, 1882.

AH 7479.32 — Bailly, Auguste. Jules César. Paris, 1932.

AH 4863.11 — Le baiser en Grèce. (Vèze, Raoul.) Paris, 1906.

Eg 972.5 — Bakchiastexte und andere Papyri. (Knudtzon, E.J.) Lund, 1946.

AH 7509.37.10 — Baker, G.P. Augustus; the golden age of Rome. N.Y., 1937.

AH 7759.30 — Baker, G.P. Constantine the Great and the Christian revolution. N.Y., 1930.

AH 7519.29 — Baker, G.P. Tiberius Caesar. N.Y., 1929.

AH 7279.34 — Baker, G.P. Twelve centuries of Rome. N.Y., 1934.

AH 7469.27 — Baker, George P. Sulla the fortunate, the great dictator. London, 1927.

AH 7449.29.15 — Baker, George Philip. Hannibal. N.Y., 1929.

AH 5673.5 — Bakhuizen, Simon Cornelis. Chalcidian studies. Proefschrift. v.2. Groningen, 1970-

AH 4859.21 — Balabanoff, A. Untersuchungen zur Geschäftsfähigkeit. Borna, 1905.

AH 4847.15 — Balaesytike. (Ginouvès, Renè.) Paris, 1962.

AH 9714.5 — Balaschev, Georgi D. Staro-trakiiski svetilishta i bozhestva v Mezek, Glava, Panega, Madara, Tsarichina i drugade i tekhnsto znachenie. Sofiia, 1932.

AH 7469.29 — Balbo, Emilio. Catilina nel giudizio della critica demagogica. Roma, 1929.

AH 7757.27 — Balduini, F. Constantinus Magnus. Lipsiae, 1727.

AH 408.69 — Baldwin, J.D. Pre-historic nations. N.Y., 1869.

AH 2109.15 — Balikçisi, Halikarnas. Anadolu'nun sesi. Istanbul, 1971.

AH 7839.61 — Balil, Albert. La ley gladiatoria de Italica. Madrid, 1961.

AH 2231.5.5 — Balkan, Kemal. Kanis Karumunun kronoloji problemleri Hakkinda Musahedeler. Ankara, 1955.

AH 2231.5 — Balkan, Kemal. Letter of King Anum-Hirbi of Mama to King Warshama of Kanish. Ankara, 1957.

AH 9707.8 — Der Balkan. 1. Aufl. (Randa, A.) Graz, 1949.

AH 3159.16 — Ball, C.J. Light from the East, or Witness of the monuments. London, 1899.

Eg 939.42 — Ball, J. Egypt in the classical geographers. Cairo, 1942.

AH 7839.38 — Das Ballspiel der Römer. (Wegner, Ernst.) Würzburg, 1938.

AH 7201.95.50 — Balog, E. Uber das alter der Ediktskommentare des Gaius. Hannover, 1914.

AH 4039.43 — Balogh, Elemér. Political refugees in ancient Greece from the period of the tyrants to Alexander the Great. Johannesburg, 1943.

AH 7529.34 — Balsdom, John Percy Vyvian D. The Emperor Gaius Caligula. Oxford, 1934.

AH 7529.34.6 — Balsdom, John Percy Vyvian D. The Emperor Gaius Caligula. Oxford, 1964.

AH 7859.7 — Balsdon, John Percy V.D. Roman women. London, 1962.

AH 7479.67 — Balsdon, John Percy Vyvian. Julius Caesar; a political biography. 1. American ed. N.Y., 1967.

AH 7819.69 — Balsdon, John Percy Vyvian Dacre. Life and leisure in ancient Rome. 1st ed. N.Y., 1969.

AH 7693.1 — Balty, Janine. Essai d'iconographie de l'empereur Clodius Albinus. Bruxelles, 1966.

AH 7210.2 — Bamberger, F. De Interregibus Romanis. Brunsvigae, 1844.

AH 4559.65 — Bamm, Peter. Alexander; oder Die Vewandlung der Welt. Zürich, 1966.

Eg 708.93 — Bandelin, Erich. De rebus inter Aegyptios et Romanos...usque ad bellum Alexandrinum a Caesare gestum. Inaug. Diss. Halis Saxonum, 1893.

AH 7239.06.7 — Bang, Martin. Die Germanen im römischen Dienst. Berlin, 1906.

AH 7239.06 — Bang, Martin. Die Germanen im römischen Dienst. Berlin, 1906.

AH 7278.18 — Bankes, H. History of Rome. London, 1818. 2v.

AH 3181.7 — Banks, E.J. Sumerisch Babylonische Hymnen. Leipzig, 1897.

AH 908.79 — Les banques dans l'antiquité. (Cruchon, G.) Paris, 1879.

AH 4889.68 — Banques et banquiers dans les cités grecques. (Bogaert, Raymond.) Leyde, 1968.

AH 908.75.3 — Les banquiers athéniens-romains. (Guillard, E.) Paris, 1875.

AH 3013.944 — Baqir, Taha. Excavations at 'Aqar Quf, 1942-1943, 1943-1944. 1st and 2nd interim report. London, 1944-45.

AH 3707.26 — Baramki, D.C. Phoenicia and the Phoenicians. Beirut, 1961.

AH 4729.05.5 — Barbaballo, C. Le declin d'une civilisation, ou La fin de la Grèce antique. Paris, 1927.

AH 7549.15 — Barbagallo, C. La catastrofe di Nerone. Catania, 1915.

AH 909.11 — Barbagallo, C. Contributo alla storia economica dell'antichità. Roma, 1907.

AH 4729.05 — Barbagallo, C. La fine della Grecia antica. Bari, 1905.

AH 7779.12 — Barbagallo, C. Giuliano l'Apostata. Genova, 1912.

AH 7299.26 — Barbagallo, C. Il problema delle origini di Roma. Milano, 1926.

AH 7299.01 — Barbagallo, C. Le relazioni politiche di Roma con l'egitto. Roma, 1901.

AH 7842.12 — Barbagallo, C. Lo stato e l'istruzione pubblica. Catania, 1911.

AH 818.71 — Barber, T.C. Aryan civilization. London, 1871.

AH 4967.88.150 — Barbié du Bocage, J.D. Maps, plans, views and coins, illustrative of the travels of Anacharsis the younger in Greece. 2. ed. London, 1793.

AH 4967.88.9 — Barbié du Bocage, J.D. Oeuvres de Barthélemy. v.1-4, Atlas. Paris, 1821. 5v.

AH 4967.88.8 — Barbié du Bocage, J.D. Oeuvres diverses. Paris, 1798. 4v.

AH 4967.88.5.10 — Barbié du Bocage, J.D. Recueil de cartes géographiques. Paris, 1807.

AH 4967.88.6 — Barbié du Bocage, J.D. Voyage du jeune Anacharsis en Grèce. Londres, 1796. 3v.

Call number	Entry
AH 4967.88.6.5	Barbié du Bocage, J.D. Voyage du jeune Anacharsis en Grèce. Londres, 1798.
AH 4967.88.10	Barbié du Bocage, J.D. Voyage du jeune Anacharsis en Grèce. 3. éd. Londres, 1806.
AH 4967.88.7	Barbié du Bocage, J.D. Voyage du jeune Anacharsis et recueil de cartes. 3. éd. Paris, 1790. 8v.
AH 4539.55	Barbieri, Guido. Conone. Roma, 1955.
AH 7207.40	Barbieri, Guido. L'albo senatorio da Settimino Severo a Carino. Roma, 1952.
AH 842.45	Barclay, William. Educational ideals in the ancient world. London, 1959.
AH 9660.7	Barco, Alejandro del. Las colonias gemelas reintegradas en la mitad de sua respectivas publaciones. Madrid, 1788.
AH 8608.7F	Bardetti, S. De primi abitatori dell'Italia; opera postuma. pt.1-2. Modena, 1769.
AH 7468.84	Bardey, Ernst. Das sechste Consulat des Marius. Brandenburg, 1884.
AH 7819.63	Bardon, H. Le génie latin. Bruxelles, 1963.
AH 7499.13	Bardt, C. Römische Charakterpöpfe in Briefen. Leipzig, 1913.
AH 3713.5	Barges, J.J.L. Colonies phéniciennes. Paris, 1878.
AH 7138.64	Barinetti, P. Dritto romano. Milano, 1864.
AH 7498.92	Baring-Gould, Sabine. The tragedy of the Caesars. London, 1892. 2v.
NEDL AH 7498.92.3	Baring-Gould, Sabine. The tragedy of the Caesars. N.Y., 1892. 2v.
AH 7498.92.6	Baring-Gould, Sabine. The tragedy of the Caesars. N.Y., 1907.
AH 7239.52.5	Barini, C. Triumphalia. Torino, 1952.
AH 4039.60.10A	Barker, E. Greek political theory. London, 1960.
AH 4039.60.11	Barker, E. Greek political theory. 5. ed. London, 1960.
AH 29.56	Barker, Ernest. From Alexander to Constantine. Oxford, 1956.
AH 7239.72	Barker, Phil. The armies and enemies of imperial Rome. Goring by Sea, 1972.
AH 3016.52	Barnett, Richard. Assyrian palace reliefs and their influence on the sculptures of Babylonia and Persia. London, 1960.
Eg 1309.56F	Barns, J.W. Five Ramesseum papyri. Oxford, 1956.
Eg 819.70.1F	Barocas, Claudio. Egypt. N.Y., 1972.
AH 7228.81.5	Baron, J. Abhandlungen aus dem römischen Civilprozess. Berlin, 1881. 3v.
AH 7138.84	Baron, J. Geschichte des römischen Rechts. Berlin, 1884.
AH 4279.61A	Barr, Stringfellow. The will of Zeus. Philadelphia, 1961.
AH 7228.58.2	Le barreau romain. (Grellet Dumageau, J.B.M.) Paris, 1858.
AH 8073.25	Barreca, Ferruccio. La civiltà di Cartagine. Cagliari, 1964.
AH 9677.2	Barros Sivélo, Ramón. Antigüedades de Galicia. Coruña, 1875.
AH 7299.49.3	Barrow, R.H. The Romans. Chicago, 1964.
AH 7299.49.2	Barrow, R.H. The Romans. Harmondsworth, 1958.
AH 7189.28	Barrow, R.H. Slavery in the Roman Empire. London, 1928.
AH 8508.12	Barruol, Guy. Les peuples préromains du Sud-Est de la Gaule. Paris, 1969.
AH 8514.10	Barry, A.E. Monographie du dieu Leherenn d'Ardiége. Paris, 1859.
Eg 879.68.10	Barta, Winfried. Aufbau und Bedeutung der altägyptischen Opferformel. Glückstadt, 1968.
AH 4158.88	Barth, B. De Graecorum Asylis. Argentorati, 1888.
AH 8549.20	Barth, C.K. Ueber die Druiden der Kelten. Erlangen, 1826.
AH 5415.5	Barth, H. Corinthiorum. Berolini, 1844.
AH 7.16.9	Barth, J.M. Mantissa...Fabricii Bibliographiam antiquariam. Ratisbonae, 1751.
AH 8013.2	Barthel, W. Zur Geschichte der römischen Städte in Africa. Griefswald, 1904.
AH 4827.96	Barthelemy, J.J. Carite et Polydore. Lausanne, 1796.
AH 4967.88.35	Barthélemy, J.J. Nouvel abrégé du Voyage du jeune Anacharsis en Grèce. v.2. Paris, 18- ?
AH 4967.88.40	Barthélemy, J.J. Periëgesis toü Néou Anacharsidos eis Ten Hellada. v.1-7, Atlas. En Bienne, 1819. 3v.
NEDL AH 4967.88.5F	Barthélemy, J.J. Recueil de cartes géographiques. Paris, 1799.
AH 4967.88.25	Barthélemy, J.J. Travels of Anacharsis the younger. Baltimore, 1829.
AH 4967.88.19A	Barthélemy, J.J. Travels of Anacharsis the younger. Philadelphia, 1804. 4v.
AH 4967.88.23	Barthélemy, J.J. Travels of Anacharsis the younger. 4. ed. London, 1806. 8v.
AH 4967.88.24	Barthélemy, J.J. Travels of Anacharsis the younger. 6. ed. London, 1825. 6v.
AH 4967.88.17	Barthélemy, J.J. Viaggio d'Anacarsi. v.1, 3-12. Venezia, 1791. 11v.
NEDL AH 4967.88.4	Barthélemy, J.J. Voyage de jeune Anacharsis. Paris, 1788.
Htn AH 4967.88*	Barthélemy, J.J. Voyage de jeune Anacharsis. Paris, 1788. 5v.
AH 4967.88.2	Barthélemy, J.J. Voyage de jeune Anacharsis. 3. éd. Paris, 1790. 7v.
NEDL AH 4967.88.3F	Barthélemy, J.J. Voyage de jeune Anacharsis. 4. éd. Paris, 1799. 7v.
AH 4967.88.11	Barthélemy, J.J. Voyage du jeune Anacharsis. Paris, 1822. 7v.
AH 4967.88.13	Barthélemy, J.J. Voyage du jeune Anacharsis. v.1-7, Atlas. Paris, 1825. 8v.
NEDL AH 4967.88.15	Barthélemy, J.J. Voyage du jeune Anacharsis en Grèce. Aux Deux-Ponts, 1791. 9v.
NEDL AH 4967.88.14	Barthélemy, J.J. Voyage du jeune Anacharsis en Grèce. Paris, 1830. 7v.
Htn AH 235.59*	Bartholin, T. De armillis veterum schedion. Amstelodami, 1676. 3 pam.
Eg 958.79	Bartlett, S.C. From Egypt to Palestine. N.Y., 1879.
AH 3159.19.10	Barton, G.A. Archaelogy and the Bible. Philadelphia, 1925.
AH 3159.19	Barton, G.A. Archaeology and the Bible. Philadelphia, 1916.
AH 3060.3.15F	Barton, George A. Haverford Library collection of cuneiform tablets. New Haven, 1918. 3v.
NEDL AH 278.75	Barton, J.A.G. The ancient world. Edinburgh, 1875.
AH 5610.14	Bartsos, Ioànnēs A. Ho Pyrros en Italia, skopoi kai drasis autou. Diss. Athènai, 1967.
AH 6108.9	Barzoni, V. I Romani nella Grecia. 11. ed. Londra, 1799.
AH 3016.5	Bas-reliefs assyriens. (Descemet, C.) Rome, 1883.
AH 7189.29	Basanoff, V. Partus ancillae. Paris, 1929.
Eg 809.26	Bases, méthodes, et résultats de la chronologie égyptienne. pt.1-2. (Weill, R.) Paris, 1926-28.
Eg 877.19	Basheysen, H. Natales XI Deo consecrat disputatione paradox de Isicle. pt.1-2. Servestae, 1719.
AH 4833.10	Basiades, C.H. De veterum Graecorum gymnastice. Berolini, 1858.
AH 7206.10	Basilicorum libri LX. (Byzantine Empire. Laws, statutes, etc.) Groningen, 1953- 13v.
AH 7206.9F	Basilicorum libri LX. Lipsiae, 1833-1850. 5v.
AH 9610.9	Bass, Josef. Dionysios I. von Syrakus. Wien, 1881.
AH 3156.8	Bassi, D. Mitologia babilonese-assira. Milano, 1899.
AH 866.5	Bastelaer, D.A. van. L'ambre taillé ou véritable. Bruxelles, 1876.
AH 4216.10	Bastid, Paul. L'hypothèque grecque et sa signification historique. Thèse. Tours, 1917.
Eg 990.16	Bataille, André. Les memnonia. Le Caire, 1952.
AH 7469.06.5	La bataille d'Aix. (Clerc, Michel.) Paris, 1906.
AH 7448.74.2	La bataille de Cannes. (Breyton, A.) Paris, 1884.
AH 4481.9	La bataille de la Marne de l'antiquité; Marathon d'aprés Hérodote. (Boucher, Arthur.) Nancy, 1920.
AH 4483.12	La bataille de Salamine. Thèse. (Rados, C.N.) Paris, 1915.
Htn AH 336.02*	Batero, G. Observations upon the lives of Alexander, Caesar, Scipio. London, 1602.
AH 3358.5F	Bates, O. The Eastern Libyans; essay. London, 1914.
AH 7449.42	La battaglia del Metauro. (Bonarelli, G.) Ancona, 1942.
AH 7449.29.12	La battaglia del Metauro. (Branchini, A.) Pesaro, 1934.
AH 7448.24	Battaglia del Ticino tra Annibale e Scipione. Appendice. (Giani, G.B.) Milano, 1824-26.
AH 7449.59.5F	La battaglia di Canne. (Ludovico, D.) Roma, 1959.
AH 3155.23	Battero, Jean. La religion babylonienne. 1. ed. Paris, 1952.
AH 819.68.5	The battle-ax people. (Vlahos, Olivia.) N.Y., 1968.
AH 7479.70.5	The battle of Actium. (Carter, John M.) London, 1970.
Eg 609.13	The battle of Megiddo. Diss. (Nelson, Harold H.) Chicago, 1921.
AH 5386.5	Battle of Plataea. v.1-2. (Stanhope, J.S.) London, 1835.
Htn AH 7203.4.7.5*	Baudoin, François. Breves commentarii, in praecipuas Justiniani imp. Novellas. Ludguni, 1548.
AH 7203.6F	Baudoin, François. Institutiones. Ingolstadt, 1573.
AH 4008.99	Bauer, A. Forsuchungen zur griechischen Geschichten. München, 1899.
AH 279.04	Bauer, A. Lehrbuch der Geschichte des Alterthums. Wien, 1904.
AH 4487.9	Bauer, Adolf. Themistokles. Merseburg, 1881.
AH 5807.5	Bauer, Edmund. Untersuchungen zur Geographie...der norwestlichen Land. Inaug. Diss. Halle, 1907.
AH 3020.55.5	Bauer, Josef. Altsumerische Wirtschaftstexte aus Lagasch. Rome, 1972.
AH 3027.5F	Bauer, Theo. Die Oskanaanäer. Leipzig, 1926.
AH 4299.64	Bauer, Walter. Lorbeer für Hallas. Stuttgart, 1964.
AH 3095.3	Die Bauinschriften Sanheribs. (Meissner, B.) Leipzig, 1893.
AH 7159.69.5	Bauman, Richard. The duumviri in the Roman criminal law. Wiesbaden, 1969.
AH 7159.67.5	Bauman, Richard A. The crimen maiestatis in the Roman Republic and Augustan Principate. Johannesburg, 1967.
AH 5666.5	Baumeister, A. Topographische Skizze der Insel Euboia. Lübeck, 1864.
Eg 409.55	Baumgärtel, E. The cultures of prehistoric Egypt. London, 1955.
AH 4819.05	Baumgarten, F. Hellenische Kultur. Leipzig, 1905.
AH 4819.05.2	Baumgarten, F. Hellenische Kultur. Leipzig, 1908.
AH 4819.05.5	Baumgarten, F. Die hellenische Kultur. 3. Aufl. Leipzig, 1913.
AH 819.13	Baumgarten, F. Die hellistisch-römische Kultur. Leipzig, 1913.
AH 4908.27	Baumstark, A. Curatoribus emporii et nautodicis. Friburgi, 1827.
AH 4848.4	Baxter, Thomas. An illustration of the Egyptian, Grecian and Roman costume. London, 1810.
AH 7817.26	Baxteri, W. Reliquiae Baxterianae. London, 1726.
AH 2648.5	Bayer, G.S. Historia osrhoëna et edessena ex numis illustrata. Petropoli, 1734.
AH 9610.26	Bayet, Jean. La Sicile greque. Paris, 1930.
AH 7759.30.5	Baynes, N.H. Constantine the Great and the Christian Church. London, 1930.
AH 4819.46.5	Baynes, Norman H. The Hellenistic civilization and East Rome. London, 1946.
AH 4200.9	Bazin, H. De Lycurgo. Paris, 1895.
AH 4216.5	Beasley, T.W. Le cautionnement. Paris, 1902.
AH 338.13.2	Beauchamp, A. de. Biographie des jeunes gens. 2. éd. Paris, 1818.
AH 4168.97.2	Beauchet, Ludovic. Histoire du droit privé de la République Athenienne. Amsterdam, 1969.
AH 7178.82.5	Beaudouin, E. Les grands domains dans l'Empire Romain. Paris, 1899.
AH 7201.95	Beaudouin, E. Le majus et le minus latium. Paris, 1879.
AH 7178.94	Beaudouin, E. La limitation des fonds de terre. Paris, 1894.
AH 7007.40	Beaufort, L. Dissertation upon uncertainty. London, 1740.
AH 7037.67	Beaufort, L. La republique romaine. Paris, 1767. 6v.
AH 7549.60	Beaujeu, J. L'incendie de Rome. Bruxelles, 1960.
AH 7498.93.5	Beaujeu, Maurice. Psychologie des premiers Césars. Lyon, 1893.
AH 7148.45	Beaujon, J.H. Specimen juridicum inaugurale, de variis modis, quibus...jus civitatis Romanae...potuerit. Lugdunum-Batavorum, 1845.
AH 7448.32	Beaujour, F. De l'expédition d'Annibal en Italie. Paris, 1832.
AH 4819.13.10	Beaunier, André. La Grèce et nous. Paris, 1913.
AH 898.98	Beaurredon, J. Voyage agricole chez les anciens. Paris, 1898.
AH 4278.53	Beautés de l'histoire grecque. 7. éd. (Durdent, René Jean.) Paris, 1853.
AH 7709.57	Bebelon, Jean. Impératrices syriennes. Paris, 1957.
AH 4039.35	Beccari, A. La fondazione delle dottrine politiche in Grecia. Napoli, 1935.
AH 7419.44	Becerra Oliva, Guillermo. La republica romana. Cordoba, 1944.
AH 138.60A	Béchard, F. Droit municipal dans l'antiquité. Paris, 1860.
AH 7168.72	Bechmann, A. Das Ius Postliminii und die Lex Cornelia. Erlangen, 1872.
AH 7228.89	Bechmann, A. Studie...Legis actio sacramenti in rem. München, 1889.
AH 7188.61	Bechmann, C.G.A. Personalservitut des Usus. Nürnberg, 1861.
AH 4842.91	Beck, F.A.G. Greek education. London, 1964.
AH 7201.4.50	Beck, I.L.G. De Fabio Mela Iuris Consulto. Lipsiae, 1806.
AH 8683.2	Becker, G.A. De Romae veteris muris...portis. Lipsiae, 1842.

Author and Title Listing

AH 6150.5   Belin de Ballu, Eugène. L'histoire des colonies grecques du littoral nord de la Mer Noire; bibliographie...1940 à 1957. Paris, 1960.

AH 6150.5.2   Belin de Ballu, Eugène. L'histoire des colonies grecques du littoral nord de la Mer Noire; bibliographie...1940 à 1962. Leiden, 1965.

AH 8549.110   Belisama, ou L'occultisme cetique. (Bosc, Ernest.) Paris, 1910.

AH 3014.5   Bell, Edward. Early architecture in western Asia: Chaldaean, Hittite, Assyrian, Persian. London, 1924.

AH 3013.913F   Bell, Gertrude. Churches and monasteries of the Tûr 'Abdîn and neighbouring districts. Heidelberg, 1913.

Eg 879.53.2   Bell, H.I. Cults and creeds in Graeco-Roman Egypt. N.Y., 1953.

Eg 885.933A   Bell, H.I. Magical texts from a bilingual papyrus in the British museum. London, 1933.

Eg 279.48A   Bell, Harold. Egypt from Alexander the Great to the Arab conquest. Oxford, 1948.

AH 7278.37   Bell, R. History of Rome. Philadelphia, 1837.

Htn AH 7816.77*   Bell, T. Roma restituta. London, 1677.

AH 7189.71.5   Bellen, Heinz. Studien zur Sklavenflucht im römischen Kaiserreich. Wiesbaden, 1971.

AH 307.87.2   Bellenden, W. De statu libri tres. 2. ed. Londini, 1787.

AH 307.87   Bellenden, W. De statu libri tres. 2. ed. Londini, 1787.

Htn AH 7276.34F*   Bellendenus, G. Supplicum libellorum August regis. Paris, 1634.

AH 7709.64.5   Bellezza, Angela. Massimino il Trace. Genova, 1964.

AH 9557.5   Bellieni, C. La Sardegna e i sardi nella civiltà del mondo antico. Cagliari, 1928-31. 2v.

AH 7137.41.15   Bello, Andrés. Institutciones de derecho romano. Santiago, 1843.

AH 4448.75   Bellum Salaminium. (Grunder, C.) Ienae, 1875.

AH 888.86   Beloch, J. Bevölkerung der griechisch-römischen Welt. Photoreproduction. Leipzig, 1886.

AH 4278.93A   Beloch, J. Grecian history. v.1-3. Strassburg, 1893- 4v.

AH 4278.93.2   Beloch, J. Grecian history. v.1-4. Strassburg, 1912-27. 8v.

AH 8610.2   Beloch, J. Der italische Bund...Roms Hegemonie. Leipzig, 1880.

AH 4408.91   Beloch, J. Storia greca. Roma, 1891.

AH 298.91   Beloch, J. Studi di storia antica. v.1-7. Roma, 1891. 3v.

AH 8857.2F   Beloch, Julius. Campanien. Geschichte und Topographie des antiken Neapel und seiner Umgebung. Atlas. Berlin, 1879.

AH 8857.2   Beloch, Julius. Campanien. Geschichte und Topographie des antiken Neapel und seiner Umgebung. Berlin, 1879.

AH 8857.3   Beloch, Julius. Campanien. Geschichte und Topogrpahie des antiken Neapel und seiner Umgebung. Breslau, 1890.

AH 9610.7   Beloch, Julius. L'imperio siciliano di Dionisio. Roma, 1881.

AH 459.33   Beloch, Julius. Le monarchie ellenistiche e la repubblica romana. Bari, 1933.

AH 7419.26   Beloch, Julius. Römische Geschichte. Berlin, 1926.

Htn AH 861.5*   Belon, P. De medicato funere. Parisiis, 1553.

AH 7888.85   Belot, E. De la révolution économique et monétaire. Paris, 1885.

AH 7114.16   Belot, E.J. Histoire des chevaliers romains. Paris, 1866.

AH 7058.72   Belot, Émile. De tribunis plebis. n.p., n.d.

AH 4518.86   Belser. Altischen Strategen in Vfahrk. v.1-2. Ellivangen, 1886.

AH 7114.6   Bemerkungen über den Census. (Burchardi, G.C.) Kiel, 1824.

AH 7888.86   Bemerkungen über die römische Volkswirtschaft. (Büchsenschütz, A.B.) Berlin, 1886.

AH 4558.61   Bemerkungen zur Geschichte Alexanders des Grossen. (Jäger.) Wetzlar, 1861.

AH 3965.18   Ben-David, Arye. Jerusalem und Tyros. Basel, 1969.

AH 3966.22   Ben-Har, Bezalel. The concealed map of the land of Israel. Jerusalem, 1964?

AH 958.90   Bencker, Max. Der Anteil der Periegese an den Kuntschrift der Alten. München, 1890.

AH 4842.69   Bendel, Paulus. Qua ratione Graeci liberos docuerint. Monasterii Guestfalorum, 1911.

AH 7818.79   Bender, H. Rom und römisches Leben im Alterthumen. Tübingen, 1879.

AH 7818.79.3   Bender, H. Rom und römisches Leben im Alterthumen. 2. Aufl. Tübingen, 1893.

AH 5157.15   Benecke, H.H. Die Seepolitik der Aitoler. Inaug. Diss. Hamburg, 1934.

AH 8534.5   Benedict, Coleman H. A history of Narbo. Thesis. Princeton, 1941.

AH 4839.71   Bengston, Hermann. Die olympischen Spiele in der Antike. Zürich, 1972.

AH 9.49   Bengtson, Hermann. Einführung in die alte Geschichte. München, 1949.

AH 9.49.2A   Bengtson, Hermann. Einführung in die alte Geschichte. 2. Aufl. München, 1953.

AH 4279.69   Bengtson, Hermann. Griechische Geschichte. 2. Aufl. München, 1969.

AH 9.49.6   Bengtson, Hermann. Introduction to ancient history. Berkeley, 1970.

AH 29.62.5   Bengtson, Hermann. Die Staatsverträge des Altertums. v.2-3. München, 1962. 2v.

AH 7238.92   Beniamin, C. De iustmiani imperatoris aetale. Berolini, 1892.

AH 4828.73   Benizelos, T.B. Peri tou idōtikou Biou. Athēnai, 1873.

AH 2957.5A   Benjamin, S. Troy. N.Y., 1880.

AH 2957.5.3   Benjamin, S. Troy. N.Y., 1893.

AH 2957.5.5   Benjamin, S. Troy. N.Y., 1895.

AH 3657.15   Benjamin, S.G.W. Story of Persia. N.Y., 1887.

AH 7469.23   Bennett, Harold. Cinna and his times. Menasha, 1923.

AH 8549.170.5   Benoît, Fernand. Le symbolisme dans les sanctuaires de la Gaule. Bruxelles, 1970.

AH 4521.19   Benson, E.F. The life of Alcibiades. N.Y., 1929.

Eg 974.5   The bent pyramid of Dahshûr. (Fakhry, A.) Le Caire, 1954.

AH 7509.45   Benuzzi, Valerio. La tragedia familiare di Augusto. Milano, 1945.

AH 7299.68   Benzinger, Josef. Invectiva in Romam. Lübeck, 1968.

VAH 3957.38   Beöthy, Leó. Júda, Izrael és Aram. Budapest, 1874.

AH 5357.10   La Béotie antique. (Guillon, P.) Paris, 1948.

AH 7039.53   Béranger, J. Recherches sur l'aspect ideologique su principat. Basel, 1953.

AH 8647.22.5   Bérard, Jean. Bibliographie topographique des principales cités grecque de l'Italie. Paris, 1941.

AH 8647.22   Bérard, Jean. La colonisation grecque de l'Italie meridionale et de la Sicile dans l'antiquité. Paris, 1957.

AH 4299.60   Berard, Jean. L'expansion et la colonisation. Paris, 1960.

AH 4148.94   Berard, V. Liberas Graecorum civitates. Lutetiae, 1894.

AH 2011.5   Le berceau de l'Islam. (Lammens, H.) Romae, 1914.

AH 4559.28A   Bercovici, Konrad. Alexander; a romantic biography. N.Y., 1928.

AH 4559.28.3   Bercovici, Konrad. La vie de Alexandre le Grand. 3. éd. Paris, 1931.

AH 7169.37   Beretta, A. L'esecuzione contro il debitore nel diritto romano ed il nexum. Udine, 1937.

AH 4478.71   Berg, C.A. Aristides. Göttingen, 1871.

AH 7207.42   Bergener, Alfred. Die führende Senatorenschicht im frühen Prinzipat. Bonn, 1965.

AH 7139.53.10F   Berger, Adolf. Encyclopedia dictionary of Roman law. Philadelphia, 1953.

AH 4039.66   Berger, Anatolii K. Politicheskaia mysl' drevnegrecheskoi demokratii. Moskva, 1966.

AH 4938.87.2   Berger, H. Geschichte der...Erdkunde der Griechen. Leipzig, 1887.

AH 4938.87   Berger, H. Geschichte der...Erdkunde der Griechen. Leipzig, 1903.

AH 3707.15   Berger, P. Phénicie. Paris, 1881.

AH 3129.8   Berger, Paul. Die neubabylonischen Königsinschriften. Kevelaer, 1973-

AH 4808.45   Bergk, T. Beiträge zur griechischen Monatskunde. Giefsen, 1845.

AH 909.52F   Berglente und Hüttenminner im Altertum. (Wilsdorf, H.) Berlin, 1952.

AH 3958.23   Bergman, A. The Israelite tribe of Half-Manasseh. Diss. Jerusalem, 1936.

AH 7509.37.25   Bergman, J. Augustus. Stockholm, 1937.

AH 3757.7   Bergmann, F.G. Les Serythes. Halle, 1858.

AH 2147.2.5   Bergmann, R. Asiae Romanorum provinciae civitatibus liberis. Berolini, n.d.

AH 2147.2   Bergmann, R. Asiae Romanorum provinciae civitatibus liberis. Brandenburg, 1855.

AH 7519.03.2   Bergmans, Jan. Die Quellen der Vita Tiberii. Bockhandel, 1903.

AH 4164.7   Bergold, Friedrich. Geschichte und Wesen des Arrabons und der Arrha im griechischen und römischen Recht. Gernsback, 1923.

AH 5390.13   Die Berichte Xenophons, Plutarchs und Diodors über die Besetzung und Befreiung. Inaug. Diss. (Schäfer, Alexander.) München, 1930.

Eg 278.83   Berkley, E. The pharaohs and their people. N.Y., 1883.

Eg 919.72.5   Berlev, Oleg D. Trudovoe naselenie Egipta v epokhn srednego tsarstva. Moskva, 1972.

AH 7478.41   Berlin. Friedrichs Werderschen Gymnasiums. Programm...De C. Iulii Caesaris Coloniis. Berlin, 1841.

Eg 1029.01.5FA   Berlin. Koniglichen Museen. Hieratische Papyrus. Leipzig, 1901- 5v.

AH 3002.120F   Berlin. Staatliche Museen. Vorderasiatische Schriftdenckmaler der Museen. Leipzig. 1-16, 1907-1917 16v.

Eg 983.10PF   Berlin. Universität. Institut für Ägyptologie. Musawwart es sufra. Humboldt-Universität zu Berlin. v.1, pt.2. Berlin, 1971.

AH 3012.4   Berliner, A. Beiträge zur Geographie und Ethnographie Babyloniens. Berlin, 1884.

AH 8008.7   Berlioux, E.F. Les atlantes. Histoire de l'Atlantis. Paris, 1883.

AH 7889.36   Bernard, Antoine. La rémunération des professions liberales en droit romain classique. Paris, 1936.

AH 7958.64   Bernard, E. Les voyages de Saint Jérome. Paris, 1864.

AH 7139.06.3   Bernard, F. First year of Roman law. Oxford, 1906.

Eg 879.57.15   Bernard, J.L. L'Égypte et la genèse du surhomme. Paris, 1957.

AH 4543.9   Bernays, J. Phokion. Berlin, 1881.

AH 238.41   Bernd, C.S.T. Die Hauptstücke der Wappenwissenschaft. Bonn, 1841.

AH 7468.29.7   Bernhardt, H. Chronologie der mithridatischen Kriege. Marburg, 1896.

AH 7708.67   Bernhardt, T. Geschichte Roms von Valerian. Berlin, 1867.

AH 7038.82   Bernhöft, F. Staat und Recht. Stuttgart, 1882.

AH 4842.60   Bernot, Alice. Recherches sur l'Ephébie attique. Paris, 1920.

AH 4559.05.3   Bernoulli, J.J. Darstellungen Alexanders des Grossen. München, 1905.

AH 7078.75   Berns, Carolus. De cometorum tributorum. Wetzlariae, 1875.

AH 3132.8   Bernstein, G. König Nebucadnezar von Babel in der judischen Tradition. Berlin, 1907.

AH 909.71   Bernstein, Weihrauch, Seide. (Raunig, Walter.) Wien, 1971.

AH 866.13.1   Der Bernstein im Altertum. (Waldmann, F.) Walluf bei Weisbaden, 1973.

AH 3187.6   Berry, George R. The letters of the Room 2 collection in the British Museum. Chicago, 1896.

AH 7569.41   Bersanetti, G.M. Vespasiano. Roma, 1941.

AH 1939.30   Berthelot, A. L'Asie ancienne, centrale et sud-orientale d'après Ptolémée. Paris, 1930.

AH 8016.9   Berthelot, André. L'Afrique saharienne et sondanaise. Paris, 1927.

AH 4298.21F   Bertocchi, F. Raccolta di 100 soggetti li piú remarche. Roma, 1821.

AH 7298.21   Bertocchi, Fulvia. Racollta...istoria romana. Roma, 1821.

AH 299.50   Bertoldi, V. Colonizzazioni nell'antico. Napoli, 1950.

AH 9313.5   Bertolé Viale, Giovanni. La civiltà latina in Abruzzo. Pescara, 1956.

AH 7279.34.15F   Bertolini, F. Storia di Roma. Milano, 1934.

Eg 609.59   Bertram, J. Echnaton der Grosse im Schauen. Hamburg, 1959.

Eg 879.54.5   Bertram, Johannes. Die Urweisheit der alten Ägypter. Hamburg, 1954.

AH 3366.5   Bertrand, Louis. Vers Cyrène, terre d'Apollon. Paris, 1935.

AH 4559.26   Berve, H. Das Alexanderreich auf prosopographischer Grundlage. v.1-2. München, 1926.

AH 7509.34.10   Berve, H. Kaiser Augustus. Leipzig, 1934.

AH 5757.15   Berve, H. Sparta. Leipzig, 1937.

AH 4459.59   Berve, Helmuf. Griechische Geschichte. Freiburg, 1959. 2v.

AH 279.49   Berve, Helmut. Gestaltende Kräfte der Antike. München, 1949.

AH 279.49.2   Berve, Helmut. Gestaltende Kräfte der Antike. 2. Aufl. München, 1966.

AH 4279.31   Berve, Helmut. Griechische Geschichte. Freiburg, 1931-33. 2v.

AH 4279.31.2 — Berve, Helmut. Griechische Geschichte. 2. Aufl. Freiburg, 1951- 2v.

AH 4043.5 — Berve, Helmut. Die Tyrannis bei den Griechen. München, 1967. 2v.

AH 7338.14 — Berwick, Edward. Lives of Caius A. Pollio. London, 1814.

AH 4559.39A — Berzunza, J. A tentative classification of books. n.p., 1939.

AH 7759.55 — Beschafsstuhl und Kaiserthron. 1. Aufl. (Instinsky, H.U.) München, 1955.

AH 7817.92.20 — Beschreibung...Zustandes der Römer. (Nitsch, P.F.) Erfurt, 1807- 2v.

AH 7817.92.18 — Beschreibung...Zustandes der Römer. (Nitsch, P.F.) Wien, 1792. 4v.

AH 4817.91.4 — Beschreibung...der Griechen. (Nitsch, P.F.A.) Erfurt, 1806. 4v.

AH 4888.69 — Besitz und Erwerb. (Büchsenschütz, B.) Halle, 1869.

AH 9286.2 — Besnier, M. De regione Paelignorum. Lutetiae Parisiorum, 1902.

AH 939.14 — Besnier, M. Lexique de géographie ancienne. Paris, 1914.

AH 9777.13 — Bessell, G. De rebus geticis. Gottingae, 1854.

AH 7939.01 — Bcsscm, E. De tcrminis ct terminationibus. Groningae, 1901.

AH 4239.69.5 — Best, Jan. Thracian Peltasts and their influence on Greek warfare. Proefschrift. Groningen, 1969.

AH 4168.62 — Bétant, C. An fuerint apud Graecos indices certi. Berolini, 1862.

AH 8908.13 — Betham, William. Etruria. Celtica Etruscan literature and antiquities. Dublin, 1842. 2v.

AH 4819.33.10 — Bethe, E. Tausend Jahre altgriechischen Lebens. München, 1933.

AH 7228.64.5 — Bethmann-Hollweg, M.A. von. Der Civilprozess des gemeinen Rechts. Bonn, 1864. 6v.

AH 7307.34.31 — Betrachtungen über die Ursachen von Grösse und Niedergang der Römer. (Montesquieu, Charles de.) Bremen, 1962.

AH 7149.01 — Betrachtungen über Majestäten. (Kuhn, F.J.) München, 1901.

AH 279.16.10 — Betten, F.S. The ancient world, from the earliest times to 800 A.D. Boston, 1916.

AH 7169.55 — Betti, Emilio. La struttura dell'obbligazione romana e il problema della sua genesi. Milano, 1955.

AH 6110.17 — Bettingen, W. König Antigonos Doson von Makedonien. Inaug. Diss. Weida, 1912.

AH 7239.03.2 — Beuchel, F. De legione Romanorum i Italica. Lipsiae, 1903.

AH 7508.68 — Beulé, C. Ernest. Auguste, sa famille et ses amis. Paris, 1868.

AH 7508.67.6 — Beulé, C. Ernest. Auguste, sa famille et ses amis. 6. éd. Paris, 1895.

AH 7518.68 — Beulé, C.E. Tibère et l'héritage d'Auguste. Paris, 1868.

AH 7518.68.3 — Beulé, C.E. Tibère et l'héritage d'Auguste. 2. éd. Paris, 1868.

AH 7518.68.4 — Beulé, C.E. Tibère et l'héritage d'Auguste. 4. éd. Paris, 1883.

AH 5957.7 — Beulé, E. Études sur Péloponésé. Paris, 1855.

AH 7498.69.2 — Beule, Ernest. Le sang de Germanicus. 2. éd. Paris, 1869.

Eg 278.94.25 — Bevan, E.R. A history of Egypt under the Ptolemaic dynasty. v.4. London, 1927.

AH 3910.7 — Bevan, E.R. The house of Seleucus. London, 1902. 2v.

AH 279.37.5 — Bevan, E.R. The world of Greece and Rome. London, 1937.

Eg 299.09 — Bevan, J.O. Egypt and the Egyptians. London, 1909.

AH 7163.20 — Beverland, H. De stolatae virginitatis. Lugdunum Batavorum, 1680.

Htn AH 7163.20.5* — Beverland, H. De stolatae virginitatis. Lugdunum Batavorum, 1680.

AH 888.86 — Bevölkerung der griechisch-römischen Welt. Photoreproduction. (Beloch, J.) Leipzig, 1886.

AH 8574.4 — Bevölkerung und Gesellschaft der römischen Provinz Dalmatien. (Alföldy, Géza.) Budapest, 1965.

AH 8458.6 — Die Bevolkerung von Pannonien bis zu den Markommenkriegen. (Mócsy, András.) Budapest, 1959.

AH 939.66 — Beyond the Pillars of Heracles. (Carpenter, Rhys.) N.Y., 1966.

Eg 269.62 — Die Beziehungen Ägyptens zu Vorderasien im 3. und 2. Jahrtausend vor Christ. (Helck, Hans Wolfgang.) Wiesbaden, 1962.

AH 4298.93 — Beziehungen zwischen Aegypten und Grieschenland. (Wiedemann, A.) Leipzig, 1883.

AH 3143.6 — Beziehungen zwischen Israel und Babylonien. (Köberle, J.) Wismar, 1908.

AH 7299.64 — Die Beziehungen zwischen Rom und dem Partherreich. (Ziegber, K.H.) Wiesbaden, 1964.

AH 7418.68 — Die Beziehungen zwischen Rom und Hellas. (Scholtze, A.) Leipzig, 1868.

AH 3009.03 — Bezold, C. Ninive und Babylon. Bielefeld, 1903.

Eg 603.7 — Bezold, C. Oriental diplomacy. London, 1893.

AH 3002.2.2 — Bezold, Carl. Die Achämenideninschriften. Leipzig, 1882.

AH 3173.12 — Bezold, Carl. Babylonisch-assyrische Texte: Die Schöpfungeslegende. Bonn, 1904.

AH 3171.6 — Bezold, E. Kurzgefasster Uberblick...Babylonisch-Assyrische Literatur. Leipzig, 1886.

AH 4147.85 — Biagi Cremonensi. De Decretis Atheniensium. Romae, 1785.

AH 4819.13.5 — Bianchi, Enrico. La Grecia nella letteratura, nella religione. Milano, 1913-14.

AH 8608.6.5 — Bianchi Giovini, Aurelio. Sulle Origini italiche di Angelo Mazzoldi; osservazioni. Milano, 1841.

AH 3159.5.20 — Bibbia e babele. (Schreiber, Emilio.) Trieste, 1904.

AH 819.61.5 — Bibby, Geoffrey. Four thousand years ago. 1. ed. N.Y., 1961.

AH 3957.30 — Die Bibel. (Ragaz, L.) Zürich, 1947-50. 7v.

AH 3075.8 — Bible. Prophets. The prophecies relating to Nineveh and the Assyrians. London, 1857.

AH 3966.2F — Bible atlas and gazetteer. N.Y., 1862.

AH 3966.4F — The Bible atlas of maps and plans to illustrate geography and topography of O.T. and N.T. and Apocrypha. (Clark, Samuel.) London, 1868.

AH 3962.22 — Bible chronology. pt.1-3. (Panin, I.N.) Lowestoft, 19- ?

AH 3963.80.2 — A bibliaí régiségtudomany kézikönyve. 2. kiadas. v.1-2. (Szeke'hyi, Lajos.) Budapest, 1896.

AH 3966.27 — Biblical topography. (Rawlinson, George.) London, 1887.

AH 7009.05 — Bibliografia dell'Italia antica. (Gamurrin, G.F.) Arezzo, 1905.

AH 7009.05.5 — Bibliografia dell'Italia antica. pt.1. (Gamurrin, G.F.) Roma, 1933.

AH 7009.53 — Bibliografia e fonti. (Arias, P.E.) Bologna, 1953?

AH 7480.2 — Bibliografia generale dell'età romana imperiale. (Sanna, G.) Firenze, 1938.

AH 4009.36 — Bibliografia historii starozytnej. pt.1-3. (Zmigryder-Konopka, Z.) Lwow, 1936-38.

AH 7008.79 — Bibliografia storica di Roma attica. (Bonghi, R.) Roma, 1879.

AH 7.16A — Bibliographia antiquaria. (Fabricius, J.A.) Hamburgi, 1716.

AH 4842.25 — Bibliographia Graeca. (Paley, F.A.) Lugdunum Batavorum, 1881.

AH 3000.6 — Bibliographie analytique de l'assyriologie et de l'archéologie du Proche-Orient. Leyde. 1,1954+

AH 8647.22.5 — Bibliographie topographique des principales cités grecque de l'Italie. (Bérard, Jean.) Paris, 1941.

AH 180.5 — Bibliographie zur antiken Sklaverei. (Vogt, Joseph.) Bochum, 1971.

Eg 1180.5 — Bibliography of Egyptian mathematics. Supplement. (Archibald, Raymond C.) Oberlin, 1927.

AH 7890.2 — A bibliography of Roman agriculture. (White, Kenneth Douglas.) Reading, 1970.

AH 3000.3.5 — A bibliography of the cuneiform tablets of the Kuyunjik collection. (British Museum. Department of Western Asiatic Antiquities.) London, 1964.

X Cg Eg 1029.32 — Biblioteca aegyptiaca. Leiden. 1-5,1932-1933

Eg 1029.32 — Biblioteca aegyptiaca. Leiden. 6-8,1936-1938 2v.

AH 9.43 — Bibliotheca orientalis. Leiden. 1,1943+ 20v.

AH 3171.7A — La bibliothèque du palais de Ninive. (Menant, J.) Paris, 1880.

AH 842.29 — Bibliothèques publiques. (Langie, A.) Fribourg, 1908.

AH 3964.34 — Bibliska städer. (Rodén, Nils.) Stockholm, 1932.

AH 809.68 — Bickerman, Elias Joseph. Chronology of the ancient world. London, 1968.

AH 4339.72 — Bicknell, P.J. Studies in Athenian politics and genealogy. Wiesbaden, 1972.

NEDL AH 7779.30.10 — Bidez, Joseph. Julian der Abtrünnige. 5. Aufl. München, 1946?

AH 7779.30.5 — Bidez, Joseph. Kaiser Julian. Hamburg, 1956.

AH 7779.30 — Bidez, Joseph. La vie de l'empereur Julien. Paris, 1930.

AH 4559.64.5 — Bieber, Margarete. Alexander the Great in Greek and Roman art. Chicago, 1964.

AH 4848.14.5F — Bieber, Margarete. Entwicklungsgeschichte der griechischen Tracht. Berlin, 1934.

AH 4848.14F — Bieber, Margarete. Griechische Kleidung. Berlin, 1928.

Eg 709.13 — Biedermann, Erhard. Studien zur ägyptischen Verwaltungsgeschichte in ptolemäisch-römischen Zeit. Berlin, 1913.

AH 5723.15 — Biedermann, Georg. Die Insel Kephallenia im Altertum. Inaug. Diss. München, 1887.

AH 4850.7 — Bielschowsky, A. De Spartanorum syssitiis. Vratislaviae, 1869.

AH 7203.41 — Biener, F.A. Geschichte der novellen Justinian's. Berlin, 1824.

AH 7799.06 — Bierbach, Karl. Die letzten Jahre Attilas. Berlin, 1906.

AH 7188.40 — Bierregaard, L. De libertinorum hominum conditione. Hauniae, 1840.

AH 9792.6A — Bigelow, Poultney. Genseric, king of the Vandals. N.Y., 1918.

AH 279.58.30 — Bignami, Ernesto. Manuale di storia orientale e greca. Milano, 1958.

AH 7279.58 — Bignami, Ernesto. Manuale di storia romana. Milano, 1958.

AH 1409.27.5 — Bilabel, Friedrich. Geschichte Vorderasiens und Ägyptens vom 16. Jahrhundert vor Christ bis auf die Neuzeit. Heidelberg, 1927.

AH 4329.20 — Bilabel, Friedrich. Die ionische Kolonisation. Leipzig, 1920.

AH 7549.48 — Das Bild Kaiser Neros bei Seneca. Inaug. Diss. (Heinz, Kurt.) Biel, 1948.

AH 3009.60.3F — Bildatlas der assyrisch-bablonischen Kultur. (Beek, Martinus A.) Gütersloh, 1961.

AH 4818.43F — Bilder Antiken Lebens. (Panofka, Theodor.) Berlin, 1843.

AH 3963.7 — Bilder Atlas zur Bibelkunde. (Frohnmeyer.) Stuttgart, 1905.

AH 4818.70 — Bilder aus dem altgriechischen Leben. (Stoll, H.W.) Leipzig, 1870.

AH 7818.71 — Bilder aus dem altrömischen Leben. (Stoll, H.W.) Leipzig, 1877.

AH 7298.65 — Bilder aus dem römischen Alterthum. (Wolterstonff, A.) Halberstadt, 1865.

AH 7898.58 — Bilder aus der römischen Landwirtschaft. (Magerstedt, A.F.) Sondershausen, 1858. 6v.

AH 3155.6.2FA — Bildermappe...zur Religion Babyloniens und Assyriens. (Jastrow, Morris.) Giessen, 1912.

AH 139.28 — Bill, August. L'évangile et la loi. Thèse. Strasbourg, 1928.

Eg 609.67.10 — Bille-de-Mot, Éléonore. The age of Akhenaten. London, 1967.

AH 3059.5 — Billerbeck, A. Das Sandschak Suliemania. Leipzig, 1898.

AH 3889.5 — Billerbeck, A. Susa. Leipzig, 1893.

AH 4299.11 — Billeter, G. Die Anschauungen von Wesen des Griechentums. Leipzig, 1911.

AH 888.98 — Billeter, G. Geschichte des Zinsfusses. Leipzig, 1898.

AH 4114.17 — Billheimer, A. Naturalization in Athenian law and practice. Diss. Gettysburg, 1922.

AH 7469.28.10 — Binder, Max. Studien zur Geschichte des zweiten Bürgerkriegs. Inaug. Diss. Uberlingen am Bodensee, 1928.

AH 9621.5 — Bindseil, R. Geschichte der Stadt Akragas. Neustettin, 1882.

Eg 845.10 — Bingmann, Lea. Die Frau in ptolemäisch-kaiserlicher Agypter. Bonn, 1939.

AH 7438.93 — Binneboessel, P. Untersuchungen über...Geschichte. Halle, 1893.

Eg 909.64 — Die Binnenwanderung. (Braunert, Horst.) Bonn, 1964.

AH 7159.06 — Binsbergen, J. De legibus ablatae Pecuniae. Trajecti ad Rhenum, 1906.

AH 4833.13 — Bintz, J. Gymnastik der Hellenen. Gütersloh, 1878.

Eg 658.98 — La biografia di un personaggio politico dell'antico Egitto scritta sopra la sua statua. (Marucchi, Orazio.) Roma, 1898.

AH 8073.6 — Biographie des Barkiden Mago. (Friedrich, T.) Wien, 1880.

AH 338.13.2 — Biographie des jeunes gens. 2. éd. (Beauchamp, A. de.) Paris, 1818.

AH 4279.34A — A biography of the Greek people. (Lavell, C.F.) Boston, 1934.

Htn AH 7655.44* — Biondo, F. Historie da la declinatione. Venetia, 1544. 2v.

Htn AH 7815.31F* — Biondo, Flavio. De Roma triumphante libri deceon. Basileae, 1531.

AH 3088.4PF — Birch, S. Bronze ornaments of the Gates of Balawat. London, 1880.

Eg 278.75.9 — Birch, S. Egypt. London, 1883.

Eg 278.75   Birch, S. Egypt. N.Y., 1875.
Eg 278.76   Birch, S. Monumental history of Egypt. London, 1876.
Eg 608.53F   Birch, S. Thothmes III. London, 1853.
AH 8222.10   Birdoswald Fort on Hadrian's Wall. (Howard, Peter.)
                 Huddersfield, 1969.
AH 936.83   Birkerod, J. Timh Timaiov. Altodorfi Noricorum, 1683.
AH 8213.4   Birley, Anthony R. Life in Roman Britain. London, 1964.
AH 7649.66   Birley, Anthony Richard. Marcus Aurelius. London, 1966.
AH 7699.71   Birley, Anthony Richard. Septimus Severus: the African
                 emperor. London, 1971.
AH 8205.4   Birley, Eric. Roman Britain and the Roman army.
                 Kendal, 1953.
AH 4299.21.4   Birt, T. Von Homer bis Sokrates. 4. Aufl. Leipzig, 1929.
AH 4559.24   Birt, Theodor. Alexander der Grosse und das
                 Weltgriechentum bis zum erscheinen Jesu. Leipzig, 1924.
AH 819.18.2   Birt, Theodor. Aus dem Leben der Antike. 2. Aufl.
                 Leipzig, 1919.
AH 7339.19.2   Birt, Theodor. Charakterbilder Spätroms. 2. Aufl.
                 Leipzig, 1920.
AH 7339.19.3   Birt, Theodor. Charakterbilder Spätroms. 3. Aufl.
                 Leipzig, 1923.
AH 7798.85   Birt, Theodor. De moribus christianis quantum Stilichonis.
                 Marburg, 1885.
AH 4819.28.5   Birt, Theodor. Das Kulturleben der Griechen und Römer in
                 ihrer Entwicklung. Leipzig, 1928.
AH 7339.13   Birt, Theodor. Römische Charakterköpfe. Leipzig, 1913.
AH 7339.13.7   Birt, Theodor. Römische Charakterköpfe. Leipzig, 1927.
AH 7339.13.3   Birt, Theodor. Römische Charakterköpfe. 3. Aufl.
                 Leipzig, 1918.
AH 7489.41   Birt, Theodor. Das römische Weltreich. Berlin, 1941.
AH 7339.13.4   Birt, Theodor. Zur Kulturgeschichte Roms. 4. Aufl.
                 Leipzig, 1919.
AH 1819.51   The birth of civilization in the Near East. (Frankfort,
                 Henri.) Bloomington, 1951.
AH 1819.51.2   The birth of civilization in the Near East. (Frankfort,
                 Henri.) Bloomington, 1954.
AH 1819.51.1   The birth of civilization in the Near East. (Frankfort,
                 Henri.) London, 1951.
AH 819.64.5F   The birth of Western civilization. (Grant, M.)
                 London, 1964.
AH 4521.5   Bischer, W. Alkibiades und Lysandros. Basel, 1845.
AH 7549.64   Bishop, John H. Nero; the man and the legend.
                 London, 1964.
AH 7549.64.2   Bishop, John H. Nero, the man and the legend. N.Y., 1965.
AH 3313.2   Bisi, Anna Maria. Kuopiaká; contributi allo studio della
                 componente cipriota della civiltá punica. Roma, 1966.
AH 7201.98.5   Bisoukides, P.K. O gaïos kai aieisègeseis autou.
                 Thessalonikè, 1937.
AH 37.96   Bisset, R. Sketch of democracy. London, 1796.
AH 4498.62   Bissing, F. Athen und die Politik seiner Staatsmeiner.
                 Heidelberg, 1862.
Eg 279.04   Bissing, F.W. von. Geschichte Ägyptens. Berlin, 1904.
Eg 819.13.5   Bissing, F.W. von. Die Kultur des alten Ägyptens. 2. Aufl.
                 Leipzig, 1919.
Eg 1129.55   Bissing, Friedrich W. von. Altägyptische Lebensweisheit.
                 Zürich, 1955.
AH 2011.9   Bistäm ibn Qais. (Bräunlich, Erich.) Leipzig, 1923.
AH 2157.2   Bithynia et Ponto. (Schoemann, A.G.O.) Gottingae, 1855.
AH 2158.5   La Bitinia - la Lidia. (Lauria, Giuseppe A.)
                 Napoli, 1874.
Eg 1159.56   Bitschai, J. A history of urology in Egypt.
                 Cambridge, 1956.
AH 2107.9A   Bittel, Kurt. Grundzüge der Vor- und Frühgeschichte
                 Kleinasiens. 2. Aufl. Tübingen, 1950.
AH 9722.9A   Bizantii v klassicheskuiu i ellinisticheskuiu epokhi.
                 (Nevskaia, V.P.) Moskva, 1953.
AH 7749.23   Bjarnason, T.H. Diocletianus keisari. Reykjavík, 1923.
AH 7168.94   Björling, C.G.E. Penning deposition enligt justiniansk
                 Rätt. Lund, 1894.
AH 329.70   Black in antiquity; Ethiopians in the Greco-Roman
                 experience. (Snowden, Frank Martin.) Cambridge, 1970.
Eg 879.00.5   Blackden, M.W. Ritual of the mystery of the judgment of
                 the soul. London, 19- .
Eg 819.23.5   Blackman, A.M. Luxor and its temples. N.Y., 1923.
Htn AH 7507.53* Blackwell, Thomas. Memoirs of the courts of Augustus.
                 Edinburgh, 1753. 3v.
Htn AH 9692.2* Blade, J.F. Géographie historique de la Vasconie
                 espagnole. Auch, 1891.
AH 8964.3   Bladé, J.F. Mémoire sur l'histoire religieuse.
                 Bordeaux, 1885.
AH 7449.45   Blaettler, Pirmin. Studien zur Regulusgeschichte.
                 Sarnen, 1945.
AH 7188.33.2   Blair, William. An inquiry into the state of slavery
                 amongst the Romans. Detroit, 1969?
NEDL AH 279.23   Blanchet, D. Histoire de l'Orient et de la Grèce. 7. éd.
                 Paris, 1923.
AH 4538.85   Blass, F.W. Die sozialen Zustände Athens. Kiel, 1885.
AH 854.7   Blatchford, C.H. Butterfly in ancient literature and art.
                 Cambridge, 1889.
AH 4279.66   Blavatskaia, Tat'iana V. Akheiskaia Gretsiia vo vtorom
                 tysiacheletii do nie. Moskva, 1966.
AH 4189.69   Blavatskaia, Tat'iana v. Rabstvo v ellinisticheskikh
                 gosudarstvakh v III-I vv do n.e. Moskva, 1969.
AH 3964.5   Blaw, L. Das altjüdische Zauberwesen. Strassburg, 1898.
AH 7508.76.7   Blaze de Bury, H. Les femmes...au temps d'Auguste. 2. éd.
                 Paris, 1876.
Eg 879.56.5   Bleeker, C.J. Die Geburt eines Gottes. Leiden, 1956.
Eg 879.73.5   Bleeker, Chaes. Hathor and Thoth. Leiden, 1973.
Eg 850.5   Bleeker, Claas J. Egyptian festivals. Leiden, 1967.
AH 7149.72   Bleicken, Jochen. Staatliche Ordnung und Freiheit in der
                 römischen Republik. Kallmünz, 1972.
AH 7114.44.2   Bleicken, Jochen. Das Volkstribunat der klassischen
                 Republik. 2e Aufl. München, 1968.
AH 9475.2   Blick in die Geschichte...Eining's von Trajan bis
                 Diocletian. v.1-2. (Schreiner, W.) Landshut, 1896.
Eg 1059.55   De blinde harpenaar. (Aafjes, B.) Amsterdam, 1955.
AH 7098.83   Bloch, G. De decretis functorum magistratum ornamentis.
                 Lutetiae Parisiorum, 1883.
AH 7489.22   Bloch, G. L'empire romain; évolution et decadence.
                 Paris, 1922.
AH 7469.13.5   Bloch, G. La République romaine. Paris, 1919.
AH 7419.13.5   Bloch, Gustave. La république romaine. Paris, 1913.
AH 7469.29.10   Bloch, Gustave. La République romaine de 133 avant J.C. à
                 la mort de César. v.1-2. 2.-3. ed. Paris, 1940-43.
AH 7818.95   Bloch, Leo. Römische Altertumskunde. Stuttgart, 1895.
AH 7818.95.5   Bloch, Leo. Römische Altertumskunde. 2. Aufl.
                 Leipzig, 1898.

AH 7889.00.2   Bloch, Leo. Soziale Kämpfe im alten Rom. 2. Aufl.
                 Leipzig, 1908.
AH 7889.00   Bloch, Leo. Die ständlichen und sozialen Kämpfe.
                 Leipzig, 1900.
AH 8913.5.8   Bloch, Raymond. The ancient civilization of the Etruscans.
                 N.Y., 1969.
AH 8913.5   Bloch, Raymond. L'art et la civilisation étrusques.
                 Paris, 1955.
AH 8913.5.6   Bloch, Raymond. The Etruscans. London, 1958.
AH 8913.5.7   Bloch, Raymond. The Etruscans. London, 1969.
AH 8907.25   Bloch, Raymond. Les Étrusques. Paris, 1954.
AH 8913.5.5   Bloch, Raymond. Le mystère étrusque. Paris, 1956.
AH 7409.58   Bloch, Raymond. Les origins de Rome. 3. ed. Paris, 1958.
AH 7409.58.5   Bloch, Raymond. The origins of Rome. London, 1960.
AH 7279.60.20   Bloch, Raymond. Rome et son destin. Paris, 1960.
AH 2014.5   Blochet, E. Le culte d'Aphrodite-Anahita.
                 Chalon-sur-Saône, 1902.
AH 7469.29.5   Block, Gustave. La République romaine de 133 avant J.C. à
                 la mort de César. Pt.1. Paris, 1929.
Eg 709.63   Bloedow, Edmund. Beiträge zur Geschichte der Ptolemaios
                 XII. Würzburg, 1963.
AH 4521.20   Bloedow, Edmund F. Alcibiades reexamined.
                 Wiesbaden, 1973.
AH 3159.34   Blome, Friedrich. Die Opfermaterie in Babylonien und
                 Israel. Thesis. Romae, 1934.
AH 7138.30.5   Bloudeau, M. Chrestomathie ou choix de textes.
                 Paris, 1830.
AH 4818.87.5   Blümner, H. Home life of ancient Greeks. London, 1893.
AH 4818.87.7A   Blümner, H. Home life of ancient Greeks. London, 1895.
AH 4818.87.3A   Blümner, H. Leben und Sitten der Griechen. Leipzig, 1887.
                 3v.
AH 908.75   Blümner, H. Technologie und Terminologie der Gewerbe.
                 v.1-4. Leipzig, 1875. 3v.
AH 908.75.2   Blümner, H. Technologie und Terminologie der Gewerbe. 2.
                 Aufl. Berlin, 1912.
AH 4949.11   Blümner, Hugo. Karte von Griechenland zur Zeit des
                 Pausanias. Bern, 1911.
Eg 279.00   Die Blütezeit des Pharaohenreichs. (Steindorff, G.)
                 Bielefeld, 1900.
AH 7201.11   Bluhme, A.F. Gaius Institutionum. Berolini, 1824.
AH 7408.28   Blum, K.L. Einleitung im Rom's alte Geschichte.
                 Berlin, 1828.
AH 328.69   Blyden, E.W. The negro in ancient history. N.Y.? 1869.
AH 328.69.2   Blyden, E.W. The negro in ancient history.
                 Washington, 1869.
AH 7799.55   Boak, A.E.R. Manpower shortage and the fall of the Roman
                 Empire in the West. Ann Arbor, 1955.
AH 7059.19   Boak, A.E.R. The master of the offices in the later Roman
                 and Byzantine empires. N.Y., 1919.
AH 7059.24A   Boak, A.E.R. Two studies in later Roman and Byzantine
                 administration. N.Y., 1924.
AH 7279.21   Boak, Arthur E.R. A history of Rome to 565 A.D.
                 N.Y., 1921.
AH 7279.21.3   Boak, Arthur E.R. A history of Rome to 565 A.D.
                 N.Y., 1929.
AH 7279.21.4   Boak, Arthur E.R. A history of Rome to 565 A.D.
                 N.Y., 1935.
AH 7279.21.4.5A Boak, Arthur E.R. A history of Rome to 565 A.D. 3. ed.
                 N.Y., 1943.
AH 7279.21.4.6   Boak, Arthur E.R. A history of Rome to 565 A.D. 3. ed.
                 N.Y., 1947.
AH 7279.21.4.9   Boak, Arthur E.R. A history of Rome to 565 A.D. 5. ed.
                 N.Y., 1965.
AH 7259.56   The boarding-bridge of the Romans. (Wallinga, Herman
                 Tammo.) Groningen, 1956.
AH 4819.39   Boas, G. The Greek tradition. Baltimore, 1939.
AH 4938.42   Bobrik, H. Griechenland. Leipzig, 1842.
AH 3716.5   Bochart, S. Geographia sacra. Francofurti, 1681.
AH 7479.62   Bocheński, J. Boski Juliusz. Wyd. 2. Warszawa, 1962.
AH 7648.68   Bodek, Arnold. Marcus Aurelius Antoninus als Zeitgenosse
                 und Freund des Rabbi Jehuda ha-Nasi. Leipzig, 1868.
AH 4498.21   Boeckh, A. De Pericle, artium et letterarum slatore.
                 Berolini, 1821.
AH 808.63   Böckh, A. Sonnenkreise der Alten. Berlin, 1863.
AH 928.38   Böckh, August. Metrologische Untersuchungen über Gewichte,
                 Münzfüsse und Masse. Berlin, 1838.
AH 4108.17.4   Böckh, August. Public economy of Athenians. Boston, 1857.
AH 4108.17.3   Böckh, August. Public economy of Athens. 2. ed.
                 London, 1842.
AH 4108.17.7F   Böckh, August. Sieben Tafeln zum 11 Bande
                 Staatshaushaltung. Berlin, 1851.
AH 4108.17   Böckh, August. Staatshaushaltung der Athener.
                 Berlin, 1817. 2v.
AH 4108.17.2   Böckh, August. Staatshaushaltung der Athener. 2. Aufl.
                 Berlin, 1851. 3v.
NEDL AH 4108.86 Böckh, August. Staatshaushaltung der Athener. 3. Aufl.
                 Berlin, 1886. 2v.
AH 4108.17.5   Böckh, August. Die Staatshaushaltung der Athener. 3. Aufl.
                 Berlin, 1967. 2v.
AH 4258.40.2F   Böckh, August. Tafeln zu Urkunden. Berlin, 1840.
AH 4258.40   Böckh, August. Urkunden. Berlin, 1840.
AH 7055.93.5   Böcking, D. Eduard. Über die Notitia Dignitatum.
                 Bonn, 1834.
AH 7188.26   Böcking, E. De mancipii causis. Berolini, 1826.
AH 7168.62   Böcking, E. Römisches Privatrecht. Bonn, 1862.
AH 7055.93.3   Böcking, Edvardus. Notitia dignitatum. Bonnae, 1839-53.
                 3v.
AH 7188.41   Böger, G. De manciporum commercio apud Romanos.
                 Berolini, 1841.
AH 3011.15   Böhl, F.M.T. Opera minora. Groningen, 1953.
AH 3002.136F   Böhl, Franz M.T. Tabulae cuneiformae a F.M.T. de Liagre
                 Böhl. v.1; 2, pt.1; 3-4. Leiden, 1957. 4v.
AH 4864.7   Boehm, C. De cottabo. Bonnae, 1893.
AH 4848.11   Boelhau, I. Quaestionum de re vestiaria graecorum
                 specimen. Diss. Wimariae, 1884.
AH 7409.51   Bömer, Franz. Rom und Troia. Baden Baden, 1951.
AH 7739.11   Boer, H.G.W. De Julia Mamaea Severi A. Matre.
                 Rhenum, 1911.
AH 5757.25   Boer, W. den. Laconian studies. Amsterdam, 1954.
AH 4819.62.20   Boer, Willem den. Eros en Amor. Den Haag, 1962.
AH 4518.94.3   Boerner, A. De rebus a Graecis. Gottingae, 1894.
AH 4846.10   Boersma, Johannes Sipko. Athenian building policy from
                 561-560 to 404-400 B.C. Groningen, 1970.
AH 7200.16   Boesch, F. De XII Tabularum Lege a Graecio Petita.
                 Gottingae, 1893.
Eg 808.45   Böskh, A. Manetho und die Hundssternperiode.
                 Berlin, 1845.
AH 4809.22   Boethius, Axel. Der argivische Kalender. Uppsala, 1922.

Author and Title Listing

AH 7109.15	Böttcher, Kurt. Die Einnahmen der römischen Republic im letzten Jahrhundert ihres Bestehens. Weida, 1915.
AH 7828.03	Böttiger, C.A. Sabina, oder Morgenscenen. Leipzig, 1803.
AH 7828.03.4	Böttiger, C.A. Sabina, oder Morgenscenen. Leipzig, 1806.
AH 7828.03.6	Böttiger, C.A. Sabine, ou Matinée d'une dame romaine. Paris, 1813.
AH 4889.68	Bogaert, Raymond. Banques et banquiers dans les cités grecques. Leyde, 1968.
AH 7448.92	Boguth, Walter. M. Valerius Laevinus (Ein Beitrag). Krems, 1892.
AH 7203.136	Boháček, Miroslav. Un esempio dell'insegnamento di Berito ai compilatori. Palermo, 1932.
AH 842.17	Bohatta, H. Erziehung und Unterricht bei den Griechen und Römern. Gütersloh, 1895.
AH 4228.72	Bohm, H. De Eisaggeliais. Inaug. Diss. Halae, 1874.
AH 7148.76	Bohn, Oscar. Qua condicione iuris reges. Berolini, 1877.
AH 4238.69.2	Bohstedt, E. Uber das Söldnerwesen. Rendsburg, 1873.
AH 3045.10	Bohtz, C. Helmut. In den Ruinen von Warka. Leipzig, 1941.
AH 3154.16F	Boissier, A. Documents assyriens relatifs aux Présages. Paris, 1894-96.
AH 3156.14	Boissier, A. Mantique babylonienne et mantique hittite. Paris, 1935.
AH 3160.5	Boissier, A. Note sur un monument babylonien. Genève, 1899.
AH 3013.912	Boissier, Alfred. Notice sur quelques monuments assyriens a l'Université de Zurich. Genève, 1912.
AH 8007.7	Boissier, Gaston. L'Afrique romaine. Paris, 1895.
AH 8007.7.4	Boissier, Gaston. L'Afrique romaine. 5. éd. Paris, 1912.
AH 7469.05	Boissier, Gaston. La conjuration de Catilina. Paris, 1905.
AH 7469.05.2	Boissier, Gaston. La conjuration de Catilina. 2. éd. Paris, 1908.
AH 7498.75.5	Boissier, Gaston. L'opposition sous les Césars. Paris, 1875.
AH 7498.85A	Boissier, Gaston. L'opposition sous les Césars. Paris, 1885.
AH 8007.7.5	Boissier, Gaston. Roman Africa. N.Y., 1899.
AH 7149.11	Boissière, G. L'accusation publique...chez les Romains. Niort, 1911.
AH 8157.3	Boissière, G. L'Algérie romaine. Paris, 1883. 2v.
AH 8157.2	Boissière, G. Esquisse d'une histoire dans la nord de l'Afrique. Paris, 1878.
AH 4843.16	Bojesen, E.F. De Tonis S. Harmoniis Graecorum commentario. Kjobenhavn, 1843.
AH 7818.66	Bojesen, E.F.C. Handbuch der römischen Antiquitaten. Wien, 1866.
AH 842.47	Bokhandel och bokforlag i antiken. (Kleberg, Tönnes.) Stockholm, 1962.
AH 3608.5	Bokshchanin, A.G. Parfiia i Rim. Moskva, 1960. 2v.
AH 7178.56.5	Bolkestein, H. De Colonatu Romano ejusque origine. Amstelodami, 1906.
AH 4889.23.3	Bolkestein, H. Economic life in Greece's golden age. Leiden, 1958.
AH 4889.23	Bolkestein, H. Het economisch leven in Griekenlands bloeitijd. Haarlem, 1923.
AH 3155.1	Bollenrücher, J. Gebete und Hymnen an Nergal. Leipzig, n.d. 6 pam.
Eg 9.10	Bollettino. (Farina, G.) Roma, 1910.
AH 7844.12	Bollinger, Traugott. Theatralis licentia. Die Publikumsdemonstrationen an den öffentlichen Spielen im Rom der früheren Kaiserzeit und ihrer Bedeutung im politischen Leben. Winterthur, 1969.
NEDL AH 8922.2	Bologne, Villanovienne et Étrusque. Thèse. (Grenier, A.) Paris, 1912.
Htn AH 7546.27*	Bolton, Edmund. Nero Caesar. London, 1627.
AH 850.9	Bommer, Sigwald. Die Gabe der Demeter. München, 1961.
AH 7089.33	Bon, Alessio de. La colonizzazione romana dal Brenta al Piave. Bassagno del Grappe, 1933.
AH 7169.64	Die bona fides des Ersitzungsbeseitzers im klassischen römischen Recht. (Hausmaninger, H.) Wien, 1964.
AH 7449.42	Bonarelli, G. La battaglia del Metauro. Ancona, 1942.
AH 7279.64.10	Bonde, Cecil von. The splendour that was Rome. Capetown, 1964.
Eg 28.97	Bondi, J.H. Aegyptiaca. Leipzig, 1897.
AH 7479.07	Bondurant, B.C. Decimus Junius Brutus Albinus. Chicago, 1907.
Htn AH 7206.1*	Bonefidius, E. Tog A'natoli. Geneva, 1573.
AH 862.14	Bones, bodies and disease. (Wells, C.) London, 1964.
AH 7008.79	Bonghi, R. Bibliografia storica di Roma attica. Roma, 1879.
AH 7008.79.3	Bonghi, R. Monografia della citta di Roma. Roma, 1881.
AH 7408.84	Bonghi, R. Storia di Roma. v.3. Milano, 1896.
AH 7203.68	Bonjean, G. Institutes de Justien. Paris, 1878. 2v.
AH 7138.76.20F	Bonjean, G. Tavleaux synoptiques de droit romain. Paris, 1876.
Htn AH 7106.12*	Bonlenger, J.C. De tributis ac vetigalis populi Romani liber. Tolosae, 1612.
AH 4819.54.5	Bonnard, André. Civilization grecque. Lausanne, 1954. 3v.
AH 4819.54.7	Bonnard, André. Civilization grecque. v.2-3. Paris, 1963. 2v.
AH 4819.54.6	Bonnard, André. Greek civilization from the Iliad to the Parthenon. London, 1957. 3v.
Eg 879.64	Bonneau, D. La crue du Nil. Paris, 1964.
AH 3759.6	Bonnell, Ernst. Beiträge zur Alterthumskunde Russlands. St. Petersburg, 1882.
AH 8513.8	Bonnemère, L. Les jeux et le théâtre chez les Gaulois en Provence. Paris, 1888.
AH 4049.33	Bonner, R.J. Aspects of Athenian democracy. Berkeley, 1933.
AH 4229.30	Bonner, Robert Johnson. The administration of justice from Homer to Aristotle. Chicago, 1930-38. 2v.
AH 4229.05	Bonner, Robert Johnson. Evidence in Athenian courts. Chicago, 1905.
AH 4229.27.1	Bonner, Robert Johnson. Lawyers and litigants in ancient Athens. N.Y., 1969.
AH 3159.12	Bonnet, E. Les découvertes assyriennes et le livre de la genèse. Montauban, 1884.
Eg 879.52	Bonnet, H. Reallexikon der ägyptischen Religionsgeschichte. Berlin, 1952.
Eg 856.2	Bonnet, Hans. Die altägyptische Schurztracht. Leipzig, 1916.
AH 7217.11	Bonolis, G. I titoli di nobiltà. Firenze, 1905.
AH 3013.32	Bonomi, J. Nineveh and its palaces. London, 1852.
AH 3013.32.3	Bonomi, J. Nineveh and its palaces. 3. ed. London, 1875.
AH 7162.13	Bonorum possessio. (Flach, J.) Paris, 1870.

AH 8200.2	Bonsen, Wilfrid. A Romano-British bibliography. Oxford, 1964. 2v.
AH 7449.25.5	Bonus, A.R. Where Hannibal passed. London, 1925.
Eg 879.56.10	Bonwick, James. Egyptian belief and modern thought. Indian Hills, 1956.
AH 8549.94	Bonwick, James. Irish Druids and old Irish religions. London, 1894.
Eg 879.63F	Book of That Which is in the Nether World. Das Amduat. v.1-3. Wiesbaden, 1963. 2v.
NEDL AH 279.23.10	The book of the ancient world for younger readers. (Mills, Dorothy.) N.Y., 1923.
NEDL AH 279.23.15	The book of the ancient world for younger readers. (Mills, Dorothy.) N.Y., 1926.
Eg 1038.86	Book of the Dead. Das ägyptische Todtenbuch. Berlin, 1886. 3v.
Eg 1039.54.5	Book of the Dead. Ägyptisches Totenbuch. München, 1955.
Eg 1038.95F	Book of the Dead. The book of the dead. London, 1895.
NEDL Eg 1038.98	Book of the Dead. The book of the dead. London, 1898. 3v.
Eg 1038.99	Book of the Dead. The book of the dead. London, 1899.
Eg 1039.13.4	Book of the Dead. The book of the dead. New Hyde Park, N.Y., 1960.
Eg 1038.99.2	Book of the Dead. The book of the dead. 2. ed. London, 1969.
Eg 1039.23A	Book of the Dead. The coming forth by day. Boston, 1923.
Eg 1039.60F	Book of the Dead. The Egyptian book of the dead. Chicago, 1960.
Eg 1039.04	Book of the Dead. The Egyptian book of the dead. London, 1904.
Eg 1039.54	Book of the Dead. Livre des morts des anciens Égyptiens. Paris, 1954.
Eg 1039.07.2	Book of the Dead. Le livre des morts des anciens Égyptiens. 2. éd. Paris, 1907.
Eg 1038.77F	Book of the Dead. Le papyrus funéraire de Soutimès. Paris, 1877.
Eg 1039.13	Book of the Dead. The papyrus of Ani. London, 1913. 2v.
Eg 1039.13.2	Book of the Dead. The papyrus of Ani. N.Y., 1913. 3v.
Eg 1039.10	Book of the Dead. Theban recension of the book of the dead. London, 1910. 3v.
Eg 1038.42	Book of the Dead. Das Todtenbuch der Ägypter. Leipzig, 1842.
Eg 1038.95F	The book of the dead. (Book of the Dead.) London, 1895.
NEDL Eg 1038.98	The book of the dead. (Book of the Dead.) London, 1898. 3v.
Eg 1038.99	The book of the dead. (Book of the Dead.) London, 1899.
Eg 1039.13.4	The book of the dead. (Book of the Dead.) New Hyde Park, N.Y., 1960.
Eg 1039.20	The book of the dead. (British Museum. Department of Egyptian and Assyrian Antiquities.) London, 1920.
Eg 1038.99.2	The book of the dead. 2. ed. (Book of the Dead.) London, 1969.
Eg 809.08	The book of the kings of Egypt. (Budge, Ernest Alfred Wallis.) London, 1908. 2v.
Eg 1309.59PF	Book of the kings of Egypt. Oxford, 1959.
Eg 1038.98.9	The book of the master. (Adams, W.M.) London, 1898.
Eg 1039.33	The book of the master of the hidden places. (Adams, W.M.) London, 1933.
Eg 879.09	The book of the opening of the mouth. (Budge, Ernest Alfred Wallis.) London, 1909. 2v.
Eg 1042.972.5	Book of Two Ways. The ancient Egyptian book of two ways. Berkeley, 1972.
NEDL AH 278.69.15	A book of worthies. (Yonge, Chrlotte M.) London, 1886.
AH 7808.72	Boor, C. de. Fasti censorii. Berolini, 1873.
AH 4162.11	Boor, Carl de. Attische Intestat Erbrecht. Hamburg, 1838.
AH 3005.5	Booth, A.J. Discovery...of trilingual cuneiform inscriptions. London, 1902.
AH 3757.12	Bor'ba plenen severnogo prichernomor'ia s rimon v III veke n.e. (Remennikov, A.M.) Moskva, 1954.
AH 5309.6	Bor'ba politicheskikh gruppirovok v Attike. (Zel'in, K.K.) Moskva, 1964.
AH 8511.18	Bordet, Marcel. La Gaule romaine. Paris, 1971.
AH 7279.69	Bordet, Marcel. Précis d'histoire romaine. Paris, 1969.
NEDL AH 278.54	Boreau, V. Historia antigua. Santiago, 1854.
AH 4278.55	Boreau, V. Historia griega. Santiago, 1855.
AH 7469.69.5	Boren, Henry Charles. The Gracchi. N.Y., 1969.
AH 7419.65	Boren, Henry Charles. The Roman republic. Princeton, 1965.
AH 78.87	Borgeaud, C. Plébiscite dans l'antiquité. Genève, 1887.
AH 3002.144	Borger, Riekele. Handbuch der Keilschriftliteratur. Berlin, 1967-
AH 7808.18	Borghesi, Bartolomeo. Nuovi frammenti dei fasti consolari capitolini. Milano, 1818.
AH 7808.18.3	Borghesi, Bartolomeo. Nuovi frammenti dei fasti consolari capitolini. Milano, 1820.
AH 4860.10	Bork, Arnold. Der junge Grieche. Zürich, 1959.
AH 4860.10.5	Bork, Arnold. Der junge Grieche. Zürich, 1961.
AH 9066.2	Bormann, A.K.E. Altlatinische Chorographie. Halle, 1852.
AH 3911.5	Bormann, E. De Syriae provinciae romanae partibus capita Nonnulla. Berolini, n.d.
AH 7819.21	Bornecque, H. Rome et les romains (littérature, histoire, antiquités publiques et privées). Paris, 1921.
AH 3017.45	Borowski, E. Cylindres et cachets orientaux conservés dans la collection suisses. Ascona, 1947.
AH 9607.23	Borzi, Salvatore. Sicilia Schiava; panoramica azione critico-storica. Paternò, 1962.
AH 9385.1	Borziani, G. Dell'antica città di Ostra. Cefalu, 1911.
VAH 4029.60	Borzsák, István. Görög történeti chrestomathia. Budapest, 1960.
AH 4817.72	Bos, L. Antiquities of Greece. London, 1772.
AH 3109.5	Bosanquet, J.W. The fall of Nineveh and the reign of Sennacherib chronologically considered. London, 1853.
AH 8549.110	Bosc, Ernest. Belisama, ou L'occultisme cetique. Paris, 1910.
AH 3021.4	Bosc, W. St. C. The first of empires. London, 1903.
AH 3008.86.5	Boscawen, William. From under the dust of ages. London, 1886.
AH 7479.62	Boski Juliusz. Wyd. 2. (Bocheński, J.) Warszawa, 1962.
AH 7108.03	Bosse, R.H.B. Grundzüge des Finanzwesens. Braunschweig, 1803.
AH 3414.15	Bossert, Helmuth. Janus und der Mann mit derer Adler; oder Greifenmaske. Istanbul, 1959.
AH 7448.91.10F	Bossi, Gaetano. La guerra d'Annibale in Italia da Canne al Metauro. Roma, 1891.
Eg 8.93	Boston, Mass. Public Library. List of works on Egypt. Boston, 1893.

AH 9675.2 — Botet y Siso, J. Noticia histórica y arqueológica de la antigua ciudad de Emporion. Madrid, 1879.

AH 4819.53 — Die Botschaft von Hellas. (Hiebel, F.) Bern, 1953.

NEDL AH 279.02.2 — Botsford, G.W. Ancient history for beginners. N.Y., 1902.

AH 4038.93.7 — Botsford, G.W. Development of the Athenian constitution. Boston, 1893.

NEDL AH 7279.01 — Botsford, G.W. History of Rome. N.Y., 1901.

AH 7279.01.10 — Botsford, G.W. A history of Rome for high schools. N.Y., 1910.

AH 7279.14.3 — Botsford, G.W. A history of Rome for high schools and academies. N.Y., 1914.

AH 279.12.2 — Botsford, G.W. History of the ancient world. N.Y., 1916.

AH 279.11.15 — Botsford, G.W. A history of the ancient world. N.Y., 1925.

AH 279.11.20 — Botsford, G.W. A history of the ancient world. N.Y., 1927.

AH 7079.09 — Botsford, G.W. The Roman assemblies. N.Y., 1909.

AH 7279.01.3 — Botsford, G.W. Story of Rome. N.Y., 1903.

AH 4279.22.9.5 — Botsford, George W. Botsford and Robinson's Hellenic history. 5. ed. N.Y., 1969.

AH 4279.15A — Botsford, George W. Hellenic civilization. N.Y., 1915.

AH 4279.22A — Botsford, George W. Hellenic history. N.Y., 1922.

AH 4279.22.2A — Botsford, George W. Hellenic history. N.Y., 1926.

AH 4279.22.4 — Botsford, George W. Hellenic history. N.Y., 1928.

AH 4279.22.3 — Botsford, George W. Hellenic history. N.Y., 1930.

AH 4279.22.5 — Botsford, George W. Hellenic history. N.Y., 1939.

AH 4279.22.8 — Botsford, George W. Hellenic history. 3. ed. N.Y., 1948.

AH 4279.22.9 — Botsford, George W. Hellenic history. 4. ed. N.Y., 1956.

AH 4278.99A — Botsford, George W. History of Greece. N.Y., 1899.

AH 4278.99.3 — Botsford, George W. A history of Greece for high schools and academies. N.Y., 1900.

AH 4278.99.5 — Botsford, George W. A history of the Orient and Greece. N.Y., 1911.

AH 4279.22.9.5 — Botsford and Robinson's Hellenic history. 5. ed. (Botsford, George W.) N.Y., 1969.

AH 3013.35.5 — Botta, P.E. Lettres de...sur ses decouvertes a Khorsabad. Paris, 1845.

AH 3013.35PF — Botta, P.E. Monument de Ninive. Text and plates. Paris, 1849-50. 5v.

Eg 1309.28F — Botti, Giuseppe. Il giornale della necropoli di Tebe. Torino, 1928.

Eg 1309.41F — Botti, Giuseppe. Testi demotici. Firenze, 1941.

AH 8073.2 — Botticher, J.F.W. Geschichte der Carthager. Berlin, 1827.

AH 7108.72 — Bouchard, L. Étude sur l'adminstration des finances. Paris, 1872.

Eg 709.03 — Bouché-Leclercq, A. Histoire des Lagides. v.4, photoreproduction. Paris, 1903. 4v.

AH 3910.8 — Bouché-Leclercq, A. Histoire des Seleucides. Paris, 1913-14. 2v.

AH 4309.00 — Bouché-Leclercq, A. Leçons d'histoire grecque. Paris, 1900.

AH 4309.00.2 — Bouché-Leclercq, A. Leçons d'histoire grecque. 2. éd. Paris, 1913.

AH 7038.86 — Bouché-Leclercq, A. Manuel des institutions romaines. Paris, 1886.

AH 4948.83 — Bouché-Leclercq, Auguste. Atlas pour servir à l'histoire grecque de E. Curtius. Paris, 1883.

AH 7279.09 — Bouché-Leclerq, A. Leçons d'histoire romaine. Paris, 1909.

AH 4481.9 — Boucher, Arthur. La bataille de la Marne de l'antiquité; Marathon d'aprés Hérodote. Nancy, 1920.

AH 8013.3 — Bouchier, E.S. Life and letters in Roman Africa. Oxford, 1913.

AH 9557.1 — Bouchier, E.S. Sardinia in ancient times. Oxford, 1917.

AH 9657.5 — Bouchier, E.S. Spain under the Roman empire. Oxford, 1914.

AH 3911.6 — Bouchier, E.S. Syria as Roman province. Oxford, 1916.

AH 4828.75 — Boudodénou, Charalampous. Dokimion. Odesso, 1875. 2v.

AH 4147.45 — Bougainville. Droits des metropolis sur colonies. Paris, 1745.

NEDL AH 278.97 — Boughton, W. History of ancient peoples. N.Y., 1896.

AH 7138.45.15 — Boujean, L.B. Traité des actions, ou Exposition historique de l'organization judiciaire. Paris, 1845. 2v.

AH 817.66.5 — Boulanger, N.A. L'antiquité dévoilée par ses usages. Amsterdam, 1766.

NEDL AH 817.66 — Boulanger, N.A. L'antiquité dévoilée par ses usages. Amsterdam, 1766. 3v.

Eg 759.06 — Boulard, L. Les instructions écrites du Magistrat au juge-commissaire dans l'Égypte Romaine. Paris, 1906.

Htn AH 7835.98* — Boulenger, J.C. De Circo Romano Ludisque. Lutetiae Parisiorum, 1598.

NEDL AH 278.44 — Boulet, Jean B.E. Manuel pratique d'histoire ancienne. Paris, 1844.

AH 3009.33 — Boulton, W.H. Babylonia. London, 1933.

AH 3966.23 — Boundary between Issachar and Naphtali. (Saarisalo, Aapeli.) Helsinki, 1927.

AH 4329.71 — Bourgeois, Alain. La Grèce antique devant la négritude. Paris, 1971.

AH 7088.85.5 — Bourgeois, Émile. Quomodo provinciarum Romanarum. Paris, 1885.

AH 6024.7 — Bourguet, Émile. De rebus Delphicis imperatoriae aetatis capita duo. Diss. Montepessulano, 1905.

AH 9090.2 — Bourne, Ella. Study of Tibur. Diss. Menasha, 1916.

AH 7279.66 — Bourne, Frank C. A history of the Romans. Boston, 1966.

AH 7499.46 — Bourne, Frank C. The public works of the Julio-Claudians and Flavians. Thesis. Princeton, 1946.

AH 7098.96.3 — Boutet, Paul. De la police et de la voirie. Paris, 1896.

AH 7509.65.1 — Bowersock, Glen Warren. Augustus and the Greek world. Oxofrd, 1966.

AH 8549.25 — Bowles, W.L. A dissertation on the Celtic deity Teutates. London, 1828.

AH 4819.65.15 — Bowra, Cecil Maurice. Classical Greece. N.Y., 1965.

AH 4819.57.10 — Bowra, Cecil Maurice. The Greek experience. London, 1957.

AH 4499.71 — Bowra, Cecil Maurice. Periclean Athens. N.Y., 1971.

AH 4819.57.12 — Bowra, Cecil Maurie. The Greek experience. 1st ed. Cleveland, 1958.

AH 39.03.2 — Boxler, A.A. Précis des institutions publiques...Grèce et Rome. Paris, 1903.

AH 7842.16 — Boyd, C.E. Public libraries and literary culture in ancient Rome. Chicago, 1915.

AH 7842.16.5 — Boyd, C.E. Public libraries and literary culture in ancient Rome. Thesis. Chicago, 1916.

AH 4860.8 — Boyhood and youth in days of Aristophanes. (Bryant, A.A.) n.p., 1907.

AH 4860.7 — Boyhood and youth in days of Aristophanes. (Bryant, A.A.) n.p., 1907.

AH 4228.86 — Boyleusis in Mordprocessen. (Heikel, I.A.) Helsingfors, 1886.

Htn AH 8514.5* — Boze, C.G. de. Explications...sacrifices...les anciens. Paris, 1705.

AH 5360.5 — Braake, G.J. Theilnahme der Böoter. Rostock, 1874.

AH 4487.15 — Braccesi, Lorenzo. Il problema del decreto di Temistocle. Bologna, 1968.

Eg 709.71.10 — Bradford, Ernle Dusgate Selby. Cleopatra. London, 1971.

AH 9777.24 — Bradley, Henry. The Goths from the earliest times to the end of the Gothic dominion. N.Y., 1899.

AH 9777.23A — Bradley, Henry. Story of the Goths. N.Y., 1888.

AH 2011.9 — Bräunlich, Erich. Bistam ibn Qais. Leipzig, 1923.

AH 1819.52 — Braidwood, Robert J. The Near East and the foundations for civilization. Eugene, 1952.

AH 4889.35 — Brake, J. Wirtschaften und Charakter in der antiken Bildung. Frankfurt, 1935.

AH 7058.39.2 — Brambach, G. De consulatus romani mutata. Bonnae, 1864.

AH 7509.63 — Brancati, Antonio. Augusto e la querra di Spagna. Urbino, 1963.

AH 7449.29.12 — Branchini, A. La battaglia del Metauro. Pesaro, 1934.

AH 7449.29.10 — Branchini, A. Studio critico-polemico su la precisazione storica della battaglia del Metauro. Fano, 1929.

AH 7239.68 — Brand, Clarence E. Roman military law. Austin, 1968.

AH 4808.57 — Brandis, J. De temporum graecorum antiquissimorum rationibus. Bonnae, 1857.

AH 3109.3 — Brandis, J. Rerum Assyriarum tempora emendata. Bonn, 1853.

AH 3004.3 — Brandis, J. Über den historischen Gewinn...assyrischen Inschriften. Berlin, 1856.

AH 879.69 — Brandon, Samuel George Frederick. Religion in ancient history: studies in ideas, men and events. N.Y., 1969.

AH 5157.10 — Brandstäter, F.A. Die Geschichten des aetolischen Landes. Berlin, 1844.

AH 5463.20 — Branigan, Keith. The foundations of palatial Crete: a survey of Crete in the early Bronze Age. London, 1970.

AH 4909.27 — Brashinskii, I.P. Afiny i Severnoe Prichernomor'e v VI-II vv. do n.e. Moskva, 1963.

AH 7159.37 — Brasiello, U. La repressione penale in diritto romano. Napoli, 1937.

AH 7139.02 — Brassloff, S. Kenntniss des Volksrechtes. Weimar, 1902.

AH 7489.33.5 — Brassloff, Stephen. Staat und Gesellschaft in der Römischen Kaiserzeit. Wien, 1933.

Htn AH 7486.36* — Brathuaite, R. The lives of all the Roman emperors. London, 1636.

Eg 609.61.5 — Bratton, Fred. The first heretic...Ikhnaton the king. Boston, 1961.

AH 8548.10 — Braudes, C. Das ethnographische Verhältniss der Kelten und Germanen. Leipzig, 1857.

AH 7709.67.5 — Brauer, George C. The young emperors, Rome, A.D. 193-244. N.Y., 1967.

AH 4519.33 — Brauer, H. Die Kriegschuldfrage in der geschichtlichen Überlieferung des peloponnesischen Krieges. Inaug. Diss. Emsdetten, 1933.

AH 9666.2 — Braun, F. Die Entwicklung der spanischen Provinzialgrenzen. Berlin, 1909.

AH 9653.2 — Braun, F. Provinzialeinteilung Spaniens in römischer Zeit. Berlin, 1908.

AH 9777.35 — Braun, F.A. Toty i ikh' sosedidov. Sankt Peterburg, 1899.

Eg 909.64 — Braunert, Horst. Die Binnenwanderung. Bonn, 1964.

AH 4848.7 — Braungarten, F. Untersuchung und der Tracht die Athener am Grundlage. n.p., 1876.

AH 4859.23 — Braunstein, O. Die politische Wirksamkeit der griechischen Frau. Leipzig, 1911.

AH 7238.94.2 — Bray, Joseph. Essai sur le droit penal militaire. Paris, 1894.

AH 9609.5.7 — Brea, L.B. Sicily before the Greeks. London, 1957.

AH 9609.5.5 — Brea, L.B. Sicily before the Greeks. N.Y., 1957.

AH 279.16A — Breasted, James H. Ancient times, a history of the early world. Boston, 1916.

AH 279.16.15 — Breasted, James H. Ancient times. 2. ed. Boston, 1935.

AH 279.15 — Breasted, James H. A short ancient history. Boston, 1915.

Eg 279.05.10 — Breasted, James Henry. Ancient records of Egypt. Chicago, 1906-07. 2v.

Eg 29.06.1 — Breasted, James Henry. Ancient records of Egypt. N.Y., 1962. 5v.

Eg 879.33A — Breasted, James Henry. The dawn of conscience. N.Y., 1933.

Eg 879.33.5A — Breasted, James Henry. The dawn of conscience. N.Y., 1934.

Eg 879.33.6 — Breasted, James Henry. The dawn of conscience. N.Y., 1935.

Eg 879.12.2 — Breasted, James Henry. Development of religion and thought in ancient Egypt. N.Y., 1912.

Eg 879.12 — Breasted, James Henry. Development of religion and thought in ancient Egypt. N.Y., 1912.

Eg 1159.31F — Breasted, James Henry. The Edwin Smith surgical papyrus. Chicago, 1931. 2v.

Eg 279.05.15 — Breasted, James Henry. Geschichte Ägyptens. Zürich, 1936.

Eg 279.05A — Breasted, James Henry. A history of Egypt. N.Y., 1905.

Eg 279.05.5 — Breasted, James Henry. A history of Egypt. N.Y., 1909.

Eg 279.05.9 — Breasted, James Henry. A history of Egypt. 2. ed. N.Y., 1912.

Eg 279.05.8 — Breasted, James Henry. A history of Egypt from the earliest times to the Persian conquest. 2. ed. London, 1950.

Eg 279.08.2 — Breasted, James Henry. A history of the ancient Egyptians. London, 1908.

Eg 279.08A — Breasted, James Henry. A history of the ancient Egyptians. N.Y., 1908.

Eg 989.10F — Breccia, E. With King Fuad to the oasis of Ammon [Siwa]. Milano, 1929.

AH 4609.03 — Breccia, Evaristo. Il diritto dinastico nelle monarchie dei successori d'Alexxandro Magno. Roma, 1903.

Eg 759.37.3 — Breccia, Evaristo. Egitto greco e romano. 3. ed. Pisa, 1957.

AH 7116.4 — Breda, O. Die Centurienverfassung des Servius Tullius. Bromberg, 1848. 2 pam.

AH 298.00 — Bredow, G.G. Untersuchungen...alten Geschichte. pt.1-2. Altona, 1800-02.

AH 3075.9 — Breiteneicher, M. Ninive und Nahum. München, 1861.

AH 4559.41 — Brelaer, B. Alexanders Bund mit Paros. Leipzig, 1941.

AH 4278.96.7 — Brelet, H. Historiae Graecae. Paris, 1896.

AH 4239.61 — Brelich, A. Guerra. Bonn, 1961.

AH 7201.75 — Bremer, F.P. Iurisprudentiae Antehadrianae. v.1-2, pt.1-2. Lipsiae, 1896. 3v.

AH 7842.6 — Bremer, F.P. Die Rechtslehrer und Rechtsschulen. Berlin, 1868.

Author and Title Listing

AH 7509.31   Brendel, Otto. Ikonographie des Kaisers Augustus. Inaug. Diss. Nürnberg, 1931.

AH 4854.7   Brendel, Otto. Die Schafzucht im alten Griechenland. Diss. Würzburg, 1934.

AH 7203.23   Brenkmann, H. Historia Pandectarum. Trajecta ad Rhenum, 1722.

AH 889.29   Brentano, Lujo. Das Wirtschaftsleben der antiken Welt. Jena, 1929.

AH 9647.5   Bres, Onorato. Malta antica illustrata cò monumenti, e coll'istoria. Roma, 1816.

AH 8207.8   La Bretagne romaine. (Sagot, François.) Paris, 1911.

AH 7201.109   Bretone, Mario. Linee dell'Enchiridion di Pomponio. Bari, 1965.

AH 7479.45.18   Breuil, Roger. Brutus. 7. éd. Paris, 1945.

AH 7058.39   Breuk, H.R. de. Dissertatio historica...de quaestione. Lugduni-Batavorum, 1839.

Htn   AH 7203.4.7.5*   Breves commentarii, in praecipuas Justiniani imp. Novellas. (Baudoin, François.) Ludguni, 1548.

AH 7139.03.5   Breviarium Alaricianum. (Conrat, M.) Leipzig, 1903.

AH 7449.14.5   Brewitz, Walther. Scipio Africanus maior in Spanien. Inaug. Diss. Tübingen, 1914.

AH 7909.17.1   Brewster, Ethel Hampson. Roman craftsmen and tradesmen of the early empire. N.Y., 1972.

AH 7448.74.2   Breyton, A. La bataille de Cannes. Paris, 1884.

AH 4939.57   Briand de Crèvecaeur, Emmanuél. Havets pionerer. København, 1957.

AH 7238.66   Briau, René. Du service de santé militaire chez les romains. Paris, 1866.

Eg 279.48.7   Brief history of ancient Egypt. 2. ed. (Iskander, Z.) Cairo, 1949.

NEDL   AH 278.81.5   A brief history of ancient peoples. (Steele, J.D.) N.Y., 1881.

AH 4298.83   Brief history of Greece. (Steele, J.D.) N.Y., 1883.

AH 4298.83.2   Brief history of Greece. (Steele, J.D.) N.Y., 1883.

NEDL   AH 7278.85.4   Brief history of Rome. (Steele, J.D.) N.Y., n.d.

Htn   AH 3980.2*   A briefe description of Hierusalem and of the suburbs thereof. (Aldrichem, C. von.) London, 1595.

AH 3155.16   Briem, Efraim. Babyloniska myter och sagor med kulturhistorisk inledning. Stockholm, 1927.

AH 4841.6   Brillant, M. Les secretaires atheniens. Paris, 1911.

AH 7139.68.5   Brink, Herman van den. Ex iure quiritium. Deventer, 1968.

AH 2757.9   Brinkgreve, I.G. De regno Pergameno deque eius dynastis. Rhenum, 1893.

AH 3075.14   Brinkman, J.A. A political history of post-Kassite Babylonia, 1158-722 B.C. Roma, 1968.

Eg 279.54   Brion, M. Histoire de l'Egypte. Paris, 1954.

AH 7469.52   Brion, M. La révolte des gladiateurs. Paris, 1952.

AH 7799.30   Brion, Marcel. La vie d'Alaric. 7. éd. Paris, 1930.

AH 7799.28   Brion, Marcel. La vie d'Attila. 2. éd. Paris, 1928.

AH 7179.27.5   Brissaud, J. Le régime de la terre dans la société étatiste du Bas-Empire. Thèse. Paris, 1927.

AH 7168.79.15   Brissaud, J.B. La notion de cause...obligations conventionnelles en droit romain et...français. Thèse. Bordeaux, 1879.

AH 7135.59.10F   Brisson, B. B. Brissonii...De verborum quae ad ivs civile pertinent significatione. Halae Magdeburgicae, 1743.

AH 3657.18   Brisson, B. De regio Persarum. Argentoratum, 1710.

Htn   AH 3657.18.5*   Brisson, B. De regio Persarum. Heidelberg, 1595.

AH 7135.59.7F   Brisson, B. De verborum quae ad jus pertinent significatione. Lipsiae, 1721.

AH 7137.21.2F   Brisson, B. Formulis et solennibul populi romani verbis. Halae, 1731.

Htn   AH 7137.49F*   Brisson, B. Opera minora. Lugdunum, 1749.

AH 8007.23   Brisson, Jean Paul. Autoñomisme et christianisme dans l'Afrique romaine de Septime Sévère à l'invasion vandale. Paris, 1958.

AH 7844.7   Brissonius, B. Commentarius de spectaculis. Lugdini Batavorum, 1742.

AH 8208.15   Britain and Rome; essays presented to Eric Birley on his sixteenth birthday. (Jarrett, Michael G.) Kendal, 1966.

AH 8213.10   Britain in the Roman empire. (Liversidge, Joan.) London, 1968.

AH 8207.34   Britain under the Romans. (Priestley, Harold E.) London, 1967.

AH 8207.21   Britain under the Romans. (Winbolt, Samuel E.) Harmondsworth, 1945.

AH 8207.35   Britannia; a history of Roman Britain. (Frere, Sheppard.) Cambridge, 1967.

AH 8207.30   Britannia, the Roman conquest. 1. ed. (Welch, G.P.) Middletown, 1963.

AHP 12.12   Britannica. London. 1,1970+ 3v.

AH 7467.21   Britannicus. Conspirators. London, 1721.

AH 3013.9   British Museum. Assyrian antiquities - guide to Koujunjik Gallery. London, 1883.

AH 3423.1F   British Museum. Carchemish: report on excavations at Djerabis. London, 1914. 3v.

AH 3000.3   British Museum. Catalog of cuneiform tablets in the Kouyunjik collection. London, 1889-99. 5v.

AH 3000.3.2   British Museum. Catalog of cuneiform tablets in the Kouyunjik collection. Supplement. London, 1914.

AH 3000.3.3   British Museum. Catalog of cuneiform tablets in the Kouyunjik collection. 2d supplement. London, 1968.

AH 3013.9.5A   British Museum. Guide to the Babylonian and Assyrian antiquities. London, 1900.

AH 3013.9.6   British Museum. Guide to the Babylonian and Assyrian antiquities. 2. ed. London, 1908.

AH 3074.5F   British Museum. Photograph of Assyrian tablet. London, n.d.

Eg 603.5A   British Museum. Tell el-Amarna tablets. London, 1892.

AH 3002.94   British Museum. Department of Egyptian and Assyrian Antiquities. Annals of the kings of Assyria. London, 1902-

AH 3191.7F   British Museum. Department of Egyptian and Assyrian Antiquities. Assyrian medical texts. London, 1923.

AH 3016.9F   British Museum. Department of Egyptian and Assyrian Antiquities. Assyrian sculptures in British Museum. London, 1914.

Eg 1039.20   British Museum. Department of Egyptian and Assyrian Antiquities. The book of the dead. London, 1920.

Eg 1300.11F   British Museum. Department of Egyptian and Assyrian Antiquities. Catalogue of demotic papyri in the British Museum. v.1-2. London, 1939-

Eg 1300.10   British Museum. Department of Egyptian and Assyrian Antiquities. Catalogue of Egyptian religious papyri in the British Museum. London, 1938.

AH 3002.26.10   British Museum. Department of Egyptian and Assyrian Antiquities. Chronicles of Chaldaean kings. London, 1956.

AH 3002.26.5F   British Museum. Department of Egyptian and Assyrian Antiquities. Cuneiform texts from Cappadocian tablets. London. 1-4,1921-1927 3v.

AH 3002.25.5F   British Museum. Department of Egyptian and Assyrian Antiquities. Cuneiform texts from Babylonian tablets. London. 13,1901+ 25v.

AH 3002.25F   British Museum. Department of Egyptian and Assyrian Antiquities. Cuneiform texts from Babylonian tablets. London. 1,1896+ 35v.

AH 3002.25.6F   British Museum. Department of Egyptian and Assyrian Antiquities. Cuneiform texts from Babylonian tablets. Index to registration numbers of texts, pt.1-25. n.p., n.d.

EgP 22.3PF   British Museum. Department of Egyptian Antiquities. Hieratic papyri in the British Museum. London. 1,1935+ 7v.

AH 3002.26F   British Museum. Department of Egytpian and Assyrian Antiquities. Hittite texts in the cuneiform character. London, 1920.

Eg 1069.58   British Museum. Department of Manuscripts. Mss. (Papyrus 10569). An ancient Egyptian book of hours. Oxford, 1958.

AH 3000.3.5   British Museum. Department of Western Asiatic Antiquities. A bibliography of the cuneiform tablets of the Kuyunjik collection. London, 1964.

AH 4333.5   Broadbent, Molly. Studies in Greek genealogy. Leiden, 1968.

AH 7138.67   Brocher, H. Del'enseignment du droit romain. Lausanne, 1867. 7 pam.

AH 7899.69   Brockmeyer, Norbert. Arbeitsorganisation und ökonomisches Denken in der Gutswirtschaft des römischen Reiches. Inaug. Diss. Bachum? 1969?

AH 4819.31.5   Brodeur, A.G. The pageant of civilization. Garden City, 1934?

AH 4819.31.6   Brodeur, A.G. The pageant of civilization. N.Y., 1931.

Eg 299.37.10   Brodrick, M. Egypt, papers and lectures. London, 1937.

AH 819.66.10   Brodskii, Boris I. Romanticheskie veduty. Moskva, 1966.

AH 7038.58   Bröcker, L. Altrömische Verfassungsgeschichte. Hamburg, 1858.

AH 7038.42.3   Bröcker, L.O. Vorarbeiten zur römische Geschichte. Tübingen, 1842.

AH 8507.10.2A   Brogan, O. Roman Gaul. Cambridge, Mass., 1953.

AH 8507.10   Brogan, O. Roman Gaul. London, 1953.

AH 7205.13   Brokate, Henricus. De Theophilinae quae fertur Iustiniani Institutionum Graecae paraphraseos compositione. Argentorati, 1886.

AH 7203.127   Bronchorst, E. In tit. digestorum de...regulis juris antiqui. Parisiis, 1672.

AH 3088.4PF   Bronze ornaments of the Gates of Balawat. (Birch, S.) London, 1880.

AH 3088.5F   Bronze reliefs from the Gates of Shalmaneser. (King, L.W.) London, 1915.

Eg 879.62F   Brooklyn Institute of Arts and Sciences. Museum. Mss. (Papyrus 47.218.3). A Saite oracle papyrus from Thebes. Providence, R.I., 1962.

AH 3155.15   Brooks, Beatrice A. A contribution to the study of moral practices of certain social groups in ancient Mesopotamia. Diss. Leipzig, 1921.

AH 850.12.5   Brothwell, Don R. Food in antiquity. N.Y., 1969.

AH 850.12   Brothwell, Don R. Food in antiquity: a survey of the diet of early peoples. London, 1969.

AH 8007.15   Broughton, T.R.S. The romanization of Africa Proconsularis. Baltimore, 1929.

AH 8007.15.5   Broughton, T.R.S. The romanization of Africa Proconsularis. Diss. Baltimore, 1929.

AH 7339.51   Broughton, Thomas R.S. The magistrates of the Roman Republic. N.Y., 1951-52. 2v.

AH 7339.51.1   Broughton, Thomas R.S. The magistrates of the Roman Republic. Supplement. N.Y., 1960.

AH 7845.9   Brouwer, P.C. De Romanorum indole e litteris cognascenda. n.p., 1911.

AH 3004.7   Brown, F. Assyriology - its use and abuse in Old Testament study. N.Y., 1885.

AH 3902.5   Brown, John Pairman. The Lebanon and Phoenicia; ancient texts illustrating their physical geography and native industries. Beirut, 1969.

AH 939.28.5   Browne, Lewis. The graphic Bible, from Genesis to Revelation in animated maps and charts. N.Y., 1941.

AH 939.28.10   Browne, Lewis. The graphic Bible. N.Y., 1942.

AH 4819.66.15   Browning, Robert. Greece - ancient and medieval: an inaugural lecture delivered at Birkbeck College, 15th June, 1966. London, 1966.

AH 162.5   Bruck, E.F. Die Schenkung auf den Todesfall. Breslau, 1909.

AH 7139.54   Bruck, E.F. Über römisches Recht im Rahmen der Kulturgeschichte. Berlin, 1954.

AH 4159.09   Bruck, E.F. Zur Geschichte der Verfügungen von Todeswegen. Breslau, 1909.

AH 4328.84   Bruck, Sylvius. De Pelasgis. Vratislaviae, 1884.

AH 4538.81   Brückler, C.A. De chronologia Belli...Corinthiaci. Halis Saxonum, 1881.

AH 6110.9   Brückner, K.A.F. König Philipp. Göttingen, 1837.

Eg 818.91   Brugsch, H. Die Ägyptologie. Leipzig, 1891.

Eg 278.59.9   Brugsch, H. Egypt under the pharaohs. London, 1891.

Eg 938.57   Brugsch, H. Geographische Inschriften. v.1-3. Leipzig, 1857. 2v.

Eg 278.59.4   Brugsch, H. Geschichte Aegypten's. Leipzig, 1877.

Eg 278.59   Brugsch, H. Histoire d'Egypte. Leipzig, 1859.

Eg 278.59.6   Brugsch, H. A history of Egypt. London, 1879. 2v.

Eg 1158.63   Brugsch, H. Notice raisonnée d'un traité médical datant du XIVme siècle. Leipzig, 1863.

Eg 878.85   Brugsch, H. Religion und Mythologie der alten Ägypter. Leipzig, 1885. 2v.

Eg 878.85.3   Brugsch, H. Religion und Mythologie der alten Ägypter. Leipzig, 1891.

NEDL   Eg 278.59.10   Brugsch, H. The true story of the exodus of Israel. Boston, 1880.

Eg 1098.81   Brugsch, H.K. Die neue Weltordnung nach Vernichtung. Berlin, 1881.

Eg 558.75   Brugsch-Bey, H. L'éxode et les monuments égyptiens. Leipzig, 1875.

AH 4833.7   Brugsma, A.L. Gymasiorum apud Graecos descriptionem. Groningae, 1855.

AH 7469.33   Brun-Laloire, Louis. La vie tragique des Gracques. Paris, 1933.

Eg 299.39   Brundage, B.C. Notes on some blocks from the excavation of Medinet Habu. Diss. Chicago, 1939.

NEDL   AH 3008.85   Brunengo, G. L'impero di Babilonia e di Ninive. v.1-2. Prato, 1885.

Author and Title Listing

AH 7828.90F   Brunet, P. Mémoires d'un romain vie. Tours, 1890.

AH 9607.7   Brunet de Presle, W. Recherches sur les établissements des grecs. Paris, 1845.

AH 8908.3   Brunet y Bellet, J. Els gregs, els etruscos. Barcelona, 1895.

AH 7158.87   Brunnenmeister, E. Das Tödtungsverbrechen im alten Rechts. Leipzig, 1887.

AH 9790.5.10   Die Brunnenschlacht. (Schneeberger, H.) Bad Kissingen, 1931.

Eg 848.5   Brunner, Hellmut. Altägyptische Erziehung. Wiesbaden, 1957.

Eg 879.64.5   Brunner, Hellmut. Die Geburt des Gottkonigs. Wiesbaden, 1964.

Eg 1009.66   Brunner, Hellmut. Grundzüge einer Geschichte der altägyptischen Literatur. Darmstadt, 1966.

Eg 1099.44F   Brunner, Hellmut. Die Lehre des Cheti. Glückstadt, 1944.

Eg 502.5   Brunner, Hellmut. Die Texte aus den Gräbern der Herakleopolitenzeit von Suit. Glückstadt, 1937.

Eg 849.5F   Brunner-Traut, E. Der Tanz im alten Ägypten nach bildlichen und inschriftlichen Zeugnissen. N.Y., 1938.

Eg 1109.59.2   Brunner-Traut, Emma. Altägyptische Tiergeschichte und Fabel. 2. Aufl. Darmstadt, 1968.

AH 7203.140.5F   Brunnermann, J. Commentoris in Pandectas. Wittenburgae, 1701.

AH 7201.47.12   Bruns, C.G. Fontes Juris Romani Antiqui. Index. Tubingae, 1912.

AH 7201.47.12F   Bruns, C.G. Fontes Juris Romani Antiqui. v.2. Plates. Tubingae, 1912.

AH 7201.47.2   Bruns, C.G. Fontes Juris Romani Antiqui. 2. ed. Tubingae, 1871.

AH 7201.47.3   Bruns, C.G. Fontes Juris Romani Antiqui. 3. ed. Tubingae, 1876.

AH 7201.47.4   Bruns, C.G. Fontes Juris Romani Antiqui. 4. ed. Friburg, 1879.

AH 7201.47.5   Bruns, C.G. Fontes Juris Romani Antiqui. 5. ed. Friburg, 1871.

AH 7201.47.6   Bruns, C.G. Fontes Juris Romani Antiqui. 6. ed. Friburg, 1893.

AH 7201.47.7   Bruns, C.G. Fontes Juris Romani Antiqui. 7. ed. Tubingae, 1909.

AH 7138.76.13   Bruns, C.G. Unterschriften in römischen Rechts-Urkunden. Berlin, 1876.

AH 4859.13   Bruns, Ivo. Frauenemancipation in Athen. Kiliae, 1900.

AH 8615.15   Brunt, Peter A. Italian manpower, 225 B.C.-A.D. 14. Oxford, 1971.

AH 7114.46   Brunt, Peter Astbury. Social conflicts in the Roman Republic. London, 1971.

AH 3017.19   Brussels. Musée des Arts Décoratifs et Industriels. Catalogue des intailles et empreintes orientales des Musées royaux du cinquantenaire. Bruxelles, 1917.

AH 3002.87   Brussels. Musées Royaux du Cinquantenaire. Recueil des inscriptions de l'Asie des Musées Royaux du Cinquantenaire à Bruxelles. Bruxelles, 1925.

AH 3001.5   Bruston, Charles. Le dechiffrement des inscriptions cuneiform. Paris, 1873. 13 pam.

AH 7479.45.10   Bruto. (Delogu, Giuseppe.) Lugano, 1945.

AH 7479.55.5   Bruto e i neo-atticisti. (Portalupi, Felicita.) Torino, 1955.

AH 7479.45.18   Brutus. 7. éd. (Breuil, Roger.) Paris, 1945.

AH 7479.38.10   Brutus et la fin de la république. (Walter, Gérard,) Paris, 1938.

AH 4279.47   Bruwaene, M. Le miracle grec. Bruxelles, 1947.

AH 7819.55   Bruwaene, M. van den. La société romaine. Bruxelles, 1955.

AH 7158.89   Bruyant, E. Juridictions criminelles à Rome. Paris, 1889.

AH 4817.34   Bruyn, C. Compendium Antiquitatum Graecum. Francofurti, 1734.

AH 7138.91.15   Bry, Georges. Principes de droit romain. 6. éd. v.1-2. Paris, 1927-30.

AH 4860.7   Bryant, A.A. Boyhood and youth in days of Aristophanes. n.p., 1907.

AH 4860.8   Bryant, A.A. Boyhood and youth in days of Aristophanes. n.p., 1907.

AH 7638.95   Bryant, E.E. Reign of Antoninus Pius. Cambridge, 1895.

AH 297.67   Bryant, J. Observations and inquiries relating to ancient history. Cambridge, 1767.

AH 7138.71.11   Bryer, J. The academical study of the civil law. London, 1871.

Eg 850.1   Brygseh, H. Drei Fest-Kalender. Leipzig, 1877.

AH 7529.30.5   Bubi Caligula. 2. Aufl. (Sachs, Hanns.) Wien, 1932.

AH 3027.10   Buccellati, Biorgio. The Amorites of the Ur III period. Naples, 1966.

AH 3909.10   Buccellati, Giorgio. Cities and nations of ancient Syria. Roma, 1967.

AH 842.46   Das Buch bei den Griechen. 3. Aufl. (Schubart, Wilhelm.) Heidelberg, 1960.

AH 842.46.5   Das Buch bei den Griechen und Römern. (Schubart, Wilhelm.) Berlin, 1907.

AH 7509.37.5A   Buchan, J. Augustus. Boston, 1937.

AH 7509.37.7   Buchan, J. Augustus. London, 1937.

AH 4103.2   Buchanan, James. Theorika. N.Y., 1962.

AH 7168.15.2   Bucher, K. Das Recht der Forderungen. 2e Aufl. Leipzig, 1830.

AH 842.47.5   Buchhandel und Verlagswesen in der Antike. (Kleberg, Tönnes.) Darmstadt, 1967.

AH 848.11   Buchholtz, F. De aulaeorum velorum que usu. Gottingae, 1876.

AH 3653.5   Buchholz, A. Quaestiones de Persarum satrapis satrapiiseque. Lipsiae, 1894.

AH 7448.72.10   Buchholz. Die Quellen des Appian und Dio Cassius für die Geschichte des zweiten punischen Krieges. Pyritz, 1872.

AH 3132.6   Buchwald, R. Nebuchodnosor II von Babylon. n.p., 1898.

Eg 1042.935.10F   Buck, Adriaan de. The Egyptian coffin texts. Chicago, 1935. 7v.

AH 9471.3   Buckhardt-Biedermann, T. Die Kolonie Augusta Raurica. Basel, 1910.

AH 3013.26   Buckingham, J.S. The buried city of the East-Nineveh. London, 1851?

AH 3667.7   Buckingham, J.S. Travels in Assyria, Media and Persia. London, 1829.

AH 7169.21.2   Buckland, W.W. A text-book of Roman law from Augustus to Justinian. 2. ed. Cambridge, Eng., 1932.

AH 7189.08   Buckland, William Warwick. The Roman law of slavery. Cambridge, Eng., 1908.

AH 7189.08.1   Buckland, William Warwick. The Roman law of slavery. Cambridge, Eng., 1970.

AH 7168.95   Buckler, W.H. Contract in Roman law. London, 1895.

AH 4858.9   Buddenhagen, F. Peri gamou. pt.1. Turici, 1919.

Htn   AH 7203.125*   Budé, G. Annotationes in quatuor et viginti Pandectarum libros. Pt.1. Basiliae, 1534.

Htn   AH 7105.22.5*   Budé, G. Extrait ou abregé du Livre de assé de feu mons. Lyon, 1554.

Htn   AH 7135.48*   Budé, G. Forensia. Lutetiae, 1548. 2 pam.

Htn   AH 7105.22.3*   Budé, G. Libri V de asse et partibus eius. Venetiis, 1522.

Htn   AH 7105.22*   Budé, G. Libri V de asse et partibus eius. Venice, 1522.

AH 3096.4   Budge, E.A. The history of Esarhaddon...681-668. London, 1880.

AH 3005.8   Budge, E.A.T.N. The rise and progress of Assyriology. London, 1925.

AH 3008.84   Budge, E.A.W. Babylonian life and history. London, 1884. 2v.

AH 3008.84.5   Budge, E.A.W. Babylonian life and history. 2. ed. London, 1925.

Eg 809.08   Budge, Ernest Alfred Wallis. The book of the kings of Egypt. London, 1908. 2v.

Eg 879.09   Budge, Ernest Alfred Wallis. The book of the opening of the mouth. London, 1909. 2v.

Eg 709.04   Budge, Ernest Alfred Wallis. The decrees of Memphis and Canopus. London, 1904. 3v.

X Cg   Eg 278.85.3   Budge, Ernest Alfred Wallis. The dwellers on the Nile. London, 1885.

Eg 278.85.3.5   Budge, Ernest Alfred Wallis. The dwellers on the Nile. London, 1926.

Eg 279.25   Budge, Ernest Alfred Wallis. Egypt. London, 1925.

Eg 879.06   Budge, Ernest Alfred Wallis. The Egyptian heaven and hell. London, 1906. 3v.

Eg 879.00   Budge, Ernest Alfred Wallis. Egyptian ideas of the future life. 2. ed. London, 1900.

Eg 885.899.4   Budge, Ernest Alfred Wallis. Egyptian magic. Evanston, 1958.

Eg 885.899.2   Budge, Ernest Alfred Wallis. Egyptian magic. London, 1901.

Eg 885.899.6   Budge, Ernest Alfred Wallis. Egyptian magic. N.Y., 1971.

Eg 1109.31   Budge, Ernest Alfred Wallis. Egyptian tales and romances, pagan, Christian and Muslim. London, 1931.

Eg 879.34   Budge, Ernest Alfred Wallis. From fetish to God in ancient Egypt. London, 1934.

Eg 879.04   Budge, Ernest Alfred Wallis. The gods of the Egyptians. Chicago, 1904.

Eg 879.04.2   Budge, Ernest Alfred Wallis. The gods of the Egyptians. London, 1904. 2v.

Eg 879.04.2.2   Budge, Ernest Alfred Wallis. The gods of the Egyptians. N.Y., 1969. 2v.

X Cg   Eg 879.04   Budge, Ernest Alfred Wallis. The gods of the Egyptians. v.2. Chicago, 1904.

Eg 1039.10.5   Budge, Ernest Alfred Wallis. A hieroglyphic vocabulary to the Theban recension of the book of the dead. London, 1911.

Eg 279.02   Budge, Ernest Alfred Wallis. A history of Egypt. London, 1902. 8v.

Eg 1029.14   Budge, Ernest Alfred Wallis. The literature of the ancient Egyptians. London, 1914.

Eg 879.09.5   Budge, Ernest Alfred Wallis. The liturgy of funerary offerings. London, 1909.

Eg 879.11   Budge, Ernest Alfred Wallis. Osiris and the Egyptian resurrection. London, 1911. 2v.

Eg 279.14   Budge, Ernest Alfred Wallis. A short history of the Egyptian people. London, 1914.

Eg 609.23   Budge, Ernest Alfred Wallis. Tutankhamen, Amenism, Atenism and Egyptian monotheism. London, 1923.

AH 7298.81.1   Budinszky, Alexander. Die Ausbreitung der lateinischen Sprache über Italien und die Provinzen des römischen Reiches. Berlin. Wiesbaden, 1973.

AH 5309.5   Büchenschütz, A.B. Könige von Athen. Berlin, 1855.

AH 7888.84   Bücher, Karl. Die Aüfstande der unfreien Arbeiter. Frankfurt, 1874.

AH 408.91   Büchner, L. Das goldene Zeitalter. Berlin, 1891.

AH 7888.86   Büchsenschütz, A.B. Bemerkungen über die römische Volkswirtschaft. Berlin, 1886.

AH 4888.69   Büchsenschütz, B. Besitz und Erwerb. Halle, 1869.

AH 7488.68   Büdinger, M. Untersuchungen zur Römischen Kaesergeschichte. Leipzig, 1868. 3v.

AH 8.95   Büdinger, Max. Die Universalhistorie. Wien, 1895.

AH 3659.3   Büdinger. Die neuentdckten Inscription über Cyrus. Wien, 1881.

AH 7809.08   Bülz, Martin. Dem Jahresberichte geht eine wissenschaftliche Abhandlung des Oberlehrers. Zittau, 1908.

AH 7468.79.5   Bürcklein, A. Quellen und Chronologie der römisch-parthischen Feldzüge in den Jahren 713-718. Inaug. Diss. Berlin, 1879.

AH 7478.61   Bürgerkrieg zwischen Cäsar und Pompejus. (Göler, F.A.) Heidelberg, 1861.

AH 7888.98   Die Buerkundung des Civilstandes. (Levison, W.) Bonn, 1898.

AH 4114.9   Buermann, H. De titulis atticis. Lipsiae, 1879.

AH 5303.7   Büttner, H. Polische Hetärieen in Athen. Leipzig, 1840.

AH 7298.76   Büttner-Wobst, Theodor. De legationibus reipublicae liberae temporibus Romam missis. Diss. Lipsiae, 1876.

AH 7198.66   Bufnoir, C. Théorie de la condition...en droit romain. Paris, 1866.

AH 7799.09   Bugiani, Carlo. L'Imperatore Avito. Pistoia, 1909.

AH 7799.05   Bugiani, Carlo. Storia di Ezio generale dell'Impero Sotto Valentiniano III. Firenze, 1905.

AH 7201.67   Buhl, H. Salvius Julianus. Heidelberg, 1886.

AH 7178.78   Buhl, Heinrich. Die agrarische Frage. Heidelberg, 1878.

AH 3129.3   Building inscriptions of the Neo-Babylonian Empire: Nabopolassar and Nebuchadnezzar. (Langdon, S.) Paris, 1905.

AH 8907.22   Bulanda, E. Etrurja i Etruskowie. Lwów, 1934.

AH 7749.18   Bulić, F. Car Dijoklecijan. Zagreb, 1918.

AH 7002.5   Bulletin analytique d'histoire romaine. Strasbourg. 1,1962+ 4v.

Eg 879.05.10   Bulletin critique des religions de l'Égypte. v.1-5. (Capart, Jean.) Leiden, 1905-39.

AH 7138.89.3   Bulletino dell'Istituto di diritto romano. Roma. 1,1889+ 41v.

AH 8525.2   Bulliot, J.G. Essai sur le système défensif...pays Éduen. Paris, 1856.

AH 889.39A   Bullock, C.J. Politics, finance, and consequences. Cambridge, 1939.

AH 4299.36   Bullock, Charles J. The new deal in ancient Greece. Cambridge, 1936.

AH 5307.9   Bulwer, E. Athens. Its rise and fall. London, 18- . 2v.

Author and Title Listing

AH 5307.14.2 — Bulwer, E. Athens. Its rise and fall. N.Y., 1837. 2v.

AH 5307.13 — Bulwer, E. Athens. Its rise and fall. Paris, 1837.

AH 5307.14.6 — Bulwer, E. Athens. Its rise and fall. v.1-2. Leipzig, 1843.

AH 938.79 — Bunbury, E.H. A history of ancient geography. London, 1879. 2v.

AH 938.79.10 — Bunbury, E.H. A history of ancient geography among the Greeks and Romans. 2. ed. N.Y., 1959. 2v.

AH 4112.5 — Bund der Amphiktyonen. (Tittman, F.W.) Berlin, 1812.

AH 4498.90.5 — Bundesrat, Bundessteuer und Kriegsdienst der delischen Bündner. (Nöthe, Heinrich.) Magdeburg, 1890.

AH 4559.37 — Bungard, R. L'expedition d'Alexandre et la conquête de l'Asie. Paris, 1937.

AH 4162.5 — Bunsen, C.C. De iure hereditario Atheniensium. Gottingae, 1813.

Eg 278.45 — Bunsen, C.C.J. Aegyptens Stelle. v.1-5. Hamburg, 1845. 3v.

Eg 278.48 — Bunsen, C.C.J. Egypt's place in universal history. London, 1848. 5v.

Eg 278.48.5 — Bunsen, C.C.J. Egypt's place in universal history. v.1,5. London, 1867. 2v.

AH 8907.16 — Buonamici, G. L'Etruria e gli Etruschi. Firenze, 1926.

AH 7759.27 — Burch, Vacher. Myth and Constantine the Great. London, 1927.

AH 7114.6 — Burchardi, G.C. Bemerkungen über den Census. Kiel, 1824.

AH 7138.41.5 — Burchardi, G.C. Lehrbuch des römischen Rechts. v.1-2, pt.1-3. Stuttgart, 1841. 3v.

AH 7158.38 — Burckhardt, Adolf. Die Kriminalgerichtbarkeit. Basel, 1838.

AH 4818.98.5A — Burckhardt, J. Griechische Kulturgeschichte. Stuttgart, 1930-31. 4v.

AH 4818.98.10 — Burckhardt, J. Griechische Kulturgeschichte. Stuttgart, 1952. 3v.

AH 4818.98.3 — Burckhardt, J. Griechische Kulturgeschichte. 3. Aufl. Berlin, 1898. 4v.

AH 4818.98.20 — Burckhardt, J. History of Greek culture. N.Y., 1963.

AH 4818.98.5.15 — Burckhardt, J. Kulturgeschichte Griechenlands. Berlin, 1934.

AH 7759.49 — Burckhardt, Jacob. The age of Constantine the Great. N.Y., 1949.

Htn   AH 7758.53.2* — Burckhardt, Jacob. Die Zeit Constantins des Grossen. Basel, 1853.

AH 7759.50 — Burckhardt, Jacob. Die Zeit Constantins des Grossen. Bern, 1950.

AH 7758.53 — Burckhardt, Jacob. Die Zeit Constantins des Grossen. Leipzig, 1853.

AH 7758.80 — Burckhardt, Jacob. Die Zeit Constantins des Grossen. Leipzig, 1880.

AH 7758.98 — Burckhardt, Jacob. Die Zeit Constantins des Grossen. Leipzig, 1898.

AH 7759.24.3 — Burckhardt, Jacob. Die Zeit Constantins des Grossen. Stuttgart, 1929.

AH 7759.24 — Burckhardt, Jacob. DieZeit Konstantins des Grossen. 4e Aufl. Leipzig, 1924.

AH 7168.89 — Burckhardt, Karl. Zur Geschichte der Socatio Conductio. Basel, 1889.

AH 7489.64 — Burdeau, François. Aspects de l'empire romain. Paris, 1964.

Eg 819.51 — The burden of Egypt. (Wilson, J.) Chicago, 1951.

Eg 1069.10 — The burden of Isis. (Dennis, J.T.) London, 1910.

AH 909.72 — Burford, Alison. Craftsmen in Greek and Roman society. London, 1972.

AH 7438.84 — Burger, Combertus P. De bello cum Samnitibus secundo. Harlemi, 1884.

AH 7438.98 — Burger, Combertus P. Der Kampf zwischen Rom und Samnium. Amsterdam, 1898.

AH 7428.94 — Burger, Combertus P. Neue Forschungen zur älteren Geschichte Roms. Amsterdam, 1894. 2v.

AH 7428.91 — Burger, Combertus P. Sechzig Jahre aus der älteren Geschichte Roms. Amsterdam, 1891.

AH 4861.6 — The burial customs of the ancient Greeks. Thesis. (Graves, F.R.) Brooklyn, 1891.

AH 8907.50 — Burian, Ján. Zagadochnye etruski. Moskva, 1970.

AH 4550.2 — Burich, Nancy J. Alexander the Great: a bibliography. 1st ed. Kent, Ohio, 1970.

AH 3013.26 — The buried city of the East-Nineveh. (Buckingham, J.S.) London, 1851?

AH 8907.26.5 — The buried people. (Cles-Reden, S.) N.Y., 1955.

AH 7107.34 — Burmani, Petro. Vectigalia Popule Romani. Leidae, 1734.

AH 8211.5 — Burn, A.R. Agricola and Roman Britain. London, 1953.

AH 4559.47.5 — Burn, A.R. Alexander the Great and the Hellenistic Empire. London, 1947.

AH 4499.48 — Burn, A.R. Pericles and Athens. London, 1948.

AH 4479.62 — Burn, Andrew. Persia and the Greeks. London, 1962.

AH 4439.60.1 — Burn, Andrew Robert. The lyric age of Greece. London, 1967.

AH 4279.68.5 — Burn, Andrew Robert. The warring states of Greece from their rise to the Roman conquest. London, 1968.

AH 4819.36.5 — Burn, Andrew Robert. The world of Hesiod. London, 1936.

AH 4819.36.6 — Burn, Andrew Robert. The world of Hesiod. 2. ed. N.Y., 1966.

AH 2057.5 — Burney, Charles Allen. The peoples of the hills: ancient Ararat and Caucasus. London, 1971.

AH 4819.17 — Burns, Cecil D. Greek ideals; study of social life. London, 1917.

Eg 759.55 — Burr, Viktor. Tiberius Iulius Alexander. Bonn, 1955.

AH 5658.5 — Bursian, C. Quaestionum Euboicarum. Lipsiae, 1856.

AH 4938.62.5 — Bursian, Konrad. Geographie von Griechenland. Leipzig, 1862-72. 2v.

AH 4938.62 — Bursian, Konrad. Geographie von Griechenland. v.1-2. Leipzig, 1862. 3v.

Htn   AH 8217.5* — Burton, William. Commentary on Antoninus...itinerary. London, 1658.

AH 279.46.5 — Burton-Brown, T. Studies in third millennium history. London, 1946.

AH 819.70.15 — Burton-Brown, Theodore. Diffusion of ideas. Wootton, 1970-

AH 7039.10 — Bury, J.B. Constitution of the later Roman empire. Cambridge, 1910.

AH 7488.93.2 — Bury, J.B. History of the Roman Empire. N.Y., 1893.

AH 7488.93 — Bury, J.B. History of the Roman Empire. N.Y., 1893.

AH 4279.00.4A — Bury, John Bagnell. History of Greece. London, 1902. 2v.

AH 4279.00.30 — Bury, John Bagnell. A history of Greece to the death of Alexander the Great. 3. ed. London, 1951.

AH 4279.00.31 — Bury, John Bagnell. A history of Greece to the death of Alexander the Great. 3. ed. London, 1972.

AH 3960.24 — Busch, Fritz-Otto. The fine Herods. London, 1958.

AH 7908.80 — Business life in ancient Rome. (Herbermann, Charles G.) N.Y., 1880.

AH 4889.26 — The business life of ancient Athens. (Calhoun, G.M.) Chicago, 1926.

AH 3014.30 — Busink, T.A. Die Babylonische Tempeltoren. Leiden, 1949.

AH 3013.938.5 — Busink, T.A. De Toren van Babel. Batavia, 1938.

AH 4278.85 — Busolt, G. Griechische Geschichte. Gotha, 1885-97. 3v.

AH 4278.85.3 — Busolt, G. Griechische Geschichte. v.1-3. Gotha, 1893-1904. 4v.

AH 4818.92 — Busolt, G. Griechischen Staats- und Rechtsaltertümer. München, 1892.

AH 5757.9 — Busolt, G. Lakedaimonier. Leipzig, 1878.

AH 7039.10.2A — Bussell, F.W. Roman empire. London, 1910. 2v.

AH 7169.33.5 — Bussmann, M. L'obligation de délivrance du vendeur. Thèse. Lausanne, 1933.

AH 4200.11 — Busson, A. Lykurgos. Innsbruck, 1887.

AH 4855.11 — Butler, Alfred J. Sport in classic times. London, 1930.

AH 930.10 — Butler, George. The public school's atlas of ancient geography. London, 1889.

AH 5307.23 — Butler, Howard C. Story of Athens. London, 1902.

AH 5307.23.5 — Butler, Howard C. Story of Athens. N.Y., 1902.

AH 938.31 — Butler, Samuel. Geographia classica. Philadelphia, 1831.

AH 854.7 — Butterfly in ancient literature and art. (Blatchford, C.H.) Cambridge, 1889.

Eg 845.5A — Buttles, Janet R. The queens of Egypt. N.Y., 1908.

AH 5760.13 — Buttmann, A. Agesilaus. Halle, 1872.

AH 4298.95 — Butzer, H. Quellenbuch. Dresden, 1895.

AH 7448.78.3 — Buzello, J. De oppugnatione sagunti quaestiones chronologicae. Inaug. Diss. Regimonti, 1886.

AH 4049.09 — Buzeskul, V. Istoria afinskoi demokratia. Sankt Peterburg, 1909.

AH 3009.72 — By the waters of Babylon. (Wellard, James Howard.) London, 1972.

AH 7137.10 — Bynkershoek, C. von. Observationum juris romani. Lugdunum Batavorum, 1710. 2v.

AH 7137.09 — Bynkershoek, C. von. Opuscula varii argumenti. Lugdunum Batavorum, 1719.

AH 8647.9 — Byvanck, A.W. De Magnae Graeciae historia antiquissima. Hagae, 1912.

AH 7468.79 — Byvanck, W.G.C. Studia in Ti. Gracchi historiam. Lugdunum Batavorum, 1879.

Eg 909.49 — Byzantine Egypt: economic studies. (Johnson, A.C.) Princeton, 1949.

AH 7206.10 — Byzantine Empire. Laws, statutes, etc. Basilicorum libri LX. Groningen, 1953- 13v.

AH 7206.34 — Byzantine Empire. Laws, statutes, etc. Ekloga. Moskva, 1965.

AH 7799.68.5 — Byzantium and the decline of Rome. (Kaegi, Walter Emil.) Princeton, 1968.

AH 9722.8 — Byzanz in der klassischen und hellenistischen Epoche. (Nevskaia, V.P.) Leipzig, 1955.

AH 7202.35 — C. Atei Capitonis fragmenta. (Capito, Caius Ateius.) Wratislaviae, 1960.

AH 7708.74 — C. Cilnius Maecenas G. Octaviano Augusto ad adipiscendum gerendumque principatum quantum profuerit. Thesis. (Feugère, A.C.) Paris, 1874.

AH 7015.11F — C. Maecenas. Rede...zur Feier der akademischen Preisvertheilung. (Götz, Georg.) Jena, 1902. 3 pam.

NEDL AH 7278.37.3 — Cabinet cyclopedia. (Lardner, D.) London, 1833. 2v.

NEDL AH 4278.35 — Cabinet of history. (Thirlwall, C.) London, 1835. 8v.

AH 7168.81 — Cabonat, J. De la Successio in locum creditorum. Paris, 1881.

AH 2589.9 — Cadaux, Cecil J. Ancient Smyrna. Oxford, 1938.

AH 7130.2 — Caes, Lucien. Collectio bibliographica operum ad ius romanum pertinetium. v.1-20. Bruxelles, 1949- 13v.

NEDL AH 7478.79.1A — Caesar; a sketch. (Froude, J.A.) London, 1879.

AH 7478.79.2A — Caesar; a sketch. (Froude, J.A.) London, 1880.

AH 7478.81.9 — Caesar; a sketch. (Froude, J.A.) London, 1893.

AH 7478.79A — Caesar; a sketch. (Froude, J.A.) N.Y., 1879.

AH 7478.81 — Caesar; a sketch. (Froude, J.A.) N.Y., 1881.

NEDL AH 7478.79.3 — Caesar; a sketch. (Froude, J.A.) N.Y., 1881.

NEDL AH 7478.81.7A — Caesar; a sketch. (Froude, J.A.) N.Y., 189-?

AH 7479.21 — Cäsar, der Politiker und Staatsmann. (Gelzer, Matthias.) Stuttgart, 1921.

AH 7479.21.7 — Cäsar, der Politiker und Staatsmann. 4. Aufl. (Gelzer, Matthias.) München, 1942.

AH 7479.21.9 — Cäsar, der Politiker und Staatsmann. 6. Aufl. (Gelzer, Matthias.) Wiesbaden, 1960.

AH 7479.24.7 — Caesar; Geschichte seines Ruhms. 2. Aufl. (Gundolf, F.) Berlin, 1925.

AH 7479.21.12 — Caesar, politician and statesman. (Gelzer, Matthias.) Cambridge, 1968.

AH 7479.24.5 — Caesar. (Gundolf, F.) Berlin, 1924.

AH 7479.58 — Caesar. (Opermann, Hans.) Göttingen, 1958.

AH 7479.52 — Caesar. (Walter, G.) N.Y., 1952.

NEDL AH 7478.92.2 — Caesar. A History of the art of war. (Dodge, T.A.) Boston, 1892.

AH 7279.44A — Caesar and Christ. (Durant, W.) N.Y., 1944.

AH 7479.71 — Caesar and Roman politics 60-50 B.C. (Sabben-Clare, James.) London, 1971.

AH 8210.5.2 — Caesar in Kent, an account of the landing of Julius Caesar and his battles with the ancient Britons. 2. ed. (Vine, Francis T.) London, 1887.

AH 8210.5 — Caesar in Kent, the landing of Julius Caesar and his battles with the ancient Britons. (Vine, Francis T.) Edinburgh, 1886.

AH 7279.71.5 — Cäsar lässt Grüssen. (Fernau, Joachim.) München, 1971.

AH 7499.58.5 — Cäsar und die julisch-claudischen Kaiser im biologisc-härztichen Blickfeld. (Esser, A.A.M.) Leiden, 1958.

AH 7489.69.10 — Caesaren, Herren am Limes. (Koch, Wilhelm.) Stuttgart, 1969.

AH 7479.14 — Cäsaren-Porträts. v.1-2, 3. (Müller, Ernst.) Bonn, 1914-27. 2v.

AH 7498.75 — Der Cäsarenwahnsinn. (Wiedemeister, F.) Hannover, 1875.

AH 7478.79.4 — Caesarfabeln des Mittelalters. (Wesemann, H.) Löwenberg, 1879.

AH 7339.56.2 — The Caesars: might and madness. (Lissner, Ivar.) N.Y., 1958.

AH 7339.72 — The Caesars: the Roman Empire and its rulers. (Saklatvala, Beram.) Newton Abbott, 1972.

AH 7659.62.5 — Caesars and saints. 1. ed. (Perowne, Stewart.) N.Y., 1963.

AH 7238.88.1 — Caesar's army; a study of the military art of the Romans in the last days of the Republic. (Judson, Harry P.) N.Y., 1961.

AH 8210.4   Caesar's campaigns in Britain. London, 1881.
AH 7478.99   Caesar's conquest of Gaul. (Holmes, T.R.E.) London, 1899.
AH 7478.99.5   Caesar's conquest of Gaul. 2. ed. (Holmes, T.R.E.) Oxford, 1911.
AH 7479.70   Caesars diplomatische Tätigkeit im gallischen Krieg. (Szidat, Joachim.) Wiesbaden, 1970.
AH 7479.38.6   Caesars Eintritt in die Geschichte. (Strasburger, Hermann.) Darmstadt, 1966.
AH 7479.45.5   Caesars Entwicklung bis zum Consulat im Urteil seiner Zeitgenossen. (Vollenweider, H.) Zürich, 1945.
AH 8536.5   Cäsars fahrt nach Britannien. (Ganter, F.L.) Düsseldorf, 1914.
AH 7478.80   Caesars gallischer Krieg. v.1-2. (Göler, F.A.) Freiburg, 1880.
AH 7469.34.5.3   Caesar's mantle. (Mainzer, Ferdinand.) N.Y., 1936.
AH 7479.18.2   Caesars Monarchie und das Principat des Pompejus. 2. Aufl. (Meyer, Eduard.) Stuttgart, 1919.
AH 7479.18.3   Caesars Monarchie und das Principat des Pompejus. 3. Aufl. (Meyer, Eduard.) Stuttgart, 1963.
AH 2007.7   Çagatay, Neş'et. Islâmdan önce Arap tarihi. Ankara, 1957.
AH 2007.7.2   Çagatay, Neş'et. Islâmdan önce Arap tarihi. 2. ed. Ankara, 1963.
AH 9379.10   Cagiano de Azenado, M. Interamna Lirenas vel Sucasina. Roma, 1947.
AH 8005.2   Cagnat, René. L'armée romaine d'Afrique. Paris, 1892.
AH 8005.2.2   Cagnat, René. L'armée romaine d'Afrique. 2. éd. Paris, 1912. 2v.
AH 8182.5   Cagnat, René. Les deux camps de la légion IIIe Auguste à Lambèse. Paris, 1908.
AH 7108.82   Cagnat, René. Étude historique sur les impots. Paris, 1882.
AH 8005.2.7   Cagnat, René. La frontière militaire de la Tripolitaine à l'époque romaine. Paris, 1912.
NEDL AH 7819.16   Cagnat, René. Manual d'archeologie romaine. Paris, 1916-20. 2v.
AH 7108.80   Cagnat, René. Le portorium...chez les Romains. Paris, 1880.
EgP 143.2   Cahier de recherches. (Université de Lille III. Institut de papyrologie et d'égyptologie.) Lille. 1,1973+ 2v.
AHP 13.8   Cahiers des études anciennes. Montréal. 1,1972+
AH 4162.15   Caillemer, E. Droit de succession légitime. v.1-2. Paris, 1879.
AH 7628.57   Caillet, Jules. De ratione in imperio Romano ordinando ab Hadriano imperatore adhibita. Diss. Parisiis, 1857.
AH 8548.145   Cailleux, Théophile. Origine celtique de la civilisation de tous les peuples: théorie nouvelle. Paris, 1878.
AH 7479.38   Caio Guilio Cesare. (Viviani, Alberto.) Firenze, 1938.
AH 7469.41   Caio Mario. (Passerini, Alfredo.) Roma, 1941.
Eg 9.70   Cairo. Musée des Antiquités Egyptiennes. Catalogue de la Bibliothek...1927-1958. Le Caire, 1970.
Eg 850.8F   Cairo. Musée des antiquités égyptiennes. M'n.(Papyrus 86637). The Cairo calendar, no. 86637. Cairo, 1966.
Eg 850.8F   The Cairo calendar, no. 86637. (Cairo. Musée des antiquités égyptiennes. M'n.(Papyrus 86637).) Cairo, 1966.
AH 7549.16   Caiti, G. Una nuova ipotesi sulle origini dell'incendio Nerone ano. Roma, 1916.
AH 7469.64   Caius Marius. (Ooteghem, Jules van.) Namur, 1964.
AH 7469.40   Cajo Mario. (Andreotti, Roberto.) Gubbio, 1940.
AH 7909.58   Calabi Limentani, Ida. Studi sulla società romana; il lavoro artistico. Milano, 1958.
AH 2102.10A   Calder, W.M. Anatolian studies presented to William H. Buckler. Manchester, 1939.
AH 4189.08   Calderini, A. Condizione dei liberti in Grecia. Milano, 1908.
AH 7419.51   Calderini, A. L'espansione romana in occidente durante la repubblica. Milano, 1951.
AH 7759.62   Calderone, S. Costantino e il cattolicesimo. Firenze, 1962.
AH 819.49   Caldwell, W.E. The ancient world. N.Y., 1949.
AH 7809.67   The calendar of the Roman republic. (Michels, Agnes Kirsopp.) Princeton, 1967.
AH 4809.47   The calendars of Athens. (Pritchett, W.K.) Cambridge, Mass., 1947.
Eg 1179.32   Calendars on coffin lids from Asyut. (Pogo, A.) Bruges, 1932.
AH 3193.8   Un calendrier babylonien des travaux des signes et des mois. (Labat, René.) Paris, 1965.
AH 7807.98   Calendriers de Rome ancienne et moderne. Paris. 1798
NEDL AH 7299.41   Calestoni, V. Origini della razza italiana. Milano, 1941.
AH 5315.25   Calhoun, G.M. Ancient Athenian mining. Cambridge, Mass., 1931.
AH 4909.26A   Calhoun, G.M. The ancient Greeks and the evolution of standards in business. Boston, 1926.
AH 5308.9   Calhoun, G.M. Athenian clubs in politics and litigation. Austin, 1913.
AH 5308.9.2   Calhoun, G.M. Athenian clubs in politics and litigation. Austin, 1913.
AH 4889.26   Calhoun, G.M. The business life of ancient Athens. Chicago, 1926.
AH 4159.27A   Calhoun, G.M. The growth of criminal law in ancient Greece. Berkeley, Calif., 1927.
AH 4130.5   Calhoun, George M. A working bibliography of Greek law. Cambridge, 1927.
AH 7529.06   Caligola. (Venturini, L.) Milano, 1906.
NEDL AH 7528.94   Caligula. (Quidde, L.) Leipzig, 1894.
AH 7529.30.15   Caligula. (Sachs, Hanns.) London, 1931.
AH 8789.5   Callaway, Joseph S. Sybaris. Baltimore, 1950.
AH 8549.104   Callegari, G.V. Il druidismo nell'antica Gallia. Padova, 1904.
AH 5207.10   Callmer, C. Studien zur Geschichte Arkadiens. Lund, 1943.
AH 4164.5   Caloziron, Georges. Die Arrha im Vermögensrecht. Leipzig, 1911.
AH 8513.9   Camau, E. Moeurs et institutions romaines. Paris, 1905.
AH 29.23.5A   The Cambridge ancient history. Cambridge, Eng., 1923-1939. 12v.
AH 29.23.7   The Cambridge ancient history. Plates. Cambridge, Eng., 1927-39. 5v.
AH 29.23.10   The Cambridge ancient history. v.3-12. Cambridge, Eng., 1923-1939. 10v.
Eg 1099.58   Caminos, R.A. The chronicle of Prince Osorkon. Roma, 1958.
Eg 1309.54   Caminos, R.A. Late-Egyptian miscellanies. London, 1954.
Eg 1109.56F   Caminos, R.A. Literary fragments in the hieratic script. Oxford, 1956.
AH 7468.70.5   Campagne de Marius dans la Gaule. (Gilles, I.) Paris, 1870.
AH 8647.11   Campagne della Società Magna Grecia, 1926 e 1927. (Società Magna Grecia.) Roma, 1928.

AH 4558.83   Les campagnes d'Alexandre; drame macédonien. (Jurien, J.P.E.) Paris, 1883. 5v.
AH 8211.2   The campaign of Aulus Plautius in Britain, A.D. 43. (Guest, Edwin.) London, 1866.
AH 4559.64   The campaign of Gaugamela. (Marsden, E.W.) Liverpool, 1964.
AH 4484.13   Campaign of Plataea. (Wright, H.B.) New Haven, 1904.
AH 3955.5A   Campaigns in Palestine from Alexander the Great. (Abrahams, Israel.) London, 1927.
AH 8857.2   Campanien. Geschichte und Topographie des antiken Neapel und seiner Umgebung. (Beloch, Julius.) Berlin, 1879.
AH 8857.2F   Campanien. Geschichte und Topographie des antiken Neapel und seiner Umgebung. Atlas. (Beloch, Julius.) Berlin, 1879.
AH 8857.3   Campanien. Geschichte und Topogrpahie des antiken Neapel und seiner Umgebung. (Beloch, Julius.) Breslau, 1890.
Eg 603.17   Campbell, E.F. The chronology of the Amarna letters. Baltimore, 1964.
AH 3407.7   Campbell, J. Hittites. London, 1891. 2v.
AH 8015.5   Camps-Fabrer, Henriette. L'olivier et l'huile dans l'Afrique romaine. Alger, 1953.
AH 3959.4   The Canaanites. (Gray, J.) London, 1964.
AH 7549.45   Cananesi, M. Nerone. Milano, 1945.
AH 4909.57   Canarache, V. Importul amforelor stampilate la Istria. Bucureşti, 1957.
NEDL AH 7299.42   Canavesi, Manlio. La politica estera di Roma antica. Milano, 1942. 2v.
Eg 847.6   Candar, Aaoni Ali. Eti hiyeroglifi üzerinde tetkikler 534 idéogramme. Ankara, 1933.
AH 4543.10   Candidus, Isaums. Vie de Phocion. Paris, 1948.
AH 4819.47.6   Cane del popolo. 2. ed. (Paoli, Ugo E.) Firenze, 1958.
AH 5303.9   Canet, V. Institutions d'Athènes. Lille, 1888. 2v.
AH 9660.5   Los Cantabras y Astures y su guerra con Roma. (Schulten, Adolf.) Madrid, 1943.
AH 7168.94.5   Cantacuzène, M.G. Droit romain de l'impot sur l'importation et l'exportation des marchandises à Rome sous la république et sous l'empire. Paris, 1894.
AH 7059.03F   Cantarelli, L. La diocesi italiana. Roma, 1901.
AH 7201.74   Cantarelli, L. Il frammento Berlinese "De Dediticus". Roma, 1894.
AH 7618.95   Cantarelli, Luigi. Le fonti per la storia dell'imperatore Traiano. Roma, 1895.
AH 7816.88.3   Cantel, P.J. De Romana Republica sive de re militari et Civili Romanorum ad explicandos scriptores antiquos. Ultrajecti, 1691.
AH 7809.10.5   Caosta, G. I Fasti Consolari Romani. Milano, 1910.
Eg 879.05.10   Capart, Jean. Bulletin critique des religions de l'Egypte. v.1-5. Leiden, 1905-39.
AH 1279.36   Capart, Jean. Histoire de l'Orient ancien. Paris, 1936.
Eg 609.23.6   Capart, Jean. The tomb of Tutankhamen. London, 1923.
Eg 609.23.6.5   Capart, Jean. Tout-Ankh-Amon. 2. éd. Bruxelles, 1950.
AH 4498.62.2   Capefigue, M. Aspasie et le siècle de Périclès. Paris, 1862.
AH 9758.7   Capelle, Wilhelm. Das alte Germanien. Jena, 1929.
X Cg AH 4842.21   Capes, W.W. University life in Athens. N.Y., 1877.
NEDL AH 7598.76   Capes, William W. The Roman Empire of the second century. London, 1876.
NEDL AH 7598.76.9   Capes, William W. The Roman Empire of the second century. N.Y., 1887.
AH 7598.76.12   Capes, William W. The Roman Empire of the second century. N.Y., 1891.
AH 7598.76.15   Capes, William W. The Roman Empire of the second century. N.Y., 1895.
AH 7498.76   Capes, William W. Roman history, early empire. London, 1876.
AH 7498.77   Capes, William W. Roman history, early empire. 2. ed. London, 1877.
AH 7498.87   Capes, William W. Roman history: the early empire. London, 1887.
AH 7498.87.4   Capes, William W. Roman history: the early empire. N.Y., 1892.
AH 7498.87.5   Capes, William W. Roman history: the early empire. N.Y., 1895.
AH 889.06   Capitalisme dans le monde antique. (Salvioli, G.) Paris, 1906.
AH 7109.00   Die Capitatio Plebeia. (Leo, Fritz.) Berlin, 1900.
AH 7109.45   La capitation du Bas-Empire. (Déléage, A.) Macon, 1945.
AH 7202.35   Capito, Caius Ateius. C. Atei Capitonis fragmenta. Wratislaviae, 1960.
AH 7201.110   Capito, G.A. Fragmenta. Wratislaviae, 1960.
AH 819.64.10   Capovilla, G. Praehomerica et praeitalica. Roma, 1964.
AH 7189.66   Capozza, Maria. Movimenti servili nel mondo romano in età repubblicana. Roma, 1966.
AH 2211.5   Cappadocia as a Roman procuratorial province. Diss. (Gwatkin, William E.) Princeton, 1930.
AH 7449.33   Cappis, F. Zum Alpenübergang Hannibals. Aarau, 1933.
Htn AH 4238.51*   The captains of the Old World. (Herbert, Henry W.) N.Y., 1851.
AH 4238.52.5   The captains of the Old World. (Herbert, Henry W.) N.Y., 1852.
AH 7238.54   The captains of the Roman republic. (Herbert, H.W.) N.Y., 1854.
AH 7749.18   Car Dijoklecijan. (Bulić, F.) Zagreb, 1918.
AH 3408.9   Cara, Cesare A. de. Gli Hethei-Palasgi. Roma, 1894. 3v.
AH 3147.5   Le caractère religieux de la royauté assyrobabylonienne. Thèse. (Labat, René.) Paris, 1939.
AH 3423.1F   Carchemish: report on excavations at Djerabis. (British Museum.) London, 1914. 3v.
AH 8940.2   Carchidio, F. Memorie storichi dell'...Telamone. Firenze, 1824.
AH 7819.41.2   Carcopino, J. Daily life in ancient Rome. New Haven, 1940.
AH 7819.41   Carcopino, J. Daily life in ancient Rome. New Haven, 1941.
AH 7819.41.10   Carcopino, J. Daily life in ancient Rome. New Haven, 1945.
AH 8107.10   Carcopino, J. Le Maroc antique. 8. éd. Paris, 1948.
AH 4039.35.5   Carcopino, J. L'ostracisme athénien. Paris, 1935.
AH 7489.34   Carcopino, J. Points de vue sur l'impérialisme romain. Paris, 1934.
AH 339.61   Carcopino, J. Profils de conquérants. Paris, 1961.
AH 7819.41.3   Carcopino, J. La vida catidiana en Roma en el apogeo del imperio. Buenos Aires, 1942.
AH 7819.39   Carcopino, J. La vie quotidienne à Rome à l'apogée de l'empire. Paris, 1939.
AH 7819.38.5   Carcopino, J. La vita quotidiana a Roma. 2. ed. Bari, 1947.

Author and Title Listing

AH 7469.28.15 Carcopino, Jérôme. Autour des Gracques, études critiques. Paris, 1928.

AH 7819.32 Carcopino, Jérôme. Ce que Rome et l'empire romain doivent à la Gaule. Oxford, 1932.

AH 7279.61 Carcopino, Jérôme. Les étapes de l'impérialisme romaine. Paris, 1961.

AH 7479.65 Carcopino, Jérôme. Jules César. Paris, 1965.

AH 7499.58 Carcopino, Jerôme. Passion et politique chez les Césars. Paris, 1958.

AH 7469.31 Carcopino, Jérôme. Sylla; ou, La monarchie manquée. Paris, 1931.

AH 3142.17 Cardascia, Guillaume. Les archives des Murašû, une famille d'hommes d'affaires babyloniens à l'époque perse (455-403 avant J.C.). Paris, 1951.

AH 7238.35 Cardinali, Clemente. Diplomi imperiali di privilegj accordatiai militari. Velletri, 1835.

AH 7179.12 Cardinali, G. Studi graccani. Roma, 1912.

AH 7409.49 Cardinali, Giuseppe. Le origini di Roma. Roma, 1949.

AH 2757.15 Cardinali, Giuseppe. Il regno di Pergamo. Roma, 1968.

AH 7279.20.5 Cardona, Chiara. Roma antica attraverso la sua storia e i suoi monumenti. 2. ed. Roma, 192-.

AH 8503.2 Carette, E. Les assemblées provinciales de la Gaule romaine. Paris, 1893.

AH 2257.5 La Carie. v.2. (Robert, L.) Paris, 1954.

AH 4827.96 Carite et Polydore. (Barthelemy, J.J.) Lausanne, 1796.

AH 7299.55 Carnuntina; Ergebnisse der Forschung über die Grenzprovinzen des Römischen Reiches. (International Congress of Roman Frontier Studies, 2d, Carnuntum, 1955.) Graz, 1956.

Htn   AH 7655.93F* Caroli Sigonii historiarum de occidentali imperio libri XX. (Sigonio, Carlo.) Francofurti, 1591-93. 2 pam.

Htn   AH 3966.8* Carpenter, L. An introduction to the geography of the New Testament. Cambridge, 1811.

AH 3966.8.5 Carpenter, L. An introduction to the geography of the New Testament. 6. ed. London, 1830.

AH 939.66 Carpenter, Rhys. Beyond the Pillars of Heracles. N.Y., 1966.

AH 4819.66.10 Carpenter, Rhys. Discontinuity in Greek civilization. Cambridge, Eng., 1966.

AH 7649.53 Carrata Thomes, Franco. Il regno di Marco Aurelio. Torino, 1953.

AH 8536.9 Carré, G. Le régime municipal à Périgueux. Périgueux, 1876.

AH 7619.40 Carrea d'Oliveira, E. Roma imperiale ai tempi di Traiano. Milano, 1940.

AH 259.59 Carson, Lionel. The ancient mariners: seafarers. N.Y., 1966.

AH 9614.5 Carta teotopiche della Sicilia antica. (Tropea, G.) Padova, 1902.

AH 8516.5 Carte de la Gaule sous le proconsulat de César. (Creuly, Casimir.) Paris, 1864.

Eg 609.23.7 Carter, Howard. The tomb of Tut-Ankh-Amen. London, 1923-33. 3v.

Eg 609.23.8A Carter, Howard. The tomb of Tut-Ankh-Amen. N.Y., 1923.

AH 7479.70.5 Carter, John M. The battle of Actium. London, 1970.

Eg 609.72.5 Carter, Michael. The golden monarch; Tutankhamun. Christchurch, 1972.

AH 8073.28 Carthage, la prestigieuse cité d'Elissa. (Fantar, Mhamed.) Tunis, 1970.

AH 8073.7.5 Carthage, or The empire of Africa. Photoreproduction. (Church, A.J.) London, 1887.

AH 8073.13 Carthage, sive Carthaginensium respublica. (Hendreich, C.) Francofurti ad Oderam, 1664.

AH 8057.5.6 Carthage. (Charles-Picard, Gilbert.) N.Y., 1965.

AH 8073.17 Carthage. (Hubac, Pierre.) Paris, 1946.

AH 8073.20 Carthage. (Picard, Colette.) Paris, 1951.

AH 8073.23 Carthage. (Warmington, Brian Herbert.) London, 1960.

AH 8073.21 Carthage. 1. éd. (Hours-Miedan, Madeleine.) Paris, 1949.

AH 8073.23.2 Carthage. 2. ed. (Warmington, Brian Herbert.) London, 1969.

AH 8073.4 Carthage and the Carthaginians. 2. ed. (Smith, R.B.) London, 1879.

AH 8073.22.5 La Carthage de Saint Augustin. (Charles-Picard, Gilbert.) Paris, 1965.

AH 939.29 Cary, Max. The ancient explorers. London, 1929.

AH 4009.27 Cary, Max. The documentary sources of Greek history. Oxford, 1927.

AH 939.49 Cary, Max. The geographic background of Greek and Roman history. London, 1949.

AH 7279.35.8 Cary, Max. A history of Rome down to the reign of Constantine. London, 1938.

AH 4659.32.20 Cary, Max. A history of the Greek world from 323-146 B.C. N.Y., 1939.

AH 4659.32.15 Cary, Max. A history of the Greek world from 323-146 B.C. 2. ed. London, 1951.

AH 4659.32.10A Cary, Max. A history of the Greek world from 325-146 B.C. London, 1932.

AH 7078.48 Casar aux elections. Paris, 1848.

AH 7339.56 Die Casaren. (Lissner, Ivar.) Olten, 1956.

AH 8907.9 Casati, Charles. Les Étrusques, leur langue...civilisation. Paris, 1914.

AH 842.15 Cassan, K. Pädagogik der Alten. Leipzig, 1882.

AH 808.79 Cassel, P.S. Phönix und seine Aera. Berlin, 1879.

AH 7889.31 Cassimatis, Grégoire. Les intérêts dans la législation de Justinien et dans le droit byzantin. Paris, 1931.

AH 7419.62 Cassola, F. I gruppi politici romani nel III secolo A.C. Triesti, 1962.

AH 2120.5 Cassola, Filippo. La Ionia nel mondo micineo. Napoli, 1957.

AH 4819.22.5 Casson, S. Ancient Greece. London, 1922.

AH 4819.22.6 Casson, S. Ancient Greece. Oxford, 1939.

AH 6113.5 Casson, Stanley. Macedinia, Thrace and Illyria. Oxford, 1926.

AH 7809.10 Casta, G. L'originale dei Fasti Consolari. Roma, 1910.

AH 8505.5 Castagne, E. Mémoire sur les ouvrages de fortification des appidum gaulois. Tours, 1875.

AH 846.36 Castagnoli, Ferdinando. Orthogonal town planning in antiquity. Cambridge, 1971.

AH 8666.5 Castagnoli, Ferdinando. Topografia e urbanistica di Roma antica. Bologna, 1969.

AH 7818.58.5 Castelar y Ripoll, E. La civilizacion en los cinco primeros siglos del cristianismo. 2. ed. Madrid, 1865. 4v.

AH 3013.949.5 Castellino, Giorgio. Corso di lezioni di assiriologia. Roma, 1949.

AH 3155.29 Castellino, Giorgio R. Mitologia sumerico-accadica. Torino, 1967.

AH 3181.14 Castellino, Giorgio R. Two Šulgi hymns [and] Be. Roma, 1972.

Htn   AH 8957.10* Castiglione, B. Gallorum Insubrum antiquae sedes. Mediolani, 1541.

AH 7161.14 Das castrense peculium. (Fitting, H.) Halle, 1871.

AH 7769.69 Castritius, Helmut. Studien zu Maximinus Daia. Diss. Kallmünz, 1969.

AH 3000.3 Catalog of cuneiform tablets in the Kouyunjik collection. (British Museum.) London, 1889-99. 5v.

AH 3000.3.2 Catalog of cuneiform tablets in the Kouyunjik collection. Supplement. (British Museum.) London, 1914.

AH 3000.3.3 Catalog of cuneiform tablets in the Kouyunjik collection. 2d supplement. (British Museum.) London, 1968.

Eg 1300.5 Catalogo de' papiri egiziani della Biblioteca Vaticana e notizia piu estesa di uno d'essi. (Champollion-Figeae, Jacques J.) Roma, 1825.

Eg 9.70 Catalogue de la Bibliothek...1927-1958. (Cairo. Musée des Antiquités Égyptiennes.) Le Caire, 1970.

AH 3013.13.5 Catalogue des antiquités chaldéennes. (Paris. Musée Nationale du Louvre.) Paris, 1902.

Eg 847.11F Catalogue des caractères d'impression hiéroglyphiques égyptiens. (Gardiner, Alan Henderson.) Bruxelles, 1928.

AH 3017.7.11F Catalogue des cylindres orientaux du cabinet royal des medailles de la Haye. (Menant, J.) La Haye, 1878.

AH 3017.19 Catalogue des intailles et empreintes orientales des Musées royaux du cinquantenaire. (Brussels. Musée des Arts Décoratifs et Industriels.) Bruxelles, 1917.

AH 8008.10 Catalogue des tribus africaines de l'antiquité classique à l'ouest du Nil. (Desanges, J.) Dakar, 1962.

Eg 8.80 Catalogue of...books on Egypt and Egyptology. (Trübner and Co.) London, 1880.

Eg 1300.11F Catalogue of demotic papyri in the British Museum. v.1-2. (British Museum. Department of Egyptian and Assyrian Antiquities.) London, 1939-

Eg 1300.10 Catalogue of Egyptian religious papyri in the British Museum. (British Museum. Department of Egyptian and Assyrian Antiquities.) London, 1938.

AH 3017.70F A catalogue of oriental cylinder seals and seal impressions in the Danish National Museum. (Ravn, Otto E.) København, 1960.

AH 3020.7.10 Catalogue of Sumerian tablets in the John Rylands Library. (John Rylands Library. Manchester.) Manchester, 1932.

Eg 9.24 Catalogue of the Egyptological library and other books from the collection of the late Charles E. Wilbour. (Cook, William B.) Brooklyn, 1924.

AH 3017.60 Catalogue sommaire des cylindres orientaux au Cabinet. (Hague. Kabinet van Munten.) La Haye, 1952.

AHP 13.1 Catania. Universita. Instituto di Storia del Diritto Romano. Annuario. Catania. 13-14,1914-1915

AH 7549.15 La catastrofe di Nerone. (Barbagallo, C.) Catania, 1915.

AH 5309.12 Cataudella, Michele R. Atene fra il VII e il VI secolo. Catania, 1966.

AH 4818.22 Catechism of Grecian antiquities. (Irving, C.) N.Y., 1822.

AH 4278.25 Catechism of history of Greece. (Pinnock, W.) London, 1822.

AH 7818.31 Catechism of Roman antiquities. 4th American ed. (Irving, C.) N.Y., 1831.

AH 7278.24 Catechism of Roman history. 2. American ed. (Irving, C.) N.Y., 1824.

AH 7469.19 Catilina in classic tradition. Thesis. (Koehler, M.A.) N.Y., 1919.

AH 7469.29 Catilina nel giudizio della critica demagogica. (Balbo, Emilio.) Roma, 1929.

AH 7468.69 Catilina und die Parteikämpfe in Rom im Jahre 63 vor Christus. (Backmund, J.) Würzburg, 1869.

AH 7468.83 Catilina und die Parterkämpfe. (Stern, Ernst von.) Dorpat, 1883.

AH 7469.71.10 The Catilinarian conspiracy. (Odahl, Charles Matson.) New Haven, 1971.

AH 7469.24 The Catilinarian conspiracy in its context. (Hardy, E.G.) Oxford, 1924.

AH 7468.78 Catiline, Clodius and Tiberius. (Beesly, E.S.) London, 1878.

AH 7469.68 Catiline; the man and his role in the Roman revolution. (Kaplan, Arthur.) N.Y., 1968.

Eg 855.1 Caton, R. Ancient Egyptian medicine. London, 1904.

AH 7277.25 Catrou, François. Histoire romaine. Paris, 1725. 17v.

AH 7277.25.3 Catrou, François. Histoire romaine. v.18-21. Paris, 1734. 4v.

AH 7277.25.5F Catrou, François. Roman history. London, 1728. 6v.

AH 7008.84 Cauer, F. De fabulis graecis ad romam. Berolini, 1884.

AH 5853.7 Cauer, F. Parteien und Politiker. Stuttgart, 1890.

AH 7279.25 Cauer, Friedrich. Römische Geschichte. München, 1925.

AH 7279.25.5 Cauer, Friedrich. Römische Geschichte. 2. Aufl. München, 1933.

AH 4178.34 Causis turbatae apud Lacedaemonios agrorum aequalitatis. (Hermann, C.F.) Marburgi, 1834.

AH 3957.25 Causse, A. Du groupe ethnique à la communaté religieuse. Paris, 1937.

Htn   AH 3958.8.20* Caussin, N. The unfortunate politique [or the life of Herod]. Oxford, 1638.

AH 4216.5 Le cautionnement. (Beasley, T.W.) Paris, 1902.

AH 279.13 Cavaignac, E. Histoire de l'antiquité. v.1-3 et index générale. Paris, 1913-20. 5v.

AH 279.46.10 Cavaignac, E. Histoire générale de l'antiquité. Paris, 1946.

AH 3407.20 Cavaignac, E. Les Hittites. Paris, 1950.

AH 889.23 Cavaignac, E. Population et capital dans le monde mediterranéen antique. Strasbourg, 1923.

AH 5757.19 Cavaignac, E. Sparte. 25. éd. Paris, 1948.

AH 3407.22 Cavaignac, Eugène. Le problème hittite. Paris, 1936.

AH 3409.5 Cavaignac, Eugène. Subbililiuma et son temps. Paris, 1932.

AH 3013.5 Cavaniol, C.H. Les monuments en Chaldée, en Assyrie. Paris, 1870.

AH 819.44 Cavazzana, J.C. Historia de la cultura. Lima, 1944.

AH 7549.02 Cavazzi, C.G. Sull'incendio di Roma. Roma, 1902.

AH 7169.33.10 Cavin, P.E. L'extinction de l'usufruit "rei mutatione". Thèse. Lausanne, 1933.

Eg 879.30.5 Cazemier, L.J. Oud-Egyptiese voorstellingen aangaande de ziel. Proefschrift. Wageningen, 1935.

AH 9777.41 Cazzaniga, I. Dispense relative alla lettura del testo di Iordanes Historia getarum. Milano, 1963.

AH 7819.32 Ce que Rome et l'empire romain doivent à la Gaule. (Carcopino, Jérôme.) Oxford, 1932.

	AH 4279.28.5	Ce qu'il faut connaître de la Grèce antique. (Puech, Aimé.) Paris, 1928.
	AH 7009.47	Ceccarelli, G. Saggio di bibliografia romana. Roma. 2-12,1946-1957// 5v.
	AH 4039.69.10	Ceechin, Sergio A. Patrios politeia. Torino, 1969.
	AH 7817.42.10	Cellarii, Christophori. Christophori Cellarii Breviarium antiquitatum romanarum, accurante. Augustae Taurinorum, 1742.
	AH 8548.75	Celt and the world. (Leslie, S.) N.Y., 1917.
	AH 8548.25	Les Celtes, la Gaule celtique. (Valroger, L. de.) Paris, 1879.
	AH 8548.55	Les Celtes. (Arbois de Jubainville, Henry d'.) Paris, 1904.
	AH 8548.154	Les Celtes au second âge du fer. (Harmond, Jacques.) Paris, 1970.
	AH 8548.125	Les Celtes au XIX. siècle. (Gaulle, C. de.) Paris, 1903.
	AH 8548.90	Les Celtes bretons et les Phocéens dans le sud ouest de la Gaule. (Paniagua, A. de.) Paris, 1926.
	AH 8548.55.1	Les Celtes depuis le temps les plus anciens. (Arbois de Jubainville, Henry d'.) Osnabrück, 1968.
	AH 8548.147	Les Celtes et la civilisation celtique; mythe et histoire. (Markale, Jean.) Paris, 1969.
	AH 8549.168.10	Les Celtes et les druides. (Serbanesco, Demeter Gérard Roger.) Paris, 1968.
	AH 8549.148	The Celtic and Scandinavian religions. (MacCulloch, John A.) London, 1948.
	AH 8549.135.5	Celtic and Teutonic religions. (MacNiell, Evin.) London, 1935.
	AH 8548.141	Celtic civilization and its heritage. (Filip, Jan.) Prague, 1960.
	AH 8549.85.5	Celtic mythology and religion. (Macbain, A.) Stirling, 1917.
	AH 8549.85	Celtic mythology and religion. Photoreproduction. (Macbain, A.) Inverness, 1885.
	AH 8548.120.5	The Celtic realms. (Dillon, Myles.) London, 1967.
	AH 8549.106.5	Celtic religion in pre-Christian times. (Arnoyl, E.) London, 1906.
Htn	AH 8548.4*	Celtic researches on the origin, traditions and languages. (Davies, E.) London, 1804.
	AH 8548.4	Celtic researches on the origin, traditions and languages. (Davies, E.) London, 1804.
	AH 8548.115	Celtische Forschungen zur Geschichte Mitteleuropas. (Mone, F.J.) Freiburg, 1857.
	AH 8548.152	The Celts. (Chadwick, Nora (Kershaw).) Harmondsworth, Eng., 1970.
	AH 8548.22	The Celts. (Maclear, George F.) London, 1878.
	AH 8548.140	The Celts. (Powell, Terence G.E.) London, 1958.
	AH 8548.142	The Celts. (Raftery, Joseph.) Cork, 1964.
	AH 8548.38	The Celts and Druids and their story from the earliest times. (Scott, A.) North Shields, 1894.
	AH 8513.16.1	Celts and Gallo-Romans. (Hatt, Jean Jacques.) London, 1970.
Htn	AH 8936.2F*	Cenotaphia Piasana Caii et Lucii Caesarum. (Noris, Enrico.) Venetiis, 1681.
	AH 842.40	Censura en el mundo antiguo. (Gil, Luis.) Madrid, 1961.
	Eg 909.38	Census and poll-tax in Ptolemaic and Roman Egypt. (Wallace, S. Le Roy.) Princeton, 1938.
	AH 7759.12	Centonze, L. L'imperatore Costantino e la chiesa cattolica. Bari, 1912.
	AH 1819.26	The centre of ancient civilization. (Daunt, Hew D.) London, 1926.
	AH 7659.62	Centro Italiano di Studi Sull'alto Medioevo. Il passaggio dall'antichita al Medioevo in occidente. Spoleto, 1962.
	AH 7116.4	Die Centurienverfassung des Servius Tullius. (Breda, O.) Bromberg, 1848. 2 pam.
	AH 3013.929.5A	A century of exploration at Nineveh. (Thompson, R.C.) London, 1929.
	AH 3921.11	Ceran, Waldemar. Rzemieslnicy i kupcy w Antiochii i ich ranga spoleczna (II polowa IV wieku). Wroclaw, 1969.
	AH 4899.25	Les céreales dans l'antiquité grecque. Thèse. (Jardé, A.) Paris, 1925.
	AH 1279.57.3	Cerfaux, Lucien. L'antiquité: le Proche-Orient. 3. éd. Tournai, 1960.
	Eg 879.52.10	Cerný, J. Ancient Egyptian religion. London, 1952.
	AH 8549.81	Cerquand, J.F. Taranis Lithobole; étude de mythologie celtique. Avignon, 1881.
	Eg 1029.57PF	Cervý, Jaroslav. Hieratic ostraca. Oxford, 1957.
	AH 7479.59	César. (Madaule, Jacques.) Paris, 1959.
	AH 7478.70.3	César. (Ramée, A.) Paris, 1870.
	AH 7478.69	César et ses contemporains. (Delorme, S.) Paris, 1869.
	AH 7498.46	Cesare, G. di. Lettere romane dall'anno 818 della 830. Prato, 1846.
	AH 7479.45	Cesare. (Ferrabino, Aldo.) Torino, 1945.
	AH 7479.36	Cesare. (Foschini, Antonino.) Milano, 1936.
	AH 7479.56	Cesare nel brimillenario della morte. (Radio Italiana.) Torino, 1956.
	AH 7488.83.5	Césarisme et Christianisme. (Proudhon, P.J.) Paris, 1883. 2v.
	AH 7498.59	Les Césars. (Champagny, F.J.M.T.) Paris, 1859.
	AH 7498.59.4	Les Césars. 4. éd. v.1-4. (Champagny, F.J.M.T.) Paris, 1867. 2v.
	AH 7709.05.1	Les Césars africains et syriens et l'anarchie militaire. [Ristampa anastatica]. (Forquet de Dorne, Charles B.) Roma, 1970.
	AH 3936.2	Césars de Palmyre. (Double, L.) Paris, 1877.
	AH 7708.70.3	Les Césars du troisieme siecle. (Champagny, F.J.M.T.) Paris, 1878. 3v.
	AH 7179.13	La cessio bonorum. (Guenoun, L.) Paris, 1913.
	AH 7698.80	Ceuleneer, A. de. Essai sur la vie et le regne de Septime Sévère. Bruxelles, 1880.
	AH 7668.76	Ceuleneer, A. de. Marcia la favorite de Commode. Paris, 1876.
	Eg 558.68	Chabas, F. Les pasteurs en Egypte. Amsterdam, 1868. 2 pam.
	Eg 958.66F	Chabas, F. Voyage d'un égyptien. Paris, 1866.
	AH 7850.2A	Chacon, P. De Triclinio rive de modo convivandi. Amsterdam, 1664.
	AH 8548.152	Chadwick, Nora (Kershaw). The Celts. Harmondsworth, Eng., 1970.
	AH 8549.166	Chadwick, Nora (Kershaw). The Druids. Cardiff, 1966.
	AH 8532.5.10	Chagny, André. Au cours de l'automne de 43 avant notre ere Lucius Munatius Plancus. Lyon, 1957.
	AH 7079.11	Chaigne, O. Sous la robe blanche. Paris, 1866.
	AH 879.60	Chakraberty, Chandra. Ancient races and myths. Calcutta, 196-.
	AH 5673.5	Chalcidian studies. Proefschrift. v.2. (Bakhuizen, Simon Cornelis.) Groningen, 1970-
	AH 3177.3F	Chaldaean account of the deluge. (Smith, George.) London, 1872.
	AH 3159.6.3.5	The Chaldean account of genesis. (Smith, George.) N.Y., 1876.
	AH 3159.6.3	The Chaldean account of genesis. 3. ed. (Smith, George.) London, 1876.
	AH 3156.5.5	Chaldean magic. (Lenormant, F.) London, 1877.
	AH 4819.42A	The challenge of the Greek. (Glover, Terrot R.) Cambridge, Eng., 1942.
	Eg 759.64	Chalon, Gérard. L'édit de Tiberius Julius Alexander; étude historique et exégétique. Olten, 1964.
	AH 7659.63	Chambers, M.H. The fall of Rome. N.Y., 1963.
	AH 279.58.20	Chambers, M.H. Greek and Roman history. Washington, 1958.
	AH 4279.73.5	Chambers, Mortimer Hardin. Ancient Greece. Washington, 1973.
	AH 7138.93	Chamier, D. Manual of Roman law. London, 1893.
	AH 4819.63.15	Chamoux, François. La civilisation grecque. Paris, 1963.
	AH 4819.63.16	Chamoux, François. The civilization of Greece. London, 1965.
	AH 3359.10	Chamoux, J. Cyrène sour la monarchie des Battiades. Paris, 1952.
	Eg 879.36	Le champ des roseaux et le champ des offrandes dans la religion funéraire. (Weill, R.) Paris, 1936.
	AH 7598.66	Champagny, F.J.M.T. Les Antonins. Paris, 1866. 3v.
	AH 7498.59	Champagny, F.J.M.T. Les Césars. Paris, 1859.
	AH 7498.59.4	Champagny, F.J.M.T. Les Césars. 4. éd. v.1-4. Paris, 1867. 2v.
	AH 7708.70.3	Champagny, F.J.M.T. Les Césars du troisieme siècle. Paris, 1878. 3v.
	AH 7558.58	Champagny, F.J.M.T.N. Rome et la Judée au temps de la chute de Néron. Paris, 1858.
	AH 3659.12	Champdor, A. Cyrus. Paris, 1952.
	AH 3009.57	Champdor, Albert. Babylone. Paris, 1957.
	Eg 1039.63	Champdor, Albert. Le livre des morts. Paris, 1963.
	Eg 708.19	Champollion, J.J. Annales des Lagides. Paris, 1819. 2v.
	Eg 291.5	Champollion, J.J. A collection of 15 tracts. Grenoble, 1806. 15 pam.
	Eg 278.14	Champollion, J.J. L'Égypte. Paris, 1814. 2v.
	Eg 278.14.3	Champollion, J.J. Égypte ancienne. Paris, 1839.
	Eg 1300.5	Champollion-Figeae, Jacques J. Catalogo de' papiri egiziani della Biblioteca Vaticana e notizia piu estesa di uno d'essi. Roma, 1825.
	AH 2957.3	Chandler, R. History of Illium or Troy. London, 1802.
	AH 4957.77	Chandler, R. Reisen in Griechenland. Leipzig, 1777.
	AH 7189.67	Chantraine, Heinrich. Freigelassene und Sklaven im Dienst der römischen Kaiser. Wiesbaden, 1967.
	AH 7469.59.5	Chantraine, Heinrich. Untersuchungen zur römischen Geschichte am Ende des 2. Jahrhunderts vor Christus. Kallmünz, 1959.
	AH 9086.5	Un chapitre d'histoire pontine. (La Blanchère, R.) Paris, 1889.
	AH 7207.7	Chapman, Thomas. An essay on the Roman senate. Cambridge, 1764.
	AH 2147.5	Chapot, V. Province romaine proconsulaire d'Asie. Paris, 1904.
	AH 7258.96	Chapot, Victor. La flotte de misène. Paris, 1896.
	AH 7489.27	Chapot, Victor. Le monde romain. Paris, 1927.
	AH 7489.27.5	Chapot, Victor. The Roman world. N.Y., 1928.
	AH 6049.5	Chapters in history of ancient Sicyon. (Skalet, Charles H.) Baltimore, 1928.
	AH 5857.11.5	Chapters in the history and civilization of ancient Megara. (Highbarger, E.L.) Baltimore, 1927.
	AH 4848.9	Chapters on Greek dress. (Evans, M.M.) London, 1893.
	AH 7478.26	Character of Julius Caesar. (Knowles, J.S.) Boston, 1826.
	AH 7819.61	The character of the Romans in their history and their literature. (Adcock, Frank Ezra.) Sydney, 1961.
Htn	Eg 876.08*	Characteres Aegyptii hoc est sacrorum. (Pignorio, L.) Francofurti, 1608.
	AH 7309.09	Characters and events of Roman history. (Ferrero, G.) N.Y., 1909.
	AH 7309.09.5	Characters and events of Roman history. (Ferrero, G.) N.Y., 1922.
	AH 7499.09	Charakterbilder römischer Kaiser. (Schmaus, J.) Bamberg, 1909.
	AH 7339.19.2	Charakterbilder Spätroms. 2. Aufl. (Birt, Theodor.) Leipzig, 1920.
	AH 7339.19.3	Charakterbilder Spätroms. 3. Aufl. (Birt, Theodor.) Leipzig, 1923.
	AH 4828.40.5	Charicles. (Becker, W.A.) London, 1845.
	AH 4828.40.7	Charicles. (Becker, W.A.) London, 1854.
	AH 4828.40.8A	Charicles. (Becker, W.A.) London, 1854.
	AH 4828.40.20	Charicles. (Becker, W.A.) London, 1899.
	AH 4828.40.11A	Charicles. 3. ed. (Becker, W.A.) London, 1866.
NEDL	AH 4828.40.12	Charicles. 4. ed. (Becker, W.A.) London, 1874.
	AH 4828.40.14	Charicles. 6. ed. (Becker, W.A.) London, 1882.
	AH 4828.40.3	Charikles. (Becker, W.A.) Berlin, 1877-78. 3v.
	AH 4828.40	Charikles. (Becker, W.A.) Leipzig, 1840.
	AH 4828.40.2	Charikles. 2. Aufl. (Becker, W.A.) Leipzig, 1854. 3v.
	AH 4049.57	Charisma. (Taeger, Fritz.) Stuttgart, 1951-60. 2v.
	AH 4218.5	Charles, John F. Statutes of limitations at Athens. Diss. Chicago, 1938.
	AH 7819.69.11	Charles-Picard, Gilbert. The ancient civilization of Rome. N.Y., 1969.
	AH 8057.5.6	Charles-Picard, Gilbert. Carthage. N.Y., 1965.
	AH 8073.22.5	Charles-Picard, Gilbert. La Carthage de Saint Augustin. Paris, 1965.
	AH 8013.4	Charles-Picard, Gilbert. La civilisation de l'Afrique romaine. Paris, 1959.
	AH 8073.22.15	Charles-Picard, Gilbert. Daily life in Carthage at the time of Hannibal. London, 1961.
	AH 8073.22.10	Charles-Picard, Gilbert. The life and death of Carthage. London, 1968.
	AH 8057.5	Charles-Picard, Gilbert. Le monde de Carthage. Paris, 1956.
	AH 8014.5	Charles-Picard, Gilbert. Les religions de l'Afrique antique. Paris, 1954.
	AH 7029.69	Charles-Picard, Gilbert. Textes et documents relatifs à la vie économique et sociale dans l'empire romain. Paris, 1969.
	AH 8073.22.9	Charles-Picard, Gilbert. Vie et mort de Carthage. Paris, 1970.
	AH 8073.22	Charles-Picard, Gilbert. La vie quotidienne à Carthage en temps d'Hannibal. Paris, 1958.
	AH 7539.39	Charlesworth, M.P. Documents illustrating the reigns of Cladius and Nero. Cambridge, Eng., 1939.

Author and Title Listing

AH 7489.36   Charlesworth, M.P. Five men. Cambridge, Mass., 1936.

AH 8207.25   Charlesworth, M.P. The lost province. Cardiff, Wales, 1949.

AH 7489.51A   Charlesworth, M.P. The Roman Empire. London, 1951.

AH 7909.24A   Charlesworth, M.P. Trade-routes and commerce of the Roman Empire. Cambridge, 1924.

AH 7909.24.5   Charlesworth, M.P. Trade-routes and commerce of the Roman Empire. Hildesheim, 1961.

AH 7489.37.5   Charlesworth, M.P. The virtues of a Roman emperor. London, 1937.

Eg 879.66F   Chassinat, Emile G. Le mystère d'Osiris au mois de Khoiak. Le Caire, 1966-68. 2v.

Eg 879.65.10F   Chassinat, Emile G. Le temple de Dendara. v.6. Le Caire, 1965-

AH 8662.5   Chastagnol, André. Les fastes de la préfecture de Rome au Bas-Empire. Paris, 1962.

AH 8653.5   Chastagnol, André. La préfecture urbaine à Rome sous le Bas-Empire. 1. éd. Paris, 1960.

AH 7498.26   Chateaubriand, François August René. Discours servant d'introduction à l'histoire de France. Paris, 1826.

AH 4309.62   Châtelet, François. La naissance de l'histoire. Paris, 1962.

AH 3302.1   Chatzeioannou, Kyriakos. He archaia Kypros eis tas Hellenikas pegas. Leukosia, 1971.

AH 4828.01   Chaussard, J.B. Fetes et courtisanes. Paris, 1801. 4v.

AH 4828.01.4   Chaussard, J.B. Fetes et courtisanes. 4. éd. Paris, 1821. 4v.

AH 7728.02   Chaussard, P.J.B. Héliogabale, ou Esquisse morale. Paris, 1802.

AH 842.16   Chauvinismus und Schulreform im Altertum. (Marr, F.) Breslau, 1894.

AH 7239.14   Cheesman, G.L. The auxilia of the Roman imperial army. Oxford, 1914.

Htn   AH 7653.10*   Chelsum, J. Remarks on 2 last chapters of Gibbon's History of Roman Empire. London, 1776.

Eg 458.61   Cheops der Pyramidenerbauer und seine Nachfolger. (Knötel, August.) Leipzig, 1861.

Eg 459.58   Cheops und die grosse Pyramide. (Muck, O.H.) Olten, 1958.

AH 7769.13   Cherniavskii, N.F. Imperator Feodosii Velikii i ego tsaratvovanie v tserkovno istoricheskom otnoshenii. Sergiev Posad, 1913.

AH 4728.78   Chevalier, L. Einfälle der Gallier in Griechen. Prag, 1878.

AH 4238.69   Chevalier, L. Entstehung...der griechischen Söldnerheere und ihre Teilnahme. Prag, 1869.

AH 2357.7   Chevalier, L. Die Gallier in Kleinasien. Prag, 1883.

AH 7114.12   Les chevaliers romains. (Gomont, H.) Paris, 1854.

AH 3160.6   Chevolson, D.A. Uber Tammuz und die Menschenverehrung. St. Petersburg, 1860.

Eg 885.959   La chiave perduta. (Piantanida, Danato.) Milano, 1959.

AH 7203.137   Chiazzese, L. Confronti testuali contributo alla dottrina delle interpolazioni giustinianee. Cortona, 1933.

AH 3013.31   Chicago, Illinois. University. Oriental Exploration Fund. Expedition of Oriental Exploration Fund (Babylonian section). Reports 1-4, 6. Chicago? 1904.

AH 3013.31.7   Pamphlet box. Chicago, Illinois. University. Oriental Exploration Fund.

AH 3011.18   Chicago. University. Studies presented to A. Leo Oppenheim, June 7, 1964. Chicago, 1964.

AHP 11.8   Chicago. University. Oriental Institute. Assyriological studies. Chicago. 1-11,1932-1939 5v.

AH 3013.958F   Chicago. University. Oriental Institute. Soundings at Tell Fakhariyah. Chicago, 1958.

AH 3020.13A   Chiera, Edward. Excavations at Nuzi. v.2-8. Cambridge, 1932-62. 7v.

AH 3002.37   Chiera, Edward. Selected temple accounts from Tellohyokha and Drehem. Philadelphia, 1921.

AH 3020.16F   Chiera, Edward. Sumerian epics and myths. Chicago, 1934.

AH 3020.15F   Chiera, Edward. Sumerian lexical texts from the temple school of Nippur. Chicago, 1929.

AH 3020.17F   Chiera, Edward. Sumerian texts of varied contents. Chicago, 1934.

AH 3143.13   Chiera, Edward. They wrote on clay. Chicago, 1938.

AH 1819.28.5   Childe, Vere G. The most ancient East. London, 1929.

AH 1819.34A   Childe, Vere G. New light on the most ancient East. London, 1934.

AH 1819.34.10   Childe, Vere G. New light on the most ancient East. N.Y., 1934.

AH 1819.34.5   Childe, Vere G. New light on the most ancient East. 4. ed. London, 1952.

AH 819.36.10A   Childe, Vere Gordon. Man makes himself. London, 1936.

AH 819.36.11   Childe, Vere Gordon. Man makes himself. London, 1948.

AH 819.42   Childe, Vere Gordon. What happened in history. Harmondsworth, 1943.

AH 819.42.6   Childe, Vere Gordon. What happened in history. Harmondsworth, 1948.

AH 819.42.5   Childe, Vere Gordon. What happened in history. London, 1960.

AH 408.87   Childhood of the world. (Clodd, E.) London, 1887.

AH 8965.5   Chilver, G.E.F. Cisalpine Gaul. Oxford, 1941.

AHP 13.7   Chiron. München. 1,1971+ 4v.

AH 7817.42   Chladenii, E.M. De gentilitate vetervm Romanorum liber singvlaris. Lipsiae, 1742.

AH 3002.29   Choix de textes cunéiformes. (Lenormant, F.) Paris, 1873-75.

Eg 132.53   Choix de textes juridiques en hiératique et en démotique. pt.1. (Malinine, Michel.) Paris, 1953-

AH 3002.84   Choix de textes religieux assyro-babylonies. (Dhorme, Paul.) Paris, 1907.

AH 8548.95   Chotzen, T.M. Primitieve Keltistiek in de Nederlanden. 's-Gravenhage, 1931.

AH 7138.30.5   Chrestomathie ou choix de textes. (Bloudeau, M.) Paris, 1830.

AH 7549.04   Les chrétiens ont-ils incendie Rome sous Néron. (Allard, Paul.) Paris, 1904.

AH 5757.21   Chrimes, K.M.T. Ancient Sparta. Manchester, 1949.

AH 4108.79   Christ, J. De publicis populi atheniensis rationibus saeculo A. Ch. quinto et quarto. Gryphiswaldiae, 1879.

AH 7509.56.5   Christ, Karl. Drusus und Germanicus. Paderborn, 1956.

AH 7659.70   Christ, Karl. Der Untergang des Romischen Reiches. Darmstadt, 1970.

AH 7549.07   Die Christenkatastrophe unter Nero. (Klette, E.T.) Tübingen, 1907.

AH 3661.5   Christensen, A. L'empire des Sassanides. København, 1907.

AH 8305.5   Christescu, V. Istoria militară a Daciei romane. Bucureşti, 1937.

AH 3013.940   Christian, V. Altertumskunde des Zweistromlandes von der Vorzeit bis zum Ende der Achamenidenherrschaft. v.1; pt.2. Leipzig, 1940.

AH 7659.16   Christianity and nationalism in...Roman Empire. Photoreproduction. (Woodward, E.L.) London, 1916.

Eg 758.79   Christianity in Egypt. (Peabody, F.G.) n.p., n.d.

AH 7469.71   Christiansen, Erik. Den romerske republiks sidste hundrede år. København, 1971.

AH 7168.43   Christiansen, J. Institutionen des römischen Rechts. Altona, 1843.

AH 7198.38   Christiansen, J. Wissenschaft des römischen Rechtsgeschichte. Altona, 1838.

Htn   AH 4864.9*   Christie, J. Inquiry into ancient Greek game. London, 1801.

AH 7817.42.10   Christophori Cellarii Breviarium antiquitatum romanarum, accurante. (Cellarii, Christophori.) Augustae Taurinorum, 1742.

AH 7279.48   Christus und die Caesaren. 2. Aufl. (Stauffer, Ethelbert.) Hamburg, 1948.

AH 507.98   Chronica medii aevi. (Roesler, C.F.) Tubingae, 1798.

Htn   AH 7495.57*   A chronicle, conteyning the lives of tenne emperours of Rome. (Guevara, A.) London, 1577.

Eg 1099.58   The chronicle of Prince Osorkon. (Caminos, R.A.) Roma, 1958.

AH 3020.22.1   Chronicles concerning early Babylonian kings. v.1-2. (King, Leonard W.) London, 1972.

AH 3002.26.10   Chronicles of Chaldaean kings. (British Museum. Department of Egyptian and Assyrian Antiquities.) London, 1956.

AH 807.52.5F   Chronicon historiam catholicam. (Simson, E.) Amstelodami, 1752.

AH 4808.84   Chronicon Parium. (Parian Chronicle.) Tubingae, 1884.

Htn   AH 805.75*   Chronicon seu Emendatio temporum. (Lucidus, J.) Venetiis, 1575.

Htn   AH 275.39F*   Chronicorum. (Freculphus.) Cologne, 1539.

Htn   AH 806.72F*   Chronicus canon. (Marcham, John.) Londini, 1672.

EgP 27.2   Chronique d'Egypte. Bruxelles. 4-11,1928-1936 4v.

AH 809.10   La chronographie. (Elia bar Sinaya.) Paris, 1910.

AH 7539.11   Chronoligisch-kritische Untersuchungen zur Geschichte des Kaisers Claudius. Diss. (Vivell, Karl.) Freiburg, 1911.

Htn   AH 805.45F*   Chronologia. (Funck, J.) Norimbergae, 1545.

AH 7808.99.3   Chronologia storica Roma. (Rolando, A.) Torino, 1899.

Htn   AH 3962.16*   Chronologiae sacrae isagoge. (Vossius, G.J.) Hagae-Comitum, 1659. 2 pam.

AH 7277.60   Chronological abridgement of Roman history. (Macquer, P.) London, 1760.

AH 807.52   Chronological antiquities. (Jackson, J.) London, 1752. 3v.

AH 4808.82A   Chronological tables of Greek history. (Peter, C.L.) Cambridge, 1882.

AH 4808.83   Chronologie. (Mommsen, A.) Leipzig, 1883.

AH 7808.91   Chronologie de l'Empire romain. (Goyau, G.) Paris, 1891.

AH 1807.38   Chronologie de l'histoire sainte. (Vignolles, A.) Berlin, 1738. 2v.

Eg 808.49F   Die Chronologie der Ägypter. (Lepsius, K.R.) Berlin, 1849.

AH 7448.78   Die Chronologie der Belagerung von Sagunt. (Sieglin, W.) Leipzig, 1878.

AH 1808.96   Die Chronologie der Geschichte Israels, Aegyptens. (Krug, Carl.) Leipzig, 1896.

Eg 603.19   Die Chronologie der internationalen Korrespondenz von El-Amarna. (Kühne, Cord.) Kevelaer, 1973.

AH 7468.29.7   Chronologie der mithridatischen Kriege. (Bernhardt, H.) Marburg, 1896.

AH 4498.90   Chronologie der Pentekontaëtie. (Mosler, I.) Berlin, 1890.

AH 3149.3   Chronologie des Assyriens et des Babyloniens. (Oppert, J.) Paris, n.d.

Eg 808.67   Chronologie des Manetho. (Unger, G.F.) Berlin, 1867.

Eg 809.62   Chronologie des préfets d'Égypte de 284 à 395. (Vanderslayen, Claude.) Bruxelles, 1962.

AH 2012.2   La chronologie des rois de Saba et dü-Raydân. (Ryckmans, Jacques.) Istanbul, 1964.

Eg 808.73   Chronologie égyptienne. (Lieblein, J.) Christiania, 1873.

AH 7808.87   Die Chronologie von 218/217 v. Chr. (Thouret, Georg.) Berlin, 1887.

AH 4708.83   Chronologische Beiträge zur Geschichte des achäischen Bundes. (Klatt, Max.) Berlin, 1883.

Eg 808.78   Das chronologisches System Manetho's. (Pessl, H. von.) Leipzig, 1878.

Htn   AH 807.28.3*   Chronology of ancient kingdoms. (Newton, Isaac.) London, 1728.

AH 807.22   Chronology of antient kingdoms. (Newton, Isaac.) Dublin, 1722.

AH 5312.5F   The chronology of Hellenistic Athens. (Pritchett, William K.) Cambridge, Mass., 1940.

Eg 603.17   The chronology of the Amarna letters. (Campbell, E.F.) Baltimore, 1964.

AH 809.68   Chronology of the ancient world. (Bickerman, Elias Joseph.) London, 1968.

AH 3022.11   Chronology of the Shuk-ad culture. (Pallis, Svend Aage.) Kobenhavn, 1941.

AH 299.30   Chuckerbutty, K. The world on the positive plate. Calcutta, 193-. 5 pam.

AH 7039.05   Chudzinski, A. Staatseinrichtungen...Kaiserreichs. Gutersloh, 1905.

AH 8073.7.5   Church, A.J. Carthage, or The empire of Africa. Photoreproduction. London, 1887.

AH 4239.00.5   Church, A.J. Helmet and spear. N.Y., 1914.

AH 4523.7   Church, A.J. Nicias and Sicilian expedition. London, 1899.

AH 8073.7   Church, A.J. Story of Carthage. Photoreproduction. N.Y., 1886.

NEDL   AH 7818.84.5   Church, Alfred J. Roman life in the days of Cicero. London, 1884.

AH 7818.84.6   Church, Alfred J. Roman life in the days of Cicero. N.Y., 1883.

AH 3013.913F   Churches and monasteries of the Tûr 'Abdîn and neighbouring districts. (Bell, Gertrude.) Heidelberg, 1913.

AH 8647.10.5   Ciaceri, E. Storia della Magna Grecia. Milano, 1927-32. 3v.

AH 7519.34   Ciaceri, E. Tiberio, successore di Augusto. Milano, 1934.

AH 7519.34.5   Ciaceri, E. Tiberio, successore di Augusto. 2. ed. Roma, 1944.

AH 9610.28   Ciaceri, Emanuele. Esame critico della storia...guerre servili. Catania, 1907.

AH 9610.28.5   Ciaceri, Emanuele. Intorno alle più antiche relazioni fra la Sicilia e la Persia. Pisa, 1912.

AH 7279.37   Ciaceri, Emanuele. Le origini di Roma. Milano, 1937.

AH 7449.40 — Ciaceri, Emanuele. Scipione Africano e l'idea imperiale di Roma. Napoli, 1940.

AH 8909.5 — Ciba Foundation. Ciba Foundation on medical biology and Etruscan origins. London, 1959.

AH 8909.5 — Ciba Foundation on medical biology and Etruscan origins. (Ciba Foundation.) London, 1959.

AH 7478.95 — Ciccotti, E. Donne e politica. Milano, 1895.

AH 819.35 — Ciccotti, Ettore. La civiltà del mondo antico. Udine, 1935. 2v.

AH 139.34 — Ciccotti, Ettore. La formazione della coscienza giuridica e le sue concrete graduali espressioni nel mondo antico. Udine, 1934.

AH 4279.20 — Ciccotti, Ettore. Griechische Geschichte. Gotha, 1920.

AH 239.01 — Ciccotti, Ettore. La guerra et la pace. Torino, 1901.

AH 109.21 — Ciccotti, Ettore. Lineamenti dell'evoluzione tributaria nel mondo antico. Milano, 1921.

AH 4279.22.10 — Ciccotti, Ettore. Storia greca. Firenze, 1922.

AH 188.99 — Ciccotti, Ettore. Il tramonto della schiavitù nel mondo antico. Torino, 1899.

AH 7419.48 — Cicero and the Roman republic. (Cowell, Frank R.) London, 1948.

AH 7419.48.5 — Cicero and the Roman republic. (Cowell, Frank R.) N.Y., 1948.

AH 7479.39 — Cicero und Caesar. (Klass, J.) Berlin, 1939.

AH 7469.38.6 — Cicero und Sallust über die Catilinarische Verschwörung. (Vogt, Joseph.) Darmstadt, 1973.

VAH 7819.58.5 — Ciceronis Jilius. (Paoli, Ugo Enrico.) Firenze, 1958.

VAH 7823.2 — Ciceronis Jilius. 5. ed. (Peoli, Ugo Enrico.) Florentiae, 1961.

AH 7299.22 — Cichorius, C. Römische Studien, historisches, epigraphisches, literargeschichtliches. Leipzig, 1922.

AH 5132.7 — Cichorius, Conrad. Rom und Mytilene. Leipzig, 1888.

AH 3020.40.5 — Çiğ, Muazzez. Eski Babill zamanina ait Nippur menşeli iki okul kitabi. Ankara, 1959.

AH 3020.75 — Çiğ, Muazzez. Istanbul arkeoloji müzelerinde bulunan Sumer edebi tablet parçalari. Ankara, 1969.

AH 3020.40 — Çiğ, Muazzez. Yeni Sumer çağina ait Nippur hukukî ve idarî belgeleri. Ankara, 1965.

AH 879.67 — Cilento, Vincenzo. Comprensione della religione antica. Napoli, 1967.

AH 9773.5 — Cimbrorum et Gothorum origines. (Pedersen, N.) Lipsiae, 1695.

AH 2108.15 — I Cimmeri. (Cozzoli, Umberto.) Roma, 1968.

AH 4479.34 — Cimone. (Lombardo, G.) Roma, 1934.

AH 7469.23 — Cinna and his times. (Bennett, Harold.) Menasha, 1923.

AH 7203.147F — Cino da Pistoia. Cyni Pistoriensis in codicem et aliquot titulos primi pandectorum tomi. Torino, 1964. 2v.

AH 3307.7 — Cipro. (Lauria, G.A.) Napoli, 1879.

AH 5409.6 — I Cipselidi. (Porzio, Guido.) Bologna, 1912.

AH 889.22 — Circolazione monetaria e prezzi nel mondo antico ed in particolare in Egitto. (Segrè, Angelo.) Roma, 1922.

AH 3013.18 — Circourt, A. de. Decouvertes dans les ruines de Ninive et de Babylone. Paris, 1854.

AH 8965.5 — Cisalpine Gaul. (Chilver, G.E.F.) Oxford, 1941.

AH 8963.5 — I Cisalpini. (Mansuelli, Guido Achille.) Firenze, 1962.

AH 8957.5 — Das cisalpinische Gallien. (Rovelli, G.) Leipzig, 1791.

AH 38.64 — La cité antique. 3. éd. (Fustel de Coulanges, N.D.) Paris, 1870.

AH 38.64.2 — La cité antique. 4. éd. (Fustel de Coulanges, N.D.) Paris, 1872.

AH 38.64.4 — La cité antique. 10. éd. (Fustel de Coulanges, N.D.) Paris, 1883.

AH 38.64.5 — La cité antique. 16. éd. (Fustel de Coulanges, N.D.) Paris, 1898.

AH 38.64.6 — La cité antique. 18. éd. (Fustel de Coulanges, N.D.) Paris, 1903.

AH 8063.5 — Les cités romaines de Tunisie. (Mahjouhi, Ammar.) Tunis, 1969?

AH 2808.5A — Cities and bishoprics of Phrygia. (Ramsay, W.M.) Oxford, 1895. 2v.

AH 3909.10 — Cities and nations of ancient Syria. (Buccellati, Giorgio.) Roma, 1967.

AH 7819.72 — Cities in the sand. (Menen, Aubrey.) N.Y., 1973.

AH 7299.37.5 — The cities of the eastern Roman provinces. (Jones, Arnold H.M.) Oxford, 1937.

AH 7299.37.6 — The cities of the eastern Roman provinces. 2. ed. (Jones, Arnold H.M.) Oxford, 1971.

AH 38.64.30 — La città antica. (Fustel de Coulanges, N.D.) Firenze, 1924.

AH 99.24 — La città antica e la sua economia. (Salvioli, G.) Napoli, 1924.

AH 9186.5 — La città di Pandosia. (Grazia, Paolo di.) Napoli, 1918.

AH 9627.2 — Città sicane, sicule e greche nella zona di Gela. (Navarra, Giuseppe.) Palermo, 1964.

AH 4847.5 — I cittadini lavoratori. (Mauri, A.) Milano, 1895.

AH 4039.64A — The city and man. (Strauss, L.) Chicago, 1964.

AH 299.72.10A — The city in the ancient world. (Hammond, Mason.) Cambridge, Mass., 1972.

AH 1812.5 — City invincible. (Symposium on Urbanization and Cultural Development in the Ancient Near East, University of Chicago, 1958.) Chicago, 1960.

AH 8657.5.3 — The city of Rome. 2. ed. (Dyer, Thomas H.) London, 1883.

Eg 971.7.20 — City of the stargazers. (Heuer, Kenneth.) N.Y., 1972.

AH 39.51 — City-state and world state in Greek and Roman political theory until Augustus. (Hammond, M.) Cambridge, Mass., 1951.

AH 48.93.5 — The city-state of the Greeks and Romans. (Fowler, W.W.) London, 1898.

AH 48.93.7 — The city-state of the Greeks and Romans. (Fowler, W.W.) London, 1921.

AH 7137.22.2F — The civil law in its natural order together with the publick law. (Domat, Jean.) London, 1737. 2v.

AH 7137.22.15 — The civil law in its natural order together with the publick law. 2. ed. (Domat, Jean.) Boston, 1850. 2v.

AH 7559.08 — Civil war and rebellion in Roman Empire. (Henderson, B.W.) London, 1908.

AH 7468.44 — Civil wars of Rome. (Plutarch.) London, 1844. 3v.

AH 3143.9 — La civilisation assyro-babylonienne. (Contenau, Georges.) Paris, 1922.

AH 818.68.5 — La civilisation au cinquième siècle. (Ozanam, A.F.) Paris, 1855. 2v.

AH 3143.9.5 — La civilisation d'Assur et de Babylone. (Contenau, Georges.) Paris, 1937.

AH 4819.32.15 — La civilisation de la Grèce antique. (Croiset, Maurice.) Paris, 1932.

AH 9563.5 — La civilisation de la Sardaigne. (Zervos, C.) Paris, 1954.

AH 8013.4 — La civilisation de l'Afrique romaine. (Charles-Picard, Gilbert.) Paris, 1959.

Eg 819.65.5 — La civilisation de l'Egypte pharaonique. (Daumas, François.) Paris, 1965.

AH 3413.12 — La civilisation des Hitties et des Mitanniens. (Contenau, Georges.) Paris, 1934.

AH 3413.12.5 — La civilisation des Hittites. (Contenau, Georges.) Paris, 1948.

AH 5463.15 — La civilisation égéenne. (Glotz, Gustave.) Paris, 1952.

AH 8913.12 — La civilisation étrusque. (Pallottino, Massimo.) Paris, 1949.

AH 4819.63.15 — La civilisation grecque. (Chamoux, François.) Paris, 1963.

AH 4819.67.10 — La civilisation grecque de l'antiquité à nos jours. Bruxelles, 1967. 2v.

AH 4819.22 — La civilisation hellénique. (Croiset, M.) Paris, 1922. 2v.

AH 4659.62 — La civilisation hellénistique. (Petit, Paul.) Paris, 1962.

AH 819.71.5 — La civilisation hellénistique et la montée de Rome. (Grimal, Pierre.) Paris, 1971.

AH 3713.10 — La civilisation phénicienne. (Contenau, G.) Paris, 1926.

AH 7819.60.10 — La civilisation romaine. (Grimal, Pierre.) Paris, 1960.

AH 7819.30.10 — La civilisation romaine. (Homs, Léon.) Paris, 1930.

AH 1819.45.4 — Les civilisations anciennes du Proche-Orient. 5. éd. (Contenau, Georges.) Paris, 1963.

AH 819.51.5 — Civilisations antiques. (Pirenne, J.) Paris, 1951.

AH 819.67 — Les civilisations de l'Europe ancienne. (Mansuelli, Guido Achille.) Paris, 1967.

AH 7138.20 — Civilistische Abhandlungen. (Dirksen, H.E.) Berlin, 1820. 2v.

AH 279.33 — La civiltà antica dal periodo preistorico. (Vicini, Antonio.) Piedimonte d'Alife, 1933.

AH 7818.58.5 — La civilizacion en los cinco primeros siglos del cristianismo. 2. ed. (Castelar y Ripoll, E.) Madrid, 1865. 4v.

AH 819.24.5 — Civilizaciones antiguas. Barcelona. 1-3

AH 7819.54 — Civilization and the Caesars. (Starr, C.G.) Ithaca, 1954.

AH 4819.54.5 — Civilization grecque. (Bonnard, André.) Lausanne, 1954. 3v.

AH 4819.54.7 — Civilization grecque. v.2-3. (Bonnard, André.) Paris, 1963. 2v.

AH 3143.8 — The civilization of Babylonia and Assyria. (Jastrow, Morris.) Philadelphia, 1915.

AH 3143.8.2 — The civilization of Babylonia and Assyria. (Jastrow, Morris.) Philadephia, 1915.

AH 4819.63.16 — The civilization of Greece. (Chamoux, François.) London, 1965.

AH 7819.60.5 — The civilization of Rome. (Dudley, Donald R.) N.Y., 1960.

AH 7819.60.6 — The civilization of Rome. (Dudley, Donald R.) N.Y., 1962.

AH 7819.60.11 — The civilization of Rome. (Grimal, Pierre.) N.Y., 1963.

Eg 819.16 — The civilization of the ancient Egyptians. (Gosse, A.B.) N.Y., 1916.

AH 1818.82.5 — Civilization of the eastern Iranians. (Geiger, W.) London, 1885.

AH 7228.64.5 — Der Civilprozess des gemeinen Rechts. (Bethmann-Hollweg, M.A. von.) Bonn, 1864. 6v.

AH 7138.72.3 — Civilrechts der Römer. (Puntschart, V.) Erlangen, 1872.

AH 819.48 — La civiltà de mondo antico. (Passerini, A.) Milano, 1948.

AH 9563.6 — La civiltà dei Sardi dal neolitico all'età dei nuraghi. (Lilliu, G.) Torino, 1963.

AH 819.35 — La civiltà del mondo antico. (Ciccotti, Ettore.) Udine, 1935. 2v.

Eg 819.63 — Civiltà dell'antico Egitto. (Nolli, G.) Tolino, 1963.

AH 8073.25 — La civiltà di Cartagine. (Barreca, Ferruccio.) Cagliari, 1964.

AH 3963.165 — La civiltà ebraica e le origini del cristianesimo, ad uso delle scuole medie. (Lattes, Aldo.) Firenze, 1924.

AH 8608.12 — La civiltà gallica in Italia. L'impero di Severo Alessandro. (Arias, Paolo E.) Bologna, 1953.

AH 8647.14 — Civiltà greca nell'Italia meridionale. (Olivieri, A.) Napoli, 1931.

AH 9313.5 — La civiltà latina in Abruzzo. (Bertolé Viale, Giovanni.) Pescara, 1956.

AH 819.71.10 — Civiltà sul Mediterraneo. (Moscati, Sabatino.) Novara, 1971.

Htn AH 7035.88* — Civitas romana. (Panvino, O.) Parisiis, 1588.

AH 7549.72 — Cizek, Eugen. L'époque de Néron et ses controverses idéologiques. Leiden, 1972.

AH 5138.17F — Clara Rhodes. 1-9, 1928-1938 10v.

AH 3002.154.5 — The claremont Ras Shamra tablets. Roma, 1971.

AH 7138.72 — Clark, E.C. Early Roman law. London, 1872.

AH 7169.06.5 — Clark, E.C. History of Roman private law. pt.1-2. Cambridge, 1906-19. 4v.

AH 7259.15 — Clark, F.W. The influence of sea power on…Roman republic. Menasha, 1915.

Eg 879.59A — Clark, R.T. Myth and symbol in ancient Egypt. v.4. London, 1959.

AH 3966.4F — Clark, Samuel. The Bible atlas of maps and plans to illustrate geography and topography of O.T. and N.T. and Apocrypha. London, 1868.

NEDL AH 5957.9 — Clark, W.G. Peloponnesus. London, 1858.

AH 7842.2 — Clarke, George. The education of children at Rome. N.Y., 1896.

AH 842.52 — Clarke, Martin Lowther. Higher education in the ancient world. London, 1971.

AH 9610.17 — Clasen, C. Timoleon, eine historische Untersuchung. Glückstadt, 1896.

AH 7148.71 — Clason, D.O. Kristische Erörterungen über den römischen Staat. Rostock, 1871.

AH 4299.47 — Class struggles in ancient Greece. (Wason, Margaret O.) London, 1947.

AH 7114.38 — Les classes sociales dans l'empire romain. (Gagé, Jean.) Paris, 1964.

AH 7818.83.15 — Classical antiquities. (Wilkins, A.S.) N.Y., 1883.

AH 8616.9A — Classical associations of places in Italy. (Sabin, Frances E.) Madison, Wis., 1921.

NEDL AH 930.7.3 — A classical atlas, to illustrate ancient geography. (Findlay, Alexander G.) London, 1854.

NEDL AH 930.7.6 — A classical atlas, to illustrate ancient geography. (Findlay, Alexander G.) N.Y., 1849.

NEDL AH 930.7.5 — A classical atlas, to illustrate ancient geography. (Findlay, Alexander G.) N.Y., 185-?

AH 930.15 — Classical atlas. (Ginn and Co., publishers.) Boston, 1894.

AH 819.40.2 — Classical civilization. (Couch, H.N.) N.Y., 1947.

AH 819.40.4 — Classical civilization. 2. ed. (Couch, H.N.) N.Y., 1950-51. 2v.

Author and Title Listing

AH 938.77A   Classical geography. (Tozer, Henry F.) N.Y., 1877.
AH 938.77.5   Classical geography. (Tozer, Henry F.) N.Y., 1877.
AH 4819.65.15   Classical Greece. (Bowra, Cecil Maurice.) N.Y., 1965.
AH 7139.51   Classical Roman law. (Schulz, Fritz.) Oxford, 1951.
AH 8667.2   Classical Rome. (Jones, H.S.) N.Y., 1910.
AH 8667.4   Classical Rome. (Stuart-Jones, H.) London, 1910.
AH 7539.32.5   Claudius, the emperor. (Momigliano, A.) Oxford, 1934.
AH 7538.58   Claudius und Nero und ihre Zeit. (Lehmann, H.) Gotha, 1858.
AH 7538.58.2   Claudius und seine Zeit. (Lehmann, H.) Leipzig, 1877.
AH 7239.71.5F   Claustra Alpium Iuliarum. Ljubljana, 1971.
AH 4408.09.5   Clavier, M. Histoire des premiers temps de la Grèce. 2. éd. Paris, 1822. 3v.
AH 3028.5   Clay, A.T. The antiquity of Amorite civilization. New Haven, 1924.
AH 3002.7.5   Clay, A.T. Hebrew deluge story in cuneiform...Morgan Library. New Haven, 1922.
AH 8914.10   Clemen, Carl. Die Religion der Etrusker. Bonn, 1936.
AH 3664.15   Clemen, Carolus. Fontes historiae religionum Persicae. Bonnae, 1920.
Eg 709.37.3   Cleopatra, Geschichte einer Königin. (Ludwig, E.) Amsterdam, 1937.
Eg 709.37.5A   Cleopatra, the story of a queen. (Ludwig, E.) N.Y., 1937.
Eg 709.71.10   Cleopatra. (Bradford, Ernle Dusgate Selby.) London, 1971.
Eg 709.72   Cleopatra. (Grant, Michael.) London, 1972.
Htn   Eg 708.90.7*   Cleopatra. (Houssaye, Henry.) N.Y., 1890.
Eg 708.90.5   Cleopatra. (Houssaye, Henry.) N.Y., 1890.
Eg 709.71   Cleopatra. (Lindsay, Jack.) London, 1971.
Eg 708.64   Cleopatra. (Stahr, Adolf.) Berlin, 1864.
Eg 708.64.2   Cleopatra. 2. Aufl. (Stahr, Adolf.) Berlin, 1879.
Eg 709.09.15   Cleopatra of Egypt. (Sergeant, P.W.) N.Y., 1909.
Eg 709.71.5   Cleopatra's children. (Desmond, Alice Curtis.) N.Y., 1971.
Eg 608.86   Cleopatra's needle. (King, James.) London, 1886.
Eg 709.03.5   Cléopâtre; sa vie, son règne. (De Bernáth, D.) Paris, 1903.
Eg 709.60   Cléopâtre. (Daix, Pierre.) Paris, 1960.
AH 7469.06.5   Clerc, Michel. La bataille d'Aix. Paris, 1906.
AH 3013.42PF   Clercq, Louis de. Collection De Clercq. Paris, 1885-1908. 2v.
AH 3013.42.2F   Clercq, Louis de. Collection De Clercq. Paris, 1912.
AH 3013.42F   Clercq, Louis de. Collection De Clercq. v.3-6, 7, pt.1-2. Paris, 1905-11. 6v.
AH 7419.55   Clerici, André. La république romaine. 1. éd. Paris, 1955.
AH 7109.43   Clerici, Luigi. Economici e finanza dei romani. Bologna, 1943-
AH 8907.26.5   Cles-Reden, S. The buried people. N.Y., 1955.
AH 8907.26   Cles-Reden, S. Les Étrusques. Paris, 1955.
AH 4818.27.4   Cleveland, C.D. Compendium of Grecian antiquities. 2. ed. Boston, 1831.
AH 4818.27   Cleveland, C.D. Epitome of Grecian antiquities. Boston, 1827.
AH 4818.27.6   Clevland, C.D. Compendium of Grecian antiquities. 2. ed. Boston, 1836.
AH 7419.08   Client princes of the Roman empire. (Sands, P.C.) Cambridge, 1908.
AH 8016.10   Le climat de l'Afrique du nord dans l'antiquité. (Gsell, Stéphane.) Alger, 1911.
AH 7659.67.5   The climax of Rome. (Grant, Michael.) Saskatoon, 1967.
AH 7489.68   The climax of Rome. 1. American ed. (Grant, Michael.) Boston, 1968.
AH 4808.51   Clinton, H.F. Epitome...civil and literary chronicle of Greece. Oxford, 1851.
AH 4808.34.3   Clinton, H.F. Fasti Hellenici. Lipsiae, 1830.
AH 4808.34   Clinton, H.F. Fasti Hellenici. Oxford, 1834. 3v.
AH 7808.53.5   Clinton, Henry Fynes. An epitome of the civil and literary chronology of Rome and Constantinople. Oxford, 1853.
AH 7808.45   Clinton, Henry Fynes. Fasti Romani, the civil and literary chronology of Rome and Constantinople. v.2. Oxford, 1845.
AH 4559.53.5   Cloché, Paul. Alexandre le Grand et les essais de fusion entre l'occident gréco-macédonien. Neuchatel, 1953.
AH 5303.14   Cloché, Paul. La démocratie athénienne. Paris, 1951.
AH 4609.59   Cloché, Paul. La dislocation d'un empire. Paris, 1959.
AH 4458.5   Cloché, Paul. Étude chronologique sur la troisième guerre sacrée. Thèse. Paris, 1915.
AH 6110.21   Cloché, Paul. Un fondateur d'empire. Saint Etienne, 1955.
AH 6107.10   Cloché, Paul. Histoire de la Macédoine. Paris, 1960.
AH 4459.58   Cloché, Paul. Le monde grec aux temps classiques. Paris, 1958.
AH 5310.15   Cloché, Paul. La politique étrangère d'Athènes de 404 à 338 avant Jesus Christ. Paris, 1934.
AH 5310.6   Cloché, Paul. Le restauration democratique à Athènes en 403 avant J.C. Paris, 1915.
AH 5390.17   Cloché, Paul. Thèbes de Béotie. Namur, 1952?
AH 408.87   Clodd, E. Childhood of the world. London, 1887.
AH 7469.54.5   Clodia. (Mainzer, Ferdinand.) Braunschweig, 1954.
AH 7469.60.10   Clodia. (Weil, Bruno.) Zürich, 1960.
AH 7848.9.10   The clothing of the ancient Romans. (Wilson, L.M.) Baltimore, 1938.
AH 8616.2F   Cluneri, P. Italiae antiquae. Lugduni Batavorum, 1624.
AH 8549.171   Coarer-Kalondan, Edmond. Le druidisme, ou La lumière del l'Occident. Paris, 1971.
AH 5308.10   Coastal demes of Attika. (Eliot, C.W.J.) Toronto, 1962.
AH 7207.35   Cobban, J.M. Senate and provinces, 78-49 B.C. Cambridge, Eng., 1935.
AH 7278.28.2   Cobbett, W. Abridged history of emperors. London, 1829.
AH 7278.28   Cobbett, W. Elements of Roman history. London, 1828.
AH 3151.10   Le code d'Hammourabi. (Colgecen, M.C.) Fribourg, 1949.
X Cg   AH 3151.9.2   The code of Hammurabi...about 2250 B.C. 2. ed. (Hammurabi, king of Babylonia.) Chicago, 1904.
AH 3151.14   The code of Hammurabi. (Hammurabi, king of Babylonia.) Chicago, 1904.
AH 7202.5F   Codex. (Codex Theodosianus.) Lugduni Batavorum, 1665. 6v.
AH 7202.7F   Codex. (Codex Theodusianus.) Lipsiae, 1743. 6v.
AH 3151.2.3F   Codex Hammurabi. (Hammurabi, king of Babylonia.) Romae, 1950.
AH 3151.1.3F   Codex Hammurabi. (Hammurabi, king of Babylonia.) Romae, 1953.
AH 7203.67   Codex Iustinianus. (Corpus juris civilis. Codex.) Berolini, 1877.
AH 7202.13   Codex Theodosianus. Antiqua summaria Codicis Theodosiani. Lipsiae, 1834.
AH 7202.5F   Codex Theodosianus. Codex. Lugduni Batavorum, 1665. 6v.
AH 7202.11   Codex Theodosianus. Codicis Theodosiani libri v priores. Lipsiae, 1825.

AH 7202.15   Codex Theodosianus. Gregorianus Hermogenianus. Bonn, 1842.
AH 7202.15.2   Codex Theodosianus. Gregorianus Hermogenianus. Bonn, 1844.
AH 7202.30F   Codex Theodosianus. The Theodosian code and novels and the Sermondian constitutions. Princeton, N.J., 1952.
AH 7202.17   Codex Theodosianus. Theodosiani. Berolini, 1905. 2v.
AH 7202.18   Codex Theodosianus. Theodosiani libri XVI. Berolini, 1905.
AH 7202.9   Codex Theodosianus. Theodosianus Codex genuina fragmenta. Bonnae, 1825.
AH 7202.20   Codex Theodosianus. Facsimile 1-2. (Rome. Laws, statutes, etc. Theodosius II.) Berolini, 1923-26.
AH 7202.7F   Codex Theodusianus. Codex. Lipsiae, 1743. 6v.
Htn   AH 7203.5*   Codicis Justiniani. (Corpus juris civilis. Codex.) Lugduni, 1571.
Htn   AH 7203.11.3*   Codicis justiniani imperiales. (Perez, A.) Amstelodami, 1671. 2v.
AH 7203.11   Codicis justiniani imperiales. (Perez, A.) Amstelodami, 1761.
AH 7202.11   Codicis Theodosiani libri v priores. (Codex Theodosianus.) Lipsiae, 1825.
Eg 1042.946A   Coffin Texts (Egyptian). Textes des cercueils du Moyen Empire égyptien. Bruxelles, 1946.
AH 98.80   Cognat, René. De municipalibus et provincialibus militus in Imperio Romano. Thesis. Lutetiae Parisiorum, 1880.
AH 7099.00.2   I cognomi delle colonie romane militari. (Leogrande, P.) Trani, 1900.
AH 7869.2   Cognomine et agnomine Romano. (Ellendt, F.) Regimontii Borussorum, 1853.
Eg 39.12   Cohen, D. De magistratibus Aegyptiis externas Lagidarum regni provincias administrantibus. 's Gravenhage, n.d.
AH 4659.24   Cohen, D. Universalisme en particularisme in den aarwang van het hellenistisch tijdperk. Groningen, 1924.
AH 5304.2   Cohen, Edward E. Ancient Athenian maritime courts. Princeton, 1973.
AH 3803.5   Cohen, Kadmi. Introduction à l'histoire des institutions sociales et politiques chez les Semites. Paris, 1922.
AH 5307.30   Cohen, R. Athènes, une démocratie. Paris, 1936.
AH 4299.34   Cohen, R. La grèce et l'hellénisation du monde antique. Paris, 1934.
AH 4299.34.5   Cohen, R. La grèce et l'hellénisation du monde antique. 3. éd. Paris, 1948.
AH 7239.38   Les cohortes pretoriennes. Thèse. (Durry, Marcel.) Paris, 1938.
AH 4238.37   Cohortis Sacrae apud Thebanos Histobiam. (Kreenen, J.J.) Arnhemiae, 1837.
AH 3250.5   Colchis, Iberien und Albanien um die Wende des 1. Jahrhunderts vor Christ. Inaug. Diss. (Margwelaschwili, T. von.) Halle, 1914.
AH 7489.50   The cold war in the Roman Empire. (Toynbee, Arnold J.) Claremont, Calif., 1950.
AH 7842.14   Cole, P.R. Later Roman education in Ausonius, Capella. N.Y., 1909.
AH 3966.3   Coleman, L. An historical text book and atlas of Biblical geography. Philadelphia, 1868.
AH 4278.98.10   Coleridge, E.P. Res graecae. London, 1898.
AH 7278.96.10   Coleridge, E.P. Res Romanae. London, 1896.
AH 3151.10   Colgecen, M.C. Le code d'Hammourabi. Fribourg, 1949.
AH 7162.34   Coli, Ugo. Lo suiluppo delle varie forme di legato nel diritto romano. Parigi, 1920.
AH 7448.18.13   Colin, J. Annibal en Gaule. Paris, 1904.
AH 8514.15   Colin, J. L'empire des Antonins et les martyrs gaulois de 177. Bonn, 1964.
AH 7099.65   Colin, Jean. Les villes libres de l'Orient gréco-romain et l'envoi au supplice par acclamations populaires. Bruxelles, 1965.
AH 8689.5F   Colini, Antonio. Stadium Domitiani. Roma, 1943.
AH 6136.10   Collart, Paul. Philippes, ville de Macédoine. Atlas. Paris, 1937. 2v.
AHP 25.4   Collectio. (Oriens antiquus.) Roma. 1,1962+ 9v.
AH 7130.2   Collectio bibliographica operum ad ius romanum pertienetium. v.1-20. (Caes, Lucien.) Bruxelles, 1949-13v.
AH 7206.7   Collectio librorum juris Graeco-Romanum. (Zacharia, K.E.) Lipsiae, 1852.
AH 3013.42PF   Collection De Clercq. (Clercq, Louis de.) Paris, 1885-1908. 2v.
AH 3013.42.2F   Collection De Clercq. (Clercq, Louis de.) Paris, 1912.
AH 3013.42F   Collection De Clercq. v.3-6, 7, pt.1-2. (Clercq, Louis de.) Paris, 1905-11. 6v.
Eg 291.5   A collection of 15 tracts. (Champollion, J.J.) Grenoble, 1806. 15 pam.
AH 3607.15   Colledge, Malcom A.R. The Parthians. London, 1967.
AH 7918.97.3   Les Collegia Juvenum. (Demoulin, H.) Louvain, 1897.
AH 8207.12   Collingwood, Robin G. Roman Britain. London, 1923.
AH 3657.46   Collins, Robert J. The Medes and Persians, conquerors and diplomats. N.Y., 1972.
AH 7653.20   Collins, William M. The student's companion to Gibbon. Melbourne, 1957.
Eg 39.26   Collomp, Paul. Recherches sur la chancellerie et la diplomatique des Lagides. Paris, 1926.
Eg 39.25   Collomp, Paul. Recherches sur la chancellerie et la diplomatique des Lagides. Thèse. Strasbourg, 1925.
AH 9773.13   Colonia Agrippinensis. 3. Aufl. (La Baume, Peter.) Köln, 1964.
AH 9273.5   La colonia Carseolana. (Passeri, T.) Roma, 1883.
AH 7168.85   Die Colonia Partiaria des römischen Rechts. (Waaser, M.) Berlin, 1885.
AH 9660.7   Las colonias gemelas reintegradas en la mitad de sua respectivas publacions. (Barco, Alejandro del.) Madrid, 1788.
AH 9658.5   Las colonias romanas de Hispania. (García y Bellido, Antonio.) Madrid, 1959.
AH 7098.96   Le colonie dei romani. (Ruggiero, E. de.) Spoleto, 1896.
AH 4298.08   Colonien der Griechen. (Hegewisch, D.H.) Altona, 1808.
AH 3713.5   Colonies phéniciennes. (Barges, J.J.L.) Paris, 1878.
AH 299.70   La colonisation dans l'antiquité. (Massé, Claude.) Paris, 1970.
AH 8647.22   La colonisation grecque de l'Italie meridionale et de la Sicile dans l'antiquité. (Bérard, Jean.) Paris, 1957.
AH 7089.33   La colonizzazione romana dal Brenta al Piave. (Bon, Alessio de.) Bassagno del Grappe, 1933.
AH 299.50   Colonizzazioni nell'antico. (Bertoldi, V.) Napoli, 1950.
AH 7409.38   Colonna di Cesaro, G.A. Il mistero delle origini di Roma. Milano, 1938.
AH 4299.64.5   Colony and mother city in ancient Greece. (Graham, Alexander John.) N.Y., 1964.

AH 2573.5 — Colophoniaca. (Pertz, C.A.) Gottingae, 1848.

AH 32.5 — Coloquios sobre teoria política de la antigüedad clásica. (Sociedad Española de Estudios Clásicos.) Madrid, 1965.

AH 7138.49 — Colquhoun, P. Summary of Roman civil law. London, 1849. 4v.

AH 7489.44.5 — Columba, G.M. L'impero romano. 3. ed. pt.1. Milano, 1944.

AH 938.93 — Columba, G.M. Gli studi geografici nel I secolo dell'impero romano. Torino, 1893.

AHP 13.5 — Columbia University. Ancient Near Eastern Society. Journal. N.Y. 1,1969+ 3v.

AH 7487.29 — Comazzi, G.B. The morals of princes. London, 1729.

AH 3160.12 — Combe, E. Histoire du culte de Sin. Paris, 1908.

AH 4278.80 — Combers, L. La Grèce. Paris, 1880.

AH 7059.66 — Combès, Robert. Imperator; recherches sur l'emploi et la signification du titre d'imperator dans la Rome republicaine. Thèse. Paris, 1966.

AH 7419.72 — Combès, Robert. La république à Rome, 509-29 avant Jésus-Christ. Paris, 1972.

AH 7201.113 — Comentarios a las Instituciones de Gayo. 1. ed. (Ortiz Márquez, Julio.) Bogota, 1968.

AH 7768.85 — Der Comes Theodosius. Inaug. Diss. (Löffler, Eduard.) Halle, 1885.

AH 7298.71A — Comic history of Rome. (À Beckett, G.A.) London, n.d.

Htn — AH 7298.52* — The comic history of Rome. (A Beckett, G.A.) London, 1852?

AH 7208.3 — Les comices à Rome. (Hallays, André.) Paris, 1890.

AH 7208.4 — Les comices électoraux. (Marlot, Emile.) Paris, 1884.

Eg 1039.23A — The coming forth by day. (Book of the Dead.) Boston, 1923.

AH 8073.5 — Comment...les sémites entrèrent. (Littré, M.P.E.) Leipzig, 1879.

AH 8522.5 — Comment la Belgique fut romanisée. (Cumont, Franz.) Paris, 1914.

AH 8549.79 — Comment le druidisme a disparu. (Fustel de Coulanges, N.D.) Paris, 1879.

AH 3159.24F — Commentaire geographique sur l'exode et les nombres. (Laborde, L. de.) Paris, 1841.

AH 3156.15 — Commentaires assyro-babyloniens sur les présages. (Labat, René.) Bordeux, 1933.

AH 7486.57F — Commentaires historiques contenans l'histoire générale des empereurs, impératrices, Caesars, et tyrans de l'Empire Romain. (Tristan, Jean.) Paris, 1657.

AH 7202.16 — Ein Commentar des Florus von Lyon zu einigen der sogenannten Sermondschen Constitutionen. (Maasen, F.) Wien, 1879.

AH 7162.17 — Commentar über den Paudie de Heeredetatis Petitione. (Franke, W.) Göttingen, 1864.

AH 7201.43 — Commentaries. (Gaius.) Cambridge, 1870.

AH 7201.49 — Commentaries. (Gaius.) Cambridge, 1874.

AH 7138.22 — Commentarii de iure civili. (Doneau, H.) Norimberg, 1822. 16v.

AH 7844.5.5F — I commentarii dei ludi secolari. (Mommsen, T.) Roma, 1891.

AH 7844.5F — Commentarium ludorum. (Mommsen, T.) Milano, 1891.

Htn — AH 7203.10F* — Commentarius ad digestorum. (Zoesius.) Bruxelles, 1717.

AH 7167.42 — Commentarius ad Leges decemvirdem. (Taylor, John.) Cantabrigiae, 1742.

Htn — AH 7203.138.6F* — Commentarius ad Pandectas. (Voet, J.) Hagae, 1731. 2v.

AH 7844.7 — Commentarius de spectaculis. (Brissonius, B.) Lugdini Batavorum, 1742.

Htn — AH 8217.5* — Commentary on Antoninus...itinerary. (Burton, William.) London, 1658.

AH 3012.3 — Commentary on cuneiform inscriptions. (Rawlinson, H.C.) London, 1850.

Htn — AH 3664.10* — Commentatio de...religionis Persarum. (Meiners, Christoph.) n.p., n.d.

AH 8549.10 — Commentatio de Druidis. (Frick, J.G.) Ulmae, 1744.

AH 3980.12.10 — Commentatio de Golgothae et sanctissimi D.N.J.C. sepulcri situ. (Scholz, J.M.A.) Bonnae, 1825.

AH 7178.41 — Commentatio de Lege Thoria Agraria. (Zeiss, Gustavo.) Vimariae, 1841.

AH 7448.70.5 — Commentatio de pace anno 201 a. Chr. Carthaginiensibus data. (Nissen, Heinrich.) Marburgi, 1870.

AH 7114.7 — Commentatio de Patronatus. (Swingar, G.H.D.) Groningae, 1823.

AH 9777.8 — Commentatio Jornande sive Jordane libellorum natalibus. (Freudensprung, S.) Monaci, 1837.

AH 3959.31 — Commentationes societati regiae scientiarum Goettingensi per armas 1758-62. (Michaelis, J.D.) Bremae, 1763.

AH 3959.31.5 — Commentationes societati regiae scientiarum Goettingensi per armas 1758-62. (Michaelis, J.D.) Bremae, 1769.

AH 7158.45.15 — Commentationis de legibus judiciisque repetundarum. (Zumpt, Karl G.) Berolini, 1845. 2 pam.

AH 7098.50 — Commentationum epigraphicarum. (Zumptii, A.W.) Berolini, 1850.

AH 7203.140.5F — Commentoris in Pandectas. (Brunnermann, J.) Wittenburgae, 1701.

AH 7909.28 — The commerce between the Roman Empire and India. (Warmington, E.H.) Cambridge, 1928.

AH 909.25 — Il commercio dei popoli antichi nel bacino del Mediterraneo. (Segre, Arturo.) Torino, 1925.

AH 908.77F — Il commercio dell'ambra. (Helbig, W.) Roma, 1877.

AH 7819.11 — The common people of ancient Rome. (Abbott, F.F.) N.Y., 1911.

AH 2147.6 — Communi asiae provinciae. (Monceaux, P.) Paris, 1885.

AH 9113.5 — Comunità rurali nell'Italia antica. (Sereni, Emilio.) Roma, 1955.

AH 4819.05.3 — Companion to Greek studies. (Whibley, Leonard.) Cambridge, 1905.

AH 4819.05.3.6 — Companion to Greek studies. (Whibley, Leonard.) Cambridge, 1916.

AH 4819.05.3.5 — Companion to Greek studies. 2nd ed. (Whibley, Leonard.) Cambridge, 1906.

AH 7819.10 — Companion to Latin studies. (Sandys, J.E.) Cambridge, 1910.

AH 7819.13 — A companion to Latin studies. 2. ed. (Sandys, J.E.) Cambridge, 1913.

AH 7819.13.3 — A companion to Latin studies. 3. ed. (Sandys, J.E.) Cambridge, 1921.

AH 7279.12A — Companion to Roman history. (Jones, H.S.) Oxford, 1912.

AH 3013.949F — The comparative archaeology of early Mesopotamia. (Perkins, Ann L.) Chicago, 1949.

AH 3013.942 — The comparative stratigraphy of prehistoric Mesopotamia. (Perkins, Ann L.) Chicago, 1942.

Eg 1009.31A — Comparative study of the literature of Egypt, Palestine and Mesopotamia. (Peet, Thomas Eric.) London, 1931.

NEDL AH 278.92 — Compendio de historia antigua, griega y romana. (Eyzaquirre, R.) Santiago de Chile, 1892.

NEDL AH 278.84.12 — Compendio de historia antigua. 4. ed. (Martinez Silva, Carlos.) Bogota, 1910.

Htn — AH 277.88* — A compendious history of the world. (Newbery, John.) London, 1788. 2v.

AH 4817.34 — Compendium Antiquitatum Graecum. (Bruyn, C.) Francofurti, 1734.

AH 937.91 — Compendium of ancient geography. (Anville, Jean B.B. d'.) London, 1791. 2v.

AH 937.91.3 — Compendium of ancient geography. (Anville, Jean B.B. d'.) N.Y., 1814. 2v.

AH 4818.27.4 — Compendium of Grecian antiquities. 2. ed. (Cleveland, C.D.) Boston, 1831.

AH 4818.27.6 — Compendium of Grecian antiquities. 2. ed. (Clevland, C.D.) Boston, 1836.

AH 7168.95.3 — Compensation en droit romain. (Appleton, C.) Paris, 1895.

AH 7168.70 — Compensation nach römischen Recht. (Schwanert, H.A.) Rostock, 1870.

AH 7168.76.5 — Compensation nach römischen und gemeinem Recht. (Eisele, F.H.) Berlin, 1876.

AH 9609.3 — Compernolle, René van. Étude de chronologie et d'historiographie siciliotes...concernant la fondation des colonies siciliotes. Bruxelles, 1960.

AH 7207.33 — La composition du sénat romain de l'accession au trône d'Hadrien à la mort de Commode, 117-192. (Lambrechts, P.) Antwerpen, 1936.

AH 879.67 — Comprensione della religione antica. (Cilento, Vincenzo.) Napoli, 1967.

AH 3123.6 — Comptabilité Chaldienne. (Virolleaud, C.) Poitiers, 1903.

AH 3966.22 — The concealed map of the land of Israel. (Ben-Har, Bezalel.) Jerusalem, 1964?

AH 3022.25 — Le concept sumérien de consommation. (Rosengarten, Yvonne.) Paris, 1960.

AH 7228.99 — Conceptio formularum, actio in factum und ipso iure-Consumption. (Erman, Karl.) Weimar, 1899.

AH 7159.34 — Les conceptions du crime politique sous la République romaine. Thèse. (Mellor, A.) Paris, 1934.

AH 4819.55.5 — El concepto del hombre en la antigua Grecia. (Fernandez-Galiano, M.) Madrid, 1955.

AH 3142.4 — Concilium Seleuciae et Ctesiphonti Habitum. (Lamy, T.J.) Levanii, 1868.

AH 4279.73 — A concise history of Ancient Greece to the close of the classical era. (Green, Peter.) London, 1973.

AH 3407.11 — Conder, C.R. Hittites and their language. N.Y., 1898.

AH 4148.78.3 — Condicione, jure...sociorum atheniensium. (Fränkel, A.) Rostochii, 1878.

AH 7228.50 — Condictiones sine causa. pt.1-2. (Erxleben, A.) Leipzig, 1850.

AH 8073.9 — La condition de Carthage. (Drapeyron, L.) Paris, 1882.

Eg 845.7 — La condition juridique. (Paturet, G.) Paris, 1886.

AH 4728.52 — Conditione Graeciae post captam Corinthun. (Hermann, C.F.) Gottingae, 1852.

AH 4189.08 — Condizione dei liberti in Grecia. (Calderini, A.) Milano, 1908.

AH 8907.3 — Conestabile, G. Degli etruschi dell'agricoltura. Perugia, 1859.

AH 4709.14 — La confederazione Achea. (Niccolini, G.) Paris, 1914.

Eg 879.60.10 — The conflict of Horus and Seth. (Griffiths, J.G.) Liverpool, 1960.

AH 7769.52 — A conflict of ideas in the late Roman Empire. (Alföldi, Andras.) Oxford, 1952.

AH 7203.137 — Confronti testuali contributo alla dottrina delle interpolazioni giustinianee. (Chiazzese, L.) Cortona, 1933.

AH 7169.30 — Die Confusio im römischen Recht. Inaug. Diss. (Hollfelder, H.) Kallmünz, 1930.

AH 7468.98.5 — La congiura catilinaria. (Tarantino, Mario.) Catania, 1898.

AH 7469.25 — La congiura di Catilina alle soglie dell'impero. (Pareti, Luigi.) Catania, 1934.

AH 3964.11 — Coniecturae historiae criticae sadducaeorum inter indaeos sectae novam lucem accendentes. (Schulze, B.) Halae, 1779.

AH 7277.53 — Conjectures sur les causes de la grandeur des Romains. (Holberg, Ludvig.) Leipzig, 1752.

AH 7469.05 — La conjuration de Catilina. (Boissier, Gaston.) Paris, 1905.

AH 7469.05.2 — La conjuration de Catilina. 2. éd. (Boissier, Gaston.) Paris, 1908.

AH 4819.61.5 — Conley, P.M. America's debt to Greece. Charleston, 1961.

AH 5303.30 — Connor, Walter Robert. The new politicians of fifth-century Athens. Princeton, 1971.

AH 4539.55 — Conone. (Barbieri, Guido.) Roma, 1955.

AH 7419.27.5 — La conquête romaine. 5. éd. (Piganiol, André.) Paris, 1967.

AH 7139.03.5 — Conrat, M. Breviarium Alaricianum. Leipzig, 1903.

AH 8574.2 — Cons, Henri. La province romaine de Dalmatie. Paris, 1881.

Eg 39.29 — Les conseils de fonctionnaires dans l'Égypte pharaonique. (Gabra, Sami.) Le Caire, 1929.

AH 4845.17F — Conservative Zug. (Curtius, E.) Berlin, 1890.

AH 7037.34.30 — Consideratione on the causes of the greatness of the Romans. (Montesquieu, Charles L.) N.Y., 1965.

AH 7148.34 — Considérations historique...sur les ambassades. (Weiske, C.A.) Zwickau, 1834.

AH 7307.34.19 — Considerations on the causes of the grandeur of the Romans. (Montesquieu, Charles de.) N.Y., 1882.

AH 7307.34.18 — Considérations sur les causes de la grandeur des Romains, et de leur décadence. (Montesquieu, Charles de.) Paris, 1771.

AH 7307.34.5 — Considérations sur les causes de la grandeur des Romains. (Montesquieu, Charles de.) Amsterdam, 1759.

AH 7307.34.7 — Considérations sur les causes de la grandeur des Romains. (Montesquieu, Charles de.) Amsterdam, 1761.

AH 7307.34.12 — Considérations sur les causes de la grandeur des Romains. (Montesquieu, Charles de.) Paris, 1876.

AH 7307.34.11 — Considérations sur les causes de la grandeur des Romains. (Montesquieu, Charles de.) Paris, 1876.

AH 7307.34.13 — Considérations sur les causes de la grandeur des Romains. (Montesquieu, Charles de.) Paris, 1887.

AH 7307.34.14 — Considérations sur les causes de la grandeur des Romains. (Montesquieu, Charles de.) Paris, 1894.

AH 7307.34.15 — Considérations sur les causes de la grandeur des Romains. (Montesquieu, Charles de.) Paris, 1896.

AH 7307.34.30 — Considérations sur les causes de la grandeur des Romains. (Montesquieu, Charles de.) Paris, 1945.

	Call No.	Entry
Htn	AH 7307.34*	Considérations sur les causes de la grandeur des Romains. 2. éd. (Montesquieu, Charles de.) Amsterdam, 1734.
Htn	AH 7307.34.3*	Considérations sur les causes de la grandeur des Romains. 2. éd. (Montesquieu, Charles de.) Amsterdam, 1935.
	Eg 879.46	Considérations sur les religions égyptiennes. (Jéquier, Gustave.) Neuchâtel, 1946.
Htn	AH 4521.16*	Considerations upon the lives of Alcibiades and Coriolanus. (Malvezzi, V.) London, 1650.
	AH 9633.7	Considerazione sopra la storia dei Mamerlini. (Giacomazzi, Rosaria.) Messina, 1935.
	AH 7059.55	Consilium principis. (Crook, J.A.) Cambridge, Eng., 1955.
	AH 7469.66	The conspiracy of Catiline. (Hutchinson, Lester.) London, 1966.
	AH 7467.21	Conspirators. (Britannicus.) London, 1721.
	AH 7467.21.2.2	The conspirators. 2. ed. (Gordon, T.) London, 1721.
	AH 7467.21.2	The conspirators. 2. ed. (Gordon, T.) London, 1721.
	AH 7469.21	Constans, L.A. Un correspondant de Cicérone. Thèse. Paris, 1921.
	AH 7759.49.5	Constantin der Grosse. (Vogt, J.) München, 1949.
	AH 7759.49.6	Constantin der Grosse und sein Jahrhundert. 2. Aufl. (Vogt, J.) München, 1960.
	AH 7759.69	Constantine. (MacMullen, Ramsay.) N.Y., 1969.
	AH 7759.60	Constantine and religious liberty. (Doerries, Hermann.) New Haven, 1960.
	AH 7759.05	Constantine the Great. (Firth, J.B.) N.Y., 1905.
	AH 7759.42A	Constantine the Great. (Holsapple, L.B.) N.Y., 1942.
	AH 7759.71	Constantine the Great. (Smith, John Holland.) London, 1971.
	AH 7759.30.5	Constantine the Great and the Christian Church. (Baynes, N.H.) London, 1930.
	AH 7759.30	Constantine the Great and the Christian revolution. (Baker, G.P.) N.Y., 1930.
	AH 7759.53	Constantiniana. (Franchi de' Cavalieri, P.) Roma, 1953.
	AH 7058.91	Der Constantinische Patriciat. (Stückelberg, E.A.) Basel, 1891.
	AH 7759.64	Constantino e il cristianesimo. (Fera, Giovanni.) Milano, 1964.
	AH 7757.27	Constantinus Magnus. (Balduini, F.) Lipsiae, 1727.
	AH 7039.10	Constitution of the later Roman empire. (Bury, J.B.) Cambridge, 1910.
	AH 7038.99.2	Constitutional and political history of Rome. (Taylor, Thomas M.) London, 1899.
	AH 7038.99.3	A constitutional and political history of Rome. (Taylor, Thomas M.) London, 1911.
	AH 4038.81.4	Constitutional antiquities. (Gilbert, G.) London, 1895.
	AH 4038.81.3	Constitutional antiquities. (Gilbert, G.) London, 1895.
	AH 7168.11	Constitutionen der römischen Kaiser. v.1-2. (Löhr, E.) Wetzlar, 1811.
	AH 4200.5	Constitutionis Lycurgae. (Kopstadt, A.) Gryphiae, 1849.
	AH 7449.63	Consules. (Lippold, A.) Bonn, 1963.
	AH 3713.10	Contenau, G. La civilisation phénicienne. Paris, 1926.
	AH 3158.7	Contenau, G. La déesse nue babylonienne. Paris, 1914.
	AH 3155.20	Contenau, G. Le déluge babylonier. Paris, 1952.
	AH 3400.5	Contenau, G. Eléments de bibliograhie Hittite. Thèse. Paris, 1922.
	AH 3400.5.5	Contenau, G. Eléments de bibliographie Hittite. Paris, 1922.
	AH 3165.10.6	Contenau, G. Everyday life. London, 1954.
	AH 3165.10.5	Contenau, G. Everyday life in Babylon and Assyria. N.Y., 1954.
	AH 3165.10	Contenau, G. La vie quotidienne à Babylone et en Assyrie. 16. éd. Paris, 1950.
	AH 3143.9	Contenau, Georges. La civilisation assyro-babylonienne. Paris, 1922.
	AH 3143.9.5	Contenau, Georges. La civilisation d'Assur et de Babylone. Paris, 1937.
	AH 3413.12	Contenau, Georges. La civilisation des Hitties et des Mitanniens. Paris, 1934.
	AH 3413.12.5	Contenau, Georges. La civilisation des Hittites. Paris, 1948.
	AH 1819.45.4	Contenau, Georges. Les civilisations anciennes du Proche-Orient. 5. éd. Paris, 1963.
	AH 3061.1	Contenau, Georges. Contribution à l'histoire économique d'Umma. Paris, 1915.
	AH 3016.45	Contenau, Georges. Monuments mésopotamiens. Paris, 1934.
	AH 3061.2	Contenau, Georges. Umma sous la dynastie d'Ur. Paris, 1916.
	AH 7168.95	Contract in Roman law. (Buckler, W.H.) London, 1895.
	AH 7169.28	Le contrat de société en droit privé romain sous la République. (Del Chiaro, E.) Paris, 1928.
	AH 7169.30.5	Il contratto di società in diritto romano classico. (Poggi, Agostino.) Torino, 1930-34. 2v.
	Eg 39.16	Contribute papirologici. (Modica, Marco.) Roma, 1916.
	AHP 23.12	Contributi. (Milan. Universita Cattolica del Sacro Cuore. Istituto di Filologia Classica. Sezione di Storia Antica.) Milano. 1,1963+
	AH 3061.1	Contribution à l'histoire économique d'Umma. (Contenau, Georges.) Paris, 1915.
	AH 4819.32.20	The contribution of ancient Greece to modern life. (Dickinson, G.L.) London, 1932.
	AH 8048.2	A contribution to the history of Hamitic peoples. (Honea, K.K.) Horn, 1958.
	AH 3155.15	A contribution to the study of moral practices of certain social groups in ancient Mesopotamia. Diss. (Brooks, Beatrice A.) Leipzig, 1921.
	AH 8549.142	Contributions à l'étude des divinités celtiques. (Lambrechts, P.) Brügge, 1942.
	AH 909.11	Contributo alla storia economica dell'antichità. (Barbagallo, C.) Roma, 1907.
	AH 7448.18.7	Die Controverse über Hannibals Alpenübergang. (Linke, Otto.) Breslau, 1873.
	AH 7138.56.15	Controversen Lexikon des römischen Civilrechts. (Matthiae, C.) Leipzig, 1856. 3v.
	AH 8902.5	Convegno di studi etruschi. Atti. Firenze. 1-2
	AH 8913.28.5	Convegno di studi sulla città etrusca e italica preromana. Studi sulla città antica. Bologna, 1970.
	AH 8647.25*	Convegno di Studi sulla Magna Grecia. Atti. Napoli. 1,1961+ 9v.
	AH 7759.48	The conversion of Constantine and pagan Rome. (Alfoldi, Andras.) Oxford, 1948.
	AH 5708.7	Cook, John. The Greeks in Ionia and the East. London, 1962.
	Eg 9.24	Cook, William B. Catalogue of the Egyptological library and other books from the collection of the late Charles E. Wilbour. Brooklyn, 1924.
	Eg 879.31.10	Cooke, Harold P. Osiris. London, 1931.
	AH 8907.17	Cooley, Julia. The forgotten Etruscans. N.Y., 1927.
	AH 3075.2	Cooper, William R. The resurrection of Assyria. London, 1875.
	AH 7214.2	Die Cooptation der Römer. (Mercklin, D.) Mitau, 1848.
	AH 7239.39	Le coorti pretorie. (Passerini, A.) Roma, 1939.
Htn	AH 7445.48*	Cope, Anthony. Historie of two the moste noble capitaines...Anniball...Scipio. Londini, 1548.
Htn	AH 7445.44*	Cope, Anthony. The historie of two the moste noble capitaines. Londini, 1544.
	AH 7108.43	Coppi, A. Discorso sopra alcune tasse...degli antichi romani. Roman, 1843.
	AH 7163.29	Corbett, Percy E. The Roman law of marriage. Oxford, 1930.
	AH 4408.89F	Corcia, N. Frammento della storia graecia. Napoli, 1889.
	Eg 609.40.5	The coregency of Ramses II with Seti I and the date of the great hypostyle hall at Karnak. (Seele, Keith C.) Chicago, 1940.
	AH 5415.5	Corinthiorum. (Barth, H.) Berolini, 1844.
	AH 5409.6.15	Corinto. (Porzio, Guido.) Padova, 1907.
	AH 3909.4	Cormack, George. Egypt in Asia; a plain account of pre-biblical Syria and Palestine. London, 1908.
	AH 1279.50	Cornelius, F. Geschichte des alten Orients. Stuttgart, 1950.
	AH 4449.29	Cornelius, Friedrich. Die Tyrannis in Athen. München, 1929.
	AH 7169.05	Cornil, G. Possession dans le droit romain. Paris, 1905.
	AH 848.17	Coronae. (Paschalius, C.) Lugduni Batavorum, 1671.
	AH 7918.95.3	Les corporations romaines. (Waltzing, J.P.) Louvain, 1895.
	AH 3020.25F	Corpus des inscriptions royales présargoniques de Lagas. (Sollberger, E.) Genève, 1956.
	AH 3002.86F	Corpus inscriptionum Chaldicarum. (Lehmann-Haupt, C.F.) Berlin, 1928-35.
	AH 7201.25F	Corpus Iuris Romani. Anteiustiniani. Bonnae, 1841.
	AH 4138.68	Corpus juris Attici. (Télfy, I.) Lipsiae, 1868.
	AH 7203.15A	Corpus juris civilis. Corpus juris civilis. Amstelaedami, 1663-64. 2v.
Htn	AH 7203.29F*	Corpus juris civilis. Corpus juris civilis. Amstelodami, 1663. 2v.
	AH 7203.19	Corpus juris civilis. Corpus juris civilis. Amstelodami, 1700. 2v.
	AH 7203.75	Corpus juris civilis. Corpus juris civilis. Berolini, 1880-95. 3v.
	AH 7203.44	Corpus juris civilis. Das Corpus Juris Civilis. Leipzig, 1831-39. 7v.
	AH 7203.44.6	Corpus juris civilis. Corpus juris civilis. Lipsiae, 1848-49. 3v.
	AH 7203.75.5	Corpus juris civilis. Corpus juris civilis. 10.-22. ed. Dublin, 1970-73. 3v.
	AH 7203.6.9	Corpus juris civilis. Corpus juris civilis in iiii partes distinctum. Genevae, 1619.
	AH 7203.12	Corpus juris civilis. Corpus juris civilis in iv partes distinctum. Lugduni, 1652. 2v.
	AH 7203.33F	Corpus juris civilis. Corpus juris civilis Romani. Coloniae Munatianae, 1781.
	AH 7203.44.5	Corpus juris civilis. Institutes. Paris, 1847.
	AH 7203.40.15	Corpus juris civilis. Juris civilis ecloga. Parisiis, 1822.
	AH 7203.6.5F	Corpus juris civilis. Juris civilis septimus tomus. Venetiis, 1610. 2v.
	AH 7203.25	Corpus juris civilis. Jurisprudentia restituta, sive Index chronologicus in totum juris Justinianaei corpus. Amstelaedami, 1727.
Htn	AH 7203.4.7*	Corpus juris civilis. Justiniani Leges de re rustica. Lobanii, 1542.
	AH 7203.4.8F	Corpus juris civilis. Leges Justiniani. Parisiis, 1559. 5v.
	AH 7203.42.10	Corpus juris civilis. Lehrbuch des Pandecten-Rechts. 4. Aufl. Halle, 1844. 3v.
	AH 7203.01	Pamphlet box. Corpus juris civilis.
	AH 7203.15A	Corpus juris civilis. (Corpus juris civilis.) Amstelaedami, 1663-64. 2v.
Htn	AH 7203.29F*	Corpus juris civilis. (Corpus juris civilis.) Amstelodami, 1663. 2v.
	AH 7203.19	Corpus juris civilis. (Corpus juris civilis.) Amstelodami, 1700. 2v.
	AH 7203.75	Corpus juris civilis. (Corpus juris civilis.) Berolini, 1880-95. 3v.
	AH 7203.44	Das Corpus Juris Civilis. (Corpus juris civilis.) Leipzig, 1831-39. 7v.
	AH 7203.44.6	Corpus juris civilis. (Corpus juris civilis.) Lipsiae, 1848-49. 3v.
	AH 7203.43	Corpus juris civilis. (Corpus juris civilis. Institutiones.) Lipsiae, 1829-37. 2v.
	AH 7203.50	Corpus juris civilis. (Corpus juris civilis. Institutiones.) Lipsiae, 1866. 3v.
	AH 7203.105	Corpus juris civilis. (Taschenwörterbuch.) Berlin, 1907.
	AH 7203.67	Corpus juris civilis. Codex. Codex Iustinianus. Berolini, 1877.
Htn	AH 7203.5*	Corpus juris civilis. Codex. Codicis Justiniani. Lugduni, 1571.
	AH 7203.107	Corpus juris civilis. Digesta. Digest of Justinian. Cambridge, Eng., 1904-09. 2v.
	AH 7203.144	Corpus juris civilis. Digesta. Digest XII...XIII...De condictionibus. Cambridge, Eng., 1937.
	AH 7203.97	Corpus juris civilis. Digesta. Digest XLI. Cambridge, Eng., 1900.
	AH 7203.101	Corpus juris civilis. Digesta. Digest XVII. Cambridge, Eng., 1902.
	AH 7203.57	Corpus juris civilis. Digesta. Digesta Iustiniani Augusti. Berolini, 1870. 2v.
	AH 7203.135	Corpus juris civilis. Digesta. Digesta Justiniani Augusti. Mediolani, 1931.
Htn	AH 7203.4PF*	Corpus juris civilis. Digesta. Digestorum seu Pandectarum codex Florentinus. v.1-2. Roma, 1902-10. 10v.
Htn	AH 7203.4.6*	Corpus juris civilis. Digesta. Digestum vetus. Colophon, 1513.
	AH 7203.134	Corpus juris civilis. Digesta. Index interpolationum. Supplement. Weimar, 1929.
	AH 7203.133	Corpus juris civilis. Digesta. Index interpolationum quae in Iustiniani Digestis inesse dicuntur. Weimar, 1929-35. 3v.
	AH 7203.24	Corpus juris civilis. Digesta. Jacobi Labitti index legum omnium. Francoforti, 1724. 2v.
	AH 7203.132	Corpus juris civilis. Digesta. Lex aquilia. Cambridge, 1929.
	AH 7203.40F	Corpus juris civilis. Digesta. Pandectae Justinianae. Parisiis, 1818. 3v.

	AH 7203.40.9	Corpus juris civilis. Digesta. Pandectae Justinianae. Parisiis, 1818-20. 5v.
	AH 7203.93	Corpus juris civilis. Digesta. Roman law of sale with modern illustrations. Digest XVIII.1 and XIX.1 translated. Edinburgh, 1892.
	AH 7203.74	Corpus juris civilis. Digesta. Select titles from the Digest of Justinian. Oxford, 1881.
	AH 7203.100.3	Corpus juris civilis. Digesta. Selected titles from the Digest...XII and XIII. Cambridge, 1881.
	AH 7203.100.2	Corpus juris civilis. Digesta. Selected titles from the Digest...XLI. Cambridge, Eng., 1880.
	AH 7203.100	Corpus juris civilis. Digesta. Selected titles from the Digest...XVII. Cambridge, Eng., 1879.
	AH 7203.65.3	Corpus juris civilis. Digesta. Das zwanzigste Buch der Pandekten. Bonn, 1877.
	AH 7203.43	Corpus juris civilis. Institutiones. Corpus juris civilis. Lipsiae, 1829-37. 2v.
	AH 7203.50	Corpus juris civilis. Institutiones. Corpus juris civilis. Lipsiae, 1866. 3v.
	AH 7203.62	Corpus juris civilis. Institutiones. Corpus juris civilis. pt.1-3. Lipsiae, 1875. 2v.
	AH 7203.31	Corpus juris civilis. Institutiones. D. Justiniani Institutionum libri quatuor. London, 1761.
	AH 7203.39.6	Corpus juris civilis. Institutiones. Einleitung in das römisch-justinianische Sbuch Recht. Hannover, 1817.
	AH 7203.19.5	Corpus juris civilis. Institutiones. Elementa juris secundum ordinem Institutionum Justiniani. Lugduni Batavorum, 1700.
	AH 7203.51	Corpus juris civilis. Institutiones. Imp. Iustiniani Institutionum libri quattuor. Lipsiae, 1868.
	AH 7203.14	Corpus juris civilis. Institutiones. Imp. Justiniani Institutionum sive Elementorum. Tremoniae, 1663.
	AH 7203.43.9	Corpus juris civilis. Institutiones. Imperatoris Justiniani Institutionum libri IV. Berolini, 1844.
	AH 7203.43.10	Corpus juris civilis. Institutiones. Imperatoris Justiniani Institutionum libri IV. 5th ed. Oxford, 1946.
	AH 7203.91.5	Corpus juris civilis. Institutiones. Imperatoris Justiniani Institutionum libri quattuor. 4th ed. Oxford, 1903.
	AH 7203.45	Corpus juris civilis. Institutiones. Institutes de Justinien. Paris, 1851. 2v.
	AH 7203.109	Corpus juris civilis. Institutiones. Les Institutes de Justinien. Paris, 1935.
	AH 7203.63	Corpus juris civilis. Institutiones. Institutes of Justinian. Cambridge, Eng., 1876.
	AH 7203.46	Corpus juris civilis. Institutiones. Institutes of Justinian. London, 1853.
	AH 7203.61A	Corpus juris civilis. Institutiones. Institutes of Justinian. Oxford, 1873.
	AH 7203.47	Corpus juris civilis. Institutiones. Institutes of Justinian. 2. ed. London, 1859.
	AH 7203.78	Corpus juris civilis. Institutiones. The institutes of Justinian. 2. ed. Oxford, 1889.
	AH 7203.46.5	Corpus juris civilis. Institutiones. Institutes of Justinian. 5. London ed. Chicago, 1876.
	AH 7203.85	Corpus juris civilis. Institutiones. Institutes of Justinian. 8th ed. London, 1888.
	AH 7203.87	Corpus juris civilis. Institutiones. Institutes of Moyle. 2. ed. Oxford, 1889.
Htn	AH 7203.4.9*	Corpus juris civilis. Institutiones. Institutionum D. Justiniani. Parisiis, 1560.
	AH 7203.90	Corpus juris civilis. Institutiones. Justinian: Institutionum libri quattuor. Oxford, 1883. 2v.
	AH 7203.36	Corpus juris civilis. Institutiones. Justiniani Institutiones. Parisiis, 1805.
	AH 7203.39	Corpus juris civilis. Institutiones. Justiniani Institutionum libri IV. Berolini, 1812.
	AH 7203.43.6	Corpus juris civilis. Institutiones. Justiniani Institutionum libri IV. Berolini, 1832.
	AH 7203.91	Corpus juris civilis. Institutiones. Justiniani Institutionum libri quattuor. 2. ed. Oxford, 1890.
	AH 7203.21	Corpus juris civilis. Institutiones. Der teutsche Justinianus...Der Grund-lehren dess römischen Rechts. Augspurg, 1718. 2v.
	AH 7203.145	Corpus juris civilis. Institutiones. Theophili antecessoris Institutionum libri quatuor. Parisiis, 1681.
	AH 7203.95	Corpus juris civilis. Novellae constitutiones. Appendix ad editionem novellarum Iustiniani. Lipsiae, 1884.
	AH 7203.60F	Corpus juris civilis. Novellae Constitutiones. Iuliani epilome latina Novellarum Iustiniani. Lipsiae, 1873.
	AH 7203.89	Corpus juris civilis. Novellae constitutiones. Justiniani Novellae. Lipsiae, 1881. 2v.
	AH 7203.62	Corpus juris civilis. pt.1-3. (Corpus juris civilis. Institutiones.) Lipsiae, 1875. 2v.
	AH 7203.75.5	Corpus juris civilis. 10.-22. ed. (Corpus juris civilis.) Dublin, 1970-73. 3v.
	AH 7203.6.9	Corpus juris civilis in iiii partes distinctum. (Corpus juris civilis.) Genevae, 1619.
	AH 7203.12	Corpus juris civilis in iv partes distinctum. (Corpus juris civilis.) Lugduni, 1652. 2v.
	AH 7203.33F	Corpus juris civilis Romani. (Corpus juris civilis.) Coloniae Munatianae, 1781.
	AH 7204.5F	Corpus legem. (Haenel, G.F.) Lipsiae, 1857.
	Eg 1042.957PF	A corpus of inscribed Egyptian funerary cones. pt.1. (Davies, Norman de Garis.) Oxford, 1957.
	Eg 1308.85F	Corpus papyrorum Egyptii. v.1-3. (Revillout, Eugène.) Parisiis, 1885-1902.
	AH 4659.29.10	Corradi, G. Studi ellenistíci. Torino, 1929.
	AH 7629.46	Corradi, Guiseppe. Adriano. Roma, 1946.
	AH 9057.5	Corradini, Pietro M. Petri Marcellini Corradini. Romae, 1748. 2v.
	Eg 603.6	Correspondance d'Amenophis III. (Halevy, J.) Paris, 1899.
	AH 7469.21	Un correspondant de Cicérone. Thèse. (Constans, L.A.) Paris, 1921.
	AH 7078.76	La corruption électorale. (Labatut, E.) Paris, 1876.
	AH 4807.44	Corsine, E. Fastiattici in quibus Archantum. Florentiae, 1744. 4v.
	AH 7097.66	Corsinii, Eduardi. De praefectis urbis. Pisis, 1766.
	AH 3013.949.5	Corso di lezioni di assiriologia. (Castellino, Giorgio.) Roma, 1949.
	AH 9666.5	Cortés y López, Miguel. Diccionario...de la Espana antigua. Madrid, 1835-36. 3v.
Htn	AH 7203.7*	Corvini, A. Digesta per aphoumos. Amstelodami, 1642.
	AH 7203.7.5	Corvini, A. Digesta per aphoumos. Amstelodami, 1664.
	AH 7203.7.10	Corvini, A. Elementa juris civilis. Amstelodami, 1664.
	AH 7203.7.15	Corvini, A. Euchiridium seu institutiones imperiales. Amstelodami, 1644.
	AH 1028.32.3	Cory, I.P. Ancient fragments. London, 1832.
	AH 298.76	Cory, I.P. Ancient fragments. London, 1876.
	AH 7059.05.2	Cosenza, M.E. Official positions after the time of Constantine. Lancaster, 1905.
	AH 7139.01.3	Costa, E. Storia del diritto romano. Bologna, 1901. 2v.
	AH 7149.06	Costa, Emilio. Storia del diritto romano. Firenze, 1906.
	AH 7749.20	Costa, Giovanni. Diocleziano. Roma, 1920.
	AH 7759.62	Costantino e il cattolicesimo. (Calderone, S.) Firenze, 1962.
	AH 7759.28	Costantino il Grande. (Salvatorelli, Luigi.) Roma, 1928.
	AH 6057.7F	Costanzi, V. Saggio di storia tessalica. Pisa, 1906.
	AH 7159.35.5	Coster, C.H. The indicium quinquevirale. Cambridge, 1935.
	AH 7659.68	Coster, Charles Henry. Late Roman studies. Cambridge, 1968.
	AH 7039.28	La costituzione romana dai gracchi a Giulio Cesare. (Levi, Mario A.) Firenze, 1928.
	AH 4848.1	Pamphlet box. Costume special.
	AH 4819.13A	Cotterill, H.B. Ancient Greece. London, 1913.
	Eg 819.55.10	Cottrell, L. Life under the pharaohs. London, 1955.
	AH 4410.30	Cottrell, L. Realms of gold; a journey in search of the Mycenaeans. 1. ed. Greenwich, 1963.
	AH 279.58	Cottrell, Leonard. The anvil of civilisation. London, 1958.
	AH 8211.7	Cottrell, Leonard. The great invasion. London, 1958.
	AH 7449.61	Cottrell, Leonard. Hannibal, enemy of Rome. 1. American ed. N.Y., 1961.
	AH 3022.28	Cottrell, Leonard. The land of Shinar. London, 1965.
	AH 5463.35	Cottrell, Leonard. The mystery of Minoan civilization. N.Y., 1971.
	Eg 239.68	Cottrell, Leonard. The warrior pharaohs. London, 1968.
	AH 819.40.2	Couch, H.N. Classical civilization. N.Y., 1947.
	AH 819.40.4	Couch, H.N. Classicai civilization. 2. ed. N.Y., 1950-51. 2v.
	AH 7239.26	Couissin, Paul. Les armes romaines. Paris, 1926.
	AH 7239.26.5	Couissin, Paul. Les armes romaines. Thèse. Paris, 1926.
	AH 7278.46.10	Coup d'oeil sur l'histoire des roumains. (Laurian, A.T.) Bucuresti, 1846.
	AH 3961.3	Couret, A. La Palestine sur les empereurs grecs, 326-636. Grenoble, 1869.
	AH 4842.77	Couroi et courètes. Thèse. (Jeanmaire, H.) Lille, 1939.
	Eg 138.84	Cours de droit égyptien. (Revillout, Eugène.) Paris, 1884.
	AH 7138.84.3	Cours de droit romain. (Appleton, C.) Paris, 1884.
	AH 7138.70.3	Cours de droit romain. (Maynz, C.) Bruxelles, 1870. 3v.
	AH 7138.76.15	Cours de droit romain. 4. éd. (Marynz, K.G.) Bruxelles, 1876. 3v.
	AH 7138.64.6	Cours d'institutes. v.1-2. (Namur, P.) Bruxelles, 1873.
	AH 7138.78	Cours élémentaire de droit romain. (Pailhé, E.D.) Paris, 1878.
	AH 7138.71.5	Cours élémentaire de droit romain. (Wetter, P.) Gand, 1871. 2v.
	AH 7138.71.6	Cours élémentaire de droit romain. (Wetter, P.) Gand, 1875. 2v.
	AH 7138.66	Cours élémentaire de droit romain. 2. ed. (Demangeat, C.) Paris, 1866. 2v.
	AH 7138.76	Cours élémentaire de droit romain. 3. éd. (Demangeat, C.) Paris, 1876. 2v.
	AH 7447.94	Course of Hannibal over the Alps. (Whitaker, J.) London, 1794. 2v.
	AH 938.60.3	Course on ancient geography. (Schmidt, H.I.) N.Y., 1860.
	AH 8011.7	Courtois, C. Les Vandales et l'Afrique. Paris, 1955.
	AH 2110.7	Cousin, J. Kyros le jeune en Asie mineure. Nancy, 1904.
	AH 8548.15	Coutzen, L. Die Wanderungen der Kelten. Leipzig, 1861.
	AH 7759.11	Couzard, R. Sainte Hélène d'après l'histoire et la tradition. Paris, 1911.
	AH 7419.48	Cowell, Frank R. Cicero and the Roman republic. London, 1948.
	AH 7419.48.5	Cowell, Frank R. Cicero and the Roman republic. N.Y., 1948.
	AH 7469.17	Cowles, F.H. Gaius Verres. Thesis. Ithaca, 1917.
	AH 3407.17	Cowley, Arthur E. The Hittites. London, 1920.
	AH 4458.76.6	Cox, George W. The Athenian empire. London, 1876.
	AH 4458.76.5	Cox, George W. The Athenian empire. N.Y., 1876.
	AH 4458.76.10	Cox, George W. Athenian empire. N.Y., 1889.
	AH 4458.76.15	Cox, George W. Athenian empire. N.Y., 1895.
	AH 4458.76.7	Cox, George W. The Athenian empire. 5. ed. London, 1887.
	AH 4458.76.9	Cox, George W. Athenian empire. 6. ed. London, 1888.
	AH 4278.76	Cox, George W. General history of Greece. N.Y., 1876.
	AH 4478.61	Cox, George W. Great Persian War. London, 1861.
	AH 4478.76.3	Cox, George W. Greeks and Persians. London, 1876.
	AH 4478.76.2	Cox, George W. Greeks and Persians. N.Y., 1876.
	AH 4478.76.5	Cox, George W. Greeks and Persians. N.Y., 1892.
	AH 4478.76A	Cox, George W. Greeks and Persians. 5. ed. London, 1886.
	AH 4278.77	Cox, George W. History of Greece. London, 1874. 2v.
	AH 4278.74.5	Cox, George W. History of Greece. London, 1878. 2v.
	AH 4338.85A	Cox, George W. Lives of Greek statesmen. N.Y., 1885. 2v.
	AH 2108.15	Cozzoli, Umberto. I Cimmeri. Roma, 1968.
	AH 4551.5	Crämer, H. Beiträge zur Geschichte Alexanders der Grossen. Marburg, 1893. 3 pam.
	AH 909.72	Craftsmen in Greek and Roman society. (Burford, Alison.) London, 1972.
	AH 3002.2.13	Craig, James A. Assyrian and Babylonian religious texts. Leipzig, 1895-97.
	AH 3002.2.14	Craig, James A. Astrological-astronomical texts. Leipzig, 1899.
	AH 7203.37	Cramer, A.W. Verborum significatione. Kiliae, 1811.
	AH 9757.6	Cramer, F. Römisch-germanische Studien. Breslau, 1914.
	AH 842.34	Cramer, Friedrich. Geschichte der Erziehung und des Unterrichts im Alterthume. Elberfeld, 1832-38. 2v.
	AH 4938.25.3	Cramer, J.A. Ancient Greece. Oxford, 1828. 3v.
	AH 8616.6	Cramer, J.A. Geographical...description of ancient Italy. Oxford, 1826. 2v.
	AH 2107.5	Cramer, J.A. Geographical and historical description of Asia Minor. Oxford, 1832. 2v.
	Eg 879.55.5	Cramer, Maria. Das altägyptische Lebenszeichen. 3. Aufl. Wiesbaden, 1955.
	AH 7567.85	Cramero, A.W.D. Vespasianus sive de vita et legislatione. Ienae, 1785.
	Eg 981.5	Crawford, Dorothy. Kerkeosiris. Cambridge, Eng., 1971.
	Eg 878.98.5	Creation records discovered in Egypt. (St. Clair, G.) London, 1898.
	AH 7419.67.5	Les Crecilii Metelli de la république. (Ooteghem, Jules van.) Namur, 1967?
	AH 862.10	Crecope, John. Medicine, magic and mythology. London, 1954.

Author and Title Listing

AH 7009.02 — Credibility of early Roman history. (Platner, S.B.) n.p., 1902.

AH 7709.11.5 — Crees, J.H.E. The reign of the Emperor Probus. London, 1911.

NEDL AH 7278.85.2.5 — Creighton, M. History of Rome. London, 1888.

AH 7278.85.3A — Creighton, M. History of Rome. N.Y., 1875.

AH 7278.85.3.4 — Creighton, M. History of Rome. N.Y., 1877.

AH 7278.85.3.5 — Creighton, M. History of Rome. N.Y., 1879.

AH 7278.85.3.6 — Creighton, M. History of Rome. N.Y., 1883.

AH 7278.85 — Creighton, M. History of Rome. N.Y., 1885.

AH 7278.85.3.8 — Creighton, M. History of Rome. N.Y., 1886.

AH 7278.85.2 — Creighton, M. History of Rome. N.Y., 1888.

AH 7278.85.3.7A — Creighton, M. History of Rome. N.Y., 189-?

AH 7278.85.3.10 — Creighton, M. History of Rome. N.Y., 1890.

NEDL AH 7278.85.3.15 — Creighton, M. Nociones de historia de Roma. N.Y., 1903.

AH 7861.12 — Cremation and burial in the Roman Empire. (Nock, A.D.) Cambridge, 1932.

AH 8673.3 — Cremera und Porta Carmentalis. (Elter, A.) Bonn, 1910.

AH 7239.66 — Crescenti, Giovanni. Obiettori di coscienza e martiri militari nei primi cinque secoli del cristianesimo. Polermo, 1966.

AH 5457.5 — Creta, Cyprus, Rhodus. (Meursius, J.) Amstelodami, 1675.

AH 5453.7A — The Cretan koinon. (Mijnsbrugge, M. van der.) N.Y., 1931.

AH 5459.5 — Crete and the Lumians. (Huxley, George Leonard.) Oxford, 1961.

AH 5460.5 — La Crète et le monde grec. (Effenterre, H. van.) Paris, 1948.

AH 8516.5 — Creuly, Casimir. Carte de la Gaule sous le proconsulat de César. Paris, 1864.

AH 5307.11 — Creuzeri, F. Oratio de civitate Athenarum. Francofurti, 1826.

AH 7818.24 — Creuzers, G.F. Abriss der römischen Antiquitäten. Leipzig, 1824.

AH 7818.24.3 — Creuzers, G.F. Abriss der römischen Antiquitäten. 2. Aufl. Leipzig, 1829.

AH 7487.50 — Crevier, J.B.L. Histoire des empereurs romains. Paris, 1750. 6v.

NEDL AH 7487.50.10 — Crevier, J.B.L. Histoire des empereurs romains. Paris, 1753-66. 12v.

AH 7487.50.3 — Crevier, J.B.L. History of Roman emperors. London, 1755. 10v.

AH 7159.61 — Crifò, Giuliano. Richerche sull'"exilium" nel periodo repubblicano. Milano, 1961.

AH 7159.67.5 — The crimen maiestatis in the Roman Republic and Augustan Principate. (Bauman, Richard A.) Johannesburg, 1967.

AH 7159.35 — Crimial trials and criminal legislation under Tiberius. (Rogers, R.S.) Middletown, Conn., 1935.

AH 7159.72 — The criminal curts of the Roman Republic and Principate. (Jones, Arnold Hugh Martin.) Oxford, 1972.

AH 7158.71 — Criminalprocess der römischen Republik. (Zumpt, A.W.) Leipzig, 1871.

AH 7158.44 — Criminalrecht der Römer. (Rein, W.) Leipzig, 1844.

AH 7158.65 — Criminalrecht der römischen Republik. v.1-2. (Zumpt, A.W.) Berlin, 1865. 4v.

AH 7659.64 — La crise de l'Empire romain. (Rémondon, Roger.) Paris, 1964.

AH 7659.64.2 — La crise de l'Empire romain de Marc Aurèle à Anastase. 2. éd. (Rémondon, Roger.) Paris, 1970.

AH 7559.39 — La crisi del principato nell'anno. (Zancan, P.) Padova, 1939.

AH 4039.51.10 — La crisi del 411 a.C. nell'Anthenaeon politeia di Aristotele. (Sartori, F.) Padova, 1951.

AH 7842.20 — La crisi della scuola nel IV secolo d.C. (Pavan, M.) Bari, 1952.

AH 7769.33 — La crisi dell'impero romano. (Solari, A.) Milano, 1933-37. 5v.

AH 7559.47 — La crisi politica del'anno 68-69 d. C. (Manfri, Guglielmo.) Bologna, 1947.

AH 8549.18 — A critical history of the Celtic religion. (Toland, John.) Edinburgh, 1815.

AH 8549.17.50 — A critical history of the Celtic religion. (Toland, John.) London, 174-?

AH 7549.20 — A critical study of the history of the Emperor Nero. Thesis. (Jahn, John Nicholas H.) N.Y.? 1920.

AH 4039.09 — Croiset, A. Les démocraties antiques. Paris, 1909.

AH 4819.22 — Croiset, M. La civilisation hellénique. Paris, 1922. 2v.

AH 4459.06.5 — Croiset, Maurice. Aristophanes and the political parties at Athens. London, 1909.

AH 4819.32.15 — Croiset, Maurice. La civilisation de la Grèce antique. Paris, 1932.

AH 4819.25.15 — Croiset, Maurice. Hellenic civilization. N.Y., 1925.

AH 7279.60.10F — Cronica romanorum. (Johannes Victoriensis.) Klagenfurt, 1960.

AH 4229.36.5 — Cronin, James F. The Athenian juror and his oath. Diss. Chicago, 1936.

AH 7809.08.5 — Cronologia romana. (Varese, P.) Roma, 1908.

AH 7059.55 — Crook, J.A. Consilium principis. Cambridge, Eng., 1955.

AH 7139.67 — Crook, John A. Law and life of Rome. Ithaca, 1967.

AH 5335.5 — Cropo et Amphiarae Sacro. (Dunbach, F.) Parisiis, 1967.

X Cg AH 3060.3.13F — Cros, Gaston. Nouvelle fouilles de Tello. Paris, 1910-14.

AH 3013.937.5 — Cross, Dorothy. Movable property in the Nuzi documents. Diss. Philadelphia, 1937.

AH 5603.5 — Cross, Geoffrey N. Epirus; a study in Greek constitutional development. Cambridge, 1932.

AH 4279.60.5 — Crossland, R.A. New background to the study of ancient Greece. Sheffield, 1960.

AH 4819.70 — Crow, John Armstrong. Greece: the magic spring. 1st ed. N.Y., 1970.

AH 7850.6 — Croyances et superstitions de table dans la Rome antique. (Deouna, Waldemar.) Bruxelles, 1961.

AH 7844.13 — Cruanté et civilisation: les jeux romains. (Auguet, Roland.) Paris, 1970.

AH 908.79 — Cruchon, G. Les banques dans l'antiquité. Paris, 1879.

Eg 879.64 — La crue du Nil. (Bonneau, D.) Paris, 1964.

AH 7189.06 — Crumley, J.J. On the social standing of freedmen. Baltimore, 1906.

AH 3863.5 — Cruveilher, P. Les principaux résultats des nouvelles fouilles de Suse. Paris, 1934.

AH 809.42 — The crux of chronology; an essay to establish the life-time of Jesus Christ and...date of Easter. (Meyer, Frank H.) Boston, 1942.

AH 8908.12 — Cserèp, J. De Pelasgis Etruscisqui. Budapestini, 1912.

AH 7138.76.11 — Cubain, R. Lois civiles de Rome. Angers, 1876.

AH 3017.9 — Cullimore, A. Oriental cylinders. London, 1842.

AH 3160.24 — The cult of Assur. (Driel, G. van.) Assen, 1969.

AH 2014.5 — Le culte d'Aphrodite-Anahita. (Blochet, E.) Chalon-sur-Saône, 1902.

Eg 989.5 — Le culte de Neit à Saïs. (Mallet, D.) Paris, 1888.

AH 8514.13 — Le culte des sources dans la Gaule antique. (Vaillat, Claudius.) Paris, 1932.

AH 8514.11 — Culte des sources thermales. (Rodet, P.) Paris, 1908.

AH 8514.14 — Cultes indigènes des Lingons. (Drioux, Georges.) Paris, 1934.

AH 8514.14.5 — Cultes indigènes des Lingons. Thèse. (Drioux, Georges.) Paris, 1934.

AH 2264.5 — Les cultes indigènes en Carie. (Laumonier, A.) Paris, 1958.

AH 7239.03.3 — Cultes militaires de Rome. Les enseignes. (Renel, Charles.) Lyon, 1903.

Eg 879.53.2 — Cults and creeds in Graeco-Roman Egypt. (Bell, H.I.) N.Y., 1953.

AH 8864.16 — The cults of Campania. (Peterson, Roy M.) Rome, 1919.

AH 7138.68 — Cultur und Recht der Römer. (Arnold W.) Berlin, 1868.

AH 4819.72.15 — La cultura de Grecia: antigua, bizantia, moderna. (Hurmuziadis, Jorge.) Buenos Aires, 1972.

AH 5763.8 — La cultura di Sparta arcaica. (Janni, Pietro.) Roma, 1965. 2v.

AH 3964.18 — Culture and conscience. (Graham, William C.) Chicago, 1936.

AH 4819.22.10A — The culture of ancient Greece and Rome. (Poland, Franz.) Boston, 1926.

AH 4819.22.9 — The culture of ancient Greece and Rome. (Poland, Franz.) London, 1926.

Eg 409.55 — The cultures of prehistoric Egypt. (Baumgärtel, E.) London, 1955.

AH 818.57 — Culturgeschichte. (Hermann, K.F.) Göttingen, 1857.

Eg 878.90.5 — Der Cultus der Aegyptischen Gottheiten. (Drexler, W.) Leipzig, 1890.

Htn AH 3965.6* — Cumberland, R. An essay towards the recovery of the Jewish measures and weights. London, 1686.

Htn AH 297.24* — Cumberland, R. Origines gentium antiquissimae. Londini, 1724.

AH 3707.5 — Cumberland, R. Sanchoniatho's Phoenician history. London, 1720.

AH 4559.40 — Cummings, L.V. Alexander the Great. Boston, 1940.

AH 8522.5 — Cumont, Franz. Comment la Belgique fut romanisée. Paris, 1914.

Eg 819.37 — Cumont, Franz. L'Égypt des astrologues. Bruxelles, 1937.

AH 3002.40 — Cuneiform documents in Smith Library. (Grant, Elihu.) Haverford, 1918.

AH 3000.5 — Cuneiform inscriptions : Chaldean, Babylonian. (Morgan, J.P.) N.Y., 1908.

AH 3159.11.5 — The cuneiform inscriptions and the Old Testament. (Schrader, E.) London, 1885-88. 2v.

AH 3002.30F — Cuneiform inscriptions of Western Asia. v.1-5. (Rawlinson, H.C.) London, 1861-64. 3v.

AH 3002.30.2F — Cuneiform inscriptions of Western Asia. v.4. (Rawlinson, H.C.) London, 1891.

AH 3002.28 — Cuneiform parallels to the Old Testament. (Rogers, R.W.) N.Y., 1912.

AH 3132.3 — Cuneiform text...cylinder of Nebuchadnezzar. (O'Connor, J.F.X.) n.p., 1885.

AH 3002.25F — Cuneiform texts from Babylonian tablets. (British Museum. Department of Egyptian and Assyrian Antiquities.) London. 1,1896+ 35v.

AH 3002.25.5F — Cuneiform texts from Babylonian tablets. (British Museum. Department of Egyptian and Assyrian Antiquities.) London. 13,1901+ 25v.

AH 3002.25.6F — Cuneiform texts from Babylonian tablets. Index to registration numbers of texts, pt.1-25. (British Museum. Department of Egyptian and Assyrian Antiquities.) n.p., n.d.

AH 3002.26.5F — Cuneiform texts from Cappadocian tablets. (British Museum. Department of Egyptian and Assyrian Antiquities.) London. 1-4,1921-1927 3v.

AH 3002.158 — Cuneiform texts from Nimrud. London. 1,1972+

AH 3002.4 — Cuneiform texts in the Metropolitan Museum. (New York Metropolitan Museum of Art.) N.Y., 1893.

AH 3002.92 — Cuneiform texts in the National Museum. (Jacobsen, T.) Copenhagen, 1939.

AH 7328.78 — Cuno, J.G. Vorgeschichte Roms. Leipzig, 1878. 2v.

AH 8617.5 — Cuoco, Vincenzo. Platone in Italia. Bari, 1916-24. 2v.

AH 8617.5.2 — Cuoco, Vincenzo. Platone in Italia. 2. ed. Parma, 1820.

AH 8617.5.5 — Cuoco, Vincenzo. Voyage de Platon en Italie. Paris, 1807. 3v.

AH 7138.91 — Cuq, E. Institutions juridiques. Paris, 1891. 2v.

AH 7138.91.2 — Cuq, E. Institutions juridiques. Paris, 1904. 2v.

AH 7139.17.2 — Cuq, Edouard. Manuel des institutions juridiques des Romains. Paris, 1928.

AH 4908.27 — Curatoribus emporii et nautodicis. (Baumstark, A.) Friburgi, 1827.

AH 7299.40 — Curotto, Ernest. Antichità classica. Torino, 1940.

NEDL AH 278.58.5 — Curso de historia antigua. 2. ed. (Flóres, Antonio.) Besanyon, 1863.

AH 7138.45.3 — Cursus der Institutionen. (Puchta, G.F.) Leipzig, 1845. 2v.

AH 7138.45.9 — Cursus der Institutionen. (Puchta, G.F.) Leipzig, 1871. 3v.

AH 7138.45.10 — Cursus der Institutionen. (Puchta, G.F.) Leipzig, 1875.

AH 7138.45.8 — Cursus der Institutionen. 6. Aufl. (Puchta, G.F.) Leipzig, 1865. 3v.

AH 7138.79.3 — Cursus des römischen Rechts. (Kuntze, J.E.) Leipzig, 1879.

NEDL AH 7488.75.3A — Curteis, A.M. History of Roman Empire. Philadelphia, 1875.

AH 6107.8 — Curteis, A.M. Rise of the Macedonian empire. London, 1877.

AH 6107.9 — Curteis, A.M. Rise of the Macedonian empire. N.Y., 1880.

AH 6107.11.5 — Curteis, A.M. Rise of the Macedonian empire. N.Y., 1896.

AH 6107.11 — Curteis, A.M. Rise of the Macedonian empire. 4. ed. London, 1886.

AH 7868.2 — Curtel, G. La vigne et le vin chez les Romains. Paris, 1903.

AH 5139.7.5 — Curtius, C. Inschriften und Studien zur Geschichte von Samos. Lübeck, 1877.

AH 5139.7 — Curtius, C. Inschriften zur Geschichte von Samos. Lübeck, 1877.

AH 5139.5 — Curtius, C. Urkunden zur Geschichte von Samos. Wesel, 1873.

AH 5333.5 — Curtius, Carl. Metroon in Athen. Berlin, 1868.

AH 938.47 — Curtius, E. Beiträge zur Terminologie...der alten Geographie. Berlin, 1888.

AH 4845.17F — Curtius, E. Conservative Zug. Berlin, 1890.

AH 5306.5 — Curtius, E. De portubus Athenarum. Halis, 1842.

Call number	Entry
AH 4938.82	Curtius, E. Die Griechen in der Diaspora. v.1-2. Berlin, 1882.
AH 4839.35.5	Curtius, E. Olympia. Berlin, 1935.
AH 214.7	Curtius, E. Der Zehnte. Berlin, 1885.
AH 4278.57.5	Curtius, Ernest. Griechische Geschichte. Berlin, 1857. 3v.
NEDL AH 4278.57.6	Curtius, Ernest. Griechische Geschichte. Berlin, 1878. 3v.
AH 4278.57.7A	Curtius, Ernest. Griechische Geschichte. 6. Aufl. Berlin, 1887. 3v.
AH 4278.57.12	Curtius, Ernest. History of Greece. London, 1868. 5v.
NEDL AH 4278.57.13.5	Curtius, Ernest. History of Greece. N.Y., 1868?-1873? 5v.
NEDL AH 4278.57.13	Curtius, Ernest. History of Greece. N.Y., 1871. 5v.
NEDL AH 4278.57.14A	Curtius, Ernest. History of Greece. N.Y., 1876. 5v.
NEDL AH 4278.57.16	Curtius, Ernest. History of Greece. N.Y., 1883. 5v.
NEDL AH 4278.57.17A	Curtius, Ernest. History of Greece. N.Y., 1886. 5v.
NEDL AH 4278.57.17.5	Curtius, Ernest. History of Greece. N.Y., 1892. 5v.
NEDL AH 4278.57.18	Curtius, Ernest. History of Greece. N.Y., 1897. 5v.
AH 6024.5	Curtius, Ernst. Anecdota Delphica. Berolini, 1843.
AH 5336.6	Curtius, Ernst. Attische Studien; Pnyx und Stadtmauer. Göttingen, 1862.
AH 4308.69	Curtius, Ernst. Festrede. Berlin, 1869.
AH 4328.55	Curtius, Ernst. Die Ionier. Berlin, 1855.
AH 48.86	Curtius, Ernst. Das Königthum bei dem Alten. Berlin, 1886.
AH 5957.5	Curtius, Ernst. Peloponnesos. Gotha, 1851. 2v.
AH 5307.22	Curtius, Ernst. Die Stadtgeschichte von Athen. Berlin, 1891.
AH 5553.7	Curtius, Ernst. Der Synoikismos von Elis. Berlin, 1895.
AH 7138.54.3	Cushing, L.S. Introduction to study of Roman law. Boston, 1854.
Htn AH 7485.61.10F*	Cuspinianus, J. De Caesaribus. Basileae, 1561?
AH 4259.19	Custance, Reginald Neville. War at sea. Edinburgh, 1919.
AH 819.05.3F	Cybulski, S. Kultur der Griechen und Römer. Leipzig, 1905.
AH 3096.7	Cylinder A of the Esarhaddon inscriptions. (Esarhaddon, king of Assyria.) New Haven, 1888.
AH 3094.3F	Die Cylinder-Inschrift Sargons II. (Lyon, D.G.) Leipzig, 1882.
AH 3017.8.1	Cylinder seals. (Frankfort, Henri.) Furnborough, 1965.
AH 3017.35	The cylinder seals of the Pontifical Institute. (Rome (City). Pontificio Instituto Biblico.) Roma, 1940.
Htn AH 3017.4F*	Cylinders and oriental seals in library. (Morgan, John P.) N.Y., 1909.
AH 3052.9F	Les cylindres de Gudéa. (Toscanne, P.) Paris, 1901.
AH 3017.45	Cylindres et cachets orientaux conservés dans la collection suisses. (Borowski, E.) Ascona, 1947.
AH 3017.7.12	Les cylindres orientaux. (Menant, J.) Paris, 1879.
AH 7203.147F	Cyni Pistoriensis in codicem et aliquot titulos primi pandectorum tomi. (Cino da Pistoia.) Torino, 1964. 2v.
AH 7098.94	Cyprès, Imbert. Droit romain de la curie. Paris, 1894.
AH 3308.5	Cyprus: its place in Bible history. (Davidson, J.T.) London, 1878.
AH 5409.5	Cypsello Corinthiorum tyranno. (Schubring, J.J.) Gottingae, 1862.
AH 3359.5	Cyrenarum origines. (Malten, L.) n.p., 1904.
AH 3359.10	Cyrène sour la monarchie des Battiades. (Chamoux, J.) Paris, 1952.
AH 3659.12	Cyrus. (Champdor, A.) Paris, 1952.
AH 3659.14	Cyrus the Great. 1st ed. (Lamb, Harold.) Garden City, N.Y., 1960.
AH 2623.7	Cyzicus. (Hasluck, Fredrick William.) Cambridge, 1910.
AH 2623.5	Cyzicus und sein Gebiet. (Marquarat, J.) Berlin, 1836.
AH 7138.99	Czyhlarz, Karl. Lehrbuch der Institutionen des römischen Rechtes. 4. Aufl. Leipzig, 1899.
AH 7138.99.2	Czyhlarz, Karl. Lehrbuch der Institutionen des römischen Rechtes. 7-8. Aufl. Wien, 1905.
AH 7138.99.3	Czyhlarz, Karl. Lehrbuch der Institutionen des römischen Rechtes. 19. Aufl. Wien, 1933.
AH 7203.31	D. Justiniani Institutionum libri quatuor. (Corpus juris civilis. Institutiones.) London, 1761.
AH 8307.5	Dacia provincia Augusti. (Király, Pál.) Nagy-Becskerek, 1893-94. 2v.
AH 8307.3	Dacii. (Daicoviciu, Hadrian.) Bucureşti, 1965.
AHP 14.8	Dacoromania. Freiburg. 1,1973+
AH 7626.92	Dadwell, Henry. Praelectiones academicae in schola historices camdeniana. Oxonii, 1692.
AH 878.22	Dämonen-Lehre der Alten. (Onymus, A.J.) Würzburg, 1822.
AH 5124.5	Daenius, A. Specimen litterarum de Insula delo. Lugdunum Batavorum, 1851. 2 pam.
AH 5757.13	Däubler, T. Sparta; ein Versuch. Leipzig, 1923.
Eg 139.14	Dagallier, Jean. Les institutions judiciaires de l'Egypte ancienne. Thèse. Paris, 1914.
AH 7269.65.1	Dahlheim, Werner. Struktur und Entwicklung des römischen Volkerrechte im dritten und zweiten Jahrhundert v. Chr. München, 1968.
AH 4109.04	Dahms, R. De atheniensium sociorum tributis quaestiones septem. Berolini, 1904.
AH 8308.5.1	Daicoviciu, Constantin. Siebenbürgen im Altertum. Bukarest, 1943.
AH 8308.5	Daicoviciu, Constantin. Le Transylvanie dans l'antiquité. Bucarest, 1938.
AH 8307.3	Daicoviciu, Hadrian. Dacii. Bucureşti, 1965.
Eg 819.64	Daily life in ancient Egypt. (Sämih, Wali al Din.) N.Y., 1964.
AH 7819.41.2	Daily life in ancient Rome. (Carcopino, J.) New Haven, 1940.
AH 7819.41	Daily life in ancient Rome. (Carcopino, J.) New Haven, 1941.
AH 7819.41.10	Daily life in ancient Rome. (Carcopino, J.) New Haven, 1945.
AH 8073.22.15	Daily life in Carthage at the time of Hannibal. (Charles-Picard, Gilbert.) London, 1961.
AH 4819.66	Daily life in Greece at the time of Pericles. (Flacelière, Robert.) N.Y., 1966.
AH 4819.54.12	Daily life in the time of Homer. (Mireaux, Émile.) London, 1959.
AH 3963.77	Daily life in the time of Jesus. (Daniel-Rops, H.) N.Y., 1962.
Eg 909.33	Dairanes, Serge. L'Égypte economique sous la XVIIIe dynastie pharaonique. Thèse. Paris, 1933.
Eg 709.60	Daix, Pierre. Cléopatre. Paris, 1960.
AH 8007.19	Dakiia v epokhu rinskoi okkupatsii. (Kruglikova, I.T.) Moskva, 1955.
Htn AH 297.02*	Dale, A. van. Dissertationes IX. antiquitatibus. Amstelodami, 1702.
X Cg Eg 308.68	Dall, C. (Mrs.). Egypt's place in history. Boston, 1868.
AH 7419.18	Dalle guerre puniche a Cesare Augusto. v.1-2. (Pais, Ettore.) Roma, 1918.
AH 279.09.5	Dalle rive del Nilo ai lidi del "mar nostro". 2. ed. (Amatucci, A.G.) Bari, 1925. 2v.
AH 8574.5	Dalmatia. (Wilkes, J.J.) Cambridge, 1969.
AH 4808.21	Dalzel, A. Substance of lecture on ancient Greece. Edinburgh, 1821.
AH 4039.70.5	Damsgaard-Madsen, Aksel. Det athenske demokrati. København, 1970.
AH 3179.14	Dan Lugalbandaepos. (Wilcke, Claus.) Wiesbaden, 1969.
AH 4843.24	The dance in ancient Greece. (Lawler, Lillian B.) London, 1964.
AH 3660.15	Dandamaev, M.A. Iran pri perviykh akhemenidakh. Moskva, 1963.
AH 3167.11	Dandamaev, Mukhammed A. Rabstvo v Vavilonii VII-IV vv. do n.e. (661-331 gg). Moskva, 1974.
AH 4212.7	D'André, J. La proxénie. Toulouse, 1911.
AH 7228.58	Daniel, C.G.F. Legisactionen und Formularprozess. Schwerin, 1858.
AH 8549.127.10	Daniel, J. The philosophy of ancient Britain. London, 1927.
AH 7509.33	Daniel, Rudolf. Mareus Vipsanius Agrippa. Inaug. Diss. Breslau, 1933.
AH 3963.77	Daniel-Rops, H. Daily life in the time of Jesus. N.Y., 1962.
AH 239.10	Daniels, Emil. Das antike Kriegswesen. Leipzig, 1910.
AH 239.20	Daniels, Emil. Das antike Kriegswesen. 2. Aufl. Berlin, 1920.
AH 7709.09	Dannhäuser, Erich. Geschichte des Kaisers Probus (276-282). Jena, 1909.
AH 9707.12	Danov, Khristo M. Drevna Trakiia. Sofiia, 1968.
AH 4843.5	Danse grecque. (Emmanuel, M.) Paris, 1896.
AH 4843.21	La danse greque antique. (Séchan, Louis.) Paris, 1930.
AH 4238.57	Dansin, H. De mercenariis militibus apud antiquas Graeciae civitates...Thesim proponebat. Argentorati, 1857.
AH 8258.1	Danubian papers. (Syme, Ronald.) Bucharest, 1971.
AH 7138.71.7	Danz, H.A.A. Lehrbuch der Geschichte des römischen Rechts. v.1-2. Leipzig, 1871.
AH 7215.6	Danz, H.A.A. Der sacrale Schutz im römischen Rechtsverkehr. Jena, 1857.
AH 4168.67	Dareste, R. Du pret a la grosse. Paris, 1867.
AH 4138.95	Dareste, R. Recueil des inscriptions juridiques grecques. Paris, 1895.
AH 4138.95.2	Dareste, R. Recueil des inscriptions juridiques grecques. Paris, 1898. 2v.
AH 9603.2	Dareste de la Chavanne, R. De forma et conditione Siciliae provinciae Romanae. Thesis. Lutetiae, 1850.
Eg 232.5	Daris, Sergio. Documenti per la storia dell'esercito romano in Egitto. Milano, 1964.
AH 8863.10	D'Arms, John Houghton. Romans and the Bay of Naples; a social and cultural study of the villas and their owners from 150 B.C. to A.D. 400. Cambridge, 1970.
AH 7827.95	D'Arnay, J.R. Habitudes et moeurs privées. Paris, 1795.
AH 7827.59.3	D'Arnay, J.R. Private life of the Romans. 2. ed. London, 1764.
AH 4861.7	Darstellung der griechische Grabsitte. (Kriesche, W.) Braunau, 1878.
AH 842.13	Darstellung des Erziehungs- und Unterrichtwesens. (Ussing, J.L.) Altona, 1870.
AH 4818.43.5	Darstellung des Religiösen...Bildungszustandes. (Schönwalder.) Brieg, 1843.
AH 4559.05.3	Darstellungen Alexanders des Grossen. (Bernoulli, J.J.) München, 1905.
AH 7818.65.6	Darstellungen aus der Sittengeschichte Roms. v.1, 4. Aufl; v.2, 3. Aufl. (Friedlaender, Ludwig.) Leipzig, 1873-1874. 2v.
AH 7818.65	Darstellungen aus der Sittengeschichte Roms. v.2-3. (Friedlaender, Ludwig.) Leipzig, 1864-1871. 2v.
AH 7818.65.2	Darstellungen aus der Sittengeschichte Roms. 2. Aufl. (Friedlaender, Ludwig.) Leipzig, 1865-1867. 2v.
AH 7818.65.3	Darstellungen aus der Sittengeschichte Roms. 3. Aufl. (Friedlaender, Ludwig.) Leipzig, 1869.
AH 7818.65.9	Darstellungen aus der Sittengeschichte Roms. 6. Aufl. (Friedlaender, Ludwig.) Leipzig, 1888. 3v.
AH 7818.65.11	Darstellungen aus der Sittengeschichte Roms. 7. Aufl. (Friedlaender, Ludwig.) Leipzig, 1901. 2v.
AH 7818.65.13	Darstellungen aus der Sittengeschichte Roms. 8. Aufl. (Friedlaender, Ludwig.) Leipzig, 1910. 4v.
AH 7818.65.15	Darstellungen aus der Sittengeschichte Roms. 9.-10. Aufl. (Friedlaender, Ludwig.) Leipzig, 1919. 4v.
AH 7818.65.16	Darstellungen aus der Sittengeschichte Roms. 10. Aufl. (Friedlaender, Ludwig.) Aalen, 1964. 4v.
AH 4908.67	Darstellungen des Handwerks. (Jahn, Otto.) Leipzig, 1868.
AH 7648.97	Dartique-Peyroux, J. Marc Aurèle dans ses rapports avec le christianisme. Paris, 1897.
AH 4482.2	Daskalakès, A.B. Problèmes historiques autour de la bataille des Thermopyles. Paris, 1962.
AH 4559.66.5	Daskalakès, Apostolos Basileiou. Alexander the Great and Hellenism. Thessalonikè, 1966.
AH 6107.6.2	Daskalakès, Apostolos Basileiou. The Hellenism of the ancient Macedonians. Thessalonikè, 1965.
AH 6107.6	Daskalakès, Apostolos Basileiou. Ho Hellenismos tes archaias Makedonias. Athènai, 1960.
AH 4559.63	Daskalakès, Apostolos Basileiou. O Mégas Alèxandros kaí o Helleniphios. Athènai, 1963.
AH 4438.92A	Date of Cylon...early Athenian history. (Wright, J.H.) Boston, 1892.
AH 7219.5	Daube, David. Studies in the Roman law of sale. Oxford, 1959.
AH 7898.57	Daubeny, Charles. Lectures on Roman husbandry. Oxford, 1857.
Eg 819.65.5	Daumas, François. La civilisation de l'Égypte pharaonique. Paris, 1965.
Eg 879.65.5	Daumas, François. Les dieux de l'Égypte. Paris, 1965.
Eg 879.58.2F	Daumas, François. Les mammisis de Dendara. Le Caire, 1959.
Eg 879.58	Daumas, François. Les mammisis des temples égyptiens. Paris, 1958.
AH 1819.26	Daunt, Hew D. The centre of ancient civilization. London, 1926.
Eg 855.2	Dauson, Warren R. Magician and leech. London, 1929.
AH 6024.11	Daux, Georges. Delphes au IIe et au Ier siècle depuis l'abaissement de l'Etolie jusqu'à la paix romaine 191-31 avant J.C. Thèse. Paris, 1936.
AH 8549.45.5	David de St. Georges, J.J.A. Histoire des druides et...Calédonie. Arbois, 1845.

Author and Title Listing

AH 4818.83.5 — De cura statuarum apud Graecos. (Kuhnert, E.) Berolini, 1883.

AH 817.03 — De cymbalis veterum. (Lampe, F.A.) Trajecti, 1703.

AH 3759.5 — De cyri expeditione in Massagetas. (Walch, G.B.) Goettingae, 1767.

AH 4147.85 — De Decretis Atheniensium. (Biagi Cremonensi.) Romae, 1785.

AH 7098.83 — De decretis functorum magistratum ornamentis. (Bloch, G.) Lutetiae Parisiorum, 1883.

AH 4098.80 — De demis atticis. (Mueller, O.) Nordhusae, 1880.

AH 4031.5 — De demorum atticae per tribus distributione. (Saal, N.) Coloniae-Agrippinensim, 1860. 3 pam.

AH 4518.70 — De Demosthenes Atheniensium. (Haussding, F.) Halae, 1870.

AH 7162.33 — De descrimine quod inter regulam Cotonianem. (Rivier, A.) Berolini, n.d.

AH 844.5 — De die natali apud veteres. (Schmidt, G.) Hannoverae, 1905.

AH 4808.79 — De Dilbus Contionum Ordmarium. (Reusch, A.) Argentorali, 1879.

AH 3914.3.8 — De dis Syris. (Selden, John.) Amsterdam, 1680.

AH 3914.3.6 — De dis Syris. (Selden, John.) Lipsiae, 1672.

AH 3914.3 — De dis Syris. (Selden, John.) Lugdunum Batavorum, 1629.

AH 3914.3.3 — De dis Syris. 3. ed. (Selden, John.) Lipsiae, 1662.

Htn AH 3914.2* — De dis Syris syntagmata II. (Selden, John.) London, 1617.

AH 3658.7 — De discriptione regni achaemenidarum. (Krumbholz, Paul.) Eisnach, 1891.

AH 4888.56 — De dogtrinae oeconomico-politicae apud Graecos primordiis. Diss. (Roscher, Wilhelm.) Lipsiae, 1856.

AH 8549.50 — De Druidibus, eine Abhandlung. (Herrig, L.) Berlin, 1853.

AH 8549.5 — De druidis occidentalium popularum philosophis. (Frick, J.G.) Ulmae, 1731.

AH 7201.22 — De duorum praecipuorum iurisprudentiae. Inaug. Diss. (Unger, F.W.) Hannoverae, 1834.

AH 4078.36 — De ecclesiis lacedaemoniorum. (Schömann, G.F.) Gryphiswaldiae, 1836.

AH 4228.72 — De Eisaggeliais. Inaug. Diss. (Bohm, H.) Halae, 1874.

Htn AH 805.83.2F* — De emendatione temporum. (Scaliger, J.) Francofurti, 1593.

Htn AH 805.83.3F* — De emendatione temporum. (Scaliger, J.) Lugduni Batavorum, 1598.

AH 4842.9 — De Ephebis Atticis. (Dittenberger, W.) Gottingae, 1863.

AH 5753.15 — De ephoris Spartanis. Diss. (Gachon, Paul.) Monspelii, 1888.

AH 861.13 — De epulis veteruno Christianorum sepulcrabibus. (Vogelives, I.G.) Viternbergae, 1710.

AH 7238.64.5 — De equitatu romano. Diss. (Steinike, Heinrich.) Halis Saxonum, 1864.

AH 7114.11 — De equitibus romanis. (Niemeyer, K.) Gryphiae, 1851.

AH 7114.31 — De equitibus Romanis. Diss. (Muhlert, Fridericus.) Hildesiae, 1831.

AH 4114.5 — De equititus atticis. (Dirichlet, G.J.) Regimonti, 1882.

AH 4842.50 — De eruditione Graecorum. v.1-2. (Möller.) Weimar, 1863.

Htn AH 8907.7* — De Etruriae regionis. (Postell, G.) Florentiae, 1551.

AH 7168.52.5 — De exceptione Disionis. (Grotefend, G.A.A.) Gottingae, 1852.

AH 4238.93 — De exercitu Laeedaemoniorum. (Ringnalda, H.F.T.) Leovardiae, 1893.

AH 7148.87 — De exilio apud Romanos. (Hartmann, L.M.) Berolini, 1887.

AH 7201.4.50 — De Fabio Mela Iuris Consulto. (Beck, I.L.G.) Lipsiae, 1806.

AH 7008.84 — De fabulis graecis ad romam. (Cauer, F.) Berolini, 1884.

AH 7161.20 — De familiari patriciorum. (Heiberg, C.F.) Slesvici, 1829.

Htn AH 7295.72* — De' fatti d'arme de' Romani. (Serdonati, Francesco.) Venetia, 1572.

AH 7808.91.3F — De feriis anni Romanorum vetustissimi observationes selectae. (Wissowa, Georgius.) Marburgi, 1891.

AH 7808.88.5 — De feriis Latinis. (Werner, C.) Coloniae, 1888.

AH 2357.16 — De fontibus. (Schmidt, G.A.) Berolini, 1834.

AH 7518.74 — De Fontibus ad Tiberii historiam pertinentibus. (Thamm, M.) Halis Saxonum, 1874.

AH 7498.66 — De fontibus historiae imperatorem Flaviorum. Diss. (Peter, Carl Eduard.) Halis, 1866.

AH 9603.2 — De forma et conditione Siciliae provinciae Romanae. Thesis. (Dareste de la Chavanne, R.) Lutetiae, 1850.

Htn AH 7861.3* — De funeribus Romanorum. (Kirchmann, J.) Hamburg, 1605.

Htn AH 7861.4* — De funeribus Romanorum cum appendice. (Kirchmann, J.) Lugduni Batavorum, 1672.

AH 7158.93 — De Furtis. (Justinianus I.) Cantabrigiae, 1893.

AH 2353.2 — De Galatarum tetarchis. (Zwintscher, A.) Lipsiae, 1892.

AH 2357.13 — De Galatia provincia romana. (Perrot, G.) Lutetiae, 1867.

AH 7118.9 — De gente valeria. (Münzer, F.) Oppoliae, 1891.

AH 4118.5 — De gentibus atticis. (Platner, E.) Marburgi, 1811.

AH 4118.7 — De gentilitate attica. (Meier, M.H.E.) Halis, 1834.

AH 4118.9 — De gentilitate attica. (Meier, M.H.E.) Halis, 1835.

AH 7817.42 — De gentilitate vetervm Romanorum liber singvlaris. (Chladenii, E.M.) Lipsiae, 1742.

AH 9777.6 — De getarum sive Gothorum. (Jordanes.) Lugduni Batavorum, 1732.

AH 7838.81 — De gladiatura romana. (Meier, P.J.) Bonnae, 1881.

AH 9777.31A — De Gotorum usque ad decium imperatorem. (Rappaport, B.) Berlin, 1899.

AH 7098.82 — De gradu et statu quaestorum im municipiis colonisque. Diss. Inaug. (Mantey, Otto.) Halis Saxonum, 1882.

AH 7818.80 — De Graecis Romanorum amicis aut praeceptoribus a secundo punico bello ad Augustum. Thesim. (Dupuy, Antoine.) Parisiis, 1880.

AH 4158.88 — De Graecorum Asylis. (Barth, B.) Argentorati, 1888.

AH 4808.92.5 — De Graecorum Magistratibus Eponymis. (Gnaedinger, G.) Argentorali, 1892.

AH 4217.5 — De Graecorum pryteneis capita Tria. (Hagemann, G.) Vrateslaviae, 1881.

AH 8017.5 — De Hannonis Carthagoniensis. (Fischer, C.T.) Lipsiae, 1893.

AH 4838.39 — De hippodromo olympiaco. (Hermanno, G.) Lipsiae, 1839.

AH 4118.11 — De historia gentium atticarum. (Petersen, J.C.G.) Slesvici, 1880.

AH 4006.51 — De historicis Graecis. (Vossius, G.J.) Lugdunum Batavorum, 1651.

AH 4206.8 — De homicidarum in Areopago Atheniensi judicio. (Gleue, H.) Gottingae, 1894.

AH 858.5 — De hymenaeo et talasio. (Schmidt, R.O.) Kiliae, 1886.

AH 7678.83 — De imperatore Pertinace; dissertatio historica. (Hundertmark, J.) Monasterii Guestfalorum, 1883.

AH 7578.83 — De Imperatoris Titi temporibus. (Hoffman, O.A.) Marpeogi, 1883.

AH 8679.2 — De incendiis urbis Romae. (Werner, P.) Lipsiae, 1906.

AH 8955.2 — De incursionibus a Gallis in Italiani factis. (Lackner, G.) Regimonti, 1887.

AH 4158.35 — De Infama jure Attico. (Lelyveld, P.) Amsterdam, 1835.

AH 4608.61 — De ingenio et fortuna Graecarum apud Thraces coloniarum. Thesim proponebat. (Nicolas, B.) Lutetiae Parisiorum, 1861.

AH 3094.6.5 — De inscriptione Sargonis. (Sargon, king of Assyria.) Berolini, 1886.

AH 4842.7 — De institutione...scholastica. (Bach, A.) Bonnae, 1841.

AH 5134.5 — De Insula Naxo. (Dugit, E.) Lutetiae Parisiorum, 1867.

AH 5140.9 — De Insula Teno Eiusque historia. (Moschatos, A.) Gottingae, 1855.

AH 7210.2 — De Interregibus Romanis. (Bamberger, F.) Brunsvigae, 1844.

AH 7058.14F — De irenarchis. (Thorlacius, B.) Aavniae, 1814.

AH 4214.17 — De iurandi apud Atheniensium formulis. (Hofmann, G.) Darmatadii, 1886.

AH 4161.9 — De iure familiarum. (Es Vanden, A.H.G.P.) Lugdunum Batavorum, 1864.

AH 4162.5 — De iure hereditario Atheniensium. (Bunsen, C.C.) Gottingae, 1813.

AH 7148.43 — De iure praetorio. (Thermann.) Lipsiae, 1843. 2 pam.

AH 4214.7 — De iureiurando in iure Graeco. (Ziebarth, E.) Gottingae, 1888.

AH 4208.5 — De iuris iurandi iudicium Atheniensium formula. (Westermann, A.) Lipsiae, 1858.

AH 7238.92 — De iustmiani imperatoris aetale. (Beniamin, C.) Berolini, 1892.

AH 7739.11 — De Julia Mamaea Severi A. Matre. (Boer, H.G.W.) Rhenum, 1911.

AH 4138.29A — De jure et Auctoritate Magistratum. (Hermann, C.F.) Heidelbergae, 1829.

AH 4162.25 — De jure hereditario Atheniensium. (Schneider, E.) Monachii, 1851.

AH 7861.13 — De jure manium. (Gautière, J.) Lipsiae, 1671.

AH 7469.06 — De L. Appuleio Saturnino Tribuno Plebis. (Mühll, F.V.) Basileae, 1906.

AH 7478.86.5 — De L. Cornelio Balbo majore. Thesim. (Jullien, Émile.) Lutetiae Parisiorum, 1886.

AH 7168.78.5 — De la cause en droit romain et en droit français. (Artur, E.) Paris, 1878.

AH 7188.78 — De la condition des esclaves. (Duchauffour, A.) Paris, 1878.

AH 7098.75 — De la condition et...chez les romains. (Houdoy, R.J.A.) Paris, 1875.

AH 7038.77 — De la constitution. (Dupond, A.) Paris, 1877.

AH 7908.74.7 — De la cura annonae. (Babled, H.) Paris, 1892.

Eg 879.60.15 — De la divinité du pharaon. (Posener, Georges.) Paris, 1960.

AH 8016.3 — De la geographie du nord de l'Afrique. (Rabusson, A.) Paris, 1856.

AH 7307.34.9 — De la grandeur des Romains. (Montesquieu, Charles de.) Paris, 1870.

AH 7307.34.12.5 — De la grandeur des Romains. (Montesquieu, Charles de.) Paris, 1879.

AH 7238.63 — De la milice romaine depuis la fondation de Rome jusqu'à Constantin. Thèse. (Lamarre, Claude.) Paris, 1863.

AH 7217.13.5 — De la noblesse chez les Romains. (Naudet, Joseph.) Paris, 1868.

AH 7217.13 — De la noblesse et des récompenses. (Naudet, Joseph.) Paris, 1863.

AH 7098.96.3 — De la police et de la voirie. (Boutet, Paul.) Paris, 1896.

AH 3407.9 — De la race...langue des Hittites. (Lantsheere, L.) Bruxelles, 1891.

AH 7168.61 — De la restitution. (Staedtler, H.) Bruxelles, 1861.

AH 7888.85 — De la révolution économique et monétaire. (Belot, E.) Paris, 1885.

AH 7168.81 — De la Successio in locum creditorum. (Cabonat, J.) Paris, 1881.

AH 9777.9 — De la succession des royaumes...les Goths. (Jordanes.) Paris, 1842.

AH 7852.5 — De lacrymatoriis sive de lagenulis. (Namur, A.) Luciliburgi, 1855.

AH 7897.88.15 — De l'agriculture des anciens. (Dickson, Adam.) Paris, 1802. 2v.

AH 7148.80.2 — De l'aquisition et de la perte. (Lindet, T.) Paris, 1880.

AH 5308.8 — De laudibus Athenarum a poetis. (Schroeder, Otto.) Gottingae, 1914.

AH 7169.09 — De l'édit sur l'alienatio judicii mutandi causa facta. (Partsch, J.) Genève, 1909.

AH 4148.85 — De legationibus Graecorum publicis. (Poland, F.) Lipsiae, 1885.

AH 7298.76 — De legationibus reipublicae liberae temporibus Romam missis. Diss. (Büttner-Wobst, Theodor.) Lipsiae, 1876.

AH 7159.06 — De legibus ablatae Pecuniae. (Binsbergen, J.) Trajecti ad Rhenum, 1906.

AH 7808.93 — De legibus et senatus consultis anno 710. (Groebe, P.) Lipsiae, 1893.

AH 7238.95.5 — De legione II adiutrice. Inaug. Diss. (Gündel, Friedrich.) Lipsiae, 1895.

AH 7239.03.2 — De legione Romanorum i Italica. (Beuchel, F.) Lipsiae, 1903.

AH 7238.30 — De legione Romanorum vicesima secunda. (Wiener, P.E.A.) Darmstadii, 1830.

AH 7238.85 — De legione Romanorum X Genima. (Ritterling, E.H.E.) Lipsiae, 1855.

AH 7238.87 — De legione Romanorum XIII Genima. (Schultze, E.) Kiliae, 1887.

AH 7448.75.5 — De legionum per alterum bellum punicum historium quae investigari posse videntur. (Schemann, Ludwig.) Bonnae, 1875.

AH 7201.90 — De legislatione decemoirali. (Haeckermann, G.A.A.G.) Gryphiae, 1843.

AH 7038.77.5 — De l'etat des personnes et des peuples sous les empereurs romains. (Naudet, Joseph.) Paris, 1877.

Eg 269.22 — De l'évolution des relations internationales de l'Égypte pharaonique. Thèse. (Lazzaridès, C.A.) Paris, 1922.

AH 7448.32 — De l'expédition d'Annibal en Italie. (Beaujour, F.) Paris, 1832.

AH 7188.40 — De libertinorum hominum conditione. (Bierregaard, L.) Hauniae, 1840.

AH 4188.96 — De libertorum conditione apud Athenienses. (Foucart, G.) Lutetiae, 1896.

AH 7138.55 — De l'influence du christianisme. (Troplong, R.T.) Paris, 1855.

AH 3017.10 — De l'intérêt de pierres gravées. (Le Brun-Dalbanne.) Besançon, 1872.

Htn AH 925.32* — De liquidorum leguminumque. (Senali, R.) Parisiis, 1532.

AH 4108.80 — De livium atheniensium. (Thumser, V.) Vindobonae, 1880.

Author and Title Listing

	AH 7168.58.10	De l'obligation naturelle. (Massol, M.) Paris, 1858.
	AH 817.58.3	De l'origine des lois, des arts, et des sciences. (Goguet, Antoine Y.) Paris, 1758. 3v.
NEDL	AH 817.58.5	De l'origine des lois. 6. éd. (Goguet, Antoine Y.) Paris, 1820. 3v.
Htn	AH 7836.00F*	De Ludis Circensibus. (Panvinio, O.) Venetia, 1600.
	AH 7844.9.2	De ludis saecularibus populi Romani quiritium. (Pighi, Giovanni B.) Amstelodami, 1965.
	AH 7838.82	De ludo Troiae. v.1-2. (Rasch, Franz.) Jena, 1882.
	AH 864.5	De ludorum memoria. (Soveri, H.F.) Helsingforsiae, 1912.
	AH 7659.51	De l'unité à la division de l'Empire romain. (Demougeot, E.) Paris, 1951.
	AH 9682.2	De Lusitania provincia Romana. (Ursin, Nils R.) Helsingiae, 1884.
	AH 2503.5	De Lyciorum communi. (Fougères, G.) Lutetiae, 1898.
	AH 4200.9	De Lycurgo. (Bazin, H.) Paris, 1895.
	AH 7478.83.5	De M. Antonii triumveri quae supersunt epistalis. Pt.1. (Schelle, Emil.) Frankenberg, 1883.
	AH 7727.11	De M. Aurelii Antonine Elaggbali tribunitici potestate V. (Valsecchi, V.) Florentiae, 1711.
	AH 7708.91	De Maecenatis oratione a Dione ficta. Inaug. Diss. (Meyer, Paul.) Berolini, 1891.
	Eg 39.12	De magistratibus Aegyptiis externas Lagidarum regni provincias administrantibus. (Cohen, D.) 's Gravenhage, n.d.
	AH 4108.90.5	De magistratibus atticis qui saeculo A. Chr. n. quarto pecunias publicas curabant. pt.1. Inaug. Diss. (Panske, Petrus Paulus.) Lipsiae, 1890.
	AH 4058.65	De magistratu decem strategorum. (Kubicki, C.) Berolini, 1865.
	AH 4138.41	De Magistratum Probatione. (Halbertsma, P.) Daventriae, 1841.
	AH 7148.75.2	De magistratuum Romanorum. (Eigenbrodt, A.) Lipsiae, 1875.
	AH 7058.94	De magistratuum romanorum. (Mentz, M.) Ienae, 1894.
	AH 7214.3	De magistratuum Romanorum iure. (Maschke, R.) Berolini, 1884.
	AH 8647.9	De Magnae Graeciae historia antiquissima. (Byvanck, A.W.) Hagae, 1912.
	AH 7148.60	De maiore ac minori latio. (Rudorff, A.) Berolini, 1860.
	AH 7188.26	De mancipii causis. (Böcking, E.) Berolini, 1826.
	AH 7188.41	De manciporum commercio apud Romanos. (Böger, G.) Berolini, 1841.
	AH 7161.7	De manu iuris romani antiquioris commentatis. (Hase, E.F.) Halis, 1847.
	AH 4189.04	De manumissionibus Delphicis. (Francke, I.) Monasterii Guestfalorum, 1904.
	AH 7204.19	De Marco Aurelio Centonio. (Malmeri, J.P.) Halae, 1772. 2v.
Htn	AH 861.5*	De medicato funere. (Belon, P.) Parisiis, 1553.
	AH 5233.5	De megalopolitarum rebus gestis. (Herthum, P.) Lipsiae, 1893.
	AH 7158.85	De memoriae damnatione quae dicitur. (Zedler, K.A.G.I.) Darmstaadiae, 1885.
	Eg 807.37	De mensibus Aegyptiorum. (Averani, N.) Florentiae, 1737.
	AH 4238.57	De mercenariis militibus apud antiquas Graeciae civitates...Thesim proponebat. (Dansin, H.) Argentorati, 1857.
	AH 4852.9	De Metallis Atticis. (Hansen, I.H.) Hamburgi, 1885.
Htn	AH 7235.96*	De militia Romana. (Lipsius, J.) Antverpiae, 1596.
	AH 3654.5	De More Pensarum aquam. (Roth, R.) Jenae, 1670.
	AH 7798.85	De moribus christianis quantum Stilichonis. (Birt, Theodor.) Marburg, 1885.
Htn	AH 4815.99*	De moribus et ritibus gentium. (Sardi, Alessandro.) Ambergae, 1599.
Htn	AH 4815.57*	De moribus et ritibus gentium. (Sardi, Alessandro.) Venetiis, 1557.
	AH 7161.5	De muliere in manu in tutela secundum Gaji Veronensis institutionum principis. (Maanen, J.M. van.) Lugdunum Batavorum, 1823.
	AH 7859.3	De mulierum romanorum cultu. (Pitacco, G.) Görz, 1907.
	AH 98.80	De municipalibus et provincialibus militus in Imperio Romano. Thesis. (Cognat, René.) Lutetiae Parisiorum, 1880.
	AH 5307.15	De munimentis Athenarum. (Müller, K.O.) Gottingae, 1836.
	AH 4843.6F	De musicis Graecorum organis. (Krüger, E.) Gottingae, 1830.
	AH 7628.83	De mutationibus in imperio romano ordinando ab imperatore Hadriano factis. pt.1. (Schurz, Wilhelm.) Bonnae, 1883.
	AH 7116.5	De mutatis centuriis servianis. (Schmidt, F.) Gissae, 1890.
	AH 4840.5	De natura familiae Graecae. (Szymanski, M.) Berolini, 1840.
	AH 168.56	De nautico foenore. (Goldschmidt, J.G.) Berolini, 1866.
	AH 5134.7	De Nesistarum republica commentatio. (Stumpf, Phil.) Monachii, 1881.
	AH 5363.5	De nominibus boeotorum propriis. (Newmann, G.) Regimonti, 1908.
	AH 4058.80	De nomophylacibus atheniensium. (Starker, J.) Nissae, 1880.
	AH 4228.77	De nomothesia Attica. (Höffler, R.J.A.) Kiliae, 1877.
	AH 7116.3	De non metata classium centuriarum. (Troll, M.J.) Asciburgi, 1830.
	AH 4161.7	De nothorum Athenis condicione. (Timmermann, R.) Mederici, 1886.
	AH 7798.41	De occupatione et divisione. (Gaupp, E.T.) Vratislaviae, 1841.
	AH 7055.93.9	De officiis domus Augustae. (Goutière, Jacques.) Parisiis, 1628.
	AH 908.66	De opificum apud veteres Graecas condicione dissertatio. (Frohberger, H.) Grimae, 1866.
	AH 7829.10	De opificum romanorum condicione privata quaestiones. Diss. inaug. (Kuehn, G.) Halis, 1910.
	AH 5858.5	De oppidis et portibus Megaridis ac Boeotiae. Thesim proponebat. (Levègue, J. A.) Parisiis, 1875.
	AH 7448.78.3	De oppugnatione sagunti quaestiones chronologicae. Inaug. Diss. (Buzello, J.) Regimonti, 1876.
	AH 4838.41.5	De ordine certaminum. (Dissenio, L.) Gottingae, 1841.
Htn	AH 844.8F*	De origine, progressu, ceremoniis. (Hospinian, Rudolph.) Tiguri, 1592.
Htn	AH 844.8.3F*	De origine, progressu, ceremoniis. (Hospinian, Rudolph.) Tiguri, 1593.
	AH 7798.82	De origine actibusque Getarum. (Jornandes.) Freiburg, 1882.
	AH 9722.5	De origine Byzantie dissertatio. (Falk, F.W.A.) Vratislaviae, 1829.
	AH 7201.29	De origine iuris. (Pomponius.) Gissae, 1848.
Htn	AH 295.53*	De originibus, seu De varia...historia. (Postel, G.) Basiliae, 1553.
	AH 7468.88A	De P. Clodis Pulchris tribuno plebis. Thèse. (Lacour-Gayet, G.) Lutetiae Parisiorum, 1888.
	AH 7448.77	De P. Cornelio Scipione Aemiliano Africano et Numantino. Thesis. (Person, Émile.) Sancti-Clodoaldi, 1877.
	AH 7458.36	De P. et L. Scipionum accusation de quaestio. (Heerwagen, H.G.) Baruthi, 1836.
	AH 4473.5	De pace quae dicitur cimonica. (Witkowski, S.) Leopoli, 1900.
	AH 2007.2	De Palaestina e Arabia. (Rohden, P.) Berolini, 1885.
	AH 857.5	De parasiti persona capita selecta. (Giese, A.) Berolini, 1908.
	AH 4857.5	De parasitis Graecorum. (Knorr, A.) Colbergae, 1873.
Htn	AH 846.5*	De partibus Aedium. (Grapaldi, F.M.) Venetiis, 1517.
Htn	AH 846.4*	De partibus Aedium dictionari. (Grapaldi, F.M.) Argentinae, 1508.
Htn	AH 846.6*	De partibus Aedium lexicon. (Grapaldi, F.M.) Basil, 1533.
	AH 7118.8	De patriciis gentibres. (Heiter, C.) Berolini, 1909.
	AH 7889.02	De Pauperum cura apud Romanos. (Esser, J.J.) Campis, 1902.
	AH 4328.84	De Pelasgis. (Bruck, Sylvius.) Vratislaviae, 1884.
	AH 8908.12	De Pelasgis Etruscisqui. (Cserèp, J.) Budapestini, 1912.
	AH 4498.21	De Pericle, artium et letterarum slatore. (Boeckh, A.) Berolini, 1821.
	AH 7238.60	De phaleris et de argenteis e arum exemplaribus haud praculcalone et Asaburgio. (Rein, A.) Romae, 1860.
	AH 4116.5	De phratriis atticis. (Sauppe, H.) Gottingae, 1886.
	AH 848.15	De pileo. (Solerius, A.) Amstelodami, 1672.
	AH 897.30	De pistrinis veterum. (Goetze, F.L.) Cygneae, 1730.
	AH 7207.31	De plebiscitis ovinio et atinio disputatio. (Lange, Ludwig.) Lipsiae, 1879.
Htn	AH 927.08.2*	De ponderibus et mensuris veterum. 2. ed. (Eisenschmid, J.C.) Argentorati, 1732.
	AH 928.21	De ponderum, numerum. (Wurm, J.F.) Stutgardaie, 1821.
	AH 7215.5	De pontificum collegii pontifisque Maximi in re publica potestate. Diss. inaug. (Schwede, C.) Lipsiae, 1875.
	AH 4328.49	De populi Atheniensis tribuum origine. (Mueller, E.H.O.) Marburgi, 1849.
	AH 5306.5	De portubus Athenarum. (Curtius, E.) Halis, 1842.
	AH 4258.55	De potentiae...maritimae Epochis. (Goodwin, G.W.) Gottingae, 1855.
	AH 258.55	De potentiae veterum...maritimae epochis. (Goodwin, J.W.) Gottingae, 1855.
	AH 214.5	De praecisis iurandi formis Graecorum. (Schröder, G.A.) Marienwerder, 1845.
	AH 7097.66	De praefectis urbis. (Corsinii, Eduardi.) Pisis, 1766.
	AH 7239.26.9	De praetoria atque amicorum cohortibus. Diss. (Vliet, Jacobus van.) Traiecti ad Rhenum, 1926.
	AH 7918.66	De pretiis frumentis apud Romanos. (Friedlaender, L.) Regimonti, 1866.
	AH 8608.7F	De primi abitatori dell'Italia; opera postuma. pt.1-2. (Bardetti, S.) Modena, 1769.
	AH 7448.64	De primis Hannibalici belli annis quaestiones. (Voigt, G.) Berlin, 1864.
Htn	AH 8548.1.100*	De prisca Celtopaedia. (Picard, Jean.) Parisiis, 1556.
	AH 7228.70	De procédure civile et des actions. (Keller, F.L. von.) Paris, 1870.
	AH 2302.2	De proconsulatu Ciceronis Ciliciensi. (Hartung, Caspar.) Wirceburgi, 1868. 3 pam.
	AH 7217.5	De professoribus et medicis eorumgue. (Gaupp, E.T.) Vratislaviae, 1827.
	AH 7058.18	De propria reipublicae romanae. (Harencarspel, R.S. van.) Trajecti ad Rhenum, 1818.
	AH 7238.83.5	De protectoribus et domesticis Augustorum. Thesis. (Jullian, C.) Paris, 1883.
	AH 8007.11	De provinciis Africanis. (Baale, C.H.) Groningae, 1896.
	AH 4212.5	De proxenia Attica. (Schubert, J.G.) Lipsiae, 1881.
	AH 5336.7	De Prytaneo. (Hagemann, G.) Vratislaviae, 1880.
	AH 7188.89	De publica romanorum servitute quaestiones. Diss inaug. (Lehmann, Eduard.) Lipsiae, 1889.
	AH 4217.7	De publicis Atheniensium honoribus ae Praemais commutaico. (Westermann, A.) Lipsiae, 1830.
	AH 7158.36	De publicis et criminalibus iudiciis Romanorum. (Invernizi, P.) Lipsiae, 1846.
	AH 4108.79	De publicis populi atheniensis rationibus saeculo A. Ch. quinto et quarto. (Christ, Johann.) Gryphiswaldiae, 1879.
	AH 7098.44	De publicis urbium Romae et Constantinapolis. (Jordans, G.H.H.) Bonnae, 1844.
	AH 7448.67.3	De Pugna ad Trebiam Flumen. Inaug. Diss. (Pohle, R.) Halis Saxonum, 1872.
	AH 7448.88	De Pugna ad Zamam Commissa. (Koehn, M.) Halis Saxonum, 1888.
	AH 7448.74	De Pugna Cannensi. (Hesselbarth, H.) Gottingae, 1874.
	AH 4481.5	De Pugnia Marathonia. (Noethe, H.) Susati, 1881.
	AH 7228.76	De quaestionum perpetuarum origine. (Lohse, S.C.) Plaviae, 1876.
	AH 7628.57	De ratione in imperio Romano ordinando ab Hadriano imperatore adhibita. Diss. (Caillet, Jules.) Parisiis, 1857.
	AH 848.9	De ratione quam veteres artifices. (Fuchs, W.H.) Gottingae, 1852.
Htn	AH 7236.57*	De re militari Romanorum. (Saumaise, C. de.) Lugdunum, 1657.
Htn	AH 7235.97*	De re militari veterum Romanorum. (Valtrimus, J.A.) n.p., 1597.
Htn	AH 255.40*	De re nautica libellus. (Geraldi, L.G.) Basiliae, 1540.
Htn	AH 255.37*	De re navali libellus. (Baif, Lazare de.) Lugdunum Batavorum, 1537.
	AH 4518.94.3	De rebus a Graecis. (Boerner, A.) Gottingae, 1894.
	AH 7458.79	De rebus a P. et Cn. Corneliis Scipionibus in Hispania gestis. Diss. inaug. (Genzken, H.) Fribergae, 1879.
	AH 5307.19	De rebus ab Atheniensibus in Thracia et in Ponto. (Hoeck, A.) Kiliae, 1876.
	AH 6024.7	De rebus Delphicis imperatoriae aetatis capita duo. Diss. (Bourguet, Émile.) Montepessulano, 1905.
	AH 9777.13	De rebus geticis. (Bessell, G.) Gottingae, 1854.
	AH 2957.11	De rebus Iliensium. (Haubold, P.) Lipsiae, 1888.
	Eg 708.93	De rebus inter Aegyptios et Romanos...usque ad bellum Alexandrinum a Caesare gestum. Inaug. Diss. (Bandelin, Erich.) Halis Saxonum, 1893.
	AH 8740.2.5	De rebus sacris et artibus veterum Tarentinorum. (Lorentz, Rudolf.) Elberfeldiae, 1836.
	AH 9610.25	De rebus Siculis ab Atheniensium expeditione usque ad prioris belli Punice finem gestia. Inaug. Diss. (Völkerling, A.) Vratislaviae, 1868.
	AH 3657.18	De regio Persarum. (Brisson, B.) Argentoratum, 1710.
Htn	AH 3657.18.5*	De regio Persarum. (Brisson, B.) Heidelberg, 1595.

Author and Title Listing

Author and Title Listing

AH 4277.84 — Denina, C. Istoria...della Graecia. Venezia, 1784. 4v.

AH 8907.46 — Denn die Entzündeten das Licht. (Keller, Werner.) München, 1970.

AH 3002.2.22 — Dennefeld, L. Babylonisch-assyrische Geburts-Omina. Leipzig, 1914.

Eg 1069.10 — Dennis, J.T. The burden of Isis. London, 1910.

AH 833.7 — Deonna, W. Le symbolisme de l'acrobatie antique. Berchem, 1953.

AH 7850.6 — Deouna, Waldemar. Croyances et superstitions de table dans la Rome antique. Bruxelles, 1961.

AH 3160.22 — Der mondgott nanna-suen in der sumerischen uberliefeung Uppsala. (Sjoeberg, Ake.) Uppsala, 1960.

AH 7448.83.15 — Der Romanorum cladibus Trasumenna et Cannensi. (Stuerenburg, Heinrich.) Leipzig, 1883.

AH 3980.9 — Derby, H.W. Selous' two grand pictures of Jerusalem. N.Y., 1872.

Eg 879.72 — Derchain, Philippe. Hathor Quadrifons. Istanbul, 1972.

AH 7239.08.5 — De Rebus Bellicis. Anonymi de rebus bellicis liber. Berlin, 1908.

AH 7239.52A — De Rebus Billicis. A Roman reformer and inventor. Oxford, 1952.

AH 3961.4 — Derenbourg, M.J. Quelques notes sur la guerre de Bar Kôzèbâ. Paris, 1878.

AH 4229.30.10 — Derenne, Eudore. Les procès d'impiété. Liége, 1930.

AH 7169.32 — Deretictio. Inaug. Diss. (Meyer-Collings, J.J.) Kallmünz, 1932.

AH 7168.50 — Dernburg, H. Emtio Bonorum. Heidelberg, 1850.

AH 7168.83.7 — Dernburg, H. Entwicklung und Begriff des juristischen Besitzes des römischen Rechts. Halle, 1883.

AH 7201.41 — Dernburg, H. Institutionen des Cajus. Halle, 1869.

AH 7149.36 — De Robertis, F.M. La espropriazione per pubblica utilità nel diritto romano. Bari, 1936.

AH 7163.23 — Dervilers, P. Des peines de l'adultère. Paris, 1893.

AH 7898.59 — Des céréales en Italie sous les Romains. (Michon, L.A.J.) Paris, 1859.

AH 7058.17 — Des changemens...de l'empire romain. (Naudet, Joseph.) Paris, 1817. 2v.

AH 7850.5 — Des coinestebles et des vins de la Grèce et de l'Italie, en usage chez les Romains. (Peignot, Gabriel.) Dijon, 1822.

Eg 879.60.5 — Des hieroglyphes à la croix. (Doresse, Jean.) Istanbul, 1960.

AH 7108.75 — Des impots indirects. (Naquet, Henri.) Paris, 1875.

AH 7008.38 — Des journaux chez les romaines. (Le Clerc, J.V.) Paris, 1838.

AH 7148.78 — Des municipes. (Grévy, L.) Versailles, 1878.

AH 7168.61.10 — Des obligations naturelles. (Machelard, E.) Paris, 1861.

AH 7168.58.5 — Des obligations solidaires. (Demangeat, C.) Paris, 1858.

AH 7419.40 — Des origines à l'achievement de la conquête. (Pais, Ettore.) Paris, 1940.

AH 819.69.10 — Des origines au vie siècle après J.C. (Lonis, Raoul.) Paris, 1969.

AH 7163.23 — Des peines de l'adultère. (Dervilers, P.) Paris, 1893.

AH 8011.9.5 — Des Vandalenreich, Aufstieg und Untergang. (Diesner, Hans J.) Stuttgart, 1966.

AH 8008.10 — Desanges, J. Catalogue des tribus africaines de l'antiquité classique à l'ouest du Nil. Dakar, 1962.

AH 4409.72 — Desborough, Vincent Robin d'Arba. The Greek dark ages. London, 1972.

AH 3016.5 — Descemet, C. Bas-reliefs assyriens. Rome, 1883.

Htn AH 4935.45F* — Descriptio Graeciae. (Gerbelius, N.) Basiliae, 1545.

AH 6116.5 — Desdevises-du-dezert. Géographie ancienne de la Macedoine. Paris, 1863.

AH 7059.63 — Désignation et investiture de l'empéreur romain, Ier et IIe siècles après J.C. (Parsi, Blanche.) Paris, 1963.

AH 4279.62 — De Silincourt, A. The world of Herodotus. London, 1962.

AH 4279.62.3 — De Silincourt, A. The world of Herodotus. 1. ed. Boston, 1963.

AH 8516.3 — Desjardins, E. Géographie de la Gaule d'après la Table de Peutinger. Paris, 1869.

AH 9066.5 — Desjardins, Ernest. Essai sur la topographie du Latium. Thèse. Paris, 1854.

Htn AH 257.68* — Déslandes, A.F.B. Essai sur la marine des anciens. Paris, 1768.

Eg 709.71.5 — Desmond, Alice Curtis. Cleopatra's children. N.Y., 1971.

AH 7489.24 — Dessau, Hermann. Geschichte der römischen Kaiserzeit. v.1-2. Berlin, 1924-30. 3v.

AH 4519.72.1 — De Ste. Croix, Geoffrey Ernest Maurice. The origins of the Peloponnesian War. Ithaca, 1972.

AH 4519.72 — De Ste. Croix, Geoffrey Ernest Maurice. The origins of the Peloponnesian War. London, 1972.

AH 8073.19 — La destruction de Carthage. 264-146. (Walter, Gerard.) Paris, 1947.

AH 3980.15 — The destruction of Jerusalem. 10. American ed. (Holford, George Peter.) Boston, 1817.

AH 5463.36 — The destruction of Knossos: the rise and fall of Minoan Crete. (Mellersh, Harold E.L.) London, 1970.

AH 7648.60 — Des Vergers, M.J.A. Essai sur Marc Aurèle. Paris, 1860.

AH 8907.4 — Des Vergers, M.J.A.N. L'Étrurie et les Étrusques. Paris, 1862-64. 2v.

AH 8907.4PF — Des Vergers, M.J.A.N. L'Étrurie et les Étrusques. v.3. Atlas. Paris, 1862-64.

AH 8016.2 — Detlefsen, D. Die Geographie Afrikas. Berlin, 1908.

AH 7138.49.5 — Deurer, E.F.F.W. Grundriss für Äussere Geschichte und Institutionen. Heidelberg, 1849.

AH 7162.31 — Deutsch, H. Die Vorläufer der heutigen Testamentsvollstrecker. Berlin, 1899.

AHP 14.7 — Deutsche Beiträge zur Altertumswissenschaft. Baden-Baden. 1,1951+ 5v.

AHP 14.5F — Deutsche Forschungsgemeinschaft. Ausgraben der deutschen Froschungsgemeinschaft in Uruk-Warka. Leipzig. 1,1936+ 6v.

AH 29.64 — Deutsche Historiker-Gesellschaft. Fachgruppe alte Geschichte. Neue Beiträge zur Geschichte der alten Welt. Berlin, 1964-65. 2v.

AH 819.61.20 — Deutsche Historiker-Gesellschaft. Sozialökonomische Verhältnisse in alter Orient. Berlin, 1961.

AH 3045.5.5F — Deutsches Archäologisches Institut. Vorläufiger Bericht über die von dem Deutschen Archäologischen Institut und der Deutschen Orient-Gesellschaft aus Mitteln der Deutschen Forschungsgemeinschaft unternommenen Ausgrabungen in Uruk-Warka. Berlin. 12,1953+ 9v.

AH 9757.7 — Deutschlands Besetzung durch die Römer. (Eidam, Heinrich.) Dinkelsbühl, 1928.

AH 7479.00 — Deux campagnes de César. (Moineville, L.) Paris, 1900.

AH 8182.5 — Les deux camps de la légion IIIe Auguste à Lambèse. (Cagnat, René.) Paris, 1908.

AH 9757.8 — Les deux Germanies cis-rhénanes. Étude d'histoire et de géographie anciennes. (Martin, Charles.) Paris, 1863.

AH 8511.10 — Deux siècles décisifs! (Grossi, Georges.) Vaison-la-Romaine, 1953.

AH 4048.86 — Development of Athenian democracy. (Jevons, F.B.) London, 1886.

Eg 879.12.2 — Development of religion and thought in ancient Egypt. (Breasted, James Henry.) N.Y., 1912.

Eg 879.12 — Development of religion and thought in ancient Egypt. (Breasted, James Henry.) N.Y., 1912.

AH 7038.86.3 — Development of Roman constitution. (Tighe, A.) N.Y., 1889.

AH 3014.19 — The development of Sumerian art. (Woolley, Charles L.) N.Y., 1935.

AH 4038.93.7 — Development of the Athenian constitution. (Botsford, G.W.) Boston, 1893.

AH 7038.86.5 — The development of the Roman constitution. (Tighe, A.) N.Y., 1886.

AH 7038.86.9 — The development of the Roman constitution. (Tighe, A.) N.Y., 1886.

Eg 138.68 — Devéria, T. Le papyrus judiciaire de Turin. Paris, 1868.

AH 7799.53 — Dévignes, G. Ici, le monde changea de maitre. Paris, 1953.

AH 3183.5 — The devils and evil spirits of Babylonia. (Thompson, Reginald C.) London, 1903- 2v.

AH 8608.10 — Devoto, Giacomo. Gli antichi italici. Firenze, 1931.

AH 8608.10.2 — Devoto, Giacomo. Gli antichi italici. 2. ed. Firenze, 1951.

AH 8513.12 — DeWitt, N.J. Urbanization and the franchise in Roman Gaul. Lancaster, Pa., 1940.

AH 7818.46.5 — Dezobry, Charles. Rome au siècle d'Auguste. Göttingen, 1850.

AH 7818.46.3 — Dezobry, Charles. Rome au siècle d'Auguste. Paris, 1846. 4v.

AH 7818.46.7 — Dezobry, Charles. Rome au siècle d'Auguste. Paris, 1870. 4v.

AH 3663.7 — Dhalla, M.N. Loroastrian civilization. N.Y., 1922.

AH 3964.19 — Dhorme, E. L'evolution religieuse d'Israël. Thèse. Bruxelles, 1937.

AH 3171.9 — Dhorme, E. La littérature babylonienne et assyrienne. Thèse. Paris, 1937.

AH 3155.18 — Dhorme, E. Les religions de Babylonie et d'Assyrie. 2. ed. Paris, 1949.

AH 3011.8 — Dhorme, E.P. Recueil Edouard Dhorme. Paris, 1951.

AH 3002.84 — Dhorme, Paul. Choix de textes religieux assyro-babylonies. Paris, 1907.

AH 8647.15 — Di Cautonia, repubblica della Magna Grecia. (Marincola Pistoja, D.) Catanzaro, 1866. 2 pam.

AH 49.65 — Diadem und Königsherrschaft. (Ritter, Hans-Werner.) München, 1965.

AH 3507.10 — Diakonov, I. Istoriia Midii. Moskva, 1956.

AH 3022.20 — D'iakonov, I.M. Obshchestvennyi i gosudarstvennyi stroi drevnego Dvurech'ia. Moskva, 1959.

AH 4559.42 — Dialoge um Alexander. (Grabowsky, Adolf.) Zurich, 1942.

AH 4819.52.10 — Diano, Carlo. Forma ed evento. 1. ed. Veneia, 1952.

AH 4819.52.12 — Diano, Carlo. Forma ed evento. 2. ed. Venezia, 1960.

AH 8548.40 — Dias Pinheiro, Alfredo. Os celtas e povos com êles relacionados. Guimarães, 1928.

AH 7207.20A — Diaz, José F. Historia del Senado romano. Barcelona, 1867.

AH 4049.72 — Díaz Tejera, Alberto. Encrucijada de lo político y lo humano, un momento histórico de Grecia. Sevilla, 1972.

AH 3964.14 — Dibelius, Martin. Die Lade Jahnes. Inaug. Diss. Göttingen, 1906.

AH 9666.5 — Diccionario...de la Espana antigua. (Cortés y López, Miguel.) Madrid, 1835-36. 3v.

AH 4819.32.20 — Dickinson, G.L. The contribution of ancient Greece to modern life. London, 1932.

AH 4819.05.12 — Dickinson, G.L. The Greek view of life. N.Y., 1916.

AH 4818.98 — Dickinson, G.L. Greek view of life. 2nd ed. London, 1898.

AH 4819.05.8 — Dickinson, G.L. The Greek view of life. 3d ed. N.Y., 1905.

AH 4818.96.15 — Dickinson, G.L. The Greek view of life. 5th ed. N.Y., 1906.

AH 4819.09.3 — Dickinson, G.L. The Greek view of life. 6th ed. N.Y., 1909.

AH 4819.05.17 — Dickinson, G.L. The Greek view of life. 7th ed. Garden City, N.Y., 1925.

AH 4819.05.20 — Dickinson, G.L. The Greek view of life. 7th ed. Garden City, N.Y., 1927.

AH 4819.05.30 — Dickinson, G.L. The Greek view of life. 22d ed. London, 1949.

AH 4819.05.31 — Dickinson, G.L. The Greek view of life. 23d ed. London, 1957.

AH 7479.63 — Dickinson, J. Death of a republic. N.Y., 1963.

AH 7897.88.15 — Dickson, Adam. De l'agriculture des anciens. Paris, 1802. 2v.

AH 7897.88 — Dickson, Adam. Husbandry of the ancients. Edinburgh, 1788.

AH 3966.38 — Dictionary of Bible place names. (Rowley, Harold Henry.) London, 1970.

NEDL AH 938.54.2 — Dictionary of Greek and Roman geography. (Smith, William.) London, 1854.

AH 938.54.3 — Dictionary of Greek and Roman geography. (Smith, William.) London, 1854.

NEDL AH 938.54.4 — Dictionary of Greek and Roman geography. (Smith, William.) London, 1856-57. 2v.

AH 938.54.5 — Dictionary of Greek and Roman geography. (Smith, William.) London, 1870. 2v.

Eg 819.59.5 — Dictionnaire de la civilisation égyptienne. (Posener, Georges.) Paris, 1959.

AH 3966.19 — Dictionnaire topographique. (Saulcy, F. de.) Paris, 1877.

AH 4112.9 — Die...Amphiktyonie. (Gürgel, H.) München, 1877.

AH 930.25 — Die Entdeckungen der Carthager und Griechen. (Lelewel, J.) Berlin, 1821.

NEDL AH 278.41.7 — Dielitz, T. Hellas und Rom. 7. Aufl. Berlin, 18- ?

AH 4499.59 — Dienelt, Karl. Die Friedenspolitik des Perikles. Wien, 1959.

AH 8011.9.5 — Diesner, Hans J. Des Vandalenreich, Aufstieg und Untergang. Stuttgart, 1966.

AH 8011.9 — Diesner, Hans J. Der Untergang der römischen Herrschaft in Nordafrika. Weimar, 1964.

AH 239.71 — Diesner, Hans-Joachim. Kriege des Altertums. Berlin, 1971.

AH 4448.40 — Dietrich, A. De Clisthene. Halis Saxonum, 1840.

AH 3095.10 — Dietrich, Manfried. Die Aramäer Südbabyloniens in der Sargonidenzeit, 700-648. Kevelaer, 1970.

AH 3054.10 — Dietrich, Manfried. Nuzi-Bibliographie. Kevelaer, 1972.

Author and Title Listing

Author and Title Listing

Htn   AH 297.02*   Dissertationes IX. antiquitatibus. (Dale, A. van.) Amstelodami, 1702.

NEDL   AH 138.83.3   Dissertations on early law and custom. (Maine, Henry S.) N.Y., 1883.

NEDL   AH 138.83.5   Dissertations on early law and custom. (Maine, Henry S.) N.Y., 1886.

AH 4865.5   Dissertations on the ancient chariot. (Pownall, Thomas.) London, 1771.

AH 8942.2   Dissertazione istorico-etrusca...della città di Volterra. (Riccobaldi del Bana, G.M.) Firenze, 1758.

AH 9621.9   Dissertazione sopra una statua di Marmo. (Torremuzza, G.L.C.) Palermo, 1749.

AH 4279.29.5   La dissoluzione della libertà nella Grecia antica. (Ferrabino, Aldo.) Padova, 1929.

AH 4299.29   La dissoluzione della libertà nella Grecia antica. (Ferrarino, Aldo.) Padova, 1929.

AH 7188.68.3   Distinctions admises. (Machelard, E.) Paris, 1868.

AH 4559.08   Dittberner, W. Issos. Ein Beiträge zur Geschichte Alexanders des Grossen. Berlin, 1908.

AH 4842.9   Dittenberger, W. De Ephebis Atticis. Gottingae, 1863.

AH 9777.18   Diversarum...historiae antiquae scriptores tres. (Jordanes.) Hamburgi, 1611.

AH 3156.16   La divination en Mésopotamie ancienne et dans les régions voisines. (Rencontre Assyriologique Internationale, 14th, Strasbourg 1965.) Paris, 1966.

AH 3156.5.9   La divination et la science des présages. (Lenormant, F.) Paris, 1875.

AH 8205.5   Divine, Arthur D. The north-west frontier of Rome: a military study of Hadrian's Wall. London, 1969.

AH 8549.168.5   Divinités et sanctuaires de la Gaule. (Thévenot, Émile.) Paris, 1968.

AH 8549.125.5   Divinités gauloises. (Hubert, Henri.) Epona, 1925.

AH 3107.3   Divisione politica e militare dell'antica Assiria. (Oberziner, L.A.) Trento, 1884.

AH 9666.7   Les divisions administratives de l'Espagne romaine. Thèse. (Albertini, E.) Paris, 1923.

Eg 878.81   Dizionario di mitologia egizia. v.1-5. (Lauzone, R.N.) Torino, 1881. 3v.

AH 4829.33   Ho dnmodios...tòn hargaiòy Hellenòn. (Demopoulos, P.N.) Athēnai, 1933.

AH 3911.7   Dobias, J. Dějiny Římské provincie Syrske. Praha, 1924.

AH 7469.23.5   Dobiás, J. Synoský prokonsulát M. Calpurnia Bibula. Praha, 1923.

AH 8453.10   Dobó, Árpád. Der Verwaltung der römischen Provinz Pannonien von Augustus bis Diocletianus. Amsterdam, 1968.

AH 4842.71   Dobson, J.F. Ancient education and its meaning to us. N.Y., 1932.

AH 7203.42   Doctriia Pandectarum. (Mühlenbruch, C.F.) Bruxelles, 1838.

AH 4162.13   Doctrin am iuris Attici de hereditatibus. (Grasshof, W.) Berolini, 1877.

AH 926.17   Doctrina de ponderibus. (Angelocrator, D.) Marpurgi Cattorum, 1617.

AH 4842.23   Doctrines pédagogiques. (Martin, A.) Paris, 1881.

AHP 14.6F   Documenta et Monumenta orientis antiqui. Leiden. 3,1948+ 11v.

AH 4009.27   The documentary sources of Greek history. (Cary, Max.) Oxford, 1927.

Eg 232.5   Documenti per la storia dell'esercito romano in Egitto. (Daris, Sergio.) Milano, 1964.

AH 3154.16F   Documents assyriens relatifs aux Présages. (Boissier, A.) Paris, 1894-96.

AH 7532.2   Documents illustrating the principates of Gaius Claudius and Nero. (Smallwood, Edith Mary.) Cambridge, 1967.

AH 7592.2   Documents illustrating the principates of Nerva Trajan and Hadrian. (Smallwood, Edith Mary.) Cambridge, Eng., 1966.

AH 7502.5.4   Documents illustrating the reigns of Augustas and Tiberius. 2. ed. (Ehrenberg, Victor.) Oxofrd, 1967.

AH 7539.39   Documents illustrating the reigns of Cladius and Nero. (Charlesworth, M.P.) Cambridge, Eng., 1939.

AH 3150.3   Documents juridiques de l'Assyrie et de la Chaldée. (Oppert, J.) Paris, 1877.

AH 3020.18F   Documents présargoniques. (Allotte de la Fuÿe, Francois N.) Paris, 1908-20. 5v.

AH 3154.2   Documents religieux. (Halevy, J.) Paris, 1882.

AH 4819.51   Dodds, Eric Robertson. The Greeks and the irrational. Berkeley, Calif., 1951.

AH 4819.51.3   Dodds, Eric Robertson. The Greeks and the irrational. Berkeley, 1959.

AH 4819.51.2   Dodds, Eric Robertson. The Greeks and the irrational. 1st ed. Boston, 1957. 2v.

NEDL   AH 7478.92.2   Dodge, T.A. Caesar. A History of the art of war. Boston, 1892.

AH 7448.91A   Dodge, T.A. Hannibal - history of the art of war. Boston, 1891.

AH 807.01   Dodwell, Henry. De veteribus Graecorum Romanorum que cyclis. Oxonii, 1701.

AH 4819.60   Doedeus, T.P. Ontmoeting met het oude Hellas. Amsterdam, 1960.

AH 8740.3   Doehle. Geschichte Tarents bis auf seine Unterwerfung unter Rom. Strassburg, 1877.

AH 6116.7   Döll, M. Studien zur Geographie des alten Makedoniens. Stadtamhof, 1891.

AH 4259.37   Döpel, G. Die attische Flotte im peloponnesischen Kriege. Inaug. Diss. Borna, 1937.

AH 4818.76   Döring, E. Hellas. Frankfurt, 1876.

AH 7759.60   Doerries, Hermann. Constantine and religious liberty. New Haven, 1960.

AH 7759.58   Doerries, Hermann. Konstantin der Grosse. Stuttgart, 1958.

AH 7508.76   Doetsch, P. Leben und Treiben am Hofe des Kaisers Augustus, nach Tacitus. Malmedy, 1876.

Eg 879.39.5   Die dogmatische Stellung des Königs. (Jacobsohn, Helmuth.) Glückstadt, 1939.

AH 4828.75   Dokimion. (Boudodénou, Charalampous.) Odèssò, 1875. 2v.

AH 7178.82.4   Die Domänen der römischen Kaiserzeit. (His, Rudolph.) Leipzig, 1896.

AH 7489.09   Domaszewski, A. von. Geschichte der Römischen Kaiser. Leipzig, 1909. 2v.

AH 7489.09.2   Domaszewski, A. von. Geschichte der Römischen Kaiser. 2. Aufl. Leipzig, 1914. 2v.

AH 7239.08.7   Domaszewski, Alfred von. Die Anlage der Limeskastelle. Heidelberg, 1908.

AH 7137.22.2F   Domat, Jean. The civil law in its natural order together with the publick law. London, 1737. 2v.

AH 7137.22.15   Domat, Jean. The civil law in its natural order together with the publick law. 2. ed. Boston, 1850. 2v.

AH 7137.22.5F   Domat, Jean. Les loix civiles. Paris, 1756.

AH 7137.35F   Domat, Jean. Les loix civiles dans leur ordre naturel. v.1-2. Paris, 1735.

AH 818.67   Dombart, Theodore. Die sieben Weltwunder des Altertums. 2. Aufl. München, 1970.

AH 7201.34   Domenget, M.L. Institutes de Gaius. Paris, 1866.

Eg 759.47   La domination romaine en Égypte aux deux premiers siècles. (Jouguet, P.) Alexandrie, 1947.

AH 4729.46   Il domino romano in Grecia dalla guerra acaica ad Augusto. (Accame, Silvio.) Roma, 1946.

AH 7589.02   Domitians Chattenkrieg. (Vieze, H.) Berlin, 1902.

AH 7589.45   Domiziano. (Arias, P.) Catania, 1945.

AH 7239.05   Die Dona Militaria. (Steiner, Paul.) Bonn, 1905.

Eg 879.55   Donadoni, S. Le religione dell'Egitto antico. Milano, 1955.

Eg 309.63   Donadoni, Sergio. Le fonti indirette della storia egiziana. Roma, 1963.

Eg 1009.68   Donadoni, Sergio. La letteratura egizia. Firenze, 1968.

AH 7162.38   Die Donatio Mortis Causa im klassischen römischen Recht. (Simonius, Pascal.) Basel, 1958.

AH 4204.15   Dondorff, H. Aphorismen zur Beurtheilung der solonischen Verfassung. Berlin, 1880.

AH 7138.22   Doneau, H. Commentarii de iure civili. Norimberg, 1822. 16v.

AH 7859.5   La donna nella storia del diritto romano. (Paternò-Paterno, S.) Roma, 1932.

AH 7478.95   Donne e politica. (Ciccotti, E.) Milano, 1895.

AH 7489.31   Doppelprinzipat und Reichsteilung im Imperium Romanum. (Kornemann, E.) Leipzig, 1931.

Eg 879.60.5   Doresse, Jean. Des hieroglyphes à la croix. Istanbul, 1960.

AH 7449.71.5   Dorey, Thomas Alan. Rome against Carthage. London, 1971.

AH 4329.56.5   Doriens et Ioniens. (Will, Edouard.) Paris, 1956.

AH 4329.56   Doriens et Ioniens. (Will, Edouard.) Strasbourg, 1956.

AH 4459.46   Dorjohn, A.P. Political forgiveness in old Athens. Evanston, 1946.

AH 7148.86   Dorsch, E. De civitatis Romanae apud Graecos. Vratislaviae, 1886.

AH 8548.57   Dottin, Georges. Manuel pour servir à l'étude de la antiquité celtique. Paris, 1906.

AH 8548.57.2   Dottin, Georges. Manuel pour servir à l'étude de l'antiquité celtique. 2. éd. Paris, 1915.

AH 8549.104.5   Dottin, Georges. La religion des Celtes. 2. éd. Paris, 1904.

NEDL   AH 7842.4   Le dottrine pedagogiche. (Gerini, G.B.) Torino, 1894.

AH 7108.88.5   Les douanes chez les romains. (Thibault, Fabien.) Paris, 1888.

AH 3936.2   Double, L. Césars de Palmyre. Paris, 1877.

AH 7538.76   Double, L. L'empereur Claude. Paris, 1876.

AH 818.74.3   Doublier, L. Geschichte des Altertums. Wien, 1874.

AH 5759.9   Doukas, P.C. He Sparte dia mesou tòn aiònon. Nea Yorkē, 1922.

AH 3407.36   Dovgialo, Gennadii I. K istorii vozniknoveniia gosudarstva. Minsk, 1968.

AH 3911.9A   Downey, G. A study of the Comites orientis and the Consulares Syriae. Diss. Princeton, 1939.

AH 3921.8.5   Downey, Glanville. Ancient Antioch. Princeton, 1963.

AH 3921.9   Downey, Glanville. Antioch in the age of Thedosius the Great. Norman, 1962.

AH 3921.8   Downey, Glanville. A history of Antioch in Syria. Princeton, 1961.

AH 7659.69   Downey, Glanville. The late Roman Empire. N.Y., 1969.

AH 15.8   Pamphlet box. Downey, Glanville 1908-   . Miscellaneous pamphlets.

AH 9757.5   Dragendorff, H. Westdeutschland zur Römerzeit. Leipzig, 1912.

AH 9757.5.5   Dragendorff, H. Westdeutschland zur Römerzeit. 2. Aufl. Leipzig, 1919.

AH 4202.15   Drakon's law on homicide. (Stroud, Ronald S.) Berkeley, 1968.

AH 4204.9   Dramburg. Verfassungskämpfe Athens. Dramburg, 1870.

Eg 559.41   Le drame d'Avaris; essai sur la pénétration des Sémites en Égypte. (Montet, Pierre.) Paris, 1941.

AH 4558.83.2   Le drame macédonien. 2. éd. (Jurien, J.P.E.) Paris, 1891.

AH 8073.9   Drapeyron, L. La condition de Carthage. Paris, 1882.

Eg 133.70   Drath, Juergen. Untersuchungen zum Wohnungseigentum auf Grund der gräko-ägyptischen Papyri. Diss. Marburg, 1970?

AH 4839.62   Drees, Ludwig. Der Ursprung der olympischen Spiele. Stuttgart, 1962.

AH 7148.91   Drei Abhandlungen zum römischen Staats- und Privatrecht. (Kappeyne van de Coppello, Johann.) Berlin, 1891.

AH 7098.60   Drei epigraphische Constitutionen. (Voigt, Moritz.) Leipzig, 1860.

Eg 850.1   Drei Fest-Kalender. (Brygseh, H.) Leipzig, 1877.

AH 7808.76   Drei synchronistische Daten der römischen Kalenders vor der julianischen Reform. (Hofmann, A.) Triest, 1876.

AH 7468.36   Die drei Volkstribunen Tib. Gracchus, M. Drusus und P. Sulpicius. (Ahrens, E.A.J.) Leipzig, 1836.

AH 4819.33   Drerup, Engelbert. Kulturprobleme des klassischen Griechentums. Paderborn, 1933-34. 2v.

AH 7478.63   Dressel, E. Uber die politische Rolle des Gnaeus Pompejus Magnus. Coburg, 1863.

AH 4842.54A   Drever, J. Greek education, its practice and principles. Cambridge, 1912.

AH 9707.12   Drevna Trakiia. (Danov, Khristo M.) Sofiia, 1968.

AH 1298.95   Drevne patriarhalnyja. (Vinogradov, Aleksy.) St. Petersburg, 1895.

AH 4819.30   Drevniaia gretsiia. (Moscow. Gosudarstvennyi Muzei Iziashchnykh Iskusstv.) Moskva, 1930.

AH 9.61   Drevniaia Gretsiia i drevnii Rim. (Voronkov, A.I.) Moskva, 1961.

AH 4299.69   Drevnie greki na ostrove Berezan'. (Gorbunova, Vseniia S.) Leningrad, 1969.

Eg 299.67   Drevnii Ēgipet i drevniaia Afrika. (Akademiia nauk SSSR. Institut Narodov Azii.) Moskva, 1967.

Eg 299.60   Drevnii Egypet; sbornik statei. (Akademiia nauk SSSR. Institut Narodov Azii.) Moskva, 1960.

AH 29.62   Drevnii mir; sbornik statei. (Akademiia nauk SSSR. Institut narodov Azii.) Moskva, 1962.

AH 7489.69   Drevnii Rim. (Utchenko, Sergei L.) Moskva, 1969.

AH 1279.37   Drevnii Vostok; atlas. (Snegirev, I.L.) Leningrad, 1937.

AH 279.72   Drevnii Vostok i antichnyi mir. Moskva, 1972.

Eg 878.90.5   Drexler, W. Der Cultus der Aegyptischen Gottheiten. Leipzig, 1890.

AH 7178.98.2   Dreyfus, Robert. Essae sur les lois agraires. Paris, 1898.

AH 3160.24   Driel, G. van. The cult of Aššur. Assen, 1969.

Author and Title Listing

	Call no.	Entry
	AH 888.49	Driot à l'oisiveté. (Moreau-Christophe, Louis-Mathurin.) Paris, 1849.
	Eg 279.59	Drioton, Etienne. L'Egypte pharaonique. Paris, 1959.
	Eg 299.57	Drioton, Etienne. Pages d'égyptologie. Le Caire, 1957.
	Eg 1009.42	Drioton, Etienne. Le théâtre egyptien. Le Caire, 1942.
	AH 8514.14	Drioux, Georges. Cultes indigènes des Lingons. Paris, 1934.
	AH 8514.14.5	Drioux, Georges. Cultes indigénes des Lingons. Thèse. Paris, 1934.
	AH 3045.5F	Dritter vorläufiger Bericht über die von der Notgemeinschaft die deutschen Wissenschaft in Uruk unternommenen Ausgrabungen. (Jordan, J.) Berlin, 1932.
	AH 7138.64	Dritto romano. (Barinetti, P.) Milano, 1864.
	AH 9639.14	Droegemueller, Hans-Peter. Syrakus; zur Topographie und Geschichte einer griechischer Stadt. Heidelberg, 1969.
	AH 139.61	Le droit antique et ses prolongements modernes. (Imbert J.) Paris, 1961.
	AH 7162.29	Droit d'accroissement. (Wetter, P.A.H.) Bruxelles, 1866.
	AH 7148.38	Droit de propriété. (Giraud, C.) Aix, 1838.
	AH 4162.15	Droit de succession légitime. v.1-2. (Caillemer, E.) Paris, 1879.
	AH 7161.21	Droit des patresfamilias. (Laënnec, R.) Saint-Amand, 1899.
	AH 7148.83	Le droit fétial et les fétiaux. (Weiss, André.) Paris, 1883.
	AH 3152.7	Droit matrimonial assyro-Babylonien. (Praag, A.) Amsterdam, 1945.
	AH 7098.75.4	Le droit municipal. (Houdoy, R.J.A.) Paris, 1876.
	AH 138.60A	Droit municipal dans l'antiquité. (Béchard, F.) Paris, 1860.
	AH 4158.75	Le droit pénal. (Thonissen, J.J.) Bruxelles, 1875.
	AH 7168.40	Droit privé des Romains. (Marezoll, T.) Paris, 1840.
	AH 4148.69	Droit public d'Athènes. (Perrot, G.) Paris, 1869.
	AH 7148.62	Droit public et administratif. (Serrigny, D.) Paris, 1862. 2v.
	AH 7148.70.2	Le droit public romain. 2e éd. (Willems, P.) Louvain, 1872.
	AH 7148.70.3	Le droit public romain. 3e éd. (Willems, P.) Louvain, 1874.
	AH 7148.70.4	Le droit public romain. 4e éd. (Willems, P.) Louvain, 1880.
	AH 7148.70.5	Le droit public romain. 5e éd. (Willems, P.) Louvain, 1883.
	AH 7148.70.6	Le droit public romain. 6e éd. (Willems, P.) Louvain, 1888.
	AH 7148.70.7	Le droit public romain. 7e éd. (Willems, P.) Louvain, 1910.
	AH 7168.92.7	Droit romain; essai sur le fondement de la protection possessoire. (Appleton, J.) Paris, 1892.
	AH 7138.82	Droit romain. (Ruben de Couder, M.J.) Paris, 1882.
	AH 7203.69	Droit romain. (Ruben der Couder.) Paris, 1878.
	AH 7108.94	Droit romain. Des impots indirectes. (Moulin, C.D.) Poitiers, 1894.
	AH 7203.59	Droit romain. 2. ed. (Thézard, L.) Paris, 1873.
	AH 7203.71	Droit romain. 3. éd. (Thézard, L.) Paris, 1878.
	AH 7098.94	Droit romain de la curie. (Cyprès, Imbert.) Paris, 1894.
	AH 7168.94.5	Droit romain de l'impot sur l'importation et l'exportation des marchandises à Rome sous la république et sous l'empire. (Cantacuzène, M.G.) Paris, 1894.
	AH 7108.87	Droit romain des douanes chez les Romains. v.1-2. (Mendes, José Amando.) Libourne, 1887.
	AH 7148.84	Droit romain des juridictions. (Roques, Charles.) Paris, 1884.
	AH 7108.88	Droit romain des magistrats monétaires. (Marsault, A.) Paris, 1888.
	AH 7148.85.2	Droit romain du droit de cité. (Pinvert, L.) Paris, 1885.
	AH 4147.45	Droits des metropolis sur colonies. (Bougainville.) Paris, 1745.
	AH 7329.12	Les droits politiques des juifs dans L'empire romain. (Juster, Jean.) Paris, 1912.
	AH 7162.22	Dropsie, M.A. Roman law of testaments. Philadelphia, 1892.
	AH 4558.85	Droysen, H. Alexanders des Grossen Heerwesen. Freiburg, 1885.
	AH 5308.5	Droysen, H. Athen und der Westen. Berlin, 1882.
	AH 4558.33	Droysen, J.G. Alexanders des Grossen. Hamburg, 1833.
	AH 4558.33.6	Droysen, J.G. Geschichte Alexanders des Grossen. Berlin, 1917.
	AH 4658.36	Droysen, J.G. Geschichte des Hellenismus. Hamburg, 1836. 2v.
	AH 4658.36.2	Droysen, J.G. Geschichte des Hellenismus. v.1-6. 2. Aufl. Gotha, 1877-78. 4v.
	AH 4658.36.5	Droysen, J.G. Histoire de l'hellénisme. Paris, 1883. 3v.
	AH 8549.161	Les druides. (Le Roux, F.) Paris, 1961.
	AH 8549.106	Les druides et les dieux celtiques. (Arbois de Jubainville, Henry d'.) Paris, 1906.
	AH 8549.42.5	Druidical remains and antiquities of the ancient Britons. (Roberts, J.) Swansea, 1842.
	AH 8549.124	Druidism; the ancient faith of Britain. (Wright, D.) London, 1924.
	AH 8549.171	Le druidisme, ou La lumière del l'Occident. (Coarer-Kalondan, Edmond.) Paris, 1971.
	AH 8549.65	Le druidisme; ou Religion des anciens gaulois. (Panchaud, Édouard.) Lausanne, 1865.
	AH 8549.104	Il druidismo nell'antica Gallia. (Callegari, G.V.) Padova, 1904.
	AH 8549.166	The Druids. (Chadwick, Nora (Kershaw).) Cardiff, 1966.
	AH 8549.127	The Druids. (Kendrick, T.D.) London, 1927.
	AH 8549.127.5	The Druids. (Kendrick, T.D.) N.Y., 1927.
	AH 8549.168	The Druids. (Piggott, Stuart.) N.Y., 1968.
	AH 8549.80.5	The Druids and their religion. (Howard, John E.) London, 1880?
	AH 4308.15	Drumann, K.U. Ideen zur Geschichte des Verfalls. Berlin, 1815.
	AH 908.60	Drumann, W. Die Arbeiter und Communisten. Königsberg, 1860.
	AH 7468.34.4	Drumann, W. Geschichte Roms. Koenigsberg, 1834. 6v.
	AH 7468.34.5	Drumann, W. Geschichte Roms. v.1-6. Berlin, 1899. 5v.
	Eg 708.23	Drumann, Wilhelm. Historisch-antiquarische Untersuchungen über Aegypten, oder Die Inschrift von Rosette. Königsberg, 1823.
	AH 1298.24	Drummond, W. Origines. London, 1824. 4v.
	AH 4047.94	Drummond, W. Review of government of Sparta and Athens. London, 1794.
	AH 7509.34.20	Druso. (Stella, L.A.) Gleno, 1934.
	AH 7509.56.5	Drusus und Germanicus. (Christ, Karl.) Paderborn, 1956.
	Eg 919.22	The "dryland" in Ptolemaic and Roman Egypt. (Westermann, W.L.) n.p., 1922.
	AH 7163.19	Du divorce. (Morael, G.L.M.) Paris, 1888.
	AH 7178.82	Du domaine public del'état. (Baillierie, P.) Paris, 1882.
	AH 7148.85	Du droit de cité romaine. (Michel, N.H.) Paris, 1885.
	AH 7168.52	Du droit privé. 2. éd. (Marezoll, T.) Paris, 1852.
	AH 3957.25	Du groupe ethnique à la communaté religieuse. (Causse, A.) Paris, 1937.
	AH 7148.59	Du municipe romain. (Quinion, L.) Paris, 1859.
	AH 7039.63	Du pouvoir dans la république romaine. (Rouvier, J.) Paris, 1963.
	AH 4168.67	Du pret a la grosse. (Dareste, R.) Paris, 1867.
	AH 7114.21	Du role des tribuns de la plebe. (Lefèvre, Eugene.) Paris, 1910.
	AH 7238.66	Du service de santé militaire chez les romains. (Briau, René.) Paris, 1866.
	AH 7468.76.2	Dubois-Guchan, E.P. Rome et Cicéron. Paris, 1880.
	AH 7498.61	Dubois Guchan, E.P. Tacite et son siècle. Paris, 1861. 2v.
	EgP 39.41	Dubois-Richard, P. Essai sur les gouvernements de l'Egypte. Le Caire, 1941.
	Eg 39.41	Dubois-Richard, Paul. Essai sur les gouvernements de l'Egypte. Le Caire, 1941.
	AH 3143.3	Dubor, Georges de. Assyrie et Chaldée. Montauban, 1878.
	AH 8607.10	Ducati, P. L'Italia antica dalle prime civiltà alla morte di Cesare, 44 a.C. Milano, 1936.
	AH 8907.15	Ducati, Pericule. Etruria antica. Torino, 1925.
	AH 8907.23	Ducati, Pericule. Le problème étrusque. Paris, 1938.
	AH 7188.78	Duchauffour, A. De la condition des esclaves. Paris, 1878.
	AH 3664.12	Duchesne-Guillemin, J. La religion de l'Iran ancien. Paris, 1962.
Htn	AH 7235.59*	Du Choul, G. Discorso...sopra la castrametatione. n.p., 1559. 2 pam.
Htn	AH 7235.59.3*	Du Choul, G. Discorso...sopra la castrametatione. n.p., 1579.
Htn	AH 7235.59.5*	Du Choul, G. Discorso...sopra la castrametatione. Vinegia, 1582. 5 pam.
	AH 7236.86	Du Choul, G. Veterum Romanorum religio. Amstelodami, 1686.
	AH 4239.68.5	Ducrey, Pierre. Le traitement des prisonniers de guerre dans la Grèce antique des origines à la conquête romaine. Paris, 1968.
	AH 7819.60.5	Dudley, Donald R. The civilization of Rome. N.Y., 1960.
	AH 7819.60.6	Dudley, Donald R. The civilization of Rome. N.Y., 1962.
	AH 8211.9	Dudley, Donald R. The Roman conquest of Britain, A.D. 43-57. London, 1965.
	AH 7279.70	Dudley, Donald Reynolds. The Romans. London, 1970.
	AH 7478.87.5	Due studî di storia romana. (Stocchi, Giuseppe.) Firenze, 1887.
	Eg 458.74	Dümichen, J. Die erste bis...aufgefundene...Angabe über die Regierungszeit...Königs...alten Reich. Leipzig, 1874.
	Eg 938.94.1	Dümichen, Johannes. Zur Geographie des alten Agypten. Wiesbaden, 1973.
	AH 7148.80.5	Dürr, F. Die Majestätsprocesse unter dem Kaiser. Heilbronn, 1880.
	AH 7168.80.5	Dürr, Julius. Die Majestätsprocesse unter dem Kaiser Tiberius. Heilbronn, 1880.
	AH 3915.5	Dürst, J.U. Die Rinder von Babylonien, Assyrien. Berlin, 1899.
	AH 7189.25.5	Duff, Arnold Mackay. Freedmen in the early Roman Empire. Cambridge, 1958.
	AH 7189.25.2	Duff, Arnold Mackay. Freedmen in the early Roman Empire. Oxford, 1928.
	AH 7479.55A	Duggan, A.L. Julius Caesar. 1. ed. N.Y., 1955.
	AH 2910.2	Duggan, Alfred Leo. He died old. London, 1958.
	AH 5134.5	Dugit, E. De Insula Naxo. Lutetiae Parisiorum, 1867.
	AH 7137.11	Duker, K.A. Opuscula varia de Latimitate. Lugdunum Batavorum, 1711.
Htn	AH 7137.11.2*	Duker, K.A. Opuscula varia de Latinate. 2. ed. n.p., 1761.
	AH 5753.5	Dum, Georg. Spartanischen Ephorats. Innsbruck, 1878.
	AH 5762.5	Dum, Georg. Spartanischen Königslisten. Innsbruck, 1878.
	AH 7207.19	Dumeril, Adfred E.S. De senatu romano sub imperatoribus Augusto Tiberioque. Duaci, 1859.
	AH 7819.69.5	Dumézil, Georges. Idées romaines. Paris, 1969.
	AH 4808.70	Dumont, A. Essai sur la chronologie des archontes athéniens. Paris, 1870.
	AH 4842.17	Dumont, A. Essai sur l'Ephébie Attique. Paris, 1876. 2v.
	AH 4808.74	Dumont, A. Fastes éponymiques d'Athènes. Paris, 1874.
	AH 8647.17A	Dunabin, T.J. The western Greeks. Oxford, 1948.
	AH 5335.5	Dunbach, F. Cropo et Amphiarae Sacro. Parisiis, 1890.
	AH 7479.31.5	Duncan, Renée. The love life of Julius Caesar. N.Y., 1931.
	AH 7889.74	Duncan-Jones, Richard. The economy of the Roman Empire: quantitative studies. Cambridge, Eng., 1924.
	AH 408.55	Duncker, M. Geschichte des Alterthums. Berlin, 1855. 4v.
	AH 278.52.15	Duncker, M. Geschichte des Alterthums. Berlin, 1863. 4v.
	AH 278.52.19	Duncker, M. Geschichte des Alterthums. 4. Aufl. Leipzig, 1874. 9v.
	AH 408.77A	Duncker, M. History of antiquity. London, 1877. 6v.
	AH 4481.7	Duncker, M. Die Schlacht von Marathon. München, 1881.
	AH 4278.83	Duncker, M.W. History of Greece. London, 1883. 2v.
	AH 4298.87	Duncker, Max. Abhandlungen aus der griechische Geschichte. Leipzig, 1887.
	AH 5905.5	Dundaczek, Raimund. Beiträge zur Geschichte der...messenischen Kriege. Czernowitz, 1882.
	AH 2583.8	Dunham, A.G. History of Miletus down to the anabasis of Alexander. Thesis. London, 1915.
Htn	AH 7037.63*	Duni, E. Origini del cittadino di Roma. Roma, 1763. 2v.
	AH 7059.24.5	Dunlap, J.E. The office of the grand chamberlain in the later Roman and Byzantine empires. London, 1924.
	AH 7200.12	Duodecim Tabulae. Legis Duodecim Tabularum. Lipsiae, 1866.
NEDL	AH 277.09	Du Pin, L.E. Universal library of historians. London, 1709. 2v.
	AH 7038.77	Dupond, A. De la constitution. Paris, 1877.
	AH 3908.5.5	Dupont-Sommer, Andre. Les Araméens. Paris, 1949.
	AH 7818.80	Dupuy, Antoine. De Graecis Romanorum amicis aut praeceptoribus a secundo punico bello ad Augustum. Thesim. Parisiis, 1880.
	AH 7168.98	Duquesne, J. Possession et de la détention en droit romain. Paris, 1898.
	AH 7279.44A	Durant, W. Caesar and Christ. N.Y., 1944.

AH 4819.39.5 — Durant, Will. The life of Greece. N.Y., 1939.
Eg 958.72 — Durch Gosen zum Sinai. (Ebers, G.) Leipzig, 1872.
AH 279.68.5 — Der Durchbruch durch die Völkerwanderung. (Passman, Franz Anton.) Bonn, 1968. 2v.
AH 4278.53 — Durdent, René Jean. Beautés de l'histoire grecque. 7. éd. Paris, 1853.
AH 7888.40 — Dureau, A.J. Économie politique des Romains. Paris, 1840. 2v.
AH 8157.7 — Dureau de la Malle, A. L'Algérie. Paris, 1852.
AH 238.19 — Dureau de la Malle, Adolphe. Poliorcéteque des anciens. Paris, 1819.
AH 7239.38 — Durry, Marcel. Les cohortes pretoriennes. Thèse. Paris, 1938.
AH 1408.88 — Duruy, J.V. Histoire ancienne des peuples de l'Orient. Paris, 1888.
NEDL AH 4278.87.5A — Duruy, J.V. Histoire des Grecs. Paris, 1887. 3v.
AH 7498.53 — Duruy, V. État du monde romain. Paris, 1853.
AH 4278.56.7 — Duruy, V. Histoire de la Grèce ancienne. Paris, 1888.
AH 7278.70 — Duruy, V. Histoire des romains. Paris, 1870. 7v.
AH 7278.70.3 — Duruy, V. Histoire des romains. Paris, 1881-90. 7v.
AH 4278.56.9 — Duruy, V. Histoire grecque. Paris, 1856.
AH 4278.56.13 — Duruy, V. Histoire grecque. Paris, 1889.
NEDL AH 4278.56.5 — Duruy, V. Histoire grecque. 4. éd. Paris, 1864.
AH 4278.56.4 — Duruy, V. Histoire grecque. 5. éd. Paris, 1866.
NEDL AH 4278.56.6 — Duruy, V. Histoire grecque. 6. éd. Paris, 1867.
AH 4278.56.25 — Duruy, V. Histoire grecque. 32. éd. Paris, 1901.
AH 7278.67 — Duruy, V. Histoire romaine. Paris, 1867.
AH 7278.67.17 — Duruy, V. Histoire romaine. Paris, 1889.
AH 7278.67.27 — Duruy, V. Histoire romaine. Paris, 1899.
NEDL AH 7278.67.3 — Duruy, V. Histoire universelle. Paris, 1876.
NEDL AH 4278.56.15 — Duruy, V. Historia de los Griegos. Barcelona, 1890. 2v.
AH 4278.56.35F — Duruy, V. History of Greece. v.1-4. Boston, 1890. 8v.
AH 7278.70.9 — Duruy, V. History of Rome. Boston, 1883. 16v.
NEDL AH 7278.70.5 — Duruy, V. History of Rome. v.1-6, pt.1-2. London, 1884-12v.
AH 7278.70.15F — Duruy, V. History of Rome. v.1-8, pt.1-2. Boston, 1884-87. 16v.
NEDL AH 278.83 — Duruy, V. Petite histoire ancienne. Paris, 1883.
AH 7278.83 — Duruy, V. Petite histoire grecque. Paris, 1883.
AH 5210.5 — Dušanić, Slobodan. Arkadski savez IV veka. Beograd, 1970.
AH 3914.6 — Dussaud, R. Notes de mythologie syrienne. Paris, 1903.
AH 3813.10 — Dussel, Enrique D. El humanismo semita. Buenos Aires, 1969.
Eg 1158.78 — Dutrieux, P.J. Egyptian ophthalmia. Cairo, 1878.
AH 7159.69.5 — The duumviri in the Roman criminal law. (Bauman, Richard.) Wiesbaden, 1969.
AH 8549.157 — Duval, Paul Marie. Les dieux de la Gaule. 1. éd. Paris, 1957.
AH 8513.13 — Duval, Paul Marie. La vie quotidienne en Gaule pendant la paix romaine. Paris, 1953.
AH 7729.03 — Duviquet, Georges. Héliogabale. Paris, 1903.
AH 3022.17.5 — Dve elegii na tablichke muzeia im A.S. Pushkina. (Kramer, S.N.) Moskva, 1960.
AH 39.66 — Dvornik, Frantisek. Early Christian and Byzantine political philosophy; origins and background. Washington, 1966. 2v.
X Cg Eg 278.85.3 — The dwellers on the Nile. (Budge, Ernest Alfred Wallis.) London, 1885.
Eg 278.85.3.5 — The dwellers on the Nile. (Budge, Ernest Alfred Wallis.) London, 1926.
AH 8657.5.3 — Dyer, Thomas H. The city of Rome. 2. ed. London, 1883.
AH 8657.5 — Dyer, Thomas H. History of the city of Rome. London, 1865.
AH 7408.68A — Dyer, Thomas H. History of the kings of Rome. London, 1868.
NEDL AH 7408.68.3 — Dyer, Thomas H. History of the kings of Rome. Philadelphia, 1868.
Eg 909.36.5 — Dykmans, G.L. Histoire économique et social de l'ancienne Égypte. Paris, 1936-37. 3v.
AH 2011.10 — La dynastie de Sarahbi il Yakuf et la documentation épigraphique sud-arabe. (Jamme, Albert.) Istanbul, 1961.
AH 3142.3.3 — Die Dynastie der Lahmiden in al-Hira. (Rothstein, G.) Berlin, 1899.
AH 3142.3 — Die Dynastie der Lahmiden in al-Hira. (Rothstein, G.) Halle, 1898.
Eg 708.97 — Die Dynastie der Ptolemäer. (Strack, M.L.) Berlin, 1897.
AH 7798.89 — Dynasty of Theodosius. (Hodgkin, T.) Oxford, 1889.
AH 6107.20 — He dytike Makedonia kata tous archaious chronous. (Kanatsoulēs, Dēmētrios.) Thessalonikē, 1958.
AH 4559.63.5 — Dzięciot, Witold. Aleksander Wielki Macedoński. Londyn, 1963.
AH 6110.13 — Dzieje upadku monarchji macedonskiej. (Wałek, T.B.) Krakow, 1924.
AH 7469.63.5 — Earl, D.C. Tiberius Gracchus; a study in politics. Bruxelles, 1963.
AH 7509.68.5 — Earl, Donald Charles. The age of Augustus. N.Y., 1968.
AH 7039.67 — Earl, Donald Charles. The moral and political tradition of Rome. London, 1967.
AH 8609.3 — Earliest inhabitants of Italy. (Mommsen, Theodor.) London, 1858.
AH 8548.105 — The earliest relations between Celts and Germans. (Elston, C.S.) London, 1934.
AH 3160.29 — The earliest Semitic pantheon. (Roberts, Jimmy J.M.) Baltimore, 1972.
AH 4409.01A — Early age of Greece. (Ridgeway, W.) Cambridge, 1901-31. 2v.
NEDL AH 408.58 — Early ancient history. (Menzies, H.) London, 1858.
AH 3014.5 — Early architecture in western Asia: Chaldaean, Hittite, Assyrian, Persian. (Bell, Edward.) London, 1924.
AH 3021.3 — Early Babylonian history. (Radar, H.) N.Y., 1899.
AH 3021.3.3 — Early Babylonian history. (Radar, H.) N.Y., 1900.
AH 39.66 — Early Christian and Byzantine political philosophy; origins and background. (Dvornik, Frantisek.) Washington, 1966. 2v.
AH 4842.73 — Early Christianity and Greek Paideia. (Jaeger, Werner Wilhelm.) Cambridge, 1961.
AH 3022.7 — The early dynasties of Sumer and Akkad. (Gadd, C.J.) London, 1921.
Eg 298.63 — Early Egyptian history, for the young. London, 1863.
AH 8913.30 — The early Etruscans. (Strong, Donald Emrys.) London, 1968.
AH 4408.91.5 — Early Grecian history. (Allcroft, A.H.) London, 1891.
AH 4409.70 — Early Greece; the bronze and archaic ages. (Finley, Moses I.) London, 1970.
AH 2109.10 — Early highland peoples of Anatolia. (Lloyd, Seton Howard.) London, 1967.

AH 2807.7 — Early historical relations between Phrygia and Cappadocia. (Ramsay, W.M.) n.p., n.d.
AH 3037.5 — Early history of Assyria to 1000 B.C. (Smith, S.M.A.) London, 1928.
Eg 278.36 — Early history of Egypt. (Sharpe, S.) London, 1836.
AH 3909.7A — The early history of Syria and Palestine. (Paton, L.B.) N.Y., 1901.
AH 4329.66 — The early Ionians. (Huxley, George.) N.Y., 1966.
AH 138.83A — Early law and custom. (Maine, Henry S.) London, 1883.
AH 3022.30 — Early Mesopotamia and Iran. (Mallowan, Max Edgar.) N.Y., 1965.
AH 7498.93 — Early principate: history of Rome 31 B.C.-96 A.D. (Allcroft, A.H.) London, 1892.
AH 7138.72 — Early Roman law. (Clark, E.C.) London, 1872.
NEDL AH 7408.78.2 — Early Rome. (Ihne, W.) London, 1876.
AH 7408.78.11 — Early Rome. (Ihne, W.) London, 1913.
NEDL AH 7408.78 — Early Rome. (Ihne, W.) N.Y., 1878.
NEDL AH 7408.78.5 — Early Rome. (Ihne, W.) N.Y., 1892.
AH 7408.78.7 — Early Rome. (Ihne, W.) N.Y., 1896.
NEDL AH 7408.77.25 — Early Rome. 2. ed. (Ihne, W.) London, 1877.
NEDL AH 7408.78.3 — Early Rome. 4th ed. (Ihne, W.) London, 1886.
AH 7409.65A — Early Rome and the Latins. (Alföldi, Andras.) Ann Arbor, 1965.
AH 5759.12A — Early Sparta. (Huxley, G.L.) Cambridge, 1962.
AH 819.33 — Early steps in human progress. (Peake, Harold.) London, 1933.
AH 4819.29 — Earp, F.R. The way of the Greeks. London, 1929.
AH 3358.5F — The Eastern Libyans; essay. (Bates, O.) London, 1914.
AH 279.04.5 — The eastern nations and Greece. (Myers, Philip Van Ness.) Boston, 1904.
AH 819.64.20 — Eastwood, Charles Cyril. Life and thought in the ancient world. London, 1964.
AH 3195.7 — Ebeling, Erich. Die babylonische Fabel. Leipzig, 1927.
AH 279.29.10 — Ebeling, Erich. Geschichte des alten Morgenlandes. Berlin, 1929.
AH 1279.39 — Ebeling, Erich. Geschichte des Orients vom Tode Alexanders des Grossen bis zum Einbruch des Islams. Berlin, 1939.
AH 3005.10 — Ebeling, Erich. Keallexikon der Assyriologie. Berlin, 1928-38. 4v.
AH 3154.27 — Ebeling, Erich. Tod und Leben nach den Vorstellungen der Babylonier. Berlin, 1931.
AH 850.7 — Eberl, G. Die Fischkonserven der Alten. Stadtamhof, 1892.
AH 7649.14 — Eberlein, Hellmut. Kaiser Mark Aurel und die Christen. Inaug. Diss. Breslau, 1914.
Eg 298.68 — Ebers, G. Aegypten und die Bücher Mose's. Leipzig, 1868.
Eg 958.72 — Ebers, G. Durch Gosen zum Sinai. Leipzig, 1872.
Htn Eg 1158.75F* — Ebers, G.M. Papyros Ebers...Arzeneimittel der alten Ägypter. Leipzig, 1875. 2v.
Eg 658.65 — Ebers, Georg. Disquisitiones de dynastia vicesima sexta regum Aegyptiarum. Berolini, 1865.
AH 7277.13 — Echard, L. Roman history. London, 1713. 5v.
Eg 609.59 — Echnaton der Grosse im Schauen. (Bertram, J.) Hamburg, 1959.
AH 4819.57 — The echo of Greece. 1st ed. (Hamilton, Edith.) N.Y., 1957.
AH 7203.27 — Eck, Cornelius van. Principia juris civilis. Trajecta ad Rhenum, 1756. 2v.
AH 7207.48 — Eck, Werner. Senatoren von Vespasian bis Hadrian. Diss. München, 1970.
AH 8516.9 — Éclaircissemens géographiques sur l'ancienne Gaule. (Anville, J.B.B.) Paris, 1741.
AH 7206.11 — Ecloga. (Leonis.) Athenis, 1889.
AH 4842.13 — L'ecole d'Athènes. (Petit de Julleville.) Paris, 1868.
AH 4842.41 — L'ecole d'Athens. (Grousset, P.) Paris, 1908.
AH 8615.7 — Economia e società nell'Italia annonaria. (Ruggini, Lallia.) Milano, 1961.
AH 5315.35 — An economic history of Athens under Roman domination. (Day, John.) N.Y., 1942.
AH 7889.20A — An economic history of Rome. (Frank, Tenney.) Baltimore, 1920.
AH 7889.20.2 — An economic history of Rome. 2. ed. (Frank, Tenney.) Baltimore, 1927.
AH 4889.23.3 — Economic life in Greece's golden age. (Bolkestein, H.) Leiden, 1958.
AH 889.30 — The economic life of the ancient world. (Toutain, J.) London, 1930.
AH 7889.33A — An economic survey of ancient Rome. (Frank, Tenney.) Baltimore, 1933-40. 3v.
AH 7889.33.5 — An economic survey of ancient Rome. (Frank, Tenney.) Paterson, N.J., 1959.
AH 7889.33.2 — An economic survey of ancient Rome. General index. (Frank, Tenney.) Baltimore, 1940.
AH 7109.43 — Economici e finanza dei romani. (Clerici, Luigi.) Bologna, 1943-
AH 4881.1 — Pamphlet box. Economics. Greece.
AH 4889.40 — The economics of ancient Greece. (Michell, Humfrey.) Cambridge, 1940.
AH 4889.40.2 — The economics of ancient Greece. 2. ed. (Michell, Humfrey.) Cambridge, 1957.
AH 889.64 — L'économie antique. (Lévy, Jean Philippe.) Paris, 1964.
AH 7888.40 — Économie politique des Romains. (Dureau, A.J.) Paris, 1840. 2v.
Eg 909.39 — L'économie royale des Lagides. (Preaux, C.) Bruxelles, 1939.
AH 4882.5 — Économies et sociétés en Grèce ancienne. (Austin, Michel.) Paris, 1972.
AH 4889.23 — Het economisch leven in Griekenlands bloeitijd. (Bolkestein, H.) Haarlem, 1923.
AH 7889.33.10 — Economische en sociale toestanden in het Romeinsche rijk. Proefschrift. (Jonkers, Engbert.) Wageningen, 1933.
AH 7889.74 — The economy of the Roman Empire: quantitative studies. (Duncan-Jones, Richard.) Cambridge, Eng., 1924.
AH 842.21 — Écrivans, pédagogues de l'antiquité. (Saffroy, (Mlle.).) Paris, 1947.
AH 4659.61 — Eddy, S.K. The king is dead. Lincoln, 1961.
AH 3181.12 — Edelkoort, A.H. Het zondebesef in de Babylonische boetepsalmen. Utrecht, 1918.
AH 7203.26 — Eden, R. Jurisprudentia Philologica. Oxonii, 1744.
AH 3159.18 — The Edenic period of man. (Mac Whorter, Alexander.) N.Y., 1880.
AH 7159.69 — Eder, Walter. Das vorsullanische Repetundenverfahren. Inaug. Diss. München, 1969.
AH 3964.17 — Edersheim, A. The temple; its ministry and services as they were at the time of Jesus Christ. 2. ed. London, 1874.
AH 3045.150 — Edessa and Harran. (Segal, Judah B.) London, 1963.
AH 3925.5F — Edesse et ses monuments. (Texier, C.F.M.) Paris, 1859.

Author and Title Listing

Eg 844.5 Edgerton, W.F. Notes on Egyptian marriage chiefly in the Plotemaic period. Chicago, 1931.

Eg 602.10 Edgerton, William F. Historical records of Ramses III. Chicago, 1936.

Eg 609.33A Edgerton, William F. The Thutmosid succession. Chicago, 1933.

AH 7908.51 Das Edict Diocletians de Pretiis Rerum Venalium. (Mommsen, Theodor.) Leipzig, 1851.

AH 7228.82 Edict und Klageform. (Wlassak, M.) Jena, 1882.

AH 7204.7 Edicti perpetui. (Julianus, S.) Lipsiae, 1869.

AH 7903.5.2 Edictum Diocletiani de pretiis rerum venalium. (Diocletianus.) Berolini, 1893.

AH 7204.9 Edictum perpetuum. (Lenel, Otto.) Leipzig, 1883.

AH 7204.13 Edictum perpetuum. 2. Aufl. (Lenel, Otto.) Leipzig, 1907.

AH 7204.4 L'édit d'Antonin Caracalla. (Lefranc, André.) Bordeaux, 1907.

AH 7903.5.5F Édit de Dioclétien, établissant le maximum dans l'Empire romain. (Diocletianus.) Paris, 1864.

Eg 759.64 L'édit de Tiberius Julius Alexander; étude historique et exégétique. (Chalon, Gérard.) Olten, 1964.

AH 7204.11 L'édit perpétuel. (Lenel, Otto.) Paris, 1901. 2v.

AH 3097.6 Editions E, B and K of the annals of Ashurbanipal. Diss. (Ashurbanapal, king of Assyria.) Chicago, 1933.

AH 4609.34 Edson, C.F. The Antigonids, Heracles, and Beroea. n.p., 1934.

AH 3668.5 Education among the ancient Iranians. (Modi, J.J.) Bombay, 1905.

AH 4842.5 L'éducation athénienne. (Girard, P.) Paris, 1889.

AH 4842.6 L'éducation athénienne. 2. éd. (Girard, P.) Paris, 1891.

AH 4842.63 An education bill from ancient Greece. (Hudson-Williams, T.) Cambridge, 1917.

AH 7842.2 The education of children at Rome. (Clarke, George.) N.Y., 1896.

AH 4842.35 Education of the Greek people. (Davidson, T.) N.Y., 1894.

AH 4842.35.5 Education of the Greek people. (Davidson, T.) N.Y., 1903.

AH 842.45 Educational ideals in the ancient world. (Barclay, William.) London, 1959.

AH 4842.58 L'educazione in Grecia. (Terzaghi, N.) Milano, 1910.

AH 7479.60 Les éduens n'ont pas trahi. (Thevenot, Emile.) Bruxelles, 1960.

AH 3005.828 Edward Hincks; a selection from his correspondence. (Hincks, Edward.) London, 1933.

AH 4117.6 Edwards, J.B. Demesman in Attic life. Thesis. Menasha, 1916.

Eg 1159.66 Edwin Smith Surgical Papyrus. Ein medizinisches Lehrbuch aus dem alten Agypten! Wund- und Unfallchirurgie. Bern, 1966.

Eg 1159.31F The Edwin Smith surgical papyrus. (Breasted, James Henry.) Chicago, 1931. 2v.

AH 3021.21 Edzard, Dietz O. Die "zweite Zwischenzeit" Babyloniens. Wiesbaden, 1957.

Htn AH 8511.5* Effects of the Germanic invasions on Gaul. (Manley, Inza J.) Berkeley, 1934.

AH 8511.5.2 Effects of the Germanic invasions on Gaul. (Manley, Inza J.) Berkeley, 1934.

AH 5460.5 Effenterre, H. van. La Crète et le monde grec. Paris, 1948.

AH 4828.93.5 Egcheiridion Archaiologias toù demosiou biou. Tom A', Teux.1-3. (Gilbert, Gustav.) Athénai, 1897-99.

AH 7449.22 Egelhauf, G. Hannibal. Stuttgart, 1922.

AH 7508.44 Egger, A.E. Examen critique des historiens anciens. Paris, 1844.

AH 7842.7 Egger, Émile. Étude sur l'éducation. Paris, 1833.

AH 120.5 Egger, Emile. Observations historiques sur la fonction de secrétaire des princes chez les anciens. Paris, 1858.

AH 148.66 Egger, Emile. Traités publics. Paris, 1886.

AH 7163.13 Eggers, F.W.T. Alt-römischen Ehe mit Manus. Altona, 1833.

VEg 279.67 Egipat. (Novak, Grga.) Zagreb, 1967.

Eg 909.65.5 Egipet na rubezhe dvukh epokh. (Fikhman, Itskhok.) Moskva, 1965.

VEg 869.09 Egiptom és a biblia. (Giesswein, Sándor.) Budapest, 1909.

Eg 758.82 L'Egitto al tempo dei Greci e dei Romani. (Lumbroso, Giacomo.) Roma, 1882.

Eg 759.37.3 Egitto greco e romano. 3. ed. (Breccia, Evaristo.) Pisa, 1957.

AH 7959.72 The Egnation Way. (O'Sullivan, Firmin.) Newton Abbot, 1972.

Eg 15.5 Pamphlet vol. Egypt, ancient and modern. 2 pam.

Eg 299.37.10 Egypt, papers and lectures. (Brodrick, M.) London, 1937.

Eg 15.3 Pamphlet box. Egypt.

Eg 15.2F Pamphlet box. Egypt.

Eg 15.1 Pamphlet vol. Egypt. 24 pam.

Eg 819.70.1F Egypt. (Barocas, Claudio.) N.Y., 1972.

Eg 278.75.9 Egypt. (Birch, S.) London, 1883.

Eg 278.75 Egypt. (Birch, S.) N.Y., 1875.

Eg 279.25 Egypt. (Budge, Ernest Alfred Wallis.) London, 1925.

Eg 855.3 Egypt. (Garry, Thomas G.) London, 1931.

Eg 279.43F Egypt. (Steindorff, G.) N.Y., 1943.

Eg 298.85.5 Egypt and Babylon. (Rawlinson, George.) N.Y., 1885.

Eg 299.11 Egypt and Israel. (Petrie, William M.F.) London, 1911.

Eg 938.85 Egypt and Syria. (Dawson, J.W.) London, 1885.

Eg 269.71 Egypt and the east Mediterranean world, 2200-1900 B.C.; studies in Egyptian foreign relations during the first intermediate period. (Ward, William A.) Beirut, 1971.

Eg 299.09 Egypt and the Egyptians. (Bevan, J.O.) London, 1909.

Eg 759.51 Egypt and the Roman Empire. (Johnson, A.C.) Ann Arbor, 1951.

Eg 819.37 L'Égypt des astroloques. (Cumont, Franz.) Bruxelles, 1937.

Eg 279.48A Egypt from Alexander the Great to the Arab conquest. (Bell, Harold.) Oxford, 1948.

AH 3909.4 Egypt in Asia; a plain account of pre-biblical Syria and Palestine. (Cormack, George.) London, 1908.

Eg 939.42 Egypt in the classical geographers. (Ball, J.) Cairo, 1942.

Eg 298.95.4 The Egypt of the Hebrews and Herodotos. (Sayce, A.H.) London, 1896.

Eg 298.95 The Egypt of the Hebrews and Herodotos. (Sayce, A.H.) N.Y., 1895.

Eg 278.81.50 The Egypt of the past. (Wilson, E.) London, 1881.

Eg 459.61 Egypt of the pharaohs. (Gardiner, Alan.) Oxford, 1961.

Eg 459.65.5 Egypt to the end of the Old Kingdom. (Aldred, Cyril.) London, 1965.

Eg 278.59.9 Egypt under the pharaohs. (Brugsch, H.) London, 1891.

Eg 708.38 Egypt under the Ptolemies. (Sharpe, S.) London, 1838.

Eg 758.42 Egypt under the Romans. (Sharpe, S.) London, 1842.

Eg 278.14 L'Égypte. (Champollion, J.J.) Paris, 1814. 2v.

Eg 278.67 Égypte. (Mariette, A.) Paris, 1867.

Eg 278.14.3 Égypte ancienne. (Champollion, J.J.) Paris, 1839.

Eg 279.49 L'Égypte ancienne. (Vercoutter, Jean.) Paris, 1949.

Eg 276.66.10 L'Égypte de Murtadi. Facsimile. (Murtada ibn al-Kafif.) Paris, 1953.

Eg 909.33 L'Égypte economique sous la XVIIIe dynastie pharaonique. Thèse. (Dairanes, Serge.) Paris, 1933.

Eg 609.59.5 L'Égypte et la Bible. (Montet, Pierre.) Neuchâtel, 1959.

Eg 879.57.15 L'Égypte et la genèse du surhomme. (Bernard, J.L.) Paris, 1957.

Eg 878.75.5 L'Égypte et Moïse. (Ancessi, Victor.) Paris, 1875.

Eg 279.59 L'Égypte pharaonique. (Drioton, Etienne.) Paris, 1959.

Eg 878.46 L'Égypte pharaonique. (Henry, D.M.J.) Paris, 1846. 2v.

Eg 409.08 L'Égypte préhistorique. (Reinach, A.J.) Paris, 1908.

Eg 1179.60F Egyptian astronomical texts. v.2-3, pt.1-2. (Neugebauer, Otto.) Providence, 1960- 3v.

Eg 879.56.10 Egyptian belief and modern thought. (Bonwick, James.) Indian Hills, 1956.

Eg 1039.60F The Egyptian book of the dead. (Book of the Dead.) Chicago, 1960.

Eg 1039.04 The Egyptian book of the dead. (Book of the Dead.) London, 1904.

X Cg Eg 8.61 Egyptian chronicles. (Palmer, W.) London, 1861. 2v.

Eg 819.30 Egyptian civilization. (Waddell, L.A.) London, 1930.

Eg 1042.935.10F The Egyptian coffin texts. (Buck, Adriaan de.) Chicago, 1935. 7v.

Eg 850.5 Egyptian festivals. (Bleeker, Claas J.) Leiden, 1967.

Eg 931.1 Pamphlet box. Egyptian geography.

Eg 879.37.5 The Egyptian gods. (Shorter, A.W.) London, 1937.

Eg 879.06 The Egyptian heaven and hell. (Budge, Ernest Alfred Wallis.) London, 1906. 3v.

Eg 1309.11 Egyptian hieratic texts. (Gardiner, A.H.) Leipzig, 1911-

Htn Eg 276.66.15* The Egyptian history. (Murtada ibn al-Kafif.) London, 1672.

Eg 691.2 Pamphlet box. Egyptian history. Persian supremacy.

Eg 879.00 Egyptian ideas of the future life. 2. ed. (Budge, Ernest Alfred Wallis.) London, 1900.

Eg 1028.97 Egyptian literature. (Griffith, Francis L.) N.Y., 1897.

Eg 1029.01.15 Egyptian literature. London, 1901.

Eg 885.899.4 Egyptian magic. (Budge, Ernest Alfred Wallis.) Evanston, 1958.

Eg 885.899.2 Egyptian magic. (Budge, Ernest Alfred Wallis.) London, 1901.

Eg 885.899.6 Egyptian magic. (Budge, Ernest Alfred Wallis.) N.Y., 1971.

Eg 839.24 Egyptian mummies. (Smith, G.E.) London, 1924.

Eg 878.63 Egyptian mythology. (Sharpe, Samuel.) London, 1863.

Eg 1158.78 Egyptian ophthalmia. (Dutrieux, P.J.) Cairo, 1878.

Eg 1309.25 Egyptian papyri and papyrus-hunting. (Baikie, James.) N.Y., 1925?

AH 2117.5F Egyptian records of travel in Western Asia. v.1-3. (Paton, David.) Princeton, 1915-18. 4v.

Eg 871.1 Pamphlet box. Egyptian religion.

EgP 41.5 Egyptian religion. N.Y., 1-4,1933-1936 3v.

Eg 1069.49 Egyptian religious poetry. (Murray, Margaret A.) London, 1949.

Eg 1029.25 Egyptian scriptures interpreted through the language of symbolism. (Gaskell, G.A.) London, 1925.

EgP 40.5 Egyptian Society of Historical Studies, Gezireh, Cairo. Proceedings. Cairo.

Eg 1109.31 Egyptian tales and romances, pagan, Christian and Muslim. (Budge, Ernest Alfred Wallis.) London, 1931.

Eg 279.61 The Egyptians. (Aldred, Cyril.) London, 1961.

Eg 818.57 The Egyptians in the time of the pharaohs. (Wilkinson, J.G.) London, 1857.

Eg 298.85 Egyptological research. (Tomkins, H.G.) London, 1885?

Eg 29.11 Egyptological tracts. (Pick, Robert F.) N.Y., 1911.

Eg 1128.76F L'égyptologie - maximes du scribe Ani. (Ani.) Paris, 1876.

X Cg Eg 308.68 Egypt's place in history. (Dall, C. (Mrs.).) Boston, 1868.

Eg 278.48 Egypt's place in universal history. (Bunsen, C.C.J.) London, 1848. 5v.

Eg 278.48.5 Egypt's place in universal history. v.1,5. (Bunsen, C.C.J.) London, 1867. 2v.

AH 7163.21 Ehe Gesetze des Augustus. (Jörs, Paul.) Marburg, 1894.

AH 7163.7 Ehescheidungen. (Wächter-Spittler, K.) Stuttgart, 1833.

AH 4279.46.5 Ehrenberg, V. Aspects of the ancient world. N.Y., 1946.

AH 299.35 Ehrenberg, V. Ost und West. Brünn, 1935.

AH 4819.64.5 Ehrenberg, V. Society and civilization in Greece and Rome. Cambridge, 1964.

AH 4559.38 Ehrenberg, Victor. Alexander and the Greeks. Oxford, 1938.

AH 7502.5.4 Ehrenberg, Victor. Documents illustrating the reigns of Augustas and Tiberius. 2. ed. Oxofrd, 1967.

AH 4449.68 Ehrenberg, Victor. From Solon to Socrates. London, 1968.

AH 4449.68.2 Ehrenberg, Victor. From Solon to Socrates. 2. ed. London, 1973.

AH 4039.60 Ehrenberg, Victor. The Greek state. Oxford, 1960.

AH 4039.60.2 Ehrenberg, Victor. The Greek state. 2. ed. London, 1969.

AH 4449.25 Ehrenberg, Victor. Neugründer des Staates. München, 1925.

AH 819.65 Ehrenberg, Victor. Polis und Imperium. Zürich, 1965.

AH 4039.57.5 Ehrenberg, Victor. Der Staat der Griechen. Leipzig, 1957- 2v.

Eg 702.10 Das Ehrendekret für den Strategen Kallimachos. (Hutmacher, Rudolf.) Meisenheim am Glan, 1965.

AH 39.59 Ehrhardt, Arnold. Politische Metaphysik von Solon bis Augustin. Tübingen, 1959-69. 3v.

AH 3653.7 Ehtécham, Mortéza. L'Iran sous les Achéménides. Fribourg, 1946.

AH 3013.24 Eichhoff, F.G. Etudes sur Ninive et Persepolis. Lyon, 1852.

AH 4840.15 Eichhoff, Karl. Ueber die Blutrache bei den Griechen. Duisburg, 1873.

AH 278.11 Eichhorn, J.G. Antiqua historia. Lipsiae, 1811. 4v.

AH 7238.64 Eichhorst, Otto. De Cohortibus urbanis imperatorum Romanorum. Danzig, 1864.

AH 3054.10.5 Eichler, Barry L. Indenture at Nuzi. New Haven, 1973.

AH 7838.25F Eichstadius, H.C.A. De Votis X, XX, et XXX Imperatoum Romanorum. Ienae, 1825.

AH 4845.5F Eichstädt, H.C. Humanitate Graecorum. Ienae, 1825.

AH 9777.38 Eicke, Hermann. Heerführer und Könige. Leipzig, 193-?

AH 4559.09.3 Eicke, L. Veterum philosophorum qualia fuerint de Alexandro Magno iudicia. Rostochii, 1909.

AH 9777.21 Eicken, H. von. Der Kampf der Westgothen und Römer. Leipzig, 1876.

AH 4214.11 Der Eid. (Hirzel, R.) Leipzig, 1902.

Eg 139.29.5 — Der Eid im ptolemäischen Recht. (Seidl, Erwin.) München, 1929.

AH 4484.16 — Der Eid von Plataiai. (Siewert, Peter.) München, 1972.

AH 9757.7 — Eidam, Heinrich. Deutschlands Besetzung durch die Römer. Dinkelsbühl, 1928.

AH 4819.62.15 — Eigenart der Griechen. (Harder, Richard.) Freiburg, 1962.

AH 7148.75.2 — Eigenbrodt, A. De magistratuum Romanorum. Lipsiae, 1875.

AH 819.52 — Eight decisive books of antiquity. (Hoare, F.R.) London, 1952.

AH 4299.10.3 — Eikones ek tēs archaias. (Syllogos pros.) Athēnai, n.d.

Eg 879.73 — Der Eine und die Vielen. (Hornung, Erik.) Darmstadt, 1973.

AH 4728.78 — Einfälle der Gallier in Griechen. (Chevalier, L.) Prag, 1878.

AH 9777.33 — Die Einfälle der Goten in der römische Reich. (Rappaport, B.) Leipzig, 1899.

AH 4108.76 — Einführung des Soldes. (Pflug, C.) Waldenburg, 1876.

AH 3150.14 — Einführung in das Studium keilschriftlicher Rechtsquellen. (Haase, Richard.) Wiesbaden, 1965.

Eg 139.51F — Einführung in die ägyptische Rechtsgeschichte. 2. Aufl. (Seidl, Erwin.) Glückstadt, 1951.

AH 9.49 — Einführung in die alte Geschichte. (Bengtson, Hermann.) München, 1949.

AH 9.49.2A — Einführung in die alte Geschichte. 2. Aufl. (Bengtson, Hermann.) München, 1953.

AH 39.68 — Einführung in die antike Staatskunde. (Meyer, Ernst.) Darmstadt, 1968.

AH 3013.971 — Einführung in die vorderasiatische Archäologie. (Moortgat, Anton.) Darmstadt, 1971.

AH 7149.14 — Die Einheit des Gewaltgedankens im römischen Staatsrecht. (Leifer, Franz.) München, 1914.

AH 298.95 — Einleitung...der alten Geschichte. (Wachsmuth, C.) Leipzig, 1895.

AH 7408.28 — Einleitung im Rom's alte Geschichte. (Blum, K.L.) Berlin, 1828.

AH 7203.39.6 — Einleitung in das römisch-justinianische Sbuch Recht. (Corpus juris civilis. Institutiones.) Hannover, 1817.

AH 299.12.2 — Einleitung in die Altertumswissenschaft. (Gercke, Alfred.) Leipzig, 1910-12. 3v.

AH 299.12 — Einleitung in die Altertumswissenschaft. (Gercke, Alfred.) Leipzig, 1912-23. 3v.

AH 299.12.5 — Einleitung in die Altertumswissenschaft. 3. Aufl. (Gercke, Alfred.) Leipzig, 1921-27. 3v.

AH 1279.19 — Einleitung und Geschichte des alten Orients. (Hanslik, E.) Gotha, 1919.

AH 7279.21.7 — Einleitung und Quellenkunde zur römischen Geschichte. (Rosenberg, Arthur.) Berlin, 1921.

AH 4845.21 — Einleitung zu einer Darstellung der nationalen Ethik. (Muller, E.) n.p., n.d.

AH 7109.15 — Die Einnahmen der römischen Republic im letzten Jahrhundert ihres Bestehens. (Böttcher, Kurt.) Weida, 1915.

AH 819.12.3 — Die Einteilungsarten der Lebens- und Weltalter bei Griechen und Römer. (Höhn, A.) Würzburg, 1912.

AH 7238.93 — Einundvierzigster Jahresbericht...Realgymnasium. (Vaders, Joseph.) Münster, 1893.

Eg 879.57.10 — Die Einweihung im alten Ägypten. (Uxkull, Woldemar.) Büdingen-Gettenbach, 1957.

AH 7138.96 — Eisele, F. Beiträge zur römischen Rechtsgeschichte. Freiburg, 1896.

AH 7228.71.5 — Eisele, F. Materielle Grundlage der Exceptio. Berlin, 1871.

AH 7228.75 — Eisele, F. Zur Geschichte der processualen Behandlung der Exceptionen. Berlin, 1875.

AH 7168.76.5 — Eisele, F.H. Compensation nach römischen und gemeinem Recht. Berlin, 1876.

AH 3739.5 — Eiselen, F.C. Sidon. N.Y., 1907.

AH 3739.5.2 — Eiselen, F.C. Sidon. N.Y., 1907.

AH 7148.29 — Eisendecher, W. Über die Entstehung...des Burgerrechts. Hamburg, 1829.

Eg 1188.77 — Eisenlohr, August. Ein mathematisches Handbuch der alten Ägypter. Leipzig, 1877. 2v.

AH 7158.58 — Eisenlohr, C. Die Provocatio ad Populum. Schwerin, 1858.

Htn AH 927.08.2* — Eisenschmid, J.C. De ponderibus et mensuris veterum. 2. ed. Argentorati, 1732.

AH 4103.3 — Eisphora; a study of direct taxation in ancient Athens. (Thomsen, Rudi.) København, 1964.

AH 4408.25 — Eissner, C.G. Die alten Pelasger und ihre Mysterien. Leipzig, 1825.

AH 3965.7 — Ejges, Simcha. Das Geld im Talmud. Diss. Wilna, 1930.

AH 7206.34 — Ekloga. (Byzantine Empire. Laws, statutes, etc.) Moskva, 1965.

Eg 603.11 — El Amarna tablets, 359-379. (Tell el-Amarna Tablets.) Neukirchen-Vluyn, 1970.

Eg 603.8 — Die el Amarna-Tafeln. (Knudtzon, J.A.) Leipzig, 1907-08. 2v.

AH 4819.43 — El genio helénico y las caracteres de sus creaciones espirituales. (Mondolfo, Rodolfo.) Tucuman, 1943.

AH 3757.22 — Elderkin, George. Migration in the Mycenaean Age. n.p., 1963.

NEDL AH 4038.91.3 — Election by lot at Athens. (Headlam-Morley, J.W.) Cambridge, 1891.

AH 4038.91.5 — Election by lot at Athens. 2. ed. (Headlam-Morley, J.W.) Cambridge, 1933.

AH 8886.5 — Les élections municipales à Pompéi. (Willems, Pierre.) Paris, 1887.

AH 7137.57 — Elementa antiquitatum iuris Romani publici et privati. (Selchow, J.H.C.) Gottingae, 1757.

AH 7203.7.10 — Elementa juris civilis. (Corvini, A.) Amstelodami, 1664.

AH 7203.32.5 — Elementa juris civilis. 5. ed. (Heineccius, J.G.) Trajecti ad Rhenum, 1772.

AH 7203.19.5 — Elementa juris secundum ordinem Institutionum Justiniani. (Corpus juris civilis. Institutiones.) Lugduni Batavorum, 1700.

AH 4842.56 — Elementary Greek education. (Lane, F.H.) Syracuse, N.Y., 1895.

AH 7818.59 — Elementary manual of Roman antiquities. (Ramsay, William.) London, 1859.

AH 7818.59.3 — Elementary manual of Roman antiquities. 3. ed. (Ramsay, William.) London, 1863.

AH 8607.2.10F — Gli elementi ilaiati sannitici e campani nella più antica civiltà romana. (Pais, Ettore.) Napoli, 1900.

AH 7844.10 — Elementi speltocolori nei rihuoli festivi Romani. (Piccoluga, Giulia.) Roma, 1965.

AH 7139.28 — Elementos de derecho romano. (Rodriguez, José S.) Caracas, 1928. 2v.

AH 7138.50 — Elementos de derecho romano. 3. ed. (Heineccius, J.G.) Paris, 1850.

NEDL AH 278.44.5 — Elementos de historia antigua. (Lista y Aragón, A.) Sevilla, 1844.

AH 3400.5 — Eléments de bibliograhie Hittite. Thèse. (Contenau, G.) Paris, 1922.

AH 3400.5.5 — Eléments de bibliographie Hittite. (Contenau, G.) Paris, 1922.

AH 7139.01.6 — Éléments de droit romain. (May, Gaston.) Paris, 1907.

AH 7139.01.5 — Éléments de droit romain. 7e éd. (May, Gaston.) Paris, 1901.

Htn AH 278.00* — Elements of ancient history. (Millot, C.F.X.) N.Y., 18- .

AH 7278.28 — Elements of Roman history. (Cobbett, W.) London, 1828.

AH 7201.45 — Elements of Roman law. (Gaius.) Oxford, 1871.

AH 7201.73 — Elements of Roman law. (Gaius.) Oxford, 1890.

AH 7138.75 — Elements of Roman law. (Harris, S.F.) London, 1875.

AH 7201.51A — Elements of Roman law. 2. ed. (Gaius.) Oxford, 1875.

Htn AH 7137.55* — Elements of the civil law. (Taylor, J.) Cambridge, 1755.

AH 7137.55.3 — Elements of the civil law. 3. ed. (Taylor, J.) London, 1769.

AH 7137.55.5 — Elements of the civil law. 3. ed. (Taylor, J.) London, 1786.

Htn AH 8207.5* — Elenchus antiquitatum albionensium. (Langhorne, D.) Londini, 1675.

AH 7078.79 — Le elezioni et il Broglio. (Gentile, I.) Milan, 1879.

Eg 659.51 — Elgood, P.G. Later dynasties of Egypt. Oxford, 1951.

Eg 709.38 — Elgood, P.G. The Ptolemies of Egypt. Bristol, 1938.

AH 809.10 — Elia bar Sinaya. La chronographie. Paris, 1910.

AH 8314.2 — Eliade, Mircea. De Zalmoxis à Gengis-Khan. Paris, 1970.

AH 8314.2.1 — Eliade, Mircea. Zalmoxis, the vanishing god. Chicago, 1972.

AH 9560.2 — Eliaeson, Ake. Beiträge zur Geschichte Sardiniens. Uppsala, 1906.

AH 5308.10 — Eliot, C.W.J. Coastal demes of Attika. Toronto, 1962.

AH 3013.950PF — Eliot, H.W. Excavations in Mesopotamia and Western Iran. Cambridge, 1950.

AH 7308.49.2 — Eliot, Samuel. History of the liberty of the ancient Romans. Boston, 1853.

AH 7308.49 — Eliot, Samuel. Liberty of Rome. N.Y., 1849. 2v.

AH 5557.5 — Elis, Arkadien, Achaja. (Schiller, L.) Erlangen, 1855.

AH 2061.3 — Elisaeus. History of Varton and of the Battle of the Armenians. London, 1830.

AH 7869.2 — Ellendt, F. Cognomine et agnomine Romano. Regimontii Borussorum, 1853.

AH 4818.55 — Ellēnikēs archaiologias. (Rousopoulos, A.S.) Patrais, 1855.

AH 8658.2 — Elliot, F.D.G. Pictures of old Rome. Leipzig, 1882.

AH 7448.18.6 — Ellis, Robert. An inquiry into the ancient routes between Italy and Gaul. Cambridge, Eng., 1867.

AH 7448.18.3 — Ellis, Robert. Treatise on Hannibal's Passage. Cambridge, 1853.

AH 7189.64 — El'nitskii, L.A. Voznknovenie i razvitie rabstva v Rime v XIII - III v do n.e. Moskva, 1964.

AH 7297.47 — Elogiorum Romae reliquae. (Zell, Carolus.) Stuttgartie, 1847.

AH 7138.87.7 — L'eloquence judiciaire. (Poiret, J.) Paris, 1887.

AH 8908.3 — Els gregs, els etruscos. (Brunet y Bellet, J.) Barcelona, 1895.

AH 6110.14 — Elson, Charles F. Perseus and Demetrius. n.p., 1935.

AH 8548.105 — Elston, C.S. The earliest relations between Celts and Germans. London, 1934.

AH 8673.3 — Elter, A. Cremera und Porta Carmentalis. Bonn, 1910.

AH 7488.25 — Elton, C.A. History of Roman emperors...to...last Constantine. London, 1825.

AH 7188.56 — Elvers, R. Römischen Servitutenlehre. Marburg, 1856.

AH 4410.38 — The emergence of civilisation: the Cyclades and the Aegean in the third millennium B.C. (Renfrew, Colin.) London, 1972.

AH 4409.66 — The emergence of Greek democracy, 800-400 B.C. (Forest, William George Grieve.) N.Y., 1966.

AH 7279.50 — The emergence of Rome as ruler of the Western world. (Starr, Chester G.) Ithaca, 1950.

AH 7279.50.3 — The emergence of Rome as ruler of the Western world. 2. ed. (Starr, Chester G.) Ithaca, 1953.

AH 4558.98 — Emerson, A. Portraiture of Alexander the Great. Baltimore, 1886.

AH 8615.10 — Emigration from Italy in the republican age of Rome. (Wilson, A.J.N.) Manchester, Eng., 1966.

AH 4843.5.10 — Emmanuel, M. The antique Greek dance. London, 1927.

AH 4843.5.8A — Emmanuel, M. The antique Greek dance. N.Y., 1916.

AH 4843.5 — Emmanuel, M. Danse grecque. Paris, 1896.

AH 4843.3 — Emmanuel, M. L'orchestique grecque. Paris, 1895.

AH 4843.2 — Emmanuel, M. Saltationis disciplina. Paris, 1895.

AH 4296.26 — Emmius, U. Vetus Graecia. Lugdunum Batavorum, 1626.

AH 4559.68.15 — Emmrich, Kurt. Alexander der Grosse. Zürich, 1968.

AH 4559.68.10 — Emmrich, Kurt. Alexander the Great: power as destiny. London, 1968.

AH 4410.40.3 — Emmrich, Kurt. An den Küsten des Lichts. 3. Aufl. München, 1961.

Htn AH 4036.32* — Emmus, Vbbonis. Graecorum republicae. Lugdunum Batavorum, 1632.

Htn AH 4036.44* — Emmus, Vbbonis. Republica Graecorum. Luden, 1644. 2v.

AH 7628.69 — L'empereur-architecte Adrien. (Lucas, Charles.) Paris, 1869.

AH 7538.76 — L'empereur Claude. (Double, L.) Paris, 1876.

AH 7539.27 — L'empereur Claude et l'idée de la domination mondiale des Juifs. (Zielinski, T.) Bruxelles, 1927.

AH 7759.32 — L'empereur Constantin. (Piganiol, A.) Paris, 1932.

AH 7629.50 — L'empereur Hadrien. (Orgeval, B.) Paris, 1950.

AH 7488.63.3 — Les empereurs romains. 2. ed. (Zeller, J.S.) Paris, 1863.

AH 7488.63.4 — Les empereurs romains. 3. ed. (Zeller, J.S.) Paris, 1869.

AH 7599.65 — Les empéreurs romains d'Espagne. Paris, 1965.

AH 7468.29 — Emperius, A.C.W. De temporum Belli Mithridatici. Gottingae, 1829.

AH 7539.40A — The emperor Claudius. (Scramuzza, V.M.) Cambridge, 1940.

AH 7529.34 — The Emperor Gaius Caligula. (Balsdom, John Percy Vyvian D.) Oxford, 1934.

AH 7529.34.6 — The Emperor Gaius Caligula. (Balsdom, John Percy Vyvian D.) Oxford, 1964.

AH 7628.98 — The Emperor Hadrian. (Gregorovius, F.A.) London, 1898.

AH 7778.79 — Emperor Julian, paganism and Christianity. (Rendall, Gerald Henry.) Cambridge, 1879.

AH 7779.19 — The emperor Julian. (Martin, Edward J.) London, 1919.

AH 7778.12.5 — The Emperor Julian and his generation. (Neander, A.) N.Y., 1850.

AH 8073.16 — L'empire carthaginois. (Schmidt, W.) Paris, 1940.

AH 7769.47.2 — L'empire chrétien (325-395). 2. éd. (Piganiol, André.) Paris, 1972.

Author and Title Listing

AH 8514.15 — L'empire des Antonins et les martyrs gaulois de 177. (Colin, J.) Bonn, 1964.

AH 3507.5 — L'empire des Mèdes. (Delattre, A.) Bruxelles, 1883.

AH 3661.5 — L'empire des Sassanides. (Christensen, A.) København, 1907.

AH 3407.5 — Empire of Hittites. (Wright, W.) London, 1884.

AH 3407.5.3 — Empire of Hittites. 2d ed. (Wright, W.) London, 1886.

Eg 708.95A — The empire of the Ptolemies. (Mahaffy, J.P.) London, 1895.

AH 7489.22 — L'empire romain; évolution et decadence. (Bloch, G.) Paris, 1922.

AH 7489.25 — L'empire romain. (Homo, Léon P.) Paris, 1925.

AH 7489.29.4 — L'empire romain. 4. éd. (Albertini, Eugène.) Paris, 1970.

AH 7488.67 — L'empire romain à Rome. (Ampère, J.J.) Paris, 1867. 2v.

AH 3659.7 — Das Emporkommen der persischen Macht. (Evers, E.) Berlin, 1884.

AH 4909.26.5 — Emporos. (Knorringa, H.) Amsterdam, 1926.

AH 3017.7.9 — Empreintes de cylindres assyro-chaldéens. (Menant, J.) Paris, 1880.

NEDL AH 7489.11A — The empresses of Rome. (McCabe, Joseph.) London, 1911.

AH 7489.10 — The empresses of Rome. (McCabe, Joseph.) N.Y., 1911.

AH 7168.50 — Emtio Bonorum. (Dernburg, H.) Heidelberg, 1850.

AH 279.41.10 — En el primer giro. (Tovar, Antonio.) Madrid, 1941.

AH 4483.9 — Hē en Salamini Naumachia. (Rediades, P.D.) Athens, 1911.

EgP 43.9 — Enchoria. Wiesbaden. 1,1971+

AH 4049.72 — Encrucijada de lo político y lo humano, un momento histórico de Grecia. (Díaz Tejera, Alberto.) Sevilla, 1972.

AH 7139.53.10F — Encyclopedia dictionary of Roman law. (Berger, Adolf.) Philadelphia, 1953.

AH 4410.34 — The end of Atlantis: a new light on an old legend. (Luce, John Victor.) London, 1969.

AH 7659.31.10 — The end of the ancient world and the beginnings of the Middle Ages. (Lot, Ferdinand.) N.Y., 1961.

AH 7769.67 — The end of the Roman world. (Perowne, Stewart.) N.Y., 1967.

AH 7799.67 — Das Ende des Kaisertums im Westen des Römischen Reichs. (Wes, Marinus Antony.) 's-Gravenhage, 1967.

AH 7169.59 — Endemann, W. Der Begriff der Delegation im klassischen, römischen Recht. Marburg, 1959.

AH 4889.37 — Endenburg, P.J. Koinoonia. Amsterdam, 1937.

AH 4559.24.5 — Endres, Heinrich. Geographischer Horizont und Politik bei Alexander der Grossen in den Jahren 330/323. Würzburg, 1924.

Eg 879.63.5 — Énel (pseud.). Les origines de la Genèse et l'enseignement des temples de l'ancienne Egypte. Paris, 1963.

AH 7299.66 — Enemies of the Roman order. (MacMullen, Ramsay.) Cambridge, 1966.

Eg 879.14 — L'enfer égyptien et l'enfer virgilien. (Amélineau, Emile.) Paris, 1914.

Eg 559.39 — Engberg, R.M. The Hyksos reconsidered. Diss. Chicago, 1939.

AH 3407.33 — Enge Schlucht und schwarzer Berg. (Marek, Kurt W.) Hamburg, 1955.

AH 3407.33.5 — Enge Schlucht und schwarzer Berg. (Marek, Kurt W.) Reinbek, 1966.

AH 3307.5 — Engel, W.H. Kypros. Berlin, 1841. 2v.

AH 7178.42 — Engelbregt, C.A. Legibus Agrariis. Lugduni Batavorum, 1842.

AH 6104.5 — Engelhardt, Hans. Das senatus consultum Macedonianum. Inaug. Diss. Bamberg, 1930.

Eg 39.09 — Engers, M. De Aegyptiarum...administratione. Groningae, 1909.

AH 4049.38 — English, B.R. The problem of freedom in Greece from Homer to Pindar. Toronto, 1938.

AH 3179.16 — Enmerkar and the Lord of Aratta. (Kramer, Samuel Noah.) Ann Arbor, 1973.

AH 4809.03 — Die enneadischen und hebdomadischen Fristen und Wochen der ältesten Griechen. (Roscher, W.H.) Leipzig, 1903.

Htn AH 7477.38* — An enquiry into the merit of assassination...character of Caesar. (Hill, Aaron.) London, 1738.

Htn AH 137.69* — An enquiry into the use and practice of juries. (Pettingal, J.) London, 1769.

AH 3659.10 — Enstehung und Blüte...des altorientalischen Kulturwelt: Cyrus. (Lindl, Ernest.) München, 1903.

AH 4819.65.10 — Enter Plato. (Gouldner, Alvin Ward.) N.Y., 1965.

AH 928.13 — Entfernungen bei den Alten. (Ukert, F.A.) Weimar, 1813.

NEDL AH 298.65 — Entretiens sur l'histoire antiquité. (Zeller, J.) Paris, 1865.

AH 4238.69 — Entstehung...der griechischen Söldnerheere und ihre Teilnahme. (Chevalier, L.) Prag, 1869.

AH 98.78 — Entstehung der Staedte der Alten. (Kuhn, Emil.) Leipzig, 1878.

AH 7178.56.3 — Die Entstehung des Colonats. (Heisterbergk, B.) Leipzig, 1876.

AH 7049.27 — Die Entstehung des römischen Principats; ein Beispiel des Wandels von Staatsformen. (Münzer, Friedrich.) Münster, 1927.

AH 3012.13 — Die Entstehung und Entwicklung der Götterwaffen im alten Mesopotamien und ihre Bedeutung. (Sulayman, Tawfiq.) Berlin, 1964.

AH 7168.80 — Die Entwickelungsformen des römischen Privatrechtes. (Hoelder, E.) Erlangen, 1880.

AH 7116.2 — Die Entwicklung. (Plüss, H.T.) Leipzig, 1870.

AH 5958.5 — Die Entwicklung der Sage von der Rückkehr der Herakliden. (Vitalis, Gerhard.) Griefswald, 1930.

AH 9666.2 — Die Entwicklung der spanischen Provinzialgrenzen. (Braun, F.) Berlin, 1909.

AH 7168.88 — Entwicklung des römischen Schiedgerichts. (Matthiass, B.) Rostock, 1888.

AH 7168.83.7 — Entwicklung und Begriff des juristischen Besitzes des römischen Rechts. (Dernburg, H.) Halle, 1883.

AH 4848.14.5F — Entwicklungsgeschichte der griechischen Tracht. (Bieber, Margarete.) Berlin, 1934.

AH 7161.19 — Entwicklungsgeschichte des römischen Rechts. (Jhering, R.) Leipzig, 1894.

AH 7139.10 — Die Entwicklungsgeschichte des römischen Rechts. (Kuhlenbeck, L.) München, 1910. 2v.

AH 883.2 — Entwicklungshilfe im Altertum. (Altheim, Franz.) Reinbeck, 1962.

AH 7161.23 — Entzug der väterlichen Gewalt. (Stockar, H.) Zürich, 1903.

AH 3179.10.2 — Enuma eliš. (Enuma eliš.) Oxford, 1966.

AH 3179.10.15 — Enuma eliš und Hexaëmeron. (Deimel, Anton.) Rom, 1934.

AH 3179.10.2 — Enuma elish. Enuma eliš. Oxford, 1966.

AH 3179.10 — Enuma elish. Le poème babylonien de la création. Paris, 1935.

AH 4269.73 — Envoys and diplomacy in ancient Greece. (Mosley, Derek J.) Wiesbaden, 1973.

AH 4539.67 — Epaminoud. (Fol, Aleksandur.) Sofiia, 1967.

AH 5607.5 — Epeirotika...Geschichte des alten Epeiros. (Schmidt, H.) Marburg, 1894.

AH 4559.32A — The Ephemerides of Alexander's expedition. (Robinson, Charles A.) Providence, 1932.

AH 2575.5 — Ephesiaca. (Guhl, Ernestus.) Berolini, 1843.

AH 4229.41 — Ephesus in Athenian litigation. Thesis. (Ralph, J.D.) Chicago, 1941.

AH 5753.9 — Ephoris Spartanis. (Frick, C.) Gottingae, 1872.

AH 3177.16 — The epic of Gilgamesh. (Gilgamesh.) Harmondsworth, 1960.

X Cg AH 3177.10F — The epic of Gilgamesh. (Gilgamesh.) Oxford, 1930.

AH 819.61.10F — The epic of man. (Life (Chicago).) N.Y., 1961.

AH 2061.3.5 — The epic of St. Vardan the brave. (Yeghisheh, Elisha Vardapet.) N.Y., 1951.

AH 8379.2 — Epigraphische Beiträge zur Geschichte Histrias in hellenistischer und römanischer Zeit. (Pippidi, D.M.) Berlin, 1962.

AH 5310.11 — Epigraphische Beiträge zur sozial-politischen Geschichte Athens im Zeitalter des Demosthenes. (Sundwall, J.) Leipzig, 1906.

AH 4079.27 — Epigraphische Untersuchungen zu den griechischen Volksbeschlüssen. (Laqueur, Richard.) Leipzig, 1927.

AH 5607.7 — Epirotische Geschichte. (Klotzsch, C.) Boston, 1911.

AH 5603.5 — Epirus; a study in Greek constitutional development. (Cross, Geoffrey N.) Cambridge, 1932.

AH 5607.8 — Epirus: the geography, the ancient remains, the history. (Hammond, Nicholas Geoffrey Lempriere.) Oxford, 1967.

AH 5616.5 — Epirus im Altertum; Studien zur historischen Topographie. Inaug. Diss. (Treidler, Hans.) Leipzig, 1917.

AH 3187.7 — Epistolary literature of Assyrians and Babylonians. (Johnston, C.) Baltimore, 1898.

Eg 39.11 — Les Epistratèges. (Martin, V.) Genève, 1911.

Eg 39.70 — Gli epistrategi nell'Egitto greco-romano. (Vandoni, Mariangela.) Milano, 1970?

AH 4808.51 — Epitome...civil and literary chronicle of Greece. (Clinton, H.F.) Oxford, 1851.

AH 4278.07 — Epitome historia tès Hellados. En Benetia, 1807. 2v.

AH 4818.27 — Epitome of Grecian antiquities. (Cleveland, C.D.) Boston, 1827.

AH 7808.53.5 — An epitome of the civil and literary chronology of Rome and Constantinople. (Clinton, Henry Fynes.) Oxford, 1853.

AH 7029.08 — Epitome rerum romanarum. (Giorni, C.) Firenze, 1908.

AH 7038.41.2 — Die Epochen der Verfassungsgeschichte. (Peter, C.L.) Leipzig, 1841.

AH 3195.10.3 — L'epopea di Erra. (Era.) Roma, 1969.

AH 7549.72 — L'époque de Néron et ses controverses idéologiques. (Cizek, Eugen.) Leiden, 1972.

AH 3177.14 — Epos o Gil'gameshe. (Gilgamesh.) Moskva, 1961.

AH 7629.17 — The equestrian officials of Trajan and Hadrian. Thesis. (Lacey, R.H.) Princeton, 1917.

AH 7239.65.10 — Die equites singulares Augusti. (Speidel, Michael.) Bonn, 1965.

AH 3195.10.3 — Era. L'epopea di Erra. Roma, 1969.

AH 3195.10F — Era. Das Era-Epos. Würzburg, 1956.

AH 3195.10.2 — Era. Das Erra-Epos. Rom, 1970.

AH 3195.10F — Das Era-Epos. (Era.) Würzburg, 1956.

AH 3657.5 — Éran. (Spiegel, F.) Berlin, 1863.

AH 7409.62 — Erasmus, Hendrik. The origins of Rome. Assen, 1962.

AH 8549.122 — Das Erbe der Druiden. 7. Aufl. (Memminger, A.) Würzburg, 1922.

AH 7162.5 — Erbrecht. (Rosshirt, K.F.) Landshut, 1831.

AH 4162.17 — Die Erbtochter. (Hafter, Eugen.) Leipzig, 1887.

AH 3966.18 — Die Erdkarte der Urbibel. (Herrmann, A.) Braunschweig, 1931.

AH 4298.83.10 — Erdmann, M. Zur Kunde der hellenistischen Städtegründungen. Strassburg, 1883.

Eg 1029.50F — Erichsen, W. Auswahl frühdemotischer Texte. Kopenhagen, 1950.

AH 38.29 — Erinnerungen aus der Staatskunst. (Reichard, H.G.) Leipzig, 1829.

AH 3013.8 — Erklärung der König Ludwig's Inschriften in der Münchner Glyptothek. (Gaugengigl, I.) München, 1870.

AH 3041.2 — Die Erlässe und Instruktionen aus dem Lande Arrapha, ein Beitrag zur Rechtsgeschichte des Alten Vorderen Orients. Inaug. Diss. (Mueller, Manfred.) Leipzig? 1968?

AH 3011.5F — Erläuterung der Keilinschriften babylonischer Backsteine. (Grotefend, G.F.) Hannover, 1852.

AH 3011.5.5F — Erläuterung einer Inschrift des letzten assyrisch-babylonischen Königs aus Nimrud. (Grotefend, G.F.) Hannover, 1853.

AH 3132.7 — Erläuterung zweier Ausschreiben des Königes Nebukadnezar. (Grotefend, G.F.) Göttingen, 1853.

AH 7114.19 — Erläuterungen...zur römischen Ritter. (Kappes, K.) Freiburg, 1855.

Eg 278.85 — Erman, A. Ägypten. Tübingen, 1885.

Eg 278.85.1 — Erman, A. Ägypten. Tübingen, 1885-87. 2v.

Eg 278.85.2A — Erman, A. Ägypten und ägyptisches Leben im Altertum. Tübingen, 1923.

Eg 879.07 — Erman, A. Handbook of Egyptian religion. London, 1907.

Eg 278.85.4A — Erman, A. Life in ancient Egypt. London, 1894.

Eg 1308.99.5 — Erman, Adolf. Aus den Papyrus der Königlichen Museen. Berlin, 1899.

Eg 1029.23A — Erman, Adolf. Die Literatur der Ägypter. Leipzig, 1923.

Eg 1029.23.5 — Erman, Adolf. The literature of the ancient Egyptians. London, 1927.

Eg 819.36 — Erman, Adolf. Die Welt am Nil. Leipzig, 1936.

AH 7228.99 — Erman, Karl. Conceptio formularum, actio in factum und ipso iure-Consumption. Weimar, 1899.

AH 4719.40.2 — Die Eröffnung des zweiten römisch-makedonischen Krieges. 2. Aufl. (Petzold, Karl E.) Darmstadt, 1968.

AH 7168.59 — Erörterungen aus dem Obligationenrecht. v.1-2. (Mommsen, Theodor.) Braunschweig, 1859.

AH 4819.62.20 — Eros en Amor. (Boer, Willem den.) Den Haag, 1962.

AH 3195.10.2 — Das Erra-Epos. (Era.) Rom, 1970.

AH 4719.69 — Errington, Robert. Philopormen. Oxford, Eng., 1969.

AH 7449.71.10 — Errington, Robert Malcolm. The dawn of empire; Rome's rise to world power. London, 1971.

Eg 458.74 — Die erste bis...aufgefundene...Angabe über die Regierungszeit...Königs...alten Reich. (Dümichen, J.) Leipzig, 1874.

AH 7449.05 — Der erste punische Krieg. (Schermann, Max.) Stuttgart, 1905.

AH 8416.5 — Ertl, Franz. Topographia Norici. Kremsmünster, 1965-69. 2v.

NEDL AH 278.26.5 — Ertov, I.D. Prodolzhenie v seobshchei istorii drevnikh prosveshchennykh narodov. Sankt Peterburg, 1826. 2v.

AH 7228.50	Erxleben, A. Condictiones sine causa. pt.1-2. Leipzig, 1850.
AH 2575.7	Erythrä. (Gaebler, H.) Berlin, 1892.
NEDL AH 298.61	Erzählungen aus der alten Geschichte in biographischer Form. 4. Aufl. v.2. (Stacke, L.) Oldenburg, 1861.
AH 842.14	Erziehung und Jugenduntericht. (Ussing, J.L.) Berlin, 1885.
AH 842.11	Erziehung und Unterricht. (Grasberger, L.) Würzburg, 1864. 3v.
AH 4558.48	Erziehung und Unterricht Alexanders des Grossen. (Geier, S.R.) Halle, 1848.
AH 842.17	Erziehung und Unterricht bei den Griechen und Römern. (Bohatta, H.) Gütersloh, 1895.
AH 842.5	Erziehungswissenschaft. (Goess, G.F.D.) Ansbach, 1808.
AH 4161.9	Es Vanden, A.H.G.P. De iure familiarum. Lugdunum Batavorum, 1864.
AH 9610.28	Esame critico della storia...guerre servili. (Ciaceri, Emanuele.) Catania, 1907.
AH 3096.7	Esarhaddon, king of Assyria. Cylinder A of the Esarhaddon inscriptions. New Haven, 1888.
AH 3096.8	Esarhaddon, king of Assyria. The Vassal-treaties of Esarhaddon. London, 1958.
AH 7228.42	Escher, J.H.A. De testium ratione. Turici, 1842.
AH 188.96	L'esclavage à Athènes et à Rome. (Keiffer, Jules.) Luxembourg, 1896.
AH 4189.28	Les esclaves publics à Athènes. (Jacob, Oscar.) Liége, 1928.
AH 7188.97	Les esclaves publics chez les Romains. (Halkin, Léon.) Bruxelles, 1897.
Eg 848.7	Las escuelas del antiquo Egipto a través de los papiros griegos. (Galé, José Miguel.) Madrid, 1961.
AH 7169.37	L'esecuzione contro il debitore nel diritto romano ed il nexum. (Beretta, A.) Udine, 1937.
AH 7203.136	Un esempio dell'insegnamento di Berito ai compilatori. (Boháček, Miroslav.) Palermo, 1932.
AH 4217.10	Eshi yunondo eşitlitove eşitsrilik. (Şenel, Alaeddin.) Ankara, 1970.
AH 3045.100.5	Eshnunna. Laws, statutes, etc. The laws of Eshnunna. Jerusalem, 1969.
AH 2110.15	Eski Anadolu tarihi. (Kinal, Füruzan.) Ankara, 1962.
AH 3020.40.5	Eski Babill zamanina ait Nippur menşeli iki okul kitabi. (Çiğ, Muazzez.) Ankara, 1959.
AH 4279.68	Eski Yunanda siyasal düşünüş. (Senel, Alâeddin.) Ankara, 1968.
AH 7138.56	Esmach, K. Römischen Rechtsgeschichte. Göttingen, 1856.
AH 7203.62.5	Esmarch, K. Pandekten-Exegeticum. Prag, 1875.
AH 7138.80	Esmarch, K. Römische Rechtsgeschichte. Kassel, 1880.
AH 7168.86.10	Esmein, A. Mélanges de l'histoire du droit et de critique. Paris, 1886.
AH 7309.61	Espadas Burgos, Manuel. La periodización de la historiagrafia romana. Madrid, 1961.
AH 9661.2	Las España del siglo primero de nustra era. (García y Bellido, Antonio.) Madrid, 1947.
AH 9646.10	L'espansione di Zande sulla costa settentrionale della Sicilia dalla metà dell'VIII secolo a.C. agli albori del V secolo a.C. (Ryolo di Maria. Domenico.) Messina, 1968.
AH 3707.12	L'espansione fenicia nel Mediterraneo. Roma, 1971.
AH 7419.51	L'espansione romana in occidente durante la repubblica. (Calderini, A.) Milano, 1951.
AH 7198.77.2A	L'esprit du droit romain. (Ihering, R.) Paris, 1877. 4v.
AH 7198.77.3	L'esprit du droit romain. v.1-2. (Ihering, R.) Paris, 1880-82.
AH 7149.36	La espropriazione per pubblica utilità nel diritto romano. (De Robertis, F.M.) Bari, 1936.
AH 8157.2	Esquisse d'une histoire dans la nord de l'Afrique. (Boissière, G.) Paris, 1878.
AH 7768.73	Essae sur la condition des barbares. (Léotard, E.) Paris, 1873.
AH 7178.98.2	Essae sur les lois agraires. (Dreyfus, Robert.) Paris, 1898.
AH 7088.77	Essai...des provinces romaines. (Person, E.) Paris, 1877.
AH 7168.86.15	Essai de restitution de l'Edit publicien. (Appleton, C.) Paris, 1886.
AH 7693.1	Essai d'iconographie de l'empereur Clodius Albinus. (Balty, Janine.) Bruxelles, 1966.
AH 7707.66	Essai historique sur la famille de l'Empereur Valérien. (Montégut, J.F.) n.p., 1766. 2 pam.
AH 7818.53	Essai historique sur la société civile. (Schmidt, C.) Strasbourg, 1853.
AH 7161.9	Essai historique sur la tutelle en droit romain. (La Fort, Charles.) Genève, 1850.
AH 7058.78.5	Essai historique sur le préteur romain. (Faure, F.) Paris, 1878.
AH 4818.05	Essai sur...supériorité des Grecs. (Leuliette, J.J.) Paris, 1805.
AH 7888.99.3	Essai sur...théories économiques. (Thomas, Paul.) Paris, 1899.
AH 4808.70	Essai sur la chronologie des archontes athéniens. (Dumont, A.) Paris, 1870.
Htn AH 257.68*	Essai sur la marine des anciens. (Déslandes, A.F.B.) Paris, 1768.
AH 7158.83	Essai sur la nature des condamnations civiles. (Montagnon, E.) Lyon, 1883.
AH 7059.33	Essai sur la préfecture du prétoire du Bas-Empire. Thèse. (Palanque, Jean-Rémy.) Paris, 1933.
AH 9066.5	Essai sur la topographie du Latium. Thèse. (Desjardins, Ernest.) Paris, 1854.
AH 7698.80	Essai sur la vie et le regne de Septime Sévère. (Ceuleneer, A. de.) Bruxelles, 1880.
AH 7088.98	Essai sur l'administration des provinces sénatoriales. (Halgan, C.) Paris, 1898.
AH 7238.94.2	Essai sur le droit penal militaire. (Bray, Joseph.) Paris, 1894.
AH 7088.46	Essai sur le nombre et l'origine des provinces romaines. (Poinsignon, A.) Paris, 1846.
AH 7618.77	Essai sur le regne de Trajan. (La Berge, C. de.) Paris, 1877.
Eg 847.5	Essai sur le symbolisme antique. Paris, 1847.
AH 8525.2	Essai sur le système défensif...pays Eduen. (Bulliot, J.G.) Paris, 1856.
AH 4842.17	Essai sur l'Ephébie Attique. (Dumont, A.) Paris, 1876. 2v.
AH 7598.00.3	Essai sur l'epoque de l'histoire romaine. (Hegewisch, D.H.) Paris, 1834.
AH 7855.2	Essai sur les chasses romaines, des origines à la fin du siècle des Antonins (Cynegetica). Thèse. (Aymard, Jacques.) Paris, 1957.
Htn AH 8549.76*	Essai sur les divinités indigètes du Vocontium. (Vallentin, F.) Grenoble, 1877.
AH 7108.86	Essai sur les finances. (Humbert, G.) Paris, 1886. 2v.
EgP 39.41	Essai sur les gouvernements de l'Egypte. (Dubois-Richard, P.) Le Caire, 1941.
Eg 39.41	Essai sur les gouvernements de l'Égypte. (Dubois-Richard, Paul.) Le Caire, 1941.
AH 8904.5	Essai sur les magistratures des républiques étrusques. (Lambrechts, R.) Bruxelles, 1959.
AH 7299.16	Essai sur les origines de Rome. Thèse. (Piganiol, André.) Paris, 1916.
AH 7088.80	Essai sur les pouvoirs du gouverneur. (Marx, Edgarel.) Paris, 1880.
AH 7114.37	Essai sur les procurateurs equestres sous le Haut-Empire romain. (Pflaum, Hans Georg.) Paris, 1950.
Eg 269.54	Essai sur les relations entre Egyptiens et Préhellènes. (Vercoutter, Jean.) Paris, 1954.
AH 7098.96.2	Essai sur l'histoire de la Praefectura Urbis. (Vigneaux, P.E.) Paris, 1896.
AH 3654.10	Essai sur l'histoire du droit persan des l'origine a l'invasion arabe. (Nasr, Taghi.) Paris, 1933.
AH 3936.9	Essai sur l'histoire politique et economique de Palmyre. (Février, J.G.) Paris, 1931.
AH 3936.9.5	Essai sur l'histoire politique et economique de Palmyre. Thèse. (Février, J.G.) Paris, 1931.
AH 115.3	Essai sur l'organisation de la tribu dans l'antiquité. (Kutorga, M.) Paris, 1839.
AH 4200.13	Essai sur Lycurgue. (Attinger, G.) Neuchatel, 1892.
AH 7648.60	Essai sur Marc Aurèle. (Des Vergers, M.J.A.) Paris, 1860.
Eg 847.3	Essai sur une stèle junéraire. (Rougé, Emman.) Berlin, 1849.
AH 3980.3	Essay on ancient topography of Jerusalem. (Fergusson, J.) London, 1847.
AH 928.36A	Essay on ancient weights and money. (Hussey, R.) Oxford, 1836.
AH 408.46.3	Essay on primaeval history. (Kenrick, J.) London, 1846.
AH 3195.3	An essay on the age and antiquity of the book of Nabathaean agriculture. (Renan, Ernest.) London, 1862.
AH 8549.71	An essay on the Druids. (Smiddy, Richard.) Dublin, 1871.
AH 8549.42	An essay on the question "Whether the British Druids offered human sacrifices". (Williams, J.) Bala, 1842.
AH 7207.7	An essay on the Roman senate. (Chapman, Thomas.) Cambridge, 1750.
AH 2007.4	Essay towards the history of Arabia. (Price, David.) London, 1824.
Htn AH 3965.6*	An essay towards the recovery of the Jewish measures and weights. (Cumberland, R.) London, 1686.
AH 7278.85.19	Essays. (Pelham, H.F.) Oxford, 1911.
AH 819.60	Essays in antiquity. (Green, Peter.) Cleveland, 1960.
AH 4279.58.5	Essays in Greek history. (Wade-Gery, H.T.) Oxford, 1958.
AH 4299.37A	Essays in Greek history and literature. (Gomme, Arnold W.) Oxford, 1937.
AH 5307.34	Essays in Greek politics. (Sealey, Raphael.) N.Y., 1967.
AH 8205.2	Essays on the invasion of Britain by Julius Caesar; the invasion of Britain by Plautius, and by Claudius Caesar; the early military policy of the Romans in Britain; the battle of Hastings. (Airy, George B.) London, 1865.
NEDL AH 279.02.5	Essentials in ancient history. (Wolfson, A.M.) N.Y., 1902.
AH 7279.57	L'essenza del romanesimo. (Ferrabino, Aldo.) Roma, 1957.
AH 7499.58.5	Esser, A.A.M. Cäsar und die julisch-claudischen Kaiser im biologisc-härztichen Blickfeld. Leiden, 1958.
AH 862.11	Esser, Alexander Albert Maria. Das Antlitz der Blindheit in der Antike. Leiden, 1961.
AH 7889.02	Esser, J.J. De Pauperum cura apud Romanos. Campis, 1902.
AH 8210.7	The establishment of Roman power in Britain. (Tamblyn, William F.) Hamilton, Ont., 1899.
AH 4039.39	El estado y las facciones en la antiquedad. (Romero, J.L.) Buenos Aires, 1938.
AHP 908.43	Estrup, H.F.J. De makariske ör og Elisa. Kjøbenhavn, 1843.
AH 7448.98.5	Estudios históricos y militares sobre las compañas de Anibal. (Garmendia, J.I.) Buenos Aires, 1898.
AH 7161.15	Estudios jurídicos. (Maranges, J.M.) Madrid, 1878.
AH 4299.71.5	Estudios sobre el mundo helenístico. Swilla, 1971.
AH 4819.65.5	Estudos de história da cultura clássica. (Pereira, Maria Helena Rocha.) Lisboa, 1965.
NEDL AH 4818.73.2	Esvanden, A.H.G.P. Griecksche antiquiteiten. Groningen, 1873.
AH 4847.7	Esveld, C. De Balneis Lavationibusque Graecorum. Amersfortiae, 1908.
AH 5372.5	Et graesk Senatsconsult om Thisbaeerne. (Aubert, L.M.B.) n.p., 1875.
AH 3127.5	L'Etalon des mesures Assyriennes. (Oppert, J.) Paris, 1875.
AH 7279.61	Les étapes de l'impérialisme romaine. (Carcopino, Jérôme.) Paris, 1961.
AH 7498.53	État du monde romain. (Duruy, V.) Paris, 1853.
AH 7038.81.4	L'etat romain. v.1-5. (Madvig, J.N.) Paris, 1882. 4v.
AH 5303.32	Eterie e gruppi politici nell'Atene del IV sec. A.C. (Pecorella Longo, Chlara.) Firenze, 1971.
AH 5303.25	Le eterie nella vita politica ateniese del VI e V secolo A.C. (Sartori, Franco.) Roma, 1957.
Eg 819.64.5	Eternal Egypt. (Montet, Pierre.) N.Y., 1969.
AH 4845.28	Ethnica, pars prima: De Graecorum civitatum proprietatibus proverbio notatis. (Goebel, Maximilianus.) Vratislaviae, 1915.
AH 328.73	Ethnogénie gauloise. (Roget de Belloguet, D.F.L.) Paris, 1873. 4v.
AH 8548.10	Das ethnographische Verhältniss der Kelten und Germanen. (Braudes, C.) Leipzig, 1857.
Htn AH 8907.5F*	Ethruscarum antiquitatum fragmenta. Francofurti, 1637.
Eg 847.6	Eti hiyeroglifi üzerinde tetkikler 534 idéogramme. (Candar, Aaoni Ali.) Ankara, 1933.
AH 8908.13	Etruria. Celtica Etruscan literature and antiquities. (Betham, William.) Dublin, 1842. 2v.
AH 8907.13	Etruria and Rome. (Fell, R.A.L.) Cambridge, Eng., 1924.
AH 8907.15	Etruria antica. (Ducati, Pericule.) Torino, 1925.
AH 8907.16	L'Etruria e gli Etruschi. (Buonamici, G.) Firenze, 1926.
AH 8907.19	Etruria past and present. (Johnstone, M.A.) London, 1930.
AH 8907.4	L'Étrurie et les Étrusques. (Des Vergers, M.J.A.N.) Paris, 1862-64. 2v.
AH 8907.4PF	L'Étrurie et les Étrusques. v.3. Atlas. (Des Vergers, M.J.A.N.) Paris, 1862-64.
AH 8907.22	Etrurja i Etruskowie. (Bulanda, E.) Lwów, 1934.

Author and Title Listing

AH 3013.924   Excavations at Kish. v.1, 3, 4. (Langdon, S.H.) Paris, 1924-34. 3v.

AH 3013.39PF   Excavations at Nippur. Pt.1-2. (Pennsylvania. University. Babylonian Expeditions.) Philadelphia, 1905.

AH 3020.13A   Excavations at Nuzi. v.2-8. (Chiera, Edward.) Cambridge, 1932-62. 7v.

AH 3013.955   Excavations at Ur. (Woolley, Charles L.) London, 1955.

AH 3013.929   The excavations at Ur and the Hebrew records. (Woolley, Charles L.) London, 1929.

AH 3013.950PF   Excavations in Mesopotamia and Western Iran. (Eliot, H.W.) Cambridge, 1950.

AH 7138.80.3   Excurse über römischen Recht. 2. Aufl. (Kuntze, J.E.) Leipzig, 1880.

AH 9684.7   Excursión a Numancia pasando por Soria. (Mélida, José R.) Madrid, 1922.

AH 9389.5.4F   Exercitatio. (Naudé, Gabriel.) Lugduni Batavorum, 1722.

AH 4299.60   L'expansion et la colonisation. (Berard, Jean.) Paris, 1960.

AH 3005.14   The expansion of Assyrian studies. (Wiseman, D.J.) London, 1962.

AH 4559.37   L'expedition d'Alexandre et la conquête de l'Asie. (Bungard, R.) Paris, 1937.

AH 4481.11   L'expédition de Marathon. (Sotiriadis, G.) Salonique, 1934.

AH 4523.5   Expedition der Athener nach Sicilien. (Rottsahl, C.) Langensalza, 1878.

AH 3013.31   Expedition of Oriental Exploration Fund (Babylonian section). Reports 1-4, 6. (Chicago, Illinois. University. Oriental Exploration Fund.) Chicago? 1904.

AH 3013.11F   Expédition scientifique en Mésopotamie. v.1-2; plates. (Oppert, J.) Paris, 1863. 3v.

AH 3013.855   L'expedition scientifique et artistique de Mésopotamie et de Médie. (Pillet, M.) Paris, 1922.

AH 3966.24F   The explanatory Bible atlas and scripture gazetteer. (Jenks, William.) Boston, 1847.

AH 938.49F   The explanatory Bible atlas and Scripture gazetteer. (Jenks, William.) Boston, 1849.

AH 7203.53   Explication..des Instituts. 8. ed. (Ortolan, J.L.E.) Paris, 1870. 3v.

AH 7203.55   Explication..des Instituts. 8. ed. (Ortolan, J.L.E.) Paris, 1870. 3v.

Htn   AH 8514.5*   Explications...sacrifices...les anciens. (Boze, C.G. de.) Paris, 1705.

AH 8066.3   Exploration scientifique de la Tunisie. Atlas. (Tissot, Charles.) Paris, 1884-88. 2v.

AH 3013.10A   Explorations in Bible lands. (Hilprecht, H.V.) Philadelphia, 1903.

AH 7168.37.2   Exposé...du droit romain sur la propriété. (Pellat, C.A.) Paris, 1853.

AH 7169.33.10   L'extinction de l'usufruit "rei mutatione". Thèse. (Cavin, P.E.) Lausanne, 1933.

Htn   AH 7105.22.5*   Extrait ou abregé du Livre de assé de feu mons. (Budé, G.) Lyon, 1554.

AH 8513.14   Eydaux, Henri. La France antique. Paris, 1962.

Htn   AH 925.55*   Eynopsis. (Neander, M.) Basileae, 1555.

AH 8549.2   Eyring, Elias M. Veterum instituta druidum. Lipsiae, 1698.

AH 2104.5   Eyuboğlu, Ismet Zeki. Tanri yaratan toprak; Anadolu. Istanbul, 1973.

NEDL   AH 278.92   Eyzaquirre, R. Compendio de historia antigua, griega y romana. Santiago de Chile, 1892.

AH 2158.2   Faber, A. Quaestionum propontiacarum. Herford, 1858.

AH 8532.5   Fabia, Philippe. La garnison romaine de Lyon. Lyon, 1918.

AH 3059.7   Fabian, E.A. De Seleucia Babylonia. Lipsiae, 1869.

AH 7168.37.7   Fabricius, C.F. Historische Forschungen im Gebiete des römischen Privat-Rechts. Berlin, 1837.

AH 5390.7   Fabricius, E. Theben. Freiburg, 1890.

AH 7039.11   Fabricius, Ernest. Uber die Entwicklung der römischen Verfassung im republikanischer Zeit. Freiburg, 1911.

AH 7.16A   Fabricius, J.A. Bibliographia antiquaria. Hamburgi, 1716.

AH 4309.65   Fabricius, Johannes. Oldtidens idéhistorie. København, 1965.

AH 1819.56.3   The face of the ancient Orient. (Moscati, Sabatino.) Chicago, 1960.

Eg 1042.970   La face sud du massif est du pylône de Ramse's II à Louxor. (Kuentz, Charles.) Le Caire, 1970.

AH 7509.69.5   Fadinger, Volker. Quellenuntersuchungen zur Geschichte des 2. Triumvirats. Inaug. Diss. München, 1969.

AH 6140.6   Fafralé, O. Thessalonique des origines au XIVe siècle. Paris, 1919.

AH 7469.55   The failure of the Roman Republic. (Smith, R.E.) Cambridge, Eng., 1955.

Eg 974.5   Fakhry, A. The bent pyramid of Dahshûr. Le Caire, 1954.

Eg 974.5.5F   Fakhry, A. The monuments of Sneferu at Dahshur. Cairo, 1959-61. 2v.

AH 958.72   Falconer, W. Dissertation on St. Paul's voyage. Photoreproduction. London, 1872.

AH 8926.2   Die Falisker, eine geschichtlich-sprachliche Untersuchung. (Deecke, W.) Strassburg, 1888.

AH 9722.5   Falk, F.W.A. De origine Byzantie dissertatio. Vratislaviae, 1829.

AH 818.78.3FA   Falke, J. von. Greece and Rome. N.Y., 1882.

AH 818.78F   Falke, J. von. Hellas und Rom. Stuttgart, 1878.

AH 3181.13   Falkenstein, Adam. Sumerische und akkadische Hymnen und Gebete. Zurich, 1953.

AH 3017.50   Falkenstein, Adams. Grammatik der Sprache Gudeas von Lagaš. Roma, 1949-50. 2v.

AH 3109.5   The fall of Nineveh and the reign of Sennacherib chronologically considered. (Bosanquet, J.W.) London, 1853.

AH 7659.63   The fall of Rome. (Chambers, M.H.) N.Y., 1963.

AH 7799.71   The fall of Rome. (Lafferty, Raphael A.) Garden City, N.Y., 1971.

AH 7658.61   The fall of Rome. (Sheppard, J.G.) London, 1861.

AH 7658.61.5   The fall of Rome. (Sheppard, J.G.) London, 1892.

AH 7468.70   Fall of the Roman Republic. (Merivale, Charles.) London, 1870.

AH 8507.13   Fallue, Léon. Annales de la Gaule avant et pendant la domination romaine. Paris, 1864.

AH 7478.65.50   Fallue, Léon. Etudes archéologiques sur l'histoire de Jules César par l'empereur Napoléon III. Paris, 1867.

AH 7499.38   La famiglia di Augusto. (Pietrangeli, Carlo.) Roma, 1938.

AH 7840.5.4   Le famiglia romana. 4. ed. (Paribeni, Roberto.) Bologna, 1948.

AH 7161.13   La famiglia secondo il diritto romano. (Schupfer, F.) Padova, 1876.

AH 840.7   Familienfeste. (Samter, Ernst.) Berlin, 1901.

AH 4850.9   Familienmahl. (Pervanoglu, P.) Leipzig, 1872.

AH 4161.11   Familienrechts. (Hruza, Ernst.) Erlangen, 1892. 2v.

AH 840.9   La famille. (Léotard, E.) Lyon, 1909.

AH 7840.2   La famille dans la société romaine. (Lacombe, P.) Paris, 1889.

Eg 1309.34F   A family archive from Siut from papyri in the British Museum. (Thompson, H.) Oxford, 1934. 2v.

AH 7189.72   Family Caesaris; a social study of the Emperor's freedom and slaves. (Weaver, Paul Richard Carey.) Cambridge, Eng., 1972.

AH 4840.8   The family in classical Greece. (Lacey, Walter K.) London, 1968.

AH 5307.5   Fanelli, F. Athene Attica. Venezia, 1707.

AH 8073.28   Fantar, Mhamed. Carthage, la prestigieuse cité d'Elissa. Tunis, 1970.

AH 3358.9   Fantoli, A. La Libia negli scritti degli antiche. Roma, 1933.

Eg 971.9   Fantomes d'Antinoe. (Gayet, A.J.) Paris, 1904.

AH 3046.5F   Fara; Ergebnisse der Ausgrabungen der Deutschen Orient-Gesellschaft in Fara. (Heinrich, Ernst.) Berlin, 1931.

Eg 984.2   Farag, Nagib. The discovery of Neferuptah. Cairo, 1971.

Eg 819.67   Faraoner och människor. (Säve-Söderbergh, Torgny.) Stockholm, 1967.

Eg 863.5   Faraos blomster. (Laurent-Täckholm, Vini.) Stockholm, 1951.

AH 3017.30F   Farbige Keramik aus Assur und ihre Vorstafen in altassyrischen Wandmalereien. (Andrae, W.) Berlin, 1923.

AH 2013.7.5   Farès, Edouard. L'honneur chez les Arabes avant l'Islam. Paris, 1932.

AH 2013.7   Farès, Edouard. L'honneur chez les Arabes avant l'Islam. Thèse. Paris, 1932.

AH 4539.59   Farina, Antonio. Il processo di Frine. Napoli, 1959.

Eg 9.10   Farina, G. Bollettino. Roma, 1910.

AH 3910.12   Farn, W.W. Selencid-Parthian studies. London, 1930.

AH 7779.34   Farney, R. La religion de l'empereur Julien et le mysticisme du temps. Paris, 1934.

AH 7649.51   Farquharson, A.S.L. Marcus Aurelius. Oxford, 1951.

AH 4819.47.15   Farrington, B. Head and hand in ancient Greece. London, 1947.

AH 4808.61   Faselius, A. Attische Kalender. Weimar, 1861.

AH 3960.5   Fassinus, V. De Alexandro Magno ingresso Hierosolyma. Florentiae, 1780.

AH 8312.2   Fasten der Provinz Dacien. (Jung, Julius.) Innsbruck, 1894.

AH 8162.5   Les fastes de la Numidie sous la domination romaine. (Pallu de Lessert, A.C.) Constantine, 1888.

AH 8662.5   Les fastes de la préfecture de Rome au Bas-Empire. (Chastagnol, André.) Paris, 1962.

AH 3094.4F   Les fastes de Sargon roi d'Assyrie. (Oppert, J.) Paris, 1863. 2 pam.

AH 3094.4.2F   Les fastes de Sargon roi d'Assyrie. (Oppert, J.) Paris, 1863.

AH 8012.2   Fastes des provinces africaines. (Pallu de Lessert, A.C.) Paris, 1896-1901. 2v.

AH 7088.72   Fastes des provinces asiatiques de l'empire romain. pt.1. (Waddington, W.H.) Paris, 1872.

AH 4808.74   Fastes éponymiques d'Athènes. (Dumont, A.) Paris, 1874.

AH 7058.28.3   Fasti aedilicii. Inaug. Diss. (Seidel, Joseph.) Breslau, 1908.

AH 7809.10.7   Fasti aediliicii inde a Caesaris nece usque ad imperium A. Severi. (Heiligenstaedt, F.) Halis Saxonum, 1910.

AH 7809.54   Fasti capitolini. 1. ed. (Degrassi, A.) Torino, 1954.

AH 7808.72   Fasti censorii. (Boor, C. de.) Berolini, 1873.

AH 7809.52   I fasti consolari dell'Impero Romano. (Degrassi, A.) Roma, 1952.

AH 7809.10.5   I Fasti Consolari Romani. (Caosta, G.) Milano, 1910.

AH 7809.09.5   Fasti Consulares. Fasti consulares imperii romani von 30 v. Chr. bis 565 n. Chr. Bonn, 1909.

AH 7808.33   Fasti consulares capitolini. Altonae, 1833.

AH 7809.09.5   Fasti consulares imperii romani von 30 v. Chr. bis 565 n. Chr. (Fasti Consulares.) Bonn, 1909.

AH 7808.81   Fasti Consularis inde a Caesaris nece usque ad imperium Diocletiani. (Klein, Joseph.) Lipsiae, 1881.

AH 7114.30   I fasti dei tribuni della plebe. (Niccolini, G.) Milano, 1934.

AH 4808.98   Fasti Ephororum spartanorum. (Solari, Arcturus.) Pisis, 1898.

Htn   AH 7805.57.2F*   Fasti et triumphi. (Panvinio, Onafrio.) Venetiis, 1557.

AH 4214.19   Fasti Graecorum sacri. (Prott, J. de.) Lipsiae, 1893.

AH 4808.34.3   Fasti Hellenici. (Clinton, H.F.) Lipsiae, 1830.

AH 4808.34   Fasti Hellenici. (Clinton, H.F.) Oxford, 1834. 3v.

AH 7808.75   Fasti Praetorii ab A.V. DLXXXVIII ad A.V. DCCX. (Wehrmann, Petrus.) Berolini, 1875.

AH 7808.75.2   Fasti Praetorii ad A.V. DLXXXVII ad A.V. DCCX. (Hölzl, M.) Lipsiae, 1876.

AH 7808.75.3   Fasti Praetorii inde ab Octaviani imperii singularis intro usque ad Hadriani Exitum. (Levison, Hans.) Vratislaviae, 1892.

AH 7808.45   Fasti Romani, the civil and literary chronology of Rome and Constantinople. v.2. (Clinton, Henry Fynes.) Oxford, 1845.

AH 7239.20   Fasti triumphales populi Romani. v.1-2. (Pais, Ettore.) Roma, 1920.

AH 4807.44   Fastiattici in quibus Archantum. (Corsine, E.) Florentiae, 1744. 4v.

AH 7806.35   Fastorum Romanorum formula post consulatum. (Nagel, J.A.M.) Altorfii, 1635.

AH 7808.57   Fastorum Romanorum Specimen. (Simon, Heinrich O.) Berlin, 1857.

AH 3017.55   The fauna of ancient Mesopotamia as represented in art. (Van Buren, Elizabeth D.) Roma, 1939.

AH 7058.78.5   Faure, F. Essai historique sur le préteur romain. Paris, 1878.

AH 3013.888   Les fausses antiquités de l'Assyrie et de la Chaldée. (Menant, J.) Paris, 1888.

AH 7203.13F   Favre, A. Rationalias in pandectas. Lugduni, 1559. 4v.

AH 7808.20F   Fea, Carlo. Frammenti di fasti consolari e trionfali ultimamente scaperti nel faro romano e altrove. Roma, 1820.

AH 4838.89.5   Fedde, F. Über den Fünfkampf der Hellenen. Leipzig, 1889.

AH 842.19   Fegerl, J. Die physikalischen Kenntnisse der Alten. Mähr, 1896.

AH 7169.10   Fehr, M. Beiträge zur römischen Pfandrecht. Upsala, 1910.

AH 7238.94   Feldheeren des Altertums. v. 1-2, 3-5. (Fröhlich, F.) Zürich, 1894. 4v.

AH 4098.85   Feldmann, W. Analecta epigraphica...synoecismorum. Argentorati, 1885.

Author and Title Listing

AH 7479.20	Der Feldrug von Dyrrhachium. (Veith, Georg.) Wien, 1920.
AH 4558.97	Feldzüge Alexanders des Grossen. (Yorck, M.G.) Berlin, 1897.
AH 4479.13	Der Feldzug des Xerxes. Kapitel V. (Obst, E.) Leipzig, 1913.
AH 9610.23	Felice-Guiffrida, G. de. Le guerre servili in Sicilia. Catania, 1911.
AH 8907.13	Fell, R.A.L. Etruria and Rome. Cambridge, Eng., 1924.
AH 4609.30	Fellmann, W. Antigonos Gonatas, König der Makedonen. Inaug. Diss. Würzburg, 1930.
AH 5307.25	Felton, C.C. Athens. n.p., 18- .
AH 4818.67A	Felton, C.C. Greece, ancient and modern. Boston, 1867. 2v.
NEDL AH 4818.67.10	Felton, C.C. Greece, ancient and modern. v.1-2. Boston, 1896.
AH 2103.2	Feminae res republicas. (Paris, P.) Paris, 1891.
AH 4859.17F	La femme. (Notor, G.) Paris, 1901.
AH 859.3	La femme dans l'antiquité et d'après la morale. (Rainneville, Joseph de.) Paris, 1865.
X Cg AH 4859.11	Femme grecque. (Bader, C.) Paris, 1872. 2v.
AH 7859.4.2	La femme romaine. 2. éd. (Bader, Clarisse.) Paris, 1877.
AH 7508.76.7	Les femmes...au temps d'Auguste. 2. éd. (Blaze de Bury, H.) Paris, 1876.
AH 7478.63.8	Les femmes de Jules César. 2. éd. (Gastineau, Benjamin.) Paris, 1865.
AH 7497.21	Les femmes des douze Cesars. (Serviez, J.R. de.) Amsterdam, 1721.
AH 7497.21.4	Les femmes des douze Cesars. 4. éd. (Serviez, J.R. de.) Amsterdam, 1722-24. 3v.
AH 4850.14	Fendius, M. Oratio de Appellationibus panum. Vitebergae, 1549.
AH 7819.55.5	Il fenomeno associativo nel mondo romano. (Robertis, Francesco Maria de.) Napoli, 1955.
AH 3011.3	Fenzi, F. Ricerche per lo Studio dell'antichità Assira. Roma, 1872.
AH 7759.64	Fera, Giovanni. Constantino e il cristianesimo. Milano, 1964.
AH 7518.90	Ferber, Curtius. Utrum metuerit Tiberius Germanicum necne quaeritur. Inaug. Diss. Hamburgi, 1890.
AH 7417.83.3	Ferguson, A. A history of...Roman republic. Dublin, 1783. 3v.
AH 7417.83	Ferguson, A. History of...Roman republic. London, 1783. 3v.
AH 7417.83.11	Ferguson, A. History of...Roman republic. London, 1825.
NEDL AH 7417.83.9	Ferguson, A. History of...Roman republic. Philadelphia, 1811. 3v.
NEDL AH 7417.83.13	Ferguson, A. History of...Roman republic. Philadelphia, 1830.
NEDL AH 7417.83.5A	Ferguson, A. A history of...Roman republic. 1. American ed. Philadelphia, 1805. 3v.
NEDL AH 7417.83.14	Ferguson, A. A history of the progress and termination of the Roman republic. N.Y., 1836.
NEDL AH 7417.83.15	Ferguson, A. A history of the progress and termination of the Roman republic. N.Y., 1841.
NEDL AH 7417.83.17	Ferguson, A. History of the progress and termination of the Roman republic. N.Y., 1852.
AH 4819.73	Ferguson, John. The heritage of Hellenism. 1st American ed. N.Y., 1973.
AH 845.10	Ferguson, John. Moral values in the ancient world. London, 1958.
AH 4809.32A	Ferguson, W.S. Athenian tribal cycles in the Hellenistic age. Cambridge, 1932.
AH 4039.13A	Ferguson, W.S. Greek imperialism. Boston, 1913.
AH 4039.13.3	Ferguson, W.S. Greek imperialism. London, 1913.
AH 4809.06	Ferguson, W.S. The priests of Asklepios; a new method of dating Athenian archons. Berkeley, 1906.
AH 5303.15	Ferguson, William S. The Athenian secretaries. Photoreproduction. N.Y., 1898.
AH 4109.32.5	Ferguson, William S. Athenian war finance. Boston, 1932.
AH 5310.5A	Ferguson, William S. Hellenistic Athens. London, 1911.
AH 5303.13	Ferguson, William S. The treasurers of Athena. Cambridge, Mass., 1932.
AH 3980.3	Fergusson, J. Essay on ancient topography of Jerusalem. London, 1847.
AH 3013.28	Fergusson, J. The palaces of Nineveh and Persepolis restored. London, 1851.
AH 8549.77	Ferk, F. Uber Driudismus in Noricum. Graz, 1877.
AH 4819.55.5	Fernandez-Galiano, M. El concepto del hombre en la antigua Grecia. Madrid, 1955.
AH 7279.71.5	Fernau, Joachim. Cäsar lässt Grüssen. München, 1971.
AH 9283.5	Fernique, Emmanuel. De regione Marsorum. Thesis. Lutetiae Parisiorum, 1880.
AH 4459.27	Ferrabino, A. L'impero ateniese. Torino, 1927.
AH 4709.21	Ferrabino, A. Il problema dell'unita nazionale nella Grecia antica I. Firenze, 1921.
AH 7479.45	Ferrabino, Aldo. Cesare. Torino, 1945.
AH 4279.29.5	Ferrabino, Aldo. La dissoluzione della libertà nella Grecia antica. Padova, 1929.
AH 7279.57	Ferrabino, Aldo. L'essenza del romanesimo. Roma, 1957.
AH 8607.11	Ferrabino, Aldo. L'Italia romana. Milano, 1934.
AH 7279.42.10	Ferrabino, Aldo. Nuova storia di Roma. Roma, 1942- 2v.
AH 3179.18	Ferrara, A.J. Nanna-Suen's journey to Nippur. Rome, 1973.
AH 4299.29	Ferrarino, Aldo. La dissoluzione della libertà nella Grecia antica. Padova, 1929.
AH 7148.95	Ferrenbach, V. Die Amici Populi Romani. Strassburg, 1895.
AH 7418.14	Ferrer, V.P. Historia de los dictadores de la republica romana. Cartagena de Indias, 1814.
AH 7188.77	Ferrero, E. Dei libertini dissertazione. Torino, 1877.
AH 7258.78.2F	Ferrero, E. Iscrizioni e ricerche nuove. Torino, 1884.
AH 7258.78F	Ferrero, E. L'ordinamento delle armate romane. Torino, 1878.
AH 7309.14	Ferrero, G. Ancient Rome and modern America. N.Y., 1914.
AH 7309.09	Ferrero, G. Characters and events of Roman history. N.Y., 1909.
AH 7309.09.5	Ferrero, G. Characters and events of Roman history. N.Y., 1922.
AH 7499.12	Ferrero, G. Die Frauen der Caesaren. Stuttgart, 1912.
AH 7309.04	Ferrero, G. Grandeur et décadence de Rome. Paris, 1904. 6v.
NEDL AH 7309.04.1	Ferrero, G. Grandeur et décadence de Rome. Paris, 1907. 5v.
AH 7309.04.2	Ferrero, G. Grandezza e decadenza di Roma. Milano, 1907. 5v.
AH 7309.04.7	Ferrero, G. Greatness and decline of Rome. London, 1909. 5v.
NEDL AH 7309.04.6	Ferrero, G. Greatness and decline of Rome. N.Y., 1908. 4v.
AH 7309.04.8A	Ferrero, G. Greatness and decline of Rome. N.Y., 1909. 5v.
AH 7309.04.4	Ferrero, G. Greatness and decline of Rome. N.Y., 1909-10. 5v.
AH 7309.04.3A	Ferrero, G. Greatness and decline of Rome. v.1-3,5. N.Y., 1907-09. 4v.
AH 7309.04.10	Ferrero, G. Grösse und Niedergang Roms. Stuttgart, 1908-09. 5v.
AH 7309.21A	Ferrero, G. The ruin of the ancient civilization and the triumph of Christianity. N.Y., 1921.
AH 7309.21.3	Ferrero, G. La ruine de la civilisation antique. Paris, 1921.
AH 7499.11A	Ferrero, G. The women of the Caesars. N.Y., 1911.
AH 7279.21.5	Ferrero, Guglielmo. Roma antica. Firenze, 1921-22. 3v.
AH 7279.21.6	Ferrero, Guglielmo. Roma antica. 2. ed. Firenze, 1933. 3v.
AH 7279.18	Ferrero, Guglielmo. Short history of Rome. N.Y., 1918-19. 2v.
AH 816.72F	Ferretti, G.B. Musae lapidariae antiquarum. Veronae, 1672.
AH 7137.18.5	Ferriere, M.C.J. The history of the Roman or civil law. London, 1724.
AH 4844.8	Feste pubbliche e private nei documenti greci. (Vandoni, Mariangela.) Milano, 1964.
AH 4308.69	Festrede. (Curtius, Ernst.) Berlin, 1869.
Eg 299.68	Festschrift für Siegfried Schott zu seinem 70. Geburtstag am 20. August 1967. Wiesbaden, 1968.
AH 4238.72	Festungen und Festungskrieg der Griechen. (Stettin, Prussia.) Stettin, 1872.
AH 4523.10	Der Festungskrieg vor Syrakus in den Jahren 414-413 v.C. Inaug. Diss. (Odermann, E.) Leipzig, 1927.
AH 7844.11	La fete des kalendes de janvier dans l'Empire romain. (Meslin, Michel.) Bruxelles, 1970.
Eg 879.31.5	Les fêtes du dieu Min. Thèse. (Gauthier, Henri.) Le Caire, 1931. 2 pam.
AH 4828.01	Fetes et courtisanes. (Chaussard, J.B.) Paris, 1801. 4v.
AH 4828.01.4	Fetes et courtisanes. 4. éd. (Chaussard, J.B.) Paris, 1821. 4v.
AH 7148.93	Les fétiaux du peuple romain. (Roy, C.) Poitiers, 1893.
Eg 885.967	Feucht-Putz, Erika. Die königlichen Pektorale; Motive, Sinngehalt und Zweck. Inaug. Diss. Bamberg, 1967.
Eg 885.971F	Feucht-Putz, Erika. Pektorale nichtköniglicher Personen. Wiesbaden, 1971.
AH 3961.5	Feuerlein, J.J. Dissertatio...de Christian orum migratione in Oppidum Pellam. Jenae, 1694.
AH 7708.74	Feugère, A.C. C. Cilnius Maecenas G. Octaviano Augusto ad adipiscendum gerendumque principatum quantum profuerit. Thesis. Paris, 1874.
AH 3936.9	Février, J.G. Essai sur l'histoire politique et economique de Palmyre. Paris, 1931.
AH 3936.9.5	Février, J.G. Essai sur l'histoire politique et economique de Palmyre. Thèse. Paris, 1931.
AH 3936.9.7	Février, J.G. La religion des Palmyrénies. Thèse. Paris, 1931.
AH 861.7F	Feydeau, E. Histoire des usages funèbres. Paris, 1856. 2v.
AH 238.88	Fickelscherer, M. Kriegswesen der Alten. Leipzig, 1888.
AH 4859.7	Fickler, C.B.A. Griechischen Frauen. Heidelberg, 1848.
AH 4938.43	Fiedler, F. Geographie und Geschichte von Altgriechenland. Leipzig, 1843.
AH 7278.39.9	Fiedler, F.A.M. Geschichte der Römer. 2. Aufl. Leipzig, 1854.
AH 7278.39.7	Fiedler, F.A.M. Geschichte des römischen Staates. Leipzig, 1839.
AH 7238.82.5	Fiegel, M. Historia legionis III. Augustae. Inaug. Diss. Berolini, 1882.
AH 4029.71	The fifth century B.C. (Lewis, Naphtali.) Toronto, 1971.
AH 7848.2	Figrelills, E. De statius illustrium Romanorum. v.1-2. Holmiae, 1656.
AH 3059.7.10	Figurines from Seleucia on the Tigris. (Van Ingen, W.) Ann Arbor, 1939.
Eg 909.65.5	Fikhman, Itskhok. Egipet na rubezhe dvukh epokh. Moskva, 1965.
AH 8617.7	Il filadelfos de Giovanni Gemelli. (Tulelli, E.) Napoli, 1882.
AH 939.12	Filek, E. von Wittinghausen. Die geographischen Vorstellungen in Altertum. Wien, 1912.
AH 8548.141	Filip, Jan. Celtic civilization and its heritage. Prague, 1960.
AH 8548.141.5	Filip, Jan. Keltská civilisace a její dědictví. Praha, 1959.
AH 6110.19	Filippo il Macedone. (Momigliano, A.) Firenze, 1934.
AH 4498.73	Filleul, E. Siècle der Périclès. Paris, 1873. 2v.
AH 4038.54.7	Filon, A. Histoire de la démocratie athénienne. Paris, 1854.
AH 199.58	La filosofía del clericho in la antigüedad cristiana. 2. ed. (Kuri Breña, Daniel.) Mexico, 1958.
AH 8355.2	Filow, B. Die Legionen der Provinz Moesia. Leipzig, 1906.
AH 4410.37	Les fils de Minos. (Harrel-Courtès, Henry.) Paris, 1967.
AH 4409.09	Fimmen, D. Zeit und Dauer der kretisch-mykenischen Kultur. Leipzig, 1909.
AH 4539.62	La fin de la démocratie athénienne. (Mossé, C.) Paris, 1962.
AH 7659.31.5	La fin du monde antique et le début du moyen âge. (Lot, Ferdinand.) Paris, 1951.
Eg 509.18	La fin du moyen empire égyptien. v.1-2. (Weill, Raymond.) Paris, 1918.
AH 8913.34	La fin du mystère étrusque; les origines, la langue et la vie des Étrusques. (Mayani, Zecharia.) Paris, 1970.
AH 7888.95	La fin d'un peuple. (Vanlaer, M.) Paris, 1895. 2v.
VAH 842.50.2	Finácsy, Ernö. Az ókori newelés törteneti. 2. kiad. Budapest, 1922.
Eg 709.05	Les finances de l'Égypte sous les Lagides. (Maspéro, Henri.) Paris, 1905.
AH 4109.09	Les finances des cités grecques. (Francotte, H.) Liège, 1909.
AH 4909.07	Finanzen und Monopole in Griechenland. (Riezler, Kurt.) Berlin, 1907.
NEDL AH 930.7.3	Findlay, Alexander G. A classical atlas, to illustrate ancient geography. London, 1854.
NEDL AH 930.7.6	Findlay, Alexander G. A classical atlas, to illustrate ancient geography. N.Y., 1849.
NEDL AH 930.7.5	Findlay, Alexander G. A classical atlas, to illustrate ancient geography. N.Y., 185-?
AH 4729.05	La fine della Grecia antica. (Barbagallo, C.) Bari, 1905.

Author and Title Listing

Author and Title Listing

AH 7279.23.10 Frank, Tenney. A history of Rome. N.Y., 1928.
AH 7279.23.4 Frank, Tenney. A history of Rome. N.Y., 1931.
AH 7279.23.5 Frank, Tenney. A history of Rome. N.Y., 1933.
AH 7489.14 Frank, Tenny. Roman imperialism. N.Y., 1914.
Eg 879.17.5 Frank-Kamenetskii, I.G. Pamiatniki egipetskoi religii v fivanskii period. Moskva, 1917- 2v.
AH 5610.20 Franke, Peter R. Alt-Epirus und des Königtum der Molosser. Kallmünz, 1954.
AH 7162.17 Franke, W. Commentar über den Paudie de Heeredetatis Petitione. Göttingen, 1864.
AH 3160.20 Frankena, R. Takultu. Leiden, 1954.
Eg 879.48.5 Frankfort, Henri. Ancient Egyptian religion. N.Y., 1961.
AH 1819.51 Frankfort, Henri. The birth of civilization in the Near East. Bloomington, 1951.
AH 1819.51.2 Frankfort, Henri. The birth of civilization in the Near East. Bloomington, 1954.
AH 1819.51.1 Frankfort, Henri. The birth of civilization in the Near East. London, 1951.
AH 3017.8.1 Frankfort, Henri. Cylinder seals. Furnborough, 1965.
AH 3014.23F Frankfort, Henri. The Gimilsin temple and the palace of the rulers at Tell Asmar. Chicago, 1940.
AH 3016.35F Frankfort, Henri. More sculpture from the Diyala region. Chicago, 1943.
AH 3016.30 Frankfort, Henri. Sculpture of the third millennium B.C. from Tell Asmar and Khafajah. Chicago, 1939.
AH 7448.83 Frantz, Johann. Die Kriege der Scipionen in Spanien. München, 1883.
AH 9.56 Franz Joseph Dölger. (Klauser, Theodor.) Münster, 1956.
AH 7409.60 Franzero, A.M. The life and times of Tarquin the Etruscan. London, 1960.
AH 7549.54 Franzero, Charles M. The life and times of Nero. London, 1954.
AH 7519.47 Franzero, Charles M. The memoirs of Pontius Pilate. London, 1947.
AH 5138.14 Fraser, P.M. The Rhodian Peraen and island. London, 1954.
Eg 971.7.25 Fraser, Peter Marshall. Ptolemaic Alexandria. Oxford, 1972. 3v.
AH 859.8 Die Frau in der antiken Welt und im Urchristentum. (Leipoldt, J.) Gütersloh, 1962.
AH 859.9 Die Frau in Hellas und Rom. (Zinserling, Verena.) Stuttgart, 1972.
Eg 845.10 Die Frau in ptolemäisch-kaiserlicher Ägypter. (Bingmann, Lea.) Bonn, 1939.
AH 7499.12 Die Frauen der Caesaren. (Ferrero, G.) Stuttgart, 1912.
AH 4859.9 Frauen des griechischen Alterthums. (Mähly, J.A.) Basel, 1853.
AH 3187.16 Frauenbriefe über Religion, Politik und Privatleben in Mari. (Römer, Willem H.P.) Kevelaer, 1971.
AH 4859.13 Frauenemancipation in Athen. (Bruns, Ivo.) Kiliae, 1900.
AH 4959.30 Frazer, James G. Graecia antiqua. London, 1930.
AH 4959.00A Frazer, James G. Pausanias and other Greek sketches. London, 1900.
AH 4959.00.2 Frazer, James G. Studies in Greek scenery, legend and history, selected from his commentary on Pausanias. London, 1919.
AH 4959.00.7 Frazer, James G. Sur les traces de Pausanias a travers la Grèce ancienne. Paris, 1923.
Htn AH 275.39F* Freculphus. Chronicorum. Cologne, 1539.
AH 7189.25.5 Freedmen in the early Roman Empire. (Duff, Arnold Mackay.) Cambridge, 1958.
AH 7189.25.2 Freedmen in the early Roman Empire. (Duff, Arnold Mackay.) Oxford, 1928.
AH 4819.66.5 Freedom in Greek life and thought. (Pohlenz, Max.) Dordrecht, 1966.
AH 1819.61A Freedom in the ancient world. 1. ed. (Muller, H.J.) N.Y., 1961.
AH 7159.40 Freedom of speech in the Roman republic. Thesis. (Robinson, L.) Baltimore, 1940.
AH 4038.63A Freeman, E.A. History of federal government. London, 1863.
AH 4038.63.2 Freeman, E.A. History of federal government. 2. ed. London, 1893.
AH 9607.13A Freeman, E.A. History of Sicily from earliest times. Oxford, 1891. 4v.
AH 9607.15A Freeman, E.A. Story of Sicily, Phoenician, Greek and Roman. N.Y., 1892.
AH 7799.04A Freeman, E.A. Western Europe in the fifth century. London, 1904.
AH 4819.52 Freeman, K. God, man and state. London, 1952.
AH 4299.50 Freeman, K. Greek city-states. London, 1950.
AH 4299.50.5 Freeman, K. Greek city-states. 1. ed. N.Y., 1950.
AH 4159.46 Freeman, Kathleen. The murder of Herodes and other trials from the Athenian law courts. London, 1946.
AH 4842.39 Freeman, Kenneth John. Schools of Hellas. London, 1907.
AH 4842.39.1 Freeman, Kenneth John. Schools of Hellas. London, 1908.
AH 4842.39.5 Freeman, Kenneth John. Schools of Hellas. N.Y., 1969.
AH 4842.39.1.2 Freeman, Kenneth John. Schools of Hellas. 2. ed. London, 1912.
AH 4842.39.2 Freeman, Kenneth John. Schools of Hellas. 3. ed. London, 1922.
AH 7776.81 Freher, Marquard. Sapphirus Constantii imp. Aug. exposita anno 1602. Heidelbergae, 1681.
AH 7079.67 Frei-Stolba, Regula. Untersuchungen zur den Wahlen in der römischen Kaiserzeit. Zürich, 1967.
AH 3132.5 Freibrief Nebukadnezars I. (Hilprecht, H.V.) Leipzig, 1883.
AH 7189.67 Freigelassene und Sklaven im Dienst der römischen Kaiser. (Chantraine, Heinrich.) Wiesbaden, 1967.
AH 7189.66.5 Freigelassene und Sklaven in der staatlichen Finanzverwaltung der römischen Kaeserzeit von Augustus bis Diokletian. (Wachtel, Klaus.) Berlin, 1966.
AH 4819.68.12 Freiheit und Freundschaft in Hellas. 2. Aufl. (Scheliha, Renata von.) Amsterdam, 1968.
AH 188.88 Der Freiheitsprozess im klassischen Altertum. (Maschke, R.) Berlin, 1888.
AH 7469.26 Der Fremdenverkehr in Rom zur Zeit Ciceros. Inaug. Diss. (Groener, Franz.) Bonn, 1926.
AH 4889.64 French, A. The growth of the Athenian economy. London, 1964.
AH 7009.57 French Bibliographic Digest. History III. Roman history. N.Y., 1957.
AH 8207.35 Frere, Sheppard. Britannia; a history of Roman Britain. Cambridge, 1967.
AH 277.96 Fréret, N. Oeuvres complètes. Paris, 1796. 20v.
AH 807.28.5 Fréret, Nicolas. Défense de la chronologie. Paris, 1758.
Eg 139.12 Frese, Benedict. Ocherki greko-egipetskago prava. Iaroslavl', 1912.

AH 3159.25 Fresh light from the ancient monuments. 2d ed. (Sayce, A.H.) London, 1884.
AH 7449.14 Freshfield, D.w. Hannibal once more. London, 1914.
AH 2008.5 Fresnel, F. Lettres sur l'histoire des Arabes. Paris, 1836.
AH 7138.54 Fresquet, R. Traité élémentaire de droit romain. Paris, 1854. 2v.
AH 3757.9 Fressl, J. Skythen-Saken. München, 1886.
AH 9777.8 Freudensprung, S. Commentatio Jornande sive Jordane libellorum natalibus. Monaci, 1837.
AH 7178.83 Freund, F. Die gesetzlichen Beschränkungen. Berlin, 1883.
AH 4498.87.3 Frey, Karl. Leben des Perikles. Bern, 1887.
AH 7518.70 Freytag, L. Tiberius und Tacitus. Berlin, 1870.
AH 5753.9 Frick, C. Ephoris Spartanis. Gottingae, 1872.
AH 8549.10 Frick, J.G. Commentatio de Druidis. Ulmae, 1744.
AH 8549.5 Frick, J.G. De druidis occidentalium popularum philosophis. Ulmae, 1731.
AH 4484.5 Frick, Otto. Plataeische Weihgeschenk. Leipzig, 1859.
AH 8858.7 Fricke, Karl. Die Hellenen in Campanien. Hildesheim, 1873.
AH 5343.2 Frickenhaus, A. Athens Mauern. Bonn, 1905.
AH 7448.74.4 Fried, F. Uber die Schlacht bei Cannä. Leipzig, 1898.
AH 7448.98.10 Fried, Friedrich. Uber Die schlacht bei Cannä. Inaug. Diss. Leipzig, 1898.
AH 4049.37 Friedel, H. Untersuchungen zum Tyrannenmord in Gesetzgebung und Volksmeinung der Griechen. Inaug. Diss. Würzburg, 1937.
AH 819.36.27 Friedell, Egon. Kulturgeschichte Ägyptens und des alten Orients. 3. Aufl. München, 1951.
AH 819.36.25 Friedell, Egon. Kulturgeschichte des Altertums. Zürich, 1936-
AH 4819.49.5 Friedell, Egon. Kulturgeschichte Griechenlands. München, 1949.
AH 4499.59 Die Friedenspolitik des Perikles. (Dienelt, Karl.) Wien, 1959.
AH 4499.19 Die Friedenspolitik des Perikles. (Schulte-Vaërting, H.) München, 1919.
AH 7838.72 Friedlaender, L. De certamine cercensi diversio appellato. Regimonti, 1872.
AH 7918.66 Friedlaender, L. De pretiis frumentis apud Romanos. Regimonti, 1866.
AH 7828.59 Friedlaender, L. Dissertatio de appellatione doninis. Regimonti Borussorum, 1859.
AH 7908.74.9 Friedlaender, L. Dissertatio de mercatura Romanorum. Regimonti Prussorum, 1874.
AH 7818.65.6 Friedlaender, Ludwig. Darstellungen aus der Sittengeschichte Roms. v.1, 4. Aufl; v.2, 3. Aufl. Leipzig, 1873-1874. 2v.
AH 7818.65 Friedlaender, Ludwig. Darstellungen aus der Sittengeschichte Roms. v.2-3. Leipzig, 1864-1871. 2v.
AH 7818.65.2 Friedlaender, Ludwig. Darstellungen aus der Sittengeschichte Roms. 2. Aufl. Leipzig, 1865-1867. 2v.
AH 7818.65.3 Friedlaender, Ludwig. Darstellungen aus der Sittengeschichte Roms. 3. Aufl. Leipzig, 1869.
AH 7818.65.9 Friedlaender, Ludwig. Darstellungen aus der Sittengeschichte Roms. 6. Aufl. Leipzig, 1888. 3v.
AH 7818.65.11 Friedlaender, Ludwig. Darstellungen aus der Sittengeschichte Roms. 7. Aufl. Leipzig, 1901. 2v.
AH 7818.65.13 Friedlaender, Ludwig. Darstellungen aus der Sittengeschichte Roms. 8. Aufl. Leipzig, 1910. 4v.
AH 7818.65.15 Friedlaender, Ludwig. Darstellungen aus der Sittengeschichte Roms. 9.-10. Aufl. Leipzig, 1919. 4v.
AH 7818.65.16 Friedlaender, Ludwig. Darstellungen aus der Sittengeschichte Roms. 10. Aufl. Aalen, 1964. 4v.
NEDL AH 7818.65.19A Friedlaender, Ludwig. Moeurs romaines du règne d'Auguste. Paris, 1865. 4v.
AH 7818.65.17 Friedlaender, Ludwig. Roman life and manners. London, 190-. 4v.
AH 7818.65.18 Friedlaender, Ludwig. Roman life and manners under the early empire. N.Y., 1968. 4v.
AH 7818.65.27 Friedlaender, Ludwig. Town life in ancient Italy. Boston, 1902.
AH 7818.65.23 Friedlaender, Ludwig. Vida íntima de los Romanos. Primera version española. Barcelona, 1876.
AH 938.87.2 Friedrich, R. Begriffsbestimmung des Orbis terearum. Leipzig, 1887.
AH 8073.6 Friedrich, T. Biographie des Barkiden Mago. Wien, 1880.
AH 2807.5 La Frigia. (Lauria, G.A.) Naples, 1874.
AH 4139.49 Frisch, Hortvig. Might and right in antiquity. København, 1949.
AH 4309.67 Fritz, Kurt von. Die griechische Geschichtsschreibung. Text und notes. Berlin, 1967- 2v.
AH 4202.7 Fritzsche, F.V. De sortitione judicum. Lipsiae, 1835.
AH 5386.7 Fritzsche, G. Geschichte Plätääs. Bautzen, 1898.
AH 7468.82 Fritzsche, Hermann. Die sulianische Gesetzgebung. Essen, 1882.
AH 7448.84 Fröhlich, F. Die Bedeutung des zweiten punischen Krieges. Leipzig, 1884.
AH 7238.94 Fröhlich, F. Feldheeren des Altertums. v. 1-2, 3-5. Zürich, 1894. 4v.
AH 8533.5 Fröhner, W. Scolies latines relatives à l'histoire...de Marseille. Paris, 1891.
AH 908.66 Frohberger, H. De opificum apud veteres Graecas condicione dissertatio. Grimae, 1866.
AH 3963.7 Frohnmeyer. Bilder Atlas zur Bibelkunde. Stuttgart, 1905.
AH 4043.5.20 Frolov, Eduard D. Grecheskie tirany IV v. do n.e. Leningrad, 1972.
AH 309.67.5 Frolov, Eduard D. Russkaia istoriografiia antichnosti do serediny XIX v. Leningrad, 1967.
AH 4459.64 Frolov, Eduard Davidovich. Sotsial'no-politicheskaia bor'ba v Afinakh v kontse V veka do n.e. Leningrad, 1964.
AH 29.56 From Alexander to Constantine. (Barker, Ernest.) Oxford, 1956.
Eg 958.79 From Egypt to Palestine. (Bartlett, S.C.) N.Y., 1879.
Eg 879.34 From fetish to God in ancient Egypt. (Budge, Ernest Alfred Wallis.) London, 1934.
AH 4410.31.5 From Mycenae to Homer. (Webster, Thomas Bertram Lonsdale.) N.Y., 1964.
AH 4410.31.7 From Mycenae to Homer. 2. ed. (Webster, Thomas Bertram Lonsdale.) London, 1964.
AH 4459.17 From Pericles to Philip. (Glover, Terrot R.) London, 1917.
AH 4459.17.5 From Pericles to Philip. (Glover, Terrot R.) N.Y., 1917.
AH 4449.68 From Solon to Socrates. (Ehrenberg, Victor.) London, 1968.
AH 4449.68.2 From Solon to Socrates. 2. ed. (Ehrenberg, Victor.) London, 1973.

Author and Title Listing

Author and Title Listing

AH 7099.63   Ganghoffer, Roland. L'evolution des institutions municipales en Occident et en Orient au Bas-Empire. Thèse. Paris, 1963.

AH 7201.7   Gans, E. Scholien zum Gajus. Berlin, 1821.

AH 7138.27   Gans, E. System des römischen Civilrechts. Berlin, 1827.

AH 3966.14   Gans, J. Kĕnaän nach der Stammeintheilung. Paderborn, 1843.

AH 7479.10.5   Gans, Maximilian E. Studien zu Schlacht bei Pharsalus. Lundenberg, 1910.

AH 8536.5   Ganter, F.L. Cäsars fahrt nach Britannien. Düsseldorf, 1914.

AH 4138.94   Gantzer, P. Verfassungs- und Gesetzevision in Athen. Halle, 1894.

AH 7899.51   García-Badell, Gabriel. La agricultura en la Roma. Madrid, 1951.

AH 3160.21   García de la Fuente, Oligario. Los dioses y el pecado en Babilonia. El Escorial, 1961.

AH 9658.5   García y Bellido, Antonio. Las colonias romanas de Hispania. Madrid, 1959.

AH 9661.2   García y Bellido, Antonio. Las España del siglo primero de nustra era. Madrid, 1947.

Eg 1309.32   Gardiner, A.H. The Astarte papyrus. London, 1932.

Eg 1309.11   Gardiner, A.H. Egyptian hieratic texts. Leipzig, 1911-

Eg 1309.31PFA   Gardiner, A.H. The library of A. Chester Beatty. London, 1931.

Eg 1309.55F   Gardiner, A.H. The Ramesseum papyri. Oxford, 1955.

Eg 459.61   Gardiner, Alan. Egypt of the pharaohs. Oxford, 1961.

Eg 879.35   Gardiner, Alan H. The attitude of the ancient Egyptians to death and the dead. Cambridge, Eng., 1935.

Eg 602.15   Gardiner, Alan H. The Kadesh inscriptions of Ramesses II. Oxford, 1960.

Eg 602.14   Gardiner, Alan H. Ramesside administrative documents. London, 1940.

Eg 847.11F   Gardiner, Alan Henderson. Catalogue des caractères d'impression hiéroglyphiques égyptiens. Bruxelles, 1928.

AH 839.30   Gardiner, Edward Norman. Athletics of the ancient world. Oxford, 1930.

AH 839.30.1   Gardiner, Edward Norman. Athletics of the ancient world. Oxford, 1971.

AH 4839.10   Gardiner, Edward Norman. Greek athletic sport. London, 1910.

AH 4839.10.1   Gardiner, Edward Norman. Greek athletic sports and festivals. London, 1973.

AH 4818.95.5   Gardner, P. A manual of Greek antiquities. Books 1-5. N.Y., 1895.

AH 4298.92.11   Gardner, P. New chapters in Greek history. London, 1892.

AH 4959.08A   Gardner, W.A. In Greece with the classics. Boston, 1908.

AH 7508.91   Gardthausen, V. Augustus und seine Zeit. Leipzig, 1891. 2v.

AH 8909.2   Gardthausen, V. Mastarna öder Servius Tullius. Leipzig, 1882.

AH 3005.15   Garelli, Paul. L'assyriologie. Paris, 1964.

AH 1279.69   Garelli, Paul. Le Proche-Orient asiatique. Paris, 1969.

AH 239.72   Garlan, Yvon. La guerre dans l'antiquité. Paris, 1972.

Eg 862.5   Garland, H. Ancient Egyptian metallurgy. London, 1927.

AH 7448.98.5   Garmendia, J.I. Estudios históricos y militares sobre las compañas de Anibal. Buenos Aires, 1898.

AH 8532.5   La garnison romaine de Lyon. (Fabia, Philippe.) Lyon, 1918.

Eg 870.1   Garnot, J. St. F. Religions égyptiennes antiques; bibliographie analytique. Paris, 1952.

Eg 879.48   Garnot, J.S.F. La vie religieuse dans l'ancienne Égypte. 1. éd. Paris, 1948.

Eg 819.59   Garnot, Jean Sainte F. Aspects de l'Égypte antique. Cairo, 1959.

AH 7229.70.5   Garnsey, Peter. Social status and legal privilege in the Roman Empire. Oxford, 1970.

AH 7299.04   Garofalo, F.P. Studi storici. Noto, 1904.

AH 5610.6.2   Garouphalias, Petros Euagelov. Pyrros, ho Basilias tès Epeirov. 2. ed. Athēnai, 1972.

AH 7478.81.15   Garrido, Luiz. L'histoire romaine au septième siècle, 622-677. Lisbonne, 1881.

Eg 855.3   Garry, Thomas G. Egypt. London, 1931.

AH 7138.88   Garsonnet, E. Textes de droit romain. Paris, 1888.

AH 7609.50   Garzetti, A. Nerva. Roma, 1950.

AH 7489.74   Garzetti, Albino. From Tiberius to the Antoninos. London, 1974.

AH 7469.54.10   Garzetti, Albino. Verso il principato. Milano, 1954.

AH 7488.43   Garzetti, G.B. Della condizione di Roma, d'Italia. Capologo, 1843. 5v.

AH 7488.42   Garzetti, G.B. Römische Geschichte von den Unruhen. Landshut, 1842.

AH 8003.1   Gascou, Jacques. La politique municipale de l'empire romain en Afrique proconsulaire de Trajan à Septime-Sévère. Rome, 1972.

Eg 1029.25   Gaskell, G.A. Egyptian scriptures interpreted through the language of symbolism. London, 1925.

AH 4839.05   Gaspar, C. Olympia. Paris, 1905.

AH 7478.63.8   Gastineau, Benjamin. Les femmes de Jules César. 2. éd. Paris, 1865.

Eg 879.54A   Der Gatt auf der Blume. (Morenz, S.) Ascona, 1954.

AH 9707.5   Gatterer, J.C. Abhandlung von Thracien. Göttingen, 1800.

AH 7469.09   Gatti, Giuseppe. Lamina di bronzo con iscrizione...guerra dei socii italici. Roma, 1909.

AH 39.67   Gaudement, Jean. Institutions de l'antiquité. Paris, 1967.

AH 39.71.5   Gaudemet, Jean. Précis des institutions de l'antiquité. Paris, 1971. 2v.

AH 8913.32   Gaudio, Attilio. Les Étrusques. Une civilisation retrouvée. Verviers, 1969.

AH 3013.8   Gaugengigl, I. Erklärung der König Ludwig's Inschriften in der Münchner Glyptothek. München, 1870.

AH 8511.18   La Gaule romaine. (Bordet, Marcel.) Paris, 1971.

AH 8548.125   Gaulle, C. de. Les Celtes au XIX. siècle. Paris, 1903.

AH 8008.9   Les gaulois en Afrique. (Leglay, Marcel.) Bruxelles, 1962.

AH 7798.41   Gaupp, E.T. De occupatione et divisione. Vratislaviae, 1841.

AH 7217.5   Gaupp, E.T. De professoribus et medicis eorumgue. Vratislaviae, 1827.

AH 862.5   Gaupp, W. Sanitätswesen in den Heeren der Alten. Blaubeuren, 1875.

AH 4498.60   Gause, A. Societatis Atheniensis historia. Berolini, 1860.

Eg 879.31.5   Gauthier, Henri. Les fêtes du dieu Min. Thèse. Le Caire, 1931. 2 pam.

AH 9792.7.5   Gautier, E.F. Geiserich, König der Wandalen. Frankfurt am Main, 1934.

AH 9792.7   Gautier, E.F. Genséric, roi des Vandales. Paris, 1932.

AH 939.02.2   Gautier, E.F. Indici oceani pars. Lutetiia, 1902.

AH 7861.13   Gautière, J. De jure manium. Lipsiae, 1671.

Eg 971.9.5   Gayet, A.J. Antinoï et les sepultures de Thaïs et Serapion. Paris, 1902.

Eg 971.9   Gayet, A.J. Fantomes d'Antinoe. Paris, 1904.

AH 3958.5.5   Gaza und die philistäische Küste. (Stark, Karl B.) Jena, 1852.

Htn   AH 4805.36*   Gaze Thessalo. Liber de Mensibus Atticis. Basileae, 1536.

AH 9777.14   The Geats of Beowulf. (Leake, Jane.) Madison, 1967.

AH 867.5   Die Gebärden der Griechen und Römer. (Sittl, C.) Leipzig, 1890.

AH 3155.1   Gebete und Hymnen an Nergal. (Bollenrücher, J.) Leipzig, n.d. 6 pam.

AH 7908.74.5   Gebhardt, E. Studien über das Verpflegungswesen. Dorpat, 1881.

AH 2928.5   Das Gebiet von Heraklea Pontica. (Steinmann, W.) Rostock, 1869.

AH 7408.71   Der Gebrauch der Schrift unter den römischen Königen. (Modestow, B.) Berlin, 1871.

AH 3143.22   Die Geburt der Hochkultur in Ägypten und Mesopotamien. (Fischer, Hugo.) Stuttgart, 1960.

Eg 879.64.5   Die Geburt des Gottkonigs. (Brunner, Hellmut.) Wiesbaden, 1964.

Eg 879.56.5   Die Geburt eines Gottes. (Bleeker, C.J.) Leiden, 1956.

Eg 1159.15   Geburts- und Wochenbettsdarstellungen auf altägyptischen Tempelreliefs. (Weindler, Fritz.) München, 1915.

AH 844.7   Geburtstag im Altertum. (Schmidt, W.) Giessen, 1908.

AH 7278.54.41   Gedächtnisrede auf Theodor Mommsen. (Hirschfeld, O.) Berlin, 1904.

AH 7779.14   Geffcken, J. Kaiser Julianus. Leipzig, 1914.

AH 7158.42   Geib, G. Römische Criminalprocesses. Leipzig, 1842.

AH 4558.48   Geier, S.R. Erziehung und Unterricht Alexanders des Grossen. Halle, 1848.

AH 7809.36   Geiger, Karl. Der römische Kalender und seine Verbesserung durch Julius Caesar. München, 1936.

AH 1818.82.5   Geiger, W. Civilization of the eastern Iranians. London, 1885.

AH 1818.82   Geiger, W. Ostiranische Kultur im Altertum. Erlangen, 1882.

AH 4818.30   Geijer, Erik Gustof. Mores heroicae aetatis apud veteres Graecas et Scandinovas comjsaroti. Upsaliae, 1830.

AH 3963.19   Geikie, J.C. The Holy Land and the Bible. N.Y., 1888. 2v.

AH 9792.7.5   Geiserich, König der Wandalen. (Gautier, E.F.) Frankfurt am Main, 1934.

AH 7198.66.8   Geist des römischen Rechts. (Ihering, R.) Leipzig, 1891. 3v.

AH 7198.66.3   Geist des römischen Rechts. v.1-3. (Ihering, R.) Leipzig, 1866. 4v.

AH 5763.3   Die Geist Spartas. 1. Aufl. (Willing, Karl.) Berlin, 1935.

AH 4499.71.5   Geistesgeschichte der Perikleischen Zeit. (Schachermeyr, Fritz.) Stuttgart, 1971.

AH 7299.38   Der geistige Widerstand gegen Rom. (Fucho, Harold.) Berlin, 1938.

AH 3002.88F   Gelb, I.J. Inscriptions from Alishar and vicinity. Chicago, 1935.

AH 3400.15F   Gelb, Ignace J. Hittite hieroglyphic monuments. Chicago, 1939.

AH 3965.7   Das Geld im Talmud. Diss. (Ejges, Simcha.) Wilna, 1930.

AH 5138.13   Gelder, H. Geschichte der alten Rhodier. Haag, 1900.

AH 2357.4   Gelder, H. van. Galatarum res in Graecia et Asia gestae. Inaug. Diss. Amstelaedami, 1888.

AH 7479.21   Gelzer, Matthias. Cäsar, der Politiker und Staatsmann. Stuttgart, 1921.

AH 7479.21.7   Gelzer, Matthias. Cäsar, der Politiker und Staatsmann. 4. Aufl. München, 1942.

AH 7479.21.9   Gelzer, Matthias. Cäsar, der Politiker und Staatsmann. 6. Aufl. Wiesbaden, 1960.

AH 7479.21.12   Gelzer, Matthias. Caesar, politician and statesman. Cambridge, 1968.

AH 7039.24   Gelzer, Matthias. Gemeindestaat und Reichsstaat in der römischen Geschichte. Frankfurt, 1924.

AH 7299.62   Gelzer, Matthias. Kleine Schriften. Wiesbaden, 1962-64. 3v.

AH 7217.15   Gelzer, Matthias. Die Nobilität der römischen Republik. Leipzig, 1912.

AH 7479.49.2   Gelzer, Matthias. Pompeius. 2. Aufl. München, 1959.

AH 7217.15.5   Gelzer, Matthias. The Roman nobility. Oxford, 1969.

NEDL   AH 7299.44A   Gelzer, Matthias. Vom romanischen Staat. Leipzig, 1944. 2v.

AH 7039.24   Gemeindestaat und Reichsstaat in der römischen Geschichte. (Gelzer, Matthias.) Frankfurt, 1924.

AH 850.5   Gemüse und Salate der Alten. (Schuch, C.T.) Rastatt, 1853.

AH 8403.2   General, civil and military administration. (Peaks, M.B.) Chicago, 1907.

AH 279.30.5   General estoria. pt.1-2. (Alfonso I, king of Castile and Leon.) Madrid, 1930- 2v.

AH 4278.76   General history of Greece. (Cox, George W.) N.Y., 1876.

AH 7278.75   General history of Rome. (Merivale, C.) N.Y., 1875.

AH 4439.52   Generale machen Politik. 1. Aufl. (Lindemann, H.) Bonn, 1952.

AH 4559.58   The generalship of Alexander the Great. (Fuller, J.F.) London, 1958.

AH 7009.11   La genesi degli annales Maximi. (Parducci, P.) Pisa, 1911.

NEDL   AH 818.82.10   Genesi dell'incivilimento. (Aguglia, S.) Napoli, 1882.

AH 7419.63   Genesi e sviluppi dell'imperialismo. (Pieri, Piero.) Torino, 1963.

AH 8542.2   Genève et la colonie de Vienne. (Morel, Charles.) Genève, 1888.

AH 818.62   Génie des civilisations. (Trottet, J.P.) Paris, 1862. 2v.

AH 7819.63   Le génie latin. (Bardon, H.) Bruxelles, 1963.

AH 3051.5F   Genouillac, H. de. Premières recherches archéologiques à Kich. Paris, 1924.

AH 3002.115F   Genouillac, Henri de. Tablettes de Dréhem. Paris, 1911.

AH 7118.2   La gens in Roma. (Ruggiero, E. de) Napoli, 1872.

AH 9792.6A   Genseric, king of the Vandals. (Bigelow, Poultney.) N.Y., 1918.

AH 9792.7   Genséric, roi des Vandales. (Gautier, E.F.) Paris, 1932.

AH 8011.2   Genséric ou la conquête vandale. (Martroye, F.) Paris, 1707.

AH 8915.2   Genthe, H.F. Ueber den etruskischen Tauschhandel. Heibronn, 1874.

AH 7078.79   Gentile, I. Le elezioni e il Broglio. Milan, 1879.

AH 8549.167   Genty, Patrice. Etudes sur le celtisme. Paris, 1967.

Author and Title Listing

AH 7114.27 — Genz, Hermann. Das patrische Rom. Berlin, 1878.

AH 7238.74 — Genz, Hermann. Die servianische Centurien-Verfassung. Sorau, 1874. 2 pam.

AH 7458.79 — Genzken, H. De rebus a P. et Cn. Corneliis Scipionibus in Hispania gestis. Diss. inaug. Fribergae, 1879.

AH 938.92 — Geografía antigua comparada. (Villar, J.) Santiago, 1892.

AH 9666.4 — La geografía de la peninsula ibérica. (Alemany y Bolufer, J.) Madrid, 1912.

AH 938.31 — Geographia classica. (Butler, Samuel.) Philadelphia, 1831.

AH 4938.53 — Geographia Graecorum antiquissima Napoleonopoli qualis ab Homero...Thesim proponebat. (Hanriot, Charles.) Pictavorum, 1853.

AH 3716.5 — Geographia sacra. (Bochart, S.) Francofurti, 1681.

AH 939.49 — The geographic background of Greek and Roman history. (Cary, Max.) Oxford, 1949.

AH 8616.6 — Geographical...description of ancient Italy. (Cramer, J.A.) Oxford, 1826. 2v.

AH 2107.5 — Geographical and historical description of Asia Minor. (Cramer, J.A.) Oxford, 1832. 2v.

AH 3966.30F — The geographical and topographical texts of the Old Testament. (Simons, Jan.) Leiden, 1959.

AH 4299.53 — Geographical history in Greek lands. (Myres, John L.) Oxford, 1953.

AH 938.29 — Geographie. v.1-10. (Mannert, K.) Leipzig, 1799-1829. 14v.

AH 8016.2 — Die Geographie Afrikas. (Detlefsen, D.) Berlin, 1908.

AH 937.68 — Geographie ancienne abrégée. (Anville, Jean B.B. d'.) Paris, 1768. 3v.

Eg 938.91 — Géographie ancienne de la Basse-Égypte. (Rougé, J. de.) Paris, 1891.

AH 6116.5 — Géographie ancienne de la Macedoine. (Desdevises-du-dezert.) Paris, 1863.

AH 8516.3 — Géographie de la Gaule d'après la Table de Peutinger. (Desjardins, E.) Paris, 1869.

Eg 938.93 — La géographie de l'Égypte. (Amélineau, Emile.) Paris, 1893.

Eg 939.57 — Géographie de l'Égypte ancienne. pt.1-2. (Montet, Pierre.) Paris, 1957. 2v.

AH 938.16 — Geographie der Griechen und Römer. v.1-3. (Ukert, F.A.) Weimar, 1816-46. 5v.

AH 4937.90F — Geographie des Grècs analysée. (Gossellin, M.) Paris, 1790.

AH 2321.2 — Géographie et l'histoire des pays d'Arzava. (Kinal, F.) Ankara, 1953.

Htn AH 9692.2* — Géographie historique de la Vasconie espagnole. (Blade, J.F.) Auch, 1891.

AH 4938.89 — Geographie und Geschichte des griechisches Altertums. (Lolling, H.G.) Athen? 1889.

AH 4938.43 — Geographie und Geschichte von Altgriechenland. (Fiedler, F.) Leipzig, 1843.

AH 4938.62.5 — Geographie von Griechenland. (Bursian, Konrad.) Leipzig, 1862-72. 2v.

AH 4938.62 — Geographie von Griechenland. v.1-2. (Bursian, Konrad.) Leipzig, 1862. 3v.

Eg 938.57 — Geographische Inschriften. v.1-3. (Brugsch, H.) Leipzig, 1857. 2v.

AH 4938.92 — Geographische Forschungen und Märchen. (Urban, K.) Gütersloh, 1892.

AH 939.12 — Die geographischen Vorstellungen in Altertum. (Filek, E. von Wittinghausen.) Wien, 1912.

AH 4559.24.5 — Geographischer Horizont und Politik bei Alexander der Grossen in den Jahren 330/323. (Endres, Heinrich.) Würzburg, 1924.

AH 939.31.5 — The geography of the Mediterranean region. (Semple, Ellen C.) N.Y., 1937.

Eg 879.70.15 — George, Beate. Zu den altägyptischen Vorstellungen vom Schatten als Seele. Bonn, 1970.

AH 3159.6.9 — George Smith's Chaldaische Genesis. (Smith, George.) Leipzig, 1876.

AH 938.38 — Georgii, L. Alte Geographie. Stuttgart, 1838. 2v.

Htn AH 925.33* — Georgii agricolae medici libri. Parisiis, 1533. 3 pam.

AH 4858.7 — Georgopoulos. Otamos ton ellennon. Tripolei, 1880.

AH 7238.72 — Geppert, P. De tribunis miletum. Berolini, 1872.

Htn AH 255.40* — Geraldi, L.G. De re nautica libellus. Basiliae, 1540.

AH 7114.13 — Gerathewohl, Bernhard. Die Reiter und die Rittercenturien. München, 1886.

Htn AH 4935.45F* — Gerbelius, N. Descriptio Graeciae. Basiliae, 1545.

AH 299.12.2 — Gercke, Alfred. Einleitung in die Altertumswissenschaft. Leipzig, 1910-12. 3v.

AH 299.12 — Gercke, Alfred. Einleitung in die Altertumswissenschaft. Leipzig, 1912-23. 3v.

AH 299.12.5 — Gercke, Alfred. Einleitung in die Altertumswissenschaft. 3. Aufl. Leipzig, 1921-27. 3v.

Eg 981.2 — Geremek, Hanna. Karanis; communsuté rurale. Wrocław, 1969.

AH 4114.18 — Gerhardt, Paul. Die attische Metoikie im vierten Jahrhundert. Inaug. Diss. Königsberg, 1933.

AH 7539.29 — Eine Gerichtsreform des Kaisers Claudius. (Stroux, J.) München, 1929.

NEDL AH 7842.4 — Gerini, G.B. Le dottrine pedagogiche. Torino, 1894.

AH 7163.15 — Gerlach, F. De romanorum conubio. Halis, 1851.

AH 7038.71 — Gerlach, F. Verfassungsgeschichte. Basel, 1871.

AH 7438.72 — Gerlach, F.D. Griechischer Einfluss in Rom. Basel, 1872.

AH 298.41 — Gerlach, F.D. Historische Studien. Hamburg, 1841. 2v.

AH 7468.34.2 — Gerlach, F.D. Marius and Sulla. Basel, 1856.

AH 6110.11 — Gerlach, F.D. Perseus König von Makedonien. Basel, 1857.

AH 7408.53 — Gerlach, F.D. Quellen der altesten römischen Geschichte. Basel, 1853.

AH 7038.42 — Gerlach, F.D. Die römische Censur. Basel, 1842.

AH 408.60 — Gerlach, F.D. Sage und Forschung. Basel, 1860.

AH 7408.51 — Gerlach, F.D. Von den Quellen der ältesten römischen Geschichte. Basel, 1853.

AH 8613.5 — Gerlach, F.D. Zaleukos, Charondas, Pythagoras. Basel, 1858.

AH 9760.1 — The German policy of Augustus: an examination of the archaeological evidence. (Wells, Colin Michael.) Oxford, 1972.

AH 7239.06 — Die Germanen im römischen Dienst. (Bang, Martin.) Berlin, 1906.

AH 7239.06.7 — Die Germanen im römischen Dienst. (Bang, Martin.) Berlin, 1906.

AH 7239.65.5 — Germanen im römischen Dienst im 4. Jahrhundert nach Christus. (Waas, Manfred.) Bonn, 1965.

AH 7769.65 — Germanentum und Spätantike. (Stroheker, Karl Friedrich.) Zürich, 1965.

AH 9765.5 — Germania oeconomica; das Bild der germanischen Wirtschaft bei Caesar und Tacitus. (Wollheim, Günther.) Freiburg, 1958.

AH 9758.8 — Germanische Frühzeit in den Berichten der Antike. (Gutenbrunner, S.) Halle, 1939.

AH 4819.68.5 — Gernet, Louis. Anthropologie de la Grèce antique. Paris, 1968.

AH 4819.17.8 — Gernet, Louis. Recherches sur le développement de la pensée juridique...en Grèce. Thèse. Paris, 1917.

AH 4098.98 — Gertz, M.C. Statog statsforfatninger. Kjøbenhavn, 1898.

AH 7138.73.10 — Gesammelte civilisatische Schriften. (Arndts, L.) Stuttgart, 1873. 3v.

AH 7139.63 — Gesammelte Schriften. (Levy, Ernst.) Köln, 1963. 2v.

AH 7299.05 — Gesammelte Schriften. (Mommsen, Theodor.) Berlin, 1905. 8v.

AH 854.9.2 — Gesamtregister von Eugen Staiger. (Keller, Otto.) Leipzig, 1920.

AH 7479.68 — Gesche, Helga. Die Vergottung Caesars. Kallmünz, 1968.

AH 8657.3 — Geschichte...der Stadt Rom im Altertum. (Gilbert, Otto.) Leipzig, 1883. 3v.

NEDL AH 7652.16 — Geschichte...des Römischen Rechts. (Gibbon, Edward.) Frankfurt, 1800. 13v.

AH 7139.03 — Geschichte...des römischen Rechts. (Kipp, T.) Leipzig, 1903.

AH 7138.24 — Geschichte...römischen Rechts. (Pernice, L.) Halle, 1824.

Eg 279.04 — Geschichte Ägyptens. (Bissing, F.W. von.) Berlin, 1904.

Eg 279.05.15 — Geschichte Ägyptens. (Breasted, James Henry.) Zürich, 1936.

Eg 278.59.4 — Geschichte Aegypten's. (Brugsch, H.) Leipzig, 1877.

AH 4558.33.6 — Geschichte Alexanders des Grossen. (Droysen, J.G.) Berlin, 1917.

AH 3008.57 — Geschichte Assur's und Babel's seit Phiel. (Niebuhr, M.K.N.) Berlin, 1857.

AH 3008.92 — Geschichte Babyloniens und Assyriens. (Winckler, H.) Leipzig, 1892.

AH 3008.82.5 — Geschichte Babyloniens und Assyriens. 2. Aufl. (Mürdter, F.) Stuttgart, 1891.

AH 2011.8 — Geschichte de Familie El-'Abbâs bin 'Abd El-Muttalib. Inaug. Diss. (Jochum, Johannes.) Berlin, 1933.

AH 4938.87.2 — Geschichte der...Erdkunde der Griechen. (Berger, H.) Leipzig, 1887.

AH 4938.87 — Geschichte der...Erdkunde der Griechen. (Berger, H.) Leipzig, 1903.

AH 5138.13 — Geschichte der alten Rhodier. (Gelder, H.) Haag, 1900.

AH 29.50 — Geschichte der alten Welt; Christomathie. (Struve, V.V.) Berlin, 1954-57. 3v.

AH 278.26 — Geschichte der alten Welt. v.1-3. (Schlosser, Friedrich Christoph.) Frankfurt, 1826. 9v.

AH 938.88 — Geschichte der antike Naturwissenschaft. (Günther, S.) Nördlingen, 1888.

AH 1408.56 — Geschichte der Assyrier und Iranier. (Krüger, J.) Frankfurt, 1856.

AH 4538.97 — Geschichte der athenischen...Politik. (Reichenbächer, W.) Halle, 1897.

AH 4843.15 — Geschichte der Aulodik bie den Griechen. (Waldenburg. Gymnasium.) Waldenburg, 1879.

AH 8073.2 — Geschichte der Carthager. (Botticher, J.F.W.) Berlin, 1827.

AH 938.39 — Geschichte der Erd- und Landerabbildungen. (Reinganum, H.) Jena, 1839.

AH 842.9 — Geschichte der Erziehung. (Krause, J.H.) Halle, 1851.

AH 842.34 — Geschichte der Erziehung und des Unterrichts im Alterthume. (Cramer, Friedrich.) Elberfeld, 1832-38. 2v.

AH 7468.01 — Geschichte der gracchischen Unruhen. (Hegewisch, D.H.) Hamburg, 1801.

AH 4278.87 — Geschichte der Griechen. (Jäger, O.E.F.) Gütersloh, 1887.

NEDL AH 4278.68.2 — Geschichte der Griechen bis zur Unterwerfung unter Rom. 2. Aufl. (Stoll, H.W.) Hannover, 1871. 2v.

NEDL AH 278.96 — Geschichte der Griechen und Römen. (Krüger, C.A.) Berlin, 1896.

AH 279.10 — Geschichte der Griechen und Römer. (Schwahn, W.) Berlin, 1910.

AH 338.72 — Geschichte der Griechen und Römer in Biographien. 2. Aufl. (Stoll, H.W.) Leipzig, 1872. 2v.

AH 279.48.15 — Geschichte der griechiesh-römischen Altertums. (Kahrstedt, Ulrich.) München, 1948.

AH 4843.4 — Geschichte der griechischen Musik. (Weitzmann, C.F.) Berlin, 1855.

AH 4109.18.5 — Geschichte der griechischen Staatswirtschaft. (Andreades, Andreas M.) Hildesheim, 1965.

AH 6107.13 — Geschichte der griechischen und makedonischen Staaten. (Niese, B.) Gotha, 1893. 3v.

AH 3357.9 — Geschichte der Gründung...des Hellenischen Staates. (Gottschick, A.F.) Leipzig, 1858.

AH 5138.7 — Geschichte der Insel Rhodus. (Schneiderwirth, J.H.) Heiligenstadt, 1868.

AH 8073.3 — Geschichte der Karthager. (Meltzer, Otto.) Berlin, 1879. 3v.

AH 2357.5 — Geschichte der kleinasiatischen Galater. (Staehelin, Felix.) Basel, 1897.

AH 2357.11.3 — Geschichte der kleinasiatischen Galater. 2. Aufl. (Staehelin, Felix.) Osnabrück, 1973.

NEDL AH 817.95 — Geschichte der Kultur der Menschheit. (Pölitz, K.H.L.) Leipzig, 1795.

AH 845.5.3 — Geschichte der Lustseuche im Alterthume. 3. Aufl. (Rosenbaum, J.) Halle, 1882.

AH 845.5.7 — Geschichte der Lustseuche im Altertume. (Rosenbaum, J.) Berlin, 1904.

AH 2507.7 — Geschichte der Lykier. (Treuber, O.) Stuttgart, 1887.

AH 3657.20 — Geschichte der Meder und Perser. (Prášek, J.V.) Gotha, 1906. 2v.

AH 7203.41 — Geschichte der novellen Justinian's. (Biener, F.A.) Berlin, 1824.

AH 3661.6.1 — Geschichte der Perser und Araber. (Tabari, Muhammed Ibn.) Leyden, 1973.

AH 5610.5 — Geschichte der Pyrrhus. (Schubert, R.) Königsberg, 1894.

AH 7138.88.5 — Geschichte der Quellen...römischen Rechts. (Krüger, Paul.) Leipzig, 1888.

AH 7278.39.9 — Geschichte der Römer. 2. Aufl. (Fiedler, F.A.M.) Leipzig, 1854.

Htn AH 7278.69.2* — Geschichte der Römer bis zum Untergange der Republik. 2. Aufl. (Stoll, H.W.) Hannover, 1871. 2v.

AH 7138.60 — Geschichte der römische Rechte. (Walter, F.) Bonn, 1860. 2v.

AH 7468.25 — Geschichte der römischen Burgerkreige. (Reiff, H.C.) Berlin, 1825.

Author and Title Listing

AH 7489.09   Geschichte der Römischen Kaiser. (Domaszewski, A. von.) Leipzig, 1909. 2v.

AH 7489.09.2   Geschichte der Römischen Kaiser. 2. Aufl. (Domaszewski, A. von.) Leipzig, 1914. 2v.

AH 7238.81   Geschichte der Römischen Kaiserlegionen. (Pfitzner, W.) Leipzig, 1881.

AH 7488.83   Geschichte der Römischen Kaiserzeit. (Schiller, K.H.F.H.) Gotha, 1883. 2v.

AH 7488.83.2   Geschichte der Römischen Kaiserzeit. v.1,pt.1-2. (Schiller, K.H.F.H.) Gotha, 1883. 2v.

AH 7489.24   Geschichte der römischen Kaiserzeit. v.1-2. (Dessau, Hermann.) Berlin, 1924-30. 3v.

AH 7168.26   Geschichte der römischen Privatrechts. v.1,3. (Zimmern, S.W.) Heidelberg, 1826. 2v.

AH 7139.46.2   Geschichte der römischen Rechtswissenschaft. (Schulz, Fritz.) Weimar, 1961.

AH 7418.84   Geschichte der römischen Republik. (Nitzsch, K.W.) Leipzig, 1884.

AH 7038.40   Geschichte der römischen Staatsverfassung. (Göttling, K.) Halle, 1840.

AH 7708.52   Geschichte der s.g. driessig Inrannen. (Hoyns, Georg.) Göttingen, 1852.

AH 7659.28   Geschichte der spätrömischen Reiches I. (Stein, Ernst.) Wien, 1928.

AH 9621.5   Geschichte der Stadt Akragas. (Bindseil, R.) Neustettin, 1882.

AH 9722.7   Die Geschichte der Städte Byzantion und Kalchedon. Inaug. Diss. (Merle, Heinrich.) Kiel, 1916.

AH 8011.3   Geschichte der vandalischen Herrschaft. (Papencordt, F.) Berlin, 1837.

AH 7658.59   Geschichte der Völkerwanderung. (Wietersheim, E. von.) Leipzig, 1859. 4v.

AH 8011.4   Geschichte der Wandalen. (Schmidt, L.) Leipzig, 1901.

AH 9777.7   Geschichte der Westgothen. (Aschbach, J.) Frankfurt, 1827.

AH 9610.11   Geschichte des Agathokles. (Schubert, R.J.W.) Breslau, 1887.

AH 4278.31   Geschichte des alten Griech. (Plass, H.G.) Leipzig, 1831. 3v.

AH 279.29.10   Geschichte des alten Morgenlandes. (Ebeling, Erich.) Berlin, 1929.

AH 1408.95   Geschichte des alten Morgenlandes. (Hommel, Fritz.) Stuttgart, 1895.

AH 1408.95.2   Geschichte des alten Morgenlandes. 2. Aufl. (Hommel, Fritz.) Leipzig, 1898.

AH 1279.50   Geschichte des alten Orients. (Cornelius, F.) Stuttgart, 1950.

AH 408.55   Geschichte des Alterthums. (Duncker, M.) Berlin, 1855. 4v.

AH 278.52.15   Geschichte des Alterthums. (Duncker, M.) Berlin, 1863. 4v.

AH 278.84.3   Geschichte des Alterthums. (Meyer, E.) Stuttgart, 1884. 5v.

AH 278.84.5   Geschichte des Alterthums. v.1-5. (Meyer, E.) Stuttgart, 1907-31. 7v.

AH 278.52.19   Geschichte des Alterthums. 4. Aufl. (Duncker, M.) Leipzig, 1874. 9v.

AH 818.74.3   Geschichte des Altertums. (Doublier, L.) Wien, 1874.

AH 278.84.10   Geschichte des Altertums. 5. Aufl. v.1,3,4. (Meyer, E.) Stuttgart, 1925-26. 4v.

AH 889.09   Geschichte des antike Sozialismus. (Wolf, H.) Gütersloh, 1909.

AH 7188.87   Geschichte des capitis deminutio. (Krüger, H.) Breslau, 1887.

AH 4498.70F   Geschichte des delisch-attischen Bundes. (Köhler, U.) Berlin, 1870.

AH 7138.40.3   Geschichte des griechisch-römischen Rechts. (Zachariä, K.E.) Berlin, 1892.

AH 4238.52   Geschichte des griechischen Kriegswesens. (Rüstow, W.) Aarau, 1852.

AH 4658.36   Geschichte des Hellenismus. (Droysen, J.G.) Hamburg, 1836. 2v.

AH 4658.36.2   Geschichte des Hellenismus. v.1-6. 2. Aufl. (Droysen, J.G.) Gotha, 1877-78. 4v.

AH 4659.01.2   Geschichte des Hellenismus. 2. Aufl. (Kaerst, Julius.) Leipzig, 1917-26. 2v.

AH 4659.01   Geschichte des hellenistischen Zeitalters. (Kaerst, Julius.) Leipzig, 1901. 2v.

AH 7698.84   Geschichte des Kaisers L. Septimius Severus. (Fuchs, C.) Wien, 1884.

AH 7709.09   Geschichte des Kaisers Probus (276-282). (Dannhäuser, Erich.) Jena, 1909.

AH 2907.2   Geschichte des Königreichs Pontos. (Meyer, E.) Leipzig, 1879.

AH 4609.00   Geschichte des Königs Lysimachos. (Hünerwadel, W.) Zürich, 1900.

AH 1279.39   Geschichte des Orients vom Tode Alexanders des Grossen bis zum Einbruch des Islams. (Ebeling, Erich.) Berlin, 1939.

AH 7548.72.7   Geschichte des Römischen Kaisereichs. (Schiller, H.) Berlin, 1872.

AH 7488.80   Geschichte des Römischen Kaiserreiches. (Hertzberg, G.F.) Berlin, 1880.

AH 7628.51   Geschichte des römischen Kaisers Hadrian. (Gregorovius, F.A.) Königsberg, 1851.

AH 7058.78   Geschichte des Römischen Postwesens. (Hudemann, E.E.) Berlin, 1878.

AH 7139.25   Geschichte des römischen Rechts; ein Lehrbuch. (Kübler, Bernhard.) Leipzig, 1925.

AH 7138.84   Geschichte des römischen Rechts. (Baron, J.) Berlin, 1884.

AH 7206.17   Geschichte des römischen Rechts. (Walter, F.) Bonn, 1840.

AH 7138.45   Geschichte des römischen Rechts. 2e Aufl. (Walter, F.) Bonn, 1845.

AH 7278.39.7   Geschichte des römischen Staates. (Fiedler, F.A.M.) Leipzig, 1839.

AH 1808.82   Geschichte des semitischen Altertums in Tabellen. (Floigl, Victor.) Leipzig, 1882.

AH 4415.5   Geschichte des trojanischen Krieges. (Uschold, Johannes N.) Stuttgart, 1836.

AH 7658.95   Geschichte des Untergangs der antiken Welt. v.1-6. Appendix. (Seeck, Otto.) Berlin, 1895. 8v.

AH 7658.95.5   Geschichte des Untergangs der antiken Welt. v.1-6. Appendix 1-6. (Seeck, Otto.) Stuttgart, 1920-23. 12v.

AH 7817.91   Geschichte des Verfalls der Sitten. (Meiners, C.) Wien, 1791.

AH 888.98   Geschichte des Zinfusses. (Billeter, G.) Leipzig, 1898.

AH 4538.40   Geschichte Griechenlandes. (Sievers, G.R.) Kiel, 1840.

AH 4728.66   Geschichte Griechenlands. (Hertzberg, G.F.) Halle, 1866. 3v.

AH 4708.33   Geschichte Griechenlands. (Schorn, W.) Bonn, 1833.

AH 4538.54   Geschichte Griechenlands. v.1-2. (Lachmann, J.H.) Leipzig, 1854.

AH 3657.17.1   Geschichte Irans. (Gutschmid, Alfred von.) Graz, 1973.

AH 7478.65.6   Geschichte Julius Cäsars. (Napoléon III, emperor of the French.) Wien, 1865. 2v.

AH 5410.5   Geschichte Korinths. (Wilisch, E.) Zittau, 1896.

AH 6107.7   Geschichte Macedoniens. (Flathe, L.) Leipzig, 1832. 2v.

AH 1279.70   Geschichte Mittelasiens im Altertum. (Altheim, Franz.) Berlin, 1970.

AH 5386.7   Geschichte Platääs. (Fritzsche, G.) Bautzen, 1898.

AH 7468.34.4   Geschichte Roms. (Drumann, W.) Koenigsberg, 1834. 6v.

AH 7468.81   Geschichte Roms. (Neumann, Carl.) Breslau, 1881.

AH 7278.53.3   Geschichte Roms. (Peter, C.) Halle, 1853. 2v.

AH 7278.53.5   Geschichte Roms. v.1-2; v.3, pt.1-2. 2. Aufl. (Peter, C.) Halle, 1865. 4v.

AH 7468.34.5   Geschichte Roms. v.1-6. (Drumann, W.) Berlin, 1899. 5v.

AH 7278.53.7   Geschichte Roms. 3. Aufl. (Peter, C.) Halle, 1870. 3v.

AH 7278.53.9   Geschichte Roms. 4. Aufl. (Peter, C.) Halle, 1881. 3v.

AH 7708.67   Geschichte Roms von Valerian. (Bernhardt, T.) Berlin, 1867.

AH 9607.9   Geschichte Siciliens in Alterthum. (Holm, A.) Leipzig, 1870. 3v.

AH 8740.3   Geschichte Tarents bis auf seine Unterwerfung unter Rom. (Doehle.) Strassburg, 1877.

AH 5390.5   Geschichte Thebens. (Müller, M.) Leipzig, 1879.

AH 7548.72   Geschichte und Bild von Nero. (Raabe, A.H.) Utrecht, 1872.

X Cg   AH 7038.84   Geschichte und System der römischen Staatverfassung. (Herzog, Ernst.) Leipzig, 1884. 3v.

AH 4164.7   Geschichte und Wesen des Arrabons und der Arrha im griechischen und römischen Recht. (Bergold, Friedrich.) Gernsback, 1923.

AH 6024.9   Geschichte von Delphi. (Hiller von Gaertringen, F.) Stuttgart, 1899.

AH 4278.79   Geschichte von Hellas und Rom. (Hertzberg, G.F.) Berlin, 1879. 2v.

AH 9684.9   Geschichte von Numantia. (Schulten, Adolf.) München, 1933.

AH 2957.7   Geschichte von Troas. (Meyer, E.) Leipzig, 1877.

AH 1409.27.5   Geschichte Vorderasiens und Ägyptens vom 16. Jahrhundert vor Christ bis auf die Neuzeit. (Bilabel, Friedrich.) Heidelberg, 1927.

AH 5157.10   Die Geschichten des aetolischen Landes. (Brandstäter, F.A.) Berlin, 1844.

AH 4298.44.5   Geschichten hellenische Stämme und Städte-Karten. (Müller, K.O.) Breslau, 1844. 4v.

AH 7488.97   Die geschichtliche Literatur...Kaiserzeit. (Peter, H.) Leipzig, 1897.

AH 9758.6   Die Geschichtschreiber der deutschen Vorzeit. (Horkel, J.) Berlin, 1847.

AH 3143.23.3   Gesellschaft und Kultur des alten Mesopotamien. (Klima, Josef.) Prag, 1964.

AH 139.68   Gesellschaft und Recht im griechisch-römischen Altertum. Berlin, 1968- 2v.

AH 8357.2   Gesellschaft und Romanisation in der römischen Provinz Moesia Superior. (Mócsy, András.) Amsterdam, 1970.

AH 7889.26.10   Gesellschaft und Wirtschaft im Römischen Reich. (Rostovtsev, M.I.) Leipzig, 1929. 2v.

AH 4659.41.5   Gesellschafts- und Wirtschaftsgeschichte der hellenistischen Welt. (Rostovtsev, Mikhail Ivanovich.) Darmstadt, 1955-56. 3v.

AH 3151.8   Die Gesetze Hammurabis. (Müller, D.H.) Wien, 1903.

AH 3151.6   Die Gesetze Hammurabis in Urnschrift. (Hammurabi, king of Babylonia.) Leipzig, 1904.

AH 7178.83   Die gesetzlichen Beschränkungen. (Freund, F.) Berlin, 1883.

AH 7188.44   Gessner, Aemilius. De servis Romanorum publicis. Berolini, 1844.

AH 7139.04.5   Die Gesta municipalia. (Hirschfeld, B.) Marburg, 1904.

AH 4339.23   Gestalten aus Hellas. (Pohlenz, M.) München, 1950.

AH 279.49   Gestaltende Kräfte der Antike. (Berve, Helmut.) München, 1949.

AH 279.49.2   Gestaltende Kräfte der Antike. 2. Aufl. (Berve, Helmut.) München, 1966.

AH 7569.11   Gestaltung des römischen Staats...Flairer Vespasian. (Menrad, K.) München, 1911.

AH 2014.6   Der Gestirndienst der alten Araber. (Hommel, Fritz.) München, 1901.

AH 867.10   Der Gestus des Aposkopein. (Jucker, Ines.) Zürich, 1956.

AH 9777.19   Getarum sive Gothorum. (Jordanes.) Stuttgart, 1861.

AH 9777.19.2   Getarum sive Gothorum. 2. ed. (Jordanes.) Stuttgart, 1866.

AH 9777.19.3   Getarum sive Gothorum. 3. ed. (Jordanes.) Reutlingen, 1888.

AH 9777.20   Die Geten und ihre Nachbarn. (Roesler, E.) Wien, 1864.

AH 4858.13   Geurts, Nico. Het huwelijk bij de Griekse en Romeinse moralisten. Proefschrift. Amsterdam, 1928.

AH 843.4   Gevaert, F.A. Mélopée antique. Gand, 1895.

AH 843.3   Gevaert, F.A. La musique de l'antiquité. Gand, 1875. 2v.

AH 4929.01   Gewichte aus Thera. (Lehmann, C.F.) Berlin, 1901.

AH 5657.5   Geyer, F. Topographie...der Insel Euboia. Berlin, 1903.

AH 5657.4   Geyer, F. Topographie...der Insel Euboia. Kirchain, 1902.

AH 7899.39   Ghigi, A. Poultry farming as described by the writers of ancient Rome. Milano, 1939.

AH 4039.70   Ghinatti, Franco. I gruppi politici ateniesi fino alle guerre persiane. Roma, 1970.

AH 7903.6   Giacchero, Marta. Note sull'Editto-calmiere di Diocleziano. Genova, 1962.

AH 7828.85   Giachi, V. Amori e costumi latini. Citta di Castello, 1885.

AH 9633.7   Giacomazzi, Rosaria. Considerazione sopra la storia dei Mamerlini. Messina, 1935.

AH 7448.24   Giani, G.B. Battaglia del Ticino tra Annibale e Scipione. Appendice. Milano, 1824-26.

AH 279.54   Giannelli, G. Le grandi correnti della storia antica. Milano, 1954.

AH 7419.37   Giannelli, Giulio. La repubblica romana. Milano, 1937.

AH 4479.24   Giannelli, Giulio. La spedizione di serse da terme a Salamina. Milano, 1924.

Author and Title Listing

Author and Title Listing

AH 7139.12.9 — Girard, P.F. Études d'histoire juridique. Paris, 1913. 2v.

AH 7229.01 — Girard, P.F. Histoire de l'organization judiciaire. Paris, 1901.

AH 7138.95.3 — Girard, P.F. Manuel élémentaire de droit romain. 3. éd. Paris, 1906.

AH 7138.95.4 — Girard, P.F. Manuel élémentaire de droit romain. 4. éd. Paris, 1906.

AH 7138.95.6 — Girard, P.F. Manuel élémentaire de droit romain. 5e éd. Paris, 1911.

AH 7138.95.10 — Girard, P.F. Manuel élémentaire de droit romain. 8e éd. Paris, 1929.

AH 7139.12 — Girard, P.F. Mélanges. Paris, 1912. 2v.

AH 7139.12.3 — Girard, P.F. Mélanges du droit romain. Paris, 1912-23. 2v.

AH 7139.06 — Girard, P.F. Short history of Roman law. Oxford, 1906.

AH 7138.89.10 — Girard, P.F. Textes de droit romain. Paris, 1895.

AH 7138.95.5 — Girard, P.F. Textes de droit romain. 3. éd. Paris, 1903.

AH 7148.38 — Giraud, C. Droit de propriété. Aix, 1838.

AH 7138.73.5 — Giraud, C. Novum enchiridion juris Romani. Paris, 1873.

AH 7118.3 — Giraud, Charles. Dissertation sur la gentilité romaine. n.p., n.d.

AH 909.10 — Girowesen im griechischen Ägypten. (Preisigke, F.) Strassburg, 1910.

AH 4559.51 — Gitti, Alberto. Alessandro Magno all'oasi di Siwah. Bari, 1951.

AH 9792.8 — Gitti, Alberto. Ricerche sui rapporti tra i vandali e l'impero romano. Bari, 1953.

AH 9639.9.5 — Giuliano, Luigi. Storia di Siracusa antica. 2. ed. Milano, 1928.

AH 7779.12 — Giuliano l'Apostata. (Barbagallo, C.) Genova, 1912.

AH 7479.30 — Giulio Cesare. (Silvagni, V.) Torino, 1930.

Htn AH 5723.7* — Giurini, A.M. Primordia Corcyrae. Brixiae, 1738.

AH 5723.5 — Giurini, A.M. Primordia Corcyrae. Lycij, 1725.

AH 48.61 — Givodan, Léon. Histoire des classes privilégiées. Paris, 1861. 2v.

AH 4844.6 — Les gladiateurs dans l'Orient grec. (Robert, Louis.) Paris, 1940.

AH 7838.69 — Les gladiateurs romains. (Goguel, Edward.) Paris, 1869.

AH 7839.67.2 — Gladiators. (Grant, Michael.) Harmondsworth, Eng., 1971.

Htn AH 7295.89F* — Glandorp. Onomasticon historicae Romanae. Francofurti, 1859.

Eg 819.42A — Glanville, S.R.K. The legacy of Egypt. Oxford, 1942.

AH 2007.3 — Glaser, E. Skizze der Geschichte und Geographie Arabiens. Berlin, 1890.

AH 4888.65 — Glaser, J.C. Wirtschafts-Verhältnisse. Berlin, 1865.

AH 7201.65 — Glasson, E. Étude sur Gaius. Paris, 1885.

AH 7168.70.5 — Glasson, E. Étude sur les donations. Paris, 1870.

AH 4559.61 — Gleixner, H.J. Das Alexanderbild der Byzantiner. München, 1961.

AH 4206.8 — Gleue, H. De homicidarum in Areopago Atheniensi judicio. Gottingae, 1894.

Eg 278.43.3 — Gliddon, G.R. Ancient Egypt. N.Y., 1843.

Eg 278.43A — Gliddon, G.R. Ancient Egypt. N.Y., 1843.

Eg 278.43.2 — Gliddon, G.R. Ancient Egypt. N.Y., 1844.

Eg 278.43.8 — Gliddon, G.R. Ancient Egypt. N.Y., 1847.

AH 3125.3 — Glimpses of Nineveh. N.Y., 1857.

AH 7819.49.5 — Glimpses of Roman culture. (Poulsen, F.) Leiden, 1950.

AH 9777.11 — Glöden, I. von. Das römische Recht im östgothischen Reiche. Jena, 1843.

AH 4819.62.10 — The glory of Greece. (Samivel.) N.Y., 1962.

AH 4840.10A — The glory of Hera. (Slater, Philip Elliot.) Boston, 1968.

AH 4819.11.3A — The glory that was Greece. (Stobart, J.C.) London, 1911.

AH 4819.11.4 — The glory that was Greece. (Stobart, J.C.) London, 1921.

AH 4819.11.5 — The glory that was Greece. (Stobart, J.C.) N.Y., 1935.

AH 4819.06 — Glotz, G. Études...sur l'antiquité grecque. Paris, 1906.

AH 4889.20 — Glotz, G. Le travail dans la Grèce ancienne. Paris, 1920.

AH 5113.15A — Glotz, Gustave. The Aegean civilization. N.Y., 1925.

AH 5463.15 — Glotz, Gustave. La civilisation égéenne. Paris, 1952.

AH 4539.36.2 — Glotz, Gustave. La Grèce au IVe siècle; la lutte pour l'hégémonie, 404-336. Paris, 1941.

AH 4161.5 — Glotz, Gustave. Solidarité de la famille. Paris, 1904.

AH 4559.38.10 — Glotz, Gustone. Alexandre et l'hellenisation du monde antique. 2. éd. Paris, 1945.

AH 279.35A — Glover, T.R. The ancient world; a beginning. N.Y., 1935.

AH 279.35.5 — Glover, T.R. The ancient world. London, 1944.

AH 4039.27.5 — Glover, T.R. Democracy in the ancient world. Cambridge, 1927.

AH 4819.42A — Glover, Terrot R. The challenge of the Greek. Cambridge, Eng., 1942.

AH 4459.17 — Glover, Terrot R. From Pericles to Philip. London, 1917.

AH 4459.17.5 — Glover, Terrot R. From Pericles to Philip. N.Y., 1917.

AH 4819.32 — Glover, Terrot R. Greek byways. Cambridge, Eng., 1932.

AH 4819.32.5A — Glover, Terrot R. Greek byways. N.Y., 1932.

AH 7203.141 — Glück, D.C.F. Ausführliche Erläuterung der Pandecten. Erlangen, 1797-1868. 46v.

AH 7203.141.2 — Glück, D.C.F. Ausführliche Erläuterung der Pandecten und Hellfeld ein Commentar. Erlangen, 1871-87. 6v.

AH 2008.12 — Glueck, Nelson. Deities and dolphins; the story of the Nabataeans. N.Y., 1965.

AH 3017.75F — La glyphique mesopotamienne archaïque. (Amiet, Pierre.) Paris, 1961.

AH 4808.92.5 — Gnaedinger, G. De Graecorum Magistratibus Eponymis. Argentorali, 1892.

AH 7138.80.4 — Gneist, R. Institutionum et regularum iuris Romani syntagma. Lipsiae, 1880.

AH 4558.22 — Gobdelas, D. Histoire d'Alexandre le Grand. Varsovie, 1822.

AH 3663.12 — Gobineau, Arthur. The world of the Persians. London, 1971.

AH 3657.7 — Gobineau, J.A. Histoire des Perses. Paris, 1869. 2v.

AH 4819.52 — God, man and state. (Freeman, K.) London, 1952.

AH 3107.5 — Godbey, A.H. Notes on some officials of the Sargonid period. Chicago, 1906.

AH 7138.06 — Godefroy, J. Manuale juris. Parisiis, 1806.

AH 4819.60.10 — Godel, Roger. Une Grèce secrete. Paris, 1960.

AH 4839.64.5 — Goden in het stadion. (Spaak, Bob.) Amsterdam, 1964.

AH 819.59 — Gods and men. 1. ed. (Parker, Henry B.) N.Y., 1959.

Eg 879.04 — The gods of the Egyptians. (Budge, Ernest Alfred Wallis.) Chicago, 1904.

Eg 879.04.2 — The gods of the Egyptians. (Budge, Ernest Alfred Wallis.) London, 1904. 2v.

Eg 879.04.2.2 — The gods of the Egyptians. (Budge, Ernest Alfred Wallis.) N.Y., 1969. 2v.

X Cg Eg 879.04 — The gods of the Egyptians. v.2. (Budge, Ernest Alfred Wallis.) Chicago, 1904.

Htn AH 7816.28* — Godwyn, Thomas. Romanae historiae anthologia. Oxford, 1628. 2 pam.

Htn AH 7816.28.5* — Godwyn, Thomas. Romanae historiae anthologia. 15th ed. London, 1689.

AH 4845.28 — Goebel, Maximilianus. Ethnica, pars prima: De Graecorum civitatum proprietatibus proverbio notatis. Vratislaviae, 1915.

AH 7478.61 — Göler, F.A. Bürgerkrieg zwischen Cäsar und Pompejus. Heidelberg, 1861.

AH 7478.80 — Göler, F.A. Caesars gallischer Krieg. v.1-2. Freiburg, 1880.

AH 818.69.4 — Göll, Hermann. Kulturbilder. Leipzig, 1880. 2v.

AH 818.69.3 — Göll, Hermann. Kulturbilder. v.1-3. Leipzig, 1869. 2v.

AH 7649.54 — Goerlitz, W. Marc Aurel, Kaiser und Philosoph. Stuttgart, 1954.

AH 7449.70.5 — Goerlitz, Walter. Hannibal; eine politische Biographie. Stuttgart, 1970.

VAH 4029.60 — Görög történeti chrestomathia. (Borzsák, István.) Budapest, 1960.

Htn AH 2058.5* — Görres, J. Die Japhetiden. München, 1844.

AH 842.5 — Goess, G.F.D. Erziehungswissenschaft. Ansbach, 1808.

Eg 879.59.10 — Die Götter am Nil. (Gollob, Hedwig.) Wien, 1959.

AH 3914.5 — Die Götter Syriens. (Korn, F.) Stuttgart, 1842.

Eg 879.38.5 — Götter und Kulte im ptolemäischen Alexandrien. (Visser, Cornelia E.) Amsterdam, 1938.

Eg 879.38 — Götter und Kulte im ptolemäischen Alexandrien. Thesis. (Visser, Cornelia E.) Amsterdam, 1938.

Eg 879.56 — Der Götterglaube im alten Ägypten. 2. Aufl. (Kees, Hermann.) Berlin, 1956.

AH 3160.19 — Die Götternamen von Ur III. (Schneider, Nikolaus.) Roma, 1939.

AH 4112.7 — Göttingen. De amphictionia delphica. Gottingae, 1873.

AH 2173.5 — Göttingen. Universitat. Index Scholarum...Academia Georgia Augusta. Gottingae, 1879.

EgP 60.5 — Göttinger Orientforschungen. Reihe IV: Ägypten. Wiesbaden. 1,1973+

AH 7038.40 — Göttling, K. Geschichte der römischen Staatsverfassung. Halle, 1840.

AH 7015.11F — Götz, Georg. C. Maecenas. Rede...zur Feier der akademischen Preisvertheilung. Jena, 1902. 3 pam.

AH 1409.36 — Götze, Albrecht. Hethiter, Churriter und Assyrer. Oslo, 1936.

AH 2109.9 — Götze, Albrecht. Kleinasien zur Hethiterzeit. Heidelberg, 1924.

AH 897.30 — Goetze, F.L. De pistrinis veterum. Cygneae, 1730.

AH 7838.69 — Goguel, Edward. Les gladiateurs romains. Paris, 1869.

AH 817.58.3 — Goguet, Antoine Y. De l'origine des lois, des arts, et des sciences. Paris, 1758. 3v.

NEDL AH 817.58.5 — Goguet, Antoine Y. De l'origine des lois. 6. éd. Paris, 1820. 3v.

NEDL AH 817.58.13 — Goguet, Antoine Y. Della origine delle leggi, delle arte...antichi popoli. Lucca, 1761. 3v.

NEDL AH 817.58.17 — Goguet, Antoine Y. The origins of laws, arts, and sciences. Edinburgh, 1775. 3v.

AH 7808.15 — Golbrig, Karl Friedrich. Über Jahrform und Jahrrechnung bei den Römern. Salzwedel, 1815.

Eg 971.7.15 — The golden age of Alexandria: from its foundation by Alexander the Great in 1331 B.C. to its capture by the Arabs in 642 A.D. (Marlowe, John.) London, 1971.

Eg 1079.72.1 — The golden goddess. (McCoy, Raymond Aloysius.) Menomonie, 1972.

Eg 609.72.5 — The golden monarch; Tutankhamun. (Carter, Michael.) Christchurch, 1972.

AH 408.91 — Das goldene Zeitalter. (Büchner, L.) Berlin, 1891.

AH 168.56 — Goldschmidt, J.G. De nautico foenore. Berolini, 1866.

AH 7203.46.10 — Goldschmidt, L. Untersuchungen. Heidelberg, 1855.

NEDL AH 7277.70.25 — Goldsmith, O. Rōmaïkēs istorias. Athēnai, 1852.

Htn AH 7277.69* — Goldsmith, O. The Roman history, from the foundation of the city of Rome to the destruction of the western empire. London, 1769. 2v.

NEDL AH 7277.70.9 — Goldsmith, O. Roman history. Dublin, 1781.

AH 7277.70 — Goldsmith, O. Roman history. London, 1770. 2v.

AH 7277.70.3 — Goldsmith, O. Roman history. London, 1786. 2v.

AH 7277.70.5 — Goldsmith, O. Roman history. London, 1805. 2v.

NEDL AH 7277.70.7 — Goldsmith, O. Roman history. London, 1821. 2v.

NEDL AH 7277.70.21 — Goldsmith, O. Roman history. 35. American ed. Philadelphia, 1853.

AH 4278.00 — Goldsmith, Oliver. Grecian history. London, 1800. 2v.

NEDL AH 4278.00.2 — Goldsmith, Oliver. Grecian history. v.1-2. Philadelphia, 1805.

NEDL AH 4278.00.3 — Goldsmith, Oliver. Grecian history. v.1-2. Philadelphia, 1808.

NEDL AH 4278.00.5 — Goldsmith, Oliver. Grecian history from earliest state. v.1-2. Hallowell, 1818.

NEDL AH 4278.00.8 — Goldsmith, Oliver. Grecian history from earliest state to the death of Alexander. Hartford, 1824.

Htn AH 4277.74* — Goldsmith, Oliver. The Grecian history from the earliest state to the death of Alexander the Great. London, 1774. 2v.

NEDL AH 4278.00.7 — Goldsmith, Oliver. History of Greece. London, 1821. 2v.

AH 4278.00.10 — Goldsmith, Oliver. History of Greece. 11. ed. London, 1825.

AH 4278.00.9 — Goldsmith, Oliver. The history of Greece from the earliest state to the death of Alexander the Great. London, 1825.

AH 4278.00.11 — Goldsmith, Oliver. Pinnock's improved edition of Goldsmith's History of Greece. Philadelphia, 1846.

AH 4278.00.15 — Goldsmith, Oliver. Pinnock's improved edition of Goldsmith's History of Greece. Philadelphia, 1854.

AH 3980.12.5 — Golgotha and the holy sepulchre. (Wilson, C.W.) London, 1906.

Eg 879.59.10 — Gollob, Hedwig. Die Götter am Nil. Wien, 1959.

AH 7519.59 — Gollub, Wilhelm. Tiberius. München, 1959.

AH 2907.4 — Gologlu, Mahmut. Anadolunun milli devleti Pontos. Istanbul, 1973.

Htn AH 9607.5F* — Goltzius, H. Sicilia et Magna Graecia. Brugis, 1576.

Htn AH 9607.6F* — Goltzius, H. Sicilia historia posterior. Brugis Flandrorum, 1576.

AH 2147.9 — Golubtsova, E.S. Ocherki sotsial'no-politicheskoi istorii Maloi Asii v I-III vv. Moskva, 1962.

AH 7449.51 — Gómez, N.P. Guerras de Anibal preparatorias del sitio de Saguntum. Valencia, 1951.

AH 9684.10 — Gómez Santa Cruz, S. El solar numantino. Madrid, 1914.

AH 5315.5 — Gomme, A.W. Population of Athens in the fifth and fourth centuries B.C. Oxford, 1933.

AH 4309.54A — Gomme, Arnold W. The attitude to poetry and history. Berkeley, 1954.

Call number	Entry
AH 4299.37A	Gomme, Arnold W. Essays in Greek history and literature. Oxford, 1937.
AH 4299.62.5	Gomme, Arnold W. More essays in Greek history and literature. Oxford, 1962.
AH 7114.12	Gomont, H. Les chevaliers romains. Paris, 1854.
AH 2963.5	Gomperz, T. Zur Entzifferung der Schliemann sehen Inschriften. Wien, 1874.
AH 7819.47.5	Gonella, Guido. Pace romana e pace cartaginese. Roma, 1947.
AH 9664.5	Gonzalez Echegaray, Joaquin. Origenes del cristianismo en Cantabria. Santander, 1969.
AH 7149.35	Goodfellow, C.E. Roman citizenship. Thesis. Lancaster, 1935.
AH 278.47	Goodrich, S.G. Ancient history. Louisville, Ky., 1847.
AH 3009.02	Goodspeed, G.S. A history of the Babylonians and Assyrians. N.Y., 1902.
AH 3009.06	Goodspeed, G.S. A history of the Babylonians and Assyrians. 2. ed. N.Y., 1906.
AH 279.04.3	Goodspeed, George S. A history of the ancient world. N.Y., 1904.
AH 279.12.3	Goodspeed, George S. A history of the ancient world. N.Y., 1912.
AH 4258.55	Goodwin, G.W. De potentiae...maritimae Epochis. Gottingae, 1855.
AH 258.55	Goodwin, J.W. De potentiae veterum...maritimae epochis. Gottingae, 1855.
AH 4108.85	Goodwin, W.W. Value of Attic talent in modern money. v.1-2. n.p., 1885.
AH 8321.5	Gooss, Carl. Die römische Lagerstadt Apulum in Dacien. Schassburg, 1878.
AH 3928.45	Goossens, Godefroy. Hiérapolis de Syrie. Louvain, 1943.
AH 4299.69	Gorbunova, Vseniia S. Drevnie greki na ostrove Berezan'. Leningrad, 1969.
AH 7539.52	Gordon, A.E. Quintus Veranius. Berkeley, 1952.
AH 862.9	Gordon, B.L. Medicine throughout antiquity. Philadelphia, 1949.
AH 819.62.10	Gordon, Cyrus. Before the Bible. London, 1962.
AH 3151.12	Gordon, Cyrus. Hammurabi's code. N.Y., 1957.
AH 1279.53.5	Gordon, Cyrus H. Introduction to Old Testament times. Ventnor, N.J., 1953.
AH 3902.3	Gordon, Cyrus H. Ugarit and Minoan Crete; the bearing of their texts on the origins of Western culture. N.Y., 1966.
AH 3189.3A	Gordon, Edmund I. Sumerian proverbs. Philadelphia, 1959.
AH 7467.21.2.2	Gordon, T. The conspirators. 2. ed. London, 1721.
AH 7467.21.2	Gordon, T. The conspirators. 2. ed. London, 1721.
AH 2209.2	Gorelli, P. Les assyriens en Cappadoce. Paris, 1963.
AH 3670.5	Goroda Irana v rannem srednevekove. (Pigulevskaia, N.V.) Moskva, 1956.
VAH 279.67.5	Goroda raskryvaint tainy. (Varshavskii, Anatolii S.) Moskva, 1967.
Eg 819.16	Gosse, A.B. The civilization of the ancient Egyptians. N.Y., 1916.
NEDL AH 3103.3	Gosse, P.H. Assyria: her manners, customs. London, 1852.
AH 3966.20	Gosse, Philip H. Sacred streams; or, The ancient and modern history of the rivers of the Bible. N.Y., 1852.
AH 4937.90F	Gossellin, M. Geographie des Grècs analysée. Paris, 1790.
AH 3052.6.5	Gosudarstvo Lagash. (Struve, Vasilii V.) Moskva, 1961.
AH 2012.4	Gosudarstvo mukarribov Saba'. (Lundin, Avraam G.) Moskva, 1971.
AH 8311.2	A gót mozgalom és Dácia feladása. (Alfoldi, András.) Budapest, 1930?
AH 9777.29.6	The Gothic history of Jordanes. (Jordanes.) N.Y., 1960.
AH 9777.29.5A	The Gothic history of Jordanes. (Jordanes.) Princeton, 1915.
AH 9777.5	Gothicarum et Langobardicarum. Lugduni Batavorum, 1618.
AH 5057.2	Gothofreedus, J. History of united provinces of Achaia. London, 1673.
AH 9777.24	The Goths from the earliest times to the end of the Gothic dominion. (Bradley, Henry.) N.Y., 1899.
AH 9777.36	I Goti illustrati o vero Istoria de Goti antichi. (Ropaligero, D.) Verona, 1679.
Eg 879.37	Der Gott Chnum. Inaug. Diss. (Badawi, Ahmod M.) Glückstadt, 1937.
AH 3014.7F	Das Gottehaus und die Urformen des Bauens im alten Orient. (Andrae, Walter.) Berlin, 1930.
AH 3357.9	Gottschick, A.F. Geschichte der Gründung...des Hellenischen Staates. Leipzig, 1858.
AH 9660.2	Gotzfried, K. Annalen der römischen Provinzen...Spanien. Erlangen, 1907.
AH 3002.38F	Goucher College cuneiform inscriptions. New Haven. 1-2,1923-1933 2v.
AH 7138.73	Goudsmit, J.E. Pandects; treatise on Roman law. London, 1873.
AH 4819.65.10	Gouldner, Alvin Ward. Enter Plato. N.Y., 1965.
AH 7055.93.9	Goutière, Jacques. De officiis domus Augustae. Parisiis, 1628.
AH 8353.2	Governors of Moesia. (Stout, S.E.) Princeton, 1911.
AH 7808.91	Goyau, G. Chronologie de l'Empire romain. Paris, 1891.
Eg 1042.944	Goyon, G. Les inscriptions et graffiti des voyageurs sur la grande pyramide. Le Caire, 1944.
AH 4559.42	Grabowsky, Adolf. Dialoge um Alexander. Zurich, 1942.
AH 7469.47	Die Gracchen. (Rimscha, Hans von.) München, 1947.
AH 7468.47	Die Gracchen und ihre...Vorgänger. (Nitzsch, K.W.) Berlin, 1847.
AH 7468.54	Die Gracchen und ihre Zeit. (Lau, Thaddeus.) Hamburg, 1854.
AH 7468.77	The Gracchi, Marius and Sulla. (Beesly, A.H.) London, 1877.
NEDL AH 7468.77.3	The Gracchi, Marius and Sulla. (Beesly, A.H.) London, 1887.
NEDL AH 7468.77.4	The Gracchi, Marius and Sulla. (Beesly, A.H.) N.Y., 1891.
NEDL AH 7468.77.4.5A	The Gracchi, Marius and Sulla. (Beesly, A.H.) N.Y., 1892.
AH 7468.77.5	The Gracchi, Marius and Sulla. (Beesly, A.H.) N.Y., 1895.
AH 7469.69.5	The Gracchi. (Boren, Henry Charles.) N.Y., 1969.
AH 7469.67	Les gracques ou Crise agraire et révolution à Rome. (Nicolet, Claude.) Paris, 1967.
Eg 709.12	Gradenwitz, O. Griechische und demotische Papyri. Strassburg, 1912.
AH 7203.83	Gradenwitz, O. Interpolationen in den Pandekten. Berlin, 1887.
AH 7202.25F	Gradenwitz, Otto. Heidelberger Index zum Theodosianus. Berlin, 1925.
AH 4959.30	Graecia antiqua. (Frazer, James G.) London, 1930.
AH 138.84	Graeco-italische Rechtsgeschichte. (Leist, B.W.) Jena, 1884.
AH 818.90	Graeco-Roman institutions. (Reich, Emil.) London, 1890.
Htn AH 4036.32*	Graecorum republicae. (Emmus, Vbbonis.) Lugdunum Batavorum, 1632.
AH 846.7	Graekernes og Romernes huse. (Ussing, J.L.) Kjøbenhavn, 1876.
AH 7026.94F	Graevio, J.G. Thesaurus antiquitatum rom. Lugdunum Batavorum, 1694. 12v.
AH 4132.5	Graezistische Abhandlungn. Weimar. 1,1965+ 2v.
AH 7308.82	Graf, A. Roma. Torino, 1882. 2v.
NEDL AH 8007.2	Graham, A. Roman Africa...Roman occupation of Africa. London, 1902.
AH 4299.64.5	Graham, Alexander John. Colony and mother city in ancient Greece. N.Y., 1964.
AH 3964.18	Graham, William C. Culture and conscience. Chicago, 1936.
AH 909.58	Grain-mills and flour in classical antiquity. (Moritz, L.A.) Oxford, 1958.
AH 7469.31.10	Graindor, P. La guerre d'Alexandrie. Le Caire, 1931.
AH 5311.7	Graindor, Paul. Athènes sous Hadrieu. Le Caire, 1934.
AH 3017.50	Grammatik der Sprache Gudeas von Lagaš. (Falkenstein, Adams.) Roma, 1949-50. 2v.
Htn AH 8549.102*	Le grand dieu gaulois...Allobroges. (Gaidoz, Henri.) n.p., 1902.
AH 8647.5	Grand-Grèce paysages. (Lenormant, F.) Paris, 1881. 3v.
AH 8647.5.3	Grande-Grèce paysages. 2. éd. (Lenormant, F.) Paris, 1881. 2v.
Eg 1038.88F	Il grande papiro egizio della Biblioteca Vaticana. (Marucchi, Orazio.) Roma, 1888.
AH 809.62	Les grandes dates de l'antiquité. (Delorme, J.) Paris, 1962.
AH 3910.26	Les grandes monarchies hellenistiques en Asie. (Aymard, André.) Paris, 1965.
AH 9666.10	As grandes vias da Lusitania. (Saa, Mário.) Lisboa, 1956-60. 5v.
AH 7309.04	Grandeur et décadence de Rome. (Ferrero, G.) Paris, 1904. 6v.
NEDL AH 7309.04.1	Grandeur et décadence de Rome. (Ferrero, G.) Paris, 1907. 5v.
AH 7819.11.5A	The grandeur that was Rome; a survey of Roman culture. (Stobart, J.C.) London, 1912.
AH 7819.11.9A	The grandeur that was Rome; a survey of Roman culture. (Stobart, J.C.) N.Y., 1935.
AH 4819.27.10	The grandeur that was Rome. (Zane, J.M.) Chicago, 1927.
AH 7819.11.12	The grandeur that was Rome. 4. ed. (Stobart, J.C.) London, 1961.
AH 7309.04.2	Grandezza e decadenza di Roma. (Ferrero, G.) Milano, 1907. 5v.
AH 279.54	Le grandi correnti della storia antica. (Giannelli, G.) Milano, 1954.
AH 7178.82.5	Les grands domains dans l'Empire Romain. (Beaudouin, E.) Paris, 1899.
AH 7039.02	Granrud, John E. Roman constitutional history, 753-44 B.C. Boston, 1902.
AH 7088.62	Grant, A. How the ancient Roman governed their provinces. Bombay, 1862.
AH 4498.93	Grant, A.J. Greece in age of Pericles. London, 1893.
AH 3152.5	Grant, Elihu. Babylonian business documents of the classical period. Philadelphia, 1919.
AH 3002.40	Grant, Elihu. Cuneiform documents in Smith Library. Haverford, 1918.
AH 1409.20	Grant, Elihu. The Orient in Bible times. Philadelphia, 1920.
AH 819.64.5F	Grant, M. The birth of Western civilization. London, 1964.
AH 279.52.5	Grant, Michael. Ancient history. London, 1952.
AH 819.69.15	Grant, Michael. The ancient Mediterranean. London, 1969.
Eg 709.72	Grant, Michael. Cleopatra. London, 1972.
AH 7659.67.5	Grant, Michael. The climax of Rome. Saskatoon, 1967.
AH 7489.68	Grant, Michael. The climax of Rome. 1. American ed. Boston, 1968.
AH 7839.67.2	Grant, Michael. Gladiators. Harmondsworth, Eng., 1971.
AH 4279.58.15	Grant, Michael. Greeks. Edinburgh, 1958.
AH 7479.69	Grant, Michael. Julius Caesar. London, 1969.
AH 7549.70	Grant, Michael. Nero. London, 1970.
AH 2108.10	Grantovskii, E.A. Ranniaia istoriia iranskikh plemen Perednei Azii. Moskva, 1970.
Htn AH 846.5*	Grapaldi, F.M. De partibus Aedium. Venetiis, 1517.
Htn AH 846.4*	Grapaldi, F.M. De partibus Aedium dictionari. Argentinae, 1508.
Htn AH 846.6*	Grapaldi, F.M. De partibus Aedium lexicon. Basil, 1533.
AH 939.28.5	The graphic Bible, from Genesis to Revelation in animated maps and charts. (Browne, Lewis.) N.Y., 1941.
AH 939.28.10	The graphic Bible. (Browne, Lewis.) N.Y., 1942.
Eg 1159.54	Grapow, H. Grundriss der Medizin der alten Ägypter. v.1-9. Berlin, 1954- 10v.
Eg 829.60	Grapow, Herman. Wie die alten Ägypter sich anredeten. Berlin, 1960.
Eg 1039.15F	Grapow, Hermann. Religiöse Urkunden. Heft 1-3. Leipzig, 1915.
AH 842.11	Grasberger, L. Erziehung und Unterricht. Würzburg, 1864. 3v.
AH 4162.13	Grasshof, W. Doctrin am iuris Attici de hereditatibus. Berolini, 1877.
AH 3159.26	Graven in the rock. (Kinns, Samuel.) London, 1895.
AH 4861.6	Graves, F.R. The burial customs of the ancient Greeks. Thesis. Brooklyn, 1891.
AH 862.6	Grawinkel, Karl J. Zähne und Zahnbehandlung der alten Aegypter, Hebräer, Inder, Babyloner, Assyrer, Griechen und Römer. Berlin, 1906.
AH 8907.6	Gray, E.C.H. History of Etruria. London, 1843. 3v.
AH 3959.4	Gray, J. The Canaanites. London, 1964.
AH 1279.62	Gray, John. Archaeology and the Old Testament world. London, 1962.
AH 7629.20	Gray, William D. A study...life of Hadrian prior...accession. Northampton, 1919?
AH 9186.5	Grazia, Paolo di. La città di Pandosia. Napoli, 1918.
AH 7449.41	Grazioli, Francesco. Scipione l'Africano. Torino, 1941.
Eg 879.42.10	Grdseloff, Bernhard. Les débuts du culte de Rechef en Egypte. Le Caire, 1942.
AH 4299.73	Great and small poleis. (Amit, M.) Bruxelles, 1973.
AH 2108.5	Great cities and islands of Asia Minor. (Vaux, W.S.W.) London, 1877.
AH 299.72.5	Great cities of the ancient world. (De Camp, Lyon S.) Garden City, N.Y., 1972.
AH 819.41A	The great cultural traditions. 1. ed. (Turner, R.C.) N.Y., 1941. 2v.
AH 3002.2.15	The great cylinder inscriptions A and B of Gudea. Pt.1-2. (Price, Ira M.) Leipzig, 1899-1927. 2v.
AH 4039.65	The great dialogue; history of Greek political thought from Homer to Polybius. (Kagan, Donald.) N.Y., 1965.
AH 8211.7	The great invasion. (Cottrell, Leonard.) London, 1958.

Eg 299.29 — Great ones of ancient Egypt. London, 1929.

AH 4478.61 — Great Persian War. (Cox, George W.) London, 1861.

AH 4479.01.1 — The great Persian War and its preliminaries. (Grundy, George Beardoe.) N.Y., 1969.

Eg 928.59 — The great pyramid. (Taylor, J.) London, 1859.

AH 4519.27 — The great war between Athens and Sparta. (Henderson, B.W.) London, 1927.

AH 7449.26.3 — A greater than Napoleon, Scipio Africanus. (Liddell Hart, B.H.) Boston, 1927.

AH 7449.26.5 — A greater than Napoleon, Scipio Africanus. (Liddell Hart, B.H.) Boston, 1928.

AH 7449.26 — A greater than Napoleon, Scipio Africanus. (Liddell Hart, B.H.) Edinburgh, 1926.

AH 7309.04.7 — Greatness and decline of Rome. (Ferrero, G.) London, 1909. 5v.

NEDL AH 7309.04.6 — Greatness and decline of Rome. (Ferrero, G.) N.Y., 1908. 4v.

AH 7309.04.8A — Greatness and decline of Rome. (Ferrero, G.) N.Y., 1909. 5v.

AH 7309.04.4 — Greatness and decline of Rome. (Ferrero, G.) N.Y., 1909-10. 5v.

AH 7309.04.3A — Greatness and decline of Rome. v.1-3,5. (Ferrero, G.) N.Y., 1907-09. 4v.

AH 8548.155 — The greatness and decline of the Celts. (Hubert, Henri.) New York, 1972.

AH 3143.15 — The greatness that was Babylon. (Saggs, H.W.) N.Y., 1962.

AH 7926.47 — Greaves, John. Pyramidographia. London, 1646. 2 pam.

AH 4278.80 — La Grèce. (Combers, L.) Paris, 1880.

AH 4498.83 — La Grèce. (Larocque, J.) Paris, 1883.

AH 4818.35 — Grèce. (Pouqueville, F.C.H.L.) Paris, 1835.

AH 4818.35.5 — Grèce. (Pouqueville, F.C.H.L.) Paris, 1843.

AH 4978.90 — Grèce. Collection des guides - Joanne. (Haussoullier, Bernard.) Paris, 1890. 2v.

AH 4978.90.2 — Grèce. Collection des guides - Joanne. (Haussoullier, Bernard.) Paris, 1896. 2v.

AH 4819.00 — Grèce antique. (Lefèvre, A.) Paris, 1900.

AH 4329.71 — La Grèce antique devant la négritude. (Bourgeois, Alain.) Paris, 1971.

AH 4279.14 — Grèce antique et la vie grecque. (Jardé, A.) Paris, 1914.

AH 4539.36.2 — La Grèce au IVe siècle; la lutte pour l'hégémonie, 404-336. (Glotz, Gustave.) Paris, 1941.

AH 4819.10 — La Grèce avant Alexandre. (Monceaux, Paul.) Paris, 1892.

AH 4299.34 — La grèce et l'hellénisation du monde antique. (Cohen, R.) Paris, 1934.

AH 4299.34.5 — La grèce et l'hellénisation du monde antique. 3. éd. (Cohen, R.) Paris, 1948.

AH 829.13 — La Grèce et l'Italie. (Ménard, René J.) Paris, 1913.

AH 4819.13.10 — La Grèce et nous. (Beaunier, André.) Paris, 1913.

AH 4410.15 — Grece et Proche Orient avant Homère. (Severyns, Albert.) Bruxelles, 1960.

AH 4299.45 — La Grèce et son héritage. (Hatzfeld, Jean.) Paris, 1945.

AH 4819.60.10 — Une Grèce secrete. (Godel, Roger.) Paris, 1960.

AH 4043.5.20 — Grecheskie tirany IV v. do n.e. (Frolov, Eduard D.) Leningrad, 1972.

NEDL AH 4818.35.9 — La Grecia. (Pouqueville, F.C.H.L.) Venezia, 1836.

AH 4819.13.5 — La Grecia nella letteratura, nella religione. (Bianchi, Enrico.) Milano, 1913-14.

AH 4818.01 — Grecian antiquities. (Harwood, T.) London, 1801.

AH 4015.10 — Pamphlet vol. Grecian history. 3 pam.

AH 4278.00 — Grecian history. (Goldsmith, Oliver.) London, 1800. 2v.

AH 4278.92 — Grecian history. (Joy, James R.) N.Y., 1892.

Htn AH 4277.51* — Grecian history. (Stanyan, T.) London, 1751. 2v.

NEDL AH 4278.00.2 — Grecian history. v.1-2. (Goldsmith, Oliver.) Philadelphia, 1805.

NEDL AH 4278.00.3 — Grecian history. v.1-2. (Goldsmith, Oliver.) Philadelphia, 1808.

AH 4278.93A — Grecian history. v.1-3. (Beloch, J.) Strassburg, 1893-4v.

AH 4278.93.2 — Grecian history. v.1-4. (Beloch, J.) Strassburg, 1912-27. 8v.

NEDL AH 4278.00.5 — Grecian history from earliest state. v.1-2. (Goldsmith, Oliver.) Hallowell, 1818.

NEDL AH 4278.00.8 — Grecian history from earliest state to the death of Alexander. (Goldsmith, Oliver.) Hartford, 1824.

Htn AH 4277.74* — The Grecian history from the earliest state to the death of Alexander the Great. (Goldsmith, Oliver.) London, 1774. 2v.

AH 4299.71 — Grecità adriatica. (Baaccesi, Lorenzo.) Bologna, 1971.

AH 4039.58.5 — La grecità politica da Jucidide ad Aristotele. (Pavar, Massiniliaro.) Roma, 1958.

AH 4279.58.20 — Grecja niepodległa. 1. wyd. (Zielinski, Tadeusz.) Warszawa, 1958.

AH 4819.60.15 — Grecja współczesna i starożytna. (Polska Akademia nauk Oddział w Krakowie.) Kraków, 1960.

AH 4842.88 — Greco, Felice. La pedagogia presso i Greci. Bologna, 1959.

AH 819.73.5 — The Greco-Roman tradition. (White, Hayden V.) N.Y., 1973.

AH 4299.61 — Grècs et barbares. Genève, 1961.

AH 4279.63 — Les Grecs et les barbares. v.1-3. (Badi, Amiz Mehdi.) Lausanne, 1963-66. 2v.

Eg 459.60.5 — Grediche, Hans. Die Stellung des Königs im alten Reich. Weisbaden, 1960.

AH 4818.67A — Greece, ancient and modern. (Felton, C.C.) Boston, 1867. 2v.

NEDL AH 4818.67.10 — Greece, ancient and modern. v.1-2. (Felton, C.C.) Boston, 1896.

AH 4298.40 — Greece; pictorial, descriptive, and historical. (Wordsworth, C.) London, 1840.

AH 4298.53 — Greece; pictorial, descriptive, and historical. (Wordsworth, C.) London, 1853.

AH 4298.53.2 — Greece; pictorial, descriptive, and historical. (Wordsworth, C.) London, 1859.

NEDL AH 4298.40.2 — Greece; pictorial, descriptive, and historical. 2. ed. (Wordsworth, C.) London, 1844.

NEDL AH 4298.53.3 — Greece; pictorial, descriptive and historical. 5. ed. (Wordsworth, C.) London, 1868.

NEDL AH 4278.46.34 — Greece. (Grote, George.) N.Y., 1899-1901. 2v.

AH 4279.26.9 — Greece. (Hamilton, M.A. (Mrs.).) Oxford, 1926.

AH 4279.06 — Greece. (Shuckburgh, E.S.) N.Y., 1906.

NEDL AH 4278.35.4 — Greece. (Thirlwall, C.) London, 1844. 2v.

AH 4721.5 — Pamphlet box. Greece. B.C. 146-A.D. 476.

AH 4842.01 — Pamphlet box. Greece. Education.

AH 4819.70 — Greece: the magic spring. 1st ed. (Crow, John Armstrong.) N.Y., 1970.

AH 4278.90.9 — Greece. v.2. (Oman, C.W.C.) Philadelphia, 1906.

AH 4819.66.15 — Greece - ancient and medieval: an inaugural lecture delivered at Birkbeck College, 15th June, 1966. (Browning, Robert.) London, 1966.

AH 4819.46 — Greece and Greek civilization as results of economic expansion. (Marinatos, S.W.) Athens, 1946.

AH 818.78.3FA — Greece and Rome. (Falke, J. von.) N.Y., 1882.

AH 4409.20 — Greece before Homer. (Forsdyke, E.J.) London, 1956.

AH 4279.06.5 — Greece from the coming of the Hellenes to A.D. 14. 1. ed. (Shuckburgh, E.S.) London, 1922.

AH 4498.93 — Greece in age of Pericles. (Grant, A.J.) London, 1893.

AH 4410.32 — Greece in the bronze age. (Vermeule, Emily.) Chicago, 1964.

AH 4410.32.1 — Greece in the bronze age. (Vermeule, Emily.) Chicago, 1964.

AH 4828.85 — Greece in times of Homer. (Timayenis, T.T.) N.Y., 1885.

AH 4819.72.5 — Greece through the ages. (Miller, Helen (Hill).) N.Y., 1972.

AH 4819.64.15 — The Greek adventure. (Lévéque, Pierre.) Cleveland, 1968.

AH 4239.57 — The Greek and Macedonian art of war. (Adcock, F.E.) Berkeley, 1957.

AH 239.69 — Greek and Roman artillery; historical development. (Marsden, Eric W.) Oxford, 1969.

AH 239.71.5 — Greek and Roman artillery; technical treatises. (Marsden, Eric W.) Oxford, 1971.

AH 279.58.20 — Greek and Roman history. (Chambers, M.H.) Washington, 1958.

AH 79.72 — Greek and Roman voting and elections. (Staveley, Eastland Stuart.) London, 1972.

AH 819.60.15 — The Greek and Roman world. (Hardy, William.) Cambridge, 1962.

AH 4018.2 — Pamphlet vol. Greek antiquities. 5 pam.

AH 4018.1 — Pamphlet vol. Greek antiquities. 6 pam.

AH 4819.59.5 — Greek art and literature, 700-530 B.C. (Webster, Thomas.) Dunedin, 1959.

AH 4839.64 — Greek athletes and athletics. (Harris, Harold Arthur.) London, 1964.

AH 4839.10 — Greek athletic sport. (Gardiner, Edward Norman.) London, 1910.

AH 4839.10.1 — Greek athletic sports and festivals. (Gardiner, Edward Norman.) London, 1973.

AH 4839.25 — Greek athletics. (New York Metropolitan Museum of Art.) N.Y., 1925.

AH 4839.25.5 — Greek athletics. (Wright, Frederick A.) London, 1925.

AH 4861.9 — Greek burial customs. (Kurtz, Donna Carol.) London, 1971.

AH 4819.32 — Greek byways. (Glover, Terrot R.) Cambridge, Eng., 1932.

AH 4819.32.5A — Greek byways. (Glover, Terrot R.) N.Y., 1932.

AH 4843.26 — The Greek chorus. (Webster, Thomas Bertram Lonsdale.) London, 1970.

AH 8647.12 — Greek cities in Italy and Sicily. (Randall-MacIver, D.) Oxford, 1931.

AH 4039.40A — The Greek city from Alexander to Justinian. (Jones, A.H.M.) Oxford, 1940.

AH 4299.50 — Greek city-states. (Freeman, K.) London, 1950.

AH 4299.50.5 — Greek city-states. 1. ed. (Freeman, K.) N.Y., 1950.

AH 4811.2 — Pamphlet box. Greek civilization.

AH 4819.54.6 — Greek civilization from the Iliad to the Parthenon. (Bonnard, André.) London, 1957. 3v.

AH 4819.11.2.5A — The Greek commonwealth. 4th ed. (Zimmern, A.E.) Oxford, 1924.

AH 4819.11.2.10A — The Greek commonwealth. 5th ed. (Zimmern, A.E.) Oxford, 1931.

AH 4038.96 — Greek constitutional history. (Greenidge, A.H.J.) London, 1896.

AH 4038.91 — Greek constitutions. (Hammond, B.E.) Cambridge, 1891.

AH 4819.58 — Greek culture and the ego. (Stokes, Adrian Durham.) London, 1958.

AH 4409.72 — The Greek dark ages. (Desborough, Vincent Robin d'Arba.) London, 1972.

AH 4848.13 — Greek dress. (Abrahams, E.B.) London, 1908.

AH 4842.54A — Greek education, its practice and principles. (Drever, J.) Cambridge, 1912.

AH 4842.91 — Greek education. (Beck, F.A.G.) London, 1964.

AH 4819.57.10 — The Greek experience. (Bowra, Cecil Maurice.) London, 1957.

AH 4819.57.12 — The Greek experience. 1st ed. (Bowra, Cecil Maurie.) Cleveland, 1958.

AH 4039.67 — Greek federal states. (Larsen, Jakob Aall Ottesen.) Oxford, 1968.

AH 4279.32.5 — Greek history. (Laistner, M.L.W.) Boston, 1932.

AH 4299.00.4 — Greek history. (Swoboda, H.) London, 1920.

AH 4279.21.5 — Greek history. (Walker, E.M.) Oxford, 1921.

AH 4015.3.5 — Pamphlet vol. Greek history. Göttingen, 1850. 7 pam.

AH 4015.3 — Pamphlet vol. Greek history. Göttingen. 12 pam.

AH 4846.8 — Greek house, its history and development from Neolithic period to Hellenistic. Thesis. (Rider, B.C.) Cambridge, 1916.

AH 4819.17 — Greek ideals; study of social life. (Burns, Cecil D.) London, 1917.

AH 4039.13A — Greek imperialism. (Ferguson, W.S.) Boston, 1913.

AH 4039.13.3 — Greek imperialism. (Ferguson, W.S.) London, 1913.

AH 4959.09A — Greek lands and letters. (Allinson, Francis Greenleaf.) Boston, 1909.

AH 4959.09.5 — Greek lands and letters. (Allinson, Francis Greenleaf.) Boston, 1912.

AH 4959.09.10 — Greek lands and letters. 3. ed. (Allinson, Francis Greenleaf.) Boston, 1931.

AH 4299.10 — Greek lands and the Greek people. (Myres, John L.) Oxford, 1910.

AH 4219.5 — The Greek law of sale. (Pringsheim, F.) Weimar, 1950.

AH 4339.18 — Greek leaders. (Hopkinson, L.W.) Boston, 1918.

AH 4009.20 — Greek life; bibliography and review questions. (Tilden, F.W.) Bloomington, 1920.

AH 4818.87.10A — Greek life and thought. (Mahaffy, J.P.) London, 1887.

AH 4829.23 — Greek life and thought. (Van Rook, La Rue.) N.Y., 1923.

AH 4818.87.11A — Greek life and thought. 2nd ed. (Mahaffy, J.P.) London, 1896.

AH 4239.33 — Greek mercenary soldiers. (Parke, H. William.) Oxford, 1933.

AH 4819.57.5 — The Greek mind. (Agard, W.R.) Princeton, N.J., 1957.

AH 4259.68 — Greek oared ships, 900-322 B.C. (Morrison, John Sinclair.) Cambridge, Eng., 1968.

AH 4048.96A — Greek oligarchies. (Whibley, L.) N.Y., 1896.

AH 4845.26 — Greek peasants, ancient and modern: a camparison of social and moral values. (Walcot, Peter.) Manchester, Eng., 1970.

AH 4842.87.1 — Greek physical education. (Forbes, Clarence Allen.) N.Y., 1971.

AH 4819.25A — The Greek point of view. (Hutton, Maurice.) London, 1925.

Author and Title Listing

AH 4038.76F Pamphlet vol. Greek political antiquities. 23 pam.
AH 4039.41 The Greek political experience. Princeton, 1941.
AH 4039.60.10A Greek political theory. (Barker, E.) London, 1960.
AH 4039.60.11 Greek political theory. 5. ed. (Barker, E.) London, 1960.
AH 4819.67 Greek realities; life and thought in ancient Greece. (Hooper, Finley Allison.) N.Y., 1967.
AH 4819.21.5A The Greek renaissance. (Ure, Percy N.) London, 1921.
AH 4829.25A Greek social life. (Wright, F.A.) London, 1925.
AH 4819.14 The Greek spirit. (Stephens, Kate.) N.Y., 1914.
AH 4039.60 The Greek state. (Ehrenberg, Victor.) Oxford, 1960.
AH 4039.60.2 The Greek state. 2. ed. (Ehrenberg, Victor.) London, 1969.
AH 4819.39 The Greek tradition. (Boas, G.) Baltimore, 1939.
AH 4043.5.5 The Greek tyrants. (Andrews, Anthony.) London, 1956.
AH 4819.05.12 The Greek view of life. (Dickinson, G.L.) N.Y., 1916.
AH 4818.98 Greek view of life. 2nd ed. (Dickinson, G.L.) London, 1898.
AH 4819.05.8 The Greek view of life. 3d ed. (Dickinson, G.L.) N.Y., 1905.
AH 4818.96.15 The Greek view of life. 5th ed. (Dickinson, G.L.) N.Y., 1906.
AH 4819.09.3 The Greek view of life. 6th ed. (Dickinson, G.L.) N.Y., 1909.
AH 4819.05.17 The Greek view of life. 7th ed. (Dickinson, G.L.) Garden City, N.Y., 1925.
AH 4819.05.20 The Greek view of life. 7th ed. (Dickinson, G.L.) Garden City, N.Y., 1927.
AH 4819.05.30 The Greek view of life. 22d ed. (Dickinson, G.L.) London, 1949.
AH 4819.05.31 The Greek view of life. 23d ed. (Dickinson, G.L.) London, 1957.
AH 4259.05 The Greek warship I-II. (Taru, William W.) n.p., 1905. 3 pam.
AH 4728.90 Greek world under Roman sway. (Mahaffy, J.P.) London, 1890.
AH 4819.67.15 The Greeks. (Andrewes, Anthony.) N.Y., 1967.
AH 4279.58.15 Greeks. (Grant, Michael.) Edinburgh, 1958.
AH 4279.51 The Greeks. (Kitto, H.D.F.) Harmondsworth, 1951.
AH 4819.72.10 The Greeks: their legacy. (Van Duyn, Janet H. (Dunning).) N.Y., 1972.
AH 4819.63.5 The Greeks. 1. ed. (Lloyd-Jones, H.) Cleveland, 1963.
AH 4819.21 Greeks and Barbarians. (Thomson, J.A.K.) London, 1921.
AH 4478.76.3 Greeks and Persians. (Cox, George W.) London, 1876.
AH 4478.76.2 Greeks and Persians. (Cox, George W.) N.Y., 1876.
AH 4478.76.5 Greeks and Persians. (Cox, George W.) N.Y., 1892.
AH 4478.76A Greeks and Persians. 5. ed. (Cox, George W.) London, 1886.
AH 4819.51 The Greeks and the irrational. (Dodds, Eric Robertson.) Berkeley, Calif., 1951.
AH 4819.51.3 The Greeks and the irrational. (Dodds, Eric Robertson.) Berkeley, 1959.
AH 4819.51.2 The Greeks and the irrational. 1st ed. (Dodds, Eric Robertson.) Boston, 1957. 2v.
AH 4659.38.5 The Greeks in Bactria and India. 2. ed. (Tarn, William W.) Cambridge, Eng., 1951.
AH 5708.7 The Greeks in Ionia and the East. (Cook, John.) London, 1962.
AH 4299.62 The Greeks in the West. (Woodhead, Arthur Geoffrey.) London, 1962.
AH 4559.70.1 Green, Peter. Alexander of Macedon, 356-323 B.C. Harmondsworth, 1974.
AH 4559.70 Green, Peter. Alexander the Great. London, 1970.
AH 4523.12 Green, Peter. Armada from Athens. 1st ed. Garden City, N.Y., 1970.
AH 4279.73 Green, Peter. A concise history of Ancient Greece to the close of the classical era. London, 1973.
AH 819.60 Green, Peter. Essays in antiquity. Cleveland, 1960.
AH 819.72.10 Green, Peter. The shadow of the Parthenon; studies in ancient history and literature. London, 1972.
AH 4483.16.5 Green, Peter. Xerxes at Salamis. N.Y., 1970.
AH 4483.16 Green, Peter. The year of Salamis, 480-479 B.C. London, 1970.
AH 7819.33A Greene, William C. Achievement of Rome. Cambridge, 1933.
AH 4819.23.5 Greene, William Chase. The achievement of Greece; a chapter in human experience. N.Y., 1967.
AH 4819.23A Greene, William Chase. The achievement of Greece. Cambridge, 1923.
AH 4819.23.2 Greene, William Chase. The achievement of Greece. Cambridge, 1924.
AH 4038.96 Greenidge, A.H.J. Greek constitutional history. London, 1896.
AH 4038.96.10 Greenidge, A.H.J. A handbook of Greek constitutional history. London, 1920.
AH 7499.04 Greenidge, A.H.J. History of Rome during later republic. London, 1904.
AH 7158.94 Greenidge, A.H.J. Infamia. Oxford, 1894.
AH 7469.03 Greenidge, A.H.J. Sources for Roman history, B.C. 133-70. Oxford, 1903.
AH 7462.5.2 Greenidge, Abel H.J. Sources for Roman history, 133-70 B.C. 2. ed. Oxford, 1960.
AH 7039.01.5 Greenidge, Abel Hendy Jones. Roman public life. London, 1922.
AH 3052.6 Grégoire, J.P. La province méridionale de l'état de Lagash. Luxembourg, 1962.
AH 4559.40.5 Gregor, Joseph. Alexander der Grosse. München, 1940.
AH 7202.15 Gregorianus Hermogenianus. (Codex Theodosianus.) Bonn, 1842.
AH 7202.15.2 Gregorianus Hermogenianus. (Codex Theodosianus.) Bonn, 1844.
AH 7628.98 Gregorovius, F.A. The Emperor Hadrian. London, 1898.
AH 7628.51 Gregorovius, F.A. Geschichte des römischen Kaisers Hadrian. Königsberg, 1851.
AH 7628.84.3 Gregorovius, F.A. Der Kaiser Hadrian. 2. Aufl. Stuttgart, 1884.
AH 3013.43 Gregory, John M. An account of the sepulchres of the antients. London, 1712.
AH 4819.50.10 Den grekiska kulturhistoriens faser. (Wifsbrand, Albert.) Stockholm, 1950.
AH 4842.85.5 Den grekiska skolan. (Nilsson, M.P.) Stockholm, 1954.
AH 7099.72 Grelle, Francesco. L'autonomia cittadina fra Traiano e Adriano. Napoli, 1972.
AH 7228.58.2 Grellet Dumageau, J.B.M. Le barreau romain. Paris, 1858.
NEDL AH 8922.2 Grenier, A. Bologne, Villanovienne et Étrusque. Thèse. Paris, 1912.
AH 2108.7 Die Grenzen der hellenistischen Staaten in Kleinasien. (Meyer, Ernst.) Zürich, 1925.
AH 7499.64 Grenzheuser, Bruno. Kaiser und Senat in der Zeit von Nero bis Nerva. Münster? 1964.

AH 7738.34 Grepps, J.G.H. Dissertation sur les laraires de l'empereur Sévère Alexandre. Belley, 1834.
AH 3159.36 Gressmann, Hugo. Altorientalische Texte zum Alten Testament. Berlin, 1965.
Eg 879.52.15F Greven, L. Der Ka in Theologie und Königs Kult. Glückstadt, 1952.
AH 7148.78 Grévy, L. Des municipes. Versailles, 1878.
AH 4938.82 Die Griechen in der Diaspora. v.1-2. (Curtius, E.) Berlin, 1882.
AH 4819.69.15 Die Griechen von Mykene bis Byzanz. (Krause, Wilhelm.) Wien, 1969.
AH 4938.42 Griechenland. (Bobrik, H.) Leipzig, 1842.
AH 4938.41 Griechenland. (Hoffmann, S.) Leipzig, 1841. 2v.
AH 4819.52.20 Griechentum. (Kranz, W.) Baden-Baden, 1952.
AH 6168.5 Griechesche Städte und einheimische Völker des Schwarzmengebietes. (Komitee zur Förderung der Klassischen Studien.) Berlin, 1961.
AH 4818.44F Griechinnnen und Griechen. (Panofka, Theodor.) Berlin, 1844.
AH 842.23 Griechisch-römische Schulwesen. (Rauschen, G.) Bonn, 1900.
AH 842.23.5 Das griechisch-römische Schulwesen zur zeit des ausgehenden Heidentums. (Rauschen, G.) Bonn, 1901.
AH 4818.51 Griechische Alterthümer. (Schoemann, G.F.) Berlin, 1855. 2v.
NEDL AH 4818.51.3A Griechische Alterthümer. 2. Aufl. (Schoemann, G.F.) Berlin, 1861.
AH 4818.51.5 Griechische Alterthümer. 3. Aufl. (Schoemann, G.F.) Berlin, 1871. 2v.
AH 4818.51.8 Griechische Alterthümer. 4. Aufl. (Schoemann, G.F.) Berlin, 1897. 2v.
AH 4818.97 Griechische Altertumskunde. (Maisch, R.) Leipzig, 1897.
AH 4159.33 Die griechische Asylie. Diss. (Schlesinger, E.) Giessen, 1933.
AH 4148.92 Griechische Bürgerrecht. (Szántó, Emil.) Freiburg, 1892.
AH 4202.9 Griechische Denkwürdigkeiten. (Hüllmann, K.D.) Bonn, 1840.
AH 4819.55 Griechische Freiheit. (Pohlenz, Max.) Heidelberg, 1955.
AH 4459.59 Griechische Geschichte. (Berve, Helmuf.) Freiburg, 1959. 2v.
AH 4279.31 Griechische Geschichte. (Berve, Helmut.) Freiburg, 1931-33. 2v.
AH 4278.85 Griechische Geschichte. (Busolt, G.) Gotha, 1885-97. 3v.
AH 4279.20 Griechische Geschichte. (Ciccotti, Ettore.) Gotha, 1920.
AH 4278.57.5 Griechische Geschichte. (Curtius, Ernest.) Berlin, 1857. 3v.
NEDL AH 4278.57.6 Griechische Geschichte. (Curtius, Ernest.) Berlin, 1878. 3v.
AH 4278.86.5 Griechische Geschichte. (Holm, Adolf.) Berlin, 1886. 4v.
AH 4309.02 Griechische Geschichte. (Pöhlmann, R.) München, 1902.
AH 4278.91.5 Griechische Geschichte. (Roth, K.L.) München, 1891.
AH 4279.60.10 Griechische Geschichte. (Schachermeyr, Fritz.) Stuttgart, 1960.
AH 4278.96 Griechische Geschichte. (Swoboda, H.) Leipzig, 1896.
AH 4279.29.10 Griechische Geschichte. (Warg, Hans.) Leipzig, 1929.
AH 4278.85.3 Griechische Geschichte. v.1-3. (Busolt, G.) Gotha, 1893-1904. 4v.
AH 4279.69 Griechische Geschichte. 2. Aufl. (Bengtson, Hermann.) München, 1969.
AH 4279.31.2 Griechische Geschichte. 2. Aufl. (Berve, Helmut.) Freiburg, 1951- 2v.
AH 4279.60.12 Griechische Geschichte. 2. Aufl. (Schachermeyr, Fritz.) Stuttgart, 1969.
AH 4278.57.7A Griechische Geschichte. 6. Aufl. (Curtius, Ernest.) Berlin, 1887. 3v.
AH 4299.07 Griechische Geschichte bis 449. (Huber, Peter.) München, 1907.
AH 4279.24 Griechische Geschichte im Rahmen der Altertumsgeschichte. (Wilcken, U.) München, 1924.
AH 4279.24.5 Griechische Geschichte im Rahmen der Altertumsgeschichte. 7. Aufl. (Wilcken, U.) München, 1951.
AH 4309.67 Die griechische Geschichtsschreibung. Text and notes. (Fritz, Kurt von.) Berlin, 1967- 2v.
AH 4828.94 Griechische Gewichte. (Pernice, E.) Berlin, 1894.
Eg 841.5 Das griechische Gymnasium in Ägypten. (Schmidt, Karl F.W.) Halle, 1926?
AH 4909.34 Der griechische Kaufmann im Altertum. (Ziebarth, Erich.) München, 1934.
AH 4848.14F Griechische Kleidung. (Bieber, Margarete.) Berlin, 1928.
AH 4238.81 Griechische Kriegsaltertümer. (Kopp, W.) Berlin, 1881.
AH 4819.14.5 Griechische Kultur im Bilde. (Lamer, Hans.) Leipzig, 1914.
AH 4818.98.5A Griechische Kulturgeschichte. (Burckhardt, J.) Stuttgart, 1930-31. 4v.
AH 4818.98.10 Griechische Kulturgeschichte. (Burckhardt, J.) Stuttgart, 1952. 3v.
AH 4818.98.3 Griechische Kulturgeschichte. 3. Aufl. (Burckhardt, J.) Berlin, 1898. 4v.
AH 4819.57.15 Griechische Miniaturen. (Kerényi, Karoly.) Zürich, 1957.
AH 4808.44 Griechische Monatskunde. (Hermann, K.F.) Göttingen, 1844.
AH 4168.95 Griechische Pfandrecht. (Hitzig, H.F.) München, 1895.
AH 4939.56 Die griechische Polis als historisch-geographisches Problem des Mittelmeerraumes. (Kirsten, Ernst.) Bonn, 1956.
AH 4843.7 Griechische Saiteninstrumente. (Karl von Jan.) Leipzig, 1882.
AH 4038.93 Griechische Staatsaltertümer. (Kopp, W.) Berlin, 1893.
AH 4169.62 Griechische Stiftungsurkunden. (Mannzmann, Anneliese.) Münster, 1962.
AH 4539.07 Griechische Studien. (Grillnberger, P.O.) Wilhering, 1906.
AH 162.3 Das griechische Testament. (Schulin, F.) Basel, 1882.
Eg 709.12 Griechische und demotische Papyri. (Gradenwitz, O.) Strassburg, 1912.
AH 7808.40 Griechische und römische Zeittafeln. (Fischer, Ernst.) Altona, 1840-46. 2v.
AH 4889.31 Griechische Wirtschafts- und Gesellschaftsgeschichte bis zur Perserzeit. (Hasebroeck, J.) Tübingen, 1931.
AH 4028.97 Griechischen Altertumswissenschaft. (Toepffer, J.) Berlin, 1897.
AH 4039.15 Die griechischen Bünde und der moderne Bundesstaat. (Swoboda, H.) Prag, 1915.
AH 4298.11 Griechischen Colonien. (Hegewisch, D.H.) Altona, 1811.
AH 4859.7 Griechischen Frauen. (Fickler, C.B.A.) Heidelberg, 1848.
AH 4833.17 Griechischen Gymnasien und Palästren. Diss. (Schneider, K.) Solothurn, 1909.

Author and Title Listing

AH 4239.61   Guerra. (Brelich, A.) Bonn, 1961.

AH 7448.91.10F   La guerra d'Annibale in Italia da Canne al Metauro. (Bossi, Gaetano.) Roma, 1891.

AH 7469.09.5   La guerra dei gladiatori (73-71 a.C.). (Paladino, G.) Napoli, 1909.

AH 239.01   La guerra et la pace. (Ciccotti, Ettore.) Torino, 1901.

AH 7449.51   Guerras de Anibal preparatorias del sitio de Saguntum. (Gómez, N.P.) Valencia, 1951.

AH 7469.31.10   La guerre d'Alexandrie. (Graindor, P.) Le Caire, 1931.

AH 239.72   La guerre dans l'antiquité. (Garlan, Yvon.) Paris, 1972.

NEDL AH 7509.00.7F   Le guerre di Augusto contro i populi alpini. (Oberziner, G.) Roma, 1900.

AH 7449.17   Une guerre d'usure. (Huvelin, Paul.) Paris, 1917.

AH 9610.23   Le guerre servili in Sicilia. (Felice-Guiffrida, G. de.) Catania, 1911.

Eg 609.71   Les guerres d'Amoses. (Vandersleyen, Claude.) Bruxelles, 1971.

AH 8211.2   Guest, Edwin. The campaign of Aulus Plautius in Britain, A.D. 43. London, 1866.

AH 8210.2   Guest, Edwin. The invasion of Britain by Julius Caesar. London, 1864.

AH 3414.10   Gueterbock, H.G. Kumarki. Zürich, 1946.

AH 3414.10.5   Gueterbock, H.G. The song of Ullikummi. New Haven, 1952.

AH 3171.12   Güterbock, Hans G. Die historische Tradition und ihre literarische Gestaltung bei Babyloniern und Hethitern bis 1200. Inaug. Diss. Glückstadt, 1934.

AH 7163.9   Güterrecht der Ehegatten. (Hasse, J.C.) Berlin, 1824.

Htn   AH 7495.57*   Guevara, A. A chronicle, conteyning the lives of tenne emperours of Rome. London, 1577.

AH 2575.5   Guhl, Ernestus. Ephesiaca. Berolini, 1843.

NEDL AH 818.62.3   Guhl, Ernst. Leben der Griechen und Römer. Berlin, 1862.

NEDL AH 818.62.5   Guhl, Ernst. Leben der Griechen und Römer. Berlin, 1876.

NEDL AH 818.62.3.5   Guhl, Ernst. Leben der Griechen und Römer. 2. Aufl. Berlin, 1864.

NEDL AH 818.62.4   Guhl, Ernst. Leben der Griechen und Römer. 3. Aufl. Berlin, 1872.

AH 818.62.6   Guhl, Ernst. Leben der Griechen und Römer. 6. Aufl. Berlin, 1893.

NEDL AH 818.62.13A   Guhl, Ernst. The life of Greeks and Romans described from antique monuments. N.Y., 1896.

NEDL AH 818.62.15   Guhl, Ernst. The life of Greeks and Romans described from antique monuments. N.Y., 1902.

AH 818.62.9   Guhl, Ernst. Life of the Greeks and Romans. London, 188-?

NEDL AH 818.62.8   Guhl, Ernst. Life of the Greeks and Romans. N.Y., 1876.

AH 7819.52   Guida allo studio della civiltà romana antica. (Ussani, Vincenzo.) Napoli, 1952-54. 2v.

AH 7819.52.5   Guida allo studio della civiltà romana antica. 2. ed. (Ussani, Vincenzo.) Torino, 1961-64. 2v.

AH 9.59   Guide de l'étudiant en histoire ancienne. (Petit, Paul.) Paris, 1959.

AH 9.59.2   Guide de l'étudiant en histoire ancienne. 2. éd. (Petit, Paul.) Paris, 1962.

AH 7279.52.5   Guide romain antique. (Hocquard, G.) Paris 1952.

AH 3013.937.10   Guide thru the ruins of Babylon and Borsippa. (Iraq. Department of Antiquities.) Baghdad, 1937.

AH 3013.9.5A   Guide to the Babylonian and Assyrian antiquities. (British Museum.) London, 1900.

AH 3013.9.6   Guide to the Babylonian and Assyrian antiquities. 2. ed. (British Museum.) London, 1908.

AH 8548.100   The Guidels and their predecessors. (O'Rahilly, T.F.) London, 1936.

AH 2013.7.8   Guidi, Ignazio. L'Arabie antéislamique. Paris, 1921.

AH 3999.59   Guignebert, Charles. The Jewish world in the time of Jesus. 7th American ed. N.Y., 1959.

Eg 298.67   Guigniaut, J.D. Progrès des etudes relatives à l'Égypte et à l'Orient. Paris, 1867.

AH 3142.20   Guild structure and political allegiance in early Achaemenid Mesopotamia. (Weisberg, David B.) New Haven, 1967.

AH 908.75.3   Guillard, E. Les banquiers athéniens-romains. Paris, 1875.

NEDL AH 278.58   Guillemin, J.J. Histoire ancienne. Paris, 1858.

AH 5357.10   Guillon, P. La Béotie antique. Paris, 1948.

Eg 879.70.5   Guilmot, Max. Le message spirituel de l'Égypte ancienne. Paris, 1970.

AH 860.5   Guiochi infantili e giocattoli. (Galante, L.) Firenze, 1904.

AH 889.05   Guiraud, P. Études économiques. Paris, 1905.

AH 4818.94   Guiraud, P. Lectures historiques. Paris, 1894.

AH 4889.00   Guiraud, P. Main d'oeuvre industrielle. Paris, 1900.

AH 4888.93   Guiraud, P. Propriété foncière. Paris, 1893.

AH 7088.87   Guiraud, Paul. Les assemblées provinciales. Paris, 1887.

AH 7478.78   Guiraud, Paul. Le différend entre César et le sénat (59-49 avant J.C.). Thèse. Paris, 1878.

AH 7278.85.23   Guiraud, Paul. Histoire romaine. Paris, 1885.

AH 7477.74   Guischard, Charles. Memoires...plusieurs points d'antiquités militaires. Paris, 1774. 4v.

AH 4237.60   Guischardt, Karl. Mémoires militaires sur les Grecs...Romains. Lyon, 1760.

AH 336.42.5   Guldene Annotatien. (Heerman, F.) Dordrecht, 1664.

AH 4819.02A   Gulick, C.B. Life of ancient Greeks. N.Y., 1902.

AH 4819.02.5   Gulick, C.B. Life of the ancient Greeks. N.Y., 1905.

AH 4819.02.3A   Gulick, Charles B. Life of the ancient Greeks. N.Y., 1902.

AH 4819.27A   Gulick, Charles B. Modern traits in old Greek life. N.Y., 1927.

AH 3661.20   Gumilev, L.N. Podvig Bakhrama Chubiny. Leningrad, 1962.

AH 3149.5   Gumpach, J. Die Zeitrechnung der Babylonier und Assyrier. Heidelberg, 1852.

AH 3008.54   Gumpach, J. von. Abriss der babylonisch-assyrischen Geschichte. Mannheim, 1854.

Eg 1042.970.10   Gundlach, Rolf. Lexikalisch-grammatische Liste zu Spruch 335a der altägyptischen Sargtexte LL/CT 335a. Darmstadt, 1970. 2v.

Eg 1042.935.20   Gundlach, Rolf. Lexikalisch-grammatische Liste zu Spruch 335a der altägyptischen Sargtexte LL/CT. Darmstadt, 1970. 2v.

AH 7479.24.7   Gundolf, F. Caesar; Geschichte seines Ruhms. 2. Aufl. Berlin, 1925.

AH 7479.24.5   Gundolf, F. Caesar. Berlin, 1924.

AH 7479.24.10   Gundolf, F. The mantle of Caesar. London, 1929.

AH 3407.30   Gurney, O.R. The Hittites. London, 1952.

AH 9758.8   Gutenbrunner, S. Germanische Frühzeit in den Berichten der Antike. Halle, 1939.

AH 9777.40   Guthones (the Goths), kinsmen of the Lithuanian people. (Rackus, A.M.) Chicago, 1929.

AH 819.60.10A   Guthrie, William K.C. Tradition and personal achievement in classical antiquity. London, 1960.

AH 3005.7   Gutschmid, A. Neue Beiträge zur Geschichte des alten Orients; die Assyriologie in Deutschland. Leipzig, 1876.

AH 28.89   Gutschmid, A. von. Kleine Schriften. Leipzig, 1889. 5v.

AH 3657.17.1   Gutschmid, Alfred von. Geschichte Irans. Graz, 1973.

AH 5307.29   Guy, Noël. Athènes. Illustrations en couleurs de Marilac. Paris, 1935.

AH 2211.5   Gwatkin, William E. Cappadocia as a Roman procuratorial province. Diss. Princeton, 1930.

AH 7842.19.5   Gwynn, Aubrey. Roman education from Cicero to Quintilian. N.Y., 1966.

AH 7842.19   Gwynn, Aubrey. Roman education from Cicero to Quintilian. Oxford, 1926.

AH 9807.6   Gyárfás, István Tihamér. A jasz-kunok története. v.1-2,4. Kecskemét, 1870-85. 3v.

VAH 4039.68   Gycie politzczne w Atenach V i IV w. przed n.e. w ocenie krytzcznej wspólczesnych autorow atenskich. 1. wyd. (Turasiewicz, Romuald.) Wrocław, 1968.

AH 4609.59.5   Gyiokos, P.K. Philippos ho He. Thessalonikē, 1959.

AH 4833.7   Gymasiorum apud Graecos descriptionem. (Brugsma, A.L.) Groningae, 1855.

AHP 17.1   Gymnasial-Bibliothek. Gütersloh. 1-58,1892-1920 4v.

AH 4833.9   Gymnasium der Griechen. (Petersen, C.) Hamburg, 1858.

AH 7238.81.2   Gymnasium zu Mühlhausen - Jahres-Bericht. (Schambach, O.) Mühlhausen, 1881.

AH 4833.13   Gymnastik der Hellenen. (Bintz, J.) Gütersloh, 1878.

AH 4833.15   Die Gymnastik der Hellenen. (Jaeger, O.H.) Stuttgart, 1881.

AH 4833.5   Gymnastik der Hellenen. (Loebker, G.) Münster, 1835.

AH 4114.19A   Haarhoff, T.J. The stranger at the gate. London, 1938.

AH 4114.19.5   Haarhoff, T.J. The stranger at the gate. Oxford, 1948.

AH 3414.20   Haas, Volkert. Der Kult von Nerik. Rom, 1970.

AH 3150.14   Haase, Richard. Einführung in das Studium keilschriftlicher Rechtsquellen. Wiesbaden, 1965.

AH 7827.95   Habitudes et moeurs privées. (D'Arnay, J.R.) Paris, 1795.

AH 3966.26   Hackett, H.B. Illustrations of scripture. Boston, 1855.

AH 7239.59   Hackl, Othmar. Die sogenannte serwianische Heeresreform. München, 1959.

AH 4459.60   Hackl, Ursula. Die oligarchische Bewegung in Athen am Ausgang des 5. Jahrhunderts. München, 1960.

AH 4559.02   Hackmann, F. Schlacht bei Gaugamela. Halle, 1902.

AH 4659.59.5   Hadas, Moses. Hellenistic culture. N.Y., 1959.

AH 7279.56.5   Hadas, Moses. A history of Rome. 1. ed. Garden City, 1956.

AH 7509.30.5   Hadas, Moses. Sextus Pompey. N.Y., 1930.

AH 3921.7   Haddad, G. Aspects of social life in Antioch in the Hellenistic Roman period. Thesis. Chicago, 1949.

AH 7509.22.3   Hadley, H.S. Rome and the world today. 3. ed. N.Y., 1934.

AH 7138.73.3.5   Hadley, James. Introduction to Roman law, in twelve academical lectures. N.Y., 1893.

AH 7138.73.3   Hadley, James. Introduction to Roman law. N.Y., 1873.

AH 7138.73.4   Hadley, James. Introduction to Roman law. New Haven, 1931.

AH 7629.60   Hadrian. (Perowne, Stewart.) London, 1960.

AH 7629.04   Hadrians Rescript an Minicius Fundanus. (Mecklin, J.M.) Leipzig, 1899.

AH 4842.33   Haebeilin, C. Beiträge zur Kenntniss des Bibliographies und Buchwesens. Leipzig, 1890.

AH 9666.9   Haebler, Albin. Die Nord- und Westküste Hispaniens; ein Beitrag zur Geschichte der antiken Geographie. Leipzig, 1886.

AH 7201.90   Haeckermann, G.A.A.G. De legislatione decemoirali. Gryphiae, 1843.

AH 4908.86   Häderli, R. Astynomen und Agoranomen. Leipzig, 1886.

AH 7204.5F   Haenel, G.F. Corpus legem. Lipsiae, 1857.

AH 7842.5.2   Haenny, L. Schriftsteller und Buchhändler. 2. Aufl. Leipzig, 1885.

AH 3109.4F   Haerdtl, E. Astronomische Beiträge zur assyrischen Chronologie. Wien, 1884.

AH 2358.5   Haerne, D. de. Les Belges en Asie-Mineure. Louvain, n.d.

AH 7118.5   Die Häupter des patrizischen Claudiergeschlechts. (Lohse, G.) Chemnitz, 1891.

AH 840.5   Häusliche Leben. (Opitz, R.) Leipzig, 1894.

AH 861.14   Haffner, G. De antiquis sepulturae ritibus. Ulmae, 1764.

AH 4162.17   Hafter, Eugen. Die Erbtochter. Leipzig, 1887.

AH 4217.5   Hagemann, G. De Graecorum prytaneis capita Tria. Vrateslaviae, 1881.

AH 5336.7   Hagemann, G. De Prytaneo. Vratislaviae, 1880.

AH 7468.54.25   Hagen, E. Untersuchungen über römische Geschichte. Königsberg, 1854.

AH 862.12   Hagen, Hansludwig. Die physiologisch und psychologisch Bedeutung der Leber in der Antike. Bonn, 1961.

AH 7508.87   Hagen, M. von. Quaestiones criticae de belle mutinensi. Marburgi Cattorum, 1887.

AH 3013.801   Hager, Joseph. A dissertation of the newly discovered Babylonian inscriptions. London, 1801.

AH 9621.7   Hagt, W. van de. De urbe Agrigentinorum. Roterodami, 1903.

AH 3017.60   Hague. Kabinet van Munten. Catalogue sommaire des cylindres orientaux au Cabinet. La Haye, 1952.

AH 819.05   Hahn, E. Das Alle wirtschaftlichen Kultur. Heidelberg, 1905.

AH 7108.79   Hahn, G. De censorum locationibus. Lipsiae, 1879.

AH 7489.13   Hahn, L. Das Kaisertum. Leipzig, 1913.

AH 8504.5   Hajje, Antoine. Histoire de la justice seigneuriale en France; les origines romaines. Paris, 1927.

AH 4138.41   Halbertsma, P. De Magistratum Probatione. Daventriae, 1841.

AH 3966.29   Halbwachs, M. La topographie légendaire des Évangiles en Terre Sainte. Paris, 1941.

AH 3027.11   Haldar, Alfred Ossian. Who were the Amorites? Leiden, 1971.

Htn   AH 316.77F*   Hale, Matthew. Primitive origination of mankind. London, 1677.

AH 4819.65   Hale, William Harlan. The Horizon book of ancient Greece. N.Y., 1965.

AH 808.30   Hales, W. New analysis of chronology and geography. London, 1830. 4v.

Eg 603.6   Halevy, J. Correspondance d'Amenophis III. Paris, 1899.

AH 3154.2   Halevy, J. Documents religieux. Paris, 1882.

AH 3808.3   Halévy, J. Melanges de critique et d'histoire. Paris, 1883.

AH 7088.98   Halgan, C. Essai sur l'administration des provinces sénatoriales. Paris, 1898.

AH 4855.13   Halieutica. Proefschrift. (Höppener, Frank.) Amsterdam, 1931.

AH 7138.36   Halifax, S. An analysis of the civil law. Cambridge, 1836.

Author and Title Listing

AH 7188.97 — Halkin, Léon. Les esclaves publics chez les Romains. Bruxelles, 1897.

AH 1409.13 — Hall, Harry R. The ancient history of the Near East from the earliest times to the Battle of Salamis. London, 1913.

AH 1409.13.1 — Hall, Harry R. The ancient history of the Near East from the earliest times to the Battle of Salamis. N.Y., 1913.

AH 1409.13.5 — Hall, Harry R. The ancient history of the Near East from the earliest times to the Battle of Salamis. 5. ed. London, 1920.

AH 3016.50F — Hall, Harry R. Babylonian and Assyrian sculpture in the British Museum. Paris, 1928.

AH 3013.927F — Hall, Harry R. Ur excavations. v.1-10. Oxford, 1927-39. 9v.

AH 8538.2 — Hall, William H. Romans on the Riviera and the Rhone. London, 1898.

AH 7208.3 — Hallays, André. Les comices à Rome. Paris, 1890.

AH 7158.95 — Hallensleben, P.W. Das Vitium Furti und seine Purgatio. Aachen, 1895.

AH 7559.63 — Hallermann, Burkhard. Untersuchungen zu den Truppenbewegungen in den Jahren 68/69 nach Christ. Inaug. Diss. Würzburg, 1963.

AH 4299.23 — Halliday, William R. The growth of the city state. Liverpool, 1923.

AH 1279.71 — Hallo, William W. The ancient Near East. N.Y., 1971.

AH 3179.13 — Hallo, William W. The exaltation of Inanna. New Haven, 1968.

AH 4279.29.15 — Hallynck, P. L'Orient et la Grèce. Paris, 1929.

AH 5313.15 — Halsberghe, Gaston. Zoeklicht op het oude Athene. Hasselt, 1960.

AH 7889.64 — Halsberghe, Gaston H. Het republikeinse Rome; de grondslagen van het antieke wirtschaftswunder (509-31 v. Chr.). Hasselt, 1964.

AH 7419.64 — Halsberghe, Gaston H. Zoeklicht op het oude Rome. Hasselt, 1964.

AH 5610.9 — Hamburger, Oswald. Untersuchungen über den pynhischen Krieg. Inaug. Diss. Würzburg, 1927.

AH 8549.135 — Hamel, Anton G. van. Aspects of Celtic mythology. London, 1935.

AH 7518.04 — Hamilton, E. Memoirs of the life of Agrippina. Bath, 1804. 3v.

AH 4819.57 — Hamilton, Edith. The echo of Greece. 1st ed. N.Y., 1957.

AH 7339.22 — Hamilton, M.A. Ancient Rome. Oxford, 1922.

AH 7279.10 — Hamilton, M.A. A junior history of Rome. Oxford, 1910.

AH 4279.26.9 — Hamilton, M.A. (Mrs.). Greece. Oxford, 1926.

AH 4038.91 — Hammond, B.E. Greek constitutions. Cambridge, 1891.

AH 4038.95 — Hammond, B.E. Political institutions of ancient Greeks. London, 1895.

AH 39.51 — Hammond, M. City-state and world state in Greek and Roman political theory until Augustus. Cambridge, Mass., 1951.

AH 7049.33.2 — Hammond, Mason. The Augustan Principate in theory and practice during the Julio-Claudian period. N.Y., 1968.

AH 299.72.10A — Hammond, Mason. The city in the ancient world. Cambridge, Mass., 1972.

AH 5607.8 — Hammond, Nicholas Geoffrey Lempriere. Epirus: the geography, the ancient remains, the history. Oxford, 1967.

AH 4279.59 — Hammond, Nicholas Geoffrey Lemprière. A history of Greece. Oxford, 1959.

AH 4279.59.5 — Hammond, Nicholas Geoffrey Lemprière. A history of Greece to 322 B.C. 2. ed. Oxford, 1967.

AH 6107.14 — Hammond, Nicholas Geoffrey Lempriere. A history of Macedonia. Oxofrd, 1972-

AH 3151.2.5 — Hammurabi, king of Babylonia. The Babylonian laws. Oxford, 1960. 2v.

X Cg AH 3151.9.2 — Hammurabi, king of Babylonia. The code of Hammurabi...about 2250 B.C. 2. ed. Chicago, 1904.

AH 3151.14 — Hammurabi, king of Babylonia. The code of Hammurabi. Chicago, 1904.

AH 3151.2.3F — Hammurabi, king of Babylonia. Codex Hammurabi. Romae, 1950.

AH 3151.1.3F — Hammurabi, king of Babylonia. Codex Hammurabi. Romae, 1953.

AH 3151.6 — Hammurabi, king of Babylonia. Die Gesetze Hammurabis in Urnschrift. Leipzig, 1904.

AH 3151.2.10 — Hammurabi, king of Babylonia. The Hammurabi code and the Sinaitic legislation. Port Washington, 1971.

AH 3151.7 — Hammurabi, king of Babylonia. Hammurabis Gesetz. v.1-6. Leipzig, 1904-23. 4v.

AH 3151.11 — Hammurabi, king of Babylonia. La loi de Hammourabi. Paris, 1904.

AH 3151.4 — Hammurabi, king of Babylonia. The oldest code of laws in the world. Edinburgh, 1903.

AH 3151.4.5 — Hammurabi, king of Babylonia. The oldest code of laws in the world. Edinburgh, 1903.

AH 3151.2.10 — The Hammurabi code and the Sinaitic legislation. (Hammurabi, king of Babylonia.) Port Washington, 1971.

AH 3030.5 — Hammurabi von Babylon. (Schnöbel, Hartmut.) München, 1958.

AH 3151.12 — Hammurabi's code. (Gordon, Cyrus.) N.Y., 1957.

AH 3151.7 — Hammurabis Gesetz. v.1-6. (Hammurabi, king of Babylonia.) Leipzig, 1904-23. 4v.

AH 6103.5 — Hampl, Franz. Der König der Makedonien. Inaug. Diss. Weida, 1934.

Htn AH 7497.85.5* — Hancarville, Pierre François Hugues. Monumens de la vie privée des douze Césars. Rome, 1786.

Htn AH 7497.85* — Hancarville, Pierre François Hugues. Monumens de la vie privée des douze Césars. pt.1-2. Rome, 1785. 2v.

Htn AH 7497.84* — Hancarville, Pierre François Hugues. Monumens du culte secret des dames romaines. Nancy, 1784.

Htn AH 7497.84.5* — Hancarville, Pierre François Hugues. Monumens du culte secret des dames romaines. Rome, 1790.

Eg 958.47 — Hand-book for travellers in Egypt. (Wilkinson, G.) London, 1847.

Eg 879.07 — Handbook of Egyptian religion. (Erman, A.) London, 1907.

AH 4038.96.10 — A handbook of Greek constitutional history. (Greenidge, A.H.J.) London, 1920.

AH 7139.27 — Handbook of Roman law. (Radin, Max.) St. Paul, 1927.

AH 7138.83 — Handbook of Roman law. v.1-2. (Mackeldey, F.) Philadelphia, 1883.

NEDL AH 278.10 — Handbuch...Geschichte...Staaten. (Heeren, Arnold Herman Ludwig.) Göttingen, 1810.

AH 278.17 — Handbuch...Geschichte...Staaten. (Heeren, Arnold Herman Ludwig.) Göttingen, 1817.

AH 808.25 — Handbuch der...Chronologie. (Ideler, L.C.) Berlin, 1825. 2v.

AH 3143.12 — Handbuch der altorientalischen Geisteskultur. (Jeremias, Alfred.) Leipzig, 1913.

AH 3143.12.5A — Handbuch der altorientalischen Geisteskultur. 2e Aufl. (Jeremias, Alfred.) Berlin, 1929.

AH 3002.2.23F — Handbuch der babylonischen Astronomus. (Weidner, Ernst F.) Leipzig, 1915.

AH 277.93.3.4 — Handbuch der Geschichte der Staaten des Alterthums. 4. Aufl. (Heeren, Arnold Herman Ludwig.) Göttingen, 1821.

AH 4818.54 — Handbuch der Griechischen Antiquitäten. (Schwalbe, K.F.H.) Magdeburg, 1854.

AH 4808.88 — Handbuch der griechischen Chronologie. (Schmidt, A.) Jena, 1888.

AH 4038.81.5 — Handbuch der griechischen Staatsalterthümer. (Gilbert, G.) Leipzig, 1893.

AH 3002.144 — Handbuch der Keilschriftliteratur. (Borger, Riekele.) Berlin, 1967-

AH 7817.92.13 — Handbuch der römischen Alterthümer. (Adam, Alexander.) Erlangen, 1805-06. 2v.

AH 7818.41 — Handbuch der römischen Alterthümer. (Ruperte, F.F.F.) Hannover, 1841. 3v.

AH 7818.64.4 — Handbuch der römischen Alterthümer. v.1-7. (Marquardt, Joachim.) Leipzig, 1871-1888. 9v.

AH 7818.43.5 — Handbuch der römischen Alterthümer. v.1-9. (Becker, W.A.) Leipzig, 1843. 5v.

AH 7818.64.7 — Handbuch der römischen Alterthümer. 2. Aufl. (Marquardt, Joachim.) Leipzig, 1876- 2v.

AH 7818.64.9 — Handbuch der römischen Alterthümer. 2. Aufl. v.1-7. (Marquardt, Joachim.) Leipzig, 1876. 10v.

AH 7818.64.11 — Handbuch der römischen Alterthümer. 3. Aufl. (Marquardt, Joachim.) Leipzig, 1887. 3v.

AH 7818.64.18 — Handbuch der römischen Alterthümer. 3. Aufl. v.1-3. (Marquardt, Joachim.) Graz, 1952-53. 5v.

AH 7818.66 — Handbuch der römischen Antiquitaten. (Bojesen, E.F.C.) Wien, 1866.

AH 3013.17A — Handcock, P.S.P. Mesopotamian archaeology. N.Y., 1912.

AH 3143.11 — Handel und Wandel in Altbabylonien. (Delitzsch, Friedrich.) Stuttgart, 1910.

Eg 971.7.5 — Der Handel von Alexandreia. (Leider, Erich.) Hamburg, 1933.

Eg 971.7.6 — Der Handel von Alexandreia. Diss. (Leider, Erich.) Hamburg, 1934.

AH 4908.39 — Handelsgeschichte. (Hüllmann, K.D.) Bonn, 1839.

AH 908.77.3 — Die Handelstrassen der Griechen und Römer. (Sadowski, J.N.) Jena, 1877.

AH 7203.98 — Die Handschriften der castilianischen Übersetzung des Codi. (Suchier, H.) Halis, 1900.

AH 5857.12 — Hanell, Krister. Megarische Studien. Lund, 1934.

AH 7899.21.5 — Hanger, A. Zur römischen Landwirtschaft und Haustierzucht. Hanover, 1921.

AH 7449.70.5 — Hannibal; eine politische Biographie. (Goerlitz, Walter.) Stuttgart, 1970.

AH 7449.61 — Hannibal, enemy of Rome. 1. American ed. (Cottrell, Leonard.) N.Y., 1961.

AH 7448.97A — Hannibal; soldier, statesman. (Morris, William C.) N.Y., 1897.

AH 7449.69 — Hannibal; the struggle for power in the Mediterranean. (De Beer, Gavin Rylands.) London, 1969.

AH 7449.29.15 — Hannibal. (Baker, George Philip.) N.Y., 1929.

AH 7449.22 — Hannibal. (Egelhauf, G.) Stuttgart, 1922.

AH 7449.47 — Hannibal. (Zeller, Eberhard.) Uberlingen, 1948.

AH 7448.91A — Hannibal - history of the art of war. (Dodge, T.A.) Boston, 1891.

AH 7449.29 — Hannibal als Politiker. (Groag, Edmund.) Wien, 1929.

AH 7448.99 — Hannibal and the Great War. (How, W.W.) London, 1899.

AH 7449.25 — Hannibal crosses the Alps 2. ed. (Torr, Cecil.) Cambridge, 1925.

AH 7449.14 — Hannibal once more. (Freshfield, D.w.) London, 1914.

AH 7448.68 — Hannibal sive disputatio. (Alames, H.) Dublin, 1868.

Htn AH 7445.02* — Hannibalis atque Scipionis...ducum historie eleganti dulcique stilo coscriptac. (Acciajuoli, D.) Swollensi, 1502.

AH 7448.18.9 — Hannibals Alpenübergang. (Fuchs, J.) Wien, 1897.

AH 7448.18.14 — Hannibals Alpenübergang. (Hesselmeyer, E.) Tübingen, 1906.

AH 7819.65 — Hannibal's legacy. (Toynbee, Arnold Joseph.) London, 1965. 2v.

AH 7449.55.5 — Hannibal's march. (De Beer, Gavin Rylands.) London, 1967.

AH 7449.71 — Hannibal's march in history. (Proctor, Dennis.) Oxford, 1971.

AH 7448.18.15 — Hannibal's march through the Alps. (Wilkinson, S.) Oxford, 1911.

AH 7448.18.10 — Der Hannibalweg. (Osiander, W.) Berlin, 1901.

AH 8073.11 — Hannon, G. Antigüedad maritima de...Cartago. Madrid, 1756.

AH 4938.53 — Hanriot, Charles. Geographia Graecorum antiquissima Napoleonopoli qualis ab Homero...Thesim proponebat. Pictavorum, 1853.

AH 4117.8 — Hanriot, Charles. Recherches sur la topographie des dèmes de l'Attique. Napoléon-Vendée, 1853.

AH 4852.9 — Hansen, I.H. De Metallis Atticis. Hamburgi, 1885.

AH 5315.7 — Hansen, J.H. Über die Bevölkerungsdichtigkeit Attika's und ihre politische Bedeutung im Altertum. Hamburg, 1885?

AH 1279.19 — Hanslik, E. Einleitung und Geschichte des alten Orients. Gotha, 1919.

AH 3013.928.5.2 — Harcourt-Smith, S. Babylonian art. N.Y., 1928.

AH 7850.3 — Harcum, C.G. Roman cooks. Diss. Baltimore, 1914.

AH 3707.28.1 — Harden, Donald B. The Phoenicians. Harmondsworth, 1971.

AH 3707.28 — Harden, Donald B. The Phoenicians. London, 1962.

AH 4819.62.15 — Harder, Richard. Eigenart der Griechen. Freiburg, 1962.

AH 7479.10 — Hardinge, Hilary. Julius Caesar. London, 191-.

AH 9613.10 — Hardouin di Belmonte, F. Trinacria olimpica. Palermo, 1951.

AH 7469.24 — Hardy, E.G. The Catilinarian conspiracy in its context. Oxford, 1924.

AH 7139.12.7 — Hardy, E.G. Roman laws and charters. Oxford, 1912.

NEDL AH 7139.11 — Hardy, E.G. Six Roman laws. Oxford, 1911.

AH 7479.24 — Hardy, E.G. Some problems in Roman history. Oxford, 1924.

AH 7299.06 — Hardy, E.G. Studies in Roman history. London, 1906.

AH 7299.06.2 — Hardy, E.G. Studies in Roman history. London, 1909.

Eg 759.31 — Hardy, E.R. The large estates of Byzantine Egypt. N.Y., 1931.

AH 819.60.15 — Hardy, William. The Greek and Roman world. Cambridge, 1962.

AH 7058.18 — Harencarspel, R.S. van. De propria reipublicae romanae. Trajecti ad Rhenum, 1818.

AH 3103.6 — Harkness, M.E. Assyrian life and history. London, 1883.

AH 7147.19 — Harlessen, A. Jure colonario. Jenae, 1719.

AH 7239.67 — Harmand, Jacques. L'armée et le soldat à Rome de 107 à 50 avant notre ere. Paris, 1967.

AH 7489.60 — Harmand, Louis. L'occident romain. Paris, 1960.

AH 7138.86 — Harmann, O.E. Ordo judiciorum. Göttingen, 1886.

Author and Title Listing

NEDL AH 298.15 Heeren, Arnold Herman Ludwig. Ideen über Politik, Verkehr und Handel. v.1-2. Göttingen, 1815. 3v.
NEDL AH 278.40.5 Heeren, Arnold Herman Ludwig. A manual of ancient history. London, 1847.
AH 278.40 Heeren, Arnold Herman Ludwig. A manual of ancient history. 3. ed. Oxford, 1840.
AH 9777.38 Heerführer und Könige. (Eicke, Hermann.) Leipzig, 193-?
AH 7769.27 Heering, Walter. Kaiser Valentinian I (364-375). Inaug. Diss. Magdeburg, 1927.
AH 336.42.5 Heerman, F. Guldene Annotatien. Dordrecht, 1664.
AH 7458.36 Heerwagen, H.G. De P. et L. Scipionum accusation de quaestio. Baruthi, 1836.
Eg 709.00.5 Das Heerwesen der Ptolemäer und Römer in Ägypten. (Meyer, Paul M.) Leipzig, 1900.
AH 4138.22 Heffter, A.W. Athenäische Gerichtsverfassung. Cöln, 1822.
AH 7228.25.3 Heffter, A.W. System des römischen und deutschen Civil-Processrechts. 2. Aufl. Bonn, 1843.
AH 4298.08 Hegewisch, D.H. Colonien der Griechen. Altona, 1808.
AH 7598.00.3 Hegewisch, D.H. Essai sur l'epoque de l'histoire romaine. Paris, 1834.
AH 7468.01 Hegewisch, D.H. Geschichte der gracchischen Unruhen. Hamburg, 1801.
AH 4298.11 Hegewisch, D.H. Griechischen Colonien. Altona, 1811.
AH 7108.04 Hegewisch, D.H. Historische Versuch. Altona, 1804.
AH 807.28A Hegewisch, D.H. Introduction to historical chronology. Burlington, 1837.
AH 7598.00 Hegewisch, D.H. Über die Menscheit...Epoche in der römischen Geschichte. Hamburg, 1800.
AH 7161.20 Heiberg, C.F. De familiari patriciorum. Slesvici, 1829.
AH 7279.62 Heichelheim, F. A history of the Roman people. Englewood Cliffs, 1962.
AH 889.38.2 Heichelheim, Fritz. An ancient economic history from the Palaeolithic age to the migrations of the Germanic, Slavic, and Arabic nations. Leiden, 1958-64. 3v.
AH 3179.7.17 Heidel, Alexander. The Babylonian Genesis. 2d ed. Chicago, 1965.
AH 3177.13 Heidel, Alexander. The Gilgamesh epic and Old Testament parallels. Chicago, 1946.
AH 3177.13.5 Heidel, Alexander. The Gilgamesh epic and Old Testament parallels. 2d ed. Chicago, 1949.
AH 7202.25F Heidelberger Index zum Theodosianus. (Gradenwitz, Otto.) Berlin, 1925.
AH 3011.20 Heidelberger Studien zum Alten Orient. Adam Falkenstein zum (60 Geburtstag) 17 September 1966. Wiesbaden, 1967.
AH 5766.5 Heidemann, L. Die territoriale Entwicklung. Berlin, 1904.
AH 3017.11 Heidenreich, R. Beiträge zur Geschichte der vorderasiatischen Steinschneidekunst. Inaug. Diss. Heidelberg, 1925.
AH 7759.08 Heidentum und Christianismus des Kaisers Konstantin des Grossen. (Jenks, J.) Sereth, 1907.
AH 4228.86 Heikel, I.A. Boyleusis in Mordprocessen. Helsingfors, 1886.
AH 7217.16 Heil, Wilhelm. Der konstantinische Patriziat. Diss. Basel, 1966.
AH 6110.12 Heiland, Paul. Untersuchungen zur Geschichte des Königs Perseus von Makedonien. Diss. Jena, 1913.
AH 7809.10.7 Heiligenstaedt, F. Fasti aedilicii inde a Caesaris nece usque ad imperium A. Severi. Halis Saxonum, 1910.
AH 4215.7 Heiliges Recht. (Latte, Kurt.) Tübingen, 1920.
AH 7201.92 Heimbach, C. Aelii Galli icti de verborum. Lipsiae, 1823.
AH 7206.27F Heimbach, G.E. Anekdota. v.1-2. Lipsiae, 1838.
AH 7138.41 Heineccius, J.G. Antiquitatum Romanarum. Francofurti, 1841.
AH 7137.41 Heineccius, J.G. Antiquitatum Romanarum iurisprudentiam. Argentorati, 1741.
AH 7137.41.5 Heineccius, J.G. Antiquitatum Romanarum jurisprudentiam. Leovardiae, 1777.
AH 7203.32.5 Heineccius, J.G. Elementa juris civilis. 5. ed. Trajecti ad Rhenum, 1772.
AH 7138.50 Heineccius, J.G. Elementos de derecho romano. 3. ed. Paris, 1850.
Eg 709.66.5 Heinen, Heinz. Rom und Ägypten vom 51 bis 47 vor Christ; Untersuchungen zur Regierungszeit der 7. Kleopatra und des 13. Ptolemäers. Tübingen, 1966.
AH 4659.72 Heinen, Heinz. Untersuchungen zur hellenistischen Geschichte des 3. Jahrhunderts. Wiesbaden, 1972.
AH 3046.5F Heinrich, Ernst. Fara; Ergebnisse der Ausgrabungen der Deutschen Orient-Gesellschaft in Fara. Berlin, 1931.
AH 3014.17F Heinrich, Ernst. Schilf und Lehm. Diss. Berlin, 1934.
AH 7549.48 Heinz, Kurt. Das Bild Kaiser Neros bei Seneca. Inaug. Diss. Biel, 1948.
AH 7008.57.5 Heinze, H. De spuriis actorum diurnorum. Gryphiae, 1860.
AH 7509.30 Heinze, Richard. Die augusteische Kultur. Leipzig, 1930.
AH 7509.30.2 Heinze, Richard. Die augusteische Kultur. 2. Aufl. Leipzig, 1933.
AH 7309.38 Heinze, Richard. Vom Geist des Römertums. Leipzig, 1938.
AH 7309.38.3 Heinze, Richard. Vom Geist des Römertums. 3. Aufl. Darmstadt, 1960.
AH 7309.21.5 Heinze, Richard. Von den Ursachen der Grösse Roms. Leipzig, 1921.
AH 7039.25 Heinze, Richard. Von den Ursachen der grösse Roms. Leipzig, 1925.
AH 7178.56.3 Heisterbergk, B. Die Entstehung des Colonats. Leipzig, 1876.
AH 7118.8 Heiter, C. De patriciis gentibres. Berolini, 1909.
AH 7309.25.5 Heitland, W.E. Iterum, or A further discussion of the Roman fate. Cambridge, 1925.
AH 7419.09 Heitland, W.E. Roman republic. Cambridge, 1909. 3v.
AH 7419.09.2 Heitland, W.E. Roman republic. Cambridge, 1923. 3v.
AH 899.21 Heitland, William E. Agricola; a study of agriculture and rustic life in the Greco-Roman world. Cambridge, 1921.
AH 7099.28 Heitland, William E. Last wards on the Roman municipalities. Cambridge, Eng., 1928.
AH 7309.22 Heitland, William E. The Roman fate; an essay. Cambridge, 1922.
AH 7099.30 Heitland, Willian E. Repetita. Cambridge, Eng., 1930.
AH 908.77F Helbig, W. Il commercio dell'ambra. Roma, 1877.
AH 908.89 Helbig, W. Sopra le relazioni commerciali. Roma, 1889.
AH 7239.03.4 Helbig, W. Sur l'ara pararium. Paris, 1903. 2 pam.
AH 7848.7 Helbig, W. Toga und Trabea. v.1-2. Berlin, 1904.
Eg 269.62 Helck, Hans Wolfgang. Die Beziehungen Agyptens zu Vorderasien im 3. und 2. Jahrtausend vor Christ. Wiesbaden, 1962.
Eg 990.21 Helck, Hans Wolfgang. Die Ritualdarstellungen des Ramesseums. [Thebes]. Wiesbaden, 1972-
Eg 1042.968.5 Helck, Hans Wolfgang. Die Ritualszenen auf der Umfassungsmauer Ramses' II. Wiesbaden, 1968.

Eg 39.54F Helck, W. Untersuchungen zu den Beamtentiteln des ägyptischen alten Reichs. Glückstadt, 1954.
Eg 279.72 Helek, Hans Wolfgang. Lexikon der Agyptologie. v.1, pt.1-6. Wiesbaden, 1972-
AH 7808.69 Helfferich, A. Der altroemische Kalender. Frankfurt, 1869.
AH 7728.02 Héliogabale, ou Esquisse morale. (Chaussard, P.J.B.) Paris, 1802.
AH 7729.34A Héliogabale. (Artaud, Antonin.) Paris, 1934.
AH 7729.03 Héliogabale. (Duviquet, Georges.) Paris, 1903.
AH 7729.57 Héliogabale. (Villeneuve, Roland.) Paris, 1957.
AH 4298.52.2 Hellas; Geographie, Geschichte und Literatur Griechenlands. (Jacobs, Friedrich.) Stuttgart, 1897.
AH 4819.42.10 Hellas; kultur og religion. v.1-5. (Grønbech, Vilhelm.) København, 1942-45. 3v.
AH 4298.52.5 Hellas; or, The home, history, literature, and art of the Greeks. (Jacobs, Friedrich.) London, 1855.
AH 4298.52 Hellas; Vorträge über Heimath, Geschichte, Literatur und Kunst der Hellenen. (Jacobs, Friedrich.) Berlin, 1852.
AH 4818.76 Hellas. (Döring, E.) Frankfurt, 1876.
AH 4819.42.15 Hellas. (Grønbech, Vilhelm.) Hamburg, 1965.
AH 4938.25 Hellas. (Kruse, F.C.H.) Leipzig, 1825. 3v.
AH 4279.46.2 Hellas. (Robinson, Cyril E.) N.Y., 1948.
AH 4819.08 Hellás. v.1-2. (Amatucci, A.G.) Bari, 1908.
AH 4818.73 Hellas. v.1-2. (Wägner, W.) Leipzig, 1873.
AH 4939.13 Hellas abs Wiege der wissenschaftliche Geographie. (Oberhummer, E.) Wien, 1913.
AH 4819.36 Hellas and Hellenism. (Vlachos, N.P.) Boston, 1936.
AH 4819.63.25 Hellas en de Westeuropese cultuur. (Peremans, Willy.) Kasterlee, 1963.
AH 818.78F Hellas und Rom. (Falke, J. von.) Stuttgart, 1878.
AH 4819.59.15 Hellas und Rom. (Zschietzschmann, Willy.) Zürich, 1959.
AH 818.76.3 Hellas und Rom. v.1-2. (Forbiger, A.) Leipzig, 1876. 6v.
NEDL AH 278.41.7 Hellas und Rom. 7. Aufl. (Dielitz, T.) Berlin, 18- ?
AH 7204.21 Hellems, F.B.R. Lex de Imperio Vespasiani. Chicago, 1902.
AH 4298.44 Hellen. (Weissenborn, J.C.) Jena, 1844.
AH 8858.7 Die Hellenen in Campanien. (Fricke, Karl.) Hildesheim, 1873.
AH 6157.5 Hellenen in Skythenlande. (Neumann, K.) Berlin, 1855.
AH 4828.42.3 Hellenes. History of manners and customs of ancient Greece. (St. John, J.A.) London, 1844. 3 pam.
AH 4279.15A Hellenic civilization. (Botsford, George W.) N.Y., 1915.
AH 4819.25.15 Hellenic civilization. (Croiset, Maurice.) N.Y., 1925.
AH 4279.22A Hellenic history. (Botsford, George W.) N.Y., 1922.
AH 4279.22.2A Hellenic history. (Botsford, George W.) N.Y., 1926.
AH 4279.22.4 Hellenic history. (Botsford, George W.) N.Y., 1928.
AH 4279.22.3 Hellenic history. (Botsford, George W.) N.Y., 1930.
AH 4279.22.5 Hellenic history. (Botsford, George W.) N.Y., 1939.
AH 4279.22.8 Hellenic history. 3. ed. (Botsford, George W.) N.Y., 1948.
AH 4279.22.9 Hellenic history. 4. ed. (Botsford, George W.) N.Y., 1956.
AH 4819.14.8 L'hellénisation du monde antique. Paris, 1914.
AH 4818.26 Hellenische Alterthumskunde. (Wachsmuth, W.) Halle, 1826. 4v.
AH 4818.26.3 Hellenische Alterthumskunde. (Wachsmuth, W.) Halle, 1846. 2v.
AH 4819.05 Hellenische Kultur. (Baumgarten, F.) Leipzig, 1905.
AH 4819.05.2 Hellenische Kultur. (Baumgarten, F.) Leipzig, 1908.
AH 4819.05.5 Die hellenische Kultur. 3. Aufl. (Baumgarten, F.) Leipzig, 1913.
AH 4819.47.10 Der hellenische Mensch. (Pohlenz, Max.) Göttingen, 1947?
AH 6057.13 Das hellenische Thessalien. (Stählin, F.) Stuttgart, 1924.
AH 4819.41.5 Hellenische Weltanschauung. (Mewaldt, J.) Wien, 1941.
AH 4338.49 Hellenischer Heldensaal. v.2. (Bässler, Ferdinand.) Berlin, 1851.
AH 4298.62 Hellenischer Heldensaal. 2. Aufl. (Bässler, F.) Berlin, 1862.
AH 4659.59 Hellenism. (Toynbee, A.J.) London, 1959.
AH 4659.59.2 Hellenism. (Toynbee, A.J.) N.Y., 1959.
AH 4299.53.7 Hellenism and the modern world. (Murray, Gilbert.) Boston, 1954.
AH 4299.53.5 Hellenism and the modern world. (Murray, Gilbert.) London, 1953.
AH 6107.6.2 The Hellenism of the ancient Macedonians. (Daskalakēs, Apostolos Basileiou.) Thessalonikē, 1965.
AH 4659.28 O hellenismo e a civilisação christan. 4. ed. (Oliveira Martins, J.P.) Lisboa, 1928.
AH 6107.6 Ho Hellenismos tes archaias Makedonias. (Daskalakes, Apostolos Basileiou.) Athēnai, 1960.
AH 4659.25 Hellenismus. (Laqueur, R.) Giessen, 1925.
AH 4659.50 Der Hellenismus und seine geschichtliche Ralle. (Ranovich, A.B.) Berlin, 1958.
AH 4659.23 The Hellenistic age. Cambridge, Eng., 1923.
AH 5310.5A Hellenistic Athens. (Ferguson, William S.) London, 1911.
AH 4659.27 Hellenistic civilization. (Tarn, William W.) London, 1927.
AH 4659.27.10 Hellenistic civilization. (Tarn, William W.) London, 1947.
AH 4659.27.3 Hellenistic civilization. 2. ed. (Tarn, William W.) London, 1930.
AH 4659.27.15 Hellenistic civilization. 3. ed. (Tarn, William W.) London, 1952.
AH 4819.46.5 The Hellenistic civilization and East Rome. (Baynes, Norman H.) London, 1946.
AH 4659.59.5 Hellenistic culture. (Hadas, Moses.) N.Y., 1959.
AH 4239.30 Hellenistic military and naval developments. (Tarn, William W.) Cambridge, Eng., 1930.
AH 4659.32A Hellenistic queens. (Macurdy, G.H.) Baltimore, 1932.
AH 4659.61.5 The Hellenistic world. Photoreproduction. (Welles, Charles B.) New Haven, 1961.
AH 4819.07 Hellenistisch-Römische Kultur. (Wendland, P.) Tübingen, 1907.
AH 4819.07.2A Hellenistisch-römische Kultur. (Wendland, P.) Tübingen, 1912.
AH 4842.85 Die hellenistische Schule. (Nilsson, M.P.) München, 1955.
AH 7549.30 Hellenistische und griechische Elemente in der Regierung Neros. Inaug. Diss. (Schumann, Gerhard.) Leipzig, 1930.
AH 4410.33 Hellenosemitica. (Astour, Michael C.) Leiden, 1965.
AH 3966.40 Det hellige land og dets Mabolande i fortid og mutid. (Kok, Johannes.) Kjøbenhavn, 1878.
AH 819.13 Die hellistisch-römische Kultur. (Baumgarten, F.) Leipzig, 1913.
AH 7819.63.5 Helm, Ruddle. Römisches Alltagsleben im 1. und 2. Jahrhundert nach Christ nach martial und juvenal. Zürich, 1963.

Author and Title Listing

Author and Title Listing

AH 4039.52.5 — Hignett, C. A history of the Athenian constitution to the end of the fifth century B.C. Oxford, 1958.

AH 4479.63 — Hignett, Charles. Xerxes' invasion of Greece. Oxford, 1963.

AH 7178.62 — Hildebrand, B. De antiquiisimae agri Romani. Jenae, 1862.

Htn — AH 7477.38* — Hill, Aaron. An enquiry into the merit of assassination...character of Caesar. London, 1738.

AH 4498.97 — Hill, G. Sources for Greek history. Oxford, 1897.

AH 4498.97.5 — Hill, G. Sources for Greek history between the Persian and Pelopormesian wars. Oxford, 1951.

AH 7218.5 — Hill, George. Treasure-trove; the law and practice of antiquity. London, 1934.

AH 7114.34.5 — Hill, Herbert. The Roman middle class in the Republican period. Ann Arbor, 1967.

AH 5308.11 — The hill of Athena. (Powers, H.H.) N.Y., 1924.

AH 4058.78 — Hille, C.A. De scribis atheniensium publicis. v.1-2. Lipsiae, 1878.

AH 5140.5 — Hiller, F. Archaische Kultur der Insel Thera. Berlin, 1897.

AH 6024.9 — Hiller von Gaertringen, F. Geschichte von Delphi. Stuttgart, 1899.

AH 3011.4 — Hilprecht, H.V. Assyriaca eine Nachlese...Assyriologie. Berlin, 1894.

AH 3013.10.7 — Hilprecht, H.V. Die Ausgrabungen in Assyrien und Babylonien. Leipzig, 1904.

AH 3013.10A — Hilprecht, H.V. Explorations in Bible lands. Philadelphia, 1903.

AH 3132.5 — Hilprecht, H.V. Freibrief Nebukadnezars I. Leipzig, 1883.

AH 3002.18 — Hilprecht, H.V. The so-called Peters-Hilprecht controversy. Pt.1-2. Philadelphia, 1908.

AH 3017.80 — Hilzheimer, Max. Animal remains from Tell Asmar. Chicago, 1941.

AH 3001.4 — Hincks, E. On the polyphony of the Assyric-Babylonian cuneiform writing. Dublin, 1863. 10 pam.

AH 3005.828 — Hincks, Edward. Edward Hincks; a selection from his correspondence. London, 1933.

AH 3163.5 — Hinke, W.J. Selected Babylonian Kudurrie inscriptions. Leiden, 1911.

AH 7418.77 — Hinstin, G. Les romains à Athènes avant l'empire. Paris, 1877.

AH 7138.71.9 — Hinterlassene Schriften. v.1-2. (Dirksen, H.E.) Leipzig, 1871.

AH 4838.90.5 — Hippodromica. (Pollack, E.) Lipsiae, 1891.

AH 4838.90 — Hippodromica. Diss. (Pollack, E.) Lipsiae, 1890.

AH 4838.76 — Hippodromos. (Lehndorff, G.G.) Berlin, 1876.

AH 3096.6 — Hirschberg, Hans. Studien zur Geschichte Esarhaddons König von Assyrien (681-669). Inaug. Diss. Ohlau, 1932.

AH 7139.04.5 — Hirschfeld, B. Die Gesta municipalia. Marburg, 1904.

AH 7278.54.41 — Hirschfeld, O. Gedächtnisrede auf Theodor Mommsen. Berlin, 1904.

AH 7059.05 — Hirschfeld, O. Die kaiserlichen Verwaltungsbeamten. Berlin, 1905.

AH 7058.77 — Hirschfeld, O. Untersuchungen...römischen Verwaltungsgeschichte. Berlin, 1877.

AH 7138.79.7F — Hirschfeld, O. Zur Geschichte des lateinischen Rechts. Wien, 1879. 2 pam.

AH 7238.68 — Hirschfeld, Otto. Das Aerarium Militare und die Verwaltung der Heeresgelder in der römischen Kaiserzeit. Leipzig, 1868.

AH 4844.2 — Hirt, A.L. Die Hierodulen. Berlin, 1818.

AH 3167.10 — Hirt, Herde, Konig; zur Hirausbildung des Königtums in Mesopotamien. (Seibert, Ilse.) Berlin, 1969.

AH 4214.11 — Hirzel, R. Der Eid. Leipzig, 1902.

AH 7178.82.4 — His, Rudolph. Die Domänen der römischen Kaiserzeit. Leipzig, 1896.

AH 3075.12 — Histoire ancienne, Égypte, Assyrie; lectures historiques. (Maspero, Gaston.) Paris, 1890.

NEDL — AH 278.58 — Histoire ancienne. (Guillemin, J.J.) Paris, 1858.

AH 278.67 — L'histoire ancienne. (Lamé-Fleury, J.R.) Paris, 1867.

AH 277.34.2.3 — Histoire ancienne. (Rollin, Charles.) Amsterdam, 1734-39. 13v.

NEDL — AH 277.34.3 — Histoire ancienne. (Rollin, Charles.) Amsterdam, 1759. 3v.

AH 277.34.2 — Histoire ancienne. (Rollin, Charles.) Paris, 1740. 5v.

NEDL — AH 278.93 — Histoire ancienne. (Seignbos, C.) Paris, 1903.

NEDL — AH 277.34.5 — Histoire ancienne. v.1-13. (Rollin, Charles.) Paris, 1758-63. 14v.

AH 277.34.4 — Histoire ancienne. v.4-13. (Rollin, Charles.) Amsterdam, 1767. 10v.

AH 8007.25 — Histoire ancienne de l'Afrique du nord. (Ayache, Albert.) Paris, 1964.

AH 8007.12.6 — Histoire ancienne de l'Afrique du nord. (Gsell, Stéphane.) Osnabrück, 1972. 8v.

AH 8007.12 — Histoire ancienne de l'Afrique du nord. (Gsell, Stéphane.) Paris, 1913-28. 8v.

AH 8007.12.5 — Histoire ancienne de l'Afrique du nord. (Gsell, Stéphane.) Paris, 1920. 4v.

AH 1278.68.7 — Histoire ancienne de l'Orient. (Lenormant, F.) Paris, 1881-86. 6v.

AH 1408.88 — Histoire ancienne des peuples de l'Orient. (Duruy, J.V.) Paris, 1888.

AH 1278.76 — Histoire ancienne des peuples de l'Orient. (Maspero, Gaston.) Paris, 1876.

AH 1278.76.4 — Histoire ancienne des peuples de l'Orient. (Maspero, Gaston.) Paris, 1886.

AH 1278.95 — Histoire ancienne des peuples de l'Orient. (Maspero, Gaston.) Paris, 1895. 3v.

NEDL — AH 1278.76.8 — Histoire ancienne des peuples de l'Orient. 3. éd. (Maspero, Gaston.) Paris, 1878.

AH 7448.26 — Histoire critique du passage des Alpes par Annibal. (Larauza, J.L.) Paris, 1826.

AH 4521.9 — Histoire d'Alcibiade. (Houssaye, H.) Paris, 1874. 2v.

AH 4558.22 — Histoire d'Alexandre le Grand. (Gobdelas, D.) Varsovie, 1822.

AH 7448.70 — Histoire d'Annibal. (Hennebert, E.) Paris, 1870. 3v.

AH 7448.70F — Histoire d'Annibal. Atlas. (Hennebert, E.) Paris, 1870.

AH 7798.56 — Histoire d'Attila. (Thierry, A.S.D.) Paris, 1856. 2v.

AH 7798.56.6 — Histoire d'Attila et de ses successeurs. 6. éd. (Thierry, A.S.D.) Paris, 1884. 2v.

AH 2110.10 — Histoire de Cyrus le jeune. (Pagi.) Paris, 1736.

AH 7478.65 — Histoire de Jules César. (Napoléon III, emperor of the French.) N.Y., 1865. 2v.

AH 7478.65.3F — Histoire de Jules César. (Napoléon III, emperor of the French.) Paris, 1865-66. 2v.

AH 7478.65.2 — Histoire de Jules César. (Napoléon III, emperor of the French.) Paris, 1865-66. 2v.

AH 7478.65.2F — Histoire de Jules César. Atlas. (Napoléon III, emperor of the French.) Paris, 1865-66.

AH 7478.87 — Histoire de Jules César. Atlas. (Stoffel.) Paris, 1887. 3v.

AH 7478.65.2.5F — Histoire de Jules César. Atlas. v.1-2. (Napoléon III, emperor of the French.) Paris, 1865-66.

AH 7038.96 — Histoire de la centralisation dans l'empire romain. Thèse. (Decley, Ferdinand.) Caen, 1896.

AH 3008.71 — L'histoire de la Chaldée et de l'Assyrie. (Robion, F.M.L.J.) n.p., 1871.

AH 7658.36 — Histoire de la chute de l'Empire romain. (Simonde de Simondi, J.C.L.) Bruxelles, 1836.

AH 819.03 — Histoire de la civilisation ancienne. (Seignobos, C.) Paris, 1903.

AH 819.03.5 — Histoire de la civilisation ancienne. 5. éd. (Seignobos, C.) Paris, 1910.

Eg 819.61 — Histoire de la civilisation de l'Égypte. (Pirenne, Jacques.) Neuchâtel, 1961. 3v.

Eg 819.25 — Histoire de la civilisation égyptienne des origines à la conquête d'Alexandre. (Jequier, Gustave.) Paris, 1925.

AH 8307.2 — Histoire de la conquête...de la Dacie. (Vaschide, V.) Paris, 1903.

NEDL — AH 7652.8 — Histoire de la décadence et de la chute de l'Empire Romain. (Gibbon, Edward.) Paris, 1812. 13v.

NEDL — AH 7652.10 — Histoire de la décadence et de la chute de l'Empire Romain. (Gibbon, Edward.) Paris, 1839. 2v.

AH 4038.54.7 — Histoire de la démocratie athénienne. (Filon, A.) Paris, 1854.

AH 8507.12 — Histoire de la Gaule romaine, 120 avant J.C. (Hatt, Jean Jacques.) Paris, 1959.

AH 4728.66.5 — Histoire de la Grèce. (Hertzberg, G.F.) Paris, 1887. 2v.

AH 4728.75 — Histoire de la Grèce. (Petit de Julleville, L.) Paris, 1875.

AH 4278.46.17 — Histoire de la Grece. v.1-19. (Grote, George.) Paris, 1864. 9v.

AH 4278.56.7 — Histoire de la Grèce ancienne. (Duruy, V.) Paris, 1888.

AH 4279.26.5 — Histoire de la Grèce ancienne. (Hatzfeld, Jean.) Paris, 1926.

AH 4279.26.5.3 — Histoire de la Grèce ancienne. (Hatzfeld, Jean.) Paris, 1950.

NEDL — AH 4278.35.5 — Histoire de la Grèce ancienne. (Thirlwall, C.) Paris, 1847.

AH 4279.26.5.4 — Histoire de la Grèce ancienne. 3. éd. (Hatzfeld, Jean.) Paris, 1962.

AH 4728.75.2 — Histoire de la Grèce sou la domination romaine. 2. éd. (Petit de Julleville, L.) Paris, 1879.

AH 8504.5 — Histoire de la justice seigneuriale en France; les origines romaines. (Hajje, Antoine.) Paris, 1927.

AH 68.17 — Histoire de la législation. (Pastoret, C.E.J.P. de.) Paris, 1817-37. 11v.

AH 9754.3 — Histoire de la legislation des anciens germains. (Davoud-Oghlou, G.A.) Berlin, 1845. 2v.

AH 7114.10 — Histoire de la lutte entre les patriciens. (Hennebert, A.) Gand, 1845.

AH 7114.9 — Histoire de la lutte entre les patriciens. (Schuermans, Henri.) Bruxelles, 1845.

AH 6107.10 — Histoire de la Macédoine. (Cloché, Paul.) Paris, 1960.

AH 7162.24 — Histoire de la novelle 118. (Jarriand, E.) Paris, 1889.

AH 3960.23 — Histoire de la Palestine. (Abel, F.M.) Paris, 1952. 2v.

AH 7228.41 — Histoire de la procédure civile. (Walter, F.) Paris, 1841.

AH 7148.89 — Histoire de la propriété prétorien. (Appleton, C.) Paris, 1889. 2v.

AH 7278.10F — Histoire de la république romaine. (Mirys, S.D.) Paris, 1810.

AH 38.54.2 — Histoire de la souveraineté. 2. éd. (Sudre, Alfred.) Paris, 1874.

AH 4863.9 — Histoire de l'amour grec. (Meier, M.H.E.) Paris, 1930.

AH 279.12.5 — Histoire de l'antiquité. (Meyer, E.) Paris, 1912.

AH 279.13 — Histoire de l'antiquité. v.1-3 et index générale. (Cavaignac, E.) Paris, 1913-20. 5v.

AH 7048.75 — Histoire de le transmission du pouvoir impérial. (Paillard, A.) Paris, 1875.

AH 842.35 — Histoire de l'éducation dans l'antiquité. (Marrow, Henri Irenée.) Paris, 1948.

AH 842.35.2 — Histoire de l'éducation dans l'antiquité. 2. éd. (Marrow, Henri Irenée.) Paris, 1950.

AH 842.35.6 — Histoire de l'éducation dans l'antiquité. 4. éd. (Marrow, Henri Irenée.) Paris, 1958.

Eg 279.54 — Histoire de l'Egypte. (Brion, M.) Paris, 1954.

AH 7787.50 — Histoire de l'Empereur Jovien. (La Bleterie.) Amsterdam, 1750.

AH 4842.89 — Histoire de l'Ephébie attique. (Pélékidis, Chrysis.) Paris, 1962.

AH 4842.90 — Histoire de l'Éphébie attique. (Pélékidis, Chrysis.) Paris, 1962.

AH 4658.36.5 — Histoire de l'hellénisme. (Droysen, J.G.) Paris, 1883. 3v.

AH 7229.01 — Histoire de l'organization judiciaire. (Girard, P.F.) Paris, 1901.

AH 1279.36 — Histoire de l'Orient ancien. (Capart, Jean.) Paris, 1936.

NEDL — AH 279.23 — Histoire de l'Orient et de la Grèce. 7. éd. (Blanchet, D.) Paris, 1923.

AH 2583.7 — L'histoire de Milet. Photoreproduction. (Haussoulier, B.) Paris, 1902.

AH 7279.39 — Histoire de Rome. (Piganiol, André.) Paris, 1939.

AH 7279.39.8 — Histoire de Rome. 3. éd. (Piganiol, André.) Paris, 1949.

AH 7279.39.9 — Histoire de Rome. 4. éd. (Piganiol, André.) Paris, 1954.

AH 7279.39.10 — Histoire de Rome. 5. éd. (Piganiol, André.) Paris, 1962.

AH 7766.81 — Histoire de Theodose le Grand. (Fléchier, E.) Paris, 1681.

Eg 278.59 — Histoire d'Égypte. (Brugsch, H.) Leipzig, 1859.

AH 7448.12F — Histoire des campagnes d'Annibal. (Vaudoncourt, F. Guillaume.) Milan, 1812. 3v.

AH 8548.3 — Histoire des Celtes. (Pelloutier, S.) Paris, 1770-71. 8v.

AH 8548.3.2 — Histoire des Celtes. (Pelloutier, S.) Paris, 1771. 2v.

AH 7114.16 — Histoire des chevaliers romains. (Belot, E.J.) Paris, 1866.

AH 48.61 — Histoire des classes privilégiées. (Givodan, Léon.) Paris, 1861. 2v.

Author and Title Listing

AH 6150.5 — L'histoire des colonies grecques du littoral nord de la Mer Noire; bibliographie...1940 à 1957. (Belin de Ballu, Eugène.) Paris, 1960.

AH 6150.5.2 — L'histoire des colonies grecques du littoral nord de la Mer Noire; bibliographie...1940 à 1962. (Belin de Ballu, Eugène.) Leiden, 1965.

AH 8549.45.5 — Histoire des druides et...Calédonie. (David de St. Georges, J.J.A.) Arbois, 1845.

AH 8549.45 — Histoire des druides et...Calédonie. (Smith, John.) Arbois, 1845.

AH 7487.20 — Histoire des empereurs. (Lemain de Tillemont.) Paris, 1720-38. 6v.

AH 7487.00 — Histoire des empereurs. (Lenain, L.S.) Paris, 1700. 6v.

AH 7487.32.2F — Histoire des empereurs. v.1-6. (Lemain de Tillemont.) Bruxelles, 1732. 3v.

AH 7487.50 — Histoire des empereurs romains. (Crevier, J.B.L.) Paris, 1750. 6v.

NEDL AH 7487.50.10 — Histoire des empereurs romains. (Crevier, J.B.L.) Paris, 1753-66. 12v.

AH 3008.65 — Histoire des empires de Chaldée et d'Assyrie. (Oppert, J.) Versailles, 1865.

AH 8508.7.2 — Histoire des Gaulois. 2. éd. (Thierry, A.S.D.) Paris, 1835. 3v.

AH 2357.9 — Histoire des Gaulois d'Orient. (Robiou, F.) Paris, 1866.

NEDL AH 4278.87.5A — Histoire des Grecs. (Duruy, J.V.) Paris, 1887. 3v.

AH 4278.86 — Histoire des Grecs. (Ménard, L.) Paris, 1886. 2v.

AH 139.56 — Histoire des institutions et des faits sociaux des origines à l'aube du Moyen Âge. (Monier, Raymond.) Paris, 1955.

Eg 39.32 — Histoire des institutions et du droit privé de l'ancienne Égypte. v.1-3. (Pirenne, Jacques.) Bruxelles, 1932-35. 4v.

AH 7228.70.5 — Histoire des institutions judiciaires. (Latreille, J.) Paris, 1870.

Eg 709.03 — Histoire des Lagides. v.4, photoreproduction. (Bouché-Leclercq, A.) Paris, 1903. 4v.

AH 3657.7 — Histoire des Perses. (Gobineau, J.A.) Paris, 1869. 2v.

AH 9307.5 — Histoire des peuples opiques. (Ring, B.J.J.M. de.) Paris, 1859.

AH 4408.09.5 — Histoire des premiers temps de la Grèce. 2. éd. (Clavier, M.) Paris, 1822. 3v.

AH 7297.20.5 — Histoire des révolutions. (Vertot, R.A.) Paris, 1796. 4v.

AH 7297.20.7 — Histoire des révolutions. (Vertot, R.A.) Paris, 1833. 4v.

AH 7297.20.6 — Histoire des révolutions. 6e éd. (Vertot, R.A.) Paris, 1767. 3v.

AH 7297.20.6.5 — Histoire des révolutions. 8e éd. (Vertot, R.A.) Paris, 1786. 2v.

AH 7278.70 — Histoire des romains. (Duruy, V.) Paris, 1870. 7v.

AH 7278.70.3 — Histoire des romains. (Duruy, V.) Paris, 1881-90. 7v.

AH 3910.8 — Histoire des Seleucides. (Bouché-Leclercq, A.) Paris, 1913-14. 2v.

AH 7138.90.5 — Histoire des sources du droit français. (Tardif, A.) Paris, 1890.

AH 4408.56 — L'histoire des temps heroïques. (Behr, Par M.) Paris, 1856.

AH 861.7F — Histoire des usages funèbres. (Feydeau, E.) Paris, 1856. 2v.

AH 8011.5 — Histoire des wandales. (Marcus, Ludwig.) Paris, 1836.

AH 7659.28.5 — Histoire du Bas-Empire. v.1-2. (Stein, Ernst.) Paris, 1949. 3v.

AH 7059.68 — L'histoire du cens jusqu'à la fin de la République romaine. (Pieri, Georges.) Paris, 1968.

AH 907.63 — Histoire du commerce et de la navigation des anciens. (Huet, Pierre D.) Lyon, 1763.

AH 907.63.2 — Histoire du commerce et de la navigation des anciens. 2. éd. (Huet, Pierre D.) Paris, 1716.

Eg 907.66 — Histoire du commerce et de la navigation des Égyptiens. (Armeilhon, H.P.) Paris, 1766.

AH 3160.12 — Histoire du culte de Sin. (Combe, E.) Paris, 1908.

AH 4168.97.2 — Histoire du droit privé de la République Athenienne. (Beauchet, Ludovic.) Amsterdam, 1969.

AH 7168.92 — L'histoire du droit romain. (Audibert, A.) Paris, 1892.

AH 7138.25 — Histoire du droit romain. (Hugo, G.) Paris, 1825. 2v.

AH 47.69 — Histoire du gouvernement des anciennes républiques. (Turpin, François H.) Paris, 1769.

AH 7448.18 — Histoire du passage des Alpes par Annibal. (DeLuc, J.A.) Genève, 1818.

Eg 909.36.5 — Histoire économique et social de l'ancienne Égypte. (Dykmans, G.L.) Paris, 1936-37. 3v.

AH 279.56 — Histoire et historiens dans l'antiquité. Genève, 1956.

AH 279.46.10 — Histoire générale de l'antiquité. (Cavaignac, E.) Paris, 1946.

AH 4278.29.13 — L'histoire grecque, racontée aux enfants. (Lamé Fleury, J.R.) Paris, 1873.

NEDL AH 4278.29.7 — L'histoire grecque, racontée aux enfants. 4e éd. (Lamé Fleury, J.R.) Paris, 1837.

AH 4278.56.9 — Histoire grecque. (Duruy, V.) Paris, 1856.

AH 4278.56.13 — Histoire grecque. (Duruy, V.) Paris, 1889.

AH 4728.80 — Histoire grecque. (Petit de Julleville, L.) Paris, 1880.

NEDL AH 4278.56.5 — Histoire grecque. 4. éd. (Duruy, V.) Paris, 1864.

AH 4278.56.4 — Histoire grecque. 5. éd. (Duruy, V.) Paris, 1866.

NEDL AH 4278.56.6 — Histoire grecque. 6. éd. (Duruy, V.) Paris, 1867.

AH 4278.56.25 — Histoire grecque. 32. éd. (Duruy, V.) Paris, 1901.

AH 7278.85.6 — Histoire intérieure de Rome. (Lange, Ludwig.) Paris, 1885. 2v.

AH 238.43 — Histoire militaire des éléphants. (Armandi, C.P.) Paris, 1843.

AH 8514.12 — Histoire morale de la Gaule. (Martin, L.A.) Paris, 1848.

NEDL AH 279.03.5 — Histoire narrative et descriptive de l'antiquité. 8. éd. (Seignobos, C.) Paris, 1910.

AH 4407.87 — L'histoire primitive de la Grèce. (Rabaut, J.P.) Paris, 1787.

AH 7279.29 — Histoire romaine. (Ambrosi, A.) Paris, 1929.

AH 7278.62 — Histoire romaine. (Ampère, J.J.) Paris, 1862. 4v.

AH 7277.25 — Histoire romaine. (Catrou, François.) Paris, 1725. 17v.

AH 7278.67 — Histoire romaine. (Duruy, V.) Paris, 1867.

AH 7278.67.17 — Histoire romaine. (Duruy, V.) Paris, 1889.

AH 7278.67.27 — Histoire romaine. (Duruy, V.) Paris, 1899.

AH 7278.85.23 — Histoire romaine. (Guiraud, Paul.) Paris, 1885.

AH 7277.52 — Histoire romaine. (Rollin, Charles.) Paris, 1752. 8v.

NEDL AH 7277.52.1 — Histoire romaine. (Rollin, Charles.) Paris, 1758-68. 16v.

AH 7277.52.2 — Histoire romaine. (Rollin, Charles.) Paris, 1803-05. 16v.

AH 7278.51 — Histoire romaine. (Segur.) Paris, 1851. 2v.

AH 7278.76.10 — Histoire romaine. (Talbot, E.) Paris, 1876.

AH 7279.30.10 — Histoire romaine. (Terrail, Gabriel.) Paris, 1930.

AH 7278.54.30 — Histoire romaine. v.1-2, 3-4, 5-6, 7. (Mommsen, T.) Paris, 1882. 4v.

AH 7278.54.29 — Histoire romaine. v.1-8. (Mommsen, T.) Paris, 1863. 4v.

AH 7277.25.3 — Histoire romaine. v.18-21. (Catrou, François.) Paris, 1734. 4v.

AH 7278.33 — Histoire romaine. 2. ed. (Michelet, J.) Paris, 1833. 2v.

AH 7278.33.3 — Histoire romaine. 3. ed. (Michelet, J.) Paris, 1843. 2v.

AH 7278.62.3 — L'histoire romaine à Rome. 3. éd. (Ampère, J.J.) Paris, 1866-72. 4v.

AH 7478.81.15 — L'histoire romaine au septième siècle, 622-677. (Garrido, Luiz.) Lisbonne, 1881.

AH 7278.32.5 — L'histoire romaine racontée aux enfants. (Lamé Fleury, J.R.) Paris, 1869-70. 2v.

NEDL AH 7278.67.3 — Histoire universelle. (Duruy, V.) Paris, 1876.

AH 278.36 — Histoire universelle. 5. éd. v.1-10. Atlas. (Ségur, L.P.) Paris, 1836. 11v.

AH 1278.83 — Histoire universelle les Asiatiques. (Fontane, M.) Paris, 1883.

AHP 18.3 — Historia. Zeitschrift für alte Geschichte. Baden-Baden. 1,1950+ 25v.

NEDL AH 278.54 — Historia antigua. (Boreau, V.) Santiago, 1854.

X Cg AH 7486.85F — L'historia Augusta. (Angeloni, F.) Roma, 1685.

AH 3357.5 — Historia Cyrenes. (Thrige, Johann P.) Hauniae, 1819.

AH 7418.85.3 — Historia da republica romana. 3. ed. v.1-2. (Oliveira Martins, J.P.) Lisboa, 1919.

AH 4881.5 — Historia das doutrinas económicas da antiga Grécia. (Amzalak, Moses B.) n.p., n.d. 3 pam.

AH 819.44 — Historia de la cultura. (Cavazzana, J.C.) Lima, 1944.

NEDL AH 7297.20.15 — Historia de las revoluciones. (Vertot, R.A.) Paris, 1825.

AH 7418.14 — Historia de los dictadores de la republica romana. (Ferrer, V.P.) Cartagena de Indias, 1814.

NEDL AH 4278.56.15 — Historia de los Griegos. (Duruy, V.) Barcelona, 1890. 2v.

AH 4279.38.7 — Historia de los griegos. (Secco Ellauri, Oscar.) Montevideo, 1945.

AH 7278.54.31 — Historia de Roma. (Mommsen, T.) Madrid, 1877.

AH 1279.63 — Historia del antiguo oriente. (Tovar, Antonio.) Barcelona, 1963.

AH 1279.31 — Historia del Oriente antiguo y Medo Persa. (Stewart-Vargas, Guillermo.) Montevideo, 1931.

AH 7207.20A — Historia del Senado romano. (Diaz, José F.) Barcelona, 1867.

AH 7138.49.9 — Historia externa del derecho romano para el uso de los estudiantes de jurisprudencia. (Warnkoenig, Leopold A.) Habana, 1849.

AH 7107.34.2 — Historia fisci judaici. (Zornii, Petri.) Altonaviae, 1734.

AH 4278.55 — Historia griega. (Boreau, V.) Santiago, 1855.

Htn AH 7485.61F* — Historia imperial y Cesarea. (Mexia, Pedro.) Anvers, 1561.

AH 2007.5 — Historia imperii vetustissimi. v.1-2. (Pocock, E.) Harderovici Gebrorum, 1786.

AH 7478.27 — Historia Iulii Caesaris. (Petrarca, F.) Lipsiae, 1827.

AH 819.64.16 — Historia kultury stroźytnej Grecji i Rzymu. wyd. 2. (Kumaniecki, Kazimierz F.) Warszawa, 1964.

AH 7238.82.5 — Historia legionis III. Augustae. Inaug. Diss. (Fiegel, M.) Berolini, 1882.

AH 7238.77 — Historia legionum auxiliorumqui ende ab execessu divi Augusti usque ad Vespasiani tempora. (Stille, Wilhelm.) Kiliae, 1877.

AH 15.2 — Historia mutationum rei...romanorum. (Lange, C.C.L.) Gottingae, 1846- 12 pam.

Htn AH 256.33* — Historia navalis antiqua. (Ryves, Thomas.) Londini, 1633.

Htn AH 256.40* — Historia navalis antiqua. (Ryves, Thomas.) Londini, 1640.

AH 2648.5 — Historia osrhoëna et edessena ex numis illustrata. (Bayer, G.S.) Petropoli, 1734.

AH 7203.23 — Historia Pandectarum. (Brenkmann, H.) Trajecta ad Rhenum, 1722.

Eg 607.04 — Historia Pharaonis. Helmstadt? 1704.

AH 198.32 — Historia philosophiae juris apud veteres. (Veder, A.) Lugduni Batavorum, 1832.

Eg 707.01 — Historia Ptolemaeorum. (Vaillant, J.) Amstelodami, 1701.

AH 7228.36 — Historia quaestionum pertormenta. (Wasserschleben, W.H.) Berolini, 1836.

AH 4278.50 — Historia tès Archaias Hellados. (Keightley, T.) En Athènais, 1850.

X Cg AH 4279.12 — Historia tès Archaiotètos. (Soteriades, G.) Athènai, 1912.

AH 6107.21 — Historia tès Makedonias. (Kanatsoulès, Dèmètrios.) Thessalonikè, 1964.

AH 5271.7 — Historia tou Argous. (Kophiniòtès, I.K.) Athènai, 1892.

NEDL AH 278.58.4 — Historia universal. (Flóres, Antonio.) Lima, 1858.

AH 7114.8 — Historiae equitum romanorum. (Marquardt, I.) Berolini, 1840.

AH 4278.96.7 — Historiae Graecae. (Brelet, H.) Paris, 1896.

AH 4158.19 — Historiae juris Attici. (Meier, M.H.E.) Berolini, 1819.

AH 7487.07F — Historicae Augusta imperatorum Rom. (Lotich, J.P.) Amstelodami, 1707.

AH 4818.26.6 — Historical antiquities of Greeks. (Wachsmuth, W.) Oxford, 1837. 2v.

AH 3957.24 — The historical background of the Bible. (Schofield, J.N.) London, 1938.

AH 3957.24.3 — The historical background of the Bible. (Schofield, J.N.) London, 1946.

Htn AH 7416.01* — An historical collection of the continuall factions...of the Romans and Italians...before Augustus Caesar. (Fulbeck, William.) London, 1601.

AH 2016.5 — The historical geography of Arabia. (Forster, Charles.) London, 1844. 2v.

AH 3966.5.3 — The historical geography of the Holy Land. 3. ed. (Smith, George A.) N.Y., 1895.

AH 3966.5.5 — The historical geography of the Holy Land. 3d ed. (Smith, George A.) London, 1897.

AH 3966.5.6 — The historical geography of the Holy Land. 4. ed. (Smith, George A.) N.Y., 1897.

AH 3966.5.7 — The historical geography of the Holy Land. 7. ed. (Smith, George A.) N.Y., 1900.

AH 3966.5.26 — The historical geography of the Holy Land. 26. ed. (Smith, George A.) N.Y., 1937?

AH 3966.25 — An historical geography of the Old Testament. (Wells, Edward.) London, 1711-12. 3v.

	AH 3159.22	Historical illustrations of the Old Testament. (Rawlinson, George.) London, 18- .
	AH 7139.03.3	Historical introduction to Roman law. (Walton, F.P.) Edinburgh, 1903.
	AH 7139.03.4	Historical introduction to Roman law. 2. ed. (Walton, F.P.) Edinburgh, 1912.
	AH 7168.86.5	Historical introduction to the private law of Rome. (Muirhead, J.) Edinburgh, 1886.
	AH 7168.86.6	Historical introduction to the private law of Rome. 2. ed. (Muirhead, J.) London, 1899.
	AH 7139.32.2	Historical introduction to the study of Roman law. 2. ed. (Jolowicz, Herbert Felix.) Cambridge, Eng., 1952.
	AH 7139.32.3	Historical introduction to the study of Roman law. 2. ed. (Jolowicz, Herbert Felix.) Cambridge, Eng., 1965.
	AH 8658.5	Historical pictures of pagan and Christian Rome. Rome, 1855.
	AH 7298.63	Historical questions. (Labberton, R.H.) Philadelphia, 1863.
	Eg 602.10	Historical records of Ramses III. (Edgerton, William F.) Chicago, 1936.
	AH 8007.5	Historical researches...politics. (Heeren, A.H.L.) Oxford, 1852. 2v.
	AH 8007.5.2	Historical researches...politics. 2. ed. (Heeren, A.H.L.) Oxford, 1838. 2v.
NEDL	AH 298.33.3	Historical researches. (Heeren, Arnold Herman Ludwig.) Oxford, 1833. 3v.
	AH 277.93.10	Historical researches into politics, intercourse and trade. (Heeren, Arnold Herman Ludwig.) London, 1866. 2v.
	AH 842.32	Historical survey of pre-Christian education. (Laurie, S.S.) London, 1895.
	AH 842.32.3	Historical survey of pre-Christian education. (Laurie, S.S.) N.Y., 1904.
	AH 842.32.2	Historical survey of pre-Christian education. 2. ed. (Laurie, S.S.) N.Y., 1900.
	AH 3966.3	An historical text book and atlas of Biblical geography. (Coleman, L.) Philadelphia, 1868.
	AH 4298.26.5	The historical works of Arnold H.L. Heeren. (Heeren, Arnold H.L.) London, 1846?-50? 6v.
	AH 1278.76.7	Historie ancienne des peuples de l'Orient. 7e éd. (Maspero, Gaston.) Paris, 1905.
Htn	AH 7655.44*	Historie da la declinatione. (Biondo, F.) Venetia, 1544. 2v.
Htn	AH 276.14.4F*	The historie of the world. (Raleigh, Walter.) London, 1628.
Htn	AH 276.14.3F*	Historie of the world and Life of the author. (Raleigh, Walter.) London, 1736. 2v.
Htn	AH 276.14.7F*	Historie of the world in five bookes. (Raleigh, Walter.) London, 1634.
	AH 276.14.2F	Historie of the world in five bookes. (Raleigh, Walter.) London, 1677.
Htn	AH 276.14F*	Historie of the world in five books. (Raleigh, Walter.) London, 1614.
Htn	AH 7445.48*	Historie of two the moste noble capitaines...Anniball...Scipio. (Cope, Anthony.) Londini, 1548.
Htn	AH 7445.44*	The historie of two the moste noble capitaines. (Cope, Anthony.) Londini, 1544.
	AH 317.93	Historie philosophique du monde primitif. (Delisle de Sales, J.C.I.) Paris, 1793. 8v.
	AH 7114.8.2	Historiea equitum romanorum. (Marquardt, I.) Berolini, 1840.
	VAH 9.65	Historiografia a bibliografia dejín prvotnopospolnej a otrokárskej spolocnosti. (Kocis, Gejza.) Bratislava, 1965.
	Eg 708.23	Historisch-antiquarische Untersuchungen über Aegypten, oder Die Inschrift von Rosette. (Drumann, Wilhelm.) Königsberg, 1823.
	AH 4408.92	Historisch-mythologischen Untersuchungen. (Müller, H.D.) Göttingen, 1892.
	AH 4479.23	Die historisch-politischen Voraussetzungen des Konigsfriedens von 386 v. Chr. (Nolte, Ferdinand.) Bamberg, 1923.
	AH 4609.67	Historische Beiträge zu den dynastischen Verbindungen in hellenistischer Zeit. (Seibert, Jakob.) Wiesbaden, 1967.
	AH 7449.07	Historische Bilder vom Bosporus. (Mordtmann, A.D.) Konstantinopel, 1907.
	AH 7168.37.7	Historische Forschungen im Gebiete des römischen Privat-Rechts. (Fabricius, C.F.) Berlin, 1871.
	AH 3018.5	Die historische Semiramis und ihre Zeit. (Lehmann-Haupt, C.F.) Tübingen, 1910.
	AH 298.41	Historische Studien. (Gerlach, F.D.) Hamburg, 1841. 2v.
	AH 3916.5	Historische Topographie von Nordsyrien im Altertum. (Honigmann, Ernst.) Leipzig, 1923.
	AH 3171.12	Die historische Tradition und ihre literarische Gestaltung bei Babyloniern und Hethitern bis 1200. Inaug. Diss. (Güterbock, Hans G.) Glückstadt, 1934.
	AH 7108.04	Historische Versuch. (Hegewisch, D.H.) Altona, 1804.
	AH 7649.23	Der historische Wert der Vita Marci bei Scriptores Historiae Augustae. Photoreproduction. (Schwendemann, J.) Heidelberg, 1923.
	AH 4328.30	History and antiquities of Dorie Race. (Müller, K.O.) Oxford, 1830. 2v.
	AH 4328.30.2	History and antiquities of Dorie Race. 2. ed. (Müller, K.O.) London, 1839. 2v.
	Eg 609.67.5	History and chronology of the eighteenth dynasty of Egypt. (Redford, Donald B.) Toronto, 1967.
	AH 5857.11	The history and civilization of ancient Megara. (Highbarger, E.L.) Baltimore, 1927.
	AH 7039.01	History and description of Roman political institutions. (Abbott, Frank F.) Boston, 1901.
	AH 7039.01.2	History and description of Roman political institutions. (Abbott, Frank F.) Boston, 1901.
	AH 3013.929.10	History and monuments of Ur. (Gadd, Cyril J.) London, 1929.
	AH 8549.149.5	The history and origins of druidism. (Spence, Lewis.) N.Y., 1949.
	AH 8549.149	The history and origins of druidism. (Spence, Lewis.) N.Y., 1949.
	AH 7138.83.3	History and principles of the civil law of Rome. (Amos, S.) London, 1883.
	AH 7009.57	History III. Roman history. (French Bibliographic Digest.) N.Y., 1957.
	AH 7417.83.3	A history of...Roman republic. (Ferguson, A.) Dublin, 1783. 3v.
	AH 7417.83	History of...Roman republic. (Ferguson, A.) London, 1783. 3v.
	AH 7417.83.11	History of...Roman republic. (Ferguson, A.) London, 1825.
NEDL	AH 7417.83.9	History of...Roman republic. (Ferguson, A.) Philadelphia, 1811. 3v.
NEDL	AH 7417.83.13	History of...Roman republic. (Ferguson, A.) Philadelphia, 1830.
NEDL	AH 7417.83.5A	A history of...Roman republic. 1. American ed. (Ferguson, A.) Philadelphia, 1805. 3v.
	AH 4558.48.5	History of Alexander the Great. (Abbott, J.) N.Y., 1848.
	AH 4559.13	History of Alexander the Great. (Kirkman, M.M.) Chicago, 1913.
	AH 4559.53	The history of Alexander the Great. v.2. (Robinson, C.A.) Providence, 1953.
	AH 819.36	History of ancient civilization. (Trever, Albert A.) N.Y., 1936-39. 2v.
NEDL	AH 818.89	History of ancient civilization. (Verschoyle, J.S.) N.Y., 1889.
	Eg 278.81.3	History of ancient Egypt. (Rawlinson, George.) Boston, 1882. 2v.
NEDL	Eg 278.81.2	History of ancient Egypt. (Rawlinson, George.) London, 1881. 2v.
	Eg 278.81.1	History of ancient Egypt. (Rawlinson, George.) London, 1881. 2v.
	Eg 278.81.5	History of ancient Egypt. (Rawlinson, George.) N.Y., 188-? 2v.
	Eg 278.81	History of ancient Egypt. (Rawlinson, George.) N.Y., 1881. 2v.
	Eg 278.81.6	History of ancient Egypt. (Rawlinson, George.) N.Y., 1886. 2v.
	AH 408.01	History of ancient Europe. (Russell, William.) Philadelphia, 1801. 2v.
	AH 938.79	A history of ancient geography. (Bunbury, E.H.) London, 1879. 2v.
	AH 938.97	History of ancient geography. (Tozer, Henry F.) Cambridge, 1897.
	AH 938.97.2	A history of ancient geography. (Tozer, Henry F.) N.Y., 1964.
	AH 938.79.10	A history of ancient geography among the Greeks and Romans. 2. ed. (Bunbury, E.H.) N.Y., 1959. 2v.
NEDL	AH 4277.86.4	History of ancient Greece. (Gillies, J.) Basil, 1790. 5v.
	AH 4277.86.3	History of ancient Greece. (Gillies, J.) Dublin, 1786. 3v.
	AH 4277.86F	History of ancient Greece. (Gillies, J.) London, 1786. 2v.
	AH 4277.68	History of ancient Greece. (Robertson, W.) Edinburgh, 1768.
NEDL	AH 4278.56	History of ancient Greece. London, 1856.
	AH 4277.86.7	History of ancient Greece. 1. American ed. (Gillies, J.) N.Y., 1814. 4v.
	AH 4277.86.12	History of ancient Greece. 2. American ed. (Gillies, J.) Philadelphia, 1822. 4v.
NEDL	AH 4277.86.5	History of ancient Greece. 4. ed. (Gillies, J.) London, 1801. 4v.
NEDL	AH 4277.86.10	History of ancient Greece. 6. ed. v.1-8. (Gillies, J.) London, 1820. 4v.
NEDL	AH 278.97	History of ancient peoples. (Boughton, W.) N.Y., 1896.
	AH 3657.29	A history of ancient Persia. (Rogers, Robert W.) N.Y., 1929.
	AH 3921.8	A history of Antioch in Syria. (Downey, Glanville.) Princeton, 1961.
	AH 408.77A	History of antiquity. (Duncker, M.) London, 1877. 6v.
	AH 3097.4	History of Assurbanipal. (Smith, George.) Leiden, 1871.
	AH 3075.13	History of Assyria. (Olmstead, Albert T.) N.Y., 1923.
	AH 5307.7	History of Athens. (Young, W.) London, 1786.
	AH 5307.7.3	History of Athens. 3. ed. (Young, W.) London, 1804.
	AH 7799.48	A history of Attila and the Huns. (Thompson, E.A.) Oxford, 1948.
	AH 3009.10	History of Babylon from foundation...to Persian conquest. (King, L.W.) N.Y., 1915.
	AH 3008.77	The history of Babylonia. (Smith, George.) London, 1877.
	AH 3009.00	A history of Babylonia and Assyria. (Rogers, R.W.) N.Y., 1900. 2v.
	AH 3008.92.7A	The history of Babylonia and Assyria. (Winckler, H.) N.Y., 1907.
	AH 3009.15	A history of Babylonia and Assyria. 6. ed. (Rogers. R.W.) N.Y., 1915. 2v.
Htn	AH 279.30*	History of civilization. (Hollins, Elizabeth C.M.) Portland, 1930.
	AH 818.68	History of civilization. (Ozanam, A.F.) London, 1868. 2v.
	AH 3963.12	A history of civilization in Palestine. (Macalister, R.A.S.) Cambridge, Eng., 1912.
	AH 3963.12.5	A history of civilization in Palestine. (Macalister, R.A.S.) Cambridge, Eng., 1921.
	AH 4842.95	History of classical scholarship from the beggining to the end of the Hellenistic age. (Pfeiffer, Rudolf.) Oxford, 1968.
	Eg 708.51	History of Cleopatra, queen of Egypt. (Abbott, Jacob.) N.Y., 1851.
	Eg 708.51.2	History of Cleopatra, queen of Egypt. (Abbott, Jacob.) N.Y., 1860.
	Eg 708.51.5	History of Cleopatra, queen of Egypt. (Abbott, Jacob.) N.Y., 1874.
	AH 3659.15	History of Cyrus the Great. (Abbott, Jacob.) N.Y., 1850.
	AH 3659.15.2	History of Cyrus the Great. (Abbott, Jacob.) N.Y., 1852.
	AH 3659.15.6	History of Cyrus the Great. (Abbott, Jacob.) N.Y., 1877.
	AH 3659.20	History of Darius the Great. (Abbott, Jacob.) N.Y., 1850.
	AH 3659.20.3	History of Darius the Great. (Abbott, Jacob.) N.Y., 1854.
	AH 3659.20.6	History of Darius the Great. (Abbott, Jacob.) N.Y., 1871.
NEDL	AH 7650.54	History of decline and fall of Roman Empire. (Gibbon, E.) Boston, 1854. 8v.
NEDL	AH 7650.46	History of decline and fall of Roman Empire. (Gibbon, Edward.) Boston, 1850.
NEDL	AH 7650.49	History of decline and fall of Roman Empire. (Gibbon, Edward.) Boston, 1851. 6v.
NEDL	AH 7650.38.5	History of decline and fall of Roman Empire. (Gibbon, Edward.) Cincinnati, 1840.
NEDL	AH 7650.24.5	History of decline and fall of Roman Empire. (Gibbon, Edward.) London, 1820. 12v.
NEDL	AH 7650.24	History of decline and fall of Roman Empire. (Gibbon, Edward.) London, 1820. 12v.
NEDL	AH 7650.25	History of decline and fall of Roman Empire. (Gibbon, Edward.) London, 1821. 2v.
NEDL	AH 7650.26	History of decline and fall of Roman Empire. (Gibbon, Edward.) London, 1821. 12v.
NEDL	AH 7650.27	History of decline and fall of Roman Empire. (Gibbon, Edward.) London, 1825. 8v.
NEDL	AH 7650.53	History of decline and fall of Roman Empire. (Gibbon, Edward.) London, 1853. 7v.

Author and Title Listing

Call number	Title
NEDL AH 7650.60	History of decline and fall of Roman Empire. (Gibbon, Edward.) London, 1872. 3v.
NEDL AH 7650.65	History of decline and fall of Roman Empire. (Gibbon, Edward.) London, 1872. 3v.
NEDL AH 7650.39	History of decline and fall of Roman Empire. (Gibbon, Edward.) N.Y., 1841-43. 4v.
NEDL AH 7650.40	History of decline and fall of Roman Empire. (Gibbon, Edward.) N.Y., 1843-44. 4v.
NEDL AH 7650.67	History of decline and fall of Roman Empire. (Gibbon, Edward.) N.Y., 1880. 6v.
NEDL AH 7650.75	History of decline and fall of Roman Empire. (Gibbon, Edward.) N.Y., 1902. 5v.
AH 7650.85	History of decline and fall of Roman Empire. (Gibbon, Edward.) N.Y., 1914. 7v.
AH 7650.32A	History of decline and fall of Roman Empire. (Gibbon, Edward.) Oxford, 1827. 8v.
NEDL AH 7650.36	History of decline and fall of Roman Empire. (Gibbon, Edward.) Paris, 1840. 8v.
NEDL AH 7650.37	History of decline and fall of Roman Empire. (Gibbon, Edward.) Paris, 1840. 8v.
AH 7650.17	History of decline and fall of Roman Empire. (Gibbon, Edward.) Philadelphia, 1804. 8v.
NEDL AH 7650.17	History of decline and fall of Roman Empire. (Gibbon, Edward.) Philadelphia, 1804. 8v.
AH 7650.80.5A	History of decline and fall of Roman Empire. v.2. (Gibbon, Edward.) London, 1910.
AH 7650.34	History of decline and fall of Roman Empire. v.2-8. (Gibbon, Edward.) London, 1862. 7v.
NEDL AH 7650.38	History of decline and fall of Roman Empire. v.3-8. (Gibbon, Edward.) Paris, 1840. 3v.
NEDL AH 7650.33	History of decline and fall of Roman Empire. 6. American ed. (Gibbon, Edward.) Philadelphia, 1830. 4v.
AH 7650.41	History of decline and fall of the Roman Empire. (Gibbon, Edward.) Chicago, 1845. 5v.
NEDL AH 7650.7	History of decline and fall of the Roman Empire. (Gibbon, Edward.) London, 1782. 3v.
NEDL AH 7650.41.5	History of decline and fall of the Roman Empire. (Gibbon, Edward.) Philadelphia, 1845. 5v.
AH 7650.3F	History of decline and fall of the Roman Empire. v.1, 2. ed. (Gibbon, Edward.) London, 1776-78. 6v.
AH 5124.7	A history of Delos. (Laidlaw, W.A.) Oxford, 1933.
AH 842.35.4	A history of education in antiquity. (Marrow, Henri Irenée.) London, 1956.
AH 1279.07	History of Egypt, Chaldea, Syria, Babylonia and Assyria in the light of recent discovery. (King, Leonard.) London, 1907.
Eg 279.05A	A history of Egypt. (Breasted, James Henry.) N.Y., 1905.
Eg 279.05.5	A history of Egypt. (Breasted, James Henry.) N.Y., 1909.
Eg 278.59.6	A history of Egypt. (Brugsch, H.) London, 1879. 2v.
Eg 279.02	A history of Egypt. (Budge, Ernest Alfred Wallis.) London, 1902. 8v.
Eg 278.36.3	History of Egypt. (Sharpe, S.) London, 1846.
Eg 278.36.4A	History of Egypt. (Sharpe, S.) London, 1859. 2v.
Eg 278.36.6	History of Egypt. (Sharpe, S.) London, 1870. 2v.
Eg 278.90A	History of Egypt. (Wendel, F.C.H.) N.Y., 1890.
Eg 279.05.9	A history of Egypt. 2. ed. (Breasted, James Henry.) N.Y., 1912.
Eg 278.36.10	History of Egypt. 6. ed. (Sharpe, S.) London, 1885. 2v.
Eg 278.94.16	A history of Egypt during the XVIIth and XVIIIth dynasties. 7. ed. (Petrie, William M.F.) London, 1924.
Eg 278.94	A history of Egypt from earliest times to the XVIth dynasty. v.1. (Petrie, William M.F.) London, 1894.
Eg 278.94.10	A history of Egypt from the earliest kings to the XVIth dynasty. 10. ed. (Petrie, William M.F.) London, 1923.
Eg 279.29	A history of Egypt from the earliest times to the end of the 18th dynasty. (Baikie, James.) N.Y., 1929. 2v.
Eg 279.05.8	A history of Egypt from the earliest times to the Persian conquest. 2. ed. (Breasted, James Henry.) London, 1950.
Eg 278.94.9	A history of Egypt from the earliest times to the XVIth dynasty. 2. ed. (Petrie, William M.F.) London, 1895.
Eg 278.94.17	A history of Egypt from the XIXth to the XXXth dynasties. 3. ed. (Petrie, William M.F.) London, 1925.
Eg 278.94.21	A history of Egypt in the Middle Ages. (Lane-Poole, Stanley.) N.Y., 1901.
Eg 278.94.6A	A history of Egypt in the Middle Ages. v.6. (Lane-Poole, Stanley.) London, 1901.
Eg 278.94.20	A history of Egypt in the Middle Ages. 4. ed. (Lane-Poole, Stanley.) London, 1925.
Eg 278.94.22	A history of Egypt in the Middle Ages. 4. ed. (Lane-Poole, Stanley.) London, 1968.
Eg 278.94.19	A history of Egypt under Roman rule. 3. ed. (Milne, Joseph G.) London, 1924.
Eg 278.94.25	A history of Egypt under the Ptolemaic dynasty. v.4. (Bevan, E.R.) London, 1927.
Eg 278.94.4	A history of Egypt under the Ptolemaic dynasty. v.4. (Mahaffy, J.P.) London, 1899.
AH 3096.4	The history of Esarhaddon...681-668. (Budge, E.A.) London, 1880.
AH 8907.6	History of Etruria. (Gray, E.C.H.) London, 1843. 3v.
AH 4038.63A	History of federal government. (Freeman, E.A.) London, 1863.
AH 4038.63.2	History of federal government. 2. ed. (Freeman, E.A.) London, 1893.
AH 4278.99A	History of Greece. (Botsford, George W.) N.Y., 1899.
AH 4279.00.4A	History of Greece. (Bury, John Bagnell.) London, 1902. 2v.
AH 4278.77	History of Greece. (Cox, George W.) London, 1874. 2v.
AH 4278.74.5	History of Greece. (Cox, George W.) London, 1878. 2v.
AH 4278.57.12	History of Greece. (Curtius, Ernest.) London, 1868. 5v.
NEDL AH 4278.57.13.5	History of Greece. (Curtius, Ernest.) N.Y., 1868?-1873? 5v.
NEDL AH 4278.57.13	History of Greece. (Curtius, Ernest.) N.Y., 1871. 5v.
NEDL AH 4278.57.14A	History of Greece. (Curtius, Ernest.) N.Y., 1876. 5v.
NEDL AH 4278.57.16	History of Greece. (Curtius, Ernest.) N.Y., 1883. 5v.
NEDL AH 4278.57.17A	History of Greece. (Curtius, Ernest.) N.Y., 1886. 5v.
NEDL AH 4278.57.17.5	History of Greece. (Curtius, Ernest.) N.Y., 1892. 5v.
NEDL AH 4278.57.18	History of Greece. (Curtius, Ernest.) N.Y., 1897. 5v.
AH 4278.83	History of Greece. (Duncker, M.W.) London, 1883. 2v.
NEDL AH 4278.78.5	History of Greece. (Fyffe, C.A.) N.Y., 1875.
AH 4278.78	History of Greece. (Fyffe, C.A.) N.Y., 1878.
NEDL AH 4278.78.4	History of Greece. (Fyffe, C.A.) N.Y., 1883.
NEDL AH 4278.78.8	History of Greece. (Fyffe, C.A.) N.Y., 1885.
NEDL AH 4278.78.7	History of Greece. (Fyffe, C.A.) N.Y., 1890.
NEDL AH 4278.00.7	History of Greece. (Goldsmith, Oliver.) London, 1821. 2v.
NEDL AH 4278.46.7	History of Greece. (Grote, George.) Boston, 1851.
AH 4278.46	History of Greece. (Grote, George.) London, 1846. 12v.
AH 4278.46.16	A history of Greece. (Grote, George.) London, 1862. 8v.
NEDL AH 4278.46.21	History of Greece. (Grote, George.) London, 1869. 12v.
AH 4278.46.23A	History of Greece. (Grote, George.) London, 1869. 12v.
AH 4278.46.36	History of Greece. (Grote, George.) London, 1906. 12v.
AH 4278.46.37	History of Greece. (Grote, George.) London, 1906. 3v.
AH 4278.46.15	History of Greece. (Grote, George.) N.Y., 1852-71. 12v.
NEDL AH 4278.46.19	History of Greece. (Grote, George.) N.Y., 1867. 12v.
AH 4279.59	A history of Greece. (Hammond, Nicholas Geoffrey Lemprière.) Oxford, 1959.
AH 4278.86.7A	History of Greece. (Holm, Adolf.) London, 1894. 4v.
NEDL AH 4278.86.8	History of Greece. (Holm, Adolf.) London, 1896-99. 4v.
NEDL AH 4278.86.10	The history of Greece. (Holm, Adolf.) London, 1899-1902. 4v.
NEDL AH 4278.86.9	The history of Greece. (Holm, Adolf.) London, 1906. 4v.
AH 4278.39	History of Greece. (Keightley, T.) Boston, 1839.
AH 4278.02	History of Greece. (Mavor, W.) London, 1802. 2v.
AH 4277.95.5	History of Greece. (Mitford, W.) Boston, 1823. 8v.
NEDL AH 4277.95.5.5	History of Greece. (Mitford, W.) Boston, 1823. 8v.
AH 4277.95	History of Greece. (Mitford, W.) London, 1795. 10v.
AH 4277.95.3	History of Greece. (Mitford, W.) London, 1814. 8v.
AH 4278.90.5	History of Greece. (Oman, C.W.C.) Rivingtons, 1890.
NEDL AH 4278.57.19.5A	A history of Greece. (Smith, William.) Boston, 1855.
NEDL AH 4278.57.19	A history of Greece. (Smith, William.) Boston, 1855.
NEDL AH 4278.57.21	History of Greece. (Smith, William.) Boston, 1857.
AH 4278.57.20	History of Greece. (Smith, William.) Boston, 1857.
NEDL AH 4278.57.22	History of Greece. (Smith, William.) Boston, 1860.
NEDL AH 4278.57.25	History of Greece. (Smith, William.) London, 1900.
NEDL AH 4278.57.23	History of Greece. (Smith, William.) N.Y., 1860.
NEDL AH 4278.57.23.10	History of Greece. (Smith, William.) N.Y., 1861.
NEDL AH 4278.57.23.15	History of Greece. (Smith, William.) N.Y., 1863.
NEDL AH 4278.57.24.7	History of Greece. (Smith, William.) N.Y., 1885.
NEDL AH 4278.57.24.9	History of Greece. (Smith, William.) N.Y., 1886.
AH 4278.35.3	History of Greece. (Thirlwall, C.) London, 1845. 8v.
AH 4278.35.3.5	History of Greece. (Thirlwall, C.) N.Y., 1845. 2v.
AH 4278.81	History of Greece. (Timayenis, T.T.) N.Y., 1881. 2v.
NEDL AH 4278.81.4	History of Greece. (Timayenis, T.T.) N.Y., 1882-83. 2v.
NEDL AH 4278.81.2	History of Greece. (Timayenis, T.T.) N.Y., 1883. 2v.
NEDL AH 4278.81.3	History of Greece. (Timayenis, T.T.) N.Y., 1884. 2v.
AH 4278.56.35F	History of Greece. v.1-4. (Duruy, V.) Boston, 1890. 8v.
NEDL AH 4278.46.29	History of Greece. v.1-6,8-10. (Grote, George.) London, 1872. 9v.
AH 4278.88	History of Greece. v.2, photoreproduction. (Abbott, Evelyn.) London, 1888-1900. 3v.
NEDL AH 4278.46.11	History of Greece. v.2-12. (Grote, George.) N.Y., 1859. 11v.
NEDL AH 4277.95.4	History of Greece. v.9-10, 3. ed. (Mitford, W.) London, 1821-22. 10v.
NEDL AH 4278.46.5	History of Greece. 2. ed. (Grote, George.) London, 1849. 12v.
AH 4278.46.3	History of Greece. 2. ed. (Grote, George.) London, 1849. 12v.
AH 4278.90.6	History of Greece. 2. ed. (Oman, C.W.C.) London, 1891.
AH 4278.90.6.3	History of Greece. 3. ed. (Oman, C.W.C.) London, 1892.
NEDL AH 4278.46.27	History of Greece. 4. ed. (Grote, George.) London, 1872. 10v.
AH 4278.90.6.4	History of Greece. 4. ed. (Oman, C.W.C.) London, 1893.
AH 4278.90.7.5	History of Greece. 7. ed. (Oman, C.W.C.) N.Y., 1901.
AH 4279.29.4.5	A history of Greece. 9. ed. (Robinson, Cyril E.) London, 1957.
AH 4278.00.10	History of Greece. 11. ed. (Goldsmith, Oliver.) London, 1825.
AH 4278.98	A history of Greece for colleges and high schools. (Myers, P. Van Ness.) Boston, 1898.
AH 4278.99.3	A history of Greece for high schools and academies. (Botsford, George W.) N.Y., 1900.
AH 4278.29	History of Greece from earliest times. (Malkin, F.) London, 1829.
NEDL AH 4277.95.6	The history of Greece from the earliest period to the death of Agesilaus. (Mitford, W.) London, 1835. 8v.
AH 4278.00.9	The history of Greece from the earliest state to the death of Alexander the Great. (Goldsmith, Oliver.) London, 1825.
AH 4278.46.75	A history of Greece from the time of Solon to 403 B.C. (Grote, George.) London, 1907.
AH 4279.00.30	A history of Greece to the death of Alexander the Great. 3. ed. (Bury, John Bagnell.) London, 1951.
AH 4279.00.31	A history of Greece to the death of Alexander the Great. 3. ed. (Bury, John Bagnell.) London, 1972.
AH 4279.59.5	A history of Greece to 322 B.C. 2. ed. (Hammond, Nicholas Geoffrey Lemprière.) Oxford, 1967.
AH 4277.95.7	History of Greece with final additions and corrections. (Mitford, W.) London, 1838. 8v.
AH 4818.98.20	History of Greek culture. (Burckhardt, J.) N.Y., 1963.
AH 4039.51	A history of Greek political thought. (Sinclair, Thomas Alan.) London, 1951.
AH 4039.51.2	A history of Greek political thought. 2. ed. (Sinclair, Thomas Alan.) Cleveland, 1968.
AH 4889.18.25A	History of Greek public finance. (Andreades, Andreas Michael.) Cambridge, 1933.
AH 7448.49	History of Hannibal the Carthaginian. (Abbott, Jacob.) N.Y., 1849.
AH 2957.3	History of Illium or Troy. (Chandler, R.) London, 1802.

Author and Title Listing

AH 7478.49	History of Julius Caesar. (Abbott, Jacob.) N.Y., 1849.
AH 7478.49.9	History of Julius Caesar. (Abbott, Jacob.) N.Y., 1877.
AH 7478.65.4	History of Julius Caesar. (Napoléon III, emperor of the French.) London, 1865. 2v.
AH 7478.65.7A	History of Julius Caesar. (Napoléon III, emperor of the French.) N.Y., 1865-66. 2v.
AH 7478.65.5F	History of Julius Caesar. Atlas. (Napoléon III, emperor of the French.) London, n.d.
AH 6110.7F	History of life and reign of Philip. (Leland, T.) London, 1758.
AH 6110.5F	History of life and reign of Philip. 2. ed. (Leland, T.) London, 1761. 2v.
AH 6110.8	History of life and reign of Philip. 2. ed. (Leland, T.) London, 1775. 2v.
AH 6107.14	A history of Macedonia. (Hammond, Nicholas Geoffrey Lempriere.) Oxofrd, 1972-
AH 4828.42	History of manners and customs of ancient Greece. (St. John, J.A.) London, 1842. 3v.
AH 818.93	History of mental growth of mankind. (Hittell, J.S.) N.Y., 1893. 4v.
AH 5910.10	A history of Messenia from 369 to 146 B.C. Thesis. (Roebuck, Carl A.) Chicago, 1941.
AH 2583.8	History of Miletus down to the anabasis of Alexander. Thesis. (Dunham, A.G.) London, 1915.
AH 8534.5	A history of Narbo. Thesis. (Benedict, Coleman H.) Princeton, 1941.
AH 7548.53	History of Nero. (Abbott, Jacob.) N.Y., 1853.
AH 7548.72.5	History of Nero. (Abbott, Jacob.) N.Y., 1872.
AH 3960.8.5	A history of New Testament times in Palestine, 175 B.C.-70 A.D. (Mathews, S.) N.Y., 1914.
AH 3957.23	History of Palestine. (Rappoport, A.S.) N.Y., 1931.
AH 3707.11.3A	History of Phoenicia. (Rawlinson, G.) London, 1889.
AH 5610.7.5	History of Pyrrhus. (Abbott, Jacob.) N.Y., 1854.
AH 5610.7	History of Pyrrhus. (Abbott, Jacob.) N.Y., 1871.
AH 7297.20	History of revolutions of the Roman Republic. (Vertot, R.A.) London, 1720. 2v.
AH 7297.20.2	History of revolutions of the Roman Republic. (Vertot, R.A.) London, 1721.
AH 7488.25	History of Roman emperors...to...last Constantine. (Elton, C.A.) London, 1825.
AH 7487.50.3	History of Roman emperors. (Crevier, J.B.L.) London, 1755. 10v.
NEDL AH 7488.75.3A	History of Roman Empire. (Curteis, A.M.) Philadelphia, 1875.
AH 7139.46	History of Roman legal science. (Schulz, Fritz.) Oxford, 1946.
AH 7169.06.5	History of Roman private law. pt.1-2. (Clark, E.C.) Cambridge, 1906-19. 4v.
AH 7259.54	A history of Roman sea-power before the second Pernic War. (Thiel, J.H.) Amsterdam, 1954.
NEDL AH 7488.52.7	History of Romans under the Empire. (Merivale, Charles.) London, 1865-68. 8v.
AH 7418.98.2	History of Rome, 390-202 B.C. (Woodhouse, Mason A.) London, 1911.
AH 7277.92	History of Rome. (Adams, J.) Dublin, 1792. 2v.
AH 7278.40	History of Rome. (Arnold, T.) London, 1840. 3v.
AH 7278.40.7	History of Rome. (Arnold, T.) N.Y., 1857.
AH 7278.18	History of Rome. (Bankes, H.) London, 1818. 2v.
AH 7278.37	History of Rome. (Bell, R.) Philadelphia, 1837.
NEDL AH 7279.01	History of Rome. (Botsford, G.W.) N.Y., 1901.
NEDL AH 7278.85.2.5	History of Rome. (Creighton, M.) London, 1888.
AH 7278.85.3A	History of Rome. (Creighton, M.) N.Y., 1875.
AH 7278.85.3.4	History of Rome. (Creighton, M.) N.Y., 1877.
AH 7278.85.3.5	History of Rome. (Creighton, M.) N.Y., 1879.
AH 7278.85.3.6	History of Rome. (Creighton, M.) N.Y., 1883.
AH 7278.85	History of Rome. (Creighton, M.) N.Y., 1885.
AH 7278.85.3.8	History of Rome. (Creighton, M.) N.Y., 1886.
AH 7278.85.2	History of Rome. (Creighton, M.) N.Y., 1888.
AH 7278.85.3.7A	History of Rome. (Creighton, M.) N.Y., 189-?
AH 7278.85.3.10	History of Rome. (Creighton, M.) N.Y., 1890.
AH 7278.70.9	History of Rome. (Duruy, V.) Boston, 1883. 16v.
AH 7279.23.1	A history of Rome. (Frank, Tenney.) London, 1923.
AH 7279.23A	A history of Rome. (Frank, Tenney.) N.Y., 1923.
AH 7279.23.10	A history of Rome. (Frank, Tenney.) N.Y., 1928.
AH 7279.23.4	A history of Rome. (Frank, Tenney.) N.Y., 1931.
AH 7279.23.5	A history of Rome. (Frank, Tenney.) N.Y., 1933.
AH 7279.14	A history of Rome. (Giles, A.F.) London, 1914.
AH 7278.39	History of Rome. (Hetherington, W.M.) Edinburgh, 1839.
AH 7278.96.7	History of Rome. (How, W.W.) London, 1898.
AH 7278.68.3A	History of Rome. (Ihne, W.) London, 1871. 5v.
AH 7278.39.5	History of Rome. (Keightley, T.) Boston, 1839.
AH 7278.79	History of Rome. (Leighton, R.F.) N.Y., 1879.
NEDL AH 7278.79.4	History of Rome. (Leighton, R.F.) N.Y., 1880.
AH 7278.79.12	A history of Rome. (Leighton, R.F.) N.Y., 1901.
AH 7278.55	History of Rome. (Liddell, H.G.) London, 1855. 2v.
NEDL AH 7278.55.2A	History of Rome. (Liddell, H.G.) N.Y., 1857.
NEDL AH 7278.55.2.5	History of Rome. (Liddell, H.G.) N.Y., 1864.
NEDL AH 7278.55.9A	History of Rome. (Liddell, H.G.) N.Y., 1879.
AH 7278.54.12	History of Rome. (Mommsen, T.) London, 1868. 4v.
AH 7478.54A	History of Rome. (Mommsen, T.) London, 1886. 2v.
AH 7278.54.28.10	The history of Rome. (Mommsen, T.) London, 1908-12. 5v.
AH 7278.54.27	The history of Rome. (Mommsen, T.) London, 1920.
AH 7278.54.16	History of Rome. (Mommsen, T.) N.Y., 1868. 4v.
NEDL AH 7278.54.15	History of Rome. (Mommsen, T.) N.Y., 1869-70. 4v.
AH 7278.54.16.5	History of Rome. (Mommsen, T.) N.Y., 1871. 4v.
NEDL AH 7278.54.17	History of Rome. (Mommsen, T.) N.Y., 1873. 2v.
AH 7278.54.18	History of Rome. (Mommsen, T.) N.Y., 1885. 4v.
AH 7278.54.18.15	History of Rome. (Mommsen, T.) N.Y., 1894. 4v.
AH 7278.54.19	History of Rome. (Mommsen, T.) N.Y., 1895. 5v.
AH 7478.54.2	History of Rome. (Mommsen, T.) N.Y., 1899. 2v.
AH 7278.54.21	History of Rome. (Mommsen, T.) N.Y., 1900. 5v.
AH 7278.54.24	The history of Rome. (Mommsen, T.) N.Y., 1908. 5v.
AH 7278.54.28	The history of Rome. (Mommsen, T.) N.Y., 1958.
AH 7278.11.13	History of Rome. (Niebuhr, B.G.) Cambridge, 1828. 3v.
AH 7278.11.21	History of Rome. (Niebuhr, B.G.) London, 1844. 2v.
AH 7278.11.18A	History of Rome. (Niebuhr, B.G.) London, 1851. 3v.
AH 7278.11.15	History of Rome. (Niebuhr, B.G.) Philadelphia, 1835. 2v.
AH 7278.11.16	History of Rome. (Niebuhr, B.G.) Philadelphia, 1844. 2v.
AH 7279.35	A history of Rome. (Robinson, C.E.) N.y., 1935.
AH 7278.47	History of Rome. (Schmitz, L.) N.Y., 1847.
NEDL AH 7278.94A	History of Rome. (Shuckburgh, E.S.) N.Y., 1894.
AH 7278.96.5	History of Rome. (Wells, J.) London, 1896.
NEDL AH 7278.54.18.9	History of Rome. Provinces of the Roman Empire from Caesar to Diocletian. (Mommsen, T.) N.Y., 1887. 2v.

AH 7278.40.3A	History of Rome. v.1-3. (Arnold, T.) N.Y., 1846. 2v.
AH 7278.30	History of Rome. v.1-5. London, 1830-
NEDL AH 7278.70.5	History of Rome. v.1-6, pt.1-2. (Duruy, V.) London, 1884-12v.
AH 7278.70.15F	History of Rome. v.1-8, pt.1-2. (Duruy, V.) Boston, 1884-87. 16v.
AH 7279.56.5	A history of Rome. 1. ed. (Hadas, Moses.) Garden City, 1956.
AH 7278.54.11.2	History of Rome. 2. ed. v.1-3; v.4, pt.1-2. (Mommsen, T.) London, 1864-67. 5v.
AH 7279.35.8	A history of Rome down to the reign of Constantine. (Cary, Max.) London, 1938.
AH 7499.04	History of Rome during later republic. (Greenidge, A.H.J.) London, 1904.
AH 7279.01.10	A history of Rome for high schools. (Botsford, G.W.) N.Y., 1910.
AH 7279.14.3	A history of Rome for high schools and academies. (Botsford, G.W.) N.Y., 1914.
AH 7278.47.2	A history of Rome from the earliest times to the death of Commodus, A.D. 192. (Schmitz, L.) Andover, 1847.
AH 7278.94.2	A history of Rome to the battle of Actium. (Shuckburgh, E.S.) N.Y., 1917.
NEDL AH 7278.96.8	A history of Rome to the death of Caesar. (How, W.W.) N.Y., 1907.
AH 7279.21	A history of Rome to 565 A.D. (Boak, Arthur E.R.) N.Y., 1921.
AH 7279.21.3	A history of Rome to 565 A.D. (Boak, Arthur E.R.) N.Y., 1929.
AH 7279.21.4	A history of Rome to 565 A.D. (Boak, Arthur E.R.) N.Y., 1935.
AH 7279.21.4.5A	A history of Rome to 565 A.D. 3. ed. (Boak, Arthur E.R.) N.Y., 1943.
AH 7279.21.4.6	A history of Rome to 565 A.D. 3. ed. (Boak, Arthur E.R.) N.Y., 1947.
AH 7279.21.4.9	A history of Rome to 565 A.D. 5. ed. (Boak, Arthur E.R.) N.Y., 1965.
AH 7408.52.5	History of Romulus. (Abbott, Jacob.) N.Y., 1852.
NEDL AH 7408.77.2	History of Romulus. (Abbott, Jacob.) N.Y., 1852.
AH 7408.77	History of Romulus. (Abbott, Jacob.) N.Y., 1877.
AH 3095.6	History of Sennacherib. (Smith, George.) London, 1878.
AH 9607.13A	History of Sicily from earliest times. (Freeman, E.A.) Oxford, 1891. 4v.
NEDL AH 9607.11	History of Sicily to the Athenian war. (Lloyd, W.W.) London, 1872.
AH 9610.13	History of Sicily 491-289 B.C. (Allcroft, A.H.) London, 1890.
AH 5757.20	A history of Sparta, 950-192 B.C. (Forrest, William George Grieve.) N.Y., 1969.
AH 3022.5	A history of Sumer and Akkad. (King, Leonard W.) N.Y., 1910?
Eg 279.08.2	A history of the ancient Egyptians. (Breasted, James Henry.) London, 1908.
Eg 279.08A	A history of the ancient Egyptians. (Breasted, James Henry.) N.Y., 1908.
AH 279.12.2	History of the ancient world. (Botsford, G.W.) N.Y., 1916.
AH 279.11.15	A history of the ancient world. (Botsford, G.W.) N.Y., 1925.
AH 279.11.20	A history of the ancient world. (Botsford, G.W.) N.Y., 1927.
AH 279.04.3	A history of the ancient world. (Goodspeed, George S.) N.Y., 1904.
AH 279.12.3	A history of the ancient world. (Goodspeed, George S.) N.Y., 1912.
AH 279.24.6	A history of the ancient world. (Rostovtsev, Mikhail Ivanovich.) Westport, 1971. 2v.
AH 279.65	A history of the ancient world. (Starr, Chester G.) N.Y., 1965.
AH 279.24.5A	A history of the ancient world. v.2. (Rostovtsev, Mikhail Ivanovich.) Oxford, 1927.
AH 817.37	History of the arts and sciences. (Rollin, Charles.) London, 1737. 4v.
AH 4039.52	A history of the Athenian constitution to the end of the fifth century B.C. (Hignett, C.) Oxford, 1952.
AH 4039.52.5	A history of the Athenian constitution to the end of the fifth century B.C. (Hignett, C.) Oxford, 1958.
AH 3009.02	A history of the Babylonians and Assyrians. (Goodspeed, G.S.) N.Y., 1902.
AH 3009.06	A history of the Babylonians and Assyrians. 2. ed. (Goodspeed, G.S.) N.Y., 1906.
AH 8657.5	History of the city of Rome. (Dyer, Thomas H.) London, 1865.
AH 7650.72	The history of the decline and fall of the Roman Empire. (Gibbon, Edward.) London, 1898-1901. 7v.
NEDL AH 7650.8	History of the decline and fall of the Roman Empire. (Gibbon, Edward.) London, 1783. 6v.
NEDL AH 7650.13	The history of the decline and fall of the Roman Empire. (Gibbon, Edward.) London, 1802. 12v.
NEDL AH 7650.29	History of the decline and fall of the Roman Empire. (Gibbon, Edward.) London, 1826-28. 4v.
NEDL AH 7650.31	The history of the decline and fall of the Roman Empire. (Gibbon, Edward.) London, 1827. 11v.
AH 7650.70	The history of the decline and fall of the Roman Empire. (Gibbon, Edward.) London, 1887. 8v.
NEDL AH 7650.40.5	History of the decline and fall of the Roman Empire. (Gibbon, Edward.) N.Y., 1845-46. 4v.
NEDL AH 7651.10.5	The history of the decline and fall of the Roman Empire. (Gibbon, Edward.) N.Y., 1860.
NEDL AH 7651.11	History of the decline and fall of the Roman Empire. (Gibbon, Edward.) N.Y., 1862.
AH 7651.19	The history of the decline and fall of the Roman Empire. v.2. (Gibbon, Edward.) London, 1899.
NEDL AH 7650.43	History of the decline and fall of the Roman Empire. v.3. (Gibbon, Edward.) N.Y., 1847.
AH 7651.26	The history of the decline and fall of the Roman Empire. 2. ed. v.2-7. (Gibbon, Edward.) London, 1926-29. 6v.
AH 3657.39	History of the early kings of Persia. (Mirkhoud.) London, 1832.
Eg 878.82	History of the Egyptian religion. (Tiele, C.R.) London, 1882.
AH 7658.35	History of the fall of the Roman Empire. (Simonde de Simondi, J.C.L.) Philadelphia, 1835.
AH 4279.26	A history of the Greek and Roman world. (Grundy, G.B.) London, 1926.
AH 4279.25	A history of the Greek and Roman world. (Grundy, G.B.) N.Y., 1925.

Author and Title Listing

Call number	Entry
AH 4459.36.3	A history of the Greek world. 3. ed. (Laistner, M.L.W.) London, 1957.
AH 4659.32.20	A history of the Greek world from 323-146 B.C. (Cary, Max.) N.Y., 1939.
AH 4659.32.15	A history of the Greek world from 323-146 B.C. 2. ed. (Cary, Max.) London, 1951.
AH 4659.32.10A	A history of the Greek world from 325-146 B.C. (Cary, Max.) London, 1932.
AH 4459.36	A history of the Greek world from 479 to 323 B.C. (Laistner, M.L.W.) London, 1936.
AH 4459.36.2	A history of the Greek world from 479 to 323 B.C. 2. ed. (Laistner, M.L.W.) London, 1947.
AH 7328.82	A history of the Jews in Rome. (Hudson, E.H.) London, 1882.
AH 7328.84	History of the Jews in Rome. (Hudson, E.H.) London, 1884.
AH 7408.68A	History of the kings of Rome. (Dyer, Thomas H.) London, 1868.
NEDL AH 7408.68.3	History of the kings of Rome. (Dyer, Thomas H.) Philadelphia, 1868.
AH 7278.46.5	History of the later Roman Commonwealth. (Arnold, T.) London, 1857. 2v.
AH 7308.49.2	History of the liberty of the ancient Romans. (Eliot, Samuel.) Boston, 1853.
AH 4278.99.5	A history of the Orient and Greece. (Botsford, George W.) N.Y., 1911.
AH 3657.31A	History of the Persian empire. (Olmstead, A.T.E.) Chicago, 1948.
Eg 279.25.5	A history of the pharaohs. (Weigall, A.E.P.B.) London, 1925-27? 2v.
Eg 279.25.7A	A history of the pharaohs. (Weigall, A.E.P.B.) N.Y., 1927. 2v.
NEDL AH 7417.83.14	History of the progress and termination of the Roman republic. (Ferguson, A.) N.Y., 1836.
NEDL AH 7417.83.15	A history of the progress and termination of the Roman republic. (Ferguson, A.) N.Y., 1841.
NEDL AH 7417.83.17	History of the progress and termination of the Roman republic. (Ferguson, A.) N.Y., 1852.
AH 9607.21	The history of the province of Sicily. (Jenison, E.S.) Boston, 1919.
AH 7278.46	History of the Roman Commonwealth. (Arnold, T.) N.Y., 1846.
AH 7488.50	The history of the Roman emperors, from Augustus to the death of Marcus Antoninus. (Lynam, R.) London, 1850. 2v.
AH 7488.41.5	History of the Roman empire, from the accession of Augustus to the end of the empire of the West. (Keightley, Thomas.) Boston, 1841.
AH 7488.93	History of the Roman Empire. (Bury, J.B.) N.Y., 1893.
AH 7488.93.2	History of the Roman Empire. (Bury, J.B.) N.Y., 1893.
AH 7338.18	History of the Roman Empire. (Rogers, Eliza.) London, 1818. 5v.
AH 7278.18.5F	History of the Roman Empire. Atlas. (Rogers, Eliza.) London, 1818.
AH 7137.18.5	The history of the Roman or civil law. (Ferriere, M.C.J.) London, 1724.
AH 7279.62	A history of the Roman people. (Heichelheim, F.) Englewood Cliffs, 1962.
AH 7278.33.5	History of the Roman Republic. (Michelet, J.) London, 1847.
AH 7278.33.6	History of the Roman Republic. (Michelet, J.) N.Y., 1847.
AH 7278.33.15	History of the Roman Republic. (Michelet, J.) N.Y., 1859.
AH 7418.89	The history of the Roman republic. (Mommsen, T.) N.Y., 1889.
AH 7419.32	A history of the Roman republic. (Robinson, Cyril E.) N.Y., 1932.
AH 7489.44.1.5	A history of the Roman world. 3. ed. (Salmon, E.T.) London, 1957.
AH 7489.35	A history of the Roman world from A.D. 138 to 337. (Parker, Henry M.D.) London, 1935.
AH 7489.35.3	A history of the Roman world from A.D. 138 to 337. (Parker, Henry M.D.) N.Y., 1939.
AH 7489.35.2	A history of the Roman world from A.D. 138 to 337. 2. ed. (Parker, Henry M.D.) London, 1958.
AH 7489.44	A history of the Roman world from 30 B.C. to A.D. 138. (Salmon, E.T.) N.Y., 1944.
AH 7469.35	A history of the Roman world from 146 to 30 B.C. (Marsh, Frank B.) London, 1935.
AH 7469.35.1	A history of the Roman world from 146 to 30 B.C. (Marsh, Frank B.) N.Y., 1939.
AH 7469.35.2	A history of the Roman world from 146 to 30 B.C. 2. ed. (Marsh, Frank B.) London, 1953.
AH 7469.35.3	A history of the Roman world from 146 to 30 B.C. 3. ed. (Marsh, Frank B.) London, 1963.
AH 7279.35.10A	A history of the Roman world from 753 to 146 B.C. (Scullard, H.H.) London, 1935.
AH 7279.35.10.6	A history of the Roman world from 753 to 146 B.C. (Scullard, H.H.) N.Y., 1939.
AH 7279.35.10.5	A history of the Roman world from 753 to 146 B.C. 2. ed. (Scullard, H.H.) London, 1951.
AH 7279.35.10.3	A history of the Roman world from 753 to 146 B.C. 3. ed. (Scullard, H.H.) London, 1961.
AH 7279.66	A history of the Romans. (Bourne, Frank C.) Boston, 1966.
NEDL AH 7488.52.2	History of the Romans. (Merivale, Charles.) London, 1850. 4v.
AH 7488.52A	History of the Romans. 2. ed. (Merivale, Charles.) London, 1852. 7v.
NEDL AH 7488.52.5	History of the Romans. 4. London ed. (Merivale, Charles.) N.Y., 1863. 7v.
AH 7488.52.10.2	History of the Romans under the Empire. (Merivale, Charles.) London, 1872-74. 8v.
NEDL AH 7488.52.10	History of the Romans under the Empire. (Merivale, Charles.) N.Y., 1872-74. 7v.
AH 7488.52.9	History of the Romans under the Empire. 4. London ed. (Merivale, Charles.) N.Y., 1866. 7v.
AH 7488.52.9.3	History of the Romans under the Empire. 4. London ed. (Merivale, Charles.) N.Y., 1866. 7v.
AH 278.28	History of the states of antiquity. (Heeren, Arnold Herman Ludwig.) Northhampton, 1828.
AH 7059.20	The history of the title imperator under the Roman empire. Thesis. (McFayden, Donald.) Chicago, 1920.
AH 458.07	History of the world. (Gillies, J.) London, 1807. 2v.
AH 458.09	History of the world. (Gillies, J.) Philadelphia, 1809. 3v.
NEDL AH 408.99	A history of the world. (Ragozin, Z.A. (Mrs.)) N.Y., 1899.
AH 276.14.9	The history of the world. (Raleigh, Walter.) London, 1971.
NEDL AH 278.85	History of the world. (Smith, P.) N.Y., 1885. 3v.
NEDL AH 278.74	History of the world. (Smith, Philip.) N.Y., 1874. 3v.
AH 6057.9	History of Thessaly. (Kent, R.G.) Lancaster, Pa., 1904.
AH 3740.8	The history of Tyre. (Fleming, Wallace B.) N.Y., 1915.
AH 5057.2	History of united provinces of Achaia. (Gothofreedus, J.) London, 1673.
Eg 1159.56	A history of urology in Egypt. (Bitschai, J.) Cambridge, 1956.
AH 2061.3	History of Varton and of the Battle of the Armenians. (Elisaeus.) London, 1830.
AH 3660.3	History of Xerxes the Great. (Abbott, Jacob.) N.Y., 1850.
AH 3660.3.2	History of Xerxes the Great. (Abbott, Jacob.) N.Y., 1852.
AH 3660.3.5	History of Xerxes the Great. (Abbott, Jacob.) N.Y., 1872.
AH 7139.02.5	Historya Prawodawstwa Rzymskiego. (Zoll, F.) Kraków, 1902. 2v.
AH 818.93	Hittell, J.S. History of mental growth of mankind. N.Y., 1893. 4v.
AH 3400.15F	Hittite hieroglyphic monuments. (Gelb, Ignace J.) Chicago, 1939.
AH 3404.5	The Hittite laws. (Hittites. Laws, statutes, etc.) London, 1951.
AH 3002.26F	Hittite texts in the cuneiform character. (British Museum. Department of Egyptian and Assyrian Antiquities.) London, 1920.
AH 3408.7	Hittiter und Amazonen. (Leonard, W.) Leipzig, 1911.
AH 3408.5	Hittiter und Armenier. (Jensen, P.) Strassburg, 1898.
AH 3400.10	The Hittites; a list of references in the New York Public Library. (Schwartz, Benjamin.) N.Y., 1939.
AH 3401.2	Pamphlet box. Hittites.
AH 3407.7	Hittites. (Campbell, J.) London, 1891. 2v.
AH 3407.20	Les Hittites. (Cavaignac, E.) Paris, 1950.
AH 3407.17	The Hittites. (Cowley, Arthur E.) London, 1920.
AH 3407.30	The Hittites. (Gurney, O.R.) London, 1952.
AH 3407.6	The Hittites. (Sayce, A.H.) London, 1888.
AH 3404.5	Hittites. Laws, statutes, etc. The Hittite laws. London, 1951.
AH 3404.6	Hittites. Laws, statutes, etc. Der Telipinu-Erlass. Diss. München? 1970?
AH 3407.6.5	The Hittites. 2d ed. (Sayce, A.H.) London, 1892.
AH 3407.11	Hittites and their language. (Conder, C.R.) N.Y., 1898.
AH 3958.5F	Hitzig, F. Zur ältesten Völker und Mythengeschichte - Urgeschichte...der Philistäer. Leipzig, 1845.
AH 4149.07	Hitzig, H.F. Altgriechische Staatsverträge. Zürich, 1907.
AH 7228.93	Hitzig, H.F. Die Assessoren der römischen Magistrate. München, 1893.
AH 4168.95	Hitzig, H.F. Griechische Pfandrecht. München, 1895.
AH 7159.09	Hitzig, H.F. Die Herkunft des Schwurgerichts. Zürich, 1909.
AH 158.99	Hitzig, H.F. Injuria. München, 1899.
AH 7628.92	Hitzig, H.F. Stellung Kaiser Hadrians. Zürich, 1892.
AH 4139.06	Hitzig, Hermann F. Die Bedeutung des altgriechischen Rechtes für die vergleichende Rechtswissenschaft. Stuttgart, 1906.
AH 279.43	Hjartarson, A. Mannkynssaga. Reykjavik, 1943.
AH 3155.21	Hoake, S.H. Babylonian and Assyrian religion. London, 1953.
AH 819.52	Hoare, F.R. Eight decisive books of antiquity. London, 1952.
AH 842.31	Hobhouse, W. Theory and practise of ancient education. N.Y., 1910.
AH 3664.16	Hochgottglaube im alten Iran. (Widengren, G.) Uppsala, 1938.
AH 4842.31	Hochheimers, C.F.A. System der griechische Pädagogik. v.1-2. Göttingen, 1788.
AH 7279.52.5	Hocquard, G. Guide romain antique. Paris 1952.
AH 819.70	Hodges, Henry W.M. Technology in the ancient world. London, 1970.
AH 7798.89	Hodgkin, T. Dynasty of Theodosius. Oxford, 1889.
AH 5307.19	Hoeck, A. De rebus ab Atheniensibus in Thracia et in Ponto. Kiliae, 1876.
AH 7488.41	Hoeck, K.F.C. Römische Geschichte. Braunschweig, 1841.
NEDL AH 7488.41.3	Hoeck, K.F.C. Römische Geschichte. Braunschweig, 1841.
AH 3013.25	Hoefer, J.C.F. Premier memoire sur les ruines de Ninive. Paris, 1850.
AH 4228.77	Höffler, R.J.A. De nomothesia Attica. Kiliae, 1877.
AH 819.12.3	Höhn, G. Die Einteilungsarten der Lebens- und Weltalter bei Griechen und Römer. Würzburg, 1912.
AH 7168.80	Hoelder, E. Die Entwickelungsformen des römischen Privatrechtes. Erlangen, 1880.
AH 7163.17	Hölder, E. Römische Ehe. Zürich, 1874.
AH 7138.84.15	Hölder, E. Zwei Abhandlungen aus dem römischen Rechte. Freiburg, 1884.
AH 3178.5	Die Höllenfahrt der Istar. (Schrader, E.) Giessen, 1874.
AH 3960.7	Hölscher, G. Palästina in der persischen und hellenistischen Zeit. Berlin, 1903.
AH 7808.75.2	Hölzl, M. Fasti Praetorii ad A.V. DLXXXVII ad A.V. DCCX. Lipsiae, 1876.
AH 4854.5	Hömschemeyer, Orloys. Die Pferdezucht im klassischen Altertum. Diss. Giessen, 1929.
AH 7729.11	Hönn, K. Quellenuntersuchungen zu den Viten des Heliogabalus. Leipzig, 1911.
AH 7509.38.5	Hönn, Karl. Augustus. 2. Aufl. Wien, 1938.
AH 7509.38.7	Hönn, Karl. Augustus und seine Zeit. 3. Aufl. Wien, 1943.
AH 7509.38.8	Hönn, Karl. Augustus und seine Zeit. 4. Aufl. Wien, 1953.
AH 7759.40.5	Hönn, Karl. Konstantin der Grosse. Leipzig, 1945.
AH 4855.13	Höppener, Frank. Halieutica. Proefschrift. Amsterdam, 1931.
AH 3095.4	Hoerning, K.J.R. Das sechsseitige Prisma des Sanherib. Leipzig, 1878.
AH 7578.83	Hoffman, O.A. De Imperatoris Titi temporibus. Marpeogi, 1883.
AH 7188.38	Hoffmann, E. Lehre von den Servituten. v.1-2. Darmstadt, 1838.
AH 7148.79	Hoffmann, E. Patricische und plebeische Curien. Wien, 1879.
AH 4938.41	Hoffmann, S. Griechenland. Leipzig, 1841. 2v.
AH 4559.07	Hoffmann, W. Literarische Porträt Alexanders des Grossen. Leipzig, 1907.
AH 4559.07.2	Hoffmann, W. Literarische Porträt Alexanders des Grossen. Quelle, 1907.
AH 5308.12	Hoffmeister, E.E.W. Kritische Untersuchung der Charakterentwicklung der Athener. Hamburg, 1932.
AH 7888.99	Hoffmeister, K. Die wirtschaftliche Entwicklung Roms. Wien, 1899.
AH 3659.9	Hoffmenn-Kutschke, A. Die Wahrheit über Kyros, Darius und Zarathuschatra. Berlin, 1910.
AH 7859.6	Hoffsten, R.B. Roman women of rank of the early empire in public life as portrayed by Dio. Diss. Philadelphia, 1939.

Htn AH 876.77* Howe, John. View of antiquity. London, 1677.
AH 7709.42A Howe, L.L. The pretorian prefect from Commodus to Diocletian (A.D. 180-305). Chicago, 1942.
AH 276.61F Howel, W. An institution of general history. London, 1661.
Htn AH 276.61.2F* Howel, W. An institution of general history. London, 1680.
AH 6024.15 Hoyle, Peter. Delphi. London, 1967.
AH 818.76 Hoyns, G. Die alte Welt. Berlin, 1876.
AH 7708.52 Hoyns, Georg. Geschichte der s.g. driessig Inrannen. Göttingen, 1852.
AH 3005.830.5 Hrozný, Bedřich. Stručný přehled mých vědeckých objevů. Praha, 1848.
AH 4161.11 Hruza, Ernst. Familienrechts. Erlangen, 1892. 2v.
AH 3657.35 Huart, Clément. La Perse antique et la civilisation iranienne. Paris, 1925.
AH 8073.17 Hubac, Pierre. Carthage. Paris, 1946.
AH 8942.5 Hubaux, Jean. Rome et Véies. Paris, 1958.
AH 7469.00 Hubel, Karl. Die Beiffragmente der Cornelia. Erlangen, 1900.
AH 3002.2.21 Huber, Engelbert. Die Personennamen in der Keilschrifturkunden. Leipzig, 1907.
AH 7833.5 Huber, Karl. Theorie des gymnischen Erziehung bei den Römern. Langensalza, 1934.
AH 7162.36 Huber, Paul. Die Ausdehnung der Normen der Senatus Consultum Juventianum auf die private Heredetatis petitio klassischen Rechts. Inaug. Diss. Erlangen, 1933.
AH 4299.07 Huber, Peter. Griechische Geschichte bis 449. München, 1907.
AH 8549.125.5 Hubert, Henri. Divinités gauloises. Epona, 1925.
AH 8548.155 Hubert, Henri. The greatness and decline of the Celts. New York, 1972.
AH 4889.03 Huch, G. Die Organisation der offentlichen Arbeit. Schlesien, 1903.
AH 4852.5 Huddilston, J.H. Lessons from Greek pottery. N.Y., 1902.
AH 7058.78 Hudemann, E.E. Geschichte des Römischen Postwesens. Berlin, 1878.
AH 7328.82 Hudson, E.H. A history of the Jews in Rome. London, 1882.
AH 7328.84 Hudson, E.H. History of the Jews in Rome. London, 1884.
AH 4842.63 Hudson-Williams, T. An education bill from ancient Greece. Cambridge, 1917.
AH 4228.12 Hudtwalcker, M.H. Privat-Schiedsrichter-Diäteten. Jena, 1812.
AH 7008.58 Hübner, E.W. De senatus populique romani actis. Lipsiae, 1858.
AH 7869.7 Hübner, Emil. Quaestiones onomatologicae Latinae. Berolini, 1874. 2 pam.
AH 7869.5 Hübner, Emil. Quaestiones onomatologicae Latinae. Bonnae, 1854.
AH 7298.90 Hübner, Emil. Römische Herrschaft in Westeuropa. Berlin, 1890.
AH 7838.68 Hübner, Émile. Revue archéologique - nouvelles tessères. Paris, 1868.
AH 4408.14 Hüllmann, K.D. Anfänge der griechische Geschichte. Königsberg, 1814.
AH 4202.9 Hüllmann, K.D. Griechische Denkwürdigkeiten. Bonn, 1840.
AH 4908.39 Hüllmann, K.D. Handelsgeschichte. Bonn, 1839.
AH 38.20 Hüllmann, K.D. Staatsrecht des Alterthums. Cöln, 1820.
AH 4108.18 Hüllmann, K.D. Ursprünge der Besteurung. Cöln, 1818.
AH 7038.32.2 Hüllmann, Karl. Römische Grundverfassung. Bonn, 1832.
AH 7038.32 Hüllmann, Karl. Römische Grundverfassung. Bonn, 1832.
AH 4609.00 Hünerwadel, W. Geschichte des Königs Lysimachos. Zürich, 1900.
AH 4862.5 Hueppe, F. Rassen und Sozialhygiene. Wiesbaden, 1897.
AH 907.63 Huet, Pierre D. Histoire du commerce et de la navigation des anciens. Lyon, 1763.
AH 907.63.2 Huet, Pierre D. Histoire du commerce et de la navigation des anciens. 2. éd. Paris, 1716.
Htn AH 7495.34* Hüttich, J. Imperatorum et Caesarum vitae. Argentorati, 1534.
Htn AH 7495.26* Hüttich, J. Romische Keyser abcontra Vegt. Strassburg, 1526.
AH 7639.33 Hüttl, Willy. Antoninus Pius. Prag, 1933-36.
AH 3921.5F Hug, A. Antiochia und der Aufstand des Jahres 387 nach Christus. Winterthur, 1863.
Eg 919.52 Hughes, George. Saite demotic land leases. Chicago, 1952.
AH 938.89.5 Hughes, Lugi. Manuali di geografia antica ad uso delle scuole secondarie. v.1-3. Torino, 1889-90.
NEDL AH 938.56.20 Hughes, William. An atlas of classical geography. N.Y., 1856.
NEDL AH 938.56.10 Hughes, William. An atlas of classical geography. N.Y., 1867.
NEDL AH 938.56.12 Hughes, William. An atlas of classical geography. N.Y., 1870.
NEDL AH 938.56.15 Hughes, William. An atlas of classical geography. N.Y., 1871.
AH 938.56 Hughes, William. An atlas of classical geography. Philadelphia, 1856.
NEDL AH 938.56.3 Hughes, William. An atlas of classical geography. Philadelphia, 1859.
NEDL AH 938.56.4 Hughes, William. An atlas of classical geography. Philadelphia, 1861.
AH 938.56.5 Hughes, William. An atlas of classical geography. Philadelphia, 1865.
AH 7138.25 Hugo, G. Histoire du droit romain. Paris, 1825. 2v.
AH 7201.6 Hugo, G. Jus civile antejustinianeum. Berolini, 1815. 2v.
AH 7138.32 Hugo, G. Lehrbuch der Geschichte des römischen Rechts. Berlin, 1832.
AH 7468.76 Hugues, G.D. Une province romaine sous la Republique. Paris, 1876.
AH 7848.8 Hula, Eduard. Die Toga der späteren Kaiserzeit. Brünn, 1895.
AH 4855.15 Hull, Denison B. Hounds and hunting in ancient Greece. Chicago, 1964.
AH 7008.55 Hullmann, I.G. Disputatio critica de Annalibus. n.p., 1855.
AH 7842.22 Hulsebos, G.A. Disputatio antiquabis de educatione et institutione apud Romanos. n.p., 1867.
AH 928.62 Hultsch, F. Metrologie. Berlin, 1862.
AH 928.62.3 Hultsch, F. Metrologie. Berlin, 1882.
Eg 909.03 Hultsch, F. Die ptolemäischen Münz und Rechnungswerte. Leipzig, 1903.
AH 819.30 Human history. (Smith, G.E.) London, 1930.
AH 408.92 Human origins. (Laing, S.) London, 1892.
AH 8549.103 Human sacrifice among the Irish Celts. (Robinson, F.N.) Boston, 1913.

AH 3813.10 El humanismo semita. (Dussel, Enrique D.) Buenos Aires, 1969.
AH 7199.60 Humanitas und Rhetorik in spät römischen Kaisergesetzen; Studien zur Gesinnungsgrundlage des Dominats. (Honig, Richard.) Göttingen, 1960.
AH 4845.5F Humanitate Graecorum. (Eichstädt, H.C.) Ienae, 1825.
AH 7108.86 Humbert, G. Essai sur les finances. Paris, 1886. 2v.
Eg 1009.69 L'humour dans la littérature et dans l'art de l'ancienne Égypte. (Walle, Baudouin van de.) Leiden, 1969.
AH 7138.54.16 Humphreys, E.R. Manual of civil law for...schools. 2. ed. London, 1856.
AH 7678.83 Hundertmark, J. De imperatore Pertinace; dissertatio historica. Monasterii Guestfalorum, 1883.
AH 3195.14 Hunger, Hermann. Babylonische und assyrische Kolophone. Neukirchen, 1968.
AH 7138.80.5A Hunter, W.A. Introduction to Roman law. London, 1880.
AH 7138.76.8 Hunter, W.A. Roman law. London, 1876.
AH 7138.76.7 Hunter, W.A. Roman law. London, 1876.
AH 7138.97 Hunter, W.A. Roman law. 3. ed. London, 1897.
Eg 819.33 Hur man levde i Faraos land. (Rydh, H.) Stockholm, 1933.
AH 8073.15 Hurd, H.P. The topography of Punic Carthage. Williamsport, 1934.
AH 4819.72.15 Hurmuziadis, Jorge. La cultura de Grecia: antigua, bizantia, moderna. Buenos Aires, 1972.
AH 1329.64 I Hurriti. (Imparati, Fiorella.) Firenze, 1964.
Eg 1159.28 Hurry, Jamieson Boyd. Imhotep. 2. ed. Oxford, 1928.
AH 8907.30.5 Hus, Alain. The Etruscans. N.Y., 1961.
AH 8907.30 Hus, Alain. Les Etrusques. Paris, 1957.
AH 7897.88 Husbandry of the ancients. (Dickson, Adam.) Edinburgh, 1788.
AH 7158.74 Huschke, E. Die Multa und das Sacramentum. Leipzig, 1874.
AH 7138.30 Huschke, E. Studien des römischen Rechts. Breslau, 1830.
AH 7038.38 Huschke, G. Die Verfassung der Servius Tullius. Heidelberg, 1838.
AH 7808.69.5 Huschke, G.P.E. Das alte römische Jahr und seine Tage. Breslau, 1869.
AH 7201.39 Huschke, P.E. Indices. Lipsiae, 1868.
AH 7201.40.2 Huschke, P.E. Iurisprudentiae anteiustinianae. Lipsiae, 1867.
AH 7201.40 Huschke, P.E. Iurisprudentiae anteiustinianae. Lipsiae, 1867.
AH 7201.40.4 Huschke, P.E. Iurisprudentiae anteiustinianae. Lipsiae, 1879.
AH 7201.40.6 Huschke, P.E. Iurisprudentiae anteiustinianae. v.1-2. Lipsiae, 1908-27. 3v.
AH 7168.46 Huschke, P.E. Ueber das Recht des Nexum. Leipzig, 1846.
AH 7108.47 Huschke, P.E. Uber den Census und die Steuerverfassung. Berlin, 1847.
AH 928.36A Hussey, R. Essay on ancient weights and money. Oxford, 1836.
AH 7469.66 Hutchinson, Lester. The conspiracy of Catiline. London, 1966.
Eg 702.10 Hutmacher, Rudolf. Das Ehrendekret für den Strategen Kallimachos. Meisenheim am Glan, 1965.
AH 7799.15.5 Hutton, Edward. Attila and the Huns. N.Y., 1915.
AH 4819.25A Hutton, Maurice. The Greek point of view. London, 1925.
AH 7159.15 Huvelin, Paul. Études sur le fortum dans le très ancien droit roman. Lyon, 1915.
AH 7449.17 Huvelin, Paul. Une guerre d'usure. Paris, 1917.
AH 4858.13 Het huwelijk bij de Griekse en Romeinse moralisten. Proefschrift. (Geurts, Nico.) Amsterdam, 1928.
AH 5759.12A Huxley, G.L. Early Sparta. Cambridge, 1962.
AH 4329.66 Huxley, George. The early Ionians. N.Y., 1966.
AH 4410.20.5 Huxley, George Leonard. Achaeans and Hittites. Belfast, 1965.
AH 5459.5 Huxley, George Leonard. Crete and the Lumians. Oxford, 1961.
AH 5463.30 Huxley, George Leonard. Minoans in Greek sources. Belfast, 1968.
AH 4819.52.5 Huxley, Michael. The root of Europe. London, 1952.
AH 4259.47 Hyde, Walter W. Ancient Greek mariners. N.Y., 1947.
Eg 559.66 The Hyksos. (Seters, John van.) New Haven, 1966.
Eg 559.39 The Hyksos reconsidered. Diss. (Engberg, R.M.) Chicago, 1939.
Eg 1068.74 Hymme à Ammon-Ra. Paris, 1874.
AH 4843.9 Hymne à Apollon. Paris, 1894.
AH 4843.8 Hymnen. (Dionysius, A.) Berlin, 1840.
Eg 1069.48F De hymnen aan Amon van papyrus Leiden I 350. (Zandee, J.) Leiden, 1948.
Eg 1069.30 Hymnes religieux du moyen empire. (Hassan, Sélim.) La Caire, 1928.
AH 4843.10F Hymnus an Apollo. Leipzig, 1896.
AH 7168.76 L'Hypothèque. (Jourdan, A.) Paris, 1876.
AH 4216.10 L'hypothèque grecque et sa signification historique. Thèse. (Bastid, Paul.) Tours, 1917.
Eg 879.71.5 I faraos land-på faraos tid. (Olsson, Albert.) Solna, 1971.
Eg 877.50 Iablonski, P.E. Pantheon Aegyptiorum. Francofurti, 1750.
AH 3053.5 Iahdun-Lim, king of Mari. L'inscription de fondation de Iahdun-Lim, roi de Mari. Paris, 1955.
AH 3020.45 Iankovskaia, N.B. Klinopisnye teksty iz Koul'-Tepe v sobraniiakh SSSR. Moskva, 1968.
Eg 298.90 Ibn Abd al Hakam, Abd al Rahman. Libellus de Historia Aegypti antiqua. Gottingae, 1856.
AH 7799.53 Ici, le monde changea de maitre. (Dévignes, G.) Paris, 1953.
AH 1233.65 L'iconografia del carro da guerra in Siria e Palestina. (Amadasi, Maria Giulia.) Roma, 1965.
AH 1879.65 L'iconographie du dieu de l'orage. (Vanal, Antoine.) Paris, 1965.
AH 7099.67 L'idea di città nel mondo romano. (Storoni Mazzolani, Lidia.) Milano, 1967.
AH 7299.71.10 The idea of Rome; from antiquity to the Renaissance. (Thompson, David.) Albuquerque, 1971.
AH 7099.67.1 The idea of the city in Roman thought. (Storoni Mazzolani, Lidia.) London, 1970.
AH 9758.5 Idealiserung der Naturvölker des Nordens. (Riese, A.) Frankfurt, 1875.
Eg 851.5 Las ideas morales en el antiquo Egipto. (Rosenvasser, A.) Santa Fé, 1938.
AH 1049.48A Ideas of divine rule in the ancient East. (Gadd, Cyril John.) London, 1948.
AH 879.14 L'idee du juste dans l'orient grec avant Socrate. (Kennebicq, Léon.) Bruxelles, 1914.
AH 277.93.4 Ideen über Politik, Verbehr und Handel. (Heeren, Arnold Herman Ludwig.) Göttingen, 1824. 6v.
NEDL AH 298.15 Ideen über Politik, Verkehr und Handel. v.1-2. (Heeren, Arnold Herman Ludwig.) Göttingen, 1815. 3v.

Author and Title Listing

Author and Title Listing

AH 7138.73.3.5 — Introduction to Roman law, in twelve academical lectures. (Hadley, James.) N.Y., 1893.

AH 7138.73.3 — Introduction to Roman law. (Hadley, James.) N.Y., 1873.

AH 7138.73.4 — Introduction to Roman law. (Hadley, James.) New Haven, 1931.

AH 7138.80.5A — Introduction to Roman law. (Hunter, W.A.) London, 1880.

AH 7139.62A — An introduction to Roman law. (Nicholas, B.) Oxford, 1962.

AH 7203.79 — Introduction to study of Justinian's Digest. (Roby, H.J.) Cambridge, 1884.

AH 7138.54.3 — Introduction to study of Roman law. (Cushing, L.S.) Boston, 1854.

Htn AH 3966.8* — An introduction to the geography of the New Testament. (Carpenter, L.) Cambridge, 1811.

AH 3966.8.5 — An introduction to the geography of the New Testament. 6. ed. (Carpenter, L.) London, 1830.

AH 7009.09.5A — Introduction to the sources relating to the Germanic invasions. (Hayes, C.H.) N.Y., 1909.

AH 7009.09.3 — Introduction to the sources relating to the Germanic invasions. (Hayes, C.H.) N.Y., 1909.

AH 938.29.2 — An introduction to the study of Greek and Roman geography. (Longe, George.) Charlottesville, 1829.

AH 817.58 — Introduction to universal history. (Holberg, Ludwig.) London, 1758.

AH 1409.63.10 — Introduzione alla storia dell'Asia anteriore antica. (Liverani, M.) Roma, 1963.

AH 279.58.25 — Introduzione alle guerre persiane e altri saggi. (Nenci, Giuseppe.) Pisa, 1958.

AH 7203.79.10 — Introduzione allo studio del Digesto giustinianeo. (Roby, H.J.) Firenze, 1887.

AH 4009.52 — Introduzione allo studio della staria greca e romana. (Manni, Eugenio.) Palermo, 1952.

AH 4009.52.2 — Introduzione allo studio della storia greca e romana. 2. ed. (Manni, Eugenio.) Palermo, 1959.

Htn AH 7817.32* — Introduzzione alla scienza d'antichita. (Vaslet, L.) Venezia, 1732.

AH 7817.32.5 — Introduzzione alla scienza d'antichita. (Vaslet, L.) Venezia, 1828.

AH 8210.2 — The invasion of Britain by Julius Caesar. (Guest, Edwin.) London, 1864.

AH 4558.93.3 — Invasion of India by Alexander the Great. (M'Crindle, J.W.) Westminster, 1893.

AH 4558.93.5A — Invasion of India by Alexander the Great. (M'Crindle, J.W.) Westminster, 1896.

AH 7299.68 — Invectiva in Romam. (Benzinger, Josef.) Lübeck, 1968.

AH 7158.36 — Invernizi, P. De publicis et criminalibus iudiciis Romanorum. Lipsiae, 1846.

AH 7214.10 — Ioachmiovici, V.E. Juspirandum...du droit romain. Paris, 1912.

AH 4136.85.5 — Ioannis Meursii Themis Attica, sive De legibus Atticii libri II. (Meurs, Johannes van.) Rhenum, 1685.

AH 2120.3 — Ionia; a quest. 1. ed. (Stark, Freya.) London, 1954.

AH 2557.7 — Ionia and the East. (Hogarth, D.G.) Oxford, 1909.

AH 2120.5 — La Ionia nel mondo miceneo. (Cassola, Filippo.) Napoli, 1957.

AH 2120.7F — Ionian trade and colonization. (Roebuck, Carl A.) N.Y., 1959.

AH 4328.55 — Die Ionier. (Curtius, Ernst.) Berlin, 1855.

AH 4329.20 — Die ionische Kolonisation. (Bilabel, Friedrich.) Leipzig, 1920.

AH 4538.45 — Iphicratis Chabriae Timothei. (Rehdantz, C.) Berolini, 1845.

AH 3660.15 — Iran pri perviykh akhemenidakh. (Dandamaev, M.A.) Moskva, 1963.

AH 3653.7 — L'Iran sous les Achéménides. (Ehtécham, Mortéza.) Fribourg, 1946.

AH 3661.15 — Iran v epokhu pervykh Sasanidov. (Lukonin, Vladimir G.) Leningrad, 1961.

AH 3664.11 — Das iranische Erlösungsmysterium. (Reitzenstein, R.) Bonn, 1921.

AH 3664.14 — Iranische Geisteswelt von der Anfängen bis zum Islam. (Widengren, George.) Baden-Baden, 1961.

AHP 19.1 — Iraq. London. 1,1934+ 16v.

AH 3013.943.5 — Iraq. Department of Antiquities. Babylon. Baghdad, 1943.

AH 3013.937.10 — Iraq. Department of Antiquities. Guide thru the ruins of Babylon and Borsippa. Baghdad, 1937.

AHP 19.1.2 — Iraq. Index, v.1-30. London, 1970.

AH 3013.930 — Iraq. Ministry of Education. Report on excavations in Iraq during the season. Baghdad. 1928-1929

AH 8549.94 — Irish Druids and old Irish religions. (Bonwick, James.) London, 1894.

AH 4818.22 — Irving, C. Catechism of Grecian antiquities. N.Y., 1822.

AH 7818.31 — Irving, C. Catechism of Roman antiquities. 4th American ed. N.Y., 1831.

AH 7278.24 — Irving, C. Catechism of Roman history. 2. American ed. N.Y., 1824.

AH 4049.45 — Isaac, Jules. Les oligarques. Paris, 1945.

AH 4049.45.5 — Isaac, Jules. Les oligarques. Paris, 1946.

AH 8879.5 — Ischia preistorica, greca, romana, paleocristiana. (Monti, Pietro.) Napoli, 1968.

AH 7258.78.2F — Iscrizioni e ricerche nuove. (Ferrero, E.) Torino, 1884.

AH 3177.8 — Ishtar and Izdubar; the epic of Babylon. London, 1884.

Eg 879.71 — Isis in the Graeco-Roman world. (Witt, Reginald Eldred.) Ithaca, N.Y., 1971.

Eg 879.63.10 — Isisfeste in griechisch-römischer Zeit; Daten und Riten. (Merkelbach, Reinhold.) Meisenheim am Glan, 1963.

Eg 279.48.7 — Iskander, Z. Brief history of ancient Egypt. 2. ed. Cairo, 1949.

AH 3016.40 — Iskusstvo drevnei Mesopotamii; ocherki. (Loseva, I.M.) Moskva, 1946.

AH 2007.7 — Islâmdan önce Arap tarihi. (Çagatay, Neş'et.) Ankara, 1957.

AH 2007.7.2 — Islâmdan önce Arap tarihi. 2. ed. (Çagatay, Neş'et.) Ankara, 1963.

Eg 863.7 — Ismail, Ismail Moustafa. Die Gärten der alten Ägypter und die Entwicklung der Bewässerung bis zum Hochdamm bei Assuan. München? 1960?

AH 9632.5 — Le isole Eolie nell'antichità greca e romana. (Libertini, Guido.) Firenze, 1921.

AH 3958.20 — Israel, kirken og verden. (Nordisk Teologkonferanse, Utstein Kloster, 1971.) Oslo, 1972.

AH 3908.5.10 — Israel and the Aramaeans of Damascus. (Unger, Merrill F.) London, 1957.

AH 4808.92 — Israel-Holtzwart, Karl. Das System der attischen Zeitrechnung auf neuer Grundlage. Frankfurt, 1892.

AH 3958.23 — The Israelite tribe of Half-Manasseh. Diss. (Bergman, A.) Jerusalem, 1936.

Eg 558.56 — Israeliten und Hyksos in Aegypten. (Uhlemann, M.) Leipzig, 1856.

AH 3958.10 — Die Israeliten und ihre Nachbarstämme. (Meyer, E.) Halle, 1906.

Eg 709.60.5 — Issledovaniia po istorii zemel'nykh otnoshenii v ellinisticheskom Egipte, II-I vv. do n.e. (Zel'in, Konstantin K.) Moskva, 1960.

AH 4559.08 — Issos. Ein Beiträge zur Geschichte Alexanders des Grossen. (Dittberner, W.) Berlin, 1908.

AH 866.7 — Ist Preussen das Bernsteinland der alten Gewesen? (Rogge, A.) Königsberg, 1880.

AH 866.6 — Ist Preuzsen das Bernsteinland der alten Gewesen? (Lohmeyer, K.) Königsberg, 1872.

AH 3020.28 — Istanbul. Asari atika Müzeleri. Nouvelles tablettes sumeriennes. Paris, 1957.

AH 3020.75 — Istanbul arkeoloji müzelerinde bulunan Sumer edebi tablet parçalari. (Çiğ, Muazzez.) Ankara, 1969.

AH 8907.40 — Istituto lombardo di scienze e lettere. Tyrrhenica. Milano, 1957.

AH 7169.61 — Istituzioni di diritto privato romano. (Volterra, Edoardo.) Roma, 1961.

AH 4277.84 — Istoria...della Graecia. (Denina, C.) Venezia, 1784. 4v.

AH 4558.58 — Istoria. (Alexandrou.) Venetia, 1858.

AH 4049.09 — Istoria afinskoi demokratia. (Buzeskul, V.) Sankt Peterburg, 1909.

AH 8305.5 — Istoria militară a Daciei romane. (Christescu, V.) Bucureşti, 1937.

AH 8307.4 — Istoria pentru începutul românillor in Dacia. (Maior, Petru.) Bucureşti, 1971. 2v.

AH 8308.10 — Istoria sclavajului in Dacia romana. (Tudor, D.) Bucureşti, 1957.

AH 4109.18 — Istoría tēs 'Ellēnikēs. (Andreadēs, Andreas M.) Athens, 1918.

AH 4109.18.2 — Istoría tēs Hellēnikēs. (Andreadēs, Andreas M.) Athēnai, 1928-30. 2v.

AH 4729.59 — Istoría tōn Ellēnistikōn chronōn. (Kordatos, G.K.) Athēnai, 1959.

AH 6107.60 — Istoriia antichnoi Makedonii. (Shofman, A.S.) Kazan', 1960- 2v.

AH 4819.29.5 — Istoriia antichnoi obshchestvennoi mysli. (Lur'e, Sol. Iak.) Moskva, 1929.

NEDL AH 409.09 — Istoriia drevnago vostoka. (Khvostov, M.M.) Kazan', 1909.

AH 1409.35 — Istoriia drevnego Vostoka. (Turaev, V.A.) Leningrad, 1935. 2v.

AH 279.41 — Istoriia drevnego mira. Izd. 2. (Adademiia nauk SSSR. Institut istorii.) Moskva, 1941.

AH 279.41.5 — Istoriia drevnego mira. Izd. 5. (Mishuls'a, A.V.) Moskva, 1946.

AH 1279.41 — Istoriia drevnego Vostoka. (Struve, Vasilii V.) Leningrad, 1941.

AH 3507.15 — Istoriia Midii. (Aliev, Igrar.) Baku, 1960.

AH 3507.10 — Istoriia Midii. (Diakonov, I.) Moskva, 1956.

AH 889.07 — Istoriia vostochoi torgovli. (Khvostov, M.) Kazan', 1907.

AH 4298.58 — Istorikai pragmateiai. v.1-6. (Paparrēgópanlos, K.) Athēnai, 1858.

AH 8615.5 — L'Italia agraria sotto Traiano. (Sirago, Vito A.) Louvain, 1958.

AH 7279.22.10 — Italia antica. (Pais, Ettore.) Bologna, 1922. 2v.

AH 8607.10 — L'Italia antica dalle prime civiltà alla morte di Cesare, 44 a.C. (Ducati, P.) Milano, 1936.

AH 8608.8.10 — Italia antica sul mare. (Stella, Luigia A.) Milano, 1930.

AH 8607.8 — L'Italia avanti il dominio dei romani. 3. ed. (Micali, G.) Milano, 1826. 3v.

AH 7408.21.5 — L'Italia avanti il Domino dei Romani. 2. ed. v.1-2, 3-4. (Micali, G.) Firenze, 1821. 2v.

AH 7489.38 — L'Italia imperiale da Ottaviano a Teodosio. (Pariheni, R.) Milano, 1938.

AH 8607.11 — L'Italia romana. (Ferrabino, Aldo.) Milano, 1934.

AH 9225.5 — Italia romana: Emilia romana. (Rome. Istituto di studi romani. Sezione emiliana.) Firenze, 1941.

AH 8616.2F — Italiae antiquae. (Cluneri, P.) Lugduni Batavorum, 1624.

AH 8615.15 — Italian manpower, 225 B.C.-A.D. 14. (Brunt, Peter A.) Oxford, 1971.

AH 8611.5 — The Italic regions. (Thomsen, Rudi.) København, 1947.

AH 8917.5 — L'Italie des Etrusques. (Harrel-Courtès, Henry.) Paris, 1960.

AH 7279.25.11 — L'Italie primitive et les débuts de l'impérialisme romain. (Homo, Léon.) Paris, 1953.

AH 7279.41 — Italien und Rom. (Altheim, Franz.) Leipzig, 1941-44. 2v.

AH 8610.2 — Der italische Bund...Roms Hegemonie. (Beloch, J.) Leipzig, 1880.

AH 8616.4 — Italische Landeskunde. v.1-2. (Nissen, H.) Berlin, 1883. 3v.

AH 8608.8F — Italy. Ministero della marina. Monografia storica dei porti dell'antichità nell'Italia insulare. Roma, 1906.

AH 7309.25.5 — Iterum, or A further discussion of the Roman fate. (Heitland, W.E.) Cambridge, 1925.

AH 4978.41 — Itineraire descriptif. (Aldenhoven, F.) Athènes, 1841.

AH 7979.16F — Itineraria romana. (Miller, Konrad.) Stuttgart, 1916.

AH 7979.29 — Itineraria romana. Lipsiae, 1929. 2v.

AH 7956.00 — Itinerarium Antonini Augusti. Coloniae Agrippinae, 1600.

AH 7203.60F — Iuliani epilome latina Novellarum Iustiniani. (Corpus juris civilis. Novellae Constitutiones.) Lipsiae, 1873.

AH 9446.5 — Iulium Carnicum (Zuglio). (Moro, Placida Maria.) Roma, 1956.

AH 4148.38 — Iuris publici Graecorum. (Schoemann, G.F.) Gryphiswaldiae, 1838.

AH 7201.75 — Iurisprudentiae Antehadrianae. v.1-2, pt.1-2. (Bremer, F.P.) Lipsiae, 1896. 3v.

AH 7201.40.2 — Iurisprudentiae anteiustinianae. (Huschke, P.E.) Lipsiae, 1867.

AH 7201.40 — Iurisprudentiae anteiustinianae. (Huschke, P.E.) Lipsiae, 1867.

AH 7201.40.4 — Iurisprudentiae anteiustinianae. (Huschke, P.E.) Lipsiae, 1879.

AH 7201.40.6 — Iurisprudentiae anteiustinianae. v.1-2. (Huschke, P.E.) Lipsiae, 1908-27. 3v.

AH 7168.72 — Das Ius Postliminii und die Lex Cornelia. (Bechmann, A.) Erlangen, 1872.

AH 4559.38.5 — Ivánka, E. Die aristotelische Politik und die Städtegründungen Alexanders des Grossen. Budapest, 1938.

Eg 847.10 — Iversen, Erik. The myth of Egypt and its hieroglyphs in European tradition. Copenhagen, 1961.

AH 7189.59 — Iz glubiny vekov. (Aleksishvili, M.M.) Tbilisi, 1959.

Eg 819.16.5 — Iz vostochykh motivov. pt.1-3. (Rozanov, V.V.) Petrograd, 1916-17.

Author and Title Listing

AH 819.08.10 — Iz zhizni idei. izd. 2. v.1-2,4, pt.2. (Zieliński, Tadeusz.) Sankt Peterburg, 1908-11. 2v.

AH 819.08.13 — Iz zhizni idei. izd. 3. (Zieliński, Tadeusz.) Petrograd, 1916.

AH 3178.6 — Izdubar-Nimrod...Heldensage. (Jeremias, A.) Leipzig, 1891.

AH 1309.61 — Izuchenie drevnei istorii Blizhnego Vostoka. (Postovskaia, N.M.) Moskva, 1961.

AH 6157.10 — Izvestiia vizantiiskikh pisatelei o Severnom Prichernomor'e. Moskva, 1934.

AH 807.52 — Jackson, J. Chronological antiquities. London, 1752. 3v.

AH 4817.69 — Jackson, R. Literatura Graeca. London, 1769.

AH 4189.28 — Jacob, Oscar. Les esclaves publics à Athènes. Liége, 1928.

AH 7203.24 — Jacobi Labitti index legum omnium. (Corpus juris civilis. Digesta.) Francoforti, 1724. 2v.

AH 9192.5 — Jacobone, Nunzio. Venusia, storia e topografia. Trani, 1909.

AH 5140.7 — Jacobs, Emil. Thasiaca. Berolini, 1893.

AH 5140.7.1 — Jacobs, Emil. Thasiaca. Inaug. Diss. Berolini, 1893.

AH 4298.52.2 — Jacobs, Friedrich. Hellas; Geographie, Geschichte und Literatur Griechenlands. Stuttgart, 1897.

AH 4298.52.5 — Jacobs, Friedrich. Hellas; or, The home, history, literature, and art of the Greeks. London, 1855.

AH 4298.52 — Jacobs, Friedrich. Hellas; Vorträge über Heimath, Geschichte, Literatur und Kunst der Hellenen. Berlin, 1852.

AH 3002.92 — Jacobsen, T. Cuneiform texts in the National Museum. Copenhagen, 1939.

AH 3013.935F — Jacobsen, T. Sennacherib's aqueduct at Jerwan. Chicago, 1935.

AH 3011.22 — Jacobsen, Thorkild. Toward the image of Tammuz, and other essays on Mesopotamian history and culture. Cambridge, 1970.

Eg 879.39.5 — Jacobsohn, Helmuth. Die dogmatische Stellung des Königs. Glückstadt, 1939.

AH 4278.87 — Jäger, O.E.F. Geschichte der Griechen. Gütersloh, 1887.

AH 4833.15 — Jaeger, O.H. Die Gymnastik der Hellenen. Stuttgart, 1881.

AH 7448.69 — Jäger, Oskar. Die punischen Kriege. Halle, 1869.

AH 4842.73 — Jaeger, Werner Wilhelm. Early Christianity and Greek Paideia. Cambridge, 1961.

AH 4842.73.15 — Jaeger, Werner Wilhelm. Das frühe Christentum und die griechische Beldung. Berlin, 1963.

AH 4842.72.20 — Jaeger, Werner Wilhelm. Paideia; the ideals of Greek culture. 2. English ed. Oxford, 1965.

AH 4842.72 — Jaeger, Werner Wilhelm. Paideia; die Formung des griechischen Menschen. Berlin, 1934.

X Cg AH 4842.72.10A — Jaeger, Werner Wilhelm. Paideia: the ideals of Greek culture. N.Y., 1939.

AH 4842.72.10A — Jaeger, Werner Wilhelm. Paideia: the ideals of Greek culture. v.2-3. N.Y., 1939-43. 2v.

AH 4842.72.15A — Jaeger, Werner Wilhelm. Paideia: the ideals of Greek culture. 2. ed. N.Y., 1945.

AH 4842.72.3A — Jaeger, Werner Wilhelm. Paideia. 2. Aufl. Berlin, 1936- 3v.

AH 4558.61 — Jäger. Bemerkungen zur Geschichte Alexanders des Grossen. Wetzlar, 1861.

AH 4855.5 — Jagd bei den Griechen. (Manns, O.) Cassel, 1888. 3 pam.

AH 855.5 — Jagdwesen der alten Griechen und Römer. (Miller, Max.) München, 1883.

AH 7059.70 — Jahn, Joachim. Intenegnum und Wahldiktatur. Kallmünz, 1970.

AH 7549.20 — Jahn, John Nicholas H. A critical study of the history of the Emperor Nero. Thesis. N.Y.? 1920.

AH 4908.67 — Jahn, Otto. Darstellungen des Handwerks. Leipzig, 1868.

AH 7488.97.2 — Jahrbuch. (Vienna. Heraldischen Gesellschaft "Adler".) Wien, 1897.

AHP 20.4 — Jahrbuch für Antike und Christentum. Münster. 1,1958+ 13v.

AHP 20.5 — Jahrbuch für Antike und Christentum. Ergänzungsband. Münster. 1,1964+ 2v.

AH 7808.53 — Jahrbücher der römischen Geschichte. (Scheiffele, A.) Nördlingen, 1853.

Eg 299.12.15 — Ein Jahrtausend am Nil. 2. Aufl. (Schubart, W.) Berlin, 1923.

AH 8549.36 — James, D. The patriarchal religion of Britain; or A complete manual of ancient British Druidism. London, 1836.

AH 1879.58 — James, E.O. Myth and ritual in the ancient Near East. London, 1958.

AH 4279.21 — James, Henry R. Our Hellenic heritage. London, 1921-30. 2v.

AH 4279.21.2 — James, Henry R. Our Hellenic heritage. v.1-2. N.Y., 1927.

AH 2011.10 — Jamme, Albert. La dynastie de Sarahbi il Yakuf et la documentation épigraphique sud-arabe. Istanbul, 1961.

AH 4559.04 — Janke, A. Alexanders des Grossen. Berlin, 1904.

AH 5758.5 — Jannet, C. Institutions sociales. Paris, 1880.

AH 5763.8 — Janni, Pietro. La cultura di Sparta arcaica. Roma, 1965. 2v.

Eg 609.48 — Janssen, J.M.A. Ramses III. Leiden, 1948.

Eg 1099.46F — Janssen, Jozef. De traditionelle egyptische autobiografie. Leiden, 1946.

Eg 1099.46 — Janssen, Jozef. De traditionelle egyptische autobiografie. v.2. Leiden, 1946.

AHP 20.1 — Janus. Wien. 1-2,1920-1921

AH 3414.15 — Janus und der Mann mit derer Adler; oder Greifenmaske. (Bossert, Helmuth.) Istanbul, 1959.

Htn AH 2058.5* — Die Japhetiden. (Görres, J.) München, 1844.

AH 5307.27 — Jardé, A. Athènes ancienne. Paris, 1930.

AH 4899.25 — Jardé, A. Les céreales dans l'antiquité grecque. Thèse. Paris, 1925.

AH 4279.14 — Jardé, A. Grèce antique et la vie grecque. Paris, 1914.

AH 7739.25.5 — Jardé, Auguste. Études critiques sur la vie et le règne de Sévère Alexandre. Paris, 1925.

AH 7739.25 — Jardé, Auguste. Études critiques sur la vie et le règne de Sévère Alexandre. Thèse. Paris, 1925.

AH 4329.26 — Jardé, Auguste. The formation of the Greek people. N.Y., 1926.

AH 8208.15 — Jarrett, Michael G. Britain and Rome; essays presented to Eric Birley on his sixteenth birthday. Kendal, 1966.

AH 7162.24 — Jarriand, E. Histoire de la novelle 118. Paris, 1889.

AH 7089.50 — Jashemski, W.M. The origins and history of the pro-consular. Chicago, 1950.

AH 899.44 — Jasny, Naum. The wheats of classical antiquity. Baltimore, 1944.

AH 3156.9 — Jastrow, M. Babylonian-Assyrian birth omens. Giessen, 1914.

AH 3179.5 — Jastrow, M. A fragment of Babylonian "Dibbarra" epic. Philadelphia, 1891.

AH 3155.6.5A — Jastrow, Morris. Aspects of religious belief and practice in Babylonia and Assyria. N.Y., 1911.

AH 3155.6.2FA — Jastrow, Morris. Bildermappe...zur Religion Babyloniens und Assyriens. Giessen, 1912.

AH 3143.8 — Jastrow, Morris. The civilization of Babylonia and Assyria. Philadelphia, 1915.

AH 3143.8.2 — Jastrow, Morris. The civilization of Babylonia and Assyria. Philadelphia, 1915.

AH 3155.6 — Jastrow, Morris. Die Religion Babyloniens und Assyriens. Giessen, 1905-12. 3v.

AH 3155.6.3 — Jastrow, Morris. The religion of Babylonia and Assyria. v.1-2. Boston, 1898.

AH 9807.6 — A jasz-kunok története. v.1-2,4. (Gyárfás, István Tihamér.) Kecskemét, 1870-85. 3v.

AH 3038.5 — Jawal, Abd al-Jalil. The advent of the era of townships in northern Mesopotamia. Leiden, 1965.

AH 3173.7 — Jean, C.F. La littérature des Babyloniens et des Assyriens. Paris, 1924.

AH 3020.11 — Jean, Charles Francois. Sumer et Akkad. Paris, 1923.

AH 4842.77 — Jeanmaire, H. Couroi et courètes. Thèse. Lille, 1939.

AH 818.84.2 — Jebb, R.C. Some ancient organs of public opinion. Cambridge, Eng., 1884.

AH 9607.21 — Jenison, E.S. The history of the province of Sicily. Boston, 1919.

AH 7759.08 — Jenks, J. Heidentum und Christianismus des Kaisers Konstantin des Grossen. Sereth, 1907.

AH 3966.24F — Jenks, William. The explanatory Bible atlas and scripture gazetteer. Boston, 1847.

AH 938.49F — Jenks, William. The explanatory Bible atlas and Scripture gazetteer. Boston, 1849.

AH 7854.2 — Jennison, George. Animals for show and pleasure in ancient Rome. Manchester, 1937.

Eg 1042.970.5 — Das Jenseitsgericht in der Sargtexten. (Grieshammer, Reinhard.) Wiesbaden, 1970.

AH 3408.5 — Jensen, P. Hittiter und Armenier. Strassburg, 1898.

AH 3155.4 — Jensen, P. Die Kosmologie der Babylonier. Strassburg, 1890.

Eg 878.94 — Jequier, G. Le livre de ce qu'il y a dans l'hadès. Paris, 1894.

Eg 879.46 — Jéquier, Gustave. Considérations sur les religions égyptiennes. Neuchâtel, 1946.

Eg 819.25 — Jequier, Gustave. Histoire de la civilisation égyptienne des origines à la conquête d'Alexandre. Paris, 1925.

AH 3159.5.12 — Jeremias, A. In Kämpfe um Babel und Bibel. 3. Aufl. Leipzig, 1903.

AH 3178.6 — Jeremias, A. Izdubar-Nimrod...Heldensage. Leipzig, 1891.

AH 3159.10.3 — Jeremias, A. Die Panbabylonisten der alte Orient. Leipzig, 1907.

AH 3143.12 — Jeremias, Alfred. Handbuch der altorientalischen Geisteskultur. Leipzig, 1913.

AH 3143.12.5A — Jeremias, Alfred. Handbuch der altorientalischen Geisteskultur. 2e Aufl. Berlin, 1929.

AH 3740.7 — Jeremias, F. Tyrus. Leipzig, 1891.

AH 7299.23 — Jerome, Thomas S. Aspects of the study of Roman history. N.Y., 1923.

AH 8857.5 — Jerome, Thomas S. Roman memories in the landscape seen from Capri. Detroit, 1914.

AH 189.03 — Jerovšek, Anton. Die antik-heidnische Sklaverei. Marburg, 1903.

AH 3965.18 — Jerusalem und Tyros. (Ben-David, Arye.) Basel, 1969.

AH 3020.23 — Jestin, Raymond. Textes économiques sumériens de la 11e dynastie d'Ur. Paris, 1935.

AH 864.1 — Les jeux des anciens. (Becq de Fouquières, L.) Paris, 1869.

AH 864.3 — Les jeux des anciens. 2. éd. (Becq de Fouquières, L.) Paris, 1873.

AH 8513.8 — Les jeux et le théâtre chez les Gaulois en Provence. (Bonnemère, L.) Paris, 1888.

AH 4048.86 — Jevons, F.B. Development of Athenian democracy. London, 1886.

AH 3999.59 — The Jewish world in the time of Jesus. 7th American ed. (Guignebert, Charles.) N.Y., 1959.

AH 7329.60 — The Jews of ancient Rome. 1. ed. (Leon, Harry J.) Philadelphia, 1960.

AH 7161.19 — Jhering, R. Entwicklungsgeschichte des römischen Rechts. Leipzig, 1894.

AH 7168.67 — Jhering, R. Schuldmoment im römischen Privatrecht. Giessen, 1867.

AH 3739.10 — Jidejian, Nina. Sidon through the ages. Beirut, 1971.

AH 3740.9 — Jidejian, Nina. Tyre through the ages. Beirut, 1969.

AH 3964.30.5 — Jirku, Anton. Der Mythus der Kanaanäer. Bonn, 1966.

AH 3963.30 — Jirku, Anton. Die Welt der Bibel. Stuttgart, 1957.

AH 3963.30.1 — Jirku, Anton. The world of the Bible. London, 1967.

Eg 878.77.5 — Job et l'Egypte, le redempteur et la vie future. (Ancessi, Victor.) Paris, 1877.

AH 7228.96 — Jobbé-Duval, E. La procédure civil. Paris, 1896.

AH 939.02.5 — Jobst, D. Scylla und Charybdis, eine geographische Studien. Würzburg, 1902.

AH 2011.8 — Jochum, Johannes. Geschichte de Familie El-'Abbâs bin 'Abd El-Muttalib. Inaug. Diss. Berlin, 1933.

AH 7163.21 — Jörs, Paul. Ehe Gesetze des Augustus. Marburg, 1894.

AH 7138.88.3 — Jörs, Paul. Römische Rechtswissenschaft. Berlin, 1888.

AH 7169.35 — Jörs, Paul. Römisches Privatrecht. 2. Aufl. Berlin, 1935.

AH 4855.9 — Johannes, R. De studio Venandi apud Graecos et Romanos. Gottingae, 1907.

AH 7279.60.10F — Johannes Victoriensis. Cronica romanorum. Klagenfurt, 1960.

AH 4861.8 — Johannis Nicolai Tractatus de Graecorum luctu. (Nicolai, J.) Thielae, 1697.

AH 3020.7.10 — John Rylands Library. Manchester. Catalogue of Sumerian tablets in the John Rylands Library. Manchester, 1932.

AH 3020.7F — John Rylands Library. Manchester. Sumerian tablets from Umma. Manchester, 1915.

AH 3009.13 — Johns, C.H.W. Ancient Babylonia. Cambridge, Eng., 1913.

AH 3150.8 — Johns, C.H.W. Babylonian and Assyrian laws, contracts and letters. N.Y., 1904.

AH 3002.2.17 — Johns, Claude H. An Assyrian doomsday book. Leipzig, 1901.

Eg 909.49 — Johnson, A.C. Byzantine Egypt: economic studies. Princeton, 1949.

Eg 759.51 — Johnson, A.C. Egypt and the Roman Empire. Ann Arbor, 1951.

AH 7229.27 — Johnson, H.D. The Roman tribunal. Baltimore, 1927.

AH 4848.13.5 — Johnson, Marie. Ancient Greek. Chicago, 1964.

Htn AH 7776.89* — Johnson, Samuel. Julian's arts to undermine and extirpate Christianity. London, 1689.

Author and Title Listing

AH 3187.7	Johnston, C. Epistolary literature of Assyrians and Babylonians. Baltimore, 1898.
AH 7829.03A	Johnston, Harold W. Private life of the Romans. Chicago, 1903.
AH 7829.03.2	Johnston, Harold W. Private life of the Romans. Chicago, 1903.
AH 7829.03.7	Johnston, Harold W. The private life of the Romans. Chicago, 1907.
AH 7829.03.9	Johnston, Harold W. The private life of the Romans. N.Y., 1973.
AH 930.5	Johnston, W. and A.K., publishers. The world; a classical atlas. Edinburgh, 18- .
AH 8907.19	Johnstone, M.A. Etruria past and present. London, 1930.
AH 3002.75F	Joint Expedition of the British Museum and the Museum of the University of Pennsylvania to Mesopotamia. Ur excavations. Texts and plates. v.1-4; 6, pt.1-2; 8. Philadelphia, 1920-35. 10v.
AH 7469.19.5	Jolliffe, Richard. Phases of corruption in Roman administration. Menasha, 1919.
AH 7139.32.2	Jolowicz, Herbert Felix. Historical introduction to the study of Roman law. 2. ed. Cambridge, Eng., 1952.
AH 7139.32.3	Jolowicz, Herbert Felix. Historical introduction to the study of Roman law. 2. ed. Cambridge, Eng., 1965.
AH 4204.20	Jonas, J. De Solone Atheniensi. Dissertatio historica. Monasterii Guestfalorum, 1884.
Eg 1159.58	Jonckheere, Frans. Les médecins de l'Égypte pharaonique. Bruxelles, 1958.
AH 4039.40A	Jones, A.H.M. The Greek city from Alexander to Justinian. Oxford, 1940.
AH 7709.64	Jones, A.H.M. The later Roman Empire. v.1-3, Atlas. Oxford, 1964. 3v.
AH 7039.60	Jones, A.H.M. Studies in Roman government and law. Oxford, 1960.
AH 889.48	Jones, Arnold. Ancient economic history. London, 1948.
AH 4039.58	Jones, Arnold H.M. Athenian democracy. N.Y., 1958.
AH 5303.16	Jones, Arnold H.M. Athenian democracy. Oxford, 1957.
AH 7299.37.5	Jones, Arnold H.M. The cities of the eastern Roman provinces. Oxford, 1937.
AH 7299.37.6	Jones, Arnold H.M. The cities of the eastern Roman provinces. 2. ed. Oxford, 1971.
AH 7509.70.5	Jones, Arnold Hugh Martin. Augustus. London, 1970.
AH 7159.72	Jones, Arnold Hugh Martin. The criminal curts of the Roman Republic and Principate. Oxford, 1972.
AH 7339.71	Jones, Arnold Hugh Martin. The prosopography of the later Roman Empire. Cambridge, Eng., 1971-
AH 5757.26	Jones, Arnold Hugh Martin. Sparta. Cambridge, 1967.
AH 8667.2	Jones, H.S. Classical Rome. N.Y., 1910.
AH 7279.12A	Jones, H.S. Companion to Roman history. Oxford, 1912.
AH 7489.08.5	Jones, H.S. Roman Empire B.C. 29-A.D. 476. N.Y., 192-?
AH 4139.56	Jones, J.W. The law and legal theory of the Greeks. Oxford, 1956.
AH 3020.30	Jones, Tom B. Sumerian economic texts from the third Ur dynasty. Minneapolis, 1961.
AH 819.63.5	Jones, Tom Bard. Ancient civilization. Chicago, 1963.
AH 309.67	Jones, Tom Bard. Paths to the ancient past: applications of the historical method to ancient history. N.Y., 1967.
AH 7819.62.5	Jones, Tom Bard. The silver-plated age. Sandoval, 1962.
AH 862.7	Jones, W.H.S. Malaria. Cambridge, 1907.
AH 930.3F	Jones and Co. Jones' classical atlas. London, 1830.
AH 930.3F	Jones' classical atlas. (Jones and Co.) London, 1830.
AH 4328.37	Jonische Stamms. (Uebelen, G.) Stuttgart, 1837.
AH 4328.61	Jonischen Städteleben. (Nitzsch, Otto.) Greifswald, 1861.
AH 7889.33.10	Jonkers, Engbert. Economische en sociale toestanden in het Romeinsche rijk. Proefschrift. Wageningen, 1933.
AH 7653.38	Jordan, David. Gibbon and his Roman Empire. Urbana, 1971.
AH 3179.12	Jordan, F. In den Lagen des Tammuz. München, 1950.
AH 7408.87	Jordan, Henri. Die Könige im alten Italien. Berlin, 1887.
AH 3045.5F	Jordan, J. Dritter vorläufiger Bericht über die von der Notgemeinschaft die deutschen Wissenschaft in Uruk unternommenen Ausgrabungen. Berlin, 1932.
AH 9777.6	Jordanes. De getarum sive Gothorum. Lugduni Batavorum, 1732.
AH 9777.9	Jordanes. De la succession des royaumes...les Goths. Paris, 1842.
AH 9777.18	Jordanes. Diversarum...historiae antiquae scriptores tres. Hamburgi, 1611.
AH 9777.19	Jordanes. Getarum sive Gothorum. Stuttgart, 1861.
AH 9777.19.2	Jordanes. Getarum sive Gothorum. 2. ed. Stuttgart, 1866.
AH 9777.19.3	Jordanes. Getarum sive Gothorum. 3. ed. Reutlingen, 1888.
AH 9777.29.6	Jordanes. The Gothic history of Jordanes. N.Y., 1960.
AH 9777.29.5A	Jordanes. The Gothic history of Jordanes. Princeton, 1915.
AH 9777.19.5	Jordanes. O proiskhozhdenii i deianiiakh getov. Moskva, 1960.
AH 9777.29A	Jordanes. Origins and deeds of the Goths. Princeton, 1908.
AH 7098.44	Jordans, G.H.H. De publicis urbium Romae et Constantinapolis. Bonnae, 1844.
AH 7798.82	Jornandes. De origine actibusque Getarum. Freiburg, 1882.
AH 9777.37	Jornandes vindiciae de Var Hunnorum. (Paulinus a Sancto Bartholomaeo.) Romae, 1800.
Eg 759.47	Jouguet, P. La domination romaine en Égypte aux deux premiers siècles. Alexandrie, 1947.
AH 4609.26.10	Jouguet, P. L'impérialism macédonien. Paris, 1961.
AH 4609.26.5	Jouguet, P. Macedonian imperialism and the Hellenization of the East. London, 1928.
Eg 709.44	Jouguet, P. Trois études sur l'hellénisme. Le Caire, 1944.
AH 4499.41	Jouguet, Pierre. L'Athènes de Périclès et les destinées de la Grèce. Le Caire, 1941.
AH 819.50	Jouguet, Pierre. Les premières civilisations. Paris, 1950.
AH 7168.76	Jourdan, A. L'Hypothèque. Paris, 1876.
EgP 6.5	Journal. (American Research Center in Egypt.) Boston. 1,1962+ 2v.
AHP 13.5	Journal. (Columbia University. Ancient Near Eastern Society.) N.Y. 1,1969+ 3v.
EgP 87.6	Journal. (Manchester Egyptian and Oriental Society.) Manchester. 1912-1938 4v.
AH 969.55	Journal. (Sestios, Maarkos.) Paris, 1955.
AHP 20.2	Journal of cuneiform studies. New Haven. 1,1947+ 10v.
AH 3917.5	Journey from Allepo to Jerusalem. (Maundrell, H.) Oxford, 1740.
Htn AH 7776.83.5*	Jovian. 2. ed. (Hickes, George.) London, 1683.
AH 4278.92	Joy, James R. Grecian history. N.Y., 1892.
AH 867.10	Jucker, Ines. Der Gestus des Aposkopein. Zürich, 1956.
VAH 3957.38	Júda, Izrael és Aram. (Beöthy, Leó.) Budapest, 1874.
AH 2110.5	Judeich, W. Kleinasiastische Studien. Marburg, 1892.

AH 3964.15	Das Judentherm in Palästina zur Zeit Christi. (Langen, Joseph.) Freiburg im Breisgau, 1866.
AH 3159.5.15	Judentum und Entwicklungslehre. (Tänzer, Aaron.) Berlin, 1903.
AH 3156.11	Judisch-Babylonische Zaubertexte. (Stübe, R.) Halle, 1895.
AH 7238.88.1	Judson, Harry P. Caesar's army; a study of the military art of the Romans in the last days of the Republic. N.Y., 1961.
AH 3964.16.5	Jüdische Theologie auf Grund des Talmud. (Weber, F.) Leipzig, 1897.
Eg 1309.07.5	Die jüische-aramëischen Papyri von Assuan. (Staerk, Willy.) Bonn, 1907.
AH 3159.10.5	Die jüngsten Kämpfer wider den Panbabylonismus. (Winckler, H.) Leipzig, 1907.
AH 7178.70	Jürgens. Ueber der Ursprung und die Werwendung. Blankeburg, 1870.
AH 7909.02	Juglar, L. Quamodo per servos libertosque negotiarentur Romani imperii temporibus. Paris, 1902.
AH 7189.02	Juglar, L. Zuomodo per servos...negotiarentur Romani. Paris, 1902.
AH 7329.14	Les juifs dans l'empire romain. (Juster, Jean.) Paris, 1914. 2v.
AH 7479.32	Jules César. (Bailly, Auguste.) Paris, 1932.
AH 7479.65	Jules César. (Carcopino, Jérôme.) Paris, 1965.
AH 7479.61	Jules César. (Madaule, Jacques.) Paris, 1961.
AH 3980.5.1	Julian, or Discourse...earthquake...temple at Jerusalem. (Warburton, William.) London, 1750.
AH 3980.5.2	Julian, or Discourse...earthquake...temple at Jerusalem. (Warburton, William.) London, 1751.
AH 3980.5	Julian. (Warburton, William.) London, 1750.
NEDL AH 7779.30.10	Julian der Abtrünnige. 5. Aufl. (Bidez, Joseph.) München, 1946?
AH 7779.56.4	Julian the Apostate. (Riciotti, Giuseppe.) Milwaukee, 1960.
AH 7779.01.4	Julian the Apostate. 2. ed. (Negri, G.) N.Y., 1905. 2v.
AH 7779.37	Julian the Apostate and the rise of Christianity. (Ridley, F.A.) London, 1937.
Htn AH 7776.89*	Julian's arts to undermine and extirpate Christianity. (Johnson, Samuel.) London, 1689.
AH 7204.7	Julianus, S. Edicti perpetui. Lipsiae, 1869.
AH 7201.54	Julianus. Fragments of the perpetual edict. Cambridge, Eng., 1877.
Eg 459.55	Julien, Max. Le tombeau du Pharaon, en l'an 2800 av. J.-C. Paris, 1955.
AH 4119.5	Julien, Paul. Zur Verwaltung der Satrapien unter Alexander dem Grossen. Leipzig, 1914.
AH 7778.77	Julien l'apostat. (Naville, Henri Adrien.) Paris, 1877.
AH 7479.67	Julius Caesar; a political biography. 1. American ed. (Balsdon, John Percy Vyvian.) N.Y., 1967.
AH 7478.81.10	Julius Caesar. (Froude, J.A.) N.Y., 1900.
AH 7479.69	Julius Caesar. (Grant, Michael.) London, 1969.
AH 7479.10	Julius Caesar. (Hardinge, Hilary.) London, 191-.
AH 7479.27	Julius Caesar. (Thaddeus, V.) N.Y., 1927.
AH 7479.55A	Julius Caesar. 1. ed. (Duggan, A.L.) N.Y., 1955.
AH 7479.04.5	Julius Caesar and the foundation of the Roman imperial system. (Fowler, W.W.) N.Y., 1891.
AH 7479.04	Julius Caesar and the foundation of the Roman imperial system. (Fowler, W.W.) N.Y., 1904.
AH 7238.83.5	Jullian, C. De protectoribus et domesticis Augustorum. Thesis. Paris, 1883.
AH 8514.8	Jullian, C. Recherches sur la religion gauloise. Bordeaux, 1903.
AH 7842.3	Jullien, E. Professeurs de littérature dans l'ane Rome. Paris, 1885.
AH 7478.86.5	Jullien, Émile. De L. Cornelio Balbo majore. Thesim. Lutetiae Parisiorum, 1886.
AH 7508.92	Jullien, Émile. Le fondateur de Lyon. Paris, 1892.
AH 7448.92.2	Jumpertz, M. Der römisch-karthagische Krieg. Berlin, 1892.
AH 3012.11	Jung, H.W.M. Demonische ziekten in Babylon en Bijbel. Leiden, 1959.
NEDL AH 7818.83	Jung, I. Leben und Sitten der Römer. Prag, 1883. 2v.
AH 8312.2	Jung, Julius. Fasten der Provinz Dacien. Innsbruck, 1894.
AH 7088.81A	Jung, Julius. Die romanischen Landschaften. Innsbruck, 1881.
AH 3757.24	Junge, Julius. Saka-Studien: der Ferne Nordasten im Weltbild der Antike. Aalen, 1962.
AH 4860.10	Der junge Grieche. (Bork, Arnold.) Zürich, 1959.
AH 4860.10.5	Der junge Grieche. (Bork, Arnold.) Zürich, 1961.
AH 7279.10	A junior history of Rome. (Hamilton, M.A.) Oxford, 1910.
Eg 879.17F	Junker, H. Die Onurislegende. Wien, 1917.
Eg 879.49	Junker, H. Pyramidenzeit. Einsiedeln, 1949.
AH 279.33.5	Junker, H. Die Völker des Antiken Orients. Freiburg, 1933.
AH 7147.19	Jure colonario. (Harlessen, A.) Jenae, 1719.
AH 7158.89	Juridictions criminelles à Rome. (Bruyant, E.) Paris, 1889.
AH 7228.98.5	Juridictions criminelles à Rome. (Louvet, F.) Paris, 1898.
AH 4558.83	Jurien, J.P.E. Les campagnes d'Alexandre; drame macédonien. Paris, 1883. 5v.
AH 4558.83.2	Jurien, J.P.E. Le drame macédonien. 2. éd. Paris, 1891.
AH 258.86	Jurien de la Graviére, J.P.E. Marine des anciens. Paris, 1886. 2v.
AH 7258.85	Jurien de la Gravière. Marine des Ptolémées et...Romains. Paris, 1885. 2v.
Htn AH 7136.60*	Juris civilis. (Zouche, R.) Oxoniae, 1660.
AH 7203.22	Juris civilis Antecessoris. (Perezl, A.) Vesaliae, 1670.
AH 7203.40.15	Juris civilis ecloga. (Corpus juris civilis.) Parisiis, 1822.
AH 7203.6.5F	Juris civilis septimus tomus. (Corpus juris civilis.) Venetiis, 1610. 2v.
Htn AH 7206.19F*	Juris Graeco-Romani tam Canonici quam Civilis. (Loewenklau, J.) Francofurti, 1596.
AH 7203.26	Jurisprudentia Philologica. (Eden, R.) Oxonii, 1744.
AH 7203.25	Jurisprudentia restituta, sive Index chronologicus in totum juris Justinianaei corpus. (Corpus juris civilis.) Amstelaedami, 1727.
AH 4136.35.4F	Jurisprudentia Romana et Attica. Lugdunum Batavorum, 1741.
AH 7201.4.2	Jurisprudentia vetus Ante-Justinianea. (Schulting, A.) Lipsiae, 1737.
AH 3150.4	Jurisprudentiae Babylonicae quae supersunt. (Peiser, F.E.) Cöthen, 1890.
AH 7203.76	Juristen-Bibliothek. (Violet, W.) Leipzig, 1882.

Author and Title Listing

AH 7138.41.10   Juristischer Nachlass. (Thibaut, A.F.J.) Berlin, 1841-42. 2v.

AH 4048.53   Jurrjens, D.H. Democratiae apud Athenienses. Rhenum, 1853.

AH 7201.6   Jus civile antejustinianeum. (Hugo, G.) Berolini, 1815. 2v.

AH 7206.5   Jus Graeco-Romanum. v.1-3. (Zacharia, K.E.) Lipsiae, 1856. 2v.

AH 7148.56   Jus naturale. (Voigt, M.) Leipzig, 1856. 4v.

AH 7148.56.3   Jus naturale. v.3-4. (Voigt, M.) Leipzig, 1871.

AH 7214.10   Juspirandum...du droit romain. (Ioachmiovici, V.E.) Paris, 1912.

AH 7329.12   Juster, Jean. Les droits politiques des juifs dans L'empire romain. Paris, 1912.

AH 7329.14   Juster, Jean. Les juifs dans l'empire romain. Paris, 1914. 2v.

AH 7203.90   Justinian: Institutionum libri quattuor. (Corpus juris civilis. Institutiones.) Oxford, 1883. 2v.

AH 7203.36   Justiniani Institutiones. (Corpus juris civilis. Institutiones.) Parisiis, 1805.

AH 7203.39   Justiniani Institutionum libri IV. (Corpus juris civilis. Institutiones.) Berolini, 1812.

AH 7203.43.6   Justiniani Institutionum libri IV. (Corpus juris civilis. Institutiones.) Berolini, 1832.

AH 7203.91   Justiniani Institutionum libri quattuor. 2. ed. (Corpus juris civilis. Institutiones.) Oxford, 1890.

Htn   AH 7203.4.7*   Justiniani Leges de re rustica. (Corpus juris civilis.) Lobanii, 1542.

AH 7203.89   Justiniani Novellae. (Corpus juris civilis. Novellae constitutiones.) Lipsiae, 1881. 2v.

AH 7203.148   Justinian's Digest. (Honoré, Antony Maurice.) Oxford, 1971.

AH 7158.93   Justinianus I. De Furtis. Cantabrigiae, 1893.

AH 8910.5   K istorii etrusskoi kolonizatsii Italii v VII-IV vv. (Zalesskii, Nikolai N.) Leningrad, 1965.

AH 3407.36   K istorii vozniknoveniia gosudarstva. (Dovgialo, Gennadii I.) Minsk, 1968.

Eg 879.52.15F   Der Ka in Theologie und Königs Kult. (Greven, L.) Glückstadt, 1952.

AH 8157.9   Kaddache, Mahfoud. L'Algérie dans l'antiquité. Alger, 1972.

AH 3981.3   Kadesh-Barnea - its importance. (Trumbull, H.C.) N.Y., 1884.

Eg 602.15   The Kadesh inscriptions of Ramesses II. (Gardiner, Alan H.) Oxford, 1960.

AH 5760.9   Kaegi, Adolph. Kritische Geschichte des spartanischen Staates von 500-431 vor Christ. Leipzig, 1873.

AH 7799.68.5   Kaegi, Walter Emil. Byzantium and the decline of Rome. Princeton, 1968.

AH 9610.24   Die Kämpfe der Karthager auf Sizilien in den Jahren 409-405 v. Chr. Inaug. Diss. (Märker, Martin.) Weida, 1930.

AH 309.03   Kaerst, J. Antike Idee der Oekumene. Leipzig, 1903.

AH 4659.01.2   Kaerst, Julius. Geschichte des Hellenismus. 2. Aufl. Leipzig, 1917-26. 2v.

AH 4659.01   Kaerst, Julius. Geschichte des hellenistischen Zeitalters. Leipzig, 1901. 2v.

AH 48.98   Kaerst, Julius. Studien zur Entwickelung...Monarchie...Altertum. Photoreproduction. München, 1898.

AH 7808.90   Kaestner, O. De aeris quae ab imperio Caesaris. Lipsiae, 1890.

AH 4519.69   Kagan, Doanld. The outbreak of the Peloponnesian War. Ithaca, 1969.

AH 7659.62.10   Kagan, Donald. Decline and fall of the Roman Empire. Boston, 1962.

AH 4039.65   Kagan, Donald. The great dialogue; history of Greek political thought from Homer to Polybius. N.Y., 1965.

AH 7162.15   Kahn, F. Römischen Frauen-Erbrechts. Leipzig, 1884.

AH 4519.10   Kahrstedt, U. Forschungen zur Geschichte des ausgehenden fünften und des vierten Jahrhunderts. Berlin, 1910.

AH 4149.22   Kahrstedt, U. Griechisches Staatsrecht. Göttingen, 1922.

AH 279.48.15   Kahrstedt, Ulrich. Geschichte der griechiesh-römischen Altertums. München, 1948.

AH 7819.44.5   Kahrstedt, Ulrich. Kulturgeschichte der römischen Kaiserzeit. München, 1944.

AH 7819.44.6   Kahrstedt, Ulrich. Kulturgeschichte der römischen Kaiserzeit. 2. Aufl. Bern, 1958.

AH 8647.21   Kahrstedt, Ulrich. Die wirtschaftliche Lage. Grossgriechenlands in der Kaiserzeit. Wiesbaden, 1960.

AH 7179.27   Kaïla, E. L'unité foncière en droit romain. Paris, 1927.

AH 7738.76   Der Kaiser Alexander Severus. (Porrath, Otto.) Halle, 1876.

AH 7509.34.10   Kaiser Augustus. (Berve, H.) Leipzig, 1934.

AH 7509.03.3   Kaiser Augustus. (Meyer, Eduard.) Heidelberg, 1903.

AH 7509.37.30   Kaiser Augustus. (Rehrmann, F.A.) Hildesheim, 1937.

AH 7509.02   Kaiser Augustus. (Seeck, Otto.) Bielefeld, 1902.

AH 7509.59   Kaiser Augustus. (Vittinghoff, Friedrich.) Göttingen, 1959.

AH 7748.69   Kaiser Diocletan. (Preuss, Theodor.) Leipzig, 1869.

AH 7709.11.3   Kaiser Gordian III. (Lehmann, Karl Friedrich Wilhelm.) Berlin, 1911.

AH 7709.11   Kaiser Gordian III. (Lehmann, Karl Friedrich Wilhelm.) Berlin, 1911.

AH 7629.05   Kaiser Hadrian. (Kornemann, E.) Leipzig, 1905.

AH 7628.84.3   Der Kaiser Hadrian. 2. Aufl. (Gregorovius, F.A.) Stuttgart, 1884.

AH 7778.97   Ein Kaiser im Kampf mit seiner Zeit. 2. Aufl. (Scholl, Karl.) Bamberg, 1897?

AH 7779.30.5   Kaiser Julian. (Bidez, Joseph.) Hamburg, 1956.

AH 7779.14   Kaiser Julianus. (Geffcken, J.) Leipzig, 1914.

AH 7759.57   Der Kaiser Konstantin. (Voelkl, Ludwig.) München, 1957.

AH 7649.14   Kaiser Mark Aurel und die Christen. Inaug. Diss. (Eberlein, Hellmut.) Breslau, 1914.

AH 7768.78   Der Kaiser Theodosius der Grosse. (Güldenpenning, A.) Halle, 1878.

AH 7579.00   Kaiser Titus. (Mayor, G.) Eger, 1900.

AH 7579.05   Kaiser Titus und der jüdische Krieg. (Wolff-Beckh, B.) Berlin, 1905.

AH 7499.64   Kaiser und Senat in der Zeit von Nero bis Nerva. (Grenzheuser, Bruno.) Münster? 1964.

AH 7769.27   Kaiser Valentinian I (364-375). Inaug. Diss. (Heering, Walter.) Magdeburg, 1927.

AH 7059.05   Die kaiserlichen Verwaltungsbeamten. (Hirschfeld, O.) Berlin, 1905.

AH 7739.12   Die kaiserlichen Verwaltungsbeamten unter Severus Alexander, 222-235. (Stein, Arthur.) Prag, 1912.

AH 7489.13   Das Kaisertum. (Hahn, L.) Leipzig, 1913.

Eg 819.71   Kak zhili egiptiane vo vremena stroitel'stva piramid. (Savel'eva, Tat'iana N.) Moskva, 1971.

VEg 885.969   Kákosy, László. Varázslás az ókori Egyiptomban. Budapest, 1969.

Eg 981.10   Kalabsha; Architektur und Baugeschichte des Tempels. (Siegler, Karl Georg.) Berlin, 1970.

AH 4809.51   Kalendarz starozy tnych Greków i Rzymian. (Winniczuh, L.) Warszawa, 1951.

AH 6107.15   Kalléris, J.N. Les anciens Macédoniens. Athènes, 1954-

AH 4039.22   Kallikles. (Menzel, Adolf.) Wien, 1922.

AH 9707.7.5   Kalopothakes, D. De Thracia provincia Romana. Berlin, 1893.

AH 9701.5   Kalopothakes, D. De Thracia provincia Romana. Lipsiae, 1893. 2 pam.

AH 9707.7   Kalopothakes, D. De Thracia provincia Romana. Lipsiae, 1893.

AH 9707.7.10   Kalopothakes, D. O chōrismos. Athēnai, 1894.

AH 2008.9   Kammerer, Albert. Pétra et la Nabatène. Plates, maps and atlas. Paris, 1929-30. 2v.

AH 7269.57   Kampe, Otto. Die römische Republik und ihre Auseinandersetzung mit den Grossmächten des Mittelmeerraumes bis 168. Stuttgart, 1957.

AH 930.42   Kampen, Albert van. Die Welt der Antike. 12. Aufl. Gotha, 1958.

AH 9777.21   Der Kampf der Westgothen und Römer. (Eicken, H. von.) Leipzig, 1876.

AH 7469.34.5   Der Kampf um Caesars Erbe. (Mainzer, Ferdinand.) Leipzig, 1936.

AH 7438.98   Der Kampf zwischen Rom und Samnium. (Burger, Combertus P.) Amsterdam, 1898.

AH 6107.20   Kanatsoulēs, Dēmētrios. He dytikē Makedonia kata tous archaious chronous. Thessalonikē, 1958.

AH 6107.21   Kanatsoulēs, Dēmētrios. Historia tēs Makedonias. Thessalonikē, 1964.

AH 6107.12   Kanatsoulēs, Dēmētrios. He Makedonia mechri tou thanatou tou Archelaou. Thessalonikē, 1964.

AH 4459.63   Kanellopoulos, Panagiōtēs. Apo ton Marathōna stēn Pydna ki'ōs tēn katastrophe tēs Korivthou 490-146 p.ch. Athēnai, 1963. 3v.

AH 4339.71   Kanellopoulos, Panagiōtēs. Five men - five centuries; essays on Solon. London, 1971.

AH 2231.5.5   Kanis Karumunun kronoloji problemleri Hakkinda Musahedeler. (Balkan, Kemal.) Ankara, 1955.

AH 7659.47.5   Kaphahn, Fritz. Zwischen Antike und Mittelalter. München, 1944.

AH 7659.47   Kaphahn, Fritz. Zwischen Antike und Mittelalter. München, 1947.

AH 7469.68   Kaplan, Arthur. Catiline; the man and his role in the Roman revolution. N.Y., 1968.

Eg 1029.63   Kaplony, Peter. Die Inschriften der ägyptischen Frühzeit. Wiesbaden, 1963. 3v.

Eg 1029.63.1   Kaplony, Peter. Die Inschriften der ägyptischen Frühzeit. Supplement. Wiesbaden, 1964.

Eg 1029.63.5   Kaplony, Peter. Kleine Beiträge zu der Inschriften der ägyptischen Frühzeit. Wiesbaden, 1966.

Eg 139.63   Kaplony-Heckel, U. Die demotischen Tempeleide. Wiesbaden, 1963. 2v.

Eg 1309.64.5F   Kaplony-Heckel, Ursula. Die demotischen Gebelen-Urkunden der Heidelberger Papyrus-Sammlung. Heidelberg, 1964.

AH 2207.5   Kappadokias. (Karolidos, G.K.) Kōnstantinople, 1874.

AH 7114.19   Kappes, K. Erläuterungen...zur römischen Ritter. Freiburg, 1855.

AH 7148.91   Kappeyne van de Coppello, Johann. Drei Abhandlungen zum römischen Staats- und Privatrecht. Berlin, 1891.

AH 7469.00.3   Kappler, Carl. Uber die unter dem Namen der Cornelia überlieferten Brieffragmente. Weiden, 1905.

Eg 981.2   Karanis; communsuté rurale. (Geremek, Hanna.) Wrocław, 1969.

AH 4838.80   Karikoulas. Peri chrēseōs toū stephanou. Erlangen, 1880.

AH 4843.7   Karl von Jan. Griechische Saiteninstrumente. Leipzig, 1882.

AH 7163.18   Karlowa, O. Die Formen der römischen Ehe. Bonn, 1868.

AH 7228.72   Karlowa, O. Der römische Civilprozess. Berlin, 1872.

AH 7138.85.3   Karlowa, O. Römische Rechtsgeschichte. Leipzig, 1885. 2v.

AH 2109.5   Karolides, Paul. Die sogenannten Assyro-Chaldäer und Hittiten. Athens, 1898.

AH 2207.5   Karolidos, G.K. Kappadokias. Kōnstantinople, 1874.

AH 4949.11   Karte von Griechenland zur Zeit des Pausanias. (Blümner, Hugo.) Bern, 1911.

AH 7201.21.10   Kaser, Max. Die Interpretatio zu den Paulussentenzen. Köln, 1956.

Eg 1029.68.1   Kaster, Joseph. The literature and mythology of ancient Egypt. London, 1970.

Eg 1029.68   Kaster, Joseph. Wings of the falcon; Life and thought of ancient Egypt. N.Y., 1968.

AH 4117.7   Kastromenos, P. Die Demen von Attika. Diss. Leipzig, 1886.

AH 3663.14   Katrak, Jamshed C. Marriage in ancient Iran. Bombay, 1965.

AH 6136.5   Katsarov, G.I. Peoniia. Sofiia, 1921.

AH 6110.22   Katsarov, G.I. Tsar Filipp II Makedonski. Sofiia, 1922.

AH 7659.55   Katz, Solomon. The decline of Rome and the rise of mediaeval Europe. Ithaca, N.Y., 1955.

AH 3013.6.2   Kaulen, Franz. Assyrien und Babylonien. 2. Aufl. Freiburg, 1882.

AH 3013.6.4A   Kaulen, Franz. Assyrien und Babylonien. 4. Aufl. Freiburg, 1891.

AH 3013.6.5   Kaulen, Franz. Assyrien und Babylonien. 5. Aufl. Freiburg, 1899.

AH 5309.9   Kausel, T. Thesei Synoecismo. Dillenburg, 1882.

AH 3008.82.7   Kausen, F. Assyrien und Babylonien. 2. Aufl. Freiburg, 1885.

AH 9713.5   Kazaroev, G.I. Beiträge zur Kulturgeschichte der Thraker. Sarajevo, 1916.

AH 6007.5   Kazarow, G. Foederis Phocensium institutis. Lipsiae, 1899.

AH 3005.10   Keallexikon der Assyriologie. (Ebeling, Erich.) Berlin, 1928-38. 4v.

AH 7037.76   Kearney, M. Lectures concerning history read during the year 1775 in Trinity College, Dublin. London, 1776.

AH 408.78.5A   Keary, C.F. The dawn of history. N.Y., 1879?

NEDL   AH 408.78.9   Keary, C.F. The dawn of history. N.Y., 1885.

AH 408.78.15   Keary, C.F. The dawn of history. N.Y., 1887.

AH 408.78.8   Keary, C.F. The dawn of history. pt.1. N.Y., 1883.

NEDL   AH 408.78.7   Keary, C.F. The dawn of history. pt.1-2. N.Y., 1883.

Eg 819.55.5   Kees, Hermann. Das alte Agypten. Berlin, 1955.

Eg 939.61   Kees, Hermann. Ancient Egypt. Chicago, 1961.

Call number	Entry
Eg 879.56	Kees, Hermann. Der Götterglaube im alten Ägypten. 2. Aufl. Berlin, 1956.
Eg 879.12.5	Kees, Hermann. Der Opfertanz des ägyptischen Königs. München, 1912.
Eg 879.26.5	Kees, Hermann. Totenglauben und Jenseitsvorstellungen der alten Ägypter. Leipzig, 1926.
Eg 879.26.7	Kees, Hermann. Totenglauben und Jenseitsvorstellungen der alten Ägypter. 2. Aufl. Berlin, 1956.
AH 188.96	Keiffer, Jules. L'esclavage à Athènes et à Rome. Luxembourg, 1896.
AH 4278.50	Keightley, T. Historia tēs Archaias Hellados. En Athēnais, 1850.
AH 4278.39	Keightley, T. History of Greece. Boston, 1839.
AH 7278.39.5	Keightley, T. History of Rome. Boston, 1839.
AH 7488.41.5	Keightley, Thomas. History of the Roman empire, from the accession of Augustus to the end of the empire of the West. Boston, 1841.
AH 4499.02	Keil, Bruno. Anonymus Argentinensis. Strassburg, 1902.
AH 3159.11	Die Keilinschriften und das Alte Testament. (Schrader, E.) Giessen, 1872.
AH 3159.11.2A	Die Keilinschriften und das Alte Testament. 2e Aufl. (Schrader, E.) Giessen, 1883.
AH 3012.6	Keilinschriften und Geschichtsforschung. (Schrader, E.) Giessen, 1878.
AH 3002.27.5	Keilinschriftliche Bibliothek. Berlin. 2-5,1890-1896 4v.
AH 3011.6	Keilinschriftliche Studien. (Witzel, M.) Leipzig. 1-7,1918-1930// 7v.
AH 3002.6.5	Keilinschriftliches Textbuch zum Alten Testament. (Winckler, H.) Leipzig, 1892.
AH 3159.8	Die Keilschrift-Urkunden und die Genesis. (Scholz, A.) Würzburg, 1877.
AH 3163.8	Keilschriftliche Actenstücke aus babylonischen Städten. (Peisir, Felix E.) Berlin, 1889.
AH 3002.105	Keilschriftliche Miscellanea. Roma, 1933.
AH 3192.5	Keilschriftmedicin. (Oefele, F.F.) Breslan, 1902.
AH 3002.2.5A	Keilschrifttexte: Sargon's Königs von Assyrien. (Sargon, king of Assyria.) Leipzig, 1883.
NEDL AH 3094.6F	Die Keilschrifttexte Sargons. (Winckler, Hugo.) Leipzig, 1889.
AH 3092.2	Die Keilschrifttexte Tiglat-Pilesers III. (Rost, P.) Leipzig, 1893. 2v.
AH 3002.82F	Keilschrifturkunden aus Boghazköi. Berlin. 1-37 14v.
Eg 856.4F	Keimer, Ludwig. Remarques sur le tatouage dans l'Egypte ancienne. Caire, 1948.
AH 3045.15	Keiser, Helen. Die Stadt der Grossen Götin 4000 Jahre Uruk. Olten, 1967.
AH 3002.83	Die Kelischin-Stele und ihre chaldisch-assyrischen Keilinschriften. (Belck, Waldemar.) Freienwald, 1904.
AH 4559.04.5	Keller, Erich. Alexander der Grosse. Berlin, 1904.
AH 7228.27	Keller, F.L. Litis Contestation und Ultheil. Zürich, 1827.
AH 7228.70	Keller, F.L. von. De procédure civile et des actions. Paris, 1870.
AH 7228.52.9	Keller, Friedrich. Der römische Civilprocess und die Actionen. Leipzig, 1883.
AH 7228.52.5	Keller, Friedrich. Der römische Civilprocess und die Actionen. Leipzig, 1876.
AH 7228.52.3	Keller, Friedrich. Der römische Civilprocess und die Actionen. 3. Aufl. Leipzig, 1863.
AH 7228.52.4	Keller, Friedrich. Der römische Civilprocess und die Actionen. 4. Aufl. Leipzig, 1871.
AH 7448.75	Keller, Ludwig. Der zweite punische Krieg. Marburg, 1875.
AH 854.9A	Keller, Otto. Der antike Tierwelt. Leipzig, 1909. 2v.
AH 854.9.2	Keller, Otto. Gesamtregister von Eugen Staiger. Leipzig, 1920.
AH 854.11	Keller, Otto. Thiere des...Altertums. Innsbruck, 1887.
AH 7798.84	Keller, Rudolf. Stilicho. Berlin, 1884.
AH 8907.46	Keller, Werner. Denn die Entzündeten das Licht. München, 1970.
AH 3073.3A	Kellner, M. The Assyrian monuments illustrating sermons of Isaiah. Boston, 1900.
AH 3073.3.5	Kellner, M. The prophecies of Isaiah. Cambridge, 1895.
AH 3177.7	Kellner, M.L. The deluge in the Izdubar epic. N.Y., 1888.
AH 7229.66	Kelly, John Maurice. Roman litigation. Oxford, 1966.
AH 8507.5	Kelten und Germanen. (Holtzmann, A.) Stuttgart, 1855.
AH 8549.173.1	Keltische Grottheit auf norischem Inschriftstein. Photoreproduction. (Lochner-Huettenbach, Fritz.) Graz, 1973.
AH 239.27	Keltisches Söldnertum in der Mittelmeerwelt bis zur Herrschaft der Römer. Inaug. Diss. (Wienicke, Arnold.) Breslau, 1927.
AH 8548.141.5	Keltská civilisace a její dědictví. (Filip, Jan.) Praha, 1959.
EgP 79.2	Kemi, revue de philologie et d'archeologie. Paris. 1,1928+ 5v.
AH 3966.14	Kěnaän nach der Stammeintheilung. (Gans, J.) Paderborn, 1843.
AH 8549.127	Kendrick, T.D. The Druids. London, 1927.
AH 8549.127.5	Kendrick, T.D. The Druids. N.Y., 1927.
AH 879.14	Kennebicq, Léon. L'idee du juste dans l'orient grec avant Socrate. Bruxelles, 1914.
AH 7816.96.16	Kennett, Basil. Romae antiquae notitia. 1st American ed. Philadelphia, 1822.
AH 7816.96.17	Kennett, Basil. Romae antiquae notitia. 2nd American ed. Baltimore, 18- .
AH 7816.96.3	Kennett, Basil. Romae antiquae notitia. 3. ed. Oxford, 1704.
NEDL AH 7816.96.6	Kennett, Basil. Romae antiquae notitia. 6th ed. London, 1717.
NEDL AH 7816.96.11	Kennett, Basil. Romae antiquae notitia. 11th ed. London, 1746.
NEDL AH 7816.96.13	Kennett, Basil. Romae antiquae notitia. 13th ed. London, 1763.
AH 7816.96.14	Kennett, Basil. Romae antiquae notitia. 14th ed. London, 1769.
AH 4214.9	Kenntnis der griechischen Eid. (Ott, Ludwig.) Leipzig, 1896.
AH 7139.02	Kenntniss des Volksrechtes. (Brassloff, S.) Weimar, 1902.
Eg 278.52	Kenrick, J. Ancient Egypt. N.Y., 1852. 2v.
AH 408.46.3	Kenrick, J. Essay on primaeval history. London, 1846.
AH 3707.9	Kenrick, J. Phoenicia. London, 1855.
AH 6057.9	Kent, R.G. History of Thessaly. Lancaster, Pa., 1904.
AH 3959.36	Kenyon, Kathleen Mary. Amorites and Canaanites. London, 1966.
AH 938.84	Keppel, T. Ansichten der alten Griechen und Römer. Schwienfurt, 1884.
AH 4159.23	Keramopoullos, A.D. Ho apotympanismos. Athēnai, 1923.
AH 6113.8	Keramopoullos, A.D. Arigia of the Macedonians. Detroit, 1946.
AH 4819.57.15	Kerényi, Karoly. Griechische Miniaturen. Zürich, 1957.
Eg 981.5	Kerkeosiris. (Crawford, Dorothy.) Cambridge, Eng., 1971.
AH 2583.5F	Kern, Otto. Magnesia am Maiandros. Berlin, 1894.
AH 4410.42	Kerschensteiner, Jula. Die mykenische Welt in ihren schriftlichen Zeugnissen. 1. Aufl. München, 1970.
AH 8516.7	Kerviler, René. Études critiques sur l'ancienne géographie armoricaine. Saint-Brieuc, 1882.
AH 7239.61	Késörómai hadügyek es társadalmi alapjaik. (Várady, Lazló.) Budapest, 1961.
AH 7636.67	Keuchenius, R. Antoninus Pius. Amstelaedami, 1667.
Eg 879.31	Kevin, Robert O. Wisdom of Amen-em-Apt and its possible dependence upon Hebrew book of proverbs. Thesis. Philadelphia, 1931.
AH 1928.75	Key to the Hebrew-Egyptian mystery in the source of measures. (Skinner, J.R.) Cincinnati, 1875.
AH 3407.34	Khettskoe obshchestvo. (Menabde, Eduard A.) Tbilisi, 1965.
Eg 459.62	Khramovaia forma tsarskogo khoz. drevnego Egypta. (Stuchevskii, Iosef A.) Moskva, 1962.
AH 889.07	Khvostov, M. Istoriia vostochoi torgovli. Kazan', 1907.
NEDL AH 409.09	Khvostov, M.M. Istoriia drevnago vostoka. Kazan', 1909.
AH 5909.59	Kiechle, Franz. Messenische Studien. Kallmünz, 1959.
AH 7279.67.5	Kiechle, Franz. Römische Geschichte. Stuttgart, 1967.
AH 7189.69.5	Kiechle, Franz. Sklavenarbeit und technischen Fortschritt im Römischen Reich. Wiesbaden, 1969.
AH 7819.33.5	Kiefer, Otto. Kulturgeschichte Roms, unter besonderer Berücksichtigung der römischen Sitten. Berlin, 1933.
AH 7819.33.5.3	Kiefer, Otto. Sexual life in ancient Rome. London, 1934.
AH 7819.33.5.2	Kiefer, Otto. Sexual life in ancient Rome. N.Y., 1935.
AH 5759.13	Kiele, F. Lakonien und Sparta. München, 1963.
AH 7468.45	Kiene, Adolf. Der römische Bundesgenossenkrieg. Leipzig, 1845.
Eg 279.53	Kienitz, F.K. Die politische Geschichte Ägyptens. Berlin, 1953.
AH 938.81	Kiepert, H. Manual of ancient geography. London, 1881.
AH 3013.19	Kiepert, J.S.H. Begleitworte zur Karte de Ruinenfelder von Babylon. Berlin, 1883.
AH 2321.2	Kinal, F. Géographie et l'histoire des pays d'Arzava. Ankara, 1953.
AH 2110.15	Kinal, Füruzan. Eski Anadolu tarihi. Ankara, 1962.
AH 4609.29	Kincaid, Charles A. Successors of Alexander. London, 1930.
Eg 608.86	King, James. Cleopatra's needle. London, 1886.
AH 3155.8	King, L.W. Babylonian religion and mythology. London, 1903.
AH 3088.5F	King, L.W. Bronze reliefs from the Gates of Shalmaneser. London, 1915.
AH 3009.10	King, L.W. History of Babylon from foundation...to Persian conquest. N.Y., 1915.
AH 3030.3	King, L.W. Letters and inscriptions of Hammourabi. London, 1898-1900. 3v.
AH 1279.07	King, Leonard. History of Egypt, Chaldea, Syria, Babylonia and Assyria in the light of recent discovery. London, 1907.
AH 3156.6.5	King, Leonard W. Babylonian magic and sorcery. Lieden, 1952.
AH 3156.6	King, Leonard W. Babylonian magic and sorcery. London, 1896.
AH 3020.22.1	King, Leonard W. Chronicles concerning early Babylonian kings. v.1-2. London, 1972.
AH 3022.5	King, Leonard W. A history of Sumer and Akkad. N.Y., 1910?
AH 3179.7.10	King, Leonard W. Seven tablets of creation. London, 1902.
AH 4519.33.5	King Agis of Sparta and his campaign in Arkadia in 418 B.C. (Woodhouse, William J.) Oxford, 1933.
AH 7208.6	The King and the comitium; a study of Rome's oldest public documents. (Palmer, Robert E.A.) Wiesbaden, 1969.
AH 4659.61	The king is dead. (Eddy, S.K.) Lincoln, 1961.
Eg 299.12	Kings and gods of Egypt. (Moret, Alexandre.) N.Y., 1912.
Eg 299.26	Kings and queens of ancient Egypt. London, 1926.
AH 2558.5	The kings of Lydia. (Alexander, L.) Oberlin, 1914.
AH 3408.13	Kings of the Hittites. (Hogarth, D.G.) London, 1926.
AH 7298.64	Kingsley, Charles. The Roman and the Teuton. Cambridge, 1864.
NEDL AH 7298.64.1	Kingsley, Charles. The Roman and the Teuton. London, 1879.
AH 7298.64.3	Kingsley, Charles. The Roman and the Teuton. London, 1881.
AH 7298.64.5	Kingsley, Charles. The Roman and the Teuton. London, 1889.
NEDL AH 7298.64.2	Kingsley, Charles. The Roman and the Teuton. London, 1890.
AH 3159.26	Kinns, Samuel. Graven in the rock. London, 1895.
AH 4486.5	Kinzl, Kourad. Miltiades-Forschungen. Wien, 1968.
AH 6057.11	Kip, G. Thessalische Studien. Halle, 1910.
AH 7139.03	Kipp, T. Geschichte...des römischen Rechts. Leipzig, 1903.
AH 7201.77	Kipp, T. Quellenkunde des römischen Rechts. Leipzig, 1896.
AH 8307.5	Király, Pál. Dacia provincia Augusti. Nagy-Becskerek, 1893-94. 2v.
AH 8307.6	Király, Pál. Ulpia Trajana Augusta colonia Dacica. Budapest, 1891.
Htn Eg 876.76F*	Kircher, A. Sphinx mystagoga. Amstelodami, 1676.
AH 7163.28	Kirchmaier, G.C. Papia Poppoea lex, e ruderibus exposita. Wittenbeergae, 1694.
Htn AH 7861.3*	Kirchmann, J. De funeribus Romanorum. Hamburg, 1605.
Htn AH 7861.4*	Kirchmann, J. De funeribus Romanorum cum appendice. Lugduni Batavorum, 1672.
AH 4559.13	Kirkman, M.M. History of Alexander the Great. Chicago, 1913.
AH 3013.928	Kirkuk excavations conducted by the Fogg Museum of Art. Preliminary report. (Harvard University. Fogg Art Museum.) n.p., 1928.
AH 3980.17	Kirmis, F. Die Lage der alten Davidsstadt und die Mauern des Alten Jerusalem. Breslau, 1919.
AH 4939.56	Kirsten, Ernst. Die griechische Polis als historisch-geographisches Problem des Mittelmeerraumes. Bonn, 1956.
Eg 659.73	Kitchen, Kenneth Anderson. The third intermediate period in Egypt. (1100-650 B.C.). Warminster, 1973.
AH 4279.51	Kitto, H.D.F. The Greeks. Harmondsworth, 1951.
AH 3964.17.10F	Kitto, John. The tabernacle and its furniture. London, 1849.

Author and Title Listing

Author and Title Listing

AH 7139.25   Kübler, Bernhard. Geschichte des römischen Rechts; ein Lehrbuch. Leipzig, 1925.

AH 3963.175   Küchenmeister, F. Die Totenbestattungen der Bibel. Stuttgart, 1893.

AH 3002.2.18   Küchler, Friedrich. Beiträge zur Kenntnis der assyrisch-babylonischen Medizin. Leipzig, 1904.

AH 7829.10   Kuehn, G. De opificum romanorum condicione privata quaestiones. Diss. inaug. Halis, 1910.

Eg 603.19   Kühne, Cord. Die Chronologie der internationalen Korrespondenz von El-Amarna. Kevelaer, 1973.

AH 1842.5   Kuehnert, F. Allgemeinbildung und Fachbildung in der Antike. Berlin, 1961.

AH 3910.14   Kümpel, Eduard. Die Quellen zur Geschichte des Krieges der Römer gegen Antiochus III. Hamburg, 1893.

Eg 1042.970   Kuentz, Charles. La face sud du massif est du pylône de Ramsè's II à Louxor. Le Caire, 1970.

AH 3160.11   Kugler, F.X. Im Bannkreis Babels. Münster, 1910.

AH 7139.10   Kuhlenbeck, L. Die Entwicklungsgeschichte des römischen Rechts. München, 1910. 2v.

AH 3910.6   Kuhn, Adolf. Beiträge zur Geschichte der Seleukiden. Altkirch, 1891.

AH 7038.49   Kuhn, E. Verfassung des römischen Reichs. Leipzig, 1849.

AH 98.78   Kuhn, Emil. Entstehung der Staedte der Alten. Leipzig, 1878.

AH 7098.64   Kuhn, Emil. Die stadtische...Verfassung. Leipzig, 1864.

AH 7149.01   Kuhn, F.J. Betrachtungen über Majestäten. München, 1901.

AH 4818.83   Kuhnert, E. De cura statuarum. Berolini, 1883.

AH 4818.83.5   Kuhnert, E. De cura statuarum apud Graecos. Berolini, 1883.

AH 866.9   Kuiper, G. Harpocrates. Trajecti, 1687.

AH 7161.32   Kuleczka, Gerard. Prawo rzymskie epoki pryncypatu wobec dzieci pozamałzeńskich. Wrocław, 1969.

AH 3414.20   Der Kult von Nerik. (Haas, Volkert.) Rom, 1970.

AH 2764.5   Die Kulte und Heiligtumer der Gotter im Pergamon. 2. Aufl. (Ohlemutz, Erwin.) Darmstadt, 1968.

AH 879.09   Kultübeitragungen. (Schmidt, E.) Giessen, 1909.

AH 819.49.5   Die Kultur der Antike. (Taeger, Fritz.) Köln, 1949.

AH 819.35.6   Die Kultur der Antike. 2. Aufl. (Howard, E.) Zürich, 1948.

AH 3143.20   Die Kultur der Babylonier und Assyrier. (Landersdorfer, Simon.) Kempten, 1913.

AH 4819.43.5   Die Kultur der Griechen. (Kranz, Walther.) Leipzig, 1943.

AH 819.05.3F   Kultur der Griechen und Römer. (Cybulski, S.) Leipzig, 1905.

Eg 819.13.5   Die Kultur des alten Ägyptens. 2. Aufl. (Bissing, F.W. von.) Leipzig, 1919.

AH 1819.72   Die Kultur des alten Orients. (Oberhuber, Karl.) Frankfurt, 1972.

AH 819.69   Die Kultur des klassischen Altertums. Frankfurt am Main, 1969.

Eg 819.07   Kultur und Denken der alten Ägypter. (Schneider, H.) Leipzig, 1907.

AH 3143.21   Kultur und Denken der Babylonier und Juden. (Schneider, Hermann.) Leipzig, 1910.

AH 819.66.5   Kul'tura antichnogo mira. (Akademiia nauk SSSR. Institut arkheologii.) Moskva, 1966.

AH 3143.17   Kultura drevnei Vavilonii. (Nikol'skii, Nikolai M.) Minsk, 1959.

AH 3013.958.10   Kul'tura i iskusstvo Dvurech'ia. (Flittner, N.D.) Leningrad, 1958.

AH 3613.5   Kul'tura Parfii. (Koshelenko, Gennadii A.) Moskva, 1966.

AH 3661.14   Kul'tura sasanidskogo Irana. (Lukonin, Vladimir G.) Moskva, 1969.

AH 818.69.4   Kulturbilder. (Göll, Hermann.) Leipzig, 1880. 2v.

AH 818.69.3   Kulturbilder. v.1-3. (Göll, Hermann.) Leipzig, 1869. 2v.

Eg 819.67.10   Die Kulturen des Niltals von Aswan bis Sennar. (Hofmann, Inge.) Hamburg, 1967.

Eg 819.67.7   Kulturgeist und Kulturleib. 2. Aufl. (Makram, Rizg.) Tübingen, 1970.

AH 7819.03.3   Kulturgeschichte...Kaiserzeit. (Grupp, G.) München, 1903. 2v.

AH 819.36.27   Kulturgeschichte Ägyptens und des alten Orients. 3. Aufl. (Friedell, Egon.) München, 1951.

AH 7819.44.5   Kulturgeschichte der römischen Kaiserzeit. (Kahrstedt, Ulrich.) München, 1944.

AH 7819.44.6   Kulturgeschichte der römischen Kaiserzeit. 2. Aufl. (Kahrstedt, Ulrich.) Bern, 1958.

AH 818.97   Kulturgeschichte des...Altertums. (Holm, A.) Leipzig, 1897.

Eg 819.62.5   Kulturgeschichte des alten Ägypten. (Wolf, Walther.) Stuttgart, 1962.

AH 1819.61.5   Kulturgeschichte des alten Orient. (Schmökel, Hartmut.) Stuttgart, 1961.

AH 819.36.25   Kulturgeschichte des Altertums. (Friedell, Egon.) Zürich, 1936-

AH 819.25.5   Kulturgeschichte des Altertums. (Otto, Walter G.A.) München, 1925.

AH 4659.67   Kulturgeschichte des Hellenismus. (Schneider, Carl.) München, 1967- 2v.

AH 4818.98.5.15   Kulturgeschichte Griechenlands. (Burckhardt, J.) Berlin, 1934.

AH 4819.49.5   Kulturgeschichte Griechenlands. (Friedell, Egon.) München, 1949.

AH 7819.33.5   Kulturgeschichte Roms, unter besonderer Berücksichtigung der römischen Sitten. (Kiefer, Otto.) Berlin, 1933.

AH 819.06   Kulturhistorische Beiträge zur Kenntnis des griechischen und römischen Altertums. (Schmidt, M.C.P.) Leipzig, 1906-12. 2v.

AH 819.06.2   Kulturhistorische Beiträge zur Kenntnis des griechischen und römischen Altertums. (Schmidt, M.C.P.) Leipzig, 1914.

AH 7819.03   Kulturhistoriska förekäsningar. (Rydberg, V.) Stockholm, 1903. 6v.

AH 3014.15F   Die Kulturichtung in Mesopotamien. Diss. (Martiny, G.) Berlin, 1932.

AH 4819.28.5   Das Kulturleben der Griechen und Römer in ihrer Entwicklung. (Birt, Theodor.) Leipzig, 1928.

AH 4819.33   Kulturprobleme des klassischen Griechentums. (Drerup, Engelbert.) Paderborn, 1933-34. 2v.

AH 819.64.16   Kumaniecki, Kazimierz F. Historia kultury strożytnej Grecji i Rzymu. wyd. 2. Warszawa, 1964.

AH 3414.10   Kumarki. (Gueterbock, H.G.) Zürich, 1946.

AH 8616.10   Die Kunde der Hellenen von dem Lande und den Völkern der Apenninenhalbinsel bis 300 v. Chr. (Wikén, Erik.) Lund, 1937.

AH 3413.9   Die Kunst der Hethiter. (Weber, Otto.) Berlin, 1922.

Eg 847.1   Die Kunst Hieroglyphen zu Lesen. (Schmidt, Karl F.W.) Breslau, 1828.

AH 29.14   Kunst und Altertum. Berlin, 1914-25. 6v.

AH 3154.17   Kunstmann, W.G. Die babylonische Gebetsbeschwörung. Inaug. Diss. Gräfenhainichen, 1930.

AH 7138.79.3   Kuntze, J.E. Cursus des römischen Rechts. Leipzig, 1879.

AH 7138.80.3   Kuntze, J.E. Excurse über römischen Recht. 2. Aufl. Leipzig, 1880.

AH 7298.82   Kuntze, J.E. Prolegomena zur Geschichte Roms. Leipzig, 1882.

AH 3313.2   Kuopiaká; contributi allo studio della componente cipriota della civiltá punica. (Bisi, Anna Maria.) Roma, 1966.

AH 3921.9.5   Kurbatov, G.L. Rannevizantiiskii gorod. Leningrad, 1962.

AH 199.58   Kuri Breña, Daniel. La filosofía del clerico in la antigüedad cristiana. 2. ed. Mexico, 1958.

AH 4861.9   Kurtz, Donna Carol. Greek burial customs. London, 1971.

AH 279.71.5   Kurze Geschichte der antiken Welt. (Lauffer, Siegfried.) München, 1971.

AH 4817.91   Kurzer Entwurf der griechischen Alterthümer. (Nitsch, P.F.A.) Altenburg, 1791.

AH 3008.82   Kurzgefasste Geschichte Babyloniens und Assyriens. (Mürdter, F.) Stuttgart, 1882.

AH 3171.6   Kurzgefasster Überblick...Babylonisch-Assyrische Literatur. (Bezold, E.) Leipzig, 1886.

AH 7231.9   Kuthe, A. Römische Kriegsaltertümer. Wismar, 1884. 4 pam.

AH 115.3   Kutorga, M. Essai sur l'organisation de la tribu dans l'antiquité. Paris, 1839.

AH 4908.59   Kutorga, M. Trapézites. Paris, 1859.

AH 4478.60   Kutorga, M.S. Parti persan dans la Grèce ancienne. Paris, 1860.

Eg 299.37   Kutter, Carl. Alt Egypten spricht. Basel, 1937.

AH 3310.5.5   Kyprioi basileis tou 4 aiv. P. Ch. (Spyridakis, K.) Leukōsia, 1963.

AH 3307.5   Kypros. (Engel, W.H.) Berlin, 1841. 2v.

AH 7759.69.5   Kyriazés, Kóstas D. Kónstantinos ho Megas. Athēnai, 1969.

AH 2110.7   Kyros le jeune en Asie mineure. (Cousin, J.) Nancy, 1904.

Htn   AH 7035.38.3*   L. Fenestellae, de magistratibus, sacerdotisq. (Fiocco, A.D.) Basileae, n.d.

Htn   AH 7035.38*   L. Fenestellae, de magistratibus, sacerdotisq. (Fiocco, A.D.) Basileae, 1538.

Htn   AH 7035.29*   L. Fenestellae, de magistratibus, sacerdotisq. (Fiocco, A.D.) Lutetiae, 1529.

Htn   AH 7035.49*   L. Fenestellae, de magistratibus, sacerdotisq. (Fiocco, A.D.) Lutetiae, 1549.

Htn   AH 7035.38.6*   L. Fenestellae, de magistratibus, sacerdotisq. (Fiocco, A.D.) Venetiis, n.d.

Htn   AH 7035.42*   L. Fenestellae, de magistrattibus, sacerdotisq. (Fiocco, A.D.) Parisiis, 1542. 4 pam.

Htn   AH 7055.10.3*   L. Fenestellae, de Romanarum magistratibus. (Fiocco, A.D.) Basileae, 1581.

Htn   AH 7055.10.2*   L. Fenestellae, de Romanorum magistratibus. (Fiocco, A.D.) Lugduni, 1551.

Htn   AH 7055.10*   L. Fenestellae, de Romanorum magistratibus. (Fiocco, A.D.) n.p., n.d.

Htn   AH 7055.10.4*   L. Fenestellae, de Romanorum magistratibus. (Fiocco, A.D.) n.p., n.d.

AH 7168.82   Le la cause dans les contrats et les obligations. (Trinbal, J.) Toulouse, 1882.

AH 7861.10   La Nenia Latina. (Santoro, B.) Acireale, 1902.

AH 4279.46.10   Laache, Rolv. Om hellener og barbarer og om Athens herlighet. Oslo, 1946.

AH 4259.57   Labarbe, Jules. La loi navale de Themistocle. Paris, 1957.

AH 3183.15   Die Labartu-Texte. Strassburg, 1902.

AH 7918.93.3   Labat, P. Etude sur les Collèges d'artisans. Toulouse, 1893.

AH 3193.8   Labat, René. Un calendrier babylonien des travaux des signes et des mois. Paris, 1965.

AH 3147.5   Labat, René. Le caractère religieux de la royauté assyrobabylonienne. Thèse. Paris, 1939.

AH 3156.15   Labat, René. Commentaires assyro-babyloniens sur les présages. Bordeux, 1933.

AH 3154.30   Labat, René. Hémérologies et ménologies d'Assur. Thèse. Paris, 1939.

AH 3154.30.5   Labat, René. Hémérologies et ménologies d'Assur. Paris, 1939.

AH 3191.9F   Labat, René. Traite akkadien de diagnostics et pronostics mestiaux. Paris, 1951. 2v.

AH 7078.76   Labatut, E. La corruption électorale. Paris, 1876.

AH 9773.13   La Baume, Peter. Colonia Agrippinensis. 3. Aufl. Köln, 1964.

AH 8516.11   Labbe, Philippe. Pharus Galliae antiquae. Molinis, 1644.

AH 7298.63   Labberton, R.H. Historical questions. Philadelphia, 1863.

AH 7618.77   La Berge, G. de. Essai sur le regne de Trajan. Paris, 1877.

AH 7258.87   La Berge, Camille de. Étude sur l'organisation des flottes romaines. Vienne, 1887.

AH 9086.5   La Blanchère, R. Un chapitre d'histoire pontine. Paris, 1889.

AH 7787.50   La Bleterie. Histoire de l'Empereur Jovien. Amsterdam, 1750.

AH 7777.46   La Bleterie. Vie de l'Empereur Julien. Paris, 1746.

AH 3012.22   Lablocha, Yulia. Stosunki agrarne w paristure Sargonidów. Wyd. 1. Poznan, 1971.

AH 3159.24F   Laborde, L. de. Commentaire geographique sur l'exode et les nombres. Paris, 1841.

AH 7158.45   Laboulaye, E. Lois criminelles des Romains. Paris, 1845.

AH 7629.17   Lacey, R.H. The equestrian officials of Trajan and Hadrian. Thesis. Princeton, 1917.

AH 4840.8   Lacey, Walter K. The family in classical Greece. London, 1968.

AH 4538.54   Lachmann, J.H. Geschichte Griechenlands. v.1-2. Leipzig, 1854.

AH 5754.11   Lachmann, K.H. Spartnisches Staatsverfassung. Breslau, 1836.

AH 8955.2   Lackner, G. De incursionibus a Gallis in Italiani factis. Regimonti, 1887.

AH 7840.2   Lacombe, P. La famille dans la société romaine. Paris, 1889.

AH 7850.4   Lacombe, Paul. Fragments d'une histoire des moeurs. Cahors, 1880.

AH 5751.1   Pamphlet box. Laconia.

AH 5757.25   Laconian studies. (Boer, W. den.) Amsterdam, 1954.

AH 7468.88A   Lacour-Gayet, G. De P. Clodis Pulchris tribuno plebis. Thèse. Lutetiae Parisiorum, 1888.

AH 3964.14   Die Lade Jahnes. Inaug. Diss. (Dibelius, Martin.) Göttingen, 1906.

AH 5760.15   Laecedaemoniorum Reipublicae. (Petit-Dutaillis, C.) Lutetiae Parisiorum, 1894.

AH 7161.21 — Laënnec, R. Droit des patresfamilias. Saint-Amand, 1899.

AH 3012.17 — Laessóe, J. People of ancient Assyria. London, 1963.

AH 3154.40 — Laessoe, Joergen. Studies on the Assyrian ritual and series lûtrimki. København, 1955.

AH 7509.44 — Laet, S.J. de. Aspects de la vie sociale et économique sous Auguste et Tibère. Bruxelles, 1944.

Htn — AH 7815.21* — Laeti, Pomponii. Opera varia - quorum catalogum. Moguntiae, 1521.

AH 7799.71 — Lafferty, Raphael A. The fall of Rome. Garden City, N.Y., 1971.

AH 7099.66 — Laffi, Umberto. Adtributio e contributio. 1a ed. Pisa, 1966.

AH 7161.9 — La Fort, Charles. Essai historique sur la tutelle en droit romain. Genève, 1850.

AH 3966.6.2 — Lagarde, Pauli. Onomastica sacra. Gottingae, 1887.

AH 3980.17 — Die Lage der alten Davidsstadt und die Mauern des Alten Jerusalem. (Kirmis, F.) Breslau, 1919.

AH 7239.12 — Das Lager und Heer der Römer. (Stolle, F.) Strassburg, 1912.

AH 5124.7 — Laidlaw, W.A. A history of Delos. Oxford, 1933.

AH 7408.72 — Laing, C.H.B. Seven kings of the seven hills. Philadelphia, 1872.

AH 408.92 — Laing, S. Human origins. London, 1892.

AH 4279.32.5 — Laistner, M.L.W. Greek history. Boston, 1932.

AH 4459.36.3 — Laistner, M.L.W. A history of the Greek world. 3. ed. London, 1957.

AH 4459.36 — Laistner, M.L.W. A history of the Greek world from 479 to 323 B.C. London, 1936.

AH 4459.36.2 — Laistner, M.L.W. A history of the Greek world from 479 to 323 B.C. 2. ed. London, 1947.

AH 279.29 — Laistner, Max L.W. Survey of ancient history to the death of Constantine. Boston, 1929.

AH 878.37F — Lajard, J.B.F. Recherches sur le culte...de Vénus. Paris, 1837-48. 2v.

AH 5757.9 — Lakedaimonier. (Busolt, G.) Leipzig, 1878.

AH 5759.13 — Lakonien und Sparta. (Kiele, F.) München, 1963.

AH 7207.40 — L'albo senatorio da Settimino Severo a Carino. (Barbieri, Guido.) Roma, 1952.

AH 8954.10F — Lama, Pietro de. Tavola legislativa della Gallia Cisalpina. Parma, 1820.

AH 8608.3 — Lamarre, C. Etude sur peuples anciens de l'Italie. Paris, 1899.

AH 7238.63 — Lamarre, Claude. De la milice romaine depuis la fondation de Rome jusqu'à Constantin. Thèse. Paris, 1863.

AH 4559.46 — Lamb, Harold. Alexander of Macedon, the journey to world's end. 1st ed. Garden City, N.Y., 1946.

AH 3659.14 — Lamb, Harold. Cyrus the Great. 1st ed. Garden City, N.Y., 1960.

AH 7200.15 — Lambert, E. L'origine des XII tables. Paris, 1902.

AH 3189.5 — Lambert, Wilfred G. Babylonian wisdom literature. Oxford, 1960.

AH 9108.2 — Lamboglia, Nino. Liguria romana; studi storico topografici. Roma, 1939-

AH 9121.2 — Lamboglia, Nino. Topografia storica dell'Ingaunia nell'antichità. Albenga, 1933.

AH 7207.33 — Lambrechts, P. La composition du sénat romain de l'accession au trône d'Hadrien à la mort de Commode, 117-192. Antwerpen, 1936.

AH 8549.142 — Lambrechts, P. Contributions à l'étude des divinités celtiques. Brügge, 1942.

AH 4819.57.20 — Lambrechts, Pierre. Wat Hellas en Rome ons gaven. 2. Druk. Antwerpen, 1957.

AH 8904.5 — Lambrechts, R. Essai sur les magistratures des républiques étrusques. Bruxelles, 1959.

AH 4838.96F — Lambros and Polites. Olympic games. Athens, 1896.

AH 278.70 — Lamé-Fleury, J.R. Ancient history. Boston, 1870.

AH 278.67 — Lamé-Fleury, J.R. L'histoire ancienne. Paris, 1867.

AH 4278.29.13 — Lamé Fleury, J.R. L'histoire grecque, racontée aux enfants. Paris, 1873.

NEDL — AH 4278.29.7 — Lamé Fleury, J.R. L'histoire grecque, racontée aux enfants. 4e éd. Paris, 1837.

AH 7278.32.5 — Lamé Fleury, J.R. L'histoire romaine racontée aux enfants. Paris, 1869-70. 2v.

NEDL — AH 278.53 — Lamé-Fleury, J.R. La storia antica. Venezia, 1853.

AH 7488.55 — Lamé Fleury, J.R. La storia romana. Milano, 1855.

AH 4819.14.5 — Lamer, Hans. Griechische Kultur im Bilde. Leipzig, 1914.

AH 7819.15 — Lamer, Hans. Römische Kultur im Bilde. Leipzig, 1915.

AH 7469.09 — Lamina di bronzo con iscrizione...guerra dei socii italici. (Gatti, Giuseppe.) Roma, 1909.

AH 2011.5.5 — Lammens, H. L'Arabie occidentale avant l'hégire. Beyrouth, 1928.

AH 2011.5 — Lammens, H. Le berceau de l'Islam. Romae, 1914.

AH 817.03 — Lampe, F.A. De cymbalis veterum. Trajecti, 1703.

AH 7607.48 — Lampe, H. Dissertatio juridica prior de Marco Coccejo Nerva Roman. Bremae, 1748? 2 pam.

AH 4298.84 — Lamprog, S. Meletellata. Athēnai, 1884.

AH 3142.4 — Lamy, T.J. Concilium Seleuciae et Ctesiphonti Habitum. Levanii, 1868.

AH 7819.25 — Lanciani, R. Ancient and modern Rome. Boston, 1925.

AH 7819.25.3 — Lanciani, R. Ancient and modern Rome. London, 1925.

AH 3044.2F — Land behind Bagyhdad. (Adams, Robert McCormick.) Chicago, 1965.

AH 3022.28 — The land of Shinar. (Cottrell, Leonard.) London, 1965.

AH 3160.8.5 — Das Land ohne Heimkehr. (Delitzsch, F.) Stuttgart, 1911.

AH 3022.29 — Das Land Sumer. 2. Aufl. (Schmökel, Hartmut.) Stuttgart, 1956.

AH 3707.21 — Landau, W. Die Phönizier. Leipzig, 1901.

AH 3187.8 — Landersdorfer, S. Altbabylonische Privatbriefe. Paderborn, 1908.

AH 3714.5 — Landersdorfer, S. Der baal tetramorphos und die Kerube des Ezechiel. Paderborn, 1918.

AH 3143.20 — Landersdorfer, Simon. Die Kultur der Babylonier und Assyrier. Kempten, 1913.

AH 3966.10 — Lands and peoples of the Bible. (Baikie, James.) London, 1914.

AH 3013.15 — Landseer, J. Sabaean researches. London, 1823.

AH 7138.95 — Landucci, L. Storia del diritto romano. 2. ed. Verona, 1898. 2v.

AH 898.56 — Landwirthschaftliche Mittheilungen. (Forchhammer, P.W.) Kiel, 1856.

AH 4842.56 — Lane, F.H. Elementary Greek education. Syracuse, N.Y., 1895.

AH 2589.5 — Lane, G.M. Smyrnaeorum res gestae et antiquitates. Gottingae, 1851.

AH 3013.923 — Lane, William H. Babylonian problems. N.Y., 1923.

Eg 278.94.21 — Lane-Poole, Stanley. A history of Egypt in the Middle Ages. N.Y., 1901.

Eg 278.94.6A — Lane-Poole, Stanley. A history of Egypt in the Middle Ages. v.6. London, 1901.

Eg 278.94.20 — Lane-Poole, Stanley. A history of Egypt in the Middle Ages. 4. ed. London, 1925.

Eg 278.94.22 — Lane-Poole, Stanley. A history of Egypt in the Middle Ages. 4. ed. London, 1968.

AH 3179.7 — Langdon, S. The Babylonian epic of creation restored from the recently recovered tablets of Assur. Oxford, 1923.

NEDL — AH 3181.10.5F — Langdon, S. Babylonian liturgies. Paris, 1913.

AH 3129.3 — Langdon, S. Building inscriptions of the Neo-Babylonian Empire: Nabopolassar and Nebuchadnezzar. Paris, 1905.

AH 3129.3.5 — Langdon, S. Die neubabylonischen Königsinschriften. Leipzig, 1912.

AH 3181.10 — Langdon, S. Sumerian and Babylonian psalms. Paris, 1909.

AH 3013.924 — Langdon, S.H. Excavations at Kish. v.1, 3, 4. Paris, 1924-34. 3v.

AH 3149.8F — Langdon, Stephen. The Venus tablets of Ammizaduga. London, 1928.

AH 15.2 — Lange, C.C.L. Historia mutationum rei...romanorum. Gottingae, 1846- 12 pam.

AH 7818.56 — Lange, C.C.L. Römische Alterthümer. Berlin, 1856-71. 3v.

AH 7818.56.3 — Lange, C.C.L. Römische Alterthümer. v.1-2, 2. Aufl; v.3, 1. Aufl. Berlin, 1863-71. 3v.

AH 7818.56.5 — Lange, C.C.L. Römische Alterthüsmer. v.1-2, 3. Aufl; v.3, 2. Aufl. Berlin, 1871-79. 3v.

AH 7408.81 — Lange, C.C.L. Das römische Königthum. Leipzig, 1881.

AH 7138.47.5 — Lange, C.F.W. Examinations über die römischen Rechtsgeschichte. Halle, 1847.

Eg 609.51 — Lange, Kurt. König Echnaton und die Amarnazeit. München, 1951.

AH 7207.31 — Lange, Ludwig. De plebiscitis ovinio et atinio disputatio. Lipsiae, 1879.

AH 7278.85.6 — Lange, Ludwig. Histoire intérieure de Rome. Paris, 1885. 2v.

AH 846.9 — Lange, W. Antike...Wohnhaus. Leipzig, 1878.

AH 3964.15 — Langen, Joseph. Das Judentherm in Palästina zur Zeit Christi. Freiburg im Breisgau, 1866.

Htn — AH 8207.5* — Langhorne, D. Elenchus antiquitatum albionensium. Londini, 1675.

AH 842.29 — Langie, A. Bibliothèques publiques. Fribourg, 1908.

AH 7818.28.3 — Lanktree, J. Synopsis of Roman antiquities. London, 1857.

Eg 879.60.20 — Lanozkowski, Guenter. Altägyptischer Prophetismus. Wiesbaden, 1960.

AH 3407.9 — Lantsheere, L. De la race...langue des Hittites. Bruxelles, 1891.

AH 7846.4 — Lanz-Liebenfels. Wie heizten die Römer ihre Wohnraume. Umschau, 1902.

AH 2147.12 — Lanza, Michele. Roma e l'eredita di Alessandro. Milano, 1971.

AH 7469.36 — Lanzani, C. Lucio Cornelio Silla, dittatore. Milano, 1936.

AH 7469.15.5 — Lanzani, C. Mario e Silla. Catania, 1915.

AH 7329.27 — La Piana, George. Foreign groups in Rome during the first centuries of the empire. Cambridge, 1927.

Htn — AH 7807.61PF* — Lapides capitolini sive fasti. (Piranesii, I.B.) Romae, 1761.

AH 299.62 — Laptev, V.V. Pervobytnoobshchinnyi i rabovladel'cheskii stroi na territorii nashei strany. Leningrad, 1962.

AH 4659.25 — Laqueur, R. Hellenismus. Giessen, 1925.

AH 4079.27 — Laqueur, Richard. Epigraphische Untersuchungen zu den griechischen Volksbeschlüssen. Leipzig, 1927.

AH 7489.30.5 — Laqueur, Richard. Probleme der Spätantike. Stuttgart, 1930.

Htn — AH 8513.11* — La Ramée, P. de. Liber de moribus veterum Gallorum. Parisiis, 1562.

AH 7448.26 — Larauza, J.L. Histoire critique du passage des Alpes par Annibal. Paris, 1826.

NEDL — AH 7278.37.3 — Lardner, D. Cabinet cyclopedia. London, 1833. 2v.

Eg 759.31 — The large estates of Byzantine Egypt. (Hardy, E.R.) N.Y., 1931.

AH 8647.13F — Larizza, Pietro. La Magna Grecia. Roma, 1929.

AH 4498.83 — Larocque, J. La Grèce. Paris, 1883.

AH 7479.34.5 — Larrouy, Maurice. Antoine et Cléopatre; La bataille d'Actium. Paris, 1934.

AH 49.55 — Larsen, Jakob A.O. Representative government in Greek and Roman history. Berkeley, 1955.

AH 4039.67 — Larsen, Jakob Aall Ottesen. Greek federal states. Oxford, 1968.

AH 3012.20 — Larsen, Morgens. Old Assyrian caravan procedures. Istanbul, 1967.

AH 308.46 — Lasaulx, E. von. Über das Studium der griechischen und römischen Alterthümer. München, 1846.

AH 4858.14 — Lasaulx, E. von. Zur Geschichte und Philosophie der Ehe bei den Griechen. München, 1852.

AH 7308.61 — Lasaulx, E. von. Zur Philosophie der römischen Geschichte. München, 1861.

AH 298.54 — Lasaulx, Ernest. Studien des classischen Alterthums. Regensburg, 1854.

AH 8549.3 — La Saussaye, L. de. Dissertation sur le lieu de l'assemblée des druides. n.p., n.d.

AH 4519.22 — Laskarus, K.A. Phòs eis tò Thoukydídeiou erhebos. Athēnai, 1922.

AH 8211.10A — The last age of Roman Britain. (Foord, Edward A.) London, 1925.

AH 7099.28 — Last wards on the Roman municipalities. (Heitland, William E.) Cambridge, Eng., 1928.

AH 3193.7 — Late Babylonian astronomical and related texts. (Pinches, T.G.) Providence, 1955.

AH 3187.12 — Late Babylonian letters. (Thompson, Reginald C.) London, 1906.

AH 2017.5 — The late Dr. Charles Beke's discoveries of Sinai in Arabia. (Beke, Charles.) London, 1878.

Eg 1309.54 — Late-Egyptian miscellanies. (Caminos, R.A.) London, 1954.

Eg 1139.67 — Late Ramesside letters. (Wente, Edward F.) Chicago, 1967.

AH 7659.69 — The late Roman Empire. (Downey, Glanville.) N.Y., 1969.

AH 7659.68 — Late Roman studies. (Coster, Charles Henry.) Cambridge, 1968.

Eg 659.51 — Later dynasties of Egypt. (Elgood, P.G.) Oxford, 1951.

AH 7842.14 — Later Roman education in Ausonius, Capella. (Cole, P.R.) N.Y., 1909.

AH 7709.64 — The later Roman Empire. v.1-3, Atlas. (Jones, A.H.M.) Oxford, 1964. 3v.

AH 7469.15A — Latin selections illustrating public life in the Roman Commonwealth in the time of Cicero. (Howard, A.A.) Boston, 1915.

AH 7148.33 — Latini Juniani. (Vaugerow, C.A.) Marburg, 1833.

AH 9057.2 — Latium und Rom. (Zoeller, Max.) Leipzig, 1878.

AH 7228.70.5 — Latreille, J. Histoire des institutions judiciaires. Paris, 1870.

AH 4843.12 — Latte, K. De saltationibus Graecorum. Giessen, 1913.

AH 4215.7 — Latte, Kurt. Heiliges Recht. Tübingen, 1920.

AH 3963.165 — Lattes, Aldo. La civiltà ebraica e le origini del cristianesimo, ad uso delle scuole medie. Firenze, 1924.

AH 3757.13 — Latyshev, B. Scythica et Cancasica. Petrograd. 1-2,1890-1906

AH 3097.3 — Lau, R.J. The annals of Ashurbanapal. Leiden, 1903.

AH 3154.7 — Lau, Robert J. Old Babylonian temple records. N.Y., 1906.

AH 9610.5 — Lau, T. Leben der Surakusaners Dion. Prag, 1860.

AH 7468.54 — Lau, Thaddeus. Die Gracchen und ihre Zeit. Hamburg, 1854.

AH 7468.34 — Lau, Thaddeus. Lucius Cornelius Sulla. Hamburg, 1855.

AH 7058.86 — Die Laufbahn der Procuratoren. (Liebenam, W.) Jena, 1886.

AH 8353.4 — Die Laufbahn der Statthalter in der römischen Provinz Moesia Inferior. (Fitz, Jenö.) Weimar, 1966.

AH 279.71.5 — Lauffer, Siegfried. Kurze Geschichte der antiken Welt. München, 1971.

AH 919.14 — Laum, Bernhard. Stiftungen in der griechischen und römischen Antike. Leipzig, 1914. 2v.

AH 919.14.1 — Laum, Bernhard. Stiftungen in der griechischen und römischen Antike. v.1-2. Aalen, 1964.

AH 919.14.5 — Laum, Bernhard. Über griechische und römische Stiftungen. Leipzig, 1913.

AH 2264.5 — Laumonier, A. Les cultes indigènes en Carie. Paris, 1958.

AH 3965.5 — Lauré, M.J. The property concepts of the early Hebrews. Iowa City, 1915.

AH 3156.7 — Laurent, A. La magie et la divination chez les chaldéo-assyriens. Paris, 1894.

Eg 863.5 — Laurent-Täckholm, Vini. Faraos blomster. Stockholm, 1951.

AH 3307.7 — Lauria, G.A. Cipro. Napoli, 1879.

AH 2807.5 — Lauria, G.A. La Frigia. Naples, 1874.

AH 2158.5 — Lauria, Guiseppe A. La Bitinia - la Lidia. Napoli, 1874.

AH 7278.46.10 — Laurian, A.T. Coup d'oeil sur l'histoire des roumains. Bucuresti, 1846.

AH 842.32 — Laurie, S.S. Historical survey of pre-Christian education. London, 1895.

AH 842.32.3 — Laurie, S.S. Historical survey of pre-Christian education. N.Y., 1904.

AH 842.32.2 — Laurie, S.S. Historical survey of pre-Christian education. 2. ed. N.Y., 1900.

Htn AH 8676.3* — Lauro, G. Antiquae urbis splendor. Romae, 1610.

AH 7449.05.3 — Lauterbach, A. Untersuchungen...Unterwerfung von Oberitalien. Breslau, 1905.

AH 1189.36 — Lauterbach, W. Der Arbeiter in Recht und Rechtspraxis des Alten Testaments und des alten Orients. Inaug. Diss. Heidelberg, 1936.

Eg 808.77 — Lauth, F.J. Agyptische Chronologie. Strassburg, 1877.

AH 2957.9 — Lauth, F.J. Troja's Epoche. München, 1877.

Eg 878.81 — Lauzone, R.N. Dizionario di mitologia egizia. v.1-5. Torino, 1881. 3v.

AH 4279.34A — Lavell, C.F. A biography of the Greek people. Boston, 1934.

AH 7819.63.10 — Lavore e lavoratori nel mondo romano. (Robertis, Francesco Maria de.) Bari, 1963.

AH 7448.18.5 — Law, William J. The Alps of Hannibal. London, 1866. 2v.

AH 4139.56 — The law and legal theory of the Greeks. (Jones, J.W.) Oxford, 1956.

AH 7139.67 — Law and life of Rome. (Crook, John A.) Ithaca, 1967.

AH 819.36.15 — The law and the prophets. (Peake, Harold.) New Haven, 1936.

AH 4139.68 — The law of Athens. (Harrison, A.R.W.) Oxford, 1968. 2v.

Eg 139.44.2 — The law of Greco-Roman Egypt in the light of the papyri. 2. ed. (Taubenschlag, R.) Warszawa, 1955.

Eg 139.44 — The law of Greco-Roman Egypt in the light of the papyri 332 B.C.-640 A.D. v.2: supplement. (Taubenschlag, R.) N.Y., 1944. 2v.

AH 7206.35 — Law of Justinian. Loi de judgement. Bucarest, 1971.

AH 7169.65 — The law of obligations in the later Roman Republic. (Watson, Alan.) Oxford, 1965.

AH 7169.67 — The law of persons in the later Roman Republic. (Watson, Alan.) Oxford, 1967.

AH 7169.68 — The law of property in the later Roman Republic. (Watson, Alan.) Oxford, 1968.

AH 7162.44 — The law of succession in the later Roman Republic. (Watson, Alan.) Oxford, 1971.

AH 4843.24 — Lawler, Lillian B. The dance in ancient Greece. London, 1964.

AH 3045.100.5 — The laws of Eshnunna. (Eshnunna. Laws, statutes, etc.) Jerusalem, 1969.

AH 4229.27.1 — Lawyers and litigants in ancient Athens. (Bonner, Robert Johnson.) N.Y., 1969.

AH 3013.33.8 — Layard, A.H. Discoveries among the ruins of Nineveh and Babylon. N.Y., 1853.

AH 3013.33.6A — Layard, A.H. Discoveries among the ruins of Nineveh and Babylon. N.Y., 1853.

AH 3013.33.7A — Layard, A.H. Discoveries among the ruins of Nineveh and Babylon. N.Y., 1853.

AH 3013.33.9 — Layard, A.H. Discoveries among the ruins of Nineveh and Babylon. 2. ed. N.Y., 1856.

AH 3013.33.15PF — Layard, A.H. The monuments of Nineveh. London, 1849.

AH 3013.33.17PF — Layard, A.H. The monuments of Nineveh. 2d series. London, 1853.

AH 3013.33.10 — Layard, A.H. Nineveh and Babylon; a narrative of a second expedition to Assyria...1849, 1850 and 1851. London, 1867.

AH 3013.33A — Layard, A.H. Nineveh and its remains. N.Y., 1849. 2v.

AH 3013.33.3 — Layard, A.H. Nineveh and its remains. N.Y., 1852.

AH 3013.33.4 — Layard, A.H. Nineveh and its remains. v.1-2. N.Y., 1853.

AH 3013.33.2 — Layard, A.H. Nineveh and its remains. 2. ed. London, 1849. 2v.

NEDL AH 3013.33.5 — Layard, A.H. Nineveh and its remains. 6. ed. London, 1854. 2v.

AH 3014.25 — Layard, A.H. The Nineveh court in the crystal palace. London, 1854.

AH 3013.33.24 — Layard, A.H. A popular account of discoveries at Nineveh. London, 1851.

AH 3013.33.25 — Layard, A.H. Popular account of discoveries at Nineveh. N.Y., 1852.

AH 3013.33.27 — Layard, A.H. A popular account of discoveries at Nineveh. N.Y., 1855.

AH 3005.855 — Layard, Austen Henry. Sir A. Henry Layard; autobiography and letters. London, 1903. 2v.

AH 3005.855.5 — Layard of Nineveh. (Waterfield, Gordon.) London, 1963.

AH 7842.8 — Lazic, G.S. Pogled na shkolu i polozhaj. Karlovuima, 1895.

AH 7085.98F — Lazius, W. Reipublicae Romanae in exteris provinciis. v.1-3. Francofurti, 1598.

AH 9646.5 — Lazonder, A. Zande-Messana. Rhenum, 1903.

Eg 269.22 — Lazzaridès, C.A. De l'évolution des relations internationales de l'Égypte pharaonique. Thèse. Paris, 1922.

AH 4238.77.5 — Le civilización griega y la ciencia militar entre los griegos. Barcelona, 1877.

AH 7201.95 — Le majus et le minus latium. (Beaudouin, E.) Paris, 1879.

AH 7207.23.1 — Le sénat de la République romaine. (Williams, Pierre.) Aalen, 1968. 2v.

NEDL AH 279.05 — Leadbetter, F. Outlines and studies to accompany Myer's Ancient history. Boston, 1905.

AH 7169.06.3 — Leage, Richard William. Leage's Roman private law. London, 1961.

AH 7169.06 — Leage, Richard William. Roman private law. London, 1906.

AH 7169.06.3 — Leage's Roman private law. (Leage, Richard William.) London, 1961.

Eg 1159.52 — Leake, C.D. The old Egyptian medical papyri. Lawrence, 1952.

AH 9777.14 — Leake, Jane. The Geats of Beowulf. Madison, 1967.

AH 938.54.20 — Leake, W.M. On some disputed questions of ancient geography. London, 1857.

AH 5967.7 — Leake, W.M. Peloponnesiaca. London, 1846.

AH 4958.35 — Leake, W.M. Travels in northern Greece. London, 1835. 4v.

AH 5967.5A — Leake, W.M. Travels in the Morea. London, 1830. 3v.

AH 7138.59 — Leapingwell, George. Manual of Roman civil law. Cambridge, 1859.

AH 3902.5 — The Lebanon and Phoenicia; ancient texts illustrating their physical geography and native industries. (Brown, John Pairman.) Beirut, 1969.

AH 2107.7 — Le Bas, P. Asie Mineure. Paris, 1878.

AH 7758.17 — Leben Constantins des Grossen. (Mauso, J.C.F.) Breslau, 1817.

NEDL AH 818.62.3 — Leben der Griechen und Römer. (Guhl, Ernst.) Berlin, 1862.

NEDL AH 818.62.5 — Leben der Griechen und Römer. (Guhl, Ernst.) Berlin, 1876.

NEDL AH 818.62.3.5 — Leben der Griechen und Römer. 2. Aufl. (Guhl, Ernst.) Berlin, 1864.

NEDL AH 818.62.4 — Leben der Griechen und Römer. 3. Aufl. (Guhl, Ernst.) Berlin, 1872.

AH 818.62.6 — Leben der Griechen und Römer. 6. Aufl. (Guhl, Ernst.) Berlin, 1893.

AH 9610.5 — Leben des Surakusaners Dion. (Lau, T.) Prag, 1860.

AH 4538.70 — Leben des Epaminondas. (Pomtow, L.) Berlin, 1870.

AH 7628.99 — Leben des Kaisers Hadrian. (Schulz, O.T.) Leipzig, 1904.

AH 4498.87.3 — Leben des Perikles. (Frey, Karl.) Bern, 1887.

AH 7519.12 — Leben und Charakter des Tiberius Claudius Nero nach Velleius. (Schwab, J.) Tetschen, 1912.

AH 4818.87.3A — Leben und Sitten der Griechen. (Blümner, H.) Leipzig, 1887. 3v.

NEDL AH 7818.83 — Leben und Sitten der Römer. (Jung, I.) Prag, 1883. 2v.

AH 7508.76 — Leben und Treiben am Hofe des Kaisers Augustus, nach Tacitus. (Doetsch, P.) Malmedy, 1876.

AHP 22.3 — Lebendiges Altertum. Berlin. 1,1963+ 3v.

AH 7159.67 — Lebigne, Arlette. Quelques aspects de la responsabilité pénale en droit romain classique. Paris, 1967.

AH 3017.10 — Le Brun-Dalbanne. De l'intérêt de pierres gravées. Besançon, 1872.

AH 7008.38 — Le Clerc, J.V. Des journaux chez les romaines. Paris, 1838.

AH 4309.00 — Leçons d'histoire grecque. (Bouché-Leclercq, A.) Paris, 1900.

AH 4309.00.2 — Leçons d'histoire grecque. 2. éd. (Bouché-Leclercq, A.) Paris, 1913.

AH 7279.09 — Leçons d'histoire romaine. (Bouché-Leclerq, A.) Paris, 1909.

AH 4058.93 — Lecoutere, C. L'archontat athénien. Louvain, 1893.

Htn AH 815.16.11* — Lectionum antiquarum libri XXX. (Ricchieri, Lodovico.) Ludguni, 1560. 3v.

AH 3155.5 — Lecture on...religion of...Babylonians. (Sayce, A.H.) London, 1887.

AH 4938.73 — Lecture on geography of Greece. (Tozer, H.F.) London, 1873.

AH 3980.8 — Lecture on Jerusalem at the commencement of the Christian era. (Meigs, Charles D.) Philadelphia, 1841. 2 pam.

AH 7037.76 — Lectures concerning history read during the year 1775 in Trinity College, Dublin. (Kearney, M.) London, 1776.

AH 4818.94 — Lectures historiques. (Guiraud, P.) Paris, 1894.

AH 4819.50A — Lectures of evaluations of the enduring qualities of Greek civilization. (Miami, Florida. University.) Miami, Fla., 1950.

AH 7278.11.26 — Lectures of Roman history. (Niebuhr, B.G.) London, 1850. 3v.

AH 3155.5.5 — Lectures on...growth of religion...ancient Babylonians. 5. ed. (Sayce, A.H.) London, 1898.

AH 938.54 — Lectures on ancient ethnography and geography. (Niebuhr, B.G.) Boston, 1854. 2v.

NEDL AH 938.53 — Lectures on ancient ethnography and geography. (Niebuhr, B.G.) London, 1853. 2v.

AH 278.52.3 — Lectures on ancient history. (Niebuhr, B.G.) London, 1852. 3v.

AH 278.52 — Lectures on ancient history. (Niebuhr, B.G.) Philadelphia, 1852. 3v.

AH 278.16 — Lectures on ancient history. (Whepley, S.) N.Y., 1816.

AH 4938.34 — Lectures on geography of ancient Greece. (Harrison, G.) Charlottesville, 1834.

Htn AH 3957.20* — Lectures on Jewish antiquities. (Tappan, David.) Cambridge, 1807.

AH 7898.57 — Lectures on Roman husbandry. (Daubeny, Charles.) Oxford, 1857.

AH 138.75.2A — Lectures on the early history of institutions. (Maine, Henry S.) London, 1875.

AH 138.75A — Lectures on the early history of institutions. (Maine, Henry S.) N.Y., 1875.

AH 138.75.7 — Lectures on the early history of institutions. (Maine, Henry S.) N.Y., 1884.

AH 138.75.3 — Lectures on the early history of institutions. (Maine, Henry S.) N.Y., 1888.

AH 138.75.5 — Lectures on the early history of institutions. 3. ed. (Maine, Henry S.) London, 1880.

AH 7278.11.24 — Lectures on the History of Rome. (Niebuhr, B.G.) London, 1848.

AH 7278.11.25 — Lectures on the History of Rome. 2. ed. (Niebuhr, B.G.) London, 1849. 3v.

AH 7278.11.27 Lectures on the History of Rome. 3. ed. (Niebuhr, B.G.) London, 1852. 3v.

AH 7278.11.29 Lectures on the History of Rome. 4. ed. (Niebuhr, B.G.) London, 1873?

Eg 878.80 Lectures on the origin and growth of religion...of ancient Egypt. (Renouf, P. le P.) London, 1880.

AH 3155.5.2 Lectures on the origin and growth of religion as illustrated by the religion of the ancient Babylonians. 2d ed. (Sayce, A.H.) London, 1888.

AH 4162.19 Ledl, Arthur. Studien zum attischen Epiklerenrechte. Graz, 1907.

AH 4039.14 Ledl, Arthur. Studien zur älteren athenischen Verfassungsgeschichte. Heidelberg, 1914.

AH 3013.29F Ledrain, E. Les antiquités chaldéennes du Louvre. Paris, 1882.

Eg 878.90 Lefébure, E. Rites égyptiens. Paris, 1890.

Eg 879.29.5 Lefebure, G. Inscriptions concernant les grands prêtres d'Amon. Thèse. v.1-2. Paris, 1929.

AH 4819.00 Lefèvre, A. Grèce antique. Paris, 1900.

AH 7114.21 Lefèvre, Eugene. Du role des tribuns de la plebe. Paris, 1910.

AH 7215.7 Lefèvre, R. Ses sacre privata en droit romain. Thèse. Paris, 1923.

AH 7459.18 Leffingwell, G.W. Social...life in Rome in the time of Plautus. N.Y., 1918.

AH 8549.69 Leflocq, J. Études de mythologie celtique. Orléans, 1869.

AH 7204.4 Lefranc, André. L'édit d'Antonin Caracalla. Bordeaux, 1907.

AH 6057.17 La lega tessala fino ad Afessundro-Magno. (Sordi, Marta.) Roma, 1958.

AH 6057.15 La lega tessalica. (Solari, Arturo.) Pisa, 1912.

Eg 819.42A The legacy of Egypt. (Glanville, S.R.K.) Oxford, 1942.

Eg 819.71.7 The legacy of Egypt. 2. ed. (Harris, James Renel.) Oxford, 1971.

AH 7819.23A The legacy of Rome. (Bailey, Cyril.) Oxford, 1923.

AH 7819.23.3 The legacy of Rome. (Bailey, Cyril.) Oxford, 1928.

AH 819.24 The legacy of the ancient world. (De Burgh, W.G.) London, 1924.

AH 29.29 The legacy of the ancient world. (Yale University.) New Haven, 1929.

AH 819.24.3 The legacy of the ancient world. v.1-2. (De Burgh, W.G.) London, 1953.

AH 3087.3 Le Gag, Y. Les inscriptions d'Assur Nasir Aplu III. Paris, 1907.

AH 4138.86 Pamphlet vol. Legal institutions. 4 pam.

AH 9090.3 Le Gall, Joël. Le Tibre, fleuve de Rome, dans l'antiquité. Thèse. Paris, 1952.

AH 7200.9 Lege XII Tabularum. (Kokkinos, E.) Heidelbergae, 1836.

AH 5757.10 The legend of Sparta in classical antiquity. (Tigerstedt, Eugène Napoleon.) Stockholm, 1965.

AH 3018.3F La legende de Sémiramis - mythologie comparative. (Lenormant, F.) Bruxelles, 1873.

AH 7468.74 La legende des Saintes Maries. (Gilles, I.) Paris, 1874.

AH 7212.2 Die Leges Annales. (Nipperdey, Karl.) Leipzig, 1865.

NEDL AH 4136.35.2F Leges Atticae. (Petitus, S.) Lugdunum Batavorum, 1742.

Htn AH 4136.35F* Leges Atticae. (Petitus, S.) Paris, 1635.

AH 7203.4.8F Leges Justiniani. (Corpus juris civilis.) Parisiis, 1559. 5v.

AH 7149.12 Leges publicae populi Romani. Photoreproduction. (Rotondi, G.) Hildesheim, 1962.

AH 7200.19.2 Leges XII Tabularum. Das Zwölftafelgesetz. 2. Aufl. München, 1953.

AH 7200.19.4 Leges XII Tabularum. Das Zwölftafelgesetz. 4. Aufl. München, 1971.

AH 7200.11 Leggi delle dodici tavole. (Valeriani, L.) Firenze, 1839.

AH 7178.42 Legibus Agrariis. (Engelbregt, C.A.) Lugduni Batavorum, 1842.

AH 7239.03 Die Legio XXII Primigenia. Ein Beitrag. (Weichert, A.) Trier, 1903.

AH 238.93 Legion und Phalanx. (Schneider, R.) Berlin, 1893.

AH 7239.07 Legionare Kriegsvexillationen. (Tschauschmer, Carl.) Breslau, 1907.

AH 8355.2 Die Legionen der Provinz Moesia. (Filow, B.) Leipzig, 1906.

AH 7238.67F Les légions du Rhin et les inscriptions des carrières. (Robert, Charles.) Paris, 1867.

AH 7200.12 Legis Duodecim Tabularum. (Duodecim Tabulae.) Lipsiae, 1866.

AH 8954.5F Legis rubriae pars superstes. (Ritschl, F.) Bonae, 1851.

AH 7158.25 Legis serviliae. (Fragmenta Klenze.) Berolini, 1825.

AH 7228.58 Legisactionen und Formularprozess. (Daniel, C.G.F.) Schwerin, 1858.

AH 69.09 Legislation of Greeks and Romans on corporations. (Radin, Max.) N.Y.? 1909.

AH 4204.11 Legislazioni di Solone e Servio Tullo. (Anfossi, P.C.) Torino, 1899.

AH 8008.9 Leglay, Marcel. Les gaulois en Afrique. Bruxelles, 1962.

AH 7178.87 Legnazzi, E.N. Del catasto romano. Verona, 1887.

AH 3020.3 Legrain, L. Le temps des rois d'Ur. Text and plates. Paris, 1912. 2v.

AH 7201.32 Legum quae ad ius civile. (Demelius, G.) Vimariae, 1857.

AH 4929.01 Lehmann, C.F. Gewichte aus Thera. Berlin, 1901.

AH 7188.89 Lehmann, Eduard. De publica romanorum servitute quaestiones. Diss inaug. Lipsiae, 1889.

AH 7538.58 Lehmann, H. Claudius und Nero und ihre Zeit. Gotha, 1858.

AH 7538.58.2 Lehmann, H. Claudius und seine Zeit. Leipzig, 1877.

AH 7449.05.2 Lehmann, K. Die Angriffe der drei Bardiken. Leipzig, 1905.

AH 7709.11.3 Lehmann, Karl Friedrich Wilhelm. Kaiser Gordian III. Berlin, 1911.

AH 7709.11 Lehmann, Karl Friedrich Wilhelm. Kaiser Gordian III. Berlin, 1911.

AH 3002.86F Lehmann-Haupt, C.F. Corpus inscriptionum Chaldicarum. Berlin, 1928-35.

AH 3018.5 Lehmann-Haupt, C.F. Die historische Semiramis und ihre Zeit. Tübingen, 1910.

AH 3013.30 Lehmann-Haupt, C.F. Materialen zur Kultur...der Chalder...Ausgrabungen. Berlin, 1901.

AH 3002.2.8 Lehmann-Haupt, C.F. Seamaššumukîn, König von Babylonien. Leipzig, 1892.

AH 4838.76 Lehndorff, G.G. Hippodromos. Berlin, 1876.

AH 4108.90 Lehner, H. Athenischen Schatzverzeichnisse. Strassburg, 1890.

AH 808.31 Lehrbuch der Chronologie. (Ideler, L.C.) Berlin, 1831.

AH 279.04 Lehrbuch der Geschichte des Alterthums. (Bauer, A.) Wien, 1904.

NEDL AH 278.93.3 Lehrbuch der Geschichte des Alterthums. (Zeehe, Andreas.) Laibach, 1893.

AH 7138.32 Lehrbuch der Geschichte des römischen Rechts. (Hugo, G.) Berlin, 1832.

AH 7138.71.7 Lehrbuch der Geschichte des römischen Rechts. v.1-2. (Danz, H.A.A.) Leipzig, 1871.

NEDL AH 4818.41.6 Lehrbuch der griechischen Antiquitäten. v.1,3. (Hermann, K.F.) Heidelberg, 1875. 2v.

AH 4818.41.9A Lehrbuch der griechischen Antiquitäten. v.1-4. 6. Aufl. (Hermann, K.F.) Freiburg, 1889. 7v.

NEDL AH 4818.41 Lehrbuch der griechischen Antiquitäten. 3. Aufl. (Hermann, K.F.) Heidelberg, 1841. 2v.

AH 4818.41.10 Lehrbuch der griechischen Antiquitäten. 4. Aufl. (Hermann, K.F.) Freiburg, 1895.

AH 4818.41.3 Lehrbuch der griechischen Antiquitäten. 4. Aufl. (Hermann, K.F.) Heidelberg, 1855. 3v.

NEDL AH 4818.41.5 Lehrbuch der griechischen Antiquitäten. 5. Aufl. (Hermann, K.F.) Heidelberg, 1875. 3v.

AH 7138.81 Lehrbuch der Institutionen. (Marezoll.) Brussel, 1881.

AH 7203.44.15 Lehrbuch der Institutionen. (Scheurl, C.G. von.) Erlangen, 1850.

AH 7168.83 Lehrbuch der Institutionen. 4. Aufl. (Salkowski, C.) Leipzig, 1883.

AH 7138.99 Lehrbuch der Institutionen des römischen Rechtes. 4. Aufl. (Czyhlarz, Karl.) Leipzig, 1899.

AH 7138.99.2 Lehrbuch der Institutionen des römischen Rechtes. 7-8. Aufl. (Czyhlarz, Karl.) Wien, 1905.

AH 7138.99.3 Lehrbuch der Institutionen des römischen Rechtes. 19. Aufl. (Czyhlarz, Karl.) Wien, 1933.

AH 7203.143.5 Lehrbuch der Pandekten. 7. Aufl. (Vangerow, K.A. von.) Marburg, 1876. 3v.

AH 7138.78.11 Lehrbuch der römischen Rechtsgeschichte. (Padelletti, G.) Berlin, 1879.

AH 7203.42.10 Lehrbuch des Pandecten-Rechts. 4. Aufl. (Corpus juris civilis.) Halle, 1844. 3v.

AH 7138.89 Lehrbuch des römischen Rechts. (Schulin, F.) Stuttgart, 1889.

AH 7138.41.5 Lehrbuch des römischen Rechts. v.1-2, pt.1-3. (Burchardi, G.C.) Stuttgart, 1841. 3v.

AH 7168.34 Lehrbuch für Institutionen und Geschichte. (Schilling, F.A.) Leipzig, 1834. 3v.

Eg 1099.44F Die Lehre des Cheti. (Brunner, Hellmut.) Glückstadt, 1944.

AH 7168.41 Lehre vom Schadensersatze nach römischen Rechte. (Wening Ingenheim, J.N. von.) Heidelberg, 1841.

AH 7188.91 Lehre vom Sklavenerwerb. (Salkowski, C.) Leipzig, 1891.

AH 7188.38 Lehre von den Servituten. v.1-2. (Hoffmann, E.) Darmstadt, 1838.

AH 7168.17.3 Die Lehre von der Cession. 3e Aufl. (Mühlenbruch, C.F.) Stuttgart, 1836.

AH 4842.11 Leiber, T. von. Professoren, Studenten und Studentleben. Bern, 1867.

AH 4833.11 Leibesübungen der alten Griechen. (Seitz, F.) Ansbach, 1872.

AH 4839.61.5 Leibesübungen und Leibeserziehung in der griechischen Antike. 3. Aufl. (Popplow, Ulrich.) Stuttgart, 1961.

AH 4559.05 Leichenwagen Alexanders des Grossen. (Müller, K.F.) Leipzig, 1905.

AH 3159.28 Das Leiden des Unschuldigen in Babylon und Israel. (Stamm, J.J.) Zürich, 1946.

Eg 971.7.5 Leider, Erich. Der Handel von Alexandreia. Hamburg, 1933.

Eg 971.7.6 Leider, Erich. Der Handel von Alexandreia. Diss. Hamburg, 1934.

AH 7149.14 Leifer, Franz. Die Einheit des Gewaltgedankens im römischen Staatsrecht. München, 1914.

AH 7278.79 Leighton, R.F. History of Rome. N.Y., 1879.

NEDL AH 7278.79.4 Leighton, R.F. History of Rome. N.Y., 1880.

AH 7278.79.12 Leighton, R.F. A history of Rome. N.Y., 1901.

AH 859.8 Leipoldt, J. Die Frau in der antiken Welt und im Urchristentum. Gütersloh, 1962.

EgP 83.25 Leipziger ägyptologische Studien. Glueckstadt. 1-8,1935-1937

AH 4139.08 Leisi, Ernst. Zeuge im attischen Recht. Frauenfeld, 1908.

AH 148.89 Leist, B.W. Alt-arisches jus Gentium. Jena, 1889.

AH 138.84 Leist, B.W. Graeco-italische Rechtsgeschichte. Jena, 1884.

AH 7168.79.5 Leist, B.W. Das römische Patronatrecht. Erlangen, 1879. 2v.

AH 7161.17 Leist, B.W. Zur Geschichte der römischen Societas. Jena, 1881.

Eg 829.65 Leisure and pleasure in Roman Egypt. (Lindsay, Jack.) London, 1965.

AH 278.35 Lektsii po Gerenu o politike. (Pogodin, Mikhail Petrovich.) Moskva, 1835.

AH 6110.7F Leland, T. History of life and reign of Philip. London, 1758.

AH 6110.5F Leland, T. History of life and reign of Philip. 2. ed. London, 1761. 2v.

AH 6110.8 Leland, T. History of life and reign of Philip. 2. ed. London, 1775. 2v.

AH 930.25 Lelewel, J. Die Entdeckungen der Carthager und Griechen. Berlin, 1821.

AH 938.36 Lelewel, J. Kleinere Schriften. Leipzig, 1836.

AH 8510.5 Lélu, Georges. Vercingétorix et la résistance gauloise. Clamecy, 1949.

AH 4158.35 Lelyveld, P. De Infama jure Attico. Amsterdam, 1835.

AH 7487.20 Lemain de Tillemont. Histoire des empereurs. Paris, 1720-38. 6v.

AH 7487.32.2F Lemain de Tillemont. Histoire des empereurs. v.1-6. Bruxelles, 1732. 3v.

AH 8548.20 Lemière, P.L. Étude sur les Celtes et les Gaulois. St. Brieuc, 187-?

Eg 878.82.4 Lemm, O. von. Studien zum Ritualbuche des Ammondienstes. Leipzig, 1882.

AH 7188.87.2 Lemonnier, H. Étude historique sur la condition des esclaves. Paris, 1887.

AH 7269.67 Lemosse, Maxime. Le regime des relations internationales dans le Haut-Empire romain. Paris, 1967.

AH 7487.00 Lenain, L.S. Histoire des empereurs. Paris, 1700. 6v.

AH 7204.9 Lenel, Otto. Edictum perpetuum. Leipzig, 1883.

AH 7204.13 Lenel, Otto. Edictum perpetuum. 2. Aufl. Leipzig, 1907.

AH 7204.11 Lenel, Otto. L'édit perpétuel. Paris, 1901. 2v.

AH 7038.99 Lengle, Joseph. Untersuchungen über die sulianische Verfassung. Freiburg, 1899.

AH 8548.150 Lengyel, Lancelot. Le secret des Celtes. 1. éd. Le Jas du Revest-Saint-Martin, 1969.

AH 3011.17 Leningrad. Universitet. Kafedra stran Drevnego Vostoka. Assiriologiia i egiptologiia. Leningrad, 1964.

AH 408.82 Lenormant, F. Beginnings of history. N.Y., 1882.

Author and Title Listing

AH 3156.5.5 — Lenormant, F. Chaldean magic. London, 1877.

AH 3002.29 — Lenormant, F. Choix de textes cunéiformes. Paris, 1873-75.

AH 3156.5.9 — Lenormant, F. La divination et la science des présages. Paris, 1875.

AH 8647.5 — Lenormant, F. Grand-Grèce paysages. Paris, 1881. 3v.

AH 8647.5.3 — Lenormant, F. Grande-Grèce paysages. 2. éd. Paris, 1881. 2v.

AH 1278.68.7 — Lenormant, F. Histoire ancienne de l'Orient. Paris, 1881-86. 6v.

AH 3018.3F — Lenormant, F. La legende de Sémiramis - mythologie comparative. Bruxelles, 1873.

AH 3156.5 — Lenormant, F. La magie chez les Chaldéens. Paris, 1874.

AH 8647.5.15 — Lenormant, F. La Magna Grecia, paesaggio e storia. Crotone, 1931-33. 3v.

AH 1408.69.3 — Lenormant, F. Manual of the ancient history of the East. London, 1869.

AH 1408.68.5 — Lenormant, F. Manual of the ancient history of the East. Philadelphia, 1869.

AH 1408.69 — Lenormant, F. Manual of the ancient history of the East. 3. ed. Paris, 1869. 3v.

NEDL AH 1408.68 — Lenormant, F. Manuel d'histoire ancienne de l'Orient. Paris, 1868. 2v.

AH 1408.80 — Lenormant, F. Les origines de l'histoire. v.1; v.2, pt.1-2. Paris, 1880. 3v.

AH 818.74 — Lenormant, F. Premières civilisations. Paris, 1874. 2v.

AH 3160.6.5 — Lenormant, F. Sur le nom de...Tammouz. Paris, 1873.

AH 4189.63.5 — Lentsman, Iakov A. Rabstvo v mikenskoi i gomerovskoi Gretsii. Moskva, 1963.

AH 7506.45 — Lentulus, Cyriaeus. Augustus. Amstelodami, 1645.

AH 4859.5 — Lenz, C.G. Weiber in heroischen Zeitalter. Hannover, 1790.

AH 4148.80 — Lenz, Emil. Synedrien der Bundesgenossen. Elbing, 1880.

AH 7109.00 — Leo, Fritz. Die Capitatio Plebeia. Berlin, 1900.

AH 7099.00.2 — Leogrande, P. I cognomi delle colonie romane militari. Trani, 1900.

AH 7329.60 — Leon, Harry J. The Jews of ancient Rome. 1. ed. Philadelphia, 1960.

AH 3408.7 — Leonard, W. Hittiter und Amazonen. Leipzig, 1911.

AH 7206.11 — Leonis. Ecloga. Athenis, 1889.

AH 7768.73 — Léotard, E. Essae sur la condition des barbares. Paris, 1873.

AH 840.9 — Léotard, E. La famille. Lyon, 1909.

AH 4049.04 — Léotard, M.E. La démocratie. Lyon, 1904.

AH 5608.2 — Lepore, Ettore. Recherche sull'antico-epiro. Napoli, 1962.

AH 7619.48 — Lepper, F.A. Trajan's Paethian war. London, 1948.

Eg 862.1 — Lepsius, C.R. Les métaux dans les inscriptions égyptiennes. Paris, 1877.

AH 3167.5F — Lepsius, K.R. Die babylonisch-assyrischen Längenmasse. Berlin, 1877.

Eg 808.49F — Lepsius, K.R. Die Chronologie der Ägypter. Berlin, 1849.

Eg 808.49.5F — Lepsius, K.R. Königsbuch der alten Agypter. Berlin, 1858.

AH 8908.7 — Lepsius, K.R. Ueber die tyrrhenischen Pelasger. Leipzig, 1842.

AH 8549.161 — Le Roux, F. Les druides. Paris, 1961.

AH 8205.3 — Le Roux, L. L'armée romaine de Bretagne. Paris, 1911.

AH 257.77 — LeRoy, J.D. La marine des anciens peuples. Paris, 1777.

AH 257.83 — LeRoy, J.D. Les navires des anciens. Paris, 1783.

AH 5132.5 — Lesbiacorum liber. (Plehn, S.L.) Berolini, 1826.

AH 8548.75 — Leslie, S. Celt and the world. N.Y., 1917.

Eg 709.11 — Lesquier, Jean. Les institutions militaires de l'Égypte sous les Lagides. Paris, 1911.

AH 39.73 — Il lessico filologico degli umanisti. (Rizzo, Silvia.) Roma, 1973.

AH 7819.29 — The lesson of imperial Rome. (MacKail, J.W.) London, 1929.

AH 4852.5 — Lessons from Greek pottery. (Huddilston, J.H.) N.Y., 1902.

AH 7639.10 — Leszynsky, R. Die Lösung des Antoninusrätsels. Berlin, 1910.

Htn AH 7655.15* — Leto, G.P. Romanae historiae compendium. Argentorati, 1515,

AH 7148.83.3 — Létourville, G. de. Étude sur le droit de cité à Rome. Paris, 1883.

AH 2231.5 — Letter of King Anum-Hirbi of Mama to King Warshama of Kanish. (Balkan, Kemal.) Ankara, 1957.

Eg 1009.68 — La letteratura egizia. (Donadoni, Sergio.) Firenze, 1968.

AH 7498.46 — Lettere romane dall'anno 818 della 830. (Cesare, G. di.) Prato, 1846.

AH 3030.3 — Letters and inscriptions of Hammourabi. (King, L.W.) London, 1898-1900. 3v.

AH 3096.10 — Letters from Assyrian scholars to the Kings Esarhaddon and Assurbanipal. (Parpola, Simo.) Neukirchen-Vluyn, 1970.

AH 3187.17 — Letters from Mesopotamia. (Oppenheim, Adolf L.) Chicago, 1967.

AH 7818.54 — Letters from Rome. (Tounsend, F.) N.Y., 1854.

AH 3187.6 — The letters of the Room 2 collection in the British Museum. (Berry, George R.) Chicago, 1896.

Eg 297.34 — Letters to Monsieur H*** [Hénrich] concerning the most ancient gods...Egypt. (Révérend, Dominique.) London, 1734.

Eg 298.28 — Lettre à M. Champollion le jeune...avant l'invasion de Cambyse. (Henry, Dominique Marie Joseph.) Paris, 1828.

AH 3013.35.5 — Lettres de...sur ses decouvertes a Khorsabad. (Botta, P.E.) Paris, 1845.

AH 3187.9 — Lettres néo-babyloniennes. (Martin, F.) Paris, 1909.

AH 2008.5 — Lettres sur l'histoire des Arabes. (Fresnel, F.) Paris, 1836.

AH 7089.12 — Letz, Emil. Die Provinzialverwaltung Caesars. Strassburg, 1912.

AH 8461.10 — Das letzte Jahrhundert Pannoniens, 376-476. (Várady, László.) Budapest, 1969.

AH 7799.06 — Die letzten Jahre Attilas. (Bierbach, Karl.) Berlin, 1906.

AH 7448.80 — Letzten Jahre des zweiten punischen Krieges. (Zielinski, T.) Leipzig, 1880.

AH 7799.00 — Die letzten Kaiser des römischen Abendlandes. (Hossner, K.) Bielitz, 1900.

AH 4818.05 — Leuliette, J.J. Essai sur...supériorité des Grecs. Paris, 1805.

AH 7039.12 — Leuze, O. Zur Geschichte der römischen Censur. Halle, 1912.

AH 7809.09 — Leuzl, Oscar. Die römische Jahrzählung. Tübingen, 1909.

NEDL AH 278.56.10 — Leva, G. de. Sommario della storia de' popoli antichi. Padova, 1856.

AH 7918.99 — Levasseur, E. L'organisation des métiers. Paris, 1899.

AH 5858.5 — Levègue, J. A. De oppidis et portibus Megaridis ac Boeotiae. Thesim proponebat. Parisiis, 1875.

AH 5610.15 — Léveque, P. Pyrrhos. Paris, 1957.

AH 4819.64.15 — Lévêque, Pierre. The Greek adventure. Cleveland, 1968.

AH 7509.33.9 — Levi, Mario A. Attaviano capoparti. Firenze, 1933. 2v.

AH 7509.29 — Levi, Mario A. Augusto. Roma, 1929.

AH 7039.28 — Levi, Mario A. La costituzione romana dai gracchi a Giulio Cesare. Firenze, 1928.

AH 7549.49 — Levi, Mario A. Nerone e i suoi tempi. Milano, 1949.

AH 7299.36.2 — Levi, Mario A. La pooitica imperiale di Roma. 2. ed. Torino, 1936.

AH 7509.51 — Levi, Mario A. Il tempo di Augusto. Firenze, 1951.

AH 7279.54.5 — Levi, Mario Attilio. Lineamenti di storia romana. 2. ed. Milano, 1954.

AH 279.55 — Levi, Mario Attilio. La lotta politica nel mondo antico. 1. ed. Milano, 1955.

AH 279.55.5 — Levi, Mario Attilio. Political power in the ancient world. London, 1965.

AH 4279.67.5 — Levi, Mario Attilio. Quattro studi spartani e altri scritti di storia greca. Milano, 1967.

AH 819.66.20 — Levi, Mario Attilio. La società nel mondo classico. Torino, 1966.

AH 7279.60 — Levi, Mario Attilio. Storia romana dagli etruschi a Tedosio. Milano, 1960.

AH 4298.90 — Lévi, Sylvain. Quid de Graecis veterum indorum. Paris, 1890.

AH 2111.5 — Levick, Barbara Mary. Roman colonies in Southern Asia Minor. Oxford, 1967.

AH 2958.6 — Levillain, Jean. Étude sur la localisation d'Ilion d'apres l'Iliade d'Homere. Istanbul, 1962.

AH 7808.75.3 — Levison, Hans. Fasti Praetorii inde ab Octaviani imperii singularis intro usque ad Hadriani Exitum. Vratislaviae, 1892.

AH 7888.98 — Levison, W. Die Buerkundung des Civilstandes. Bonn, 1898.

AH 4049.43 — Levitt, Bella. Supreme political power in Greek literature of the fourth century B.C. Thesis. Philadelphia, 1943.

AH 7139.63 — Levy, Ernst. Gesammelte Schriften. Köln, 1963. 2v.

AH 7201.21.5 — Levy, Ernst. Pauli sententiae. Ithaca, 1945.

AH 7169.51A — Levy, Ernst. West Roman vulgar law. Phildelphia, 1951.

AH 889.64 — Lévy, Jean Philippe. L'économie antique. Paris, 1964.

AH 7519.01.5 — Lévy, L. Quo modo Tiberius Claudius Nero. Paris, 1901.

AH 7468.96 — Lewandowski, M. La question sociale à Rome. Paris, 1896.

AH 7298.55 — Lewis, George C. An inquiry...early Roman history. London, 1855. 2v.

AH 7298.55.3 — Lewis, George C. Untersuchungen...altrömischen Geschichte. Hannover, 1863.

AH 7419.13 — Lewis, J.H. The two great republics - Rome and the United States. Chicago, 1913.

AH 7819.51 — Lewis, N. Roman civilization. N.Y., 1955-67. 2v.

AH 4029.71 — Lewis, Naphtali. The fifth century B.C. Toronto, 1971.

Eg 909.35 — Lewis, Naphtali. L'industrie du papyrus dans l'Egypte gréco-romaine. Thèse. Paris, 1934.

AH 3002.65F — Lewy, Julius. Studien zu den altassyrischen Texten aus Kappadokien. Berlin, 1922.

AH 7212.5 — The Lex Annalis before Sulla. (Astin, A.E.) Brussells, 1958.

AH 7203.132 — Lex aquilia. (Corpus juris civilis. Digesta.) Cambridge, 1929.

AH 3354.5 — La "Lex Cathartica" di Cirene. (Luzzatto, G.I.) Milano, 1936.

AH 7204.21 — Lex de Imperio Vespasiani. (Hellems, F.B.R.) Chicago, 1902.

AH 7228.61 — Die Lex Hieronica. (Degenkolb, H.) Berlin, 1861.

AH 7201.115 — Lex Rubria. Studien zur der Lex Rubria. Utrecht? 1971?

AH 7162.9 — Lex voconia. (Bachofen, J.J.) Basel, 1843.

Eg 885.925 — Lexa, Frantisek. La magie dans l'Égypte antique. v.1-2, Atlas. Paris, 1925. 3v.

Htn AH 7817.13F* — Lexicon antiquitatum Romanarum. (Pitisco, Samuel.) Leovardiae, 1713. 2v.

AH 7817.13.5F — Lexicon antiquitatum Romanarum. (Pitisco, Samuel.) Venetiis, 1719. 3v.

Eg 1042.935.20 — Lexikalisch-grammatische Liste zu Spruch 335a der altägyptischen Sargtexte LL/CT. (Gundlach, Rolf.) Darmstadt, 1970. 2v.

Eg 1042.970.10 — Lexikalisch-grammatische Liste zu Spruch 335a der altägyptischen Sargtexte LL/CT 335a. (Gundlach, Rolf.) Darmstadt, 1970. 2v.

Eg 279.72 — Lexikon der Agyptologie. v.1, pt.1-6. (Helek, Hans Wolfgang.) Wiesbaden, 1972-

AH 939.14 — Lexique de géographie ancienne. (Besnier, M.) Paris, 1914.

Eg 558.75 — L'éxode et les monuments égyptiens. (Brugsch-Bey, H.) Leipzig, 1875.

Eg 849.10 — Lexová, Irena. Ancient Egyptian dances. Praha, 1935.

AH 7839.61 — La ley gladiatoria de Italica. (Balil, Albert.) Madrid, 1961.

AH 8607.9 — Lezioni di storia patria. (Panciera, D.) Grosseto, 1867.

AH 3921.10F — Libanius et la vie municipale à Antioche au IV. siècle après J.-C. (Petet, Paul.) Paris, 1955.

Eg 298.90 — Libellus de Historia Aegypti antiqua. (Ibn Abd al Hakam, Abd al Rahman.) Gottingae, 1856.

Htn AH 4805.36* — Liber de Mensibus Atticis. (Gaze Thessalo.) Basileae, 1536.

Htn AH 8513.11* — Liber de moribus veterum Gallorum. (La Ramée, P. de.) Parisiis, 1562.

AH 4039.57 — The liberal temper in Greek politics. (Havelock, E.A.) London, 1957.

AH 4148.94 — Liberas Graecorum civitates. (Berard, V.) Lutetiae, 1894.

AH 7039.57 — Libertas. (Wirszubski, C.) Bari, 1957.

AH 7039.50 — Libertas as a political idea. (Wirszubski, C.) Cambridge, 1950.

AH 4298.56 — Libertati apud veteres Graeciae populos quid defuerit. (Reynald, H.) Parisiis, 1856.

AH 9632.5 — Libertini, Guido. Le isole Eolie nell'antichità greca e romana. Firenze, 1921.

AH 7308.49 — Liberty of Rome. (Eliot, Samuel.) N.Y., 1849. 2v.

AH 3358.9 — La Libia negli scritti degli antiche. (Fantoli, A.) Roma, 1933.

Eg 1309.31PFA — The library of A. Chester Beatty. (Gardiner, A.H.) London, 1931.

Htn AH 7105.22.3* — Libri V de asse et partibus eius. (Budé, G.) Venetiis, 1522.

Htn AH 7105.22* — Libri V de asse et partibus eius. (Budé, G.) Venice, 1522.

Htn AH 4135.43* — Libro de magistrati de gli Atheniesi. (Postel, G.F.) Venetia, 1543.

Htn AH 816.45* Licetus, F. De anulis antiquis. Utini, 1645.
X Cg AH 4829.34 Licht, Hans. Sexual life in ancient Greece. N.Y., 1934.
Htn AH 4829.26F*A Licht, Hans. Sittengeschichte Griechenlands. Dresden, 1926-28. 3v.
AH 846.10 Lichtenberg, F. Haus, Dorf, Stadt. Leipzig, 1909.
AH 3309.5 Lichtenberg, R.F. Beiträge zur...Geschichte von Kypros. Berlin, 1906.
Eg 1029.73 Lichtheim, Miriam. Ancient Egyptian literature; a book of readings. Berkeley, 1973-
AH 7278.55 Liddell, H.G. History of Rome. London, 1855. 2v.
NEDL AH 7278.55.2A Liddell, H.G. History of Rome. N.Y., 1857.
NEDL AH 7278.55.2.5 Liddell, H.G. History of Rome. N.Y., 1864.
NEDL AH 7278.55.9A Liddell, H.G. History of Rome. N.Y., 1879.
AH 7478.60 Liddell, H.G. Life of Julius Caesar. N.Y., 1860.
AH 7478.81.20 Liddell, H.G. Life of Julius Caesar. Biographical series. Boston, 1881.
AH 7449.26.3 Liddell Hart, B.H. A greater than Napoleon, Scipio Africanus. Boston, 1927.
AH 7449.26.5 Liddell Hart, B.H. A greater than Napoleon, Scipio Africanus. Boston, 1928.
AH 7449.26 Liddell Hart, B.H. A greater than Napoleon, Scipio Africanus. Edinburgh, 1926.
AH 7918.93 Liebenam, W. Aus dem Vereinswesen im römischen Reiche. Berlin, 1893.
AH 7058.86.2 Liebenam, W. Beiträge zur Verwaltungsgeschichte. Jena, 1886.
AH 7058.88 Liebenam, W. Forschungen zur Verwaltungsgeschichte. Leipzig, 1888.
AH 7058.86 Liebenam, W. Die Laufbahn der Procuratoren. Jena, 1886.
AH 7099.00.4 Liebenam, W. Stadtsverwaltung in römischen Kaiserreiche. Leipzig, 1900.
AH 7918.90 Liebenam, W. Zur Geschichte...des römischen Vereinswesens. Leipzig, 1890.
AH 7008.40 Lieberkuehn, Wilhelm. Inest commentatio de diurnis. Vimariae, 1840.
Eg 1079.55 Liebeslieder der Pharaonenzeit. (Schott, Siegfried.) Zürich, 1959.
Eg 1078.99F Die Liebespoisie der alten Ägypter. (Müller, W.M.) Leipzig, 1899.
Eg 808.63 Lieblein, J. Ägyptische Chronologie. Christiania, 1863.
Eg 808.73 Lieblein, J. Chronologie égyptienne. Christiania, 1873.
Eg 819.10 Lieblein, J. Recherches sur l'histoire et la civilisation de l'ancien Égypte. Leipzig, 1910. 3v.
AH 3921.12 Liebsschuetz, John Hugo Wolfgang Gideon. Antiochi city and imperial administration in the later Roman Empire. Oxford, 1972.
AH 7823.3 Liefeld, Walter Lewis. The wandering preacher as a social figure in the Roman Empire. Ann Arbor, 1974.
AH 238.95 Liers, Hugo. Kriegswesen der Alten. Breslau, 1895.
AH 879.09.5 Lietzmann, H. Der Weltheiland. Bonn, 1909.
AH 7509.11.5 Le lieu de la rencontre de Lépide et d'Antoine. (Poupé, E.) Droguignan, 1911.
AH 819.61.10F Life (Chicago). The epic of man. N.Y., 1961.
AH 4558.29.6 Life and actions of Alexander the Great. (Williams, John.) N.Y., 1836.
AH 4558.29.50 The life and actions of Alexander the Great. (Williams, John.) N.Y., 1900.
AH 7477.24 The life and actions of Caius Julius Caesar. London, 1724.
AH 8073.22.10 The life and death of Carthage. (Charles-Picard, Gilbert.) London, 1968.
AH 7819.69 Life and leisure in ancient Rome. 1st ed. (Balsdon, John Percy Vyvian Dacre.) N.Y., 1969.
AH 8013.3 Life and letters in Roman Africa. (Bouchier, E.S.) Oxford, 1913.
AH 7599.03 Life and principate of Emperor Nero. (Henderson, B.W.) London, 1903.
AH 7629.23 The life and principate of the Emperor Hadrian. (Henderson, B.W.) London, 1923.
AH 7699.18A Life and reign of the Emperor Lucius Septimius Severus. (Platnauer, Maurice.) London, 1918.
AH 7699.18.2 The life and reign of the Emperor Lucius Septimius Severus. (Platnauer, Maurice.) Westport, 1970.
AH 819.64.20 Life and thought in the ancient world. (Eastwood, Charles Cyril.) London, 1964.
Eg 609.11.5 The life and times of Akhnaton, pharaoh of Egypt. (Weigall, Arthur E.P.B.) Edinburgh, 1911.
Eg 609.23.9 The life and times of Akhnaton, pharaoh of Egypt. (Weigall, Arthur E.P.B.) London, 1923.
Eg 609.23.10A The life and times of Akhnaton. (Weigall, Arthur E.P.B.) N.Y., 1923.
Eg 709.14 The life and times of Cleopatra, queen of Egypt. (Weigall, Arthur E.P.B.) N.Y., 1914.
Eg 709.14.7 The life and times of Cleopatra. (Weigall, Arthur E.P.B.) London, 1926.
Eg 709.14.5A The life and times of Cleopatra. (Weigall, Arthur E.P.B.) N.Y., 1924.
AH 7469.31.5 The life and times of Marc Antony. (Weigall, Arthur E.P.B.) Garden City, 1931.
AH 7469.31.4 The life and times of Marc Antony. (Weigall, Arthur E.P.B.) N.Y., 1931.
AH 7549.54 The life and times of Nero. (Franzero, Charles M.) London, 1954.
AH 7409.60 The life and times of Tarquin the Etruscan. (Franzero, A.M.) London, 1960.
Eg 609.23.15 The life and times of Tut-Ankh-Amen. (Nahas, Bishara.) N.Y., 1923.
NEDL AH 968.55 Life and travels of Herodotus. (Wheeler, J.) London, 1855. 2v.
AH 968.55.5 Life and travels of Herodotus. (Wheeler, J.) N.Y., 1856. 2v.
AH 4819.06.3A Life in ancient Athens. (Tucker, T.G.) N.Y., 1906.
AH 4819.06.7 Life in ancient Athens. Handbooks of archaeology and antiquities. (Tucker, T.G.) Chautauqua, 1917.
Eg 278.85.4A Life in ancient Egypt. (Erman, A.) London, 1894.
AH 3103.4 Life in ancient Egypt and Assyria. (Maspero, G.) N.Y., 1899.
Eg 818.92.2 Life in ancient Egypt and Assyria. (Maspéro, Gaston.) N.Y., 1895.
AH 8213.4 Life in Roman Britain. (Birley, Anthony R.) London, 1964.
AH 7819.10.2 Life in the Roman world of Nero and St. Paul. (Tucker, T.G.) London, 1910.
AH 7819.10.4A Life in the Roman world of Nero and St. Paul. (Tucker, T.G.) N.Y., 1917.
AH 7819.10.5 Life in the Roman world of Nero and St. Paul. (Tucker, T.G.) N.Y., 1929.
AH 4521.19 The life of Alcibiades. (Benson, E.F.) N.Y., 1929.
AH 7739.07A Life of Alexander Severus. (Hopkins, R.V.N.) Cambridge, 1907.

AH 4819.02A Life of ancient Greeks. (Gulick, C.B.) N.Y., 1902.
AH 4819.39.5 The life of Greece. (Durant, Will.) N.Y., 1939.
NEDL AH 818.62.13A The life of Greeks and Romans described from antique monuments. (Guhl, Ernst.) N.Y., 1896.
NEDL AH 818.62.15 The life of Greeks and Romans described from antique monuments. (Guhl, Ernst.) N.Y., 1902.
AH 7478.60 Life of Julius Caesar. (Liddell, H.G.) N.Y., 1860.
AH 7478.81.20 Life of Julius Caesar. Biographical series. (Liddell, H.G.) Boston, 1881.
AH 1819.23A The life of the ancient East. (Baikie, James.) N.Y., 1923.
AH 4819.02.5 Life of the ancient Greeks. (Gulick, C.B.) N.Y., 1905.
AH 4819.02.3A Life of the ancient Greeks. (Gulick, Charles B.) N.Y., 1902.
AH 4810.5 Life of the ancient Greeks. (Wheeler, B.I.) Ithaca, 1890.
AH 818.62.9 Life of the Greeks and Romans. (Guhl, Ernst.) London, 188-?
NEDL AH 818.62.8 Life of the Greeks and Romans. (Guhl, Ernst.) N.Y., 1876.
Eg 819.55.10 Life under the pharaohs. (Cottrell, L.) London, 1955.
AH 279.46 Light from the ancient past. (Finegan, Jack.) Princeton, N.J., 1946.
AH 279.46.4 Light from the ancient past. (Finegan, Jack.) Princeton, 1947.
AH 279.46.2 Light from the ancient past. 2. ed. (Finegan, Jack.) Princeton, N.J., 1959.
AH 3159.16 Light from the East, or Witness of the monuments. (Ball, C.J.) London, 1899.
AH 3663.9 The light of ancient Persia. (Pithawalla, M.) Adyar, 1923.
AH 8549.87 The light of Britannia. (Morgan, O.) Cardiff, 1894.
Eg 819.09 The light of Egypt. (Rustafjaell, R. de.) London, 1909.
AH 9108.2 Liguria romana; studi storico topografici. (Lamboglia, Nino.) Roma, 1939-
AH 2507.15 Likya tarihi. (Akşit, Oktay.) Istanbul, 1967.
AH 9563.6 Lilliu, G. La civiltà dei Sardi dal neolitico all'età dei nuraghi. Torino, 1963.
AH 3017.65 Limet, Henri. Le travail du métal au pays de Sumer au temps de la III dynastie d'Ur. Paris, 1960.
AH 7178.94 La limitation des fonds de terre. (Beaudouin, E.) Paris, 1894.
AH 7779.56 L'imperatore Giuliano l'Apostata secondo i documenti. (Ricciotti, Giuseppe.) Milano, 1956.
AH 3140.4 Lincke, A.A. Assyrien und Ninive...Mittelmeervölker. Berlin, 1894.
AH 7458.98 Lincke, E. Martin. P. Cornelius Scipio Ämilianus. Dresden, 1898.
AH 4439.52 Lindemann, H. Generale machen Politik. 1. Aufl. Bonn, 1952.
AH 7468.96.5 Linden, E. De bello civili Sullano. Friburgi Brisigavorum, 1896.
AH 7238.82 Lindenschmit, Ludwig. Tracht und Bewaffnung. Braunschweig, 1882.
AH 3977.5 Linder, Sven. Sauls Gibea. Uppsala, 1922.
AH 7469.60.5 Linderski, Jerzy. Państwo a kolegia. Kraków, 1961.
AH 7079.66 Linderski, Jerzy. Rzymskie zgromadzenie wyborcze od Sulli do Cezara. Wrocław, 1966.
AH 7148.80.2 Lindet, T. De l'aquisition et de la perte. Paris, 1880.
AH 3659.10 Lindl, Ernest. Enstehung und Blüte...des altorientalischen Kulturwelt: Cyrus. München, 1903.
AH 3147.3 Lindl, Ernest. Das Priester- und Beamtentum der altbabylonischen Kontrakte. Paderborn, 1913.
AH 4819.68 Lindsay, Jack. The ancient world; manners and morals. London, 1968.
Eg 709.71 Lindsay, Jack. Cleopatra. London, 1971.
Eg 829.65 Lindsay, Jack. Leisure and pleasure in Roman Egypt. London, 1965.
AH 7469.37 Lindsay, Jack. Marc Antony; his world and his contemporaries. N.Y., 1937.
Eg 879.68 Lindsay, Jack. Men and gods on the Roman Nile. London, 1968.
AH 8207.27 Lindsay, Jack. The Romans were here. London, 1956.
AH 109.21 Lineamenti dell'evoluzione tributaria nel mondo antico. (Ciccotti, Ettore.) Milano, 1921.
AH 7279.54.5 Lineamenti di storia romana. 2. ed. (Levi, Mario Attilio.) Milano, 1954.
AH 7201.109 Linee dell'Enchiridion di Pomponio. (Bretone, Mario.) Bari, 1965.
AH 7448.18.7 Linke, Otto. Die Controverse über Hannibals Alpenübergang. Breslau, 1873.
AH 7408.58 Linker, G. Die älteste Sagengeschichte Roms. Wien, 1858.
AH 7058.53 Linker, G. Über die Wahl...Praefectus urbis feriarum. Wien? 1853.
AH 7529.09 Linnert, U. Beiträge zur Geschichte Caligulas. Nürnberg, 1909.
AH 7419.68 Lintott, Andrew W. Violence in republican Rome. Oxford, 1968.
AH 828.53 Lionnet, A. Palaion, die alte Welt. Berlin, 1853.
AH 8903.6 Liou, Bernard. Praetores Etruriae XV populorum (étude d'épigraphie). Bruxelles, 1969.
AH 7449.63 Lippold, A. Consules. Bonn, 1963.
AH 7769.68 Lippold, Adolf. Theodosius der Grosse und seine Zeit. Stuttgart, 1968.
Htn AH 7235.96* Lipsius, J. De militia Romana. Antverpiae, 1596.
AH 4139.05 Lipsius, Justus Hermann. Attische Recht. Leipzig, 1905. 4v.
AH 4139.05.1 Lipsius, Justus Hermann. Das attische Recht und Rechtsverfahren. v.1-3. Hildesheim, 1966.
Htn AH 7495.98* Lipsus, Justus. Admiranda. v.1-2. Antwerpen, 1598.
AH 3011.21 Lišan Mithurti. Festschrift Wolfram Freiherr von Soden. Kevelaer, 1969.
AH 7339.56.2 Lissner, Ivar. The Caesars: might and madness. N.Y., 1958.
AH 7339.56 Lissner, Ivar. Die Casaren. Olten, 1956.
AH 819.61.25 Lissner, Ivar. Rätselhafte Kulturen. Olten, 1961.
AH 819.62.5 Lissner, Ivar. The silent past. N.Y., 1962.
Eg 8.93 List of works on Egypt. (Boston, Mass. Public Library.) Boston, 1893.
NEDL AH 278.44.5 Lista y Aragón, A. Elementos de historia antigua. Sevilla, 1844.
Eg 841.10 Liste des gymnasiarques des métropoles de l'Égypte romaine. (Sijpesteijn, Pieter Johannes.) Amsterdam, 1967.
Eg 879.36.5 Die Listen des grossen Papyrus Harris. (Schaedel, Herbert D.) Glückstadt, 1936.
AH 4819.52.15 Der listensinnede Trug des Gottes. (Deichgräber, Karl.) Göttingen, 1952.
Eg 1069.64F The litany of Re. N.Y., 1964.
AH 3173.10 Literarische Keilschrifttexte aus Assur. (Eveling, Erich.) Berlin, 1953.

Author and Title Listing

Author and Title Listing

Author and Title Listing

AH 4859.9 — Mähly, J.A. Frauen des griechischen Alterthums. Basel, 1853.

AH 9610.24 — Märker, Martin. Die Kämpfe der Karthager auf Sizilien in den Jahren 409-405 v. Chr. Inaug. Diss. Weida, 1930.

AH 7199.47 — Magdelain, A. Auctoritas principis. Paris, 1947.

AH 7149.68 — Magdelain, André. Recherches sur l'imperium. 1e éd. Paris, 1968.

AH 7898.58 — Magerstedt, A.F. Bilder aus der römischen Landwirtschaft. Sondershausen, 1858. 6v.

AH 8708.5 — Maggiulli, Pasquale. Sull'origine dei Messapi. Lecce, 1934.

AH 8549.145 — The magic arts in Celtic Britain. (Spence, Lewis.) London, 1945.

Eg 1159.52.5F — A magical statue base. (Klasens, Adolf.) Leiden, 1952.

Eg 885.933A — Magical texts from a bilingual papyrus in the British museum. (Bell, H.I.) London, 1933.

Eg 855.2 — Magician and leech. (Dauson, Warren R.) London, 1929.

AH 2147.8 — Magie, D. Roman rule in Asia Minor. Princeton, 1950. 2v.

AH 3156.10 — La magie assyrienne. (Fossey, C.) Paris, 1902.

AH 3156.5 — La magie chez les Chaldéens. (Lenormant, F.) Paris, 1874.

Eg 885.925 — La magie dans l'Égypte antique. v.1-2, Atlas. (Lexa, Frantisek.) Paris, 1925. 3v.

AH 3156.7 — La magie et la divination chez les chaldéo-assyriens. (Laurent, A.) Paris, 1894.

Eg 885.925.5 — De magische beteekenis van den naam inzonderheid in het oude Egypte. (Obbink, H.W.) Amsterdam, 1925.

AH 7339.51 — The magistrates of the Roman Republic. (Broughton, Thomas R.S.) N.Y., 1951-52. 2v.

AH 7339.51.1 — The magistrates of the Roman Republic. Supplement. (Broughton, Thomas R.S.) N.Y., 1960.

AH 7058.29 — Magistratum et sacerdotiorum. Vratislaviae, 1829.

AH 8647.5.15 — La Magna Grecia, paesaggio e storia. (Lenormant, F.) Crotone, 1931-33. 3v.

AH 8647.13F — La Magna Grecia. (Larizza, Pietro.) Roma, 1929.

AH 2583.5F — Magnesia am Maiandros. (Kern, Otto.) Berlin, 1894.

AHP 23.4 — Magyar keleti Társaság Kiadvanyai. Budapest. 5,1945+

AH 8313.5 — Magyarország hépei es a Római biródolom. (Alfoldi, András.) Budapest, 1936.

AH 4558.87A — Mahaffy, J.P. Alexander's empire. London, 1887.

NEDL AH 4818.76.5 — Mahaffy, J.P. Antiguedades clasicas I. Antiguedades griegas. N.Y., 1889.

Eg 708.95A — Mahaffy, J.P. The empire of the Ptolemies. London, 1895.

AH 4818.87.10A — Mahaffy, J.P. Greek life and thought. London, 1887.

AH 4818.87.11A — Mahaffy, J.P. Greek life and thought. 2nd ed. London, 1896.

AH 4728.90 — Mahaffy, J.P. Greek world under Roman sway. London, 1890.

Eg 278.94.4 — Mahaffy, J.P. A history of Egypt under the Ptolemaic dynasty. v.4. London, 1899.

AH 4842.26 — Mahaffy, J.P. Old Greek education. N.Y., 188-.

AH 4842.27A — Mahaffy, J.P. Old Greek education. N.Y., 1882.

AH 4842.29 — Mahaffy, J.P. Old Greek education. N.Y., 1905.

NEDL AH 4818.76.4 — Mahaffy, J.P. Old Greek life. N.Y., 18- .

NEDL AH 4818.76.2.5 — Mahaffy, J.P. Old Greek life. N.Y., 1876.

NEDL AH 4818.76.2.9 — Mahaffy, J.P. Old Greek life. N.Y., 1885.

NEDL AH 4818.76.3 — Mahaffy, J.P. Old Greek life. N.Y., 1888.

AH 818.69 — Mahaffy, J.P. Primitive civilization. London, 1869.

AH 4298.92A — Mahaffy, J.P. Problems in Greek history. Photoreproduction. London, 1892.

AH 4659.05 — Mahaffy, J.P. Progress of Hellenism in Alexander's empire. Chicago, 1905.

AH 298.71 — Mahaffy, J.P. Prolegomena to ancient history. London, 1871.

AH 4659.06 — Mahaffy, J.P. Silver age of the Greek world. Chicago, 1906.

AH 4659.06.5 — Mahaffy, J.P. The silver age of the Greek world. Chicago, 1911.

AH 4828.74A — Mahaffy, J.P. Social life in Greece. London, 1874.

AH 4828.74.5 — Mahaffy, J.P. Social life in Greece. London, 1898.

AH 4828.74.2A — Mahaffy, J.P. Social life in Greece. 2. ed. London, 1875.

AH 4828.74.8 — Mahaffy, J.P. Social life in Greece from Homer to Menander. London, 1902.

AH 4828.74.12 — Mahaffy, J.P. Social life in Greece from Homer to Menander. London, 1925.

AH 4828.74.4 — Mahaffy, J.P. Social life in Greece from Homer to Menander. 5. ed. London, 1883.

AH 4558.87.3 — Mahaffy, J.P. Story of Alexander's empire. N.Y., 1887.

AH 4818.96A — Mahaffy, J.P. Survey of Greek civilization. N.Y., 1896.

AH 4818.96.5A — Mahaffy, J.P. Survey of Greek civilization. N.Y., 1899.

AH 4819.09 — Mahaffy, J.P. What have the Greeks done for modern civilization? N.Y., 1909.

AH 8063.5 — Mahjouhi, Ammar. Les cités romaines de Tunisie. Tunis, 1969?

AH 7299.71.5 — Maiak, I.L. Vzaimsotnosheniia Rima i italiitsev v III-II vv. do n.e. (do grakhanskogo dvisheniia). Moskva, 1971.

AH 39.71 — Maillet, Jean. Institutions politiques et sociales de l'antiquité. 2. éd. Paris, 1971.

AH 4889.00 — Main d'oeuvre industrielle. (Guiraud, P.) Paris, 1900.

NEDL AH 138.61 — Maine, Henry S. Ancient law. London, 1861.

AH 138.61.7 — Maine, Henry S. Ancient law. London, 1905.

AH 138.61.18 — Maine, Henry S. Ancient law. London, 1920.

AH 138.61.19 — Maine, Henry S. Ancient law. London, 1965.

AH 138.61.2 — Maine, Henry S. Ancient law. 1. American ed. N.Y., 1864.

AH 138.61.2.5 — Maine, Henry S. Ancient law. 1. American ed. N.Y., 1867.

AH 138.61.4 — Maine, Henry S. Ancient law. 3. American ed. N.Y., 1875.

AH 138.61.9 — Maine, Henry S. Ancient law. 10. ed. London, 1906.

NEDL AH 138.83.3 — Maine, Henry S. Dissertations on early law and custom. N.Y., 1883.

NEDL AH 138.83.5 — Maine, Henry S. Dissertations on early law and custom. N.Y., 1886.

AH 138.83A — Maine, Henry S. Early law and custom. London, 1883.

AH 138.83.8 — Maine, Henry S. Études sur l'ancien droit. Paris, 1884.

AH 138.75.2A — Maine, Henry S. Lectures on the early history of institutions. London, 1875.

AH 138.75A — Maine, Henry S. Lectures on the early history of institutions. N.Y., 1875.

AH 138.75.7 — Maine, Henry S. Lectures on the early history of institutions. N.Y., 1884.

AH 138.75.3 — Maine, Henry S. Lectures on the early history of institutions. N.Y., 1888.

AH 138.75.5 — Maine, Henry S. Lectures on the early history of institutions. 3. ed. London, 1880.

AH 7469.34.5.3 — Mainzer, Ferdinand. Caesar's mantle. N.Y., 1936.

AH 7469.54.5 — Mainzer, Ferdinand. Clodia. Braunschweig, 1954.

AH 7469.34.5 — Mainzer, Ferdinand. Der Kampf um Caesars Erbe. Leipzig, 1936.

AH 8307.4 — Maior, Petru. Istoria pentru începutul românilor in Dacia. Bucureşti, 1971. 2v.

AH 4818.97 — Maisch, R. Griechische Altertumskunde. Leipzig, 1897.

AH 3909.8 — Maisler, Benjamin. Untersuchungen zur alten Geschichte und Ethnographie Syriens und Palästinas. Giessen, 1930.

AH 4807.32F — Maittaire, M. Marmorum. London, 1732.

AH 8647.26 — Maiuri, Amedeo. Passeggiate in Magna Grecia. Napoli, 1963.

Eg 848.3.2 — Majer-Leonhard, E. Agrammatoi. Marpurgi Chattorum, 1913.

Eg 848.3 — Majer-Leonhard, E. Agrammatoi in Aegypto qui litteras sciverint qui nesciverint ex papyris graecis quantum fieri potest exploratur. Francofurti, 1913.

AH 7148.80.4 — Der Majestätsgedanke. (Pollack, Erich.) Leipzig, 1908.

AH 7148.80.5 — Die Majestätsprocesse unter dem Kaiser. (Dürr, F.) Heilbronn, 1880.

AH 7168.80.5 — Die Majestätsprocesse unter dem Kaiser Tiberius. (Dürr, Julius.) Heilbronn, 1880.

AH 3910.9 — Majo, U. Antioco IV Epifane re di Siria. Sassari, 1907.

AH 908.43 — De makariske ör og Elisa. (Estrup, H.F.J.) Kjøbenhavn, 1843.

AH 6107.12 — He Makedonia mechri tou thanatou tou Archelaou. (Kanatsoulès, Dèmètrios.) Thessalonikè, 1964.

AH 6107.5 — Makedonien. (Abel, O.) Leipzig, 1847.

AH 819.29 — The makers of civilization in race and history. (Waddell, L.A.) London, 1929.

AH 4458.98 — The making of Athens; a history of Greece, 495-431 B.C. Photoreproduction. (Allcroft, Arthur H.) London, 1898.

Eg 819.39 — The making of Egypt. (Petrie, William M.F.) London, 1939.

AH 7478.93 — Making of the monarchy. (Allcroft, A.H.) London, 1893.

AH 7409.14 — The making of the Roman people. (Lloyd, Thomas.) London, 1914.

Eg 819.67.7 — Makram, Rizg. Kulturgeist und Kulturleib. 2. Aufl. Tübingen, 1970.

AH 4204.17 — Makrygianne, E.S. Meletè peri tès politeias tou Solonos. Ermoupolei, Syrou, 1888.

AH 862.7 — Malaria. (Jones, W.H.S.) Cambridge, 1907.

Eg 132.53 — Malinine, Michel. Choix de textes juridiques en hiératique et en démotique. pt.1. Paris, 1953-

AH 4278.29 — Malkin, F. History of Greece from earliest times. London, 1829.

Eg 989.5 — Mallet, D. Le culte de Neit à Saïs. Paris, 1888.

AH 3022.30 — Mallowan, Max Edgar. Early Mesopotamia and Iran. N.Y., 1965.

AH 7204.19 — Malmeri, J.P. De Marco Aurelio Centonio. Halae, 1772. 2v.

AH 9647.5 — Malta antica illustrata cò monumenti, e coll'istoria. (Bres, Onorato.) Roma, 1816.

AH 3359.5 — Malten, L. Cyrenarum origines. n.p., 1904.

AH 4850.11 — Maltou. Ton Symposion. Athènai, 1842.

AH 8972.5 — Maluasia, C.C. Marmora felsinea...Bononiae senatu. Bononiae, 1690.

Htn AH 4521.16* — Malvezzi, V. Considerations upon the lives of Alcibiades and Coriolanus. London, 1650.

Htn AH 7406.36* — Malvezzi, V. Princeps, eiusque arcana. n.p., n.d. 2 pam.

Htn AH 7406.47* — Malvezzi, V. Il Romulo. Geneva, 1647. 5 pam.

Htn AH 7406.37* — Malvezzi, V. Romulus and Tarquin. London, 1637.

Htn AH 7406.38* — Malvezzi, V. Romulus and Tarquin. London, 1638.

Htn AH 7406.48* — Malvezzi, V. Romulus and Tarquin. 3. ed. London, 1648.

Htn AH 7406.32* — Malvezzi, V. Il Tarquinio superbo. Bologna, 1632.

Eg 879.58.2F — Les mammisis de Dendara. (Daumas, François.) Le Caire, 1959.

Eg 879.58 — Les mammisis des temples égyptiens. (Daumas, François.) Paris, 1958.

AH 7819.47A — The man in the Roman street. (Mattingly, Harold.) N.Y., 1947.

AH 819.36.10A — Man makes himself. (Childe, Vere Gordon.) London, 1936.

AH 819.36.11 — Man makes himself. (Childe, Vere Gordon.) London, 1948.

AH 7779.71 — Manacorda, Mario Alighiero. La paideia di Achille. Roma, 1971.

AH 2060.10 — Manandian, I. Tigran Vtoroi i Rim. Erevan, 1943.

AH 3002.100 — Manchester cuneiform studies. Manchester. 1-3,1951-1953 2v.

EgP 87.6 — Manchester Egyptian and Oriental Society. Journal. Manchester. 1912-1938 4v.

AH 7169.04.3 — Mancipatio. (Stintzing, W.) Leipzig, 1904.

Eg 808.45 — Manetho und die Hundssternperiode. (Böskh, A.) Berlin, 1845.

Eg 808.65 — Manethós...Geschichte und Chronologie. (Henne, A.) Gotha, 1865.

AH 7559.47 — Manfri, Guglielmo. La crisi politica del'anno 68-69 d. C. Bologna, 1947.

AH 7888.92.2 — Les manieurs d'argent à Rome. 2. éd. (Deloume, Antonin.) Rome, 1970.

Htn AH 8511.5* — Manley, Inza J. Effects of the Germanic invasions on Gaul. Berkeley, 1934.

AH 8511.5.2 — Manley, Inza J. Effects of the Germanic invasions on Gaul. Berkeley, 1934.

AH 8202.8 — Mann, John C. The northern frontier in Britain from Hadrian to Honorius; literary and epigraphic sources. Newcastle-upon-Tyne, 1969.

AH 4818.44.3 — Manners and customs of Greeks. (Panofka, Theodor.) London, 1849.

Eg 818.37.10 — The manners and customs of the ancient Egyptians. (Wilkinson, J.G.) Boston, 1883. 3v.

Eg 818.37 — Manners and customs of the ancient Egyptians. (Wilkinson, J.G.) London, 1837. 3v.

Eg 818.37.6A — Manners and customs of the ancient Egyptians. (Wilkinson, J.G.) London, 1878. 3v.

Eg 818.37.2 — Manners and customs of the ancient Egyptians. 2. series. (Wilkinson, J.G.) London, 1841. 3v.

Eg 818.37.3 — Manners and customs of the ancient Egyptians. 3. ed. (Wilkinson, J.G.) London, 1847. 5v.

AH 938.29 — Mannert, K. Geographie. v.1-10. Leipzig, 1799-1829. 14v.

AH 7617.93 — Mannert, K. Res Traiani imperatoris ad Danubium gestae. Norimbergae, 1793.

AH 4609.51 — Manni, E. Demetrio Paliorcete. Roma, 1951.

AH 7709.49 — Manni, Eugenio. L'impero di Gallieno. Roma, 1949.

AH 4009.52 — Manni, Eugenio. Introduzione allo studio della staria greca e romana. Palermo, 1952.

AH 4009.52.2 — Manni, Eugenio. Introduzione allo studio della storia greca e romana. 2. ed. Palermo, 1959.

AH 7469.39.15 — Manni, Eugenio. Lucio Sergio Catilina. Firenze, 1939.

AH 279.43 — Mannkynssaga. (Hjartarson, A.) Reykjavik, 1954.

AH 4855.5 — Manns, O. Jagd bei den Griechen. Cassel, 1888. 3 pam.

Htn AH 7207.2* — Mannuccius, P. Antiquitatum Romanarum...Liber de Senatu. Venetiis, 1581.

Author and Title Listing

AH 4169.62 — Mannzmann, Anneliese. Griechische Stiftungsurkunden. Münster, 1962.

AH 7799.55* — Manpower shortage and the fall of the Roman Empire in the West. (Boak, A.E.R.) Ann Arbor, 1955.

AH 39.64* — Man's quest for political knowledge. (Anderson, W.) Minneapolis, 1964.

AH 5757.5 — Manso, J.K.F. Sparta. v.1-3. Leipzig, 1800. 5v.

AH 8963.5 — Mansuelli, Guido Achille. I Cisalpini. Firenze, 1962.

AH 819.67 — Mansuelli, Guido Achille. Les civilisations de l'Europe ancienne. Paris, 1967.

AH 9639.12 — Mansuelli, Guido Achille. La politica estera di Siracusa. Bologna, 1958.

AH 7201.94 — Mantellini, G. Papiniano. 2. ed. Roma, 1885.

AH 7098.82 — Mantey, Otto. De gradu et statu quaestorum im municipiis coloniaue. Diss. Inaug. Halis Saxonum, 1882.

AH 3156.14 — Mantique babylonienne et mantique hittite. (Boissier, A.) Paris, 1935.

AH 7.16.9 — Mantissa...Fabricii Bibliographiam antiquariam. (Barth, J.M.) Ratisbonae, 1751.

AH 7479.24.10 — The mantle of Caesar. (Gundolf, F.) London, 1929.

NEDL AH 7819.16 — Manual d'archeologie romaine. (Cagnat, René.) Paris, 1916-20. 2v.

NEDL AH 7818.64.13 — Manual des antiquités romaines. v.1-19. (Marquardt, Joachim.) Paris, 1887-1907. 20v.

AH 7138.48.5 — Manual histórico de directo romano. (Secco, A.L. de S.H.) Coimbra, 1848.

AH 938.81 — Manual of ancient geography. (Kiepert, H.) London, 1881.

AH 938.57 — Manual of ancient geography. (Schmitz, L.) Philadelphia, 1857.

NEDL AH 278.40.5 — A manual of ancient history. (Heeren, Arnold Herman Ludwig.) London, 1847.

NEDL AH 278.69.6 — Manual of ancient history. (Rawlinson, G.) N.Y., 1871.

NEDL AH 278.69.6 — Manual of ancient history. (Rawlinson, G.) N.Y., 1871.

NEDL AH 278.69 — Manual of ancient history. (Rawlinson, G.) Oxford, 1869.

AH 278.69A — Manual of ancient history. (Rawlinson, G.) Oxford, 1869.

NEDL AH 278.55 — A manual of ancient history. (Schmitz, L.) Philadelphia, 1855.

AH 278.45 — A manual of ancient history. (Taylor, W.C.) N.Y., 1845.

NEDL AH 278.72.5 — A manual of ancient history. (Thalheimer, M.E.) Cincinnati, 1872.

AH 7278.72 — Manual of ancient history. Pt.3. (Thalheimer, Mary Elsie.) Cincinnati, 1872.

AH 278.40 — A manual of ancient history. 3. ed. (Heeren, Arnold Herman Ludwig.) Oxford, 1840.

AH 7138.54.16 — Manual of civil law for...schools. 2. ed. (Humphreys, E.R.) London, 1856.

AH 4818.95.5 — A manual of Greek antiquities. Books 1-5. (Gardner, P.) N.Y., 1895.

AH 4818.75 — Manual of Greek archaeology. (Rousopoulos, A.S.) Athens, 1875?

AH 7818.48.10 — Manual of Roman antiquities. 10th ed. (Ramsay, William.) London, 1876.

AH 7818.48.15 — Manual of Roman antiquities. 15th ed. (Ramsay, William.) N.Y., 1895.

NEDL AH 7818.48.17A — Manual of Roman antiquities. 17th ed. (Ramsay, William.) London, 1901.

AH 7138.59 — Manual of Roman civil law. (Leapingwell, George.) Cambridge, 1859.

AH 7138.93 — Manual of Roman law. (Chamier, D.) London, 1893.

AH 1408.69.3 — Manual of the ancient history of the East. (Lenormant, F.) London, 1869.

AH 1408.68.5 — Manual of the ancient history of the East. (Lenormant, F.) Philadelphia, 1869.

AH 1408.69 — Manual of the ancient history of the East. 3. ed. (Lenormant, F.) Paris, 1869. 3v.

AH 3980.7 — Manual to accompany the pictorial view of ancient Jerusalem and its vicinity. n.p., n.d.

AH 7206.13 — Manuale Basilicorum. (Haubold, G.G.) Lipsiae, 1819.

AH 8.98 — Manuale di fonti letterarie. (Tropea, Giacomo.) Messina, 1898.

AH 279.58.30 — Manuale di storia orientale e greca. (Bignami, Ernesto.) Milano, 1958.

AH 7279.58 — Manuale di storia romana. (Bignami, Ernesto.) Milano, 1958.

AH 7138.37F — Manuale iuris civilis Romani. (Dirksen, H.E.) Berolini, 1837.

AH 7138.06 — Manuale juris. (Godefroy, J.) Parisiis, 1806.

AH 7138.74 — Manuale juris synopticum. (Pellat, C.A.) Paris, 1874.

AH 938.89.5 — Manuali di geografia antica ad uso delle scuole secondarie. v.1-3. (Hughes, Lugi.) Torino, 1889-90.

AH 3005.6 — Manuel d'Assyriologie. v.1-2. (Fossey, Charles.) Paris, 1904-26. 3v.

AH 7139.17.2 — Manuel des institutions juridiques des Romains. (Cuq, Edouard.) Paris, 1928.

AH 7038.86 — Manuel des institutions romaines. (Bouché-Leclercq, A.) Paris, 1886.

AH 7138.89.15 — Manuel des textes de droit romain. (Mispoulet, J.B.) Paris, 1889.

NEDL AH 1408.68 — Manuel d'histoire ancienne de l'Orient. (Lenormant, F.) Paris, 1868. 2v.

AH 7138.95.3 — Manuel élémentaire de droit romain. 3. éd. (Girard, P.F.) Paris, 1906.

AH 7138.95.4 — Manuel élémentaire de droit romain. 4. éd. (Girard, P.F.) Paris, 1906.

AH 7138.95.6 — Manuel élémentaire de droit romain. 5e éd. (Girard, P.F.) Paris, 1911.

AH 7138.95.10 — Manuel élémentaire de droit romain. 8e éd. (Girard, P.F.) Paris, 1929.

AH 4038.36 — Manuel of political antiquities. (Hermann, C.F.) Oxford, 1836.

AH 8548.57 — Manuel pour servir à l'étude de la antiquité celtique. (Dottin, Georges.) Paris, 1906.

AH 8548.57.2 — Manuel pour servir à l'étude de l'antiquité celtique. 2. éd. (Dottin, Georges.) Paris, 1915.

NEDL AH 278.44 — Manuel pratique d'histoire ancienne. (Boulet, Jean B.E.) Paris, 1844.

AH 7139.58 — Manuele di storia del dirito romano. (Scherillo, Gaetano.) Milano, 1958.

Htn AH 7135.69* — Manuzio, P. Antiquitatem romanarum. Venetiis, 1569.

AH 7035.85 — Manuzio, Paolo. Antiquitatum romanorum. Romae, 1585.

Htn AH 7516.34* — Manzini, G.B. Political observations upon the fall of Seianus. London, 1634.

AH 4967.88.150 — Maps, plans, views and coins, illustrative of the travels of Anacharsis the younger in Greece. 2. ed. (Barbié du Bocage, J.D.) London, 1793.

AH 930.44 — Maps illustrating ancient history. (Iliff, John G.) Topeka, 1915.

AH 7161.15 — Maranges, J.M. Estudios jurídicos. Madrid, 1878.

AH 7519.52.3 — Marañón, G. Tiberius. London, 1956.

AH 7519.52 — Marañón, G. Tiberius. München, 1952.

AH 4481.13 — Marathon and Salamis. Photoreproduction. (Mackenzie, C.) London, 1934.

AH 7469.37 — Marc Antony; his world and his contemporaries. (Lindsay, Jack.) N.Y., 1937.

AH 7649.54 — Marc Aurel, Kaiser und Philosoph. (Goerlitz, W.) Stuttgart, 1954.

AH 7649.62 — Marc Aurèle. (Proyart, Pierre de.) Paris, 1962.

AH 7648.97 — Marc Aurèle dans ses rapports avec le christianisme. (Dartique-Peyroux, J.) Paris, 1897.

Htn AH 7448.18.2* — March of Hannibal from Rome. (Long, H.L.) London, 1831. 4 pam.

Htn AH 806.72F* — Marcham, John. Chronicus canon. Londini, 1672.

AH 7448.18.8 — Marche d'Annibal. (Perrin, J.B.) Paris, 1887.

AH 7819.31.5 — Marchi, Attilio de. I romani nelle istituzioni e nel costume. Milano, 1931.

AH 7668.76 — Marcia la favorite de Commode. (Ceuleneer, A. de.) Paris, 1876.

AH 7479.59.5 — Marco Antonio nella lotta politica della tarda republica romana. (Rossi, Ruggero F.) Trieste, 1959.

AH 8011.5 — Marcus, Ludwig. Histoire des wandales. Paris, 1836.

AH 7509.37A — Marcus Agrippa, organizer of victory. (Wright, F.A.) N.Y., 1937.

AH 7509.33.5 — Marcus Agrippa. (Reinhold, M.) Geneva, 1933.

AH 7201.48 — Marcus Antistius Labeo. v.2. (Pernice, A.) Halle, 1873. 3v.

AH 7449.70.10 — Marcus Atilius Regulus; exemplum historicum. (Mix, Erving R.) The Hague, 1970.

AH 7649.35 — Marcus Aurelius, a saviour of men. (Hayward, F.H.) London, 1935.

AH 7648.90 — Marcus Aurelius; an address...1890. (Dimmock, Thomas.) St. Louis, 1890.

AH 7649.66 — Marcus Aurelius. (Birley, Anthony Richard.) London, 1966.

AH 7649.51 — Marcus Aurelius. (Farquharson, A.S.L.) Oxford, 1951.

AH 7648.68 — Marcus Aurelius Antoninus als Zeitgenosse und Freund der Rabbi Jehuda ha-Nasi. (Bodek, Arnold.) Leipzig, 1868.

AH 7479.39.5 — Marcus Brutus. (Radin, Max.) N.Y., 1939.

AH 7469.66.5 — Marcus Crassus, millionaire. (Adcock, Frank Ezra.) Cambridge, 1966.

AH 3160.26F — Marduk, Urtyp Christi? (Paulus, Witold.) Romae, 1928.

AH 3407.33 — Marek, Kurt W. Enge Schlucht und schwarzer Berg. Hamburg, 1955.

AH 3407.33.5 — Marek, Kurt W. Enge Schlucht und schwarzer Berg. Reinbek, 1966.

AH 819.08 — Marett, R.R. Anthropology and the classics. Oxford, 1908.

AH 9221.5 — Maretti, N. Ancona. Roma, 1945.

AH 7509.33 — Mareus Vipsanius Agrippa. Inaug. Diss. (Daniel, Rudolf.) Breslau, 1933.

AH 7168.40 — Marezoll, T. Droit privé des Romains. Paris, 1840.

AH 7168.52 — Marezoll, T. Du droit privé. 2. éd. Paris, 1852.

AH 7138.81 — Marezoll. Lehrbuch der Institutionen. Brussel, 1881.

AH 2008.7 — Margoliouth, D.S. The relations between Arabs and Israelites prior to the rise of Islam. London, 1924.

AH 3020.6 — Margolis, E. Sumerian temple documents. N.Y., 1915.

AH 3013.965.5 — Margueron, Jean Claude. Mesopotamia. London, 1965.

Eg 509.63 — Margulies, H. Der Pharao Josefs. Herrenalb, 1963.

AH 3250.5 — Margwelaschwili, T. von. Colchis, Iberien und Albanien um die Wende des 1. Jahrhunderts vor Christ. Inaug. Diss. Halle, 1914.

Eg 278.67.3 — Mariette, A. Aperçu de l'histoire d'Égypte. 2. éd. Paris, 1870.

Eg 278.67.5 — Mariette, A. Aperçu de l'histoire d'Égypte. 3. éd. Alexandrie, 1872.

Eg 278.67 — Mariette, A. Égypte. Paris, 1867.

Eg 278.67.10A — Mariette, A. Outline of ancient Egyptian history. N.Y., 1892.

AH 9668.2 — La marina vándala. (Morales Belda, Francisco.) Barcelona, 1969.

AH 4819.46 — Marinatos, S.W. Greece and Greek civilization as results of economic expansion. Athens, 1946.

AH 8647.15 — Marincola Pistoja, D. Di Cautonia, repubblica della Magna Grecia. Catanzaro, 1866. 2 pam.

AH 258.86 — Marine des anciens. (Jurien de la Gravière, J.P.E.) Paris, 1886. 2v.

AH 257.77 — La marine des anciens peuples. (LeRoy, J.D.) Paris, 1777.

AH 7258.85 — Marine des Ptolémées et...Romains. (Jurien de la Gravière.) Paris, 1885. 2v.

AH 259.64 — Marines antiques de la Mediterranée. (Meirat, Jean.) Paris, 1964.

AH 7469.15.5 — Mario e Silla. (Lanzani, C.) Catania, 1915.

AH 7468.34.2 — Marius and Sulla. (Gerlach, F.D.) Basel, 1856.

AH 7468.71 — Marius et Jules César. (Gilles, I.) Marseille, 1871.

AH 8548.147 — Markale, Jean. Les Celtes et la civilisation celtique; mythe et histoire. Paris, 1969.

AH 7208.4 — Marlot, Emile. Les comices électoraux. Paris, 1884.

Eg 971.7.15 — Marlowe, John. The golden age of Alexandria: from its foundation by Alexander the Great in 1331 B.C. to its capture by the Arabs in 642 A.D. London, 1971.

AH 8972.5 — Marmora felsinea...Bononiae senatu. (Maluasia, C.C.) Bononiae, 1690.

AH 4807.32F — Marmorum. (Maittaire, M.) London, 1732.

AH 8107.10 — Le Maroc antique. 8. éd. (Carcopino, J.) Paris, 1948.

AH 8116.5 — Le Maroc chez les auteurs anciens. (Roget, Raymond.) Paris, 1924.

AH 2623.5 — Marquarat, J. Cyzicus und sein Gebiet. Berlin, 1836.

AH 4838.86 — Marquardt, R. Zum Pentathlon der Hellenen. Güstrow, 1886.

AH 7114.8 — Marquardt, I. Historiae equitum romanorum. Berolini, 1840.

AH 7114.8.2 — Marquardt, I. Historiea equitum romanorum. Berolini, 1840.

AH 7828.79 — Marquardt, J. Das Privatleben der Römer. Leipzig, 1879.

AH 7818.64.4 — Marquardt, Joachim. Handbuch der römischen Alterthümer. v.1-7. Leipzig, 1871-1888. 9v.

AH 7818.64.7 — Marquardt, Joachim. Handbuch der römischen Alterthümer. 2. Aufl. Leipzig, 1876- 2v.

AH 7818.64.9 — Marquardt, Joachim. Handbuch der römischen Alterthümer. 2. Aufl. v.1-7. Leipzig, 1876. 10v.

AH 7818.64.11 — Marquardt, Joachim. Handbuch der römischen Alterthümer. 3. Aufl. Leipzig, 1887. 3v.

AH 7818.64.18 — Marquardt, Joachim. Handbuch der römischen Alterthümer. 3. Aufl. v.1-3. Graz, 1952-53. 5v.

NEDL AH 7818.64.13 — Marquardt, Joachim. Manual des antiquités romaines. v.1-19. Paris, 1887-1907. 20v.

AH 7818.64.15 — Marquardt, Joachim. Römische Privatalterthümer. Leipzig, 1864-67.

AH 842.16 — Marr, F. Chauvinismus und Schulreform im Altertum. Breslau, 1894.

AH 3913.5	Marriage and family life in Ugaritic literature. (Selms, A. van.) London, 1954.
AH 3663.14	Marriage in ancient Iran. (Katrak, Jamshed C.) Bombay, 1965.
AH 842.35	Marrow, Henri Irenée. Histoire de l'éducation dans l'antiquité. Paris, 1948.
AH 842.35.2	Marrow, Henri Irenée. Histoire de l'éducation dans l'antiquité. 2. éd. Paris, 1950.
AH 842.35.6	Marrow, Henri Irenée. Histoire de l'éducation dans l'antiquité. 4. éd. Paris, 1958.
AH 842.35.4	Marrow, Henri Irenée. A history of education in antiquity. London, 1956.
AH 7108.88	Marsault, A. Droit romain des magistrats monétaires. Paris, 1888.
AH 4559.64	Marsden, E.W. The campaign of Gaugamela. Liverpool, 1964.
AH 239.69	Marsden, Eric W. Greek and Roman artillery; historical development. Oxford, 1969.
AH 239.71.5	Marsden, Eric W. Greek and Roman artillery; technical treatises. Oxford, 1971.
AH 7469.22	Marsh, F.B. The founding of the Roman empire. Austin, 1922.
AH 7469.22.2A	Marsh, F.B. The founding of the Roman empire. 2. ed. London, 1927.
AH 7469.35	Marsh, Frank B. A history of the Roman world from 146 to 30 B.C. London, 1935.
AH 7469.35.1	Marsh, Frank B. A history of the Roman world from 146 to 30 B.C. N.Y., 1939.
AH 7469.35.2	Marsh, Frank B. A history of the Roman world from 146 to 30 B.C. 2. ed. London, 1953.
AH 7469.35.3	Marsh, Frank B. A history of the Roman world from 146 to 30 B.C. 3. ed. London, 1963.
AH 7519.31	Marsh, Frank Burr. The reign of Tiberius. London, 1931.
AH 5315.40A	Marsh, T.B. Modern problems in the ancient world. Austin, 1943.
AH 4539.05	Marshall, F.H. Second Athenian Confederacy. Cambridge, 1905.
AH 5306.7F	Marstand, Vilhelm. Arsenalet i Piraeus og oldtidens byggereqler. København, 1922.
AH 4842.23	Martin, A. Doctrines pédagogiques. Paris, 1881.
AH 4214.5	Martin, Albert. Foedera publica. Lutetiae Parisiorum, 1886.
AH 9757.8	Martin, Charles. Les deux Germanies cis-rhénanes. Étude d'histoire et de géographie anciennes. Paris, 1863.
AH 7779.19	Martin, Edward J. The emperor Julian. London, 1919.
AH 3187.9	Martin, F. Lettres néo-babyloniennes. Paris, 1909.
AH 3154.5	Martin, F. Textes religieux assyriens et babyloniens. Paris, 1900.
AH 8549.12	Martin, Jacques. La religion des Gaulois, tirée des plus pures sources de l'antiquité. Amsterdam, 1750. 2v.
AH 7279.73	Martin, Jean Pierre. La Rome ancienne. 1. éd. Paris, 1973.
AH 8514.12	Martin, L.A. Histoire morale de la Gaule. Paris, 1848.
AH 7899.71	Martin, René. Recherches sur les agronomes latins et leurs conceptions économiques et sociàles. Paris, 1971.
AH 4299.56	Martin, Roland. L'urbanisme dans la Grèce antique. Paris, 1956.
Eg 39.11	Martin, V. Les Épistratèges. Genève, 1911.
NEDL AH 278.84.12	Martinez Silva, Carlos. Compendio de historia antigua. 4. ed. Bogota, 1910.
AH 27.65	Martini, J.C. Thesaurus dissertationum. Norimbergae, 1766. 3v.
AH 879.58	Martino, Ernesto de. Morti e pianto rituale nel mondo antico dal lamento pagano al pianto di Maria. Torino, 1958.
AH 7039.58	Martino, Francesco de. Storia della costituzione romana. v.1-6. Napoli, 1958-72. 7v.
AH 3014.15F	Martiny, G. Die Kulturichtung in Mesopotamien. Diss. Berlin, 1932.
AH 8011.2	Martroye, F. Genséric la conquête vandale. Paris, 1707.
Eg 658.98	Marucchi, Orazio. La biografia di un personaggio politico dell'antico Egitto scritta sopra la sua statua. Roma, 1898.
Eg 1038.88F	Marucchi, Orazio. Il grande papiro egizio della Biblioteca Vaticana. Roma, 1888.
Eg 1308.91	Marucchi, Orazio. Monumenta papyracea. Romae, 1891.
Eg 278.99	Marucchi, Orazio. Lo scarabeo onorario di una regina d'Egitto nel Museo egizio vaticano. Roma, 1899.
AH 7088.80	Marx, Edgarel. Essai sur les pouvoirs du gouverneur. Paris, 1880.
AH 4860.9	Mary Rosaria, sister. The nurse in Greek life. Diss. Boston, 1917.
AH 7138.76.15	Marynz, K.G. Cours de droit romain. 4. éd. Bruxelles, 1876. 3v.
AH 7228.98	Marzo, D.S. Procedura criminale romana. Palermo, 1898.
AH 7214.3	Maschke, R. De magistratuum Romanorum iure. Berolini, 1884.
AH 188.88	Maschke, R. Der Freiheitsprozess im klassischen Altertum. Berlin, 1888.
AH 7179.06.5	Maschke, R. Zur Theorie und Geschichte der römischen Agrargesetze. Tübingen, 1906.
AH 7509.56	Mashkin, N.A. Il principato di Augusto. Roma, 1956. 2v.
AH 7279.53.5	Mashkin, Nikolai A. Römische Geschichte. Berlin, 1953.
NEDL AH 7468.95	Masom, W.F. Decline of the oligarchy: History of Rome. London, 1895.
AH 7448.94.2	Masom, W.J. The struggle for Empire. London, 1894.
AH 3177.15	Mason, Herbert. Gilgamesh: a verse narrative. Boston, 1971.
Eg 298.79	Maspero, G. Études égyptiennes. Paris, 1879-86. 2v.
AH 3103.4	Maspero, G. Life in ancient Egypt and Assyria. N.Y., 1899.
Eg 608.86.10F	Maspero, G. Mummy of Rameses II. Boston, 1886.
Eg 818.93A	Maspéro, Gaston. The dawn of civilization. N.Y., 1894.
Eg 818.94.4	Maspéro, Gaston. The dawn of civilization. N.Y., 1897.
Eg 818.94.6	Maspéro, Gaston. The dawn of civilization. 2. ed. London, 1896.
AH 3075.12	Maspero, Gaston. Histoire ancienne, Égypte, Assyrie; lectures historiques. Paris, 1890.
AH 1278.76	Maspero, Gaston. Histoire ancienne des peuples de l'Orient. Paris, 1876.
AH 1278.76.4	Maspero, Gaston. Histoire ancienne des peuples de l'Orient. Paris, 1886.
AH 1278.95	Maspero, Gaston. Histoire ancienne des peuples de l'Orient. Paris, 1895. 3v.
NEDL AH 1278.76.8	Maspero, Gaston. Histoire ancienne des peuples de l'Orient. 3. éd. Paris, 1878.
AH 1278.76.7	Maspero, Gaston. Historie ancienne des peuples de l'Orient. 7e éd. Paris, 1905.
Eg 818.92.2	Maspéro, Gaston. Life in ancient Egypt and Assyria. N.Y., 1895.
AH 1279.00	Maspero, Gaston. The passing of the empires, 850 B.C.-330 B.C. London, 1900.
AH 1278.76.15	Maspero, Gaston. Struggle of the nations, Egypt, Syria and Assyria. N.Y., 1897.
Eg 709.05	Maspéro, Henri. Les finances de l'Égypte sous les Lagides. Paris, 1905.
Eg 239.12	Maspero, J. Organisation militaire de l'Egypte Byzantine. Paris, 1912.
AH 7238.64.10	Masquelez, Alfred Émile A.E. Étude sur la castramétation des romains. Paris, 1864.
AH 5313.12	Massachusetts Institute of Technology. Department of English and History. Athens in the fifth century B.C. Cambridge, Mass., 1950.
NEDL AH 3075.4	Massaroli, G. Phiel e Tuklatpalasar II. Roma, 1882.
AH 299.70	Massé, Claude. La colonisation dans l'antiquité. Paris, 1970.
NEDL Eg 318.83	Massey, G. The natural genesis. London, 1883. 2v.
Eg 318.81.5	Massey, G. Preface to, with extracts from, A book of the beginnings. London, 1881.
Eg 879.07.5	Massey, Gerald. Ancient Egypt, the light of the world. London, 1907. 2v.
Eg 879.07.10	Pamphlet vol. Massey, Gerald. Lectures. 6 pam.
AH 7709.64.5	Massimino il Trace. (Bellezza, Angela.) Genova, 1964.
AH 7138.76.5	Massol, H. La règle catonienne. Toulouse, 1876. 2 pam.
AH 7168.58.10	Massol, M. De l'obligation naturelle. Paris, 1858.
AH 7279.73.10	Masson, Georgina. Ancient Rome, from Romulus to Augustus. N.Y., 1974.
AH 3207.6	Masson, Vadim M. Strana tysiachi gorodov. Moskva, 1966.
AH 8909.2	Mastarna öder Servius Tullius. (Gardthausen, V.) Leipzig, 1882.
AH 7059.19	The master of the offices in the later Roman and Byzantine empires. (Boak, A.E.R.) N.Y., 1919.
AH 239.10.10	Mastropasqui, O. Assedi e battaglie memorabili dai tempi più remoti al 476. Molfetti, 1910.
AH 3013.30	Materialen zur Kultur...der Chalder...Ausgrabungen. (Lehmann-Haupt, C.F.) Berlin, 1901.
AH 3002.2.19	Materials for a Sumerian lexicon. (Prince, John D.) Leipzig, 1905-08.
AH 7228.71.5	Materielle Grundlage der Exceptio. (Eisele, F.) Berlin, 1871.
Eg 1189.72.5	Mathematics in the time of the pharaohs. (Gillings, Richard J.) Cambridge, 1972.
Eg 1188.77	Ein mathematisches Handbuch der alten Ägypter. (Eisenlohr, August.) Leipzig, 1877. 2v.
AH 4818.80	Mather, R.H. Abstract of lectures upon Greek life. n.p., 188-.
AH 7279.22A	Matheson, P.E. The growth of Rome. London, 1922.
AH 7279.22.5A	Matheson, P.E. The growth of Rome. London, 1925.
AH 7278.84	Matheson, P.E. Skeleton outline of Roman history. London, 1884.
AH 7278.84.10	Matheson, P.E. Skeleton outline of Roman history down A.D. 180. London, 1922.
AH 3960.8.5	Mathews, S. A history of New Testament times in Palestine, 175 B.C.-70 A.D. N.Y., 1914.
AH 3005.830	Matouš, Lubor. Bedřich Hrozný; the life and work of a Czech Oriental scholar. Prague, 1949.
AH 2013.5	Het matriarchaat bij de Oude Arabieren. (Wilken, G.A.) Amsterdam, 1884.
AH 2013.5.7	Das Matriarchat...bei den Alten Arabern. (Wilken, G.A.) Leipzig, 1884.
AH 3408.17	Matter, E.P. Die Bedeutung der Hethiter für das Alti Testament. Diss. Bottrop, 1933.
AH 7138.56.15	Matthiae, C. Controversen Lexikon des römischen Civilrechts. Leipzig, 1856. 3v.
AH 4859.19	Matthies, T. Stellung der griechischen Frau. Zittau, 1893.
AH 7168.88	Matthiass, B. Entwicklung des römischen Schiedgerichts. Rostock, 1888.
AH 7178.82.7	Matthiass, B. Die römische Grundsteuer. Erlangen, 1882.
AH 7516.18.10	Matthieu, P. Aelius Seianus. Rouen, 1642.
AH 7516.18.6	Matthieu, P. Aelius Sejanus. Histoire romaine. Rouen, 1628.
AH 7516.18.4	Matthieu, P. Aelius Sejanus. Histoire romaine. 4. éd. Rouen, 1626.
Htn AH 7516.28*	Matthieu, P. The powerfull favorite...Aelius Seianus. Paris, 1628.
Htn AH 7516.28.2*	Matthieu, P. Unhappy prosperity express'd in History of Aelius Sejanus. 2. ed. London, 1639.
AH 7059.10	Mattingly, H. The imperial civil service of Rome. Cambridge, 1910.
AH 279.14	Mattingly, H. Outlines of ancient history. Cambridge, Eng., 1914.
AH 7819.47A	Mattingly, Harold. The man in the Roman street. N.Y., 1947.
AH 7819.57	Mattingly, Harold. Roman imperial civilization. London, 1957.
AH 4410.10.15	Matz, Friedrich. Kreta, Mykene, Troja. 5. Aufl. Stuttgart, 1962.
AH 4410.10.5	Matz, Friedrich. Le monde egéen. Paris, 1956.
AH 7808.83	Matzat, H. Römische Chronologie. Berlin, 1883. 2v.
AH 7808.89	Matzat, Heinrich. Römische Zeitrechnung für die Jahre 219 bis 1 v. Chr. Berlin, 1880.
AH 7918.87	Maué, H.C. Der Praefectus Fabrum. Halle, 1887.
AH 3917.5	Maundrell, H. Journey from Allepo to Jerusalem. Oxford, 1740.
AH 4847.5	Mauri, A. I cittadini lavoratori. Milano, 1895.
AH 7758.17	Mauso, J.C.F. Leben Constantins des Grossen. Breslau, 1817.
AH 7509.21	Mausoleum und Tatenbericht des Augustus. (Kornemann, Ernst.) Leipzig, 1921.
AH 4278.02	Mavor, W. History of Greece. London, 1802. 2v.
Eg 1129.56F	Les maximes de Ptahhotep. (Ptah-Hetep.) Prague, 1956.
AH 7139.01.6	May, Gaston. Éléments de droit romain. Paris, 1907.
AH 7139.01.5	May, Gaston. Éléments de droit romain. 7e éd. Paris, 1901.
AH 8913.34	Mayani, Zecharia. La fin du mystère étrusque; les origines, la langue et la vie des Étrusques. Paris, 1970.
Eg 1039.55	Mayassis, S. Le livre des morts de l'Égypte ancienne est un livre d'initiation. Athènes, 1955.
Eg 879.57	Mayassis, S. Mystéres et initiations de l'Egypte ancienne. Athènes, 1957.
Eg 1029.38	Mayer, Josephine. Never to die; the Egyptians in their own words. N.Y., 1938.

Author and Title Listing

AH 3017.7.9   Menant, J. Empreintes de cylindres assyro-chaldéens. Paris, 1880.

AH 3013.888   Menant, J. Les fausses antiquités de l'Assyrie et de la Chaldée. Paris, 1888.

AH 3094.5F   Menant, J. Inscriptions...du palais de Khorsabad. Paris, 1865.

AH 3030.4   Menant, J. Inscriptions de Hammourabi. Paris, 1863.

AH 3143.4   Menant, J. Ninive et Babylone. Paris, 1888.

AH 3017.7.15   Menant, J. Notice sur quelques cylindres orientaux. Paris, 1878.

AH 3017.7.5   Menant, J. Notice sur quelques empreintes de cylindres. Paris, 1879.

AH 3030.4.5F   Menant, J. Une novelle inscription de Hammourabi. Paris, 1880.

AH 3017.7.18   Menant, J. Observations sur trois cylindres orientaux. Paris, 1880.

AH 3000.4   Ménant, J. Rapport...sur les inscriptions assyriens. v.1-2. Paris, 1862.

AH 3017.7   Menant, J. Recherches sur la glyphique orientale. Pt.1-2. Paris, 1883. 2v.

AH 4278.86   Ménard, L. Histoire des Grecs. Paris, 1886. 2v.

AH 829.13   Ménard, René J. La Grèce et l'Italie. Paris, 1913.

AH 828.80.4   Ménard, René J. Le travail dans l'antiquité. Paris, 1913? 2v.

AH 3658.6   Menaut, J. Les achemenides et les inscriptions de la Perse. Paris, 1872.

AH 3173.15   Mendelsohn, I. Religions of the ancient Near East. N.Y., 1955.

AH 1189.49A   Mendelsohn, I. Slavery in the ancient Near East. N.Y., 1949.

AH 7458.73   Mendelssohn, L. De senati consulti Romanorum. Lipsiae, 1873.

AH 808.74   Mendelssohn, L. Parallel-Tabellen zur grieschischrömischen Chronologie. Leipzig, 1874.

AH 7108.87   Mendes, José Amando. Droit romain des douanes chez les Romains. v.1-2. Libourne, 1887.

AH 7819.72   Menen, Aubrey. Cities in the sand. N.Y., 1973.

AH 7569.11   Menrad, K. Gestaltung des römischen Staats...Flairer Vespasian. München, 1911.

Htn   Eg 876.69*   Mensa isiaca qua sacrorum. (Pignorio, L.) Amstelodami, 1669.

AH 3016.58   Die menschliche Rundskulptur in der sumero-akkadischen Kunst. (Potratz, J.A.H.) Istanbul, 1960.

AH 7114.24   Menser, C.F. Dissertatio de annua equitum romanorum. Lipsiae, 1734.

AH 7058.94   Mentz, M. De magistratuum romanorum. Ienae, 1894.

Eg 139.70   Menu, Bernadette. Le regime juridique des terres et du personnel attaché à la terre dans le Papyrus Wilbour. Lille, 1970.

AH 4039.22   Menzel, Adolf. Kallikles. Wien, 1922.

NEDL   AH 408.58   Menzies, H. Early ancient history. London, 1858.

AH 4239.35   The mercenaries of the Hellenistic world. (Griffith, G.T.) Cambridge, Eng., 1935.

Eg 879.42   Mercer, S.A.B. Horus, royal god of Egypt. Grafton, 1942.

Eg 603.10.5   Mercer, S.A.B. The Tell el-Amarna tablets. Toronto, 1939. 2v.

Eg 609.23.11   Mercer, S.A.B. Tutankhamen and Egyptology. Milwaukee, 1923.

AH 3149.10   Mercer, Samuel A. Lumero-Babylonian year-formulae. London, 1946.

AH 3155.13   Mercer, Samuel A. Religious and moral ideas in Babylonia and Assyria. Milwaukee, 1919.

AH 2147.3   Merckens, G. De Asia Provincia. Vratislaviae, 1860.

AH 7214.2   Mercklin, D. Die Cooptation der Römer. Mitau, 1848.

Htn   AH 833.3*   Mercuriale, G. Arte gymnastica. Amstelodami, 1672.

Htn   AH 833.1*   Mercuriale, G. Artis gymnasticae. Venetijs, 1569.

Htn   AH 833.6*   Mercuriale, G. De arte gymnastica. Venetiis, 1587.

Htn   AH 833.2*   Mercuriale, G. Hieronymi...de arte gymnastica. Venetijs, 1601.

Htn   AH 833.4*   Mercuriale, G. Hieronymi...de arte gymnastica. 2. ed. Venetiis, 1573.

AH 8514.9   Mérimée, E. De antiquis aquarum religionibus. Parisiis, 1886.

AH 7468.44.2   Mérimée, P. Etudes sur l'histoire romaine. Paris, 1844. 2v.

AH 7468.44.3   Mérimée, P. Etudes sur l'histoire romaine. Paris, 1853.

AH 4109.32   Meritt, B.D. Athenian financial documents of the 5th century. Ann Arbor, 1932.

AH 4109.26   Meritt, B.D. Studies in the Athenian tribute lists. Diss. Princeton, N.J., 1926.

AH 4809.61   Meritt, Benjamin Dean. The Athenian year. Berkeley, Calif., 1961.

AH 7278.75   Merivale, C. General history of Rome. N.Y., 1875.

AH 7468.70   Merivale, Charles. Fall of the Roman Republic. London, 1870.

NEDL   AH 7488.52.7   Merivale, Charles. History of Romans under the Empire. London, 1865-68. 8v.

NEDL   AH 7488.52.2   Merivale, Charles. History of the Romans. London, 1850. 4v.

AH 7488.52A   Merivale, Charles. History of the Romans. 2. ed. London, 1852. 7v.

NEDL   AH 7488.52.5   Merivale, Charles. History of the Romans. 4. London ed. N.Y., 1863. 7v.

AH 7488.52.10.2   Merivale, Charles. History of the Romans under the Empire. London, 1872-74. 8v.

NEDL   AH 7488.52.10   Merivale, Charles. History of the Romans under the Empire. N.Y., 1872-74. 7v.

AH 7488.52.9.3   Merivale, Charles. History of the Romans under the Empire. 4. London ed. N.Y., 1866. 7v.

AH 7488.52.9   Merivale, Charles. History of the Romans under the Empire. 4. London ed. N.Y., 1866. 7v.

NEDL   AH 7478.77.2   Merivale, Charles. Roman triumvirates. London, 1876.

NEDL   AH 7478.77.5   Merivale, Charles. Roman triumvirates. N.Y., 1889.

NEDL   AH 7478.77.6   Merivale, Charles. Roman triumvirates. N.Y., 1893.

AH 7478.77.7   Merivale, Charles. Roman triumvirates. N.Y., 1895.

AH 7478.77.3A   Merivale, Charles. Roman triumvirates. 5. ed. London, 1887.

AH 7138.81.8   Merkel, J. Abhandlungen aus dem Gebiete des römischen Rechts. v.1-3. Halle, 1888. 2v.

AH 7168.77.3   Merkel, J. Konkurs der Abtionen. Halle, 1877.

AH 7168.92.10   Merkel, R. Der römisch-rechtliche Begriff. Strassburg, 1892.

Eg 879.63.10   Merkelbach, Reinhold. Isisfeste in griechisch-römischer Zeit; Daten und Riten. Meisenheim am Glan, 1963.

AH 9722.7   Merle, Heinrich. Die Geschichte der Städte Byzantion und Kalchedon. Inaug. Diss. Kiel, 1916.

Eg 983.5   Meroe; a civilization of the Sudan. (Shinnie, Peter L.) London, 1967.

Eg 758.83   Merriam, A.C. The Obelisk-Crab. N.Y., 1883.

AH 818.90.5   Merrians, A.C. Telegraphing among the ancients. Cambridge, 1890.

AH 8232.5   Merrifield, Ralph. Roman London. N.Y., 1969.

AH 3977.3   Merrill, S. Galilee in the time of Christ. 2. ed. London, 1886.

AH 7709.68   Merten, Elke W. Zwei Herrscherfeste in der Historia Augusta. Thesis. Bonn, 1968.

Eg 279.64   Mertz, Barbara. Temples, tombs, and hieroglyphs. N.Y., 1964.

AH 7844.11   Meslin, Michel. La fete des kalendes de janvier dans l'Empire romain. Bruxelles, 1970.

AH 8058.5   Mesnage, R.J. Romanisation de l'Afrique, Tunisie. Paris, 1913.

AH 3143.18.1   Mesopotamia; the Babylonian and Assyrian civilization. (Delaporte, Louis.) N.Y., 1970.

AH 3013.936   Mesopotamia. (Lloyd, Seton.) London, 1936.

AH 3013.965.5   Mesopotamia. (Margueron, Jean Claude.) London, 1965.

AH 3013.17A   Mesopotamian archaeology. (Handcock, P.S.P.) N.Y., 1912.

AH 3017.40   Mesopotamian art in cylinder seals of the Pierpont Morgan Library. (Pierpont Morgan Library, New York.) N.Y., 1947.

AH 3012.9A   Mesopotamian origins. (Speiser, Ephraim A.) Philadelphia, 1930.

AH 3012.9.1   Mesopotamian origins. Philadelphia, 1930. (Speiser, Ephraim A.) Ann Arbor, 1973.

Eg 879.70.5   Le message spirituel de l'Égypte ancienne. (Guilmot, Max.) Paris, 1970.

AH 5910.5   Messenien und der achäische Bund. (Seeliger, K.) Zittau, 1897.

AH 5909.59   Messenische Studien. (Kiechle, Franz.) Kallmünz, 1959.

AH 3181.6   Messerschmidt, L. Tabula Babylonica V.A. Th 246 Musei Berolinensis. Kirchain, 1896.

AH 4819.59   Messinesi, X.L. Meet the ancient Greeks. Caldwell, 1959.

AH 4039.49   Metabolē politeiōn. (Ryffel, Heinrich.) Bern, 1949.

AH 909.50   Metallurgy in antiquity. (Forbes, R.) Leiden, 1950.

Eg 862.1   Les métaux dans les inscriptions égyptiennes. (Lepsius, C.R.) Paris, 1877.

AH 4189.59   Metaxy eleutherōn kai doulōn. (Lotze, D.) Berlin, 1959.

AH 889.28   Metrologia e circolazione monetaria degli antichi. (Segrè, Angelo.) Bologna, 1928.

AH 928.62   Metrologie. (Hultsch, F.) Berlin, 1862.

AH 928.62.3   Metrologie. (Hultsch, F.) Berlin, 1882.

AH 928.38   Metrologische Untersuchungen über Gewichte, Münzfüsse und Masse. (Böckh, August.) Berlin, 1838.

AH 5333.5   Metroon in Athen. (Curtius, Carl.) Berlin, 1868.

AH 4518.58   Metropulos, C. Schacht bei Mantinea. Göttingen, 1858.

AH 2107.10   Metzger, Henri. Anatolia II. London, 1969.

AH 4169.14   Meurs, Johann van. Rechtsgedingen over Bepaalde Goederen. Amsterdam, 1914.

AH 4136.85.5   Meurs, Johannes van. Ioannis Meursii Themis Attica, sive De legibus Atticii libri II. Rhenum, 1685.

AH 4136.85   Meurs, Johannes van. Themis Attica. Rhenum, 1685. 4 pam.

AH 4136.84   Meurs, Johannes van. Theseus. n.p., 1684. 3 pam.

AH 4056.22   Meursius, J. Archontes athenienses. Lugdunum Batavorum, 1622.

AH 5457.5   Meursius, J. Creta, Cyprus, Rhodus. Amstelodami, 1675.

AH 4117.5   Meursius, J. Populis atticae. Lugdunum Batavorum, 1616.

AH 4819.41.5   Mewaldt, J. Hellenische Weltanschauung. Wien, 1941.

Htn   AH 7485.61F*   Mexia, Pedro. Historia imperial y Cesarea. Anvers, 1561.

AH 278.84.7   Meyer, E. Die ältere Chronologie Babyloniens, Assyriens und Ägyptens. Stuttgart, 1925.

AH 278.84.7.2   Meyer, E. Die ältere Chronologie Babyloniens. Stuttgart, 1931.

AH 4298.92.7   Meyer, E. Forschungen zur alten Geschichte. Halle, 1892. 2v.

AH 278.84.3   Meyer, E. Geschichte des Alterthums. Stuttgart, 1884. 5v.

AH 278.84.5   Meyer, E. Geschichte des Alterthums. v.1-5. Stuttgart, 1907-31. 7v.

AH 278.84.10   Meyer, E. Geschichte des Altertums. 5. Aufl. v.1,3,4. Stuttgart, 1925-26. 4v.

AH 2907.2   Meyer, E. Geschichte des Königreichs Pontos. Leipzig, 1879.

AH 2957.7   Meyer, E. Geschichte von Troas. Leipzig, 1877.

AH 279.12.5   Meyer, E. Histoire de l'antiquité. Paris, 1912.

AH 3958.10   Meyer, E. Die Israeliten und ihre Nachbarstämme. Halle, 1906.

AH 299.10   Meyer, E. Kleine Schriften. Halle, 1910.

AH 299.10.2   Meyer, E. Kleine Schriften. v.1, 2. Aufl. Halle, 1924. 2v.

Eg 878.75   Meyer, E. Set-Typhon. Leipzig, 1875.

AH 888.95.3   Meyer, E. Die wirtschaftliche Entwickelung. Jena, 1895.

AH 7479.18.2   Meyer, Eduard. Caesars Monarchie und das Principat des Pompejus. 2. Aufl. Stuttgart, 1919.

AH 7479.18.3   Meyer, Eduard. Caesars Monarchie und das Principat des Pompejus. 3. Aufl. Stuttgart, 1963.

AH 7509.03.3   Meyer, Eduard. Kaiser Augustus. Heidelberg, 1903.

AH 39.68   Meyer, Ernst. Einführung in die antike Staatskunde. Darmstadt, 1968.

AH 2108.7   Meyer, Ernst. Die Grenzen der hellenistischen Staaten in Kleinasien. Zürich, 1925.

AH 7039.48   Meyer, Ernst. Römischer Staat und Staatsgedanke. Zurich, 1948.

AH 809.42   Meyer, Frank H. The crux of chronology; an essay to establish the life-time of Jesus Christ and...date of Easter. Boston, 1942.

AH 188.98   Meyer, G. Die Sklaverei im Altertum. Dresden, 1898.

AH 7449.08   Meyer, P. Der Ausbruch des ersten punischen Krieges. Berlin, 1908.

AH 8.85   Meyer, P. Premières compilations françaises d'histoire ancienne. Paris, 1885.

AH 7708.91   Meyer, Paul. De Maecenatis oratione a Dione ficta. Inaug. Diss. Berolini, 1891.

AH 7161.2   Meyer, Paul. Der römische Konkubinat. Leipzig, 1895.

Eg 709.00.5   Meyer, Paul M. Das Heerwesen der Ptolemäer und Römer in Ägypten. Leipzig, 1900.

AH 7169.32   Meyer-Collings, J.J. Deretictio. Inaug. Diss. Kallmünz, 1932.

AH 2583.9   Mezger, Fridericus. Inscriptio milesiaca de pace cum magnetibus facta. Inaug. Diss. Monaci, 1913.

AH 4819.50A   Miami, Florida. University. Lectures of evaluations of the enduring qualities of Greek civilization. Miami, Fla., 1950.

AH 7408.21.6F   Micali, G. Antichi monumenti per servire all'opera intitolata l'Italia. Firenze, 1821.

AH 8607.8   Micali, G. L'Italia avanti il dominio dei romani. 3. ed. Milano, 1826. 3v.

Author and Title Listing

	AH 7408.21.5	Micali, G. L'Italia avanti il Domino dei Romani. 2. ed. v.1-2, 3-4. Firenze, 1821. 2v.
	AH 7204.15	Michaelis, H. Kritische Nürdigung der Kriese. Köln, 1895.
	AH 3959.31	Michaelis, J.D. Commentationes societati regiae scientiarum Goettingensi per armas 1758-62. Bremae, 1763.
	AH 3959.31.5	Michaelis, J.D. Commentationes societati regiae scientiarum Goettingensi per armas 1758-62. Bremae, 1769.
	AH 7819.70	Michaux, Maurice. L'antiquité, Rome et les debuts du Moyen Âge. 6. éd. Paris, 1970.
	AH 7039.69	Michel, Alain. La philosophie politique à Rome d'Auguste à Marc Aurèle. Paris, 1969.
	AH 4559.67	Michel, Dorothea. Alexander als Vorbild für Pompeius. Brussel, 1967.
	AH 7148.85	Michel, N.H. Du droit de cité romaine. Paris, 1885.
	AH 7278.33	Michelet, J. Histoire romaine. 2. ed. Paris, 1833. 2v.
	AH 7278.33.3	Michelet, J. Histoire romaine. 3. ed. Paris, 1843. 2v.
	AH 7278.33.5	Michelet, J. History of the Roman Republic. London, 1847.
	AH 7278.33.6	Michelet, J. History of the Roman Republic. N.Y., 1847.
	AH 7278.33.15	Michelet, J. History of the Roman Republic. N.Y., 1859.
NEDL	AH 4524.9	Micheli, Horace. Révolution oligarchique des quatre-cents. Genève, 1893.
	AH 3909.9	Michelini, T.F. La Siria nell'eta di Mari. Roma, 1960.
	AH 4889.40	Michell, Humfrey. The economics of ancient Greece. Cambridge, 1940.
	AH 4889.40.2	Michell, Humfrey. The economics of ancient Greece. 2. ed. Cambridge, 1957.
	AH 5763.5A	Michell, Humfrey. Sparta. Cambridge, Eng., 1952.
	AH 5763.6	Michell, Humfrey. Sparta. Cambridge, Eng., 1964.
	AH 7809.67	Michels, Agnes Kirsopp. The calendar of the Roman republic. Princeton, 1967.
	AH 7898.59	Michon, L.A.J. Des céréales en Italie sous les Romains. Paris, 1859.
	AH 1879.63	Middle Eastern mythology. (Hooke, S.H.) Harmondsworth, 1963.
	AH 8233.5	Middlesex in British, Roman and Saxon times. (Sharpe, Montagu.) London, 1919.
	AH 7207.5	Middleton, Conyers. A treatise on the Roman senate. London, 1747.
	AH 4838.88	Mie, F. Quaestiones Agonisticae. Rostochii, 1888.
	AH 7089.26	Mierow, Herbert E. The roman provincial governor as he appears in the Digest and Code of Justinian. Colorado Springs, 1926.
	AH 4139.49	Might and right in antiquity. (Frisch, Hortvig.) København, 1949.
	AH 5708.5	La migration grecque en Ionie. (Sakellariou, M.B.) Athènes, 1958.
	AH 3757.22	Migration in the Mycenaean Age. (Elderkin, George.) n.p., 1963.
	AH 5453.7A	Mijnsbrugge, M. van der. The Cretan koinon. N.Y., 1931.
	AH 9707.14	Mikhailov, Georgei I. Trakite. Sofiia, 1972.
	AH 5460.10	Mikrogiannakes, E.I. Hē Krētē kara toys Ellēnistikoys chronoys. Thesis. Athēnai, 1967.
	AHP 23.12	Milan. Universita Cattolica del Sacro Cuore. Istituto di Filologia Classica. Sezione di Storia Antica. Contributi. Milano. 1,1963+
	AH 6157.9	Die milesischen Kolonien im Skythenlande his zum III. nachchristliche Jahrhundert. (Klym, P.) Czernowitz, 1914.
	AH 2583.10	Milet. (Kobylina, Mariia M.) Moskva, 1965.
	AH 7628.97	Die Militärreorganisation Hadrians. (Schurz, Wilhelm.) Leipzig, 1897.
	AH 4231.1	Pamphlet box. Military affairs. German Dissertations.
	AH 4409.15	The military annals of Greece from the earliest times to the beginning of the Pelopormesian War. (Snyder, William L.) Boston, 1915. 2v.
	AH 3933.2	The military establishments at Mari. (Sasson, Jack Murad.) Rome, 1969.
	AH 4239.70	Military theory and practice in the age of Xenophon. (Anderson, John Kinloch.) Berkeley, 1970.
	AH 7489.66.1	Millar, Fergus. The Roman Empire and its neighbours. London, 1967.
	AH 4819.72.5	Miller, Helen (Hill). Greece through the ages. N.Y., 1972.
	AH 7979.16F	Miller, Konrad. Itineraria romana. Stuttgart, 1916.
	AH 855.5	Miller, Max. Jagdwesen der alten Griechen und Römer. München, 1883.
	AH 4809.70	Miller, Molly. The Sicilian colony dates. Albany, 1970.
	AH 4809.71	Miller, Molly. The Thalassocracies; studies in chronography. Albany, 1971.
Htn	AH 278.00*	Millot, C.F.X. Elements of ancient history. N.Y., 18- .
NEDL	AH 279.23.10	Mills, Dorothy. The book of the ancient world for younger readers. N.Y., 1923.
NEDL	AH 279.23.15	Mills, Dorothy. The book of the ancient world for younger readers. N.Y., 1923.
	Eg 848.6	Milne, J.G. Relics of Graeco-Egyptian schools. n.p., 1908.
	Eg 278.94.19	Milne, Joseph G. A history of Egypt under Roman rule. 3. ed. London, 1924.
	AH 7653.16	Milner, Joseph. Gibbon's account of Christianity. York, 1781.
	AH 4559.68	Milns, R.D. Alexander the Great. London, 1968.
	AH 4486.5	Miltiades-Forschungen. (Kinzl, Kourad.) Wien, 1968.
	Eg 1307.85F	Mingarelli, Giovanni L. Aegyptiorum codicum reliquae. Bononiae, 1785.
	Eg 1307.85.2F	Mingarelli, Giovanni L. Aegyptiorum codicum reliquae. Bononiae, 1785.
	AH 4839.35	The Minoan-Mycenaean background of Greek athletics. Diss. (Ridington, William R.) Philadelphia, 1935.
	AH 5463.25	The Minoans. (Hood, Sinclair.) N.Y., 1971.
	AH 5463.30	Minoans in Greek sources. (Huxley, George Leonard.) Belfast, 1968.
	AH 5757.47	Le miracle grec. (Bruwaene, M.) Bruxelles, 1947.
	AH 5757.11.5	Le mirage spartiate. (Ollier, F.) Paris, 1943.
	AH 5757.11	Le mirage spartiate. Thèse. (Ollier, F.) Paris, 1933.
	AH 4819.54.12	Mireaux, Émile. Daily life in the time of Homer. London, 1959.
	AH 4819.54.10	Mireaux, Émile. La vie quotidienne du temps d'Homère. Paris, 1954.
	AH 3657.39	Mirkhoud. History of the early kings of Persia. London, 1832.
	AH 8358.5	Mirković, Miroslava. Rimski gradovi no Dunavu u Gornjoi Meziji. Thesis. Beograd, 1968.
	AH 7278.10F	Mirys, S.D. Histoire de la république romaine. Paris, 1810.
	AH 136.45	Miscellae defensiones pro Cl. Salmasio. Lugduni Batavorum, 1645.
	AH 7818.91	Miscellanea archeologica. (Lovatelli, E.C. (Contessa).) Roma, 1891.
Htn	AH 816.85F*	Miscellanea eruditae antiquitatis. (Spon, J.) Lugduni, 1685.
	AH 3073.4	Miscellaneous Assyrian texts on the British Museum. (Smith, S.A.) Leipzig, 1887.
	AH 15.6	Pamphlet vol. Miscellany on archaeology. Frankfurt, 1817. 8 pam.
	AH 8608.11	Miscosi, G. Origini italiche; testimonianze storiche sull'esistenza di Roma e Genova prerumulee. Genova, 1934.
	AH 279.41.5	Mishuls'a, A.V. Istoriia drevnego mira. Izd. 5. Moskva, 1946.
	AH 8608.9	Misiano, D.B. I popoli preistorici dell'Italia. Bova Marina, 1930.
	AH 7038.87	Misporelet, J.B. Études d'institutions romaines. Paris, 1887.
	AH 7038.82.2	Mispoulet, J.B. Les institutions politiques. Paris, 1882. 2v.
	AH 7138.89.15	Mispoulet, J.B. Manuel des textes de droit romain. Paris, 1889.
	AH 7068.99	Mispoulet, J.B. La vie parlementaire a Rome. Paris, 1899.
	AH 7409.38	Il mistero delle origini di Roma. (Colonna di Cesaro, G.A.) Milano, 1938.
	AH 3179.10.8	Mite babilonesi e assiri. (Furlani, Giuseppe.) Firenze, 1958.
NEDL	AH 4277.95.5.5	Mitford, W. History of Greece. Boston, 1823. 8v.
	AH 4277.95.5	Mitford, W. History of Greece. Boston, 1823. 8v.
	AH 4277.95	Mitford, W. History of Greece. London, 1795. 10v.
	AH 4277.95.3	Mitford, W. History of Greece. London, 1814. 8v.
NEDL	AH 4277.95.4	Mitford, W. History of Greece. v.9-10, 3. ed. London, 1821-22. 10v.
NEDL	AH 4277.95.6	Mitford, W. The history of Greece from the earliest period to the death of Agesilaus. London, 1835. 8v.
	AH 4277.95.7	Mitford, W. History of Greece with final additions and corrections. London, 1838. 8v.
	AH 7468.29.5	Mithradates Eupator. (Reinach, T.) Leipzig, 1895.
X Cg	AH 7468.29.3	Mithradates Eupator. (Reinach, T.) Paris, 1890.
	Eg 879.61	I miti e i luoghi dell'antico Egitto. (Rachewiltz, Boris de.) Milano, 1961.
	AH 7509.53	Il mito di Alessandro e la Roma d'Augusto. (Treves, Piero.) Milano, 1953.
	AH 3914.7.5	Il mito di Shre Slm. Saggio sulla mitologia ugaritica. (Xella, Paolo.) Roma, 1973.
	AH 3156.8	Mitologia babilonese-assira. (Bassi, D.) Milano, 1899.
	AH 3155.29	Mitologia sumerico-accadica. (Castellino, Giorgio R.) Torino, 1967.
	AH 863.15	Mitos, ritos y costumbres sexuales en las sociedades antiguas. (Reynes-Lyons, P.) Buenos Aires, 1964.
	AH 7138.91.3	Mitteis, L. Reichsrecht und Volksrecht. Leipzig, 1891.
	AH 7169.08	Mitteis, L. Römisches Privatrecht. Leipzig, 1908.
	AH 3160.23	Mity i legendy drevnego Dvurech'ia. (Reder, Dimitrii G.) Moskva, 1965.
	AH 7449.70.10	Mix, Erving R. Marcus Atilius Regulus; exemplum historicum. The Hague, 1970.
	EgP 89.5F	Mizraim. N.Y. 1-3,1933-1936
	AH 3983.5	The Moabites. (Zwl, A.D. van.) Leiden, 1960.
	AH 8458.6	Mócsy, András. Die Bevolkerung von Pannonien bis zu den Markommenkriegen. Budapest, 1959.
	AH 8357.2	Mócsy, András. Gesellschaft und Romanisation in der römischen Provinz Moesia Superior. Amsterdam, 1970.
	Eg 829.55	Models of daily life in ancient Egypt. (Winlock, H.E.) Cambridge, Mass., 1955.
	AH 5315.40A	Modern problems in the ancient world. (Marsh, T.B.) Austin, 1943.
	AH 4819.27A	Modern traits in old Greek life. (Gulick, Charles B.) N.Y., 1927.
	AH 8609.5	Modestov, V.I. Introduction à l'histoire romaine. Paris, 1907.
	AH 8609.4	Modestov, V.I. Vvednie v rimskuiu. Sankt Peterburg, 1902-04. 2v.
	AH 7408.71	Modestow, B. Der Gebrauch der Schrift unter den römischen Königen. Berlin, 1871.
	AH 3668.5	Modi, J.J. Education among the ancient Iranians. Bombay, 1905.
	AH 3663.5	Modi, J.J. Wine among the ancient Persians. Bombay, 1888.
	Eg 39.16	Modica, Marco. Contribute papirologici. Roma, 1916.
	AH 4819.67.20	Moebius, Hans. Studia varia. Auftsätze zur Kunst und Kultur der Antike mit Nachträgen. Wiesbaden, 1967.
	Eg 847.4.10	Möller, G. Hieratische Lesestücke für den akademischen Gebrauch. v.1-3. Berlin, 1961.
	Eg 847.4F	Möller, G. Hieratische Paläographie. Leipzig, 1909-12. 3v.
	Eg 847.4.5F	Möller, G. Hieratische Paläographie. Ergänzungsheft zu Bd. 1-2. Leipzig, 1936.
	AH 4842.50	Möller. De eruditione Graecorum. v.1-2. Weimar, 1863.
	AH 4843.22	Moens, P.W. De twee delphische hymnen. Purmerend, 1930.
	AH 3910.9.5	Mørkholm, Otto. Antiochus IV of Syria. Thesis. København, 1966.
	AH 8513.9	Moeurs et institutions romaines. (Camau, E.) Paris, 1905.
	AH 7818.99	Moeurs romaines. (Thomas, Paul.) Bruxelles, 1899.
NEDL	AH 7818.65.19A	Moeurs romaines du règne d'Auguste. (Friedlaender, Ludwig.) Paris, 1865. 4v.
	AH 7479.00	Moineville, L. Deux campagnes de César. Paris, 1900.
	AH 7114.28	Moinier, Gilbert. Les pérégrins déditices dans les premiers siècles de la Republique et sous le Haut-Empire. Thèse. Paris, 1930.
	AH 3002.4.5	Moldenke, A.B. Babylonian contract tablets in the Metropolitan Museum of Art. N.Y., 1893.
	AH 7138.74.3	Molitor, J.P. Obligations en droit romain. Paris, 1874. 3v.
	AH 7539.32.5	Momigliano, A. Claudius, the emperor. Oxford, 1934.
	AH 6110.19	Momigliano, A. Filippo il Macedone. Firenze, 1934.
	AH 7539.32	Momigliano, A. L'opera dell'imperatore Claudio. Firenze, 1932.
	AH 7309.38.5	Momigliano, Arnaldo. La formazione della moderna storiografia sull'impiro romano. Torino, 1938.
	AH 4808.83	Mommsen, A. Chronologie. Leipzig, 1883.
	AH 7844.5.5F	Mommsen, T. I commentarii dei ludi secolari. Roma, 1891.
	AH 7844.5F	Mommsen, T. Commentarium ludorum. Milano, 1891.
	AH 7058.46	Mommsen, T. De apparitoribus magistratum romanorum. Romae, 1846.
	AH 7818.43	Mommsen, T. De Collegiis et Sodaliciis Romanorum. Kiliae, 1843. 3 pam.
	AH 7201.69	Mommsen, T. Fragmenta Vaticana III. Berolini, 1890.
	AH 7278.54.30	Mommsen, T. Histoire romaine. v.1-2, 3-4, 5-6, 7. Paris, 1882. 4v.
	AH 7278.54.29	Mommsen, T. Histoire romaine. v.1-8. Paris, 1863. 4v.
	AH 7278.54.31	Mommsen, T. Historia de Roma. Madrid, 1877.

Author and Title Listing

AH 7278.54.12 Mommsen, T. History of Rome. London, 1868. 4v.
AH 7478.54A Mommsen, T. History of Rome. London, 1886. 2v.
AH 7278.54.28.10 Mommsen, T. The history of Rome. London, 1908-12. 5v.
AH 7278.54.27 Mommsen, T. The history of Rome. London, 1920.
AH 7278.54.16 Mommsen, T. History of Rome. N.Y., 1868. 4v.
NEDL AH 7278.54.15 Mommsen, T. History of Rome. N.Y., 1869-70. 4v.
AH 7278.54.16.5 Mommsen, T. History of Rome. N.Y., 1871. 4v.
NEDL AH 7278.54.17 Mommsen, T. History of Rome. N.Y., 1873. 2v.
AH 7278.54.18 Mommsen, T. History of Rome. N.Y., 1885. 4v.
AH 7278.54.18.15 Mommsen, T. History of Rome. N.Y., 1894. 4v.
AH 7278.54.19 Mommsen, T. History of Rome. N.Y., 1895. 5v.
AH 7478.54.2 Mommsen, T. History of Rome. N.Y., 1899. 2v.
AH 7278.54.21 Mommsen, T. History of Rome. N.Y., 1900. 5v.
AH 7278.54.24 Mommsen, T. The history of Rome. N.Y., 1908. 5v.
AH 7278.54.28 Mommsen, T. The history of Rome. N.Y., 1958.
NEDL AH 7278.54.18.9 Mommsen, T. History of Rome. Provinces of the Roman Empire from Caesar to Diocletian. N.Y., 1887. 2v.
AH 7278.54.11.2 Mommsen, T. History of Rome. 2. ed. v.1-3; v.4, pt.1-2. London, 1864-67. 5v.
AH 7418.89 Mommsen, T. The history of the Roman republic. N.Y., 1889.
AH 7278.54.13 Mommsen, T. Index to History of Rome. London, 1870.
AH 7278.54.5 Mommsen, T. Inhalts-Verzeichniss. Römische Geschichte. n.p., n.d.
AH 7478.57 Mommsen, T. Die Rechtsfrage zwischen Caesar und dem Senat. Breslau, 1857.
AH 7818.63 Mommsen, T. Römische Forschungen. Berlin, 1864-79. 2v.
AH 7818.63.3 Mommsen, T. Römische Forschungen. v.1, 2. Aufl.; v.2, 1. Aufl. Berlin, 1864. 2v.
AH 7278.54.30.10 Mommsen, T. Römische Geschichte. Wien, 1932.
AH 7278.54.30.12 Mommsen, T. Römische Geschichte. Wien, 1934.
AH 7278.54.30.15 Mommsen, T. Römische Geschichte. Wien, 1954.
AH 7278.54.10.15 Mommsen, T. Römische Geschichte. v.1-3, 5. Berlin, 1933. 4v.
Htn AH 7278.54* Mommsen, T. Römische Geschichte. v.1-3, 5. Leipzig, 1954. 4v.
AH 7278.54.9.5 Mommsen, T. Römische Geschichte. v.1-3, 7. Aufl. v.5, 3. Aufl. Berlin, 1881-86. 4v.
AH 7278.54.10 Mommsen, T. Römische Geschichte. v.5. Berlin, 1885.
AH 7278.54.3 Mommsen, T. Römische Geschichte. 2. Aufl. Berlin, 1856. 3v.
AH 7278.54.6 Mommsen, T. Römische Geschichte. 3. Aufl. Berlin, 1861. 3v.
AH 7278.54.4 Mommsen, T. Römische Geschichte. 4. Aufl. Berlin, 1865. 4v.
AH 7278.54.7 Mommsen, T. Römische Geschichte. 5. Aufl. v.1, pt.1-2; v.2-3. Berlin, 1868. 4v.
NEDL AH 7278.54.9 Mommsen, T. Römische Geschichte. 6. Aufl. Berlin, 1874. 3v.
AH 7115.2 Mommsen, T. Die römischen Tribus. Altona, 1844.
AH 7278.54.23 Mommsen, T. Rome. v.3. Philadelphia, 1906.
AH 9654.5 Mommsen, T. Die Stadtrechte der latinischen Gemeinden Salkensa und Malaca. Leipzig, 1855.
AH 7278.54.32.5 Mommsen, T. Storia di Roma antica. Torino, 1943. 3v.
AH 7278.54.32 Mommsen, T. Storia romana. Torino, 1857-63. 3v.
AH 7278.54.30.5A Mommsen, T. Das Weltreich der Caesaren. Wien, 1933.
AH 159.05 Mommsen, T. Zum ältesten Strafrecht der Kulturvölker. Leipzig, 1905.
AH 7149.07 Mommsen, Theodor. Abriss des römischen Staatsrechts. Leipzig, 1907.
AH 7148.43.5 Mommsen, Theodor. Ad legem de scribis et viatoribus et de anectoritate commentationes. Kiliae, 1843.
AH 7918.43 Mommsen, Theodor. De Collegiis et sodalicis Romanorum. Kiliae, 1843.
AH 8609.3 Mommsen, Theodor. Earliest inhabitants of Italy. London, 1858.
AH 7908.51 Mommsen, Theodor. Das Edict Diocletians de Pretiis Rerum Venalium. Leipzig, 1851.
AH 7168.59 Mommsen, Theodor. Erörterungen aus dem Obligationenrecht. v.1-2. Braunschweig, 1859.
AH 7299.05 Mommsen, Theodor. Gesammelte Schriften. Berlin, 1905. 8v.
AH 7298.86.2 Mommsen, Theodor. The provinces of the Roman empire, from Caesar to Diocletian. N.Y., 1899. 2v.
AH 7298.86.5 Mommsen, Theodor. The provinces of the Roman Empire; the European provinces. Chicago, 1968.
AH 7298.86.3 Mommsen, Theodor. The provinces of the Roman empire from Caesar to Diocletian. London, 1909. 2v.
AH 7299.05.4 Mommsen, Theodor. Reden und Aufsätze. Berlin, 1905.
AH 7299.05.7 Mommsen, Theodor. Reden und Aufsätze. Berlin, 1912.
AH 7299.05.5 Mommsen, Theodor. Reden und Aufsätze. 2. Aufl. Berlin, 1905.
AH 7808.58.3 Mommsen, Theodor. Römische Chronologie bis auf Caesar. 2. Aufl. Berlin, 1859.
AH 7158.99 Mommsen, Theodor. Römisches Strafrecht. Leipzig, 1899.
AH 7748.61 Mommsen, Theodor. Uber die Zeitfolge der Verordnungen Diocletians. Berlin, 1861.
AH 7278.54.35 Mommsen's Darstellung der römische Herrschaft. (Nöldeke, T.) Leipzig, 1885.
AH 7279.20.7 Monaci, Ernesto. Storie de Troja et de Roma altrimenti dette Liber ystoriarum Romanorum. Roma, 1920.
AH 6103.7 Il monarcato ellenistico nei suoi elementi federativi. (Zancan, P.) Padova, 1934.
AH 7709.39 La monarchia militare di Gallieno. (Regibus, L.) Recco, 1939.
AH 459.33 Le monarchie ellenistiche e la repubblica romana. (Beloch, Julius.) Bari, 1933.
AH 2147.6 Monceaux, P. Communi asiae provinciae. Paris, 1885.
AH 4212.6 Monceaux, P. Les proxénies grecques. Paris, 1885.
AH 4819.10 Monceaux, Paul. La Grèce avant Alexandre. Paris, 1892.
AH 459.61 Le monde a la mort de Socrate. (Mourre, Michel.) Paris, 1961.
AH 8057.5 Le monde de Carthage. (Charles-Picard, Gilbert.) Paris, 1956.
AH 4410.10.5 Le monde egéen. (Matz, Friedrich.) Paris, 1956.
AH 5107.5 Le monde égéen avant les Grècs. (Waltz, Pierre.) Paris, 1934.
AH 4459.58 Le monde grec aux temps classiques. (Cloché, Paul.) Paris, 1958.
AH 4545.5 Le monde grec aux temps de Philippe II de Macédoine et d'Alexandre le Grand (359-323 avant J.-C.). (Aymard, André.) Paris, 1964.
AH 7489.27 Le monde romain. (Chapot, Victor.) Paris, 1927.
AH 4819.43 Mondolfo, Rodolfo. El genio helénico y las caracteres de sus creaciones espirituales. Tucuman, 1943.

AH 4278.57 Mone, F. Kritische Bemerkung von Ernest Curtius. Berlin, 1858.
AH 8548.115 Mone, F.J. Celtische Forschungen zur Geschichte Mitteleuropas. Freiburg, 1857.
AH 139.56 Monier, Raymond. Histoire des institutions et des faits sociaux des origines à l'aube du Moyen Âge. Paris, 1955.
Eg 971.15 Monneret de Villard, Ugo. Aksum. Roma, 1938.
Eg 971.11F Monneret de Villard, Ugo. La Necropoli musulmana di Aswán. Le Caire, 1930.
AH 7008.79.3 Monografia della citta di Roma. (Bonghi, R.) Roma, 1881.
AH 8608.8F Monografia storica dei porti dell'antichità nell'Italia insulare. (Italy. Ministero della marina.) Roma, 1906.
AH 8514.10 Monographie du dieu Leherenn d'Ardiége. (Barry, A.E.) Paris, 1859.
AH 842.25 Monroe, Paul. Source book of the history of education. N.Y., 1901.
AH 842.25.5 Monroe, Paul. Source book of the history of education for the Greek and Roman period. N.Y., 1906.
AH 8548.7 Le Mont-Glonne; ou Recherches historiques sur l'origine des Celtes. (Robin, Claude C.) Paris, 1774. 2v.
AH 7158.83 Montagnon, E. Essai sur la nature des condamnations civiles. Lyon, 1883.
AH 307.59 Montagu, E.W. Reflections on the rise and fall of the ancient republic. London, 1759.
AH 307.60 Montagu, E.W. Reflections on the rise and fall of the ancient republic. London, 1759.
AH 7449.01 Montanari, T. Annibale. Rovigo, 1900-01.
AH 7448.18.12 Montanari, T. Punto per Punto. Mantova, 1903.
AH 279.36 Monteath, K.M. The antiquity of mankind and the modernity of religions. 3. ed. York, 1936.
AH 3661.15.5 La montée des Sassanides et l'heure de Palmyre. (Gagé, Jean.) Paris, 1964.
AH 7707.66 Montégut, J.F. Essai historique sur la famille de l'Empereur Valérien. n.p., 1766. 2 pam.
AH 7307.34.31 Montesquieu, Charles de. Betrachtungen über die Ursachen von Grösse und Niedergang der Römer. Bremen, 1962.
AH 7307.34.19 Montesquieu, Charles de. Considerations on the causes of the grandeur of the Romans. N.Y., 1882.
AH 7307.34.18 Montesquieu, Charles de. Considérations sur les causes de la grandeur des Romains, et de leur décadence. Paris, 1771.
Htn AH 7307.34* Montesquieu, Charles de. Considérations sur les causes de la grandeur des Romains. 2. éd. Amsterdam, 1734.
Htn AH 7307.34.3* Montesquieu, Charles de. Considérations sur les causes de la grandeur des Romains. 2. éd. Amsterdam, 1935.
AH 7307.34.5 Montesquieu, Charles de. Considérations sur les causes de la grandeur des Romains. Amsterdam, 1759.
AH 7307.34.7 Montesquieu, Charles de. Considérations sur les causes de la grandeur des Romains. Amsterdam, 1761.
AH 7307.34.12 Montesquieu, Charles de. Considérations sur les causes de la grandeur des Romains. Paris, 1876.
AH 7307.34.11 Montesquieu, Charles de. Considérations sur les causes de la grandeur des Romains. Paris, 1876.
AH 7307.34.13 Montesquieu, Charles de. Considérations sur les causes de la grandeur des Romains. Paris, 1887.
AH 7307.34.14 Montesquieu, Charles de. Considérations sur les causes de la grandeur des Romains. Paris, 1894.
AH 7307.34.15 Montesquieu, Charles de. Considérations sur les causes de la grandeur des Romains. Paris, 1896.
AH 7307.34.30 Montesquieu, Charles de. Considérations sur les causes de la grandeur des Romains. Paris, 1945.
AH 7307.34.9 Montesquieu, Charles de. De la grandeur des Romains. Paris, 1870.
AH 7307.34.12.5 Montesquieu, Charles de. De la grandeur des Romains. Paris, 1879.
AH 7307.34.17 Montesquieu, Charles de. Reflections on the causes of the rise and fall of the Romans. London, 1752.
AH 7037.34.30 Montesquieu, Charles L. Consideratione on the causes of the greatness of the Romans. N.Y., 1965.
Eg 559.41 Montet, Pierre. Le drame d'Avaris; essai sur la pénétration des Sémites en Égypte. Paris, 1941.
Eg 609.59.5 Montet, Pierre. L'Égypte et la Bible. Neuchâtel, 1959.
Eg 819.64.5 Montet, Pierre. Eternal Egypt. N.Y., 1969.
Eg 829.46.5 Montet, Pierre. Everyday life in Egypt in the days of Ramesses the Great. N.Y., 1958.
Eg 939.57 Montet, Pierre. Géographie de l'Égypte ancienne. pt.1-2. Paris, 1957. 2v.
Eg 829.25 Montet, Pierre. Les scènes de la vie privée dans les tombeaux égyptiens de l'ancien empire. Londres, 1925.
Eg 829.25.5 Montet, Pierre. Les scènes de la vie privée dans les tombeaux égyptiens de l'ancien empire. Thèse. Strasbourg, 1925.
Eg 829.46 Montet, Pierre. La vie quotidienne en Égypt au temps des Ramsès (XIII-XII siècles avant J.C.). Paris, 1946.
AH 2008.14 Montgomery, James Alan. Arabia and the Bible. N.Y., 1969.
AH 7489.70 Montherlant, Henry de. Le treizieme César. Paris, 1970.
AH 8879.5 Monti, Pietro. Ischia preistorica, greca, romana, paleocristiana. Napoli, 1968.
Htn AH 7497.85.5* Monumens de la vie privée des douze Césars. (Hancarville, Pierre François Hugues.) Rome, 1786.
Htn AH 7497.85* Monumens de la vie privée des douze Césars. pt.1-2. (Hancarville, Pierre François Hugues.) Rome, 1785. 2v.
Htn AH 7497.84* Monumens du culte secret des dames romaines. (Hancarville, Pierre François Hugues.) Nancy, 1784.
Htn AH 7497.84.5* Monumens du culte secret des dames romaines. (Hancarville, Pierre François Hugues.) Rome, 1790.
AH 3013.35PF Monument de Ninive. Text and plates. (Botta, P.E.) Paris, 1849-50. 5v.
AH 8548.65 Monumenta historica celtica. (Dinan, W.) London, 1911.
Eg 1308.91 Monumenta papyracea. (Marucchi, Orazio.) Romae, 1891.
Htn AH 5958.10* Monumenta Peloponnesia. (Pasiaudi, P.M.) Romae, 1761. 2v.
Eg 278.76 Monumental history of Egypt. (Birch, S.) London, 1876.
Eg 278.54 The monumental history of Egypt. (Osburn, W.) London, 1854. 2v.
AH 7339.35A Monuments and men of ancient Rome. (Showerman, G.) N.Y., 1935.
AH 3159.15.5 The monuments and the Old Testament. (Price, I.M.) Chicago, 1899.
AH 3159.15 The monuments and the Old Testament. 2. ed. (Price, I.M.) Chicago, 1900.
AH 3013.5 Les monuments en Chaldée, en Assyrie. (Cavaniol, C.H.) Paris, 1870.
AH 3016.45 Monuments mésopotamiens. (Contenau, Georges.) Paris, 1934.
AH 3013.33.15PF The monuments of Nineveh. (Layard, A.H.) London, 1849.

AH 3013.33.17PF — The monuments of Nineveh. 2d series. (Layard, A.H.) London, 1853.

Eg 974.5.5F — The monuments of Sneferu at Dahshur. (Fakhry, A.) Cairo, 1959-61. 2v.

Htn AH 7206.31* — Monvéron, Charles Sabatino. Observationes et emendationes in synopsim Basilicum. Paris, 1607.

AH 4410.1 — Moon, Brenda Elizabeth. Mycenaean civilization, publications...1935-1960, a bibliography. v.1-2. London, 1957-61.

AH 959.20 — Mooney, William West. Travel among the ancient Romans. Boston, 1920.

AH 4842.75A — Moore, E.C. The story of instruction. N.Y., 1936.

AH 3129.7 — Moore, Ellen W. Neo-Babylonian business and administrative documents. Ann Arbor, 1935.

AH 3129.7.5A — Moore, Ellen W. Neo-Babylonian documents in the University of Michigan collection. Ann Arbor, 1939.

AH 7819.36A — Moore, F.G. The Roman's world. N.Y., 1936.

AH 7819.42.5 — Moore, R.W. The Roman commonwealth. London, 1942.

AH 8202.5 — Moore, Ralph W. The Romans in Britain; a selection of Latin texts. London, 1938.

AH 3965.6.9 — Moors, B.P. Le système des poids, mesures et monnaies des israélites d'apres la Bible. Paris, 1904.

AH 3013.959 — Moortgat, Anton. Archäologische Forschungen der Max Freiherr von Oppenheim - Stiftung in nördlichen Mesopotamien 1956. Köln, 1959.

AH 3013.971 — Moortgat, Anton. Einführung in die vorderasiatische Archäologie. Darmstadt, 1971.

AH 3016.55 — Moortgat, Anton. Tammuz. Berlin, 1949.

AH 3017.85 — Moortgat, Anton. Vorderasiatische Rollsiegel; ein Beitrag zur Geschichte der Steinschneidekunst. 2. Aufl. Berlin, 1966.

AH 7163.19 — Morael, G.L.M. Du divorce. Paris, 1888.

AH 7039.67 — The moral and political tradition of Rome. (Earl, Donald Charles.) London, 1967.

AH 845.10 — Moral values in the ancient world. (Ferguson, John.) London, 1958.

AH 9668.2 — Morales Belda, Francisco. La marina vándala. Barcelona, 1969.

AH 7487.29 — The morals of princes. (Comazzi, G.B.) London, 1729.

AH 7449.07 — Mordtmann, A.D. Historische Bilder vom Bosporus. Konstantinopel, 1907.

AH 4299.62.5 — More essays in Greek history and literature. (Gomme, Arnold W.) Oxford, 1962.

AH 4861.5 — More Humandi and Concremandi Mortuos. (Nathusius, C.H.A.) Halis Saxonum, 1864?

AH 3016.35F — More sculpture from the Diyala region. (Frankfort, Henri.) Chicago, 1943.

AH 8548.135 — Moreau, Jacques. Die Welt der Kelten. Stuttgart, 1958.

AH 888.49 — Moreau-Christophe, Louis-Mathurin. Driot à l'oisiveté. Paris, 1849.

AH 8542.2 — Morel, Charles. Genève et la colonie de Vienne. Genève, 1888.

AH 4543.5 — Morell, L.J. Vita Phocionis. Lugdunum Batavorum, 1869.

AH 4278.19 — Morell, T. Studies in history...Greece. Philadelphia, 1819.

Eg 879.54A — Morenz, S. Der Gatt auf der Blume. Ascona, 1954.

AH 4818.30 — Mores heroicae aetatis apud veteres Graecas et Scandinovas comjsaroti. (Geijer, Erik Gustof.) Upsaliae, 1830.

Eg 659.03 — Moret, A. De Bocchori Rege. Paris, 1903.

Eg 279.13.5 — Moret, A. Mystères égyptiens. Paris, 1927.

Eg 299.11.10 — Moret, Alexandre. Au temps des pharaons. 5. éd. Paris, 1925.

Eg 299.12 — Moret, Alexandre. Kings and gods of Egypt. N.Y., 1912.

Eg 819.26.5 — Moret, Alexandre. The Nile and Egyptian civilization. N.Y., 1927.

Eg 299.12.3 — Moret, Alexandre. Rais et dieux d'Égypte. 5. éd. Paris, 1925.

AH 4299.62.10 — Moretti, Luigi. Ricerche sulle leghe greche: peloponnesiaca-beotica-licia. Roma, 1962.

Eg 848.4 — Moreux, T. La science mystérieuse des pharaons. Paris, 1923.

Eg 848.4.5 — Moreux, T. La science mystérieuse des pharaons. Paris, 1926.

Eg 848.4.10 — Moreux, T. La science mystérieuse des pharaons. Paris, 1938.

NEDL AH 279.06.5 — Morey, William Carey. Outlines of ancient history. N.Y., 1906.

AH 819.09 — Morgan, J. Premières civilisations. Paris, 1909.

AH 819.25 — Morgan, J. de. La préhistoire orientale. Paris, 1925-27. 3v.

AH 3002.7F — Morgan, J.P. Babylonian records in the library of J.P. Morgan. N.Y., 1912. 4v.

AH 3000.5 — Morgan, J.P. Cuneiform inscriptions : Chaldean, Babylonian. N.Y., 1908.

Htn AH 3017.4F* — Morgan, John P. Cylinders and oriental seals in library. N.Y., 1909.

AH 818.77.5 — Morgan, L.H. Ancient society. Chicago, 1877.

AH 818.77.4 — Morgan, L.H. Ancient society. N.Y., 1877.

AH 7847.2 — Morgan, M.H. Remarks on water supply of ancient Rome. Boston, 1902.

AH 8549.87 — Morgan, O. The light of Britannia. Cardiff, 1894.

AH 3813.7 — Morgenstern, Julian. Rites of birth, marriage, death, and kindred occasions among the Semites. Cincinnati, 1966.

AH 7239.56 — Morin y Peña, Manuel. Instituciones militares romanas. Madrid, 1956.

NEDL AH 7817.91.5 — Moritz, K.P. Anthoysa, oder Roms Alterthümer. Berlin, 1791.

AH 7817.91.5 — Moritz, K.P. Anthoysa, oder Roms Alterthümer. Berlin, 1791. 2v.

AH 909.58 — Moritz, L.A. Grain-mills and flour in classical antiquity. Oxford, 1958.

AH 9446.5 — Moro, Placida Maria. Iulium Carnicum (Zuglio). Roma, 1956.

AH 7448.97A — Morris, William C. Hannibal; soldier, statesman. N.Y., 1897.

AH 4259.68 — Morrison, John Sinclair. Greek oared ships, 900-322 B.C. Cambridge, 1968.

AH 7478.62 — La mort de César. (De Damas, Nicolas.) Paris, 1862.

AH 879.58F — Morti e pianto rituale nel mondo antico dal lamento pagano al pianto di Maria. (Martino, Ernesto de.) Torino, 1958.

AH 7845.15* — Mos maiorum; Wesen und Wirkung der Tradition in Rom. Inaug. Diss. (Rech, H.) Marburg, 1936.

AH 4278.83.5 — Mosaics of Grecian history. (Willson, M.) N.Y., 1883.

AH 3807.15.2 — Moscati, Sabatino. Ancient Semitic civilizations. London, 1957.

AH 3807.15 — Moscati, Sabatino. Ancient Semitic civilizations. 1st American ed. N.Y., 1957.

AH 3813.8 — Moscati, Sabatino. Le antiche civiltà semitiche. Bari, 1958.

AH 819.71.10 — Moscati, Sabatino. Civiltà sul Mediterraneo. Novara, 1971.

AH 1819.56.3 — Moscati, Sabatino. The face of the ancient Orient. Chicago, 1960.

AH 3959.35 — Moscati, Sabatino. I predecessori d'Israele. Roma, 1956.

AH 1819.56 — Moscati, Sabatino. Il profilo dell'Oriente mediterraneo. Torino, 1956.

AH 3807.20 — Moscati, Sabatino. The Semites in ancient history. Cardiff, 1959.

AH 3807.10 — Moscati, Sabatino. Storia e civiltà dei Semiti. Bari, 1949.

AH 3707.22 — Moscati, Sabatino. The world of the Phoenicians. London, 1968.

AH 5140.9 — Moschatos, A. De Insula Teno Eiusque historia. Gottingae, 1855.

AH 4819.30 — Moscow. Gosudarstvennyi Muzei Iziashchnykh Iskusstv. Drevniaia gretsiia. Moskva, 1930.

AH 4498.90 — Mosler, I. Chronologie der Pentekontaëtie. Berlin, 1890.

AH 4269.73 — Mosley, Derek J. Envoys and diplomacy in ancient Greece. Wiesbaden, 1973.

AH 4539.62 — Mossé, C. La fin de la démocratie athénienne. Paris, 1962.

AH 4043.5.15 — Mossé, Claude. La tyrannie dans la Grèce antique. Paris, 1969.

AH 1819.28.5 — The most ancient East. (Childe, Vere G.) London, 1929.

AH 4539.03 — Motzki, A. Eubulos von Probalinthos. Königsberg, 1903.

AH 3960.16 — Motzo, B. Saggi di storia e letteratura guideo-ellenistica. Firenze, 1925.

AH 7418.60 — Moule, H. The Roman republic. London, 1860.

AH 7108.94 — Moulin, C.D. Droit romain. Des impots indirectes. Poitiers, 1894.

AH 459.61 — Mourre, Michel. Le monde a la mort de Socrate. Paris, 1961.

AH 3964.25 — Le mouvement baptiste en Palestine et Syrie. (Thomas, Joseph.) Gembloux, 1935.

AH 3013.937.5 — Movable property in the Nuzi documents. Diss. (Cross, Dorothy.) Philadelphia, 1937.

AH 3707.7 — Movers, F.K. Die Phönizier. v.1-2, pt.1-3. Bonn, 1841. 4v.

AH 7189.66 — Movimenti servili nel mondo romano in età repubblicana. (Capozza, Maria.) Roma, 1966.

Eg 609.26F — Mr. Howard Carter's triumph: the superb coffins of Tutankhamen. London, 1926.

Eg 279.27 — Much, Hans. Das ewige Agypten. Dresden, 1927.

AH 8407.2 — Muchar, A.A. Das römische Norikum. Gratz, 1825. 2v.

AH 9790.5 — Muchau, H. Das 4000 Jährige alter des Volkes der Hermunduringer (Thüringer). Jena, 1910.

AH 7738.73 — Muche, Eugenius. Forschungen über den römischen Kaiser M.A. Severus Alexander. Schweidnitz, 1873.

Eg 459.58 — Muck, O.H. Cheops und die grosse Pyramide. Olten, 1958.

AH 4329.27 — Mucke, J.R. Die Urbevölkerung Griechenlands und ihre allmähliche Entwickelung zu Volksstämen. Leipzig, 1927-29.

AH 298.99 — Mücke, C. Vom Euphrat zum Tiber. Leipzig, 1899.

AH 7203.42 — Mühlenbruch, C.F. Doctriia Pandectarum. Bruxelles, 1838.

AH 7168.17.3 — Mühlenbruch, C.F. Die Lehre von der Cession. 3e Aufl. Stuttgart, 1836.

AH 8908.15 — Mühlestein, H. Uber die Herkunft der Etrusker. Berlin, 1929.

AH 7469.06 — Mühll, F.V. De L. Appuleio Saturnino Tribuno Plebis. Basileae, 1906.

AH 4239.08 — Müller, B. Beiträge zur Geschichte...Söldnerwesens. Frankfurt am Main, 1908.

AH 5121.5 — Mueller, C. Aegineticorum. Berolini, 1817.

AH 939.02 — Müller, C. Studien zur Geschichte der Erdkunde. Breslau, 1902.

AH 818.52 — Müller, C.O. Ancient art and its remains. London, 1852.

AH 3151.8 — Müller, D.H. Die Gesetze Hammurabis. Wien, 1903.

AH 4328.49 — Mueller, E.H.O. De populi Atheniensis tribuum origine. Marburgi, 1849.

AH 4518.94 — Müller, Emil. Sokrates in der Volksversammlung. Zittau, 1894.

AH 7479.14 — Müller, Ernst. Cäsaren-Porträts. v.1-2, 3. Bonn, 1914-27. 2v.

AH 3936.7 — Müller, F. Studien über Zenobia und Palmyra. Kirchain, 1902.

AH 7448.67 — Müller, H. Die Schlacht an der Trebia. Berlin, 1867.

AH 928.59 — Müller, H. Uber die heilige Masse des Alterthums. Freiburg, 1859.

AH 4408.92 — Müller, H.D. Historisch-mythologischen Untersuchungen. Göttingen, 1892.

Eg 299.12.5F — Müller, Hugo. Die formale Entwicklung der Titulatur der ägyptischen Könige. Inaug. Diss. Glückstadt, 1938.

AH 4559.05 — Müller, K.F. Leichenwagen Alexanders des Grossen. Leipzig, 1905.

AH 4258.82 — Müller, K.K. Griechischen Schrift über Seekrieg. Würzburg, 1882.

AH 4238.82 — Müller, K.K. Griechisches Fragment über Kriegswesen. Würzburg, 1882.

AH 5307.17 — Müller, K.O. Attica and Athens. London, 1842.

AH 5307.15 — Müller, K.O. De munimentis Athenarum. Gottingae, 1836.

AH 4298.44.5 — Müller, K.O. Geschichten hellenische Stämme und Städte-Karten. Breslau, 1844. 4v.

AH 4328.30 — Müller, K.O. History and antiquities of Dorie Race. Oxford, 1830. 2v.

AH 4328.30.2 — Müller, K.O. History and antiquities of Dorie Race. 2. ed. London, 1839. 2v.

AH 8907.8.10 — Müller, Karl O. Die Etrusker. Graz, 1965. 2v.

AH 8907.8.5 — Müller, Karl O. Die Etrusker. Stuttgart, 1877. 2v.

AH 8907.8 — Müller, Karl O. Die Etrusker. v.1-2. Breslau, 1828.

AH 5390.5 — Müller, M. Geschichte Thebens. Leipzig, 1879.

AH 3041.2 — Mueller, Manfred. Die Erlässe und Instruktionen aus dem Lande Arrapha, ein Beitrag zur Rechtsgeschichte des Alten Vorderen Orients. Inaug. Diss. Leipzig? 1968?

AH 4098.80 — Mueller, O. De demis atticis. Nordhusae, 1880.

AH 4609.73 — Müller, Olaf. Antigonos Monophthalmos und "Das Jahr der Könige". Bonn, 1973.

AH 4848.5.5 — Müller, V.K. Der Polos, die griechische Gotterkrone. Inaug. Diss. Berlin, 1915.

AH 279.58.35 — Mueller, W.F. Aufstieg und Untergang der Grossreiche des Altertums. 2. Aufl. Stuttgart, 1959.

Eg 298.93 — Müller, W.M. Asien und Europa nach altägyptischen Denkmälern. Leipzig, 1893.

Eg 1078.99F — Müller, W.M. Die Liebespoisie der alten Ägypter. Leipzig, 1899.

AH 48.51 — Natalia Caroli Friderici. Inaug. Diss. (Zell, Karl.) Heidelbergae, 1851.

AH 9221.5.5 — Natalucci, Mario. Ancona antica. Città di Castello, 1960.

AH 4861.5 — Nathusius, C.H.A. More Humandi and Cencremandi Mortuos. Halis Saxonum, 1864?

AH 4842.15 — National education in Greece. (Wilkins, A.S.) London, 1873.

AH 819.51 — National Geographic Magazine. Everyday life in ancient times. Washington, 1951.

AH 7909.09 — Die Nationalität der Kaufleute. (Parvan, Vasile.) Breslau, 1909.

NEDL Eg 318.83 — The natural genesis. (Massey, G.) London, 1883. 2v.

AH 4114.17 — Naturalization in Athenian law and practice. Diss. (Billheimer, A.) Gettysburg, 1922.

AH 7168.61.5 — Die Naturalobligationen der römischen Recht. (Schwanert, H.A.) Göttingen, 1861.

AH 8016.5F — Nau de Champlouis, A.V. Notice sur la carte de l'Afrique. Paris, 1864.

AH 9389.5.4F — Naudé, Gabriel. Exercitatio. Lugduni Batavorum, 1722.

AH 7217.13.5 — Naudet, Joseph. De la noblesse chez les Romains. Paris, 1868.

AH 7217.13 — Naudet, Joseph. De la noblesse et des récompenses. Paris, 1863.

AH 7038.77.5 — Naudet, Joseph. De l'etat des personnes et des peuples sous les empereurs romains. Paris, 1877.

AH 7058.17 — Naudet, Joseph. Des changemens...de l'empire romain. Paris, 1817. 2v.

AH 7238.70 — Naudet, Joseph. Études d'histoire romaine. Paris, 1870.

AH 4483.15 — Hē naumachia tēs Salaminos. (Papadopoulos, Nikos M.) Athēnai, 1961.

AH 9627.2 — Navarra, Giuseppe. Città sicane, sicule e greche nella zona di Gela. Palermo, 1964.

AH 4859.15 — Navarre, O. Mulieres Athenienses. Tolosae, 1900.

AH 8548.110 — Navarro, J.M. de. A survey of research on an early phase of Celtic culture. London, 1936.

AH 959.17 — Navigation to the Far East under the Roman Empire. (Schoff, Wilfred H.) Boston, 1917.

AH 7778.77 — Naville, Henri Adrien. Julien l'apostat. Paris, 1877.

AH 257.83 — Les navires des anciens. (LeRoy, J.D.) Paris, 1783.

AH 9634.5 — Naxos siceliota. (Rizzo, P.) Catania, 1894.

AH 7778.12.5 — Neander, A. The Emperor Julian and his generation. N.Y., 1850.

Htn AH 925.55* — Neander, M. Eynopsis. Basileae, 1555.

AH 1819.52 — The Near East and the foundations for civilization. (Braidwood, Robert J.) Eugene, 1952.

AH 3966.17 — Nebo, undi tota perlustratur Terra Sancta. (Quistorpius, J.) Rostochi, 1663.

AH 3132.6 — Nebuchodnosor II von Babylon. (Buchwald, R.) n.p., 1898.

AH 7188.38.5 — Necessitudine cum moralitum civili. (Schüller, C.L.) Rhenum, 1838.

AH 7419.72.5 — Nechai, Fedor M. Obrazovanie rimskogo gosudarstva. Minsk, 1972.

Eg 971.11F — La Necrapoli musulmana di Aswán. (Monneret de Villard, Ugo.) Le Caire, 1930.

AH 3002.135A — Nederkands Institut voor het Nabije Oosten, Leyden. Studia ad tabulas cuneiformas collectas ab De Liagre Böhl pertinentia. v.1, pt.1-2; 3. Leiden, 1952- 3v.

AH 4498.89.5 — Nedwed, E. Perikles. Iglau, 1889.

Eg 609.64.5 — Nefertiti. (Wells, Evelyn.) Garden City, N.Y., 1964.

AH 854.12 — Negelini, J. Das Pferd im arischen Altertum. Königsberg, 1903.

AH 308.64 — Negri, C. Memorie storico-politiche. Torino, 1864.

AH 7779.01.3 — Negri, G. L'imperatore Giuliano l'Apostata. Milano, 1902.

AH 7779.01.4 — Negri, G. Julian the Apostate. 2. ed. N.Y., 1905. 2v.

AH 328.69 — The negro in ancient history. (Blyden, E.W.) N.Y.? 1869.

AH 328.69.2 — The negro in ancient history. (Blyden, E.W.) Washington, 1869.

AH 846.31 — Neikhardt, Aleksandra A. Sem' chudes drevnego mira. Leningrad, 1966.

Eg 609.13 — Nelson, Harold H. The battle of Megiddo. Diss. Chicago, 1921.

AH 309.07 — The nemesis of nations. (Paterson, W.R.) London, 1907.

AH 7799.40 — Németh, Gyula. Attila és hunjai. Budapest, 1940.

AH 7799.40.5 — Németh, Gyula. Attila ve Hunlari. Istanbul, 1962.

AH 7819.64.5 — Nemirovskii, Aleksandr. Ideologiia i kul'tura rannego Rima. Voronezh, 1964.

AH 8907.48 — Nemirovskii, Aleksandr I. Etruski. Voronezh, 1969.

AH 279.58.25 — Nenci, Giuseppe. Introduzione alle guerre persiane e altri saggi. Pisa, 1958.

AH 3129.7 — Neo-Babylonian business and administrative documents. (Moore, Ellen W.) Ann Arbor, 1935.

AH 3129.7.5A — Neo-Babylonian documents in the University of Michigan collection. (Moore, Ellen W.) Ann Arbor, 1939.

AH 4839.33 — Neoi. (Forbes, C.A.) Middletown, Conn., 1933.

AH 7549.30.5 — Nero, emperor of Rome. (Weigall, Arthur E.P.B.) London, 1930.

AH 7549.64 — Nero; the man and the legend. (Bishop, John H.) London, 1964.

AH 7549.64.2 — Nero, the man and the legend. (Bishop, John H.) N.Y., 1965.

AH 7549.30.11 — Nero, the singing emperor of Rome. (Weigall, Arthur E.P.B.) N.Y., 1930.

AH 7549.70 — Nero. (Grant, Michael.) London, 1970.

AH 7549.55.2 — Nero. (Walter, Gérard.) London, 1957.

AH 7549.30.10 — Nero. (Weigall, Arthur E.P.B.) N.Y., 1930.

AH 7549.69 — Nero: reality and legend. (Warmington, Brian Herbert.) London, 1969.

Htn AH 7546.27* — Nero Caesar. (Bolton, Edmund.) London, 1627.

AH 7549.55 — Néron. (Walter, Gérard.) Paris, 1955.

AH 7549.62 — Néron et le mystère des origines chrétiennes. (Pichon, Jean Charles.) Paris, 1971.

AH 7549.45 — Nerone. (Cananesi, M.) Milano, 1945.

AH 7549.23 — Nerone. (Pascal, Carlo.) Milano, 1923.

AH 7549.49 — Nerone e i suoi tempi. (Levi, Mario A.) Milano, 1949.

AH 7609.50 — Nerva. (Garzetti, A.) Roma, 1950.

AH 3152.3 — Nesbit, William M. Sumerian records from Drehem. N.Y., 1914.

AH 5136.5 — Hē Nēsos Peparēthos. (Oikonomos, S.A.) Ienae, 1883.

AH 808.79.10 — Neteler, Bernhard. Zusammenhang der alttestamentlichen Zeitrechnung mit der Profangeschichte. v.1-3. Münster, 1879-86.

AH 3150.13 — Neubabylonische Achtsurkunden aus den Berliner Staatlichen Museum. v.1-2. (Pohl, Alfred.) Roma, 1933-34.

AH 3129.8 — Die neubabylonischen Königsinschriften. (Berger, Paul.) Kevelaer, 1973-

AH 3129.3.5 — Die neubabylonischen Königsinschriften. (Langdon, S.) Leipzig, 1912.

AH 5311.5 — Neubauer, F. Atheniensium Reipublicae quaenam romanorum temporibus fuerit condicio. Halis Saxonum, 1882.

Eg 819.54.4 — Neubert, Otto. Tutankhamun and the Valley of the Kings. London, 1972.

AH 819.19.15 — Neuburger, Albert. The technical arts and sciences of the ancients. London, 1930.

AH 819.19.16 — Neuburger, Albert. The technical arts and sciences of the ancients. N.Y., 1969.

AH 819.19.10 — Neuburger, Albert. Die Technik des Altertums. 2. Aufl. Leipzig, 1921.

AH 29.64 — Neue Beiträge zur Geschichte der alten Welt. (Deutsche Historiker-Gesellschaft. Fachgruppe alte Geschichte.) Berlin, 1964-65. 2v.

AH 3005.7 — Neue Beiträge zur Geschichte des alten Orients; die Assyriologie in Deutschland. (Gutschmid, A.) Leipzig, 1876.

AHP 24.15 — Neue deutsche Forschungen. Abteilungen alte Geschichte. Berlin. 1-7,1935-1939 8v.

AH 7428.94 — Neue Forschungen zur älteren Geschichte Roms. (Burger, Combertus P.) Amsterdam, 1894. 2v.

Eg 1098.81 — Die neue Weltordnung nach Vernichtung. (Brugsch, H.K.) Berlin, 1881.

AH 3659.3 — Die neuentdckten Inscription über Cyrus. (Büdinger.) Wien, 1881.

AH 3154.14 — Ein neuer Ninkarrak. (Nikel, Johannes.) Paderborn, 1918.

AH 3407.10 — Neuere Hethiterforschung. (Walser, G.) Wiesbaden, 1964.

AH 8908.14 — Neues über die Herkunft der Etrusker und über Homer. (Haury, Jacob.) Kaiserslautern, 1926.

Eg 1179.60F — Neugebauer, Otto. Egyptian astronomical texts. v.2-3, pt.1-2. Providence, 1960- 3v.

AH 4449.25 — Neugründer des Staates. (Ehrenberg, Victor.) München, 1925.

AH 7448.73 — Neuling, I. De belli punici primi scriptorum. Gottingae, 1873.

AH 7468.81 — Neumann, Carl. Geschichte Roms. Breslau, 1881.

AH 6157.5 — Neumann, K. Hellenen in Skythenlande. Berlin, 1855.

AH 7179.00 — Neumann, K.J. Die Grundherrschaft der Römischen Republik. Strassburg, 1900.

AH 7448.83.10 — Neumann, Karl. Das Zeitalter der punischen Kriege. Breslau, 1883.

AH 7469.02.5 — Neunheuser, J. Aemilius Lepidus. Essen, 1902.

AH 889.09.5 — Neurath, A. Antike Wirtschaftsgeschichte. Leipzig, 1909.

AH 889.06.5 — Neurath, Otto. Zur Anschauung der Antike über Handel, Gewerbe und Landwirtschaft. Jena, 1906.

Eg 1029.38 — Never to die; the Egyptians in their own words. (Mayer, Josephine.) N.Y., 1938.

AH 9722.9A — Nevskaia, V.P. Bizantii v klassicheskuiu i ellinisticheskuiu epokhi. Moskva, 1953.

AH 9722.8 — Nevskaia, V.P. Byzanz in der klassischen und hellenistischen Epoche. Leipzig, 1955.

AH 808.30 — New analysis of chronology and geography. (Hales, W.) London, 1830. 4v.

AH 4279.60.5 — New background to the study of ancient Greece. (Crossland, R.A.) Sheffield, 1960.

AH 4298.92.11 — New chapters in Greek history. (Gardner, P.) London, 1892.

AH 4299.36 — The new deal in ancient Greece. (Bullock, Charles J.) Cambridge, 1936.

AH 7299.39 — The new deal in old Rome; how government in the ancient world tried to deal with modern problems. (Haskell, Henry J.) N.Y., 1939.

AH 7277.27 — A new essay on the Roman history. London, 1727.

AH 1819.34A — New light on the most ancient East. (Childe, Vere G.) London, 1934.

AH 1819.34.10 — New light on the most ancient East. (Childe, Vere G.) N.Y., 1934.

AH 1819.34.5 — New light on the most ancient East. 4. ed. (Childe, Vere G.) London, 1952.

AH 7207.52 — New men in the Roman senate 139 B.C. - A.D. 14. (Wiseman, Timothy Peter.) London, 1971.

AH 5303.30 — The new politicians of fifth-century Athens. (Connor, Walter Robert.) Princeton, 1971.

AH 298.21 — New researches in ancient history. (Volney, C.F.) London, 1821. 2v.

Eg 9.25.5A — New York. Public Library. Ancient Egypt, 1925-1941. Supplement. N.Y., 1942.

Eg 9.25A — New York. Public Library. Ancient Egypt. N.Y., 1925.

AH 3002.4 — New York Metropolitan Museum of Art. Cuneiform texts in the Metropolitan Museum. N.Y., 1893.

AH 4839.25 — New York Metropolitan Museum of Art. Greek athletics. N.Y., 1925.

Eg 279.07 — Newberry, P.E. Ancient Egypt. London, 1907.

Eg 1308.99 — Newberry, R.E. The Amherst papyri. London, 1899.

Htn AH 277.88* — Newbery, John. A compendious history of the world. London, 1788. 2v.

AH 7408.52 — Newman, F.W. Regal Rome. London, 1852.

AH 5363.5 — Newmann, G. De nominibus boeotorum propriis. Regimonti, 1908.

Htn AH 807.28.3* — Newton, Isaac. Chronology of ancient kingdoms. London, 1728.

AH 807.22 — Newton, Isaac. Chronology of antient kingdoms. Dublin, 1722.

AH 3708.5 — Nibbi, Alessandra. The Tyrrhenians. Cowley, 1969.

AH 4709.14 — Niccolini, G. La confederazione Achea. Paris, 1914.

AH 7114.30 — Niccolini, G. I fasti dei tribuni della plebe. Milano, 1934.

AH 7114.29 — Niccolini, G. Il tribunato della plebe. Milano, 1932.

AH 7058.87.3 — Niccolini, I. Tasti tribunorum plebis. Pisis, 1898.

AH 808.77 — Nichol, J. Tables of ancient literature and history. Glasgow, 1877.

AH 7139.62A — Nicholas, B. An introduction to Roman law. Oxford, 1962.

AH 4523.7 — Nicias and Sicilian expedition. (Church, A.J.) London, 1899.

Eg 809.28 — Nicklin, T. Studies in Egyptian chronology. v.1-2. Blackpool, 1928-29.

AH 7779.40 — Nicolaas, T.W.J. Praetextatus. Proefschrift. Nijmegen, 1940.

AH 4861.8 — Nicolai, J. Johannis Nicolai Tractatus de Graecorum luctu. Thielae, 1697.

Eg 137.06 — Nicolai, J. Tractatus de Synedrio Aegyptiorum. Lugdunum Batavorum, 1706.

AH 4608.61 — Nicolas, B. De ingenio et fortuna Graecarum apud Thraces coloniarum. Thesim proponebat. Lutetiae Parisiorum, 1861.

AH 4719.09 — Nicolaus, M. Zwei Beiträge zur Geschichte König Philipps V. von Makedonien. Berlin, 1909.

AH 7509.23.5 — Nicolaus Damascenus. Nicolaus of Damascus' life of Augustus. Menasha, 1923.

Author and Title Listing

Author and Title Listing

NEDL AH 4818.76.2.5 — Old Greek life. (Mahaffy, J.P.) N.Y., 1876.
NEDL AH 4818.76.2.9 — Old Greek life. (Mahaffy, J.P.) N.Y., 1885.
NEDL AH 4818.76.3 — Old Greek life. (Mahaffy, J.P.) N.Y., 1888.
AH 7818.67 — The old Roman world. (Lord, John.) N.Y., 1867.
AH 3159.14 — The Old Testament in the light of the historical records. (Pinches, T.G.) London, 1902.
AH 3966.33 — The Old Testament world. (North, Martin.) Philadelphia, 1966.
Eg 1128.87.8 — "The oldest book in the world"...Papyrus Prisse. n.p., 1888.
AH 3151.4 — The oldest code of laws in the world. (Hammurabi, king of Babylonia.) Edinburgh, 1903.
AH 3151.4.5 — The oldest code of laws in the world. (Hammurabi, king of Babylonia.) Edinburgh, 1903.
Eg 138.99 — Oldest known will. (Uah.) Philadelphia, 19- .
AH 4309.65 — Oldtidens idéhistorie. (Fabricius, Johannes.) København, 1965.
AH 4459.60 — Die oligarchische Bewegung in Athen am Ausgand des 5. Jahrhunderts. (Hackl, Ursula.) München, 1960.
AH 4524.11 — Die oligarchische Revolution vom Jahre 411. (Sadl, A.) Pola, 1910.
AH 4524.5 — Oligarchische Umwälzung. (Scheibe, J.F.) Leipzig, 1841.
AH 4049.45 — Les oligarques. (Isaac, Jules.) Paris, 1945.
AH 4049.45.5 — Les oligarques. (Isaac, Jules.) Paris, 1946.
AH 8457.6 — Oliva, Pavel. Pannonia and the onset of crisis in the Roman empire. Praha, 1962.
AH 8457.5 — Oliva, Pavel. Pannonie a počátky krize Řemskeho imperia. Praha, 1959.
AH 4403.54 — Oliva, Pavel. Raná řecká tyrannis. Praha, 1954.
AH 5758.16.1 — Oliva, Pavel. Sparta and her social problems. Amsterdam, 1971.
AH 5758.16 — Oliva, Pavel. Sparta and her social problems. Prague, 1971.
AH 4659.28 — Oliveira Martins, J.P. O hellenismo e a civilisação christan. 4. ed. Lisboa, 1928.
AH 7418.85.3 — Oliveira Martins, J.P. Historia da republica romana. 3. ed. v.1-2. Lisboa, 1919.
AH 7889.07 — Oliver, E.H. Roman economic conditions. Toronto, 1907.
AH 4215.9 — Oliver, James H. The Athenian expounders of sacred and ancestral law. Baltimore, 1950.
AH 4039.60.5 — Oliver, James H. Demokratia, the gods and the free world. Baltimore, 1960.
AH 7478.61.2 — Oliver y Hurtado, J. y D. Munda Pompeiana. Madrid, 1861.
AH 7769.15.5 — Olivetti, Alberto. Osservazioni storiche cronologiche sulla guerra di Costanzo II contro i Persiani. Torino, 1915.
AH 7769.15 — Olivetti, Alberto. Sulle stragi di Costantinopoli succedute alla morte di Costantino il Grande. n.p., n.d.
AH 8015.5 — L'olivier et l'huile dans l'Afrique romaine. (Camps-Fabrer, Henriette.) Alger, 1953.
AH 8647.14 — Olivieri, A. Civiltà greca nell'Italia meridionale. Napoli, 1931.
AH 5757.11.5 — Ollier, F. Le mirage spartiate. Paris, 1943.
AH 5757.11 — Ollier, F. Le mirage spartiate. Thèse. Paris, 1933.
AH 3657.31A — Olmstead, A.T.E. History of the Persian empire. Chicago, 1948.
AH 3075.13 — Olmstead, Albert T. History of Assyria. N.Y., 1923.
AH 1409.06.1 — Olmstead, Albert T. Western Asia in the days of Sargon of Assyria, 722-705 B.C. N.Y., 1908.
AH 1409.06 — Olmstead, Albert T. Western Asia in the days of Sargon of Assyria. Thesis. Lancaster, Pa., 1908.
AH 4484.11 — Olsen, W. Schlacht bei Plataeae. Greifswald, 1903.
Eg 879.71.5 — Olsson, Albert. I faraos land-på faraos tid. Solna, 1971.
AH 808.52 — Olymiadòn anagra. (Scaliger, J.) Berolini, 1852.
AH 4839.35.5 — Olympia. (Curtius, E.) Berlin, 1935.
AH 4839.05 — Olympia. (Gaspar, C.) Paris, 1905.
AH 4838.38 — Olympia. (Krause, J.H.) Wien, 1838.
AH 4839.65 — Olympia und seine Spiele. (Schöbel, Heinz.) Berlin, 1965.
AH 4838.96.5 — Pamphlet box. Olympian Games at Athens, 1896.
AH 4559.36 — Olympias, die Mutter Alexanders des Grossen; das Schicksal eines Weltreiches. (Tritsch, Walther.) Frankfurt, 1936.
AH 4838.96F — Olympic games. (Lambros and Polites.) Athens, 1896.
AH 4839.71 — Die olympischen Spiele in der Antike. (Bengston, Hermann.) Zürich, 1972.
AH 4839.65.5 — Olympischer Kampfsport in der Antike. (Rudolph, Werner.) Berlin, 1965.
AH 5673.10 — Olynth und die Chalkidier. (Zahrnt, Michael.) München, 1971.
AH 4279.46.10 — Om hellener og barbarer og om Athens herlighet. (Laache, Rolv.) Oslo, 1946.
AH 4278.90.9 — Oman, C.W.C. Greece. v.2. Philadelphia, 1906.
NEDL AH 4278.90.5 — Oman, C.W.C. History of Greece. Rivingtons, 1890.
AH 4278.90.6 — Oman, C.W.C. History of Greece. 2. ed. London, 1891.
AH 4278.90.6.3 — Oman, C.W.C. History of Greece. 3. ed. London, 1892.
AH 4278.90.6.4 — Oman, C.W.C. History of Greece. 4. ed. London, 1893.
AH 4278.90.7.5 — Oman, C.W.C. History of Greece. 7. ed. N.Y., 1901.
AH 7469.02 — Oman, Charles. Seven Roman statesmen of the later Republic. London, 1902.
AH 7469.02.3.5 — Oman, Charles. Seven Roman statesmen of the later Republic. London, 1927.
AH 7469.02.4 — Oman, Charles. Seven Roman statesmen of the later Republic. London, 1929.
AH 7469.02.2 — Oman, Charles. Seven Roman statesmen of the later Republic. N.Y., 1902.
AH 7469.02.3 — Oman, Charles. Seven Roman statesmen of the later Republic. N.Y., 191-?
AH 7469.02.6 — Oman, Charles. Seven Roman statesmen of the later Republic: the Gracchi, Sulla, Crassus, Cato, Pompey and Caesar. Freeport, 1971.
Eg 509.62 — Omlin, J. Amenemhet I. und Sesostris I. Heidelberg, 1962.
AH 7055.93.6 — Omont, H. Le plus ancien manuscrit de la Notitia dignitatum. Paris, 1891.
AH 938.54.20 — On some disputed questions of ancient geography. (Leake, W.M.) London, 1857.
AH 3001.4 — On the polyphony of the Assyric-Babylonian cuneiform writing. (Hincks, E.) Dublin, 1863. 10 pam.
AH 7189.06 — On the social standing of freedmen. (Crumley, J.J.) Baltimore, 1906.
AH 4114.13 — On the structure of the Greek Tribal Society. (Seebohm, H.E.) London, 1895.
AH 4308.65 — Oncken, W. Athen und Hellas. Leipzig, 1865.
AH 3020.13.9A — One hundred new selected Nuzi texts. (Pfeiffer, R.H.) n.p., 1936.
AH 3966.6.2 — Onomastica sacra. (Lagarde, Pauli.) Gottingae, 1887.
Htn AH 7295.89F* — Onomasticon historicae Romanae. (Glandorp.) Francofurti, 1859.
AH 4819.63.10F — Ontieke cultuur in beeld. 7. Druk. (Zadoks, A.N.) Bussum, 1963.

AH 4819.60 — Ontmoeting met het oude Hellas. (Doedeus, T.P.) Amsterdam, 1960.
AH 7836.81F — Onuphrii Panvinii Veronensis. Patanii, 1681.
Eg 879.17F — Die Onurislegende. (Junker, H.) Wien, 1917.
AH 878.22 — Onymus, A.J. Dämonen-Lehre der Alten. Würzburg, 1822.
AH 4719.54 — Oost, S.I. Roman policy in Epirus and Acarmania in the age of the Roman conquest of Greece. Dallas, 1954.
AH 7799.68 — Oost, Stewart Irvin. Galla Placidia Augusta. Chicago, 1968.
AH 7469.64 — Ooteghem, Jules van. Caius Marius. Namur, 1964.
AH 7419.67.5 — Ooteghem, Jules van. Les Crecilii Metelli de la république. Namur, 1967?
AH 7469.59 — Ooteghem, Jules van. Lucius Licinius Lucullus. Namur, 1959.
AH 7469.61 — Ooteghem, Jules van. Lucius Marcius Phillipus et sa famille. Namur, 1961.
AH 7479.54 — Ooteghem, Jules van. Pompée le grand, bâtisseur d'empire. Namur, 1954.
AH 7201.98 — Opera. v.1-3, pt.1-2. (Gaius. 1937. Bizoukides.) Thessalonicae, 1937-39. 5v.
AH 7539.32 — L'opera dell'imperatore Claudio. (Momigliano, A.) Firenze, 1932.
AH 3011.15 — Opera minora. (Böhl, F.M.T.) Groningen, 1953.
Htn AH 7137.49F* — Opera minora. (Brisson, B.) Lugdunum, 1749.
Htn AH 7815.21* — Opera varia - quorum catalogum. (Laeti, Pomponii.) Moguntiae, 1521.
AH 7478.86 — Les operations militaires de Jules César. (Heuzey, L.A.) Paris, 1886.
AH 7138.96.5F — Opere giuridiche e storiche. (Alibrandi, I.) Roma, 1896.
AH 7479.58 — Opermann, Hans. Caesar. Göttingen, 1958.
AH 3159.34 — Die Opfermaterie in Babylonien und Israel. Thesis. (Blome, Friedrich.) Romae, 1934.
Eg 879.12.5 — Der Opfertanz des ägyptischen Königs. (Kees, Hermann.) München, 1912.
AH 840.5 — Opitz, R. Häusliche Leben. Leipzig, 1894.
Eg 1029.58 — Opowiadaniia egipskie. (Andrzejewski, Tad.) Warszawa, 1958.
Eg 298.68.5 — Oppel, K. Wunderland der Pyramiden. Leipzig, 1868.
AH 3187.17 — Oppenheim, Adolf L. Letters from Mesopotamia. Chicago, 1967.
AH 3013.943F — Oppenheim, Max. Tell Halaf. Berlin, 1943. 4v.
AH 3013.931.5 — Oppenheim, Max. Der Tell Halaf. Leipzig, 1931.
AH 1866.5 — Oppert, J. L'ambre jaune chez les Assyriens. Paris, 1880.
AH 3008.67 — Oppert, J. Babylone et les Babyloniens. Paris, 1867.
AH 3149.3 — Oppert, J. Chronologie des Assyriens et des Babyloniens. Paris, n.d.
AH 3150.3 — Oppert, J. Documents juridiques de l'Assyrie et de la Chaldée. Paris, 1877.
AH 3127.5 — Oppert, J. L'Etalon des mesures Assyriennes. Paris, 1875.
AH 3013.11F — Oppert, J. Expédition scientifique en Mésopotamie. v.1-2; plates. Paris, 1863. 3v.
AH 3094.4F — Oppert, J. Les fastes de Sargon roi d'Assyrie. Paris, 1863. 2 pam.
AH 3094.4.2F — Oppert, J. Les fastes de Sargon roi d'Assyrie. Paris, 1863.
AH 3013.38 — Oppert, J. Grundgüge des Assyrischen Kunst. Basel, 1872.
AH 3008.65 — Oppert, J. Histoire des empires de Chaldée et d'Assyrie. Versailles, 1865.
AH 3160.8 — Oppert, J. L'inmortalité de l'âme chez les chaldéens. Paris, 1875.
AH 3163.7 — Oppert, Jules. Les inscriptions commerciales en caractères cuneiformes. Paris, 1866.
AH 7498.75.5 — L'opposition sous les Césars. (Boissier, Gaston.) Paris, 1875.
AH 7498.85A — L'opposition sous les Césars. (Boissier, Gaston.) Paris, 1885.
AH 7729.69 — Optendrenk, Theo. Die Religionspolitik des Kaisers Elagabal im Spiegel der Historia Augusta. Bonn, 1969.
AH 7619.26 — Optimus princeps. (Paribeni, R.) Messina, 1926-27.
Eg 807.65 — Opuscula Aegyptiacae. (Schmidt, F.S. de.) Caroleruhae, 1765.
AH 7137.11 — Opuscula varia de Latimitate. (Duker, K.A.) Lugdunum Batavorum, 1711.
Htn AH 7137.11.2* — Opuscula varia de Latinate. 2. ed. (Duker, K.A.) n.p., 1761.
AH 7137.09 — Opuscula varii argumenti. (Bynkershoek, C. von.) Lugdunum Batavorum, 1719.
AH 8548.100 — O'Rahilly, T.F. The Guidels and their predecessors. London, 1936.
AH 4850.14 — Oratio de Appellationibus panum. (Fendius, M.) Vitebergae, 1549.
AH 5307.11 — Oratio de civitate Athenarum. (Creuzeri, F.) Francofurti, 1826.
AH 279.60.5 — Orbis. (Vogt, Joseph.) Freiburg, 1960.
AH 7037.03 — Orbis romanus. (Spanhem, Ezekiel.) London, 1703.
AH 4843.3 — L'orchestique grecque. (Emmanuel, M.) Paris, 1895.
AH 7258.78F — L'ordinamento delle armate romane. (Ferrero, E.) Torino, 1878.
AH 7138.86 — Ordo judiciorum. (Harmann, O.E.) Göttingen, 1886.
AH 7228.59 — Ordo judiciorum. (Hartmann, O.E.) Göttingen, 1859.
AH 4889.03 — Die Organisation der offentlichen Arbeit. (Huch, G.) Schlesien, 1903.
AH 7918.99 — L'organisation des métiers. (Levasseur, E.) Paris, 1899.
Eg 239.12 — Organisation militaire de l'Egypte Byzantine. (Maspero, J.) Paris, 1912.
AH 889.42 — L'organizzazione del lavoro nel mondo antico. (Palumbo, P. Fausto.) Firenze, 1942.
AH 7629.50 — Orgeval, B. L'empereur Hadrien. Paris, 1950.
AHP 25.4 — Oriens antiquus. Collectio. Roma. 1,1962+ 9v.
AHP 25.3 — Oriens antiquus. Roma. 1,1962+ 10v.
AH 1801.1 — Pamphlet box. The Orient. Chronology.
AH 3911.10 — L'Orient des premiers chrétiens. (Sournia, Jean Charles.) Paris, 1966.
AH 4279.29.15 — L'Orient et la Grèce. (Hallynck, P.) Paris, 1929.
AH 279.36.5 — L'Orient et la Grèce. (Sêcher, J.) Paris, 1936.
AH 1409.20 — The Orient in Bible times. (Grant, Elihu.) Philadelphia, 1920.
AH 3910.25 — Orient und Hellas in den Denkmälern und Inschriften des Königs Antiochos I. von Kommagene. (Krüger, F.) Greifswald, 1937.
AH 1299.67 — Oriental and Biblical studies. (Speiser, Ephraim A.) Philadelphia, 1967.
AH 3017.9 — Oriental cylinders. (Cullimore, A.) London, 1842.
Eg 603.7 — Oriental diplomacy. (Bezold, C.) London, 1893.
Eg 278.67.20 — L'oriente antico. (Regaldi, G.) Torino, 1867.
AH 9664.5 — Origenes del cristianismo en Cantabria. (Gonzalez Echegaray, Joaquin.) Santander, 1969.
AH 8549.111 — The origin of druidism. (Pokorny, J.) Washington, 1911.

AH 4842.72.20 — Paideia; the ideals of Greek culture. 2. English ed. (Jaeger, Werner Wilhelm.) Oxford, 1965.

AH 4842.72 — Paideia: die Formung des griechischen Menschen. (Jaeger, Werner Wilhelm.) Berlin, 1934.

X Cg — AH 4842.72.10A — Paideia: the ideals of Greek culture. (Jaeger, Werner Wilhelm.) N.Y., 1939.

AH 4842.72.10A — Paideia: the ideals of Greek culture. v.2-3. (Jaeger, Werner Wilhelm.) N.Y., 1939-43. 2v.

AH 4842.72.15A — Paideia: the ideals of Greek culture. 2. ed. (Jaeger, Werner Wilhelm.) N.Y., 1945.

AH 4842.72.3A — Paideia. 2. Aufl. (Jaeger, Werner Wilhelm.) Berlin, 1936- 3v.

AH 7779.71 — La paideia di Achille. (Manacorda, Mario Alighiero.) Roma, 1971.

AH 7138.78 — Pailhé, E.D. Cours élémentaire de droit romain. Paris, 1878.

AH 7048.75 — Paillard, A. Histoire de le transmission du pouvoir impérial. Paris, 1875.

AH 7149.15 — Pais, E. Ricerche sulla storia e sul diritto pubblico di Roma. Roma, 1915. 4v.

AH 7659.13 — Pais, E. Storia critica di Roma durante i primi cinque secoli. v.1-4. Roma, 1913- 5v.

AH 8607.2 — Pais, Ettore. Ancient Italy. Chicago, 1908.

AH 7278.98.5 — Pais, Ettore. Ancient legends of Roman history. London, 1906.

AH 7278.98.3 — Pais, Ettore. Ancient legends of Roman history. N.Y., 1905.

AH 7419.18 — Pais, Ettore. Dalle guerre puniche a Cesare Augusto. v.1-2. Roma, 1918.

AH 7419.40 — Pais, Ettore. Des origines à l'achievement de la conquête. Paris, 1940.

AH 8607.2.10F — Pais, Ettore. Gli elementi ilaliati sannitici e campani nella più antica civiltà romana. Napoli, 1900.

AH 7239.20 — Pais, Ettore. Fasti triumphales populi Romani. v.1-2. Roma, 1920.

AH 7279.22.10 — Pais, Ettore. Italia antica. Bologna, 1922. 2v.

AH 7278.54.37 — Pais, Ettore. Ottantaduesimo anniversario di Theodor Mommsen. Messina, 1899.

AH 7809.02 — Pais, Ettore. Saggio di illustrazione del calendario romano. Napoli, 1902.

AH 9558.2 — Pais, Ettore. La Sardegna prima del dominio romano. Roma, 1881.

AH 7449.27 — Pais, Ettore. Storia de Roma durante le guerre puniche. 2. ed. Torino, 1935. 2v.

AH 9558.3 — Pais, Ettore. Storia della Sardegna e della Corsica durante il dominio romano. Roma, 1923. 2v.

AH 9607.17 — Pais, Ettore. Storia della Sicilia. Torino, 1894.

AH 8607.2.5 — Pais, Ettore. Storia dell'Italia antica. Roma, 1925. 2v.

AH 8607.2.7 — Pais, Ettore. Storia dell'Italia antica e della Sicilia per l'età anteriore al dominio romano. 2. ed. Torino, 1933. 2v.

AH 7278.98 — Pais, Ettore. Storia di Roma. v.1, pt.1-2. Torino, 1898. 2v.

AH 3966.32 — Los paises legendarios de la Biblia. (Pidal Rios, Carlos.) Buenos Aires, 1962.

AH 276.16A — Paiva d'Andrada, Diogo de. Exame d'antiquidades. Lisboa, 1616.

AH 7489.67.5 — La paix romaine. (Petit, Paul.) Paris, 1967.

AH 3013.28 — The palaces of Nineveh and Persepolis restored. (Fergusson, J.) London, 1851.

AH 7469.09.5 — Paladino, G. La guerra dei gladiatori (73-71 a.C.). Napoli, 1909.

AH 3960.7 — Palästina in der persischen und hellenistischen Zeit. (Hölscher, G.) Berlin, 1903.

AH 828.53 — Palaion, die alte Welt. (Lionnet, A.) Berlin, 1853.

AH 3060.3.5 — Un palais Chaldéen. (Heuzey, L.) Paris, 1888.

Eg 879.03 — Palanque, C. Le Nil...son rôle et son culte en Égypte. Paris, 1903.

AH 49.60 — Palanque, Jean R. Les imperialismes antiques. Paris, 1960.

AH 7059.33 — Palanque, Jean-Rémy. Essai sur la préfecture du prétoire du Bas-Empire. Thèse. Paris, 1933.

AH 7203.146 — Palazzini Fivetti, Luigi. Storia della ricerca delle interpolazioninel Corpus iuris Giustinianeo. Milano, 1953.

AH 3951.1 — Pamphlet box. Palestine.

AH 3951.2 — Pamphlet box. Palestine.

AH 3959.23A — Palestine in general history. (Robinson, T.H.) Oxford, 1929.

AH 3961.3 — La Palestine sur les empereurs grecs, 326-636. (Couret, A.) Grenoble, 1869.

AH 4842.25 — Paley, F.A. Bibliographia Graeca. Lugdunum Batavorum, 1881.

AH 4859.25 — Pallake proef. (Vries, M. de.) Amsterdam, 1927.

AH 3013.956 — Pallis, Svend Aage. The antiquity of Iraq. Copenhagen, 1956.

AH 3022.11 — Pallis, Svend Aage. Chronology of the Shuk-ad culture. Kobenhavn, 1941.

AH 8913.12 — Pallottino, Massimo. La civilisation étrusque. Paris, 1949.

AH 8907.11.5 — Pallottino, Massimo. The Etruscans. 3d Italian ed. Harmondsworth, 1955.

AH 8907.11.10 — Pallottino, Massimo. Etruscologia. 6. ed. Milano, 1968.

AH 8908.16 — Pallottino, Massimo. L'origine degli Etruschi. Roma, 1947.

AH 8162.5 — Pallu de Lessert, A.C. Les fastes de la Numidie sous la domination romaine. Constantine, 1888.

AH 8012.2 — Pallu de Lessert, A.C. Fastes des provinces africaines. Paris, 1896-1901. 2v.

AH 8012.5 — Pallu de Lessert, A.C. Vicaires et comtes d'Afrique. Constantine, 1892.

AH 7208.8A — Palmer, Robert E.A. The archaic community of the Romans. Cambridge, 1970.

AH 7208.6 — Palmer, Robert E.A. The King and the comitium; a study of Rome's oldest public documents. Wiesbaden, 1969.

X Cg — Eg 8.61 — Palmer, W. Egyptian chronicles. London, 1861. 2v.

AH 3936.5 — Palmyra and Zenobia. (Wright, W.) N.Y., 1895.

AH 3936.10 — Palmyre. (Starcky, J.) Paris, 1952.

AH 889.42 — Palumbo, P. Fausto. L'organizzazione del lavoro nel mondo antico. Firenze, 1942.

AH 889.52 — Palumbo, P. Fausto. L'unità economica del mondo antico. Roma, 1952.

Eg 879.17.5 — Pamiatniki egipetskoi religii v fivanskii period. (Frank-Kamenetskii, I.G.) Moskva, 1917- 2v.

AH 3159.10.3 — Die Panbabylonisten der alte Orient. (Jeremias, A.) Leipzig, 1907.

AH 8548.52 — La panceltisme universel et pacifique contre le pangermanisme envahisseur et l'imperialisme anglais. (Sculfort de Beaurepas, Serge.) Paris, 1903. 2v.

AH 8549.65 — Panchaud, Édouard. Le druidisme; ou Religion des anciens gaulois. Lausanne, 1865.

AH 8607.9 — Panciera, D. Lezioni di storia patria. Grosseto, 1867.

AH 9421.10 — Panciera, Silvio. Vita economica de Aquileia in età romana. Venezia, 1957.

AH 7203.40F — Pandectae Justinianae. (Corpus juris civilis. Digesta.) Parisiis, 1818. 3v.

AH 7203.40.9 — Pandectae Justinianae. (Corpus juris civilis. Digesta.) Parisiis, 1818-20. 5v.

AH 7138.73 — Pandects; treatise on Roman law. (Goudsmit, J.E.) London, 1873.

AH 7203.62.5 — Pandekten-Exegeticum. (Esmarch, K.) Prag, 1875.

AH 8548.90 — Paniagua, A. de. Les Celtes bretons et les Phocéens dans le sud ouest de la Gaule. Paris, 1926.

AH 3962.22 — Panin, I.N. Bible chronology. pt.1-3. Lowestoft, 19- ?

AH 8458.5 — Pannonia. (Kovrig, Ilona.) Budapest, 1939.

AH 8457.6 — Pannonia and the onset of crisis in the Roman empire. (Oliva, Pavel.) Praha, 1962.

AH 8457.5 — Pannonie a počátky krize Remskeho imperia. (Oliva, Pavel.) Praha, 1959.

AH 4844.3 — Panofka, T. Die griechischen Trinkhörner. Berlin, 1851.

AH 4818.43F — Panofka, Theodor. Bilder Antiken Lebens. Berlin, 1843.

AH 4818.44F — Panofka, Theodor. Griechinnnen und Griechen. Berlin, 1844.

AH 4818.44.3 — Panofka, Theodor. Manners and customs of Greeks. London, 1849.

AH 9684.5.2F — Panorama von Numantia. (Hofmann, H.) München, 1922.

AH 4108.90.5 — Panske, Petrus Paulus. De magistratibus atticis qui saeculo A. Chr. n. quarto pecunias publicas curabant. pt.1. Inaug. Diss. Lipsiae, 1890.

AH 7469.60.5 — Państwo a kolegia. (Linderski, Jerzy.) Kraków, 1961.

AH 7278.81 — Pantaleoni, D. Storia...di Roma. Torino, 1881.

AH 7207.21 — Pantaleoni, Diomede. Dell'auctoritas patrum. Bologna, 1882.

Eg 877.50 — Pantheon Aegyptiorum. (Iablonski, P.E.) Francofurti, 1750.

AH 3154.13 — Pantheon Babylonicum. Nomina deorum. (Deimel, Anton.) Romae, 1914.

Htn — AH 7836.00F* — Panvinio, O. De Ludis Circensibus. Venetia, 1600.

Htn — AH 7805.57.2F* — Panvinio, Onafrio. Fasti et triumphi. Venetiis, 1557.

Htn — AH 7035.88* — Panvino, O. Civitas romana. Parisiis, 1588.

AH 3964.32 — Paoli, P.A. Della religione de Gentili per riguardo ad alcuni animali e specialmente a topi. Napoli, 1771.

AH 4229.33 — Paoli, U.E. Studi sul processo attico. Padova, 1933.

AH 7279.40.2 — Paoli, U.E. Vita romana. 2. ed. Paris, 1960.

AH 7279.40.5 — Paoli, U.E. Vita romana. 4. ed. Firenze, 1945.

AH 7279.40.7 — Paoli, U.E. Vita romana. 6. ed. Firenze, 1951.

AH 4819.47.6 — Paoli, Ugo E. Cane del popolo. 2. ed. Firenze, 1958.

AH 4819.47.5 — Paoli, Ugo E. Uomini e cose del mondo antico. Firenze, 1947.

VAH 7819.58.5 — Paoli, Ugo Enrico. Ciceronis Jilius. Firenze, 1958.

AH 4139.30 — Paoli, Ugo Enrico. Studi di diritto attico. Firenze, 1930.

AH 4483.15 — Papadopoulos, Nikos M. Hē naumachia tēs Salaminos. Athēnai, 1961.

AH 4298.58 — Paparrēgópanlos, K. Istorikai pragmateiai. v.1-6. Athēnai, 1858.

AH 4708.44 — Paparrēgopoulos, Konstantinos. To telegtaion etos tēs ellēnikēs eleutherias. Athēnai, 1844.

AH 7899.42 — Papàsogli, G. L'agricoltura degli etruschi e dei Romani. Roma, 1942.

AH 8011.3 — Papencordt, F. Geschichte der vandalischen Herrschaft. Berlin, 1837.

AH 7163.28 — Papia Poppoea lex, e ruderibus exposita. (Kirchmaier, G.C.) Wittenbeergae, 1694.

AH 7201.94 — Papiniano. 2. ed. (Mantellini, G.) Roma, 1885.

Eg 1309.31.5F — Papyri der Universität München. (Otto, Walter.) München. 1,1931

Eg 752.10 — Papyri from Panopolis in the Chester Beatty Library. (Skeat, T.C.) Dublin, 1964.

Eg 1158.90.1 — Papyros Ebers; das älteste Buch über Heilkunde. Berlin 1890. (Papyrus Ebers.) Berlin, 1973.

Htn — Eg 1158.75F* — Papyros Ebers...Arzeneimittel der alten Ägypter. (Ebers, G.M.) Leipzig, 1875. 2v.

Eg 1309.21F — Papyrus démotiques de Lille. (Sottas, Henri.) Paris, 1921.

Eg 1109.00.5 — Papyrus d'Orbiney. Papyrus d'Orbiney. The hieroglyphic transcription. Watchung, N.J., 1900.

Eg 1108.90 — Papyrus d'Orbiney. The tale of the two brothers. [Egyptian fairy-tale]. n.p., 189-?

Htn — Eg 1108.98* — Papyrus d'Orbiney. The tale of the two brothers. Watchung, N.J., 1898.

Eg 1109.00.5 — Papyrus d'Orbiney. The hieroglyphic transcription. (Papyrus d'Orbiney.) Watchung, N.J., 1900.

Eg 1158.90.1 — Papyrus Ebers. Papyros Ebers; das älteste Buch über Heilkunde. Berlin 1890. Berlin, 1973.

Eg 1159.37 — Papyrus Ebers. The Papyrus Ebers. Copenhagen, 1957.

Eg 1159.37 — The Papyrus Ebers. (Papyrus Ebers.) Copenhagen, 1957.

Eg 1038.77F — Le papyrus funéraire de Soutimès. (Book of the Dead.) Paris, 1877.

Eg 1309.26F — Papyrus Insinger. Papyrus Insinger. v.1-2. Paris, 1926.

Eg 1309.26F — Papyrus Insinger. v.1-2. (Papyrus Insinger.) Paris, 1926.

Eg 138.68 — Le papyrus judiciaire de Turin. (Devéria, T.) Paris, 1868.

Eg 1309.62F — Le papyrus Jumilhac. (Vandier, Jacques.) Paris, 1962.

Htn — Eg 1309.39PF* — Papyrus Leopold II. Le papyrus Leopold II. N.Y., 1939.

Htn — Eg 1309.39PF* — Le papyrus Leopold II. (Papyrus Leopold II.) N.Y., 1939.

Eg 1309.07 — Der Papyrus Libbey. (Spiegelberg, W.) Strassburg, 1907.

Eg 879.59.15 — Le papyrus mythologique de Te-hem-en-Mout. (Andrzejewski, Tadeusz.) Warszawa, 1959.

Eg 1039.13 — The papyrus of Ani. (Book of the Dead.) London, 1913. 2v.

Eg 1039.13.2 — The papyrus of Ani. (Book of the Dead.) N.Y., 1913. 3v.

Eg 1309.27F — Papyrus Prachov. (Turaev, B.A.) Leningrad, 1927.

Eg 1128.87.15PF — Papyrus Prisse. Le papyrus Prisse et ses variantes. Paris, 1911.

Eg 1128.87.15PF — Le papyrus Prisse et ses variantes. (Papyrus Prisse.) Paris, 1911.

Eg 1309.63PF — Papyrus Reimer I. Papyrus Reimer I. Boston, 1963.

Eg 1309.63PF — Papyrus Reimer I. (Papyrus Reimer I.) Boston, 1963.

Eg 502.12PF — Papyrus Reisner II; accounts of the dockyard workshop at This in the reign of Sesostris I. (Papyrus Reisner II.) Boston, 1965.

Author and Title Listing

AH 4408.90 Die Pelasgerfrage und ihre Lösbarkeit. (Hesselmeyer, E.) Tübingen, 1890.

AH 6082.5 He pelasgis Larissa kai he archaia Thessalia. (Axenidēs, T.D.) Athēnai, 1947.

AH 4329.06 Pelasgove'. (Peroutka, E.) Praze, 1906.

AH 4842.89 Pélékidis, Chrysis. Histoire de l'Éphébie attique. Paris, 1962.

AH 4842.90 Pélékidis, Chrysis. Histoire de l'Éphébie attique. Paris, 1962.

AH 7278.85.19 Pelham, H.F. Essays. Oxford, 1911.
AH 7278.85.7A Pelham, H.F. Outlines of Roman history. N.Y., 1893.
AH 7278.85.7.5 Pelham, H.F. Outlines of Roman history. N.Y., 1893.
NEDL AH 7278.85.13 Pelham, H.F. Outlines of Roman history. 4. ed. London, 1905.

AH 7278.85.15 Pelham, H.F. Outlines of Roman history. 4. ed. N.Y., 1905.

AH 7278.85.25 Pelham, H.F. Outlines of Roman history. 5. ed. London, 1928.

AH 7178.82.3 Pelham, Henry. Imperial domains and the Colonate. London, 1890.

AH 7168.37.2 Pellat, C.A. Exposé...du droit romain sur la propriété. Paris, 1853.

AH 7138.74 Pellat, C.A. Manuale juris synopticum. Paris, 1874.

AH 7203.52 Pellat, C.A. Textes choisis des pandectes. 2. ed. Paris, 1866.

AH 7163.27.2 Pellat, C.A. Textes sur la dot. 2e éd. Paris, 1853.

AH 8857.4 Pellegrini, C. Apparato alle antichità di Capua o vero discorsi della campania. Napoli, 1651.

AH 8857.4.5 Pellegrini, C. Apparato alle antichità di Capua o vero discorsi della campania. Napoli, 1771. 2v.

AH 7114.4 Pellegrino, D. Andeutungen...der römischen Patricier. Leipzig, 1842.

AH 7828.82 Pellisson, M. Les Romains au temps de Pline. Paris, 1882.

AH 7828.82.3A Pellisson, M. Roman life in Pliny's time. Meadville, Pa., 1897.

AH 7618.86 Pellisson, M. Rome sous Trajan. Paris, 1886.

AH 8548.3 Pelloutier, S. Histoire des Celtes. Paris, 1770-71. 8v.

AH 8548.3.2 Pelloutier, S. Histoire des Celtes. Paris, 1771. 2v.

AH 8549.15 Pelloutier, S. Die Religion der Celten. Frankfurt am Mayn, 1784.

AH 5967.7 Peloponnesiaca. (Leake, W.M.) London, 1846.
AH 4511.6 Pamphlet box. Peloponnesian War.
AH 4518.95 Peloponnesian War. (Allcroft, A.H.) London, 1895.
AH 5957.5 Peloponnesos. (Curtius, Ernst.) Gotha, 1851. 2v.
NEDL AH 5957.9 Peloponnesus. (Clark, W.G.) London, 1858.
AH 239.37A Pen and sword in Greece and Rome. (Spaulding, O.L.) Princeton, 1937.

Eg 603.10 Pendleburg, J.D.S. Tell el-Amarna. Photoreproduction. London, 1935.

AH 328.83 Penka, K. Origines ariacae. Wien, 1883.
AH 4409.11 Penka, K. Die vorhellenische Bevölkerung Griechenlands. Hildburg, 1911.

NEDL AH 4278.76.4 Pennell, R.F. Ancient Greece. Boston, 1876.
AH 4278.76.5 Pennell, R.F. Ancient Greece. Boston, 1886.
AH 4278.76.10 Pennell, R.F. Ancient Greece from the earliest times down to 146 B.C. Boston, 1895.

AH 7278.76.2 Pennell, R.F. Ancient Rome. Boston, 1890.
AH 7278.76 Pennell, R.F. Rome. Boston, 1876.
AH 7278.76.1 Pennell, R.F. Rome. Boston, 1886.
AH 7168.94 Penning deposition enligt justiniansk Rätt. (Björling, C.G.E.) Lund, 1894.

AH 3013.39PF Pennsylvania. University. Babylonian Expeditions. Excavations at Nippur. Pt.1-2. Philadelphia, 1905.

Htn Eg 708.58* Pennsylvania. University. Philomathean Society. Report of the committee...to translate...the Rosetta Stone. Philadelphia, 1858.

Htn Eg 708.58.5* Pennsylvania. University. Philomathean Society. Report of the committee. Manuscript. n.p., n.d.

AH 3022.15 Pensamiento idiomatico šumero-akkadico. Series 1. v.1, pt.1-2. (Aldrey Pereira, M.L.) Madrid, 1953. 2v.

AH 4838.92 Pentathlon der Griechen. (Henrich, K.E.) Würzburg, 1892.
VAH 7823.2 Peoli, Ugo Enrico. Ciceronis Jilius. 5. ed. Florentiae, 1961.

AH 6136.5 Peoniia. (Katsarov, G.I.) Sofiia, 1921.
AH 3012.17 People of ancient Assyria. (Laessøe, J.) London, 1963.
AH 2057.5 The peoples of the hills: ancient Ararat and Caucasus. (Burney, Charles Allen.) London, 1971.

AH 3965.15 Peppercorne, J.W. Testimonies to the fertility of ancient Palestine. London, 1838.

AH 7909.32 Perali, P. Le origini artigiane industriali e mercantili di Roma. Roma, 1932.

AH 7909.32.5 Perali, P. Vestigia dell'antico artigianato nelle regioni dell 'Egeo e dell'Italia. Roma, 1934.

AH 7114.28 Les pérégrins déditices dans les premiers siècles de la Republique et sous le Haut-Empire. Thèse. (Moinier, Gilbert.) Paris, 1930.

AH 4819.65.5 Pereira, Maria Helena Rocha. Estudos de história da cultura clássica. Lisboa, 1965.

AH 3707.17 Pereira de Lima, J.M. Phenicios a carthaginezes. Lisboa, 1904.

Eg 709.37.10 Peremans, W. Vreemdelingen en Egyptenaren. Louvain, 1937.
AH 4819.63.25 Peremans, Willy. Hellas en de Westeuropese cultuur. Kasterlee, 1963.

Eg 609.67 Perepelkin, Iurii I. Perevorot Amen-Khotpa IV. Moskva, 1967.

Eg 609.68.5 Perepelkin, Iurii I. Taina zolotogo groba. Moskva, 1968.
Eg 609.67 Perevorot Amen-Khotpa IV. (Perepelkin, Iurii I.) Moskva, 1967.

Htn AH 7203.11.3* Perez, A. Codicis justiniani imperiales. Amstelodami, 1671. 2v.

AH 7203.11 Perez, A. Codicis justiniani imperiales. Amstelodami, 1761.

AH 7203.9 Perez, A. Institutiones imperiales erotematibus. Amstelodami, 1657.

AH 7203.9.2 Perez, A. Institutiones imperiales erotematibus. Amstelodami, 1662.

AH 7203.22 Perezl, A. Juris civilis Antecessoris. Vesaliae, 1670.
AH 2763.5 Pergamon und seine Kunstschätze. (Reifferscheid, August.) Breslau, 1881-82.

AH 2757.5 Pergamos. (Thraemer, E.) Leipzig, 1888.
AH 4838.80 Peri chrēseōs toū stephanou. (Karikoulas.) Erlangen, 1880.

AH 4858.9 Peri gamou. pt.1. (Buddenhagen, F.) Turici, 1919.
AH 4842.47 Peri tes Latinikes glosses kai philologias. (Sakellaropoulou, S.K.) Athēnai, 1878.

AH 4828.73 Peri tou idotikou Biou. (Benizelos, T.B.) Athēnai, 1873.

AH 9727.15 Peri Zamolxidos. Inaug. Diss. (Rousopoulos, A.S.) Gottingae, 1852.

AH 4499.44 Pericle. (Sanctis, G. de.) Milano, 1944.
AH 4499.71 Periclean Athens. (Bowra, Cecil Maurice.) N.Y., 1971.
AH 4499.40 Périclès. (Delcourt, Marie.) Paris, 1940.
AH 4499.54 Périclès. (Homo, León.) Paris, 1954.
AH 4499.37 Pericles. (Mackenzie, Compton.) London, 1937.
AH 4499.48 Pericles and Athens. (Burn, A.R.) London, 1948.
AH 4498.91 Pericles and golden age of Athens. (Abbott, E.) N.Y., 1891.

AH 4967.88.40 Periēgesis toū Néou Anacharsidos eis Ten Hellada. v.1-7, Atlas. (Barthélemy, J.J.) En Bienne, 1819. 3v.

AH 4498.77 Perikleische Zeitalter. (Schmidt, A.) Jena, 1877. 2v.

AH 4498.89.5 Perikles. (Nedwed, E.) Iglau, 1889.
AH 4499.69 Perikles. (Schachermeyr, Fritz.) Stuttgart, 1969.
AH 4499.36 Perikles. (Willrich, Hugo.) Göttingen, 1936.
AH 4498.84 Perikles als Feldherr. (Pflugk-Harttung, A.) Stuttgart, 1884.

AH 7309.61 La periodización de la historiagrafia romana. (Espadas Burgos, Manuel.) Madrid, 1961.

AH 309.70 Periodizatsiia drevnei istorii v sovetskoi istoriografii. (Slonimskii, Mikhail M.) Voronezh, 1970.

AH 4839.34 Die Periodoniken. Diss. (Knab, Rudolf.) Boltrop, 1934.
AH 4139.46 Périphanakis, C. La théorie grecque du droit et le classicisme actuel. Athènes, 1946.

Htn AH 307.69* Perisonius, J. Animadversiones historicae. Amstelodami, 1685.

AH 7297.71 Perizonius, I. Animadversiones historicae. Altenburgi, 1771.

AH 7163.5 Perizonius, J. Dissertationes. Lugdunum Batavorum, 1710.
AH 3007.11A Perizonius, J. Origines Babylonicae et Aegypticae. Lugdunum Batavorum, 1711. 2v.

AH 3013.949F Perkins, Ann L. The comparative archaeology of early Mesopotamia. Chicago, 1949.

AH 3013.942 Perkins, Ann L. The comparative stratigraphy of prehistoric Mesopotamia. Chicago, 1942.

AH 279.36.10 Perkins, C. Ancient history. N.Y., 1936.
AH 6110.26 Perlman, Samuel. Philip and Athens. Cambridge, 1973.
AH 4819.48.5 Permanence de la Grèce. Paris, 1948.
AH 7201.48 Pernice, A. Marcus Antistius Labeo. v.2. Halle, 1873. 3v.

AH 4828.94 Pernice, E. Griechische Gewichte. Berlin, 1894.
AH 7138.24 Pernice, L. Geschichte...römischen Rechts. Halle, 1824.
AH 4329.06 Peroutka, E. Pelasgove'. Praze, 1906.
AH 7659.62.5 Perowne, Stewart. Caesars and saints. 1. ed. N.Y., 1963.
AH 7469.68.5 Perowne, Stewart. Death of the Roman republic. 1. ed. Garden City, 1968.

AH 7769.67 Perowne, Stewart. The end of the Roman world. N.Y., 1967.
AH 7629.60 Perowne, Stewart. Hadrian. London, 1960.
AH 7629.29 Perret, Louis. La titulature impériale d'Hadrien. Paris, 1929.

AH 7448.18.8 Perrin, J.B. Marche d'Annibal. Paris, 1887.
Htn AH 9610.3* Perrinchief, Richard. The Sicilian tyrant. London, 1676.
AH 2357.13 Perrot, G. De Galatia provincia romana. Lutetiae, 1867.
AH 4148.69 Perrot, G. Droit public d'Athènes. Paris, 1869.
AH 9607.19 Perry, W.C. Sicily in fable, history, art and song. London, 1908.

AH 3657.35 La Perse antique et la civilisation iranienne. (Huart, Clément.) Paris, 1925.

AH 7778.92 Der Perserkreig des Kaisers Julian. (Reinhardt, G.) Dessau, 1892.

AH 4478.87 Die Perserkriege. (Delbrück, H.) Berlin, 1887.
AH 6110.14 Perseus and Demetrius. (Elson, Charles F.) n.p., 1935.
AH 6110.11 Perseus König von Makedonien. (Gerlach, F.D.) Basel, 1857.

AH 3657.11 Persia. (Vaux, William Sandys Wright.) London, 1875.
AH 3657.11.5 Persia. (Vaux, William Sandys Wright.) London, 1893.
AH 4479.62 Persia and the Greeks. (Burn, Andrew.) London, 1962.
AH 3657.44 The Persian empire. (Herzfeld, Ernst Emil.) Wiesbaden, 1968.

AH 3660.10 Die persische Politik gegen die Griechen seit dem Ende der Perserkriege. (Schneiderwirth, J.H.) Heiligenstadt, 1863.
AH 7088.77 Person, E. Essai...des provinces romaines. Paris, 1877.
AH 7448.77 Person, Emile. De P. Cornelio Scipione Aemiliano Africano et Numantino. Thesim. Sancti-Clodoaldi, 1877.

AH 169.06 Persona und Prosópon im Recht. (Schlossmann, S.) Kiliae, 1906.

AH 4819.27.8A Personalities of antiquity. (Weigall, A.) Garden City, N.Y., 1928.

AH 7188.61 Personalservitut des Usus. (Bechmann, C.G.A.) Nürnberg, 1861.

AH 3002.2.21 Die Personennamen in der Keilschrifturkunden. (Huber, Engelbert.) Leipzig, 1907.

AH 2573.5 Pertz, C.A. Colophoniaca. Gottingae, 1848.
AH 7409.70.5 Peruzzi, Emilio. Origini di Roma. Firenze, 1970- 2v.
AH 4850.9 Pervanoglu, P. Familienmahl. Leipzig, 1872.
AH 299.62 Pervobytnoobshchinnyi i rabovladel'cheskii stroi na territorii nashei strany. (Laptev, V.V.) Leningrad, 1962.

AH 9713.6 Pesenta za Sitalk. (Fol, Aleksandur.) Sofiia, 1968.
AH 3177.9 Peserico, Luigi. Indagini sul poema di Gilgames. Vicenza, 1919.

AH 8907.12 Peserico, Luigi. Ricerche di storia etrusca. Vicenza, 1919.

Eg 808.78 Pessl, H. von. Das chronologisches System Manetho's. Leipzig, 1878.

AH 4889.01 Pestalozza, U. Vita economica Ateniese. Milano, 1901.
AH 7278.53.3 Peter, C. Geschichte Roms. Halle, 1853. 2v.
AH 7278.53.5 Peter, C. Geschichte Roms. v.1-2; v.3, pt.1-2. 2. Aufl. Halle, 1865. 4v.

AH 7278.53.7 Peter, C. Geschichte Roms. 3. Aufl. Halle, 1870. 3v.

AH 7278.53.9 Peter, C. Geschichte Roms. 4. Aufl. Halle, 1881. 3v.

AH 4808.82A Peter, C.L. Chronological tables of Greek history. Cambridge, 1882.

AH 7038.41.2 Peter, C.L. Die Epochen der Verfassungsgeschichte. Leipzig, 1841.

AH 4808.35 Peter, C.L. Zeittafeln der griechischen Geschichte. v.1-2. Halle, 1835.

AH 4808.35.3 Peter, C.L. Zeittafeln der griechischen Geschichte. 3. Aufl. v.1-2. Halle, 1866.

AH 4808.35.4 Peter, C.L. Zeittafeln der griechischen Geschichte. 4. Aufl. Halle, 1873.

AH 4808.35.6 Peter, C.L. Zeittafeln der griechischen Geschichte. 6. Aufl. Halle, 1886.

AH 7808.41 Peter, C.L. Zeittafeln der römischen Geschichte. 6. Aufl. Halle, 1882.

Author and Title Listing

AH 7278.54.33 — Peter, Carl. Studien zur römische Geschichte. 2. Aufl. Halle, 1863.

AH 7808.35.5 — Peter, Carl. Zeittafeln der römischen Geschichte. Halle, 1864.

AH 7808.35.7 — Peter, Carl. Zeittafeln der römischen Geschichte. Halle, 1882.

AH 7808.35.6 — Peter, Carl. Zeittafeln der römischen Geschichte. 5. Aufl. Halle, 1875.

AH 7498.66 — Peter, Carl Eduard. De fontibus historiae imperatorem Flaviorum. Diss. Halis, 1866.

AH 7488.97 — Peter, H. Die geschichtliche Literatur...Kaiserzeit. Leipzig, 1897.

AH 7008.61 — Peter, K. Mommsen. Studien zur römischen Geschichte. Naumburg, 1861.

AH 7214.5 — Peter, R. Quaestionum pontificatium specimen. Argentorati, 1886. 2 pam.

AH 1819.70.1 — Peters, Francis E. The harvest of Hellenism. N.Y., 1971.

AH 3013.37 — Peters, J.P. Nippur or explorations...on the Euphrates. N.Y., 1898. 2v.

AH 4833.9 — Petersen, C. Gymnasium der Griechen. Hamburg, 1858.

AH 4818.26.7 — Petersen, F.C. De statu culturae. Havniae, 1826.

AH 4118.11 — Petersen, J.C.G. De historia gentium atticarum. Slesvici, 1880.

AH 8864.16 — Peterson, Roy M. The cults of Campania. Rome, 1919.

AH 3921.10F — Petet, Paul. Libanius et la vie municipale à Antioche au IV. siècle après J.-C. Paris, 1955.

AH 4659.62 — Petit, Paul. La civilisation hellénistique. Paris, 1962.

AH 9.59 — Petit, Paul. Guide de l'étudiant en histoire ancienne. Paris, 1959.

AH 9.59.2 — Petit, Paul. Guide de l'étudiant en histoire ancienne. 2. éd. Paris, 1962.

AH 7489.67.5 — Petit, Paul. La paix romaine. Paris, 1967.

AH 279.62 — Petit, Paul. Précis d'histoire ancienne. Paris, 1962.

AH 4728.75 — Petit de Julleville, L. Histoire de la Grèce. Paris, 1875.

AH 4728.75.2 — Petit de Julleville, L. Histoire de la Grèce sou la domination romaine. 2. éd. Paris, 1879.

AH 4728.80 — Petit de Julleville, L. Histoire grecque. Paris, 1880.

AH 4842.13 — Petit de Julleville, L. L'ecole d'Athènes. Paris, 1868.

AH 5760.15 — Petit-Dutaillis, C. Laecedaemoniorum Reipublicae. Lutetiae Parisiorum, 1894.

AH 4818.87.2 — Petit manuel d'archéologie grecque. (Gache, F.) Paris, 1887.

AH 4408.27 — Petit-Radel, C.F. Examen analytique...de l'histoire...de la Grèce. Paris? 1827.

Eg 971.15PF — Le petit temple d'Abou Simbel. (United Arab Republic. Centre of Documentation and Studies on Ancient Egypt.) Le Caire, 1968. 2v.

NEDL AH 278.83 — Petite histoire ancienne. (Duruy, V.) Paris, 1883.

NEDL AH 1278.78 — Petite histoire ancienne des peuples de l'Orient. (Van Den Berg, E.) Paris, 1878.

AH 1278.78.2 — Petite histoire ancienne des peuples de l'Orient. 2. éd. (Van Den Berg, E.) Paris, 1881.

AH 4278.80.5 — Petite histoire des Grecs. (Van den Berg.) Paris, 1880.

AH 7278.83 — Petite histoire grecque. (Duruy, V.) Paris, 1883.

NEDL AH 4136.35.2F — Petitus, S. Leges Atticae. Lugdunum Batavorum, 1742.

Htn AH 4136.35F* — Petitus, S. Leges Atticae. Paris, 1635.

AH 4559.28.5 — Petković, Živko D. Aleksandr Veliki. Beograd, 1928.

AH 2008.9 — Pétra et la Nabatène. Plates, maps and atlas. (Kammerer, Albert.) Paris, 1929-30. 2v.

AH 7478.27 — Petrarca, F. Historia Iulii Caesaris. Lipsiae, 1827.

AH 9057.5 — Petri Marcellini Corradini. (Corradini, Pietro M.) Romae, 1748. 2v.

AH 4279.32 — Petrie, Alexander. An introduction to Greek history. London, 1932.

AH 819.19 — Petrie, W.M.F. Some sources of human history. London, 1919.

AH 3909.5 — Petrie, W.M.F. Syria and Egypt from the Tell el Amarna letters. London, 1908.

Eg 299.11 — Petrie, William M.F. Egypt and Israel. London, 1911.

Eg 278.94.16 — Petrie, William M.F. A history of Egypt during the XVIIth and XVIIIth dynasties. 7. ed. London, 1924.

Eg 278.94 — Petrie, William M.F. A history of Egypt from earliest times to the XVIth dynasty. v.1. London, 1894.

Eg 278.94.10 — Petrie, William M.F. A history of Egypt from the earliest kings to the XVIth dynasty. 10. ed. London, 1923.

Eg 278.94.9 — Petrie, William M.F. A history of Egypt from the earliest times to the XVIth dynasty. 2. ed. London, 1895.

Eg 278.94.17 — Petrie, William M.F. A history of Egypt from the XIXth to the XXXth dynasties. 3. ed. London, 1925.

Eg 819.39 — Petrie, William M.F. The making of Egypt. London, 1939.

Eg 878.98 — Petrie, William M.F. Religion and conscience in ancient Egypt. London, 1898.

Eg 879.06.5 — Petrie, William M.F. The religion of ancient Egypt. London, 1906.

Eg 819.23A — Petrie, William M.F. Social life in ancient Egypt. Boston, 1923.

Eg 819.23.2 — Petrie, William M.F. Social life in ancient Egypt. London, 1932.

AH 3156.18 — Pettinato, Giovanni. Die Ölwahrsagung bei den Babyloniern. Roma, 1966. 2v.

AH 3002.152 — Pettinato, Giovanni. Texte zur Verwaltung der Landwirtschaft in der Ur-III Zeit. Habilitationsschrift. Roma, 1969.

AH 3022.38 — Pettinato, Giovanni. Untersuchungen zur neusumarischen Landwirtschaft. Napoli, 1967.

Htn AH 137.69* — Pettinger, J. An enquiry into the use and practice of juries. London, 1769.

AH 4719.40.2 — Petzold, Karl E. Die Eröffnung des zweiten römisch-makedonischen Krieges. 2. Aufl. Darmstadt, 1968.

AH 1279.38 — Les peuples de l'Orient méditerranée. Paris, 1938. 2v.

AH 8508.12 — Les peuples préromains du Sud-Est de la Gaule. (Barruol, Guy.) Paris, 1969.

AH 4819.25.10 — Peyronnet, Raymond. Méditerranée au temps de l'Iliade; civilisation hellène. Paris, 1924.

NEDL AH 276.28 — Pezelio, T. Mellificium historicum. Francofurti, 1628.

AH 8548.2 — Pezron, P. Antiquité de la nation et de la langue des Celtes. Paris, 1706.

AH 8548.2.5 — Pezron, P. Antiquities of nations. London, 1706.

AH 7519.56 — Pezzella, Federico. L'imperatore Tiberio. Santa Maria, 1956.

AH 7888.97 — Pfaff, Ivo. Über den rechtlichen Schutz. Weimar, 1897.

AH 7179.14 — Pfeifer, Gerhard. Agrargeschichtlicher Beitrag. Inaug. Diss. Altenburg, 1914.

AH 3020.13.7 — Pfeiffer, R.H. Nuzi and the Hurrians. Washington, 1936.

AH 3020.13.9A — Pfeiffer, R.H. One hundred new selected Nuzi texts. n.p., 1936.

AH 3105.5A — Pfeiffer, R.H. State letters of Assyria. New Haven, 1935.

AH 4842.95 — Pfeiffer, Rudolf. History of classical scholarship from the beggining to the end of the Hellenistic age. Oxford, 1968.

AH 854.12 — Das Pferd im arischen Altertum. (Negelini, J.) Königsberg, 1903.

AH 4854.5 — Die Pferdezucht im klassischen Altertum. Diss. (Hömschemeyer, Orloys.) Giessen, 1929.

AH 7228.88 — Pfersche, E. Interdicte des römischen Civilprocesses. Graz, 1888.

AH 8903.5 — Pfiffig, Ambros Josef. Die Ausbreitung des römischen Städtewesens in Etrurien und die Frage der Unterwerfung der Etrusker. Firenze, 1966.

AH 4559.56 — Pfister, F. Alexander der Grosse in den Offenbarungen der Griechen. Berlin, 1956.

AH 8907.27 — Pfister, Kurt. Die Etrusker. München, 1940.

AH 7238.81 — Pfitzner, W. Geschichte der Römischen Kaiserlegionen. Leipzig, 1881.

AH 7114.37 — Pflaum, Hans Georg. Essai sur les procurateurs equestres sous le Haut-Empire romain. Paris, 1950.

AH 4860.5 — Pflege der Kinder bei den Griechen. (Sureçicki, H.) Breslau, 1877.

AH 7188.68 — Pflichttheilsrecht. (Schmidt, A.) Heidelberg, 1868.

AH 7299.11 — Pflüger, P. Die soziale Frage im alten Rom. Zürich, 1911.

AH 4108.76 — Pflug, C. Einführung des Soldes. Waldenburg, 1876.

AH 4498.84 — Pflugk-Harttung, J. Perikles als Feldherr. Stuttgart, 1884.

AH 7138.47 — Pfund, T.G. Rechts Alterthümer. Weimar, 1847.

Eg 509.63 — Der Pharao Josefs. (Margulies, H.) Herrenalb, 1963.

Eg 278.83 — The pharaohs and their people. (Berkley, E.) N.Y., 1883.

Eg 609.65 — Pharaohs of Egypt. 1. ed. (Hawkes, Jacquetta Hopkins.) N.Y., 1965.

Eg 278.87.5 — The pharaohs of the bondage and the Exodus. (Robinson, Charles S.) N.Y., 1887.

AH 8516.11 — Pharus Galliae antiquae. (Labbe, Philippe.) Molinis, 1644.

AH 7469.19.5 — Phases of corruption in Roman administration. (Jolliffe, Richard.) Menasha, 1919.

AH 3707.15 — Phénicie. (Berger, P.) Paris, 1881.

AH 3707.25 — La Phenicie et l'Asie occidentale. (Weill, R.) Paris, 1939.

AH 3707.19F — Phéniciens. (Autran, C.) Paris, 1920.

AH 3707.17 — Phenicios a carthaginezes. (Pereira de Lima, J.M.) Lisboa, 1904.

AH 1028.35A — The Phenix. N.Y., 1835.

NEDL AH 3075.4 — Phiel e Tuklatpalasar II. (Massaroli, G.) Roma, 1882.

AH 4845.19 — Philanthropie bei den Griechen. (Wolff, E.) Berlin, 1902.

AH 4558.97.3 — Philip and Alexander of Macedon. (Hogarth, D.G.) N.Y., 1897.

AH 6110.26 — Philip and Athens. (Perlman, Samuel.) Cambridge, 1973.

AH 4609.40 — Philip V of Macedon. (Walbank, F.W.) Cambridge, Eng., 1940.

AH 6110.10 — Philipp II. (Wüst, F.R.) München, 1938.

AH 6136.10 — Philippes, ville de Macédoine. Atlas. (Collart, Paul.) Paris, 1937. 2v.

AH 4206.7 — Philippi, A. Areopagu...Epheten. Berlin, 1874.

AH 4148.70 — Philippi, A. Attischen Bürgerrechtes. Berlin, 1870.

AH 6110.24 — Philippos deuteros ho Makedon. (Naltsas, Christophoros A.) Thessalonike, 1970.

AH 4609.59.5 — Philippos ho He. (Gyiokos, P.K.) Thessalonike, 1959.

AH 3968.1 — The Philistines. (Macalister, Robert Alexander Stewart.) London, 1914.

AH 7168.63 — Phillimore, J.G. Private law among Romans. London, 1863.

AH 1329.65 — Phillips, Eustace Dockray. The royal hordes. London, 1965.

AH 878.80 — Phillips, H. Worship of the sun. The story told by a coin of Constantine. Philadelphia, 1880.

AH 149.11 — Phillipson, C. International law and custom. London, 1911. 2v.

AH 7238.39 — Philologische Abhandlungen. (Klenze, C.A.C.) Berlin, 1839.

AH 4719.69 — Philopormen. (Errington, Robert.) Oxford, Eng., 1969.

AH 4307.87.5 — Philosophical dissertations on the Greeks. (Pauw, C.) London, 1793. 2v.

AH 7039.69 — La philosophie politique à Rome d'Auguste à Marc Aurèle. (Michel, Alain.) Paris, 1969.

AH 8549.127.10 — The philosophy of ancient Britain. (Daniel, J.) London, 1927.

Htn AH 307.66* — The philosophy of history. (Voltaire, François Marie Arouet de.) London, 1766.

AH 3707.9 — Phoenicia. (Kenrick, J.) London, 1855.

AH 3713.15 — Phoenicia and Israel. (Wilkins, A.S.) London, 1871.

AH 3707.26 — Phoenicia and the Phoenicians. (Baramki, D.C.) Beirut, 1961.

AH 3707.25.5 — Phoenicia and western Asia to the Macedonian conquest. (Weill, R.) London, 1940.

AH 3707.28.1 — The Phoenicians. (Harden, Donald B.) Harmondsworth, 1971.

AH 3707.28 — The Phoenicians. (Harden, Donald B.) London, 1962.

AH 808.79 — Phönix und seine Aera. (Cassel, P.S.) Berlin, 1879.

AH 3707.21 — Die Phönizier. (Landau, W.) Leipzig, 1901.

AH 3707.7 — Die Phönizier. v.1-2, pt.1-3. (Movers, F.K.) Bonn, 1841. 4v.

AH 3715.5 — Der phönizische Handel in den griechischen Gewässern. (Schmülling, T.) Münster, 1884-85.

AH 4543.9 — Phokion. (Bernays, J.) Berlin, 1881.

AH 6007.10 — Phokis. Inaug. Diss. (Schober, Friedrick.) Crossen, 1924.

AH 6009.5 — Der phokische Krieg. (Flathe, Theodor.) Plauen, 1854.

AH 4519.22 — Phos eis tò Thoukydídeiou erhebos. (Laskarus, K.A.) Athenai, 1922.

AH 3074.5F — Photograph of Assyrian tablet. (British Museum.) London, n.d.

Eg 1029.06PF — Photographische Reproduktionen der Inschriften. (Dedekind, A.) Wien, 1906.

AH 5409.8 — Phouriotes, Angelos. Korinthos. Athenai, 1972.

AH 842.19 — Die physikalischen Kenntnisse der Alten. (Fegerl, J.) Mähr, 1896.

AH 4845.13 — Physiognomik der Griechen. (Foerster, R.) Kiel, 1884.

AH 3156.13 — Die physiognomischen Omina der Babylonier. Inaug. Diss. (Kraus, F.R.) Gräfenhainichen, 1935.

AH 862.12 — Die physiologisch und psychologisch Bedeutung der Leber in der Antike. (Hagen, Hansludwig.) Bonn, 1961.

AH 7207.38 — Piaget, Robert. Le sénatus-consulte neronien. Thèse. Lausanne, 1936.

AH 7279.63 — Pialouse, B. De Romulus à Romulus. Paris, 1963.

Eg 885.959 — Piantanida, Danato. La chiave perduta. Milano, 1959.

AH 4829.31A — Picard, Charles. La vie privée dans la Grèce classique. Paris, 1931.

AH 8073.20 — Picard, Colette. Carthage. Paris, 1951.

AH 7509.62.5	Picard, G.C. Auguste et Néron. Paris, 1962.
AH 7489.65	Picard, Gilbert Charles. Augustus and Nero. N.Y., 1966.
Htn AH 8548.1.100*	Picard, Jean. De prisca Celtopaedia. Parisiis, 1556.
AH 7509.39	Piccarolo, A. Augusto e seu século. São Paulo, 1939.
AH 7844.10	Piccoluga, Giulia. Elementi speltocolori nei rihuoli festivi Romani. Roma, 1965.
AH 7549.62	Pichon, Jean Charles. Néron et le mystère des origines chrétiennes. Paris, 1971.
Eg 29.11	Pick, Robert F. Egyptological tracts. N.Y., 1911.
AH 278.46	Pictorial ancient history of the world. (Frost, J.) Philadelphia, 1846.
AH 7498.52	Pictorial history of Rome. (Arnold, Thomas.) London, 1852.
Eg 847.9	Picture writing in ancient Egypt. (Davies, N.M.) London, 1958.
AH 8658.2	Pictures of old Rome. (Elliot, F.D.G.) Leipzig, 1882.
AH 3966.32	Pidal Rios, Carlos. Los paises legendarios de la Biblia. Buenos Aires, 1962.
Htn AH 805.97*	Pie, Thomas. An houreglasse. London, 1597.
AH 7059.68	Pieri, Georges. L'histoire du cens jusqu'à la fin de la République romaine. Paris, 1968.
AH 7419.63	Pieri, Piero. Genesi e sviluppi dell'imperialismo. Torino, 1963.
AH 3017.40	Pierpont Morgan Library, New York. Mesopotamian art in cylinder seals of the Pierpont Morgan Library. N.Y., 1947.
AH 3155.31	Piesl, Helga. Vom Präanthropomorphismus zum Anthropomorphismus. Innsbruck, 1969.
AH 7499.38	Pietrangeli, Carlo. La famiglia di Augusto. Roma, 1938.
AH 7759.32	Piganiol, A. L'empereur Constantin. Paris, 1932.
AH 7839.23	Piganiol, A. Recherches sur les jeux romains. Strasbourg, 1923.
AH 7419.27.5	Piganiol, André. La conquête romaine. 5. éd. Paris, 1967.
AH 7769.47.2	Piganiol, André. L'empire chrétien (325-395). 2. éd. Paris, 1972.
AH 7299.16	Piganiol, André. Essai sur les origines de Rome. Thèse. Paris, 1916.
AH 7279.39	Piganiol, André. Histoire de Rome. Paris, 1939.
AH 7279.39.8	Piganiol, André. Histoire de Rome. 3. éd. Paris, 1949.
AH 7279.39.9	Piganiol, André. Histoire de Rome. 4. éd. Paris, 1954.
AH 7279.39.10	Piganiol, André. Histoire de Rome. 5. éd. Paris, 1962.
AH 7109.16	Piganiol, André. L'impot de capitation sons le Bas-Empire romain. Chambéry, 1916.
AH 7299.73	Piganiol, André. Scripta varia. Bruxelles, 1973. 3v.
AH 7908.74.3	Pigeonneau, H. De convectione urbanae annonae. Sancti-Clodoaldi, 1876.
AH 819.61.4F	Piggott, Stuart. Aux portes de l'histoire. Paris, 1962.
AH 819.61F	Piggott, Stuart. The dawn of civilization. N.Y., 1961.
AH 8549.168	Piggott, Stuart. The Druids. N.Y., 1968.
AH 7844.9.2	Pighi, Giovanni B. De ludis saecularibus populi Romani quiritium. Amstelodami, 1965.
Htn AH 7805.99F*	Piglius, S.V. Annales magistratuum. Antverpiae, 1599.
AH 7805.99.2F	Piglius, S.V. Annales romanorum qui commentarii vicem supplent in omnes veteres historiae romanae scriptores. Antverpiae, 1599-1615. 3v.
AH 186.74	Pignoria, L. De servis. Amstelodami, 1674.
AH 186.56	Pignoria, L. De servis. Patavii, 1656.
Htn Eg 876.08*	Pignorio, L. Characteres Aegyptii hoc est sacrorum. Francofurti, 1608.
Htn Eg 876.69*	Pignorio, L. Mensa isiaca qua sacrorum. Amstelodami, 1669.
AH 7168.96	Pignus in causa judicati captum. (Fleischmann, M.) Breslau, 1896.
AH 3670.5	Pigulevskaia, N.V. Goroda Irana v rannem srednevekove. Moskva, 1956.
AH 3670.5.5	Pigulevskaia, N.V. Les villes de l'état iranien. Paris, 1963.
AH 7863.7	Pike, Edgar R. Love in ancient Rome. London, 1965.
Eg 919.72	Pikus, Nikolai N. Tsanskie zemledel'tsy (nepossedstvennye proisvoditeli) i nemeslenniki v Egipte III v. do n.e. Moskva, 1972.
AH 3013.855	Pillet, M. L'expedition scientifique et artistique de Mésopotamie et de Médie. Paris, 1922.
AH 3005.913	Pillet, Maurice. Un pionnier de l'assyriologie: Victor Place. Paris, 1962.
AH 3163.6	Pinches, T.G. The Babylonian tables of the Berens collection. London, 1915.
AH 3193.7	Pinches, T.G. Late Babylonian astronomical and related texts. Providence, 1955.
AH 3159.14	Pinches, T.G. The Old Testament in the light of the historical records. London, 1902.
AH 3155.7	Pinches, T.G. The religion of Babylonia and Assyria. London, 1906.
AH 3004.5	Pinches, Theodore G. The Babylonian chronicle. London, 1887.
AH 4838.67	Pinder, E. Fünfkampf der Hellenen. Berlin, 1867.
AH 7203.128	Pinelus, Arius. Ad constitutiones codicis de bonis maternis doctissimus. Venetiis, 1573.
AH 3757.5	Pinkerton, J. Seythians or Goths. London, 1787.
AH 4278.25	Pinnock, W. Catechism of history of Greece. London, 1822.
AH 4278.00.11	Pinnock's improved edition of Goldsmith's History of Greece. (Goldsmith, Oliver.) Philadelphia, 1846.
AH 4278.00.15	Pinnock's improved edition of Goldsmith's History of Greece. (Goldsmith, Oliver.) Philadelphia, 1854.
AH 7148.85.2	Pinvert, L. Droit romain du droit de cité. Paris, 1885.
AH 3005.913	Un pionnier de l'assyriologie: Victor Place. (Pillet, Maurice.) Paris, 1962.
Eg 759.22	Piotrowicz, L. Stanowisko nomarchów w administracji Egiptu. Poznan, 1922.
AH 8379.2	Pippidi, D.M. Epigraphische Beiträge zur Geschichte Histrias in hellenistischer und römanischer Zeit. Berlin, 1962.
Htn AH 7807.61PF*	Piranesii, I.B. Lapides capitolini sive fasti. Romae, 1761.
AH 819.51.5	Pirenne, J. Civilisations antiques. Paris, 1951.
Eg 819.61	Pirenne, Jacques. Histoire de la civilisation de l'Égypte. Neuchâtel, 1961. 3v.
Eg 39.32	Pirenne, Jacques. Histoire des institutions et du droit privé de l'ancienne Égypte. v.1-3. Bruxelles, 1932-35. 4v.
Eg 879.65	Pirenne, Jacques. La religion et la morale dans l'Égypte antique. Neuchâtel, 1965.
AH 7438.98.5	Pirro, A. La seconda guerra samnitica. Salerno, 1898.
AH 4228.93	Pischinger, A. De arbitris Atheniensium publicis. München, 1893.
Htn AH 3958.2.5F*	A Pisgah-sight of Palestine. (Fuller, T.) London, 1662.
AH 4449.03	Pisistrato. (Oddo, Antonio.) Palermo, 1903.
AH 7114.42	Pistor, Hans Henning. Prinzeps und Patriziat in den Zeit von Augustus bis Commodus. Thesis. Freiburg, 1965?
Eg 1009.62	Pistsy Drevnego Egipta. (Korostovtsev, M.A.) Moskva, 1962.
AH 7859.3	Pitacco, G. De mulierum romanorum cultu. Görz, 1907.
AH 3663.9	Pithawalla, M. The light of ancient Persia. Adyar, 1923.
Htn AH 7817.13F*	Pitisco, Samuel. Lexicon antiquitatum Romanarum. Leovardiae, 1713. 2v.
AH 7817.13.5F	Pitisco, Samuel. Lexicon antiquitatum Romanarum. Venetiis, 1719. 3v.
AH 5403.5	La più antica aristocrazia Corintiaca. (Porzio, Guido.) Milano, 1919.
AH 3013.36PF	Place, V. Ninive et l'Assyrie. Paris, 1867. 3v.
AH 2958.5	The plain of Troy described. (Maclaren, Charles.) Edinburgh, 1863.
AH 7838.66	Planck, M. Über den Ursprung der römischen Gladiatorenspiele. Ulm, 1866.
AH 3014.16	Plano-convex bricks and the methods of their employment. (Delougaz, Pinhas.) Chicago, 1933.
AH 4278.31	Plass, H.G. Geschichte des alten Griech. Leipzig, 1831. 3v.
AH 4043.5.10	Plass, Hermann. Die Tyrannis in ihren beiden Perioden. Bremen, 1852. 2v.
AH 4043.5.12	Plass, Hermann. Die Tyrannis in ihren beiden Perioden. v.1-2. 2. Ausg. Leipzig, 1859.
AH 4484.15	Platää. (Winter, L.) Berlin, 1909.
AH 4484.5	Plataeische Weihgeschenk. (Frick, Otto.) Leipzig, 1859.
AH 7478.82	Plathner, J. Zur Quellenkritik der...Bürgerkrieges. Bernburg, 1882.
AH 7699.18.2	Platnauer, Maurice. The life and reign of the Emperor Lucius Septimius Severus. Westport, 1970.
AH 7699.18A	Platnauer, Maurice. Life and reign of the Emperor Lucius Septimius Severus. London, 1918.
AH 4118.5	Platner, E. De gentibus atticis. Marburgi, 1811.
AH 4228.24	Platner, E. Process und Klagen. Darmstaat, 1824. 2v.
AH 7009.02	Platner, S.B. Credibility of early Roman history. n.p., 1902.
AH 4888.95	Platon, G. Socialisme en Grèce. Paris, 1895.
AH 8617.5	Platone in Italia. (Cuoco, Vincenzo.) Bari, 1916-24. 2v.
AH 8617.5.2	Platone in Italia. 2. ed. (Cuoco, Vincenzo.) Parma, 1820.
Eg 986.5A	Plaumann, G. Ptolemais in Oberägypten. Leipzig, 1910.
Eg 709.10	Plaumann, Gerhard. Ptolemais in Oberägypten. Leipzig, 1910.
AH 78.87	Plébiscite dans l'antiquité. (Borgeaud, C.) Genève, 1887.
AH 7114.15	Die Plebs. (Vinder, Julius.) Leipzig, 1909.
AH 7114.40	Plebs and princeps. (Yavetz, Z.) London, 1969.
AH 7114.25	The plebs in Cicero's day. Diss. (Park, Marion E.) Cambridge, 1918.
AH 5132.5	Plehn, S.L. Lesbiacorum liber. Berolini, 1826.
AH 817.87	Plessing, F.V.L. Memnonium. Leipzig, 1787. 2v.
AH 4215.5	Ploeg, G.L.J. De veterum Graecorum. Groningae, n.d. 3 pam.
AH 4842.80	Die plotonische Akademie. (Seel, Otto.) Stuttgart, 1953.
AH 7116.2	Plüss, H.T. Die Entwicklung. Leipzig, 1870.
AH 4838.98	Plummer, E.M. Athletics and games of ancient Greece. Cambridge, Mass., 1898.
AH 7055.93.6	Le plus ancien manuscrit de la Notitia dignitatum. (Omont, H.) Paris, 1891.
AH 7468.44	Plutarch. Civil wars of Rome. London, 1844. 3v.
AH 819.70.5	Po co Homer? wyd. 1. (Zieliński, Tadeusz.) Kraków, 1970.
AH 4819.49.10	Počátky helénské civilozace. (Solle, Miloš.) Praha, 1949.
AH 2007.5	Pocock, E. Historia imperii vetustissimi. v.1-2. Harderovici Gebrorum, 1786.
AH 4318.51.1	Pococke, Edward. India in Greece. Delhi, 1972.
AH 2147.10	Podstawy gospodarcze anatolijskiej arystokraeji w świetle inskrypcji fundacyjnych okresu wczesnegocesarstwa. Wyd. 1. (Zablocka, Julia.) Poznań, 1968.
AH 3661.20	Podvig Bakhrama Chubiny. (Gumilev, L.N.) Leningrad, 1962.
AH 308.95	Pöhlmann, R. Aus Altertum und Gegenwart. München, 1895.
AH 308.95.2	Pöhlmann, R. Aus Altertum und Gegenwart. München, 1911.
AH 4309.02	Pöhlmann, R. Griechische Geschichte. München, 1902.
AH 279.11	Pöhlmann, R. von. Aus Altertum und Gegenwart. München, 1911.
AH 4279.09.5	Pöhlmann, R. von. Grundriss der griechischen Geschichte nebst Quellenkunde. 4. Aufl. München, 1909.
AH 7408.21	Pöhlmann, Robert. Die Anfange Roms. Erlangen, 1887.
NEDL AH 817.95	Pölitz, K.H.L. Geschichte der Kultur der Menschheit. Leipzig, 1795.
AH 3179.10	Le poème babylonien de la création. (Enuma elish.) Paris, 1935.
AH 3177.5	Le poème Chaldéen du deluge. (Gilgamesh.) Paris, 1885.
Eg 1059.29	Le poème dit de Pentaour et le rapport officiel. (Hassan, S.) Le Caire, 1929.
Eg 1058.85	Un poeme satyrique. (Revillout, E.) Paris, 1885.
AH 3175.10	Poemetti mitologici babilonesi e assiri. Firenze, 1954.
AH 3175.20A	Poems of heaven and hell from ancient Mesopotamia. (Sanders, Nancy K.) Harmondsworth, 1971.
Eg 819.11.3	Poertner, D.B. Die agyptischen Totenstelen. Paderborn, 1911.
AH 299.45	La poesía amatoria en el antiguo egipto. (Rosenvasser, Abraham.) Buenos Aires, 1945.
Eg 1059.59.5	La poesia dell'Egitto e della Mesopotamia. (Flora, Francesco.) Milano, 1959.
AH 7169.30.5	Poggi, Agostino. Il contratto di società in diritto romano classico. Torino, 1930-34. 2v.
AH 819.68	Pogibskie tsivilizatsii. (Kondratov, Aleksandr M.) Moskva, 1968.
AH 7842.8	Pogled na shkolu i polozhaj. (Lazic, G.S.) Karlovuima, 1895.
AH 3095.5	Pognon, H. L'inscription de Bavian. Paris, 1879.
AH 3154.3	Pognon, H. Les inscriptions babyloniennes du Wade Brissa. Paris, 1887.
Eg 1179.30	Pogo, A. Astronomical ceiling decoration in the tomb of Senmut. Bruges, 1930.
Eg 1179.32	Pogo, A. Calendars on coffin lids from Asyut. Bruges, 1932.
Eg 1179.31	Pogo, A. Zum Problem der Identifikation der nördlichen Sternbilder der alter Ägypter. Bruges, 1931.
AH 278.35	Pogodin, Mikhail Petrovich. Lektsii po Gerenu o politike. Moskva, 1835.
AH 3020.19F	Pohl, A. Vorsargonische und sargonische Wirtschaftstexte. Leipzig, 1935.
AH 3150.13	Pohl, Alfred. Neubabylonische Achtsurkunden aus den Berliner Staatlichen Museum. v.1-2. Roma, 1933-34.
AH 7448.67.3	Pohle, R. De Pugna ad Trebiam Flumen. Inaug. Diss. Halis Saxonum, 1872.
AH 4339.23	Pohlenz, M. Gestalten aus Hellas. München, 1950.

Author and Title Listing

AH 4817.06.4   Potter, J. Antiquities of Greece. 5th ed. London, 1728. 2v.

NEDL AH 4817.06.5   Potter, J. Antiquities of Greece. 6th ed. London, 1740.

AH 4817.06.5   Potter, J. Antiquities of Greece. 6th ed. London, 1740. 2v.

AH 4817.06.6   Potter, J. Antiquities of Greece. 8th ed. London, 1764. 2v.

AH 4817.06.8   Potter, J. Antiquities of Greece. 9th ed. London, 1775. 2v.

AH 4817.06.15   Potter, J. Archaeologia Graeca. Edinburgh, 1813. 2v.

NEDL AH 4817.06.16   Potter, J. Archaeologia Graeca. Edinburgh, 1832. 2v.

NEDL AH 4817.06.17   Potter, J. Archaeologia Graeca. v.2. Edinburgh, 1818.

AH 4817.06.18   Potter, J. Archaeologia Graeca. 3. ed. London, 1837.

AH 3413.5   Pottier, E. L'art hittite. Paris, 1926.

AH 7409.67   Poucet, Jacques. Recherches sur la légende sabine des origines de Rome. Louvain, 1967.

AH 8107.5   Poulle, M.A. A travers la Mauritanie sétifienne. Constantine, 1863.

AH 7819.49.5   Poulsen, F. Glimpses of Roman culture. Leiden, 1950.

AH 7819.49   Poulsen, F. Römische Kulterbilder. Københagen, 1949.

AH 819.36.20   Poulsen, Frederik. Fra stille aftener. København, 1936.

AH 7899.39   Poultry farming as described by the writers of ancient Rome. (Ghigi, A.) Milano, 1939.

Eg 1079.62   Pound, Ezra. Love poems of ancient Egypt. Norfolk, Conn., 1962.

AH 7509.11.5   Poupé, E. Le lieu de la rencontre de Lépide et d'Antoine. Droguignan, 1911.

AH 4818.35   Pouqueville, F.C.H.L. Grèce. Paris, 1835.

AH 4818.35.5   Pouqueville, F.C.H.L. Grèce. Paris, 1843.

NEDL AH 4818.35.9   Pouqueville, F.C.H.L. La Grecia. Venezia, 1836.

AH 8548.140   Powell, Terence G.E. The Celts. London, 1958.

Htn AH 7516.28*   The powerfull favorite...Aelius Seianus. (Matthieu, P.) Paris, 1628.

AH 5308.11   Powers, H.H. The hill of Athena. N.Y., 1924.

AH 4865.5   Pownall, Thomas. Dissertations on the ancient chariot. London, 1771.

AH 3152.7   Praag, A. Droit matrimonial assyro-Babylonien. Amsterdam, 1945.

AH 7918.87   Der Praefectus Fabrum. (Maué, H.C.) Halle, 1887.

AH 819.64.10   Praehomerica et praeitalica. (Capovilla, G.) Roma, 1964.

AH 7626.92   Praelectiones academicae in schola historices camdeniana. (Dadwell, Henry.) Oxonii, 1692.

AH 7779.40   Praetextatus. Proefschrift. (Nicolaas, T.W.J.) Nijmegen, 1940.

AH 8903.6   Praetores Etruriae XV populorum (étude d'épigraphie). (Liou, Bernard.) Bruxelles, 1969.

AH 7206.15   Pragmateia. (Hertzog, Emil.) Monacho, 1837.

AH 7653.35   Pragmatismus in Edward Gibbons Geschichte vom Verfall und Untergang des romischen Reiches. Inaug. Diss. (Ringeling, Hans G.) Schönberg, 1915.

AH 4809.43   Prakken, D.W. Studies in Greek genealogical chronology. Lancaster, Pa., 1943.

AH 4204.5   Prantl, C. De Solonis legibus. Monachii, 1841.

AH 3659.5   Prášek, J.V. Forschungen zur Geschichte des Alterthums. Leipzig, 1897. 3v.

AH 3657.20   Prášek, J.V. Geschichte der Meder und Perser. Gotha, 1906. 2v.

AH 4819.12   Prato, E. Vita e civilta digh Elleni. Livorno, 1912.

AH 7161.32   Prawo rzymskie epoki pryncypatu wobec dizeci pozamałżeńskich. (Kuleczka, Gerard.) Wrocław, 1969.

AH 4408.75   Pre-historic Greece. (Pyne, J.) N.Y., 1875.

AH 408.69   Pre-historic nations. (Baldwin, J.D.) N.Y., 1869.

AH 3013.942F   Pre-Sargonia temples in the Diyala region. (Delougaz, Pinhas.) Chicago, 1942.

Eg 909.39   Preaux, C. L'économie royale des Lagides. Bruxelles, 1939.

AH 7168.78   Il precarium nel diritto romano. (Scialoja, V.) Roma, 1878.

AH 8157.5F   Précis analytique de l'histoire ancienne de l'Afrique septent. (France. Ministère de la guerre.) Paris, 1842.

AH 7138.72.5   Précis de droit romain. (Accarias, C.) Paris, 1872.

NEDL AH 7138.71.3   Précis de droit romain. v.1-2. (Accarias, C.) Paris, 1871. 3v.

NEDL AH 278.11.5   Précis de l'histoire ancienne. 2. éd. (Royou, J.C.) Paris, 1811. 4v.

AH 278.27.12   Précis de l'histoire ancienne. 12. éd. (Poirson, A.) Paris, 1853. 2v.

AH 7478.36.3   Précis des guerres de César. (Napoléon III, emperor of the French.) Bruxelles, 1836.

AH 7478.36   Précis des guerres de César. (Napoléon III, emperor of the French.) Paris, 1836.

AH 39.71.5   Précis des institutions de l'antiquité. (Gaudemet, Jean.) Paris, 1971. 2v.

AH 39.03.2   Précis des institutions publiques...Grèce et Rome. (Boxler, A.A.) Paris, 1903.

AH 279.62   Précis d'histoire ancienne. (Petit, Paul.) Paris, 1962.

AH 7279.69   Précis d'histoire romaine. (Bordet, Marcel.) Paris, 1969.

AH 7161.4   Précis du droit de famille romain. (Rivier, Alphonse.) Paris, 1891.

AH 3959.35   I predecessori d'Israele. (Moscati, Sabatino.) Roma, 1956.

Eg 318.81.5   Preface to, with extracts from, A book of the beginnings. (Massey, G.) London, 1881.

AH 8653.5   La préfecture urbaine à Rome sous le Bas-Empire. 1. éd. (Chastagnol, André.) Paris, 1960.

AH 819.25   La préhistoire orientale. (Morgan, J. de.) Paris, 1925-27. 3v.

Eg 860.5F   Prehistoric pottery and civilization in Egypt. (Raphael, M.) N.Y., 1947.

AH 7829.08.6   Preibisch, J. De sermonis cotidiani formulis. Halis Saxonum, 1908.

AH 909.10   Preisigke, F. Girowesen im griechischen Ägypten. Strassburg, 1910.

Eg 39.03   Preisigke, Friedrich. Städtisches Beamtenwesen im römischen Ägypten. Halle, 1903.

AH 3013.931   Preliminary report upon excavations at Tel Umar, Iraq. (Waterman, Leroy.) Ann Arbor, 1931-33. 2v.

AH 299.20   Preller, Hugo. Das Altertum seine staatliche und geistige Entwicklung und deren Nachwirkungen. Leipzig, 1920.

AH 3013.25   Premier memoire sur les ruines de Ninive. (Hoefer, J.C.F.) Paris, 1856.

AH 7479.57   La première campagne de César contre les Germaines. (Schmittlein, Raymond.) Paris, 1957.

AH 819.50   Les premières civilisations. (Jouguet, Pierre.) Paris, 1950.

AH 818.74   Premières civilisations. (Lenormant, F.) Paris, 1874. 2v.

AH 819.09   Premières civilisations. (Morgan, J.) Paris, 1909.

AH 819.41.8   Les premières civilisations de la Mediterranée. 6. éd. (Gabriel-Leroux, Jacqueline.) Paris, 1958.

AH 8.85   Premières compilations françaises d'histoire ancienne. (Meyer, P.) Paris, 1885.

AH 3051.5F   Premières recherches archéologiques à Kich. (Genouillac, H. de.) Paris, 1924.

AH 4709.38.5   Les premiers rapports de Rome et de la confédération achaienne, 198-189 avant J.C. Thèse. (Aymard, A.) Bordeaux, 1938.

AH 4279.40A   Prentice, William K. The ancient Greeks. London, 1940.

AH 279.65.10   Preobrazhenskii, Petr F. V mire antichnykh idei i obrazov. Moskva, 1965.

AH 8548.130   Présence des Celtes. (Rivoallan, A.) Paris, 1957.

Eg 839.13   La préservation de la propriété funéraire. (Sottas, H.) Paris, 1913.

AH 7828.93   Preston, H.W. Private life of the Romans. Boston, 1893.

AH 7819.30.15   Preston, H.W. The private life of the Romans. Chicago, 1930.

AH 7709.42A   The pretorian prefect from Commodus to Diocletian (A.D. 180-305). (Howe, L.L.) Chicago, 1942.

Eg 879.57.5   Les prêtres de l'ancienne Égypte. (Sauneron, Serge.) Paris, 1957.

AH 7748.69   Preuss, Theodor. Kaiser Diocletan. Leipzig, 1869.

AH 2007.4   Price, David. Essay towards the history of Arabia. London, 1824.

AH 3159.15.5   Price, I.M. The monuments and the Old Testament. Chicago, 1899.

AH 3159.15   Price, I.M. The monuments and the Old Testament. 2. ed. Chicago, 1900.

AH 3052.5A   Price, I.M. Some literary remains of Rim-Sin...king of Larsa. Chicago, 1904.

AH 3002.2.15   Price, Ira M. The great cylinder inscriptions A and B of Gudea. Pt.1-2. Leipzig, 1899-1927. 2v.

Eg 878.19   Prichard, J.C. An analysis of Egyptian mythology. London, 1819.

Eg 878.19.5   Prichard, J.C. An analysis of Egyptian mythology. London, 1838.

AH 5390.15   Prickard, A.O. The return of the Theban exiles, 379-378 B.C. Oxford, 1926.

Htn AH 457.16.20*   Prideaux, H. The Old and New Testament connected in the history of the Jews. Charlestown, 1815-16. 4v.

AH 457.49   Prideaux, H. The Old and New Testament connected in the history of the Jews. v.3-4. London, 1749. 2v.

AH 457.16.5F   Prideaux, H. The Old and New Testament connected in the history of the Jews. 5. ed. London, 1718-19. 2v.

AH 457.16.10   Prideaux, H. The Old and New Testament connected in the history of the Jews. 10. ed. v.1-2. London, 1729. 4v.

AH 457.16.15   Prideaux, H. The Old and New Testament connected in the history of the Jews. 13. ed. v.1-2. Glasgow, 1763. 4v.

AH 3147.3   Das Priester- und Beamtentum der altbabylonischen Kontrakte. (Lindl, Ernest.) Paderborn, 1913.

AH 7409.12   Der Priester Codex in der Regia. (Kornemann, E.) Tübingen, 1912.

Eg 879.05   Priester und Tempel im Hellenistischen Ägypten. (Otto, Walter.) Leipzig, 1905. 2v.

AH 8207.34   Priestley, Harold E. Britain under the Romans. London, 1967.

AH 819.27.10   Priests and kings. (Peake, Harold.) New Haven, 1927.

Eg 879.57.7   The priests of ancient Egypt. (Sauneron, Serge.) N.Y., 1960.

AH 4809.06   The priests of Asklepios; a new method of dating Athenian archons. (Ferguson, W.S.) Berkeley, 1906.

AH 4408.91.7   Prigge, E. De thesei rebus gestis quaestionum. Marpurgi, 1891.

AH 819.54   La prima umanità. (Turone, Mario.) Milano, 1954.

AH 2011.6   Primae lineae historiae regnorum arabicorum. (Reiske, J.J.) Gottingae, 1847.

AH 3143.19   A primer of Assyriology. (Sayce, Archibald H.) London, 1894.

AH 3143.19.1   A primer of Assyriology. (Sayce, Archibald H.) N.Y., 1894.

AH 8548.95   Primitieve Keltistiek in de Nederlanden. (Chotzen, T.M.) 's-Gravenhage, 1931.

AH 818.69   Primitive civilization. (Mahaffy, J.P.) London, 1869.

AH 818.94   Primitive civilizations. (Simcox, E.J.) London, 1894. 2v.

AH 4819.25.5   Primitive culture in Greece. (Rose, H.J.) London, 1925.

AH 7819.26   Primitive culture in Italy. (Rose, Herbert J.) London, 1926.

AH 407.89   Primitive history. (Williams, W.) Chichester, 1789.

Htn AH 316.77F*   Primitive origination of mankind. (Hale, Matthew.) London, 1677.

Htn AH 295.64*   Il primo volume delle cagioni delle guerre antiche. (Porcacchi, T.) Vinegia, 1564.

AH 7409.59.5   Primordia civitates. (Francisci, Pietro.) Romae, 1959.

Htn AH 5723.7*   Primordia Corcyrae. (Giurini, A.M.) Brixiae, 1738.

AH 5723.5   Primordia Corcyrae. (Giurini, A.M.) Lycij, 1725.

AH 3002.2.19   Prince, John D. Materials for a Sumerian lexicon. Leipzig, 1905-08.

Htn AH 7406.36*   Princeps, eiusque arcana. (Malvezzi, V.) n.p., n.d. 2 pam.

AH 7509.36   Princeps; Studien zur Geschichte des Augustus. (Weber, W.) Stuttgart, 1936.

AH 7509.56   Il principato di Augusto. (Mashkin, N.A.) Roma, 1956. 2v.

AH 3863.5   Les principaux résultats des nouvelles fouilles de Suse. (Cruveilhier, P.) Paris, 1921.

AH 7039.53.5   Principe e magistrati repubblicani. (Tibiletti, G.) Roma, 1953.

AH 7138.91.15   Principes de droit romain. 6. éd. v.1-2. (Bry, Georges.) Paris, 1927-30.

AH 7237.64.5   Principes de l'art de la guerre. (Stierneman.) Strasbourg, 1765.

AH 7203.27   Principia juris civilis. (Eck, Cornelius van.) Trajecta ad Rhenum, 1756. 2v.

AH 7139.34.15   Principles of Roman law. (Schulz, Fritz.) Oxford, 1936.

AH 4219.5   Pringsheim, F. The Greek law of sale. Weimar, 1950.

AH 7206.33   Pringsheim, Fritz. Zum Plan einer neuen Ausgabe der Basiliken. Berlin, 1956.

AH 7114.42   Prinzeps und Patriziat in den Zeit von Augustus bis Commodus. Thesis. (Pistor, Hans Henning.) Freiburg, 1965?

AH 7139.34.20   Prinzipien des römischen Rechts. (Schulz, Fritz.) München, 1934.

AH 3096.3   Le prisme d'Assaraddon...681-668. (Scheil, V.) Paris, 1914.

AH 3097.7   Le prisme du Louvre AO 19.939. (Ashurbanapal, king of Assyria.) Paris, 1957.

Author and Title Listing

Author and Title Listing

AH 4559.34.5   Ptolemaios und Alexander. (Strasburger, H.) Leipzig, 1934.

Eg 986.5A   Ptolemais in Oberägypten. (Plaumann, G.) Leipzig, 1910.

Eg 709.10   Ptolemais in Oberägypten. (Plaumann, Gerhard.) Leipzig, 1910.

AH 4818.36   Public and private life of ancient Greeks. (Hase, H.) London, 1836.

AH 4229.36   Public arbitration in Athenian Law. (Harrell, Hansen C.) Chicago, 1936.

AH 4229.36.3   Public arbitration in Athenian Law. (Harrell, Hansen C.) Columbia, 1936.

AH 4108.17.4   Public economy of Athenians. (Böckh, August.) Boston, 1857.

AH 4108.17.3   Public economy of Athens. 2. ed. (Böckh, August.) London, 1842.

AH 7178.91A   Public lands and agrarian laws. (Stephenson, A.) Baltimore, 1891.

AH 7842.16   Public libraries and literary culture in ancient Rome. (Boyd, C.E.) Chicago, 1915.

AH 7842.16.5   Public libraries and literary culture in ancient Rome. Thesis. (Boyd, C.E.) Chicago, 1916.

AH 930.10   The public school's atlas of ancient geography. (Butler, George.) London, 1889.

AH 7499.46   The public works of the Julio-Claudians and Flavians. Thesis. (Bourne, Frank C.) Princeton, 1946.

AH 7889.72   Publicans and sinners; private enterprise in the service of the Roman Republic. (Badian, Ernst.) Ithaca, N.Y., 1972.

EgP 133.15F   Publications. Textes et documents. (Société fouadier de papyrologie.) Caire. 1-6,1931-1945 3v.

EgP 133.15   Publications. Textes et documents. (Société fouadier de papyrologie.) Caire. 7-9,1947-1949

AH 3002.70   Publications - Texts. (American Schools of Oriental Research.) Paris. 1-6,1927-1939 6v.

AH 3002.8   Publications of the Babylonian section...Museum. (University of Pennsylvania.) Philadelphia. 1-16,1911-1930 20v.

AH 7469.39.10   Publius Cornelius Dolabella. (Sheldon, E.L.) N.Y., 1939.

AH 7138.45.3   Puchta, G.F. Cursus der Institutionen. Leipzig, 1845. 2v.

AH 7138.45.9   Puchta, G.F. Cursus der Institutionen. Leipzig, 1871. 3v.

AH 7138.45.10   Puchta, G.F. Cursus der Institutionen. Leipzig, 1875.

AH 7138.45.8   Puchta, G.F. Cursus der Institutionen. 6. Aufl. Leipzig, 1865. 3v.

AH 7138.51   Puchta, G.F. Kleine civilistische Schriften. Leipzig, 1851.

AH 4279.28.5   Puech, Aimé. Ce qu'il faut connaître de la Grèce antique. Paris, 1928.

AH 8549.86.1A   Pufendorf, E. A dissertation upon the Druids. Edinburgh, 1886.

AH 8549.86   Pufendorf, E. A dissertation upon the Druids. Edinburgh, 1886.

AH 4279.67   Pugliese Carratelli, Giovanni. Storia greca. Milano, 1967.

AH 7139.67.5   Puglisi Cosentino, Alfio. Influenza del primo cristianesino sul diritto romano dell'epoca classica. Palermo, 1967?

AH 9609.5   Puglisi Marino, S. Siculi e greci nella Sicilia orientale. Catania, 1909.

AH 8607.7   Puglisi-Marino, S. Sul nome Italia. Catania, 1901.

AH 7448.69   Die punischen Kriege. (Jäger, Oskar.) Halle, 1869.

AH 7448.18.12   Punto per Punto. (Montanari, T.) Mantova, 1903.

AH 7138.72.3   Puntschart, V. Civilrechts der Römer. Erlangen, 1872.

Eg 959.60   Puteshestvie Un-Amuna v Bibl; egipetskii ieraticheskii papirus no.120. (Unamun.) Moskva, 1960.

AH 4408.75   Pyne, J. Pre-historic Greece. N.Y., 1875.

Eg 1042.908   Pyramid Texts. Die altägyptischen Pyramidentexte. v.1-4. Leipzig, 1908-22. 3v.

Eg 1042.969   Pyramid Texts. The ancient Egyptian pyramid texts. Oxford, 1969.

Eg 1042.969.2   Pyramid Texts. The ancient Egyptian pyramid texts. Supplement of hieroglyphic texts. Oxford, 1969.

Eg 1042.952   Pyramid Texts. The pyramid texts in translation and commentary. 1. ed. N.Y., 1952. 4v.

Eg 1042.923F   Pyramid Texts. Les textes des pyramides egyptiennes. v.1-2. Bruxelles, 1923-24.

Eg 1042.935F   Pyramid Texts. Übersetzung und Kommentar zu den altägyptischen Pyramidentexten. Glückstadt, 1935-1962. 6v.

Eg 1042.968F   Pyramid texts: the pyramid of Unas. Princeton, 1968.

Eg 1042.952   The pyramid texts in translation and commentary. 1. ed. (Pyramid Texts.) N.Y., 1952. 4v.

Eg 879.49   Pyramidenzeit. (Junker, H.) Einsiedeln, 1949.

AH 7926.47   Pyramidographia. (Greaves, John.) London, 1646. 2 pam.

AH 5610.15   Pyrrhos. (Léveque, P.) Paris, 1957.

AH 5610.12   Pyrrhus. (Hassell, Ulrich von.) München, 1947.

AH 5610.6.2   Pyrros, ho Basilias tēs Epeirov. 2. ed. (Garouphalias, Petros Euagelov.) Athēnai, 1972.

AH 5610.14   Ho Pyrros en Italia, skopoi kai drasis autou. Diss. (Bartsos, Ioannes A.) Athēnai, 1967.

AH 4838.41   Pythien, Nemeen und Isthmien. (Krause, J.H.) Leipzig, 1841.

AH 2575.9   Qua condicione Ephesii. (Menadier, J.) Berolini, 1880.

AH 7148.76   Qua condicione iuris reges. (Bohn, Oscar.) Berolini, 1877.

AH 4842.69   Qua ratione Graeci liberos docuerint. (Bendel, Paulus.) Monasterii Guestfalorum, 1911.

AHP 27.5   Quaderni dell'impero; La scienza e la tecnica di tempi di Roma imperiale. Roma. 10-20 2v.

AH 4524.7   Quadringentorum Athenis factione. (Wattenbach, G.) Berolini, 1842.

AH 7448.72   Quaeritur unde belli punici secundi. (Vollmer, A.) Gottingae, 1872.

AH 4838.88   Quaestiones Agonisticae. (Mie, F.) Rostochii, 1888.

AH 7508.87   Quaestiones criticae de belle mutinensi. (Hagen, M. von.) Marburgi Cattorum, 1887.

AH 7448.48   Quaestiones criticae de belli punici. (Wijmre, J.A.) Groningae, 1848.

AH 7055.93.6.5   Quaestiones de Notitia dignitatum. (Seeck, Otto.) Berolini, 1872.

AH 3653.5   Quaestiones de Persarum satrapis satrapiiseque. (Buchholz, A.) Lipsiae, 1894.

AH 3361.5   Quaestiones de rebus Cyrenarum. (Rossberg, W.) Frankenbergae, 1876.

Eg 709.00   Quaestiones de rebus militaribus...in regno Lagidarum. (Schubart, W.) Trebnitz, 1900.

AH 4108.73   Quaestiones fiscales iuris attici. (Schoell, R.) Berolini, 1873.

AH 4328.91F   Quaestiones Ionicas. (Schwartz, E.) Adleranis, 1891.

AH 7038.42.2   Quaestiones literariae. (Terpstra, D.) Rotterdami, 1842.

AH 4858.11   Quaestiones nonnullae ad Atheniensium matrimonia vetamque conjugalem pertinentes. Inaug. Diss. (Mulder, J.J.B.) Traiecti ad Rhenum, 1920?

AH 7869.7   Quaestiones onomatologicae Latinae. (Hübner, Emil.) Berolini, 1874. 2 pam.

AH 7869.5   Quaestiones onomatologicae Latinae. (Hübner, Emil.) Bonnae, 1854.

AH 4448.86   Quaestiones pisistrateae. (Toepffer, J.) Dorpati, 1886.

AH 7698.88   Quaestiones severianae. (Wirth, A.) Lipsiae, 1888.

AH 4848.11   Quaestionum de re vestiaria graecorum specimen. Diss. (Boelhau, I.) Wimariae, 1884.

AH 5658.5   Quaestionum Euboicarum. (Bursian, C.) Lipsiae, 1856.

AH 7214.5   Quaestionum pontificatium specimen. (Peter, R.) Argentorati, 1886. 2 pam.

AH 2158.2   Quaestionum propontiacarum. (Faber, A.) Herford, 1858.

AH 7059.09   Die Quästoren der Römischen Republik. (Sobeck, T.) Trebnitz, 1909.

AH 7909.02   Quamodo per servos libertosque negotiarentur Romani imperii temporibus. (Juglar, L.) Paris, 1902.

AH 1298.61   Quatremère, Etienne M. Mélanges d'histoire et de philologie orientale. Paris, 1861.

AH 4279.67.5   Quattro studi spartani e altri scritti di storia greca. (Levi, Mario Attilio.) Milano, 1967.

Eg 845.5A   The queens of Egypt. (Buttles, Janet R.) N.Y., 1908.

AH 7408.53   Quellen der altesten römischen Geschichte. (Gerlach, F.D.) Basel, 1853.

AH 7519.03.2   Die Quellen der Vita Tiberii. (Bergmans, Jan.) Bockhandel, 1903.

AH 7448.72.10   Die Quellen des Appian und Dio Cassius für die Geschichte des zweiten punischen Krieges. (Buchholz.) Pyritz, 1872.

AH 7138.79   Quellen des römischen Rechts. (Heumann, H.G.) Jena, 1879.

AH 7139.53F   Die Quellen des römischen Rechts. (Wenger, L.) Wien, 1953.

AH 7468.79.5   Quellen und Chronologie der römisch-parthischen Feldzüge in den Jahren 713-718. Inaug. Diss. (Bürcklein, A.) Berlin, 1879.

Eg 809.17F   Quellen und Forschungen zur Zeitbestimmung der ägyptischen Geschichte. Berlin. 1-2,1917-1935 2v.

AH 4609.14   Die Quellen zur Geschichte der Diadochenzeit. (Schubert, R.) Leipzig, 1914.

AH 3910.14   Die Quellen zur Geschichte des Krieges der Römer gegen Antiochus III. (Kümpel, Eduard.) Hamburg, 1893.

AH 4543.7   Quellen zur Geschichte Phokions. (Klotz, W.O.R.) Zittau, 1877.

AH 4298.95   Quellenbuch. (Butzer, H.) Dresden, 1895.

AH 7201.77   Quellenkunde des römischen Rechts. (Kipp, T.) Leipzig, 1896.

AH 9610.15   Quellenuntersuchung zur Geschichte des jüngeren Dionys. (Krug, Otto.) Kattowitz, 1891.

AH 7729.11   Quellenuntersuchungen zu den Viten des Heliogabalus. (Hönn, K.) Leipzig, 1911.

AH 7509.69.5   Quellenuntersuchungen zur Geschichte des 2. Triumvirats. Inaug. Diss. (Fadinger, Volker.) München, 1969.

AH 7159.67   Quelques aspects de la responsabilité pénale en droit romain classique. (Lebigne, Arlette.) Paris, 1967.

AH 3961.4   Quelques notes sur la guerre de Bar Kôzèbâ. (Derenbourg, M.J.) Paris, 1878.

AH 4819.33.16   Quennell, M.C. Everday things in ancient Greece. 2. ed. London, 1954.

AH 4819.33.15   Quennell, M.C. Everday things in classical Greece. N.Y., 1933.

AH 861.9   Quenstedt, J.A. Septultura veterum. Wittenberge, 1660.

AH 7468.96   La question sociale à Rome. (Lewandowski, M.) Paris, 1896.

AH 7468.98   Questioni cronologiche. (Tarantino, Mario.) Catania, 1898.

AH 4148.99   Questioni di diritto Attico. (Arvanitopullo, A.) Roma, 1899.

AH 279.52.10   Questioni di storia antica. (Passerini, Alfredo.) Milano, 1952.

AH 4708.94   Questioni politiche e reforme sociali. v.1-2. (Sanctis, G.) Roma, 1894.

AH 7169.45   Questions and answers on Roman law. (Hornby, J.A.) London, 1945.

AH 4298.90   Quid de Graecis veterum indorum. (Lévi, Sylvain.) Paris, 1890.

AH 3407.13   Quid de Hethaeis. (Fossey, C.) Versailles, 1902.

AH 8557.7   Quid praicipue apud Romanos adusque Diocletiani tempora Illyricum fuerit breviter disseritur. (Poinsignon, A.M.) Parisiis, 1896.

NEDL AH 7528.94   Quidde, L. Caligula. Leipzig, 1894.

AH 7179.08   Quillfeldt, W. Altrömisches Landwirtschaftsrecht. Inaug. Diss. Heidelberg? 1908?

AH 7148.59   Quinion, L. Du municipe romain. Paris, 1859.

AH 7539.52   Quintus Veranius. (Gordon, A.E.) Berkeley, 1952.

AH 3966.17   Quistorpius, J. Nebo, undi tota perlustratur Terra Sancta. Rostochi, 1663.

AH 7519.01.5   Quo modo Tiberius Claudius Nero. (Lévy, L.) Paris, 1901.

AH 7088.85.5   Quomodo provinciarum Romanarum. (Bourgeois, Émile.) Paris, 1885.

AH 7548.72   Raabe, A.H. Geschichte und Bild von Nero. Utrecht, 1872.

AH 4169.12   Raape, L. Der Verfall des griechischen Pfandes. Halle, 1912.

AH 4483.7   Raase, Hans. Beitrag zur Darstellung der Schacht bei Salamis. Rostock, 1904.

AH 7918.41   Rabanis, J.F. Recherches sur les dendrophores et sur les corporations romaines en général. Bordeaux, 1841.

AH 4833.19   Rabath, Joseph. Artis gymnicae quae fuerit origo. Gleiwitz, 1851.

AH 4407.87   Rabaut, J.P. L'histoire primitive de la Grèce. Paris, 1787.

AH 7189.71   Rabovladel'cheskie otnosheniia v romner Rimskoi imperii (Italiia). (Shtaerman, Elena.) Moskva, 1971.

AH 4189.68   Rabstvo na periferii antichnogo mira. Leningrad, 1968.

AH 4189.69   Rabstvo v ellinisticheskikh gosudarstvakh v III-I vv do n.e. (Blavatskaia, Tat'iana v.) Moskva, 1969.

AH 4189.63.5   Rabstvo v mikenskoi i gomerovskoi Gretsii. (Lentsman, Iakov A.) Moskva, 1963.

AH 3167.11   Rabstvo v Vavilonii VII-IV vv. do n.e. (661-331 gg). (Dandamaev, Mukhammed A.) Moskva, 1974.

AH 7238.50   Rabus, J.M. Ad solemia anniversaria gymnasii. n.p., 1850.

AH 8016.3   Rabusson, A. De la geographie du nord de l'Afrique. Paris, 1856.

Call number	Entry
AH 4298.21F	Raccolta di 100 soggetti li piú remarche. (Bertocchi, F.) Roma, 1821.
AH 8048.3	La race chamitique. (Vibert, Théodore.) Paris, 1916.
AH 4329.37	Race mixture among the Greeks before Alexander. (Diller, A.) Urbana, 1937.
Eg 819.51.5	Race-relations in ancient Egypt. (Davis, Simon.) London, 1951.
AH 3807.5	La race sémitique. (Vibert, C.T.) Paris, 1883.
AH 3963.76	The races of the Old Testament. (Sayce, A.H.) London, 1891.
AH 8011.10	Rachet, Marguerite. Rome et les berbères. Bruxelles, 1970.
Eg 879.61	Rachewiltz, Boris de. I miti e i luoghi dell'antico Egitto. Milano, 1961.
AH 7329.67	Racial prejudice in imperial Rome. (Sherwin-White, Adrian N.) Cambridge, 1967.
AH 9777.40	Rackus, A.M. Guthones (the Goths), kinsmen of the Lithuanian people. Chicago, 1929.
AH 7298.21	Racollta...istoria romana. (Bertocchi, Fulvia.) Roma, 1821.
AH 3021.3	Radar, H. Early Babylonian history. N.Y., 1899.
AH 3021.3.3	Radar, H. Early Babylonian history. N.Y., 1900.
AH 3155.14	Radau, Hugo. Bel, the Christ of ancient times. Chicago, 1908.
AH 4559.31.10A	Radet, Georges. Alexandre le Grand. 5. éd. Paris, 1931.
AH 4559.31.12	Radet, Georges. Alexandre le Grand. 7. éd. Paris, 1950.
AH 6108.7	Radet, Georges. De coloniis a Macedonibus in Asiam cis Taurum deductis. Thesim. Parisiis, 1892.
AH 4559.25	Radet, Georges. Notes critiques sur l'histoire d'Alexandre. Bordeaux, 1925-27.
AH 7139.27	Radin, Max. Handbook of Roman law. St. Paul, 1927.
AH 69.09	Radin, Max. Legislation of Greeks and Romans on corporations. N.Y.? 1909.
AH 7479.39.5	Radin, Max. Marcus Brutus. N.Y., 1939.
AH 7479.56	Radio Italiana. Cesare nel brimillenario della morte. Torino, 1956.
AH 4483.12	Rados, C.N. La bataille de Salamine. Thèse. Paris, 1915.
AH 4539.08	Radüge, E. Zur Zeitbestimmung des euböischen...Krieges. Giessen, 1908.
AH 4038.93.3	Raeder, A. Athens politiske udvikling. Christiania, 1893.
AH 4189.69.5	Rädle, Herbert. Untersuchungen zum griechischen Freilassungswesen. Inaug. Diss. München, 1969.
AH 819.61.25	Rätselhafte Kulturen. (Lissner, Ivar.) Olten, 1961.
AH 7200.5	Rättshistoriska studier till den tolf taflanaslag. (Wolff, Emil.) Göteborg, 1883.
AH 8548.142	Raftery, Joseph. The Celts. Cork, 1964.
AH 3957.30	Ragaz, L. Die Bibel. Zürich, 1947-50. 7v.
AH 3507.7.5	Ragozin, Z.A. Media, Babylon, and Persia. N.Y., 1900.
AH 3507.7.7	Ragozin, Z.A. Media, Babylon, and Persia. N.Y., 1903.
AH 3507.7	Ragozin, Z.A. Story of Media, Babylon and Persia. N.Y., 1888.
AH 3075.10	Ragozin, Z.A. The story of the nations: story of Assyria. N.Y., 1887.
NEDL AH 408.99	Ragozin, Z.A. (Mrs.). A history of the world. N.Y., 1899.
AH 3021.2.5	Ragozin, Zénaide A. The story of Chaldea. 2. ed. N.Y., 1890.
AH 3021.2.10	Ragozin, Zénaide A. The story of Chaldea from the earliest times to the rise of Assyria. 2. ed. N.Y., 1896.
AH 3021.2A	Ragozin, Zénaide A. The story of the nations: story of Chaldea. N.Y., 1886.
AH 859.3	Rainneville, Joseph de. La femme dans l'antiquité et d'après la morale. Paris, 1865.
Eg 299.12.3	Rais et dieux d'Egypte. 5. éd. (Moret, Alexandre.) Paris, 1925.
AH 7138.78.5	Raisini, G. Programma di diritto romano. Bologna, 1878.
Htn AH 276.14.5*	Raleigh, Walter. An abridgment of Raleigh's Historie of the world. London, 1700.
Htn AH 276.14.4F*	Raleigh, Walter. The historie of the world. London, 1628.
Htn AH 276.14.3F*	Raleigh, Walter. Historie of the world and Life of the author. London, 1736. 2v.
Htn AH 276.14.7F*	Raleigh, Walter. Historie of the world in five bookes. London, 1634.
AH 276.14.2F	Raleigh, Walter. Historie of the world in five bookes. London, 1677.
Htn AH 276.14F*	Raleigh, Walter. Historie of the world in five books. London, 1614.
AH 276.14.9	Raleigh, Walter. The history of the world. London, 1971.
AH 4229.41	Ralph, J.D. Ephesus in Athenian litigation. Thesis. Chicago, 1941.
AH 7168.74	Rambaud de Larocque, Marcel. Étude sur la société de crédit foncier de France. Paris, 1874.
AH 7478.70.3	Ramée, D. César. Paris, 1870.
Eg 608.70	Rameses the Great. (Tugnot de Lanoye, Ferdinand.) N.Y., 1870.
Eg 1309.55F	The Ramesseum papyri. (Gardiner, A.H.) Oxford, 1955.
Eg 602.14	Ramesside administrative documents. (Gardiner, Alan H.) London, 1940.
AH 4139.71	Ramilly, Jacqueline de. La loi dans la pensée grecque des origines à Aristote. Paris, 1971.
AH 930.30	Ramsauer, F. Die antike Vulkankunde. Burghausen, 1906.
AH 4819.27.5A	Ramsay, W.M. Asianic elements in Greek civilization. London, 1927.
AH 4819.27.7	Ramsay, W.M. Asianic elements in Greek civilization. New Haven, 1928.
AH 2808.5A	Ramsay, W.M. Cities and bishoprics of Phrygia. Oxford, 1895. 2v.
AH 2807.7	Ramsay, W.M. Early historical relations between Phrygia and Cappadocia. n.p., n.d.
AH 2147.7	Ramsay, W.M. The social basis of Roman power in Asia Minor. Aberdeen, 1941.
AH 7818.59	Ramsay, William. Elementary manual of Roman antiquities. London, 1859.
AH 7818.59.3	Ramsay, William. Elementary manual of Roman antiquities. 3. ed. London, 1863.
AH 7818.48.10	Ramsay, William. Manual of Roman antiquities. 10th ed. London, 1876.
AH 7818.48.15	Ramsay, William. Manual of Roman antiquities. 15th ed. N.Y., 1895.
NEDL AH 7818.48.17A	Ramsay, William. Manual of Roman antiquities. 17th ed. London, 1901.
Eg 609.48	Ramses III. (Janssen, J.M.A.) Leiden, 1948.
AH 4403.54	Raná řecká tyrannis. (Oliva, Pavel.) Praha, 1954.
AH 9707.8	Randa, A. Der Balkan. 1. Aufl. Graz, 1949.
AH 8647.12	Randall-MacIver, D. Greek cities in Italy and Sicily. Oxford, 1931.
AH 6110.20	Rane, H.O. Untersuchungen zur Geschichte des koituthischen Bundes. Inaug. Diss. Marburg, 1937.
AH 7239.13.5	Die Rangordnung der römischen Centurionen. (Wegeleben, Theodor.) Berlin, 1913.
Eg 459.60	Rank and title in the Old Kingdom. (Baer, Klaus.) Chicago, 1960.
AH 278.84	Ranke, L.F. von. Universal history. London, 1884.
AH 278.84.2	Ranke, L.F. von. Universal history. N.Y., 1884.
AH 288.85	Ranke, L.F. von. Universal history. N.Y., 1885.
AH 4850.13	Rankin, E.M. Role of Mageiroi in life of ancient Greece. Chicago, 1907.
AH 3921.9.5	Rannevizantiiskii gorod. (Kurbatov, G.L.) Leningrad, 1962.
AH 2108.10	Ranniaia istoriia iranskikh plemen Perednei Azii. (Grantovskii, E.A.) Moskva, 1970.
AH 4659.50	Ranovich, A.B. Der Hellenismus und seine geschichtliche Ralle. Berlin, 1958.
Eg 860.5F	Raphael, M. Prehistoric pottery and civilization in Egypt. N.Y., 1947.
AH 9777.31A	Rappaport, B. De Gotorum usque ad decium imperatorem. Berlin, 1899.
AH 9777.33	Rappaport, B. Die Einfälle der Goten in die römische Reich. Leipzig, 1899.
AH 3957.23	Rappoport, A.S. History of Palestine. N.Y., 1931.
AH 3000.4	Rapport...sur les inscriptions assyriens. v.1-2. (Ménant, J.) Paris, 1862.
AH 7114.36	I rapporti romano-ceriti e l'origine della civitas sino suffragio. (Sardi, Marta.) Roma, 1960.
Eg 139.02	Les rapports historiques et legaux des Quirites et des Egyptiens. (Revillout, Eugène.) Paris, 1902.
AH 7838.82	Rasch, Franz. De ludo Troiae. v.1-2. Jena, 1882.
AH 3002.155	Rashid, Fawzi. Archiv des Nûrsâmâs und andere Darlehensurkunden aus der altbabylonischen Zeit. Inaug. Diss. Heidelberg, 1965.
AH 3088.3	Rasmussen, N. Salmanasser den II's Indskrifter. Kjøbenhavn, 1897.
AH 3013.7	Rassam, H. Asshur and the land of Nimrod. N.Y., 1897.
AH 3013.40	Rassam, H. Babylonian cities. London, 1884?
AH 1879.30	Rassen und Religionen im alten Vorderasien. (Semper, Max.) Heidelberg, 1930.
AH 4862.5	Rassen und Sozialhygiene. (Hueppe, F.) Wiesbaden, 1897.
AH 4329.29	Rassengeschichte des hellenischen und des römischen Volkes. (Günther, H.F.K.) München, 1929.
AH 7189.64.5	Rastzvet rabovladel'cheskikh otnoshenii v Rimskoi respublike. (Shtaerman, Elena.) Moskva, 1964.
AH 4559.71	Der rationale Alexander. (Kraft, Konrad.) Kallmünz, 1971.
AH 7203.13F	Rationalia in pandectas. (Favre, A.) Lugduni, 1559. 4v.
AH 818.84.5	Rauber, August. Urgeschichte des Menschen. v.1-2. Leipzig, 1884.
AH 9615.5	Rauber, H. Die agrarischen Verhaltnisse Siziliens in Altertume besonders zur Zeit Ciceros. Bayreuth, 1919.
AH 7448.18.4	Rauchenstein, F. Nochmals Hannibals Alpenübergang. Aarau, 1864.
AH 7038.46	Raumer, F. Die römische Staatsverfassung. Berlin, 1846.
AH 7114.5	Raumer, R. De. De servii tullii censu. Erlangae, 1840.
AH 909.71	Raunig, Walter. Bernstein, Weihrauch, Seide. Wien, 1971.
AH 842.23	Rauschen, G. Griechisch-römische Schulwesen. Bonn, 1900.
AH 842.23.5	Rauschen, G. Das griechisch-römische Schulwesen zur zeit des ausgehenden Heidentums. Bonn, 1901.
AH 8013.6	Raven, Susan. Rome in Africa. London, 1969.
AH 3017.70F	Ravn, Otto E. A catalogue of oriental cylinder seals and seal impressions in the Danish National Museum. København, 1960.
AH 1278.62	Rawlinson, G. Five great monarchies of the ancient Eastern World. London, 1862-1867. 4v.
AH 1278.62.4	Rawlinson, G. Five great monarchies of the ancient Eastern World. N.Y., 1880. 3v.
NEDL AH 1278.62.6	Rawlinson, G. Five great monarchies of the ancient Eastern World. N.Y., 1881. 3v.
AH 1278.62.6	Rawlinson, G. Five great monarchies of the ancient Eastern World. N.Y., 190-? 3v.
NEDL AH 1278.62.2A	Rawlinson, G. Five great monarchies of the ancient Eastern World. 2. ed. London, 1871. 3v.
AH 3707.11.3A	Rawlinson, G. History of Phoenicia. London, 1889.
NEDL AH 278.69.6	Rawlinson, G. Manual of ancient history. N.Y., 1871.
AH 278.69.6	Rawlinson, G. Manual of ancient history. N.Y., 1871.
NEDL AH 278.69	Rawlinson, G. Manual of ancient history. Oxford, 1869.
AH 278.69A	Rawlinson, G. Manual of ancient history. Oxford, 1869.
AH 818.77.3	Rawlinson, G. Origin of nations. N.Y., 1881.
AH 818.77.3.5	Rawlinson, G. Origin of nations. N.Y., 1881.
AH 818.77	Rawlinson, G. Origins of nations. London, 1877.
AH 3607.12	Rawlinson, G. Parthia. N.Y., 1903.
AH 878.82.3	Rawlinson, G. The religions of the ancient world. N.Y., 1883.
AH 878.84	Rawlinson, G. Religions of the ancient world. N.Y., 1884.
AH 878.85	Rawlinson, G. Religions of the ancient world. N.Y., 1885.
AH 3657.12	Rawlinson, G. Seventh great oriental monarchy. London, 1876.
NEDL AH 3657.13	Rawlinson, G. Seventh great oriental monarchy. N.Y., 1882. 2v.
AH 3657.13.5	Rawlinson, G. Seventh great oriental monarchy. v.1-2. N.Y., 190-?
AH 3607.9A	Rawlinson, G. Sixth great oriental monarchy. London, 1873.
AH 3607.9.5	Rawlinson, G. Sixth great oriental monarchy. N.Y., 190-?
AH 3607.11A	Rawlinson, G. Story of Parthia. N.Y., 1893.
AH 3707.11A	Rawlinson, G. Story of Phoenicia. N.Y., 1889.
AH 3707.11.2	Rawlinson, G. Story of Phoenicia. N.Y., 1896.
Eg 278.91	Rawlinson, George. Ancient Egypt. N.Y., 1891.
AH 3966.27	Rawlinson, George. Biblical topography. London, 1887.
Eg 298.85.5	Rawlinson, George. Egypt and Babylon. N.Y., 1885.
AH 3159.22	Rawlinson, George. Historical illustrations of the Old Testament. London, 18- .
Eg 278.81.3	Rawlinson, George. History of ancient Egypt. Boston, 1882. 2v.
NEDL Eg 278.81.2	Rawlinson, George. History of ancient Egypt. London, 1881. 2v.
Eg 278.81.1	Rawlinson, George. History of ancient Egypt. London, 1881. 2v.
Eg 278.81.5	Rawlinson, George. History of ancient Egypt. N.Y., 188-? 2v.
Eg 278.81	Rawlinson, George. History of ancient Egypt. N.Y., 1881. 2v.
Eg 278.81.6	Rawlinson, George. History of ancient Egypt. N.Y., 1886. 2v.
AH 7408.68.5	Rawlinson, George. Recent histories of early Rome. London, 1868.
Eg 278.87	Rawlinson, George. The story of ancient Egypt. N.Y., 1887.

Author and Title Listing

	Call no.	Entry
	AH 8453.5	Reidinger, Walter. Die Statthalter der ungeteilten Pannonien und Oberpannoniens von Augustus bis Diokletian. Bonn, 1956.
	AH 7468.25	Reiff, H.C. Geschichte der römischen Burgerkreige. Berlin, 1825.
	AH 2763.5	Reifferscheid, August. Pergamon und seine Kunstschätze. Breslau, 1881-82.
	AH 7638.95	Reign of Antoninus Pius. (Bryant, E.E.) Cambridge, 1895.
	AH 7699.45	The reign of the Emperor L. Septimius Severus. (Murphy, G.J.) Philadelphia, 1945.
	AH 7709.11.5	The reign of the Emperor Probus. (Crees, J.H.E.) London, 1911.
	AH 7519.31	The reign of Tiberius. (Marsh, Frank Burr.) London, 1931.
	Eg 909.13.5	Reil, Theodor. Beiträge zur Kenntnis des Gewerbes im hellenistischen Ägypten. Borna, 1913.
	AH 5390.19	Reimer, P.J. Zeven tegen Thebe. Gouda, 1953.
	AH 7238.60	Rein, A. De phaleris et de argenteis e arum exemplaribus haud praculcalone et Asaburgio. Romae, 1860.
	AH 7158.44	Rein, W. Criminalrecht der Römer. Leipzig, 1844.
	AH 7168.58	Rein, W. Privatrecht...der Römer. Leipzig, 1858.
	AH 7168.36	Rein, W. Römisches Privatrecht. Leipzig, 1836.
	AH 9633.5F	Reina, Placido. Delle notizie istoriche della città della Messina. Messina, 1739.
	Eg 409.08	Reinach, A.J. L'Egypte préhistorique. Paris, 1908.
X Cg	AH 7468.29.5	Reinach, T. Mithradates Eupator. Leipzig, 1895.
	AH 7468.29.3	Reinach, T. Mithradates Eupator. Paris, 1890.
	AH 7488.63	Reinaud, J.T. Relations politiques...de la empire romain. Paris, 1863.
	AH 3053.10	Reinaud, Joseph T. Mémoire sur le commencement et la fin de la Mésène et de la Kharacène. Paris, 1861.
	AH 5857.5	Reinganum, H. Alte Megaris. Berlin, 1825.
	AH 938.39	Reinganum, H. Geschichte der Erd- und Landerabbildungen. Jena, 1839.
	AH 9639.5	Reinganum, H. Selinus und sein Gebiet. Leipzig, 1827.
	AH 7778.92	Reinhardt, G. Der Perserkreig des Kaisers Julian. Dessau, 1892.
	AH 7548.39	Reinhold, K.W. Die Römische Kaisergeschichte. Pasewalf, 1839.
	AH 7509.33.5	Reinhold, M. Marcus Agrippa. Geneva, 1933.
	AH 7098.47.5	Reinii, W. Dissertatio de Romanorum Municipiis. Eisenach, 1847.
	AH 4842.67	Reinmuth, O.W. The foreigners in the Albanian Ephebia. Lincoln, Neb., 1929.
	AH 7085.98F	Reipublicae Romanae in exteris provinciis. v.1-3. (Lazius, W.) Francofurti, 1598.
	AH 4958.43	Reise durch...nördlichen Griechenlandes. (Stephani, L.) Leipzig, 1843.
	AH 3143.25	Reise in das alte Babylon. 1. Aufl. (Klengel, Evelyn.) Leipzig, 1970.
	AH 4957.77	Reisen in Griechenland. (Chandler, R.) Leipzig, 1777.
	AH 2011.6	Reiske, J.J. Primae lineae historiae regnorum arabicorum. Gottingae, 1847.
	Eg 847.7	Reisner, M. Inscribed monuments from Gebel Barkal. Leipzig, 1934.
	AH 7114.13	Die Reiter und die Rittercenturien. (Gerathewohl, Bernhard.) München, 1886.
NEDL	AH 819.07	Reitzenstein, R. Werden und Wesen der Humanität. Strassburg, 1907.
	AH 3664.11	Reitzenstein, R. Das iranische Erlösungsmysterium. Bonn, 1921.
	AH 2008.7	The relations between Arabs and Israelites prior to the rise of Islam. (Margoliouth, D.S.) London, 1924.
	AH 7488.63	Relations politiques...de la empire romain. (Reinaud, J.T.) Paris, 1863.
	AH 7299.01	Le relazioni politiche di Roma con l'egitto. (Barbagallo, C.) Roma, 1901.
	Eg 848.6	Relics of Graeco-Egyptian schools. (Milne, J.G.) n.p., 1908.
	Eg 1039.15F	Religiöse Urkunden. Heft 1-3. (Grapow, Hermann.) Leipzig, 1915.
	AH 1818.72	Religiösen, politischen und socialen Ideen. v.1-2. (Twesten, C.) Berlin, 1872.
	Eg 878.98	Religion and conscience in ancient Egypt. (Petrie, William M.F.) London, 1898.
	AH 3155.23	La religion babylonienne. 1. ed. (Battero, Jean.) Paris, 1952.
	AH 3155.6	Die Religion Babyloniens und Assyriens. (Jastrow, Morris.) Giessen, 1905-12. 3v.
	Eg 879.10	La religion de l'ancienne Égypte. (Virey, P.) Paris, 1910.
	AH 7779.34	La religion de l'empereur Julien et le mysticisme du temps. (Farney, R.) Paris, 1934.
	AH 3664.12	La religion de l'Iran ancien. (Duchesne-Guillemin, J.) Paris, 1962.
	AH 3155.3	Religion der Babylonier. (Münter, D.F.) Kopenhagen, 1827.
	AH 8549.15	Die Religion der Celten. (Pelloutier, S.) Frankfurt am Mayn, 1784.
	AH 8914.10	Die Religion der Etrusker. (Clemen, Carl.) Bonn, 1936.
	AH 8064.1	Religion der Karthager. (Münter, F.) Kopenhagen, 1816.
	AH 8064.1.5	Religion der Karthager. (Münter, F.) Kopenhagen, 1821.
	AH 8549.163.1	La religion des Celtes. (Vries, Jan de.) Paris, 1963.
	AH 8549.104.5	La religion des Celtes. 2. éd. (Dottin, Georges.) Paris, 1904.
	AH 8549.12	La religion des Gaulois, tirée des plus pures sources de l'antiquité. (Martin, Jacques.) Amsterdam, 1750. 2v.
	AH 3936.9.7	La religion des Palmyrénies. Thèse. (Février, J.G.) Paris, 1931.
	Eg 879.44	La religion égyptienne. (Vondier, Jacques.) Paris, 1944.
	Eg 879.65	La religion et la morale dans l'Egypte antique. (Pirenne, Jacques.) Neuchâtel, 1965.
	AH 8549.80	La religion gauloise et de Gui de Chêne. (Gaidoz, Henri.) Paris, 1880.
	AH 879.69	Religion in ancient history: studies in ideas, men and events. (Brandon, Samuel George Frederick.) N.Y., 1969.
	Eg 879.06.5	The religion of ancient Egypt. (Petrie, William M.F.) London, 1906.
	AH 3155.7	The religion of Babylonia and Assyria. (Pinches, T.G.) London, 1906.
	AH 3155.19	The religion of Babylonia and Assyria. (Rogers, R.W.) N.Y., 1908.
	AH 3155.6.3	The religion of Babylonia and Assyria. v.1-2. (Jastrow, Morris.) Boston, 1898.
	AH 8549.111.5	The religion of the ancient Celts. (MacCullock, John A.) Edinburgh, 1911.
	Eg 879.05.5	The religion of the ancient Egyptians. (Steindorff, Georg.) N.Y., 1905.
	Eg 878.97A	Religion of the ancient Egyptians. Photoreproduction. (Wiedemann, A.) N.Y., 1897.
	AHP 28.6	Religion und Kultur der alten Arier. Frankfurt a.M. 1,1935 2v.
	AH 8914.20	Religion und Kultur der Etrusker. (Herbig, G.) Breslau, 1922.
	Eg 878.85	Religion und Mythologie der alten Ägypter. (Brugsch, H.) Leipzig, 1885. 2v.
	Eg 878.85.3	Religion und Mythologie der alten Ägypter. (Brugsch, H.) Leipzig, 1891.
	AH 3414.5	La religione degli Hittite. (Furlani, G.) Bologna, 1936.
	Eg 879.55	Le religione dell'Egitto antico. (Donadoni, S.) Milano, 1955.
	AH 2014.8	Les religiones arabes préislamiques. 2. éd. (Ryckmans, G.) Louvain, 1951.
	AH 3155.18	Les religions de Babylonie et d'Assyrie. 2. ed. (Dhorme, E.) Paris, 1949.
	AH 8014.5	Les religions de l'Afrique antique. (Charles-Picard, Gilbert.) Paris, 1954.
	Eg 870.1	Religions égyptiennes antiques; bibliographie analytique. (Garnot, J. St. F.) Paris, 1952.
	Eg 879.69.5	Religions en Égypte hellenistique et romaine, colloque de Strasbourg, 16-18 mai 1967. Paris, 1969.
	Eg 879.02.5	The religions of ancient Egypt and Babylonia. (Sayce, Archibald H.) Edinburgh, 1903.
	AH 3964.01	Pamphlet box. Religions of ancient Palestine.
	AH 3173.15	Religions of the ancient Near East. (Mendelsohn, I.) N.Y., 1955.
	AH 878.82.3	The religions of the ancient world. (Rawlinson, G.) N.Y., 1883.
	AH 878.84	Religions of the ancient world. (Rawlinson, G.) N.Y., 1884.
	AH 878.85	Religions of the ancient world. (Rawlinson, G.) N.Y., 1885.
	AH 7729.69	Die Religionspolitik des Kaisers Elagabal im Spiegel der Historia Augusta. (Optendrenk, Theo.) Bonn, 1969.
	AH 3155.13	Religious and moral ideas in Babylonia and Assyria. (Mercer, Samuel A.) Milwaukee, 1919.
	AH 7817.26	Reliquiae Baxterianae. (Baxteri, W.) London, 1726.
	AH 7459.66	The reluctant warriors. (Armstrong, Donald Budd.) N.Y., 1966.
	AH 842.4	Reluire des livres. (Peignot, E.G.) Dijon, 1834.
	AH 842.4.2	Reluire des livres. (Peignot, E.G.) Dijon, 1834.
	AH 1808.30	Remarks of Bible chronology. (Yeates, T.) London, 1830.
	AH 7847.2	Remarks on water supply of ancient Rome. (Morgan, M.H.) Boston, 1902.
Htn	AH 7653.10*	Remarks on 2 last chapters of Gibbon's History of Roman Empire. (Chelsum, J.) London, 1776.
	Eg 856.4F	Remarques sur le tatouage dans l'Égypte ancienne. (Keimer, Ludwig.) Caire, 1948.
	AH 3757.12	Remennikov, A.M. Bor'ba plenen severnogo prichernomor'ia s rimon v III veke n.e. Moskva, 1954.
	AH 7279.68	Remeslenniki drevnego Rima. (Sergeenko, Mariia E.) Leningrad, 1968.
	AH 7659.64	Rémondon, Roger. La crise de l'Empire romain. Paris, 1964.
	AH 7659.64.2	Rémondon, Roger. La crise de l'Empire romain de Marc Aurèle à Anastase. 2. éd. Paris, 1970.
	AH 7889.36	La rémunération des professions liberales en droit romain classique. (Bernard, Antoine.) Paris, 1936.
	AH 3195.3	Renan, Ernest. An essay on the age and antiquity of the book of Nabathaean agriculture. London, 1862.
	AH 8515.10	Renard, Marcel. Technique et agriculture en pays trévire et rémois. Bruxelles, 1959.
	AH 3177.4	Rencontre assyriologique, 7, Paris, 1958. Gilgames et sa légende. Paris, 1960.
	AH 3156.16	Rencontre Assyriologique Internationale, 14th, Strasbourg 1965. La divination en Mésopotamie ancienne et dans les régions voisines. Paris, 1966.
	AH 7778.79	Rendall, Gerald Henry. Emperor Julian, paganism and Christianity. Cambridge, 1879.
	AH 7239.03.3	Renel, Charles. Cultes militaires de Rome. Les enseignes. Lyon, 1903.
	AH 4410.38	Renfrew, Colin. The emergence of civilisation: the Cyclades and the Aegean in the third millennium B.C. London, 1972.
	AH 7578.67	Renier, Léon. Mémoire sur les officiers qui assistèrent au conseil de guerre. Paris, 1867.
	Eg 878.80	Renouf, P. le P. Lectures on the origin and growth of religion...of ancient Egypt. London, 1880.
	AH 7008.57	Renssen, J.G. Disputatio de diurnis aliisque. Groningen, 1857.
	AH 3020.50	Répertoire commenté des signes présargoniques sumériens de Lagaš. (Rosengarten, Yvonne.) Paris, 1967.
	AH 7099.30	Repetita. (Heitland, Willian E.) Cambridge, Eng., 1930.
	AH 7138.64.10	Repetitorium der ausseren römischen Rechtsgeschichte. (Beckhaus, F.W.K.) Berlin, 1873.
	AH 7653.8	Reply to Gibbon's vindication. (Davis, H.E.) London, 1779.
Htn	Eg 708.58*	Report of the committee...to translate...the Rosetta Stone. (Pennsylvania. University. Philomathean Society.) Philadelphia, 1858.
Htn	Eg 708.58.5*	Report of the committee. Manuscript. (Pennsylvania. University. Philomathean Society.) n.p., n.d.
	AH 3013.930	Report on excavations in Iraq during the season. (Iraq. Ministry of Education.) Baghdad. 1928-1929
	AH 3154.7.5	The reports of the magicians and astrologers of Nineveh and Babylon in the British Museum. (Thompson, Reginald Campbell.) Ann Arbor, 1974.
	AH 49.55	Representative government in Greek and Roman history. (Larsen, Jakob A.O.) Berkeley, 1955.
	AH 7159.37	La repressione penale in diritto romano. (Brasiello, U.) Napoli, 1937.
	AH 7419.37	La repubblica romana. (Giannelli, Giulio.) Milano, 1937.
	AH 459.51	La repubblica romana e gli ultimi re di Macedonia. (Regibus, Luca de.) Genova, 1951.
	AH 5857.9	Republica ac Magistratibus Megarensium. (Thamm, M.) Halis Saxonum, 1885.
	AH 2357.15	Republica Galatarum. (Wernsdoff, G.) Norimbergae, 1743.
Htn	AH 4036.44*	Republica Graecorum. (Emmus, Vbbonis.) Luden, 1644. 2v.
	AH 5138.11	Republica Rhodiorum commentatio. (Schumacher, C.) Heidelbergae, 1886.
	AH 7419.44	La republica romana. (Becerra Oliva, Guillermo.) Cordoba, 1944.
Htn	AH 7036.29*	Republica romana. (Schrijver, Pieter.) Lugdunum Batavorum, 1629.
	AH 7419.11	La república romana. (Vargas Vila, J.M.) Paris, 1911.
Htn	AH 5303.5*	Republica seu magistratibus. (Postel, G.) Lugdunum Batavorum, 1635.

Author and Title Listing

Htn AH 5303.5.3* Republica seu magistratibus Atheniensium. (Postel, G.) Lugdunum Batavorum, 1645.

AH 7469.63 The Republican empire. (Hawthorn, J.R.) London, 1963.

AH 7419.14.2A Republican Rome. (Havell, Herbert L.) London, 1914.

AH 7419.14 Republican Rome. (Havell, Herbert L.) N.Y., 1914.

AH 7419.66 Republican Rome. (McDonald, Alex.) London, 1966.

AH 7889.64 Het republikeinse Rome; de grondslagen van het antieke wirtschaftswunder (509-31 v. Chr.). (Halsberghe, Gaston H.) Hasselt, 1964.

AH 7419.72 La république à Rome, 509-29 avant Jésus-Christ. (Combès, Robert.) Paris, 1972.

AH 7037.67 La republique romaine. (Beaufort, L.) Paris, 1767. 6v.

AH 7469.13.5 La République romaine. (Bloch, G.) Paris, 1919.

AH 7419.13.5 La république romaine. (Bloch, Gustave.) Paris, 1913.

AH 7419.55 La république romaine. 1. éd. (Clerici, André.) Paris, 1955.

AH 7469.29.5 La République romaine de 133 avant J.C. à la mort de César. Pt.1. (Block, Gustave.) Paris, 1929.

AH 7469.29.10 La République romaine de 133 avant J.C. à la mort de César. v.1-2. 2.-3. ed. (Bloch, Gustave.) Paris, 1940-43.

AH 3109.3 Rerum Assyriarum tempora emendata. (Brandis, J.) Bonn, 1853.

Htn AH 7276.25* Rerum patriae libri IIII. (Alciati, Andrea.) Mediolani, 1625.

AH 4498.65 Rerum post Bellum Persicum. (Schaefer, A.) Lipsiae, 1865.

AH 3910.13 Res ab Antiocho III Magno. (Heyden, E.A.) Monasterii, 1877.

AH 3357.7 Res Cyrenensium. (Thrige, Johann P.) Hauniae, 1828.

AH 3357.7.5 Res Cyrenensium. (Thrige, Johann P.) Verbania, 1940.

AH 4278.98.10 Res graecae. (Coleridge, E.P.) London, 1898.

AH 7039.66.5 Res publica amissa. Eine Studie zu Verfassung und Geschichte der späten römischen Republik. (Meier, Christian.) Wiesbaden, 1966.

AH 7278.96.10 Res Romanae. (Coleridge, E.P.) London, 1896.

AH 7617.93 Res Traiani imperatoris ad Danubium gestae. (Mannert, K.) Norimbergae, 1793.

AH 1958.38 Researches in Assyria...Euphrates expedition. (Ainsworth, W.) London, 1838.

AH 3012.5 Researches in Assyrian and Babylonian geography. (Tofteen, O.A.) Chicago, 1908.

AH 3022.24 Resina, Guiseppe. Sumer e Akkad; la vita economica. Catania, 1958.

Htn AH 5057.5* Respublicae Achaeorum. (Schoockius, M.) Trajani ad Rhenum, 1664.

AH 5310.6 Le restauration democratique à Athènes en 403 avant J.C. (Cloché, Paul.) Paris, 1915.

AH 2014.7.2 Reste arabischen Heidentums. (Wellhausen, Julius.) Berlin, 1897.

AH 2014.7.5 Reste arabischen Heidentums. (Wellhausen, Julius.) Berlin, 1927.

AH 3020.9PF Restitution matérielle de la stèle des vautours. (Heuzey, Léon A.) Paris, 1909.

AH 7779.33 Das Restitutions-Edict Kaiser Julians. Inaug. Diss. (Weis, B.K.) Bruchsal, 1933.

AH 3075.2 The resurrection of Assyria. (Cooper, William R.) London, 1875.

AH 4521.11 Rettungen des Alkibiades. (Fokke, A.) Emden, 1883.

AH 5390.15 The return of the Theban exiles, 379-378 B.C. (Prickard, A.O.) Oxford, 1926.

AH 4808.79 Reusch, A. De Dilbus Contionum Ordmarium. Argentorali, 1879.

AH 4479.02 Reuther, H. Pausanias, Sohn des Kleombrotos. Bonn, 1902.

AH 9607.9.25 Revelli, P. La storia della Sicilia nell'antichità. Pinerolo, 1902.

Eg 297.34 Révérend, Dominique. Letters to Monsieur H*** [Hénrich] concerning the most ancient gods...Egypt. London, 1734.

AH 4047.94 Review of government of Sparta and Athens. (Drummond, W.) London, 1794.

AH 7139.12.5 Revillont, E. Les origines égyptiennes. Paris, 1912.

AH 7178.56 Revillout, Charles. Etude sur l'histoire du Colonat. Paris, 1856.

Eg 1058.85 Revillout, E. Un poeme satyrique. Paris, 1885.

Eg 1308.85F Revillout, Eugène. Corpus papyrorum Egyptii. v.1-3. Parisiis, 1885-1902.

Eg 138.84 Revillout, Eugène. Cours de droit égyptien. Paris, 1884.

Eg 928.95 Revillout, Eugène. Mélanges sur la métrologie, l'économie politique et l'histoire de l'ancienne Egypte. Paris, 1895.

Eg 138.86 Revillout, Eugène. Les obligations en droit égyptien. Paris, 1886.

Eg 138.82 Revillout, Eugène. Le procès d'Hermias d'après les documents démotiques et grecs. pt.1-2. Paris, 1882.

Eg 139.02 Revillout, Eugène. Les rapports historiques et legaux des Quirites et des Egyptiens. Paris, 1902.

AH 7469.52 La révolte des gladiateurs. (Brion, M.) Paris, 1952.

NEDL AH 4524.9 Révolution oligarchique des quatre-cents. (Micheli, Horace.) Genève, 1893.

AH 7838.68 Revue archéologique - nouvelles tessères. (Hübner, Émile.) Paris, 1868.

AHP 28.2 Revue d'assyriologie. Paris. 1,1884+ 31v.

EgP 120.3 Revue de l'Égypte ancienne. Paris. 1-3,1927-1931 3v.

EgP 120.4 Revue d'Egyptologie. Paris. 1,1933+ 8v.

AHP 28.5 Revue des études semitiques et babyloniaca. Paris. 1934-1945 3v.

EgP 120.1 Revue egyptologique. Paris. 1-9,1880-1924 5v.

AH 3407.25 Revue hittite et asianique. Paris. 1,1930+ 10v.

Eg 879.69 Reymond, Eve A.E. The mythical origin of the Egyptian temple. N.Y., 1969.

AH 4298.56 Reynald, H. Libertati apud veteres Graeciae populos quid defuerit. Parisiis, 1856.

AH 4048.60 Reynald, M.H. Recherches sur ce qui manquait a la liberté...mircouvch. Paris, 1860.

AH 863.15 Reynes-Lyons, P. Mitos, ritos y costumbres sexuales en las sociedades antiguas. Buenos Aires, 1964.

AH 7099.26 Reynolds, P.K.B. The vigiles of imperial Rome. London, 1926.

AH 4229.08.2 Die Rezeption des attischen Prozessrechts. (Weber, Hans.) Paderborn, 1908.

AH 9633.6 Rhégion et Zancle. (Vallet, Georges.) Paris, 1958.

AH 4200.15 La Rhètre de Lycurgue. (Tsopanakis, A.) Tyrtée, 1954.

Eg 1189.23F The Rhind mathematical papyrus. (Papyrus Rhind.) London, 1923.

Eg 1189.23.5FA The Rhind mathematical papyrus. British Museum, 10057 and 10058. (Papyrus Rhind.) Oberlin, 1927-29. 2v.

AH 4819.48.3 Rhodakanakes, K.P. Athens and the Greek miracle. 1. American ed. Boston, 1951.

AH 5303.6 Rhodes, P.J. The Athenian boule. Oxford, 1972.

AH 5138.9 Rhodes in ancient times. Photoreproduction. (Torr, Cecil.) Cambridge, 1885.

AH 5138.15 Rhodian law. (Nomos Rodiön, Nautikos.) Oxford, 1909.

AH 5138.14 The Rhodian Peraen and island. (Fraser, P.M.) London, 1954.

Htn AH 815.16.9F* Rhodigini lectionum antiquarum...XXX. (Ricchieri, Lodovico.) Basileae, 1542.

Htn AH 815.16.15F* Rhodigini lectionum antiquarum. (Ricchieri, Lodovico.) n.p., 1599.

AH 4819.48 Rhodokanakès, K.P. Athens and the Greek miracle. London, 1948.

Eg 1159.55 Riad, Naguib. La médecine au temps des pharaons. Paris, 1955.

AH 4857.9 Ribbeck, O. Kolax. Leipzig, 1883.

AH 4845.15 Ribbeck, O.J.K. Agroikos. Leipzig, 1885.

AH 8942.9 Ricchi, Antonio. La reggia de' Volsci. Bologna, 1967.

Htn AH 815.16.3F* Ricchieri, Lodovico. Digini lectionum antiquarum libri XVI. Basileae, 1517.

Htn AH 815.16.11* Ricchieri, Lodovico. Lectionum antiquarum libri XXX. Ludguni, 1560. 3v.

Htn AH 815.16.9F* Ricchieri, Lodovico. Rhodigini lectionum antiquarum...XXX. Basileae, 1542.

Htn AH 815.16.15F* Ricchieri, Lodovico. Rhodigini lectionum antiquarum. n.p., 1599.

AH 7779.56 Ricciotti, Giuseppe. L'imperatore Giuliano l'Apostata secondo i documenti. Milano, 1956.

AH 8942.2 Riccobaldi del Bana, G.M. Dissertazione istorico-etrusca...della città di Volterra. Firenze, 1758.

AH 7139.56 Riccobono, Salvatore. Profilo storico del diritto romano. Palermo, 1956.

AH 3757.15 Rice, Tamara. The Scythians. London, 1957.

AH 8907.12 Ricerche di storia etrusca. (Peserico, Luigi.) Vicenza, 1919.

AH 4409.65 Ricerche di storia greca. (Accame, Silvio.) Napoli, 1965?

AH 4539.51 Ricerche intorno alla guerra corinzia. (Accame, Silvio.) Napoli, 1951.

AH 4499.68 Ricerche intorno alla Pentecontaetia. (Accame, Silvio.) Napoli, 1968.

AH 3011.3 Ricerche per lo Studio dell'antichità Assira. (Fenzi, F.) Roma, 1872.

AH 5754.13 Ricerche spartane. (Solari, Arturo.) Livorno, 1907.

AH 7099.00 Ricerche storiche-epigrafiche. (Tanfani, L.) Taranto, 1900.

AH 7163.32 Ricerche sui Conubia tra romani e germani nei secoli IV-VI. (Soraci, Rosario.) Catania, 1968.

AH 9792.8 Ricerche sui rapporti tra i vandali e l'impero romano. (Gitti, Alberto.) Bari, 1953.

AH 7099.56 Ricerche sulla praefectura urbi in età imperiale. (Vitucci, Giovanni.) Roma, 1956.

AH 7149.15 Ricerche sulla storia e sul diritto pubblico di Roma. (Pais, E.) Roma, 1915. 4v.

AH 4299.62.10 Ricerche sulle leghe greche: peloponnesiaca-beotica-licia. (Moretti, Luigi.) Roma, 1962.

AH 3013.20.3 Rich, C.J. Memoir on the ruins of Babylon. 3. ed. v.1-2. London, 1818.

AH 3013.20.7 Rich, C.J. Narrative of a journey to the site of Babylon. London, 1839.

AH 8913.25 Richardson, Emeline H. The Etruscans; their art and civilization. Chicago, 1964.

AH 7162.35 Richerche di diritto ereditario romano. (Segrè, Angelo.) Roma, 1930.

AH 7163.30 Richerche sulle diverse maniere di contrarre matrimonio. (Spagnolo, C.A.) Roma, 1807.

AH 7159.61 Richerche sull'"exilium" nel periodo repubblicano. (Crifò, Giuliano.) Milano, 1961.

AH 846.25FA Richter, G.M.A. Ancient furniture; a history of Greek. Oxford, 1926.

AH 7768.65 Richter, H. Das weströmische Reich. Berlin, 1865.

AH 838.87.3 Richter, W. Die Spiele der Griechen und Römer. Leipzig, 1887.

AH 7779.56.4 Riciotti, Giuseppe. Julian the Apostate. Milwaukee, 1960.

AH 4846.8 Rider, B.C. Greek house, its history and development from Neolithic period to Hellenistic. Thesis. Cambridge, 1916.

AH 4409.01A Ridgeway, W. Early age of Greece. Cambridge, 1901-31. 2v.

AH 4839.35 Ridington, William R. The Minoan-Mycenaean background of Greek athletics. Diss. Philadelphia, 1935.

AH 7779.37 Ridley, F.A. Julian the Apostate and the rise of Christianity. London, 1937.

Eg 990.7 Riefstahl, E. Thebes in the time of Amunhotep III. 1. ed. Norman, 1964.

AH 819.64 Riemschneider, M. Von Olympia bis Ninive im Zeitalter Homeis. Heidelberg, 1964.

AH 3413.15 Riemschneider, M. Die Welt der Hethiter. Stuttgart, 1954.

AH 9508.5 Riese, A. Forschungen zur Geschichte der Rheinlande in der Römerzeit. Frankfurt am Main, 1889.

AH 9758.5 Riese, A. Idealiserung der Naturvölker des Nordens. Frankfurt, 1875.

AH 4819.62 Riesterer, Peter P. Griechisches Erbe. Zürich, 1962.

Eg 1029.61 Riesterer, Peter P. Kostbarkeiten aus Ägypten. Zürich, 1961.

AH 7118.4 Rieu, G.N. du. Dissertatio...de gente fabia. Lugduni-Batavorum, 1856.

AH 4909.07 Riezler, Kurt. Finanzen und Monopole in Griechenland. Berlin, 1907.

Htn AH 7861.6* Rigalt, N. Funus Parasiticum. Lutetiae, 1601. 4 pam.

AH 819.69.5 Riley, Carroll L. The origins of civilization. Carbondale, 1969.

AH 7479.33F Rimini e Giulio Cesare. (Pasquini, Luigi.) Rimini, 1933.

AH 7469.47 Rimscha, Hans von. Die Gracchen. München, 1947.

AH 8358.5 Rimski gradovi no Dunavu u Gornjoi Meziji. Thesis. (Mirkovič, Miroslava.) Beograd, 1968.

AH 3171.10 Rinaldi, Giovanni. Storia delle letterature dell'antica mesopotamia. Milano, 1957.

AH 3915.5 Die Rinder von Babylonien, Assyrien. (Dürst, J.U.) Berlin, 1899.

AH 9307.5 Ring, B.J.J.M. de. Histoire des peuples opiques. Paris, 1859.

AH 9505.2 Ring, B.J.J.M. de. Mémoire sur les établissements romains. Paris, 1852. 2v.

AH 7653.35 Ringeling, Hans G. Pragmatismus in Edward Gibbons Geschichte vom Verfall und Untergang des romischen Reiches. Inaug. Diss. Schönberg, 1915.

AH 4238.93 Ringnalda, H.F.T. De exercitu Laeedaemoniorum. Leovardiae, 1893.

AH 4844.4 Ringwood, I.C. Agonistic features of local Greek festivals chiefly from inscriptional evidence. Poughkeepsie, N.Y., 1927.

Author and Title Listing

AH 7659.39.5	Il rinnovamento dell'impero romano. (Solari, A.) Milano, 1938-
AH 4299.58.5	Riot in Ephesus; writings on the heritage of Greece. (Seltman, Charles T.) London, 1958.
AH 808.87.5	Riposta alle osservazione...della civiltà cattolica sulla chronologia rivendicata. (Paganelli, A.) Prato, 1889.
AH 8608.6.10	Riposta alle osservazioni di Bianchi-Giovini sulle Origini. (Mazzoldi, Angelo.) Milano, 1841.
Eg 509.47A	The rise and fall of the middle kingdom in Thebes. (Winlock, H.E.) N.Y., 1947.
AH 3005.8	The rise and progress of Assyriology. (Budge, E.A.T.N.) London, 1925.
AH 4323.5	The rise of the Dorians. (Nixon, Ivor G.) N.Y., 1968.
AH 6107.8	Rise of the Macedonian empire. (Curteis, A.M.) London, 1877.
AH 6107.9	Rise of the Macedonian empire. (Curteis, A.M.) N.Y., 1880.
AH 6107.11.5	Rise of the Macedonian empire. (Curteis, A.M.) N.Y., 1896.
AH 6107.11	Rise of the Macedonian empire. 4. ed. (Curteis, A.M.) London, 1886.
AH 4559.32.5	Risi, Arnaldo de. Alessandro Magno, 356-331. Roma, 1932.
Eg 878.90	Rites égyptiens. (Lefébure, E.) Paris, 1890.
AH 3813.7	Rites of birth, marriage, death, and kindred occasions among the Semites. (Morgenstern, Julian.) Cincinnati, 1966.
AH 8954.5F	Ritschl, F. Legis rubriae pars superstes. Bonae, 1851.
AH 7838.64	Ritschl, F. Die Tessarae Gladiatoriae. München, 1864.
AH 8548.5	Ritson, J. Memoirs of the Celts or Gauls. London, 1827.
AH 6158.5	Ritter, C. Vorhalle europäischer Völkerges. Berlin, 1820.
AH 7468.85	Ritter, Georg. Untersuchungen zu dem allobrogischen Krieg. Hof, 1885.
AH 49.65	Ritter, Hans-Werner. Diadem und Königsherrschaft. München, 1965.
AH 7238.85	Ritterling, E.H.E. De legione Romanorum X Genima. Lipsiae, 1855.
AH 9379.5	Ritual and cults of pre-Roman Iguvium. (Rosenzweig, I.) London, 1937.
Eg 879.00.5	Ritual of the mystery of the judgment of the soul. (Blackden, M.W.) London, 19- .
Eg 990.21	Die Ritualdarstellungen des Ramesseums. [Thebes]. (Helck, Hans Wolfgang.) Wiesbaden, 1972-
Eg 1042.968.5	Die Ritualszenen auf der Umfassungsmauer Ramses' II. (Helck, Hans Wolfgang.) Wiesbaden, 1968.
AH 3154.15	Rituels accadiens. (Thureau-Dangin, F.) Paris, 1921.
AH 7817.12.3	Rituum qui olim apud Romanos. 3rd ed. (Nieupoort, W.H.) Rhenum, 1723.
AH 7817.12.13	Rituum qui olim apud Romanos obtinuerunt. (Nieupoort, W.H.) Berolini, 1767.
NEDL AH 7817.12.9	Rituum qui olim apud Romanos obtinuerunt. 9. ed. (Nieupoort, W.H.) Berolini, 1751.
AH 7817.12.6	Rituum qui olim apud Romanos obtinuerunt. 13. ed. (Nieupoort, W.H.) Venetiis, 1748.
AH 139.00	Rivalta, V. Atticarum et Romanarum legum collatio. Ravennae, 1900.
AH 7162.33	Rivier, A. De descrimine quod inter regulam Cotonianem. Berolini, n.d.
AH 7138.71	Rivier, A. Introduction historique au droit romain. Bruxelles, 1871.
AH 7138.81.3	Rivier, A. Introduction historique au droit romain. Bruxelles, 1881.
NEDL AH 7138.72.2	Rivier, A. Introduction historique droit romain. Paris, 1872.
AH 7162.21	Rivier, A. Traité élémentarie des successions. Bruxelles, 1878.
AH 7161.4	Rivier, Alphonse. Précis du droit de famille romain. Paris, 1891.
AHP 28.3	Rivista di storia antica e scienze affini. Messina. 1-13 13v.
AHP 28.4	Rivista storica dell'antichità. Bologna. 1,1971+
AH 8548.130	Rivoallan, A. Présence des Celtes. Paris, 1957.
AH 7469.34	La rivolta di Catalina. (Pavano Amato, Giovanni.) Messina, 1934.
AH 9634.5	Rizzo, P. Naxos siceliota. Catania, 1894.
AH 39.71	Rizzo, Silvia. Il lessico filologico degli umanisti. Roma, 1973.
NEDL AH 7829.13A	Roads from Rome. (Allinson, A.C.E.) N.Y., 1913.
AH 7238.67F	Robert, Charles. Les légions du Rhin et les inscriptions des carrières. Paris, 1867.
AH 2257.5	Robert, L. La Carie. v.2. Paris, 1954.
AH 4844.6	Robert, Louis. Les gladiateurs dans l'Orient grec. Paris, 1940.
AH 7819.55.5	Robertis, Francesco Maria de. Il fenomeno associativo nel mondo romano. Napoli, 1955.
AH 7819.63.10	Robertis, Francesco Maria de. Lavore e lavoratori nel mondo romano. Bari, 1963.
AH 8549.42.5	Roberts, J. Druidical remains and antiquities of the ancient Britons. Swansea, 1842.
AH 3160.29	Roberts, Jimmy J.M. The earliest Semitic pantheon. Baltimore, 1972.
AH 5357.5A	Roberts, W.R. Ancient Bocotians. Cambridge, 1895.
AH 3075.7	Robertson, H.S. Voices of the past from Assyria and Babylonia. London, 1900.
AH 4807.88	Robertson, Joseph. Parian chronicle. London, 1788.
AH 4277.68	Robertson, W. History of ancient Greece. Edinburgh, 1768.
Eg 990.5F	Robichon, C. Le temple du scribe royal Amenhotep. pt.1. Le Caire, 1936.
AH 8548.7	Robin, Claude C. Le Mont-Glonne; ou Recherches historiques sur l'origine des Celtes. Paris, 1774. 2v.
AH 4559.47A	Robinson, C.A. Alexander the Great. 1st ed. N.Y., 1947.
AH 279.51	Robinson, C.A. Ancient history from prehistoric times to the death of Justinian. N.Y., 1951.
AH 4559.53	Robinson, C.A. The history of Alexander the Great. v.2. Providence, 1953.
AH 4829.16.5	Robinson, C.E. The days of Alkibiades. 3. ed. London, 1925.
AH 4819.33.5	Robinson, C.E. Everyday life in ancient Greece. Oxford, 1934.
AH 7279.35	Robinson, C.E. A history of Rome. N.y., 1935.
AH 5313.10	Robinson, Charles. Athens in the age of Pericles. 1st ed. Norman, 1959.
AH 4559.32A	Robinson, Charles A. The Ephemerides of Alexander's expedition. Providence, 1932.
Eg 278.87.5	Robinson, Charles S. The pharaohs of the bondage and the Exodus. N.Y., 1887.
AH 4279.46.2	Robinson, Cyril E. Hellas. N.Y., 1948.
AH 4279.29.4.5	Robinson, Cyril E. A history of Greece. 9. ed. London, 1957.

AH 7419.32	Robinson, Cyril E. A history of the Roman republic. N.Y., 1932.
AH 4279.46	Robinson, Cyril E. Zîto Hellas. London, 1946.
AH 4279.36	Robinson, D.M. A short history of Greece. N.Y., 1936.
AH 8549.103	Robinson, F.N. Human sacrifice among the Irish Celts. Boston, 1913.
AH 4818.07.2	Robinson, J. Antiquities of Greece. London, 1807.
AH 7139.05.5	Robinson, J.J. Selections from the public and private law of the Romans. N.Y., 1905.
AH 7139.05	Robinson, J.J. Selections from the public and private law of the Romans. N.Y., 1905.
AH 7159.40	Robinson, L. Freedom of speech in the Roman republic. Thesis. Baltimore, 1940.
AH 4839.27	Robinson, Rachel Louisa. Sources for the history of Greek athletics. Cincinnati, 1955.
AH 3959.23A	Robinson, T.H. Palestine in general history. Oxford, 1929.
AH 3008.71	Robion, F.M.L.J. L'histoire de la Chaldée et de l'Assyrie. n.p., 1871.
AH 2357.9	Robiou, F. Histoire des Gaulois d'Orient. Paris, 1866.
AH 4818.89	Robiou, F. Les institutions de la Grèce antique. Paris, 1889.
Eg 708.52	Robiou, Felix. Aegypti regimen quo anno susceperunt et qua ratione tractaverint Ptolemai. Rhedonis, 1852.
AH 7818.84.3	Robiow, F.M.C.J. Les institutions de l'ancienne Rome. Paris, 1884. 3v.
AH 4559.29.5	Robson, Edgar. Alexander the Great. London, 1929.
AH 9708.5	Robstvoto v Trakiia i Miziia prez antichnostta. (Velkov, Velizar I.) Sofiia, 1967.
AH 7203.79	Roby, H.J. Introduction to study of Justinian's Digest. Cambridge, 1884.
AH 7203.79.10	Roby, H.J. Introduzione allo studio del Digesto giustinianeo. Firenze, 1887.
AH 7169.02	Roby, H.J. Roman private law. Cambridge, 1902. 2v.
AH 8549.174	"Les roches aux fées" dans l'ancienne Gaule. (Gilbert, Max.) Fécamp, 1971.
AH 7819.09.5	Rockwell, J.C. Private Baustiftungen. Jena, 1909.
AH 7769.72	Ród konstantgna. Wyd. 1. (Krawczuk, Aleksander.) Warszawa, 1972. 2v.
AH 3964.34	Rodén, Nils. Bibliska städer. Stockholm, 1932.
AH 8514.11	Rodet, P. Culte des sources thermales. Paris, 1908.
AH 7139.28	Rodriguez, José S. Elementos de derecho romano. Caracas, 1928. 2v.
AH 5910.10	Roebuck, Carl A. A history of Messenia from 369 to 146 B.C. Thesis. Chicago, 1941.
AH 2120.7F	Roebuck, Carl A. Ionian trade and colonization. N.Y., 1959.
Eg 819.12.3	Röder, G. Aus dem Leben vornehmer Ägypter. Leipzig, n.d.
Eg 879.52.5	Roeder, G. Volksglaube in Pharaonenreich. Stuttgart, 1952.
Eg 879.59.5	Roeder, Günther. Die ägyptische Religion in Texten und Bildern. v.1-3. Zürich, 1959-
AH 7469.69.10	Roedl, Bernd. Das Senatus Consultum Ultimun und der Tod der Gracchen. Thesis. Bonn, 1969.
AH 7038.41	Römer, H.G. De consulum Romanorum auctoritate. Trajecti ad Rhenum, 1841.
AH 7148.40	Römer, J.W. Defensaibus plebis seu civitatium. Trajecti ad Rhenum, 1840.
AH 3187.16	Römer, Willem H.P. Frauenbriefe über Religion, Politik und Privatleben in Mari. Kevelaer, 1971.
AH 3181.15	Römer, Willem H.P. Sumerische Königshymnen, der Isin-Zeit. Leiden, 1965.
AH 8257.7	Die Römer im Gebiete des ehenmaligen Österreich-Ungarn. (Nischer, Ernst.) Wien, 1923.
AH 9773.13.5	Die Römer in Köln. (Signon, Helmut.) Frankfurt, 1971.
AH 188.40	Römerthum, Christenthum und Germanenthum. (Venedey, J.) Frankfurt, 1840.
AH 8411.5	Die Römerzeit in Österreich und in den augreuzenden Gebieten von Slowenien. 2. Aufl. (Schober, Arnold.) Wien, 1955.
AH 9757.6	Römisch-germanische Studien. (Cramer, F.) Breslau, 1914.
AH 7448.92.2	Der römisch-karthagische Krieg. (Jumpertz, M.) Berlin, 1892.
AH 7168.92.10	Der römisch-rechtliche Begriff. (Merkel, R.) Strassburg, 1892.
AH 7114.26	Römische Adelsparteien und Adelsfamilien. (Münzer, F.) Stuttgart, 1920.
AH 7178.91.6	Die römische Agrargeschichte in ihrer Bedeutung für das Staats- und Privatrecht. (Weber, Max.) Amsterdam, 1966.
AH 7818.56	Römische Alterthümer. (Lange, C.C.L.) Berlin, 1856-71. 3v.
AH 7818.56.3	Römische Alterthümer. v.1-2, 2. Aufl; v.3, 1. Aufl. (Lange, C.C.L.) Berlin, 1863-71. 3v.
AH 7818.56.5	Römische Alterthüsmer. v.1-2, 3. Aufl; v.3, 2. Aufl. (Lange, C.C.L.) Berlin, 1871-79. 3v.
AH 7818.95	Römische Altertumskunde. (Bloch, Leo.) Stuttgart, 1895.
AH 7818.95.5	Römische Altertumskunde. 2. Aufl. (Bloch, Leo.) Leipzig, 1898.
AH 7008.73	Die römische Annalistik. (Nitzsch, K.W.) Berlin, 1873.
AH 9508.6	Die römische Besiedlung von Rheingau und Welterau. (Schell, Günther.) Mainz, 1962.
AH 7468.45	Der römische Bundesgenossenkrieg. (Kiene, Adolf.) Leipzig, 1845.
AH 7038.42	Die römische Censur. (Gerlach, F.D.) Basel, 1842.
AH 7339.13	Römische Charakterköpfe. (Birt, Theodor.) Leipzig, 1913.
AH 7339.13.7	Römische Charakterköpfe. (Birt, Theodor.) Leipzig, 1927.
AH 7339.13.3	Römische Charakterköpfe. 3. Aufl. (Birt, Theodor.) Leipzig, 1918.
AH 7499.13	Römische Charakterpöpfe in Briefen. (Bardt, C.) Leipzig, 1913.
AH 7808.85	Römische Chronologie. (Holzapfel, L.) Leipzig, 1885.
AH 7808.83	Römische Chronologie. (Matzat, H.) Berlin, 1883. 2v.
AH 7808.89.15	Römische Chronologie. (Soltau, Wilhelm.) Freiburg, 1889.
AH 7808.58.3	Römische Chronologie bis auf Caesar. 2. Aufl. (Mommsen, Theodor.) Berlin, 1859.
AH 7228.52.9	Der römische Civilprocess und die Actionen. (Keller, Firedrich.) Leipzig, 1883.
AH 7228.52.5	Der römische Civilprocess und die Actionen. (Keller, Friedrich.) Leipzig, 1876.
AH 7228.52.3	Der römische Civilprocess und die Actionen. 3. Aufl. (Keller, Friedrich.) Leipzig, 1863.
AH 7228.52.4	Der römische Civilprocess und die Actionen. 4. Aufl. (Keller, Friedrich.) Leipzig, 1871.
AH 7228.72	Der römische Civilprozess. (Karlowa, O.) Berlin, 1872.
AH 7158.42	Römische Criminalprocesses. (Geib, G.) Leipzig, 1842.
AH 7163.17	Römische Ehe. (Hölder, E.) Zürich, 1874.
AH 7162.11	Römische Erbrecht. (Vering, F.H.) Heidelberg, 1861.

AH 7818.91.3 Römische Essays. (Lovatelli, E.C. (Contessa).) Leipzig, 1891.

AH 7161.11 Die römische Familie. (Thön, Karl.) Kronstadt, 1857.

AH 7818.63 Römische Forschungen. (Mommsen, T.) Berlin, 1864-79. 2v.

AH 7818.63.3 Römische Forschungen. v.1, 2. Aufl.; v.2, 1. Aufl. (Mommsen, T.) Berlin, 1864. 2v.

AH 8676.2 Römische Forum als Mittelpunkt. (Schulze, E.) Gütersloh, 1893.

AH 7279.48.10 Römische Geschichte. (Altheim, Franz.) Berlin, 1948. 2v.

AH 7279.51 Römische Geschichte. (Altheim, Franz.) Frankfurt, 1951-53. 2v.

AH 7419.26 Römische Geschichte. (Beloch, Julius.) Berlin, 1926.

AH 7279.25 Römische Geschichte. (Cauer, Friedrich.) München, 1925.

AH 7279.19 Römische Geschichte. (Hartmann, Ludo.) Gotha, 1919.

AH 7279.60.5 Römische Geschichte. (Heuss, Alfred.) Braunschweig, 1960.

NEDL AH 7488.41.3 Römische Geschichte. (Hoeck, K.F.C.) Braunschweig, 1841.

AH 7488.41 Römische Geschichte. (Hoeck, K.F.C.) Braunschweig, 1841.

AH 7279.67.5 Römische Geschichte. (Kiechle, Franz.) Stuttgart, 1967.

AH 7278.98.15 Römische Geschichte. (Koch, Julius.) Berlin, 1932. 2v.

AH 7279.42 Römische Geschichte. (Kornemann, Ernst.) Stuttgart, 1941-42. 2v.

AH 7278.43 Römische Geschichte. (Kortüm, F.) Heidelberg, 1843.

AH 7279.53.5 Römische Geschichte. (Mashkin, Nikolai A.) Berlin, 1953.

AH 7278.54.30.10 Römische Geschichte. (Mommsen, T.) Wien, 1932.

AH 7278.54.30.12 Römische Geschichte. (Mommsen, T.) Wien, 1934.

AH 7278.54.30.15 Römische Geschichte. (Mommsen, T.) Wien, 1954.

Htn AH 7278.11* Römische Geschichte. (Niebuhr, B.G.) Berlin, 1811. 2v.

AH 7278.11.11 Römische Geschichte. (Niebuhr, B.G.) Berlin, 1873. 3v.

AH 7278.11.23 Römische Geschichte. (Niebuhr, B.G.) Jena, 1844. 2v.

AH 7278.53.10 Römische Geschichte. (Schwegler, A.) Tübingen, 1853. 4v.

AH 7279.32 Römische Geschichte. Freiburg, 1932. 2v.

AH 7278.54.10.15 Römische Geschichte. v.1-3, 5. (Mommsen, T.) Berlin, 1933. 4v.

Htn AH 7278.54* Römische Geschichte. v.1-3, 5. (Mommsen, T.) Leipzig, 1954. 4v.

AH 7278.54.9.5 Römische Geschichte. v.1-3, 7. Aufl. v.5, 3. Aufl. (Mommsen, T.) Berlin, 1881-86. 4v.

AH 7278.44 Römische Geschichte. v.1-4. (Roth, C.L.) Nürnberg, 1844. 3v.

AH 7278.68 Römische Geschichte. v.1-6, 7-8. (Ihne, W.) Leipzig, 1868. 7v.

AH 7278.54.10 Römische Geschichte. v.5. (Mommsen, T.) Berlin, 1885.

AH 7279.25.5 Römische Geschichte. 2. Aufl. (Cauer, Friedrich.) München, 1933.

AH 7279.60.5.2 Römische Geschichte. 2. Aufl. (Heuss, Alfred.) Braunschweig, 1964.

AH 7278.54.3 Römische Geschichte. 2. Aufl. (Mommsen, T.) Berlin, 1856. 3v.

AH 7278.11.5 Römische Geschichte. 2. Aufl. (Niebuhr, B.G.) Berlin, 1827.

AH 7278.53.11 Römische Geschichte. 2. Aufl. (Schwegler, A.) Tubingen, 1867-1872. 3v.

AH 7278.68.7 Römische Geschichte. 2. Aufl. v.1-2. (Ihne, W.) Leipzig, 1893.

AH 7278.54.6 Römische Geschichte. 3. Aufl. (Mommsen, T.) Berlin, 1861. 3v.

NEDL AH 7278.11.7 Römische Geschichte. 3. Aufl. (Niebuhr, B.G.) Berlin, 1828. 3v.

AH 7279.32.5 Römische Geschichte. 3. Aufl. (Vogt, Joseph.) Freiburg, 1955.

AH 7279.42.4 Römische Geschichte. 4. Aufl. (Kornemann, Ernst.) Stuttgart, 1960. 2v.

AH 7278.54.4 Römische Geschichte. 4. Aufl. (Mommsen, T.) Berlin, 1865. 4v.

AH 7278.54.7 Römische Geschichte. 5. Aufl. v.1, pt.1-2; v.2-3. (Mommsen, T.) Berlin, 1868. 4v.

NEDL AH 7278.54.9 Römische Geschichte. 6. Aufl. (Mommsen, T.) Berlin, 1874. 3v.

AH 7488.42 Römische Geschichte von den Unruhen. (Garzetti, G.B.) Landshut, 1842.

AH 7229.70 Die römische Geschworenenverfassung. Diss. (Behrends, Okko.) Göttingen, 1970.

AH 7178.82.7 Die römische Grundsteuer. (Matthiass, B.) Erlangen, 1882.

AH 7038.32.2 Römische Grundverfassung. (Hüllmann, Karl.) Bonn, 1832.

AH 7038.32 Römische Grundverfassung. (Hüllmann, Karl.) Bonn, 1832.

AH 7239.06.5 Römische Heeresverfassung und Timokratie. (Smith, F.) Berlin, 1906.

AH 8557.2 Römische Herrschaft in Illyrien. (Zippel, B.) Leipzig, 1877.

AH 7298.90 Römische Herrschaft in Westeuropa. (Hübner, Emil.) Berlin, 1890.

AH 7161.12 Römische Hochzeits- und Ehedenkmäler. (Rossbach, August.) Leipzig, 1871.

AH 7809.09 Die römische Jahrzählung. (Leuzl, Oscar.) Tübingen, 1909.

AH 7719.09 Der römische Kaiser Caracalla. (Schulz, O.T.) Leipzig, 1909.

AH 7214.12 Der römische Kaisereid. Habilitationsschrift. (Herrmann, Peter.) Göttingen, 1968.

AH 7498.65 Römische Kaiserfrauen. (Stahr, Adolf.) Berlin, 1865.

AH 7548.39 Die Römische Kaisergeschichte. (Reinhold, K.W.) Pasewalf, 1839.

AH 7808.82 Der römische Kalender. (Hartmann, O.E.) Leipzig, 1882.

AH 7809.36 Der römische Kalender und seine Verbesserung durch Julius Caesar. (Geiger, Karl.) München, 1936.

AH 7489.51.5 Römische Kinderkaiser. (Hartke, W.) Berlin, 1951.

AH 7408.81 Das römische Königthum. (Lange, C.C.L.) Leipzig, 1881.

AH 7161.2 Der römische Konkubinat. (Meyer, Paul.) Leipzig, 1895.

AH 7231.9 Römische Kriegsaltertümer. (Kuthe, A.) Wismar, 1884. 4 pam.

AH 7819.49 Römische Kulterbilder. (Poulsen, F.) Kobenhagen, 1949.

AH 7819.15 Römische Kultur im Bilde. (Lamer, Hans.) Leipzig, 1915.

AH 7819.64 Römische Kunst als religioses Phänomen. (Schefold, K.) Reinbek, 1964.

AH 7239.14.4 Das römische Lager insbesondere nach Livius. (Fischer, W.) Leipzig, 1914.

AH 8321.5 Die römische Lagerstadt Apulum in Dacien. (Gooss, Carl.) Schassburg, 1874.

AH 7168.41.6 Römische Lehre der dinglichen Rechte. (Sell, K.) Bonn, 1852.

AH 7239.20.5 Römische Militärgeschichte. (Grosse, Robert.) Berlin, 1920.

AH 8407.2 Das römische Norikum. (Muchar, A.A.) Gratz, 1825. 2v.

AH 7168.79.5 Das römische Patronatrecht. (Leist, B.W.) Erlangen, 1879. 2v.

AH 7148.87.5 Das römische Pfandrecht. (Bachofen.) Baseel, 1887.

AH 7279.67.10 Römische Politik und römische Politiker. (Hoffter, Heinz.) Heidelberg, 1967.

AH 7818.64.15 Römische Privatalterthümer. (Marquardt, Joachim.) Leipzig, 1864-67.

AH 7228.88.5 Römische Processgesetze. (Wlassak, M.) Leipzig, 1888.

AH 9777.11 Das römische Recht im östgothischen Reiche. (Glöden, I. von.) Jena, 1843.

AH 7138.80 Römische Rechtsgeschichte. (Esmarch, K.) Kassel, 1880.

AH 7138.85.3 Römische Rechtsgeschichte. (Karlowa, O.) Leipzig, 1885. 2v.

AH 7138.32.3 Römische Rechtsgeschichte. (Schweppe, A.) Göttingen, 1832.

AH 7138.92 Römische Rechtsgeschichte. (Voigt, M.) Leipzig, 1892. 3v.

AH 7139.71 Römische Rechtsgeschichte. 1e Aufl. (Soellner, Alfred.) Freiburg, 1971.

AH 7138.88.3 Römische Rechtswissenschaft. (Jörs, Paul.) Berlin, 1888.

AH 7449.35 Die römische Republik um das Jahr 225 vor Christus. (Nap, J.M.) Leiden, 1935.

AH 7269.57 Die römische Republik und ihre Auseinandersetzung mit den Grossmächten des Mittelmeerraumes bis 168. (Kampe, Otto.) Stuttgart, 1957.

AH 7808.61 Der römische Schalttag seit Julius Caesar. (Hermann, F.C.) Berlin, 1861.

AH 7207.17 Der römische Senat. (Hofmann, Friedrich.) Berlin, 1847.

AH 7038.95 Römische Staats und Rechtsaltertümer. (Zoeller, Max.) Breslau, 1895.

AH 7038.46 Die römische Staatsverfassung. (Raumer, F.) Berlin, 1846.

AH 7299.22 Römische Studien, historisches, epigraphisches, literargeschichtliches. (Cichorius, C.) Leipzig, 1922.

AH 7239.13 Die römische Taktik zur Zeit der Manipularstellung. (Steinwender, T.) Danzig, 1913.

AH 7139.05.3 Römische und antike Rechtsgeschichte. (Wenger, L.) Graz, 1905.

AH 7846.5 Der römische Villenbesitz in Italien zur Keiserzeit. Inaug. Diss. (Becker, Philipp.) Bonn, 1925.

AH 7228.45 Der römische Vindicationsprocess. (Wetzell, G.W.) Leipzig, 1845.

AH 7489.41 Das römische Weltreich. (Birt, Theodor.) Berlin, 1941.

AH 7808.89 Römische Zeitrechnung für die Jahre 219 bis 1 v. Chr. (Matzat, Heinrich.) Berlin, 1880.

AH 7808.88 Die römischen Amstjahre auf ihren natürlichen Zeitwerth reducirt. (Soltau, Wilhelm.) Freiburg, 1888.

AH 7861.8 Die römischen Collegia Funeraticia. (Schiess, T.) München, 1888.

AH 7162.15 Römischen Frauen-Erbrechts. (Kahn, F.) Leipzig, 1884.

AH 7178.96 Die römischen Grundherrschaften. (Schulten, A.) Weimar, 1896.

AH 7198.97 Römischen Institutionen-System. (Affolter, F.X.) Berlin, 1897.

AH 7498.00F Die Römischen Kaiser. Leipzig, 18- .

AH 7488.28 Die Römischen Kaiser. v.1-4. Leipzig, 1828-29.

AH 7238.95 Die römischen Legionen und Kriegsschiffe. (Luterbacher, F.) Burgdorf, 1895.

AH 7168.62 Römischen Privatrecht. (Böcking, E.) Bonn, 1862.

AH 7168.77 Römischen Privatrecht. (Zródlowski, F.) Prag, 1877. 2v.

AH 7138.70.5 Römischen Rechts, kritische Versuche. (Krüger, P.) Berlin, 1870.

AH 7138.56 Römischen Rechtsgeschichte. (Esmach, K.) Göttingen, 1856.

AH 7138.57 Römischen Rechtsgeschichte. (Rudorff, A.F.) Leipzig, 1857.

AH 7188.56 Römischen Servitutenlehre. (Elvers, R.) Marburg, 1856.

AH 7115.2 Die römischen Tribus. (Mommsen, T.) Altona, 1844.

AH 7229.04 Römischen Zivilprozess. (Schott, R.) München, 1904.

AH 7039.48 Römischer Staat und Staatsgedanke. (Meyer, Ernst.) Zurich, 1948.

AH 7819.63.5 Römisches Alltagsleben im 1. und 2. Jahrhundert nach Christ nach martial und juvenal. (Helm, Ruddle.) Zürich, 1963.

AH 7819.69.15 Römisches Gesellschaftsdenken. (Schottlaender, Rudolf.) Weimar, 1969.

AH 7169.08 Römisches Privatrecht. (Mitteis, L.) Leipzig, 1908.

AH 7168.36 Römisches Privatrecht. (Rein, W.) Leipzig, 1836.

AH 7169.35 Römisches Privatrecht. 2. Aufl. (Jörs, Paul.) Berlin, 1935.

AH 7139.26 Römisches Recht in Grundzügen für die Vorlesung. (Siber, Heinrich.) Berlin, 1925-28. 2v.

AH 7158.99 Römisches Strafrecht. (Mommsen, Theodor.) Leipzig, 1899.

AH 7178.98 Römisches Wasserrecht. (Ossig, A.) Leipzig, 1898.

AH 3813.5 Röntsch, J. Indogermanen und Semitenthum. Leipzig, 1872.

AH 5390.20 Roesch, Paul. Thespies et la confédération béotienne. Paris, 1965.

AH 507.98 Roesler, C.F. Chronica medii aevi. Tubingae, 1798.

AH 9777.20 Roesler, E. Die Geten und ihre Nachbarn. Wien, 1864.

AH 8548.50 Roessler, C. Les influences celtiques. Paris, 1902.

AH 7338.18 Rogers, Eliza. History of the Roman Empire. London, 1818. 5v.

AH 7278.18.5F Rogers, Eliza. History of the Roman Empire. Atlas. London, 1818.

AH 7159.35 Rogers, R.S. Crimial trials and criminal legislation under Tiberius. Middletown, Conn., 1935.

AH 7519.43 Rogers, R.S. Studies in the reign of Tiberius. Baltimore, 1943.

AH 3002.28 Rogers, R.W. Cuneiform parallels to the Old Testament. N.Y., 1912.

AH 3009.00 Rogers, R.W. A history of Babylonia and Assyria. N.Y., 1900. 2v.

AH 3155.19 Rogers, R.W. The religion of Babylonia and Assyria. N.Y., 1908.

AH 3657.29 Rogers, Robert W. A history of ancient Persia. N.Y., 1929.

AH 3009.15 Rogers, R.W. A history of Babylonia and Assyria. 6. ed. N.Y., 1915. 2v.

AH 8116.5 Roget, Raymond. Le Maroc chez les auteurs anciens. Paris, 1924.

AH 328.73 Roget de Belloguet, D.F.L. Ethnogénie gauloise. Paris, 1873. 4v.

AH 866.7 Rogge, A. Ist Preussen das Bernsteinland der alten Gewesen? Königsberg, 1880.

AH 8557.10 Rogošić, Roko. Veliki Illirik (284-395) i njegova konačna dioba (396-437). Zagreb, 1962.

AH 2007.2 Rohden, P. De Palaestina e Arabia. Berolini, 1885.

AH 7808.99.3 Rolando, A. Chronologia storica Roma. Torino, 1899.

AH 7859.8	Le role judiciaire et politique des femmes sous la République romaine. (Herrmann, Claudine.) Bruxelles, 1964.
AH 4850.13	Role of Mageiroi in life of ancient Greece. (Rankin, E.M.) Chicago, 1907.
AH 812.10	The role of the Phoenicians in the interaction of Mediterranean civilizations. (Archaeological Symposium, American University of Beirut, 1967.) Beirut, 1968.
AH 3957.35	Rolla, Armando. L'ambiente biblico. Brescia, 1959.
NEDL AH 277.34.11	Rollin, Charles. Ancient history. Boston, 1801. 8v.
AH 277.34.12	Rollin, Charles. Ancient history. Boston, 1807. 8v.
NEDL AH 277.34.13	Rollin, Charles. Ancient history. Boston, 1807. 8v.
NEDL AH 277.34.14	Rollin, Charles. Ancient history. Boston, 1823. 2v.
AH 277.34.10	Rollin, Charles. Ancient history. Glasgow, 1800. 6v.
NEDL AH 277.34	Rollin, Charles. Ancient history. London, 1734. 10v.
NEDL AH 277.34.6	Rollin, Charles. Ancient history. London, 1774. 8v.
NEDL AH 277.34.8	Rollin, Charles. Ancient history. London, 1788. 10v.
NEDL AH 277.34.14.3	Rollin, Charles. Ancient history. N.Y., 1828. 2v.
NEDL AH 277.34.14.9	Rollin, Charles. Ancient history. N.Y., 1839. 2v.
NEDL AH 277.34.15	Rollin, Charles. Ancient history. N.Y., 1841. 2v.
NEDL AH 277.34.10.8	Rollin, Charles. Ancient history. Portland, 1805. 8v.
AHP 277.34.30	Rollin, Charles. Ancient history. Atlas. n.p., 1738-40.
NEDL AH 277.34.21	Rollin, Charles. Ancient history. v.1-4. Cincinnati, 1860. 2v.
NEDL AH 277.34.19	Rollin, Charles. Ancient history. v.1-4. N.Y., 1857. 2v.
NEDL AH 277.34.14.5	Rollin, Charles. Ancient history. v.2-4,6-8. Philadelphia, 1829. 6v.
AH 277.34.10.9	Rollin, Charles. Ancient history. v.6. Philadelphia, 1805.
NEDL AH 277.34.10.5	Rollin, Charles. Ancient history. 10. ed. London, 1804. 8v.
AH 277.34.17	Rollin, Charles. The ancient history of the Egyptians. Cincinnati, 1850. 2v.
AH 277.34.23	Rollin, Charles. The ancient history of the Egyptians. London, 1826. 8v.
NEDL AH 277.34.16	Rollin, Charles. Ancient history of the Egyptians. N.Y., 1843-44. 8v.
AH 277.34.22	Rollin, Charles. The ancient history of the Egyptians. N.Y., 1883. 4v.
AH 277.34.2.3	Rollin, Charles. Histoire ancienne. Amsterdam, 1734-39. 13v.
NEDL AH 277.34.3	Rollin, Charles. Histoire ancienne. Amsterdam, 1759. 3v.
AH 277.34.2	Rollin, Charles. Histoire ancienne. Paris, 1740. 5v.
NEDL AH 277.34.5	Rollin, Charles. Histoire ancienne. v.1-13. Paris, 1758-63. 14v.
AH 277.34.4	Rollin, Charles. Histoire ancienne. v.4-13. Amsterdam, 1767. 10v.
AH 7277.52	Rollin, Charles. Histoire romaine. Paris, 1752. 8v.
NEDL AH 7277.52.1	Rollin, Charles. Histoire romaine. Paris, 1758-68. 16v.
AH 7277.52.2	Rollin, Charles. Histoire romaine. Paris, 1803-05. 16v.
AH 817.37	Rollin, Charles. History of the arts and sciences. London, 1737. 4v.
AH 7277.52.3	Rollin, Charles. Roman history. 2. ed. London, 1754. 16v.
NEDL AH 277.34.25	Rollin, Charles. Storia antica. Livorno, 1835. 11v.
NEDL AH 277.34.27	Rollin, Charles. Storia antica e romana. 1. ed. Firenze, 1828-32. 49v.
AH 4239.03	Roloff, G. Probleme aus der griechischen Kriegsgeschichte. Berlin, 1903.
AH 5807.7	Roltsch, Otto. Die Westlokrer. Inaug. Diss. Weida, 1914.
AH 7599.37	Rom; Herrschertum und Reich in zweiten Jahrhundert. (Weber, William.) Stuttgart, 1937.
AH 7479.07.5	Rom im Übergange von der Republik. (Volquardsen, C.) Kiel, 1907.
AH 7269.33	Rom und Aegypten im 2. Jahrhundert v. Chr. (Winkler, Heinz.) Engelsdorf, 1933.
Eg 709.66.5	Rom und Ägypten vom 51 bis 47 vor Christ; Untersuchungen zur Regierungszeit der 7. Kleopatra und des 13. Ptolemäers. (Heinen, Heinz.) Tübingen, 1966.
AH 7819.42.10	Rom und der Hellenismus. (Atheim, F.) Amsterdam, 1942.
AH 7419.13.10	Rom und Eturien von der Eroberung Vejis bis zur Mitte des 3. Jahrhunderts vor Christus. (Gröseling, Johannes.) Borna, 1913.
AH 8073.18	Rom und Karthago. (Vogt, Josef.) Leipzig, 1943.
AH 7448.76	Rom und Karthago in ihren gegenseitigen Veziehungen 513-536 von Christus. (241-218 von Christus). (Gilbert, Otto.) Leipzig, 1876.
AH 5132.7	Rom und Mytilene. (Cichorius, Conrad.) Leipzig, 1888.
AH 7818.79	Rom und römisches Leben im Alterthumen. (Bender, H.) Tübingen, 1879.
AH 7818.79.3	Rom und römisches Leben im Alterthumen. 2. Aufl. (Bender, H.) Tübingen, 1893.
AH 7409.51	Rom und Troia. (Bömer, Franz.) Baden Baden, 1951.
AHP 28.8	Roma, guida allo studio della civilta romana. Roma.
AH 7308.82	Roma. (Graf, A.) Torino, 1882. 2v.
AH 7769.67.5	Roma aeterna. (Paschoud, François.) Rome, 1967.
AH 7279.21.5	Roma antica. (Ferrero, Guglielmo.) Firenze, 1921-22. 3v.
AH 7279.21.6	Roma antica. 2. ed. (Ferrero, Guglielmo.) Firenze, 1933. 3v.
AH 7279.20.5	Roma antica attraverso la sua storia e i suoi monumenti. 2. ed. (Cardona, Chiara.) Roma, 192-.
AH 7449.31	Roma e Cartagine sul mare. (Guarnieri, L.) Roma, 1931.
AH 7148.87.7	Roma e isuoi municipi. (Taddei, A.) Firenze, 1887.
AH 2147.12	Roma e l'eredita di Alessandro. (Lanza, Michele.) Milano, 1971.
AH 7298.99F	Roma e l'Oriente. (Gubernatis, A. de.) Roma, 1899.
AH 7619.40	Roma imperiale ai tempi di Traiano. (Carrea d'Oliveira, E.) Milano, 1940.
AH 7276.64	Roma in ogni stato. (Alveri, Gasparo.) Roma, 1664. 2v.
Htn AH 7816.77*	Roma restituta. (Bell, T.) London, 1677.
AH 7816.96.16	Romae antiquae notitia. 1st American ed. (Kennett, Basil.) Philadelphia, 1822.
AH 7816.96.17	Romae antiquae notitia. 2nd American ed. (Kennett, Basil.) Baltimore, 18- .
AH 7816.96.3	Romae antiquae notitia. 3. ed. (Kennett, Basil.) Oxford, 1704.
NEDL AH 7816.96.6	Romae antiquae notitia. 6th ed. (Kennett, Basil.) London, 1717.
NEDL AH 7816.96.11	Romae antiquae notitia. 11th ed. (Kennett, Basil.) London, 1746.
NEDL AH 7816.96.13	Romae antiquae notitia. 13th ed. (Kennett, Basil.) London, 1763.
AH 7816.96.14	Romae antiquae notitia. 14th ed. (Kennett, Basil.) London, 1769.
NEDL AH 7277.70.25	Rōmaïkēs istorias. (Goldsmith, O.) Athēnai, 1852.
AH 7818.40.3	Les Romains...République romaine. 2. éd. (Ozaneaux, J.G.) Paris, 1845.
AH 7418.77	Les romains à Athènes avant l'empire. (Hinstin, G.) Paris, 1877.
AH 7828.82	Les Romains au temps de Pline. (Pellisson, M.) Paris, 1882.
NEDL AH 8007.2	Roman Africa...Roman occupation of Africa. (Graham, A.) London, 1902.
AH 8007.01	Pamphlet box. Roman Africa.
AH 8007.7.5	Roman Africa. (Boissier, Gaston.) N.Y., 1899.
AH 7298.64	The Roman and the Teuton. (Kingsley, Charles.) Cambridge, 1864.
NEDL AH 7298.64.1	The Roman and the Teuton. (Kingsley, Charles.) London, 1879.
AH 7298.64.3	The Roman and the Teuton. (Kingsley, Charles.) London, 1881.
AH 7298.64.5	The Roman and the Teuton. (Kingsley, Charles.) London, 1889.
NEDL AH 7298.64.2	The Roman and the Teuton. (Kingsley, Charles.) London, 1890.
AH 7015.13F	Pamphlet box. Roman antiquities.
AH 7817.92.7	Roman antiquities. (Adam, Alexander.) N.Y., 1826.
NEDL AH 7817.92.9	Roman antiquities. (Adam, Alexander.) N.Y., 1830.
NEDL AH 7817.92.11	Roman antiquities. (Adam, Alexander.) N.Y., 1837.
AH 7818.20.6	Roman antiquities. (Fuss, J.D.) Oxford, 1840.
NEDL AH 7818.84	Roman antiquities. (Wilkins, A.S.) N.Y., 1884.
NEDL AH 7818.84.2A	Roman Antiquities. (Wilkins, A.S.) N.Y., 1892?
AH 7817.92.5	Roman antiquities. 1st American ed. (Adam, Alexander.) Philadelphia, 1807.
AH 7817.92.6	Roman antiquities. 2nd American ed. (Adam, Alexander.) N.Y., 1814.
AH 7817.92.2	Roman antiquities. 2nd ed. (Adam, Alexander.) Edinburgh, 1792.
AH 7817.92.10	Roman antiquities. 6th ed. (Adam, Alexander.) Glasgow, 1835.
AH 7817.92.12	Roman antiquities. 7th ed. (Adam, Alexander.) N.Y., 1836.
AH 7818.32.3	Roman antiquities and ancient mythology. 2nd ed. (Dillaway, C.K.) Boston, 1833.
AH 7239.56.5	The Roman army. (Webster, Graham.) Chester, 1956.
AH 7239.40	The Roman art of war under the republic. (Adcock, F.E.) Cambridge, 1940.
AH 7079.09	The Roman assemblies. (Botsford, G.W.) N.Y., 1909.
AH 8207.12	Roman Britain. (Collingwood, Robin G.) London, 1923.
AH 8205.4	Roman Britain and the Roman army. (Birley, Eric.) Kendal, 1953.
AH 7099.39	The Roman citizenship. (Sherwin-White, A.N.) Oxford, 1939.
AH 7149.35	Roman citizenship. Thesis. (Goodfellow, C.E.) Lancaster, 1935.
AH 7819.18	The Roman civilization. (Gilis, Alexander A.) Edinburgh, 1918.
AH 7819.51	Roman civilization. (Lewis, N.) N.Y., 1955-67. 2v.
AH 2111.5	Roman colonies in Southern Asia Minor. (Levick, Barbara Mary.) Oxford, 1967.
AH 7299.69	Roman colonization under the Republic. (Salmon, Edward T.) London, 1969.
AH 7819.42.5	The Roman commonwealth. (Moore, R.W.) London, 1942.
AH 8211.9	The Roman conquest of Britain, A.D. 43-57. (Dudley, Donald R.) London, 1965.
AH 7039.02	Roman constitutional history, 753-44 B.C. (Granrud, John E.) Boston, 1902.
AH 7297.97	Roman conversations. (Wilcocks, J.) London, 1797. 2v.
AH 7850.3	Roman cooks. Diss. (Harcum, C.G.) Baltimore, 1914.
AH 7909.17.1	Roman craftsmen and tradesmen of the early empire. (Brewster, Ethel Hampson.) N.Y., 1972.
AH 7818.79.5	Roman days. (Rydberg, V.) N.Y., 1879.
AH 7029.69.5	Roman documents from the Greek East; senatus consulta and epistolae to the age of Augustus. (Sherk, Robert K.) Baltimore, 1969.
AH 7889.07	Roman economic conditions. (Oliver, E.H.) Toronto, 1907.
AH 7842.10A	Roman education. (Wilkins, A.S.) Cambridge, 1905.
AH 7842.10.5	Roman education. (Wilkins, A.S.) Cambridge, 1914.
AH 7842.19.5	Roman education from Cicero to Quintilian. (Gwynn, Aubrey.) N.Y., 1966.
AH 7842.19	Roman education from Cicero to Quintilian. (Gwynn, Aubrey.) Oxford, 1926.
AH 7481.01	Pamphlet box. Roman empire.
AH 7039.10.2A	Roman empire. (Bussell, F.W.) London, 1910. 2v.
AH 7489.51A	The Roman Empire. (Charlesworth, M.P.) London, 1951.
AH 7278.45	The Roman Empire. (Society for Promoting Christian Knowledge, London.) London, 1845.
AH 7489.30	The Roman Empire. (Stevenson, G.H.) London, 1930.
AH 7489.66.1	The Roman Empire and its neighbours. (Millar, Fergus.) London, 1967.
AH 7489.08.5	Roman Empire B.C. 29-A.D. 476. (Jones, H.S.) N.Y., 192-?
NEDL AH 7598.76	The Roman Empire of the second century. (Capes, William W.) London, 1876.
NEDL AH 7598.76.9	The Roman Empire of the second century. (Capes, William W.) N.Y., 1887.
AH 7598.76.12	The Roman Empire of the second century. (Capes, William W.) N.Y., 1891.
AH 7598.76.15	The Roman Empire of the second century. (Capes, William W.) N.Y., 1895.
AH 7497.21.6	Roman empresses, or History of lives. (Serviez, J.R. de.) Dublin, 1752. 3v.
Htn AH 7497.21.7*	Roman empresses, or History of lives. (Serviez, J.R. de.) London, 1752. 3v.
AH 7497.21.25	The Roman empresses. (Serviez, J.R. de.) London, 1899. 2v.
AH 7899.70	Roman farming. (White, Kenneth Douglas.) London, 1970.
AH 7309.22	The Roman fate; an essay. (Heitland, William E.) Cambridge, 1922.
AH 7189.69	Roman freedmen during the late republic. (Treggiari, Susan.) Oxford, 1969.
AH 8515.5	Roman Gaul; the objects of trade. (West, L.C.) Oxford, 1935.
AH 8507.10.2A	Roman Gaul. (Brogan, O.) Cambridge, Mass., 1953.
AH 8507.10	Roman Gaul. (Brogan, O.) London, 1953.
AH 7081.1	Pamphlet box. Roman government.
AH 7101.1	Pamphlet box. Roman government and finance.
AH 7029.04	Roman historical sources. (Sanders, Henry.) N.Y., 1904.
AH 7859.1	Pamphlet box. Roman history, civilization, condition of women.
AH 7498.76	Roman history, early empire. (Capes, William W.) London, 1876.

Author and Title Listing

	Call no.	Title
	AH 7498.77	Roman history, early empire. 2. ed. (Capes, William W.) London, 1877.
Htn	AH 7277.69*	The Roman history, from the foundation of the city of Rome to the destruction of the western empire. (Goldsmith, O.) London, 1769. 2v.
	AH 7819.42	Roman history, life and literature. (White, George W.) London, 1942.
	AH 7015.9	Pamphlet box. Roman history. 7 pam.
	AH 7015.10	Pamphlet vol. Roman history. 10 pam.
	AH 7015.6	Pamphlet vol. Roman history. 14 pam.
	AH 7277.25.5F	Roman history. (Catrou, François.) London, 1728. 6v.
	AH 7277.13	Roman history. (Echard, L.) London, 1713. 5v.
NEDL	AH 7277.70.9	Roman history. (Goldsmith, O.) Dublin, 1781.
	AH 7277.70	Roman history. (Goldsmith, O.) London, 1770. 2v.
	AH 7277.70.3	Roman history. (Goldsmith, O.) London, 1786. 2v.
	AH 7277.70.5	Roman history. (Goldsmith, O.) London, 1805. 2v.
NEDL	AH 7277.70.7	Roman history. (Goldsmith, O.) London, 1821. 2v.
	AH 7277.38.9	The Roman history. (Hooke, N.) London, 18- . 3v.
	AH 7277.38.2	The Roman history. (Hooke, N.) London, 1745-64. 3v.
	AH 7277.38.3	The Roman history. (Hooke, N.) London, 1757. 4v.
	AH 7811.2	Pamphlet box. Roman history. Civilization.
	AH 7842.01	Pamphlet box. Roman history. Civilization. Books and education.
	AH 7881.2	Pamphlet box. Roman History. Economics.
	AH 7899.10	Pamphlet box. Roman History. Economics. Agriculture.
	AH 8908.01	Pamphlet box. Roman history. Etruria.
	AH 7031.01	Pamphlet box. Roman history. Government.
	AH 7051.1	Pamphlet box. Roman history. Government. Administration.
	AH 7091.1	Pamphlet box. Roman history. Government. Municipal.
	AH 7131.1	Pamphlet box. Roman history. Law.
	AH 7231.01	Pamphlet box. Roman history. Military affairs.
	AH 7581.01	Pamphlet box. Roman history. The Caesars. Domitian.
	AH 7571.01	Pamphlet box. Roman history. The Caesars. Titus.
	AH 7751.01	Pamphlet box. Roman history. The Decline.
	AH 7498.87	Roman history: the early empire. (Capes, William W.) London, 1887.
	AH 7498.87.4	Roman history: the early empire. (Capes, William W.) N.Y., 1892.
	AH 7498.87.5	Roman history: the early empire. (Capes, William W.) N.Y., 1895.
	AH 7277.52.3	Roman history. 2. ed. (Rollin, Charles.) London, 1754. 16v.
	AH 7278.61	Roman history. 3. ed. (Turner, D.W.) London, 1861.
NEDL	AH 7277.70.21	Roman history. 35. American ed. (Goldsmith, O.) Philadelphia, 1853.
	AH 7029.10	Roman history and mythology. (Sanders, Henry.) N.Y., 1910.
	AH 7239.69	The Roman Imperial Army of the first and second centuries, A.D. (Webster, Graham.) London, 1969.
	AH 7819.57	Roman imperial civilization. (Mattingly, Harold.) London, 1957.
	AH 7259.41.5	The Roman imperial navy. 2. ed. (Starr, Chester G.) N.Y., 1960.
	AH 7489.14	Roman imperialism. (Frank, Tenny.) N.Y., 1914.
	AH 7469.68.12	Roman imperialism in the late republic. 2. ed. (Badian, Ernst.) Oxford, 1968.
	AH 7138.76.8	Roman law. (Hunter, W.A.) London, 1876.
	AH 7138.76.7	Roman law. (Hunter, W.A.) London, 1876.
	AH 7139.51.5	Roman law. (Wolff, Hans J.) Oklahoma, 1951.
	AH 7138.97	Roman law. 3. ed. (Hunter, W.A.) London, 1897.
	AH 7168.86.3	Roman law of damage to property. (Grueber, E.) Oxford, 1886.
	AH 7163.29	The Roman law of marriage. (Corbett, Percy E.) Oxford, 1930.
	AH 7203.93	Roman law of sale with modern illustrations. Digest XVIII.1 and XIX.1 translated. (Corpus juris civilis. Digesta.) Edinburgh, 1892.
	AH 7189.08	The Roman law of slavery. (Buckland, William Warwick.) Cambridge, Eng., 1908.
	AH 7189.08.1	The Roman law of slavery. (Buckland, William Warwick.) Cambridge, Eng., 1970.
	AH 7162.22	Roman law of testaments. (Dropsie, M.A.) Philadelphia, 1892.
	AH 7139.12.7	Roman laws and charters. (Hardy, E.G.) Oxford, 1912.
	AH 7239.28	The Roman legions. (Parker, Henry M.D.) Oxford, 1928.
	AH 7818.65.17	Roman life and manners. (Friedlaender, Ludwig.) London, 190-. 4v.
	AH 7818.65.18	Roman life and manners under the early empire. (Friedlaender, Ludwig.) N.Y., 1968. 4v.
	AH 7828.82.3A	Roman life in Pliny's time. (Pellisson, M.) Meadville, Pa., 1897.
NEDL	AH 7818.84.5	Roman life in the days of Cicero. (Church, Alfred J.) London, 1884.
	AH 7818.84.6	Roman life in the days of Cicero. (Church, Alfred J.) N.Y., 1883.
	AH 7818.97.5	Roman life under the Caesars. (Thomas, Émile.) N.Y., 1899.
	AH 7229.66	Roman litigation. (Kelly, John Maurice.) Oxford, 1966.
	AH 8232.5	Roman London. (Merrifield, Ralph.) N.Y., 1969.
	AH 8857.5	Roman memories in the landscape seen from Capri. (Jerome, Thomas S.) Detroit, 1914.
	AH 7114.34.5	The Roman middle class in the Republican period. (Hill, Herbert.) Ann Arbor, 1967.
	AH 7239.68	Roman military law. (Brand, Clarence E.) Austin, 1968.
	AH 7239.71	Roman military records on Papyrus. (Fink, Robert O.) Cleveland, 1971.
	AH 7819.58	The Roman mind at work. (McKendrick, Paul Lachlan.) Princeton, N.J., 1958.
	AH 7251.01	Pamphlet box. Roman Naval affairs.
	AH 7217.15.5	The Roman nobility. (Gelzer, Matthias.) Oxford, 1969.
	AH 8207.15	The Roman occupation of Britain. (Haverfield, F.J.) Oxford, 1924.
	AH 9085.5	Roman Ostia. (Meiggs, Russell.) Oxford, 1960.
	AH 7819.44	Roman panorama. (Grose-Hodge, Hamfrey.) Cambridge, Eng., 1944.
	AH 4719.54	Roman policy in Epirus and Acarmania in the age of the Roman conquest of Greece. (Oost, S.I.) Dallas, 1954.
	AH 7039.59	Roman political ideas and practice. (Adcock, Frank.) Ann Arbor, 1959.
	AH 7039.29	Roman political institutions from city to state. (Homs, Léon.) London, 1929.
	AH 7462.10.2	Roman politics, 80-44 B.C.; a selection of Latin passages. (Hawthorn, John R.) London, 1965.
	AH 7459.51	Roman politics, 220-150 B.C. (Scullard, Howard Hayes.) Oxford, 1951.
	AH 7459.51.2	Roman politics, 220-150 B.C. 2. ed. (Scullard, Howard Hayes.) Oxford, 1973.
	AH 7039.23A	Roman politics. (Abbott, Frank F.) Boston, 1923.
	AH 7159.68	Roman politics and criminal courts, 149-78 B.C. (Gruen, Erich Stephen.) Cambridge, 1968.
	AH 7169.06	Roman private law. (Leage, Richard William.) London, 1906.
	AH 7169.02	Roman private law. (Roby, H.J.) Cambridge, 1902. 2v.
	AH 7168.86	Roman private law. (Salkowski, C.) London, 1886.
	AH 7169.71	Roman private law around 200 B.C. (Watson, Alan.) Edinburgh, 1971.
	AH 7829.24	Roman private life and its survivals. (McDaniel, W.B.) Boston, 1924.
	AH 7829.24.5	Roman private life and its survivals. (McDaniel, W.B.) N.Y., 1929.
	AH 7829.24.6	Roman private life and its survivals. (McDaniel, W.B.) N.Y., 1963.
	AH 7089.39A	Roman provincial administration. (Stevenson, G.H.) Oxford, 1939.
	AH 7089.26	The roman provincial governor as he appears in the Digest and Code of Justinian. (Mierow, Herbert E.) Colorado Springs, 1926.
	AH 7039.01.5	Roman public life. (Greenidge, Abel Hendy Jones.) London, 1922.
	AH 7239.52A	A Roman reformer and inventor. (De Rebus Billicis.) Oxford, 1952.
	AH 7411.01	Pamphlet box. Roman republic.
	AH 7419.65	The Roman republic. (Boren, Henry Charles.) Princeton, 1965.
	AH 7419.72.10	The Roman republic. (Gruen, Erich Stephen.) Washington, 1972.
	AH 7419.09	Roman republic. (Heitland, W.E.) Cambridge, 1909. 3v.
	AH 7419.09.2	Roman republic. (Heitland, W.E.) Cambridge, 1923. 3v.
	AH 7418.60	The Roman republic. (Moule, H.) London, 1860.
	AH 7419.23	The Roman republic and the founder of the empire. (Holmes, T. Rice E.) Oxford, 1923. 3v.
	AH 7469.39	The Roman revolution. (Syme, Ronald.) Oxford, 1939.
	AH 7469.39.3	The Roman revolution. (Syme, Ronald.) Oxford, 1956.
	AH 2147.8	Roman rule in Asia Minor. (Magie, D.) Princeton, 1950. 2v.
	AH 7819.74	Roman social relations, 50 B.C. to A.D. 284. (MacMullen, Ramsay.) New Haven, 1974.
	AH 7819.56	Roman society. (Dill, Samuel.) N.Y., 1956.
	AH 7819.04A	Roman society from Nero to Marcus Aurelius. (Dill, Samuel.) London, 1904.
	AH 7819.04.5	Roman society from Nero to Marcus Aurelius. (Dill, Samuel.) London, 1920.
	AH 7819.04.7A	Roman society from Nero to Marcus Aurelius. (Dill, Samuel.) London, 1925.
	AH 7819.04.2	Roman society from Nero to Marcus Aurelius. 2. ed. (Dill, Samuel.) London, 1905.
	AH 7819.04.3	Roman society from Nero to Marcus Aurelius. 2. ed. (Dill, Samuel.) London, 1911.
	AH 7818.98	Roman society in the last century of the Western Empire. (Dill, Samuel.) London, 1898.
	AH 7818.98.5A	Roman society in the last century of the Western Empire. (Dill, Samuel.) London, 1906.
	AH 7818.98.3A	Roman society in the last century of the Western Empire. 2. ed. (Dill, Samuel.) London, 1905.
	AH 7818.98.10	Roman society in the last century of the Western Empire. 2. ed. (Dill, Samuel.) London, 1919.
	AH 7239.65	The Roman soldier. (Mellersh, Harold Edward Leslie.) N.Y., 1965.
	AH 7239.69.5	The Roman soldier. (Watson, G.R.) London, 1969.
	AH 7088.79A	Roman system of provincial administration. (Arnold, W.T.) London, 1879.
	AH 7088.79.5	Roman system of provincial administration. (Arnold, W.T.) Oxford, 1906.
	AH 7088.79.9	Roman system of provincial administration. 3rd ed. (Arnold, W.T.) Oxford, 1914.
	AH 7848.9	The Roman toga. (Wilson, L.M.) Baltimore, 1924.
	AH 7229.27	The Roman tribunal. (Johnson, H.D.) Baltimore, 1927.
	AH 7238.50.3	Pamphlet box. Roman triumph. 2 pam.
NEDL	AH 7478.77.2	Roman triumvirates. (Merivale, Charles.) London, 1876.
NEDL	AH 7478.77.5	Roman triumvirates. (Merivale, Charles.) N.Y., 1889.
NEDL	AH 7478.77.6	Roman triumvirates. (Merivale, Charles.) N.Y., 1893.
	AH 7478.77.7	Roman triumvirates. (Merivale, Charles.) N.Y., 1895.
	AH 7478.77.3A	Roman triumvirates. 5. ed. (Merivale, Charles.) London, 1887.
	AH 7079.66.5	Roman voting assemblies from the Hannibalic war to the dictatorship of Caesar. (Taylor, Lily Ross.) Ann Arbor, 1966.
	AH 7859.7	Roman women. (Balsdon, John Percy V.D.) London, 1962.
	AH 7859.6	Roman women of rank of the early empire in public life as portrayed by Dio. Diss. (Hoffsten, R.B.) Philadelphia, 1939.
	AH 7489.27.5	The Roman world. (Chapot, Victor.) N.Y., 1928.
Htn	AH 7816.28*	Romanae historiae anthologia. (Godwyn, Thomas.) Oxford, 1628. 2 pam.
Htn	AH 7816.28.5*	Romanae historiae anthologia. 15th ed. (Godwyn, Thomas.) London, 1689.
Htn	AH 7655.15*	Romanae historiae compendium. (Leto, G.P.) Argentorati, 1515.
	AH 819.32	The romance of life in the ancient world. (Wright, Frederick A.) London, 1932?
	AH 8007.21	Romanelli, P. Storia delle province romane dell'Africa. Roma, 1959.
	AH 6108.9	I Romani nella Grecia. 11. ed. (Barzoni, V.) Londra, 1799.
	AH 7819.31.5	I romani nelle istituzioni e nel costume. (Marchi, Attilio de.) Milano, 1931.
	AH 8058.5	Romanisation de l'Afrique, Tunisie. (Mesnage, R.J.) Paris, 1913.
	AH 8208.10	Romanisation in Scotland. (Young, Douglas.) Tayport, 1955?
	AH 7088.81A	Die romanischen Landschaften. (Jung, Julius.) Innsbruck, 1881.
	AHP 28.11	Romanitas. Rio de Janeiro. 1-5 5v.
	AH 8007.15	The romanization of Africa Proconsularis. (Broughton, T.R.S.) Baltimore, 1929.
	AH 8007.15.5	The romanization of Africa Proconsularis. Diss. (Broughton, T.R.S.) Baltimore, 1929.
	AH 8213.2	The romanization of Roman Britain. (Haverfield, Francis J.) London, 1906.
	AH 8213.2.2	The romanization of Roman Britain. 2. ed. (Haverfield, Francis J.) Oxford, 1912.
	AH 8213.2.4	The romanization of Roman Britain. 4. ed. (Haverfield, Francis J.) Oxford, 1923.

Author and Title Listing

AH 8548.80   Rott, Joseph. Ueber die Nationalität der Kelten. Passau, 1866?

AH 4523.5   Rottsahl, C. Expedition der Athener nach Sicilien. Langensalza, 1878.

Eg 608.58   Rougé, E. de. Etude sur une stèle égyptienne. Paris, 1858.

Eg 847.3   Rougé, Emman. Essai sur une stèle junéraire. Berlin, 1849.

Eg 938.91   Rougé, J. de. Géographie ancienne de la Basse-Égypte. Paris, 1891.

Eg 938.65   Rougé, J. de. Textes geógraphiques du temple d'Edfou. Paris, 1865.

Eg 1008.83   Rouge, Jacques de. Littérature de l'ancienne Égypte. Paris, 1883.

AH 7909.66   Rougé, Jean. Recherches sur l'organisation du commerce maritime en Méditerranée sous l'Empire romain. Thèse. Paris, 1966.

AH 3809.5   Rougemont, F. L'age du bronze ou Semites en occident. Paris, 1866.

Eg 39.23   Rouillard, G. L'administration civile de l'Égypte Byzantine. Thèse. Paris, 1923.

AH 7148.36   Roulez, J. Observations sur divers points de l'histoire de la constitution. Bruxelles, 1836.

AH 4818.55   Rousopoulos, A.S. Ellènikès archaiologias. Patrais, 1855.

AH 4818.75   Rousopoulos, A.S. Manual of Greek archaeology. Athens, 1875?

AH 9727.15   Rousopoulos, A.S. Peri Zamolxidos. Inaug. Diss. Gottingae, 1852.

AH 5124.6.5   Roussel, Pierre. Délos. Paris, 1925.

AH 7039.63   Rouvier, J. Du pouvoir dans la république romaine. Paris, 1963.

AH 3009.64   Roux, Georges. Ancient Iraq. London, 1964.

AH 8957.5   Rovelli, G. Das cisalpinische Gallien. Leipzig, 1791.

AH 7038.24   Rovers, J.A.C. De censaum apud romanos auctoritate. Trajecti ad Rhenum, 1824.

AH 7509.62   Rowell, H.T. Rome in the Augustan Age. Norman, 1962.

AH 8207.36   Rowland, Thomas Henry. The Romans in North Britain. Newcastle upon Tyne, 1970.

AH 3966.38   Rowley, Harold Henry. Dictionary of Bible place names. London, 1970.

AH 7148.93   Roy, C. Les fétiaus du peuple romain. Poitiers, 1893.

AH 3002.81   Royal correspondence of the Assyrian empire. (Waterman, L.) Ann Arbor, 1930-36. 4v.

AH 1329.65   The royal hordes. (Phillips, Eustace Dockray.) London, 1965.

AH 4609.65   Le royaume de Macédoine de la mort d'Alexandre à sa disparition, 323-168 avant J.-C. (Aymard, André.) Paris, 1965.

NEDL AH 278.11.5   Royou, J.C. Précis de l'histoire ancienne. 2. éd. Paris, 1811. 4v.

Eg 819.16.5   Rozanov, V.V. Iz vostochykh motivov. pt.1-3. Petrograd, 1916-17.

AH 298.42.2   Rozbiór krytyczny zazad historii. wyd.1. (Kołłątaj, Hugo.) Warszawa, 1972.

NEDL AH 298.42   Rozbiór krytyczny zazad historyi. (Kołłątaj, Hugo.) Krakow, 1842. 3v.

AH 7299.71   Rozwòj polityczny roli jednostki w republice rsymskiej i jego olkicije w literaturze. Wyd. 1. (Korpanty, Jósef.) Wrocław, 1970.

AH 7138.82   Ruben de Couder, M.J. Droit romain. Paris, 1882.

AH 7203.69   Ruben der Couder. Droit romain. Paris, 1878.

AH 8609.2   Rubino, J. Beiträge zur Vorgeschichte Italiens. Leipzig, 1868.

AH 7038.39   Rubino, J. Untersuchungen und römische Verfassung. Cassel, 1839.

AH 4484.9   Rudolph, F. Schlacht von Platää. Dresden, 1895.

AH 7099.35   Rudolph, Hans. Stadt und Staat im römischen Italien. Leipzig, 1935.

AH 4839.65.5   Rudolph, Werner. Olympischer Kampfsport in der Antike. Berlin, 1965.

AH 7148.60   Rudorff, A. De maiore ac minori latio. Berolini, 1860.

AH 7178.39   Rudorff, A.A.F. Ackergesetz der S. Thorius. Berlin, 1839.

AH 7138.57   Rudorff, A.F. Römischen Rechtsgeschichte. Leipzig, 1857.

AH 4521.17   Die Rückkehr des Alcibiades. (Herbst, L.F.) Hamburg, 1843.

AH 4539.10   Rügg, A. Thermaenes. Basel, 1910.

AH 8908.5   Rühle, J.J.O.A. Zur Geschichte der Pelasger und Etrusker. Berlin, 1831.

AH 4238.52   Rüstow, W. Geschichte des griechischen Kriegswesens. Aarau, 1852.

AH 7148.75   Ruggier de Ettore. Diritto publico romano. Firenze, 1875.

AH 7148.93.5   Ruggiero, E. de. L'arbitrato pubblico. Roma, 1893.

AH 7098.96   Ruggiero, E. de. Le colonie dei romani. Spoleto, 1896.

AH 7118.2   Ruggiero, E. de. La gens in Roma. Napoli, 1872.

AH 8615.7   Ruggini, Lallia. Economia e società nell'Italia annonaria. Milano, 1961.

AH 7309.21A   The ruin of the ancient civilization and the triumph of Christianity. (Ferrero, G.) N.Y., 1921.

AH 7099.43   Ruina y extención del municipio. (Sanchez-Albornoz y Menduiña, C.) Buenos Aires, 1943.

AH 7309.21.3   La ruine de la civilisation antique. (Ferrero, G.) Paris, 1921.

AH 7309.25   La ruine du monde antique. 2e éd. (Sorel, Georges.) Paris, 1925.

AH 3013.942.12   Ruined cities of Iraq. 3. ed. (Lloyd, Seton.) London, 1945.

AH 307.96.3   Les ruines...révolutions des empires. (Volney, C.F.) Paris, 1826.

AH 3013.23   Ruins of Nineveh. (Smith, A.) n.p., 1845?

AH 7769.03   Runkel, F. Schlacht bei Adrianapel. Rostock, 1903.

AH 7818.41   Ruperte, F.F.F. Handbuch der römischen Alterthümer. Hannover, 1841. 3v.

AH 3012.21   Rupper, Jean R. Les nomades en Mésopotamia au temps des rois de Mari. Paris, 1957.

AH 408.01   Russell, William. History of ancient Europe. Philadelphia, 1801. 2v.

AH 309.67.5   Russkaia istoriografiia antichnosti do serediny XIX v. (Frolov, Eduard D.) Leningrad, 1967.

AH 1409.27   Russkaia nauka odrevnem Vostoke do 1917 g. (Turaev, V.A.) Leningrad, 1927.

Eg 819.09   Rustafjaell, R. de. The light of Egypt. London, 1909.

AH 4609.06   Rutgers, A. De Eumene Cardiano. Amsterdam, 1906.

AH 7539.24   Ruth, Thomas De C. The problem of Claudius. Diss. Baltimore, 1924.

AH 3009.58   Rutten, M. Babylone. Paris, 1958.

AH 2014.8   Ryckmans, G. Les religiones arabes préislamiques. 2. éd. Louvain, 1951.

AH 2012.2   Ryckmans, Jacques. La chronologie des rois de Saba et dü-Raydän. Istanbul, 1964.

AH 2003.5   Ryckmans, Jacques. L'institution monarchique en Arabie méridionale avant l'Islam. Louvain, 1951.

AH 7819.03   Rydberg, V. Kulturhistoriska förekäsningar. Stockholm, 1903. 6v.

AH 7818.79.5   Rydberg, V. Roman days. N.Y., 1879.

AH 4039.65.5   Ryder, Timothy Thomas Bennett. Koine Eirene. London, 1965.

Eg 819.33   Rydh, H. Hur man levde i Faraos land. Stockholm, 1933.

AH 4039.49   Ryffel, Heinrich. Metabolè politeiön. Bern, 1949.

AH 3740.5   Ryhinerus, E. De Tyro. Basilae, 1715.

AH 9646.10   Ryolo di Maria, Domenico. L'espansione di Zande sulla costa settentrionale della Sicilia dalla metà dell'VIII secolo a.C. agli albori del V secolo a.C. Messina, 1968.

Htn   AH 256.33*   Ryves, Thomas. Historia navalis antiqua. Londini, 1633.

Htn   AH 256.40*   Ryves, Thomas. Historia navalis antiqua. Londini, 1640.

AH 3921.11   Rzemieslnicy i kupcy w Antiochii i ich ranga społeczna (II połowa IV wieku). (Ceran, Waldemar.) Wrocław, 1969.

AH 7079.66   Rzymskie zgromadzenie wyborcze od Sulli do Cezara. (Linderski, Jerzy.) Wrocław, 1966.

AH 9666.10   Saa, Mário. As grandes vias da Lusitania. Lisboa, 1956-60. 5v.

AH 7438.42   Saal, N. De appio Claudio Caeco commentatio historica. Köln, 1842.

AH 4031.5   Saal, N. De demorum atticae per tribus distributione. Coloniae-Agrippinensim, 1860. 3 pam.

AH 7818.84.10   Saalfeld, G.A.E.A. Haus und Hof in Rom im Spiegel griechischen Kultur. Paderborn, 1884.

AH 3966.23   Saarisalo, Aapeli. Boundary between Issachar and Naphtali. Helsinki, 1927.

AH 3013.15   Sabaean researches. (Landseer, J.) London, 1823.

AH 7549.00   Sabatini, F. Pascal. L'incendio di Roma. Roma, 1901. 5 pam.

AH 817.76   Sabbathier, F. Institutions, manners and customs of ancient nations. London, 1776. 2v.

AH 7479.71   Sabben-Clare, James. Caesar and Roman politics 60-50 B.C. London, 1971.

AH 8616.9A   Sabin, Frances E. Classical associations of places in Italy. Madison, Wis., 1921.

AH 7828.03   Sabina, oder Morgenscenen. (Böttiger, C.A.) Leipzig, 1803.

AH 7828.03.4   Sabina, oder Morgenscenen. (Böttiger, C.A.) Leipzig, 1806.

AH 7828.03.6   Sabine, ou Matinée d'une dame romaine. (Böttiger, C.A.) Paris, 1813.

AH 7201.85   Sabinus, M. Fragmente in Ulpians Sabinus Commentar. Halle, 1906.

AH 7529.30.5   Sachs, Hanns. Bubi Caligula. 2. Aufl. Wien, 1932.

AH 7529.30.15   Sachs, Hanns. Caligula. London, 1931.

AH 3133.1   Sack, Ronald Herbert. Amel-Marduk, 562-560 B.C. Kevelaer, 1972.

AH 7215.6   Der sacrale Schutz im römischen Rechtsverkehr. (Danz, H.A.A.) Jena, 1857.

AH 277.27.25   The sacred and profane history of the world connected. (Shuckford, Samuel.) London, 1858. 2v.

Htn   AH 277.27.3*   The sacred and prophane history of the world connected. (Shuckford, Samuel.) London, 1731-37. 3v.

Htn   AH 3966.9*   Sacred geography: or, A gazetteer of the Bible. (Parish, Elijah.) Boston, 1813.

AH 3160.25   The sacred marriage rite. (Kramer, Samuel N.) Bloomington, 1969.

AH 3966.15   The sacred mountains. (Headley, J.T.) N.Y., 1847.

AH 3966.16.3   The sacred plains. (Headley, J.T.) Buffalo, 1856.

AH 3966.20   Sacred streams; or, The ancient and modern history of the rivers of the Bible. (Gosse, Philip H.) N.Y., 1852.

AH 3963.150.5F   Sacrorum elaeochrismatwn myrothecia tria. (Scaccho, F.) Amstelaedami, 1701.

AH 4524.11   Sadl, A. Die oligarchische Revolution vom Jahre 411. Pola, 1910.

AH 908.77.3   Sadowski, J.N. Die Handelsstrassen der Griechen und Römer. Jena, 1877.

AH 7844.3   Die Saecularfeier des Augustus. (Wissowa, G.) Marburg, 1894.

Eg 819.67   Säve-Söderbergh, Torgny. Faraoner och människor. Stockholm, 1967.

AH 842.21   Saffroy, (Mlle.). Ecrivans, pédagogues de l'antiquité. Paris, 1897.

AH 408.60   Sage und Forschung. (Gerlach, F.D.) Basel, 1860.

Eg 1128.76.5   La sagesse d'Ani. (Ani.) Roma, 1935.

AH 3190.5.1   La sagesse suméro-accadienne. (Dijk. Johannes J.A. van.) Leiden, 1953.

AH 3190.5   La sagesse suméro-accadienne. Proefschrift. (Dijk, Johannes J.A. van.) Leiden, 1953.

AH 299.10.3   Saggi di storia antica e di archeologia. Roma, 1910.

AH 3960.16   Saggi di storia e letteratura guideo-ellenistica. (Motzo, B.) Firenze, 1925.

AH 8900.5   Saggio di bibliografia etrusca. (Lopes Pegna, M.) Firenze, 1953.

AH 7009.47   Saggio di bibliografia romana. (Ceccarelli, G.) Roma. 2-12,1946-1957// 5v.

AH 7809.02   Saggio di illustrazione del calendario romano. (Pais, Ettore.) Napoli, 1902.

AH 6057.7F   Saggio di storia tessalica. (Costanzi, V.) Pisa, 1906.

AH 8716.5   Saggio sulla geografia storica del Japigia. (Lucarelli, Antonio.) Trani, 1903.

AH 3143.15   Saggs, H.W. The greatness that was Babylon. N.Y., 1962.

AH 3005.16   Saggs, Henry William. Assyriology and the study of the Old Testament. Cardiff, 1969.

AH 3165.15   Saggs, Henry William Frederick. Everyday life in Babylonia and Assyria. London, 1967.

AH 8207.8   Sagot, François. La Bretagne romaine. Paris, 1911.

Eg 878.98.5   St. Clair, G. Creation records discovered in Egypt. London, 1898.

AH 259.35   Saint-Denis, E. de. Le vocabulaire des manoeuvres nautiques en Latin. Thèse. Macon, 1935.

AH 4828.42.3   St. John, J.A. Hellenes. History of manners and customs of ancient Greece. London, 1844. 3 pam.

AH 4828.42   St. John, J.A. History of manners and customs of ancient Greece. London, 1842. 3v.

AH 37.99   Sainte Croix, G.E.J.G. de. Anciens gouvernemens fédératifs. Paris, 1799.

AH 4558.04   Sainte-Croix, Guillaume Emmanuel Joseph de. Examen critique. Paris, 1804.

AH 4558.04.2   Sainte-Croix, Guillaume Emmanuel Joseph de. Examen critique. 2. éd. Paris, 1810.

Eg 879.54.10   Sainte Fare Garnot, Jean. L'hommage aux dieux sous l'ancien empire egyptien. 1. éd. Paris, 1954.

Author and Title Listing

AH 7759.11 — Sainte Hélène d'après l'histoire et la tradition. (Couzard, R.) Paris, 1911.

Eg 919.52 — Saite demotic land leases. (Hughes, George.) Chicago, 1952.

Eg 879.62F — A Saite oracle papyrus from Thebes. (Brooklyn Institute of Arts and Sciences. Museum. Mss. (Papyrus 47.218.3).) Providence, R.I., 1962.

AH 3757.24 — Saka-Studien: der Ferne Nordasten im Weltbild der Antike. (Junge, Julius.) Aalen, 1962.

AH 5708.5 — Sakellariou, M.B. La migration grecque en Ionie. Athènes, 1958.

AH 4842.47 — Sakellaropoulou, S.K. Peri tes Latinikes glōssēs kai philologias. Athēnai, 1878.

AH 7339.72 — Saklatvala, Beram. The Caesars: the Roman Empire and its rulers. Newton Abbott, 1972.

AH 7844.4 — Das Sakularfest des Augustus. (Vollbrecht, W.) Gütersloh, 1900.

AH 9639.8 — Salinas, A. Soluto ricordi storici. Palermo, 1884.

AH 7168.83.2 — Salkowski, C. Institutionen. 8. Aufl. Leipzig, 1902.

AH 7168.83 — Salkowski, C. Lehrbuch der Institutionen. 4. Aufl. Leipzig, 1883.

AH 7188.91 — Salkowski, C. Lehre vom Sklavenerwerb. Leipzig, 1891.

AH 7168.86 — Salkowski, C. Roman private law. London, 1886.

AH 7168.66.5 — Salkowski, C. Zur Lehre von der Novation. Leipzig, 1866.

AH 7027.16F — Sallengre, Albert Hendrik de. Novus thesaurus antiquitatum. Hagae, 1716-19. 3v.

AH 3088.3 — Salmanasser den II's Indskrifter. (Rasmussen, N.) Kjøbenhavn, 1897.

AH 7489.44.1.5 — Salmon, E.T. A history of the Roman world. 3. ed. London, 1957.

AH 7489.44 — Salmon, E.T. A history of the Roman world from 30 B.C. to A.D. 138. N.Y., 1944.

AH 7299.69 — Salmon, Edward T. Roman colonization under the Republic. London, 1969.

AH 9307.10 — Salmon, Edward Togo. Samnium and the Samnites. Cambridge, 1967.

AH 8986.5 — Salomonius, J. Agri Patavini inscriptiones sacrae et prophanae. Patavius, 1696.

AH 4843.2 — Saltationis disciplina. (Emmanuel, M.) Paris, 1895.

Htn AH 7488.92* — Saltus, E. Imperial purple. Chicago, 1892.

AH 7478.89 — Salvatierra. Lo mundo de los romanos. Ronda, 1889.

AH 7759.28 — Salvatorelli, Luigi. Costantino il Grande. Roma, 1928.

AH 889.06 — Salvioli, G. Capitalisme dans le monde antique. Paris, 1906.

AH 99.24 — Salvioli, G. La città antica e la sua economia. Napoli, 1924.

AH 7178.99 — Salvioli, G. Sulla distribuzione della proprietà fondiaria in Italia al tempo dell'impero romano. Modena, 1899.

AH 7201.67 — Salvius Julianus. (Buhl, H.) Heidelberg, 1886.

AH 8208.20 — Salway, Peter. The frontier people of Roman Britain. Cambridge, Eng., 1965.

AH 4848.12 — Sambon, A. La toilette des femmes grecques. Paris, 1904.

Eg 819.64 — Sāmih, Wali al Din. Daily life in ancient Egypt. N.Y., 1964.

AH 4819.62.10 — Samivel. The glory of Greece. N.Y., 1962.

AH 3002.27 — Sammlung von assyrischen und babylonsichen Texten. (Schrader, E.) Berlin. 1-6,1889-1915 6v.

AH 3002.6FA — Sammlung von Keilschrifttexten. (Winckler, H.) Leipzig, 1893. 2v.

AH 9307.10 — Samnium and the Samnites. (Salmon, Edward Togo.) Cambridge, 1967.

AH 840.7 — Samter, Ernst. Familienfeste. Berlin, 1901.

AH 3110.5 — San Nicoló, Mariano. Beiträge zur Rechtsgeschichte im Brereiche der keilschriftlichen Rechtsquellen. Cambridge, 1931.

AH 7099.43 — Sanchez-Albornoz y Menduiña, C. Ruina y extención del municipio. Buenos Aires, 1943.

AH 3707.5 — Sanchoniatho's Phoenician history. (Cumberland, R.) London, 1720.

AH 5309.11 — Sanctis, G. Atthis. Roma, 1898.

AH 5309.11.2 — Sanctis, G. Atthis. 2. ed. Torino, 1912.

AH 4708.94 — Sanctis, G. Questioni politiche e reforme sociali. v.1-2. Roma, 1894.

AH 4499.44 — Sanctis, G. de. Pericle. Milano, 1944.

AH 279.32 — Sanctis, G. de. Problemi di storia antica. Bari, 1932.

AH 4279.42 — Sanctis, G. de. Storia dei greci dalle origini alla fine del secolo V. 3. ed. Firenze, 1942. 2v.

AH 7279.07 — Sanctis, G. de. Storia dei Romani. v.1-4, pt.1-3. Torino, 1907. 8v.

AH 279.66 — Sanctis, Gaetano de. Scritti minori. Roma, 1966- 3v.

AH 5610.21 — Sandberger, Frank. Prosopographie zur Geschichte des Pyrrhos. Diss. Stuttgart, 1970.

AH 7859.9 — Sandels, Friedrich. Die Stellung der kaiserlichen Frauen aus dem julisch-claudischen Wause. Darmstadt, 1912.

AH 7029.04 — Sanders, Henry. Roman historical sources. N.Y., 1904.

AH 7029.10 — Sanders, Henry. Roman history and mythology. N.Y., 1910.

AH 3175.20A — Sanders, Nancy K. Poems of heaven and hell from ancient Mesopotamia. Harmondsworth, 1971.

AH 7419.08 — Sands, P.C. Client princes of the Roman empire. Cambridge, 1908.

AH 3059.5 — Das Sandschak Suliemania. (Billerbeck, A.) Leipzig, 1898.

AH 7819.10 — Sandys, J.E. Companion to Latin studies. Cambridge, 1910.

AH 7819.13 — Sandys, J.E. A companion to Latin studies. 2. ed. Cambridge, 1913.

AH 7819.13.3 — Sandys, J.E. A companion to Latin studies. 3. ed. Cambridge, 1921.

Eg 1109.52PF — Sanehet. The Ashmolean ostracon of Sinuhe. London, 1952.

AH 299.38 — Sanford, E.M. The Mediterranean world in ancient times. N.Y., 1938.

AH 299.38.5 — Sanford, E.M. The Mediterranean world in ancient times. N.Y., 1951.

AH 7498.69.2 — Le sang de Germanicus. 2. éd. (Beule, Ernest.) Paris, 1869.

AH 862.5 — Sanitätswesen in den Heeren der Alten. (Gaupp, W.) Blaubeuren, 1875.

AH 4538.84.2 — Sankey, C. Spartan and Theban supremacies. N.Y., 1886.

AH 4538.84.5 — Sankey, C. Spartan and Theban supremacies. N.Y., 1894.

AH 4538.84 — Sankey, C. Spartan and Theban supremacies. 3. ed. London, 1884.

AH 7449.14.7 — Sann, Georg. Untersuchungen zu Scipios Feldzug in Afrika. Inaug. Diss. Berlin, 1914.

AH 7480.2 — Sanna, G. Bibliografia generale dell'età romana imperiale. Firenze, 1898.

AH 4842.92 — Sant'Anna Dionisio, J.A. Pedagogia culminante dos gregos. Porto, 1962.

AH 7861.10 — Santoro, B. La Nenia Latina. Acireale, 1902.

AH 7776.81 — Sapphirus Constantii imp. Aug. exposita anno 1602. (Freher, Marquard.) Heidelbergae, 1681.

AH 9557.5 — La Sardegna e i sardi nella civiltà del mondo antico. (Bellieni, C.) Cagliari, 1928-31. 2v.

AH 9558.2 — La Sardegna prima del dominio romano. (Pais, Ettore.) Roma, 1881.

Htn AH 4815.99* — Sardi, Alessandro. De moribus et ritibus gentium. Ambergae, 1599.

Htn AH 4815.57* — Sardi, Alessandro. De moribus et ritibus gentium. Venetiis, 1557.

AH 7114.36 — Sardi, Marta. I rapporti romano-ceriti e l'origine della civitas sino suffragio. Roma, 1960.

AH 9551.1 — Pamphlet box. Sardinia and Corsica.

AH 9557.1 — Sardinia in ancient times. (Bouchier, E.S.) Oxford, 1917.

AH 2589.10 — Sardis in the age of Croesus. 1. ed. (Pedley, John.) Norman, 1968.

AH 4189.23.5 — Sargent, R.L. The size of the slave population at Athens. Urbana, 1924.

AH 4189.23 — Sargent, R.L. The size of the slave population at Athens during the 5th and 4th century B.C. Thesis. Urbana? 1923?

AH 3094.6.5 — Sargon, king of Assyria. De inscriptione Sargonis. Berolini, 1886.

AH 3002.2.5A — Sargon, king of Assyria. Keilschrifttexte: Sargon's Königs von Assyrien. Leipzig, 1883.

AH 4239.53 — Sarikakēs, Theodóros Christou. The hoplite general in Athens. Athens, 1953.

AH 919.09 — Sarrazin, Albert. Étude sur les fondations dans l'antiquité en particulier à Rome et à Byzance. Thèse. Paris, 1909.

AH 4039.51.10 — Sartori, F. La crisi del 411 a.C. nell'Anthenaeon politeia di Aristotele. Padova, 1951.

AH 8647.20 — Sartori, F. Problemi di storia costituzionale italiata. Roma, 1953.

AH 5303.25 — Sartori, Franco. Le eterie nella vita politica ateniese del VI e V secolo A.C. Roma, 1957.

AH 4838.93 — Sartori, K. Studien...der griechischen Privataltertümer. München, 1893.

AH 3013.45PF — Sarzec, E. de. Decouvertes en Chaldée. Facsimile. Paris, 1884-93.

AH 7204.4.5 — Sasse, Christoph. De Constitutio Antoniniana. Wiesbaden, 1958.

AH 3933.2 — Sasson, Jack Murad. The military establishments at Mari. Rome, 1969.

AH 7509.60 — Sattler, Peter. Augustus und der Senat. Göttingen, 1960.

AH 4838.48 — Satyrspiel. (Wieseler, F.) Göttingen, 1848.

AH 3966.19 — Saulcy, F. de. Dictionnaire topographique. Paris, 1877.

AH 3977.5 — Sauls Gibea. (Linder, Sven.) Uppsala, 1922.

AH 162.7 — Saumaise, A. Specimen confutationis...sive tractatus. Lugdunum Batavorum, 1648.

Htn AH 7236.57* — Saumaise, C. de. De re militari Romanorum. Lugdunum, 1657.

Eg 879.57.5 — Sauneron, Serge. Les prêtres de l'ancienne Égypte. Paris, 1957.

Eg 879.57.7 — Sauneron, Serge. The priests of ancient Egypt. N.Y., 1960.

AH 4116.5 — Sauppe, H. De phratriis atticis. Gottingae, 1886.

AH 4228.83 — Sauppe, Herman. Atheniensium...suffragia. Gottingae, 1883.

AH 3061.5 — Sauren, Herbert. Topographie der Provinz Umma nach den Urkunden der Zeit der III. Dynastie von Ur. Bamberg, 1966.

AH 3020.70 — Sauren, Herbert. Wirtschaftsurkunden aus der Zeit der III. Dynastie von Ur im Besitz des Musée d'Art et d'Histoire in Genf. Napoli, 1969.

AH 4161.13 — Savage, C.A. The Athenian family. Baltinore, 1907.

Eg 299.41 — Savē-Soderbergh, T. Ägypten und Nubien. Lund, 1941.

Eg 919.62 — Savel'eva, T.N. Agrarnyi stroi Egipta. Moskva, 1962.

Eg 819.71 — Savel'eva, Tat'iana N. Kak zhili egiptiane vo vremena stroitel'stva piramid. Moskva, 1971.

AH 4559.55 — Savill, A.F. Alexander the Great and his time. Rockliff, 1955.

AH 1278.89A — Sayce, A.H. Ancient empires of the East. London, 1884.

NEDL AH 1278.89.5 — Sayce, A.H. Ancient empires of the East. N.Y., 1904.

NEDL AH 1278.89.7 — Sayce, A.H. Ancient empires of the East. N.Y., 1907.

AH 1279.06 — Sayce, A.H. Ancient empires of the East. Philadelphia, 1906.

AH 3012.7 — Sayce, A.H. The archaeology of cuneiform inscriptions. London, 1907.

AH 3075.6 — Sayce, A.H. Assyria, its princes, priests and people. London, 1885.

AH 3171.5.5 — Sayce, A.H. Babylonian literature. London, 1877.

AH 3171.5 — Sayce, A.H. Babylonian literature. London, 1879.

AH 3143.7 — Sayce, A.H. Babylonians and Assyrians. N.Y., 1899.

Eg 298.95.4 — Sayce, A.H. The Egypt of the Hebrews and Herodotos. London, 1896.

Eg 298.95 — Sayce, A.H. The Egypt of the Hebrews and Herodotos. N.Y., 1895.

AH 3159.25 — Sayce, A.H. Fresh light from the ancient monuments. 2d ed. London, 1884.

AH 3407.6 — Sayce, A.H. The Hittites. London, 1888.

AH 3407.6.5 — Sayce, A.H. The Hittites. 2d ed. London, 1892.

AH 3155.5 — Sayce, A.H. Lecture on...religion of...Babylonians. London, 1887.

AH 3155.5.5 — Sayce, A.H. Lectures on...growth of religion...ancient Babylonians. 5. ed. London, 1898.

AH 3155.5.2 — Sayce, A.H. Lectures on the origin and growth of religion as illustrated by the religion of the ancient Babylonians. 2d ed. London, 1888.

AH 3963.76 — Sayce, A.H. The races of the Old Testament. London, 1891.

AH 3165.5 — Sayce, A.H. Social life among the Assyrians and Babylonians. London, 1893.

AH 3143.19 — Sayce, Archibald H. A primer of Assyriology. London, 1894.

AH 3143.19.1 — Sayce, Archibald H. A primer of Assyriology. N.Y., 1894.

Eg 879.02.5 — Sayce, Archibald H. The religions of ancient Egypt and Babylonia. Edinburgh, 1903.

AH 3963.150.5F — Scaccho, F. Sacrorum elaeochrismatwn myrothecia tria. Amstelaedami, 1701.

AH 3963.150F — Scaccho, F. Thesaurus antiquitas sacro-prophanarum. Hagae-Comitum, 1725.

AH 28.98 — Scala, Rudolf von. Die Staatsverträge des Altertums. Leipzig, 1898.

Htn AH 805.83.2F* — Scaliger, J. De emendatione temporum. Francofurti, 1593.

Htn AH 805.83.3F* — Scaliger, J. De emendatione temporum. Lugduni Batavorum, 1598.

AH 808.52 — Scaliger, J. Olymiadōn anagra. Berolini, 1852.

Eg 278.99 — Lo scarabeo onorario di una regina d'Egitto nel Museo egizio vaticano. (Marucchi, Orazio.) Roma, 1899.

AH 3052.3F — Les sceaux de Longalanda. (Allotte, C.) Paris, 1907.

Eg 829.25 — Les scènes de la vie privée dans les tombeaux égyptiens de l'ancien empire. (Montet, Pierre.) Londres, 1925.

Author and Title Listing

Eg 829.25.5   Les scènes de la vie privée dans les tombeaux égyptiens de l'ancien empire. Thèse. (Montet, Pierre.) Strasbourg, 1925.

AH 7819.52.10   Scenes de la vie romaine sous la République. (Homo, Léon.) Paris, 1952.

AH 4559.49.5   Schachermeyer, F. Alexander der Grosse. Graz, 1949.

AH 8907.18   Schachermeyer, F. Etruskische Frühgeschichte. Berlin, 1929.

AH 4410.5   Schachermeyr, Fritz. Die ältesten kulturen Griechenlands. Stuttgart, 1955.

AH 4499.71.5   Schachermeyr, Fritz. Geistesgeschichte der Perikleischen Zeit. Stuttgart, 1971.

AH 4279.60.10   Schachermeyr, Fritz. Griechische Geschichte. Stuttgart, 1960.

AH 4279.60.12   Schachermeyr, Fritz. Griechische Geschichte. 2. Aufl. Stuttgart, 1969.

AH 4499.69   Schachermeyr, Fritz. Perikles. Stuttgart, 1969.

AH 4518.58   Schacht bei Mantinea. (Metropulos, C.) Göttingen, 1858.

AH 4484.15.2   Die Schacht von Platää. (Winter, L.) Berlin, 1909.

Eg 879.36.5   Schaedel, Herbert D. Die Listen des grossen Papyrus Harris. Glückstadt, 1936.

AH 4498.65   Schaefer, A. Rerum post Bellum Persicum. Lipsiae, 1865.

AH 7058.29.3   Schaefer, A. Zur Geschichte des römischen Consulates. Leipzig, 1876.

AH 5390.13   Schäfer, Alexander. Die Berichte Xenophons, Plutarchs und Diodors über die Besetzung und Befreiung. Inaug. Diss. München, 1930.

AH 298.82   Schaefer, Arnold. Abrisz der Quellenkunde der griechischen und römischen Geschichte. Leipzig, 1882.

AH 298.82.4   Schaefer, Arnold. Abrisz der Quellenkunde der griechischen und römischen Geschichte. v.1, 4. Aufl; v.2, 2. Aufl. Leipzig, 1885-89. 2v.

AH 4116.7   Schaefer, C. Die attischen Phratrien. Naumburg, 1888.

AH 279.63.5   Schaefer, Hans. Probleme der alten Geschichte. Göttingen, 1963.

AH 4039.32   Schaefer, Hans. Staatsform und Politik. Leipzig, 1932.

AH 3804.5   Schaeffer, Henry. The social legislation of the primitive Semites. N.Y., 1971.

AH 4854.7   Die Schafzucht im alten Griechenland. Diss. (Brendel, Otto.) Würzburg, 1934.

AH 4808.85   Das Schaltjahr in der grossen Rechnungs-Urkunde. v.1-2. (Kubicki, K.) Ratibor, 1885.

AH 7238.81.2   Schambach, O. Gymnasium zu Mühlhausen - Jahres-Bericht. Mühlhausen, 1881.

AH 7238.83.2   Schambach, O. Sechsundsiebenzigste Nachricht. Altenburg, 1883.

AH 7449.29.5   Scharf, Alfred. Der Ausgang des tarentinischen Krieges als Wendepunkt. Inaug. Diss. Bremen, 1929.

AH 1407.50   Scharff, A. Ägypten und Vorderasien im Altertum. München, 1950.

Eg 1189.20F   Scharff, A. Ein Rechnungsbuch des königlichen Hofes aus der 13 Dynastie. Berlin, 192-.

AH 7844.2   Die Schauspiele zur Unterhaltung. (Schulze, E.) Gütersloh, 1895.

AH 3188.5   Schawe, Joseph. Untersuchung der Elambriefe aus dem Archiv Assurbanîpals. Inaug. Diss. Berlin, 1927.

AH 7819.64   Schefold, K. Römische Kunst als religioses Phänomen. Reinbek, 1964.

AH 4524.5   Scheibe, J.F. Oligarchische Umwälzung. Leipzig, 1841.

AH 7808.53   Scheiffele, A. Jahrbücher der römischen Geschichte. Nördlingen, 1853.

AH 3096.3   Scheil, V. Le prisme d'Assaraddon...681-668. Paris, 1914.

AH 3005.13   Scheil, Vincent. Au service de Clio. Chalon-sur-Saone, 1937.

AH 4819.68.12   Scheliha, Renata von. Freiheit und Freundschaft in Hellas. 2. Aufl. Amsterdam, 1968.

AH 939.31   Scheliha, Renata von. Die Wassergrenze im Altertum. Breslau, 1931.

AH 9508.6   Schell, Günther. Die römische Besiedlung von Rheingau und Wetterau. Mainz, 1962.

AH 3089.3   Schell, P. Inscription Assyrienne...de Sămší-Ramman IV. Paris, 1889.

AH 7478.83.5   Schelle, Emil. De M. Antonii triumveri quae supersunt epistalis. Pt.1. Frankenberg, 1883.

AH 4204.7   Schelling, H. De Solonis legibus. Berolini, 1842.

AH 7448.75.5   Schemann, Ludwig. De legionum per alterum bellum punicum historium quae investigari posse videntur. Bonnae, 1875.

Eg 809.32   A scheme of Egyptian chronology. (Macnaughton, D.) London, 1932.

AH 7203.123   Schemmelpfeng, T. Hommel Redivivus. Cassel, 1858. 3v.

AH 7489.48   Schenk von Stauffenberg, A. Das Imperium und die Völkerwanderung. München, 1948.

AH 9610.27   Schenk von Stauffenberg, Alexander. König Hieron der Zweite von Syrakus. Stuttgart, 1933.

AH 299.72   Schenk von Stauffenberg, Alexander. Macht und Geist. München, 1972.

AH 9607.24   Schenk von Stauffenberg, Alexander. Trinakria. München, 1963.

Eg 452.6   Schenkel, Wolfgang. Memphis, Herakleopolis, Theben; die epigraphischen Zeugnisse der 7.-11. Dynastie Ägyptens. Wiesbaden, 1965.

AH 162.5   Die Schenkung auf den Todesfall. (Bruck, E.F.) Breslau, 1909.

AH 8647.16   Schereschewsky, J. Die politischen Beziehungen der unter italischen Griechenstädte. Inaug. Diss. Leipzig, 1934.

AH 7139.58   Scherillo, Gaetano. Manuele di storia del dirito romano. Milano, 1958.

AH 7449.05   Schermann, Max. Der erste punische Krieg. Stuttgart, 1905.

AH 7203.44.15   Scheurl, C.G. von. Lehrbuch der Institutionen. Erlangen, 1850.

AH 7138.53   Scheurl, C.G.A. Beiträge zur...römischen Rechts. Erlangen, 1853. 2v.

Eg 878.77.10   Schiaparelli, Ernesto. Del sentimento religioso degli antichi Egiziani secondo i monumenti. Torino, 1877.

AH 279.65.5   Schieder, Oscar. Die alte Welt. Wiesbaden, 1965-69. 2v.

AH 7214.9   Schiedseid und Beweiseid. (Demelius, G.) Leipzig, 1887.

NEDL AH 278.72.3   Schieffelin, S.B. Ta themelia tes istorias. Athens, 1872.

AH 7861.8   Schiess, T. Die römischen Collegia Funeraticia. München, 1888.

AH 1909.24   Schiffahrt und Handelsverkehr des östlichen Mittelmeeres. (Köster, A.) Leipzig, 1924.

AH 3908.5   Schiffer, Sina. Die Aramäer. Leipzig, 1911.

AH 7798.97   Schild, W. Galla Placidia. Halle, 1897.

AH 3014.17F   Schilf und Lehm. Diss. (Heinrich, Ernst.) Berlin, 1934.

AH 7548.72.7   Schiller, H. Geschichte des Römischen Kaisereichs. Berlin, 1872.

AH 7488.83   Schiller, K.H.F.H. Geschichte der Römischen Kaiserzeit. Gotha, 1883. 2v.

AH 7488.83.2   Schiller, K.H.F.H. Geschichte der Römischen Kaiserzeit. v.1,pt.1-2. Gotha, 1883. 2v.

AH 5557.5   Schiller, L. Elis, Arkadien, Achaja. Erlangen, 1855.

AH 7201.64   Schilling, F.A. Dissertatio critica de Ulpiani fragmentis. Vratislaviae, 1824. 3 pam.

AH 7168.34   Schilling, F.A. Lehrbuch für Institutionen und Geschichte. Leipzig, 1834. 3v.

AH 4511.5   Schimmelpfeng, G. De Brasidae Spartani. Marburgi Cattorum, 1857. 4 pam.

AH 7159.26   Schisas, P.M. Offences against the state in Roman law. London, 1926.

AH 5309.7   Schjøtt, P.O. Athen for Solon. Kristiania, 1880.

AH 7448.67   Die Schlacht an der Trebia. (Müller, H.) Berlin, 1867.

AH 7769.03   Schlacht bei Adrianapel. (Runkel, F.) Rostock, 1903.

AH 7448.74.6   Die Schlacht bei Cannä. (Schutz, Karl.) Donaueschingen, 1899.

AH 7448.74.3   Die Schlacht bei Cannae. (Wilms, A.) Hamburg, 1895.

AH 4518.55   Die Schlacht bei den Arginusen. (Herbst, L.F.) Hamburg, 1855.

AH 4559.02   Schlacht bei Gaugamela. (Hackmann, F.) Halle, 1902.

AH 4484.11   Schlacht bei Plataeae. (Olsen, W.) Greifswald, 1903.

AH 4481.7   Die Schlacht von Marathon. (Duncker, M.) München, 1881.

AH 4484.9   Schlacht von Platää. (Rudolph, F.) Dresden, 1895.

AH 7448.74.5   Das Schlachtfeld von Cannä. (Schwab, Otto.) München, 1898.

AH 4559.05.7   Das Schlachtfeld von Issus. (Gruhn, Albert.) Jena, 1905.

AH 7459.68   Schlag, Ursula. Regnum in senatu; das Wirken römischer Staatsmänner von 200 bis 191 vor Christus. Stuttgart, 1968.

Htn   AH 7278.11.3*   Schlegel, August W. Recension von Niebuhr's Römische Geschichte. n.p., 1816.

AH 4159.33   Schlesinger, E. Die griechische Asylie. Diss. Giessen, 1933.

AH 278.15   Schlosser, Friedrich Christoph. Alte Geschichte bis zum Untergang des weströmischen Reiche. Frankfurt am Main, 1815.

AH 278.26   Schlosser, Friedrich Christoph. Geschichte der alten Welt. v.1-3. Frankfurt, 1826. 9v.

AH 7169.04   Schlossmann, S. Altrömische Schuldrecht und Schuldverfahren. Leipzig, 1904.

AH 7229.05.5   Schlossmann, S. Litis Contestatio. Leipzig, 1905.

AH 169.06   Schlossmann, S. Persona und Prosôpon im Recht. Kiliae, 1906.

AH 7059.37   Schmähling, E. Untersuchungen zur Sittenaufsicht der Censoren. Inaug. Diss. Würzburg, 1937.

AH 7499.09   Schmaus, J. Charakterbilder römischer Kaiser. Bamberg, 1909.

AH 4818.98.25   Schmid, Wilhelm. Über den kulturgeschichtlichen Zusammenhang. Leipzig, 1898.

AH 298.88.3   Schmidt, A. Abhandlungen zur alten Geschichte. Leipzig, 1888.

AH 4808.88   Schmidt, A. Handbuch der griechischen Chronologie. Jena, 1888.

AH 4498.77   Schmidt, A. Perikleische Zeitalter. Jena, 1877. 2v.

AH 7188.68   Schmidt, A. Pflichttheilsrecht. Heidelberg, 1868.

AH 7818.53   Schmidt, C. Essai historique sur la société civile. Strasbourg, 1853.

AH 938.87   Schmidt, C.P. Zur Geschichte der geographischen Litteratur bei Griechen und Römer. Breslau, 1887.

AH 879.09   Schmidt, E. Kultübeitragungen. Giessen, 1909.

AH 7116.5   Schmidt, F. De mutatis centuriis servianis. Gissae, 1890.

Eg 807.65   Schmidt, F.S. de. Opuscula Aegyptiacae. Caroleruhae, 1765.

AH 844.5   Schmidt, G. De die natali apud veteres. Hannoverae, 1905.

AH 2357.16   Schmidt, G.A. De fontibus. Berolini, 1834.

AH 5607.5   Schmidt, H. Epeirotika...Geschichte des alten Epeiros. Marburg, 1894.

AH 938.60.3   Schmidt, H.I. Course on ancient geography. N.Y., 1860.

AH 7161.27   Schmidt, K.A. Das Hauskind in Mancipio. Leipzig, 1879.

AH 7228.53   Schmidt, K.A. Interdiktenverfahren der Römer. Leipzig, 1853.

Eg 841.5   Schmidt, Karl F.W. Das griechische Gymnasium in Ägypten. Halle, 1926?

Eg 847.1   Schmidt, Karl F.W. Die Kunst Hieroglyphen zu Lesen. Breslau, 1828.

AH 4259.31   Schmidt, Kurt. Die Namen der attischen Kriegsschiffe. Inaug. Diss. Engelsdorf, 1931.

AH 8011.4   Schmidt, L. Geschichte der Wandalen. Leipzig, 1901.

AH 819.06   Schmidt, M.C.P. Kulturhistorische Beiträge zur Kenntnis des griechischen und römischen Altertums. Leipzig, 1906-12. 2v.

AH 819.06.2   Schmidt, M.C.P. Kulturhistorische Beiträge zur Kenntnis des griechischen und römischen Altertums. Leipzig, 1914.

Eg 809.00   Schmidt, Orlando P. A self-verifying chronological history of ancient Egypt. Cincinnati, 1900.

AH 9071.2   Schmidt, Otto Eduard. Arpinum, eine topographischhistorische Skizze. Meissen, 1900.

AH 9071.2.5   Schmidt, Otto Eduard. Arpinum. Arpino, 1907.

AH 858.5   Schmidt, R.O. De hymenaeo et talasio. Kiliae, 1886.

AH 7468.74.5   Schmidt, Robert. Kritik der Quellen...gracchischen Unruhen. Berlin, 1874.

AH 298.72   Schmidt, V. Assyriens og Aegyptiens gamle historie. Kjøbenhavn, 1872-77.

AH 3909.6   Schmidt, V. Indledning til Syriens historie i oldtiden. Kjobenhavn, 1872.

AH 8073.16   Schmidt, W. L'empire carthaginois. Paris, 1940.

AH 844.7   Schmidt, W. Geburtstag im Altertum. Giessen, 1908.

AH 7098.36   Schmidt. Über römische Colonien. pt.1-2. Potsdam, 1836.

AH 3096.5   Schmidtke, Friedrich. Asarhaddons Statthalterschaft in Babylonien und seine Thronbesteigung in Assyrien. Inaug. Diss. Leiden, 1916.

AH 3149.13   Schmidtke, Friedrich. Der Aufbau der babylonischen Chronologie. Münster, 1952.

AH 3910.16   Schmitt, H.H. Untersuchungen zur Geschichte Antiochos des Grossen. Wiesbaden, 1964.

AH 4217.9   Schmitthenner, W. De coronarum apud Athenienses honoribus. Berolini, 1891.

AH 7509.69   Schmitthenner, Walter. Augustus. Darmstadt, 1969.

AH 7479.57   Schmittlein, Raymond. La première campagne de César contre les Germaines. Paris, 1957.

AH 7278.47   Schmitz, L. History of Rome. N.Y., 1847.

AH 7278.47.2   Schmitz, L. A history of Rome from the earliest times to the death of Commodus, A.D. 192. Andover, 1847.

Author and Title Listing

AH 938.57 — Schmitz, L. Manual of ancient geography. Philadelphia, 1857.

NEDL AH 278.55 — Schmitz, L. A manual of ancient history. Philadelphia, 1855.

AH 4842.19 — Schmitz, W. Schriftsteller und Buchshändler. Heidelberg, 1876.

AH 3009.55 — Schmökel, H. Ur, Assur und Babylon. Stuttgart, 1953.

AH 1819.61.5 — Schmökel, Hartmut. Kulturgeschichte des alten Orient. Stuttgart, 1961.

AH 3022.29 — Schmökel, Hartmut. Das Land Sumer. 2. Aufl. Stuttgart, 1956.

AH 3715.5 — Schmülling, T. Der phönizische Handel in den griechischen Gewässern. Münster, 1884-85.

AH 4843.18 — Schnabel, H. Kordap. München, 1910.

AH 9790.5.10 — Schneeberger, H. Die Brunnenschlacht. Bad Kissingen, 1931.

AH 7188.92.1 — Schneider, Albert. Zur Geschichte der Sclaverei im alten Rom. Frankfurt, 1970.

AH 7718.90 — Schneider, C. Beiträge zur Geschichte Caracallas. Marburg, 1890.

AH 4659.67 — Schneider, Carl. Kulturgeschichte des Hellenismus. München, 1967- 2v.

AH 4162.25 — Schneider, E. De jure hereditario Atheniensium. Monachii, 1851.

Eg 819.07 — Schneider, H. Kultur und Denken der alten Ägypter. Leipzig, 1907.

AH 3143.21 — Schneider, Hermann. Kultur und Denken der Babylonier und Juden. Leipzig, 1910.

AH 4855.7 — Schneider, K. Fischer in der antiken Literatur. Aachen, 1892.

AH 4833.17 — Schneider, K. Griechischen Gymnasien und Palästren. Diss. Solothurn, 1909.

AH 7228.35 — Schneider, K.A. De centumviralis judicii apud romani origine. Rostochii, 1835.

AH 3149.12 — Schneider, N. Die Zeitbestimmungen der Wirtschaftsurkunden von Ur. III. Rom, 1936.

AH 3160.19 — Schneider, Nikolaus. Die Götternamen von Ur III. Roma, 1939.

AH 7478.86.2 — Schneider, R. Ilerda. Beitrag zur römische Kriegsgeschichte. Berlin, 1886.

AH 238.93 — Schneider, R. Legion und Phalanx. Berlin, 1893.

AH 5138.7 — Schneiderwirth, J.H. Geschichte der Insel Rhodus. Heiligenstadt, 1868.

AH 3660.10 — Schneiderwirth, J.H. Die persische Politik gegen die Griechen seit dem Ende der Perserkriege. Heiligenstadt, 1863.

AH 5271.5 — Schneiderwirth, J.H. Polische Geschichte des dorischen Argos. v.1-2. Heiligenstadt, 1865.

AH 818.97.2 — Schneidewin, Max. Antike Humanität. Berlin, 1897.

AH 818.97.5 — Schneidewin, Max. Offener Brief au Herrn Professor Theobald Ziegler über "Antike Humanität". Leipzig, 1897.

AH 3016.48 — Schnitzler, Ludwig. Frühe Plastik im Zweistromland. 1. Aufl. Stuttgart, 1959.

AH 3030.5 — Schnöbel, Hartmut. Hammurabi von Babylon. München, 1958.

AH 8411.5 — Schober, Arnold. Die Römerzeit in Österreich und in den augreuzenden Gebieten von Slowenien. 2. Aufl. Wien, 1955.

AH 6007.10 — Schober, Friedrick. Phokis. Inaug. Diss. Crossen, 1924.

AH 4839.65 — Schöbel, Heinz. Olympia und seine Spiele. Berlin, 1965.

AH 4108.73 — Schoell, R. Quaestiones fiscales iuris attici. Berolini, 1873.

AH 2157.2 — Schoemann, A.G.O. Bithynia et Ponto. Gottingae, 1855.

AH 4328.56 — Schoemann, G.F. Animadversiones de Ionibus. Gryphisivaldiae, 1856.

AH 4818.51.10 — Schoemann, G.F. Antiquities of Greece. Oxford, 1879.

AH 4078.19.3 — Schoemann, G.F. Assemblies of the Athenians. Cambridge, 1838.

AH 4038.54.3 — Schömann, G.F. Athenian constitutional history. Oxford, 1878.

AH 4078.19 — Schömann, G.F. De comitiis atheniensium. Gryphiswaldiae, 1819.

AH 4078.36 — Schömann, G.F. De ecclesiis lacedaemoniorum. Gryphiswaldiae, 1836.

AH 7408.47 — Schoemann, G.F. De tullo hostilio. Gryphiswaldiae, 1847.

AH 4818.51 — Schoemann, G.F. Griechische Alterthümer. Berlin, 1855. 2v.

NEDL AH 4818.51.3A — Schoemann, G.F. Griechische Alterthümer. 2. Aufl. Berlin, 1861.

AH 4818.51.5 — Schoemann, G.F. Griechische Alterthümer. 3. Aufl. Berlin, 1871. 2v.

AH 4818.51.8 — Schoemann, G.F. Griechische Alterthümer. 4. Aufl. Berlin, 1897. 2v.

AH 4148.38 — Schoemann, G.F. Iuris publici Graecorum. Gryphiswaldiae, 1838.

AH 4114.7 — Schömann, G.F. Recognitio quaestionis de Spartanis Homoeis. Gryphiswaldiae, 1855.

AH 4845.9 — Schömann, G.F. Sittlich-religiöse Verhalten. Greifswald, 1848.

AH 4038.54 — Schömann, G.F. Verfassungsgeschichte Athen's. Leipzig, 1854.

AH 7809.05 — Schön, Georg. Die Differenzen zwischen der kapitolinischen Magistrats- und Triumphliste. Wien, 1905.

AH 7309.66 — Schoenlein, Peter Wilhelm. Sittliches Bewusstsein als Handlungsmotiv bei römischen Historiken. Erlangen, 1966.

AH 4818.43.5 — Schönwalder. Darstellung des Religiösen...Bildungszustandes. Brieg, 1843.

AH 8548.6 — Schoepflin, J.D. Vindiciae Celticae. Argentorati, 1754.

AH 959.17 — Schoff, Wilfred H. Navigation to the Far East under the Roman Empire. Boston, 1917.

AH 3957.24 — Schofield, J.N. The historical background of the Bible. London, 1938.

AH 3957.24.3 — Schofield, J.N. The historical background of the Bible. London, 1946.

AH 7201.7 — Scholien zum Gajus. (Gans, E.) Berlin, 1821.

AH 7778.97 — Scholl, Karl. Ein Kaiser im Kampf mit seiner Zeit. 2. Aufl. Bamberg, 1897?

AH 3181.9 — Schollmeyer, A. Sumerisch-babylonische Hymnen und Gebete an Samas. Paderborn, 1912.

AH 7418.68 — Scholtze, A. Die Beziehungen zwischen Rom und Hellas. Leipzig, 1868.

AH 3159.8 — Scholz, A. Die Keilschrift-Urkunden und die Genesis. Würzburg, 1877.

AH 3980.12.10 — Scholz, J.M.A. Commentatio de Golgothae et sanctissimi D.N.J.C. sepulcri situ. Bonnae, 1825.

Htn AH 5057.5* — Schoockius, M. Republicae Achaeorum. Trajani ad Rhenum, 1664.

AH 3195.12 — Schooldays. (Kramer, Samuel Noah.) Philadelphia, 1950?

AH 4842.39 — Schools of Hellas. (Freeman, Kenneth John.) London, 1907.

AH 4842.39.1 — Schools of Hellas. (Freeman, Kenneth John.) London, 1908.

AH 4842.39.5 — Schools of Hellas. (Freeman, Kenneth John.) N.Y., 1969.

AH 4842.39.1.2 — Schools of Hellas. 2. ed. (Freeman, Kenneth John.) London, 1912.

AH 4842.39.2 — Schools of Hellas. 3. ed. (Freeman, Kenneth John.) London, 1922.

AH 4708.33 — Schorn, W. Geschichte Griechenlands. Bonn, 1833.

AH 3150.9 — Schorr, M. Urkunden des altbabylonischen Zivil- und Prozessrechts. Leipzig, 1913.

AH 7229.04 — Schott, R. Römischen Zivilprozess. München, 1904.

Eg 1079.50 — Schott, Siegfried. Altägyptische Liebeslieder. Zürich, 1950.

Eg 1079.55 — Schott, Siegfried. Liebeslieder der Pharaonenzeit. Zürich, 1959.

Eg 1042.926F — Schott, Siegfried. Untersuchungen zur Schriftgeschichte der Pyramidentexte. Inaug. Diss. Heidelberg, 1926.

Eg 872.10 — Schott, Siegfried. Urkunden mythologischen Inhalts. Heft 1-2. Leipzig, 1929-39.

AH 7518.93 — Schott, W. Kriminaljustiz und des Kaisers Tiberius. Erlangen, 1893.

AH 7819.69.15 — Schottlaender, Rudolf. Römisches Gesellschaftsdenken. Weimar, 1969.

AH 3159.11.5 — Schrader, E. The cuneiform inscriptions and the Old Testament. London, 1885-88. 2v.

AH 3178.5 — Schrader, E. Die Höllenfahrt der Istar. Giessen, 1874.

AH 3159.11 — Schrader, E. Die Keilinschriften und das Alte Testament. Giessen, 1872.

AH 3159.11.2A — Schrader, E. Die Keilinschriften und das Alte Testament. 2e Aufl. Giessen, 1883.

AH 3012.6 — Schrader, E. Keilinschriften und Geschichtsforschung. Giessen, 1878.

AH 3002.27 — Schrader, E. Sammlung von assyrischen und babylonsichen Texten. Berlin. 1-6,1889-1915 6v.

AH 7201.9 — Schrader, E. Wasgewimit die römische Rechtsgeschichte. Heidelberg, 1823.

AH 3092.3 — Schrader, E. Zur Kritik der Inschriften Tiglath-Pilesers II des Asarhaddon. Berlin, 1880.

AH 3159.5.20 — Schreiber, Emilio. Bibbia e babele. Trieste, 1904.

AH 279.57 — Schreiber, H. Throne unter Schutt und Sand. Wien, 1957.

AH 4559.03.7 — Schreiber, T. Studien über das Bildniss Alexanders des Grossen. Leipzig, 1903.

AH 4204.12 — Schreiner, Iosephus: de corpore iuris Atheniensium. Bonn, 1913.

AH 9475.2 — Schreiner, W. Blick in die Geschichte...Eining's von Trajan bis Diocletian. v.1-2. Landshut, 1896.

AH 7649.68 — Schrempf, Claus. Weisheit und Weltherrschaft. München, 1968.

AHP 29.5 — Schriften zur Geschichte und Kultur der Antike. Berlin. 1,1970+ 3v.

AH 7752.5 — Schriftenreihe. (Internationaler Konstantinorden.) Zürich. 1,1959+

AH 7229.05 — Schriftformel im römischen Provinzialprozesse. (Partsch, J.) Breslau, 1905.

AH 7842.5.2 — Schriftsteller und Buchhändler. 2. Aufl. (Haenny, L.) Leipzig, 1885.

AH 4842.19 — Schriftsteller und Buchshändler. (Schmitz, W.) Heidelberg, 1876.

Htn AH 7036.29* — Schrijver, Pieter. Republica romana. Lugdunum Batavorum, 1629.

AH 839.27 — Schröder, B. Der Sport im Altertum. 1. Aufl. Berlin, 1927.

AH 214.5 — Schröder, G.A. De praecisis iurandi formis Graecorum. Marienwerder, 1845.

AH 4538.42 — Schröder, H. Abbildungen des Demosthenes. Braunschweig, 1842.

AH 5308.8 — Schroeder, Otto. De laudibus Athenarum a poetis. Gottingae, 1914.

AH 5138.5 — Schryver, P.A. Loi Rhodia de Jactu. Bruxelles, 1844.

Eg 279.26 — Schubart, F. Von der Flügelsonne zum Halbmond. Leipzig, 1926.

Eg 299.22.5 — Schubart, W. Ägypten von Alexander dem Grossen bis auf Mohammed. Berlin, 1922.

Eg 299.12.15 — Schubart, W. Ein Jahrtausend am Nil. 2. Aufl. Berlin, 1923.

Eg 709.00 — Schubart, W. Quaestiones de rebus militaribus...in regno Lagidarum. Trebnitz, 1900.

AH 842.46 — Schubart, Wilhelm. Das Buch bei den Griechen. 3. Aufl. Heidelberg, 1960.

AH 842.46.5 — Schubart, Wilhelm. Das Buch bei den Griechen und Römern. Berlin, 1907.

AH 7058.28 — Schubert, F.G. De romanorum aedilibus. Regimontii, 1828.

AH 4212.5 — Schubert, J.G. De proxenia Attica. Lipsiae, 1881.

AH 5610.5 — Schubert, R. Geschichte der Pyrrhus. Königsberg, 1894.

AH 4609.14 — Schubert, R. Die Quellen zur Geschichte der Diadochenzeit. Leipzig, 1914.

AH 6110.15 — Schubert, R. Untersuchungen über die Quellen zur Geschichte Philipps II von Macedonien. Konigsberg, 1904.

AH 9610.11 — Schubert, R.J.W. Geschichte des Agathokles. Breslau, 1887.

AH 2557.5 — Schubert, R.J.W. Könige von Lydien. Breslau, 1884.

AH 5409.5 — Schubring, J.J. Cypsello Corinthiorum tyranno. Gottingae, 1862.

AH 850.5 — Schuch, C.T. Gemüse und Salate der Alten. Rastatt, 1853.

AH 7828.42 — Schuch, C.T. Privatalterthümer. Karlsruhe, 1842.

AH 4523.9 — Schübeler, P. De Syracusarum oppugnatione quaestiones criticae. Geestemüde, 1910.

AH 4188.75 — Schück, J. Sklaverei bei den Griechen. Breslau, 1875.

AH 7188.38.5 — Schüller, C.L. Necessitudine cum moralitum civili. Rhenum, 1838.

AH 7114.9 — Schuermans, Henri. Histoire de la lutte entre les patriciens. Bruxelles, 1845.

AH 8557.4 — Schütt, C. Untersuchungen zur Geschichte der alten Illyrien. Inaug. Diss. Breslau, 1910.

AH 4558.86F — Schuffert. Alexanders des Grossen indischer Feldzug. Colberg, 1886.

AH 7168.67 — Schuldmoment im römischen Privatrecht. (Jhering, R.) Giessen, 1867.

AH 162.3 — Schulin, F. Das griechische Testament. Basel, 1882.

AH 7138.89 — Schulin, F. Lehrbuch des römischen Rechts. Stuttgart, 1889.

AH 4499.19 — Schulte-Vaërting, H. Die Friedenspolitik des Perikles. München, 1919.

AH 7178.96 — Schulten, A. Die römischen Grundherrschaften. Weimar, 1896.

AH 9660.5 — Schulten, Adolf. Los Cantabras y Astures y su guerra con Roma. Madrid, 1943.

AH 7098.92 — Schulten, Adolf. De conventibus civium romanorum. Berolini, 1892.

Author and Title Listing

AH 7098.92.1 Schulten, Adolf. De conventibus civium romanorum. Diss. Lipsiae, 1892.

AH 9684.9 Schulten, Adolf. Geschichte von Numantia. München, 1933.

AH 9684.5F Schulten, Adolf. Numantia...1905-1912. v.1-4 and atlas. München, 1914-31. 7v.

AH 938.16.5 Schulthess, J. Das Paradies. Zürich, 1816.

AH 4229.21 Schulthess, Otto. Das attische Volksgericht. Bern, 1921.

AH 7201.4.2 Schulting, A. Jurisprudentia vetus Ante-Justinianea. Lipsiae, 1737.

AH 7203.35 Schultingii, A. Notae ad...pandectas. v.1-7, pt.1-2. Lugdunum Batavorum, 1804. 8v.

AH 7038.33 Schultz, C.L. Grundlegung-Staatswissenschaft. Köln, 1833.

AH 7238.87 Schultze, E. De legione Romanorum XIII Genima. Kiliae, 1887.

AH 9722.6 Schultze, V. Altchristliche Städte und Landschaften. Leipzig, 1913-22. 3v.

AH 7139.51 Schulz, Fritz. Classical Roman law. Oxford, 1951.

AH 7139.46.2 Schulz, Fritz. Geschichte der römischen Rechtswissenschaft. Weimar, 1961.

AH 7139.46 Schulz, Fritz. History of Roman legal science. Oxford, 1946.

AH 7139.34.15 Schulz, Fritz. Principles of Roman law. Oxford, 1936.

AH 7139.34.20 Schulz, Fritz. Prinzipien des römischen Rechts. München, 1934.

AH 7628.99 Schulz, O.T. Leben des Kaisers Hadrian. Leipzig, 1904.

AH 7719.09 Schulz, O.T. Der römische Kaiser Caracalla. Leipzig, 1909.

AH 7659.03.5 Schulz, Otto. Beiträge zur Kritik unserer litterarischen Überlieferung fur die Zeit von Commodus' Sturze bis auf den Tod des M. Aurelius Antonius. Leipzig, 1903.

AH 7709.19 Schulz, Otto T. Vom Prinzipat zum Dominat. Das Wesen des römischen Kaisertums. Paderborn, 1919.

AH 7489.16 Schulz, Otto T. Das Wesen des Römischen Kaisertums. Paderborn, 1916.

AH 3964.11 Schulze, B. Coniecturae historiae criticae sadducaeorum inter inadeos sectae novam lucem accendentes. Halae, 1779.

AH 7078.15 Schulze, C.F. Von den Volksdersammlungen. Gotha, 1815. .

AH 8676.2 Schulze, E. Römische Forum als Mittelpunkt. Gütersloh, 1893.

AH 7844.2 Schulze, E. Die Schauspiele zur Unterhaltung. Gütersloh, 1895.

AH 9792.5 Schulze, H. De testamento Genserici (Vandali). Jenae, 1859.

AH 5138.11 Schumacher, C. Republica Rhodiorum commentatio. Heidelbergae, 1886.

Eg 877.73 Schumacher, J.H. De cultu animalium. Brunsvigiis, 1773.

AH 7549.30 Schumann, Gerhard. Hellenistische und griechische Elemente in der Regierung Neros. Inaug. Diss. Leipzig, 1930.

AH 7161.13 Schupfer, F. La famiglia secondo il diritto romano. Padova, 1876.

AH 7168.68 Schupfer da Chioggia, F. Il diritto delle obbligazioni. Padova, 1868.

AH 7509.34.5 Schur, Werner. Augustus. Lübeck, 1934.

AH 7628.83 Schurz, Wilhelm. De mutationibus in imperio romano ordinando ab imperatore Hadriano factis. pt.1. Bonnae, 1883.

AH 7628.97 Schurz, Wilhelm. Die Militärreorganisation Hadrians. Leipzig, 1897.

AH 7448.74.6 Schutz, Karl. Die Schlacht bei Cannä. Donaueschingen, 1899.

AH 4038.84 Schvarcz, J. Die Demokratie. v.1-2. Leipzig, 1884. 3v.

AH 5207.5 Schwab, C.T. Arkadien. Stuttgart, 1852.

AH 7519.12 Schwab, J. Leben und Charakter des Tiberius Claudius Nero nach Velleius. Tetschen, 1912.

AH 7448.74.5 Schwab, Otto. Das Schlachtfeld von Cannä. München, 1898.

AH 279.10 Schwahn, W. Geschichte der Griechen und Römer. Berlin, 1910.

AH 4818.54 Schwalbe, K.F.H. Handbuch der Griechischen Antiquitäten. Magdeburg, 1854.

AH 7168.70 Schwanert, H.A. Compensation nach römischen Recht. Rostock, 1870.

AH 7168.61.5 Schwanert, H.A. Die Naturalobligationen der römischen Recht. Göttingen, 1861.

AH 1409.65 Schwantes, Siegfried J. A short history of the ancient Near East. Grand Rapids, 1965.

AH 3400.10 Schwartz, Benjamin. The Hittites; a list of references in the New York Public Library. N.Y., 1939.

AH 7009.03 Schwartz, E. Ad praemiorum...publicam renuntiationem. Gottingae, 1903.

AH 4328.91F Schwartz, E. Quaestiones Ionicas. Adleranis, 1891.

Eg 847.2 Schwartze, Moritz Gotthilf. Das alte Ägypten...altägyptischen Original-Schriften und den Mittheilungen der nichtägyptischen alten Schriftsteller bearbeitet. Leipzig, 1843. 2v.

AH 4558.93 Schwarz, F. Alexanders des Grossen Feldzüge in Turkestan. München, 1893.

AH 4558.93.2 Schwarz, F. Alexanders des Grossen Feldzüge in Turkestan. 2. Aufl. Stuttgart, 1906.

AH 7899.12 Schwarze, K. Beiträge zur Geschichte altrömische Agrarprobleme. Halle, 1912.

AH 7215.5 Schwede, C. De pontificum collegii pontifisque Maximi in re publica potestate. Diss. inaug. Lipsiae, 1875.

AH 7278.53.10 Schwegler, A. Römische Geschichte. Tübingen, 1853. 4v.

AH 7278.53.11 Schwegler, A. Römische Geschichte. 2. Aufl. Tubingen, 1867-1872. 3v.

Eg 878.46.5 Schwenck, K. Die Mythologie der Aegypter für gebildete und die studirende Jugend. Frankfurt am Main, 1846. 5v.

AH 7649.23 Schwendemann, J. Der historische Wert der Vita Marci bei Scriptores Historiae Augustae. Photoreproduction. Heidelberg, 1923.

AH 7138.32.3 Schweppe, A. Römische Rechtsgeschichte. Göttingen, 1832.

AH 7168.78 Scialoja, V. Il precarium nel diritto romano. Roma, 1878.

AH 9604.5 Scicilano-Villanueva, L. Sul diritto greco-romano (privato) in Sicilia. Palermo, 1902.

AH 862.13.5 Science and secrets of early medicine. (Thorwald, Jürgen.) London, 1962.

Eg 1189.27 La science égyptienne; L'arithmetique au Moyen Empire. (Gillain, O.) Bruxelles, 1927.

Eg 848.4 La science mystérieuse des pharaons. (Moreux, T.) Paris, 1923.

Eg 848.4.5 La science mystérieuse des pharaons. (Moreux, T.) Paris, 1926.

Eg 848.4.10 La science mystérieuse des pharaons. (Moreux, T.) Paris, 1938.

AH 7446.17 Scipio, L.C. Vetustissima inscriptio. Romae, 1617.

AH 7459.67 Scipio Aemilianus. (Astin, A.E.) Oxford, 1967.

AH 7449.70 Scipio Africanus: soldier and politician. (Scullard, Howard Hayes.) Ithaca, 1970.

AH 7449.30 Scipio Africanus in the second Punic War. (Scullard, Howard Hayes.) Cambridge, Eng., 1930.

AH 7449.14.5 Scipio Africanus maior in Spanien. Inaug. Diss. (Brewitz, Walther.) Tübingen, 1914.

AH 7449.40 Scipione Africano e l'idea imperiale di Roma. (Ciaceri, Emanuele.) Napoli, 1940.

AH 7449.41 Scipione l'Africano. (Grazioli, Francesco.) Torino, 1941.

AH 7449.48 Scipione l'Africano. (Valori, F.) Torino, 1948.

AH 3757.14 Gli sciti. (Gibellino Krasceninnicowa, Maria.) Roma, 1942.

AH 8533.5 Scolies latines relatives à l'histoire...de Marseille. (Fröhner, W.) Paris, 1891.

AH 8548.38 Scott, A. The Celts and Druids and their story from the earliest times. North Shields, 1894.

AH 7448.73.10 Scott, Austin. Macedonien und Rom während des Hannibalischen Krieges. Berlin, 1873.

AH 7479.03 Scott, F.J. Portraitures of Julius Caesar. London, 1903.

Eg 819.44 Scott, N.E. The home life of the ancient Egyptians. N.Y., 1944.

AH 7539.40A Scramuzza, V.M. The emperor Claudius. Cambridge, 1940.

AH 7015.20 Pamphlet vol. Scramuzza, V.M. Roman studies. 14 pam.

AH 9440.5 Scrinari, V. Tergeste. Roma, 1951.

AH 7299.73 Scripta varia. (Piganiol, André.) Bruxelles, 1973. 3v.

AH 3159.23F The scripture chronology demonstrated by astronomical calculations. (Bedford, A.) London, 1730.

AH 279.66 Scritti minori. (Sanctis, Gaetano de.) Roma, 1966- 3v.

AH 7138.85 Scrutton, T.E. Influence of Roman law on the law of England. Cambridge, 1885.

AH 8548.52 Sculfort de Beaurepas, Serge. La panceltisme universel et pacifique contre le pangermanisme envahisseur et l'imperialisme anglais. Paris, 1903. 2v.

AH 7279.35.10A Scullard, H.H. A history of the Roman world from 753 to 146 B.C. London, 1935.

AH 7279.35.10.6 Scullard, H.H. A history of the Roman world from 753 to 146 B.C. N.Y., 1939.

AH 7279.35.10.5 Scullard, H.H. A history of the Roman world from 753 to 146 B.C. 2. ed. London, 1951.

AH 7279.35.10.3 Scullard, H.H. A history of the Roman world from 753 to 146 B.C. 3. ed. London, 1961.

AH 8913.28 Scullard, Howard. The Etruscan cities and Rome. Ithaca, 1967.

AH 7489.59 Scullard, Howard Hayes. From the Gracchi to Nero. London, 1959.

AH 7489.59.2 Scullard, Howard Hayes. From the Gracchi to Nero. 2. ed. N.Y., 1963.

AH 7489.59.3 Scullard, Howard Hayes. From the Gracchi to Nero. 3. ed. London, 1970.

AH 7459.51 Scullard, Howard Hayes. Roman politics, 220-150 B.C. Oxford, 1951.

AH 7459.51.2 Scullard, Howard Hayes. Roman politics, 220-150 B.C. 2. ed. Oxford, 1973.

AH 7449.70 Scullard, Howard Hayes. Scipio Africanus: soldier and politician. Ithaca, 1970.

AH 7449.30 Scullard, Howard Hayes. Scipio Africanus in the second Punic War. Cambridge, Eng., 1930.

AH 3016.30 Sculpture of the third millennium B.C. from Tell Asmar and Khafâjah. (Frankfort, Henri.) Chicago, 1939.

AH 939.02.5 Scylla und Charybdis, eine geographische Studien. (Jobst, D.) Würzburg, 1902.

AH 3757.15 The Scythians. (Rice, Tamara.) London, 1957.

AH 3757.13 Scythica et Cancasica. (Latyshev, B.) Petrograd. 1-2,1890-1906

AH 4259.60 The sea as a factor of the Greek life. (Potamianos, Phòkiòn.) Athens? 1960?

AH 259.24 Sea power in ancient history. (Shepard, A.M.) Boston, 1924.

AH 7519.72 Seager, Robin. Tiberius. London, 1972.

AH 5307.34 Sealey, Raphael. Essays in Greek politics. N.Y., 1967.

AH 3017.27 Seals of ancient Indian style found at Ur. (Gadd, Cyril J.) London, 1933.

AH 3002.2.8 Šeamaššumukîn, König von Babylonien. (Lehmann-Haupt, C.F.) Leipzig, 1892.

AH 7138.48.5 Secco, A.L. de S.H. Manual histórico de directo romano. Coimbra, 1848.

AH 4279.38.7 Secco Ellauri, Oscar. Historia de los griegos. Montevideo, 1945.

AH 4843.21 Séchan, Louis. La danse greque antique. Paris, 1930.

AH 279.36.5 Sêcher, J. L'Orient et la Grèce. Paris, 1936.

AH 7279.37.5 Sécher, J. Rome. Paris, 1937.

AH 3095.4 Das sechsseitige Prisma des Sanherib. (Hoerning, K.J.R.) Leipzig, 1878.

AH 7468.84 Das sechste Consulat des Marius. (Bardey, Ernst.) Brandenburg, 1884.

AH 7238.83.2 Sechsundsiebenzigste Nachricht. (Schambach, O.) Altenburg, 1883.

AH 7428.91 Sechzig Jahre aus der älteren Geschichte Roms. (Burger, Combertus P.) Amsterdam, 1891.

AH 4539.05 Second Athenian Confederacy. (Marshall, F.H.) Cambridge, 1905.

AH 7448.86 The second Punic War. (Arnold, Thomas.) London, 1886.

AH 7438.98.5 La seconda guerra samnitica. (Pirro, A.) Salerno, 1898.

Eg 708.68 Seconda lettera al Gaspare Garresio intorno ad alcuni punti della storia dei Tolemei. (Lumbroso, Giacomo.) Torino, 1868.

AH 7509.00 Il secondo viaggio di Augusto in Oriente. (Gabrici, E.) Napoli, 1900.

AH 8548.150 Le secret des Celtes. 1. éd. (Lengyel, Lancelot.) Le Jas du Revest-Saint-Martin, 1969.

AH 4841.6 Les secretaires atheniens. (Brillant, M.) Paris, 1911.

AH 4114.13 Seebohm, H.E. On the structure of the Greek Tribal Society. London, 1895.

AH 7658.95 Seeck, Otto. Geschichte des Untergangs der antiken Welt. v.1-6. Appendix. Berlin, 1895. 8v.

AH 7658.95.5 Seeck, Otto. Geschichte des Untergangs der antiken Welt. v.1-6. Appendix 1-6. Stuttgart, 1920-23. 12v.

AH 7509.02 Seeck, Otto. Kaiser Augustus. Bielefeld, 1902.

AH 7055.93.6.5 Seeck, Otto. Quaestiones de Notitia dignitatum. Berolini, 1872.

AH 7659.19F Seeck, Otto. Regesten der Kaiser und Päpste für die Jahre 311 bis 476 nach Christ. Stuttgart, 1919.

AH 3011.16 The seed of wisdom. (McCullough, W.S.) Toronto, 1964.

AH 168.93 Seedarlehen. (Sieveking, H.) Leipzig, 1893.

AH 959.61 Seel, Otto. Antike Entdeckerfahrten. Zürich, 1961.

AH 4842.80 Seel, Otto. Die plotonische Akademie. Stuttgart, 1953.

Author and Title Listing

Author and Title Listing

AH 7709.45   I Severi da Caracalla ad Alessandro Severo. (Passerini, Alfredo.) Roma, 1945.

AH 8011.8   Severnaia Afrika v IV-V vekakh. (Diligenskii, G.G.) Moskva, 1961.

AH 7693.5   Severus, Lucius Septimius. Apokrimata; decisions of Septimius Severus on legal matters. N.Y., 1954.

AH 4410.15   Severyns, Albert. Grece et Proche Orient avant Homère. Bruxelles, 1960.

AH 7509.30.5   Sextus Pompey. (Hadas, Moses.) N.Y., 1930.

X Cg   AH 4829.34   Sexual life in ancient Greece. (Licht, Hans.) N.Y., 1934.

AH 7819.33.5.3   Sexual life in ancient Rome. (Kiefer, Otto.) London, 1934.

AH 7819.33.5.2   Sexual life in ancient Rome. (Kiefer, Otto.) N.Y., 1935.

AH 7202.36   Seyfarth, W. Soziale Fragen der spätrömischen Kaiserzeit im Spiegel des Theodosianus. Berlin, 1963.

Eg 8.50   Seyffarth, G. Altertumskunde. n.p., 1850?

Eg 278.59.12   Seyffarth, G. Summary of recent discoveries in biblical chronology. 2. ed. N.Y., 1859.

Eg 878.55   Seyffarth, G. Theologische Schriften der alten Aegypter. Gotha, 1855.

AH 3757.5   Seythians or Goths. (Pinkerton, J.) London, 1787.

AH 819.72.10   The shadow of the Parthenon; studies in ancient history and literature. (Green, Peter.) London, 1972.

Eg 1058.77   Shaï-en-Sinsin. Le livre des respirations. Paris, 1877.

AH 3088.10   Shalmaneser II, king of Assyria. Les inscriptions de Salmanasar II, roi d'Assyrie, 860-824. Paris, 1890.

AH 8233.5   Sharpe, Montagu. Middlesex in British, Roman and Saxon times. London, 1919.

Eg 278.36   Sharpe, S. Early history of Egypt. London, 1836.

Eg 708.38   Sharpe, S. Egypt under the Ptolemies. London, 1838.

Eg 758.42   Sharpe, S. Egypt under the Romans. London, 1842.

Eg 278.36.3   Sharpe, S. History of Egypt. London, 1846.

Eg 278.36.4A   Sharpe, S. History of Egypt. London, 1859. 2v.

Eg 278.36.6   Sharpe, S. History of Egypt. London, 1870. 2v.

Eg 278.36.10   Sharpe, S. History of Egypt. 6. ed. London, 1885. 2v.

Eg 878.63   Sharpe, Samuel. Egyptian mythology. London, 1863.

Eg 1059.25   Sharpley, C.E. Anthology of ancient Egyptian poems. London, 1925.

AH 7469.39.10   Sheldon, E.L. Publius Cornelius Dolabella. N.Y., 1939.

NEDL   AH 298.90   Sheldon, Mary D. Studies in Greek and Roman history. Boston, 1890.

AH 259.24   Shepard, A.M. Sea power in ancient history. Boston, 1924.

AH 930.43   Shepherd, William Robert. Atlas of ancient history. N.Y., 1913.

AH 7658.61   Sheppard, J.G. The fall of Rome. London, 1861.

AH 7658.61.5   Sheppard, J.G. The fall of Rome. London, 1892.

AH 7029.69.5   Sherk, Robert K. Roman documents from the Greek East; senatus consulta and epistolae to the age of Augustus. Baltimore, 1969.

AH 7099.39   Sherwin-White, A.N. The Roman citizenship. Oxford, 1939.

AH 7329.67   Sherwin-White, Adrian N. Racial prejudice in imperial Rome. Cambridge, 1967.

AH 8073.24   Shifman, I.S. Vozniknovenie Karfagenskoi derzhavy. Leningrad, 1963.

AH 3707.29   Shifman, Il'ia. Finikliskie morekhody. Moskva, 1965.

AH 3757.20   Shifskoe vosstanie na Bospore. (Shikov, A.F.) Voronezh, 1960.

AH 3757.20   Shikov, A.F. Shifskoe vosstanie na Bospore. Voronezh, 1960.

Eg 983.5   Shinnie, Peter L. Meroe; a civilization of the Sudan. London, 1967.

AH 7509.33.7   Shipley, F.W. Agrippa's building activities in Rome. St. Louis, 1933.

AH 6107.60   Shofman, A.S. Istoriia antichnoi Makedonii. Kazan', 1960-2v.

AH 279.15   A short ancient history. (Breasted, James H.) Boston, 1915.

Eg 279.34   A short history of ancient Egypt. (Weigall, A.E.P.B.) London, 1934.

NEDL   AH 279.03   Short history of ancient peoples. (Souttar, R.) London, 1903.

NEDL   AH 279.03.2   Short history of ancient peoples. (Souttar, R.) N.Y., 1904.

AH 279.06   A short history of ancient times. (Myers, Philip Van Ness.) Boston, 1906.

AH 4279.36   A short history of Greece. (Robinson, D.M.) N.Y., 1936.

AH 7139.06   Short history of Roman law. (Girard, P.F.) Oxford, 1906.

AH 7279.18   Short history of Rome. (Ferrero, Guglielmo.) N.Y., 1918-19. 2v.

AH 1409.65   A short history of the ancient Near East. (Schwantes, Siegfried J.) Grand Rapids, 1965.

AH 279.39.10   A short history of the ancient world. (Smith, C.E.) N.Y., 1939.

Eg 279.14   A short history of the Egyptian people. (Budge, Ernest Alfred Wallis.) London, 1914.

AH 7489.31.5   A short history of the Roman Empire to the death of Marcus Aurelius. (Wells, Joseph.) N.Y., 1931.

NEDL   AH 7278.90.5   A short history of the Roman people. (Allen, W.T.) Boston, 1895.

Eg 879.37.5   Shorter, A.W. The Egyptian gods. London, 1937.

Eg 829.32   Shorter, Alan W. Everyday life in ancient Egypt. London, 1932.

AH 7339.35A   Showerman, G. Monuments and men of ancient Rome. N.Y., 1935.

AH 7819.31.2   Showerman, Grant. Rome and the Romans. N.Y., 1931.

Eg 609.55F   The shrines of Tut-Ankh-Amen. N.Y., 1955.

AH 7189.57.5   Shtaerman, Elena. Krizis rabovladel'cheskogo stroia v zapadn'ikh provinschchiiakh rimskoi imperii. Moskva, 1957.

AH 7189.71   Shtaerman, Elena. Rabovladel'cheskie otnosheniia v romner Rimskoi imperii (Italiia). Moskva, 1971.

AH 7189.64.5   Shtaerman, Elena. Rastzvet rabovladel'cheskikh otnoshenii v Rimskoi respublike. Moskva, 1964.

AH 7509.03.5A   Shuckburgh, E.S. Augustus...(B.C. 63-A.D. 14). London, 1903.

AH 4279.06   Shuckburgh, E.S. Greece. N.Y., 1906.

AH 4279.06.5   Shuckburgh, E.S. Greece from the coming of the Hellenes to A.D. 14. 1. ed. London, 1922.

NEDL   AH 7278.94A   Shuckburgh, E.S. History of Rome. N.Y., 1894.

AH 7278.94.2   Shuckburgh, E.S. A history of Rome to the battle of Actium. N.Y., 1917.

AH 277.27.25   Shuckford, Samuel. The sacred and profane history of the world connected. London, 1858. 2v.

Htn   AH 277.27.3*   Shuckford, Samuel. The sacred and prophane history of the world connected. London, 1731-37. 3v.

AH 8663.2   Shumway, E.S. A day in ancient Rome. Boston, 1897.

AH 7818.85   Shumway, E.S. A day in ancient Rome. N.Y., 1885.

AH 7139.26   Siber, Heinrich. Römisches Recht in Grundzügen für die Vorlesung. Berlin, 1925-28. 2v.

AH 9610.26   La Sicile greque. (Bayet, Jean.) Paris, 1930.

AH 9608.5.5F   Sicilia antica. (Pareti, Luigi.) Palermo, 1959.

Htn   AH 9607.5F*   Sicilia et Magna Graecia. (Goltzius, H.) Brugis, 1576.

Htn   AH 9607.6F*   Sicilia historia posterior. (Goltzius, H.) Brugis Flandrorum, 1576.

AH 9610.19   La Sicilia romana. (Loncao, E.) Palermo, 1905.

AH 9607.23   Sicilia Schiava; panoramica azione critico-storica. (Borzi, Salvatore.) Paternò, 1962.

AH 4809.70   The Sicilian colony dates. (Miller, Molly.) Albany, 1970.

Htn   AH 9610.3*   The Sicilian tyrant. (Perrinchief, Richard.) London, 1676.

AH 9609.4   Sicily and the Greeks. (Sjoeqvist, Erik.) Ann Arbor, 1973.

AH 9609.5.7   Sicily before the Greeks. (Brea, L.B.) London, 1957.

AH 9609.5.5   Sicily before the Greeks. (Brea, L.B.) N.Y., 1957.

AH 9607.19   Sicily in fable, history, art and song. (Perry, W.C.) London, 1908.

AH 9609.5   Siculi e greci nella Sicilia orientale. (Puglisi Marino, S.) Catania, 1909.

AH 3149.7   Sidersky, David. Etude sur la chronologie Assyro-Babylonienne. Paris, 1916.

AH 3739.5.2   Sidon. (Eiselen, F.C.) N.Y., 1907.

AH 3739.5   Sidon. (Eiselen, F.C.) N.Y., 1907.

AH 3739.10   Sidon through the ages. (Jidejian, Nina.) Beirut, 1971.

AH 4108.17.7F   Sieben Tafeln zum 11 Bande Staatshaushaltung. (Böckh, August.) Berlin, 1851.

AH 818.67   Die sieben Weltwunder des Altertums. 2. Aufl. (Dombart, Theodore.) München, 1970.

AH 8308.5.1   Siebenbürgen im Altertum. (Daicoviciu, Constantin.) Bukarest, 1943.

AH 7438.63   Siebert, W. Ueber Appius Claudius Caecus. Kassel, 1863.

AH 7509.55   Le siècle d'Auguste. 1. éd. (Grimal, Pierre.) Paris, 1955.

AH 4498.73   Siècle der Périclès. (Filleul, E.) Paris, 1873. 2v.

AH 7449.53   Le siècle des Scipions. (Grimal, P.) Paris, 1953.

AH 7599.47.2   Le siècle d'or de l'empire romain. (Homo, Léon P.) Paris, 1969.

AH 7599.47   Le siècle d'or de l'empire romain. 3. éd. (Homo, Léon P.) Paris, 1947.

VAH 5390.21   Siedurin pneciw Tebom. 1. wyd. (Krawczuk, Aleksander.) Warszawa, 1968.

AH 3980.50   Siege de Jotapata. (Parent, A.) Paris, 1866.

AH 4838.91   Sieger in den olympischen Spielen. (Förster, H.) Zwickau, 1891.

AH 7059.69   Die Siegestitulatur der römischen Kaiser. (Kneissl, Peter.) Göttingen, 1969.

Eg 981.10   Siegler, Karl Georg. Kalabsha; Architektur und Baugeschichte des Tempels. Berlin, 1970.

AH 7448.78   Sieglin, W. Die Chronologie der Belagerung von Sagunt. Leipzig, 1878.

AH 7438.90   Sieke, Carl. Appius Claudius Caesar Censor. Marburg, 1890.

Eg 609.22F   Siemens, Clara. Koenig Echnaton in el-Amarna. Leipzig, 1922.

AH 168.93   Sieveking, H. Seedarlehen. Leipzig, 1893.

AH 4538.40   Sievers, G.R. Geschichte Griechenlandes. Kiel, 1840.

AH 7488.70   Sievers, G.R. Studien zur Geschichte der Römischen Kaiserreiches. Berlin, 1870.

AH 4484.16   Siewert, Peter. Der Eid von Plataiai. München, 1972.

AH 849.5   Sigismund, R. Die Aromata. Leipzig, 1884.

AH 9773.13.5   Signon, Helmut. Die Römer in Köln. Frankfurt, 1971.

AH 8907.44   Signorelli, Mario. Storia degli Etruschi. Roma, 1969.

Htn   AH 7135.73*   Sigonio, C. De antiquo iure civium romanorum. Paris, 1573.

AH 7135.74F   Sigonio, C. De antiquo iure populi romani. Bononiae, 1574.

AH 7137.15   Sigonio, C. De antiquo iure populi romani. Lipsiae, 1715. 2v.

Htn   AH 7135.68*   Sigonio, C. De antiquo iure provinciarum. Venetiis, 1568.

Htn   AH 7655.93F*   Sigonio, Carlo. Caroli Sigonii historiarum de occidentali imperio libri XX. Francofurti, 1591-93. 2 part.

Htn   AH 3953.9*   Sigonio, Carlo. De republica hebralarum libri VII. Francofurti, 1585.

AH 7808.01   Sigonio, Carlo. Mutinensis fasti consulares ac triumphi acti. Oxonii, 1801.

Eg 841.10   Sijpesteijn, Pieter Johannes. Liste des gymnasiarques des métropoles de l'Égypte romaine. Amsterdam, 1967.

AH 819.62.5   The silent past. (Lissner, Ivar.) N.Y., 1962.

AH 7469.56   Silla e la crisi repubblicana. 1. ed. (Valgiglio, E.) Firenze, 1956.

AH 7499.09.5   Silvagni, K. L'impero e le donne dei Cesari. 2. ed. Torino, 1909.

AH 7479.30   Silvagni, V. Giulio Cesare. Torino, 1930.

AH 4659.06   Silver age of the Greek world. (Mahaffy, J.P.) Chicago, 1906.

AH 4659.06.5   The silver age of the Greek world. (Mahaffy, J.P.) Chicago, 1911.

AH 7819.62.5   The silver-plated age. (Jones, Tom Bard.) Sandoval, 1962.

AH 3659.8   Silvestre de Sacy, A.I. Memoires sur diverses antiquités de la Perse. Paris, 1793.

Eg 758.92   Simaika, A. Province Romaine d'Égypte. Paris, 1892.

AH 818.94   Simcox, E.J. Primitive civilizations. London, 1894. 2v.

AH 7889.16A   Simklovich, V.G. Rome's fall reconsidered. N.Y., 1916.

AH 7468.74.7   Simon, H.O. Vita Q. Lutatii Q.F. Catuli. Berlin, 1874.

AH 7808.57   Simon, Heinrich O. Fastorum Romanorum Specimen. Berlin, 1857.

AH 7658.36   Simonde de Simondi, J.C.L. Histoire de la chute de l'Empire romain. Bruxelles, 1836.

AH 7658.35   Simonde de Simondi, J.C.L. History of the fall of the Roman Empire. Philadelphia, 1835.

AH 9777.15   Simonis, Carl. Versuch einer Geschichte des Alarich. Göttingen, 1858.

AH 7203.142   Simonius, A. Was bedeuten für uns die Pandekten? Basel, 1934.

AH 7162.38   Simonius, Pascal. Die Donatio Mortis Causa im klassischen römischen Recht. Basel, 1958.

AH 3966.30F   Simons, Jan. The geographical and topographical texts of the Old Testament. Leiden, 1959.

AH 7238.51   Simpson, J.Y. Was the Roman army provided with any medical officers? Edinburgh, 1851.

Eg 1029.72   Simpson, William Kelly. The literature of ancient Egypt; an anthology of stories, instructions, and poetry. New Haven, 1972.

AH 807.52.5F — Simson, E. Chronicon historiam catholicam. Amstelodami, 1752.

AH 4039.51 — Sinclair, Thomas Alan. A history of Greek political thought. London, 1951.

AH 4039.51.2 — Sinclair, Thomas Alan. A history of Greek political thought. 2. ed. Cleveland, 1968.

AH 3005.855 — Sir A. Henry Layard; autobiography and letters. (Layard, Austen Henry.) London, 1903. 2v.

AH 9639.15 — Siracusa greca. (Fiori, Alberto.) Roma, 1971.

AH 7799.61 — Sirago, V.A. Galla Placidia e la trasformazione politica dell'Occidente. Louvain, 1961.

AH 8615.5 — Sirago, Vito A. L'Italia agraria sotto Traiano. Louvain, 1958.

AH 3909.9 — La Siria nell'eta di Mari. (Michelini, T.F.) Roma, 1960.

AH 3907.3F — Siria sacra. (Terzidi Lavria, B.) Roma, 1695.

AH 7200.17 — Sistema i teket "XII tablin". (Nikol'skii, B.V.) Sankt Peterburg, 1897.

AH 818.86 — Sitte und Sitten der alten Völker. (Spitzer, S.) Budapest, 1886.

Htn AH 4829.26F*A — Sittengeschichte Griechenlands. (Licht, Hans.) Dresden, 1926-28. 3v.

AH 867.5 — Sittl, C. Die Gebärden der Griechen und Römer. Leipzig, 1890.

AH 8.96 — Sittl, Karl. Anschauungsmethode...Altertumswissenschaft. Gotha, 1896.

AH 4845.9 — Sittlich-religiöse Verhalten. (Schömann, G.F.) Greifswald, 1848.

AH 7309.66 — Sittliches Bewusstsein als Handlungsmotiv bei römischen Historiken. (Schoenlein, Peter Wilhelm.) Erlangen, 1966.

NEDL AH 7139.11 — Six Roman laws. (Hardy, E.G.) Oxford, 1911.

AH 3607.9A — Sixth great oriental monarchy. (Rawlinson, G.) London, 1873.

AH 3607.9.5 — Sixth great oriental monarchy. (Rawlinson, G.) N.Y., 190-?

AH 4189.23.5 — The size of the slave population at Athens. (Sargent, R.L.) Urbana, 1924.

AH 4189.23 — The size of the slave population at Athens during the 5th and 4th century B.C. Thesis. (Sargent, R.L.) Urbana? 1923?

AH 9610.29 — Sizilien und Athen. (Wentker, Hermann.) Heidelberg, 1956.

AH 3160.22 — Sjoeberg, Ake. Der mondgott nanna-suen in der sumerischen uberliefeung Uppsala. Uppsala, 1960.

AH 9609.4 — Sjoeqvist, Erik. Sicily and the Greeks. Ann Arbor, 1973.

AH 6049.5.5 — Skalet, Charles H. Ancient Sicyon, with a prosopographia Sicyonia. Baltimore, 1928.

AH 6049.5 — Skalet, Charles H. Chapters in history of ancient Sicyon. Baltimore, 1928.

Eg 752.10 — Skeat, T.C. Papyri from Panopolis in the Chester Beatty Library. Dublin, 1964.

AH 959.01 — Skeel, C.A.J. Travel in the first century after Christ. Cambridge, 1901.

AH 7278.84 — Skeleton outline of Roman history. (Matheson, P.E.) London, 1884.

AH 7278.84.10 — Skeleton outline of Roman history down A.D. 180. (Matheson, P.E.) London, 1922.

AH 37.96 — Sketch of democracy. (Bisset, R.) London, 1796.

NEDL AH 4278.24.2 — Sketch of political history of ancient Greece. (Heeren, A.H.L.) Oxford, 1829.

AH 7828.22 — Sketches of domestic manners. Philadelphia, 1822.

AH 7828.22.3A — Sketches of domestic manners. 2. American ed. Philadelphia, 1823.

AH 1928.75 — Skinner, J.R. Key to the Hebrew-Egyptian mystery in the source of measures. Cincinnati, 1875.

AH 2007.3 — Skizze der Geschichte und Geographie Arabiens. (Glaser, E.) Berlin, 1890.

AH 7189.69.5 — Sklavenarbeit und technischen Fortschritt im Römischen Reich. (Kiechle, Franz.) Wiesbaden, 1969.

AH 189.34 — Sklaverei. (Westermann, W.L.) Stuttgart, 1934.

AH 4188.75 — Sklaverei bei den Griechen. (Schück, J.) Breslau, 1875.

AH 188.98 — Die Sklaverei im Altertum. (Meyer, G.) Dresden, 1898.

AH 842.33 — Skolens og opdragelsens historie. (Rordam, H.F.) Kjobenhavn, 1866.

Eg 879.38.10 — The sky-religion in Egypt. (Wainwright, G.A.) Cambridge, Eng., 1938.

AH 3757.10 — Die Skythen in Südrussland. (Potratz, Johannes A.H.) Basel, 1963.

AH 3757.9 — Skythen-Saken. (Fressl, J.) München, 1886.

AH 4840.10A — Slater, Philip Elliot. The glory of Hera. Boston, 1968.

AH 189.55A — The slave systems of Greek and Roman antiquity. (Westermann, W.L.) Philadelphia, 1955.

AH 189.71 — Slavery: from the rise of Western civilization to the Renaissance. 1. ed. (Meltzer, Milton.) N.Y., 1971.

AH 189.60 — Slavery in classical antiquity. (Finley, Moses I.) Cambridge, Eng., 1960.

AH 1189.49A — Slavery in the ancient Near East. (Mendelsohn, I.) N.Y., 1949.

AH 7189.28 — Slavery in the Roman Empire. (Barrow, R.H.) London, 1928.

AH 309.70 — Slonimskii, Mikhail M. Periodizatsiia drevnei istorii v sovetskoi istoriografii. Voronezh, 1970.

NEDL AH 4278.57.28 — Smaller history of Greece. (Smith, William.) N.Y., 1860.

NEDL AH 4278.57.32 — Smaller history of Greece. (Smith, William.) N.Y., 1886.

AH 7278.74 — Smaller history of Rome. (Smith, William.) N.Y., 1874.

NEDL AH 7278.74.8 — A smaller history of Rome. (Smith, William.) N.Y., 1881.

AH 1278.71.4 — Smaller history of the East. (Smith, Philip.) N.Y., 1872.

AH 7532.2 — Smallwood, Edith Mary. Documents illustrating the principates of Gaius Claudius and Nero. Cambridge, 1967.

AH 7592.2 — Smallwood, Edith Mary. Documents illustrating the principates of Nerva Trajan and Hadrian. Cambridge, Eng., 1966.

AH 8549.71 — Smiddy, Richard. An essay on the Druids. Dublin, 1871.

Eg 919.60 — Smiderkówna, Anna. La propriété foncière privée dans l'Egypte de Vespasien et technique agricole d'après. Wroclaw, 1960.

AH 3013.23 — Smith, A. Ruins of Nineveh. n.p., 1845?

AH 279.39.10 — Smith, C.E. A short history of the ancient world. N.Y., 1939.

AH 7519.42 — Smith, Charles E. Tiberius and the Roman Empire. Baton Rouge, 1942.

AH 7239.06.5 — Smith, F. Römische Heeresverfassung und Timokratie. Berlin, 1906.

AH 3013.23.15 — Smith, G. Assyrian discoveries. N.Y., 1875.

Eg 819.11 — Smith, G.E. Egyptians. London, 1911.

Eg 839.24 — Smith, G.E. Egyptian mummies. London, 1924.

AH 819.30 — Smith, G.E. Human history. London, 1930.

Eg 609.23.5 — Smith, G.E. Tutankhamen and the discovery of his tomb. London, 1923.

AH 3075.3 — Smith, George. Ancient history...Assyria. London, 1875.

AH 3075.3.3 — Smith, George. Ancient history...Asyria. N.Y., 1876.

AH 3075.3.2 — Smith, George. Assyria from the earliest time to the fall of Nineveh. London, 1875.

AH 3013.41 — Smith, George. Assyrian discoveries. London, 1875.

AH 3109.6 — Smith, George. Assyrian Eponym Canon. London, 1875.

AH 3177.3F — Smith, George. Chaldaean account of the deluge. London, 1872.

AH 3159.6.3.5 — Smith, George. The Chaldean account of genesis. N.Y., 1876.

AH 3159.6.3 — Smith, George. The Chaldean account of genesis. 3. ed. London, 1876.

AH 3159.6.9 — Smith, George. George Smith's Chaldaische Genesis. Leipzig, 1876.

AH 3097.4 — Smith, George. History of Assurbanipal. Leiden, 1871.

AH 3008.77 — Smith, George. The history of Babylonia. London, 1877.

AH 3095.6 — Smith, George. History of Sennacherib. London, 1878.

AH 408.47.5 — Smith, George. The patriarchial age. N.Y., 1851.

AH 3966.5.3 — Smith, George A. The historical geography of the Holy Land. 3. ed. N.Y., 1895.

AH 3966.5.5 — Smith, George A. The historical geography of the Holy Land. 3d ed. London, 1897.

AH 3966.5.6 — Smith, George A. The historical geography of the Holy Land. 4. ed. N.Y., 1897.

AH 3966.5.7 — Smith, George A. The historical geography of the Holy Land. 7. ed. N.Y., 1900.

AH 3966.5.26 — Smith, George A. The historical geography of the Holy Land. 26. ed. N.Y., 1937?

AH 4229.24 — Smith, Gertrude. The administration of justice from Hesiod to Solon. Diss. Chicago, 1924.

Eg 839.56 — Smith, J.L. Tombs, temples and ancient art. 1. ed. Norman, 1956.

AH 4848.10 — Smith, J.M. Ancient Greek female costume. London, 1882.

AH 4848.10.3 — Smith, J.M. Ancient Greek female costume. 2. ed. London, 1883.

AH 808.39 — Smith, J.T. Observations on chronological eras. Boston, 1839.

AH 8549.45 — Smith, John. Histoire des druides et...Calédonie. Arbois, 1845.

AH 7759.71 — Smith, John Holland. Constantine the Great. London, 1971.

AH 4279.60 — Smith, Morton. The ancient Greeks. Ithaca, N.Y., 1960.

NEDL AH 278.85 — Smith, P. History of the world. N.Y., 1885. 3v.

AH 1278.71.3 — Smith, Philip. Ancient history of the East. N.Y., 1871.

NEDL AH 278.74 — Smith, Philip. History of the world. N.Y., 1874. 3v.

AH 1278.71.4 — Smith, Philip. Smaller history of the East. N.Y., 1872.

AH 1278.71.7 — Smith, Philip. The student's ancient history. The ancient history of the East. N.Y., 1894.

AH 8073.4 — Smith, R.B. Carthage and the Carthaginians. 2. ed. London, 1879.

AH 7448.81 — Smith, R.B. Rome and Carthage. N.Y., 1880.

AH 7448.81.5 — Smith, R.B. Rome and Carthage. N.Y., 1896.

NEDL AH 7448.81.2A — Smith, R.B. Rome and Carthage. 5. ed. London, 1887.

AH 7469.55 — Smith, R.E. The failure of the Roman Republic. Cambridge, Eng., 1955.

AH 7239.58 — Smith, Richard. Service in the past - Marian Roman Army. Manchester, 1958.

AH 3149.9 — Smith, S. Alalakh and chronology. London, 1940.

AH 3073.4 — Smith, S.A. Miscellaneous Assyrian texts on the British Museum. Leipzig, 1887.

AH 3037.5 — Smith, S.M.A. Early history of Assyria to 1000 B.C. London, 1928.

AH 3002.80 — Smith, Sidney. Babylonian historical texts relating to the capture and downfall of Babylon. London, 1924.

AH 938.54.3 — Smith, William. Dictionary of Greek and Roman geography. London, 1854.

NEDL AH 938.54.2 — Smith, William. Dictionary of Greek and Roman geography. London, 1854.

NEDL AH 938.54.4 — Smith, William. Dictionary of Greek and Roman geography. London, 1856-57. 2v.

AH 938.54.5 — Smith, William. Dictionary of Greek and Roman geography. London, 1870. 2v.

NEDL AH 4278.57.19 — Smith, William. A history of Greece. Boston, 1855.

NEDL AH 4278.57.19.5A — Smith, William. A history of Greece. Boston, 1855.

NEDL AH 4278.57.21 — Smith, William. History of Greece. Boston, 1857.

AH 4278.57.20 — Smith, William. History of Greece. Boston, 1857.

NEDL AH 4278.57.22 — Smith, William. History of Greece. Boston, 1860.

NEDL AH 4278.57.25 — Smith, William. History of Greece. London, 1900.

NEDL AH 4278.57.23 — Smith, William. History of Greece. N.Y., 1860.

NEDL AH 4278.57.23.10 — Smith, William. History of Greece. N.Y., 1861.

NEDL AH 4278.57.23.15 — Smith, William. History of Greece. N.Y., 1863.

NEDL AH 4278.57.24.7 — Smith, William. History of Greece. N.Y., 1885.

NEDL AH 4278.57.24.9 — Smith, William. History of Greece. N.Y., 1886.

NEDL AH 4278.57.28 — Smith, William. Smaller history of Greece. N.Y., 1860.

NEDL AH 4278.57.32 — Smith, William. Smaller history of Greece. N.Y., 1886.

AH 7278.74 — Smith, William. Smaller history of Rome. N.Y., 1874.

NEDL AH 7278.74.8 — Smith, William. A smaller history of Rome. N.Y., 1881.

AH 2589.5 — Smyrnaeorum res gestae et antiquitates. (Lane, G.M.) Gottinge, 1851.

AH 1279.37 — Snegirev, I.L. Drevnii Vostok; atlas. Leningrad, 1937.

NEDL AH 279.08 — Snider, D.J. European history, chiefly ancient. St. Louis, 1908.

AH 329.70 — Snowden, Frank Martin. Black in antiquity; Ethiopians in the Greco-Roman experience. Cambridge, 1970.

AH 4409.15 — Snyder, William L. The military annals of Greece from the earliest times to the beginning of the Pelopormesian War. Boston, 1915. 2v.

AH 3002.18 — The so-called Peters-Hilprecht controversy. Pt.1-2. (Hilprecht, H.V.) Philadelphia, 1908.

AH 7059.09 — Sobeck, T. Die Quästoren der Römischen Republik. Trebnitz, 1909.

AH 7459.18 — Social...life in Rome in the time of Plautus. (Leffingwell, G.W.) N.Y., 1918.

AH 4659.41A — The social and economic history of the Hellenistic world. (Rostovtsev, Mikhail Ivanovich.) Oxford, Eng., 1941. 3v.

AH 4659.41.2 — The social and economic history of the Hellenistic world. (Rostovtsev, Mikhail Ivanovich.) Oxford, 1967. 3v.

AH 7889.26A — The social and economic history of the Roman Empire. (Rostovtsev, M.I.) Oxford, 1926.

AH 2147.7 — The social basis of Roman power in Asia Minor. (Ramsay, W.M.) Aberdeen, 1941.

AH 7114.46 — Social conflicts in the Roman Republic. (Brunt, Peter Astbury.) London, 1971.

AH 3804.5 — The social legislation of the primitive Semites. (Schaeffer, Henry.) N.Y., 1971.

AH 3165.5 — Social life among the Assyrians and Babylonians. (Sayce, A.H.) London, 1893.

AH 7829.08.3 — Social life at Rome in the age of Cicero. (Fowler, W.W.) N.Y., 1909.

Author and Title Listing

AH 7829.08.4 Social life at Rome in the age of Cicero. (Fowler, W.W.) N.Y., 1922.

AH 7829.08.5 Social life at Rome in the age of Cicero. (Fowler, W.W.) N.Y., 1933.

Eg 819.23A Social life in ancient Egypt. (Petrie, William M.F.) Boston, 1923.

Eg 819.23.2 Social life in ancient Egypt. (Petrie, William M.F.) London, 1932.

AH 4828.74A Social life in Greece. (Mahaffy, J.P.) London, 1874.

AH 4828.74.5 Social life in Greece. (Mahaffy, J.P.) London, 1898.

AH 4828.74.2A Social life in Greece. 2. ed. (Mahaffy, J.P.) London, 1875.

AH 4828.74.8 Social life in Greece from Homer to Menander. (Mahaffy, J.P.) London, 1902.

AH 4828.74.12 Social life in Greece from Homer to Menander. (Mahaffy, J.P.) London, 1925.

AH 4828.74.4 Social life in Greece from Homer to Menander. 5. ed. (Mahaffy, J.P.) London, 1883.

AH 7229.70.5 Social status and legal privilege in the Roman Empire. (Garnsey, Peter.) Oxford, 1970.

AH 819.36.5 The social thought of the ancient civilization. 1. ed. (Hertzler, J.O.) N.Y., 1936.

AH 4888.95 Socialisme en Grèce. (Platon, G.) Paris, 1895.

AH 32.5 Sociedad Española de Estudios Clásicos. Coloquios sobre teoria política de la antigüedad clásica. Madrid, 1965.

AH 8647.11 Società Magna Grecia. Campagne della Società Magna Grecia, 1926 e 1927. Roma, 1928.

AH 819.66.20 La società nel mondo classico. (Levi, Mario Attilio.) Torino, 1966.

AH 4498.60 Societatis Atheniensis historia. (Gause, A.) Berolini, 1860.

EgP 133.15F Société fouadier de papyrologie. Publications. Textes et documents. Caire. 1-6,1931-1945 3v.

EgP 133.15 Société fouadier de papyrologie. Publications. Textes et documents. Caire. 7-9,1947-1949

AH 7819.55 La société romaine. (Bruwaene, M. van den.) Bruxelles, 1955.

AH 4819.64.5 Society and civilization in Greece and Rome. (Ehrenberg, V.) Cambridge, 1964.

AH 7819.09.3 Society and politics in ancient Rome. (Abbott, F.F.) London, 1912.

AH 7819.09.10 Society and politics in ancient Rome. (Abbott, F.F.) N.Y., 1910.

NEDL AH 7819.09.2 Society and politics in ancient Rome. (Abbott, F.F.) N.Y., 1918.

AH 7278.45 Society for Promoting Christian Knowledge, London. The Roman Empire. London, 1845.

AH 7818.88A Society in Rome under the Caesars. (Inge, W.R.) N.Y., 1888.

AH 3145.5 Soden, W.F. von. Herrscher im alten Orient. Berlin, 1954.

AH 4238.77 Sölderei bei den Griechen. (Lorenz, A.) Eichstätt, 1876-77.

AH 8073.8 Der Söldner-Krieg der Karthager. (Seibel, V.) Dilingen, 1848.

AH 7139.71 Soellner, Alfred. Römische Rechtsgeschichte. 1e Aufl. Freiburg, 1971.

AH 7239.59 Die sogenannte servianische Heeresreform. (Hackl, Othmar.) München, 1959.

AH 2109.5 Die sogenannten Assyro-Chaldäer und Hittiten. (Karolides, Paul.) Athens, 1898.

AH 7138.92.5 Sohm, R. Institutes of Roman law. Oxford, 1892.

AH 7138.84.5 Sohm, R. Institutionen des römischen Rechts. Leipzig, 1884.

AH 7138.83.5.3 Sohm, R. Institutionen des römischen Rechts. 3e Aufl. Leipzig, 1888.

AH 4518.94 Sokrates in der Volksversammlung. (Müller, Emil.) Zittau, 1894.

AH 9684.10 El solar numantino. (Gómez Santa Cruz, S.) Madrid, 1914.

AH 7769.33 Solari, A. La crisi dell'impero romano. Milano, 1933-37. 5v.

AH 7659.39.5 Solari, A. Il rinnovamento dell'impero romano. Milano, 1938-

AH 9710.5 Solari, A. Sui dinasti degli Odrisi (V-IV secolo a.C.). Pisa, 1912.

AH 4808.98 Solari, Arcturus. Fasti Ephororum spartanorum. Pisis, 1898.

AH 7489.40 Solari, Arturo. L'impero romano. Genova, 1940.

AH 6057.15 Solari, Arturo. La lega tessalica. Pisa, 1912.

AH 5754.13 Solari, Arturo. Ricerche spartane. Livorno, 1907.

AH 7799.16 Solari, Arturo. Gli uomi e Attila. Pisa, 1916.

AH 8907.21F Solari, Arturo. Vita pubblica e privata degli Etruschi. Firenze, 1931.

AH 7909.05 Solbisky. Voraus geht eine Abhandlung. Weimar, 1905.

AH 7131.7 Soldan, A. De reipublicae romanae legatis. Marburg, 1854. 6 pam.

AH 299.39 Die Soldatinkaiser. (Altheim, F.) Frankfurt am Main, 1939.

AH 7239.63A Soldier and civilian in the later Roman Empire. (MacMullen, R.) Cambridge, 1963.

AH 848.15 Solerius, A. De pileo. Amstelodami, 1672.

AH 4161.5 Solidarité de la famille. (Glotz, Gustave.) Paris, 1904.

AH 3020.25F Sollberger, E. Corpus des inscriptions royales présargoniques de Lagas. Genève, 1956.

AH 3002.154 Sollberger, Edmond. Inscriptions royales sumériennes et akkadiennes. Paris, 1971.

AH 4819.49.10 Solle, Miloš. Počátky helénské civilozace. Praha, 1949.

AH 4819.28A Solon and Croesus, and other Greek essays. (Zimmern, A.E.) London, 1928.

AH 5315.20 Solon the liberator; a study of the Agrarian problem in Attika in the seventh century. (Woodhouse, William J.) London, 1938.

AH 7009.09 Soltau, W. Anfänge der roemischen Geschichtsschreibung. Leipzig, 1909.

AH 7078.80 Soltau, W. Uber Entstehung und Zusammensetzung der altrömischen Volksversammlungen. Berlin, 1880.

AH 7808.86 Soltau, Wilhelm. Prolegomena zu einer römische Chronologie. Berlin, 1886.

AH 7808.89.15 Soltau, Wilhelm. Römische Chronologie. Freiburg, 1889.

AH 7808.88 Soltau, Wilhelm. Die römischen Amstjahre auf ihren natürlichen Zeitwerth reducirt. Freiburg, 1888.

AH 9639.8 Solunto ricordi storici. (Salinas, A.) Palermo, 1884.

AH 818.84.2 Some ancient organs of public opinion. (Jebb, R.C.) Cambridge, Eng., 1884.

AH 7139.34 Some aspects of Roman law. (Mackintosh, J.) Patna, 1934.

AH 3167.7 Some aspects of the hiring of workers in the Sippar region at the time of Hammorati. (Weitemeyer, M.) Copenhagen, 1962.

AH 3052.5A Some literary remains of Rim-Sin...king of Larsa. (Price, I.M.) Chicago, 1904.

AH 7889.15A Some observations on the economic interpretation of early Roman history. (MacFarlane, Charles W.) Philadelphia, 1915.

AH 7479.24 Some problems in Roman history. (Hardy, E.G.) Oxford, 1924.

AH 4819.69.20 Some problems of Greek history. (Toynbee, Arnold Joseph.) London, 1969.

AH 819.19 Some sources of human history. (Petrie, W.M.F.) London, 1919.

NEDL AH 278.56.10 Sommario della storia de' popoli antichi. (Leva, G. de.) Padova, 1856.

AH 3414.10.5 The song of Ullikummi. (Gueterbock, H.G.) New Haven, 1952.

AH 4148.88 Sonne, E. De arbitris externis. Gottingae, 1888.

AH 808.63 Sonnenkreise der Alten. (Böckh, A.) Berlin, 1863.

AH 7479.32.5 Sonnet, Paul. Gaius Trebatius Testa. Diss. Jena, 1932.

AH 339.63 Sonnet-Altenburg, Helene. Hetären, Mütter, Amazonen. Heidenheim, 1963.

AH 7163.25 Sontag, C.R. De sponsalibus apud Romanos. Halae, 1860.

AH 908.89 Sopra le relazioni commericali. (Helbig, W.) Roma, 1889.

AH 9608.7 Soraci, Rosario. I proconsoli di Sicilia da Augusto a Traiano. Catania, 1958?

AH 7163.32 Soraci, Rosario. Ricerche sui Conubia tra romani e germani nei secoli IV-VI. Catania, 1968.

AH 6057.17 Sordi, Marta. La lega tessala fino ad Afessundro-Magno. Roma, 1958.

AH 7309.25 Sorel, Georges. La ruine du monde antique. 2e éd. Paris, 1925.

X Cg AH 4279.12 Soteriades, G. Historia tēs Archaiotētos. Athēnai, 1912.

AH 7709.61 Sotgiu, Giovanna. Studi sull'epigrafia di Aureliano. Palmero, 1961.

AH 4481.11 Sotiriadis, G. L'expédition de Marathon. Salonique, 1934.

AH 819.72.5 Sotsial'no-ekonomicheskie problemy istorii drevnego mira i srednikh vekov. Moskva, 1972.

AH 4459.64 Sotsial'no-politicheskaia bor'ba v Afinakh v kontse V veka do n.e. (Frolov, Eduard Davidovich.) Leningrad, 1964.

Eg 839.13 Sottas, H. La préservation de la propriété funéraire. Paris, 1913.

Eg 1309.21F Sottas, Henri. Papyrus démotiques de Lille. Paris, 1921.

AH 7203.149 Soubie, André. Recherches sur les origines des rubriques du Digeste. Tarbes, 1960.

AH 3013.958F Soundings at Tell Fakhariyah. (Chicago. University. Oriental Institute.) Chicago, 1958.

AH 7009.04 Source book of Roman history. (Munro, D.C.) Boston, 1904.

AH 842.25 Source book of the history of education. (Monroe, Paul.) N.Y., 1901.

AH 842.25.5 Source book of the history of education for the Greek and Roman period. (Monroe, Paul.) N.Y., 1906.

AHP 29.10 Sources and monographs. Monographs in history: ancient Near East. Los Angeles. 1,1974+

AH 7204.2 Les sources des Institutes de Justinien. (Appleton, Charles.) Paris, 1891.

AH 4498.97 Sources for Greek history. (Hill, G.) Oxford, 1897.

AH 4498.97.5 Sources for Greek history between the Persian and Pelopormesian wars. (Hill, G.) Oxford, 1951.

AH 7469.03 Sources for Roman history, B.C. 133-70. (Greenidge, A.H.J.) Oxford, 1903.

AH 7462.5.2 Sources for Roman history, 133-70 B.C. 2. ed. (Greenidge, Abel H.J.) Oxford, 1960.

AH 4839.27 Sources for the history of Greek athletics. (Robinson, Rachel Louisa.) Cincinnati, 1955.

AH 3911.10 Sournia, Jean Charles. L'Orient des premiers chrétiens. Paris, 1966.

AH 818.77.6 Soury, J. Études historiques sur les religions, les arts, la civilisation. Paris, 1877.

AH 7079.11 Sous la robe blanche. (Chaigne, G.) Paris, 1911.

AH 3100.5 Southern Mesopotamia in the time of Ashurbanipal. (al-Ahmad, Sami S.) The Hague, 1968.

NEDL AH 279.03 Souttar, R. Short history of ancient peoples. London, 1903.

NEDL AH 279.03.2 Souttar, R. Short history of ancient peoples. N.Y., 1904.

AH 864.5 Soveri, H.F. De ludorum memoria. Helsingforsiae, 1912.

AH 1309.58 Sovietskaia nauka s drevnene Vostoke za 40 let. (Avdiëv, Vsevolod I.) Moskva, 1958.

AH 7299.11 Die soziale Frage im alten Rom. (Pflüger, P.) Zürich, 1911.

AH 7202.36 Soziale Fragen der spätrömischen Kaiserzeit im Spiegel des Theodosianus. (Seyfarth, W.) Berlin, 1963.

AH 7889.00.2 Soziale Kämpfe im alten Rom. 2. Aufl. (Bloch, Leo.) Leipzig, 1908.

AH 4538.85 Die sozialen Zustände Athens. (Blass, F.W.) Kiel, 1885.

AH 819.61.20 Sozialökonomische Verhältnisse in alter Orient. (Deutsche Historiker-Gesellschaft.) Berlin, 1961.

AH 4839.64.5 Spaak, Bob. Goden in het stadion. Amsterdam, 1964.

AH 8907.2 Spadoni, O.L. The Etruscans. Rome, 1887.

Eg 1042.973 Die spätägyptischen Totenstelen. v.1-2. (Munro, Peter.) Glückstadt, 1973.

AH 7439.26 Spaeth, John W. A study of the causes of Rome's wars from 343 to 265 B.C. Diss. Princeton, 1926.

AH 7163.30 Spagnolo, C.A. Richerche sulle diverse maniere di contrarre matrimonio. Roma, 1807.

AH 9657.5 Spain under the Roman empire. (Bouchier, E.S.) Oxford, 1914.

AH 4608.84 Spangenberg, E. De Atheniensium publicis institutis aetate Macedonum commutatis. Diss. inaug. Halis Saxonum, 1884.

AH 7037.03 Spanhem, Ezekiel. Orbis romanus. London, 1703.

AH 4112.14 Sparta, Delphoi und die Amphiktyonen im 5. Jahrhundert. (Zulhofer, Gerhard.) Erlangen? 1959?

AH 5757.13 Sparta; ein Versuch. (Däubler, H.) Leipzig, 1923.

AH 5757.17 Sparta, Lebensordnung und Schicksal. (Lüdemann, Hans.) Leipzig, 1939.

AH 5757.15 Sparta. (Berve, H.) Leipzig, 1937.

AH 5757.26 Sparta. (Jones, Arnold Hugh Martin.) Cambridge, 1967.

AH 5760.7 Sparta. (Löwy, A.) Rostock, 1873.

AH 5763.5A Sparta. (Michell, Humfrey.) Cambridge, Eng., 1952.

AH 5763.6 Sparta. (Michell, Humfrey.) Cambridge, Eng., 1964.

AH 5763.10 Sparta. Geschiedenis en cultuur der Spartanen van praehistorie tot Perzische oorlogen. (Stibbe, C.M.) Bussum, 1969.

AH 5757.5 Sparta. v.1-3. (Manso, J.K.F.) Leipzig, 1800. 5v.

AH 5758.16.1 Sparta and her social problems. (Oliva, Pavel.) Amsterdam, 1971.

AH 5758.16 Sparta and her social problems. (Oliva, Pavel.) Prague, 1971.

AH 4538.95 Sparta and Thebes. (Allcroft, A.H.) London, 1895.

	AH 7259.41.5	Starr, Chester G. The Roman imperial navy. 2. ed. N.Y., 1960.
	AH 3013.937F	Starr, R.F.S. Nuzi; report on the excavations at Yorgan Tepa near Kirkuk, Iraq, conducted by Harvard University. Cambridge, 1937-39. 2v.
	AH 4279.53.5	Stasis. (Loenen, Dirk.) Amsterdam, 1953.
	AH 3105.5A	State letters of Assyria. (Pfeiffer, R.H.) New Haven, 1935.
	AH 7842.12	Lo stato e l'istruzione pubblica. (Barbagallo, C.) Catania, 1911.
	AH 4098.98	Statog statsforfatninger. (Gertz, M.C.) Kjøbenhavn, 1898.
	AH 8453.5	Die Statthalter der ungeteilten Pannonien und Oberpannoniens von Augustus bis Diokletian. (Reidinger, Walter.) Bonn, 1956.
	AH 8161.2	Die Statthalter Numidiens von Gallien bis Konstantin, 268-320. (Kolbe, H.G.) München, 1962.
	AH 3155.30	Les statues de culte dans les textes mésopotamiens, des origines à la 1er dynastie de Babylone. (Spycket, Agnès.) Paris, 1968.
	Eg 879.26	Les statues vivantes. (Weynants-Ronday, M. (Mrs.).) Bruxelles, 1926.
	AH 3965.13	The status of labor in ancient Israel. (Sulzberger, M.) Philadelphia, 1923.
	AH 7217.18	Le statut obligatoire des décurions dans le droit constantinien. (Nuyens, Michel.) Louvain, 1964.
	AH 4218.5	Statutes of limitations at Athens. Diss. (Charles, John F.) Chicago, 1938.
	AH 5308.7	Stauffer, A. Zwölf Gestalten der Glanzzeit Athens. München, 1896.
	AH 7279.48	Stauffer, Ethelbert. Christus und die Caesaren. 2. Aufl. Hamburg, 1948.
	AH 79.72	Staveley, Eastland Stuart. Greek and Roman voting and elections. London, 1972.
	AH 3020.20	Steele, Francis Rue. Nuzi real estate transactions. Thesis. Philadelphia, 1943.
NEDL	AH 278.81.5	Steele, J.D. A brief history of ancient peoples. N.Y., 1881.
	AH 4298.83.2	Steele, J.D. Brief history of Greece. N.Y., 1883.
	AH 4298.83	Steele, J.D. Brief history of Greece. N.Y., 1883.
NEDL	AH 7278.85.4	Steele, J.D. Brief history of Rome. N.Y., n.d.
	AH 4162.9	Steigertahl, G.H.C.L. De vi et usu Parachatabolès in causis Atheniensium hereditariis commentatio. Cellis, 1832.
	AH 7739.12	Stein, Arthur. Die kaiserlichen Verwaltungsbeamten unter Severus Alexander, 222-235. Prag, 1912.
	Eg 759.15	Stein, Arthur. Untersuchungen zur Geschichte und Verwaltung Ägyptens unter roemischer Herrschaft. Stuttgart, 1915.
	AH 7659.28	Stein, Ernst. Geschichte der spätrömischen Reiches I. Wien, 1928.
	AH 7659.28.5	Stein, Ernst. Histoire du Bas-Empire. v.1-2. Paris, 1949. 3v.
	AH 4200.7	Stein, H.K. Kritik der Überlieferung über...Lykurg. Glatz, 1882.
	AH 8873.10	Stein, J.J. De Capuae gentisque Campanorum. Diss. Vratislaviae, 1838.
	AH 4559.29	Stein, Mark Aurel. Alexander's campaign on the Indian north-west frontier. London, 1929.
	AH 7207.46.1	Stein, Paul. Die Senatssitzungen der ciceronischen Zeit 68-43. Photoreproduction. Münster, 1930.
	Eg 909.10.1	Steinbrüche und Bergwerke im ptolemäischen und römischen Ägypten. (Fitzler, Kurt.) Leipzig, 1910.
	Eg 909.10	Steinbrüche und Bergwerke im ptolemäischen und römischen Ägypten. Thesis. (Fitzler, Kurt.) Leipzig, 1910.
	Eg 279.00	Steindorff, G. Die Blütezeit des Pharaonenreichs. Bielefeld, 1900.
	Eg 279.43F	Steindorff, G. Egypt. N.Y., 1943.
	Eg 299.42	Steindorff, G. When Egypt ruled the East. Chicago, 1942.
	Eg 299.42.5	Steindorff, G. When Egypt ruled the East. Chicago, 1957.
	Eg 879.05.5	Steindorff, Georg. The religion of the ancient Egyptians. N.Y., 1905.
	Eg 709.13.3	Steiner, A. Der Fiskus der Ptolemaeer. v.1-3. Leipzig, 1913.
	AH 7239.05	Steiner, Paul. Die Dona Militaria. Bonn, 1905.
	AH 7238.64.5	Steinike, Heinrich. De equitatu romano. Diss. Halis Saxonum, 1864.
	AH 2114.2	Steinleitner, Franz Seraph. Die Beicht im Zusammenhange mit der sakralen Rechtspflege in der Antike. Inaug. Diss. München, 1913.
	AH 2928.5	Steinmann, W. Das Gebiet von Heraklea Pontica. Rostock, 1869.
	AH 3017.15.1	Steinmetzer, Franz Xaver. Die babylonischen Kudurru (Grenzsteine) als Urkundenform. Paderborn, 1968.
	AH 7239.13	Steinwender, T. Die römische Taktik zur Zeit der Manipularstellung. Danzig, 1913.
	AH 7239.08	Steinwender, T. Ursprung und Entwickelung. Danzig, 1908.
	AH 3017.5F	La stèle des vautours. (Heuzey, L.) Paris, 1884.
	Eg 609.40F	Die Stelen der thebanischen Felsgräber. (Hermann, Alfred.) Glüchstadt, 1940.
	AH 7509.34.20	Stella, L.A. Druso. Gleno, 1934.
	AH 8608.8.10	Stella, Luigia A. Italia antica sul mare. Milano, 1930.
	AH 7058.87.5	Stella Maranca, F. Il tribunato della Plebe. Lanciano, 1901.
	AH 859.7	Die Stellung der Frau und der vorgriechischen Mittelmeerkultur. (Kornemann, Ernst.) Heidelberg, 1927.
	AH 4859.19	Stellung der griechischen Frau. (Matthias, T.) Zittau, 1893.
	AH 7859.9	Die Stellung der kaiserlichen Frauen aus dem julisch-claudischen Wause. (Sandels, Friedrich.) Darmstadt, 1912.
	Eg 459.60.5	Die Stellung des Königs im alten Reich. (Grediche, Hans.) Weisbaden, 1960.
	AH 7628.92	Stellung Kaiser Hadrians. (Hitzig, H.F.) Zürich, 1892.
	AH 4958.43	Stephani, L. Reise durch...nördlichen Griechenlandes. Leipzig, 1843.
	AH 3002.65.5	Stephens, Ferris J. Studies of the cuneiform tablets from Cappadocia. n.p., 1925.
	AH 4819.14	Stephens, Kate. The Greek spirit. N.Y., 1914.
	AH 7178.91A	Stephenson, A. Public lands and agrarian laws. Baltimore, 1891.
	AH 409.28	The steppe and the sown. (Peake, Harold.) New Haven, 1928.
	AH 5157.20	Stergiopoulos, K.D. He archaia aitōlia. En Athēnais, 1939.
	AH 7468.83	Stern, Ernst von. Catilina und die Parterkämpfe. Dorpat, 1883.
	AH 4238.72	Stettin, Prussia. Festungen und Festungskrieg der Griechen. Stettin, 1872.
	AH 849.6	Steuer, R.O. Myrrhe und Stakte. Wien, 1933.
	Eg 1159.59	Steuer, Robert. Ancient Egyptian and Cnidian medicine. Berkeley, 1959.
	AH 7489.30	Stevenson, G.H. The Roman Empire. London, 1930.
	AH 7089.39A	Stevenson, G.H. Roman provincial administration. Oxford, 1939.
	AH 3150.7A	Stevenson, J.H. Assyrian and Babylonian contracts. N.Y., 1902.
	AH 819.66	Stewart, Z. The ancient world. Englewood Cliffs, 1966.
	AH 1279.31	Stewart-Vargas, Guillermo. Historia del Oriente antiguo y Medo Persa. Montevideo, 1931.
	AH 5763.10	Stibbe, C.M. Sparta. Geschiedenis en cultuur der Spartanen van praehistorie tot Perzische oorlogen. Bussum, 1969.
	AH 848.5	Stieglitz, C.L. Archäologische Unterhaltungen. Leipzig, 1820.
	AH 4499.34	Stier, Hans E. Eine Grosstat der attischen Geschichte, die sog. Schlacht bei Oinoë. Stuttgart, 1934.
	AH 7237.64.5	Stierneman. Principes de l'art de la guerre. Strasbourg, 1765.
	AH 919.14	Stiftungen in der griechischen und römischen Antike. (Laum, Bernhard.) Leipzig, 1914. 2v.
	AH 919.14.1	Stiftungen in der griechischen und römischen Antike. v.1-2. (Laum, Bernhard.) Aalen, 1964.
	AH 7798.84	Stilicho. (Keller, Rudolf.) Berlin, 1884.
	AH 7238.77	Stille, Wilhelm. Historia legionum auxiliorumqui ende ab execessu divi Augusti usque ad Vespasiani tempora. Kiliae, 1877.
	AH 7169.04.3	Stintzing, W. Mancipatio. Leipzig, 1904.
	AH 4819.11.3A	Stobart, J.C. The glory that was Greece. London, 1911.
	AH 4819.11.4	Stobart, J.C. The glory that was Greece. London, 1921.
	AH 4819.11.5	Stobart, J.C. The glory that was Greece. N.Y., 1935.
	AH 7819.11.5A	Stobart, J.C. The grandeur that was Rome; a survey of Roman culture. London, 1912.
	AH 7819.11.9A	Stobart, J.C. The grandeur that was Rome; a survey of Roman culture. N.Y., 1935.
	AH 7819.11.12	Stobart, J.C. The grandeur that was Rome. 4. ed. London, 1961.
	AH 7058.72.5	Stobbe, H.F. Zum Capitel von den Consules Suffecti unter den Kaisern. n.p., n.d.
	AH 7478.87.5	Stocchi, Giuseppe. Due studî di storia romana. Firenze, 1887.
	Eg 509.42F	Stock, Hanns. Studien zur Geschichte und Archäologie. Glüchstadt, 1942.
	AH 7161.23	Stockar, H. Entzug der väterlichen Gewalt. Zürich, 1903.
	AH 3963.162	Stockholm. Statens Historiska Museum. Från bibelns land. 2. uppl. Stockholm, 1955.
	AH 7478.87	Stoffel. Histoire de Jules César. Atlas. Paris, 1887. 3v.
	AH 4819.58	Stokes, Adrian Durham. Greek culture and the ego. London, 1958.
	AH 4818.70	Stoll, H.W. Bilder aus dem altgriechischen Leben. Leipzig, 1870.
	AH 7818.71	Stoll, H.W. Bilder aus dem altrömischen Leben. Leipzig, 1877.
NEDL	AH 4278.68.2	Stoll, H.W. Geschichte der Griechen bis zur Unterwerfung unter Rom. 2. Aufl. Hannover, 1871. 2v.
	AH 338.72	Stoll, H.W. Geschichte der Griechen und Römer in Biographien. 2. Aufl. Leipzig, 1872. 2v.
Htn	AH 7278.69.2*	Stoll, H.W. Geschichte der Römer bis zum Untergange der Republik. 2. Aufl. Hannover, 1871. 2v.
	AH 7239.12	Stolle, F. Das Lager und Heer der Römer. Strassburg, 1912.
	AH 7238.50.2	Stolze, F. Triumph and ovation. Rostock, 1874.
	AH 3016.13F	The stones of Assyria. (Gadd, C.J.) London, 1936.
	AH 3151.3	Stooss, Carl. Das babylonische Strafrecht Hammurabis. Bern, 1903.
	AH 7278.81	Storia...di Roma. (Pantaleoni, D.) Torino, 1881.
NEDL	AH 278.53	La storia antica. (Lamé-Fleury, J.R.) Venezia, 1853.
NEDL	AH 277.34.25	Storia antica. (Rollin, Charles.) Livorno, 1835. 11v.
NEDL	AH 278.47.10	Storia antica. Torino, 1847.
NEDL	AH 277.34.27	Storia antica e romana. 1. ed. (Rollin, Charles.) Firenze, 1828-32. 49v.
	AH 7659.13	Storia critica di Roma durante i primi cinque secoli. v.1-4. (Pais, E.) Roma, 1913- 5v.
	AH 7449.27	Storia de Roma durante le guerre puniche. 2. ed. (Pais, Ettore.) Torino, 1935. 2v.
	AH 8907.44	Storia degli Etruschi. (Signorelli, Mario.) Roma, 1969.
	AH 4279.42	Storia dei greci dalle origini alla fine del secolo V. 3. ed. (Sanctis, G. de.) Firenze, 1942. 2v.
	AH 9157.5	Storia dei lucani. (Tropea, G.) Messina, 1894.
	AH 7279.07	Storia dei Romani. v.1-4, pt.1-3. (Sanctis, G. de.) Torino, 1907. 8v.
	AH 7139.01.3	Storia del diritto romano. (Costa, E.) Bologna, 1901. 2v.
	AH 7149.06	Storia del diritto romano. (Costa, Emilio.) Firenze, 1906.
	AH 7138.78.10	Storia del diritto romano. (Padelletti, G.) Firenze, 1878.
	AH 7138.95	Storia del diritto romano. 2. ed. (Landucci, L.) Verona, 1898. 2v.
	AH 7039.58	Storia della costituzione romana. v.1-6. (Martino, Francesco de.) Napoli, 1958-72. 7v.
	AH 8647.10.5	Storia della Magna Grecia. (Ciaceri, E.) Milano, 1927-32. 3v.
	AH 7203.146	Storia della ricerca delle interpolazioninel Corpus iuris Giustinianeo. (Palazzini Fivetti, Luigi.) Milano, 1953.
	AH 9558.3	Storia della Sardegna e della Corsica durante il dominio romano. (Pais, Ettore.) Roma, 1923. 2v.
	AH 9607.17	Storia della Sicilia. (Pais, Ettore.) Torino, 1894.
	AH 9607.9.25	La storia della Sicilia nell'antichità. (Revelli, P.) Pinerolo, 1902.
	AH 8990.5	Storia dell'antica Torino, Julia Augusta Taurinorum. (Promis, Carlo.) Torino, 1869.
	AH 279.13.4	Una "storia dell'antichità". (Porzio, G.) Milano, 1919.
	AH 3171.10	Storia delle letterature dell'antica mesopotamia. (Rinaldi, Giovanni.) Milano, 1957.
	AH 8007.21	Storia delle province romane dell'Africa. (Romanelli, P.) Roma, 1959.
	AH 8607.2.5	Storia dell'Italia antica. (Pais, Ettore.) Roma, 1925. 2v.
	AH 8607.5.5	Storia dell'Italia antica. 3. ed. (Vannucci, A.) Milano, 1873-76. 4v.
	AH 8607.2.7	Storia dell'Italia antica e della Sicilia per l'età anteriore al dominio romano. 2. ed. (Pais, Ettore.) Torino, 1933. 2v.
	AH 3357.8	Storia di Cirene. (Thrige, Johann P.) Verbania, 1948.
	AH 7799.05	Storia di Ezio generale dell'Impero Sotto Valentiniano III. (Bugiani, Carlo.) Firenze, 1905.

AH 7279.34.15F — Storia di Roma. (Bertolini, F.) Milano, 1934.

AH 7279.38 — Storia di Roma. (Rome. Instituto di Studi Romani.) Bologna, 1938.

AH 7278.98 — Storia di Roma. v.1, pt.1-2. (Pais, Ettore.) Torino, 1898. 2v.

AH 7279.38.5 — Storia di Roma. v.1-. (Rome. Instituto di Studi Romani.) Bologna, 1938- 23v.

AH 7408.84 — Storia di Roma. v.3. (Bonghi, R.) Milano, 1896.

AH 7278.54.32.5 — Storia di Roma antica. (Mommsen, T.) Torino, 1943. 3v.

AH 7279.52 — Storia di Roma e del mondo romana. (Pareti, L.) Torino, 1952- 6v.

AH 9639.9.5 — Storia di Siracusa antica. 2. ed. (Giuliano, Luigi.) Milano, 1928.

AH 5759.7 — Storia di Sparta arcaica. (Pareti, Luigi.) Firenze, 1917.

AH 3941.5 — Storia di Ugarit nell'età degli archivi politici. (Liverari, Mario.) Roma, 1962.

AH 8607.5 — Storia d'Italia. (Vannucci, A.) Firenze, 1851. 4v.

AH 8607.12 — Storia d'Italia dalle origini alla conquista romana. (Sesti, Luigi.) Milano, 1960.

AH 3807.10 — Storia e civiltà dei Semiti. (Moscati, Sabatino.) Bari, 1949.

AH 7889.26.15 — Storia economica e sociale dell'Impero romano. (Rostovtsev, M.I.) Firenze, 1946.

AH 4408.91 — Storia greca. (Beloch, J.) Roma, 1891.

AH 4279.22.10 — Storia greca. (Ciccotti, Ettore.) Firenze, 1922.

AH 4279.67 — Storia greca. (Pugliese Carratelli, Giovanni.) Milano, 1967.

AH 9308.5 — Storia politica civile...di Trentani. (Del Rosso, G.) Campobasso, 1887.

AH 7488.55 — La storia romana. (Lamé Fleury, J.R.) Milano, 1855.

AH 7278.54.32 — Storia romana. (Mommsen, T.) Torino, 1857-63. 3v.

AH 7279.60 — Storia romana dagli etruschi a Tedosio. (Levi, Mario Attilio.) Milano, 1960.

AH 7309.54 — Storia romana e storiografia moderna. (Mazzarino, Santo.) Napoli, 1954.

AH 8986.10 — Storia romana 1962-63. Epigrafia latina; il Piemonte preromano e romano. Milano, 1962.

AH 7279.20.7 — Storie de Troja et de Roma altrimenti dette Liber ystoriarum Romanorum. (Monaci, Ernesto.) Roma, 1920.

VAH 7278.20 — Stories from Roman history, by a lady. Boston, 182-?

Eg 1109.00 — Stories of the high priests of Memphis. [Sethon-Khamuas]. v.1, Atlas. (Griffith, F.L.) Oxford, 1900. 2v.

AH 4309.54.5 — Storiografia e fonti della storia greca. (Arias, Paolo E.) Bologna, 1954.

AH 7299.72 — Storoni Mazzolani. L'impero sena fine. Milano, 1972.

AH 7099.67 — Storoni Mazzolani, Lidia. L'idea di città nel mondo romano. Milano, 1967.

AH 7099.67.1 — Storoni Mazzolani, Lidia. The idea of the city in Roman thought. London, 1970.

AH 4558.87.3 — Story of Alexander's empire. (Mahaffy, J.P.) N.Y., 1887.

Eg 278.87 — The story of ancient Egypt. (Rawlinson, George.) N.Y., 1887.

Eg 278.87.3 — The story of ancient Egypt. (Rawlinson, George.) N.Y., 1889.

Eg 278.93 — The story of ancient Egypt. (Rawlinson, George.) N.Y., 1893.

AH 279.12.7 — The story of ancient nations. (Westermann, William L.) N.Y., 1912.

AH 5307.23 — Story of Athens. (Butler, Howard C.) London, 1902.

AH 5307.23.5 — Story of Athens. (Butler, Howard C.) N.Y., 1902.

AH 8073.7 — Story of Carthage. Photoreproduction. (Church, A.J.) N.Y., 1886.

AH 3021.2.5 — The story of Chaldea. 2. ed. (Ragozin, Zénaide A.) N.Y., 1890.

AH 3021.2.10 — The story of Chaldea from the earliest times to the rise of Assyria. 2. ed. (Ragozin, Zénaide A.) N.Y., 1896.

AH 4278.85.5 — The story of Greece. (Harrison, J.A.) N.Y., 1885.

AH 4278.85.7 — The story of Greece. (Harrison, J.A.) N.Y., 1887.

AH 8229.5 — The story of Ilkley in Roman times. (Fletcher, Elsie.) Skipton, 1966.

AH 4842.75A — The story of instruction. (Moore, E.C.) N.Y., 1936.

AH 3507.7 — Story of Media, Babylon and Persia. (Ragozin, Z.A.) N.Y., 1888.

AH 3607.11A — Story of Parthia. (Rawlinson, G.) N.Y., 1893.

AH 3657.15 — Story of Persia. (Benjamin, S.G.W.) N.Y., 1887.

AH 3707.11A — Story of Phoenicia. (Rawlinson, G.) N.Y., 1889.

AH 3707.11.2 — Story of Phoenicia. (Rawlinson, G.) N.Y., 1886.

NEDL AH 7278.96 — Story of Romans. (Guerber, H.A.) N.Y., 1896.

AH 7279.01.3 — Story of Rome. (Botsford, G.W.) N.Y., 1903.

AH 7278.85.21 — Story of Rome. (Gilman, A.) N.Y., 1885.

NEDL AH 7278.88 — The story of Rome. (Gilman, A.) N.Y., 1888.

AH 9607.15A — Story of Sicily, Phoenician, Greek and Roman. (Freeman, E.A.) N.Y., 1892.

AH 9777.23A — Story of the Goths. (Bradley, Henry.) N.Y., 1888.

AH 3075.10 — The story of the nations: story of Assyria. (Ragozin, Z.A.) N.Y., 1887.

AH 3021.2A — The story of the nations: story of Chaldea. (Ragozin, Zénaide A.) N.Y., 1886.

Eg 279.08.5 — The story of the pharaohs. (Baikie, James.) London, 1908.

Eg 279.17 — The story of the pharaohs. 2. ed. (Baikie, James.) London, 1917.

AH 3012.22 — Stosunki agrarne w paristure Sargonidów. Wyd. 1. (Lablocha, Yulia.) Poznan, 1971.

AH 8353.2 — Stout, S.E. Governors of Moesia. Princeton, 1911.

AH 7159.12A — Strachan-Davidson, J.L. Problems of the Roman criminal law. Oxford, 1912. 2v.

Eg 708.97 — Strack, M.L. Die Dynastie der Ptolemäer. Berlin, 1897.

AH 7278.54.46 — Straeuli, Hans Heinrich. Theodor Mommsen's Römische Geschichte. Zuerich, 1948.

AH 7114.18 — Strafser, G. Versuch über die römische Plebejer. Elberfeld, 1832.

AH 3207.6 — Strana tysiachi gorodov. (Masson, Vadim M.) Moskva, 1966.

AH 4114.19A — The stranger at the gate. (Haarhoff, T.J.) London, 1938.

AH 4114.19.5 — The stranger at the gate. (Haarhoff, T.J.) Oxford, 1948.

AH 7489.39 — Strank, J.A. Vom Herrscherideal in der Spätantike. Stuttgart, 1939.

AH 4559.34.5 — Strasburger, H. Ptolemaios und Alexander. Leipzig, 1934.

AH 7479.38.6 — Strasburger, Hermann. Caesars Eintritt in die Geschichte. Darmstadt, 1966.

AH 3002.2.4 — Strassmaier, J.N. Alphabetisches Verzeichniss. Leipzig, 1886.

AH 4149.32 — Strateegas autokrator. Inaug. Diss. Engelsdorf, 1932. 4v.

AH 7059.18 — Stratēgos Ypatos. Thèse. (Holleaux, M.) Paris, 1918.

AH 808.37 — Strauchius, G. Treatise...in chronology. London, 1722.

AH 4039.64A — Strauss, L. The city and man. Chicago, 1964.

AH 3075.5 — Strauss, Otto. Ninive und das Wort Gottes. Berlin, 1855.

Eg 878.89 — Strauss, V. von. Der altägyptische Götterglaube. Heidelberg, 1889. 2v.

AH 3013.22 — Streber, F. Über die Mauern von Babylon. München, 1849.

AH 3097.5 — Streck, Maximilian. Assurbanipal und die letzen assyrischen Könige. Leipzig, 1916. 3v.

NEDL AH 299.01 — Strehl, Willy. Grundriss der alten Geschichte. Breslau, 1901. 2v.

AH 299.13 — Strehl, Willy. Grundriss der alten Geschichte und Quellenkundl. 2. Aufl. Breslau, 1913. 2v.

AH 7468.87 — Strehl, Willy. M. Livius Drusus. Marburg, 1887.

AH 9610.22 — Stroheker, Karl. Dionysios I. Wiesbaden, 1958.

AH 7769.65 — Stroheker, Karl Friedrich. Germanentum und Spätantike. Zürich, 1965.

AH 8503.4 — Stroheker, Karl Friedrich. Der senatorische Adel in spätaniken Gallien. Tübingen, 1948.

AH 4039.22.5 — Strohm, Gustav. Demos und Monarch. Stuttgart, 1922.

AH 8913.30 — Strong, Donald Emrys. The early Etruscans. London, 1968.

Eg 27.82 — Stroth, F.A. Aegyptiaca sev veterum scriptorum. Gothae, 1782.

AH 4202.15 — Stroud, Ronald S. Drakon's law on homicide. Berkeley, 1968.

AH 7539.29 — Stroux, J. Eine Gerichtsreform des Kaisers Claudius. München, 1929.

AH 3005.830.5 — Stručný přehled mých vědeckých objevů. (Hrozný, Bedřich.) Praha, 1848.

AH 3151.5 — Structure of the Hammurabi code. (Lyon, D.G.) New Haven, 1904.

AH 7448.94.2 — The struggle for Empire. (Masom, W.J.) London, 1894.

AH 1278.76.15 — Struggle of the nations, Egypt, Syria and Assyria. (Maspero, Gaston.) N.Y., 1897.

AH 7269.65.1 — Struktur und Entwicklung des römischen Volkerrechte im dritten und zweiten Jahrhundert v. Chr. (Dahlheim, Werner.) München, 1968.

AH 7169.55 — La struttura dell'obbligazione romana e il problema della sua genesi. (Betti, Emilio.) Milano, 1955.

AH 7867.5 — Struve, B.G. Antiquitatum Romanorum syntagma. Jenae, 1701.

AH 7203.143.2 — Struve, G.A. Syntagmatis juris civilis. 2. ed. Francofurti, 1718.

AH 29.50 — Struve, V.V. Geschichte der alten Welt; Christomathie. Berlin, 1954-57. 3v.

AH 1299.68 — Struve, Vasilii V. Etudy po istorii Severnogo Prichernomor'ia, Kavkazo i Srednei Azii. Leningrad, 1968.

AH 3052.6.5 — Struve, Vasilii V. Gosudarstvo Lagash. Moskva, 1961.

AH 1279.41 — Struve, Vasilii V. Istoriia drevnego Vostoka. Leningrad, 1941.

AH 7539.38 — Stuart, Meriwether. Portraiture of Claudius. Thesis. N.Y., 1938.

AH 8667.4 — Stuart-Jones, H. Classical Rome. London, 1910.

AH 9423.5 — Stucchi, S. Forum Iulii (Cividale del Friuli). Roma, 1951.

Eg 459.62 — Stuchevskii, Iosef A. Khramovaia forma tsarskogo khoz. drevnego Egypta. Moskva, 1962.

Eg 299.66 — Stuchevskii, Iosif A. Zavisimoe naselenie drevnego Egipta. Moskva, 1966.

AH 850.3F — Stuck, J.G. Antiquitatum convivialium. Lugduni Batavorum, 1695.

AH 1278.71.7 — The student's ancient history. The ancient history of the East. (Smith, Philip.) N.Y., 1894.

AH 7653.20 — The student's companion to Gibbon. (Collins, William M.) Melbourne, 1957.

NEDL AH 7651.10A — Student's Gibbon. (Gibbon, Edward.) N.Y., 1857.

NEDL AH 7651.15 — Student's Gibbon. History of Roman Empire. (Gibbon, Edward.) London, 1868.

NEDL AH 7651.12 — Student's Gibbon. History of Roman Empire. (Gibbon, Edward.) N.Y., 1859.

NEDL AH 7651.12.5 — Student's Gibbon. History of Roman Empire. (Gibbon, Edward.) N.Y., 1867.

NEDL AH 7651.13 — Student's Gibbon. History of Roman Empire. (Gibbon, Edward.) N.Y., 1868.

AH 4139.30 — Studi di diritto attico. (Paoli, Ugo Enrico.) Firenze, 1930.

AH 298.91 — Studi di storia antica. v.1-7. (Beloch, J.) Roma, 1891. 3v.

AH 279.69 — Studi di storia antica in memoria di Luca de Regibus. Genova, 1969.

AH 299.71 — Studi di storiografia antica. In memoria di Leonardo Ferrero. Torino, 1971.

AH 4659.29.10 — Studi ellenistíci. (Corradi, G.) Torino, 1929.

AH 938.93 — Gli studi geografici nel I secolo dell'impero romano. (Columba, G.M.) Torino, 1893.

AH 7509.37.20 — Gli studi germanici sulla figura e l'opera di Augusto e sulla fondazione dell'Impero romano. (Kornemann, E.) Spoleto, 1937.

AH 7179.12 — Studi graccani. (Cardinali, G.) Roma, 1912.

AH 279.58.5 — Studi minori di storia antica. (Pareti, Luigi.) Roma, 1958-69. 4v.

AH 899.27F — Studi reassuntivi di agricoltura antica. (Acerbo, Giacomo.) Roma, 1927.

AH 8507.3 — Studi Romana. (Zumpt, A.W.) Berolini, 1859.

AH 7458.96 — Studi romani. (Pascal, Carlo.) Torino, 1896.

AH 9608.5 — Studi siciliani ed italioti. (Pareti, Luigi.) Firenze, 1920.

AH 7299.04 — Studi storici. (Garofalo, F.P.) Noto, 1904.

AH 4229.33 — Studi sul processo attico. (Paoli, U.E.) Padova, 1933.

AH 8913.28.5 — Studi sulla città antica. (Convegno di studi sulla città etrusca e italica preromana.) Bologna, 1970.

AH 7169.33 — Studi sulla derelizione nel diritto romano. (Romano, S.) Padova, 1933.

AH 7909.58 — Studi sulla società romana; il lavoro artistico. (Calabi Limentani, Ida.) Milano, 1958.

AH 7709.61 — Studi sull'epigrafia di Aureliano. (Sotgiu, Giovanna.) Palmero, 1961.

AH 7469.14 — Studi sull'età dei Gracchi. (Fraccaro, P.) Città di Castello, 1914.

AH 3963.140 — Studi sull'Oriente e la Bibbia. Genova, 1967.

AH 3002.135A — Studia ad tabulas cuneiformas collectas ab De Liagre Böhl pertinentia. v.1, pt.1-2; 3. (Nederkands Institut voor het Nabije Oosten, Leyden.) Leiden, 1952- 3v.

Eg 459.49F — Studia aegyptiaca. v.1-2. Roma, 1938-49.

AH 1130.36.5 — Studia et documenta ad iura orientia antiqui pertinentia. Leiden. 1-9 7v.

AH 7201.1.5 — Studia Gaiana. Leiden. 1,1948+ 4v.

AH 7468.79 — Studia in Ti. Gracchi historiam. (Byvanck, W.G.C.) Lugdunum Batavorum, 1879.

AH 4819.67.20 — Studia varia. Auftsätze zur Kunst und Kultur der Antike mit Nachträgen. (Moebius, Hans.) Wiesbaden, 1967.

Author and Title Listing

Author and Title Listing

AH 8708.5 — Sull'origine dei Messapi. (Maggiulli, Pasquale.) Lecce, 1934.

AH 7168.64 — Sulpius, B. von. Novation und Delegation. Berlin, 1864.

AH 7239.20.7 — Sulser, Jakob. Disciplina, Beiträge zur inneren Geschichte des römischen Heeres von Augustus bis Vespasian. Inaug. Diss. Dachau, 1920.

AH 3965.13 — Sulzberger, M. The status of labor in ancient Israel. Philadelphia, 1923.

NEDL AH 278.48.5 — Sumario de la historia de Grecia i de Roma. (Vendel-Heyl, L.A.) Santiago, 1848. 2 pam.

AH 3013.960.5 — Sumer. (Parrot, André.) London, 1960.

AH 3022.24 — Sumer e Akkad; la vita economica. (Resina, Guiseppe.) Catania, 1958.

AH 3020.11 — Sumer et Akkad. (Jean, Charles Francois.) Paris, 1923.

AH 3020.76 — Sumerian and Akkadian cuneiform texts in the collection of the World Heritage Museum of the University of Illinois. Urbana, 1972. 2v.

AH 3181.10 — Sumerian and Babylonian psalms. (Langdon, S.) Paris, 1909.

AH 3020.30 — Sumerian economic texts from the third Ur dynasty. (Jones, Tom B.) Minneapolis, 1961.

AH 3020.16F — Sumerian epics and myths. (Chiera, Edward.) Chicago, 1934.

AH 3181.5.2 — Sumerian hymns. (Vanderburgh, F.A.) N.Y., 1908.

AH 3181.5 — Sumerian hymns. Thesis. (Vanderburgh, F.A.) N.Y., 1908.

AH 3020.15F — Sumerian lexical texts from the temple school of Nippur. (Chiera, Edward.) Chicago, 1929.

AH 3155.28 — Sumerian mythology. (Kramer, Samuel N.) Philadelphia, 1944.

AH 3189.3A — Sumerian proverbs. (Gordon, Edmund I.) Philadelphia, 1959.

AH 3152.3 — Sumerian records from Drehem. (Nesbit, William M.) N.Y., 1914.

AH 3020.7F — Sumerian tablets from Umma. (John Rylands Library. Manchester.) Manchester, 1915.

AH 3020.10FA — Sumerian tablets in the Harvard Semitic Museum. Pt.1-2. (Harvard University. Semitic Museum.) Cambridge, Mass., 1912. 2v.

AH 3020.6 — Sumerian temple documents. (Margolis, E.) N.Y., 1915.

AH 3020.14 — Sumerian temple records of the late Ur dynasty. (Lutz, H.F.) Berkeley, 1928.

AH 3020.17F — Sumerian texts of varied contents. (Chiera, Edward.) Chicago, 1934.

AH 3022.9A — The Sumerians. (Woolley, Charles L.) Oxford, 1928.

AH 3022.17.10 — The Sumerians: their history. (Kramer, S.N.) Chicago, 1963.

AH 3181.11.1 — Sumerisch-akkadische Parallelen zum Aufbau alttestamentlicher Psalmen. Diss. (Stummer, Friedrich.) Paderborn, 1968.

AH 3181.7 — Sumerisch Babylonische Hymnen. (Banks, E.J.) Leipzig, 1897.

AH 3181.9 — Sumerisch-babylonische Hymnen und Gebete an Samas. (Schollmeyer, A.) Paderborn, 1912.

AH 3181.15 — Sumerische Königshymnen, der Isin-Zeit. (Römer, Willem H.P.) Leiden, 1965.

AH 3176.2 — Sumerische Kultlyrik. (Krecher, Joachim.) Wiesbaden, 1966.

AH 3181.13 — Sumerische und akkadische Hymnen und Gebete. (Falkenstein, Adam.) Zurich, 1953.

AH 3020.4 — Die sumerische und akkadischen Königsinschriften. (Thureau-Dangin, F.) Leipzig, 1907.

AH 3020.5 — Die sumerischen Familiengesetze. (Haupt, Paul.) Leipzig, 1879.

AH 3022.27 — Sümeroloji arastirmalari, 1940-1941. (Ankara. Universite.) Istanbul, 1941.

Eg 278.59.12 — Summary of recent discoveries in biblical chronology. 2. ed. (Seyffarth, G.) N.Y., 1859.

AH 7138.49 — Summary of Roman civil law. (Colquhoun, P.) London, 1849. 4v.

AH 7137.32 — Summary of the Roman law. (Taylor, J.) London, 1772.

AH 2816.5 — A summer in Phrygia. (Anderson, J.G.C.) n.p., 1897.

AH 7809.44 — Sunday in Roman paganism, a history of the planetary week and its "day of the sun". (Odom, R.L.) Washington, D.C., 1944.

AH 5310.11 — Sundwall, J. Epigraphische Beiträge zur sozial-politischen Geschichte Athens im Zeitalter des Demosthenes. Leipzig, 1906.

AH 7799.15 — Sundwall, J. Weströmische Studien. Berlin, 1915.

Htn AH 7276.34F* — Supplicum libellorum August regis. (Bellendenus, G.) Paris, 1634.

AH 4049.43 — Supreme political power in Greek literature of the fourth century B.C. Thesis. (Levitt, Bella.) Philadelphia, 1943.

AH 7239.03.4 — Sur l'aes pararium. (Helbig, W.) Paris, 1903. 2 pam.

AH 3160.6.5 — Sur le nom de...Tammouz. (Lenormant, F.) Paris, 1873.

AH 4959.00.7 — Sur les traces de Pausanias a travers la Grèce ancienne. (Frazer, James G.) Paris, 1923.

AH 4860.5 — Suręcicki, H. Pflege der Kinder bei den Griechen. Breslau, 1877.

AH 279.29 — Survey of ancient history to the death of Constantine. (Laistner, Max L.W.) Boston, 1929.

AH 4818.96A — Survey of Greek civilization. (Mahaffy, J.P.) N.Y., 1896.

AH 4818.96.5A — Survey of Greek civilization. (Mahaffy, J.P.) N.Y., 1899.

AH 8548.110 — A survey of research on an early phase of Celtic culture. (Navarro, J.M. de.) London, 1936.

AH 3889.5 — Susa. (Billerbeck, A.) Leipzig, 1893.

AH 3867.5F — A Suse journal des fouilles, 1884-86. (Dieulafoy, J.A.) Paris, 1888.

AH 5123.5 — Susini, Giancarlo. Nuove scoperte sulla storia di Coo. Bologna, 1957.

AH 7139.01.8 — Susthema pomaikou dikaiou. (Theophanopoulos, D.) Athens, 1900. 3 pam.

Eg 1099.53 — Suys, Émile. Etude sur le Conte du Fellah Plaideur. Roma, 1933.

AH 7819.65.5 — Suzdal'skii, Jurii P. Na semi kholmakh. 2. izd. Moskva, 1965.

AH 8913.20F — Svenska Institutet i Rom. Etruscan culture, land and people. N.Y., 1963.

AH 9777.19.10 — Svensson, Jacob Vilhelm. De sydsvenska folknammen hos Jordanes. Karlstad, 1914.

AH 279.63.10 — Sverdlovsk, Russia (City). Ural'skii gosudarstvennyi universitet. Antichnaia drevnost' i srednie veka. v.1-2,4-5,7. v.1,5; Photoreproduction. Sverdlovsk, 1963-5v.

AH 7039.45 — Lo sviluppo costituzionale di Roma dalle origini alla fine della repubblica. (Lombardi, Gabrio.) Roma, 1945.

AH 4808.99 — Svoronos, J.M. Der athenische Volkskalender. Athens, 1899.

AH 279.50A — Swain, J.W. The ancient world. N.Y., 1950. 2v.

AH 7114.7 — Swingar, G.H.D. Commentatio de Patronatus. Groningae, 1823.

AH 4299.00.4 — Swoboda, H. Greek history. London, 1920.

AH 4278.96 — Swoboda, H. Griechische Geschichte. Leipzig, 1896.

AH 4039.15 — Swoboda, H. Die griechischen Bünde und der moderner Bundesstaat. Prag, 1915.

AH 4078.90 — Swoboda, H. Griechischen Volksbeschlüsse. Leipzig, 1890.

AH 8789.7 — Sybaris, les grecs en Italie. (Tabouis, Geneviève R.) Paris, 1958.

AH 8789.5 — Sybaris. (Callaway, Joseph S.) Baltimore, 1950.

AH 5308.6 — Sycophancy in Athens. Thesis. (Lofberg, John O.) Chicago, 1917.

AH 9777.19.10 — De sydsvenska folknammen hos Jordanes. (Svensson, Jacob Vilhelm.) Karlstad, 1914.

AH 7469.31 — Sylla; ou, La monarchie manquée. (Carcopino, Jérôme.) Paris, 1931.

AH 3002.98 — Syllabaire cunéiforme. (Fossey, C.) Paris, 1901.

AH 279.37 — A syllabus for ancient history. (Finkelstein, M.I.) N.Y., 1937.

AH 4299.10.3 — Syllogos pros. Eikones ek tès archaias. Athēnai, n.d.

AH 2760.5 — Symbolae ad Eumenis II. Pergamenorum regis historiam. Inaug. Diss. (Meischke, Kurt.) Lipsiae, 1892.

AH 8549.170.5 — Le symbolisme dans les sanctuaires de la Gaule. (Benoît, Fernand.) Bruxelles, 1970.

AH 833.7 — Le symbolisme de l'acrobatie antique. (Deonna, W.) Berchem, 1953.

AH 3160.16 — Symbols of the gods in Mesopotamian art. (Van Buren, Elizabeth.) Roma, 1945.

AH 8258.1 — Syme, Ronald. Danubian papers. Bucharest, 1971.

AH 7469.39 — Syme, Ronald. The Roman revolution. Oxford, 1939.

AH 7469.39.3 — Syme, Ronald. The Roman revolution. Oxford, 1956.

AH 1812.5 — Symposium on Urbanization and Cultural Development in the Ancient Near East, University of Chicago, 1958. City invincible. Chicago, 1960.

AH 7132.10 — Sympotica Franz Wieacker sexagenario Sasbachwaldeni a suis libata. Göttingen, 1970.

AH 4148.80 — Synedrien der Bundesgenossen. (Lenz, Emil.) Elbing, 1880.

AH 5553.7 — Der Synoikismos von Elis. (Curtius, Ernst.) Berlin, 1895.

AH 7818.28.3 — Synopsis of Roman antiquities. (Lanktree, J.) London, 1857.

AH 7469.23.5 — Synoský prokonsulát M. Calpurnia Bibula. (Dobiás, J.) Praha, 1923.

AH 7203.143.2 — Syntagmatis juris civilis. 2. ed. (Struve, G.A.) Francofurti, 1718.

AH 7162.7 — Syntrophius, T.F. Instrumentum donationis ineditum. Vratislaviae, 1838.

AH 9639.14 — Syrakus; zur Topographie und Geschichte einer griechischer Stadt. (Droegemueller, Hans-Peter.) Heidelberg, 1969.

AH 9639.6 — Syrakus im zweiten peinischen Kriege. (Arendt, A.) Königsberg, 1899.

AH 3909.5 — Syria and Egypt from the Tell el Amarna letters. (Petrie, W.M.F.) London, 1908.

AH 3911.6 — Syria as Roman province. (Bouchier, E.S.) Oxford, 1916.

EgP 137.50 — Syro-Egyptian Society of London. Original papers read before. London, 1845.

Eg 808.57 — System der ägyptischen Chronologie. (Knötel, A.) Leipzig, 1857.

AH 4808.92 — Das System der attischen Zeitrechnung auf neuer Grundlage. (Israel-Holtzwart, Karl.) Frankfurt, 1892.

AH 4842.31 — System der griechische Pädagogik. v.1-2. (Hochheimers, C.F.A.) Göttingen, 1788.

AH 3964.16 — System des Altsynagogalen palästinischen Theologie aus Targum. (Weber, F.) Leipzig, 1880.

AH 7138.03.9 — System des Pandekten-Rechts. (Thibaut, F.J.) Jena, 1846. 2v.

AH 7138.27 — System des römischen Civilrechts. (Gans, E.) Berlin, 1827.

AH 7228.25.3 — System des römischen und deutschen Civil-Processrechts. 2. Aufl. (Heffter, A.W.) Bonn, 1843.

AH 3965.6.9 — Le système des poids, mesures et monnaies des israélites d'apres la Bible. (Moors, B.P.) Paris, 1904.

AH 4148.92 — Szántó, Emil. Griechische Bürgerrecht. Freiburg, 1892.

AH 4148.81.3 — Szántó, Emil. Untersuchungen über die attische Bürgerrecht. Wien, 1881.

AH 3963.80.2 — Szeke'hyi, Lajos. A bibliaí régiségtudomany kézikönyve. 2. kiadas. v.1-2. Budapest, 1896.

AH 7479.70 — Szidat, Joachim. Caesars diplomatische Tätigkeit im gallischen Krieg. Wiesbaden, 1970.

AH 819.70.10 — Szkice antyezne. wyd. 1. (Zieliński, Tadeusz.) Kraków, 1971.

AH 4840.5 — Szymanski, M. De natura familiae Graecae. Berolini, 1840.

AH 7478.83 — T. Labienus. Inaug. Diss. (Wendelmuth, Richard.) Marburg, 1883.

AH 4038.86 — Ta teah et oi en telei. Diss. (Koenig, C.) Jenae, 1886.

AH 8918.1 — Tabanelli, Mario. La medicina nel mondo degli Etruschi. Firenze, 1963.

AH 3661.6.1 — Tabari, Muhammed Ibn. Geschichte der Perser und Araber. Leyden, 1973.

AH 3964.17.10F — The tabernacle and its furniture. (Kitto, John.) London, 1849.

AH 7168.79.7 — La table de bronze d'Aljustrel. (Flach, J.) Paris, 1879.

AH 7203.138.25F — Table des Commentaires. (Voet, J.) Bruxelles, 1841.

AH 7179.20 — La table hypothécaire de Valeia. (Pachtere, F.G.) Paris, 1920.

AH 7308.76.2 — Tableau de l'Empire Romain. (Thierry, A.S.D.) Paris, 1862.

NEDL AH 7308.76A — Tableau de l'Empire Romain. (Thierry, A.S.D.) Paris, 1876.

AH 7308.65 — Tableau de l'Empire Romain. (Thierry, M. Amédée.) Paris, 1865.

AH 7308.76.3A — Tableau de l'Empire Romain. 6e éd. (Thierry, A.S.D.) Paris, 1872.

AH 1457.5 — Tableau historique de l'Asie. (Klaproth, J.) Paris, 1826.

AH 1457.5F — Tableau historique de l'Asie. Atlas. (Klaproth, J.) Paris, 1826.

AH 3657.3 — Tableau historique de l'Orient. (Ohsson.) Paris, 1804. 2v.

AH 808.77 — Tables of ancient literature and history. (Nichol, J.) Glasgow, 1877.

AH 3002.115F — Tablettes de Dréhem. (Genouillac, Henri de.) Paris, 1911.

AH 3020.55 — Tablettes économiques de Lagash (époque de la IIIe dynastie d'Ur). (Virolleaud, Charles.) Paris, 1968.

AH 8789.7 — Tabouis, Geneviève R. Sybaris, les grecs en Italie. Paris, 1958.

AH 3181.6 — Tabula Babylonica V.A. Th 246 Musei Berolinensis. (Messerschmidt, L.) Kirchain, 1896.

AH 3002.136F — Tabulae cuneiformae a F.M.T. de Liagre Böhl. v.1; 2, pt.1; 3-4. (Böhl, Franz M.T.) Leiden, 1957. 4v.

Author and Title Listing

	Call No.	Entry
	AH 3002.125F	Tabulae signorum cuneiformium in usum scholae. (Deimel, Anton.) Romae, 1910.
	AH 7498.61	Tacite et son siècle. (Dubois Guchan, E.P.) Paris, 1861. 2v.
	AH 7148.87.7	Taddei, A. Roma e isuoi municipi. Firenze, 1887.
	AH 4521.15.5	Taeger, Fritz. Alkibiades. München, 1943.
	AH 4521.15	Taeger, Fritz. Alkibiades. Stuttgart, 1925.
	AH 279.39.5	Taeger, Fritz. Das Altertum. 3. Aufl. v.2. Stuttgart, 1942.
	AH 279.39.7	Taeger, Fritz. Das Altertum. 4. Aufl. Stuttgart, 1950.
	AH 279.39.9	Taeger, Fritz. Das Altertum. 6. Aufl. Stuttgart, 1958. 2v.
	AH 4499.32	Taeger, Fritz. Ein Beitrag zur Geschichte der Pentekontaetie. Stuttgart, 1932.
	AH 4049.57	Taeger, Fritz. Charisma. Stuttgart, 1951-60. 2v.
	AH 279.48.5	Taeger, Fritz. Grundzüge der alten Geschichte. Oberursel, 1948.
	AH 819.49.5	Taeger, Fritz. Die Kultur der Antike. Köln, 1949.
	AH 7469.28.5	Taeger, Fritz. Untersuchungen zur römischen Geschichte und Quellenkunde. Stuttgart, 1928.
	AH 3159.5.15	Tänzer, Aaron. Judentum und Entwicklungslehre. Berlin, 1903.
	AH 7489.13.3	Täubler, E. Imperium Romanum. Leipzig, 1913.
	AH 7200.18	Täubler, Eugen. Untersuchungen zur Geschichte des Decemvirats und der zwölft Afdu. Berlin, 1921.
	AH 7449.21	Täubler, Eugen. Die Vorgeschichte des zweiten punischen Krieges. Berlin, 1921.
	AH 6140.2	Tafel, F. Thessalonica. Berolini, 1839.
	AH 4258.40.2F	Tafeln zu Urkunden. (Böckh, August.) Berlin, 1840.
	AH 4818.94.3	Ein Tag in alten Athen. (Kleemann, M.) Gütersloh, 1894.
	AH 4958.65	Tagebuch einer griechische Reise. (Welcker, F.G.) Berlin, 1865.
	Eg 609.68.5	Taina zolotogo groba. (Perepelkin, Iurii I.) Moskva, 1968.
	AH 3407.35	Tainy khettov. (Zamarovsky, Voitech.) Moskva, 1968.
	AH 3160.20	Takultu. (Frankena, R.) Leiden, 1954.
	AHP 30.5	Talanta; proceedings of the Dutch Archaeological and Historical Society. Groningen. 1,1969+
	AH 7278.76.10	Talbot, E. Histoire romaine. Paris, 1876.
Htn	Eg 1108.98*	The tale of the two brothers. (Papyrus d'Orbiney.) Watchung, N.J., 1898.
	Eg 1108.90	The tale of the two brothers. [Egyptian fairy-tale]. (Papyrus d'Orbiney.) n.p., 189-?
	AH 3187.10F	Tallquist, K.L. Babylonische Schenkungsbriefe. Helsingfors, 1891.
	AH 3154.11	Tallqvist, K.L. Die assyrische Beschwörungsserie Maqlû. Leipzig, 1895.
	AH 8210.7	Tamblyn, William F. The establishment of Roman power in Britain. Hamilton, Ont., 1899.
	AH 3016.55	Tammuz. (Moortgat, Anton.) Berlin, 1949.
	AH 3160.18	Tammuz-Liturgien und Verwandtes. (Witzel, M.) Roma, 1935.
	AH 7099.00	Tanfani, L. Ricerche storiche-epigrafiche. Taranto, 1900.
	Eg 990.10F	Tanis und Theben. (Beckerath, J. von.) Glückstadt, 1951.
	AH 2104.5	Tanri yaratan toprak; Anadolu. (Eyuboğlu, Ismet Zeki.) Istanbul, 1973.
	Eg 849.5F	Der Tanz im alten Ägypten nach bildlichen und inschriftlichen Zeugnissen. (Brunner-Traut, E.) N.Y., 1938.
	AH 4843.20F	Der Tanz in der Antike. (Weege, Fritz.) Halle, 1926.
Htn	AH 3957.20*	Tappan, David. Lectures on Jewish antiquities. Cambridge, 1807.
	AH 8549.81	Taranis Lithobole; étude de mythologie celtique. (Cerquand, J.F.) Avignon, 1881.
	AH 7468.98.5	Tarantino, Mario. La congiura catilinaria. Catania, 1898.
	AH 7468.98	Tarantino, Mario. Questioni cronologiche. Catania, 1898.
	AH 3740.10	Tarbox, Increase N. Tyre and Alexandria. Boston, 1865.
	AH 7138.90.5	Tardif, A. Histoire des sources du droit français. Paris, 1890.
	AH 7228.81.9	Tardif, E.J. Étude sur la Litis Contestatio en droit romain. Paris, 1881.
	AH 29.65	Tarih, devrim, sosyalizm. (Kivilcimli, Hikmet.) Istanbul, 1965.
	AH 4039.59	Tarkiainen, Tuttu. Demokratia. Helsinki, 1959.
	AH 4559.33	Tarn, W.W. Alexander the Great and the unity of mankind. London, 1933.
	AH 4609.13	Tarn, W.W. Antigonos Gonatas. Oxford, 1913.
	AH 4559.48	Tarn, William W. Alexander the Great. Cambridge, 1948. 2v.
	AH 4659.38.5	Tarn, William W. The Greeks in Bactria and India. 2. ed. Cambridge, Eng., 1951.
	AH 4659.27	Tarn, William W. Hellenistic civilization. London, 1927.
	AH 4659.27.10	Tarn, William W. Hellenistic civilization. London, 1947.
	AH 4659.27.3	Tarn, William W. Hellenistic civilization. 2. ed. London, 1930.
	AH 4659.27.15	Tarn, William W. Hellenistic civilization. 3. ed. London, 1952.
	AH 4239.30	Tarn, William W. Hellenistic military and naval developments. Cambridge, Eng., 1930.
Htn	AH 7406.32*	Il Tarquinio superbo. (Malvezzi, V.) Bologna, 1632.
	AH 4259.05	Taru, William W. The Greek warship I-II. n.p., 1905. 3 pam.
	AH 7519.02	Tarver, J.C. Tiberius the tyrant. N.Y., 1902.
	AH 7203.105	Taschenwörterbuch. Corpus juris civilis. Berlin, 1907.
	AH 9662.5	Tasti Hispaniarum provinciarum. Inaug. Diss. (Wilsdorf, D.) Lipsiae, 1878.
	AH 7058.87.3	Tasti tribunorum plebis. (Niccolini, I.) Pisis, 1898.
	Eg 819.72	Tatankhamun's Egypt. (Aldred, Cyril.) London, 1972.
	Eg 139.44.2	Taubenschlag, R. The law of Greco-Roman Egypt in the light of the papyri. 2. ed. Warszawa, 1955.
	Eg 139.44	Taubenschlag, R. The law of Greco-Roman Egypt in the light of the papyri 332 B.C.-640 A.D. v.2: supplement. N.Y., 1944. 2v.
	AH 4819.33.10	Tausend Jahre altgriechischen Lebens. (Bethe, E.) München, 1933.
	AH 889.19	Le taux du "fenus unciarum". (Appleton, C) Paris, 1919.
	AH 7138.76.20F	Tavieaux synoptiques de droit romain. (Bonjean, G.) Paris, 1876.
	AH 8954.10F	Tavola legislativa della Gallia Cisalpina. (Lama, Pietro de.) Parma, 1820.
	Eg 759.38	Taxation in Egypt from Augustus to Diocletian. (Wallace, S.L.) Princton, 1938.
	AH 308.96	Taylor, H.O. Ancient ideals. N.Y., 1896. 2v.
	AH 308.96.2	Taylor, H.O. Ancient ideals. v.2. N.Y., 1896.
	AH 308.96.5A	Taylor, H.O. Ancient ideals. 2. ed. N.Y., 1921. 2v.
Htn	AH 7137.55*	Taylor, J. Elements of the civil law. Cambridge, 1755.
	AH 7137.55.3	Taylor, J. Elements of the civil law. 3. ed. London, 1769.
	AH 7137.55.5	Taylor, J. Elements of the civil law. 3. ed. London, 1786.
	Eg 928.59	Taylor, J. The great pyramid. London, 1859.
	AH 7137.32	Taylor, J. Summary of the Roman law. London, 1772.
	AH 7167.42	Taylor, John. Commentarius ad Leges decemvirdem. Cantabrigiae, 1742.
	AH 8914.16	Taylor, Lily R. Local cults in Etruria. Rome, 1923.
	AH 7479.49.5	Taylor, Lily Ross. Party politics in the age of Caesar. Berkeley, 1949.
	AH 7079.66.5	Taylor, Lily Ross. Roman voting assemblies from the Hannibalic war to the dictatorship of Caesar. Ann Arbor, 1966.
	AH 7038.99.2	Taylor, Thomas M. Constitutional and political history of Rome. London, 1899.
	AH 7038.99.3	Taylor, Thomas M. A constitutional and political history of Rome. London, 1911.
	AH 278.45	Taylor, W.C. A manual of ancient history. N.Y., 1845.
	AH 4410.31	Taylour, William. The Mycenaeans. London, 1964.
	AH 7842.24	Teachers and administrators. (Norman, Albert Francis.) Hall, 1969.
	Eg 879.24	The teaching of Amen-em-Apt. (Amenopĕ.) London, 1924.
	Eg 879.39	The teaching of Amen-em-Apt. (McGlinchey, J.M.) Washington, 1939.
	AH 819.19.15	The technical arts and sciences of the ancients. (Neuburger, Albert.) London, 1930.
	AH 819.19.16	The technical arts and sciences of the ancients. (Neuburger, Albert.) N.Y., 1969.
	AH 819.19.10	Die Technik des Altertums. 2. Aufl. (Neuburger, Albert.) Leipzig, 1921.
	AH 8515.10	Technique et agriculture en pays trévire et rémois. (Renard, Marcel.) Bruxelles, 1959.
	AH 908.75	Technologie und Terminologie der Gewerbe. v.1-4. (Blümner, H.) Leipzig, 1875. 3v.
	AH 908.75.2	Technologie und Terminologie der Gewerbe. 2. Aufl. (Blümner, H.) Berlin, 1912.
	AH 819.70	Technology in the ancient world. (Hodges, Henry W.M.) London, 1970.
	AH 299.39.5	Teggart, F.J. Rome and China. Berkeley, 1939.
	AH 7418.99	Tegge, August. Die Staatsgewalten der römischen Republik. Bunzlau, 1899.
	AHP 30.6	Teiresias. Montreal. 1,1971+
	AHP 30.7	Teiresias. Supplement. Montreal. 1,1972+
	AH 818.90.5	Telegraphing among the ancients. (Merrians, A.C.) Cambridge, 1890.
	AH 4708.44	To telegtaion etos tès ellēnikēs eleutherias. (Paparrēgópoulos, Konstantinos.) Athēnai, 1844.
	AH 4138.68	Télfy, I. Corpus juris Attici. Lipsiae, 1868.
	AH 3404.6	Der Telipinu-Erlass. Diss. (Hittites. Laws, statutes, etc.) München? 1970?
	Eg 603.10	Tell el-Amarna. Photoreproduction. (Pendleburg, J.D.S.) London, 1935.
	Eg 603.11	Tell el-Amarna Tablets. El Amarna tablets, 359-379. Neukirchen-Vluyn, 1970.
	Eg 603.5A	Tell el-Amarna tablets. (British Museum.) London, 1892.
	Eg 603.10.5	The Tell el-Amarna tablets. (Mercer, S.A.B.) Toronto, 1939. 2v.
	AH 3013.943F	Tell Halaf. (Oppenheim, Max.) Berlin, 1943. 4v.
	AH 3013.931.5	Der Tell Halaf. (Oppenheim, Max.) Leipzig, 1931.
	AH 3060.3.20	Tello. (Parrot, André.) Paris, 1948.
	Eg 971.2F	The temper of Ramesses I at Abydos. (Winlock, H.E.) N.Y., 1937.
	AH 3964.17	The temple; its ministry and services as they were at the time of Jesus Christ. 2. ed. (Edersheim, A.) London, 1874.
	Eg 879.65.10F	Le temple de Dendara. v.6. (Chassinat, Emile G.) Le Caire, 1965-
	Eg 990.5F	Le temple du scribe royal Amenhotep. pt.1. (Robichon, C.) Le Caire, 1936.
	AH 3014.21F	The temple oval at Khafājah. (Delougaz, Pinhas.) Chicago, 1940.
	Eg 279.64	Temples, tombs, and hieroglyphs. (Mertz, Barbara.) N.Y., 1964.
	AH 3964.17.15F	The temples in Jerusalem. (Eversull, H.K.) Cincinnati, Ohio, 1946.
	AH 7509.51	Il tempo di Augusto. (Levi, Mario A.) Firenze, 1951.
	AH 3020.3	Le temps des rois d'Ur. Text and plates. (Legrain, L.) Paris, 1912. 2v.
	AH 4039.54	Ténékidès, G. La notion juridique d'independance et la tradition hellenique. Athenes, 1954.
	AH 4259.15	Tenne, A. Kriegsschiffe zu den zeiten der alten Griechen. Oldenburg, 1915.
	AH 863.10	Tennodrac, M.J. L'antiquité érotique. Paris, 1952.
	AH 4559.39A	A tentative classification of books. (Berzunza, J.) n.p., 1939.
	AH 9440.5	Tergeste. (Scrinari, V.) Roma, 1951.
	AH 4889.34	De terminologie van het crediet-wezen in het Grieksch. (Korver, J.) Amsterdam, 1934.
	AH 7038.42.2	Terpstra, D. Quaestiones literariae. Rotterdami, 1842.
	AH 7279.30.10	Terrail, Gabriel. Histoire romaine. Paris, 1930.
	Eg 817.67	Terrasson, J. Sethos. Paris, 1767. 2v.
	AH 5766.5	Die territoriale Entwicklung. (Heidemann, L.) Berlin, 1904.
	AH 4206.9	Terwen, J.J. De Areopago Atheniensium. Ultraiecti, 1894.
	AH 4842.58	Terzaghi, N. L'educazione in Grecia. Milano, 1910.
	AH 3907.3F	Terzidi Lavria, B. Siria sacra. Roma, 1695.
	AH 7838.64	Die Tessarae Gladiatoriae. (Ritschl, F.) München, 1864.
	Eg 1309.41F	Testi demotici. (Botti, Giuseppe.) Firenze, 1941.
	AH 3965.15	Testimonies to the fertility of ancient Palestine. (Peppercorne, J.W.) London, 1838.
	AH 3910.15	Tetzlaff, N.J. De Antiochi III. Magni Syriae. Monasterii, 1874.
	AH 4228.94	Teusch, T. De sortitione indicum apud Atheniensis. Gottingae, 1894.
	AH 8008.11	Teutsch, Leo. Das Stadtewesen in Nordafrika. Berlin, 1962.
	AH 7203.21	Der teutsche Justinianus...Der Grund-lehren dess römischen Rechts. (Corpus juris civilis. Institutiones.) Augspurg, 1718. 2v.
	AH 3925.5F	Texier, C.F.M. Edesse et ses monuments. Paris, 1859.
	AH 7169.21.2	A text-book of Roman law from Augustus to Justinian. 2. ed. (Buckland, W.W.) Cambridge, Eng., 1932.
	Eg 502.5	Die Texte aus den Gräbern der Herakleopolitenzeit von Suit. (Brunner, Hellmut.) Glückstadt, 1937.
	Eg 1042.972	Die Texte zum Begrabensritual in den Pyramiden des alten Reiches. (Altenmüller, Hartwig.) Wiesbaden, 1972.
	AH 3154.35	Texte zum Studium sumerischer Tempel und Kulturzentren. (Witzel, M.) Roma, 1932.

Author and Title Listing

Author and Title Listing

Eg 1309.34F   Thompson, H. A family archive from Siut from papyri in the British Museum. Oxford, 1934. 2v.

AH 3964.36   Thompson, Henry O. Mekal, the God of Beth-Shan. Leiden, 1970.

AH 3013.929.5A   Thompson, R.C. A century of exploration at Nineveh. London, 1929.

AH 3183.5   Thompson, Reginald C. The devils and evil spirits of Babylonia. London, 1903- 2v.

AH 3187.12   Thompson, Reginald C. Late Babylonian letters. London, 1906.

AH 3154.7.5   Thompson, Reginald Campbell. The reports of the magicians and astrologers of Nineveh and Babylon in the British Museum. Ann Arbor, 1974.

AH 4103.3   Thomsen, Rudi. Eisphora; a study of direct taxation in ancient Athens. København, 1964.

AH 8611.5   Thomsen, Rudi. The Italic regions. København, 1947.
AH 4819.49A   Thomson, G.D. Studies in ancient Greek society. London, 1949. 2v.

AH 4819.49.2   Thomson, G.D. Studies in ancient Greek society. London, 1954. 2v.

AH 4819.21   Thomson, J.A.K. Greeks and Barbarians. London, 1921.
AH 4158.75   Thonissen, J.J. Le droit pénal. Bruxelles, 1875.
AH 7058.14F   Thorlacius, B. De irenarchis. Aavniae, 1814.
AH 862.13   Thorwald, Jürgen. Macht und Geheimnis der frühen Ärzte. München, 1962.

AH 862.13.5   Thorwald, Jürgen. Science and secrets of early medicine. London, 1962.

AH 8907.41   Those mysterious Etruscans. 1. ed. (Vaughan, A.C.) Garden City, N.Y., 1964.

Eg 848.2   Thoth oder die Wissenschaft der alten Ägypter. (Uhlemann, M.) Göttingen, 1855.

Eg 608.53F   Thothmes III. (Birch, S.) London, 1853.
AH 7808.87   Thouret, Georg. Die Chronologie von 218/217 v. Chr. Berlin, 1887.

AHP 30.8   Thracia. Serdicae. 1,1972+
AH 4239.69.5   Thracian Peltasts and their influence on Greek warfare. Proefschrift. (Best, Jan.) Groningen, 1969.

AH 2757.5   Thraemer, E. Pergamos. Leipzig, 1888.
AH 9707.9   Die Thraker. (Wieser, J.) Stuttgart, 1963.
AH 3357.5   Thrige, Johann P. Historia Cyrenes. Hauniae, 1819.
AH 3357.7   Thrige, Johann P. Res Cyrenensium. Hauniae, 1828.
AH 3357.7.5   Thrige, Johann P. Res Cyrenensium. Verbania, 1940.
AH 3357.8   Thrige, Johann P. Storia di Cirene. Verbania, 1948.
AH 279.57   Throne unter Schutt und Sand. (Schreiber, H.) Wien, 1957.
AH 7488.97.5   Die Thronfolge von Augustus bis Constantin. (Stueckelberg, Ernst Alfred.) Wien, 1897.

AH 4459.66   Thueydides and the politics of bipolarity. (Fliess, Peter J.) Baton Rouge, 1966.

AH 4108.80   Thumser, V. De livium atheniensium. Vindobonae, 1880.
AH 3154.15   Thureau-Dangin, F. Rituels accadiens. Paris, 1921.
AH 3020.4   Thureau-Dangin, F. Die sumerische und akkadischen Königsinschriften. Leipzig, 1907.

AH 7148.83.2   Thurm, A.A. De Romanorum legatis. Lipsiae, 1883.
Eg 609.33A   The Thutmosid succession. (Edgerton, William F.) Chicago, 1933.

Htn   AH 276.46*   Thysius, Antonius. Memorabilia celebriorum veterum rerumpublicarum. Lugduni Batavorum, 1646.

AH 7518.68   Tibère et l'héritage d'Auguste. (Beulé, C.E.) Paris, 1868.

AH 7518.68.3   Tibère et l'héritage d'Auguste. 2. éd. (Beulé, C.E.) Paris, 1868.

AH 7518.68.4   Tibère et l'héritage d'Auguste. 4. éd. (Beulé, C.E.) Paris, 1883.

AH 7519.34   Tiberio, successore di Augusto. (Ciaceri, E.) Milano, 1934.

AH 7519.34.5   Tiberio, successore di Augusto. 2. ed. (Ciaceri, E.) Roma, 1944.

AH 7519.59   Tiberius. (Gollub, Wilhelm.) München, 1959.
AH 7519.60   Tiberius. (Kornemann, Ernst.) Stuttgart, 1960.
AH 7519.52.3   Tiberius. (Marañón, G.) London, 1956.
AH 7519.52   Tiberius. (Marañón, G.) München, 1952.
AH 7519.72   Tiberius. (Seager, Robin.) London, 1972.
AH 7518.63   Tiberius. (Stahr, Adolf.) Berlin, 1863.
AH 7518.63.3   Tiberius. 2. Aufl. (Stahr, Adolf.) Berlin, 1873.
AH 7519.42   Tiberius and the Roman Empire. (Smith, Charles E.) Baton Rouge, 1942.

AH 7519.29   Tiberius Caesar. (Baker, G.P.) N.Y., 1929.
AH 7469.63.5   Tiberius Gracchus; a study in politics. (Earl, D.C.) Bruxelles, 1963.

Eg 759.55   Tiberius Iulius Alexander. (Burr, Viktor.) Bonn, 1955.
AH 7519.02   Tiberius the tyrant. (Tarver, J.C.) N.Y., 1902.
AH 7518.96   Tiberius und die Verschwörung des Sejan. (Willenbucher, H.) Gütersloh, 1896.

AH 7519.01   Tiberius und Germanicus. (Viertel, A.) Göttingen, 1901.
AH 7518.70   Tiberius und Tacitus. (Freytag, L.) Berlin, 1870.
AH 7039.53.5   Tibiletti, G. Principe e magistrati repubblicani. Roma, 1953.

AH 9090.3   Le Tibre, fleuve de Rome, dans l'antiquité. Thèse. (Le Gall, Joël.) Paris, 1952.

AH 3155.11   Tiele, C.P. Die Assyriologie...verleichende Religionsgeschichte. Leipzig, 1878.

AH 3008.86A   Tiele, C.P. Babylonisch-assyrische Geschicte. Gotha, 1886. 2v.

AH 3155.11.5   Tiele, C.P. De vrucht der assyriologie. Amsterdam, 1877.
Eg 878.82   Tiele, C.R. History of the Egyptian religion. London, 1882.

Eg 879.14.5F   Der Tierkult der alten Ägypter. (Hopfner, Theodor.) Wien, 1913.

AH 5757.10   Tigerstedt, Eugène Napoleon. The legend of Sparta in classical antiquity. Stockholm, 1965.

AH 7038.86.3   Tighe, A. Development of Roman constitution. N.Y., 1889.
AH 7038.86.9   Tighe, A. The development of the Roman constitution. N.Y., 1886.

AH 7038.86.5   Tighe, A. The development of the Roman constitution. N.Y., 1886.

AH 2060.10   Tigran Vtoroi i Rim. (Manandian, I.) Erevan, 1943.
AH 2060.5   Tigranes the Great. (Armen, H.K.) Detroit, 1940.
AH 4009.20   Tilden, F.W. Greek life; bibliography and review questions. Bloomington, 1920.

AH 4299.14   Tillyard, E. The Athenian empire and the great illusion. Cambridge, 1914.

AH 9610.21   Tillyard, H.J.W. Agathocles. Cambridge, 1908.
AH 4828.85   Timayenis, T.T. Greece in times of Homer. N.Y., 1885.
AH 4278.81   Timayenis, T.T. History of Greece. N.Y., 1881. 2v.
NEDL   AH 4278.81.4   Timayenis, T.T. History of Greece. N.Y., 1882-83. 2v.

NEDL   AH 4278.81.2   Timayenis, T.T. History of Greece. N.Y., 1883. 2v.
NEDL   AH 4278.81.3   Timayenis, T.T. History of Greece. N.Y., 1884. 2v.

AH 936.83   Timh Timaiov. (Birkerod, J.) Altodorfi Noricorum, 1683.
AH 4161.7   Timmermann, R. De nothorum Athenis condicione. Mederici, 1886.

AH 9610.17   Timoleon, eine historische Untersuchung. (Clasen, C.) Glückstadt, 1896.

AH 9610.18   Timoleon and his relations with tyrants. (Westlake, H.D.) Manchester, Eng., 1952.

AH 7039.62   Timpe, D. Untersuchungen zur Kontinuität. Wiesbaden, 1962.

AH 8914.5   Il tipo e l'ufficio del charun etrusco. (Rossi, S.) Messina, 1900.

AH 7206.23   Tipucitus. M. Kritoy Patzë Tipoy Keitos. Romae, 1914-29. 5v.

AH 8066.3   Tissot, Charles. Exploration scientifique de la Tunisie. Atlas. Paris, 1884-88. 2v.

AH 7217.11   I titoli di nobiltà. (Bonolis, G.) Firenze, 1905.
AH 4112.5   Tittman, F.W. Bund der Amphiktyonen. Berlin, 1812.
AH 4038.22   Tittmann, F.W. Staatsverfassungen. Leipzig, 1822.
AH 7629.29   La titulature impériale d'Hadrien. (Perret, Louis.) Paris, 1929.

AH 4149.13   Tod, Marcus N. International arbitration amongst the Greeks. Oxford, 1913.

AH 7548.96   Der Tod Neros in der Legende. (Nordmeyer, G.) Mors, 1896.
AH 3154.27   Tod und Leben nach den Vorstellungen der Babylonier. (Ebeling, Erich.) Berlin, 1931.

Eg 1038.42   Das Todtenbuch der Agypter. (Book of the Dead.) Leipzig, 1842.

AH 7158.87   Das Tödtungsverbrechen im alten Rechts. (Brunnenmeister, E.) Leipzig, 1887.

AH 4114.11   Toepffer, J. Attische Genealogie. Berlin, 1889.
AH 4028.97   Toepffer, J. Griechischen Altertumswissenschaft. Berlin, 1897.

AH 4448.86   Toepffer, J. Quaestiones pisistrateae. Dorpati, 1886.
AH 3149.6   Toffteen, O.A. Ancient chronology. Chicago, 1907.
AH 3012.5   Toffteen, O.A. Researches in Assyrian and Babylonian geography. Chicago, 1908.

Htn   AH 7206.1*   Tog A'natoli. (Bonefidius, E.) Geneva, 1573.
AH 7848.8   Die Toga der späteren Kaiserzeit. (Hula, Eduard.) Brünn, 1895.

AH 7848.7   Toga und Trabea. v.1-2. (Helbig, W.) Berlin, 1904.
AH 4848.12   La toilette des femmes grecques. (Sambon, A.) Paris, 1904.

AH 8549.18   Toland, John. A critical history of the Celtic religion. Edinburgh, 1815.

AH 8549.17.50   Toland, John. A critical history of the Celtic religion. London, 174-?

AH 856.5   Tomasini, J.P. De tesseris hospitalitatis. Utini, 1647.
Eg 1069.39   The tomb of Canefer at Thebes (no.158). (Seele, K.C.) Chicago, 1939.

Eg 990.20PF   The tomb of Tjanefer at Thebes. (Seele, Keith.) Chicago, 1959.

Eg 609.23.7   The tomb of Tut-Ankh-Amen. (Carter, Howard.) London, 1923-33. 3v.

Eg 609.23.8A   The tomb of Tut-Ankh-Amen. (Carter, Howard.) N.Y., 1923.
Eg 609.23.6   The tomb of Tutankhamen. (Capart, Jean.) London, 1923.
Eg 459.55   Le tombeau du Pharaon, en l'an 2800 av. J.-C. (Julien, Max.) Paris, 1955.

Eg 839.56   Tombs, temples and ancient art. 1. ed. (Smith, J.L.) Norman, 1956.

Eg 298.85   Tomkins, H.G. Egyptological research. London, 1885?
AH 5257.1   Tomlinson, Richard Allan. Argos and the Argolid. Ithaca, N.Y., 1972.

AH 7138.67.5   Tompkins, F. The institutes of the Roman law. London, 1867.

AH 3013.931.10F   Tompson, Reginald C. The prisms of Esarhaddon and Ashurbanipal found at Nineveh. London, 1931.

AH 4850.11   Tòn Symposion. (Maltou.) Athênai, 1840.
AH 3155.17   Tooke, W. The loves of Othniel and Achsah. London, 1769. 2v.

NEDL   AH 298.88   Topics in ancient history. (Wood, C.W.) Boston, 1888.
AH 8666.5   Topografia e urbanistica di Roma antica. (Castagnoli, Ferdinando.) Bologna, 1969.

AH 9121.2   Topografia storica dell'Ingaunia nell'antichità. (Lamboglia, Nino.) Albenga, 1933.

AH 8416.5   Topographia Norici. (Ertl, Franz.) Kremsmünster, 1965-69. 2v.

AH 5657.5   Topographie...der Insel Euboia. (Geyer, F.) Berlin, 1903.
AH 5657.4   Topographie...der Insel Euboia. (Geyer, F.) Kirchain, 1902.

AH 3061.5   Topographie der Provinz Umma nach den Urkunden der Zeit der III. Dynastie von Ur. (Sauren, Herbert.) Bamberg, 1966.

AH 3966.29   La topographie légendaire des Evangiles en Terre Sainte. (Halbwachs, M.) Paris, 1941.

AH 5666.5   Topographische Skizze der Insel Euboia. (Baumeister, A.) Lübeck, 1864.

AH 4484.7   Topography of Battle of Plataea. (Grundy, G.B.) London, 1894.

AH 8073.15   The topography of Punic Carthage. (Hurd, H.P.) Williamsport, 1934.

AH 3013.938.5   De Toren van Babel. (Busink, T.A.) Batavia, 1938.
AH 806.11.5F   Tornielli, A. Annales sacri. Lucae, 1756-57. 4v.
Eg 808.96   Torr, C. Memphis and Mycenae. Cambridge, Eng., 1896.
AH 7449.25   Torr, Cecil. Hannibal crosses the Alps 2. ed. Cambridge, 1925.

AH 5138.9   Torr, Cecil. Rhodes in ancient times. Photoreproduction. Cambridge, 1885.

AH 9621.9   Torremuzza, G.L.C. Dissertazione sopra una statua di Marmo. Palermo, 1749.

AH 279.45   Tôrres, Flausino. O mundo mediterrânico do séc. XII a.C. ao séc. III d.C. Lisboa, 1945.

AH 3052.9F   Toscanne, P. Les cylindres de Gudéa. Paris, 1901.
AH 3963.175   Die Totenbestattungen der Bibel. (Küchenmeister, F.) Stuttgart, 1893.

Eg 879.26.5   Totenglauben und Jenseitsvorstellungen der alten Ägypter. (Kees, Hermann.) Leipzig, 1926.

Eg 879.26.7   Totenglauben und Jenseitsvorstellungen der alten Ägypter. 2. Aufl. (Kees, Hermann.) Berlin, 1956.

AH 9777.35   Toty i ikh' sosedidov. (Braun, F.A.) Sankt Peterburg, 1899.

AH 4303.6   Touloumakos, Johannes. Zum Geschichtsbewusstsein der Griechen in der Zeit der römischen Herrschaft. Bonn, 1971.

AH 7818.54   Tounsend, F. Letters from Rome. N.Y., 1854.
Eg 609.23.6.5   Tout-Ankh-Amon. 2. éd. (Capart, Jean.) Bruxelles, 1950.
AH 889.30   Toutain, J. The economic life of the ancient world. London, 1930.

Eg 609.61   Toutankhamon dans les archives hittites. (Vergote, J.) Istanbul, 1961.

AH 279.41.10   Tovar, Antonio. En el primer giro. Madrid, 1941.

	AH 7239.07	Tschauschmer, Carl. Legionare Kriegsvexillationen. Breslau, 1907.
	AH 4200.15	Tsopanakis, A. La Rhètre de Lycurgue. Tyrtée, 1954.
	AH 4819.06.3A	Tucker, T.G. Life in ancient Athens. N.Y., 1906.
	AH 4819.06.7	Tucker, T.G. Life in ancient Athens. Handbooks of archaeology and antiquities. Chautauqua, 1917.
	AH 7819.10.2	Tucker, T.G. Life in the Roman world of Nero and St. Paul. London, 1910.
	AH 7819.10.4A	Tucker, T.G. Life in the Roman world of Nero and St. Paul. N.Y., 1917.
	AH 7819.10.5	Tucker, T.G. Life in the Roman world of Nero and St. Paul. N.Y., 1929.
	AH 8308.10	Tudor, D. Istoria sclavajului in Dacia romana. Bucureşti, 1957.
	EgP 142.2	Tübinger ägyptologische Beiträge. Bonn. 1,1973+
	Eg 608.70	Tugnot de Lanoye, Ferdinand. Rameses the Great. N.Y., 1870.
	AH 8617.7	Tulelli, E. Il filadelfos de Giovanni Gemelli. Napoli, 1882.
	Eg 1309.27F	Turaev, B.A. Papyrus Prachov. Leningrad, 1927.
	Eg 1109.15	Turaev, B.A. Razskaz Egiptiianina Sinukheta. Moskva, 1915.
	AH 1409.35	Turaev, V.A. Istoriia drevnago Vostoka. Leningrad, 1935. 2v.
	AH 1409.27	Turaev, V.A. Russkaia nauka odrevnem Vostoke do 1917 g. Leningrad, 1927.
	AH 4189.63	Turasiewicz, R. De servis testibus in Atheniensium. Wrocław, 1963.
	VAH 4039.68	Turasiewicz, Romuald. Gycie politzczne w Atenach V i IV w. przed n.e. w ocenie krytzcznej wspófczenych autorow atenskich. 1. wyd. Wrocław, 1968.
	AH 3160.13	Turibuli Assyrii descriptio. (Walz, C.) Tubingae, 1856.
	AH 4298.53.5	Turner, D.W. Heads of an analogy of the history of Greece. 2. ed. London, 1860.
	AH 7278.61	Turner, D.W. Roman history. 3. ed. London, 1861.
	AH 819.41A	Turner, R.C. The great cultural traditions. 1. ed. N.Y., 1941. 2v.
	AH 819.54	Turone, Mario. La prima umanità. Milano, 1954.
	AH 47.69	Turpin, François H. Histoire du gouvernement des anciennes républiques. Paris, 1769.
	AH 9458.5	"Tusca origo Raetis". (Whatmough, J.) n.p., 1937.
	Eg 609.23	Tutankhamen, Amenism, Atenism and Egyptian monotheism. (Budge, Ernest Alfred Wallis.) London, 1923.
	Eg 609.23.11	Tutankhamen and Egyptology. (Mercer, S.A.B.) Milwaukee, 1923.
	Eg 609.23.5	Tutankhamen and the discovery of his tomb. (Smith, G.E.) London, 1923.
	Eg 819.54.4	Tutankhamun and the Valley of the Kings. (Neubert, Otto.) London, 1972.
	Eg 603.15	Tut'ankhomien's tomb series. Oxford. 1,1963+ 9v.
	AH 4279.58.10	The tutorial history of Greece. 3. ed. (Woodhouse, W.J.) London, 1958.
	AH 7279.52.12	Tutorial history of Rome (to A.D. 69). 6. ed. (Allcroft, Arthur.) London, 1961.
	AH 4843.22	De twee delphische hymnen. (Moens, P.W.) Purmerend, 1930.
	AH 7279.34	Twelve centuries of Rome. (Baker, G.P.) N.Y., 1934.
	AH 339.52.5	Twelve men of action in Graeco-Roman history. (Toynbee, Arnold Joseph.) Freeport, N.Y., 1969.
	AH 1818.72	Twesten, C. Religiösen, politischen und socialen Ideen. v.1-2. Berlin, 1872.
	AH 5463.5	The twilight of history. (Hogarth, D.G.) London, 1926.
Htn	AH 4807.41*	Two essays, a defense of ancient Greek chronologies. (Squire, Samuel.) Cambridge, 1741.
	AH 7419.13	The two great republics - Rome and the United States. (Lewis, J.H.) Chicago, 1913.
	AH 7059.24A	Two studies in later Roman and Byzantine administration. (Boak, A.E.R.) N.Y., 1924.
	AH 3181.14	Two Sulgi hymns [and] Be. (Castellino, Giorgio R.) Roma, 1972.
	AH 9640.2	Tyndaris. (Parisi, G.) Messina, 1950.
X Cg	AH 4559.02.3F	Type physique d'Alexandre le Grand. (Ujfalvy, C. d'.) Paris, 1902.
	AH 4043.5.15	La tyrannie dans la Grèce antique. (Mossé, Claude.) Paris, 1969.
	AH 4043.5	Die Tyrannis bei den Griechen. (Berve, Helmut.) München, 1967. 2v.
	AH 4449.29	Die Tyrannis in Athen. (Cornelius, Friedrich.) München, 1929.
	AH 4043.5.10	Die Tyrannis in ihren beiden Perioden. (Plass, Hermann.) Bremen, 1852. 2v.
	AH 4043.5.12	Die Tyrannis in ihren beiden Perioden. v.1-2. 2. Ausg. (Plass, Hermann.) Leipzig, 1859.
	AH 3740.6.3	Tyre; its rise, glory, and desolation. Nashville, 1856.
	AH 3740.6	Tyre; its rise, glory, and desolation. Philadelphia, 1852.
	AH 3740.10	Tyre and Alexandria. (Tarbox, Increase N.) Boston, 1865.
	AH 3740.9	Tyre through the ages. (Jidejian, Nina.) Beirut, 1969.
	AH 3708.5	The Tyrrhenians. (Nibbi, Alessandra.) Cowley, 1969.
	AH 8907.40	Tyrrhenica. (Istituto lombardo di scienze e lettere.) Milano, 1957.
	AH 3740.7	Tyrus. (Jeremias, F.) Leipzig, 1891.
	Eg 138.99	Uah. Oldest known will. Philadelphia, 19- .
	AH 7168.70.10	Ubbelohde, A. Zur Geschichte der...Realcontracte auf Rückgabe. Marburg, 1870.
	AH 4238.69.2	Uber das Söldnerwesen. (Bohstedt, E.) Rendsburg, 1873.
	AH 7448.74.4	Uber die Schlacht bei Cannä. (Fried, F.) Leipzig, 1898.
	AH 4328.37	Uebelen, G. Jonische Stamms. Stuttgart, 1837.
	AH 7208.2	Über Abstimmung des römischen Volks. (Zumpt, Karl G.) Berlin, 1837.
	AH 7438.63	Ueber Appius Claudius Caecus. (Siebert, W.) Kassel, 1863.
	AH 3017.6F	Über Babylonische "Talismane". (Fischer, H.) Stuttgart, 1881.
	AH 4038.63.9	Ueber C.A. Freeman's History of federal governemnt. (Vischer, W.) n.p., 1864.
	AH 7201.95.50	Über das alter der Ediktskommentare des Gaius. (Balog, E.) Hannover, 1914.
	AH 7168.46	Ueber das Recht des Nexum. (Huschke, P.E.) Leipzig, 1846.
	AH 308.46	Über das Studium der griechischen und römischen Alterthümer. (Lasaulx, E. von.) München, 1846.
	AH 7188.90	Über das Verhaltnis der späteren Stoa zur Sklaverei im römischen Reiche. (Vollmann, Franz.) Stadtamhof, 1890.
	AH 7108.47	Über den Census und die Steuerverfassung. (Huschke, P.E.) Berlin, 1847.
	AH 8915.2	Ueber den etruskischen Tauschhandel. (Genthe, H.F.) Heibronn, 1874.
	AH 4838.89.5	Über den Fünfkampf der Hellenen. (Fedde, F.) Leipzig, 1889.
	AH 3004.3	Über den historischen Gewinn...assyrischen Inschriften. (Brandis, J.) Berlin, 1856.
	AH 4818.98.25	Über den kulturgeschichtlichen Zusammenhang. (Schmid, Wilhelm.) Leipzig, 1898.
	AH 7888.97	Über den rechtlichen Schutz. (Pfaff, Ivo.) Weimar, 1897.
	AH 888.41	Über den Stand der Bevölkerung. (Zumpt, K.G.) Berlin, 1841.
	AH 7838.66	Über den Ursprung der römischen Gladiatorenspiele. (Planck, M.) Ulm, 1866.
	AH 7178.70	Ueber der Ursprung und die Werwendung. (Jürgens.) Blankeburg, 1870.
	AH 5315.7	Über die Bevölkerungsdichtigkeit Attika's und ihre politische Bedeutung im Altertum. (Hansen, J.H.) Hamburg, 1885?
	AH 4840.15	Ueber die Blutrache bei den Griechen. (Eichhoff, Karl.) Duisburg, 1873.
	AH 2013.10	Über die Blutrache bei den vorislamischen Arabern und Mohammeds Stellung zu Christ. (Proksch, Otto.) Leipzig, 1899.
	AH 7114.3	Über die Clientel und Libertinität. (Voigt, Moritz.) Leipzig, 1878.
	AH 7228.62	Ueber die condictiones ob causam. (Voigt, M.) Leipzig, 1862.
	AH 8549.20	Ueber die Druiden der Kelten. (Barth, C.K.) Erlangen, 1826.
	AH 7148.29	Über die Entstehung...des Burgerrechts. (Eisendecher, W.) Hamburg, 1829.
	AH 7039.11	Über die Entwicklung der römischen Verfassung im republikanischer Zeit. (Fabricius, Ernest.) Freiburg, 1911.
	AH 928.59	Über die heilige Masse des Alterthums. (Müller, H.) Freiburg, 1859.
	AH 8908.14.5	Über die Herkunft der Etrusker. (Haury, Jacob.) Kaiserslautern, 1922.
	AH 8908.15	Über die Herkunft der Etrusker. (Mühlestein, H.) Berlin, 1929.
	AH 4409.06	Über die ionische Wanderung. (Wilamowitz-Moellendorff, Ulrich von.) n.p., 1906.
	AH 7138.93.5F	Über die Leges Iuliae iudiciorum privatorum et publicorum. (Voigt, M.) Leipzig, 1893.
	AH 3013.22	Über die Mauern von Babylon. (Streber, F.) München, 1849.
	AH 7598.00	Über die Menscheit...Epoche in der römischen Geschichte. (Hegewisch, D.H.) Hamburg, 1800.
	AH 8548.80	Ueber die Nationalität der Kelten. (Rott, Joseph.) Passau, 1866?
	AH 7055.93.5	Über die Notitia Dignitatum. (Böcking, D. Eduard.) Bonn, 1834.
	AH 7207.15	Über die Patres Conscripti. (Ihne, W.) n.p., n.d.
	Eg 878.18	Über die philosophische Historiographie der neuesten Zeit. (Babor, Johann.) Olmütz, 1818.
	AH 7031.7F	Über die Politik des Marcus Agrippa. (Frandsen, P.S.) Altona, 1833. 5 pam.
	AH 7478.63	Über die politische Rolle des Gnaeus Pompejus Magnus. (Dressel, E.) Coburg, 1863.
	AH 7148.81	Über die rechtliche Grundlage der Leges contractus. (Heyrovský, Leopold.) Leipzig, 1881.
	AH 7162.32	Über die regula Catoiana. (Wöll, W.) Strassburg, 1894.
	AH 7114.32	Über die römischen Ritter und den Ritterstand in Rom. v.1-2. (Zumpt, Karl G.) Berlin, 1841.
	AH 7448.98.10	Über Die schlacht bei Cannä. Inaug. Diss. (Fried, Friedrich.) Leipzig, 1898.
	AH 7188.66	Über die Sklaverie und Sklavenentlassung bei den Römern. (Adams.) Tübingen, 1866.
	AH 2009.6.5	Über die südarabische Sage. (Kremer, A. von.) Leipzig, 1866.
	AH 2009.6	Über die südarabische Sage. (Kremer, A. von.) Leipzig, 1866.
	AH 4478.76.15	Ueber die Tradition der Perserkriege. (Wecklein, N.) München, 1876.
	AH 8908.7	Ueber die tyrrhenischen Pelasger. (Lepsius, K.R.) Leipzig, 1842.
	AH 7469.00.3	Über die unter dem Namen der Cornelia überlieferten Brieffragmente. (Kappler, Carl.) Weiden, 1905.
	AH 9758.3	Ueber die Völker und Völkerbundnisse des alten Teutschlands. (Wersebe, August von.) Hannover, 1826.
	AH 7058.53	Über die Wahl...Praefectus urbis feriarum. (Linker, G.) Wien? 1853.
	AH 7748.61	Über die Zeitfolge der Verordnungen Diocletians. (Mommsen, Theodor.) Berlin, 1861.
	AH 8549.77	Über Driudismus in Noricum. (Ferk, F.) Graz, 1877.
	AH 7078.80	Über Entstehung und Zusammensetzung der altrömischen Volksversammlungen. (Soltau, W.) Berlin, 1880.
	AH 919.14.5	Über griechische und römische Stiftungen. (Laum, Bernhard.) Leipzig, 1913.
	AH 7808.15	Über Jahrform und Jahrrechnung bei den Römern. (Golbrig, Karl Friedrich.) Salzwedel, 1815.
	AH 7158.88	Über Lex Plantia de VI und Lex Lutatia. (Weihmayr, W.) Augsburg, 1888.
	AH 7098.36	Über römische Colonien. pt.1-2. (Schmidt.) Potsdam, 1836.
	AH 7139.54	Über römisches Recht im Rahmen der Kulturgeschichte. (Bruck, E.F.) Berlin, 1954.
	AH 7827.76.2	Ueber Sitten und Lebensart der Römer. (Meierotto, J.H.L.) Berlin, 1802.
	AH 7827.76.3	Ueber Sitten und Lebensart der Römer. (Meierotto, J.H.L.) Berlin, 1814.
	AH 3160.6	Über Tammuz und die Menschenverehrung. (Chevolson, D.A.) St. Petersburg, 1860.
	AH 7138.38	Über Ursprung, Form und Bedeutung. (Zumpt, C.G.) Berlin, 1838.
	AH 7168.53	Uebernahme fremder Schulden. (Delbrück, E.L.B.) Berlin, 1853.
	Eg 1042.935F	Übersetzung und Kommentar zu den altägyptischen Pyramidentexten. (Pyramid Texts.) Glückstadt, 1935-1962. 6v.
	AHP 31.6	Übersetzungen ausländischer Arbeiten zur antiken Sklaverei. Wiesbaden. 1,1966+ 4v.
	AH 3902.3	Ugarit and Minoan Crete; the bearing of their texts on the origins of Western culture. (Gordon, Cyrus H.) N.Y., 1966.
	AHP 31.3	Ugarit-Forschungen. Neukirchen. 1,1969+ 5v.
	AH 3914.7	Ugaritic mythology. (Obermann, Julian.) New Haven, 1948.
	Eg 558.56	Uhlemann, M. Israeliten und Hyksos in Aegypten. Leipzig, 1856.
	Eg 848.2	Uhlemann, M. Thoth oder die Wissenschaft der alten Ägypter. Göttingen, 1855.
X Cg	AH 4559.02.3F	Ujfalvy, C. d'. Type physique d'Alexandre le Grand. Paris, 1902.
	AH 928.13	Ukert, F.A. Entfernungen bei den Alten. Weimar, 1813.
	AH 938.16	Ukert, F.A. Geographie der Griechen und Römer. v.1-3. Weimar, 1816-46. 5v.

NEDL	AH 279.09	Ulbricht, E. Grundzüge der alten Geschichte. Weissen, 1909. 2v.
	AH 5853.5	Ullrich, F.W. Megarische Psephisma. Hamburg, 1838.
	AH 308.57	Ulm. Gymnasium. Parallelen römischer und griechischen Entwicklungsgeschichte. Ulm, 1857.
	AH 8307.6	Ulpia Trajana Augusta colonia Dacica. (Király, Pál.) Budapest, 1891.
	AH 7201.23	Ulpiani, D. Fragmenta. Bonnae, 1836.
	AH 7201.23.4	Ulpiani, D. Fragmenta. Leipsiae, 1855.
	AH 7201.5	Ulpiani, D. Fragmenta. v.1-2. Berolini, 1811.
	AH 7201.4.35	Ulpianus. Fragmenta. Notas adjecit Joannes Canregieter. Trajecti ad Rhenum, 1768.
	AH 7201.57A	Ulpianus. Fragmenta minora. Berolini, 1878.
	AH 3061.2	Umma sous la dynastie d'Ur. (Contenau, Georges.) Paris, 1916.
	Eg 959.60	Unamun. Puteshestvie Un-Amuna v Bibl; egipetskii ieraticheskii papirus no.120. Moskva, 1960.
Htn	AH 3958.8.20*	The unfortunate politique [or the life of Herod]. (Caussin, N.) Oxford, 1638.
	AH 3013.938	Unger, E. Altindogermanisches Kulturgut in Nordmesopotamien. Leipzig, 1938.
	AH 3042.3.10	Unger, Eckhard. Babylon. Berlin, 1931.
	AH 3042.3.12	Unger, Eckhard. Babylon. 2e Aufl. Berlin, 1970.
	AH 819.39	Unger, Eckhard. Welt und Mensch im alten Orient. v.4. Berlin, 1939.
	AH 7201.22	Unger, F.W. De duorum praecipuorum iurisprudentiae. Inaug. Diss. Hannoverae, 1834.
	Eg 808.67	Unger, G.F. Chronologie des Manetho. Berlin, 1867.
	AH 3908.5.10	Unger, Merrill F. Israel and the Aramaeans of Damascus. London, 1957.
	AH 7207.50	Ungern-Sternberg von Pürkel, Jürgen. Untersuchungen zum spatrepublikanischen Notstandsrecht. Diss. München, 1970.
	AH 3020.8	Ungnad, A. Babylonische Briefe aus der Zeit der Hammurapidynastie. Leipzig, 1914.
	AH 1819.36	Ungnad, Arthur. Subartu; Beiträge zur Kulturgeschichte und Völkerkunde Vorderasiens. Berlin, 1936.
	AH 3177.11	Ungnod, Arthur. Gilgamesch - Epos und Odysee. Breslau, 1923.
Htn	AH 7516.28.2*	Unhappy prosperity express'd in History of Aelius Sejanus. 2. ed. (Matthieu, P.) London, 1639.
	AH 889.52	L'unità economica del mondo antico. (Palumbo, P. Fausto.) Roma, 1952.
	AH 7179.27	L'unité foncière en droit romain. (Kaïla, E.) Paris, 1927.
	Eg 971.15PF	United Arab Republic. Centre of Documentation and Studies on Ancient Egypt. Le petit temple d'Abou Simbel. Le Caire, 1968. 2v.
	AH 278.84	Universal history. (Ranke, L.F. von.) London, 1884.
	AH 278.84.2	Universal history. (Ranke, L.F. von.) N.Y., 1884.
	AH 288.85	Universal history. (Ranke, L.F. von.) N.Y., 1885.
NEDL	AH 277.09	Universal library of historians. (Du Pin, L.E.) London, 1709. 2v.
	AH 8.95	Die Universalhistorie. (Büdinger, Max.) Wien, 1895.
	AH 4659.24	Universalisme en particularisme in den aarwang van het hellenistisch tijdperk. (Cohen, D.) Groningen, 1924.
	EgP 143.2	Université de Lille III. Institut de papyrologie et d'égyptologie. Cahier de recherches. Lille. 1,1973+ 2v.
	AH 7469.31.11	Pamphlet vol. Université Égyptienne. Recueil de travaux par la faculté des lettres. 2 pam.
X Cg	AH 4842.21	University life in Athens. (Capes, W.W.) N.Y., 1877.
	AH 4842.43A	University of ancient Greece. (Walden, J.W.H.) N.Y., 1909.
	AH 4842.43.2	University of ancient Greece. (Walden, J.W.H.) N.Y., 1912.
	AH 3002.8	University of Pennsylvania. Publications of the Babylonian section...Museum. Philadelphia. 1-16,1911-1930 20v.
	AH 3002.12	University of Pennsylvania. Babylonian Expedition. The Babylonian expedition. Series A: Cuneiform texts. Philadelphia. 1-29,1893-1913 10v.
	AH 3002.12F	University of Pennsylvania. Babylonian Expedition. The Babylonian expedition. Series A: Cuneiform texts. Philadelphia. 30-31,1913-1914 2v.
	AH 3002.15	University of Pennsylvania. Babylonian Expedition. Babylonian expedition. Series D: Researches and treatises. Philadelphia. 1-4,1904-1907 3v.
	AH 7799.16	Gli unni e Attila. (Solari, Arturo.) Pisa, 1916.
	AH 842.27	Die Unsicherheit literarischen Eigentums. (Adam, L.) Düsseldorf, 1906.
	AH 7659.03	Untergang der antiken Welt. (Hartmann, L.M.) Wien, 1903.
	AH 7659.03.2	Untergang der antiken Welt. (Hartmann, L.M.) Wien, 1910.
	AH 8011.9	Der Untergang der römischen Herrschaft in Nordafrika. (Diesner, Hans J.) Weimar, 1964.
	AH 7659.70	Der Untergang des Romischen Reiches. (Christ, Karl.) Darmstadt, 1970.
	AH 7659.39	Der Untergang Roms. (Werner, H.) Stuttgart, 1939.
	AH 7659.30	Der Untergang Roms im abendländischen Denken. (Rehm, Walther.) Leipzig, 1930.
	AH 898.54	Unterhaltungen aus der alten Welt. (Wüstemann, E.F.) Gotha, 1854.
	AH 7138.76.13	Unterschriften in römischen Rechts-Urkunden. (Bruns, C.G.) Berlin, 1876.
	AH 3188.5	Untersuchung der Elambriefe aus dem Archiv Assurbanîpals. Inaug. Diss. (Schawe, Joseph.) Berlin, 1927.
	AH 4848.7	Untersuchung und der Tracht die Athener am Grundlage. (Braungarten, F.) n.p., 1876.
	AH 7239.36	Untersuchung zum Prätorium. Inaug. Diss. (Lorenz, H.) Halle, 1936.
	AH 298.00	Untersuchungen...alten Geschichte. pt.1-2. (Bredow, G.G.) Altona, 1800-02.
	AH 7298.55.3	Untersuchungen...altrömischen Geschichte. (Lewis, George C.) Hannover, 1863.
	AH 7058.77	Untersuchungen...römischen Verwaltungsgeschichte. (Hirschfeld, O.) Berlin, 1877.
	AH 7449.05.3	Untersuchungen...Unterwerfung von Oberitalien. (Lauterbach, A.) Breslau, 1905.
	AH 7203.46.10	Untersuchungen. (Goldschmidt, L.) Heidelberg, 1855.
	AH 7438.93	Untersuchungen über...Geschichte. (Binneboessel, P.) Halle, 1893.
	AH 5610.9	Untersuchungen über den pynhischen Krieg. Inaug. Diss. (Hamburger, Oswald.) Würzburg, 1927.
	Eg 856.3	Untersuchungen über die ägyptischen Kronen. Inaug. Diss. (Abubakr, Abdel Monem Jooussef.) Glückstadt, 1937.
	AH 4148.81.3	Untersuchungen über die attische Bürgerrecht. (Szántó, Emil.) Wien, 1881.
	AH 4049.71	Untersuchungen über die Natur und die Anfange der bundesstaatlichen Sympolitie in Griechenland. (Giovannini, Adalberto.) Göttingen, 1971.
	AH 6110.15	Untersuchungen über die Quellen zur Geschichte Philipps II von Macedonien. (Schubert, R.) Konigsberg, 1904.
	AH 7161.3	Untersuchungen über die römische Ehe. (Rossbach, A.) Stuttgart, 1853.
	AH 7038.99	Untersuchungen über die sulianische Verfassung. (Lengle, Joseph.) Freiburg, 1899.
	AH 7468.54.25	Untersuchungen über römische Geschichte. (Hagen, E.) Königsberg, 1854.
	AH 7038.39	Untersuchungen und römische Verfassung. (Rubino, J.) Cassel, 1839.
	AH 7509.34	Untersuchungen zu Augustus' Politik und Staatsauffassung nach den autobiographischen Schriften. Inaug. Diss. (Vaubel, T.) Düsseldorf, 1934.
	AH 7468.85	Untersuchungen zu dem allobrogischen Krieg. (Ritter, Georg.) Hof, 1885.
	Eg 39.54F	Untersuchungen zu den Beamtentiteln des ägyptischen alten Reichs. (Helck, W.) Glückstadt, 1954.
	AH 7559.63	Untersuchungen zu den Truppenbewegungen in den Jahren 68/69 nach Christ. Inaug. Diss. (Hallermann, Burkhard.) Würzburg, 1963.
	AH 4539.70	Untersuchungen zu der Zeit der thebanischen Hegemonie. Inaug. Diss. (Beister, Hartmut.) Bonn, 1970.
	AH 7449.14.7	Untersuchungen zu Scipios Feldzug in Afrika. Inaug. Diss. (Sann, Georg.) Berlin, 1914.
	AH 8008.12	Untersuchungen zum afrikanischen Senatsadel in der Spätantike. (Overbeck, Hechtild.) Kallmünz, 1973.
	AH 4189.69.5	Untersuchungen zum griechischen Freilassungswesen. Inaug. Diss. (Rädle, Herbert.) München, 1969.
	AH 3910.27	Untersuchungen zum Partherkrieg. Diss. (Fisher, Thomas.) Tübingen, 1970.
	AH 9653.5F	Untersuchungen zum römischen Städtewesen auf der iberieschen Halbinsel. (Galsterer, Hartmut.) Berlin, 1971.
	AH 7207.50	Untersuchungen zum spatrepublikanischen Notstandsrecht. Diss. (Ungern-Sternberg von Pürkel, Jürgen.) München, 1970.
	AH 4049.37	Untersuchungen zum Tyrannenmord in Gesetzgebung und Volksmeinung der Griechen. Inaug. Diss. (Friedel, H.) Würzburg, 1937.
	Eg 133.70	Untersuchungen zum Wohnungseigentum auf Grund der gräko-ägyptischen Papyri. Diss. (Drath, Juergen.) Marburg, 1970?
	AH 3909.8	Untersuchungen zur alten Geschichte und Ethnographie Syriens und Palästinas. (Maisler, Benjamin.) Giessen, 1930.
	AH 1298.89	Untersuchungen zur altorientalischen Geschichte. (Winckler, H.) Leipzig, 1889.
	AHP 31.5	Untersuchungen zur Assyriologie und vorderasiatischen Archäologie. Berlin. 1,1960+ 5v.
	Eg 609.64	Untersuchungen zur Chronologie und Geschichte des Neuen Reiches. (Hornung, E.) Wiesbaden, 1964.
	AH 7079.67	Untersuchungen zur den Wahlen in der römischen Kaiserzeit. (Frei-Stolba, Regula.) Zürich, 1967.
	AH 5807.5	Untersuchungen zur Geographie...der norwestlichen Land. Inaug. Diss. (Bauer, Edmund.) Halle, 1907.
	AH 4859.21	Untersuchungen zur Geschäftsfähigkeit. (Balabanoff, A.) Borna, 1905.
	Eg 278.96F	Untersuchungen zur Geschichte...Aegyptens. v.1-10. Leipzig, 1896-1928. 5v.
	AH 7629.07	Untersuchungen zur Geschichte...Hadrianus. (Weber, W.) Leipzig, 1907.
	AH 3910.16	Untersuchungen zur Geschichte Antiochos des Grossen. (Schmitt, H.H.) Wiesbaden, 1964.
	AH 8557.4	Untersuchungen zur Geschichte der alten Illyrien. Inaug. Diss. (Schütt, C.) Breslau, 1910.
	AH 7499.69	Untersuchungen zur Geschichte der julisch-claudischen Dynastie. (Meise, Erkhard.) München, 1969.
	AH 7200.18	Untersuchungen zur Geschichte des Decemvirats und der zwölft Afdu. (Täubler, Eugen.) Berlin, 1921.
	AH 7699.21	Untersuchungen zur Geschichte des Kaisers Septimius Severus. (Haselroeck, J.) Heidelberg, 1921.
	AH 6110.12	Untersuchungen zur Geschichte des Königs Perseus von Makedonien. Diss. (Heiland, Paul.) Jena, 1913.
	AH 6110.20	Untersuchungen zur Geschichte des koituthischen Bundes. Inaug. Diss. (Rane, H.O.) Marburg, 1937.
	Eg 759.15	Untersuchungen zur Geschichte und Verwaltung Ägyptens unter roemischer Herrschaft. (Stein, Arthur.) Stuttgart, 1915.
	AH 4659.72	Untersuchungen zur hellenistischen Geschichte des 3. Jahrhunderts. (Heinen, Heinz.) Wiesbaden, 1972.
	AH 7039.62	Untersuchungen zur Kontinuität. (Timpe, D.) Wiesbaden, 1962.
	AH 3022.38	Untersuchungen zur neusumarischen Landwirtschaft. (Pettinato, Giovanni.) Napoli, 1967.
	Eg 509.64	Untersuchungen zur politischen Geschichte der Zweiten Zwischenzeit in Ägypten. (Beckerath, Jürgen von.) Glückstadt, 1964.
	AH 7769.69.5	Untersuchungen zur römischen Aussenpolitik in der Spätantike (306-395). (Stallknecht, Bernt.) Bonn, 1969.
	AHP 31.4	Untersuchungen zur römischen Geschichte. Frankfurt a.M. 1,1961+ 4v.
	AH 7469.59.5	Untersuchungen zur römischen Geschichte am Ende des 2. Jahrhunderts vor Christus. (Chantraine, Heinrich.) Kallmünz, 1959.
	AH 7469.28.5	Untersuchungen zur römischen Geschichte und Quellenkunde. (Taeger, Fritz.) Stuttgart, 1928.
	AH 7488.68	Untersuchungen zur Römischen Kaesergeschichte. (Büdinger, M.) Leipzig, 1868. 3v.
	AH 7116.6	Untersuchungen zur römischen Zenturienverfassung. (Rosenberg, A.) Berlin, 1911.
	Eg 1042.926F	Untersuchungen zur Schriftgeschichte der Pyramidentexte. Inaug. Diss. (Schott, Siegfried.) Heidelberg, 1926.
	AH 7059.37	Untersuchungen zur Sittenaufsicht der Censoren. Inaug. Diss. (Schmähling, E.) Würzburg, 1937.
	AH 7189.65	Untersuchungen zur Stellung der kaiserlichen Freigelassenen und Sklaven in Italien und der Westprovinzen. (Wolf, Manfred.) Munster? 1965.
	AH 8073.14	Untersuchungen zur Verfassungsgeschichte Karthagos bis auf Aristoteles. Inaug. Diss. (Lüdemann, Hans.) Bottrop, 1933.
	AH 5271.10	Untersuchungen zur Verfassungsgeschichte von Argos im 5. Jahrhundert vor Christus. Diss. (Woerrle, Michael.) Erlangen? 196-.
	AH 4819.47.5	Uomini e cose del mondo antico. (Paoli, Ugo E.) Firenze, 1947.
	AH 3009.55	Ur, Assur und Babylon. (Schmökel, H.) Stuttgart, 1953.
	AH 3002.2.25	Ur dynasty tablets. (Nies, James B.) Leipzig, 1920.

Author and Title Listing

AH 3002.75F — Ur excavations. Texts and plates. v.1-4; 6, pt.1-2; 8. (Joint Expedition of the British Museum and the Museum of the University of Pennyslvania to Mesopotamia.) Philadelphia, 1920-35. 10v.

AH 3013.927F — Ur excavations. v.1-10. (Hall, Harry R.) Oxford, 1927-39. 9v.

AH 3013.930.10 — Ur of the Chaldees. (Woolley, Charles L.) N.Y., 1930.

AH 3013.930.5 — Ur of the Chaldees. (Woolley, Charles L.) Washington, 1930.

AH 4938.92 — Urban, K. Geographischen Forschungen und Märchen. Gütersloh, 1892.

AH 4299.56 — L'urbanisme dans la Grèce antique. (Martin, Roland.) Paris, 1956.

AH 8513.12 — Urbanization and the franchise in Roman Gaul. (DeWitt, N.J.) Lancaster, Pa., 1940.

AH 4329.27 — Die Urbevölkerung Griechenlands und ihre allmähliche Entwickelung zu Volksstämen. (Mucke, J.R.) Leipzig, 1927-29.

AH 299.22 — Ure, Percy. The origin of tyranny. Cambridge, 1922.

AH 299.22.2 — Ure, Percy. The origin of tyranny. N.Y., 1962.

AH 4819.21.5A — Ure, Percy N. The Greek renaissance. London, 1921.

AH 8257.5 — Urgeschichte der österreichischen Länder. (Gross-Hoffinger, A.) Meissen, 1846.

AH 818.84.5 — Urgeschichte des Menschen. v.1-2. (Rauber, August.) Leipzig, 1884.

AH 4258.40 — Urkunden. (Böckh, August.) Berlin, 1840.

AH 3002.96 — Urkunden aus der Zeit der dritten babylonischen Dynastie. (Peiser, F.) Berlin, 1905.

Eg 602.5.2 — Urkunden der 18. Dynastie. Übersetzung zu den Heften 17-22...von Wolfgang Helck. (Sethe, Kurt.) Berlin, 1961.

AH 3150.9 — Urkunden des altbabylonischen Zivil- und Prozessrechts. (Schorr, M.) Leipzig, 1913.

Eg 602.5 — Urkunden des 18. Dynastie. (Heft 1-22). (Sethe, Kurt.) Leipzig, 1906- 6v.

Eg 872.10 — Urkunden mythologischen Inhalts. Heft 1-2. (Schott, Siegfried.) Leipzig, 1929-39.

AH 5139.5 — Urkunden zur Geschichte von Samos. (Curtius, C.) Wesel, 1873.

AH 3664.17.1 — Urmensch und Seele in der iranischen Überlieferung. (Wesendonk, Otto Günther von.) Osnabrück, 1971.

AH 9682.2 — Ursin, Nils R. De Lusitania provincia Romana. Helsingiae, 1884.

AH 4108.18 — Ursprünge der Besteurung. (Hüllmann, K.D.) Cöln, 1818.

AH 8908.17 — Der Ursprung der Etrusker. (Altheim, F.) Baden, 1950.

AH 4839.62 — Der Ursprung der olympischen Spiele. (Drees, Ludwig.) Stuttgart, 1962.

AH 3964.12 — Der Ursprung des Monotheismus. (Popper, Julius.) Berlin, 1879.

AH 7239.08 — Ursprung und Entwickelung. (Steinwender, T.) Danzig, 1908.

AH 3045.20 — The Uruk countryside. (Adams, Robert McCormick.) Chicago, 1972.

Eg 879.54.5 — Die Urweisheit der alten Ägypter. (Bertram, Johannes.) Hamburg, 1954.

AH 4415.5 — Uschold, Johannes N. Geschichte des trojanischen Krieges. Stuttgart, 1836.

AH 7819.52 — Ussani, Vincenzo. Guida allo studio della civiltà romana antica. Napoli, 1952-54. 2v.

AH 7819.52.5 — Ussani, Vincenzo. Guida allo studio della civiltà romana antica. 2. ed. Torino, 1961-64. 2v.

Htn AH 276.50.8F* — Ussher, James. Annales Veteris et Novi Testamenti. Genevae, 1722.

Htn AH 276.50* — Ussher, James. Annales Veteris Testamenti a prima mundi origine deducti. Londini, 1650-54. 2v.

Htn AH 276.58F* — Ussher, James. The annals of the Old and New Testament. London, 1658.

AH 842.13 — Ussing, J.L. Darstellung des Erziehungs- und Unterrichtwesens. Altona, 1870.

AH 842.14 — Ussing, J.L. Erziehung und Jugendunterricht. Berlin, 1885.

AH 846.7 — Ussing, J.L. Graekernes og Romernes huse. Kjøbenhavn, 1876.

AH 5253.5 — Ustrój państwowy w starożytnym Argos. (Zwolski, Edward.) Lublin, 1967.

AH 7469.65 — Utchenko, S. Krizis; padenie Rimskoi respubliki. Moskva, 1965.

AH 7459.56 — Utchenko, S.L. Der weltanschaulich politische Kampf in Rom. Berlin, 1956.

AH 7489.69 — Utchenko, Sergei L. Drevnii Rim. Moskva, 1969.

AH 3661.10.5 — Utopie und Wirtschaft. (Altheim, Franz.) Frankfurt, 1957.

AH 7518.90 — Utrum metuerit Tiberius Germanicum necne quaeritur. Inaug. Diss. (Ferber, Curtius.) Hamburgi, 1890.

Eg 879.57.10 — Uxkull, Woldemar. Die Einweihung im alten Ägypten. Büdingen-Gettenbach, 1957.

AH 819.68.15 — Uygarlik çizgisi. (Şenel, Alâeddin.) Ankara, 1968.

AH 279.65.10 — V mire antichnykh idei i obrazov. (Preobrazhenskii, Petr F.) Moskva, 1965.

AH 8913.10.10 — Vacano, Otto Wilhelm von. The Etruscans in the ancient world. N.Y., 1960.

AH 8913.10 — Vacano, Otto Wilhelm von. Die Etrusker. Stuttgart, 1955.

AH 8913.10.5 — Vacano, Otto Wilhelm von. Die Etrusker in der Welt der Antike. Hamburg, 1957.

AH 7844.6.15 — Vaccari, A. Il natale de Roma nelle leggende e nella storia. Verona, 1934.

AH 7238.93 — Vaders, Joseph. Einundvierzigster Jahresbericht...Realgymnasium. Münster, 1893.

AH 2271.5 — Vagts, Rudolph. Aphrodisias in Karien. Diss. Borna, 1920.

Eg 707.01 — Vaillant, J. Historia Ptolemaeorum. Amstelodami, 1701.

AH 3607.5 — Vaillant, J.F. Regum Parthorum historia. Parisiis, 1725. 2v.

AH 3607.7 — Vaillant, J.F. Regum Parthorum historia. Parisiis, 1728.

AH 8514.13 — Vaillat, Claudius. Le culte des sources dans la Gaule antique. Paris, 1932.

AH 7200.11 — Valeriani, L. Leggi delle dodici tavole. Firenze, 1839.

AH 819.72 — Valeurs antiques et temps modernes. Classical values and the modern world. Ottawa, 1972.

AH 7469.56 — Valgiglio, E. Silla e la crisi repubblicana. 1. ed. Firenze, 1956.

Htn AH 8549.76* — Vallentin, F. Essai sur les divinités indigètes du Vocontium. Grenoble, 1877.

AH 8516.12 — Vallentin, Florian. Les Alpes cottiennes et graies; géographie gallo-romaine. Paris, 1883.

AH 9633.6 — Vallet, Georges. Rhégion et Zancle. Paris, 1958.

AH 5916.5 — Valmin, M.N. Études topographiques sur la Messénie ancienne. Lund, 1930.

AH 4189.37 — Valmin, N.S. Arbete och slaveri i antiken. Stockholm, 1937.

AH 7449.48 — Valori, F. Scipione l'Africano. Torino, 1948.

AH 8548.25 — Valroger, L. de. Les Celtes, la Gaule celtique. Paris, 1879.

AH 7727.11 — Valsecchi, V. De M. Aurelii Antonine Elaggbali tribunitici potestate V. Florentiae, 1711.

Htn AH 7235.97* — Valtrimus, J.A. De re militari veterum Romanorum. n.p., 1597.

AH 4108.85 — Value of Attic talent in modern money. v.1-2. (Goodwin, W.W.) n.p., 1885.

AH 1879.65 — Vanal, Antoine. L'iconographie du dieu de l'orage. Paris, 1965.

AH 3160.16 — Van Buren, Elizabeth. Symbols of the gods in Mesopotamian art. Roma, 1945.

AH 3017.55 — Van Buren, Elizabeth D. The fauna of ancient Mesopotamia as represented in art. Roma, 1939.

AH 3016.25 — Van Buren, Elizabeth D. The flowing vase and the god with streams. Berlin, 1933.

AH 3016.15F — Van Buren, Elizabeth D. Foundation figurines and offerings. Berlin, 1931.

AH 8011.7 — Les Vandales et l'Afrique. (Courtois, C.) Paris, 1955.

NEDL AH 1278.78 — Van Den Berg, E. Petite histoire ancienne des peuples de l'Orient. Paris, 1878.

AH 1278.78.2 — Van Den Berg, E. Petite histoire ancienne des peuples de l'Orient. 2. éd. Paris, 1881.

AH 4278.80.5 — Van den Berg. Petite histoire des Grecs. Paris, 1880.

AH 3181.5.2 — Vanderburgh, F.A. Sumerian hymns. N.Y., 1908.

AH 3181.5 — Vanderburgh, F.A. Sumerian hymns. Thesis. N.Y., 1908.

Eg 809.62 — Vanderslayen, Claude. Chronologie des préfets d'Égypte de 284 à 395. Bruxelles, 1962.

Eg 609.71 — Vandersleyen, Claude. Les guerres d'Amoses. Bruxelles, 1971.

Eg 1309.62F — Vandier, Jacques. Le papyrus Jumilhac. Paris, 1962.

Eg 39.70 — Vandoni, Mariangela. Gli epistrategi nell'Egitto greco-romano. Milano, 1970?

AH 4844.8 — Vandoni, Mariangela. Feste pubbliche e private nei documenti greci. Milano, 1964.

AH 4819.72.10 — Van Duyn, Janet H. (Dunning). The Greeks: their legacy. N.Y., 1972.

AH 7569.65 — Vanella, Giovanni. L'Adventus di Vespasiano nei suoi aspetti mistico-religiosi e giundico-costituzionali. Napoli, 1965.

AH 7819.48 — Vangenechten, K. Het antieke Rome. Antwerpen, 1948.

AH 7203.143.5 — Vangerow, K.A. von. Lehrbuch der Pandekten. 7. Aufl. Marburg, 1876. 3v.

AH 3059.7.10 — Van Ingen, W. Figurines from Seleucia on the Tigris. Ann Arbor, 1939.

AH 819.63F — Vanished civilizations of the ancient world. (Bacon, Edward.) N.Y., 1963.

AH 7888.95 — Vanlaer, M. La fin d'un peuple. Paris, 1895. 2v.

AH 409.20 — Van Loon, Hendrik Willem. Ancient man. N.Y., 1920.

AH 409.22 — Van Loon, Hendrik Willem. Ancient man. N.Y., 1922.

AH 8607.5.5 — Vannucci, A. Storia dell'Italia antica. 3. ed. Milano, 1873-76. 4v.

AH 8607.5 — Vannucci, A. Storia d'Italia. Firenze, 1851. 4v.

AH 4829.23 — Van Rook, La Rue. Greek life and thought. N.Y., 1923.

AH 7499.02A — Van Santvoord, S. The house of Caesar. Troy, 1902.

AH 279.47 — Van Sickle, C.E. A political and cultural history of the ancient world from prehistoric times to the dissolution of the Roman Empire in the West. Boston, 1947-

AH 8461.10 — Várady, László. Das letzte Jahrhundert Pannoniens, 376-476. Budapest, 1969.

AH 7239.61 — Várady, Lazló. Késórómai hadügyek es társadalmi alapjaik. Budapest, 1961.

VEg 885.969 — Varázslás az ókori Egyiptomban. (Kákosy, Lászl.) Budapest, 1969.

AH 7809.08.5 — Varese, P. Cronologia romana. Roma, 1908.

AH 7419.11 — Vargas Vila, J.M. La república romana. Paris, 1911.

VAH 279.67.5 — Varshavskii, Anatolii S. Goroda raskryvaint tainy. Moskva, 1967.

AH 8307.2 — Vaschide, V. Histoire de la conquête...de la Dacie. Paris, 1903.

Htn AH 7817.32* — Vaslet, L. Introduzzione alla scienza d'antichita. Venezia, 1732.

AH 7817.32.5 — Vaslet, L. Introduzzione alla scienza d'antichita. Venezia, 1828.

AH 7489.37A — Vassal-queens and some contemporary women in Roman Empire. (Macurdy, G.H.) Baltimore, 1937.

AH 3096.8 — The Vassal-treaties of Esarhaddon. (Esarhaddon, king of Assyria.) London, 1958.

AH 7479.34 — Vassalli, Pietro. Lucio Munazio Planco, generale di Giulio Cesare, console 42 a. C. Cassino, 1934.

AH 3160.7 — Vater, Sohn und Fursprecher. (Zimmern, H.) Leipzig, 1896.

AH 7114.48 — Der Vater des Vaterlandes im römischen Denken. (Alföldi, Andras.) Darmstadt, 1971.

AH 7201.17 — Vaticana fragmenta. Borussorum, 1828.

AH 4858.17 — Vatin, Claude. Recherches sur le mariage et la condition de la femme mariée à l'epoque hellénistique. Thèse. Paris, 1970.

AH 4858.17.1 — Vatin, Claude. Recherches sur le mariage et la condition de la femme mariée à l'epoque hellénistique. Paris, 1970.

AH 7509.34 — Vaubel, T. Untersuchungen zu Augustus' Politik und Staatsauffassung nach den autobiographischen Schriften. Inaug. Diss. Düsseldorf, 1934.

AH 7448.12F — Vaudoncourt, F. Guillaume. Histoire des campagnes d'Annibal. Milan, 1812. 3v.

AH 7148.33 — Vaugerow, C.A. Latini Juniani. Marburg, 1833.

AH 8907.41 — Vaughan, A.C. Those mysterious Etruscans. 1. ed. Garden City, N.Y., 1964.

AH 2108.5 — Vaux, W.S.W. Great cities and islands of Asia Minor. London, 1877.

AH 3013.27.4 — Vaux, W.S.W. Nineveh and Persepolis. 4. ed. London, 1855.

AH 3657.11 — Vaux, William Sandys Wright. Persia. London, 1875.

AH 3657.11.5 — Vaux, William Sandys Wright. Persia. London, 1893.

AH 3009.71 — Vavilon legendarnyi i Vavilon istoricheskii. (Beliavskii, Vatalii A.) Moskva, 1971.

AH 9682.4 — Vázquez Seijas, M. Lugo bajo el imperio romano. Lugo, 1939.

AH 7107.34 — Vectigalia Popule Romani. (Burmani, Petro.) Leidae, 1734.

AH 198.32 — Veder, A. Historia philosophiae juris apud veteres. Lugduni Batavorum, 1832.

AH 8060.5 — Vega, Luis A. de. Amilcar Barca. Madrid, 1960.

AH 7479.20 — Veith, Georg. Der Feldrug von Dyrrhachium. Wien, 1920.

AH 7449.59 — Veitskivs'kyi, I.I. Zovnishnia polityka krain Zakhidnogo Ceredzemnomor'ia v 264-219 rr. do n.e. L'viv, 1959.

AH 8557.10 — Veliki Illirik (284-395) i njegova konačna dioba (396-437). (Rogošić, Roko.) Zagreb, 1971.

AH 279.52A — Velikovsky, I. Ages in chaos. 1. ed. Garden City, 1952.

AH 809.45 — Velikovsky, I. Thesis for the reconstruction of ancient history. N.Y., 1945.

Author and Title Listing

Author and Title Listing

AH 7118.10 — Wende, Martin. De Caeciliis metellis commentationis pars I. Inaug. Diss. Bonnae, 1875.

Eg 278.90A — Wendel, F.C.H. History of Egypt. N.Y., 1890.

AH 7478.83 — Wendelmuth, Richard. T. Labienus. Inaug. Diss. Marburg, 1883.

AH 4819.07 — Wendland, P. Hellenistisch-Römische Kultur. Tübingen, 1907.

AH 4819.07.2A — Wendland, P. Hellenistisch-römische Kultur. Tübingen, 1912.

AH 7139.53F — Wenger, L. Die Quellen des römischen Rechts. Wien, 1953.

AH 7139.05.3 — Wenger, L. Römische und antike Rechtsgeschichte. Graz, 1905.

Eg 759.22.5 — Wenger, L. Volk und Staat in Ägypten am Ausgang der Römerherrschaft. München, 1922.

AH 7168.41 — Wening Ingenheim, J.N. von. Lehre vom Schadensersatze nach römischen Rechte. Heidelberg, 1841.

Eg 1139.67 — Wente, Edward F. Late Ramesside letters. Chicago, 1967.

AH 9610.29 — Wentker, Hermann. Sizilien und Athen. Heidelberg, 1956.

Eg 879.53.5 — Das Werden der Altägyptischen Hochkultur. (Spiegel, J.) Heidelberg, 1953.

NEDL AH 819.07 — Werden und Wesen der Humanität. (Reitzenstein, P.) Strassburg, 1907.

AH 5390.11 — Werenka, D. Kritische Bemerkungen. Czernowitz, 1907.

AH 7808.88.5 — Werner, C. De feriis Latinis. Coloniae, 1888.

AH 7659.39 — Werner, H. Der Untergang Roms. Stuttgart, 1939.

AH 8679.2 — Werner, P. De incendiis urbis Romae. Lipsiae, 1906.

AH 7419.63.5 — Werner, Robert. Der Beginn der römischen Republik. München, 1963.

AH 2357.15 — Wernsdoff, G. Republica Galatarum. Norimbergae, 1743.

AH 9758.3 — Wersebe, August von. Ueber die Völker und Völkerbundnisse des alten Teutschlands. Hannover, 1826.

Eg 709.30 — Wertheimer, O.V. Kleopatra. Zürich, 1930.

AH 7799.67 — Wes, Marinus Antony. Das Ende des Kaisertums im Westen des Römischen Reichs. 's-Gravenhage, 1967.

AH 7478.79.4 — Wesemann, H. Caesarfabeln des Mittelalters. Löwenberg, 1879.

AH 7489.16 — Das Wesen des Römischen Kaisertums. (Schulz, Otto T.) Paderborn, 1916.

Eg 819.69 — Wesen und Wandel der ägyptischen Kultur. (Otto, Eberhard.) Berlin, 1969.

AH 3664.17.1 — Wesendonk, Otto Günther von. Urmensch und Seele in der iranischen Überlieferung. Osnabrück, 1971.

AH 7957.35 — Wesseling, P. Vetera Romanorum itineraria. Amstelodami, 1735.

AH 4818.23 — Wessenberg, I.H. Volksleben zu Athen. Zürich, 1823.

AH 8515.5 — West, L.C. Roman Gaul; the objects of trade. Oxford, 1935.

AH 9665.5 — West, Louis C. Imperial Roman Spain; the objects of trade. Oxford, 1929.

AH 279.13.10 — West, Willis M. The ancient world. Boston, 1913.

NEDL AH 279.05.5 — West, Willis M. The ancient world from the earliest times to 800 A.D. Boston, 1905.

AH 7169.51A — West Roman vulgar law. (Levy, Ernst.) Phildelphia, 1951.

AH 9757.5 — Westdeutschland zur Römerzeit. (Dragendorff, H.) Leipzig, 1912.

AH 9757.5.5 — Westdeutschland zur Römerzeit. 2. Aufl. (Dragendorff, H.) Leipzig, 1919.

AH 4208.5 — Westermann, A. De iuris iurandi iudicium Atheniensium formula. Lipsiae, 1858.

AH 4217.7 — Westermann, A. De publicis Atheniensium honoribus ae Praemais commutaico. Lipsiae, 1830.

Eg 919.22 — Westermann, W.L. The "dryland" in Ptolemaic and Roman Egypt. n.p., 1922.

AH 189.34 — Westermann, W.L. Sklaverei. Stuttgart, 1934.

AH 189.55A — Westermann, W.L. The slave systems of Greek and Roman antiquity. Philadelphia, 1955.

AH 279.12.7 — Westermann, William L. The story of ancient nations. N.Y., 1912.

AH 1409.06.1 — Western Asia in the days of Sargon of Assyria, 722-705 B.C. (Olmstead, Albert T.) N.Y., 1908.

AH 1409.06 — Western Asia in the days of Sargon of Assyria. Thesis. (Olmstead, Albert T.) Lancaster, Pa., 1908.

AH 7799.04A — Western Europe in the fifth century. (Freeman, E.A.) London, 1904.

AH 8647.17A — The western Greeks. (Dunabin, T.J.) Oxford, 1948.

AH 7239.38.5 — Westington, M.M. Atrocities in Roman warfare to 133 B.C. Diss. Chicago, 1938.

AH 9610.18 — Westlake, H.D. Timoleon and his relations with tyrants. Manchester, Eng., 1952.

AH 6060.5.2 — Westlake, Henry Dickinson. Thessaly in the fourth century B.C. Groningen, 1969.

AH 6060.5 — Westlake, Henry Dickinson. Thessaly in the fourth century B.C. London, 1935.

AH 5807.7 — Die Westlokrer. Inaug. Diss. (Roltsch, Otto.) Weida, 1914.

AH 3966.28F — The Westminster historical atlas to the Bible. (Wright, G.E.) Philadelphia, 1945.

AH 3966.28.2F — The Westminster historical atlas to the Bible. (Wright, G.E.) Philadelphia, 1956.

AH 7768.65 — Das weströmische Reich. (Richter, H.) Berlin, 1865.

AH 7799.15 — Weströmische Studien. (Sundwall, J.) Berlin, 1915.

AH 7161.29 — Westrup, Carl W. Introduction to early Roman law; the patriarchal joint family. London, 1934-55. 5v.

AH 7138.71.5 — Wetter, P. Cours élémentaire de droit romain. Gand, 1871. 2v.

AH 7138.71.6 — Wetter, P. Cours élémentaire de droit romain. Gand, 1875. 2v.

AH 7162.29 — Wetter, P.A.H. Droit d'accroissement. Bruxelles, 1866.

AH 888.95 — Wetzel, M. Bedeutung des klassischen Altertums. Paderborn, 1895.

AH 7228.45 — Wetzell, G.W. Der römische Vindicationsprocess. Leipzig, 1845.

AH 8873.5 — Weyer, G.A. Die staatsrechtlichen Beziehungen Kapuas zu Rom. Inaug. Diss. Bonn, 1913.

Eg 879.26 — Weynants-Ronday, M. (Mrs.). Les statues vivantes. Bruxelles, 1926.

AH 4049.42A — What democracy meant to the Greeks. (Agard, W.R.) Chapel Hill, 1942.

AH 819.42 — What happened in history. (Childe, Vere Gordon.) Harmondsworth, 1943.

AH 819.42.6 — What happened in history. (Childe, Vere Gordon.) Harmondsworth, 1948.

AH 819.42.5 — What happened in history. (Childe, Vere Gordon.) London, 1960.

AH 4819.09 — What have the Greeks done for modern civilization? (Mahaffy, J.P.) N.Y., 1909.

AH 9458.5 — Whatmough, J. "Tusca origo Raetis". n.p., 1937.

AH 899.44 — The wheats of classical antiquity. (Jasny, Naum.) Baltimore, 1944.

AH 4559.00.2 — Wheeler, B.I. Alexander the Great. London, 1925.

AH 4558.99.5 — Wheeler, B.I. Alexander the Great. n.p., n.d.

AH 4559.00A — Wheeler, B.I. Alexander the Great. N.Y., 1900.

AH 4810.5 — Wheeler, B.I. Life of the ancient Greeks. Ithaca, 1890.

NEDL AH 968.55 — Wheeler, J. Life and travels of Herodotus. London, 1855. 2v.

AH 968.55.5 — Wheeler, J. Life and travels of Herodotus. N.Y., 1856. 2v.

Eg 299.42 — When Egypt ruled the East. (Steindorff, G.) Chicago, 1942.

Eg 299.42.5 — When Egypt ruled the East. (Steindorff, G.) Chicago, 1957.

AH 278.16 — Whepley, S. Lectures on ancient history. N.Y., 1816.

AH 7449.25.5 — Where Hannibal passed. (Bonus, A.R.) London, 1925.

AH 4048.96A — Whibley, L. Greek oligarchies. N.Y., 1896.

AH 4518.89 — Whibley, L. Political parties in Athens. 2. ed. Cambridge, 1889.

AH 4819.05.3 — Whibley, Leonard. Companion to Greek studies. Cambridge, 1905.

AH 4819.05.3.6 — Whibley, Leonard. Companion to Greek studies. Cambridge, 1916.

AH 4819.05.3.5 — Whibley, Leonard. Companion to Greek studies. 2nd ed. Cambridge, 1906.

AH 7447.94 — Whitaker, J. Course of Hannibal over the Alps. London, 1794. 2v.

AH 7653.18 — Whitaker, J. Gibbon's History of decline and fall of Roman Empire. London, 1791.

AH 7659.27 — White, Edward L. Why Rome fell. N.Y., 1927.

AH 7819.42 — White, George W. Roman history, life and literature. London, 1942.

AH 819.73.5 — White, Hayden V. The Greco-Roman tradition. N.Y., 1973.

Eg 279.52A — White, Jon M. Ancient Egypt. London, 1952.

AH 7899.67 — White, K.D. Agricultural implements of the Roman world. Cambridge, 1967.

AH 7890.2 — White, Kenneth Douglas. A bibliography of Roman agriculture. Reading, 1970.

AH 7899.70 — White, Kenneth Douglas. Roman farming. London, 1970.

AH 819.59.5 — White, Leslie A. The evolution of culture. N.Y., 1959.

AH 7653.17 — White, Lynn Townsend. The transformation of the Roman world; Gibbon's problem after two centuries. Berkeley, 1966.

AH 3027.11 — Who were the Amorites? (Haldar, Alfred Ossian.) Leiden, 1971.

AH 4299.30 — Who were the Greeks? (Myres, John L.) Berkeley, Calif., 1930.

AH 7659.27 — Why Rome fell. (White, Edward L.) N.Y., 1927.

AH 7448.20 — Wickham, Henry L. A dissertation on the passage of Hannibal over the Alps. Oxford, 1820.

AH 3664.16 — Widengren, G. Hochgottglaube im alten Iran. Uppsala, 1938.

AH 3182.5 — Widengren, Georg. The Accadian and Hebrew Psalms of lamentation as religious documents. Inaug. Diss. Uppsala, 1936.

AH 3664.14 — Widengren, George. Iranische Geisteswelt von der Anfängen bis zum Islam. Baden-Baden, 1961.

Eg 829.60 — Wie die alten Ägypter sich anredeten. (Grapow, Herman.) Berlin, 1960.

AH 7846.4 — Wie heizten die Römer ihre Wohnraume. (Lanz-Liebenfels.) Umschau, 1902.

Eg 278.84 — Wiedemann, A. Ägyptische Geschichte. Gotha, 1884. 2v.

Eg 278.84.2 — Wiedemann, A. Ägyptische Geschichte. Supplement. Gotha, 1888.

Eg 819.20 — Wiedemann, A. Das alte Ägypten. Heidelberg, 1920.

Eg 878.95.15 — Wiedemann, A. The ancient Egyptian doctrine of the immortality of the soul. London, 1895.

Eg 878.95 — Wiedemann, A. The ancient Egyptian doctrine of the immortality of the soul. N.Y., 1895.

AH 4298.93 — Wiedemann, A. Beziehungen zwischen Aegypten und Griechenland. Leipzig, 1883.

Eg 878.97A — Wiedemann, A. Religion of the ancient Egyptians. Photoreproduction. N.Y., 1897.

AH 7498.75 — Wiedemeister, F. Der Cäsarenwahnsinn. Hannover, 1875.

AH 3013.925 — Das wieder erstehende Babylon. (Koldewey, Robert.) Leipzig, 1925.

AH 3013.925.3 — Das wieder erstehende Babylon. 3. Aufl. (Koldewey, Robert.) Leipzig, 1914.

AH 7478.98 — Wiegandt, L. Studien zur staatsrechtlichen Stellung. Dresden, 1898.

AH 7508.66 — Wiegestaltete sich der Caesarismus. (Wutzdorff, R.) Langensalza, 1866.

AH 7238.30 — Wiener, P.E.A. De legione Romanorum vicesima secunda. Darmstadii, 1830.

AH 239.27 — Wienicke, Arnold. Keltisches Söldnertum in der Mittelmeerwelt bis zur Herrschaft der Römer. Inaug. Diss. Breslau, 1927.

AH 4838.48 — Wieseler, F. Satyrspiel. Göttingen, 1848.

AH 9707.9 — Wieser, J. Die Thraker. Stuttgart, 1963.

AH 409.43 — Wiesner, J. Vor- und Frühzeit der Mittelmeerländer. Berlin, 1943. 2v.

AH 7658.59 — Wietersheim, E. von. Geschichte der Völkerwanderung. Leipzig, 1859. 4v.

AH 4819.50.10 — Wifsbrand, Albert. Den grekiska kulturhistoriens faser. Stockholm, 1950.

AH 7448.48 — Wijmre, J.A. Quaestiones criticae de belli punici. Groningae, 1848.

AH 8616.10 — Wikén, Erik. Die Kunde der Hellenen von dem Lande und den Völkern der Apenninenhalbinsel bis 300 v. Chr. Lund, 1937.

AH 4409.06 — Wilamowitz-Moellendorff, Ulrich von. Über die ionische Wanderung. n.p., 1906.

Eg 1309.41.5PF — The Wilbour papyrus. London, 1941.

Eg 1309.41.5F — The Wilbour papyrus. v.2-4. London, 1941-52. 3v.

AH 4168.95.5 — Wilbrandt, M. De rerum privatarum ante solonis tempus. Rostochii, 1895.

AH 3179.14 — Wilcke, Claus. Dan Lugalbandaepos. Wiesbaden, 1969.

AH 4279.24 — Wilcken, U. Griechische Geschichte im Rahmen der Altertumsgeschichte. München, 1924.

AH 4279.24.5 — Wilcken, U. Griechische Geschichte im Rahmen der Altertumsgeschichte. 7. Aufl. München, 1951.

AH 7088.85 — Wilcken, U. Observationes ad historiam Aegypti. Berolinii, 1885.

AH 4559.31 — Wilcken, Ulrich. Alexander der Grosse. Leipzig, 1931.

AH 4559.31.5 — Wilcken, Ulrich. Alexander the Great. London, 1932.

AH 7297.97 — Wilcocks, J. Roman conversations. London, 1797. 2v.

AH 7909.70 — Wild, J.P. Textile manufacture in the northern Roman provinces. Cambridge, Eng., 1970.

Author and Title Listing

Author and Title Listing

AH 2009.5	Die Wohnsetze und Wanderungen der arabischen Stämme. (Abu Ubaid al-Bakri.) Göttingen, 1869.
AH 4199.50	Wolf, E. Griechisches Rechtsdenken. v.1-4. Frankfurt am Main, 1950-52. 5v.
AH 889.09	Wolf, H. Geschichte des antike Sozialismus. Gütersloh, 1909.
Eg 709.06	Wolf, Josef. Aus Inschriften und Papyren der Ptolemaierzeit. Feldkirch, 1906.
AH 7189.65	Wolf, Manfred. Untersuchungen zur Stellung der kaiserlichen Freigelassenen und Sklaven in Italien und der Westprovinzen. Munster? 1965.
Eg 279.71	Wolf, Walther. Das alte Ägypten. München, 1971.
Eg 819.62.5	Wolf, Walther. Kulturgeschichte des alten Ägypten. Stuttgart, 1962.
Eg 819.55	Wolf, Walther. Die Welt der Ägypter. Stuttgart, 1955.
AH 4487.7	Wolff, E. De vita Themiestoclis Atheniensis. Monasteii, 1871.
AH 4845.19	Wolff, E. Philanthropie bei den Griechen. Berlin, 1902.
AH 7200.5	Wolff, Emil. Rättshistoriska studier till den tolf taflanaslag. Göteborg, 1883.
AH 163.10	Wolff, H.J. Written and unwritten marriages in Hellenistic and postclassical Roman law. Haverford, 1939.
AH 7139.51.5	Wolff, Hans J. Roman law. Oklahoma, 1951.
AH 7579.05	Wolff-Beckh, B. Kaiser Titus und der jüdische Krieg. Berlin, 1905.
NEDL AH 279.02.5	Wolfson, A.M. Essentials in ancient history. N.Y., 1902.
AH 819.16	Wolfson, Arthur M. Ancient civilization. N.Y., 1916.
AH 7239.08.9	Wolks, Josef. Beiträge zur Geschichte der Legio XI Claudia. Breslau, 1908.
AH 9765.5	Wollheim, Günther. Germania oeconomica; das Bild der germanischen Wirtschaft bei Caesar und Tacitus. Freiburg, 1958.
AH 7201.111	Wołodkiewicz, Witold. Obligationes ex variis causarum figuris. Warszawa, 1968.
AH 7298.65	Wolterstonff, A. Bilder aus dem römischen Alterthum. Halberstadt, 1865.
AH 3954.11	Women, slaves and the ignorant in rabbinic literature. (Zucrow, S.) Boston, 1932.
AH 859.9.1	Women in Greece and Rome. (Zinserling, Verena.) N.Y., 1973.
AH 7499.11A	The women of the Caesars. (Ferrero, G.) N.Y., 1911.
NEDL AH 298.88	Wood, C.W. Topics in ancient history. Boston, 1888.
AH 4299.62	Woodhead, Arthur Geoffrey. The Greeks in the West. London, 1962.
AH 7418.98.2	Woodhouse, Mason A. History of Rome, 390-202 B.C. London, 1911.
AH 4279.58.10	Woodhouse, W.J. The tutorial history of Greece. 3. ed. London, 1958.
AH 4519.33.5	Woodhouse, William J. King Agis of Sparta and his campaign in Arkadia in 418 B.C. Oxford, 1933.
AH 5315.20	Woodhouse, William J. Solon the liberator; a study of the Agrarian problem in Attika in the seventh century. London, 1938.
AH 7659.16	Woodward, E.L. Christianity and nationalism in...Roman Empire. Photoreproduction. London, 1916.
AH 3014.19	Woolley, Charles L. The development of Sumerian art. N.Y., 1935.
AH 3013.955	Woolley, Charles L. Excavations at Ur. London, 1955.
AH 3013.929	Woolley, Charles L. The excavations at Ur and the Hebrew records. London, 1929.
AH 3022.9A	Woolley, Charles L. The Sumerians. Oxford, 1928.
AH 3013.930.10	Woolley, Charles L. Ur of the Chaldees. N.Y., 1930.
AH 3013.930.5	Woolley, Charles L. Ur of the Chaldees. Washington, 1930.
AH 4298.40	Wordsworth, C. Greece; pictorial, descriptive, and historical. London, 1840.
AH 4298.53	Wordsworth, C. Greece; pictorial, descriptive, and historical. London, 1853.
AH 4298.53.2	Wordsworth, C. Greece; pictorial, descriptive, and historical. London, 1859.
NEDL AH 4298.40.2	Wordsworth, C. Greece; pictorial, descriptive, and historical. 2. ed. London, 1844.
NEDL AH 4298.53.3	Wordsworth, C. Greece; pictorial, descriptive and historical. 5. ed. London, 1868.
AH 4130.5	A working bibliography of Greek law. (Calhoun, George M.) Cambridge, 1927.
AH 930.5	The world; a classical atlas. (Johnston, W. and A.K., publishers.) Edinburgh, 18- .
AH 4819.66.21F	The world of classical Athens. London, 1970.
AH 279.37.5	The world of Greece and Rome. (Bevan, E.R.) London, 1937.
AH 4279.62	The world of Herodotus. (De Silincourt, A.) London, 1962.
AH 4279.62.3	The world of Herodotus. 1. ed. (De Silincourt, A.) Boston, 1963.
AH 4819.36.5	The world of Hesiod. (Burn, Andrew Robert.) London, 1936.
AH 4819.36.6	The world of Hesiod. 2. ed. (Burn, Andrew Robert.) N.Y., 1966.
AH 4819.54.2	The world of Odysseus. (Finley, Moses I.) Harmondsworth, 1962.
AH 4819.54.1	The world of Odysseus. (Finley, Moses I.) Harmondsworth, 1972.
AH 4819.54	The world of Odysseus. (Finley, Moses I.) N.Y., 1954.
AH 3963.30.1	The world of the Bible. (Jirku, Anton.) London, 1967.
AH 3663.12	The world of the Persians. (Gobineau, Arthur.) London, 1971.
AH 3707.22	The world of the Phoenicians. (Moscati, Sabatino.) London, 1968.
AH 299.30	The world on the positive plate. (Chuckerbutty, K.) Calcutta, 193-. 5 pam.
AH 878.80	Worship of the sun. The story told by a coin of Constantine. (Phillips, H.) Philadelphia, 1880.
Eg 879.04.5	Wreszinski, W. Die Hohenpriester des Amon. Berlin, 1904.
AH 8549.124	Wright, D. Druidism; the ancient faith of Britain. London, 1924.
AH 4843.19	Wright, F.A. The arts in Greece. London, 1923.
AH 4829.25A	Wright, F.A. Greek social life. London, 1925.
AH 7509.37A	Wright, F.A. Marcus Agrippa, organizer of victory. N.Y., 1937.
AH 4559.34	Wright, Frederick A. Alexander the Great. London, 1934.
AH 4839.25.5	Wright, Frederick A. Greek athletics. London, 1925.
AH 819.32	Wright, Frederick A. The romance of life in the ancient world. London, 1932?
AH 3966.28F	Wright, G.E. The Westminster historical atlas to the Bible. Philadelphia, 1945.
AH 3966.28.2F	Wright, G.E. The Westminster historical atlas to the Bible. Philadelphia, 1956.
AH 4484.13	Wright, H.B. Campaign of Plataea. New Haven, 1904.
AH 4438.92A	Wright, J.H. Date of Cylon...early Athenian history. Boston, 1892.
AH 3407.5	Wright, W. Empire of Hittites. London, 1884.
AH 3407.5.3	Wright, W. Empire of Hittites. 2d ed. London, 1886.
AH 3936.5	Wright, W. Palmyra and Zenobia. N.Y., 1895.
AH 1298.86	Wright, William B. Ancient cities from dawn to the daylight. Boston, 1886.
AH 163.10	Written and unwritten marriages in Hellenistic and postclassical Roman law. (Wolff, H.J.) Haverford, 1939.
AH 7168.97	Wünsch, P. Zur Lehre vom Beneficium Competentiae. Diss. Leipzig, 1897.
AH 6110.10	Wüst, F.R. Philipp II. München, 1938.
AH 898.54	Wüstemann, E.F. Unterhaltungen aus der alten Welt. Gotha, 1854.
AH 8532.5.5	Wuilleumier, P. Lyon. Paris, 1953.
AH 4558.98.3	Wulff, Oskar. Alexander mit der Lanze. Berlin, 1898.
Eg 298.68.5	Wunderland der Pyramiden. (Oppel, K.) Leipzig, 1868.
AH 7135.59.20F	Wunderlich, I. Additamentorum ad Barnabae Brissonii. Hamburgi, 1778.
AH 4410.36	Wundsam, Klaus. Die politische und soziale Struktur in den mykenischen Residenzen nach den Linear B. Texten. Wien, 1968.
AH 7898.98	Wurm, A. De villa rustica. Kempten, 1898.
AH 928.21	Wurm, J.F. De ponderum, numerum. Stutgardiae, 1821.
AH 7508.66	Wutzdorff, R. Wiegestaltete sich der Caesarismus. Langensalza, 1866.
VAH 1402.5	Wybór źrodet do historii starozytnego wschodu do pol. Wyd. 2. (Zabłocka, Julia.) Poznań, 1966.
AH 4846.9	Wycherley, Richard Ernest. How the Greeks built cities. 2. ed. London, 1967.
Eg 609.72	Wynne, Barry. Behind the mask of Tutankhamen. London, 1972.
AH 3914.7.5	Xella, Paolo. Il mito di Šhre Šlm. Saggio sulla mitologia ugaritica. Roma, 1973.
AH 4483.16.5	Xerxes at Salamis. (Green, Peter.) N.Y., 1970.
AH 4479.63	Xerxes' invasion of Greece. (Hignett, Charles.) Oxford, 1963.
AH 7200.13	Die XII Tafeln. (Voigt, M.) Leipzig, 1883. 2v.
AH 1239.63	Yadin, Y. The art of warfare in Biblical lands. N.Y., 1963. 2v.
AH 818.82	Yaggy, Levi M. Museum of antiquity, a description of ancient life. N.Y., 1882.
AH 3002.32F	Yale Oriental series. Babylonian texts. New Haven. 1-10,1915-1947 10v.
AH 3002.33	Yale Oriental series. Researches. New Haven. 2-24,1916-1949 20v.
AH 29.29	Yale University. The legacy of the ancient world. New Haven, 1929.
AH 7114.40	Yavetz, Z. Plebs and princeps. London, 1969.
AH 4483.16	The year of Salamis, 480-479 B.C. (Green, Peter.) London, 1970.
Eg 278.35	Yeates, T. Ancient Egypt. London, 1835.
AH 1808.30	Yeates, T. Remarks of Bible chronology. London, 1830.
AH 2061.3.5	Yeghisheh, Elisha Vardapet. The epic of St. Vardan the brave. N.Y., 1951.
AH 3020.40	Yeni Sumer çağina ait Nippur hukukî ve idarî belgeleri. (Çiğ, Muazzez.) Ankara, 1965.
NEDL AH 278.69.15	Yonge, Chrlotte M. A book of worthies. London, 1886.
AH 4558.97	Yorck, M.G. Feldzüge Alexanders des Grossen. Berlin, 1897.
AH 8208.10	Young, Douglas. Romanisation in Scotland. Tayport, 1955?
AH 5307.7	Young, W. History of Athens. London, 1786.
AH 5307.7.3	Young, W. History of Athens. 3. ed. London, 1804.
AH 7709.67.5	The young emperors, Rome, A.D. 193-244. (Brauer, George C.) N.Y., 1967.
AH 4039.72	Yunan arkeolojisinin ana çirgileri. (Akarca, Aşkidil.) Ankara, 1972.
AH 819.71.2	Z antycznego świata. wyd. 2. (Parandowski, Yan.) Warszawa, 1971.
Eg 879.68.5	Žabkar, Louis V. A study of the Ba concept in ancient Egyptian texts. Chicago, 1968.
AH 2147.10	Zabłocka, Julia. Podstawy gospodarcze anatolijskiej arystokraeji w świetle inskrypcji fundacyjnach okresu wczesnegocesarstwa. Wyd. 1. Poznań, 1968.
VAH 1402.5	Zabłocka, Julia. Wybór źrodet do historii starozytnego wschodu do pol. Wyd. 2. Poznań, 1966.
AH 7206.7	Zacharia, K.E. Collectio librorum juris Graeco-Romanum. Lipsiae, 1852.
AH 7138.40.3	Zachariä, K.E. Geschichte des griechisch-römischen Rechts. Berlin, 1892.
AH 7206.6	Zacharia, K.E. Innere Geschichte des griechisch römische Rechts. Leipzig, 1856.
AH 7206.5	Zacharia, K.E. Jus Graeco-Romanum. v.1-3. Lipsiae, 1856. 2v.
AH 7468.34.6	Zacharia, K.S. Lucius Cornelius Sulla. Heidelberg, 1834.
AH 7468.34.7	Zacharia, K.S. Lucius Cornelius Sulla. Mannheim, 1850.
AH 7908.65	Zacharia von Lingenthal, K.E. Eine Verordnung Justinian's über den Seidenhandel. v.1-2. St. Petersburg, 1865. 2 pam.
AH 4819.63.10F	Zadoks, A.N. Ontieke cultuur in beeld. 7. Druk. Bussum, 1963.
AH 862.6	Zähne und Zahnbehandlung der alten Aegypter, Hebräer, Inder, Babyloner, Assyrer, Griechen und Römer. (Grawinkel, Karl J.) Berlin, 1906.
AH 4410.41	Zafiropulo, Jean. Mead and wine. N.Y., 1966.
AH 8907.50	Zagadochnye etruski. (Burian, Ján.) Moskva, 1970.
AH 4498.94	Zahl der Bürger von Athen. (Östlye, P.) Kristiania, 1894.
AH 5673.10	Zahrnt, Michael. Olynth und die Chalkidier. München, 1971.
AH 8907.35	Zalesskii, Nikolai N. Etruski v severnoi Italii. Leningrad, 1959.
AH 8910.5	Zalesskii, Nikolai N. K istorii etrusskoi kolonizatsii Italii v VII-IV vv. Leningrad, 1965.
AH 8613.5	Zaleukos, Charondas, Pythagoras. (Gerlach, F.D.) Basel, 1858.
AH 8314.2.1	Zalmoxis, the vanishing god. (Eliade, Mircea.) Chicago, 1972.
AH 4559.71.5	Zalokóstas, Chrēstos Petrou. Megas Alexandros. Athēnai, 1971?
AH 3407.35	Zamarovsky, Voitech. Tainy khettov. Moskva, 1968.
AH 36.08	Zamosci, J. De senatu romano. Argen, 1608.
AH 7179.35	Zancan, L. Ager publicus. Padova, 1935.
AH 7559.39	Zancan, P. La crisi del principato nell'anno. Padova, 1939.
AH 6103.7	Zancan, P. Il monarcato ellenistico nei suoi elementi federativi. Padova, 1934.
AH 9646.5	Zande-Messana. (Lazonder, A.) Rhenum, 1903.
Eg 1069.48F	Zandee, J. De hymnen aan Amon van papyrus Leiden I 350. Leiden, 1948.
Eg 879.60	Zandee, Jan. Death as an enemy. Leiden, 1960.
AH 4845.7	Zander, A.G.B. Luxu Atheniensium. Gryphiae, 1828.

Author and Title Listing

AH 4819.27.10   Zane, J.M. The grandeur that was Rome. Chicago, 1927.
AH 7278.54.39   Zangmeister, K. Theodor Mommsen als Schriftsteller. Berlin, 1905.
AH 4559.60   Zarathustra und Alexander. (Altheim, F.) Frankfurt, 1960.
Eg 299.66   Zavisimoe naselenie drevnego Egipta. (Stuchevskii, Iosif A.) Moskva, 1966.
AH 7158.85   Zedler, K.A.G.I. De memoriae damnatione quae dicitur. Darmstaadiae, 1885.
NEDL AH 278.93.3   Zeehe, Andreas. Lehrbuch der Geschichte des Alterthums. Laibach, 1893.
AH 214.7   Der Zehnte. (Curtius, E.) Berlin, 1885.
Eg 659.44F   Zeisel, Helene von. Athiopen und Assyrer in Ägypten. Glüchstadt, 1944.
AH 7178.41   Zeiss, Gustavo. Commentatio de Lege Thoria Agraria. Vimariae, 1841.
Htn   AH 7758.53.2*   Die Zeit Constantins des Grossen. (Burckhardt, Jacob.) Basel, 1853.
AH 7759.50   Die Zeit Constantins des Grossen. (Burckhardt, Jacob.) Bern, 1950.
AH 7758.53   Die Zeit Constantins des Grossen. (Burckhardt, Jacob.) Leipzig, 1853.
AH 7758.80   Die Zeit Constantins des Grossen. (Burckhardt, Jacob.) Leipzig, 1880.
AH 7758.98   Die Zeit Constantins des Grossen. (Burckhardt, Jacob.) Leipzig, 1898.
AH 7759.24.3   Die Zeit Constantins des Grossen. (Burckhardt, Jacob.) Stuttgart, 1929.
AH 7759.24   DieZeit Konstantins des Grossen. 4e Aufl. (Burckhardt, Jacob.) Leipzig, 1924.
AH 4409.09   Zeit und Dauer der kretisch-mykenischen Kultur. (Fimmen, D.) Leipzig, 1909.
AH 7448.83.10   Das Zeitalter der punischen Kriege. (Neumann, Karl.) Breslau, 1883.
AH 3149.12   Die Zeitbestimmungen der Wirtschaftsurkunden von Ur. III. (Schneider, N.) Rom, 1936.
AH 3149.5   Die Zeitrechnung der Babylonier und Assyrier. (Gumpach, J.) Heidelberg, 1852.
EgP 149.5   Zeitschrift für ägyptische Altertumskunde. Leipzig. 1,1863+ 43v.
EgP 149.5.2   Zeitschrift für ägyptische Altertumskunde. Index, 1863-1943. Osnabrück, 1970.
AH 298.99.3   Zeitschrift für Altegeschichte. Leipzig, 1899.
AHP 36.2   Zeitschrift für Assyriologie. Leipzig. 1886+ 31v.
AHP 36.3   Zeitschrift für die alttestamentliche Wissenschaft. Giessen. 1881+ 58v.
AHP 36.3.5   Zeitschrift für die alttestamentliche Wissenschaft. Beihefte. Giessen. 1,1896+ 75v.
AHP 36.3.3   Zeitschrift für die alttestamentliche Wissenschaft. Register, Bd. 1-25. Giessen, 1910.
AHP 36.3.4   Zeitschrift für die alttestamentliche Wissenschaft. Register, 26-50 (1906-1932). Berlin, 1970.
AHP 36.1   Zeitschrift für Keilschriftforschung. Leipzig. 1-2,1884-1885
AH 4808.35   Zeittafeln der griechischen Geschichte. v.1-2. (Peter, C.L.) Halle, 1835.
AH 4808.35.3   Zeittafeln der griechischen Geschichte. 3. Aufl. v.1-2. (Peter, C.L.) Halle, 1866.
AH 4808.35.4   Zeittafeln der griechischen Geschichte. 4. Aufl. (Peter, C.L.) Halle, 1873.
AH 4808.35.6   Zeittafeln der griechischen Geschichte. 6. Aufl. (Peter, C.L.) Halle, 1886.
AH 7808.35.5   Zeittafeln der römischen Geschichte. (Peter, Carl.) Halle, 1864.
AH 7808.35.7   Zeittafeln der römischen Geschichte. (Peter, Carl.) Halle, 1882.
AH 7808.35.6   Zeittafeln der römischen Geschichte. 5. Aufl. (Peter, Carl.) Halle, 1875.
AH 7808.41   Zeittafeln der römischen Geschichte. 6. Aufl. (Peter, C.L.) Halle, 1882.
AH 5309.6   Zel'in, K.K. Bor'ba politicheskikh gruppirovok v Attike. Moskva, 1964.
AH 7189.69.10   Zel'in, Konstantin K. Formy zavisimosti v Vostochnom Sredi zemnomor'e ellinisticheskogo perioda. Moskva, 1969.
Eg 709.60.5   Zel'in, Konstantin K. Issledovaniia po istorii zemel'nykh otnoshenii v ellinisticheskom Egipte, II-I vv. do n.e. Moskva, 1960.
AH 7297.47   Zell, Carolus. Elogiorum Romae reliquae. Stuttgartie, 1847.
AH 48.51   Zell, Karl. Natalia Caroli Friderici. Inaug. Diss. Heidelbergae, 1851.
AH 7449.47   Zeller, Eberhard. Hannibal. Uberlingen, 1948.
NEDL AH 298.65   Zeller, J. Entretiens sur l'histoire antiquité. Paris, 1865.
AH 7488.63.3   Zeller, J.S. Les empereurs romains. 2. ed. Paris, 1863.
AH 7488.63.4   Zeller, J.S. Les empereurs romains. 3. ed. Paris, 1869.
AH 3013.935.5F   Zervos, C. L'art de la Mésopotamie de la fin du quatrième millénaire au XVe siècle avant notre ère. Paris, 1935.
AH 9563.5   Zervos, C. La civilisation de la Sardaigne. Paris, 1954.
AH 4139.08   Zeuge im attischen Recht. (Leisi, Ernst.) Frauenfeld, 1908.
AH 5390.19   Zeven tegen Thebe. (Reimer, P.J.) Gouda, 1953.
AH 7279.64.5   Zhizn' drevnego Rima. (Sergeenko, Mariia E.) Leningrad, 1964.
AH 3187.15   al-Zibari, Akram. Altbabylonische Briefe des Iraq-Museums. Köln, 1964.
AH 4842.45   Ziebarth, E. Aus dem griechischen Schulwesen. Leipzig, 1909.
AH 4842.45.2   Ziebarth, E. Aus dem griechischen Schulwesen. 2. Aufl. Leipzig, 1914.
AH 4214.7   Ziebarth, E. De iureiurando in iure Graeco. Gottingae, 1892.
AH 4909.29   Ziebarth, Erich. Beiträge zur Geschichte des Seeraubs und Seehandels im alten Griechenland. Hamburg, 1929.
AH 4909.34   Ziebarth, Erich. Der griechische Kaufmann im Altertum. München, 1934.
AH 7299.64   Ziegber, K.H. Die Beziehungen zwischen Rom und dem Partherreich. Wiesbaden, 1964.
AH 7538.85   Ziegler, A. Die Regierung des Kaisers Claudius I. Wien, 1885.
AH 7539.27   Zielinski, T. L'empereur Claude et l'idée de la domination mondiale des Juifs. Bruxelles, 1927.
AH 7448.80   Zielinski, T. Letzten Jahre des zweiten punischen Krieges. Leipzig, 1880.
AH 4279.58.20   Zieliński, Tadeusz. Grecja niepodległa. 1. wyd. Warszawa, 1958.
AH 819.08.10   Zieliński, Tadeusz. Iz zhizni idei. izd. 2. v.1-2,4, pt.2. Sankt Peterburg, 1908-11. 2v.

AH 819.08.13   Zieliński, Tadeusz. Iz zhizni idei. izd. 3. Petrograd, 1916.
AH 819.70.5   Zieliński, Tadeusz. Po co Homer? wyd. 1. Kraków, 1970.
AH 819.70.10   Zieliński, Tadeusz. Szkice antyezne. wyd. 1. Kraków, 1971.
AH 3013.949.10   Ziggurats et Tour de Babel. (Parrot, André.) Paris, 1949.
AH 3012.10   Zimmermann, Carl. Babylon. Basel, 1859.
Eg 879.12.3   Zimmermann, F. Die ägyptische Religion. Paderborn, 1912.
AH 4819.11.2.5A   Zimmern, A.E. The Greek commonwealth. 4th ed. Oxford, 1924.
AH 4819.11.2.10A   Zimmern, A.E. The Greek commonwealth. 5th ed. Oxford, 1931.
AH 4819.28A   Zimmern, A.E. Solon and Croesus, and other Greek essays. London, 1928.
AH 3160.7   Zimmern, H. Vater, Sohn und Fursprecher. Leipzig, 1896.
AH 3155.4.5   Zimmern, Heinrich. The Babylonian and the Hebrew genesis. London, 1901.
AH 3002.2.6   Zimmern, Heinrich. Babylonische Busspsalmen. Leipzig, 1885.
AH 3002.2.12   Zimmern, Heinrich. Beiträge zur Kenntnis der babylonischen Religion. Leipzig, 1901.
AH 7168.26.5   Zimmern, M. Traité des actions, ou Théorie de la procédure privée. Paris, 1843.
AH 7168.26   Zimmern, S.W. Geschichte der römischen Privatrechts. v.1,3. Heidelberg, 1826. 2v.
AH 859.9   Zinserling, Verena. Die Frau in Hellas und Rom. Stuttgart, 1972.
AH 859.9.1   Zinserling, Verena. Women in Greece and Rome. N.Y., 1973.
AH 8557.2   Zippel, B. Römische Herrschaft in Illyrien. Leipzig, 1877.
AH 7058.83   Zippel, Gustav. Die Losung der konsularischen Prokonsuln in der früheren Kaizerzeit. Königsberg, 1883.
AH 7203.131   Zitelmann, E. Digestenexegese; 20 Fälle aus dem Römischen Recht. Berlin, 1925.
AH 4279.46   Zíto Hellas. (Robinson, Cyril E.) London, 1946.
AH 9707.11   Zlatkovskaia, Tat'iana D. Vozniknovenie gosudarstva u trakiitsev. VII-V vv do n.e. Moskva, 1971.
AH 4009.36   Zmigryder-Konopka, Z. Bibliografia historii starozytnej. pt.1-3. Lwow, 1936-38.
AH 5313.15   Zoeklicht op het oude Athene. (Halsberghe, Gaston.) Hasselt, 1960.
AH 7419.64   Zoeklicht op het oude Rome. (Halsberghe, Gaston H.) Hasselt, 1964.
AH 3657.42   Zoeklicht op Oud-Perzie. (Verbruggen, Hendrick.) Hasselt, 1964.
AH 7098.66   Zoeller, M. De civitate sine suffragio et municipio Romanorum. Heidelbergae, 1866.
AH 9057.2   Zoeller, Max. Latium und Rom. Leipzig, 1878.
AH 828.87   Zoeller, Max. Privataltertümer. Breslau, 1887.
AH 7038.95   Zoeller, Max. Römische Staats und Rechtsaltertümer. Breslau, 1895.
AH 8873.2   Zoeller, Max. Das Senatusconsultum über Capua. Mulhausen, 1875.
Htn   AH 7203.10F*   Zoesius. Commentarius ad digestorum. Bruxelles, 1717.
AH 7139.02.5   Zoll, F. Historya Prawodawstwa Rzymskiego. Kraków, 1902. 2v.
AH 4558.75.3   Zolling, T. Alexanders des Grossen Feldzug in centralischen Asien. Leipzig, 1875.
AH 3181.12   Het zondebesef in de Babylonische boetepsalmen. (Edelkoort, A.H.) Utrecht, 1918.
AH 7107.34.2   Zornii, Petri. Historia fisci judaici. Altonaviae, 1734.
Htn   AH 7136.60*   Zouche, R. Juris civilis. Oxoniae, 1660.
AH 7449.59   Zovnishnia polityka krain Zakhidnogo Ceredzemnomor'ia v 264-219 rr. do n.e. (Veitskivs'kyi, I.I.) L'viv, 1959.
AH 7168.77   Zródlowski, F. Römischen Privatrecht. Prag, 1877. 2v.
AH 4833.22   Zschietzschmann, W. Weltkampf- und Übungsstätten in Griechenland. Schomdorf, 1961. 2v.
AH 4819.59.15   Zschietzschmann, Willy. Hellas und Rom. Zürich, 1959.
Eg 879.70.15   Zu den altägyptischen Vorstellungen vom Schatten als Seele. (George, Beate.) Bonn, 1970.
AH 7238.89   Zu den Schlachtfeldern am trasionenischen See. (Stürenburg, H.) Leipzig, 1889.
AH 3954.11   Zucrow, S. Women, slaves and the ignorant in rabbinic literature. Boston, 1932.
AH 7098.47   Zuder öffentlichen Prüsung der Zöglinge. (Potsdam. Gymnasiums.) Potsdam, 1847.
AH 3024.5   Der Zug Sargons von Akkad nach Kleinasien. (Weidner, Ernst F.) Leipzig, 1922.
AH 4112.14   Zulhofer, Gerhard. Sparta, Delphoi und die Amphiktyonen im 5. Jahrhundert. Erlangen? 1959?
AH 7449.33   Zum Alpenübergang Hannibals. (Cappis, F.) Aarau, 1933.
AH 3150.11F   Zum altbabylonischen Gerichtswesen. Inaug. Diss. (Walther, Arnold.) Leipzig, 1915.
AH 159.05   Zum altesten Strafrecht der Kulturvölker. (Mommsen, T.) Leipzig, 1905.
AH 7058.72.5   Zum Capitel von den Consules Suffecti unter den Kaisern. (Stobbe, H.F.) n.p., n.d.
AH 4303.6   Zum Geschichtsbewusstsein der Griechen in der Zeit der römischen Herrschaft. (Touloumakos, Johannes.) Bonn, 1971.
AH 8908.11   Zum heutigen Stand der etruskischen Frage. (Herbig, G.) München, 1907.
AH 4838.86   Zum Pentathlon der Hellenen. (Marquardt, H.) Güstrow, 1886.
AH 7206.33   Zum Plan einer neuen Ausgabe der Basiliken. (Pringsheim, Fritz.) Berlin, 1956.
Eg 1179.31   Zum Problem der Identifikation der nördlichen Sternbilder der alten Ägypter. (Pogo, A.) Bruges, 1931.
AH 7808.60   Zum römischen Kalender. Eine Entgegnung auf Th. Mommsen's Angriffe. (Hartmann, O.E.) Göttingen, 1860.
AH 7158.71   Zumpt, A.W. Criminalprocess der römischen Republik. Leipzig, 1871.
AH 7158.65   Zumpt, A.W. Criminalrecht der römischen Republik. v.1-2. Berlin, 1865. 4v.
AH 8507.3   Zumpt, A.W. Studi Romana. Berolini, 1859.
AH 7138.38   Zumpt, C.G. Über Ursprung, Form und Bedeutung. Berlin, 1838.
AH 808.38   Zumpt, K.G. Annales. Berolini, 1838.
AH 808.38.3   Zumpt, K.G. Annales. Berolini, 1862.
AH 888.41   Zumpt, K.G. Über den Stand der Bevölkerung. Berlin, 1841.
AH 7158.45.15   Zumpt, karl G. Commentationis de legibus judiciisque repetundarum. Berolini, 1845. 2 pam.
AH 7208.2   Zumpt, Karl G. Über Abstimmung des römischen Volks. Berlin, 1845.
AH 7114.32   Zumpt, Karl G. Über die römischen Ritter und den Ritterstand in Rom. v.1-2. Berlin, 1841.